IDENTIFICATION AND VALUE GUIDE

Old Fishing Lures & Tackle

5th edition

Carl F. Luckey

Published by

700 E. State Street • Iola, WI 54990-0001
Telephone: 715/445-2214

Please call or write for our free catalog.
Our toll-free number to place an order or obtain a free catalog is 800-258-0929
or please use our regular business telephone 715-445-2214
for editorial comment and further information.

Library of Congress Catalog Number: 98-87368
ISBN: 0-87341-728-3

Printed in the United States of America

FOREWORD

Friend Luckey spent several years compiling, organizing and writing this useful and entertaining work about the growing hobby of collecting old plugs and tackle. During a recent visit with me, he told me it was a labor of love, saying further: "My greatest liability while working on the manuscript was my bass boat, always in full view, sittin' in the water and ready to go. It caused many enjoyable delays." Luckey, a lifetime member of B.A.S.S., is an incurable fisherman and it shows in his work.

Although there have already been fine books written for the serious collectors of old plugs and tackle, this is the first and most comprehensive collectors guide aimed at the smaller and/or more casual collectors. With 60 million or so fishermen in the United States today, there are at least thousands who have a treasured item or two of Dad's or Grandad's original fishing tackle. The book has been written for them as well as those who have a few dozen to thousands of items in their collections. All will benefit somehow. It is easy to understand and use, and should provide countless hours of entertainment for all of us inveterate fishermen.

Take the book read, learn, enjoy and discover. Your own tackle box will be appreciated even more by understanding the history and development of its contents. You enjoyment of fishing will be expanded by this unique book.

By Ray Scott
Founder and President,
Bass Anglers Sportsman Society
(B.A.S.S.)

DEDICATION

To my father, who first took me fishing. Thank you sir.
To my dear friend Walter Murphy, without whom this book might never have been.
To the Tennessee River, where it all started and still goes on for me.
And all for Mary Frances, who sees with island eyes.

PASS IT ON

What magic there is
in togetherness alone.
Unshared. Undivided.
Far away in your soft, green world
of solitude
of things to fill the dreams
of childhood;
The music of wind in the pines.
Firelight. Night sounds.
Only for a little while
will you stand
the tallest tree in the forest.
Capture those fleeting moments!
While the child is catching fish
fishing will catch the child.
And the child will need the green world
someone else gave to you.
Pass it on.

Reprinted from an advertisement by Eagle Claw/Wright and McGill Co., Denver, Colorado with their permission.

ACKNOWLEDGMENTS FOR THE FIFTH EDITION

Two people deserve special recognition for their contributions to the fifth edition.

Ken Bernoteit of Joliet, IL
Jim Muma of Belleville, IL

These two decided that there were a number of lures and reels that needed to be in the book and individually undertook the task to photograph those they had in their collections. They didn't know it, but they saved me many days of travel time when I desperately needed to, as a result of losing two months of work time due to illness. In addition to the photographs, they also took the time to write out everything they knew about the lures and reels they photographed. This gave me a nice jump start in my research efforts. Jim Muma also contributed a descriptive color table that will help the collector identify some of the more esoteric names that companies chose to describe their colors and patterns.

Two others who contributed many photocopies of old fishing tackle catalogs to my research files are George Chrisman of Allen, Texas and Harvey Garrison of Ft. Lauderdale, Florida.

The following is a list of those who helped me in some way. I thank you all. I hope I haven't left anyone out.

Gene Abney, Springfield, IL; Dave & Judy Anderson, Clayton, NY; James Arnold, New Lennox, IL; Artemborski, Rochester, MI; Phil Baker, Tampa, FL; Herb Berry, Cedar Rapids, IA; Dave Burns, Alpine, UT; Wayne Butler, Ft. Worth, TX; Tom Campbell; Ralph Doss, Winston-Salem, NC; Joseph T. Evans, Little Genesee, NY; Michael D. Frazier, Baltimore, MD; Tim Garrison, Decatur, AL; Dick Hall, Portland, CT; David Jorgensen, Central City, NE; Albert Kadet, Painesville, OH; Earl Keirstead, Madison, CT; Fred Kerr, Orlando, FL; Brett Kramer, Aplington, IA; Richard Leamon, Riceville, TN; Peter Leavitt, New Bern, NC; Bill Leonard, Lexington, KY; Buddy, Link, Ocala, FL; J.A. Lundquist, Oil City, PA; Wayne Marquis, Charlton, MA; Jerry Madson, Smelterville, ID; Walt Maynard, Greensboro, NC; Robert Minch, Marion IN; Billy Prince, Decatur, AL; Paul W. Snider, Pensacola, FL; John J. Thomas, Ventura, CA; Ken Volz, Baraboo, WI; Steve Wecker, Olpe, KS; Darr Wellman, Bark River, MI .

Thank you all.

ACKNOWLEDGMENTS FOR THE FOURTH EDITION

Books that deal with collectibles of any sort are rarely the product of a single mind and this one is certainly no exception. In the years past as a writer in the collectibles field I have traveled thousands of miles visiting dealers and collectors in order to gain the necessary knowledge and research materials to produce my books. I have made many good friends and had many good times. This time I had the very lucky accident to stumble upon Clyde Harbin, "The Bassman," and his collection. I know now that it was inevitable. Anyone, then or now, pursuing information about old fishing would eventually come upon Clyde and his incredible collection. In my opinion it is one of the most important collections of American fishing tackle in the United States. That he has thousands of lures is a well-known fact among serious collectors. What many don't realize is that in addition to the lures he has scores of rods, reels, tackle boxes, along with slides, photographs, and documentation of his collection, but one of the most important aspects of his collection, thousands of pages of old fishing tackle catalogs, magazines, references and patent illustrations an applications. He spent over 30 years gathering these materials, organizing and cataloging them. He is rightfully proud of it and I can personally testify that it is a pleasure to use for research.

The collection was sold to Bass Pro Shops in 1995. They have been in the process of assembling antique fishing tackle for some time now toward establishing a museum and this important acquisition should put them close to their goal. We can only hope that they will make it available for others to study as Clyde Harbin did for me over the years.

I am indebted to the following people who contributed to the fourth edition of this book. Some contributed quite a lot and others only a little. Whatever the contribution, big or small, makes the book a better tool for the collector. Many of the names on this list are also on the list of former contributors.

Michael Bacon, Shreveport, LA; Bob Bales, Locanto, FL; Dan Basore, Warrenville, IL; Keith and Sandra Bogardus, Stony Point, NY; Doug Brace, Concord, NC; Homer Circle, Ocala, FL; Gary Claxon, Grayson, KY; Chris Crawford, Ft. Wayne, IN; Bob Daniels, Hamilton, VA; Dennis Emerson, New Paltz, NY; Roy Fedewa, St Johns, MI; Bob Fawl, Scottsdale, AZ; Steve Fussell, Winter Park, FL; Steve Gamble, Norwich, Norfolk, England; Frederick Greene, Louisville, KY; Tom Harwood, Tacoma, WA; Phil Henderson, Garber, OK; Harold "Doc" Herr, Ephrata, PA; Roger Hinders, Belmond, IA; J.H. Holleman, M.D., Columbus, MS; Dennis "Doc" Hyder, Seymour, MO; William J. Hylton, Warren, MI; Lloyd Isotaho, Tucson, AZ; Martin Kane, Lake Hopatcong Historical Society, Landing, NJ; Denny Koppen, Spirit Lake, IA; Edward and Virginia Kieffer, Homosassa, FL; Brian Kot, Flushing, MI; John Kruzan, Carthage, TN; Edwin A. Legg, Melvindale, MI; John Lusardi, Escondido, CA; Albert Maher, Knoxville, IL; Dave Marske, Appleton, WI; Ron Matthews, Garrett, IN; Bobby Matt, Tackle Service Center, Mooresville, IN; Brian Mayer, Porter, IN; Gary McCord, Grand Junction, CO; Mike Meadows, Waconia, MN; Tim Mosher, Emporia, KS; Jim Muma, Belleville, IL; John Nash, Burlington, NC; Dan Onchuck, Phillips, WI; Alex Porubyansk, Whiting, IN; Wilfred H. Reinholz, Hubbard Lake, MI; Kevin Richards, Henley, MO; Paul Rilenge, MI; Frank Sheriff, Hopewell, NJ; Art Sereque, Downers Grove, IL; Thomas Skarupa, Belleair, FL; Dan Slagle, Coeur d'Alene, ID; Tom Smith, Florence, AL; Calky Sorrells, Ft. Worth, TX; Don Spause, Willow Grove, PA; Craig Surdy, Minnetonka, MN; Gary Tomlinson, Poynette, WI; Wilbur N. Toutloff, Pound, WI; Gary Ward, North Brunswick, NJ; Ken Webb, Shreveport, LA; Elena W. Weldon, Akron, OH; Jerry Whitten, Florence, AL; Gary Willis, Listowel, Ontario, Canada; Dick Wilson, Kent, OH; Curt Wykstra, Maravia, NY; John Yashinski, Red Lodge, MT.

Clyde Harbin, "THE BASSMAN"

ACKNOWLEDGMENTS FOR THE FIRST THREE EDITIONS

I owe a great debt of special thanks to three men who went beyond the call with generous contributions of research and photography. Their kindness and generosity has made this a much better book.

JIM BOURDON, Croton-on-Hudson, New York
DENNIS "DOC" HYDER, Seymour, Missouri
CLARENCE ZAHN, Ann Arbor, Michigan

It is never possible to acknowledge all those individuals who contribute to a work of this sort. There are always so many helpful and cooperative people in on an endeavor such as this that is not practical to thank them all in print. This is especially so when the work has gone through five editions over a period of almost 30 years. The following is a list of those I have been able to keep up with over the years. I sincerely hope I have not omitted a deserving person, but at the same time realistically expect I have. To those folks I proffer my most heartfelt apologies. It is you and the rest of these folks that make this book possible. My continuing gratitude and good wishes to you all.

Frank Baron, Livonia, MI; Ray Barzee, Sumpter, OR; Ronald Bash, Lancaster, OH; Ed Blazek, Wadena, MN; Stu Bonney, Falmouth, ME; Charlie Brown, Sand Point, ID; Bruce Boyden, Providence, RI; Rex Butel, Apache Junction, AZ; Jim Cantwell, Lake Forrest, IL; Harold Dickert, Muskegon, MI; Bruce Dyer, Labradore City, Newfoundland; Jim Frazier, Hollywood, FL; Ron Fritz, Fife Lake, MI; Steve Fussell, Winter Park, FL; Clarence Grimm, Columbia, MO; W. F. Hamilton, Port New Richey, FL; Paul W. Haudrich, Bridgeton, MO; Emerson Heilman, Kunkleton, PA; Harry Heinzerling, Garrett, IN; Ed Henckel, San Antonio, TX; Harold G. Herr, Ephrata, PA; Randy Hilst, Peking, IL; Ray Homme, Bloomington, MN; Clark Hunholz, Milwauki, MI; Dan Long, Rogersville, AL; Rick Loucks, Ashley, IN; Don C. Ludy, West Chicago, IL; Trygue C. Lund, Dowagiac, MI; James F. Mallory of the American Fishing Tackle Manufacturers Association; Brain J. McGrath, Plano, TX; Dave McCleski, Hoover, AL; Russ Mumford, West LaFayette, IN; Walter G. Murphy, Florence, AL; Leo J. Pachner, Momence, IL; Stehpen K. Peterson, Denver, CO; Bill Potts, Cincinnati, OH; A. Barton Pride, Killen, AL; George Richey, Honor, MI; E. Nelson Robinson (dec.), Killen, AL; Ray Scott, Montgomery, AL; Doug Schelske, Minneapolis, MN; Jeromw Schopp, Chenoa, IL; T. Layton Shepherd, Antigo, WI; John Schoffner, Fife Lake, MI; Richard E. Shook, Youngstown, OH; Tim Smith, Florence, AL; Tim Stalling, Orlando, FL; Jim Stoker, Hastings, MN; Oscar Strausborge, Edon, OH; John Thomas, Laramie, WY; Rich Treml, Detroit, MI; Robert V. Vermillion, Huntington Woods, MI; Buck Vest, Claremore, OK; Tim Waits, Urbana, IL; Bill Wetzel, Hampton, SC; Dave Whisman, Prestonsburg, KY; Dick Wilson, Kent, OH.

REMEMBERING CARL LUCKEY

Sadly, author Carl Luckey passed away prior to the publication of this, the Fifth Edition of Old Fishing Lures and Tackle.

Those who knew Carl are well aware that he touched many lives beyond the scope of his books. In addition to his research and writing, Carl was a genuine hero, an ambitious volunteer and a patron of the arts. The following is portion of Carl's obituary as it appeared in the Nov. 4, 1998 edition of The Florence (Alabama) TimesDaily.

Capt. Carl Freeman Luckey Jr. died Monday, Nov. 2 1998, unexpectedly at his home in Killen, Alabama. He was born in Nashville, Tennessee, March 4, 1941.

He attended Georgia Tech in Atlanta for two years, and received a bachelor of science degree from the University of North Alabama with double major in biology and chemistry and was inducted into the Beta Biological Honor Society. He entered the U.S. Air Force immediately afterward.

During his much-decorated career in the Air Force, he flew 197 reconnaissance missions over enemy territory during the Vietnam War. He was awarded the Distinguished Flying Cross, the Air Medal with 12 oak leaf clusters, and the National Defense Medal for bravery and efficiency in his duties.

After completing his tour of duty in the Air Force, he returned to his home in Florence where for five years he owned and operated a fine arts gallery. He worked for several years with the Tennessee Valley Authority as a biologist; was editor of a local newspaper and a national collectors' periodical; worked as a designer and artist, and finally set to his career as a professional writer on art, antiques, and collectibles. He now has more than 25 books to his credit.

His public service activities among many others include work for the Tennessee Valley Art Center, the Alabama Assembly of Community Arts Councils, The Kennedy-Douglass Art Center and the U.S. Coast Guard Auxiliary.

Since the 1980s he has been a member of the United States Coast Guard Auxiliary, a civilian volunteer arm of the Coast Guard with primary activities including teaching boating safety classes, coordinating, conducting and participating in search and rescue operations and safety patrols on the Tennessee River. He served as commander of the Florence Flotilla and has served on District And Division Staff of the Second Southern.

He achieved status as an Auxiliary Vessel Crewman and Vessel Operator in 1989, as an Auxiliary Coxswain in 1996 and distinguished as an AuxOp member in 1996. In 1992 he received the Award of Operational Merit for saving a life in a boating incident on the Tennessee River. In 1995 he received the second highest award presented by the Coast Guard to a civilian, THE PLAQUE OF MERIT, for preventing the loss of life at the risk of his own life.

He is a U.S. Coast guard licensed captain; member of the Sons of the American Revolution; a communicant of Trinity Episcopal Church; past commodore of Turtle Point Yacht Club; member of the Turtle Point bridge and marina committee; member of the Muscle Shoals Amateur Radio Club, KD4HPK, Sky Warn, Alabama Emergency Net J.

He leaves his wife, Dr. Mary Frances Werner-Luckey; his parents, Dr. and Mrs. Carl Freeman Luckey; his brother, Dr. George Luckey; niece and nephew, Elizabeth and Arthur Luckey.

Carl's enduring accomplishments are many. He was a professional in every sense of the word and he will be missed.

Krause Publications

TABLE OF CONTENTS

INTRODUCTION

Between these covers lies what has evolved into a singularly valuable reference for the collector of old fishing tackle, particularly those whose interest is in the old fishing lure. The lure is a device made of some material, organic or inorganic, bearing a hook, a facility for tying it to a line and made in such a way as to deceive a fish into thinking it to be a delicacy worthy of pursuit. If successfully made and properly used, it will often net the user on the other end of the line a bit of fun and perhaps, turning the table on the fish's interest, a bit of good eating.

Since the first edition was published in 1980 much has been learned and a tremendous additional amount of material has been turned up. Everybody who has had a serious interest has been generous with their information and material. Indeed, they have been anxious to share it with their fellow collectors. First edition publications have been revised and released and the National Fishing Lure Collectors Club (NFLCC) members have been at the fore in this effort. Their excellent newsletter and members' research efforts (shared enthusiastically by the way) have been excellent to say the least. Many of them have been of incredible help in providing new research materials for this fifth edition. Membership in this fine organization is inexpensive and an absolute must for any collector of old fishing tackle. It cannot be recommended highly enough.

There have always been collectors. You name it and someone, somewhere, collects it. The collectors of old fishing tackle number in the many, many thousands, if the number of sales of the first four editions of this book is any indication. For every serious collector member of the NFLCC (genus and species, HOARDPLUGENS ENMASSUS), there are hundreds of casual collectors. Any one of these folks can become as engrossed in this fascinating hobby as the above-mentioned critter, Hoardplugens Enmassus.

The fascination with old lures and tackle is understandable and contagious. It is most likely that the first lures were conceived and fashioned when early thinking man first began to formulate ways of outwitting his prey in fishing. Whether early man's piscatorial pursuits were of a sporting nature or to supplement his diet is an academic point. What it does indicate is how long man has had to dream up new ways of tempting our fishy friends (foes?).

The province of this book is primarily that of manufactured artificial lures used since the earliest days of their production in the United States. There are only a few artificial flies in the listings, nor will you find many metal or metal spinner type lures. There have been numerous fine works about flies and fly-tying already produced and the inclusion of all the spinner baits and other metal lures would present quite a problem. There are enough old plugs and related lures to fill two or three volumes this size and the metal spinners, etc., just may outnumber the plugs, not to mention the tremendous difficulty in identifying and cataloging them. I'll just stick with the old plugs, add a few important metal items, some fly rod lures and reels. I have been writing this book for almost 20 years now, so I feel like I have something of a say about what goes into it. You will find some companies and their lures this time that have never appeared before for various and sundry reasons.

The first edition contained a section on old rods. You will find that the listing and pricing of rods has been eliminated, but the history of rod development has been retained. The author and his publisher felt that the small listing was woefully inadequate to serve the needs of the rod collector. The enormous numbers of styles, types, materials, jobbers, manufacturers and habit of manufacturers supplying numbers of companies with their own trademarks make it all but impossible for it to be covered sufficiently here. A whole book for rods themselves would be required. There have been a few published. Please turn to the recommended reference section for a list of these and other interesting publications related to the fishing collectibles hobby.

Reels have been retained and expanded a bit, but the section covers a small number of earlier products and a representation of some of those more commonly found by collectors are here for those of you who may be interested. It may also help to give a plug collector an impetus to begin a reel collection. The comments made above with regard to rods apply here to reels as well. There are several good books on reels to be had. Just consult the list of collector references elsewhere in this book.

Given the above you can see that the greatest majority of information presented is about fishing lures made beginning around 1890-1900 and ending in the early 1970s.

Think of it. Think how many thousands of fishermen have tried to think of a "better mousetrap" in those 70 or 80 years! Most producers of plugs in those years have experimented with myriad designs in the continuing battle to make the "secret weapon." The producers are represented by hundreds upon hundreds of operations, from the one-man shop and Mom and Pop businesses to the large manufacturer, that have come and gone during this time. The types of lures that have come down the pike range from the sublime to the ridiculous, from the ineffective to the explosively successful fish-getter. Every single one of them, if you believe the advertisements, have been the proverbial secret weapon, the fabled supreme achievement. For example there is an old (1911) Ans. B. Decker advertisement which boasts that he can catch more bass over 14 inches with his bait "...than you can!", and backs up his boast with a wager of "$1,000 against $500.". Now that's a real challenge when you consider what a prodigious sum of money $1,000 was in those days! It would probably be prudent to suspect that Mr. Decker's skill was more likely the source of such confidence than was his bait design. Of course it is quite possible the bait was responsible, at least in part, for all fishermen are painfully aware of the apparent changing preferences of our fickle and apparently fashion-conscious, fishy foes.

For the collector of old tackle there follows here a guide to the hobby. There is a history of artificial lures, a history of reel and rod development, a glossary of terms specific to the subject, illustrations of major developments and improvements, an illustrated guide to the identification and valuation of old reels and lures, lists of clubs, related books, interesting periodicals, experts, appraisers and restorers. There is a section on care and practical, convenient display, and a very useful section on how to snag new items for your collection.

HISTORY AND SIGNIFICANT DEVELOPMENTS IN THE EVOLUTION OF AMERICAN FISHING TACKLE

This section is designed to give the collector some important general background information and some specifics in the development of fishing tackle in the United States. Knowledge of general history and significant events in the evolution of tackle will enable collectors to better understand and use this guide to properly identify, classify and possibly date the items in his or her collection. These first pages are devoted to a general chronology and is followed by a separate, somewhat more detailed history of the lure, rod and reel.

While there has never been any revolutionary event in the history of fishing to compare with what the invention of gun powder did for hunting, there have been significant technical advances in lure and tackle manufacture over the years. These can sometimes be identified as to an approximate date and are listed following.

A GENERAL CHRONOLOGY OF DEVELOPMENT

PRE-COLONIAL TIMES

1. The Indians used their hands, traps, spears and lights at night. The latter, as we know and use them today, obviously attracted some fish. Light could be said to be one of the first artificial "lures."
2. Primitive American Indians as well as primitive peoples of other parts of the world used a "Gorge," the crude forerunner of today's modern barbed hook. The gorge, still used by some primitive people, is a straight bar made of bone, shell, stone or wood, sometimes with a groove around it near the center for tying a line. It was utilized by inserting it lengthwise in the bait. When the fish swallows the bait, the line is tugged and the gorge becomes lodged lengthwise in the fish.
3. Eskimos and Indians used artificial lures made of ivory or bone. They were customarily used as decoys while ice fishing and/ or spear fishing.
4. Eskimos and Indians used gill nets and seines.

EARLY COLONIAL TIMES

The first colonists had little interest in sport fishing as their immediate need was survival. History proves that there was much commercial fishing from the very earliest days of settlement in America.

18th CENTURY

First appearance of fishing for sport in America. Sport fishing probably pre-dates this era, but it was likely to be European aristocrats who brought their fly fishing gear with them.

1800-1810

1. First appearance of the Phantom Minnow in America.

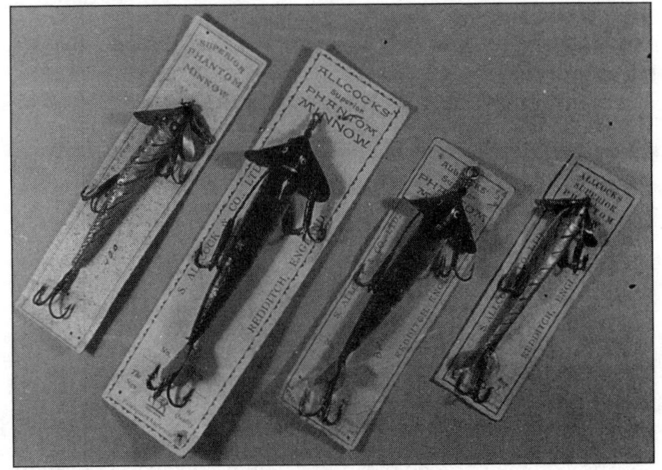

The Phantom Minnow

Various parts of Buel spoons and spinners. They may be found with either J.T. or H.W. Buel (Julio's half brother) and patent date, 1852 or 1854 markings. The metal strips and spoons in the photo here are the 1854 patent. The spinner body/blade is from the 1852 patent. Only that was provided. The angler had to attach his own hook and wire armature.

2. George Snyder made the first "Kentucky Reels"

1835-1840

The first commercial manufacture of the "Kentucky Reels" by the Meeks Brothers.

1844-1925

The development of the "Henshall Rod".

*1848

Julio T. Buel began commercial manufacture of the spoon lure. He is credited with its invention.

1852

Julio T. Buel - First U.S. patent on spinner bait.

1859

First known patent for a lure that mentions wood as possible material for the lure body. Riley Haskell, Painesville, Ohio.

Riley Haskell Minnow. This metal minnow lure measures 4-9/16" in body and 5-5/8" overall (including the hook and line tie). *See page XXX and page XXX.*

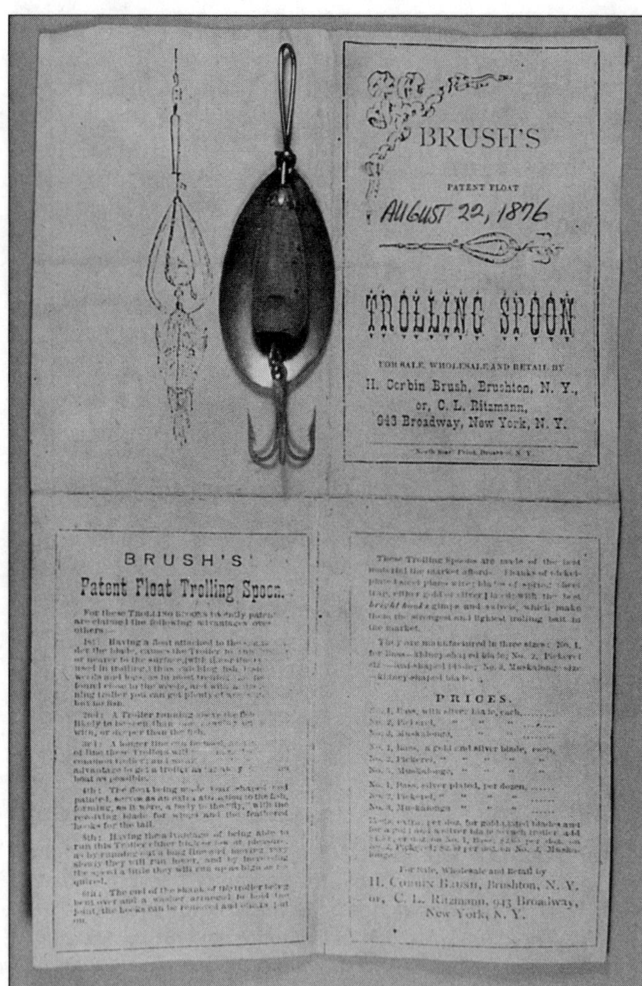

The Brush Floating Spinner and papers.

FLYING HELLGRAMMITE

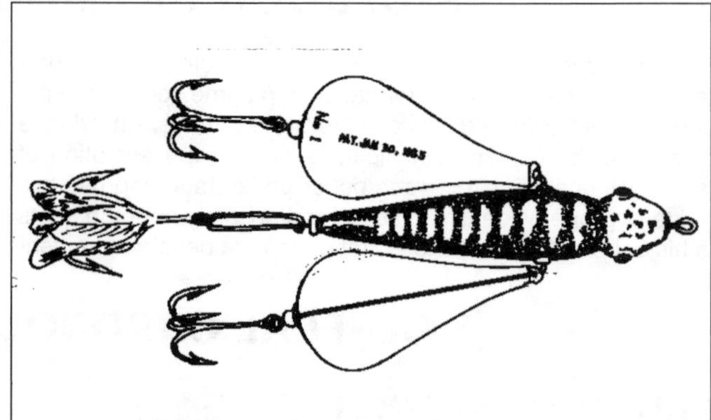

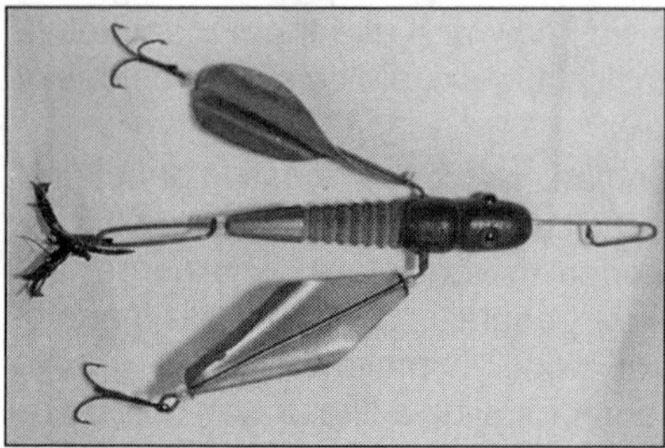

A Flying Hellgrammite. This particular example has red eyes. Photo courtesy Elena W. Weldon.

1874

First granted patent for an artificial lure specifying the use of wood for the lure body. Patented May 26, 1874 by David Huard and Charles M. Dunbar of Ashland Wisconsin

1876

Early manufactured artificial lure incorporating wood as a component. Listed in U.S. patent records as patented by H. C. Brush**, August 22, 1876.

**Buel was actually fishing with his invention as early as 1821 and made many for friends and neighbors over the years. The 1848 date is subject to speculation as there is a 1904 ad stating "Over 60 Years in Use."*

***The 1876 H. C. Brush patent has heretofore been thought to be the first wooden plug. However study of patent records reveal the Huard and Dunbar patent precedes Brush by two years. It is not known if it was ever produced.*

1880

First known granted patent for an artificial lure specifying glass for the lure body. J. Irgens, Sept. 7, 1880 (see page XXX for illustration).

1883

Patent for "artificial bait" called The Flying Hellgrammite by Harry Comstock, Fulton, New York, January 30,1883. See page XXX for the patent illustration.

1883

Patent granted to Earnest F. Pflueger for artificial lures coated with luminous paint for fishing at night.

1885

The development of the "Chicago Rod".

1890

The beginning of widespread bait-casting in the United States. Although the bait casting reel was invented about 75 years previously, it wasn't until the 1890s that casting plugs were born in the U.S.

1869-1898

James Heddon is generally credited with the first artificial lure we know as the "plug" today.

1900-1905

The beginnings of major plug manufacturers in the United States.

1907

The first appearance of jointed wooden plugs - the "K and K Animated Minnows".

1910-1920

The first widespread use of luminous paint on plugs began sometime during this period. Pflueger was given the first patent on a luminous lure on Feb. 3, 1883 (see page XXX for an illustration of the patent).

c. 1912

The first water sonic plugs appeared. Probably the 1912 "Diamond Wiggler". Please turn to the Diamond Wiggler listing for an illustration of this lure.

c. 1914

The first appearance of fluted plugs, probably the Lockhart "Wobbler Wizard." It was later followed by the Wilson "Fluted

A 1908 advertisement for the K & K Animated Minnow.

Wobbler" around 1917 These are illustrated in their respective company listings.

c. 1914

The Detroit Glass Minnow Tube was introduced; the first of the few and rare glass fishing lures.

1915

First appearance of a self-illuminated plug to utilize a battery-operated bulb. It was called "Dr. Wasweyler's Marvelous Electric Glow Casting Minnow".

An advertisement for the Detroit Glass Minnow Tube from the March, 1814 issue of The Outer's Book magazine.

c.1917

Earliest known advertisement of a lure made of celluloid. The first advertisement found was in a May 1917 issue of National Sportsman magazine. It was for an Al Foss "Oriental Wiggler" - a pork rind minnow. Soon after his ads began to say Pyralin instead of celluloid. These may be the first plastic lures.

c. 1922

The Vesco Bait Company of New York City advertised baits and spoons made of Dupont Pyralin. One of the first plastic plugs.

1932

Heddon introduced their "Fish Flesh" plastic lure. The first lures were produced in the #9100 and #9500 (Vamp) series. Soon thereafter came plastic "Spooks".

1940

Appearance of the first American-built spinning reels.

THE TACKLE COLLECTOR'S PRIMER

WHERE TO FIND IT

This business of collecting old fishing tackle is one of the most interesting and natural extensions to the sport of fishing. Until recent years it has been one of the most unexploited areas of collecting old Americana. If you are interested in joining in the collecting of old tackle get cracking, because the ranks are growing rapidly. Luckily there have been millions upon millions of pieces of tackle hand-crafted and manufactured since the early days so there should still be plenty of nice examples to go around. Some collectors are mistaken in their claim that the sources are drying up. Don't you believe it. Every day new and fabulous finds are being made. In fact, the newsletter of the National Fishing Lure Collectors Club has a section in every issue entitled *It's Still Out There* where great new finds are chronicled.

Try the oldest general stores, drugstores (used to carry bass plugs), bait shops and hardware stores in your area, especially their storerooms and basements if they have such. There has been many-a treasure turned up by feeling around a dusty top shelf in a storage room. Anywhere tackle has been sold over a period of 40 years or more, there could be some oldies. Some of these places may have sold tackle one time or another. Even if they don't now, they may have some old unsold stock stuck away somewhere. A friend of mine paid $1.29 for a Millsite "Rattle Bug" in an old general store near the Alabama gulf coast. That plug possibly dates back to 1940 and had apparently been laying around unsold for all that time.

Remember trading boards? Well there are some shops that still use them. For an old or unwanted lure you pay a quarter or half a buck, put your plug on the board and take another of your choice. There is one right near my home but alas, the owner is a collector. Many shops sell used rods and reels. You may find an old one or two this way.

Ask your family and friends if they know of an old-timer who left his tackle box or other fishing gear in the cellar or attic. If they say no, ask them to look anyway. They may not know or have simply forgotten. Look in your own box, there may be one in there under all that junk you haven't used or even seen for years.

The garage sales and flea markets of today are good places to try, but so far they haven't been very good hunting grounds. Few of these folks think of old tackle as being very marketable. This source is growing, but often the prices are way out of line. I have noticed over the past five or six years that more and more flea marketeers and junk shop owners are offering old tackle and plugs at grossly inflated prices and most of those I have seen are beaters or common items. There are exceptions, however, so keep your eyes open at the flea market. Garage sales, on the other hand, have grown to be a productive source for many. As mentioned before, most people don't think of old tackle as marketable at garage sales and don't display it. Ask them if they have any old fishing tackle or boxes. I have been surprised more than once after asking.

Another possible source for lures is the banks of old favorite fishing lakes and rivers. The latter are the best because of fluctuating water levels. I live on the banks of the Tennessee River and during low water periods, I have spent many enjoyable hours searching for lures among the driftwood, etc., deposited by the retreating water. The lake impoundments around here are 60 to 70 years old and most lures don't fare too well when exposed to the elements for a long time. The search is pleasant, however, and I have found dozens of salvageable modern lures that are in my tackle box now. I feel it's an even trade because I know a few submerged stumps around here that must look like Christmas trees the way I have decorated them with lost lures over the years.

Make up a want list with pictures or drawings and pass the list out among friends and relatives or post it on public bulletin boards such as provided by many grocery stores and in senior citizen centers. Don't use names or numbers, just pictures. Names and numbers will just confuse some people. On the other hand, when sending your want list to other collectors provide all the information you can; name, numbers, pictures, dimensions and complete descriptions.

The National Fishing Lure Collectors Club (NFLCC) holds many regional shows each year. Join the NFLCC to get an annual schedule of these and other organization events. Chances are you will find one within a reasonable distance from your home. These events are fabulous sources for everything connected to collecting old fishing tackle. The least of this is meeting other folks with a common interest. This is a great way to build your list of contacts for trading and purchasing items for your collection.

A new source for contact with collectors who want to buy, sell, trade or just talk about old tackle is the Internet. There are hundreds of sites on the Web now. Some are absolutely dazzling sources that are incredibly rich with information.

In short, just use your imagination to come up with both likely and unlikely sources.

NOW YOU'VE FOUND IT - WHAT DO YOU PAY?

Now this is mighty sticky wicket, this business of pricing old tackle. It is an area probably as full of unseen hazards as there are standing hairs on a mad cat's back.

It would be safe to say that many tackle collectors, particularly among lure collectors, would much prefer swapping and buying. For the most part collectors are "swappers and/or buyers", but generally not sellers. The swap is by far the best way to expand your collection when other sources dry up. The problem is there are precious few instances when one can pin down a value in swapping terms. You just can't say that a "Doctor Catchum's Surefire Killer Diller Spinner" is worth two "Magic Molly Gogglers" and half a "Big Bass Basher". Each swap is an individual negotiation between two collectors which ends in satisfying both. Most of the time, the only way to avoid the unsatisfactory alternative is to know your business. That takes study.

When hunting for old tackle, most of the time you find it already marked with a price at shows, in stores, garage sales, etc., and that's generally what you pay unless you're that enviable type, the "silver-tongued devil." In the above instances the price is usually more than a fair one, sometimes being a downright steal. The other sources discussed, Grampa's tackle box, etc., usually end up in no monetary outlay at all or if so, an insignificant one. I went prospecting a few years ago and came up with a beat up old metal tackle box with 22 old lures and a reel in it for 20 bucks. That comes to less than $1 per plug. There were only two good collectible plugs in the box, but worth a good bit more than what I paid and the others, while beaters, were still good for parts and a couple went right into my tackle box. The reel was too far gone to count. I keep hearing collectors talk of their sources drying up; that there isn't much left to find. Since it had been several years since that last foray, I decided to try again. I put a couple of ads in local give-away shoppers and waited for the calls. Two weeks later I spent one day on the road visiting the folks who had called. This time the monetary outlay was higher, $255, but some of the lures I came up with were a Heddon blue nose No. 200 Surface, a glass-eyed Lucky-13 and a glass-eyed Creek Chub Plunker and Dingbat, all in great condition. Also included were a couple of dozen lesser baits in varying condition and a sack of Heddon plastics, a metal tackle box in good shape, a nice Bronson Commander reel in the box and a battery-operated toy Mercury outboard motor. You add it up. It wasn't a bad haul especially when you consider how far Alabama is from the mother load of the Midwest. All that for this: Don't tell me it's not out there!

Generally speaking, the older the item the more it's worth, simply because the older it is the less there are available in most cases. The simple law of supply and demand comes into important play in this case. Some old lures, reels, and especially old split cane fly rods can and sometimes do soar into the hundreds, even thousands of dollars. "Older-worth-more" is not necessarily set in concrete. Some lures of the 1920's and 1930's were made for a short period of time and are quite rare and valuable. Some others made in the 1940's through the 1970's are also valuable

Another important consideration is just how bad you want it. It matters not a flit what someone or some book says it's worth if you're in a "I gotta have it" frame of mind. Let's say you have but one more necessary to complete a color set and you're looking right at it but - it belongs to another collector who prizes it also. In this extreme case you probably will walk away empty-handed, but for the sake of argument, the conversation might go something like this:

"Charlie, ole buddy, I just gotta have that Purple Plunker."

"Aw, Bill, I can't part with it. Just look at it, it's mint,"

"Yeah I know Charlie, but you know that's the one I need to complete my set and it's the only one you got like that. It looks lonesome on your board."

"Well, what'll you gimme?"

"How about two Topless Torpedo Twisters and a couple of six-packs of suds?"

"No way, Charlie, I gotta have some long green. You know I've been savin' for one of those new super-charged boat trailers. Tell you what, a portrait of Mr. Grant and you can take it home."

"Charlie! 50 bucks?! Gimme a break, the book says it's only worth twenny. Holy catfish!"

"That's my price, Bill, take it or leave it."

" Awright you old skinflint, here's your bounty."

Charlie paid over two times what the book said the plug was worth but he really didn't get ripped off. In the final analysis, to you, something is worth what you're willing to pay for it. If Charlie already had his Purple Plunker, then Bill might not have gotten even the $20 it was supposed to be worth. Or - if Bill had wanted the two Topless Torpedo Twisters more than the money, Charlie would have still gotten his Purple Plunker. In either case, the swap or the purchase, both were satisfied in the end.

All that for this: Take the value guide presented in this book or any other book, as exactly that - a guide. It is, after all, only one man's opinion. I couldn't say how many times I have heard: "This is worth about $20 or so, but I wouldn't take three times that for it." You are the final authority. Don't forget it.

SOME HINTS FOR SUCCESSFUL BUYING, SELLING, TRADING

1. Arm yourself with knowledge. Get and study every piece of printed information you can get your paws on.
2. Mutual cooperation builds better collections, good friends and sources. Ask for help from knowledgeable collectors and give an edge to those who helped you in the beginning, after you get smart.
3. If you find you have a treasure, don't be greedy, be fair. If you don't deal fairly you may find many of your sources drying up.
4. If you find you have made a bad deal, don't worry over it - learn from it. Turn lemons into lemonade by knowing better next time.
5. Always make an offer. Nothing ventured, nothing gained. Remember one man's trash is another man's treasure.
6. Honest mistakes are made. If you have built up a good rapport with and a good reputation among your collector friends, most mistakes can be rectified. Keep in mind, however, that it is not possible to make all your deals mutually fair, only mutually acceptable. Don't squawk if you find later the deal wasn't so good. You can't win them all.

One last note about the way the values are presented in the individual listings. You will note that they are presented as "Collector Value Range". In many cases the range is quite wide. You may reasonably place the lower limits of the range as the approximate value of a newer item in less than perfect condition and the upper limit on those older or more rare pieces in excellent condition. The final judgment is yours even to the extent that your opinion places the value outside the printed range. All the value ranges in this book are for lures in very good to mint condition. Any in less than very good condition will fall out the lower side range. Valuation of these is strictly a matter of negotiation between individual buyers/sellers or traders.

NEVER MISS A CHANCE

How many times have you been out on the water only to lose that special plug? I mean the only one that works; or worse, you and your fishing buddy are having a bad day and he starts hauling 'em in like he was bailing out a sinking boat. He found today's secret weapon and he's only got one copy and you're zeroed out in that type. Whatever the reason, we all have modified plugs in our tackle boxes in a sometimes vain attempt to land a lunker. Therein lies a problem the plug collector will invariably encounter. I have replaced spinners, hooks, lips, hook hardware, swivels, etc. and yes, even repainted favorite plugs. Think of the strange concoctions you might run across in an old timer's tackle box! Some may even defy the most expert collector but, most can be identified and eventually the proper hardware may be obtained and the plug restored to its original configuration (more about this later). Moral: Never discard old, beat up, mistreated plugs you find. Throw them in a box for cannibalization. The same applies to rods and reels.

SOME MISCELLANEOUS CONSIDERATIONS

INSURANCE - If you find yourself with a collection of old tackle that you cherish and/or is valuable then please consider some insurance. In the unfortunate event of a house fire those old wooden plugs and bamboo rods will be great kindling. Many reels have hard rubber and plastic parts and fires can reach temperatures high enough to melt some metals.

Check your homeowners insurance policy or personal effects rider. Most contain a clause that limits or excludes collectibles. I am not qualified to delve into the intricacies of insurance policies, but do emphasize the importance of proper coverage. It is important to discuss your particular collecting situation with a trusted agent. Alternatively, the National Fishing Lure Collectors Club (NFLCC) has made reasonable insurance available to its members. You might want to look into that possible opportunity.

PROTECTION - There are numerous ways to protect and safeguard your collection which you can accomplish with ease if you will just take the time to do so. In the unfortunate circumstance of theft or destruction, the law enforcement authorities and/or insurance companies will be able to handle recovery, replacement or reimbursement much more efficiently if you have done your homework before the fact. This "homework" can be rewarding in itself by increasing your knowledge of the very things you collect.

WRITE IT DOWN - Inventory your collection. Put it on your "Things To Do Today" list. Get yourself some index cards and file box, a loose leaf notebook, or whatever may be easiest for you to use to catalog your collection. Some of the important things to record in your inventory are when, where and how you obtained each piece. Record the price you paid or what you traded for it. Describe each with name, company name, catalog number, material, measurements, all signatures and other marks. It would be good even to assign each item a number in your collection and describe the location on the premises. The number may be your own or in the event there is a universal number such as from a company catalog, you may prefer to use it.

PHOTOGRAPH IT - Photographs are evidence of original condition, should a piece be damaged. They are a positive means of identification by which items may be traced if stolen and assurance for insurance purpose. They can serve as a valuable tool in either case.

Many collectors find it convenient to use the back of each photo to record the description, etc., for their inventory. It is advisable to maintain duplicates of each, one set in a safe place at home so that you may use them when you wish, and the other set somewhere off the premises, such as in a safe deposit box at a bank. There is a primer on photographing lures in Appendix B at the back of this book.

IDENTIFICATION MARKS - An additional safeguard is to mark each item individually. If a piece is lost or stolen, the ability to point out a distinctive mark identifying it as your property is quite helpful.

If you are a purist, reluctant to permanently mark an object because it alters the original state, then there are other slightly more difficult ways.

You may want to use descriptions of unique properties of each item such as repairs, imperfections or areas of wear.

Should you choose to mark, do so in an unobtrusive location. However you mark, make sure it is permanent and very small. You could also use an ink that is visible only under ultraviolet or black light.

REPRODUCTIONS OR COPIES - The forgery is a copy or reproduction of an item specifically for the purpose of deceiving the purchaser. There are a lot of talented folks in this world of ours and some of them capable of doing an incredible job of copying. That in itself is fine, but where that talent belongs to a dishonest individual his product, the reproduction, becomes a forgery. The purpose of these few pages is not to help that nefarious forger, but to help the collector protect himself against the varmint, and have a little fun to boot.

There is no substitute for intimate familiarity with the nature and characteristics of what you collect, but the author has found another way to at least add a little to the understanding. *Try to make a lure yourself.* Reels are just about out of the question. Although not altogether impossible, it would not be economically feasible for anyone to try to forge an old reel. Do watch out for altered markings, however. The same applies to rods.

Old lures are a completely different proposition for obvious reasons. By attempting to reproduce an old plug yourself you will gain some insight into the problems a potential forger may encounter and that might help you to identify counterfeits.

A more enjoyable and satisfying experience however, is the making of lures that catch fish. Some of those old plugs actually were "performing fools." If fish do, as some insist, learn and remember lures which are constantly jerked by their noses then you will present them with a new, unfamiliar delicacy that they might just select for their breakfast. Many of those old successful plugs are not made anymore simply because the making of them costs the manufacturer too much to sell at a profit.

The best way to begin is in a book. There are three that I am familiar with. The most recent one is a pamphlet, *Hooked on Lure Crafting* by Ronald F. Mirabile, *Tackle Craft* by C. Boyd Pfieffer and *The Book of Old Lures* by Charles K. Fox. The latter two are out of print, but I found both of them in my smallish hometown library. The Mirabile book is excellent, but too new to have made it to most libraries. You can order it from the author at the address given in the Recommended Reference section of this book. The Pfieffer book is a highly detailed, excellent work dealing with fashioning your own tackle. The Fox book deals primarily with old lures, with some great directions for making plugs like the old ones.

If you like the idea and are fairly handy with your hands, try it. There can't be any greater satisfaction in fishing than landing a lunker with a lure made with your own hands.

DEFINING YOUR COLLECTION

Sooner or later, you will have to decide what kind of collection you are building. The collector may approach his hobby in one of several different ways. You may want to specialize in wooden lures only, lures or reels or rods made by just one manufacturer or even specialize in only one type. Some collectors "color collect". They attempt to find every color and finish option ever offered on a particular lure. Another direction is attempting to collect only lures in one pattern, such as those with a white body red head. Almost all the companies offered that color. The choices are many. A collector I know, who began over 30 years ago, started out trying to obtain one example of every single lure from one company. His collecting expanded to the same goal for products of several other companies. The collection eventually surpassed 10,000 lures!

An interesting and very attractive collection would be one made up of only those lures, rods, or reels in good to mint condition or collect only those lures that can be found in the original box. This would be difficult but challenging. Some collectors collect *only* the boxes. To add some variety to your collection and display, even the specialist collector should have a few pieces from other areas of collectible tackle. There are hundreds of accessories to be found illustrated in old catalogs, some quite cu-

A small collection of old-style hunting and fishing licenses ranging from 1935 to 1955. Could make a nice addition to a display of a collection of old lures and tackle.

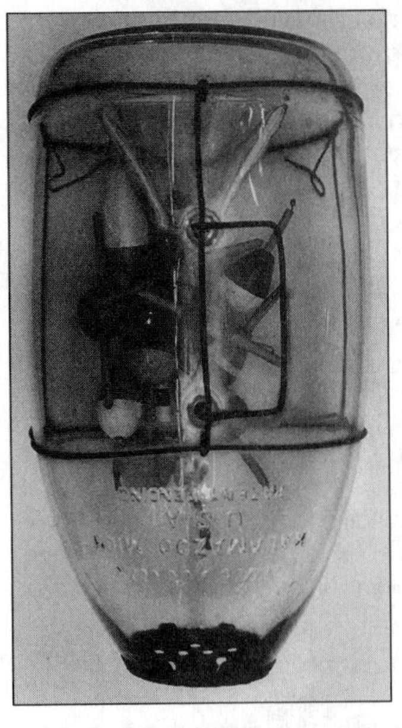

A very early glass minnow trap/bucket offered by Shakespeare. Note the old wooden floaters or bobbers inside. An interesting addition to any collection.

rious, others interesting but unsuccessful attempts at making the fisherman more comfortable under adverse conditions. The old catalogs themselves are fascinating, incredibly entertaining to read and some are works of art in themselves.

An old Marshall Field and Company catalog (c. 1915) advertises a FISHING BELL ALARM at five cents, saying "It is called the sleepy fisherman's friend." A 1919 catalog shows that for $1.35 the unlucky fisherman may obtain a LINE RELEASER complete with leather case. The advertisement states, in part: "Ever have your fly in a tree? Got mad of course." It goes on to claim that the device will not only save your temper but will save your line, leader, lure and possibly the tip of your rod to boot. It is placed on the tip of the rod, cuts the twig and "down comes twig and your belongings." I've seen many a day when I could have used one of those. Sometimes I think I should be casting for our feathered friends instead of the fishy variety.

NOW THAT YOU HAVE IT HOW DO YOU DISPLAY IT?

There can be no end to methods of display if you use your imagination. To name but a few: the professionally made, glassed and sealed shadow box; open frames with burlap or other decorative, appropriate substances; custom-made shadow box types with removable glass or Plexiglas; an arrangement on a wall; display shelves and cabinets; hung from ceilings or beams; in antique or modern display fixtures used by tackle shops or, in the case of some collectors, whole rooms or more, entirely devoted to display and enjoyment. The list is limited only by your imagination and individual requirements. All have advantages, but one will suit your needs.

For the serious or would-be serious collector, I would recommend a method that both protects and allows ease of access and removal. If you don't you'll regret it later.

One very effective method for lure display is the use of tray-like cases with fabric covered foam rubber backing and a sliding or hinged Plexiglas cover. It is quite easy to remove, add and rearrange plugs on the using upholsterers "T pins". The Plexiglas protects from dust and the box itself can be hung on the wall or transported if you wish. If you're handy with your hands you can build them yourself. For reels, almost any cabinet with glass fronts and or sides would be very handy. Lights in the interior can add a very dramatic and decorative element to the room as the various metals and surfaces of the reels reflect it.

Rods could be shown to great advantage hung on your walls (removable of course) or perhaps a gun cabinet would be attractive. I have seen some beautiful old wooden rod racks that came out of tackle shops of bygone days. These are ideal for display and ease of removal. Do remember that rods should always be displayed or stored vertically.

You might add interest and contrast to your collection by displaying some of the very old with the very new, modern versions of the same thing.

If you are into rods, reels or lures alone, the inclusion of some example of the others will add enjoyment and interest to your display. An old rod looks a lot nicer with a vintage reel mounted on it.

Most of you are fishermen. Add trophy mounts to your collection. Old tackle boxes, patches and gadgets and accessories add even more interest.

Old catalogs or reproductions of them serve two purposes. One is that they make fascinating reading and more importantly, they are the single most important source of information from which to learn about your hobby. Many of these old catalogs are rare and eminently collectible in themselves. A word about using the catalogs as reference material: The manufacturers were not always entirely accurate when listing. This is especially true with regard to sizes. Frequently the size is rounded to the nearest half or quarter-inch. Some companies used the same illustration for years even though there may have been significant changes in hardware or design. Use them as a guide only.

Whatever method or scope of collection and display you arrive at, you will always find it necessary to change, add or delete. That's part of the fun.

YOU HAVE IT, IT'S BROKEN, BEAT UP OR MISSING PARTS. WHAT DO YOU DO?

Restoration and repair? Your first thought should be" "Wait a minute now." "How is this going to affect the value and does it really matter to me?" Each individual must make up his mind as to what he prefers.

Itis safe to say most collectors would rather have a lure with a beat-up or half missing original paint than a perfect looking repaint. Repaints are out except for the demonstration, or the fun of fishing an old lure and you would rather not risk those fine examples in your collection. Whatever the reason, all repaints of old lures, *no exception*, should be permanently marked as such, somewhere on the body. More about this later.

Save the old beat up plugs that are beyond help. Collectors have assigned a most appropriate name to these, "Beaters." Keep the beaters for hardware. They are good source for replacing bent or broken hardware, eyes, etc., with authentic parts should you come up with a nice body and not-so-nice hardware. There's nothing wrong with that as long as you don't change the original configuration.

Rods in their original, "mint" condition are quite rare and highly sought by collectors. This is especially true of the old split cane rods. It is so unusual to find any old rod in new condition that repair and restoration is permissible under certain conditions.

If the rod is rebuilt and refinished by a recognized rod smith in such a way that the original integrity of it is preserved, then it does not devalue it.

Old reels are frequently found in near perfect working condition. There is usually a good bit of dirt or deposit of some sort, but this can be cleaned off without disturbing original condition. Just don't use any sort of abrasive cleaner or steel wool and *never* use a power polishing wheel. They will damage the finish. If it is not working, take it to a competent professional for repair. Just make sure he knows you don't want any new parts unless they are authentic or taken from another older reel made by the same company. I know two good repair folks in my area and both have a lot of interest in old reels, each keeping a few busted down examples around for just such a case. If they are typical, I don't imagine you will have much trouble in this regard. Keep your reels oiled and free from dust. Operate the mechanisms occasionally. Lubrication has a tendency to pool over time. For heavens sake if you want to load the spool with line, use some old black line or braided line. Never use today's monofilament lines or the new super strong synthetics. These can cause irreparable damage to an old reel.

SOME PITFALLS YOU MAY ENCOUNTER

It may be that most collectors are interested in but one particular type of lure, or merely accumulating an interesting collection of plugs for nostalgia, or even just an attractive colorful display for the den or study. These and other casual collectors are not so concerned with authenticity as is the serious collector. However, all would be well-advised to acquire at least a basic knowledge of the techniques of identification and authentication. There are many items worth hundreds of dollars and a lot more worth $50 to a hundred bucks to a serious collector, although that serious collector would probably be more interested in swapping several attractive and interesting pieces out of his collection or trade box to obtain one.

There are some areas all must be aware of. We have already talked about modifying lures while fishing. This generally takes the form of bending a diving blade or taking a deep diving blade off one plug and placing it on another which happens to be our finny foe's favorite flavor of the day. The same sort of thing went on 60, 70 or more years ago. You may find a South Bend plug with Heddon or Barracuda brand-marked propeller spinners, or a Creek Chub with a Brooks-style diving lip and, woe is me, you might even find all four or more on one body. In the case of hook hardware, there may have been some good and valid reasons for a fisherman to modify a newer plug with older hardware. He wasn't thinking of future collectors of tackle, but of his fishing luck that past spring day on the lake. How about that old sure fire fish-getter that the paint has just plumb wore off? He might spend a winter afternoon doing an absolutely splendid job of repainting it, using another brand plug as his model. Illustrated here is a genuine old plug and another just as genuine in body and hardware, but repainted.

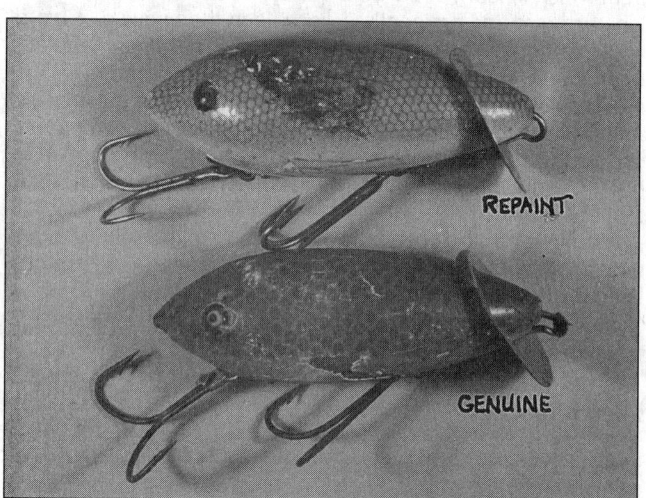

For the purpose of demonstration here, I took a badly beat up Heddon CRAB WIGGLER, removed the hardware and repainted it. I then "aged" the repaint job and replaced the hardware. At first glance it looks genuine. As a matter of fact, if there were no other Heddon plugs of the same vintage to compare it you might reasonable take it for the "real McCoy". However, if you are only casually familiar with the size of the scale pattern of that Heddon vintage, it would jump out and holler "REPAINT!" at you. Repaints are interesting, but collectors do not value them as much as an original paint job in poor condition. If you were able to hold that lure in your hand right now, and know of the many layers of thick, baked enamel and quality and size of the genuine scale finish, there would be no doubt in you mind as to its nature.

NOTE. The demonstration repaint shown in these photos was removed. The plug again repainted, plainly marked Repaint and now resides in my collection.

There is wide availability of modern hardware on the market today. Fortunately it is easy to spot it, but the collector should be acutely aware that out of all the people in and around the tackle collecting hobby, there are bound to be one or two bad apples in

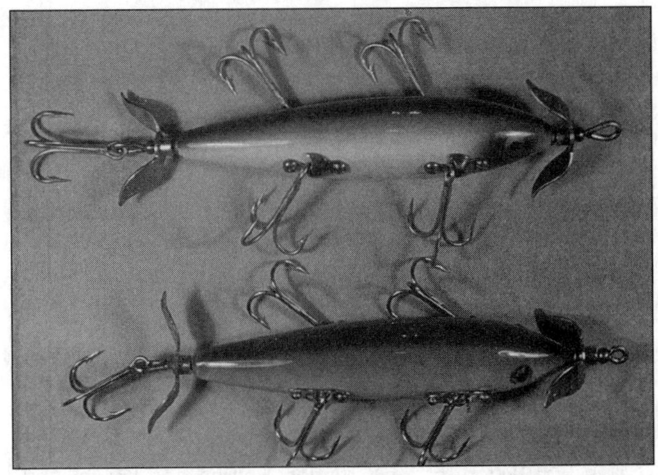

Upper plug in the photo is a mint condition late model Heddon lure. The lower plug is a genuine wood-bodied, glass-eyed older Heddon with an extraordinarily good repaint in the original Heddon rainbow paint pattern.

A wood body, injured minnow type lure made from scratch by the author.

the barrel. With the rapidly increasing interest in collecting plugs, there naturally follows an increasing market for the items that are both genuine and old. There are some, unfortunately, who attempt to take advantage of that. This is not peculiar to tackle collecting, but has followed virtually every area of collecting that has gained in popularity. Sounding somewhat negative here, I hasten to point out that all the dealers and collectors I have had any contact with are completely honest and trustworthy. It has happened, however, and collectors and dealers who are aware of it deplore the situation and vociferously condemn the guilty parties. It is exceedingly rare, but occasionally a theft or misrepresentation happens at swap meets or shows. When it does, you will hear this condemnation over the PA system. There is further discussion of this issue later.

RECOMMENDED REFERENCES AND SELECTED BIBLIOGRAPHY

When I first began writing this book back in 1979 there were only five references to list as devoted to collecting old tackle. As you can see, the 20 years since have seen an enormous increase in those references. Some of these have even gone out of print, but most can be found in a library of any significant size.

You will find six of these references marked with a star. Those books plus the one you are holding in your hand now are probably the minimum any collector should have in his library. It may be more money than you wish to shell out all at once, but any one of them might net you that money back with the identification of just one lure that can be had at a bargain. You could buy them one at a time or split the cost with a buddy.

Your local bookseller can probably locate and order any of the books that are still in print. There is an excellent mail-order source that carries many of the books in this list. The HIGHWOOD BOOKSHOP, P.O. Box 1246, Traverse City, MI 49685, 1-800-425-3966. This shop not only stocks the books, but has reprinted some that have gone out of print.

AMAZING LURES & FLIES by Dickson Schneider, Copyright 1997. Penguin Books USA, Inc., 375 Hudson Street, New York, NY 10014.

Schneider takes us on an illustrated tongue-in-cheek tour of "forty-eight lost masterpieces" of lure making. Illustrations of whimsical, imaginary lures along with descriptive text takes you on a very enjoyable journey all the way to the censored and banned lure and fly. Banned by the government for fear they would result in the depletion of fish in our waters.

AMERICAN SPORTING COLLECTOR'S HANDBOOK, New Revised Edition by Allan J. Liu. Copyright 1982, Winchester Press, P.O. Box 1260, Tulsa, Oklahoma 74101.

This volume is available in soft or hard-bound edition. It covers a wide range of sporting collectibles including rods, reels, lures and decoys. Useful to the collector and fascinating reading. It is currently out of print.

ANTIQUE & COLLECTIBLE FISHING REELS by Harold Jellison and D. B. Homel. Copyright 1996. Published by Forrest Park Publishers, P.O. Box 29775, Bellingham, WA 98228.

Numerous large and detailed photographs. The book includes 200 pages with eight in full color. A guide to the identification and values of all types of reels including some specialty/unusual reels. Realistic price listings.

ANTIQUE & COLLECTIBLE FISHING RODS by D. B. Homel. Copyright 1997. Published by Forrest Park Publishers, P.O. Box 29775, Bellingham, WA 98228.

An identification and value guide for split bamboo, wood, steel and fiberglass rods. Much detailed photography, illustrations and patent details. Particularly handy are the close-up photos of reel seats, ferrules and other distinguishing features.

ANTIQUE FISHING REELS by Steven K. Vernon. Copright 1995. Stackpole Books, P.O. Box 1831, Harrisburg, Pennsylvania 17105.

The first comprehensive reference for fishing reel collectors. Out of print.

BENEATH THE ICE by Ben Apfelbaum, Eli Gottlieb and Steve Michean. Copyright 1990, Museum of American Fork Art, 2 Lincoln Square, New York, NY 10023.

This is the exhibit catalog of a traveling exhibit of fish decoys. It includes a history of the decoy and is profusely illustrated with color photography. 9 x 11 format, 87 pages.

THE BEST OF BRITISH BAITS by Chris Sanford, copyright 1997. Published privately by the author, P.O. Box 256, Esher, Surrey, KT10 9WA, England.

This is the first in-depth study of artificial baits made in the British Isles. It traces their development from Izaak Walton's description of a silk minnow in 1653 through to the 1930's. It is a scholarly work replete with excellent full color photographs, related patent illustrations and text. If one is interested in English lures, this buck is a must. It is of general interest to all lure collectors as European lures are the forerunners of American lures.

THE BOOK OF BLACK BASS, James A. Henshall, M.D. Copyright 1881, revised 1904. The Robert Clarke Company, Cincinnati, Ohio. Out of Print.

You may be able to obtain a reprint of the wonderful old book from the Highwood Bookshop.

THE BOOK OF OLD LURES, Charles K. Fox. Copyright 1975 by Fox Publishers: Freshet Press, New York. Out of print.

A very interesting treatment of old lures and good instructions on how to fashion your own wooden lures for fishing.

CLASSIC & ANTIQUE FLY-FISHING TACKLE, A Guide for Collectors and Anglers by A. J. Campbell. 1997. Available from Highwood Bookshop, P.O. Box 1246, Traverse City, MI 49685.

History, construction, design and identification of old rods and reels. Eight pages of color and over 350 black and white photographs and drawings. Covers the years 1860 to the 1960's. 360 pages.

CLASSIC FISHING LURES AND ANGLING COLLECTIBLES by Dan Homel. Released in 1998 this is a 144-page softcover book in the 8-1/2" x 11" format. It covers the waterfront of collectible lures, tackle and accessories. It also includes many important design patents from 1852 to 1938. Highwood Bookshop, P.O. Box 1246, Traverse City, MI 49685.

COLLECTING FISHING and COLLECTING FLY FISHING by Carl Caiati, copyright 1997. Alliance Publishing, Inc., P.O. box 080377, Brooklyn, NY 11208-0002.

These two books are sized at 4" x 8 1/2" to fit handily in the pocket or purse. Billed as "Instant Expert" books, both are 100-page books giving both the beginning and seasoned collector a handy reference easily carried. Surprisingly comprehensive for their size, they are still limited by that small size. You will, however, be surprised at how much information Caiati has managed to cram into them. Recommended for any collector.

COLLECTING OLD FISHING TACKLE by John Muma. Copyright 1987, National Child Publishing Company, P.O. Box 3452, Lubbock, Texas 79452.

A great little book crammed full of information. It would be useful to both the beginner and the veteran collector.

COLLECTOR'S GUIDE TO CREEK CHUB LURES & COLLECTIBLES by Harold E. Smith, M.D. Copyright 1997. Published by Collector Books, Paducah, KY. Available from Harold E. Smith, 3366 Eskew Road, Boonville, IN 47601.

This is a the great reference book for anyone interested in Creek Chub lures. It is a large-format, full-color hard bound book. It is well researched including some catalog reproductions, a listing of the lures and when production began and ended, plus much more. Highly recommended.

A COLLECTORS GUIDE TO THE HELIN TACKLE COMPANY by Jack L. Turner. Copyright 1996, Jack L. Turner. Available from him at 4348 Palo Verde Ave., Lakewood, CA 90713.

If you are, or are an aspiring collector of Helin Tackle, makers of the famous Flatfish and Fishcake lures, this is the book for you. Turner is a Helin collector extraordinaire and has compiled the most complete work on Helin lures to date.

A COLLECTOR'S REFERENCE GUIDE TO HEDDON FISHING PLUGS by Bill Wetzel and Clyde A. Harbin, Sr. Copyright 1984. Bill Wetzel, 700 Ann Street, Hampton, South Carolina 29924 or CAH Enterprises, 1105 Marlin Road, Memphis, Tennessee 38116.

Super handy little guide for the Heddon collector. Reprinted 1995 by the HIGHWOOD BOOK SHOP and available from them.

THE COLLECTOR'S GUIDE TO ANTIQUE FISHING GEAR by Silvio A. Calabi. Copyright 1989, Wellfeet Press.

A scholarly, full-color hard bound, 9-1/2" x 12-1/2" format book. It covers rods, reels, lures, art and accessories. A very informative and beautiful book. Recommended for any collector.

COLLECTORS GUIDE TO OLD REELS by Dan Homel. Copyright 1991, Forest Park Publishers. Available from Dan Homel, 5163 Ranchos Road, Bellingham, WA 98226.

Covers both British and American reels of all types from wood to metal. Good photography, values.

COLORADO CLASSIC CANE, A History of the Colorado Bamboo Rod Makers by Dick Spurr and Michael Sinclair. Copyright 1992. Centennial Publications, 2835 B Lexington Lane, Grand Junction, CO 81503

This is a history of the Granger, Phillips and Wright and McGill companies. Contains interesting data and many photos and illustrations including early catalog pages. A must for the collector of old bamboo rods.

COLORADO REELS & OLD FISHING TACKLE: A Collector's Guide by Gary Carbaugh and Dick Spurr. Soft cover, 5" x 9", 128 pages.

Covers such companies as Fre-Line, Magic, Wright $ McGill, Humphreys and Humpal.

COYKENDALL'S SPORTING COLLECTIBLES PRICE GUIDE by Ralf Coykendall, Jr. Copyright 1992, Lyons & Burford. Publishers, 31 West 21st Street, New York, NY 10010.

This guide covers a large area including lures, rods, reels, books, prints, decoys and many more. It is a good guide as far as it can go. One book cannot cover all of these subjects, but it is a good starting point and its size makes it handy to carry on the hunt.

***EARLY FISHING PLUGS OF THE U.S.A. Revised Second Edition by Art and Scott Kimball. Copyright 1989, Aardvark Publications, Inc., P.O. Box 252, Boulder Junction, Wisconsin 54512.**

This updated edition of their superb 1985 book is a classic for collectors. It has added some great information about the early days of the Heddon Company with photographs of the family and new lure information. This information was uncovered and provided to the Kimballs by collector Clyde A. Harbin, Sr. Out of print. Reprint available from the Highwood Bookshop, P.O. Box 1246, Traverse City, MI 49685.

ESQUIRE'S BOOK OF FISHING, Robert Scharff. Copyright 1933, Harper and Row, New York.

FIELD AND STREAM TREASURY, Greg and McCluskey. Copyright 1955, Henry Holt and Company, New York.

THE FISH DECOY by Art, Brad and Scott Kimball. Volumes I, II, III. Latest copyright 1993. Aardvark Publication, P.O. Box 252, Boulder Junction, Wisconsin 54512.

This excellent series is an absolute necessity for the fish decoy collector. It is definitive and exhaustive. The Kimballs have worked constantly since the publication of Volume I and each successive book is an addition to the first with each providing new information on the identification of makers and their products.

FISHING IN AMERICA, Charles F. Waterman. Copyright 1975, Holt, Rhinehart and Winston, New York.

FISHING AND COLLECTING OLD REELS AND TACKLE AND HISTORY by Albert J. Munger.

Includes histories and photos of old reels such as Meek, Milam, Talbot, Leonard and more. Out of print

***FISHING LURE COLLECTIBLES by Dudley Murphy and Rick Edmisten. Copyright 1994, published by Collector Books, Paducah, KY. Available from Rick Edmisten, 3736 Sunswept Drive, Studio City, CA 91604.**

This 330-page book is available in a regular and a limited-edition (450) hard bound version. A very good, full-color book dedicated to the "...Most Collectible Antique Fishing Lures." It is an identification and value guide. Every collector should have a copy.

FISHING REEL MAKERS OF KENTUCKY by Steven K. Vernon and Frank M. Stewart, 111. Copyright 1992, Thomas B. Reel Company, P.O. Box 2797, Kenebunkport, ME 04046.

This is a limited edition (950), hard bound book detailing the history of the early Kentucky reel makers and identification of the reels. Covers the years 1813 to 1940. Should be in every reel collector's library.

FISHING TACKLE, A COLLECTOR'S GUIDE by Graham Turner.

This is a large hardcover book that goes into great detail about the history of fishing and tackle. An exhaustively researched work. It is presently available from the author in England, but by the time this book is released it may be available in the states. The address is Hammerton's 55 Hammerton Street, Burnley Lanchashire, England BB 11 1LT.

***FISHING TACKLE ANTIQUES, Revised Edition by Karl T. White. Copyright 1995. Available from Karl T. White, P.O. Box 169, Arcadia, OK 73007.**

A really good reference that has been around quite a while. This latest revision (1995) is thorough and makes it even better. One of the classics for the collector's library. An excellent research tool and highly recommended.

***FISHING TACKLE COLLECTIBLES by George S. (Stu) Lawson. Copyright 1998. Available from Monterey Bay Publishing, P.O. Box 798, Capitola, CA 95010-0796.**

An excellent book for new collectors who need to learn how to navigate in the world of collecting tackle. It is also a very useful book for the old-timer collector. It has lists of shows, organizations, dealer, reference books. appraisers, publications, etc. It also has a great glossary of terms peculiar to this area of collecting. There is a section on grading tackle and detecting fakes as well as good advice on what makes a collectible.

FISHING TACKLE OF YESTERYEAR-A COLLECTOR'S GUIDE by Jamie Maxtone Graham. Copyright 1989. Available from Graham at Lyne Haugh, Lyne Station, Peebles, Scotland EH45 8NP.

This 219-page book is literally crammed with information about every aspect of English fishing tackle and accessories.

FISHING TACKLE MADE IN MISSOURI, by Dean A. Murphy. Copyright 1993. Available from the Damma Publishing Company, 7076 North Shore Drive, Hartsburg, MO 65039.

This book is a fine effort to document early Missouri tackle manufacturer and makers. There are some familiar companies discussed, but many others not covered in references so far. A good reference for the collector. Contains numerous patent application drawings.

FLORIDA LURE MAKERS AND THEIR LURES, Volumes I, II and III, by Bill Stuart, Doug Brace and Russ Riddle. Copyright 1995, 1996, 1997. Available from Bill Stuart, 205 East Hooker Street, Bartow, FL 33830

This is an ambitious project to catalog over 300 lure makers thus far uncovered by their research. It is a comprehensive history and identification guide for the collector of antique Florida lures and their makers. These are the first three of five planned volumes. The fourth may have been released by the publication of this list. A few of them have been made available in a signed, limited edition.

FLY REELS OF THE PAST by John Orrelle. Copyright 1987. American Museum of Fly Fishing, P.O. Box 42, Manchester, Vermont 05254.

Early history and evolution of fly fishing reels is covered as well as many photos. It covers construction of the old reels and the various clicks and drags. All in all, a very complete book belonging in the library of any fly reel collector.

FOLK ART FISH DECOYS by Donald Petersen. Highwood Bookshop, P.O. Box 1246, Traverse City, MI 49685.

Detailed history of early 20th Century and contemporary carvers of the state of Minnesota. Over 500 color photographs. Value guide.

FRESHWATER FISHING, Arthur H. Carhart, Copyright 1949 by Carhart. Publishers: A. S. Barnes and Company, New York.

GREAT FISHING TACKLE CATALOGS OF THE GOLDEN AGE by Samuel Meiner and Herman Kessler with a commentary by Sparse Grey Hackle. Out of print.

A wonderful compendium of old tackle catalog pages and advertising. The accompanying commentary is both informative and entertaining.

GREAT TACKLE ADVERTISEMENTS BOOK I 1882-1930, 1990 revised edition. Larry M. Smith, Editor, 3907 Wedgewood Drive, Portage, Michigan 49008.

A great collection of old tackle advertisements in book form. Good research material. Out of print

GREAT TACKLE ADVERTISEMENTS BOOK II 1874-1955. L. M. Smith, Editor. Copyright 1985. 3907 Wedgewood Drive, Portage, Michigan 49008.

A wonderful collection of old tackle advertisements reproduced in book form. A veritable treasure of information.

HEDDON HISTORICAL FOOTPRINTS BY Clyde A. Harbin, Sr, Copyright 1996. Available from Harbin at 1105 Marlin Road, Memphis, TN 38116.

This is a comprehensive history of the Heddon family and the company they founded. Additionally it reproduces the catalogs from the first in 1902 through 1907. It also covers lures Heddon made for the Edward K. Tryon Company, Von Lengerke & Antoine (VL&A) and Abbey & Imbrie. A prodigious volume useful to any serious collector of Heddon tackle.

HEDDON, THE ROD WITH THE FIGHTING HEART

JAMES HEDDON'S SONS CATALOGUES by The Bassman (C) Copyright 1977, Clyde A. Harbin, CAH Enterprises, 1105 Marlin Road, Memphis, Tennessee 38116.

This is a large book containing reprints of old Heddon catalogs beginning in 1903. In addition to the catalog reprints, the author has provided the collector of Heddon lures with a veritable treasure by meticulously describing and classifying each Heddon lure in organized charts throughout the book. A must for any collector of Heddon lures. Available in reprint form from the Highwood Bookshop.

HISTORY OF THE SPORT OF CASTING, People, Events, Records, Tackle and Literature by Cliff Netherton. Copyright 1981. American Casting Education Foundation, Inc., P.O. Box 182, Herndon, Virginia 22070.

A HISTORY OF ANGLING, Charles Chevevix Trench. Copyright 1974. Follet, Chicago.

A HISTORY OF ANGLING AND ANGLING LITERATURE IN AMERICA by Charles M. Wetzel, Newark, Delaware.

ICE FISHING SPEAR BOOK by Marcel Salive. Copyright 1993. Marcel Salive, 1483 Dunster Lane, Potomac, MD 20854.

This book gives the collector sage information on gauging the quality of construction of ice fishing spears. It includes much information on the construction of the various types with photographs of hundreds of examples. You really can't appreciate the beauty of these spears until you see them.

IDENTIFICATION GUIDE TO HOOKS AND HARNESSES by Tom Minarik. Copyright 1992. Available from Tom Minarik, 16890 Barbara Line, Tinley Park, IL 60477.

For those of you who have ever been stumped or puzzled about the various weird contraptions that seem to be some sort of fishing apparatus, this is the book for you. A really well constructed reference including some 80 pages of illustrations from original patents.

INTRODUCTION TO THE KENTUCKY REEL by Malcolm Clark, Sr. Soft bound, 5 1/2" x 8 1/2" format, 17 pages.

A pretty good little book that does what the tile says. Many black and white photos showing various styles of Kentucky Reels.

LAWSON'S PRICE GUIDE TO OLD FISHING LURES, 1996 Edition. Monterey Bay Publishing, P.O. Box 796, Capitola, CA 95010.

This guide is essentially the same as the one below for reels except this one covers lures. Neither guide is for identification so use of them with ID guides is essential. Over 4,300 listings. It is periodically updated so look for the latest edition.

LAWSON'S PRICE GUIDE TO OLD FISHING REELS, 1997 Edition. Monterey Bay Publishing, P.O. Box 796, Capitola, CA 95010.

This guide is a list of over 5,900 reel prices. If you can't find it here, where else do you look? It is well organized and easy to use. It is periodically updated so look for the latest edition.

LAWSON'S PRICE GUIDE TO OLD FISHING RODS & MISC. TACKLE, 1997 Edition. Monterey Bay Publishing, P.O. Box 796, Capitola. CA 95010.

This is a listing of over 2,600 fishing rods and about 2,000 additional old catalogs, lure boxes, hunting & fishing licenses and miscellaneous other fishing collectibles. It is periodically updated so look for the latest edition.

THE LURE OF FISHING by Herb Berry, copyright 1988. Publishers Xln, 4214 F Avenue N.E., Cedar Rapids, Iowa 52402.

This little-known book about old fishing tackle should be well known. Berry is an excellent writer who presents humor, philosophy and history in a very entertaining manner. His book is full of great detail regarding important patents, illustrations of important lures as well as a few obscure ones. A section of historical sketches of old lure making companies is particularly interesting and useful. Any collector would enjoy this book.

***MADE IN MICHIGAN FISHING LURES by George Richey. Copyright 1995, George Richey, P.O. Box 619, Honor, Michigan 49640.**

A fine reference book for any collector. It is a history and identification guide for the over 400 fine Michigan lure makers and their products. A real plus for any collectors library.

McGINTYS by Richard K. Nissley. 1995. McGintys and Whammies. These are defined and covered comprehensively in this enormous photocopied collection of information. Anyone interested in them cannot do without this book. 325 pages. Available only through the NFLCC Library, 22325 B Drive South, Marshall, MI 49068.

THE MEEKS by Malcolm Clark. Copyright 1988, published by The Kentucky Reel Company, P. 0. Box 3175, Frankfort, KY 40602.

This is a soft bound 20-page booklet crammed full of information about the early Meeks reels in Kentucky. A good reference.

MEISSELBACH & MEISSELBACH-CATUCCI FISHING REELS by Phil White.

Detailed collector's guide with information and illustrations for identification and evaluation of the reels. Well illustrated with old catalog copy and illustrations and advertising.

MICHIGAN'S MASTER CARVER, OSCAR W. PETERSON, 1887-1951 by Ronald J. Fritz. Aardvark Publications, Inc., P.O. Box 252, Boulder Junction, Wisconsin 54512.

Complete information on the identification and dating of the work by this popular carver of lures, decoys, animals, plaques, signs and more. 300 color photos. 104 pages, 8 1/2" x 11".

MONTEGUE RODS. Highwood Bookshop, P.O. Box 1246, Traverse City, MI 49685.

A quality reprint of the 1939 Montegue catalog. 5" x 7 1/2", soft cover, 48 pages.

NFLCC PATCH HISTORY by Kathy Carver. 1993. Available from Carver at 22325 B. Drive S., Marshall, MI 49068.

This is a 22-page booklet containing photographs of and background information on each patch issued by the National Fishing Lure Collectors Club from 1982 through 1993.

OLD FISHING TACKLE AND COLLECTIBLES by Dan Homel. Copyright 1995, second printing, 1996. Published by Forrest-Park Publishers, Bellingham WA.

This 95-page, softcover book covers the waterfront. It touches on split bamboo and antique wood rods, reels, Bass plugs and metal lures and much more. It is impossible for a small book to cover all these subjects comprehensively, but it is a good overview of the hobby.

OLD FISHING TACKLE AND TALES by Albert J. Munger. Copyright 1987 Albert J. Munger.

A good book for any collector of Heddon lures, but out of print and very difficult to obtain.

OLD FLY-ROD LURES by John R. Muma. Copyright 1991. Natural Child Publisher, Lubbock, TX 79413. Available from John R. Muma, 3811 62nd Street, Lubbock, TX 79413.

Muma, along with nine other noted Fly-rod experts has compiled a super book for the collector. It is an exhaustive work containing photographs of 900 lures in 600 full color photographs. A comprehensive work for any fly-rod lure collector. Highly recommended.

ONE FISH, TWO FISH, GREEN FISH, BLUE FISH by Frank Baron. Copyright 1992. Available from Frank Baron, 35824 West Chicago, Livonia, Michigan 48150.

This is a booklet crammed full of information about early Michigan carvers and their fish decoys. Over 60 carvers are represented. A good historical background. Any collector, of fish decoys, especially new collectors, should have this book.

E. F. PAYNE ROD COMPANY, Catalog Reprints. Highwood Bookshop. P.O. Box 1246, Traverse City, MI 49685.

Three catalogs, 1931, 1951, 1975, reproduced in one 88-page softcover book. 6" x 9".

SALMON FISHING PLUGS, A History of Wood Salmon Fishing Plugs from Washington, Idaho and British Columbia by Jim Lone. Copyright 1983. 610 8th Avenue South, Edmonds, Washington 98020.

THE SPOONERS, Harvey W. Thompson. Copyright 1979, Eppinger Manufacturing Company, Dearborn, Michigan.

BUD STEWART, MICHIGAN'S LEGENDARY LURE MAKER by Frank Baron and Raymond L. Carver. Copyright. A limited edition 228-page hard bound book available from Raymond L. Carver, 22325 B Drive South, Marshall, MI 49068.

Essentially a history of Stewart's products from his early folk period through the mass production era to the present where most of the products are made for collectors and not primarily for practical use. Color and black and white photo illustrations.

***STREATER'S REFERENCE CATALOG OF OLD FISHING LURES by Richard L. Streater. Copyright 1978, Richard L. Streater, Mercer Island, Washington 98040.**

The author has provided the collector with a large, loose leaf bound and index-tabbed book dealing with many different companies that produced lures over the years, illustrated. Highly recommended for any new or experienced collector of old lures. Revised 1981. It may be old but it is still the original classic for collectors and extremely useful.

TACKLE TINKERING, H. G. Tappley. Copyright 1946. A. S. Barnes and Company, NY Out of print.

THOSE OLD FISHING REELS by Albert J. Munger. Out of print.

TOP OF THE LINE FISHING COLLECTIBLES by Donna Tonelli, copyright 1997. Schiffer Publishing, 77 Lower Valley Road, Atglen, PA 19310. Tel: (610) 593-1777.

A beautiful, full-color book chock full of the best and most interesting pieces of fishing tackle you could ever dream of owning. This is not just a pretty face, however. It is well written, both entertaining and informative. As an additional plus, there is a collector value range assigned to each item in every photograph. Any collector would love this book.

A TREASURY OF REELS by Jim Brown. Copyright 1990. The American Museum of Fly Fishing, P.O. Box 42, Manchester, VT 05254

An illustrated catalog of the museum's collection of more than 750 reels. Also includes a lengthy introductory essay on the history of reels. 8-1/2 x 11 format, 285 pages.

U.S. FISHING ROD PATENTS AND OTHER TACKLE by Mary Kefover Kelly. Copyright 1993. Thomas B. Reel Company, P.O. Box 2797, Kennebunkport, ME 04046.

A well organized, easy-to-use reference. Limited edition (750), hard bound, a great tool for the identification of antique fishing rods and rod and reel combinations. Hundreds of patents are included.

WINCHESTER CATALOG Reprints. Highwood Bookshop, P.O. Box 1246, Traverse City MI 49685.

1926-27 Winchester Product Catalog - Contains reels along with other sporting goods. 292 pages.

1924 Winchester Fishing Tackle Catalog - Comprehensive catalog covers all their fishing tackle products with 32 illustrated pages.

1933 Winchester Fishing Tackle Catalog - Contains bamboo rods fly rods and casting rods. 35 pages.

WINCHESTER FISHING TACKLE - A Collector's Guide by Phil White. New in 1998 this is a history of Winchester's 10-year foray into the fishing tackle business. It is illustrated with several hundred black and white pictures and drawings of Winchester tackle. It also contains a price guide. 8-1/2" x 11" format. Highwood Bookshop, P.O. Box 1246, Traverse City, MI 49685.

THE WRIGHT PRICE GUIDE FOR THE REEL MAN by Ben Wright. 1997. Highwood Bookshop, P.O. Box 1246, Traverse City, MI 49685.

This 44-page, soft bound book is billed as "A No-Nonsense Straight-Forward Price Guide for Open Face Spinning Reels and Fixed Spool Reels." History and valuation from 1884 to date including 80 photos with over 800 reels listed.

PAUL H. YOUNG COMPANY catalog. Highwood Bookshop, P.O. Box 1246, Traverse City, MI 49685.

A reprint of their 1956 issue of *Catalog of Fine Fishing Tackle* More Fishing Less Fussing. 5" x 7 1/2", soft bound, 61 pages.

VIDEOTAPES

Clyde Harbin has put together a series of eight interesting video tapes that any collector would find useful. They are available in VHS from the following: Antique Lures - VHS tapes, P.O. Box 154087, Irving, Texas 75015 Telephone: 1-800-634-8917. The tapes available are as follows:

Volume 1

Antique and Collectibles: An Overview

Volume 2

Antique Lures: Over 40 of the Rarest

Volume 3

Antique Lures: The Heddon Collection

Volume 4

Antique Lures: Heddon/Stokes Heritage

Volume 5

Heddon Un-cataloged Lures

Volume 6

1903-1916 Heddon Catalogs

Volumes 7 & 8

Heddon/Pradco Lure Collection I and II, Ft. Smith, Arkansas

R.L. (DICK) STREATER, the first to produce a guide for collectors of all brands of fishing lures has produced a wild and wacky 70 minute videotape presenting his collection of novelty lures. *Dick Streater - The Return of the Henny Youngman of Fishing Lures* was taped at a live presentation and is most enjoyable. Copies are available from Dick at P.O. Box 393, Mercer Island, WA 98040.

There is a group of very informative scholarly studies privately published by the active members of the National Fishing Lure Collectors Club. While these were produced for other members of the club and may not be generally available, you might contact the authors or the club about the possibility. They are professionally prepared and are very detailed, valuable illustrated references for the particular companies chosen.

AL FOSS. A history of the company and their lures. By Jim Frazier. Copyright 1985. 312 North 46th Avenue, Hollywood, FL 33021.

THE BOMBER BAIT COMPANY. A study of the company's lures, particularly the Bomber. Copyright 1983 by Jim Bourdon, Nordica Drive, Croton-on-Hudson, NY 10520.

EARLY FISHING TACKLE OF NEW YORK STATE. Anyone with an interest in old tackle would be interested in this study chock full of old advertisements and a plethora of old patent application drawings. Copyright 1985. Jim Bourdon, Nordica Drive, Croton-on-Hudson, NY 10520.

FISHING REEL PATENTS OF THE UNITED STATES, 1838-1940 by Jim Brown. Copyright 1985. 97 Franklin Street, Stamford, CT 06902.

This is a comprehensive, 112-page, indexed list of over 800 fishing reel patents with instructions on how to order copies of them. Available through interlibrary loan from the NFLCC Library.

HENDRYX. This is essentially a reproduction of catalog entries of Hendryx metal lures made prior to the 1919 acquisition of the company by Winchester. Copyright 1986. Harold D. Herr, D.D.S.

CHARLEY LANE. Copyright 1987 by Rich Metcalf. This book shows a New York lure maker in detail. Available from Metcalf, 112 Sutton Drive, Syracuse, NY 13219.

HENRY LOFTIE, FLY FISHERMAN, INVENTOR, TACKLE MAKER. Copyright 1987 by Richard R. Metcalf, 112 Sutton Drive, Syracuse, NY 13219

A HISTORY OF THE ERWIN WELLER COMPANY by Harold G. Dickart. Copyright 1984. This very good study was written specifically for members of The National Fishing Lure Collectors Club and says so on the cover. Contact the club. May not be available to the general public.

JOHN H. MANN, THE MANN FROM SYRACUSE. A history of the man and his lures. Copyright 1986 by Richard R. Metcalf, 112 Sutton Drive, Syracuse, NY 13219

MEMBERS OF THE CREEK CHUB PIKIE AND SURFSTER FAMILIES by Bruce Boyden. A good study that was produced specifically for members of The National Fishing Lure Collectors Club. Copyright 1984. Bruce Boyden, P.O. Box 752, Annex Station, Providence, RI 02901.

THE PONCA CITY BAIT CARVERS. Copyright 1986 by Jim Bourdon, Nordica Drive, Croton-on-Hudson, NY 10520.

SOUTH BEND-THEIR ARTIFICIAL BAITS AND REELS as reflected by the company's catalogs between 1912 and 1953. Copyright 1985 by Jim Bourdon, Nordica Drive, Croton-on-Hudson, NY 10520. Reprinted in 1995 by John Shoffner, P.O. Box 250, Fife Lake, MI 49633

THE WATER SCOUT AND OTHER CLARK BAITS, A Preliminary Report by Ray Barzee and Jim Bourdon. Copyright 1984. Nordica Drive, Croton-on-Hudson, NY 10520.

SOME USEFUL PERIODIC PUBLICATIONS

SPECIFIC TO OLD FISHING TACKLE AND OTHER SPORTING COLLECTIBLES

FISHING COLLECTIBLES. Brian J. McGrath, editor. P.O. Box 2797, Kennebunkport, ME 04046.

This publication is devoted entirely to tackle and issued quarterly. Well worth subscribing to. A must for the collector.

THE FISHERMAN'S TRADER. Joe A. Arches, Publisher/ Editor. P.O. Box 203, Gillette, NJ 07933. Telephone: (908) 647-9356.

I have just become aware of this bimonthly publication through a letter from Joe A. Arches. He states that they are in their third year of publication and that "Many of our readers are collectors of used and antique fishing tackle..." This could be another way to reach collectors. The sample page he sent was interesting and it looks like it might be enjoyable.

SPORTING COLLECTOR'S MONTHLY. RW Publishing, P.O. Box 305, Camden, DE 19934. Telephone: (302) 678-0113.

This primarily a classified and display ad newsletter for sporting collectibles, but occasionally contains short, but interesting articles. The ads are grouped by category of collectibles. It is an excellent source for making new contacts in sale or trade of fishing collectibles

THE CLASSIC FISHING TACKLE MARKET INFORMER. Marc Dixon, 114 East Poplar, Arkansas City, KS 67005

A general interest newsletter covering all aspects of collecting old fishing tackle. Show coverage, history, "the hunt" and editorial content are some of the subjects covered. Edited by a very knowledgeable collector.

SPORTING CLASSICS. Chuck Wechsler, Editor. Editorial offices: 3031 Scotsman Road, Columbia, SC 29223. Subscriber Service Center, same address. Telephone: (803) 736-2424.

This is an excellent bimonthly, up-scale fishing, hunting and wildlife art magazine full of interesting richly illustrated articles and stories. Any hunter or fisherman would find it interesting. It was founded 16 years ago and devoted exclusively to collectibles. It has evolved over the years to make it more widely interesting. I spoke with the editor and he says they are starting to get back into more collectibles.

CANADIAN OUTDOOR COLLECTOR

A publication devoted to Canadian outdoor collectibles. It has been on the internet and in print. The Editor/Publisher is outdoor writer Don Stokes. The publication is undergoing a transition as of this writing. Stokes says it "...is being switched to book form..." What has been published so far has been worthwhile and interesting. For further information contact: Don Stokes, R.M.R.R. Co., 101 Bridge Street W., Napanee, Ontario, Canada, K7R-2C8. Tel: 1-613-354-5768.

THE AMERICAN FLYFISHER. P.O. Box 42, Manchester, VT.

The magazine of the American Museum of Fly Fishing. Published Quarterly.

GENERAL TO COLLECTING

ANTIQUE TRADER WEEKLY
P.O. Box 1050
Dubuque, IA 52004
Weekly tabloid

ANTIQUE WEEK
P.O. Box 90
Knightstown, IN 46148
Weekly tabloid

COLLECTORS JOURNAL
P.O. Box 601
Vinton, IA 52349
Weekly tabloid

MAINE ANTIQUES DIGEST
P.O. Box 1429
Waldoboro, ME 05254
Quarterly tabloid

SOURCES FOR OLD BOOKS AND MAGAZINES ABOUT FISHING AND TACKLE

Many of the old publications from catalogs and magazines to hardcover books are rich in information about tackle from the time they were printed. Many of the sources named here will be glad to supply you with lists of those they have available upon request. Be sure to specify type wanted and include a legal size stamped, self-addressed envelope (SASE). When writing to them, also don't forget to try your own public library. It can sometimes turn out to be very rich source of material.

Highwood Bookshop
Louis Razek
P.O. Box 1246
Traverse City, MI 49685

Kenneth Anderson-Books
38 Silver Street
Auburn, MA 01501

The Anglers Art
P.O. Box 148
Plainfield, PA 17081

Angler's and Shooter's Bookshelf
Goshen, CT 06756

Avocet Books
827 South Homer
Sanford, NC 27330

Judith Bowman Books
Pound Ridge Road
Bedford, NY 10506

Gary L. Esterbrook - Books
P.O. Box 61453
Vancouver, WA 98666

Gunnerman Books
Box 429a
Auburn Heights, NE 48057

Hampton Books
Rt. 1, Box 202
Newberry, SC 29108

Henderson and Park
500 Main
Greenwood, MO 64030

Melvin Marcher
6204 North Vermont
Oklahoma City, OK 73112

MUSEUMS AND ORGANIZATIONS OF INTEREST TO COLLECTORS

A nice display of antique tackle surrounding the NFLCC collector patch of the Luny Frog. These patches are issued annually and are very collectible. A few of them were sold at auction in April of 1995. The prices realized varied from $5 to the $75 the Luny Frog patch brought.

National Fishing Lure Collectors Club (NFLCC)
HC #3, Box 4012
Reeds Spring, MO 65737

The premier organization of fishing tackle collectors. The National Fishing Lure Collectors Club (NFLCC) was founded originally by three lure collectors in the mid-1970s. It has since grown to include several thousand members who collect not only lures, but all sorts of fishing tackle, accessories and ephemera. The NFLCC publishes a very interesting quarterly newsletter very useful to collectors, with a BUY/SELL/TRADE section for members and numerous articles dedicated to the hobby. In addition there is a slick, well-written, well-produced magazine, The National Fishing Lure Collectors Club Magazine and a growing research library that provides much valuable information for the collector. Membership is an absolute must for any collector.

Florida Antique Tackle Collectors, Inc.(FATC)
P.O. Box 420703
Kissimmee, FL 34742-0703

This is a very active organization for those collectors specializing in antique Florida tackle, but it is not limited to that. Anyone interested in old tackle is a welcome member.

Carolina Antique Tackle Collectors (CATC)
619 Elm Avenue
Columbia, SC 29205

A group of collectors from North and South Carolina. They publish a newsletter.

Old Reel Collectors Association (ORCA)
849 NE 70th Avenue
Portland, OR 97213

A helpful organization for collectors of antique fishing reels. Publishes a newsletter.

Antique Outboard Motor Club, Inc.
224 W. Houston
Sherman, TX 75090
George Jacobs, Pres.
(903) 892-2607

American Fish Decoy Association
P.O. Box 252
Boulder Junction, WI 54512

This is an organization of fish decoy collectors. Art and Scott Kimball are the editors of the association newsletter. This club and the newsletter are invaluable assets to this newest, fast-growing segment of fishing tackle collecting.

International Game Fish Association (IGFA) World Fishing Center
Library of Fishes
1301 East Atlantic Blvd.
Pompano Beach, FL 33060

More than just an association, among other things, the IGFA is also a museum of fishing. Since its creation for promulgation of standard and ethical sport fishing regulations and for the establishing of a central clearing house of world records. The IGFA has expanded to include many necessary services and worthwhile objectives over the years. In 1973 they established The International Library of Fishes. In addition to a library of 10,000 books on fishing and tackle, it also has an extensive collection of fishing tackle and angling artifacts, art, photographs, etc. A marvelous place to browse or conduct major research. Their hours are 9:00 AM to 4:30 PM, Monday-Friday. Telephone: (315) 941-3474.

As of this writing big changes are happening to the IGFA. They are building a new $25 million facility in Dania, Florida and planning to move in 1998. Among the new attractions will be a hands-on, interactive museum, a Sportfishing Hall of Fame and an antique and modern fishing tackle gallery. There will be an exhibit showing simulated natural freshwater and saltwater habitats with emphasis on the environmental impact of human activity and many more attractions. There will also be an associated marina and a Bass Pro Shop super store. Bass Pro Shops donated the land upon which the center is being built.

Museum of Fishing
4000 Recker Highway
Winter Haven, FL 33882

This great little museum was born out of necessity, not to house a collection outgrowing its owner, but to deflect the occasional retail customer from disrupting operations at the Bagley Bait Company plant in Winter Haven. At first it was a small retail counter, then a video was added, showing the plant operation without disturbing production and finally, after Bill Stuart, President and CEO of Bagley, made an extensive collecting trip for the museum, the museum was opened up in

1990. It is open to the public, 8:00 AM to 4:00 PM, Monday-Friday. Telephone: (813) 294-4271. There is a small charge for admission, a portion of which goes to a youth fishing program and the Florida Conservation Association.

American Museum of Fly Fishing
P.O. Box 42
Manchester, VT 05354

This museum is dedicated primarily to fly fishing, but should be of interest to other fishermen. Their exhibits also include the tackle of such famous fishermen as Daniel Webster, Bing Crosby, Babe Ruth, all the fishing presidents like Dwight Eisenhower and more. They maintain a growing library of almost 3,000 volumes and an extensive magazine and periodical collection that goes back to 1830. The hours are 10:00 AM to 4:00 PM, Monday-Friday. In the summer between May 1 and Columbus Day they are also open on Saturdays and Sundays. Telephone: (802) 362-3300.

National Freshwater Hall of Fame
Hayward, WI 54843

This is a 7-acre museum complex of several buildings displaying antique fishing tackle and equipment. They have a collection of more than 7,000 lures, 2,000 reels, 400 old outboard motors, fish mounts of different species numbering about 400, some antique fishing boats and just about anything else associated with the sport. The Hall of Fame is also the keeper of the world freshwater fish records. The grounds include several huge (bigger than an automobile) fish models including, a bass, trout, and a bluegill. There is also a muskie measuring half a city block long, standing 4-1/2 stories high, with an observation deck in its open mouth. Hours of operation are 10:00 AM to 5:00 PM, seven days a week from April 15 to November 1.

Nation Heddon Museum
Dowagiac, Michigan

This is a wonderful display of Heddon historical artifacts and examples of almost everything Heddon produced; lures, reels and rods. Housed in the Heddon factory building in Dowagiac Michigan, this is a must see in the home of Heddon lures. The hours are 6:30 to 8:30 on Tuesday evenings and 1:30 to 4:30 Sunday afternoons. They will open the doors just about anytime with a telephone call. The museum telephone is (616) 782-4068. If there is no one there, a recorded message give you another number to call. Don and Joan Lyons, the folks who put this museum together, graciously allow telephone calls at their home for an appointment. Their number is (616) 782-5698.

Bass Pro Shops Fishing and Wildlife Museum
1935 South Campbell
Springfield, MO 65898

This is a commendable effort on the part of the Bass Pro Shops folks. Presently it is a very nice facility showcasing wildlife taxidermy with thousands of animals, old boats, and several thousand fishing lures and other tackle. They have been buying collections for some time now, both major and minor and are presently in the process of sorting and cataloging the items. The museum is well worth a visit now, but when they have finished with the new acquisitions the collection should be nothing less than spectacular. The hours of the museum are 8:00 AM to 9:00 PM, Monday through Saturday and 9:00 AM to 5:00 PM on Sundays. Telephone: (417) 8871915, ext. 4350.

TACKLE MANUFACTURERS PAST AND PRESENT

Research and Reference List

The following list of American Fishing Tackle Manufacturers and/or distributors contains hundreds of names and addresses of firms that no longer exist and some presently in business. Over the years many of these firms went out of business, were bought by other companies, merged or changed their names. The primary reason for the inclusion of unknown or defunct companies is to allow those collectors who may live in or near the addresses given to embark on a little research of their own. Some detective work might ferret out the original owners, their children or relatives or maybe even some former employees. This kind of effort might net the collector a veritable treasure trove of unsold tackle, catalogs, records, etc., socked away in an attic, basement, or garage.

There are many more in the individual company and lure listings later in the book. Don't forget them. There are also some duplications of those in this listing.

A

ABBEY AND IMBRIE — **MIXED**
New York, New York

ABC MFG., CO — **LURES**
Detroit, Michigan

ABERCROMBIE and FITCH CO. — **MIXED**
New York, New York

TONY ACCETTA — **LURES**
853 E. 144th St.
Cleveland, Ohio

ACTION LURE CO — **LURES**
Hollywood, California

ADOLF ARNTZ — **LURES**
24 W. Western Ave.
Muskegon, Michigan

W. and J.M. AIKENHEAD — **REELS**
55 Front St.
Rochester, New York

ALCOE LURE CO. — **LURES**
Fern Park, Florida

FRANKLIN A. ALGER — **LURES**
Grand Rapids, Michigan

ALLSTAR BAIT CO. — **LURES**
1303 W. Jackson Blvd.
Chicago, Illinois

FORREST ALLEN — **LURES**
1658 Summer St.
Stamford, Connecticut

ALLIANCE MFG., CO. — **LURES**
Alliance, Ohio

AMERICAN DISPLAY CO. — **LURES**
Akron, Ohio

AMERICAN ROD AND GUN — **LURES**
Stamford, Connecticut

J.E. ANDERSON RODS — **RODS**
6224 May St.
Chicago, Illinois

ANGLER'S SUPPLY CO — **MIXED**
Utica, New York

FRED ARBOGAST CO., INC — **LURES**
313 W. North St. and
43 Water St.
Akron, Ohio 44303

ASSOCIATED SPECIALTIES — **LURES**
Chicago, Illinois

T.F. AUCLAIR AND ASSOC., INC. — **LURES**
279 Highland Ave.
Detroit, Michigan

B

BARR-ROYER CO. — **LURES**
Waterloo, Iowa

BARRACUDA BRAND — **MIXED**
(Florida Fishing Tackle Co.)
St. Petersburg, Florida

BASS-KING — **LURES**
Brushton, New York

THOMAS H. BATE and CO. — **MIXED**
7 Warren St.
New York, New York

BEAR CREEK BAIT CO. — **LURES**
Kaleva, Michigan

BECKER SHEWARD MFG. CO. — **LURES**
Council Bluffs, Iowa

BENSON-VAILE CO. — **REELS**
Kokomo, Indiana

BERRY-LEBECK MFG. CO. — **LURES**
California, Missouri

BIEK MFG. CO. — **LURES**
Dowagiac, Michigan

BIFF BAIT CO. — **LURES**
4101 Meinecke Ave.
Milwaukee, Wisconsin

A.F. BINGENHEIMER — **LURES**
142 Second St.
Milwaukee, Wisconsin

BITE-EM BAIT CO. — **LURES**
Warsaw, Indiana
Ft. Wayne, Indiana

BLEEDING BAIT MFG. CO. — **LURES**
3404-06 Main St.
Dallas, Texas

BOMBER BAIT CO. — **LURES**
326 Lindsay St.
Gainesville, Texas 76240

T.J. BOULTON — **LURES**
32 Lauderdale St.
Detroit, Michigan

BRAINARD BAIT CO. — **LURES**
St. Paul, Minnesota

BRIGHT-EYE LURE PRODUCTS LURES
19646 Chalmers Ave.
Detroit, Michigan

BRISTOL RODS HORTON MFG. CO. RODS
23 Horton St.
Bristol, Connecticut

BROADCASTER LURES LURES
224 Phelps St.
Youngstown, Ohio

BRONSON REEL CO. REELS
145 State St.
Bronson, Michigan

BROOK SHINER BAIT CO. LURES
Milwaukee, Wisconsin

BROWN'S FISHERETTO CO. LURES
Alexandria, Minnesota
Osakis, Minnesota

H. CORBIN BRUSH LURES
Brushton, New York

JULIO T. BUEL SPINNERS
Whitehall, New York

PAUL BUNYAN BAIT CO. LURES
1307 Glenwood
Minneapolis, Minnesota

BURKE BAIT CO. LURES
2314 West 12th St.
Chicago, Illinois

AL BYLER LURES
Seattle, Washington

C

CARTER'S BESTEVER BAIT CO. LURES
25-1/2 W. Washington St.
Indianapolis, Indiana

CASE BAIT CO. LURES
208 E. Perry St.
Detroit, Michigan

CHARMER MINNOW CO. LURES
Springfield, Missouri

CHICAGO TACKLE CO. MIXED
2725 W. Windsor
Chicago, Illinois

THOMAS H. CHUBB MIXED
Post Mills, Vermont

CISCO KID TACKLE, INC. LURES
2630 N.W. 1st Ave.
Boca Raton, Florida

C.A. CLARK CO. LURES
Springfield, Missouri

COLDWATER BAIT CO. LURES
Coldwater, Michigan

HARRY COMSTOCK SPINNERS
Fulton, New York

THOMAS J. CONROY REELS
28 John Street
New York, New York

MAX COOK MIXED
1608 Glenarm
Denver, Colorado

DAVE COOK SPORTING GOODS MIXED
Denver, Colorado

CRALL BROTHERS LURES
Chicago Junction, Ohio

CREEK CHUB BAIT CO. LURES
Garret, Indiana 46738

D.J. CRITTENBERGER RODS
3210 Ruckle St.
Indianapolis, Indiana

D

DAME, STODDARD and KENDALL MIXED
374 Washington St.
Boston, Massachusetts

DAVID LURE CO. LURES
Peoria, Illinois

ANS B. DECKER LURES
Nolan's Point
Lake Hopatcong, New Jersey

DECKER BAIT CO.
6 Henry St.
45 E. Willoughby St.
Brooklyn, New York

DETROIT BAIT CO. LURES
12248 Woodrow Wilson
Detroit, Michigan

DETROIT GLASS MINNOW TUBE CO. LURES
55 W. Lafeyette Blvd.
Detroit, Michigan

DETROIT WEEDLESS BAIT CO. LURES
6906 W. Lafeyette
Detroit, Michigan

DIAMOND MFG. CO. MIXED
St. Louis, Missouri

DICKENS BAIT CO. LURES
714 W. Superior St.
Ft. Wayne, Indiana

LYLE DICKERSON RODS
Detroit, Michigan

DILLON-BECK CO LURES
Address unknown

FRED D. DIVINE CO. RODS
505 Robert St.
Utica, New York

JAMES L. DONALY LURES
137 Court St.
Newark, New Jersey and
Bloomfield, New Jersey

HARRY F. DRAKE LURES
900 S. 20th St.
Milwaukee, Wisconsin

DRULY'S RESEARCH PRODUCTS LURES
Prescott, Wisconsin

DUNK'S LURES
4186 Vira Road
Stowe, Ohio 44224

E

EAGLE CLAW MIXED
(WRIGHT and McGILL)
4245 E. 46th St.
Denver, Colorado

ECKFIELD BOAT CO. LURES
Algonac, Michigan

EGER BAIT MFG. CO. LURES
Bartow, Florida

ELECTRIC LUMINOUS SUBMARINE LURES
Milwaukee, Wisconsin

R.S. ELLIOT ARMS CO. LURES
Kansas City, Missouri

ENTERPRISE MFG. CO. LURES
Akron, Ohio

LOU J. EPPINGER MFG. CO. LURES
301 Gratiot St.
310-16 E. Congress St.
Detroit, Michigan

ESSENTIAL PRODUCTS CO. LURES
201 Fifth Ave.
New York, New York

ETCHEN TACKLE CO. LURES
Detroit, Michigan

EUREKA BAIT CO. LURES
Coldwater, Michigan

F

FENNER WEEDLESS BAIT CO. LURES
Oxford, Wisconsin

FISCHER-SCHUBERTH CO. LURES
5820 S. Wentworth Ave.
Chicago, Illinois

FISHATHON BAIT MFG. CO., INC. LURES
Okumlgee, Oklahoma and
Ypsilanti, Michigan

FLORIDA FISHING TACKLE CO. MIXED
St. Petersburg, Florida

H. and D. FOLSOM ARMS CO. MIXED
314 Broadway
New York, New York

AL FOSS LURES
1716-1736 Columbus Road
Cleveland, Ohio

FOUR TEES LURES
Tampa, Florida

C.J. FROST LURES
300 Ellis St. and
200 Normal Ave.
Stevens Point, Wisconsin

H.J. FROST and CO MIXED
90 Chambers St.
New York, New York

G

GARLAND BROTHERS LURES
Plant City, Florida

GEORGE GAYLE and SON LURES
Frankfort, Kentucky

GEN-SHAW LURES
Kankakee, Illinois

GENERAL MERCHANDISE CO. MIXED
243 N. Water St.
Milwaukee, Wisconsin

STAN GIBBS LURES
35-39 Old Plymouth Road
Sagamore, Massachusetts

GLADDING CORP. MIXED
(SOUTH BEND)
5985 Tarbell Road
Syracuse, New York 13217

GO-ITE MFG. CO. REELS
Kokomo, Indiana

GOULD and GOULD MIXED
Boston, Massachusetts

GOODWIN GRANGER and COMPANY RODS
1240 E. 9th Ave.
Denver, Colorado

GRAND LAKE FISHING TACKLE MIXED
Springfield, Ohio

J.F. GREGORY LURES
St. Louis, Missouri

H

HASS TACKLE CO. MIXED
8-10 N. Poplar St.
Sapulpa, Oklahoma

F.B. HAMILTON MFG. LURES
Pasadena, California

JACOB HANSON LURES
11 Ottawa St.
30 Manz Ave.
1700 Manz Sts.
Muskegan, Michigan

WILLIAM B. HANSON CO. LURES
939 Pollmey St.
Pittsburgh, Pennsylvania

C.R. HARRIS LURES
449 River St.
Manistee, Michigan
Niles, Michigan
Mackinaw City, Michigan

HASTINGS SPORTING GOODS WORKS LURES
418 Michigan Ave.
Hastings, Michigan

HARDY SMAIL CO., INC. MIXED
Fulton St.
New York, New York

W.B. HAYNES LURES
274 Park St.
Akron, Ohio

JAMES HEDDON'S SONS MIXED
414 W. St.
Dowagiac, Michigan 49047

HELIN TACKLE CO. LURES
333 Elmwood
Troy, Michigan

J.G. HENZEL LURES
1313 S. Fairfield Ave.
Chicago, Illinois

BILL HERRINGTON BAIT CO. LURES
2323 Greenshaw St.
Green City, Missouri

HIBBARD, SPENCER, BARTLETT and CO. MIXED
State Street Bridge
Chicago, Illinois

JOHN J. HILDEBRANDT CO. MIXED
816-1/2 High St.
Logansport, Indiana

JOE HINKLE LURES
505 Augustus Ave.
Louisville, Kentucky

HOLLAND ROD CO. RODS
St. Joseph, Michigan

J.C. HOLZWARTH LURES
(SPRING, HOLZWARTH and CO.)
Alliance, Ohio

HOM-ART BAIT CO. LURES
310 N. Howard St.
Akron, Ohio

HOOKZEM BAIT CO. — **LURES**
3443 N. Harding Ave.
Chicago, Illinois

HORROCKS-IBBOTSON CO. — **MIXED**
Rome, New York
Utica, New York

HORTON MFG. CO. — **MIXED**
245 Horton St.
Bristol, Connecticut

I

IMMELL BAIT CO. — **LURES**
26 Main St.
Blair, Wisconsin

ISLE ROYALE BAIT CO. — **LURES**
Jackson, Michigan

J

JACK'S TACKLE MFG. CO. — **LURES**
Oklahoma City, Oklahoma

W.J. JAMISON — **MIXED**
736 S. California Ave.
2751 Polk St.
Chicago, Illinois

JENNINGS FISHING TACKLE CO. — **LURES**
Olympia, Washington

JENSON DISTRIBUTING CO. — **LURES**
Waco, Texas

LOUIS JOHNSON CO. — **LURES**
40-B N. Wells St.
Chicago, Illinois
Highland Park, Illinois

JOY BAIT CO. — **LURES**
221 W. Maple St.
Lansing, Michigan

K

KALAMAZOO FISHING TACKLE MFG. — **LURES**
610 Douglas Ave.
Kalamazoo, Michigan

KAUTZKY MFG. CO. — **LURES**
Ft. Dodge, Iowa

FRED C. KEELING and CO — **LURES**
Rockford, Illinois

H.H. KIFFE CO. — **MIXED**
521 Broadway
New York, New York

KING BAIT CO. — **LURES**
4312 Chicago Ave.
Minneapolis, Minnesota

M.F. KIRWAN MFG. — **LURES**
O'Neil, Nebraska

K & K MFG. CO. — **LURES**
Toledo, Ohio

A. KLEINMAN — **REELS**
250 8th Ave.
New York, New York

S.E. KNOWLES — **LURES**
72 4th St.
San Francisco, California

JOHN KRIDER — **MIXED**
Second and Walnut Sts.
Philadelphia, Pennsylvania

ARTHUR J. KUMM — **LURES**
Dearborn, Michigan

L

LAUBY LURE CO. — **LURES**
Marshfield, Wisconsin

LAZY DAZY BAIT CO. — **LURES**
Preston, Minnesota

LAZY IKE CORP. (KAUTZKY) — **LURES**
P.O. Box 4827
Des Moines, Iowa 50309

HIRAM L. LEONARD — **RODS and REELS**
Bangor, Maine
Central Valley, New York

LEX BAITS — **LURES**
Louisville, Kentucky

E.J. LOCKHART CO. — **LURES**
Galesburg, Michigan

LOTZ BROTHERS — **LURES**
169 N. Main St.
St. Louis, Missouri

W.T.J. LOWE — **SPINNER BAITS**
Buffalo, New York

M

MAKINEW TACKLE CO. — **LURES**
Kaleva, Michigan

MANTA-RAY CO., INC. — **LURES**
304 E. Wabash St.
Montpelier, Ohio 43543

MARATHON BAIT CO. — **LURES**
Wausau, Wisconsin

MARINAC TACKLE CO — **LURES**
Kaleva, Michigan

MARTIN REEL CO. — **REELS**
(Martin Automatic Fishing Reel Co.)
30 East Main St.
Mohawk, New York

McCLEAN SPORTING GOODS CO. — **MIXED**
400 S. 7th St.
St. Louis, Missouri

McCORMIC BAIT CO. — **LURES**
Kalamazoo, Michigan
Warsaw, Indiana

E.C. MEACHAN ARMS CO. — **MIXED**
St. Louis, Missouri

B.F. MEEK and SONS, INC. — **REELS**
Louisville, Kentucky

A.F. MEISSELBACH and BRO. — **REELS**
10 Congress St.
Newark, New Jersey

MEPPS (SHELDON'S INC.) — **LURES**
Box 508
Antigo, Wisconsin 54409

MERMADE BAIT CO., INC. — **LURES**
Platteville, Wisconsin

H.H. MICHAELSON — **MIXED**
912-914 Broadway
Brooklyn, New York

MICHIGAN TACKLE CO. — **MIXED**
2550 Blaine
Detroit, Michigan

B.C. MILAN — **REELS**
Frankfort, Kentucky

WILLIAM MILLS and SON MIXED
New York, New York
Central Valley, New York

MILLSITE FISHING TACKLE LURES
1415 Michigan Ave.
Howell, Michigan

MOONLIGHT BAIT CO. LURES
Paw Paw, Michigan

H.C. MOORE LURES
432 N. Huron St.
Ypsilanti, Michigan

PHILIP MORRIS CO. MIXED
Nashua, New Hampshire

M

MYERS and SPELLMAN LURES
Shelby, Michigan

N

NATIONAL SPORTSMAN STORE MIXED
75 Federal St.
Boston, Massachusetts

NATIONAL SUPPLY CO. MIXED
Minneapolis, Minnesota

NATURALURE BAIT CO. LURES
104 E. Colorado
1218 Fair Oaks Ave.
Pasadena, California

NEAL BAIT MFG. CO. LURES
320 So. Cherry Street
Columbus, Indiana

NEW YORK SPORTING GOODS Co. MIXED
15-17 Warren St.
New York, New York

FRANK T. NIXON LURES
107 Mt. Vernon Ave.
Grand Rapids, Michigan

O

ROBERT OGILVY CO. MIXED
78 Chambers St.
New York, New York

ORCHARD INDUSTRIES, INC. LURES
18404 Morang Rd.
Detroit, Michigan

ORVIS CO. MIXED
Manchester, Vermont 05254

W.E. OSTER MFG LURES
1620 N. Karlov Ave.
Chicago, Illinois

OUTING MFG. CO LURES
Elkhart, Indiana

OZARK LURE CO. LURES
Tulsa, Oklahoma

F.A. PARDEE and CO. LURES
Kent, Ohio

P

PAW PAW BAIT CO. LURES
Paw Paw, Michigan

PAYNE BAIT CO. LURES
3142 Edgewood Ave.
Chicago, Illinois

E.F. PAYNE ROD CO. RODS
Highland Mills, New York

JOE E. PEPPER LURES
Rome, New York

PEQUEA WORKS, INC. LURES
Strasburg, Pennsylvania

PERRINE MFG. CO. REELS
704 S. Fourth St.
Minneapolis, Minnesota

JIM PFEFFER LURES
Orlando, Florida

PFEIFFER LIVE BAIT HOLDER CO. LURES
52 Clark Court
Detroit, Michigan

PFLUEGER SPORTING GOODS MIXED
1801 Main St.
P.O. Box 185
Columbia, South Carolina

PHILLIPS FLY and TACKLE CO. LURES
Alexandria, Pennsylvania

PICO LURES LURES
P.O. Box 5310
2617 N. Zaryamora
San Antonio, Texas 78201

P and K LURES
122 N. Dixie Hwy.
Momence, Illinois

PONTIAC MFG. CO. LURES
Pontiac, Michigan

EDDIE POPE and CO. LURES
Montrose, California

P and S BALL BEARING BAIT CO. LURES
Whitehall, New York

R

R.K. TACKLE CO. LURES
Grand Rapids, Michigan

RAWLINGS SPORTING GOODS, CO. MIXED
620 Locust St.
St. Louis, Missouri

REDIFOR ROD and REEL CO. REELS
Warren, Ohio

LOUIS RHEAD NATURE LURES LURES
Brooklyn, New York
Amityville, New York

FRED RHODES LURES
Kalamazoo, Michigan

RICE ENG. CO. LURES
912 Stephenson Bldg.
Detroit, Michigan

RIDER CASTING REEL CO. LURES
St. Wayne, Indiana

C.L. RITZMANN LURES
943 Broadway
New York, New York

C.C. ROBERTS LURES
Mosinee, Wisconsin

ROD and CREEL TACKLE CO. LURES
630 Helen Ave.
Detroit, Michigan

H.C. ROYER LURES
335 Wilson Block
Terminal Island
Los Angeles, California

J.K. RUSH LURES
914 S. A. and K. Bldg.
Syracuse, New York

RUSSELURE MFG. CO., INC. LURES
2514 S. Grand Ave.
Los Angeles, California

S

SCHMELZER'S MIXED
Kansas City, Missouri

SCHOENFELD GUTTER, INC. LURES
63 Park Row
New York, New York

JOHN RAY SCHOONMAKER LURES
Kalamazoo, Michigan

SHAKESPEARE CO. MIXED
3801 Westmore Drive
Columbia, South Carolina 29204

SHANNON LURES
816 Chestnut St.
Philadelphia, Pennsylvania

SHAPLEIGH HARDWARE CO. MIXED
St. Louis, Missouri

SHOFF FISHING TACKLE CO. MIXED
407 W. Gowe St.
Kent, Washington

SHURE-BITE INC. LURES
Bronson, Michigan

SILVER CREEK NOVELTY WORKS LURES
Dowagiac, Michigan

SIMMONS HARDWARE CO. MIXED
St. Louis, Missouri

T.S. SKILTON MFG. HOOKS
Winstead, Connecticut FLIES

G.M. SKINNER LURES
Clayton, New York

BOB SMITH SPORTING GOODS MIXED
75 Federal St.
Boston, Massachusetts

JACK K. SMITHWICK LURES
Shreveport, Louisiana

SOUTH BEND TACKLE CO. (GLADDING) MIXED
1950 Stanley St.
Northbrook, Illinois 60065

SPRINGFIELD NOVELTY MFG. CO. LURES
Springfield, Missouri

CHARLES STAPF LURES
Prescott, Wisconsin

BUD STEWART TACKLE MIXED
1032 Ann Arbor St.
Flint, Michigan

STOCKFORD REEL CO. REELS
328 W. Kinzie St.
Chicago, Illinois

SUNNYBROOK LURE CO. LURES
Tyler, Texas

SURE-CATCH BAIT CO. LURES
Versailles, Ohio

T

TALBOT REEL and MFG. CO. REELS
314-316 E. Eighth St.
Kansas City, Missouri
Nevada, Missouri

FRED E. THOMAS RODS
117 Exchange St.
Bangor, Maine

TOLEDO BAIT CO. LURES
1944 Broadway
Toledo, Ohio

TRAPPERS SUPPLY CO. LURES
Oak Park, Illinois

G. ED TREBING CO. MIXED
Address Unknown

TRENTON FISHING TACKLE and EQUIPMENT LURES
429 Greenup
Covington, Kentucky

EDWARD K. TRYON, JR. and CO. MIXED
10-12 N. 6th St.
220 N. 2nd St.
Philadelphia, Pennsylvania

TRUE TEMPER (American Fork and Hoe) LURES
Geneva, Ohio

L.J.TOOLEY LURES
251 Hartford Ave.
Detroit, Michigan

TULSA FISHING TACKLE CO. LURES
1402 East 6th St.
Tulsa, Oklahoma

O.A. TURNER LURES
Coldwater, Michigan

O.C. TUTTLE LURES
13 Tuttle Bldg.
Old Forge, New York

U

UNION SPRINGS SPECIALTY CO. LURES
Union Springs
Cayuga Lake, New York

V

VACUUM BAIT CO LURES
307 Walnut St.
North Manchester, Indiana

VAUGHN'S TACKLE CO. LURES
Cheboygan, Michigan

VESCO BAIT CO. LURES
154 West 18th St.
New York, New York

VEX BAIT CO. LURES
1917 N. Main St.
Dayton, Ohio

VOEDISCH BROTHERS LURES
3429 N. Clark St.
Chicago, Illinois

EDWARD VOM HOFE and CO. MIXED
II 2 Fulton St.
New York, New York

VON LENGERKE and ANTOINE MIXED
33 South Wabash Ave.
Chicago, Illinois

VON LENGERKE and DETMOLD, INC. MIXED
349 Madison Ave.
New York, New York

W

WALTON SUPPLY CO. **LURES**
St. Louis, Missouri

DR. C.S. WASWEYLER **LURES**
461 Mitchell St.
Milwaukee, Wisconsin

WATT TACKLE CO. **LURES**
8500 Nottingham

W.C. MFG. CO. **REELS**
1142 Main St.
Racine, Wisconsin

WEBER TACKLE CO. **MIXED**
(WEBER LIFELIKE FLY CO.)
Stevens Point, Wisconsin 54481

ERWIN WELLER CO. **LURES**
2105 Clark St.
Sioux City, Iowa 51104

WEEZEL BAIT CO. **LURES**
6006 Wooster Pike Fairfax
Cincinnati, Ohio

WIGGLE TAIL MINNOW CO. **LURES**
162 Canfield Ave
Detroit, Michigan

WILKINSON CO. **MIXED**
83 Randolph St.
Chicago, Illinois

L.A. WILFORD and SON **LURES**
Jackson, Michigan

WILMARTH TACKLE CO. **MIXED**
Roosevelt, New York

THOMAS E. WILSON and CO. **MIXED**
WILSON-WESTER W. SPORTING GOODSCO.
New York, Chicago, and
San Francisco, California

CLINTON WILT MFG. CO. **LURES**
Springfield, Missouri

WINCHESTER ARMS CO. **MIXED**
New Haven, Connecticut

ALBERT WINNIE **LURES**
Traverse City, Michigan

F. C. WOODS and CO. **LURES**
Alliance, Ohio

*** WRIGHT and McGILL** **MIXED**
(Eagle Claw)
4245 E. 46th St.
Denver, Colorado

Y

YAKIMA BAIT CO. **LURES**
Granger, Washington

YAWMAN and ERBE **REELS**
Rochester, New York

Z

ZINK ARTIFICIAL BAIT CO. **LURES**
Dixon, Illinois

ZOLI, INC. **LURES**
280 Hobart St.
Perth Amboy, New Jersey

HISTORY OF FISHING REELS

Reels, as we know them today, are direct descendants of the single-action reels used by American anglers in the 18th and early 19th Centuries. There can be no doubt however that reels in some crude form were used several hundred of years ago. In fact, perhaps thousands of years ago, the ancient Egyptians had a reel of sorts. It was a spool-like affair, attached to the "rod" and apparently was merely for storing the line. In the 15th Century an English angler Thomas Barker wrote a book entitled "The Art of Angling". In the first edition he spoke of a "wind" and his expanded second edition (1657) even illustrated this apparatus. He stated, describing the affair, in part: "Within two foot of the bottom of the rod there was a hole made for to put in a wind to turn with a barrell to gather up his line, and loose at his pleasure". It may be of interest to note here that in recent years manufacturers have begun to offer and represent as "the latest" or "newest", rods with reels built right into the handles or butts of the rig.

With the increase in popularity of these rods and reels in pursuing the black bass came the phenomenally rapid growth of the American fishing tackle manufacturing industry.

During the first decade of the 1900s, the manufacturers seemed to compete furiously, almost to the point of the ridiculous. Some companies actually advertised more than 200 reel models and sizes as being available. By the 1920s this situation had generally settled down to more reasonable numbers.

During the Expansion Age came widespread use of the level-wind mechanism, free spooling, and various experiments with anti-backlash devices. The old catalogs are full of various attempts to provide a preventative for this frustrating phenomenon which still plagues today's angler. Even with the highly efficient reels of modern manufacture, it takes practiced skill to avoid the lamentable "bird's nest".

The Spinning Reel

The forerunner of today's modern spinning reels is the Peter Malloch reel. Made by Malloch in 1884 in Scotland and subsequently improved upon in England and France, the Malloch principle was incorporated in the first American-built spinning reels. These reels began to become available in the 1940s, but American manufacturers continued to import European models and often offered them under their own name rather than the European company name.

The American spinning reel came into its own shortly after World War II and immediately became the most popular.

Spinning reels were used exclusively in salt water fishing until the late 1940s when anglers finally discovered its great potential in casting lightweight, artificial lures long distances.

The Four Ages of American Fishing Reels

In the fine book, **The American Sporting Collector's Handbook*, Mr. Warren Shepard has set down "The Three Ages of Fine Reels". He has divided the history and development of reels very logically and in the interest and need of standardization we shall define these ages, add a fourth and use the same natural divisions in the discussion of reel history. The four ages are: THE SMITH AGE - Reels & Rods that were handcrafted by American reelsmiths (usually signed) from about 1800 to roughly 1875. Reels from this period are represented by reelsmiths such as Clark, Conroy, Hardman**, Krider**, Meek**, Milam**, Noel**, Sage**, Shipley and Snyder**.

**Edited by Allan J. Liu, Copyright 1976 by Winchester Press.*

***Kentucky reelsmiths fashioning the earliest brass and silver multiplying reels.*

These three reels, various pieces of fishing gear and award medals were the property of Mr. Fred N. hite of Chicago, Illinois. White at one time held the casting championship for all weights of plugs in the late 1920s. The reels are identified in the photograph value section. All items came from White's tackle box.

THE GOLDEN AGE - The beginning of the Golden Age is represented by the early machine-made reels. The period from 1875 to 1900 saw the development of high-quality manufactured reels, usually made on a lathe, fitted and assembled by hand. Some of the best of this period are represented by makers such as Conroy, Vom Hofe, Leonard, Meek, Meisselbach, Milam, Orvis, Perry, and Talbot.

THE EXPANSION AGE - So called because of the surge in growth of American tackle manufacture. Mr. Shepard defines this period as being from 1900 to 1930. The most notable companies representing this period are Heddon, Hendryx, Horrocks Ibbotson, Pflueger, Shakepeare, South Bend and Creek Chub.

THE TECHNOLOGY AGE - The period of time from 1930 to the early 1950s saw the beginning of spin fishing and spinning tackle manufacture in the U.S. (about 1935-1940). It was during years that great technical advances in use of materials were made, modern plastics and alloys. Light-weight, high-speed reels were manufactured on highly mechanized assembly lines. The earliest reels of this period are collectible, but not quite so desirable as those from the earlier three ages. The exception of course would be the fine hand-made products of Bogdan, FinNor, Vom Hofe, and Zwarg.

Undoubtedly the first mechanical reels in America were single-action models brought from Europe. The first known American-made were hand-made and dated from about 1800. The hand-made reels of George Snyder, dating about 1800-1810, are the most notable among the first.

Snyder was a Kentucky fisherman who was also a watchmaker and silversmith. He made spool reels in his shop and is credited with the development of the first multiplying reel. The reel has a four to one gear ratio. Snyder never went into a commercial enterprise but remained in his chosen profession. He fashioned the reels only for himself and friends. This was the birth of the Kentucky Reel.

The first Kentucky Reels were made commercially available through the efforts of another watchmaker, Mr. Jonathan F. Meek who, with his brother Benjamin F. Meek, went into the business of commercial manufacture in 1835. An apprentice reelsmith, Benjamin C. Milam later became a partner also, leaving the company in 1851 to make reels on his own.

The Meeks developed the first mechanically actuated, adjustable clicks and drags, but both were rather crude at first and cumbersome to operate.

J. L. Sage, A.B. Shipley, and Thomas Conroy, all of Kentucky are other notable reelsmiths working during this period.

Until the end of the Civil War most reel bodies were made of brass and some were of silver. Thereafter the better reels were made of nickel or "German Silver", an alloy of nickel, copper and zinc.

Before the advent of machine-made reels around 1875 most were unmarked, but many were signed by the reelsmith, ie: "J. CONROY, MAKER". Many of the truly fine old reels will also be found with a dated presentation inscription engraved in the beautiful script style of the day.

Reels from the Golden Age (1875-1900) are much more easily found than the early hand-made ones. This era saw the advent of the "Henshall Rod" and the "Chicago Rod". These were the first rods with which the multiplying reels could be used efficiently in bait casting. Used with these rods, the reels experienced an increased popularity and more widespread acceptance and use. This development is responsible, in the main, for the rapid growth of the fishing tackle beginning around 1900, the birth of the Expansion Age of tackle manufacture.

Toward the end of the Golden age a new reel was patented (1887). It was called the "Henshall-Van Antwerp Black Bass Reel" and incorporated what is thought to be the forerunner of today's Star Drag.

IDENTIFICATION AND LISTING OF OLD REELS

Many of the early craftsman and manufacturers identified their products by engraving or stamping their names and/or patent dates, etc., on them but later years saw the advent of decals, hot stamps, stencils, etc. The trouble is many others did not bother with this identification and those can defy the most knowledgeable to the point of frustration. Here we will discuss some general and some specific methods of determining dates and origins of reels.

The scarcest and most valuable reels are those that were hand-crafted from about 1800 to 1875. After that, more modern mechanized production methods were prevalent in the industry. Those early reels were usually signed by the reelsmith. Often they also had beautiful presentation engravings: "Presented to so and so by so and so, dated".

George Snyder, the man usually credited with the beginning of the Kentucky reels, made his earliest reels of brass and all where quadruple multipliers (4:1 ratio). They incorporated jewel pivots and square, steel gears. Watchmaker Snyder knew the jeweled movements to be the most advanced state of pivots at the time. These early models had the ends of the pillars riveted to one of the base plates and the other ends secured by wire. Later this was improved by Milam and Hardman. They introduced screws to fasten them for easier dismantling for repairs and lubrication. The screws on Meek reels made after about 1840-45 were each numbered to match the number stamped beside each screw hole. After about 1865, the reels were also made larger and in a double multiplier model for the saltwater fisherman.

The reels of this period are exceedingly rare and valuable. The collector who obtains one should consider himself a lucky individual indeed, for few will ever possess even one example.

There are today six basic types of reels. They are the bait-casting reel, spinning reel, spin casting reel, fly casting, saltwater reel, and the special use reels. Of these, the bait-casting, the fly-casting and the salt water reels are the most popularly collected types. Early spinning reels are beginning to enjoy popularity as well.

The following pages will aid the collector in identification of reels and where possible indicate an earliest possible date of manufacture. It is of necessity, only a sampling. Because of the great variety of reels made prior to the 1800s, they are not listed individually. The early Kentucky reels of the 1840s are also quite scarce, but the collector may get lucky and happen upon one.

The reel listing is set up according to manufacturer. All reels that could be found listed and priced, and reasonably attributed to that company as the actual manufacturer are listed as such. Because there were literally hundreds that had reels manufactured by others, but bearing only the distributor's name, there is much room for error. It is hoped however that the lists will be of help in identifying reels in your collecting efforts.

ANATOMY OF A REEL

The National Fishing Lure Collectors Club (NFLCC) has set up a standard for rating reels in both appearance and mechanical condition. It is set forth here in the hope that we will all adhere to these standards. At the very least it might eliminate some confusion in communicating with fellow collectors.

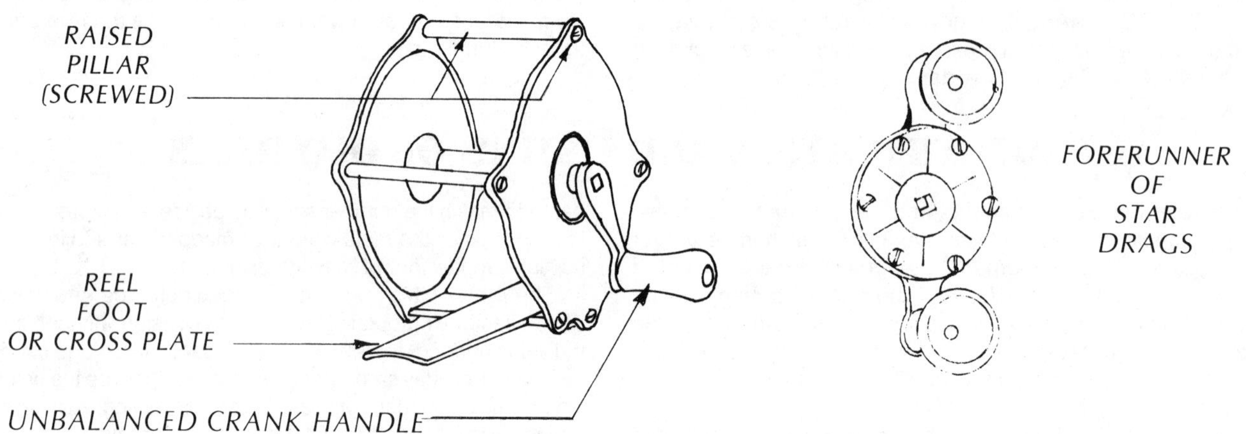

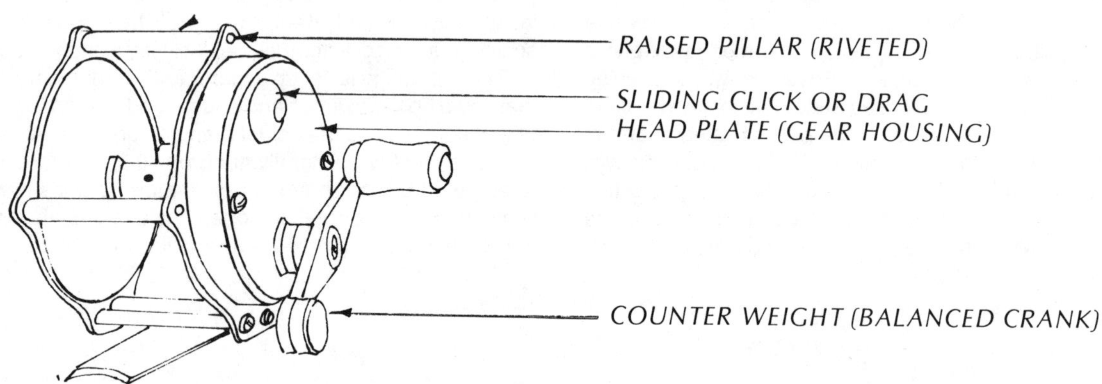

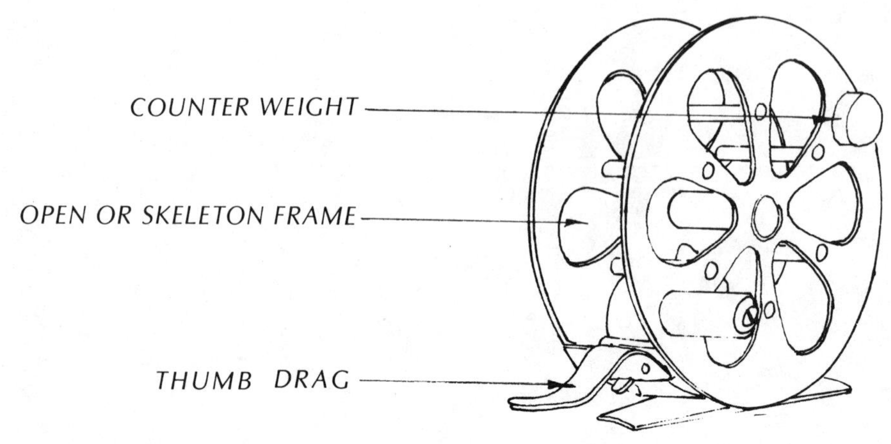

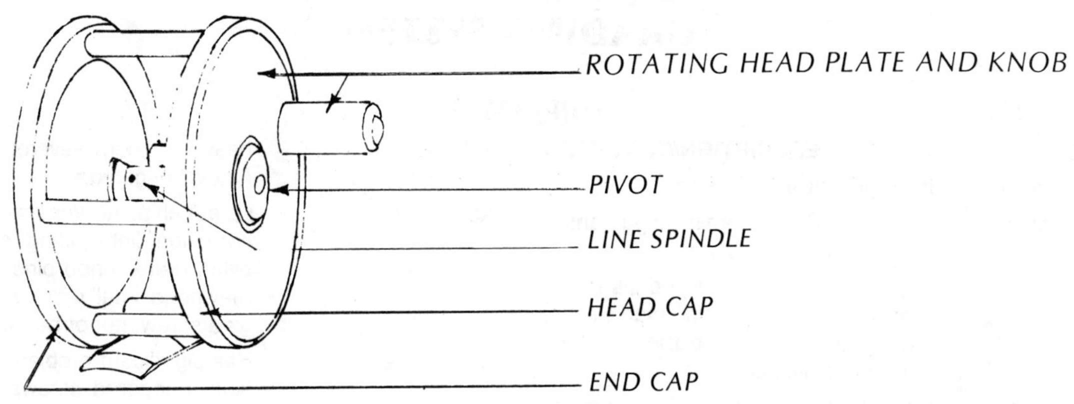
ROTATING HEAD PLATE AND KNOB
PIVOT
LINE SPINDLE
HEAD CAP
END CAP

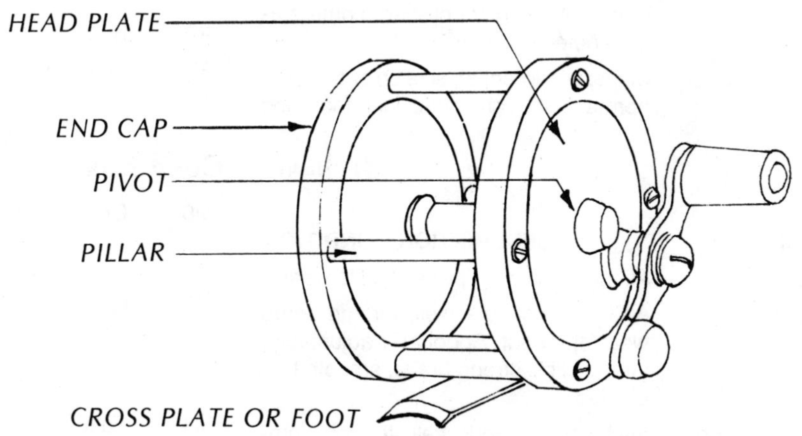
HEAD PLATE
END CAP
PIVOT
PILLAR
CROSS PLATE OR FOOT

NFLCC STANDARD REEL GRADING SYSTEM

Appearance

CONDITION		DESCRIPTION/CONDITION
Mint	Never used	In original factory condition.
A10	Unflawed	Looks "Mint", but there is no guarantee as to whether it was used.
A9	Excellent	Hard rubber still polished; edges sharp; marking sharp; machining marks crisp; plating intact; no corrosion, pitting, chips or scratches.
A8	Very Good	Occasional light scratch; minor normal plating wear; rubber edges may not be sharp; minor foot imperfections; clean; crank knobs tight.
A7	VG	Small chips; some plating wear; screw slots obviously used; light cleaning required; if recently polished, some surface defects.
A6	Good	Chips; small dent(s); scratch or two from normal use, light corrosion; foot filed heavily or bent severely; some screw heads buggered.
A5	G-	Larger chips and/or scratches; heavier corrosion, light pitting; slight bends in pillar, crank; knob pins bent or loose; may need small replacement part such as a screw, nut or bearing cap.
A4	Fair	Has significant problem. Heavy corrosion; buggered screws; cracked rubber plate; small broken part; missing major part(s)such as pillar, line guide, click button; foot seriously damaged.
A3	F-	More serious problems. Broken foot or other frame part; bent or badly dented plates.
A2	Poor	May be useful for parts.
A1	Valueless	No aesthetic value.

Mechanical Condition

SCALE OF CONDITION		DESCRIPTION/CONDITION
M10	Excellent	All functions work perfectly. No wear.
M9	Exc-	All functions work well, though some wear apparent. Spool fully adjustable; strong click, strong brake; smooth level-wind.
M8	Very Good	All functions work well, though complete adjustment may not be possible. Slight spool, dinging; some click wear; brake pressure may not be maximal.
M7	VG-	Normal use and wear. Spool "sloppy", click weakening; level-wind slight wobble.
M6	Good	All functions work, but some may be fairly worn; some gear noise; click may slip or be very weak; needs new pawl.
M5	G-	All functions work, but with some difficulty; click or brake not functional; level-wind jams; broken gear tooth or worn gears.
M4	Fair	Functional problems requiring replacement parts to make operable.
M3	F-	Major functional problems, possibly due to missing or broken parts that are not easily replaced.
M2	Poor	Major problems.
M1	Valueless	No mechanical value.

ILLUSTRATED REELS

The 56 wonderful illustrations of reels on the next few pages were taken from a 1928 Diamond Brand Fishing Tackle catalog published by Shapleigh's in St. Louis Missouri. They should be a great aid in identifying some reels that may be found. The copy from each reel listing in the catalog is also reproduced here. Those marked as UNKNOWN were not identified in the catalog. They were only described beneath the illustration.

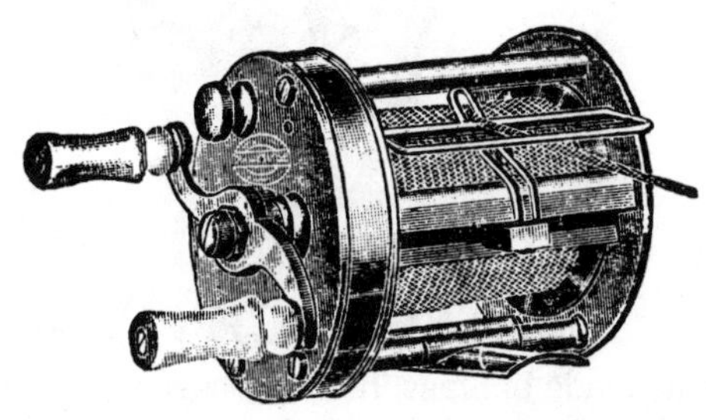

SOUTH BEND

LEVEL WINDING ANTI-BACK-LASH REEL

Made of German silver with double ivoroid grip; jewel spool caps, one of which is adjustable; diameter of spool, 1-1/2 inches; Quadruple multiplying.

Thumbing and spooling are entirely eliminated; Absolutely cannot back-lash or tangle; and upon reeling in it automatically spools itself, winding the line perfectly smooth and even. Adjustment screw on side of reel which allows drag on anti-back lash device to be taken off; thereby this reel level can be converted into a free-winding type.

SOUTH BEND 550

No. 550 LEVEL WINDING ANTI-BACK-LASH REEL

Frame is highly nickel and plated brass with double grip of black ivoroid riveted to crank. Quadruple multiplying gears of Hunting-tooth train type, that equalizes the wear on all teeth. Spool bearings run in bronze bushings; adjustable spool caps; spool diameter is 1-1/2 inches; width, 1-3/4 inches.

SOUTH BEND

ANTI-BACK-LASH REEL

Made of German silver with double ivoroid grips and jewel spool caps, one of which is adjustable; diameter of spool, 1-1/2 inches; Quadruple multiplying.

Anti-back lash enables beginner to cast with precision. The brake action applies itself only for a fraction of a second when the bait hits the water; there is no continuous drag to retard the cast; adjustment screw on side, which allows this reel to be converted into the free-running type of reel.

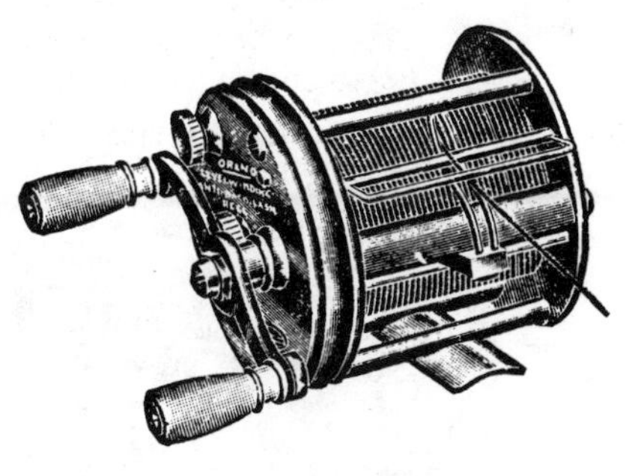

SOUTH BEND-ORENO

LEVEL WINDING ANTI-BACK-LASH REEL

Highly nickel plated with Ivoroid double grips, jewel spool caps, one of which is adjustable; diameter of spool, 1-1/2 inches; quadruple multiplying.

Thumbing and spooling are entirely eliminated; absolutely cannot back-lash or tangle; and upon reeling in it automatically spools itself, winding the line perfectly smooth and even. Adjustable screw on side of reel which allows drag on anti-back lash device to be taken off; thereby this reel can be converted into a free running, level-winding type.

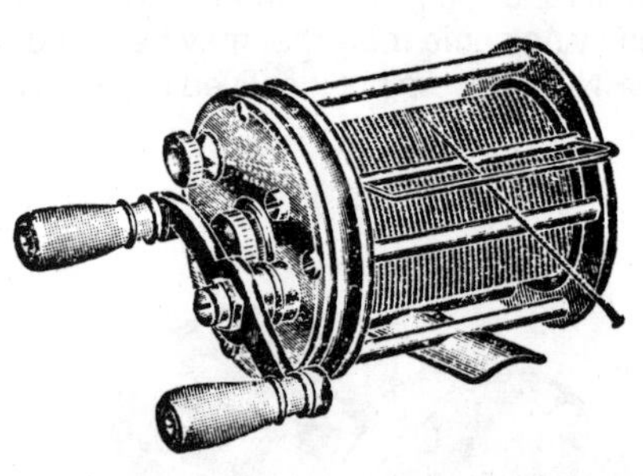

SOUTH BEND-ORENO

NO. 900 ANTI-BACK-LASH REEL

Nickel plated, brass with double Ivoroid grips and jewel spool caps, one of which is adjustable; diameter of spool, 1-1/2 inches; Quadruple multiplying.

Anti-back lash enables beginner to cast with precision. The brake action applied itself only for a fraction of a second when the bait hits the water; there is no continuous drag to retard the cast. Adjustable screw on side, which allows this reel to be converted into the free-running type of reel.

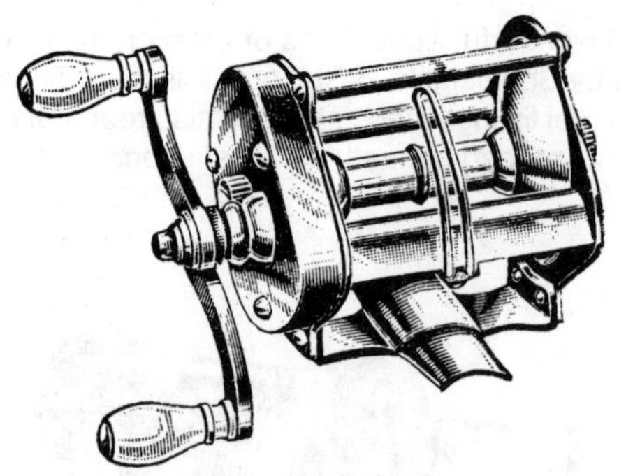

MEISSELBACH FLYER

Frame made of brass, heavily nickel plated; spool flanges; nickel silver; brass arbor; nickel steel pivots running in phosphor bronze bearings; adjustable end bearings; Pin which travels in groove of level wind shaft is made of long-wearing hardened steel. Copper-coated to prevent rust; back sliding click; double handle with white celluloid thumb pieces.

HEDDON CHIEF DO-WA-GIAC

THE REEL WITH THE MECHANICAL THUMB

The mechanical thumb is an effective anti-back lash device, adjustable to any weight of bait and does away with constant thumbing of spool. Parts of level winding mechanism are chromium plated, therefore non-rusting and non-corroding. Click made of hardened steel with phosphor bronze spring. jeweled adjustable screw caps; reel has a highly nickeled finish; double handle with Ivoroid grips.

MEISSELBACH NO. 100

BULL'S EYE LEVEL WINDING REEL

Heavy nickel plated brass frame; brass arbor and nickel silver spool flanges; nickel steel, rust resisting pivots run in phosphor bronze bearings; both adjustable and removable; the end plates are made of "Permo", a tough, tenacious (not brittle) material; it is light and strong; highly polished and not affected by water or oil.

The one piece seat is a cross bar type; "Permo" end plates come in assorted colors of green, red, brown or black.

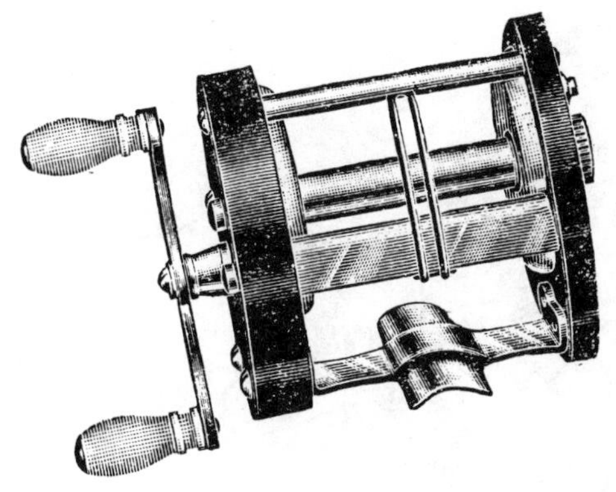

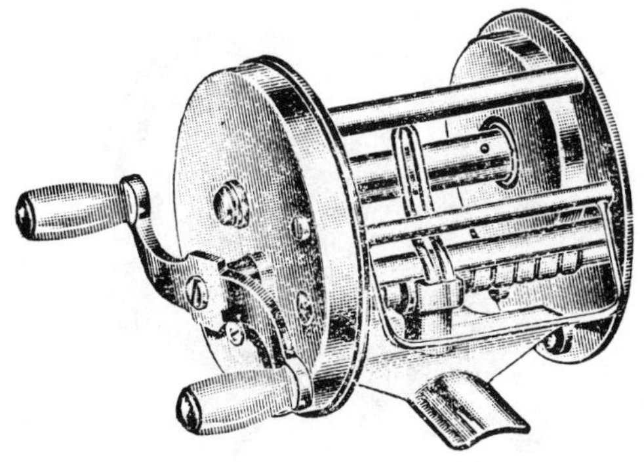

MEISSELBACH

LEVEL WINDING REEL

Frame constructed of heavy nickel plated brass; brass arbor and nickel silver spool flanges; nickel steel rust-resisting pivots; genuine Bakelite end plates guaranteed against breakage; large double handle with tension adjusting end cap; full quadruple action; a substantial and well made reel.

MEISSELBACH

ALUMINUM LEVEL-WINDING TAKE DOWN

Cast aluminum head cap and tail plate frosted finish, perfectly balanced double crank handle , special take down feature; bearings of nickel alloy, phosphor bronze; click level winding screw of phosphor bronze and tool steel pawl; click and drag combined in one unit; Quadruple multiplying.

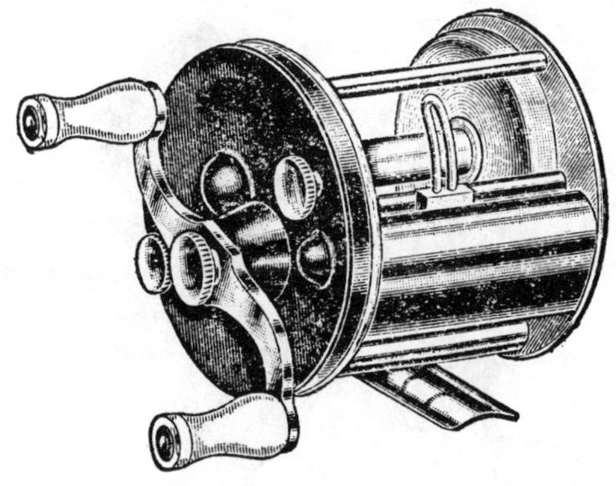

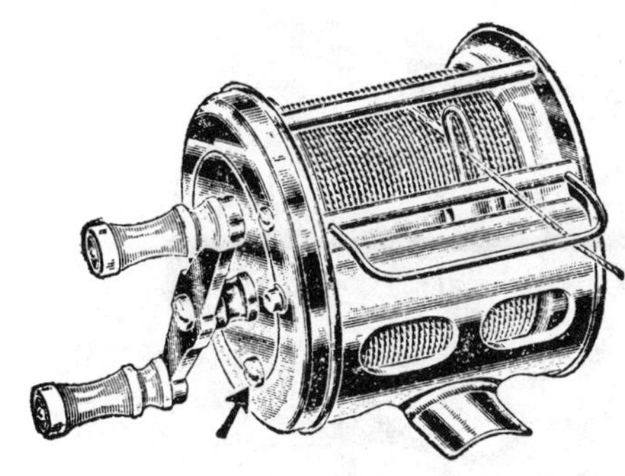

MEISSELBACH

PEERLESS LEVEL WINDING REEL TAKE DOWN

Gears of tempered metal; line carriage of special alloy; bushings of best material; click and drag combined in one member. Head cap made of Bakelite; balance nickel finished.

Transverse screw made phosphor bronze, pawl of tool steel. Slightly more than quadruple multiplying. Length of spool, 1-7/8 inches; diameter, 1-1/2 inches; weight each, 7 1/4 oz.

MEISSELBACH

MODERN LEVELWIND AND ANTI-BACK LASH

Polished nickel finish scribed panels plated; perfectly balanced crank handle, celluloid grips; tempered and hardened gears; transverse screw and line carriage of special alloy; Bushings made of metal; drag lever made of nickel silver alloy; drag lever adjusting spring made of finest tempered bronze; Crank and drag combined in one member; length of spool, 1-7/8 inches; diameter, 1-1/2 inches.

MEISSELBACH

LION ANTI-BACK LASH LEVEL WINDING

Satin finish, equipped with adjustment screw for regulating anti-back lash device whereby, any tension desired may be put on back-lash drag. Also can be set to release anti-back lash device entirely; equipped with double crank handle, tempered gears; transverse screw of phosphor bronze; line carrier of a special alloy; spool shaft of tempered steel running in metal alloy bushings. Quadruple multiplying click and drag combined in one unit.

MEISSELBACH

LION LEVEL WINDING REEL

Satin finish throughout; equipped with perfectly balanced double crank handles; tempered gears; transverse screw of phosphor bronze; line carriage of a special alloy to give best possible service; spool shaft of tempered steel, running in metal alloy housings; quadruple multiplying; click and drag combined in one unit.

MEISSELBACH

MODERN LEVEL WINDING

Plate frame supports; polished nickel head and tail plates; perfectly balanced crank handle with two celluloid grips; tempered and hardened gears; transverse screw and line carriage of a special alloy; bushing of both screw and spool made of special alloy metal; slightly more than quadruple multiplying; click and drag are combined in one member; length of spool, 1-7/8 inches; diameter, 1-1/4 inches.

DIAMOND KING

LEVEL WINDING REEL

TAKE DOWN

Plate frame construction with inserted heads; riveted gears; riveted steel plate; polished and buffed; head and tail plated; perfectly balanced letter "S" handles; Ivory grips; special head screw take down feature permits taking apart the reel without tools; tempered and hardened bronze transverse screw with special alloy steel pawls; full quadruple action.

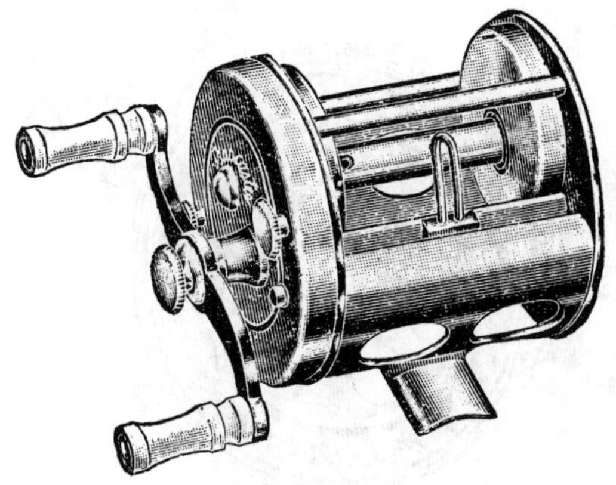

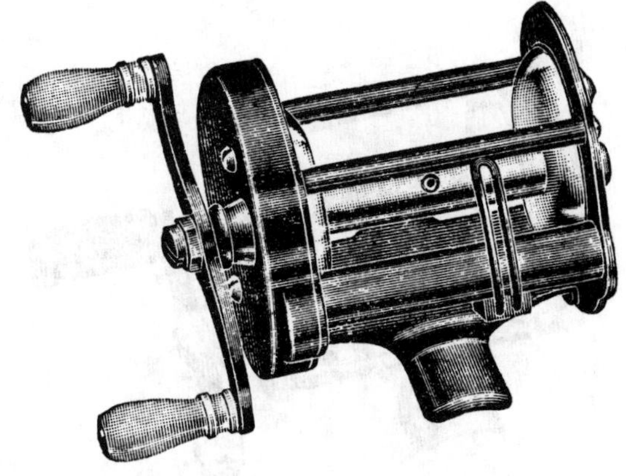

DIAMOND KING

BASS CASTER LEVEL WINDING

Take Down

Plate frame construction; polished nickel head and plates; perfectly balanced crank handle celluloid grips; special head take down feature permits taking apart without tools. Riveted gears, tempered and hardened bronze transverse screw with special alloy steel pawl; click and drag are combined in one member quadruple action.

UNKNOWN

Frame constructed of heavy brass gun-metal finish, with nickel silver spool; double celluloid handle; tempered and hardened gears; has good substantial click; quadruple multiplying; diameter of spool, 1-3/8 inches; Length of spool, 1-7/8 inches.

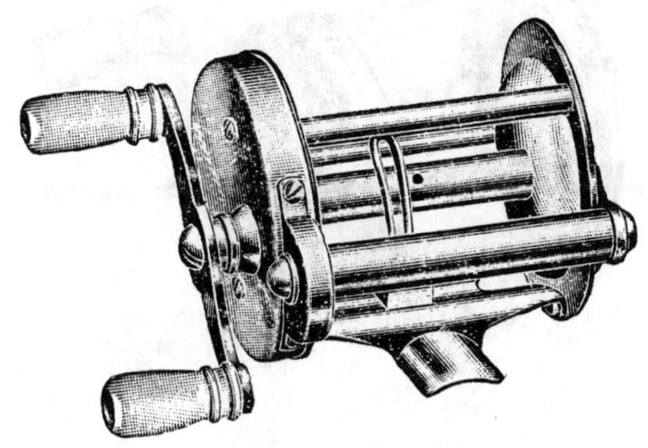

DIAMOND KING

UNION

Polished nickel finish, with smooth head and end plate. Perfectly balanced crank handle with celluloid grips, tempered and hardened gears; hardened transverse screw; line carriage of special alloy hardened bushing of both screw and spool; good substantial click; stamped brass plate riveted and reinforced, set in with screws.

Diameter, 2 inches; length of spool 1-7/8 inches.

MEEK

B.F. MEEK and SONS BLUE GRASS No. 3

German silver throughout, satin and hand burnished finished; spiral gears; gear cut from finest bronze; steel cut spiral pinion; tempered tool steel pivots and stud; box pattern front head; absolutely dust and water proof; fine scroll counter balanced handle with genuine ivory thumb piece; accurately and smooth working adjustable steel click and drag on front head plate; screw-off oil caps; all parts handsomely milled, knurled and finished. Diameter of end plates, 2 inches; length of spool, 1-5/8 inches.

B.F. MEEK AND SONS

BLUE GRASS SIMPLEX IMPROVED TAKE DOWN STYLE

With New Style Thumb Rest

Brass nickel plated frame; one piece seamless drawn tubing; German silver plates and spool with polished brass shaft; spiral gear; gear cut from one piece hard drawn brass rod; pivots tempered, ground and polished; front plate rigidly fixed in frame; rear plate screwed into frame; sliding click drag on back plate, diameter of plates; 1-3/4 inches; length of spool, 1-3/8 inches; quadruple action; with plain German silver pivot bearings.

BOYER

WINONA

Spool made of one piece cast aluminum; finely machined to insure perfect balance and true running; entire reel highly nickel plated; bronze bearing; tool steel shaft; hard brass plate; very easily taken apart without tools; has only one place to oil; adjustable drag which can be set for heavy trolling; capacity, approximately 100 yards.

B.F. MEEK AND SONS

BLUE GRASS

German silver take-apart improved design; German silver spool with hardened and polished brass shaft; hardened steel axles; Bronze gear and steel pinion; German silver sliding steel click with steel pinion, pawl and spring; No drag; German silver balance handle with celluloid thumb piece. Diameter of plates, 1-7/8; length of spool, 1-1/2 inches.

MEISSELBACH

TRI-PART No. 80

Tubular brass frame; brass end plates and ring frame cut from drawn brass tube; all nickel plated and polished; satin finish end plates; German silver spool; polished brass shaft and hardened steel axles; bronze gear and steel pinion; back sliding steel click; with steel pinion, pawl and spring; milled oil and friction adjusting cap on tail plate. Quadruple action; diameter of plates, 2 inches; width of spool, 1-3/8 inches.

MEISSELBACH

TAKAPART

Tubular brass frame; brass end plates and rings; frame cut from drawn brass tube; all nickel plated and polished; German silver spool, polished brass shaft and hardened steel axles; bronze gear and steel pinion; back sliding steel click with steel pinion, pawl and spring; milled oil and friction adjusting cap on end plate. Quadruple action; diameter of plates 2 inches; width of spool, 1-5/8 inches.

DIAMOND BRAND

ST. LOUIS CASTING

Highest quality German silver frame; spool and shaft steel axles running in hardened brass bearings; phosphor bronze gear; German silver double handles with celluloid thumb pieces; back sliding steel click accurately milled and nicely knurled.

DIAMOND BRAND

ULTRA CASTING

Highest quality German silver frame; German silver spool with hardened and polished brass shaft; Steel axles running in phosphor bronze bearings; Phosphor bronze gear; double German silver balance handle, with celluloid thumb pieces; Back sliding steel click; accurately milled and handsomely knurled. Diameter of plates, 2 inches; length of spool, 1-7/8 inches; Quadruple action, with agate jeweled end bearing oil cups.

DIAMOND BRAND

MAYFAIR CASTING

German silver finish; highest quality German silver frame and spool with hardened brass shaft; steel axis running in hardened brass bearings; phosphor bronze gear; German silver balance handle with white celluloid thumb pieces; back sliding steel click; knurled disc; oil caps and handle hub. Diameter of plates, 2 inches; length of spool, 1-7/8 inches. Quadruple action; with large ruby jeweled end bearings oil caps.

DIAMOND BRAND

SENECA

Brass, nickel plated and polished; brass spool and shaft; steel axles running in hardened brass bearings; machine cut gears; spring steel click and drag; knurled oil caps and handle hub. Diameter of plates, 2 inches; length of steel spool, 1-7/8 inches. Quadruple action; with agate jeweled oil caps.

DIAMOND BRAND

ROYAL

Brass, nickel plated and polished; well balanced handle with white thumb piece; brass spool and shaft; back sliding steel click; all parts carefully milled, and the reel very nicely finished; will stand much use and hard service.

DIAMOND BRAND

BLUE HERON

Heavy brass frame; brass spool and shaft; steel axle running in hardened brass bearings; phosphor bronze gear; brass balance handle with white thumb piece; sliding steel click; knurled oil caps; nickel plated and polished. Diameter of plates, 2 inches; length of spool, 1-7/8 inches. Triple action; with agate jeweled end bearing oil caps.

PENNELL

EAGLE

Nickel plated brass frame; solid side plates with three cross bars; extension plate on right hand side for housing; solid one-piece base; extra axle reinforcement; white handle; brass gears and pinions; adjustable steel plate with agate jeweled end bearing oil cups.

UNKNOWN

DOUBLE ACTION

Made of brass, nickel plated and polished; solid side plates with three cross bars; complete with screws; extension plate on right hand side for housing; solid one piece base; extra axle reinforcement; complete with genuine bone handle; brass hubs; brass gears and pinions; adjustable steel click; knurled housing makes the reel more attractive.

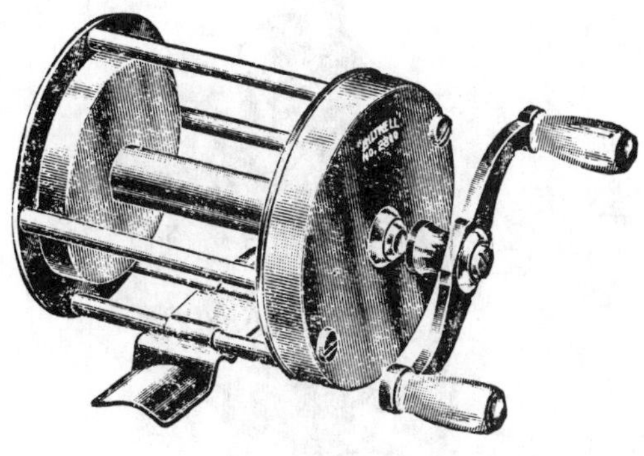

BILTWELL

No. 2800 QUADRUPLE MULTIPLYING

Made of nickel plated brass; special "S" shaped crank insures a balanced double handle and evenness of action. Frame is very staunchly constructed; bearings are all tempered metal securely spun into the plates of the reel. Diameter of spool, 1-1/2 inches; length of plates, 1-7/8 inches.

UNION

Double action; highly polished; raised pillars; back sliding steel click; well balanced handle with white wood thumb piece; 1-5/8 inch spool; substantially made.

UNKNOWN

SINGLE ACTION

Brass; nickel plated; riveted; raised pillars; black thumb piece; permanent click; end plate and bearings in one piece; size of plates, 2-1/4 inches; size of pillars, 1 inch.

UNKNOWN SINGLE ACTION

Diameter of plate, 2-1/2 inches; width of spool, 3/4 inch; line-carrying to attach to top or bottom or rod; made of cold rolled sheet steel; bright finish.

UNKNOWN
SINGLE ACTION

A remarkably staunch and rigid reel, entirely new, and something different in construction; rod clip has drilled holes for attaching reel to bamboo pole; Also designed to fit the reel seat of any bait casting rod; tail plate and head plate embossed; hub is provided with a line notch for fastening the line in the reel; diameter of spool 1-1/2 inch; length of pillars, 1 inch; assorted colors: Red, green, orange, blue and brown.

UNKNOWN
SINGLE ACTION

A combination trout and casting reel; rod clip has drilled holes which may be used for attaching reel to a bamboo rod; it will also fit the reel seat of any bait casting or fly rod; guide arms for winding accurately to the width of the spool and guide it properly when retrieving diameter of spool, 2 inches; width, 7/8 inch; height of reel, 2-1/4 inches; assorted colors: Red, green, orange, blue and brown.

UNKNOWN
SINGLE ACTION

A new and distinctively novel construction of reel; rod clip had drilled holes which may be used for attaching reel to a bamboo pole; also designed to fit the reel seat of any bait casting rod; diameter of spool, 2 inches; width 7/8 inch; assorted colors: Red, green, orange, blue and brown.

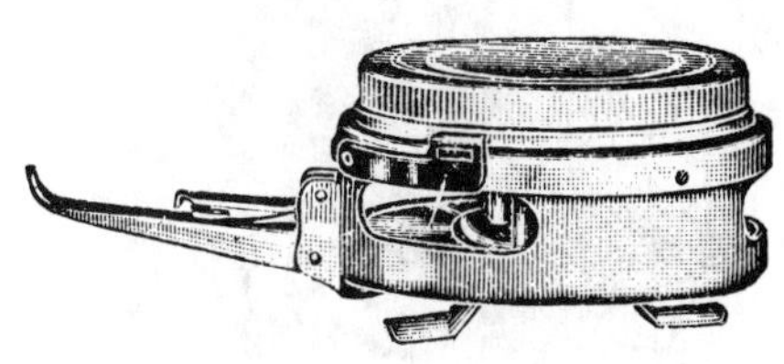

MARTIN AUTOMATIC

FLY-WATE REEL

For Fly Fishing

Made of duraluminum, a light, strong metal; milled brass gears that have large teeth insuring long life. The spindle is of hardened steel and the line spool is of light aluminum, fitted with a large, hardened steel, reversible line guide made the full size of the opening for the line which prevents piling and snarling of the line. The new spring tension throw-off is made practically flush with the side of the reel and operated by lifting the release with the thumb nail and allowing the drum to revolve slowly in the palm of the hand. Capacity 90 feet of "G" line; diameter of spool, 2-1/2 inches; width of spool, 3/8 inch; weight 6 oz.

UNKNOWN

Automatic Fly Reel

No. 1-Capacity, 75 feet; diameter of spool, 3 inches; width of spool, 1/2 inch; weight, 11 oz.

No. 2-Capacity, 90 feet; diameter of spool, 3 inches; width of spool, 5/8 inch; weight, 12-1/2 oz.

No. 3-Capacity, 150 feet; diameter of spool, 3 inches; width of spool, 3/4 inch; weight, 14 oz.

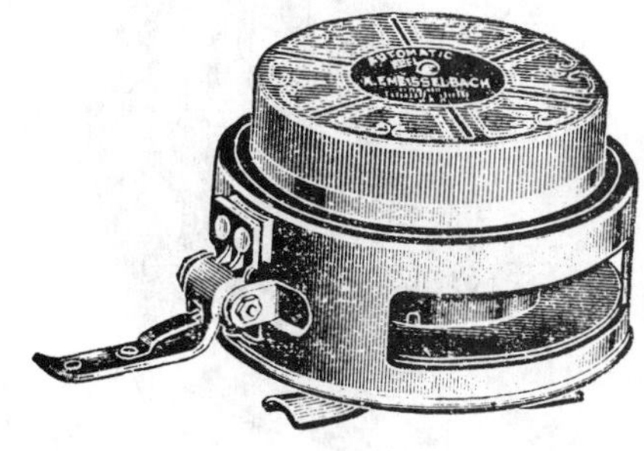

MEISSELBACH

Automatic Reel

Beautiful in design, as light as a good automatic reel can be made; it embodies all the Meisselbach strength of construction and is built to give the everlasting service which made Meisselbach Reels famous; constructed of special metal light as aluminum; strong as steel and most important of all, it is rust proof; the strongly constructed winding mechanism is completely enclosed; paying out the line winds up the reel and a feather touch on the lever reels in the fish. Easy to disassemble for oiling and cleaning. Diameter of spool, 3 inches; width of spool, 112 inch; actual weight each 12 oz.

MEISSELBACH

RAINBOW

For Trout or Bass Fishing

Made of special alloy which combines lightness and strength; frame and reel seat strong and rigidly constructed; hardened and tempered steel click wheel and spring; phosphor bronze bearings; runs true and smooth under all conditions; every part is instantly accessible for oiling and cleaning; dull black finish; German silver trimmings. Capacity, 35 yards; diameter, 2-7/8 inches; width, 3/4 inch.

MEISSELBACH

WANITA FLY

Built of a special alloy metal combining both lightness and strength; Phosphor bronze bearings, click and gear of hardened steel; nickel silver reel seat; easily taken apart; dull black finish; wt. 3-7/8 oz.

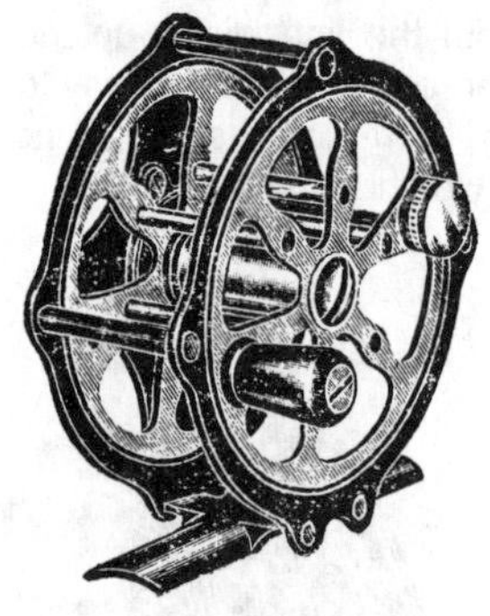

DIAMOND BRAND

Very practical high class single action casting reel; very light in weight; the holes in the spool and frame insure lightness and permit the line to dry quickly; had adjustable back sliding click; outside frame finished in dull black; inside is polished nickel finish.

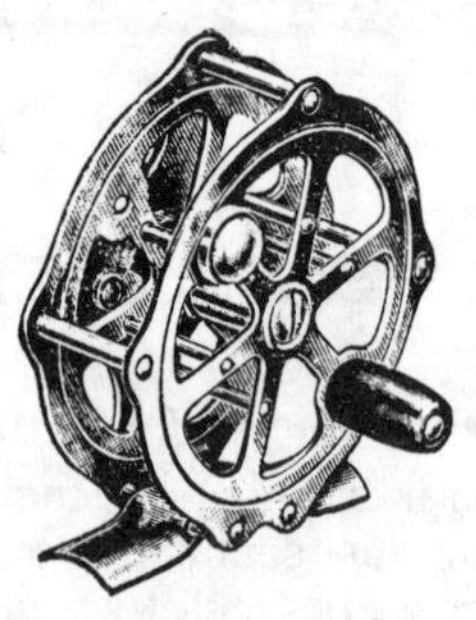

DIAMOND BRAND

Brass; skeleton frame model; removable spool; back sliding steel click; white thumb piece; very light in weight; weight, 4 oz. Nos. 90N and 90B capacity, 80 yards; balance 60 yards.

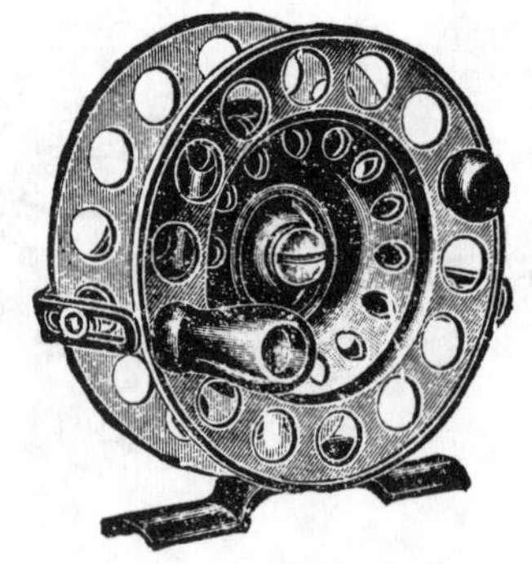

DIAMOND BRAND

SINGLE ACTION

Made of brass; black Japanese finish; steel bearing; Wood handle; Metal ball balance; two line sleeve with loose ring line guides; Frame and base all one piece stamped metal. Diameter of spool, 2-1/4 inches; Width of spool, 1 inch.

CATALINA FREE SPOOL

(Salt Water)

German silver, hard rubber side plates; metal bound; adjustable steel click; large well balanced handle with black rubber thumb piece; lever on side of top plate to adjust free spool action; all parts carefully milled and highly polished; leather thumb brake.

CATALINA FREE SPOOL

(Salt Water)

Steel pivot; adjustable click; fancy crank with specially shaped rubber handle; hard rubber plate reinforced with metal bands; fitted with leather thumb brake; lever on side of top plate to adjust free spool action; double multiplying metal disc on top plate with gear bridge and pivot bearing; all parts nickeled silver.

GULF SURF CASTING

(Salt Water)

German silver, hard rubber side plates; metal bound; steel pivots- adjustable steel click; black rubber thumb piece; all parts carefully milled and highly polished; leather thumb brake.

MIAMI FREE SPOOL

(Salt Water)

Best medium priced reel made for surf casting; extra heavy rubber side pieces; metal bound; lever free spool on handle side of reel; new style large handle, black rubber thumb piece; all parts carefully milled and highly nickel plated; leather thumb brake.

PACIFIC SURF CASTING

(Salt Water)

Double multiplying, hard rubber side plates; metal bound, thereby giving extra strength; steel pivot bearings; all parts carefully milled and highly nickel plated; large new style handle with black rubber thumb piece; adjustable steel click; leather thumb brake.

CALIFORNIA FREE SPOOL

(Salt Water)

Steel pivot; adjustable click; well balanced handle; black rubber thumb piece; lever on side of top plate to adjust free spool action; double multiplying; highly polished bronze finish; nickel plated spool; all parts carefully milled; leather thumb brake.

FAVORITE

(Salt Water)

Double multiplying, steel pivots; adjustable click and well balanced handle with black rubber thumb piece; Nicely nickel plated.

YANKEE

(Salt Water)

Double multiplying; steel pivots; adjustable click; well balanced handle with black rubber thumb piece; all parts nickel plated; built exceptionally strong.

PHOTOS AND DETAILS OF REELS WITH COLLECTOR VALUES

Here are several pages of photos of reels. Where possible, markings on the reel are described plus any other information that could be found. Following the photo section is an expanded, descriptive listing of reels with collector values.

ABU 1750 A, Ambassadeur with original leather case. 2-1/4" in diameter. Made in Sweden. Collector value range: $40-$80.

Ambassadeur No. 5000. "Record" with oil holes on the right. Collector value range: $60-$80.

Ambassadeur No. 5000-C with original leather case, black in color. Collector value range: $90-$130.

ABU Ambassadeur No. 6000 free spool. Collector value range: $80-$100.

Ambassadeur No. 6000. Note large crank handle. Collector value range: $80-$100.

Airex (Lionel Corporation) Spinning reels. Collector value range: N.A.

Alcedo spinning reel. Markings: ALCEDO (on handles) Erie 2C (stamped on side). Collector value range: N.A.

Basscaster. No company name probably Bronson. Collector value range: $10-$15.

Left.- Arrow. No other markings, raised pillar. Right: Unmarked raised reel. Collector value range: $15-$20.

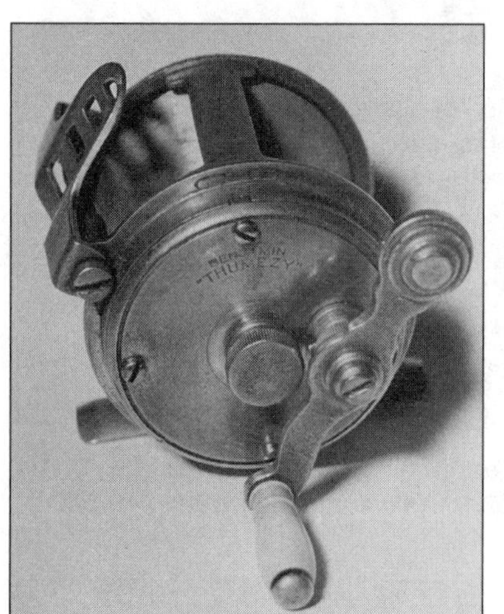

Benjamin "THUMEZY". Collector value range: $400-$600.

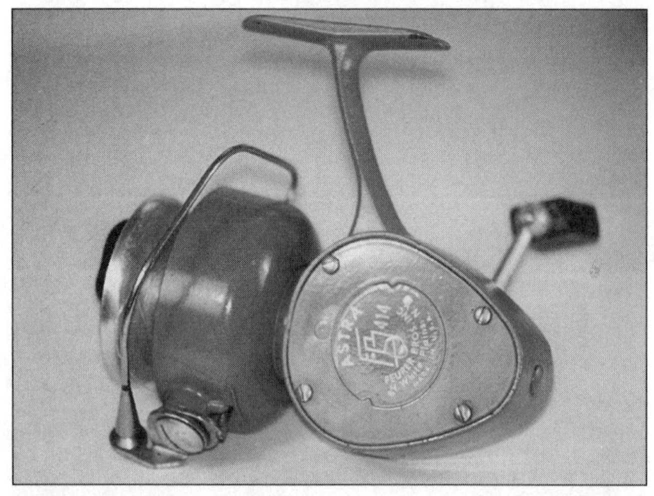

Astra spinning reel. Markings: ASTRA FEURER BROS. INC., N. White Plains, N.Y. MADE IN U.S.A. Collector value range: $10-$12.

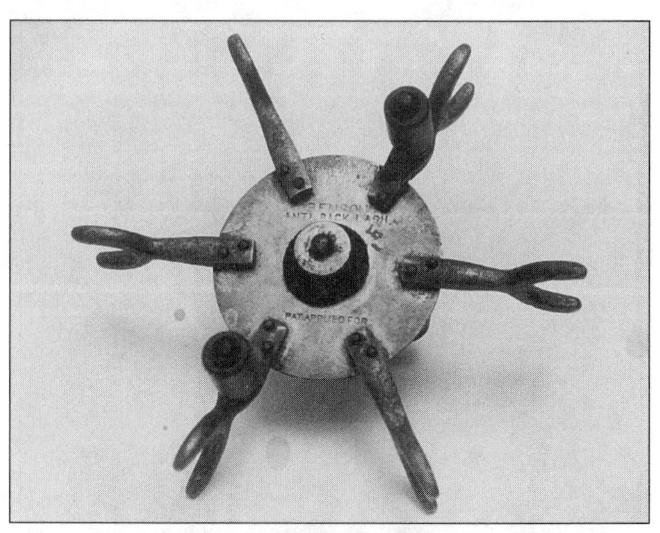

Markings: BENSON ANTI BACKLASH. PAT APPLIED FOR. Collector value range: $40-$60.

Billinghurst, Rochester, NY. Patent 1896. Collector value range: $600-$1,200.

Left reel is a Bronson Biltwell #3300. Jeweled. "Bronson, Mich." Collector value range: $10-$15. Right: Bronson Comet #2400R. Collector value range: $8-$15.

Bronson Commander. Markings: BRONSON Commander NO 3600. PAT. APP. FOR MADE IN U.S.A. under the foot. Collector value range: $10-$15.

Two Bronson Coronets. Markings include "Bronson Reel Go., Bronson Mich. J.A. Coxe" on both reels. Left reel is the #25N and the right is the #25. Collector value range for the #25N: $50-$80.; for the #25: $30-$50.

Bronson Fleetwings #2475. Collector value range: $10-$20.

Bronson Lion. Markings include "Bronson Reel Co. LION, L W, No. 1800". Collector value range: $10-$15.

Bronson Mercury No. 2550. Fishing scenes on each side. Collector value range: $5-$10.

Chamberlain Cartridge Company, c. 1904. Collector value range: $250-$350.

Markings: COZZONE. "200 YD" on foot. A saltwater reel with star drag. Collector value range: $100-$200.

Conroy, Thomas, 1860. Collector value range: $350-$600.

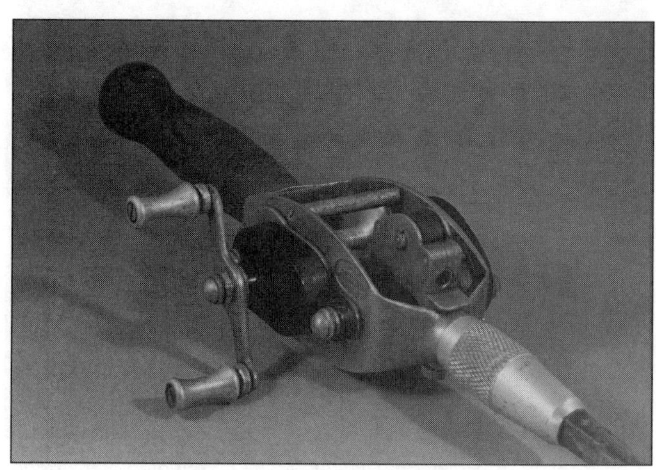

Chicago Fishing Equipment Company. "Gentleman Streamliner" #1372. Collector value range: $100-$150.

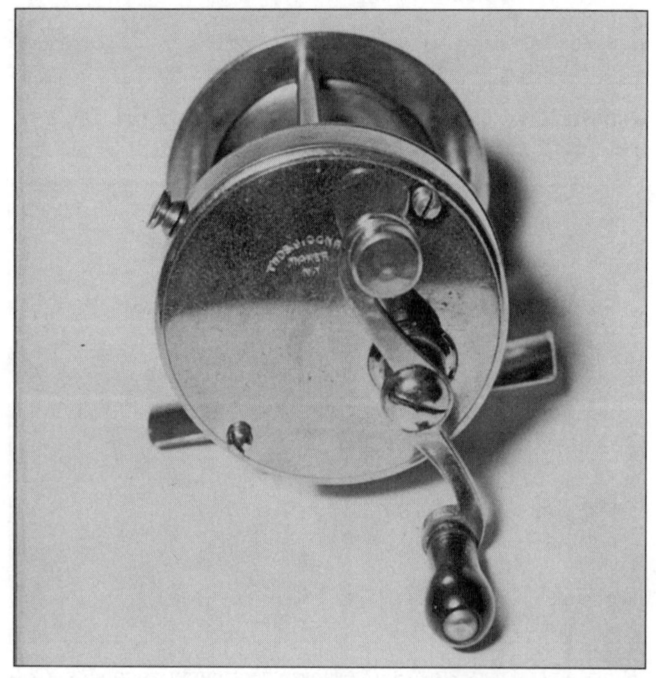

Conroy, Thomas. Collector value range: $250-$350.

Both reels marked "Defiance". No company name. Collector value range: $15-$25.

"The Elite" 80 yard capacity with steel pivot bearings. Collector value range: $40-$55.

Markings: FREE no tangle spool. Lou F. Eppinger DETROIT MODEL EE. Collector value range: $75-$100.

Fin-Nor #3 fly rod reel. Collector value range: $300-$600.

Go-Ite with original box and pocket catalog. Collector value range: $50-$75. with box, $30-$50. without box.

Markings; GAYLE "SYMPLICITY" No. 2 FRANKFORT, KY USA. Collector value range: $20-$35.

Good-All fly reel. Markings: America's Finest Reels. Ogallala, Nebr. Good-All Reel Mfg. Co, R. A. Goodall, Pres. Good-All's Goods are Always Good For 30 Years. Collector value range: $20-$25.

Markings: THE "St. JOHN" FLY REEL. HARDY'S PAT No. 9261 SIZE 3-7/8" MADE BY HARDY BROS LTD. ALNWICK, ENGLAND. It has a metal plate attached to it that says MADE FOR ABERCROMBIE & FITCH, NEW YORK. Collector value range: $100-$200.

Markings: MADE BY JAMES HEDDON'S SONS DOWAGIAC, MICH. 3-15. Collector value range: $100-$175.

Heddon's Dowagiac. Non-level wind. Markings: Heddon'S DOWAGIAC. A.F MEISSELBACH & BRO. 80 yards. This reel was in the first Heddon catalog to feature a Heddon reel (1912). Collector value range: $100-$200.

Heddon Pal #P-41 with original box. Collector value range: $30-$50. Add $25 for new in the box.

Markings: Made by JAMES HEDDON'S SONS. DOWAGIAC, MICH. Heddon No. 45. Carters Patent July 6, 1904 and Nov. 28, 1905. "#2" on bottom of the foot. Collector value range: $300-$400.

Heddon level wind. Markings: JAMES HEDDON'S SONS DOWAGIAC, MICH. MADE IN U.S.A. 3-35. Collector value range: $150-$200.

Markings: Made by JAMES HEDDON'S SONS. DOWAGIAC, MICH. This reel has a wooden spool. Documented as once belonging to Fred N. White. Possibly made special for White. Collector value range: No trade data found.

Markings: HEDDON LONE-EAGLE JAMES HEDDON'S SONS, DOWAGIAC, MICH. "Made in USA Patented" on bottom of foot. A No. 208 level wind reel that was offered in the 1932 catalog as a kit. May have been available earlier. Collector value range: $30-$45.

Markings: WINONA JAMES HEDDON'S SONS DOWAGIAC, MICH. The one with the line guide (left) is marked No. 105-SS. The other is marked No. 105-FF. Collector value range: $25-$35.. Double that for new in the box.

Heddon. Markings: HEDDON WHITE HOUSE ANGLER Snarl Free No. 215 JAMES HEDDON'S SONS DOWAGIAC MICH. Collector value range: $75-$85.

Heddon automatic fly reel. Markings: HEDDON MARK IV, Model 10. Collector value range: $15-$25.

Hendryx raised pillar reel. 1-1/2" diameter. Markings: HENDRYX PAT Mar 21, 1876 PAT July 10, 1888. Collector value range: $25-$35.

Left: Hendryx, raised pillar, 25 yd. capacity. Collector value range: $20-$25.
Middle: Hendryx #4906, raised pillar. Collector value range: $25-$40.
Right: Hendryx double multiplier. Marked "4-21-76 and 7-10 88" Collector value range: $35-$50.

Horrocks and Ibbotson Vernley Trout Reel, Plastic. Collector value range: $18-$22.

J.C. Higgins (Sears & Roebuck) Model No. 2882. Collector value range: $8-$10.

Left: Unmarked Horrocks and Ibbotson raised pillar brass reel. Collector value range: $10-$20. Right: Empire City, brass, raised pillar. Collector value range: $15-$25.

Markings: No. 34 BLUE GRASS SIMPLEX FREE SPOOL. THE HORTON MFG CO. BRISTOL, CONN. The opposite side has an arrow with the word SCREWOFF under it. The letter J appears under the foot. Collector value range: $100-$160.

Markings: No. 25 BLUE GRASS SIMPLEX. THE HORTON MFG CO. BRISTOL, CONN. The opposite side has an arrow with the word SCREWOFF under it. The letter E appears under the foot. Collector value range: $150-$200.

"The Ideal Casting Reel". No other markings. Collector value range: $10-$20.

Marked: "United States. INDIANA." No other markings. Collector value range: $10-$15.

Kalamazoo Tackle Company automatic fly reel. Markings: WOLVERINE NO 1695 Kalamazoo Tackle Co. MADE IN U.S.A. Patented MODEL E. Collector value range: $5-$10.

Johnson LAKER Model 140. Dennison-Johnson, Inc., Mankato MN. 1950s. Collector value range: $15-$20.

Markings: Keystone Casting Reel. The number 60 appears beneath the foot Collector value range: $25-$35.

Johnson SABRA Model 130B, Johnson SABRA Model 130A. Collector value range: $15-$20.

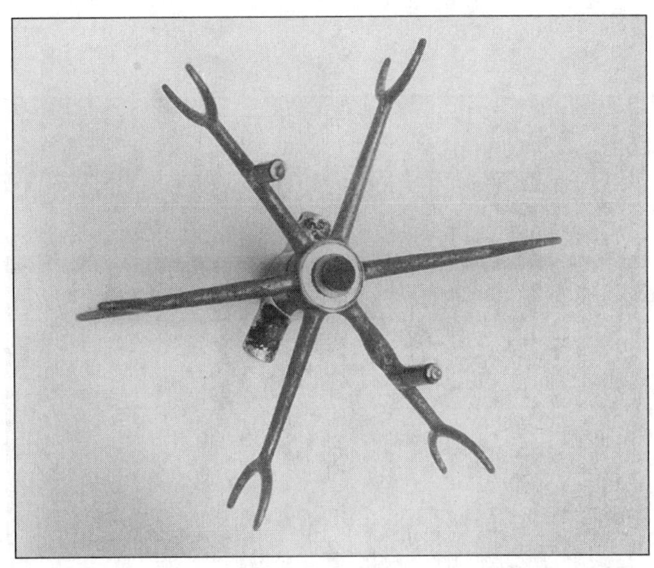

Markings: HENRY A KIEST MF'R KNOX, IND. PATENTED. Collector value range: $45-$65.

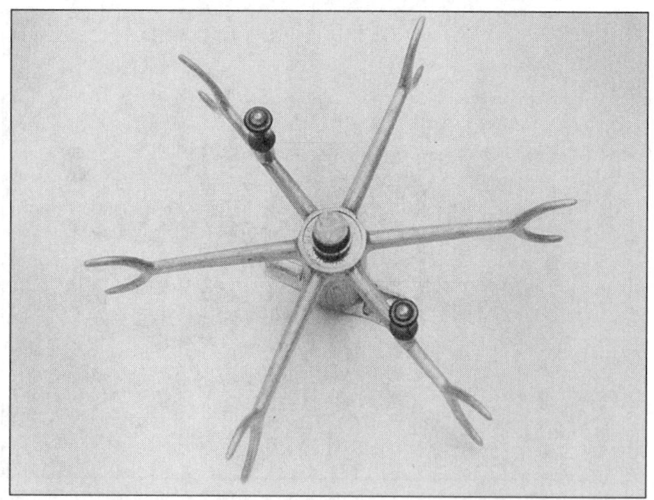

Markings: KIEST REEL CO MFRS KNOX IND PATENTED. Collector value range: $45-$65.

Markings: LANGLEY LAKECAST Model 350. The box is not correct. It is marked Model 505. Collector value range: $10-$15.

Langley Streamlite. Model #310-KB. Collector value range: $10-$20. Add $10. with box.

Leonard-Mills, c. 1884. Early free spool lever. Collector value range $500-$1,000.

Longfellow CR 2000. Collector value range: $8-$12.

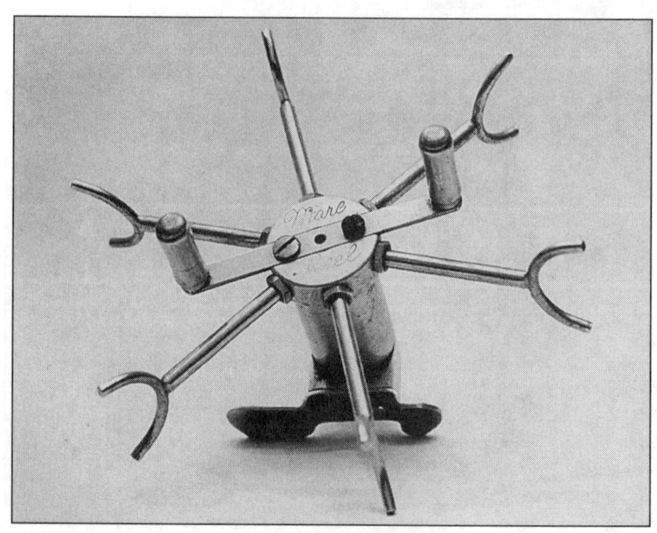

Markings: "Marc Reel" in script PAT PEND. Collector value range: $20-$40.

Markings: MARTIN AUTFISH REEL CO. MOHAWK, N.Y. PAT APPLIED FOR FS No. 2. Collector value range: $10-$20.

Markings: MARTIN AUT'SHORE CO. MOHAWK, N. Y. No. 3 PAT NO 2-175-756. Black in color. Collector value range: $20-$30.

Markings: An arrow with the words SCREWOFF under it. "J. F Hamiltion, Chicago" in script. CARTERS PAT July 5.04 Nov 28.05. Markings on the other side: B.F MEEK & SONS, LOUISVILLE, KY. No. 33 BLUE GRASS. Collector value range: $175-$190.

Markings: BLUE GRASS REEL. MADE BY B.F. MEEK A SONS, LOUISVILLE, KY. No. 38 "H.B. Locker" in script markings on other side: CARTER'S PAT JUL 5.04 NOV 21.05. The number 7 appears on the bottom of the foot. Collector value range: $175-$200.

Markings: B. F. MEEK & SONS, LOUISVILLE, KY. No. 38. The numbers 3550 appear on the bottom of the foot. Collector value range: $250-$425.

Markings: B. F. MEEK & SONS, LOUISVILLE, KY. No. 2. The numbers 4237 appear on the bottom of the foot. Collector value range: $275-$450.

Markings: No. 34 FREE SPOOL PAT NOV 26.01 NOV 28.05. Markings on opposite side: an arrow with SCREWOFF under it. B.F. MEEK & SONS, LOUISVILLE, KY. The letter C appears on the bottom of the foot. Collector value range: $250-$300.

Markings: MEEK No. 3 FREE SPOOL. THE HORTON MFG CO. BRISTOL, CONN. The numbers 10570 appear on the bottom of the foot. Collector value range: $350-$400.

Meisselbach and Co., Rainbow. Collector value range: $15-$30.

Meisselbach and Co., Tripart No. 580. Collector value range: $25-$35.

Montgomery Ward Sport King, Model 150. Probably made by Meisselbach. Collector value range: $8-$10.

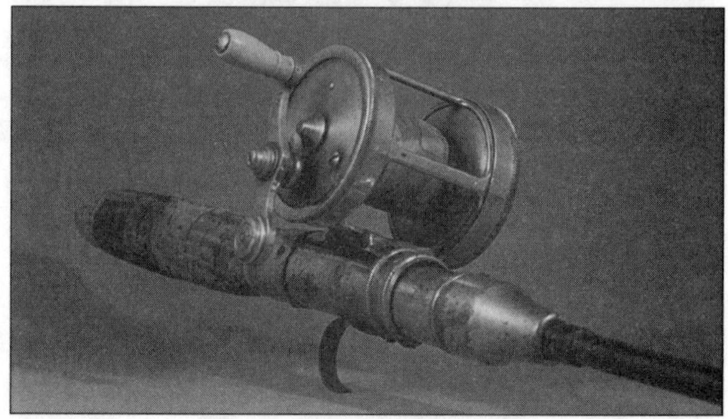

Meisselbach and Co., Simmons Special Tripart Free Spool mounted on a 3-1/2' Royal Steel Rod. (Simmons Hardware Co.) Collector value range: $50-$60. (rod is not included)

Left: Meisselbach and Bro., Tripart, Pat. dates marked "04, 04, 05, 07, Newark, N.J.' Middle: Meisselbach and Co., Tripart #580. Pat. dates marked "04, 04, 05, 07, 09" Right. Meisselbach and Co., Tripart #581, Free Spool. Pat, dates marked '04, 04, 05, 07, 09' Collector value range: $20-$30.

Markings: MEISSELBACH-AUTOMATIC. A.F MEISSELBACH & BRO NEWARK N.J. PAT PENDING. Collector value range: $15-$20.

Markings: The Frankfort Kentucky Reel. No. 3 B.C. Milam & Son. Frankfort, Kentucky. Collector value range: $500-$1,000.

Montegue YANKEE saltwater reel with leather thumb drag, click and drag, 200 yards cap. Mint, unused condition with original box. Collector value range: $10-$20.

Unmarked English wooden reel with brass fittings. It has been identified as a c 1880-1920 Nottingham with a Bicker Dyke line guard. Collector value range: $150-$250.

Ocean city fly reel. Markings: OCEAN CITY NO. 36 MADE IN PHILADELPHIA USA. Collector value range: $6-$12.

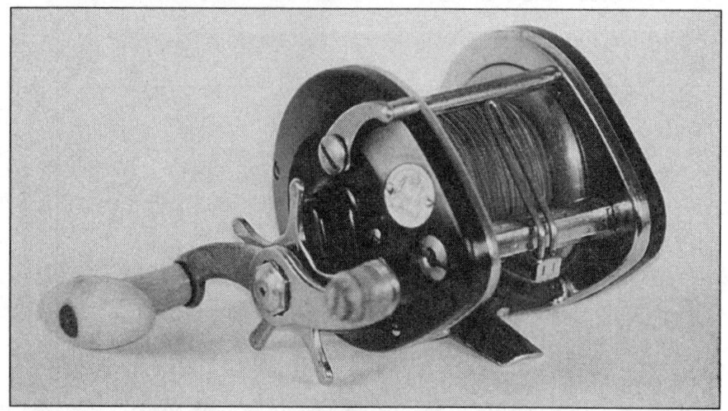

Ocean City. Markings: 922 Ocean City MADE IN PHILA. USA. Collector value range: $15-$20.

Orvis Model 50 A spinning reel. Collector value range: $80-$100.

Pelican. No company name. Collector value range: $14-$20.

Penn Delmar #285. Collector value range: $10-$12.

Penn SUPER-MARINER #49M. Collector value range: $25-$40.

Penn Senator #112H. Markings: Penn Reel 3/0 H, Special Senator. Collector value range: $20-$30. Double that for new in the box.

Penn #430 SS. Collector value range: $40-$50.

Left: Pennell, serial number 752. Right: Pennell Peerless. Collector value range: $15-$30.

Perrine automatic fly reels. Left: Model 50 with retrieve and brake levers. Collector value range: $15-$18. Right: Model 30. Collector value range: $10-$15. Both are marked PERRINE MFG. CO. Pat No 1, 810,573. FREE STRIPPING Minneapolis, Minn.

Perrine Automatic fly rod reel. Collector value range: $8-$15.

Pflueger INTEROCEAN. Close-up of the leather thumb piece to regulate casting speed and protect from burn. Collector value range: $40-$50.

Pflueger AUTOPLA No. 2475-S with original box and papers. Collector value range: $70-$100.

Pflueger Saltwater, 250 yards capacity. Has Pflueger's Bull Dog trademark. Marked: TEMCO Free Spool SURF CASTING. Collector value range: $15-$20.

Pflueger. Marked SKILKAST No. 1953. The round, screwed affair on the crank handle is marked PFLUEGER CUB No. 2542. Has plastic spool. Collector value range: $15-$20.

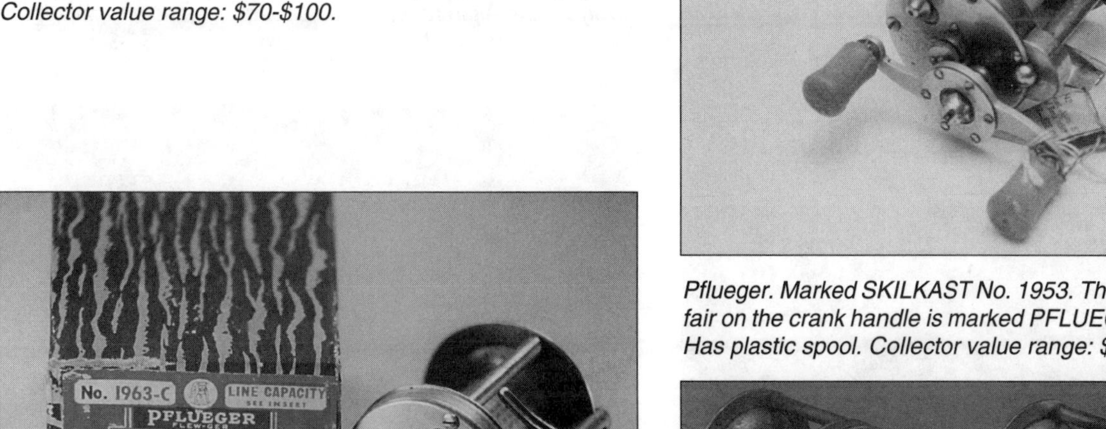

Pflueger Nobby. Model 1963-C with original box. Collector value range: $15-$20.

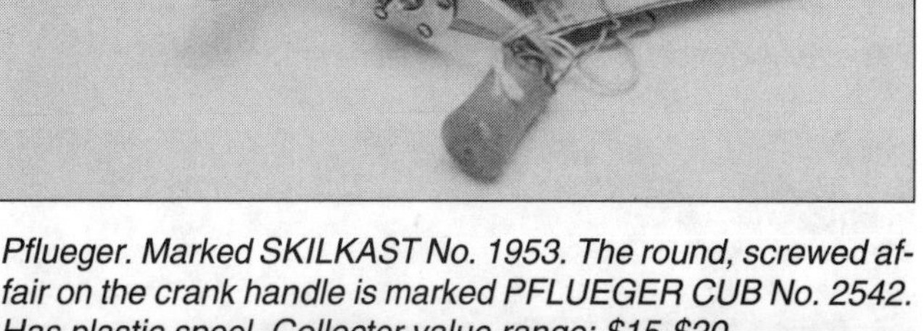

Pflueger Akron. Left: is marked "4-3-1923 and others" Right: #1893. Marked. "Patd and pat pend". Collector value range: $8-$18.

Pflueger Akron #1893-L. Collector value range: $8-$18.

Pflueger Akron #1894. Collector value range: $8-$18.

Pflueger Akron #1895. Collector value range: $25-$35.

Pflueger Knobby #1963. Collector value range: $8-$15.

Pflueger Progress #1774 fly rod reel with box and papers. Collector value range: $20-$25.

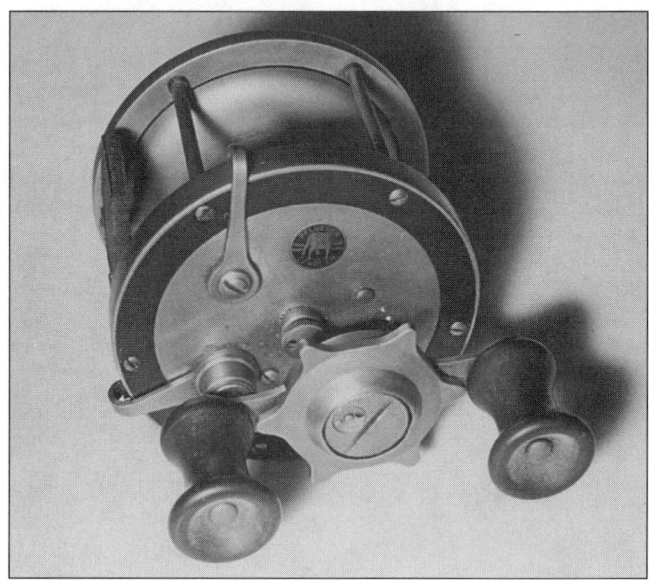

Pflueger Saltwater Casting reel. The first integrated Star Drag. This is the Pflueger-Williams patented drag. It was used extensively on the Alpin reel. It could be retrofitted as a replacement for the regular handle. Collector value range: $35-$65.

Pflueger Skilcast #1953 with original box. Collector value range: $20-$25.

Pflueger Summit #1294 fly reel. Collector value range: $15-$25.

Pflueger Summit. Left reel has no number, but is a #1983M. Collector value range: $25-$35. Right reel is the #1993-L Summit. Collector value range: $15-$25.

Pflueger Summit #1993-L. Rubber guard on tailplate. Original box and chamois sack. Engraved Collector value range: $50-$60. new with everything.

Pflueger Summit #1993-L new with box and papers. Collector value range: $50-$60., reel only: $15-$25.

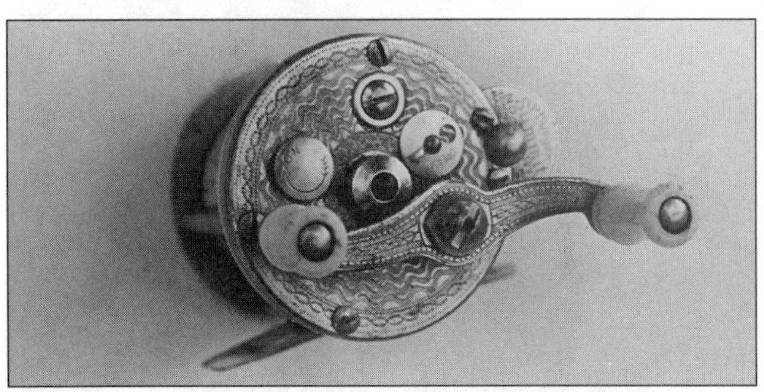

Pflueger. Marked SUMMIT, No. 1993. Beautiful "engraving". Collector value range: $15-$25.

Pflueger Supreme No. 510, free spool. Collector value range: $25-$35.

Pflueger Supreme with push button free spool. Collector value range: $30-$40.

Pflueger Supreme. Collector value range: $30-$40.

Pflueger Supreme No. 1573. New with the box. Collector value range: $35-$50.

Pflueger Supreme Model No. 1576. Mint in original box with zippered plastic pouch (in box). Leaping bass on end plate. Collector value range: $35-$55.

Pflueger Taxie #3128 loaded with braided copper line. Collector value range: $25-$40., with box and papers: add $10-$20.

Pflueger TRUMP #1943 level wind. Collector value range: $10-$18.

Pflueger Worth, 60 yd capacity. Marked. "5039 Pat 1-22-07,4-10-08, 12-29-14" Collector value range: $50-$100.

Popeil Brothers, Inc., Chicago. Year: 1972. Pocket Fisherman Spin Casting Outfit. Collector value range: $15-$25.

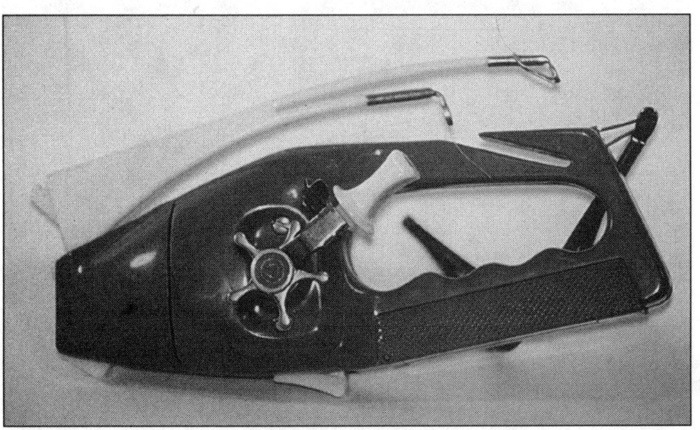

Pflueger Trusty #1933. Collector value range: $15-$20.

Quick Model 1001. Made in West Germany. This company made seven models of this reel, each with a different gear ratio. Collector value range: $15-$20.

Russell Flyrod Reel #1895, Model NF. Collector value range: $15-$20.

Russell Flyrod Reel #1889, Model GE Green finish. Collector value range: $20-$30.

Shakespeare Model 26, 100 yards capacity. Collector value range: No trade data found.

Shakespeare #1924, DIRECT DRIVE. Note the star drag. Collector value range: $10-$20.

Shakespeare # 1950, DIRECT DRIVE Model ED. Mint condition. Collector value range: $10-$18.

Shakespeare Triumph #1958, Model GE. Collector value range: $10-$15.

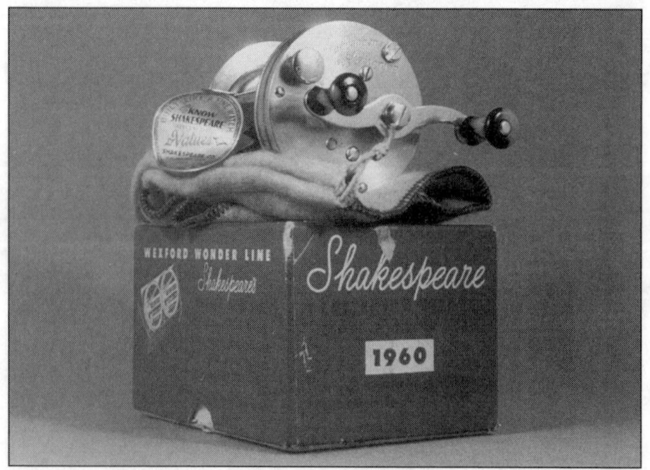

Shakespeare Criterion Deluxe #1960. Model GE. Original box and cloth sack. Collector value range: $15-$20, $30. with box and papers

Shakespeare Criterion #1961. Model HO. Engraved. Collector value range: $15-$25.

Shakespeare Criterion Deluxe #1960. Model GE. Collector value range: $15-$20.

Shakespeare Deuce #1905. Model GA. 100 yard capacity. Original box. Collector value range: $10-$15, $20 with box.

Shakespeare Precision (23041) 1914 Model Jeweled. 100 yd capacity. Collector value range: $25-$50.

Shakespeare Marhoff #1964. Model HE. Jeweled. Collector value range: $20-$30.

Shakespeare Leader #1909, Model FD. Collector value range: $8-$12.

Shakespeare President #1970, Model 31, 100 yd capacity, original leather case. Collector value range: $40-$50. with leather case.

Shakespeare President #1970, Model FK. Collector value range: $25-$35.

Shakespeare Tournament #1922, 100 yard capacity. Collector value range: $15-$25.

Shakespeare Wondereel #1920. Model GA. range: Collector value: $10-$20.

Markings: SHAKESPEARE STANDARD REEL No. 2 - 60 YDS - QUAD. PATENTED. Opposite side is marked Wm. SHAKESPEARE, JR. KALMAZOO, MICH. The numbers 1902-02 appear on the bottom of the foot. Collector value range: $50-$90.

Markings: SHAKESPEARE UNIVERSAL 23038. Beneath the foot is a fancy trademark with these words within it: 1918 MODEL PATENTED 80 YDS KALAMAZOO, MICH. Collector value range: $60-$70.

Markings: SHAKESPEARE "1918" MODEL MARHOFF PATENT LEVEL WINDING REEL 1964. Collector value range: $20-$30.

Markings: SHAKESPEARE STANDARD PROFESSIONAL 13053. Under the foot appears a fancy trademark with the words: 1912 MODEL PATENTED 80 YDS KALAMAZOO, MICH within the mark. Collector value range: $75-$90.

Markings: SHAKESPEARE CLASSIC 23054. Beneath the foot is a fancy trademark with these words within it: 1918 MODEL PATENTED 80 YDS KALAMAZOO, MICH. Collector value range: $50-$70.

South Bend automatic fly reel. OREN-O-MATIC No 1125. Collector value range: $15-$20.

South Bend #20. Model A. Collector value range: $15-$20.

South Bend #30, Model D. Collector value range: $10-$15.

South Bend #300, Model E, anti-backlash. Collector value range: $10-$15.

South Bend #400, Model D, anti-backlash with original box. Collector value range: $15-$20, $25-$30 with box.

South Bend No. 400, anti-backlash Model E. Collector value range: $20-$30.

South Bend No. 550-C, anti-backlash model. Collector value range: $10-$15.

South Bond #666 Free Cast. Collector value range: $10-$15; $25 with box.

South Bend Perfectoreno #750. Collector value range: $10-$15, $20 with box.

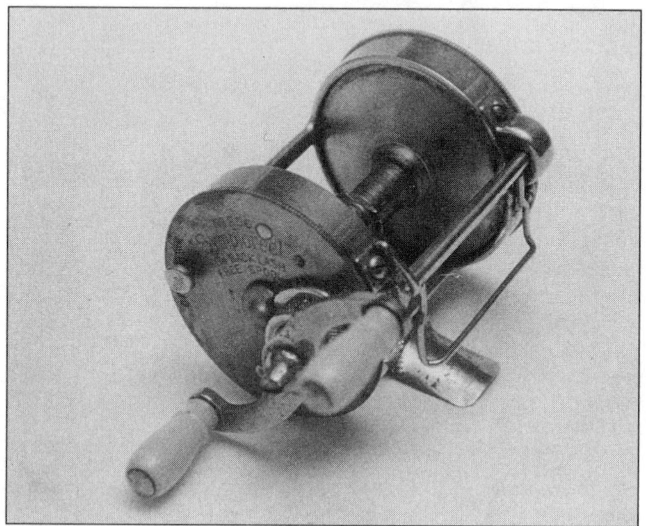

Markings: No. 256 Symploreel NON BACK LASH FREE SPOOL. Markings on opposite side: STANTON ST. NEWARK N.J. PAT. PENDING. Collector value range: $25-$50.

Markings: NIANGUA. Wm. H. TALBOT CO., NEVADA, MO. U.S.A. Markings on opposite side: SMELZER ARMS CO., KANSAS CITY, MO. Collector value range: $500-$600.

Four reels by William H. Talbot. Left to right: Meteor; Star; Niangua, Nevada, MO, Star. Collector value range: Meteor, $350-$450; Star, $200-$300; Niangua, $500-$600; Starr, $200-$300.

Markings: FREE SPOOL "Tripart" 581. Has three patent dates on it: 04, 07, 09. Collector value range: $25-$35.

Only markings on this reel are the letters U T K in a diamond. The diamond is surrounded with the words TRADE MARK Reg. US PAT OFF with MADE IN USA beneath it. Collector value range: $10-$20.

Left: Union Hardware Sunnybrook. Raised pillar, 60-yard capacity; Right. The identical reel but totally unmarked. This was apparently a trade model used by salesman. Collector value range: $10-$20 each

Union Hardware Samson. Collector value range: $20-$40.

Markings: EDWARD VOM HOFE MAKER -N.Y.- Patent July 1896. Model 550. Collector value range: $300-$400.

Vom Hofe, Edward.No. 423, Restigouche, size 4/0. Collector value range: $500-$700.

Vom Hofe, Julius. (1885,1889 patents) Collector value range: $100-$125.

Vom Hofe, Julius, No 5. Collector value range: $1,000-$1,300.

Vom Hofe. C. 1906 with leather case. Collector value range: $300-$400.

Von Lengerke and Antoine. Marked "V.L.& A. Peerless". Collector value range: $100-$150.

Wayne. No other markings. Collector value range: $10-$15.

Winchester #4450 Takapart mounted on a Winchester steel rod #5047. Collector value range: $100-$150. (reel). The rod is valued at about $100..

Wright and McGill Eagle Claw, Stream & Lake Model 88-A. Closed face spinning reel. Collector value range: $20-$25.

Wright and McGill Eagle Claw Model No. 102. Collector value range: $10-$15.

Markings: AUTOMATIC REEL PA'TD FEBY 28, 1888. JUNE 16, 1891, YAWMAN & ERBE MFG. CO ROCHESTER, NY, USA PATENT AUG 1, 1899. There is another illegible patent date starting "JUNE 16..." Collector value range: $40-$55.

Zebco Model 202 spinning reel. Collector value range: $4-$7, with box $5-$10.

Unknown wooden reel with brass fittings. It measures 6" across. Collector value range: $50-$60.

Unknown reel appears to be made of Bakelite, wood knobs on a brass crank handle, 4-1/4" in diameter. Marked "U-Need-A-Reel". Insufficient trade data to determine value.

REELS-REPRESENTATIVE VALUES

The following list is a sampling of several company's reels. The values were taken from actual advertised asking prices in various published and private collector's lists of those available for sale. Because many appeared in more than one list the values are placed in ranges rather than one specific figure. Where a reel falls in this range depends upon condition. It is impossible to assign a value to each and every one of the many thousands.

COLLECTOR

MAKER	NAME, DESCRIPTION and MARKINGS	VALUE RANGE
Abbey & Imbrie	"Beverly"	$30-$40
Abbey & Imbrie	"Lakeside," engraved	$20-$40
Abbey & Imbrie	"St. Lawrence"	$30-$40
Abbey & Imbrie	"Silver King"	$75-$100
Abu Ambassadeur	1000, red	$45-$55
Abu-Matic	#330, Red spinner	$35-$45
Abu-Matic	Spin casting reel, #550	$35-$45
Acme	"The Acme"	$10-$25
Airex	Apache, open face spinning reel	$20-$30
Airex	"AIREX LARCHMONT," Lionel Corp.	$25-$40
Airex	Bache-Brown Spinster	$15-$30
Airex	Mastercast #320, closed face spinning	$15-$20
Airex	Spinster, open face spinning reel	$15-$25
Airex	Standard	$10-$18
Allison fly reel	"Boston"	$80-$120
American	Reel, Indianapolis	$200-$300
Arrow	No. 60, raised pillar	$20-$25
Ashaway	Slipcast	$20-$30
Atlas	Portage, sliding click, raised pillar, 100 yard	$12-$18
Atlas	Portage, sliding click, raised pillar, 40 yard	$12-$18
Atlas	Portage, sliding click, raised pillar, 60 yard	$12-$18
Atlas	Portage, sliding click, raised pillar, 80 yard	$12-$18
Atlantic	"Surf Caster," nickel plate and bakelite	$15-$20
Atlantic	"Surf Caster," same as above, c. 1925	$15-$20
Bill Ballan	Fly reel	$100-$200
Bass Caster	"Bass Caster," 80 yd.	$8-$15
Bate	T. H., No. 3, Ball handle reel, brass with case	$375-$450
Beetzel	Washington, D.C.	$50-$60
Benjamine	"Thumezy"	$400-$600
Berkley	Specialist	$10-$15
Berkley	Castamatic	$10-$15
Billinghurst, Wm.	Fly reel, very early 19th Century	$600-$1,200
Biltwell	"Biltwell" No. 2800, metal bearings	$8-$14
Bogdan	Steelhead fly reel	$750-$1500
Boyer	Winona	$50-$60
Bradford & Anthony		$350-$500
Bristol	"Bristol No. 65," 3-1/2" x 1-1/8"	$8-$16
Bristol-Horton	Reels	$20-$40
Bronson	"Comet No. 2400R"	$8-$15
Bronson	"Fleetwing No. 2475," jeweled, levelwind	$9-$17

Maker	Description	Value
Bronson	"Biltwell No. 3300," jeweled, "Bronson, Mich."	$10-$15
Bronson	"Lion LW No. 1800, Bronson Reel Co."	$10-$18
Bronson	"Mercury No. 2550," engraved, jeweled	$7-$12
Bronson	"Top Flight"	$8-$10
Bronson	"Lashless No. 1700-A"	$10-$12
Bronson	"Meadowbrook"	$10-$12
Bronson	"Rouge No. 300"	$10-$12
Bronson	"Meteor," jeweled	$8-$15
Bronson	"Jolly Roger"	$8-$12
Bronson	"Spartan," jeweled	$12-$16
Bronson	"Green Hornet"	$5-$8
Bronson	"Torrent," free spool, star drag	$20-$30
Bronson	"X-Pert," jeweled	$12-$18
Brookline	"Brookline No. 16"	$8-$12
Bunyan	Paul Model No. 66	$14-$16
Burlington Metal Products	"BURLINGTON," level wind	$20-$30
Carlton	No. 4, jeweled, multiplier, pat. 1903	$140-$150
Carlton	"GEM" fly rod reel	$40-$50
Carlton	"IDEAL" flyrod reel	$50-$60
Centaure Pacific		$12-$20
Chamberlain Cartridge	"THE HUNTER"	$250-$350
Champion	"Champion, Model 805," pivoting base	$20-$30
Champion	Wide spool, 40 yds.	$20-$30
Chicago Fishing Equipment Co.	Gentleman Streamliner, No.1372, rod w/ built-in reel & wooden pistol-grip handle	$100-$125
Chief		$10-$15
Chubb, Thomas H.		$150-$350
Climax	Reels	$25-$60.
Clinton, C. M.	Very rare side-mount fly reel	$4,000-$4,500
Congress	Reels	$25-$50.
Conroy, Thomas J.	"Ball handle, 3," New York	$300-$400
Conroy, Thomas J.	"JVH-PAT OCT 8, 89," fly reel	$450-$500
Conroy, Thomas J.	Bait casting size, S-handle, multiplier	$250-$300
Cortland		$20-$40
Coxe, J. A.	(Very early, Los Angeles, CA)	$400-$450
Coxe, J. A.	No. 65C Do-All	$30-$40
Coxe, J. A.	Coronet No. 25, c. l940, aluminum	$50-$60
Coxe, J. A.	Coronet No. 25N with case	$75-$95
Coxe, J. A.	Invader No. 26, level wind	$15-$20
Coxe, J. A.	Sea Wolf No. 400B	$40-$60
Coxe and Bronson	"Crusader" No. 30	$30-$45
Cozzone		$75-$200
Creek Chub	"WAWASEE"	$175-$225
Cycloid	Reels	$20-$50
Defiance	"Defiance," 60 yd.	$20-$30
Defiance	"Defiance," 80 yd.	$20-$30
Diktator	"Diktator No. D-1706,", jeweled	$20-$40
Drop-liner	Rod and reel combo	$20-$30
Duncan-Briggs	Fly reels	$15-$25
Eclipse	Reels	$20-$25
Edwards	Fly reels	$10-$18
Empire City	"Empire City," raised pillars, sliding click and drag, 40 yd.	$20-$25
Empire City	"Empire City," raised pillars, 60 yd.	$20-$25
Empire City	"Empire City," sliding click and drag, 80 yd.	$15-$25
Eppinger, Lou	No-Tangle Free Spool	$85-$95
Eveready, Rex		$35-$40
Expert	"The Expert, Casting Reel"	$15-$25

Farlow		$50-$250
Favorite		$10-$25
Fenwick	Reels	$100-$400
Ferris-Lingren Aluminum	"Ferris-Lingren Mohawk, New Rochelle, NY"	$30-$40
Feurer Bros.	Spinning reels	$25-$40
Fin-Nor	Reels	$150-$400
Fin-Nor	Wedding Cake design fly reels	$300-$800
Follett	Fly reel	$600-$750
Folsom Arms	"St George" fly reel by Hardy	$400-$480
Four Brothers	BEACON	$20-$30
Four Brothers	CASTWELL	$20-$25
Four Brothers	CAPITOL	$40-$50
Four Brothers	COMRADE	$125-$150
Four Brothers	DELITE	$125-$175
Four Brothers	ECLIPSE	$30-$50
Four Brothers	ELINOR	$30-$40
Four Brothers	MOHAWK	$20-$30
Four Brothers	PARD	$10-$15
Four Brothers	PASTIME	$30-$45
Four Brothers	PONTIAC	$20-$35
Four Brothers	REGAL	$25-$40
Four Brothers	SENTRIE	$15-$20
Four Brothers	SUMCO	$20-$40
Four Brothers	TAXIE	$15-$20
Four Brothers	TRUSTY	$10-$15
Four Brothers	VICTORY	$20-$30
Fox Gun Company		$15-$30
Franklin	"Franklin" 100 yd., sliding click and drag	$14-$18
Frost, H. J.	Kelso Automatic Fly Reel	$20-$25
Frost, H. J.	Kelso Takapart	$30-$45
Garcia Mitchell	Reels	$20-$50
Gayle	SIMPLICITY	$20-$40
Go-Ite Mfg. Co.	"Go-Ite Real Reels Patent Pending," aluminum	$30-$50
Good-all Mfg.	"Good-all El. Mfg., Co.," R. A. Goodall,	
Pres., Good-For	30 years Ogalla, Nebr.," spinning reel, c. 1955	$20-$25
Great Lakes	Reels	$10-$40
Haywood Mfg. Co.	Humphrey Denver Model 3A	$25-$30
Hart Reel Company		$300-$600
Hawk Ogilvy	Brass w/ ball handle, very rare	$400-$500
Heddon	"Heddon No. 3-15 Dowagiac, Mich.," silver	$150-$250
Heddon	"Heddon No. 3-25 Dowagiac, Mich."	$100-$200
Heddon	Imperial No. 125	$100-$200
Heddon	Heritage No. 30	$50-$80
Heddon	Lone Eagle No. 206	$30-$50
Heddon	"Winona No. 105SS," has line guide arm	$30-$40
Heddon	"Winona No. 105FF," has line guide arm	$30-$40
Heddon	"Winona No. 105H"	$20-$30
Heddon	"Winona No. 105F"	$20-$30
Heddon	"Pal No. P-$41"	$25-$50
Hendryx	Very early brass reel, c. 1880	$40-$50
Hendryx	"No. 4906," raised pillar, 60 yd.	$30-$45
Hendryx	"4-21-78/7-10-88," 2-multiplier, raised pillar	$30-$45
Hendryx	Nickel plated, raised pillar, 25 yd.	$20-$30
Hendryx	Nickel plated, raised pillar, 40 yd.	$25-$40
Herters	Reels	$20-$40
Higgins, J.C.	"300," made by Bronson	$10-$15
Higgins, J.C.	"537-31010," made by Bronson	$8-$10

Maker	Description	Price
Higgins, J.C.	"537-3105," made by Bronson	$10-$12
Higgins, J.C.	"537-3101," engraved	$10-$15
Higgins, J.C.	"312-3101 No. 489	$10-$14
Higgins, J.C.	"312-3111 engraved, jeweled	$14-$20
Horrocks-Ibbotson	"No. 1" on foot, made by Julius Vom Hofe	$200-$300
Horrocks-Ibbotson	"The Captain" No. 1863 model B, aluminum	$20-$25
Horrocks-Ibbotson	Vernley Trout Reel, bakelite	$20-$25
Horrocks-Ibbotson	Commodore No. 1865	$10-$15
Horrocks-Ibbotson	Minute Man No. 1810	$15-$25
Horrocks-Ibbotson	Mohawk No. 1106, aluminum fly reel	$15-$20
Horton	Reels	$100-$500
Horton-Bristol	Reels	$10-$30
Horton-Meek	Reels	$100-$400
Humphrey	"Denver Model 3A," Haywood Mfg. Co.	$25-$30
Hurd Super Caster	Rod and reel combo	$90-$100
Ideal	Casting reels	$15-$20
Ideal	Fly reels	$50-$75
Indian	"Indian," 60 yd., raised pillar	$15-$20
Jamison	PRACTICAL	$35-$50
Johnson, Iver	Hardy PERFECT fly reel	$200-$250
Johnson, Iver	Hardy UNIQUA fly reel	$100-$140
Johnson	Reels	$10-$25
Kalamazoo Tackle Co.	"American Boy" No. 1709	$10-$15
Kalamazoo Tackle Co.	"Empress No. 1689" (fly)	$20-$25
Kalamazoo Tackle Co.	"Miracle Silent Automatic, No. 1698 Model Co."	$8-$12
Kaufman Manufacturing		$20-$55
Keen Kaster		$20-$30
Kenebuc Reels		$20-$30
Kentucky Blue Grass Reel Works	No. 3	$400-$500
Kentucky Blue Grass Reel Works	No. 33	$175-$200
Kerr	Rod and reel combo	$70-$80
Keystone		$25-$30
Kiest, Henry A.	Aluminum reel	$45-$65
Kiffe, H.	H. Reels	$75-$125
Killian Neocaster		$50-$80
Kingfisher		$40-$60
Koph	Reels	$70-$80
Kosmic Reel		$100-$300
Langley	"Reelcast" No. 500A	$10-$15
Langley	"Streamlite Model 310KB"	$10-$20
Langley	"Streamlite Model 310"	$10-$20
Langley	"Target" No. 340	$20-$40
Langley	"Whitecap" No. 410, star drag, free spool	$15-$25
Langley	"Model No. 191-B" fly reel	$10-$15
Lawson Machine Works		$5-$15
Leonard, H. L.	Reels	$300-$1500
Liberty Bell Reel Co		$250-$350
Lionel Corporation (Airex)	"Airex Larchmont"	$25-$40
Longfellow		$8-$10
Louisville Casting Reel Company		$30-$50
Malloch Brass Spinning Reel	Very early	$220-$300
Malloch	Reels	$100-$300
Martin	Martin Automatic No. 1, aluminum	$10-$20
Martin	Martin Automatic No. 2, aluminum	$6-$12
Martin	Martin Automatic No. 3, aluminum	$10-$12
Martin	Martin Automatic No. 27/0, aluminum	$10-$15
Martin	Martin Automatic No. 28/0, aluminum	$15-$25

Maker	Model	Price
Martin	Martin Automatic No. 53, aluminum	$10-$15
Meadowbrook	No. 3123460, engraved	$10-$15
Meek, B.F. and Son	"No. 3"	$200-$500
Meek and Sons	"Bluegrass No. 3"	$200-$350
Meek and Milam	Hand made, brass, c. 1850	$1,000-$1,500
Meek-Horton	Reels	$250-$375
Meisselbach	No. 19 "Expert" fly reel, c. 1890	$45-$75
Meisselbach	No. 250 "Featherlight" fly reel, c. 1890	$40-$80
Meisselbach	No. 480 "Takapart," nickel	$25-$35
Meisselbach	"Takapart," nickel, free spool	$25-$40
Meisselbach	No. 6 "Good Luck" (wood reel)	$50-$100
Meisselbach	"Rainbow" fly reel, aluminum	$15-$30
Meisselbach	"Triton," triple multiplier	$30-$70
Meisselbach	"Elyria, Ohio," no number, level/wind	
Bakelite	End plates	$10-$20
Meisselbach, A.F. and Bro.	Horizontal wire line trolling reel	$40-$60
Meisselbach, A.F. and Bro.	Tripart style, no number, 80 yd.	$40-$50
Meisselbach and Co.	"Tripart No. 580, 04, 05, 07"	$30-$40
Meisselbach and Co.	"Tripart No. 581, 04, 05, 07," free spool	$30-$40
Meisselbach and Co.	Tripart style, no number, 80 yd.	$20-$30
Meisselbach and Co.	"Simmons Special, Tripart," free spool	$30-$50
Meteor		$10-$12
Milam	"Milam, The Frankfort Kentucky No. 1	$1,800-$2,500
Milam, B.C.	"Frankfort, Kentucky"	$1,800-$2,500
Milam, B.C. and Son	"No. 3, Frankfort, Ky".	$900-$1,500
Mills, William & Son	(Leonard reels)	$500-$1,000
Montgomery-Ward		$5-$20
Ny-O-Lyte (Waltco)		$30-$50
Ocean City	No. 35	$15-$20
Ocean City	No. 305	$5-$10
Ocean City	No. 306	$8-$12
Ocean City	No. 1529	$5-$10
Ocean City	"Interstate," jeweled, level wind	$10-$15
Ocean City	"Nile"	$10-$20
Ocean City	No. 970	$5-$15
Ocean City	No. 1600	$5-$10
Ocean City	No. 1810	$5-$10
Orvis	1874 patent in script, Silver fly reel	$800-$1,200
Orvis	1874 patent in script, Nickel fly reel	$500-$650
Orvis	1876 patent fly reel	$350-$500
Orvis	1920 patent fly reel	$250-$400
Orvis	Reels	$30-$120
Penn	Long Beach	$10-$20
Penn	Jigmaster	$15-$35
Penn	Senator	$150-$200
Pennell	"Peerless," 80 yd.	$20-$30
Pennell	Eagle	$20-$30
Pennell	Tournament	$30-$40
Pflueger	"Akron No. 1893-L," jeweled, level wind and made of nickel plated brass	$15-$20
Pflueger	"Capitol No. 1988," star drag, free spool, made of nickel plate and bakelite	$25-$35
Pflueger	"Captain," wire line trolling reel,wood knobs	$15-$30.
Pflueger	"Gem No. 2094," c. 1940	$10-$20
Pflueger	"Golden West," early fly reel	$200-$300
Pflueger	"Knobby No. 1963"	$10-$15
Pflueger	"Medalist No. 1495"	$20-$50

Maker	Model	Price
Pflueger	“Oceanic No. 2859” patented 1907 and 1923	$25-$50
Pflueger	“Pontiac”	$10-$30
Pflueger	“Progress,” open frame, raised pillar	$40-$60
Pflueger	“Progress,” anodized brass, raised pillar and wood knob	$50-$75
Pflueger	“Rocket No. 1375,” nickel plate	$15-$30
Pflueger	Sal-Trout No. 1554”	$15-$20
Pflueger	“Sal-Trout No. 1558”	$15-$25
Pflueger	Sea Star No. 1050”	$15-$25
Pflueger	Skilcast No. 1953”	$10-$15
Pflueger	“Summit No. 1993”	$15-$20
Pflueger	“Superex Automatic No. 775 pat. 1907,” fly	$25-$50
Pflueger	“Supreme” fly reel, Mod. No. 578	$150-$175
Pflueger	“Taxie No. 3138” wire line trolling reel	$25-$40
Pflueger	“Trump No. 1943”	$10-$20
Pflueger	“Worth No. 5039,” jeweled nickel silver	$75-$125
Portage	Atlas	$10-$15
Portage	Seminole	$20-$40
Precisionbilt		$20-$40
Ranger		$10-$15
Record		$20-$40
Redifor		$100-$300
Rev-O-Noc		$15-$25
Rohester-Carleton		$30-$80
Sage		$150-$175
Schmelzer		$25-$50
Seamaster		$1,000-$1,400
Sears		$10.20
Shakespeare	“Acme No. 1904”	$8-$10
Shakespeare	“Automatic No. 1815”	$10-$12
Shakespeare	“Criterion No. 1960 Mod. GE”	$10-$18
Shakespeare	“Criterion No. 1961, Mod. HO,” engraved	$14-$20
Shakespeare	“Deuce No. 1905, Mod. GA”	$8-$14
Shakespeare	“Favorite No. 1733”	$12-$22
Shakespeare	“Imperial No. 1951”	$20-$25
Shakespeare	“Intrinsic No. 1903”	$20-$30
Shakespeare	“Intrinsic No. 1959 Mod. GK”	$12-$15
Shakespeare	“Leader No. 1731”	$12-$18
Shakespeare	“Leader No. 1909,” level wind	$10-$20
Shakespeare	“Marhoff No. 1964, Mod. GE,” level wind	$15-$25
Shakespeare	“Marhoff No. 1964, Mod. HE,” jeweled	$20-$30
Shakespeare	“President,” c. 1940, bakelite	$20-$30
Shakespeare	“President No. 1970, Mod. 31,” engraved	$30-$40
Shakespeare	“Russell No. 1895, Model GE,” fly reel	$20-$30
Shakespeare	“Russell No. 2062”	$15-$20
Shakespeare	“Service No. 1944, Model GK”	$15-$20
Shakespeare	“Service No. 13042”	$35-$75
Shakespeare	“Tournament No. 1740”, 1743, 1744	$100-$200
Shakespeare	“True Blue No. 1956”	$8-$15
Shakespeare	“Wondereel No. 1920, Mod. GA”	$8-$15
Shakespeare	“Light Wondereel No. 1921”	$12-$20
Shapleigh		$10-$25
Sheldon		$8-$12
Shipley, M. A.		$150-$300
Simplicity		$25-$50
South Bend	No. 400 level wind, anti-back-lash casting reel	$15-$25
South Bend	“No. 666 Free Cast”	$15-$20
South Bend	“No. 350-B Level Winding Anti-Back-Lash”	$8-$12

Maker	Description	Price
South Bend	Oreno Saltwater Reel #850, free spool, star drag	$12-$16
South Bend	No. 30 level wind Model D	$12-$18
South Bend	No. 300 Anti backlash, level wind	$7-$15
Spiral Wind		$40-$80
Sport King		$8-$20
Star Reel Company		$10-$20
Staro		$25-$40
Sterling		$20-$50
Stubby Brand	American Display, rod & reel combo	$30-$45
Talbot, WM	"No. 3, Nevada, Mo.", silver, early 1800s	$500-$800
Talbot	"Kansas City, Mo.", silver, early 1900s	$300-$400
Talbot	No. 3 Nianqua-Nevada, Mo., c. 1901, jeweled	$500-$600
Trimline		$10-$18
True Temper		$8-$20
UTK		$15-$20
UCO		$20-$30
Union Hardware	"Sunnybrook" fly reel	$10-$20
Union Hardware	"No. 71155" fly reel	$10-$14
Union Hardware	"Sunnybrook", brass, raised pillar	$10-$15
Union Hardware	"Sunnybrook", bright finish, raised pillar	$10-$15
Union Hardware	"No. 7169" aluminum, raised pillar	$18-$25
Union Hardware	Very small brass, raised pillar reel	$20-$30
Union Hardware	"No. 7225S"	$8-$12
Union Hardware	"Samson", 60-$80 yd.	$20-$28
V.L. and A.	"Peerless", jeweled, 60 yd.	$50-$60
Vom Hofe, Edward	No. 355 Peerless fly reel	$1,000-$2,000
Vom Hofe, Edward	No. 360 Perfection	$2,000-$4,000
Vom Hofe, Edward	No. 423 4/0, multiplier w/ leather case	$600-$900
Vom Hofe, Edward	No. 621 6/0	$400-$500
Vom Hofe, Julius	"B Ocean", c1918	$200-$400
Vom Hofe, Julius	No. 2	$100-$200
Vom Hofe, Julius	No. 3	$100-$300
Vom Hofe, Julius	No. 4	$100-$200
Walker, Arthur		$300-$800
Waltco Ny-O-Lyte		$20-$30
Water Witch		$25-$35
Weber		$10-$20
Western Auto		$5-$10
Winchester	No. 2726, wood knob	$110-$135
Winchester	No. 4253, 80 yd.	$80-$100
Winchester	No. 4290	$90-$100
Winchester	No, 4296 Armax	$70-$80
Winchester	No. 4350, 100 yd., takapart	$100-$150
Wright and McGill	"Stream and Lake", No. 14	$5-$10
Wright and McGill	"Fre-Line, Mod. 10 BC", side-mount spinning reel	$8-$15
Yankee		$10-$20
Yawman & Erbe		$25-$50
Young, J. W.		$25-$75
Zebco		$5-$20
Zebco	Cardinal spinning reels (made in Sweden)	$50-$75
Zebco	Zero Hour Bomb Co. reels	$15-$25

THE AMERICAN FISHING ROD:

A BRIEF HISTORY

It has been said that the first fishing rod was the human arm. Soon after early man began to fish with primitive 'hooks' it probably occurred to him that if he attached his line to the end of a pole, he could increase his reach therefore increase his catch.

The first sport fishermen in America were few in the early colonial days. Generally most of them were visiting European aristocrats. Fishing as a pastime was looked upon with disdain by the hard-working early colonists for theirs was the strenuous business of surviving and building. They had little time in which to pursue such frivolous activities.

The first fishing rods used in America were undoubtedly English-made. The first native American rod was more likely a long pole with a short line which allowed the presentation of the bait. This long pole is the only American device that can have the remotest claim to being an ancestor of the fly rod as we know it today. That we try to claim any of the original history of rods at all is vanity, for the English had already developed fly rods far superior to this crude pole and line. In actuality the first true claim we can make to any revolution in rod design, as the case with reels, is found in Kentucky history.

Until sometime in the late 1800s most American rods were of solid wood. They were cumbersome affairs of great length and casting or presentation of the bait with them required two hands. They were stiff and not well suited to fly casting or any type of casting for that matter.

About 1846-1848 a Pennsylvanian, Sam Philippi, improved on an English rod maker's innovation of using flexible bamboo or cane for their rod tips. Philippi made an all bamboo fly rod by gluing four long strips of split bamboo together. Sometime in the 1860's Hiram Leonard improved the Philippi innovation by using six strips instead of four.

American rod makers can claim the history of today's fine bait casting rods as theirs. In the 1880s, a Kentuckian, James Henshall (1836-1925), introduced a new rod that can be said to be the true forerunner of the bait casting rod. It was made by the Orvis company. Although it was designed primarily for live bait presentation, when anglers used the new Kentucky reel with this shorter, lighter rod, it became extremely popular. The Hensall rod was still long by today's standards. The original rod was eight feet three inches long and made of wood.

About 1885 James M. Clark introduced a rod for bait casting. Called the "Chicago Rod", it was made of split bamboo and only six feet long. It took this rod a short five years to replace the longer Henshall rod almost completely. It was of course this very same time that we have noted that the artificial plug began its meteoric rise in popularity.

With the "Chicago Rod", the "Kentucky Reel" and the "Plug", there was no stopping the phenomenal growth in the popularity of bait casting. This was the beginning of the Expansion Age in the American fishing tackle industry.

From then until 1946 rods were made of bamboo, some other wood material or metal with steel being the most common. Then came the invention of the fiberglass rod by Arthur M. Howald and first manufactured as the WONDEROD in 1946. Its introduction revolutionized the rod making industry and rendered the steel rod obsolete. Bamboo persists to this day, because it is considered the premier material for the purist fly fisherman.

IDENTIFICATION OF OLD RODS

Markings

Most old hand-made rods were signed by their makers. The signature is usually found stamped on the butt cap, but some actually signed them on the shaft itself, just forward of the handle.

If there are no markings to be found at all, the collector should then check the metal fittings. If the fittings are of "German silver", the rod is probably an early hand-crafted one. "German silver" typically tarnishes to a dull gray, sometimes tending toward green. There is occasionally found a greenish corrosion in crevices or joints. There early rods may also be found with nickel or brass fittings.

Later models were almost always marked with the maker's or manufacturer's name on the shaft or the reel seat.

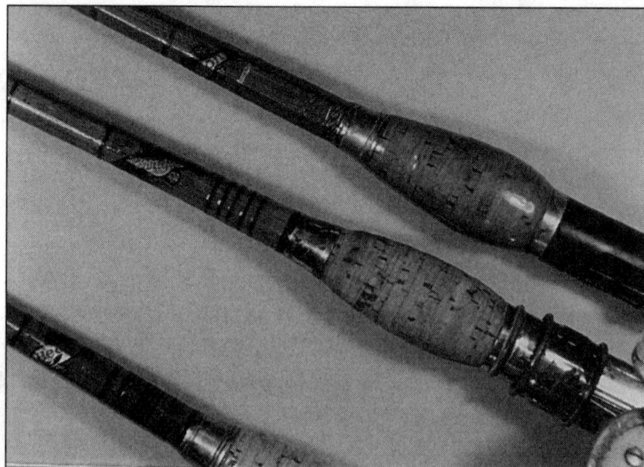

Three rods with the Bass/Heddon mark on the shafts.

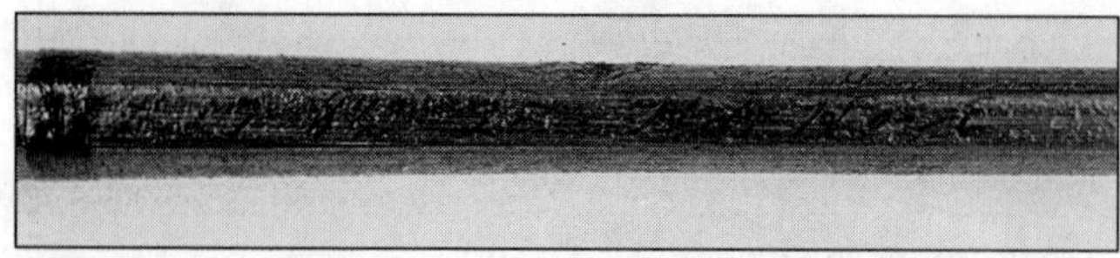

Here is an example of a hand-signed identification on a rod shaft. It reads: "#17- 8 1/2'-2F-H.D. Howe".

Bindings

Early split cane rods had to be bound at short intervals for the entire length of the rod for glues & materials used prior to World War I were inferior. After WW I better glues and higher quality cane was used and the wrapped bindings were not as numerous. Frequently the bindings were necessary only at the ends of the rods.

Length

Length of rods is a good clue to age. Most fly rods made prior to the early 1900s were 10, 12 or more feet long while those made afterward are found in 6- to 10-foot lengths.

While in general, bait casting rods can be examined with the above length guide lines in mind, the collector should be aware that most are shorter and stiffer than fly rods.

Hardware and Handles

Another, but not dependable, way to date a rod is by examining the other hardware, the line guides, and handle styles.

Most of the earliest casting rods were made for a two-handed grip. The handles were wooden, mostly ribbed for a better grip. Long about 1900 or so cork handles became popular, but smooth or ribbed wooden handles continued in wide use. Trigger type additions to the grip were added occasionally to the one-handed rods. These, of course, are still used today on some rods.

Early eye guides were sometimes made collapsible to protect them from breakage in transporting the rod. Snake guides and soldered eye or ring guides were developed early on with the snake guide probably coming first. For those of us who believe the ceramic eye guides are a recent development there is a surprise. Several early catalogs illustrate and offer agate eye guides. These are virtually the same except the inserts were made of natural agate rather than ceramic. The reason for them was the same. Trumpet guides were also an early development not found on today's rods.

Reel Seats

Earliest reel seats were simply a place to tie the reel to the handle with line. Quickly thereafter came the slide locking and screw type locking devices.

The collector should be aware that rebuilding rods, changing broken hardware, etc. is nothing new. Be wary of an old rod with brand new fittings unless the rod has been rebuilt by a competent rodsmith.

In the final analysis the business of identifying a casting rod by maker is almost impossible in the absence of an actual maker trademark or signature.

ANATOMY OF A ROD

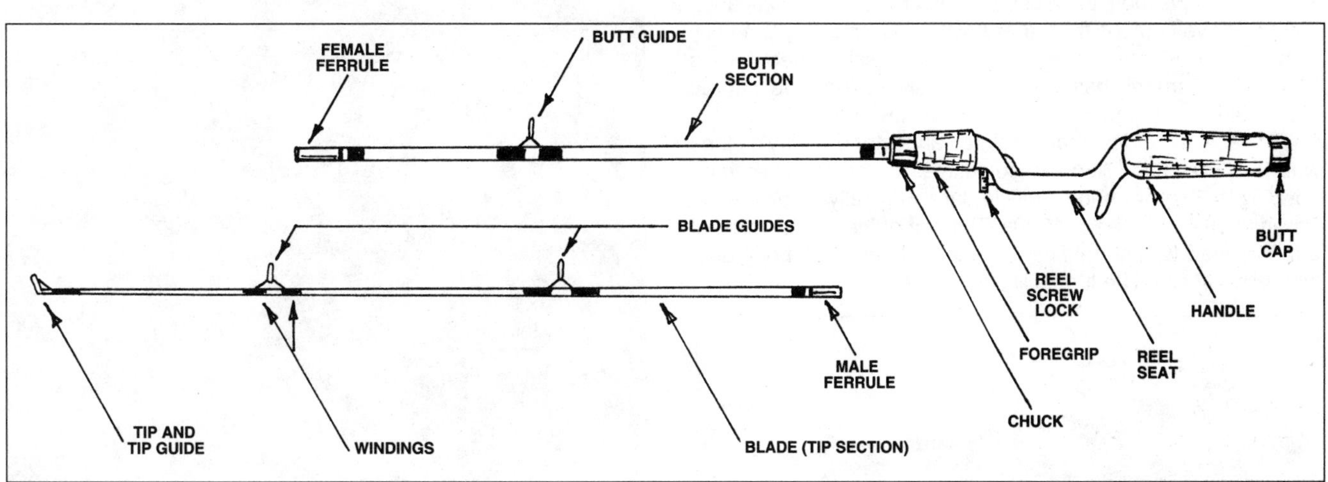

LURES

A History of Lure Development in the United States

Legend has it that many years ago, after hours of fruitless hard work, a rather disgusted and altogether unhappy fisherman sat in his boat lamenting that all-too-familiar moan: "Why the heck aren't they biting?!"

After pondering his situation, punctuating his thoughts with muttered remarks about fish, luck and everything else connected with the sport of fishing, he made his final decision. He emphasized its frustrating impact by angrily flinging an empty cigarette box into the water. After the package landed, causing a small disturbance in the water, something happened. Something unseen jabbed hard at the box sending it several inches into the air. Not a little unsettled, the angler watched as the box was struck again. This time however, the force was seen. It was a big black bass that had smashed up through the surface hitting the box with such fury. An idea was born.

Perhaps this tale is a bit far-fetched, but who's to say? Whatever the case, there are some hard facts to follow the original idea and there is a story, said to be true, concerning a similar happening to James Heddon, the founder of the Heddon lure company.

Lure development from that point, was probably painfully slow at first. It was a gradual process crossing many years from the first crudely painted, haphazardly hook-rigged, carved blocks of wood to the works of art we fish with today.

Probably the oldest manufactured ancestor of today's plugs was the "Phantom Minnow," sometimes called the false minnow. This English-made artificial lure originally appeared in America during the early 1800s. The first of these consisted of a metal head with metal fins on either side and soft body usually made of silk. The lure is illustrated here.

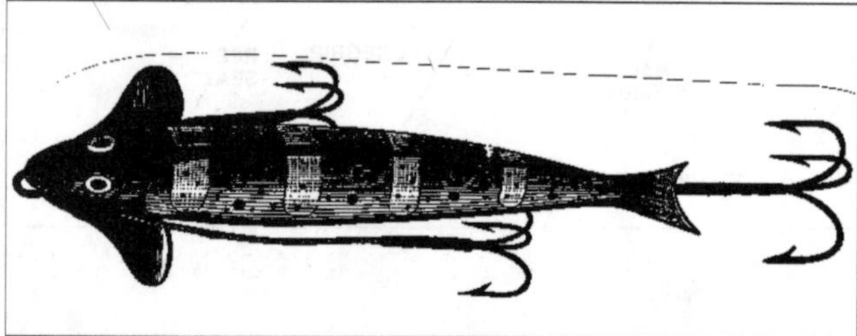

The Phantom Minnow remained essentially the same for the next 75 to 80 years. The lure was one of the first artificial baits to sport both the barbed and the treble hook together. The only significant changes in it for those years, was the addition and/ or deletion of the number and type of hooks. An 1890s William Mills and Sons catalog shows a "Celebrated Phantom Minnow", available in twelve lengths, describing the lure as being "... made of silk, coated with rubber, very light, very fine for black bass and pickerel."

The Phantom Minnow can be found in several catalogs under various "Phantom" names until the 1940s. It appears that manufacturers settled upon three treble hooks as the best design. Most of the illustrations in these old catalogs show three treble hooks in various configurations.

The first American artificial bait incorporating wood as a component and known to have actually been manufactured, is listed in the United States' patent records is H. C. Brush's "Floating Spinners," manufactured in Brushes Mills, New York. The patent was granted to Brush August 22, 1876. The bait is essentially a spinner bait, not a plug. It consists of a red painted natural wood (cork) float, center-mounted on the shaft of a revolving spinner.

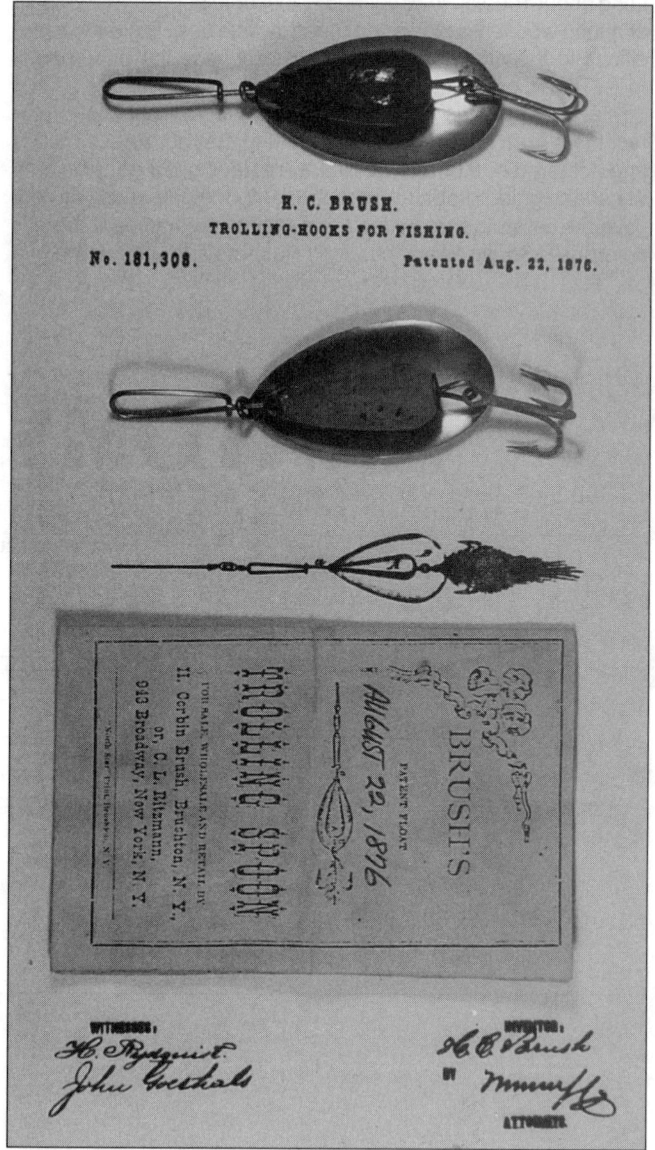

Here are two actual Brush Floating Spinners and a paper flyer that came with the lure. They are lying on a photo of part of the original patent.

There were no further major innovations in artificial lures until around 1890. About this time, the first U.S.-made artificial minnows that reflected the look of a natural minnow began to appear This bait was usually made of wood and is the first manufactured bait known to be purposely made to actually look the like a live minnow. Early copies of the original are sometimes found made of hollow aluminum. This particular bait can be said to be the first "plug". Early on, artificial baits were fashioned to look like other critters and made of other materials. Frogs, mice, crawfish and minnows seem to have been the most popular ones imitated.

Although they were very eclectic in their offerings, American fishing tackle companies had but a small stock to offer the bait casting fisherman prior to 1890. These early catalogs catered primarily to the fly fisherman, but did offer limited choices for those who wished to troll or cast spoons and spinners. The plug was rarely mentioned. It was just too new and not yet widely popular. Plugs began to appear more frequently in catalogs around 1892. Along with the "Phantom Minnow" such things as the Caledonian Minnow, the Protean Minnow, the Devon Minnow and various hard and soft rubber minnows began to appear. The rubber minnows were usually offered in a luminous or non-luminous version.

James Heddon, the founder of James Heddon's Sons tackle company, was one of the early pioneers in the lure manufacturing industry that still flourishes in the United States today. There is no concrete evidence to support the contention that he was the first to manufacture what we today refer to as the plug and certainly his company was not the first to produce artificial baits. His story, however, serves well to illustrate what was happening in that era.

In the years 1898 to 1901, Mr. Heddon whittled out a few wooden frogs and minnows for himself and some friends. These early plugs became the basis for the establishment of the Heddon company founded in 1901.

Naturally these baits were extremely limited in number and precious few exist today. A version of each was made commercially available by the infant Heddon company, but no early catalogs were found that illustrated them.

Along about the same time, or very shortly thereafter, the other bait companies were beginning to show a few plugs in their catalogs. One of the first was a revolutionary concept developed by the William Shakespeare company. This is the famous Shakespeare "Revolution" Bait and a variation, the Shakespeare-Worden "Bucktail Spinner." Both were made of wood.

Shakespeare writes in a 1902 catalog that the Revolution Bait "... takes its name from the fact that it has revolutionized fishing in the vicinity of Kalamazoo (Michigan), where it was developed. Whereas formerly all anglers used live bait for bass, pickerel, pike and other game fish, now nothing is used but the Shakespeare baits. The reason is very apparent, as these baits catch good strings of fish were every other kind of bait fails."*

The variation, the Shakespeare-Worden Bucktail Spinner derives its name from Shakespeare's modification of the Revolution Bait by adding the bucktail originated from Mr. F. G. Worden of South Bend, Indiana, the founder of the South Bend Bait Company.

There were many other developments in the first decade of the 1900s. Mr. Ans B. Decker originated a top-water plug which was and still is the old "Lake Hapatcong" plug.

There were several close copies of this design, not the least of which was the Mills Yellow Kid. Named after a popular comic strip character of the times, this lure was made of copper. Mills also

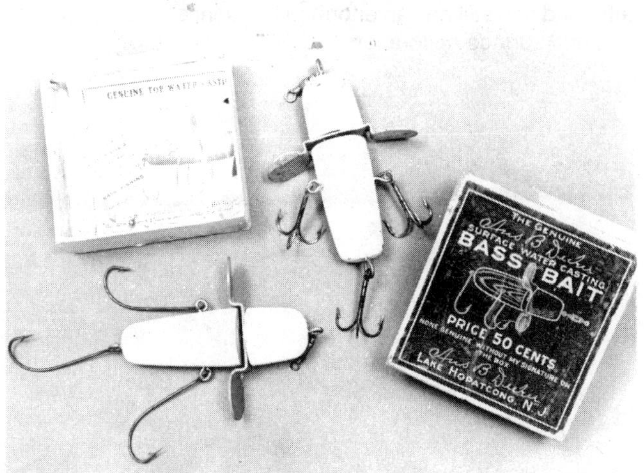

These are two Deckers and an original Decker box. Both have his name stamped on the propeller blades.

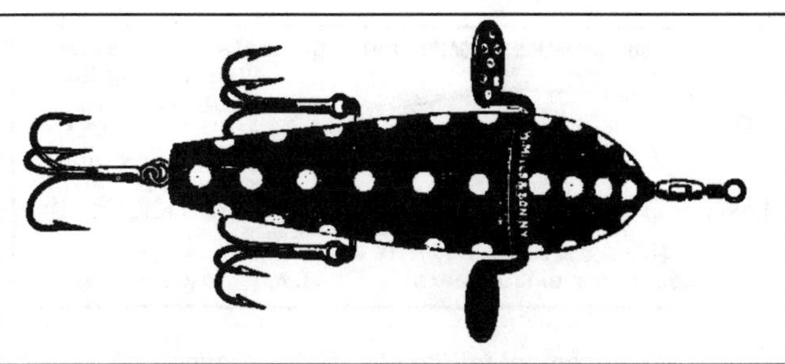
A Jersey Queen lure from a 1924 Marshall Field catalog.

brought out a similar plug made of wood called the Jersey Queen.

Also during this period were born the famed "Dowagiac Minnows" by Heddon, the "Coaxer" and the "Teaser".

The "Coaxer" and "Teasers" were developed by the W. J. Jamison Company. The original models were made of cork enameled white with wings of red felt and the tail was composed of a number of red feathers.

*From *Fine Points About Tackle-Being a Catalog of Fine Fishing Tackle, suited to the Needs of Anglers Who Follow the "Art of Bait-Casting.* Copyright 1902 by William Shakespeare, Jr., Kalmazoo, Michigan.

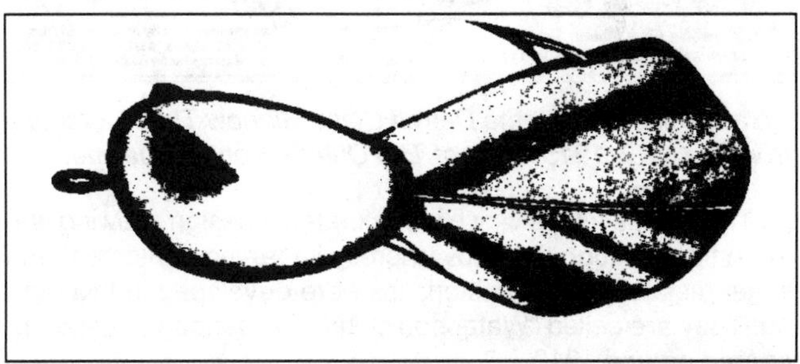
A Jamison Coaxer from a 1909 Abercrombie & Fitch catalog.

Variations of the original "Phantom Minnow" continued. 1906 saw the first Bing's "Weedless Nemahbin Minnow" by A. F. Bingenheimer of Milwaukee and in 1907 the K and K Manufacturing Company of Toledo, Ohio touted their "Animated Minnows" as an unprecedented development. They consisted of a divided wooden minnow, jointed at about the middle so that they wriggled along in the water.

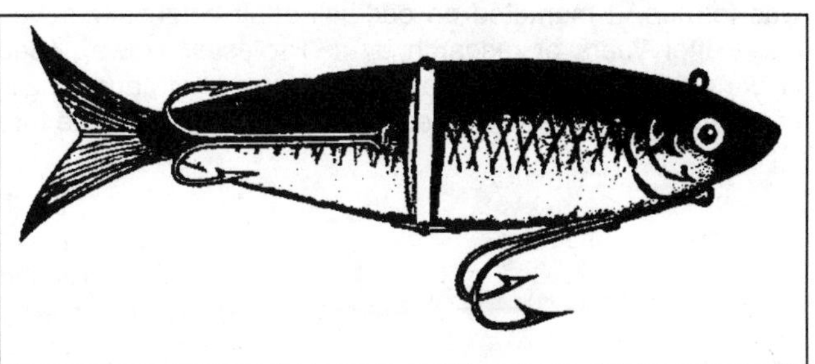
The 1910 Abercrombie & Fitch catalog illustration of the K & K Animated Minnow mentioned in the text.

A 1907 Abercrombie and Fitch catalog illustrated a soft rubber mouse covered with real skin. "A splendid bait for black bass. Mounted with single hook of proper size and watch-spring swivel."

1910-1920

The "Famous Moonlight Floating Bait" appeared advertised first in a 1910 copy of the *Angler's Guide*. This curious bait was

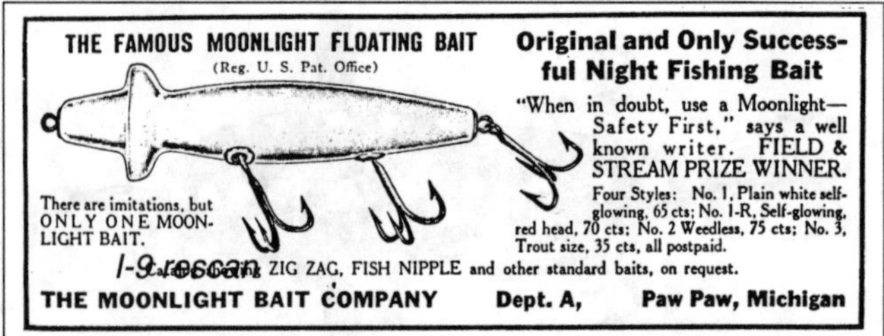

A 1915 advertisement for the Moonlight Floating Bait.

called by its maker, the "Original and only successful night fishing bait." This apparently because it was painted with a luminous paint which allegedly glowed in the dark.

About the same time, the Detroit Glass Minnow Tube Company introduced a lure in which one could place a live minnow. It was a glass test tube-like affair with a cap allowing circulation of water and four treble hooks. According to their advertisement in the May 1915 issue of Field and Stream the bait had a "Magnifying glass tube" and the minnow would remain alive all day.

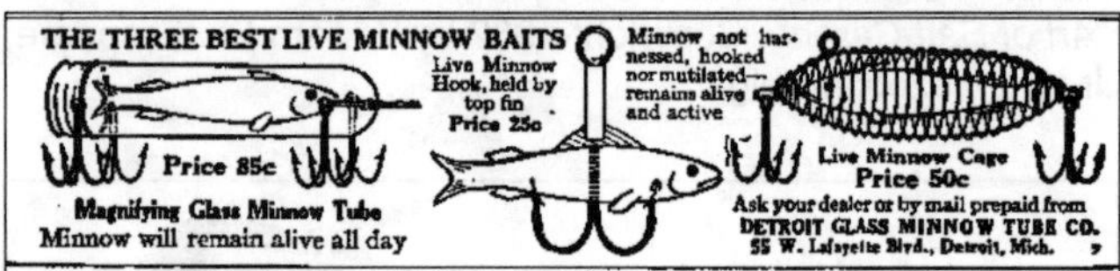

An advertisement by the Detroit Glass Minnow Tube Company from the May, 1915 issue of The Outer's Book magazine.

The earliest plugs which incorporated a design allowing water to flow through the body, thereby imparting movement and water disturbance characteristics were developed in this period. They are called "Water sonic" lures. It is thought these appeared around 1912.

There are several other interesting and curious plug developments during this decade. For instance there is "The Booster Bait." The advertisement in a pre-1915 Bob Smith Tackle and Camping Goods catalog states it was a prize winner at the Seattle Exposition. It was a plug " ... filled with edible matter and containing a capsule which, when placed in water, dissolves, throwing off a strong taste and smell." One can only assume the taste and smell was irresistible to the fish.

Somewhere in this time period the Vacuum Bait Company was formed. It marketed an odd-ball affair ostensibly developed after years of research by a "Professor Howe". (See Howe's Vacuum Bait Company listing for a photo and details of the lure and its development.) The plug was a surface lure and the shape caused a spray, when retrieving, that attracted fish. It was later produced by South Bend.

A particularly clever weedless plug developed around 1914 was called "The Captor". It was invented by J. B. Fischer of Chicago and is detailed in the Fischer-Schuberth Co. listing later in this volume.

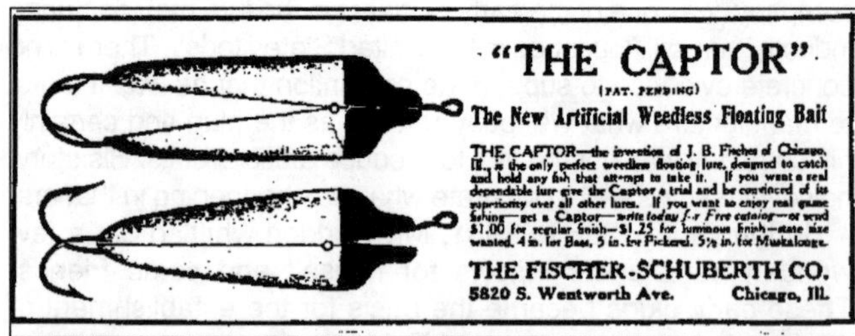

A 1914 advertisement for "The Captor".

Another ingenious invention, a "Spinner" plug was the "Chippewa" introduced in 1913 by the Immell Bait Company in Blair, Wisconsin. It is a wooden plug with the center portion cut out and a piece of twisted metal placed on an armature in such a way as to revolve when retrieved causing a flashing effect by reflecting light. It is illustrated in the Immell Bait Company section.

It was during the years between 1900 and 1920 that Creek Chub, South Bend, Heddon, Pflueger, Jamison, Rush, Mills, etc., established themselves firmly in the lure business. Many of the designs developed then are still in use today! Perhaps modified but nevertheless the same basic concept is utilized.

1920-1950s

We have discussed most of the major developments in plugs in the early days. There were, of course many more produced in that era, but almost all were merely variations on a theme. Most will be discussed and illustrated in the expanded Collector's Identification and Value Guide.

From 1920 on, there were other developments in plugs but these were more of a technical nature such as improved swivel designs and better hook hardware. The experimentation with materials other than wood and metal such as the use of Tenite and mother of pearl are good examples. Perhaps one of the most important influencing design and manufacture was the advent of plastics.

Other important influences were better and better paints and increasing interest in researching the habits of fish. The latter had and still has an enormous influence on plug body design and surface decoration.

ILLUSTRATIONS OF EARLY PATENTS IN THE DEVELOPMENT OF LURES AND THEIR COMPONENTS

From the early 1890's on there were a number of rather amusing attempts at animation of artificial lures. Some of them would rival the fabled "Rube Goldberg Apparatus". A few of them were so complicated that the angler would have had to be an experienced mechanical engineer to repair and maybe even to operate the crazy things. Some of the patent drawings of these contraptions are illustrated on the following pages.

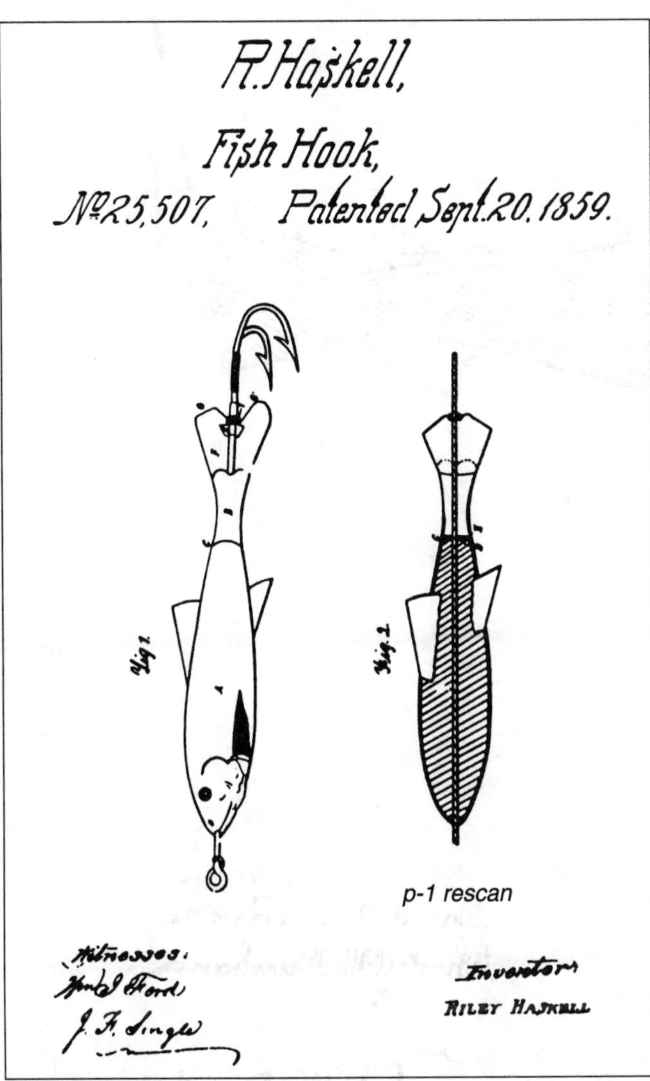

R. Haskell,
Fish Hook,
No. 25,507, Patented Sept. 20, 1859.
p-1 rescan
Witnesses:
Inventor
Riley Haskell

Drawing accompanying the patent application for the famous Haskell Minnow. It is the first known American patent for a lure that mentions wood as a possible material for the body. A wooden version was apparently never made, but the metal version is well known. Originally silver-plated, this very rare lure has brought low five-figure prices in the past, but has dropped to a lower, mid to high four-figure amount. There are only about 30 known to exist.

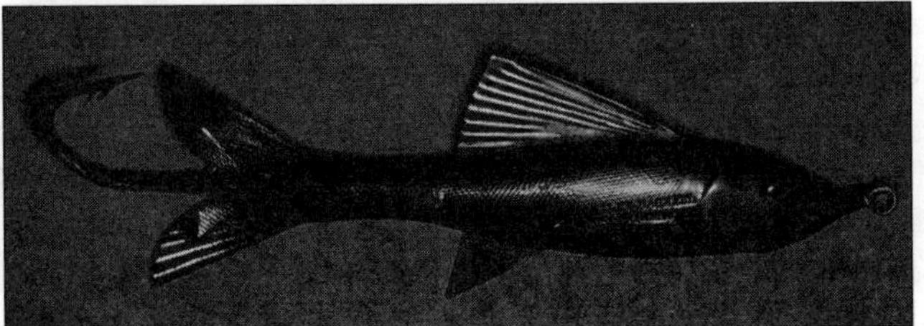

A Haskell Minnow. This example measures 5-5/8" overall (including hook and line tie). The body measures 4-9/16". The overall length varies from lure to lure. The other side of the lure is stamped "R. HASKELL PAINESVIL, O. PAT'D. DEC. 20, 1859". The fin and scale finish are beautifully rendered, due probably to the fact that Haskell was a gunsmith.

D. HUARD & C. M. DUNBAR.

Trolling Fish-Hooks.

No. 151,394. **Patented May 26, 1874.**

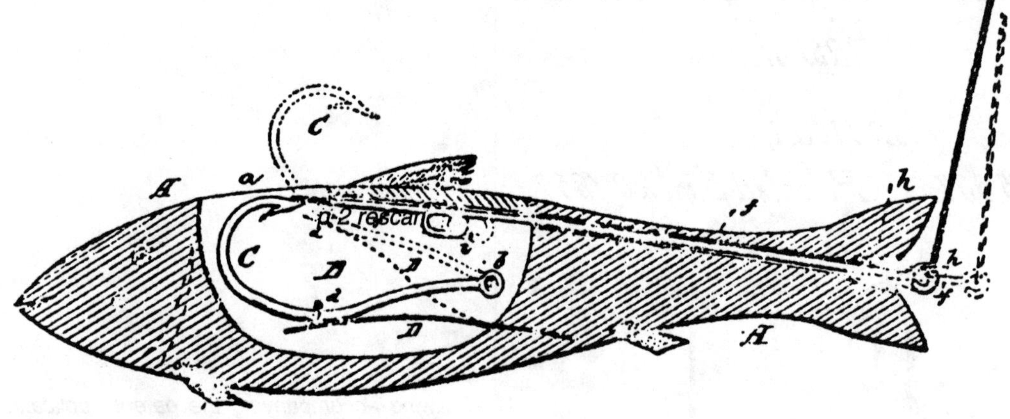

WITNESSES:

INVENTORS

David Huard

Charles M. Dunbar

per C. H. Watson & Co.
ATTORNEYS.

Illustration accompanying the application for the first known granted patent for an artificial lure specifying "... wood or other suitable material" for the body.

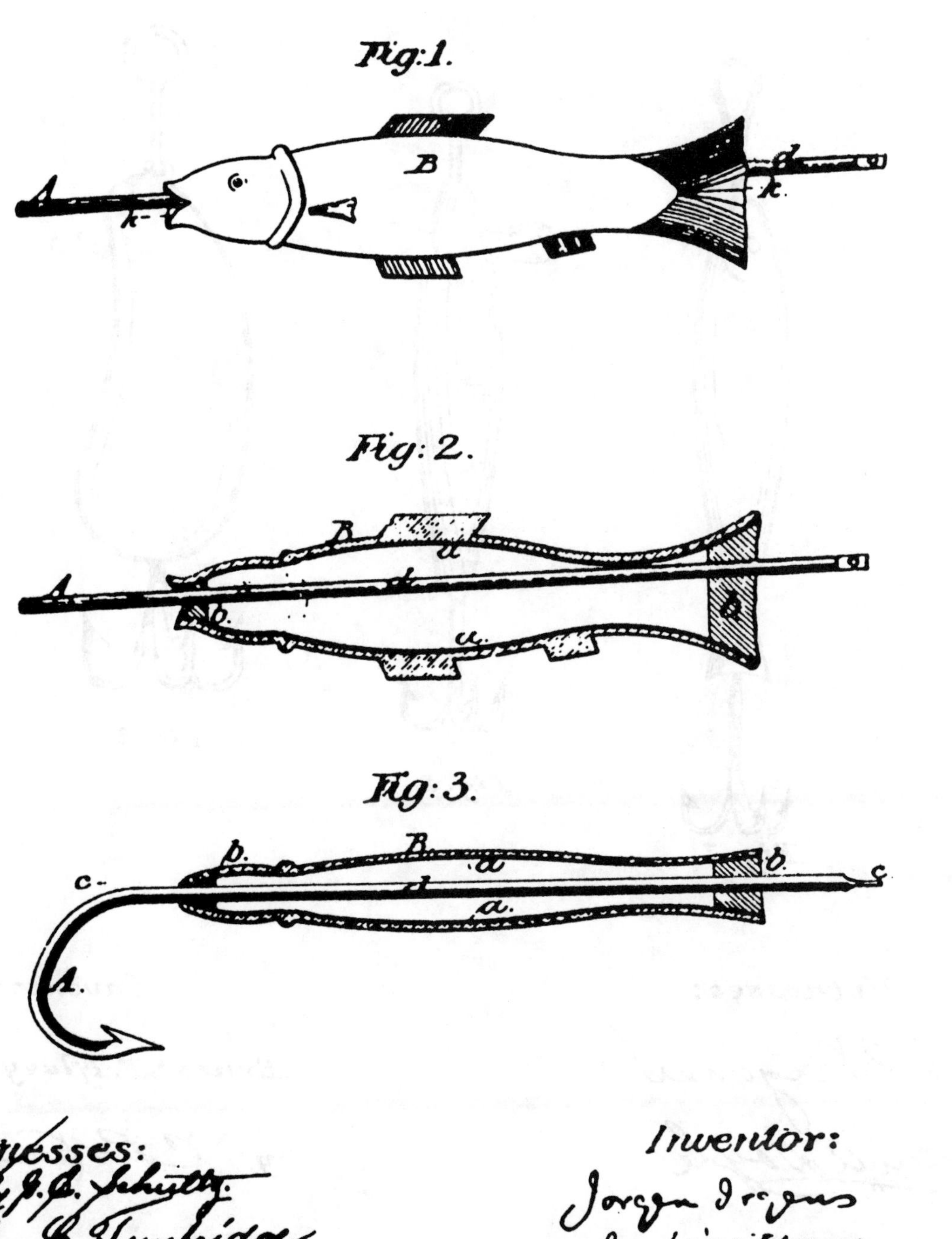

Illustration accompanying the U.S. patent application for the first known artificial lure specifying glass for the lure body. Granted Sept. 7, 1880 to Jorgen Irgens of Bergern, Norway.

(No Modél.)

E. F. PFLUEGER.

ARTIFICIAL FISH BAIT.

No. 272,317. Patented Feb. 13, 1883.

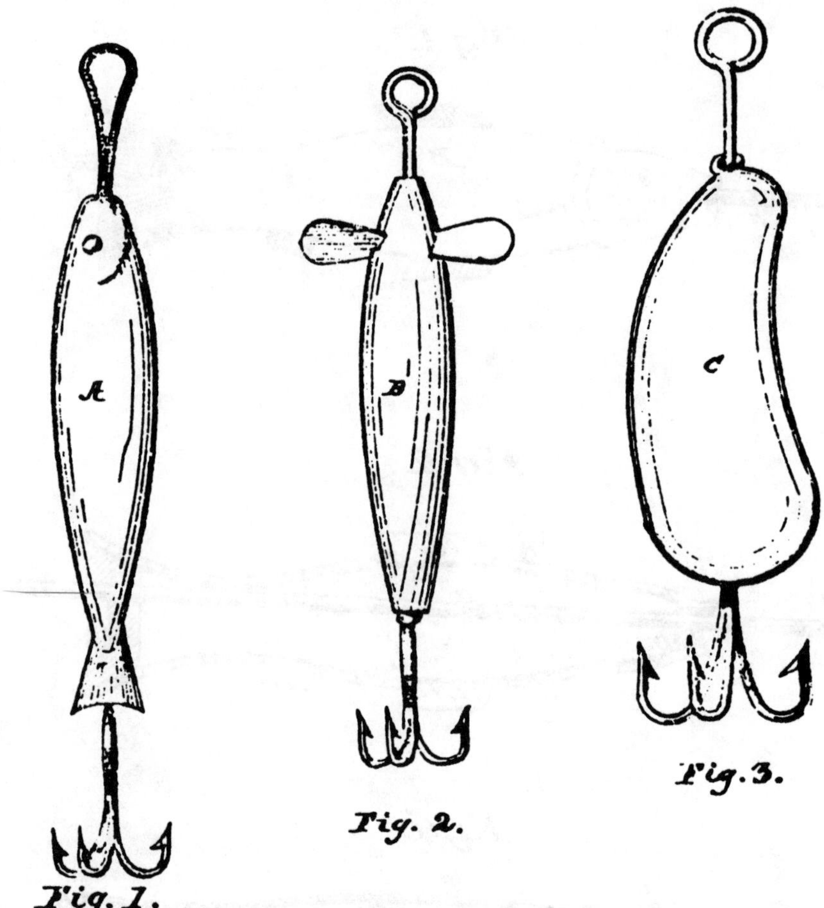

Witnesses:

C. F. Wagoner

Dayton A Doyle

Inventor:

Ernest F. Pflueger,

by C. P. Humphrey

Atty.

Lures on which Pflueger obtained the first patent for a lure coated with luminous paint. Granted Feb. 13, 1883.

(No Model.)

C. J. W. GAIDE.

ARTIFICIAL FISHING BAIT.

No. 567,310. Patented Sept. 8, 1896.

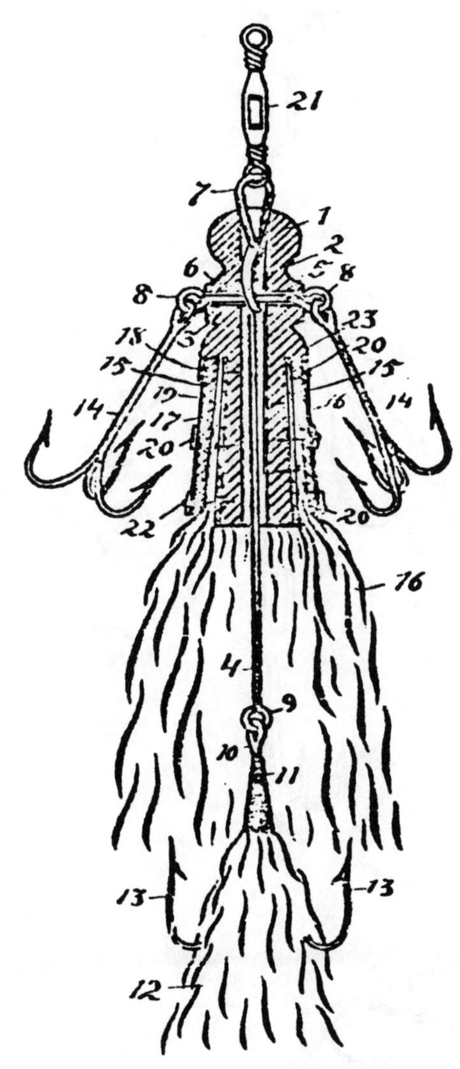

WITNESSES: Carl J. W. Gaide INVENTOR

J. W. Wilson

BY H. G. Burns

Emmett V. Harris

his ATTORNEY.

A very early wood body lure patented September 8, 1896 by Carl J. W. Gaide. Found advertised in a 1898 Smelzer and Son sporting goods catalog.

(No Model.)

H. COMSTOCK.

ARTIFICIAL BAIT.

No. 271,424. Patented Jan. 30, 1883.

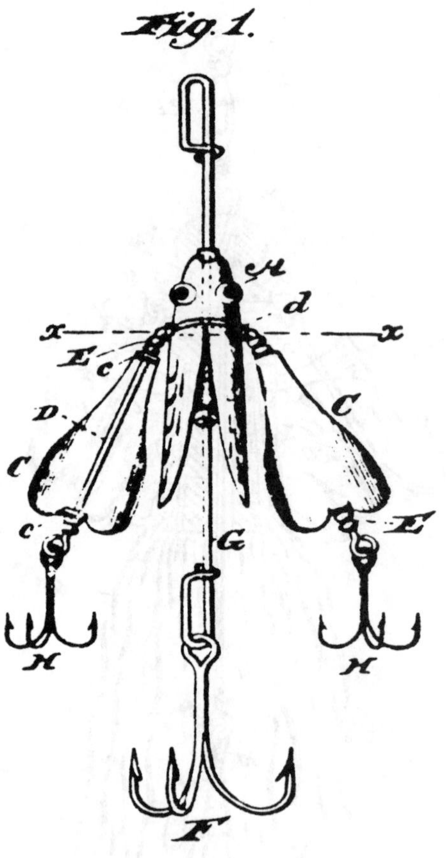

Fig. 2.

Fig. 3

A d

D

G

Witnesses.

Robert Everett

J. A. Rutherford

Inventor.

Harry Comstock.

By James L. Norris.

Atty.

This is the original patent drawing accompanying the patent application for Harry Comstock's wood body Flying Hellgrammite. Granted January 30, 1883.

No. 777,488. PATENTED DEC. 13, 1904.

F. D. RHODES.

FISH BAIT OR LURE.

APPLICATION FILED NOV. 2, 1903.

NO MODEL.

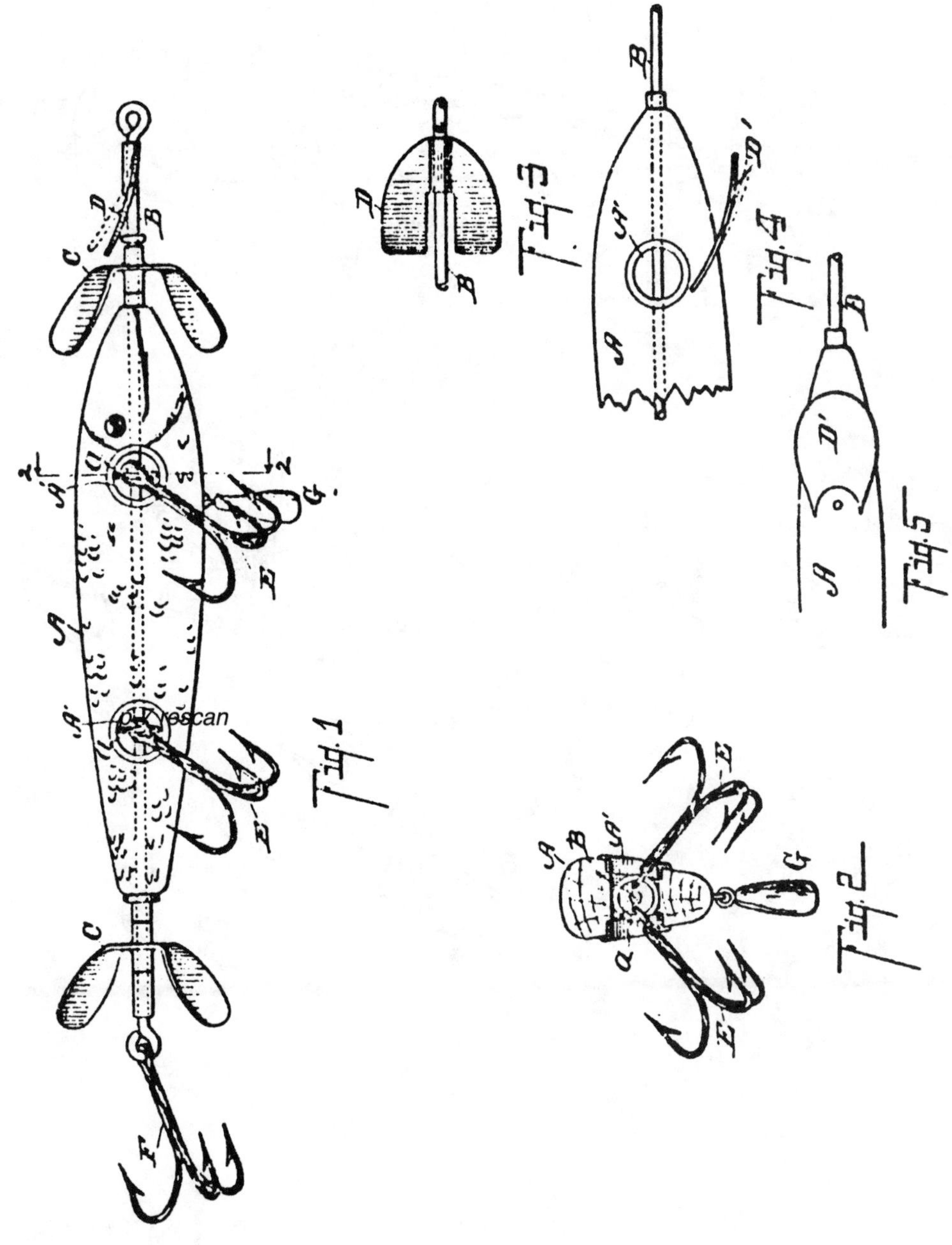

Witnesses:

A. Irene Adams

Otto O. Earl

Inventor.

Fred D Rhodes

This patent drawing illustrates the first time the see-through hook hanger shows up in patent applications and it is fully described in the text of the patent. The patent was granted to Fred D. Rhodes of Kalamazoo, Michigan on Dec. 13, 1904 and full rights were assigned to Frederick C. Austin of Chicago. The Shakespeare Company marketed the Rhodes Wooden Minnow.

J. E. PFLUEGER.

ARTIFICIAL BAIT.

APPLICATION FILED APR. 16, 1908

954,691. Patented Apr. 12, 1910.

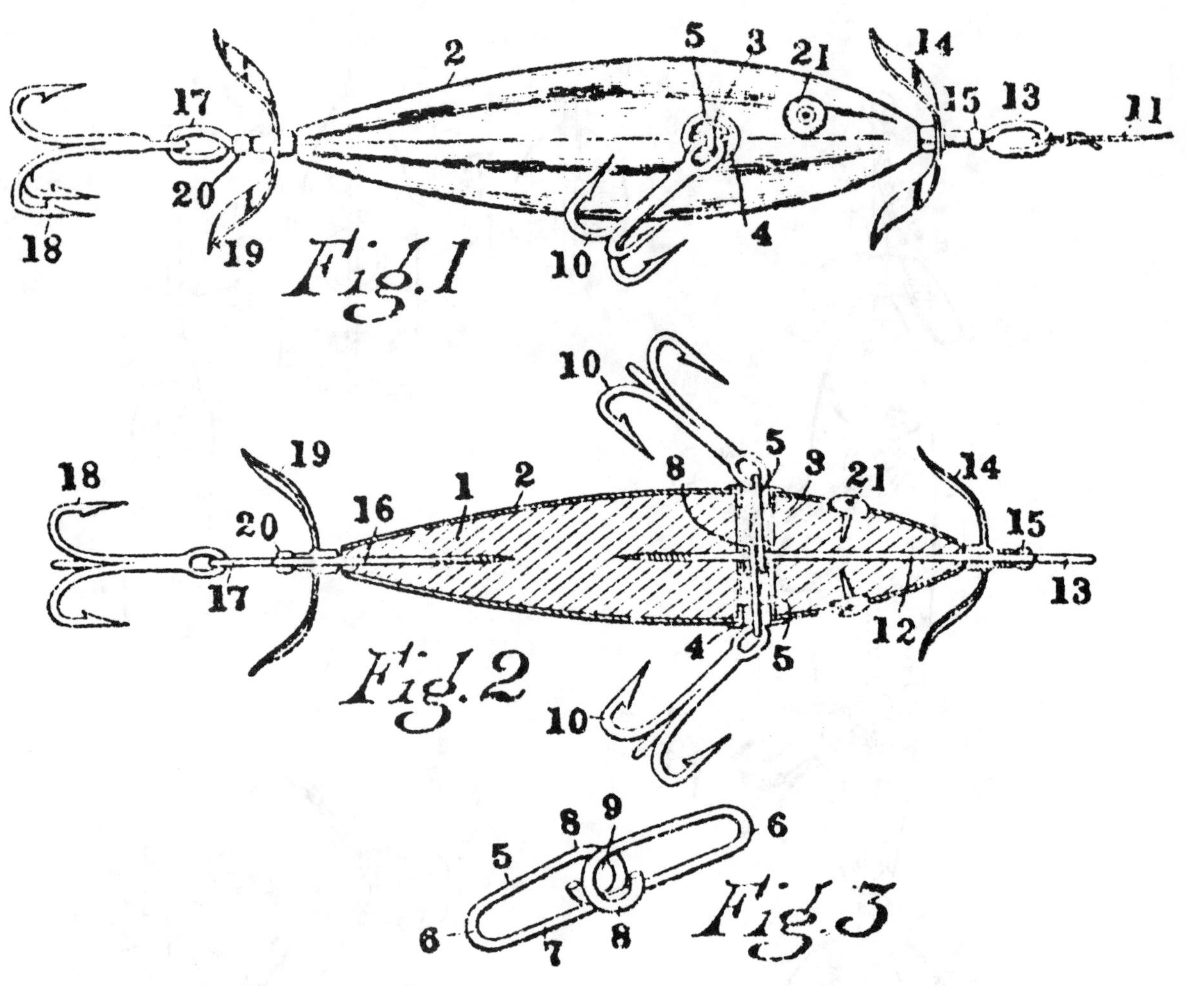

Witnesses:

INVENTOR–

Joseph E. Pflueger,

By C. E. Humphrey, Attorney.

This patent drawing illustrates another see-through hook hanger claimed by Pflueger and granted on April 12, 1910. However there is a "disclaimer" attached to the end of the text. It is dated August 6, 1914, and withdraws the claim to the patent rights. This was, apparently, because of the prior patent granted to Rhodes in 1904.

E. A. PFLUEGER.
ARTIFICIAL BAIT.
APPLICATION FILED MAY 18, 1911.

1,007,007. Patented Oct. 24, 1911.

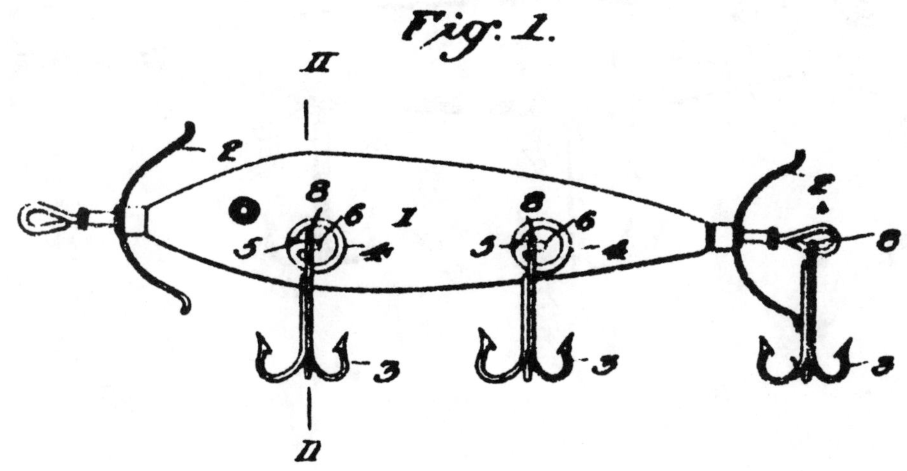

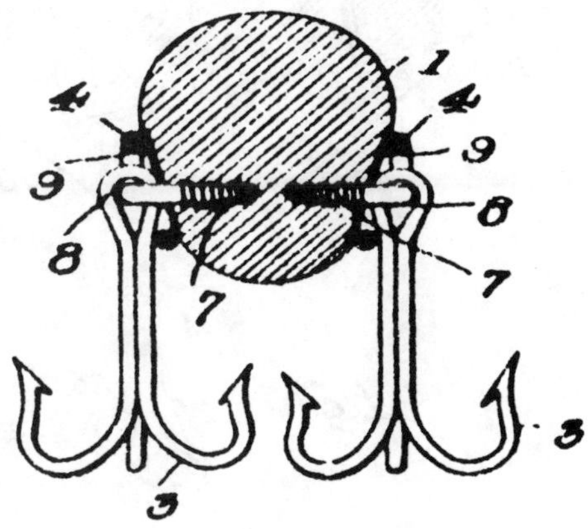

Fig: 3.

Witnesses

Inventor

By

Attorney

Patent illustration of the Pflueger patent of the "Neverfail" Hook hanger. Granted Oct. 24,1911.

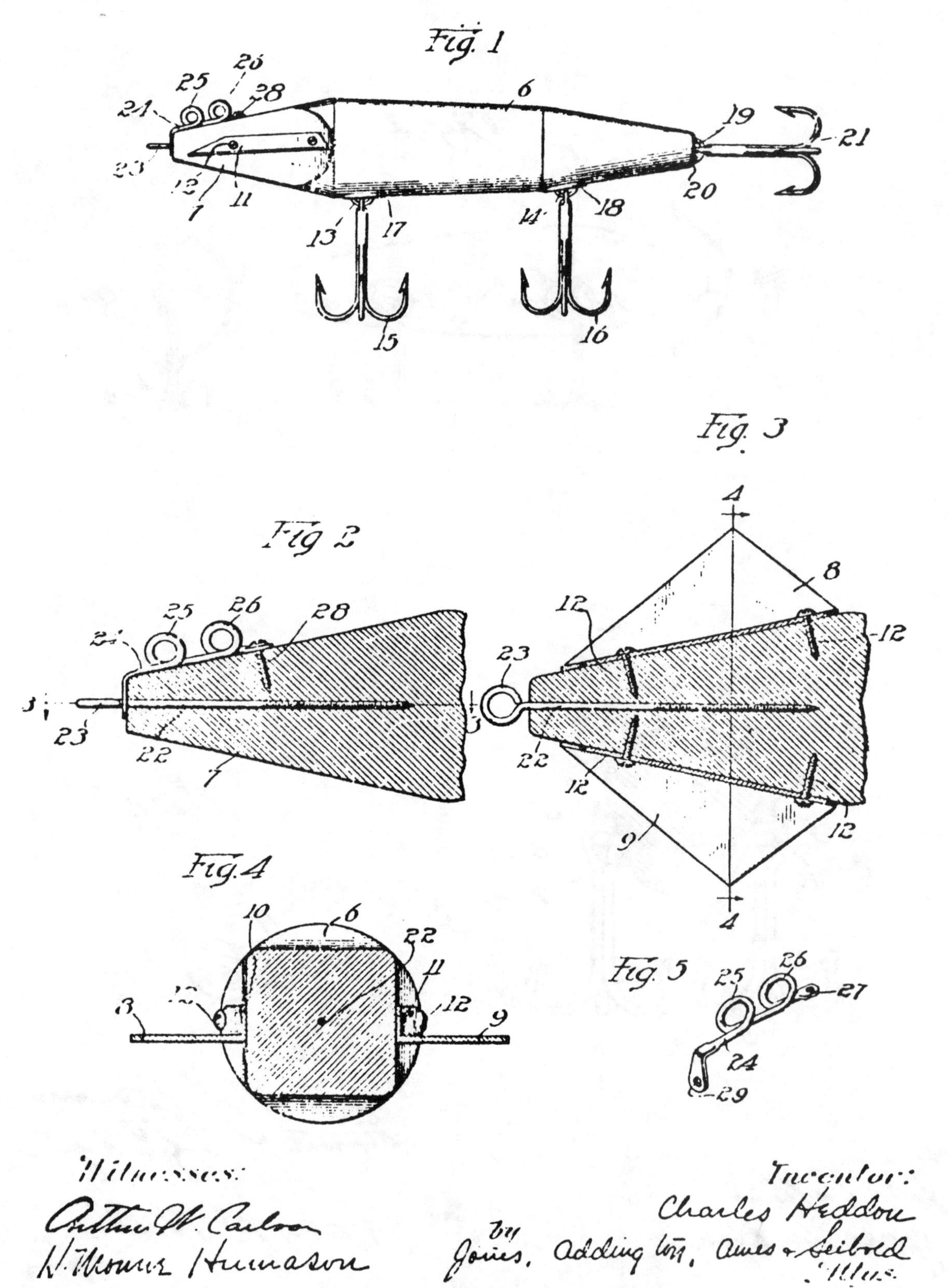

Patent illustration of Heddon's claim for the "pigtail" type Variable Line Tie. Granted Oct. 20, 1914.

C. HEDDON.

FISH HOOK.

APPLICATION FILED DEC. 26, 1912.

1,133,724. Patented Mar. 30, 1915.

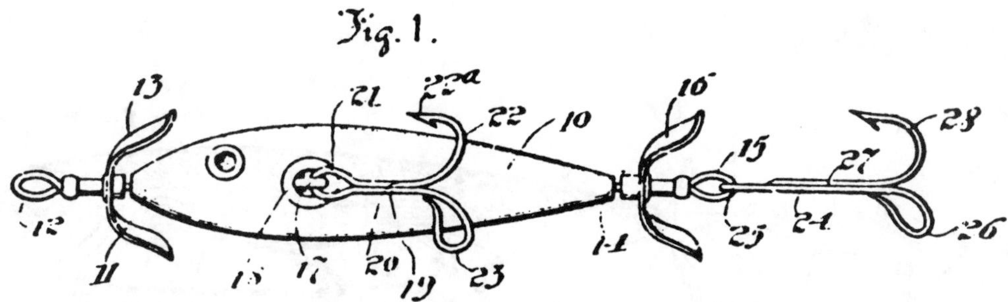

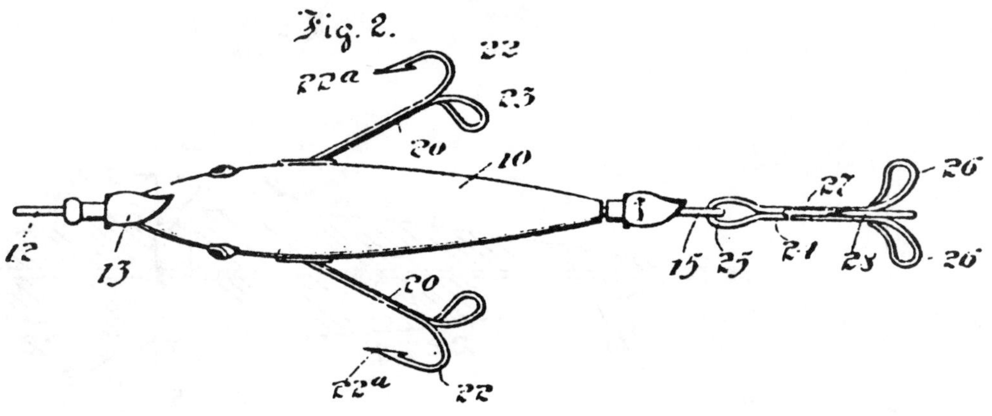

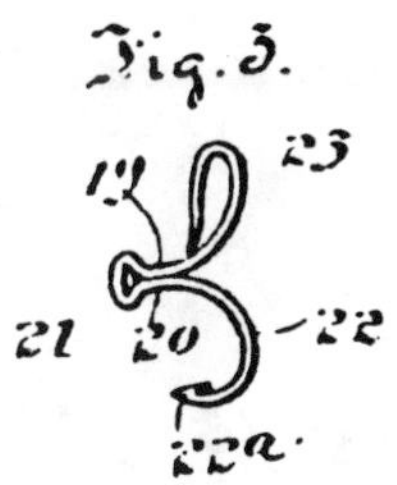

Witnesses
Charles J. Cope
Mae Hanover

Inventor
Charles Heddon
By Jones, Addington & Ames Seibold
Attys.

Patent illustration of Heddon's "Dummy Double" detachable double hook. Granted March 30, 1915.

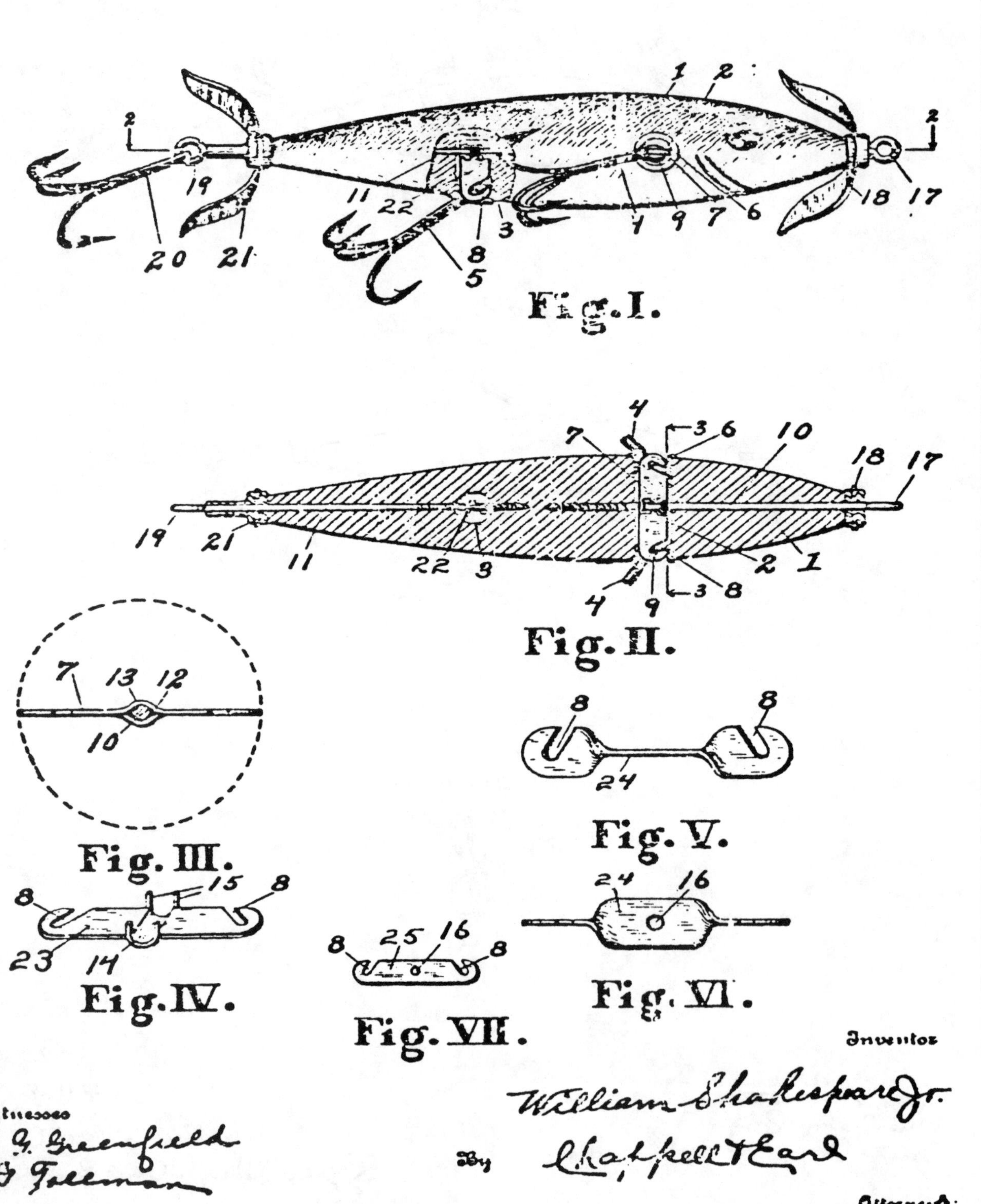

The Shakespeare patent for the one-piece plate-style hook hanger. Note there are four different types in the drawing. Granted August 17, 1915.

C. HEDDON.

FISH LURE.

APPLICATION FILED MAY 20, 1915.

1,276,062. Patented Aug. 20, 1918.

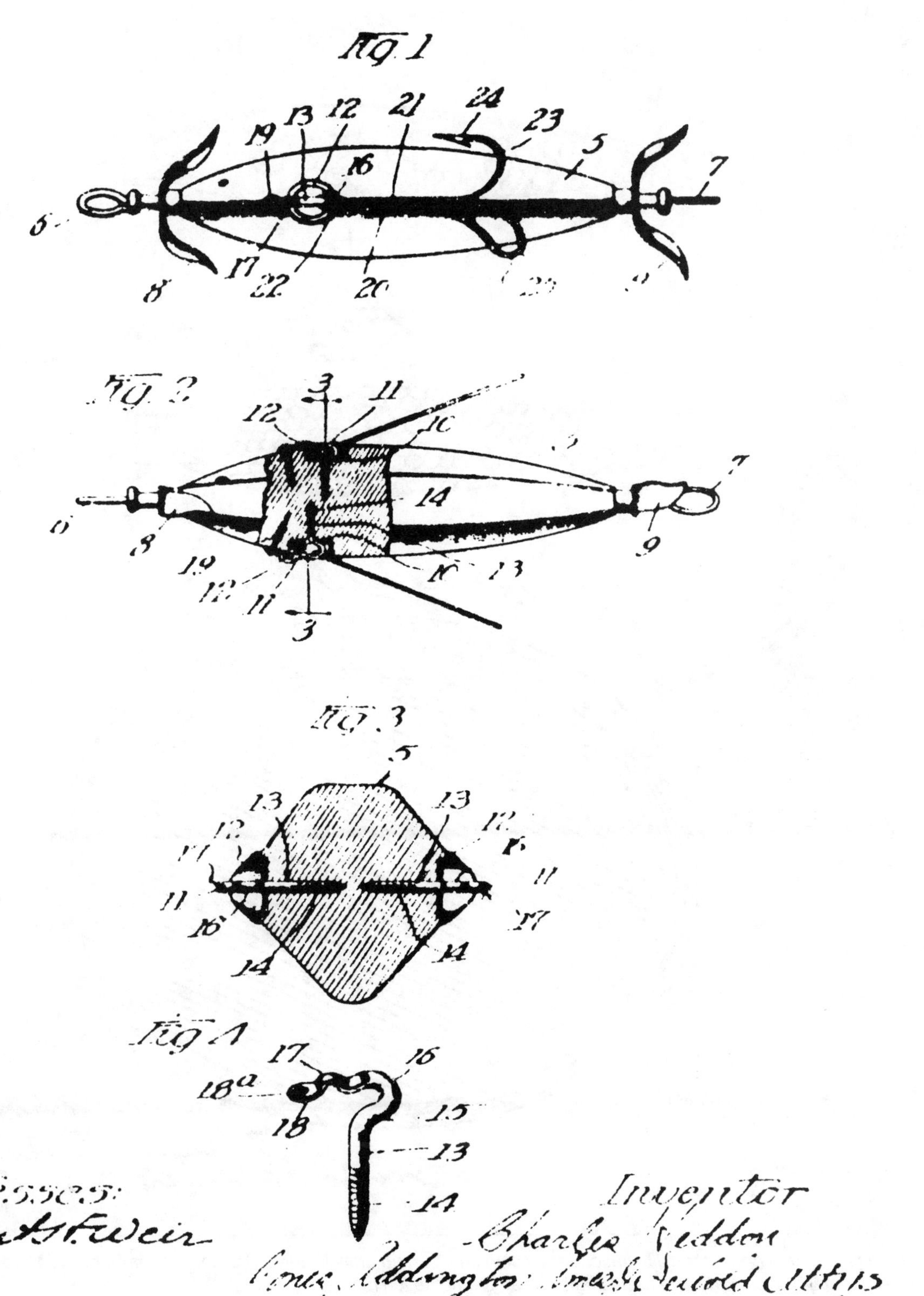

Illustration accompanying the patent application for Heddon's "L-rig" hook hanger. Granted to Charles Heddon August 20, 1918.

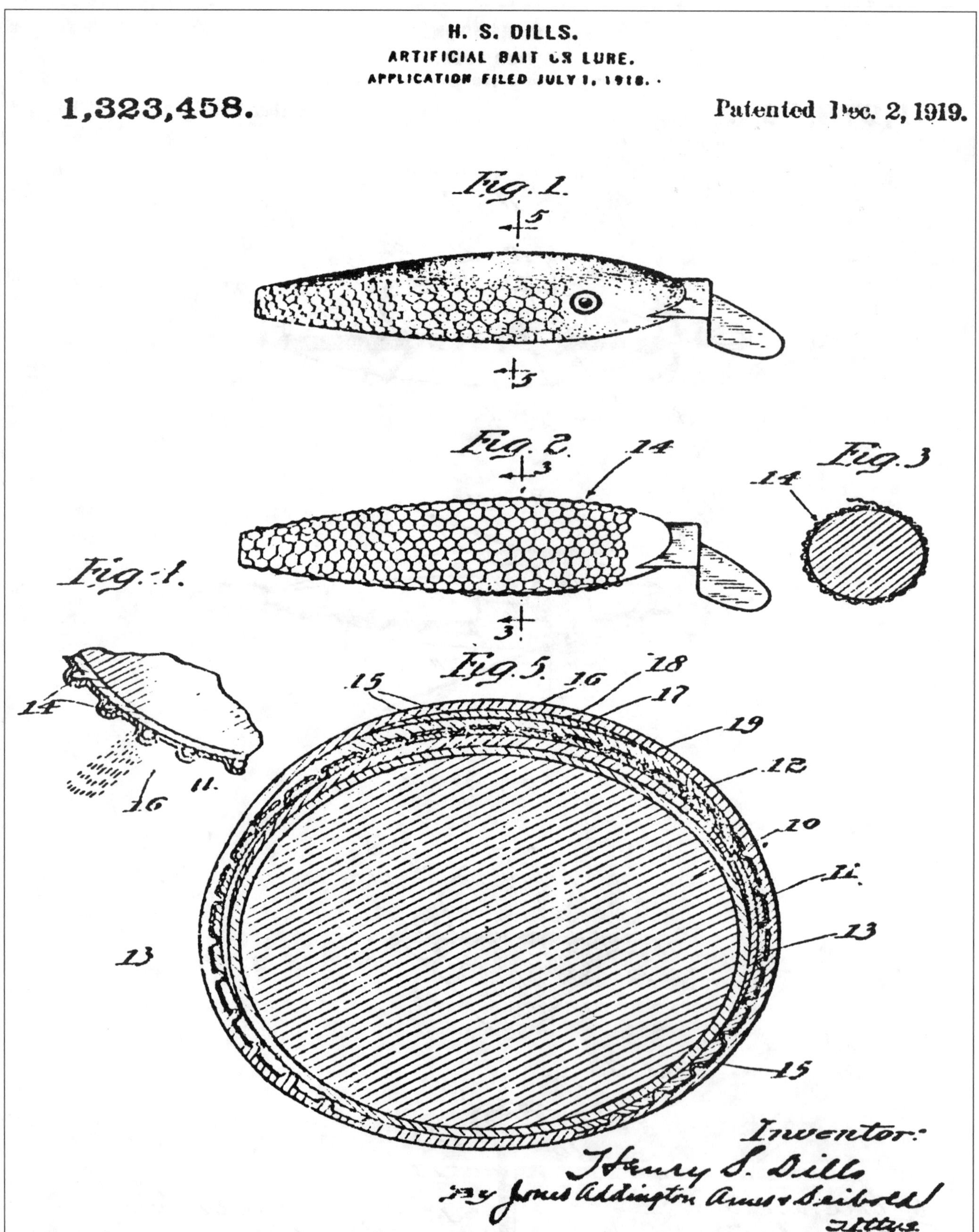

The original patent application illustration for a scale finish on an artificial lure. Granted December 2, 1919 to Henry S. Dills of the Creek Chub Bait Company and assigning one-half the rights to Heddon.

W. A. STOLLEY.

ARTIFICIAL BAIT.

APPLICATION FILED JAN. 22, 1917.

1,376,590. Patented May 3, 1921.

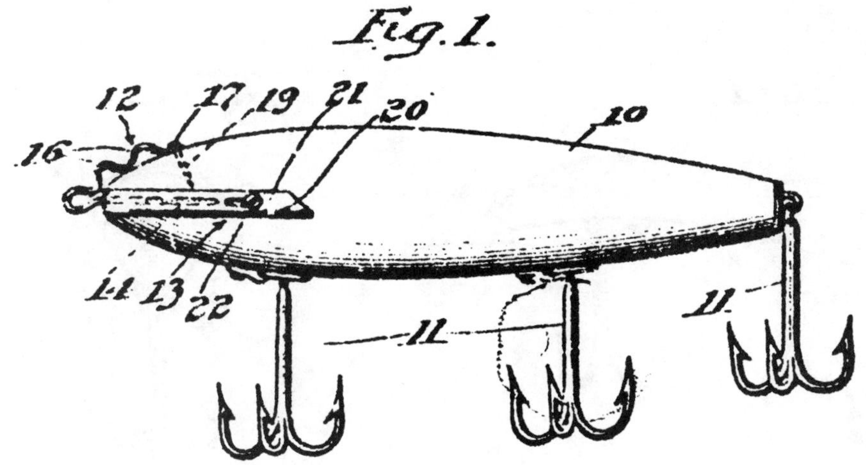

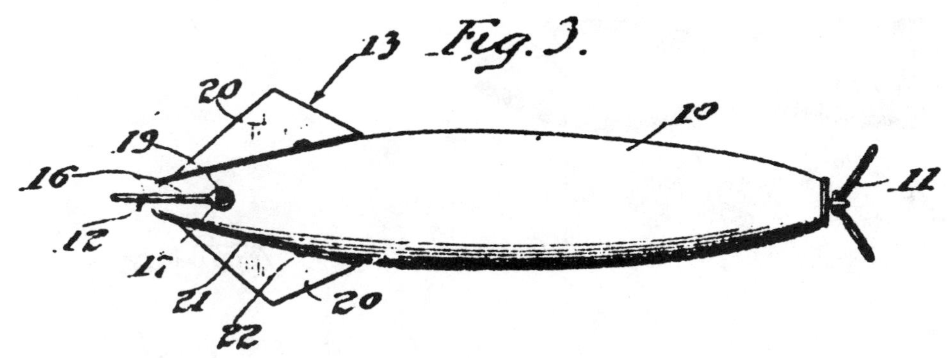

Fig. 2.
17
18
16
14
15
12

Witnesses:
W. T. Smith

Inventor.
William A. Stolley.
By Jones, Addington, Ames & Seibold
Attys.

The drawing accompanying Heddon's patent application for the "inchworm" type variable line tie. Granted May 3, 1921 to William A. Stolley, a Heddon employee, and assigned to Heddon.

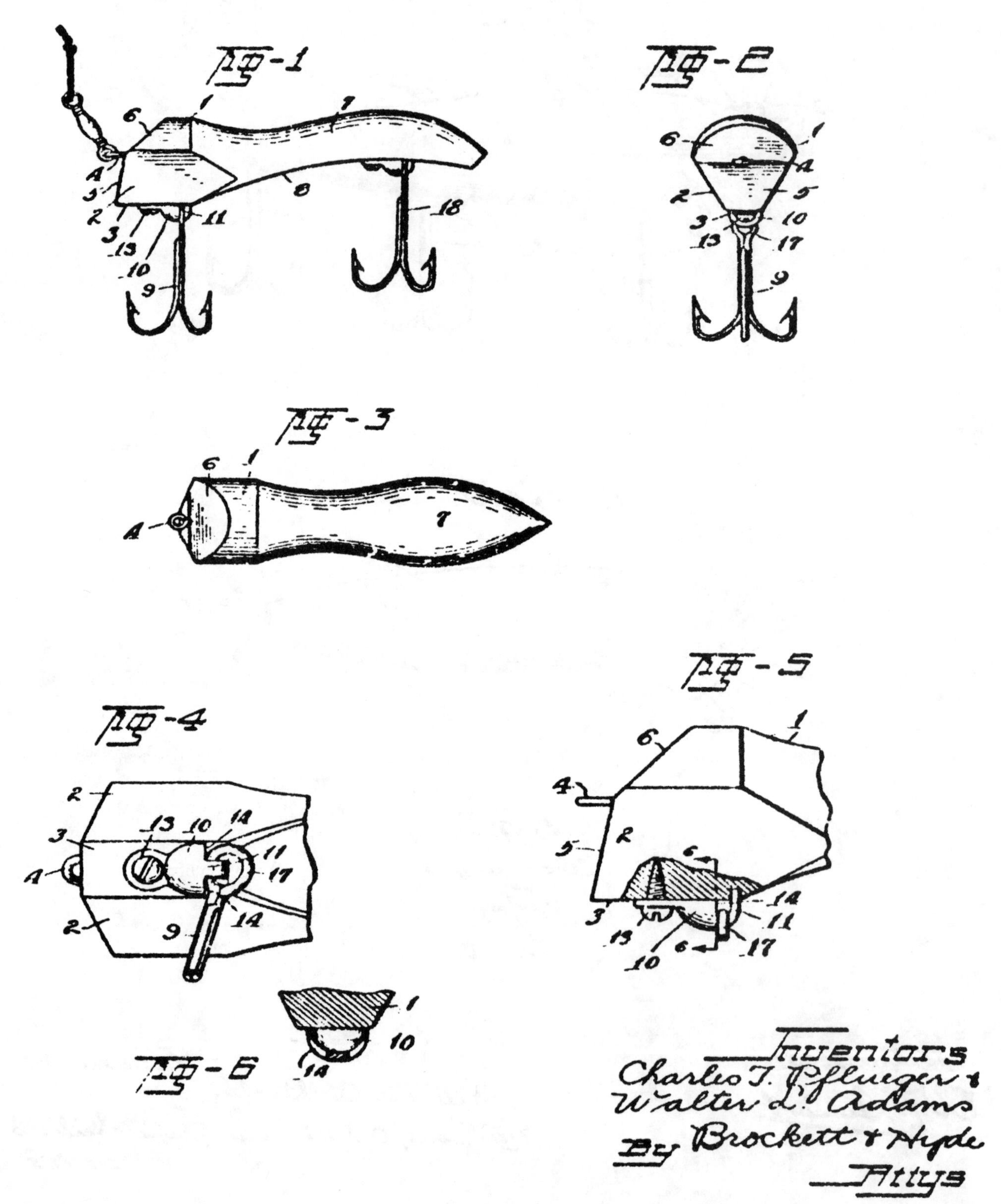

First patent of the one-piece hook hanger. Granted and assigned to Pflueger on June 6, 1922.

Aug. 5, 1930. J. T. WELCH 1,772,058

ARTIFICIAL MINNOW

Filed Jan. 26, 1929

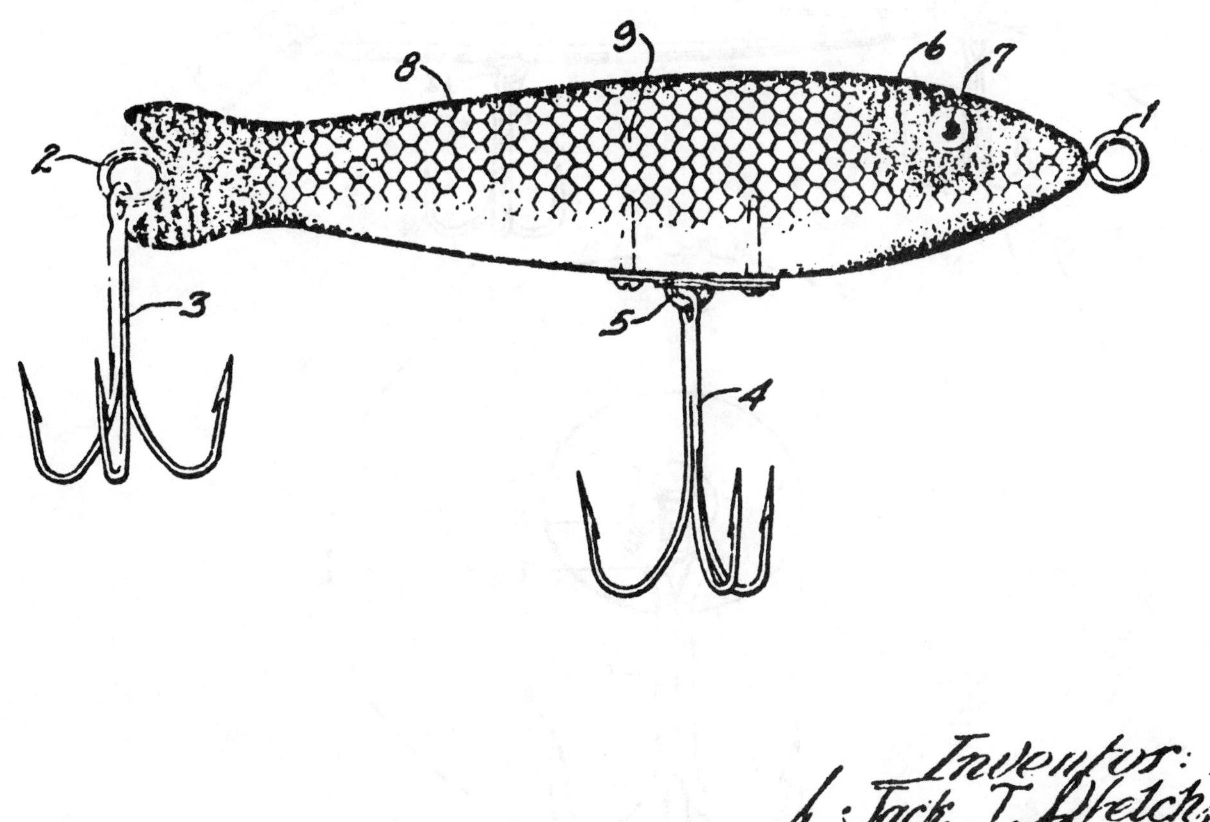

This Heddon patent drawing is the earliest found illustrating a lure with the first two-piece hook fastener. It is also the earliest application Heddon made for a plastic lure. The text stated that it may be made "... of celluloid or pyralin". Applied for in January 1929 and granted August 5, 1930.

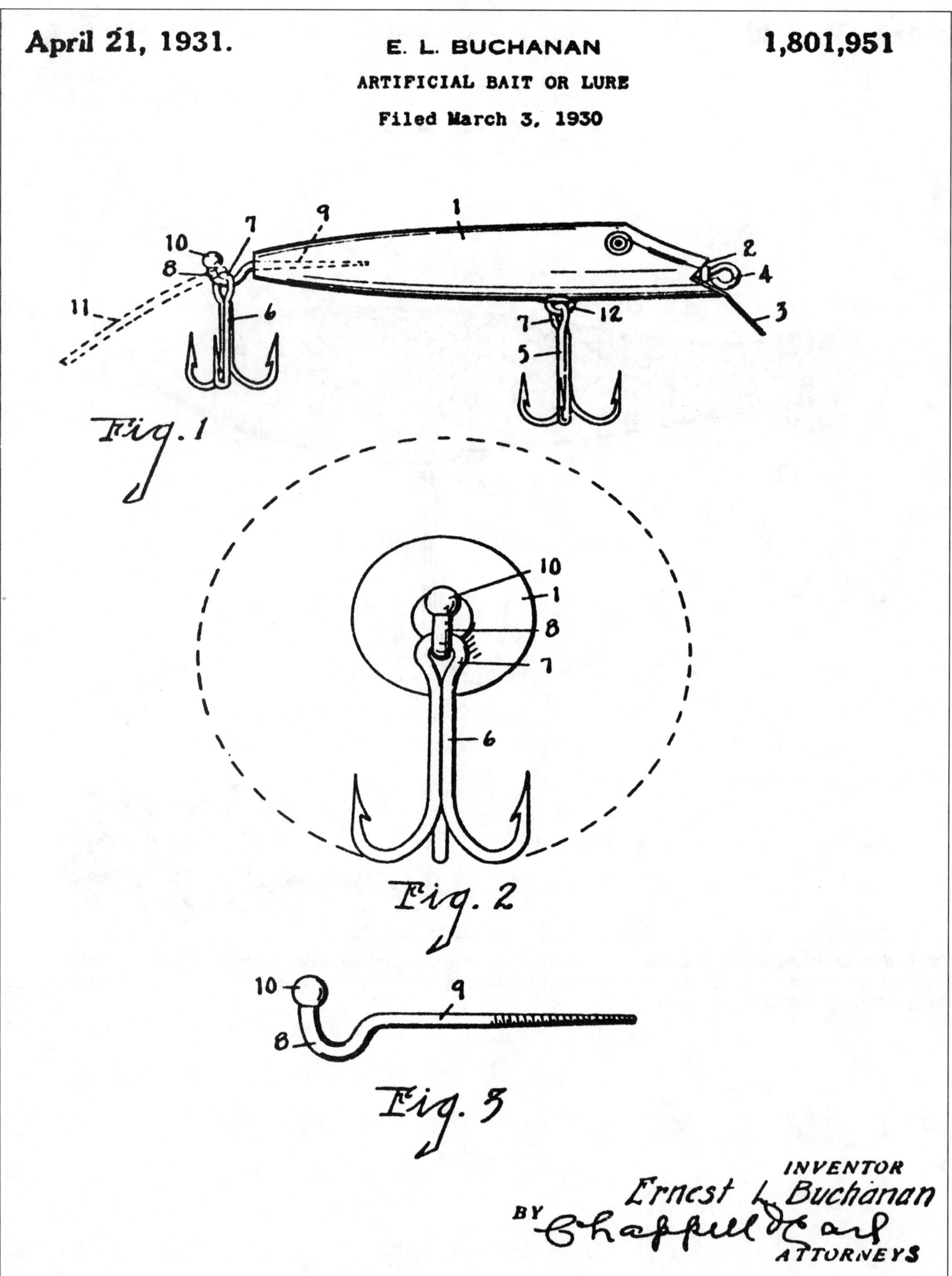

Shakespeare's "Ball Head Hook Retainer" patent. Granted April 21, 1931.

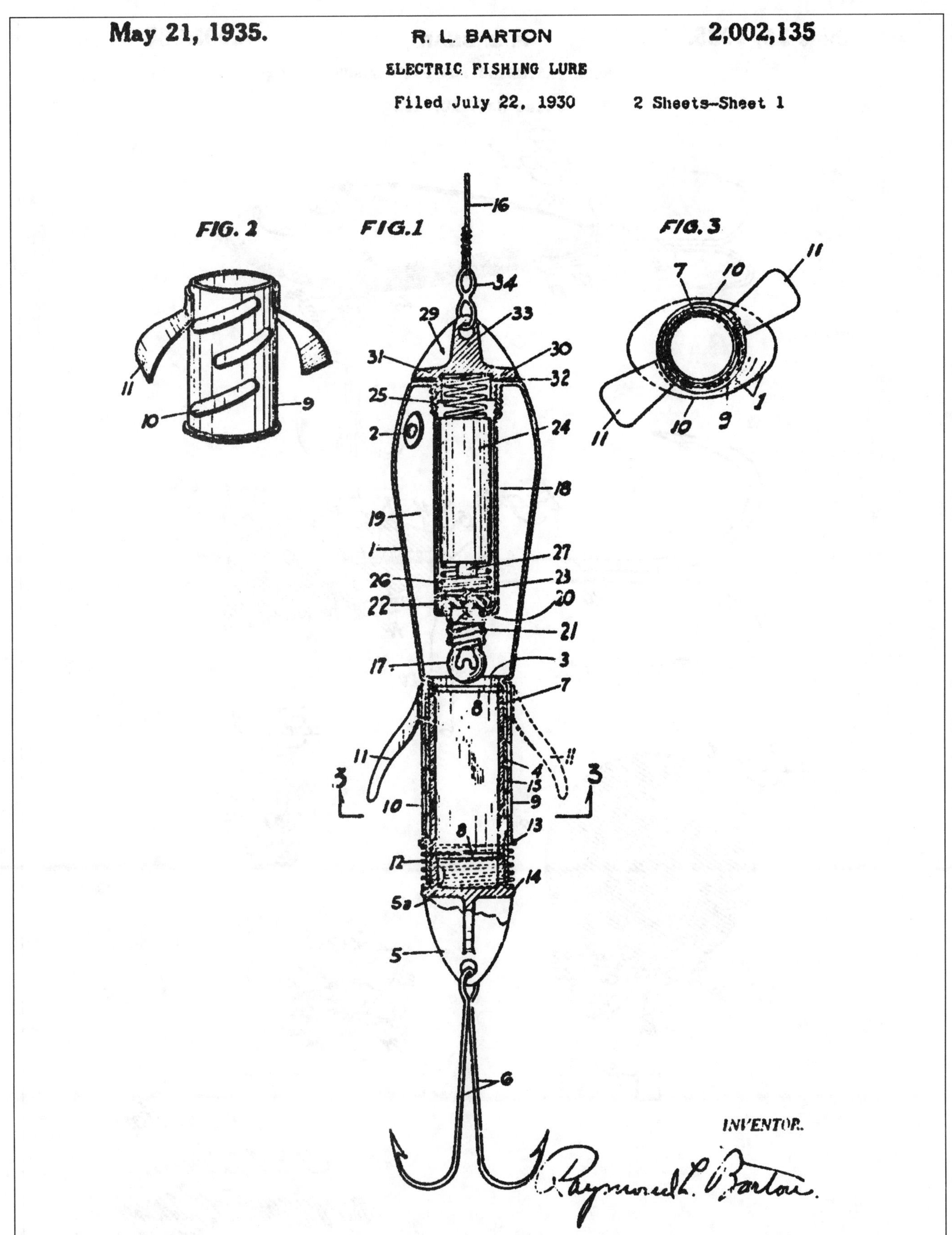

May 21, 1935.
R. L. BARTON
2,002,135
ELECTRIC FISHING LURE
Filed July 22, 1930
2 Sheets-Sheet 1
FIG. 2
FIG. 1
FIG. 3
INVENTOR.
Raymond L. Barton.

One of the many ingenious attempts at a self-illuminating lure using a battery and light bulb. This is the earliest one I ran across in patent records. Granted May 21, 1935 to Raymond L. Barton, San Diego, California.

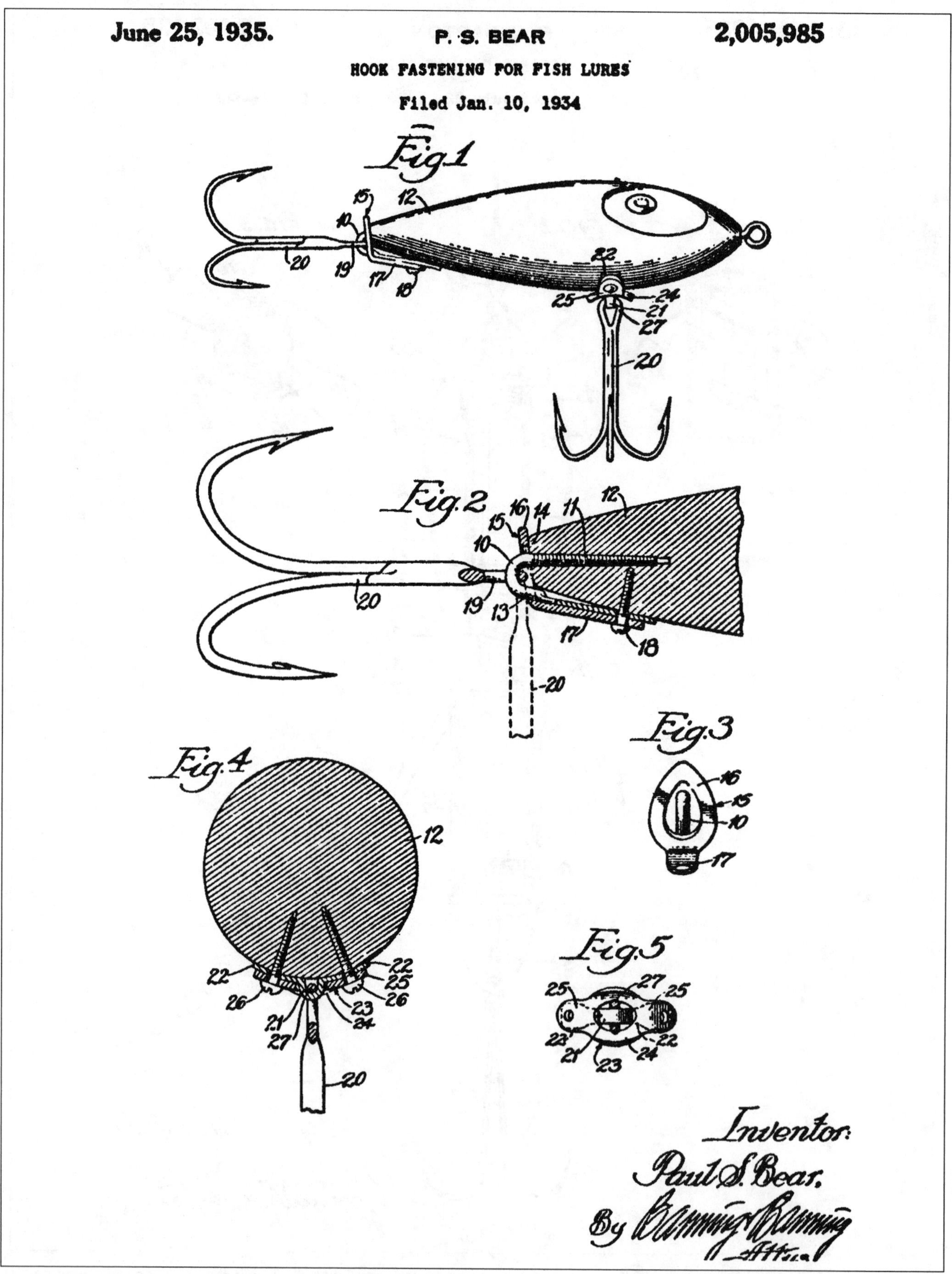

Granted to Heddon in 1935 the two-piece tail hook fastener is familiar, but the cross-wise orientation of the two-piece belly hook hanger has never been seen on a Heddon lure (See fig. 4 in drawing).

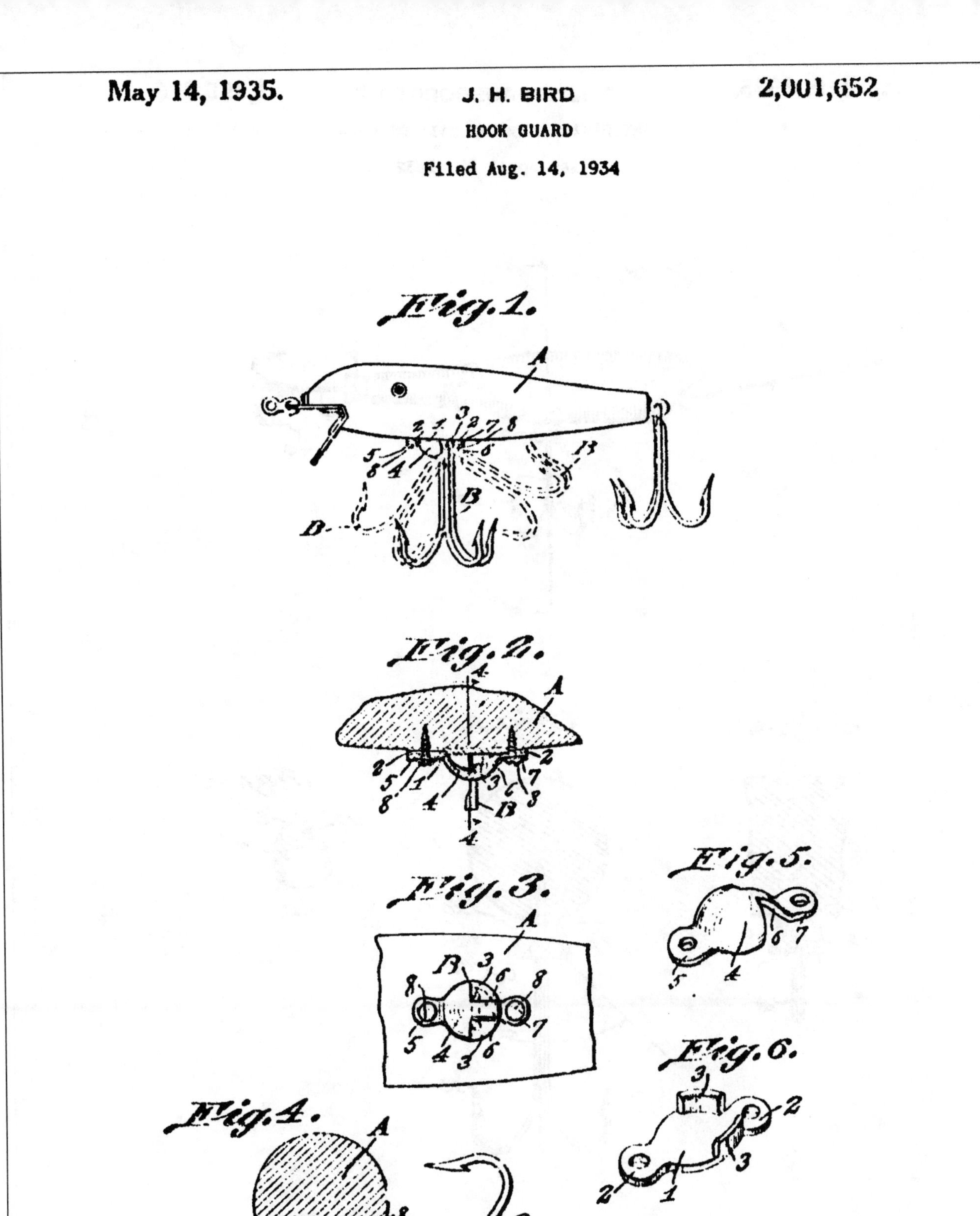

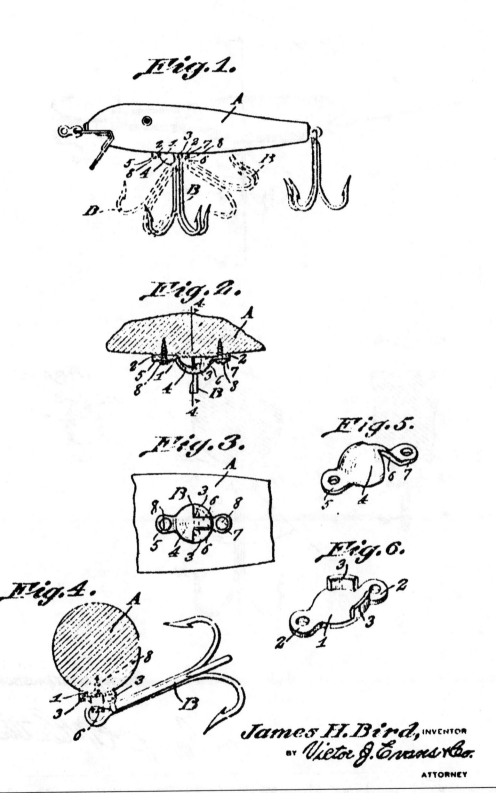

This patent was granted to a James H. Bird of San Antonio on May 14, 1935. It is an interesting variation on the familiar one-piece hanger patented by Pflueger 13 years before. As you can see it has the addition of a base plate.

April 9, 1935. **O. L. STRAUSBORGER** **1,996,776**

ARTIFICIAL FISHING BAIT OR LURE

Filed April 28, 1932

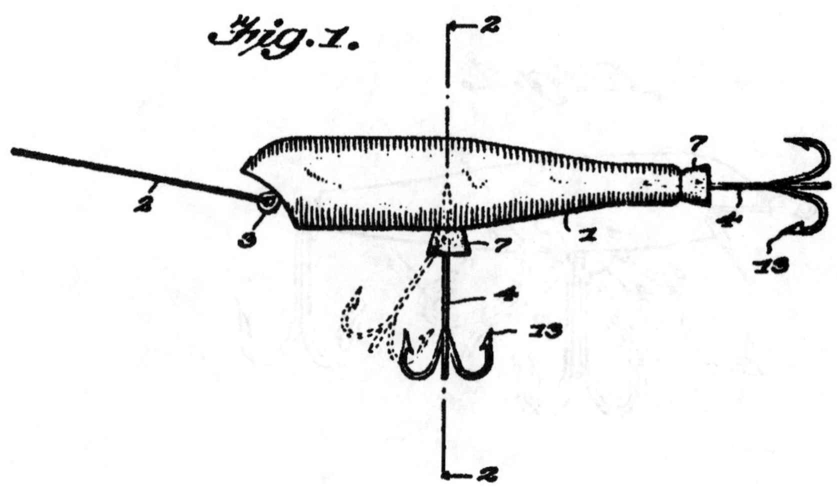

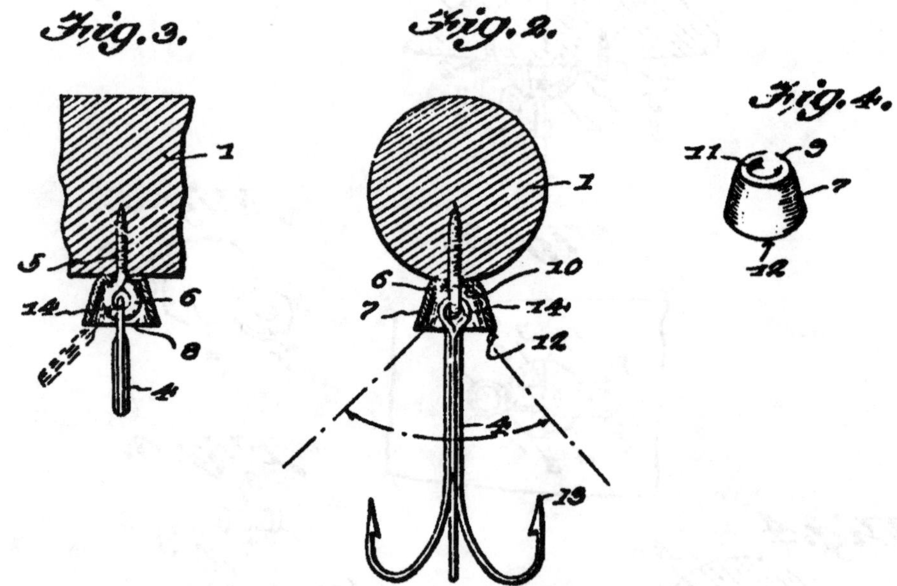

Inventor
OSCAR L. STRAUSBORGER

By [signature]

This illustration accompanied a patent filed in 1932 and granted to Oscar L. Strausborger of Edon, Ohio in 1934. It is a hook limiter made to prevent the hook from damaging the finish on the lure body. It is really an externally mounted cup. Many companies use this relatively inexpensive protective hook hanger even today, over 50 years later.

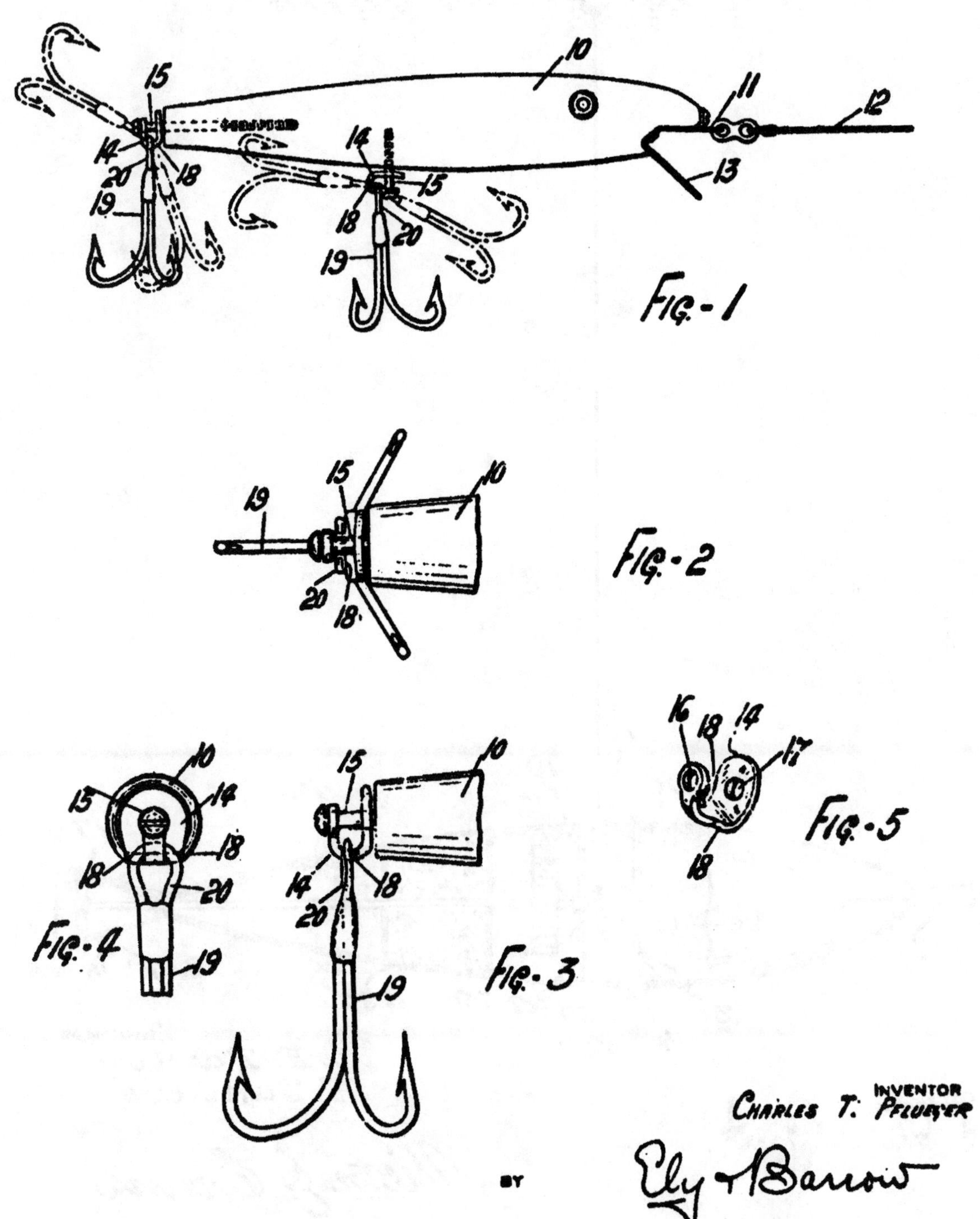

Patent of the Pflueger swiveled hook fastener. Granted August 13, 1935.

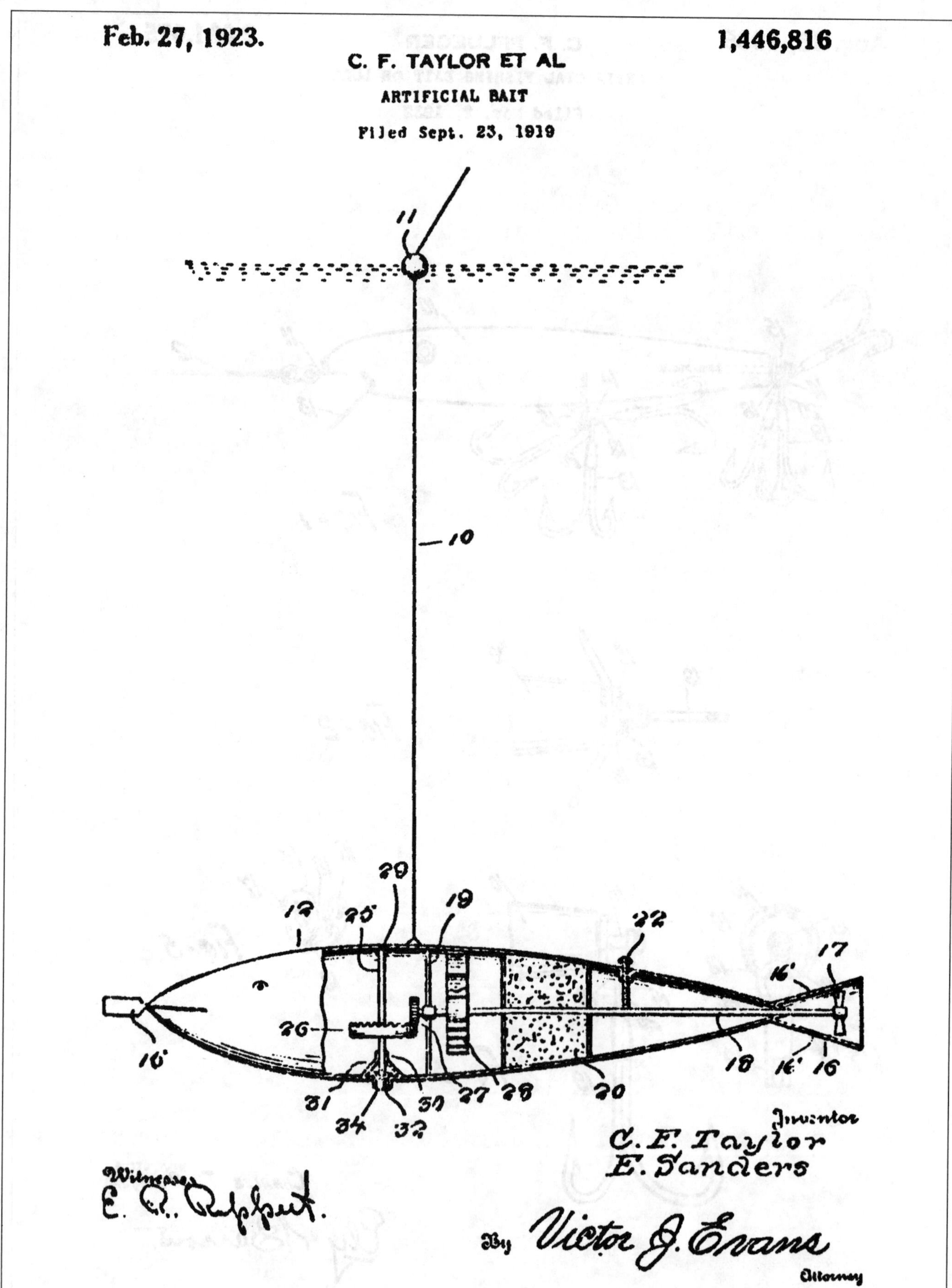

Feb. 27, 1923.
1,446,816
C. F. TAYLOR ET AL
ARTIFICIAL BAIT
Filed Sept. 23, 1919
Inventor
C. F. Taylor
E. Sanders
Witnesses
By Victor J. Evans
Attorney

SELF-PROPELLED!

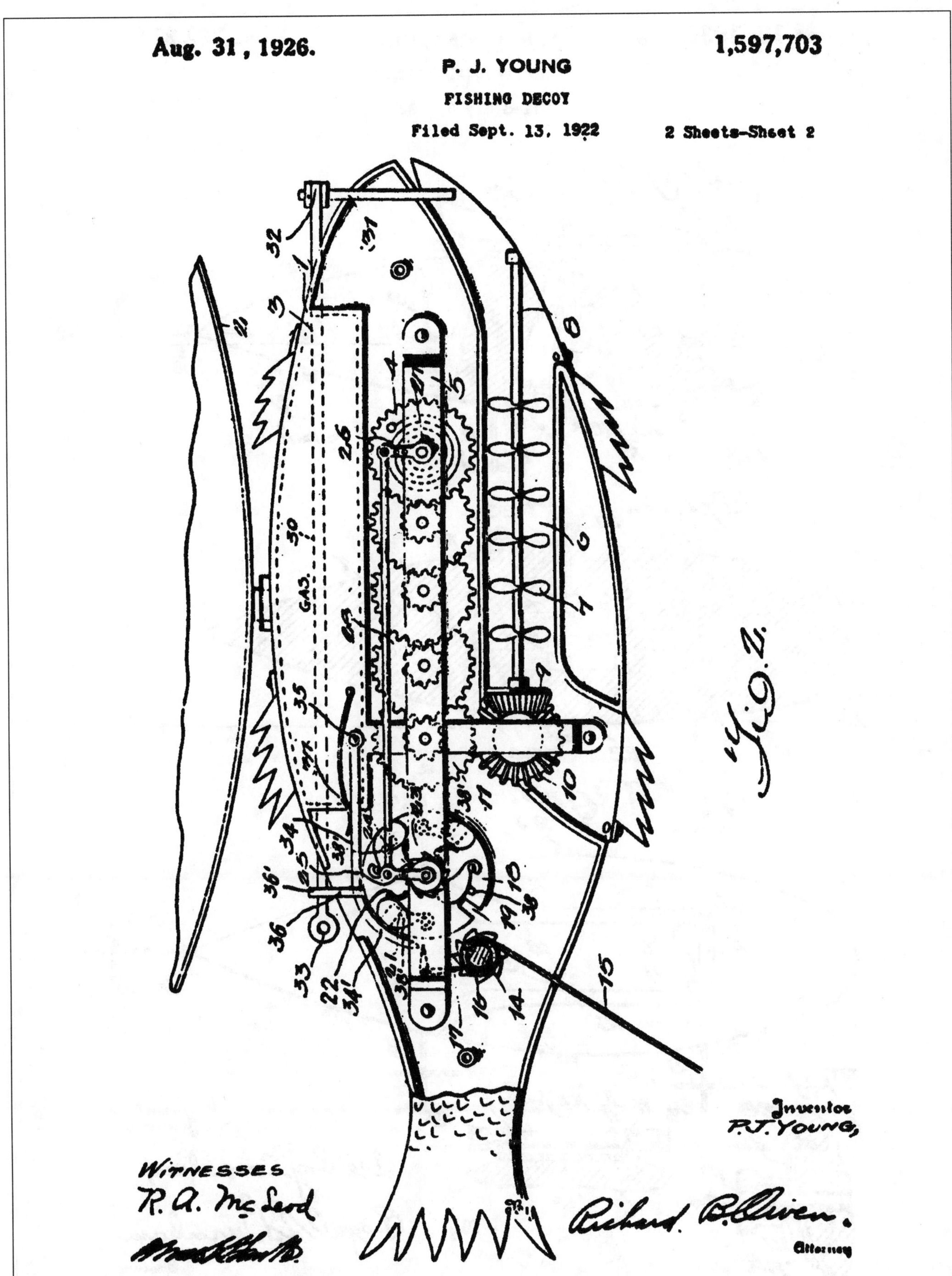

THIS FISH DECOY WOULD BE A WATCH REPAIRMAN'S NIGHTMARE.

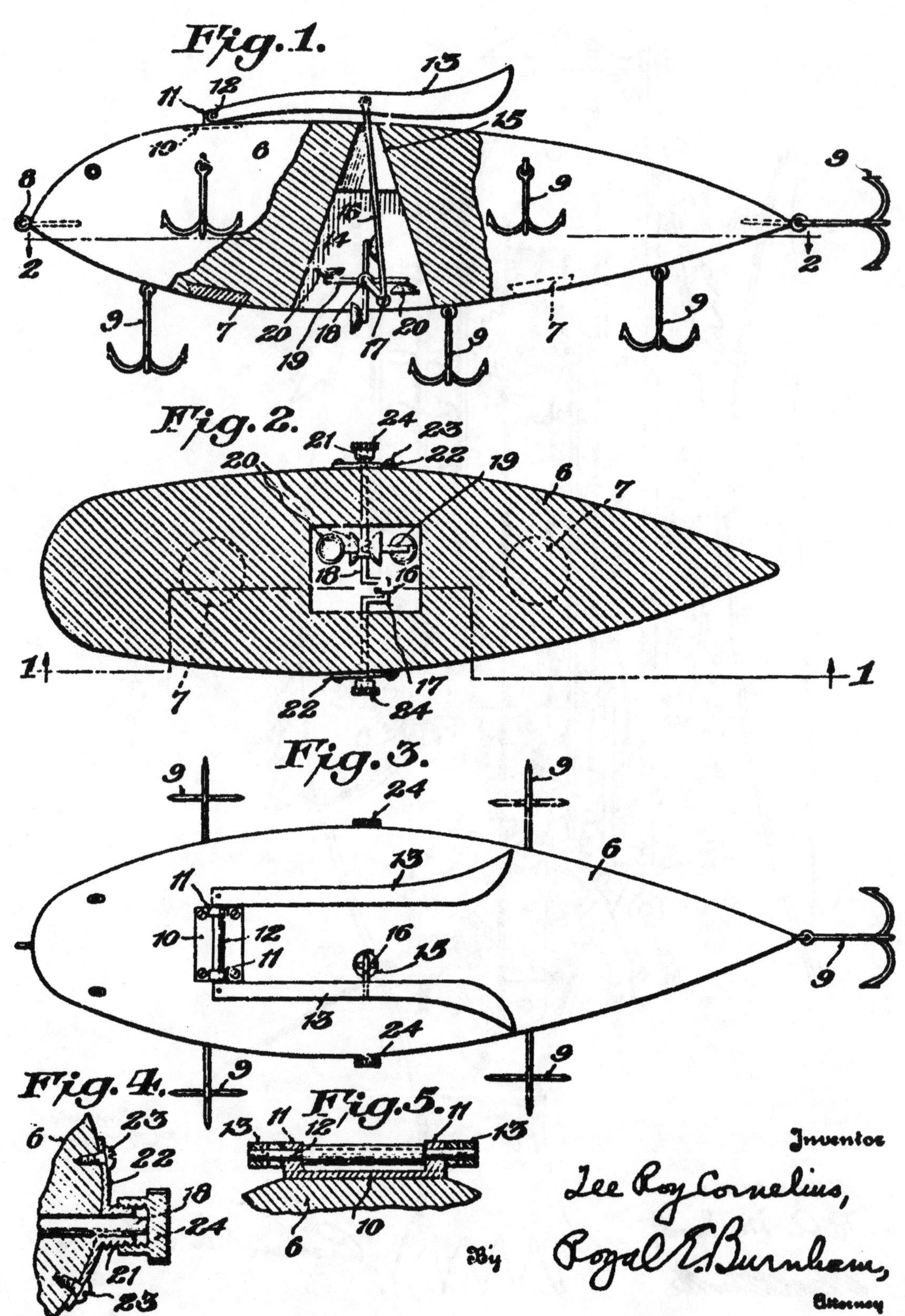

A PADDLE-WHEELER YET!

Feb. 11, 1930. E. R. WHITNEY 1,746,753

ARTIFICIAL BAIT

Filed July 24, 1928 2 Sheets-Sheet 2

Fig. 4

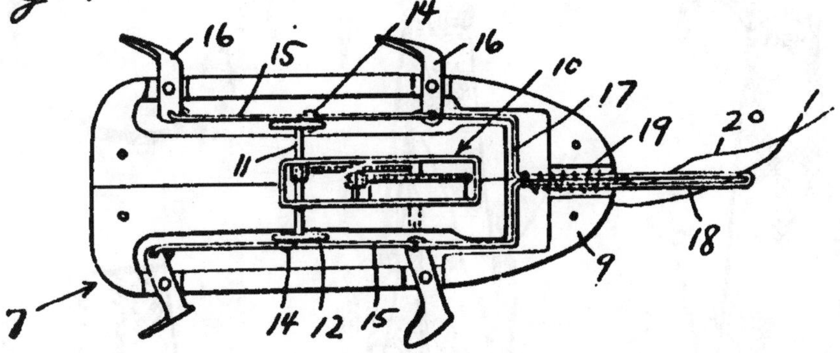

Fig. 5.

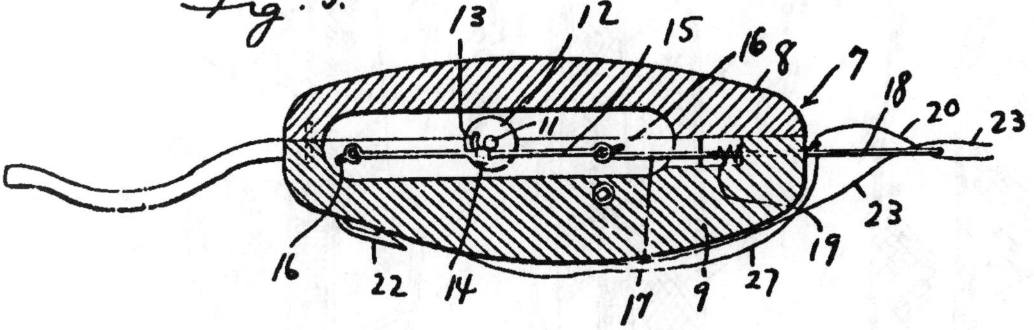

Fig. 6.

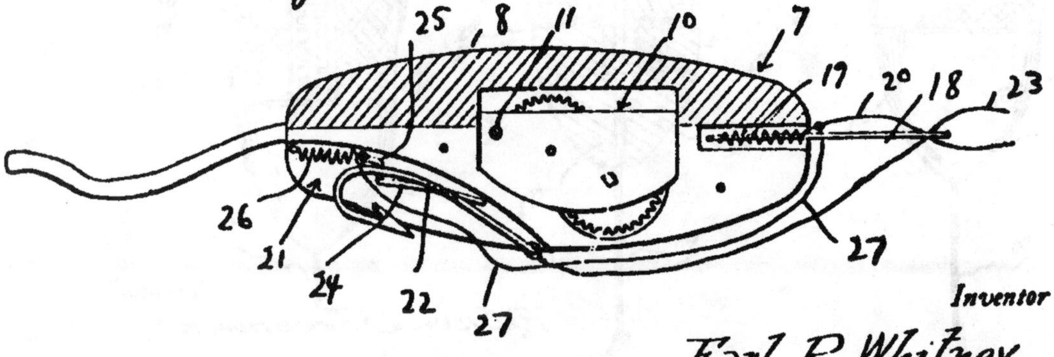

Inventor

Earl R. Whitney

By Clarence A. O'Brien, Attorney

COULD THIS BE THE SAME E. WHITNEY OF COTTON GIN FAME? THE INTERIOR LOOKS LIKE IT COULD BALE COTTON.

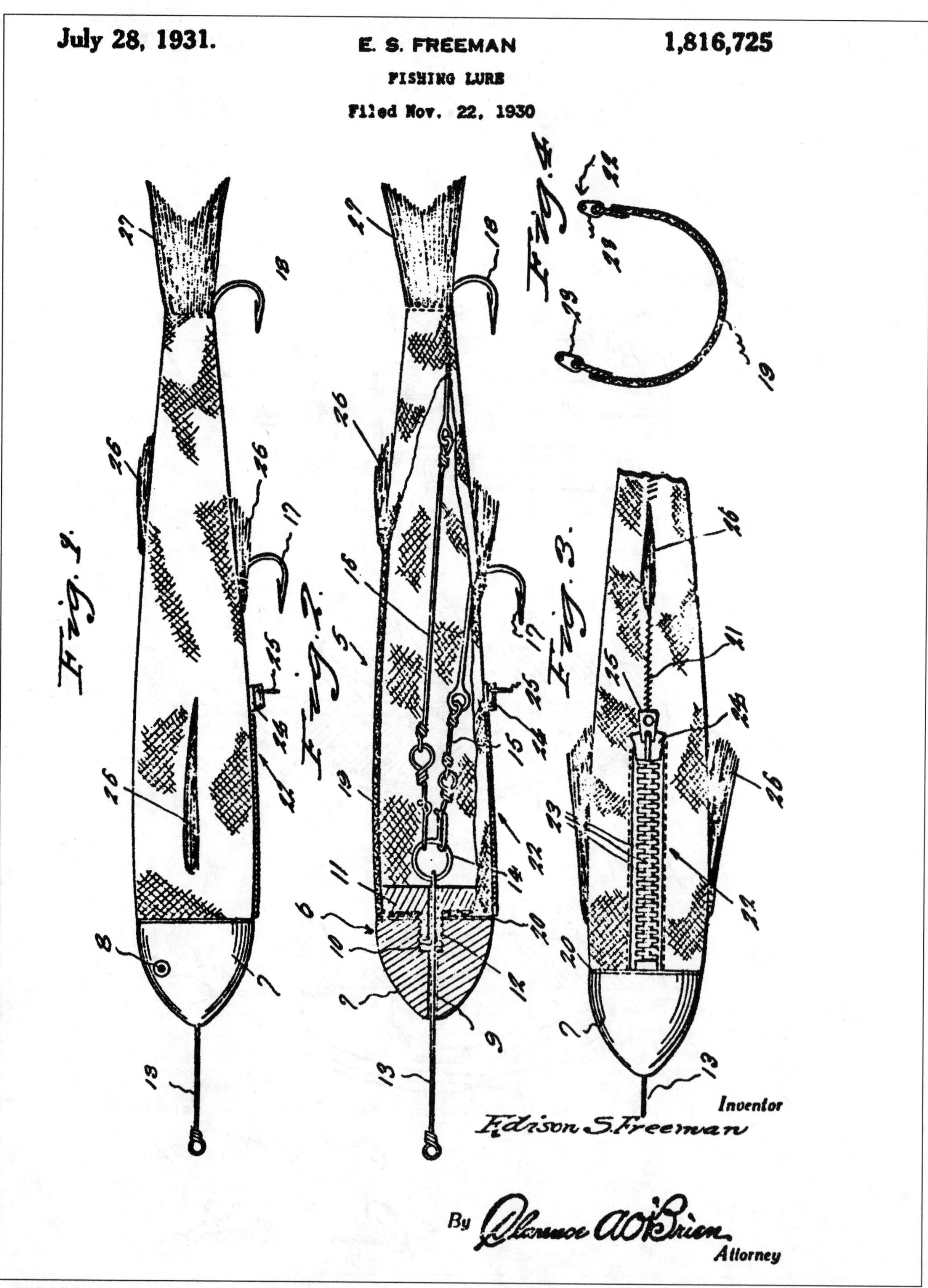

A ZIPPER! ONE CAN ONLY WONDER WHAT SALTWATER MIGHT DO TO IT. THE INVENTOR WAS FROM MIAMI.

C. W. LANE.

ARTIFICIAL FISH BAIT.

APPLICATION FILED JAN. 14, 1913.

1,068,908. Patented July 29, 1913.

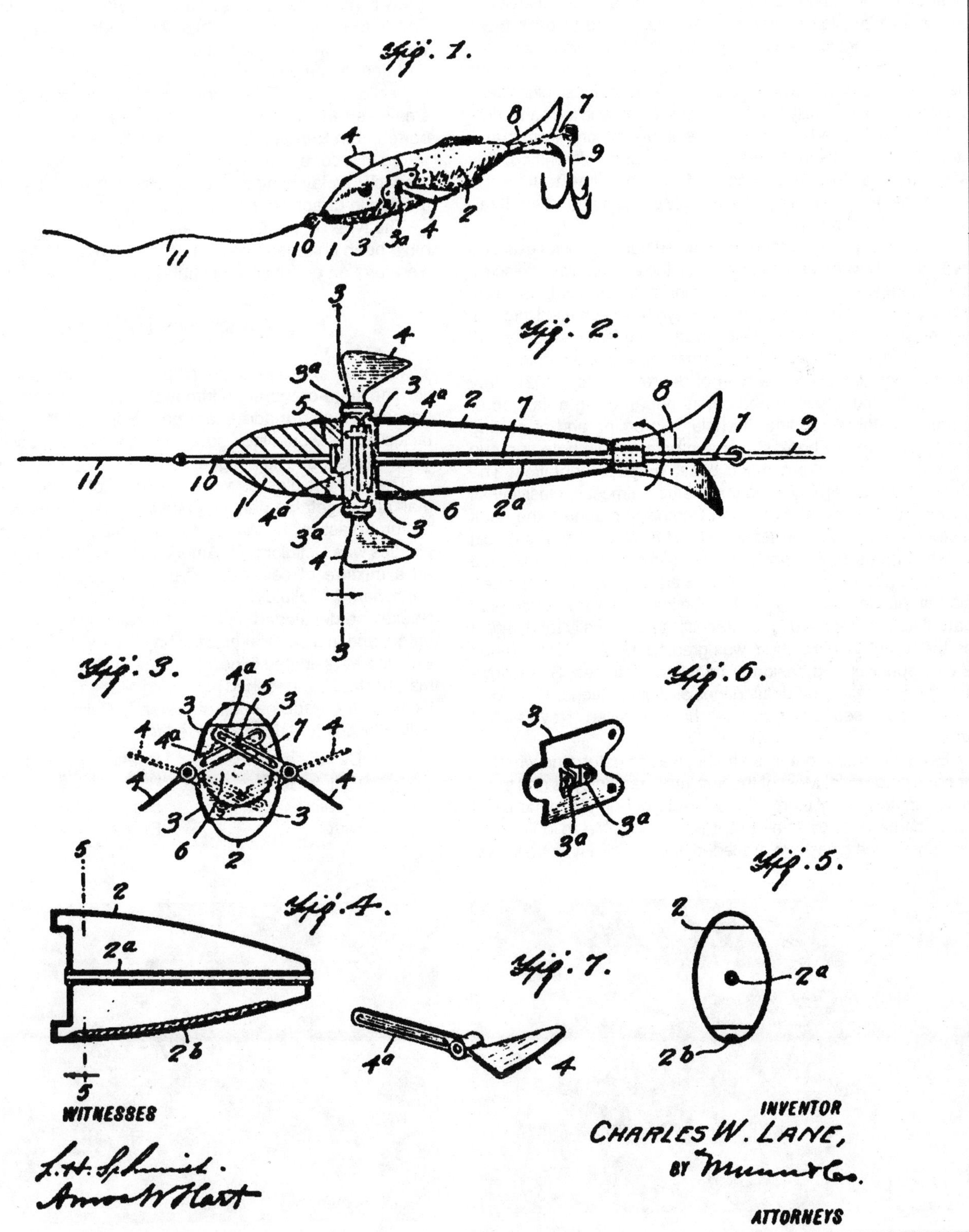

WITH THOSE FLAPPING WINGS IT MIGHT EVEN BE A FLYING FISH. THIS IS ACTUALLY A VERY DESIRABLE COLLECTIBLE LURE (See page 495??).

THE FISHING LURE

Some General Guidelines For Identification and Dating

The first thing to do is study the overall appearance of the plug. Most of the older ones were made of wood and real marvels of craftsmanship. High quality enamels were used to paint them, most with several coats. Over the years this paint often has a tendency to "check" or "craze". This is the appearance of hair-line cracks in the paint. Be aware however that not all these plugs demonstrate the high quality production used by most in the early days.

The metals used in the first days of lure making were brass, steel, nickel, and sometimes even silver and gold plating. You will encounter the term "Nickel Silver" from time to time. Be aware that this is an alloy and actually contains no silver. It tarnished to a dull gray.

The earliest hook fastener and line-tie hardware was usually a through-body wire twisted into loops on the ends or a simple screw eye. There were many, many different methods, but those were the most common. The simple screw eye has been used throughout the years and is still in use by many manufacturers today.

Heddon, as far as can be determined, was the first to use a screw *hook* recessed in a hole or depression (c. 1902). Very soon after that, Heddon and others began using a flanged or rimmed metal cup to line the hole, reinforcing and protecting the body from the hook shank and points. This hole and cup served also to make a much better hook presentation. The Creek Chub Company used this method almost exclusively all through the years. The Heddon Company patented the hook fastener known as the "L-rig" in 1917. Careful study of old patent records shows that it is possible that even though he did not try to patent it, Edward J. Lockhart used a very close version of the Heddon "L-rig" in his application for a wooden plug patent in October of 1913. Heddon filed specifically for a patent on the "L-rig" in 1915 and it was granted in 1917. Heddon has a very specific progression of hardware changes. See following pages for detailed descriptions and illustrations.

Pflueger used a unique hook hanger called "Neverfail". It was patented Oct. 24, 1911.

Eye type and/or detail is another way to determine whether or not a plug is old. Most of the first lures had no eyes and there was a limited use of painted eyes. Probably simple round-head tacks came next as eyes but it is not possible to determine presently if the glass eye preceded or coincided with their use. It is known that tacks were often used, painted or unpainted, by a few companies at the same time others were utilizing glass. The first glass eyes were slightly rounded having an opaque yellow iris and a small black pupil. The second was more rounded, has a clear outer section and yellow-tinted iris and a larger black pupil. The yellow eyes varied in size generally the smaller size being the oldest. Often these glass eyes were imported from Europe. Then came the "Tack on Eye" which consisted of a cone shape plastic eye with a hole in the middle for the tack. Today almost all eyes are simply decals, painted on, molded in or applied photographically.

The types of hooks found are really of no use as these may have been changed one or more times over the years as they were broken or bent out of shape, etc.

PLASTIC LURES

With few exceptions, the plugs we fish with today are plastic. The state-of-the-art in lure manufacture is astounding with advances being made every day. Some of the plugs in our tackle boxes would look good enough to clean, cook, and eat if they were just a little bigger.

The earliest plastics were made up of compounds of animal- and vegetable-derived materials. Many consider these as "natural plastics" because of their makeup. The first of these plastics was Celluloid. An American named John Hyatt patented a mixture of cellulose, nitrate and camphor giving it the trade name "Celluloid". It was 40 years later before Dr. Leo Baekeland developed a phenol-formaldehyde material he patented and called "Bakelite". The early years of the use of Bakelite were limited to darker colors, but by the mid-1930s the material had been refined and could be made in lighter shades. Some of the trade names of the early Cellulose Nitrate, Phenolic Plastics and their improved formulas are as follows:

Cellulose Nitrates	Phenolic Plastics
Celluloid	Bakelite
Pyralin	Durite
Nitro	Durex
	Catalin

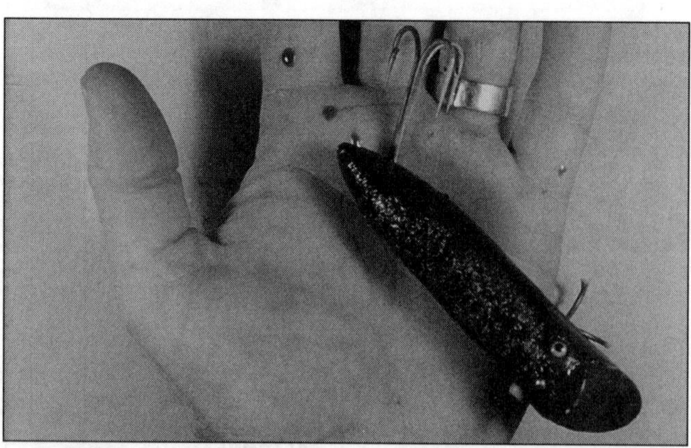

Some early plastics were not perfected. They were unstable and had a tendency to break down. Photo shows a messy example of this. An occurrence as bad as this does not happen often fortunately.

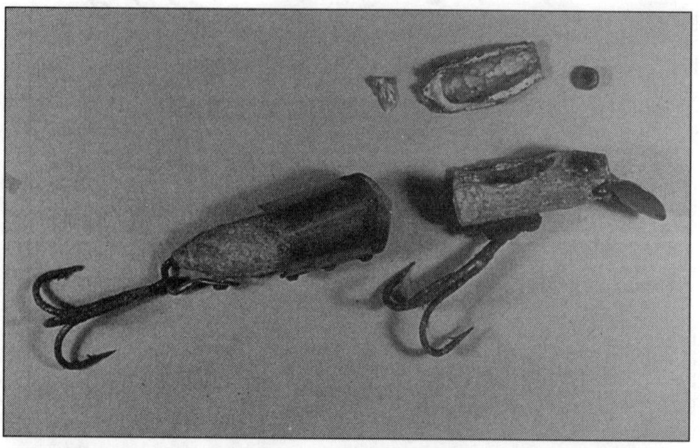

This happened to a new lure while in its box. The proper mixture of ingredients for the plastic was apparently not carefully prepared resulting in the breakdown. It is thought that heat may accelerate the breakdown.

The Celluloid plugs were made in many colors and transparent as well. One of its properties is that it is highly flammable and subject to melting under heat or chemical reaction with other materials. It has tendency to yellow and become brittle with age.

Lure manufacturers experimented with many different plastics over the years and many of them were unstable. Illustrated here is an example of what can happen to some of those early plastics. Most of the earlier plastics are highly susceptible to damage from the compounds used in the plastic worms of today. Take care not to mix them.

SPECIFIC GUIDELINES FOR IDENTIFICATION AND DATING LURES

When trying to describe the type and condition through written or voice communication, confusion frequently reigns. I am a firm believer in the hands-on or photographic examination of a lure, but we all know that can be impractical. For whatever reason, there needs to be some standard way of describing what a lure is and what its condition may be. Some abbreviations of a few long-winded parts or component names and descriptions would also be helpful, especially if you are preparing a long list of lures described in detail. Before you attempt that you must first familiarize yourself with how a lure is made, what its parts are and how they are described by collectors already active in the hobby.

The individual company histories, hints for identifying and dating there, and the detailed lure listings will give you information specific to the companies and/or their lures. There is one universal way to date boxes and other materials to the 1933-36 years. The NATIONAL RECOVERY ACT of 1933 was one of Roosevelt's attempt to bring the country back after the Great Depression. It was the first "Buy American" campaign. Participating companies would sticker or stamp their literature or boxes with the NRA logo. It consisted of an American Eagle with "NRA" in big block letters over the eagle and the slogan "WE DO OUR PART" below. It was a failure, deemed unconstitutional and was repealed in 1936.

ANATOMY OF A LURE AND ITS COMPONENTS

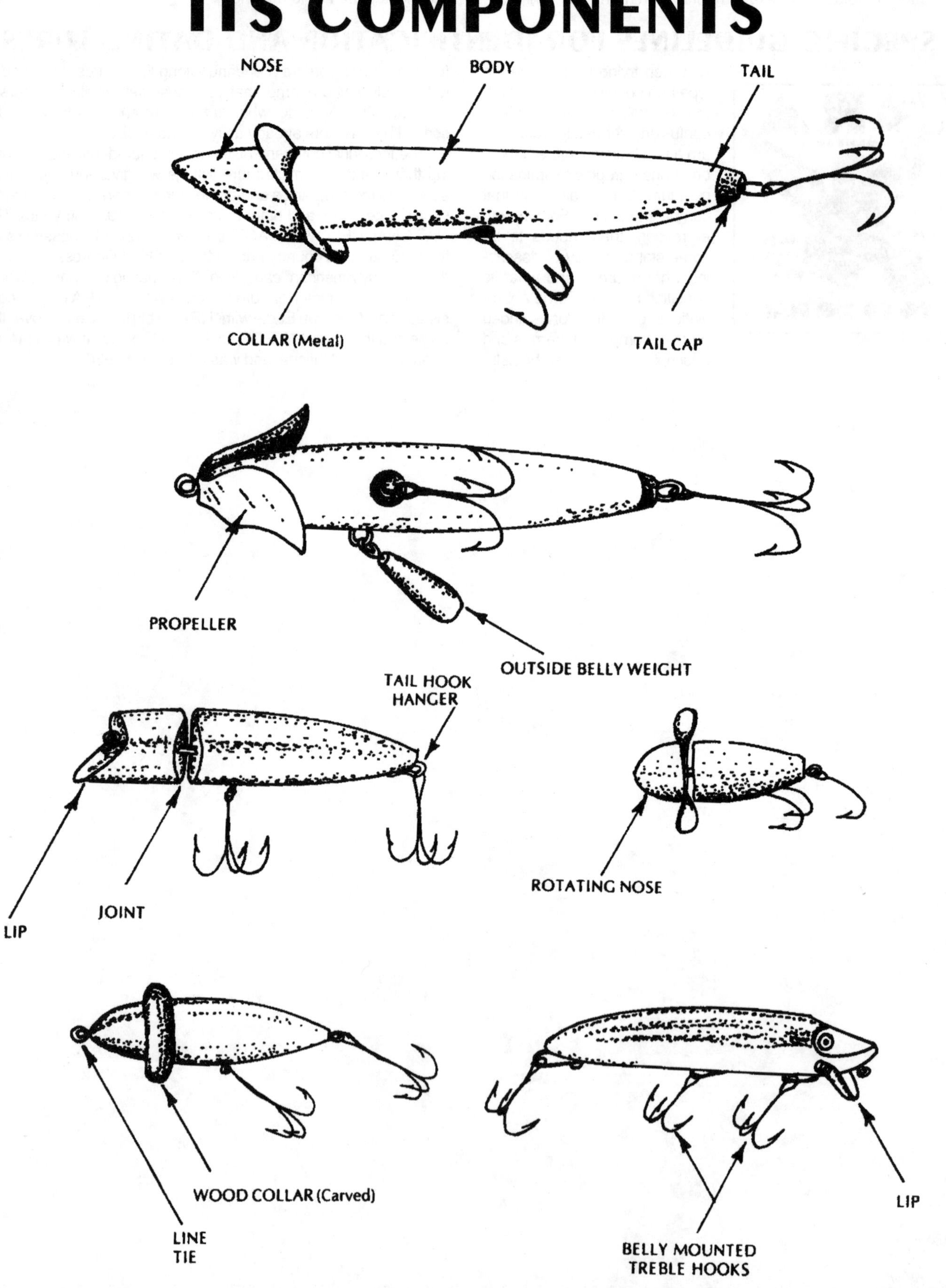

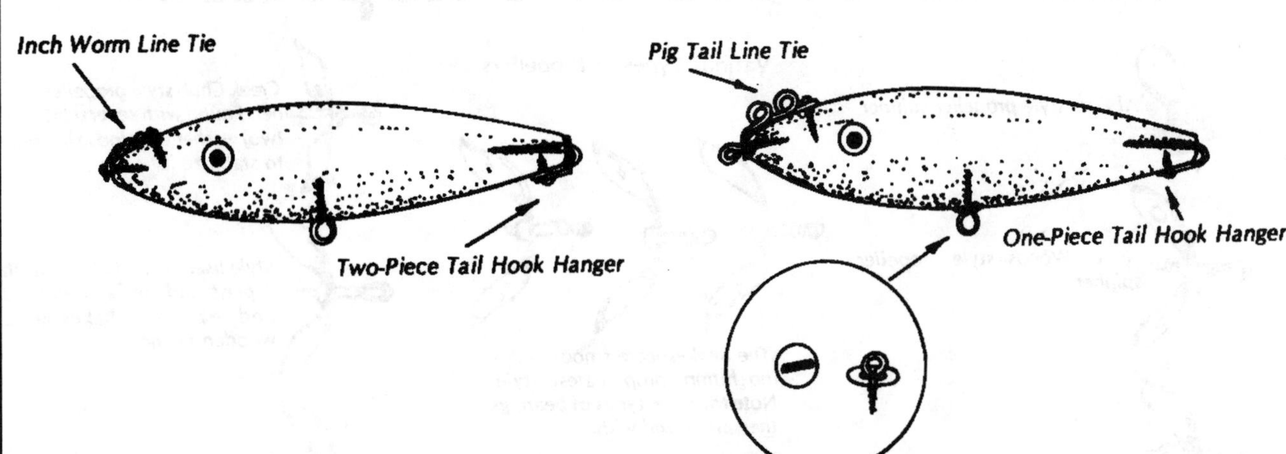

Detail of the Screw Eye and Washer style hook hanger

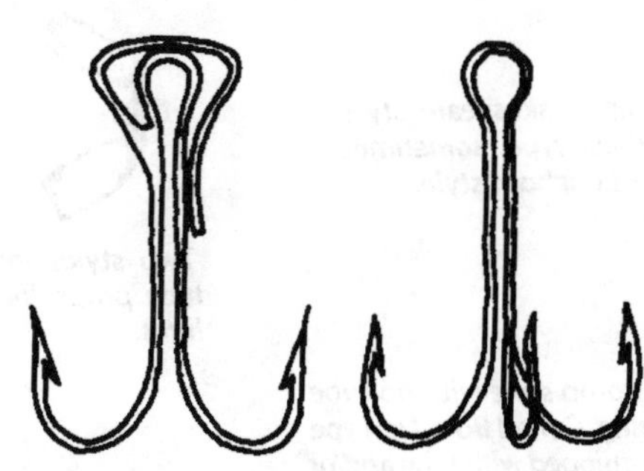

Heddon's patented Dummy Double detachable double hook

F. C. Woods patented detachable double and treble hooks

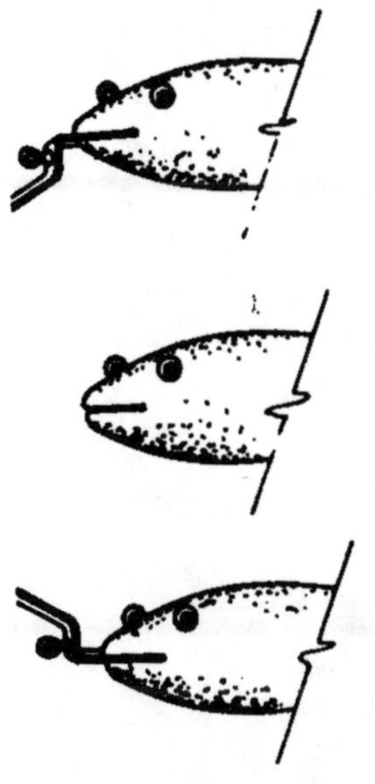

The Creek Chub convertible metal lip, three choices and two line tie options

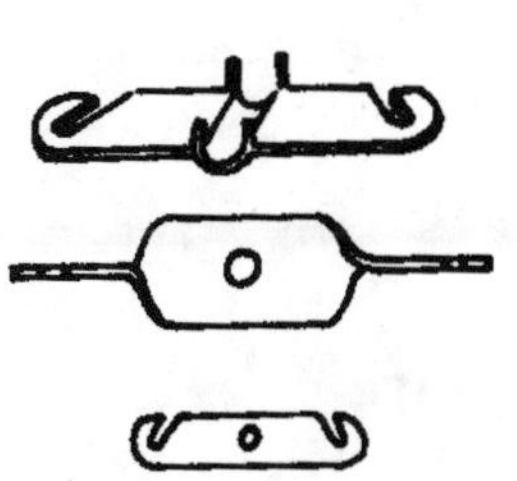

Three styles of plate hardware used in See-thru Plate Hook Hangers

Gem Clip style hook hanger. Usually utilized with a see-thru type.

Various Types of Propellers

Various Types of Propellers

Al Foss style propeller spinner

F. C. Woods style propeller spinner

Clark and Keeling Expert style.

One hump Shakespeare style prop. Earliest type, sometimes called the Longhorn style.

Floppy prop style with no tube or bearing. Called Bow Tie Type when equipped with tube and/or bearings.

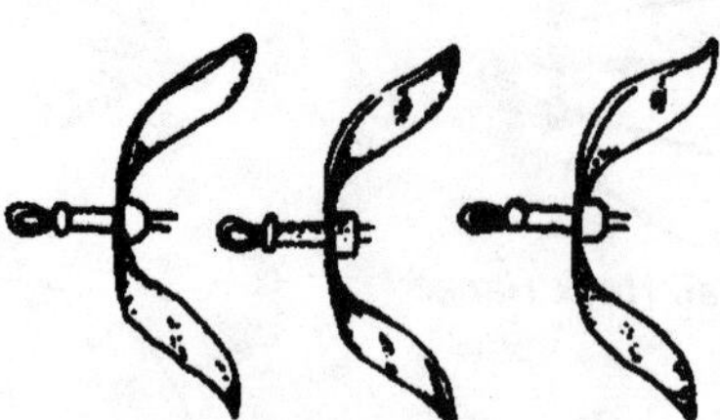

The Shakespeare smooth edge (no hump) prop. Latest style. Note the three types of bearings they are found with.

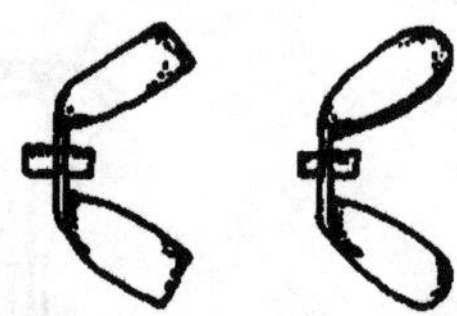

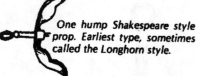

Two styles inexpensive tube type props found on various lures.

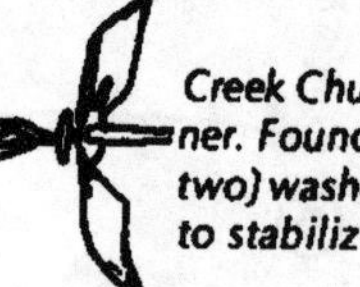

Creek Chub style propeller spinner. Found with several (at least two) washer type loose bearings to stabilize it.

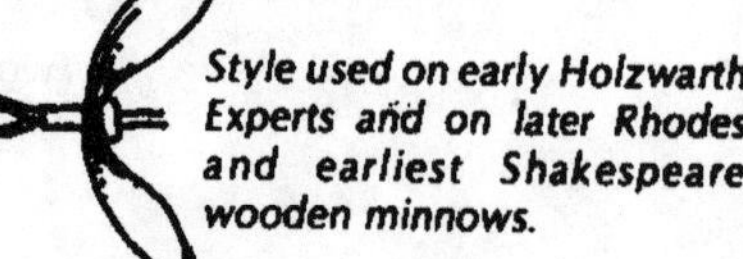

Style used on early Holzwarth Experts and on later Rhodes and earliest Shakespeare wooden minnows.

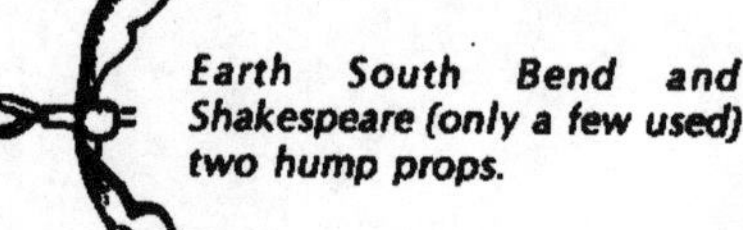

Earth South Bend and Shakespeare (only a few used) two hump props.

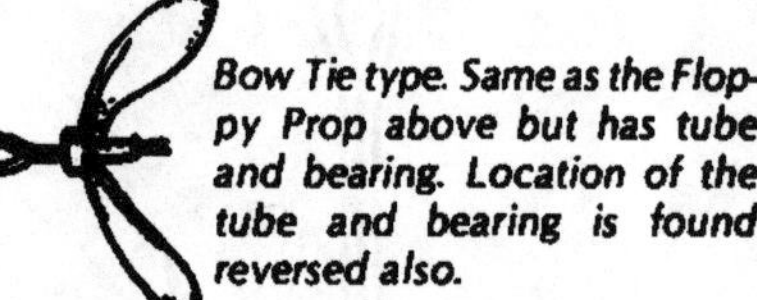

Bow Tie type. Same as the Floppy Prop above but has tube and bearing. Location of the tube and bearing is found reversed also.

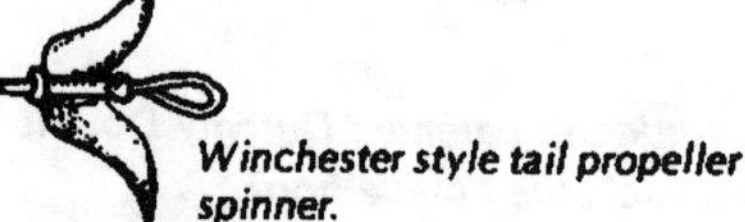

Winchester style tail propeller spinner.

TYPES OF HOOK HANGERS

Screw Hook

Screw Eye (recessed)

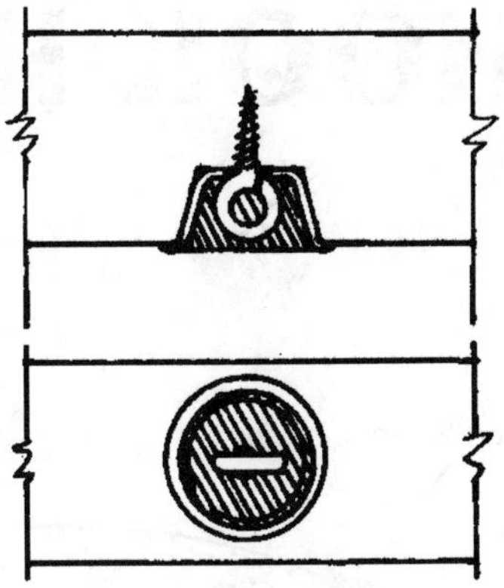

Cup (Metal cup and screw eye)

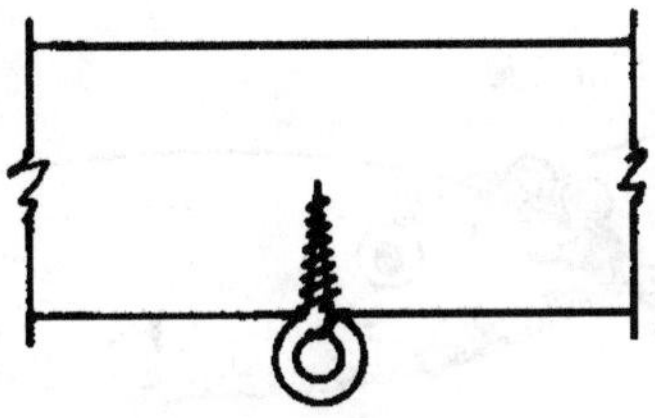

Screw Eye (found with and without washer)

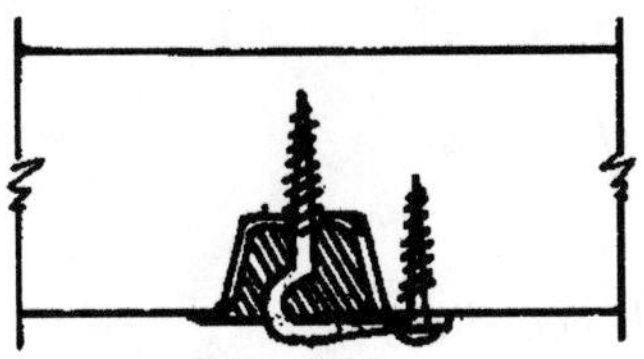

L-Rig (variation)

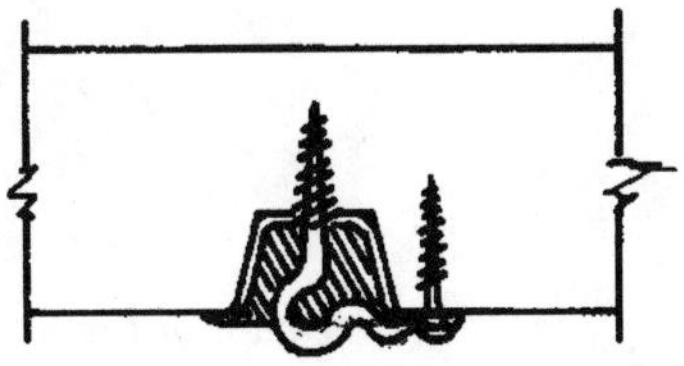

L-Rig (Heddon style, most common)

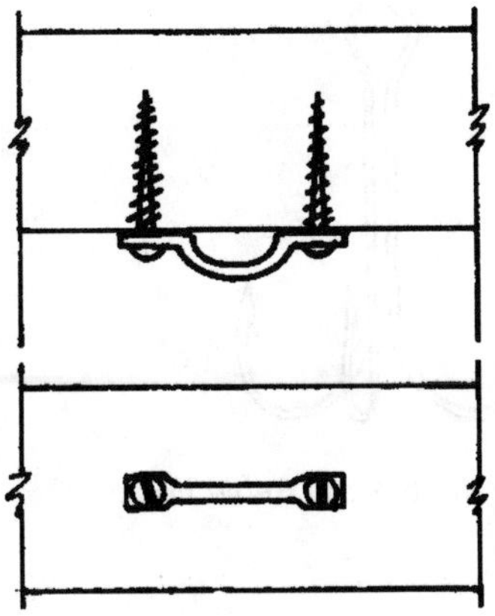

Bar (one-piece bar)

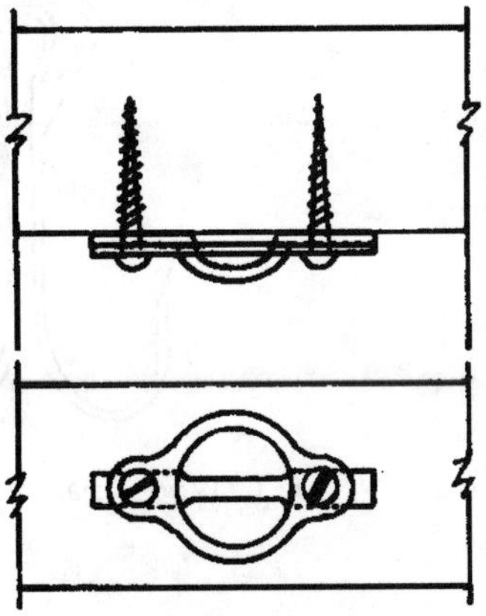

2-Pc Surface or Toilet Seat (First style of Heddon Two-Piece)

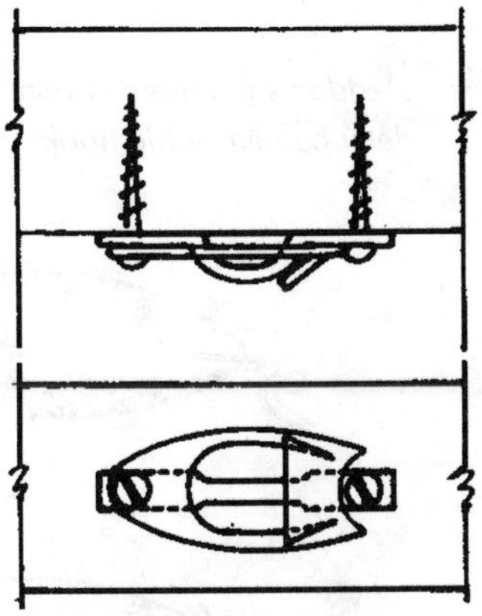

*2-PC Surface or Flap Rig (*Second style of Heddon 2-PC)*

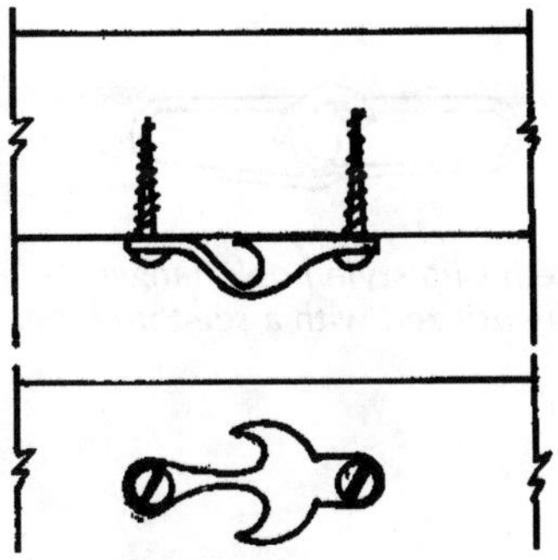

1-Pc (one-piece surface)

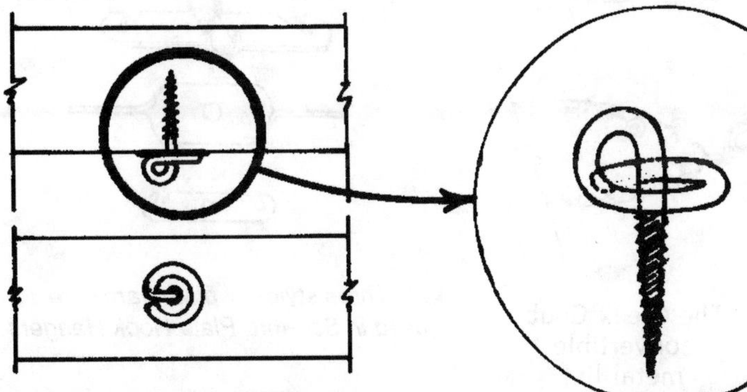

Pflueger NEVERFAIL

**Pflueger used a slightly different type of this 2-PC hanger.*

VARIOUS STYLES OF HOOK-HANGER AND LINE-TIE HARDWARE

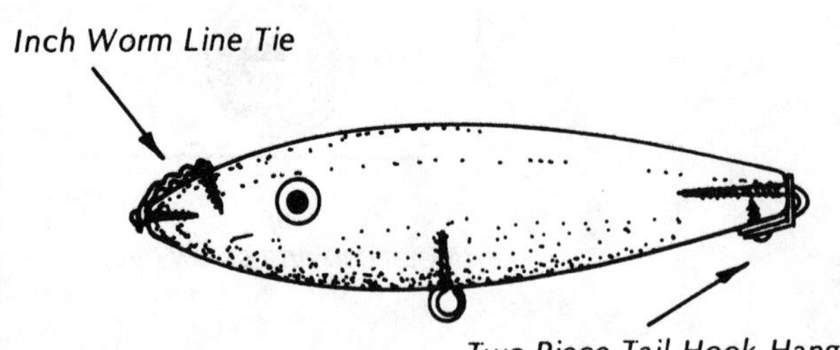

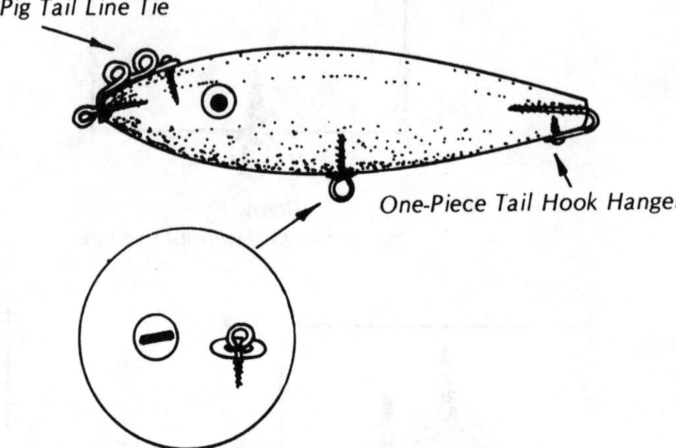

Detail of the Screw Eye and Washer style hook hanger

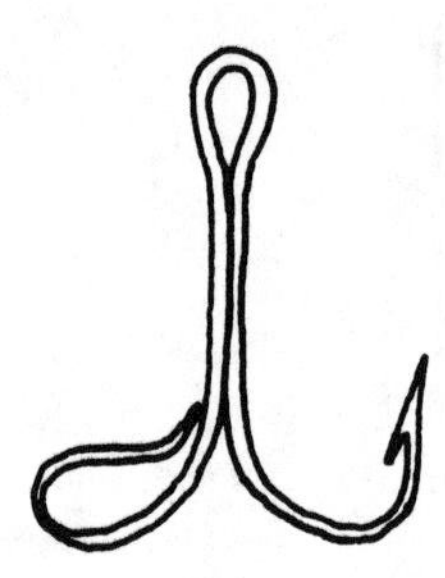

Heddon's patented Dummy Double detachable double hook

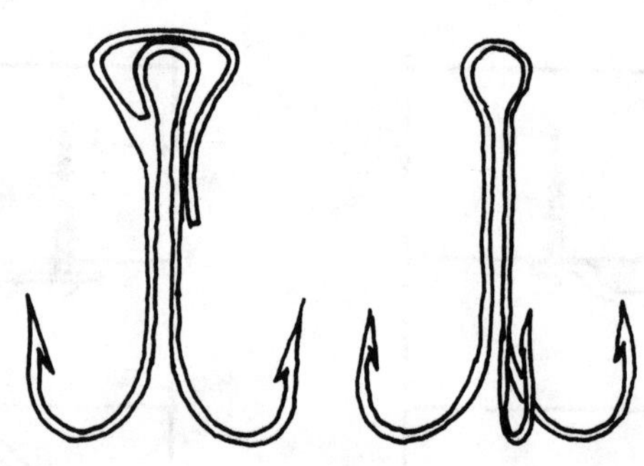

F. C. Woods patented detachable double and treble hooks

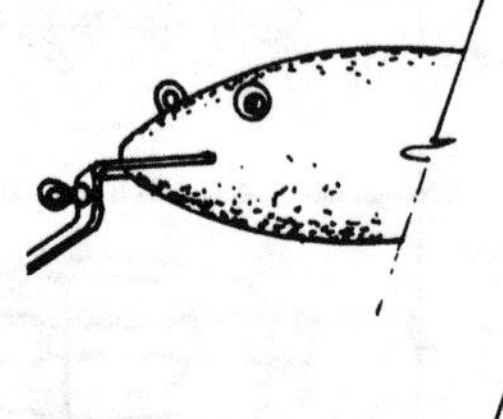

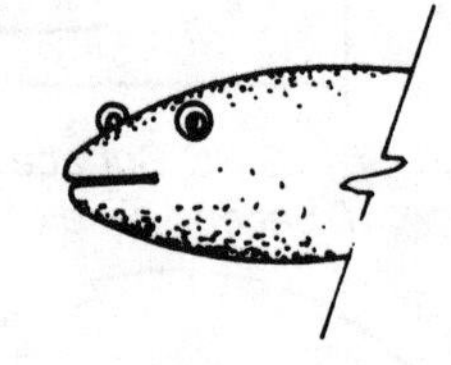

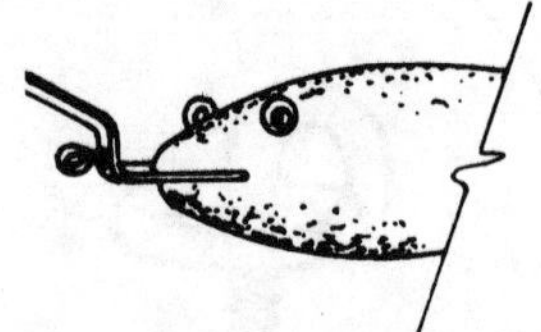

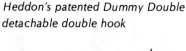

The Creek Chub convertible metal lip, three choices and two line tie options

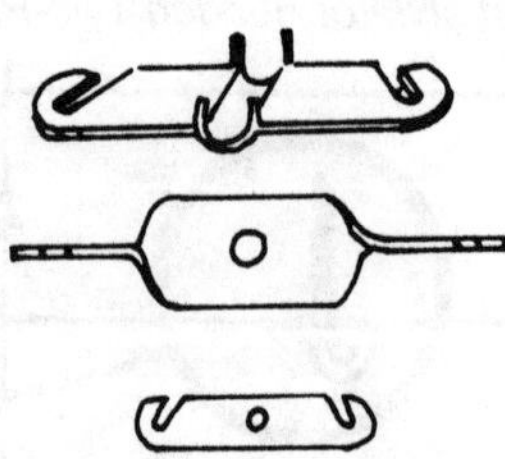

Three styles of plate hardware used in See-thru Plate Hook Hangers

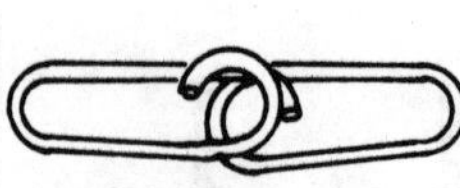

Gem Clip style hook hanger. Usually utilized with a see-thru type.

COLORS OF FISHING LURES

Colors can be very confusing, especially to the beginning collector. Often, companies would name a color that is unfamiliar to the collector, For instance: DACE. What would that mean to a collector who had never seen a dace, which is a type of minnow. COACH DOG is another that one might wonder about. The following should help to allay some of the confusion. There is also much help in this area in the color sections.

The following is a descriptive list of the colors, patterns or finishes you will most often encounter in the lure listings in this and other books and publications, lure company-published catalogs and other literature and collector sale/trade lists. It will help you to understand what is being described. The listing was first published, in edited form, in the March, 1990 issue (Vol. 13, No. 44) of the N.F.L.C.C. Gazette, pages 12-13. It is used here with their kind permission and the author, Jim Muma of Belleville, Illinois. Jim asked that I use his original, unedited manuscript and that is what follows here. Jim also asked that the following people be acknowledged for their help in compiling the color list. Jim Frazier, Jack Looney, John Shoffner and Dick Wilson.

FISHING LURE COLOR PATTERNS

By Jim Muma

This list covers fishing lure color patterns which are most frequently misunderstood.

1. **Allen Stripey** - Silver or white scale body with red head and a single red stripe along each side.
2. **Arrowhead** - Red or black arrow design on the head of South Bend lures.
3. **Blue Eel** - Dark blue back blended to white belly.
4. **Blue Flash** - Blue body with silver sparkle added.
5. **Bonehead Finish** - Two-tone brown pattern with imitation jewel eyes. Lure is plastic with horizontal corrugated sides. Used by Paw Paw.
6. **Bug Finish** - A bug design used on Creek Chub Bait Co. Big Creek Wiggler and Wee Dee.
7. **Bumble Bee** - Alternating yellow and black stripes on a lure body.
8. **Butterfly**-Yellow body with black/red stripes and black/red spots. Used on South Bend WhirlOreno and Truck-Oreno.
9. **Chipmunk** - Flocked, light brown body with dark brown horizontal stripes on the top and sides. Stripes have white dots. Head is dark brown.
10. **Christmas Tree** - (Eger Bait Co.)? See Strawberry.
11. **Coach Dog** - White or yellow body with irregular black spots.
12. **Dace** - Silver scale over blended red and green/blue.
13. **Day-N-Nite** - Luminous body with silver sparkle.
14. **Decoration** - Vertical side design which simulates ribs. Used by Pflueger.
15. **Dragon Fly** - An imitation dragon fly design on one side of a South Bend Vacuum Bait.
16. **Fancy Back** - A crackle-back color used on a lure top only.
17. **Fireplug** - A fluorescent paint finish with an orange belly.
18. **Flocked** - A lure surface texture which simulates fur.
19. **Florida Vertical Red Bars** - White body with black back stripe and red vertical bars/eyes. Used by Shur-Strike.
20. **Frog** - Dark green body and yellow spots with black centers. Early pattern had *small* yellow/black spots.
21. **Frog Scale** - A Heddon term for "Snake" pattern. See Snake.
22. **Frog Skin** - Real frog skin covers a lure. Primarily used by Paw Paw, Shakespeare and Eger.
23. **German Silver** - A shiny metal alloy, but *not* real silver.
24. **Glow Worm** - A Heddon Crazy Crawler pattern. Green body with black wings and star on nose, and white luminous belly ribs.
25. **Gold Scale** - Gold color with decal eyes and scales. Used by Winchester.
26. **Green Cracked Back** - Distinctive dark green diamonds on white body with red side spots. Looks like an argyle sock pattern. A Pflueger color which followed the early Green Crackle back.
27. **Green Crackle back** - Dark green back on white body. The green paint was dried quickly to produce cracks which show the white paint.
28. **Hex** - White or yellow body with red and black spots, and black horizontal stripes on the top and sides. Stripes imitate a multiple flat-sided lure on a rounded body.
    Hex - Same as above with red body and black spots/stripes.
29. **Horned Ace** - Red body with black eye shade, black stripe and tail. Nose and belly is white with red on the nose tip. Used by Moonlight.
30. **Imperial Spoon** - A small frog or crawfish painted on the concave side of a spoon. Used by Pflueger.
31. **Jimmy Skunk** - Black body with yellow stripe. Used by Shakespeare.
32. **Lightning Flash** - A jagged design imitating a lightning bolt.
33. **Meadow Frog** - Dark green body and irregular yellow spots with black centers. Sometimes called the "Luny Frog" pattern.
34. **Metalized Finish** - Metal plated lures. Pflueger used nickel plate. Shakespeare used nickel, copper and gold plate.
35. **Moss Back** - Brown body with green scales, black, white belly and red mouth and chin.
36. **Mottled** - Colors blotched on or overlapping to give a "camouflage" effect.
37. **Mud Puppy** - Gray body with tangerine striped belly. Used by Shakespeare.
38. **Muskrat Skin** - Real muskrat skin covers a lure. Used by Bud Stewart.
39. **Natural Chub** - Light green or brown scale pattern. No vertical stripes.
40. **Natural Mullet** - Light blue scale blended to white or yellow belly.
41. **Natural Perch** - See Perch.
42. **Natural Pickerel** - Yellow body with several vertical stripes compared to a few stripes of a perch pattern. Stripes are usually brown.
43. **Natural Pike** - Same as Natural Pickerel.
44. **Natural Pollywog** - Olive green body with light green-gold spots. Used on the Creek Chub Bait Co. Pollywog.
45. **Parrot** - White body with green back and large red eye shade. Used by Winchester.
46. **Peanut Butter Scale** - Light pink-silver scale with back stripe and eyes tan on yellow. Chin is red. Used by Shur-Strike.
47. **Perch** - Usually yellow body with few vertical stripes compared to the number of stripes on a pike or pickerel. Stripes are usually green, brown or black.

48. **Photo-Scale -** Simulated scales, gills, tail marks and side fins. Pattern applied by rolling a matt over the body. Used by Shakespeare.
49. **Purple Eel** - Dark purple back blended to white belly.
50. **Rainbow Fire -** Blended fluorescent rainbow stripes with white belly.
51. **Rainbow Trout -** Black or green back with silver-white scale and white belly. A single side stripe is light red or pink.

    Rainbow Trout - Dark green top with white sides and belly. A single blended light-red stripe on the sides. Back and sides have several black dots. Used by Paw Paw.
52. **Red Devil -** Red scale Weller Classic Minnow.
53. **Red, Green and Yellow Scramble -** A random mix of red, green and yellow covering a lure. Used by Pflueger.
54. **Red-White Luminous -** Luminous body and red design on a Heddon Crazy Crawler.
55. **Red Wing (Blackbird) -** Black body and red wings with blended white on the wings. Used by the Creek Chub Bait Co.
56. **River Peeler -** A steel blue Crawdad by the Creek Chub Bait Co.
57. **Salt-N-Pepper** - White body with specks of sparkle and red head.
58. **Saw-Tooth Perch** - Yellow body with heavy black, triangular stripes.
59. **Serpentine Stripe -** A wavy line along both sides of a lure.
60. **Sha-Zam -** White body with red horizontal lightning bolts on top, bottom. Also Black body with yellow lightning bolts. Used on Shakespear's Swimming Mouse.
61. **Shore Minnow -** A color pattern which simulates "ribs" and "backbone" of a minnow and produces a skeleton effect.
62. **Sienna Crackle back -** Dark orange-brown color used in place of green in Green Crackle back. See Green Crackle back.
63. **Silver Flash -** Usually white body with green trim on top and around eyes and silver sparkle added.
64. **Silver Herring -** Silver-gray scale body with black back and cream belly.
65. **Silver Scale -** Silver color with decal eyes and scales. Used by Winchester.
66. **Slate Back -** Light gray back. Primarily used by Heddon and Pflueger.
67. **Smokey Joe -** (Wood's Lures)?
68. **Snake -** Green scale and yellow spots with black centers. Heddon calls it "Frog Scale."
69. **Snake Skin -** Real snake skin (copperhead, rattlesnake, etc.) covers a lure.
70. **Splotch Frog Finish -** South Bend frog color. See Frog.
71. **Spotlite -** A Pflueger color used on metal lures. It is dull metallic with gold spots.
72. **Squid -** Light red-pink blended to white belly.
73. **Star-Burst Spot Pattern -** Tan, yellow or red body with multiple black ring-spots. Each ring-spot has an inner solid black circle and an outer concentric, black ring. Ring-spots vary in size. Belly is usually white. Normally some red (simulating blood) is on the head or body. Used by Bud Stewart.
74. **Strawberry -** White or yellow body and black top stripe with large red and small black side spots. (Early Pflueger) White body and black top stripe with large red and small black side spots.

    Strawberry (Early Pflueger) - White body and black top stripe with large red and small green side spots.

    Strawberry (Late Pflueger) - White body and black top stripe with large red and small yellow spots with black centers on the sides. Sometimes called "Christmas Tree."
75. **Target Spot -** (Jamison, #1500)?
76. **Tiger -** Yellow body with distinctive irregular black vertical stripes.
77. **Variegated Dots -** Different colored dots on the Shakespeare Floating Spinner.
78. **Victory Finish** (World War I) - Iridescent gold scale over blended red and green. Used on Rush Tangos.

    Victory Finish (World War II) - A Creek Chub Bait Co. Finish. Yellow or white body with black back stripe and black or red "V" with Morse Code for V, dit dit dit dah, along the side of their large-size Bomber. The smaller size Bomber has the "V" and dah dit dit dit along the side.
79. **Water Wave** - Scrambled mix of red and white or green and white. Used on Heddon River runt Spooks.

80\. **White, Red, Yellow and Black Spots -** See Strawberry. Late Pflueger pattern.

80\. **Zebra -** Black and white alternating, vertical stripes. Primarily used by Shakespeare, Paw Paw and Eger.

CONDITION GRADING

The National Fishing Lure Collectors Club (NFLCC) established a code of ethics for members some years ago. It is a good standard and one to which we should all adhere. Part of that code is the NFLCC Standard Lure Grading System. The code states, in part, that the system "...should be used on all sale and bid lists and verbal discussions of tackle grading. Bid or sale lists should include a minimum of 5-day return privilege." It is a 1 to 10 grading system. If the numerical scale condition needs further clarification, they state that a 1/2 can be added to this end. Also you may add a (+) or (-) to the regular description, ie. "AVG+" meaning better than "Average", but not quite up to "Good". The system is printed here for your use.

NUMERICAL SCALE OF CONDITION	DESCRIPTION/CONDITION	
10	NEW-IN-BOX (NIB)	Unused with original box or carton.
9	MINT(M)	Unused without box or carton.
8	EXCELLENT (EXC)	Very little age or no age cracks; very minor defects.
7	VERY GOOD (VG)	Little age cracks; some minor defects.
5-6	GOOD (G)	Some age cracks; starting to chip, small defects.
3-4	AVERAGE (AVG)	Some paint loss and/or chipping; showing age.
2	FAIR(F)	Major paint loss and/or defects; much chipping.
1	POOR(P)	Parts missing, poor color and/or major chipping.
0	REPAINT (R)	Original paint covered over in part or all.

IDENTIFICATION NOMENCLATURE

Clyde Harbin, a charter member of the N.F.L.C.C., devised a system of short-hand description of lures early in the development of the hobby. He published and utilized the system in his book *James Heddon's Sons Catalogues. It is reproduced in the next few pages with his permission. It is arranged in two forms, the first according to category and the second, alphabetically.

Listing by Category

BODY SHAPES & COMPOSITION

FBL Fat Body Lure
FSB Flat Sided Body
HEX Hexagonal (Six-sided body)
PEN Pentagonal (Five-sided body)
TSB Tapered Smaller Body
WFF Webbed Foot Frog
PB Plastic Body
PPB Pyralin Plastic Body

**Copyright 1977, Clyde A. Harbin, published by CAH Enterprises, Memphis, Tennessee.*

WB Wooden Body
RR Reverse Running Lure
DEB Double Ended Body (line tie on each end)
TenB Tenite Body
BB Bakelite Body

COLLARS

NC Narrow Collar (oldest type)
NP No Pen (friction fit)-Oldest Type
O Type of Collar (completely encircles the lure body)
PNC Penned or Nailed Collar (second oldest method of attachment)
S&FC Screw and Flanged Collar
U Type of Collar (similar to the 'O' collar above, but older and stops short of complete encirclement, thus: 'U' collar)

EYES

BE Bead Eye
GE Glass Eye
NE No Eye
PE Painted Eye
TOE Tack, Peg, or Nail-on Eye
TBGE Teddy Bear Glass Eye
TPE Tack Painted Eye

HEAD TYPES

2 SH Two Slanted (Sided) Head
4 SH Four Slanted (Sided) Head

HOOK FASTENER HARDWARE TYPES

BHHF Ball Head Hook Fastener (Shakespeare)
CUP Metal Cup and Screw-eye Hook Fastener
HD"L" Heavy Duty Double Screw Hook Fastener
"L" Double Screw Hook Fastener. Frequently called the "L" rig
SH Screw-hook Fastener (used with CUP hardware)
SE Screw-eye Hook Fastener
SEW Screw-eye Hook Fastener with Washer
WH Wood Hole (screw-eye) Hook Fastener
BAR One Piece Bar Hook Fastener
1PC One Piece (surface) Hook Fastener
2PC(1) Two Piece Metal Hook Fastener. Frequently called the "Toilet Seat" Fastener. (first Heddon style)
2PC(2) Second Style of Above (Heddon*)

HOOK TYPE AND POSITIONS

BH Belly Hook
DBL Double Hook
DHOT Double Hook on Tail
NBH No Belly Hook
SGL Single Hook
SHOT Single Hook on Tail
STH Side Treble Hooks
1-T One Treble Hooks
2-T Two Treble Hooks
3-T Three Treble Hooks
4-T Four Treble Hooks
5-T Five Treble Hooks
6-T Six Treble Hooks

LINE TIE TYPES

LTHD Line Tie Hump Down
LTHU Line Tie Hump Up
SELT Screw Eye Line Tie

TL&SELT Two Loop and Screw Eye Line Tie

VLF Variable Line Fastener-known variously as the '3-Loop', the 'Pigtail', or the 'Lunch Worm'

LIP TYPES

APL Adjustable Position Lip
BSL Bell Shape Lip
HSL Heart Shape Lip (appears somewhat like the profile shape of an inverted apple)
LLL Long Lower Lip
PPL Pyralin Plastic Lip

NAME PLACEMENT

NNBP No Name on Big Propeller
NNLP No Name of Little Propeller
NNOC No Name on Collar
NNOL No Name of Lip
NOBS Name on Both Sides (collar or lip)
NOCF Name on Collar Front
NOL Name on Lip
NOLP Name on Little Propeller
NOB Name on Body

NOSES

PN Pencil Nose
SN Slant or Slope Nose

MISCELLANEOUS

PRA Pork Rind Attachment
Pwts Pennyweight (24 grams or .05 ounces)

TAIL TYPES

BT Buck Tail
FS Florida Special
FT Feather Tail
NTC No Tail Cap
TC Tail Cap
THI Tail Hook Metal Insert

NUMBERS

1PC One Piece Surface Fastener
2PC(1) Two Piece Metal Hook Fastener. Frequently called the "Toilet Seat" fastener (first Heddon style)
2PC(2) *Second Style of Above (Heddon)
2 SH Two Slanted (Sided) Head
4 SH Four Slanted (Sided) Head
1-T One Treble Hook
2-T Two Treble Hooks
3-T Three Treble Hooks
4-T Four Treble Hooks
5-T Five Treble Hooks
6-T Six Treble Hooks

**Pfluger used a slightly different style of 2 pc. hardware*

Alphabetical Listing

A

APL Adjustable Position Lip

B

BAR One Piece Bar Hook Fastener
BE Bead Eye
BH Belly Hook
BHHF Ball Head Hook Fastener (Shakespeare)
BSL Bell Shape Lip
BT Buck Tail

C

CUP Metal Cup and Screw Eye Hook Fastener

D

DBL Double Hook (two point on one hook)
DEB Double Ended Body (line tie on each end)
DHOT Double Hook on Tail

F

FBL Fat Body Lure
FS Florida Special
FSB Flat Sided Body
FT Feather Tail

G

GE Glass Eye

H

HD"L" Heavy duty Double Screw Hook Fastener
HEX Hexagonal (six-sided body)
HSL Heart Shape Lip (appears somewhat Like the profile shape of an inverted apple)

L

"L" Double Screw Hook Fastener. Frequently called the "L" Rig.
LLP Long Lower Lip
LTHD Line Tie Hump Down
LTHU Line Tie Hump Up

N

NBH No Belly Hook
NC Narrow Collar (oldest type)
NE No Eye
NNBP No Name on Big Propeller
NNLP No Name on Little Propeller
NNOC No Name on Collar
NNOL No Name on Lip
NOB Name on Body
NOBP Name on Big Propeller
NOBS Name on Both Sides (collar or lip)
NOCF Name on Collar Front
NOL Name on Lip
NOLP Name on Little Propeller
NTC No Tail Cap

O

O Type of Collar (completely encircles the lure body)

P

PB Plastic Body
PE Painted Eye
PEN Pentagonal (five-sided body)
PN Pencil Nose
PNC Penned or Nailed Collar (second oldest method of attachment)
PPB Pyralin Plastic Lip
Pwts Pennyweight (24 grams or .05 ounces)

S

SE Screw Eye Hook Fastener
SELT Screw Eye Line Tie
SEW Screw Eye Hook Fastener with washer
S&FC Screw and Flanged Collar

SGL Single Hook (one point)
SH Screw Hook Fastener
SHOT Single Hook on Tail
SN Slant or Slope Nose
STH Side Treble Hooks

T

TBGE Teddy Bear Glass Eye
TC Tail Cap
TL&SELT Two Loop and Screw Eye Line Tie
TOE Tack, Peg, or Nail-on Eye (no paint)
TPE Tack Painted Eye
TSB Tapered Smaller Body
THI Tail Hook Metal Insert

U

U Type of Collar (similar to the 'O' collar above, but older and stops short of complete encirclement, thus: 'u' collar)

V

VLF Variable Line Fastener-known variously as the "3 Loop", the "Pigtail", or the "Inch Worm"

W

WB Wooden Body
WFF Webbed Foot Frog
WH Wood Hole (screw eye) Hook Fastener

UNDERSTANDING PATENTS AND THEIR USE IN IDENTIFYING LURES

The United States Patent System was created by Act of Congress in 1790. On April 10 of that year, President George Washington signed "An Act to Promote the Progress of Useful Arts". Its purpose was and is to protect the rights of inventors to the exclusive use of their inventions for a "limited" amount of time. This was, simply put, a way of preventing others from taking commercial advantage of the inventor's creation without the inventor's permission. The requirements for being granted a patent were the submission of a drawing, a written description and a working model, built to scale. Times were tough for the new young government and three years later the requirement for the scale model was eliminated and replaced with a flat fee of $30.00. That was a prodigious amount of money for those days and that, along with the elimination of the model requirement, effectively destroyed any protection for the inventor. Anyone with the wherewithal could swipe a design and reap the benefit. Eli Whitney realized very little profit from his invention of the cotton gin as a result of this. Forty-three years later, in 1836, this problem was finally solved with the passage of The Patent Act.

The new patent act reinstated the requirement for the model stating in part "...furnish a model of his invention in all cases which admit of a representation by model, of a convenient size to exhibit advantageously its several parts. The model, not more than twelve inches square, should be neatly made, the name of the inventor should be printed or engraved upon, or affixed to it, in a durable manner." As you can imagine, the patent office was inundated with new applications and December 15 of that same year disaster struck. A fire destroyed most of the models and all of the Patent Office records. An Act of Congress was immediately passed appropriating $100,000 for the restoration of 3,000 of the most important models. At the same time they decided to change the manner of keeping up with the inventions by the inventor's name in favor of a numerical system. Thus, the patent number system was born with the issuance of Patent Number 1 in 1836. The patent number 1 was, incidentally, the only patent number issued in 1836.

As the years went by, the models piled up and room to store them ran out. They were stacked on window sills, desks and anywhere else space could be found. In 1877 fire struck once again, this time destroying an estimated 76,000 models. Still, many survived and by 1880 the Patent Office was overflowing with them again. At that point, the Patent Office modified the model requirement to those only requested by the Commissioner of Patents "...along with all flying, and perpetual motion machines." Despite them no longer being required, some inventors continued to submit models even up into the 1900s. Around 1893 the existing models were put into storage and in 1907 the Smithsonian obtained more than 1,000 of the most famous patents models. Over the years, families of the inventors were given opportunities to reacquire the models and a huge number were disposed of to other private parties.

Now, all of that for this. There are an unknown, but probably large number of these patent models to be found. Only a few have so far turned up. Think what treasures these would be.

The most useful aspect of the patent system is its practice of the assigning of sequential numbers to patent applications since Number 1 in 1836. The following chart is helpful in determining the earliest possible date of a lure if the patent number is stamped on it somewhere. Two words of caution. First is that the date derived from the number or the date actually on the lure is only the date the patent was granted, not the date of the lure manufacture. Many patented lures continued to be made for ten, twenty or more years. The other caveat is that sometimes the patent number is for only the component it is stamped on and not necessarily the lure itself. Remember also that many makers were fashioning their lures long before the patent was granted. From time to time you will encounter the inscription on a lure or in the literature the words "PAT PENDING", "PAT PEND" or some other similar wording. That means that a patent had been applied for, but not yet granted as of the time of manufacture of the lure.

FAKES, COPIES AND REPRODUCTIONS

We have discussed the fakes, copycats and reproductions to a small degree so far. It behooves us to elaborate because, unfortunately, the problem has risen to a point where it has become a controversial issue. So much so that the NFLCC has been forced to address the problem formally through an addition to their *Bylaws and Procedures.*

What are the differences? First of all it is unfortunate to have to lump the legitimate reproduction with the others, but some would argue that if it is a reproduction it is not legitimate. We needn't get into a semantic argument here, but we do need to define the term. To reproduce a lure is just that, to make an exact copy. The method of fashioning the reproduction may differ greatly from the original, but the outcome is the same. Now, if the lure has been exactly copied is it a fake? The answer is yes

Patent Dating Chart

Patent Number	Year	Patent Number	Year	Patent Number	Year
1	1836	223,211	1880	1,478,996	1924
110	1837	236,137	1881	1,521,590	1925
546	1838	251,685	1882	1,568,040	1926
1,106	1839	269,820	1883	1,612,700	1927
1,465	1840	291,016	1884	1,654,521	1928
1,923	1841	310,163	1885	1,696,897	1929
2,413	1842	333,494	1886	1,742,181	1930
2,901	1843	355,291	1887	1,787,424	1931
3,395	1844	375,720	1888	1,839,190	1932
3,873	1845	395,305	1889	1,892,663	1933
4,348	1846	418,665	1890	1,941,449	1934
4,914	1847	443,987	1891	1,985,878	1935
5,409	1848	466,315	1892	2,026,516	1936
5,993	1849	488,976	1893	2,066,309	1937
6,981	1850	511,744	1894	2,104,004	1938
7,865	1851	531,619	1895	2,142,080	1939
8,622	1852	552,502	1896	2,185,170	1940
9,512	1853	574,369	1897	2,227,418	1941
10,358	1854	596,467	1898	2,268,540	1942
12,117	1855	616,871	1899	2,307,007	1943
14,009	1856	640,167	1900	2,338,081	1944
16,324	1857	664,827	1901	2,366,154	1945
19,010	1858	690,385	1902	2,391,856	1946
22,477	1859	717,521	1903	2,413,675	1947
26,642	1860	748,567	1904	2,433,824	1948
31,005	1861	778,834	1905	2,457,797	1949
34,045	1862	808,618	1906	2,492,944	1950
37,266	1863	839,799	1907	2,536,016	1951
41,047	1864	875,679	1908	2,580,379	1952
45,685	1865	908,436	1909	2,624,046	1953
51,784	1866	945,010	1910	2,664,562	1954
60,658	1867	980,178	1911	2,698,434	1955
72,959	1868	1,013,095	1912	2,728,913	1956
85,503	1869	1,049,326	1913	2,775,752	1957
98,460	1870	1,083,267	1914	2,818,973	1958
110,617	1871	1,123,212	1915	2,866,973	1959
122,304	1872	1,166,419	1916	2,919,443	1960
134,504	1873	1,210,389	1917	2,966,681	1961
146,120	1874	1,251,458	1918	3,015,103	1962
158,350	1875	1,290,027	1919	3,070,801	1963
171,641	1876	1,326,899	1920	3,116,487	1964
185,813	1877	1,364,063	1921	3,163,865	1965
198,733	1878	1,401,948	1922		
211,078	1879	1,440,362	1923		

and no. If it is clearly marked as a reproduction then it is a "legitimate" reproduction and marketed as such. If it is not marked, but represented as what it is, a reproduction, then where are we? I suppose the legitimacy of this initial transaction is without question, but the problem rears its ugly head later when through misrepresentation, intentional or otherwise, the unmarked reproduction makes its way into the collector market. So now you can see why it is of paramount importance that any reproduction be marked in such a way as to leave no doubt as to its origin.

A fake is a reproduction clearly made from the get-go with the intent to pass it off as the real thing. The unmarked reproduction, however legitimate in its origin, becomes a fake if misrepresented.

Legitimate reproductions have a place in the market, especially when they are older. This has been going on for decades. A good example is the Wallace Nutting reproductions of early American furniture. These reproductions will sometimes bring almost as much as the originals. I have written extensively about fakes and reproductions in another of my books, pointing out that fakes,

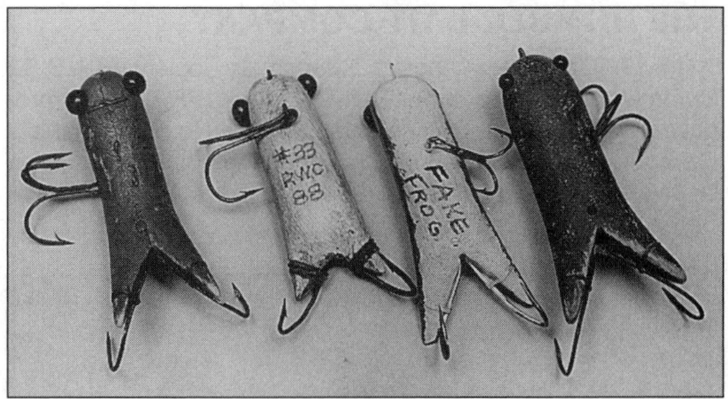

Four frogs. The one on the left is an authenticated original hand-carved frog lure by James Heddon. The next one (belly up) is a reproduction. The inscription indicates it is #33 made by RWC in 1988. The third and fourth are fakes. The owner of these unidentified, unmarked reproductions has, as you can see, prominently marked them as fakes.

and "copycats" can also be collectibles. Indeed, Lawrence L. Wonsch has written of their inherent value as collectibles in his *Hummel Copycats with Values* (Wallace-Homestead, 1987).

A "copycat" is merely the use of the original "style" of an object, an imitation if you will, in the production of another. It is an attempt to make a profit by marketing a product imitating a successful product playing on the popularity of that usually more expensive original. These imitations are usually inferior to the real thing and readily identifiable as such.

The fishing lure collector must be cognizant of a practice unique to fishermen. From the beginning there have been fishermen who fashioned their own lures for whatever the reason, be they unable to afford the real thing, skinflint or the inveterate tinkerer. Many would simply copy the popular lure of the time. Some were better than others, some added their own ideas. Whatever the case, there are hundreds of examples of lures that are unidentifiable or only attributable at best, to one company or another. There can be no doubt that the majority of these were a product of fishermen and not the company that they appear to have been made by. Beware the category "prototype". A prototype is an early experiment in the development of a product. There may be more than one in the development. There is a tendency to lump any strange configuration of otherwise familiar lures into the prototype category. I have seen entirely too many of these so-called "prototypes" for them all to be genuine. Most are probably the result of tinkering or copying with "a better idea" or two added. Let us not forget the tinkerer for sure. Many a fisherman, myself included, have modified a lure by the addition or deletion of hooks, types of hooks, repainting, repairing. Sometimes this is an expedient on a fishing trip and sometimes just an irresistible modification by a fisherman looking for the proverbial "secret weapon" that no one else has. There is no telling what you might run across.

NFLCC BYLAWS AND PROCEDURES CONCERNING:

F. Reproductions, Reprints, Restorations, Folk Art and Contemporary Guidelines for Lures, Decoys, Rods and Reels, not excluding any items related to the hobby of Fishing Collectibles.

1. Definitions:

A. *REPRODUCTIONS:* A contemporary imitation of a rod, lure, decoy or fishing related item by a craftsman or company intended to appear identical or nearly identical to an original or commercially produced object;

B. *REPAINTS:* An authentic lure, decoy or fishing related item that has been repainted in any manner after the craftsman or company originally marketed or manufactured said item;

C. *RESTORATION:* An authentic lure, decoy, rod or fishing related item restored to the original condition of up to but not exceeding 20% of the item. Restorations exceeding 20% shall be considered a repaint;

D. *FOLK ART:* A unique lure or fishing related item, regardless of size or color, by an individual reflecting personal craftsmanship and unique regional style; and

E. *CONTEMPORARY:* A modern lure, decoy, or related item manufactured by a present day craftsman or company.

2. Identification of Reproductions, Repaints and Restorations

A. *REPRODUCTIONS:* The NFLCC does not support the reproduction of antique fishing tackle since it is harmful to the hobby. Reproductions shall not be displayed or sold at any sanctioned NFLCC show or event with but one exception. *A marked reproduction may be included in an educational display only. The display or reproduction cannot be sold or traded during any sanctioned show or event.*

B. *REPAINTS:* Shall be marked deeply into the lure or item with the artists initial or trademark, in such a manner making it impossible to remove without altering the item. The artists identifying mark or marks should be registered with the NFLCC secretary, to be published annually for identification and educational purposes.

C. Any known restoration or alteration must be pointed out to a prospective buyer or trader. An identifying tag should be attached to the item to avoid misunderstandings. Failure to do so will void a sale or trade at the option of the buyer or trader within a 14-day exam period.

A FEW EXAMPLES OF SOME REALLY FINE REPRODUCTIONS

There are a number of individuals making and marketing reproductions of the classic old lures and many who make them in the manner of the old style. A good example of the former is theWEIR CLASSIC LURES of Ronald F. Mirabile. As we have discussed, it is imperative that these reproductions be clearly marked as such. A partial quote from a promotional letter from Mr. Mirabile: "Weir Classic Lures are hand-crafted from furniture grade woods ... They are produced in the same manner as the originals ... These lures capture not only the quality but also the art of those old lures and the 'Lure master' that created them. My task is only to honor them."

Some of the names of people and companies whose lures are reproduced by Weir are, Alger, Bidwell, Brown Brothers, Comstock, Donaly, Egar, Haynes, Heddon, Pflueger and Shakespeare.

Mr. Mirabile states clearly and emphatically in his literature: "Weir Classic Lures are signed 'W E I R', so that they are not confused with originals."

Mr. Mirabile also sell kits for anyone wishing to try their hand.

THE HEDDON 1894-1994 CENTENNIAL EDITION

In 1994 Heddon (Pradco) released a series of wooden replicas of some of their more famous lures, the Zaragossa, the River Runt and the Lucky-13. Note the identification as such on the box. The lures are so marked as well. The edition is reported by the company to be 10,000 each.

Heddon Centennial Edition Wood River Runt.

Heddon Centennial Edition Wood Zaragossa.

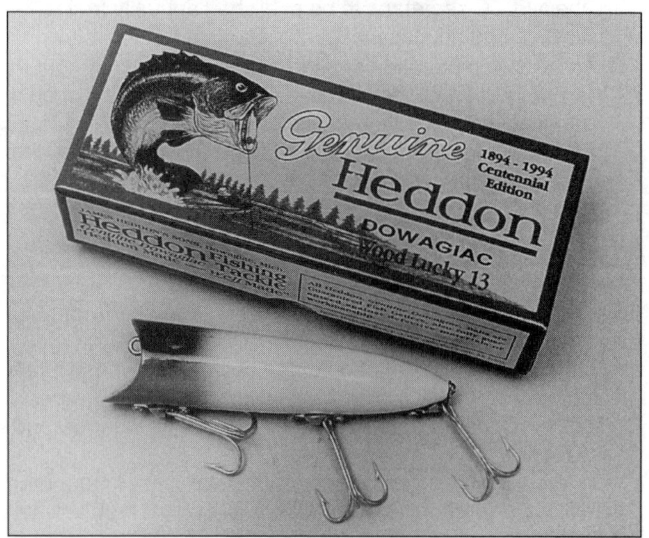

Heddon Centennial Edition Wood Lucky-13.

THE BOMBER BAIT COMPANY

In 1997 the Bass Anglers Sportsman Society (B.A.S.S.) Commissioned the Bomber Bait Company (PRADCO)to produce a reproduction of their famous Spinstick to commemorate the 30th Anniversary of B.A.S.S. This is the lure that was used by the winner of the first All-American Bass Tournament at Beaver Lake, Arkansas in 1967.

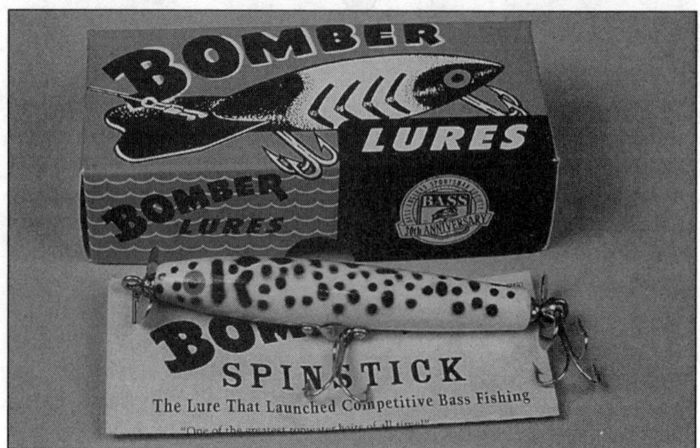

The Bomber Bait Company reproduction Spinstick in the Coach Dog color finish used by the winner in 1967 of the first All-American Bass Tournament.

THE CREEK CHUB BAIT COMPANY

In 1992 the Creek Chub Co. released "Collector's Limited Editions" of its famous Wiggle Fish and Creek Darter. Each of the boxes are so marked. The edition is said to be limited to 10,000 lures each.

The Collector's Limited Edition Creek Chub Bait Co. wooden #2000 series Darter.

EARLY FISHING LURES AND THEIR MAKERS

The following pages list thousands of old fishing lures and their makers. The lures and companies are listed alphabetically. In most cases if there was only one lure found, its name, if known, heads the listing. In the case of companies with multiple products the company and its known history head up the listing. If you have any trouble locating a lure or company, turn to the index for additional help. If the lure or company is not listed there, it's not in the

The Collector's Limited Edition Creek Chub Bait Co. wooden #2400 series Wiggle Fish.

book. Just because it is not in the book doesn't mean it wasn't important and/or interesting. It simply means I have to cut it off somewhere or the book would never get finished.

At the end of the listings you will also find several pages of photographs and descriptions of lures that have so far defied attempts at identification.

IMPORTANT NOTICE

The value ranges listed in this book are for lures in Very Good to Excellent condition. The values of those lures not in Very Good to Excellent condition can and probably will be worth considerably less. The values are meant to be a guide only.

A-B-C MINNOW

George W. Bolton — Detroit, Michigan

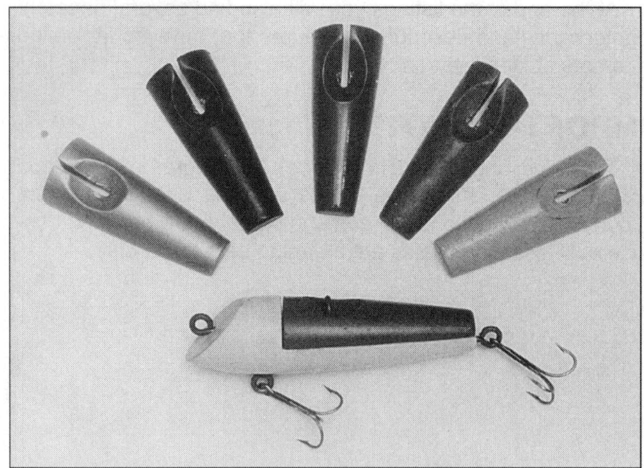

An A-B-C MINNOW with all of its back inserts.

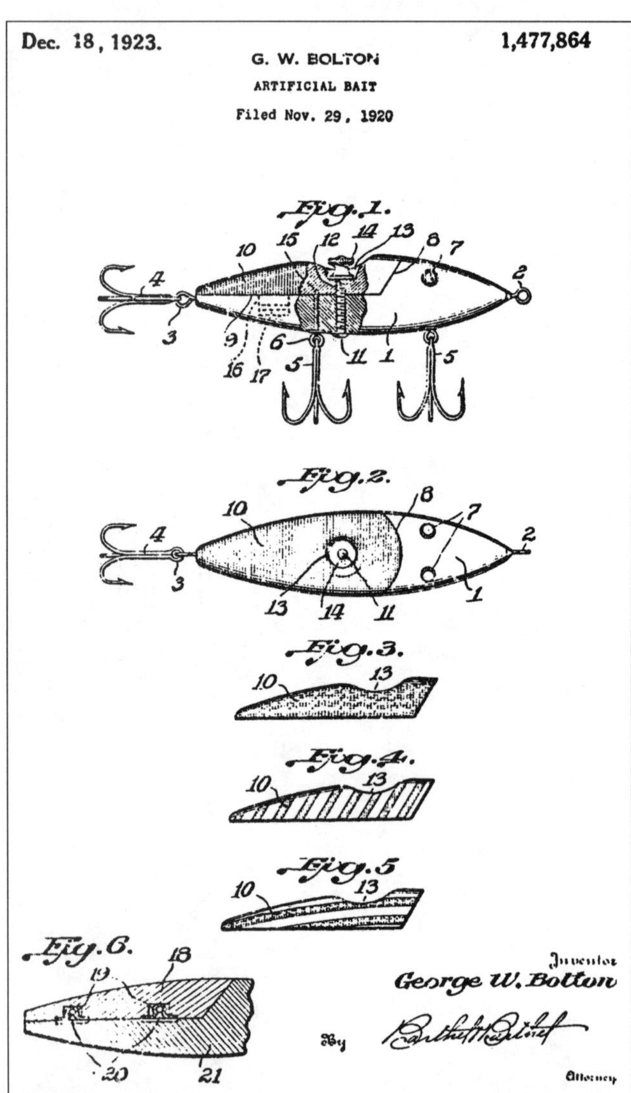

The A-B-C Minnow Patent Drawing.

There are two models of this clever lure. Each has interchangeable back pieces. The available colors were black, white, red, green and silver. The photo of the single lure here is No. 100. As you can see it has a carved mouth and a pointed nose. Not very evident in the photo are glass eyes and cup/screw eye hook hangers. The accompanying illustration is of the patent granted to Bolton in December of 1923. As you can see, neither of the production models are exactly like the patent drawing. They are, however, close enough that the patent protected them. No patent models have, as yet, shown up. That would be a treasure indeed. Note the knurled nut and bolt fastener for the removable backs used rather than the screw eye fastener on the production models. Collector value range: $200 to $350 with all parts. The glass-eyed model will bring a bit more than the eyeless model.

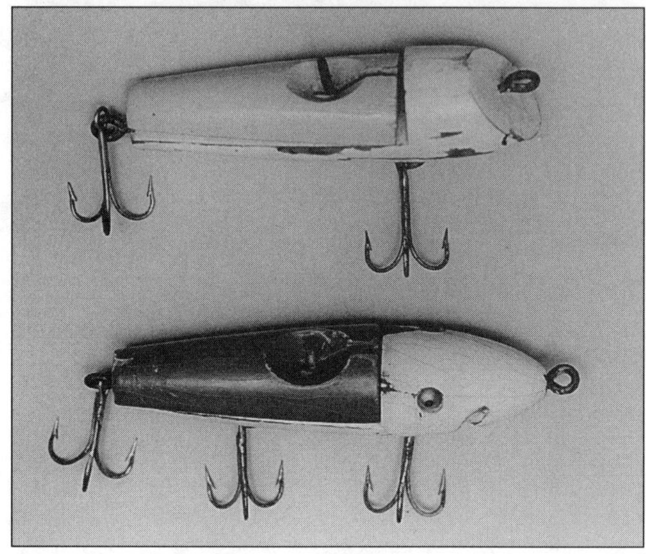

The two different models.

ABBEY AND IMBRIE FISHING TACKLE

This famous New York company was in business long before they began to market fishing tackle to any great degree. They were founded in 1875 as the successors to Andrew Clerk and Company, purveyors of fishing tackle in New York since 1820. Abbey & Imbrie lasted until Horrocks-Ibbotson of Utica, NY bought the company in 1930.

If you examine the advertising and tackle catalogs of the era, with any knowledge of old lures from other companies, you will find striking similarities. In fact it has long been established that the company had many well-known lure manufacturers to produce their products with the Abbey & Imbrie (A&I) imprint.

The photo of the lure with its original box here is a good example of this. It is no doubt a lure made by J.K. Rush (Rush Tango). The box is labeled "Go-Getter", but there is no identifying imprint anywhere on the plug itself. Collector value range: $20-$50.

I can't say with any sure evidence at this time that they ever actually manufactured lures themselves, but my inclination is to doubt it. The company was established in 1820 and earliest advertisements uncovered so far, that includes lures, date in the mid to late 1880s.

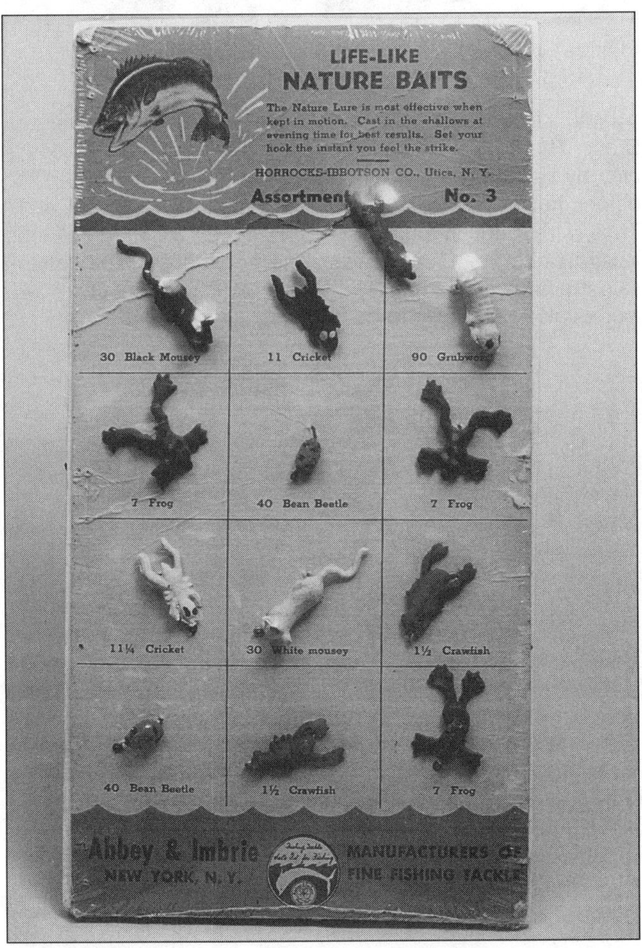

A display card of Abbey & Imbrie rubber lures.

JOINTED METAL MINNOW

The accompanying illustration was found in Henshall's Book of Black Bass and identified there as a "Jointed Metal Minnow (Abbey & Imbrie)". The book was copyrighted in 1881 so the lure must be somewhat older than that. I have never seen one exactly as in the illustration, but have seen some quite similar to it. This may have been an import from Europe.

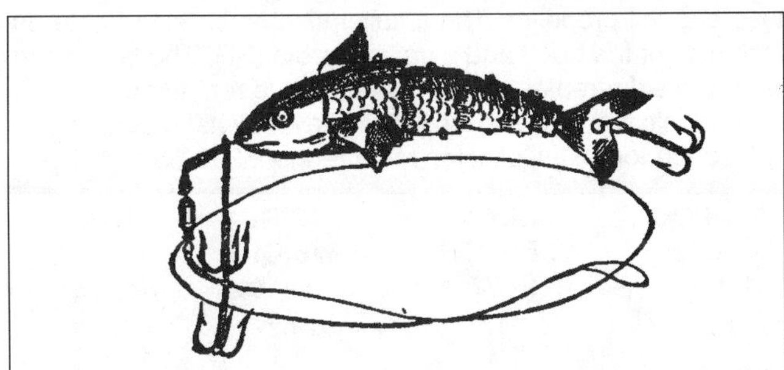

An Abbey and Imbrie jointed metal minnow.

THE GHOST

Measuring 6" overall, this lure dates back into the late 1800s to the early 1900s. The A&I logo on the box began use in 1893 and the lure looks much like the P&S Ball Bearing Company Lures of around 1900. In the box were an extra set of snelled hooks and an extra "Weedless Fly Gang". This is probably the No. 2 as the printing on the box indicates that the No. 1 and No. 3 were fitted with "Extra Treble Hooks"; no mention of the Weedless Fly Gang, which utilizes a weedless treble hook. Collector value range: $150-$250. The box is worth more than the lure. It can easily be worth double that.

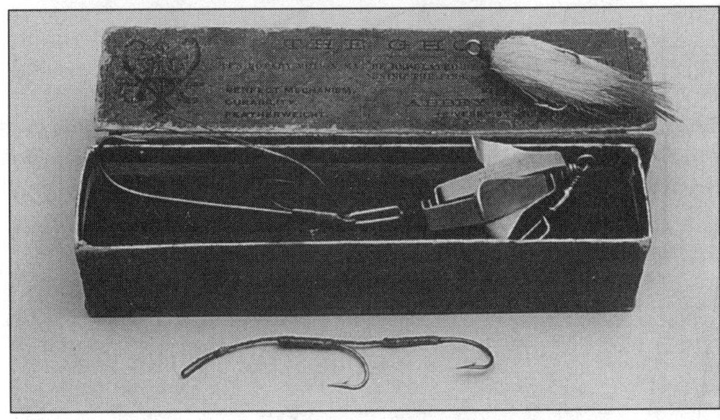

ABBEY AND IMBRIE MADE by HEDDON

The lures in the following photos are known to have been made by Heddon but marketed by A&I under their own brands and names. What is not presently known is what many of those were. Almost all the Heddon manufactured A&I lures will have "Abbey & Imbrie" stenciled on the belly. When fitted with metal plates, propeller spinners or diving lips they will have the same imprinted in place of the "Heddon Dowagiac" imprint.

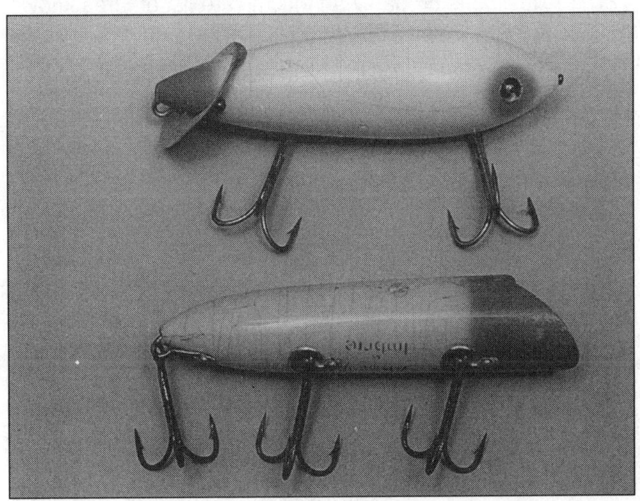

The top lure here is a dead ringer for the Heddon 1800 Series CRAB WIGGLER with glass eyes. The lower lure is obviously a Heddon BASSER. It has no eyes and the Heddon L-rig hook hangers. It bears the Abbey & Imbrie imprint on the belly. Collector value range: $55-$125 for each.

An A&I lure based on the Heddon TRIPLE TEASE. The metal minnow flippers are imprinted with 'Abbey & Imbrie'. The center flipper is missing on this particular lure. Collector value range: $35-$50.

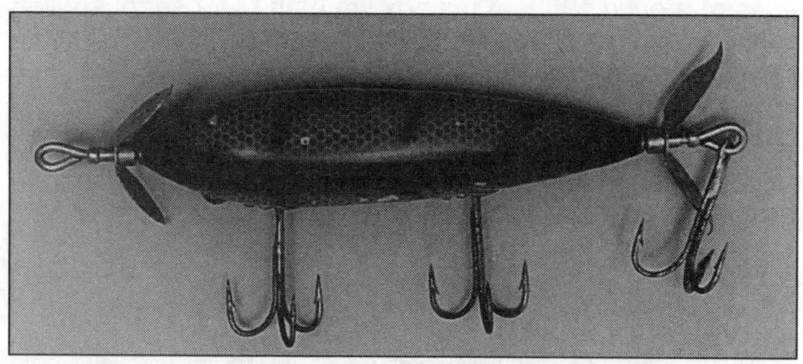

This 3-7/8" glass-eyed A&I lure was made by Heddon utilizing their #140 FLIPPER body. The A&I version has the L-rigged hooks mounted on the side rather than the belly as Heddon did. Both the propeller spinners are marked with the Abbey & Imbrie imprint. Collector value range: $200-$400.

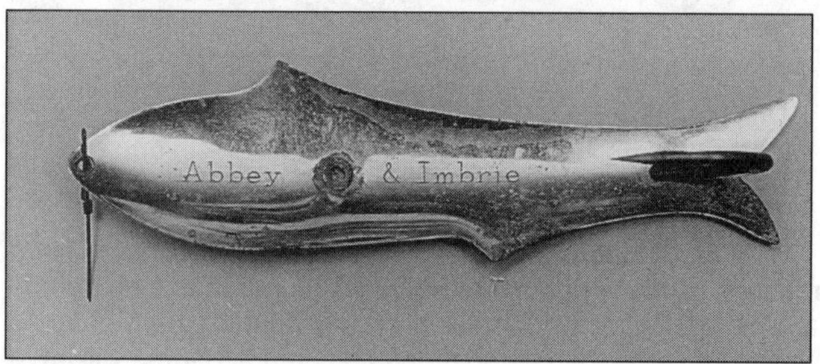

Another Heddon-made lure with the Abbey & Imbrie imprint A 5-1/2" metal fish spoon. Collector value range: $300-$400.

The following is probably an incomplete list of lures known to have been made for Abbey and Imbrie by Heddon:

Lucky-13 and Lucky-13 Jr.	Basser
#175 Heavy Casting Minnow	Triple Tease
#700 Musky Minnow	Series #150
Flipper (side hook)	Vamp (jointed)
Series #150 Injured Minnow style	Series "O" Minnow
Meadow Mouse	#1800 Crab Wiggler
(3T, no belly weights)	

MOUSE

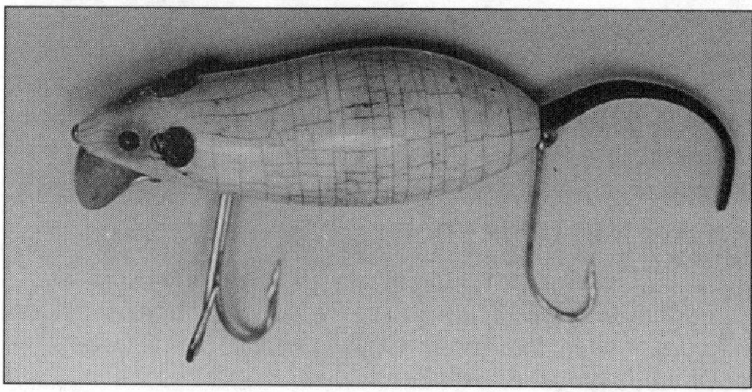

This is an A&I mouse lure made by Heddon from their MEADOW MOUSE design. The metal lip on this lure is imprinted "Abbey & Imbrie." It has black bead eyes, leather ears and tail and sports and L-rig belly hook hanger and the Heddon one-piece short loop (Stolley patent) tail hanger. It measures 2-3/4" without the tail. It was made in the following finishes: Gray mouse color, White body with red blush around eyes and chin. Collector value range: $40-$80.

THE GRIFFITHS MINNOW

A 1923 Edition of an Abbey & Imbrie catalog illustrated this lure. It was supplied with "several detachable fins of different

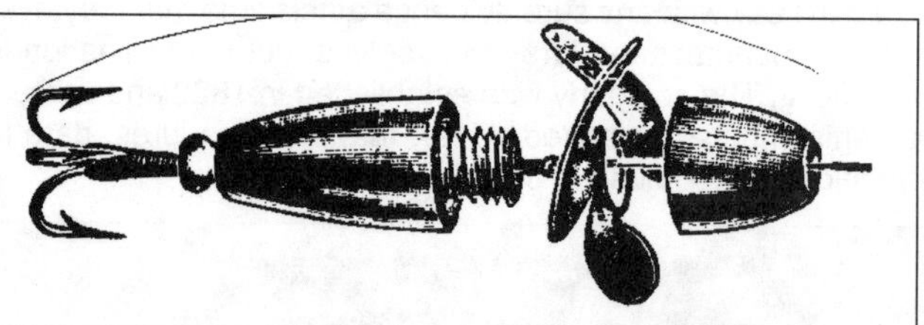

colors...". The only "colors" mentioned were Copper, Silver and Brass. The entry went on to say "The fin already on the body is already bent up to what is considered the best position. The others, however, are left flat for the angler to experiment with." They were made in four sizes: 1", 2", 2-1/2", 3". The one in the illustration is the 1" model with one treble hook. The catalog said the larger sizes had "two treble hooks, tandem style. Collector value range: No trade data found.

THE "GLOWBODY" MINNOW

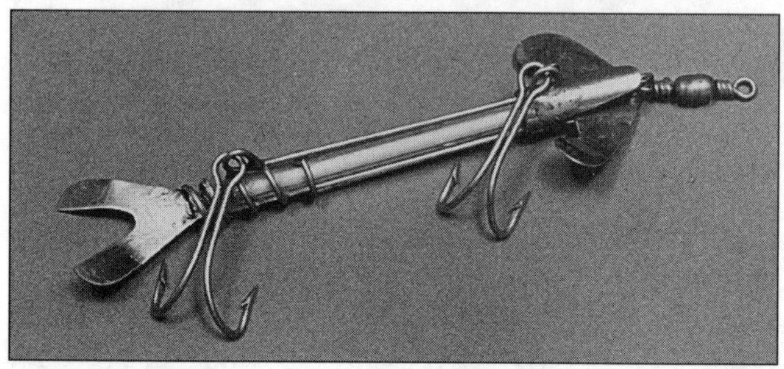

This dandy was introduced in 1920. It has nickel plated hardware made so that the changing of hooks is easy. The body is a glass tube with a smaller tube inside that is coated with a luminous material so that it could be fished at night. Length is about 3-1/2". Collector value range: $60-$100.

HIAWATHA WOODEN MINNOW

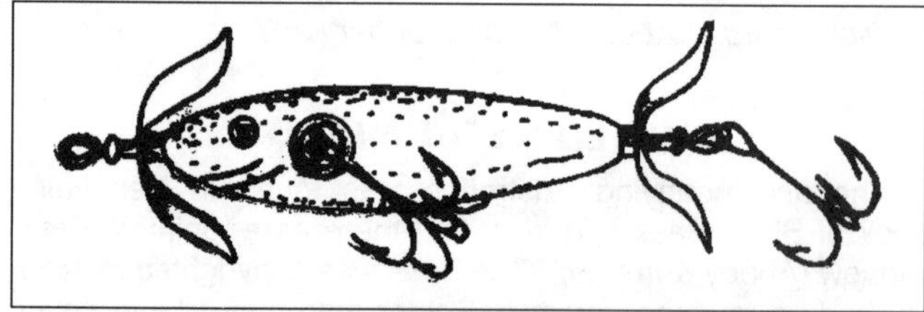

A 1914 Abbey and Imbrie catalog illustrates this plug as available in two sizes and hook configurations. Both sizes have nose and tail propeller. The smaller size and a side treble on each side of the body and a trailing treble (3T). The larger had two more side trebles (5T), these baits are remarkably similar to Heddon's No. 100 and No. 150. They may have been made by Heddon for A&I. Collector value range: $300-$500.

CATALOG SERIES	BODY LENGTH	LURE WEIGHT	HOOKS
1100	2-1/2"	3/4 oz.	3T
1150	3-1/2"	1 oz.	5T

COLOR OR FINISH: Fancy back; Rainbow Solid White; Solid red; Blended green; Yellow perch.

THE OCTOPUS WOODEN MINNOWS

These plugs were first observed in a 1911 catalog as available in two sizes: The No. 1 was 3-1/2" long and had a pair of trebles on each side and a trailing treble (5T); the No. 2 was 2-

OCTOPUS MINNOW. Note the unique soldered, reinforced propellers and white cylindrical bearing beads. The hook hangers are staple-type.

1/2" long and had only one treble on each side and a trailing treble (3T). Each sported nose and tail propeller spinners. Collector value range: $300-$500.

CRIPPLED MINNOW

Some time in the 1920s this plug became available. It was wood and shaped somewhat like a minnow with a realistic tail fin shape. It has one left-side-mounted treble and left mounted trailing tail treble (2T). Collector value range: $40-$85.

CATALOG SERIES	BODY LENGTH	LURE WEIGHT
3400	4"	3/4 oz.

COLOR OR FINISH: White with red head, Silver scale finish, Frog finish.

BASS-CATCHER

This is a 1920s vintage plug with a slope nose and 1" wire leader attached. It has one belly treble and trailing treble hook (2T). It is the same as the BASS SEEKER made by Moonlight Bait Company. Moonlight also made them for Abbey & Imbrie. Collector value range: $150-$175.

CATALOG SERIES	BODY LENGTH	LURE WEIGHT
2700	3-1/2"	1 oz.

COLOR OR FINISH: White with red head, Gold scale finish, Silver with red head.

WHIPPET

This lure first came along in 1929. It had nose- and tail-mounted propellers, a belly treble and trailing treble hook (2T). Collector value range: $15-$20.

CATALOG SERIES	BODY LENGTH	LURE WEIGHT
2400	4"	5/8 oz.

COLOR OR FINISH: White with red head; Gold scale finish; Perch finish.

FLASH-HEAD WOBBLER

This deep-water plug was first put in the line about 1929. It had a nickel plated metal head, a wire leader, belly mounted and trailing treble hooks (2T). It was made for Abbey & Imbrie by the Moonlight Bait Company. Collector value range: $25-$40.

CATALOG SERIES	BODY LENGTH	LURE WEIGHT
3700	3-1/2"	1 oz.

COLOR OR FINISH: Gold scale finish; Frog finish.

WHIRLING CHUB

First found in late 1920s catalogs, this is a minnow shaped plug with a nose propeller. It has one belly treble and a trailing

treble hook (2T). Measuring 4-1/4", this lure was made for Abbey & Imbrie by the Moonlight Bait Company. Moonlight probably never marketed it under its own name. Moonlight also made a 3-1/4" BABY WHIRLING CHUB. It has only a trailing treble. Collector value range: $100-$150. Photo courtesy Jim Muma.

CATALOG SERIES	BODY LENGTH	LURE WEIGHT
3200	4-1/2"	1 oz.

COLOR OR FINISH: White with redhead, Silver scale finish; Frog finish.

EZY-KATCH WOOD MINNOW

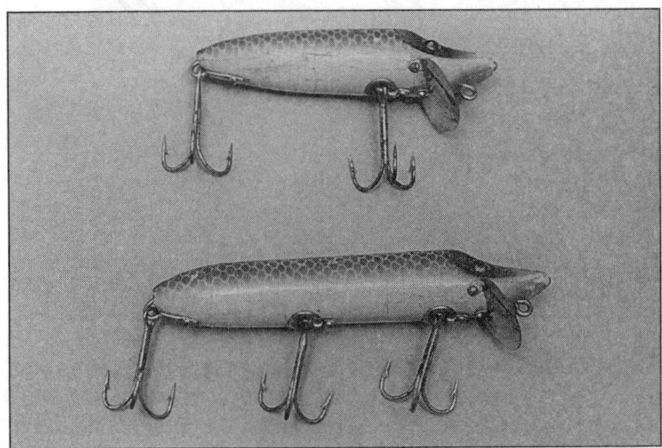

This late 1920s plug was available in two distinctly different body designs even though both bore the same catalog number (No. 50). They were available to dealers in six-plug counter display boxes (3 of each type). Colors were assorted. One style is more or less tear drop-shaped with a nose propeller, belly treble and trailing treble (2T) and 3-1/2" long.

The other EZY-KATCH minnows were made by Heddon. The lure is actually a Heddon VAMP series plug. The two in the photo here have the Abbey & Imbrie imprint on the metal diving lips, glass eyes, "L-rigs" and the Heddon (Stolley patent) drop loop tail hook hangers. Collector value range: $75-125.

"JIGOLET"

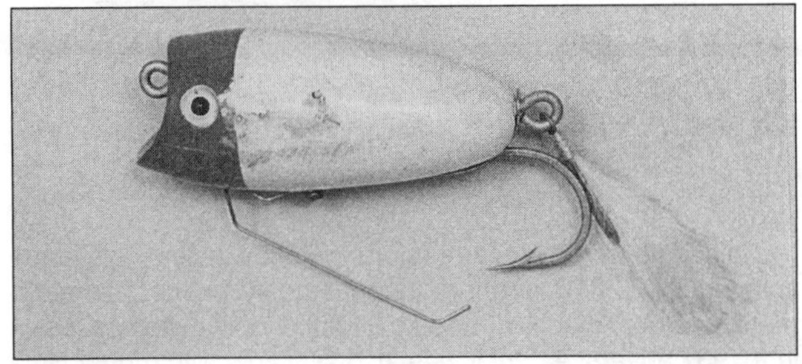

TONY ACCETTA — Cleveland, Ohio

Accetta formed his company sometime in the late 1930s.

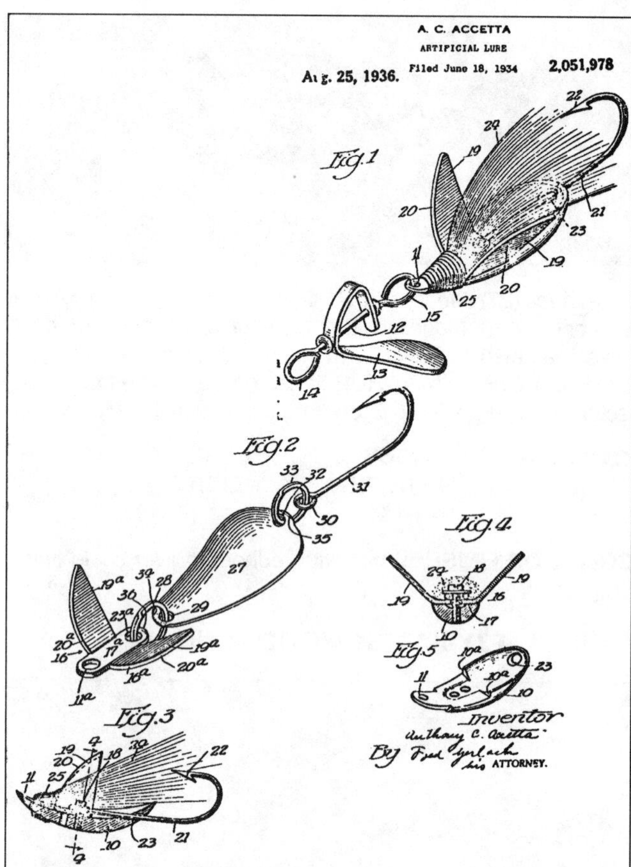

A patent filed in 1934 and granted to Accetta in August of 1936. Fig. 1 is the RIVER DEVIL and Fig. 2 has components of the BUG SPOON and the FLY ROD BUG SPOONET.

The last reference I could find in catalogs and magazines was in 1957. There was an advertisement for a new lure in a 1957 issue of *Outdoor Life.* Presumably the company continued in operation after that, but for how long is not known to the author.

This lure was introduced at the end of the 1930s. It is a 2-3/4" Tenite plug. It was available with a single belly hook rigged snagless and with belly and trailing trebles. The tail trails a wiggling skirt on both and the head is concave vertically. Colors available were: White with red head, white with black head, green, yellow, black and pearl. Collector value range: $10-$20

RIVER DEVIL

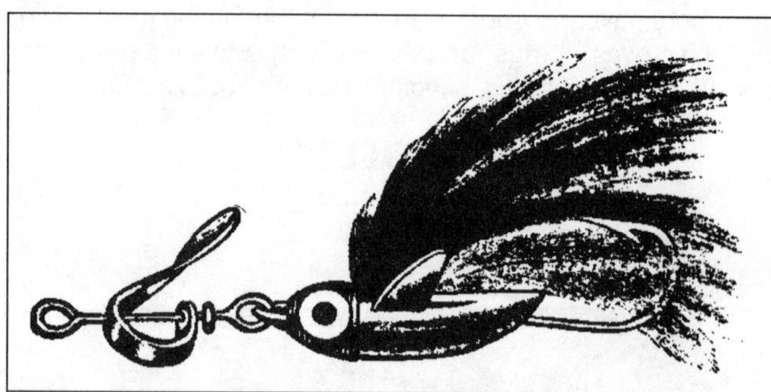

This feathered metal lure sports a Ponca style single blade spinner. It is 3-3/4" long including the hook, but not the feathers. It was also made with a size 3 treble hook. Listed as "New" in a 1937 advertisement it was also available with rubber Hula skirts attached to each side. Illustrations indicate that the body styles for the rubber skirt model and the feather model were a bit different. Each is well identified with its name. Color finishes available were red and white, black and white, black and yellow, black, yellow, brown. Collector value range: $6-$12.

HOBO

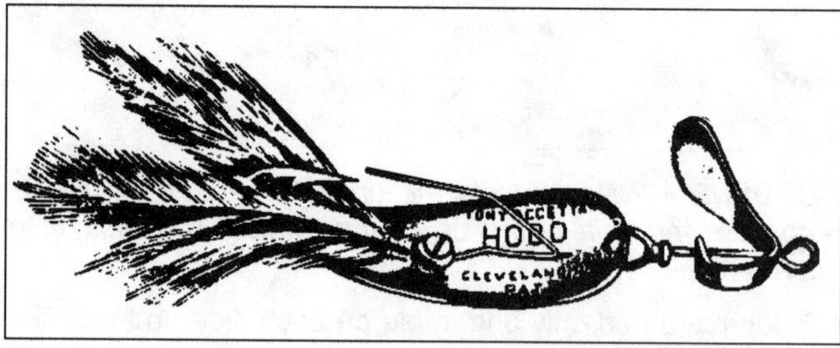

This feathered spoon also uses a Ponca style single blade spinner. It is a 1/2-ounce lure measuring 3-1/2" long disregarding the feathers. It is rigged weedless and as you can see by the illustration, well marked for identification. Collector value range: $4-$8.

BUG SPOON AND BUG SPOONET

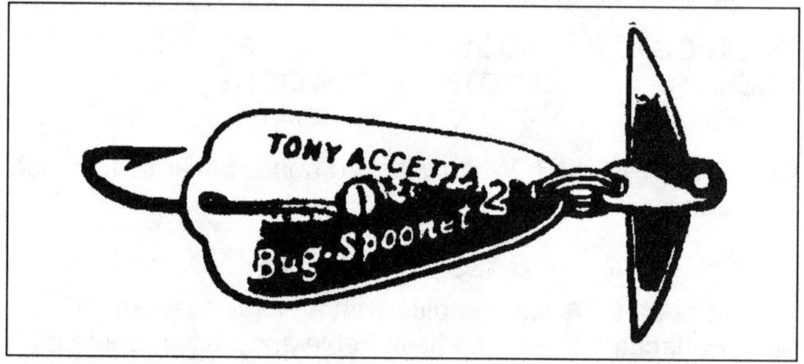

Both of these are thought to have been introduced around 1939. The Bug Spoonet in the accompanying illustration measures 2" from nose to the end of the single hook. Size of the Bug Spoon was not available. Collector value range: $8-$12.

HOLI-HEAD OR HOLLOW HEAD

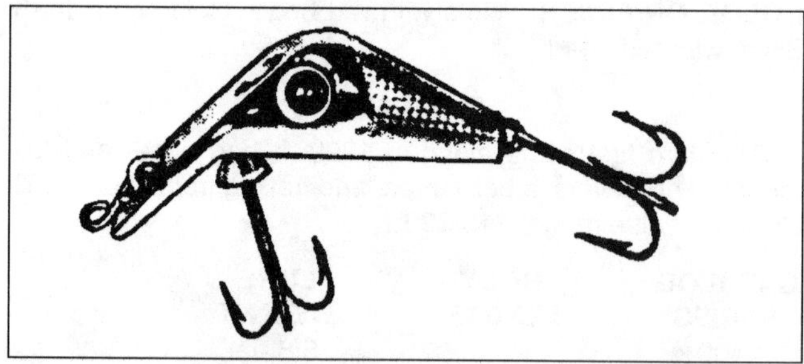

This plastic lure was advertised as "New" in a 1957 issue of *Outdoor Life*. There was a hole through the head. According to one advertisement this "Attracts fish by sound waves...". Weighing 1/2 ounce it was 2" long according to the ad. Colors available were red and white, gold, yellow, Perch finish, Silver Shiner and Green Shiner. Collector value range: $20-$25.

OTHER ACCETTA LURES

There are at least 18 other lures from the Accetta Company. Perhaps collectors can fill the gaps for the next edition. They are all listed below with the earliest date found advertised. In a few cases the vintage of the ad or catalog was obscure for one reason or another. In that case the year date is left blank.

LURE NAME	EARLIEST AD DATE FOUND	COLLECTOR VALUE RANGE
Bug Spoon	1939	$12-20

LURE NAME	EARLIEST AD DATE FOUND	COLLECTOR VALUE RANGE
Fly Rod Bug Spoonet	1939	$8-$15
Green Spoon		$4-$10
Jig-A-Roo	1956	$3-$8
Jigit Eel	1938	$3-$8
Jigit & Skirt	1951	$3-$8
Mr. Eel	1956	$3-$8
Pet Spoon	1946	$3-$8
Weedless Pet Spoon	1946	$4-$8
Fly Rod Pet Spoon	1947	$7-$14
Fly Rod Weedless Pet Spoon	1942	$6-$12
Sea King Trolling Spoon		$3-$8
Spin Dodger	1942	$7-$14
Weedless Spin Dodger	1942	$7-$14
Super-Mop Sea Worm		$5-$10
Tony	1949	$2-$6
Wacky	1946	$5-$12
Weed Dodger	1946	$5-$12

ACTION LURE

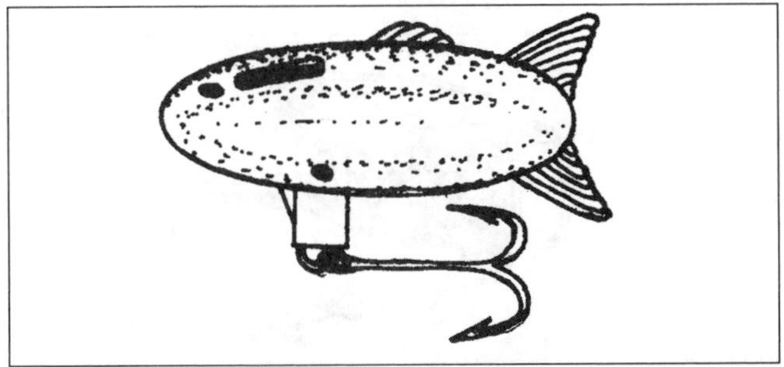

Action Lure — Hollywood, California

Billed as the "WORLD'S FIRST SELF-PROPELLED LURE!", this crazy contraption was chemically propelled by the combination of a "blue pellet" and a "white pellet" in the "fuel tank", and presumably water. The plug was supposed to emit a buzzing sound while swimming "..various depths to 15 feet for up to one hour or more..." One can only guess at its effectiveness. Collector value range: $5-$10

ACTUAL LURE

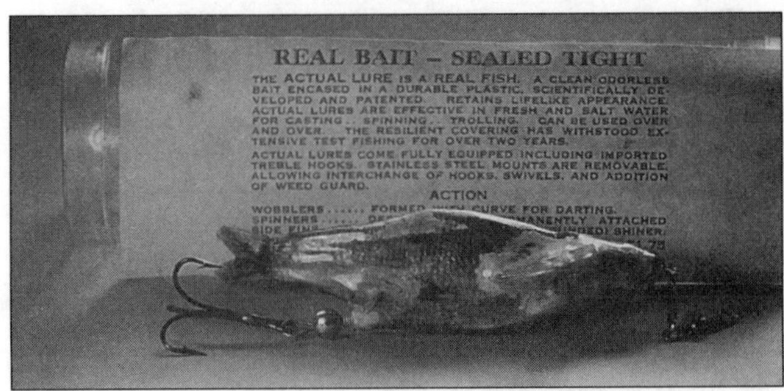

This photo of an ACTUAL LURE with its original plastic tube and papers. The lure is finely made with much detail given to the scales.

The Actual Lure, Inc — New York, New York

There were advertisements found in *Sports Afield* in the early 1950s and catalog entries at the same time. These lures are actual shiner minnows; "Clean, odorless bait encased in durable plastic." The ads went on to say they were scientifically developed and patented. There were three basic types of the ACTUAL LURES based on size. They were the TINY at 2-1/4", the SMALL at 3-1/2" and MEDIUM at 4-1/2". Then they developed the WOBBLER by forming the minnow in a curved configuration. The SKIP-DIP SPIN-STER and HI-LOW GLIDER were made by placing a plane on each side of the body. The only color ever referenced was the addition of red paint to simulate a wounded minnow. Although used with some of the others they had one other lure called the TINY TROUTER where the red paint was an option. It included a long leader and was billed as "PERFECT FOR FLYROD". Collector value range: $5-$10. Photo courtesy Ken Bernoteit.

ADJUSTABLE WING LURE

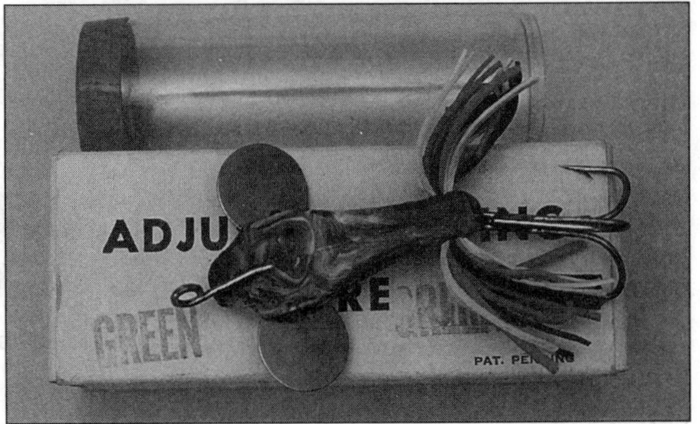

Challenge Tackle, Inc. — Meadville, Pennsylvania

Two advertisements for this lure were found in 1951 issues of sportsman's magazines. It is made of two fused halves of solid molded plastic. There are two round metal blades attached to each other by a spring inside the head. There are two slots on the sides where the fisherman could choose to make the plug a top-water, a diver or, by placing the blades one up and one down, it became a spinner. It measures 2-1/4". Colors are not known, but it is reported that it was made in pink and the others were all different color versions of the marbleized or swirled plastic as in the accompanying photo. They were packed in a plastic cylinder in a box as shown. Collector value range: $5-$10.

AEROPLANE BAIT

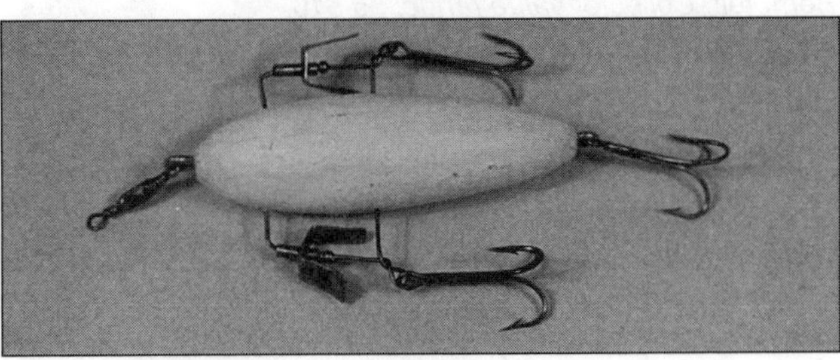

H. G. Parker and Son — Battle Creek, Michigan.

An advertisement from about 1910 reads "The newest and most attractive bait on the market. It floats for casting. It sinks for trolling." Apparently, it came only in white. The spinners are brass. I know of only two in private collections. Collector value range: $1,000-$1,500.

AIREX CORPORATION

A DIVISION OF THE LIONEL CORPORATION

Long Island City, New York — Hillsdale, New Jersey
New York, New York

Yes, that's the same famous company that made the model trains. They also owned the Airex Corporation. Airex made spinning lures and reels. In researching catalogs and magazines three different locations turned up for Lionel/Airex. It never was clear whether they were talking about the home office or about Airex itself. We have to assume the latter. The three locations, with the dates the ads appeared were: Long Island City, New York, 1949; Hillsdale, New Jersey, 1951 and New York, New York, 1954. A search of the available materials turned up advertising and catalog entries as early as 1949 and as late as 1958. It is likely that they were in the tackle business much longer, but those were the only years found.

The list of their reels and lures is extensive.

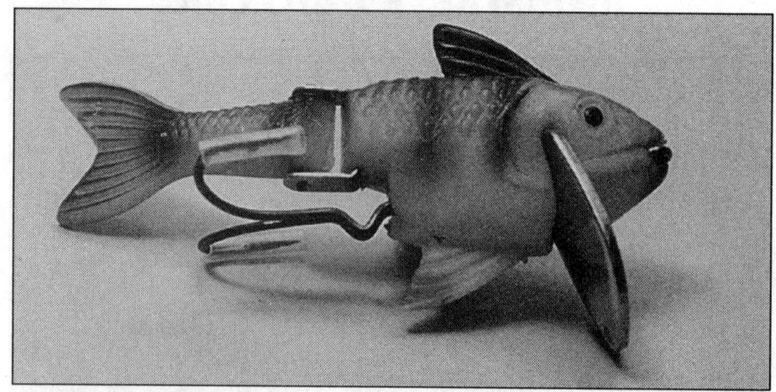

The Lionel/Airex PIXIE MINNOW LURE, 3". Collector value range: $5-$10.

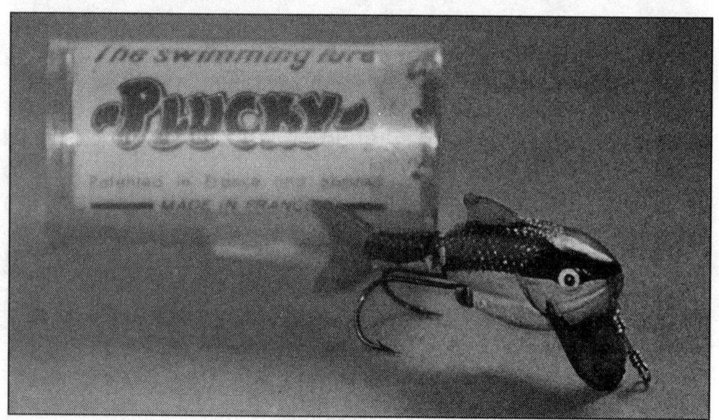

THE PLUCKY from Charles Garcia & Company, New York City. This particular lure measures 1-7/8". Photo courtesy Ken Bernoteit. Collector value range: $5-$10.

PIXIE MINNOW LURE

This is the only Airex lure that seems to interest some collectors presently. As you can see by the photos accompanying, there are two almost identical lures offered by different companies. They are both made of rubber and each one bears the phrase "Made in France" molded into the body. The same can be said for the Garcia version also. Airex did not seem to advertise theirs as much as Garcia. Both companies, however, ran their ads in the same period of time. They were found in magazines and catalogs in the early 1950s. Airex never detailed the finishes and sizes available. Garcia ads seemed also a little sketchy on details beyond offering three different weights. One entry did indicate that there were two color patterns available. A 1953 General Merchandise Company catalog, inexplicably calling it the "MITCHELL PLUCKY". The colors were described as follows: 1. Seaweed green back, silver belly and stripe, buff tail and fin; 2. Maroon back, gold stripe, pink belly and maroon fin and tail. The entry also stated the lure was 3-1/4" in length. The various lengths of these lures is difficult to sort out because of the dearth of detailed data available. Sizes that have been found run from the small 1-7/8" PLUCKY in the accompanying photo to 4-1/4" quoted as the largest PLUCKY size in Karl White's book *Fishing Tackle Antiques and Collectibles.* One 1955 catalog listed the following four weights: 1/9 oz., 1/6 oz., 1/3 oz. and 1/2 oz. No size data for the Airex PIXIE MINNOW LURE was found in any catalog or other publications. Collector value range for either: $5-$10.

AIREX POPIT RED WHITE LURE

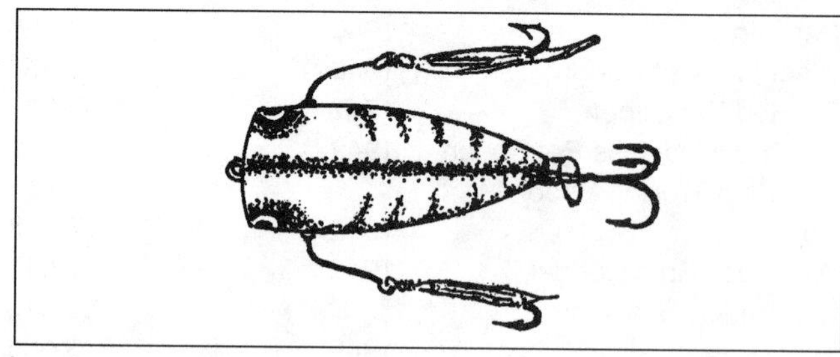

A plastic popper with deer hair outriggers making it appear as a fallen moth or June bug. Weight 1/3 ounce. Collector value range: $2-$5.

AIREX FROG POPIT

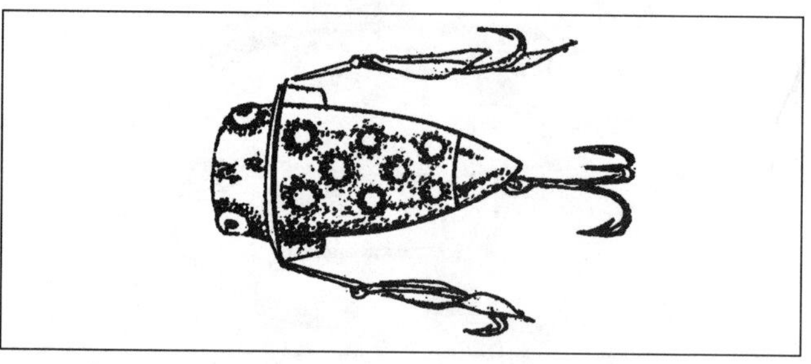

Plastic body lure with side-riding hooks camouflaged with palmer flies. It also sports a tail treble hook. Collector value range: $2-$5.

AIREX DEVIL DOG.

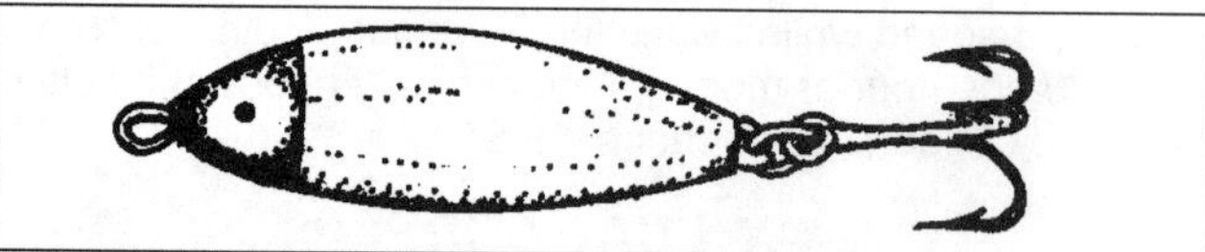

This is a curved plastic body lure with a red painted metal head. The body is silver on one side and gold on the other. Collector value range: $2-$5.

ALCOE MAGIC MINNOW No. 401

Alcoe Lure Company Fern Park, Florida

This lure is made of wood with flexible dorsal, ventral and tail fins. Found in its original box as in the photograph, nothing else is presently known about this lure. Collector value range: $20-$35.

FRANKLIN A. ALGER

(1862-1940) Grand Rapids, Michigan

Franklin A. Alger was a sportsman and an extraordinary craftsman/inventor. Besides making lures he also carved and painted bird decoys, made split bamboo rods and gun stocks. He fashioned his lure bodies on a lathe he made from a foot-operated treadle-type sewing machine. His metal spinners were stamped out on a small home-made hand-operated apparatus. He must have been an inveterate tinkerer for it is said that he designed and made over 50 styles of lures. I have seen photos of over 40 of these myself. Few of these, however, were ever patented and marketed in any quantity as far as is presently known.

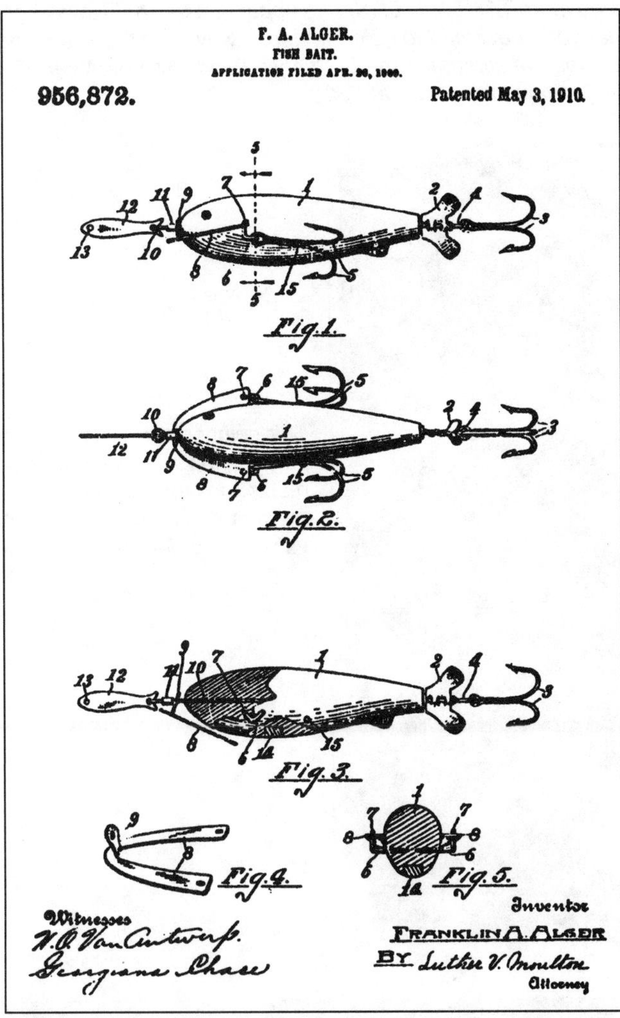

This is the lure that is in the patent illustration. The name is unknown. It has yellow glass eyes, measures 3-1/4" long and has a small metal ventral fin. The hardware is brass. At present this is the only known example. Collector value range: $150-$250.

I am truly indebted to Clarence Zahn of Ann Arbor, Michigan for providing the aforementioned photographs many of which will appear following. Space constraints did not permit me to use all of them, but what is here is representative. Mr. Zahn was fortunate enough to have acquired Alger's personal tackle box after his death. It is those lures that appear in these photographs. These lures serve well to illustrate Alger's tremendous versatility and in-

ventiveness in style and function. There really are no constants, no rules for identifying his products because of his versatility. There are a few things that appear from time to time, and I will point these out as we go along. Just don't take them for gospel. He was apparently forever modifying his lures and their hardware.

Although it is thought that he made most of his lures for his own and friends' use, he did have some commercial aspirations. He took the time and trouble to obtain patents on at least two of his lures. The only actual patent papers I was able to lay my hands on were filed in 1909 and the patent was granted to him on May 3, 1910. The other patent was for the GETSEM. He filed for it in 1914 and it was granted him May 9, 1916. You will also see, in the following photos, he had boxes made up for at least two of his lures. He was in commercial manufacture to some degree for an unknown period sometime around 1916-1918. These years are strictly speculation, but probable. Because of the boxes and printed card, we know that, however limited, he marketed at least the GETSEM, TANTALIZER and the MICHIGAN TROUT SPINNER.

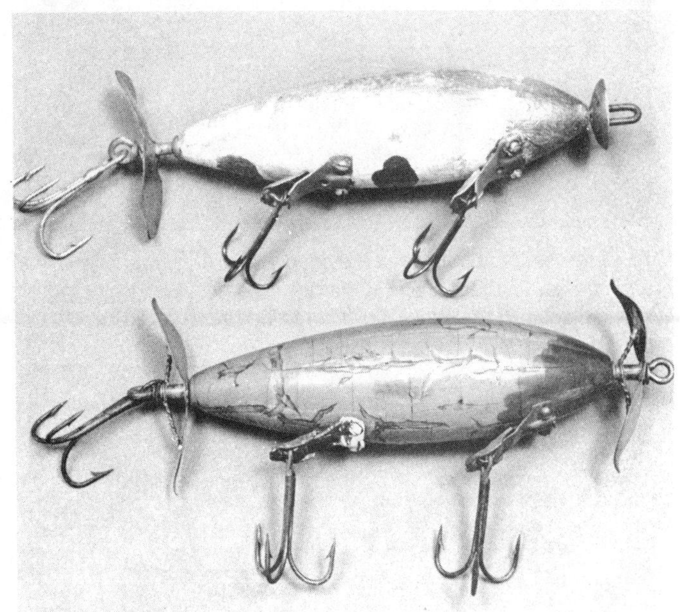

These two lures are from Alger's personal tackle box. Note the unique reinforced propeller spinners on the bottom plug and the hook hanger/guard hardware. It is obvious from the wear that Alger used these two quite a bit. The years have taken their toll on the paint jobs.

ALGER'S GETSEM

This particular lure apparently gained in popularity and success because shortly after Alger began selling it, he and Hastings Sporting Goods Works came to some agreement giving them the rights to the patent. An ad by Hastings, featuring the

GETSEM, appeared in the April, 1917 issue of *The Outer's Book* magazine. The Hastings company modified the lure by placing a metal protective plate on the belly.

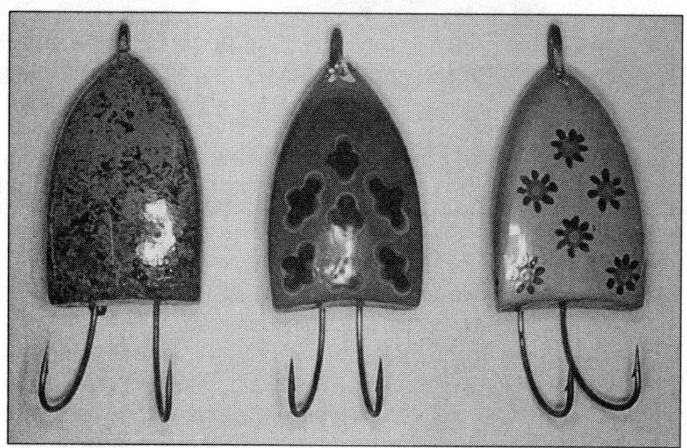

Three GETSEMS from Alger's personal tackle box. Left to right. Spatter finish, frog finish and then flowers. We can only speculate on the reason for the flowers. Perhaps it was to please a visitor to his workshop. Collector value range: $100-$300.

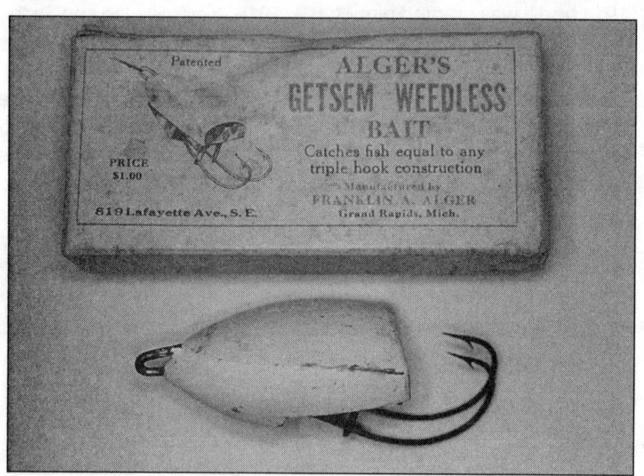

This lure with the printed box is evidence that Alger manufactured and marketed the GETSEM before Hastings Sporting Goods Works acquired the rights. Collector value range: $150-$250.

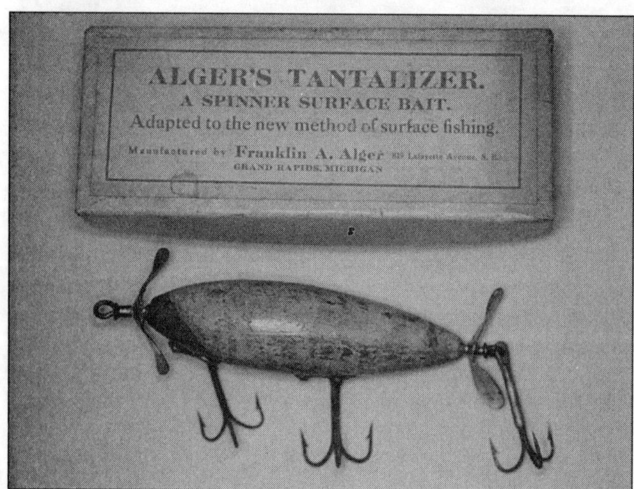

Another lure that was obviously manufactured and marketed by Alger as evidenced by the printed lure box. This 3-1/2"plug has crude L-rig style hangers and no eyes. The L-rig is, perhaps, the forerunner to the Heddon version. Collector value range: $100-$300.

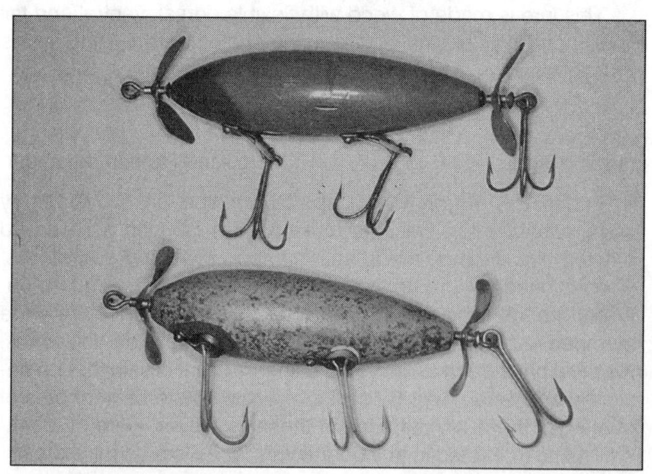

Two more TANTALIZERS. The upper lure has hold away hook hangers (designed to hold the hook away from the lure body). Lower lure illustrates the L-rig style used often by Alger. Collector value range: $100-$300.

This spinner bait made by Alger plainly shows the spinner blade made and used by Alger on numerous of his lures. Collector value range: $40-80

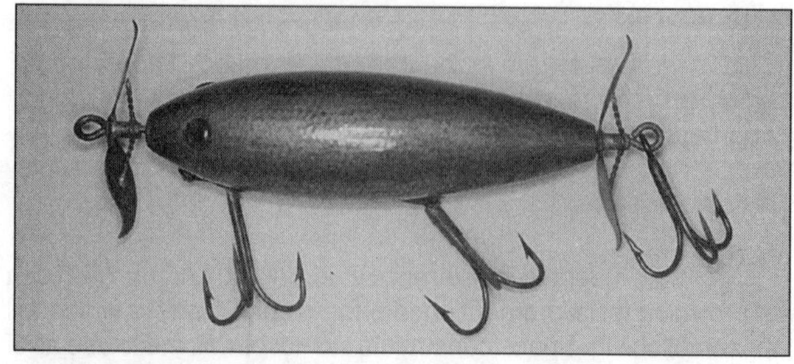

Another TANTALIZER, but this one is unusual with recessed, flattened glass eyes and propeller spinners reinforced with soldered twisted wire blade braces. Collector value range: $100-300.

An Alger bug-type lure measuring 2-3/4". The logs are made of metal and there are two line ties. Collector value range: $100-$300.

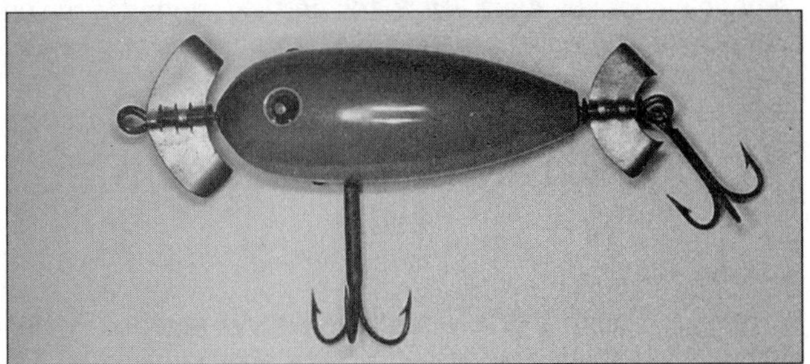

This is a small, 2-5/8", floating lure with recessed glass eyes. It clearly shows the often used Alger spinner. Collector value range: $100-$300.

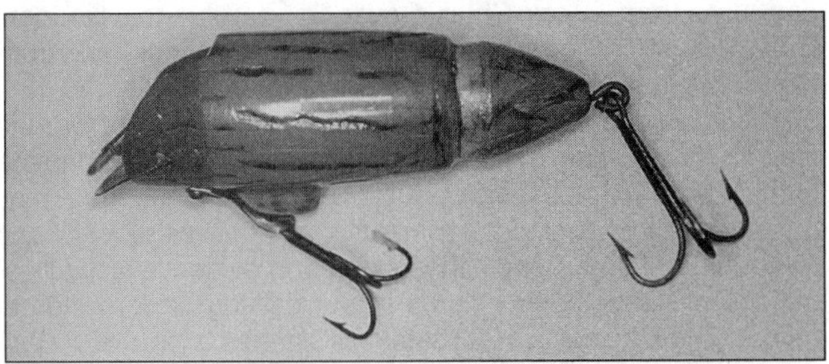

It is strongly suspected that this is a one-of-a-kind or prototype lure. It just doesn't have the polish of a production lure. It measures 3-1/4", has a metal lip and a grooved head to make it dive upon retrieve. It also has the GETSEM external belly weight and stand away hook hangers. Collector value range: $100-$300.

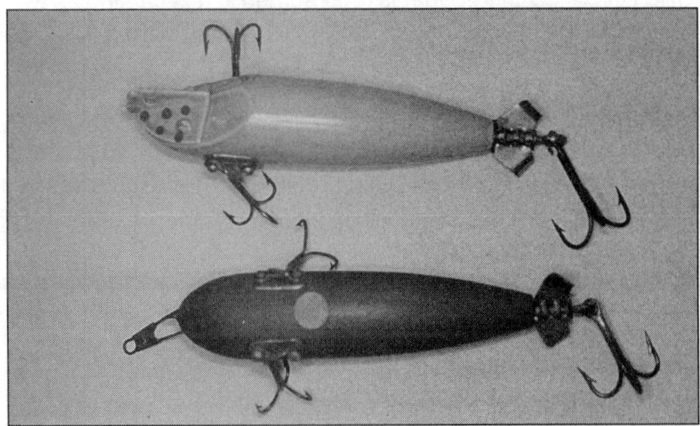

These 3-1/2" no eyed lures (top and bottom view) have the Alger spinners at the tail and an unusual head plate incorporated the line tie. They have internal belly weights (unpainted lure at bottom of above photo) and side hook hangers made by twisting wire and screwing it to the body with two screws through a metal backing plate. This is frequently found on Alger lures. Collector value range: $100-$300.

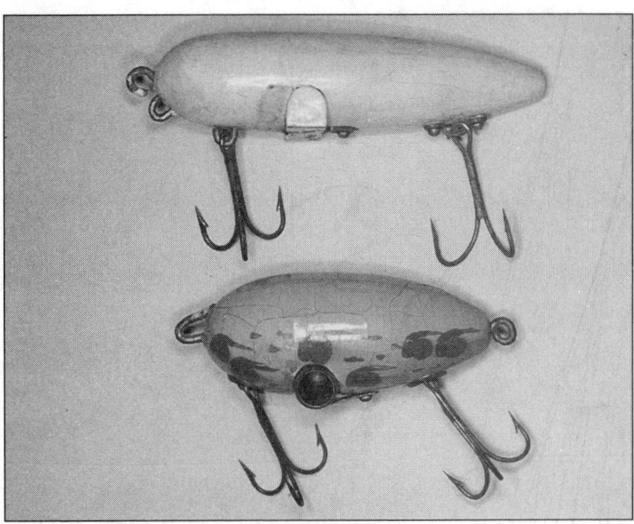

These two lures have chambers containing metal balls or shot attached to the belly. They could be the fist of the rattle baits. They measure 3-5/8" and 2-5/8" respectively. Collector value ranges: $100-300.

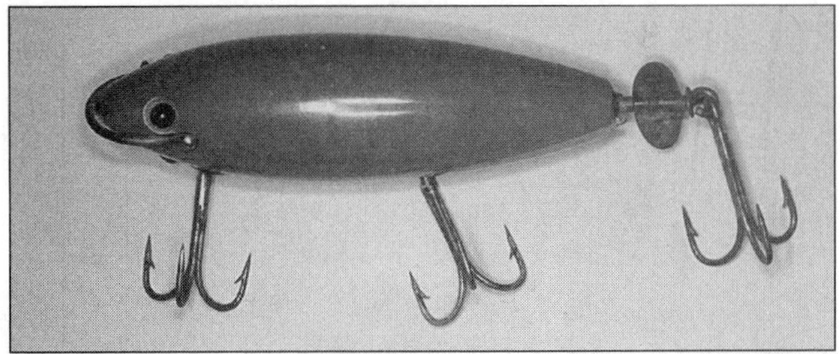

This lure has an unusual U-shaped heavy metal wire around its nose on which a line tie slides. Note the odd single round blade spinner at the tail. Collector value range: $100-$300.

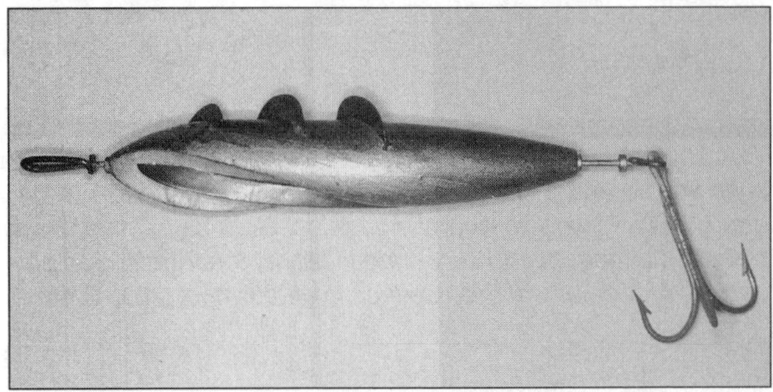

A 4" lure with fins set into the body so as to make it spiral or revolve around the through-body wire armature on retrieve. Green, white and red in colors. collector value range: $100-$300.

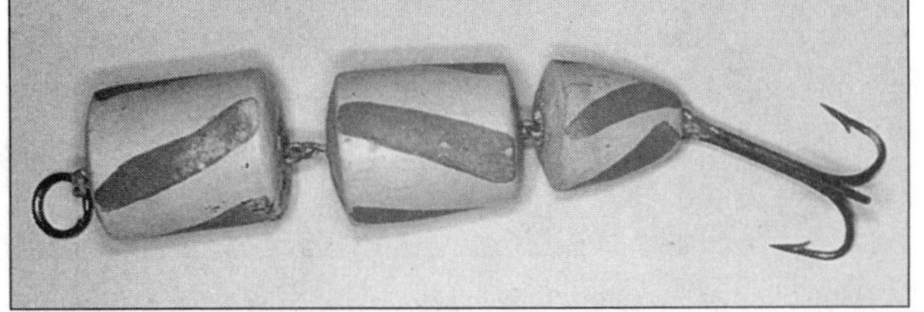

This double jointed Alger lure is painted in a red and white candy cane style. It measures 3-1/8" long. Collector value range: $100-$300.

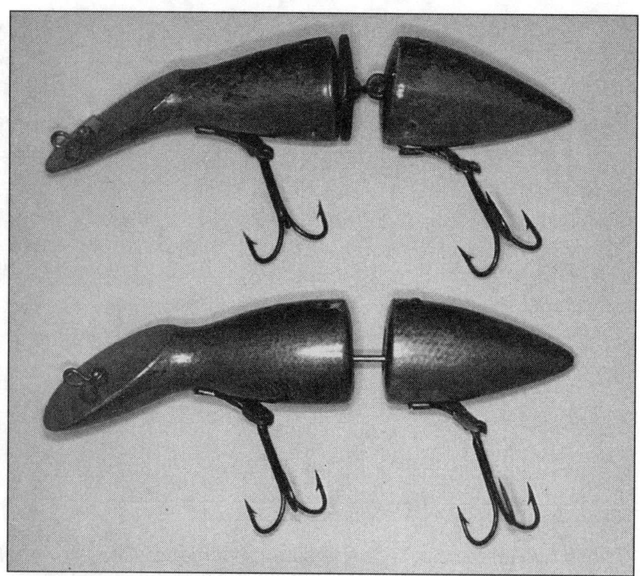

Two jointed TANGO type lures with the stand-away hook hanger. They each measure 5-1/4" in length. Collector value range: $100-$300.

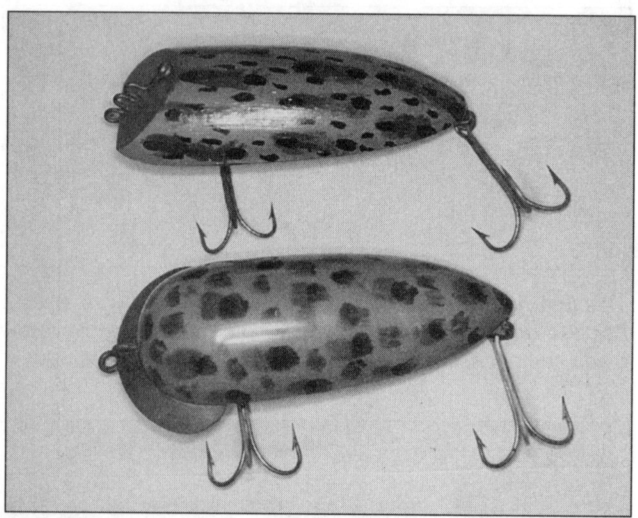

Two flat belly Alger lures. The upper is 3-1/2". has an Inch Worm style line tie and a slant head. The lower lure measures 3-3/4", has a metal diving lip and two line ties. Both have stand away belly hook hangers and very curious tail hook hangers. See photo below for details of this. Collector value range: $100-$300.

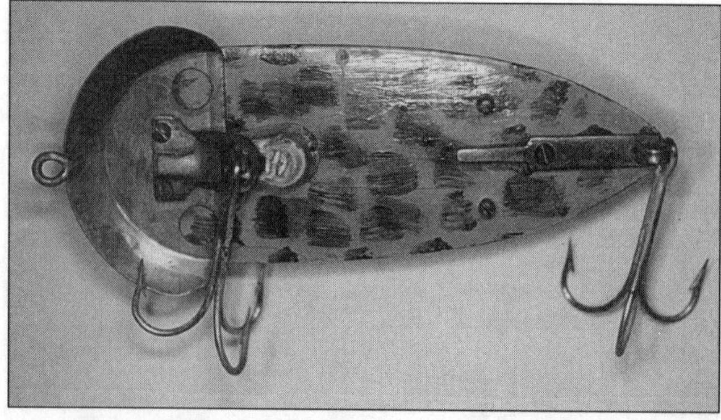

A belly view of the lower lure in above photo. It shows the stand away belly hook hardware and the tail hook hanger. The metal strip is installed with the screw so that the whole strip can swing from side to side.

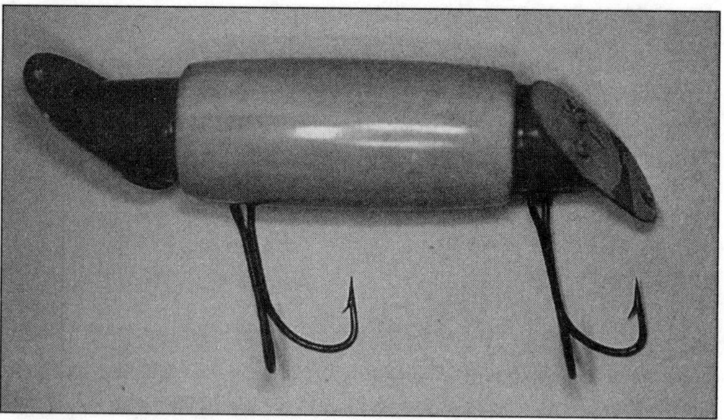

A double ender by Alger. It is 3-1/2" and is designed to run underwater or top water depending upon which end you tie your line to. Collector value range: $100-$300.

ALLCOCK, LAIGHT & WESTWOOD CO., LTD.

Toronto, Canada

Allcock, Laight & Westwood (AL&W) was founded in 1854 primarily to provide sporting equipment and clothing and also serious supplies for hunters and trappers of the day. In the early 1900's, coincidental with the development of the casting lure in the United States, they began carrying U.S. made tackle. By 1928 their catalogs were rife with U.S. fishing tackle. They carried lures from Creek Chub, South Bend, Pflueger, Heddon, Outing, Rush Tango and Rhodes. Later they would ad Arbogast, Weller, Helin and True Temper among others.

We know that AL&W and the Creek Chub Bait Co. of Garrett, Indiana made a formal agreement in 1928 for the company to manufacture some of Creek Chub's lures in Canada. There may have been other similar agreements made between AL&W and Heddon and South Bend although the only evidence is the illustrations of some of their lures in the catalog under different names. For instance a 1932 catalog illustrates a No. 7500 Heddon VAMP or VAMPIRE and calls it their VENUS MINNOW. Curiously, a few pages later in the same catalog, the Heddon VAMPIRE is also illustrated and it notes that it is indeed a Heddon lure. The only difference is the VENUS MINNOW is offered in color finishes not offered on the Heddon lure. Another Heddon lure, the No. 175 MINNOW is offered as the AL&W PERFECT CASTING PLUG. Pflueger is represented in this catalog as well. Their less expensive line of PELICAN PEERLESS WOODEN MINNOWS is offered on a different Point-of-Purchase display card. Here is a comparison of the two display cards.

Page 17 of that 1932 catalog is headed "CREEK CHUB BAITS MANUFACTURED IN CANADA BY THE ALLCOCK, LAIGHT & WESTWOOD CO., Limited". They illustrated ten lures as follows:

The Famous Pikie Minnow
The Jointed Pikie Minnow
The Baby Pikie Minnow
The Baby Jointed Pikie
The Marvel of 1932 (The Sucker Minnow)
The New Wiggle Fish
The Crawdad
The Husky Musky
The Husky Pike Minnow
Fly Rod Flexible Floating Feather Minnow

Confusing is the fact that on the previous page they are offered as regular Creek Chub lures with the exception of the

Left: The AL&W "Beaver Brand" PILOT MINNOWS display card. Right: The South Bend Bait Co. PEERLESS WOODEN MINNOW display card.

The AL&W catalog illustration for the BASS-OH.

SUCKER MINNOW and the fly rod lure. The SUCKER MINNOW is the only one that states "Manufactured in Canada" beneath the name on that page and the fly rod lure doesn't appear there at all.

Here is another example of how confusing their catalogs can be. The AL&W BASS-OH lure is the same as the Creek Chub/Shur-Strike Company BO Series. This is another case where they seem to be contradicting themselves. The BASS-OH was offered at 75 cents on one page and the almost identical South Bend BASS-ORENO on the very next page at $1.20. The copy describing the lures was identical, word-for-word. The only difference was that the color patterns offered were not the same. Shur-Strike was a Creek Chub program to sell mail order to other companies in quantities so that a less expensive, quality lure could be made available to the public through them. Western Auto and Sear and Roebuck sold Shur-Strike lures under the brands "Western" and "Meadow Brook" respectively. Please turn to Creek Chub/Shur-Strike for an more in-depth discussion. The Shur-Strike BO Series lure was an unabashed copy of the South Bend Bass-Oreno. The lure name had changed to the TEDDY WIGGLER in the 1941 AL&W catalog and BASSKILL by 1955.

According to Harold E, Smith, M.D., in his very fine book *Creek Chub Lures and Collectibles*, AL&W only manufactured the various PIKIE MINNOWS. He says one good way to tell the difference between them and the Creek Chub PIKIES, if the diving lips are not marked, is to look at the hooks. AL&W used quality English hooks that were made of a smaller gauge wire and the shanks were longer and a bit thinner than the hooks used by Creek Chub.

The next lure is shrouded in mystery. The lure was boxed in AL&W packaging. The patent date is August 6, 1929 and was granted to F.M. McLaughlin, a Canadian. Recently I have found patents ranging from 1929 to 1932 for six additional variations of body and spring-loaded weedless hook methods. The one in the photo is probably the only one to be placed in production but be alert to these variations. They might turn up.

The problem is that the lure never appeared in any AL&W catalog and the paint pattern is unlike typical AL&W patterns.

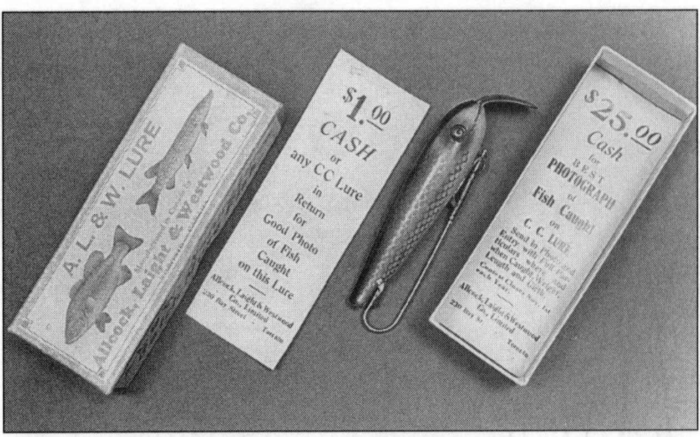

AL&W lure with original box. Each and of the box with the lure number and one side states: "A.L. & W. Nature Lures catch more fish". Collector value range $150-$200.

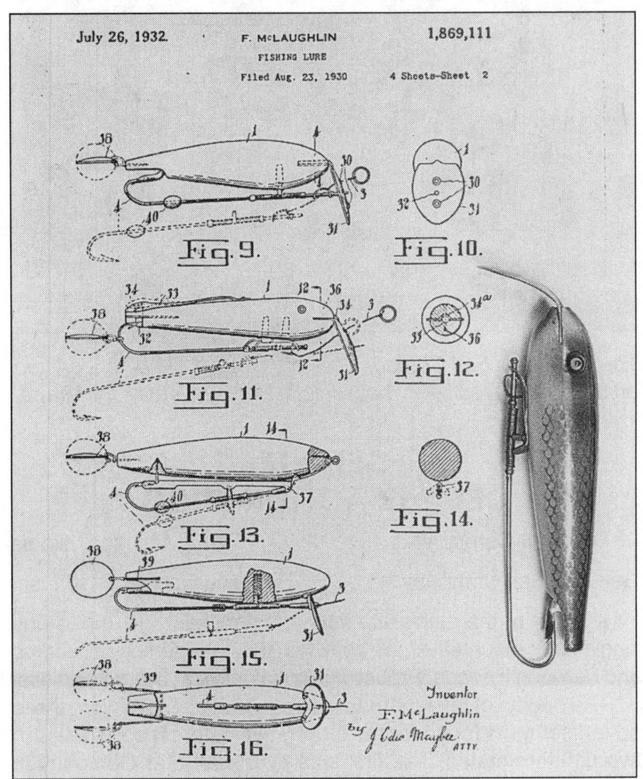

The same lure is pictured on a copy of the patent drawing for the lure. The patent was granted to F. McLaughlin. Who was McLaughlin?

It is speculated that the lure may have been made for them by another company, but never went into mass production. Perhaps time will tell.

Allcock, Laight & Westwood lures are a challenge and may interest collectors looking for new areas to pursue. Anyone interested should pick up a copy of the aforementioned *Collector's Guide to Creek Chub Lures & Collectibles*. It contains the most complete coverage, with full color photos, of the company and its history that you can find anywhere. The address is found in the Recommended References section back towards to front of this book.

UBANGI c.1955

Forrest Allen — Stamford, Connecticut

A small stubby plastic plug with a belly treble hook and a long deep diving lip blade. Collector value range: $6-$9.

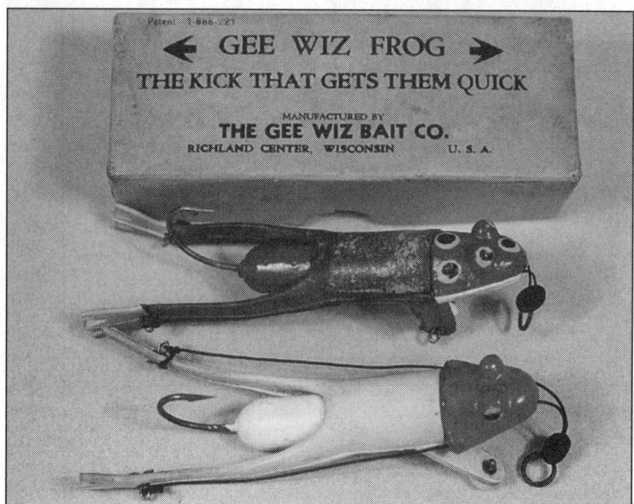

The Gee Whiz Bait Company box top has a 1932 patent printed on it. The lures represent both colors. Photo courtesy Jim Muma.

GEE WIZ
GEE WIZ ACTION FROG

All Star Bait Company — Chicago, Illinois

Gee Wiz Bait Company — Richland Center, Wisconsin

Another of the many attempts at animated frogs. It had one single hook mounted on the belly with the barb portion pointed up and between the legs. Probably fairly effective at being weedless.

The origins of the lure may a bit confusing. There were three advertisements found for the lure by two different companies in two different states. The first was by the All Star Company in 1931 and the other was by the Gee Wiz Company in 1949 and 1950. There is a patent number on the box that was granted in 1932. Perhaps All Star sold to Gee Wiz. Anybody's guess is good until we get more concrete data. The lures appear to be identical. The 1931 ad said it was available in two sizes, but did not specify. It also said it was available in three patterns:

Red and White; Musky size, Natural Green; Natural Green. They did not describe or illustrate these. Collector Bob Guist wrote of his collection of these lures in the December, 1992 issue of the *NFLCC Gazette*. He described some of the colors in it :"I know most came in frog color with others having white bodies and red heads. I know others were made with frog colored bodies with red heads; and some frog bodies with red/white heads. Some had white feet, others did not."

The 1949 and 1950 Gee Wiz ads listed no colors and stated the lure was available in only one size, 4-1/2". Collector value range: $50-75 in green, in white with red head: $150-$250.

WEEDLESS WONDER

Anderson & Son, Inc. — Hope Valley, Rhode Island

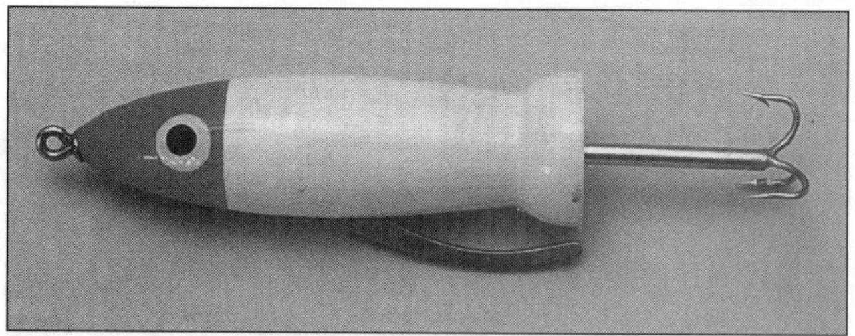

Everybody makes the same claim about their weedless baits: "The Only 100% Weedless Fishing Plug in the World!". This claim was in a 1969 advertisement. It has a balsa wood body and all metal parts are stainless steel or nickel plated. It is a spring loaded lure that you cock by pushing the hook and tube shaft into the body. This conceals the barbs rendering it weedless. It was supplied in three finises according to the ad: "Red & White, Green back & Black back." Collector value range: $20-$40.

ANDERSON MINNOW

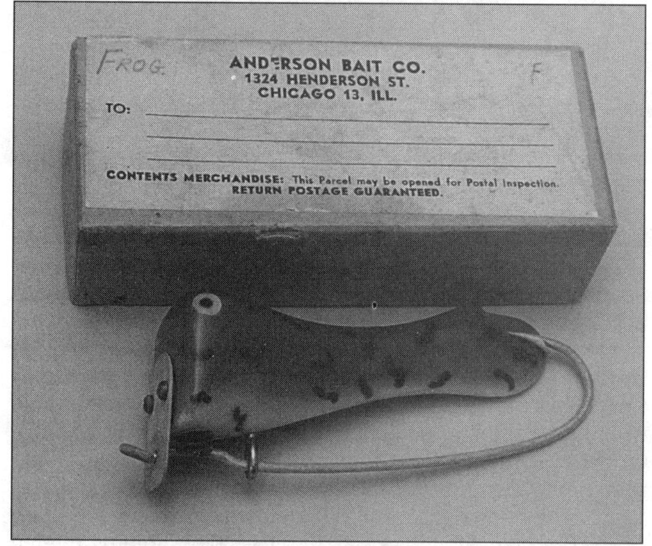

Anderson Bait Company — Chicago, Illinois

Measuring 3-3/4", this lure is weedless. An advertisement in a 1949 issue of *Field & Stream* magazine says the lure is "So Tricky-Games Laws Prohibit Use in Minnesota, Missouri, and Pennsylvania". That seems a tall claim, but maybe it was so because they also printed it on the descriptive literature that came with the lure. The New Jersey three point hook law was a peculiar one also so maybe they did that sort of thing back then. The also listed three finishes that were available. These were Frog (in photograph), Perch and Red head. Presumably the latter meant White body with Red head. Collector value range: $20-$30.

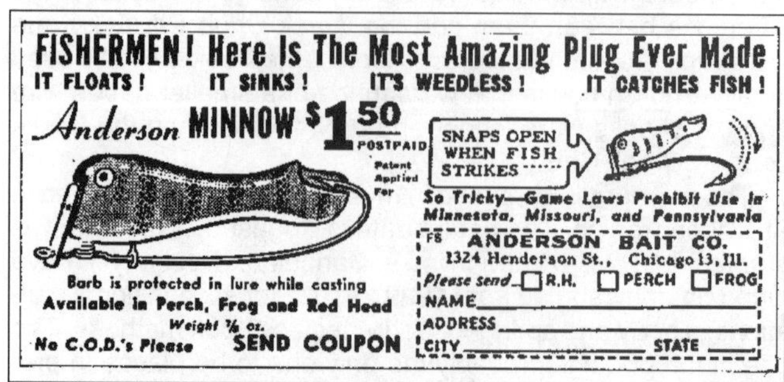

Advertisement for the ANDERSON MINNOW from the June, 1949 issue of Field & Stream.

APEX BULL NOSE AND APEX BULL NOSE, JR.

The Apex Bait Company — Chicago, Illinois

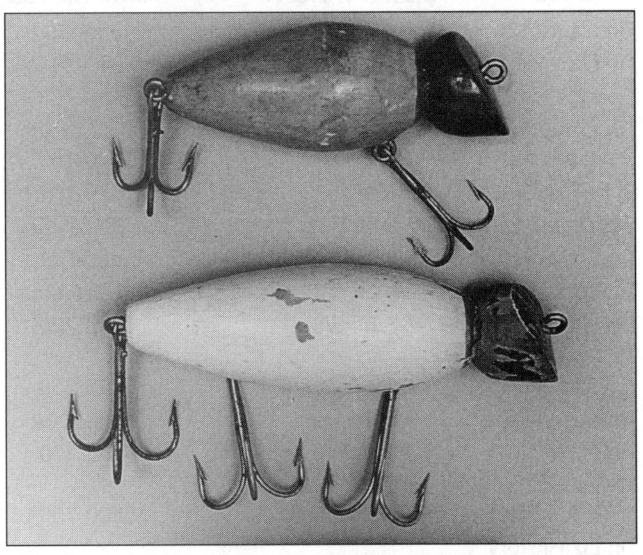

These Apex BULL NOSE lures measures 3", 4" and 3-7/8" from top to bottom. The upper two have washer and screw eye type hook hangers and the lower has the cup and screw eye hardware.

The earliest advertisement found for the BULL NOSE was in a March 1916 issue of *The Outers Book* magazine, but it is reported to have been seen advertised as early as 1913. The 1916 ad pictured the large lure in the accompanying photo and noted the availability of a smaller one (APEX JR.). Both have screw eye and washer type hook hangers. The three available colors in that ad were White with Red Head, Yellow with Red Head and Red white Yellow Head. The ad also mentioned an APEX UNDERWATER available in white or yellow with red head or green back version with green or yellow spots. It is not clear, but the ad seems to infer that this is an underwater version of the BULL NOSE that has those color patterns only. Time will tell.

There is another lure extremely similar to the BULL NOSE called the ALGONAC SNEAK BAC. It was illustrated in an ad placed in 1921 by the Eckfield Boat Company of Algonac, Michigan. The one in the ad seems to have a more narrow neck and slightly smaller head. I have never actually seen one so it may be easily distinguishable from the BULL NOSE. In any case be on the look out. Collector value range: $85-130.

AQUA SPORT, INC.

Noble, Oklahoma — DIVING DOODLE BUG cl960

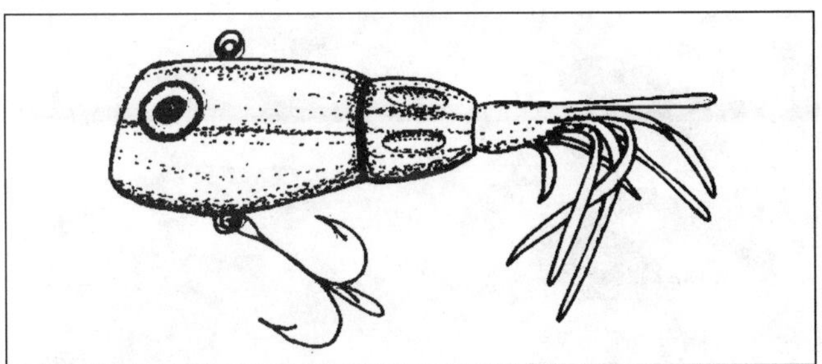

This crazy plug had provision for inserting a "Power Tab" to make it move erratically. Apparently it was caused by a chemical reaction between the tablet and water. It had one belly treble and a trailing rubber wiggler skirt, 2-1/2" long. Collector value range: $8-$16.

FRED ARBOGAST BAITS

Akron, Ohio

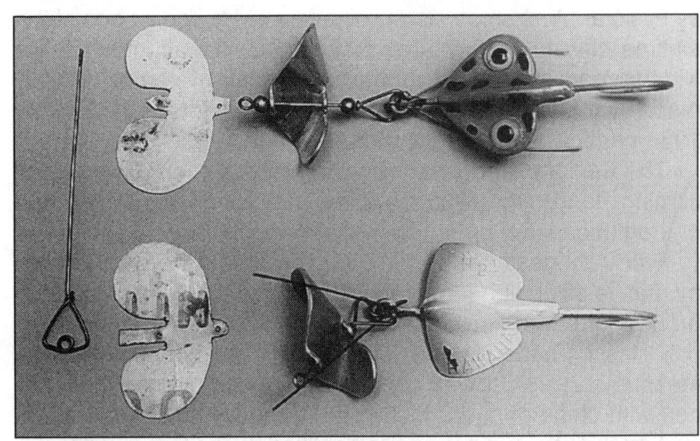

Earliest SPUTTER FUSSES had handmade spinner blades and a three-corner wire armature as shown here. Bottom is earliest manufactured.

Until recently most collectors have thought that the Arbogast Company was founded in 1928. It is now known he was in business as early as 1926. There is an advertisement for "FRED ARBOGAST'S Spin-tail Kicker" in the June, 1926 issue of Hunting & Fishing magazine. This was the first lure he offered commercially. One can deduce from this that he might have been active in business some time before that. Some place the date around 1924, but it is known that he did not leave his job at the Goodyear Rubber Company until 1926. He was a bait casting champion winning competitions in 1922, 1923 and 1924.

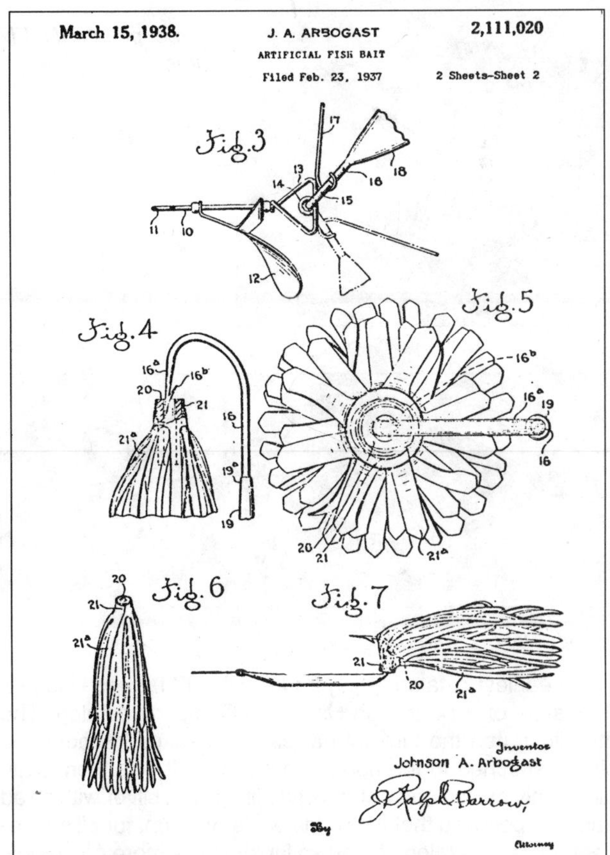

The original patent illustration for Arbogast's invention of the rubber 'Hula Skirt' for lures. It was filed in 1937 and granted in 1938.

His most important contributions to the development of the artificial lure are the invention of the rubber "Hula Skirt" and the famous "JITTERBUG". In fact the "JITTERBUG" was selected by Popular Mechanics magazine a few years ago as one of the all-time classic fishing lures in America. We all know of the wide-spread use of the rubber skirt today of course, mostly made synthetic materials. He filed his patent for the skirt in mid 1938 and it was granted to him August 8, 1939.

The earliest Arbogast lures were mostly metal, with wood coming along in the 1930's. The original wood lures were made of aromatic cedar.

Fred Arbogast died in 1947, but the Fred Arbogast Company, Inc. is still going strong in Akron, Ohio today. In 1980 they brought out "... a limited edition collector's replica of the original, classic, cedar Musky Jitterbug."* The body of the lure measures 2-5/8". It was packed in a "wood grain" cardboard box with chips of cedar included. There are no special markings on the lure, but it is easily identified by the fact that it is unfinished cedar; no paint or decoration at all.

The Arbogast company is still going strong today, almost seventy years of continuous operation.

**From an Arbogast ad in the Sept/Oct. 1980 issue of Rod and Reel magazine.*

TIN LIZ

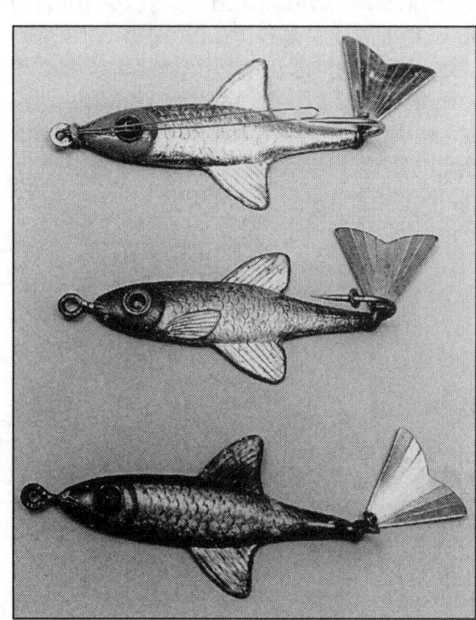

Three plain TIN LIZ lures

Sunfish TIN LIZ with glass eyes.

The earliest catalog listing for the TIN LIZ I found was in a 1928 issue of a Shapliegh Hardware Company catalog. The entry illustrated the lure with a tear drop shaped spoon-type spinner attached to the hook with a swivel. It was then available in only two colors: natural chub finish and silver with a red head. It is believed that this is the earlier version, for all subsequent ads and catalogs found so far show the more commonly found life-like fluted tail fins attached to the lure's hook.In the first years of production the lure sported glass eyes with the subsequent ones having painted eyes. All were made of metal and had a single hook with the trailing fin tail attached. There were several versions made available after the initial plain Tin Liz. They are all listed following, with photo when available.

NAME	LURE SIZE & WEIGHT	COLLECTOR VALUE RANGE
Tin Liz, c1924	2-1/4", 5/8 oz.	$30-40
Tin Liz, glass eyes	2-1/4", 5/8 oz	$40-70
Tin Liz (3 fins)	2-1/4"	$50-75
Tin Liz (3 fins) weedless	2-1/4"	$100-150
Spin Tail Tin Liz	2-1/4"	$60-70
Big Tin Liz	2-3/4",1 oz.	$200-400
Tin Liz, Weedless	5/8 oz.	no trade data
Tin Liz Perch	5/8 oz.	no trade data
Tin Liz Sunfish	1-5/8", 5/8 oz.	$175-225
Tin Liz Sunfish (3 fins)	1-3/4"	$225-250
Tin Liz Walleye	2-3/8"	$800-1000
Tin Liz Muskie	2-1/2"	$200-300
Tin Liz Snake (Baby Pike)	2-5/8", 5/8 oz.	$500-750
Tin Liz Hickory Shad	2-1/4", 5/8 oz.	$20-30
Fly rod Tin Liz	1-1/8",1/64 oz.; 1-5/8", 1/32 oz.; 2", 1/16 oz.	no trade data
Tin Liz Twins	5/8 oz.	no trade data
Tin Liz Minnow	5/8 oz.	no trade data
Spin Tin Liz	1", 1-1/2", 1-3/4", 2-1/4"	no trade data

BIG TIN LIZ (musky size, 2-1/2"). This rare Arbogast lure is valued at $200-300; with the box can double that. Photo courtesy Jim Muma.

Top left is TIN LIZ SUNFISH. Bottom left: Three fin SUNFISH. Top to bottom at right: TIN LIZ WALLEYE, TIN LIZ SNAKE, Three fin TIN LIZ WEEDLESS. Photo courtesy Jim Muma.

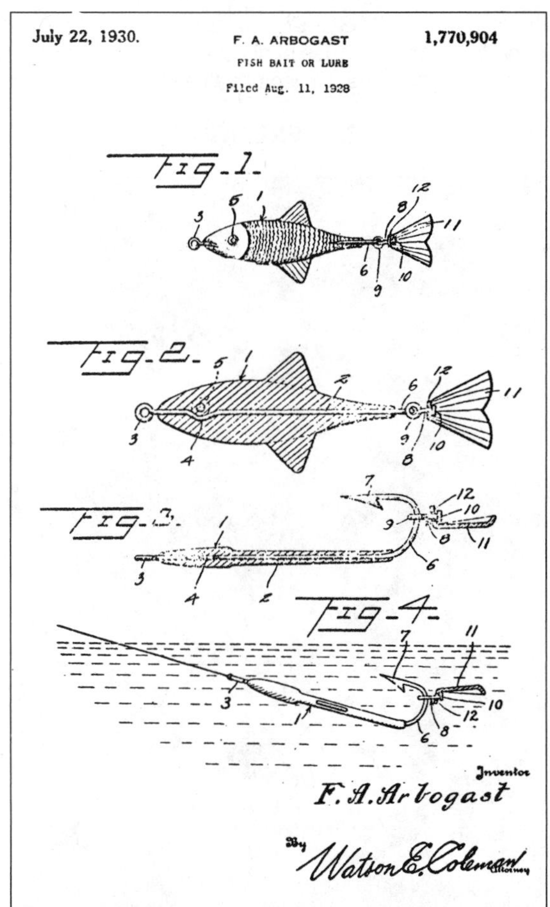

The original patent illustration for the TIN LIZ filed in 1928 and granted to Arbogast in 1930.

Top to bottom: Old style TIN LIZ with stamped eyes; later version with glass eyes. SPIN TAIL TIN LIZ, TIN LIZ HICKORY SHAD. Photo courtesy Jim Muma.

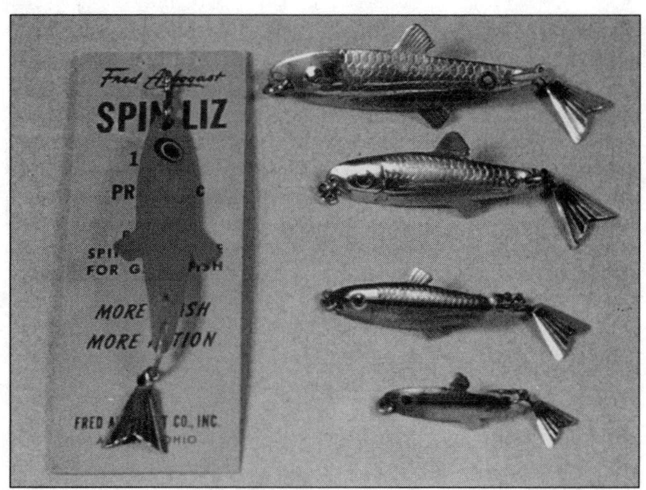

The four sizes of the SPIN LIZ.

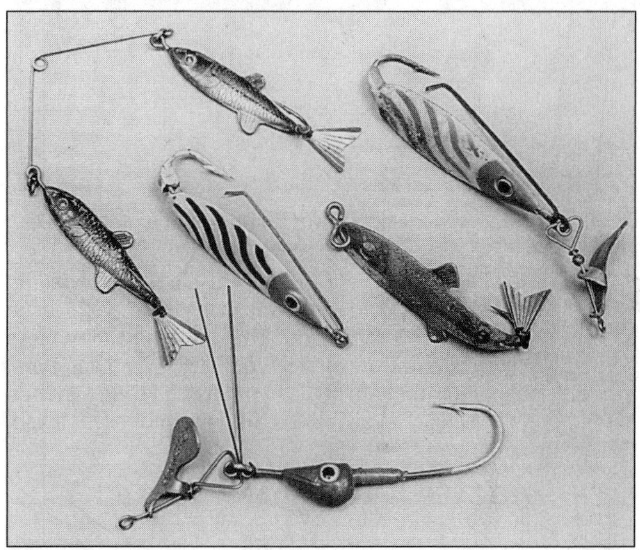

Top left: TIN LIZ TWIN; Top right. #3 HAWAIIAN WEEDLESS WIGGLER with spinner, Middle/left: #3 HAWAIIAN WEEDLESS WIGGLER, Middle right: plain TIN LIZ; Bottom: #1 HAWAIIAN WEEDLESS SINGLE SPINNER.

IMPORTANT NOTICE

The value ranges listed in this book are for lures in Very Good to Excellent condition. The values of those lures not in Very Good to Excellent condition can and probably will be worth considerably less. The values are meant to be a guide only.

WEEDLESS KICKER

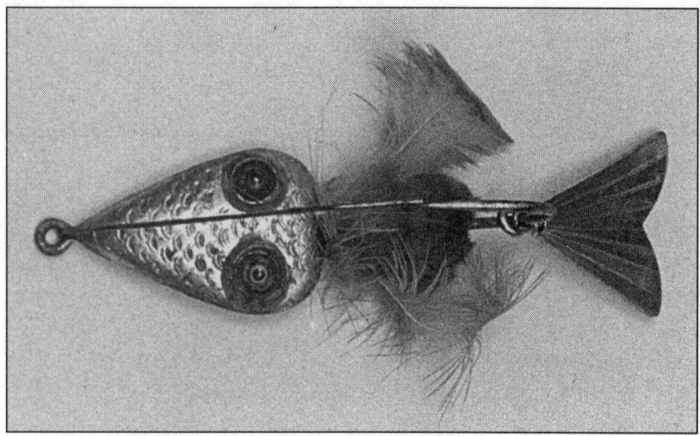

This is an early WEEDLESS KICKER dating from around l926.

First called the WEEDLESS SPIN-TAIL KICKER in ads, the earliest advertisement found so far was in the June, 1926 issue of *Hunting and Fishing* magazine. The ad stated they were available in two sizes, 1/2-oz. and 5/8-oz. They had glass eyes, a single hook, fancy feathers and a free-flipping tail fin attached to the hook. They were available in a frog finish or silver finish. Collector value range: $40-$60.

WIGGLER OR HAWAIIAN WIGGLER

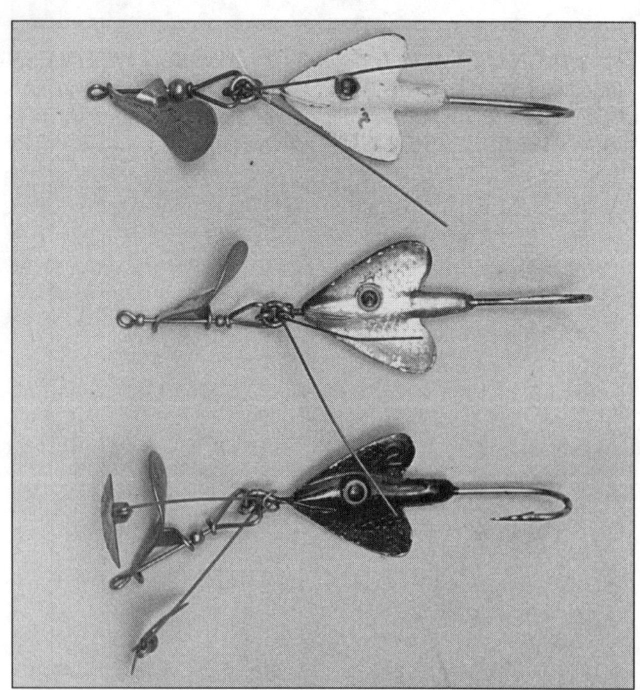

New in about 1930, this famous lure was preceded by the Al Foss Shimmy Wiggler (c. 1918) which had a bucktail attached to the hook. Then came Arbogast's WIGGLER, quite similar. He then patented the rubber skirt, hung it on the hook and thus was born the HAWAIIAN WIGGLER. He used this skirt on various other of his lures and because of his patent, he had an exclusive on its use for many years. Collector value range: $5-15.

JITTERBUG

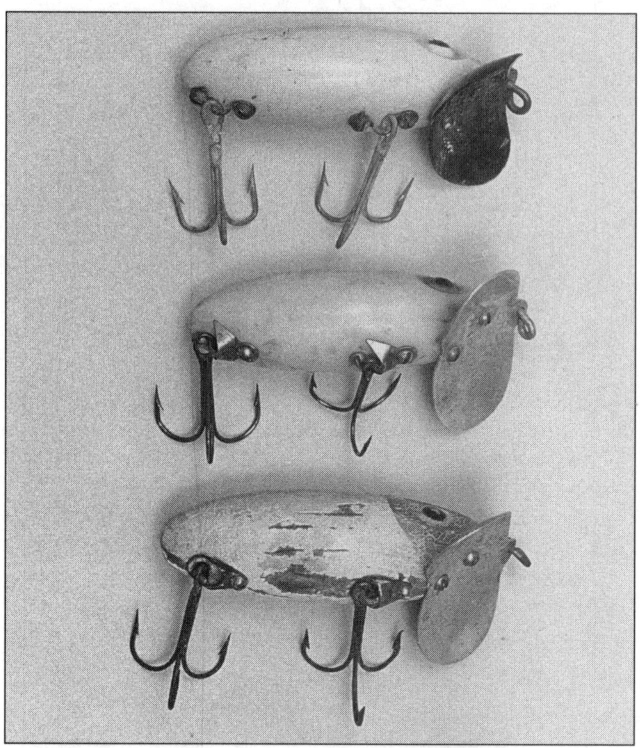

This is perhaps, one of the most famous of the Arbogast lures. It was first introduced to the fisherman about 1937. It was first patented on July 9, 1940. The first JITTERBUGS were made of cedar and initially had glass eyes. None in the photo here have glass eyes. The bottom lure in the photo with three is made of wood. The name was derived from the dance craze of the time. The upper lure has a plastic nose blade. This was done because of the metal shortage during World War II. The plastic blades lacked the weight of the metal ones and the resulting plug did not perform as well as the other.

The story of the origin of the Jitterbug is interesting. It seems that Arbogast whittled a plug out of a piece of broomstick in the early 1920s, attached a spoon to the nose crosswise in attempt to make a deep diving lure. It was a miserable failure gyrating wildly out of control on retrieve. As the story goes he tossed it in a drawer at home only to have it found during the visit of an old friend in 1934. Asked what it was, Arbogast said it was an underwater plug that didn't work. The two of them fooled around with it eventually coming up with the Jitterbug.

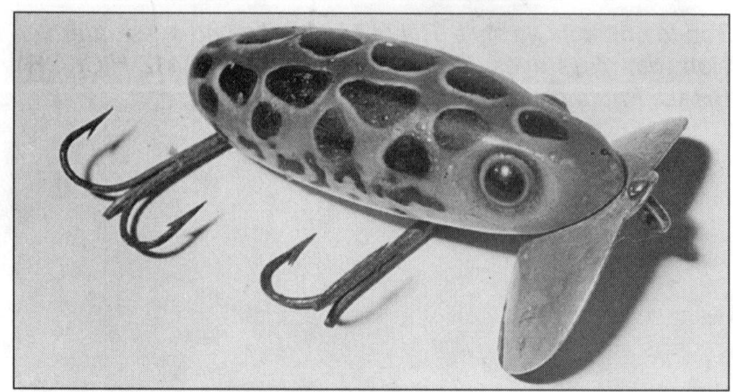

A Frog finish JITTERBUG.

Today there are nine different models and sizes available including a jointed version. There were eight finishes listed in a 1941 catalog. They were black and silver scale, white and silver scale, perch, solid black, white body with red head, frog, yellow with herringbone stripes, pearl with herringbone stripes. By 1949 only one other had been added, a luminous finish with a blue head. In 1950 Arbogast announced three new "FIRE PLUG DAYLIGHT FLUORESCENT FINISHES". Color collecting JITTERBUGS can be a lot of fun with 25 or more different finishes to be found. Some others to be found are: red-winged black bird, frog with white belly, frog with yellow belly, shad, coach dog, yellow coach dog, silver on body, silver flash, brown scale, sparrow, mouse, chipmunk, leopard frog.

Collector value range for metal-lipped, wooden Jitterbugs: $15-$50.

Collector value range for plastic and metal-lipped plastic Jitterbugs: $10-$20.

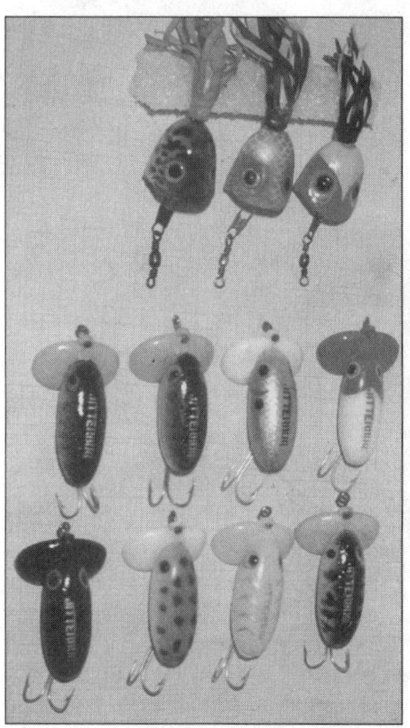

Left: Three 3/4" fly rod size wooden HULA POPPERS. Right: Eight 1-1/4" plastic JITTERBUGS with the WORLD WAR II era plastic lips. Photo courtesy Jim Muma.

HULA POPPER

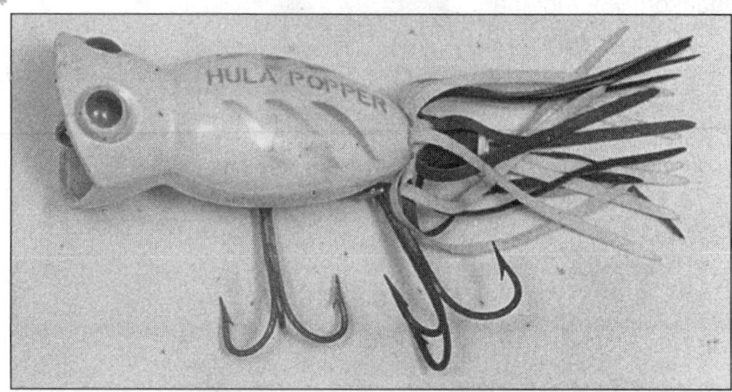

This lure was never manufactured in wood, only plastic, and it was introduced by Arbogast in 1948. It is known, however, that Brooke Ortell, a consultant to Arbogast, whittled possibly as many as 100 models before he and Arbogast finally settled on the production design. These prototypes were carved from white poplar and it is reasonable to assume that toward the end of this prodigious effort, there were a few that came close to the final product. Whether or not any of these have made their way out of company hands isn't known. If any have landed in a collector's hands, he possesses a true gem.

The original plastic Hula Poppers were made in only one size, a casting weight for bass. They now come in four sizes from the smallest 3/16-oz. to the largest, 5/6-oz. Collector value range for the earliest Hula Poppers: $3-$6.

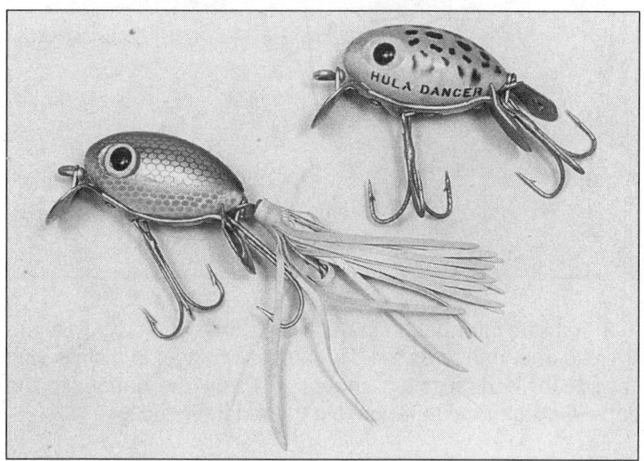

HULA DANCERS. Collector value range: $3-$6.

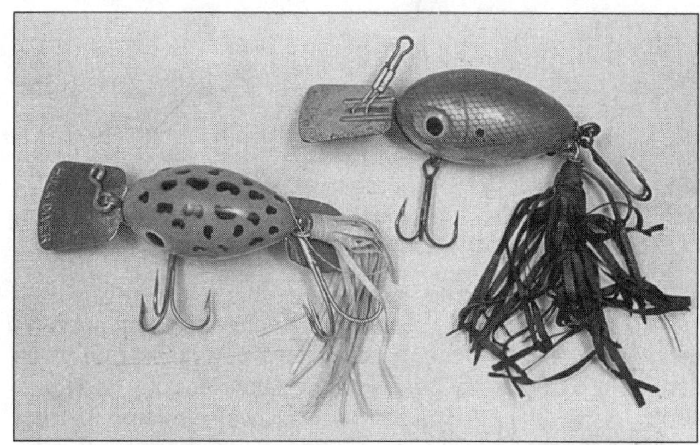

Right: ARBO-GASTER. Left: HULA DIVER. Collector value range: $3-$6.

Two examples of the smaller size HUSTLER lure. Notice the metal reinforced lip. Dark color on bottom. Photo courtesy Ken Bernoteit.

HUSTLER

This plastic lure came along in the 1960s. As with many companies superlative claims were made. Arbogast was no exception calling it "The most revolutionary lure ever developed." This lure was cataloged in two sizes, 2-1/2" and 4-1/2". That is overall size including the lip. They were made in 12 finishes: white body with red head, frog with white belly, solid black, yellow herringbone, perch, shad, coach dog, yellow coach gog, willow cat, orange with spots, silver on body, silver flash. Collector value range: $15-$20.

ARBY'S FIRE FISH

Arby's Bait Manufacturing Company Hicksville, New York

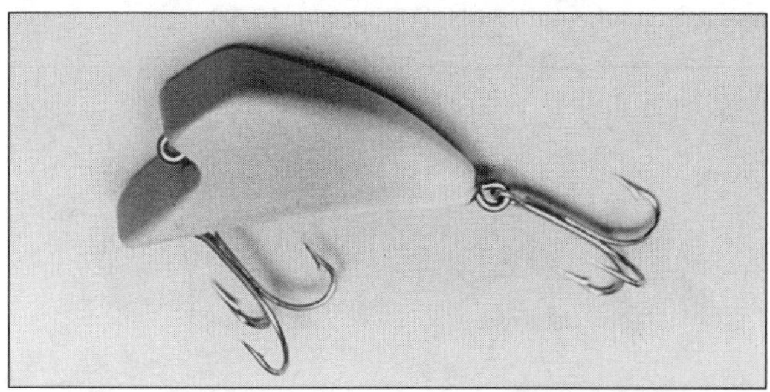

What little information there is came from the box. This lure is white and measures 2-1/4". The hook hanger is a strap with flat square ends just big enough to screw the hanger to the body. Collector value range: No trade data found.

ARKANSAS "TRENCH-BACK POPPER"

Perry's Fish Lure Co. Camden, Arkansas

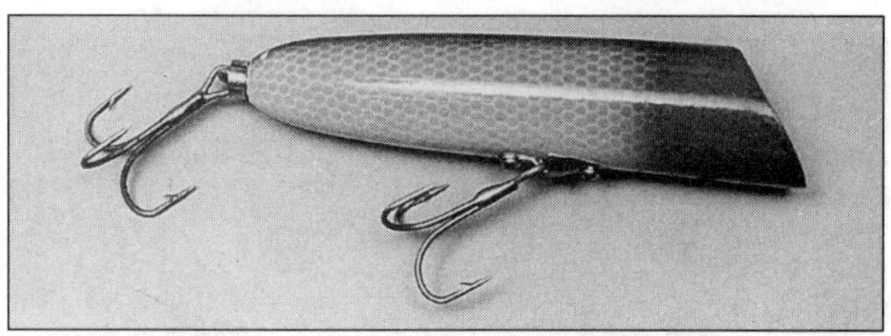

I was unable to turn up any data on this company and their lures. The name of the lure above is exactly as it appeared on the box. The lure is wood, measures 3-7/8" and has one-piece surface belly hook hanger. Note the tail-protecting hook preventer at the tail end. The paint finish is well rendered. Collector value range: $20-$30.

IMPORTANT NOTICE

The value ranges listed in this book are for lures in Very Good to Excellent condition. The values of those lures not in Very Good to Excellent condition can and probably will be worth considerably less. The values are meant to be a guide only.

ARNOLD LURES

Arnold Tackle Company Paw Paw, Michigan

Mr. Delavan 'Del' Arnold founded the company sometime in the late 1930s or early 1940s. Three Arnold lures were listed in a 1953 *General Merchandise Company* catalog. The Paw Paw, Michigan address was found on the metal diving lip of the wood body JOINTED PIKE (upper lure). It measures 3-1/2" and has tack painted eyes (TPE). It was cataloged as available in four finishes: Red head, white body; frog green; pike scale; golden flash. The catalog listed the size as 4-1/4" so we know there are two sizes to be found.

The other two lures in the accompanying photo were not listed in the catalog. They are wood body, side hook lures in the injured minnow style. They have TPE and measure 3" and 3-1/2" respectively.

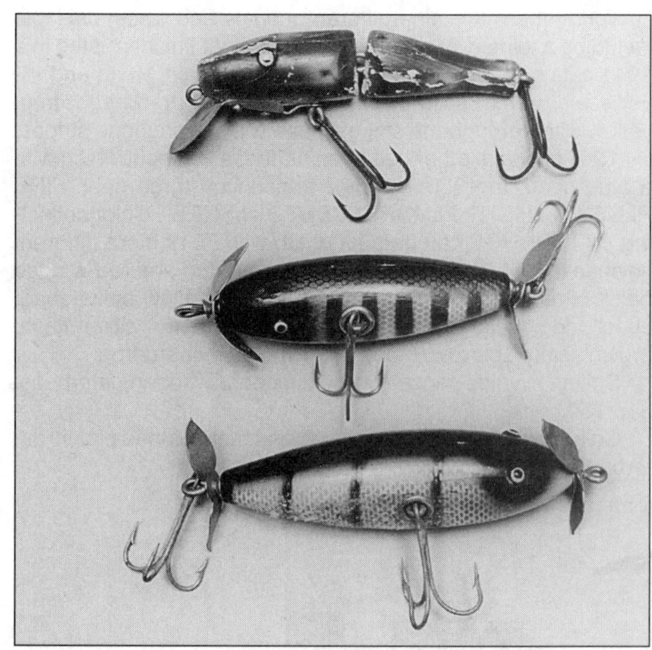

The photo above is of an Arnold HOPALONG BAIT. It measures 2-1/2", weighs 5/8 oz. and was available in three finishes: Red head, green frog and perch scale. Note that it is stamped HOPALONG on top. Collector value range for Arnold lures: $20-$50.

B-W SPINNER

Bill Watters Bait Company Humphrey Bait Company
Jacksonville, Indiana

Both company names were found on the box with no explanation. It is a 3" wood body lure with indented painted eyes. Notice the fancy back finish. It sports a one-piece surface belly hook hanger and fairly high quality tube type propeller spinners. No realistic collector value can presently be assigned.

BAIT-CASTER

Deluxe Mfg. Co, Inc Rome, Georgia

This is a clever contraption made, ostensibly, to enable the fisherman to cast a live minnow on a hook a long distance un-

harmed. It is red in color with an aluminum cylinder into which you place the hooked minnow and leader at the depth you wish to fish. When it lands it automatically turns over dumping the minnow and leader out. It then becomes a bobber. It came in three sizes: 3/4" cylinder, 2-1/4"; 7/8" cylinder, 3"; 1" cylinder, 3-1/4". Insufficient data to establish a collector value range.

BASS BIRD c. 1946

J.J. Gill and Associates — Huntington Park, California

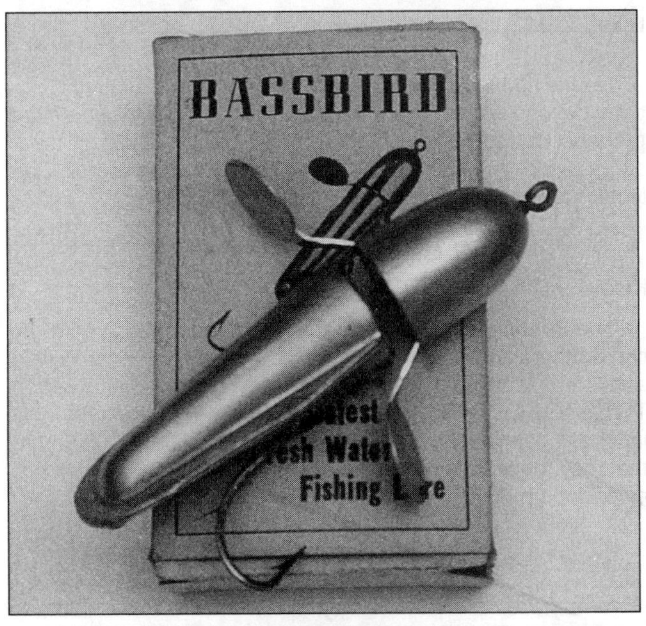

Found in its original box, little is known about this metal lure. The illustration on the box is of a two-hooker.

The lure in the previous photo is missing the tail hook. Collector value range: $30-$50.

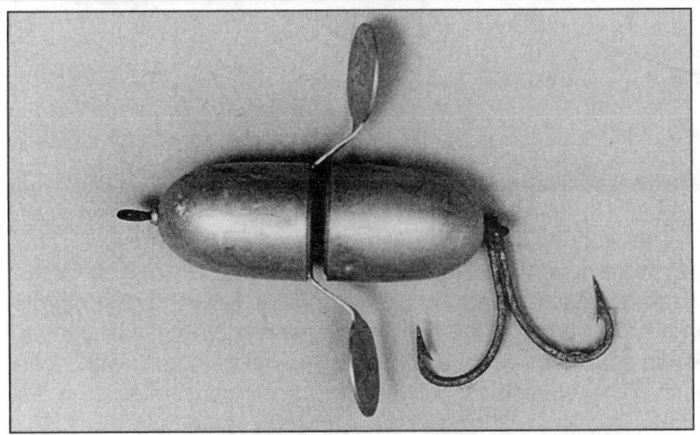

This lure measures 2-1/2". It is not known what the name is if any. It is placed here because the front half (spinning portion) is precisely the same as the BASS BIRD above. Collector value range: $30-$40.

BASS CALLER

Detroit Bait Company — Detroit, Michigan

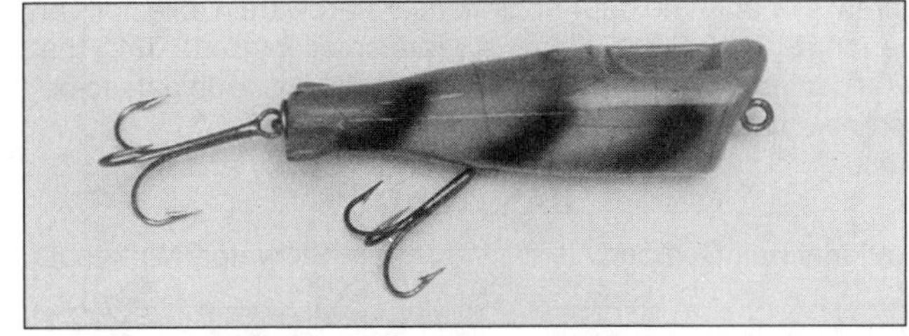

This top-water popper-type lure has an interesting innovation. It has a scoop-out on top of its head that the company called a "vacuum cup" in a 1940 advertisement. It isn't too clear in the photograph here, but the tail end sports a pair of aircraft type tail planes that appear to be an integral part of the body, not attached to the surface. Body length is 3-1/2". Colors: red, green, cream, red head and luminous. Collector value range: $60-$80.

BASS HOG

T.J. Boulton — Detroit, Michigan

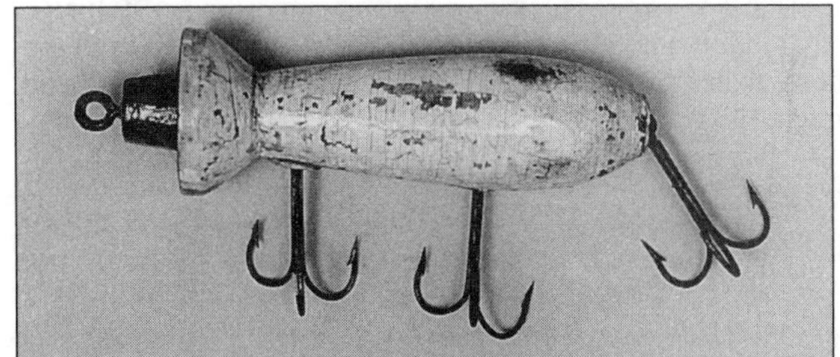

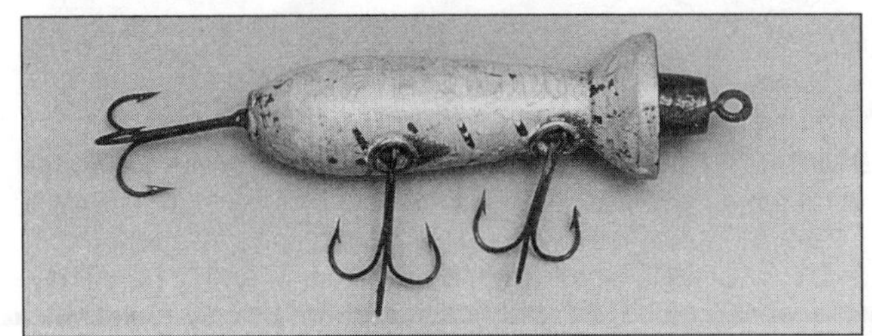

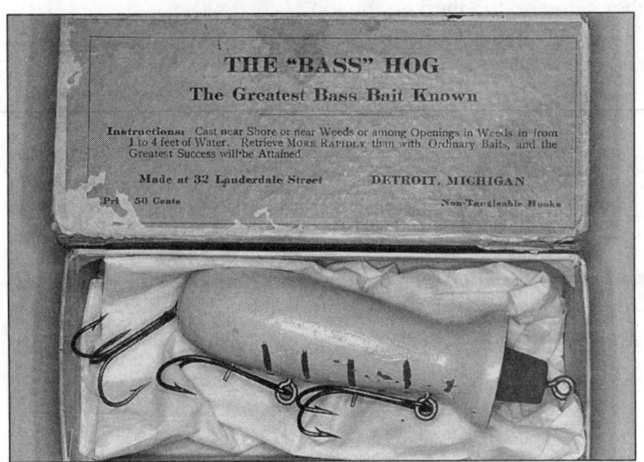

A BASS HOG in its original box. A new-in-the-box example like this one sold for $451 at auction in 1997.

This lure was first found referenced in a 1911 publication. The upper lure is 4-1/2" and painted white with a red head and red stripes and dots on the belly. It has cup and screw eye hardware with a reinforcing metal tail insert. The lower lure in the photo of two is suspected to be a later model of the BASS HOG although this is not yet substantiated. It is 3-7/8", has screw eye only (no cup) hook hanger hardware. Collector value range: $100-$200. There is a rare smaller size (2-1/4") that would bring a premium. There was insufficient trade date to establish a value for the smaller lure.

BASS KING

National Bait Company Stillwater, Minnesota

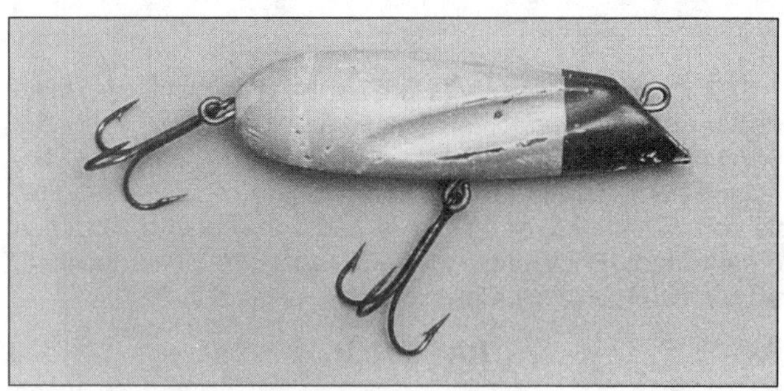

This is thought to be the earliest version of the BASS KING. Note that the flute on the body side is slanted down from the nose. It utilized the simple screw eye hardware. Collector value range. $50-$75.

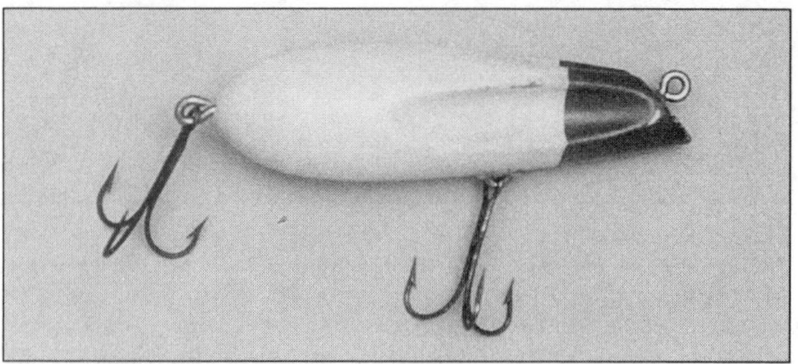

BASS KING JR. with cup and screw eye hardware. Collector value range: $25-$50.

These c. 1927 lures came in two sizes, 3" and 3-1/2". They were white-bodied with red heads and are usually found with cup and screw eye hardware. There are three flutes, one on either side and the third on the top.

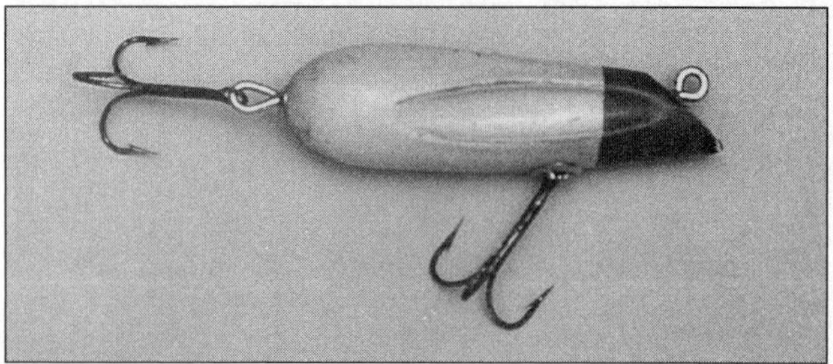

A later model BASS KING with cup and screw eye hardware and non-slanted flutes. Collector value range: $25-$40.

BASS KING

Red & Green Tackle Company Detroit, Michigan

Thought to be of 1940s vintage, this 2-3/4" lure has tack painted eyes and a screw eye/washer belly hook hanger. There is a protecting tail cap and the odd shaped diving lip has a cotter key for a line tie. The pamphlet in the box said it is a near surface bait to be reeled in very slowly. Collector value range: $25-$35.

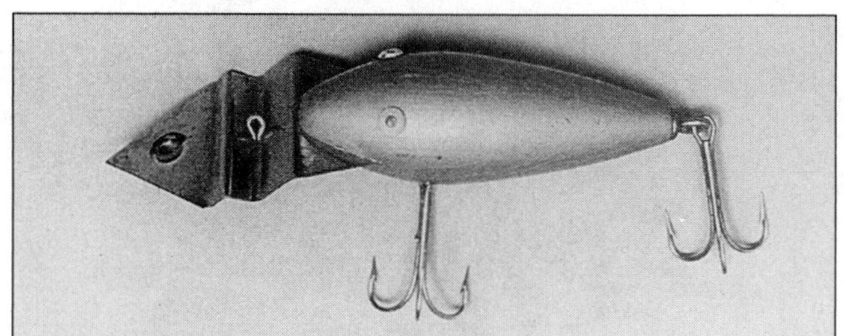

BASSNIK

Ross Manufacturing Company Old Hickory, Tennessee

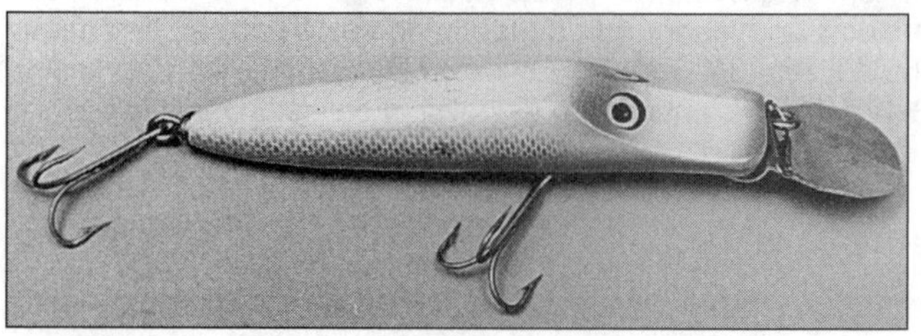

I found nothing with regard to the Ross Manufacturing Company beyond what was on the box. This is a quality wood lure probably dating from the late 1950s or early 1960s. It measures 3-1/2" and utilizes one-piece belly hook hardware. Collector value range: $6-$12.

BEAR CREEK BAIT COMPANY

Keleva, Michigan

The Bear Creek Bait Company was established in 1946 by two brothers and a friend. They were Walter and Elmer Wiitala and Leo Manilla. They made three lures, the wooden TWEEDLER, COHO KING and the SUCKER MINNOW. The latter are both plastic lures with metal diving lips. It is reported that they made fewer than 1,000 of each of them. The company ended up making primarily ice fishing decoys.

TWEEDLER

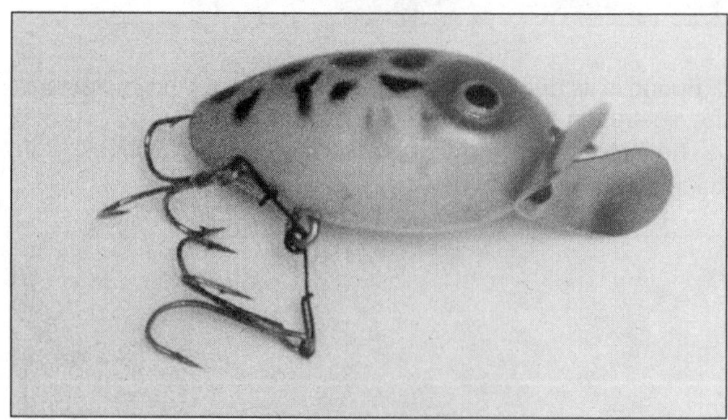

The wooden TWEEDLER was available in six finishes, but they were never listed in the advertisements. The five observed so far are described as: Frog pattern, white belly with black spots on a brown back, white belly with brown spots on yellow back, brown scale with white belly and a green scale back with white belly. They were furnished with the outrigger hooks as in the photo. Two sizes: 2" and 2-1/2". Collector value range: $15-30.

SUCKER MINNOW

The SUCKER MINNOW was a solid plastic lure made in two sizes. They were 2-3/4" and 3-1/2". They were reportedly made

in two colors described as a light yellowish green scale and a slightly darker scale finish with a very dark back. A 1952 advertisement illustrated a very dark scale finish. Collector value range: $15-$25. Photo courtesy Tom Jacomet.

COHO KING LURE

This plastic lure is essentially an elongated version of the SUCKER MINNOW at 5-1/4". It carried three treble hooks, two on the belly and one trailing. The only finish reported in a heavy glitter. Collector value range: N.A.

BERRY-LEBECK MFG. CO., "OZARKA LURES"

Robert Berry, Paul Lebeck — California, Missouri

Until the fourth edition I reported that little was known about this company and its products. Thanks to collector Kevin Richards, who sent me some super info, and the ably written Fishing Tackle Made in Missouri, by Dean A. Murphy we now know more about the company.

The company marketed their lures under the trade name "Ozarka Lures". The first lure was the #100 Series, 3" TALKY-TOPPER. Thecompany was in business until the death of one of the partners in 1951.

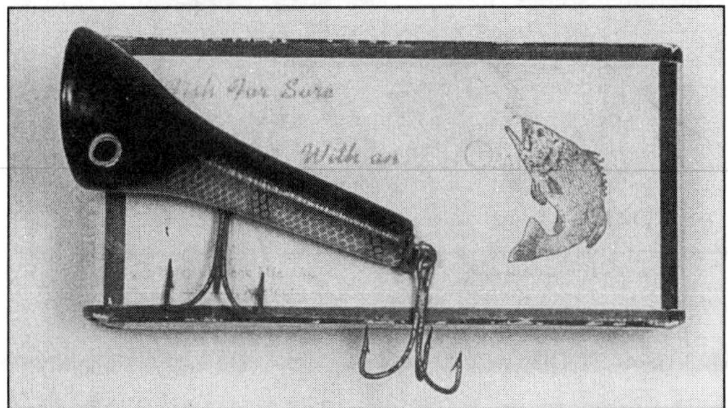

An Ozarka Lure, TALKY-TOPPER.

The patent was applied for in 1945 so we know it is at least that old. It may have been made for some time before that. It is a very well made and painted wooden lure. A company flyer states it was available in the following nine finishes: Red head, white body; solid black; salmon red shiner, red etching and white scales; steelhead shiner, black etching and white scales; green shiner, green etching with gold scales; yellow perch scale, green etching with yellow and gold scales; perch scale, red etching with dark green scales; pick scale, light brown etching with gold scales; frog finish. It had a tail hook preventer to keep it from tangling with the belly treble. If you will look at the photo of the two TALKIE-TOPPERS here you will see one with a tail prop. Each time this configuration is found there is no preventer present. Collector value range: $15-$30.

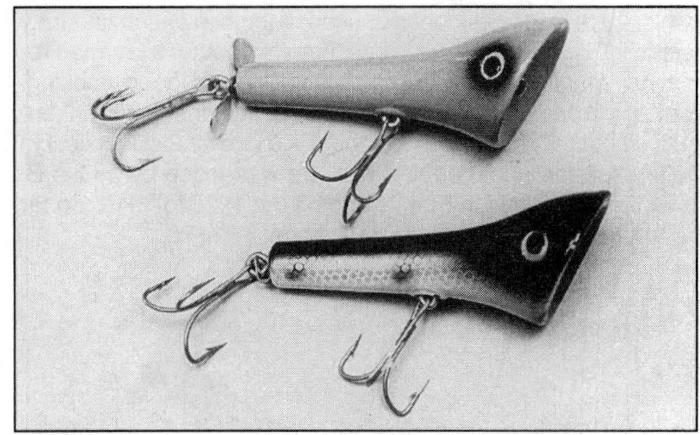

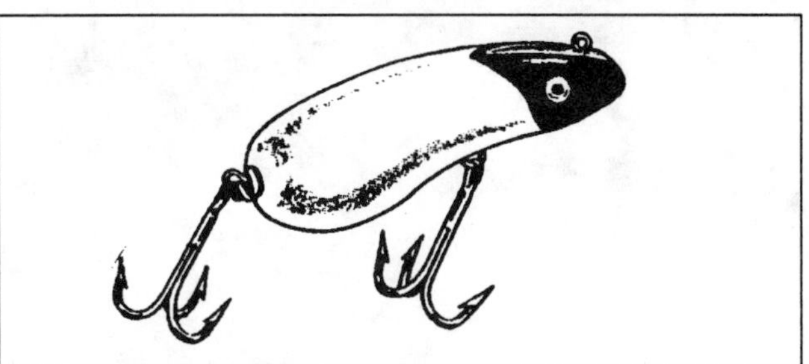

This is the wooden WEE GEE.

The plastic (Tenite) WEE GEE

The Series 200, WEE GEE was an underwater lure available in the same color patterns as listed above for the TALKIE-TOPPER. The illustration above is a 2" wooden version. About 1949 they attempted to make both this one and the TALKIE-TOPPER in plastic. The attempts were not particularly successful for the TALKIE-TOPPER. They did market a plastic WEE GEE, but you can see from the photo that the result was not the same as the original lure. Collector value range for wooden Ozarka lures: $10-$20.

At one time the lure pictured here was thought to be a Berry-Lebeck product because it was found in this box. It is no longer considered so. The photo is left here for you to see the Ozarka Lure box.

THE BEYERLEIN LURE

Gus B. Beyerlein Frankenmuth, Michigan

In an earlier edition of this book the lures in the above photo were in the "UNKNOWN" section as "...attributed to a company in South Haven, Michigan". While there still may be something to this, there is also evidence to support the contention that they belong in Frankenmuth, Michigan. Frankenmuth is a German resort community famous for its hospitality and good cooking. They are proud of their heritage and maintain the fine Frankenmuth Historical Museum where there is a lure almost identical to the lures in the photo above. The lure was made by a Gus B. Beyerlein, who lived in Frankenmuth from 1928 to 1940. So far that's all we know. Collector value range: $40-$80.

Side and belly view of two lures attributed to Gus Beyerlein. They measure 4-3/8' and 4-3/4' respectively and are paintea bright gold with red heads.

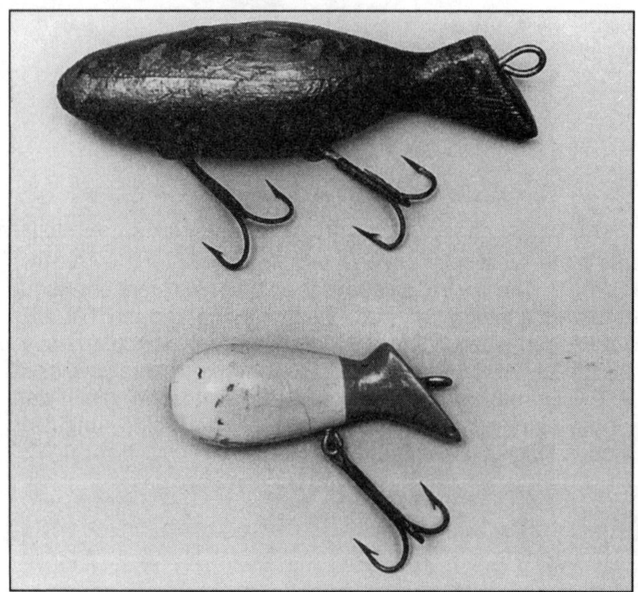

The lures in the above photo are also attributed to Beyerlein. They measure 4-1/2" and 2-3/4" respectively.

BIDWELL BAIT

Clifford W. Bidwell Kalamazoo, Michigan

The name "BIDWELL BAIT" is used by collectors to identify the above lure. The patent was granted to Bidwell in 1915 and the lower lure in the above photo is a match to the patent illustration. None of these lures have yet been found in a box, nor has any advertising or any other identifying literature been located. We have no other name for it. We do have a patent, however, so we do know that there was a least a serious intent to produce them. We also know that it's a rare one that's hard to find, so it may have never gone into large scale production. Take note of the brass plate on the bottom extending slightly up the tail. Also note the large brass washer-like hook preventer attached to the hooks. These appear in the patent, but several lures have surfaced without these two features. It is speculated widely that they may have discontinued making them with the plate and preventers as a means of reducing manufacturing costs. It measures 3-1/2" in length.

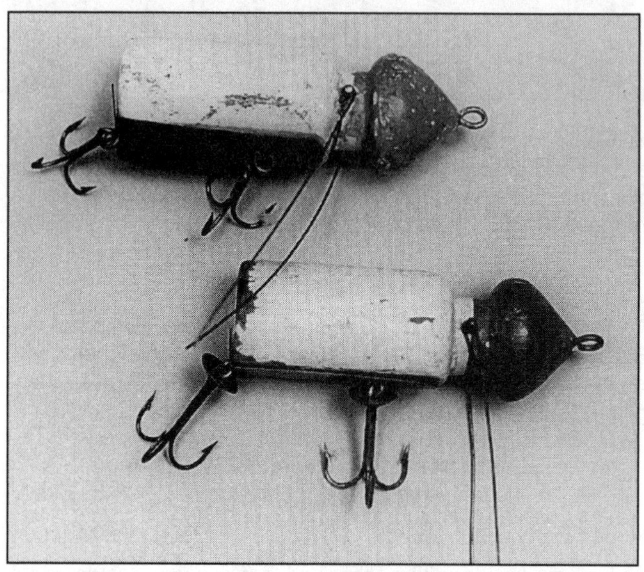

There has been another lure found that is attributed to Bidwell. It is 3" long and called the "BOTTLE BAIT" by collectors because of its shape. The shape is almost identical to the old miniature cream containers served with coffee back in the 1950s and 1960s. Collector value range for either: $200-$400.

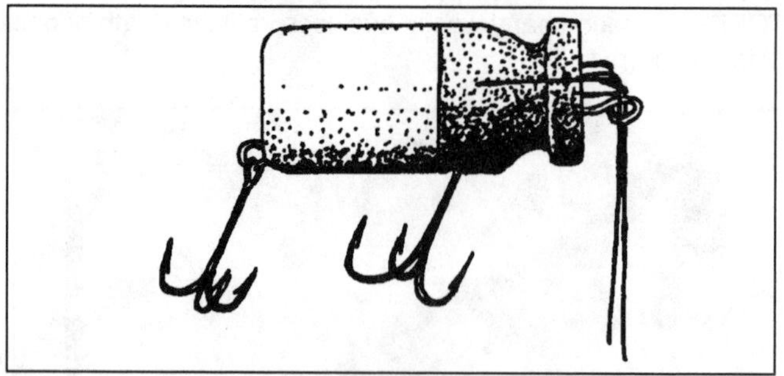

BIEK

MANUFACTURING COMPANY Dowagiac, Michigan

This company was founded in 1930. I was unable to find but one small catalog dated 1941. It illustrated eight wood lures and five fly rod bugs and flies. There were also a number of other items such as bobbers, landing nets, gaff hooks, etc. The lure entries gave no sizes, finishes or weights. The bottom right lure added to the card in the photo below is THE AGITATOR. It measures 2-5/8", has painted eyes, a recessed screw eye hook hanger (no cup), is marked "Biek" and is black with red scale finish. Other lures cataloged were a chunky surface popper named the TOPPER, A jointed PIKER looking something like a Creek Chub Bait Co. jointed PIKE MINNOW and a Biek MAJOR that looks like a Heddon BASSER. Collector value range for Biek lures: $25-$55.

This card of 12 lures says "Serving You since 1930" at the bottom. The lures are assorted colors and the bodies measure 3/4'. The one at bottom right has been added. It is a small AGITATOR.

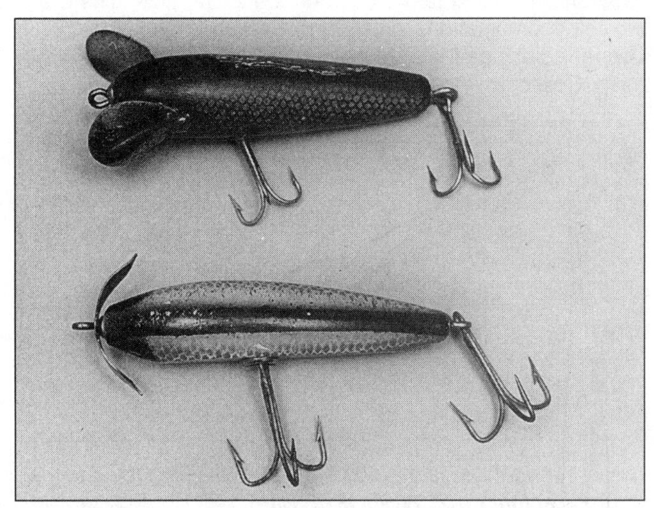

Upper lure is cataloged as "THE NEW WINGED WOBBLER." It measures 31/4", has cup and screw eye hardware, a green scale finish and is marked "BIEK". The lower lure is another uncataloged lure measuring 3-1/2", the same hook hardware, a green and red scale finish and indented painted eyes. It is also marked "BIEK".

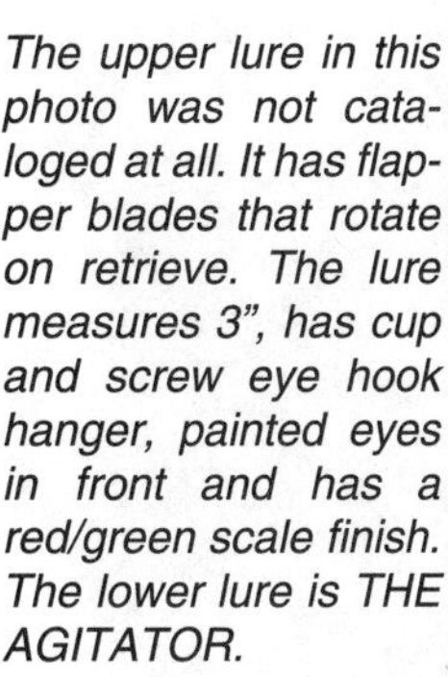

The upper lure in this photo was not cataloged at all. It has flapper blades that rotate on retrieve. The lure measures 3", has cup and screw eye hook hanger, painted eyes in front and has a red/green scale finish. The lower lure is THE AGITATOR.

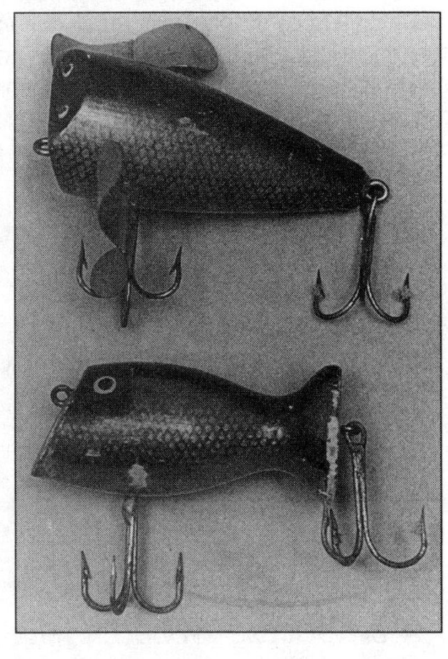

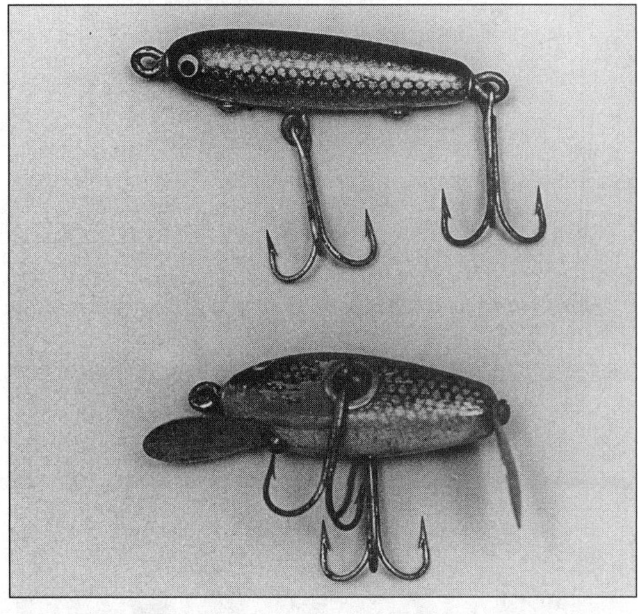

Two more Biek lures that did not appear in the one catalog I was able to find. The upper lure is a small 2-1/4" size in green scale finish with painted eyes and cup and screw eye hook hardware. It has two screws in the belly for no apparent reason. The lower lure measures 2" and has the same hardware, a red/green scale finish and indented painted eyes.

The top lure in the photo above is another, smaller version of THE AGITATOR measuring 2". This one has glass eyes and cup and screw eye hook hardware. It has a white body with red head. The other lure (lower) is not cataloged. It measures 2-3/4" and has the same finish as the upper lure. The double hook is recessed into the tail.

BIFF BAIT COMPANY

Albert R. Bayer — Milwaukee, Wisconsin

It is known that this company was doing business during the 1920s from catalog references. However the dates before and after are not presently known to the author.

THE MASTER BIFF PLUG c. 1926*

This lure was a "Water Sonic" type That is a plug with hole or holes to admit water at one point and expel it at the other end. It was cataloged as made in 2-1/2" and 2" lengths but there is also a 4-1/2" known. It has a treble mounted under the head and a trailing treble hook on the 2-1/2" size. There are two color combinations to be found: Red head with white body; Copper color head with aluminum color body; Natural Perch finish. Collector value range: $35-$80.

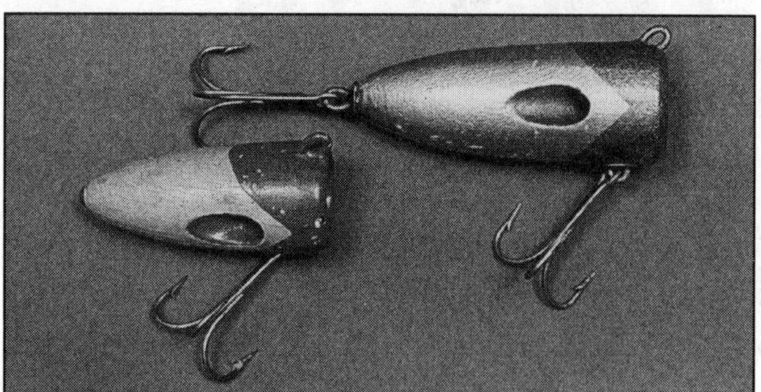

The upper right lure is a 2-1/2" MASTER BIFF PLUG. The lower lure is actually a 2" WHOOPEE BIFF.

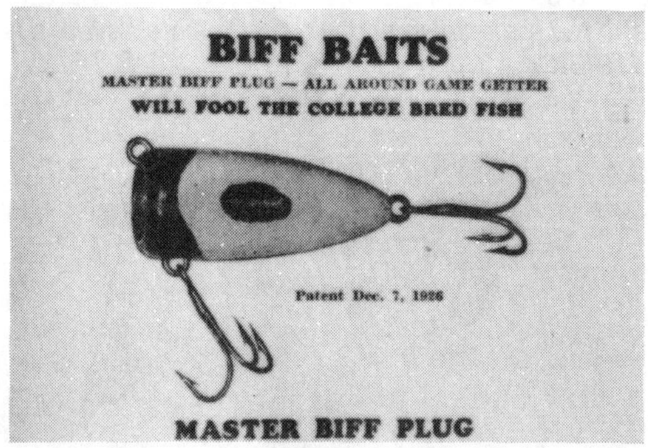

BIFF BAITS
MASTER BIFF PLUG — ALL AROUND GAME GETTER
WILL FOOL THE COLLEGE BRED FISH
Patent Dec. 7, 1926
MASTER BIFF PLUG

**Advertised in June, 1926 issue of Hunting & Fishing magazine, page 20. Patent date on box is Dec. 7, 1926.*

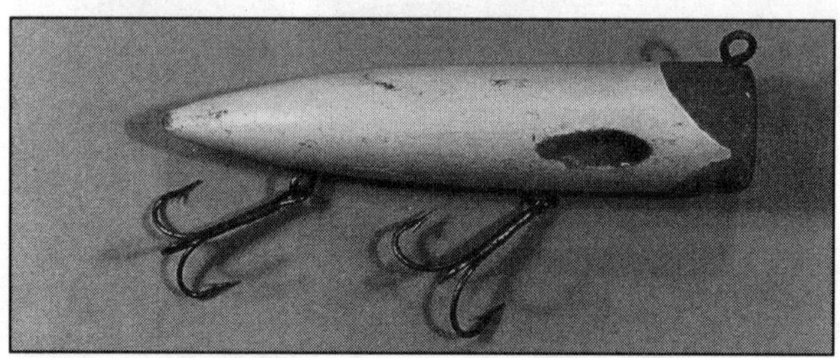

This 4-1/2' Biff plug was not found cataloged anywhere. It is placed here because of its similarity to the MASTER BIFF PLUG. It may turn out to have a separate identity.

SPIRAL SPINNER

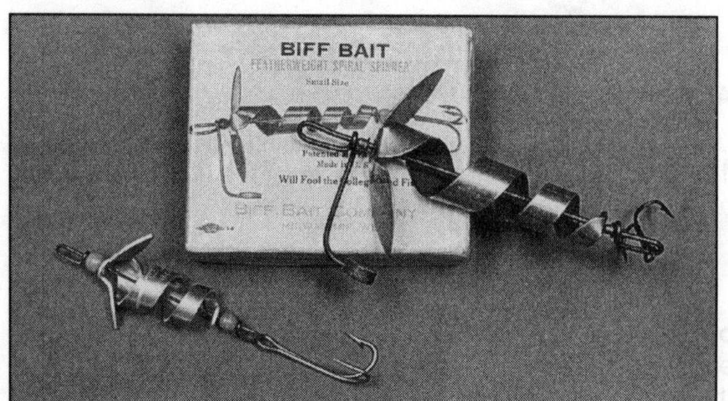

This lure was patented March 17, 1925 and marketed in two sizes, 2" and 3". The photo is of both sizes. Both were nickel plated brass and the interior of the spiral body was painted red. The larger size was also available in gold plate and brass. Collector value range: $65-$90.

BASSEY BIFF SURFACE, SINGLE WOBBLER

SINGLE WOBBLER on top of its original box. The box name is SURFACE SINGLE WOBBLER.

What a mouth full that looks like! The BASSEY was patented December 22, 1925, but may have been available prior to that. It has a cork body mounted on an aluminum plate, red beads at either end and a big counterweight at the nose. This plug was available in a swirling spattered-type paint finish in green on white or red on white backgrounds. A double body version of the same lure was also available. Collector value range of each: $200-$300.

BRINGS SUCCESS BIFF BAITS GIVES SATISFACTION
ALL BAITS ADAPTABLE FOR CASTING & TROLLING
Ptd. Dec. 22, 1925
BIFF SURFACE DOUBLE WOBBLER
Flashey Splashey Biff Double Wobbler
Very attractive at long distance

A Biff DOUBLE WOBBLER. From a pocket catalog Page, c. 1925.

GODEVIL BIFF

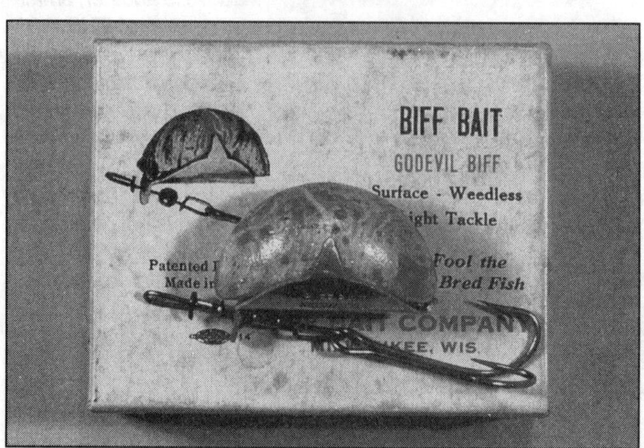

Patented December 22, 1925 this little devil was available in two colors, red and white swirled as in the photo and the same in green and white. It measures 1" long. Collector value range: $75-$100.

BING'S NEMAHBIN WEEDLESS MINNOW

A. F. Bingenheimer — Milwaukee, Wisconsin

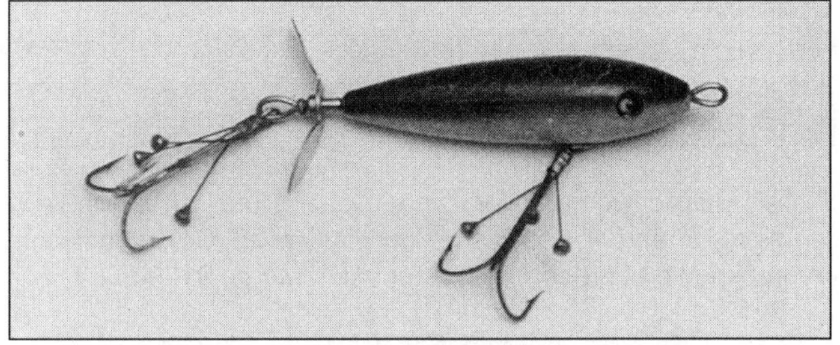

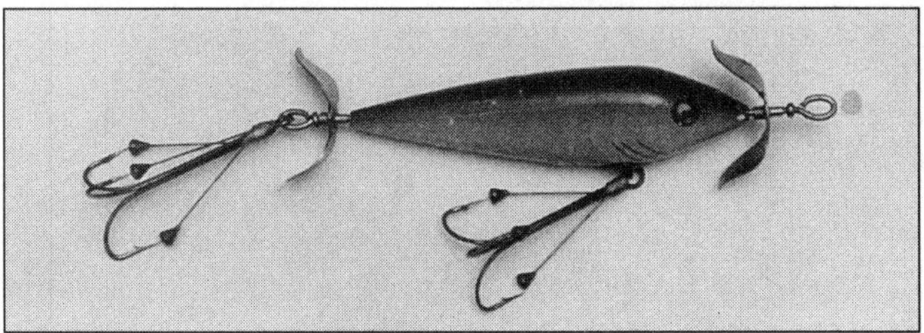

These particular plugs can be placed as early as 1905. An ad in a tackle dealers periodical of that year touts the lure as being "A NEW BAIT". The company can be found advertising tackle earlier, but not the NEMAHBIN lure. The lures pictured here are not the earliest. They are, however, 1906-vintage and the most commonly found though all are rare. Earlier versions (pictured in the 1905 ad) show the weedless wires with loops at the end that attach to the hook points. Those hooks are single point and rigidly attached to the body. They have been found with nose- or tail-mounted propellers on both. Finishes available were: Gold, silver, metallic, crackle back and green back with red or white belly. All I have observed so far have had glass eyes and hand-painted gill marks. Their lengths vary from 3" to 6". The weedless treble hooks, like those in the photos above, apparently were quite successful, as they are seen offered on lures in catalogs from other well-known companies. In the NEMAHBIN MINNOW the hooks are attached with the gem clip type fasteners to the thru-body wire. Collector value range: $250-$350.

BITE-EM-BATE COMPANY

Warsaw, Indiana (1917) — Ft. Wayne, Indiana (1920)

The dates with the two company locations above represent the dates of periodicals in which their advertisements with the addresses appeared. The name of the company had changed a bit in the 1920 advertisement. The name is found two ways prior to that: "BITE-EM-BATE" and "BITE-EM-BAIT". The 1920 ad read: "BITE-EM-BAIT SALES COMPANY" and the address was Ft. Wayne.

The earliest Bite-Em lure patent I have found so far was applied for in mid-1921 and granted mid-1922. The patent was granted to Claude M. Rodgers and Arthur W. Wenger. Some think Bite-Em became Wenger Manufacturing Company in the mid-1920s. The Wenger name on the patent and the change in address may have something to do with that. Only time and additional data will tell. The latest ads I have found for Bite-Em were in 1920 publications.

BITE-EM-BATE

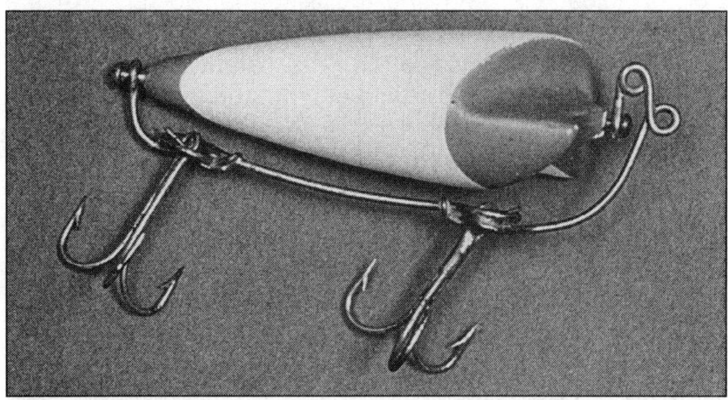

1920 vintage BITE-EM-BATE, 2-7/8'. Second style line tie.

This wooden plug was shaped so that it would rotate on retrieve. The body pivoted on an exterior wire half-loop extending from the nose to the tail. The first (c.1917) version had a treble hook attached to the wire loop and another attached directly to the tail end of the body. Later (c.1920) the trailing treble was moved to the wire loop just beneath the tail. The method of hook attachment to the wire had also changed by this time. It was available in seven different colors: White body, red head and red tail; red body, white head; gold body, red head and red tail; aluminum body, red head and gold tail; black body, white head and gold tail; yellow body, red head and red tail; choc. green, red head and red tail. Catalog entries state the size as 3-/12" overall length. Collector value range: $100-$200.

LIPPED WIGGLER

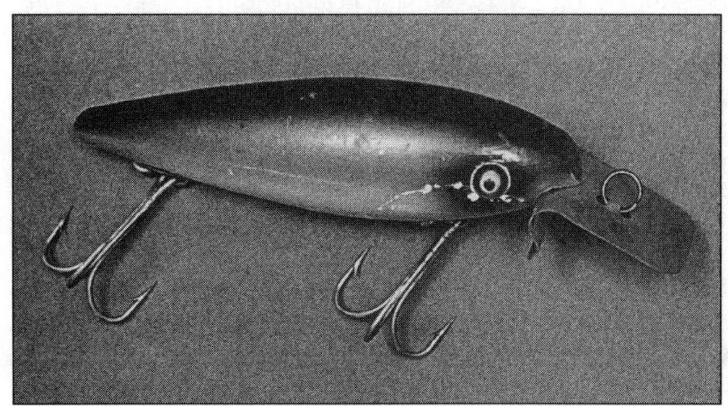

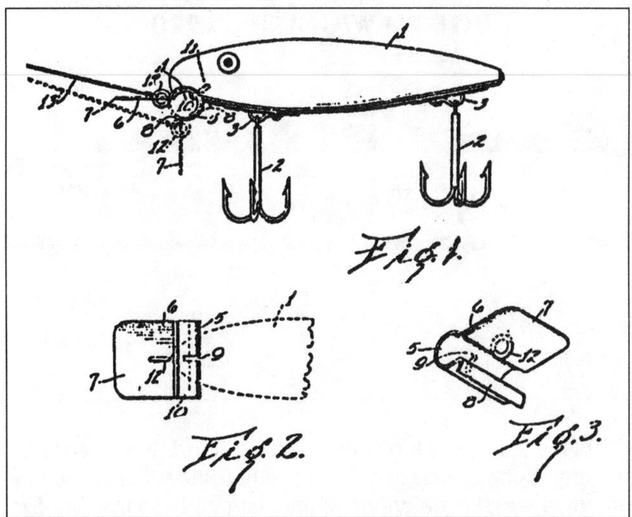

Detail from the patent illustration for the LIPPED WIGGLER. It was granted to C.M. Rodgers and A. W. Wenger in 1922.

It isn't obvious in the photo here, but the diving lip on this plug is adjustable, enabling the fisherman to run it at the depth of his choice. Refer to the patent illustration to find a clear illustration of this feature. The patent was granted in 1922. Hook hangers are a type of L-rig and the eyes are yellow glass. It was available with two or three treble hooks. Length of the one pictured is 3-3/4". Colors available are unknown. Collector value range: $60-$150.

THE BITE-EM WATER-MOLE c. 1920

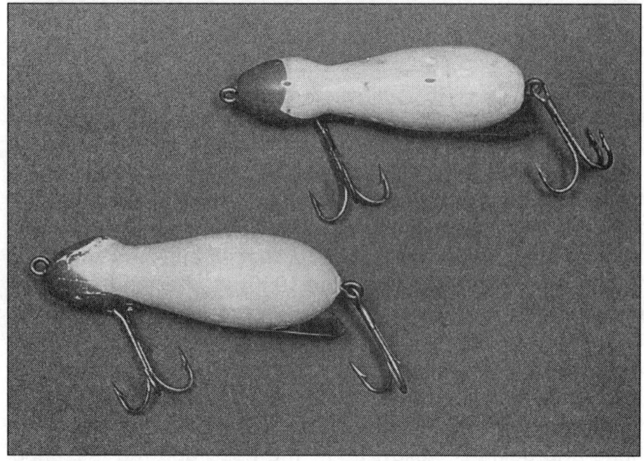

This 3" plug is shaped somewhat like a mole. As you can see in the photo it is found with a round head or with a flattened head and slightly chubbier body (lower plug). It is not presently known which version is the older. Though it has not so far been seen, a 1920 ad indicates the availability of this lure with a second line tie, ie. "...by tying the line in the upper line hitch...". It has a nickel plated metal PIECE attached along the belly extending in a spoon shape slightly past the tail end. A treble hook is attached just aft of the head on the bottom and there is a trailing treble. Colors available were: White body, red head; white body, red head and red tail; black body, white head and gold tail; black body, red head and gold tail; yellow body, red head and red tail; yellow body, green head and green tail; choc. green body, white and red head; gold body, white and red head and red tail; red body, white head; aluminum body, red head and red tail. Collector value range: $50-$150.

BITE-EM WIGGLER c.1920

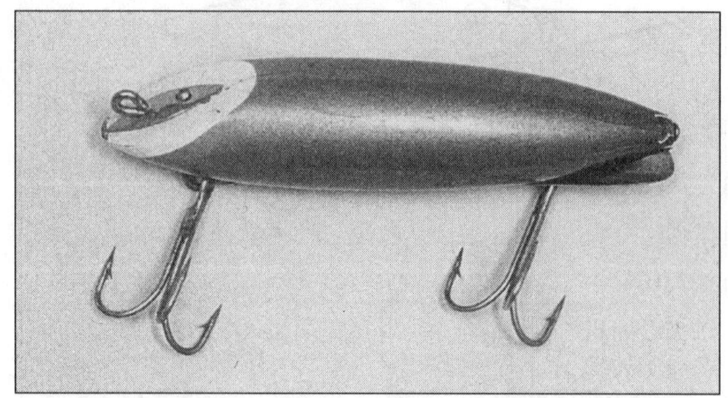

This is a 3-7/8" plug with a sloping head. It has a treble mounted beneath the nose and another under the tail. It has the same metal plate/spoon attachment as does the Bite-Em WATER-MOLE. The colors available were the same also with the addition of cream white. Collector value range: $75-$170.

BITE-EM FLOATER MINNOW

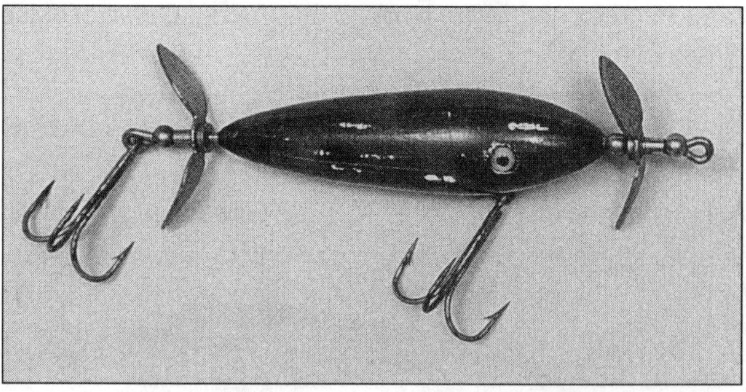

This classic two propeller spinner floating lure was available in two sizes, 3" and 4" and has yellow glass eyes. Colors available are not known at present. Collector value range: $100-$200.

BITE-EM BUG

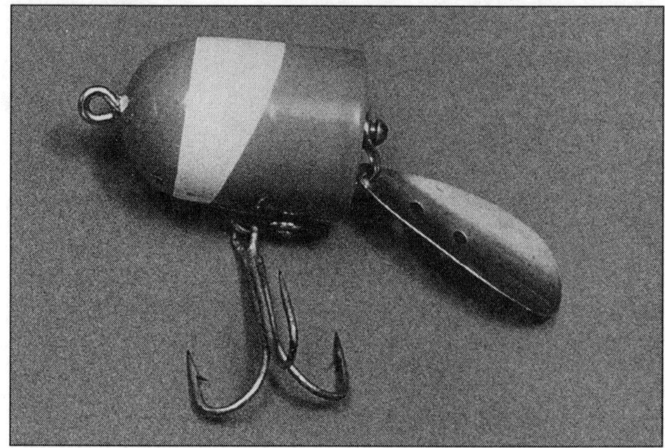

Only one illustrated reference to this lure was found. The lure in the accompanying photo is a genuine Bite-Em product, but differs from the one in the catalog illustration in some subtle and not-so-subtle ways. The catalog illustration shows a simple screw eye attachment of the trailing spoon, not as in the photo here. The body in the catalog is shaped a bit differently and its paint design is simpler. It utilizes the same L-rig type hook hanger, but it is mounted in the opposite direction from the one here. The available colors were: White body, red head; black body, red and white head; yellow body, red head; choc. green body, white head; roman gold body, red and white head; red body, white head; aluminum body, redhead. Collector value range: $100-$190.

BASS-ENTICER

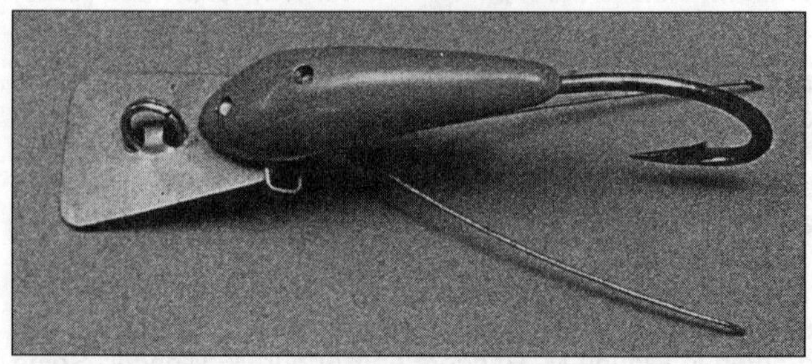

This lure has been reported as an unknown Bite-Em-Bait product. We now know its name and the fact that it is actually a product of the Wenger Manufacturing Company of Warsaw also. We are still not sure which came first, Wenger or Bite-Em. Collector value range: $20-$40.

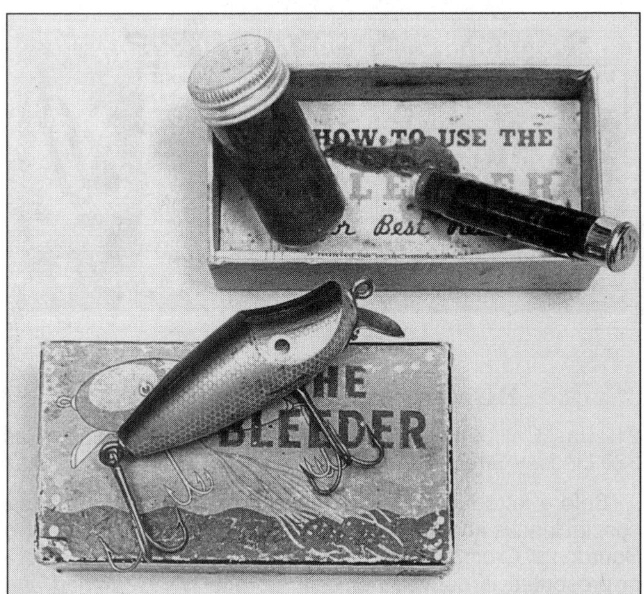

THE BLEEDER. It is unusual to find the bait new in the box with original papers and the blood pellets.

BLEEDING BAIT MANUFACTURING COMPANY

Beaumont, Texas

BLEEDER BAIT MANUFACTURING COMPANY

Dallas, Texas

BIG STATE BAIT COMPANY

Beaumont, Texas

AMERICAN TACKLE COMPANY/NATIONAL TACKLE COMPANY

Tulsa, Oklahoma

This Dallas, Texas firm is known to have been doing business in the late 1930s, but the exact dates of existence are presently unknown to the author. All the plugs were designed with a receptacle hole and pivoting cover in which you placed a special tablet that simulated the bleeding of a wounded bait fish when worked properly in the water. There were eight styles of lure and a hookless teaser. Some were available as a floater, diver or sinker making 16 different plug types including the Teaser, for the collector to find. It would be a rare moment indeed to find a BLEED-LURE in the box with the vial of tablets, for most are found without them. Each plug also came with detachable hook guards. They are listed in alphabetical order on the following pages.

We know that there was also the existence of a Big State Bait Co., in Beaumont, Texas that also made bleeding baits. A collector found a glass-eyed version in its original box along with the bleeding tablets. He reports that his is called THE SURVIVOR. It is very likely that this company was the forerunner of Bleeding Bait. The patent for the Bleeding Bait was applied for in 1935 and granted in 1939 to a Cortez E. Peck of Beaumont, Texas. THE SURVIVOR resembles the patent illustration

The company apparently moved to Dallas toward the end on the 1930s, becoming the Bleeder Bait Manufacturing Co. The company moved to Tulsa, Oklahoma at some point around or after 1939. At the same time the name of the company was changed to AMERICAN TACKLE COMPANY and then to NATIONAL TACKLE COMPANY. Collector value range for Bleeding Baits from Big State Bait Co: $150-$290; for all others: $20-$50.

THE B.P.S. 100

Made in floating, sinking and diving models, this plug is 4" long and weights 3/4 ounce. It has two side-by-side belly trebles and a trailing treble. This larger plug exhibits all the features of a RANGER though larger. A very poor photo copy of an old but undated advertisement shows a lure that appears to be the same as the one in this photo. We will tentatively identify this as the B.P.S. 100 until better evidence surfaces to confirm or discredit the assumption.

BROKEN BACK

This is a jointed lure weighing 3/4 ounce and is 4" long. It has one belly treble mounted on the rear section and a trailing treble hook.

BUBBLER

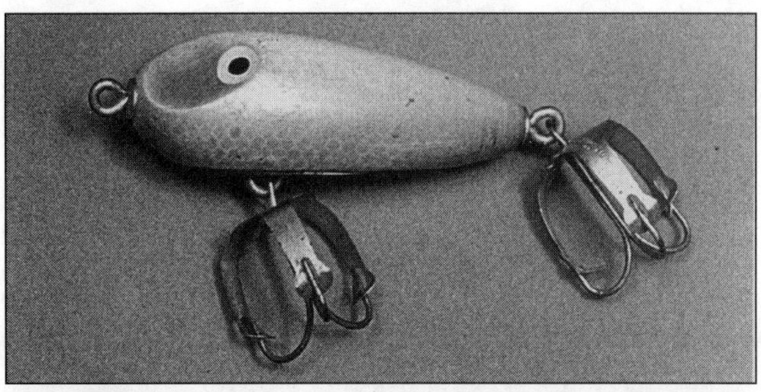

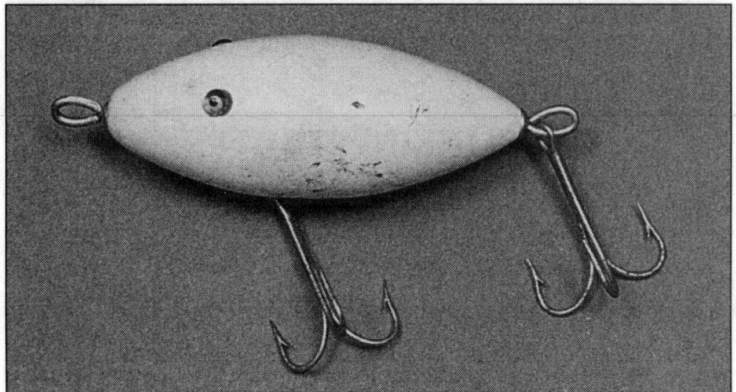

The lure on the top is a BUBBLER. The one on the bottom is interesting in that it has the bleeder feature, but was not found in catalogs or ads for the company. Could be a very early production or a prototype lure. Note that it has glass eyes, a feature not normally associated with the Bleeding Bait Company products. Painted eyes are the norm.

Available in floating (1/2 oz.) and sinking (5/8 oz.) models. Both plugs are 2-5/8". They each have one belly treble and a trailing treble hook.

CHUNKER

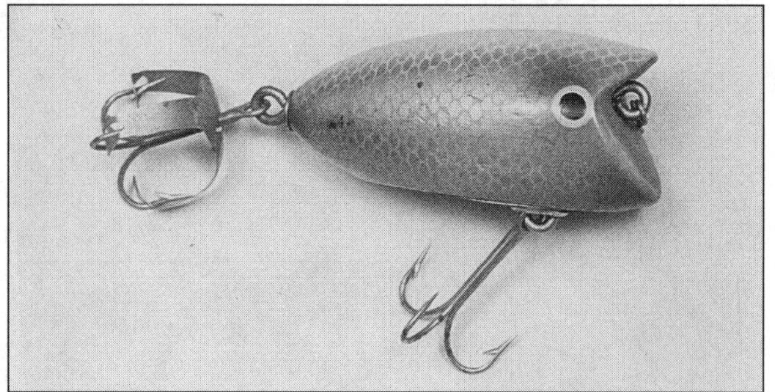

This lure has a notched mouth with the line tie in the roof of the mouth. It is 2-1/4" long and weighs 5/8 oz. It has one belly treble and a trailing treble hook. Note the unusual weedless features on the trailing treble hook. This is often found on Bleeding Baits.

DIDO

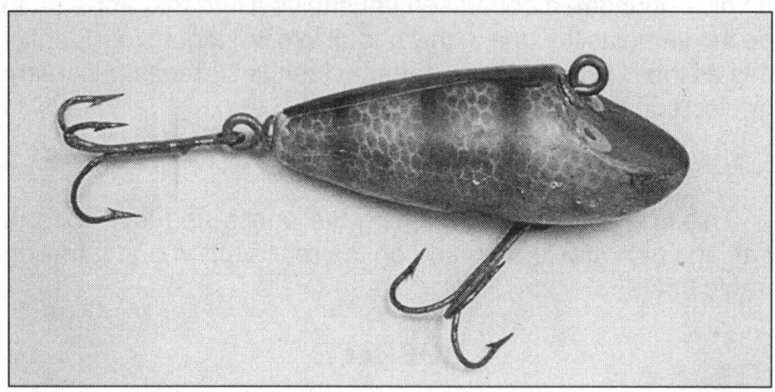

This DIDO is a slow sinking plug weighing 1/2 oz. and 2-5/8" long. It was made with a belly treble and trailing treble hook only and a scooped out head where the line tie is located.

FISH KING

Made in diving, sinking or floating models, this lure is 2-7/8 ounces and 6-1/4" long. It sports three trebles, two belly-mounted and one trailing, and a metal lip blade.

MOUSE

This is a 2-5/8", 1/2-ounce mouse-shaped plug complete with flexible tail. It had one belly treble and a trailing treble hook.

BLINKIN' BEAUTY

Glo-Lure Company — Chicago, Illinois

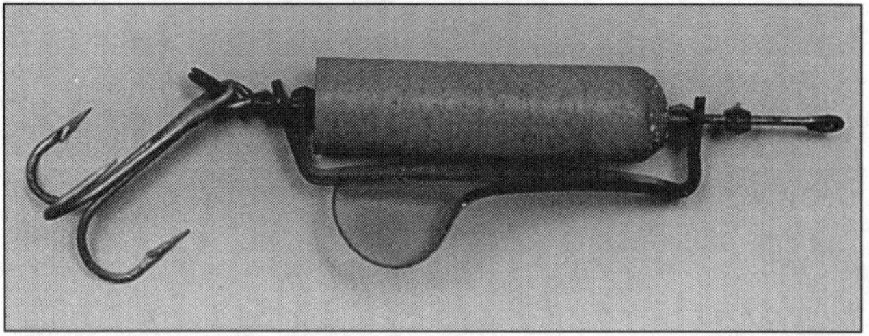

Advertised in 1944 as the "Revolutionary New 'BLINKIN' BEAUTY'", this lure has a "fluorescent" plastic spinner that revolves around a luminous body. This supposedly made the luminous light appear to blink on and off. This one measures 2", but it was made in a smaller size also. Collector value range: $10-$20.

BOMBER BAIT COMPANY

212 East California Street — Gainesville, Texas
326 Lindsay Street — Gainesville, Texas

Before introducing you to this company and its products, special thanks and recognition for his original work goes to Jim Bourdon of Croton-on-Hudson, New York. Much of the material presented is derived from his thoroughly researched and comprehensive work, The Bomber Bait Company. It is absolutely indispensable for any collector of the Bomber Company products. His address is listed in the recommended references section at the front of the book. Other materials such as boxes, brochures and lures were provided by other collectors.

The Bomber Company has its origins in the early 1940s in Texas with two fishing buddies and the proverbial "better idea". Ike Walker and C.S. "Turby" Turbeville wanted a plug to dive deeper than those commercially available at the time. They began by modifying and changing the diving lip on a Creek Chub Bait Company #300 CRAW DAD. From these early experiments came the very first "Bombers"; so named because of someone remarking that they looked like bombs.

The evolutionary history of the Bombers is interesting, but is also an important method of dating the lures so the history will be presented by years of change.

A few other wooden Bomber Bait Company lures will be covered after the Bombers.

1942-1943
Made for Personal Use
Collector value range: $40-$60.

Just about every part except the hooks was fashioned by hand from materials they could scrounge up locally. The bodies were turned on a hand lathe. To protect the edges of the cup from the hook they utilized shoe string eyelets from old shoes, flush mounted around the cup. The lips were fashioned from an old cook stove and the line ties were made out of paper clips and old tobacco tins. They were painted all black by dipping them, hooks and all, in black enamel and hung out to dry. As they dried, the paint would, of course, flow downward to the pointed nose making it particularly vulnerable to chipping.

1944-1946
Hand-made Production Lures
Collector value range: $40-$50.

When the new, small company went into business they had to find a dependable source of the right kind of wood for the large number of lures they were to produce. Old white cedar utility poles from the local company were just the ticket. The lures were still hand-turned on a lathe, but they began to make the diving lips on a hand-operated punch. This made the metal lips uniform. The lures were made with and without painted eyes (black pupil on a yellow iris) and a few were even made with glass eyes. The latter were deemed too much trouble and too expensive to produce so the glass eyes were abandoned. It is because of this, that there are not many around. They applied for a patent during this time although it was not granted until 1947. The lures were made in three sizes, 2-1/2", 2-3/4" and 3-1/8" (sizes approximate). They began to make color finishes available during this period and the final list was of 14 listed here: White, white with black shadow strip, black, pearl, gray scale, white with red tail, red head, frog, green perch, yellow with black ribs, white with black ribs, red scale, yellow scale, black with white ribs.

1946-1947
Formal Organization of the Company
Collector value range: $30-$40.

There are a couple of significant developments that took place when they formally organized as a legal corporation. For some reason they began making the lures exclusively without eyes. This was also the first use of a commercially available line tie, the "LUXON". That name was stamped on each line tie. They also added three new colors to those available: White with silver scale, black with silver flakes, rainbow.

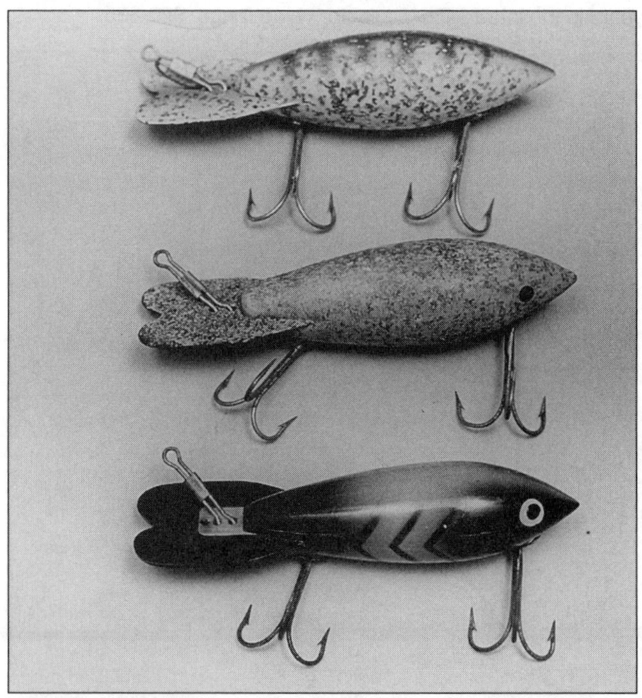

The three BOMBERS in this photo represent the transition from early to plastic, top to bottom. They each measure 3-1/8" to 31/4"' body and 4-1/4"to 4-1/2" overall. Note the metal reinforcing inserts in the plastic (lower) Bomber. Note also the change in body shape discussed in the text.

1947-1949
A Transition Era
Collector value range: $20-$30.

Several changes came about in this period. The first lures during this transition were essentially the same as those produced in the previous period except that they put the painted eyes back on the BOMBERS.

Other changes taking place were the replacement of the flush mount, eyelet style cup protector with the more familiar and conventional rimmed cup and screw eye hook hardware and the modification of the diving lips. Up until this transition period the center gap on the leading edge of the metal lips was what is referred to as the "wide gap". During this period the gap narrowed up. The difference is obvious in the next photo.

This is an example of a transition period BOMBER and the box. Note the gap at the center of the leading edge of the diving lip collectors refer to as the "Wide Gap". It changed to the "Narrow Gap" during this period so both versions can be found. Two more colors were added: (1) shad finish and (2) yellow with silver flakes, making the total 19. Two more, smaller, sizes were added to the line.

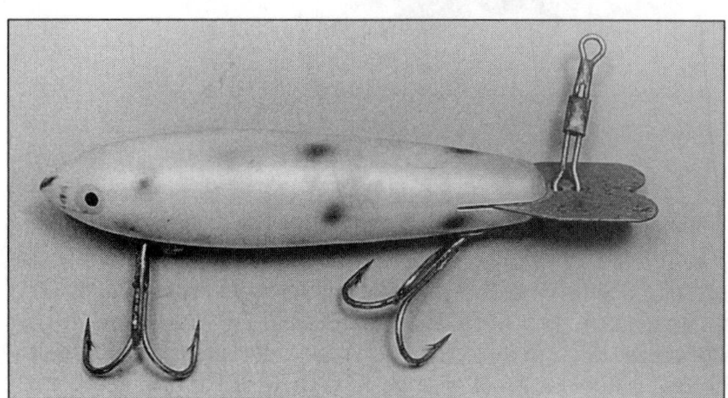

This is an unusual, probably prototype, very large (4", 5" overall) pearl finish BOMBER. Note that the sleeve and wire of the line tie has been soldered. It sports the strong "L-rig" hook hangers and orange and black painted eye.

1949
The Plastic Bomber
Collector value range: $5-$15.

The new plastic Bomber was introduced for 1949, but the wooden versions were still available. The shape of the new lure reflected a major change. If you look at the side profile of the 1949 plastic lure it is shaped with the fatter portion of the body forward of the center, unlike the more symmetrical shape of the previous wood versions.

This first plastic Bomber proved to be a "bomb", and was only in production for less than one year. The 1949 plastic Bombers are easily identified by the integral plastic diving lip with the metal reinforced insert with a "LUXON" marked line tie and the molded in "pressed" eye indent with a centered pupil. The plastic Bomber was not to reappear until about 1971 when it replaced the wood version permanently.

1950-1971
The Last Wooden Year
Collector value range: $15-$20.

Coincidental with the dramatic change in BOMBER shape in the 1949 plastic version came the same change in the wooden ones that continued in production. Sometimes called the "Fatter Forward" or "Weight Forward" version this had disappeared by the late 1950s and the older, more familiar form was back. Before the "Fatter Forward" shape disappeared, however, there was a large (approximately 4-3/4") and strong, heavy-duty version developed that utilized "L-rig" hook hanger hardware and a "LUXON" marked line tie. It was developed for saltwater use.

OTHER WOODEN LURES BY THE BOMBER BAIT COMPANY

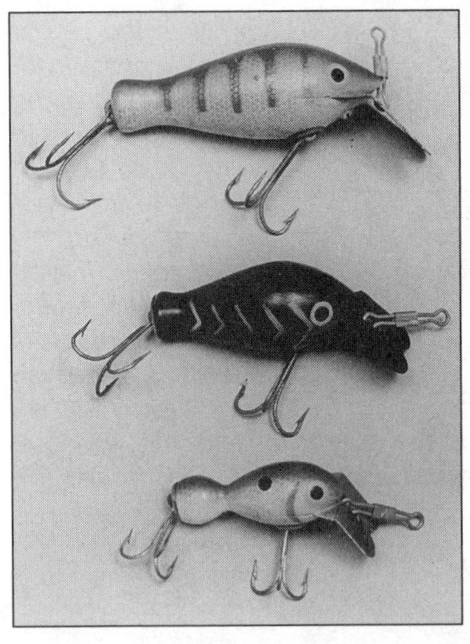

The upper lure represents the smaller (2-3/4") size of the two sizes the BOMBERETTE was supposedly available in. The middle one measures 2" and is not found cataloged. The bottom lure is the MIDGET BOMBERETTE measuring 1-5/8".

BOMBERETTE
MIDGET BOMBERETTE

These two were introduced into the line around 1948. The BOMBERETTE was supposed to be available in only two sizes, 2-3/4" and 3-1/4", but they are known to appear in more sizes (see above photo). The MIDGET BOMBERETTE was made in one size only, 1-5/8". The lures can only be dated pre or post 1950 by the use of the "LUXON" line tie. The BOMBERETTE is the forerunner of the company's famous MODEL A. It was only made for about four years, but the MIDGET BOMBERETTE was available at least into the 1960s. Collector value range for BOMBERETTES: $5-$10, for early MIDGET BOMBERETTES: $10-$15.

JERK

These lures were introduced into the line in 1953 and continued in constant production until the present time. It is interesting to note that the lure was described as "new" in the 1971 catalog. The catalog description went on to describe it as ". . a wooden body encased in durable plastic." One can only guess that the "new" referred to the use of plastic as a covering. 1971-72 marks the end of the Bomber Bait Company wooden era. From the very beginning these lures were strongly rigged for salt water use. All utilized the "L-rig" hook hanger. Collector value range: $5-$10.

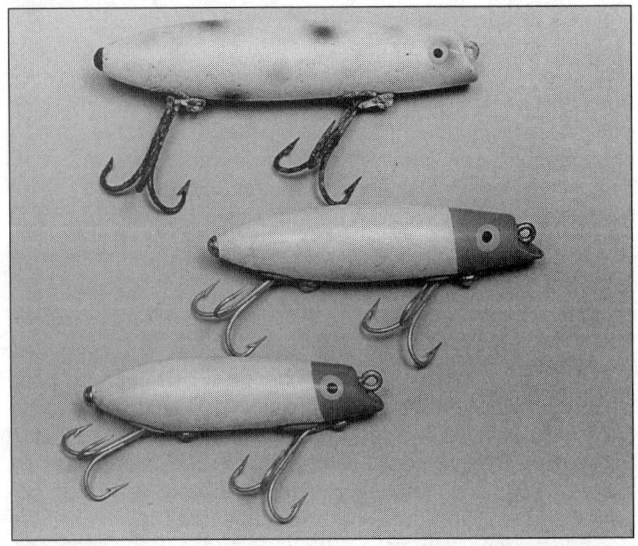

These three JERKS represent the three sizes available, 3, 3-1/2", and 4-1/8" respectively.

KNOT HEAD

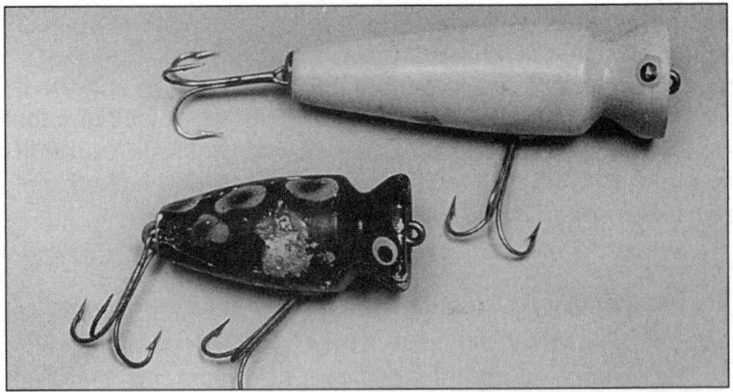

These two KNOT HEADS measure 2-1/8" and 3-1/4" respectively.

KNOT HEADS were cataloged in two sizes, 2-1/4" and 3-1/4", but there is a 4" size known to exist. The heads are concave at the face and the ones in the above photo both sport cup and screw eye hook hardware. KNOT HEADS were offered only about two years in the late 1940s. Collector value range: $20-$25.

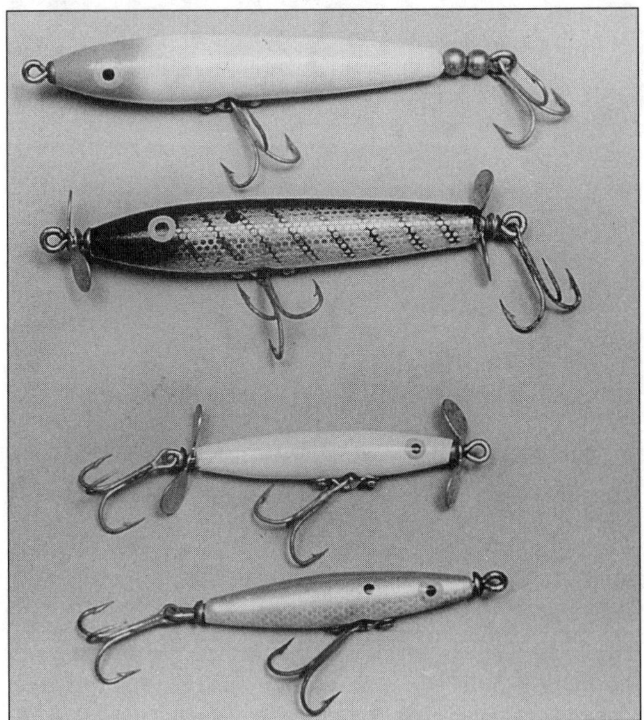

The upper lure is a 3-1/2" STICK. Immediately under is a 3-1/2" SPIN STICK. The third is the 2-1/4" size of the SPIN STICK and the bottom lure appears to be a SPIN STICK with a floppy prop spinners removed.

STICK AND SPIN STICK

Both lures were introduced in the mid-1950s and continued in production thereafter. As far as can be determined they have had the one-piece surface hook hangers since day one. There is the existence of what may be a prototype STICK, 3-7/8" long and sporting cup and screw eye hook hangers. It has two belly trebles instead of the normal configuration of one belly treble. Collector value range: $5-$10.

Collectors should be aware that there is a contemporary wood version of this lure, but it shouldn't make much difference as the SPIN STICK remained in production until it was discontinued in 1989. The new one was made in 1997. It was commissioned by Bass Anglers Sportsman Society (B.A.S.S.) in

TOP BOMBER

Two sizes of TOP BOMBERS measuring 2-3/8" and 3-1/8" respectively.

commemoration of the 30th anniversary of the first bass tournament organized by Ray Scott, founder of B.A.S.S. Stan Sloan won using this lure in a coach dog finish. A brochure accompanying the lure states, in part: "...is virtually indistinguishable from its predecessor."

WATER DOG

This lure was introduced in 1954 and continued into the plastic era beginning around 1971-72. They were made in the three sizes listed with the above photo. Collector value range $4-$8.

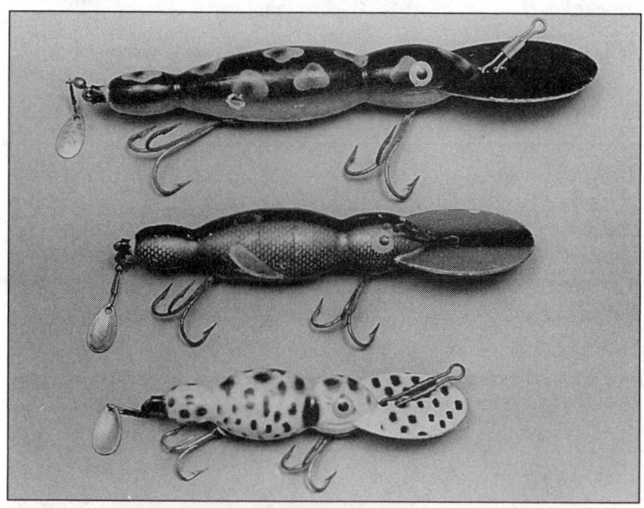

Three sizes of WATER DOGS measuring 4, 5-1/2" OA; 3-1/2", 4-5/8" OA; 2-1/4", 3-1/4" OA respectively.

Belly view of a 3-1/4" WATER DOG showing hook hardware. Photo courtesy Ken Bernoteit

This lure was made in two basic sizes in the early to mid 1950s for approximately three years. As inferred by its name it was a top-water lure. The tail propeller spinner was to kick up a fuss like an injured minnow. Collector value range: $15-$20.

BONAFIDE ALUMINUM MINNOW

Bonafide Manufacturing Company — Plymouth, Michigan

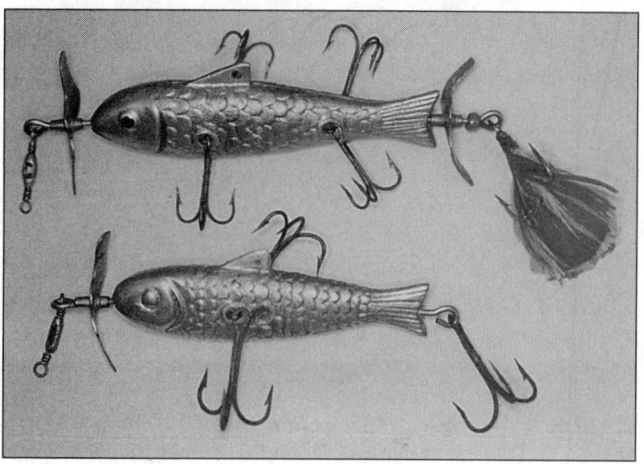

Patented in 1907 by Hiram H. Passage this little gem was available in two sizes: a 3-3/4" 5-hooker and a 3-1/4" 3-hooker as in the above photo. It is made in two halves of cast aluminum held together by a screw about mid-body. It is not solid but hollow, allowing the fisherman to make it a floater or adjust buoyancy by adding water or other interior weight. Note that there is a hole through the dorsal fin. This is to allow the lure to be used as an ice fishing decoy. The lures are rare. Collector value range is as follows: 3-hooker $800-$1,000.; 5-hooker $1,000-$1,500. Photo courtesy Clarence Zahn.

BONNER CASTING MINNOW

Leo Albert Bonner — Okeechobee, Florida

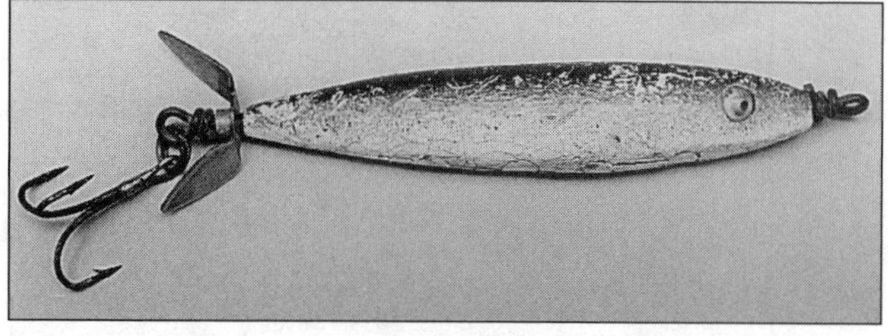

This c.1931 Florida lure looks very much like the SOUTH COAST MINNOW. There are so many of these coast minnow types, it's hard to know which came first. In any case, this lure is extremely well built and strong; obviously for salt water use. It has glass eyes, four internal belly weights and a twisted, through-body line tie/tail hook hanger. It measures 4" long. There are probably few to be found as it was the product of one man. It is thought that they were sold only by Bonner and through a bait shop in the town of Okeechobee. Insufficient trade data to determine collector value.

BOSHEARS TACKLE COMPANY

Little Rock, Arkansas

These are four very well made, very heavy plastic lures. They each measure 2-1/8" and the metal lips are attached to the body with screws. The hook hardware is cup and screw

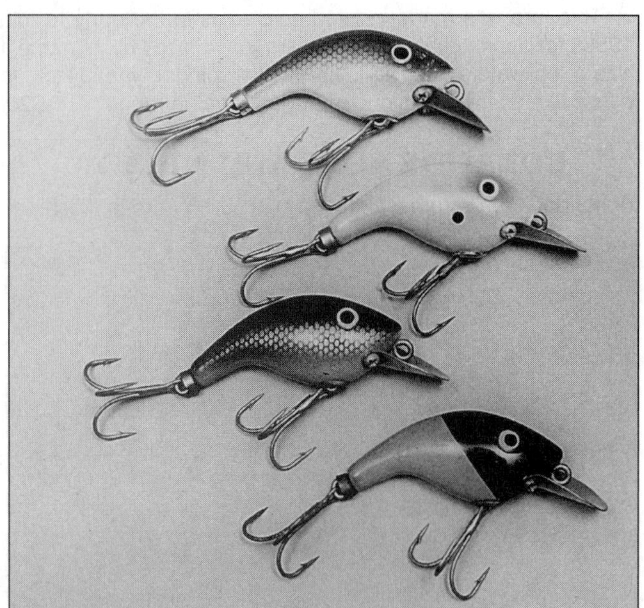

eye. The original boxes they were in called the lure a RAZZLE DAZZLE. This short-lived company was owned by brothers Raymond and Herman Boshears. The company was small, the work force largely made up of the brothers and their families. These high quality plastic lures were made for only two years, 1949-50. Collector value range: $10-$18.

BRAINARD BAIT COMPANY

St. Paul, Minnesota

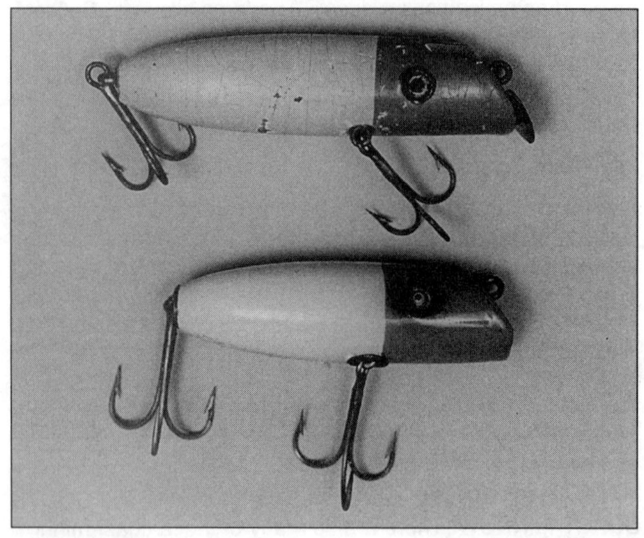

The lures in this photo are GOLD CUP DODGERS. The upper plug measures 3-3/8", has glass eyes and a screw eye only, belly hook hanger. The lower one is 2-7/8" long with yellow glass eyes and a cup and screw eye belly hook hanger. It also has a different design metal head plate. Collector value range: $75-$150.

This photo illustrates an interesting historical aside. It seems that everybody was watching everybody, with some even physically checking out the competition's products. The upper lure in the previous photo came from the Pflueger factory with this tag attached. Not only did they obtain a competitor's lure for examination, but they actually tested it. The flip side of the tag indicated that the test took place five days after obtaining it. It bears the notation "poor action. Bait turns over." It is initialed and dated by the tester and three witnesses.

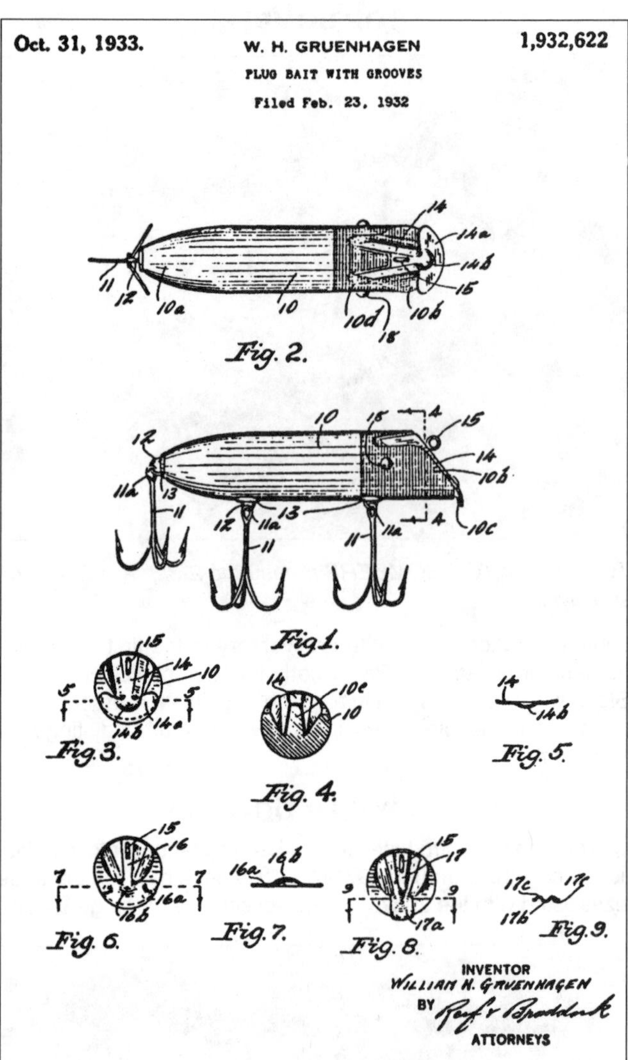

This patent illustration shows two possible designs of the metal plane (see Fig. 6 and Fig. 8). That might explain the different planes on the preceding lures. The patent was granted to William H. Gruenhagen of St. Paul on October 31, 1933, but it was filed in February, 1932 so we can date it as early as that. It was likely in full production a good bit earlier than that.

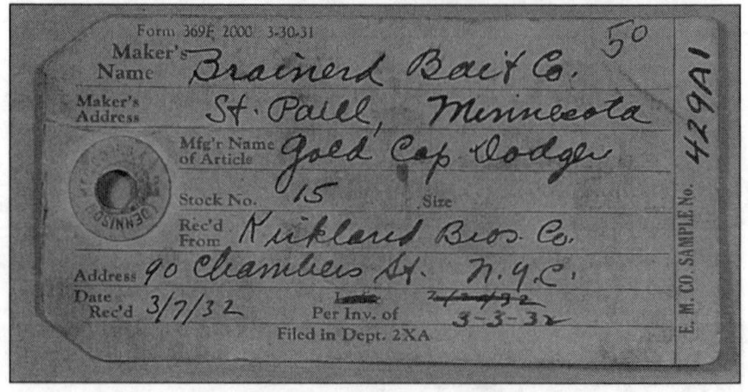

Form 369F 2000 3-30-31 50
Maker's Name Brainerd Bait Co.
Maker's Address St. Paul, Minnesota
Mfg'r Name of Article Gold Cap Dodger
Stock No. 15 Size
Rec'd From Kirkland Bros. Co.
Address 90 Chambers St. N.Y.C.
Date Rec'd 3/7/32 Per Inv. of 3-3-32
Filed in Dept. 2XA
E. M. CO. SAMPLE No. 429A1

THE DOCTOR

This 4-3/8" metal spoon by Brainard is marked "DOCTOR" and "10,000 LAKES ST. PAUL". The box it came in states "The Big 'Doc' No. 285". This is an indication that there may have been other sizes made. The spoon has a pearlized finish and trails a brass treble hook. The company was in operation in the early 1930s. Collector value range: $10-$15.

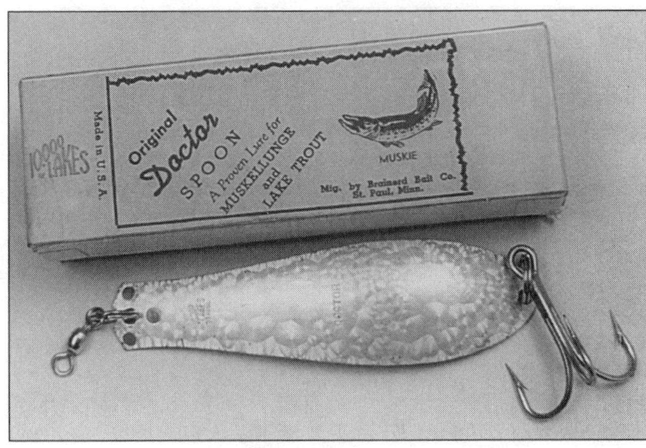

BRIGHT-EYE-LURE

Bright-Eye-Lure Products — Detroit, Michigan

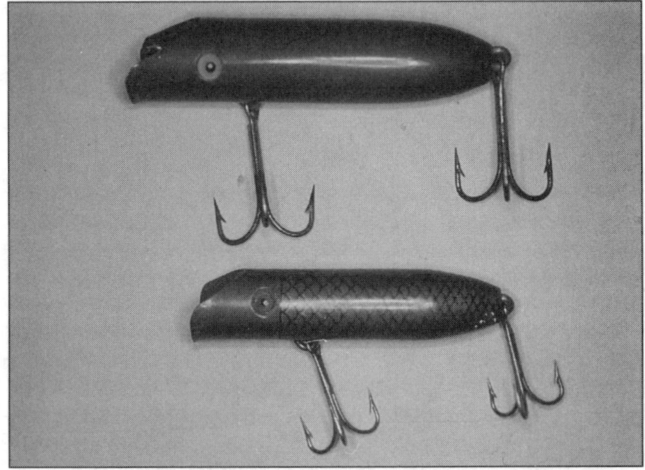

These lures are unique and are also difficult to find. Their construction is what makes them so unusual. They are made of an aluminum shell around a wooden core. There are holes in the outer shell to accommodate the glass eyes so that they may be mounted in the wood portion of the body. The two in the above photo measure 2-3/4" and 3-1/4" respectively. There is a third size, 4-1/4", also known to exist. They are thought to date around 1933, but little else is presently known. Collector value range: $50-$75.

BROADCASTER LURES

Youngstown, Ohio

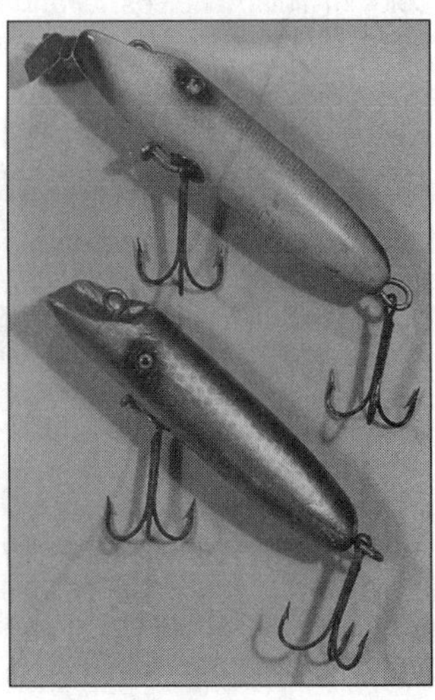

This plug, called the 4-IN-1 BROADCASTER, came along around 1933. A 1933 advertisement called it new in the text. The nose plane was adjustable so that the fisherman could change the lure into a deep diver, a wiggler, a darter or a surface teaser. Note that the metal plane is missing on the lower lure in the photo. The ones in the photo measure 3-1/2", but they also offered one in a 4-1/2". Most are easily identifiable by the unusual nose plane and the peculiar belly hook hardware that makes hook exchange or replacement handy and the stamped or stenciled "4-IN-1 BROADCASTER" on the belly. The latter may or may not be readily discernible. The eyes are yellow glass. The color patterns offered are not known. Collector value range: $50-$100.

BROOK'S BAITS
R-Jay Industries, Inc.

234 Portage Trail — Cuyahoga Falls, Ohio

BROOK'S BAITS
Division of Harrison Industries, Inc.

250 Passaic Street — Newark, New Jersey

A thorough search of the old catalogs and ads have turned up only five dated short references to Brook's Baits. The earliest was a catalog thought to be dated somewhere around 1947-50, and the latest was found in *The Fisherman's Handbook For 1954*. The 1954 ad was the only one carrying the first address above. The latest reference found was a pocket catalog or box flyer that talked about a lure being used to win the "Texas Eliminations of World Series of Fishing, Sept. 1962." This is where the second address above came from. The two companies would have been considered unrelated except for the appearance of several of the same lures as the earlier Brooks company. Perhaps Harrison Industries bought Brooks out and continued to offer a portion of the line. There were several lures from other companies in the little catalog.

The 1954 advertisement listed 15 lures as available. As far as I can determine, all Brook's lures were molded of Tenite (plastic) or made of metal. Considerable help came when NFLCC member and Brooks collector Dave Burns generously shared his knowledge and a 1950s pocket catalog from the company. It illustrated 18 baits, six of which were all metal spinners or jigs that would be almost impossible to identify unless found in Brooks boxes or on cards. One of the ads I uncovered named some other as yet unfound Brook's lures and this one is likely to be one of them. They are: BROOK'S STUD SPINNER,BROOK'S JUMPER SPINNER,BROOK'S 1/4 OZ. STRIPER JIG,BROOK'S PORK POD,BROOK'S NYLON LEADER (Bait)

The list is worded exactly as it was printed in the advertisement. In addition to those five there was also a BUZZER, that may have made a buzzing sound on retrieve, and a RANGER in two sizes.

BROOK'S No. 5 TOP WATER

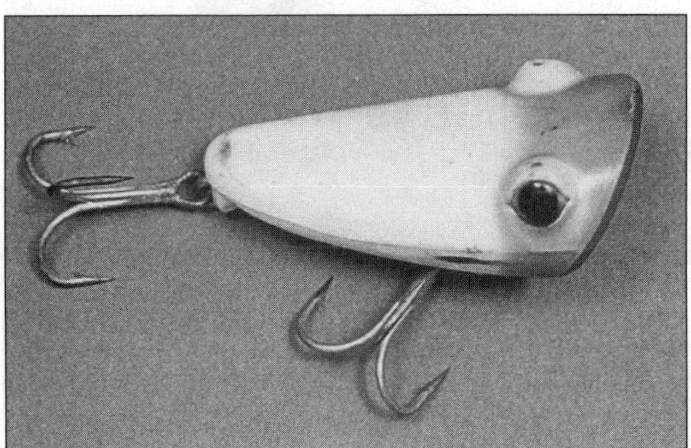

This is a 1/2-ounce popper type plug with concave mouth and bulging eyes. It is illustrated with a belly treble and a under-tail treble hook. It has been reported that it was available with single hooks as well. That is probably the very small llow, frog, scale, black. Collector value range: $5-$8.

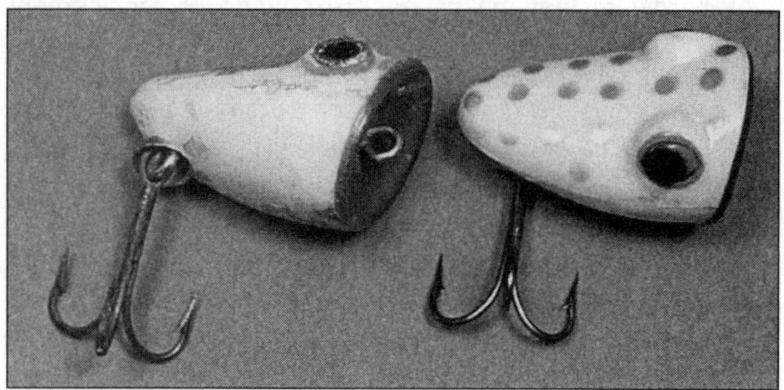

These are two Brooks No. SP-5 spinning size BABY TOPWATERS. Collector value range: N.A.

BROOK'S JOINTED TOP WATER

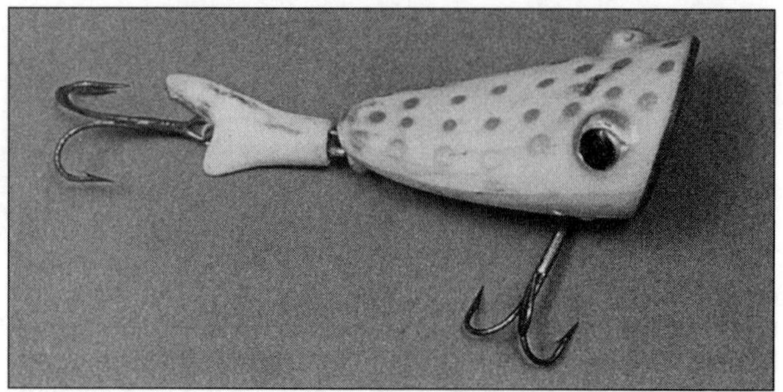

References turned up the following: Brook's JOINTED TOP WATER, JTW Series; BABY JOINTED TOP WATER also available. They came in four colors or finishes. They are: Red head, yellow, frog and black. Collector value range: $5-10.

BROOK'S DOUBLE O AND BROOK'S JOINTED DOUBLE O

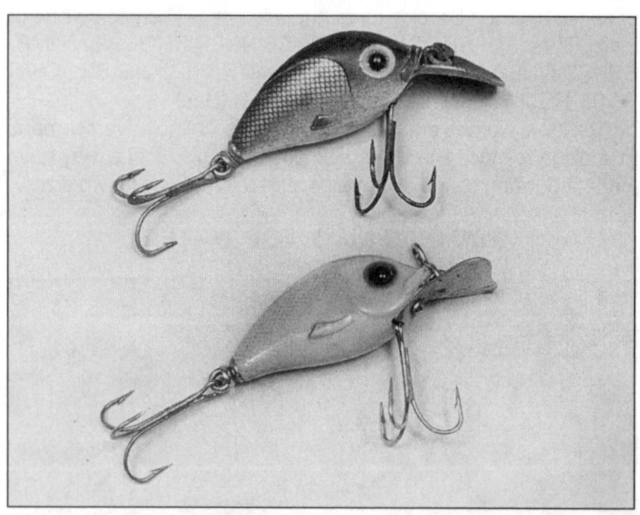

These lures had a spoon type lip blade and a short wire leader attached to the nose-mounted line tie. Each has a treble hook beneath the nose and another one trailing. Both weight 1/2 ounce and the jointed model (photo at left) has a tail-fin shaped second section.

Collector value range: $5-$10.

CATALOG SERIES	BODY LENGTH	LURE WEIGHT
00	2-1/2"	1/2 oz.
J-00	3-1/3"	1/2 oz.

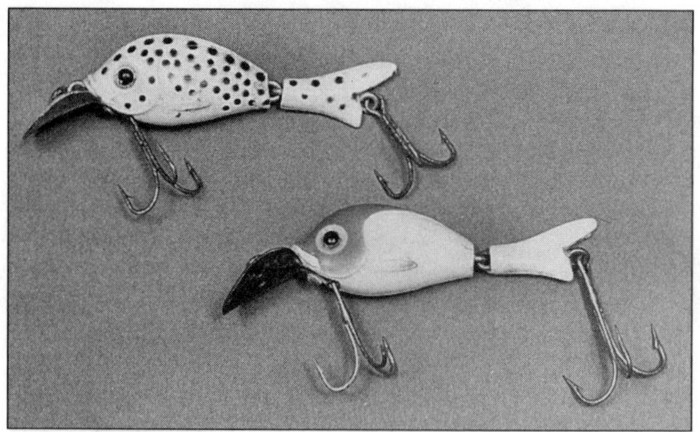

Note the two different lip styles on these DOUBLE O's and jointed DOUBLE O's.

COLOR OR FINISH: Red head, black scale, yellow shad, shiner, perch; pearl, black dotted.

BROOK'S No. 6 REEFERS

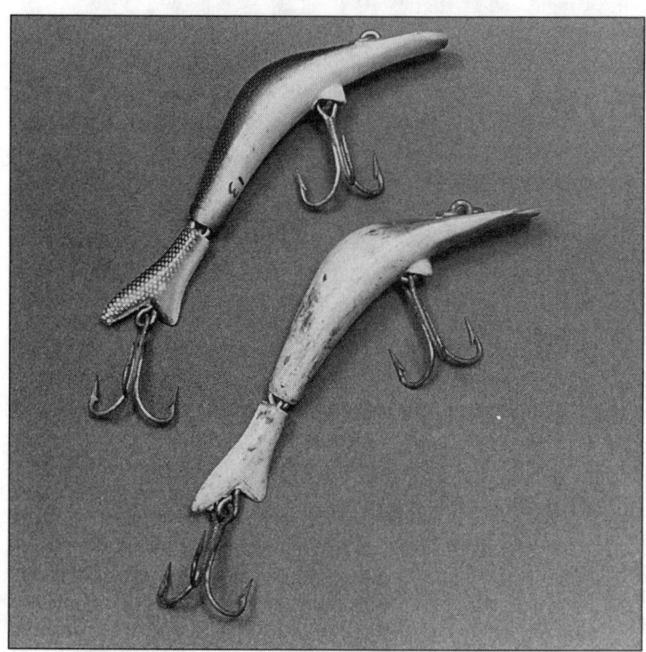

There are four types of Reefers found: The Unjointed REEFER at 3", BABY REEFER at 2-1/4", the JOINTED REEFER at 4" and BABY JOINTED REEFER. Each was available in seven color or finish choices: Orange, yellow, frog, shiner, perch, red head, black and white. Collector value range: $5-10.

BROOK'S JOINTED DIGGER

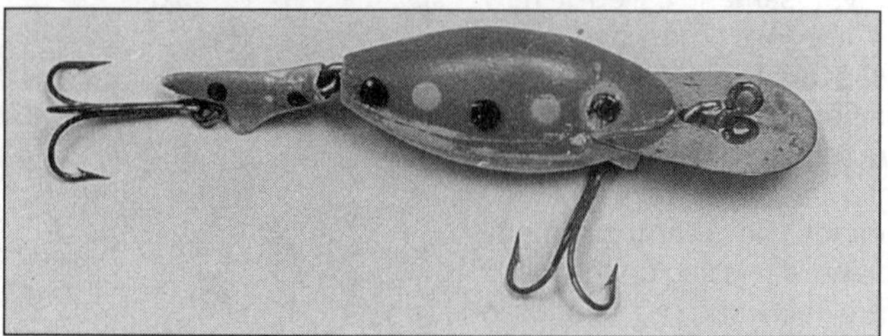

Identified in literature as Brook's Jointed DIGGER, JO Series, 1/2 oz. Eight colors or finishes found: Red head, black scale, yellow, shad, shiner, perch, pearl and black dotted. Collector value range: $4-$7.

BROOK'S No. 4 WEEDLESS

This lure has a tail-mounted single hook molded into the body during production. The hook is covered with a flexible rubber skirt and a wire weed guard extending back from the nose. There is a wire leader that has a single blade spinner mounted on it. Collector value range: $4-$6.

CATALOG SERIES #	BODY LENGTH	LURE WEIGHT
400	1-3/4"	5/8 oz.

COLOR OR FINISH: Red head, black scale, yellow, frog, shiner, perch.

BROOK'S No. 7 WEEDLESS

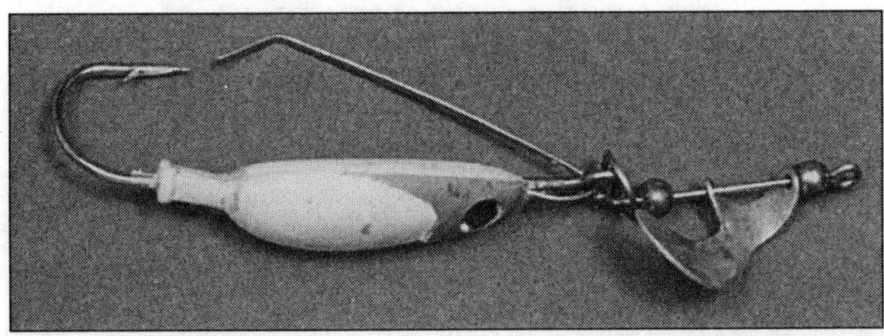

This essentially the same lure as the Brook's No. 4 except smaller and lighter (1/2 ounce). It was made in the same six colors. Collector value range: $3-$6.

BROOKS FLUTTERTAIL SPOON

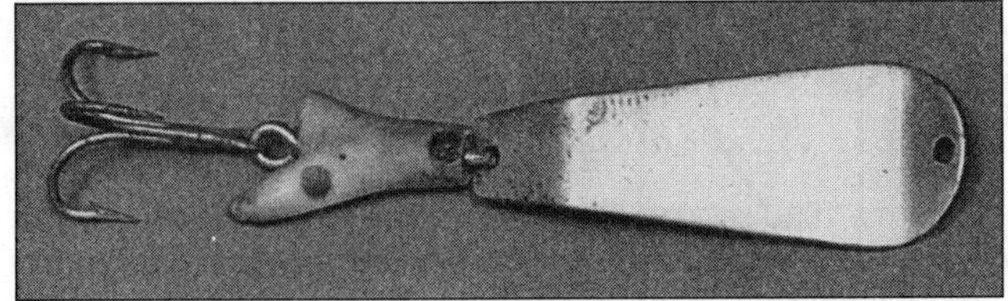

This nickel metal flasher body lure has the same type of plastic tail as the jointed TOP WATERS. It was made in three sizes: 1/4 oz., 3/8 oz. And 1/2 oz. Collector value range $00-00.

BROOK SHINER BAIT COMPANY

Milwaukee, Wisconsin

One 1926 advertisement was found. The ad inferred these were the only two lures they made. Called new they were available in two sizes, "LARGE" and "SMALL." The ones in the photo measure 3-1/2" and 4" respectively. The have aluminum-colored bodies and red heads. The "adjusting tongue and tail will make the baits shimmy, wiggle, dart or imitate a shiner in fear and distress." Collector value: $150-$200.. Photo courtesy Jim Muma.

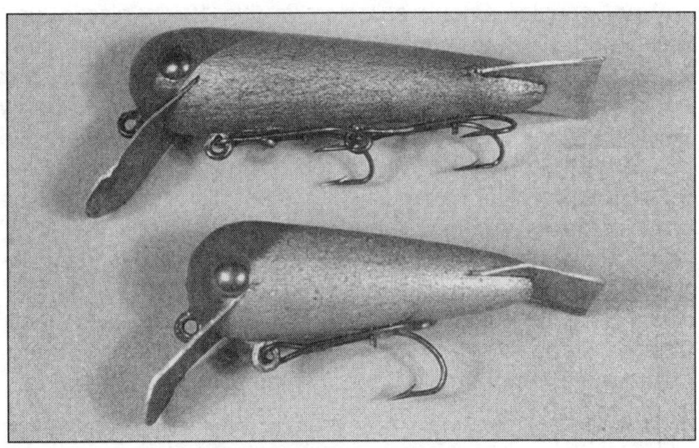

VIBRA BAT SONIC LURE

Harrison Industries — Newark, New Jersey

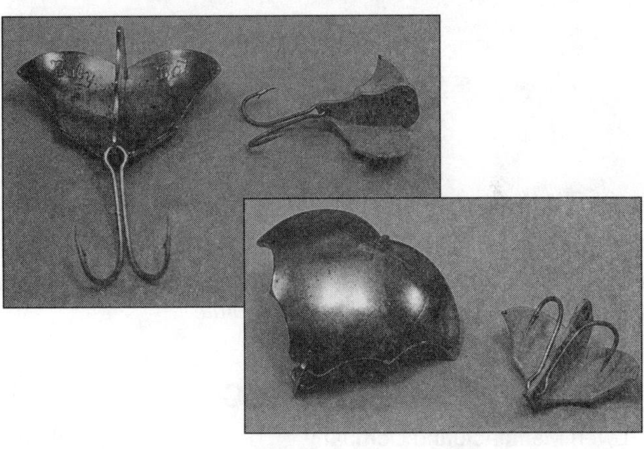

These all-metal lures are made so the double hooks could be stored in a manner rendering them safe and tangle-free. The larger one has the words "Baby Bat" stamped under the wings and "PAT PEND" on the body. It measures 2-13/16" x 1-1/4". The smaller one measures 1-1/8" x 7/8" and is painted yellow. The only listing and illustration found was in a post 1962 catalog of Brook's Baits. It was called a VIBRA BAT there and described it as a "Sonic Lure,' that, "Vibrates up to 200 times a minute! Sends out sound waves that drive fish frantic!" Colors listed were nickel, brass, orange, yellow, and black. No other catalog information was found. Collector value range: No trade data found.

BUG-N-BASS

Buckeye Bait Corporation — Council Bluff, Kansas

Very popular among collectors is this 1960s plastic lure. Measuring 3-1/2", there is a slit on the right side of the body where the double wire line tie holding the fly out front can be slid back. The only reason for it seems to be for storage of the fly while in the box or, perhaps, to protect the fly while in the tackle box. There are 16 finishes to be found. Four were added to the list of 12 below just before Buckeye went out of business. See photo of four lures below. There were two sizes made: the 3-3/8" and a smaller 2-1/2" spinning size. Collector value range: $20-$30, with the spinning size being a little more.

Finishes for the BUG-N-BASS: large mouth, sand bass, bluefish, rainbow trout, brown trout, perch, white coach dog, black with silver rib, mullet, shad, crappie, yellow coach dog.

The three red-headed baits and the black lure are four additional colors that were released just before the company went out of business. Photo courtesy Jim Muma.

BUMBLEBUG

Gowen Manufacturing Company Gowen, Michigan

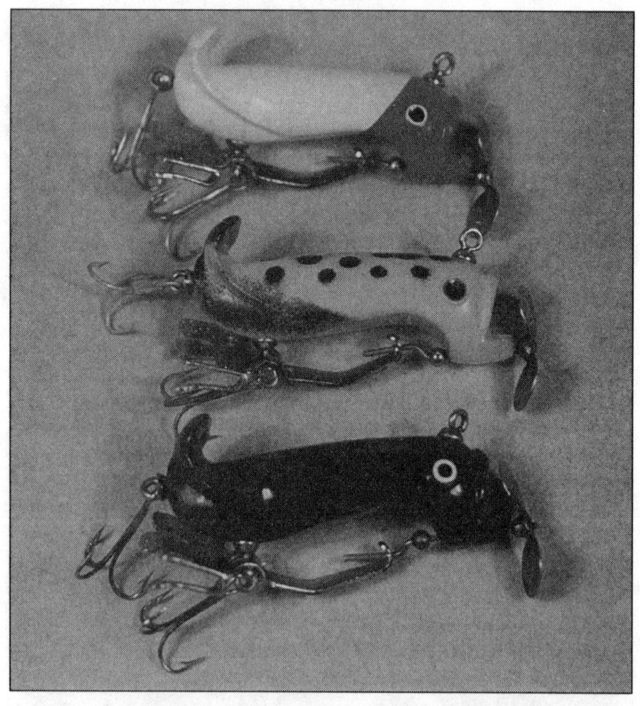

Measuring 2-1/2", this plastic lure is probably from the 1950s-1960s. It has a propeller driven mechanism that causes the metal under belly/tail assembly to move up and down on retrieve. Collector value range: $10-$15.

COLOR OR FINISH: Black, gold, silver, white with red head, white with black head, frog.

PAUL BUNYAN BAIT COMPANY

Minneapolis, Minnesota

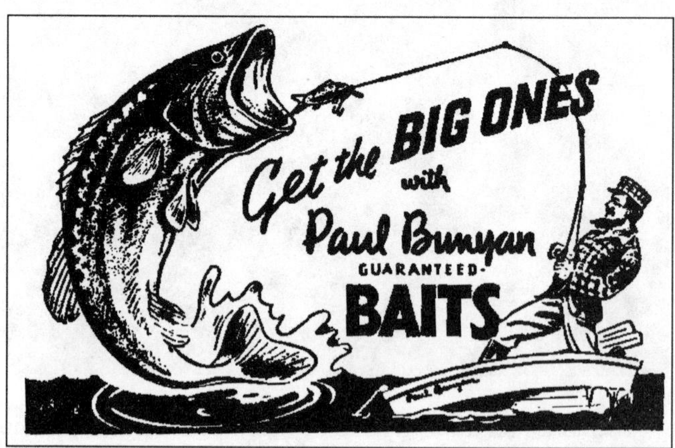

This company made lures in the 1930s, 1940s and 1950s. I found a patent for the MINNOW below that was filed in 1938 and granted to a Karl R. Larson of Minneapolis so we at least have a name attached to the company finally. The last advertisement found in fishing magazines was in 1952. Little else is known presently concerning details of its existence. They manufactured and marketed several collectible plastic plugs, some wooden lures, and some metal spoon or spinner types. It is known that they purchased the patents from the Bates Baits company when the latter ceased operations in 1938.

DOUBLE ACTION TWIRL BUG

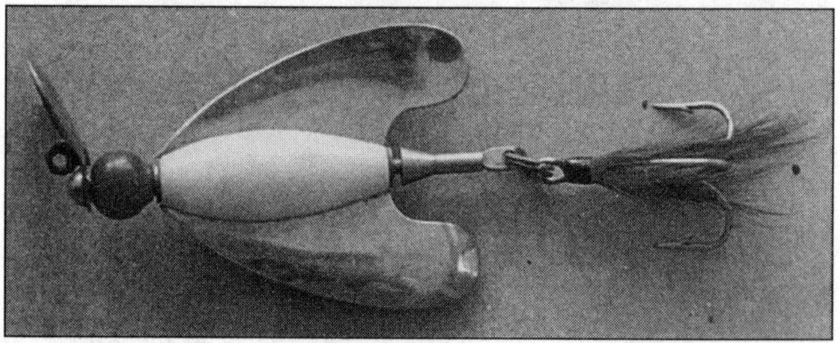

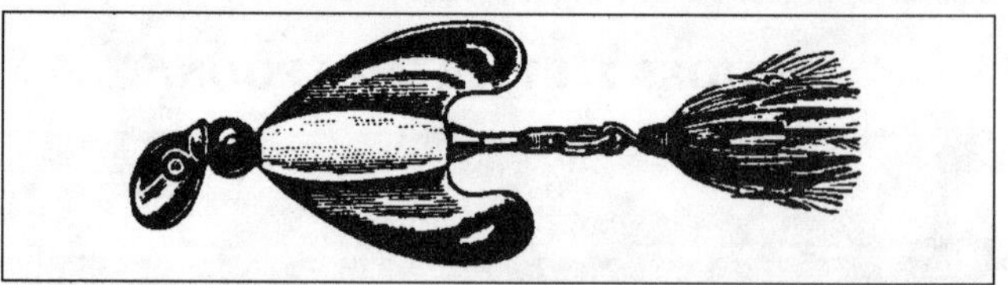

From a 1940 catalog: "This bait has a white body with nickel or copper wings which revolve on machine screw bearings." It has a red head with a scoop "...which causes the bait to wobble and dive and the wings to spin...practically weedless. Split ring attachments make it easy to put on any hook." The wings were available in either Nickel or Copper. The lure measures 3" without the bucktail. Photo courtesy Jim Muma. Collector value range: $35-$50.

TWIRL BUG WIGGLER

There is no illustration here because this lure is very similar in appearance to the DOUBLE ACTION TWIRLBUG above. The body is white and the head red, but the wings are made of celluloid. The wings are finished in either red, gold or silver. It has a spinner at the head. It spins fast in one direction while the body spins slowly in the opposite direction. It also has the split ring hook attachment and measures 3" without the bucktail. Collector value range: $25-$50.

FLOATING WEAVER

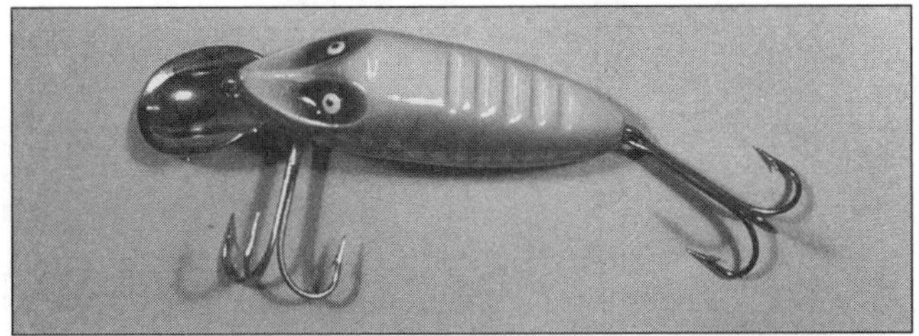

This plug had a series of grooves across the back of the body, a more or less flat belly and metal diving blade mounted under the nose. It sported one treble hook on the belly. The lure was 2-3/4" and weighed 3/8 ounce. Colors available were: White, pike scale, silver or yellow. The lure body was apparently slightly re-designed later without the flat belly. Collector value range: $25-$35.

TRANSPARENT DODGER (No. 900) AND ARTFUL DODGER (No. 2100)

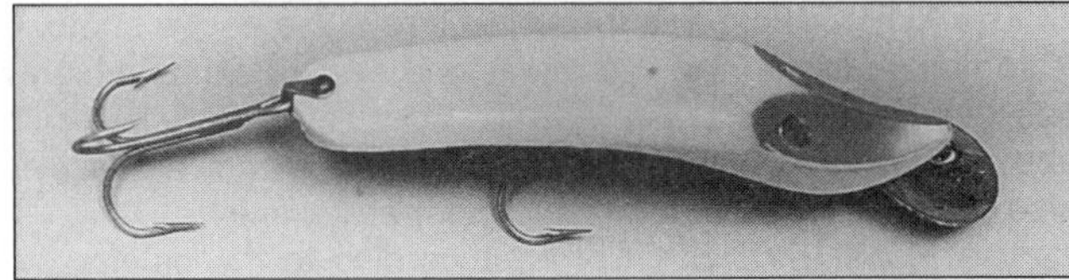

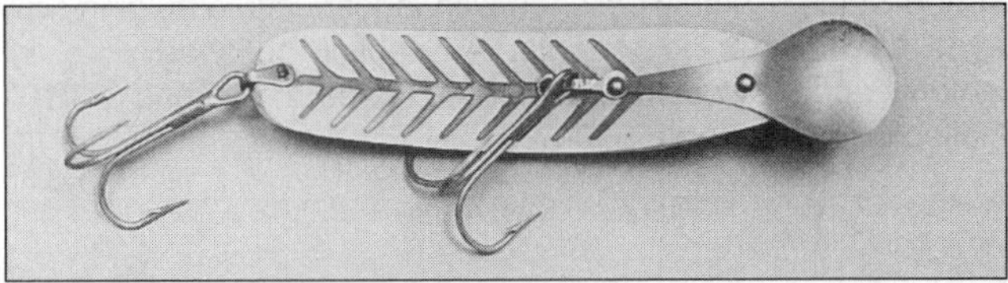

Top and belly views of the white body, red head TRANSPARENT DODGER. It measures 3-3/4". This one and the black version are not transparent as are the six other patterns.

The two sizes this plastic lure was available in were the #900, 4", and the #2100, fly-rod-size 1-1/4". The little fly-rod-size, the ARTFUL DODGER, has rhinestone eyes. Colors available were transparent clear, ruby, amber, blue and green. Each of these have a yellow face, a red nose and ribs on the belly as in the photograph. There is also: solid black with violet ribs, face and a red nose; opaque white with red ribs and head. Collector value range: $20-$30.

ELECTRO LURE c. 1938

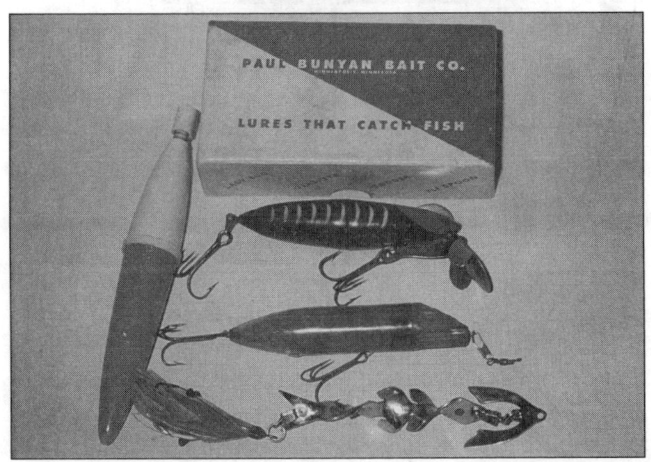

Left: A red and white plastic bobber. Top: A red and white Paul Bunyan box. Center: a 3-3/4" ELECTROLURE, a 4" TRANSLURE and on the bottom, a 4-1/4" CENTIPEDE SPINNER.

Here is another of those battery-powered electric light lures. The hollow plastic body unscrews for access to the battery and bulb. There is a clear plastic piece on top of its head through which the light shines. It had a cumbersome-looking metal diving blade affair. It came in white, green, yellow, or silver. Each of these have a red head. No trade data found to determine value. Photo courtesy Jim Muma.

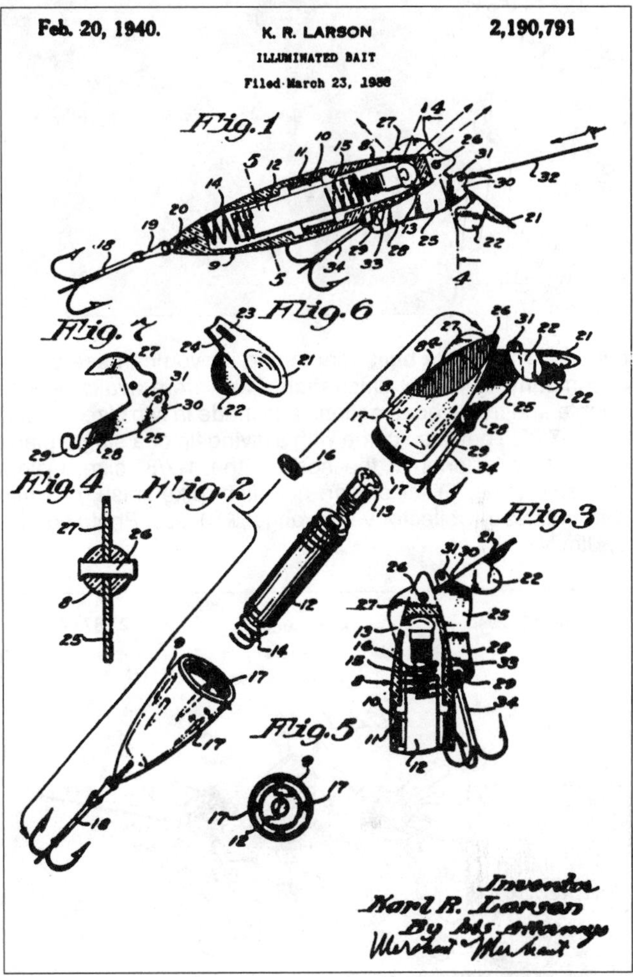

The patent illustration for the Paul Bunyan ELECTROLURE. It was granted to Karl R. Larson. He designed other baits for the company.

CENTIPEDE SPINNER

This handsome spinner has a head that remains motionless while the body spins. The bucktail is attached utilizing a split ring making it easy to replace with another color or any other type hook. It is 4-1/2" long and was made in five different finishes. They are: nickel, copper, white, yellow, perch. Collector value range: $50-$75.

TRANS-LURE

An interesting hollow plastic plug made so that you could place a live minnow inside or, if you preferred, one of twelve color combinations of body and head inserts that came along with the lure. It was made in two sizes, 4" and 1-3/4". Both had a belly treble hook. It is most unlikely the collector will find all the inserts unless lucky enough to find an un-fished lure in the original package. Collector value range: $10-$20.

SILVER SHINER GOLD FISH

Both of these lures were in the same body design. They were made of pyralin with a metal dorsal fin, ventral fins and tail fins. They were built very strong as you can see by the accompanying patent illustration. They were available with double and treble hook options and made in two sizes, 3-5/8" and 1-7/8". They also came with a diving lip or a single-blade spoon type spinner at the nose in the 1-7/8" size. Colors available were: Silver shiner, gold fish, pike finish, or white with red head. Collector value range: $10-$30. Photo courtesy Jim Muma

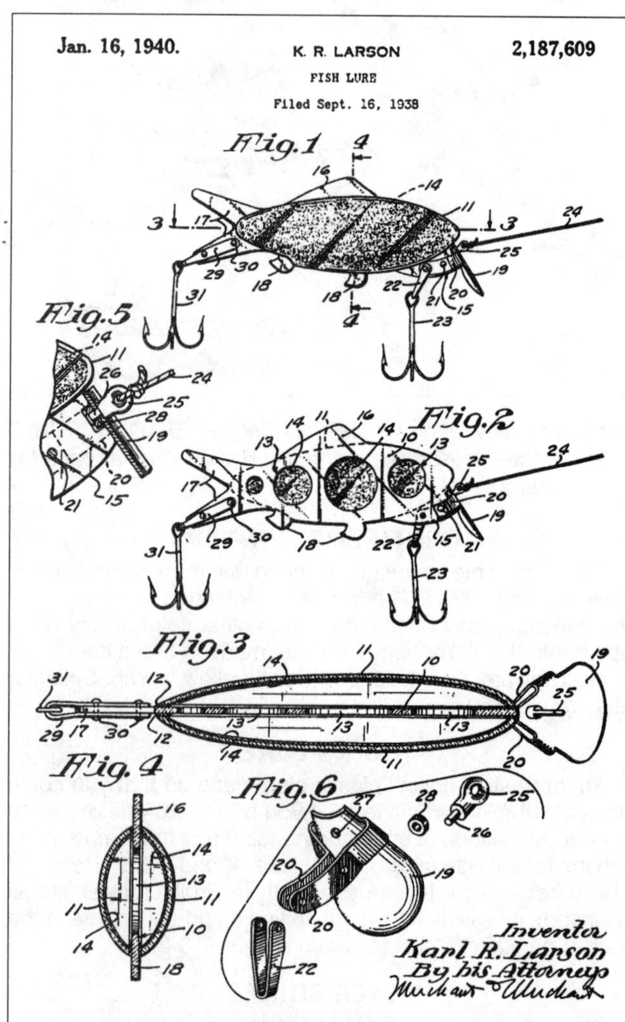

The original patent illustration for the SILVER SHINER and GOLDFISH.

RUBY SPOON AND FLASHEYE SPOON

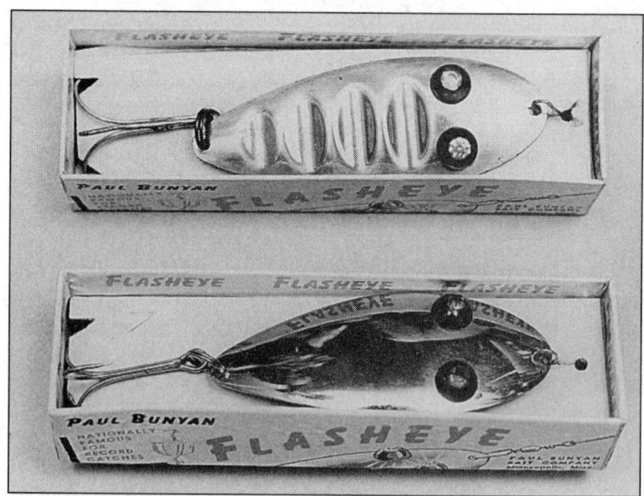

The RUBY SPOON is the upper lure in the above photo. It is so named for its ruby-red rhinestone eyes. It came in highly polished nickel or copper and in two sizes, the 3-1/2" size above and the GIANT RUBY SPOON, a 4-1/2" size that was also available in a combination copper/nickel finish.

The FLASHEYE SPOON is, according to the catalog, "a spoon which is highly polished with indestructible bulging ruby eyes set with flashing brilliants." Available in polished nickel finish only and they could be had in two sizes, 2-3/4" and 3-3/16". Collector value range: $10-$20.

A "66" spinner. Photo courtesy Ken Bernoteit.

PAUL BUNYAN'S 66

An original 66 box in red, black and white. Detailed instructions for using the lure are printed on the bottom.

This is a spinner and fly combination. First offered in eight color combinations in the late 1940s the choice increased to 12 by 1951. None of the colors were ever listed, but the advertising did say they were available with either a "...bright or dark nickel spinner" and in hackle or bucktail. They were available in four sizes. The sizes were not specified, but they were described as trolling, bait casting, spinning and fly rod sizes. A 1951 ad said you could send for a free folder showing all of them in full color. Wouldn't a Bunyan collector love one of those! Collector value range: $10-$15.

LADYBUG

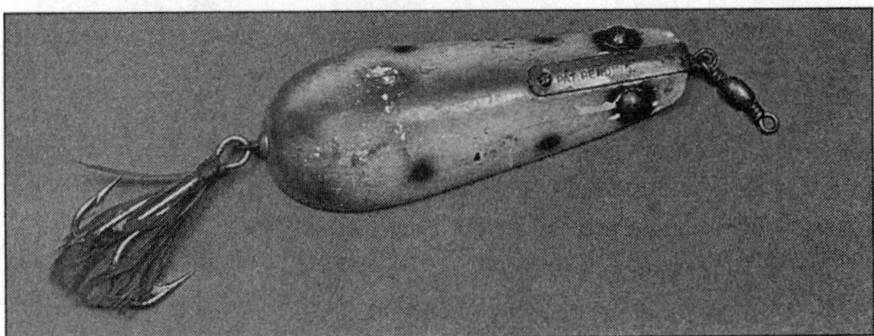

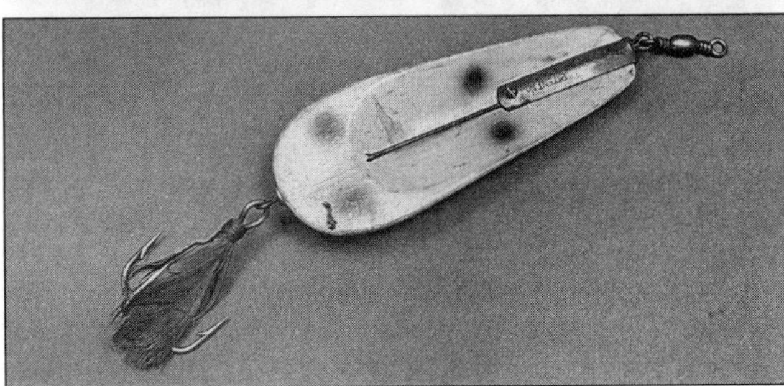

This 2-1/2" Tenite lure came in weedless or diving versions. The weedless lure had a belly double hook and was a reverse running surface plug. The diving version had a trailing treble and ran pointed end first. The body design for each was the same, having a dorsal fin running the entire body length and eyes on each end. It looks a lot like a Lauby Bait. Collector value range: $15-$25.

MINNOW

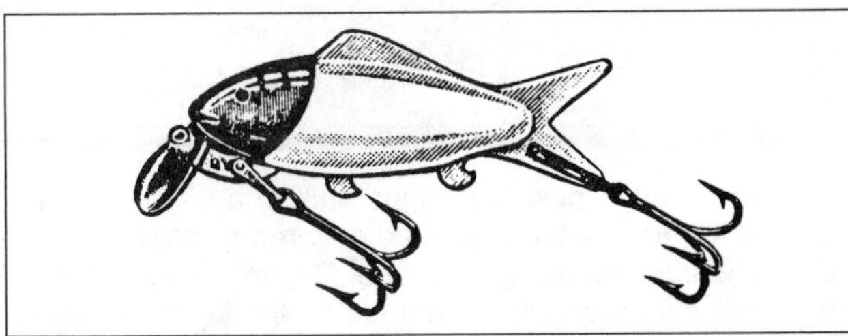

There is an indication in an advertisement that this was a new lure in 1939-40. Indeed, I found a patent that was both filed and granted in 1938. It is a floater with a diving plane. A description from an April 1940 ad in *Sports Afield* reads as follows: "...finished in red head, or in black, perch or pike scale body; length 3-5/8", weight. 9/16 oz." It is also known to have been made in a Silver Shiner finish. Collector value range: $00-00.

IMPORTANT NOTICE

The value ranges listed in this book are for lures in Very Good to Excellent condition. The values of those lures not in Very Good to Excellent condition can and probably will be worth considerably less. The values are meant to be a guide only.

BURKE FLEXO-PRODUCTS

A Division of McClellan Industries, Inc. Traverse City, Michigan

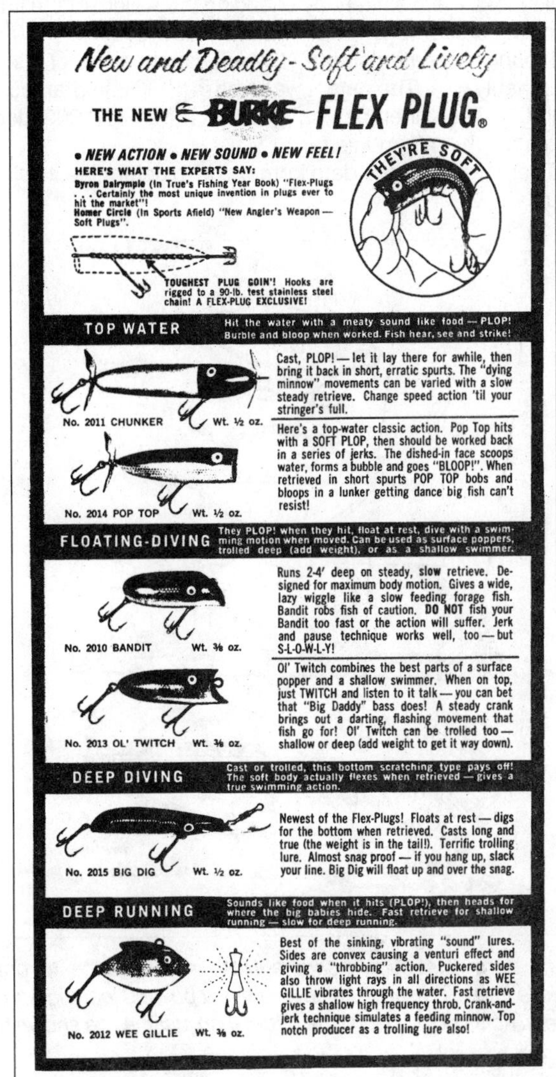

The age of these unique rubber lures is not known. The only clue we have is a pocket catalog with an address that does not include a Zip Code. Since the U.S. Postal service introduced Zip Codes in 1963 we can be reasonably sure these predate 1963-64. They are flexible rubber lures made in classic lure designs. The catalog page with the designs is reproduced here. Collector value range: $5-$8.

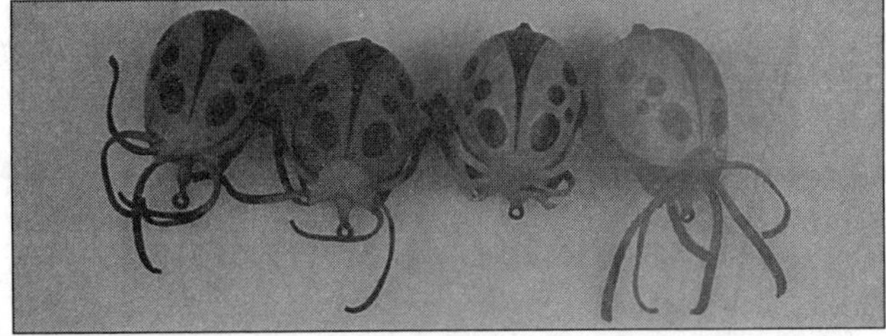

Four hollow rubber bugs measuring 1-1/8" each. Patterns are red on yellow black on orange, black on green and black on brown. Photo courtesy Jim Muma.

BURKE BAIT COMPANY

Benjamin F. Burke Chicago, Illinois

The earliest and only advertisements found for Burke Bait

Company lures were in 1913 and 1914 editions of *The Outer's Book* magazine. They made at least three different lures, each of rubber. They were floaters constructed so the fisherman could make them sinkers by changing the weight of the lure by admitting amounts of water into the hollow body.

I found two patents, one of which matches one of his lures reasonably well. The patent was filed in 1906 and granted April 9, 1907. The other patent, granted Burke in 1909 doesn't match anything found so far.

There was no trade data from which to determine a collector value.

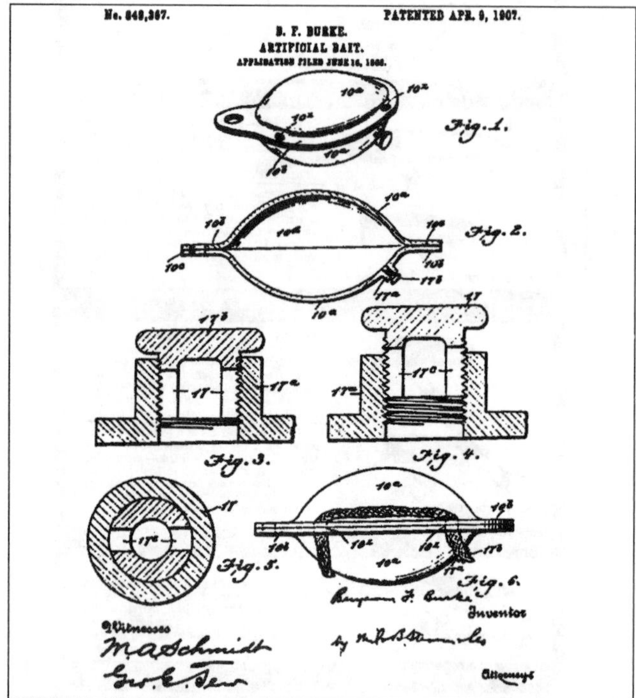

This patent illustration bears a close resemblance to one of Burke's lures. The production lure has a pointed leading end and several holes down each side rather than just the two shown here.

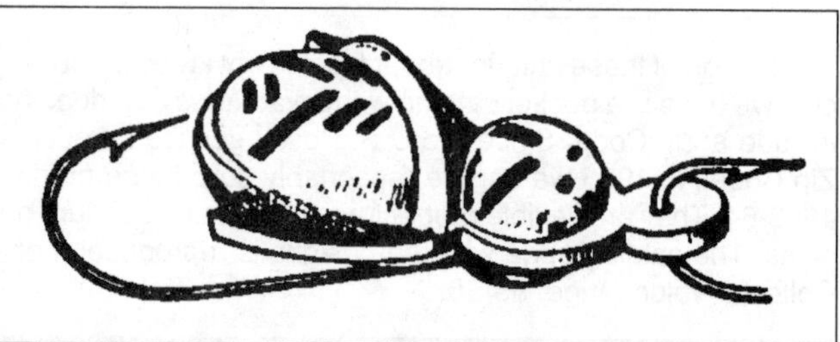

A drawing of Burke's hollow rubber BUG BAIT. It is 2-1/4" long and according to one catalog entry was available "...with fancy colorings...".

F.S. BURROUGHS & COMPANY

Dover, New Jersey

AQUA-BAT

Called "The sensational new 'AQUA-BAT'" in the May, 1949 issue of *OUTDOORS* magazine, this plastic lure moves by itself. You were to insert what they called an "Aqua Tab" pellet and when you cast it into the water the tab reacted, releasing a gas. It measures 2-7/8" long and was made in eight colors. They are gold scale, green frog, yellow perch, gray mouse, orange spot, silver scale, red head and all black. Photo courtesy Jim Muma. Collector value range: $10-$15.; $30-$40. new in the box.

CROAKER

Called "Another new Burroughs bait" in a 1950 advertisement these hard plastic frogs had a "three place line attachment" underneath, giving the lure "Three built-in actions." There was also a cup there, formed by the legs and belly to cause erratic action on retrieve. They measure 2-1/2" and were made in four color patterns: White body with red head, white body with green head, spotted green, spotted brown. They also made a fly rod size at 1-1/2". Either size is difficult to find. Collector value range: $50-$75., Fly rod size: $75-$100.

ALBYLER BASGETER SURFACE c. 1935

Al Byler — Seattle, Washington

Al Byler made and sold his lures under the name ALBYLER BASGETERS. He was a one-man operation in business somewhere around the 1930s. So far there have been only three different lures of his to turn up. All the colors that were available are not known, but probably limited. Those plugs that have so far been found all have a paint job that includes the use of glitter. Various types of hardware may be found on the lures. Apparently Byler used what he could find.

The three lures in the photo are identified as follows: the lure on the left is the BASGETER STRAIGHTAIL and is 4-5/ 8",

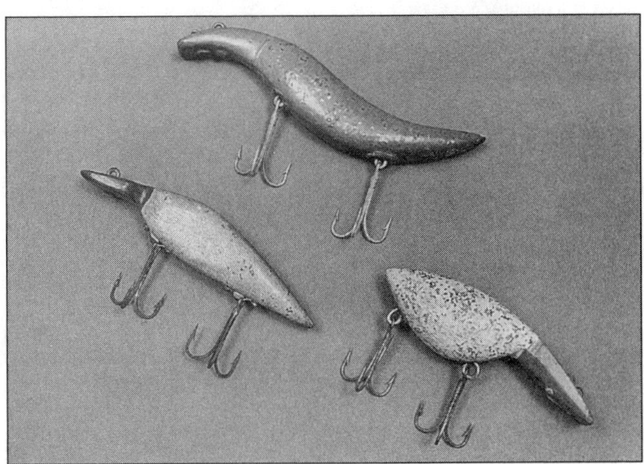

top center plug is the BASGETER SURFACE and is 5-/12" and the right plug is the BASGETER UNDERWATER, 3-1/2". Collector value range: $100-$150.

JACK CARNES LURES

Little Rock, Arkansas

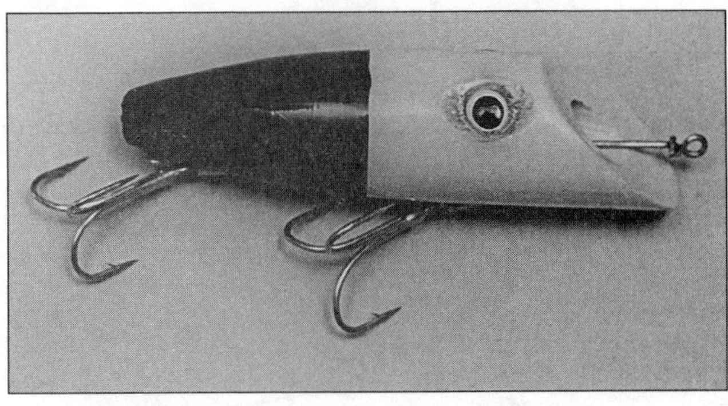

They made at least two different lures, the FANCY-DANCER and the LITTLE STINKER, in the late 1940s. They are wood-body baits. The FANCY-DANCER pictured here measures 3-1/4". It came in a nice box with the name and number S-102, printed on it, but no company name or address. It has a hole all the way through the body longitudinally. The line tie has a long shank, passes through the body and is integrated with the screw holding the tail hook hanger beneath the tail. Unfortunately I have never seen the other lure. Collector value range: $15-$25.

CARTER'S BESTEVER BAIT CO.

Indianapolis, Indiana — DUNK'S

American Display Company — Dayton, Ohio

In the beginning these two companies were entirely independent of each other. Patent application dates indicate Thomas J. Carter was in or at least preparing to go into business as early as the late 1910s. The earliest Carter patent found so far was for the Carter's BESTEVER. It was applied for on April 3, 1919 and granted February 12, 1924. The 5-year hiatus between application and patent grant remains unexplained. Mr. Milton S. Dunkelberger was apparently the owner of the American Display Company of Dayton, Ohio. They were in the tackle business in at least the early 1920s. They were either manufacturing and/or distributing lures under the name "STUBBY BRAND FISHING TACKLE" in advertising that also carried the American Display Company name. A 1933 Dunk's catalog makes the statement that they had been producing lures for the "...last twenty years." That puts Carter back to around 1913.

Advertising date studies seem to indicate Dunkelberger either bought Carter's company or obtained his lure patents around 1932. In fact it was 1932 that saw the first ads for "Dunk's-Carters" and then just "Dunk's". Both carry the American Display Company name and address. They did buy the Carter company out in 1932.

Once the Carter lures were taken over by Dunk's, there were improvements and additions to the line. An important improvement was the addition of glass eyes to the Carter lures. As far as is presently known there were never any eyes at all on the Carter lures prior to the takeover.

See accompanying photos for more hints on identification. The first two photos show the Carter's and Dunk's boxes.

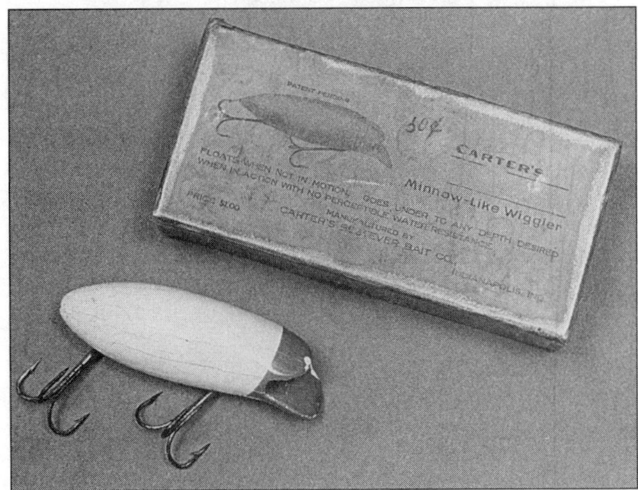

It's hard to see in the photo, but this is a Carter's Bestever Bait Company box. The lure is called a "Minnow-Like Wiggler" on the label.

A BESTEVER with original Dunk's box.

BESTEVER

There were several sizes and hook configurations available in this plug type. It has a very distinctive nose design that looks much like a bird's beak. Most of the advertising copy and illustrations indicate they were available mostly with treble or single hooks only. However one ad clearly states the three basic sizes were available in a double hook configuration too. The location of the aft hook seems to be arbitrarily placed on the belly or at the tail end.

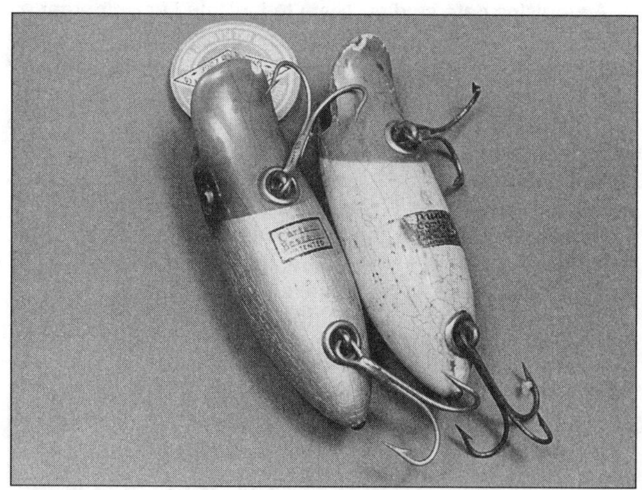

The label on the left plug says CARTER'S BESTEVER and the one on the right has the DUNK'S/CARTER'S label. As noted earlier the addition of glass eyes was a Dunk's innovation, but here we have a Carter with glass eyes and a Dunk's without. These two must represent lures produced during the transition. The round tag is for the Shapleigh Hardware Co., distributors of tackle.

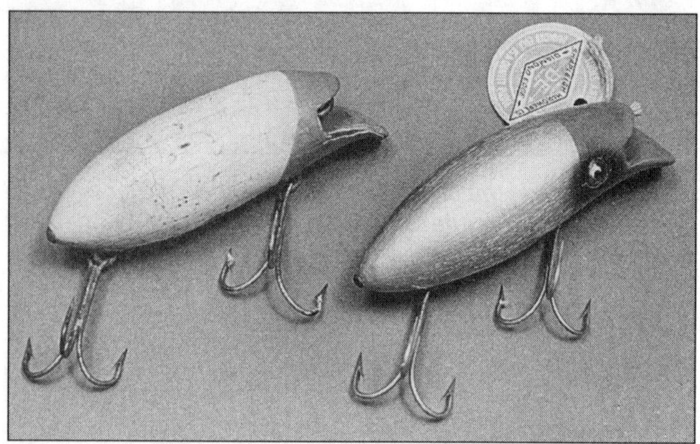

Same lure as above in side view.

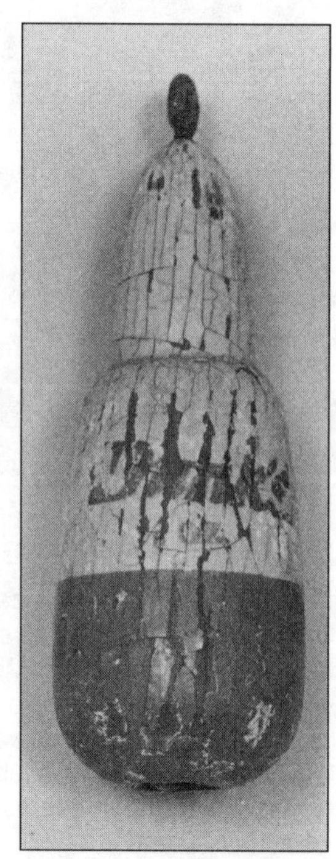

Dunk's tournament casting weight. For some reason it came in four different color schemes: White body with red or green heads, yellow body with red or green heads.

This plug appears to be a BESTEVER, but measures 2". There were no 2" BESTEVERS. It is, in fact, a copy that was made by Humphries Industries, Jacksonville, Indiana.

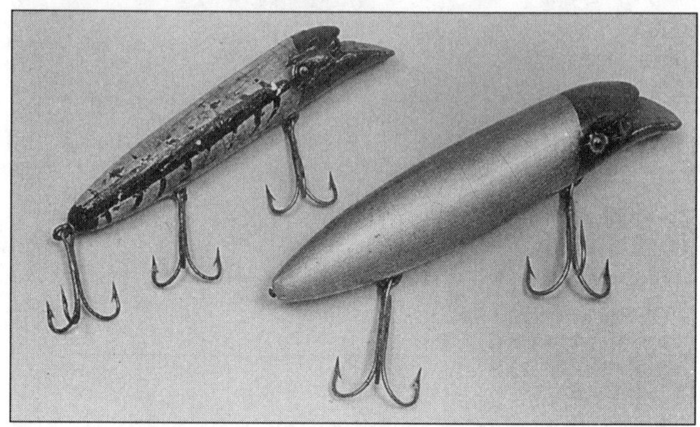

Pike and Muskie size BESTEVERS. Left lure is a fisherman repaint.

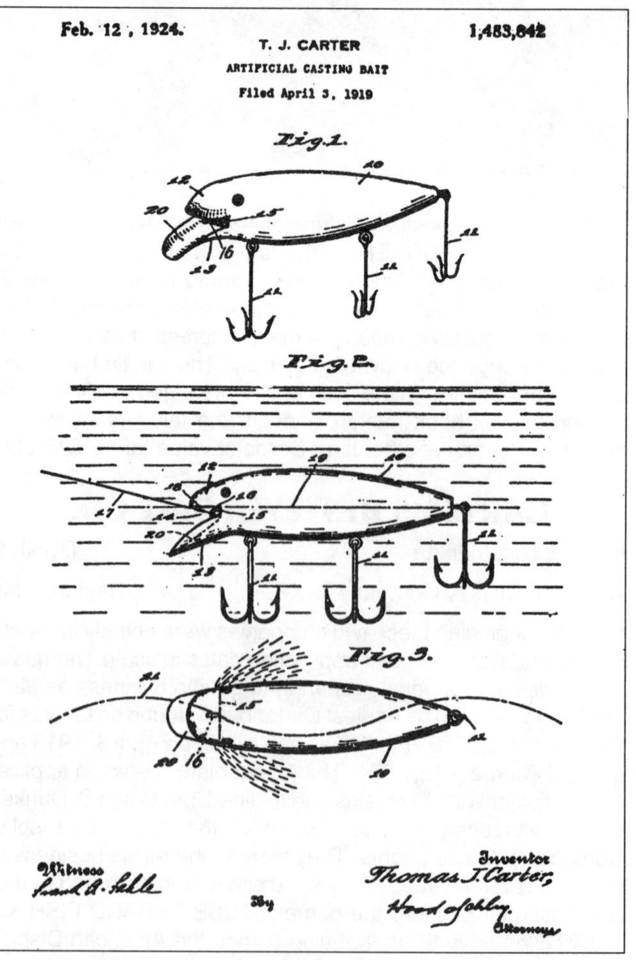

Illustration of the patent for Carter's BESTEVER lure. Granted Feb. 12, 1924.

NAME	BODY LENGTH	LURE WEIGHT	HOOKS	VALUE RANGE
Muskie	5-1/2"	1-1/2 oz.	2T	No trade data found
Pike	4-1/2"	3/4 oz.	2T or 3T	$100-$200.
Big Boy	4-1/2"	1-3/4 oz.	2T	No trade data found
Large	3-5/8"	1-1/2 oz.	2T or 2D	$75-$125.
Medium	3"	3/8 oz.	2T or 2D	$50-$60.
Midget	2-3/4"	1/2 oz.	1T or 1D	$40-$50.
Baby	1-3/4"	1/8 oz.	2T	$25-$40.
Fly rod	1-1/4	1/16 oz.	1D	$50-$75.

COLOR OR FINISH: White with red head*, red with black head, silver color with red head*, gold with red head, yellow with red head, solid red, solid black**, half black and half white***.

These two plus all black were the only colors available on the Muskie size.

***Known as the "Old Black Joe".*

****Known as the DAY-R-NIGHT. Made in Midget, Medium and Large sizes.*

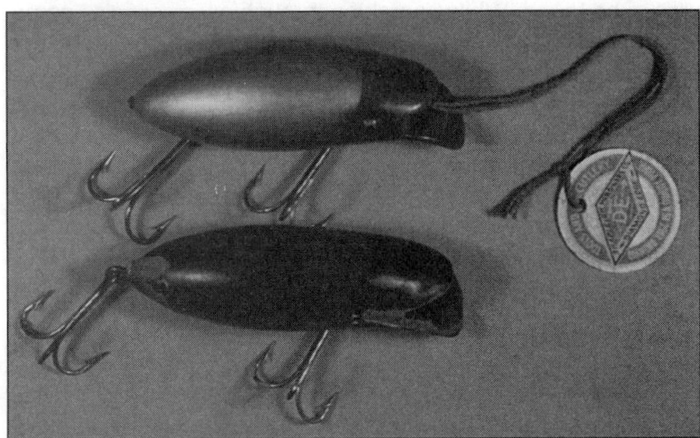

Two BESTEVERS; one in the solid black finish and the other in gold with red head.

CARTER'S MOUSE

This is the same lure as the BESTEVER midget size but has a flexible tail. It has a single belly-mounted treble hook. Collector value range: $30-$40.

COLOR OR FINISH: Gray back with white belly and red lower lip, all black, all gray.

DUNK'S DUNKIT

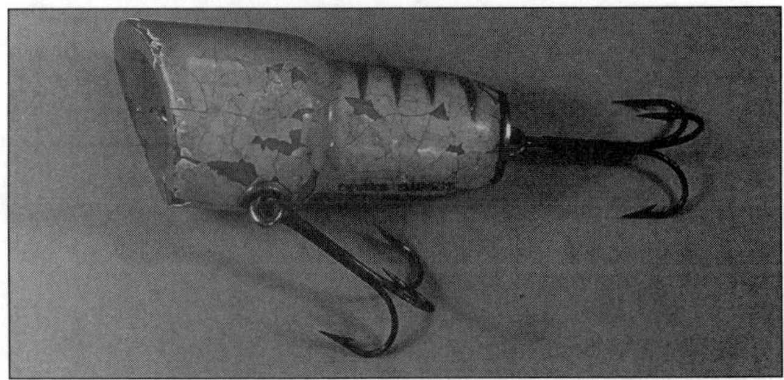

This is a 2-1/2" popper-type plug with a concave (scooped) head, a belly treble and trailing treble hook. Collector value range: $30-$50.

COLOR OR FINISH: White body with red head, tiger finish (green-brown striped back with silver sides and white belly), leopard finish (green-brown striped back with silver sides and white belly with brown spots), all black.

SINGLE HOOK WEEDLESS

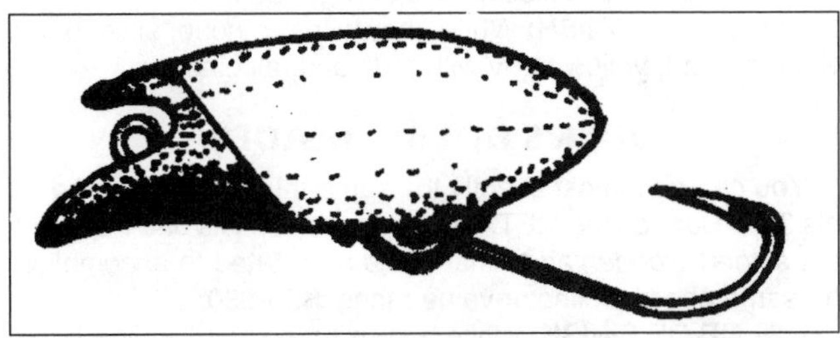

This is the very much like the MIDGET BESTEVER except that it has a single hook with a special guard to prevent the hook from turning to either side. The patent was applied for in 1923 and granted in 1927. Available in all the colors listed with the BESTEVER plugs except half black/half white. Collector value range: $40-$60.

CARTER'S CRAW

This lure used the same body style as the BESTEVER lure with the addition of side-mounted flashers to make it appear something like a craw fish. It is a 3", 3/4 ounce surface bait with one bally treble and one trailing treble hook. Collector value range: $40-60.

COLOR OR FINISH: White body with red tail, green back with yellow belly, black back with silver belly, all black with red eye shading.

DUNK'S CRAW

An all-metal lure in the shape of a crawfish. It has a flasher attached to each side emulating pincers and one trailing treble hook. It is 4" long. Collector value range: $40-$50.

COLOR OR FINISH: Red and white, nickel plate, copper plate.

SURFACE TWIN

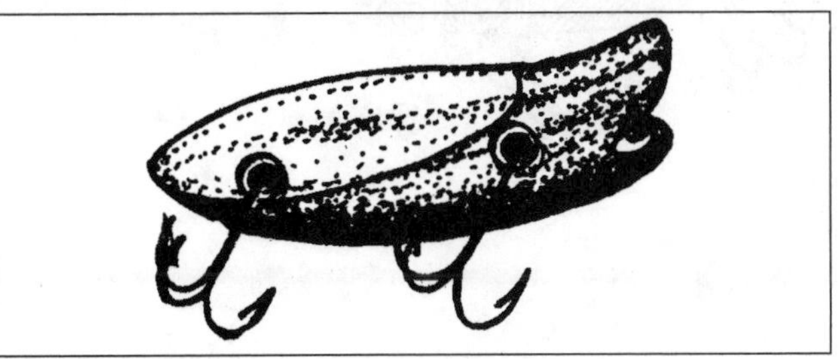

This lure is similar in design to the BESTEVER type, but inverted. It is a surface-running plug with two same-side mounted treble hooks in the "injured minnow" manner. It was available in two sizes, 3", 3-1/2" and only in a black and white color combination. Collector value range: $30-$50.

CARTER'S METALHED

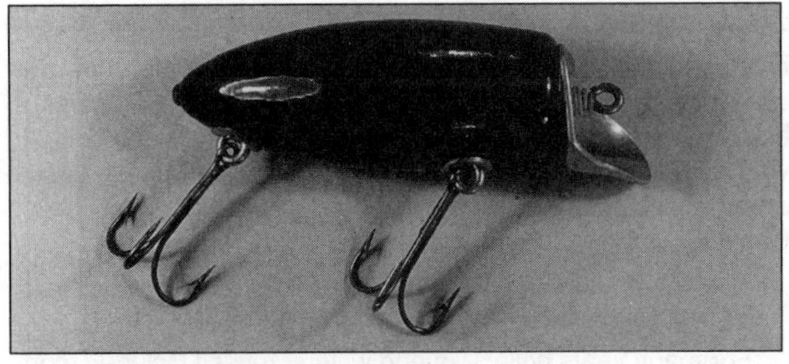

This was cataloged as a 3", ting metal plate made so that is could be rendered a top-water or an underwater lure at the will of the fisherman. Please see the next entry for a lure that could do the same thing. Collector value range: $55-$85.

COLOR OR FINISH: White body with red head, silver body with red head, yellow body with red head, all black.

DUNK'S DOUBLE HEADER

You can do almost exactly the same thing with the head of this 3-1/4" lure as the METALHED above. On this one the head is a sloped *wooden* affair that could be rotated to accomplish the same effect. Collector value range: $50-$80.

COLOR OR FINISH: White body with red head, yellow body with red head, green body with red head, all black.

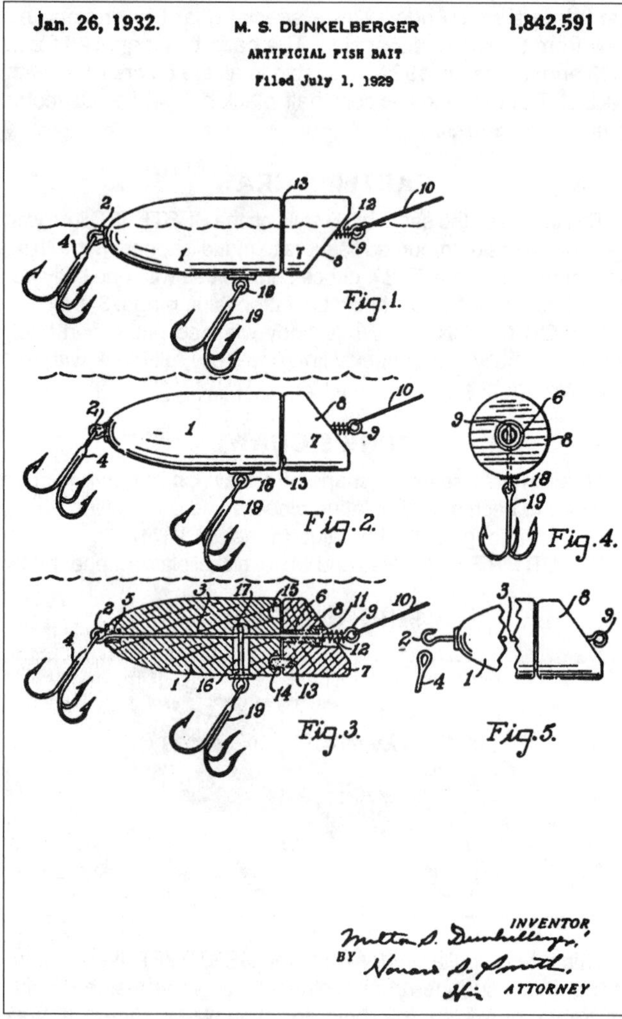

The 1932 patent illustration for Dunk's DOUBLE HEADER.

DUNK'S SHORE MINNOW
DUNK'S PIKE BAIT

The same lure as the DOUBLE HEADER except the body has been fashioned with flat sides. The only difference between these two is the colors. The SHORE MINNOW has a black head and back, silver sides, red gills and white belly. It was available in 2-1/2" and 3" sizes. The PIKE BAIT has a green head and back, silver sides, red gills and a yellow belly. Collector value range: No trade data found.

SWIM-A-LURE c. 1941

For many years collectors and writers, myself included, considered this only one lure. This because of an old (c. 1941) Dunk's advertisement that carried only one illustration. (reproduced in the accompanying drawing) It was of the Swim-A-Lure CHIPMUNK. With the illustration was a list of what we thought were simply different paint jobs and finishes. on the same lure. In the course of research several years ago, I discovered that the advertisement actually read "Eleven models" not 11 finishes or colors. At that point I began to suspect there were 11 different lures to be found. While searching through my materials I came across a photocopy of a 1933 Dunk's catalog that confirmed my suspicions. There were indeed 11 different styles of lures. All but the FROG version have a metal head plate that can be adjusted to make the lure surface swimmers or divers. All were floaters if left at rest in the water. It looks like you better look in that bunch of unidentified lures you have and see if one of these is there. Look for the distinctive adjustable lip as rendered in the drawing. Collector value range: $100-$300.

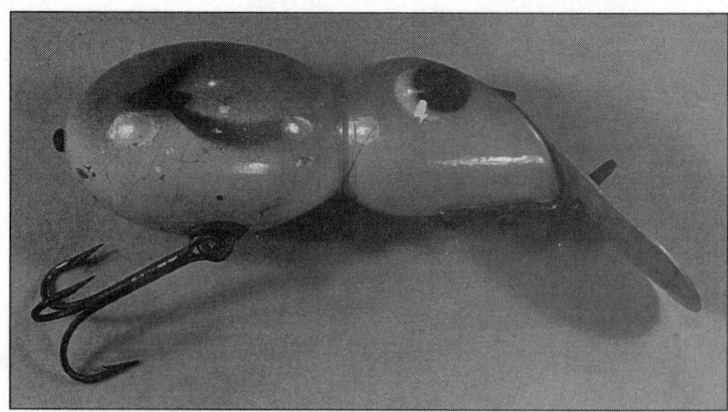

A 2-7/8" Swim-A-Lure BABY DUCK.

1. SUNFISH - 1/oz., 2". Shaped somewhat like and similar to Heddon Punkinseeds.
2. BLUEGILL - 5/8 oz., 2-1/2". Shaped same as above, but elongated.
3. BIG CHUB - 3/4 oz., 3-1/4". Body shaped like a Heddon Lucky 13 with a slope nose.
4. STRIPED MINNOW - 5/8 oz., 3". Minnow-like shape
5. RED SHRIMP - 1/2 oz., 2-1/2". Reverse running. Shaped a bit like a Carter's Bestever with a bird-like bill
6. JOINTED PIKE - 3/4 oz., 4". Body shaped somewhat like a Creek Chub Jointed Pikie Minnow
7. YELLOW JACKET - 1/2 oz., 3-1/2". Shaped like a Heddon Moonlight Radiant
8. FROG - 3/4 oz., 2-1/2". Body similar to No. 5 above and reverse running
9. BABY DUCK model of the Dunk's Swim-A-Lure. This one measures 2-7/8".
10. PIKE - 3/4 oz., 4-1/4". Body same as No. 6 above but not jointed
11. CHIPMUNK - 7/8 oz., 4-1/2". See accompanying drawing.

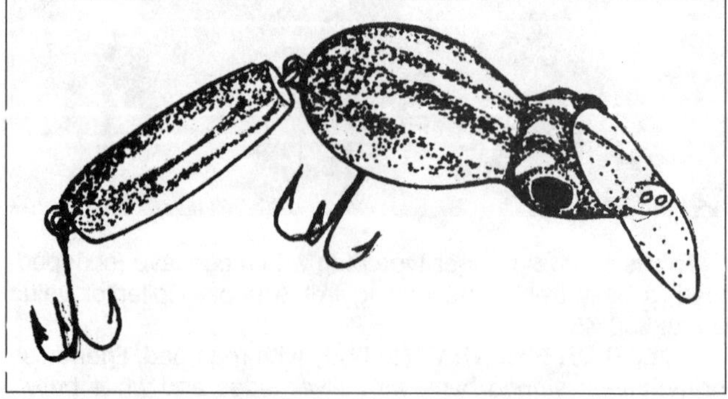

A Swim-A-Lure CHIPMUNK.

Top is a Swim-A-Lure STRIPED MINNOW. Bottom is a Swim-A-Lure SUNFISH. Note the distinctive adjustable lip.

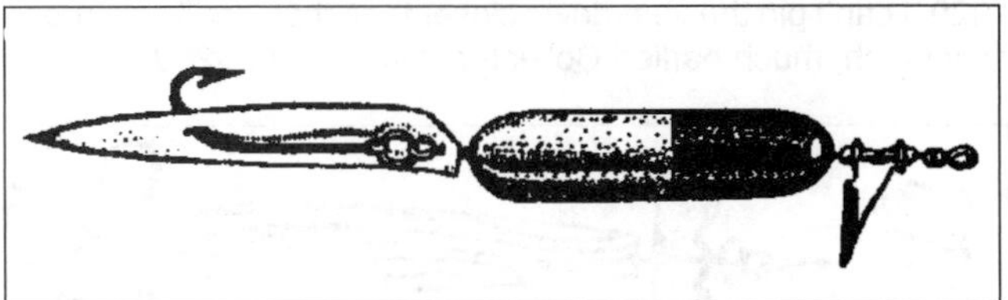

STUBBY'S HYDROPLUG BAIT

This is a unique lure which was made so you could weight it for casting by filling it with water. Dry weight is 5/8 ounce. It has a single hook with provision for attaching feathers, pork rind or live bait. The only color available was a red and aluminum combination. An ad in a 1923 sportsman's magazine infers this was a new lure by saying: "Entirely a new principle in artificial baits." Collector value range: $40-$60.

DUNK'S WORRY-WART

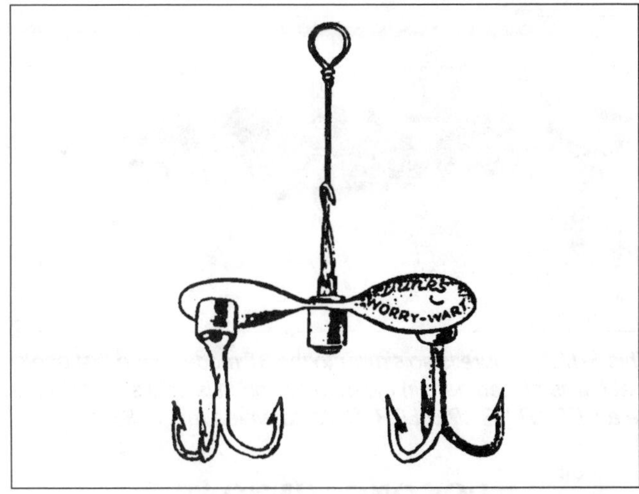

A rather peculiar bait, this was represented as "A NEW LURE FOR A NEW WAY OF FISHING...It SPINS BOTH WAYS- Going DOWN and coming UP! For those Deep Holes where the BIG BOYS silk. It worries them into striking!" Length overall was given as 3-3/4", measured from the end of the shank to the bottom of the treble hooks. Collector value range: $20-$30.

DUNK'S SPOONFISH

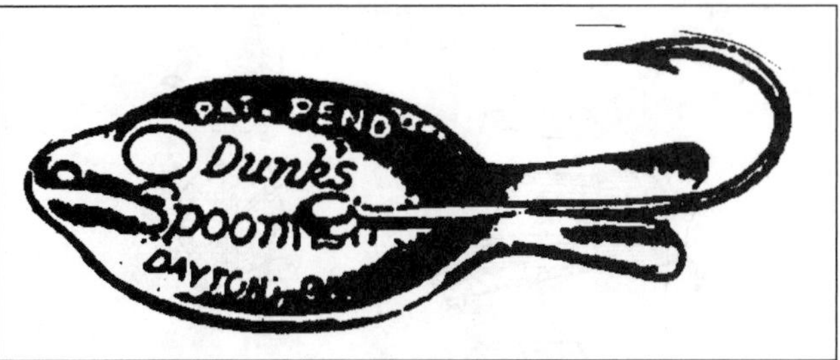

There were four sizes of this metal spoon. They were: 2-3/4" (overall), 2-7/8", 3-1/2", 4-3/8". The smallest (2-3/4 overall.) had a rigid-mount single hook as in the illustration here. The three larger sizes were made with trailing trebles. They are well marked with stamped identification in the metal. Collector value ranger: $15-$20.

CATCH-ALL, INC.

Sales Office: Milwaukee, Wisconsin Factory: Hiles, Wisconsin

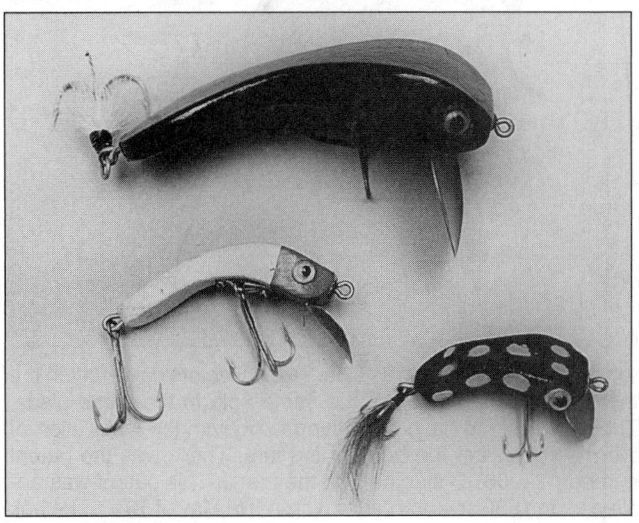

These wooden lures all have large plastic eyes. The boxes they came in indicated they came in four sizes and five colors. A recently found paper flyer from the company confirms this and infers, but does not say, that this may be their only lure. The colors listed were: Green frog, yellow frog, white with red head, black, black and orange, scale. yellow and brown has also reportedly been found. Each size was available in any of the six colors making it possible to find at least 16 different CATCH-ALL lures. If they used the seventh color on all four, that number would increase to 20. The flyer illustrates the dive plane is adjustable to two different positions, "SPOON UP" and "SPOON DOWN" rendering it a surface lure or one that runs at a depth of approximately 12 inches. The lures in the above photo measure 2", 2-3/4" and 4-1/2" respectively. Collector value range: No trade data found.

CAT'S PAW

Wilson W. Hargrett Detroit, Michigan

This interesting lure was patented by Wilson W. Hargrett of Wyandotte, Michigan, a suburb of Detroit. A detail of his patent, reproduced here, shows the mechanism plainly and that it is the same used on the lure in the photo above. The body, however is dissimilar. Mr. Hargrett either changed his mind about the lure body or he considered the mechanism the most important aspect of his patent. If you look closely at the lure in the photo you

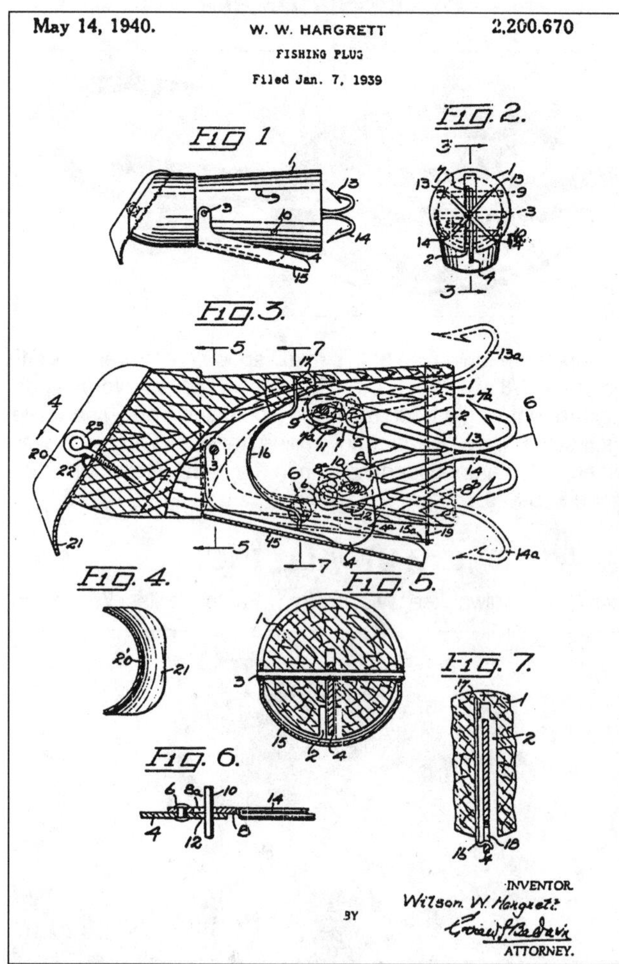

will see two tiny holes on its side. Two collectors have written me that their examples exhibit the same hole in the same place. They are likely to have something to do with the installation of the mechanism in the body of the lure. There was the patent number "2200670" stamped on the metal. This patent was applied for in 1939 and granted to Hargrett in May of 1940. The box was a simple white with green lettering: "CAT'S PAW Guaranteed Weedless Casting Bait, 2623 River Ave., Detroit, Mich." Colors seen so far are: Orange body with red spots, Black body with yellow spots, Black body with green spots, Green body with black spots and White body with red head as in the lure pictured here. Collector value range: $25-$50.

An orange body, red spotted CAT'S PAW with its original box.

CEDAR PROPELLER AND POCONO MINNOW

Malcolm A. Shipley — Philadelphia, Pennsylvania

J.L. Boorse — Allentown & Easton, Pennsylvania

CEDAR PROPELLER

Most of the information I was able to find regarding the CEDAR PROPELLER was in an article by Sam S. Stinson in a 1921 issue of The American Angler. About the plugs he says in part, "Malcolm A. Shipley, a Philadelphia tackle manufacturer, made a surface plug in the late nineties..." It was illustrated in the article. I have copied the illustration and placed it here. As you can see, it is quite similar to the one in the photo following the illustration. The only big difference is the location of the second treble hook. The one in the photo may be a little later model. Stinson said he came across Shipley's retail outlet in Philadelphia about 1901-02 and bought half a dozen of them. He describes the lure as follows: "It was a plain uncolored cedar wood ... equipped with two very light-weight metal propellers, one fore and one aft, connected by a copper wire that extended laterally through the conical body. It bore three treble hooks." We don't know for how long Shipley made his CEDAR PROPELLOR, but it is certain they were off the market by 1920. I can't pin the year down closer than that, but it was probably much, much earlier. Collector value range: $200-$300.

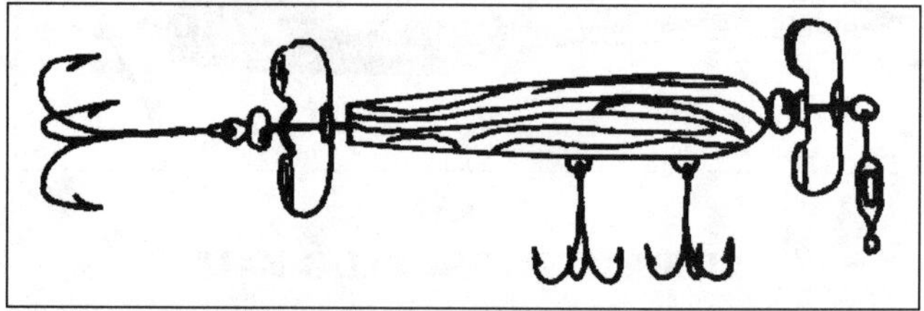

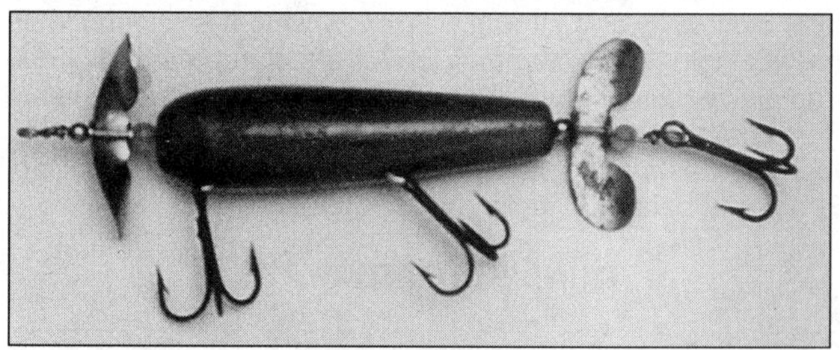

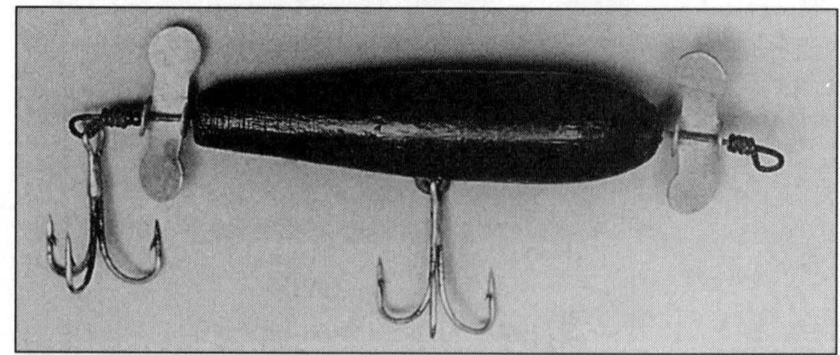

This 3-1/2", 2T lure is so similar to the 3T model in the first photo that it was placed here in the third edition. It is only suspected to be a CEDAR PROPELLER. Collector value range: $120-$200.

POCONO MINNOWS

The two lures in the photo here are POCONO MINNOWS. They are 3-1/8" long. The upper lure is natural varnished wood and the other is painted white. The only printed reference I could find attributed POCONO MINNOW to a J.L. Boorse and stated that they were manufactured in Easton and Allentown, Pennsylvania. Both cities are 30-40 miles north of Philadelphia where Shipley lived. Some collectors attribute the POCONOS to Ship-

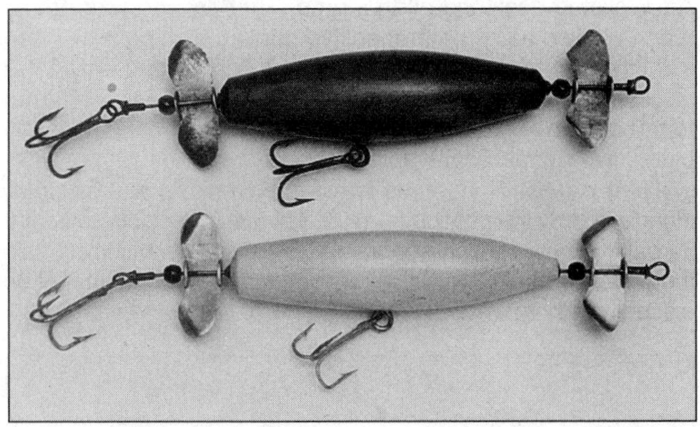

ley because of the similarity of the rigging and propeller spinners. I don't believe they were connected in any way other than one or the other copying the rigging. The body styles are significantly different and the strong, well-soldered eye construction at either end of the POCONOS suggest a more polished manufacturing operation than that of Shipley's apparently hand-made production method. Collector value range: $50-$90.

CHASE-A-BUG

Leon Tackle Company — Detroit, Michigan

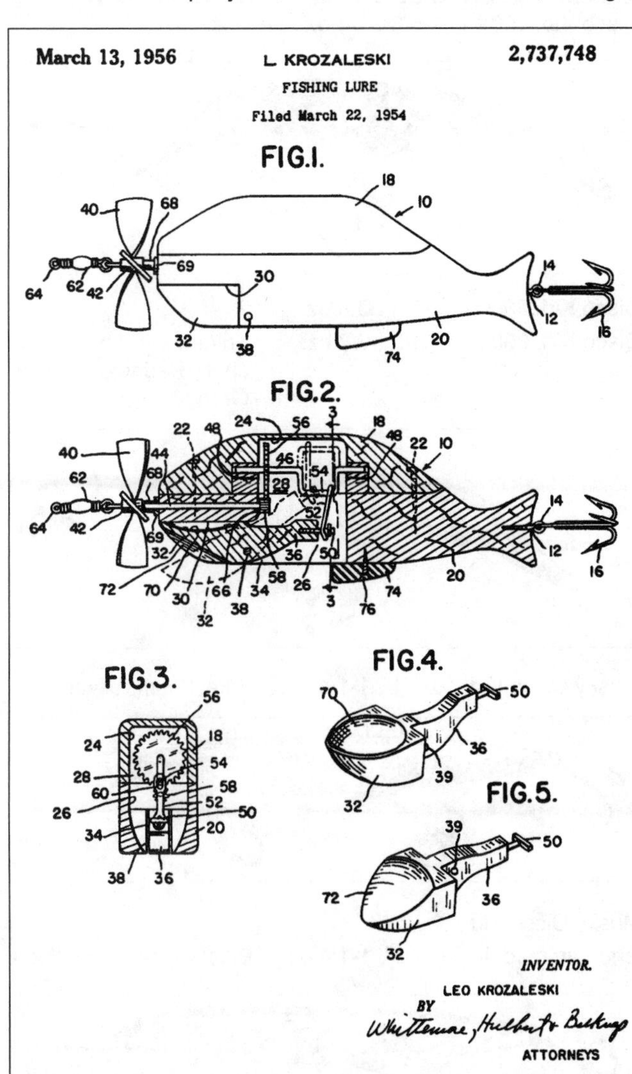

The simple appearance of the CHASE-A-BUG belies the moderate complexity shown in this patent illustration.

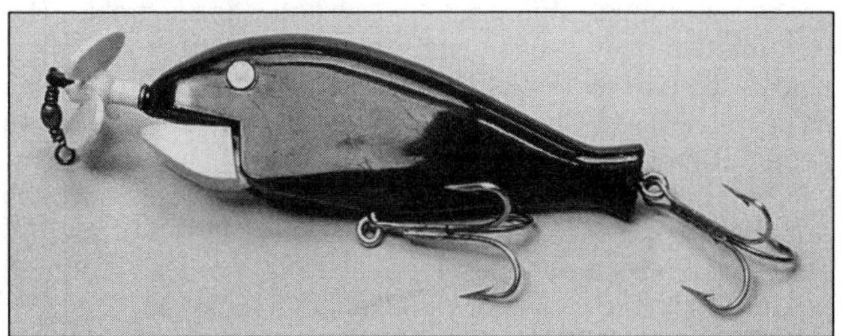

This is a really cute little plastic action lure. The lower jaw is articulated and when the plastic propeller at the nose rotates on retrieve, the mouth opens and closes. It was patented in 1956 by Leo Krozaleski of Detroit. The only color I have seen is the black and white of the one in the photograph here. It measures 3-15/16" overall including the propeller. Collector value range: $20-30.

THE CHARMER MINNOW COMPANY

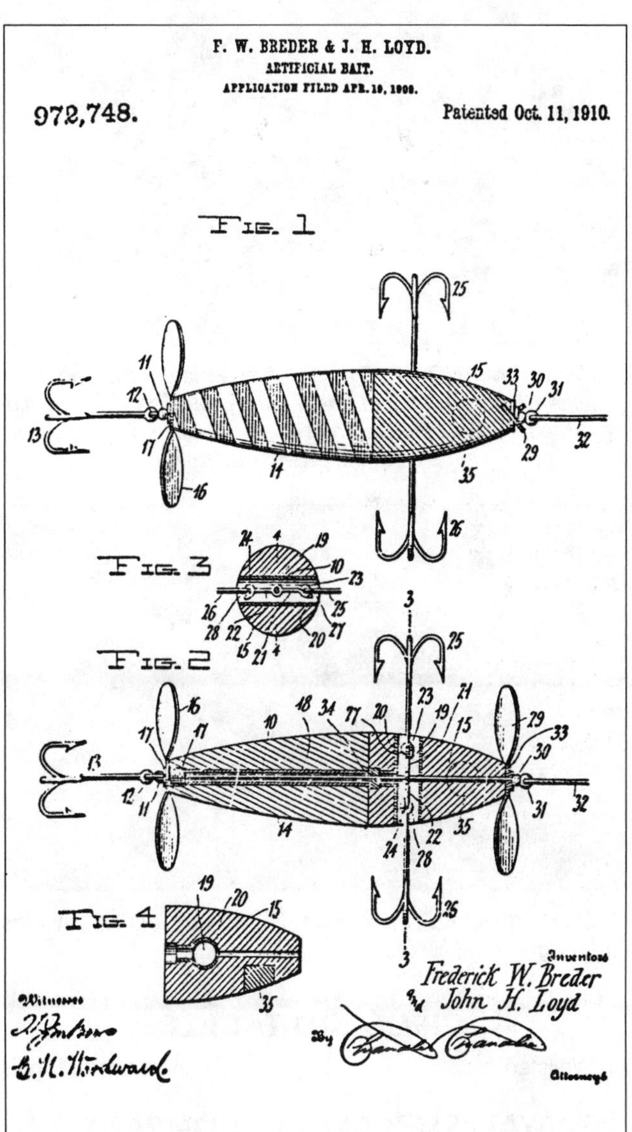

Original patent drawing for the CHARMER MINNOW. Note no eyes and see-thru hook hangers. Granted October 11, 1910.

Springfield, Missouri — Patent granted Oct. 11, 1910

These early wooden plugs had a nose-mounted propeller and a tail propeller mounted to rotate the rear section of the lure body. The lures are usually found with eyes, have two opposite see-through mount side trebles and a trailing treble. The rear rotating body section was painted with barber pole style stripes. It must have looked a little dizzy to fish. Maybe that was its secret. A 1912 Charmer advertisement states "Body of red cedar, all mountings genuine German Silver."

CHARMERS were available in eight different color finishes and there are three sizes to be found: 2-5/8", 3-3/8" and 5". There was also a surface model that has no nose-mounted propeller spinner. Collector value range: $150-$250.

COLOR OR FINISH: Gold body, green stripes; gold body, red stripes; white body, red stripes; white body, green stripes; brass body, green stripes; brass body, green stripes; brass body, red stripes; red body, white stripes; green body, white stripes. Some have been found with air-brushed stripes and a rare few have only air-brushed dots instead of the stripes on one or both sections.

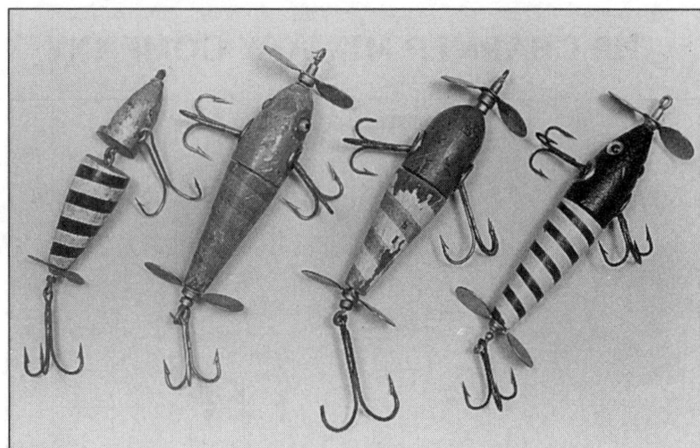

CHARMER MINNOWS. The far left lure may or may not be a genuine Charmer. It could be an early prototype. The remaining three exhibit all the Charmer characteristics. The third from the left has no eyes as in the patent illustration.

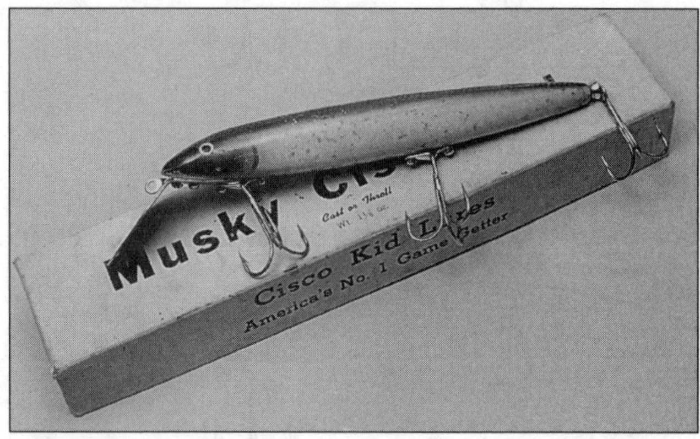

MUSKY CISCO KID measuring 6". The box it is on says the lure weighs 1-1/8 ounce.

CISCO KID TACKLE

Art Wallsten — Kenilworth, Illinois

WALLSTEN TACKLE COMPANY

Chicago, Illinois

The Kenilworth, Illinois location changed to Chicago between 1951 ads and 1952 ads. All Cisco Kid plugs are plastic. They were found advertised in sporting magazines consistently from 1949 to 1958. That's about as late my collection goes, so they were probably around after that. I found one un-dated catalog that had nine lures illustrated. According to the catalog Art Wallsten designed all the lures. That catalog was not so much catalog as a comprehensive guide to fishing with Cisco Kid lures. It was 20 pages in a 5" x 8" format and only 2-1/2 pages illustrated lures. The point here is that the text referred to the lures by number and the numbers add up to at least 15 plugs, five jigs and three spinner baits.

Here is a list of the lures found in advertising and catalogs, along with any information from the listings. The colors listed are verbatim. They were only partially listed. One advertisement said there were 11 colors available. The illustration from them will be placed with them when available. Collector value range: $15-$25.

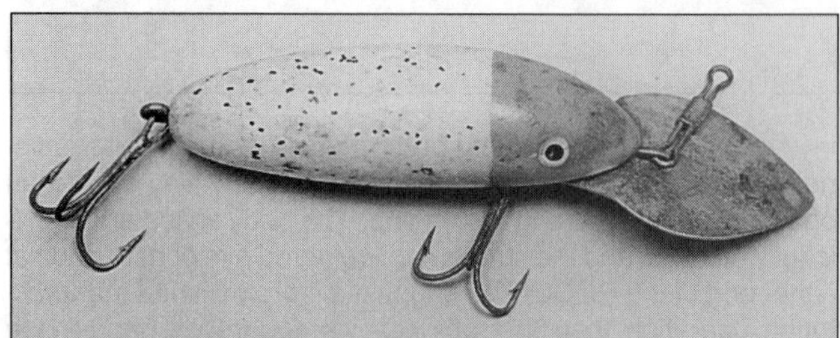

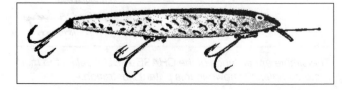

Cisco Kid DIVER with red head and white body with flitters. The body measures 3" and the lip is marked with the name.

NAME/NUMBER	SIZE & WEIGHT	COLOR/FINISH
Cisco Kid, 100	1-5/8", 1/4 oz.	?

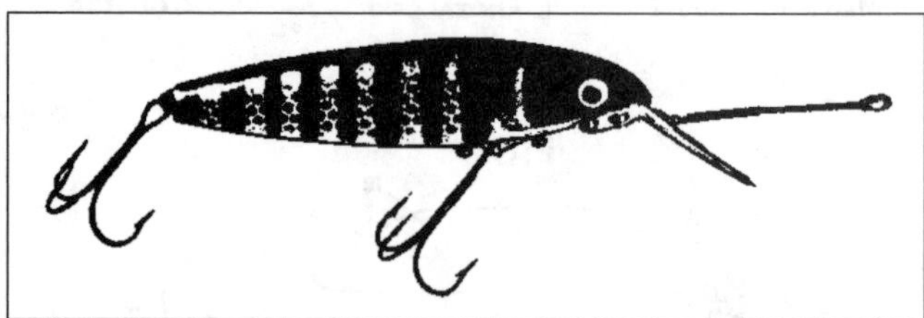

Cisco Kid, 200 — 2-1/4", 3/8 oz. — ?

Cisco Kid, 300 — 3-1/2", 5/8 oz. — Shiner, Pike, Black chub, Redhead, Yellow, Orange.

Musky Cisco Kid — 6-1/4", 1-1/4 oz. — Pike, Black, Silver flash.

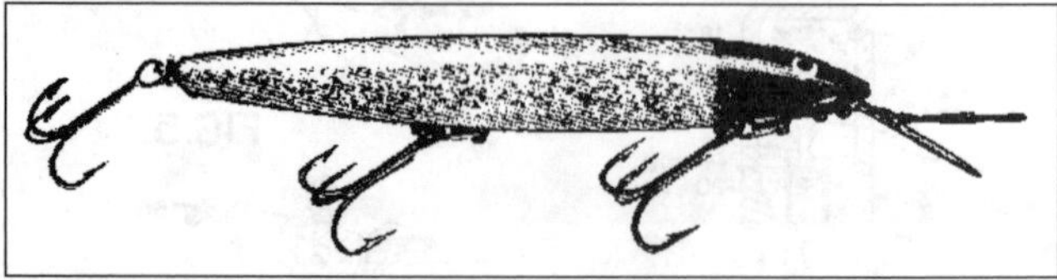

Musky Cisco Kid short lip model — 6-1/4", 1-1/4 oz. — Pike, Black, Silver flash.

NAME/NUMBER	SIZE & WEIGHT	COLOR/FINISH
Cisco Kid Diver	2-1/4", 3/8 oz.	?

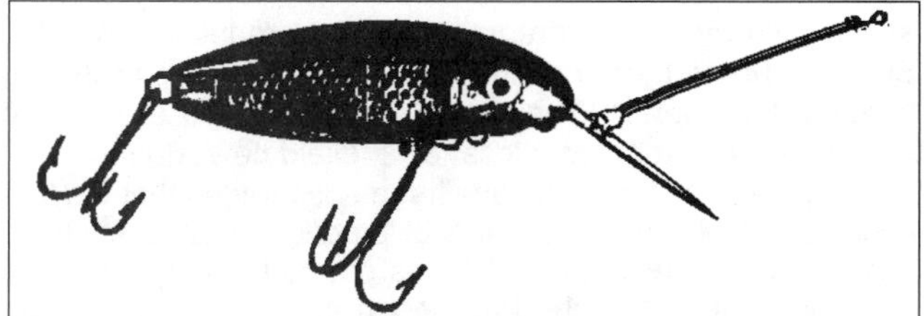

NAME/NUMBER	SIZE & WEIGHT	COLOR/FINISH
Flash Kid,	2-7/8", 1/4 oz.	?

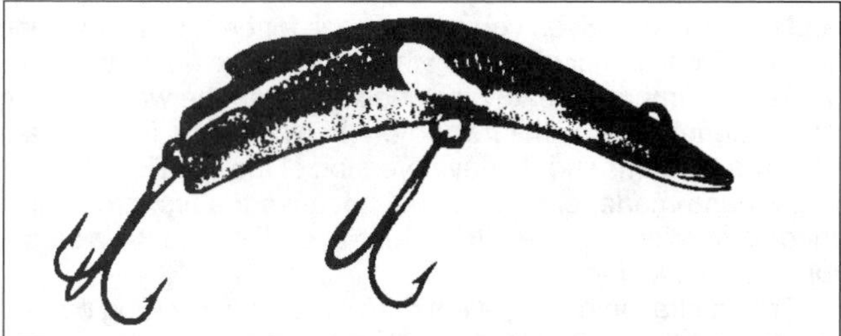

NAME/NUMBER	SIZE & WEIGHT	COLOR/FINISH
Skip-N-Cisco.	2-1/2", 1/4 oz.	?

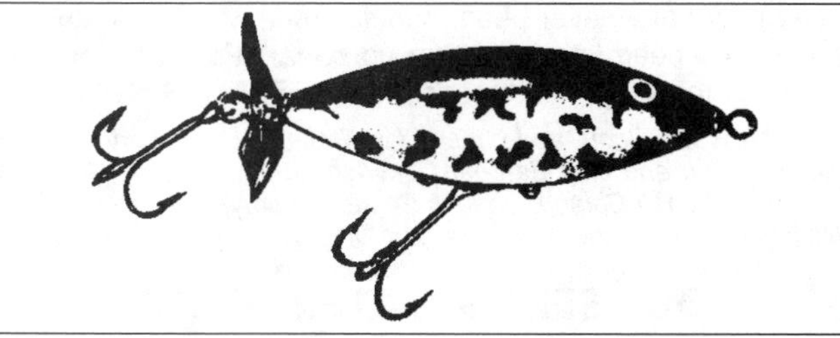

NAME/NUMBER	SIZE & WEIGHT	COLOR/FINISH
Injured Cisco	3-1/2", 1/2 oz.	Black chub, Shiner, Pike.

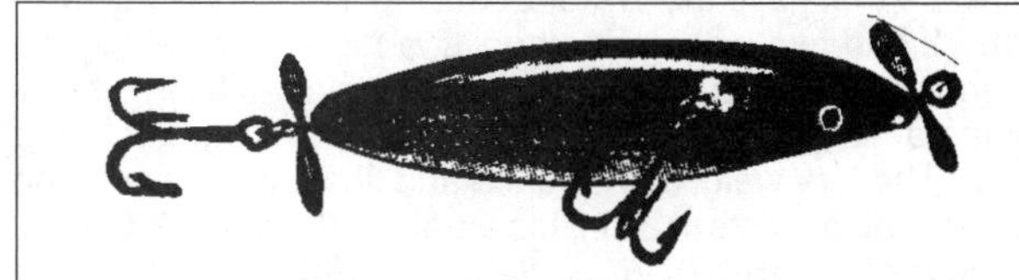

NAME/NUMBER	SIZE & WEIGHT	COLOR/FINISH
Spin Cisco Kid	?, 1/4 oz.	?

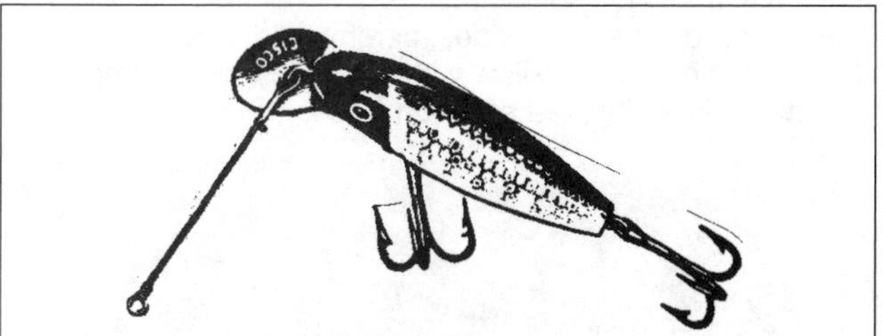

NAME/NUMBER	SIZE & WEIGHT	COLOR/FINISH
Spin Cisco	(jtd) ?, 1/4 oz.	?
Spin Cisco	(sfc) ?,	3/16 oz.?
No. 700		4-1/2", 1 oz.?

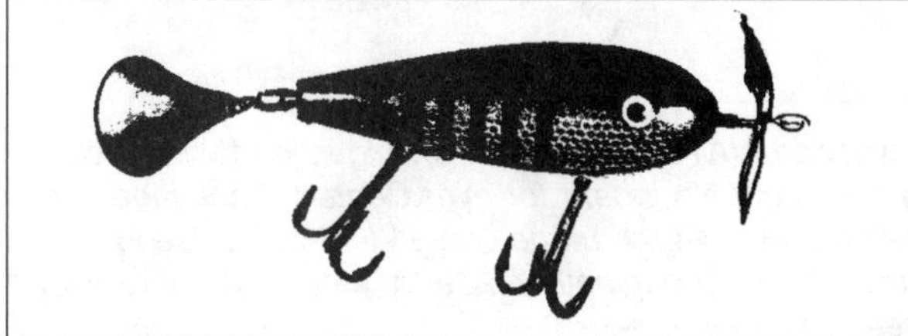

NAME/NUMBER	SIZE & WEIGHT	COLOR/FINISH
No. 700-PT	4-1/2", 1 oz.	?

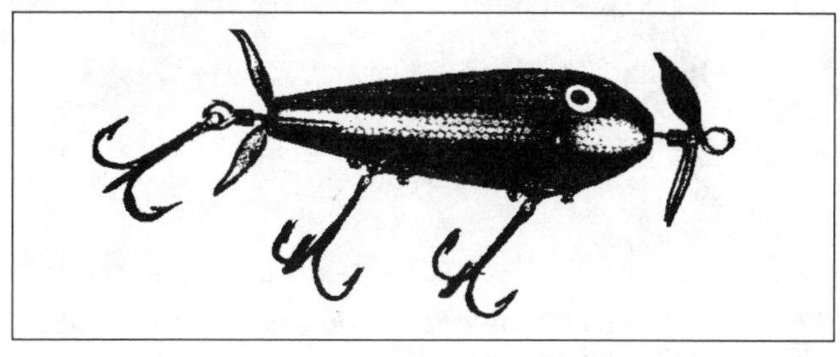

NAME/NUMBER	SIZE & WEIGHT	COLOR/FINISH
No. 1100		3-1/4", 1/4 oz.?

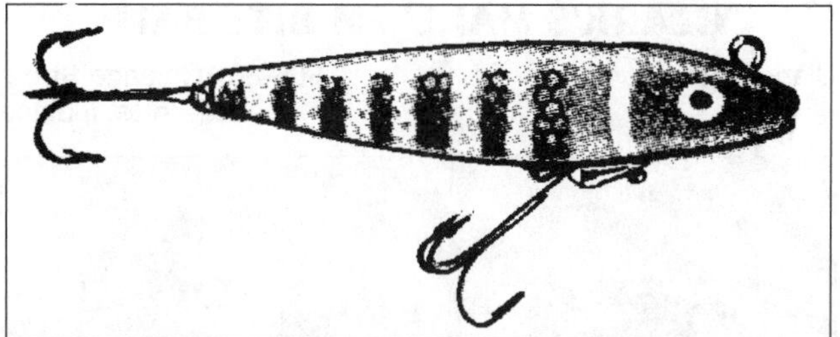

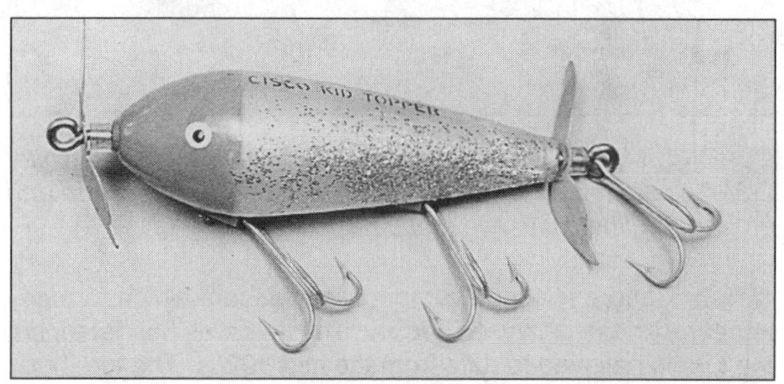

A Cisco Kid TOPPER measuring 4".

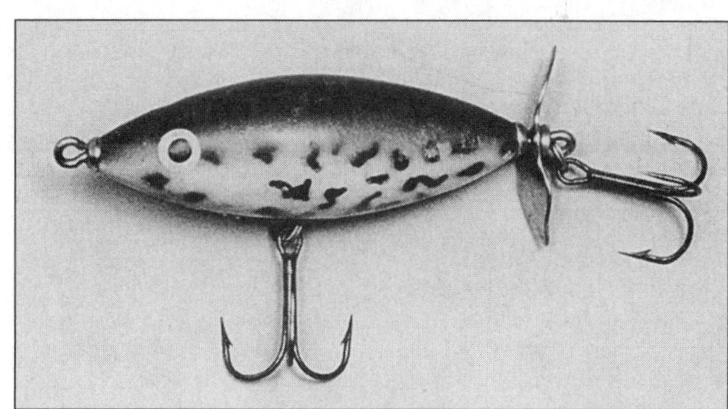

SKIP-N-CISCO. Measures 2-1/2".

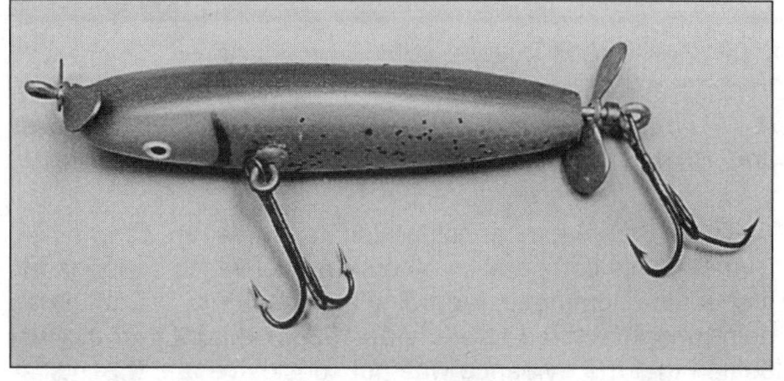

An INJURED CISCO with floppy bow tie-type propeller spinners. It measures 3-1/4".

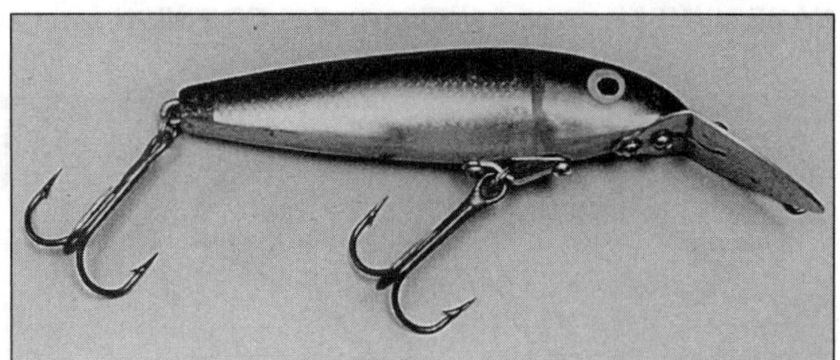

A lip marked Cisco Kid identifies this lure as probably a CISCO KID, No. 300. It measures 3-1/4".

CLARK'S MAKE' EM BITE BAIT

Clark Brothers — 805-807 Chicago Street, La Porte, Indiana

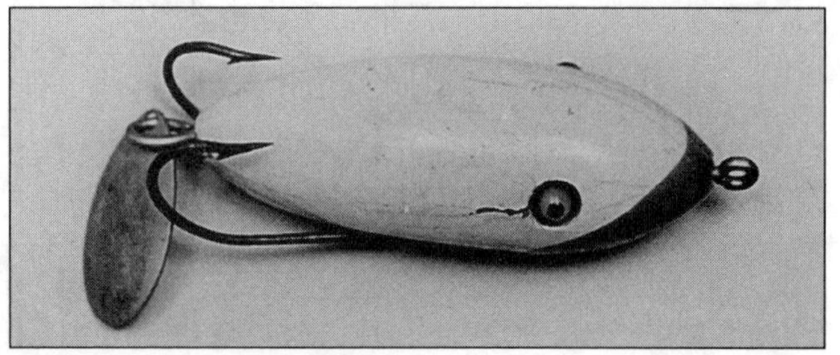

CLARK'S MAKE' EM BITE BAIT. A glass-eyed red and white, 2-3/4" wooden lure. It has two single hooks that swing fore and aft and a willow leaf style metal tail flasher.

A box and enclosed flyer identifies this lure which formerly appeared in the Unknown section. The flyer was not dated, but the lure is believed to date from the mid-1920s. The lure body measures 2-3/4". Collector value range: $200-$300.

COLOR OR FINISH: White body with red head, green body with red head, black body with red head, red body with black head.

CLARK

C.A. Clark Company
C.A. Clark Manufacturing Company
Water Scout Company — Springfield, Missouri

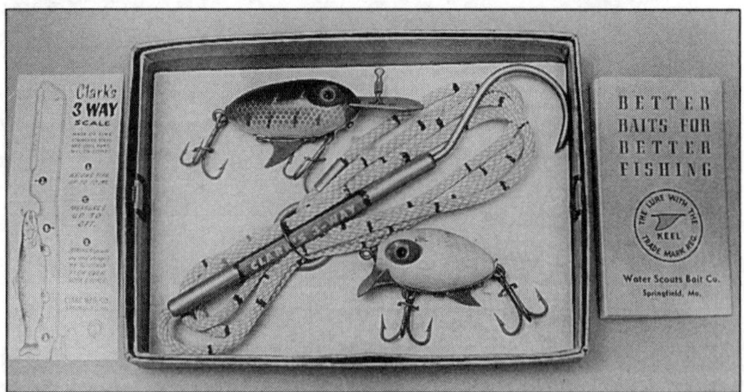

A WATER SCOUT kit containing a scale, stringer, two lures and fishing instructions.

There has been considerable research on Charles A. Clark and his company by others*, part of which supports my first edition comments regarding the possibility of Clark lures being manufactured as early as 1926. I reported in the last edition that the evidence was not conclusive and the indications were that a more accurate estimate was the 1930s. Well, we now know a bit more. Mr. Clark began experimenting with making lures in the mid-1920s and finally came up with what he and friends thought was a good design some time in the late 1920s or early 1930s. These are known to collectors as the "No eye," the forerunner of the production WATER SCOUT. Made by hand, they were mostly given to fishing buddies and friends. They were, however, also sold to the public, available only at a local Springfield newsstand.

At some point he must have been encouraged that the lure might be viable as a commercial product. He applied for a patent January 16,1934 and it was granted at the end of the same year. It is thought they began manufacturing them in some quantities in 1933.

There is a reference in a c. 1950 catalog that states in part "...an example of where twenty-five years of doing one thing and doing it well, gives you a better bait for better fishing." One would have to conclude, given the evidence so far, that the "25 years" statement probably includes the years he was whittling and experimenting with lures before beginning the formal manufacture of them. The "No-eye" version of the WATER SCOUT is the hand-made, earliest model because the first production models sported the so-called "Dent-eye", the indent was fashioned with a knife in production.

The illustration of the patent drawing on the following page is for the WATER SCOUT. Note that the drawing shows three small holes drilled in the large screw-eye line tie. This would give the fisherman three options for the running depth of the lure. They may have never been manufactured with this feature for none have been known to turn up so far. The collector value range for the early, hand-made WATER SCOUTS: $175-$275.

**The Water Scout and Other Clark Baits, A preliminary report by Jim Bourdon and Ray Barzee. Copyright 1984 and C.A. Clark Bait Company by Bill Calhoun, pages 24-28, January, 1994 issue of The National Fishing Lure Collectors Club Magazine, copyright 1994.*

300 SERIES WATER SCOUT

A small, undated pocket catalog entitled the "Water Scouts Bait Company", Springfield, Missouri, states this lure is "The original lure that gave the Water Scout family its worldwide reputation." It had two belly treble hooks, a metal band along the belly ending in a shaped metal diving lip plane. There was a small metal fin attached to the belly sort of like the keel on a sailboat. The lure weighs 1/2 ounce and floats when not being retrieved. It also exists in a sinking version (400 series). Collector value range: $15-$25.

COLOR OR FINISH: White with red head, black with white head, dace scale, black, red, yellow and silver, deep green scale, blended with yellow, rainbow, shiner scale; silver scale over white, red sheen on sides; perch scale; pike scale; pearl, black with white ribs; yellow with white ribs; green frog spot,, white with silver ribs, red scale on sides.

Early wooden WATER SCOUTS. Arranged left to right according to age. Left: No indent for eye; Center: Small indent with flat, painted eye; Right: Large oval indent with raised painted eye. Indents were originally made by striking the lure with a ball-peen hammer.

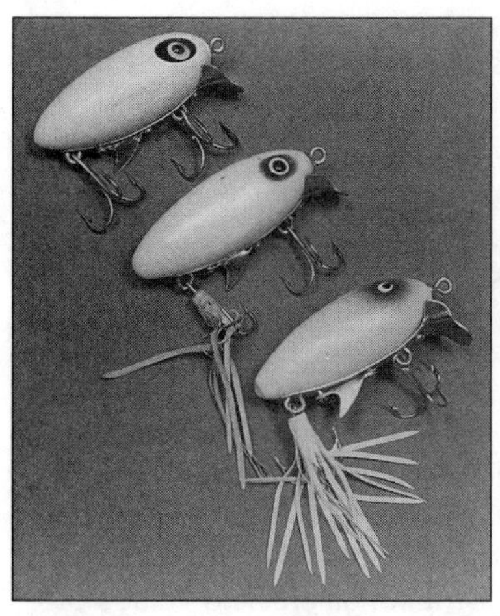

Shown here from left to right: an original WATER SCOUT, a handmade copy of the same lure, and on the far right is a modern version of the lure. This effective new plug is called the SPENCE SCOUT and is manufactured by the Strike King Lure Company.

500 Series DUCKLING

(Water Scout Duckling)
(Water Scout Duck Bill) 600 Series DUCK BILL

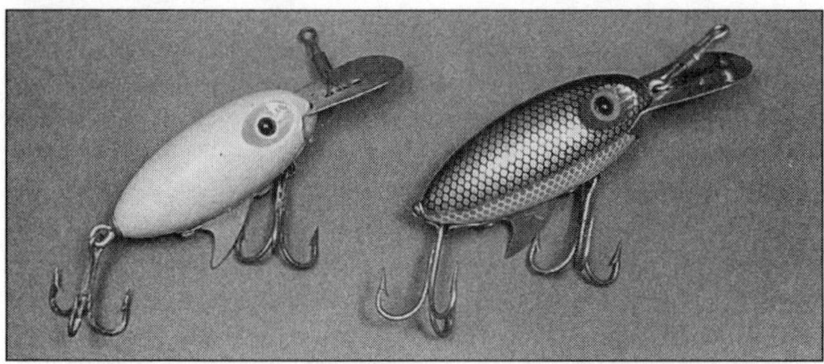

Right: Water Scout DUCK BILL. Left: Water Scout DUCKLING.

Both of these plugs are of the same design and configuration. The catalog listing of these plugs is the one in which the "25 years" reference quote was found. They are each the same basic design as the original WATER SCOUT with the exception of the nose plane design. It is flat and longer than that found on the 300 Series WATER SCOUT. The smaller one is 2" and weighs 3/8 ounce, the larger one is 2-3/8" and 1/2 ounce. Collector value range: $30-$40.

COLOR OR FINISH: White with red head; black with white head, deep green scale blended with yellow, rainbow, shiner scale; perch scale; pike scale; pearl, black with white ribs; yellow with white ribs; green frog spot, white with silver ribs, red scale on sides; fluorescent red, fluorescent yellow.

700 SERIES CLARK'S POPPER SCOUT

The ly hook. Collector value range: $10-$15.

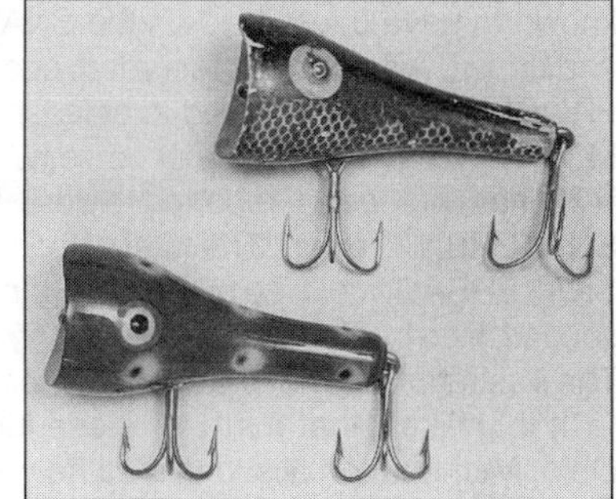

COLOR OR FINISH: Pearl; rich green scale etched with black; perch scale; green frog spot, solid black, solid yellow.

900 SERIES DARTER SCOUT

(Top Scout)

This wooden plug has a scoop nose shape, a belly and trailing treble hook. It weighs 1/2 ounce and was about 2-3/4" long.

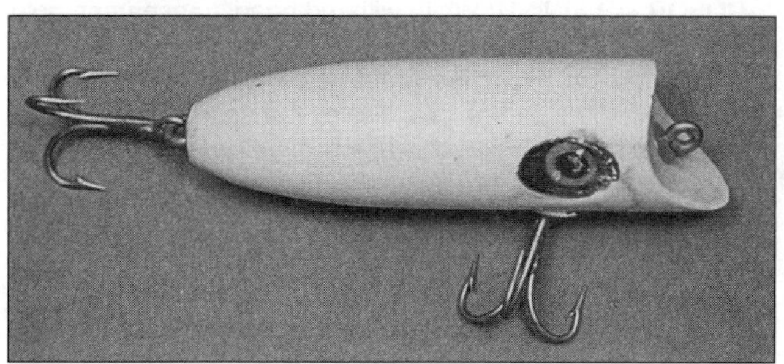

It was available in exactly the same colors as the POPPER SCOUT. Collector value range: $20-$50.

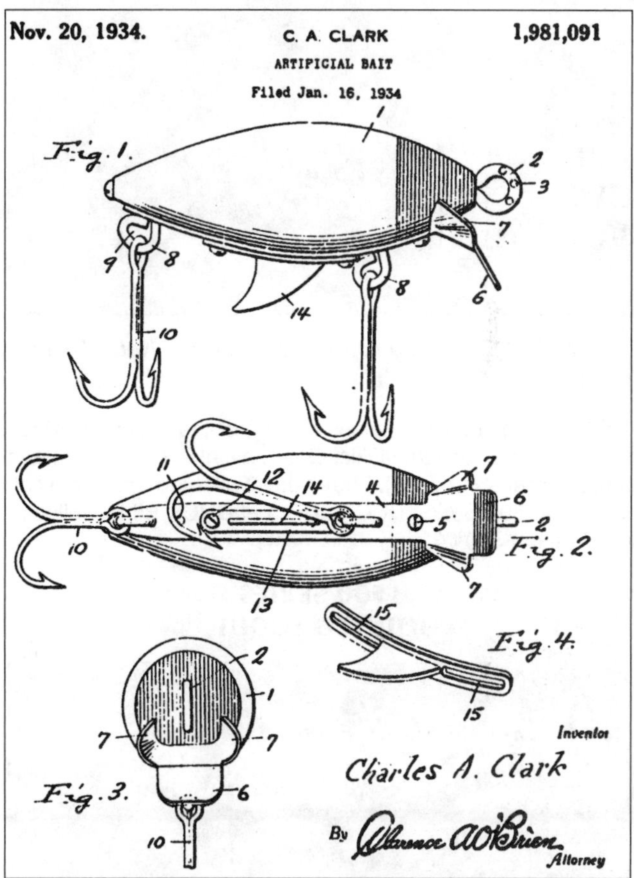

Patent drawing for Clark's WATER SCOUT showing the typical Clark keel piece and the large screw-eye line tie with holes for changing line tie position on the screw eye. None have ever shown up with this particular line tie as yet. Patent granted November 20, 1934.

800 SERIES WATER SCOUT STREAMLINER

Water Scout STREAMLINER. Shown here are examples of special-order lures that could be obtained in quantity with the angler's name or advertising on the body. Center lure says "Dale Allmon" and the left lure, "George Jordan, Furrier".

This is a sinking plastic Water Scout type lure weighing 5/8 ounce. Collector value range: $20-$30.

COLOR OR FINISH: White with red head; transparent, gold ribs, silver scale on sides; transparent, silver ribs, red scale on sides; transparent, silver ribs, green scale; rainbow; transparent shiner scale; transparent pike scale; transparent frog spots; perch scale; pearl; black with white ribs; yellow with white ribs; fluorescent green; fluorescent yellow, fluorescent red.

1000 SERIES LITTLE EDDIE (Sinker)
2000 SERIES LITTLE EDDIE (Floater)
(Little Eddie Water Scouts)

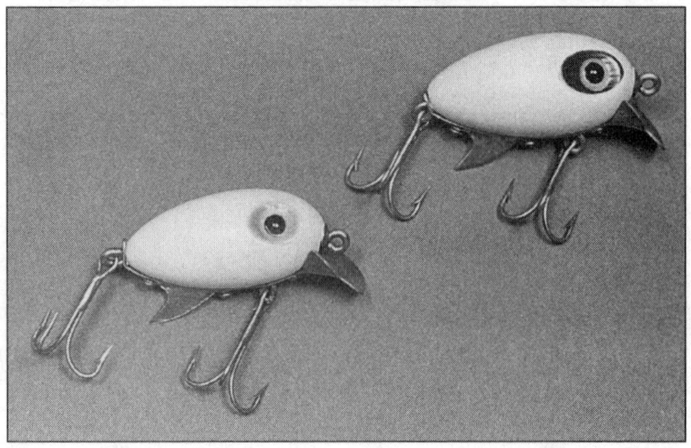

LITTLE EDDIE. Right: a floater, Left: a sinker. Note slight difference in sizes.

These are smaller versions (1-5/8") of the original WATER SCOUT, made for light tackle. One is a sinker (1/2 ounce) and one, a floater (1/4 ounce). They were available in the same colors as the 500 Series DUCKLING and DUCK BILL. Collector value range: $20-$30.

1500 SERIES
JOINTED SCOUT

This is a 3", 1/2-ounce, jointed plastic plug with essentially the same design and configuration as the 600 Series DUCK BILL. Collector value range: $20-$40.

COLOR OR FINISH: White with redhead; transparent, silver ribs, red scale on sides; rainbow, transparent, green scale, silver ribs; shiner scale; brown scale; perch scale; pearl scale; black with white ribs; yellow with white ribs; transparent pike scale; frog spot, green-yellow and black spots; fluorescent green; fluorescent yellow; fluorescent red.

2600 SERIES "GOOFY GUS"

This 1/2 ounce lure has an oddly shaped body. It is long and thin in the middle something like an hour glass. It has nose- and tail-mounted propeller spinners and is a surface bait. Collector value range: $50-$75.

COLOR OR FINISH: Deep green scale, blended with yellow, shiner scale; perch scale; pike scale; pearl with red eyes; pearl with blue eyes; black with white ribs; yellow with white ribs; yellow with black ribs; white with black ribs.

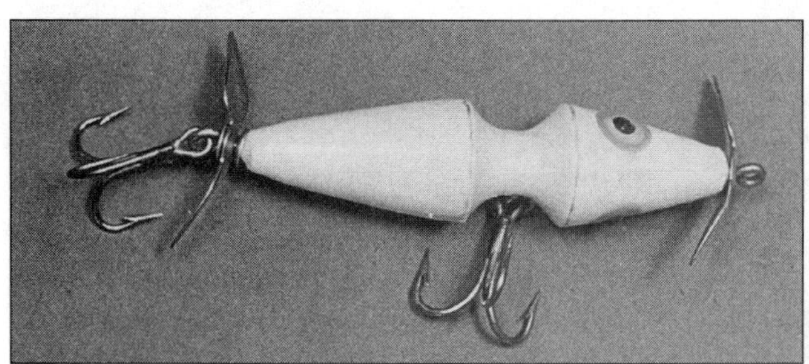

IMPORTANT NOTICE

The value ranges listed in this book are for lures in Very Good to Excellent condition. The values of those lures not in Very Good to Excellent condition can and probably will be worth considerably less. The values are meant to be a guide only.

THE SNAKERBAIT and THE FROGERBAIT

Robert L. Clewell Mfg. — Canton, Ohio

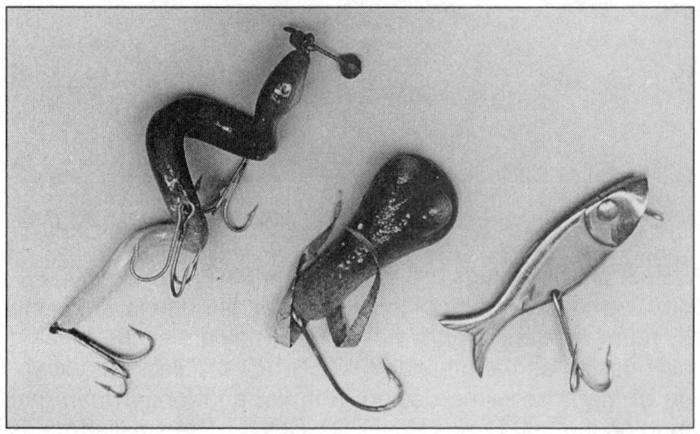

Top to bottom: The SNAKERBAIT, 4-1/2 "; the FROGERBAIT 21/4" and the BIG MOUTH MIN 2-3/4". Measurements actual, exclusive of hooks.

This one-man company existed for just a few years; mostly in Clewell's home. Beginning in 1926 and closing in 1934 when he moved to another home in Ohio. Clewell's output included several fly rod lures and a couple of other, unusual lures. It is the latter that interests collectors. The SNAKERBAIT and the FROGERBAIT were made of molded rubber and then spray painted. The colors known to have been used on the SNAKERBAIT are: red, green and brown. Although not recorded, one can only surmise that the FROGERBAIT was offered in at least a green version. The BIG MOUTH MINS were made of brass with a silver finish.

It has not been reported before that two patents for the SNAKERBAIT exist. The first, filed in 1926, for the existing SNAKERBAIT was filed by Robert L. and Charles W. Clewell. The second, filed by Robert L. alone in 1927, was for a jointed version. The illustration shows one joint, just behind the head of the snake.

It is unlikely that many of these lures will be found outside Ohio, Michigan or Wisconsin as he was not known to have actively promoted them anywhere else. The SNAKERBAIT is the only one of the three that any trade data was found for. Collector value range: $350-$450.

COLDWATER BAIT COMPANY

Willis E. Phinney — Coldwater, Michigan

W. E. PHINNEY.

ARTIFICIAL BAIT.

APPLICATION FILED SEPT. 7, 1916.

1,239,956. Patented Sept. 11, 1917.

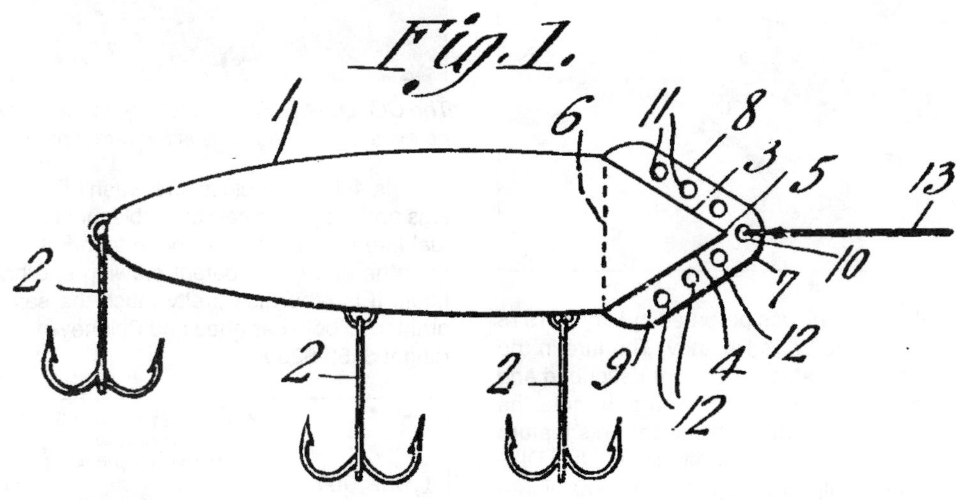

A detail from the original patent drawing for the COLDWATER KING. Note the seven holes (line ties) in the metal lip. The one in the photo has only five.

EUREKA BAIT COMPANY

Samuel O. Larrabee — Coldwater, Michigan

It really is not yet known just what the nature of the relationship between these two men and their companies was, but research of what material has been uncovered so far proves that they were connected in some way at some time in their early days. A look at patent dates and the grantees will demonstrate this.

LUREAPPLIC. DATEGRANT DATEGRANTEE

Eureka Wiggler
June 2, 1913 June 9, 1914

Larrabee
Coldwater Weedless
July 18, 1916Sept. 11, 1917

Phinney & Larrabee
Coldwater King
Sept. 7,1916Sept. 11, 1917

Phinney
Coldwater Hell Diver
May 17,1917 May 14, 1918

Note that the EUREKA WIGGLER is the earliest and granted only to Larrabee (Eureka Bait Company), but about two years later we find the COLDWATER WEEDLESS being patented with the rights being granted to both gentlemen. Furthermore, a Coldwater Bait Company (The Phinney Company) advertisement from 1931 offers the EUREKA WIGGLER (The Larrebee Bait), but calls it the COLDWATER WEEDLESS. From that it would appear that Phinney ended up in control by some means that only time will reveal to us.

Identifying which lure was made by which company is not always an easy task. A couple of general, though not always reliable rules are that the Coldwater products will often have a washer-like tail protector device and most will have cup and screw eye belly hook hardware. The Eureka products are also found with simple screw eye hook hangers. Color patterns could help to separate them, but there are some known to be common to both. The colors found in lists and on the lures themselves so far are as follows:

COLDWATER COLORS: Fancy potted, frog back with white belly, white with red throat, white luminous, white with sprayed red head, red back with white belly,

EUREKA COLORS: Green crackle back with white belly and red painted mouth, red crackle back with white belly and red painted mouth, orange crackle back with white belly and red painted mouth

The Eureka Crackle back finish is very unusual. Once you have seen an example you will recognize it from then on.

COLDWATER KING

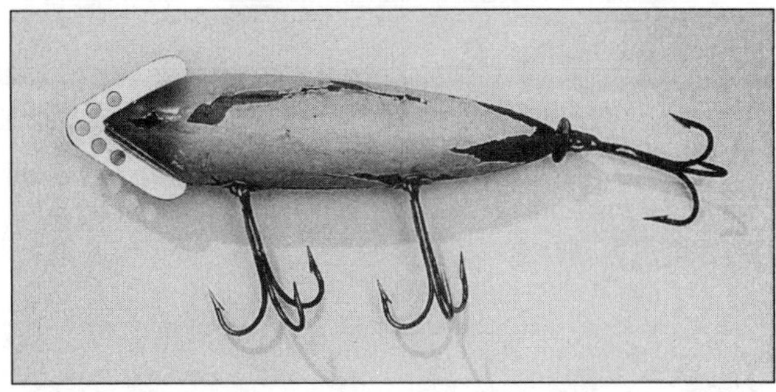

The patent for this plug was granted to Willis Phinney in 1917 and the example in the photo here conforms almost exactly to the patent drawing. Not evident in the photo is that the

metal plate is installed at an angle so that the lure is erratic on retrieve. Note the typical Coldwater use of the slightly cupped washer at the tail hook attachment. Collector value range: $150-$250.

COLDWATER HELL DRIVER

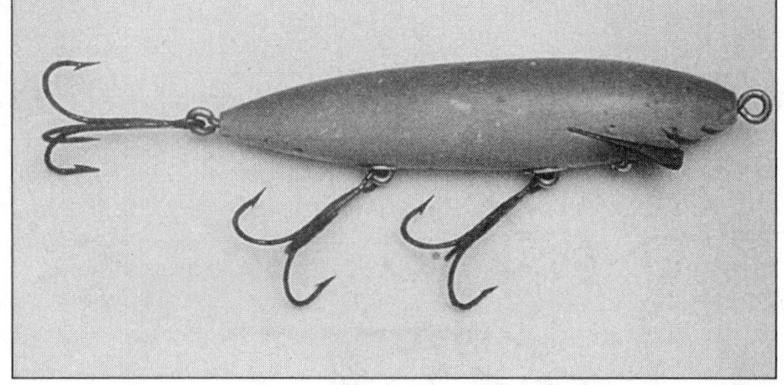

This lure, about 4-1/4" long, was patented in May of 1918 with rights being assigned to Willis Phinney. The lure in the photo here is essentially the same as the lure described and drawn in the original patent application. You may note the patent drawing shows vertical fins at the nose. This feature has not been found to date. The major feature of the hell DIVER is the adjustable diving lip. It is adjusted by loosening a screw under the nose and sliding the lip back and forth. This plug is similar to the Shakespeare HYDROPLANE so be careful not to confuse them. The Coldwater HELL DIVER has been found with glass eyes (rare) but usually has no eyes. Collector value range: $105-$175.

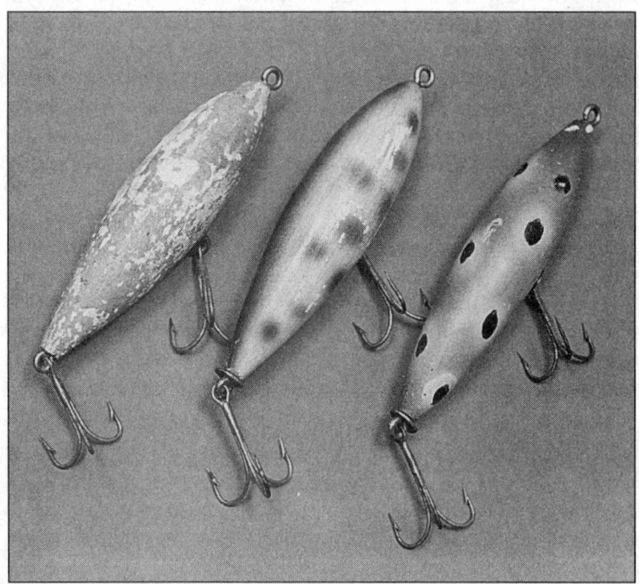

These are lures that could be either Eureka or Coldwater products. The body shape and cup hardware are the reasons they are placed here. No ads or catalog references were found for them under the Eureka Bait Company name. Lure on far right has glass eyes.

COLDWATER WEEDLESS

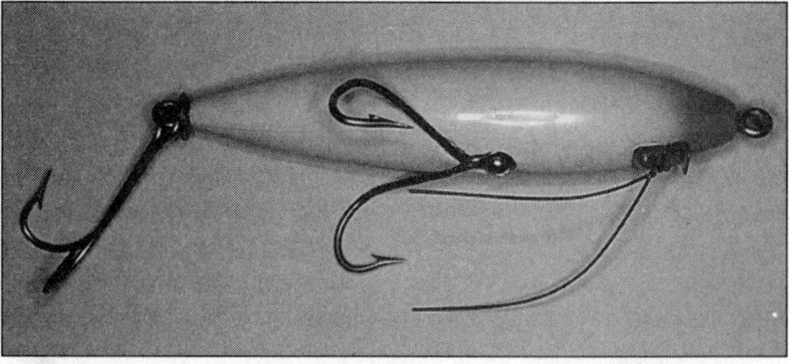

The COLDWATER WEEDLESS. White body with red head and no eyes 4-1/4' long. This is the rarest of the Coldwater lures.

This 4-1/2" weedless lure wasn't found in any of the catalogs and old periodicals available for study, but at least one actual lure (see photo) has been found. It is somewhat slimmer than the one in the patent drawing and has a trailing double hook. It is otherwise pretty much the same. The patent was granted to both Larrabee and Phinney in 1917. Collector value range: $150-$200.

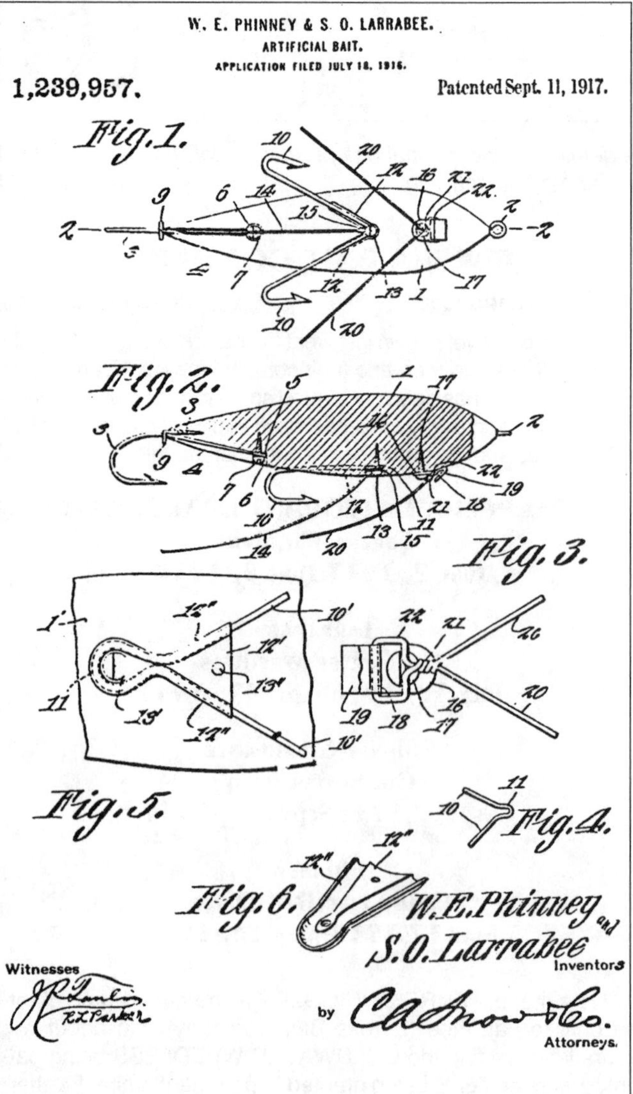

Original patent application drawing for the COLDWATER WEEDLESS.

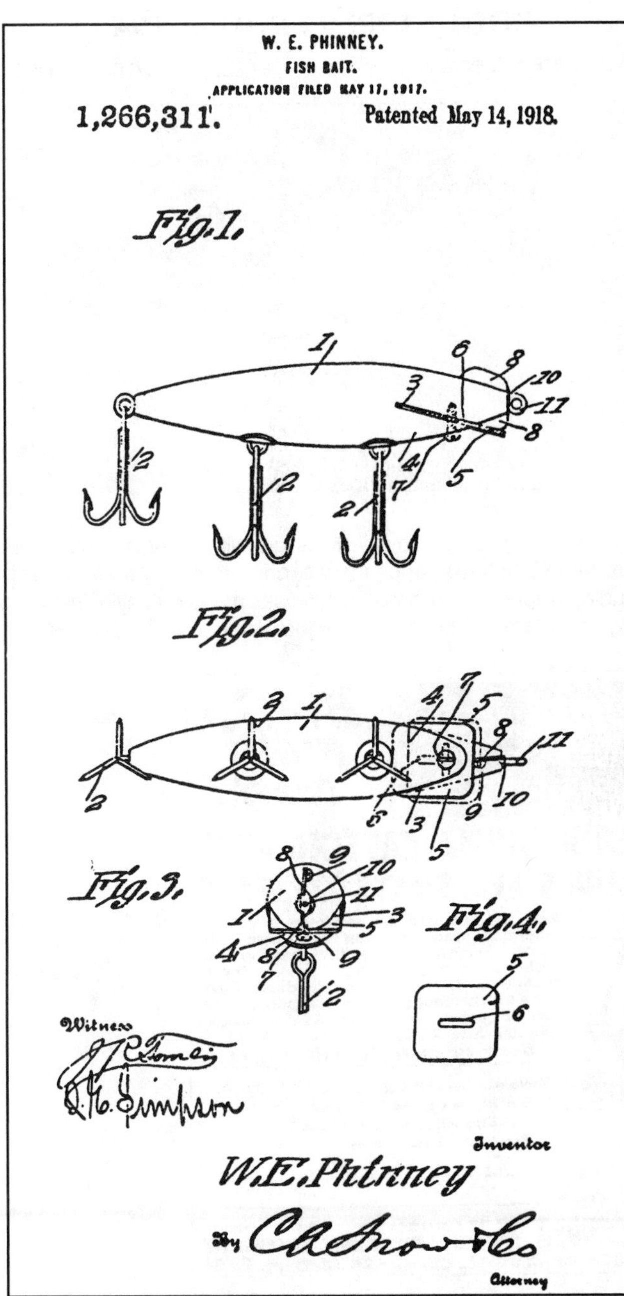

Original patent drawing of the COLDWATER HELL DIVER. Granted to Willis E. Phinney May 14, 1918.

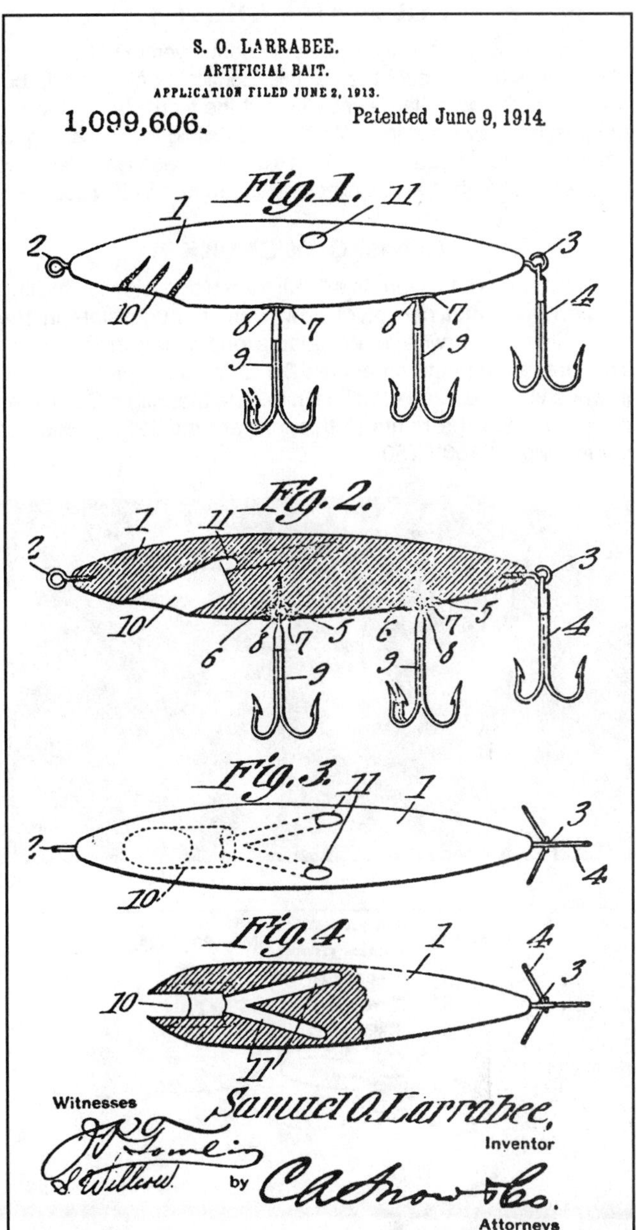

Original patent drawing for the EUREKA WIGGLER. Granted to Samuel O. Larrabee, June 9, 1914.

COLDWATER WIGGLER AND EUREKA WIGGLER

The EUREKA WIGGLER was the original name for this lure. It was the first of the Coldwater/Eureka products to be patented by Larrabee in 1914 as we have seen. As you can see by studying the accompanying patent illustration it is designed with a "Y" shaped water passageway so that as the lure is retrieved water passes through making the lure wiggle. Note that the mouth (usually painted red) is larger than the two exit holes on the sides. In the photo here, the lure measures 3-7/8" and is known to be a COLDWATER WIGGLER. Note the typical Coldwater cup and screw eye hardware. This lure is often confused with the LOCKHART WATER WITCH, another lure with an internal waterway. They are distinguished by the lack of cup hardware on the Water Witch and the fact that the Wiggler has an exit hole on each side while the other has only one (on the back). Collector value range for the Eureka Wiggler or the Coldwater Wiggler: $150-$200.

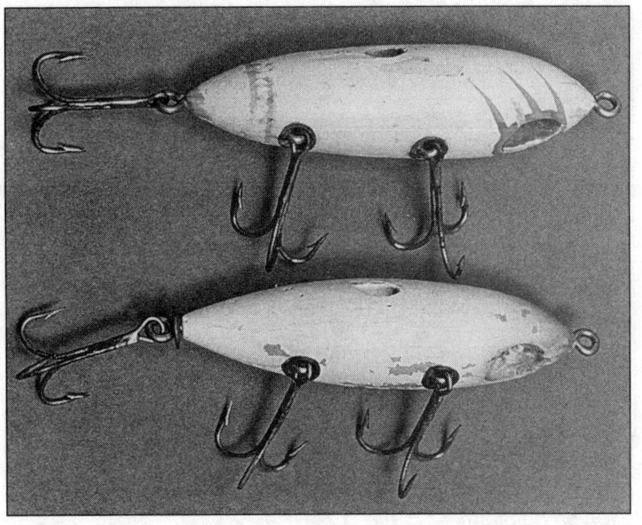

COLDWATER GHOST

This lure is in actuality, merely a curious version of the Wigglers above, or is thought to be. It is identical in all respects but one. It has the same large entry hole at the mouth but instead of the passageway splitting into a "Y" and exiting the sides, it gets smaller like the "Y", but it remains a single passage way and turns up to exit out at the back. Collector value range: $150-$200.

COMSTOCK CHUNK

Aptly named, this lure is a "chunk" of wood with two trailing single hooks that can pivot downward through slots in the body. It has two wire weed guards originating at the nose. The lure in the photo measures 2-1/2" body length. Available in white with red head or solid white. The Moonlight Bait Company obtained the rights to this lure around 1928. Collector value range: $100-$150.

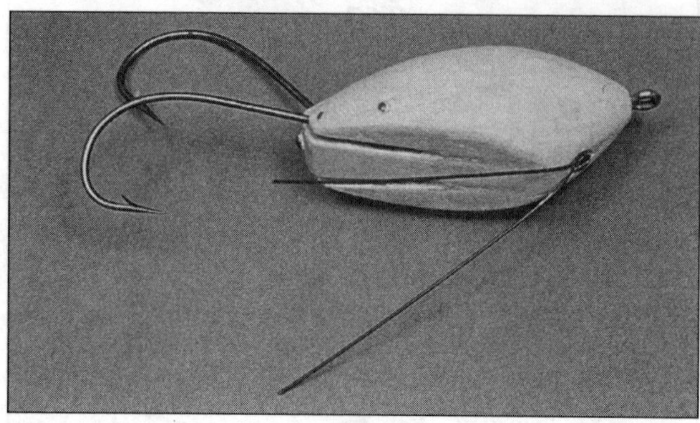

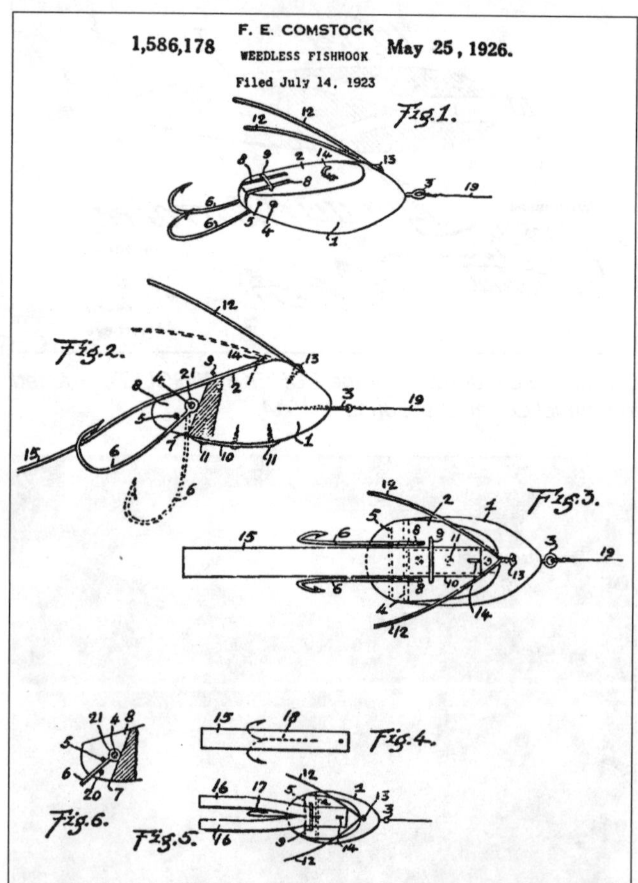

Original patent drawing of the Comstock Chunk. Filed in 1923 and granted three years later on May 25, 1926. Notice the Staple type hook limiter in Fig. 1.

COOL RIPPLE FROG c. 1947

Associated Specialties Chicago, Illinois

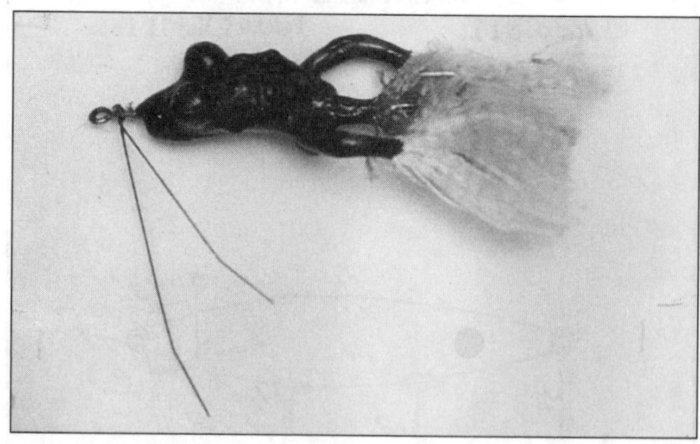

This is a frog-shaped weedless lure with a single hook. There are three brush-type appendages, one protruding from the belly and two representing legs. The lure was made with nylon skin and rayon and weighs 5/8 ounce. Collector value range: $20-$30.

Advertisement from the March, 1948 issue of Field & Stream.

The small advertisement reproduced here is for a Cool Ripple Frog that is similar, but not the same as the one in the photo. It could, I suppose, be a later or earlier model. The ad was found in the March, 1948 issue of *Field and Stream* magazine so the time frame matches.

GENTLEMAN JIM c. 1949

Associated Specialties Chicago, Illinois

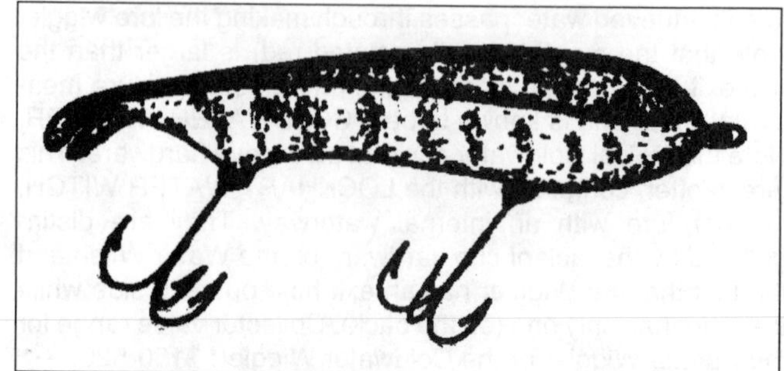

Made of plastic (Tenite), this lure has two belly-mounted trebles and a twin tail molded in. The twin tail appears fragile, therefore the collector may encounter broken examples. Collector value range: $8-$15.

THE CRA-BUG BAIT COMPANY

Forrest Craig   Charlotte, Michigan

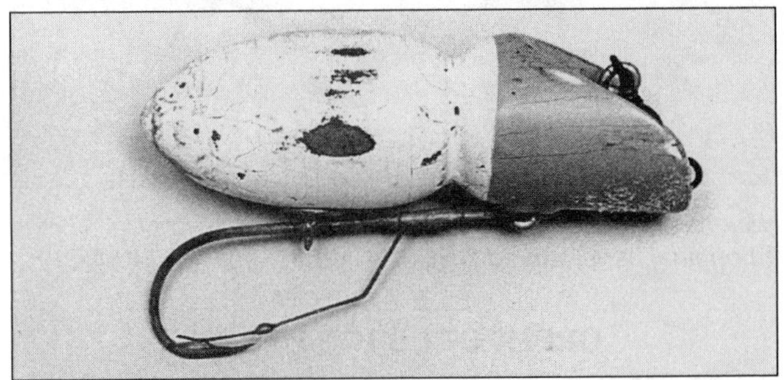

This company was a real "Mom and Pop" operation. Craig and his wife were the sole employees. The two of them, with the help of their son, did all the assembly and painting. Craig contracted out the turning of the bodies on a lathe. The company began operation in 1939 and ceased operation three years later when metal parts got scarce as the result of the U.S. entering World War II. In those three years it is estimated that less than 2,000 lures were made, so they are difficult to find. The CRA-BUG was available in three hook styles and six colors. There was one version where there were two treble hooks on the body, another with a long shank weedless hook attached along the belly and the third was a double hook that was held to the body by a screw eye and a pin. The six colors available were: White body with red head, Frog, Mouse with a tail, Tiger striped scale finish, Solid white and Solid black. Collector value range: $50-$80.

CRAZY LEGS

Mueller-Perry Company, Inc.   St. Louis, Missouri

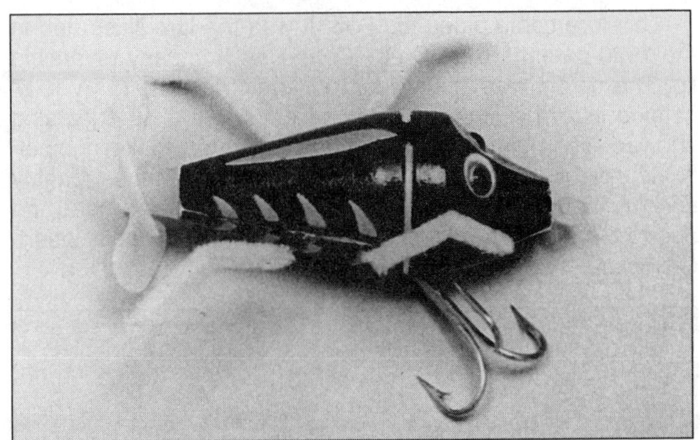

This 2" plastic lure has pipe cleaner-like legs that wiggle as the result of a plastic tail-mounted spinner turning on retrieve. There is at least one other style of this contraption known that is 3" long. Collector value range: $10-$30.

CREEK CHUB BAIT COMPANY

Garrett, Indiana

The Creek Chub Company began doing business in 1906 in Garrett, Indiana. The original three founders were George Schultress, Carl Heinzerling, and Henry S. Dills. Dills was the design genius behind the lures and Heinzerling and Schultress were the business end of the venture and provided the capital. The first Creek Chub lure was the No. 100 Wiggler. While they began producing and selling lures in 1906 they were not able to ship them in any significant numbers until 1908. A very significant contribution to the industry was their development of the natural scale finish for artificial lures. This finish was offered at least as early as 1917 and perhaps earlier. Like many other companies many of their earliest models lacked eyes, then glass eyes and so forth in the eye evolution of most companies' products. Creek Chub, however, stuck to the use of the cup and screw eye hardware from its initial development and used it from then on. The first hook hardware was the simple screw eye with a flat washer. The earliest metal diving blades were plain with no name stamped on them. Next came the plain lip with their name (CCBCO) and usually a patent date of 9-7-20. The next change was the reinforced lip produced by stamping two parallel ridges in the lip for extra strength.

Creek Chub was sold to the Lazy Ike Corp., Des Moines, in 1978.

Anyone with an interest in collecting Creek Chub lures must have the book *Collector's Guide to Creek Chub Lures & Collectibles* by Harold E. Smith, M.D. It is a full-color, indispensable book for the Creek Chub collector. Please see the section on recommended books for a source.

OBSERVATIONS REGARDING IDENTIFICATION AND DATING CREEK CHUB LURES

1. Hardware
   a. First lures had no metal reinforcing tail insert. This came along about 1920. Not all Creek Chub Bait Company lures utilized this.
   b. Earliest (1906-about 1915) hook hardware was a screw eye and small washer. Next came the small cup (shallow) and screw eye. These were always placed on the lures during hardware assembly *after* painting so cups are never found painted over as in the case of many other companies such as South Bend.
   c. The reversible metal lip plane was unmarked at first. The late teens to about 1920 saw the first of the lips with the company name stamped on them. At first the planes were fastened with a screw eye in the head. This was for ease of removal and reversal but provided a second line tie as well. Later this was replaced with a slotted screw. The double screw fastener came along in the early to mid-1930s. Most of the marked lips have a patent date stamped on them. Don't confuse this with dating the lure. The date reflects only when the blade was patented, not when it was made.
   d. Propeller spinners are unique. They were die cut and stamped out with a short raised rib on each blade extending from the pivot hole. You could call them "floppy" but the company used small discs on either side as bearings to help-them stay straight and spin easily.

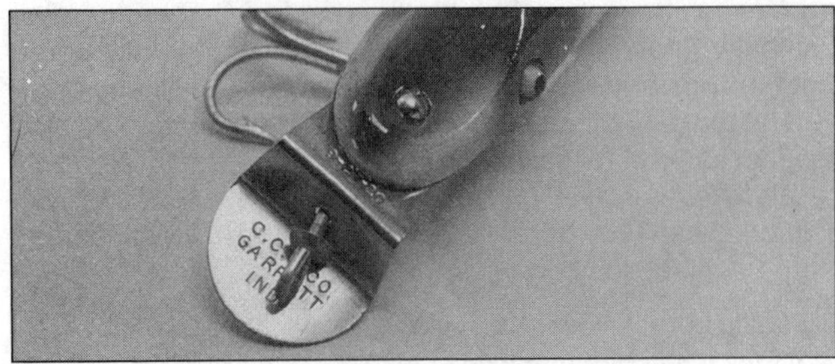

An example of the second style of the reversible lip.

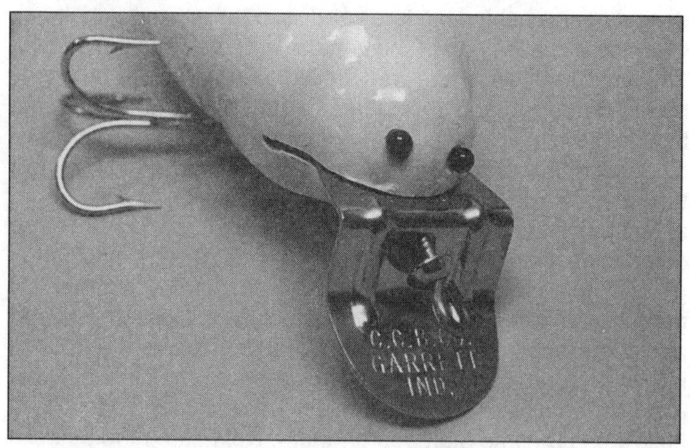

This reinforced version came along in 1935 and was used on most of their very large lures from then on.

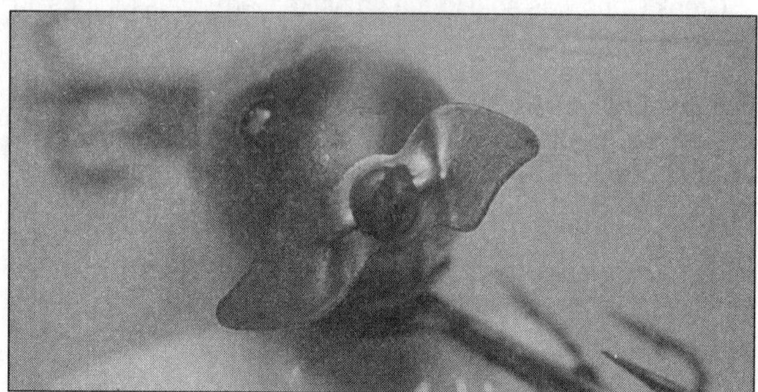

The Creek Chub Bait Company style propeller spinner.

2. Colors and Finishes
   a. Any time you find a lure with hand brushed gill marks you have a real early prize. These are found on pre-1924 lures.
   b. Henry S. Dills patented the spray-through-netting method of attaining scale finish on lures in 1919, assigning half the rights to the Heddon Company. The scale finish was used on Creek Chub Bait Company lures at least as early as 1917.
   c. The company was very liberal with special order colors. Anyone who wanted a special pattern or color could get it if a dozen or more lures were ordered, so don't be surprised if you find some real strange combinations and patterns.
   d. They introduced new colors in 1949 called "Fire Plug with Gantron Fire Laquer". The advertisement, complete with the mis-spelled word appeared in the October, 1949 issue of *Field & Stream.* The lures were painted with combinations of bright yellow, orange, fluorescent green and sometimes black. They discontinued these in 1954 and only existing stock was sold after that.
3. Eyes

Eye type is not a very good method of identification or dating. We can be reasonably sure the very first Creek Chub Bait Company lures had no eyes, but collectors generally agree that the company was producing lures with no eyes and glass eyes at the same time early on. Painted eyes were commonly used on some of these lures very early also. The rarities would be glass eyes found on lures that were usually made with painted eyes. They began using Tack Eyes in 1960 and used them from that point on.

4. Plastic Lures

Creek Chub began making plastic lures starting with the NIKIE in 1956. They added three more plastic lures the next year, the SNARK, SNARKIE and SNARK EEL. In 1960 they added several more and by the time the company was sold in 1978 the line had 42 plastic baits. The individual listings will give you a better timeline for dating the lures.

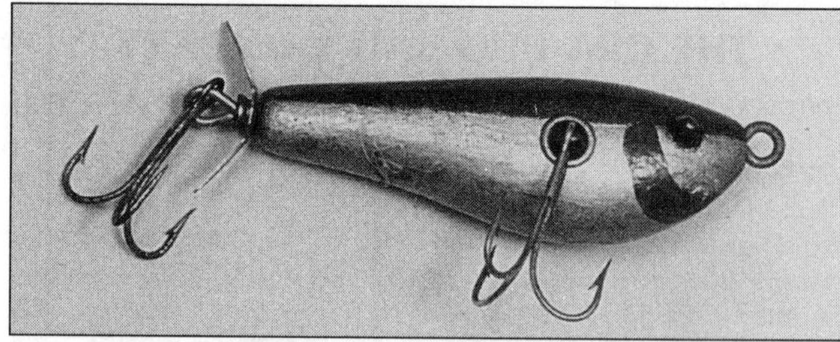

Handmade injured minnow from the Heddon archives. This is an original hand-carved CREEK CHUB INJURED MINNOW.

CREEK CHUB ICE DECOY

This is a very rare Creek Chub product. Not found in any catalog to date it is 4-1/2" long including tail fin. It has glass eyes, metal tail fin and opposite mounted side fins in line with the line tie. The body is that of the Creek Chub FIN TAIL SHINER. There is a photo of the ICE DECOY in the Creek Chub color section. Collector value range: $1,000-$1,500.

THE CREEK CHUB WIGGLER 1906-1964

This lure came along in 1906. It was the lure illustrated in the 1920 patent for the Creek Chub Bait Company reversible lip. The patent was applied for in December of 1915. A 1917 catalog illustrates the lure with no eyes, but a 1918 catalog showed eyes. They have always had the treble hooks, one belly mounted and one trailing. The collector may be reasonably sure he has the earliest version if it has flattened head, no eyes, no name stamped on the lip and no tail hook metal insert. Collector value range: $25-$50.

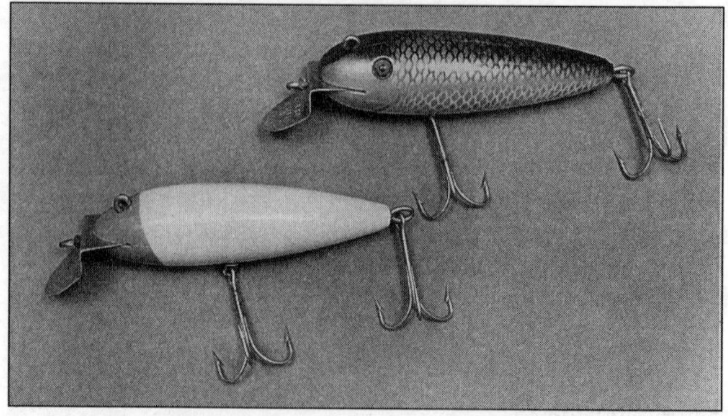

WIGGLERS. Lower is oldest with no eyes and no name on lip. Upper has glass eyes and name stamped on the lip. Neither one has the tail hook metal reinforcing insert.

Original box for the Creek Chub Wiggler. The lure came in this box. It is 3-1/2", has glass eyes and utilizes the cup and screw eye hook hardware. The finish is Natural Perch scale and the box is so marked. Having the original box can add to the value of the lure. In this case it adds roughly $50 to the lure value range of $25-$50.

CATALOG SERIES #	BODY LENGTH	LURE WEIGHT
100	3-1/2"	3/4 oz.

COLOR OR FINISH: *Natural chub, scale finish, *perch with scale finish, *dark gold with scale finish, *red side minnow with scale finish, *white with red head, *solid red, goldfish with scale finish, natural mullet with scale finish, green back with scale finish, black with white head, silver flash, frog finish, silver shiner.

**The patterns shown as available in the 1917 catalog.*

WIGGLER, yellow glass eyes, red dace scale, name on lip. What appears to be a second line tie (on top of head) is, in fact, the means of holding the reversible hook and making it easy to change it.

THE BABY CHUB
1917-1955

Known in later catalogs as the BABY CHUB WIGGLER, the 1917 listing shows this plug to be essentially the same as the Creek Chub WIGGLER but in a smaller, lighter version. It has the same hook configuration and the reversible metal lip blade is smaller. A 1953 catalog illustrates it as still being available. It is one of the first three lures available from the company. The Collector value range: $25-$40.

CATALOG SERIES #	BODY LENGTH	LURE WEIGHT
100	3/12"	3/4 oz.

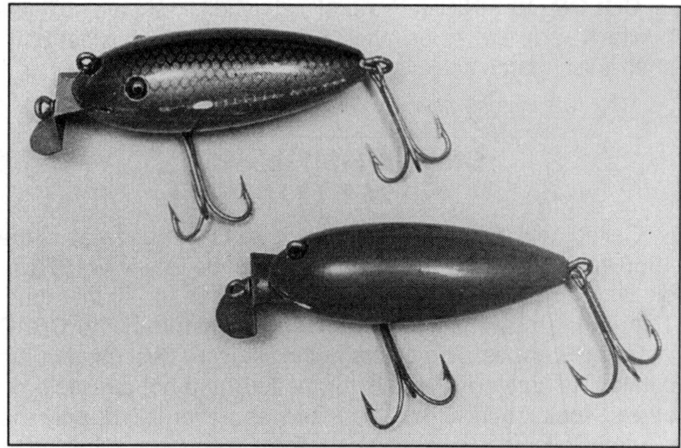

BABY CHUB. Lower has no eyes, upper has glass eyes. Neither has name stamped on lip.

COLOR OR FINISH: *Natural chub scale finish; *perch, scale finish; *red side, scale finish; *dark gold, scale finish; *white with red head; *green back, scale finish; *solid red; gold finish, scale finish; black with red head; solid red; silver flash; silver shiner, scale finish; natural mullet, scale finish; frog finish.

**The finishes first available on the plug.*

THE CREEK CRAB WIGGLERS OR THE CRAWDAD, 300 SERIES

BABY CRAWDAD, 400 SERIES
1917-1964

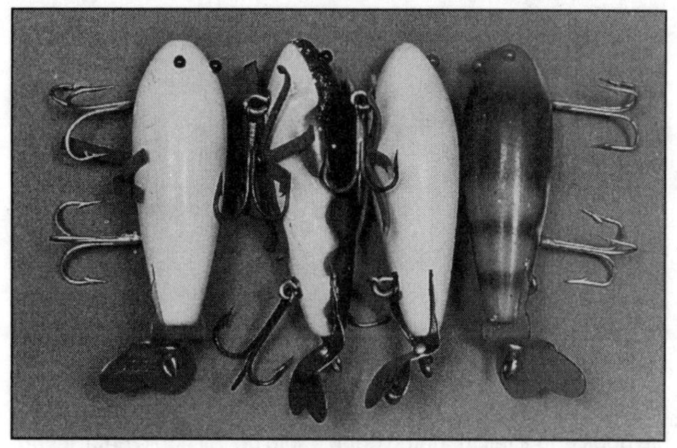

New in the late 1910s, the Creek Crab Wiggler was renamed THE CRAWDAD by 1920. At first only one size (2-3/4") and one finish (natural crab) was available. In 1919 they added the BABY CRAB at 2-1/2" and two more finishes, "Albino" and "Tan Color, Shell Finish". Both sport bead eyes. They had added the "River Peeler" (steel blue shell finish) by 1924. A 1917 catalog said this lure was the "Only Bait Without Nickel Plate." Presumably they were talking about the reversible diving plane, for earliest examples have a painted dive plane. It has eight flexible rubber legs protruding from the belly. The regular CRAWDAD is equipped with two belly trebles and the Baby size has two double hooks. The very earliest of these critters will have painted dive planes with no markings, red eyes, screw eye and washer hook rig. Collector value range: $25-$65.

CATALOG SERIES #	BODY LENGTH	LURE WEIGHT
300	2-3/4"	3/4 oz.
400	2-1/2"	1/2 oz.

COLOR OR FINISH: *Natural crab, shell finish; albino finish (white & red); tan color, shell finish; river peeler, steel blue, shell finish; perch scale; silver flash.

**This was the only finish available until around 1918-1920.*

CRAY-Z-FISH (plastic) 1964-1978

Called new in the 1964 catalog, it was last illustrated in the 1968 edition. It remained in the catalog price lists until 1978 indicating it may have remained in production for all that time. This lure is obviously the plastic replacement for the CRAB WIGGLER above. The colors in the list were described in the catalog as created specially for the lure and not available on other Creek Chub lures. The size was never listed, only the weight. Collector value range: $5-$10.

CATALOG SERIES #	BODY LENGTH	LURE WEIGHT
9900	?	1/4 oz.

COLOR OR FINISH: White with red head, natural crab, shrimp crab, tan crab, silver shad, tiger stripe.

OPEN MOUTH SHINER 1918-1933

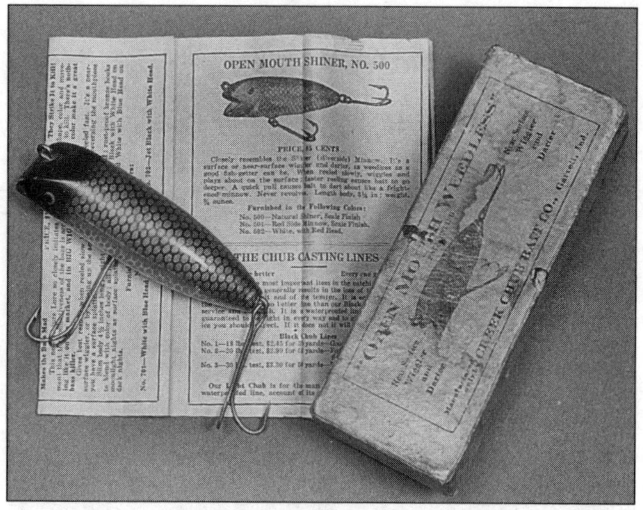

New in 1918, this plug closely resembles a Shiner or Silverside Minnow. It has cut-out notch mouth, a belly-mounted double hook and a tail mounted double with no tail hook metal insert. The 1931 catalog is the last one in the author's possession to illustrate this plug as available. Collector value range: $55-$75.

CATALOG SERIES #	BODY LENGTH	LURE WEIGHT
500	3-1/4"	3/4 oz.

COLOR OR FINISH: Natural shiner, scale finish; red side minnow, scale finish; white with red head, silver flash.

TOP 'N POP (plastic) 1960-1967

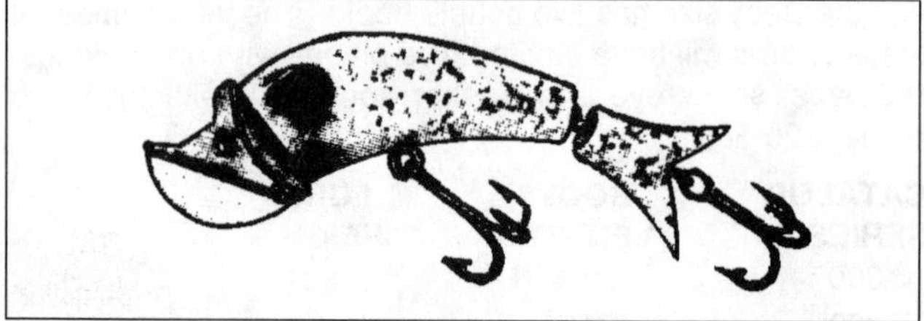

This plastic lure "Plunks, pops, short jerks, walks, jumps, frantic swimming with slow retrieve." They sure covered the waterfront. It has a peculiarly shaped metal lip that apparently is designed to enable the fisherman all those action options. First illustrated in the 1960 catalog, it was last illustrated in the 1967 edition. It was listed in the price list of the 1968 catalog, but was not detailed and illustrated. Collector value range: $5-$10.

CATALOG SERIES #	BODY LENGTH	LURE WEIGHT
500-P	?	1/4 oz.

COLOR OR FINISH: Perch scale, white with red head, yellow spotted, silver flash frog.

HUSKY MUSKY 1919-1955

This is another very early Creek Chub lure. A large plug for musky fishing, it has the reversible metal lip blade, a belly-mounted and a trailing treble hook. Prior to 1915 this hook hardware was the simple washer and screw eye. All after have the cup and anchored hook hardware. They must have made a few 3T models because several have turned up. In the 1936 they offered the "IMPROVED HUSKY MUSKY." Up until then they sported two line ties, one on top of the head and the one on the dive plane. The head-top line tie was eliminated and the Thru-body hook hangers and reinforced dive plane were added. They appeared continuously in catalogs until 1955. The Collector value range: $25-$50.

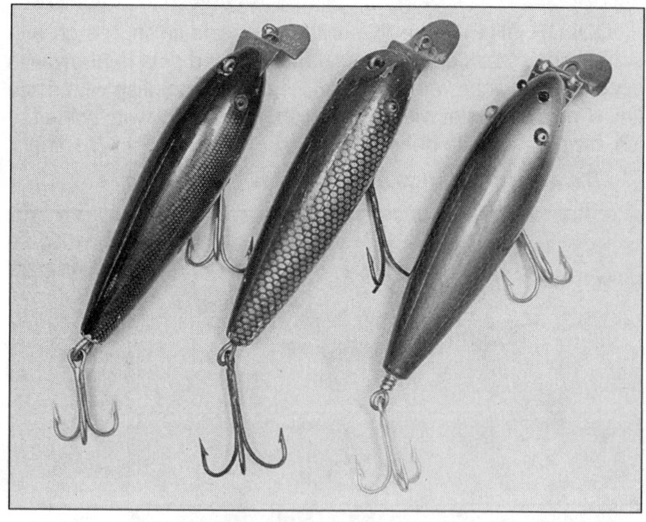

Newest on right (note 2 screws holding lip). Lip is reinforced (ribbed) and unmarked. This is the IMPROVED HUSKY MUSKY introduced in 1936.

CATALOG SERIES #	BODY LENGTH	LURE WEIGHT
600	5"	1-1/2 oz.

COLOR OR FINISH: *Natural chub, scale finish; *natural mullet, scale finish; natural perch, scale finish; white with red head; silver flash.

**The original two finishes available.*

MITIE MOUSE (plastic) 1963-1978

This little fellow floats at rest, but runs deep upon retrieve. The metal dive lip is always equipped with a snap swivel. It's size was never listed, only its weight. The colors in the list are non-standard and do not match any other Creek Chub colors.

They were unique. A couple of them are shared by the CRAY-Z-FISH, 9900 Series. Collector value range: $5-$10.

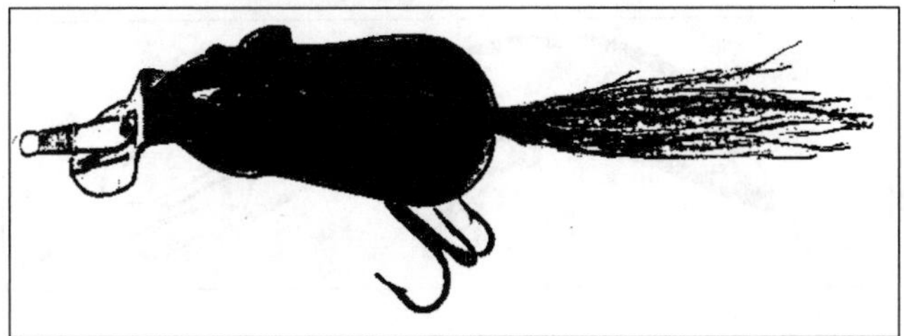

CATALOG SERIES #	BODY LENGTH	LURE WEIGHT
600-P	?	1/4 oz.

COLOR OR FINISH: Field mouse, black, gray tiger, silver flash.

THE FAMOUS PIKIE MINNOW 1920-1978 (Plastic, 1961-78)

A undated pocket catalog of around 1919-1921 illustrates this plug with the reversible metal lip blade, slope nose, two belly mounted treble hooks and a trailing treble. The listing states "all hooks set in sockets". This plug appears to have been available throughout the years. Earliest models had no eyes, hand painted gill marks and two line ties. The plastic PIKIE MINNOW came along in 1961. The plastic model was also available with the Deep Diving lip from 1961 on.

Collector value range in wood: $40-$60. Rare finishes such as black with white head, white with blue head or frog can easily double or even triple that value. Collector value range for plastic: $5-$10.

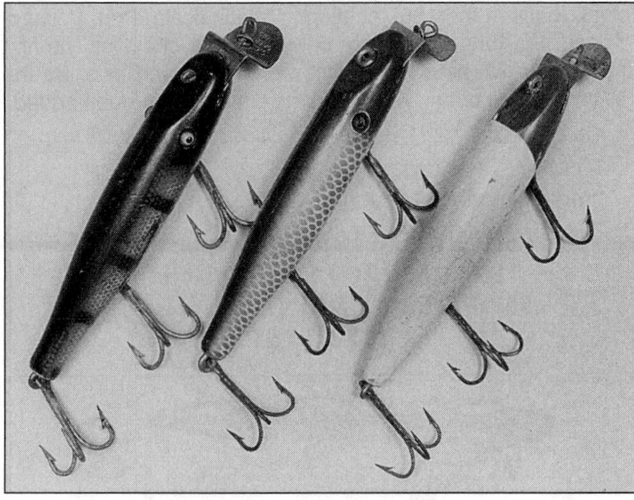

Left: Name on wide lip. Middle: Narrow lip, no name on lip. Right: Narrow lip, no name on lip, no eyes (oldest).

CATALOG SERIES #	BODY LENGTH	LURE WEIGHT
700	4-1/2"	3/4 oz.
700-P	4-1/4"	3/4 oz.
700-P-DD	4-1/4"	3/4 oz.

COLOR OR FINISH (wood): *Pikie Minnow, scale finish; *white with blue head; *black with white head, *white with red head, *natural perch, scale finish; *golden shiner, silver shiner, mullet, rainbow, silver flash; orange and black spots; "new black scale", "rainbow fire", "fire plug".

**The original finishes available (c. 1920).*

COLOR OR FINISH (plastic): Pike scale, perch scale. white with red head, silver shiner, silver flash, black, *mullet, mackerel, **fluorescent red, blue flash, ***chrome, amber.

**Deep Diving model only.*

***Available only from 1971 on.*

****Only from 1973 on.*

DELUXE WAG TAIL CHUB c. 1918-1953

This lure appears in an early (c. 1918) pocket catalog as available with the reversible metal lip blade, two belly-mounted double hooks (reversible to make the plug weedless), and a metal tail fin hinged to the lure so that it could flap on retrieve. It is illustrated in catalogs throughout the years as the "DELUXE WAG TAIL", but the listing in the 1953 catalog is rubber stamped "DISCONTINUED". Collector value range: $20-$40.

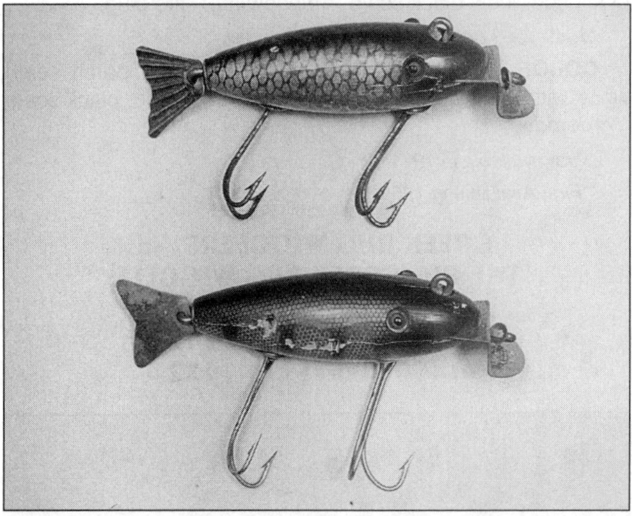

Top is newer, Bottom is oldest WAG TAIL CHUB.

CATALOG SERIES #	BODY LENGTH	LURE WEIGHT
800	2-3/4"	1/2 oz.

COLOR OR FINISH: Natural creek chub, scale finish; natural perch, scale finish; red side minnow, scale finish; golden shiner, scale finish; white with redhead, *dace; **silver flash.

**First available on this lure c. 1950.*

***Became available between 1926-1932.*

THE BABY PIKIE MINNOW 1921-1963 (Plastic 1963-1978)

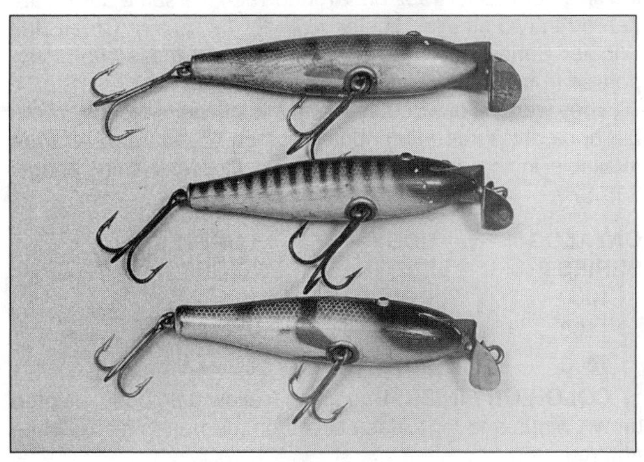

This is a smaller version of the famous Pikie Minnow No. 700. The other basic difference is the elimination of one of the belly-mounted treble hooks. Note the slightly differing body shapes and the absence of the painted fins on the middle lure in the photo. The other comments regarding the No. 700 apply to this plug as well.

The plastic version was cataloged first in the 1964 edition and was available right through to 1978. Collector value range for wood: $15-$30, plastic: $5-$10.

CATALOG SERIES #	BODY LENGTH	LURE WEIGHT
900	3-1/4"	1/2 oz.
900-P	3-3/4"	1/2 oz.

COLOR OR FINISH (wood): Natural Pikie finish, scale; white with red head, natural perch, scale; golden shiner, scale; silver shiner, scale; silver, rainbow; silver flash; orange and black spot, new black scale; *rainbow fire; *fire plug.

**1949-1953 only.*

COLOR OR FINISH (plastic): Pike scale, perch scale, white with red head, silver flash, *fluorescent red, black scale, **chrome.

**First available in 1971.*

***First Available in 1969.*

CREEK BUG WIGGLERS AND THE BIG CREEK BUG WIGGLER
1000 Series 1924-1947
1100 Series 1924-1947
1400 Series 1920-1932

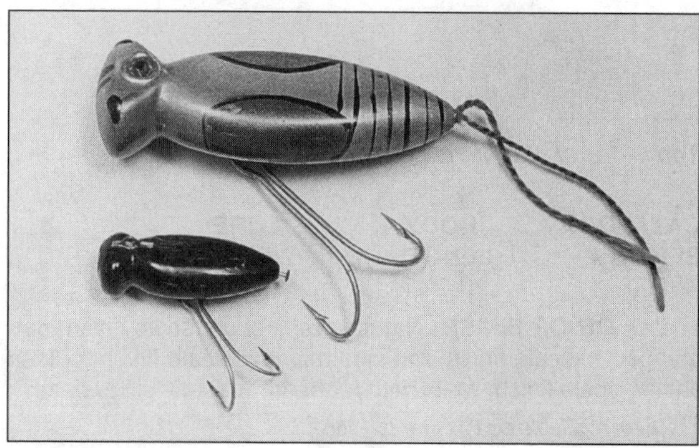

These BIG CREEK BUG WIGGLER originally appeared around 1919-1920 in three finishes, weights and lengths. It was a bass plug, but apparently wasn't offered in the bait casting size from about 1932 on. Around 1924 the same design appeared in two smaller, lighter sizes for fly fishing (Creek Bug Wiggler Series No. 1000 & No. 1100), but these two disappeared from the catalogs around 1945.

They were all of wood, had a reversible belly-mounted double hook and three tail-mounted strings or red cord. All were available in the same three finishes. Collector value range: $50-$70.

CATALOG SERIES #	BODY LENGTH	LURE WEIGHT
1000	7/8"	?
1100	1-1/4"	?
1400	2-1/2"	1/2 oz.

COLOR OR FINISH: Bug finish (yellow gold body, painted brown wings and legs, dash of red on the head); black; white and red.

NIKIE
1956-1978

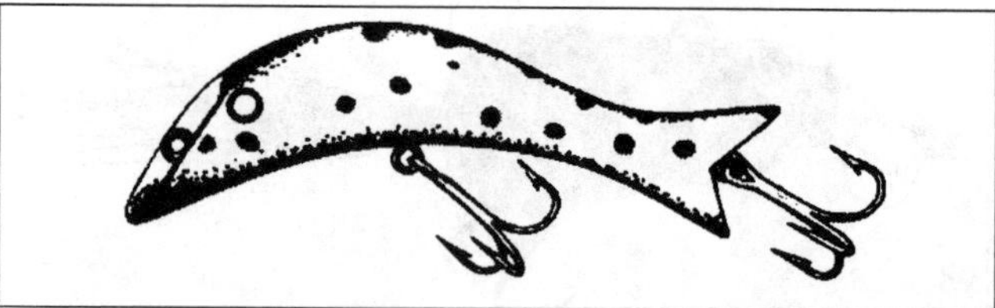

Creek Chub devoted two full pages of description and promotion in 1956 ballyhooing this new plastic lure: "NIKIE ... THE MOST IMPORTANT ADVANCE IN LURES IN A DECADE". By 1962 the larger Series 1000 was gone from the catalog. Remaining was the "Improved Model" in the smaller size, presumably because the description now includes the words "Slow Sinker". The original NIKIES floated at rest. By 1964 a smaller size had been added and both were referred to as "Ultra-Light Lures". Only the smaller size, however, carried the UL suffix denoting ultra-light lures. These two were actually first listed in the 1960 catalog, on a separate page from the larger NIKIE. They stayed in the line right up to 1978. As you can see by the color list, they apparently couldn't decide what were the best colors, because they kept changing their minds; often. Collector value range, 1000 Series: N/A, 9700 Series: $5-$10.

CATALOG SERIES #	BODY LENGTH	LURE WEIGHT
1000	3-1/2"	1/2 oz.
9700	2-1/4"	1/4 oz.
9700-UL	1-5/8"	1/8 oz.

COLOR OR FINISH: Perch, white with red head, yellow spotted, silver flash, *orange spotted (back in the 1964 catalog), *black (back in the 1962 catalog), **black scale, frog, ***shad, ***pearl. By 1964 there were only five color choices: The first three in the list here plus black, silver flash and frog. By the 1970s orange spotted was back and Chrome had been added.

**Deleted in the 1961 catalog and replaced by black scale frog.*

***Deleted in the 1962 catalog.*

****Added in the 1964 catalog.*

SNARKIE, 1100 Series (plastic)
SNARK, 1200 Series (plastic)
SNARK EEL, 1300 Series (plastic)
1957-1961

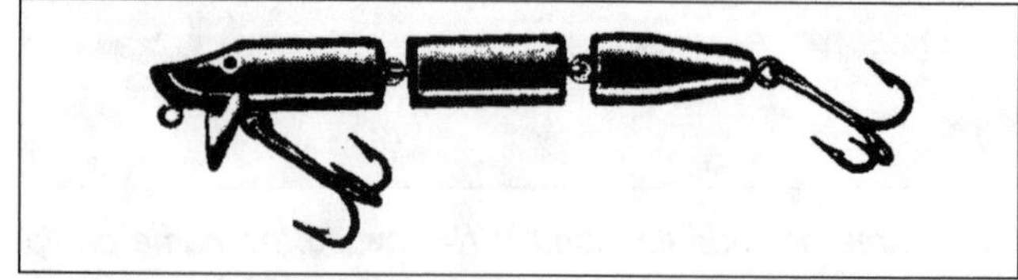

All three of these little lures are jointed with the SNARK EEL having three sections. All three are deep-running sinkers and available in the same colors. The 1961 catalog was the last to list them as available. The SNARK EEL was listed in the 1962 edition, but it was stamped "DISCONTINUED". They were produced for such a short time they are fairly hard to find. Collector value range: $5-$10.

CATALOG SERIES #	BODY LENGTH	LURE WEIGHT
1100	1-1/2"	1/8 oz.
1200	2"	1/4 oz.
1300	3"	3/8 oz.

COLOR OR FINISH: Perch scale, white with red head, solid black, silver flash, frog, orange with black spots.

FLY ROD PIKIE
1924-1925

The drawing with the graceful taper at the top of the nose and the tail above was copied from a 1931 catalog illustration. While they used the same illustration in the catalogs throughout the years of production, the actual lure never looked just like the cut. The earliest examples found do have a cylindrical tapered tail and a scooped nose, but not nearly as nice as the catalog cut. Later the nose and tail grew more blunt. The nose was still scooped a bit, but the tail just became smaller in diameter as the body neared the tail and ended with a blunt rounding. The wire leader was consistent through the years of production. Collector value range: $150-$175. If you are lucky enough to find one in its original box, add another $30-$40.

CATALOG SERIES #	BODY LENGTH	LURE WEIGHT
1200	1-1/4"	?
1300	1-5/8"	?

COLOR OR FINISH: Natural Pikie scale finish, white with red head, red side scale finish, dace.

THE ORIGINAL INJURED MINNOW OR FLAT SIDE CHUB
1924-1963, 1973-78 (PLASTIC, 1964-78)

THE BABY INJURED MINNOW
1924-1963 (PLASTIC, 1964-78)

This plug is shown in a catalog as "...new for 1924", and was then called the "Flat Side Chub" and a smaller version, the "Baby Flat Side Chub". The larger one had three treble hooks, two *side-mounted, and one trailing. The smaller is equipped with one *side-mounted double hook and a trailing double, but the catalog states it could be ordered with treble hooks, therefore the collector may find it either way. The double hooks were reversible so as to make the plug weedless. Both sizes had nose- and tail-mounted propeller spinners. The design of the earliest models incorporated a flattened side so that the plugs swam on the side like an injured minnow. Much later models do not have this flat side.

The accompanying photo of two lures shows a significant change in the width of the body. The lower plug, is the oldest of the two. Still in catalogs of the 1950s and sometimes known as "The Crip". They are still made in five sizes.

Collector value range for the wooden model: $25-$50, plastic: $5-$10.

**Technically these could be called belly-mounted hooks because of the way the plug floats (side down).*

CATALOG SERIES #	BODY LENGTH	LURE WEIGHT
1500	3-3/4"	3/4 oz.
1500-P	3-3/4"	5/8 oz.
1600 (Baby)	2-3/4"	1/2 oz.
1600-P (Baby)	2-3/4"	1/2 oz.

COLOR OR FINISH (wood): Dark green, silver and red, scale finish; natural perch, scale finish; golden shiner, scale finish; red side, scale finish; silver flash; white and red, "day-n-nite" (luminous); rainbow fire; fire plug; dace; yellow spotted, frog finish; red wing; white scale.

COLOR OR FINISH (plastic): Pike scale, perch scale, white with red head, *purple, golden shiner, dace scale, shad, silver flash, frog, black scale, **black.

**First available for a lure color in 1967.*

***Had replaced black scale in the 1967 catalog.*

SPINNING INJURED MINNOW
1952-1963 (PLASTIC, 1964-78)

This lure was among four Creek Chub classics that were new releases in a spinning model in the 1952 edition of the catalog. They remained in the line continuously in wood and then in plastic until 1978 when the company sold. The plastic, 1-7/8" version does not usually have the classic Creek Chub propeller spinners, but has smaller round blade spinners. Collector value range for wood: N/A, plastic: $5-$10.

CATALOG SERIES #	BODY LENGTH	LURE WEIGHT
9500 wood	2"	1/4 oz.
9500-P	1-7/8"	1/4 oz
9500-P-UL	1-5/8"	1/8 oz. (Ultralight)

COLOR OR FINISH (wood): Pike scale, perch scale, white with red head, silver flash, frog, *solid black, *pearl, *silver, **black scale, **shad.

**Added in 1956, but pearl was missing by 1960.*

***Added in 1962. Black scale replaced solid black.*

COLOR OR FINISH (plastic): Pike scale, perch scale, white with red head, silver flash, frog, black scale, *shad, **coach dog.

**Regular plastic 9500 Series only.*

***Ultralight only.*

THE POLLY WIGGLE
1923-1931

Introduced in 1923 this lure apparently didn't enjoy much success, It was gone from the catalogs by 1931. It was a

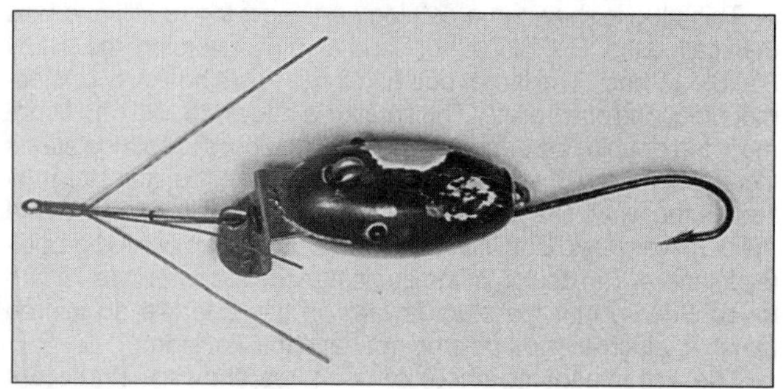

weighted bait which would not float, but had the reversible metal lip blade so it could be used as a surface plug. It had a long wire leader at the nose which had a three-wire weed guard. The single hook was mounted near the tail. There is a provision for attaching a pork rind but came with an artificial ribbon rind attached. They have been found with black and red eyes and often without the weed guard. This depresses the value considerably. The photo shows one that was left in a tackle box in contact with a plastic worm. The damage to the finish is the result. These are fairly scarce because of its short-lived production. Collector value range: $75-$100.

CATALOG SERIES #	BODY LENGTH	LURE WEIGHT
1700	1-3/4"	1/2 oz.

COLOR OR FINISH: Natural pollywog; white with red head.

SILVER SIDE 1957-1961

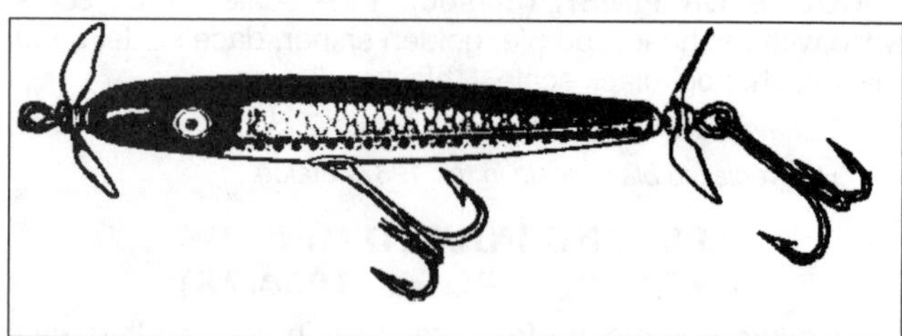

Although 1957 is the earliest catalog listing for this slim 4-3/4" lure, it may have been around a little longer. The copy describing the lure in that catalog states "Silver Side has established a great record in both fresh and salt water." It has the sturdy thru-body construction making it quite strong. Collector value range: $5-$10.

CATALOG SERIES #	BODY LENGTH	LURE WEIGHT
1700	4-3/4	7/8 oz.

COLOR OR FINISH: Pike Scale, Perch Scale, White with Red Head, Silver Flash, Blue Flash.

WIGGLE DIVER, 1800 Series 1957-1962 (Plastic, 1963-78)

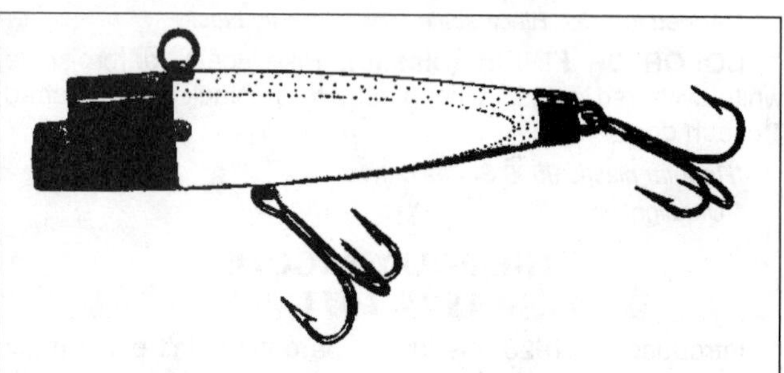

SPINNING WIGGLE DIVER, 5000 Series 1960-1962 (Plastic 1963-?)

Sometime in the 1950s Creek Chub acquired the rights to manufacture and sell Shakespeare's WIGGLE DIVER. Creek Chub modified it by making it a little longer. The earliest of these sport a tail-reinforcing metal cap as in the accompanying illustration. By 1960 this tail cap was gone. It has through-body wire construction for strength. The 1961 catalog is the first that lists the SPINNING WIGGLE DIVER. The 1962 catalog lists it, but it is stamped "DISCONTINUED." This spinning model was never listed again, but we know they were made in plastic because they are found. The small ones have a V-notch at the tail. Collector value range: Wood:$10-$20., Plastic: $5-$10.

CATALOG SERIES #	BODY LENGTH	LURE WEIGHT
1800	5"	1-1/2 oz.
1800-P	5"	1-1/2 oz.
5000	2-1/4"	1/2 oz.
5000-P	2-1/4"	1/2 oz.

COLOR OR FINISH (wood): White body with red head, silver flash, tiger stripe, yellow with red head, *yellow with black head.

**Not listed as an option in the 1961 catalog.*

COLOR OR FINISH (plastic): White with red head, silver flash, tiger stripe.

THE UNDERWATER SPINNER MINNOW 1800 Series 1824-1934

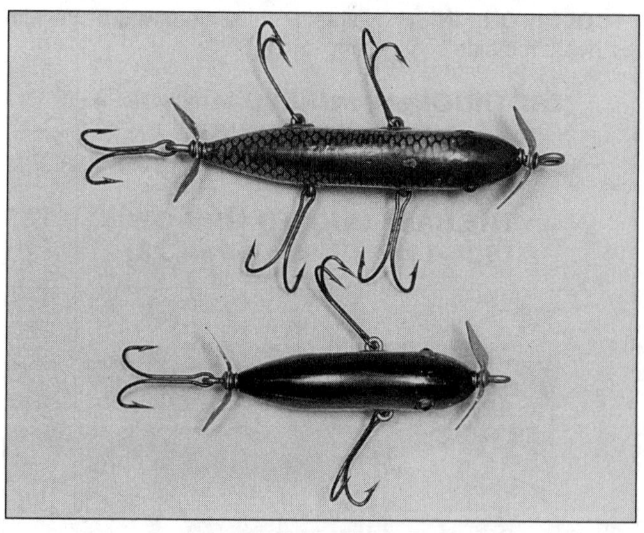

THE CREEK and RIVER FISHING LURE 1900 Series 1924-1934

A 1924 catalog listing states this plug is weighted and both the larger and smaller versions are available in the same three color designs. Both sizes have flattened sides, and propeller spinners at nose and tail. Early catalogs show round-body lures in illustrations. The larger version has two double hooks mounted on each side and one trailing double hook. The smaller one has the trailing double, but only one double hook on each side. It had disappeared from the catalog by 1935. Collector value range: $250-$350.

CATALOG SERIES #	BODY LENGTH	LURE WEIGHT
1900	2-3/4"	1/2 oz.
1800	3-3/4"	3/4 oz.

COLOR OR FINISH: Red side, scale finish; green back, scale finish; rainbow; silver flash.

STRIPER STRIKE (plastic)

Series 1900
1960-1978

Series 2100
1961-1978

Series 2200
1962-1978

Series 2400
1962-1978

Series 2500
1962-1978

Introduced in the 1960 catalog as the STRIPER STRIKER it had become the STRIPER STRIKE in the next year's catalog. This plastic popper caught on fast as an explosively successful lure. Creek Chub quickly added four new models. All five had the very strong through-body hardware. Collector value range: $5-$10.

CATALOG SERIES#	BODY LENGTH	LURE WEIGHT
1900-P	5-1/4"	2-1/4 oz.
2100-P	4-1/2"	1-1/2 oz.
2200-P	4-1/2"	1 oz.
2400-P	2-1/2"	1/2 oz.
2500-P	3"	3/4 oz.

COLOR OR FINISH: *Silver flash, *blue flash, *gray, **amber, **chrome, **silver shiner, **red eye, ***mackerel, banana, fluorescent red (these last two appeared in the early 1970s, but didn't last long).

**The only three colors available on the 1900-P Series when first released in 1960. Gray was eliminated in the 1961 catalog and the remaining two colors were the only ones available on any of the Striper Strikes until 1968.*

***Added to the color options in 1968. At the same time gray was removed as an option.*

****Added in 1969.*

CREEK DARTER
("The Two Thousand")
1924-1978 (Plastic, 1960-78)

Appearing around 1924, this plug has two belly-mounted treble hooks and one trailing treble. Just about all the Darters are found with painted eyes but a rare few have turned up with glass eyes. It continued in production in four sizes and a jointed model. Some time between 1956 and 1960 the wood SALT WATER DARTER, Series 2000-SW appeared. It was gone by the time plastic DARTERS were on the scene. Collector value range for wood: $20-$25, plastic: $5-$10.

CATALOG SERIES #	BODY LENGTH	LURE WEIGHT
2000	3-3/4"	5/8 oz.
2000-P	3-3/4"	5/8 oz.
2000-SW	4"	1 oz.

Above is a wooden reproduction of the Creek Darter the Creek Chub Company released in 1992 in a limited edition of 10,000.

COLOR OR FINISH (wood): *Frog, *white with red head, *yellow with black and red spots, **silver flash; ***dace scale (red side), ***black with nite head (glows in the dark), pikie scale, perch scale, rainbow fire and fire plug were available from 1949 to 1953 only. Pearl finish was added in 1955 or 1956; coach dog in 1961 and shad in 1962.

**The original finishes available.*

***Added in 1931.*

****Added in 1936.*

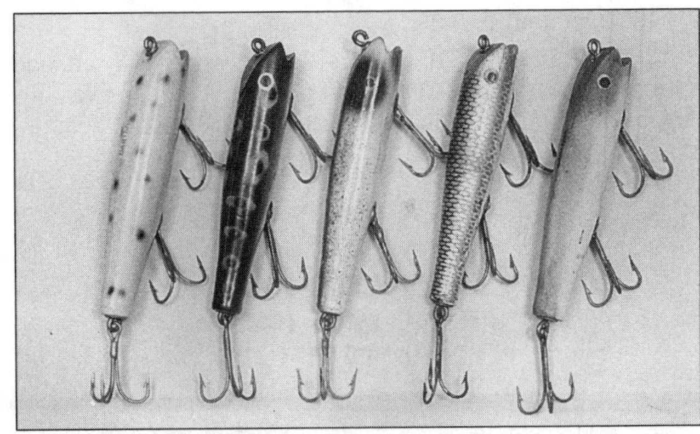

COLOR OR FINISH (Saltwater Darter): White body with red head, silver flash, blue flash, purple eel.

COLOR OR FINISH (plastic): Pike scale, perch scale, white with red head, *shad, yellow spotted, silver flash, frog, *black scale, *coach dog, **solid black

**These colors were not listed in the 1966 catalog.*

***First listed in 1967.*

THE JOINTED DARTER, 4900 Series
1938-1964, 1970-1978

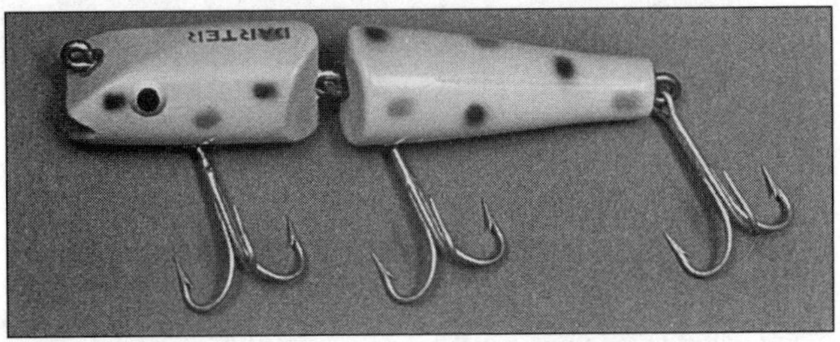

Jointed Darter

THE MIDGET DARTER, 8000 Series 1938-1978

Midget Darter

These two first appeared in the 1938 edition of the Creek Chub catalog. The JOINTED DARTER is the same plug as the original CREEK DARTER above, but is jointed. The MIDGET DARTER is smaller version of the CREEK DARTER and has one less treble hook. Collector value range: $15-$25.

CATALOG SERIES #	BODY LENGTH	LURE WEIGHT
8000(Midget)	3"	3/8 oz.
4900(Jointed)	3-3/4"	1/2 oz.

COLOR OR FINISH: *Natural Pikie; *white with redhead, *yellow spotted, *silver flash; *frog finish, **perch, **rainbow fire (1950-52), **fire plug (1950-52), ***black scale, ***pearl.

**The original colors.*

***Added in 1950.*

****Added in 1957*

THE NUMBER 8000-CB Wood, 1946-1978 Plastic, 1961-1973

This lure appeared on the market around 1946 and continued in production until 1978. It was the same body design as the 8000 Series DARTER except the belly was made concave (C.B.). It sports two belly treble hooks instead of one. The plastic model came on the scene in the 1961 catalog listed right along with the original wood model until 1973. Collector value range for wood: $10-$15, plastic $5-$10.

CATALOG SERIES #	BODY LENGTH	LURE WEIGHT
8000-CB	3"	3/8 oz.
8000-CB-P	3"	3/8 oz.

COLOR OR FINISH (wood & plastic): Pike scale, perch scale, white with red head, yellow spotted, silver flash, frog, *coach dog, ***black scale, **shad ***black,

**Added in 1964.*

***Added in 1962, but shad was absent from the 1964 catalog.*

****Not listed in the 1964 catalog, but black was listed as an option once again in 1967.*

SPINNERED DARTER 1946-1978

This is the same plug as the No. 2000 Series Creek Darter with the addition of a tail-mounted propeller. It was introduced sometime around 1946 continuing in production into the 1950s. Collector value range: $15-$25.

CATALOG SERIES #	BODY LENGTH	LURE WEIGHT
2000 S	3-3/4"	1/2 oz.

COLOR OR FINISH: Natural Pikie; white with redhead, yellow spotted; silver flash; frog finish.

SPINNING DARTER 1952-1961 (Plastic, 1962-78)

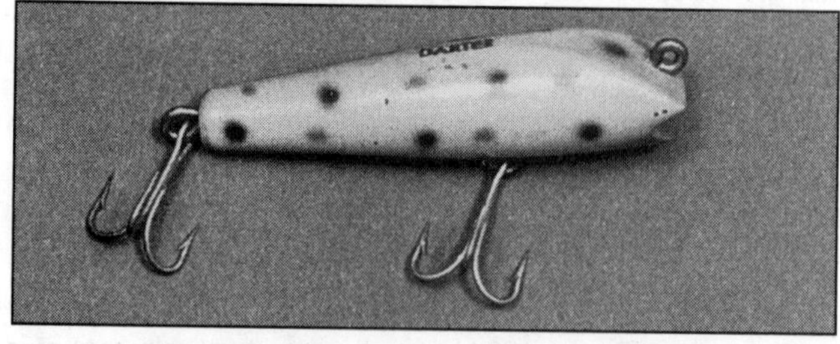

New in the line in 1952, this lure stayed in continuous production until the company sold in 1978. It was introduced with a group of five Creek Chub classics to be made in spinning size. Collector value range for wood: $10-$20, plastic: $5-$10.

CATALOG SERIES #	BODY LENGTH	LURE WEIGHT
9000	2-1/4"	1/4 oz.
9000-P	2-1/4"	1/4 oz.
9000-P-UL	1-5/8"	1/8 oz (ultralight)

COLOR OR FINISH (wood): Yellow spotted, silver flash, frog, *pike scale, *perch scale, *white with red head, *solid black, *pearl, **black scale,

*In the 1956 catalog, but gone by 1961.

**Replaced Solid Black in 1961.

COLOR OR FINISH (plastic): Pike scale, perch scale, white with red heard, yellow spotted, silver flash, frog, black scale, *shad, **pearl.

*Not available on the Ultralight.

**In the 1964 catalog. Not available on the Ultralight.

FIN TAIL SHINER 1924-1947

The lower lure has plain unstamped lip, two line ties and fiber dorsal and tail fins (oldest). The upper lure has a loose fluted metal, flopping tail fin, metal dorsal fin, unmarked lip and small metal flashers opposite mounted at sides of belly about one-third back from the nose.

New in 1924, this lure underwent a few significant changes before it was eliminated from the line. The entry for it in the 1947 catalog is printed with the notation "NOT AVAILABLE." First available with rubber fins they had trouble with deterioration and/or hardening. They were then made as in the lower lure in photo, with flexible fiber dorsal and tail fins. About 1930 another flexible fiber fin was added to each side of the head just under the eyes. The 1938 catalog is the first time the lure description mentioned metal fins although they used the same catalog illustration they had been using previously. Collector value range: Metal fins: $25-$40; fiber fins: $40-$60.

CATALOG SERIES #	BODY LENGTH	LURE WEIGHT
2100	4"	3/4 oz.

COLOR OR FINISH: *Red side shiner, scale finish; *silver shiner, scale finish; *golden shiner, scale finish; *yellow perch, scale finish; *white and red, silver flash.

MIDGET PIKIE MINNOW 1924-1960

Same body shape as the other "Pikies" but considerably smaller. Appearing in 1924, this floating plug continued in production throughout the years. It has two line ties on the older models, a belly treble hook, a trailing treble, and the reversible metal lip blade. The newer models lack the screw eye line tie on the head. Collector value range: $15-$30.

CATALOG SERIES #	BODY LENGTH	LURE WEIGHT
2200	2-3/4"	1/4-3/8 oz.

COLOR OR FINISH: *Natural Pikie, scale finish; *white with redhead, scale finish; *natural yellow perch, scale finish; *golden shiner, scale finish; *rainbow, *solid black; white and red, silver shiner, silver flash; rainbow fire; fire plug.

*Original finishes available.

SPINNING PIKIE, 9300 SERIES 1952-1963 (PLASTIC, 1964-78)

SPINNING JOINTED PIKIE, 9400 SERIES 1952-1963 (PLASTIC, 1964-78)

These two were among five classics that were released in a new size in 1952. The same page illustrated one of them in a "NEW TRANSPARENT PLASTIC TOP BOX". Collector value range: Wood, $10-$20, plastic: $5-$10.

CATALOG SERIES #	BODY LENGTH	LURE WEIGHT
9300 wood	2-1/4"	1/4 oz.
9300 plastic	2-1/4"	1/4 oz.
9300 plastic	1-5/8"	1/8 oz (ultralight)

COLOR OR FINISH (wood): Pike scale, perch scale, white with red head, silver flash, black scale, *solid black, **frog, orange with black spots (added in 1957 for the jointed lure only), ***shad

*Replaced Black Scale in 1956. Black Scale was added back 1962.

**Added in 1961

***Added in 1962

COLOR OR FINISH (Plastic): Pike scale, perch scale, white with red head, shad, silver flash, frog, *orange with black spots, black scale.

*Jointed version only.

HUSKY PIKIE MINNOW, 2300 SERIES 1924-1978

JOINTED HUSKY PIKIE MINNOW, 3000 SERIES 1930-1978 (PLASTIC, 1964-78)

An early Husky Pikie Minnow with stamped lip and two line ties.

This plug came along in 1924 and appears in the line throughout the years. It is a large plug and has two belly-mounted treble hooks and one trailing treble and the reversible metal lip blade and the sloped nose typical of all the Creek Chub Pikie Minnow plugs. It was in continuous production right up to 1978.

The 1931 catalog states that the JOINTED HUSKY PIKIE MINNOW is a "new" lure. It is a 6" jointed version of the No. 2300 Series Husky Pikie Minnow weighing in at 1-1/2 ounces. It was available continuously until 1978 when the company sold. They redesigned the hook hardware in 1936 to utilize the rugged through-body rig making it considerably stronger. The available colors and finishes are the same.

A plastic version of the JOINTED HUSKY PIKIE MINNOW was introduced around 1962-64 and continued in production right along with the wooden model until the company sold in 1978.

Collector value range for the Husky Pikie Minnow, 2300 Series: $20-$35, Jointed Husky Pikie Minnow, 3000 Series: $20-$30, $100 plus with the box; plastic Jointed Husky Pikie Minnow: $5-$10.

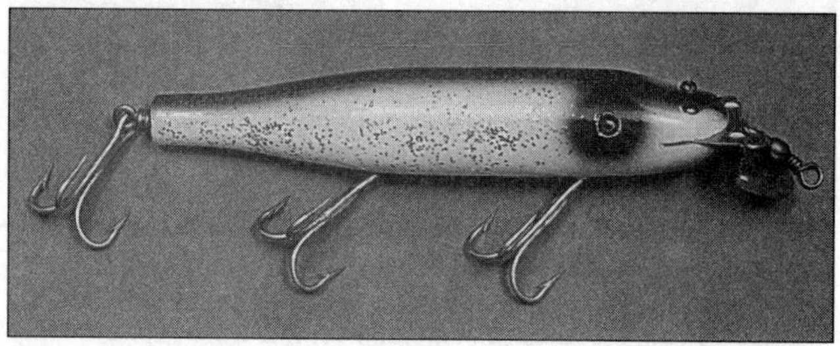

This is an improved Husky Pikie Minnow introduced in 1936. Note reinforced (ribbed) lip and two screws in head to hold the lip in.

CATALOG SERIES #	BODY LENGTH	LURE WEIGHT
2300	6"	1-1/2 oz.
3000	6"	1-1/2 oz.
3000-P	6"	1-1/2 oz.

COLOR OR FINISH (wood): *Natural Pikie, scale finish; *natural perch, scale finish; *golden shiner, scale finish; *white with red head, *rainbow; mullet, silver flash; orange and black spots; black scale finish; blue flash; purple eel; yellow flash; rainbow fire; fire plug.

**These are the original finishes available.*

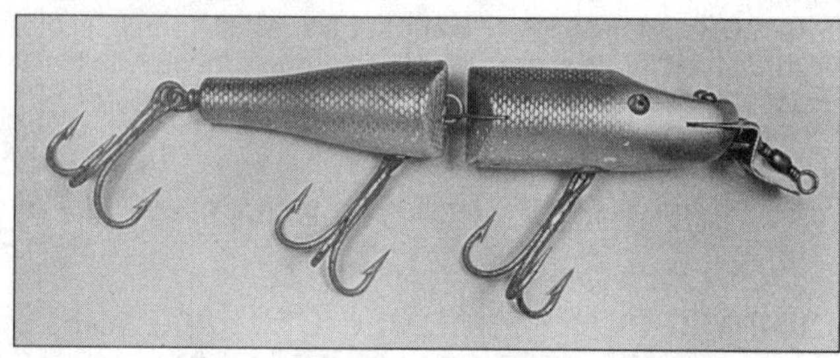

The 1936 vintage "Improved" Jointed Husky Pikie Minnow introduced in the 1936 catalog.

COLOR OR FINISH (plastic 3000 Series): Pike scale, perch scale, white with red head, rainbow, silver flash, black scale, blue flash, *tiger stripe, *solid black.

**Added to the catalog color list by 1967.*

GIANT PIKIE MINNOW (STRAIGHT PIKIE)
1960-1978

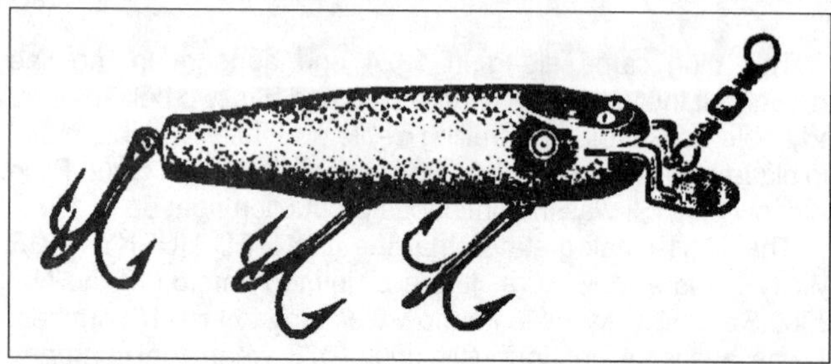

This large version of the PIKIES is not widely known. The reason for its obscurity is that it was apparently only illustrated once in the catalogs. It is listed and illustrated, along with the TOP 'N POP as new in the 1960 catalog. It was merely in a list of different PIKIE models available from then on. It lasted all the way through the years until the company sold in 1978. It was never made in plastic. Collector value range: No trade data found.

CATALOG SERIES #	BODY LENGTH	LURE WEIGHT
6000	8"	3-1/2 oz.

COLOR OR FINISH: Pike scale, perch scale, white with red head, gray, silver flash, blue flash, *gold scale, **black.

**Added in 1964.*

***Added in 1967.*

GIANT JOINTED PIKIE MINNOW
1956-1978

This is a huge lure. It is the biggest lure ever made by Creek Chub. Measuring 14 inches, it could be a formidable weapon for self defense. The first appearance of this monster was in the 1956 edition of the catalogs. There was no illustration, just an innocuous entry in a list of available PIKIE models. The lure was illustrated in the catalogs after that, but it's size didn't make much of an impact because the illustration was printed at the same scale as the other lures on the page. It was made of wood and remained so in the line right up to the time when the company was sold. Glass eyes indicate the earliest of these lures. Collector value range: $40-$80.

CATALOG SERIES #	BODY LENGTH	LURE WEIGHT
800	14"	4 oz.

COLOR OR FINISH: Pike scale, perch scale, white with red head, solid black, silver flash, orange with black spots, blue flash, *purple eel.

**Deleted in the 1962 catalog and gone from then on.*

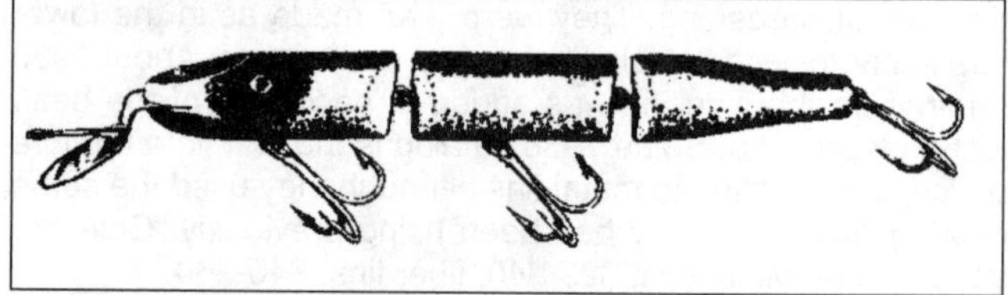

THREE JOINTED PIKIE (plastic)
1960-1978

The THREE JOINTED PIKIE is more accurately called the THREE SECTION PIKIE as indeed it was called in catalogs later. It took them 12 years, however, before they changed the name. It has the deep-diving lip developed by Creek Chub in the late 1940s. The lure remained in production until 1978 as far as we can tell. Toward the end it was listed but not illustrated. Collector value range: $5-$15.

CATALOG SERIES #	BODY LENGTH	LURE WEIGHT
2800 P	6-1/2"	1-1/2 oz.

COLOR OR FINISH: Pike scale, perch scale, silver shiner, *white with red head, *solid black, silver flash, black scale

**Gone from the 1964 catalog. Both were back by 1967 and black scale was added.*

WIGGLE FISH
1925-1957

Appearing in 1925, this is a jointed plug with a fluted nickel tail, mounted so as to let it wag. WIGGLE FISH has been found

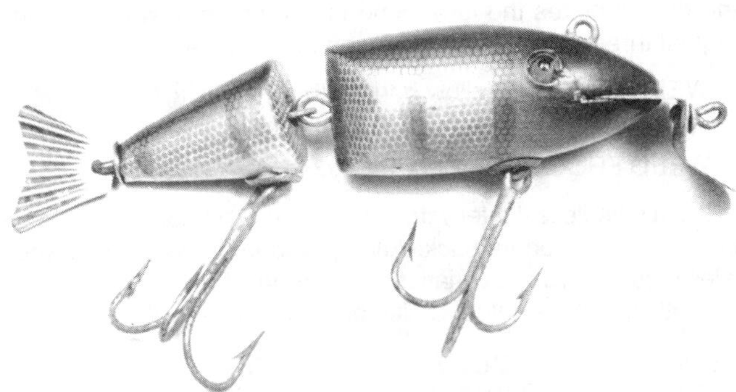

The No. 2400 WIGGLE FISH has been found with a plain tail. Those are thought to be the oldest.

with a plain tail. That variation is thought to be the oldest. It appears to have remained in production continuously through 1957. It has been reported that production resumed in 1974, but my catalog collection doesn't support that. Perhaps production resumed, but it was not cataloged. It has two line ties, two belly-mounted treble hooks and the reversible metal lip blade. Collector value range: $40-$80.

A wooden replica of the Wiggle Fish the Creek Chub Company released in a limited edition of 10,000 in 1992.

CATALOG SERIES #	BODY LENGTH	LURE WEIGHT
2400	3-1/2"	3/4 oz.

COLOR OR FINISH: *Natural perch, scale finish; *silver shiner, scale finish; *golden shiner, scale finish; *red side, scale finish; *white and red; natural pikie; dace; silver flash.

**The original colors available in 1925.*

BABY WIGGLE FISH 1925-1933

This is essentially the same lure as the No. 2400 WIGGLE FISH. It is a smaller version and has only one belly treble hook*. The same comments apply otherwise. The BABY WIGGLE FISH was however, missing from the catalogs from 1935 on. Collector value range: $30-$40.

CATALOG SERIES #	BODY LENGTH	LURE WEIGHT
2500	2-1/2"	1/2 oz.

The one on the bottom has been erroneously called a JOINTED WIGGLER NO. 100. It is either a BABY WIGGLE FISH that has had its tail fin replaced by a treble hook or a new in 1936 WIGGLE WIZARD with its belly treble replaced with a double hook. Note the difference in the size of the slant sides of the forward body section.

COLOR OR FINISH: Natural perch, scale finish; silver shiner, scale finish; golden shiner, scale finish; red side, scale finish: white and red, silver flash.

**Could be ordered with a belly double hook.*

THE JOINTED PIKIE MINNOW 1926-1978 (Plastic, 1961-78)

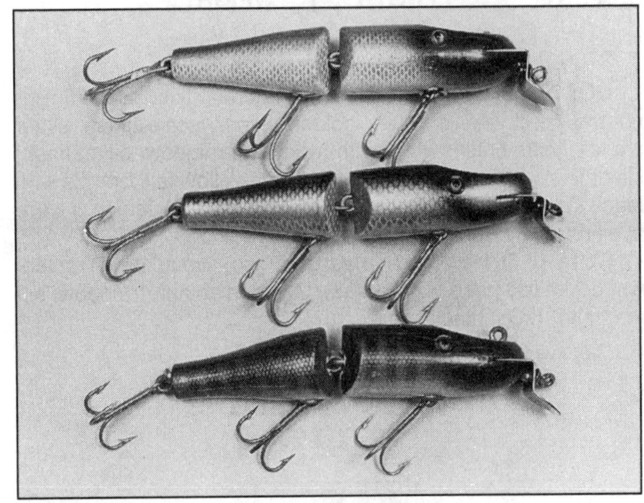

New in 1926 the JOINTED PIKIE MINNOW stayed in production throughout the years. It is a jointed version of the No. 700 Series PIKIE MINNOW. It was also available from 1950 with the Deep-Diving lip. Plastic versions of both models were first available in 1961. Collector value range for wood: $20-$50, plastic: $20-$50.

CATALOG SERIES #	BODY LENGTH	LURE WEIGHT
2600	4-1/2"	3/4 oz.
2600-DD	4-1/2"	3/4 oz.
2600-P	4-1/2"	3/4 oz.
2600-DD-P	4-1/2"	3/4 oz.

COLOR OR FINISH (wood): Natural Pikie, scale finish; natural perch, scale finish; silver shiner, scale finish; golden shiner, scale finish; white with red head, silver flash; rainbow, mullet, black scale; orange and black spots; rainbow fire; fire plug.

COLOR OR FINISH (plastic): Pike scale, perch scale, white with red head, golden shiner, *mullet, rainbow, silver flash, *frog, **orange with black spots, black scale.

**Missing from the 1966 catalog.*

***Absent in the 1962 catalog, but back in the list by 1964.*

THE BABY JOINTED PIKIE MINNOW 1926-1963 (Plastic 1964-78)

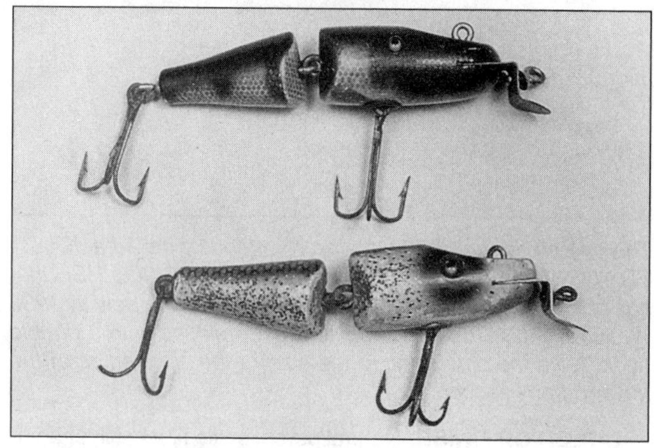

New in 1926, this plug is a jointed version of the Baby Pikie Minnow. The photo shows two older plugs. They have a line tie on the head that doubles as the securing device for the metal lip. Collector value range: Wood, $10-$20, plastic: N/A.

CATALOG SERIES #	BODY LENGTH	LURE WEIGHT
2700	3-1/2"	1/2 oz.
2700-P	3-1/4"	1/2 oz.

COLOR OR FINISH (wood): Natural Pikie, scale finish; natural perch, scale finish; golden shiner, scale finish; silver shiner, scale finish; white with red head, rainbow; silver flash; silver flash with red tail, silver flash with yellow tail, orange with black spots; black scale finish; rainbow fire and fire plug were available only from 1949 to 1953.

COLOR OR FINISH (plastic): Pike scale, perch scale, white with red head, silver shiner, *golden shiner, *rainbow, silver flash, *frog, black scale

**Not available in the 1966 catalog.*

THE WEED BUG 1927-1935

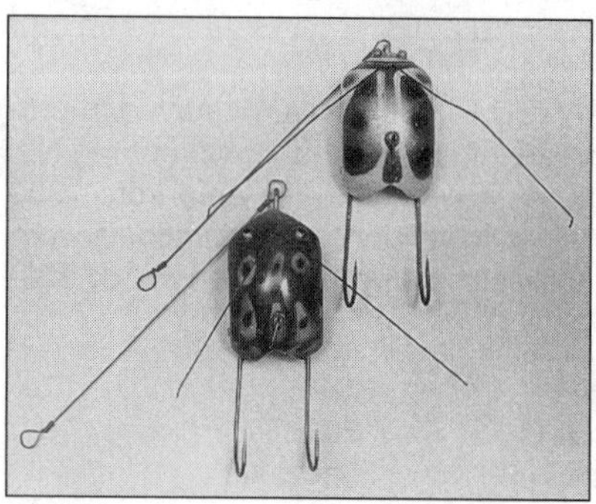

Upper left is the oldest. Note the location of the eyes (red) and pork rind attachment. The paint finish is old style.

This lure appeared in 1927 and the last catalog to list it was the 1935 edition. It was variously called the WEED BUG, WEED FROG or WEED CHUNK in Creek Chub advertising and on the boxes the lure came in according to which of the original three colors it was released in. Those are:

WEED BUG	Yellow body with green wings
WEED CHUNK	White body with red eyes
WEED FROG	Meadow Frog colors

It is a weedless floater with two single-point hooks and a pork rind attachment on its back. Attempts to improve the lure and sales resulted in three variations to be found, but they do not significantly affect the value. Collector value range: $200-$400.

CATALOG SERIES #	BODY LENGTH	LURE WEIGHT
2800	2"	3/4 oz.

THE GAR UNDERWATER MINNOW 1927-1946, 1950-1952

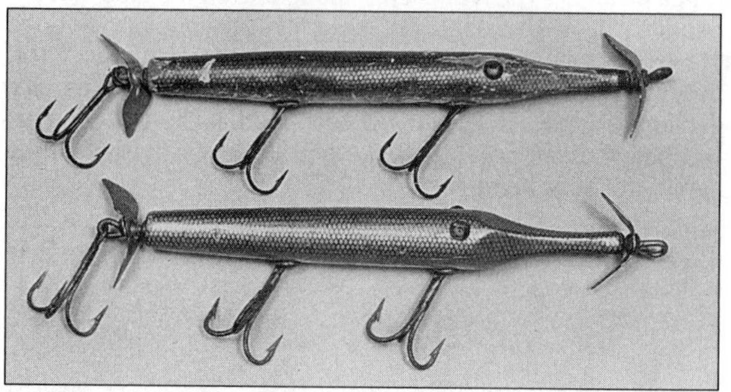

Upper lure is older version. Note the difference in head and snout dimensions and shape.

This lure was introduced in 1927 and was offered continuously until 1946. The 1947 catalog lists it but is overprinted "NOT AVAILABLE." It appears again in catalogs until the listing for it in 1952 where the word "Discontinued" appears. It has a slender body almost pointed at each end (gar shape). It sports a propeller spinner at nose and tail, two belly-mounted treble hooks and a trailing treble. Collector value range: $100-$155.

CATALOG SERIES #	BODY LENGTH	LURE WEIGHT
2900	5-1/4"	3/4 oz.

COLOR OR FINISH: Natural gar with scale finish; green gar with scale finish.

THE CASTROLA 1927-1942

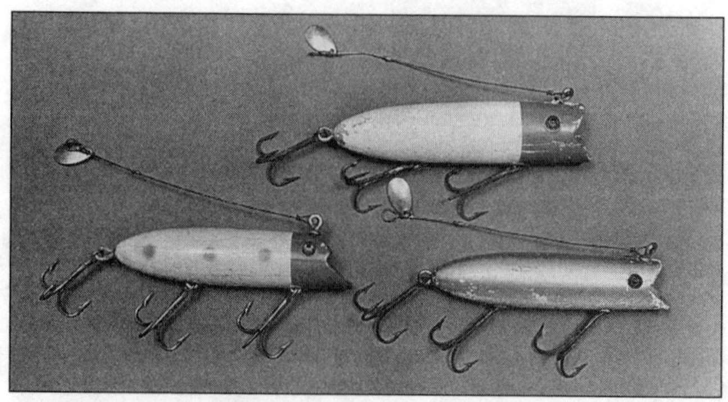

The left lure with the slant head is a variation of unknown origin. The upper lure is a larger (4") version of the CASTROLA thought to be a musky model. It was not found in any Creek Chub catalogs. The lower right is the standard 3-5/8" model.

This lure appeared on the market in 1927 and was absent from catalogs from about 1942 on. The lure has two belly treble hooks and one trailing treble. There is a long wire leader extension attached at the top of the nose with a small spinner blade mounted toward the end of it. The lure is not considered complete without this rig. Collector value range: $75-$100.

CATALOG SERIES #	BODY LENGTH	LURE WEIGHT
3100	3-5/8"	3/4 oz.
3100	4"	?

COLOR OR FINISH: Natural Pikie, scale finish; natural perch, scale finish; golden shiner, scale finish; silver flash; white with red head, rainbow.

THE PLUNKER, 3200 Series
Wood, 1926-1978
Plastic, 1964-78

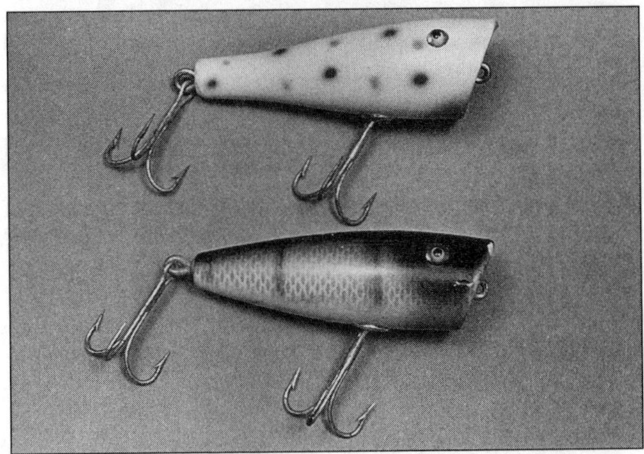

The top bait is a PLUNKER. The other is actually a Shur-Strike, but it illustrates the oldest body shape for PLUNKERS.

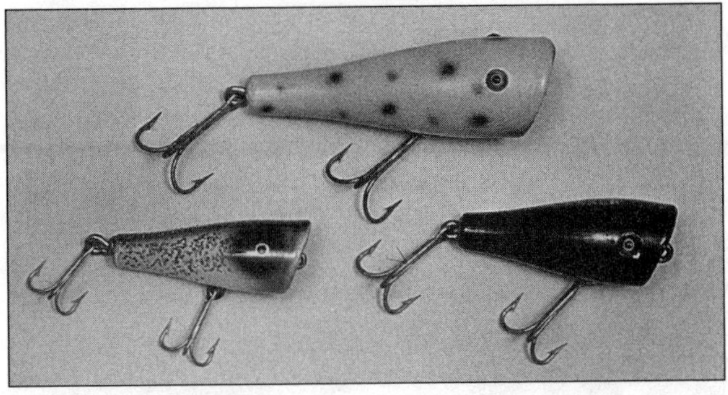

The upper plug is a Creek Chub PLUNKER. Lower: Two SPINNING PLUNKERS.

Appearing around 1926 this plug continues in production for the entire period covered in this book. Sometime around the late 1930s it underwent a slight body design change. The original design had a fatter body whereas the later bodies were slimmed a bit toward the tail. All had a trailing treble and a belly mounted treble hook.

In 1964 a plastic model was added to the line. It coexisted right along with the wood model until the company sold in 1978.

Collector value range for wood: $25-$35, for plastic: N/A.

CATALOG SERIES #	BODY LENGTH	LURE WEIGHT
3200	3"	5/8 oz.
3200	3'	1/2 oz.

COLOR OR FINISH (wood): Natural Pikie with scale finish, natural perch with scale finish, golden shiner with scale finish, white with red head, rainbow, silver flash, solid black, frog, yellow spotted, red wing with white scale, rainbow fire, fire plug.

COLOR OR FINISH (plastic): Pikie scale, perch scale, white body with red head, black, silver flash, frog.

SPINNING PLUNKER
1952-1964 (Plastic, 1965-78)

Introduced in 1952 with four other classics, all in 1/4 ounce weight. Inexplicably the sizes were not given in the catalogs until the 1957 edition. The 1964 catalog was the last to list it in wood. All after that were plastic. Collector value range: Wood, $10-$20, plastic, $5-$10.

CATALOG SERIES #	BODY LENGTH	LURE WEIGHT
9200 Wood	2"	1/4 oz.
9200 Plastic	1-5/8"	1/8 oz. (Ultralight)

COLOR OR FINISH (Wood): Pike scale, perch scale, white with red head, silver flash, frog, *pearl, *solid black, **golden shiner, **black scale, ***shad. By the time wood models were discontinued in 1964 they had added coach dog.

**Added in 1956.*

***Added in 1960.*

****Added in 1962.*

COLOR OR FINISH (Plastic): Pike scale, perch scale, white with red head, solid black, silver flash, frog, black scale, yellow spotted.

SNOOK PLUNKER
1953-1962

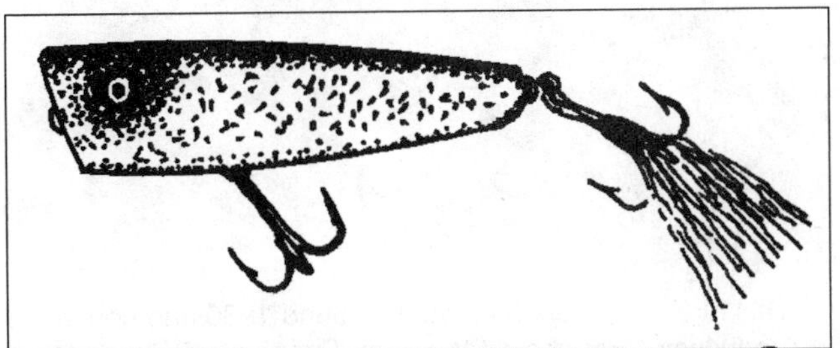

The original name in the 1953 catalog is listed above. Over the years it was also called the SPINNING POPPER, SALT SPINNING POPPER and finally simply the SALT POPPER in the 1962 catalog. This is probably a replacement for the "SEVEN THOUSAND." The SNOOK PLUNKER was available with and without the bucktail on the trailing treble hook. They originally had glass eyes, but these became painted eyes around 1959. In 1961 and 1962 the only two finishes available on it were Blue Flash and Silver Flash. Collector value range: $80-$125.

CATALOG SERIES #	BODY LENGTH	LURE WEIGHT
7100	5"	1-1/2 oz.

COLOR OR FINISH: Pikie scale, perch scale, *white with red head, mullet, yellow spotted, *silver flash, *blue flash, *eel, *yellow flash

**The only colors available from 1957 through 1960. The Yellow flash was added in 1957. The others were the original colors.*

THE "SARASOTA" MINNOW
1927-1934

This lure was introduced into the line in 1927. It had disappeared from catalogs by 1935. It was rather slender, had a belly-

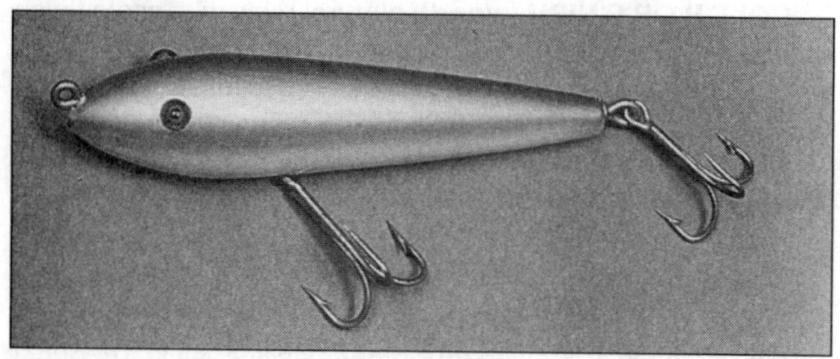

mounted treble hook and a trailing treble. There is another model with a different hook configuration. After Creek Chub ceased manufacturing the lure in 1934 the SARASOTA SPECIAL showed up. It had a treble hook on each side and a trailing treble. The line tie was located beneath the nose rather than on top as in the regular lure. There was also additional internal weight in the tail. This lure was described as a lure specially designed for the Louisville, Kentucky sporting goods firm, Sutcliffe Co., Inc. It was listed in their 1936 catalog. Collector value range: Standard Sarasota, $100-$175, Sarasota Special, can be worth as much as double the standard model. Both are scarce.

CATALOG SERIES #	BODY LENGTH	LURE WEIGHT
300	4-1/2"	3/4 oz.

COLOR OR FINISH: Natural Pikie, scale finish; natural perch, scale finish; golden shiner, scale finish; rainbow, silver flash; white with red head.

THE SNOOK PIKIE
1930-1978

This lure shows up in catalogs around 1930 and continued in production throughout the years. Eventually it came to be known as the "Straight Pikie." It was made exactly like the No. 700 Series PIKIE MINNOW except larger and much stronger. The belly hooks are swiveled and anchored entirely through the body. Collector value range: $20-$30.

CATALOG SERIES #	BODY LENGTH	LURE WEIGHT
3400	4-7/8"	1-1/8 oz.

COLOR OR FINISH: Pike scale, perch scale, golden shiner, white with red head, rainbow, silver flash, silver shiner, mullet.

THE HUSKY INJURED MINNOW
1930-1960

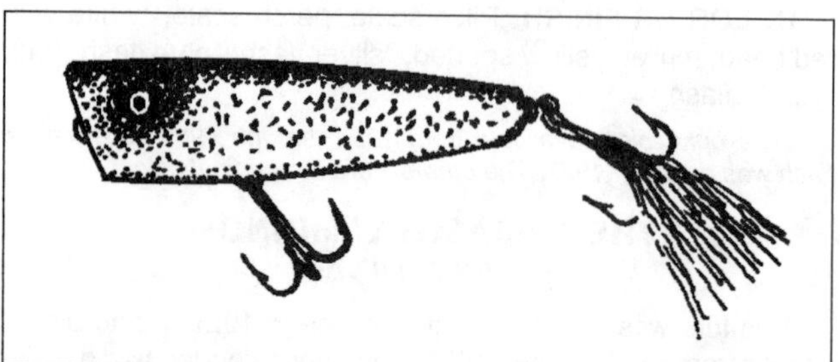

In production from around 1930 until 1960. This is the same lure as the No. 1500 Series Injured Minnow except made larger and stronger. Collector value range: $25-$55.

CATALOG SERIES #	BODY LENGTH	LURE WEIGHT
3500	5"	1-1/2 oz.

COLOR OR FINISH: Natural perch, scale finish; golden shiner, scale finish; red side, scale finish; white with red head; silver flash; Pikie scale; dace.

LUCKY MOUSE
1930-1946

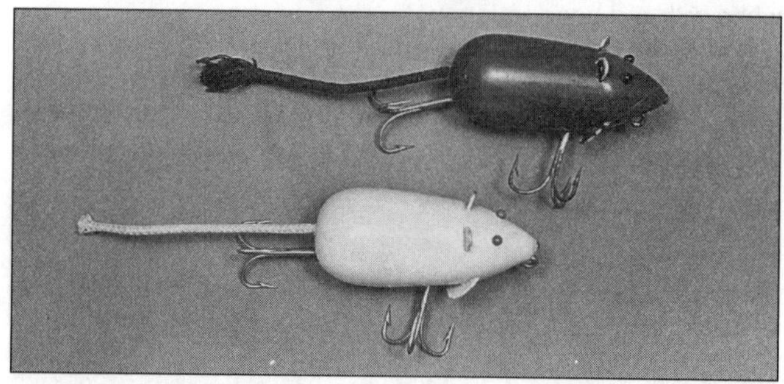

This lure first appears available around 1930 and is listed in catalogs up through 1947. The 1947 listing, however, was over printed with "NOT AVAILABLE". The lure had aluminum ears, bead eyes, a flexible braided fabric tail, a belly treble and a tailing treble hook. Collector value range: $45-$75.

CATALOG SERIES #	BODY LENGTH	LURE WEIGHT
3600	*2"	3/4 oz.

COLOR OR FINISH: Natural gray mouse; black mouse; white mouse with red eyes.

**The catalog listings all say 2", but collectors usually list them at 2-1/2" and 3".*

RIVER RUSTLER
1931-1935

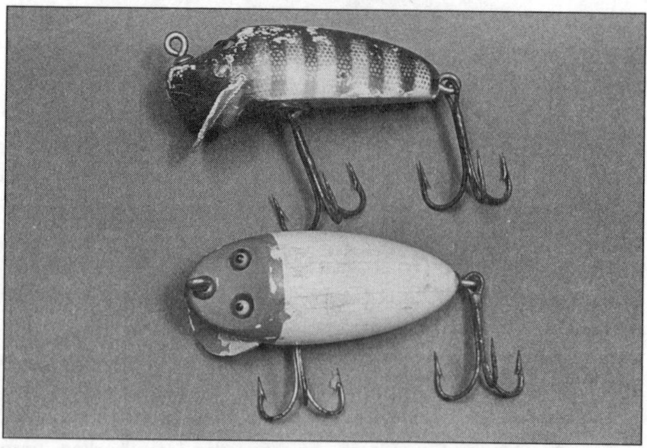

Called "new" in a 1931 catalog, it had disappeared by 1936. It has a sloped nose, protruding eyes, a lip, one belly treble hook and a trailing treble. Collector value range: $35-$50.

CATALOG SERIES #	BODY LENGTH	LURE WEIGHT
3700	2-5/8"	5/8 oz.

COLOR OR FINISH: Natural pike, scale finish; natural perch, scale finish; golden shiner, scale finish; white with red head; rainbow; silver flash.

THE BEETLE
1931-1954

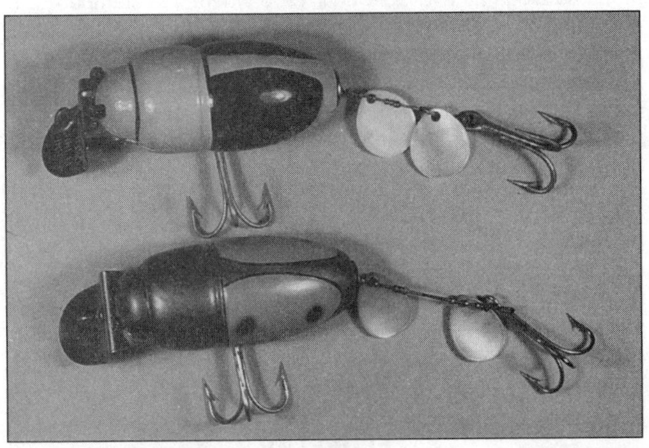

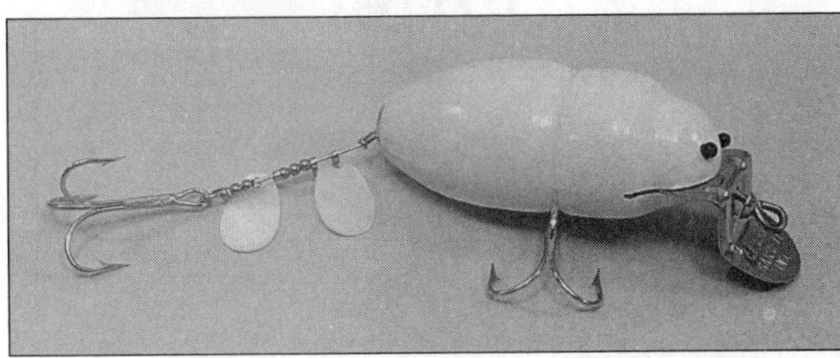

An all-white BEETLE. This is an unfinished primed, but unpainted example. See text for explanation.

This plug appears in a 1931 catalog as "The New Creek Chub Beetle" and continued in production until sometime in 1954. It is a deep-running plug with a non-reversible metal lip plane. Its bead eyes protrude from the face plate portion of the lip plane It has one belly treble and a trailing treble mounted on a wire extension which has two pearl-finished blade spinners attached. The colors listed below are unique to this lure. The solid white BEETLE in the photograph is not a legitimate one. This is a primed, but unpainted version. Many of these somehow got out of the factory when it closed in 1977. Although never cataloged, Creek Chub did give this and other lures a white finish. All, however, have some small bit of red or black on them somewhere, ie: a splash of red at the throat or black around the eyes. Collector value range: $50-$100.

CATALOG SERIES #	BODY LENGTH	LURE WEIGHT
3800	2-1/2"	3/4 oz.

COLOR OR FINISH: Yellow beetle; green beetle; white and red beetle; orange beetle; gold beetle; black beetle; pike scale; white and green.

THE MIDGET BEETLE
1939-1954

This small version of the 3800 Series BEETLE and was in production for the same years. Besides being smaller, the major difference is there is but one pearl spinner on the rear whereas there were two of them on the larger version.

CATALOG SERIES #	BODY LENGTH	LURE WEIGHT
6000	2"	1/2 oz.

COLOR OR FINISH: Yellow beetle, green beetle, white and red beetle, orange beetle, gold beetle, black beetle.

SUCKER SERIES 3900
1932-1933

Called new in 1932, it was listed again in 1933 but not in any subsequent catalogs. It is available in only two finishes: Natural yellow or natural blue sucker scale. Note the unusual corrugated metal lip. The catalog lists the size as 3-1/2", but all those found so far measure 4-1/2". Looks as if the catalog size is a misprint. Collector value range: $100-$200.

TARPON PIKIE
1933-1960

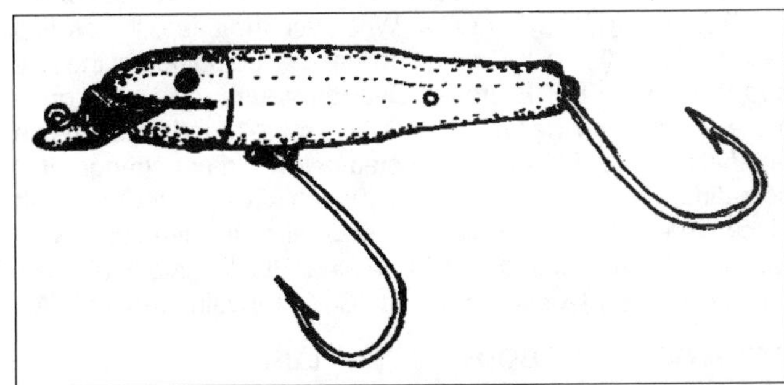

New around 1933 this lure is a large strongly built lure made for heavy saltwater use. The metal lip is heavily reinforced and the hook hangers are extremely heavy-duty and anchored all the way through the body. It was available with either single or treble hooks and is listed in catalogs into the 1960s. Collector value range: $100-$150 with the rarer single-hook version bringing about 50% more.

CATALOG SERIES #	BODY LENGTH	LURE WEIGHT
4000	6-/12"	3 oz.

COLOR OR FINISH: *White with red head, *natural mullet, scale finish; *silver flash; Pikie scale; perch scale.

**These finishes were the only ones offered until 1951. The 1951 catalog shows the addition of the last two listed above.*

THE CREEK CHUB JIGGER
1933-1946

Introduced in 1933 this is Creek Chub's first and only "Water Sonic" plug. There was a hole with a metal scoop on the bottom to cause water to flow through the body on retrieve. It had a belly-mounted treble hook and a trailing treble. It is illustrated as late as 1947 but listed as "NOT AVAILABLE." Collector value range: $60-$90. There is also a very rare BABY JIGGER at 3-1/4". Auction results and price lists range from $200 to $510.

CATALOG SERIES #	BODY LENGTH	LURE WEIGHT
4100	3-5/8"	3/4 oz.
?	3-1/4"	3/4 oz.

COLOR OR FINISH: White with red head, red side, scale finish; yellow body, black and red spots; silver flash; frog finish; black body with luminous head.

MIDGET JOINTED PIKIE
1934-1961

Why it took 10 years to come up with a jointed version of the No. 2200 is anybody's guess. Whatever the case, it was first available in 1934. In the beginning the forward portion of the lure had the classic PIKIE profile. Over the years the scoop grew more shallow and the head fatter with a more rounded nose. The original six color selections denoted below did not change until sometime between 1948 and 1950 when silver shiner and solid black were added. The bright rainbow fire and fireplug colors were available also in the 1951 catalog. Black scale was available only in 1956 for some reason. Collector value range: N/A.

CATALOG SERIES #	BODY LENGTH	LURE WEIGHT
4200	2-3/4"	1/4 oz.

COLOR OR FINISH: *Natural pike scale finish, *natural perch scale finish, *white with red head, *golden shiner scale finish, *rainbow, *silver flash, silver shiner, solid black, fireplug, rainbow fire, black scale finish.

**The original six colors offered.*

THE RIVER SCAMP
1933-1953

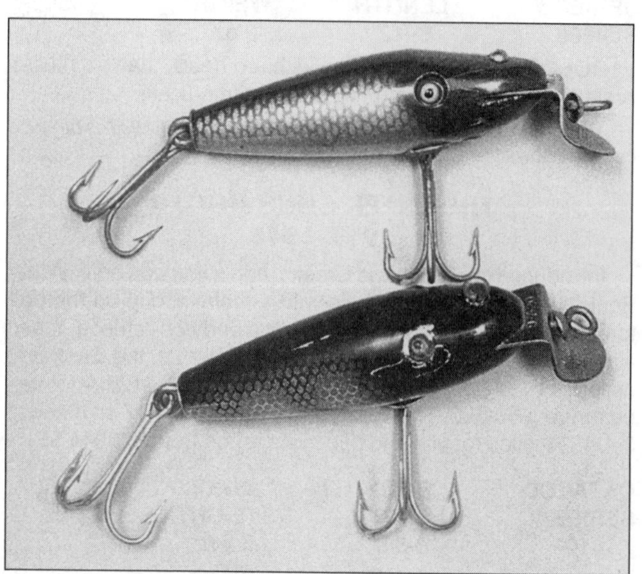

New in 1933 the earliest RIVER SCAMPS had two line ties. After 1936 the name became THE SCAMP. It continued to be listed in the catalogs as available until 1953 where it is stamped "Discontinued." They are easily confused with a PIKIE, but this lure is a sinker with an internal weight. All PIKIES are floaters at rest.

That same 1953 catalog lists a "Deep Diving Scamp" as the same as the River Scamp except with a "Deep diving mouth piece". All had a metal lip, a belly treble and a trailing treble hook. Collector value range: $15-$30.

CATALOG SERIES #	BODY LENGTH	LURE WEIGHT
4300	3-1/4"	5/8 oz.

COLOR OR FINISH: White body with red head, dace scale finish, silver flash, chub scale finish, natural perch scale finish, rainbow.

FLIP FLAP
1935-1941

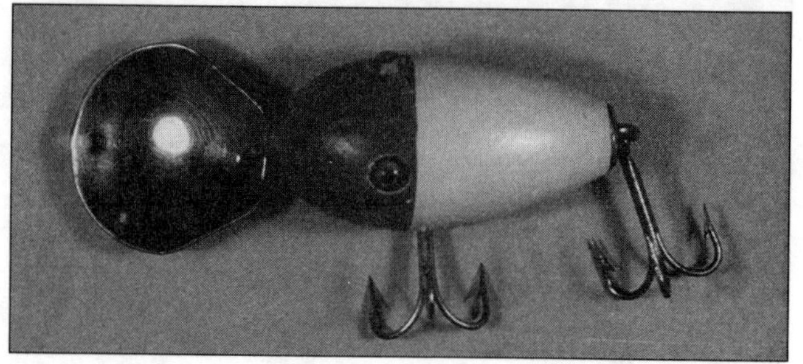

The first page of the 1935 catalog illustrates "Creek Chub's new FLIP FLAP! The Only Lure That Swims With and Up-and-Down Movement". This new "Startling Creation" must not have lived up to expectations for it was conspicuously absent from catalogs from 1942-43 on. It has a loose flapping spoon-like lip attached to the line tie at the nose. There was a belly treble hook and a trailing treble. The spoon was nickel-plated but could be ordered with a copper spoon if desired. Collector value range: $10-$20.

CATALOG SERIES #	BODY LENGTH	LURE WEIGHT
4400	3-1/4"	5/8 oz.

COLOR OR FINISH: White body with red head, dace finish; silver flash; frog finish.

WIGGLE WIZARD
1936-1938

Introduced in 1936 this jointed plug had two line ties on the earliest models, the reversible metal lip, a belly treble, and a trailing treble hook. The 1938 catalog contains the last listing of the plug. This lure replaced the BABY WIGGLE FISH, discontinued in 1935. Collector value range $30-$40.

CATALOG SERIES #	BODY LENGTH	LURE WEIGHT
4500	2-1/2"	1/2 oz.

COLOR OR FINISH: Natural perch, scale finish; silver shiner, scale finish; golden shiner, scale finish; red side, scale finish; silver flash; white with red head.

THE SKIPPER
1936-1947

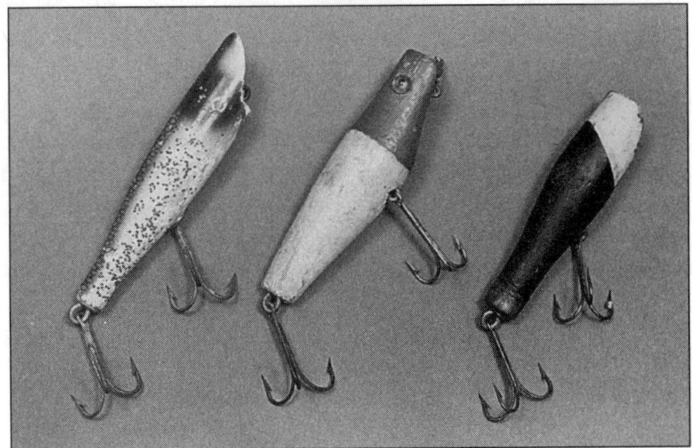

Three different body styles. Read the newest to oldest, left to right.

This lure is listed as new in a 1936 catalog and as "Not Available" in the 1947 catalog. It has a weighted tail, a belly treble hook, and a trailing treble. Note the redesigned body of the later model (on the left in the photo). Collector value range: $20-$40.

CATALOG SERIES #	BODY LENGTH	LURE WEIGHT
4600	3"	5/8 oz.

COLOR OR FINISH: Pikie finish, perch finish; white with redhead, natural frog, black with white head, solid black, silver flash.

FETHI-MIN
1936

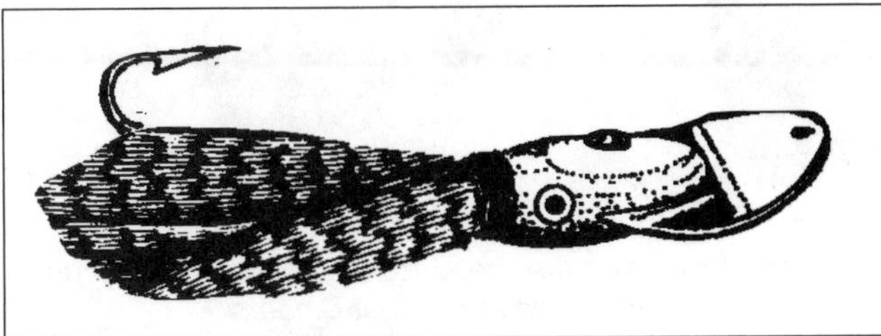

This is probably the most elusive lure ever *maybe* produced by Creek Chub. I know of no example in any collection. It was offered as new in a 1936 catalog, but never seen again in any subsequent catalogs. Was it produced? Data is non-existent. There is some indication that it may have been seen as a patent infringement by another company and never produced. Unique. No market data from which to draw a conclusion as to collector value. Data below is from the catalog.

CATALOG SERIES #	BODY LENGTH	LURE WEIGHT
4700	2-1/2"	5/8 oz.

COLOR OR FINISH: Chub finish, perch finish, brown.

THE WEE DEE, 4800 Series
1936-1946

THE WEE DEE, Series 200-P
1962-1968

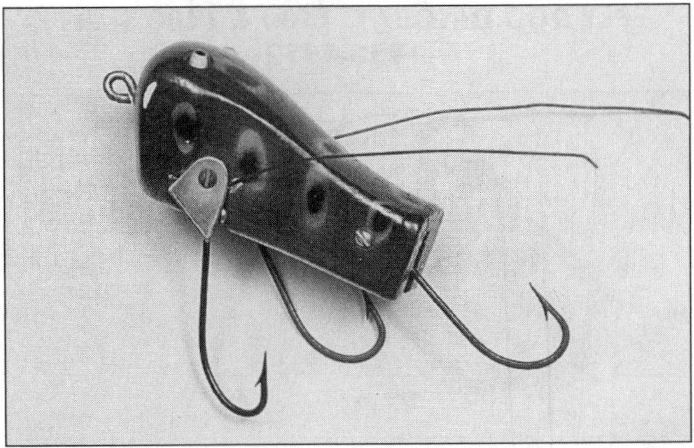

Introduced as new in the 1936 catalog, this lure had three single hooks rigged up with swinging pivots to be weedless. The 1947 catalog lists the WEE DEE but is marked as "Not Available". The WEE DEE shows up again in 1962 in a new design in spinning size and made of plastic. It was never illustrated in catalogs again, but remained in the price list through 1968. Collector value range: Wooden 4800 Series: $150-$200, plastic 200-P Series: $5-$15.

CATALOG SERIES #	BODY LENGTH	LURE WEIGHT
4800	2-1/2"	5/8 oz.
200-P	1-1/2"	1/4 oz.

COLOR OR FINISH: Bug finish, frog finish, white with red head, *yellow frog, *green frog.

**These are the only colors the plastic WEE DEE is listed as available in. Green frog and frog in the list are the same.*

THE CLOSE-PIN
1937-1947

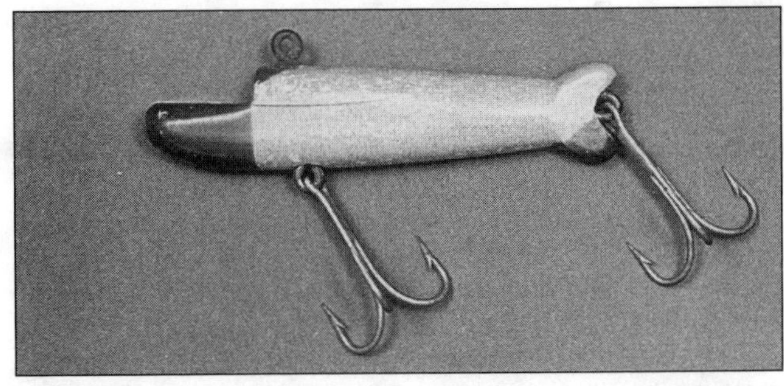

There are some very similar lures to the CLOSE-PIN. The Creek Chub model has red paint on the bottom of the tail fin and yellow in the top part. The others do not have the yellow.

This lure was called new in the 1937 catalog and continued to be offered until 1947. It was made in only one finish, white body with a red head and yellow and red tail fins. The lure has two gold-plated treble hooks and was made for saltwater fishing. It measures 3-1/4" and weighs 1-1/2 oz. Collector value range: $150-$200.

THE DINGBAT, 5100 Series
Wood, 1937-1956
Plastic, 1956-1978

MIDGET DINGBAT, 5200 Series
1938-1957

HUSKY DINGBAT, 5300 Series 1938-1946

FLY ROD DINGBAT, 1300 & 1400 Series 1938-1952

Left to Right: The HUSKY DINGBAT, new in 1943; DINGBAT, MIDGET DINGBAT and the larger of the two fly sizes introduced in 1943.

New in 1937 these plugs had fluttering hair legs protruding from each side, a metal blade lip, one belly-mounted treble and a trailing treble hook. The fly rod sizes were stamped "DISCONTINUED" in the 1953 catalog. The various DINGBATS continue to be found in catalogs until 1958. Please see above for detail of year dates.

A plastic DINGBAT was first listed in the 1965. It sported a straight diving lip rather the classic Creek Chub lip.

Collector value range for the: wooden DINGBAT: $30-$50.

Plastic DINGBAT: $5-$10.
MIDGET DINGBAT: $50-$70.
HUSKY DINGBAT: $30-$50.
FLY ROD DINGBAT: $50-$75.

CATALOG SERIES #	BODY LENGTH	LURE WEIGHT
1300	5/8"	?
1400	7/8"	1/2 oz.
5100	2"	5/8 oz.
5200	1-5/8"	1/2 oz.
5300	2-1/2"	1-1/8 oz.
5300-P	2"	1/4 oz.

COLOR OR FINISH (fly rod sizes): Pike scale with brown legs, perch scale with green legs, golden shiner scale with yellow legs, white with red head and red legs, all black, silver flash with red legs, frog with green legs

COLOR OR FINISH (wood): Pike scale with brown legs, perch scale with green legs, golden shiner scale with yellow legs, white with red head with red legs, solid black, silver flash with red legs; frog with green legs.

COLOR OR FINISH (plastic, 5300 Series): Pike Scale With Brown Legs, Perch Scale With Green Legs, White With Red Head And Red Legs, Black, Silver Flash With Red Legs, Frog With Green Legs.

THE SURFACE DINGBAT #5400 Series 1938-1955

This lure was new in 1938. It is quite similar to the other DINGBATS, but is designed without the metal lip. It has two double hooks, one at the belly and one trailing. The lure was available in exactly the same finish designs as the others but, around 1942-43 two more were added as available on the SURFACE DINGBAT only, red wing and white scale, length 1-3/4", weight 5/8 oz. Collector value range: $20-$30.

JOINTED SNOOK PIKIE MINNOW 1939-1964, 1969-1978

The first catalog description said "Shaped just like the regular JOINTED PIKIE, No. 2600, only it's a little larger and built very strong to withstand heavy fishing for Pike, Muskies, lake trout and all the varieties of lighter salt water fish - the construction is such that no strain comes on the body. Its metal, line to hook construction, makes it amply strong for any fish except the heavier salt water species." Collector value range: No trade data found.

CATALOG SERIES #	BODY LENGTH	LURE WEIGHT
5500	4-7/8"	1-1/8 oz.

COLOR OR FINISH: Natural pike scale finish, natural perch scale finish, white with red head, golden shiner scale finish, rainbow, silver flash.

THE CREEK CHUB DINGER #5600 Series 1934-1954

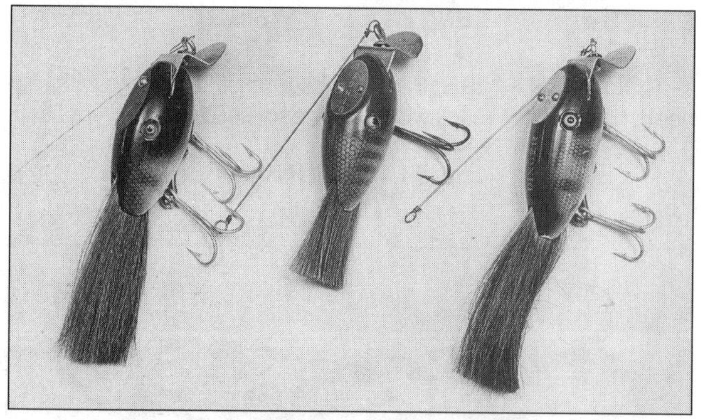

Note the absence of the metal top head plate on the upper plug. The upper two plugs are Midget Dingers

THE MIDGET DINGER #6100 Series 1940-1947

This DINGER was introduced in 1939 and continued to be available on into the early to mid-1950s. It has a metal lip, two ventrally located treble hooks, and a broom-like tail. A distinctive feature of this plug is a metal plate covering the top of the head although it is not always present. Note the design differences in the photo. Collector value range: $50-$60.

Called "NEW" in a 1940 Creek Chub catalog the MIDGET DINGER was just a smaller version available in the same colors. Collector value range: $50-$75.

CATALOG SERIES #	BODY LENGTH	LURE WEIGHT
5600	4"	1/2 oz.
6100	3-1/2"	3/8 oz.

COLOR OR FINISH: Natural Pikie, scale finish; natural perch, scale finish; natural dace, scale finish; golden shiner, scale finish; white body, red head, solid black; silver flash; natural frog finish.

THE HUSKY DINGER #5700 Series 1939-1946

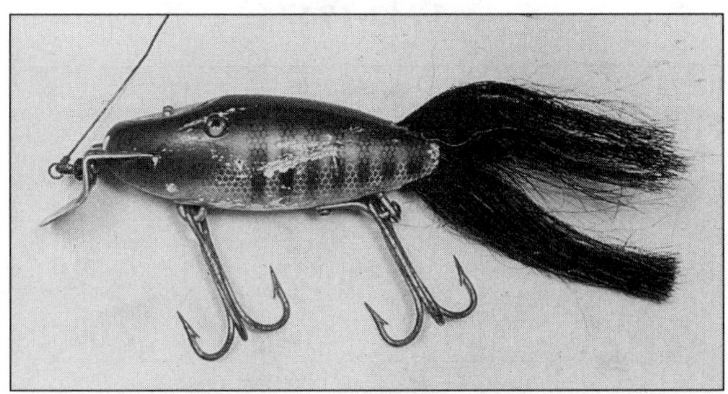

Appearing at the same time as the Creek Chub DINGER, 5600 Series, this is merely a larger, stronger version. It was listed and illustrated in the 1947 catalog but "NOT AVAILABLE" was printed under the name of the lure. Collector value range: $100-$150.

CATALOG SERIES #	BODY LENGTH	LURE WEIGHT
5700	5-1/2"	1 oz.

COLOR OR FINISH: Natural Pikie, scale finish; natural perch, scale finish; natural dace, scale finish; golden shiner, scale finish; white body with redhead, silver flash; natural frog finish.

THE PLUNKING DINGER 1940-1952

"New" in the 1940 catalog this is the same design as the original Plunker but with the addition of the broom-like hair tail of the DINGERS. The 1953 catalog lists it but it is stamped "DISCONTINUED." It was equipped with two treble hooks. Collector value range: $30-$40.

CATALOG SERIES #	BODY LENGTH	LURE WEIGHT
6200	4"	5/8 oz.

COLOR OR FINISH: Natural Pikie, scale finish; natural perch, scale finish; golden shiner, scale finish; natural dace, scale finish; white body with red head, solid black; silver flash; natural frog finish; red wing; white scale.

THE POP'N DUNK 1941-1954

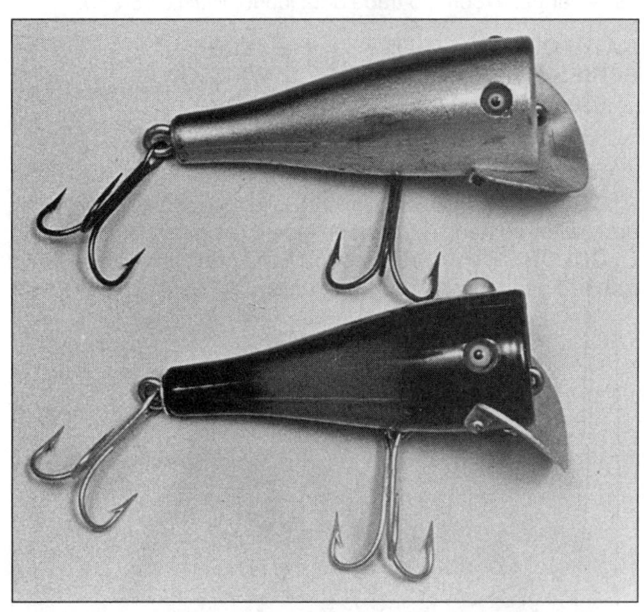

New around 1941, the POP 'N DUNK was essentially the same as the PLUNKER with a metal lip added. It was stamped "DISCONTINUED" in the 1953 catalog. The upper plug in the photo is the older of the two (note the large glass eye). Collector value range: $25-$50.

CATALOG SERIES #	BODY LENGTH	LURE WEIGHT
6300	2-3/4"	5/8 oz.

COLOR OR FINISH: Natural Pikie scale; natural perch scale; natural frog finish; dace scale; white with red head, silver flash; red wing; white scale.

MOUSE, 6380 Series
MOUSE, 6577 Series
MOUSE, 6580 Series
c. 1950-1962 (Plastic, 1963-78)

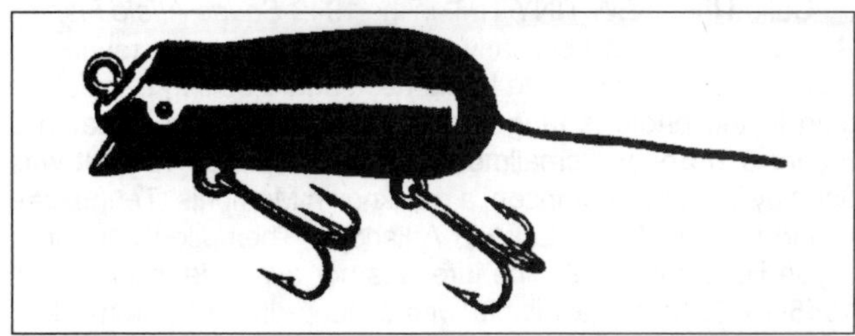

Sometime in the 1950s Creek Chub acquired the right to manufacture and sell Shakespeare's SWIMMING MOUSE. They retained the Shakespeare numbers for the lures. That explains why the numbers don't match the Creek Chub system. It can be difficult telling the difference between the Shakespeare product and the one made by Creek Chub. One good way is to know that the pure Creek Chub MOUSE was never made with internal belly weights, glass or tack eyes. They were always painted eyes. When Shur-Strike is covered the plot will thicken.

Although the first catalog to list these lure was the 1957 edition, there is good reason to suspect they were around before that. A descriptive entry in the 1957 catalog reads: "...Man, what success stories have been told about this famous Creek Chub Lure. Long a favorite, the Creek Chub Mouse has enjoyed increased popularity in the last year." So we know they were around at least as early as 1956 and probably earlier. Collector value range: Wood, no trade data found; Plastic $5-$10.

CATALOG SERIES #	BODY LENGTH	LURE WEIGHT
6380	2-1/4"	1/4 oz.
6577	2-1/2"	3/8 oz.
6580	2-3/4"	1/2 oz.

COLOR OR FINISH (wood): Solid gray, solid black, white body with red head, tiger stripe, pearl, glo-pearl.

COLOR OR FINISH (plastic): Solid gray, solid black, white with red head, tiger stripe, glo-pearl.

TINY TIM
1942-1954, 1970-1974

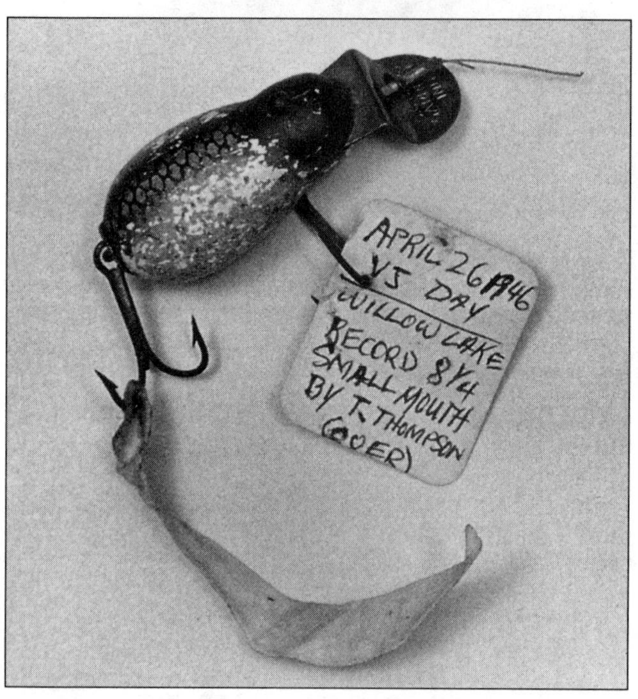

Called the "NEW TINY TIM" in the 1942 *Sports Afield Fishing Annual* this was a peculiarly shaped plug. It has a reversible metal lip, a belly-mounted treble hook and a trailing treble. The plug in the photo is tagged as having been used to catch a record 8-1/4 pound smallmouth bass on April 26,1946. It was used by Tommy Thompson, a well known Memphis, Tennessee fisherman, on Willow Lake in Arkansas. Thompson gave it to Clyde Harbin in 1969. The lure was not available in the years 1955-1969. It was available with a deep-diving lip from 1950 through 1953. The colors marked with an asterisk (*) in the color list below were developed specifically for the TINY TIM in 1942. The first eight colors in the list were those originally offered. The lure was taken out of production in 1955. After a 15-year hiatus, it was placed back in production in 1970. The only colors available on these later models are perch scale, white with red head, silver flash, fluorescent yellow, fluorescent green and fluorescent red. Collector value range: $15-$30. This will double if they are found in the specially designed colors.

CATALOG SERIES #	BODY LENGTH	LURE WEIGHT
6400	1-3/4"	1/2 oz.

COLOR OR FINISH: Natural Pikie scale, natural perch scale, white scale, white with red head, silver flash, red wing, *white and red with wings, *spot, gray.

THE BABY BOMBER SERIES NO. 6500
1942-1947

THE DIVE BOMBER SERIES NO. 6600
1942-1954 AND

THE BIG BOMBER SERIES NO. 6700
1942-1947

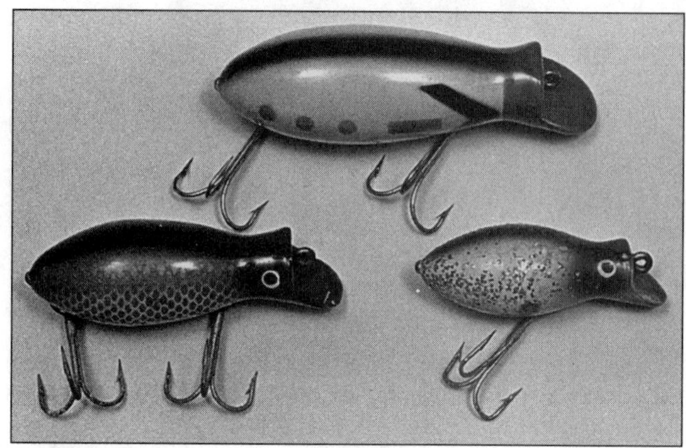

The BOMBER was new in 1942 and by 1950 the name had been changed to the "KREEKER" although most collectors refer to all of them as BOMBERS. At its introduction two of the color designs were called "Victory" finish (shown in photo). The normal color codes used by the Creek Chub Company would indicate that these had either a white body with a red head or a yellow body with a red head. The illustration in the catalog shows the addition of three dots and one dash in black and a chevron in red, all oriented to form an arrow along the side of the body. Apparently this alluded to the spirit of the country during WWII. Indeed the Morse code for "V" (Victory) is three dots and a dash, "dit, dit, dit, dah". The "Victory" finish wasn't found in catalogs subsequent to 1947. The lure had two belly-mounted treble hooks and lip that is part of the lure, not attached with screws.

The BABY BOMBER had only one belly treble hook. It first appeared in the 1942 catalog, but was marked "NOT AVAILABLE" in the 1947 catalog. It was available in the same finish designs as the DIVE BOMBER including the "Victory" finish. Collector value range: $50-$75.

CATALOG SERIES #	BODY LENGTH	LURE WEIGHT
6500	2-1/4"	3/8 oz.
6600	2-7/8"	5/8 oz.
6700	3-3/4"	7/8 oz.

COLOR OR FINISH: Pikie scale; perch scale; golden shiner, silver flash; white with red head*, yellow with red head*.

**These two were preceded by the words "Victory finish" in the 1942 catalog.*

STRIPER PIKIE AND JOINTED STRIPER PIKIE
1950-1978

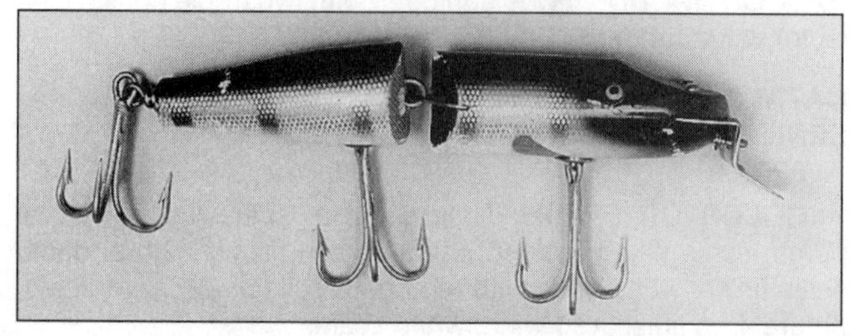

New in 1950 this is an extra-strong, bigger and heavier version of the PIKIE MINNOW that was made for saltwater or very heavy fish. The photo is of the jointed model. Collector value range: $25-$40.

CATALOG SERIES #	BODY LENGTH	LURE WEIGHT
6900	6-1/4"	3-1/4 oz.
6800 Jtd.	6-1/4"	3-3/4 oz.

COLOR OR FINISH: Pikie scale; perch scale; white with red head; mullet; rainbow; silver flash; fire plug; rainbow fire.

THE "SEVEN THOUSAND"
1950-1952

Introduced "NEW" in the 1950 catalog, this plug is a very deep runner. It was a reverse running plug with a metal diving lip. It had legs attached to the belly similar to the ones on the No. 300 Series CRAWDAD, and two belly-mounted treble hooks. Although the catalogs don't mention any size difference, the two plugs in the photo measure 2-3/8" and 2-7/8". The lure was in the 1953 catalog, but it was stamped "DISCONTINUED." Collector value range: $20-$30.

CATALOG SERIES #	BODY LENGTH	LURE WEIGHT
7000	2-3/4"	3/4 oz.

COLOR OR FINISH: Pikie scale; perch scale; white with redhead, solid black; silver flash; rainbow fire; fire plug.

POCKET ROCKET
1957-1961

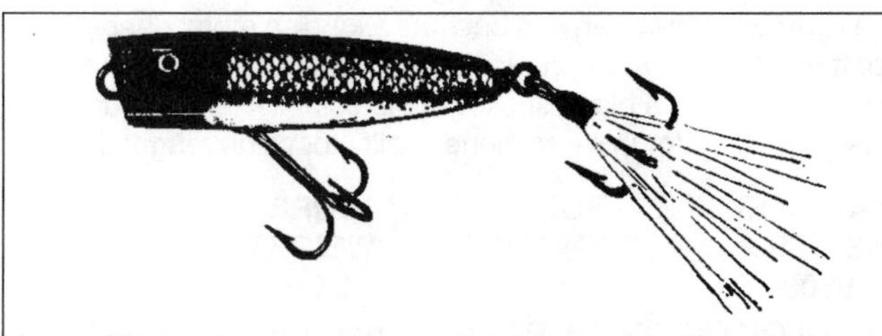

First appearing in the 1957 catalog, it also was advertised in the April, 1957 issue of *Field & Stream*. The lure is equipped with extra heavy hooks and the strong through-body wire construction. It was listed and illustrated in the 1962 catalog, but it was stamped "DISCONTINUED." It was probably because of its similarity to the SALT POPPER. It was never made in plastic. Collector value range: $5-$10.

CATALOG SERIES #	BODY LENGTH	LURE WEIGHT
7000	4"	1-1/8 oz.

COLOR OR FINISH: Silver flash, blue flash.

SURFSTER, 7200 Series
Wood, 1953-1968
Plastic, 1964-1965

SURFSTER, 7300 Series
1953-1959

SALT WATER SURFSTER, 7400 Series
1953-1959

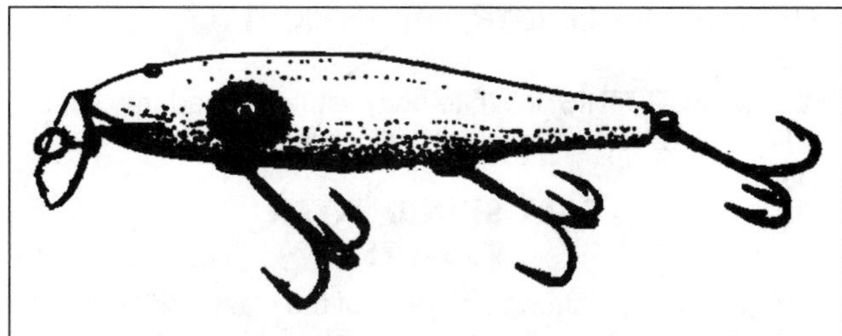

Only the SALTWATER SURFSTER was billed as new in the 1953 catalog, but none of the SURFSTER series lures were in the 1952 edition so they must have been new also. They were all three listed as new in a Creek Chub advertisement in the March, 1953 issue of *Outdoor Life*. The 7200 Series SURFSTER is the only one of the series to also be made in plastic. Inexplicably they were offered only in the 1964 and 1966 catalogs along with the wooden version. The colors offered on the plastic version were the same as on the wooden lure with the exception of Mullet. Collector value range for SURFSTER: $25-$50., Plastic, $5-$10.

CATALOG SERIES #	BODY LENGTH	LURE WEIGHT
7200	4-1/4"	3/4 oz.
7300	6"	1-7/8 oz.
7400	7-1/4"	2-1/2 oz.

COLOR OR FINISH (wood): *Pikie scale, *perch scale, white with red head, *silver flash, blue flash, purple eel, yellow flash, **mullet, ***solid red.

**Removed in 1957.*

***Added in 1957 and removed in 1967.*

****This very rare Creek Chub color was added in 1964.*

COLOR OR FINISH (plastic): White with red head, silver shiner, red eye, silver flash, blue flash.

SURF POPPER
1955-1959

This is a fairly difficult lure to find due to its short-lived production time. It was designed for surf casting from the beach. It is a very large version of the 7100 Series SNOOK PLUNKER/SALT POPPER. Collector value range: N/A.

CATALOG SERIES #	BODY LENGTH	LURE WEIGHT
7500	7-1/8"	4 oz.

COLOR OR FINISH: White body with red head, silver flash, blue flash, purple eel, yellow flash.

SURF DARTER
1955-1959

The 1956 catalog calls this lure new. It is listed among several others under the heading SALT WATER LURES. It is a very big plug designed for the surf caster, It is made strong with the through-body harness construction. Collector value range: N/A.

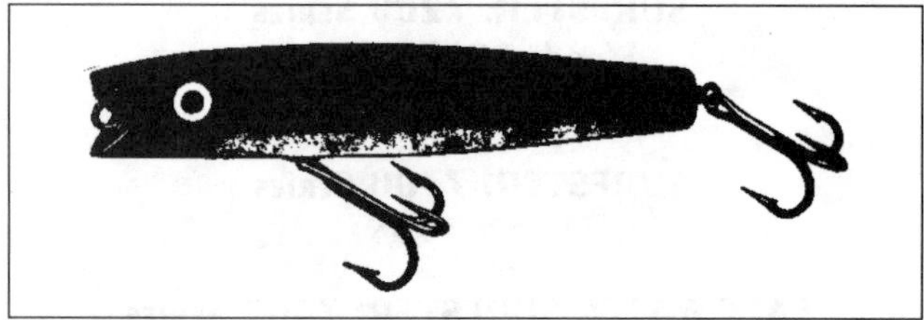

CATALOG SERIES #	BODY LENGTH	LURE WEIGHT
7600	7"	4 oz.

COLOR OR FINISH: White body with red head, mullet, silver flash, blue flash, purple eel, yellow flash.

SALT SPIN DARTER
1955-1959

This is a longer, stronger version of the classic 2000 Series DARTER made for salt water use. The catalog listing says "Spinning and squidding, darts and splashes on surface." Collector value range: $100-$200.

CATALOG SERIES #	BODY LENGTH	LURE WEIGHT
7700	5-1/2"	2-1/4 oz.

COLOR OR FINISH: White with red head, mullet, silver flash, blue flash, purple eel, yellow flash.

VIPER (plastic)
1965-1971

Promoted in the catalog: "Viper will be the sensation of the 1965 fishing season." The last catalog it was illustrated in was the 1971 edition, but the lure remained in the price list until 1978. Collector value range: N/A.

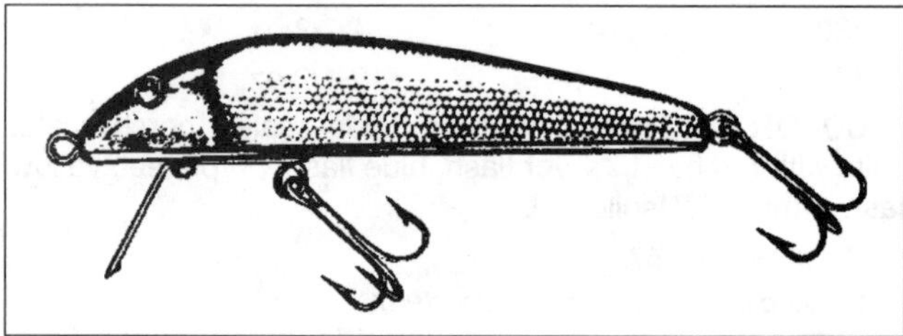

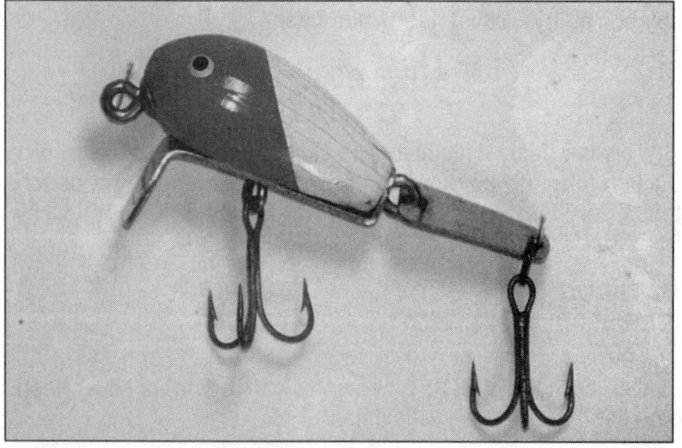

There is absolutely no doubt that this is a 2-1/4" SPOONTAIL. It is identical to all other SPOONTAILS save one thing. The lip plane portion of the metal under plate is stamped "SHAKESPEARE". It is known that Creek Chub made lures for Shakespeare for a time, but this was never cataloged by them and it was a Creek Chub production lure. Photo courtesy Ken Bernoteit.

CATALOG SERIES #	BODY LENGTH	LURE WEIGHT
8800-P	3-1/2"	1/4 oz.

COLOR OR FINISH: White with red head, silver shiner, silver flash, blue flash, *chrome.

**Chrome finish was in the color option list all along despite the fact that the 1968 catalog states "Viper has gone Chrome by popular demand".*

SPOONTAIL
1954-1956

There are two sizes of the SPOONTAIL. For some reason this handsome wood-bodied lure wasn't around very long. The body is attached to a metal plate that serves as the lip, underbelly and tail piece all in one. The metal piece trailing with a treble hook is hardly a spoon, but perhaps they used the term for lack of a better one. An advertisement in the April, 1954 issue of *Field & Stream* magazine stated the SPOONTAIL was "NEW" and that it was available in "...5 finishes." Only four were found in the catalogs. The sizes below include the metal tail. Collector value range: $30-$40.

CATALOG SERIES #	BODY LENGTH	LURE WEIGHT
9100	2-1/4"	1/4 oz.
500	3-1/2"	1/2 oz.

COLOR OR FINISH: Pikie, perch, white body with red head, silver flash.

SPINNING DEEPSTER
1953-1955

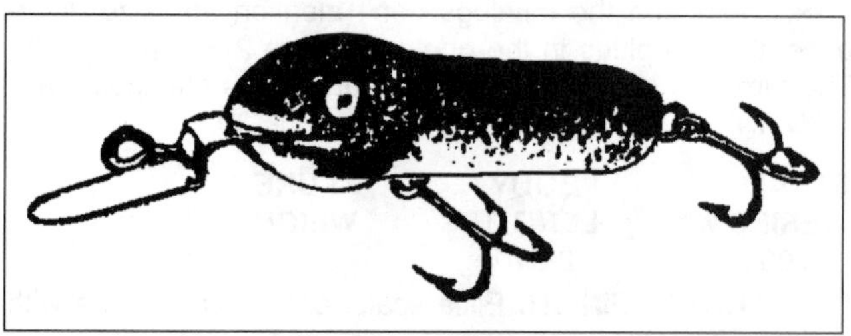

The illustration accompanying is a poor quality photocopy, but its all that was available. This 2-1/4" bulbous head plug reminds one of Eger Bait Company's BULL NOSE FROG. Unlike the Eger bait, however, this one has a longish metal deep-diving lip. It must not have been much of a seller because it lasted two years or less. The black sucker in the color list is a unique color design created for this lure alone. Collector value range: $5-$10.

CATALOG SERIES #	BODY LENGTH	LURE WEIGHT
9600	2-1/4"	1/4 oz.

COLOR OR FINISH: Pike scale, perch scale, white with red head, silver flash, black sucker.

FEATHER CASTING MINNOW
1924-1927

New in 1924 this lure disappears as a casting lure by 1928. It was then apparently redesigned for use with a fly rod. It has a propeller spinner at the nose and trails fancy feathers. The catalog listing states "Hook drops in slot behind body, making same more weedless and a better hooker." Collector value range: $100-$150.

CATALOG SERIES #	BODY LENGTH	LURE WEIGHT
F10 or F11	1-5/8"	1/2 oz.

COLOR OR FINISH: White and red; creek chub, scale finish; yellow perch, scale finish; gold fish, scale finish.

STREEKER (plastic)

S Series
1971-1978

LS Series
1973-1978

This plastic lure was introduced as new in the 1971 catalog. It is a plastic underwater lure that "...casts like a bullet." Equipped with two propeller spinners and two treble hooks. Collector value range: $5-$10.

CATALOG SERIES #	BODY LENGTH	LURE WEIGHT
S	3"	3/8 oz.
LS	4-1/2"	1 oz.

COLOR OR FINISH: Pike scale, perch scale, white with red head, silver shiner, *purple, silver flash, chrome.

**Never listed in catalogs as available on the LS Series.*

THE "WICKED WIGGLER" (S Series)
1926-1940

COHOKIE
1968-1978

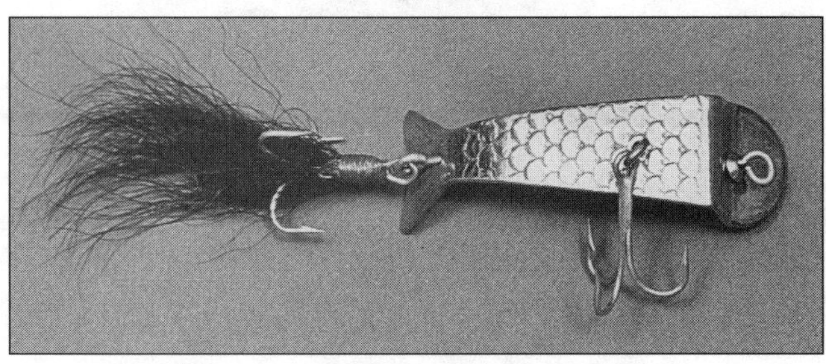

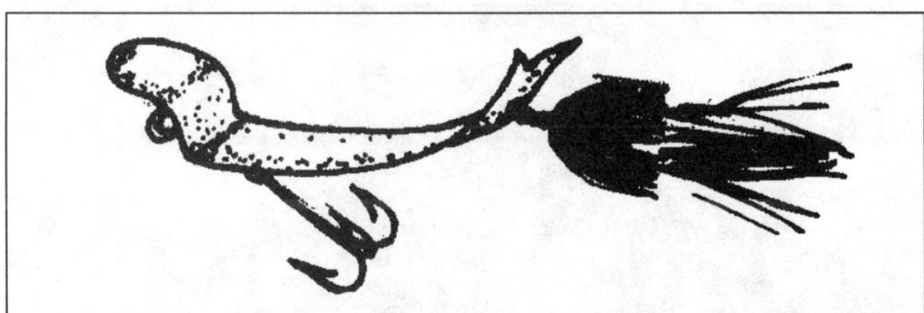

This 2-1/4" WIGGLING SPOON (original name) was new in 1926. Creek Chub advertised a contest in 1926 saying in the ad: "This new Wiggling Spoon wants to be rechristened!" and that the winner would be awarded $100. It continued to be offered until the very early 1940s. The design original never changed but initially the lure was offered in two hook styles, a feathered treble (S1) or a hook for pork rind (S2). In the 1935 catalog, a third option was offered, a single-pointed rigid hook (S3). In 1967 this lure was re-released more than 20 years after it was discontinued. Somebody must have found it in the bottom of "old possum belly" and started catching fish with it. The new version, now called the COHOKIE, was listed in the catalogs in a larger and smaller size than the earlier model. The larger size, however, was actually the same size as the original. The later versions do not have the typical early Creek Chub washer on the hook holder hardware. Collector value range for the old model: $10-$30, the new model: $5-$10.

CATALOG SERIES #	BODY LENGTH	LURE WEIGHT
S	2-1/2"	3/4 oz.
1000	2-1/2"	1/2 oz
1100	2"	1/4 oz.

WIGGLE-JIG
1966-1967

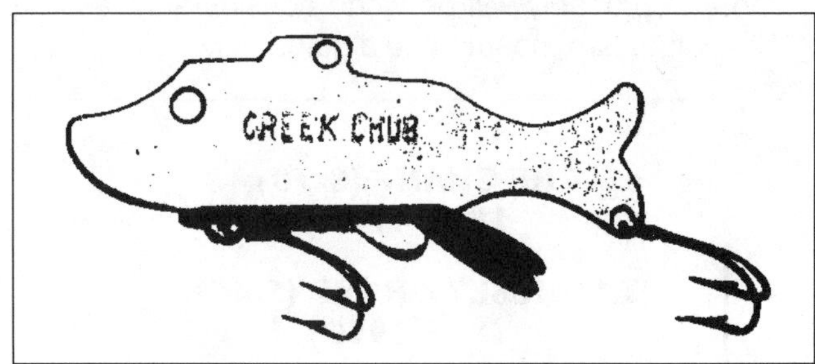

It must not have been a hot seller. It was announced as "NEW FOR 1966," was listed and illustrated in the 1967 edition of the catalog and gone in the 1968 edition. An all-metal lure of two-piece construction it had two holes, one as an eye and the other in the dorsal fin. The listing said to snap a swivel in the eye for casting or trolling and in the fin for ice jigging. Listed as the JIGGLE-JIG in 1967 it was available in Silver or Gold sides. The lower metal belly plate was Pink. The listings gave no length, but it did say it weighed 1/8 ounce and said it was for spin casting or "...ultra-light fly rod casting" so it must have been pretty small. Collector value range: $30-$40.

CATALOG SERIES #	BODY LENGTH	LURE WEIGHT
11-S (silver)	?	1/8 oz.
11-G (gold)	?	1/8 oz.

SINFUL SAL
1930-1940

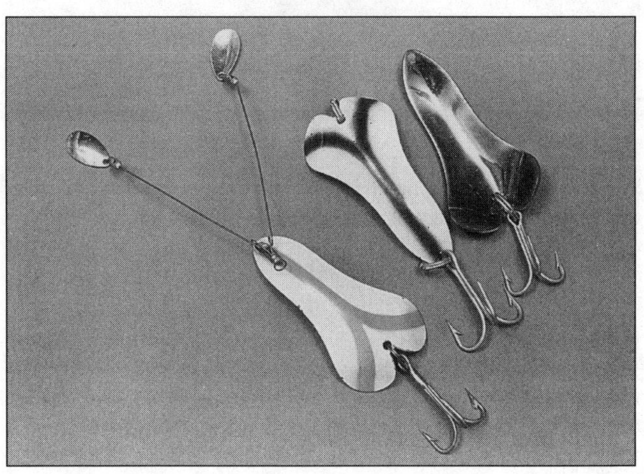

New in 1930-31, this is a wobbling spoon with twin blade spinners, and a single treble hook attached to the trailing edge of the spoon. The catalogs do not list this lure as available from about 1941-42. Collector value range: $25-$50.

CATALOG SERIES #	BODY LENGTH	LURE WEIGHT
S-20	2-3/4"	3/4 oz.

COLOR OR FINISH: All nickel, nickel inside, white & red outside; copper inside, white & red outside; nickel inside, white & black outside; nickel inside, yellow spotted outside; nickel inside, frog finish outside.

IMPORTANT NOTICE

The value ranges listed in this book are for lures in Very Good to Excellent condition. The values of those lures not in Very Good to Excellent condition can and probably will be worth considerably less. The values are meant to be a guide only.

THE CHAMP (S-30) 1937-1946

THE MUSKY CHAMP (S-40) 1937-1950

THE SALTWATER CHAMP (S-50) 1937-1950

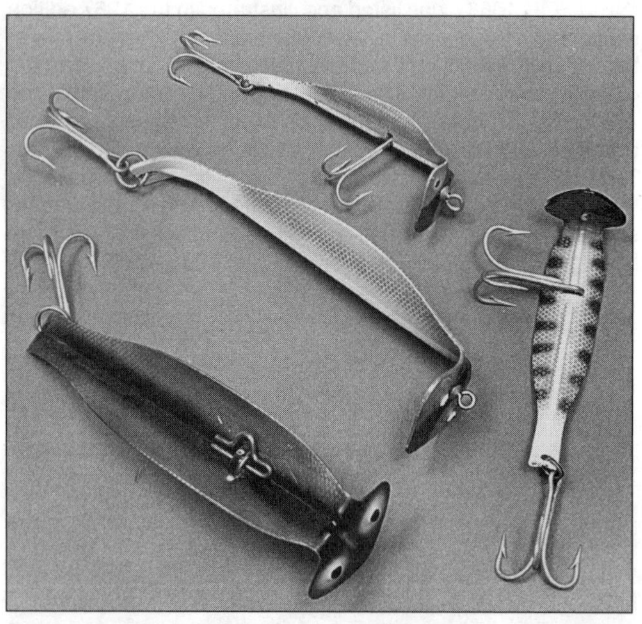

These three lures are first illustrated as "A new metal Pikie" in the 1937 catalog. The CHAMP had disappeared in the 1946 edition but the two larger sizes persisted until 1950 after which they were apparently also discontinued. They are all-metal lures with a belly treble hook and a trailing treble. Collector value range: $20-$35.

CATALOG SERIES #	BODY LENGTH	LURE WEIGHT
S-30	3-1/4"	5/8 oz.
S-40	5"	1-1/2 oz.
S-50	5"	3 oz.

COLOR OR FINISH: Pikie; nickel, copper, white with red head, yellow scale, green scale, *mullet

**Salt Water Champ only.*

CREEK CHUB/SHUR-STRIKE

Sometime in the late 1920s, the Creek Chub Bait Company initiated the Shur-Strike line in order to offer the fisherman a less expensive lure and to compete with other companies. In addition to retailing them as Shur-Strike, they sold them wholesale to other companies for distribution under their own brand. Some of them but probably not all are listed following:

COMPANY	BRAND NAME
W. Bingham Co.	UNCLE TOM LURES
True Value	TRUE VALUE
Montgomery-Ward	WARD'S, HAWTHORN
Sears and Roebuck	MEADOW BROOK

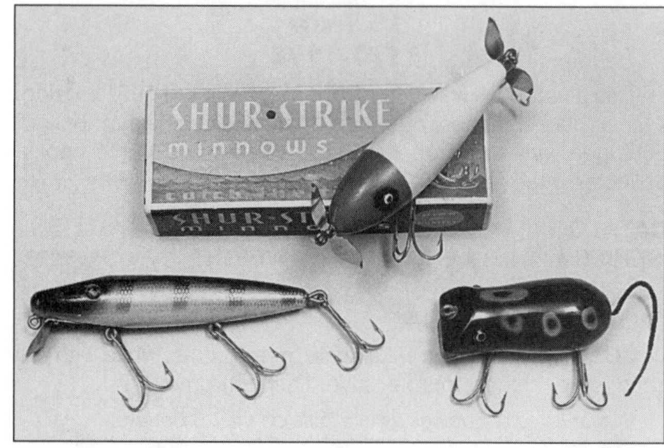

SHUR-STRIKE lures by Creek Chub. The plug on the box is a UW SERIES. Lower left: P SERIES. Lower right: MO SERIES.

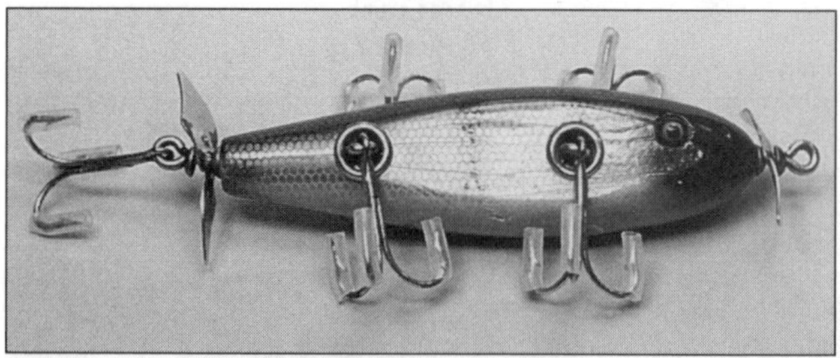

This five hook model used the injured minnow type body is very rare. It was never cataloged.

A beautiful, new with box, two-hook. Western Auto Shur-Strike IM Series wounded minnow. It measures 3-5/8". Photo courtesy Ken Bernoteit.

They each had their own distinctive box. Creek Chub was not mentioned as the manufacturer.

The baits were not cheaply made. They were high-quality products, but didn't go though the stringent quality control process that the Creek Chub lures did. They have glass eyes or tack eyes and cup/screw eye hardware. They never used the signature Creek Chub dive lip. When called for they used a "thumb print," round and cupped style.

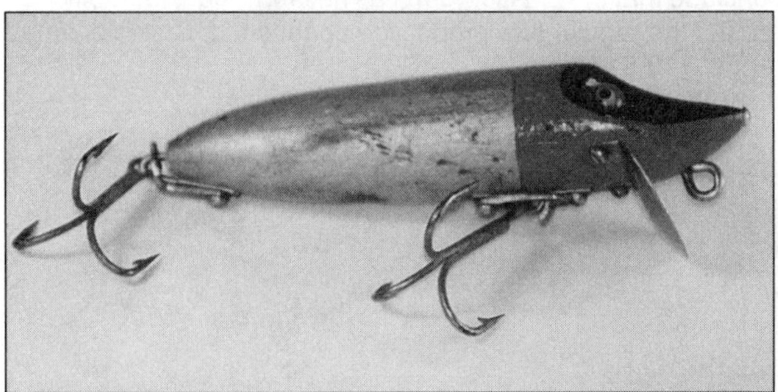

A Series HR with glass eyes and Heddon two-piece hook hardware on belly and tail. Note the black face. The finish is aluminum-colored body with red head and black face; an unusual pattern. This is an obvious Heddon RIVER RUNT copy. Photo courtesy Ken Bernoteit.

They didn't use the Creek Chub series numbering system using only combinations of letters or letters and numbers. They apparently copied many lures from other companies. Sometimes you can tell which company or which lure was copied by the number assigned to it. For instance the designation BO is for a lure that is very similar to a South Bend BASS-ORENO. Another example is their HR Series does a good job of imitating a Heddon RIVER RUNT and Series PP is a Paw Paw MOUSE look-a-like.

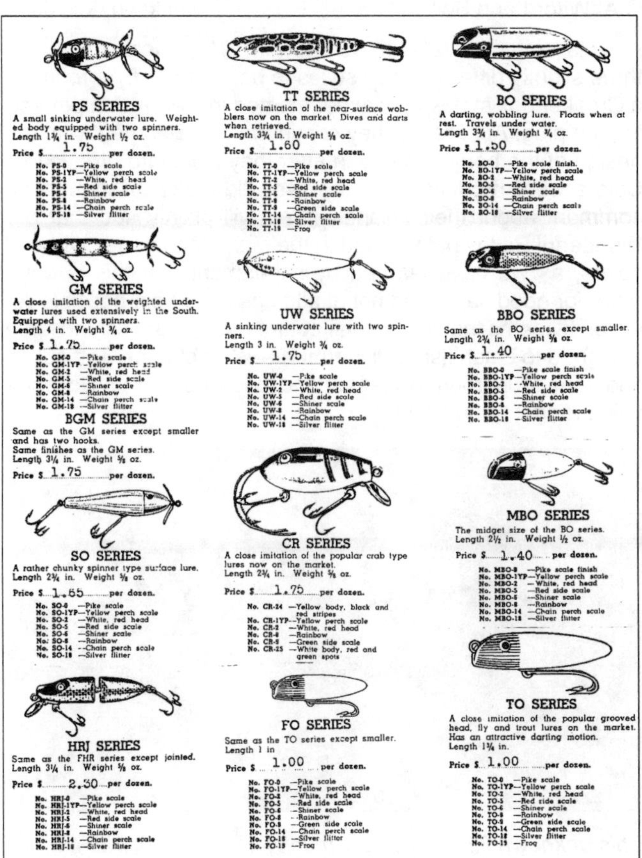

PS SERIES
A small sinking underwater lure. Weighted body equipped with two spinners.
Length 1¾ in. Weight ½ oz.
Price $ 1.75 per dozen.
No. PS-0 —Pike scale
No. PS-1YP—Yellow perch scale
No. PS-2 —White, red head
No. PS-5 —Red side scale
No. PS-6 —Shiner scale
No. PS-8 —Rainbow
No. PS-14 —Chain perch scale
No. PS-18 —Silver flitter

GM SERIES
A close imitation of the weighted underwater lures used extensively in the South. Equipped with two spinners.
Length 4 in. Weight ¾ oz.
Price $ 1.75 per dozen.
No. GM-0 —Pike scale
No. GM-1YP—Yellow perch scale
No. GM-2 —White, red head
No. GM-5 —Red side scale
No. GM-6 —Shiner scale
No. GM-8 —Rainbow
No. GM-14 —Chain perch scale
No. GM-18 —Silver flitter

BGM SERIES
Same as the GM series except smaller and has two hooks.
Same finishes as the GM series.
Length 3¼ in. Weight ⅝ oz.
Price $ 1.75 per dozen.

SO SERIES
A rather chunky spinner type surface lure.
Length 2¾ in. Weight ⅝ oz.
Price $ 1.65 per dozen.
No. SO-0 —Pike scale
No. SO-1YP—Yellow perch scale
No. SO-2 —White, red head
No. SO-5 —Red side scale
No. SO-6 —Shiner scale
No. SO-8 —Rainbow
No. SO-14 —Chain perch scale
No. SO-18 —Silver flitter

HRJ SERIES
Same as the FHR series except jointed.
Length 3¼ in. Weight ⅝ oz.
Price $ 2.30 per dozen.
No. HRJ-0 —Pike scale
No. HRJ-1YP—Yellow perch scale
No. HRJ-2 —White, red head
No. HRJ-5 —Red side scale
No. HRJ-6 —Shiner scale
No. HRJ-8 —Rainbow
No. HRJ-14 —Chain perch scale
No. HRJ-18 —Silver flitter

TT SERIES
A close imitation of the near-surface wobblers now on the market. Dives and darts when retrieved.
Length 3¾ in. Weight ⅝ oz.
Price $ 1.60 per dozen.
No. TT-0 —Pike scale
No. TT-1YP—Yellow perch scale
No. TT-2 —White, red head
No. TT-5 —Red side scale
No. TT-6 —Shiner scale
No. TT-8 —Rainbow
No. TT-9 —Green side scale
No. TT-14 —Chain perch scale
No. TT-18 —Silver flitter
No. TT-19 —Frog

UW SERIES
A sinking underwater lure with two spinners.
Length 3 in. Weight ¾ oz.
Price $ 1.75 per dozen.
No. UW-0 —Pike scale
No. UW-1YP—Yellow perch scale
No. UW-2 —White, red head
No. UW-5 —Red side scale
No. UW-6 —Shiner scale
No. UW-8 —Rainbow
No. UW-14 —Chain perch scale
No. UW-18 —Silver flitter

CR SERIES
A close imitation of the popular crab type lures now on the market.
Length 2¾ in. Weight ⅝ oz.
Price $ 1.75 per dozen.
No. CR-24 —Yellow body, black and red stripes
No. CR-1YP—Yellow perch scale
No. CR-2 —White, red head
No. CR-8 —Rainbow
No. CR-9 —Green side scale
No. CR-25 —White body, red and green spots

FO SERIES
Same as the TO series except smaller.
Length 1 in
Price $ 1.00 per dozen.
No. FO-0 —Pike scale
No. FO-1YP—Yellow perch scale
No. FO-2 —White, red head
No. FO-5 —Red side scale
No. FO-6 —Shiner scale
No. FO-8 —Rainbow
No. FO-9 —Green side scale
No. FO-14 —Chain perch scale
No. FO-18 —Silver flitter
No. FO-19 —Frog

BO SERIES
A darting, wobbling lure. Floats when at rest. Travels under water.
Length 3¾ in. Weight ¾ oz.
Price $ 1.50 per dozen.
No. BO-0 —Pike scale finish.
No. BO-1YP—Yellow perch scale
No. BO-2 —White, red head
No. BO-5 —Red side scale
No. BO-6 —Shiner scale
No. BO-8 —Rainbow
No. BO-14 —Chain perch scale
No. BO-18 —Silver flitter

BBO SERIES
Same as the BO series except smaller.
Length 2¾ in. Weight ⅝ oz.
Price $ 1.40 per dozen.
No. BBO-0 —Pike scale finish
No. BBO-1YP—Yellow perch scale
No. BBO-2 —White, red head
No. BBO-5 —Red side scale
No. BBO-6 —Shiner scale
No. BBO-8 —Rainbow
No. BBO-14 —Chain perch scale
No. BBO-18 —Silver flitter

MBO SERIES
The midget size of the BO series.
Length 2½ in. Weight ½ oz.
Price $ 1.40 per dozen.
No. MBO-0 —Pike scale finish
No. MBO-1YP—Yellow perch scale
No. MBO-2 —White, red head
No. MBO-5 —Red side scale
No. MBO-6 —Shiner scale
No. MBO-8 —Rainbow
No. MBO-14 —Chain perch scale
No. MBO-18 —Silver flitter

TO SERIES
A close imitation of the popular grooved head, fly and trout lures on the market. Has an attractive darting motion.
Length 1¾ in.
Price $ 1.00 per dozen.
No. TO-0 —Pike scale
No. TO-1YP—Yellow perch scale
No. TO-2 —White, red head
No. TO-5 —Red side scale
No. TO-6 —Shiner scale
No. TO-8 —Rainbow
No. TO-9 —Green side scale
No. TO-14 —Chain perch scale
No. TO-18 —Silver flitter
No. TO-19 —Frog

They made dozens of Shur-Strike baits and you can run into almost anything. On the next couple of pages is a reproduction of two pages of Shur-Strike lure listings in a 1940 edition of the H & D Folsom Arms Company trade catalog. It should help with identification of the 24 lures listed and illustrated. The lures were re-arranged to fit a vertical format. The end of the listing contained the following statement:

All lures are equipped with best quality hardware, Mustad extra-strength hooks and have a very high grade finish. Each lure is individually boxed in a three color set-up box, packed one dozen of a kind and color to a package, packages not broken. Approximate shipping weight-two pounds per dozen lures.

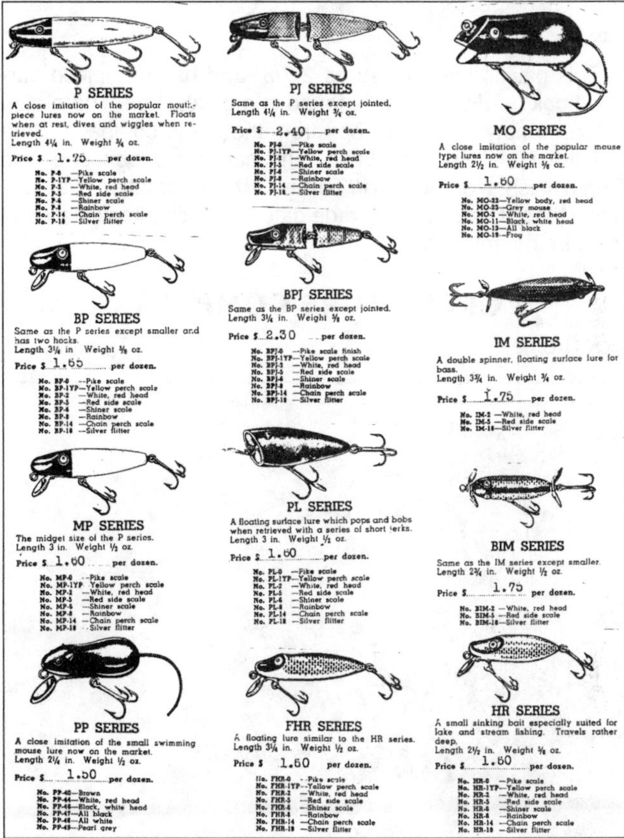

P SERIES
A close imitation of the popular mouth-piece lures now on the market. Floats when at rest, dives and wiggles when retrieved.
Length 4¼ in. Weight ¾ oz.
Price $ 1.75 per dozen.
No. P-0 —Pike scale
No. P-1YP—Yellow perch scale
No. P-2 —White, red head
No. P-5 —Red side scale
No. P-6 —Shiner scale
No. P-8 —Rainbow
No. P-14 —Chain perch scale
No. P-18 —Silver flitter

BP SERIES
Same as the P series except smaller and has two hooks.
Length 3¼ in Weight ⅝ oz.
Price $ 1.65 per dozen.
No. BP-0 —Pike scale
No. BP-1YP—Yellow perch scale
No. BP-2 —White, red head
No. BP-5 —Red side scale
No. BP-6 —Shiner scale
No. BP-8 —Rainbow
No. BP-14 —Chain perch scale
No. BP-18 —Silver flitter

MP SERIES
The midget size of the P series.
Length 3 in. Weight ½ oz.
Price $ 1.60 per dozen.
No. MP-0 —Pike scale
No. MP-1YP Yellow perch scale
No. MP-2 —White, red head
No. MP-5 —Red side scale
No. MP-6 —Shiner scale
No. MP-8 —Rainbow
No. MP-14 —Chain perch scale
No. MP-18 —Silver flitter

PP SERIES
A close imitation of the small swimming mouse lure now on the market.
Length 2¼ in. Weight ½ oz.
Price $ 1.50 per dozen.
No. PP-40—Brown
No. PP-44—White, red head
No. PP-46—Black, white head
No. PP-47—All black
No. PP-48—All white
No. PP-49—Pearl grey

PJ SERIES
Same as the P series except jointed.
Length 4¼ in. Weight ¾ oz.
Price $ 2.40 per dozen.
No. PJ-0 —Pike scale
No. PJ-1YP—Yellow perch scale
No. PJ-2 —White, red head
No. PJ-5 —Red side scale
No. PJ-6 —Shiner scale
No. PJ-8 —Rainbow
No. PJ-14 —Chain perch scale
No. PJ-18 —Silver flitter

BPJ SERIES
Same as the BP series except jointed.
Length 3¼ in. Weight ⅝ oz.
Price $ 2.30 per dozen.
No. BPJ-0 —Pike scale finish
No. BPJ-1YP—Yellow perch scale
No. BPJ-2 —White, red head
No. BPJ-5 —Red side scale
No. BPJ-6 —Shiner scale
No. BPJ-8 —Rainbow
No. BPJ-14 —Chain perch scale
No. BPJ-18 —Silver flitter

PL SERIES
A floating surface lure which pops and bobs when retrieved with a series of short jerks.
Length 3 in. Weight ½ oz.
Price $ 1.60 per dozen.
No. PL-0 —Pike scale
No. PL-1YP—Yellow perch scale
No. PL-2 —White, red head
No. PL-5 —Red side scale
No. PL-6 —Shiner scale
No. PL-8 —Rainbow
No. PL-14 —Chain perch scale
No. PL-18 —Silver flitter

FHR SERIES
A floating lure similar to the HR series.
Length 3¼ in. Weight ½ oz.
Price $ 1.60 per dozen.
No. FHR-0 —Pike scale
No. FHR-1YP—Yellow perch scale
No. FHR-2 —White, red head
No. FHR-5 —Red side scale
No. FHR-6 —Shiner scale
No. FHR-8 —Rainbow
No. FHR-14 —Chain perch scale
No. FHR-18 —Silver flitter

MO SERIES
A close imitation of the popular mouse type lures now on the market.
Length 2½ in. Weight ⅝ oz.
Price $ 1.60 per dozen.
No. MO-22—Yellow body, red head
No. MO-23—Grey mouse
No. MO-2 —White, red head
No. MO-11—Black, white head
No. MO-13—All black
No. MO-19—Frog

IM SERIES
A double spinner, floating surface lure for bass.
Length 3¾ in. Weight ¾ oz.
Price $ 1.75 per dozen.
No. IM-2 —White, red head
No. IM-5 —Red side scale
No. IM-18—Silver flitter

BIM SERIES
Same as the IM series except smaller.
Length 2¾ in. Weight ½ oz.
Price $ 1.75 per dozen.
No. BIM-2 —White, red head
No. BIM-5 —Red side scale
No. BIM-18—Silver flitter

HR SERIES
A small sinking bait especially suited for lake and stream fishing. Travels rather deep.
Length 2½ in. Weight ⅝ oz.
Price $ 1.60 per dozen.
No. HR-0 —Pike scale
No. HR-1YP—Yellow perch scale
No. HR-2 —White, red head
No. HR-5 —Red side scale
No. HR-6 —Shiner scale
No. HR-8 —Rainbow
No. HR-14 —Chain perch scale
No. HR-18 —Silver flitter

Anyone wishing to learn more about this Creek Chub line should get a copy of *SHUR-STRIKE, Color Chart and Lures* by Bob Minch. It is a great study of the lures with all the lures pictured in full color. Unfortunately it is out of print, but you might be able to get a copy from the Highwood Bookshop in Traverse City, Michigan.

It is difficult to price these lures as there is so much confusion about them. I have seen lists that usually run about the same as the Creek Chub counterparts. The rest run from around $10 to $40. There was one Shur-Strike UNDERWATER MINNOW that sold at auction in 1997 at just under $20.

CREEK KING LURES

C K Manufacturing Co. Little Rock, Arkansas

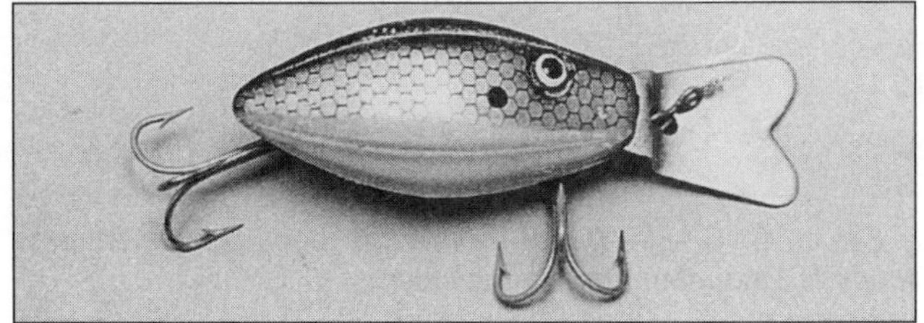

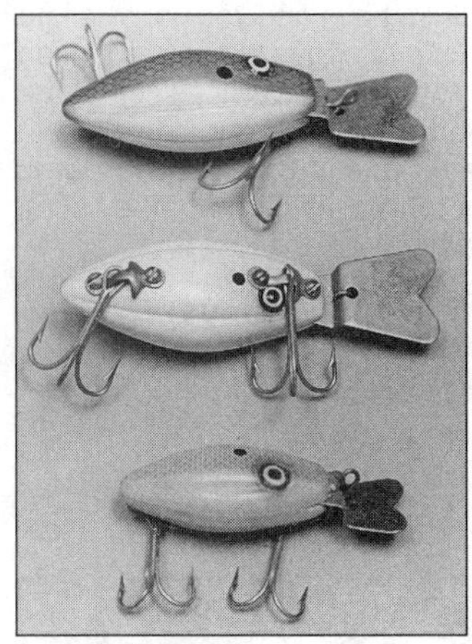

Three CREEK KING lures. The top and middle (belly view) lures have 2" bodies and measure 2-7/8" overall. The bottom lure is smaller and measures 1-1/2", 2" overall. Notice the black dot apparently used on all their lures.

This plastic lure measures 2-7/8" and has one-piece surface hook hardware. It was found in a plastic box. There also was an empty cardboard box from the same company. Both had the Little Rock address. The cardboard box end had "Perch finish" stamped on it. This is all the information available at this time. There was no trade date for which a realistic value could be determined.

CREME LURE COMPANY

Nick Creme — Tyler, Texas

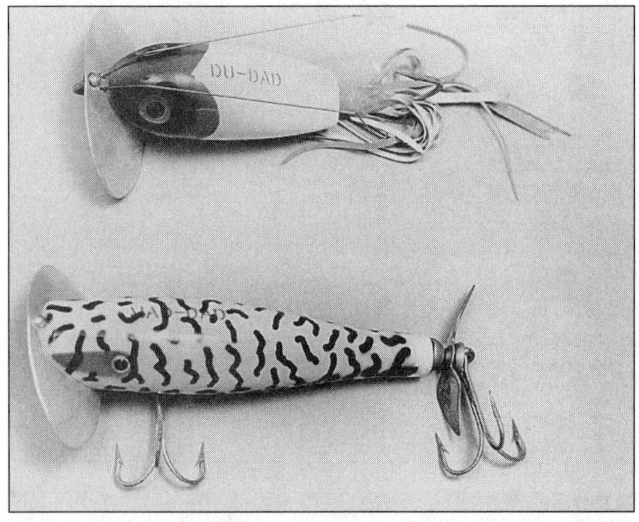

Upper lure here is a Creme Weedless DU-DAD, 6200 Series. It was available in nine finishes and two sizes, 2-1/4" and 2-1/2". The lower lure here is a MAD-DAD. It measures 3-1/2" long and has the same hook preventer more visible on the CAST-ATEM in the other photo.

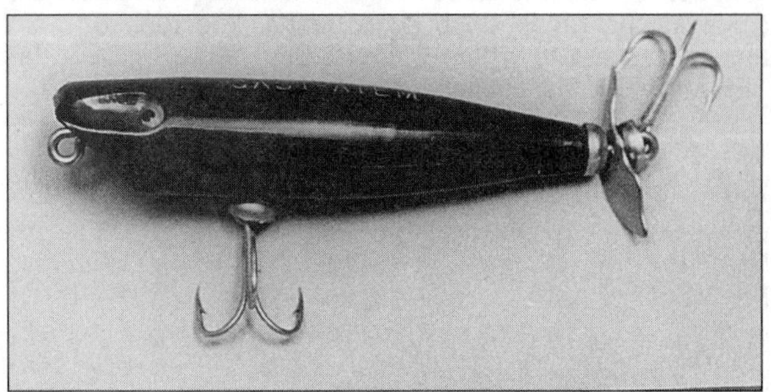

A Creme 3" CAST-AT-TEM. Note the hook presenters ana floppy tail-mounted propeller spinner.

I had only a 1971-72 catalog and it featured plastic worms and other soft plastic lures, a couple of dozen hand-made fly rod lures and a few metal spinner baits. As a matter of fact the cover of the catalog stated that Creme was "THE ORIGINATOR OF THE PLASTIC WORM." It is known that the company was doing business as early as 1960 and the three plastic lures in the accompanying photos are some of their products of that time. Since they were absent from the 1971 catalog we might conclude that the plastic worm business was considerablly better and the regular lure production abandoned. Collector value range: $10-$15.

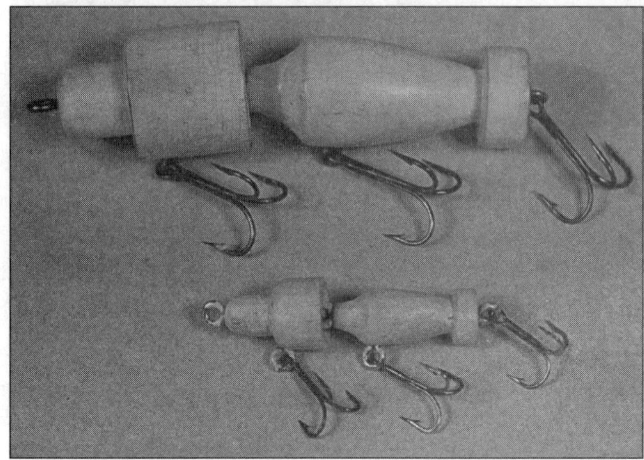

THE CROAKER. Two sizes at 2-1/4" and 4-3/8". Photo courtesy Jim Muma.

THE CROAKER
Croaker Bass Bait Company

C.A. Wiford and Son — Jackson, Michigan

This jointed 4-1/2" plug was new in 1910. There are a least three slightly different body styles to be found. A flyer found in a Croaker box states they experimented for "weeks" in perfecting the plug. Apparently they continued to experiment with the design of the body parts even after they went into production. Colors were not listed, but the flyer did make an interesting comment about their finishes. "You will plainly see that our Wonderful Bait is not finished in the most handsome style and colors, as we have learned by experiment that this is done more for good sales and not at all to give the best possible results." It seems that the familiar controversy — are fishing lures designed to catch fish or fisherman —is an old one. Difficult to find. (see Mushroom Bass Bait and following photo). Collector value range: $300-$400.

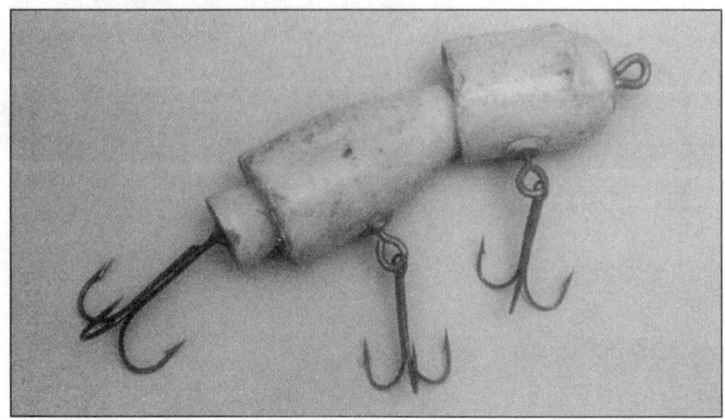

This unknown lure looks very much like the CROAKER. It has Moonlight Bait Company style hardware and measures 3-1/4".

CRUTCH'S LIZARD

William O. Crutchfield — Elizabethton, Tennessee

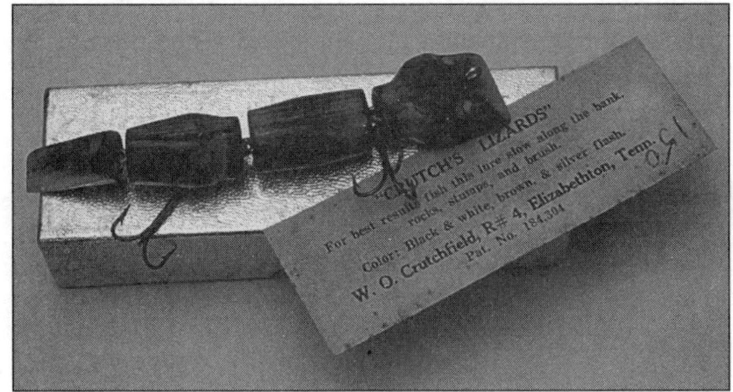

A unique triple-joint wooden lure. The example in the photo measures 5" long and is finished in a burnished natural wood. The eyes appear to be ceramic beads no doubt meant to be strung as a necklace. The made very effective eyes with the holes being the pupils. Crutchfield made these lures by hand over a period of years from probably the late 1940s or early 1950s until the 1960s. He actually took the trouble to patent the lure and a design patent was granted in 1958. The lure was offered in three finishes: the Burnished wood, Black with White stripes, White with sparkles. Collector value range: $20-$30.

ED CUMINGS, INC.

Flint, Michigan

ED'S WAIKIKI
ED's HULA HULA

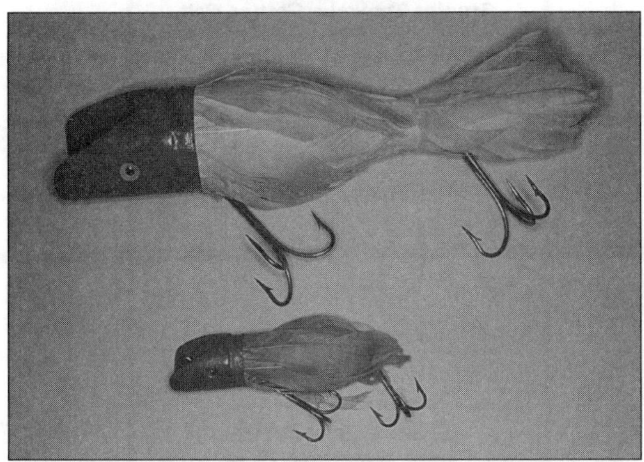

The Cummings company is still in business to this day, well known for net making. Sometime in the late 1930s the company made these two lures. They apparently didn't make them beyond the early 1940s. I found a couple of their ads in 1940 issues of *Sports Afield.* The ads were for fly line, a creel, mosquito head nets and a "NEVERSINK" wood frame landing net. There was an illustration of a beautiful fly called the "LITE-RITE FLY." The two lures in the photo are ED'S WAIKIKI, a huge (9") glass-eyed, wood-bodied musky lure and the smaller bass bait, ED'S HULA HULA, glass-eyed at 4". Both are decorated with chicken feathers. Collector value range: $25-$35.

DANDY LURES

Lonn's Sales Organization — Tampa, Florida

There is a connection between Dandy Lures and the Florida Fishing Tackle Mfg. Co. Apparently Mr. E.J. Lonn contracted them to make lures while also buying standard lures. Many companies marketed different lines of lures under different names in the earlier days and it is a marketing technique still used today. It is known that there were at least eight lures in the Dandy line. Many of their names were the same as the Florida Tackle name. So if you run across any Dandy Lures, you are most likely looking at the same products as those of the Florida Tackle Company lures. It is thought Lonn marketed Dandy Lures in the early to mid-1950s. So far the only sure way to identify these lures is to find them in a Dandy box. Collector values for those found in Dandy Boxes were not found.

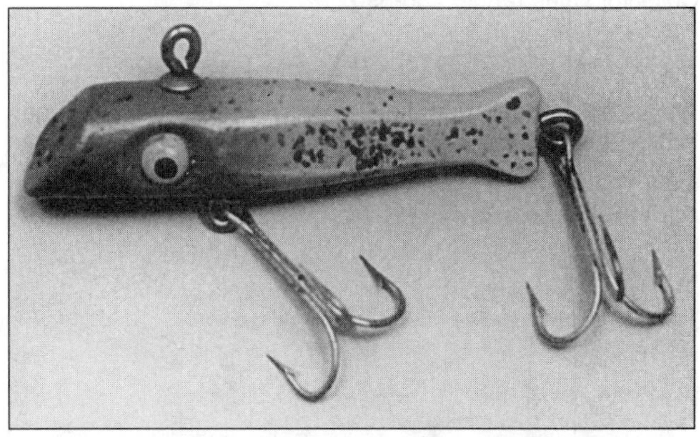

DARBY WEEDLESS
SPIN HEAD WEEDLES(S)

T & M Darby or M. L. Darby — Whiting, Indiana

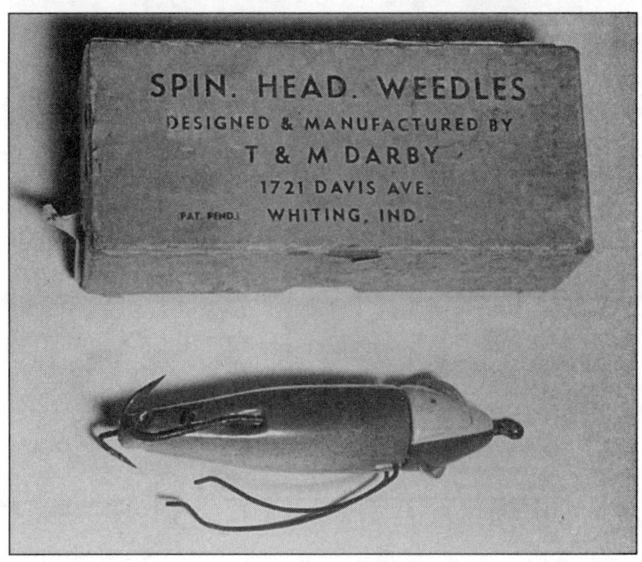

Note the box name for this lure is different from the name found in advertising. The same is true for the manufacturer's name.

This lure dates from sometime around 1934-1937. There were two advertisements found, one from each year. The latest was from the May, 1937 issue of the *Southern Sportsman*. No other references were found. The lure is wood-bodied with one single hook protruding from each side. They are rigged so the shanks could be attached to the body so they would spring out upon a fish striking the lure. It has a spinner head with metal fins inlet into the wood. Colors are White body with a half White, half Red head or Green Back body with a half White, half Green spinner head. The reason for the T & M or M. L. Darby above is that the box said one thing and the advertisements said another. The street addresses were, however, the same. Collector value range: $60-$90.

TRIGGER-FISH

Davis Tackle Manufacturing Company — Detroit, Michigan
Mittig Manufacturing Company — Dearborn, Michigan

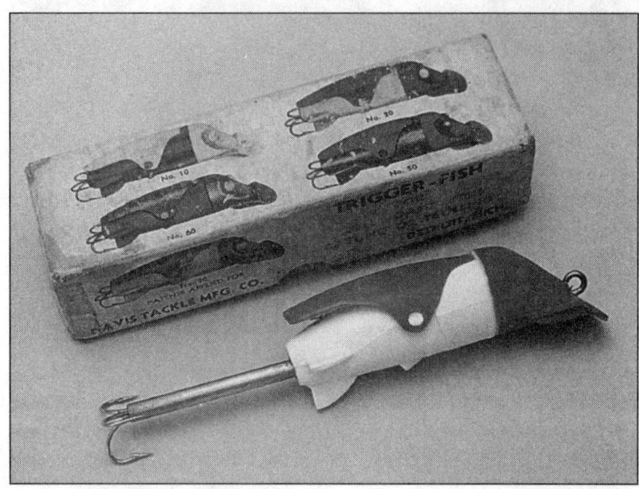

All that was found was the lure in the box and a promotional flyer. This ingenious plastic bait was rigged so the fisherman could cock it by pushing the hook/tube arrangement into the body. This rendered it weedless. When the fish strikes, pushing down on the trigger-back piece it releases the hook which rapidly and powerfully snaps back.

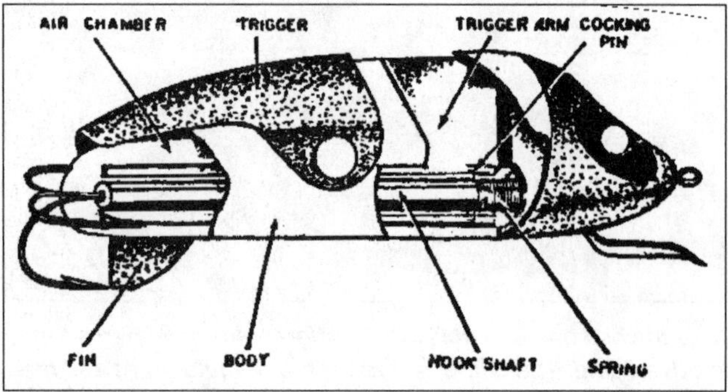

A cutaway drawing of the TRIGGER-FISH showing the mechanism.

The box said that a patent had been applied for but a search of almost 4,000 patents didn't turn up anything. Intriguing is the fact that the flyer was from Mittig Manufacturing Company and the box said Davis Manufacturing Company. Dearborn is a suburb of Detroit. We don't know yet which company was the first to make the lure. It is thought it was sometime in the late 1940s or early 1950s. As far as can be told there were six possible color combinations. The one in the photo is the # 20, white body with red head and back. The box illustration gives us an idea of the other colors. The #10 is Red body with white head and back, #30 is black body with white head and back, #40 is white body with black head, #50 is black body with red head and # 60 is red body with black head. There has also been found a version with a white body, red head and a frog finish back. The back was the trigger. Collector value range: $20-$30.

DEAN'S LURE

Nashville, Tennessee

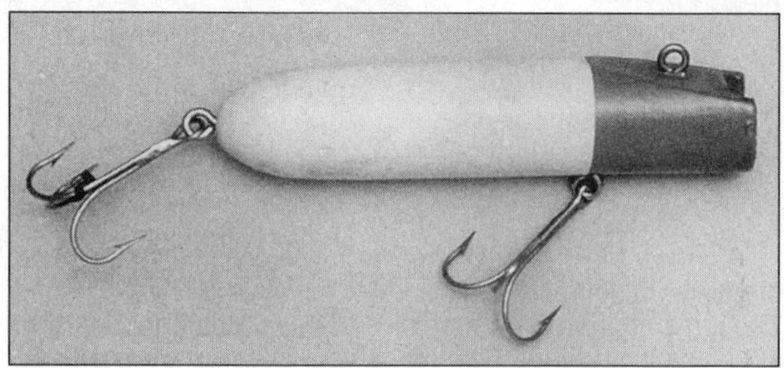

Little is known about this lure other than they were made by a man named Dean in Nashville, Tennessee. It is reported that only a couple of hundred were produced. Dean died sometime prior to 1939. Collector value range: $10-$20.

DECKER LURES

Anson B. (Ans) Decker — Lake Hopatcong, New Jersey

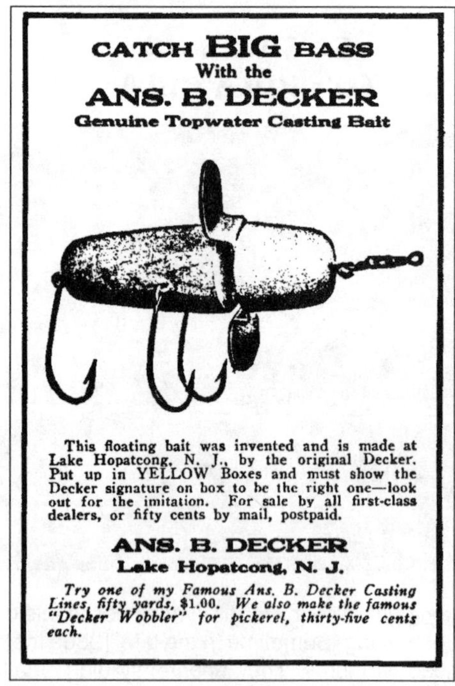

Mr. Decker was in business from the early 1900s to sometime prior to his death in 1940. One of his lures was in the celebrated fish-off with Jamison (see page XXX). His plugs are found in advertising and catalogs as early as 1907 and perhaps before. Decker lures are fairly rare and there are many look-alikes and copies. It is know that three body styles were produced by Decker because of illustrations in early to later ads. The first examples showed a blunt nose version. As the years went by the nose became more tapered. To date, about the only sure way to identify a real Decker is to find his name stamped somewhere on the propeller blade. Even this is not foolproof owing to

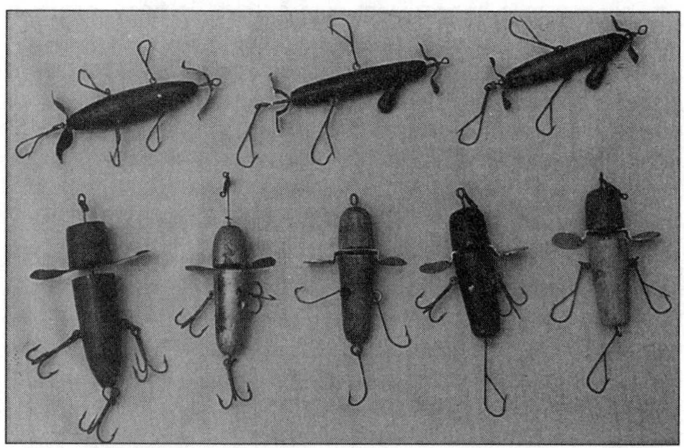

The three lures in the upper row are thought to be Decker prototypes because of their construction and elements. The three lures on the bottom right are Deckers. Note that the same unusual weedless single hooks are present on all six Decker products. The left two on the same row are identified with the name G. Cummings. Photo courtesy John J. Thomas

the unfortunate possibility of the blades being switched around. A collector sent some photographs of several Deckers that sport a weedless single hook (see accompanying photo). These hooks are made of one piece of metal for ease of installation and removal. The weedless portion is constructed like a spring so you could slide the hook off and on.

Since earlier editions of the book I have come across an advertisement in a 1905 issue of National Sportsman that offers a very Decker-like lure available in two sizes (not given, only "medium" or "Large") and three colors; red, white or yellow. The illustration shows single side hooks, one on either side and a trailing single. The manufacturer is Jacob Mick, 524 River Street, Paterson, New Jersey. Paterson is not too far from Lake Hapatcong and Mick likely fished the lake. There may be some connection between him and Decker or Decker may have swiped and patented the idea. All is subject to speculation at this time but it appears that Mick's plug predates Decker's plug for now.

To further confuse the issue regarding the "Which came first" problem, an 1899 Wm. Mills and Son catalog lists the "Yellow Kid" as available. This is a very similar lure to the Decker lure and is made of copper. Also available in a 1906 catalog from the same company is a "Jersey Queen" made of cedar; very Decker-like and may be the Jacob Mick lure. Both of these were advertised well into the 1920s where they then disappeared from catalogs and magazines. Both are considered by some to be copies of Decker's plug. More yet: In a 1902 Schoverling, Daly and Gales (NYC) catalog there is a listing as follows: "Snyder Floating Spinner or Yellow Kid" inferring that they are both the same plug known by two different names.

There is a September, 1912 advertisement that gives the Decker Company address as 45-B Willoughby Street, Brooklyn, New York.

THE "DECKER PLUG" BAIT

This wooden lure was first found illustrated in a 1907 Abercrombie and Fitch Co. catalog as available in two sizes either in white or yellow. The propeller blades were aluminum and the buyer had the option of three single or three treble hooks. It was illustrated with a box swivel attached. In a 1909 catalog from the same company there was an additional size option and a new color option, gray. The c. 1910 advertisement reproduced here, however, clearly shows the lure in the unfinished wood state.

Martin Kane, President of the Lake Hapatcong Historical Society was kind enough to send along some documentation of Mr. Decker's lure. Among other things, he provided a transcript of a

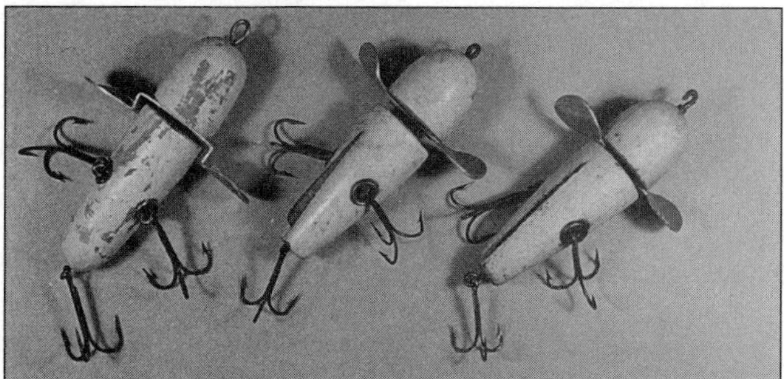

Left: DECKER PLUG BAIT. Center and Right: MANHATTANS (Decker look-a-likes).

recording of a talk Decker gave in 1933, to a sportsman's organization. In it Decker himself states that in 1882 "... On August 27th of that year I perfected what is known as the Ans B. Decker top water bait ... none of these were sold or placed on the market under ten years from the time the bait was perfected. We kept it a secret for that length of time." He and his father were guides and commercial fishermen and were not anxious to let their competition in on the secret of their success. That dates the first commercial availability of the lure at 1902.

So now we know that the lure was being actively used as early as 1882 and, according to the transcript, he made his first wooden lure by using the metal head from an old silk body Phantom Minnow whose body had been shredded by Pickerel teeth, replacing that body with one of wood. This was in 1880. He experimented with the lure until it "...was perfected" in 1882. Collector value range: $60-$80.

CATALOG SERIES #	BODY LENGTH	LURE WEIGHT
No. 1	2-3/4"	unk.
No. 2	3-1/2"	unk.
No. 3	3-3/4"	unk.

COLOR OR FINISH: White; gray; yellow, white with red head*, unfinished wood**.

**This finish had apparently been eliminated by 1950 for that catalog does not list it as available.*

***Never found cataloged.*

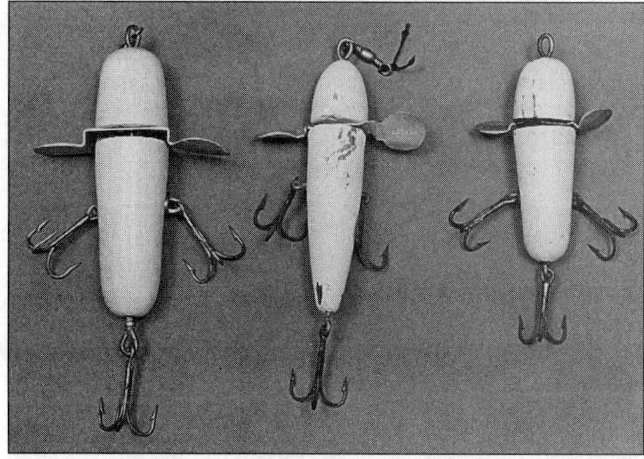

These three Deckers have his name stamped on the propeller blades.

TOPWATER CASTING BAIT

Found advertised in catalogs and sporting magazines from about 1908 on. This plug was shaped a bit differently from the DECKER PLUG BAIT. It was available with three single or double hooks. As with all Decker plugs the hooks with screw eyes

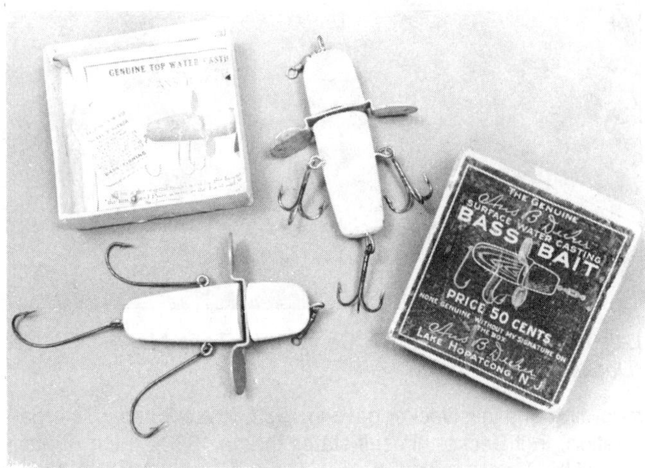

These are two Deckers and an original Decker box. Both have his name stamped on the propeller blades.

alone are oldest and those with "cups" around the screw eye mounts are newer. No catalog or lure numbers nor weights were found anywhere. Collector value range: $50-$200.

CATALOG SERIES #	BODY LENGTH	LURE WEIGHT
?	2-3/4"	?
?	3-/12"	?

COLOR OR FINISH: White; yellow, mouse color, red, blue; green; yellow mottled, white with redhead, white with red painted blades; sienna gray.

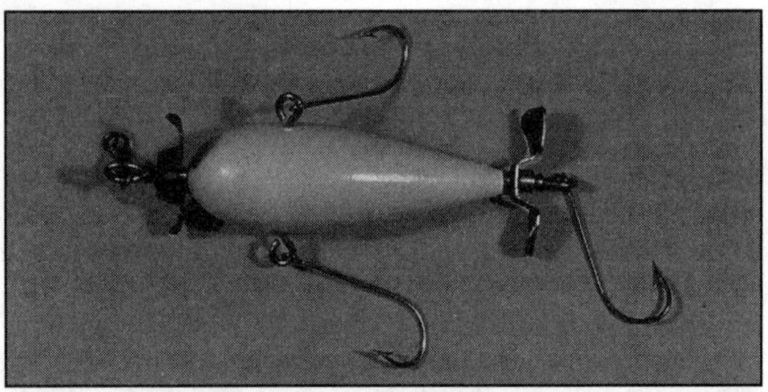

Another model of the DECKER TOP WATER measuring 2-5/8". It has screw eye hook hangers and each heavy gauge metal prop is marked "Decker". Collector value range: $100-200.

DECKER UNDERWATER

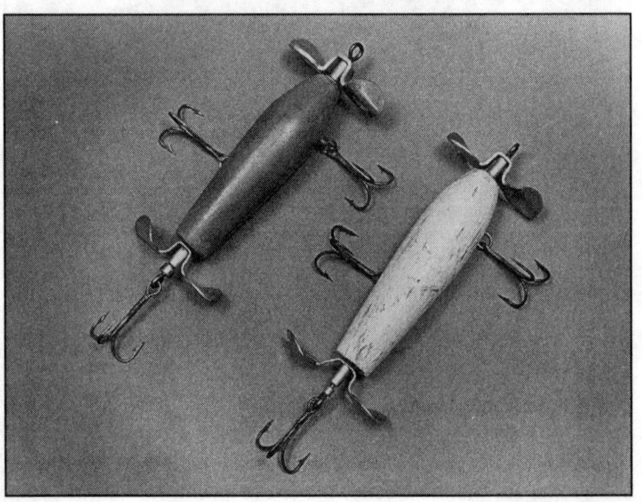

This is a little known Decker lure 3-1/8" in body length. It sported two propeller spinners made of heavy-gauge metal, a trailing treble hook and two opposite side trebles that were offset. One was toward the nose and the other mounted about mid-way on the other side of the body. Available colors are presently unknown. Collector value range: $90-$150.

DECKER LOOK ALIKES

There are so many variations on the theme they are almost impossible to sort out. Many are identified as to maker, but many are not. It seems every year more turn up. Perhaps one of you collectors could undertake a study and help straighten the rest of us out. In the meantime the following photos and information might be of some help.

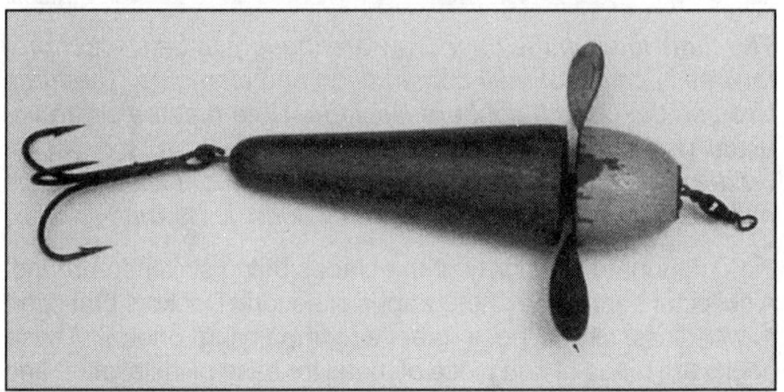

This single trailing treble plug has a round metal plate on the front of the nose. It is attached to the nose by four brads. This one conforms to the New Jersey three-point hook(s) limitation law. Collector value range: $20-$30.

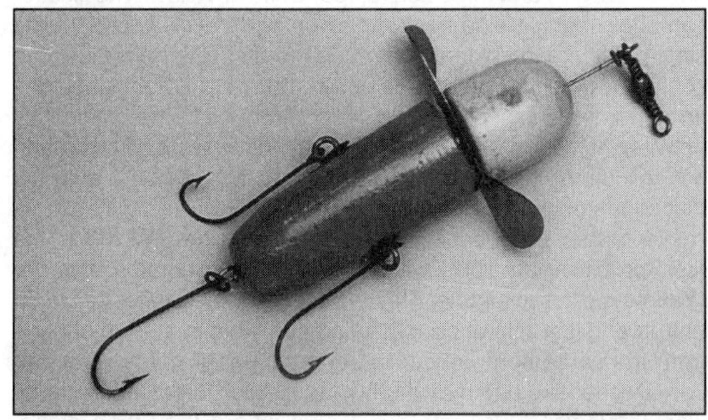

This Decker look-a-like is a 1926 vintage lure made by George Cummings of New Jersey. Conforms to the Now Jersey hook limitation law of the time. Has screw eye and washer hardware. Collector value range: $50-$60.

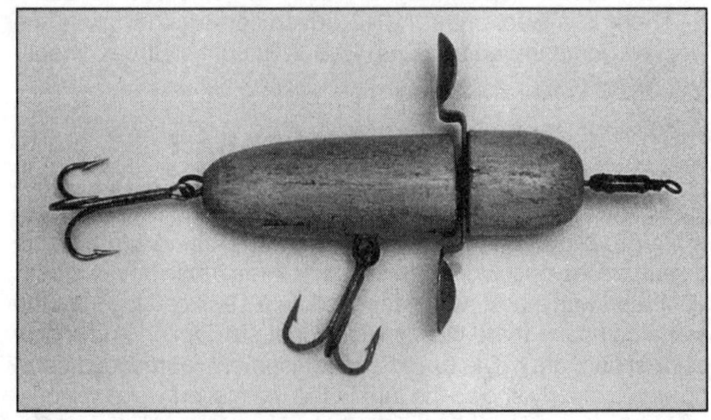

All white Decker type with a fixed box swivel at the nose. Collector value range: $20-$30.

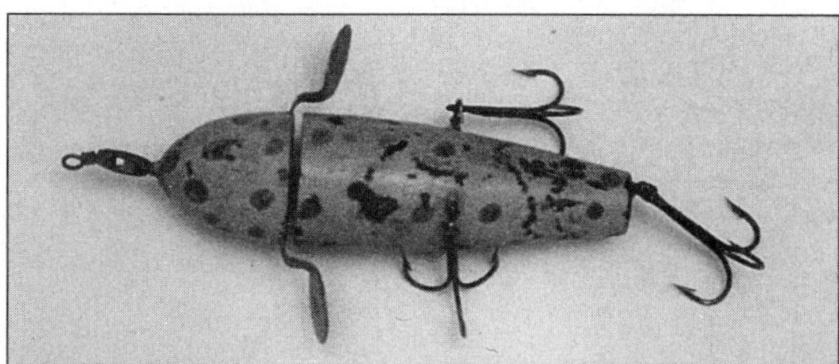

The MILLS YELLOW KID. It is made of copper and painted yellow with gold spots. The earliest listing found was in an 1899 William Mills Catalog. Named after a popular comic strip character of the era, it continued to be offered in various catalogs up into 1920s when it disappeared from listings. A 1902 Schoverting and Gales catalog offered the same lure as follows: SNYDER FLOATING SPINNER, or YELLOW KID. Collector value range: $30-$50.

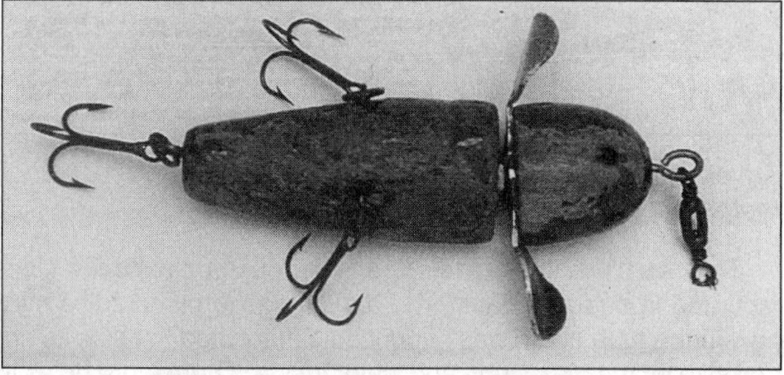

These are two wooden JERSEY QUEENS. They are the same as the MILLS YELLOW KID except made of red cedar instead of copper. Hangers are staples with O-ring hook attachments. Collector value range: $40-$45.

A partially disassembled JERSEY QUEEN showing the two-screw attachment of the spinner blade and the unique screwed armature. This is a small (2-5/8") version of the lure.

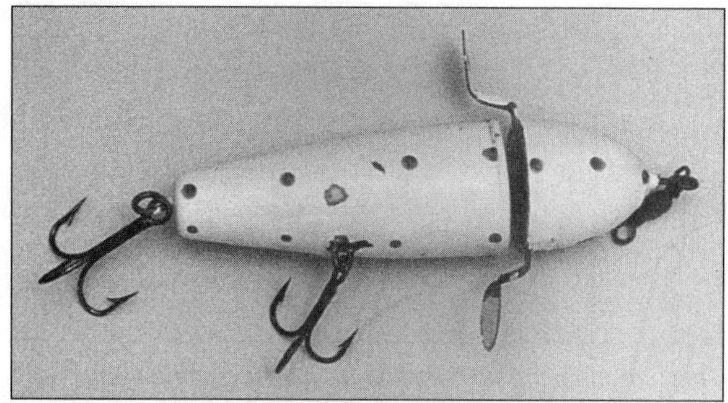

Two SUCCESS SPINNERS. One is white with gold spots and the other is white with gold spots and red head. Both are made of metal. Note one with 3-T and one with 2-T. They are also reported to have been available with single hooks. They are 1910-20s vintage and at least nine different color schemes can be found. Collector value range: $40-$45.

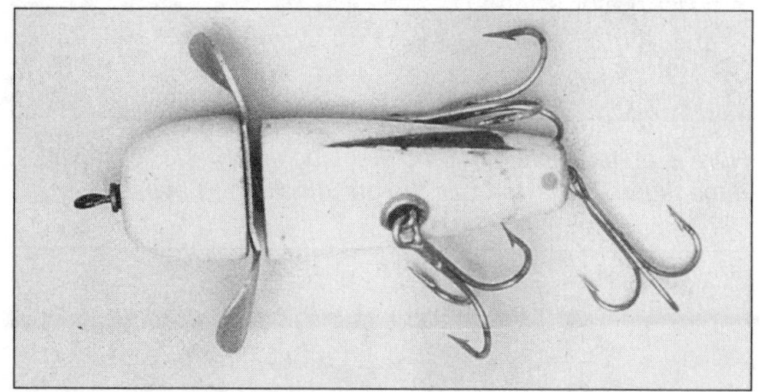

Decker look-a-like that is known as the MANHATTAN. It measures 3-3/4" with raised cup hardware. Note the metal keel ventrally. Collector value range: $40-$45.

DELEVAN OR NORTH CHANNEL MINNOW

Detroit Bait Co. — Detroit, Michigan

This 3-1/2" lure has all the characteristics discussed in the text. It also has DELEVAN inscribed on its side.

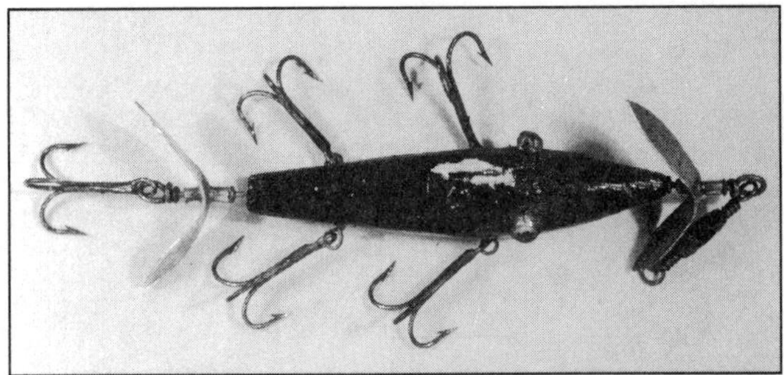

This lure measures 3-1/4" and exhibits the same characteristics as above, but has no name inscribed.

Very little is known about this lure. It is said to be made and/or distributed by the Detroit Bait Company around 1903-04. Whether the company is the same as the one operating later and producing the BASS CALLER in the 1940s is not known. They are found in a three treble and a five treble version. The 3T model is usually around 3" and 3-1/2" for the 5T. They have unusual large glass eyes with gold flecks in the glass. The line tie and hook hardware is through-body twisted wire. Most are found with a bow tie type tube propeller spinners although some will be found with the more crude prop as in the third photo below. DELEVAN or NORTH COAST is occasionally found stamped or stenciled on the side of the 5T model though not as yet on the smaller one. Collector value range: $200-$300.

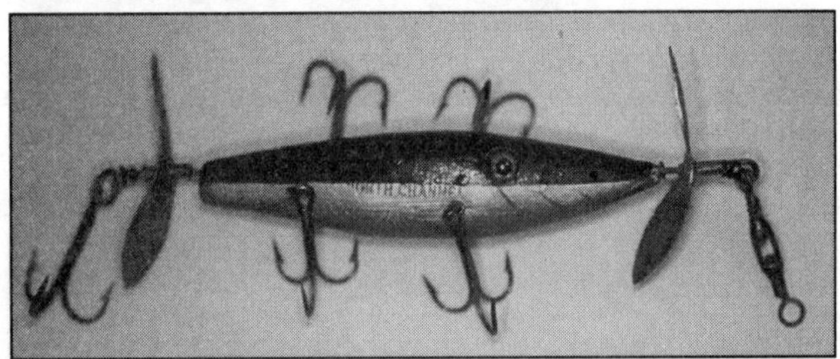

Here is an example of a 5-hooker labeled NORTH CHANNEL. It measures 3-1/2'and has the gold fleck glass eyes.

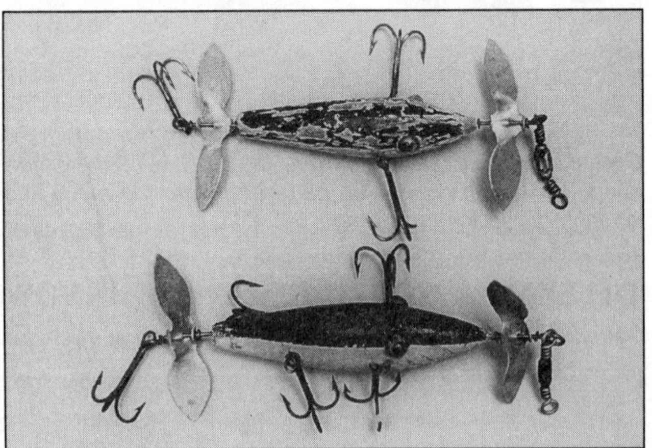

A 3T, 3" and a 5T, 3-1/4" model of the DELEVAN. Note the crude propeller spinners. Some are reluctant to identify this lure with the Delevans because of the props, but the other characteristics do match.

DETROIT GLASS MINNOW TUBE CO.

Detroit, Michigan DETROIT GLASS MINNOW TUBE c. 1914

The earliest advertisement I was able to find for this lure was in March 1914 issue of The Outer's Book reproduced

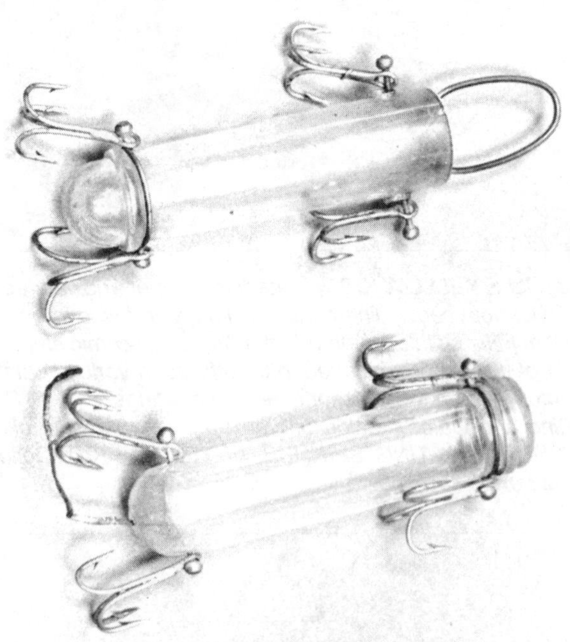

here. It illustrates a glass lure like the upper lure in the photo above. Beneath the ad illustration is the inscription "Patent Pending". With a magnifying glass, clearly visible are the words DETROIT MINNOW (with two more words unreadable) on the metal plug at the forward end of the lure. The company was the Detroit Glass Minnow Tube Company.

Advertisement from the March, 1914 issue of The Outer's Book magazine.

This was a hollow glass lure with four treble hooks side-mounted in opposite pairs. The angler was to place a live minnow in the tube and it was supposedly magnified to twice its actual size by the glass tube and water inside. There were holes in the front and rear so that the "Minnow will remain alive all day". It is the upper one in the photo and measures 3-1/4" body length.

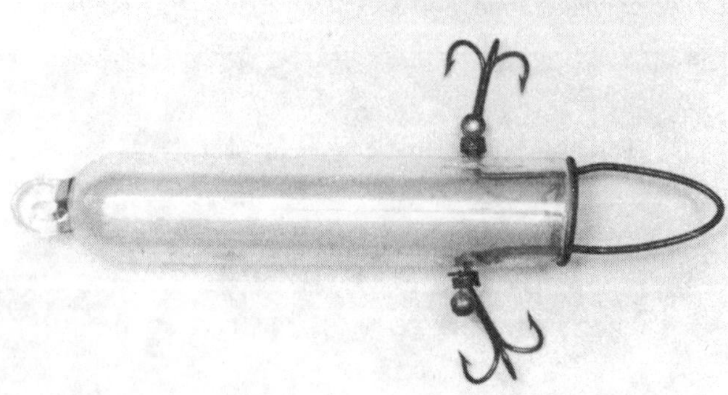

This is the rare 2-3/4" trout size of the DETROIT GLASS MINNOW TUBE. Collector value range: $400-650.

In an April 1915 issue of the same magazine is another advertisement, this time for another type of glass minnow tube, looking much like a test tube. This one has a screwcap type rear end closure (see lower lure in the previous photo. The hooks are oriented wrong). This ad was also from the Detroit Glass Minnow Tube Company so there are two styles of this lure. Also found in that issue is an advertisement for the PHEIFFER LIVE BAIT HOLDER. It appears to be identical to the first DETROIT MINNOW TUBE discussed and illustrated above.

Other minnow tube type lures are C.E. Henning, the c. 1911 Henning Minnow Tube; Welsh & Graves; Pfeiffer Live Bait Company and Charles C. Kellman.

Seems like there was a lot of interest in this oddity in lure development for awhile. I sure wouldn't want to cast one of 'em toward any rocks. Collector value range: $250-$400. Much more with original box.

One wonders if this idea ever caught on. At least it wasn't as breakable as the glass tube. This scarce item has a collector value range: $300-500. Photo courtesy Clarence Zahn.

DIAMOND JIM TACKLE COMPANY

Evanston, Illinois

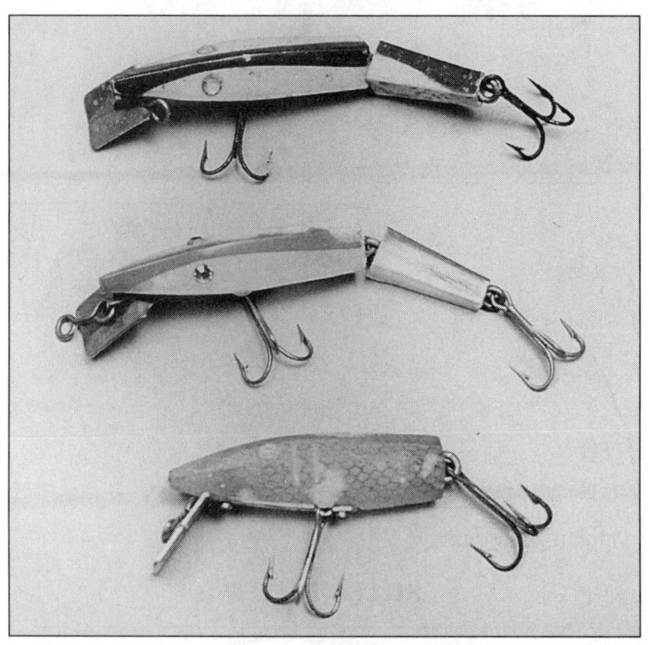

These three plastic lures each sport rhinestone eyes. The jointed one measures 3" and the smaller one, 2".

What little information here was derived from the boxes and an advertisement that said they were "NEW" in the April, 1955 issue of *Field & Stream* magazine. They are diamond shaped plastic lures with rhinestone eyes, hence the name "Diamond Jim". The boxes did not name the lures, but had only numbers. Example: "S-3". They were available in a 1/4 oz. spinning size and 1/2 oz. casting size. The advertisement said there were seven colors to choose from, but did not name them. Collector value range: $5-$15.

DIAMOND WIGGLER

Bignall and Schaaf — Grand Rapids, Michigan

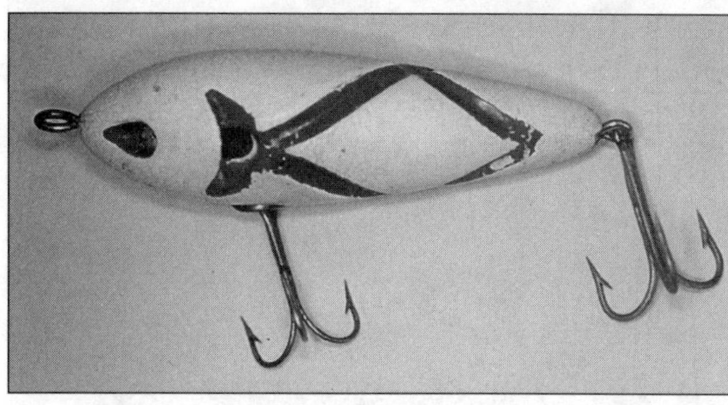

This is another "Water Sonic" type lure that seems to be a close cousin to the lures of the Eureka Bait Company and the Coldwater Bait Company, both of Coldwater, Michigan. This one measures 3-5/8" and has holes and flutes through which water may pass upon retrieve. It has cup and screw eye hook hardware. The lure dates about 1912-14. Collector value range: $100-$200.

THE DICKENS BAIT CO.

John W. Dickens — Fort Wayne, Indiana

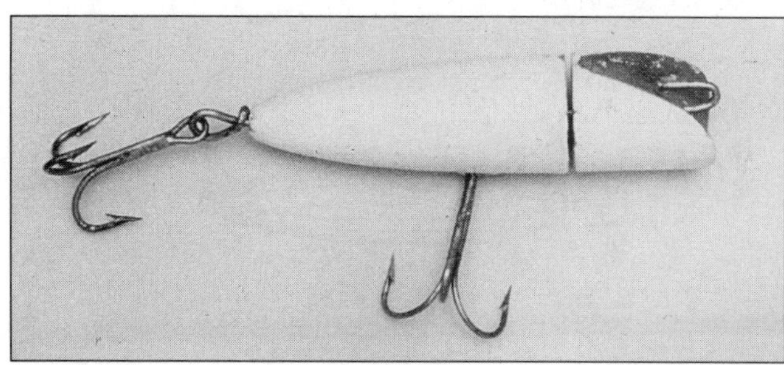

This company was started around the time of the granting of Dickens' first patent in January of 1916. It was for a lure with a head that could be turned up or down by means of a spring-loaded apparatus making it a surface or diving lure at will. The lure in the photo here is almost exactly like that 1916 patent. It has not yet been named in any printed material found so far. Because the effect gained by turning the head is the same as that of the LIAR CONVERTIBLE MINNOW below, it may have been a forerunner to that lure. Collector value range for the patent model: $50-$90.

THE LIAR CONVERTIBLE MINNOW
DICKENS' DUPLEX DARTER

Patented in 1919 this plug had sloped nose, a trailing treble and another, removable treble, that could be attached to the back or belly thereby causing the slope to be down or up. This made it either a surface or underwater wobbler.

I have had an opportunity to examine the above lure in its original box. It measures 3-1/2" and this one has a red body with white head. It seems that lure was called two different names at some point by the company. The box labels this one as a DICKENS' DUPLEX DARTER. The box has the April 8,1919 date on it. Collector value range: $75-$100.

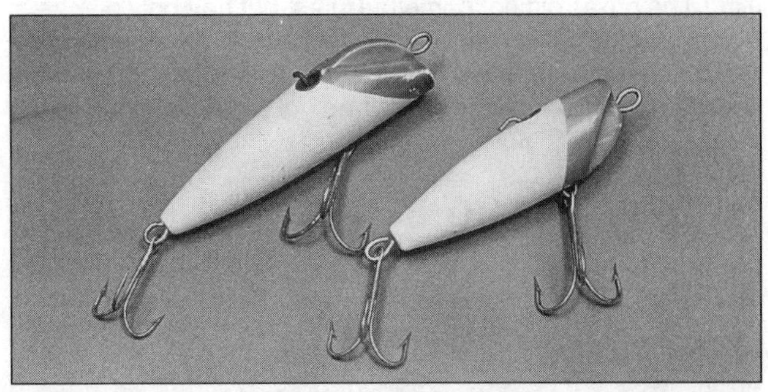

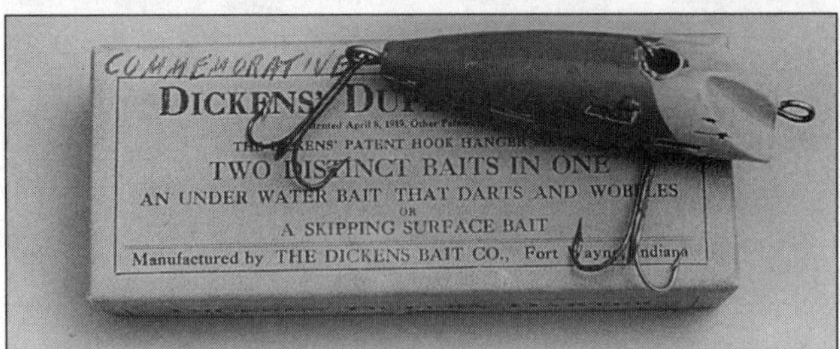

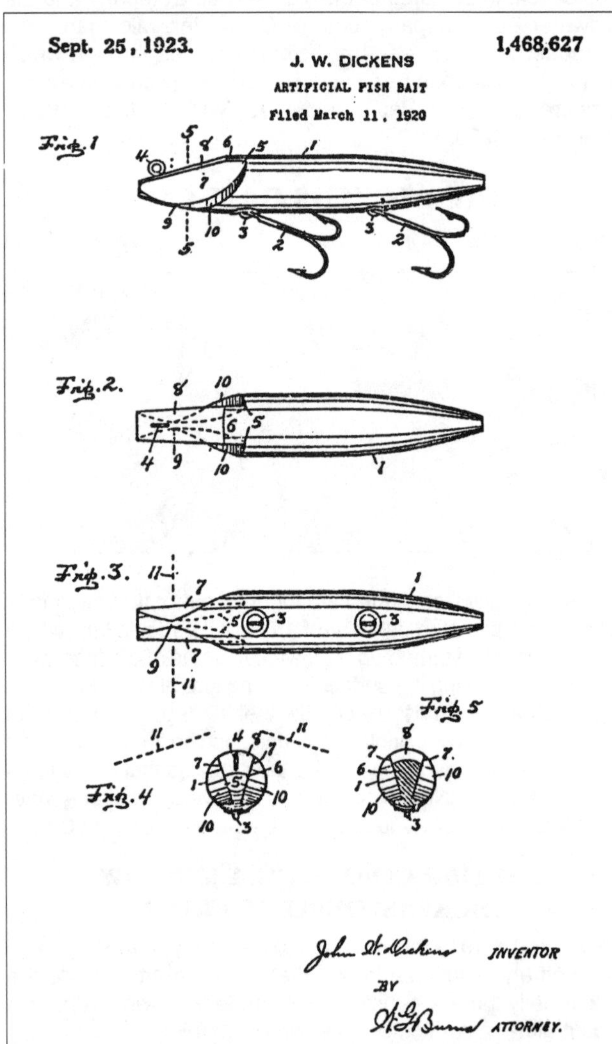

This 1923 patent illustration is of a lure similar to the LIAR or DUPLEX DARTER. It apparently is an attempt to improve on the mechanism for reversing the hook position, but to date it has not been found. They may have never put it into production.

THE WEEDLESS WONDER c. 1920

I have measured various examples of this lure and the size varies from 1-1/2" to 1-5/8". There is also a small 1/2 oz. fly rod size that is similar, but not exactly like it that is also called a WEEDLESS WONDER. The ones in the photo here differ slightly in design and utilize different hardware. The upper lure is slightly larger, has a flat tail end and twisted or bend wire line tie and hook hanger. The lower lure has a rounded tail end with a knob where the screw eye hook hanger is and a screw eye and washer line tie. Most came with the red feathered tail hook but were available with a leather tail. Colors are white with red head and feathers, red with white head and feathers, red with white head and red feathers, white with black head and feathers. Collector value range: $30-$60.

Top: A bass size at 1-1/2". Lower is the fly rod size measuring 1". Photo courtesy Jim Muma.

UNKNOWN DICKENS PLUG

This Dickens plug remains unnamed until we can find it listed in a catalog or advertisement. It measures 2-1/8" long and is obviously a deep diver. Note the unusual line tie treatment. Back and belly views. Collector value range: $35-$50.

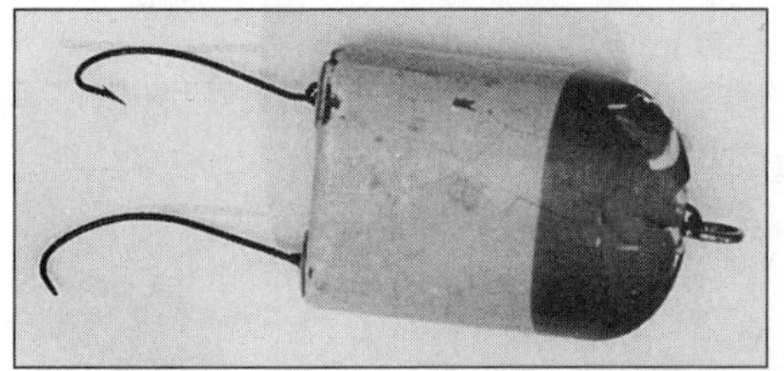

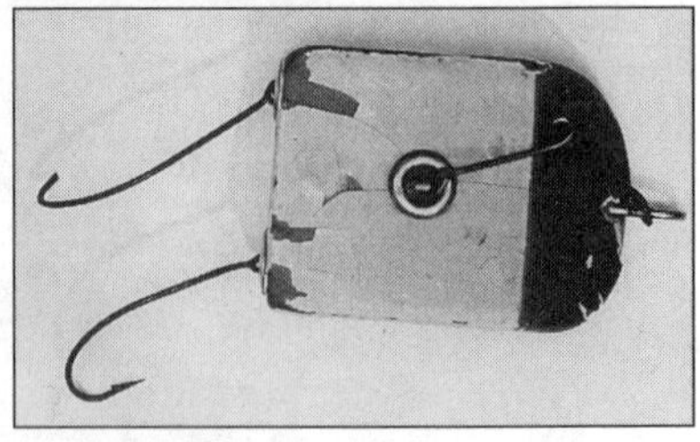

DILLON-BECK MFG. CO.

Irvington, New Jersey

KILLER-DILLER

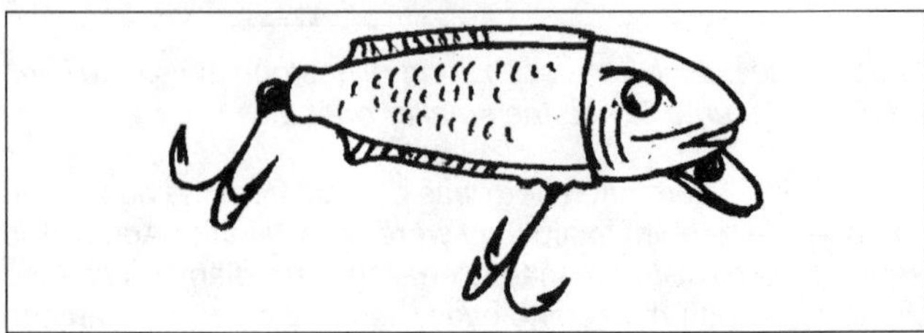

This c. 1940s company manufactured a line of about a dozen plastic lures. Some of them are duplicates of older Jamison lures such as the QUIVERLURE, BEETLE PLOP and LUR-0-LITE. The drawing above represents one of their other lures, the KILLER-DILLER. It was made of transparent plastic and very fish-like in appearance. It has a belly treble, a trailing treble hook and the body length was 3-1/4". It was available in red and white, goldfish, pike, or rainbow finishes. Collector value range: $5-$10.

QUIVERLURE

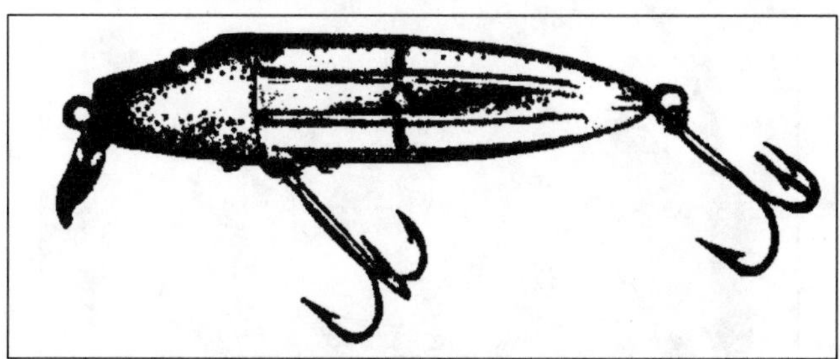

The QUIVERLURE illustrated here has heretofore been listed with the W. J. Jamison Company. This because it appeared in their catalogs more than once, with their own series numbering system. It has been found illustrated and described in a Dillon-Beck advertisement for 1940. Although the ad mentioned only one size, the 3-1/4" size, the Jamison catalogs list three sizes with the addition of 2-1/2" and 4-3/4". It is made of transparent plastic with a black, yellow or red head. There is a visible internal iridescent bar that rotates on retrieve. The color combinations are as follows:

Red head, chrome bar
Red head, red bar
Black head, chrome bar
Yellow head, chrome bar
Yellow head, green bar

The two smaller sizes had two treble hooks and the larger one had three trebles. Collector value range: $10-$20.

DINKINS RATTALUR/MARSH RATTALURE

Lewis Dinkins — St Augustine, Florida/Sanford, Florida
Johnny Marsh — Daytona Beach, Florida

Beyond the photograph a collector sent I could find virtually nothing regarding these lures in my research files. I did find the information I needed in two volumes of the three-volume set of FLORIDA LURE MAKERS AND THEIR LURES by Douglas J. Brace, Russell D. Riddle, Jr. and W. H. Bill Stuart, Jr. Anyone interested in Florida lures could not do without this excellent reference. Their treatment of these lures is much more comprehensive than what follows here.

In the late 1930s and throughout the 1940s Lewis Dinkins hand-made this lure out of wood. For all those years he made the lures for himself and gave them to friends. He may have had a name for it, but it is lost to history. At some point (probably the late 1940s) he had a mold made so he could make them out of plastic. Despite this move, he still made his 4" bait only for himself and his friends. When he made the plastic models he would put a BB inside before gluing the halves together; thus the name RATTALUR. Sometime around 1957 he made an agreement with Johnny Marsh, a lure maker in Daytona Beach, to produce the lures commercially. Marsh used very nice, colorful boxes for the lure. The boxes carried his trademark slogan "Marsh Makes Better Baits" on the top with a hooked, leaping bass. The lure was now called the RATTALURE, with an 'E'. The venture didn't last long, apparently ending in 1958.

Dinkins then found another lure maker to take over production. It was produced in Arcadia, Indiana under the HUBS-CHUB trademark. The name became RATTALUR, without the 'E' once again. The lure is still manufactured under the HUBS-CHUB trademark today. There was insufficient trade data to establish a collector value for an original wooden Dinkins product. Collector value range for the plastic models: $5-$10. This would increase considerably if one was found mint in a Marsh box.

The lures in this photo are not actually RATTALURS. They are, however, almost identical. These are contemporary JOHNNY RATTERLERS, being made by York Sports Products in Sanford, Florida. Take special note the notch in the nose. This feature is never found on the RATTALUR(E)S. Photo courtesy Ken Bernoteit.

DOC'S MENHADEN

Minnow Motion Lure
Sanford Metal Bait Company — Sanford, Florida

A 2-3/4" DOC'S MENHADEN MINNOW on its original box. This particular lure the "S" hook line tie at the head is missing.

This little aluminum lure is made in the shape of a Florida bait fish, the Menhaden minnow. It was developed by a doctor, William D. "Doc" Gardiner, in Sanford, Florida in the late 1930s. The story goes that he never intended to go into the commercial lure business, but had a hundred copies cast and tumble-polished at a local foundry. These he took home and hand-polished to the sheen he felt they should have. Apparently those he used or gave away proved so popular that demand grew to the point where he decided to go into the manufacture of them. He founded the Sanford Metal Bait Company in 1952 and began hand-finishing the lures that he had cast elsewhere just as he had done originally. The company lasted about ten years and "Doc" Gardiner died in 1965.

I have not been able to find any lists with sizes or colors, but it is known that they were made in at least three sizes and that he did paint some of them. The largest size is 2-3/4" as is the one in the above photo. The only paint finish I found reference to was a scale finish with black back and yellow belly. Most are found in the bare metal state with painted eyes. Collector value range: No trade data found.

THE DOLLY ROTATOR

This photograph was sent in by a collector. The lure is plastic and this one is red with a white head. The back, rotating part, is one-half red and one-half white longitudinally. The tail hook hardware appears to be quite strong. There was no further identification on the box beyond the name of the bait and the words "PATENT PENDING". Collector value range: $5-$10.

IMPORTANT NOTICE

The value ranges listed in this book are for lures in Very Good to Excellent condition. The values of those lures not in Very Good to Excellent condition can and probably will be worth considerably less. The values are meant to be a guide only.

JIM DONALY BAITS

James L. Donaly — Newark & Bloomfield, New Jersey

Donaly was active at least as early as 1908. He marketed his lures under the REDFIN brand. Resources so far have turned up a patent application made in 1911 (The REDFIN MINNOW). The earliest advertisement I was able to find was in a 1912 issue of *The Outer's Book.* It featured the No. 27 REDFIN MINNOW and the No. 57 CATCHUMBIG BAIT. One could deduce from these numbers that Donaly had been doing business for some time, if he numbered his lures sequentially. If so, the Donaly line could be more substantial than those found so far.

One of Donaly's lures, the WOW, is the forerunner of Heddon's CRAZY CRAWLER (see the Heddon section). The original patent was applied for in 1926 and granted to Donaly in 1928 (see patent illustration). It is known that Heddon acquired the rights sometime prior to 1940 when it first appeared in their catalogs. Donaly died in the mid-1930s. His wife and daughter continued to paint and sell already assembled lures for a while after his death. Apparently they were not able to run the business without Donaly so they began selling the rights to some of his patents to others. Heddon obtained the rights to the WOW and it became their CRAZY CRAWLER. At about the same time Barney McCagg, of Mt. Kisco, New York was granted the patent rights to Donaly's REDFIN FLOATER and it became the McCAGG BARNEY.

REDFIN No. 27

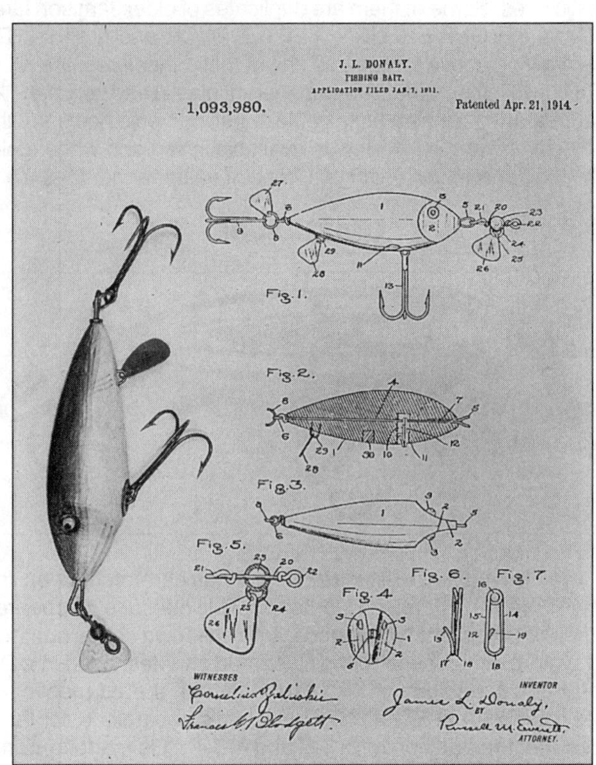

This lure was around at least as early as 1911 (patent applied for January 1911). It is a 3-1/4", 3/4 oz. lure that was made with three flasher blades and available in single-hook or treble-hook models. Colors available were: No. 27, white with red band; No. 37, green back with white belly; and No. 47, white with red stripes. Lower plug in the photo is probably a repaint. Collector value range: $300-$500.

REDFIN MINNOW box. Photo courtesy Ken Webb.

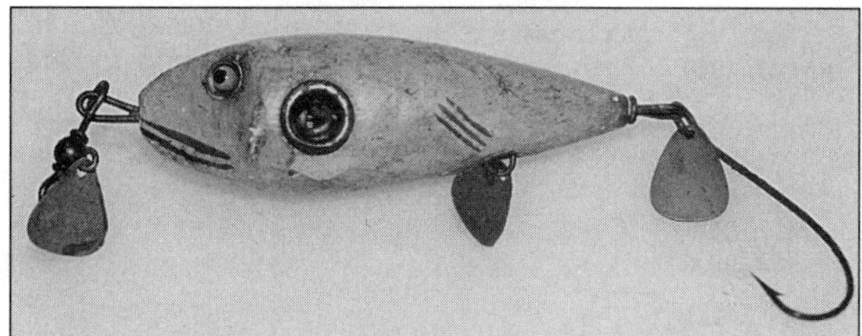

A 3-1/8" REDFIN with side hooks (removed here) and nose and tail flashers. The hook hanger is the see-through type. Photo courtesy Harold G. "Doc" Herr.

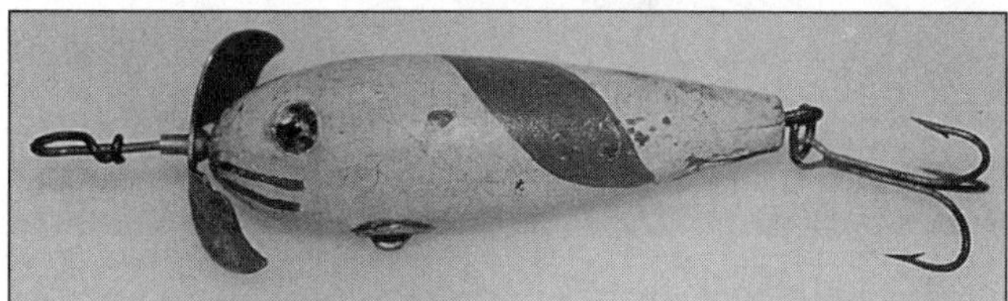

A type of REDFIN MINNOW utilizing second style Shakespeare type propeller spinner on the nose. The body measures 3-1/8". The belly hook is missing. Photo courtesy Harold G. "Doc" Herr.

THE DONALY MOUSE BAIT

The Donaly MOUSE BAIT. Photo courtesy Ken Webb.

The MOUSE BAIT is about as elusive as its namesake. They were very early Donaly lures that I have not yet found in catalogs or advertising. They were available in a gray or white finish, with and without the large propeller spinner and in various hook rigs. The white example in the accompanying photos measures 2-3/4" and has the three-point New Jersey hook rig to comply with that states law of the time. There was no trade data from which a realistic collector value could be derived.

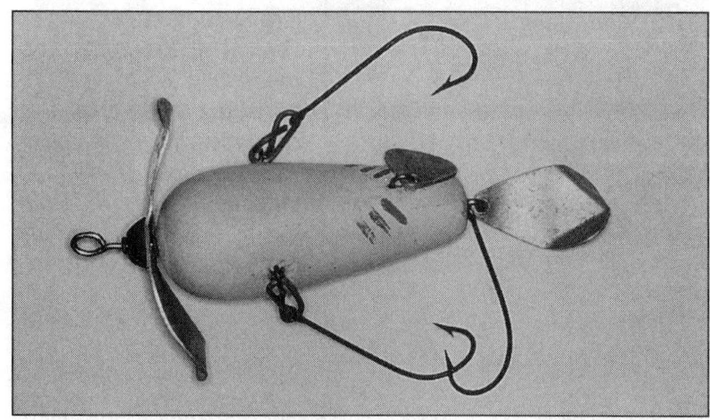

A rare 2-5/8" Donaly MOUSE BAIT. Photo courtesy Harold G. "Doc" Herr.

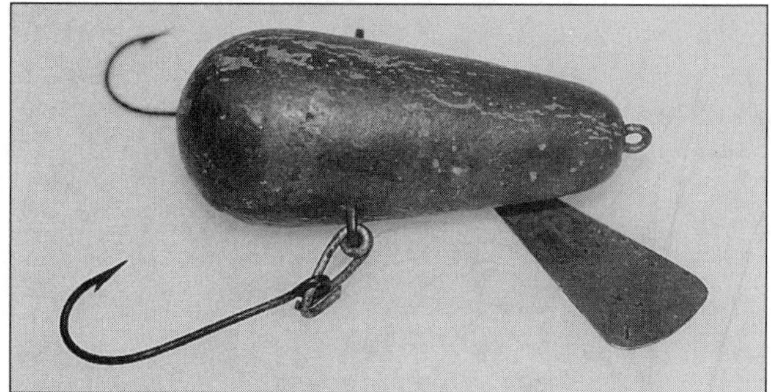

A variation of the rare Donaly MOUSE BAIT. The body on this one also measures 2-5/8". Note the unusual propeller with round blades (one blade is missing). Photo courtesy Harold G. "Doc" Herr.

DONALY WOW AND JERSEY WOW

This lure was patented July 17, 1928. Both the WOW and the JERSEY WOW utilized the same body with the difference being in hook and line tie arrangement. Note these differences in the photo above. The Jersey model has only a treble hook or sometimes three single hooks (New Jersey 3-point hook law) and was rigged for reverse running. The aluminum flapper blades are marked with Donaly's name and the Bloomfield, New Jersey, location. The regular WOW was made in two sizes, 2-3/4" and 3". The Jersey WOW was made in 3" only.

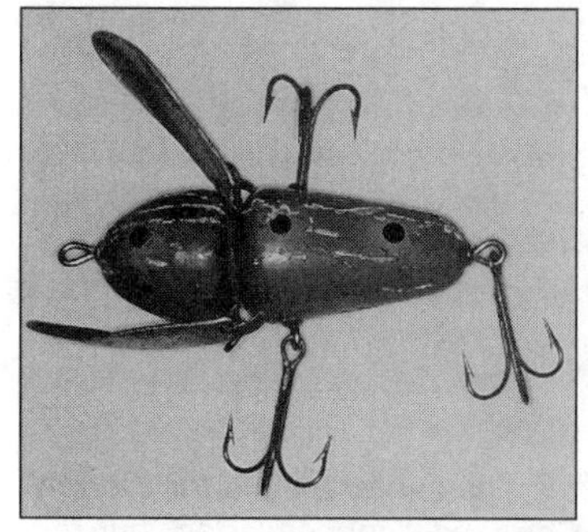

This is a photo of a Donaly WOW with, inexplicably, a genuine South Bend frog finish. Could be a South Bend factory painter did a friend a favor. It could also be that South Bend was considering the purchase at the same time Heddon was, and a few Donaly WOW's got painted at the South Bend factory. Photo courtesy Ken Webb.

Left: DONALY WOW; Right: JERSEY WOW.

The following photo of the three lures represents the transition from Donaly's WOW to Heddon's CRAZY CRAWLER.

Colors available on the Donaly WOW's: red back, white belly; yellow body, white belly. Collector value range: $125-$175.

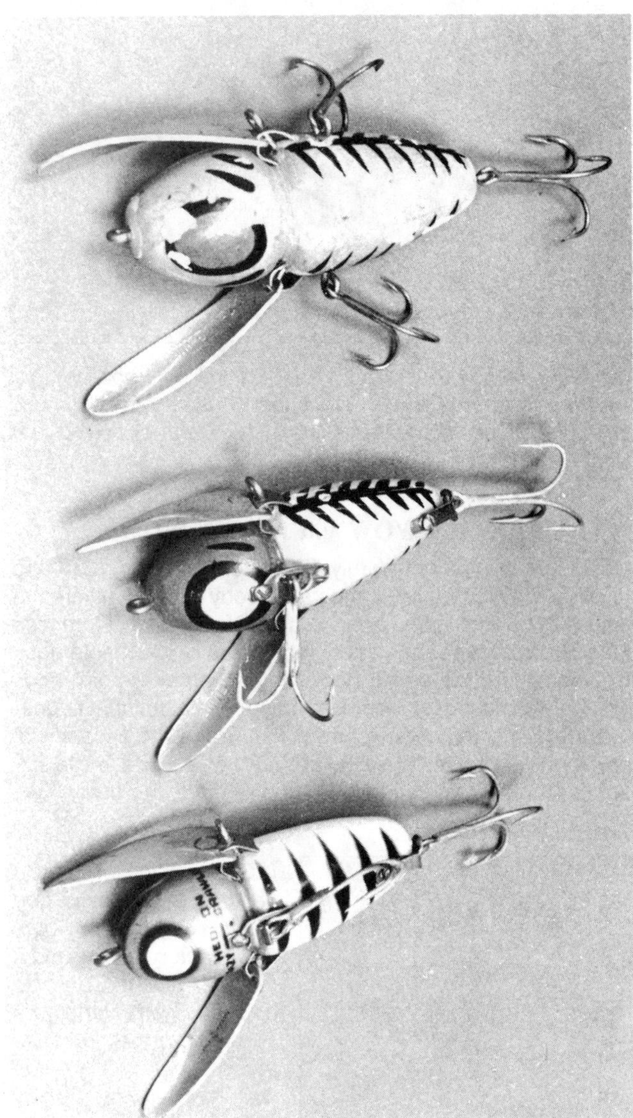

The top lure is a Donaly WOW. The center plug is the Donaly lure body, paint pattern and marked flapper blades, but the hook hardware is genuine Heddon. The lure on the bottom is the pure Heddon product.

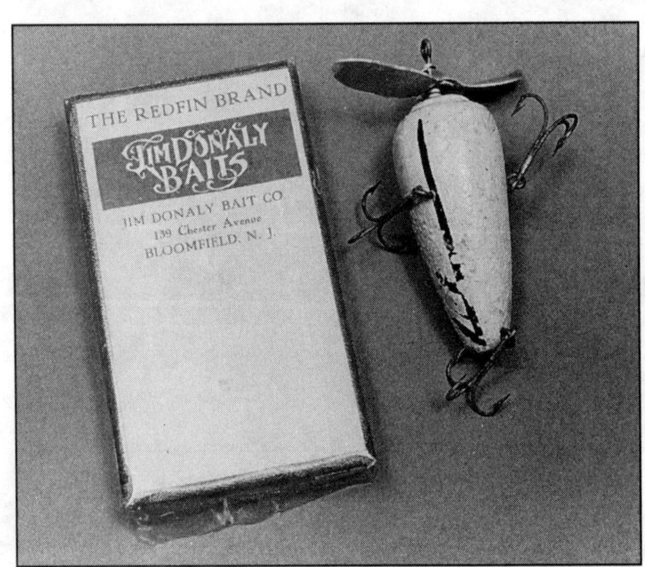

REDFIN FLOATER with original box.

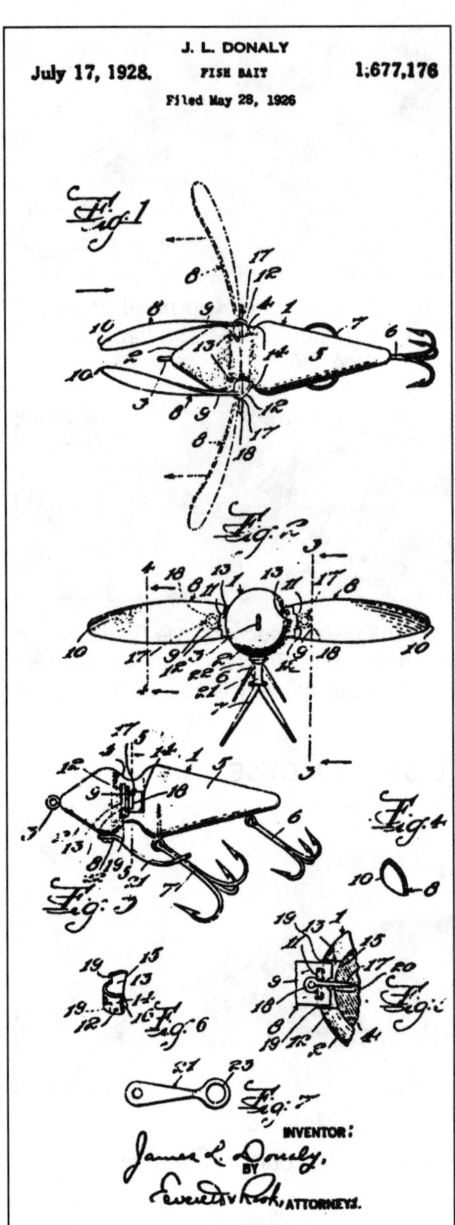

Original patent drawing for the Donaly "WOW"

REDFIN FLOATER

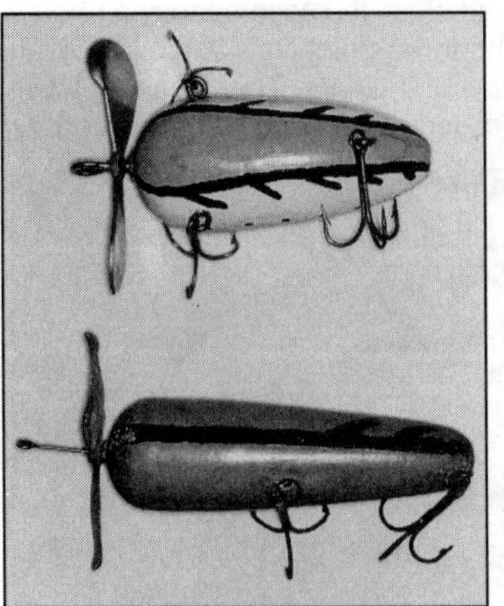

The upper lure is the 3" MUSKY REDFIN FLOATER No. 77. The propeller is not marked. The lower lure is an earlier, larger version of the same lure measuring 3-3/4". The unmarked propeller on this one appears to be much less carefully fashioned than the later one. Both exhibit typical Donaly paint. Photo courtesy Ken Webb.

Advertised in 1916 issue of The Outer's Book is the "New Redfin No. 77". The illustration in the ad shows a couple of features not often seen. The side hooks are attached to the screw eyes with a safety pin or paper clip type affair and there is a small triangular flapper blade hung just beneath the tail of the lure. An illustration in an editorial look at several lures refers to it as the "REDFIN 77" also.

The REDFIN FLOATER was made in two sizes, 2-1/4" and 2-7/8". It has two opposite-mounted side treble or single hooks and a large nose-mounted propeller spinner, usually marked with the Donaly name. It was available in red, yellow, gray, white or black. The white was luminous. Collector value range: $75-$150. (See Spinning Barney)

CATCHUMBIG BAIT #57

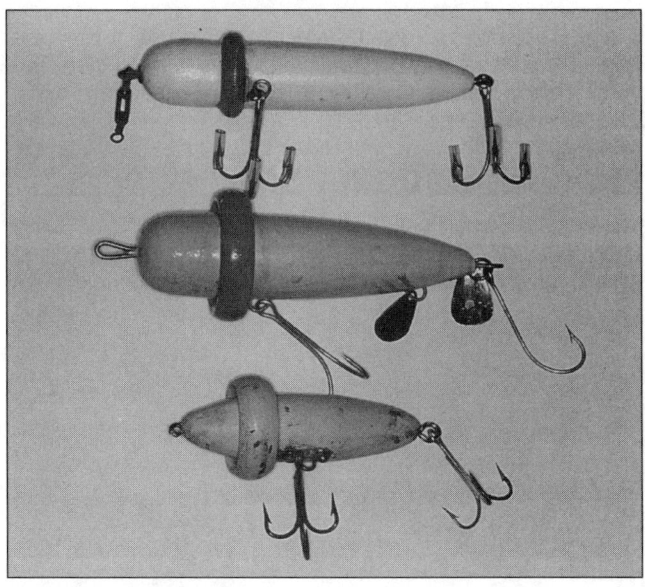

The earliest reference to this lure was in an advertisement in a 1912 issue of *The Outer's Book* magazine. It was a floating lure painted with a red collar normally. It was available in a 4" and a 3" size. The smaller size is very rare. The three in the accompanying photo are described here. The top one measures 3-15/16", has simple screw eye hardware and an early brass box swivel. The center lure is exactly like the one in the advertisement referred to above (The drawing here was made from that ad. It measures 4", has a brass wire line tie/rear hook hanger and staple type hardware. Both of them have white bodies with red collars. The small one measures 2-15/16", is solid white with red gill marks and has a belly hook hanger that appears to have been fashioned out of brass wire. This rare small version is presently the only one known and a realistic value cannot be assigned to it. The 4" models have a collector value range of $300-$700. Photo courtesy Ken Webb.

THE WEEDLESS REDFIN BAIT No. 67

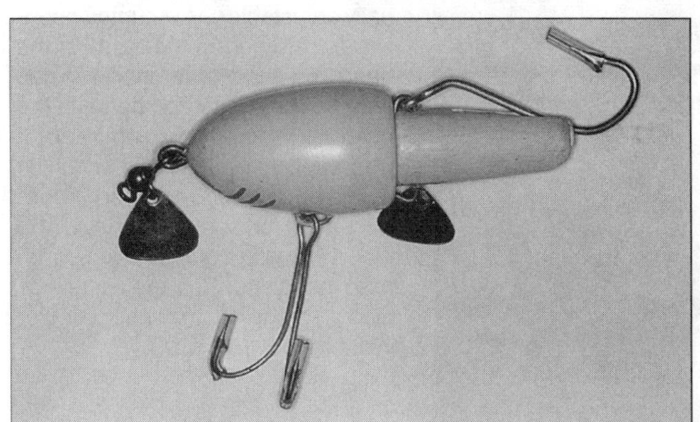

For the first three editions of this book a photo of this lure eluded me. Now, thanks to collector Ken Webb, of Shreveport, Louisiana, here is a photo. I found an advertisement in the April 1915 issue of *The Outer's Book* magazine that shows a lure that is almost identical to the patent application drawing. The application for the patent was filled in 1913 so we can be reasonably sure they date from then or before. The one in Ken's photo measures 3-1/8". It has heavy staple type hardware and the characteristic Donaly flapper blades. This one has typical painted red gill marks. Some early models had more gill marks and a painted red eye. These seem to be inconsistent in the earliest days. This is a rare, early Donaly lure with a collector value range of $300-$400.

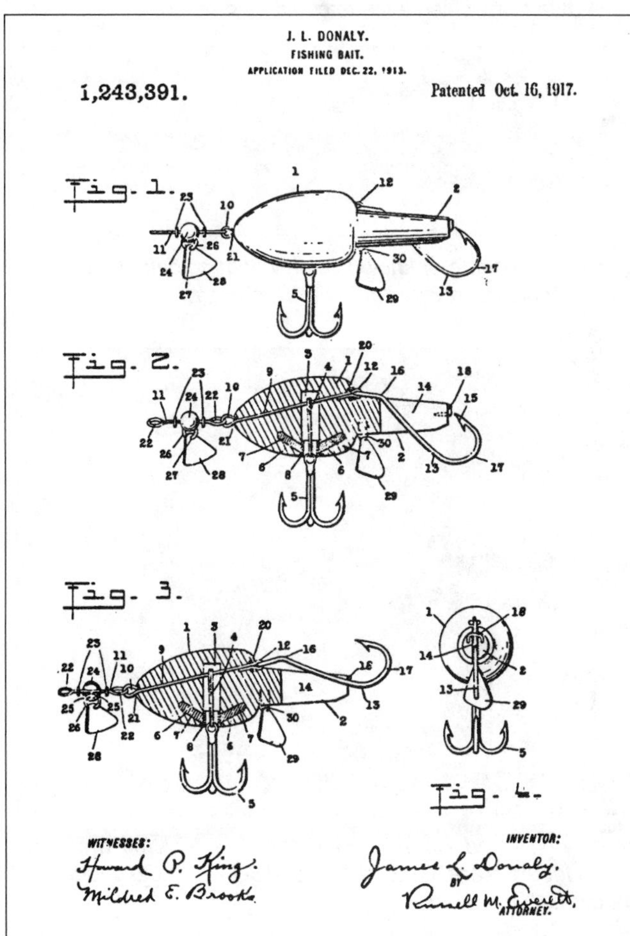

Original patent drawing for the Donaly WEEDLESS REDFIN.

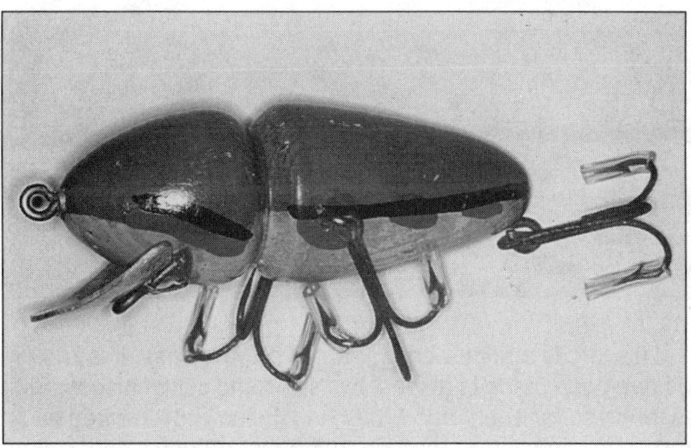

A 3" Donaly DIVER. Photo courtesy Ken Webb.

DIVER

This 3-inch wooden plug has a mid-body groove entirely encircling the body. There are two side trebles mounted offset opposite and an under-tail trailing treble. It has a metal diving plane mounted under the head, the colors available were: Green back, white belly and yellow with white belly. Both had red and black stripes.

The DIVER in the photo here measures 3". This is a rare, limited production Donaly plug. The metal lip is attached in such a way as to allow it to flap up and down. It has two line ties, one at the nose and another beneath the flapper. This one has a green back, white belly and black and red decorations on the sides. One of the rarest of the Donaly baits, there was no trade data from which a value could be derived.

A really nice name-unknown Donaly floating bait. It measures 3-1/8". Photo courtesy Harold G. "Doc" Herr.

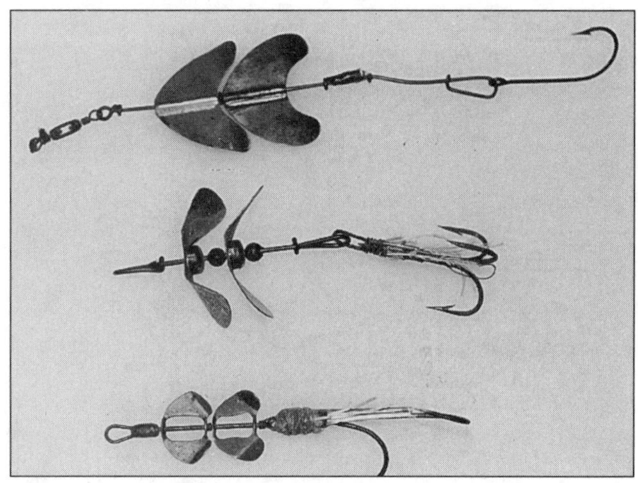

Three unmarked Donaly metal spinners. Overall measurements for them are 3-1/8", 4-1/4" and 6-1/4". Photo courtesy of Harold G. "Doc" Herr.

DOOFER

Uncle Hub's Enterprises | Ft. Lauderdale, Florida

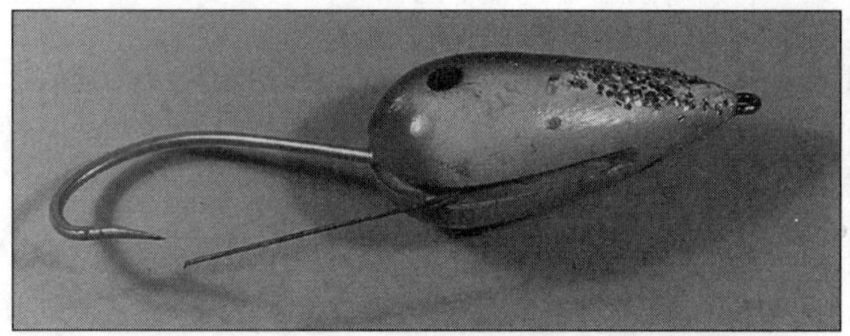

This lure is a floater and meant to be weedless. It is known to have been made in at least two sizes and color finishes. Sizes found so far are 2" and 2-3/8" and the finishes are frog back and as in the case of the one in the picture here, dark green back with glitter and pale green belly with a red flash at the broad end. Collector value range: $30-$50.

DOUBLE CYCLONE

Puls and Wencks Bait Company | Milwaukee, Wisconsin

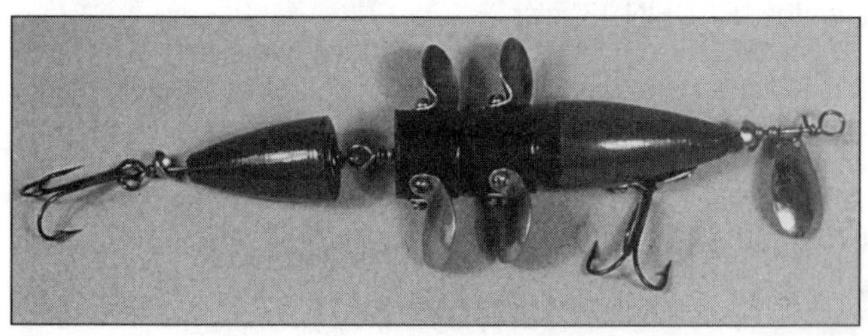

A c. 1955 four-section jointed lure. This one must have kicked up quite a fuss when retrieved. There is no further information on this company or the lure. Photo courtesy Jim Muma. Collector value range: $10-$20.

DOZEY BOY

Accepted Lures Hasand, Inc. | Cleveland, Ohio

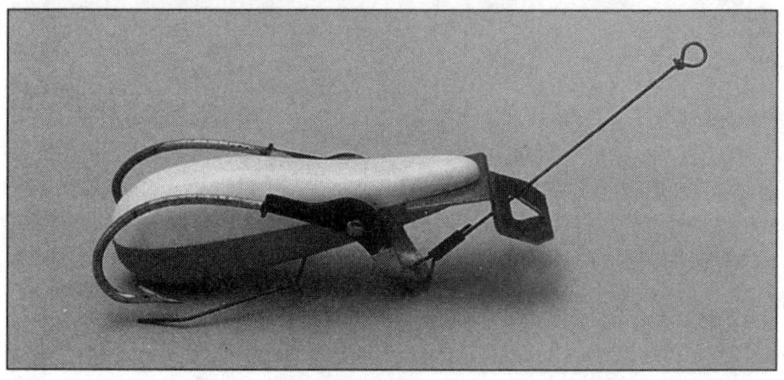

This plastic lure measures 3" long overall and is called the DOZEY BOY. In the box was a piece of paper slightly smaller than a business card describing the lure, the colors available and its action. The colors were "...Color Combinations of Red, White, Green and Yellow." Presumably this means white with any of the other three choices, but it could literally mean *any* combination. If the latter is so, there are nine possible combinations to be found. The reverse side of the paper described another lure, the BACHELOR BOY. We know that the picture here is of the DOZEY BOY because it is described as weedless and the other was not. The name "Accepted Lures" has come to be associated with this company somehow. This may or may not be in error. Only time will tell. For the moment all we can do is place the vintage of this lure as pre-1963. Collector value range: $10-$20.

SEA-BAT c.1932

HARRY F. DRAKE | Milwaukee, Wisconsin

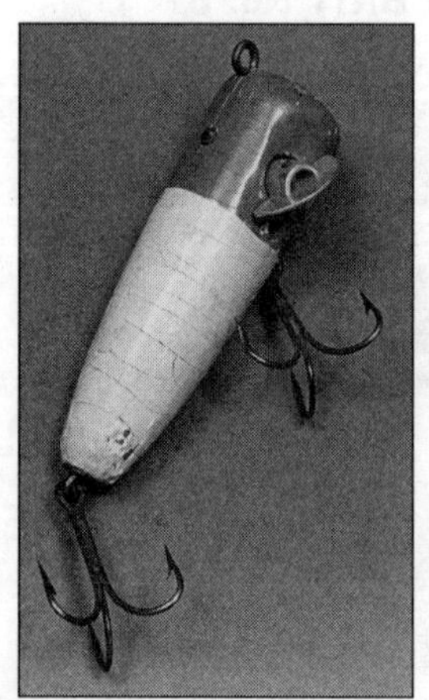

This 3-1/8" lure had two individually adjustable fins mounted opposite each other on the sides of the head and a BB rattler inside. It had a treble hook mounted beneath the head portion and a trailing treble. It was apparently available only with a white body and red head. There was a advertisement for it in the May 1932 issue of *National Sportsman* magazine. See the accompanying patent illustration. Collector value range: $50-$100.

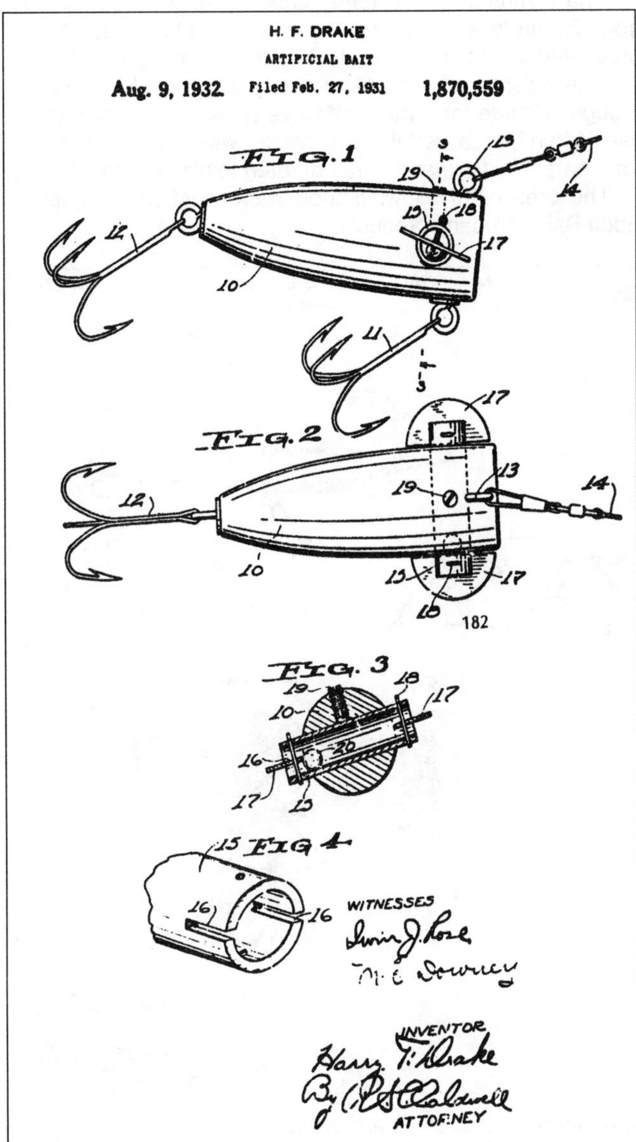

Original patent application illustration for Harry Drake's SEA-BAT. Granted August 9, 1932.

THE DRONE BAIT

L. B. Huntington Company — Baltimore, Maryland

THE DRONE BAIT in the No. O size, 2-1/4" and its original box. Photos courtesy Ken Bernoteit.

There are two patent numbers stamped into this spoon. While I couldn't find the 1923 patent I did find the 1930 patent. The spoon appears to be identical to the patent drawing. It was applied for in 1928 and granted March 25, 1930. It had a unique method of holding the hook making the hook replaceable. No catalog listings or advertising was found. It was made in 10 sizes from the tiny 1-1/4" to a very big 6-1/4". The name of the company and the lure are stamped on the bait. Collector value range: $6-$10.

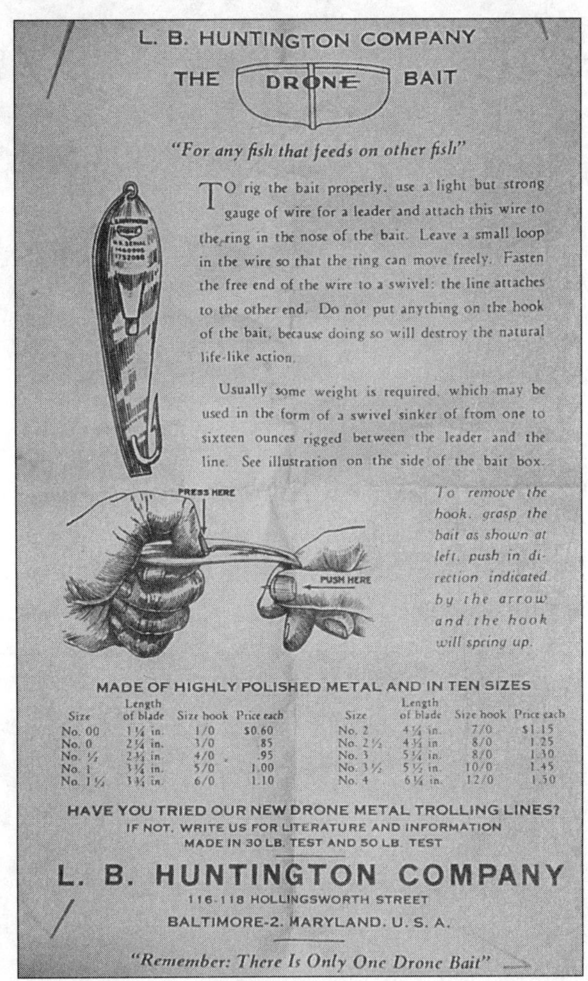

L. B. HUNTINGTON COMPANY

THE DRONE BAIT

"For any fish that feeds on other fish"

To rig the bait properly, use a light but strong gauge of wire for a leader and attach this wire to the ring in the nose of the bait. Leave a small loop in the wire so that the ring can move freely. Fasten the free end of the wire to a swivel: the line attaches to the other end. Do not put anything on the hook of the bait, because doing so will destroy the natural life-like action.

Usually some weight is required, which may be used in the form of a swivel sinker of from one to sixteen ounces rigged between the leader and the line. See illustration on the side of the bait box.

PRESS HERE

PUSH HERE

To remove the hook, grasp the bait as shown at left, push in direction indicated by the arrow and the hook will spring up.

MADE OF HIGHLY POLISHED METAL AND IN TEN SIZES

Size	Length of blade	Size hook	Price each	Size	Length of blade	Size hook	Price each
No. 00	1¼ in.	1/0	$0.60	No. 2	4¼ in.	7/0	$1.15
No. 0	2¼ in.	3/0	.85	No. 2½	4¾ in.	8/0	1.25
No. ½	2¾ in.	4/0	.95	No. 3	5¼ in.	8/0	1.30
No. 1	3¼ in.	5/0	1.00	No. 3½	5½ in.	10/0	1.45
No. 1½	3¾ in.	6/0	1.10	No. 4	6¼ in.	12/0	1.50

HAVE YOU TRIED OUR NEW DRONE METAL TROLLING LINES?
IF NOT, WRITE US FOR LITERATURE AND INFORMATION
MADE IN 30 LB. TEST AND 50 LB. TEST

L. B. HUNTINGTON COMPANY
116-118 HOLLINGSWORTH STREET
BALTIMORE-2, MARYLAND, U. S. A.

"Remember: There Is Only One Drone Bait"

DRULEY'S RESEARCH PRODUCTS

Prescott, Wisconsin

One Druley advertisement was found in the May, 1937 issue of *Sports Afield* magazine. It illustrated one lure and listed two others. They were MINNIE THE SWIMMER, HUMPY and LITTLE SQUIRT. The later has not been found. The other two are pictured here. They are made of plastic. Collector value range: $5-$10.

MINNIE THE SWIMMER. This one measures 1-1/4". They also made a 2-3/4", 3-1/2" and 5" sizes.

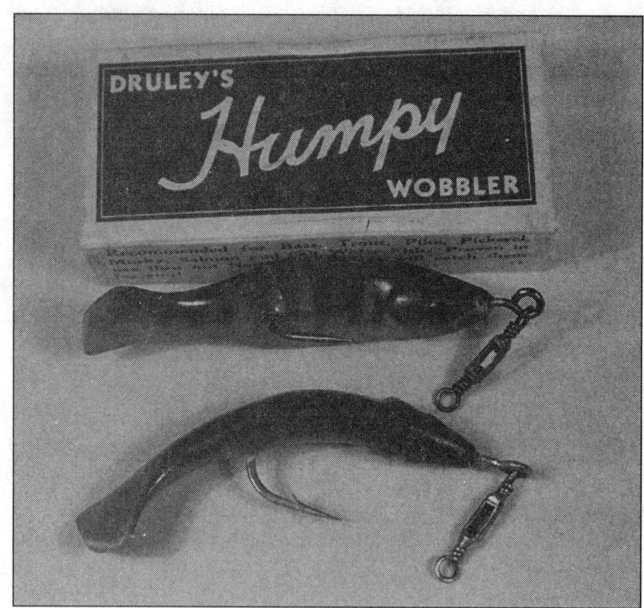

HUMPY WOBBLER and box. Notice the curve in the body.

EDGREN SPINNING MINNOW

William W. Shulean Isanti, Minnesota

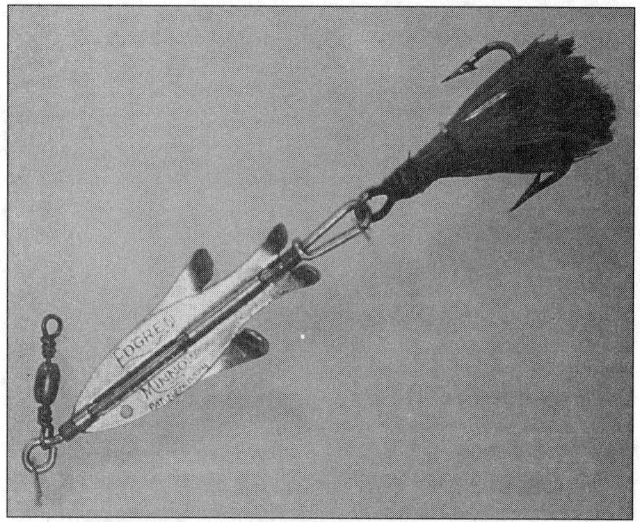

EDGREN SPINNING MINNOW measuring 1-1/4". Photo courtesy Ken Bernoteit

This metal minnow was patented by William W. Shulean in 1904. It was found in a 1914 advertisement by the Voedisch Brothers, Chicago in *The Outer's Book* magazine. It was also found in a 1919 sporting goods catalog. It was made in three sizes, 1-1/4", 2-1/4" and 1-1/2". The sizes are for the minnow. The patent was for the minnow body only. Any type of hook could be attached. They were furnished with the feather treble shown in the photo. Collector value range: $35-$55.

EDON BAIT COMPANY

Oscar L. Strausborger Edon, Ohio

Through the early development years of Strausborger lure making he experimented a good bit, carving many shapes and creating various finishes. Because of this diversity his early experiments would seem to be difficult to identify. Not so, because he consistently used a unique hook hanger apparatus that he invented. The external cup-like affair was fashioned from copper tubing. The result was a preventer/presenter that prevented the hook from contacting the lure body and damaging the finish but, perhaps more importantly, Strausborger thought it made for a more effective hook presentation to the fish. When he realized that his system was unique he applied for a patent in 1932 and it was granted to him in April of 1935.

The lures in the following photo represent typical models of Edon Bait Company products.

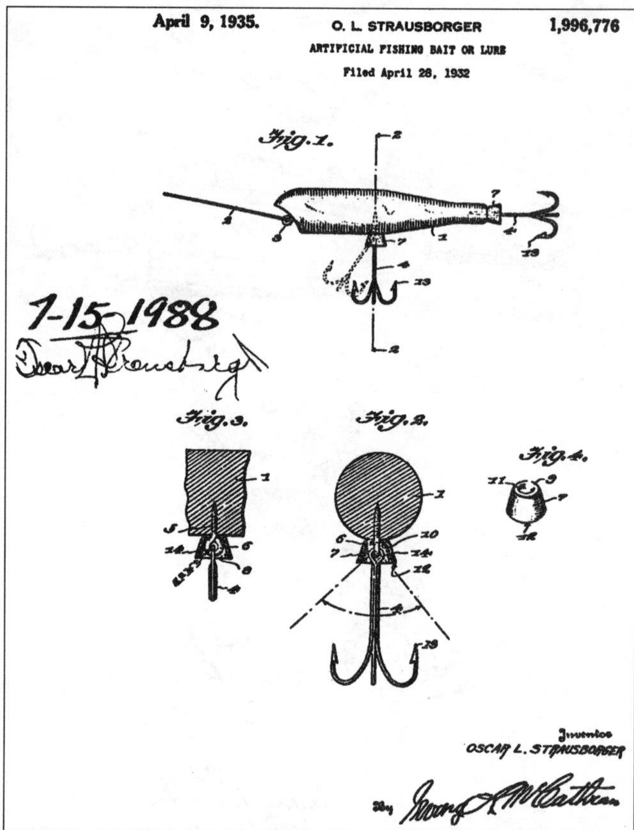

The patent illustration clearly shows the hook limiter.

By the mid 1930s he had a number of people working for him. The lure bodies were then being turned on lathes for him by a wood-working company and they were hand finished. In 1938 he sold all rights and inventory to the South Bend Tackle Company thus ending the company's existence. Collector value range: $60-$100.

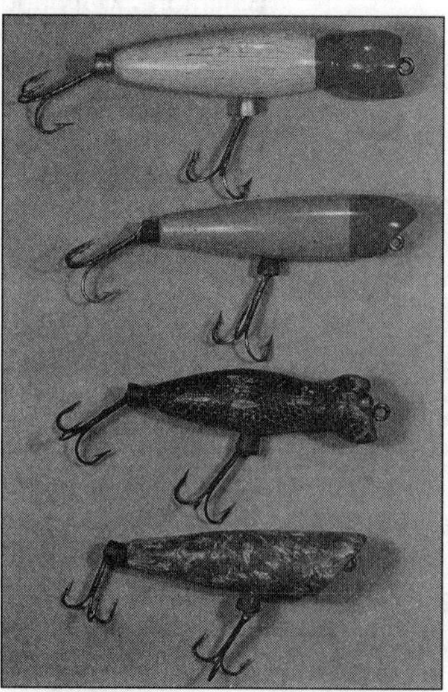

Top to Bottom: 4" long, red head with white body, no eyes; 3-1/2" long, red head with yellow body, no eyes; 3-1/8" long, dark green scale finish, this one has yellow glass eyes (glass eyes on any Edon lure is rare); 3-1/4" long, mottled red and green finish.

EGER BAIT MANUFACTURING CO.

Bartow, Florida c. 1930-1950s

William F. Eger retired in Florida after a career in a area unrelated to fishing tackle. Sometime in the early 1930s he apparently began offering fishing lures commercially. His company, however, doesn't seem to have been formally organized until 1936. Although his lures were offered in a 1932 catalog later Eger catalogs make no reference to this early effort. As a matter of fact the 1941 catalog contains a page headed 'THE ORIGIN AND PROGRESS OF EGER BAITS". The first sentence reads: "Less than five years ago Mr. W. F. Eger, prominent engineer and lifetime sportsman offered the Tackle Trade the first bait of his design." A little simple math puts the date at 1936, not 1932. So far we have found no records to explain it. Eger ran the business until 1945-46 when the company he had worked for asked him to go back to work for them. He sold the company to his grandson Leroy Eger who ran it for a very short time. The Eger company continued in business with a succession of owners. Apparently a Lake Wales, Florida company, Rhoden Enterprises, ended up with at least the rights to the DILLINGER and a few others for they are still producing some of them today.

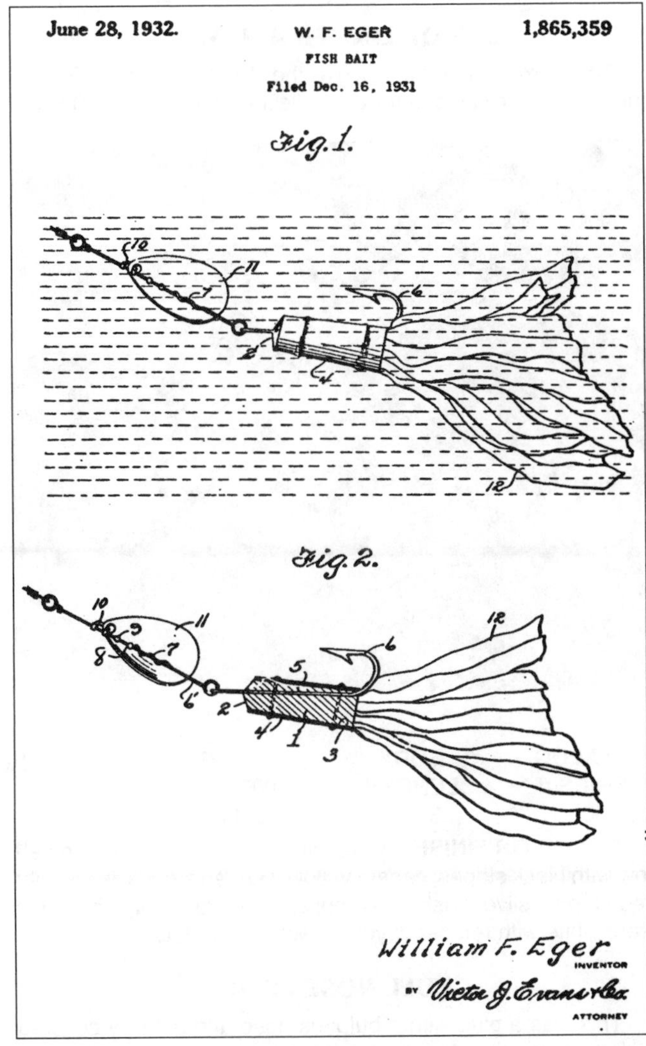

A patent granted to William Eger in 1932.

It is known that sometime in the late 1940s that Western Auto and Sears and Roebuck were Eger customers. The excellent book, *Florida Lure Makers and their Lures* illustrates a six-pack of JUNIOR DILLINGERS that are called Eger BROOKLURES. This may be packaging made up for Sears as Sears bought lures from other companies and marketed them under the BROOK WOOD brand. Those boxes share at least one design element, the use of a wave pattern. That and the similar names lends some support to the hypothesis.

Although all that is covered here are the wooden lures, it is known that Eger produced metal lures also. At least five are known (from a 1941 catalog). They are a weedless buck tail spoon with a front single blade spinner, a weedless spoon, a weedless spoon with rubber skirt and a front single-blade spinner, the same without the spinner, and a 1/2-oz. squirrel-tail spinner bait with a willow leaf-shaped single spinner forward. This latter lure is much like the Mepps or Rooster Tail spinners of today. The wooden DILLINGERS and the frog skin BULL NOSE FROG are the first two lures to be made by Eger.

This special Eger Victory box alone is valued at more than the lure. Lure: $20-$30., Box: $80-$100. Photo courtesy Jim Muma.

MASTER DILLINGER 300 Series

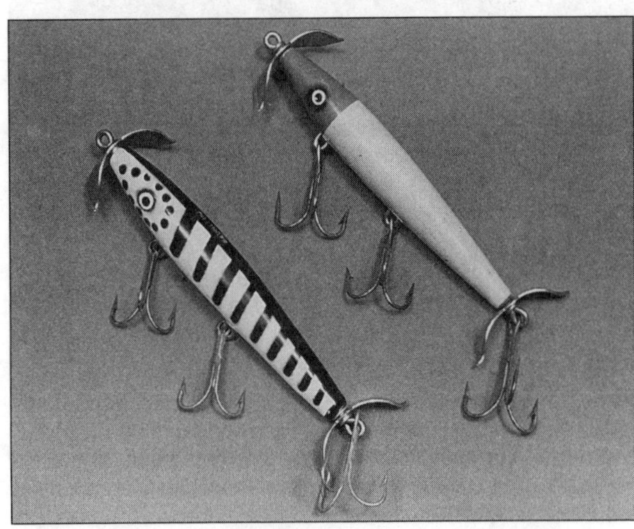

A slim wooden plug with two belly trebles and trailing treble. It had nose- and tail-mounted propeller spinners. It was one of the first two lures Eger marketed commercially. Originally called the JOHN DILLINGER, it could be that the first finish, white with black stripes reminded someone of prison bars or the prison uniform of the day and named it after the most infamous bank robber of the time. He kept getting caught. He was finally killed in Chicago in a 1934 shoot-out with FBI agents. Collector value range: $20-$30.

CATALOG SERIES #	BODY LENGTH	LURE WEIGHT
300	3-7/8"	3/4 oz.

COLOR OR FINISH (from the 1941 catalog):

DILLINGER	White body, black stripes
SILVER STREAK	Silver body, black stripes
CANDY KID	White body, brilliant red stripes
TIGER	Chrome yellow body, black stripes
GREEN DRAGON	Deep green body, black stripes
GRAY DEMON	Gray and green scale
RAINBOW	All colors of the rainbow, horizontal stripes
SHINER	Green body, chrome yellow and white spots w/ silver specks
BLUE SCALE	no description given
SILVER SCALE	no description given

COLOR OR FINISH (from the 1950 catalog): White with black stripes, red with red stripes, canary yellow with red stripes, chrome yellow with black stripes, green with black stripes, green scale, silver flash, gray scale, gray mullet scale, rainbow, Christmas tree, yellow with polka dots.

Master Dillinger with the addition of pearl and vamp spot. These colors were not listed as available in the 1950 catalog. Collector value range: $15-$25.

JUNIOR DILLINGER 200 Series
BABY DILLINGER 0 Series

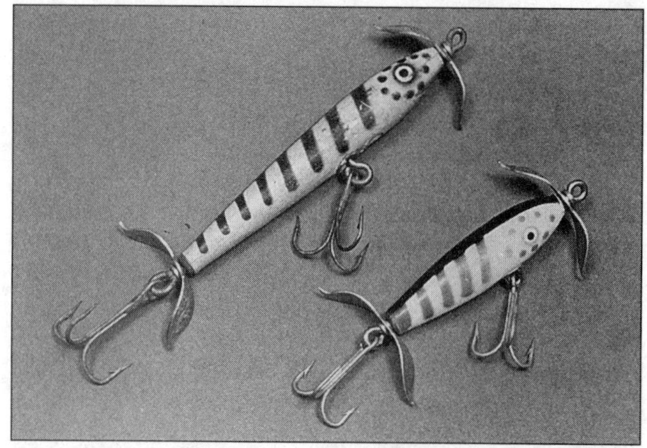

These are smaller versions of the MASTER DILLINGER above and each has only one belly treble and trailing treble hook. Collector value range: $10-$25.

CATALOG SERIES #	BODY LENGTH	LURE WEIGHT
200	3-3/8"	5/8 oz.
0	2-1/2"	1/2 oz.

COLOR OR FINISH (from the 1941 catalog): Pearl, white with black stripes, silver body with black stripes, white body with brilliant red stripes, chrome yellow body with black stripes, deep green body with black stripes, gray and green scales, silver scale, green body, chrome yellow and white spots w/ silver specks, blue scale.

COLOR OR FINISH (from the 1950 catalog): White with black stripes, canary yellow with red stripes, white with red stripes, chrome yellow with black stripes, opalescent pearl, green scale, gray scale, silver flash, rainbow, Christmas tree.

WEEDLESS DILLINGER 100 Series

This was a 2-1/8", 5/8 oz. plug with a single black spinner mounted on a wire leader. There was a hook-protecting steel wire from the nose down over the point of the rigid, single-point tail hook. The colors available were the same as the 200 Series

SEA DILLINGER 400 Series

This is exactly the same plug as the MASTER DILLINGER with the propeller spinners removed. Collector value range: $10-$25.

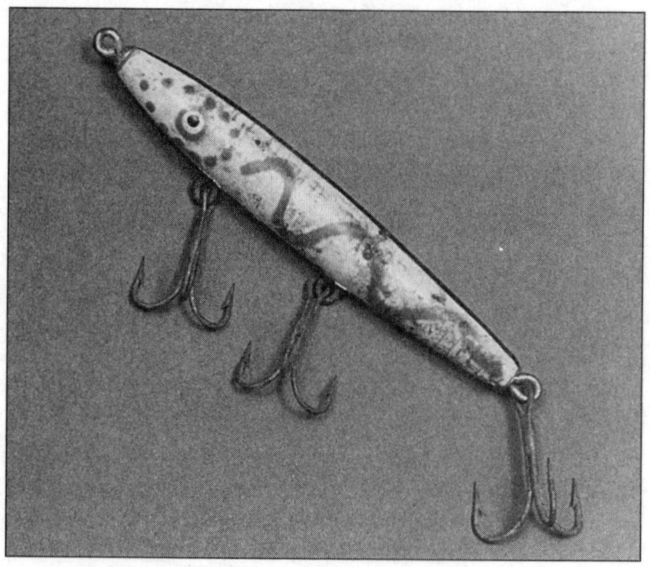

CATALOG SERIES #	BODY LENGTH	LURE WEIGHT
400	3-7/8"	3/4 oz.

COLOR OR FINISH: White with black stripes; chrome yellow with black stripes; canary yellow with red stripes; white with red stripes; silver flash; gray mullet scale; rainbow; Christmas tree; white with red head; yellow with, polka dots.

BULL NOSE FROG

This was a plug with a bulbous nose and actually covered with real frog skin. Be careful not to confuse it with a Shakespeare lure, No. 6505 FROG SKIN BAIT. Eger made Shakespeare's Frog Skin Baits for them. It has a belly treble and trailing treble hook, is 3" long and weighs 3/8 oz. Most are identified by the word Eger stamped on the belly in red ink. The belly-up lure in the photo has faint red markings and the other has none. Collector value range: $25-$40.

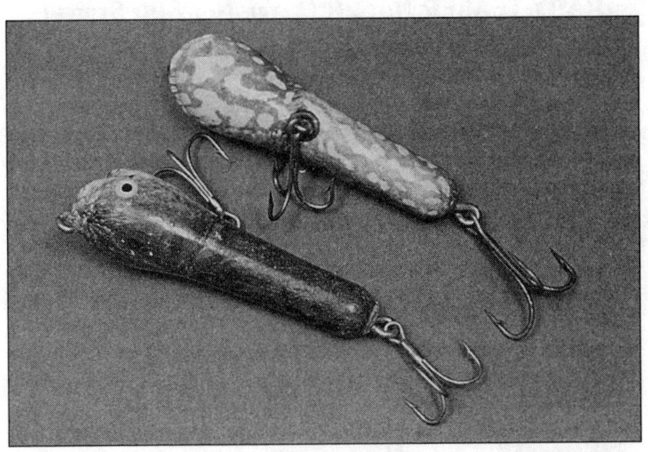

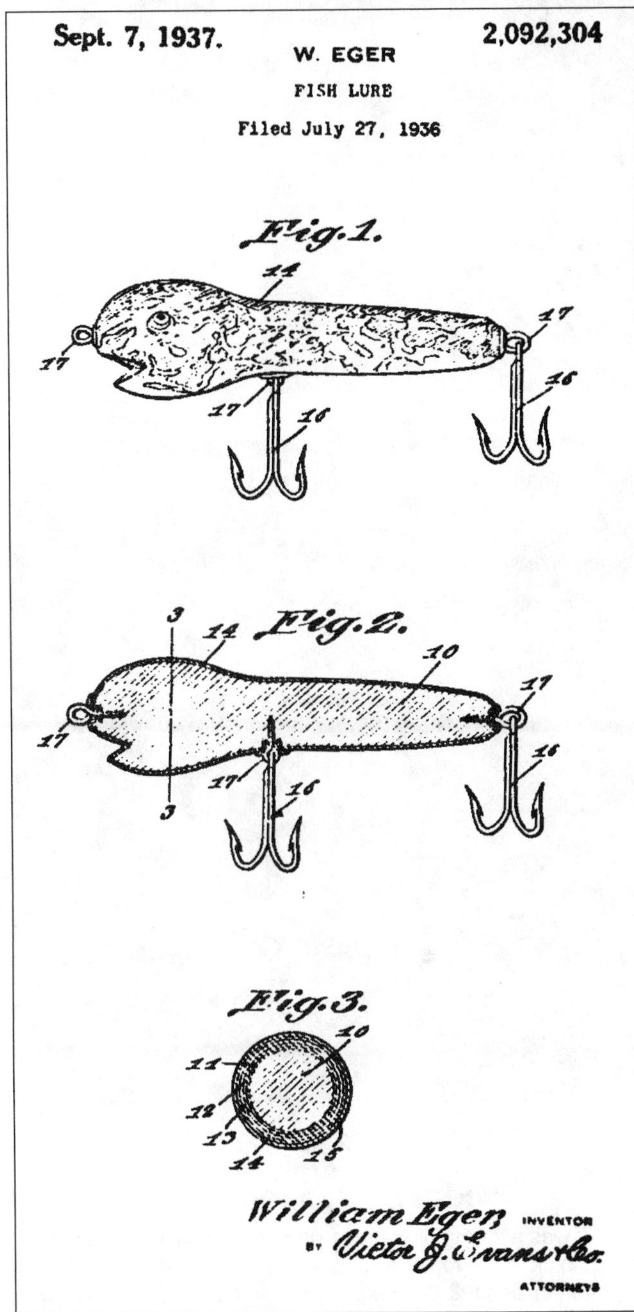

William Eger's patent for using natural frog skin stretched over a lure body. Granted on September 7, 1937.

FROG PAPPY

This is another plug covered with real frog skin. It is a top-water plug with two belly trebles and a trailing treble hook; has a notched mouth and normally, a tail-mounted propeller spinner. Weight: 5/8 oz.; Body length: 3-7/8". Collector value range: $25-$40.

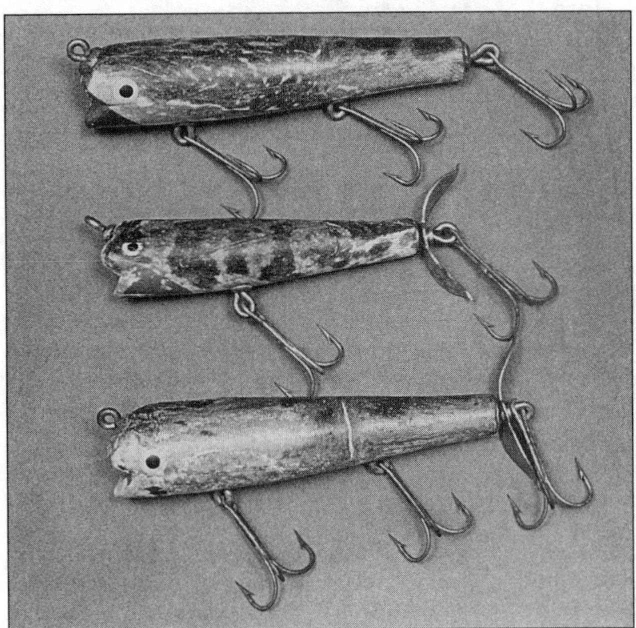

FROGGIE JUNIOR

A small version of the Frog Pappy. It has only one belly treble (2T) and no propeller spinner. Body length was 3-1/8", weight 3/8 oz. Collector value range: $20-$30.

EGER DARTER 1500 SERIES

This lure appears to have the same body as the FROG PAPPY above, with painted finish only; same weight, length and hook configuration. A tail propeller spinner was optional. Collector value range: $20-$30.

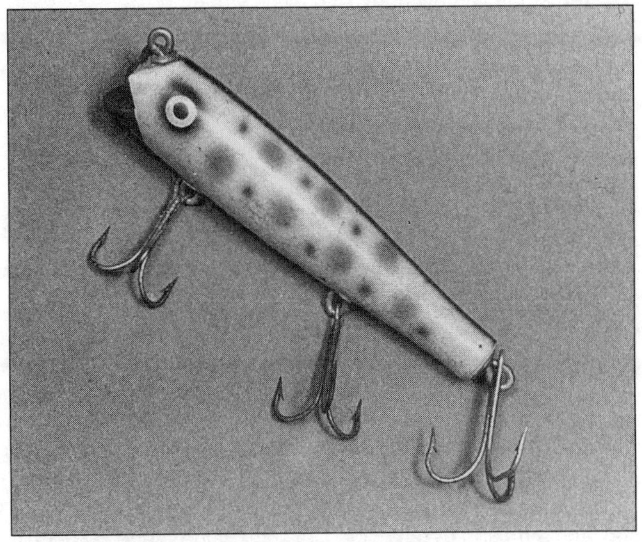

CATALOG SERIES #	BODY LENGTH	LURE WEIGHT
1500	3-7/8"	5/8 oz.

COLOR OR FINISH: Green scale; perch scale; gray mullet scale; frog spot, yellow with polka dots; silver flash.

EGER 1200 SERIES

The EGER 1200 is a larger plunker type lure. It had a belly treble and trailing treble hook (2T). Collector value range: $10-$15.

CATALOG SERIES #	BODY LENGTH	LURE WEIGHT
1200	4-1/2"	1 oz.

COLOR OR FINISH: Silver flash; gray mullet scale; rainbow, perch scale; blue mullet scale; white with red head.

MAMMOTH DILLINGER 4000 SERIES

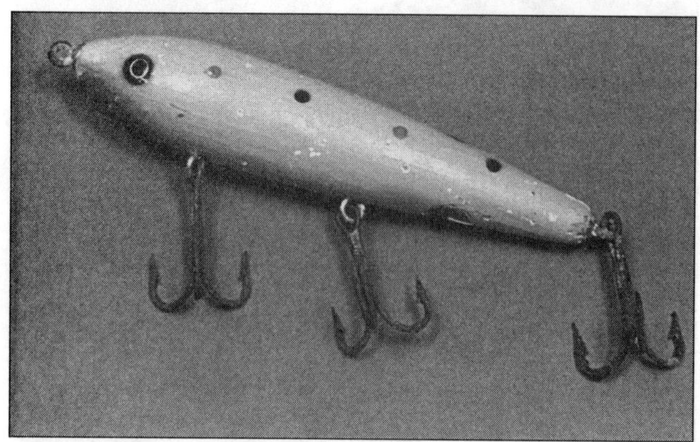

A 1941 catalog entry states "This Mammoth Dillinger has proven a wonderful big game fish bait and is very popular among big fish sportsmen." It is a large shaped-body lure with a diving plane and three treble hooks, two belly-mounted and one at the tail. The shape of the body is much like the Eger DARTER, but the shape rounds down to form a head where a metal dive lip is inserted low on that head and bent downwards where the mouth might be. The line tie is on the head, not the lip. Collector value range: $15-$30.

CATALOG SERIES #	BODY LENGTH	LURE WEIGHT
4000	5"	2-1/2 oz.

COLOR OR FINISH: *"Mammoth Dillinger", White body with red stripe, yellow body with black stripe.

**Listed as a color or finish choice, this is a white body with black stripes.*

STUMP KNOCKER 1400-1/2 SERIES

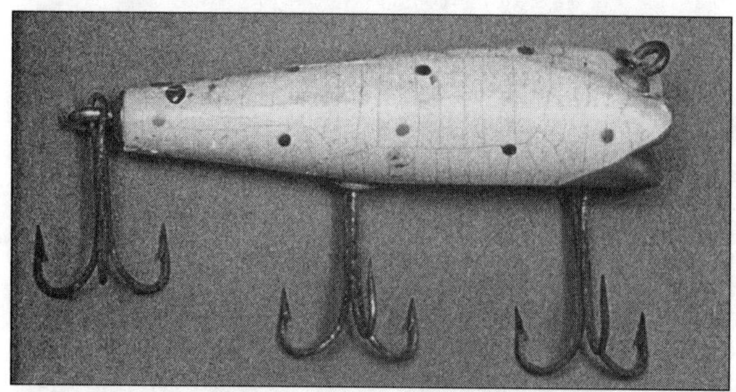

This plug had a concave belly, notched mouth, two belly trebles and a trailing treble hook. Collector value range: $10-$20.

CATALOG SERIES #	BODY LENGTH	LURE WEIGHT
1400-1/2	3-1/8"	1/2 oz.

COLOR OR FINISH: Green scale; silver flash; gray mullet scale; frog spot, yellow with polka dots.

BABY TEASER No. 20 (LATER No. 600 SERIES)

The plug in the photo with original box is 2-3/8" long and clearly marked "EGER" on the belly. It has painted eyes and cup and screw eye hook hardware. One might speculate that because they used the word "Baby" in the name that there might be a larger model out there. A larger model, however, was not found in any catalogs. Collector value range: $10-$20.

COLOR OR FINISH: Perch scale, green frog spot, white body with red head, silver sheen, white body with green trim, natural scale.

Three BABY TEASERS.

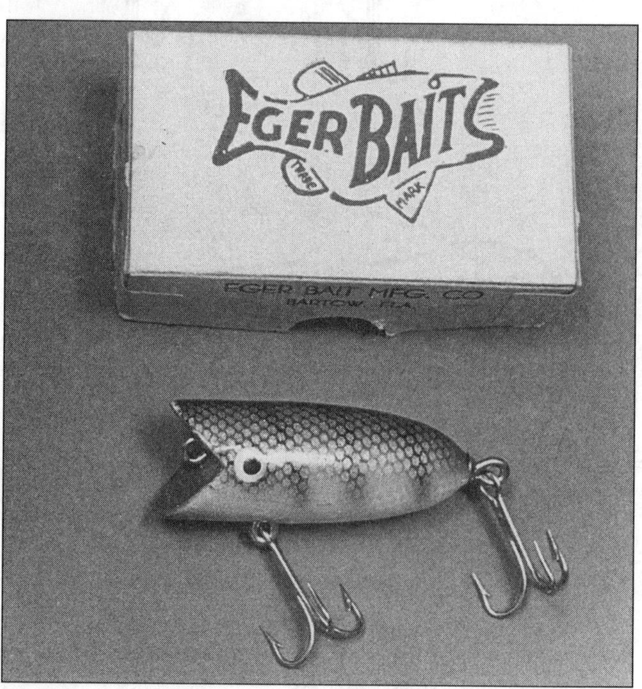

A BABY TEASER with its original box.

WIGGLE TAIL 1100 SERIES

This was a strong plug made primarily for saltwater fishing. It had a notch in the top of the nose, line tie on top of the head, a belly and trailing treble hooks. Collector value range: $10-$15.

CATALOG SERIES #	BODY LENGTH	LURE WEIGHT
1100	2-1/2"	1 oz.

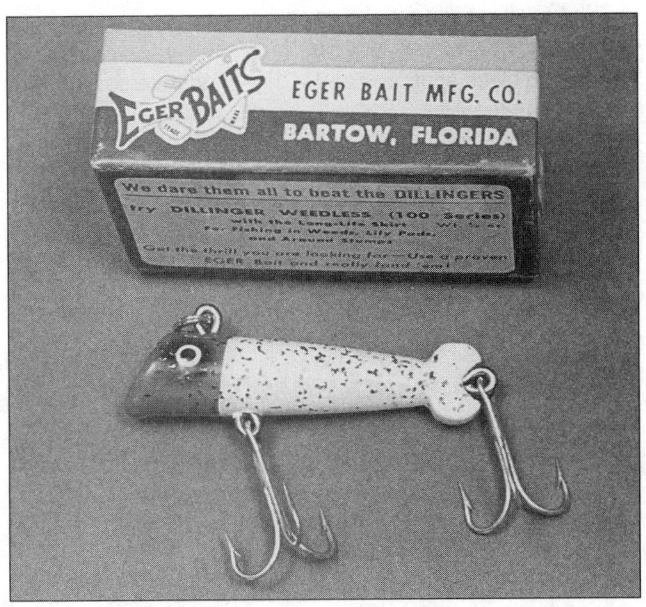

COLOR OR FINISH: White with red head; white with red head and flecks; yellow with red head and flecks; yellow with red head.

UNCATALOGED 5-HOOK DILLINGER

This 4-1/4" lure is clearly marked "Dillinger" on the back of the body, but is not listed in any of the old catalogs. It is considerably wider or fatter than the other Dillinger plugs from Eger. The colors are unknown. Collector value range: $15-$25.

EGER'S FROG WITH TAIL SPINNER
FROG
WEEDLESS FROG
FUSS BUDGET

The three baits in the photo each measure 3-3/8" in body length. Only the left lure was found illustrated in a catalog. A 1941 catalog entry infers this is the name for the lure, but a second color option at the bottom, "Silver Flash", is decidedly not a frog color. Later the lure was called FROG and then FUSS BUDGET. There were several more colors listed in a 1947 catalog. The fact that they tagged the name of the lure with the words "with spinner" infers that the lure was available without the spinner. The middle lure in the photo confirms this. There was also a weedless single hook version called the WEEDLESS FROG. Collector value range: $5-$10.

COLOR OR FINISH: Frog spot, silver flash, green scale, gray scale, perch scale, blue scale, white with red head, white with red head and fleck, yellow body with red head, yellow body with red head and fleck.

THE GLOW WORM c. 1915

The Electric Luminous Submarine Bait Co., Milwaukee, Wisconsin

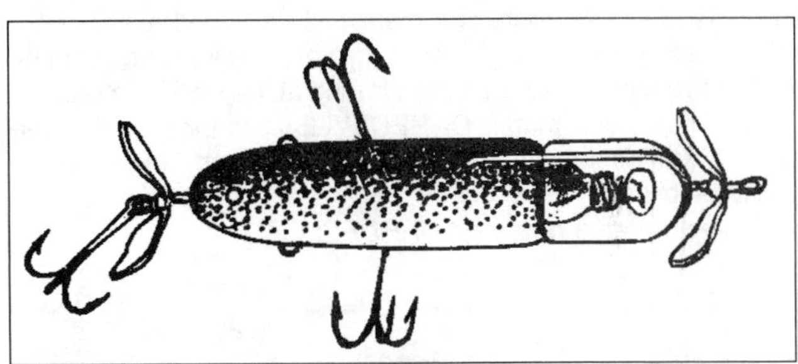

This has to be one of the earliest of the many attempts at the battery operated lighted fishing lure. The battery/light unit in this one was reversible. One way it throws the light forward and reversed it shines through little port holes in the tail. What a sight that must have been. It may even have worked! It had nose and tail propeller spinners, a belly and trailing treble hooks.

There seems to be either some confusion among collectors or there is a connection between this company and DR. WASWEYLER'S ELECTRIC GLOW CASTING BAIT that I have not yet found. The drawing accompanying this text was made from an illustration in a 1915 Electric Luminous Submarine Bait Co. advertisement. The drawing accompanying the Wasweyler listing matches the illustration in the 1914 Wasweyler advertisement. Both companies were located in Milwaukee. Collector value range: $500-$700 for either of these lures.

ELECTROLURE

The Electrolure Company, Chicago, Illinois

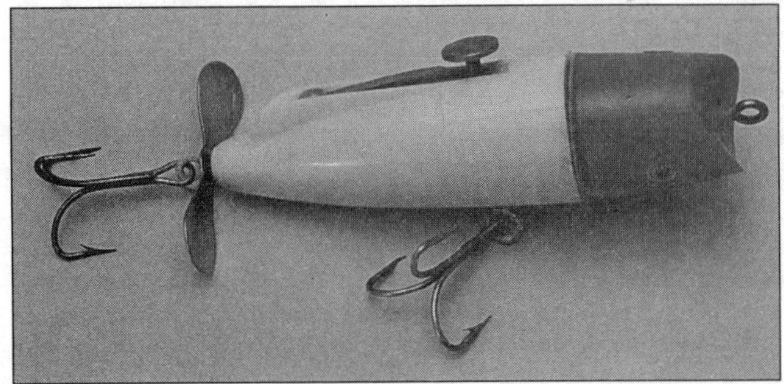

A plastic battery-powered lighted lure, it measure 3-1/3" in length and was available only in white with red body. Two different advertisements were found in 1946 and 1947 issues of *Sports Afield* magazine. The illustrations and ad copy infer that

there was a design change in the way the light worked. Note the Round metal device on the back of the bait. The illustration in the 1946 ad did not show this. The 1947 ad, however, did show it. The 1946 ad copy said it would light up only while under water. The 1947 ad copy said it would light up only *when in motion* under water. The head unscrews to replace the battery when needed. Collector value range: $25-$40.

LOU EPPINGER

Dearborn, Michigan

Eppinger made his first DAREDEVLE spoon in 1906. He called it the OSPREY at the time. It stayed that way until he changed it in 1918. I've heard a couple of stories, but the best one seems to be that he changed it to honor the U.S. Marines called returning from overseas after the end of World War I. They were called Dare Devils. The name DARE DEVIL apparently was changed to protect the sensitivities of church folk.

Over the years a few other lures were added to the line, the most desirable of these being the KLINKER. Unfortunately I have no photo of it. It consists of a metal plate rounded at the head, side edges turned down slightly, a rigid-mount single hook points up and two small metal minnows trailing at the back corners.

The most sought after DAREDEVLES are those with three cartoon likenesses of the Axis leaders, Emperor Hirohito, Hitler and Mussolini.

Collector value range for DARDEVLES: N/A.

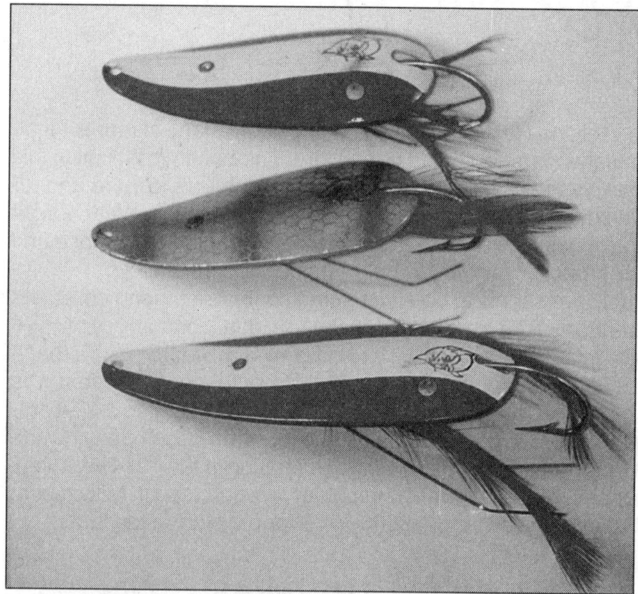

Top two lures are Eppinger DAREDEVLETS and the lower one 's a 3-1/2" DAREDEVEL. Photo courtesy Ken Bernoteit.

CATALOG SERIES NAME	BODY LENGTH	LURE WEIGHT
Daredevle's Imp	2-1/8"	2/5 oz.
Daredevlet	2-7/8"	3/5 oz.
Daredevle	3-1/2"	1 oz.
Huskie Devle, Jr.	4-1/2"	2 oz.
Huskie Devle	5-1/2"	2 oz.

COLOR OR FINISH (1926 catalog):

Black with white V, nickel on reverse side

**Black with white stripe, nickel on reverse side*

Red with white V, copper on reverse side

Red with white V, nickel on reverse side

**Red with white stripe, copper on reverse side*

**Red with white stripe, nickel on reverse side*

Green with white stripe, nickel on reverse side

Yellow with black spots and red V, nickel on reverse side

Frog coloration, nickel on reverse side

**Polished nickel on both sides*

**Polished copper on both sides*

Pearl

Mouse

**Herring finish, nickel on reverse side.*

**Huskie Devle Junior colors. Herring finish was not listed for the other sizes*

OSPREY NOTANGLE CASTING SPINNER

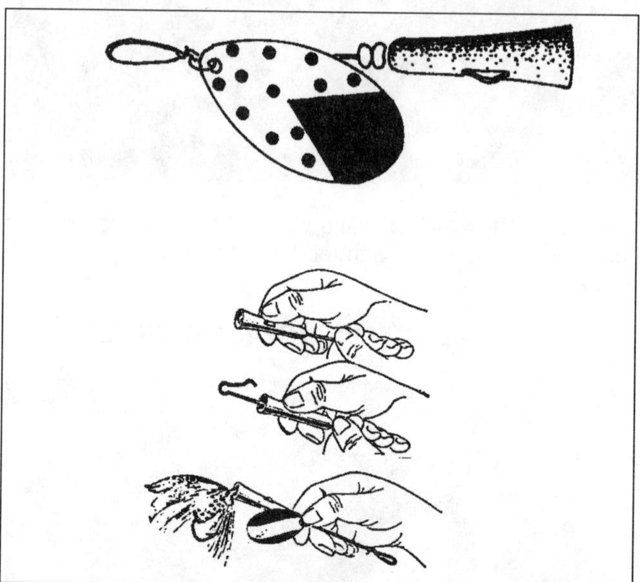

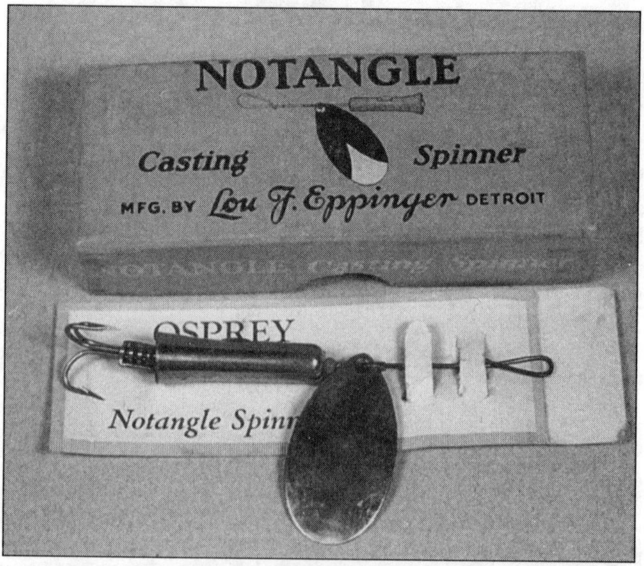

A Lou Eppinger OSPREY "Notangle" CASTING SPINNER and the illustration from the instructions on its use. Collector value range: $15-$20., with the box, $50-$75. Photo courtesy Jim Muma.

This interesting gadget is not a lure until you add some sort of hook or other lure. In the demonstration illustration they are using a feather treble. The bell that encloses the hook harness also acts as a hook preventer keeping it from interfering with the spinner blade. There are two sizes to find. Collector value range: $15-$20, with box: $50-$100.

CATALOG SERIES #	BODY LENGTH	LURE WEIGHT
400	1-1/8"	5/8 oz.
600	1-1/2"	3/4 oz.

COLOR OR FINISH (1926 catalog):

Black with white V, nickel on reverse side
Black with white stripe, nickel on reverse side
Red with white V, nickel on reverse side
Red with white stripe, nickel on reverse side
Yellow with black spots and red V, nickel on reverse side
Frog coloration, nickel on reverse side
Polished nickel on both sides
Polished brass on both sides
Polished copper on both sides
Polished copper with polished nickel on reverse side

SIX IN ONE PLUG c. 1955

Essential Products Company — New York

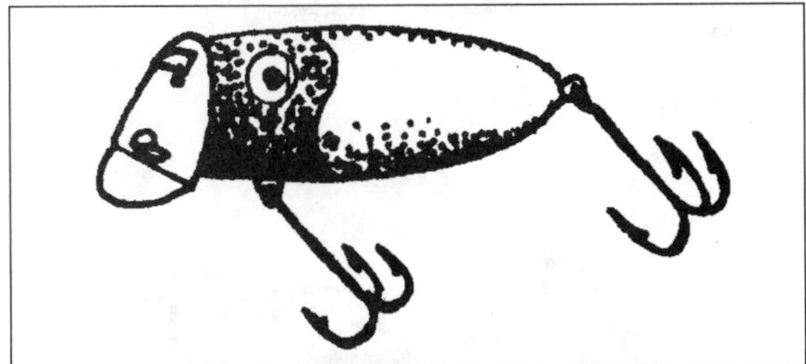

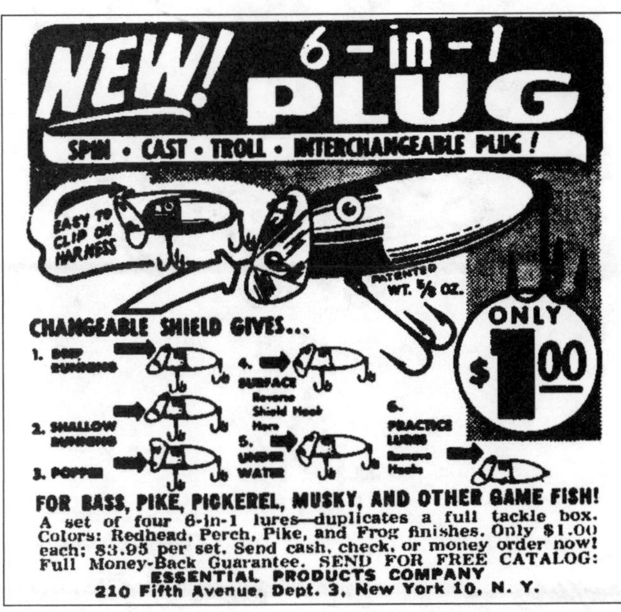

This was a plastic plug that came packed with six different metal head plates. Each was supposed to impart a different action to the plug. It is unlikely you will come across the lure with all six plates unless you find one new in the box. It came in four color finishes: Red head, perch, pike or frog. Collector value range: $10-$20.

HELGA DEVIL c. 1946

Etchen Tackle Company — Detroit, Michigan

This lure consisted of six white plastic beads and a red head strung on a wire. It had two treble hooks mounted on a cross wire between the first and second beads, and a trailing treble. Collector value range: $20-$30.

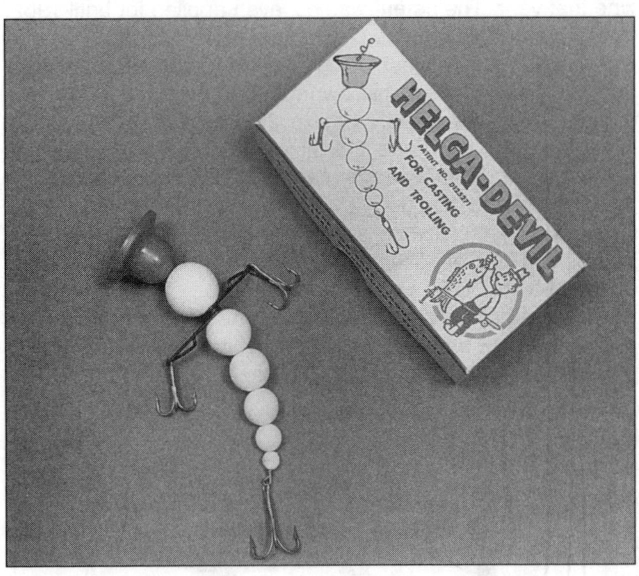

EVANS WEED QUEEN

E.S. Evans & Sons — Detroit, Michigan

The patent for this very fine lure was applied for in 1934 and issued March 12,1935. This lure is rendered weedless by placing the hooks beneath the metal plate at the rear. When a fish strikes the lure a lever on the belly is pushed in releasing the hooks to the position shown in the photo. To find one of these with the original box is uncommon. They were most often marketed on 12-lure point of purchase display cards. It has glass eyes and measures 2-1/2" in length. This particular one is in a red scale finish. Collector value range: $30-$50.

THE "EXPERT" WOODEN MINNOWS

F. (Franklin) C. Woods and Company — Charles C. Shaffer, Alliance, Ohio

J.L. Clark Manufacturing Company — Fred C. Keeling, Rockford, Illinois

The four names above represent the transition of EXPERTS from *1901 to the 1930s (1928 was the date of the latest advertisement or catalog entry found). The 1901 date comes from the advertising of Experts in *Outers Book* magazine that year. The patent was not even applied for until 1902. It was granted to Charles C. Shaffer March 17, 1903. Shaffer was working for the Post Office at the time and apparently felt that he should not use his own name in connection with the company. That is probably the explanation for his name not being in the company name. Franklin C. Woods was a relative, it is thought, and they became partners. There is a variation of the EXPERT that has "HOLZWARTH" imprinted on the side. J. C. Holzwarth of Alliance apparently sold them, buying from Woods and marketing them under his own name. His ads show up in 1903 and 1904.

The lure here is a close match for the one illustrated in an article in a 1918 article by Sam S. Stinson in *The American Angler* entitled *Whence the Plug?* and reproduced here.

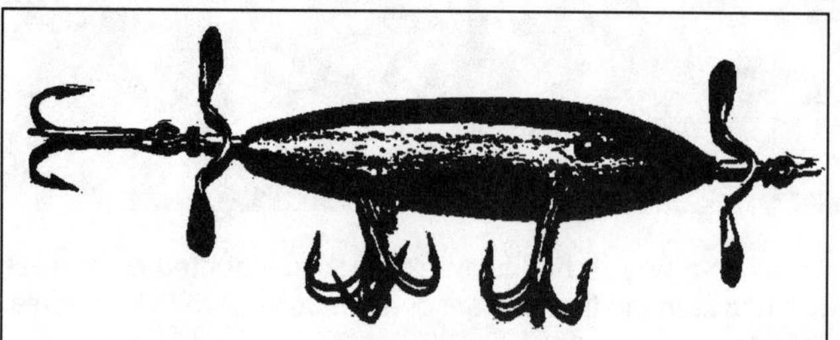

The first wooden minnow made by C.C. Shaffer.

Stinson had contacted many of the pioneers in the industry trying to ascertain the true beginnings of the "plug." He was referred to Charles Shaffer of Alliance, Ohio at one point. Shaffer informed him that he did indeed put a wooden plug on the market and that it was about 1885. Stinson says: "Mr. Shaffer disclaims any intention as the father of the plug, but he does insist that the "Expert" was the first to be advertised and offered for sale through the medium of advertising. 'From the best information I can obtain,' writes Mr. Shaffer, 'the first wooden minnow was made by a file maker somewhere in New Jersey, and he got the idea from the Indians along the Maine cost.'"

Although we know that there are others who lay a better claim to being the first, we can be sure that Shaffer was one of the earliest.

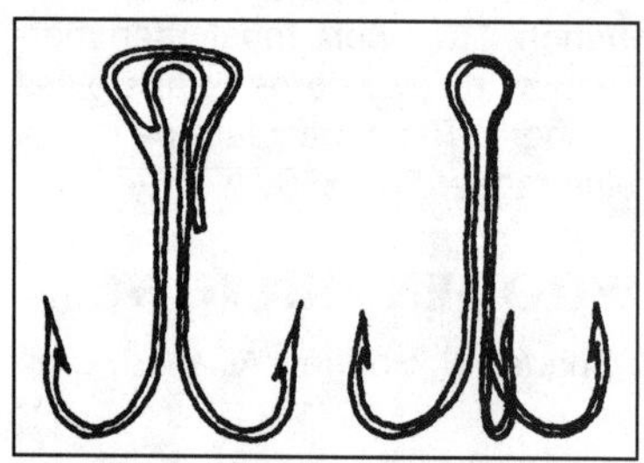

F. C. Woods patented detachable double and treble hooks.

During the F.C. Woods era of the EXPERT there were at least three patents granted, the basic EXPERT patent to Shaffer and two more to F.C. Woods. One was for a detachable treble hook in 1904 and the other, for a detachable double hook in 1906. It is interesting to note that the EXPERT used to illustrate the detachable double hook (1906) in the patent sports a newer, improved style of propeller spinner. All ads with illustrations beginning in 1906 and after, show this newer prop. The new prop came along sometime between 1904 and 1906.

Thought to be a F. C. Woods or a J. C. Holzwarth lure. The finish, the hook hangers, body style or configuration, hardware and the rear tube/bow tie propeller all are Woods or Holzworth, either with holes in propeller or not. The front propeller styles could be a fisherman change or company transitional propeller.

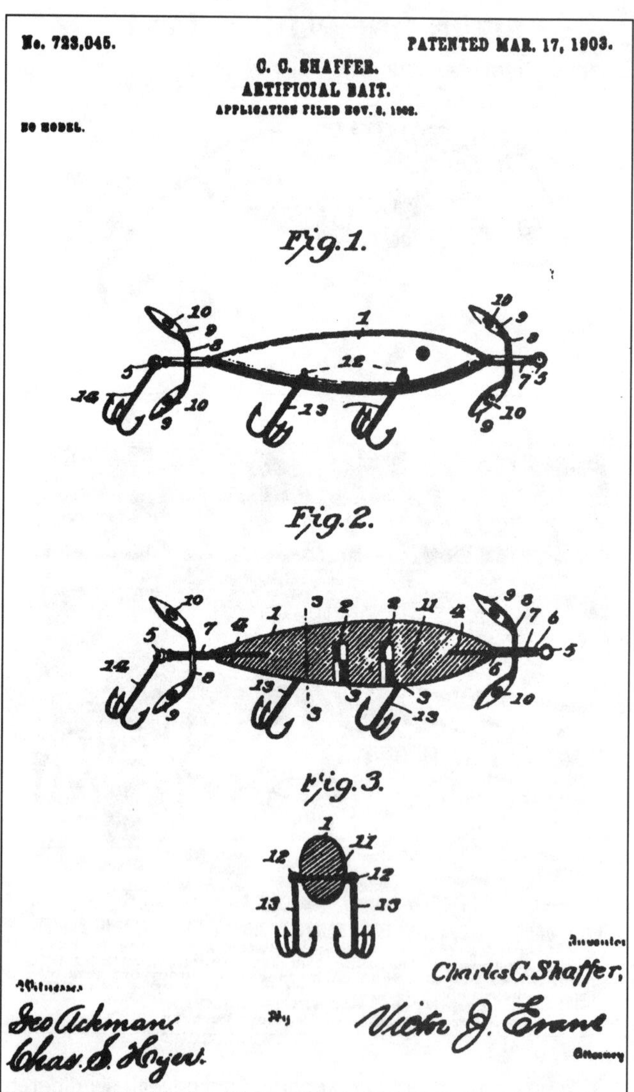

No. 723,045. PATENTED MAR. 17, 1903.

C. C. SHAFFER.

ARTIFICIAL BAIT.

APPLICATION FILED NOV. 8, 1902.

NO MODEL.

Fig. 1.

Fig. 2.

Fig. 3.

Witnesses: Geo Ackman, Chas. S. Hoyer.

Inventor: Charles C. Shaffer, By Victor J. Evans, Attorney

The Shaffer patent for his wooden minnow.

The next step in the transition took place somewhere around 1907-08. J.L. Clark Manufacturing of Rockford, Illinois began making EXPERTS. The reason or exact date for this is

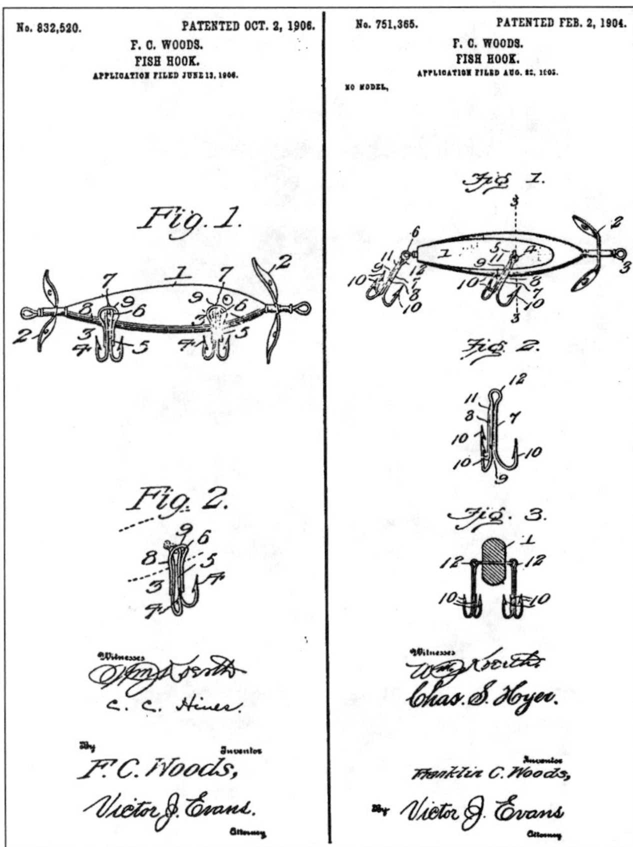

These two patents are for Keeling detachable double and treble hooks.

not known presently, but the EXPERTS continued to be made. The Clark EXPERTS are generally thought to be of better quality than the F.C. Woods lures.

About 1914 Fred K. Keeling, also of Rockford, obtained the rights to the EXPERT, continued to make them and added several other style lures. The Keeling company remained in operation until sometime in the 1930s when the company was sold to Horrocks-Ibbotson (see Keeling section).

Collector value range:
Keeling Experts \$200-400.
Holzwarth Experts \$300-500.
Woods Experts \$1000-1200.

Some Tips For Identification of Experts

1. F.C. Woods/Shaffer EXPERTS will almost always have larger holes in the propeller spinner blades. The props themselves are tube-type with blunted or rounded blade points until about 1904-06. The line tie and trailing hook hanger are through-body twisted wire.
2. It is my contention that the no-hole prop EXPERTS are either pre-production models or possibly not made by Woods/Shaffer at all. This latter observation is tempered by the fact that some of the Holzwarth models have shown up with no-hole props.
3. All Classic EXPERTS I have observed and photographed so far have yellow glass eyes.
4. Most Experts have 'THE EXPERT'" imprinted on the body side. Many may have had the two words to wear off over the years.
5. 99% of all EXPERTS sport fore and aft propeller spinners.
6. J.L. Clark EXPERTS are found with four painted gill stripes as opposed to three being found on Woods and Keeling products. A few Keeling models have been found with four gill stripes, but this is most uncommon and likely to be a result of Clark's inventory left over at the time of the takeover.
7. EXPERTS of all three makers are found in both a round body and a shaped, slimmer body. Some of the latter are actually flat-sided.
8. Earliest classic EXPERTS will have through-body twisted wire hook hangers and through-body wire line tie and trailing hook hangers.

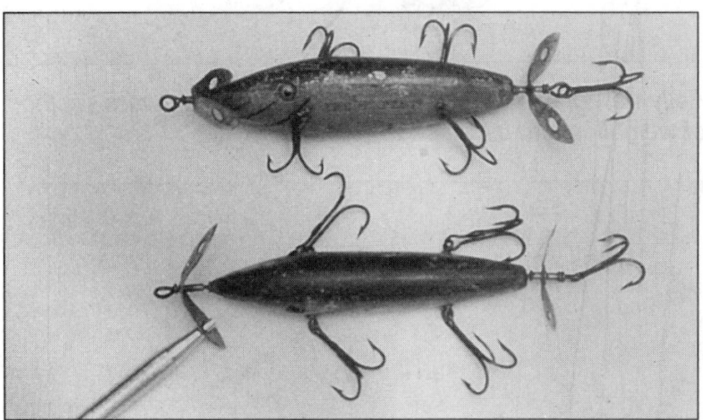

Two shaped body Woods EXPERTS. The Cross pen point is inserted to show the larger diameter hole. Later EXPERTS made by others have smaller diameter holes. Pen point will barely fit the hole on the latter.

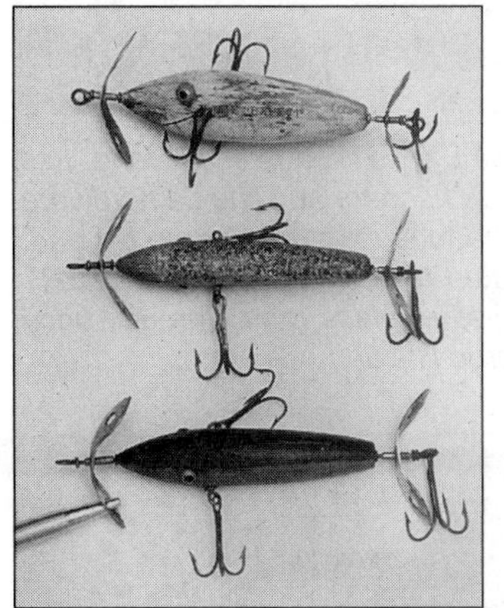

Three Woods EXPERTS. Note the flat sides on the center lure. Cross pen explained in the caption for previous photo.

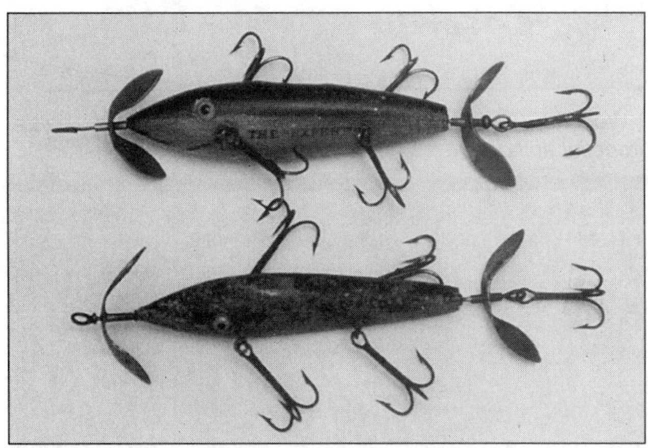

Two 5-T model EXPERTS. It looks like the upper lure has its longitudinal through-body wire and propeller spinner replaced by a fisherman.

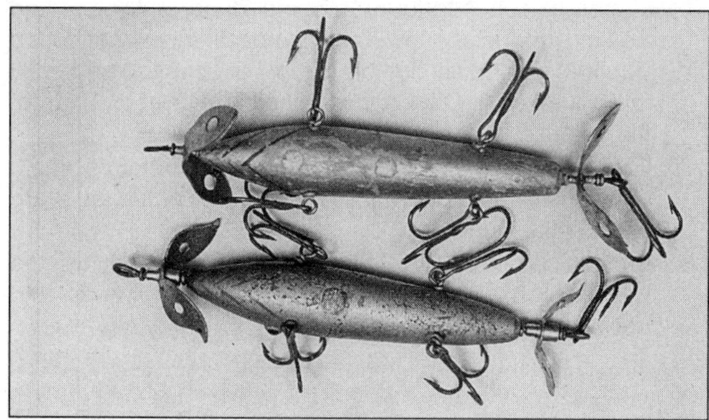

Belly view of two EXPERTS showing typical hardware, method of weighting and gill stripes.

Top: A 3-T model F C. Woods EXPERT. It is 2-1/2" long, has through-body twisted wire hook hangers and line tie hardware and yellow glass eyes. Not the tube extension at the tail end. Bottom: Another lure suspected to be F C. Woods EXPERT 5T, 2 belly weights, 3-5/8", yellow glass eyes, through-body wire hook hangers and soldered line tie.

A Woods EXPERT with typical pre-1904-06 tube-type bow tie propeller spinners.

A round-body Keeling EXPERT showing second style prop forward and no prop aft. This appears to be a production lure.

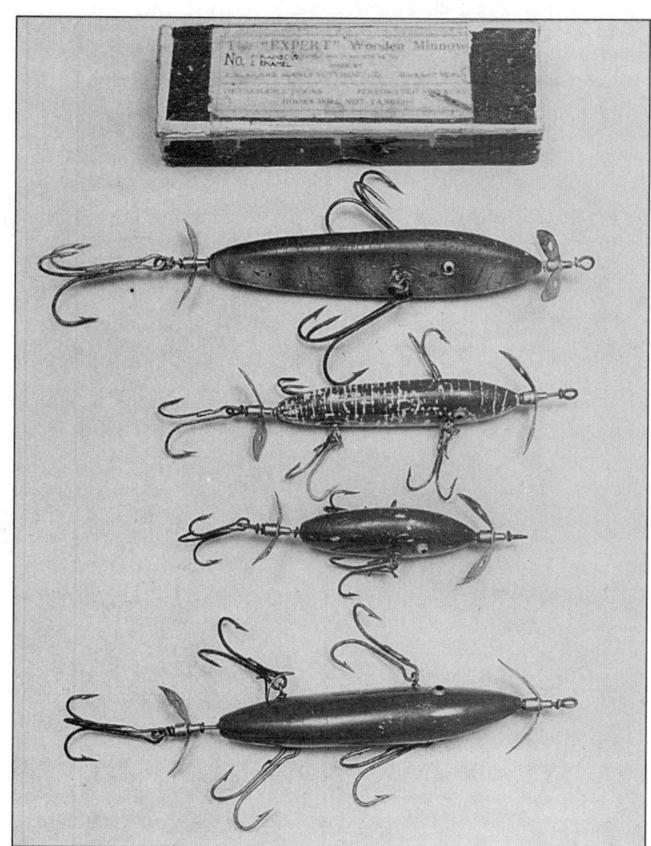

J.L. Clark box and EXPERTS. Shows detachable double and treble hooks. Some of the doubles are broken.

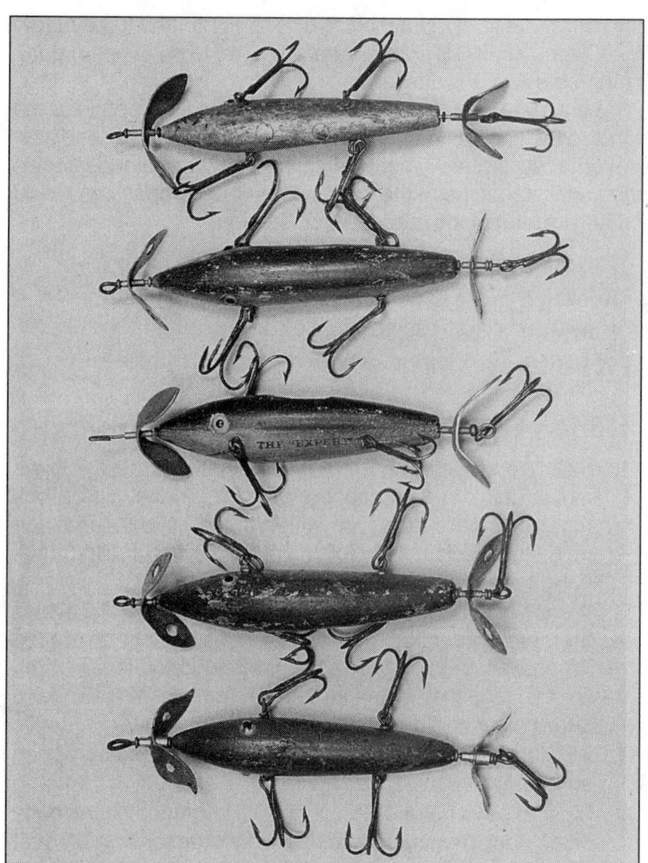

Five shaped-body EXPERTS. Bottom plug in this photo shows the second style 1904-06 pointed-blade propeller spinners.

FALLS CITY BAIT COMPANY c. 1946

Louisville, Kentucky

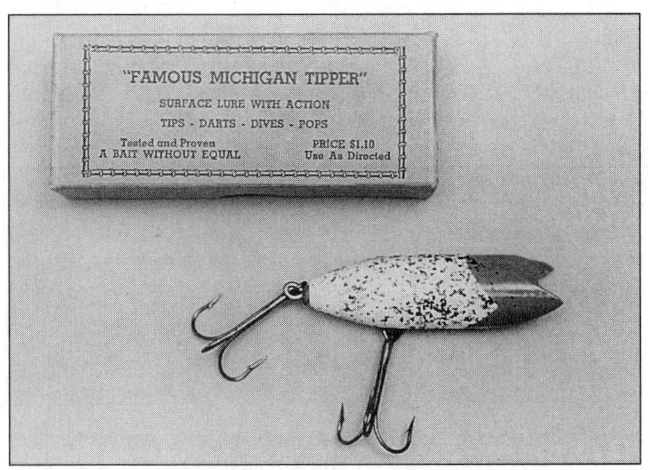

The lure pictured here is one of five that could be identified as being offered by this company. It is a MICHIGAN TIPPER. It measures 2-5/8", has a red head and white body with gold flitters. The hook hanger hardware is screw eye and brass cup. This particular lure is mint in the box. A search through the available research turned up a number of advertisements in the early 1930s, but most were for minnow buckets and tackle boxes. There was a small reference to lures offered by the company. In it, five lures are noted. They are as follows:

SNAFU - a 2-1/4" popper with two treble hooks
MICHIGAN TIPPER - pictured in the above photo
DEEP SIX - a 2-1/4" underwater lure with a metal tip
S & W SPINNER -2-7/8", typical 2-prop spinner minnow
HINKY - 2-5/8" plug with slant dive plane cut in nose

All five of these plugs are wooden. Collector value range for any of the Falls City lures: $15-$30.

WAB c. 1926

Fenner Weedless Bait Co. — Oxford, Wisconsin

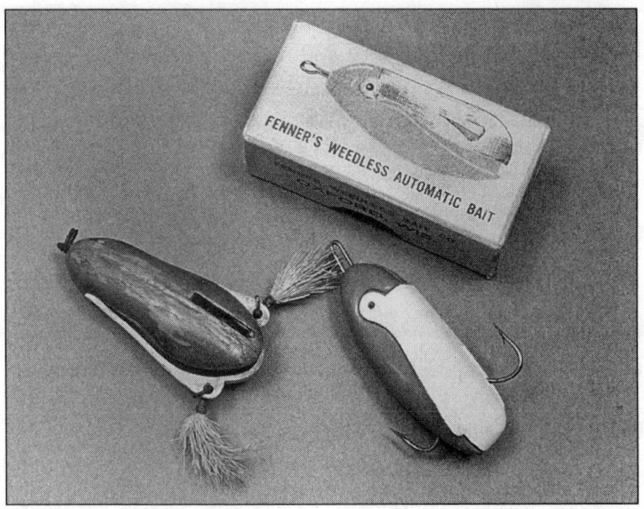

The name is taken from the first letters of "Weedless Automatic Bait." The lure was made of Pyralin, is 2-1/4" long, and the two single hooks were concealed in the body. Upon a strike the hooks came out the slots on the side. It was available in white and red only. Collector value range: $25-$50.

AUTOMATIC WEEDLESS BAIT.

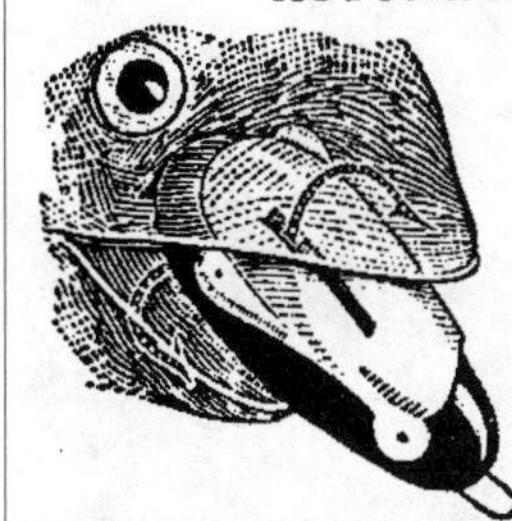

The bodies of Automatic Weedless baits are made of indestructible pyralin. The interior mechanism is made of brass, rustproof and non-corrosive, and is built with watchlike precision. The hooks are incased in the body of the bait and are automatically released when the bait is struck by a fish. Color: Red and White. Weight, ⅝ oz.

T13449 Price, each ....$1.50 net

A really neat catalog entry for the WAB.

FINCHEROO

Robfin — Scottsdale, Arizona

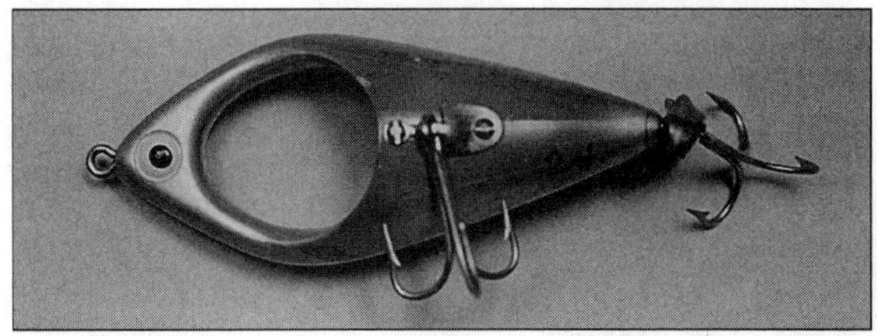

This unusual plastic lure dates from sometime in the early 1970s. It measures 3-1/2" and is marked "FINCHEROO" on the body. It utilizes a one-piece surface belly hook hanger. It is not very easily seen in this photo, but there is a tail-mounted propeller spinner. The eyes are painted indents. Looks like you could reach down and boat your fish very easily, eh?. There were three sizes made, 2-3/4", 3" and 3-1/2". Collector value range: $10-$25.

FINNEY FERRET

Vogels of California — Artesia, California

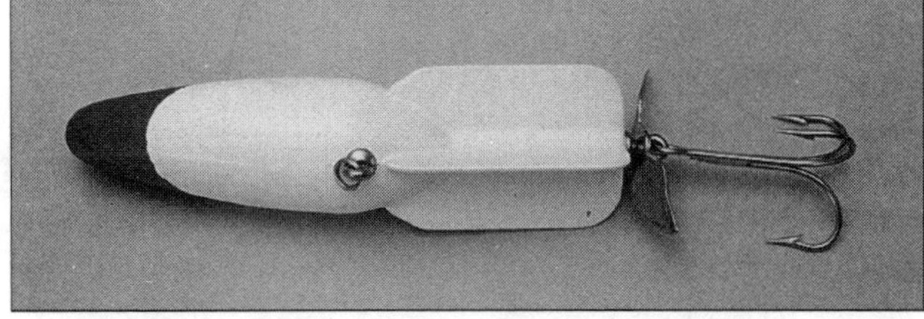

The lure box brochure contained patent numbers that were granted in 1964 and 1965. That puts the lure as early as that and probably two or three years earlier. It often took that long to obtain a patent. A check with Directory Assistance yielded no listing so they are probably no longer in business. This interesting 4" plastic lure was promoted as "The Worlds ONLY GUIDABLE Lure." The design made the lure turn either to the right or left on retrieve. To make it turn the opposite direction all you did was stop reeling, it would flip over and swim in the other direction when you began reeling in again. There were no colors listed. The one in the photo is red and white. Collector value range $5-$10.

FIN-WING

Michigan Lakes Tackle Company — Grand Rapids, Michigan

The box yielded all the information we have. It is a glass eyed wooden plug measuring 3-1/4. As you can see it is an injured minnow type. Collector value range: $25-$50. Photo courtesy Jim Muma.

THE CAPTOR c. 1914

The Fischer-Schuberth Co. Chicago, Illinois

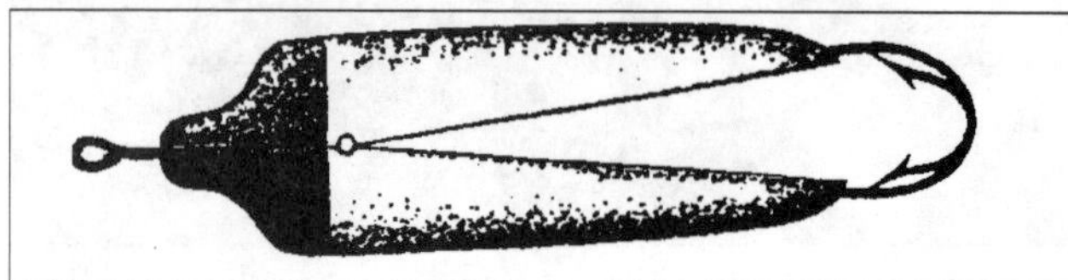

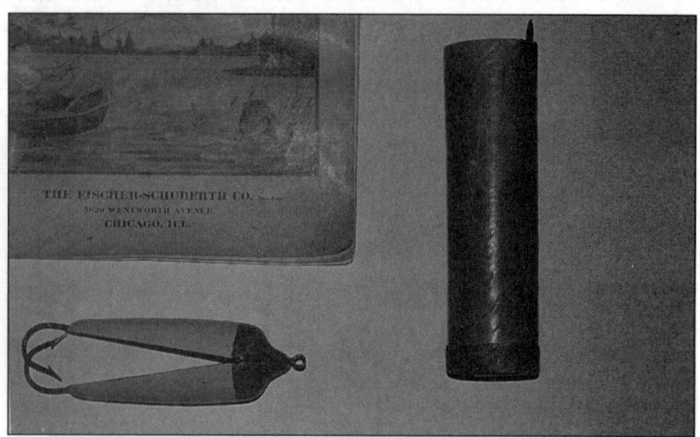

This is a white body, blue head CAPTOR with its original round box and a portion of the Fischer-Schuberth catalog. Photo courtesy Dan Basore.

This was an ingenious wooden plug made so that on casting and retrieve the two hard-mounted single hooks on the tail protected each other making the lure weedless. If a fish strikes it, the hinged plug closes at the tail and exposes the business portion of the hooks. It came in three sizes 4", 5" and 5-1/2".

Those of you who are sharp discovered that the wrong plug was in the photo with this listing in the first three editions. Collector and NFLCC member Dan Basore wrote of the Fischer-Schuberth Company in the September 1992 issue of the N.F.L.C.C. Gazette. In his article he described how he had come upon a treasure trove of company history. Among other things he has discovered that company records indicate that only 403 of the Captors were sold and that 1914 was the only year it was sold. They may have made a few more that remained unsold. There were at least two sizes made along with at least four color combinations. Be careful not to confuse this lure with the Johnson WEEDO. They are strikingly similar except for the nose design. Collector value range: $100-$300.

FISHALLURE

The Halik Company Moose Lake, Minnesota

A Halik JUNIOR FROG. It measures 3-1/4" long and has a plastic body and rubber legs. It has articulated rear legs allowing them to kick back upon retrieve. Collector value range: $15-30.

A brochure in the box shown in the photo states in part, "Every Halik Fishallure is fully guaranteed". This infers that Halik offered a line of lures they called "Fishallures". I have found evidence of none so far, but the three known Halik FROGS, 1-1/2", 3-1/4" and 4-3/8". Halik is thought to have been in business in the late 1940s to the early 1950s. A 1948 advertisement in the April, 1948 issue of *Sports Afield* magazine calls the lure "New" in a Regular and Junior size, but did not give the measurements. The fly rod size was called new in two different sportsman's magazine in April and May of 1949. The same ads now called the larger sizes the "Senior" and "Junior" sizes for casting.

FISHATHON BAIT MFG. CO., INC.

Okmulgee, Oklahoma

I was unable to uncover much information about Fishathon beyond its location and that its probable time of operation was in the 1940s and 1950s. It is thought that the early wooden models were the 1940s lures and the plastic, later of course.

Collector value range for

Wooden Fishathon Lures: $20-$30.

Plastic Fishathon Lures: $10-$20.

A box pamphlet lists the following colors with company names for each of them.

**RED HEAD - White body, red head*

**PERCH - Ivory body, green and gold scales, red stripes.*

SILVER SHAD - Silver body, green scales, yellow eyes

**BLACK JACK - Yellow with gold/green scales, red dots on sides*

**BASS CANDY - White with large red & green spots, black dots and red eyes*

LITTLE JOE - Yellow with red scales, silver scale belly, black stripe on back

CRAWDAD - Orange body with black body stripes. Interestingly, although the pamphlet doesn't say so, these are rigged out with black bead eyes toward the tail end of the body

WHITE DIVER - Pure white body with pink eyes

PURE BLACK - Black body with yellow eyes

SILVER SCALE BLACK - Black body, silver scales, yellow eyes

**SILVER KING - White body, green back with silver scales and silver tinsel on sides*

BROWN TROUT - Brown, bronze body, red, black, yellow spots

BLACK AND WHITE - Black body, white head, yellow eyes

MOUSE - A very life-like mouse color

***DIXIE CHUB - Yellow body, black scales, red ribs*

***BLACK WIDOW - White ribs, silver scale belly*

***YELLOW JACKET - Yellow body, silver scale belly, silver ribs*

***BLUEGILL - Dark green body, black scales, white belly, gold side scales*

***RED HEAD FROG FINISH*

***CRACKERJACK - Light cream body, green head, crackle back*

**These are the finishes found on both the DIZZY FLOATERS and DIZZY DIVERS.*

***These finishes are found on the DIZZY FLOATER only.*

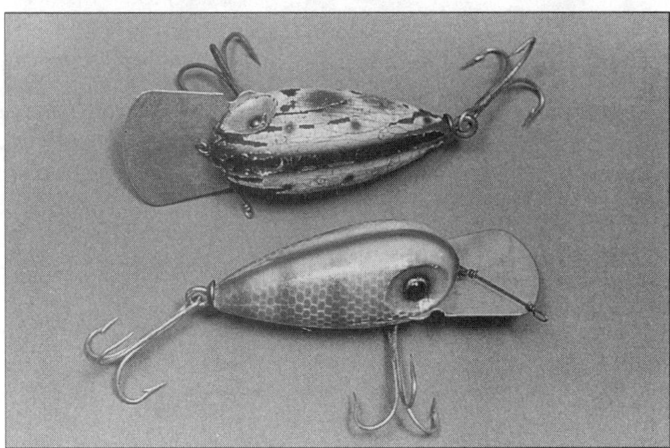

These are small 1-1/2", 1/2 oz. DIZZY DIVERS with 5/8" deep diving lips. They each have a belly treble and trailing treble hook.

A 2" wooden Fishathon DIZZY DIVER. It is stamped as such on the back. Most Fishathon lures are marked on the back.

DIZZY FLOATER

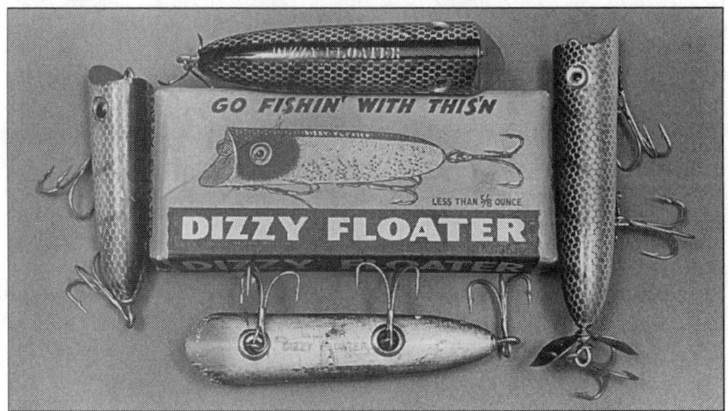

This 3-3/4", 5/8 oz. DIZZY FLOATER has a scooped out those with a lower lip. It has two belly-mounted treble hooks and one trailing treble.

FISHERETTO
c. 1918-1945

Brown's Fisheretto Co. — Alexandria, Minnesota; Osakis, Minnesota

This company was formed sometime in the 1910s. In 1910, six brothers, Sam, John, Bill, Mike, Tom and Ed Brown opened a general store in Osakis, Minnesota. At some point between then and 1918 they began making and selling lures. Sam Brown applied for a lure patent in 1918 and it was granted to him February 24, 1920. That is evidence that they were serious about the lure business at least as early as 1918. They continued actively making and selling them until 1945.

They fashioned four basic styles of lures and two of ice fishing or spearing decoys. The following photographs represent these.

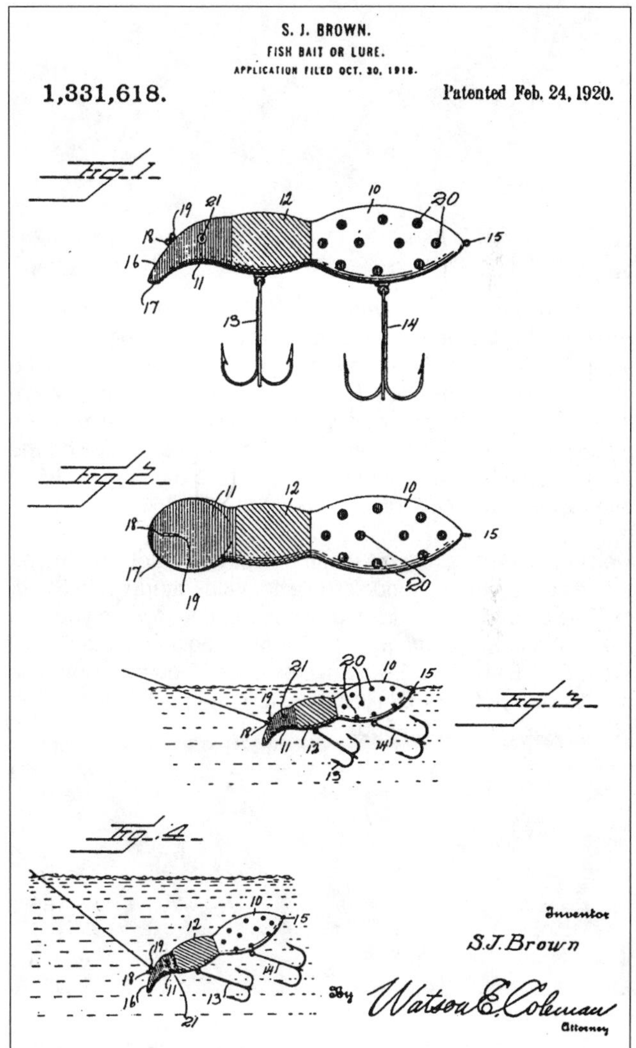

Copyright illustration for the FISHERETTO.

The illustration here was taken from a Brown's letterhead. It is thought to be the original FISHERETTO. It is shaped somewhat like the patent drawing; at least more so than any of the others. It is most commonly found in a white body with red head finish, but has been found in other colors. I have not seen one of these personally so I can't say what type of hardware is common. I can say, however, that the one in the illustration not only appears to have cup and screw eye hook hardware, but also glass eyes. This is contrary to the norm for most of their lures. The usual hardware is a screw eye and washer and the

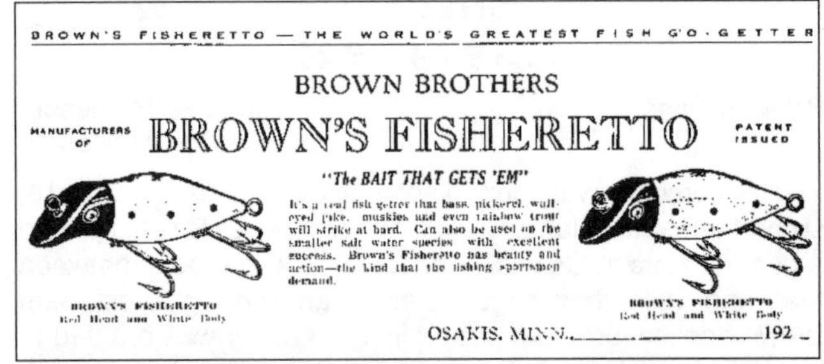

These two lures are examples of the most commonly found FISHERETTOS. Notice the distinctive concave belly. The upper lure has a frog finish and the lower has tiger stripes on a white body with a red head. These have the typical screw eye and washer line tie and hook hardware. The painted eye on the upper one is also typical, but the glued-on washer eye on the lower one isn't often found. They measure 3-3/4" and 3-5/8" long respectively. Collector value range: $25-$50.

eyes are painted. It may be that the illustration is of a prototype or early experimental model. Collector value range: $75-$150.

They also made ice fishing or spearing decoys as you can see by these two photographs. The first photo is of the DARK HORSE SPEARING DECOY. It measures 5" long. The other is the FISHERETTO SPEARING DECOY. It is 5-1/2" long. Collector value range: $25-$50.

For the most part these represent the line fairly well. Typical characteristics are screw eye and washer hook and line tie hardware and painted eyes. The lures were all hand-painted and no two were exactly alike. Most of the paint jobs would be considered crude by collectors, but they must have been successful fish getters for they were made for a least 26 years. It is possible for one of them to show up with the cup and screw eye hardware and glass eyes.

This is a minnow shape body with a floppy bow tie type propeller spinner at the tail. Note the use of cup and screw eye hook hardware. This is considered rare. This lure can be found in many different colors, some downright strange. For instance the upper lure in the above photo is white and pink! The other one is black and gold paint. They are 4-1/8" long. Collector value range: $50-$80.

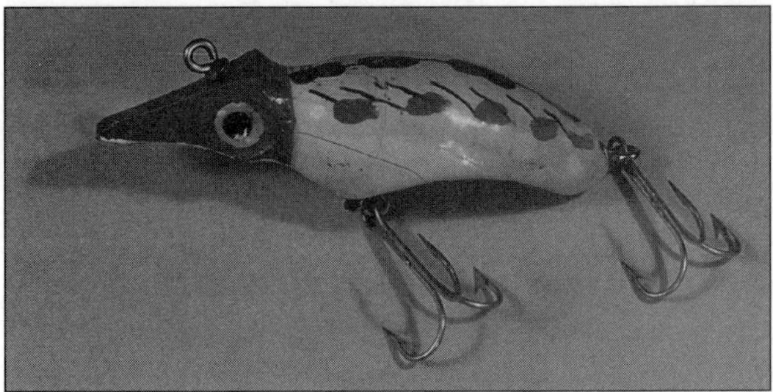

This 3-1/2" plug is considered the rarest of the FISHERETTO lures. The one in the photo sports a Lady Bug paint pattern with painted eyes and screw eye/washer hook hardware. Collector value range: $60-$120.

FISHER'S JIG

Maker Unknown

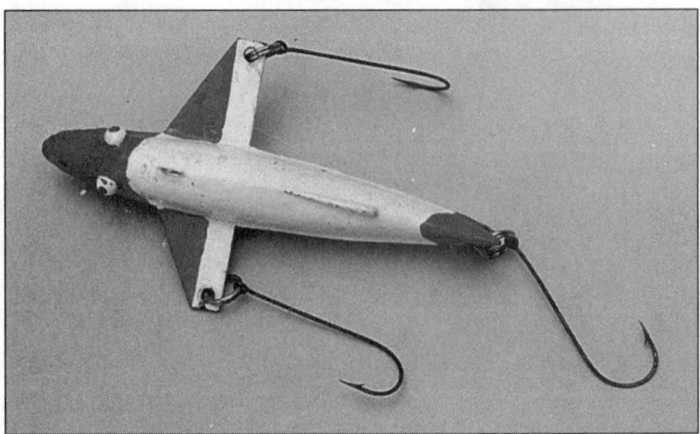

This is a fairly heavy metal lure with wing-like side fins and bulbous eyes. Little is known about this lure except for the words "FISHERS JIG" printed in blue on the belly. It has a dorsal fin and bulging eyes. It was apparently truly meant to be jigged. The line tie is on the back and lure appears to be weighted slightly nose heavy so it would glide forward on its wings when dropped down. This example appears to be a fisherman repaint. There was no trade data from which to derive a collector value.

FISHMASTER SPORTING GOODS COMPANY

Wollaston, Massachusetts

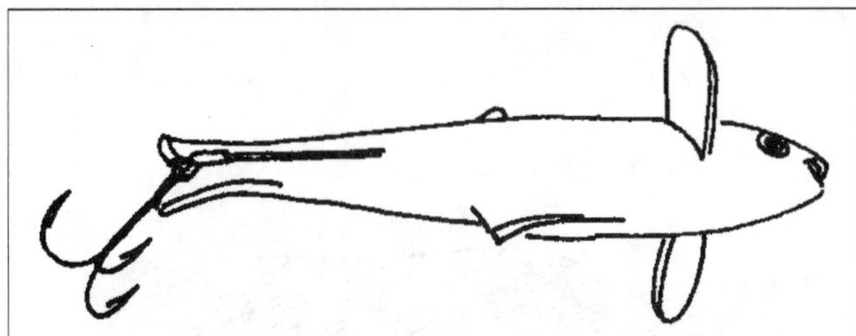

The side fins in the photo are not obvious. This sketch of the lure is turned a bit giving a better view of the fins.

This is an obscure company that was doing business sometime during the 1940s. They were not actually manufacturers of lures. They bought lures or represented lures made by others in New England.

FISHMASTER

FISHMASTER MINNO-CASTER

SURE DEATH For All Minnow-Eating Fish

Bass, pickerel, large trout, walleyes and salt water game fish go for its sparkling flash and tantalizing wiggle-wobble-waggle. One dealer guaranteed 'em to catch fish or money refunded. He sold 96 dozen to local anglers without a comeback! For bait casting, #4500-4½ in. ¼ to ½ oz.—$1.50; for spinning rod #3000-3 in. ¼ oz.—$1.25. Both are also good trollers. Your choice of gold, silver, salmon, green, red or black. Ask your dealer or postpaid direct. Specify color and size.

FISHMASTER CO., Wollaston 71, Mass.

This advertisement for the MINNO-CASTER was in the July, 1950 edition of Outdoorsman magazine.

The lure in the photo above is called FISHMASTER. It is a plastic material one advertisement called "...tough Nitron". Sounds dangerous doesn't it? It was featured in a 1944 advertisement for the company. Ad copy said the "New Indestructible Plastic FISHMASTER TOPS 'EM ALL FOR TROLLING". The ad also offered accessories for the lure; something called an INVISIBLE PLASTIC KEEL and a MULTISWIVEL. Each was offered for 25 cents. It was available in 3", 4-1/2" and 6" sizes. According to a couple of ads it was made in seven colors, but there was a total of only five actually listed.

There are three distinct models of this lure to be found. One is like the photo, with the tail hook on a long wire that protrude through the side of the body about two thirds of the way back. Another, probably older, model is made with the combination line tie/hook hanger on a wire through the center of the body. The lure rotated around the wire in both cases. The third type is the smaller 3" spinning or fly rod model that did not spin, but wobbled. Collector value range: $15-$25.

LISTED FISHMASTER COLORS

- Snapper Red
- Gold
- Smelt Blue
- Silver
- Moss Green

FISHMASTER MINNO-CASTER

Here is a heretofore unlisted Fishmaster lure. Appearing in a 1950 advertisement the ad copy stated that "...fish go for its sparkling flash and wiggle-wobble-waggle." It was made in two sizes, 3" and 4-1/2". There were six colors to choose from. Collector value range: No trade data found.

MINNO-CASTER COLORS

- Gold
- Silver
- Salmon
- Green
- Red
- Black

FISHMASTER MINNOW

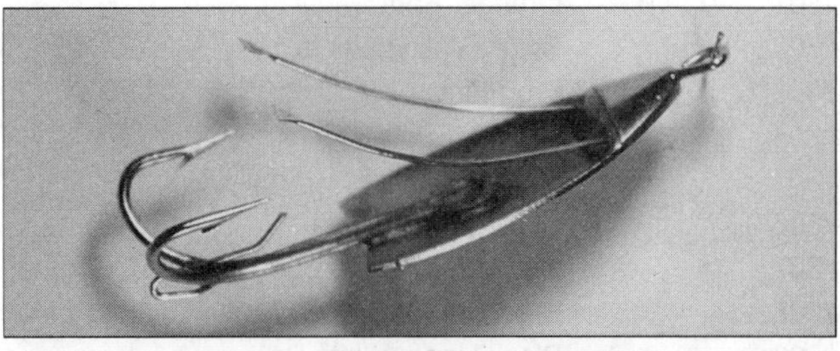

The FISHMASTER MINNOW was found in a 1940 Von Lengerke and Antoine Sporting Good catalog. It is all metal and was available in two sizes, 2-1/2" and 3". It has two weed guards and a pork rind retainer that could also be used to hang another hook. Photo above courtesy Ken Bernoteit. Collector value range: $5-$12.

FLIKO

Makall Corporation — Detroit, Michigan

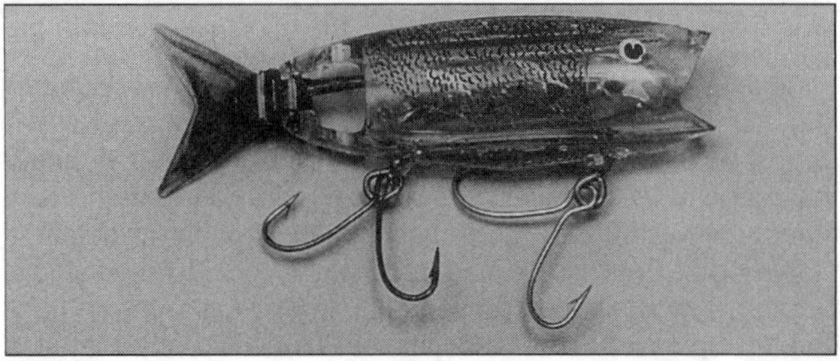

Nothing more than the name of the lure, the company and its location was found. This information was on the box this plastic lure came in. The lure is interesting with an internal metal armature that turns as water passes through it on retrieve. The armature is integrated with the metal tail fin in such away as to make the fin wag. The body is clear plastic and measures 3-3/4". No trade information was found from which a collector value could be derived.

FLIPPER FISH

Michigan Tackle Company — Detroit, Michigan

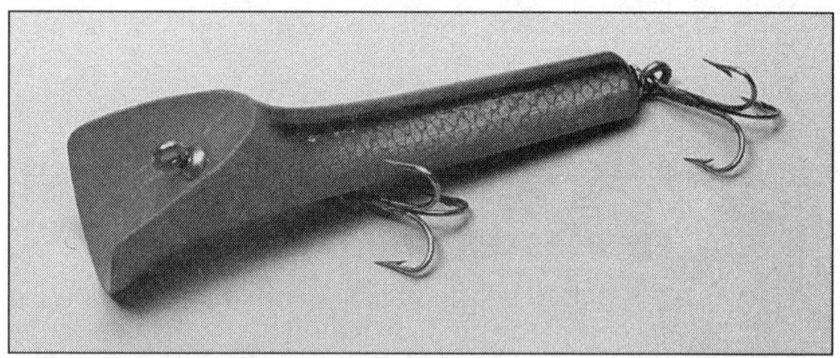

The FLIPPER fish has been reported as being made of plastic. I have only one and it is most assuredly wood. The finish was badly damaged on the underside so I scraped paint away there and found wood. It was introduced in the June 1950 issue of *Outdoorsman* "After months of experimental tests...". It was heavily advertised in just about all the fishing magazines in 1950-51. The one in the photograph measures 3-1/2". They also made a 1-1/2" fly rod model. They said there were 15 colors available, but there were actually 16 listed. Some of them are a bit vague. The list follows here exactly as the colors were listed in the advertisement. Collector value range: $20-$30. A new-in-the-box example sold for $50 at auction in 1997.

#301	Orange, Spots
#302	Black, Yellow Spots
#303	Frog Finish
#304	Yellow, Spots
#305	Orange back, Silver belly, Spots
#306	Silver, Black Scale
#307	Red Head, White Body
#308	Black Head, Orange Body
#309	Black Head, White Body
#310	Orange, Black Scale, Spots
#311	Bright Red, Cream Belly, Spots
#312	Dark Red, Black Back, Spots
#313	Orange, Silver Scale
#314	Blue, White Bell, Scale
#315	White, Spots
#316	Silver, Black Spots

FLOOD MINNOW

Frederick L.B. Flood — Frostproof, Florida

The lure in the photo here is a particularly well made, carefully painted example of the FLOOD MINNOW or SHINNER, as Flood preferred to call them. The misspelling is his. It is said that Flood never went into commercial production with his lure though one wonders why he went to the trouble to obtain a patent on it. Perhaps he had intentions to go into production, but some circumstance prevented it. In any case, they all appear to be hand-made and painted. Consequently they are each unique and all are fairly difficult to obtain. If you wanted to buy one of his lures back when he was making them, you had to go to his house. There were no commercial sources.

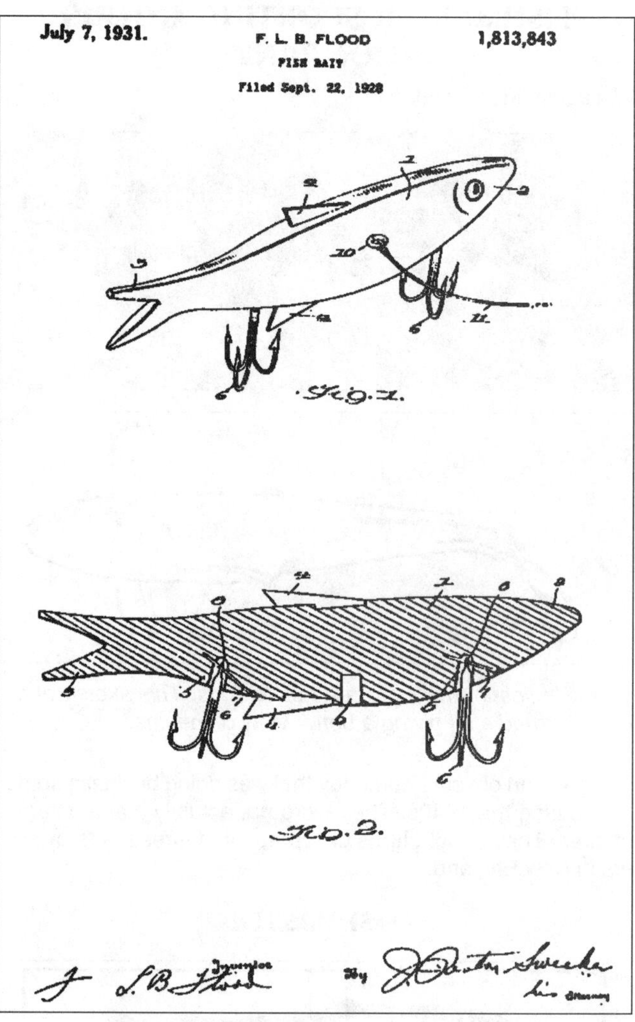

Flood began making the lures shortly after building a house on which the back porch extended out over a lake. He began fashioning them about 1922 and had perfected his design by 1925. The earliest of his shinners had leather tails, but sometime between 1925 and 1928 the leather was eliminated and the tails became wooden, carved integral with the body as in the example here. The dorsal and ventral fins are made of metal and are imbedded into the body and the pectoral fins are painted on. Two odd characteristics that are unique to Flood's lures are the rigid-mount belly hooks and the side mounted line tie. The latter is barely perceptible in the photos, but if you look at the upper end of the painted pectoral fin you might be able to pick it out. About 1932 Flood made a deal with a man named Achter to produce bodies for him. These were essentially the same as the ones Flood produced except that the Flood bodies had a more blunt, flat-topped nose as in the accompanying patent illustration. They remained pointed until Flood ceased production in 1935. Collector value range: $250-$350. The value can be as much as double that if new in the original box.

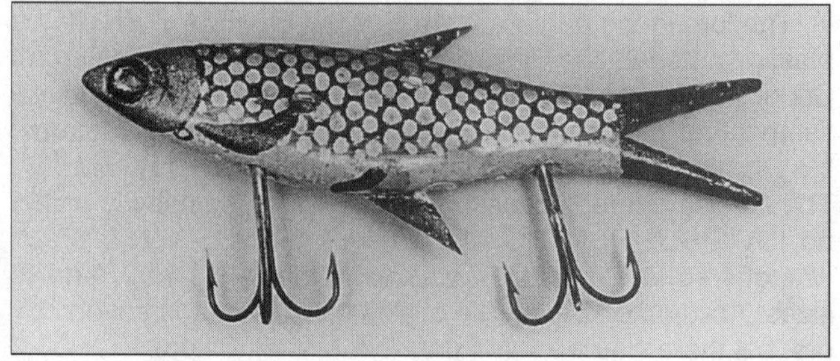

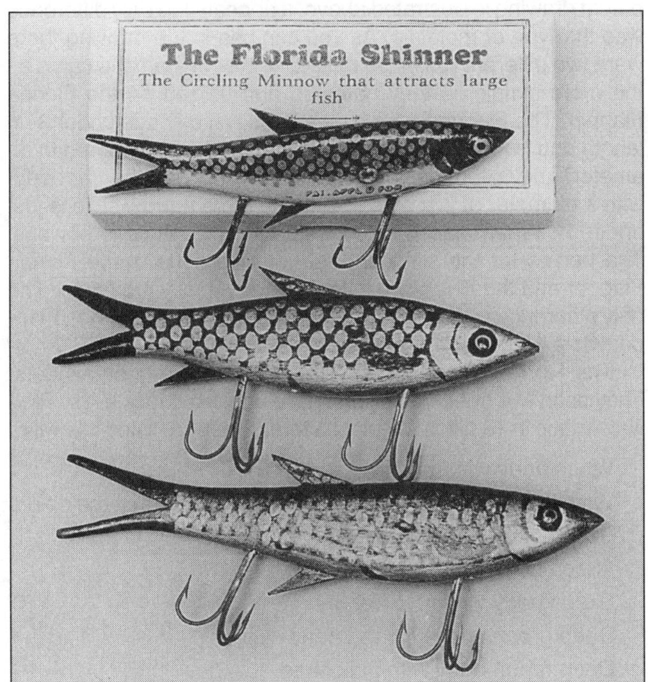

Three FLOOD SHINNERS measuring 4-7/8" (on box), 5-7/8" and 6-1/2" respectively.

FLORIDA ARTIFICIAL BAIT COMPANY

St. Augustine, Florida

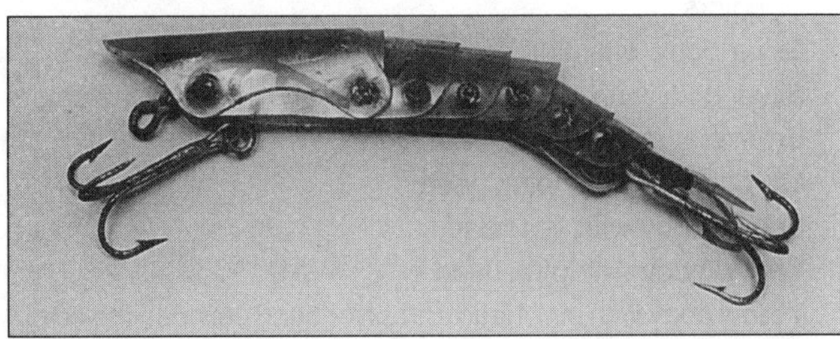

The only catalog reference to this unique lure was found in a 1940 edition of the Von Lengerke & Antoine Sporting Goods (VL&A) catalog. It is an articulated celluloid lure with eight sections. The catalog said it was available in two choices of color, "White body with red head or green and white body with red head." Those I have seen are yellowish clear celluloid with red decorations on the head and tail sections. They have black bead eyes and are 5" long. The fisherman could get it either in a "light casting" version and two treble hooks as in the above photo or it was available mounted with a "...single Tarpon hook." Collector value range: $190-$225.

FLORIDA CASTING BAIT COMPANY
UZ. C. PEMBERTON & SONS

Seffner, Florida — Tampa, Florida

This company began doing business sometime in the mid to late 1920s under the name Uz. C. Pemberton & Sons.

As was the case so many times in the early days, Pemberton had been hand-making lures for some years and was encouraged to start making them commercially. Apparently, shortly after forming his company, a friend with means joined him and founded the Florida Casting Bait Company in 1930. This was Joseph B. Johnson. His name appears on patent applications along with Pemberton on four out of five patents that

Pemberton's Bug Bait
"HAS THE MOVEMENT THEY CANNOT RESIST"
Manufactured Exclusively By
UZ. C. PEMBERTON & SONS
Pat. Pend — **Seffner, Florida**

This box top design for the Bug Bait is for the only known box made for a Pemberton bait. Each of them found so far has been made by modifying another bait company box. This design is found printed in red or black ink. These boxes are very scarce.

were filed. Over the years there was much experimentation, but it is believed that they only actively marketed five lures: the Bug Bait, the Underwater Bait, the Florida Flapper, the Busy Bait and the Rat Bait. All but the Rat Bait were originally equipped with a unique tail hook patented by Pemberton. They were either single, double or treble and fitted with a pork rind device as illustrated here. It was soldered to the hook shank. Many of them have been found without this feature. Apparently fishermen changed the hooks or perhaps the lures were so equipped from the company.

The company went out of business in the mid-1930s. The lures are rare and not likely found outside of Florida. The Collector value range for any of their lures is $80-$130..

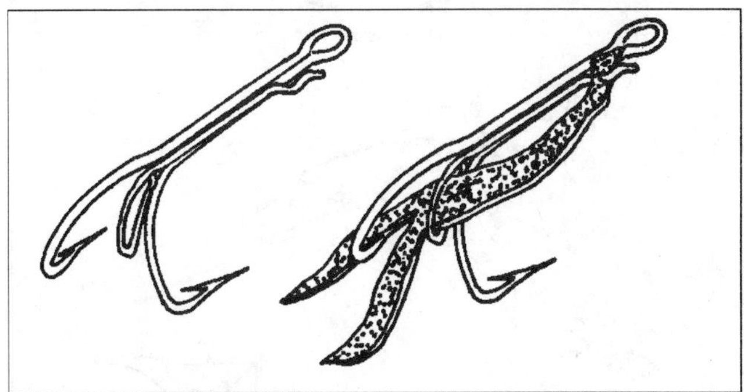

The patented Pemberton pork rind hook; double hook version.

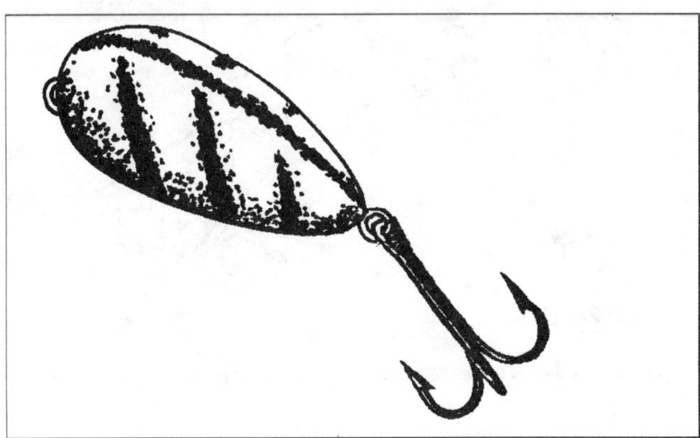

THE UNDERWATER BAIT

It is thought that the Underwater Bait pictured here is the first bait Pemberton offered as it most resembles the first patent he applied for. At about 2 1/2" the bodies are painted gold primarily with a stripe down the middle of the back and three stripes on each side. The stripes can be found in black, green or red. There has also been a yellow body found with a design similar to the Bug Bait below.

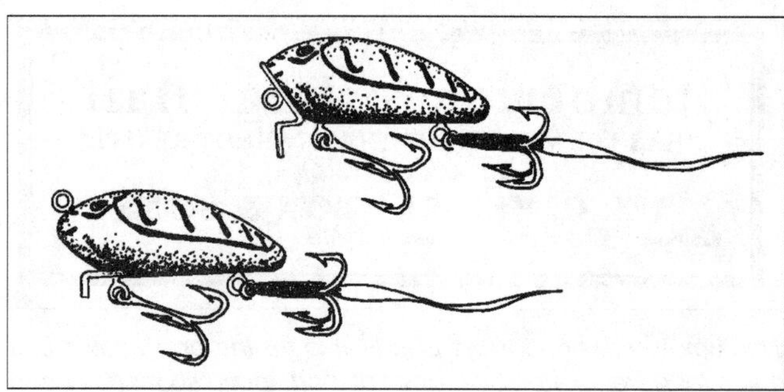

THE BUG BAIT

Above is a drawing of the two types of Bug Baits to be found. Note the flat bellies. On the left is the earliest version. It's not clear in my drawing, but the metal lip is placed in a slot cut into the body. They utilize cup and screw eye hook hardware and the aft hook is sometimes found at the tail rather than on the belly. The drawing on the right is the later version with the lip held to the nose by the screw eye line tie; much simpler to fashion the body and assemble. Colors found are gold body or yellow and white. The have a wing design on the back and legs painted on the bottom. This bug design is found in green or red.

FLORIDA FLAPPER

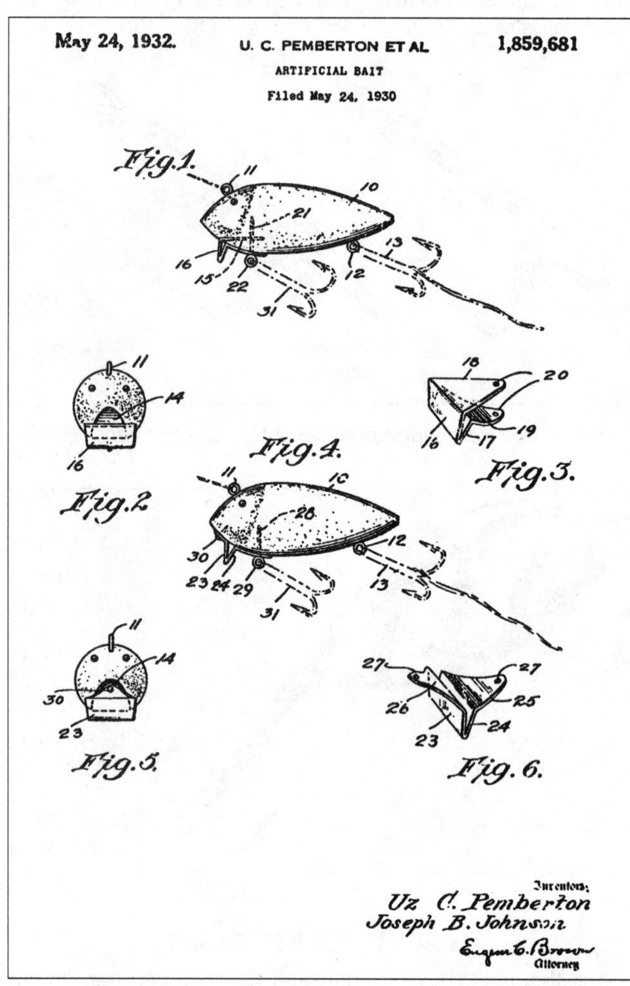

The patent illustration discussed in the text. This particular lure has not been found. It is unlikely to have been produced due to its similarity to the Florida Flapper.

Pemberton and Johnson filed for a patent on this lure in 1930. They filed for another patent at exactly the same time. The patent drawing is illustrated above. It appears the only difference was the type of metal lip. As you can see in the drawing there were two different lips in the patent, neither of them the same as the more simple lip they patented and utilized on the Florida Flapper. The Florida Flapper measures just a shade under 3" in length and is found in two different body styles with regard to diameter. The patent design is sometimes dubbed the "fat body" with a diameter of just over 1" and the more narrow style is just under 1". When placed side by side the difference is obvious. The bodies for the slim- and fat-body versions of the Florida Flapper and the Busy Bait following are virtually the same. The only difference is that glitter was *never* used on the Florida Flapper while it was *always* applied to the Busy Bait.

The Florida Flappers have simple screw eye hook hangers. They sport two treble hooks and have unpainted tack eyes. They were made in 19 different color patterns. They are listed following:

White body with red head
White body with pink head and red band between the colors
Green body with red head
Green body with pink head
Green body with gold head
Deep green body with red head
Deep green body with pink head
Deep green body with pink head and silver band between the colors
Gold body with red head
Gold body with pink head
Gold body with bronze head
Dark gold body with light gold head & red band between the colors
Silver body with pink head
Silver body with pink head and red band between the colors
Bronze body with red head
Maroon body with pink head
Yellow body with red head
Yellow body with pink head
Yellow body with pink head and silver band between the colors

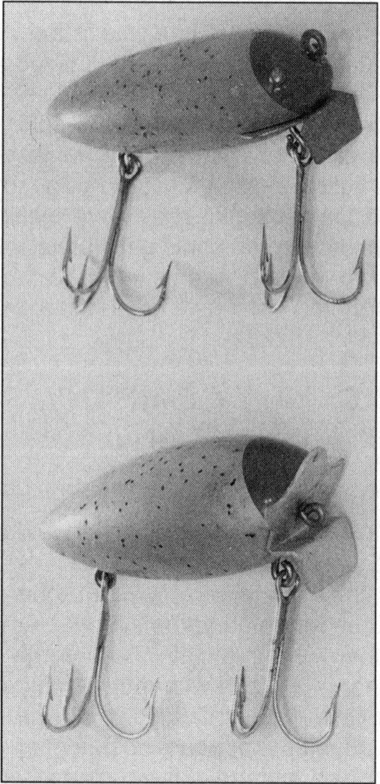

This photo is of two styles of BUSY BAIT metal lips on the "Fat Body" version. The collector may use the upper lure in the photo to identify either the FLORIDA FLAPPER or the BUSY BAIT. The bodies and lips are the same. The only difference is that glitter is always found on the BUSY BAIT and never on the FLORIDA FLAPPER.

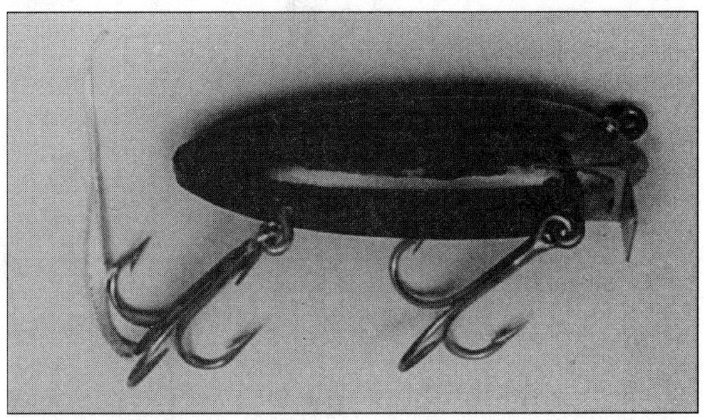

This lure is a later, c. 1940, vintage of the FLORIDA FLAPPER. It measures 2-5/8", has tack eyes, simple screw eye hook hangers and a metal lip turned almost straight down. The earlier (c. 1930) lures had the same hardware, but the bodies were fatter. They were packed with different color strips of fabric attached at the rear hook. Collector value range: $50-$90.

The attractive point of purchase box display for the Busy Bait.

BUSY BAIT

About a year after Pemberton and Johnson filed for the Florida Flapper patent, Pemberton alone applied for another patent. This was for the Busy Bait. There are four varieties of the Busy Bait to be found. As noted above they utilize the same fat and slim bodies as the Florida Flapper. Many collectors confuse them. There are two different styles of metal lips used on each of the body styles. One of them is the same as that used on the Flapper. The only difference in the two is that the Busy Bait *always* had glitter applied to its paint pattern and glitter was *never* used on the Florida Flapper. The other style lip is attached to the front of the lure by means of the screw eye line tie. See accompanying photo for examples of the two styles. There are also two different sizes to encounter. The larger, 2 3/4", size is the only one that sports eyes. They are unpainted tack eyes. The following list will help you sort out the four different versions of the Busy Bait:

1. Fat body, lip in slot, tack eyes 2 3/4"
2. Fat body, screw eye attached lip 2 1/2"
3. Slim body, lip in slot 2 1/2"
4. Slim body, screw eye attached lip 2 1/2"

THE RAT BAIT

This lure is the same lure as the Fat Body Busy Bait with the fancier face plate/lip attached with the screw eye line tie. Number two in the list above and the lower lure in the photo. The difference is that the body is left in the raw, unfinished wood state and a leather tail is attached by the same unpainted tacks used for eyes on the other lures. As in the case of the Busy Bait and Florida Flapper simple screw eye hook hardware is use. These have no eyes. As far as is presently known there were five colors offered. These are white with red head, green with red head, silver with red head, gold color with red head and yellow with red head. They always have glitter applied.

FLORIDA FISHING TACKLE MFG. CO., INC. (SEE DANDY LURES)

Barracuda Brand — Tampa, Florida

St. Petersburg, Florida — Clearwater, Florida

Florida Fishing Tackle Company (FFTCo) was formed sometime around between 1925-27 by Charles Fletcher Clark in St. Petersburg. An official announcement didn't come until 1929 when the newspaper ran a story about his grand opening. The company did not make any wood lures in this first incarnation. They made very fine fishing rods, jigs, lead weights and other such fishing paraphernalia. The wooden lures they sold were made by other companies such as the Creek Chub Bait Company.

C. J. Reynolds had been hired by Clark to be the general manager in 1928. He probably reorganized the company into a more efficient organization and was likely behind the announcing of the grand opening as a marketing ploy. They had been making the rods and thousands of Clothes Pin lures. They are probably the inventors of this type lure. They literally bought wooden clothes pins, modified them, adding lead weights, hooks, hardware and paint to make them into lures.

A 23-1/2" x 8-1/2" tin sign promoting the REFLECTO SPOONS

Reynolds bought the FFTCo from Clark in 1933. He and two brothers, Carl and B.T., were now operating the company. They designed a new metal lure, the REFLECTO SPOON and were soon making and marketing eight different sizes and weights.

The BARRACUDA BRAND was born in 1934. The company operated successfully for almost forty years after that until Jack Reynolds died in 1974.

There are precious few of their catalogs around. The following is a color listing from two of the catalogs.

A 1940s catalog color list:

Natural frog
Red head & white body
Red head & yellow body
White body, red, yellow & black spots
Yellow body, red head & black back
Yellow body with red & black spots
Golden perch
Brown perch
Green gar
Silver flash

Zebra (white body with black stripes)
Rainbow
Silver king
White body, red, yellow & black spots
Same as above with silver flash
Same as above with blue sides.

1950 catalog color list:

Frog scale
Frog spot
Red head
Golden perch
Xmas tree
Zebra
Yellow spot
Blue boy
Silver flash
Blue green
Rainbow

REFLECTO SPOONS

IT FLASHES! IT WIGGLES!
The Famous BARRACUDA Brand
REFLECTO
SPOON
The choice of America's most famous anglers —this sparkling lure with its scientifically designed ridges produce the maximum reflection and such an erratic motion in the water that big Mr. Fish never fails to strike hard and often.
CHROME FINISH
INDESTRUCTABLE
Sizes 1 to 7
The REFLECTO SPOON designed by fishermen for fishermen has been pre-tested under rugged conditions and proved a sure fire fish-getter.
If your sporting goods dealer cannot supply you with BARRACUDA BRAND lures, write us direct including his name.
FLORIDA FISHING TACKLE MANUFACTURING COMPANY INC.
ST. PETERSBURG FLORIDA
Home of the Famous "BARRACUDA BRAND" Lures

These are the first new manufactured products of the company after Reynolds took over. They made eight different weights and sizes. The catalogs describe them as having a "...step-down series of ridges on this brilliant chrome finished spoon...". Collector value range: $5-$10.

CATALOG NUMBER	BLADE LENGTH	BLADE WIDTH	HOOK SIZE/WEIGHT
R0	1-3/8"7/16"	#4	1/16 oz.
R1	1-3/4"1/2"	#2/0	1/8 oz.
R2	2-1/4"11/16"	#3/0	1/4 oz.
R3	2-3/4"3/4"	#5/0	5/16 oz.
R4	3-1/4"1"	#6/0	1/2 oz.
R5	3-3/4"1-1/8"	#7/0	5/8 oz.
R6	4-1/4"1-3/8"	#8/0	7/8 oz.
R7	4-3/4"1-1/2"	#9/0	1-1/8 oz.

NAPPANEE "Ypsi" BAIT

This lure was developed or invented by a J.O. Kantz of Nappanee, Indiana in the early 1900s and was distributed first exclusively through the A.H. Kaufman Company of Nappanee, Indiana.

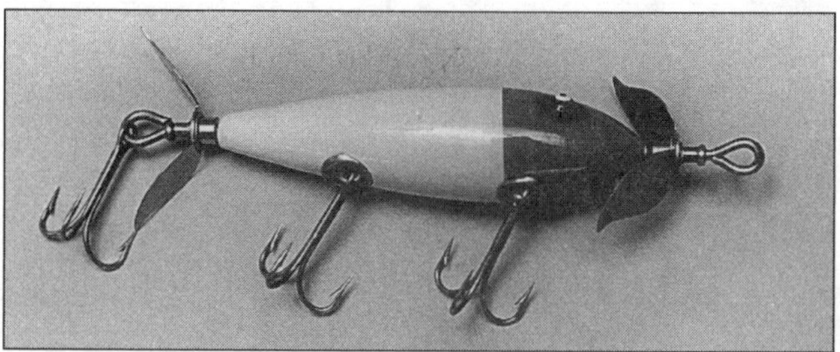

From about 1915 until the 1960s the lures were contracted out to several other companies for manufacturing. Florida Fishing Tackle had the contract to make them from 1945 until 1952.

The "Ypsi" pictured above measures 3" long, utilizes cup and screw eye hook hanger hardware and has tack painted eyes. This one has a red head and yellow body. It was available in a surface and semi-surface and an underwater version in six color combinations each: Plain yellow, yellow with red head, plain aluminum, aluminum with red head, plain black and plain red. Collector value range: $50-$75.

DALTON SPECIAL

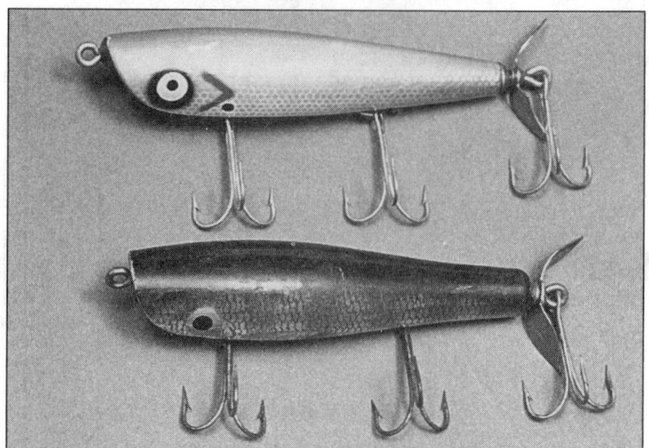

Lower lure is made by Florida Fishing Tackle Company. Upper lure is a Shakespeare product labeled Dalton Special.

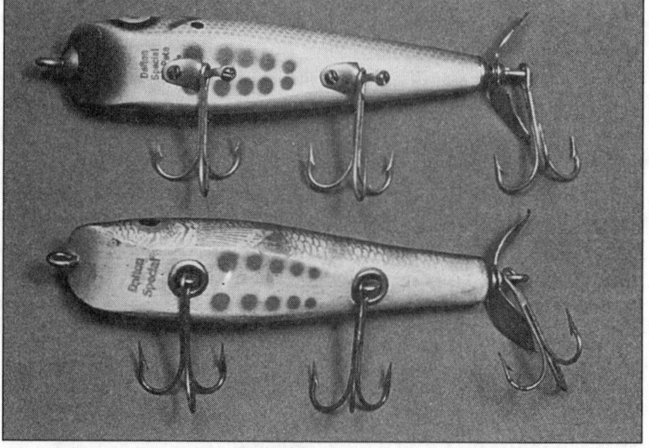

Belly view of the Shakespeare, (lower) and Florida Fishing Tackle Company (upper) Dalton Specials.

The story of how the "Dalton Special" came to be is an interesting one. Back in the late 1920s Phillip Porter "Perry" Dalton of Tampa, Florida wanted a good bass lure for his fishing friends in Florida. After experimenting awhile he finally found what he wanted. He hand-carved them out of soft, white sugar pine readily available to him. The lure, named the DALTON SPECIAL proved to be such a fish-getter at the time that it came into great demand. It soon became obvious that he was going to be unable to keep up with the demand. Sometime in the early 1930s he made arrangements for Shakespeare to manufacture them for him, retaining the DALTON SPECIAL name. In 1942 Dalton had a disagreement with Shakespeare over some design changes they wanted to make so he terminated the relationship. He then took the lure to Florida Fishing Tackle to be made and sold under their Barracuda Brand. Some time in the 1950s Dawson sold the patent rights to FFTCo. They added several sizes to the line. In 1958-59 plastic molds for the lure were made and a few manufactured in plastic in two sizes. The plastic DALTON FLASH was advertised in a 1959 as new and available in "10 COLOR COMB." The plastic version didn't perform well so back to wood they went in short order.

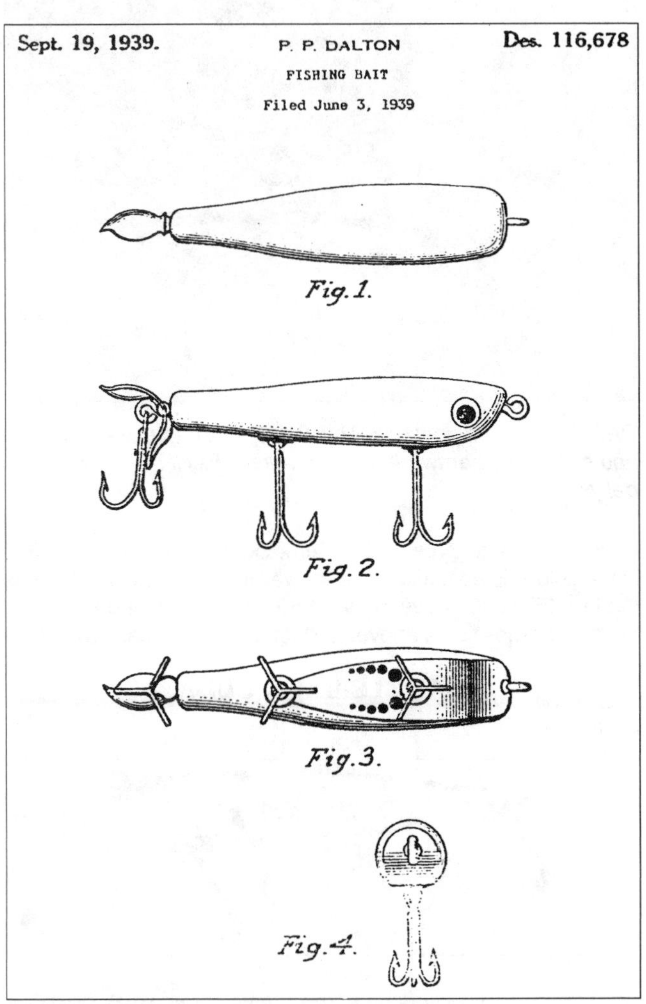

This is the original design patent granted to Perry Dalton. It was filed June 3, 1939.

In 1975 Clark Lea, of Marine Metal Products, Clearwater, Florida acquired the equipment for manufacturing, the trademark and the rights to make the DALTON SPECIAL. The rights were subsequently sold to Luhr Jensen and Son.

Collector value range:

Hand-carved Dalton Specials: no trade data found.
Shakespeare Dalton Specials: $20-$30.
FFTCo Dalton Specials (stamped "St. Pete"): $10-$20.
Dalton Flash (plastic): $5-$10.

FFTCo

FFTCo NAME	CATALOG SERIES #	BODY LENGTH	LURE WEIGHT
Big Dalton special	543	2"	3/16 oz.
Tiny Dalton Special	544	2-3/4"	1/4 oz.
Baby Dalton Special	545	3"	5/16 oz.
Med. Dalton Special	546	3-1/2"	1/2 oz.
Dalton Special	547	4"	3/4 oz.
Dalton Flash	644	2-1/2"	1/4 oz.
Dalton Flash	645	3"	7/16"

DALTON TWIST

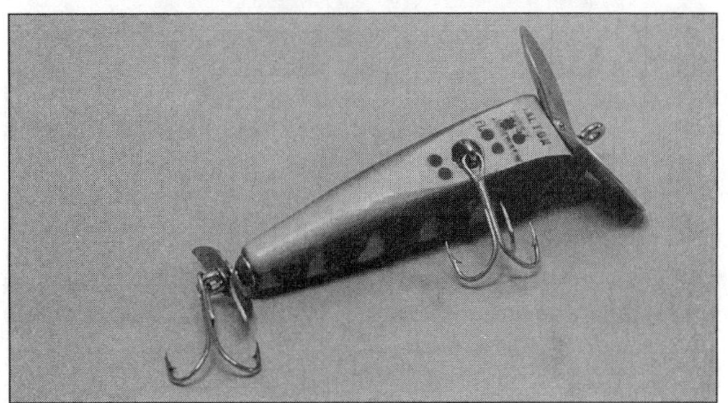

This wood body lure made by Florida Fishing Tackle measures 3" in length. The lure is essentially the same as the DALTON SPECIAL with the addition of the metal wobble plane. This one has a green frog finish. The cup in the belly hook hanger is rimless. The metal lip is marked with the Barracuda Brand and "DALTON TWIST". It is also marked as such on the belly along with the word "Clearwater." FFTCo must have been located in Clearwater, Florida at some point. Collector value range: $10-$20.

LURE SERIES #	LENGTH	WEIGHT
644	2-1/2"	1/2 oz
645	3"	5/16 oz.

BABY WAMPUS or SEA TROUT

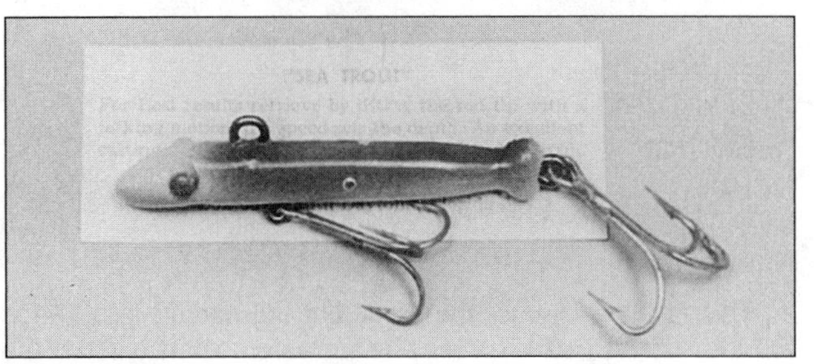

A 1940s catalog lists this as BABY WAMPUS and in a lure box flyer as a SEA TROUT. The catalogs says it is similar to their "famous May Wes except smaller". It originally was equipped with a 9-inch stainless steel leader. The colors available were the 15 listed at the beginning of this Florida Fishing Tackle section. Collector value range: $5-$10.

The following list is of the colors that were available in a 1940s catalog. The next six lures were available in these finishes.

- Natural frog
- Red head & white body
- Red head & yellow body
- White body, red, yellow & black spots
- Yellow body, red head & black back
- Yellow body with red & black spots
- Golden perch
- Brown perch
- Green gar
- Silver flash
- Zebra (white body with black stripes)
- Rainbow
- Silver king
- White body, red, yellow & black spots
- Same as above with silver flash
- Same as above with blue sides.

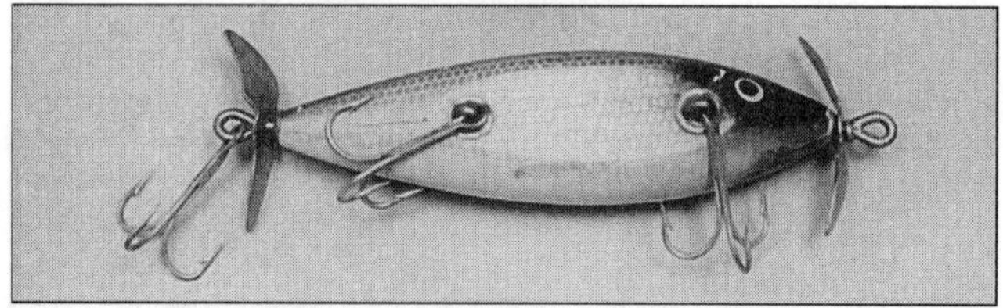

TIPSY CUDA. This wooden lure measures 3-3/4" and has cup and screw eye hook hardware. The propeller spinners are marked "BARRACUDA BRAND".

TIPSY CUDA

Number 10

This lure is 3-3/4" long and is a floater in the injured minnow style. It was new in 1933. The colors available in the 1940s are listed above. Collector value range: $15-$25.

When listed in a 1950 catalog the lure was available in the following finishes:

- Amber scale
- Frog scale
- Frog spot
- Red head
- Golden perch
- Christmas tree
- Zebra
- Yellow spot
- Blue boy
- Silver flash
- Blue green
- Rainbow

SURFACE POPPER

Number 35

This lure was found numbered but not named in a 1940s Florida Fishing Tackle catalog. There were no data given in the listing, only the following notation: "A surface lure so designed to give a popping noise." Collector value range: $10-$20.

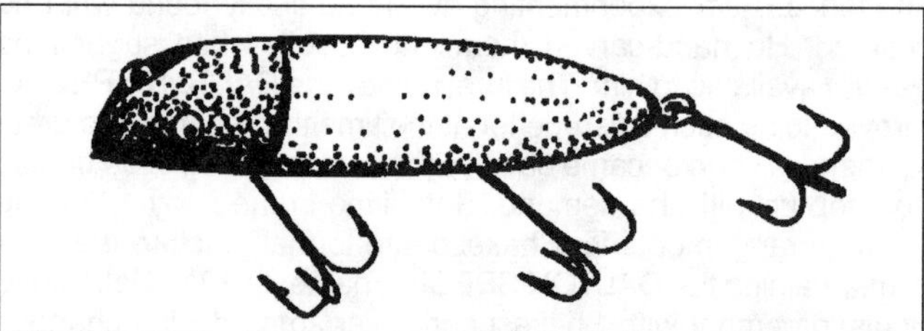

DARTER TWITCHIN' CUDA JERK

Number 40

DARTER with original box. This 3-7/8" lure has glass eyes, cup and screw eye hardware and is marked "BARRACUDA" on the belly.

A 3-3/4" darter type surface lure. Originally released in 1933 in the colors listed earlier. The list was limited to the same list as the NUMBER 35 above in the 1950 catalog. It has been called all three names listed above. Collector value range: $10-$20.

DANGLE-BACK CUDA

Number 40 J

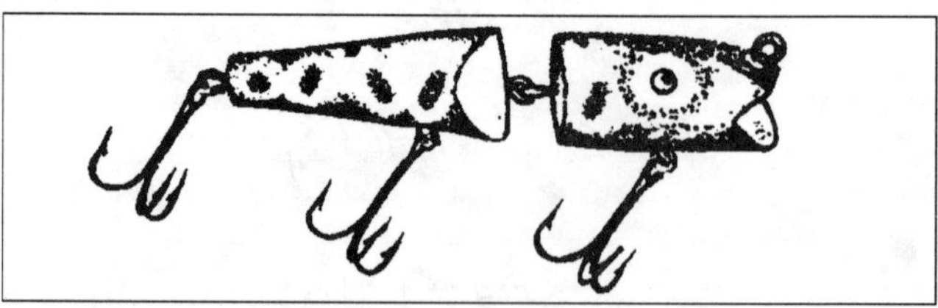

This is a jointed version of the above Number 40 TWITCHIN' CUDA. It was available in the colors listed from the 1950 catalog. Collector value range: $15-$25.

TORPECUDA

Number 50

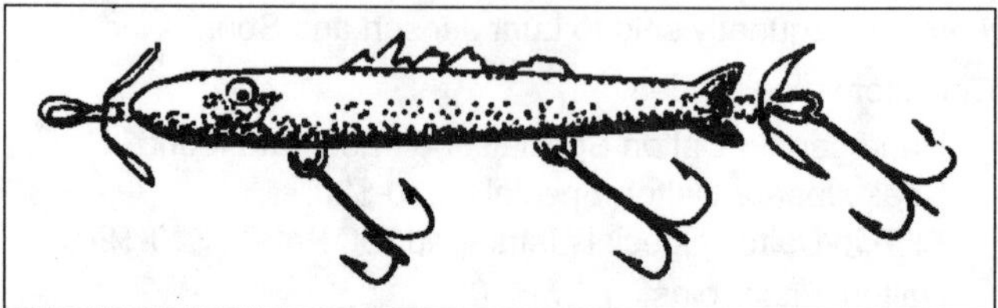

This lure was listed in a 1940s catalog, but not thereafter. Notice the dorsal fin and sculptured tail. The dorsal fin is made of a feather. This slim minnow-shaped lure was cataloged at 4-1/2". It was available only in the colors listed at the beginning of this section. Collector value range: $20-$25.

TORPECUDA

Number 60

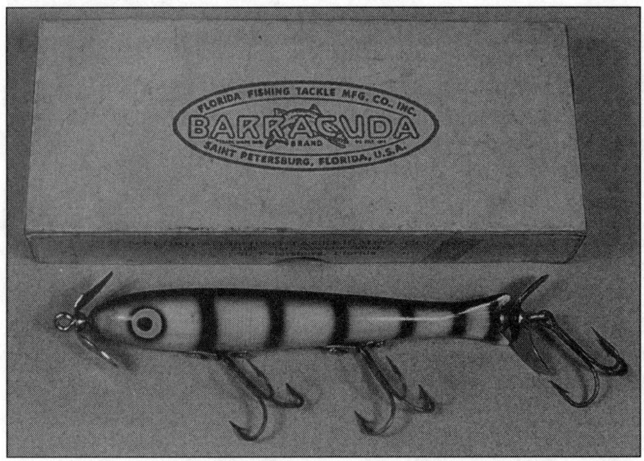

This lure is essentially the same as the Number 50 above except that it has no dorsal fin. In the 1950 catalog colors are as listed for the Number 10, TIPSY CUDA above. Collector value range: $20-$30. Photo courtesy Jim Muma.

SLIM TWIN CUDA

Number 80

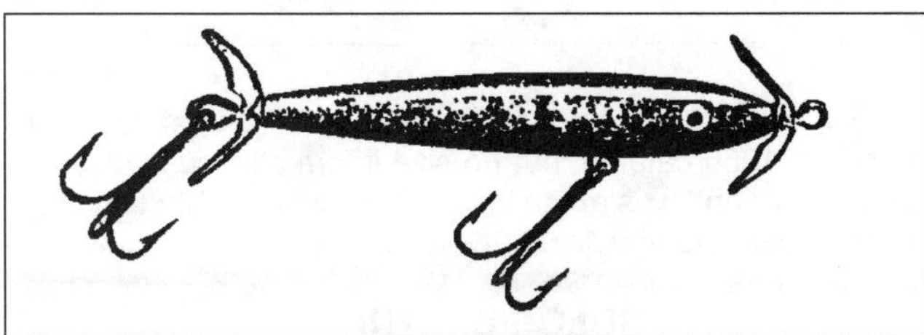

When found in the 1940s catalog, this 3-3/4" lure was not named. It was available in the colors first listed in this section. In the 1950 catalog the color list was the same as the Number 10. Collector value range: $1520.

The color list following is of the colors available on each of the remaining lures illustrated and discussed unless otherwise stated.

- Red head
- Amber scale
- Golden perch
- Frog scale
- Frog spot
- Christmas tree
- Zebra
- Yellow spot
- Blue boy
- Silver flash
- Blue green
- Rainbow

SKINNY CUDA

Number 100

A 3-3/4" underwater lure with two propeller spinners and three treble hooks. Colors available are listed above. Collector value range: $15-$20.

9999 CONVICT

Number 9999

You have to wonder what the story is behind the name of this lure. Could be interesting. One good guess is that it was a play on Eger's DILLINGERS. They were in competition with each other and the CONVICT is similar to Eger's SEA DILLINGER. It is a weighted lure that was available only in the design shown in the illustration. It was a white body with the black "9999" on the sides and a black chain down its back. It was made in a 3-3/4" size. There are examples of this lure around having fore- and aft-mounted propeller spinners. This was not found in the catalogs available for study. Collector value range: $25-$40. Photo courtesy Jim Muma.

SCO-BO

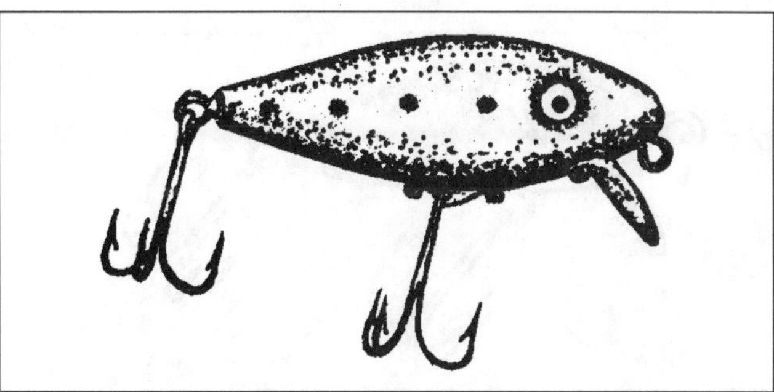

This is a 2-3/4" plastic lure with a polished metal dive plane. It has a one-piece surface belly hook hanger. It was available in any of the colors listed from a 1950 catalog. Collector value range: $10-$25.

THE MAY WES

Number 66 THE BABY MAY WES

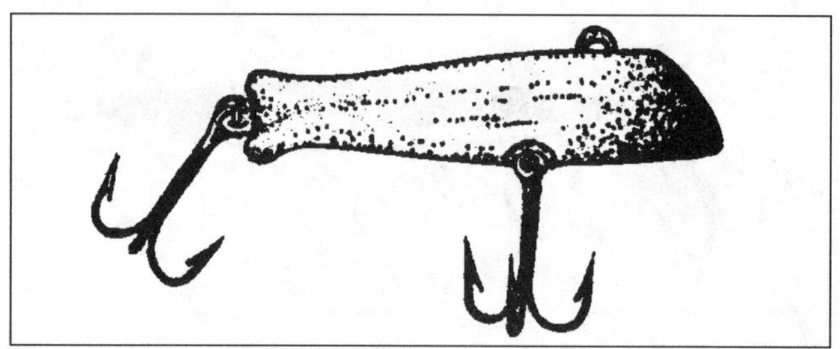

An underwater runner with a weighted head. When introduced (1940s) it was not named, but referred to as a "clothes pin type". It was 2-3/4" overall and weighed 3/4 oz. There was no data given for the BABY version. It was available in the colors listed. A 1953 listing infers it was available only in the following four finishes: Red head, frog, yellow scale and scale. Collector value range: $10-$20.

FLORIDA SHINER

BABY FLORIDA SHINER

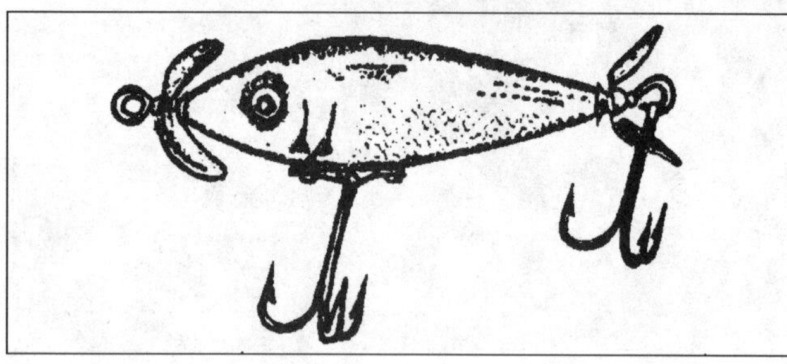

The Florida Shiner and the Baby Florida Shiner were cataloged at 3-3/4" and 2-3/4" respectively. The one in the illustration is the Baby version with two treble hooks. The larger size has three treble hooks. The lures are made of plastic and available in the 1950 colors of a gold scale or a silver scale finish only. There is a 1953 listing of a plastic lure, the SPARK-A-LURE. It appears to be the identical lure, but it is called a "new lure ... sparkles from inside out. ..reflecting material imbedded (sic) inside where light reaches it from the transparent, scale finish back." Colors available in this listing were: "silver, yellow, black". There is no trade data found for a SPARK-A-LURE. Collector value range: $20-$30.

SUPER MIDGET

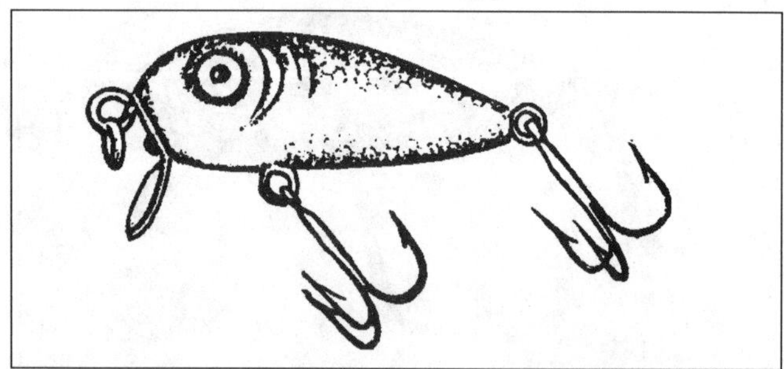

An internal entry for this lure in a 1950 catalog states "This little plastic marvel has proved such a sensation, wherever used, that we are featuring it on the back cover of the catalog." It was made in a 1 3/4" length and weighed 5/16 oz. The only colors available were gold scale or silver scale. Like the FLORIDA SHINER listed above, a lure identical in shape and hardware was found in a 1953 listing calling it a SPARK-A-MIDGET. It also had the "reflecting material imbedded." The colors listed there were yellow, silver and black. Collector value range: $15-$25.

FLORIDA SHAD

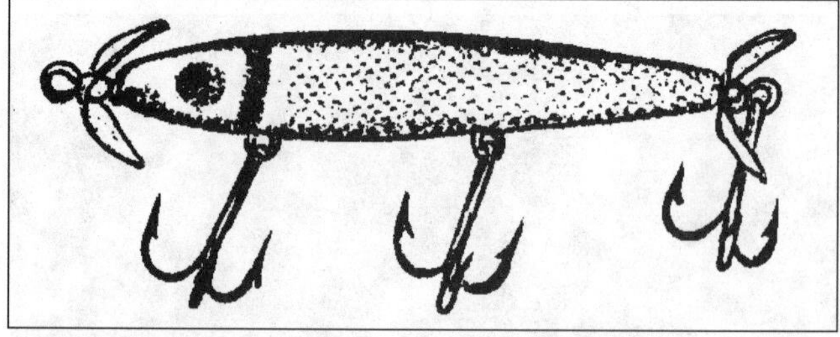

This is a slim, flat-side double spinner lure 4-1/2" in length. It was made in both a floating and sinking model. There were only two finishes available: Silver scale or silver flash. Collector value range: $15-$25.

FLORIDA PEE WEE

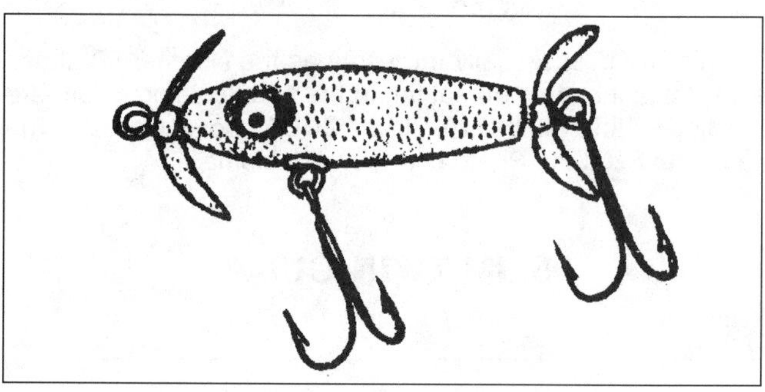

Very little information was found about this small lure. It is listed in a 1950 catalog, but no size information was given. It measures 3" and was made in the colors listed for that catalog. Collector value range: $15-$25.

BULGE EYE FROG

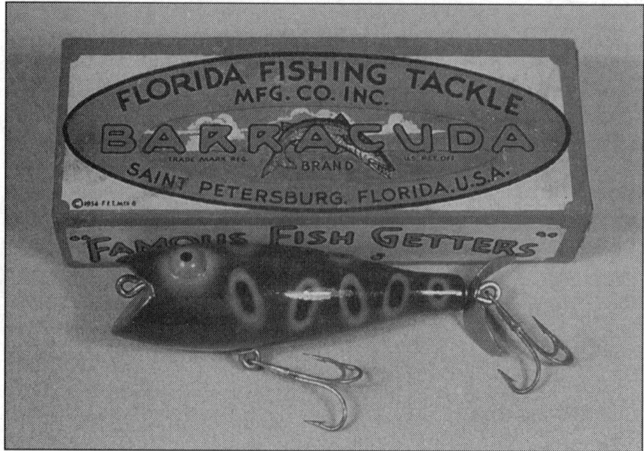

The 1950 catalog that illustrated this lure did not list any size information. All it said was that it was one of their most popular lures and that it floats. It measures 4" and was probably available in all the 1950 colors. Collector value range: $40-$75. Photo courtesy Jim Muma.

TOPPER

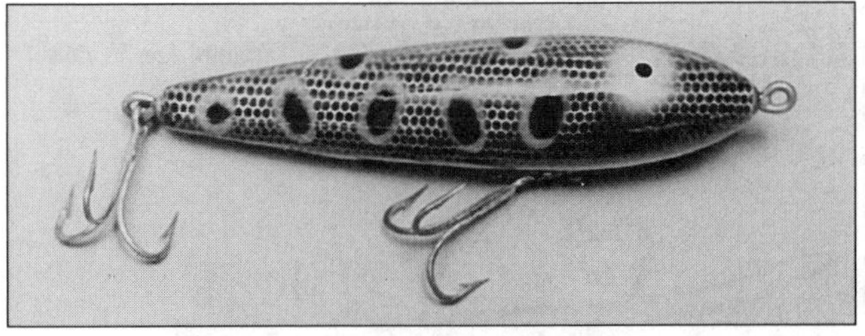

The 1950 catalog lists and illustrated this lure at 4-1/4". It is a top-water lure and has been found with an additional treble hook making it a three treble hook model. Collector value range: $10-$20.

REYHU

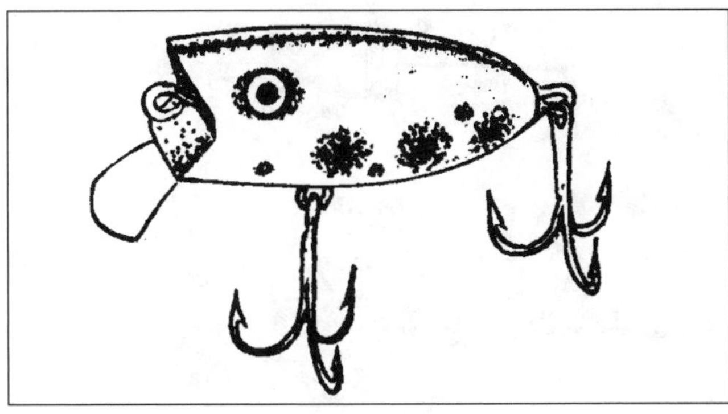

A Barracuda Brand Reyhu. A 1950s lure of the Florida Fishing Tackle Co. Little was found in available catalogs. It measures 2-1/2" and was probably available in the 1950 colors listed earlier. Collector value range: $5-$10.

KING CUDA

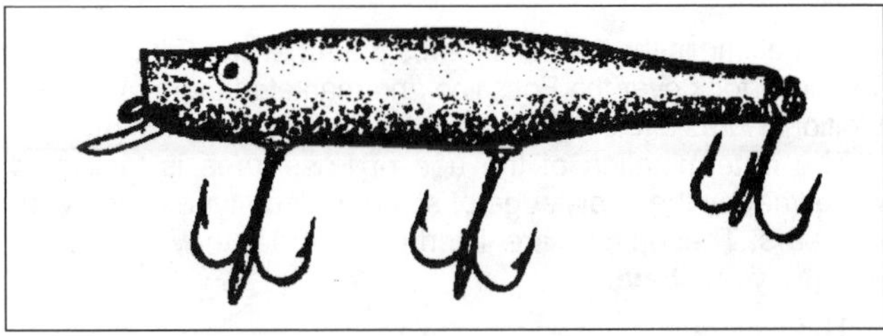

The King Cuda. A large husky lure with a strong through-body wire hook hanger/line tie. It is 6" long, weighs 1-1/2 oz. Collector value range: No trade data found.

BLOOPER

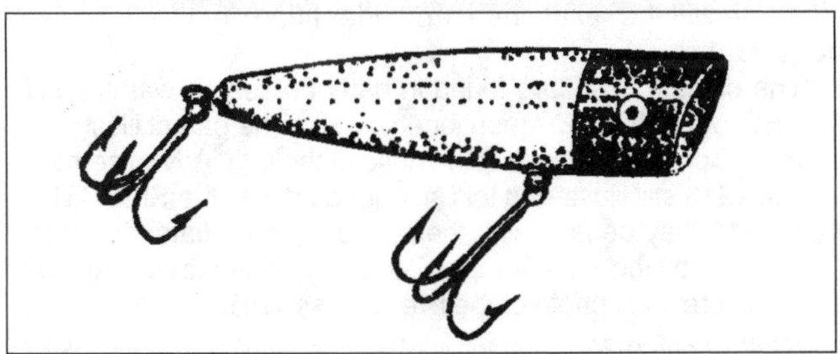

A Barracuda Brand, Florida Fishing Tackle 4-1/2" Blooper. Collector value range: No trade data found.

IMPORTANT NOTICE

The value ranges listed in this book are for lures in Very Good to Excellent condition. The values of those lures not in Very Good to Excellent condition can and probably will be worth considerably less. The values are meant to be a guide only.

FLUTTER-FIN

Worth Fishing Tackle
(The Worth Company) Stevens Point, Wisconsin

This unusual top-water lure is a 1960s-1970s plastic Worth product. Its box says it "FLUTTERS, POPS AND RIDES THE SURFACE". Worth products were primarily spinners, jigs, spoons and flies. They made the famous Anchormate reel for deploying and winding in your anchor. This lure is included because of its unusual shape and the fact it was the only lure of its kind in their catalog. It was featured in full color. The lure measures 1" in diameter, weighs 1/4 oz. and was made in the following six finishes:

- White with red scales
- Brown with yellow scales
- Orange with black scales
- Yellow with black scales
- Green with yellow scales
- Black with white scales

It was probably meant to be a cash register point of purchase, tempting the fisherman to make an impulse buy. It was patented in 1962. Collector value range: $15-$20.

AL FOSS

Cleveland, Ohio AMERICAN FORK and HOE CO.
(True Temper)
Cleveland, Ohio Geneva, Ohio

Al Foss began making his famous pork rind lures first, then was later bought out by the American Fork and Hoe Company, now known as True Temper. Al Foss was making (or at least experimenting with design) in 1915 or earlier. There is an ad in a 1916 issue of *The Outer's Book* offering the "Little Egypt Wiggler" and the "Skidder", both being all-metal pork rind type lures. The 1915 or before date is derived from the fact that although his patent was not granted until 1918, Foss applied for the patent on his "Little Egypt Wiggler" on December 29, 1915. That is the earliest date patent research has turned up so far. Please turn to Mill Run Products Company for related information.

An AL FOSS POCKET KIT. It included the tin box, any two lures, a package of pork rinds, a single hook and the pamphlet. Collector value for the intact box and all its contents is $100-$150. Photo courtesy Jim Muma.

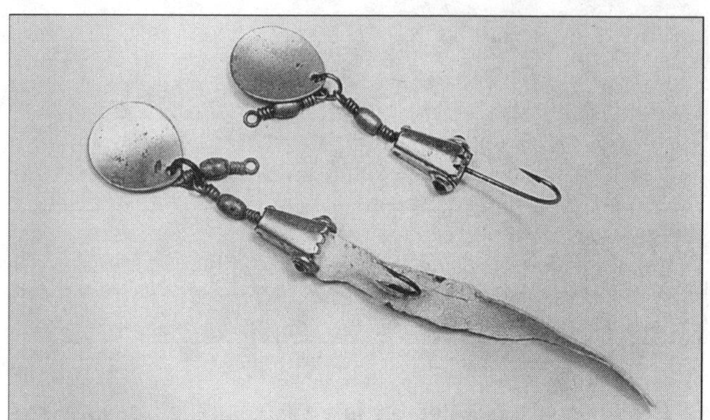

LITTLE EGYPT Earliest style, with Colorado type spinner.

Dating Al Foss lures was made a little easier than many other company lure by Foss himself. He provided some valuable data for dating on an ad page in a 1929 issue of *The Sporting Goods Dealer* whereupon he provided an illustration with lure names and dates. "AL'S PORK RIND MINNOW TREE." "A stanch-sturdy oak filled with good things for you". His listing follows:

LITTLE EGYPT - 1916

SKIDDER - 1916, retired, exact date unknown, probably c. 1918.

ORIENTAL - 1917

MUSKY ORIENTAL - 1918

SHIMMY - 1919

SHIMMYETTE - 1922

JAZZ - 1923

FROGS - 1926

DIXIE - 1928

NEW EGYPT - 1928

The patent for the now famous ORIENTAL WIGGLER was applied for on April 22, 1916 and granted to Foss two years later on April 30, 1918. The text of the original application infers that there may be some wood body "Orientals" to be found. It says, in part: "... preferably formed of wood (my emphasis), celluloid or other suitable material." No examples of a wood-body ORIENTAL WIGGLER have yet been found to my knowledge. It is not inconceivable, but is highly unlikely that the collector will ever find a genuine one made of wood. The possibility of wooden prototype designs or a patent model exists. Until about 1920 all patent applications required the inventor to supply an actual working model with the paperwork. Almost all Foss lures were designed to be used with pork rind or similar materials.

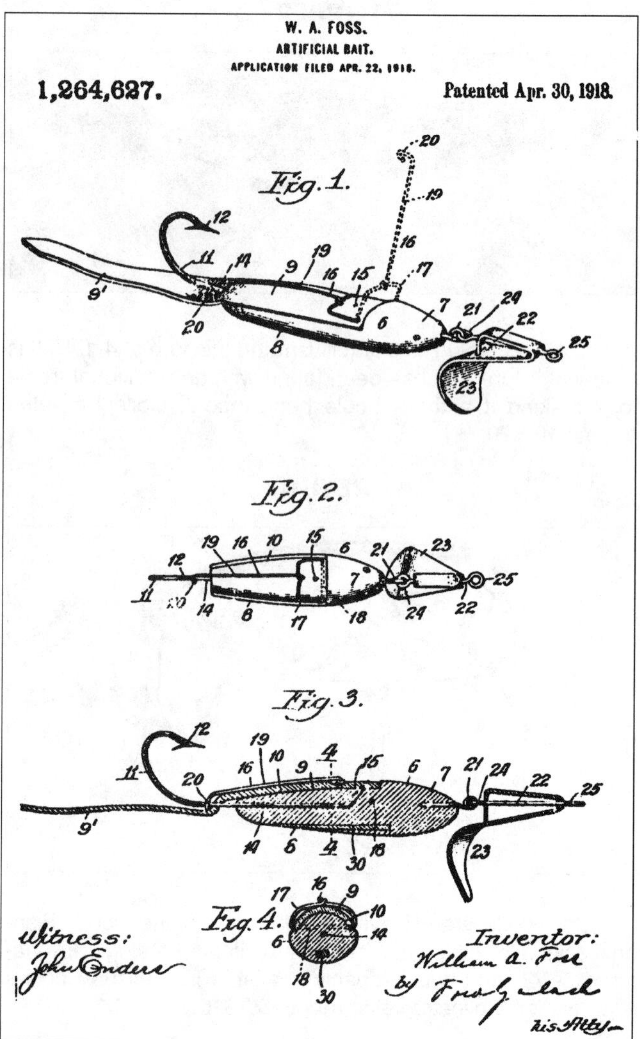

The original patent illustration for the ORIENTAL WIGGLER.

Some time in the 1930s to 1940s the American Fork and Hoe Company took over the Foss line and marketed them and a few additional lures of their own under the True Temper trademark.

The determination of the age of Foss lures is facilitated somewhat by the knowledge of spinner blade types used over the years. These types are listed in the order they were used over the years here:

The Colorado spinner

The unmarked regular spinner

The "AL FOSS" regular spinner

The Adam spinner

The "AL FOSS" regular with 1918 patent date

The Ponca 1928 spinner

They will be explained and identified in the following paragraphs.

The earliest Foss lure found in patent research was the LITTLE EGYPT WIGGLER mentioned above. The patent illustration shows a Colorado spinner at the nose of the lure. Advertisements for it in 1916 still illustrated this spinner as did all the SKIDDERS. After 1916 they began using the regular spinner (later called the "four" blade by the True Temper Company). This blade is illustrated in the previous photo of the five Al Foss WIGGLERS.

**Until about 1920 all patent applications required the inventor to supply an actual working model with the paperwork.*

Early Foss spinner blades were unmarked and then he began stamping them "AL FOSS". Later, when True Temper took over,

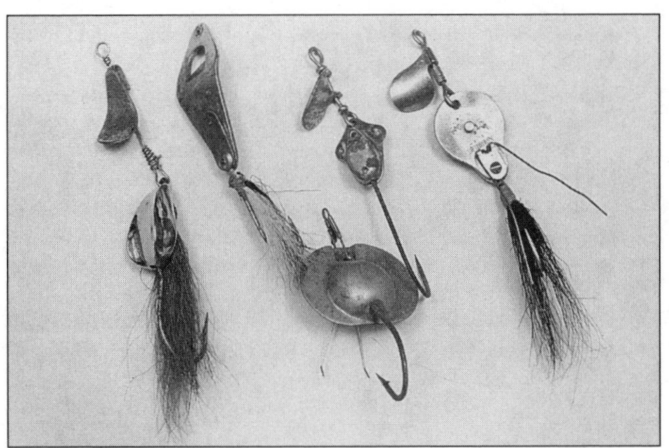

Various Al Foss Lures. Left to Right: THE SHEIK, SHIMMY SPOON, BASS POP (a True Temper product), NEW EGYPT WIGGLER, SHIMMY WIGGLER with the "Adam" type blade. Collector value range: $10-$25.

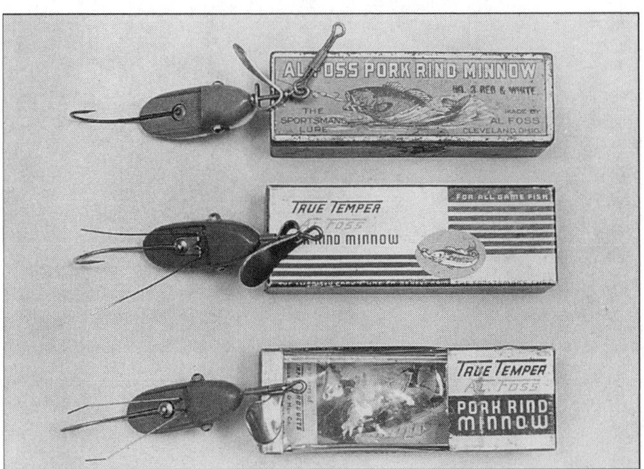

This photo shows the early 'AL FOSS' spinner blade (top), the American Fork and Hoe Company blade (center) with patent dates and the last blade (bottom) with no identification on the blade at all. Each lure is shown with its original package. Collector value range: $15-$25.

the patent dates from 1918 were added. This is true of all the Foss regular or "four" blades regardless of the type of lure on which they are used.

ORIENTAL WIGGLERS are found with unmarked regular, the "AL FOSS", the "AL FOSS" with 1918 patent dates and the "Adam" type blades. The latter can be see on the far right lure in the previous photograph.

The SHIMMY WIGGLER came out about 1919 and has been found with five blade types: The unmarked regular, the "AL FOSS" regular, the "AL FOSS" with 1918 patent dates, The "Adam", and the "Ponca 1928". The "Ponca" type spinner can be seen on the left three lures in the photo below. The Ponca blades have a 1928 patent date on them.

The JERSEY WIGGLER was new around 1923 and has so far been found with the "AL FOSS" 1918 patent date blades only.

FROG WIGGLERS became available in 1926 and as with the JERSEY WIGGLERS, have been found with the "AL FOSS" 1918 patent date blades only.

DIXIE WIGGLERS, new around 1928, can be found with the regular "AL FOSS", the "AL FOSS" 1918 patent date, the Ponca and a unique spinner that appears to be an unbalanced, two-blade Ponca spinner.

The NEW EGYPT, also out in 1928, has so far been found with the "AL FOSS" 1918 and the Ponca blades.

AL FOSS WIGGLERS. Left to Right: DIXIE WIGGLER, THE MOUSE WIGGLER, SHIMMY WIGGLER, Unidentified Wiggler. Each has the "Ponca" type blade except the far right. It appears to have a modified ponca type blade. Collector value range: $10-$25. The unidentified wiggler has now been identified. It is not a Foss product as previously thought, but is a lure called ART'S FROG made by Arthur Tuck, Tuck's Tackle Shop of Ft. Worth, Texas in the late 1940s to the early 1950s.

THE SHEIK has shown up with the "AL FOSS" 1918 and another unique spinner, this one appeared somewhat like a modified Ponca blade but with a single blade only.

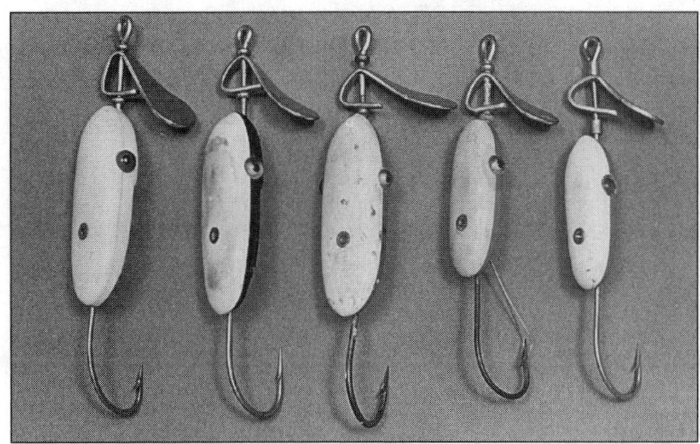

Belly view of various ORIENTAL WIGGLERS. Collector value range: $25-$35.

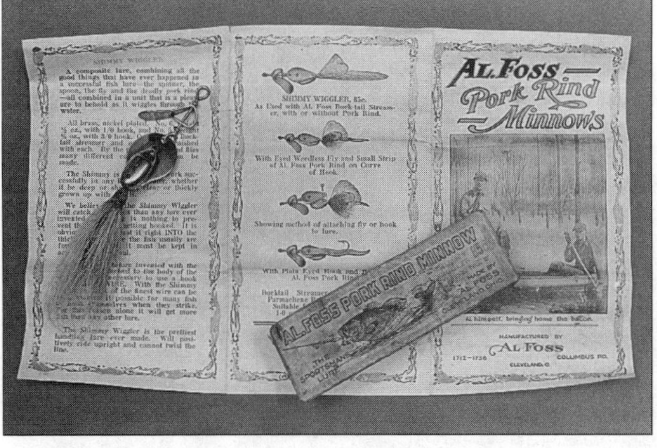

Al Foss SHIMMY No. 5 with original box and packet catalog packed with it.

The HELL CAT has been found only with this latter spinner.

The chart below provides a synopsis of much of the above spinner blade data.

	Colorado Spinner	Unmarked Regular	"AL FOSS" Regular	"AL FOSS" 1918 patent	ADAM	PONCA 1928	UNIQUE
SKIDDER	X	X		X			
LITTLE EGYPT	X	X		X			
ORIENTAL WIGGLER		X	X	X	X	X	
SHIMMY WIGGLER		X	X	X	X	X	
JAZZ WIGGLER				X			
FROG WIGGLER				X			
DIXIE WIGGLER			X	X		X	*
THE MOUSE						X	
NEW EGYPT WIGGLER				X		X	
THE SHEIK				X			**
THE HELL CAT							

**A Unique spinner appearing to be an unbalanced two-blade Ponca type.*

***Unique spinner appearing to be somewhat like a modified version of the single-blade Ponca type.*

For those of you who are or want to become more familiar with Al Foss lures there is an excellent comprehensive reference available, *AL FOSS, A History of the Company and their Lures* by Jim Frazier. You can find the address in the Recommended References section in the front of this book.

The photo here shows the evolution of boxes from earliest tin to the later cardboard. Reading top to bottom, the first four are tin boxes and the bottom two are cardboard.

FROG WIGGLERS. Left is top view, right two lures are belly view. All have the regular patent blade. Collector value range: $90-$120.

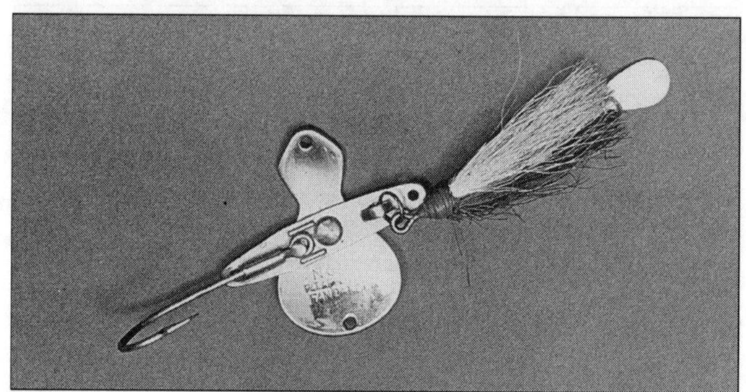

FAN DANCER ... open and closed positions.

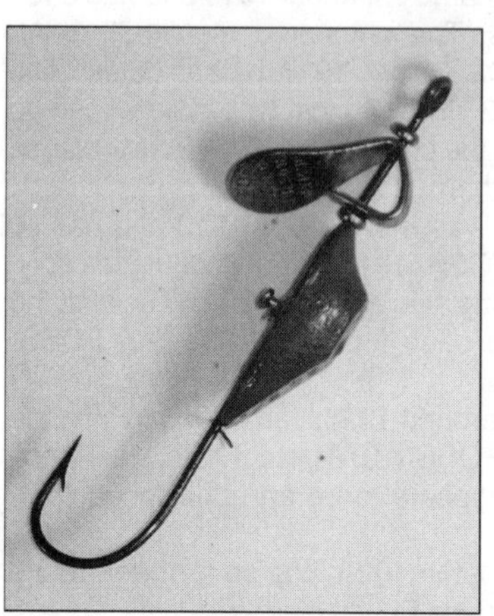

JAZZ WIGGLER. Photo courtesy Ken Bernoteit.

FOUR TEES BAIT COMPANY
1935-1953

William Robinson "Bob" Bales — Tampa, Florida

Those of you who have purchased previous editions of this book know that at the back is a section of unknown lures pictured and described in hopes someone out there can help to identify them. Over the past 20 years it has worked well. This company listing is a result of that section.

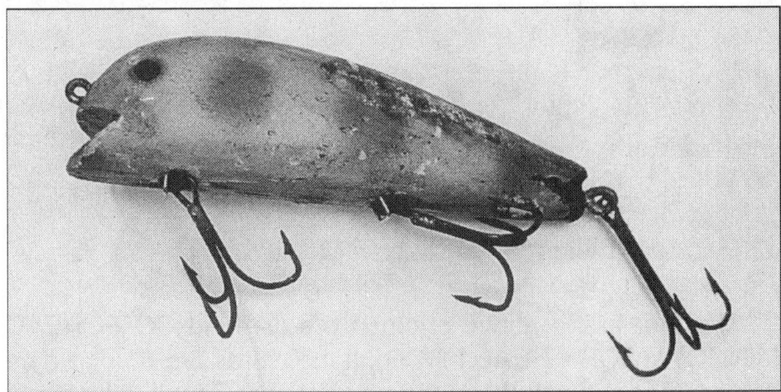

Yellow body with red spots and black stripe down the back, 3-3/4" long, painted eyes. Hook hardware is screw eye with staples mounted forward as hook restrainers. Stenciled on the belly is XXUR-TEES. The X's represent two letters that are illegible.

The above photo and caption elicited a response from the company founder's grandson, R.S. (Bob) Bales. His letter said in part "...page 441, 'UNKNOWN LURES', top left hand corner, was made by my late Grandfather, W.R. (Bob) Bales. The illegible letters are F & O in Four Tees, standing for his company name and logo 'The Topper That's Tops' each word beginning with T, thus FOUR TEES."

According to Bob Bales, in the early 1930s his grandfather, an avid fisherman, was having a bit of financial trouble and unable to afford buying lures any longer. He turned to his woodworking hobby to fashion his own. After experimentation he found a shape that satisfied him and caught fish. In fact, they worked so well and so many of his friends wanted them that he was spending all of his spare time carving and painting free lures for his friends. A fishing buddy asked why he didn't make them to sell. The short of it is he didn't have the money so his friend arranged a small loan and Four Tees was born. Starting with a scroll saw, sanding and painting supplies and equipment, Bales, with help from his wife, son and daughter-in-law, began making his first lures for sale to the public in 1935. Over the years, as the company grew more successful better equipment such as a lathe and duplicating lathe equipment was added (mid to late 1940s)

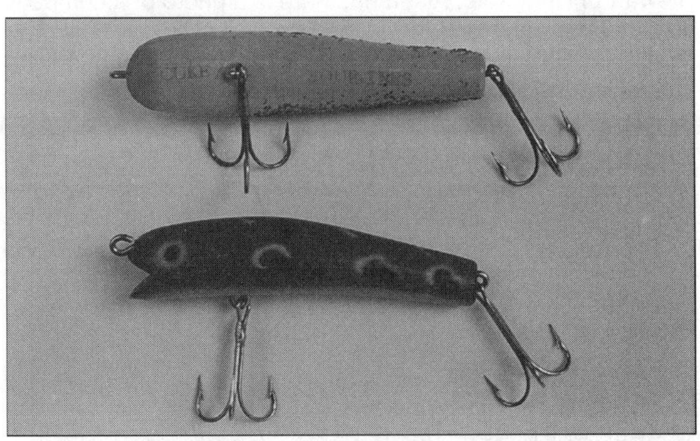

Two Four Tees CUKES measuring 3-1/2" each. Lower is the Frog finish and upper has the beige body with glitter.

The first lures, the DOLPHINS and CUKES were hand-carved and the notch mouths were located higher than the location seen on the lures in the accompanying photos. After he obtained the scroll saw he apparently made a few with this same "High mouth". They had no eyes and the hook hangers were simple recessed screw eyes. The two belly trebles on DOLPHINS had a tendency to foul with each other at first. He solved this problem by placing a staple preventer in the recesses, just forward of the screw eyes.

A Four Tees DOLPHIN in Frog finish, 3-3/4".

The next stage in production saw the lowering of the mouth position. The lures were still without eyes. The last stage lures have painted eyes and toward the end of production in the 1950s gill marks were added.

The lures were marked by stamping the undersides with "FOUR TEES" and more often than not, with the model name such as "CUKE".

The first models made were the DOLPHIN and the CUKE (short for cucumber). Then came the TORP (short for torpedo), the FROG, SHRIMP and the MINI DOLPHIN. Also made, were single-jointed and doublejointed DOLPHINS.

DOLPHIN paint finishes are almost any body color you can think of, just about all with a black back (stopping short of the head), but some with a green back and a yellow belly. A red flashed mouth is also the norm. The rarest of the colors is the green (almost black) body. There is also a frog finish and a few with a green scale finish, a brown stripe, a beige and yellow, and a glitter finish. The CUKES are mostly found with a frog, a dark green or a beige and yellow finish.

The values of these lures is affected by age of course, if you can readily determine it, and often by the color of the lure. The ranges below reflect the rarest green at the high end for the DOLPHINS, CUKES and TORPS. The others are unique or found in only one or two color finishes.

DOLPHIN	$25- $150.
MINI-DOLPHIN	*
CUKE	$25- $150.
TORP**	$15- $45.
FROG (rare)	$275-$500.
SHRIMP (rare)	$900-$1,200.

**There was insufficient trade data for a realistic determination of value in this case.*

***Usually found with an orange body and a Eger DILLINGER-style rib design.*

GABBARD TACKLE COMPANY

Detroit, Michigan

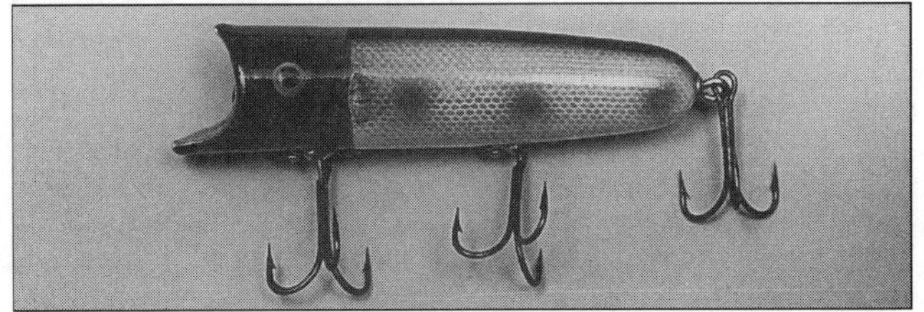

The lure in the photo was in a box that had the line "A Genuine GAB-LURE Bait" printed on it. The box end was marked "E-4". It is a 3-3/4" plastic lure from around the late 1940s. It has one-piece surface hook hardware on the bell. Collector value range: $10-$15.

THE GAMEFISH LURE
THE MYSTERY LURE

Seal Tackle Company — Union Lake, Michigan
Lakeland Products — Detroit, Michigan

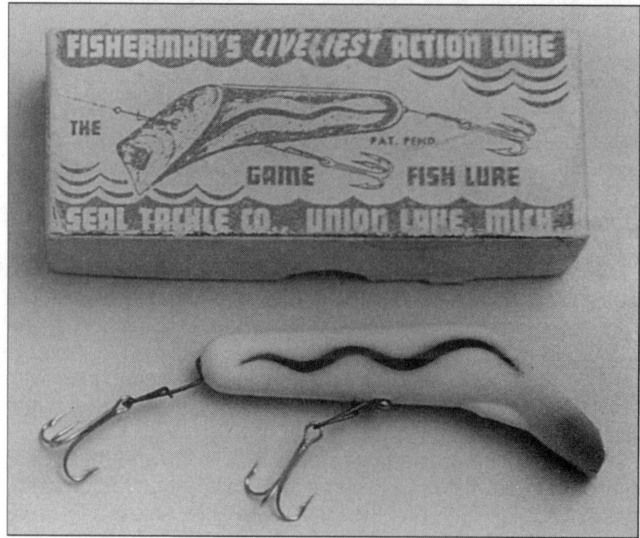

This plastic lure was marketed under two different names in the late 1940s by the Seal Tackle Company. It was also sold under the Lakeland Products label in the 1950s. Why the two names? It's anybody's guess. It could be that the MYSTERY LURE moniker was a bright idea to promote the bait; perhaps thought more catching than GAMEFISH LURE. There is no known connection between the companies beyond the likelihood of the Lakeland Products company assuming control through a business deal.

The bait was made in four sizes: 2", 2-1/2", 3", 3-1/2". There were six finishes: Orange, Frog (yellow and green with black stripe), White, Yellow, White with red head, Yellow with red head. Collector value range: $10-$15.

TWIN DANCER

Gardner Specialty Company — Gardner, Massachusetts

This lure was placed under the Arbogast listing in the first edition of this book because of its extreme similarity to Arbogast lures. It was otherwise unidentified. Little is yet known about the Gardner Specialty Company, but thanks to one of the many helpful collectors who have written me regarding previous editions we have the lure properly identified. The lure was likely made in the 1950s and is 3" long and the nose blade rotates to make it a surface or diving plug. Collector value range: $10-$20.

GARLAND BAITS

Plant City, Florida

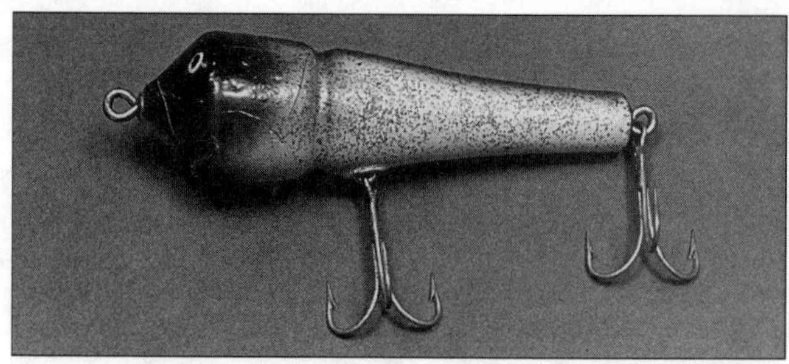

The lure in the above photo is the Garland CORK HEAD MINNOW (CORK HEAD FROG). It measures 3-5/8" long. The body is made of wood and the head of cork. The line tie has a very long shank screw eye passing through a small diameter armature (part of the body) around which the cork head is secured and into the main part of the wood body.

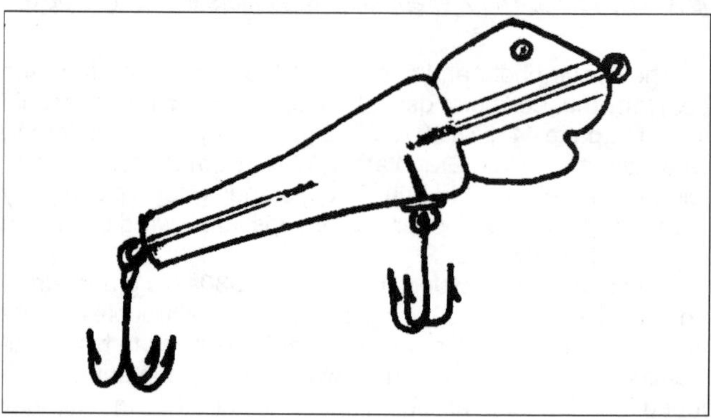

Garland lures were made from 1934 to 1940. A lure box pamphlet listed the available finishes as "Light Green Frog Finish, Dark Green Frog Finish, Green Silver Splash, and Red Silver Splash." Interestingly the pamphlet and box called the above lure the CORKHEAD MINNOW. A 1939 ad lists the following finishes: Green head with frog spots; Green head with silver sides; White with red head; White with red, yellow and green spots. This ad also called the lure CORK-HEAD MINNOW.

In an interesting article in the March 1987 issue of The *N.F.L.C.C. Gazette,* the club newsletter, by member Frank Stewart of Huntsville, Alabama, there is a photo of a company display board showing the same lure and calling it "THE FAMOUS CORK HEAD FROG." The board shows 11 other lures in the Garland line. The entire list follows:

CORK HEAD FROG
DOCK MODEL
CRIPPLE MINNOW
BABY CRIPPLE
THE ZIG ZAG
BABY ZIG ZAG
SUBMARINE
BABY SUBMARINE
SEA BITCH
SEA TROUT SPECIAL
SEA SERGEANT
FLORIDA FROG

Though the lures are small in the picture, you could probably make out enough for identification if you had a copy of the newsletter. Perhaps by the time the next edition is released I will have photos of the rest of the Garland lures. Collector value range for the CORK HEAD FROG: $90-$170.

GEORGE W. GAYLE & SON REELWORKS

Frankfort, Kentucky

Primarily reel makers George Gayle and his son, Clarence Gayle also produced a small line of wooden lures in the 1930s and possibly into the early 1940s.

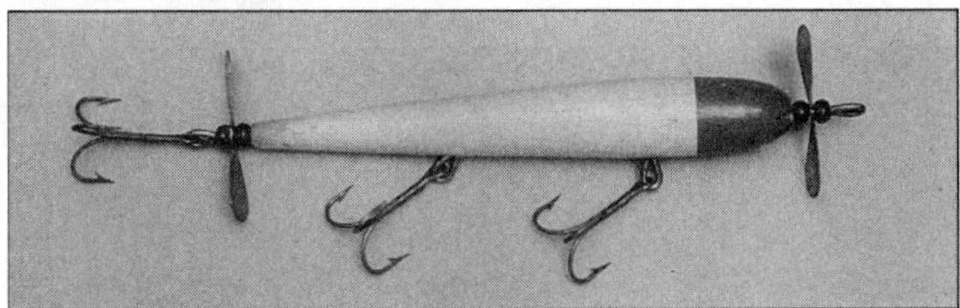

The long slim lure pictured here is a Gayle KENTUCKY STEELBACK. It is approximately 6" long and has two bead bearings at each end. Collector value range: $50-75.

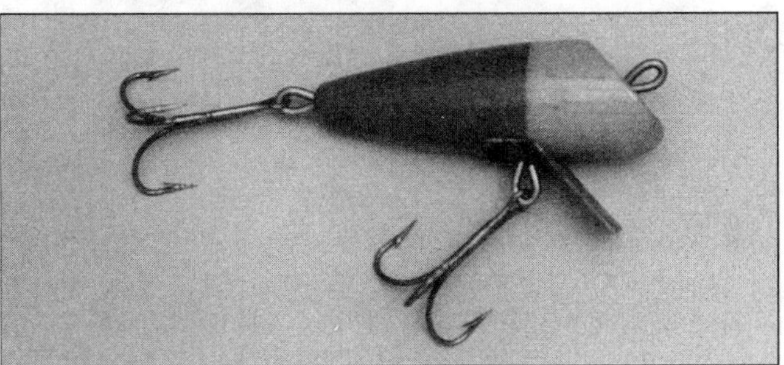

The other lure pictured here appears to be a modification of the Gayle SHORTY. It is about 3-1/4" long and has the same shape as the lure, but the problem is that the SHORTY is assembled with the line tie at the small end and the broad end is not cut off at an angle as the one in the photo is. I am fairly sure the one in this picture is a Gayle product. Collector value range: $40-$60.

GEN-SHAW BAIT COMPANY

Kankakee, Illinois

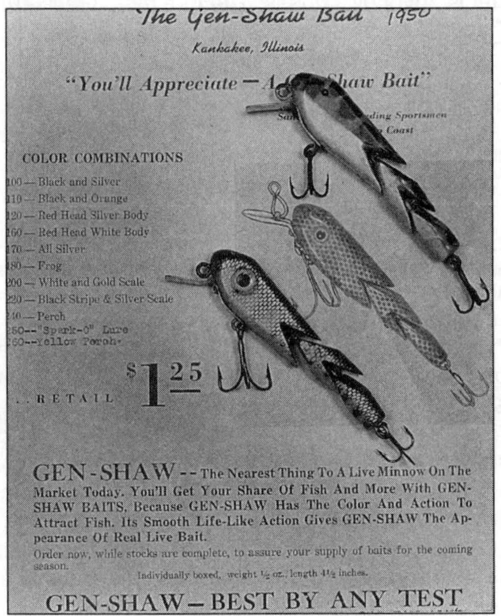

It was reported in a previous edition that the company apparently made only one lure. It is now known that they produced at least two. The WIGGLE-LURE and the L & G LURE. The photo of the two WIGGLE-LURES on 1950 catalog page are undoubtedly the same as the lure illustrated on the catalog page, but with a couple of small differences. Note the different line ties, eye size and diving lips.

WIGGLE-LURE

This is a triple jointed lure of plastic, 4-1/2" long*. Note that it is the same as the lure illustrated in the advertisement above including the one-piece surface hook hanger integrated with the diving lip. The lure in the photo is in mint condition with the original box.

It is now known that the lure was also made of wood. To my knowledge at least two have been found. The hook hardware is the simple screw eye. The eyes are very large as in the lower lure in the photo of two. The wood lure is otherwise identical to the plastic examples. A 1949 advertisement was found that stated clearly the lure was made of plastic. All that can be assumed now is that the wood most likely preceded the plastic version. Collector value range for plastic: $10-$20, for wood: $20-$30.

COLOR OR FINISH: Black and silver, black and orange, red head and silver body, red head and white body, all silver color, frog, white with gold scale, black stripe and silver scale, perch, "spark-o" lure, yellow perch.

The only reference to size found says the lure is 4-1/2". The lure in the photo measures 3-1/2". Therefore there may be two sizes to be found.

THE "L & G" LURE

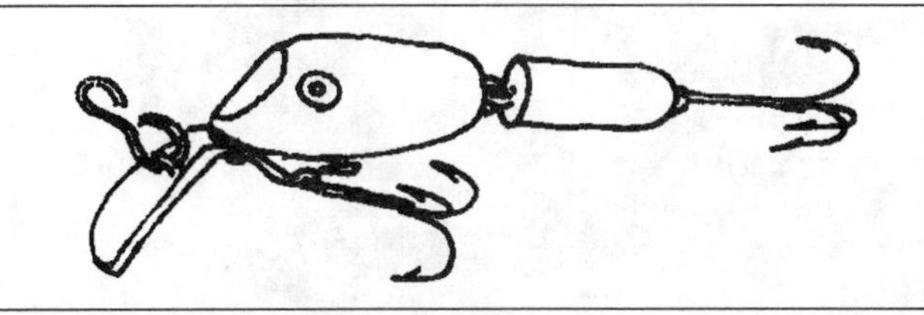

This 3-5/8" plastic lure from Gen-Shaw showed up in a 1953 catalog from General Merchandise Company, Milwaukee, Wisconsin. It is a single-jointed lure with the same hardware as on the WIGGLE-LURE. It was made in the following colors: Red head, black and orange, green sparkle, gold scale. Collector value range: $10-$15.

IMPORTANT NOTICE

The value ranges listed in this book are for lures in Very Good to Excellent condition. The values of those lures not in Very Good to Excellent condition can and probably will be worth considerably less. The values are meant to be a guide only.

GEE WIZ
GEE WIZ ACTION FROG

All Star Bait Company — Chicago, Illinois

Gee Wiz Bait Company — Richland Center, Wisconsin

Another of the many attempts at creating an animated frog. It has one single hook mounted on the belly with the barb pointed up between the legs. This probably made it pretty effective at being weedless.

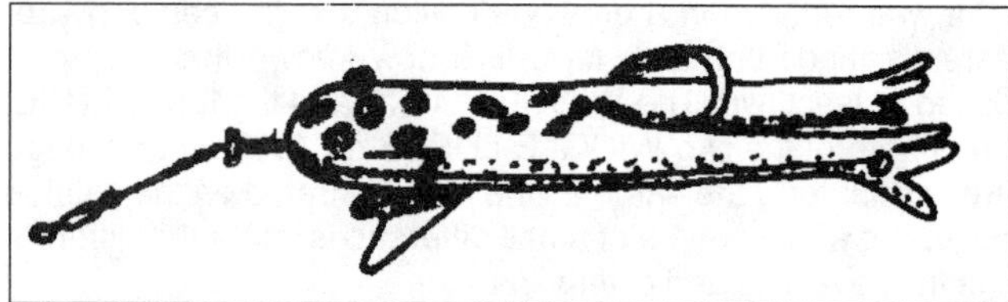

The origin of the lure is a bit confusing. There were two advertisements found by two different companies located in two different states. The first was the All Star company in 1931. The other was the Gee Wiz ad in 1949. Perhaps the company was sold to Gee Wiz. Anybody's guess is good until we learn more. The lures appear to be identical. The 1931 ad stated it was available in two sizes, but did not specify. It also said they were made in three finishes: "Red and White," "Musky size, Natural Green," and "In Natural Green". The 1949 Gee Wiz ad listed no colors and stated the lure was available in only one size, 4-1/2". Collector value range: $50-$100.

MAGNETIC WEEDLESS

General Tool Company St. Paul, Minnesota

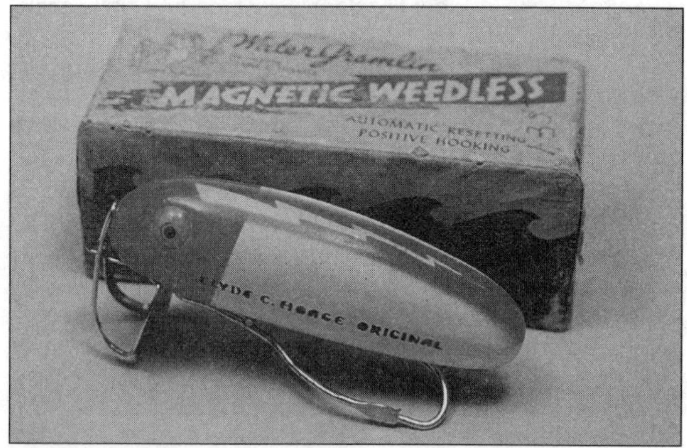

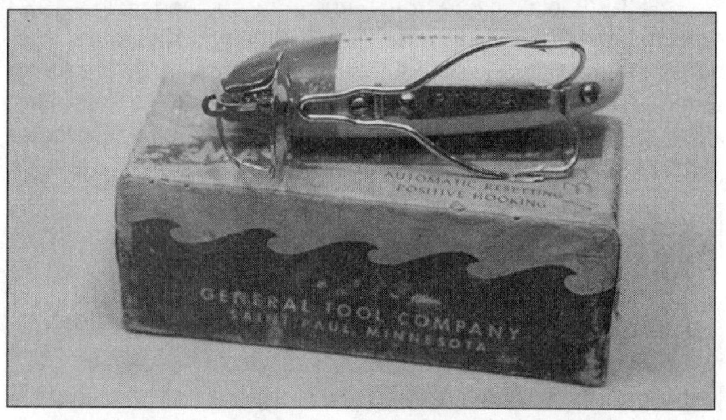

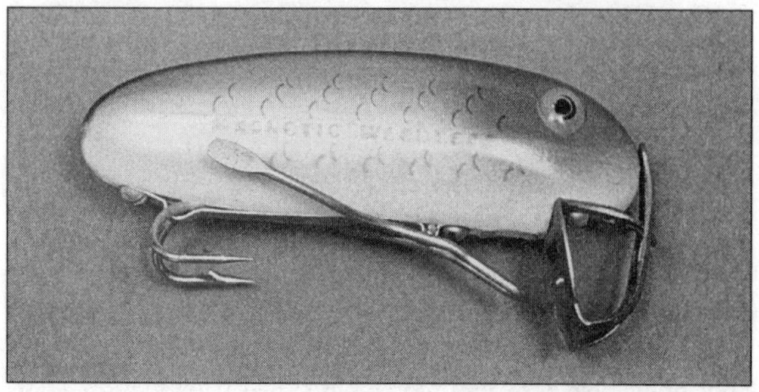

This view shows the weed guard in the open (after a fish strikes) position.

They are well identified on the body most of the time, with the inventor's name. Clyde C. Hoage applied for the patent in 1946 and it was granted January 25, 1949. As you can see by the pictures Mr. Hoage must have been proud of his lure although the lures are also found with only the name of the lure, without his name. It has a unique weed guard utilizing a magnet in the body that holds the guard out (weedless position) until a fish strikes it. It was available in four color combinations. Collector value range: $15-$20.

THE GERE BAIT COMPANY

Harry G. Gere New York, New York

This lure, the GERE FEATHERBAIT BASS LURE, would ordinarily go in the unknown section, but we do know a little about it. The photo above was provided by collector Craig Surdy. He also provided photocopies of the pamphlet included in the box. We are therefore able to provide the name and city of the maker and a patent date of June 15, 1926. I couldn't find any further reference to it in any of my research material.

The box pamphlet stated it was available in four colors, #1 - Brown for use on regular or bright days; #2 Yellow, for use when #1 fails; #3 - White, for very dark days or night fishing or when #1 fails; #4 - Brown for use the same as #1. Why the #1 and #4 are both brown and recommended as a substitute for each other is anybody's guess. The lure measures 1-1/2" long and 3/4" wide in the middle. The left one in the photo is yellow and the other, white. At this point there is insufficient data to establish a realistic collector value.

GETS-EM

Keller Rochester, Indiana

For years now, this particular plug has been grouped in with an assortment of lures all under the name Myers and Spellman. These lures were bunched together under that name because of their similarity in design, hardware and paint. They all resembled each other, but they never seemed quite close enough to me. It was a matter of convenience for there was really no other way to classify them. At best it was thought they were related. Now some of this confusion has been sorted out (see Myers and Spellman and Jacob Hansen). We now know that the lures with KELLER stamped on the back were made by a Keller in Rochester, Indiana. We have a couple more we believe to be Keller products also. Little else is known presently, but there are folks digging around in the area. Perhaps we will know more soon.

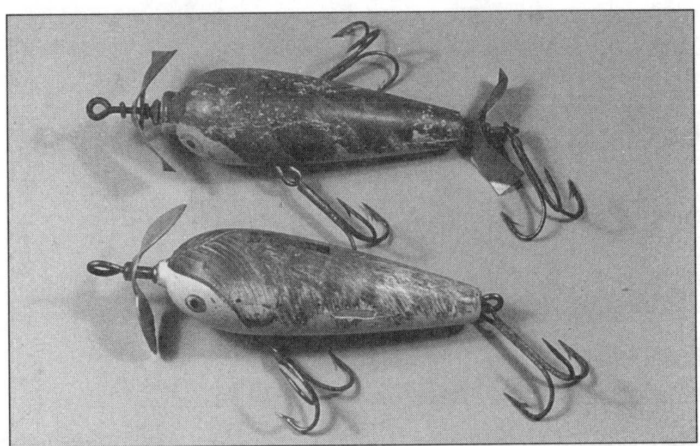

The photo above is of a Keller GETS-EM at the top and a Myers at the bottom for comparison. Note the much larger knob at the nose of the Keller plug and its soldered, reinforced propeller spinners. It also has KELLER stamped along its back in all capital letters. Its side hooks are fastened by utilizing a through-body twisted wire hanger. Collector value range: $200-$300.

Both of these Keller GETS-EMS are 3-1/4", have metal nose caps (note different types) at the knobs, tail washers, through-body twisted wire, painted eyes. Upper is blue/white, lower is orange.

The two lures in this photo are attributed to Keller because they have the same shape, same hardware and the fact that one just like the upper one in the picture has been found bearing a KELLER back stamp. The red paint at the tail end was added by a fisherman. The smaller treble hook wired near the tail end of the lower lure appears to have been added by a fisherman also. Both are 3-1/2" and have metal nose and tail protectors usually found painted over, but could be loosened with use. Collector value range: $200-$300.

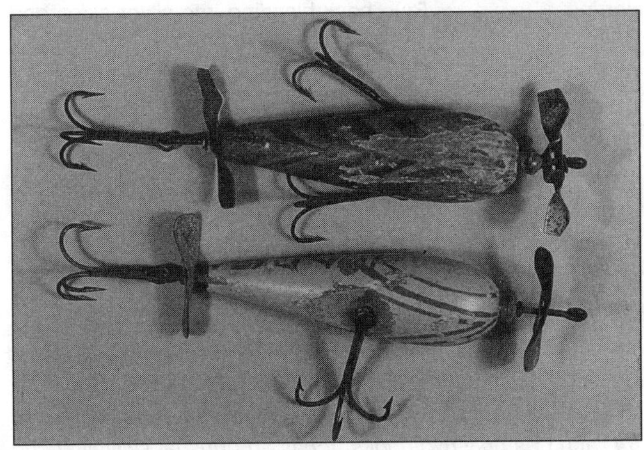

Some collectors attribute these two lures to Keller, others to Myers and some to neither. They are here because there is really no other place to put them. As you see, the confusion goes on. They are essentially the same except the hook arrangement and hanging method of the body. They have the same shape as the Keller GETS-EM and the similar Myers, but the propeller spinners are more like those used on the Keller lures. Both measure 3-1/8" and have the through-body twisted wire arrangement. Collector value range: $180-$220.

STAN GIBBS LURES

Old Plymouth Road — Buzzard's Bay, Massachusetts

Gibbs began making his lures in about 1947 after the end of WW II. His son took over the company in the 1970s and sold it about 10 years later. The Gibbs lures that collector are interested in are those he made from 1947 to the early 1960s. They are strongly rigged with through-body hardware. Some have a swiveling hook arrangement. The larger models have decal eyes. All that could be found cataloged and/or described are listed below. Photographs with this section provided by Ken Bernoteit except where noted. Collector value range: $20-$75.

COLOR OR FINISHES

Blue	Blue back blending into white belly, red face
White	All white w/ silver sparkle, blue eye spot & red face
Squid	Squid brown back blending into white belly, red face
Silver-eel	Green back blending into silver belly, red face

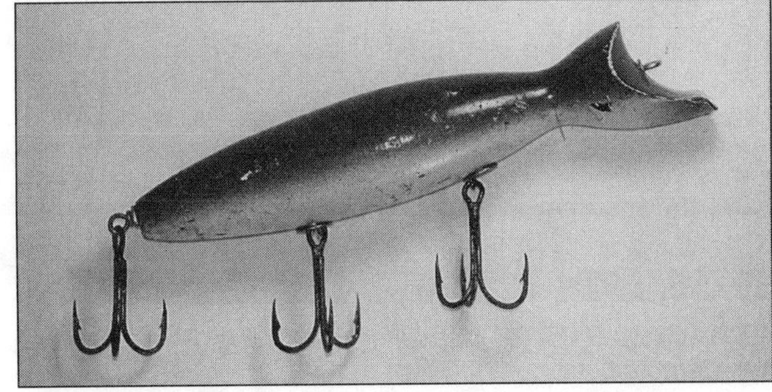

A Stan Gibbs three hook CASTING SWIMMER measuring 7-1/4" long. Photo courtesy Ken Bernoteit.

Mackerel	Iridescent green back with black mackerel markings on back blending into silver and white. Sparkle added.

Herring	Blue back blending into silver sides and white belly. Scale finish
Whiting	Squid-brown back blending into silver sides and white belly. Scale finish
Fluorescent orange	Solid color fluorescent orange

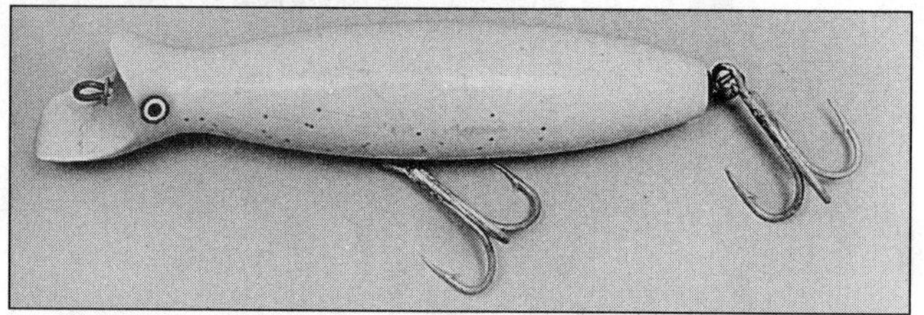

Another Gibbs CASTING SWIMMER. This one measures 6-1/4" and has only two hooks. It has an unusual swiveling cup and screw eye belly hook hanger.

CASTING SWIMMER Sizes

3"	5/8 oz.
5-1/4"	1 oz.
6-1/4"	2 oz.
7-1/4"	3 oz.

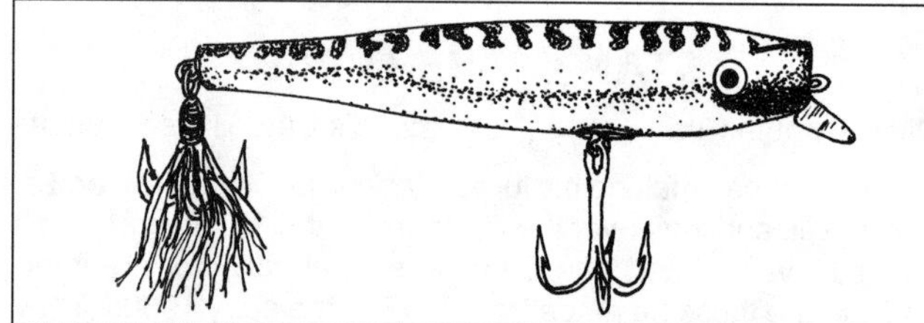

A drawing of the Gibbs TROLLING SWIMMER. There are two versions of this lure. One has a flattened nose as here. The other style has a pointed nose.

TROLLING SWIMMER Sizes

3-3/4"	7/8 OZ.
5-3/4"	1-1/2 oz.
6-1/2"	2 oz.
8"	3 oz.
10"	?

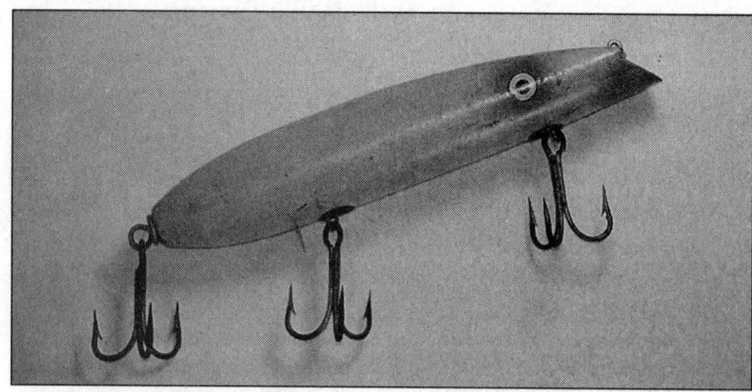

A Stan Gibbs DARTER measuring 6-1/2" long. Photo courtesy Ken Bernoteit.

DARTER Sizes

3-1/2"	1/2 oz (discontinued in the late 1960s)
4-1/4"	1 oz.
4-3/4"	1-5/8 oz.
6-1/2"	2-1/2 oz

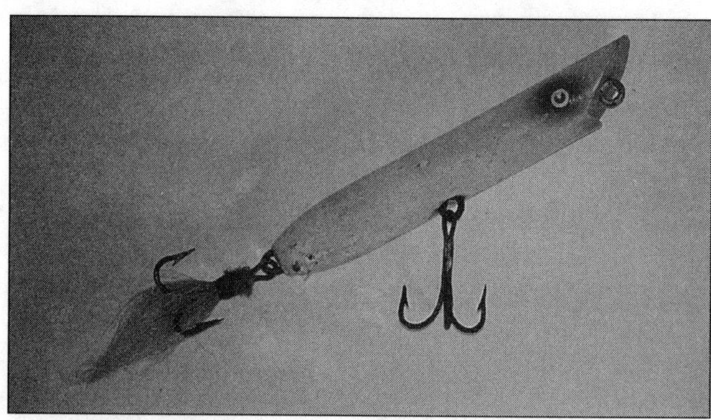

Stan Gibbs POPPER measuring 4-1/2" long. Photo courtesy Ken Bernoteit.

POPPER Sizes

3-5/8"	5/8 oz.
3-7/8"	1 oz.
4-1/2"	1-1/4 oz.
5"	1-1/2 oz.
5-1/4"	2 oz.
5-3/4"	2-1/2 oz.
6-3/4"	3 oz.

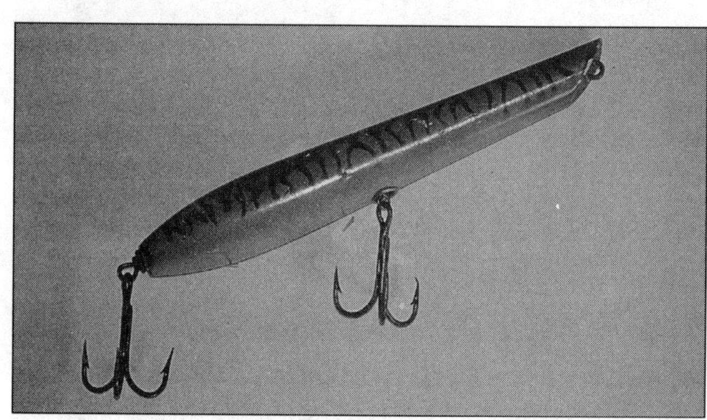

A 6-3/4" Stan Gibbs PENCIL POPPER in Mackerel finish. Photo courtesy Ken Bernoteit.

PENCIL POPPER

4-3/8"	1/2 oz.
5-1/8"	3/4 oz.
6"	1-1/8 oz.
6-3/16"	1-1/2 oz.
6-3/4"	2 oz.
7-1/2"	2-3/4 oz.

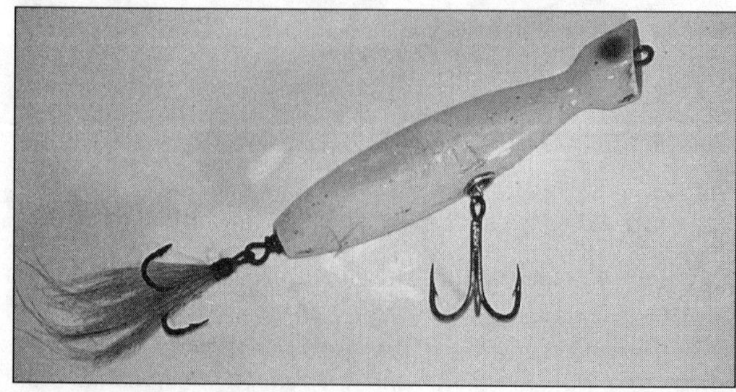

A Stan Gibbs POLARIS measuring 4-1/2" long. Photo courtesy Ken Bernoteit.

POLARIS Sizes

3-5/8"	1 oz.
4-1/2"	1-1/2 oz.
5-3/8"	2-1/4 oz
6-3/8"	3-1/2 oz.

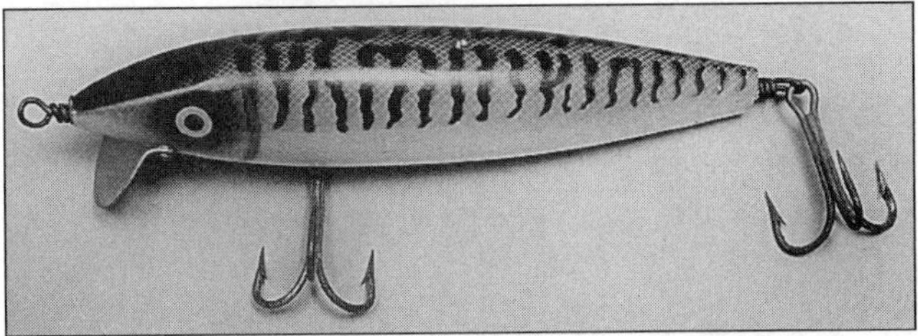

A Stan Gibbs POINT JUDE CUTLASS. This wooden body lure is very light for its size. It measures 6-1/4", has cup and screw eye hook hangers. The line tie/tail hook hanger is the strong, integrated through-body twisted wire type. It has a beautifully rendered mackerel finish.

GLOWURM

Oliver and Gruber
James Gruber

Alfred Oliver
Medical Lake, Washington

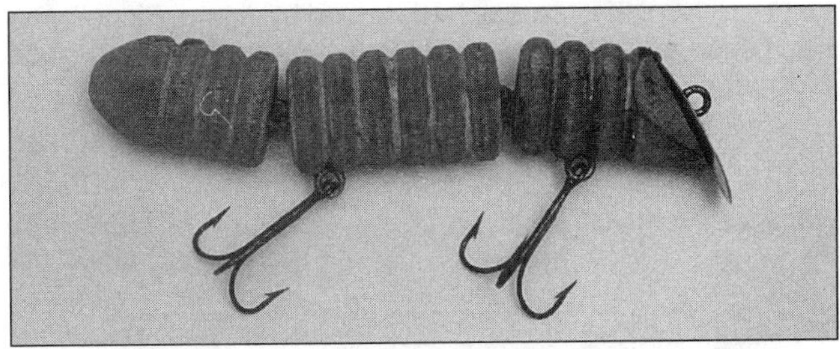

Advertisements for this 4-1/4" lure began to appear in the early 1920s. One ad contained a 1920 patent date. It was made in red and white stripes or yellow and green stripes. The one in the photo here has very little paint left on it. The lure is double jointed with three body sections. The head has a metal plate protruding slightly below forming a diving lip. The original box was very interesting. It was a long block of wood drilled out and cut in half longitudinally to accommodate the lure. It had slots in the bottom section to make room for the protruding third hook of trebles.

The lures were only made for a short time. Oliver and Gruber were employed by a home/hospital for the retarded in Medical lake. They devised this simple lure for therapy. The patients made and painted the lures for a couple of years. Apparently the folks who ran the hospital took a dim view of this enterprise because Oliver and Gruber were making money and none was going to the hospital. The ultimatum was given: The lure goes or you go. The Glowurm was dead in 1923. Collector value range: $125-$160.

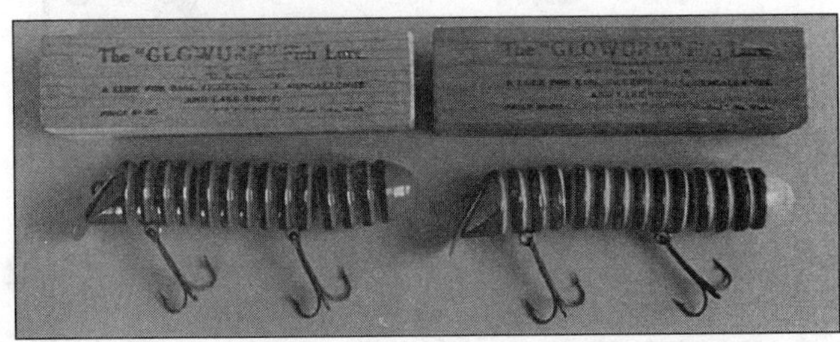

Two new GLOWURMS with their unique boxes. Photo courtesy Jim Muma.

GLUTTON DIBBLER

Clyde E. Key

Arkadelphia, Arkansas

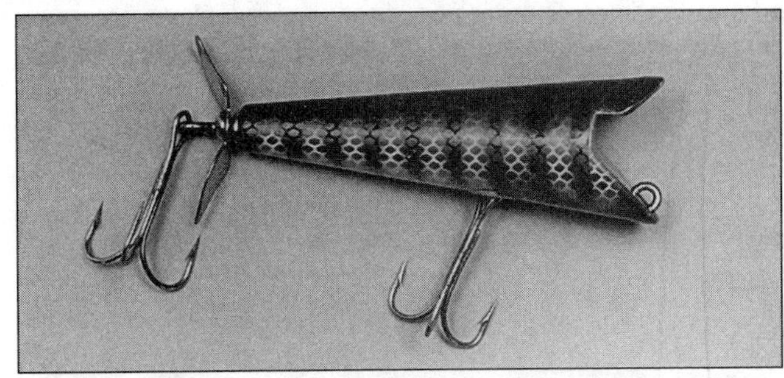

This lure was born in the late 1940s. Clyde E. Key first carved the lure himself, but as the familiar story goes, it was such a successful fish-getter, he decided to have them manufactured. He patented the lure in 1950 and contracted a company in Michigan to make them for him. They were 3" long, made of cedar and available in six finishes: Yellow, frog, black, perch, white, pike.

There were 24,000 of them made. They must not have sold as well as he thought they would for the story is that he ended up giving more of them away than he sold. Collector value range: $25-$40.

GOBLE BAIT

Bert G. Goble

Tulsa, Oklahoma

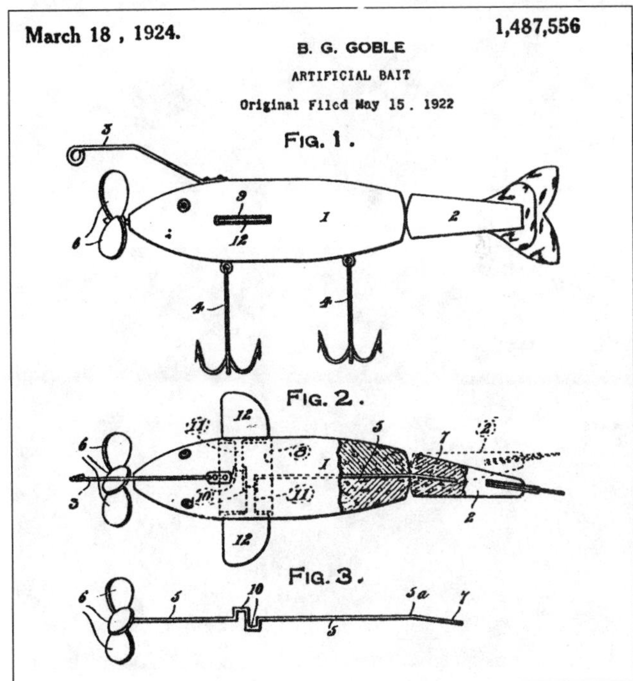

A patent illustration of a lure design filed in 1922 and granted to Goble in 1924.

Very little is known about this particular lure or its maker. A search turned up patents for two lures by Bert Goble neither of which bears any resemblance to this one. The applications were filed in 1922 and 1924 and granted to Goble in 1924 and 1929. No examples of either have been uncovered as yet. The lure in the drawing here is handsome and well made. It is very sturdily built and measures 5-1/2" long. It has cup and screw eye hardware and clear glass eyes with yellow irises. The yellow scale finish is nicely done. The remaining paint has been careful sprayed and the pectoral fins are brush painted. The metal diving lip is somewhat bell shaped, held in place by a screw and the screw eye line tie. The box says "patents granted and pending". There is no indication of model name or number. Collector value range: $150-$300.

Photo courtesy of John W. Thomas.

THE GO-GETTER

Hayes Bait Company — Indianapolis, Indiana
John J. Hildebrandt Company — Logansport, Indiana

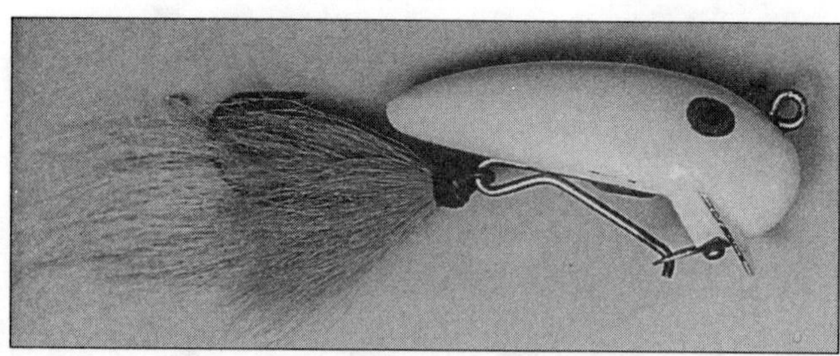

Sometimes known as the HILDEBRANT WOOD BAIT in the literature this lure was manufactured by The Hayes Bait Company and distributed by Hildebrandt, a company known widely for its metal spinners and other metal lures. Why they took on this one rather odd wooden lure is anybody's guess until more is learned. If you are lucky enough to find one in a box it may be in its original box. Others have been found in the same box with Hildebrandt labels pasted on. The lures date around 1927-30 as best as can be determined presently. There is a provision for easily removing and replacing hooks at will. It measures 2-5/8" and has painted eyes. All so far found have been painted white. Collector value range: $100-$200.

GOOD LUCK LURES

Good Luck Enterprises — Jackson, Mississippi

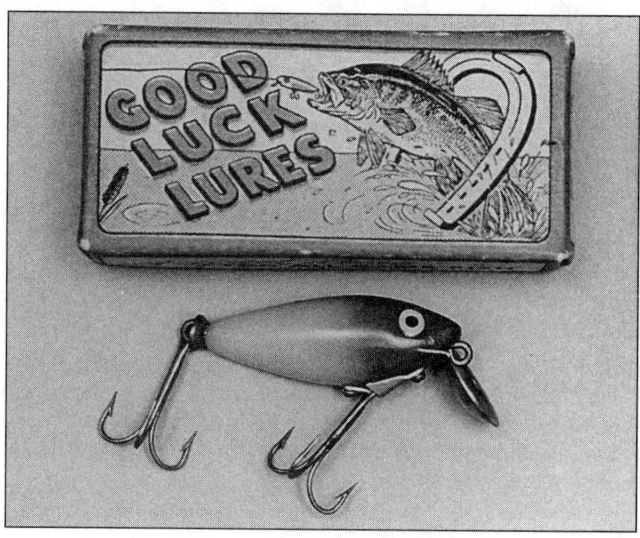

A well-made plastic lure. It has a white body and red head, measures 2-1/4" and is quite heavy. Little is known about the Good Luck Company or its products beyond what is printed on the box. It says the lure was "...designed by Jimmy Riddell, veteran fisherman". Riddell is said to also have made pretty good duck calls. Collector value range: $5-$10.

GOO GOO EYES

Stamford Products Ltd.
C. Cooper, Inc.
Stamford, Connecticut

This is a wooden lure with big, bulging plastic eyes. The advertisement said it came in 12 different sizes from ompanying measures 4-1/2". The ad said you could buy a 6" size for $2. For some unknown reason the box said the lure was from the Cooper Company listed above. There was no mention of colors either place. Collector value range: $10-$15.

THE GOPHER

Elmer J. Deuster — Milwaukee, Wisconsin
Gopher Baits — Sheboygan, Wisconsin

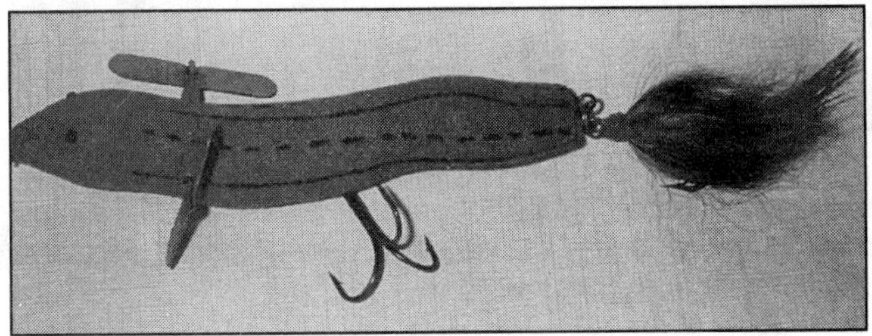

This big (5-3/4") funky-looking lure was originally available in a brown, black, gray or yellow flocked finish. Sometime in the last 10 years red was added to the choices. It is a musky or pike lure built quite strongly with an under belly wire comprising the line tie, the belly hook hanger and the bucktail hook at the tail. There are two metal paddle wheels, one at either side. An older box indicated that Mr. Deuster was the inventor, manufacturer and distributor. A later box has only the Gopher Baits name, but says "...All thanks go to E.J. Deuster, Milwaukee Inventor...". The address on that later box includes a Zip Code so one could presume that if they are not still in business they did last at least until the advent of the Zip Code in 1963. Photo courtesy Jim Muma. Collector value range: $30-$40.

EARL PARKER GRESH 1896-1977

St. Petersburg, Florida

It isn't likely that you will come across many of Earl Gresh's lures very far away from St. Pete. All his lures were hand-made by him alone. He is a legendary figure around the St. Petersburg area. He was a true artist in wood. He built his home with his own hands during the Great Depression, making it a showplace in English cottage style. There he also established his shop, The Wood Parade, where he pursued his passion for woodworking.

Among his many talents were violinist, orchestra leader (many recordings with Columbia Records), boat builder and racer, avid conservationist with much recognition, and fisherman. With a flair for fly tying, he made more than one for President Herbert Hoover, with whom he often fished. He also presented Hoover with a custom-made wooden tackle box. Mamie Eisenhower saw this box and asked Gresh if he would make one for Ike, which he did. He was invited to dine at the White House as a result.

What we are interested in here are his lures. There is no accurate estimate as to how many he might have made, but the number must be fairly limited due to the fact that they were all hand-made. Perhaps in the hundreds, perhaps more. The lures are the highest quality, professional products. They were usually put up in sets in beautiful wooden boxes. He gave a few to friends and sold the rest. He must have made a number of sets of six (see above photo) for he went to the trouble to have a set of instructions printed laying out the time and conditions under which to use the lures, providing one with each set. The lures are easily identified as made by him because he stamped each one with his name somewhere on the underside of the lure (see accompanying photos).

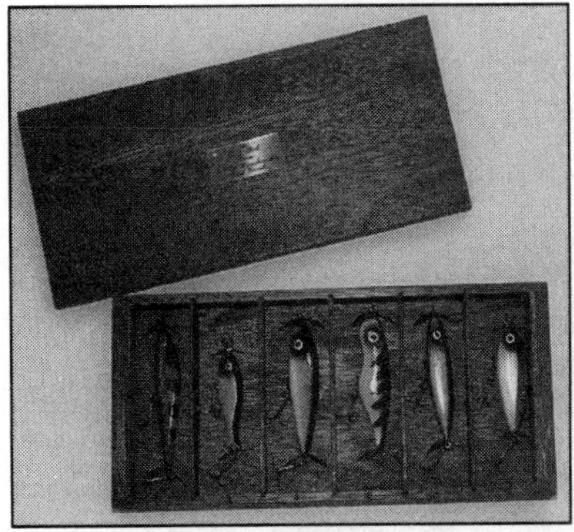

Box of six Gresh lures. The brass plate on top is inscribed "To (name) From the Old Woodworker, Earl Gresh." It apparently was a gift.

Presently it would probably not be fair to place a collector value on any of Gresh's lures due to his relative anonymity among collectors outside the Tampa/St. Pete area, but I suspect this will change. I can, however, report that the large wooden box full of his lures in the photo at right sold for $450 at auction a few years ago. I doubt that figure would touch it now.

WATER COVERAGE

WATER COVERAGE

☆ ☆ ☆ ☆

The lures in this mahogany bait box are designed to meet weather and water conditions. If the angler using these plugs will follow the numbers and directions he will obtain a maximum of results. Each of the lures has been carefully tested as to balance and usage conditions with coloration to meet outlined specifications.

No. 1 - Medium deep - - for dark days.
No. 2 - Deep sinking - - bright day fishing.
No. 3 - Slow sinking - for shoreline fishing around grass.
No. 4 - Top water - for dark days.
No. 5 - Bright day - top water, fish slowly.
No. 6 - Late evening lure - agitate by working rod tip.

Earl Gresh
The Wood Parade
St. Petersburg, Florida

This set of instructions was included in each boxed set of six lures.

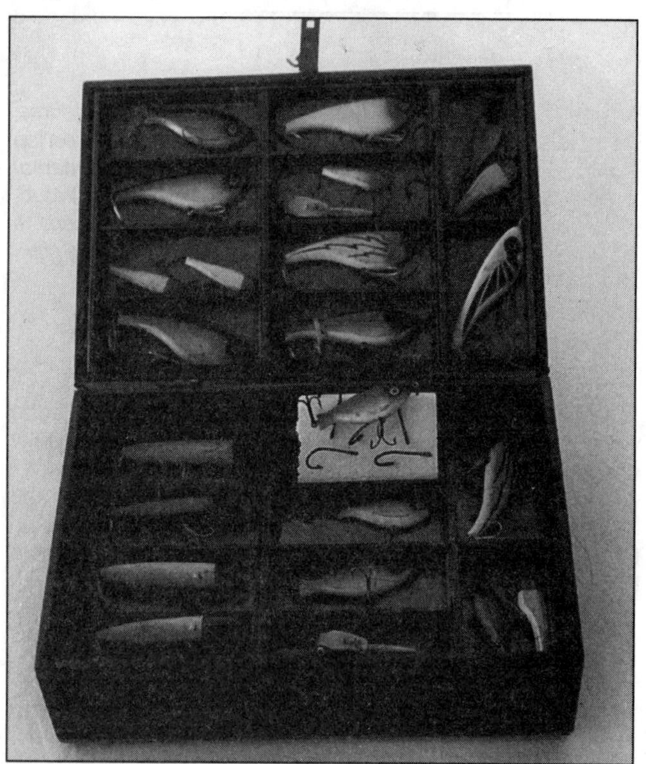

This beautiful mahogany box of Earl Gresh lures has three trays of lures. It sold at action for $450. several years ago. That figure probably wouldn't touch it today.

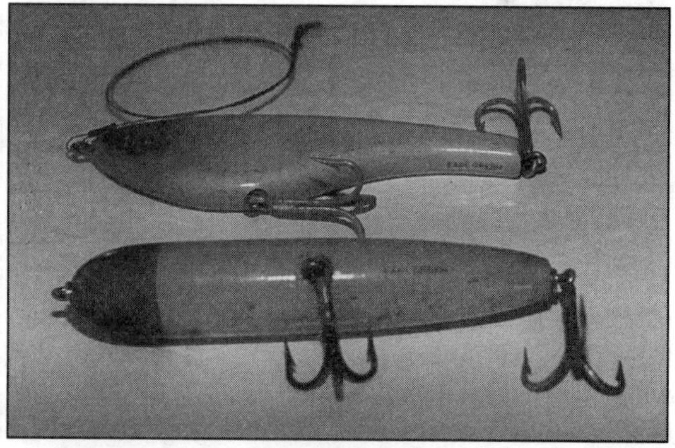

Both of these have recessed (no cup hardware) screw hook belly hook hangers. It appears the Gresh used this method most of the time. Note the swiveling tail hook on the lower plug.

A good looking minnow with wire leader. Note the nose and tail cap protectors and the three internal belly weights.

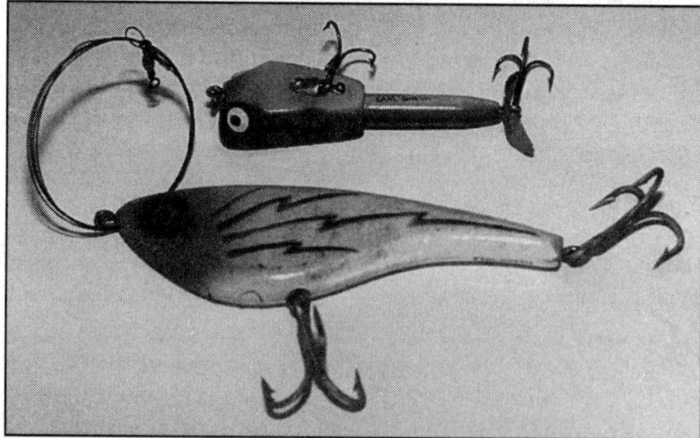

The upper lure has a tail propeller spinner and a one-piece, surface belly hook hanger. Note the large plastic eye. This probably tags the lure as one of his later products. All others appear to have painted eyes.

GROOVE HEAD

Colger Manufacturing Co. Van Dyke, Michigan

White with red head, 3-3/4" long, painted eyes. Belly hooks are mounted on a wire bridle extending the hooks out to either side.

GROOVE HEAD was listed as an unknown until the last edition. As you can see from the photo here it has now been identified, but the years of manufacture still remain a mystery. It is thought to be the 1950s. The box states it was an underwater or top water depending upon the speed of the retrieve. According to the box they were "Made in red and white orange perch scale, frog and black and white." It would be reasonable to assume that the comma was inadvertently left out between "white" and "orange." Collector value range: $25-$50.

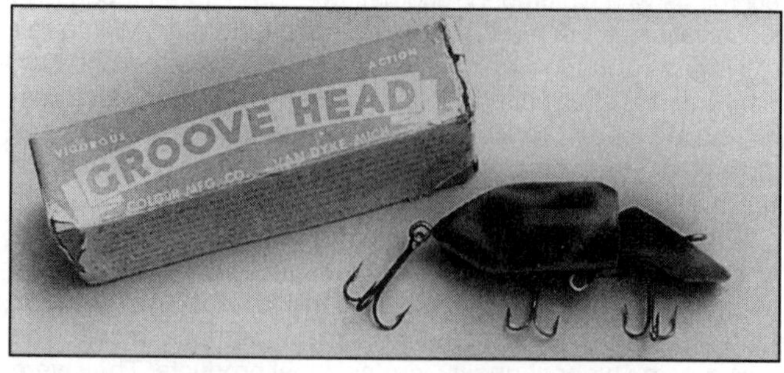

HAAS TACKLE COMPANY

Sapulpa, Oklahoma

HAAS' LIV-MINNOW

Pictured here are three lures from Haas and a reproduction of the original patent illustration. The patent was applied for in

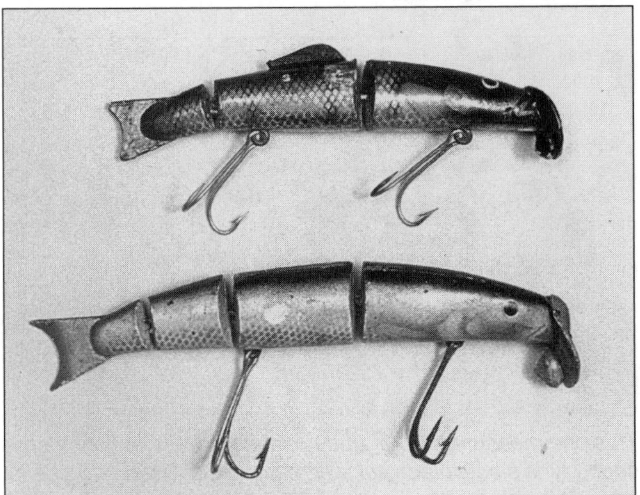

1933 and granted to Harry R. Haas on July 16, 1935. If you compare the photo with the patent you will note that the single lure in the upper photo is the one most like the patent. The other two have different types of lips, hook hardware and tail fin styles. They are however, so similar otherwise that they are most likely Haas lures was well. You may also notice that the patent shows a double jointed lure as do the two in the lower photo. A 1930s advertisement illustrates a lure substantially similar to the one in the photo here except that the one in the ad is double-jointed. The protrusions at the lower edge of the lips are weights. The ad stated they were available in a 4" single-joint and a 5" double-jointed model. No colors were given. The upper lure has glass eyes while the other two are painted-eye types. We can reasonably place the glass eye version in the earliest category. Collector value range: $100-$200.

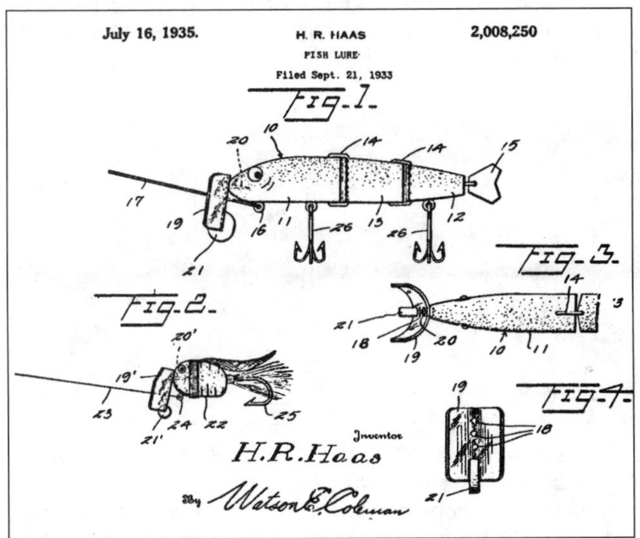

Patent on the Haas LIV-MINNOW. Granted to Harry R. Haas on July 16, 1935.

JACOB HANSEN
1866-1945

Muskegon, Michigan

For a long time there was very little concrete information to be had regarding this man. His name, along with Adolph Arntz, Edward Myers, Jack Spellman and a man named Keller were all associated with a sort of generic group of similar lures lumped under the name Myers and Spellman. When we found a lure that looked like any of those in the group, we just put it there for lack of anywhere else to put it. With the help of a few folks we can now sort this mess out for the most part. At the head of the list of these folks stands George Richey of Honor, Michigan. It was his research that uncovered much valuable information about Jacob Hansen thereby enabling us to cut through the fog.

Until now, the only thing we knew for certain was his association with Adolph Artnz with regard to the MICHIGAN LIFE-LIKE and the fact that Hansen was granted the patent on February 20, 1908. I reported in a previous edition that Arntz was the manufacturer, as a result of the advertisement I found in a 1910 issue of *The Anglers Guide* that clearly stated the lure was "Manufactured by Adolph Arntz." We have known that Arntz was a sporting goods dealer in Muskegon and now know that Hansen made the lures and Arntz marketed them. Arntz bailed out after a couple of years saying it was a good lure, but just too difficult to make.

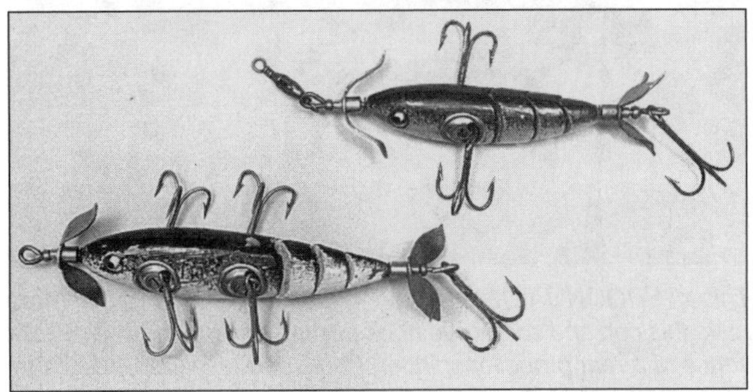

The photo here shows the MICHIGAN LIFELIKE in both versions that were made. The smaller one is 2-3/4" long and has three treble hooks and the larger one comes in a 3-3/4" with five trebles. Both sported glass eyes and three-blade tail spinners. The articulated bodies were extraordinarily well-made. The side hook hangers shown on these two lures are of the style more commonly found and are thought to represent the oldest style. The second style protrudes further and although the same principle is in use, the design is somewhat different. The third style is illustrated in the drawing of the MUSKEGON SPOON JACK MINNOW. It looks somewhat like the common one-piece surface hanger that so many companies began using around the mid 1940s. It is, however, used as a hook swing limiter and covers the screw eye hook hanger. Collector value range for the MICHIGAN LIFE-LIKE: $400-$500.

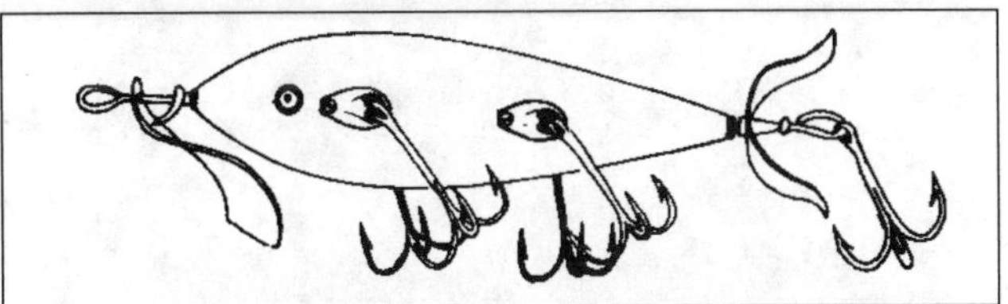

Illustrates one of the many types of forward single-blade spinners used by Hansen on the SPOON JACK MINNOW. It was fashioned by punching out and bending back a portion of the metal and boring a hole through which the through-body wire passed. This rendered the spinner more stable and held it away from the lure body.

COLOR OR FINISH: Light green with speckled back and white belly, dark green with speckled back and white belly, aluminum color with dark back, brook trout, dark back with yellow belly, solid aluminum color, perch, green back with yellow sides and red belly, natural wood finish.

MUSKEGON SPOON JACK MINNOW

The drawing of the Spoon Jack Minnow shows what might be a typical one, if indeed you can call any one of them typical. Hansen was known to be an inveterate tinker and it appears he couldn't keep from changing things about the lure. The majority are configured, as in the drawing, with either three or five hooks. They have a round body tapered to a nose and tail, a two-blade propeller spinner at the tail, a single-blade spoon-type spinner at the nose, and a through-body twisted wire line tie and tail hook hanger. The three-hooker is found either in an opposite side mount or a two belly-mount configuration. To add to the confusion there also exist, although fairly rare, two-hook and four-hook models. The two-hooker has one belly treble and the four-hooker has two side hooks on one side with a single mounted toward the tail on the opposite side. Both, of course, have tail hooks.

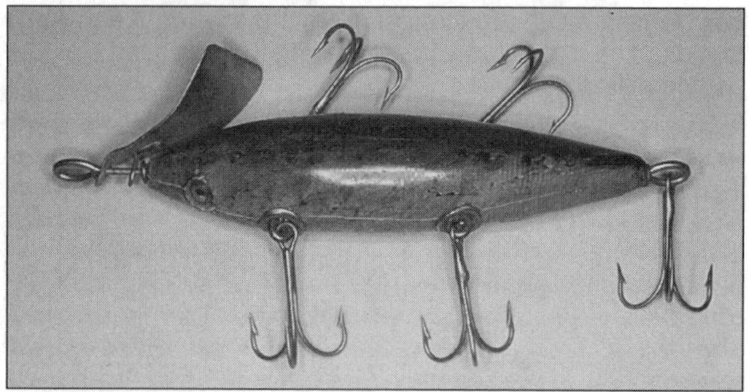

This 4" SPOON JACK MINNOW is pretty typical. Probably more have this cup and screw eye hook rig than any other. Note the absence of a rear propeller spinner. Photo courtesy Clarence Zahn.

Sizes vary from 3-1/4" to 4-1/2" usually, but there is one known unusual 5" version that has flat sides.

With regard to eyes, they are found with no eyes, yellow or amber glass eyes and painted eyes.

The single-blade spoon-type nose spinner is found made three ways. The first is illustrated in the drawing. Another type is made by simply drilling a hole in the tapered end of the spoon and the last is made by bending the small end back on itself and drilling through making two holes. Some collectors believe the simple single hole blade to be the earliest, but at the present time there is no way of being certain which of the types of blades or hook hangers came first.

This SPOON JACK MINNOW on its original box measures 3-15/16' and is configured the same as in the previous drawing. It does not have the twisted wire through-body fixture common to Hansen lures, however, it is characteristic of his lures in other ways.

Most SPOON JACK MINNOWS have a tail spinner also. For the most part these are the propeller spinner type, but from time to time you will find any of the three single-blade spoon-type spinners. With Hansen almost anything can happen. All of these variations will be illustrated in the photos to follow. Collector value range for SPOON JACK MINNOWS: $150-$200, unless otherwise noted.

This one measures 3-5/8" and has the single-hole floppy-style spoon-type single blade spinner at the nose. The rear propeller spinner is one made for use on the nose.

Measuring 3-1/4" this one is easily identifiable as it is stenciled "Spoon Jack Minnow" on the belly. You don't find that very often. It has one internal belly weight.

This is a very typical SPOON JACK MINNOW. It is the only 5" long to be found so far. It has flat sides and oddball wire extenders from the hook hangers to hold the hook away form the lure body. Note the presence of the single-blade spoon-type spinner at both ends of the lure. From the George Richey collection. Photo courtesy Clarence Zahn.

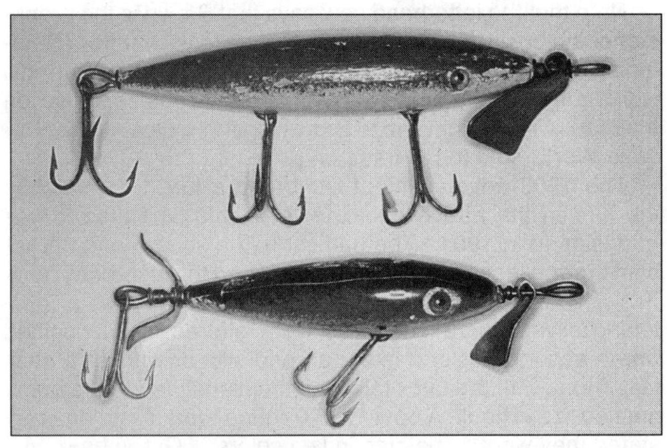

The upper is 4-3/8". The front prop is brass. Note no rear spinner. The lower lure measures 3-1/4". It has the typical spinners, but is the somewhat uncommon two-hooker. Photo courtesy Clarence Zahn.

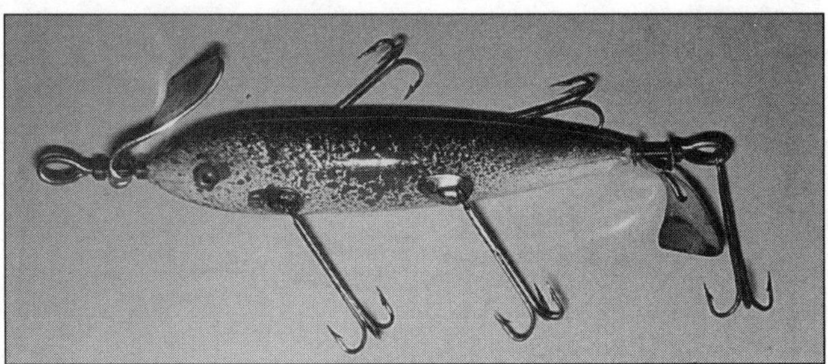

This is an unusual SPOON JACK MINNOW in several ways. It sports two styles of single-blade spinners, has long shank hooks and a spatter type paint job. Photo courtesy Clarence Zahn.

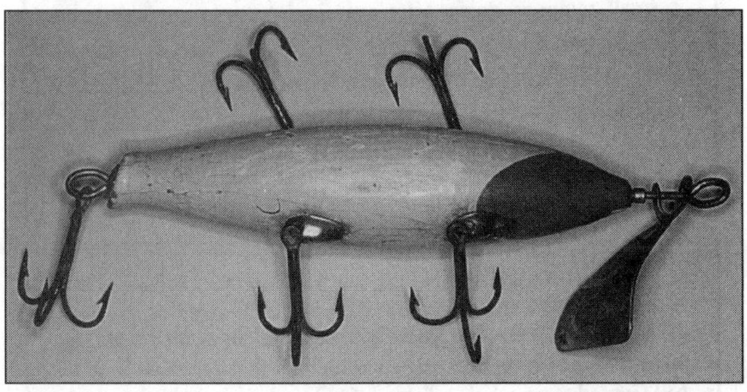

This 4-1/4" beauty exhibits a couple of unusual characteristics. This white body, red head pattern is not often found. Note the odd curved carving at the tail. It has no eyes, painted or otherwise. Photo courtesy Clarence Zahn.

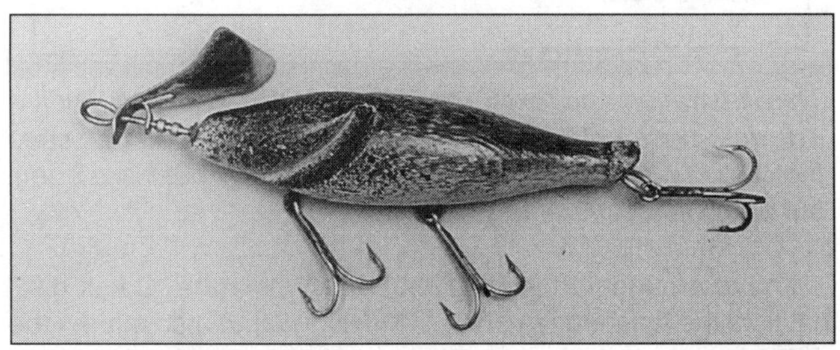

This is an unusual SPOON JACK MINNOW. It measures 4" and has a tail shaped a lot like the one in the previous photo. Note also the flutes at the head. This style Hansen is very scarce. Collector value range: $200-$250.

PULL ME SLOW

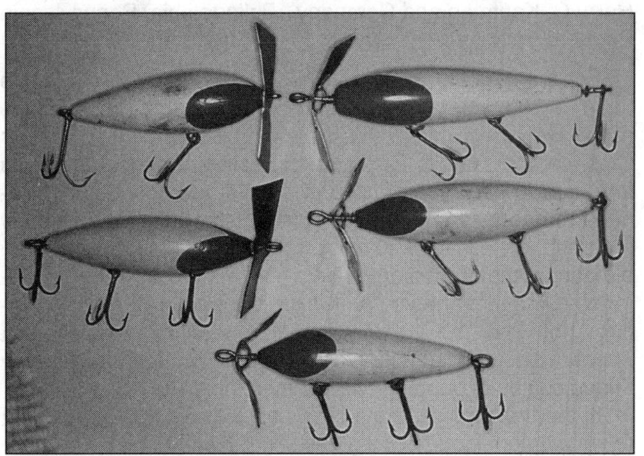

Hansen, true to his nature, made fat and fatter versions of this lure in sizes varying from 2-3/4" to more than 4-1/2". There are at least three versions of the large nose-mounted spinners. They vary with the manner of mounting them on the armature, line tie. All the lures are cup and screw eye belly-hook-rigged. None have been found with other than a white body, red head paint job. They are found with three treble hooks, two treble hooks and a third version with only a trailing treble hook (rare). Collector value range: $100-$150.

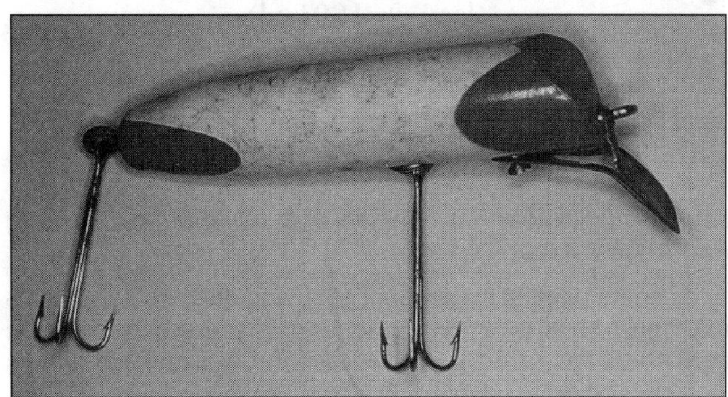

This is an unknown Hansen lure. Collector value range: $75-$100.

HANSON'S IRRESISTIBLE MINNOW

Wm. B. Hanson and Company Pittsburgh, Pennsylvania

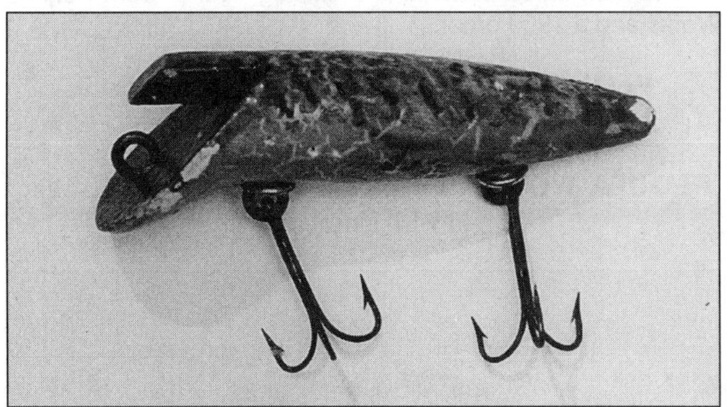

This c. 1919 odd-looking wooden lure was available as in the photo and was also furnished with two double hooks. It has a raised cup and screw hook hardware. Colors available were: Brown mottled back with red painted mouth as in above photo; green; red and green. Collector value range: $300-$400.

HARKAUF MINNOWS

Harry C. Kaufman and Company Philadelphia, Pennsylvania
Pequea Works Strasburg, Pennsylvania

For many years all of us who are interested in old tackle have had a mystery on our hands when it came to the origins of the HARKAUF MINNOW. National Fishing Lure Collectors Club member Harold "Doc" Herr of Ephrata, Pennsylvania was fortunate to be at the auction of the old and now defunct Pequea (pronounced peck-way) Works Fishing Tackle Company in Strasburg, less than 20 miles from his home. He found some old papers that turned out to be a gold mine of information. After studying them he wrote an excellent article about the company for The *N.F.L.C.C. Gazette*, the club newsletter. It appeared in the December, 1987 issue. Through his courtesy I have copies of some of those papers now.

In the first three editions of this book I said that the earliest advertisement I found was a 1903 H.C. KAUFMAN & COMPANY ad for the "Harkauf Wooden Minnow". The company had a Philadelphia address in that ad. This name is apparently the first manifestation of the Kaufman tackle business. "Doc" Herr observed in his article that the name of the lure was likely derived from the first letters of Harry Kaufman's first and last name. I don't think that can be disputed.

A series of dated invoices, bills, etc. with various headings and logos in the papers found at the auction easily show the evolution of the names.

H.C.KAUFMAN & COMPANY, Philadelphia
(from the 1903 ad)

PHILADELPHIA BAIT MANUFACTURING COMPANY

January 1907 order HARRY C. KAUFMAN, Strasburg
April 1908 invoice

At some point between April 1908 and January 1909 Kaufman must have taken on a partner or made some sort of an agreement with a Edwin Brown and the Philadelphia names was once again used, but with a twist. An invoice with an elaborate new head was used that curiously, used Edwin Brown's name prominently, but didn't mention Kaufman:

EDWIN BROWN PHILADELPHIA BAIT
MANUFACTURING CO, Strasburg, Pa.

The next dated material is a catalog "No. 9" from Pequea Works and a 1909 order.

PEQUEA WORKS, Strasburg, Pennsylvania
(1909 order)

PEQUEA WORKS, Edwin Brown, Prop., Strasburg
(1911 letterhead)

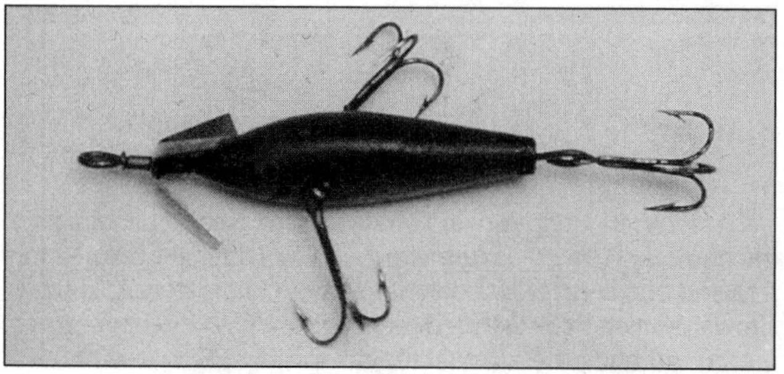

Note that the letterhead now says that Brown is the proprietor of the business. So, it seems that he took over from Kaufman in the last half of 1908. Kaufman, however, was still working in the company, apparently as a representative on the road. A letter from him to Brown in 1911 indicates this. Pequea Works sold to the trade only.

The 1903 advertisement illustrated a lure that matches the lure in the above photo. A later catalog stated it was "...designed in 1901." The earliest had a square-end, three-blade propeller spinner, painted eyes and through-body hook hangers. They were available in three finishes with a "glistening silver belly." The lures were offered in unspecified "three assorted colors" in the ad and with or without a buck tail. Those with the buck tail have them attached to the body, not tied to the hook. A post 1913 Pequea Works catalog entry stated they were "...painted in two colors ... Green back with white belly, and all white...". They have been found with glass eyes and may or may not be the earliest. The verdict is not in yet. Later versions will be found with a tube-type simple two-blade propeller spinner. Some are found with red painted gill marks and most have "THE HARKAUF" printed on the side.

Harkauf Trout Minnow

Far Superior to the Natural Insects or Artificial Flies

and is entirely different from any other Trout Bait on the market. It is the most natural bait ever made, it represents a small minnow going after a fly and if there are any trout in the stream where this bait is used, you are sure to get some, as no trout or other game fish will watch a small minnow get an insect or any other food, without interfering and the consequence is that you will get the trout on the first strike at this bait.

CONSTRUCTION

We are offering the public the best trout lure that can be had at a moderate cost. The workmanship of this bait is the very best, the body of the minnow is made of best quality wood, nicely painted with best waterproof paints, the wire rod extending through this minnow is of the best German silver, which will not rust. The fly is tied with best quality silk and natural color feathers. This bait is fitted with best brass barrel swivel (imported) with two best hollow point treble hooks. This bait is so constructed that the head hook cannot interfere with the bait whatever and is always in such a position that they have never been known to miss a strike. Size of minnow 1¼ inches long. Each bait separate in a box.

This illustration and text for the HARKAUF TROUT MINNOW is from a post-1913 Pequea Works catalog. As you can see, they did not list any finish options. There may not have been but one. Collector value range: $100-$200.

I have an undated (circa 1930) J.E. Wilmarthe "Catalog M" that lists the finished HARKAUF MINNOW, but also makes the parts available so that you could paint and assemble them yourself. You may therefore, find some crazy versions of the lure out there. Collector value range: $250-$400.

The finish on the BASS MINNOW in the photo here is in poor condition, but the lure is obviously a high quality product.

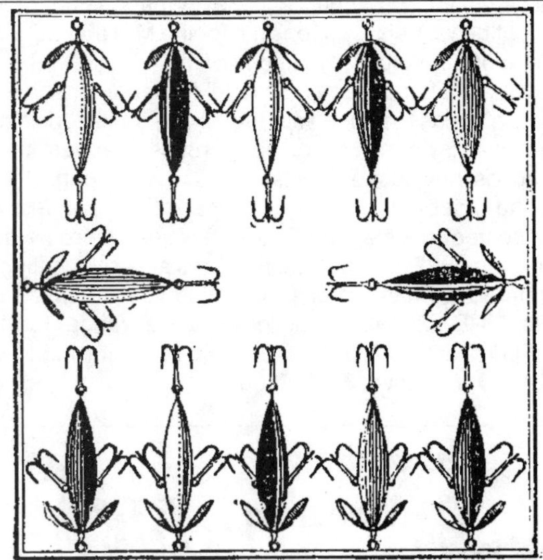

This assortment consists of three of each color as follows: Red Back with White Belly, Green Back with White Belly, Yellow Back with White Belly, Red Head with White Body.

Wood bodies are 2½ inch long, with three treble Hooks, and **one** spinner on head of minnow.

Susquehanna minnows retail at 25c each, one assortment in box.

Price $30.00 per gross.

Harkauf Wood Plug Bait

A Floater or surface bait and attracts the fish by the splashing of the fins and revolving head when drawn through the water.

Another of the old time baits that brings home the fish, made in two sizes, each Plug packed in box, 1 dozen in carton, in the following color combinations:

No. 300, 2¾ inch long, all White.
No. 301, 2¾ inch long, Red Head, White Body.
No. 302, 2¾ inch long, All Yellow with Gold Dots.
No. 303, 2¾ inch long, Mouse Head, Pearl Body.
No. 350, 3¼ inch long, All White.
No. 351, 3¼ inch long, Red Head, White Body.
No. 352, 3¼ inch long, All Yellow with Gold Dots.
No. 353, 3¼ inch long, Mouse Head, Pearl Body.

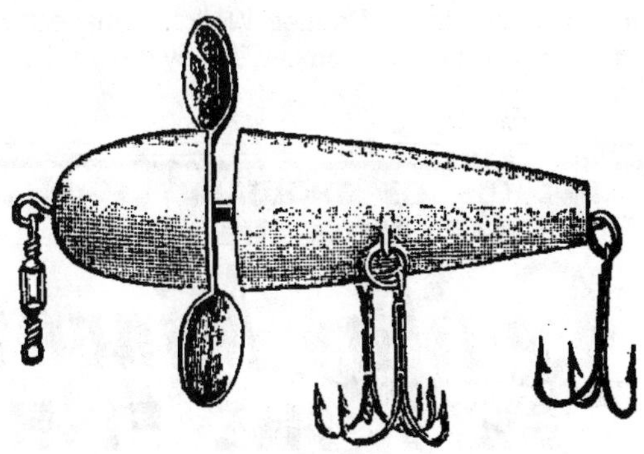

Showing exact size of No. 300

Wood Minnows

No. 6½

No. 6½, Round body minnow 3½ inches long, five treble hooks, two nickel plated spinners, no detachable hooks, painted in green back and white belly only.

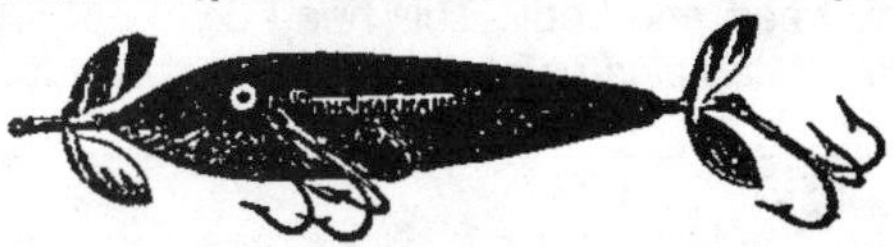

No. 5½

No. 5½, Same as our No. 6½ only smaller size with three treble hooks, length of body 3 inches.

Price per dozen $6.00.

No. 4½, Same as No. 3½ only has one spinner and body 2½ inches long, three treble hooks.

Harkauf Bass Spinners

Harkauf Spinner

Unequalled for Black Bass and Pickerel

The new Harkauf Spinner is made of brass, highly nickel plated. The body revolves on a brass wire extending through the body. It is fitted with one best Hollow Point Feathered Hook at rear end of bait. This hook can be taken off in a few seconds and another put on. It is also fitted with a swivel to assure the user that it positively will not twist the line.

This spinner is made in one size and painted in the two following colors: Green, the upper half of minnow is painted with a rich French Green enamel which is waterproof, lower half is nickel plated. Yellow, is painted with a bright yellow and has silver dots on body of spinner.

The lures in this composite of entries from two post-1913 Pequea Works catalog were a surprise to many collectors. There is another Decker look-a-like, a nickel-plated brass Harkauf spinner, three sizes of two-propeller 3T and 5T wood minnows and what appears to be a line of less expensive wood lures, 2-1/2" three hookers. So it looks like there are a lot more Harkauf/Pequea lures to look for out there than was previously thought.

It measures 2-1/2", has glass eyes and very well made propeller spinner aft. It has a beautiful feather fly mounted forward of the nose. The lure was introduced in 1913. Collector value range: $250-$400.

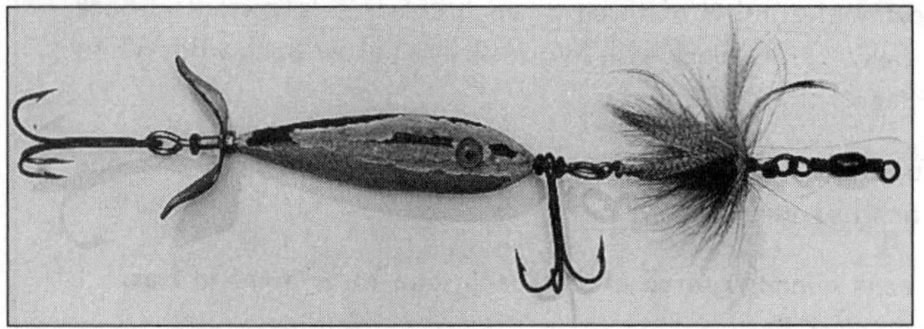

A 2-1/2" HARKAUF BASS MINNOW. The paint is in sad shape.

THE QUILBY MINNOW by Pequea Works

This is a bait made from turkey quills. It was made in five sizes from 1-1/2" to 2-1/2". The advertisement reproduced here reads an astounding "60 sizes and colors."

The lure was invented by William Miles. He made them himself until demand was too much for him to handle. He then made arrangements for Pequea Works to make them. They added two more styles as you can see by the ad. Collector value range: $5-$10.

An ad for the QUILBY MINNOW in the May, 1949 issue of THE OUTDOORSMAN.

CHARLES R. HARRIS 1848-1922

Mackinaw City, Michigan | Niles, Michigan | Manistee, Michigan

For years collectors have known Harris to be the inventor and maker of the HARRIS FLOATING CORK FROG. He was granted a patent for it on August 24, 1897. What was not widely known is that he was also responsible for the MANISTEE MINNOW, a lure of heretofore mysterious origin.

Harris was a railroad man and a hotel manager for some 20 years prior to his association with the fishing tackle business. Sometime during the 1880s or early 1890s, he was in the sporting goods business in Mackinaw City, Michigan. It was there that he first began making and marketing his lures. He later was located in Niles, and finally Manistee where he died at the age 74 in 1922. Besides the two lures already mentioned he also offered a Phantom or Devon type lure he called the FEATHERBONE MINNOW. Collector value range for the HARRIS FLOATING CORK FROG: $150-$200; for the MANISTEE MINNOW (below): $400-$600.

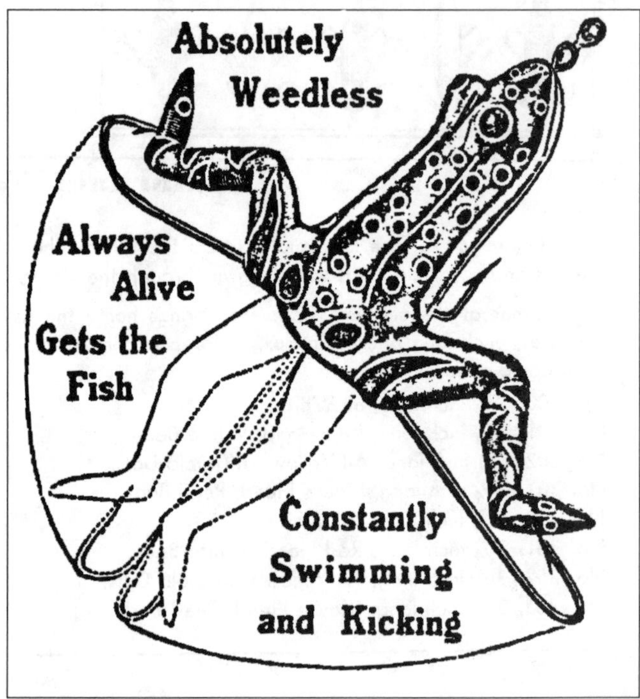

A catalog illustration for the HARRIS FLOATING CORK FROG.

MANISTEE MINNOW

This very rare lure has the words "The Manistee" on one side of the body. The photo here isn't too clear, but if you look closely you may be able to see the brass wire extending along the belly to the trailing treble hook and over the top of the tail where it is attached. There are metal hook restraining cups at the belly and tail. The spinner revolves on the armature connecting the head and body. This head does not rotate, only the spinner. It has zinc-painted eyes. See above for value.

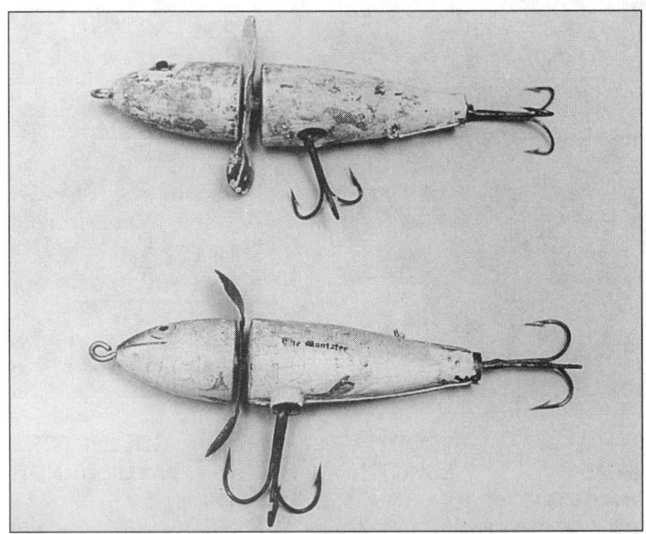

This photo shows belly views of two MANISTEE MINNOWS. Both are 3-3/4". The upper lure has a slightly different method of hanging the tail and belly hooks. You may notice glass eyes on this lure. This is not the norm. These are obviously modern and have been added in recent times.

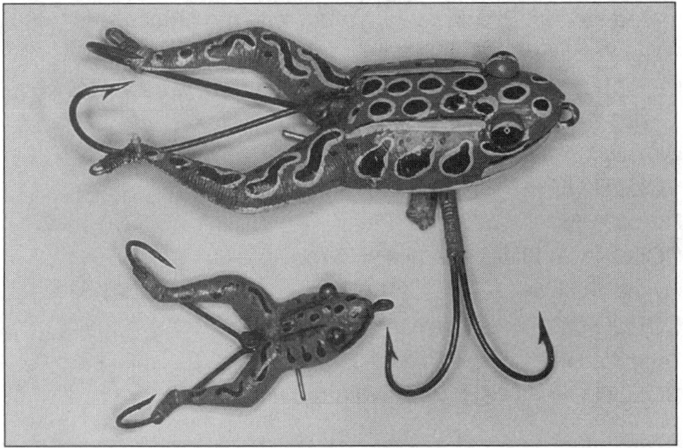

HARRIS FLOATING CORK FROG. The upper lure measures 3-1/8" and the small fly rod size, 1-1/2". Each came with an external belly weight attached by a brass wire at the belly. The weight is missing from the small one in the photo.

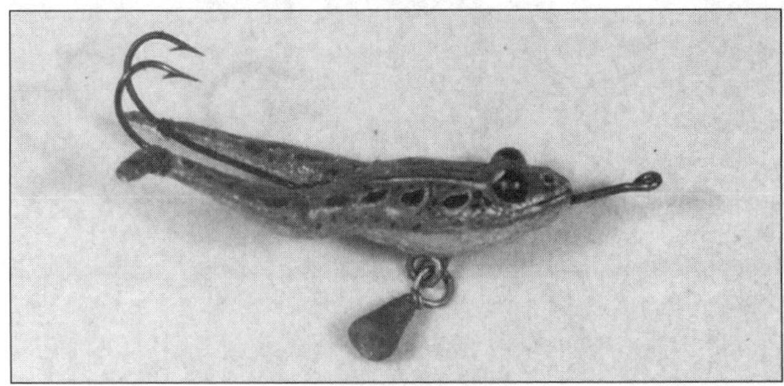

This is a third, fly rod size of the Harris frog lure. It measures 2-1/8". Photo courtesy Jim Muma.

HASKELL MINNOW

Riley Haskell — Painesville, Ohio

When Riley Haskell applied for the patent on this lure it was called, simply, "TROLLING BAIT FOR CATCHING FISH" in

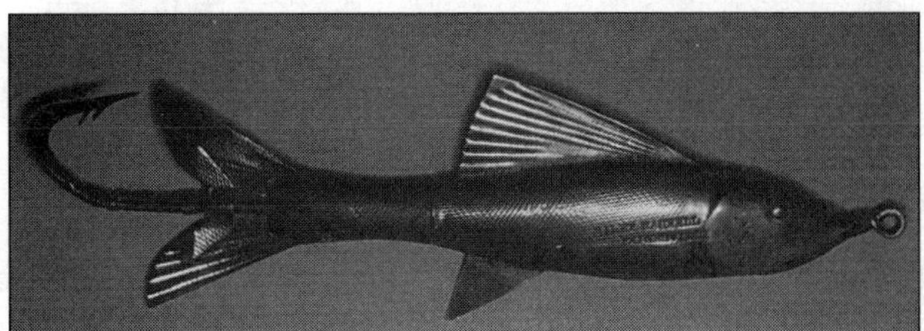

the arcane language of the U.S. patent office. Since we know of no other commercial name for the lure collectors call it the HASKELL MINNOW. This is probably the most famous lure in the antique tackle collecting world. An example sold for $22,000 at an auction about 10 years ago. That extraordinarily high price was an aberration, however, because it was so very rare then. About 30 or so have been found since. The collector value is lower as a result, but no one seems willing to part with them. There has been little known activity in this regard.

While there are many other lures more attractive or unusual, there are none that can compare. What makes this lure important is the fact that the 1859 patent is the first American patent to *mention* wood as a possible material for it to be made from. It, in fact, does use wood for the inner core over which the copper halves are soldered. It would be 15 years later, in 1874, before a patent *specified* wood as the material from which a lure was to be made. The lure is finely made with much detail given to the scales. This is probably due to Haskell's skill as a gunsmith. He was well known and highly regarded in this trade.

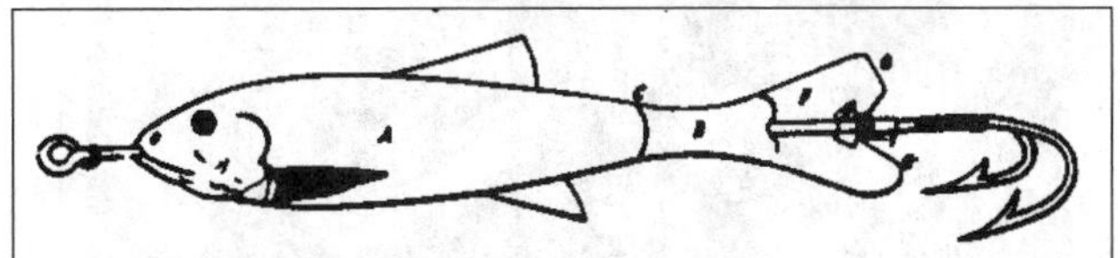

A detail from the illustration with the original 1859 patent.

There are two slightly different designs to be found. The smaller one is 3-3/4" long (nose to tail). It appears slimmer than the larger one, but is about the same shape proportionally. It has no ventral fin as does its big brother. It sports a trailing treble hook. The larger (patent model) measures 4-9/16" (nose to tail) and 5-5/8" overall. It is rigged with two rigid-mount single hooks, effectively becoming a double hook. It has a ventral fin. About the back one third of both models rotates around an armature upon retrieve. Please turn to page XX to see the original 1859 patent drawing. There was insufficient trade data to establish a realistic collector value.

WILSON WOBBLERS

Hastings Sporting Goods Company — Hasting, Michigan

The company has its origins in the early 1900s, probably around 1910-11. The first of their patents I could find was for the WILSON FLUTED WOBBLER. It was applied for in 1911 and granted to Richard T. Wilson and Aben E. Johnson on May 6, 1913. It has been reported that an advertisement for this lure appeared in a 1911 publication the name of which is unknown at this time. The earliest ad that I found for this lure was in a 1912 issue of *The Outer's Book* magazine. What is interesting about this particular ad is that the company advertising was JOHNSON SPORTING GOODS WORKS, Hastings, Michigan. It specifically stated "Wilson's Fluted Wobbler" and illustrated same. The point here is that the next ad I found was in a 1913 *Outers Book* that used the same illustration and some of the same text, but the company was then the familiar HASTINGS SPORTING GOODS WORKS. In addition to the above,

A 1917 advertisement from The Outer's Book magazine.

I came across a pocket catalog from "Good Luck Fishing Tackle" that featured a four-leaf clover trademark with a WILSON FLUTED WOBBLER superimposed. It said "Wobbler Brand." The catalog offered various Hastings company lures and said the company was located in Hastings, Michigan. In any case all patents for "Wilson's" lures so far found have been granted to both Wilson and Johnson. Wilson was obviously the creative end of the company and Johnson the business end. It appears that all but one of the Hastings lures with Wilson's name as the prefix were invented by Wilson. Others will be discussed under the individual lure entries.

Around 1927-28 Hastings Company advertising disappeared from catalogs and periodicals and about the same time the WILSON WOBBLERS and CUPPED WOBBLERS showed up in Moonlight Bait Company (Paw Paw) catalogs and advertisements. It therefore follows that Hastings went out of business either merging with or selling their rights to Moonlight.

WILSON'S FLUTED WOBBLERS
(Good Luck Wobblers)

The picture here shows four different bodies that were introduced. All had the distinctive four grooves or "flutes" in the forward portion of the body. They were available over the years mostly in two- and three-treble hook configurations and differing hook hanger hardware. It is possible that one or more copies or imitations were made because many individuals or companies were jumping on the band wagon. There were floating and sinking models.

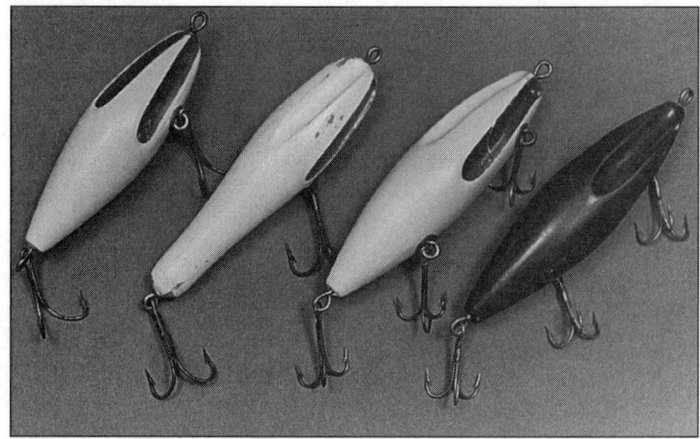

NAME	BODY LENGTH	HOOKS	COLLECTOR VALUE RANGE
Wilson's Wobbler	5"	2T	$125-$150
COLOR OR FINISH: White with red flutes, Yellow with red flutes, White with black flutes.			
Musky Wobbler	4-3/4"	3T	$125-$150
COLOR OR FINISH: Unknown			
Wilson's Wobbler	4"	3T	$40-$60
COLOR OR FINISH: White with red flutes, Black with white flutes, Rainbow, Red and green spots, Solid red, Green with red stripes, Brown scale, Yellow with red flutes.			
Super Wobbler	3-1/2"	2D	$50-$70
COLOR OR FINISH: Luminous with red flutes, Rainbow, Brown scale finish.			
Luminous Wobbler	4"	3T	$40-$60
COLOR OR FINISH: Luminous w/ red flutes			
Fly rod Wobbler	2"	2T	$200-$300
COLOR OR FINISH: White with red flutes.			
Fly rod Wobbler	2-1/2	2T	$200-$300
COLOR OR FINISH: White with red flutes.			
Trout Wobbler	1-3/4"	2T	$200-$300
COLOR OR FINISH: White with red flutes.			

A WILSON'S FLUTED WOBBLER in a rainbow-like finish (green, yellow and red) and its original box. Collector value range: $20-$40, with the box: $200 plus.

There have been Wobblers found with gold- and copper-painted flutes but it is not known if they were produced that way or were repainted by others later. Additional colors are green and silver, both with red flutes.

Two fly-rod size Wobblers at 1-7/8" and 2-1/2" respectively.

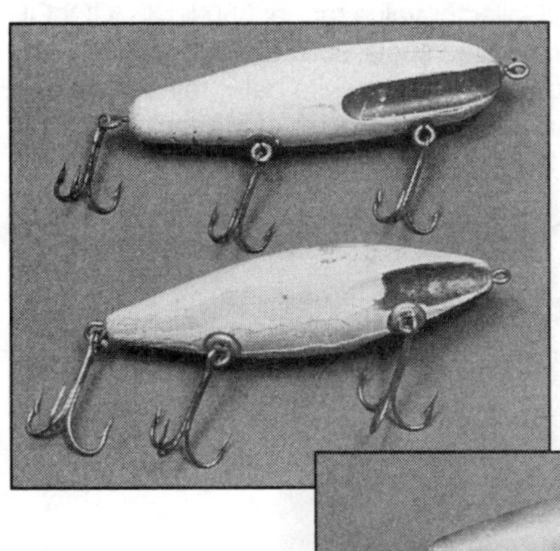

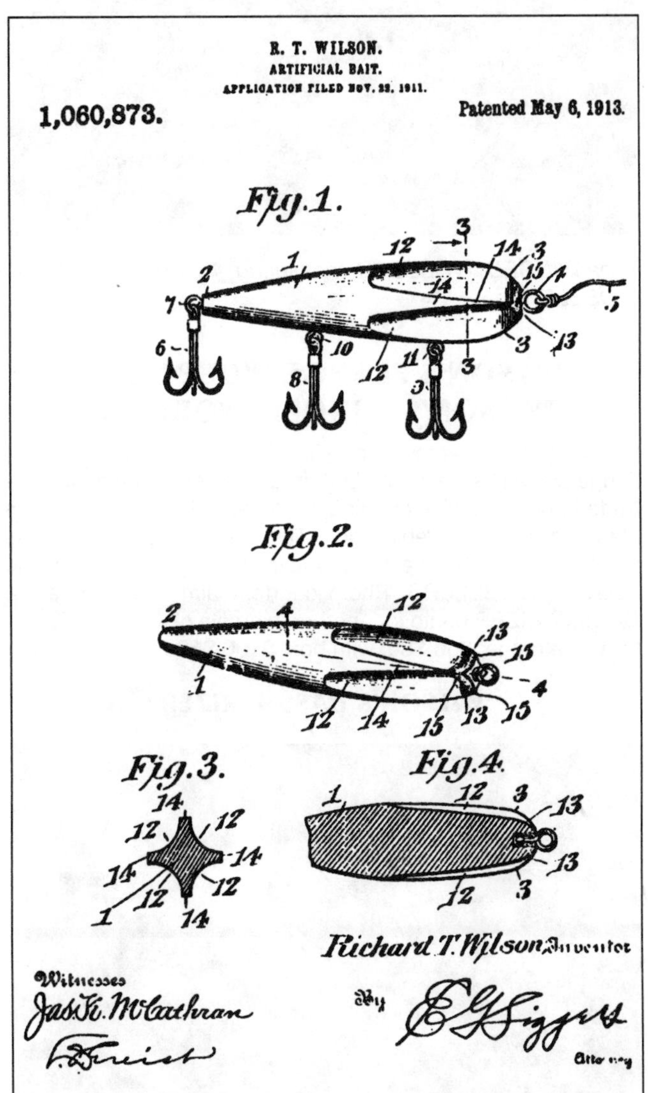

The illustration filed with patent application for WILSON'S FLUTED WOBBLER. Granted May 6, 1913 to Richard T. Wilson and assigning one-half the rights to Aben E. Johnson, both of Hastings, Michigan.

WILSON'S SIZZLER

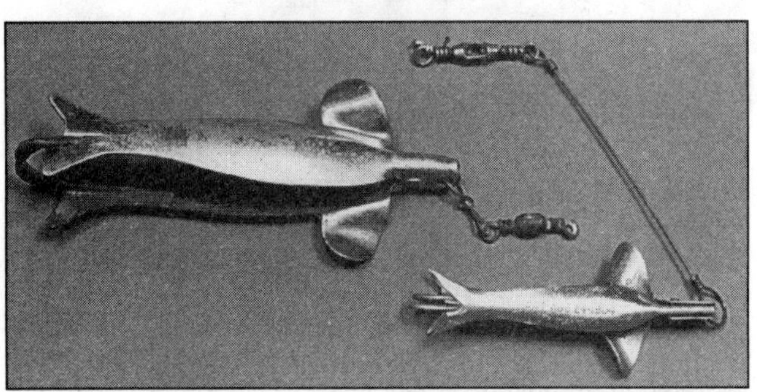

The WILSON'S SIZZLER is the only known incidence where Wilson's name was attached to a lure he did not invent. The inventor was John Hedlund of St. Cloud, Minnesota.

This is an all metal lure with a peculiar winged metal piece hinged at the nose and trailing under the body. It had two single hooks attached in a weedless manner. There were two sizes, 3-1/4" and 2-1/2" and both are plainly stamped "PAT. AUG. 24-1904" on the back. Collector value range: N.A.

WILSON'S GRASS WIDOW

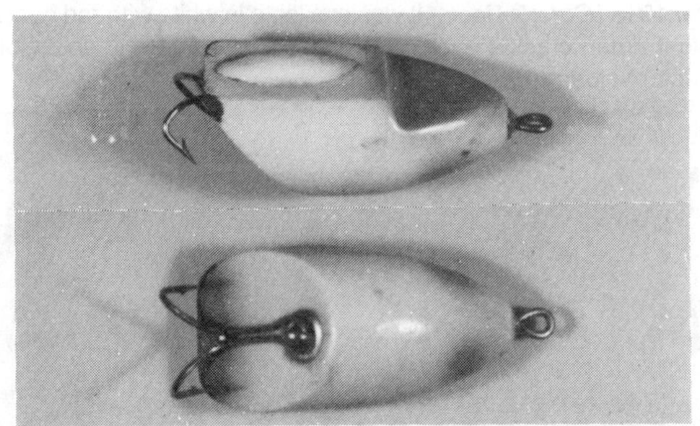

This 2-1/2" plug had an oddly shaped belly. It had one double hook. A 1921 advertisement in *Field & Stream* said it was "Weedless - but not fishless." Collector value range: $80-$135. COLOR OR FINISH: Red body, mottled spots; solid red, solid white; luminous; solid green; fancy green back, white belly; rainbow, brown scale. These colors are common to most of Wilson's lures but may or may not apply to all plugs including the GRASS WIDOW.

WILSON'S CUPPED WOBBLER or BASS SEEKER

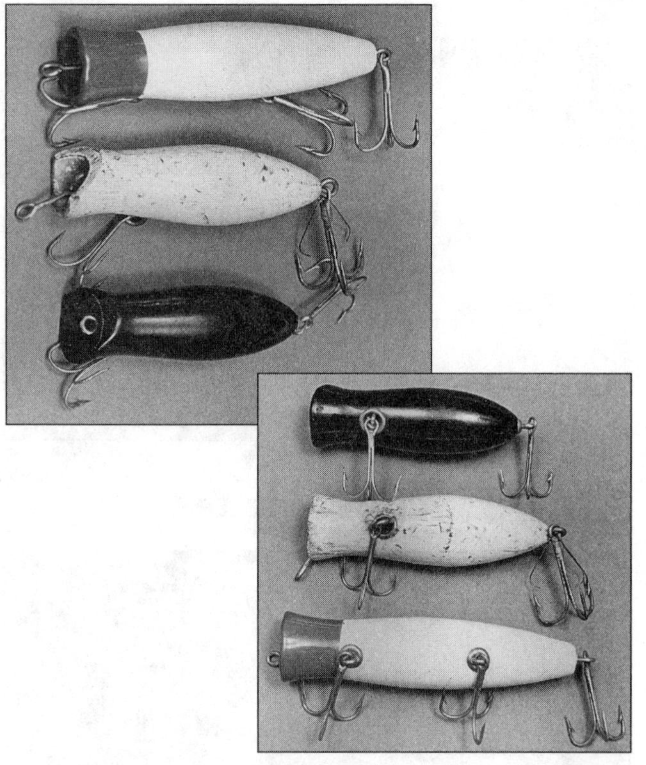

The three lures in the photos measure 4-1/2", 3-1/2" and 3-1/8" respectively. The center lure is identical to the one illustrated in an advertisement in a 1921 issue of *Forest and Stream* magazine. It was called the WILSON BASS SEEKER there. The ad stated the lure was available in white luminous only. Note the top of the cupped head end is sliced off at the top. It is also found without the cut-off as in the upper lure. They are found in various colors (listing under GRASS WIDOW). They were new around 1915. Collector value range: $60-$90.

WILSON SIX-IN-ONE WOBBLER

This lure was patented March 27, 1917 and has a unique six-position adjustable diving lip at its head. It was first marketed in 1916, found advertised and written up in an article as new for 1916 (*Outer's Book*). It was available in white with red head, light green crackle back, or red stripes on a green back. Collector value range: $250-$300.

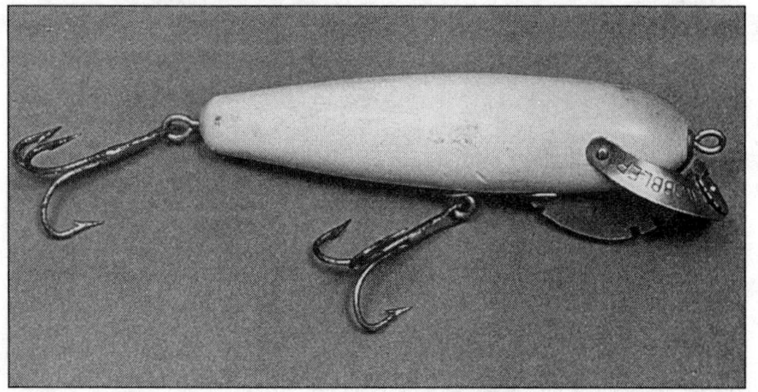

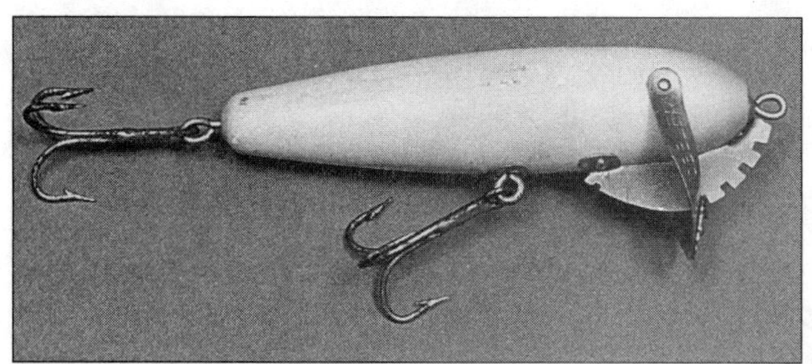

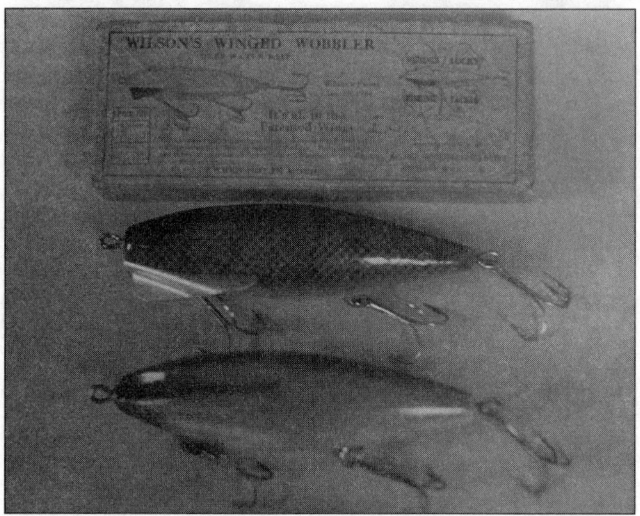

Top: WINGED WOBBLER measuring 4". Bottom: FLUTED WOBBLER.

WILSON'S FLANGE WOBBLER or WILSON'S WINGED WOBBLER

This plug, patented Jan. 13, 1914, had a metal wing or flange piece fitted onto the bottom of the nose. The metal protruded from each side creating the "wings." It had two belly trebles and a trailing treble hook. The flanges were sometimes painted red and the lure was made in all the same colors as the FLUTED WOBBLERS. Photo courtesy Jim Muma. See the BASSMERIZER photo for another example of this lure. Collector value range: $60-$80; with box: $100-$120.

WILSON'S BASSMERIZER

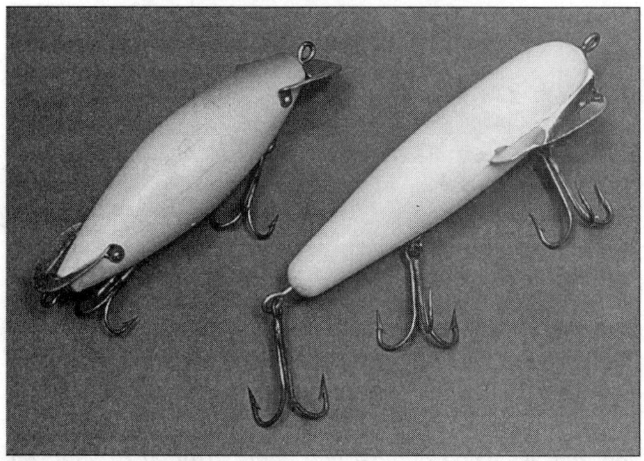

Photo shows BASSMERIZER on left and FLANGED WOBBLER on the right.

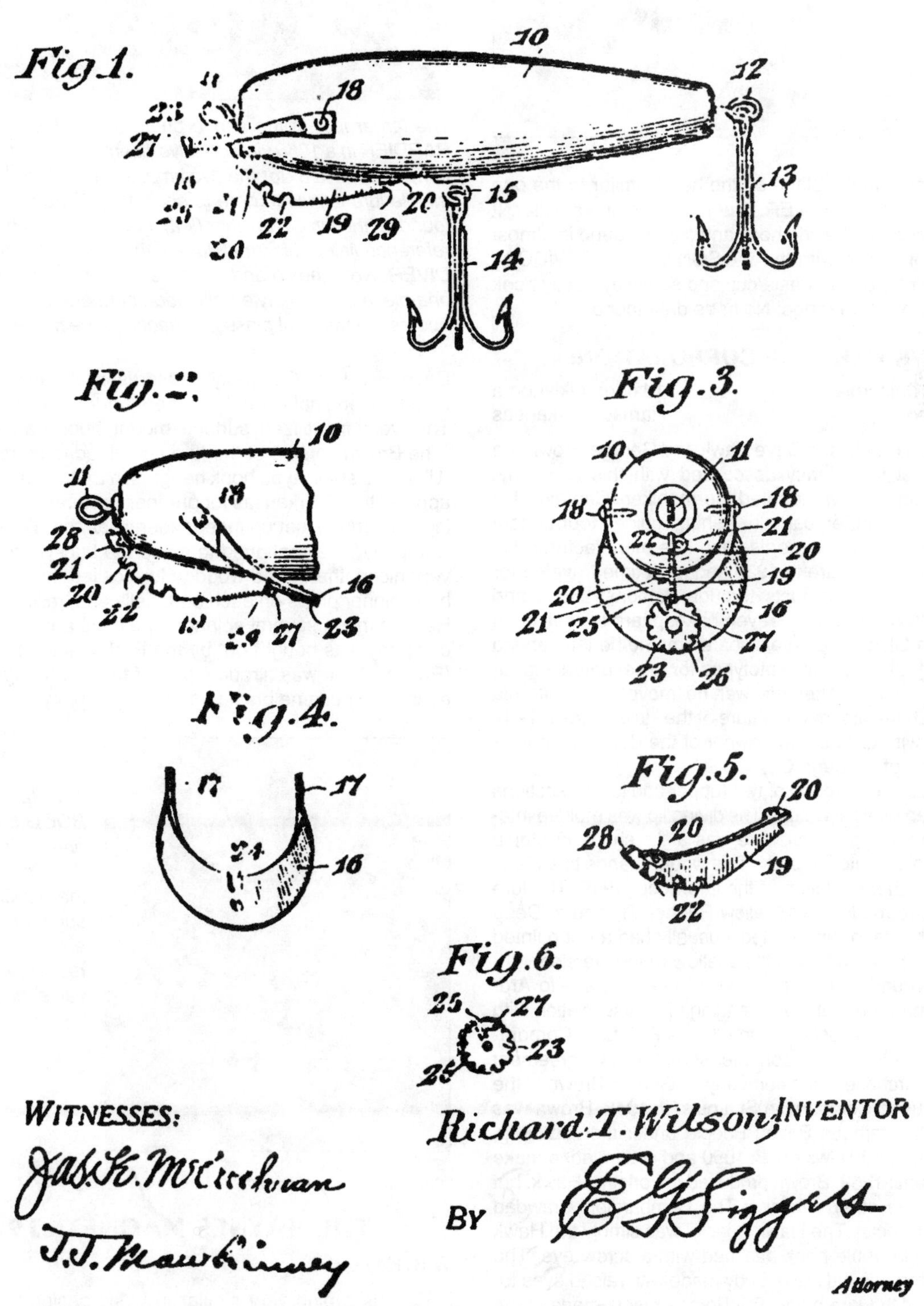

Patent for the WILSON SIX-IN-ONE WOBBLER granted March 27, 1917.

This is a 3-5/8" double-ended lure with a metal plane on each end. The angler may choose either end to render the plug action diving or surface. It had two belly mounted treble hooks. Collector value range: $100-150.

THE STAGGER BUG

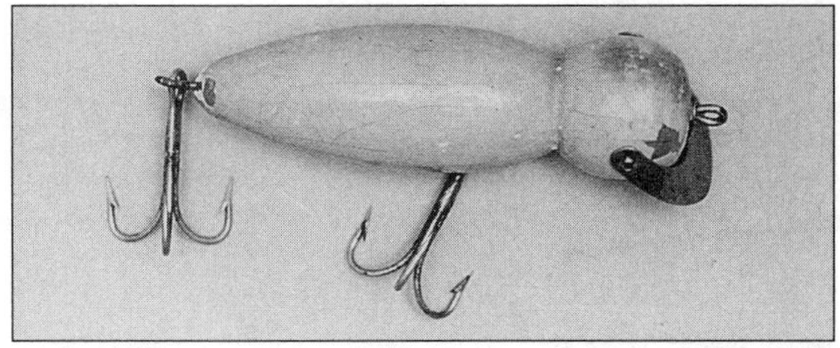

This lure has a metal plane on the head similar to the one on the SIX-IN-ONE WOBBLER. The head is much smaller. It has one belly and one trailing hook and can be found in almost any of the colors listed with the WILSON'S GRASS WIDOW. The one in the photo here has a cup and screw eye belly hook hanger. Collector value range: No trade data found.

HAWK FISH LURE CORPORATION

Verdugo City, California — Ardmore, Oklahoma
St. Louis, Missouri — Harrison, Arkansas

Olan La Vern Hawk, son Dave Hawk and George Brown are the names most importantly associated with this company. Early on, the elder Hawk adopted the moniker "Captain." He was variously a charter captain, fishing guide, tournament caster with considerable expertise and lure manufacturer. He was hired by Shakespeare in 1936 and for a time traveled for them promoting their products through demonstrations and competitions. WW II saw him leave Shakespeare to work in an aircraft plant in Oklahoma. In his spare time he began carving wooden lures that would be prototypes for his eventual manufactured plastic lures. After the war he moved to California where he began the first manufacture of the Hawk Lure in 1947 in partnership with L. A. Brown, owner of the Culver Manufacturing Company of Verdugo City.

The Hawk Lure was made of two (upper and lower) sections of plastic with an internal weight. The diving lip was molded integral with the body. Hook hardware was a "U" shape or staple type hanger molded into the body. This would change to surface hardware in another evolution of the lure about 1949. The lure was made in two models, a "Shallow Runner #1" and a "Deep Runner #2". The deep runner model usually had a dot painted on its face to distinguish it from the shallow runner version.

At a time around 1947, Hawk moved the company to Ardmore, Oklahoma for about a year ending up in association with Clyde W. Bailey and J. Boling as the "Hawk Fish Lure Corporation of St. Louis, Missouri". Soon after somehow an agreement was made for purchase of the company by George Brown of the A.D. Manufacturing Company in St. Louis, in 1948. Brown was the maker of the famous Bayou Boogie under the A.D. Mfg. Brand. Brown bought Hawk out in 1950 and continued to make the Hawk lure until 1959. Brown produced the original Hawk, but also offered three other versions: The Bombardier, Crawdad and the Hawk Special. The Hawk Special was simply the Hawk with only a single treble hook attached with a screw eye. The Crawdad was the original Hawk body made with raised eyes toward the back of the lure body. The Bombardier is made of the original Hawk body with a deep diving metal lip at the nose instead of the integral plastic diving lip.

In 1949 Captain Hawk and son Dave moved to Bull Shoals Lake in Arkansas. They set up a new company, the "Capt. And

The larger lure in the above photo was called a DEEP BOMBARDIER in a 1950 vintage advertisement. The ones in the photo measure 1-5/8" for the two smallest and 2" for the other. The middle lure is placed here to show the different lip that may be found on the lure. The other (left) lure is a BASS HAWK. Another reference listed this small lure with the straight lip as a HAWK DIVER. Note the lip and line tie are integrated. The lures have one-piece surface-style belly hook hangers and tack eyes. The bodies are made of plastic. Collector value range: $5-$10.

Dave Fish Lure Company" in Harrison, Arkansas. They marketed the original Hawk Lure there under the name Luckybug. This version utilized surface mount hook hanger hardware (The Brown version of the lure continued to be made with the "U" shape staple type hook hangers in St. Louis). Captain Dave apparently left Arkansas for greener pastures. His son, remaining in Harrison, set up independently as the "Dave Hawk Lure Company." He continued to make the Luckybug and added a very nice lathe-turned wooden lure called the Injured Shad. It had spinner props on each end, belly and trailing treble hooks. He also made several spinner type baits and jigs. In 1956 the company was bought out by the Padre Island Lure Company (PICO). Hawk was hired as part of the buyout agreement and eventually became president of the company

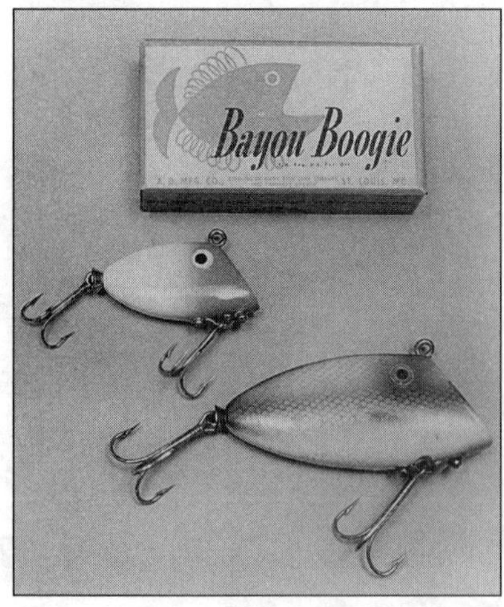

The famous BAYOU BOOGIE is one of several lipless vibrators that were developed in the 1950s. The measurements of these are 1-1/2" and 2-1/2" respectively. Collector value range: $5-$10.

THE HAYNES MAGNET c1908

W.B. Haynes — Akron, Ohio

This is a plug very similar in basic design to the MOONLIGHT FLOATING BAIT. The wood body is shaped with a carved collar behind the head. There is a small spoon attached to the line tie on the nose, a trailing treble and two belly trebles. Collector value range: $300-$500.

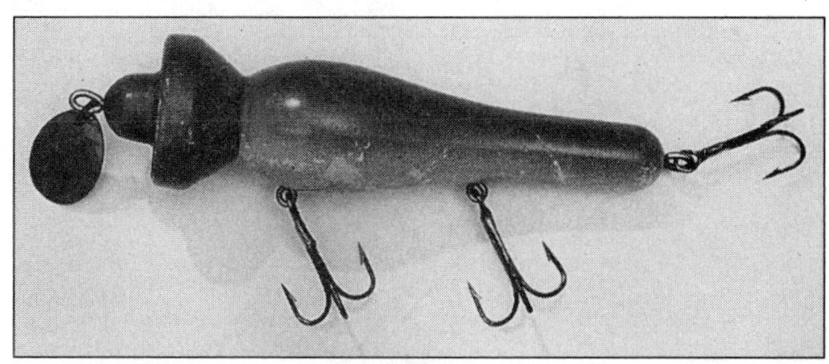

THE HAYNES PEARL CASTING MINNOW c. 1907

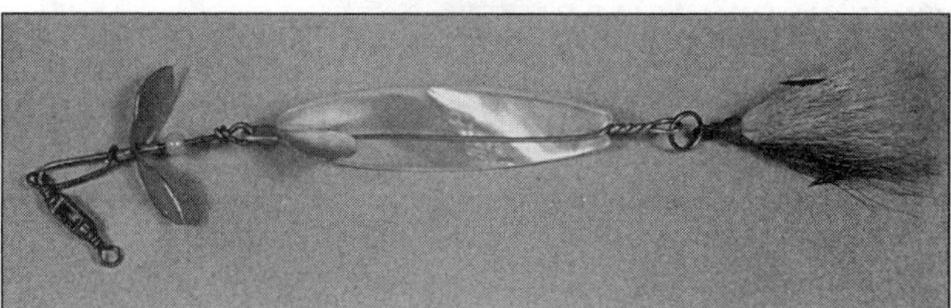

Illustrated in a 1907 advertisement, the body of this lure is made of Mother-of-Pearl. The odd-looking protrusion at the head in the drawing above are actually stabilizer fins. They are affixed in such a way as to hold the lure in an upright position and prevent spinning. The ad says they are made of "German Silver". Don't let that fool you into believing it is real silver. That was a trade name of the day to describe an alloy that was shiny but anything but real silver. 3-1/2" in length. Collector value range: $50-$100. Photo courtesy Jim Muma

A 1/16-scale limited edition model of a 1916 Studebaker. It was a specially painted delivery truck promoting the ZIG WAG. It was use in the mid to late 1930s.

JAMES HEDDON AND SONS

Dowagiac, Michigan — James Heddon, 1845-1911
Will T. Heddon, 1870-1955 — Charles Heddon, 1874-1941

The Heddon Company began humbly and became one of the giants of the tackle industry in its 80 plus years. Founded by James Heddon and his son W.T. (Will) Heddon. The elder Heddon was quite an accomplished gentleman before he ever got in to the tackle business. He was an inventor recognized nationally as an expert on bee-keeping. He invented several devices and methods in this discipline and was widely published in the journals. He was into publishing (newspaper) and politics (Mayor of Dowagiac) also. Son Will was something of an adventurer having done, among other things, hot air balloon ascents returning to the ground by parachute. The latter was particularly hazardous in those early days of its development. At the time he worked for his father in the newspaper business and became the manager of the Dowagiac electricity generating plant. At some point shortly thereafter, he organized the Dowagiac Telephone Company which he sold to the Bell Telephone Company in 1897. It was about this time that James Heddon started the company.

These are six of twenty-four blank lures found in Mineola, Florida by Heddon specialist Clyde Harbin. He carefully documented the find and authenticated them as having belonged to W.T. and Laura Heddon.

The story is old and has been told many times with little significant variation. It seems that Mr. Heddon was waiting for a fishing buddy one day by the side of the lake. To while away the time he whittled on a chunk of wood and upon satisfying the whittling urge casually tossed the result into the water. What happened next is the legend. To his amazement a big bass attacked the chunk so violently that it was knocked into the air. Some say the bass did this repeatedly. Whatever the exact event the idea of making artificial baits out of wood (hence the name "plug") was born in Heddon's mind in that moment. In Sam S. Stinson's *Whence The Plug?** he says according to James Heddon's son Charles, his father was using wooden plugs as early as 1890 and carved a few for family and friends. It was not until 1901 that Heddon Plugs were commercially available. The company was under several ownerships after the Heddons and is presently under the ownership of Pradco in Ft. Smith, Arkansas where they maintain an extensive archive of Heddon products from the earliest to latest days.

A common story related in reference to the beginnings of the company is that early on in the production of lures, there was a rush order for some lures whose paint was still wet and that to hurry up the drying process the lures were placed in Mrs. Heddon's oven. The result was a crackling of the paint on the back of the lures. Supposedly this was the birth of the so-called fancy-back paint finishes. Whatever the case, the company was started in a small upstairs room at 303 Green Street in Dowagiac by James Heddon. He was soon joined by his son Will who brought with him a $1,000 investment. This is thought to be about 1902. The 1903 catalog reads *James Heddon and Son.* Subsequent catalogs read that way until the 1908 catalog. That catalog reads James Heddon and *Sons.* It seems that Charles turned out to be the one with the talent for business and Will the tinker. It was about 1903 that Will and his wife

Laura went to Florida to experiment with various lure types and finishes. Apparently they and the company found that arrangement to their liking for it wasn't long after that they took up permanent residence in Mineola. They were both very talented fishermen and worked as a team in the experimentation and development of new lures. They also became important contributors to their newly adopted community. Each served in various community service and political capacities including terms as mayor. Will once and Laura three times. When James died in 1911, Will continued to serve in the research and development end and Charles continued to run the company. Upon the death of the father the company became known as James Heddon's Sons. At some point Charles did become president. Upon his death in 1941 his son John took over as president. Will continued in his research and development capacity until 1945. No member of the Heddon family was associated with the company after 1955.

**From an article in a 1921 issue of American Angler.*

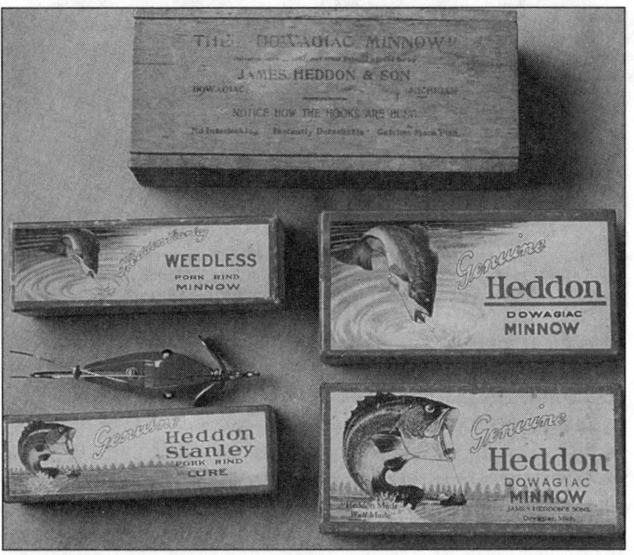

Miscellaneous early boxes. The boxes of all the companies are desirable collectibles themselves, but when you find a new lure in its original box it can add considerably to the value of the lure itself. Photo courtesy Dennis "Doc" Hyder.

A c. 1927-31 box. Note the VAMP that the bass is hooked on.

A box with the new 1949 Heddon logo on it.

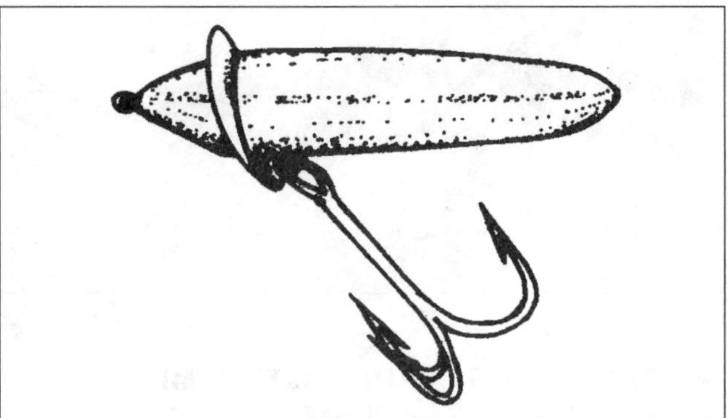

ORIGINAL DOWAGIAC BAIT. The first made by James Heddon.

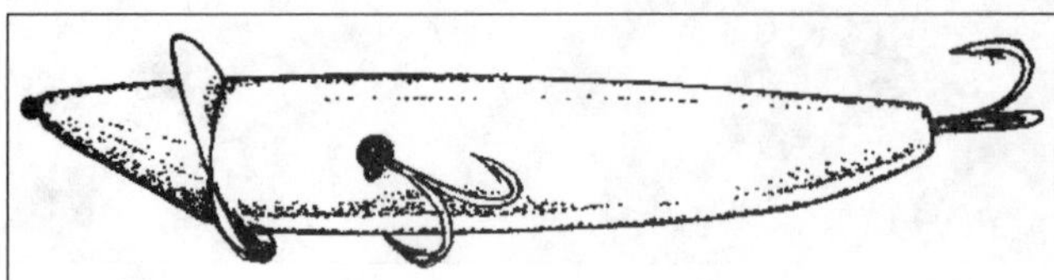

A drawing of one of the first wooden baits made by James Heddon.

The following pages list the old Heddon lures by ascending catalog series number and date where possible.

Before getting into the listings, it is important to note three early lures, the Heddon hand-carved frog, the model of the original Dowagiac bait, and the model of the first Heddon wooden bait.

JAMES HEDDON'S WOODEN FROG c. 1898.

Body Length: approximately 3"

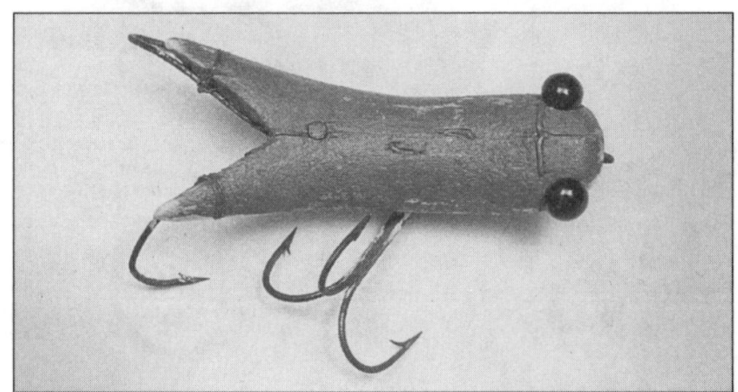

Pictured here are three views of one of the first plugs used by James Heddon. He carved this plug for himself and a few others for friends, therefore it is extremely rare and valuable. It would not be prudent to place a value on it. It is simply too rare to price. The collector who finds one should consider himself lucky, indeed.

Side view.

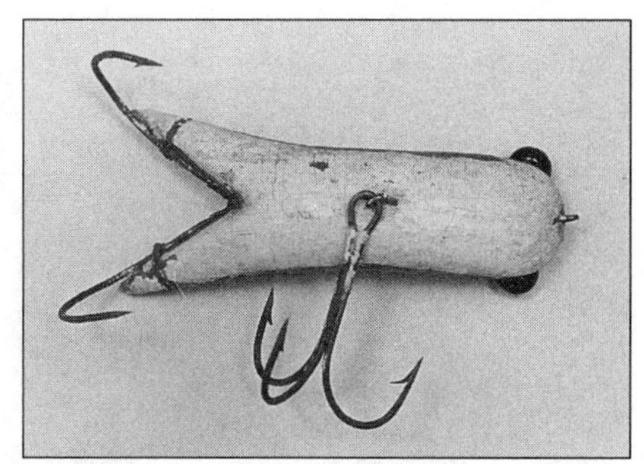

Belly view.

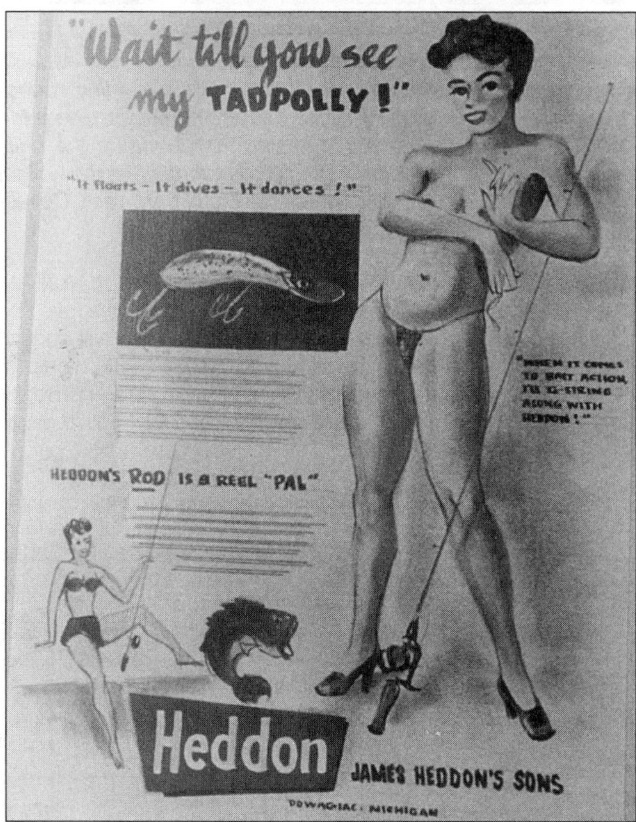

This rare risque' advertising layout may have been a joke from their advertising agency or it may have been a genuine proposal. It is full of innuendo. There is a story that the boys' wives got wind of it and squelched the idea. Whatever the case, it's fun and a humorous bit of Heddon history.

Some Specific Tips On Dating Heddon Lures

As will be discussed under the listing for the sloped-nose EXPERTS, the first commercially produced Heddon lures had hook fasteners that were screw hooks recessed in a hole in the body (see patent drawing).

Shortly after this the recesses were fitted with metal flanged cups to protect the outside edges of the recess from the hook shanks. The first of these had a very thin flange or rim. Later the cup was made a bit larger and with broader rims or flanges. This "Cup" hardware is still use by some companies today. A Heddon catalog of 1915 or 1916 illustrated and described "The new Heddon Double Screw Hook Fastening now used on all 'Dowagiac Minnows ...'". It is headed "Heddon Patent Hook Fastening", but there is a patent number 1,276,062, applied for May 20, 1915 and not granted to Heddon until August 20, 1918. Although the statement said "...all Dowagiac Minnows", it is reasonable to note the possibility of many old types still in warehouse inventory. Therefore one can only date the first use of this double screw fastener (known to collectors as the "L-rig") approximately. The patent described and illustrated the L-rig as having two humps, but there have been one hump versions, and even a no hump* version found (probably pre-dates the patented rig).

**Only one is known to the author, There may be more. Possibly a modification by a fisherman.*

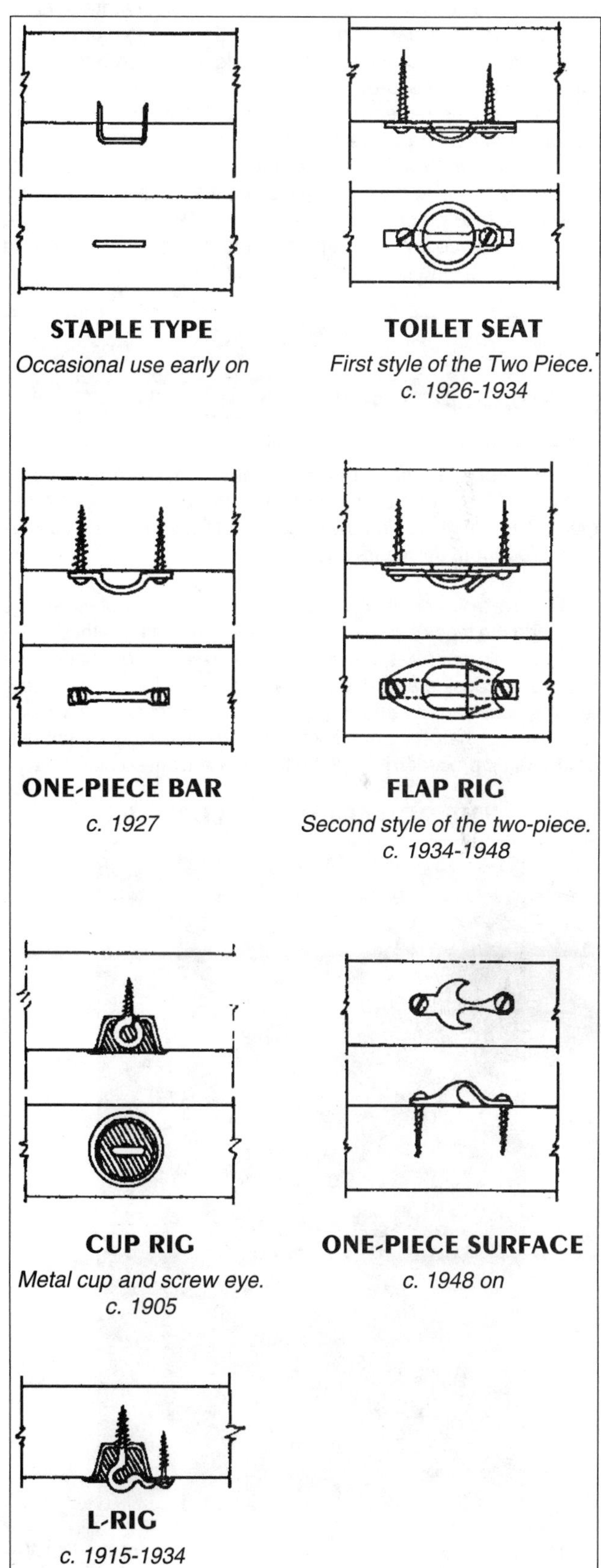

The above illustrations and dates can help you identify the vintage of your Heddon lure, but the dates are not hard and fast rules. There were also two styles of cup rigs, three if you count the earliest gold-colored cups. The early (1903 & 1904) catalogs also illustrated lures with no cup in the hole. The first cup rig is referred to as the SHALLOW CUP. Then came the standard cup rig that is sometimes referred to as the DEEP CUP. Remember also, that there may have been older vintage hardware leftover, still in the bins and placed on later vintage plugs along with newer hardware. There could also have been some mixing on the same lure.

There have been some plugs with the "one-piece bar", but generally collectors place the "two-piece rig" as next in line. There were two versions. The first, referred to as the "toilet seat" for obvious reasons, began around 1930 and the second style two-piece rig came into use around 1935. The final style is the "one-piece surface" replacing the "two-piece rig" around the mid 1940s and is in general use today.

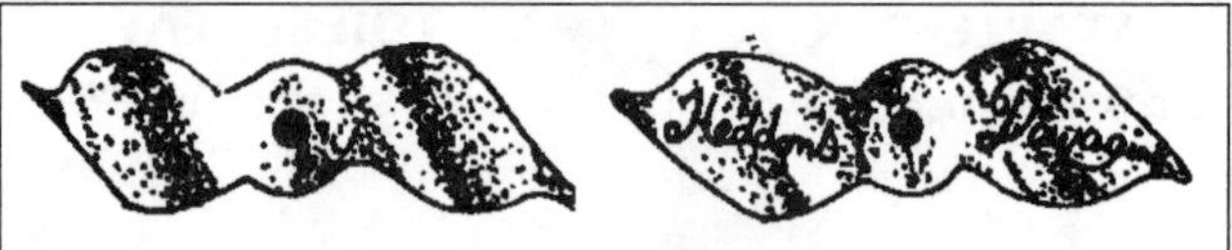

The left propeller spinner is the earliest, dating from 1903 to 1911-1912. The one on the right is marked "Heddon's Dowagiac". They began using these around 1912-1913 and continued throughout the years after.

There are other more general rules, but they are not as reliable as noting the type of hardware. Even the hardware method is not entirely foolproof for it is possible to change some or all of the hardware, causing a lure to appear older than it really is. There are methods that enable the collector to reasonably determine whether this has happened, but they are the highly technical, complicated procedures used by the very advanced collector.

THE DOWAGIAC UNDERWATER

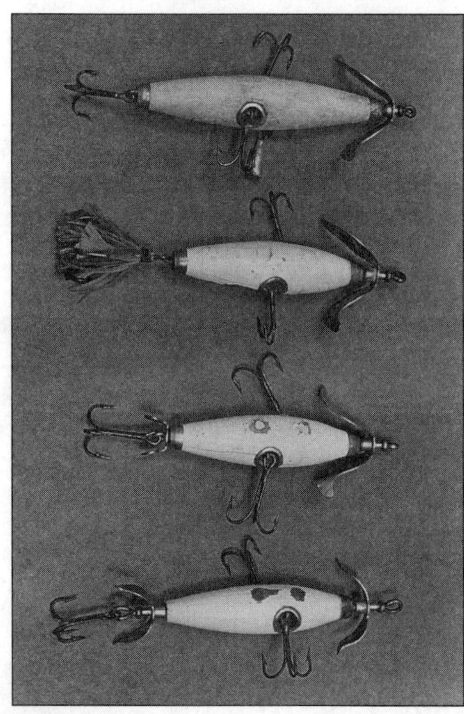

The four lures above represent the evolution of the DOWAGIAC UNDERWATER to what is thought to be its ultimate form,

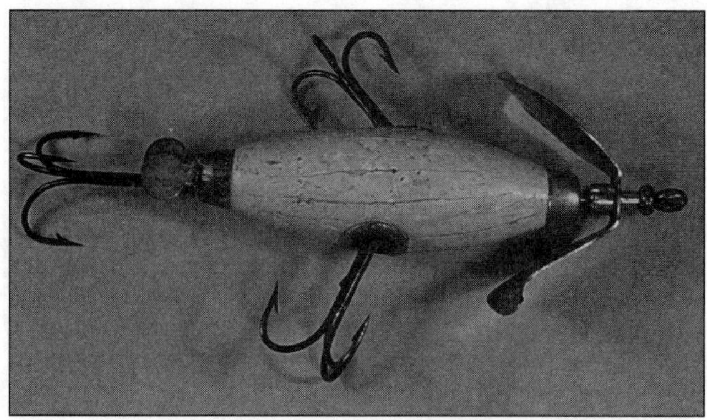

This short version of the 1903 DOWAGIAC UNDERWATER is 2-3/8" long, has marine brass hardware, no eyes, the earliest, sweeping nose-mounted propeller and the early tiny round-blade tail spinner. It has no name or trade markings. The earliest version has a lead weight swung from beneath the belly (see top lure in previous photo). Later versions have the weight inside the body. The hook hangers have cup hardware. Collector value range: $200-$300.

the No. 100. The first lure in the photo (top) is earliest. Note the external belly weight. The next down has a smaller body. The third is the same body, but it has the addition of a small oddball prop at the tail. The last is the same body with No. 100 type propeller spinner and brass cup hardware. This is believed to be the transitional plug to the No. 100. Collector value range for the earliest Dowagiac Underwaters: $500-$1,000.

DOWAGIAC "EXPERT"

SURFACE LURE and The 200 Series

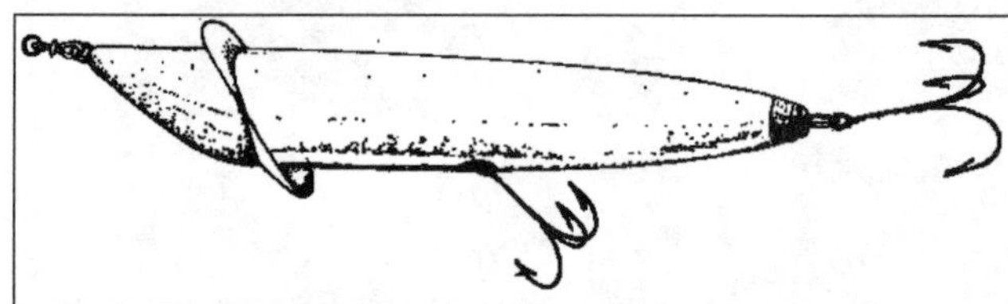

This drawing copies the illustration in the first Heddon catalog in 1902.

First called the "'Dowagiac' Perfect Surface Casting Bait" the EXPERT had evolved into the 200 Series by 1912.

The EXPERT patent was applied for January 9, 1902 and granted to Heddon on April 1, 1902.

This patent described four features as follows:

1. The metal angling collar (B on patent drawing)
2. The hook socket (A on patent drawing)
3. The screw hook or open-eye screw (B on patent drawing)
4. The sloped-up nose (A on patent drawing).

The EXPERT was featured in the 1902 catalog and incorporated all specifications in the patent. It was first marketed in a second model in 1904. The original had one belly-mounted treble and a trailing (2T) treble hook and the second ("Dowagiac No. 2") had two additional treble hooks, opposite side-mounted (4T). Interestingly that 1904 catalog states, "We do not advocate the use of the 'No. 2', but offer this pattern to those who hold the false theory of 'more hooks, more fish'." The No. 2 did not appear in subsequent catalogs. All the catalog entries until 1912 stated it was available only in a white body, red painted collar and a blue nose*. The 1912 edition of the catalog said: "White body, blue snout and nickel plated collar; Frog colors, consisting of white belly, green spotted back." By then it was called the "No. 200 Special Series." The same catalog entry said it could be had with two, three or four treble hooks if preferred. By 1913 they had added a luminous finish. Most interesting to note in the 1913 catalog is that both the slope nose style and the round pencil nose style bodies are used in illustrations. The round pencil nose style was used to illustrate the Frog finish. All EXPERT and No. 200 catalog illustrations prior were of the slope nose type. The double body style illustration remained this way at least through 1916. There is a gap in the catalog section here until in 1921 where only the round nose model was available.

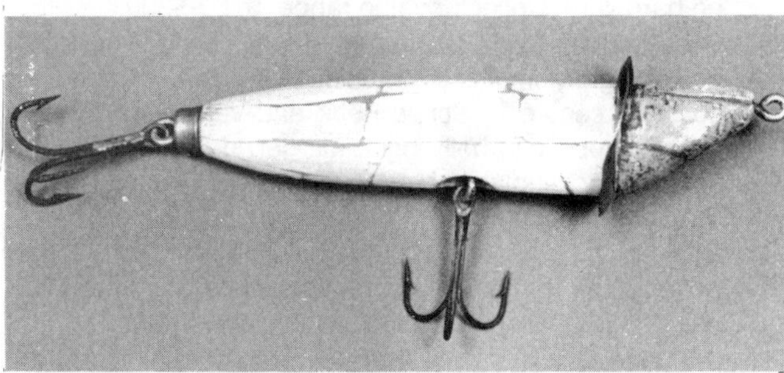

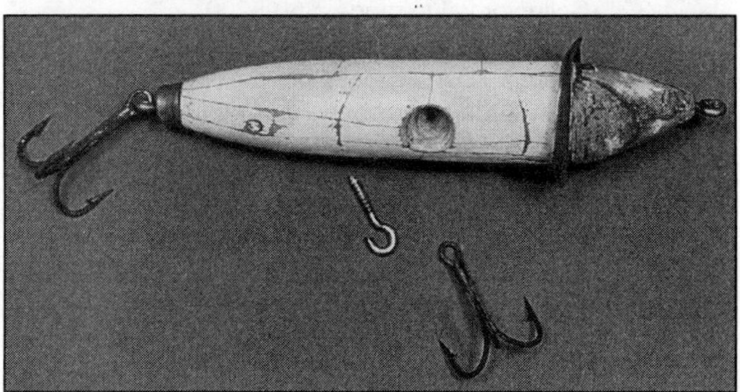

This is the 1902 vintage EXPERT in side and belly view. Note the addition of the metal reinforcing tail cap. The recess for the screw hook without any cup hardware is clearly visible. Collector value range for this particular Expert is: $50-$200.

One last note about colors. A collector wrote me of having a yellow nose No. 200. They are in scarce supply. Heddon, like most of the companies, would paint or configure lures almost any way asked if there was a sufficient number ordered that way. The yellow nose is probably one of those.

**1906 was actually the first catalog to state red collar and blue nose. All previous catalogs simply stated: "...glistening white enamel."*

The following is a set of guidelines, observations and conclusions I have arrived at regarding the EXPERTS and No. 200 Series lures:

1. It is *possible* that the earliest Experts were all white (c. 1902-03).
2. The first reference to other colors was in 1906 where it said "red painted collar and blue snout".
3. By 1912 the collar was described as nickel plated
4. Regarding collars:
   a. First was friction mount (no pins).
   b. Next was a one-pin mount under the nose.
   c. About 1912 came the two-pin collar mount simultaneous with the first of the nickel plated cup hardware and tail cap.
   d. About 1915-17 came the three-pin collar attachment and the L-rig. The collar was marked "Heddon Dowagiac". Prior to this collars were not marked in any way.
   e. Screws instead of pins were used to attach collars.
5. At some point (c1912) they were made available with the belly trebles.
6. They lost the metal tail cap sometime during the L-rig period
7. All were without eyes until about the first two-piece toilet seat hook hardware period when they acquired glass eyes
8. Deviations from the above have been found but this is extremely rare. Consider yourself fortunate if you snag one.

EVOLUTION OF THE HEDDON EXPERT TO THE No. 200 SURFACE

Letter designations beside the descriptions are keys to the photos.

A. The original EXPERT. It was the only lure listed in the first (1903) Heddon catalog. 4-1/2" long, brass screw hook in the recess, friction mount collar (no screws or pins), brass tail cap, blue painted nose. Collector value range: $650-$850.

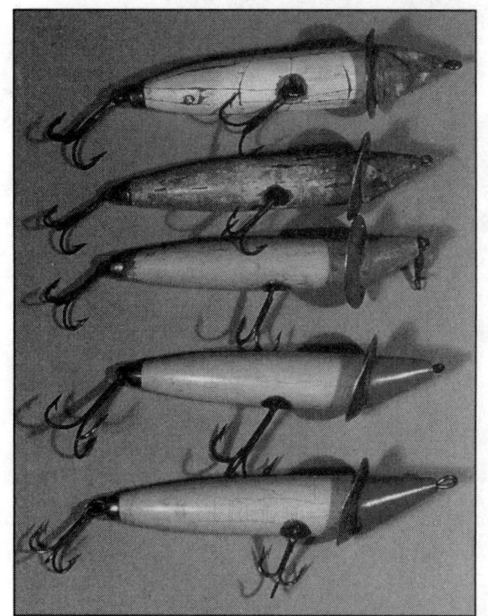

(A-E)

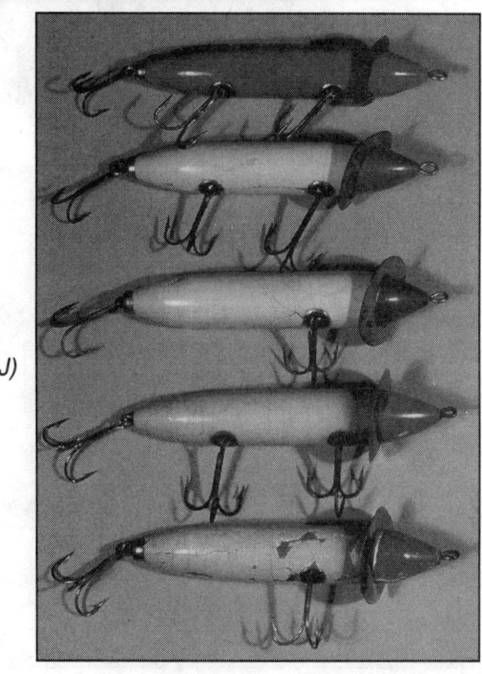

(F-J)

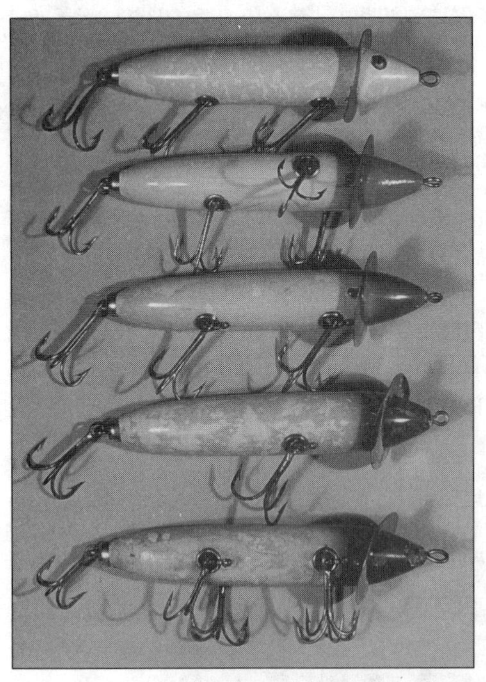

(K-O)

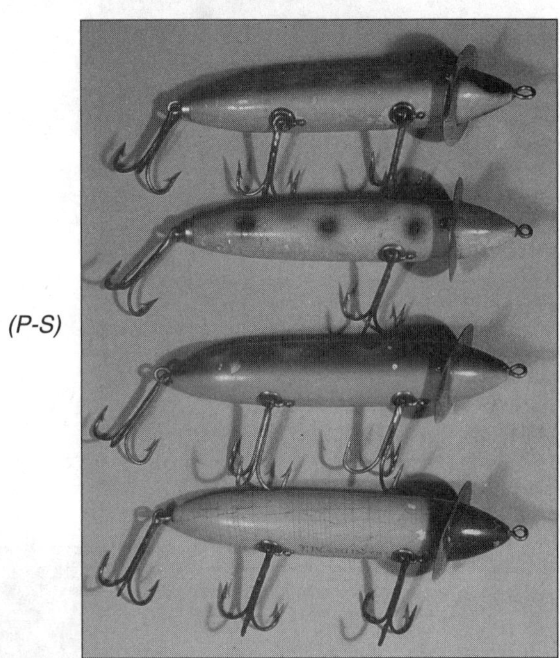

(P-S)

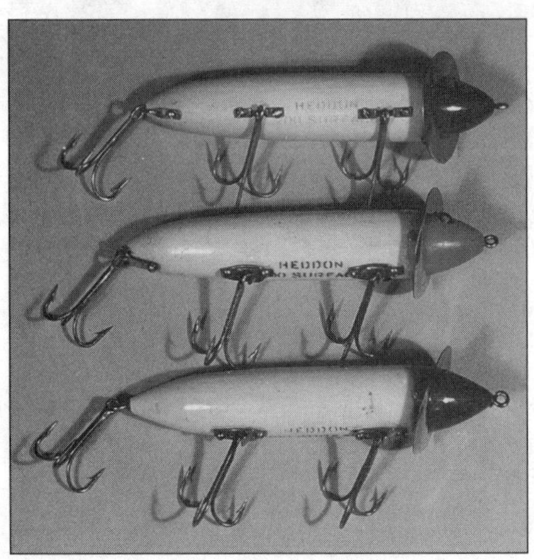

(T-V)

B. Second model of the EXPERT. Slightly thinner body. Smaller line tie. Friction fit collar painted red. Collector value range: $650-$850.

C. Same as B above except that the brass cup on this lure is rimmed. 4-3/8". Collector value range: $400-$650.

D. Same as C above except that this one has one pin at the front bottom of the collar holding it secure to the lure body. The collar is painted red. This is the last EXPERT to use the small line tie. Collector value range: $200-$400.

E. The earliest model to utilize the nickel-plated deep cup and screw hook hardware. Two pins, at the top and bottom of the collar, secure it to the body (not through the body collar but adjacent). Large line tie and all nickel plated hardware. Collector value range: $150-$300.

F. Solid red painted, cigar-shaped (pencil nose, c.1915) body. Slightly smaller collar using two pins adjacent to the collar to secure it. Screw hook and very deep, almost cone-shaped cup belly hook hanger, deep tail hook insert. All nickel-plated hardware. 4-3/4". Collector value range: $150-$300.

G. Same as F above with but a slightly larger collar attached by a pin through the collar. It has a white body with blue nose. 4-5/8". Collector value range: $150-$300.

H. Same as G above except the collar is not painted at all. 4-3/4". Collector value range: $50-$200.

I. This is the first EXPERT to utilize a flanged collar (illustrated on lure M). This is that there are two nibs or flanges on the collar through which the pins go to secure the collar to the body. Heretofore there was no flange; the pins simply went through the collar itself (illustrated on lure H.) The tail cap on this lure is missing. 4-3/4". Collector value range: $150-$200.

J. Same as above, but is a 2T model. 4-5/8". Collector value range: $150-$200.

K. This may be an experimental or prototype lure. It came from the Heddon factory archives. Oddities are the glass eyes, brass tail cap and friction-fit collar. It is placed here because of body shape and hook hardware. The glass-eyed models don't show up with any regularity until around 1930-35. 4-3/4". Collector value range: $150-$200.

L. First use of the three-flange pinned collar. 4T. Deep cup and screw hook hangers, all nickel plated hardware and red painted collar. 4-3/4". Collector value range: $75-$150.

M. First use of the L-rig hook hanger on the EXPERT. This is also the first appearance of the Heddon imprint on the collar. It appears on both sides. The other characteristics are the same as L above. Post-1915. 4-3/4". Collector value range: $50-$75.

N. Same as M above except that it is a 2T model. 4-3/4". Collector value range: $25-$75.

O. Same as N above except that it is a 5T model. 4-3/4". Collector value range: $50-$100.

P. This is the first frog finish for Heddon and it helps to estimate the vintage of this lure at c. 1915. It is easy to distinguish the difference between the two frog finishes by noting the presence or absence of the mustache type marking at the nose. The mustache is the earliest. The Heddon imprint appears on both sides of the collar. L-rig hardware. Collector value range: $50-$75.

Q. Same as P above except for finish and the fact that this is the first appearance of the flange collar held to the body with screws. 4-3/4". Collector value range: $25-$75.

R. Second frog finish (no mustache). Tail caps disappear from the lures at this point in time. The Heddon imprint now appears only on the front side of the collar. Other characteristics are the same as Q above. 4-3/4". Collector value range: $50-$75.

S. Same as R above except for "HEDDON 200 SURFACE" stenciled on the belly of the lure. 4-3/4". Collector value range: $50-$75.

T. Glass eyes, three-flange screwed unmarked collar, one-piece bar hook hanger, one-piece no-hump tail hook hanger (P.S. Bear patent), "HEDDON 200 SURFACE" stenciled on belly. 4-3/4". Collector value range: $50-$75.

U. Same as T above except for the utilization of the two-piece toilet seat style belly hook hanger and the two-piece rectangular tail hook hanger. 4-3/4". Collector value range: $50-$75.

V. Same as U above except for the screw eye tail hook hanger and lack of eyes. Collector value range: $50-$75.

SERIES NO. 1001 RH

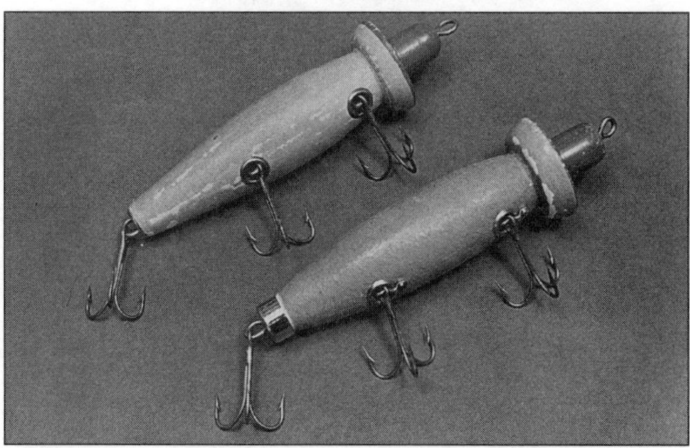

The upper lure measures 4-1/2" and sports cup and screw hook hardware and a protective/ hook preventer tail cup insert. The lower lure measures 4-5/8", utilizes the 2-hump "L-rig" hook hardware and is equipped with a polished metal tail cap. Note the fatter body. They have luminous white bodies with long, red painted heads.

These woodpecker type lures are Heddon products. Information about them is elusive. They have never been found cataloged or advertised by Heddon. There is one obscure reference in a 1917 catalog that some collectors think may be this lure. It was a list of recommended lures for various fishing conditions. Under the list for night fishing there is an entry for the 1001 RH. This number appears nowhere in catalogs for a lure that could have a red head. The number 1000 is for the metal Triple Tease, but a red head is not practical for this type lure. Collector value range: $200-$600.

NIGHT-RADIANT MOONLIGHT BAIT c. 1908-11

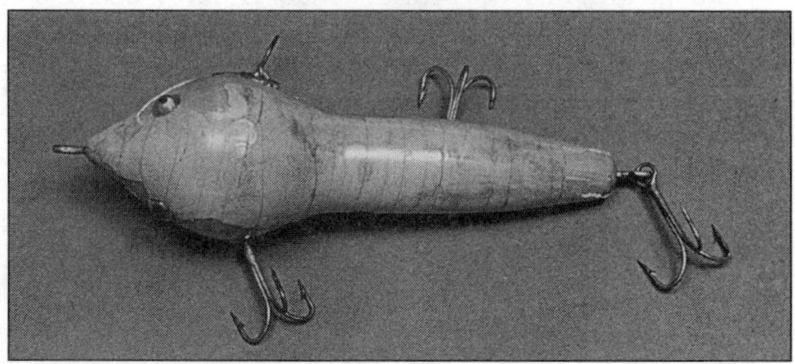

This interesting plug is 5" long and sports glass eyes. Two opposite side trebles on the bulbous head, a belly treble and trailing treble (4T). There is also a shorter, 4" version with only three treble hooks. There has been only one reference to this lure in Heddon catalogs uncovered so far. It is only a photograph as part of the back page design of the 1965 edition of a Heddon catalog. Collector value range: $2,000-$3,000.

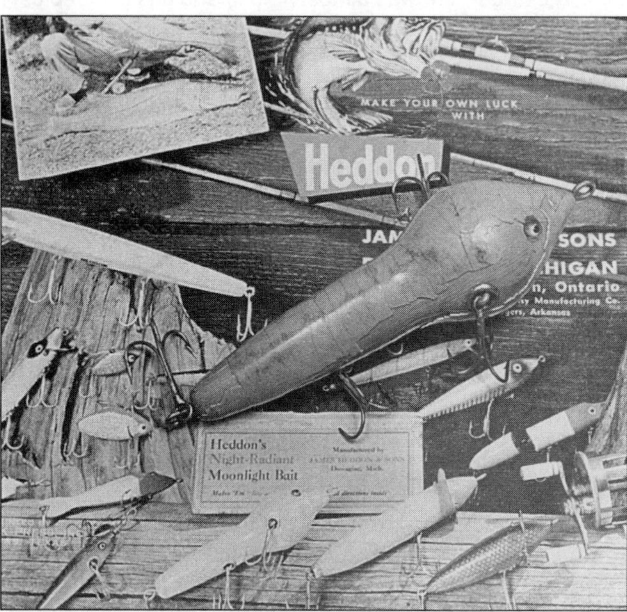

A detail from the back cover of the 1965 Heddon catalog showing the night-radiant MOONLIGHT BAIT.

DOWAGIAC MINNOW SERIES "0" AND "00"

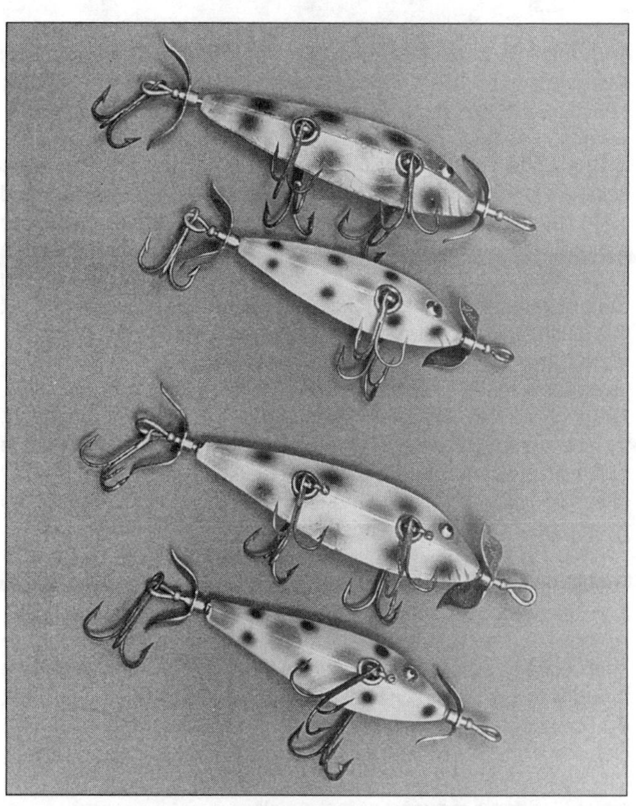

Top two DOWAGIAC MINNOWS show cup hardware. The two on the bottom have the L-rig hardware. Although the L-rig version is a later model, it is the rarest of the two. The later two-piece toilet seat style hanger is also difficult to find.

A 1912 Heddon catalog says "Here's The New One." The photo shows the earliest at the top. They were first produced with the cup and screw hook hardware. The later versions had the "L-rig" as illustrated on the bottom two plugs. The "0" was about 3-3/4" long, has three trebles as in photo and two propellers. The larger "00" was almost 4" long and has five trebles. It was otherwise the same. They were in catalogs until about 1927. The color offerings were: White body, red and green decorations; yellow body, red, green and black decorations; and red body with black decorations. Collector value range: $175-$300. Some of the rare colors such a red with black spots will bring more than double the high range figure.

DOWAGIAC MINNOW
No. 100 Series and No. 150 Series

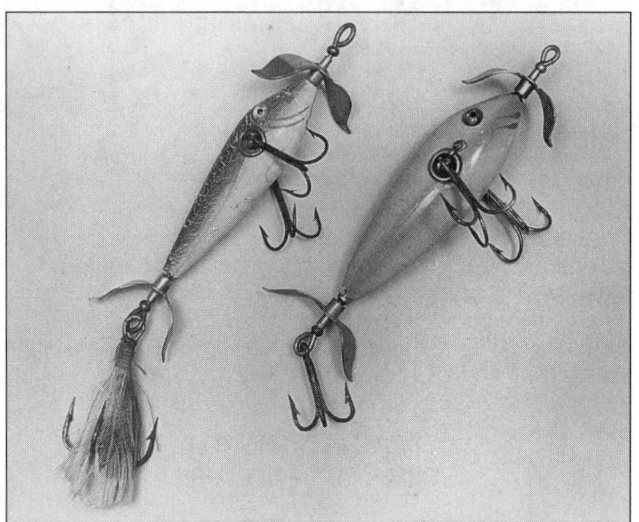

Left is an early No. 100 with high forehead, unmarked props and brass cup hook hanger hardware. Right lure is a later No. 100. Fatter body and L-rig hardware.

It is quite obvious that Heddon made no lures with propeller spinners in 1903 or prior for there is a paragraph in the 1903 and 1904 catalogs that says, "These devices, while churning water to a more or less extent, do not perform the very important function of throwing water into the air as does the 'Dowagiac'." It went on to denigrate the "spinners" and "paddle wheels" vociferously, all this, curiously, just before and in the same 1904 catalog that introduced the first Dowagiac Underwater with a forward-mounted propeller spinner. That brings us to the No. 100 and the No. 150. Although the No. 100 was first found in a 1905 edition catalog, there is an advertisement for the No. 100 in the May, 1904 issue of *National Sportsman* magazine. The same 1905 catalog and all after make no reference to the DOWAGIAC UNDERWATER, so presumably the 100s and 150s replaced it.

The No. 150 in the photo has the light GREEN FANCY BACK finish, unmarked nickel props, rear screw eye, screw hook hangers, and cups of brass. The glass eyes have YELLOW IRIS. There are three hand-painted gill marks, and three internal belly weights. The Heddon three-belly-weight lures are thought to be the first style. So is the light green fancy back (notice very faint white crackles). The wood box marked James Heddon and "SONS" came about in 1908.

The 100s and 150s are probably the first shaped-body minnows Heddon produced commercially.

The very earliest of these have what is called a high forehead body configuration as in the photo of the two No. 100s here.

The 100s were normally equipped with two opposite-mount side trebles and a trailing treble (3T) and the 150s have five trebles (two on each side). There is a 1907 Abercrombie and Fitch catalog that offers it in a belly treble and trailing treble model (2T). The 2T is rarely found. The 100s lasted until about 1942-43, but the 150s continued in production for many years after, still being made of wood with glass eyes as late as 1953. It was brought out in wood again in the late 1970s as part of Heddon's Wooden Classic Series. Collector value range: $150-$450.

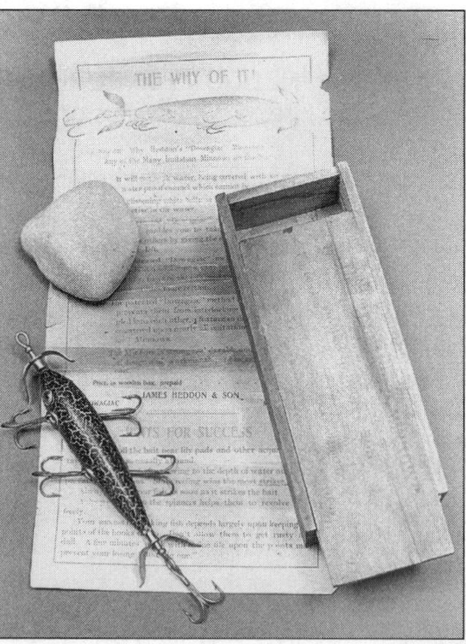

This is a No. 150 with cup and screw hook rigging with original wooden box. The stone in the photo is from Dowagiac Creek.

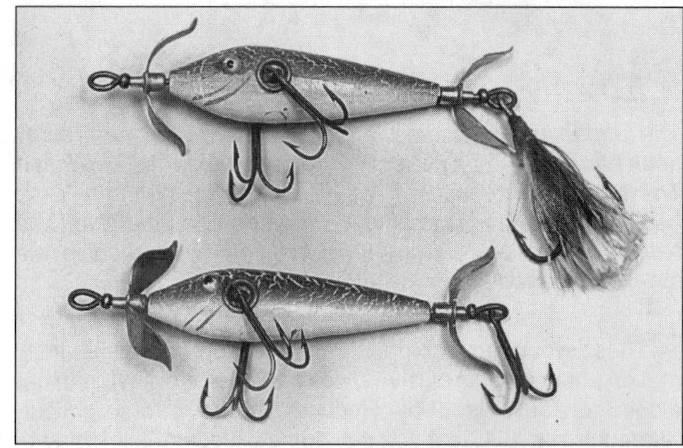

This photograph of the early 100s shows difference in gill marks. Upper lure gill marks are curved. This is oldest manner. Bottom lure has more or less straight painted gill marks. This is the newer of the two.

THE JEANETTE HAWLEY MOHAWK

For some unknown reason around 1906-08, Heddon marketed the 150s and 100s as the MOHAWK (floater or underwater) and the MOHAWK CRACKER under Laura Heddon's pen name, "Jeanette Hawley". According to the copy of a brochure I have, the MOHAWK was apparently only available in the "Fancy Back" finish as in the above photo and the MOHAWK CRACKER could be had in "Glossy White, Yellow, Aluminum or Red." Collector value range: No trade data found.

CATALOG NAME	BODY LENGTH	LURE WEIGHT
Mohawk	3-3/5"	7/10 oz.
Mohawk Cracker	2-3/4"	2/3 oz.

COLOR OR FINISH: Fancy green back, white belly; rainbow, white body, red eyes; aluminum; red body; yellow, gold; fancy sienna yellow.

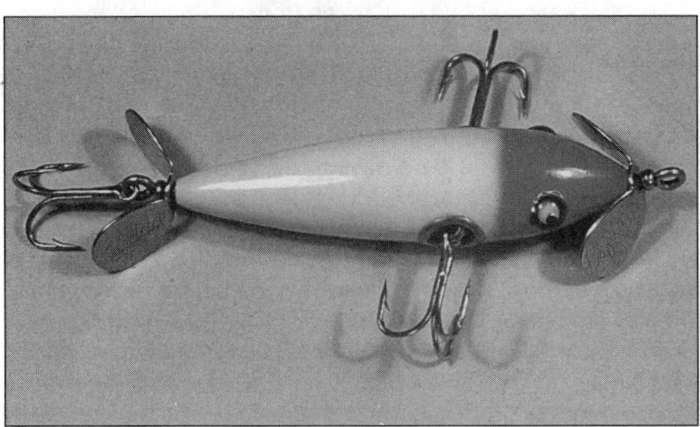

The nickel plated, large shallow cup hook hanger hardware and glass eyes should place this No. 100 in the 1905 to 1915 era. The problem here is the presence of the unique Heddon Stanley propeller spinners. As far as can presently determined, Heddon didn't acquire the Stanley company until the early 1920s. Perhaps the props were obtained from Stanley prior to Heddon buying the company.

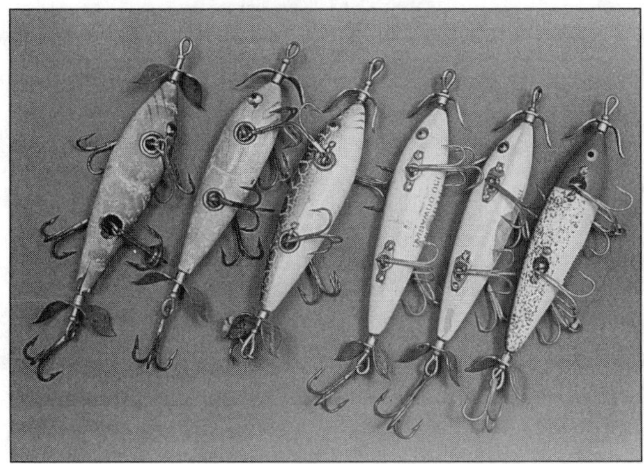

This photo shows hardware progression for the No. 150s from left to right. The first lure has see-through hardware. This is not typical of Heddon. It is not seen elsewhere and may have been an experimental prototype. The remaining lures show the classic hardware progression right up to the one-piece surface on the reissue No. 150 in the late 1970s Heddon Wooden Classic Series. Collector value range: from bottom to top: $200-$300 for the earlier examples; $75-$150 for later ones.

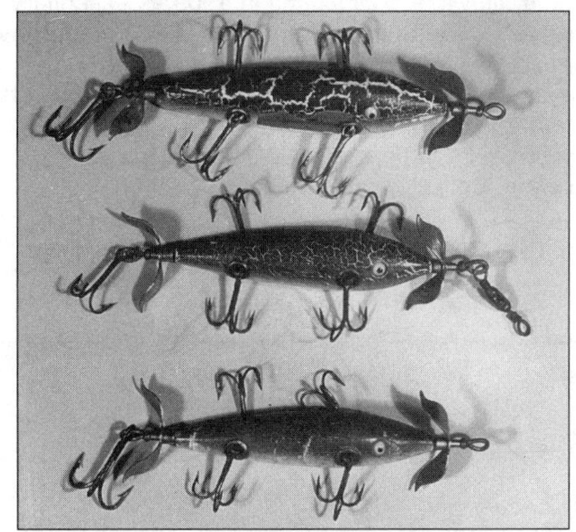

Heddon No. 150 Series. All three have opaque yellow iris glass eyes, unmarked big props and cup/screw hook hardware. The upper lure has two internal belly weights, nickel plated hardware and three long sweeping red painted gill marks, 4-1/4". The middle lure has two belly weights, brass hardware and a spray painted red throat, 3-5/8". The last has only brass cup and screw hook. The other hardware is nickel plate. It has three belly weights and measures 3-9/16". Collector value range: $200-$300.

CATALOG SERIES #	BODY LENGTH	LURE WEIGHT
150	3-3/8"	9/10 oz.
3-3/4"	3/4 oz.	

COLOR OR FINISH: Aluminum color, solid red, yellow, gold color, fancy sienna yellow, red body, dark blended back, yellow perch; yellow perch, scale finish; frog colors; frog scale finish; green scale finish; red scale finish; goldfish, scale finish; copper, white.

DOWAGIAC MINNOW
No. 175 Series

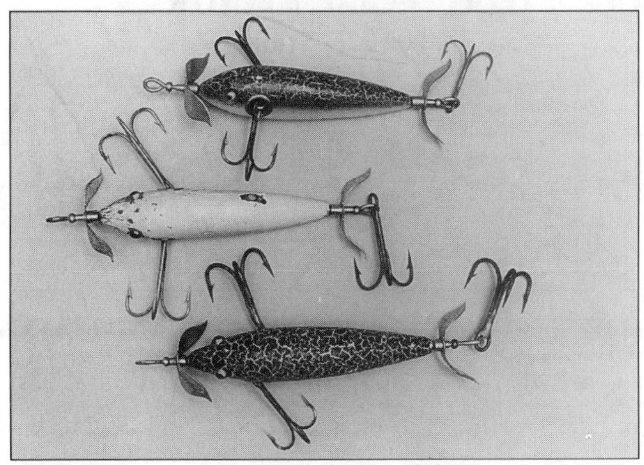

Top to bottom: oldest to newest 175's. Top lure has: large nickel plate cups with screw hooks, one internal belly weight, glass eyes and large unmarked props it measures 3-3/8". Be careful, for it is easy to confuse this one with the #100 Series. The middle lure has the same hardware, but the body is slightly bigger all round. It is 3-3/4" long. The lower lure is the same except that the props are marked with the Heddon imprint and it is 3-7/8" long.

This lure, first found cataloged in 1909, is essentially the same as the No. 150 Series except that it is a 3T model having only two opposite-mounted side trebles. It has the same specifications as the 150s and was available in fancy green back with white belly, rainbow, and blended white (gray back). Earliest models are 3-3/4" long and have larger than standard size cup hardware. Collector value range: $200-$400.

HEDDON "DOWAGIAC" MINNOW
No. 10 Series

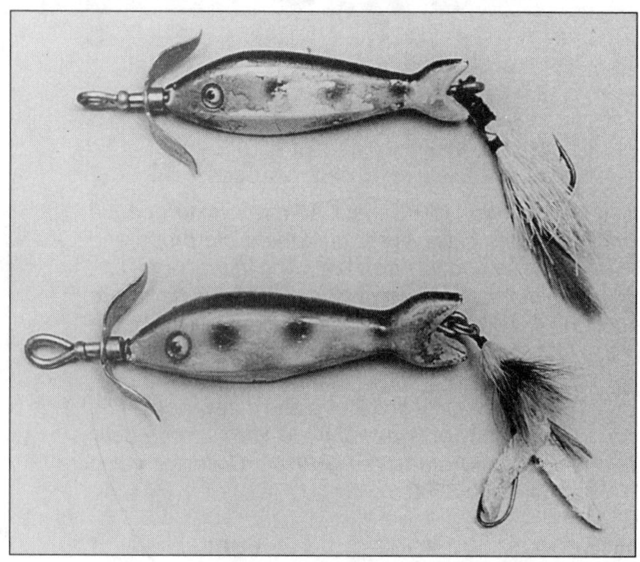

The upper lure measures 2-1/2" and the lower, 2-5/8". Each has glass eyes and marked propeller spinners.

New in the 1912 catalog this little beauty was 2-3/8" long. My drawing here is a copy of the illustration in the 1912 catalog. One single-feathered trailing hook and what they called "...the new Heddon Hexagon form...". This entry said it was available in a yellow body with red and brown spots, and white body with red and green spots. It was no longer available in the 1927 catalog. Collector value range: $300-$450.

DOWAGIAC MINNOW
No 20. Series

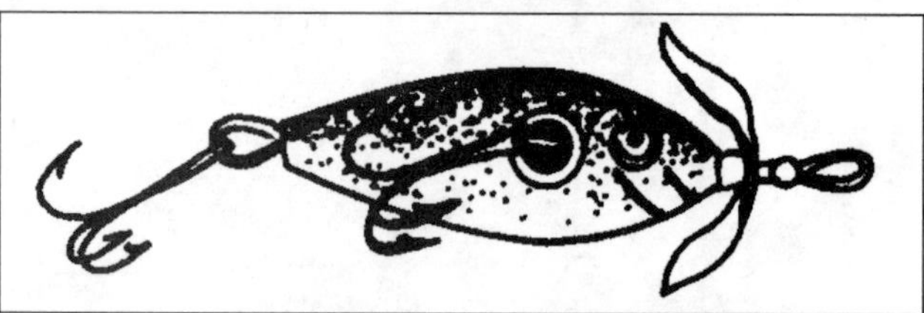

No. 20 Series. The top two lures here are DOWAGIAC MINNOWS measuring 1-7/8" and 1-13/16" respectively. The other two are BABY DOWAGIACS. The glass-eyed model measures 2-1/8" and the lower example, 2-1/4". It has plastic tack eyes.

This tiny (1-3/4", 1/2 oz.) plug first appeared in a 1909 Heddon catalog and promptly disappeared, not to turn up in catalogs again until 1922. It is the same size and weight as the ARTISTIC MINNOW and has a nose mounted propeller spinner. That is where this little critter's similarity ends though. The No. 20 has three treble hooks, one trailing and one on each side. That's a lot of artillery for such a small lure. Colors were: Fancy back sienna, yellow finish, fancy green back, white, red, gold and silver white in 1909. In 1922 they were available in all the colors of the No. 150 Minnow. The 1930 edition of the catalog is the last place this particular lure was offered for sale. Collector value range for this early model: $100-$300.

BABY DOWAGIAC
No. 20 Series

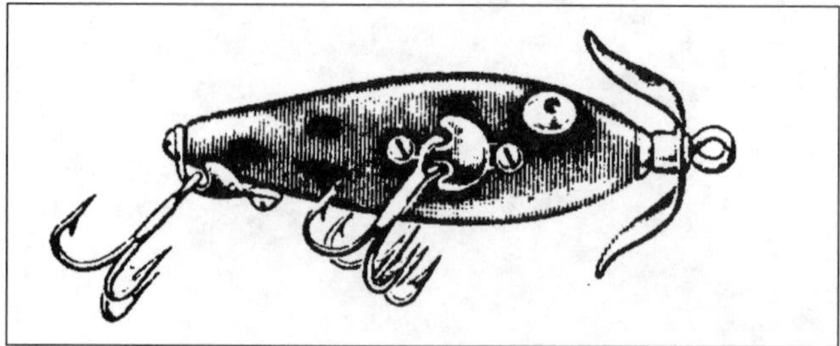

The illustration above was taken from a 1953 Heddon catalog. The lure was found in a 1952 catalog that featured it as "NEW". The listing said, in part: "This is a midget size of the famous lure that produced memorable results for your Dad and Grandad, the original 'Dowagiac'." The lure is made of wood and 2-1/2" long. There is a similar three-hooker in the 1909 catalog that is called "Dowagiac Minnow No. 20", but the listing says it is only 1-3/4" (see previous DOWAGIAC MINNOW entry). It is likely that they didn't realize that there had been a small size of the Dowagiac Minnow made before. After all, the lure had not been made for over 20 years.

This "NEW" 2-1/2" Dowagiac in the 1952 catalog is exactly that. It has tacked-on plastic eyes, one-piece surface style hook hangers and three no. 6 treble hooks. The seven colors or finishes listed are: Rainbow; shiner scale; red head, flitter; spotted orange; yellow perch scale; green crackle back; white with red eyes and tail. A thorough search of catalogs from that point into the 1970s produced no further evidence that they were made after the early 1950s, not even in a plastic "Spook" version. Collector value range: $75-$120.

LAGUNA RUNT
No. 10 Series

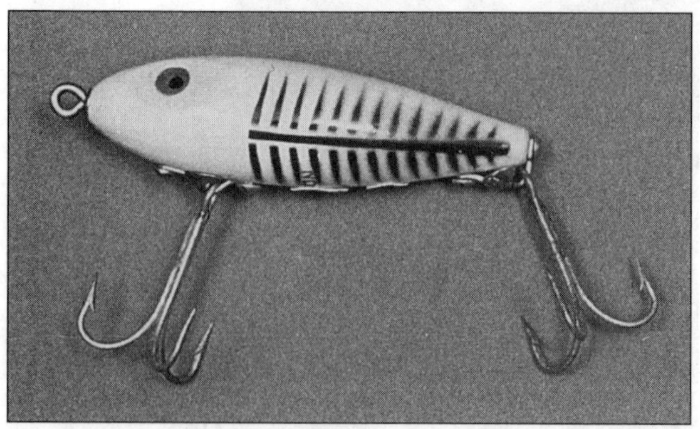

The 1939 catalog states that this is the "same body as the River Runt but without collar" (diving lip). It was made in two models, a sinker and a floater. The colors were exactly the same as the RIVER RUNT colors. It was still around in a 2-5/8" wood body, sinking version in 1949. Colors listed in the that catalog were: White with a red head and a pearl and black shore minnow finish. Collector value range for the earliest LAGUNA RUNTS: $60-$120; the later ones will bring much less.

SEA RUNT
Series #610

This is essentially the same lure as the LAGUNA RUNT above except for the line tie. On the SEA RUNT the line tie is placed on top of the nose instead of at the point of the nose. This lure was still available into the 1950s in the following colors or finishes: White with red head, yellow with red head and white body with red and green spots. It was 2-5/8" long. Collector value range: $60-$120.; the later ones will bring less.

WALTON FEATHER TAIL
No. 40 Series

This smaller plug was first found in a 1924 catalog and last found referenced in a 1926 catalog. It had a tail-mounted single hook covered with feathers. There was a nose-mounted propeller spinner. It has glass eyes, and came in four color designs. The colors were: Red and white; black body, orange tail; shiner scale, gray tail; and pike scale with green and yellow tail. Collector value range: $75-$150.

A belly view of two WALTON FEATHER TAILS showing the two styles of tail hook hangers to be found.

ARTISTIC MINNOW
#50 Series

This 1-3/4" lure first appears around 1905 and seems to have been removed from the Heddon line by the publication of the 1910 catalog. The catalog states it was available in a fancy back sienna-yellow finish and a gold finish. At some point they added a gold body with greenish cast back. All metal hardware except the hook is gold plated. The trailing treble is tied with fancy feathers or buck tail. It has glass eyes. It is thought the name was derived from the Artistic Wood Turning Works, Chicago, Illinois. This company turned out a lot of bodies for various companies in the early 1900s.

Collectors of Heddon and Pflueger should be aware of the almost identical features of the Heddon ARTISTIC MINNOW and the Pflueger SIMPLEX. Pflueger may have used the same company, for the bodies are identical. The best way to tell the difference is to compare the two and note the belly weights.

Heddon ARTISTIC MINNOWS invariably have only one belly weight whereas the Pflueger SIMPLEX is often found with two. There are some belly weight (later model)SIMPLEXES around, but the Pflueger weights are larger in diameter than those on the Heddon lure. The Heddon plug was sold with a weight to tie on in front if desired. To find the weight with the lure is rare. Collector value range: $150-$300.

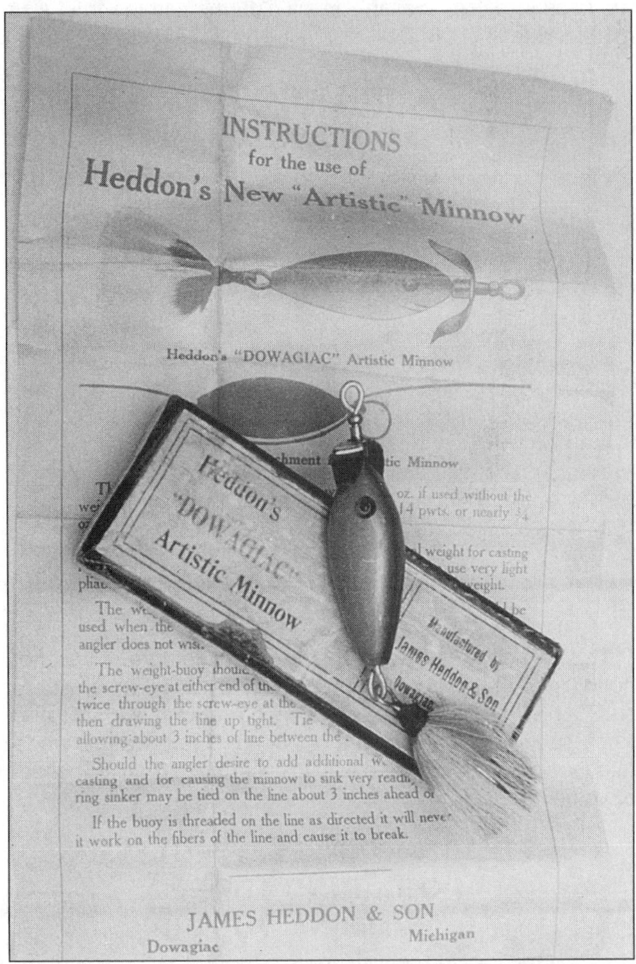

WILDER-DILG
No. 30 Series (cork)
No. 910 & No. 930 Series (plastic)

Introduced in the 1923 catalog this cork-bodied, feathered lure was invented by a Louis B. Adams of New York City and named after B. F. Wilder, also of New York City and William H. Dilg of Chicago. The latter two gentlemen were credited

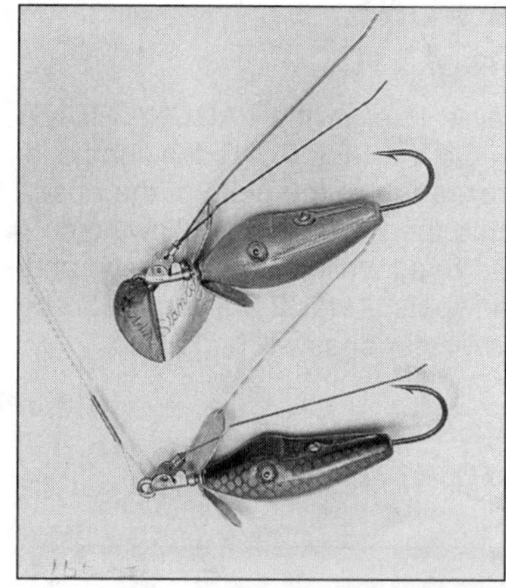

Two WEEDLESS PORK-RIND LURES. The upper lure has the scarce surface wiggler attachment.

with experimenting with and perfecting the lure in the 1924 catalog. In 1939 Heddon changed the body composition from cork to plastic and renamed it the Wilder-Dilg Spook. It was dropped from the line in 1953 after a 30-year run. It was made in two sizes, a bass size at 3-1/4" overall and a trout size at 2" overall. The bass size was available in six patterns and the trout size in 12 for a total of 18. Collector value range: $25-$40.

DREWCO
Series No. 70

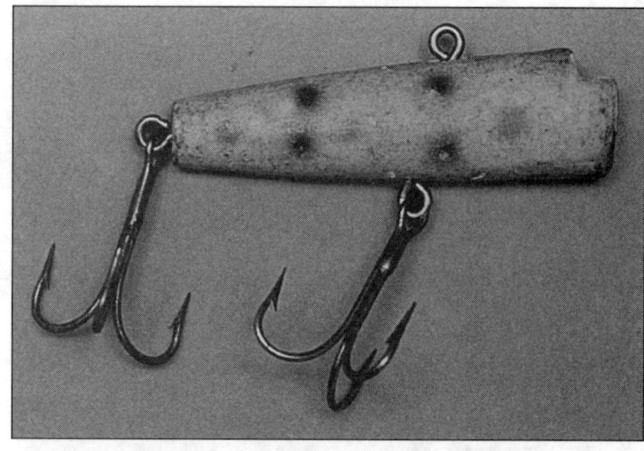

This is a c. 1934 Heddon plastic saltwater lure. It was not found listed or illustrated in any 1930s catalogs. It measures 2-1/2" and the only colors I have seen are white with red and green spots and white with a red head. There was no trade data found so there was no way to ascertain a realistic collector value.

HEDDON-STANLEY WEEDLESS PORK-RIND LURE
Series No. 70

This lure was made of Bakelite and new about 1923 (changed to Pyraline in 1925). It had glass eyes and was available with or without the wire weed guard and surface attachment. Both are pictured belly-down in the above photo. Collector value range: $25-$70.

CATALOG SERIES #	BODY LENGTH	LURE WEIGHT
70	1-1/8"	5/8 oz.

COLOR OF FINISH: Solid white; white body, red top; solid red; green scale; pike scale; shiner scale.

FUZZI-BUG
Series #74 & #75

Left: Series #74 (small size, 7/8" overall, Right: Series #75 (bass size), 1-1/2" overall.

These flies look like a moth on the water. They have beady eyes and fuzzy bodies. The colors they were made available in were: Brown body wings and hackle; white body and wings, red hackle; gray body, wings and hackle; solid yellow; dark green body and wings, black hackle; red body and wings, yellow hackle. Collector value range: $15-$50

TINY TEASE
Series No. 80

The TINY TEASE first showed up in Heddon catalogs in the 1928 issue. The entry puts the lure at 1-3/4", but it actually measures closer to 1-7/8". It is a fly rod lure weighing only

1/10 of an ounce. Collector value range: $125-$170. The brook trout finish can bring up to $200.

COLOR OR FINISH: Rainbow, white and red, red dace scale; natural scale; shiner scale; brook trout.

POP-EYE-FROG
Series No. 85

The lure was being made at least as early as 1937 and probably before. I have a copy of a letter dated July 6, 1937, in response to a claim that Heddon was infringing on a patent with the POP-EYE-FROG. Charles Heddon wrote "...we are therefore discontinuing immediately, the manufacture of our present model and will manufacture this Frog in the future with the commonly accepted hair legs." It seems there is an earlier model with a "rigid or stiffening member" referred to in the letter. The fly measures 1-5/8" body length and 3-1/2" overall. You can't see it with the lure in the box, but the single hook has a weed guard. It was available in two color finishes: Green frog and yellow frog. Collector value range: $25-$75. New in the box could be valued as much a double or more.

BUBBLE BUG or BUBBLING BUG
Series No. 90

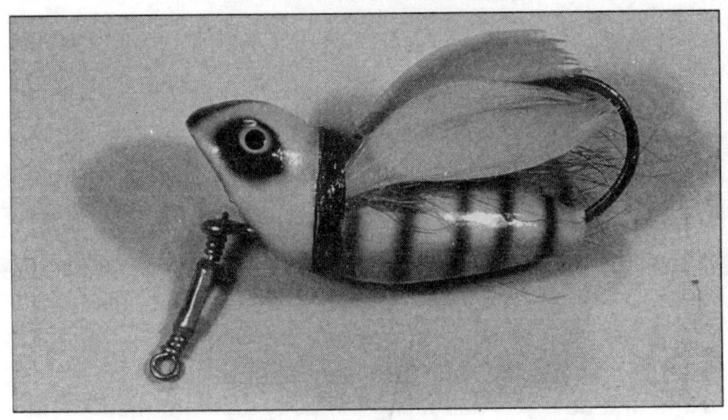

Called the BUBBLE BUG on the box, a 1936 catalog listed it as the BUBBLING BUG. The one in the photo is yellow and black with yellow feathers. It measures 1-3/4". The catalog states 2", but that probably includes hook. The catalog also notes that it could be had with the hook turned down "On special order". All I have seen have the old style (1910-20) brass box swivel. It could date these farther back or it could be that Heddon had a large inventory of them and thought the lure would have better action with their use. Collector value range: $100-$150.

COLOR OF FINISH: White body, red stripes, white wings; yellow body, black stripes, yellow wings; gold body, green stripes, green-black wings.

RIVER RUNT
Series No.110

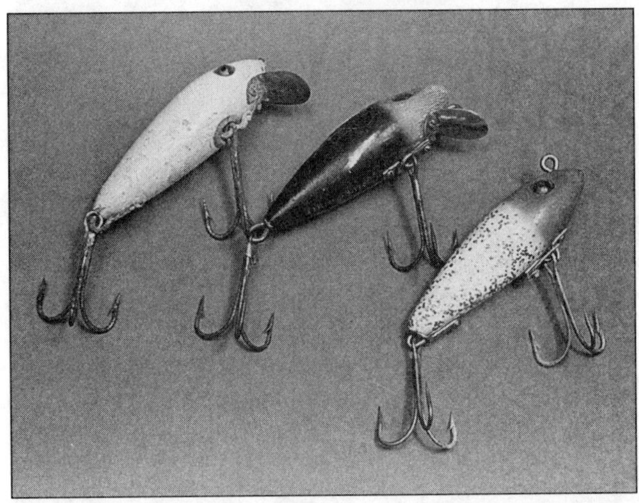

These lures illustrate hardware and style differences. Left lure is round-nosed with no eye depression and 2-hump L-rig. Center has zinc eyes and toilet seat hardware. Right lure is a glass-eyed SEA RUNT, and an early salt water No. 610.

New in 1929 the earliest models have the "L-rig" hook hardware. The photos here illustrate the subtle body style changes and the hook hardware progression over the years. It was made of wood all the way into the early 1950s. Collector value range: $20-$60.

These RIVER RUNTS illustrate the hook hardware progression left to right, from L-rig to one-piece surface. Note the pork rind attachment on the trailing treble of the third lure.

CATALOG SERIES #	BODY LENGTH	LURE WEIGHT
110	2-5/8"	1/2 oz.

COLOR OR FINISH: Rainbow, white with red head, white with red head and silver specks; solid red, yellow perch scale; red dace scale; silver scale; natural scale; shiner scale; shiner scale with red head; pearl, silver with red head, solid black; silver herring; black with white head, solid white; Allen stripey.

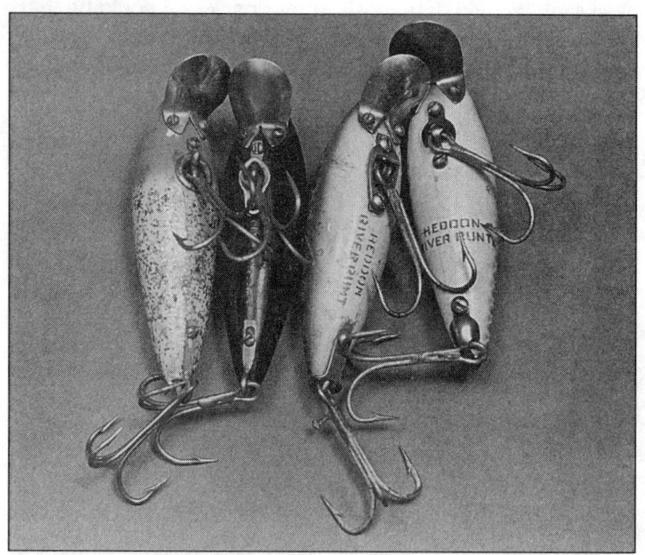

Belly view of the RIVER RUNTS in the previous picture.

A commemorative re-issue of the wooden RIVER RUNT released in an edition of 10,000 in 1994. It was a Centennial Edition (see box) celebrating the 100th anniversary of Heddon.

RIVER RUNT SPOOK
Series No. 9010, Series No. 9110 (Standard), Series No. 9400, Series No. 9430

The SPOOKS (plastic lures) were introduced in 1932, but the plastic version of the RIVER RUNT was not in the catalog until 1934. This plastic lure was offered through the years along with the wooden one. The plastic line was considerably more versatile with many different models offered such as jointed. The initial colors offered are listed following: Rainbow, white body with red head, solid red, yellow perch scale, red dace scale, natural scale, shiner scale, green scale, pearl.

By 1938 the list had expanded considerably to include the addition of the following: Spotted, silver flitter with red head, silver scale, gold fish shore minnow, glow worm (see below), silver shore minnow, black with white head, yellow shore minnow, perch scale, red and white shore minnow, pike scale, black and white shore minnow,

A 3" RIVER RUNT SPOOK floater.

Everlasting Colors: Red and white water wave, yellow and black water wave, green and black water wave.

By 1957 the list had dwindled to the eight colors listed below: pike scale, silver shore minnow, shiner scale, yellow shore minnow, white with red head, red and white shore minnow, yellow perch scale, black and white shore minnow.

The hardware started out in the second style of Heddon's two-piece surface hardware. The first RIVER RUNT SPOOK was a sinking model, but by 1938 they had added a Floating Model, Series No. 9400 and a JOINTED RIVER RUNT, Series No. 9430. They also added a fly rod size Series No. 950 in 1938 that will be covered in another listing. Collector value range for the RIVER RUNT SPOOKS: $20-$30. Some of the rare early colors will double that or more.

GLOW WORM RIVER RUNT SPOOK
No. 9409GW

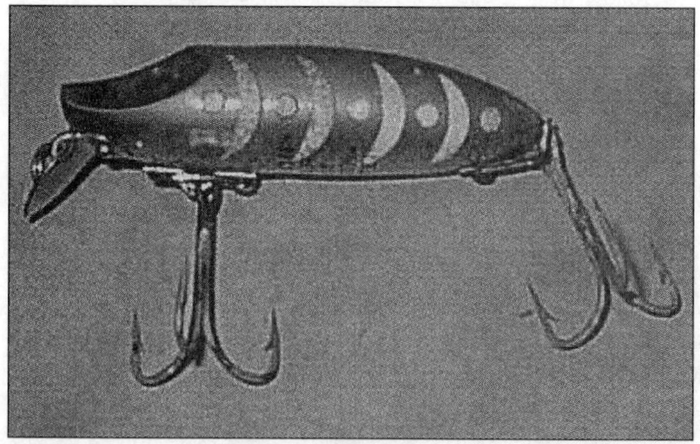

This was a luminous RIVER RUNT SPOOK. It was introduced in the late 1930s. The base color is green. The half moons and dots you see along the body side are made of luminous material. The pieces are glued on. The material would glow in the dark if you exposed it to light for a period of time. It was produced for only a few years as the company discontinued it at the request of the U.S. government. They were worried that the material might give off radiation! Thanks to Tom Jacomet for the photograph and information presented here. Collector value range: $30-$40.

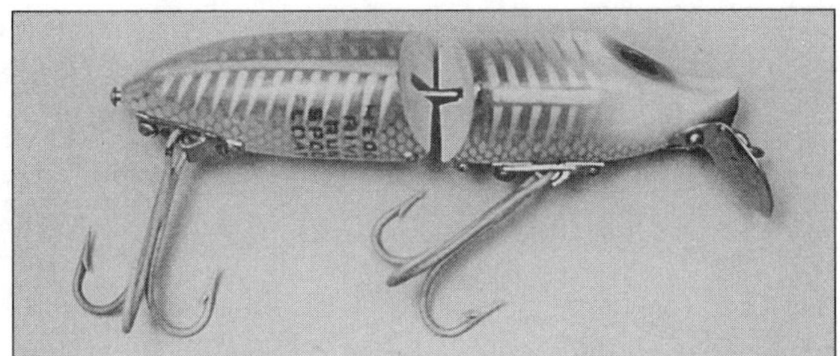

An early 3-3/4" JOINTED RIVER RUNT SPOOK floater. Note the two-piece surface hardware.

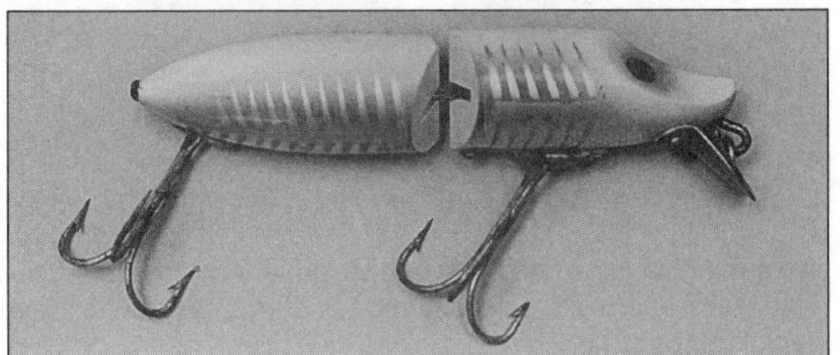

A 3-3/4" JOINTED RIVER RUNT SPOOK floater with one-piece surface hardware.

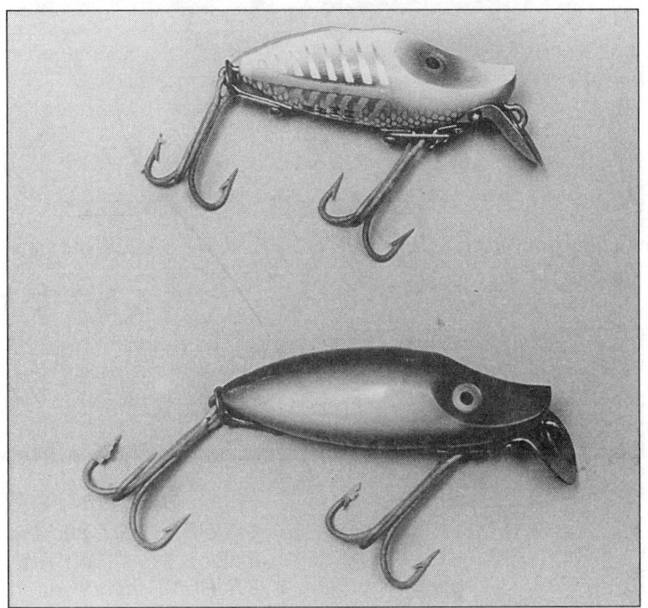

The upper lure is a MIDGET RIVER RUNT SPOOK measuring 2-1/8". The lower lure is a standard Series #9110 sinking model.

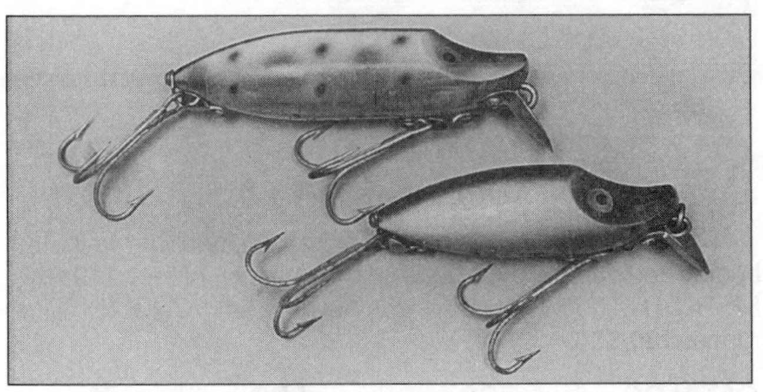

The upper lure is a 3" floater and the lower, a 2-1/4" sinking RIVER RUNT SPOOK. Both have the one-piece surface hardware.

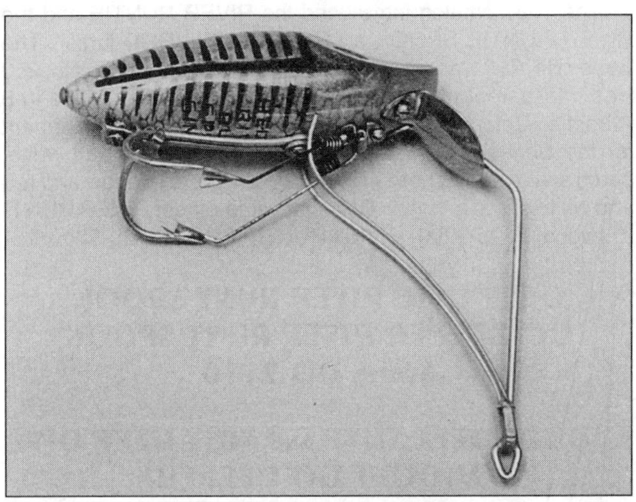

This is a really peculiar snagless arrangement that came out in 1942 on a 2-5/8" lure marked "RIVER RUNT SPOOK FLOATER". Interestingly the catalog stated that it was the "...standard sinking model..." that was equipped with this "NO-SNAG" hardware. Collector value range: $30-$70.

SALMON RIVER RUNT
Series No. 8850

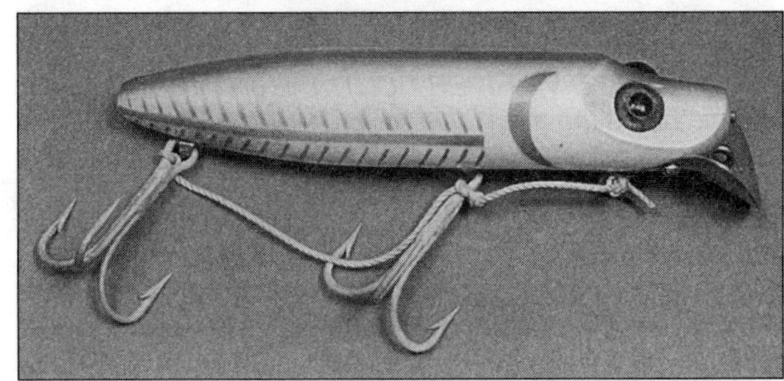

This strong, 5-1/2" wooden plug is obviously from the RIVER RUNT family, but no catalog references could be found. In the photo, you will note the string arrangement in the hook hardware and a different type metal diving lip. The photo doesn't show it well but this particular example has "Teddy Bear Glass Eyes." It does state "Heddon Salmon River Runt" on the belly. Collector value range: No trade data found. It was reported at $9-$20 in the last edition.

RIVER RUNTIE Series No. 750

RIVER RUNTIE SPOOK Series No. 950

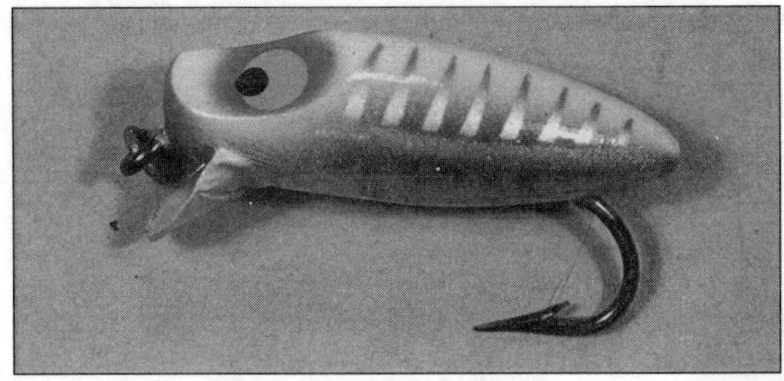

A Series No. 95 RIVER RUNTIE SPOOK.

The 1937 catalog introduced the RIVER RUNTIE and the RIVER RUNTIE SPOOK as "Two New FLYROD lures". The Series No. 750 was a 1" wood body lure and the Series No. 950 was transparent plastic. The entry said they were "Made in 8 Attractive Colors", but did not list them. A 1937 advertisement for the Series #950 listed six of the colors: Red and white, perch scale, silver shore minnow, green shore minnow and red and white shore minnow. Collector value range: RIVER RUNTIE (wood) $125-$200, RIVER RUNTIE SPOOK $20-$30.

DEEP DIVE RIVER RUNT SPOOK
GO-DEEPER RIVER RUNT SPOOK
Series DD 9110

MIDGET DEEP DIVE and TINY DEEP DIVE
MIDGET GO-DEEPER
Series DD 9010
Series DD 350

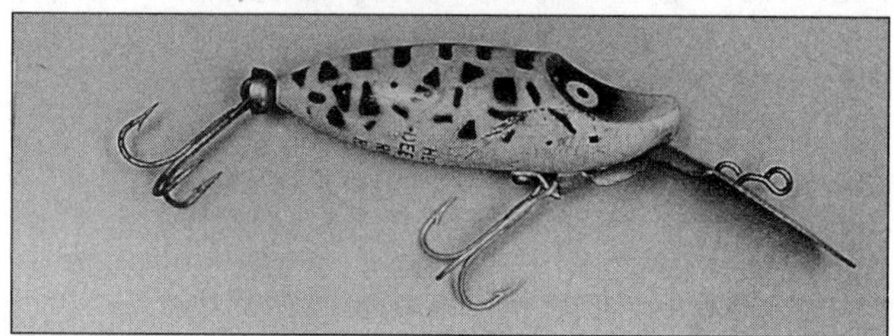

A 2-1/2" DEEP DIVE RIVER RUNT. The belly hook line tie is integrated with the metal dive lip.

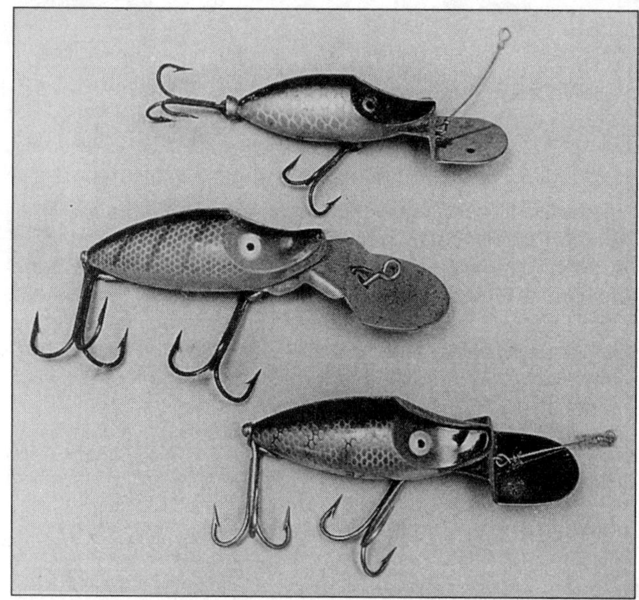

These are "Spook" or plastic deep running RIVER RUNTS. They are cataloged 2-1/2", 2-1/4" and 1-3/4" respectively. They are labeled on the belly. The belly hook hanger is integrated with the dive lip. There were six finishes available: Perch, coach dog, red head, green shad, yellow coach dog and black, white shore minnow.

The first GO-DEEPER models came out with the second style of the two-piece surface hook hangers. They were offered in a MIDGET size at 3-1/4" and a Standard size at 3-1/2". Collector value range for all: $20-$30. The colors offered were: White with red head, shad, pike, green shore minnow, yellow shore minnow, silver shore minnow, red and white shore minnow, black and white shore minnow, natural, rainbow, yellow perch, shiner scale.

A standard 2-1/2" GO-DEEPER and the 2-1/4" MIDGET model.

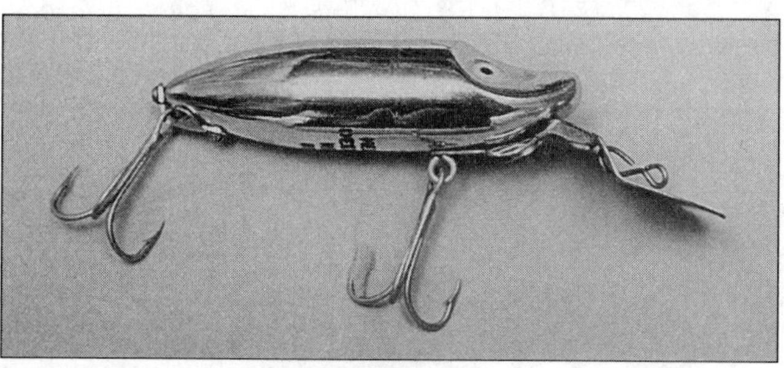

A shiny gold finish DEEP DIVE RIVER RUNT SPOOK measuring 3".

Upper lure is a 1-5/8" MIDGET DIGIT and the lower, a 1-3/4" TINY RIVER RUNT introduced in 1952.

MIDGET DIGIT
Series No. B-110

The gang of plugs in the photo are all wooden with weighted bodies and painted eyes. This is a tiny version of the #110 RIVER RUNT. The Midget Digit was new in 1941. Collector value range: $20-$30.

CATALOG SERIES #	BODY LENGTH	LURE WEIGHT
B-110	1-1/2"	2/5 oz.

COLOR OR FINISH: White body, spotted; white with red head, black with white head, yellow perch scale, red dace scale, shiner scale, blue pearl, red head with silver flitters, silver scale, black and white shore minnow, yellow shore minnow.

TORPEDO
Series No. 120 and No. 130

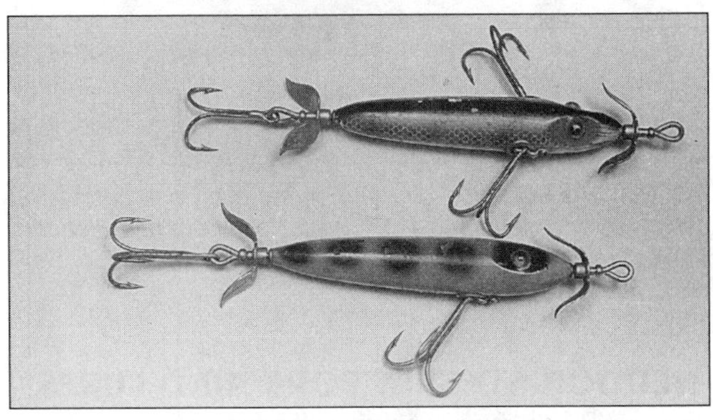

The first reference I could find for these two was in 1925. The entry, however, implied that it had been around long enough to become a "favorite." By 1930 the smaller size was no longer offered in the catalogs.

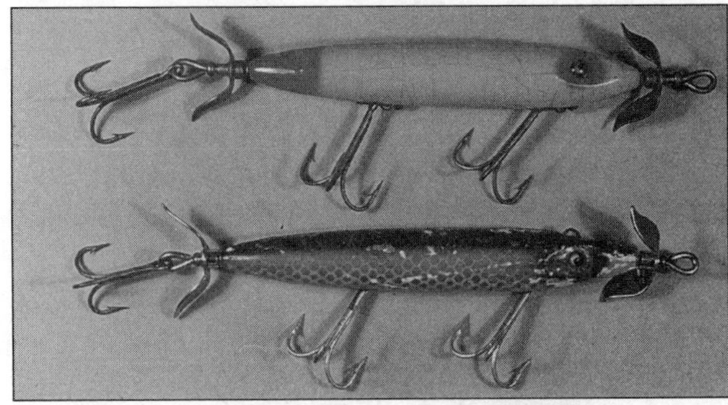

Of these two TORPEDOES the upper one is the oldest. It sports tube type propeller spinners, has the L-rig hook hardware and "HEDDON TORPEDO" is stenciled on the belly. Note the later props on the lower lure. Both have glass eyes, the props are marked with the Heddon name and the bodies each measure 4-1/8".

The 2T model in the photo above is the normal No. 120, 3" TORPEDO. The upper lure with two opposite-mount side trebles is a rare bird. It was not found cataloged anywhere. The standard TORPEDO No. 130 is larger (4-1/2") and has two belly-mounted treble hooks. All TORPEDOES so far found have L-rig, two-piece or surface hardware. They are also found with the small round-blade floppy Heddon/Stanley propeller spinners. They were offered in catalogs in wood until 1936. Collector value range: $30-$75.

CATALOG SERIES #	BODY LENGTH	LURE WEIGHT
120	3"	1/2 oz.
130	4-1/2"	3/4 oz.

COLOR OR FINISH: White body, red eyes; yellow perch scale finish; green scale finish; pike scale finish; shiner scale finish; rainbow scale finish; natural scale finish; blue scale finish; rainbow scale, purple back; orange black spots.

These two represent the next two in line of age. The upper lure here has the one-piece bar hanger. This was the first style after the cup and screw eye was abandoned. The lower lure is next in line with the two-piece toilet seat style belly hook hardware. Both measure 4-1/8", have one internal belly weight, glass eyes, marked propeller spinners and "HEDDON TORPEDO" stenciled on the belly.

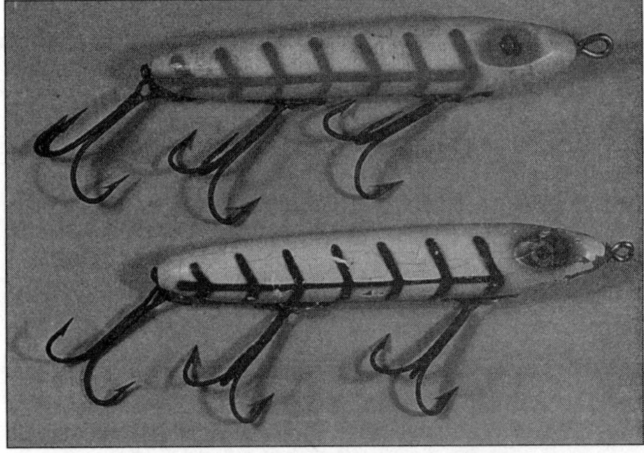

This is a pair of saltwater TORPEDOES (#30). The upper, glass-eyed version is the oldest. Note it has a slightly fatter body and more blunt nose. The newer one measures 4-1/4" with the older being just a bit shorter.

TORPEDO-SPOOK (plastic)

In 1933, when Heddon introduced a plastic, "Spook", line they offered a new TORPEDO, the No. 9130 Series TORPE-

DO-SPOOK in a 4-3/4" size and very slim. The wood body TORPEDO continued in the line along with the plastic version until plastic had replaced it altogether in 1936. Collector value range: *Series #9100 (plastic) $15-$30.

This value applies to those with the early style hardware.

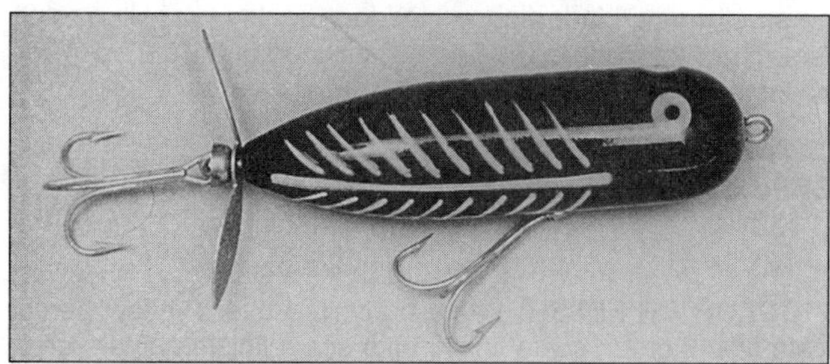

A 3-1/4" plastic MAGNUM TORPEDO.

The evolution of the TORPEDO in plastic didn't end up with nearly as handsome a lure as the original. It was available in a TINY TORPEDO spinning size at 2-1/8" and the larger one in the photo above. A 1959 catalog listed the colors available as: Perch, bullfrog, red head with flitter, white with red head, silver shore minnow, yellow shore minnow, red and white shore minnow and black and white shore minnow. Collector value range for the plastic TORPEDO: $3-$7.

THE S.O.S. WOUNDED MINNOW
Series No. 140, No. 160 and No. 170

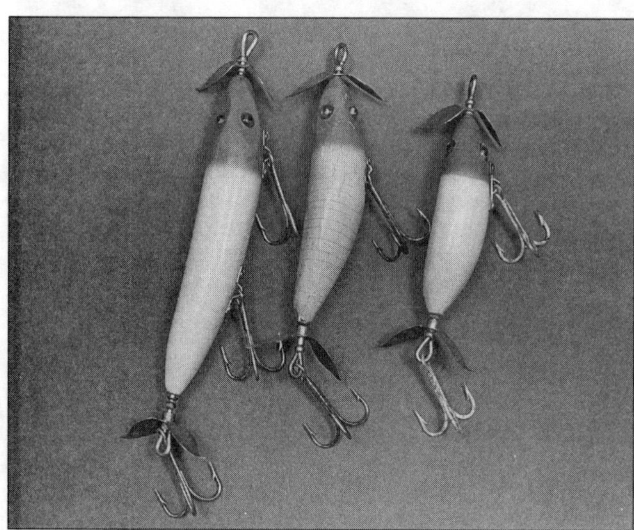

The photo shows the unique "banana" shape of all three sizes of this plug. If you look closely you will see from left to right, the one-piece bar, the L-rig and the first style of the two-piece hook hangers. The No. 370 is the Musky size. It has the same length as the No. 170 (4-3/4"), but is much heavier. Hooks and hanger hardware are bigger and stronger. There is only one belly treble on it. S.O.S. means Swims On Side. All early plugs illustrated have glass eyes. They came on the market around 1927-28 and lasted until the 1950s. Collector value range: $60-$120.

CATALOG SERIES #	BODY LENGTH	LURE WEIGHT
*140	3"	1/2 oz.
160	3-1/2"	3/5 oz.
170	4-3/4"	4/5 oz.
370	4-3/4"	1-1/6 oz.

COLOR OR FINISH: White with redhead, green scale; perch scale; shiner scale; silver scale; dace scale; luminous.

**The smallest size wasn't on the market 1937 and by then a pike scale finish had been added.*

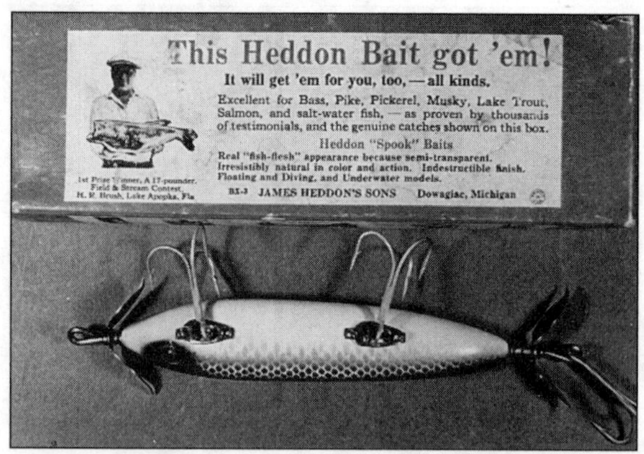

This 7-3/16" Heddon box is marked: Heddon-Dowagiac 179P. Both sides feature many pictures of fish. This No. 170 SOS has heavy duty through-body line tie/tail hook hanger hardware.

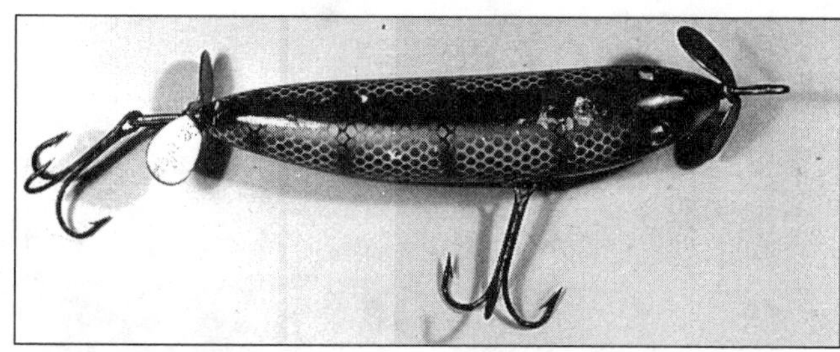

This No. 370 SOS has cup and screw eye hook hardware, glass eyes and measures 4-3/4" long. Note that it has "Heddon Stanley" marked floppy props. This is a rare occurrence. Collector value range: $150-$200.

HEDDON-STANLEY PORK RIND LURES
Ace - Series #190
Queen - Series #280
King - Series #290

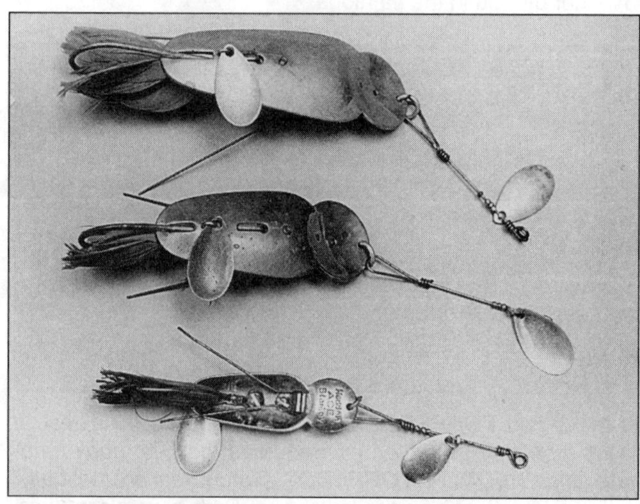

Top to bottom: KING, 3-5/8" with hook, QUEEN, 3" with hook, ACE, 2-1/2" with hook.

The smallest, the ACE, was the first to be introduced, appearing around 1925. They were available in either nickel or copper finish in four versions: Weedless or Non-Weedless, with or without a fly. By 1927 the other two sizes, the KING and QUEEN were in the catalogs. They had added three enamel finishes, white and red, pike scale and shiner scale to the back or convex side of the spoon body. The had also added a Muskie size, SILVER KILL, that was 6-1/2" overall and available in the same finishes. By the 1930s they had added gold plate to all four and silver flitter to the KING and QUEEN. In 1938 the two scale finishes had disappeared from the catalog. That may help in dating your lures. In the same catalog they introduced as "New", the DEVIL ACE, DEVIL KING and DEVIL QUEEN. "Handsomely decorated in a beetle design in two colors with contrasting colored buck tails." The colors listed were: Yellow and black, white and red, black and yellow, white and black, nickel plate.

A 1941 catalog lists the ACE, KING and QUEEN, but the DEVIL versions were not listed. All were absent from the late 1950s catalogs I studied. Collector value range: $20-$30.

WOUNDED-SPOOK
Series No. 9140
Series No. 9160

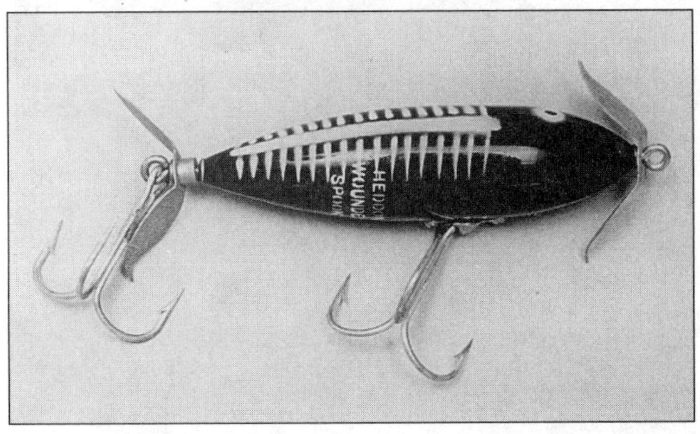

Introduced in the 1939 catalog, these two lures are 3" and 4-1/4" respectively. The two illustrated in the catalog bear the second style of the Heddon two-piece surface hook hangers. The one in the photo has the one piece surface hanger and an unmarked floppy propeller spinner at the nose and a slightly different one at the tail. The propellers in the catalog illustration are the same. Collector value range: $15-$20.

COLOR OR FINISH: Yellow perch; yellow shore minnow, silver scale; green shore minnow, silver shore minnow; red and white shore minnow.

By 1949 the color list had changed and numbered only four: Bullfrog; yellow perch scale; white with red head, pike with red head.

FLIPPER
Series No. 140

The FLIPPER came along about 1927. It is 3-3/4" long and weighs 3/4 oz. The lure shows up again in the 1928 catalog, but is missing in listings from 1929 on. It must have been retired when stocks were exhausted. Whatever the case, the number 140 was then given to the smallest S.O.S. WOUNDED MINNOW which was added to that line around 1937. All of these I have seen are glass eyed and have L-rig hook hardware. Collector value range: $125-$200.

These four FLIPPERS are arranged oldest to newest, left to right. Each has glass eyes and the normal Heddon props of the era. The center two are 3-7/8", the left one 3-3/4" and the right one is 3-1/2". Far left has cup and screw eye hardware, center two have the two-hump L-rig hardware and the far right sports the one-piece surface hangers.

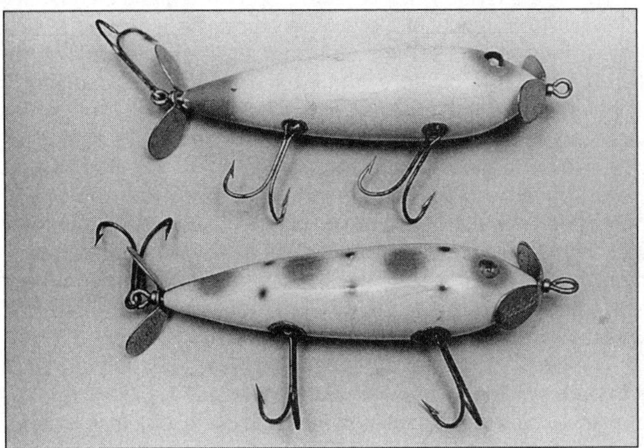

These 4-1/4" FLIPPERS have a fatter body than usual, but what really makes them unusual is the presence of the "Heddon Stanley" marked floppy props. Each has glass eyes and the shallow, big cup and screw eye hook hangers. There was insufficient trade data from which to derive a realistic value.

YOWSER SPINNER BAIT
Series No. 195

This lure came along about 1935 and only lasted until around 1939. The weight is 4/5-oz and overall length is 4" without measuring the fancy feather tail. It came in a single-hook version only. Very rare. Collector value range: $50-$100.

DOWAGIAC SURFACE MINNOW
Series No. 210

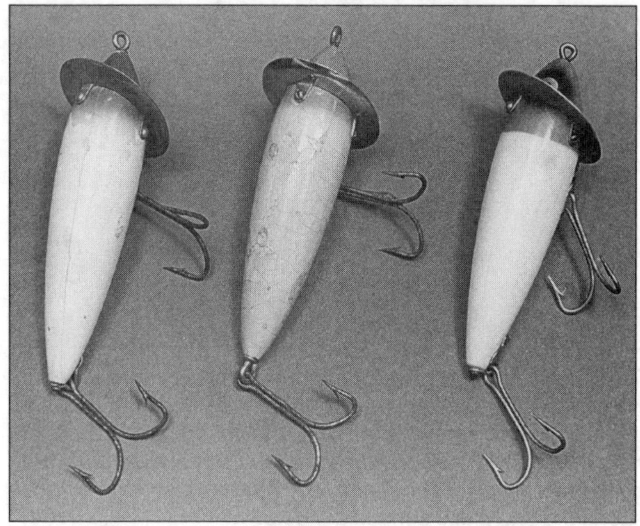

This is a short (3-1/2") version of the Series 200 DOWAGIAC MINNOW. It was first available somewhere around 1917-20, was gone in 1947-48 and back again in 1949 through 1955. Earliest hook hardware I have observed is the L-rig. They are found with no eyes, glass eyes and painted eyes. As far as can be determined to date, they were always equipped with two double hooks as shown in the photo. Colors in 1921 were: White body with blue head, white body with red head, frog, green scale. In 1936 the colors listed were the same four plus three new finishes: Luminous with red head, brown mouse with leather ears, whiskers and tail and gray mouse with ears, whiskers and tail. In 1949 there were only three finishes: White with red head, gray mouse and Frog.

The No. 210 was reintroduced in a plastic version in 1975. It lasted until the sale of the company in 1977. Colors for the plastic version were: black, blue head, bone, bull frog, coach dog, silver flitter, silver shad, yellow.

Collector value range for wood: $50-$100, for plastic: $15-$30.

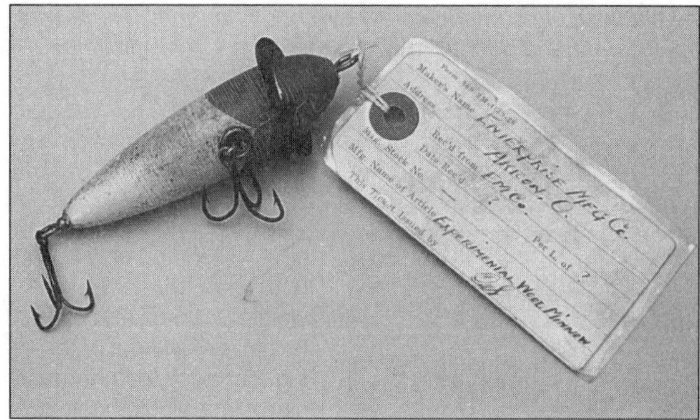

Experimental Pflueger Lure

It looks as if Pflueger was looking into the possibility of competing with Heddon's No. 210 DOWAGIAC MINNOW. The lure never went into production. It has the Neverfail hardware so that dates it contemporary with the Heddon No. 210. The card attached to the lure was dated, but the year has been obscured. Unique. No trade data from which to draw any conclusion as to collector value.

WEEDLESS WIDOW
Series No. 220

Bottom view of the WEEDLESS WIDOW.

The first time this lure was offered was in a 1928 Heddon flyer as the WEEDLESS WIZARD (2-1/2", 3-1/4 oz., six colors). The text called it new. It had only a rigid, feathered, single hook on the tail. The 1928 catalog, however, named it the WEEDLESS WIDOW. The story is that Pflueger got a bit upset because of their own rather well-known WIZARD lures, so Heddon changed the name. In 1930 they made them with a detachable belly double hook addition.

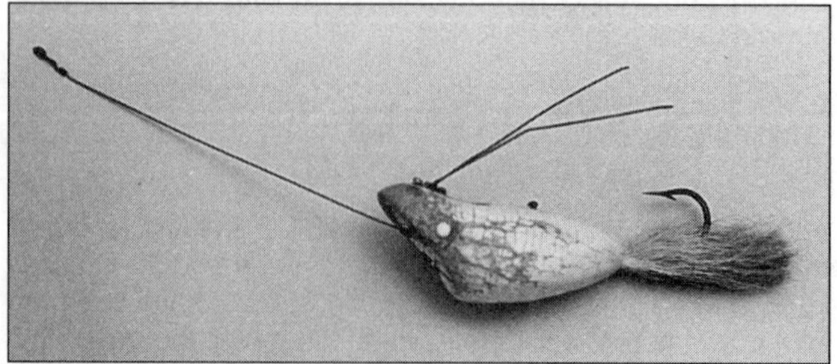

This side-view photo of the white one with bead eyes is thought to be a prototype. There is a hole bored in the back. The reason for this is unknown.

Colors available were: White with red head, bullfrog, green scale, pike scale, shiner scale and silver scale. There was a JUNIOR offered in 1940 at 2-1/4" in the same colors and by 1949 this smaller size was the only one available. Collector value range: $30-$60.

This Frog finish Heddon WEEDLESS WIZARD (note flyer in box) is the early single rigid hook model. It measures 2-3/4" (body) and 3-5/8" overall.

SURFACE MINNY
Series No. 260

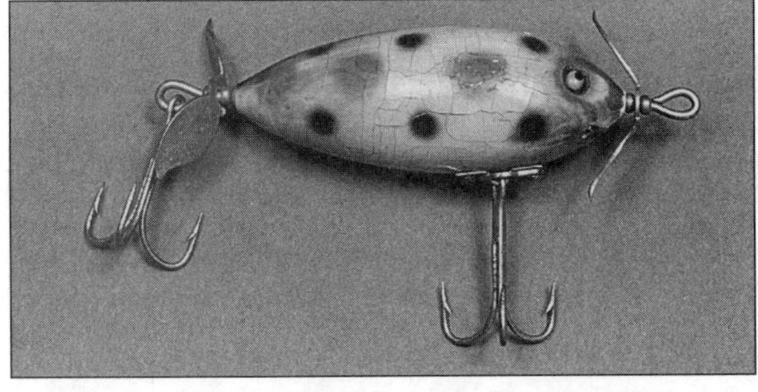

This scarce lure was in production only a short time. It appeared around 1934 and is absent from the 1936 and subsequent catalogs. It has been found only in the old two-piece hardware so far. Collector value range: $200-$300.

WIDGET
Series #300

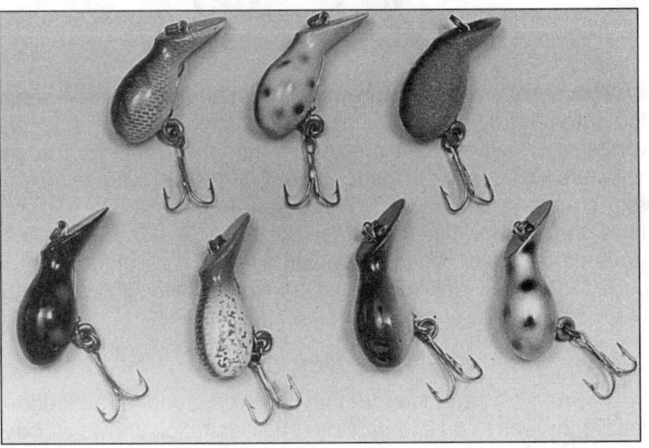

This lure looks like a tiny version of the TADPOLLY. It was first found in a 1953 catalog. The line tie is reinforced with a wire connecting it to the hook mount. It is a fly rod lure cataloged at 5/16 of an ounce and 1-1/4" long. Collector value range: $20-$40.

HEDDON SURFACE MINNOW
MUSKY SURF
Series No. 300

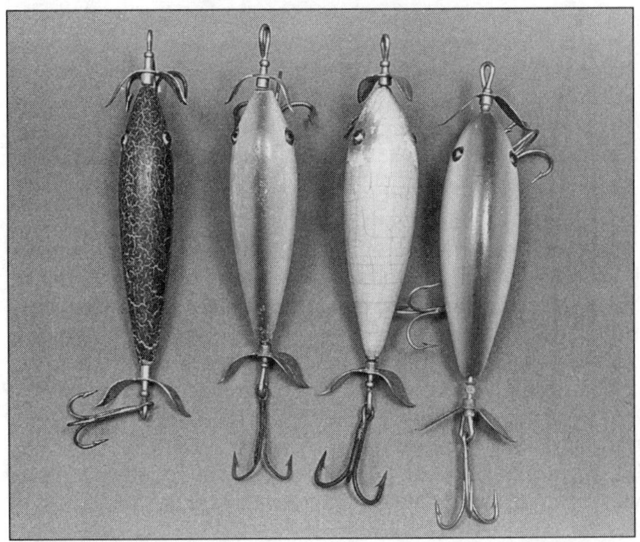

It was called new in a 1905 catalog. The 1905 model is the left lure in the photo showing body style progression to the right. The 1905 colors were: Rainbow*, frog green back*, white*, aluminum, red, yellow or copper. The early 300s were 4" and had one belly treble with cup hardware and a trailing treble. In 1911 the body had grown a bit fatter and shorter (3-1/2") according to a catalog listing of that year. It also noted the availability of a 3T model on special order. By 1922 the No. 300 is listed at 3-3/4" and they had added two finishes: White body with red and green spots; white body, red eyes. The 3T model was still available on special order. The 1925 catalog had renamed the No. 300 Series, the MUSKY MINNOW, and it had grown even fatter at 3-3/4". 1927 saw yet another name, the MUSKY SURF.

This early No. 300 has one internal belly weight, glass eyes, brass cup screw hook hardware, unmarked props and measures 3-3/4".

The No. 300 Series was around for about 30 years and can be found with a classic progression of Heddon hook hardware from the brass cup to the one-piece surface. All had glass eyes. A 1937 catalog said it was "...regularly finished with three heavy trebles, also with six trebles or two trebles on special order." It had been renamed yet again. This time it is called the MUSKY SURFUSSER. It was gone after 1941. Collector value range: $150-$300.

**The only three finishes offered from 1906 through 1916.*

HI-TAIL
Series No. 305

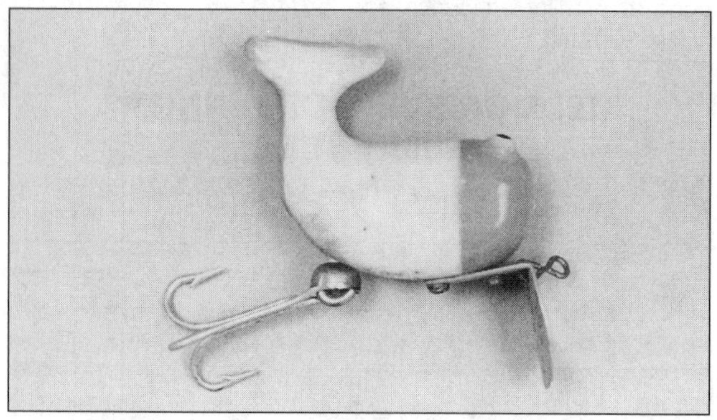

This 1960s plastic lure measures 2" in length. Called a "...new type of surface lure..." in the 1961 edition of the catalog, it was available in the following six colors: Frog, silver flitter, black, yellow, perch, white with red head. Noted collector Clyde Harbin tells me that Homer Circle keeps one in his tackle box, but calls it a "TOP-KICK." Perhaps that was what he wanted to call it when it was first introduced. There was another plastic lure by that name around 1958. It was made by a Miller Company and was a Shakespeare REVOLUTION type. That may be why the name wasn't used. The hook is rigged with an inverse cup as a preventer. Collector value range: $20-$30.

DEEP 6
Series No. 345 and Series No. 9345

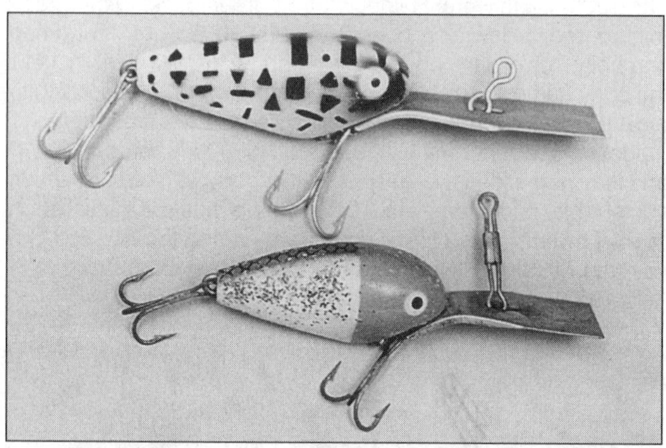

The series numbers have only to do with size. They are 1-3/4" and 2-1/4" respectively. These plastic lures may have been available earlier, but they first appeared in catalogs in the 1965 edition. They are floating divers. Collector value range: $4-$10.

COLOR OR FINISH: Black, perch, yellow, red head with flitter, spotted orange, natural crab, green shad, coach dog.

MUSKY SURFACE
MUSKY SURFUSSER
Series No. 350

Apparently this was a short-lived lure in the Heddon line. It is cataloged consistently from 1933 through 1936, but is conspicuously absent from then on. They may have been made long before 1933. The upper plug has unmarked big propellers, the same as found on early No. 700s. Collector value range: $200-$300.

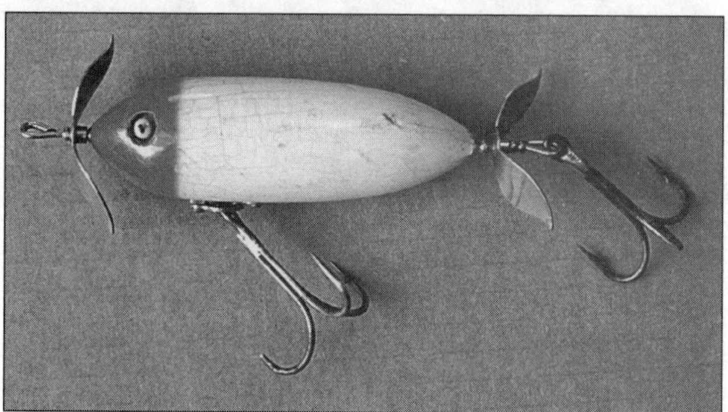

This No. 350 MUSKY SURFUSSER has the early first style of the Heddon two-piece surface hook hanger collectors call "Toilet seat". Photo courtesy Dennis "Doc" Hyder.

COLOR AND FINISH: Spotted, White with red head, green scale and shiner scale.

MUSKY SURFACE SPOOK
Series #9170

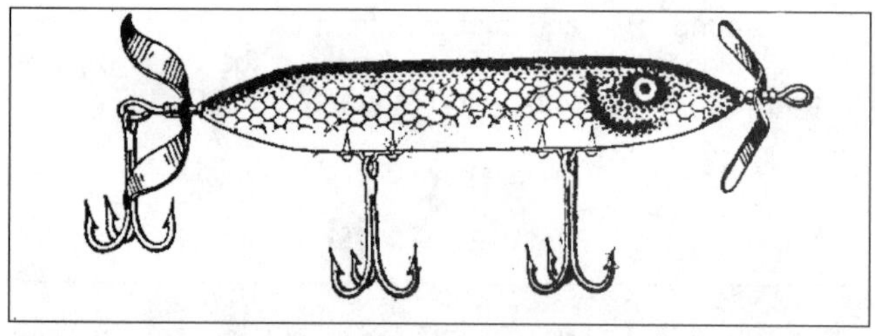

This 5-1/2", 1-1/2 oz. lure was, according to the 1934 catalog entry, "Made especially for Muskies and large Great Northern Pike, this lively bait answers a long-felt want. Two large spinners kick up a fuss on the surface of the water, it rides high, and creates a big wake ... Three sets of large treble hooks." Note the odd propeller spinner on the nose. There was no trade data from which to determine a realistic collector value.

COLOR OR FINISH: White and red, white with red and black spots; natural pike; shiner scale.

ICE DECOY

The earliest catalog entry that could be found for a Heddon Ice Decoy was in a 1913 catalog. The illustration shows a body

The decoy at the top is referred to by collectors as the BAT WING. For our purposes here, we will refer to the other as the REGULAR decoy.

much like the top decoy in the photo above. It had a small screw eye line tie, much larger metal side fins than this one and two additional metal fins (dorsal and ventral) and a natural (wooden) tail. It was listed as 5-1/8" and available in fancy green back with white belly, or yellow perch finish. By 1916 the lure was listed as 4-3/8". The illustration was the same. One length may have been overall and the other the body only. A 1923 catalog shows fins like those on the lower decoy in the above photo. This also is the first catalog illustration showing the inch worm line tie. By then they had added six more finishes: Rainbow, white body with red eyes, green scale, perch scale, shiner scale and natural scale. They had disappeared from the catalogs by 1928. All have glass eyes and fins are plainly marked Heddon.The lure in the above photo is a real

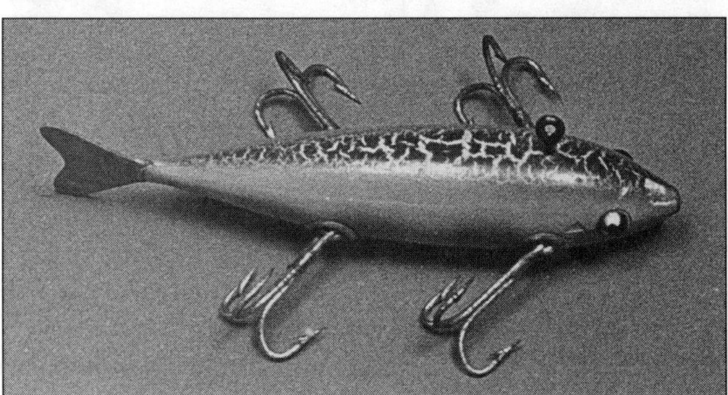

HEDDON ICE SPOOK with its box. This is a rare, un-cataloged Ice Decoy. It has a flat plastic body with metal planes and tail fin. The mass beneath the head is a painted metal weight with decal on the bottom saying "Heddon Ice Spook". It measures 4-5/8" overall. Photo courtesy Jim Muma. The ice decoy new in its box will double its collector value.

This is an example in another finish. It is very rare to find one without flaking paint on the metal weight; even new in the box.

curiosity. It is generally the same body as the Heddon 150s and has the Heddon sienna fancy crackle-back finish. Decoy or lure? It is 4-1/4" overall with a 3-3/4" body with a metal tail fin obviously installed at the factory. There is a hole in the nose, but no screw eye. The screw eye in the top is not typical of Heddon quality and may have been added later. The four treble hooks are installed utilizing cup and screw hook hardware. Eyes are glass. There are three weights beneath the nose.

Collector value range:

Bat Wing Model - $500-$750
Regular Model - $250-$500
Ice Spook - $200-$400

FIDGET
FIDGET FEATHER
FIDGET FLASHER
Series No. 400

Top: FIDGET No.400, 1-3/4" overall, jointed body, Bottom: FIDGET FEATHER, 1-1/2" overall.

These are Heddon spinning lures. The one not pictured, the FIDGET FLASHER, is the same as the FIDGET except it has a corrugated or fluted flasher as the second part of the jointed body. The ones in the photo are colored red head with white body and black respectively. Each of the metal head plates are inscribed with the Heddon name. Collector value range: $10-$20.

SPINFIN
Series No. 411, No. 412, and No. 413

The series numbers have only to do with the three sizes of the SPINFIN spinning lures. They were made in 2-1/4", 2-1/2" and 2-

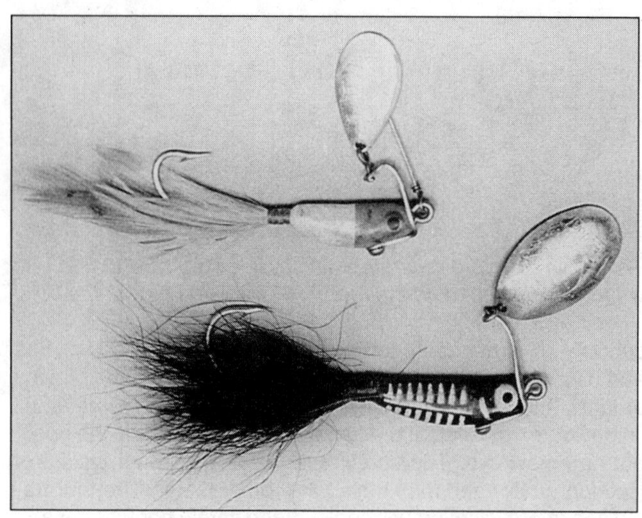

5/8" sizes. They may have been made before the early 1950s, but they didn't appear in the catalogs. They were available in the following colors in a 1957 catalog: Red head, white body; silver flitter; white head, black body; perch scale. The same colors persisted into the 1960s. Collector value range: $5-$15.

GAMBY SPINNERS
Series No. 421 and Series No. 423

The series numbers have only to do with sizes, 2-3/4" and 3-3/4" respectively. Found in a 1957 catalog and no where else. This lure was probably around longer than one year, but it wasn't cataloged. Finishes available were: Silver, Gold or Copper. Collector value range: $5-$15.

WHIS-PURR
Series No. 420 and Series No. 425

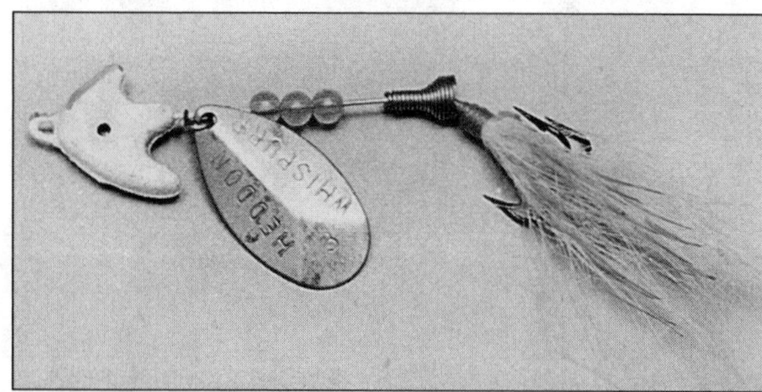

Listed as "NEW" in the 1961 catalog this metal spinning lure was available in two sizes, 3" and 3-1/2", Series #420 and Series #425 respectively. They were made in two colors, silver with white head and buck tail; gold with yellow head and buck tail. Collector value range: $5-$15.

SONAR
Series No. 431
Series No. 433
Series No. 435

The 1959 catalog features this lure as a "...new way to FIND fish and CATCH them!" The series numbers have only to do with the size. The lures are made of metal and the sizes are 1-7/8", 2-3/8" and 3-1/4" respectively. The three holes along the back are line ties. Each hole would take the lure to a different depth on re-

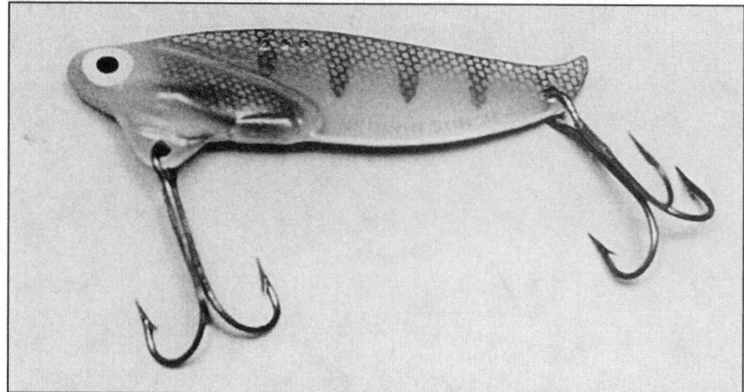

trieve. The color choices for the lures are listed following: Silver finish; yellow; red and white; black; gold finish; perch; gray shad; hot orange. Hot orange and black were not available on the larger Series No. 435 SONAR. Collector value range: $5-$15.

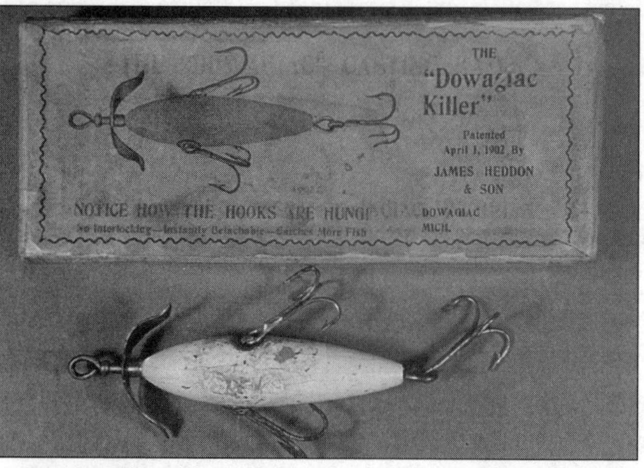

KILLER No. 400 with its original box. This particular box was originally made for the DOWAGIAC CASTING BAIT. A new label was pasted over it. Over the years the old name has bled through. If you look closely you may be able to see it just over the lure illustration.

KILLER
Series No. 400

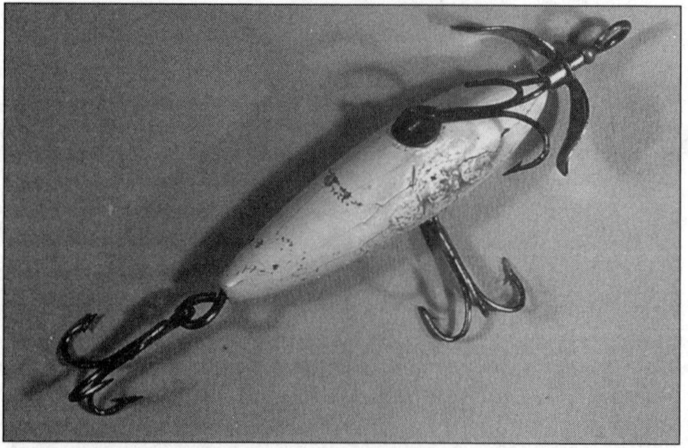

This early KILLER No. 400 is 2-5/8" long, has unmarked prop, brass screw hook and cup hardware and three internal belly weights.

A caption in the 1905 Heddon catalog states that the KILLER No. 400 is "...in all essential respects the same as our No. 100 Minnow, excepting that it has but one propeller, is round

Two 2-5/8" DOWAGIAC MINNOWS (KILLER). The upper lure is a white finish (number unknown) and the lower has a rainbow finish No. 401.

instead of Minnow shaped in body, and is without eyes or other decorations." By the time the 1909 catalog came out the KILLER name was left off and it was called simply, the DOWAGIAC MINNOW, No. 402. Why the "402" instead of the "400" is anybody's guess. This is probably why most collectors call these "402's" regardless of color. It is thought that the "2" in the number actually referred to the color listed in the 1909 catalog illustrating the lure: "Fancy Sienna Yellow finish." The other colors listed there were: Fancy Back, 400 and rainbow, 401. It did not mention white, but they have been found and in the same catalog the No. 402 example was a white lure. By this 1909 catalog they had been given glass eyes and a buck tail. The particular type of buck tail used is said to be unique to Heddon.

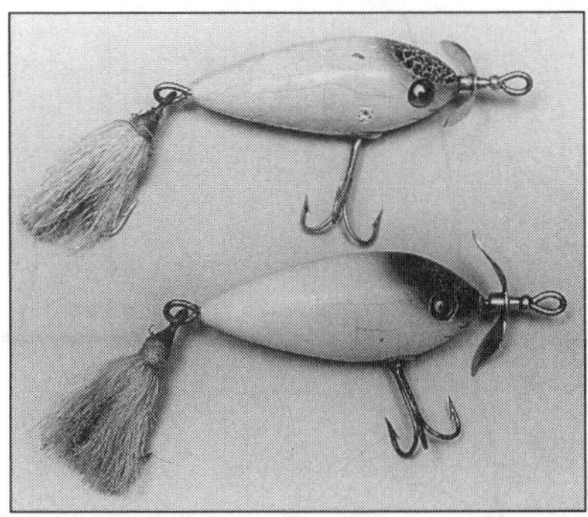

Two 2-5/8" DOWAGIAC MINNOWS (KILLER) in #400 Fancy Back finish.

Three Heddon No. 400 Series KILLERS (402's). Each has cup and screw eye hook hangers, glass eyes and the same paint finish illustrated in the 1909 catalog. Photo courtesy Dennis "Doc" Hyder.

If you spread the feathers and buck tail you will find a red chenille center. The 1909 listing said each had "... a handsome tri-color buck tail and feather tying..." This lure was absent from all subsequent catalogs. Collector value range: $300-$500.

KILLER
Series No. 450

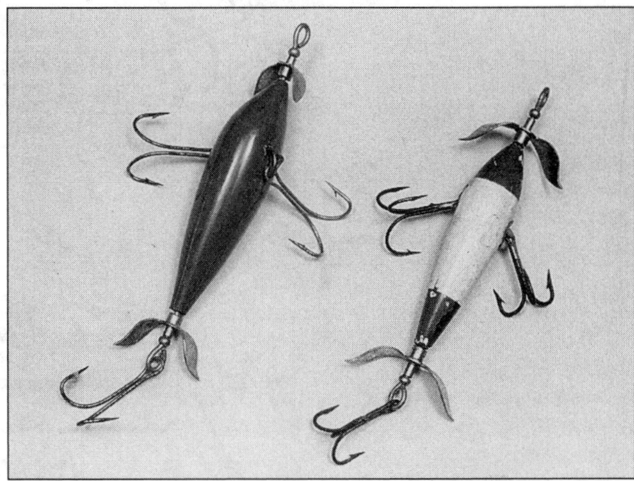

This is a 1905-vintage lure that is exactly the same as the No. 400 except that it has an additional propeller at the tail. The lures in the photo are arranged with the oldest on the left. The key to age is the number of internal belly weights. The more belly weights (up to three), the older the lure. The left lure is so well painted that it is impossible to determine whether there are any belly weights at all. It is larger than the newer model. It is 3" long, round-bodied and red in color with unmarked Heddon props and double-staple hook hangers. It could be a prototype for these 400s and 450s in this rather short-lived, inexpensive line. The other is 2-5/8" long and has only one belly weight. They are found with one, two and three internal belly weights. Colors available: White, red, yellow, copper, aluminum, white body with red head and tail. Collector value range: $300-$500.

MULTIPLE METAL MINNOW
Series No. 500

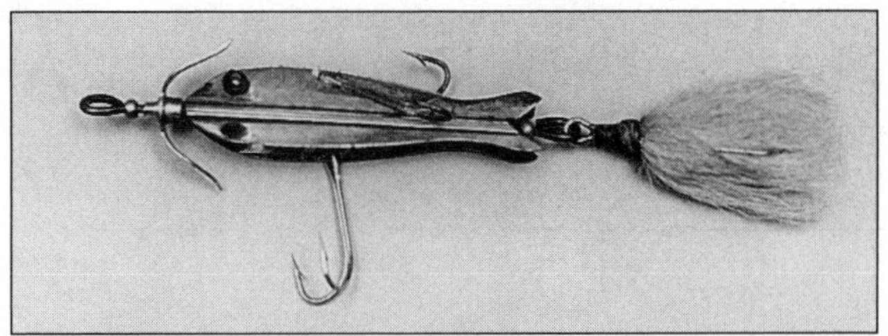

This lure is so similar to the patent illustration here that it is reasonable to presume it to be at least derived from the original patent. It first shows up as available in the early 1900s, some say as early as 1909. It didn't last long. If you look at the pictures or examples of the #500 and #600 Series Heddon SALT WATER SPECIALS you will note a striking similarity of body shape. In fact there is a listing in the 1934 catalog directly under the illustration and technical data listing for the Series 9600 SALT-SPOOK that states "Metal-Minn No. 510 Series (all-metal body). Similar to No. 9600 in shape and weight..." Now this may seem confusing until you realize that the SALT-SPOOK is merely the same-shape plastic version of the old Series #500 and #600 SALTWATER

No. 861,116. PATENTED JULY 23, 1907.

J. HEDDON.

FISH BAIT OR LURE.

APPLICATION FILED FEB. 4, 1907.

3 SHEETS—SHEET 1.

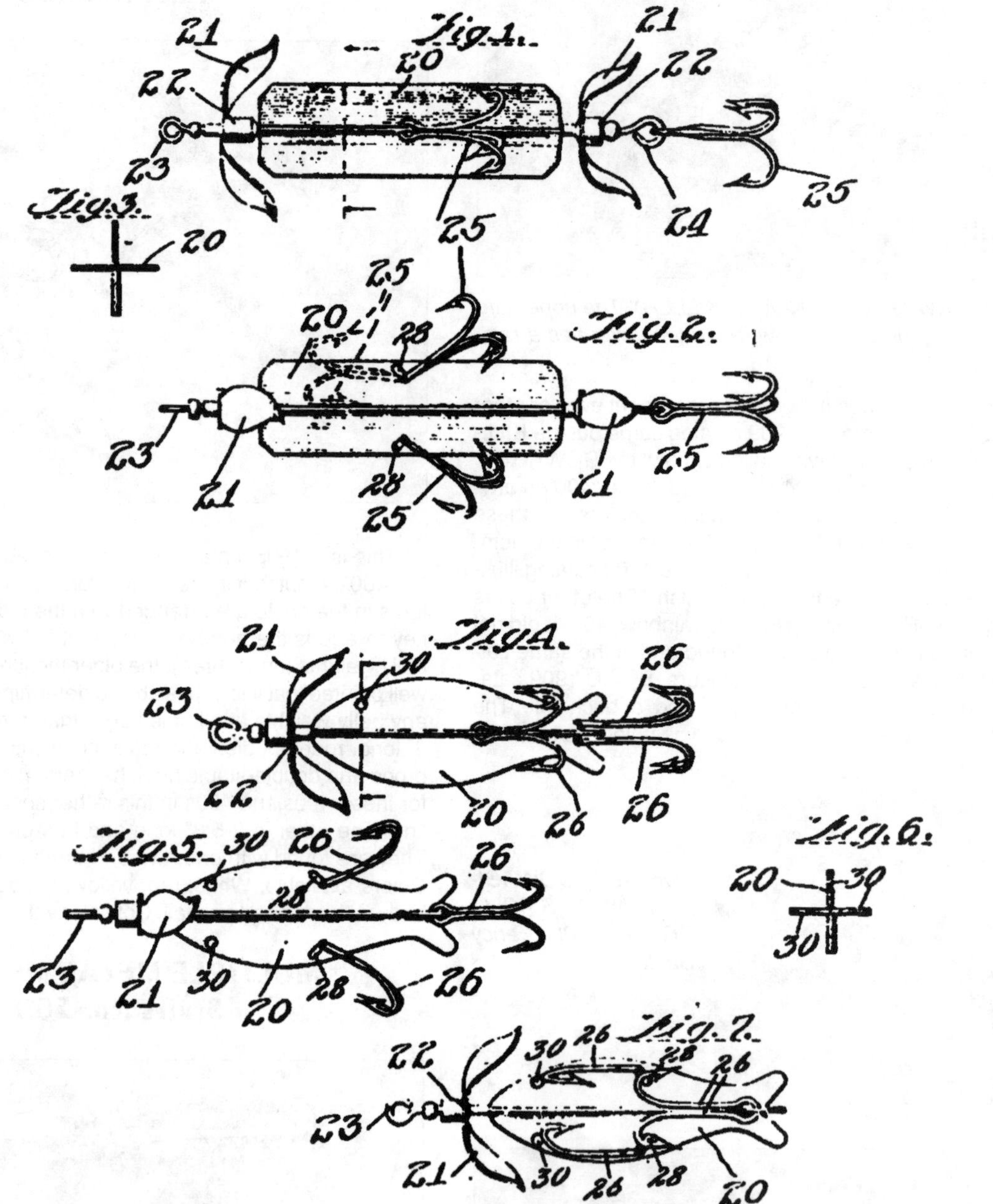

Witnesses:

W. Perry Hahn

Inventor:

James Heddon

The patent drawing for the Heddon MULTIPLE METAL MINNOW. There were actually three sheets of drawing with the patent. Each showed different versions of what appears to be essentially the same lure.

SPECIALS. In fact just under the listing for the METAL-MINN is another listing for "Old Reliables ... The same model as shown above except in wooden bodies." Listed there are the #500 and #600 Series and the colors available. All that for this: The similarity of series number and the stated body shape could mean that the original metal remained in production, albeit limited, for 25 years or so. The lure in the photo here is 2-1/2" long and nickel plated. They are known to have also been available in a gold finish and a larger, musky version at about 4-3/4". They may also be found with glass eyes. The one in the photo has rivet-like eyes. Collector value range: $300-$600.

SALTWATER SPECIAL
Series No. 500, No. 600, and No. 850

The catalog information regarding these wooden lures is confusing. They first appear around 1924 (#600 Series - second from the left) in four sizes and five color designs. By 1925 another series number (#500) appeared and the only sizes were as follows: #500 Series: 1/2-oz., 2"; #600 Series: 2-1/2", 3-1/2", 4-1/2" and 5". In 1926, another style was added (third from left), the #850 Series and #800 Series. In 1932 a "plastic" plug identical to the #800 Series was introduced as the #9600 "Salt Spook". All were gone from catalogs by 1949.

The lure at the left in the photo is not a SALTWATER SPECIAL, but is a 3-1/2" FLORIDA SPECIAL No.10 B. There was also a smaller version, the No.10 S at 2-3/4". These were found only in a 1922 Heddon catalog. Collector value range: Saltwater Special $100-$125, Florida Special $100-$300.

CATALOG SERIES #	BODY LENGTH	LURE WEIGHT
500	2"	1/2 oz.
600	2-1/2"-5"	3/4 oz.
800	3-7/8"	3/4 oz.
850	3"	1/2 oz.

COLOR OR FINISH: White body with red head; white body, gold speckled, red head; white body, silver speckled, red head; *yellow perch scale; **white body, red eyes; **white body, gold speckled; *white body, silver speckled; *solid black; *shiner scale; ***aluminum color body, bronze back.

**No. 600 Series only*

***Pre-1930 only.*

****No. 800 Series only.*

WEE WILLIE Series Number Unknown

Called WEE WILLIE by some collectors, this lure is placed here because of its similarity to the SALTWATER SPECIALS. The red head, white body plug in the photo (bottom) is 3-1/2"

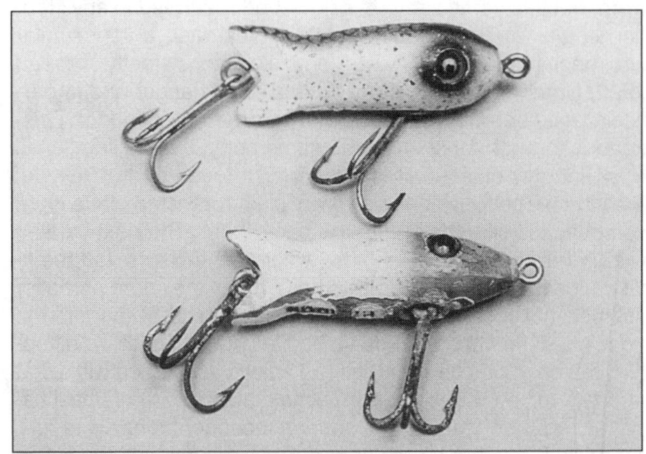

long and has "HEDDON" stenciled on the belly. The other (top) measures 2-1/8". Each has three internal belly weights and cup/screw hook hardware. Collector value range: $75-$150.

SEA RUNT Series #610

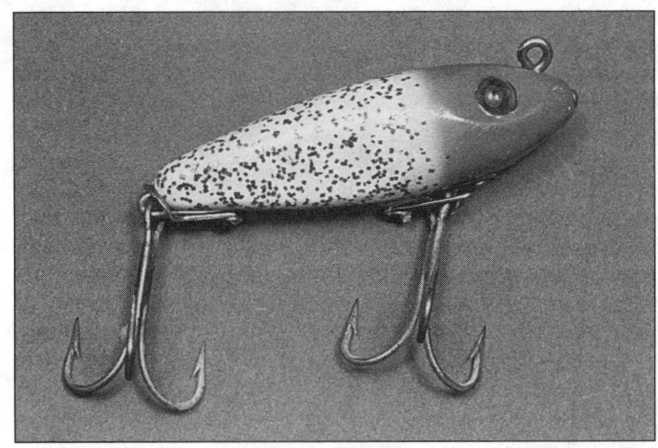

This lure was introduced as "New" in a 1937 catalog. It is somewhat similar to the #110 RIVER RUNT, but has no diving lip and the line tie is located at the top of the nose. Collector value range: $100-$150.

CATALOG SERIES #	BODY LENGTH	LURE WEIGHT
610	2-5/8"	2/3 oz.

COLOR OR FINISH: Spotted, white with red head, white with silver flitter and red head, silver scale; yellow with red head.

COAST MINNOW
No. 1, No. 2, No. 3, No. 4

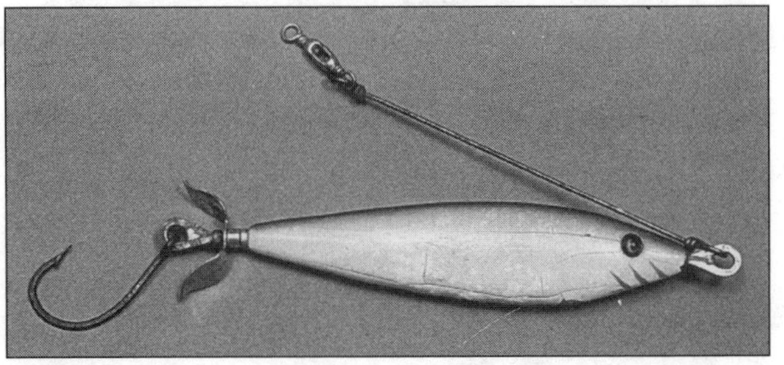

Appearing around 1913, the Coast Minnow was available in four sizes. The one in the photo had Heddon paint and hardware, but this particular lure is not found illustrated in any Heddon catalogs. The Heddon catalogs illustrated a very similar lure beginning in 1913 and continuing consistently through 1922. Note the flat metal line tie and hook hanger and in particular the rear-mounted propeller spinner. The Heddon illustrations through 1922 show the same body, but the line tie/tail hook hangers on them all is the twisted through-body wire type. Also the propeller spinner is a very plain untwisted blade type, completely unlike the one in the photo here. The next catalog (1923) listed the same lengths, weights and colors, but the illustration is more like the photo here. It has the same propeller spinner, but it is mounted at the nose instead of the tail and does have the flat metal line tie and tail hook hanger. Additionally, the openings on each end are heavily reinforced with what appears to be wire wrapping. The text accompanying the illustration described this as "...a square phosphor bronze wire running thru the entire length of body." This same catalog listing and illustration continued until 1927 when it had disappeared.

Interestingly there was an almost identical lure called the SOUTH COAST WOODEN MINNOW available at least as early as 1910. It was offered by a Dr. H.C. Royer of Terminal Island, Los Angeles, California. Perhaps it wasn't patented and Heddon appropriated the design or acquired the rights. Pflueger's CATALINA(later BEAR CAT) is also remarkably like Royer's product. This was a popular design used by many companies with only subtle differences most of the time. Collector value range: $200-$400.

CATALOG SERIES #	BODY LENGTH	LURE WEIGHT
1	4-4-1/2"	1-3/4 - 2-1/2 oz.
2	3-3-1/2"	1 oz.
3	2-1/2"-2-3/4"	1/2 oz.
4	5"	2-1/2 oz.

COLOR OR FINISH: Fancy green back, white body, red and green spots; rainbow, green scale; dark green back, gold speckles.

DOWAGIAC MUSKOLLONGE* MINNOW
Series No. 700

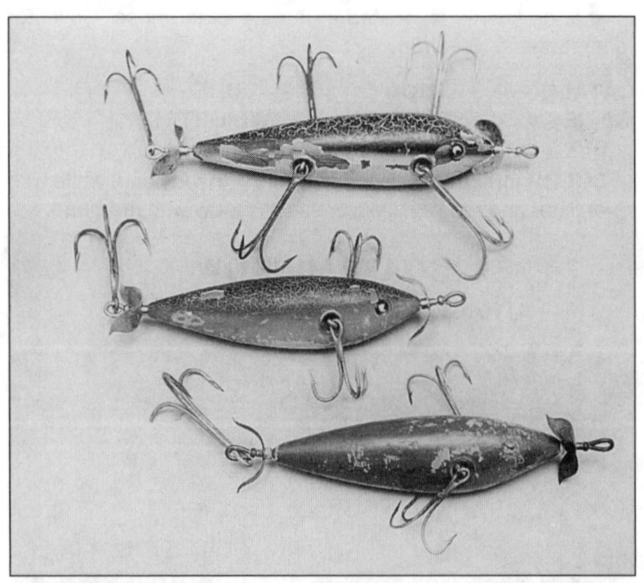

The catalog entry in 1910 said "This minnow is designed specially for catching muskollonge and is entirely too heavy for bait casting...". The #700 Series was made in 3T and 5T versions. The 5T was the first to be offered (1909) and is the rarest. The 3T model was introduced about two years later in the 1911 catalog and continued to be available until 1928 when the catalog no longer listed them. They were cataloged at 4-3/4", but the top lure in the photo measures 5-1/2". It has four internal belly weights, glass eyes, cup and screw eye hardware and no name on props. The center lure has the same characteristics and measures the standard 4-3/4". It has only three belly weights. The lower lure has the same characteristics as the center, but has four belly weights and the props have the "Heddon Dowagiac" imprint on them. Collector value range: $500-$750.

COLOR OR FINISH: Fancy back, white belly; fancy green back, white belly, rainbow, fancy sienna back, yellow belly, red sides, **yellow perch, white body, red eyes.

**1909 catalog spelling.*

***1922 on.*

HEDDON UNDERWATER MINNOW
No. "747"
VL&A No. 7000

This is a huge 8", 9-oz. version of the Series No. 700 above. It was never cataloged by Heddon, or sold by them to the public as far as can be determined. It was apparently specially made for the Von Lengerke & Antoine company (VL&A). It appeared in the VL&A catalogs in 1915 and 1916 as available in two finishes: Fancy green back and rainbow (green back with red sides blending to white belly). Collector value range: No trade data found.

SPOONY-FISH
Series No. 490, No. 590, Np. 790

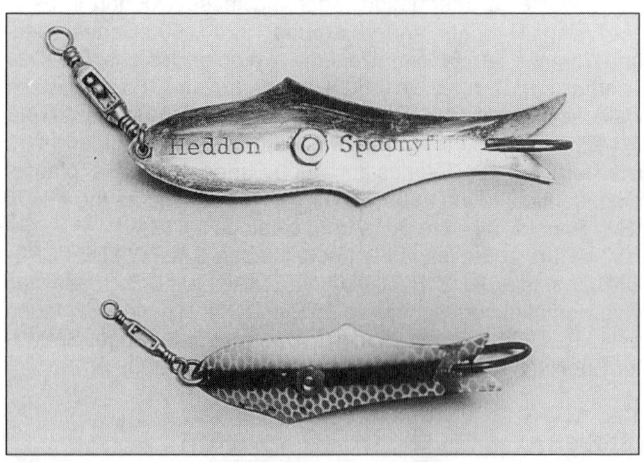

This metal spoon-type lure in the shape of a fish is found listed in the Heddon trade catalogs of 1930 and 1931 only. It measures 2-3/4". The catalog entry implies that it was available only in a heavy nickel plate finish, but as you can plainly see in the photo here it was made in at least one scale finish. The three series numbers listed above denote the sizes it was made in. As listed in the catalog they are 2-5/8", 4-1/4" and 5-3/4". Collector value range: $275-$350.

PUNKINSEED
Series No. 730, 740, 380 and 980

A new lure in 1940 and made in floating and sinking models. It was a real departure from the traditional standard shapes for lures. Made of wood it was a remarkably realistic looking "Sunfish" type lure. The original version has the line tie located *under* the notched mouth while a short time later

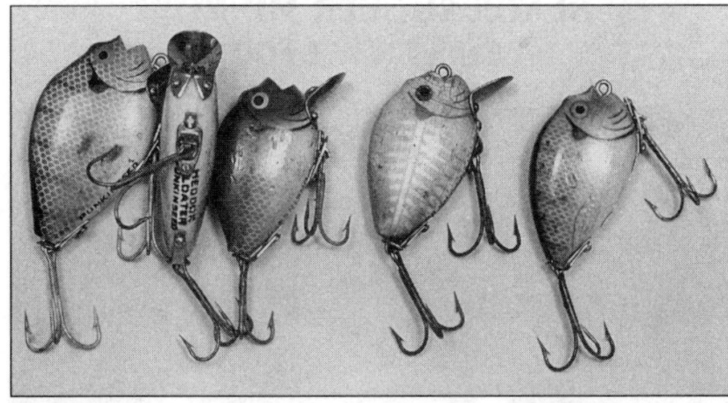

Lower lure in this photo is a renegade. As yet unknown as to why the lure was made with no lip. It may have been a prototype or an experiment. Notice the line tie location on the lure at the top of the photo. This is discussed in the text.

it was moved *into* the mouth. There is a story that the famous Homer Circle, while working for Heddon suggested this change to Heddon to impart better action to the lure and indeed later catalog photos reflect this change. A 1949 catalog calls the lure "The New Punkinseed...Do not confuse this lure with any previous model." It goes on to say that the new model is strictly a sinking plug.

Very shortly after the line tie location changed they began making the lure in plastic. The 1950 catalog offered "THE NEW 'PUNKINSEED SPOOK'." Collector value range: $50-$250. They, like many others, can sell extraordinarily high in rare finishes. For instance, one in rainbow finish hammered down at $1,320 at the 1998 Lang auction.

CATALOG SERIES #	BODY LENGTH	LURE WEIGHT
730 (sinking)	2-1/4"	2/3 oz.
740 (floating)	2-1/2"	3/5 oz.

COLOR OR FINISH: Bluegill, crappie, shad, rock bass, sunfish, *perch, red and white shore minnow, *black and white shore minnow, *yellow shore minnow.

**Sinking only.*

TINY PUNKINSEED
Series No. 380

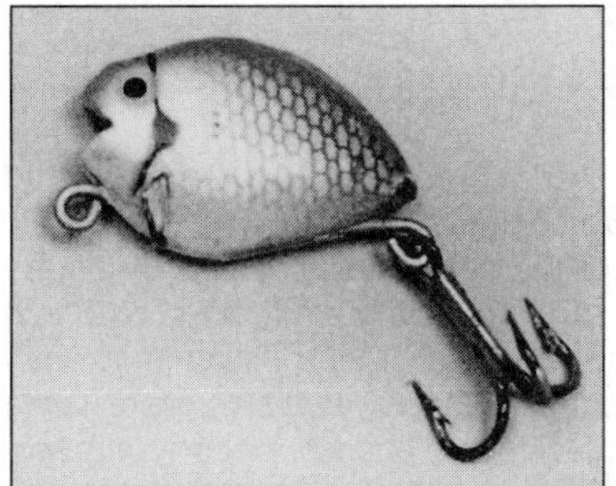

A No. 980 fly rod size. PUNKINSEED.

The fly rod size was made in plastic in 1947 and still in 1957. Available colors were shad, bluegill, sunfish or a crappie finish in the 1947 catalog. The colors had expanded to also include red and white shore minnow and rock bass by 1957. Collector value range. $45-$70.

PUNKINSEED SPOOK
Series No. 9630

The PUNKINSEED SPOOK was featured as new in the 1950 Heddon catalog the entry states in part: "The lure is now made of Tenite, making it as indestructible as the other Heddon 'Spook' baits." This infers there are no more wooden PUNKINSEEDS being made. 2-1/8" was the only size listed. The smaller, TINY PUNKINSEED, 1-3/4" size showed up in a 1956 catalog. Collector value range: $30-$75.

CATALOG SERIES #	BODY LENGTH	LURE WEIGHT
9360	2-1/8"	5/8 oz.
380 (Tiny)	1-3/4"	1/3 oz.
980 (Fly rod)	7/8"	1/20 oz.

COLOR OR FINISH (plastic): Shad, crappie, red and white shore minnow, black and white shore minnow, yellow shore minnow, sunfish, bluegill.

HEDDON SWIMMING MINNOW
DOWAGIAC SWIMMING MINNOW
No. 800 and No. 900

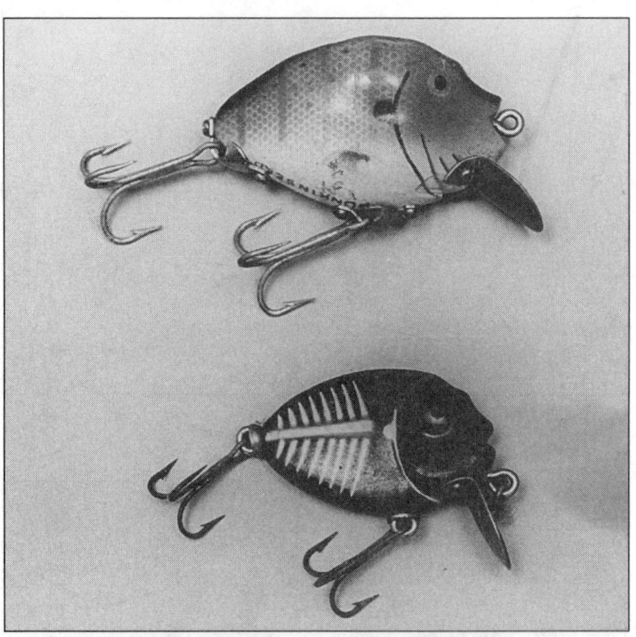

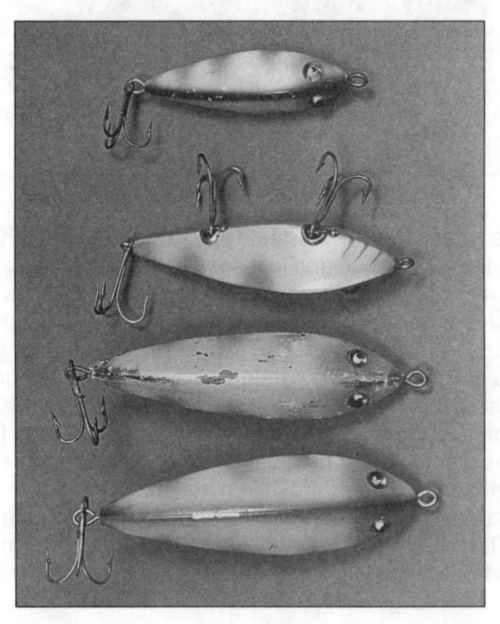

The 800s are sinkers and the 900s are floating divers. First found cataloged in a 1910 edition (900 only, 800 appeared in 1911). The No. 800 was listed at 3-1/4" with a trailing treble only. The No. 900 was 4-1/2" and had a trailing treble and a belly double with a locking pin. The 1912 and 1913 catalogs list only the large size (4-1/2") and by 1914 it had disappeared altogether. I was unable to find any catalog reference at all regarding the 3T model in the photo here. It is 3-5/8" long and equipped with L-rig hook hangers as you can see in the photo. The L-rig patent wasn't applied for until 1915 so this may be simply a prototype never put in to production or it could be a production model. It is known that Heddon didn't always catalog all their lures. The lures were available in two finishes: White body, green and red spots; yellow body, green and red spots. Collector value range: No. 800, $150-$400; No. 900, $150-$500.

TRIPLE TEASER Series No. 1000

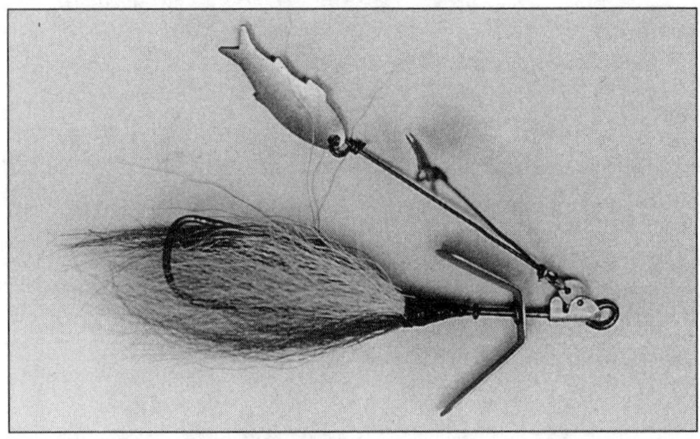

This unusual lure was first found listed in Heddon catalogs in the 1929 issue and last seen in the 1933 issue. It was made with either white, red, red and white, or natural buck tail and red or yellow feathered single hook. The example in the photo below is a typical in two ways. The spinner on the shaft is not shown in any catalog illustrations nor is it present on most of the TRIPLE TEASERS found. It appears to have been placed there at the factory. If it was done by a fisherman, he went to a great deal of trouble. The other difference is the absence of the third little metal minnow. It normally is found at the intersection of the two wires bearing the other two. It has been lost from this one. Each of the little minnow blades have "Heddon Triple Teaser" stamped on them. Collector value range: $30-$50.

BLACK SUCKER MINNOW
Series No. 1300

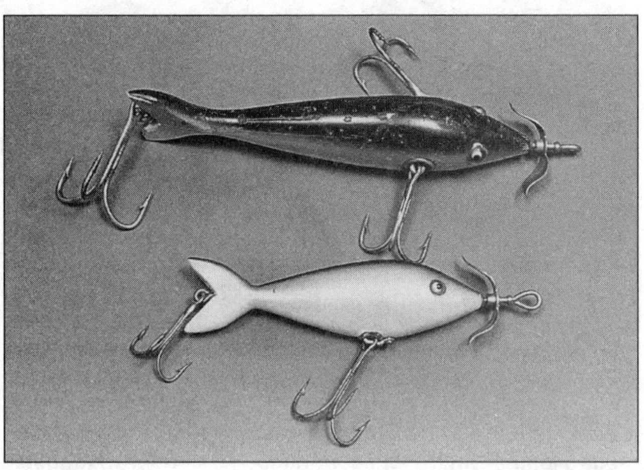

This lure was first listed in a 1913 catalog. It was described as being 5-3/4" long, weight 2-1/2 oz. Catalog entries consistently stated it was available in one color only. It has a very dark, almost black back blending down the sides into a light tint of red, ending in white down to the belly. Despite the one color statement they have been found in rainbow finish and natural scale finish. Never was there any mention of the smaller size (3-7/8") shown in the photo here or of any other colors or models. They are found with cup and two types of L-rig hook hardware, belly treble, side trebles . All found so far have glass eyes. It is missing from Heddon catalogs from 1927 on. Collector value range: $2,000-$3,000.

HEDDON DOWAGIAC MINNOW
Series No. 1400

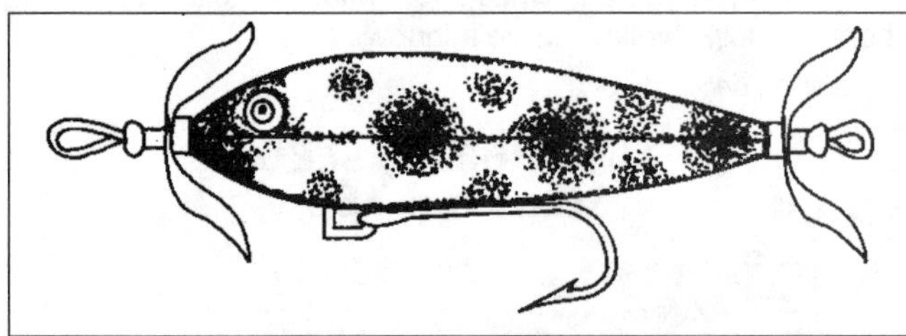

First found in a 1913 Heddon catalog it was never listed again although it may have continued in production for a time. The illustration above is of the same hexagonal body as the Series 1500 DUMMY DOUBLE below, but equipped only with a belly single hook with a unique attachment. The catalog entry said the hook was detachable. Colors available were white body with red, green and black spots and yellow body with red, green and black spots. Body length 3". There are only six known to exist in collectors' hands. One of them was sold at Lang's 1998 auction for $9,900. That was twice the estimate of its value and it set a record for the sale of a wooden lure.

DUMMY DOUBLE
Series No. 1500

Ballyhooed as new in a 1913 catalog entry, this rare 3-1/4" plug cannot be found listed in catalogs any later than 1916. It, like the No. 1400 Series, utilizes the hexagonal body of the Series No. 0 DOWAGIAC MINNOW. The lure was first made with the "Football" style side hook hangers (upper lure), but the 1914

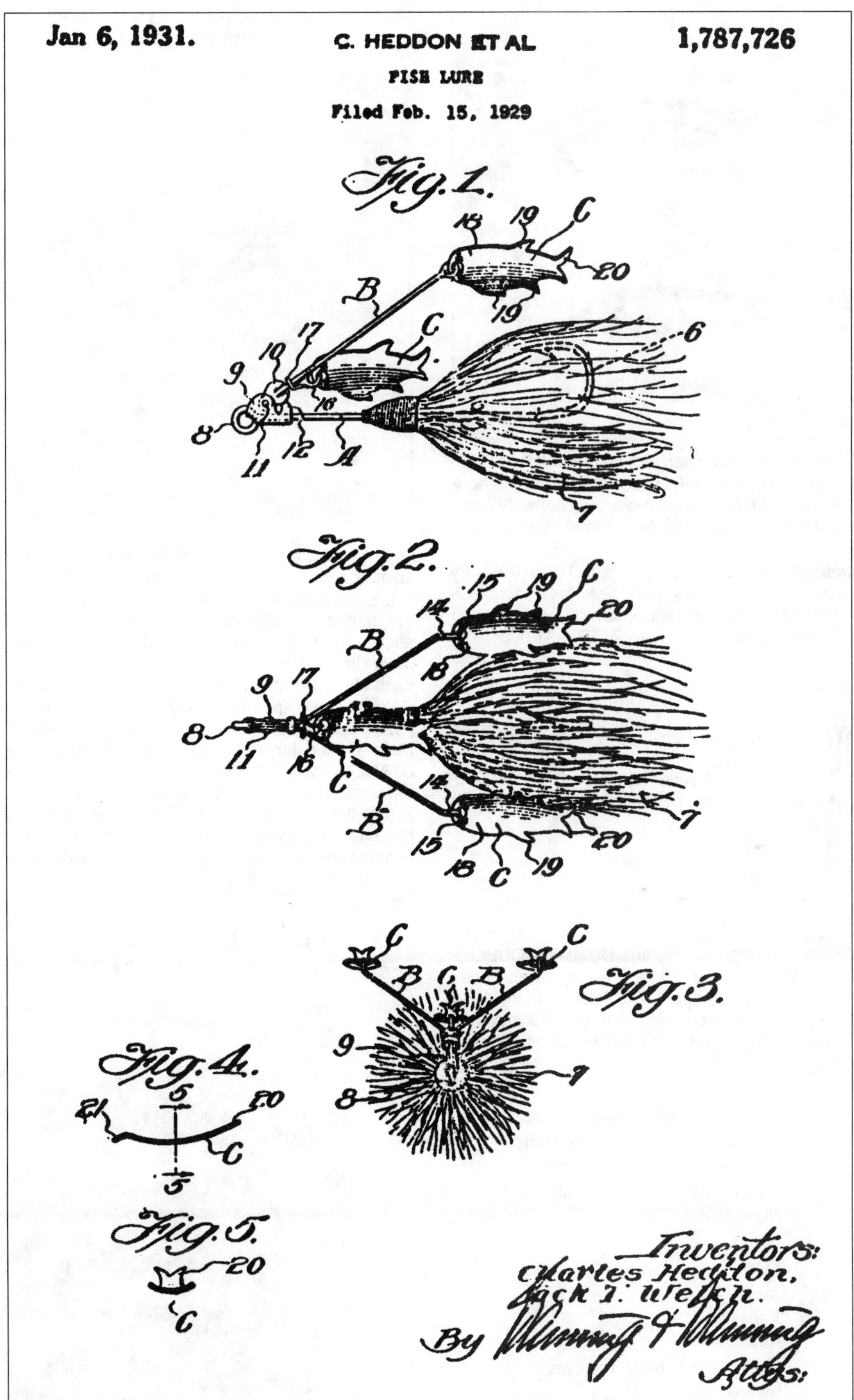

Drawing from the original patent for the TRIPLE TEASER.

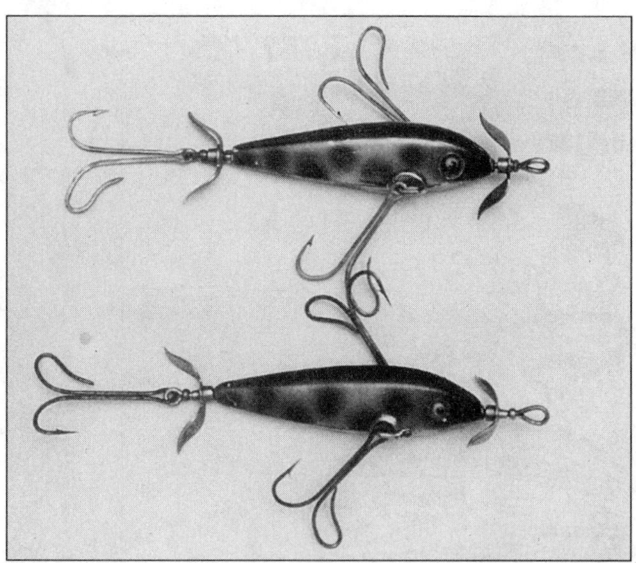

Two styles of the earliest hook hangers on the DUMMY DOUBLE. An interesting note about the upper lure is that the hook hardware and the hooks were hand-made by a collector just a few years ago. He found a good body and went from there.

catalog illustrates the lure with an L-rig hanger. Text in the entry says this is a "new" type of screw hook. Note the very unique "Dummy Double" hooks. It came equipped with one on either side and one trailing. Collector value range: $600-$1,000.

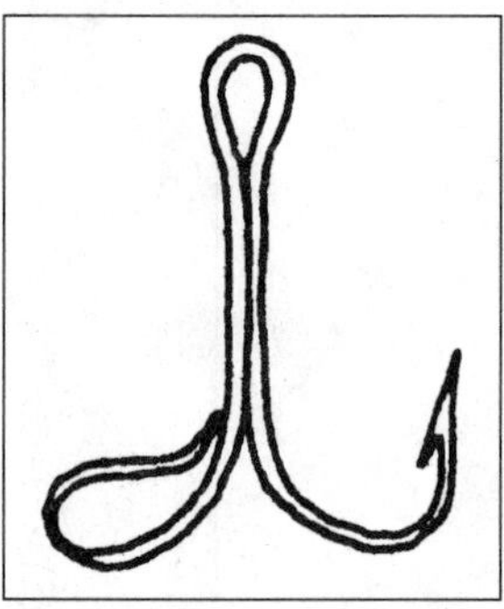

Heddon's patented Dummy Double detachable double hook.

Colors available in 1913 on the first DUMMY DOUBLES were limited to just three: Red, white, green spotted. These also had the "football" style hangers. The color list in the 1914 catalog had expanded to seven colors and in 1915 they had the same number of colors, but those listed were a bit different. See the following lists.

1914 COLORS

1500	White body, red and green spots
1501	Yellow body, red and green spots
1502	Blended white body, red eyes
1503	Fancy green back, white belly
1504	Blended red
1505	Rainbow
1509	Frog

1915 COLORS

1500	Fancy back
1501	Rainbow
1502	Blended white body, red eyes
1504	Blended red
1505	Yellow body, red and green spots
1509A	Yellow Perch
1509B	Spotted frog

STANLEY PERFECTION WEEDLESS HOOKS

These are weedless hooks made in several variations and sizes according to application. The two in the photo here are a No. 2 with spinner and another No. 2 with buck tail. The others are rigged variously with or without weights on the hook shanks, pork rind attachments, spoons and even one that is meant to be fitted with a live frog. The essential element of each of them is the unique hinged wire weedless hook guard. Details of this apparatus may be seen in the accompanying patent illustration. Note that the patent is dated 1931 having been applied for in 1929. If you will look at the HEDDON STANLEY WEEDLESS PORK RIND LURE entry you will see the same apparatus is utilized on that lure. What is interesting is that the catalog entry for that lure in 1924 stated that the hinged weed guard was patented, fully five years before the patent was actually even applied for. Perhaps it was a bluff. We may never know. Another use for the weed guard was on the TRIPLE TEASER. Collector value range: $10-$20.

DEEP DIVING WIGGLER
Series No. 1600

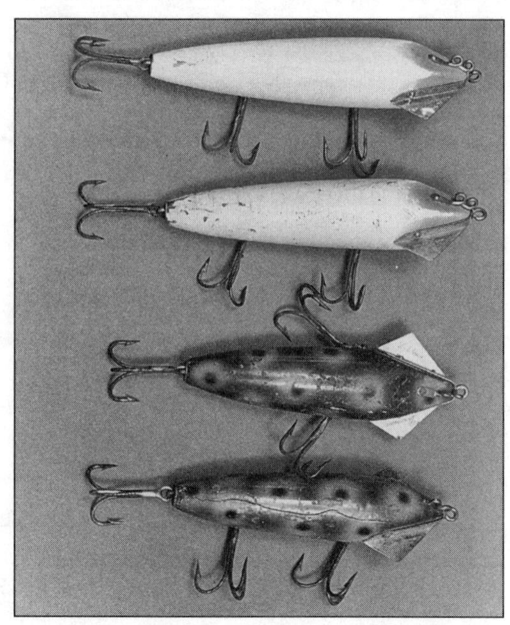

This lure and the following No.1700 Series were the first Heddon production lures to utilize the L-rig hook hanger patented by Heddon in 1918 (applied for May 20, 1915). Both also sport the 1914-patent inch worm line tie. The DEEP DIVING WIGGLER was patented October 20,1914. This patent included the aforementioned pigtail line tie. It was manufactured in two different 3T configurations. There was one with two belly trebles and a trailing treble and other had two opposite-side mounted trebles and a trailing treble. The plug body is found with subtle differences in the two or four slants cut into the nose portion. Each had two triangular fins, one mounted horizontally on each side of the head. Each had triple line ties, but are found with slightly different designs. The very latest body design (c. 1926) had no slope cut into the top of the head, but did retain the slopes on the head sides. This is seen on the bottom lure in the photograph. The photo shows the evolution of the lures oldest to the latest (top to bottom). The first three have the combination pigtail/ screw eye line tie and the other has the inch worm/screw eye line tie. These four all have the L-rig hook hangers, but there is a rare early one with the cup and screw hook hardware. None had eyes. Collector value range: $100-$200.

CATALOG SERIES #	BODY LENGTH	LURE WEIGHT
1600	4-1/2	3/4 oz.

COLOR OR FINISH: Fancy green back with white belly, white body with red and green spots; white body with red head; yellow body with red and green spots; yellow perch; frog finish; rainbow, shiner scale.

Two styles of No. 1600 WIGGLERS and an original box. The upper lure with the top of the head rounded is the newer of the two (c. 1926). The other, with the flattened or slant at the top of the head is the early production model. Both have the "pigtail" line ties. Photo courtesy Dennis "Doc" Hyder.

NEAR SURFACE WIGGLER
Series No. 1700

This lure was first introduced in 1915 and lasted until about 1926. All found so far have had glass eyes. The multiple line tie changed several times over the years. The earliest catalog illustration (1916) I found showed a double pigtail type line tie

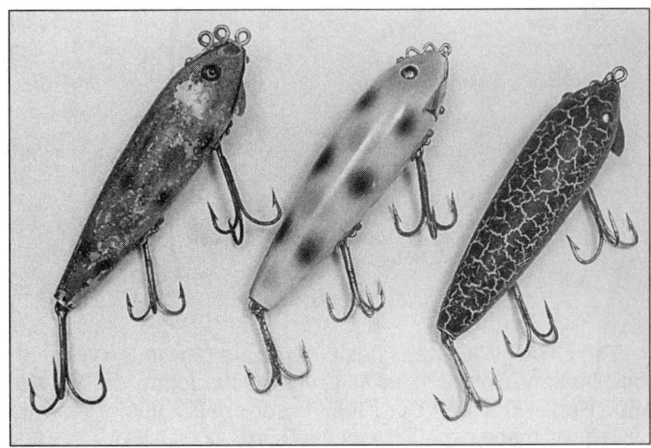

fastened at the nose with a screw eye (left lure). The photo shows the transition from oldest to newest. The left lure also has cup and L-rig hardware. Center plug has inch worm line tie and L-rig hardware. Right has a combination inch-worm/screw eye line tie. All of these have reinforcing tail cup hardware although it has been reported that the latest did not have this feature. All have the metal under-nose plate with two side protruding fins. Earliest were mounted with two screws. Later ones have only one screw with the other fastener being integrated with the line tie fastener. Colors available were the same as listed with the #1600 Series DEEP DIVING WIGGLER. Length 4-1/2", weight 7/8 oz. Collector value range: $125-$200. Rare finishes can bring much more. A perfect one in frog scale finish sold for $1,980 at a Lang auction in 1998.

A new in the box NEAR SURFACE WIGGLER with instructions attached, the original box and the enclosed pamphlet promoting the "New" DUMMY DOUBLE. It has the early "Pig-Tail" line tie. Photo courtesy Dennis "Doc" Hyder.

CRAB WIGGLER
Series No. 1800

This reverse-running plug was first introduced in 1915. The earliest models had the variable line tie and 'U' shaped collar as shown on the top plug in the photo. Then came the 'O' collars shown on the bottom. There was a slight modification of the 'U' collar before being changed to the 'O' type which completely surrounded the tail. The line tie had been changed to a single tie type and was moved to the bottom of the tail* and utilized one of the same screws as the collar to secure it to the lure.

The CRAB WIGGLER has been found new in the box with the "Dummy Double" similar to the hooks found on the No. 1500 Series DUMMY DOUBLE. These special hooks seem to have been made especially for the CRAB WIGGLER. They are heavier gauge than the others, have a shorter shank and seem to have been made curved to conform with the body. These have not been found in any catalogs. Collector value range for regular CRAB WIGGLERS: $50-$100.

CATALOG SERIES #	BODY LENGTH	LURE WEIGHT
1800	**4-1/2"	9/10 oz.
1800	3-1/2	1 oz.
3-3/4"	7/8 oz.	
4"	7/8 oz.	

COLOR OR FINISH: Fancy green back; white body, red and green spots; rainbow; white body with red head; yellow body, green back, red and green spots; yellow perch; imitation frog; imitation crab; green scale finish' red scale finish; goldfish, scale; yellow perch scale finish.

**Actually the front, as this is a reverse-running plug.*

***Earliest size.*

Two early CRAB WIGGLERS with box. The upper lure in this photo has the earlier, slimmer body. They each have the "pigtail" line tie, the U-shaped metal collar and glass eyes. Photo courtesy Dennis "Doc" Hyder.

UNKNOWN HEDDON PLUG
c. 1915
CRAB WIGGLER?

This 4-1/8" lure is very like the #1800 CRAB WIGGLER*, but enough difference to consider it another type. It is possible

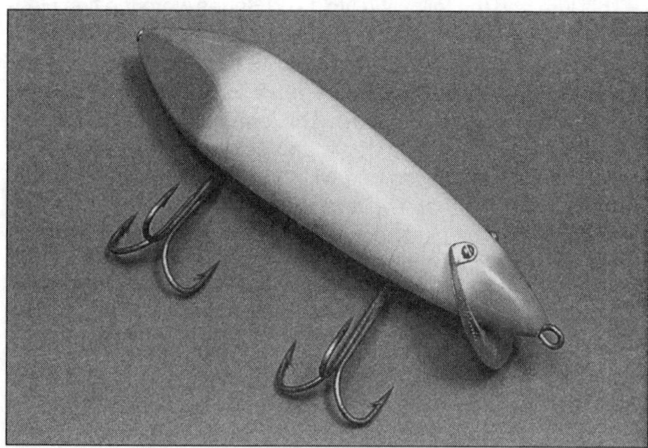

that it was an experiment or prototype of the No. 1800. Note the flattened sides of the tail. There were no references to it in any catalogs and presently only a few are known to be in collectors hands. This one has white body with red head and tail and no eyes. Collector value range: Insufficient trade data.

**It is also quite similar to the #1600 with a two-slant head.*

BABY CRAB WIGGLER (3")
Series No. 1900

MIDGET CRAB WIGGLER (2-1/2")
Series No. 1950

These are smaller versions of the #1800 CRAB WIGGLER. They were introduced in 1915 and 1921 respectively. The earliest had 'U' collars and variable line ties as on the left two lures in the photo. The last U-collar on this lure (before transition to the later O-collar) can be identified by noting that the script stamped on the collar is larger than on the earlier ones. Later plugs also utilize a single line tie secured to the body by using the same screw used to hold the center flange of the collar on. The colors are the same as the #1800 CRAB WIGGLER. The MIDGET CRAB WIGGLER model can be seen in the photo of the GO-DEEPER CRAB below. Collector value range: $40-$60.

DEEP-0-DIVER
Series No. 7000

This is an unusual version of the MIDGET CRAB WIGGLER. It has the same body with a unique line tie and a different style O-collar metal diving lip that is pointed. It sports only one double hook. New around 1919 it was first made with a pin type pork rind attachment on the body. By 1921 this was integrated into the double hook. This later version came with an imitation pork rind attachment. It is a 2/3-oz. sinker. The 1926 catalog was the last to offer the DEEP-0-DIVER. Collector value range: $150-$300.

CATALOG SERIES #	BODY LENGTH	LURE WEIGHT
7000	2-1/2"	2/3 oz.

COLOR OR FINISH: White body, redhead, white body, greenish black spots; yellow body, black head, green scale finish; red, scale finish; frog, scale finish; goldfish, scale finish; yellow perch, scale finish.

The left two lures are GO-DEEPER CRABS. The lure on the right is a MIDGET CRAB WIGGLER

GO-DEEPER CRAB
Series No. D-1900

These four GO-DEEPER CRABS are illustrative of the various names to be found stenciled on their bellies. Left to right they read: HEDDON BABY CRAB, HEDDON CRAB, HEDDON DIGGER CRAB and HEDDON GO-DEEPER CRAB. The one on the left has yellow glass eyes and all four sport the one-piece surface hardware.

The GO-DEEPER CRAB is the same as the #1900 BABY CRAB, but has a deep-diving lip instead of the collar and an optional spinner attached to the rear. These plugs came along in 1952. Collector value range: $20-$50

CATALOG SERIES #	BODY LENGTH	LURE WEIGHT
D-1900	3-1/2"	1/2 oz.

COLOR OR FINISH: Natural crab; white with redhead, green crackle back; black and white crab; yellow shore minnow, orange body, red and black spots.

CRAB-SPOOK
Series No. 9900

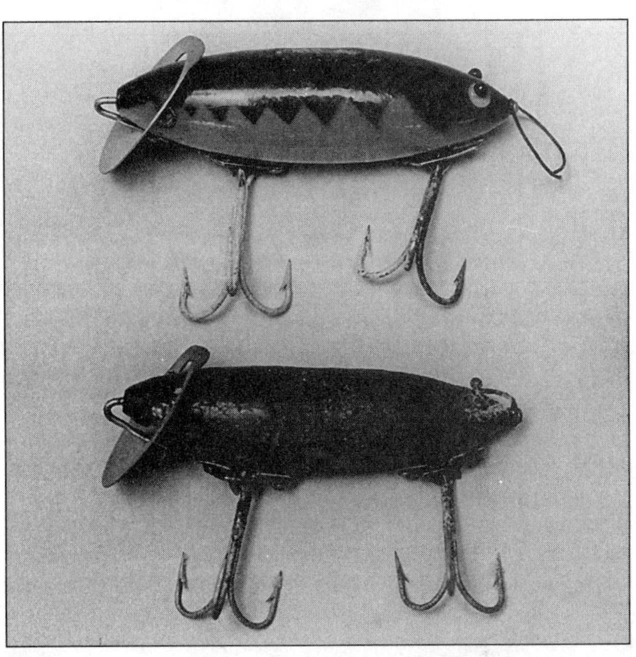

The 1936 edition of the Heddon catalog calls this lure new. This plastic version and the wood CRAB WIGGLERS continued in production into the early 1940s at least. Catalogs after that failed to list either. The photo above illustrates two early plastic CRAB-SPOOKS. They have protruding black bead eyes, feelers and the second style of the Heddon two-piece surface hook hardware. The lower lure in the photo has deteriorated considerably. The early plastics could be very unstable and the lures sometimes literally destroy themselves. They were listed as being 3" long and those in the photo measure the same. The lure exists in a 2-1/2" size, but a careful search of the catalogs on hand turned up no listing for it. Collectors refer to is as the BABY CRAB SPOOK. Collector value range: $20-$50.

WIGGLE KING
Series No. 2000

The WIGGLE KING is very similar to both the LUCKY-13 and the BASSER. It probably represents the first stage in the development of both. It came along in 1918. The LUCKY-13 was new about 1920 and the BASSER came out in 1922. The difference in the WIGGLE KING and the LUCKY-13 is found in the shape of the face of the lures. The WIGGLE KING has no upper overhang at the top of the carved out head and LUCKY-13's always do have a bit of an overhang. Please compare the photo here to the ones accompanying the LUCKY-13. The WIGGLE KING is 3-7/8" long. Collector value range: $150-$350.

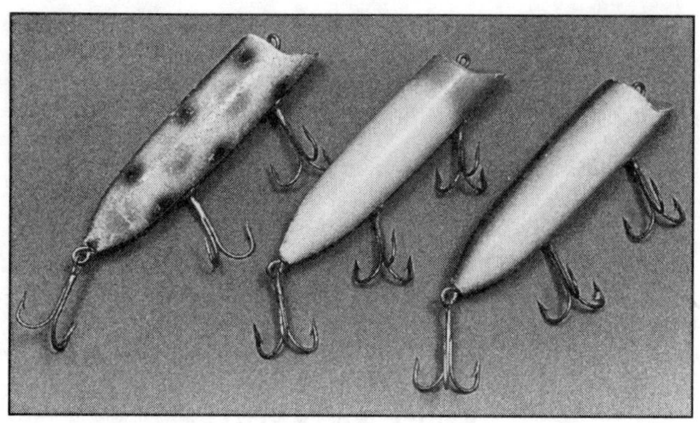

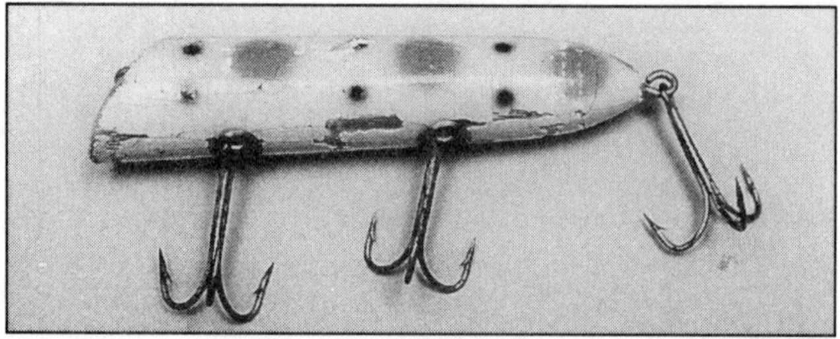

This 4-1/8" lure is probably the earliest model of the WIGGLE KING. It was not found in any Heddon catalogs, but was found listed as THE NEW HEDDON 'WIGGLE-KING' in a 1918 Von Legerke & Antoine sporting goods catalog.

Belly and side view of a CRAZY CRAWLER with two-piece surface hardware.

COLOR OR FINISH: White body with red head; white body with spots; rainbow; frog; green scale.

CRAZY CRAWLER Series No. 2100

This surface lure appeared in the Heddon catalog first in 1940. It is interesting to note its startling similarity to the James Donaly "WOW" lure. Indeed, upon closer examination collectors have noted some interesting facts. In the photo above the lure on the right is the Donaly "WOW." The center plug is the Donaly lure body, paint pattern and flapper blades, but the hook hardware is genuine Heddon. The far left plug is the Heddon product. This evidence served to convince most collectors that Heddon either bought the patent or the Donaly Company at some point prior to 1940. It is now known the Heddon did indeed acquire the Donaly patent. It was first available in two sizes, but quickly a third size was produced.

Belly view showing the hardware progression over the years. The example at the top is a flocked finish with mouse markings. Note the ears, tail and beady eyes.

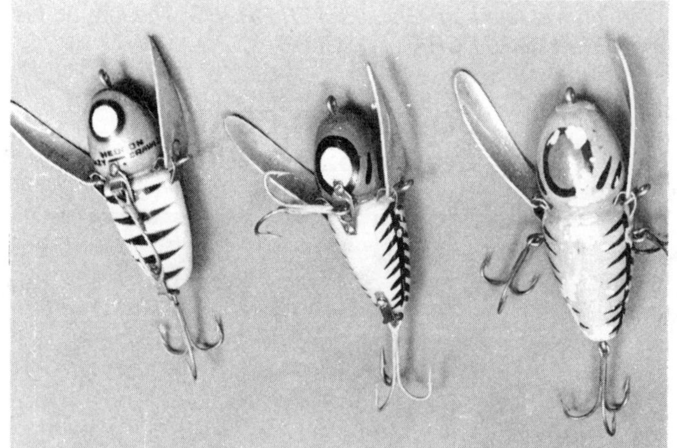

CATALOG SERIES #	BODY LENGTH	LURE WEIGHT	COLLECTOR VALUE RANGE*
2100	2-3/4"	3/4 oz.	$25-$50
2120	2-1/2"	3/5 oz.	$20-$40
2150	3-1/2"	1 oz.	$50-$75

COLOR OR FINISH: **Silver shore minnow, **gray mouse, **glow worm (luminous lines on belly), **bullfrog, **red and white shore minnow, **yellow with red head, black shore minnow, yellow shore minnow, black with white head, white with red head, luminous white with red wings, chipmunk.

**The Glow Worm finish can as much as triple the collector value.*

***The only six colors listed in the 1940 catalog.*

CRAZY CRAWLER SPOOK
Series No. 9120

Note the huge eyes on this late model CRAZY CRAWLER. It measures 2-3/4" and is black with a white head.

The plastic, "Spook" version of the classic CRAZY CRAWLER was introduced in the 1957 catalog. It was 2-3/8" and weighed 5/8 oz. A listing and illustration for a 1-3/4" TINY CRAZY CRAWLER, No. 320 was first found in the 1962 catalog along with the larger one. It was advertised, however, in the May 1955 issue of *Sports Afield* along with several other baits that were called new. It was not. Collector value range: $10-$20.

COLOR OR FINISH: Bullfrog, Yellow with red head, gray mouse, silver shore minnow, black with white head, red and white shore minnow.

SAM-SPOON
Series No. 2160

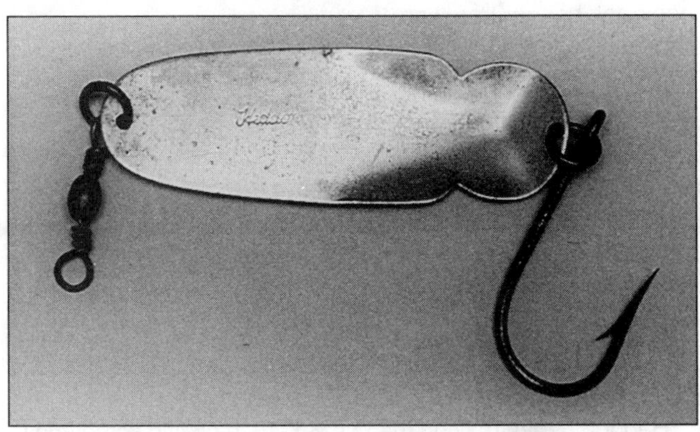

This lure was new about 1936 and was in the line regularly into the 1940s. It was available in either a single hook or a treble hook model. Length is 6-1/2" and it was available in Allen stripey, shiner scale, red and white or plain nickel-plated. Collector value range: $50-$80.

LUCKY-13
Series No. 2400 and No. 2500

The LUCKY-13 was preceded by the WIGGLE KING. They are quite similar. The difference is the LUCKY-13 always has a bit of an overhang at the top of the scooped out nose. The WIGGLE KING does not. The LUCKY-13's appeared in the line about 1920 in two sizes, the regular at 3-7/8" and the JUNIOR LUCKY-13 at 3". The regular size seems to have grown a bit by 1927 when listings begin to say they are 4" long. The oldest

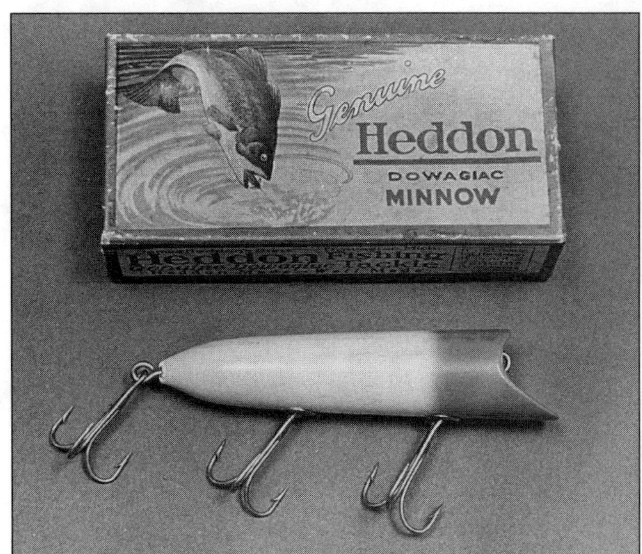

A mint condition early LUCKY-13 with its original box. Note the long lower lip and no eyes.

examples sport cup hardware and follow the classic hardware changes over the years. The photos following illustrate the changes. Collector value range: $30-$70.

CATALOG SERIES #	BODY LENGTH	LURE WEIGHT
2400 (Jr.)	3"	?
2400 (Jr. & Baby)	2-3/4"	3/8 oz.
2400 (Reg.)	4"	5/8 oz.
2500 (Reg.)	3-7/8"	5/8 oz.
*2400 (Classic Baby)	2-5/8"	5/8 oz.
*2500 (Classic)	**3-3/4"	5/8 oz.

COLOR OR FINISH: ***White body, redhead, ***green scale finish, red scale finish, frog scale finish, goldfish scale finish, ***yellow perch scale finish, ***white body with red and green spots, ***pike scale, shiner scale, mullet scale, orange with black spots blue scale finish, rainbow, ***frog scale with red head, ***shiner scale with red head, ***silver flitter with red head, natural scale.

**The classics came out about 1965 in these colors only: Bullfrog, perch, frog scale, red head, silver flitter and red head with shiner scale.*

***Actual measurement. Listed as 4" in catalogs.*

****These were the only finishes available in 1931.*

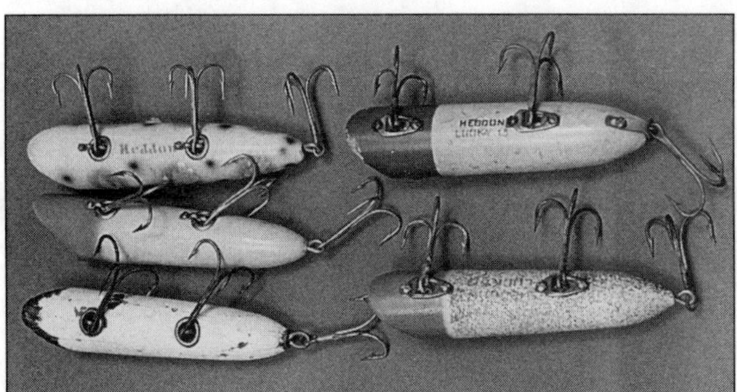

Bottom left shows the oldest with simple cup and screw eye. Above that are two with the L-rig hardware, the next style hardware. The two on the right have the next step, the 2-piece hook hangers. Note the upper right also has the 2-piece tail hook hanger.

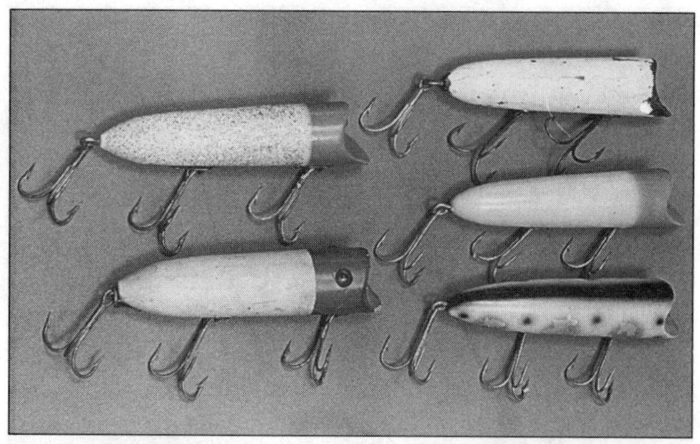

Profile view of the five lures in the previous photo.

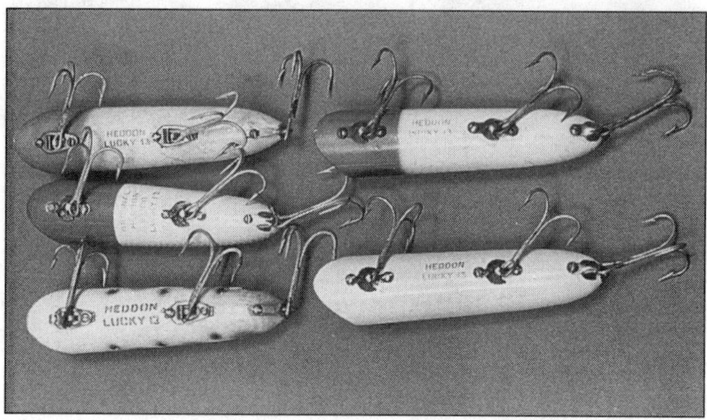

Continued progression of hardware. Upper and lower left lures have the 2-piece hardware and the other three have the final stage surface mounts.

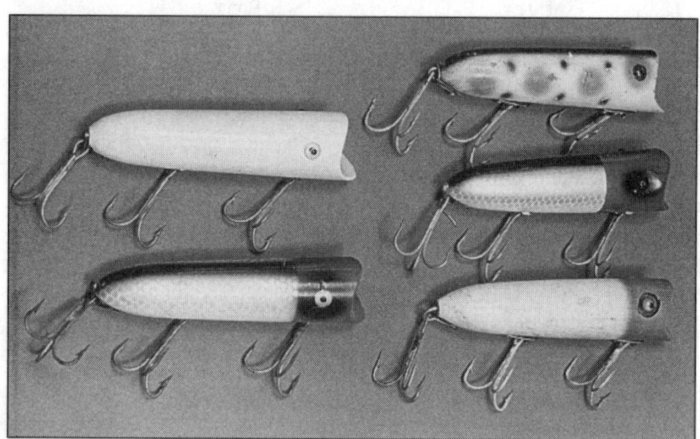

Profile view of the previous five LUCKY-13's.

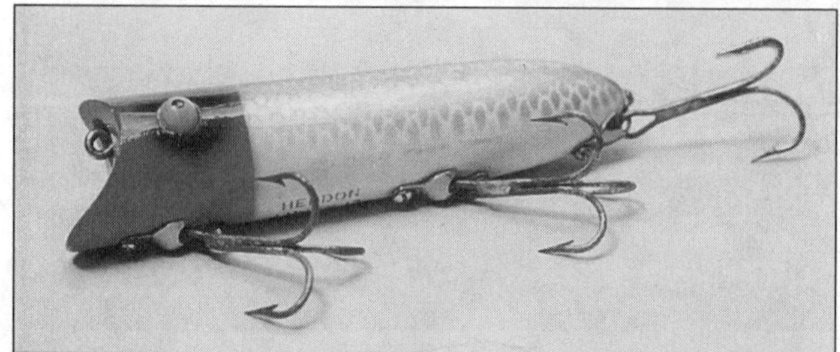

This is a 4-1/8" wooden LUCKY-13 with the last stage one-piece surface hardware. Note the huge bulging eyes. They are yellow in color.

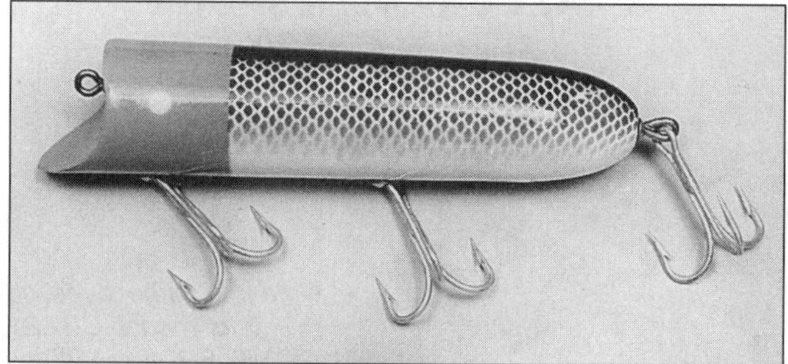

This is a wooden Centennial Edition reproduction of the LUCKY-13 produced as part of a group of classics by Heddon in 1994.

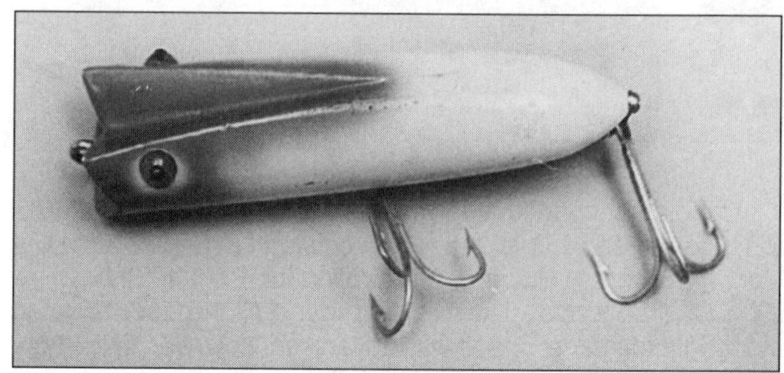

Pictured above is an interesting lure. It is a reworked LUCKY-13. It was apparently fashioned as an experiment after Heddon acquired the Makinen Tackle Company in 1951. It looks more Makinen than Heddon. It was obtained from a former Heddon employee. The body is the same shape as a LUCKY-13. It shows evidence of being a body pre-drilled for LUCKY-13 hardware, but the holes have been filled. It measures 3-1/2", has Heddon tack/plastic eyes and one-piece surface hook hanger hardware.

PLASTIC LUCKY-13's

Heddon began making the LUCKY-13 in plastic sometime in the 1950s. The LUCKY-13 in the above photo is 3-3/4" long and has plastic eyes fastened with a tack. They also made a 2-5/8" BABY LUCKY-13. The lure in the photo below is a TINY LUCKY-13 that measures 1-7/8" long. It was introduced in 1952.

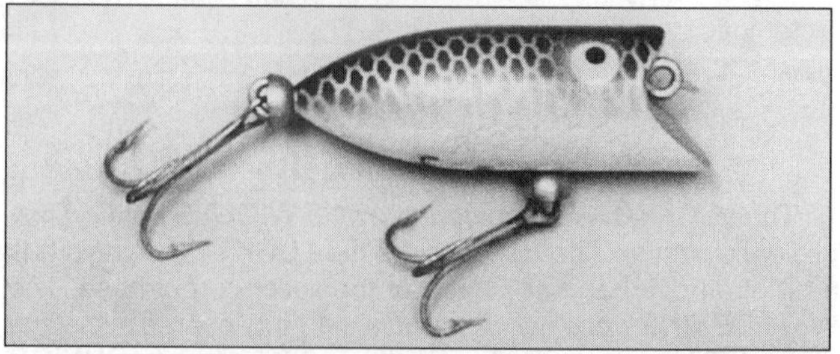

TINY LUCKY-13, Series No. 370. This little critter measures a very small 1-7/8" and weighs in at 1/5 oz.

Collector value range for plastic LUCKY-13's:
TINY LUCKY-13 $3-$10
BABY LUCKY-13 $3-$5
LUCKY-13 $5-$10

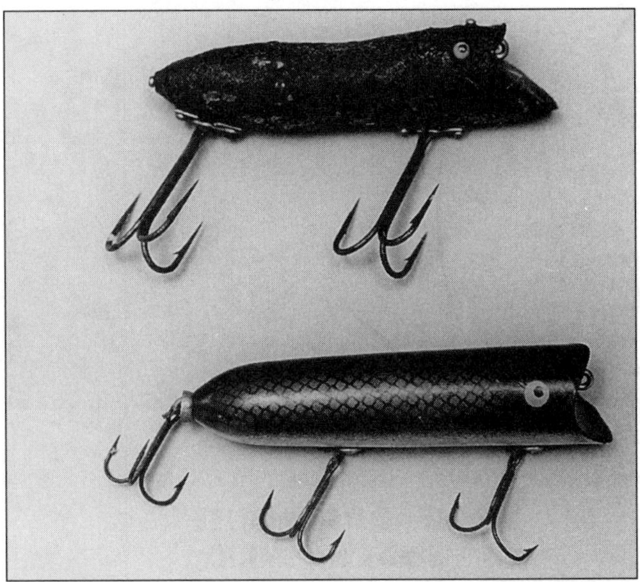

The lower lure is a plastic LUCKY-13 SPOOK measuring 3-5/8". The unfortunate early glass-eye plastic LUCKY-13 is an example of how unstable some early plastic production was.

SPIN-DIVER
Series No. 3000

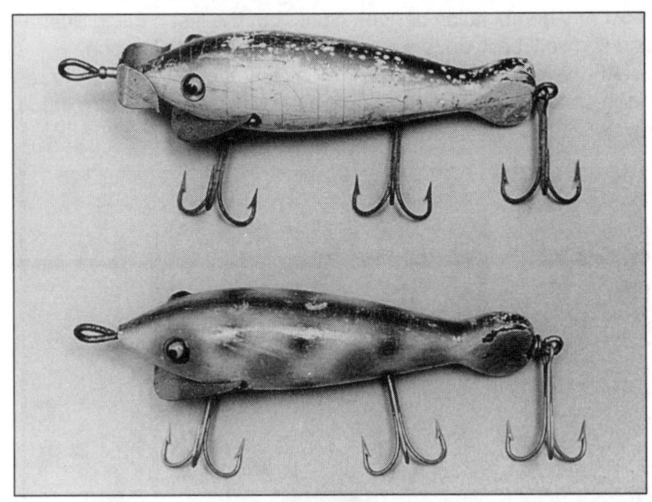

These are propped and no-prop versions of the SPIN-DIVER. Both measure 4-1/2" and have glass eyes. The no-prop model here has plain unmarked metal lip and the other has a lip with the Heddon imprint.

New around 1918 this lure disappeared from catalogs after 1926. It has been found only in L-rig hardware to date. It has been found with no prop and unmarked lip. A handsome 3T glass-eyed, 4-3/8", nose-spinnered plug. It was available in many colors: Green, red, frog, gold scale, yellow scale finish, fancy green back, white body with red and green spots, rainbow, yellow perch, white body with red spot on tail fin and enamel eyes. Collector value range: $300-$600. Rare finishes can bring incredible prices. As an example a SPIN-DIVER in green fancy back finish (crackle-back) brought $1,650 at a Lang auction in 1998.

SPOONY FROG
Series No. 3200

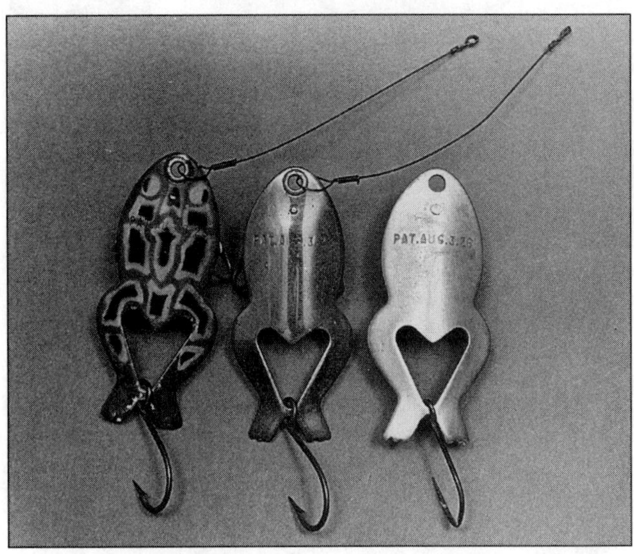

New in 1928 and gone from production two years later, this all-metal lure was offered in four color designs. They were gold-plated, silver-plated, red and white striped, and green frog. They ran belly-up on retrieve. The photo here shows the lures belly down. They are 3" in length and weigh 4/5 oz. Collector value range: $45-$75.

LITTLE LUNY FROG
Series No. 3400

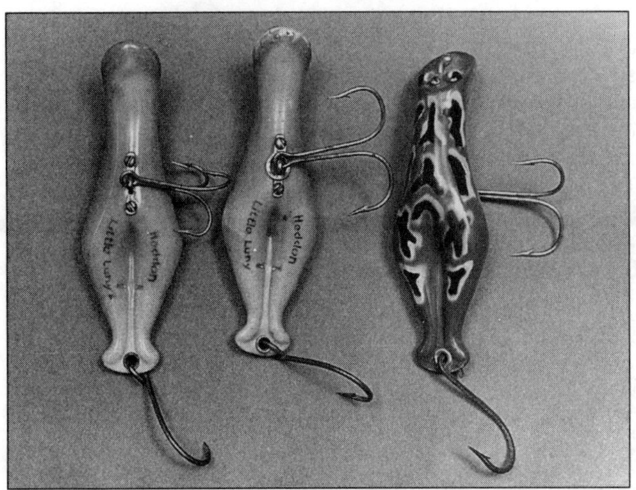

One year after Heddon introduced the No. 3500 LUNY FROG they made this lighter, smaller version available (1928). It was also made of Pyralin and subject to the same brittleness for it too had disappeared from catalogs by 1932. It was available in the same *colors as the larger one below. Collector value range: $75-$125.

**No white body, red head LITTLE LUNY FROG is known to have been found yet.*

LUNY FROG
Series No. 3500

This interesting bait was introduced in the 1927 catalog and by 1932 it was no longer listed as available. The lure was made

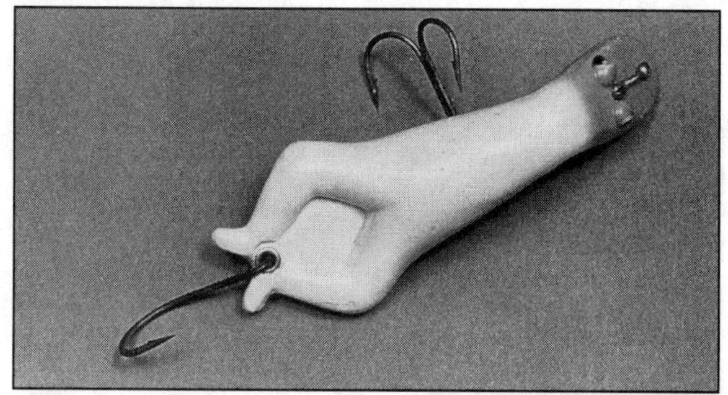

Although never listed as available in catalogs this is a rare red head, white body LUNY FROG. Collector value range: $400-$500.

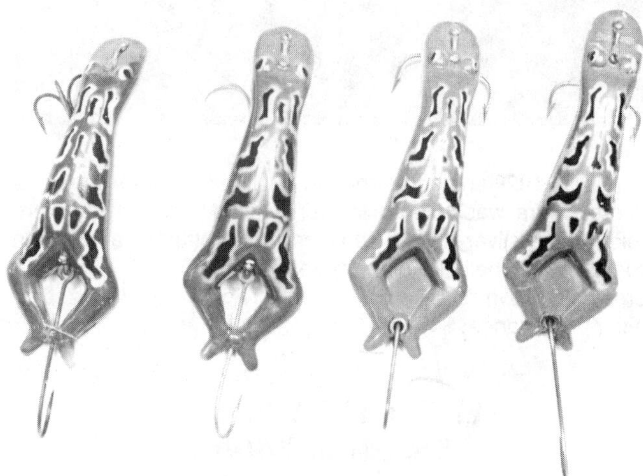

of Pyralin and is known to be a very brittle. It would shatter into several pieces if cast against rocks or other hard surfaces. The lure underwent a design change during its brief appearance in the Heddon line. The two photos above illustrate the "web" that was added apparently attempting to strengthen the design. The plugs are arranged from left to right according to age. Note the hook hardware, identification style and location, and the webbed leg design. They were available with double or treble belly hooks. Collector value range: $50-$150.

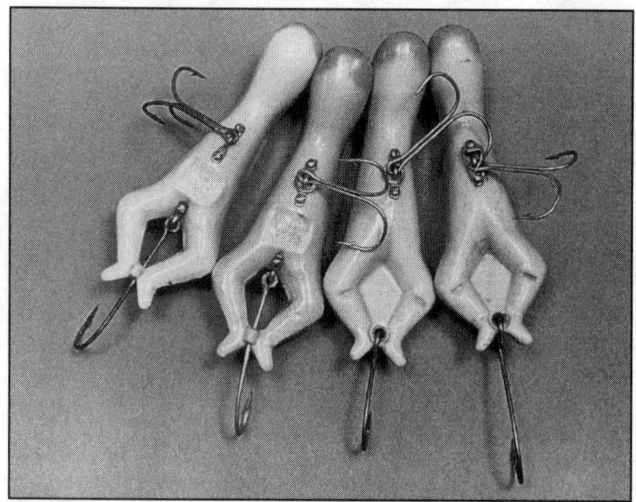

Belly view. Notice the difference. The right two have the space between the legs filled in, in an attempt to strengthen the lure.

CATALOG SERIES #	BODY LENGTH	LURE WEIGHT
3500	4-1/2"	7/8 oz

COLOR OF FINISH: Green Frog, meadow frog, white body with red head (rare).

Back and belly view of the MEADOW MOUSE.

MEADOW MOUSE
Series No. 4000

A 1929 catalog clearly states that this was a new plug for that year. The illustration also clearly shows the L-rig (post-1917) hook hardware. However, if you will examine the first photo you will note the use of the pre-1917 cup hardware. The two lures are otherwise identical to the 1929 catalog illustration. Their metal diving lips say Heddon. They could be prototypes, but they are found so often that it's doubtful. The lures are found with and without the name on the RIVER RUNT-type diving lip. They are found with almost any combination of hook types, but the first catalog illustration shows a belly double and a trailing single hook option.

All have black bead eyes. Most any type of Heddon hardware can be found on the MEADOW MOUSE. Collector value range: $50-$100.

Arranged oldest to newest, left to right according to hook hanger hardware. Note the last two have Vamp type lips. They have been found with this particular lip reversed, making it a surface plug.

CATALOG SERIES #	BODY LENGTH	LURE WEIGHT
4000	2-3/4"	2/3 oz.

COLOR OR FINISH: Brown mouse, gray mouse with white belly, white and red, *black body with white head, **fur finish brown mouse, **fur finish gray mouse, **fur finish white mouse.

**New in 1930*

***Fur finish was new in 1934.*

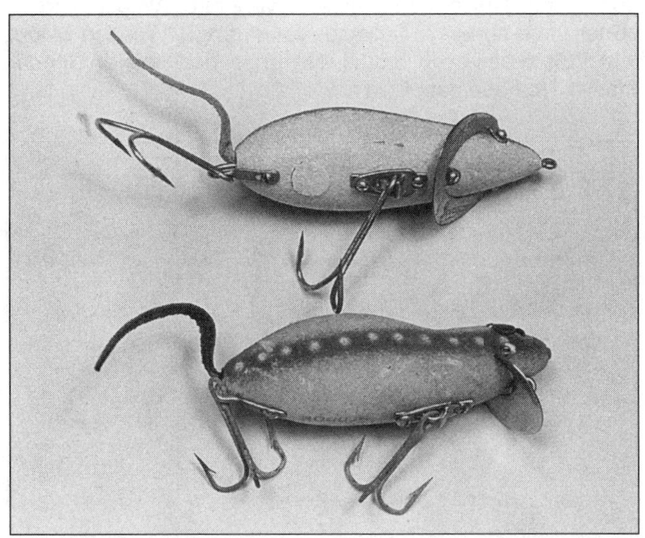

Upper is a MEADOW MOUSE with a Crab Wiggler type metal collar lip. Lower lure is the No. 4200 MUNK-MOUSE with a reversed Vamp type lip.

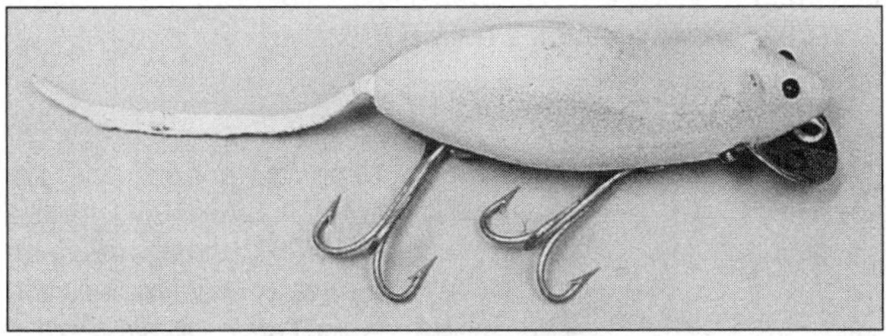

A fur finish white measuring 2-5/8".

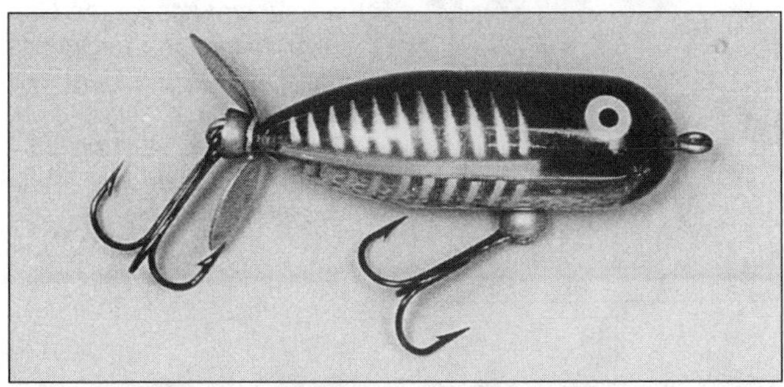

A 2-5/8" plastic MEADOW MOUSE SPOOK of a completely different design. Listed in a 1957 catalog at 2-3/4", the only size listed, has one-piece surface hook hardware. Catalog states "Durable Tenite replacing wood..." Collector value range: $10-$18.

TAD POLLY
Series No. 5000 and No. 6000

The smaller version (Series No. 5000) was the first to be introduced (1919) and the Series No. 6000 came along in 1920-21. The Series No. 6000 only lasted for seven or eight years disappearing after 1929. The Series No. 5000 was continuously in production until about 1941. There are at least two slightly differing body styles to be found; one is a bit fatter than the other as seen in above photo. A more significant difference is the metal plate shape and the position of the identifying marks on the plate. The oldest is the "Heart shape" or apple-like shape then came the "bell-shape". The words "Heddon Dowagiac" are arranged in an inverted "V" shape on the bell plate and next, the words are in the upright "V" position then later rearranged to a curve following the rounded edge of the plate. The latter two arrangements are found only on the "bell shape" plate and are not illustrated in the photo of four (top left photo). They are found with double and treble hooks. Collector value range: $25-$50.

Introductory cardboard box. No number marked on end. The 1918 Von Lengerke & Antoine (VL&A) catalog shows the No.6000 "HEART (or apple) SHAPED" lip with the lip engraved or stamped "Heddon Dowagiac" parallel to the high hump (very first style) line tie. This box, the 1918 VL&A and 1920 Heddon catalog illustrations show this style line tie. Collector value range with box: $60-$120.

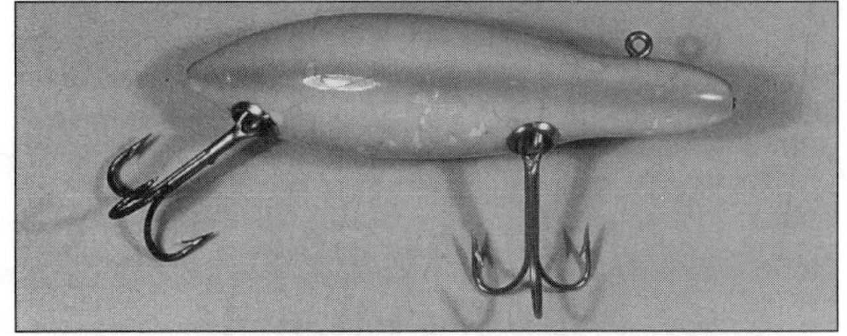

This unknown, un-cataloged lure is placed here because it bears a closer resemblance to the TAD POLLY than any other Heddon Lure. It measures 4" long. Some collectors call them by the name "Bottle Nose". Collector value range: $200-$300.

CATALOG SERIES #	BODY LENGTH	LURE WEIGHT	COLLECTOR VALUE RANGE
5000	3-7/8"	5/8 oz.	$40-90
5100 (Runt)	3"	1/2 oz.	$200-300
6000	4-5/8"	3/4 oz.	$40-90

COLOR OR FINISH: Fancy green back, white body with red and green spots, rainbow, white body with red head and tail, *yellow perch, frog coloration, green scale finish, *red scale finish, *frog scale finish, *gold fish scale finish, yellow perch scale finish, **shiner scale.

**Eliminated by 1930.*

***Added by 1930.*

TAD POLLY SPOOK
Series No. 9000

TINY TAD
Series No. 390

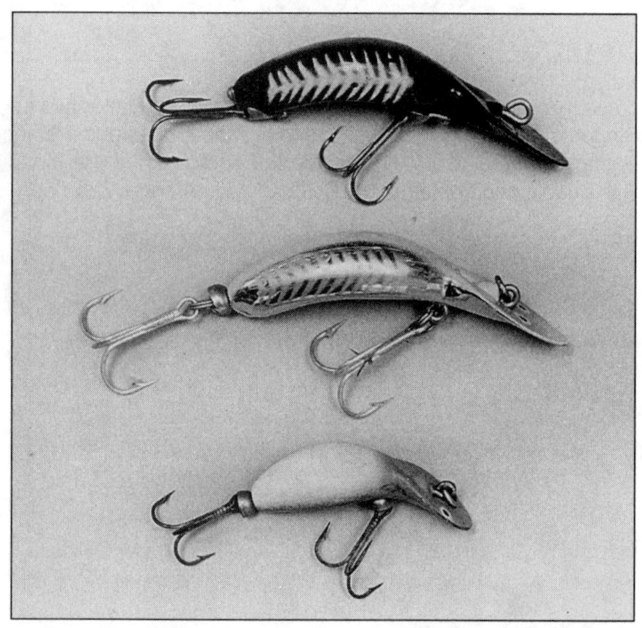

The 3" plastic TAD POLLY SPOOK floater/diver was new in 1952. The colors listed in that catalog follow: Bullfrog, yellow perch scale, golden shiner, silver shore minnow, spotted orange, yellow shore minnow, white w/red head, yellow body with red head, red head w/flitter, black and white shore minnow, light green scale, silver body, red & black spots.

The 2-1/8" plastic TINY TAD spinning lure came along a year later. It was a sinker and the catalog listed the following eight colors: Bullfrog, red head with flitter, golden shiner, yellow perch scale, spotted orange, yellow shore minnow, white w/red head, black and white shore minnow. Collector value range: TINY TAD, $5-$15; TAD POLLY SPOOK, $10-$20.

GAME FISHER
Series No. 5500

BABY GAME FISHER
Series No. 5400

The No. 5500 GAME FISHER came out in 1923 and had disappeared from catalogs from 1934 on. The smaller (No. 5400) came along about a year later. The BABY GAME FISHER was only a two-segment jointed plug. Both were missing from the 1934 and subsequent catalogs. The photos show both plugs and the three different metal lip plate styles.

The lure was patented December 18, 1923. You will note the patent drawing has eyes on the face. The patent text actually specifies glass eyes. Glass-eyed GAME FISHERS are seldom found. These are considered very rare. Almost all found so far have no eyes. Collector value range: Wooden Model, $40-$80; Glass-eyed model, No trade data found; German Plastic, No trade data found.

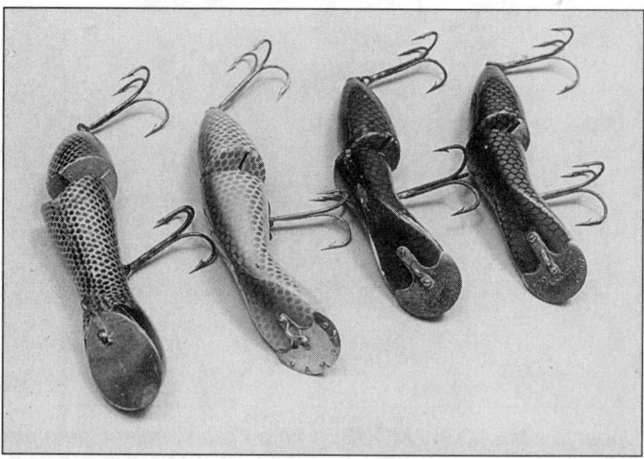

Left to right: The first has a plate that covers the face. Probably a prototype. The next has a the typical face plate but this one is stamped "VAMPIR" (very rare). The other two are stamped with the normal "Heddon's GAME FISHER".

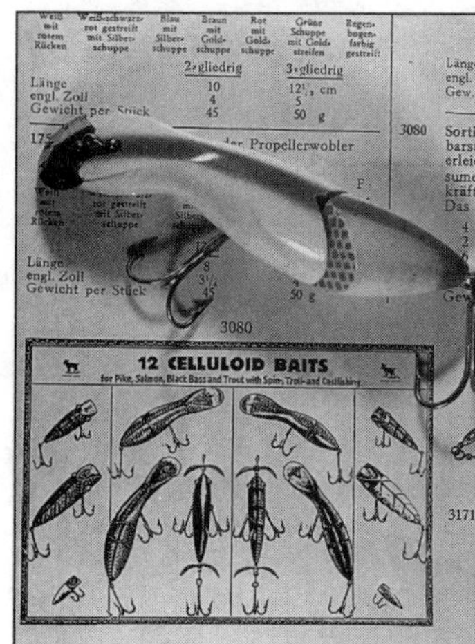

Here is another of the GAME FISHERS marked "VAMPIR" photographed on a page of a German fishing tackle catalog illustrating it. It looks as if Heddon either made these and several other of their lures for the German market or authorized their manufacture there. Notice the nicely fitted joint. This is not typical of the U.S.-made wooden model. Photo courtesy Clyde Harbin.

A belly view of the U.S. made wooden GAME FISHER at the top and the German plastic model at the bottom. A good comparison of the joints. Photo courtesy Clyde Harbin.

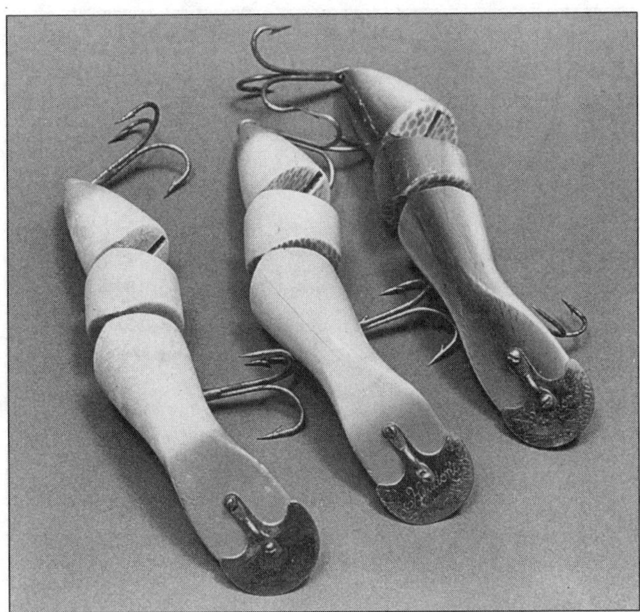

It is difficult to tell in the photo, but the major difference in the lips are: Left lure: No writing; thought to be the very first model of the GAME FISHER. The other have the words "Heddon's GAME FISHER" stamped into the metal.

ZARAGOSSA MINNOW
Series No. 6500

Originating around 1922 the earliest found so far have the L-rig hardware. They continue in production right into the 1950s and on.

The photo of the lure on the patent drawing is of the so-called "no-chin" model. As you can see, it matches the original patent.

The top row illustrates the lure progression from the earliest. Top left lure has glass eyes and L-rig hardware; the top center has glass eyes and two-piece hardware and top right has painted eyes and one-piece surface hardware. The bottom row shows three reissue ZARAGOSSAS from the Heddon Wooden Classic Series of the late 1960s. Each of the Classics has stenciled on the belly "Original Heddon Wood Zaragossa."

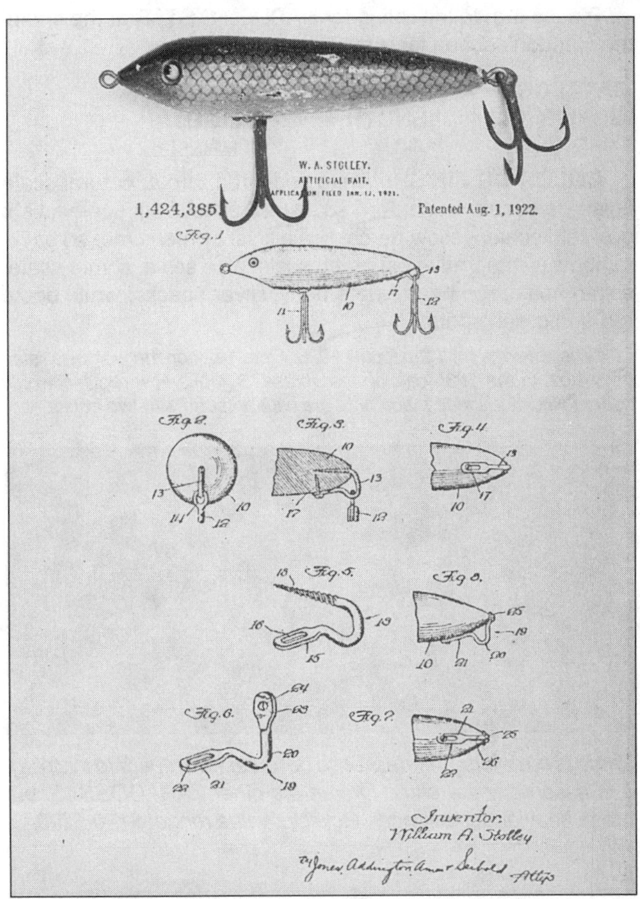

A "no chin" model of the ZARAGOSSA MINNOW with L-rig hook hardware. Beneath the lure is the patent drawing of the lure. The patent is actually for the Stolley hook hardware.

Heddon released a series of Centennial Reproductions of some of their classic lures. The ZARAGOSSA was one of them. They are glass eyed and were very nice, but don't be fooled if one is represented as the old lure. The new ones with glass eyes also have the one-piece surface hardware. You are not likely to find that combination on an early example. Collector value range for the original ZARAGOSSAS: $90-$150.

This 4-1/2" cardboard box pictures a leaping fish with a RIVER RUNT in its mouth. It has the oddly shaped regular Heddon logo (red on black) that first appeared on the cover of the 1949 Heddon Catalog. This is a 3-1/3", glass-eyed wooden lure with screw eye hook hangers and line tie made only for the Japanese market. Notice the No. 6400 ZARAGOSSA JR. box pamphlet written in Japanese.

Please turn to the listing for HARDEN'S STAR at the end of the Heddon section for a related lure.

CATALOG SERIES #	BODY LENGTH	LURE WEIGHT
6500	4-1/4"	*1/2-3/4-oz.

COLOR OR FINISH: White body, red throat, natural scale finish; red scale finish; frog scale, red eyes; frog, scale finish; goldfish, scale; yellow perch, scale finish; green cracked back; rainbow, white, red eyes; green scale; pike scale; shiner scale; shiner scale, red head, white body, silver specks; white body, red and green spots.

**The catalogs list 1/2-oz. until 1926. From 1927 on the weight is listed as 3/4-oz. In the 1935 catalog the phrase "3 hooks now regular" would seem to indicate those made prior are usually found with two hooks.*

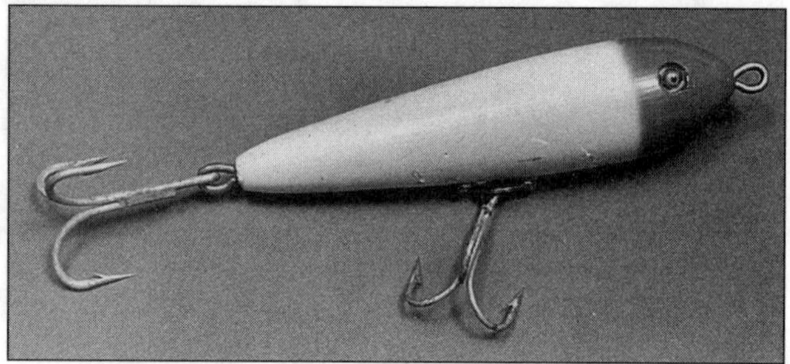

There is no catalog information to be found with regard to this plug. It is essentially the same lure as the other ZARAGOSSAS, but made heavier and stronger. Collector value range: $150-$200.

A commemorative re-issue of the wooden ZARAGOSSA MINNOW released in an edition of 10,000 in 1994. It was a Centennial Edition (see box) celebrating the 100th anniversary of Heddon.

ZARA-SPOOK
Series No. 9260

ZARA-SPOOK JR.
Series No. 9240

This plastic lure was introduced in two sizes in the 1939 catalog, 4-1/4" and 3". The photo of the lures shows that they had the second style of the two Heddon two-piece surface hook hangers. There is no clear picture of when the reinforced, molded-in hook hangers were introduced in the catalogs. They were probably introduced as an option at some point, in addition to the regular hardware. Old-time fishermen say it didn't fish well. Apparently the weight of the reinforcement threw the lure off balance. Collector value range: $25-$50.

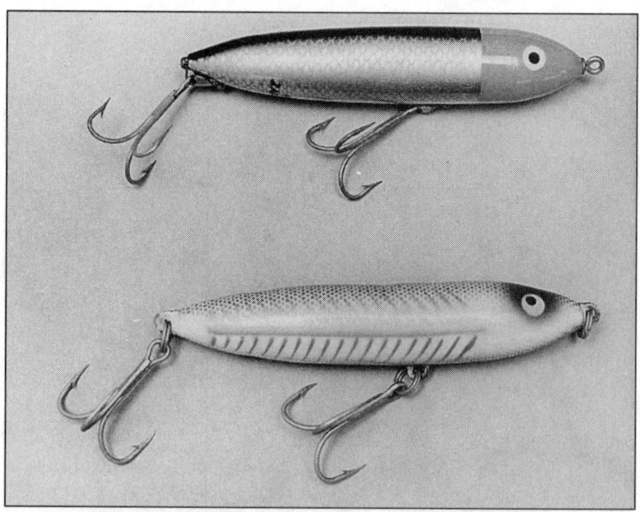

The upper ZARA-SPOOK has one-piece surface style hook hangers and the other has very strong molded-in hangers.

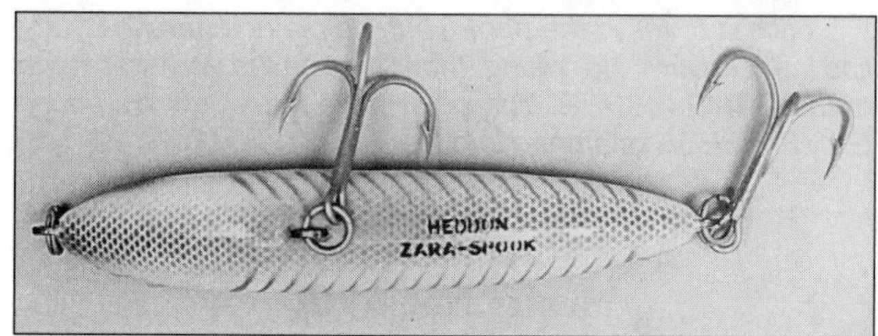

Belly view of the above showing the reinforced hook hangers and typical split ring used with salmon and other large fish lures. This was the only way the lure was made in the 1970s.

The examples with the one-piece surface hardware would be valued considerably less. Colors available into the 1940s are listed following: Bullfrog, green shore minnow, yellow perch, silver shore minnow, yellow shore minnow, red and white shore minnow.

By 1949 there were only three colors offered: silver flash, yellow shore minnow, red and white shore minnow. Only a 4-1/4" size was listed.

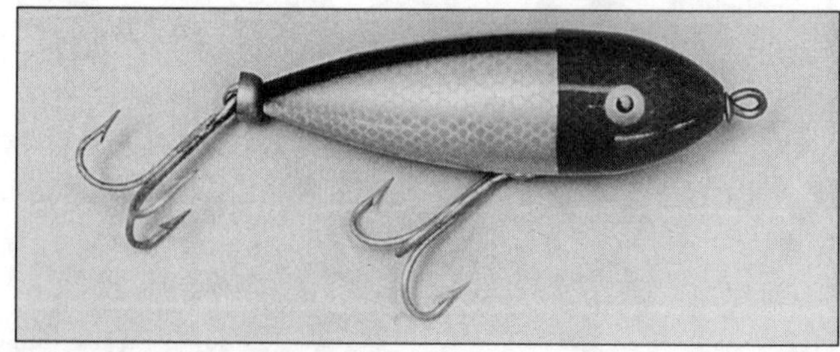

BABY ZARA SPOOK measuring 2-1/2" with one-piece surface hardware.

DARTING ZARA
Series No. 6550 and No. 6600

This lure dates back to at least 1928. A 1933 catalog says it was used to catch "two prize winning bass ... in (the) 1928

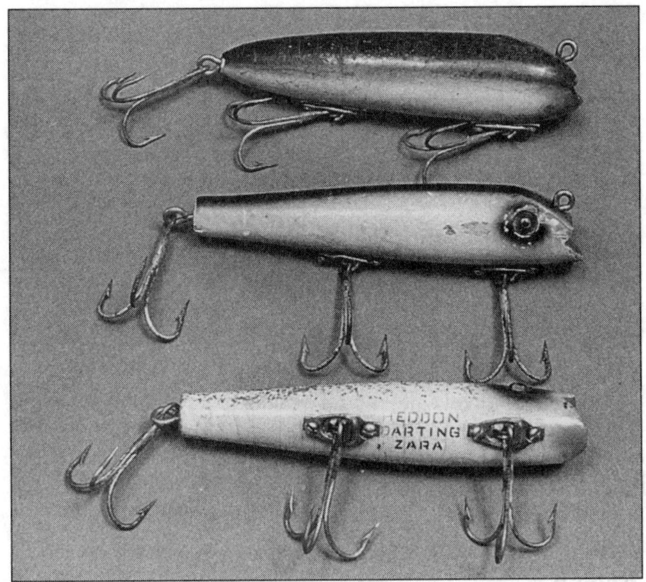

Field and Stream Contest." They were made of wood up until the late 1930s when they became the ZARA SPOOK. In the photo of the three ZARAS here they are arranged by age from oldest at the top. All these have the second style two-piece hook hangers. The lure at the top inexplicably has a nail in the middle of the notch mouth. Collector value range: $100-$200.

CATALOG SERIES #	BODY LENGTH	LURE WEIGHT
6550	3-3/4"	?
6600	4-1/2"	5/8 oz.

COLOR OR FINISH: Orange with red spots, bullfrog; green scale, silver scale.

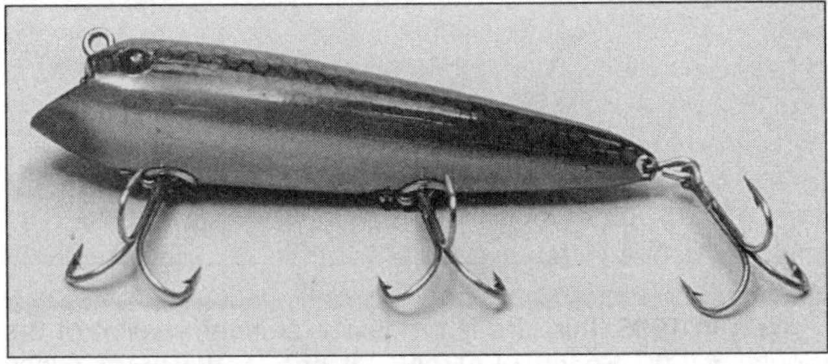

This is a DARTING ZARA with glass eyes, L-rig hardware and green scale finish. What makes this one significant is that it measures 3", an un-cataloged size.

JOINTED DARTING ZARA?

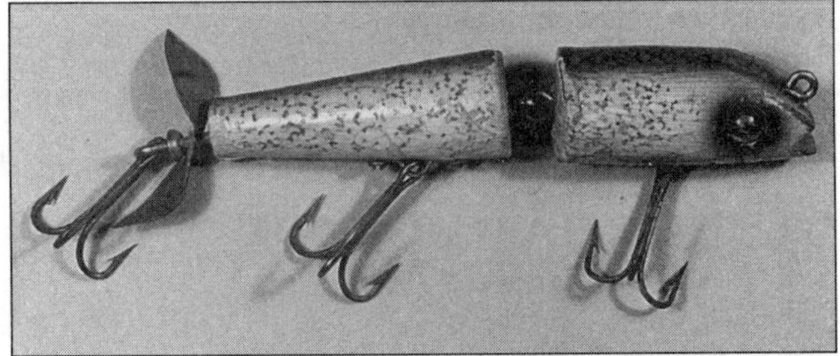

This jointed wooden version of the DARTING ZARA was not found referenced in any Heddon Catalogs. A case could be made that it is an altered unjointed DARTING ZARA except that the paint on the inside of the joint is an exact match to the remaining paint. Would you go to that much trouble if all you were doing was altering a lure in your possum-belly tackle box? This is a Heddon production model be it ever so rare. It measures 4-1/8", has glass eyes, one-piece bar hook hardware, tail spinner and has "HEDDON" stenciled on the belly. Collector value range: $150-$250.

DARTING ZARA-SPOOK
Series No. 9200 and No. 9210

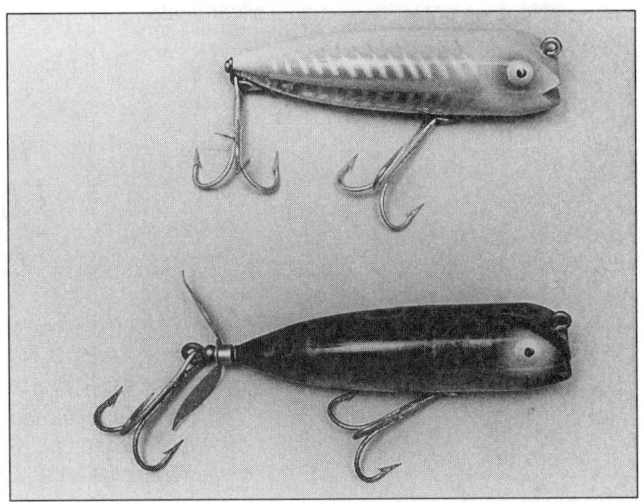

This plastic version of the DARTING ZARA was new in 1939. The only size listed was 3-1/4", but there was another size, The BABY DARTING ZARA at 3-1/4", introduced a year or two later. The upper lure in the above photo measures 3-1/4". The other one is a bit longer at 3-1/2", but the significant thing about it is the tube type rear-mounted propeller spinner. This lure is the Series No. 9210.

There were only three colors initially available for the 4-1/4" size: Bullfrog, silver scale and silver flitter with red head. Interestingly, when the smaller size was introduced it was available in the same colors, but in addition two other finishes were available only on the small size, silver shore minnow and yellow shore minnow. By 1949 the list was limited to only three colors on only one size: silver flash, yellow shore minnow and bullfrog. Collector value range: $15-$25.

FLAPTAIL
Series No. 7000

FLAPTAIL JR.
Series No. 7110

These two were introduced about 1935. Although never cataloged this way, when it was first released it had FLAPTAIL VAMP on its belly. The FLAPTAIL JR. size is found with both one and two treble hooks. The regular FLAPTAILS have two trebles. Collector value range: $25-$75.

CATALOG SERIES #	BODY LENGTH	LURE WEIGHT
7000	4"	4/5 oz.
7110	3-1/4"	5/8 oz.

COLOR OR FINISH: White with redhead, frog, green scale, perch scale, pike scale, dace scale, silver scale, gray mouse, *brown mouse, **chipmunk (fur finish).

**Junior only.*

***Added in 1942.*

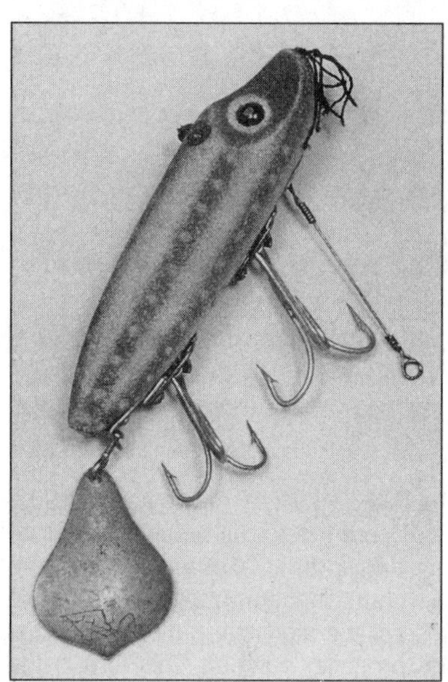

Chipmunk finish FLAPTAIL with glass eyes and two-piece surface hardware. Notice the ears.

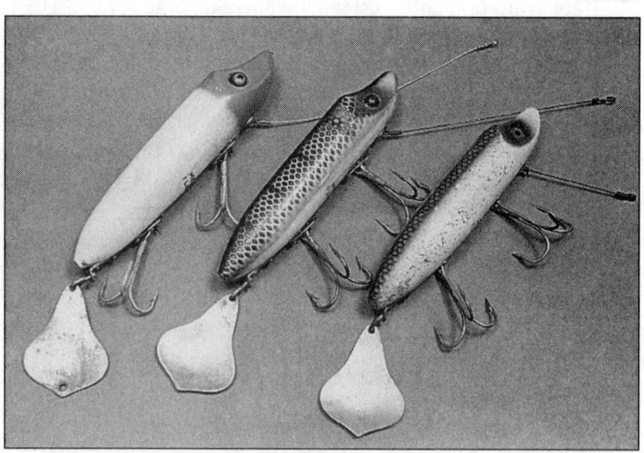

FLAPTAILS. The two on the left sport glass eyes and two-piece hook hardware. The one on the right is a later painted eye model.

FLAP-TAIL-BUG
Series No. 720

This fly rod lure has a body that is shaped somewhat like the head of the larger FLAPTAILS. It is feathered, has a single hook and the distinctive metal flap tail. It was listed in a 1947 catalog at 1-1/4" and available in three finishes: Red and white, gray mouse and solid yellow. Collector value range: $40-$80.

GIANT FLAPTAIL
Series No. 7050

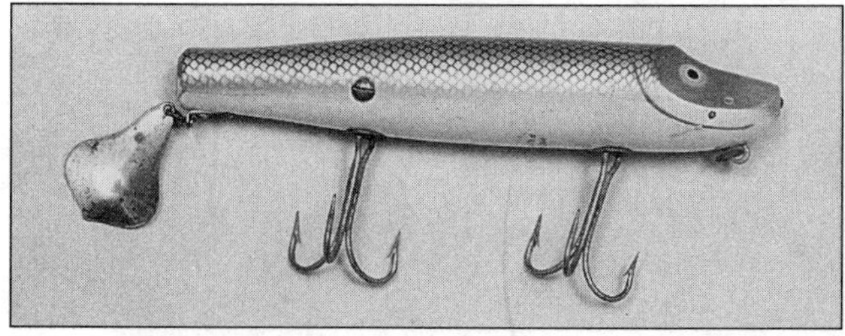

This is a relatively late model wooden plug coming out in the late 1940s. It is an exceptionally strong lure and is the same basic design as the earlier MUSKY FLAPTAIL Series #7050, but much bigger. All have painted eyes. The lure in the photo measures exactly 7". Collector value range: $50-$100.

CATALOG SERIES #	BODY LENGTH	LURE WEIGHT
7959	6-3/4"	2-1/4 oz.

COLOR OR FINISH: Shad, white red head, blue herring scale; shiner scale with red head and stripes.

FLAPTAIL MUSKY
Series No. 7050

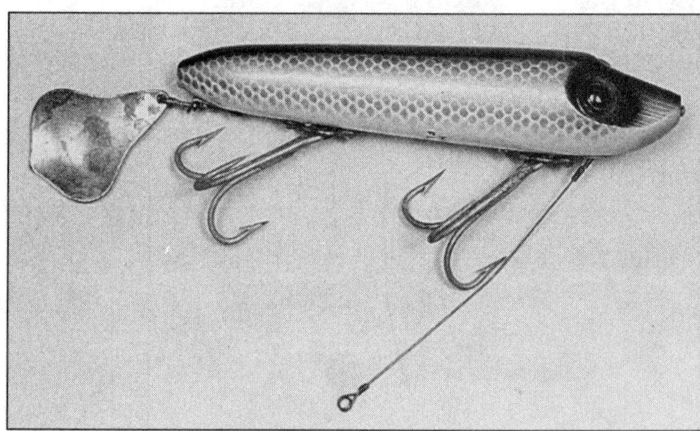

New in 1935, this lure is a heavier, sturdier version of the regular #7000 Series FLAPTAIL. It has 'Teddy Bear Glass Eyes'. Collector value range: $60-$110.

CATALOG SERIES #	BODY LENGTH	LURE WEIGHT
7050	5-1/4"	1 oz.

COLOR OR FINISH: White with red head, **copper sheen, natural scale, shiner scale, silver scale, spotted, *gray mouse, ***chipmunk (fur finish).

**Added in 1936. Had ears and whiskers. Fur finish added in 1939.*

***Removed by 1939.*

****Added in 1942.*

FLAPTAIL SPOOK
Series #7200 and

FLAPTAIL SPOOK, JR.
Series #9700

This is the plastic, "Spook" version of the wooden FLAPTAIL. The lures measure 3" and 2-3/4" respectively. They were not found in catalogs after 1953. That catalog actually lists only the FLAPTAIL, JR. and inexplicably lists it at 3". Collector value range: No trade data found. The range of $10-$15 was reported in the last edition.

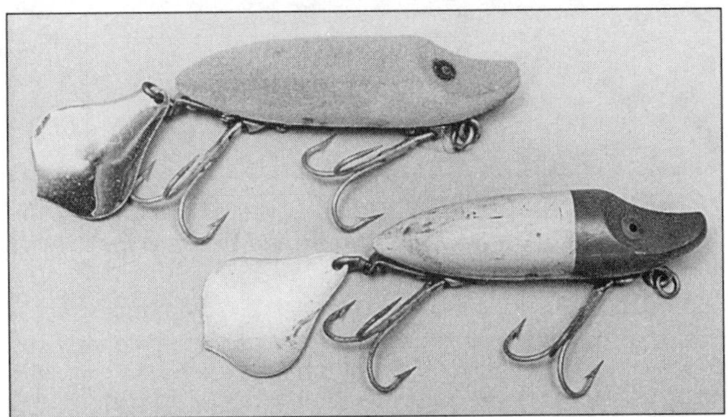

JOINTED VAMP
SWIMMING VAMP
Series #7300

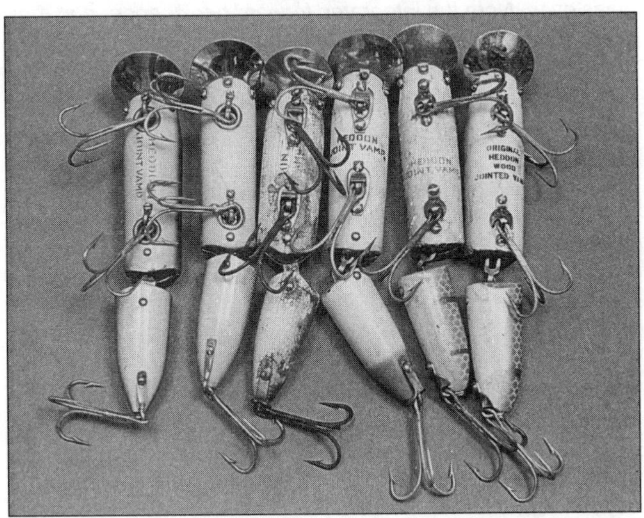

A 1927 catalog says "...newest member of the Vamp family". The 1928 catalog and those after refer to this lure as "The Swimming Vamp Jointed." They are the same design as the #7500 VAMP except jointed. The oldest JOINTED VAMPS can be identified by the single bar type connector at the joint. The newer ones utilize a two-piece connector. The photo shows the oldest at the left to the newest at the right. It does not include the single bar type connector. Note joint connectors, hook hardware, body sizes, and identification word styles and orientation. All good indicators of age. The shorter front section of this jointed lure is considered rare. The left lure is a reissue "Classic" from 1964. Collector value range: $35-$90.

CATALOG SERIES #	BODY LENGTH	LURE WEIGHT
7300	4-1/2"	3/4 oz.
**7300 (Classic)	5"	3/4 oz.

COLOR OR FINISH: Rainbow, white body with red head, green scale, perch scale, pike scale, shiner scale, natural scale, rainbow scale, *white body with silver specks and red head.

**Added in 1934*

***Classic is found only in pike scale, perch, white with red head, shiner scale, yellow shore minnow, white with red and green spots.*

JOINTED MUSKY VAMP
GIANT JOINTED VAMP
Series #7350

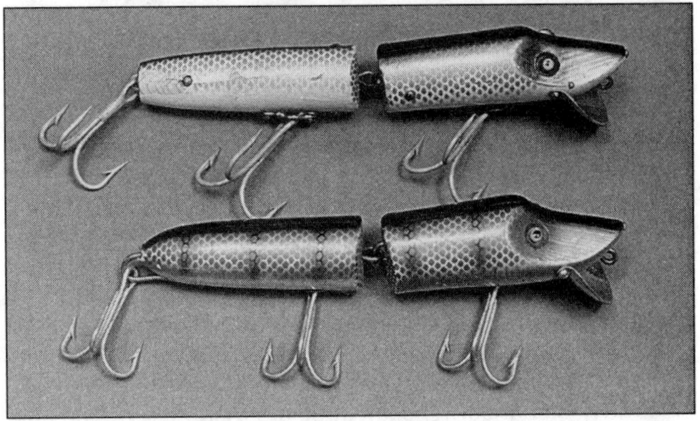

Upper lure measures 6-3/8", has glass eyes, name on metal lip and L-rig hook hangers. The lower one measures 6-7/8", has HEDDON JOINT VAMP stenciled on the belly, glass eyes and cup/screw eye style hook hangers.

This is a jointed version of the #7550 MUSKY VAMP. Prior to 1935 it was called a JOINTED MUSKY VAMP. From 1935 to the 1950s it is known as the GIANT JOINTED VAMP. They are all listed as 6" in length, but the lures in the photo above actually measure longer. Colors are the same as the MUSKY VAMPS. Collector value range: $60-$100.

BABY VAMP
Series No.7400

New around 1925, this is essentially the same as the #7500 series VAMP, but smaller. It is occasionally found with the metal lip in the two-piece hook hardware vintage. Collector value range: $30-$60.

CATALOG SERIES #	BODY LENGTH	LURE WEIGHT
7400	3-1/2"	1/2 oz.

COLOR OR FINISH: White body red and green spots, rainbow, white body with red eyes and tail, green scale, pike scale, shiner scale, mullet scale, orange with black spot, blue scale.

VAMPIRE/VAMP
Series No.7500

The Vamp was born in 1920 as the VAMPIRE MINNOW. First available in 4-1/2" and five colors. The very earliest have

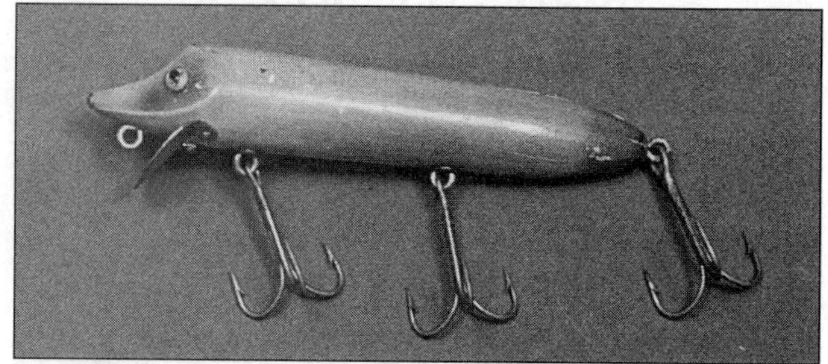

Earliest VAMPIRE. It has cup hook hanger hardware. Collector value range: $50-$100 for this particular version.

cup hardware, but the early VAMPIRES are more often found with the "L-rig." Refer to photo of four lures. Another way to distinguish these early VAMPIRES is by the manner of attaching the diving lip. In the photo you can see that it is integrated with the L-rig hook hanger. The left three are VAMPIRES. The right lure is a later VAMP. By 1922 they were all VAMPS. The diving lips are marked "Heddon." Collector value range: $75-$125.

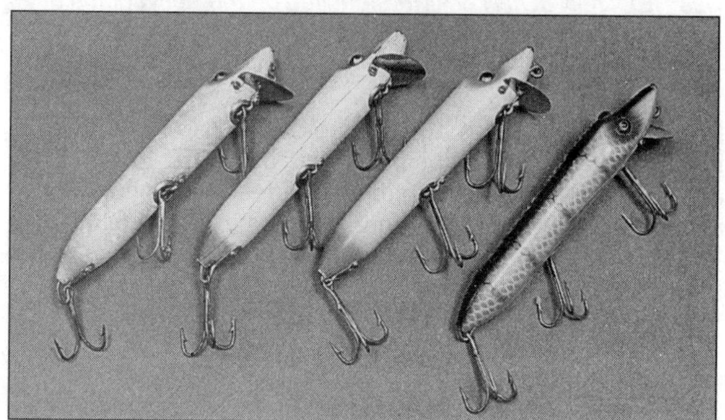

Three No. 7500 VAMPIRES and one VAMP.

CATALOG SERIES #	BODY LENGTH	LURE WEIGHT
7500	4-/12"	5/8 oz.

COLOR OR FINISH: *White body with red and green spots, *rainbow, *white body with red eyes and tail, *green scale, *pike scale, **mullet scale, **red scale; **frog scale; **yellow perch scale; **orange, black spots; **blue scale, silver scale, white with silver specks and red head, luminous with red head and tail, natural scale.

**The original colors in 1920-21. Pike scale was a new color for Heddon in 1921.*

***Added in 1925.*

****Added in 1926. The Frog, Blue scale and Orange finishes were not listed after 1934.*

GREAT VAMP
Series No. 7540

MUSKY VAMP
Series No. 7550

VAMPIRE MUSKY
Series No. 7600

The first of these to come along was the 8" model in 1925 and the 6" version came along shortly thereafter. The large one was gone by about 1930 and the smaller one had disappeared by 1932. The 5" version was in the line from 1937 to 1939. They were made quite large and strong to handle the big muskies.

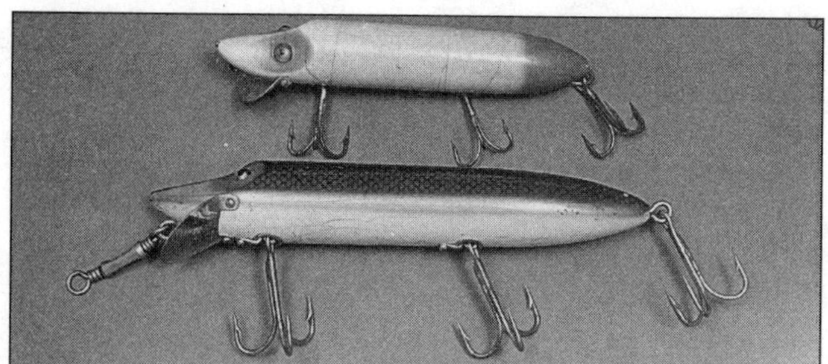

Upper lure is a 6" MUSKY VAMP. Lower lure is an 8" VAMPIRE MUSKY. The MUSKY VAMP had become the GIANT VAMP by 1939.

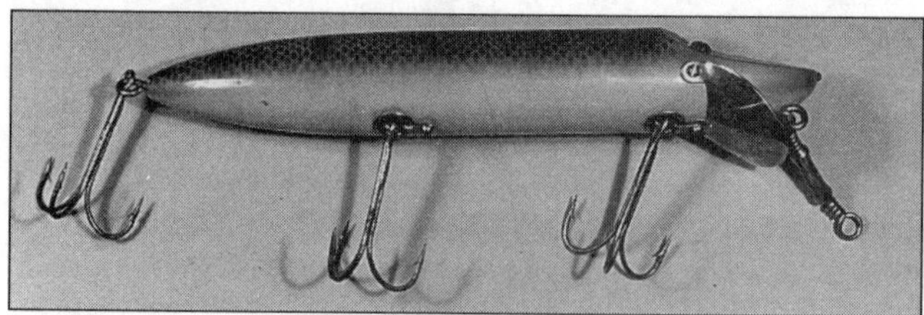

This is a VAMPIRE MUSKY No.7600. It is 8" long and has glass eyes. Note the integrated forward hook hanger and metal lip hardware. This is an important clue in determining whether a lure is a VAMPIRE (pre-1922) or a VAMP (1922 or later).

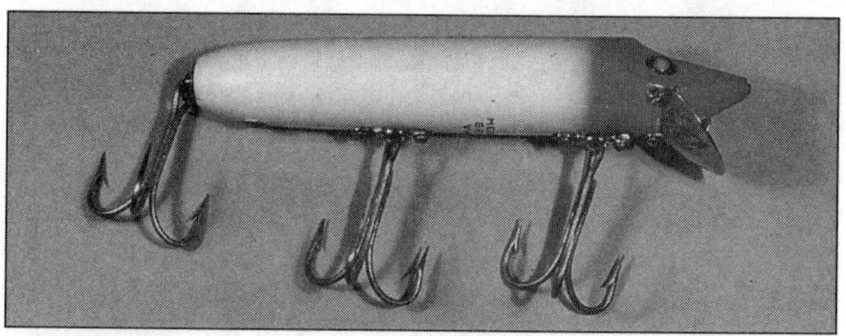

The 5" long GREAT VAMP No.7540. It has glass eyes, no name on metal lip, but the name is found stenciled on the belly. It has heavy duty two-piece toilet seat style hook hangers and a flat metal tail hook hanger held in by a screw from the bottom; metal tail hook insert.

CATALOG SERIES #	BODY LENGTH	LURE WEIGHT	COLLECTOR VALUE RANGE
7540	5"	1-1/3 oz.	$100-$200
7550	6"	1-4/5 oz.	$75-$175
7600	8"	3-1/4 oz.	$175-$265

COLOR OR FINISH: White body, red eyes and tail, green scale, pike scale, shiner scale, natural scale, white body with spots.

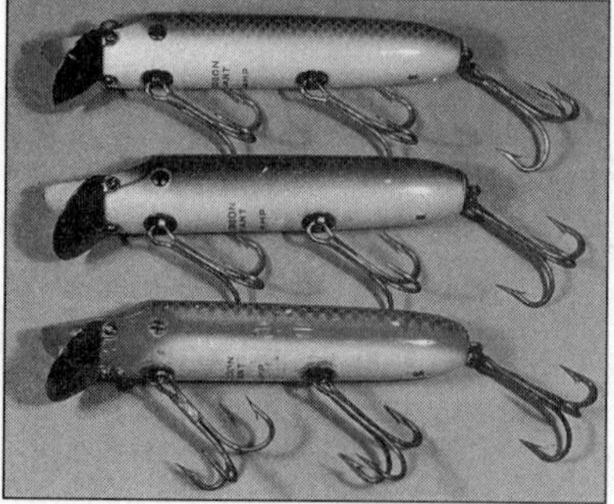

Three 5-3/4" GIANT VAMPS representing an evolution from glass-eye to painted eye models. Oldest is at the top. It has glass eyes, heavy-duty metal ribbon hook hangers, reinforcing tail hook insert. Middle has all the above except the eyes are painted. Lower lure is probably the newest due to the more economical use of screw hook and cup hook hangers.

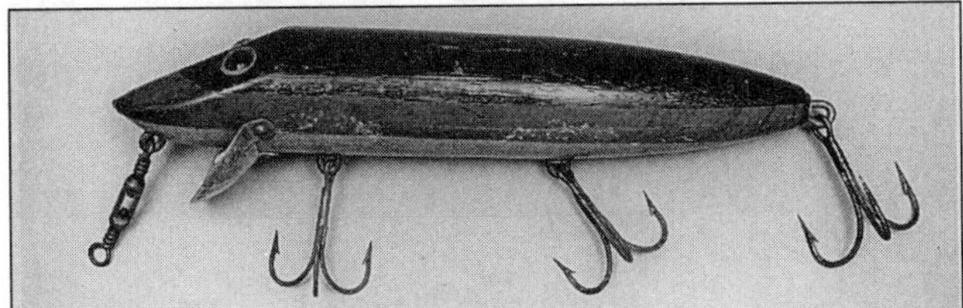

A huge 7-1/2" VAMP with cup and screw eye hook hardware and big glass eyes. It is made of laminated wood and finished in the natural wood. There is no explanation for this un-cataloged monster lure.

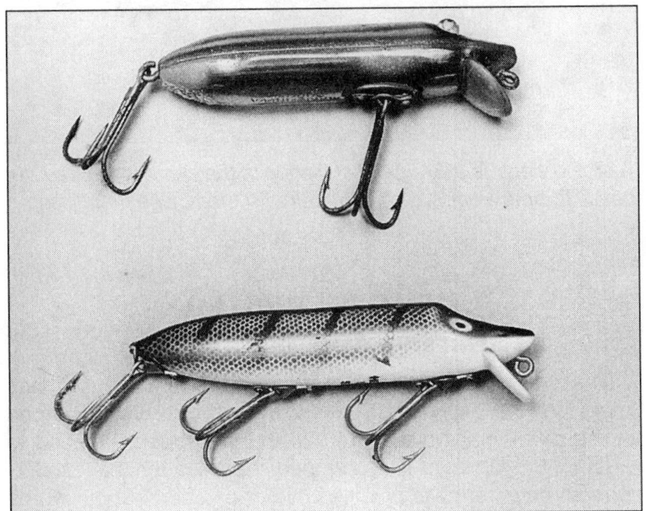

The upper lure is a fine example of the original 4" VAMP SPOOK. Note the hook hardware as the early toilet seat style. Take note of the glass eyes and a molded-in plastic lip. The lower lure is an example of a much later model.

FLOATING VAMP-SPOOK
Series No. 9500
Series No. 9750

JOINTED VAMP-SPOOK
Series No. 9730

KING FISH VAMP-SPOOK
Series No. KF9750

Heddon first introduced the plastic "SPOOK" line of lures in 1932. This was the first of any of the wooden lures listed as available in plastic. It was a hollow floater weighing log introduction of a three-hook floating model, the Series #9750 and a Series #9730 JOINTED VAMP SPOOK. In 1934 the KING FISH model was listed in the catalog. They were still offering their wooden VAMPS elsewhere in the same catalog.

By 1938 the only two remaining in the catalog were the No. 9750 three hooker and the No. 9730 jointed model.

Collector value range for the early plastic VAMP SPOOKS: $35-$110.

CATALOG SERIES #	BODY LENGTH	LURE WEIGHT
9500	3-3/4"	3/4 oz.
9750	3-3/4"	3/4 oz.
9730 (Jtd.)	4-1/2"	4/5 oz.
KF9750	4-1/2"	1 oz.

COLOR OR FINISH: Rainbow, *white with red head, gold flitters with red head, pike scale, *shiner scale, silver scale, **green scale, **yellow perch scale, x-ray green, x-ray silver scale, *silver herring.

By 1938 the color choices were white with red head, green scale, glow worm, yellow perch scale, pike scale, shiner scale green shore minnow, silver shore minnow, yellow shore minnow, red and white shore minnow, black and white shore minnow, goldfish shore minnow,

**The only three colors offered on the KING FISH model in 1934*

***The JOINTED VAMP-SPOOK only in 1933.*

An early Series No. 9730 JOINTED VAMP SPOOK measuring 4-1/2". It has the second style of the two Heddon two-piece style of surface hook hangers.

ZIG-WAG
Series #8300

ZIG-WAG JUNIOR
Series #8340

KING-ZIG WAG
Series #8360

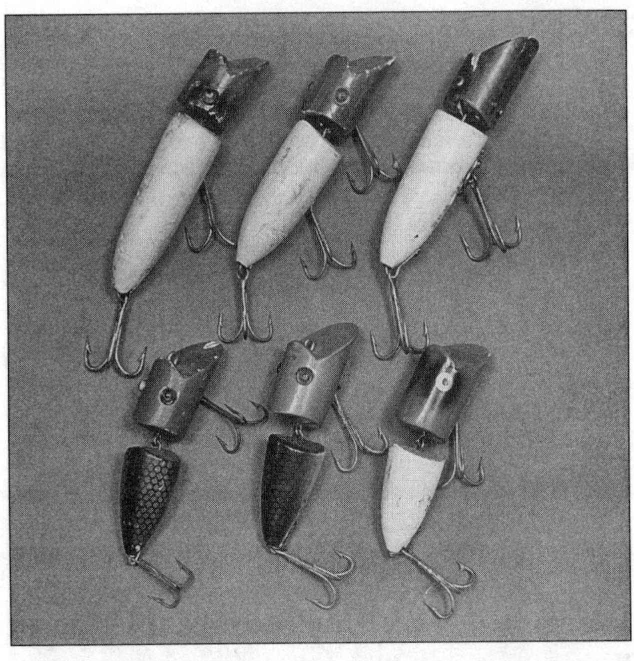

The #8300 was the first to come along (1928), then the #8340 ZIG-WAG JUNIOR in 1937. The #8360 KING-ZIG WAG was last, becoming available in 1939. All three were still being offered in the late 1940s and early 1950s. When first encountered in catalogs (1928) the listing states "ZIG-

WAG (Improved)." This seems to indicate that the plug was already being produced. Even though the author found absolutely no earlier reference to the lure, it is possible that it can be found in an earlier and different design.

CATALOG SERIES #	BODY LENGTH	LURE C WEIGHT	OLLECTOR VALUE RANGE
8300	4-1/2"	3/4 oz.	$35-$65.
8340	3-1/2"	1/2 oz.	$40-$60.

COLOR OR FINISH: White body with red head, *green frog, *green scale, green scale with red head, *pike scale, pike scale with red head, *shiner scale with red head, *natural scale, natural scale with red head, bullfrog, white body with silver specks and red head.

**Eliminated by about 1934. Shiner scale finish was added again in 1937.*

A KING ZIG-WAG.

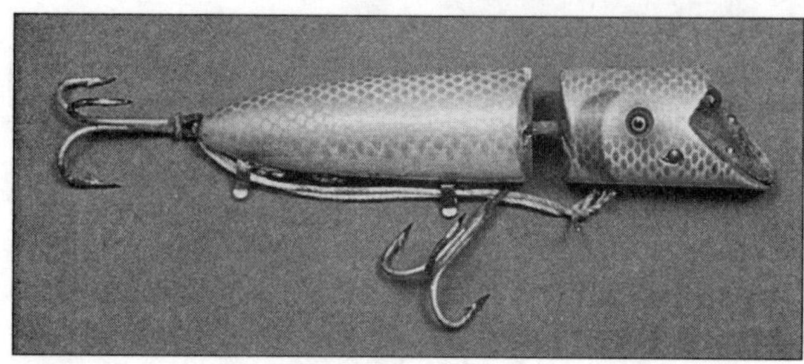

The KING ZIG-WAG sometimes came with a type of thumb tack attaching an imitation leather pork rind to its belly. It was made in two different sizes and had string hook arrangements. Both characteristics are evident in the above photo. Collector value range: $25-$65.

CATALOG SERIES #	BODY LENGTH	LURE WEIGHT
8350	5"	1-1/8 oz.
8360	6"	1-1/2 oz.

COLOR OR FINISH: White with red head, white with red gills, shiner scale, Allen stripey, blue herring, yellow scale, pearl x-ray shore minnow, yellow x-ray shore minnow, spotted with red head.

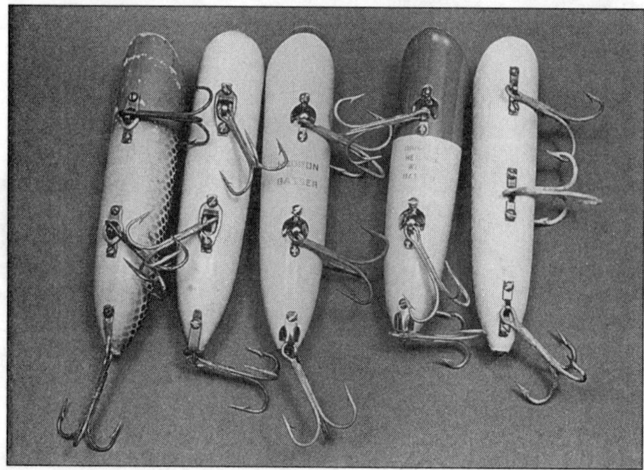

Above shows the progression of hook hanger hardware on the BASSER. Not shown are the first two, the plain no-hump L-rig and the regular L-rig. Next (far left in the photo) came the 2-piece toilet seat style, then the second style two-piece, one-piece surface and the one-piece bar.

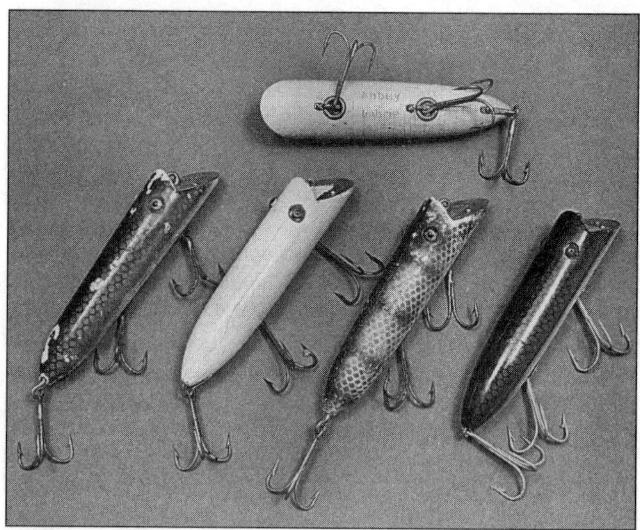

A profile view. The BASSER at the top of the photo is marked Abbey & Imbrie. Heddon made the lure for them. See their listing.

HEDDON BASSER
Series #8400 and #8500

The original or first BASSER came out in 1922 and was called the HEAD-ON-BASSER and these words were stamped on the metal head plate. In 1924 this had been changed to HEDDON BASSER. The stamped identification has undergone some other style changes over the years, but the words have remained the same. Note the body style changes over the years illustrated in the accompanying photos. The BASSER is another of those that were reissued as Classics around 1965 in wooden body and labeled "Original". Collector value range for the HEAD-ON-BASSER : $50-$150.

CATALOG SERIES #	BODY LENGTH	LURE WEIGHT	COLLECTOR VALUE RANGE
*8400 (Plunking)	3"	5/8 oz.	$100-$150.
8500 (Regular)	4"	3/4 oz.	$25-$60.
*8510 (Salmon)	4"	7/8 oz.	$30-$60.
*8520 (Salmon or Deluxe)	4-1/2"	7/8 oz.	$30-$60.
*8540 (King Basser)	4-1/2"	1 oz.	$35-$75.
*8550 (King Basser)	5"	1-1/10 oz.	$50-$90.
*9560 (King Basser)	6"	2-1/4 oz.	$50-$90.

KING BASSER Series #8560. This lure is large and strong. It was obviously made for heavy fishing. Note the strong wire hook hardware. Size: 6-1/8".

COLOR OR FINISH: Rainbow, **white body with red head and tail, **white body with silver specks, white body with silver specks and red head, green scale, **red scale, frog scale,

**goldfish scale, yellow perch scale, pike scale, shiner scale, white spotted, **mullet scale, **orange with black spots, **blue scale, luminous, luminous with red head,

**These were made no earlier than 1935 and all but the #8550 were out of production by the early 1950s.*

***These colors were gone from he 1933 catalog.*

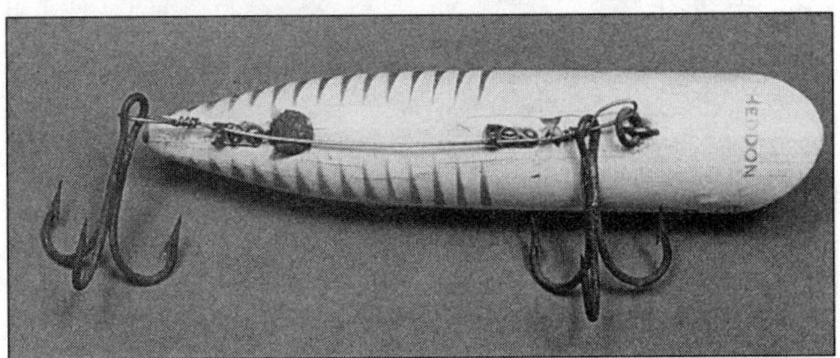

Belly view of the KING BASSER.

BASSER-SPOOK
SEA-BASSER SPOOK
Series #9850

The plastic version of the BASSER was introduced in the 1933 edition of the Heddon catalog. The wooden version was still available in the same catalog. The BASSER-SPOOK was listed at 3/4 oz., 4-1/4". The SEA-BASSER SPOOK was described as "... special salt-water model, with two heavy double hooks for Salmon and Striped Bass." There was no mention of size or weight. It may have been a plastic version of the Series No. 8560 KING BASSER.

In the 1934 catalog they had added a second size, the BASSER-SPOOK JR., Series #9840 at 3-1/4" and 2/3-oz. There is a cryptic note in this listing inferring that there is a different mouth arrangement. "Note the striking feature of an 'open mouth' on models with red beads." The note was accompanied by the following illustration:

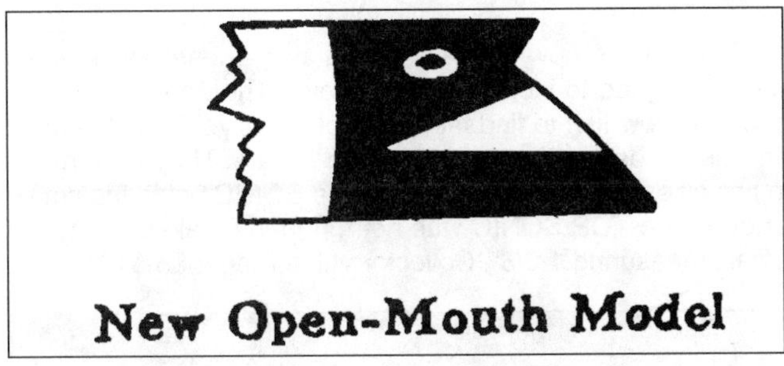

There was also a comment regarding the available special salt water model, the SEA BASSER-SPOOK with no specifications other than colors.

Collector value range for the plastic BASSER SPOOKS: N.A.

Color choices for these 1930s are listed following:

BASSER-SPOOK and BASSER-SPOOK JR.: Rainbow, shiner scale, red and white, silver flitter with red head, green scale, x-ray green, x-ray silver scale, yellow perch scale,

SEA BASSER-SPOOK JR.: White with red head, yellow perch, shiner scale, shiner herring.

SHRIMPY-SPOOK Series #9000

This lure was introduced in the 1930 Heddon catalog. The hook hardware on the one in the photo here and the illustration in the catalog both sport the first of the two Heddon styles of two-piece surface types called the "toilet seat" by collectors. It has black bead eyes, an internal belly weight and measures 4-3/4". There were two colors listed at that time, "White back, Gold Flitter, Red Head" and "Natural Shrimp Transparent Body." The 1931 catalog was the last to list the lure. The catalog listed the lure as available in a 4" size. They measure 4-3/4". Collector value range: $150-$250.

SUPER DOWAGIAC
SUPER DOWAGIAC SPOOK
Series No. 9100

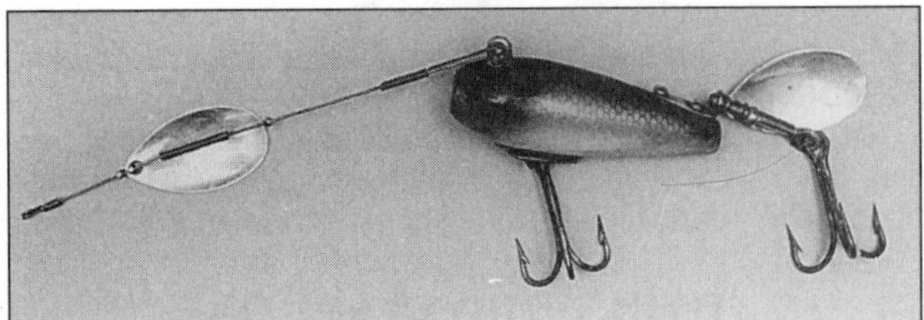

A wood body SUPER DOWAGIAC.

This particular lure is not found cataloged by Heddon in a wood body version. They were introduced in a plastic body model in a 1930 catalog, so it would not be unreasonable to say the lures were produced prior to 1930 even though this cannot presently be proven. The name in that 1930 catalog was "New SUPER DOWAGIAC Spook." The body of the wooden model here measures 2". It has two-piece hook hanger hardware, painted eyes and is drilled from the nose and filled with lead so that it is quite heavy.

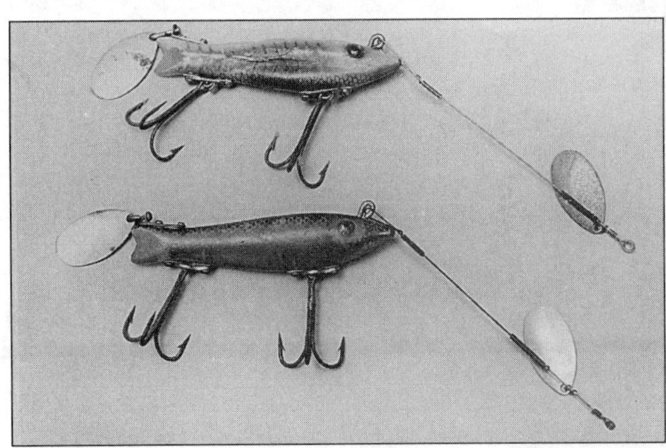

The SUPER DOWAGIAC SPOOK (plastic) was new in 1930 and considerably longer than the wooden version at 3-1/4". It was first available in the following colors: Red and green spots, rainbow, white head and tail with red decorations, perch scale, gold specks with red head, shiner scale,

According to the catalog all had a "Transparent Body" except the white head and tail version. By 1961 the color list had dwindled to the following four: Perch, yellow shore minnow, white with red eyes and tail, red and white shore minnow,

When first introduced, it had the first style, two-piece, "toilet seat" hook hangers and glass eyes. Over the years the normal progression of changes took place until it disappeared from catalogs in the early 1960s after more than 30 years in the line. Collector value range: Wood $50-$90, Plastic $20-$30.

TINY SPOOK
Series #310

This small, 1-7/8" plastic lure is the spinning version of the SUPER DOWAGIAC SPOOK. It was listed as a new bait in the

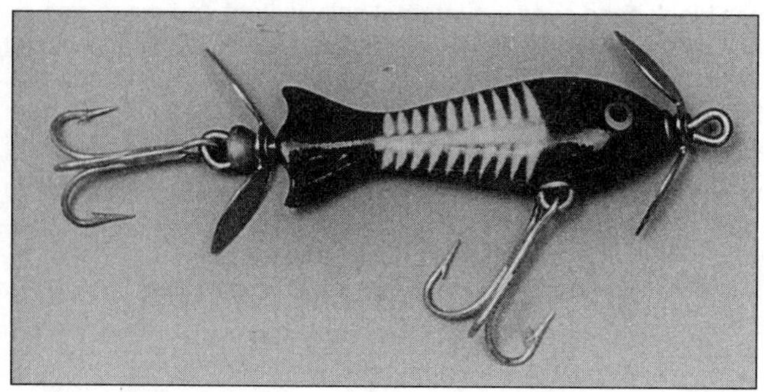

1955 catalog. It is a sinker. Both propeller spinners are marked "HEDDON". Collector value range: $5-$15.

COLOR OR FINISH: Crappie; yellow shore minnow, sunfish; black and white shore minnow, bluegill, white with red head, yellow perch scale; silver shore minnow.

DYING QUIVER SPOOK
Series No. 9200

DYING FLUTTER SPOOK
Series No. 9205

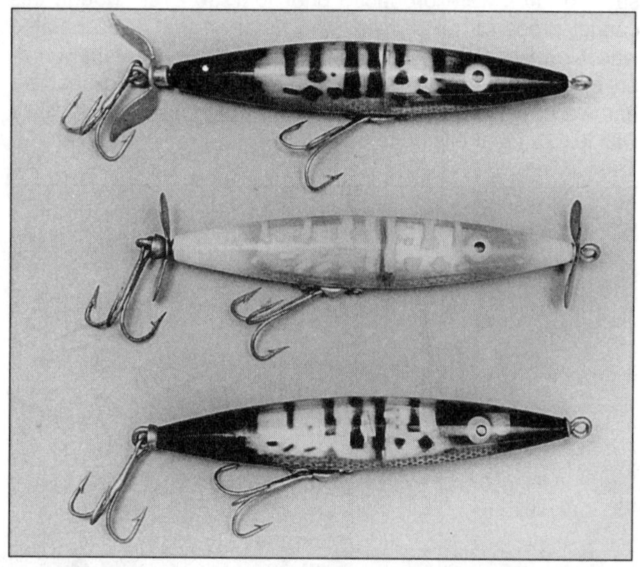

New in 1958, the 3-1/2" plastic bodies for these two lures are the same. The only difference is the presence of floppy propeller spinners at the nose and tail of the DYING FLUTTER. The one with the rear-mounted, tube type, propeller spinner in the above photo was not in the catalogs as it is marked, HEDDON DYING FLOATER, on the belly and the propeller spinner blades are stamped HEDDON DOWAGIAC. It was found listed and illustrated as a No. 9207 DYING FLUTTER, not FLOATING FLOATER in the 1962 catalog. Collector value range: $5-$10.

FIRETAIL SONIC
Series No. 395 and

SUPER SONIC
Series No. 9385

TOP SONIC
Series No. unknown

Sonic Series
No.385

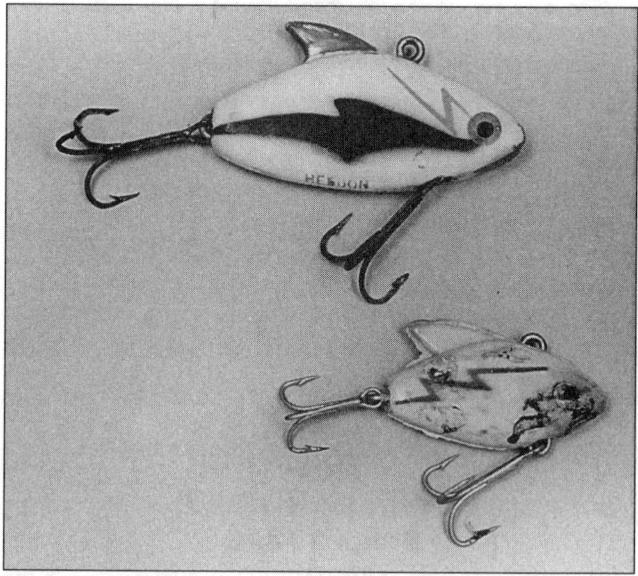

SONIC Series No. 385

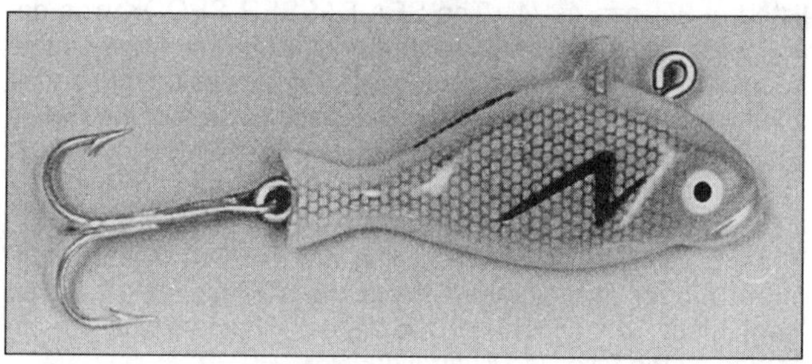

TOP SONIC. Measures 1-3/8".

Featured as new in the 1957 catalog, these plastic lures were designed to vibrate upon retrieve. The sound was suppose to allow fish to find the lure more easily. The little dorsal fin was the device that made the lure vibrate. They were made in two sizes: 1-5/8" and 2-1/8" with the SONIC being the smaller one. The TOP SONIC was not found in catalogs. It is very small, measuring 1-3/8". Collector value range: $5-$10.

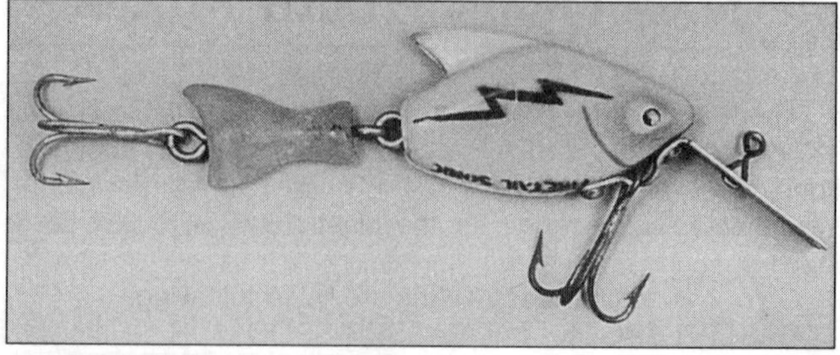

FIRETAIL SONIC Series No. 395.

There is an interesting story connected with this lure related to me by the famous "Uncle Homer" AKA Homer Circle, Angling Editor for *Sports Afield* magazine. He said of lipless vibrators, that he first ran across this type in about 1948 in Tennessee. It was called the CEDAR STUMP BAIT and weighed about two ounces and you "...had to crank like blazes to get it to wiggle. I was with Heddon at the time and I said 'Well, that bait will never make it.'" He went on to say that in the early 1950s, when the PICO PERCH and THE BAYOU BOOGIE hit the scene, "Our salesmen at Heddon insisted we get in this market so we had Conrad Wood, the genius lure maker from El Dorado, Arkansas design the SONIC and SUPER SONIC... which proved to be the hottest first-year seller Heddon ever made."

The FIRETAIL SONIC was the same lure with a separate "Flame-Glo" tail section. The colors available varied from one to the other. They are listed below:

SONIC	FIRETAIL SONIC	SUPER SONIC
yellow	white with red head	yellow
shad	black	yellow perch
black	coach dog	crystal shad
perch	perch	red and white
dark dace	yellow	black crappie
silver fish	shad	crystal rainbow

Collector value range: $5-$10.

CHUGGER
Series No. 9540

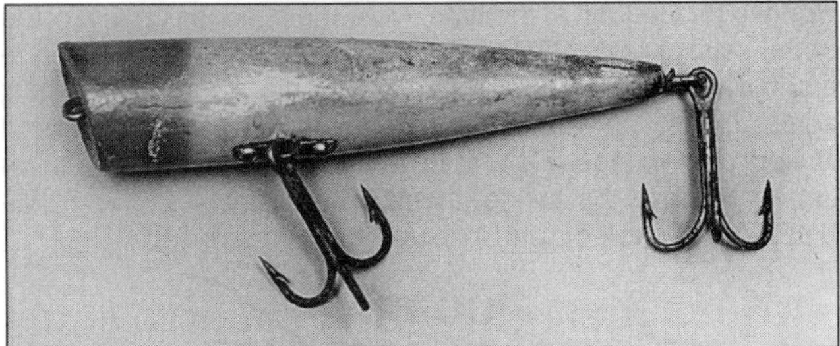

A wooden CHUGGER with the one-piece bar type hook hanger.

This is an interesting situation in that the first CHUGGERS were the #9540 Series CHUGGER SPOOKS. Spook means plastic in the Heddon line. The first CHUGGER SPOOK was released in 1938-39 and definitely was plastic. However there are several wooden CHUGGERS in collectors' hands that were found purchased in the "Classic" boxes of 1964-65. They are definitely later models because of the eyes and hardware. The "Classic" lure was to be a reissue of four old-time favorites in wood. The circular enclosed in the boxes state clearly that this style lure has been used "...for over 50 years and is one of the four great Heddon Wood Classics currently available." Perhaps the wooden Chugger was a mistake or it may be representative of a prototype for several proven old timers to be reissued in wood regardless of age or original body material. They are not marked "Original" on the lure body as are the other four classics. In any case here they are. Collector value range: $40-$80; Plastic "Spook" Chuggers: $10-$20.

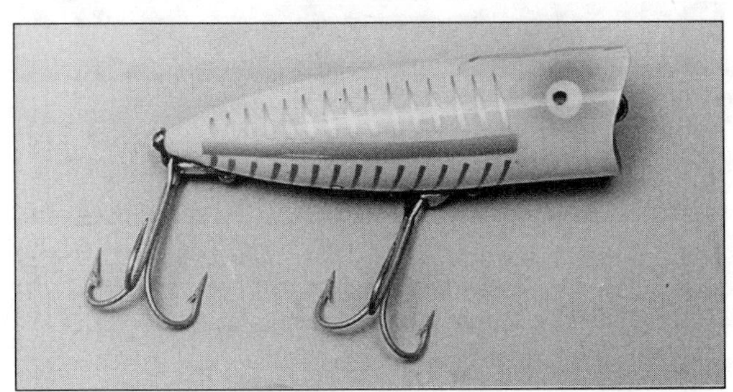

A TINY CHUGGER SPOOK measuring 3" long.

A Heddon BIG CHUG SPOOK measuring 4-7/8". The tail treble is attached by the use of a split ring.

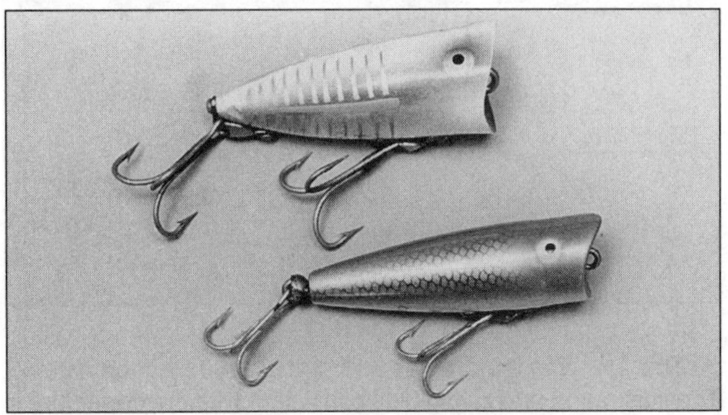

The upper lure is marked CHUGGER JR. and the lower one is marked TINY CHUGGER. Both measure 2-1/4", but the bodies are shaped slightly differently.

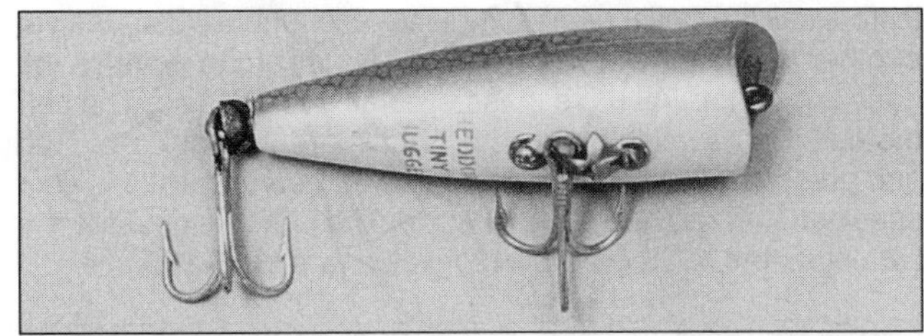

This is a belly view of the previous TINY CHUGGER. Note the modification of the standard one-piece surface style hook hanger.

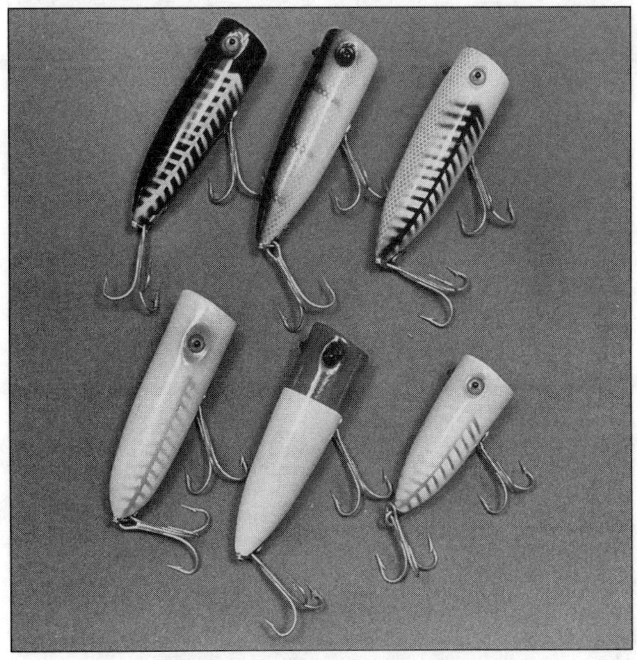

Six examples of the classic series CHUGGERS with the modern surface hook hardware and glass eyes.

SEA SPOOK
Series #9800

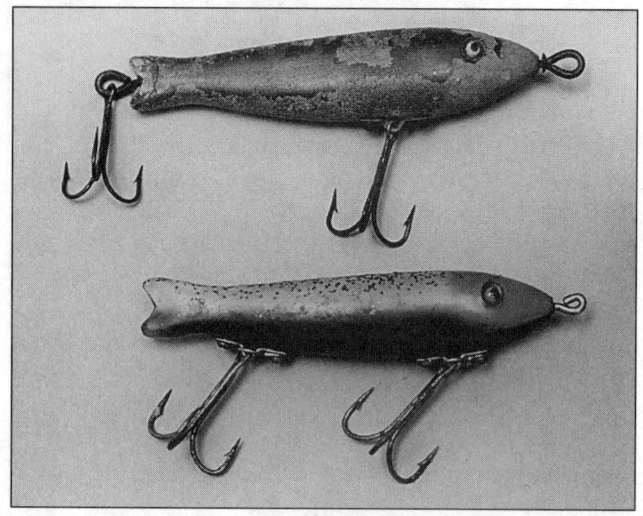

This lure was featured as new in the 1930 Heddon catalog. The illustration and listing was consistent with the upper lure in the photo; 3-3/4" long with a belly treble hook and one trailing, with the line tie at the nose. That particular lure has the one-piece bar style belly hook hanger. The other one measures the same, but the hook arrangement is different. That one sports the first style of the two, two-piece surface hook hangers collectors call the "toilet seat" style. The other photo illustrates yet another variation, where the line tie is not at the point of the nose but on top. All have glass eyes as you can see. The colors listed as available, all with "Transparent Body" are: Red and green spots, white head and tail with red decorations gold speckled with red head, shiner scale. The lure was absent from catalogs from 1932 on. Collector value range: $5-$10.

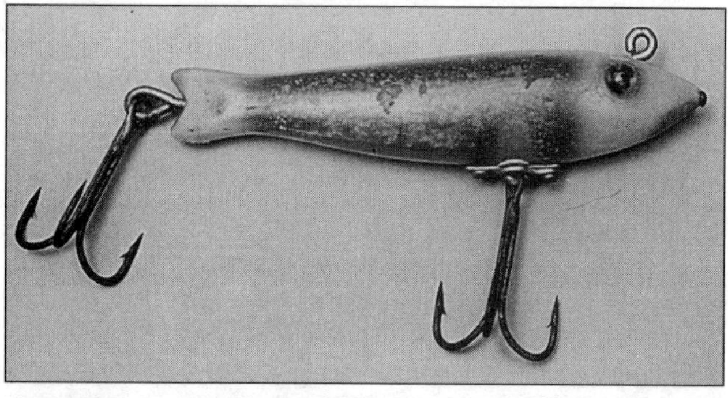

SCISSORTAIL
Series No. 9830

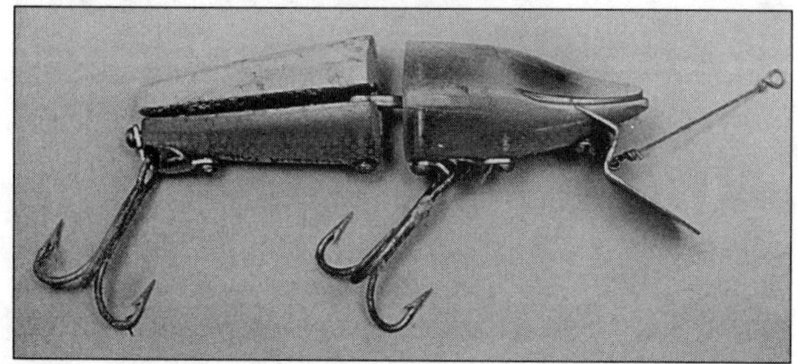

Profile view with scissor tails closed.

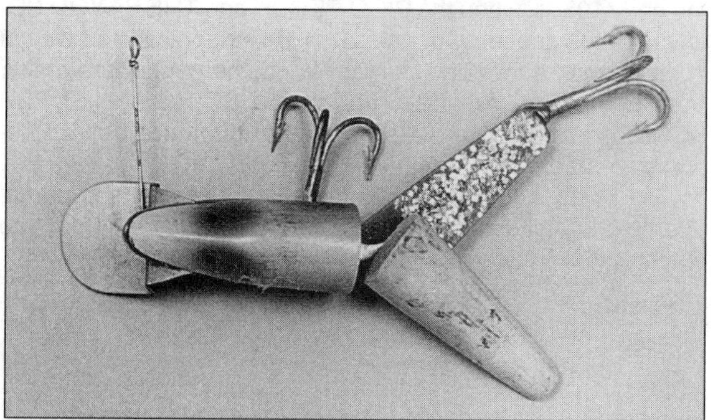

View of the back with the scissor tails open.

The SCISSORTAIL was called "A startlingly new lure" in the 1953 catalog. It is cataloged at 3-1/2", but measures 3-1/8" long. It is plastic and has one-piece surface hook hangers and the catalog illustration shows the same hardware and bug eyes. The one in the photos is almost eyeless and marked "SCISSOR TAIL" on the belly.

"Uncle Homer" Circle, Angling Editor of *Sports Afield* was working for Heddon at the time. Note the sparkles on the inside of the scissor tails. Circle said it was a last minute decision to apply the sparkles and the lure went out without field testing again. The result was the sparkles caught on each other and locked up the legs. Fishermen all over the United State returned them to the tackle shops. This terminated the SCISSORTAIL in short order. Collector value range: $15-$30.

COBRA
Series #9900

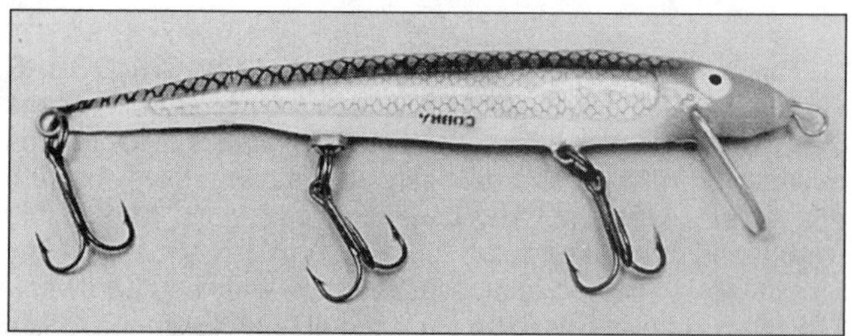

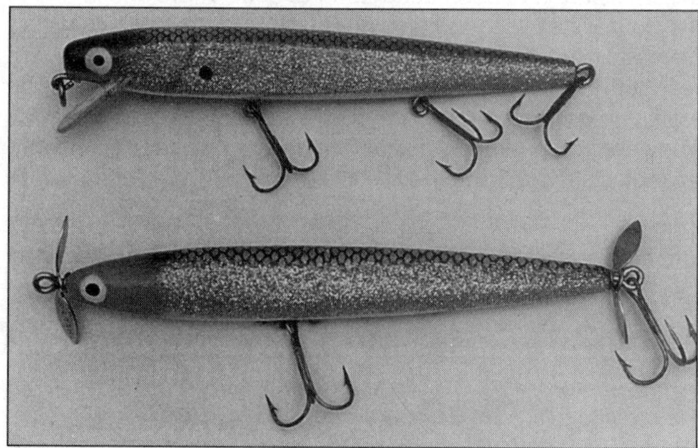

The upper lure is a wooden COBRA measuring 4-7/16". The lip is plastic. The lower lure measures 4-5/8" and is the SURFACE COBRA with fore and aft spinners marked "HEDDON" on both blades of each.

This wooden lure was first found in the 1965 edition of the Heddon catalog. There were several sizes and two types, each with a different Cobra name, Vibra-Flash (glitter) color and size:

#9905	BABY COBRA	Red and white	3"
#9910	COBRA	Gold	4"
#9930	COBRA	Perch	5"
#9940	KING COBRA	Yellow	8"
#9960	SURFACE COBRA	Shad	4"
#9970	SURFACE COBRA	Silver	5"

The SURFACE COBRA has a propeller spinner fore and aft and the other COBRAS have no spinners, but do have a plastic lip at the nose. Collector value range: $10-$15.

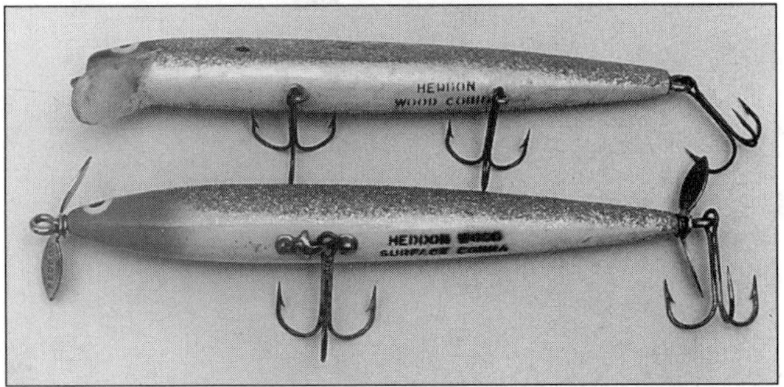

Belly view of the COBRA and SURFACE COBRA showing the hook hardware and markings.

This is a 2-1/2" STINGAREE No. 9930 L with its original box.

STINGAREE
Series #9930

TINY STINGAREE
Series #330

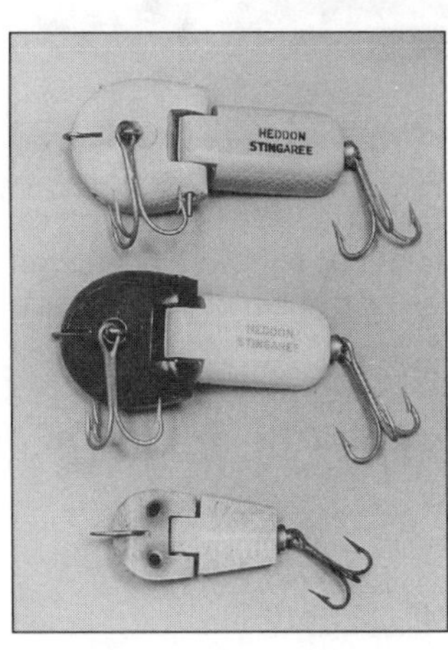

This plastic lure first appeared in catalogs in 1957 in a 2-1/2" and a spinning size, the TINY STINGAREE at 1-1/2". The photo shows two examples of the larger size, belly up. This was a unique bait with an up and down undulating motion something like a sting ray. The catalog copy said this was a "...fish attracting action". It wasn't. The lure was a failure and gone from the catalog the following year. Collector value range: $10-$20.

COLOR OR FINISH: White with red head, yellow perch scale, red and white shore minnow, bullfrog, black and white shore minnow, yellow shore minnow.

COMMANDO

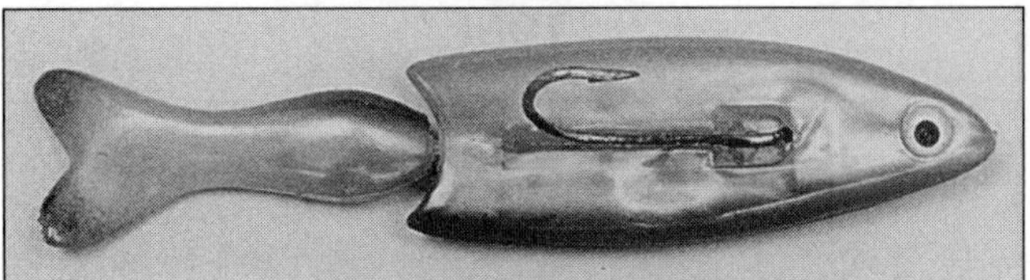

This is a soft plastic lure introduced in 1968 after "Ten years in the testing..." according to the catalog. When the fish strikes, the hook is supposed to snap away from the body which then ostensibly runs up the line so "...there is no weight attached to the hook to help your fish throw the plug." The tail portion spins upon retrieve. Length is 4-1/2", weight, 5/8 oz. Collector value range: $5-$10.

COLOR OR FINISH: Purple, green, red and white, gold, blue and silver, black and silver.

HEP SPINNERS
Series #460 through #464

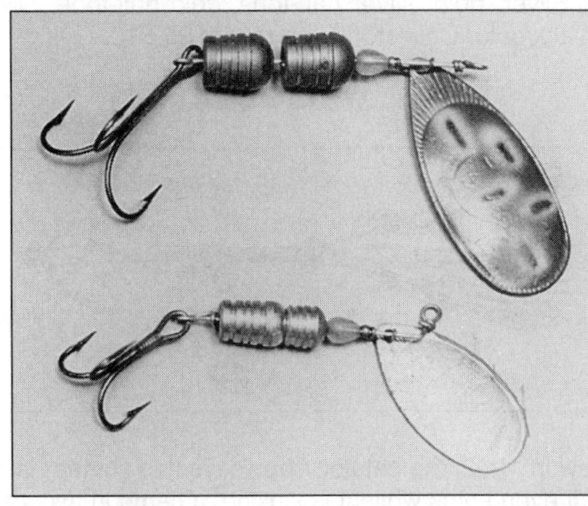

These series numbers have only to do with the sizes. These are brass-bodied spinners marked "HEP" on the blades. There is as yet no explanation for the name.

They were available in five sizes: 1-3/4", 2", 2-3/8", 2-5/8" and another, heavier 2-5/8". The colors of the blades were given as gold finish and silver finish. There were four other finishes that were available only on the lighter 2-5/8" size for some reason. Those finishes are: Smokey black, bullfrog, spotted orange and red and white. Collector value range: $5-$10.

SPOON KIT and HEP KIT

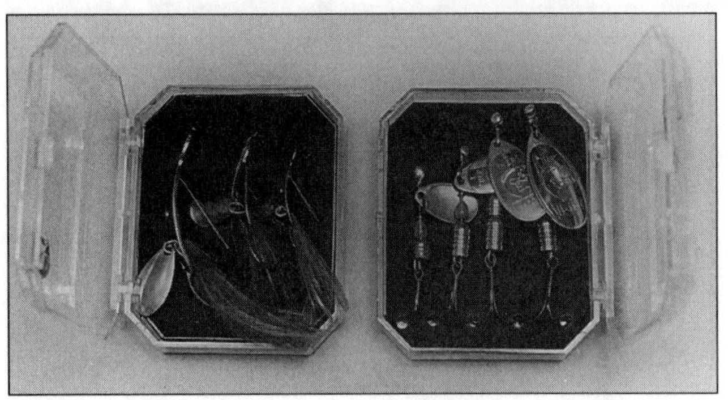

Heddon marked these attractive little kits of their various spoons and spinners. The two pictured above are two of a total of five kits they offered in plastic boxes. The other three are the FIDGET THREE, the SPINFIN KIT and the GAMBY FOUR KIT. Intact they would each be valued at about $25-$50.

TONI

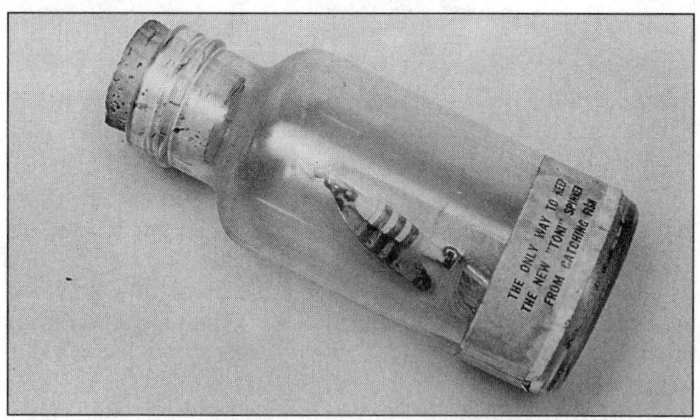

A promotional gimmick for marketing the TONI spinners. These metal-bodied lures were available in four sizes in the 1965 catalog. Sizes were given in weights: 1/6-oz., color: Black, white or yellow. The blades were available in six patterns: Silver, gold, silver half-tone, gold half-tone, silver/gold and black/gold. Collector value range: $5-$10.

WHIS-PURR

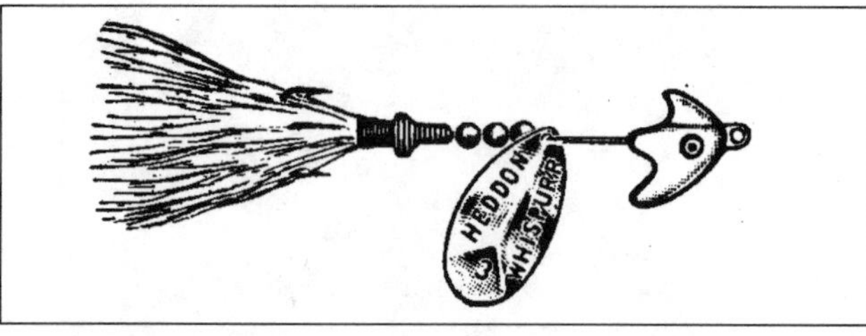

New in 1962, the catalog copy says this spinner is so sensitive it even spins while it is sinking. It came in two sizes and two colors. The colors are silver with white head and gold with yellow head. It was made so hooks could be easily changed. Collector value range: $5-$10.

CATALOG SERIES #	BODY LENGTH	LURE WEIGHT
420	3-3/4"	1/8 oz.
425	4"	1.4 oz.

WAG SPINNING LURE
Series #451

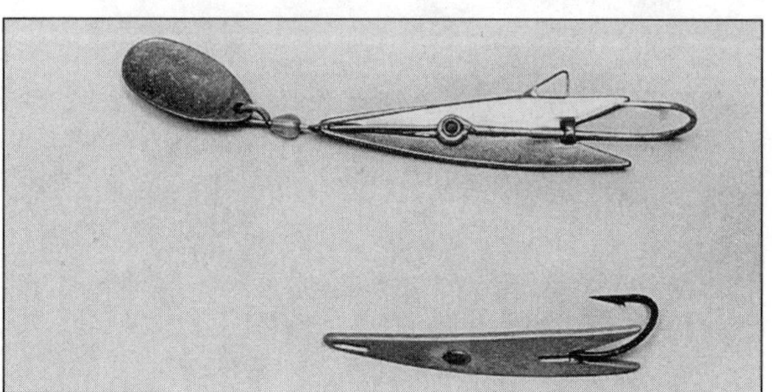

It is difficult to see in the photo, but there is a weed guard. The lower lure is an incomplete WAG. A fisherman may have modified it. They were available only in one size, 3". The plastic bead bearing is red and the willow leaf type spinner blade identifies this lure as a WAG. Colors available were: Silver, gold or smokey black. Collector value range: $5-$10.

TWIN PAL
Series #405 & 410

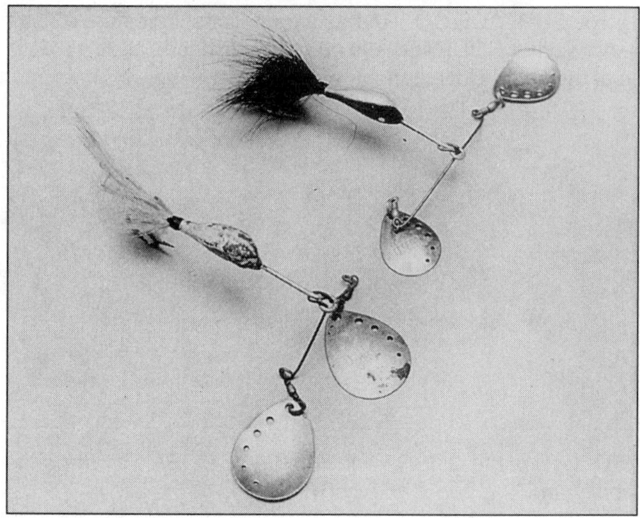

New for 1964, this is a twin blade spinner bait. It has a keel type body. It was made in two sizes and four colors. Collector value range: $5-10.

CATALOG SERIES #	LURE LENGTH	LURE WEIGHT
405	2-3/4"	3/8 oz.
410	3-3/4"	5/8 oz.

COLOR OR FINISH: Black, blue shad, perch, silver flitter.

TIGER

TIGERS came along in the late 1960s and were numbered according to size of the plastic lure and number of treble hooks. Collector value range: $5-$10.

CATALOG SERIES #	BODY NAME	LENGTH	HOOK
#1010	TIGER CUB	2-3/8"	2 No. 8 T
#1020	TIGER3-1/4"	2 No. 4 T	
#1030	TIGER4-1/4"	2 No. 4 T	
#1040	BIG TIGER5-1/4"	2 No. 0 T	

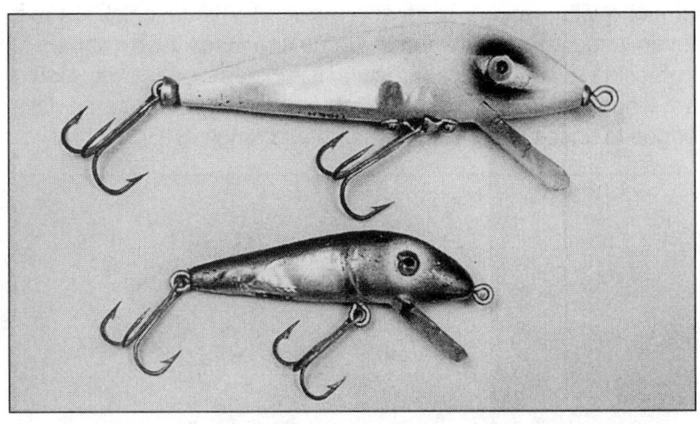

DEEP TIGER

There are DEEP DIVE TIGERS as shown in the photo, but no catalog information was found. Collector value range: $5-$10.

COLOR OR FINISH: Silver finish; purple; gold finish; shad, yellow, tiger (see photo above); perch; red head.

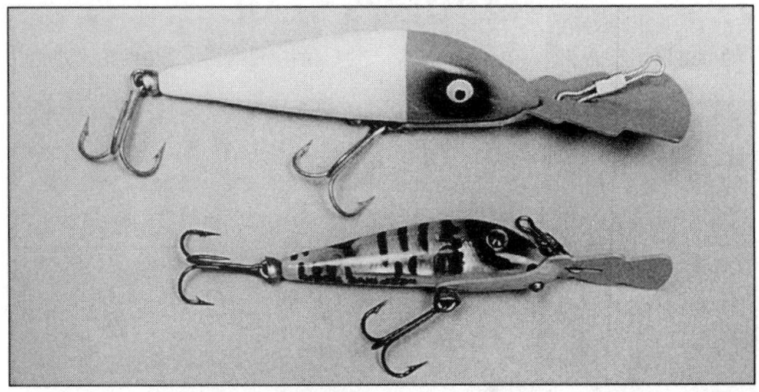

Two DEEP DIVE TIGERS so marked on their bellies. They measure 3-1/4" and 2-1/4". Note the distinctive dive planes.

PROWLER

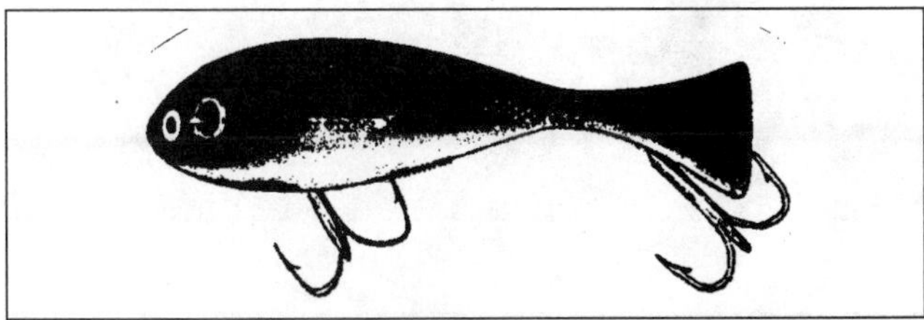

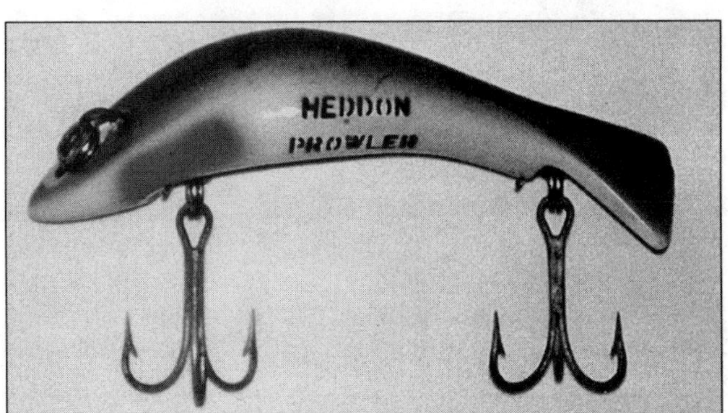

PROWLER. Belly view. Photo courtesy Ken Bernoteit.

The PROWLER was new in 1972. This plastic lure had different numbers according to length, weight and the size of treble hooks. The No. 7075 was called the BIG PROWLER

A wooden PROWLER prototype sold at auction in early 1995 for $525. The collector value range for plastic PROWLERS: $5-$10.

CATALOG SERIES #	LURE WEIGHT	BODY LENGTH	HOOKS
7015	1/4 oz.	2-5/8"	2 No. 6 T
7025	3/8 oz.	3-5/8"	2 No. 4 T
7050	5/8 oz.	4-5/8"	2 No. 2/0 T
7075	1-5/8 oz.	6-1/2"	2 No. 3/0 T

COLOR OR FINISH: Green scale with dark back, silver shad, bronze and brown scale with white belly, green/gray, black/black; blue/white/black.

BIG PROWLER ONLY: Chrome, chrome blue, mackerel, yellow with silver ribs black, sucker bronze.

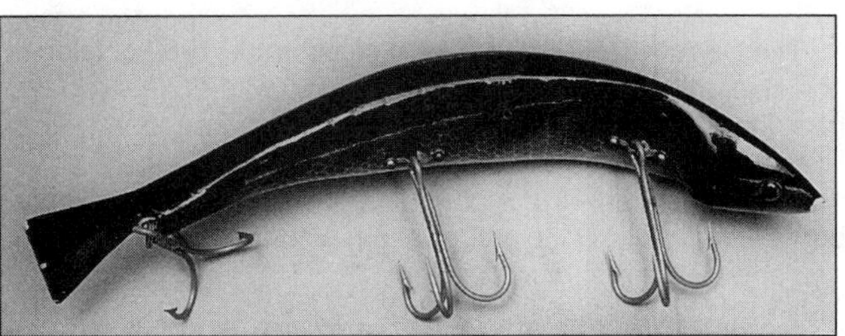

This is a rare wood-bodied, glass-eyed, 8" long hand-made test prototype for the PROWLER. As you can see, it was not exactly like the finished production model.

COUSIN I AND COUSIN II

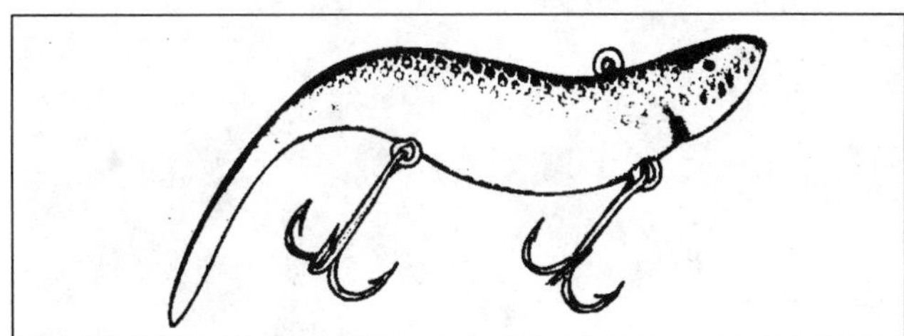

A 3-1/2" COUSIN II.

The 1/2-oz. COUSIN I with two No. 2 treble hooks is a bent plastic eel or snake-shaped lure introduced in 1973. There was a smaller size, COUSIN II with two No. 4 treble hooks introduced a year later. The lengths are 4-1/2" for the COUSIN I and 3-1/2" for the COUSIN II. Collector value range: $10-$15.

COLOR OR FINISH: Pink shrimp, barfish, rattlesnake, black, green bar, *silver shad, *green shad, *bullfrog, *pearlescent belly with purple back and red spots.

** Available on the COUSIN I only.*

CRAW/SHRIMP and a commemorative wood box. Daisy owned Heddon at the time. "HEDDON NO. 375 CRAW SHRIMP SER. NO. 520".

CRAW/SHRIMP

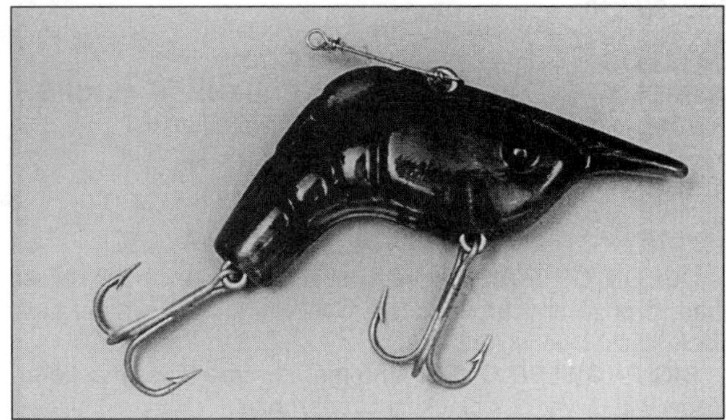

The CRAW/SHRIMP was introduced in the 1969 catalog in one size only, 2-7/8" at 1/2 oz. It is plastic with "...an exclusive body design which sends out waves of high frequency vibrations...". Collector value range: under $10.

COLOR OR FINISH: Amber, amber gold, amber yellow amber green, amber white amber pearl, amber red, amber black, amber pink, purple, blue, rainbow.

CRACKLE BACK

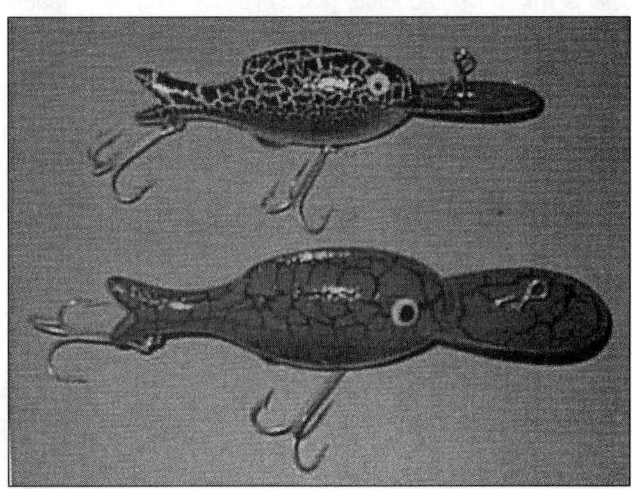

New in 1972, this plastic lure came in two sizes. It was gone from the line by 1977. Although called CRACKLE BACK, not all the finishes were crackled as in the photo. There are three with a standard finish: the green shad, silver shad and the barfish patterns. There are a total of 11 paint finishes to be found. Collector value range: $5-10. Photo courtesy Tom Jacomet.

CATALOG SERIES #	BODY LENGTH	LURE WEIGHT
8000	3-7/8"	3/8 oz.
8050	4-1/2"	5/8 oz.

COLOR OR FINISH: The first color in this list is the base paint and the second color is the crackled color: White and yellow, *white and black, *yellow and black, yellow and orange, green and black, black and orange, white and green, *white and brown. *standard patterns: green shad, silver shad, barfish.

**The only finishes available in the 1973 catalog.*

BIG BUD

This is not a particularly old lure, but it is seen at just about every tackle show for sale. At 2-3/4", 5/8-ounce, it was brought out by Heddon in 1976-77. It is, of course, a novelty plug, but it is listed along with serious lures and included a testimonial: "I have never fished with a better lure." Name and home town withheld to protect the guilty. It even stated that it had been extensively tested in Florida, Missouri, Texas, Michigan and Minnesota. A little tongue in cheek maybe? Collector value range: $10-$20.

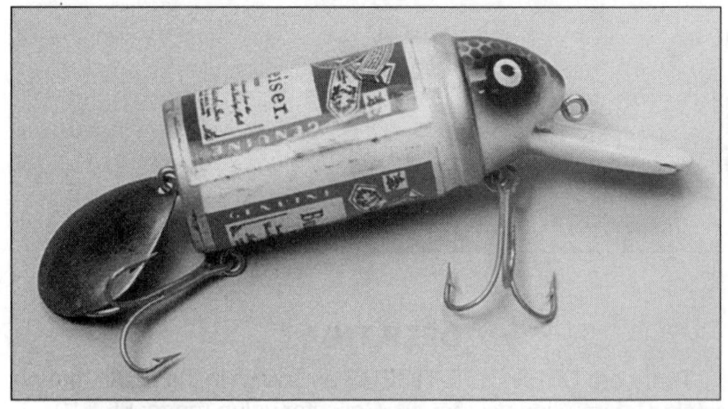

HARDEN'S SPECIAL
HARDEN'S STAR

Walter Harden, Connellsville, Pennsylvania

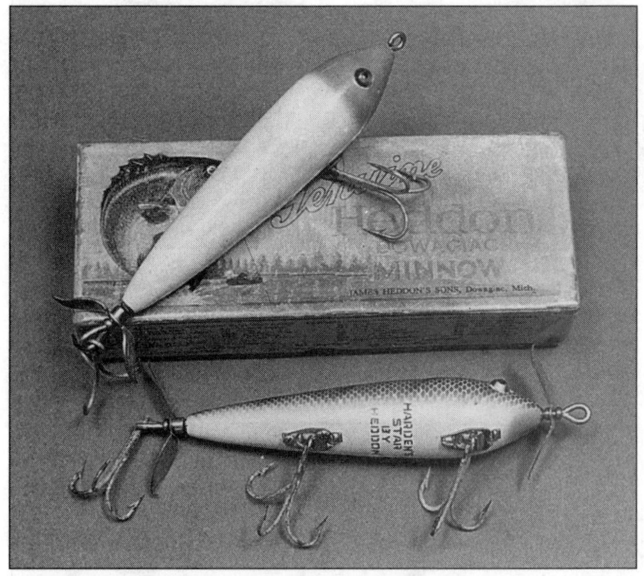

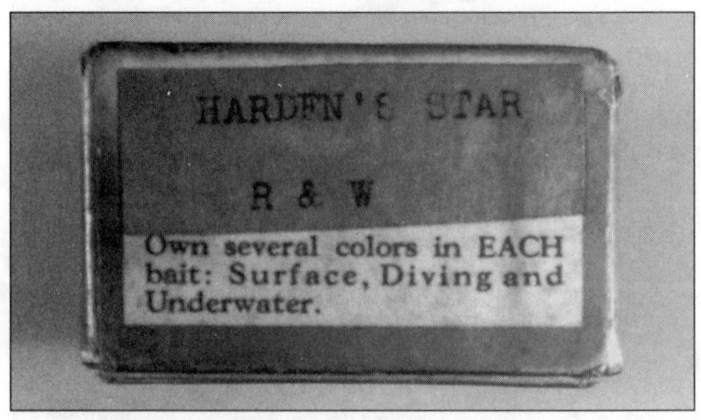

This lure is in actuality, a Heddon product, at least in part. The story is that sometime in the late 1920s to early 1930s, Mr. Harden took a Heddon ZARAGOSSA and modified it for his particular brand of Florida bass fishing. It proved so successful that Heddon put the modified ZARAGOSSA on the market. The photos show both of Harden's modified baits along with a box with brown paper labels pasted over a regular Heddon label. Collector value range: Hardens's Special, $20-$30.; Harden's Star, $300-$400.

HARDEN'S WHIZ

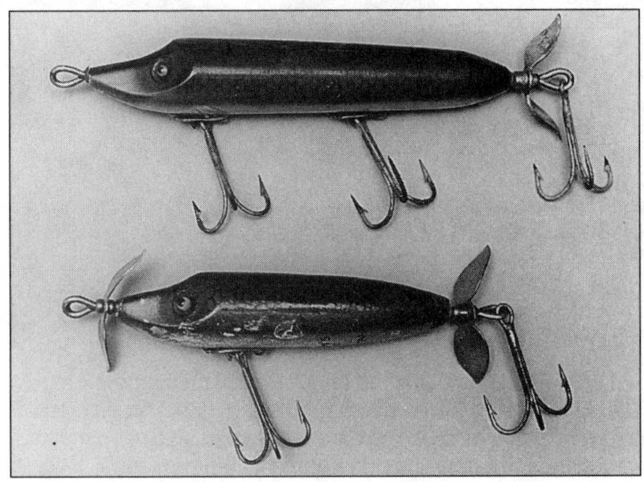

Both have glass eyes and the second style of the two-piece surface hook hangers. The upper lure measures 4-1/2" and the lower, 3-1/2". The lower lure is marked HEDDON'S HARDEN WHIZ on its belly.

This is known to be a Heddon product. It is essentially a Heddon BABY VAMP body with floppy props, yellow glass eyes and two-piece "toilet seat" style hook hardware. It measures in at 3-1/2". There is another, larger one in existence measuring 4-1/2". It is not marked on the belly as is the 3-1/2" "HARDEN'S WHIZ BY HEDDON." The large one has only a tail propeller spinner. Collector value range: $200-$300.

SOME UNUSUAL HEDDON LURES

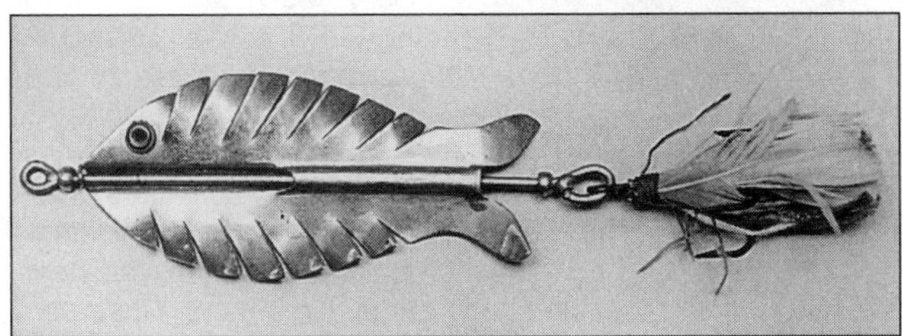

Found in the Heddon archives, this interesting c. 1908 metal minnow revolves around a shaft. Its body measures 2-3/4" and overall it measures 5-1/2". Note the feather-dressed tail treble hook and the fact that the loop it is attached by is soldered closed. The line tie is soldered closed as well. There is at least one other, in a private collection. It is smaller than this one and has a tail treble hook dressed in a striped leather skirt. Certainly that would be more durable and long lasting than the feathers. There was no recorded trade data, therefore it is impossible to establish a realistic collector value for the lure.

These two lures came from the Heddon factory archives. The lower lure is a dead ringer for a lure attributed to Leroy Yakely of Syracuse, New York. It is almost identical to a lure in a series of drawings that were exhibits in one law suit in a series of law suits from 1913 to 1915 involving several men and companies. Yakely, J.K. Rush, Moonlight, Heddon and others were involved. Heddon may simply have bought one of these for examination. It is included here because of where it came from and its possible influence on the design of the Heddon early No. 100 prototype on top.

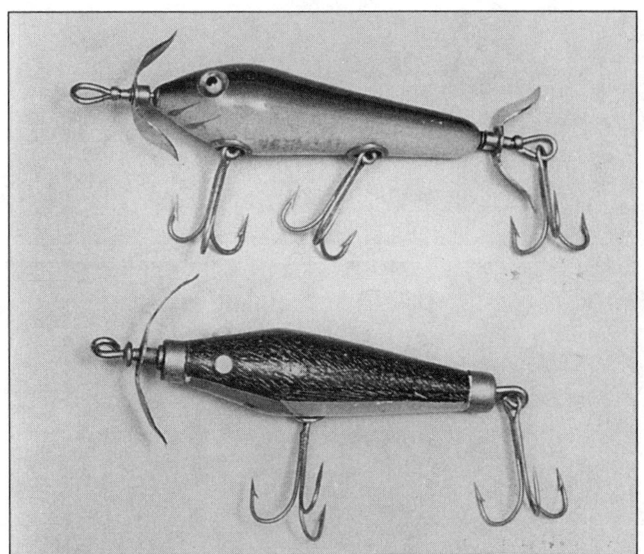

These two lures are also from the Heddon factory. Both are probably experimental or early prototypes. The upper lure has the No. 1600 Series WIGGLER metal nose fins. The lower lure could be a prototype of the MUSKY TAD POLLY.

The upper lure in the photo is the 1905 SMITH MINNOW. The lower lure is from the Heddon factory archives. The latter is an obvious variation from the SMITH MINNOW. It was never placed in production.

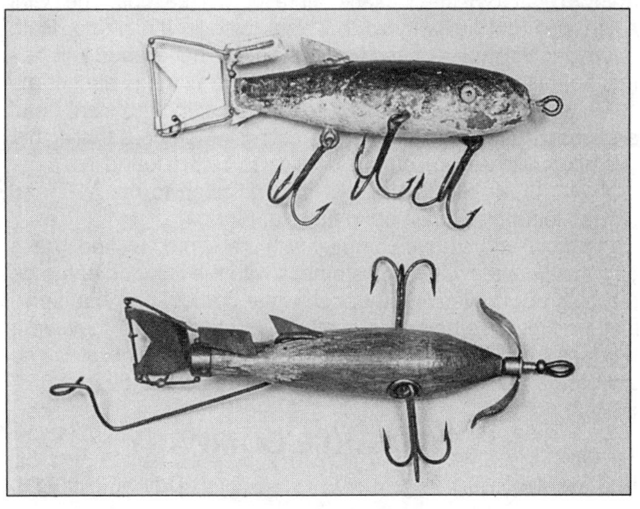

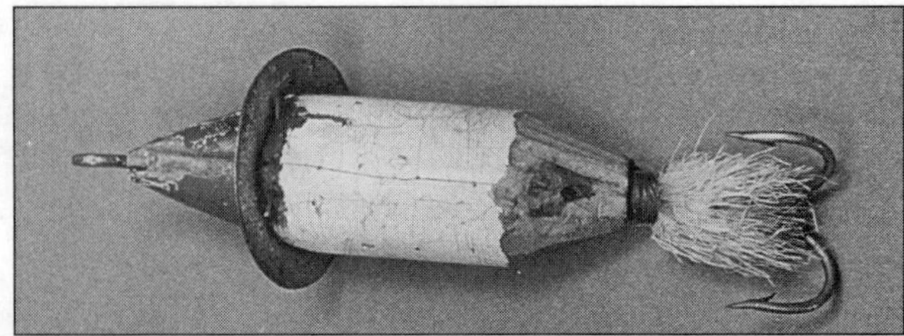

Two very early experimental Heddon lures from the factory archives. The top is obviously an old slope nose EXPERT that has been rather crudely whittled down short and fitted with a rigid-mount buck tail double hook. Note the very crude propeller spinner on the bottom plug.

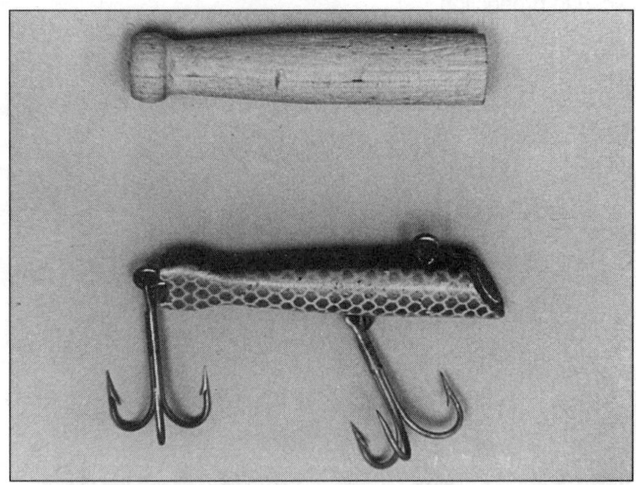

I have not been able to find any reference to this lure in all the Heddon catalogs in my collection and I'm not missing many. This 2-5/8" lure is placed here for two reasons: The paint finish and the similarity to the blank also in the photo. Both have identical holes drilled from the nose. The finished lure has this hole filled with lead. The shape of the blank is almost exactly the same as the finished one after cutting the slant head and shaping the tail. A most interesting thing about this is that this blank and several others identical to it were found in a cigar box with other Heddon blanks in what used to be W.T. and Laura Heddon's workshop in Oceola, Florida.

Two collectors have come up with the same finished lure in different finishes. One was stamped with the Heddon name on the belly. Both were red-headed white bodies, one had sparkles on the white portion of the body. It seems as if they were produced, but apparently not to any great extent. There was no trade data from which to draw a realistic value range.

HELIN TACKLE COMPANY

Charles Helin — Detroit, Michigan

A group of Helin lures. Photo courtesy Jack Turner.

Charles Helin first applied for the patent on the now famous FLATFISH in 1934 and it was granted in 1936. An inveterate fisherman since he was 16 years old, he had also been making lures since the same time, in search of the proverbial "secret weapon". Tinkering with and making lures for years, in 1933 he found what he thought was it. The FLATFISH was born.

The Helin Tackle Company remained in continuous operation until bought out in 1990 by the Yakima Bait Company. They continue production of the plastic FLATFISH.

Any Helin collector will have to have a copy of Jack L. Turner's excellent book *The Collectors Guide to the Helin Tackle Company.* It is a thorough, exhaustive treatment of Helin and his lures. There is no other reference as complete.

THE FLATFISH

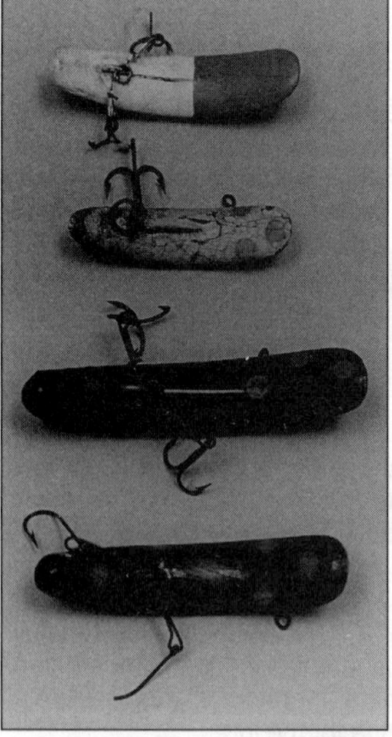

Belly view of four Helin FLATFISH. The top two illustrate the older of the hook hanger style utilizing split rings (called "O" rings by some collectors. Although not clear in this photo, a newer style, the bent wire hanger, is illustrated by the two lower lures in the photo (see next photo).

The earliest listing of Helin lures I could find was in a c. 1937 McClean Sporting Goods Catalog. There were three models of regular FLATFISH and three fly rod sizes. They ranged in size from 1-1/2" to 2-3/4". No colors or finishes were listed, but it is reported that there were at least 12 colors available at the time. A 1947 list shows 28 colors available. They were: Orange; light orange, red head, black top; light orange; bottom silver, top gold foil; white, red head, blacktop; orange top, silver belly, foil; green frog imitation; small aluminum scale; large aluminum scale; silver bronze; gold bronze; silver, gold bronze; black with orange spots; large scale; scale finish, natural; white; silver metallic foil; gold metallic foil; orange, red head, black top; orange, white belly, black top; orange top, silver bottom; yellow, red head, black top; white and red; orange top, gold bottom; yellow; orange top, gold belly, foil.

There are only 26 finishes listed, but there was also a list of fly rod finish options. They are listed as follows: orange; frog; lt. orange; yellow; white; white and red; black; aluminum;

Black and aluminum were apparently not available on any but the fly rod lures. Jack Turner lists over sixty colors in his book, but said only Helin actually new how many there were.

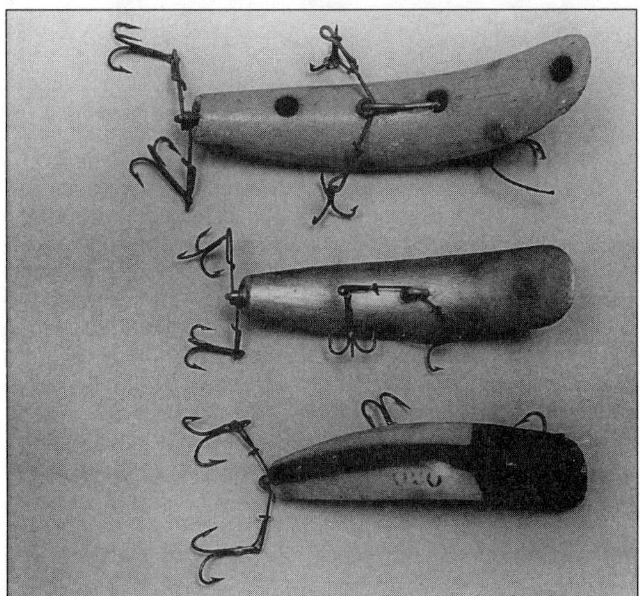

The upper FLATFISH here demonstrates the later of the hook hanger styles. The center is yet another variation of hook hanger styles. The lower lure with the "U20" stamped on its back indicates it is a 3-1/4" underwater model although it actually measures closer to 3-1/2".

FLATFISH were all made of wood through 1948, with the transition to plastic taking place in 1949. A 1948 box pamphlet states that "over 4,000,000 (were) sold by (the) end of 1947". A million more were sold in 1948. Don't make the mistake, however, of thinking because yours is made of wood, it is pre-1949. A few of the models were always made of wood and in the early 1970s, Helin reissued the FLATFISH in wood for a very short period of time. These latter are easily distinguishable from the early wood example for they were marked "Wood" and had the FLATFISH logo on the top of the diving bill portion of the lure.

Many of the Flatfish have the model marked on the body. As a matter of interest, the following is a key to some of the marks:

S	Surface
SU	Standard Underwater
SPS	Standard Pike Surface
SPU	Standard Pike Underwater
M	Musky (and Lake Trout on earlier models)
L	Lake Trout
P	Pike
T	Troller
U	Underwater
LU	Light Underwater
E	Expert
F	Fly Rod and Baby

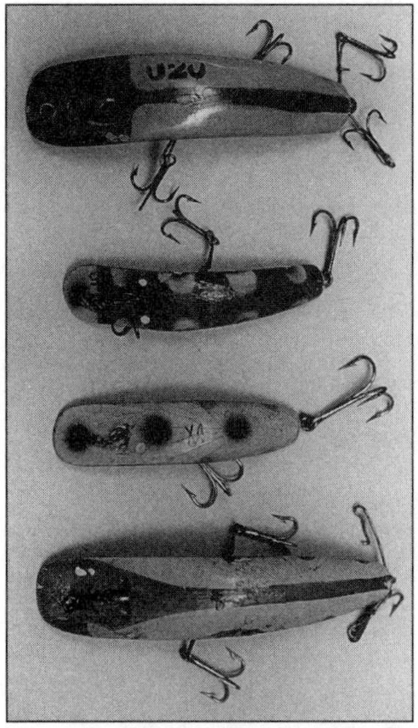

Four FLATFISH, three of which demonstrate the model code found stamped on most early wooden versions. The top one "U20" indicates it is a 3-1/2" underwater model, the second lure reads "SPU" meaning Standard Pike Underwater and the third reads "X4" meaning an underwater model 2-1/2" in length. The bottom lure has a code that is obscured and unreadable.

The numbers found with the letters refer to the size. There were 13 sizes offered in 1948 ranging from the BABY FLATFISH fly rod at 1-1/2" to the MUSKY FLATFISH size at 4-1/4". Collector value range for Early wooden FLATFISH: $15-$25, Plastic: N.A.

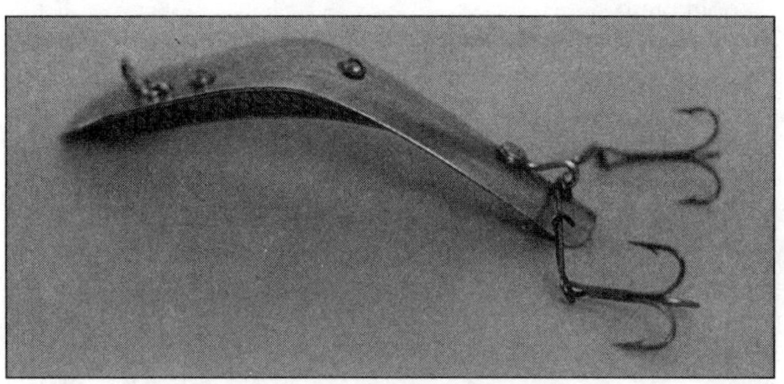

THE SWIMMERSPOON

In addition to the FLATFISH, Helin made and marketed at least two other lures, the SWIMMERSPOON and the FISHCAKE. The SWIMMERSPOON was available in 11 sizes ranging from 1-1/2" to a huge 6" model. Introduced in 1960, it comprised two parts. The lure was made up of a curved metal spoon, concave from the bottom at the head end and making a transition to convex on the bottom at the tail end. The second piece was a removable plastic back piece. The plastic insert was available in 16 patterns. The metal spoon portion was available painted or in a shiny plated finish. They were sold separately so the fisherman could choose his combination of colors. Collector value range: $5-$12.

COLOR/FINISH OPTIONS

PLATED METAL PORTION

silver
gold
copper crystal
pearl crystal

PAINTED METAL PORTION

black with silver flecks

PAINTED METAL PORTION

- white with red spots
- orange with spots
- yellow with red spots
- white with red head
- coach dog
- frog
- pearl yellow
- natural scale
- silver scale
- perch scale
- fluorescent red

INSERTS

- black with silver flecks
- orange with spots
- yellow with spots
- white with red spots
- frog
- natural scale
- perch scale
- silver scale
- pearl yellow
- coach dog
- silver plate
- gold plate
- copper crystal
- pearl crystal

THE FISHCAKE

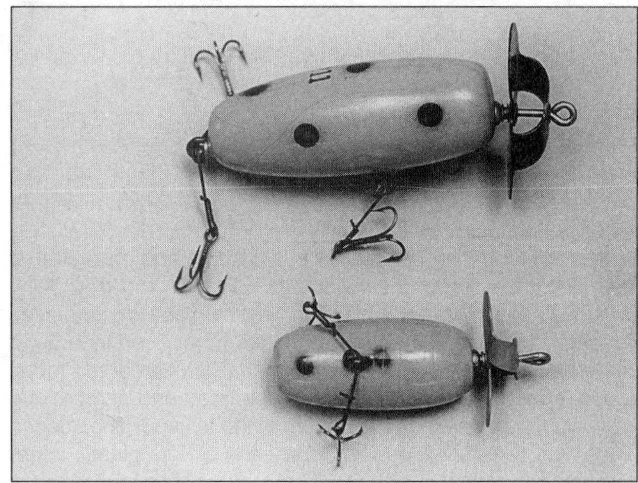

Two sizes of the Helin FISHCAKE. The larger, a No. 11, measures 2-5/8" in length and the smaller (belly view), a No. 7, 1-3/4".

Introduced in 1956, the FISHCAKE is a wooden lure with a nose-mounted spinner that was always painted either black or red. Curiously the different colored spinners rotated in opposite directions from each other. This was a top water lure designed to kick up a fuss on retrieve. It was made in three sizes, the No. 7 at 1-3/4", the No. 9 at 2-1/2" and the No. 11 at 2-5/8". It was available in 12 finishes. Collector value range: $10-$18.

Available finishes for the FISHCAKE: Orange with black spots; light orange with black spots; yellow with red spots; frog; black with orange spots; black with silver flecks; white with red spots; red with white belly; silver with red spots; silver scale; scale finish with white belly; fluorescent red with yellow belly.

HELLIONFISH

Hellion Lure Products — Detroit, Michigan

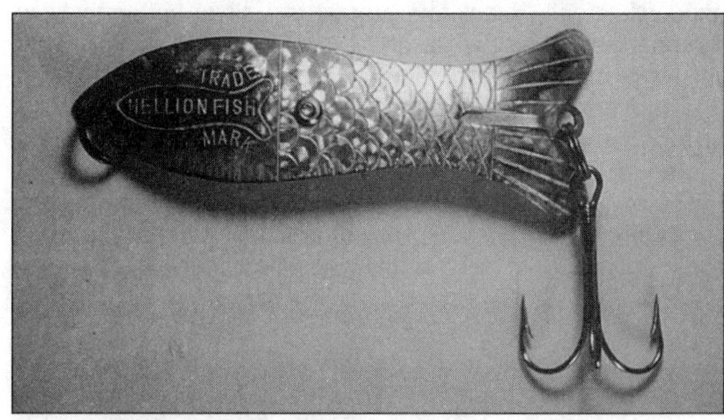

HELLIONFISH. Photo courtesy Ken Bernoteit.

This fish-shaped metal spoon was found advertised as "NEW" in the March 1950 issue of *Field & Stream* magazine. It said the lure was "Firelacquered" and available in three sizes and 12 colors, but did not list them. The one in the accompanying photograph has a gold finish and measures 3-5/8". By 1952 the ads read 7 sizes, "FLY ROD, SPINNING, CASTING, TROLLING" sizes. The one in the ad illustration was a "#4" and had weed guards. It has also been found with a smaller, plastic minnow-shaped flasher attached to the trailing hook. Collector value range: $5-$10.

THE ANDREW B. HENDRYX COMPANY

New Haven, Connecticut

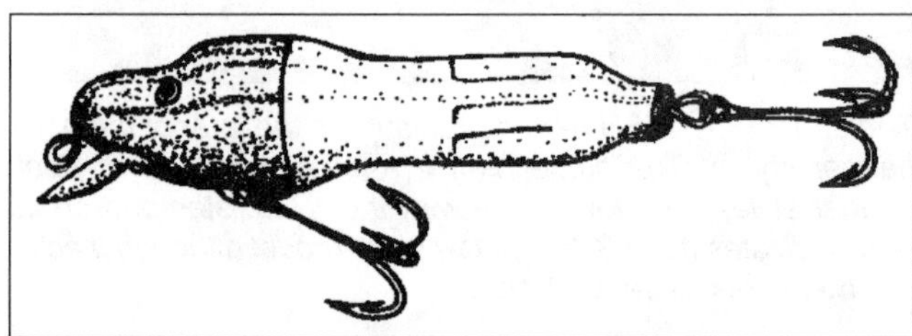

The Hendryx Company, a major manufacturer of metal spinner and spoon type lures also offered at least three wooden lures, the WEEDLESS MINNOW, the HENDRYX PLUG and the WEEDLESS SNAKE WOOD MINNOW, the latter being better known among collectors as the SNAKE BAIT. While all three are eminently collectible the SNAKE BAIT is the best known of the three.

The SNAKE BAIT has a slender body (approx. 1/2" in diameter) that is 3" in length. It has a metal ribbon (fin) wrapped around it in a spiral such that when pulled through the water it rotates around a through-body twisted wire line tin/hook hanger. It was available with a single trailing hook or a weedless treble dressed with feathers. The overall length of each is 5" and 6" respectively. They were available in two color combinations: white or green with the metal spiral fin painted red in both cases. Although it is thought the SNAKE BAIT was only made for about two to three years, 1905-1907, the company was in business as early as 1887 and was absorbed by the Winchester Repeating Arms Company in 1919. Collector value range: THE SNAKE BAIT $150-$225; THE HENDRYX PLUG $250-$450; THE WEEDLESS MINNOW $150-$225.

HEP BAIT COMPANY

Minneapolis, Minnesota

The lure here is a HEP'S BLOOEY LOOY. The lure, in its original box, was sent to me from collector Mike Meadows of

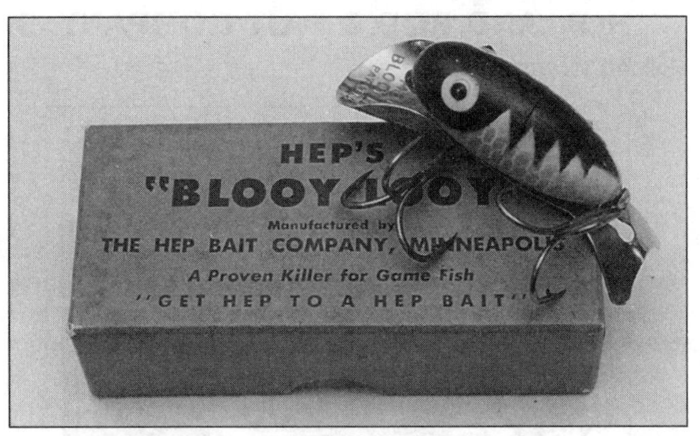

Waconia, Minnesota. He said that an elderly neighbor of his had the boxes and unassembled lures and that he obtained them from the retired company owner, who said they were made in the 1940s. I have been unable to uncover any information in a long search of the material available to me for research. The body of the lure is made of Tenite and measures 4" long. The single-piece metal nose and tail plane doubles as the treble hook holder. It is held to the body by standard straight-slot screws, one right on the tail end and on the chin. The nose end plane is stamped "HEP'S BLOOEY LOOY PAT. PEND." Collector value range: $5-$15.

COLOR OR FINISH: Yellow spider, scale; white spider, scale; yellow rib, scale; white rib, scale; yellow dot, scale; yellow dot, plain; white dot, scale; red head.

BILL HERRINGTON BAIT COMPANY

Green City, Missouri

BAG-O-MAD

An advertisement stating that the lure was new for 1932 illustrates this lure as available in two sizes, the regular at 3-3/4" three-hooker and the BAG-0-MAD JUNIOR at 2-3/4" with two trebles. They had two holes in the notch at the nose, each of which went separately through the body exiting on each side of the lure. There are five color designs offered in the ad. Collector value range: $25-$40.

COLOR OR FINISH: Red head and white body, Black head and yellow body, Red head and yellow body, Black head and white body, Solid black.

HI-YO

Activated Lure Company — Barberton, Ohio

This odd lure had its genesis about 1941 when a fisherman named Charles E. Hiltabidel observed a grasshopper that had

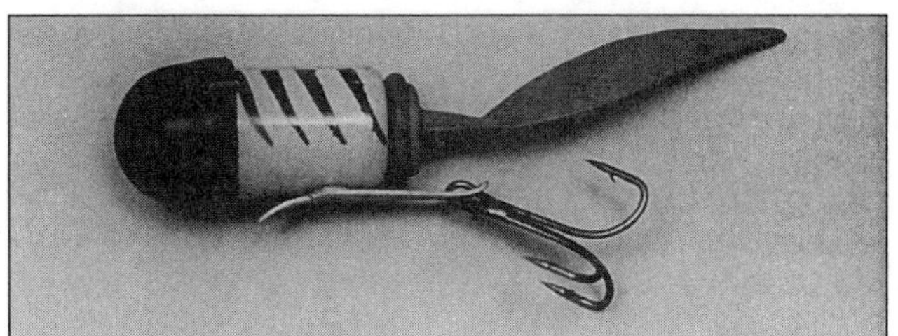

fallen into the water. Nothing happened until the hapless insect kicked. He was then taken explosively by a bass. Hiltabidel determined that he would develop a lure that emulated that action. He took his idea to a friend, David M. Yoder who was an engineer and together they invented the lure. They applied for a patent in 1945 and it was granted to them on February 11, 1947. The lure was made of a cylindrical aluminum body with a rubber cap and a balloon-like rubber tail. The fisherman was instructed to put dry ice and water in the rubber capped body. The reaction would then result in gas being forced out the tail, propelling the lure in a forward and diving motion. Seems more likely to scare all the fish out of the area to me.

I received a number of newspaper clippings and a letter from the grandson of the one of the inventors. In his letter he said that the lure would act for about 10 minutes on one charge of dry ice. He went on to say that they did not sell well, adding that he felt the selling price of $2.50 was probably a factor inasmuch as that was high for the 1940s and 1950s.

The bodies were made of anodized aluminum in at least four colors, blue, green, gold and red. Pictures and lures I have seen had painted bodies in six different patterns. There may be more patterns, but what they are is not known. They were packed in a box with three of the rubber jets, each a different color, yellow, red and green. Although hundreds were manufactured it is reported that there are only 8-10 known to exist. There could be more around. The quantities to be found are probably limited as it is known that upon the two inventors' deaths, all the remaining aluminum bodies were sold to a scrap dealer for the value of the metal. There was no trade information found from which a realistic value range could be determined.

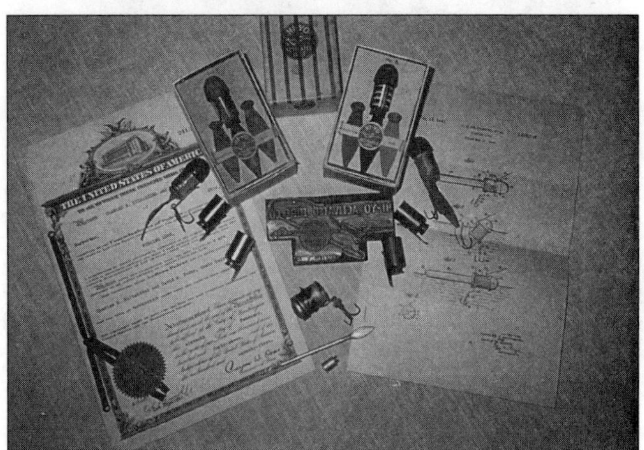

This photo shows the manner in which the lures were packed, a few examples of the lures and their aluminum bodies, the patent and the patent illustration. At lower center you can see the original prototype. Photo courtesy of Terry Grimes.

LIVINGSTON S. HINCKLEY

Newark, New Jersey

Mr. Hinckley applied for a patent on a PHANTOM FLOAT late 1896 and it was granted January 12, 1897. The opening sentences of the patent application says in part "...have invented

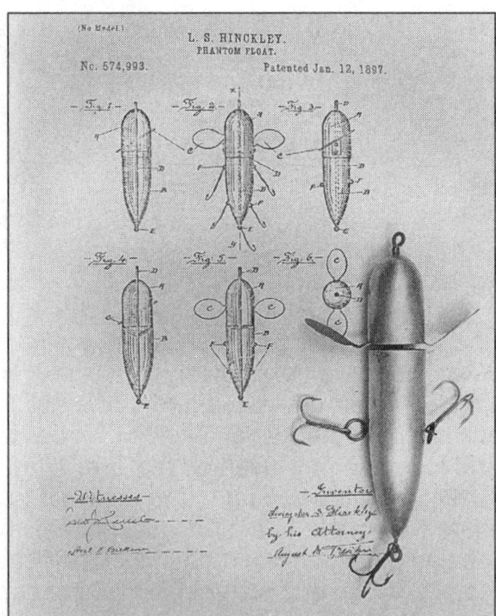

certain new and useful improvements in Phantom Floats." This seems to imply that this particular lure had been around a while. Whether the lure itself was invented by Hinckley or someone else and Hinckley merely improved it is not clear. A search of patent records does not, however, reveal a previous patent of the PHANTOM FLOAT. The photo of three lures illustrates the PHANTOM FLOAT and two sizes of the YELLOW BIRD also attributed to Hinckely. Collector value range: $50-$100.

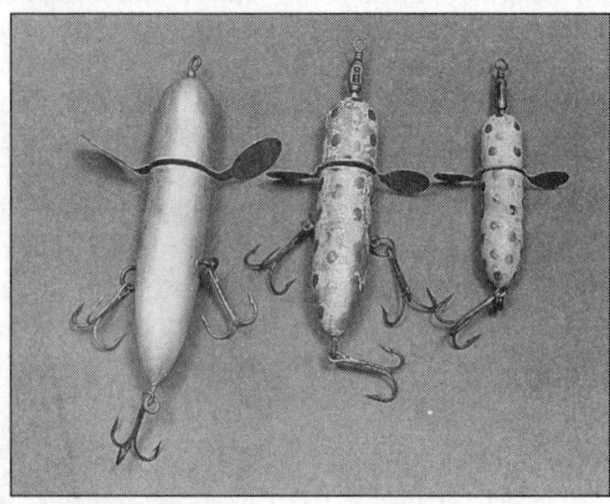

THE HINKLE LIZARD

Joe Hinkle — Louisville, Kentucky

This is a three-section jointed plastic lure made to look like a lizard. The line tie is at the throat. There are two opposite side mounted treble hooks and another treble on the tail section but not trailing the end. It was about 6" long. Collector value range: $40-60.

HOLLAND ROD & BAIT COMPANY

Holland Michigan

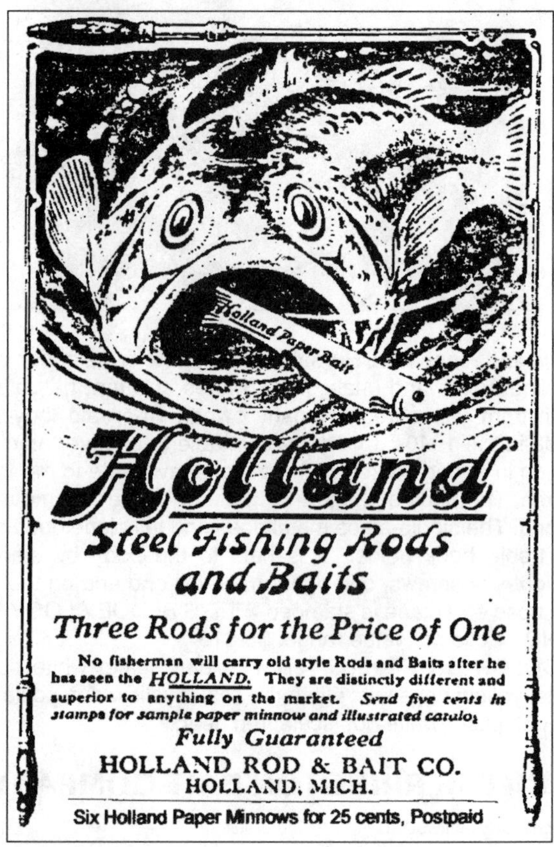

This advertisement is from page 660 of the 1911 volume of The Outer's Book magazine. It is an ad for the "Holland Paper Bait." If you look closely, you can see an illustration of it near the center of the ad. This company, more famous for its fishing rods than lures, was called simply, "Holland Rod Company" by 1914 in their advertising. It looks as if they may have gotten out of the lure business altogether and concentrated on rod-making. At the bottom of the ad is the phrase "Six Holland Paper Minnows for 25 cents, Postpaid". Might there be some lurking out there somewhere? The hunt is on!

HI-SPORT

Staley Marine, Inc. — Fort Wayne, Indiana

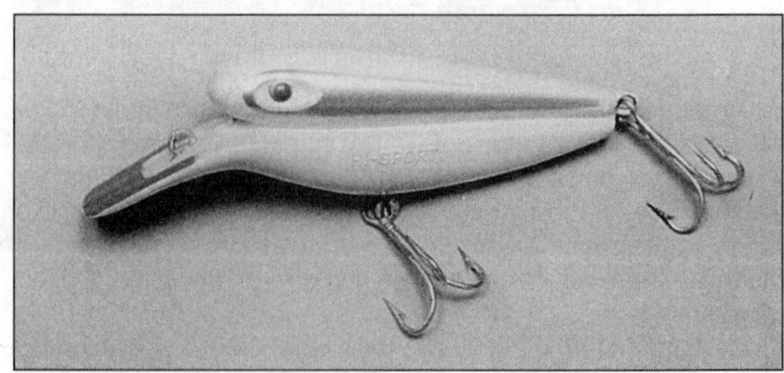

This plastic lure is easy to identify with the name molded into the side during the manufacturing process. The only ad I found for it was in a 1957 issue of *Outdoor Life* magazine. It was made in two sizes, but they gave only weights, 1/4 and 1/2 ounce. The six finishes offered were red and white, black, yellow, orange, perch and frog. Collector value range: N.A.

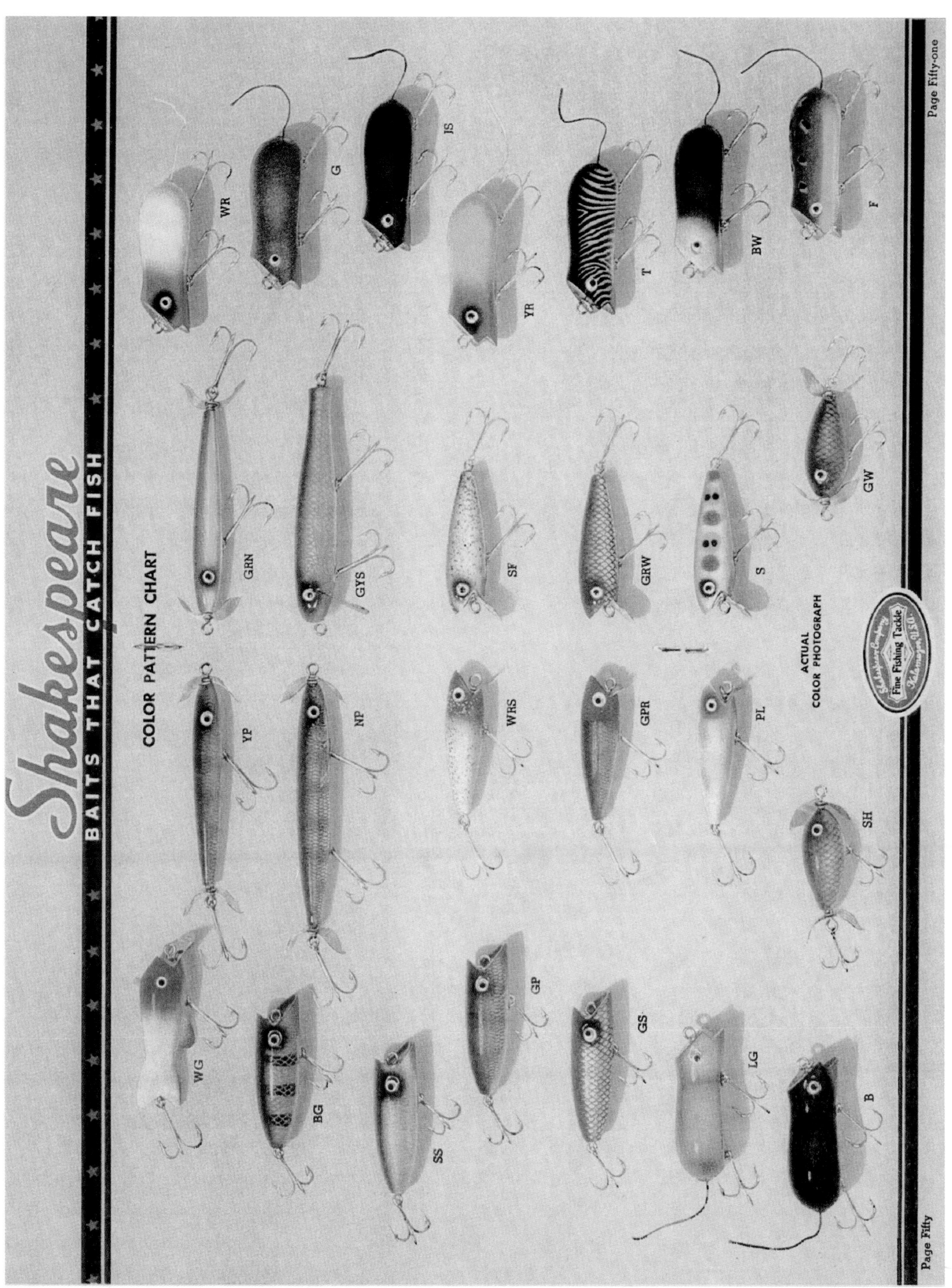

The color chart from a 1941 Shakespeare catalog. Contributed by Shakespeare of Columbia, South Carolina and reprinted here with their permission.

Shakespeare Helps You Fool 'Em

FAMOUS FISHING LURES . . . SOME STILL IN WOOD BY POPULAR DEMAND

Back in our "Tackle Selection" section we promised you straight talk. So its on this level we want to tell you about our Shakespeare line of lures.

Years back we were one of the top lure houses in the country. When World War II came along, and skilled woodworkers — especially lure makers — were scarce, we de-emphasized our lure line.

When the war ended, so much of our time was expended in the development of fiberglass rods that lures just didn't get much of our attention.

Now we're back in the business. And the honest truth is, it's because of public demand. Old timers have written telling us they've lost their last Shakespeare mouse and younger folks want Shakespeare lures — "the kind the old timers use."

So they're back — Our 16 most popular old timers plus a hot bait called Big (S)haker.

Of these 16, six are lures no guide or expert fisherman should be without. Five of these, "Swimming Mouse," "Slim Jim," "The Brawlers," "Krazy Kritter," and "Lucky Dog" are lures that have proved themselves everywhere. They're still made the way the guides demand. We include our new Big (S) haker because we've tested it extensively.

Shakespeare's LUCKY SIX—MOST EFFECTIVE LURES MADE

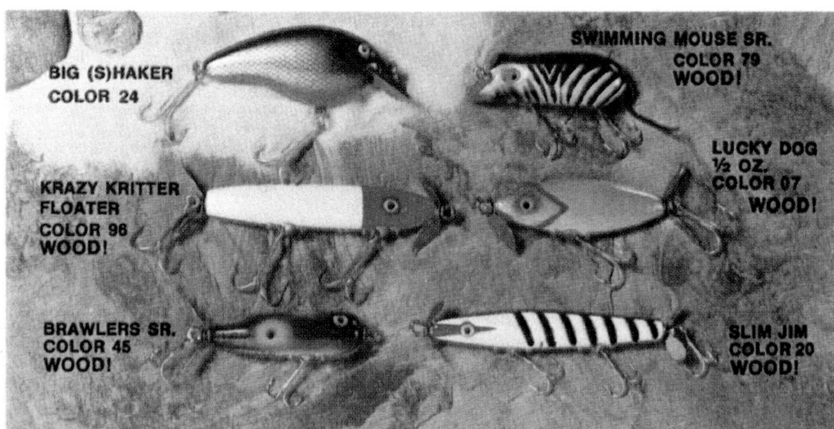

BIG (S)HAKER. This newest Shakespeare lure has wild action plus its own built-in lunker caller. Shake and listen! The rattle you hear drums fish in for a closer look, then Big (S)haker's fish-appealing action grabs 'em. Unmatched for bass! Pike and Walleye's can't resist. Raises havoc on muskie water. Absolutely the most fantastic lure you'll ever use. Length 3½ in. Weighs ¾ oz.

L4100 Series. COLORS: 24, 29, 57, 76, 79, 80.

KRAZY KRITTER. Krazy Kritter is another of our fantastic 6. He's a famous pike, muskie and big bass lure who gets big fish hopping when nothing else will do the job. Secret is a combination of wood lure action and spinner turbulance that big fish find fascinating. Comes in two models — floater and sinker. Try the floater fished slowly on calm days — fast when it's rough. The sinker's a sure cure when there's a "walleye chop." Krazy Kritter Sinker — 3¾" (¾ oz.); Krazy Kritter floater — 3¾" (½ oz.)

L2400 F (Floater), L2400 S (Sinker).

COLORS: 06, 07, 20, 45, 93, 96.

THE BRAWLERS. Be careful if you use them. These wood bodied lures start stirring up action the moment they smack the surface. Fish 'em slow for injured-minnow action. Pop 'em. Or use a fast retrieve to simulate a panic stricken minnow. They stir up bass, muskies, walleyes, pike, even stream trout. Big ones. So for gosh sakes, hold on to your rod. Comes in two dangerous sizes: Brawler, Sr. — 2½" (½ oz.); Brawler, Jr. — 2" (¼ oz.)

L9900 Sr., L9900 Jr.

COLORS: 03, 06, 33, 45, 93, 96.

SWIMMING MOUSE. A Number One, world-wide best seller and the most famous, fish-catching-est mouse of them all. Two bass-busting models, both still made in wood so they're the real McCoy. Floating action. Great in the lily pads and for fishing shore lines. Slow'n easy does it. They'll float and dip on command and they'll catch fish like you won't believe. Swimming Mouse, Sr. — 2⅝" (½ oz.); Swimming Mouse, Jr. — 2" (¼ oz.)

L4600 Sr., L4700 Jr.

COLORS: 40, 42, 43, 48, 79, 96.

LUCKY DOG. Here's another of our big 6. An excellent "up top" lure for big bass and other surface feeders. Lucky Dog's fore 'n aft props stir up fuss that attracts the big ones from all over the river or pond. Vary slow, steady retrieve with stop, twitch and go action. And keep a tight line. Lucky Dog doesn't fool around with small fry. Two sizes: 2¾" (½ oz.); 4⅛" (⅝ oz.)

L8400 Little Lucky Dog, L8500 ⅝ oz. size.

COLORS: 03, 04, 06, 07, 45, 96.

SLIM JIM. A classic American lure that ranks high among the most productive lures ever made. Slim Jim's props turn in opposite directions creating wild, fish-attracting commotion. Yet, they make Slim Jim ride straight and sure. For best results, put him in a good spot, rest him, and twitch. Vary this with a steady retrieve and you'll knock 'em for sure. Slim Jim measures 3¾", weighs ⅜ oz.

L1100 Series.

COLORS: 06, 20, 45, 92, 93, 96.

03 Silver Flitter
04 Pike Scale
20 White, Black Stripes
21 White
25 Orange, Black & Red Spots
26 Chartruese with Red Spots
40 Brown
42 Zebra
47 Shiner Scale, Red Head
48 Black
51 Black with Gold Sound Wave
59 Black, Red on Gold Spots
61 Silver Shore Minnow
69 Strawberry
70 Chrome, Blue Scale
74 Green Back, Red Belly
76 Pearl
77 Black Widow
80 Chrome & Black Top
92 White Coach Dog

LURE COLOR CHART

Please note that the last two digits of the lure numbers indicate color. For example midget Flap Jack is orange with black and red spots, as shown by the "25".

This and the facing page are taken from the 1975 edition of the Shakespeare catalog. Contributed by Shakespeare of Columbia, South Carolina and reprinted with their permission.

06 Perch Scale
07 Green Shad
23 Shad
24 Orange Belly
30 Yellow, Red & Black Spots
33 Black Scale with Yellow Belly
45 Frog
43 Yellow
46 Frog Scale, Red Head
57 Silver Mist
58 Silver, Black Spots
62 Black & White Shore Minnow
63 Yellow Shore Minnow
71 Day Glow Orange
73 Rainbow
78 Pearl Body, Mottled
79 Yellow Tiger
93 Yellow Coach Dog
96 Red Head

Shown above are lure color patterns with proper two-number designations. Remember—last two digits indicate color pattern. (Color 29, Chartreuse with green scale—not shown).

MORE Shakespeare WOOD LURES

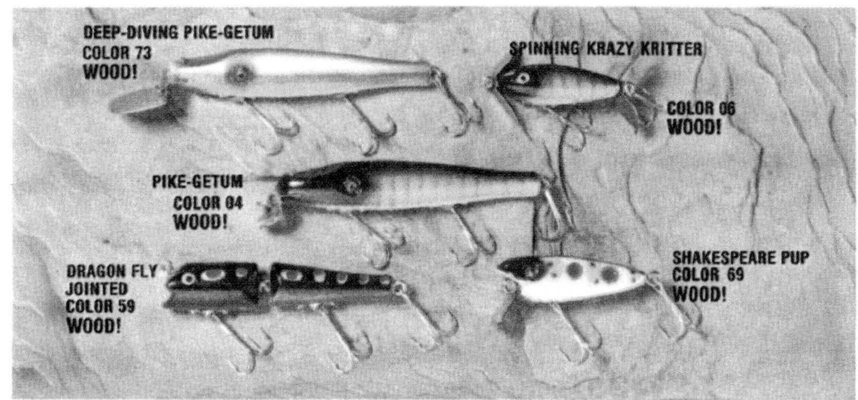

DEEP-DIVING PIKE-GETUM. Amazing what a difference wood bodies make. Pike-Getum has a distinctive action that lunkers can't resist. And this digger gets down deep where the big ones sit out those doldrum days. Wood body means he'll float or sink on command. So, you'll get precisely where the fish are by controlling retrieve speed. Length — 4¼″, weight — ¾ oz.

L2800 Series. COLORS: 03, 04, 06, 30, 45, 73, 92, 96.

PIKE-GETUM. Still made of wood . . . and the guides who use them wouldn't have it any other way. Retrieve steady to fish deep. Jerk tip for float-dip action. ¾ oz. lures have 3 trebles, others have 2. Comes in 3 sizes: Pike Getum — 4¼″ (¾ oz.); Pike Getum — 3¼″ (½ oz.); and Baby Pike Getum — 2⅝″ (¼ oz.)

L1000 Series, ¾ oz.; L2100 Series ½ oz., L9500 Series, ¼ oz.

COLORS: 03, 04, 06, 30, 45, 73, 92, 96.

DRAGON FLY. Fantastic pike, walleye and muskie lures. Our jointed Dragonfly is one of the world's finest trolling lures and it's dynamite on giant muskies. Both jointed and solid are extra effective fished slowly on calm days. Give 'em fast action in a chop. Both measure 3¾″, weigh in at ½ oz.

L9200 S (Solid), L9200 J (Joint).

COLORS: 03, 23, 30, 45, 59, 96.

SPINNING KRAZY KRITTER. One of the most famous, most productive lures in the world. Has a spinning prop and wiggle action that drive lunkers wild. Made of wood for perfect balance and that special action only wooden lures produce. Try it fished slowly with occasional tip jerks to tease 'em or with a faster retrieve for walleyes. It's a truly great spinning bait. Measures 2″, weighs ⅜ oz.

L2400 F (Floater), L2400 S (Sinker).

COLORS: 06, 07, 20, 45, 93, 96.

Shakespeare PUP. Another famous Shakespeare wood-body lure. A proved, deep swimmer for river and lake fishing that's found prime space in fishing guides' tackle boxes everywhere. Clobbers bass and walleyes with fantastic regularity. Gives a big, fish-tickling wiggle at any speed retrieve. Measures 2⅝″, weighs ½ oz.

L8800 Series. COLORS: 03, 69, 74, 77, 78, 96.

MORE Shakespeare FAVORITES

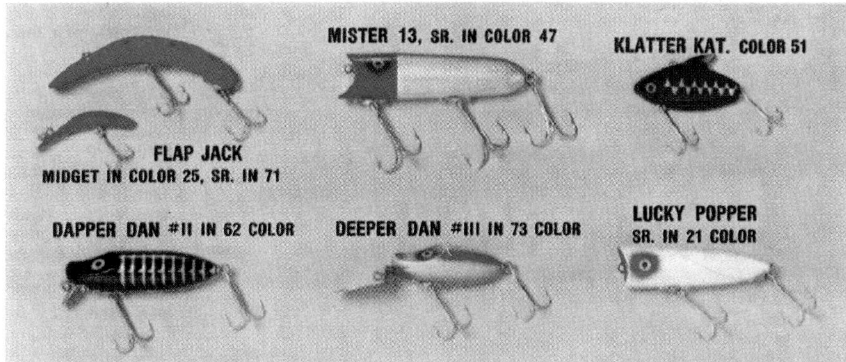

FLAP JACK. One of the most effective lake trout lures ever designed and it gets big action on walleye and bass as well. A sound addition to any angler's tackle box. Slow retrieve gets big 'wobble' action big fish really go for. Comes in three sizes: Flap Jack, Sr. — 3½″ (¾ oz.); Flap Jack, Jr. — 2½″ (¼ oz.); Flap Jack, Midget — 2″ (1/16 oz.)

L3600 Sr.; L6500 Jr.; L6600 Midget.

COLORS: 03, 06, 07, 25, 26, 45, 58, 70, 71, 76.

DAPPER DAN. Another Shakespeare Guide's favorite. Dapper Dan is a floating-diving lure with a wild wiggle that's attractive to all game fish, but downright devastating on pike and muskies. Comes in three irresistable sizes, Dapper Dan I — 3″ (½ oz.); Dapper Dan II — 2½″ (½ oz.); Dapper Dan III — 2¼″ (⅜ oz.).

L3700 Series, 3″ length, L3900 Series, 2½″ length, L4000 Series, 2¼″ length.

COLORS: 06, 62, 63, 73, 93, 96.

MISTER 13. Retrieved slowly, Mister 13's big mouth creates a ruckess that no self-respecting lunker can ignore. So they sock 'em. Retrieved steadily, he darts minnow-style, charms big ones out of their socks. Fantastic for pike and bass anywhere. Jr. has two trebles. Sr. has three. Mister 13, Jr. — 2⅝″ (⅜ oz.); Mister 13, Sr. — 3⅝″ (⅝ oz.).

DEEPER DAN. Deeper Dan lures are noted for their ability to reach the cool depths, an extra good feature on hot days. Deeper Dan I (3″ — ½ oz.) floats until retrieved, then digs deep to tease the big ones. Deeper Dan II (2½″ — ½ oz.) sinks slowly, (lets you "count-off" for probing different depths). Deeper Dan III (2¼″ — ⅜ oz.) sinks fast.

L3700 Series, 3″ length; L3900 Series, 2½″ length; L4000 Series, 2¼″ length.

COLORS: 06, 62, 63, 73, 93, 96.

KLATTER KAT. Works great in muddy, turbulent water because Klatter Kat has a built-in fish caller. Try it yourself. Shake him near your ear. The rattle you detect sends out high frequency vibrations that brings lunkers from fantastic distances. Cast it in any good looking lunker lair and bring it back fast. (If you've a strong heart and the courage of a lion.) Measures 2⅛″, weighs ½ oz.

L700 Series. COLORS: 03, 06, 23, 30, 42, 51, 73, 96.

LUCKY POPPER. Fantastic "long wait" surface specialist. Cast, let it set and set and set (or is it sit, sit, sit?) . . . then twitch your tip. Slowly. "Pops" and "smacks" all over the place. Consistently grabs bass—even when nothing else works. Comes in two fish-busting sizes: Lucky Popper, Jr. — 2¼″ (⅜ oz.); Lucky Popper, Sr. — 3″ (½ oz.)

Pike-Oreno Series

Pike-Oreno is one of the greatest artificial lures. Deep traveling, these lures float when at rest. Their realistic wiggling, swimming minnow action is unsurpassed.

No. 955 Midget Pike-Oreno—The smallest of the Pike-Oreno lures—perfect for the light tackle angler. A consistent result-getter. Extensively used with sinker for trolling. Length 2¾ inches, weight 3/10 ounce. Two No. 1 treble hooks. Patterns: RW-SH-SF-YP-P-SSS-S and SSY. Packed 12 in container. Weight per container ¾ pound. Per dozen.......**$9.00**

No. 956 Baby Pike-Oreno—Similar to No. 955 but 3¾ inches in length and weight ½ ounce. Two No. 2 treble hooks. Patterns: RW-SH-SF-YP-P-S-SSY and SSS. Packed 6 in container. Weight per container ⅞ pound. Per dozen.......**$9.00**

No. 957 Pike-Oreno—Similar to No. 955 except 4¾ inches long and weight ⅝ ounce. Three No. 1 treble hooks. Patterns: RW-SH-SF-YP-P-S-SSY and SSS. Packed 6 in container. Weight per container 1 pound. Per dozen.......**$10.20**

No. 2955 Jointed Midget Pike-Oreno—A deep diving midget wiggler with extremely fast action. Big Blue-gills, Perch and Rock Bass go for this bait as well as Bass and Pike! Length 3 inches, weight ⅜ ounce. Two No. 3 treble hooks. Patterns: RW-YP-P-SH-S-SF-SSY and SSS. Packed 12 in container. Weight per container ¾ pound. Per dozen.......**$10.20**

No. 2956 Jointed Baby Pike-Oreno—Similar to No. 2955 except 4 inches in length and weight ½ ounce. Two No. 2 treble hooks. Patterns: RW-YP-P-SH-S-SF-SSY and SSS. Packed 6 in container. Weight per container ⅞ pound. Per dozen.......**$10.20**

No. 2957 Jointed Pike-Oreno—Similar to No. 2955 except 5 inches in length and weight ⅝ ounce. Three No. 1 treble hooks. Patterns: RW-YP-P-SH-S-SF-SSY and SSS. Packed 6 in container. Weight per container 1 pound. Per dozen.......**$12.00**

Pike-Oreno Displays and Easels—Great sales producers.

No. 357—Contains 6 No. 957 Pike-Orenos.......**$5.10**

No. 356—Contains 6 No. 956 Pike-Orenos.......**$4.50**

No. E-955 Easel—Contains eight No. 955, one each pattern. Per easel.......**$6.00**

No. E-956 Easel—Contains eight No. 956, one each pattern. Per easel.......**$6.00**

No. E-957 Easel—Contains six No. 957, one each of patterns RW-YP-P-SH-S-SSY. Per easel.......**$5.10**

No. E-2955 Easel—Contains eight No. 2955, one each pattern. Per easel.......**$6.80**

No. E-2956 Easel—Contains eight No. 2956, one each pattern. Per easel.......**$6.80**

No. E-2957 Easel—Contains six No. 2957, one each of patterns RW-YP-P-SH-S-SSY. Per easel.......**$6.00**

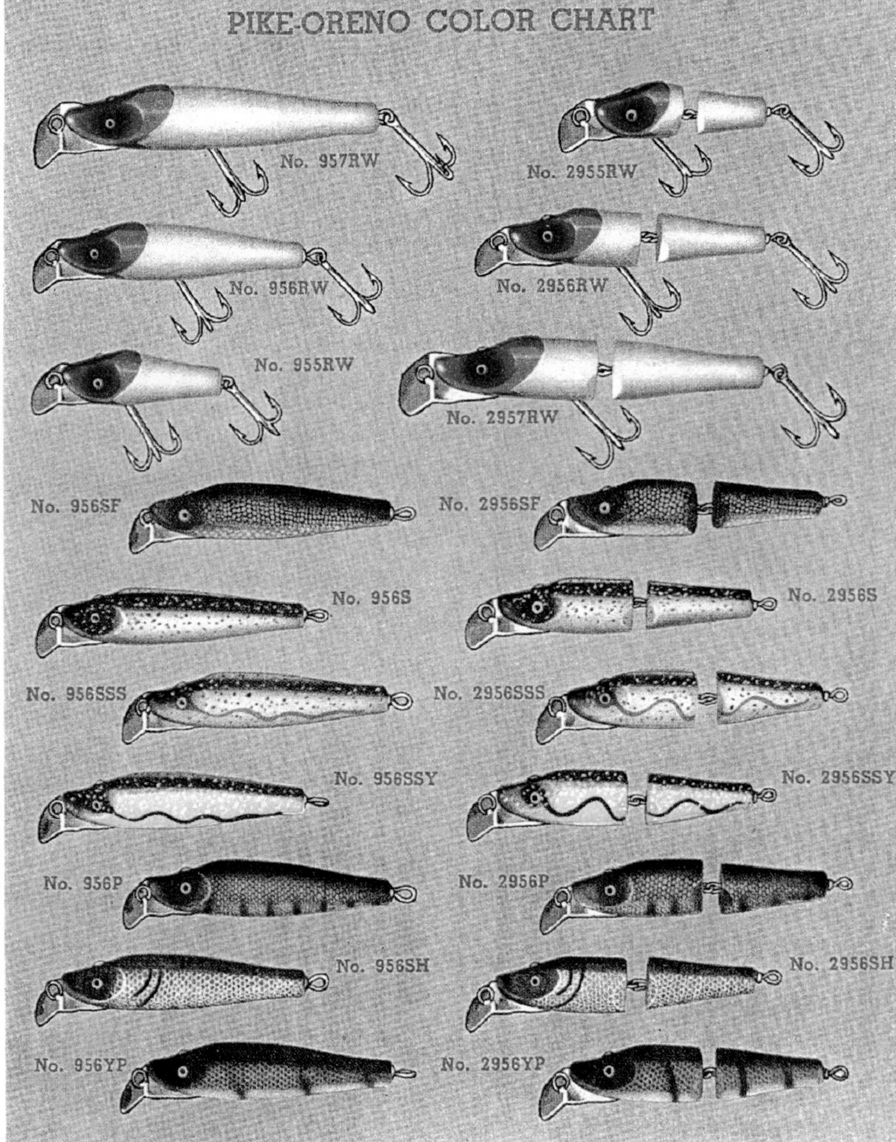

No. 969RSF

No. 969MS

No. 960GS

No. 958RW

Big Pike-Oreno Baits

No. 958 Big Pike-Oreno—For such salt water fish as Striped Bass and, in fresh water, big Great Northern Pike and Muskies. Strong soldered steel ring through Stainless Steel head plate. Three treble hooks, size 1/0. Length 5⅜ inches. Weight 1½ ounces. Patterns RW-YP-P-SH-SSY and SSS. Packed 12 in container. Weight per container 3 pounds. Per dozen.......**$12.00**

No. 960 Giant Jointed Pike-Oreno—A husky lure for record Muskies and salt water fishing. Sturdily built throughout. Metal parts of Stainless Steel are not affected by salt water. Extra strong wire extends through entire body. Three No. 5/0 extra heavy treble hooks. Length 7 inches, weight 2⅛ ounces. Patterns: RW-MS-SF-GS-RSF-SS. Packed 6 in container. Weight per container 1½ pounds. Per dozen......**$18.00**

No. 969 Big Jointed Pike-Oreno—Introduced originally for Striped Bass, it's now a favorite wherever big fish are taken. Extra strong construction; perfect action. Three No. 5/0 extra heavy treble hooks. Length 6 inches, weight 1½ ounces. Patterns: RW-MS-SF-RSF-SS-GS. Packed 12 in container. Weight per container 1½ pounds. Per dozen.......**$15.00**

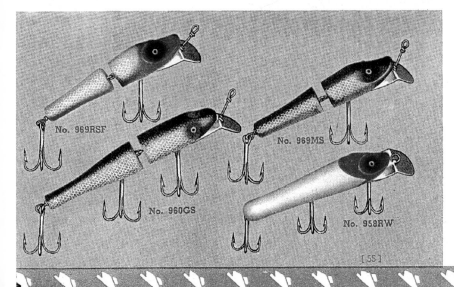

A page from the 1941 South Bend trade catalog illustrating the Pike-Oreno patterns available that year. Reprinted by permisssion of Luhr Jensen & Sons, Inc., Hood River, Oregon.

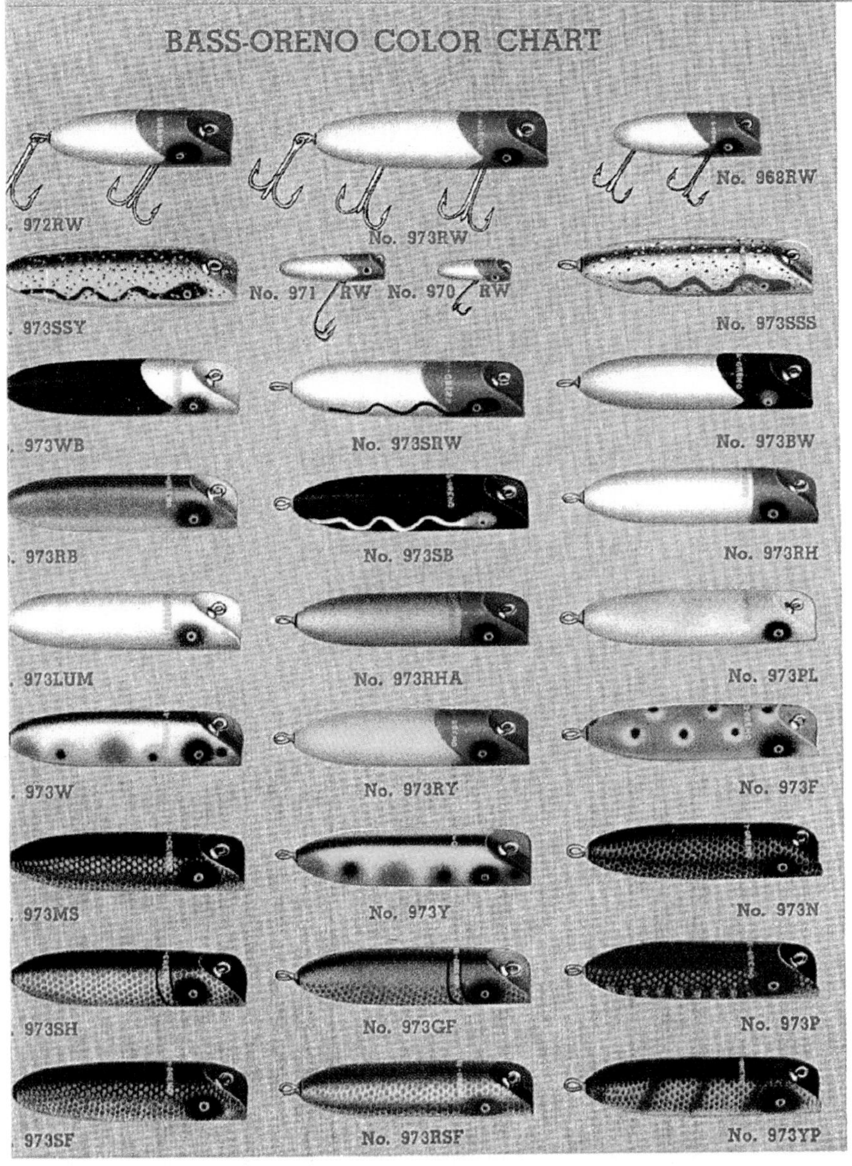

Bass-Oreno Series

No. 973 Bass-Oreno—The original and genuine world-famous South Bend Bass-Oreno—for more than a generation the world's greatest game fish lure and the most widely imitated bait ever designed. Its record of consistent results has created for the Bass-Oreno a reputation famous in the angling world. Its darting, diving Bass-Oreno action never fails to lure and land the big ones. Length 3¾ inches, weight ¾ ounce. Three No. 1 treble hooks. Patterns: RW-BW-RH-RY-W-RB-F-RHA-SF-RSF-YP-LUM-Y-P-PL-MS-N-WB-SH-GF and "Shad-O-Wave" patterns SRW-SB-SSY-SSS. Packed 12 in container. Weight per container 1½ pounds. Per dozen........ **$9.00**

No. 973 Wdls. Weedless Bass-Oreno—Same as No. 973 Bass-Oreno except weedless hooks. Patterns RH and LUM. Per dozen........ **$12.00**

No. 973SD Bass-Oreno—Same as No. 973 except single detachable hooks. Same patterns as No. 973. Per dozen........ **$9.00**

No. 972 Babe-Oreno—A small size Bass-Oreno weighing ½ ounce, perfect for use with the popular light action rods. One of the most effective small lures ever created. Has that irrestibly alluring Bass-Oreno action. Length 2¾ inches, weight ½ ounce. Two No. 1 treble hooks. Patterns RW-BW-RY-RH-RB-W-F-RHA-SF-RSF-YP-LUM-Y-P-PL-MS-N-WB and "Shad-O-Wave" patterns SRW-SB-SSY-SSS. Packed 12 in container. Weight per container 1¼ pounds. Per dozen........ **$7.80**

No. 972SD Babe-Oreno—Same as No. 972 except single detachable hooks. Same patterns as No. 972. Per dozen........ **$7.80**

No. 968 Midg-Oreno—The smallest casting lure of the Bass-Oreno type made by South Bend. Weighing but ⅜ ounce, it casts beautifully with a six-foot light action rod, 9 or 12-pound test Black-Oreno line and a No. 60, No. 65 or No. 760 South Bend reel. Length 2¼ inches, weight ⅜ ounce. Two No. 5 bronze treble hooks. Patterns RH-RY-YP-SF-P-RW-PL-MS and "Shad-O-Wave" patterns SB-SSS-SRW and SSY. Packed 12 in container. Weight per container 1¼ pounds. Per dozen........ **$7.20**

No. 976 Musk-Oreno—A Muskie size lure of the Bass-Oreno type with the same unequalled attraction and luring power. Length 4½ inches, weight 1½ ounces. Three extra strong No. 1/0 treble hooks. Patterns: SF-YP-RW. Packed 12 in container. Weight per container 2¼ pounds. Per dozen........ **$12.00**

No. 971 TROUT-ORENO

The Trout-Oreno is extremely strong yet light in weight—easy to cast and easy to pick up. A very popular and dependable lure for a great variety of fish, including trout, bass and panfish. An aluminum plate, cemented into the body, connects hook and line. Length 1⅝ inches, weight 1/10 ounce. Packed one on a card, four connected, three cards per container. Weight per container 6 ounces. Patterns: SSS-SRW-SY-RH-Y-W-RB-F-RHA-SF-YP-RSF-LUM-RW-RY-G-MS and N. Per dozen........ **$6.00**

No. 970 FLY-ORENO

Constructed along the same lines and having the same wobbling, diving, zig-zag action as the Trout-Oreno. An aluminum plate connects line tie with hook and runs through body of lure, thereby eliminating any possibility of losing fish because of loosened hooks or line tie. Very light weight (1/20 ounce) and easy to cast. Length 1⅛ inches. Packed one on a card, four connected, three cards per container. Weight per container 5 ounces. Patterns: SSS-SRW-SY-RH-Y-W-RB-F-RHA-SF-YP-RSF-LUM-RW-RY-G-MS and N. Per dozen........ **$5.40**

TROUT-ORENO AND FLY-ORENO DISPLAYS

Fifteen lures to display. Packed one display to container. Weight per container, ¼ pound.
No. E971 Easel—Contains 18 lures, 1 each color, per easel........ **$9.00**
No. E970 Easel—Contains 18 lures, 1 each color, per easel........ **$8.10**

EASEL DISPLAYS

No. E973 Bass-Oreno Easel—Contains one each of RW-RB-F-RY-W-P-SF-YP-MS-N-WB and BW colors. Weight 1 pound. Per easel........ **$9.00**

No. 382 Bass-Oreno Box Display—An attractive box display for window or counter, containing six genuine Bass-Oreno lures. Colors: RH-RSF-SF-RHA-RB and F. Packed one display in a container. Weight one pound. Each........ **$4.50**

No. 384 Babe-Oreno Box Display—An attractive box display containing six Babe-Oreno lures. Colors: RH-W-YP-RHA-RB-F. Packed one display in a container. Weight one pound. Each........ **$3.90**

No. E968 Easel—Contains one each of RH-SRW-RY-YP-SF-P-RW-SSS-SSY-PL-MS-SB colors. Per easel........ **$7.20**

A page from the 1941 South Bend trade catalog showing the Bass-Oreno patterns available that year. Reprinted by permission of Luhr Jensen & Sons, Inc., Hood River, Oregon.

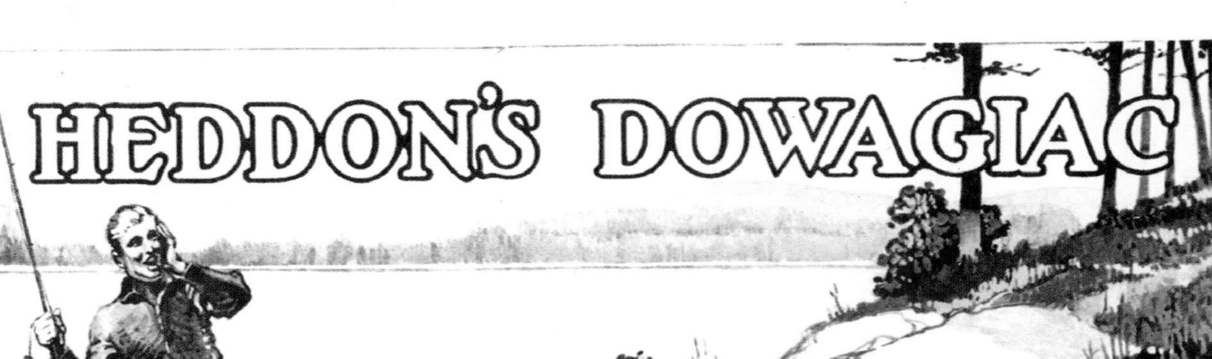

Heddon's Dowagiac Minnows

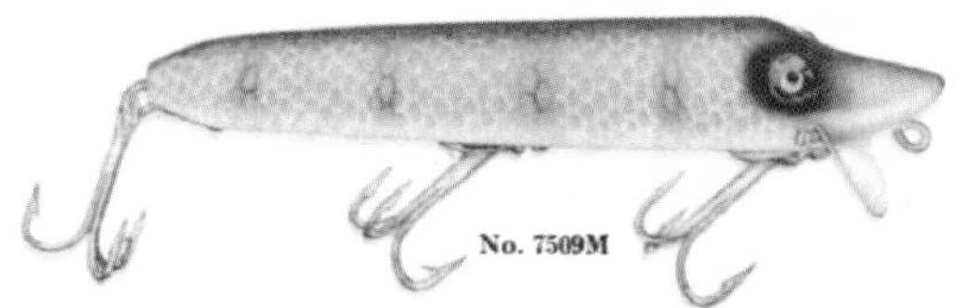

"Vampire" Minnow No. 7500 Series

The **"Vampire"** is Heddon's latest bait. Flat-nosed to resemble the baby pike and beautifully enameled in natural fish colors, the "Vampire" looks more like a real live minnow than any bait manufactured. Three treble gangs of sharp barbs make the "Vampire" a deadly hooker. A wonder for pike and all game fish. Weighs $\frac{5}{8}$ oz.; length, $4\frac{1}{2}$ inches; made only in the following colors:

No. 7500S	White body, red and green spots	**Price, each, $1.00**
No. 7501	Rainbow	
No. 7502	White body, red eyes and tail	
No. 7509D	Green scale finish	
No. 7509M	New pike scale	

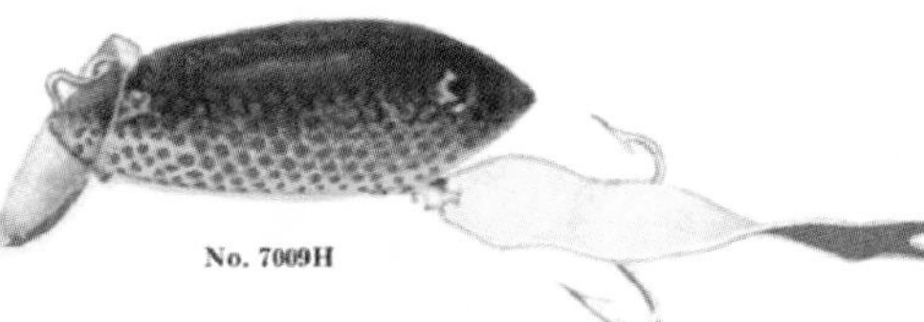

The Heddon "Deep-O-Diver," No. 7000 Series

Specially designed to dive very deep, where the bass are found in midsummer in northern lakes. Does not float. Sinks and dives, and has active swimming or wiggling movement, to which rubber pork rind attachment adds attractiveness. Is a deadly killer with one double hook equipment. Especially good for stream fishing. Weight $\frac{2}{3}$ oz.; length of body $2\frac{1}{2}$ inches.

Supplied in the following attractive colorations:

No. 7002	White body, red head	**No. 7009H**	Scale finish, red	**Price, each, $1.00**
No. 7009D	Green scale finish	**No. 7009J**	Frog, scale finish	
No. 7009E	White body, greenish black spots	**No. 7009K**	Goldfish, scale	
No. 7009F	Yellow body, black head	**No. 7009L**	Scale finish, yellow perch	

No. 5009D

The Heddon "Tad-Polly," Nos. 5000-6000 Series

Has a wonderful wiggling movement in the water, floats when at rest, dives and runs rather deep when retrieved.

Series 5000 weighs $\frac{1}{2}$ oz.; length, over all, $3\frac{7}{8}$ inches, equipped with two double hooks.

Series 600 weighs $\frac{3}{4}$ oz.; length, over all, $4\frac{5}{8}$ inches, equipped with two treble hooks.

Furnished in the following beautifully blended colors:

Small Size		Large Size	
No. 5000	Fancy green back	**No. 6000**	**Price, each, $1.10**
No. 5000S	White body, red and green spots	**No. 6000S**	
No. 5001	Rainbow	**No. 6001**	
No. 5002	White body, red head and tail	**No. 6002**	
No. 5009A	Yellow perch	**No. 6009A**	
No. 5009B	Frog colors	**No. 6009B**	
No. 5009D	Green scale finish	**No. 6009D**	
No. 5009H	Scale finish, red	**No. 6009H**	
No. 5009J	Scale finish, frog	**No. 6009J**	
No. 5009K	Scale finish, goldfish	**No. 6009K**	
No. 5009L	Scale finish, yellow perch	**No. 6009L**	

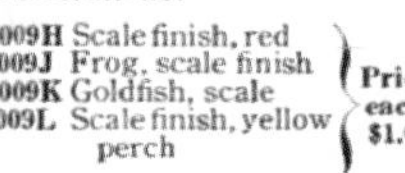

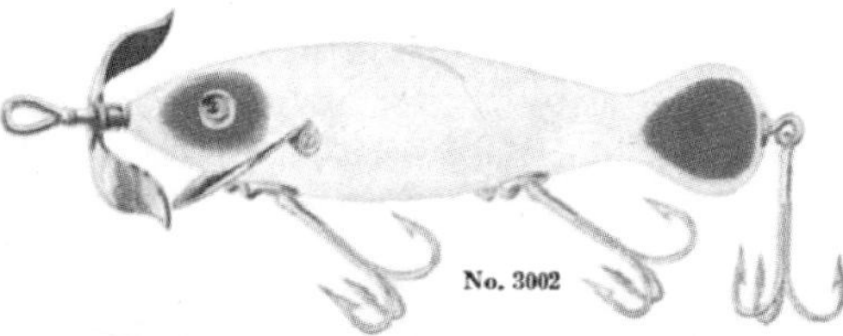

The Heddon "Spin-Diver," No. 3000 Series

This new three treble hook bait has the straight revolving spinner movement in the water, but unlike other baits of this type, floats when at rest, instead of sinking into the weeds. It is equipped with a patented fin device, which causes it to submerge to a nice depth when retrieved. Weighs 1 oz.; length, over all, $4\frac{3}{8}$ inches.

Supplied in the following harmonious colors:

No. 3000	Fancy green back	**No. 3009D**	Green scale finish	**Price, each, $1.00**
No. 3000S	White body, red and green spots	**No. 3009H**	Red scale finish	
No. 3001	Rainbow	**No. 3009J**	Frog, scale finish	
No. 3002	White body, red head	**No. 3009K**	Goldfish, scale	
No. 3009A	Yellow perch	**No. 3009L**	Scale finish, yellow perch	
No. 3009B	Frog colors			

The "Dowagiac" Minnow, Nos. 100 and 150 Series

Sinking minnow, two spinners. **No. 100 Series** has three treble hooks, weighs $\frac{2}{3}$ oz.; length of body $2\frac{3}{4}$ inches. **No. 150 Series,** same as illustration except has five treble hooks, weighs $\frac{3}{4}$ oz.; length of body $3\frac{3}{4}$ inches. Not new models but great favorites.

Furnished in the following variety of beautiful colors:

No. 100 Series, Price, each, 95c		No. 150 Series, Price, each, $1.00
No. 100	Fancy green back, white belly	**No. 150**
No. 101	Rainbow	**No. 151**
No. 102	White body with red eyes	**No. 152**
No. 104	Red body with dark blended back	**No. 154**
No. 109A	Yellow perch	**No. 159A**
No. 109B	Frog colors	**No. 159B**
No. 109D (Price, each, $1.00)	Green scale finish	**No. 159D**
No. 109H (Price, each, $1.00)	Red scale finish	**No. 159H**
No. 109J (Price, each, $1.00)	Frog, scale finish	**No. 159J**
No. 109K (Price, each, $1.00)	Goldfish, scale	**No. 159K**
No. 109L (Price, each, $1.00)	Scale finish, yellow perch	**No. 159L**

For description of other Heddon "Dowagiac" baits refer to the supplementary insert.

"Made by Heddon ~ and well made"

This and the facing page are pages 6 and 7 from a 1921 Heddon catalog.

HEDDON'S DOWAGIAC

Heddon's Dowagiac Minnows

"Baby Crab" Minnow
No. 1900 Series

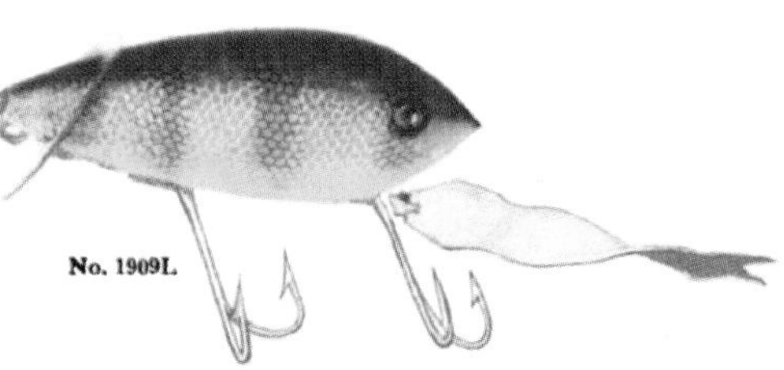

No. 1909L.

The **"Baby Crab"** is regarded by the Heddon factory as the supreme achievement in casting baits.
An entirely new principle in hook designing has made this popular lure practically snagless and weedless—yet deadly to fish.
Here are the eight features which have made "Baby Crab" a favorite:

1. Great attractive power due to excessive wiggling movement, the improved "porker" attachment, and the natural color effects.
2. Scientific arrangement of the two double hooks making bait snagless and weedless—yet deadly effective.
3. "Porker" attachment hides rear hooks.
4. You can cast the "Baby Crab" into the lily pads, where the fish hide, without fear of its snagging in the weeds.
5. No heavy back drag in retrieving.
6. Patent detachable hook fastenings—non-fouling hooks—can't scratch the enamel.
7. Artistic enamel finish that never cracks nor peels.
8. Minimum wind resistance, correct weight.

No. 1900	Fancy green back	**No. 1909B**	Frog colors
No. 1900S	White body, red and green spots	**No. 1909C**	Imitation crab
		No. 1909D	Green scale finish
No. 1901	Rainbow	**No. 1909H**	Red scale finish
No. 1902	White body with red head	**No. 1909J**	Frog, scale finish
No. 1905	Yellow body, spotted	**No. 1909K**	Goldfish, scale
No. 1909A	Yellow perch	**No. 1909L**	Yellow perch scale finish

Price, each, $1.00

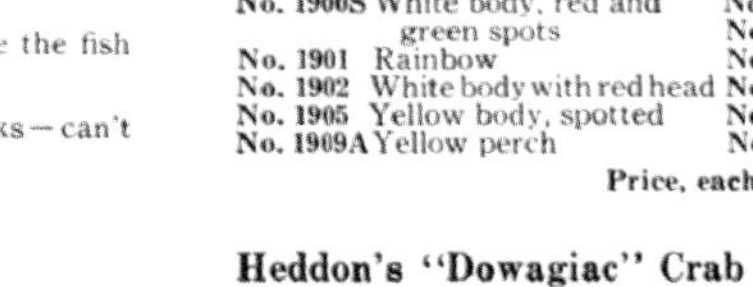

No. 1959K

"Midget Crab Wiggler," No. 1950 Series

Many anglers prefer a small bait. At their request we are now making this new minnow identical with the "Baby Crab," but much smaller.

Weighs ½ oz., length 2½ inches, made in the same colors as the No. 1900 Series. (For instance, to order **Midget Crab Wiggler** in "yellow perch scale finish," specify "1959L.")

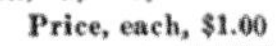

Price, each, $1.00

Heddon's "Dowagiac" Crab Wiggler, No. 1800 Series

This is a larger size of the Baby Crab and a record breaker on bass wherever tested, equally deadly on muskellunge, pike, pickerel and other fresh water game fish. Equipped with two treble hooks.

This bait is painted in close resemblance to a fresh water crab or crawfish, floats when not in motion, dives under when retrieved, the movement being a pronounced wiggle, simulating the movement of a crab when moving backwards away from danger. This novel, new bait is drawn through the water tail first and the movement so closely resembles that of the live crab that it is irresistible to game fishes.

Furnished in the following striking colors:

No. 1800	Fancy green back	**No. 1809A**	Yellow perch	**Price, each, $1.00**
No. 1800S	White body, red and green spotted effect	**No. 1809B**	Imitation frog	
		No. 1809C	Imitation crab	
No. 1801	Rainbow	**No. 1809D**	Green scale finish	
No. 1802	White body with red head	**No. 1809H**	Red scale finish	
		No. 1809J	Frog, scale finish	
No. 1805	Yellow body, red and green spots and green back	**No. 1809K**	Goldfish, scale	
		No. 1809L	Yellow perch scale finish	

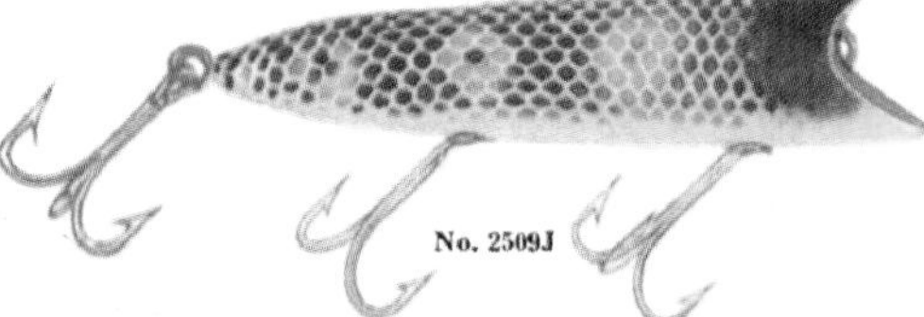

No. 2509J

The Heddon "Lucky 13," Nos. 2400-2500 Series

While resembling in appearance and principle baits of standard popular acceptance, the **"Lucky 13"** possesses certain subtle improvements in balance, stream outline and head-planes that intensify the erratic swimming movements associated with baits of similar type.

The "Lucky 13" casts straight and true and floats on the surface until retrieved. Under the line pull, it drops to an average depth of eighteen inches below the surface, and comes in with an undulating, weaving motion, interrupted by short, quick darts that excite the curiosity of any bass in the vicinity. Equipped with three treble hooks.

"Lucky 13" is made in two sizes, as listed below.

No. 2500 Series Large size weighs ⅝ oz. Length, 3⅞ inches over all	**Price, each, 85c**	**No. 2400 Series** Junior size weighs ½ oz. Length, 3 inches over all
No. 2502	White body, red head	**No. 2402**
No. 2509D	Green scale finish	**No. 2409D**
No. 2509H	Red scale finish	**No. 2409H**
No. 2509J	Frog, scale finish	**No. 2409J**
No. 2509K	Goldfish, scale	**No. 2409K**
No. 2509L	Yellow perch scale finish	**No. 2409L**

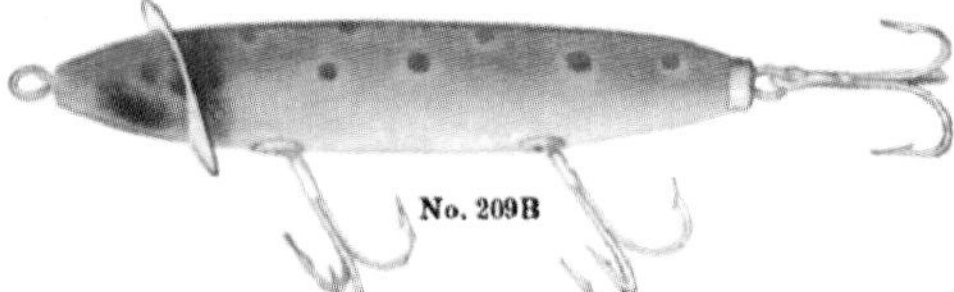

No. 209B

Heddon's "Dowagiac" Minnow, Nos. 200-210 Series

The old original "Dowagiac" surface casting or skittering bait without revolving parts; semi-weedless with two trebles on bottom and one at tail. Nickeled collar. Weight ⅘ oz.; length of body, 4¾ inches.

No. 200BH	White body, blue head	**Price, each, $1.00**
No. 200RH	White body, red head	
No. 209B	Frog coloration	
No. 209D	Scale finish, natural green	

No. 210 Series—Same as No. 200 except weight ⅗ oz.; length of body 3½ inches. One double hook on bottom, one at tail. Ideal weedless surface minnow.

No. 210BH	White body, blue head	**Price, each, $1.00**
No. 210RH	White body, red head	
No. 219B	Frog coloration	
No. 219D	Scale finish, natural green	

For description of other Heddon "Dowagiac" baits refer to the supplementary insert.

"Made by Heddon ~ and well made"

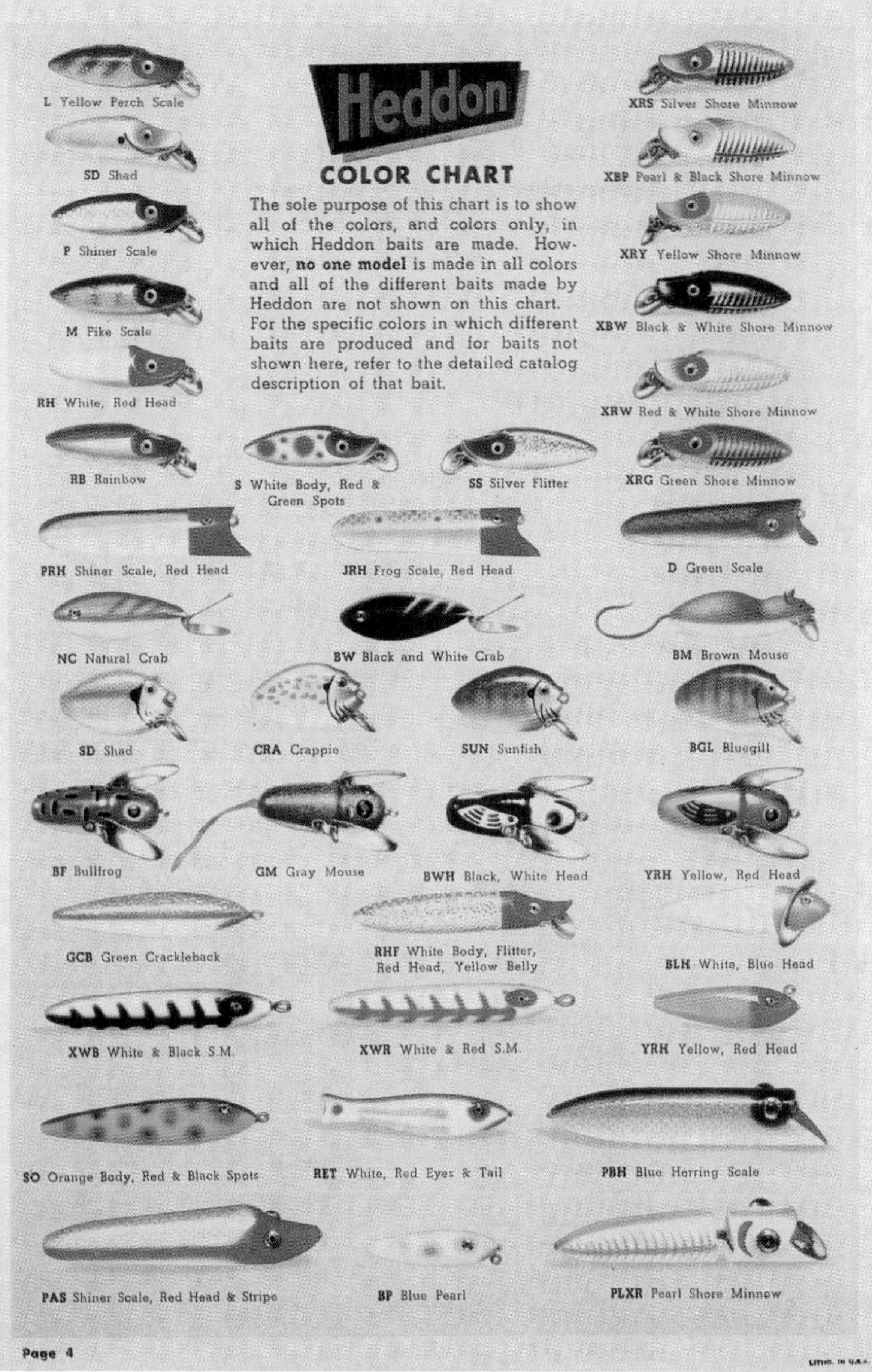

A color chart from the 1951 edition of the Heddon catalogs. Provided by Billy Prince of Decatur, Alabama and reprinted by permission of Pradco, Inc., Ft. Smith, Arkansas.

See "Punkinseed" Colors Page 37

Heddon Color Chart (For Colors only, not body shape)

NO Bait is made in ALL colors below. Baits are made only in the colors listed under **each** Series in the catalog. Some colors apply to wood-bodied baits only. Other colors apply to "Spook" or Transparent baits only; and many to both constructions. The "River-Runt" body is used below, but this model is NOT made in ALL colors shown below, only as catalogued and **listed** under **each** bait Series.

KEY TO COLOR NUMBERS: The LAST number and letters designates the Color. For example: No. 9110 Series represents the "River-Runt-Spook" (Sinking Model), and No. 91M is "Rainbow." Likewise, No. 9119P is "Shiner Scale," etc.

0	Green Crackle Back	**9D**	Green Scale	**9SH**	Silver Herring	**WH**	White Head
0LUM	Luminous	**9G**	All Black	**9SS**	Silver Scale	**RH**	Red Head
0S	White; Red and Green Spots	**9GW**	Glow Worm	**9W**	All White	**BH**	Blue Head
1	Rainbow	**9J**	Frog Scale	**9YRH**	Yellow-Red-Head	**CP**	Copper Plate
2	White and Red	**9L**	Perch Scale	**9X**	Blue Scale	**GP**	Gold Plate
2LUM	Luminous White and Red	**9M**	Pike Scale	**9XRG**	Green Shore-Minnow	**NP**	Nickel Plate
4	All Red	**9N**	Dace Scale	**9XRS**	Silver Shore-Minnow	**GM**	Grey Mouse
9	Silver Specks	**9P**	Shiner Scale	**9XRY**	Yellow Shore-Minnow	**BM**	Brown Mouse
9A	Yellow Perch	**9PAS**	Allen Stripey	**2XS**	White and Red Shore-Minnow	**GC**	Green Crab
9B	Frog	**9PL**	Pearl	**9XBW**	Black and White Shore-Minnow	**LC**	Luminous Crab
9C	Natural Crab	**9R**	Natural Scale	**9XSK**	Gold-fish Shore-Minnow	**NC**	Natural Crab

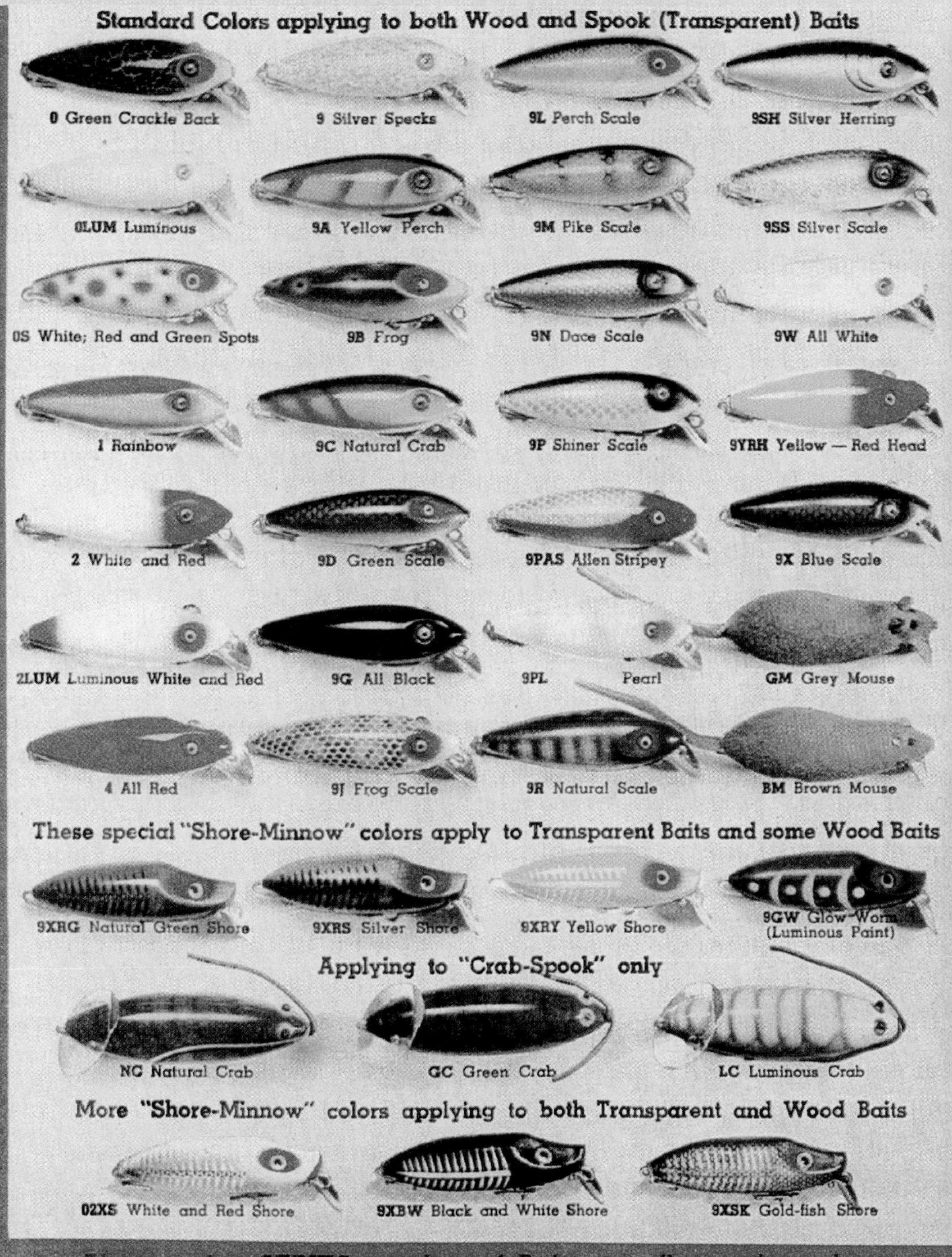

The color chart from a 1941 Heddon catalog. Note that it states this chart is for colors only, not body shape. The chart was provided by Terry Wong and is from his book Collector's Guide To Antique Fishing Lures Colors, Copyright 1997. It is reproduced by permission of Pradco, Inc., Ft. Smith, Arkansas.

eighteen new Heddon colors

18 new colors this year. No one has better colors than Heddon. And that's a fact!

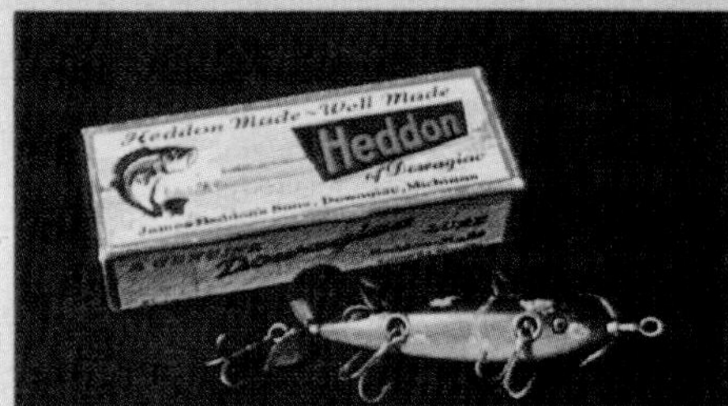

The famous "Dowagiac" bait.

Heddon painted that historic first lure in 1898. The famous "Dowagiac" bait. And we've come a long way since. Our satiny colors have Heddon's exclusive space-age plastic finish for durability. High-gloss or matte, they're all tough.

We study each of our color patterns in detail to determine if we're bringing the fishermen the best, most productive colors. As their needs change, so do our patterns and colors . . . resulting in the most effective lures on the market today. Take our improved perch and red crawdad colors, we've beefed up these designs so they are more realistic than ever.

Our new Naturals are so real that even the fish won't know until it's too late. Every gill, fin and scale resembles perfectly the markings of a perch, shad or sucker.

Try our new Phosphorescents that actually glow-in-the-dark. They're matte finish to absorb light so the glow is even brighter down deep where it's really dark.

Fluorescents are available in hot day-glo colors that really radiate down deep. These are some of the neatest colors to come along this year!

Plus the beautiful new Pearls. Modern, soft, muted colors that are particularly popular today.

New Chromes are designed to give off the ultimate reflection of light. Hot, silvery colors duplicating the silver flash of a darting minnow.

Shore Minnows have a rib pattern that simulates the natural look of a bait fish. They're translucent too, like real minnows. You know how minnows look in light or shallow water.

Plus, furry, fuzzy Meadow Mouse finishes that are soft to the touch.

Eighteen brand new colors—in a family of over a hundred different Heddon colors to choose from. That's why we're still No. 1 in lures!

11

BABY BASS

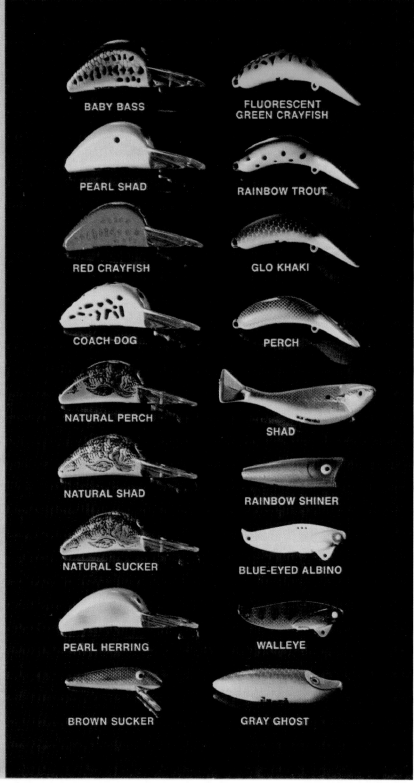

FLUORESCENT GREEN CRAYFISH

PEARL SHAD

RAINBOW TROUT

RED CRAYFISH

GLO KHAKI

COACH DOG

PERCH

NATURAL PERCH

SHAD

NATURAL SHAD

RAINBOW SHINER

NATURAL SUCKER

BLUE-EYED ALBINO

PEARL HERRING

WALLEYE

BROWN SUCKER

GRAY GHOST

In this color chart from the 1979 edition of the Heddon catalog they announce 18 new colors. This chart should be of help to the collectors of the later vintage plastic lures from Heddon. Provided by Billy Prince of Decatur, Alabama and reprinted by permission of Pradco, Inc., Ft. Smith, Arkansas.

twenty-six new Heddon colors

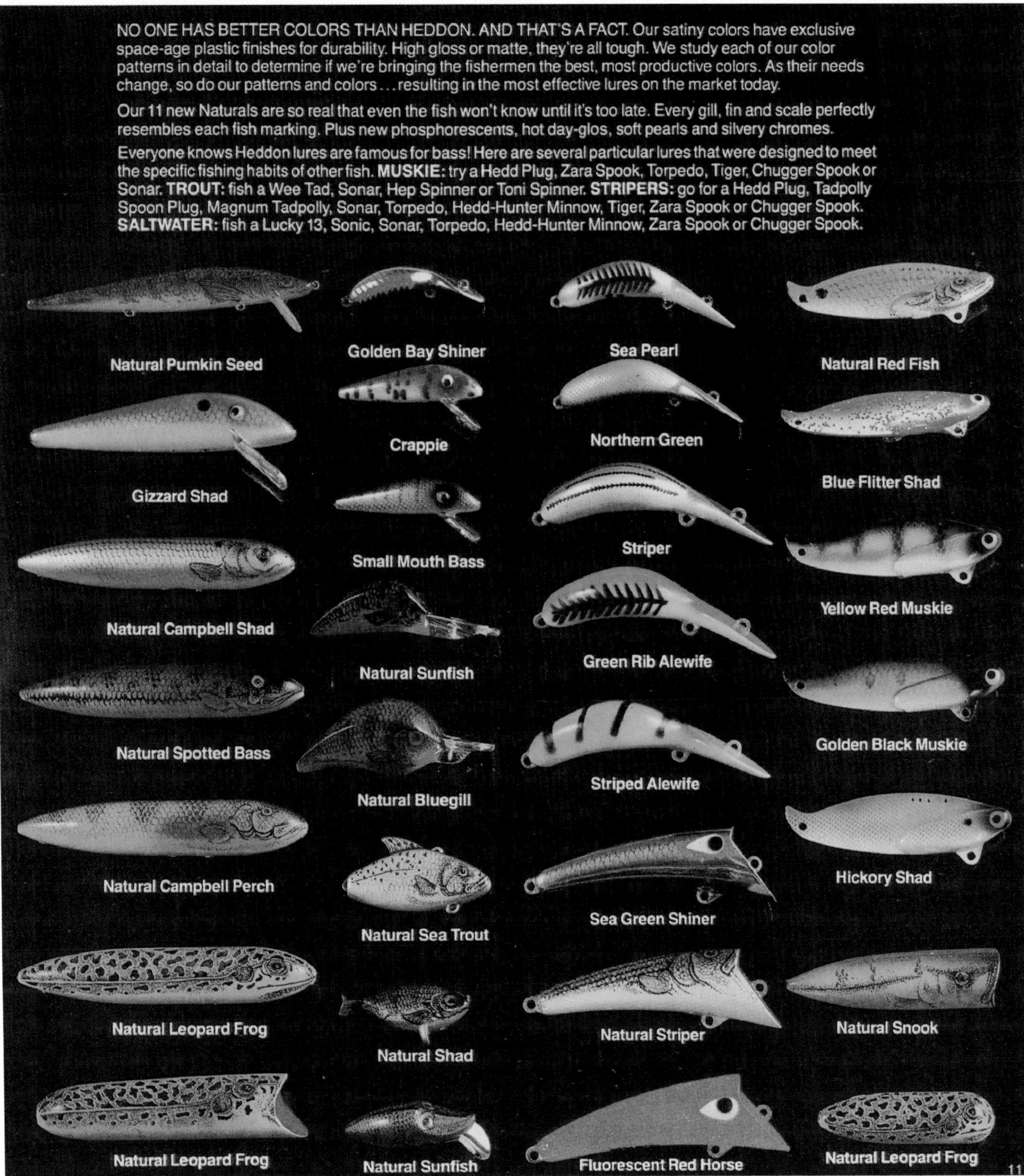

NO ONE HAS BETTER COLORS THAN HEDDON. AND THAT'S A FACT. Our satiny colors have exclusive space-age plastic finishes for durability. High gloss or matte, they're all tough. We study each of our color patterns in detail to determine if we're bringing the fishermen the best, most productive colors. As their needs change, so do our patterns and colors . . . resulting in the most effective lures on the market today.

Our 11 new Naturals are so real that even the fish won't know until it's too late. Every gill, fin and scale perfectly resembles each fish marking. Plus new phosphorescents, hot day-glos, soft pearls and silvery chromes.

Everyone knows Heddon lures are famous for bass! Here are several particular lures that were designed to meet the specific fishing habits of other fish. **MUSKIE:** try a Hedd Plug, Zara Spook, Torpedo, Tiger, Chugger Spook or Sonar. **TROUT:** fish a Wee Tad, Sonar, Hep Spinner or Toni Spinner. **STRIPERS:** go for a Hedd Plug, Tadpolly Spoon Plug, Magnum Tadpolly, Sonar, Torpedo, Hedd-Hunter Minnow, Tiger, Zara Spook or Chugger Spook. **SALTWATER:** fish a Lucky 13, Sonic, Sonar, Torpedo, Hedd-Hunter Minnow, Zara Spook or Chugger Spook.

This color chart from the 1980 edition of the Heddon catalog announces 26 new colors. This chart should also help the collectors of plastic lures from Heddon. Provided by Billy Prince of Decatur, Alabama and reprinted by permission of Pradco, Inc., Ft. Smith, Arkansas.

CREEK CHUB COLORATION CHART

Pictured below are the standard finishes and colorations used on Creek Chub True-to-Nature Lures! All lures, however, are not made in all colorations! For particular colorations used on each lure, refer to listing shown in Creek Chub catalog! The numbers in "hundreds" designate the shape and size of lure! The last two numerals designate the finish or coloration! Example, No. **701** is the Famous Pikie Minnow in the (No. 01) Yellow Perch Finish; No. 1618 is the Original Injured Minnow in the (No. 18) Silver Flash Finish, etc.

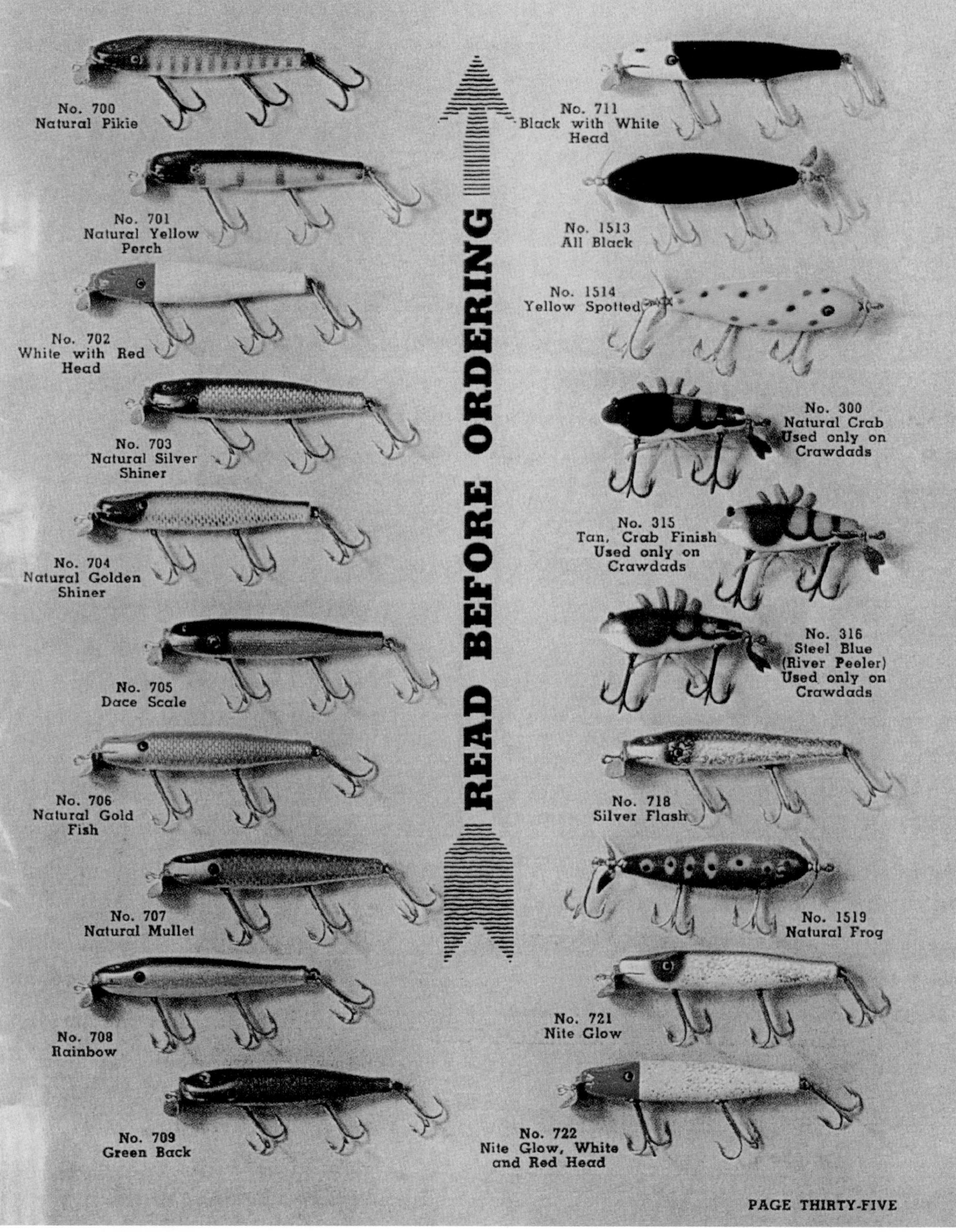

A color chart from a 1941 Creek Chub Bait Company catalog. The chart was provided by Terry Wong and is from his book Collector's Guide To Antique Fishing Lures Colors, Copyright 1997. It is reproduced by permission of Pradco, Inc., Ft. Smith, Arkansas.

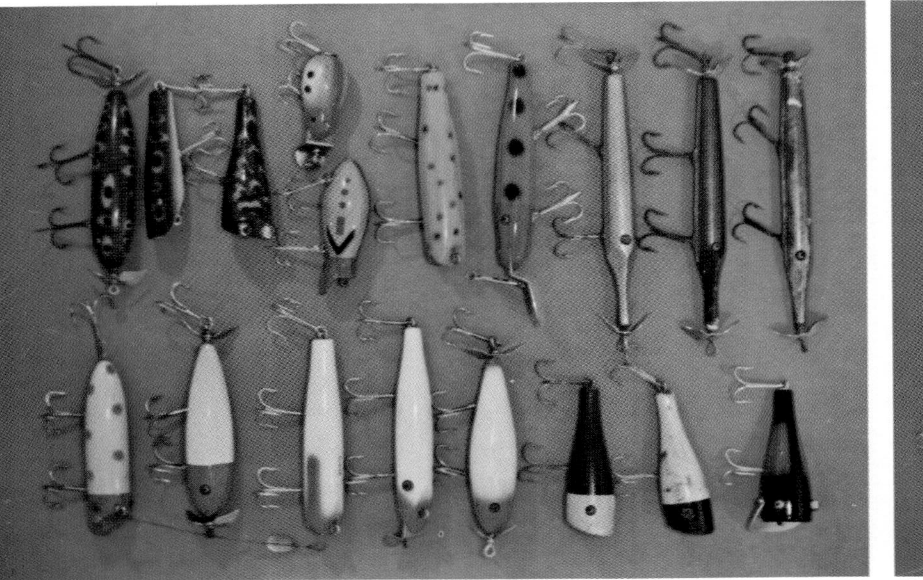

CREEK CHUB PATTERNS. *Illustrates various two-color finishes, dot patterns, scale finishes and, frog types to be found. Note the "Victory Finish" demonstrated on the lower lure of the two lures appearing fourth from the left on the top row.*

SOUTH BEND PATTERNS. *Photo illustrates various solid colors found and the several two color combinations with the "arrowhead" and "straight line" head color paint.*

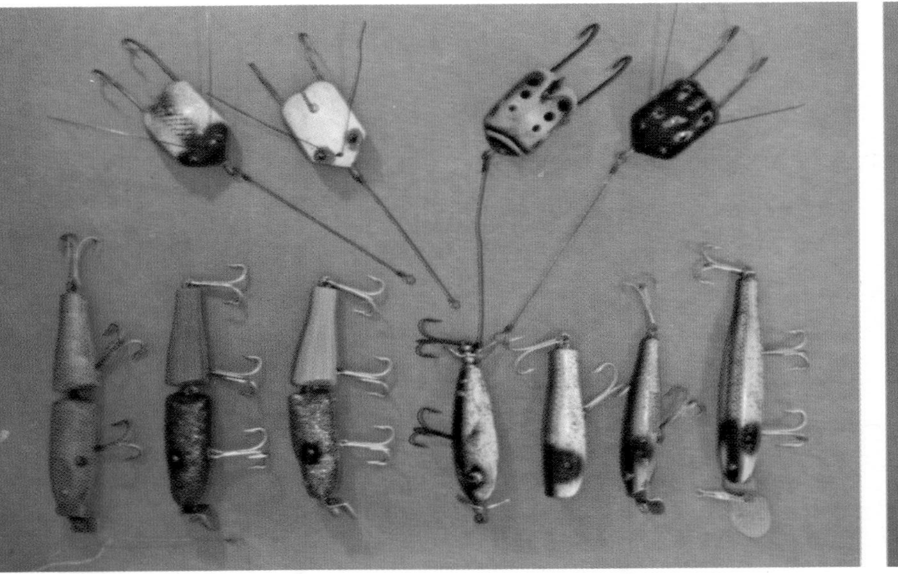

CREEK CHUB PATTERNS. *Bottom row illustrates various types of "glitter" or "sparkle" finishes to be found. Occurs in gold and silver glitter. Far left lure in bottom row is a fuzzy or flock finish. Top row is of the four patterns found so far on the "Wee Dee".*

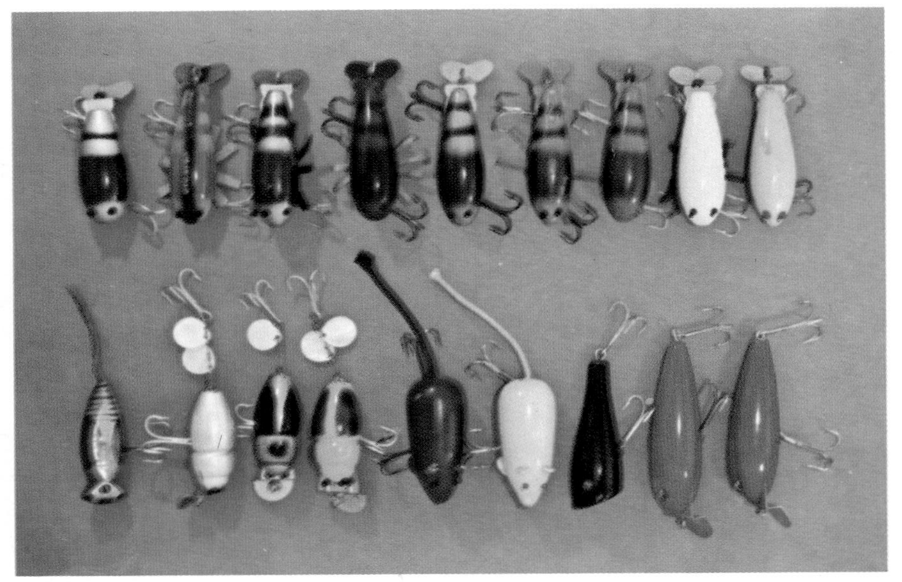

CREEK CHUB PATTERNS. *Illustrates solid colors, pearl finish (bottom row, second from left), and all patterns found on the "Crawdad" so far.*

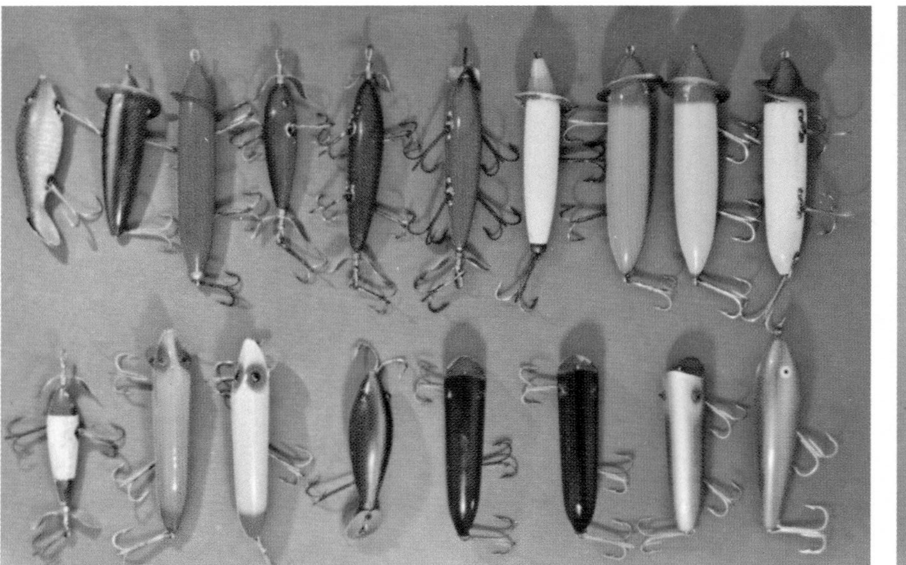

HEDDON PATTERNS. *Various early color designs. Note subtle body shape changes demonstrated by two or three of the same lures placed side by side in the photo. They are placed in order from oldest on left to newer on the right.*

HEDDON PATTERNS. *Photo shows a few of the very rare Heddon lures. Note the fish decoy at bottom right and the extremely rare frog, at bottom center, hand carved by James Heddon himself. See Heddon section text for identification of the others.*

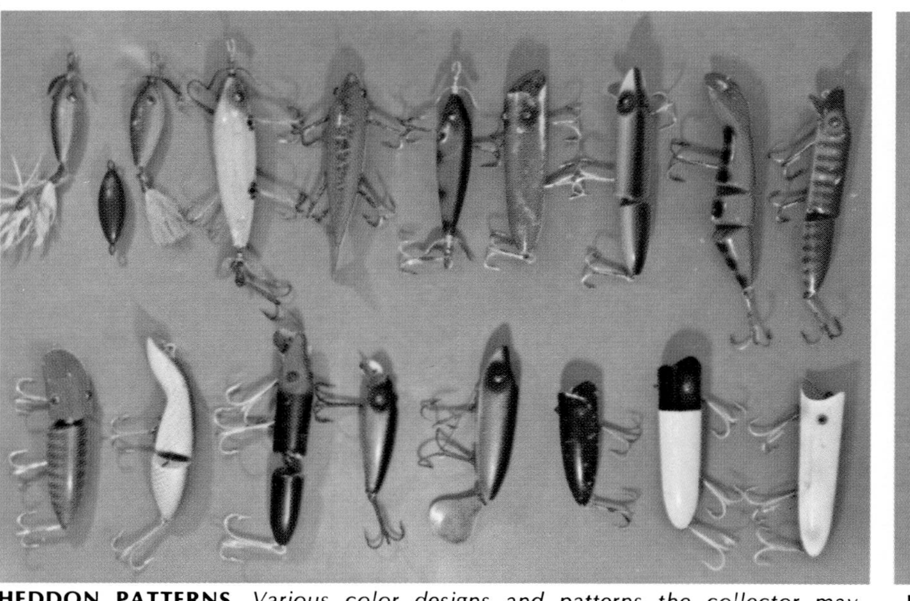

HEDDON PATTERNS. *Various color designs and patterns the collector may encounter.*

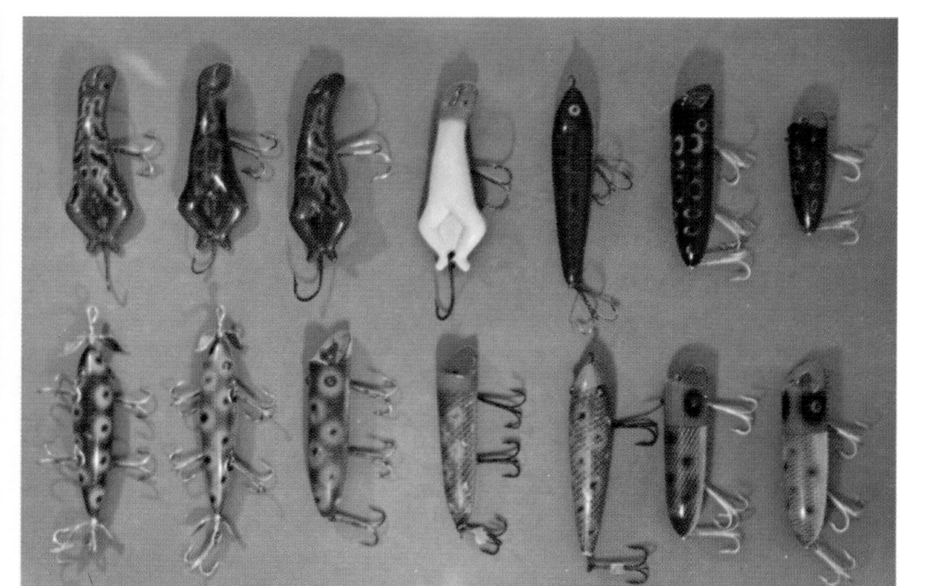

HEDDON PATTERNS. *Photo illustrates various frog and frog spot type finishes the collector may find. The top row, center lure is the very scarce red head, white body "Luny Frog" (Note webbed legs).*

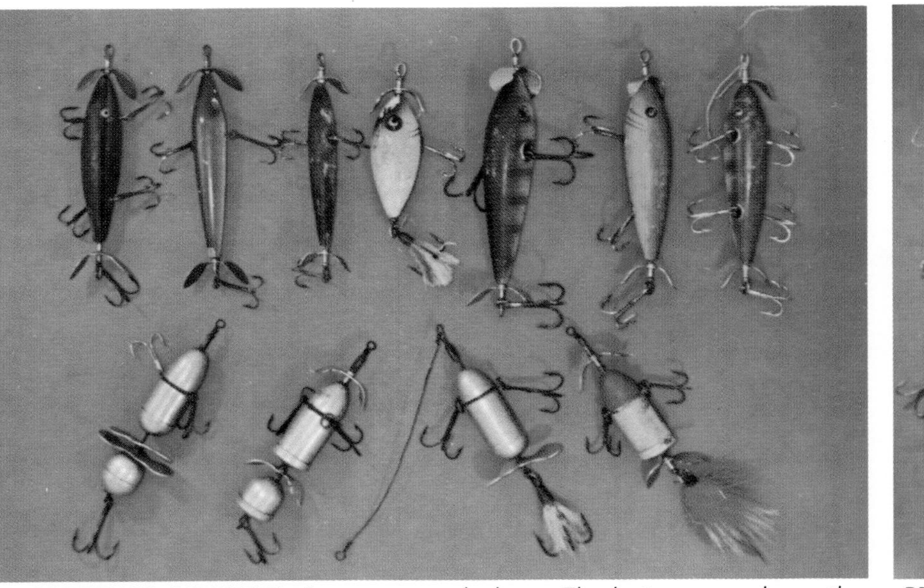

SHAKESPEARE PATTERNS. *Some very early lures. The bottom row shows the "Revolution" and "Bucktail Spinners".*

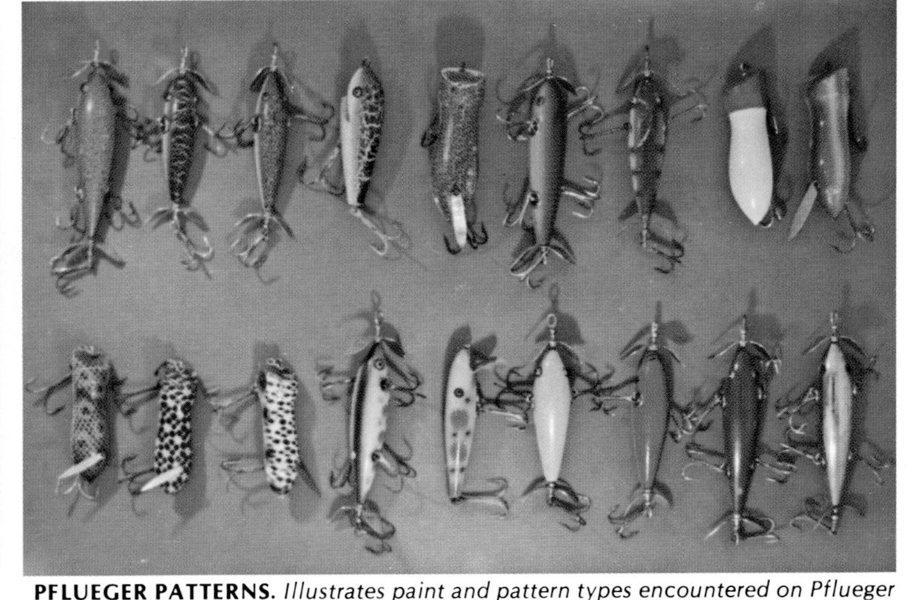

PFLUEGER PATTERNS. *Illustrates paint and pattern types encountered on Pflueger lures.*

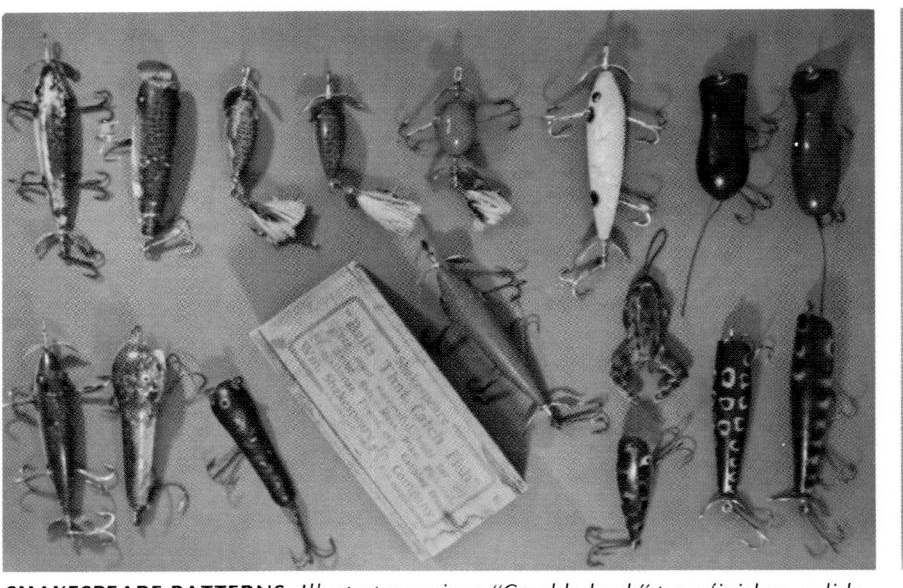

SHAKESPEARE PATTERNS. *Illustrates various "Crackle back" type finishes, solids, frog finishes and an early wooden box. Bottom row, second from left is a lure covered with actual frog skin.*

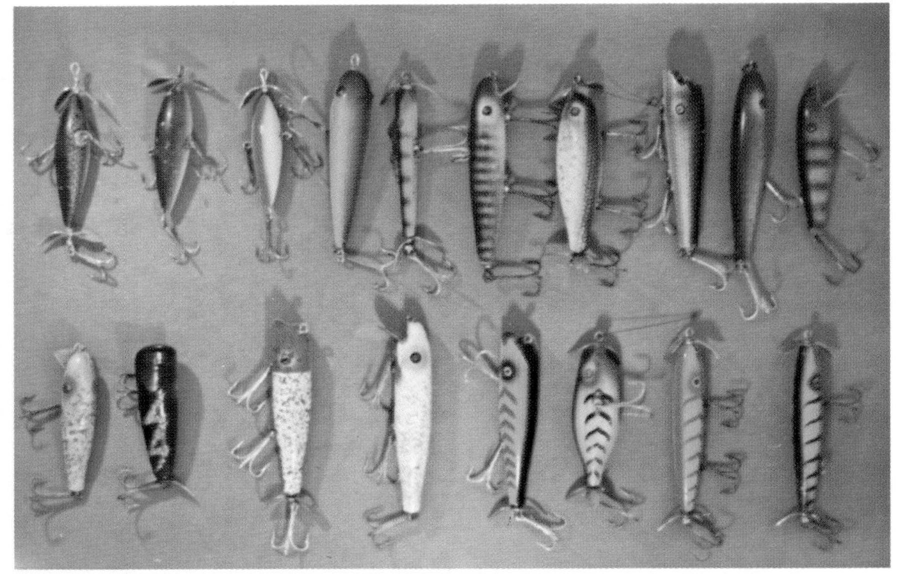

PFLUEGER PATTERNS. *Illustrates paint and pattern types encountered on Pflueger lures.*

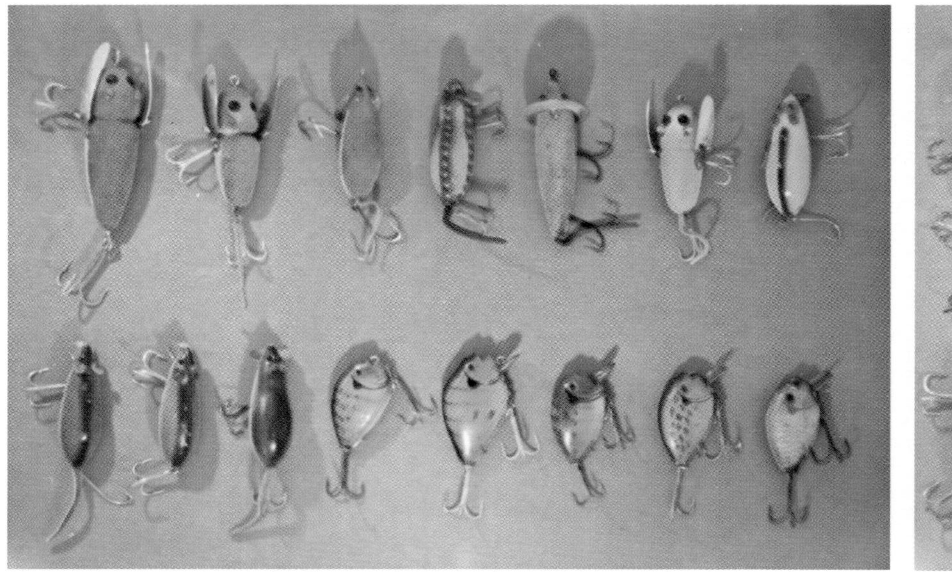

HEDDON PATTERNS. *The first six lures in the top row are the various fuzzy or flocked type finishes to be found. Bottom row includes five patterns of the "Punkin Seed" lure.*

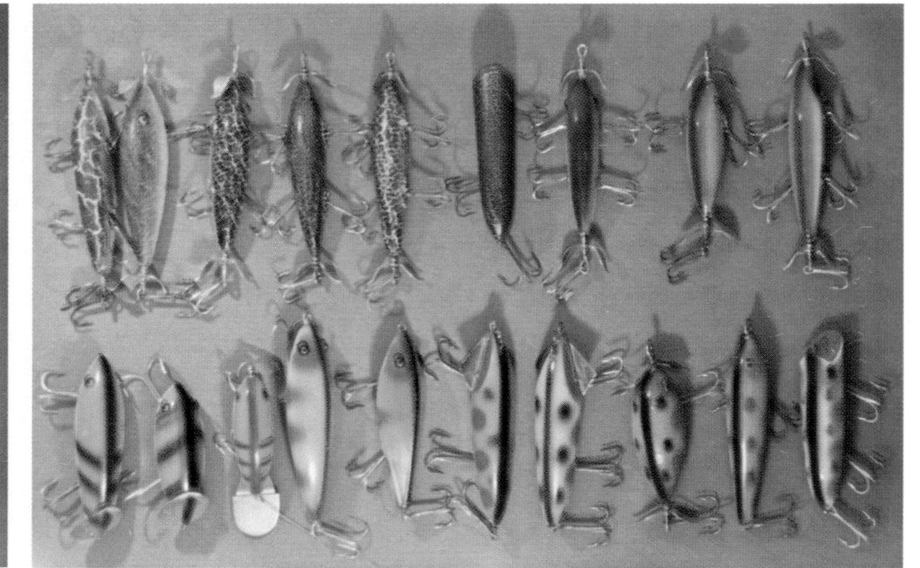

HEDDON PATTERNS. *Illustrates various types of "Fancy Back" or crackle finish to be found. Remainder of the lures show several rainbow and spot multicolor patterns.*

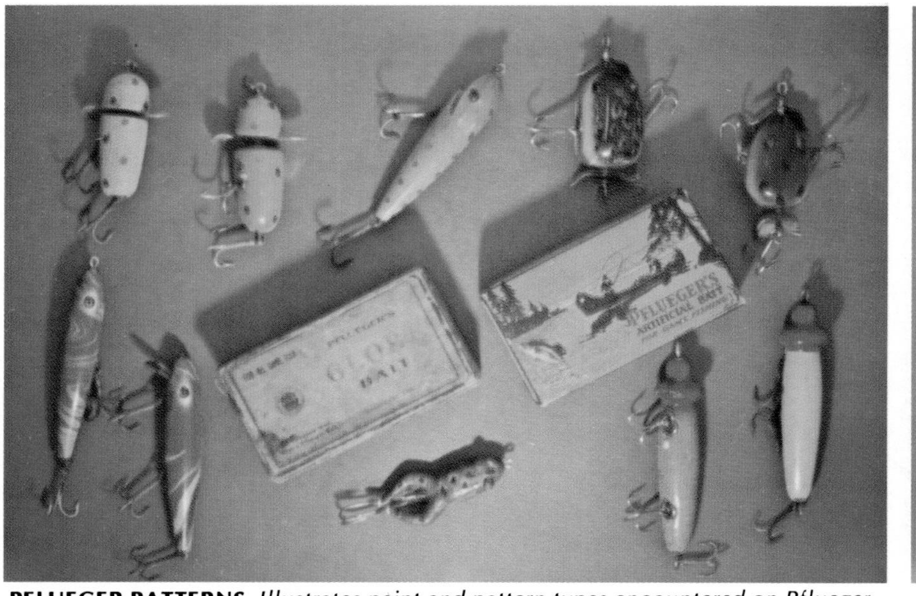

PFLUEGER PATTERNS. *Illustrates paint and pattern types encountered on Pflueger lures.*

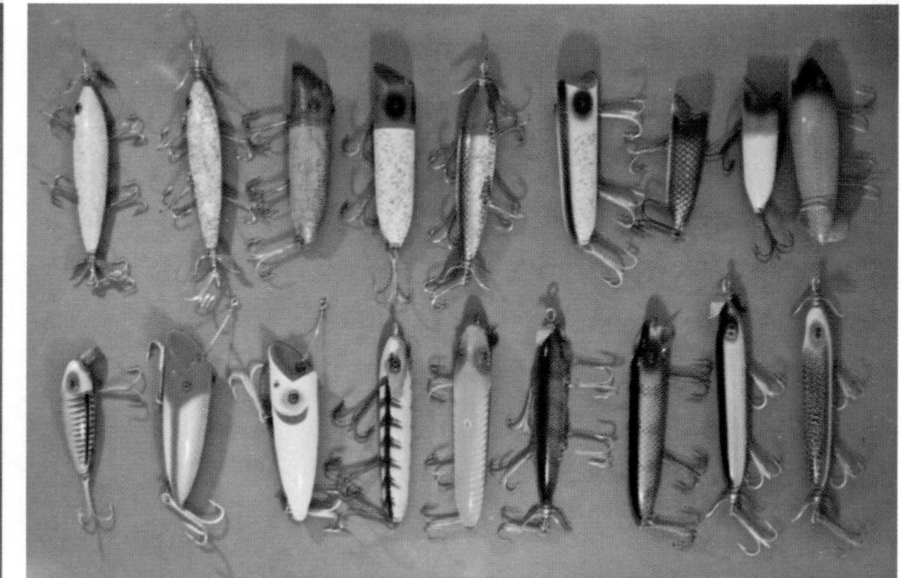

HEDDON PATTERNS. *Illustrates several types of glitter type finish. The remaining lures show assorted paint and patterns to be found.*

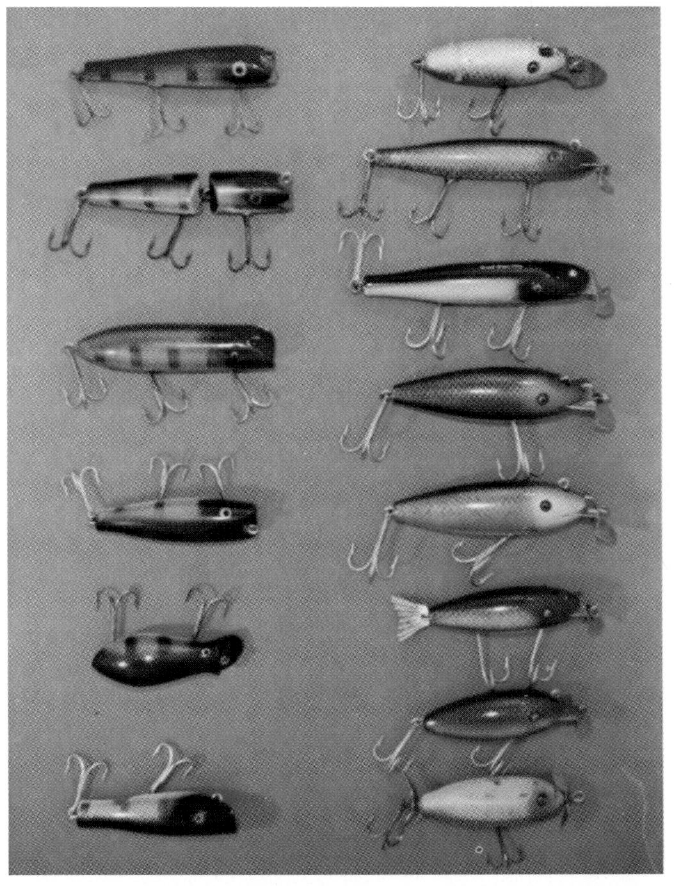

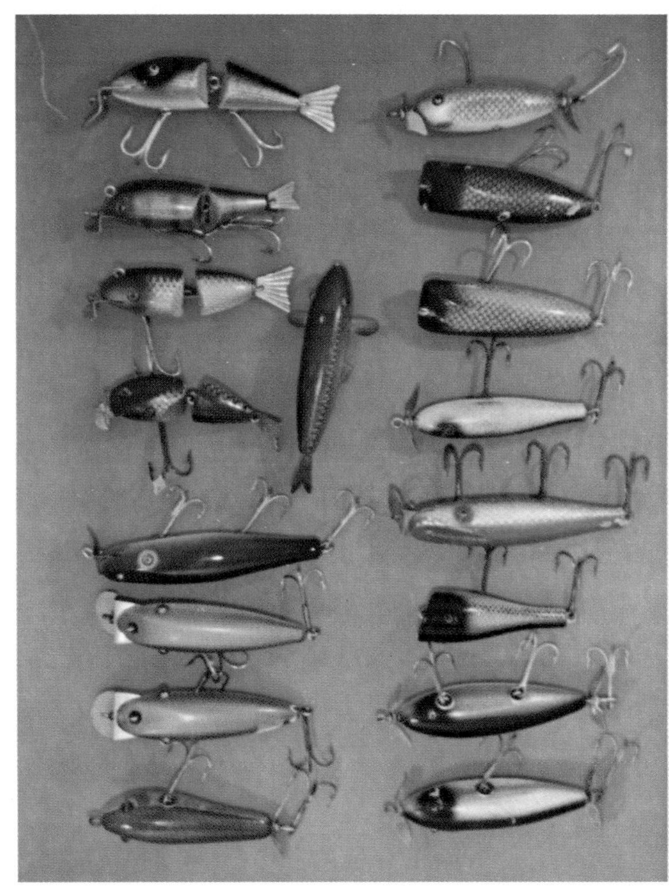

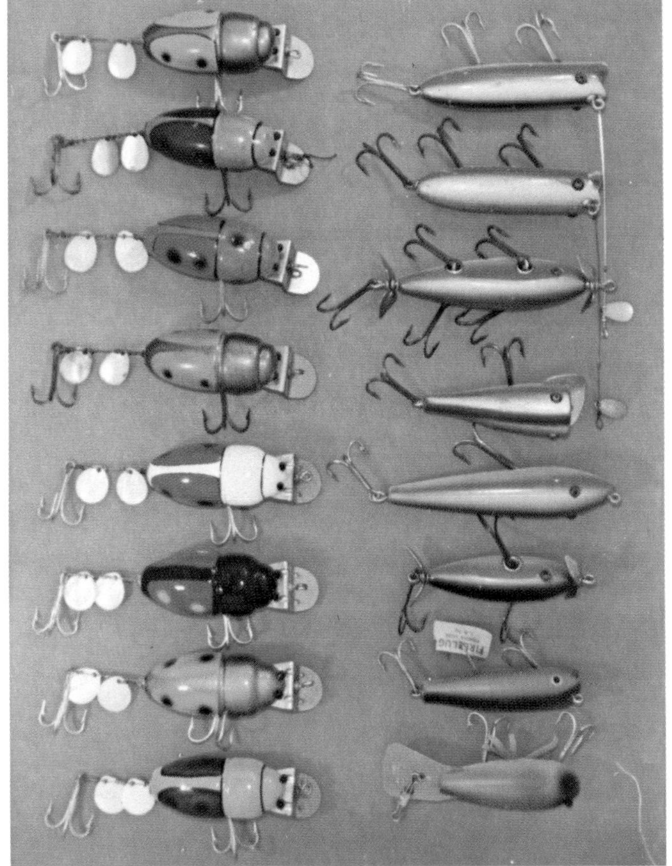

TOP LEFT: **CREEK CHUB PATTERNS.** *Illustrates various types of scale finishes found.*

TOP RIGHT: **CREEK CHUB PATTERNS.** *Bottom four lures in left row are four types of finishes found without scale pattern. The remainder are scale finish types to be found.*

BOTTOM LEFT: **CREEK CHUB PATTERN.** *Right row illustrates several rainbow type patterns to be found. Left row is of all patterns so far found on the "Beetle".*

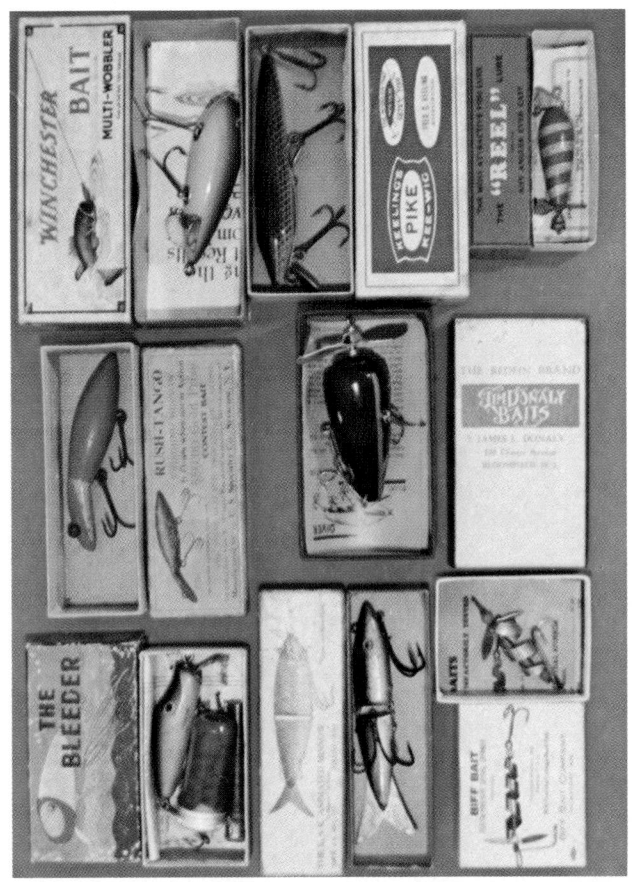

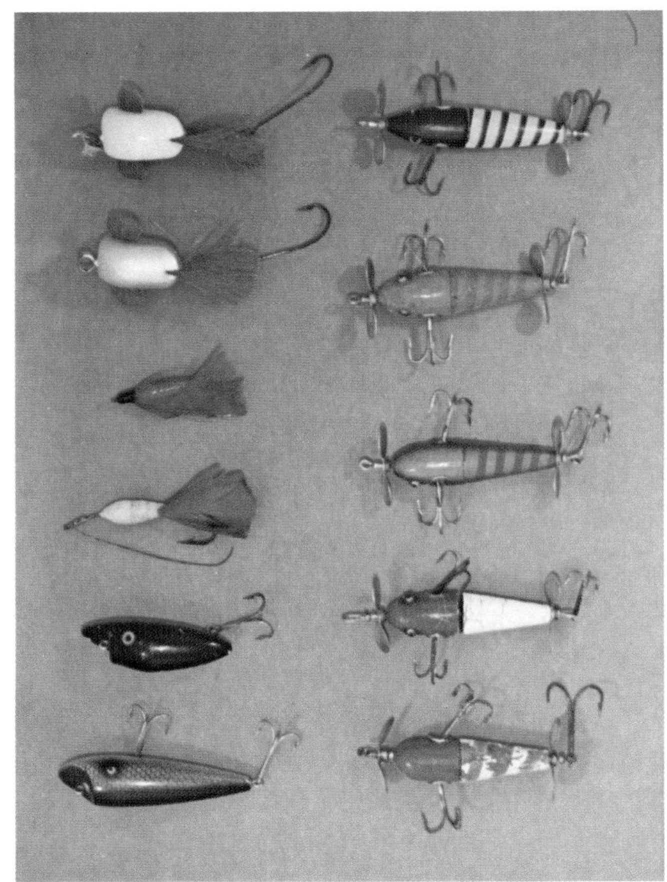

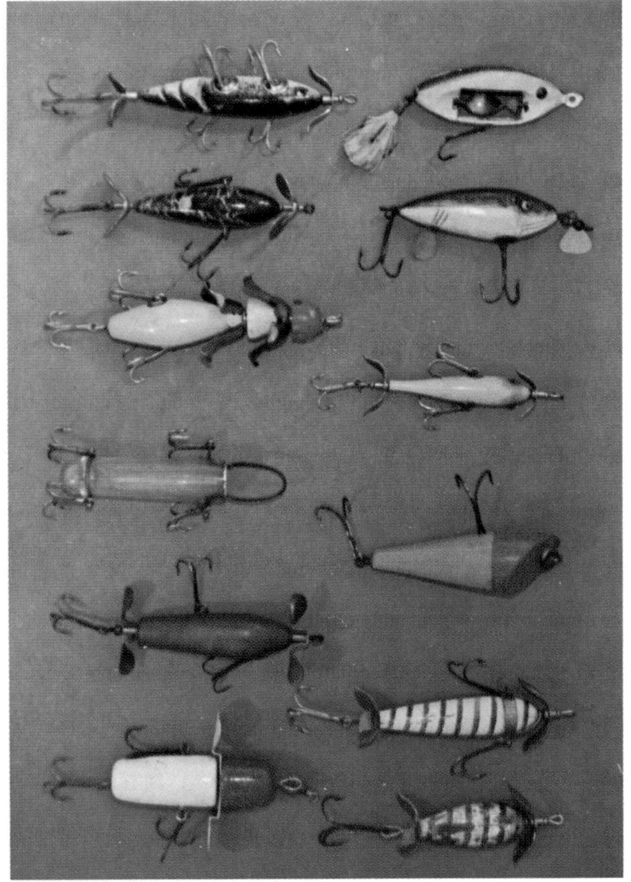

TOP LEFT: Assorted lures in original boxes.

TOP RIGHT: Bottom two lures in left row are **MOONLIGHT BAIT COMPANY** *products. Remaining four are from* **JAMISON**. *Right Row: All are* **CHARMER MINNOWS**.

BOTTOM LEFT: Left row, top to bottom: **MICHIGAN LIFE-LIKE; WORDEN** *lure;* **MILLER'S REVERSIBLE MINNOW; DETROIT GLASS MINNOW TUBE; DECKER UNDERWATER;** *and* **DECKER** *surface plug. Right row, top to bottom:* **CHIPEWAH** *from Immel Bait Co.;* **REDFIN MINNOW** *from Donaly;* **NIXON UNDERWATER; ZIG ZAG** *from Moonlight; and two* **CLINTON WILT MFG. CO.** *lures.*

SOUTH BEND PATTERNS. *Assorted styles to be found.*

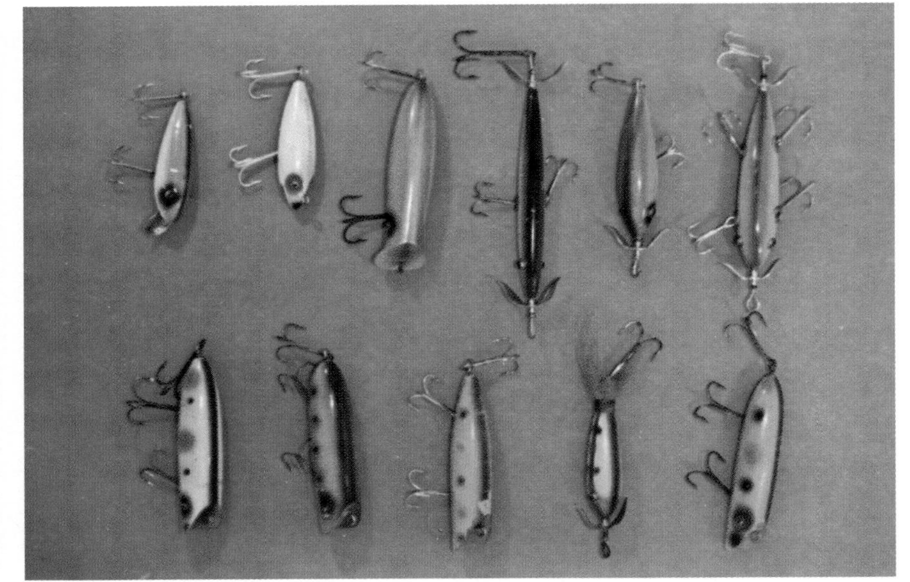

SOUTH BEND PATTERNS. *Assorted spot and rainbow type styles.*

TOP ROW: **RUSH TANGO PATTERNS.** *Bottom Row: First five illustrate* **MEDLEY'S** *Wiggly Crawfish paint styles. Last three are typical* **KEELING** *paint patterns.*

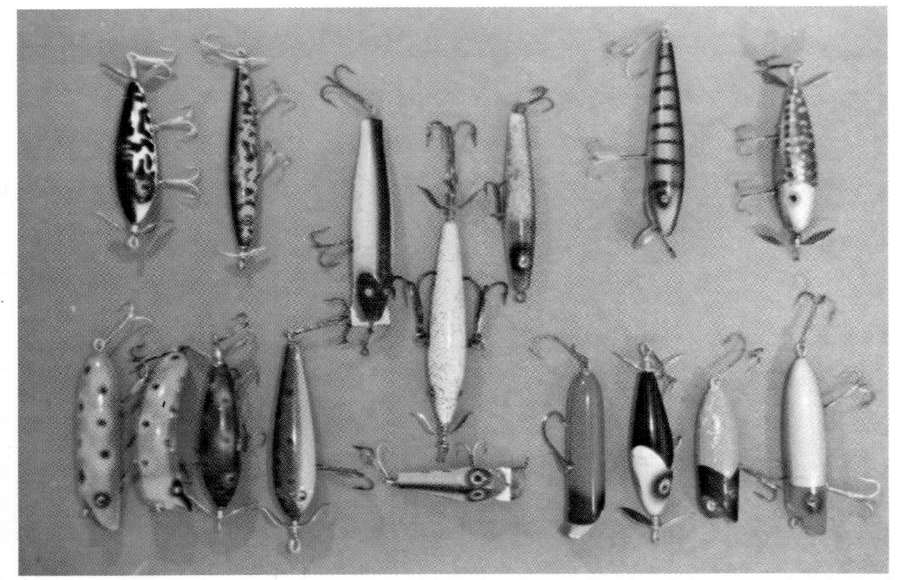

SOUTH BEND PATTERNS. *Types of head paint styles (straight, arrowhead, and blended), glitter styles, spots and frog spots, and miscellaneous.*

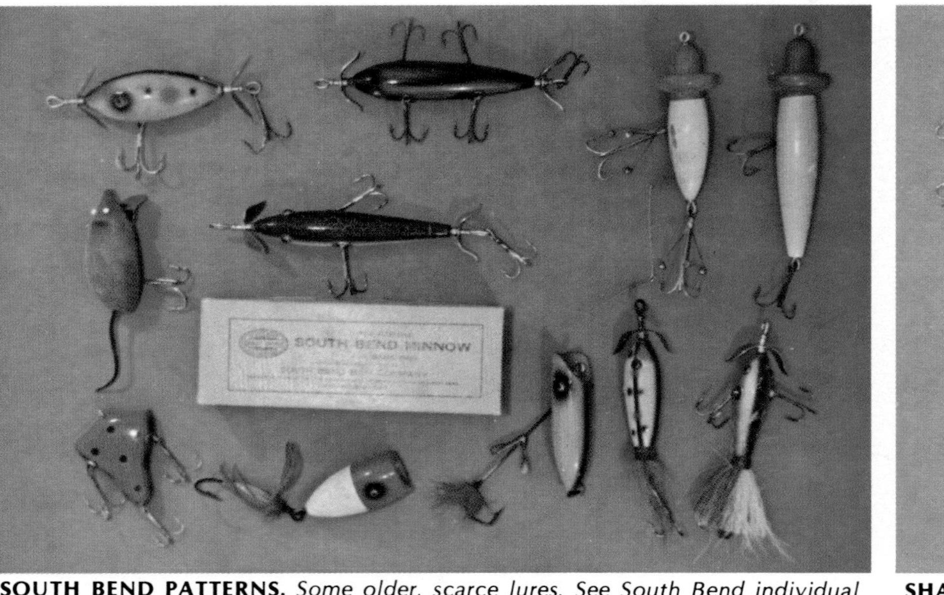

SOUTH BEND PATTERNS. *Some older, scarce lures. See South Bend individual plug listing text for identification.*

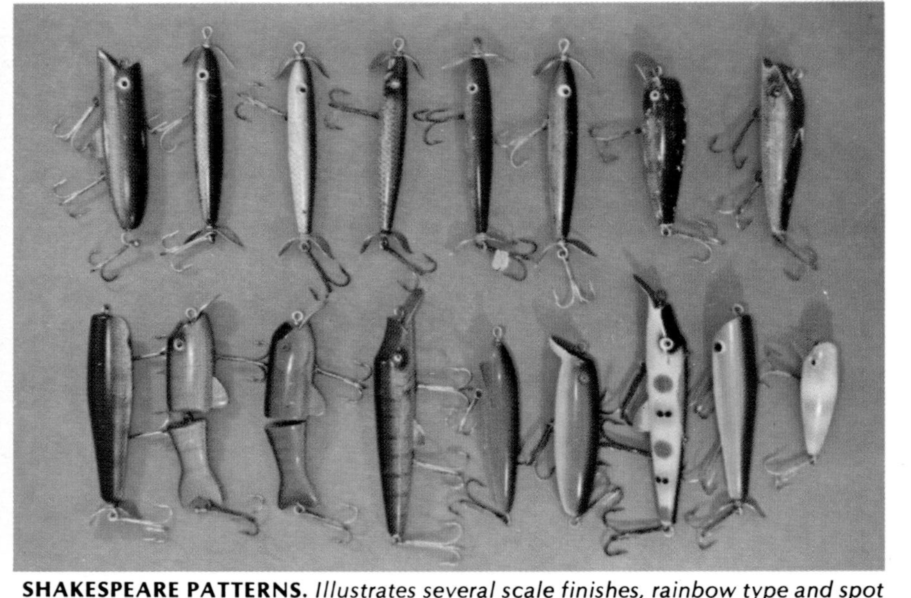

SHAKESPEARE PATTERNS. *Illustrates several scale finishes, rainbow type and spot color patterns.*

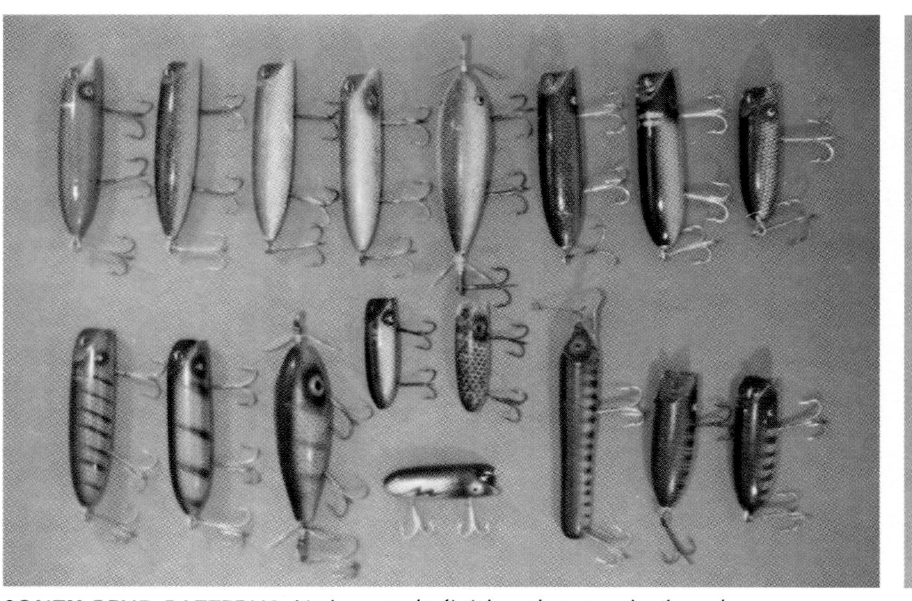

SOUTH BEND PATTERNS. *Various scale finishes that may be found.*

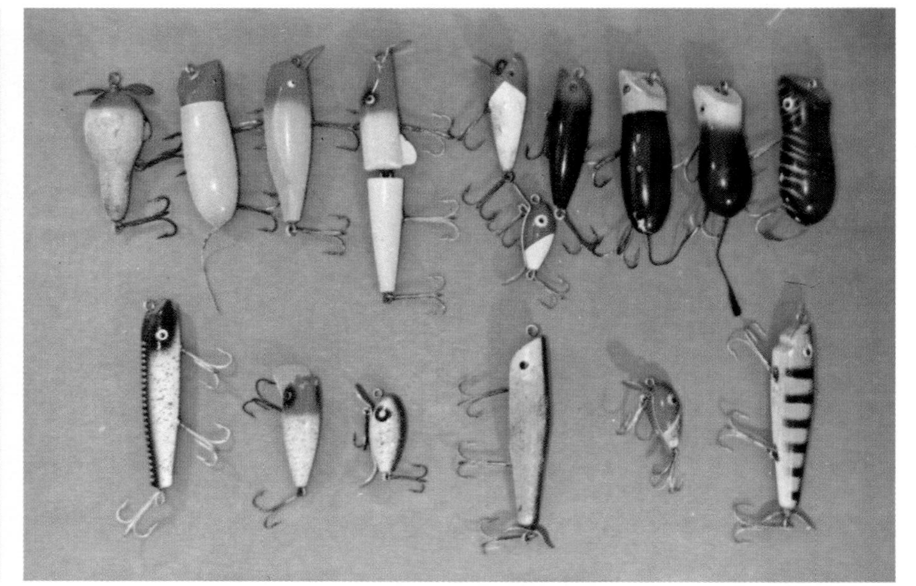

SHAKESPEARE PATTERNS. *Red and white, black and white, and other assorted styles including those found with glitter.*

TOP to BOTTOM

A Shakespeare No. 33 RHODES WOODEN MINNOW.

Slim Sweeney's TWINMINNOW.

A glass eyed Shakespeare DARTING SHRIMP.

THE MERMAID by Shakespeare.

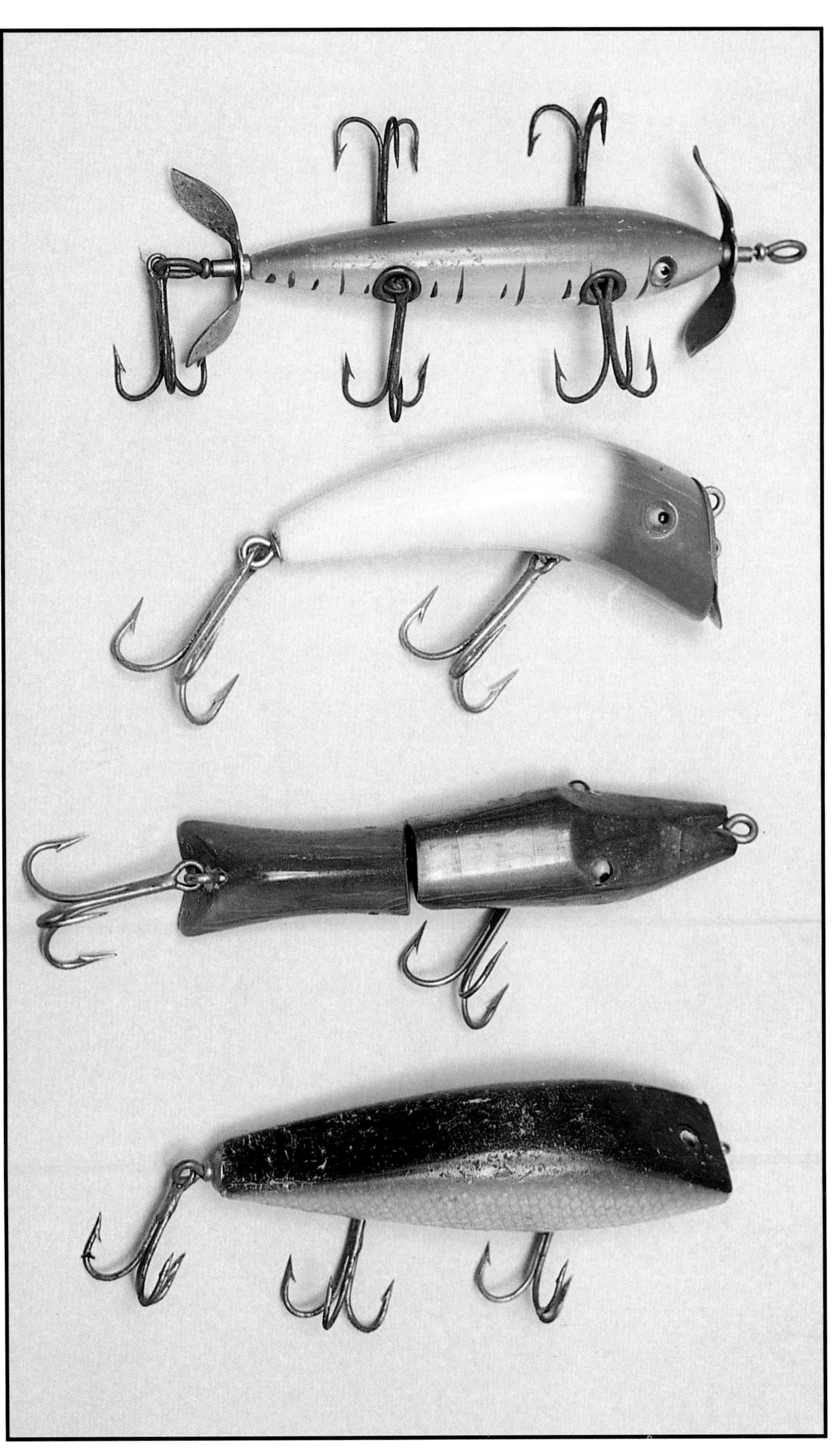

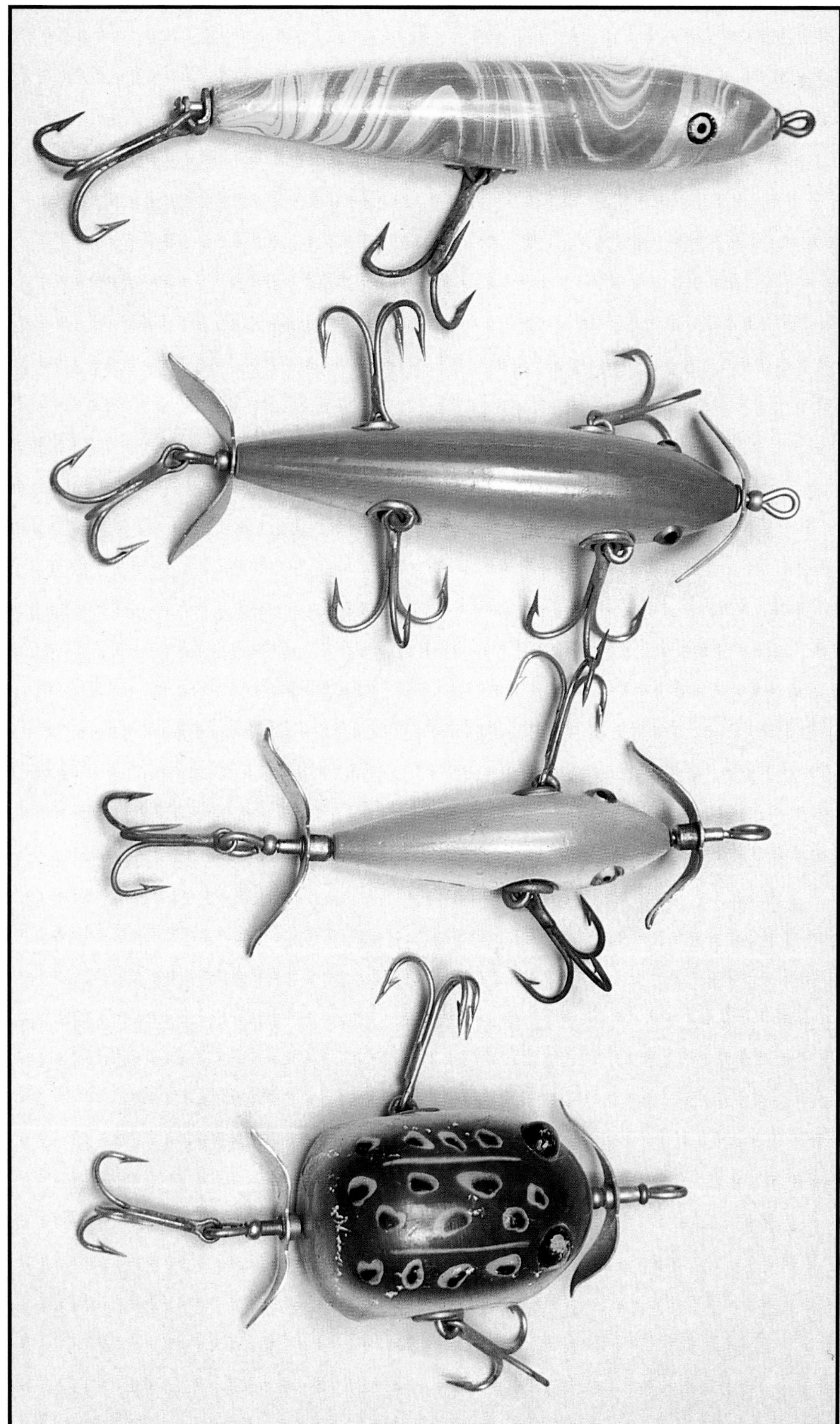

TOP to BOTTOM

A glass eyed Pflueger BALLERINA #5400 Series.

A Pflueger 5 hook NEVERFAIL #3100 Series.

A Pflueger 3 hook NEVERFAIL #3100 Series.

A Pflueger Kent Frog.

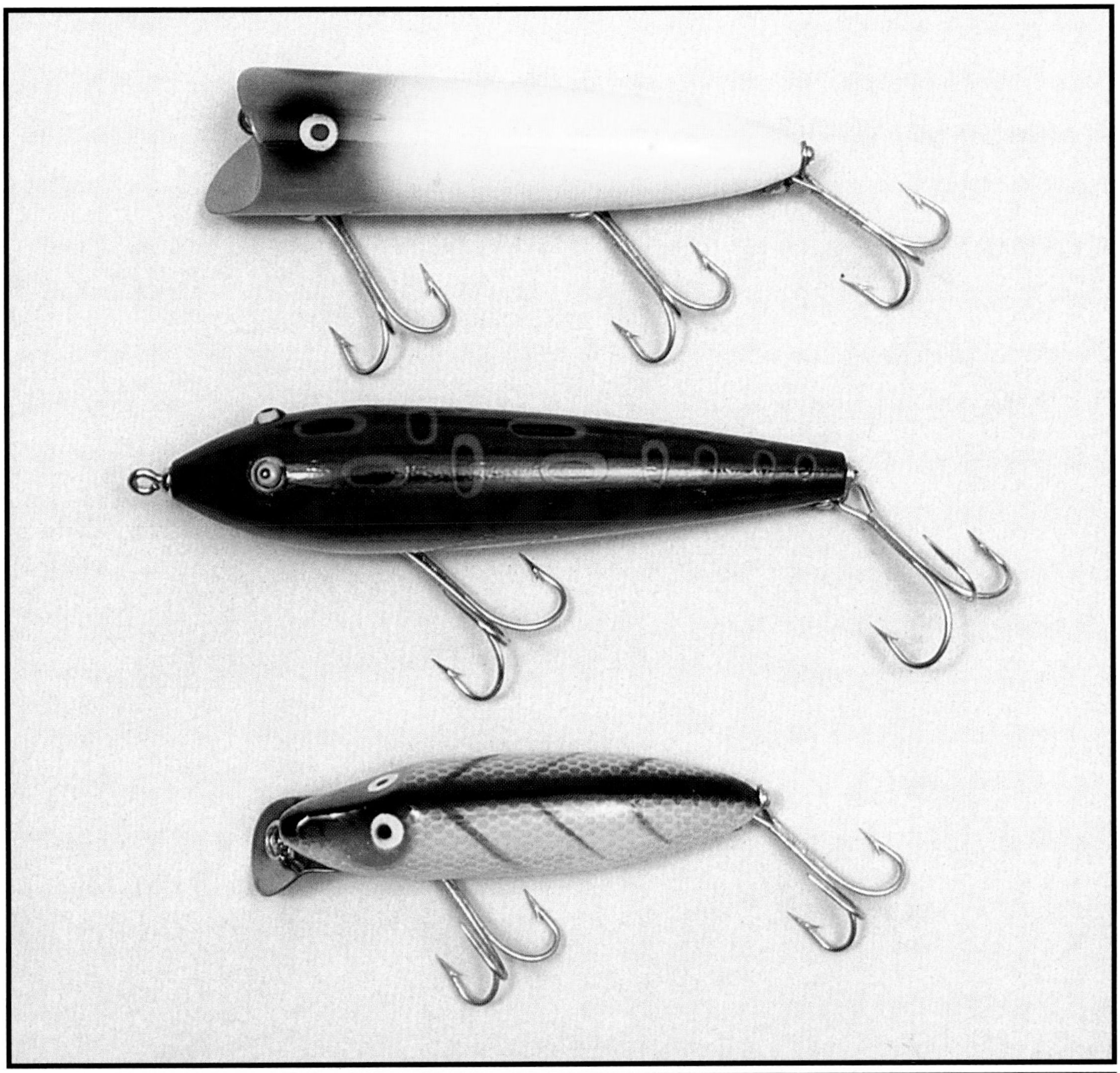

TOP to BOTTOM

This LUCKY-13 is part of a set of lures reissued in wood in 1994 by PRADCO, the present owner of Heddon. The issue was called the Centennial Edition and limited to 10,000. They are identified by a stenciled belly.

This RIVER RUNT is part of a set of lures reissued in wood in 1994 by PRADCO, the present owner of Heddon. The issue was called the Centennial Edition and limited to 10,000. They are identified by a stencil on the belly.

A Centennial Edition wooden ZARAGOSSA issued by PRADCO, the present owner of Heddon, in a limited edition of 10,000 in 1994. They are marked as such on the belly.

A Creek Chub Bait Company limited edition, wooden reissue of the Series #2000 DARTER. This lure was released in 1993 by PRADCO, the present owner of the Creek Chub Company.

A Creek Chub Bait Company wooden Wiggle Fish reissue. It was released by PRADCO, the present owner of the Creek Chub Company.

TOP to BOTTOM

This is a 4 7/8" Heddon EXPERT. This is the first use of the frog finish so the lure can be dated c1915. The Heddon imprint appears on both sides of the collar and the hook hardware is an L-rig.

A 5" Heddon EXPERT with a three flange collar, cup and screw eye hook hardware and a metal tail cap.

This is a 4 7/8" Heddon EXPERT. This is the first use of the frog finish so the lure can be dated c1915. The Heddon imprint appears on both sides of the collar and the hook hardware is an L-rig.

This is a 4 7/8" Heddon EXPERT. The Heddon imprint appears on both sides of the collar and the hook hardware is an L-rig.

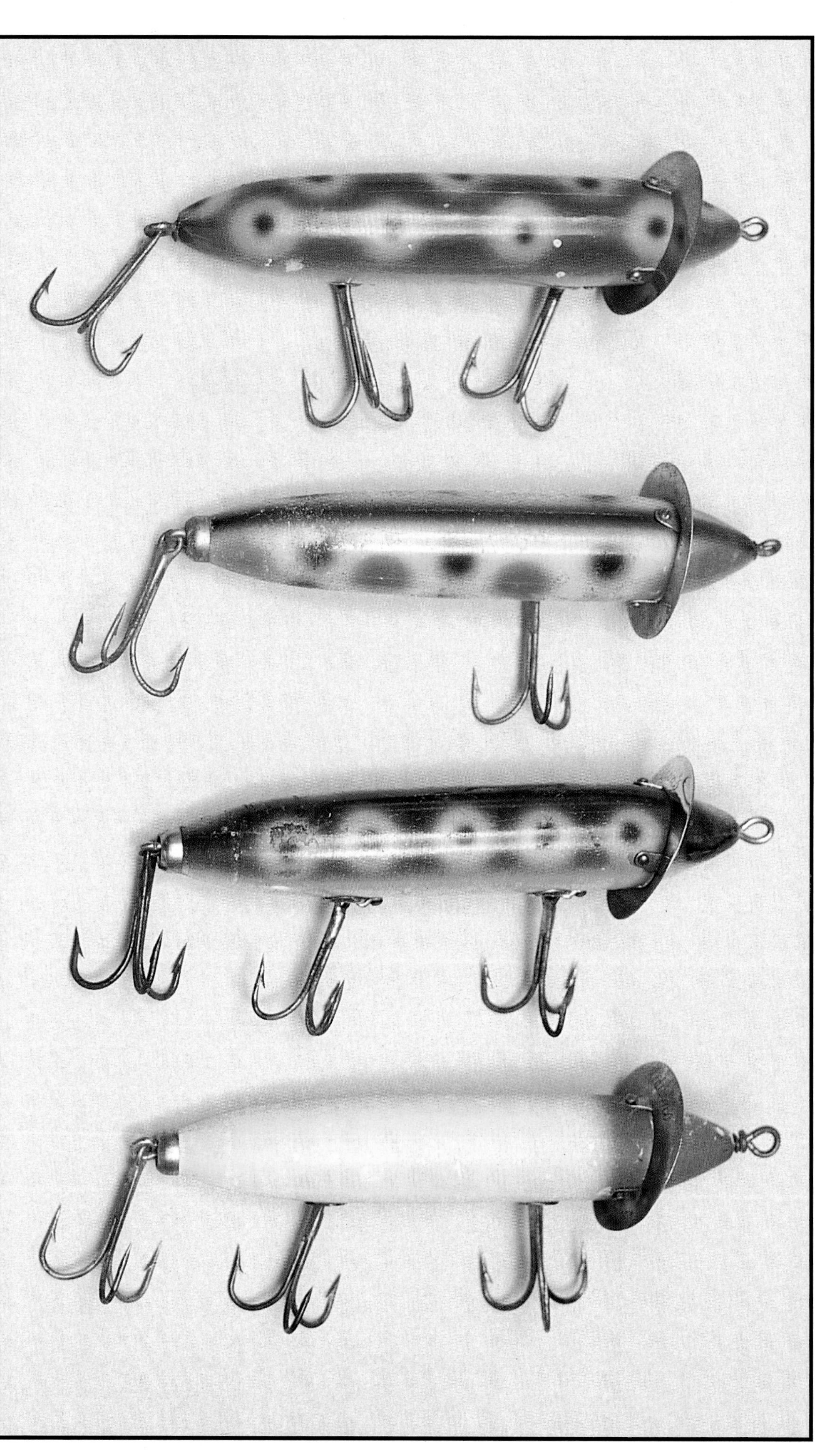

TOP to BOTTOM

A Heddon Series #6000 TAD POLLY with glass eyes, marked, bell shape metal face plane and Game Fisher type line tie. It has the L-rig hook hardware.

Heddon #1800 Series CRAB WIGGLER with glass eyes, "0" type collar and L-rig hook hardware.

A 1966 Heddon commemorative wood body reissue of the VAMP. It has painted eyes and one-piece surface hook hardware. Marked "Heddon Wood Original Classic" on the belly.

A Heddon Series #7300 JOINTED VAMP with glass eyes, L-rig hook hangers and the Stolley patent style rear hook hanger.

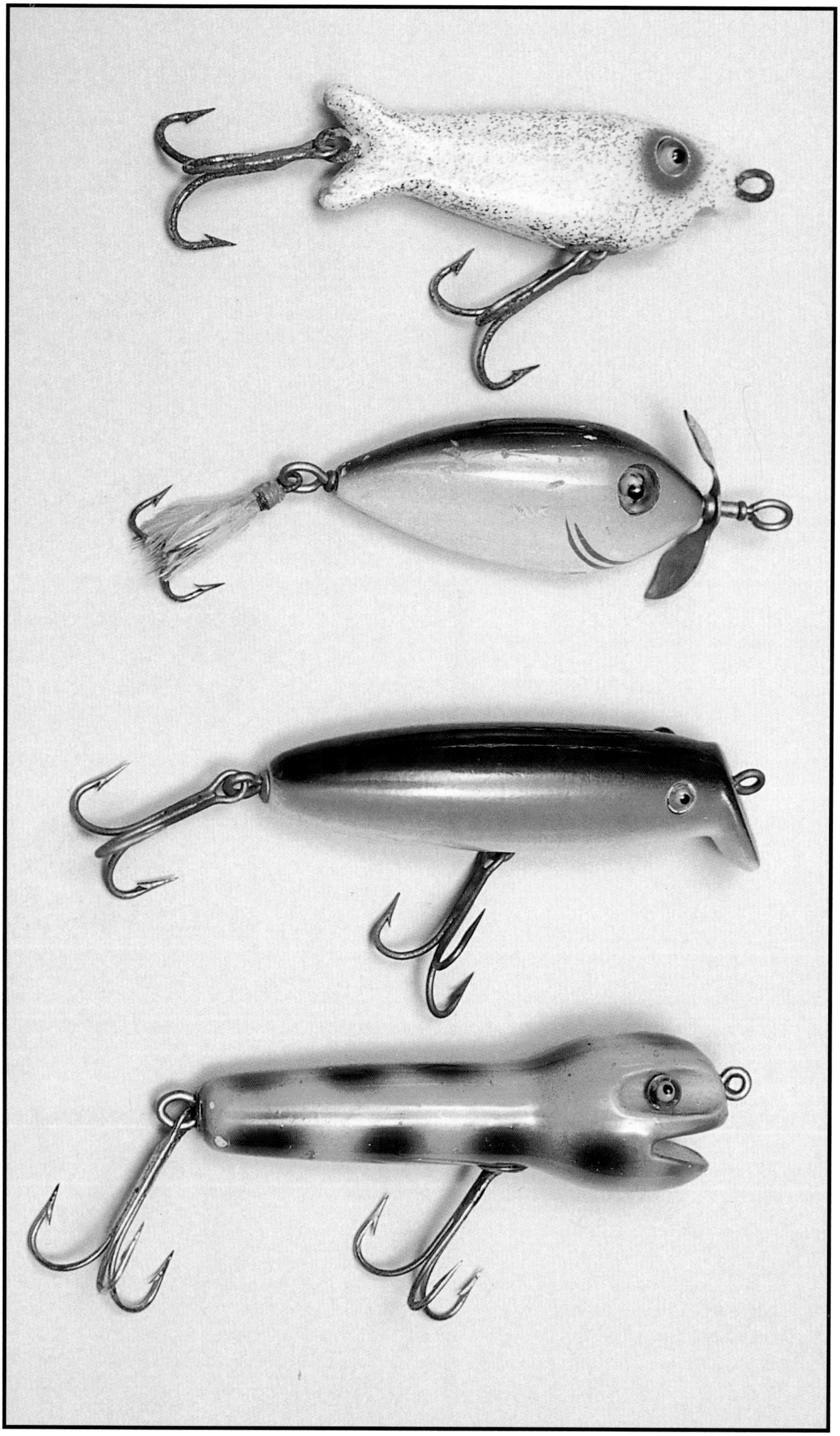

A Shakespeare SARDINIA Salt Water Minnow #7212. The glass eyes peg this as the oldest model.

A PUNKIN-SEED by Shakespeare. This particular one is a sinking model with no belly hook. It has glass eyes and the early two hump propeller spinner.

A Shakespeare Jim Dandy SPOON BILL WOBBLER.

A Shakespeare glass eyed lure shaped just like their FROG SKIN BAIT except with a painted finish instead of the frog skin normally found.

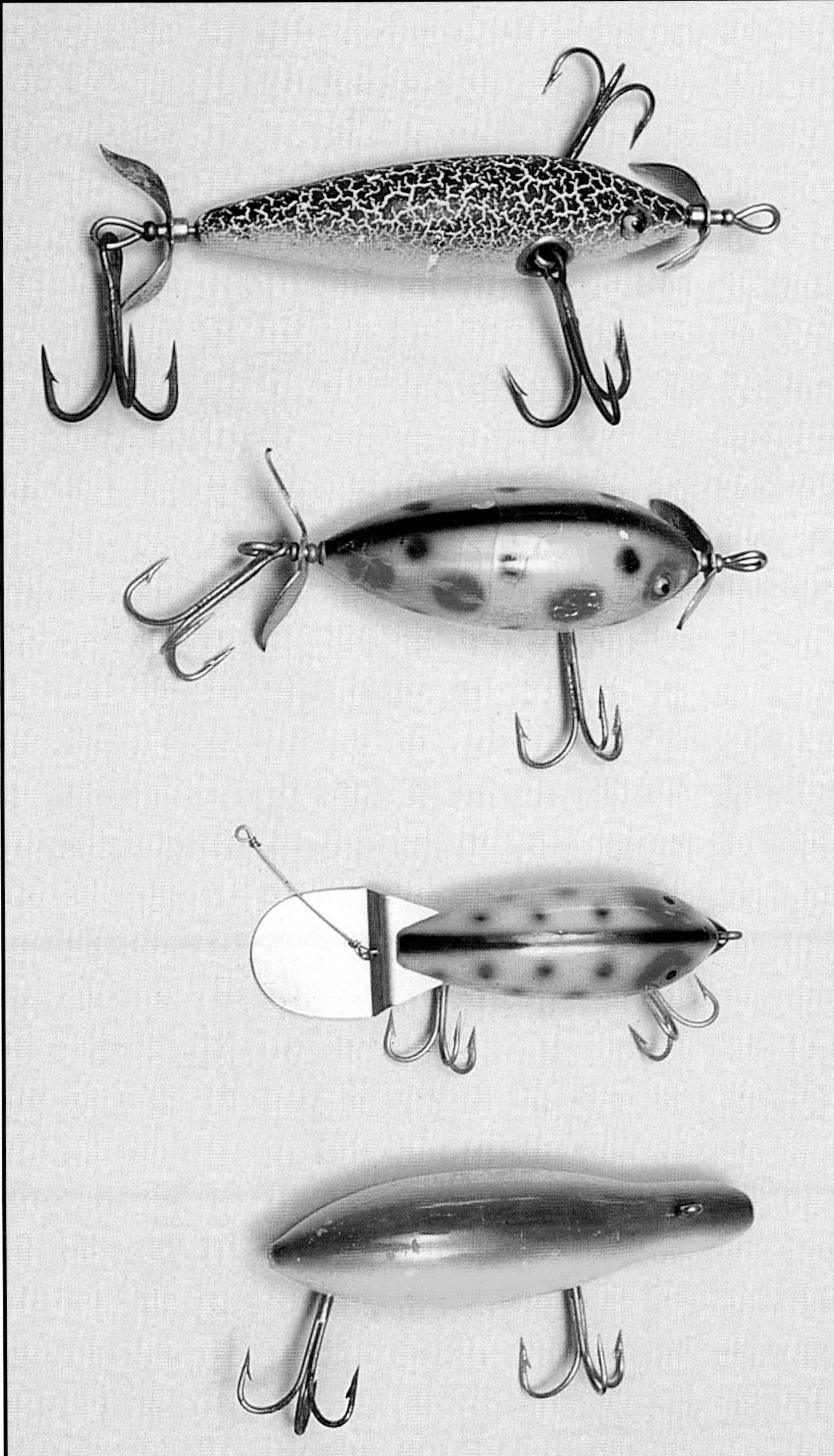

TOP to BOTTOM

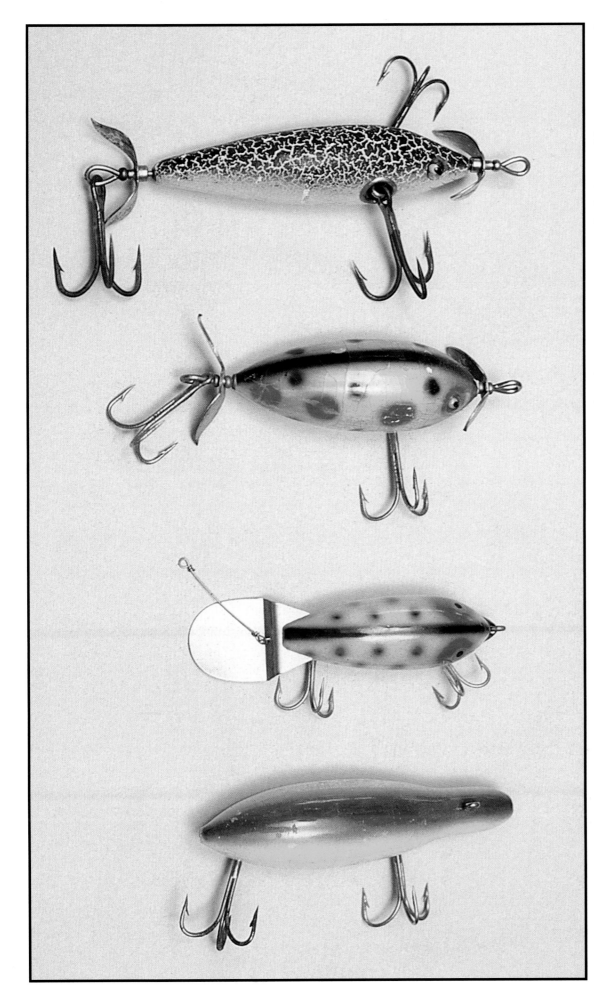

A #175 Series by Heddon. It has marked propeller spinners, glass eyes and large cup and screw *hook* hardware.

A Heddon SURFACE MINNOW with glass eyes.

A Heddon GO-DEEPER CRAB Series #D1900 with painted eyes.

A "Bottle Nose" TAD POLLY by Heddon.

TOP to BOTTOM

A Heddon #401 Rainbow finish DOWAGIAC MINNOW, c1908.

A Heddon SOS WOUNDED MINNOW, Series #140 with glass eyes and the two-piece Flap rig side hook hardware.

A Heddon Series #120 TORPEDO with glass eyes.

LEFT to RIGHT

A Heddon CRAZY CRAWLER with Donaly wing hardware and Donaly marked flapper wings.

This is a normally configured Heddon CRAZY CRAWLER with a very scarce color finish.

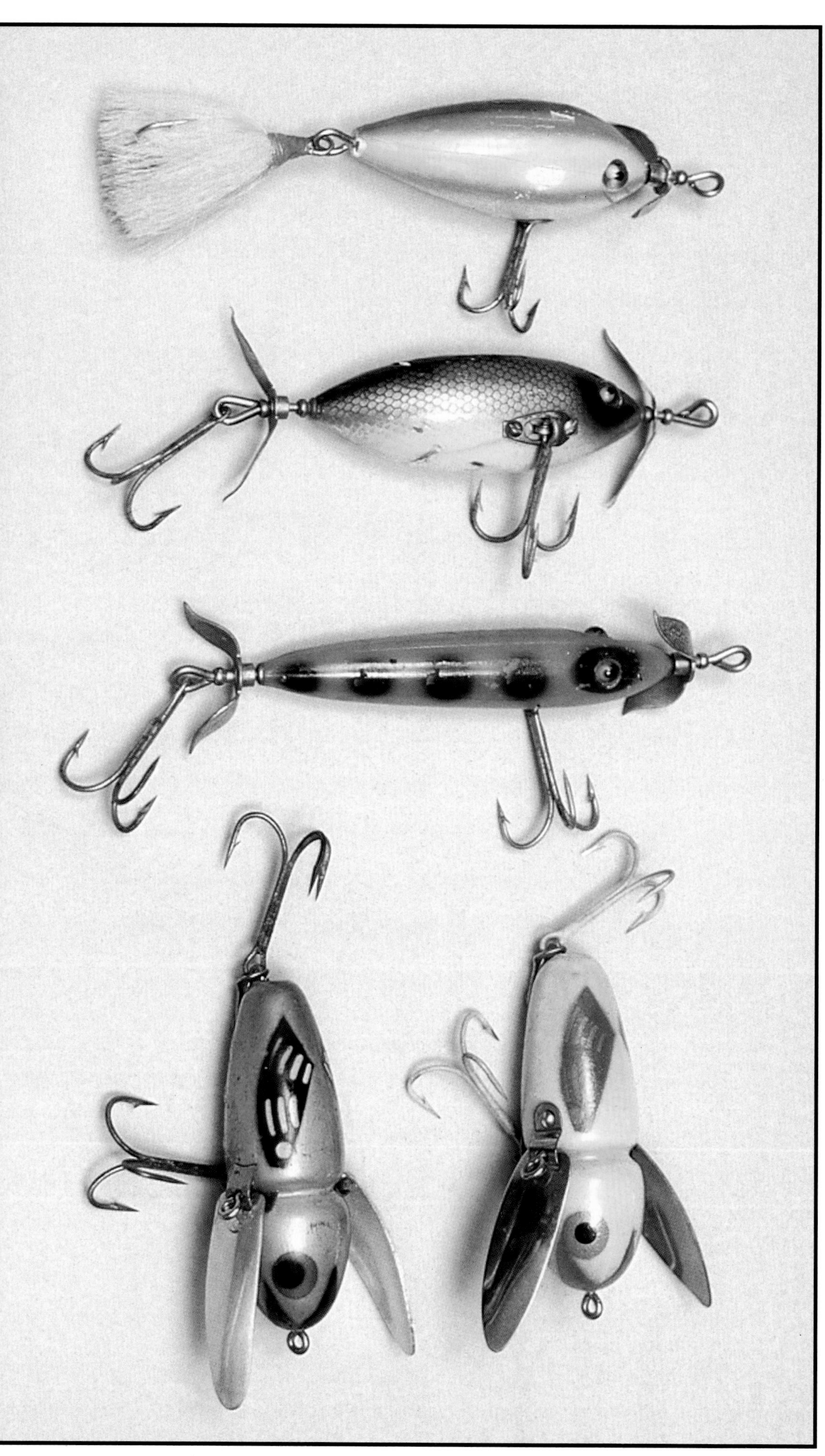

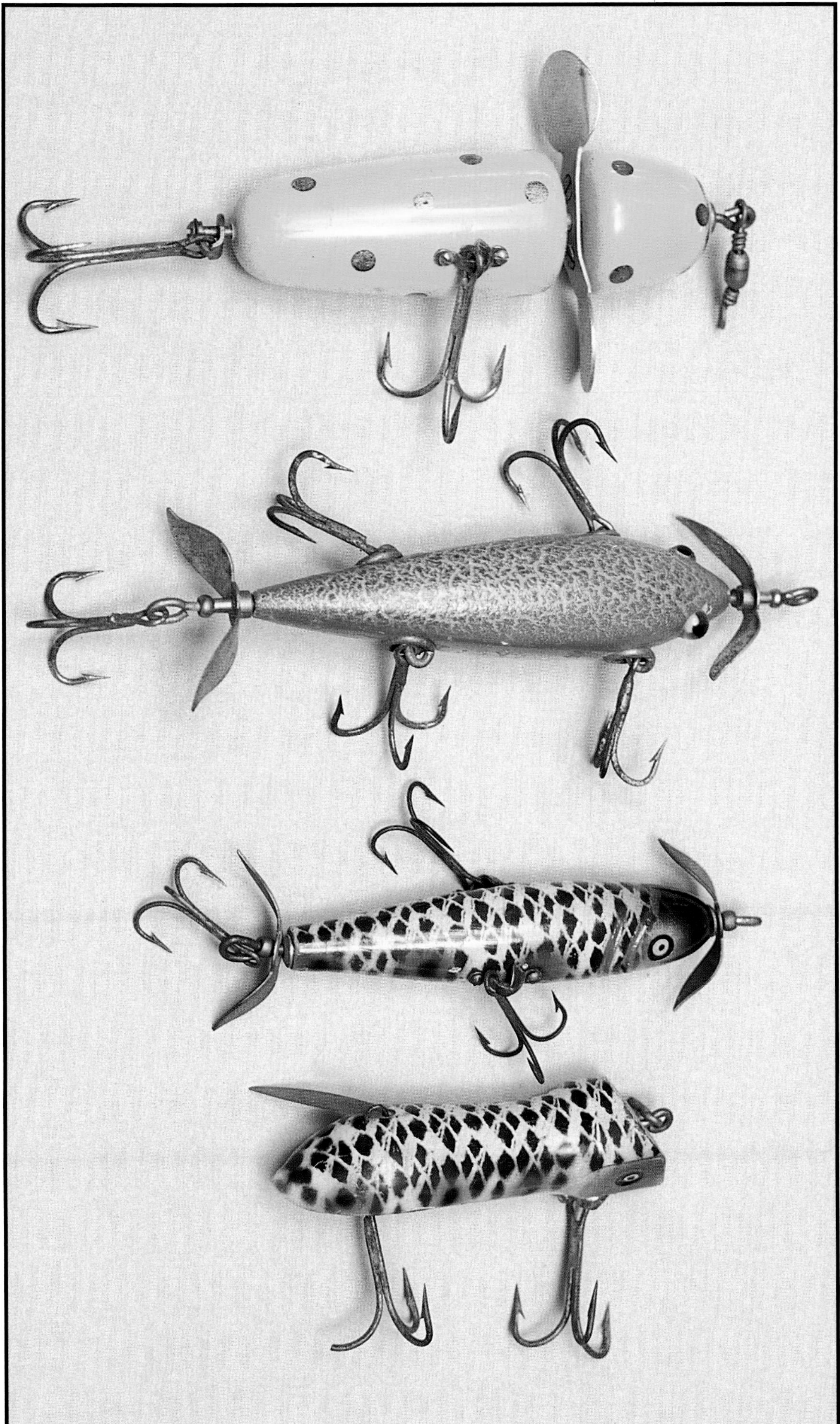

TOP to BOTTOM

A fine example of a Pflueger GLOBE.

A glass eyed Pflueger MONARCH MINNOW.

A Pflueger NEVERFAIL with painted eyes and their Natural Frog, Scale finish and surface hardware.

A Pflueger WIZARD WIGGLER with painted eyes and their Natural Frog, Scale finish and surface hardware.

TOP to BOTTOM

A TURNER CASTING BAIT measuring 4 1/8".

Medley's WIGGLY CRAWFISH.

LAKE GEORGE FLOATER.

Pepper ROMAN SPIDER.

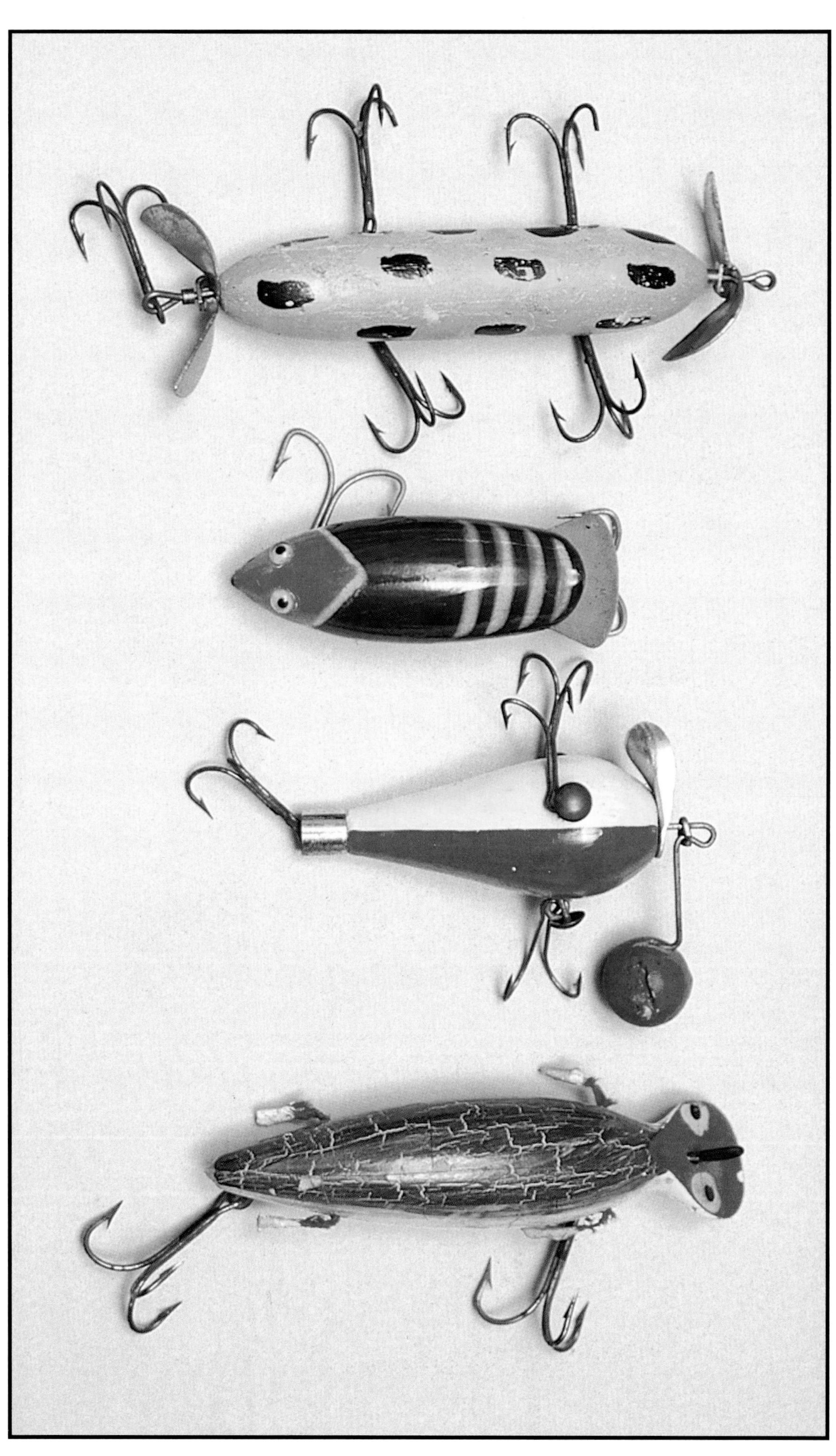

TOP to BOTTOM

A VANN-CLAY MINNOW, c1928, measuring 3 1/2".

The HAYNES MAGNET, c1908, W.B. Haynes, Akron, Ohio.

SCHOONIE'S SCOOTER, measures 4 1/2", patented in 1916 by John Ray Schoonmanker of Kalamazoo, Michigan.

This interesting lure remains unknown as to name and origins. It measures 4", has grooves carved along its back from the head rearward about one half way back. Its face is a rather complicated shade and has a polished metal plate conforming to the shape.

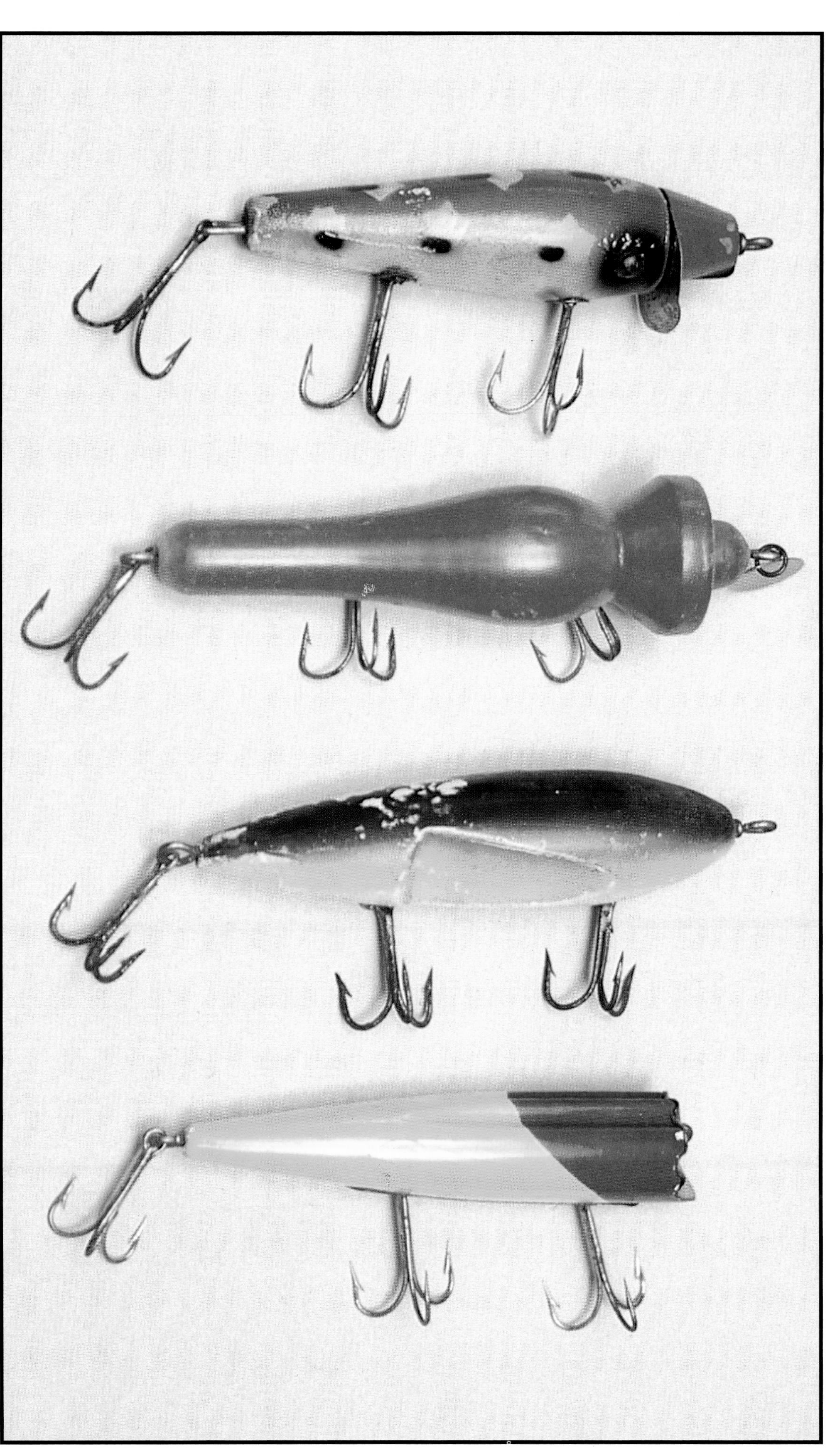

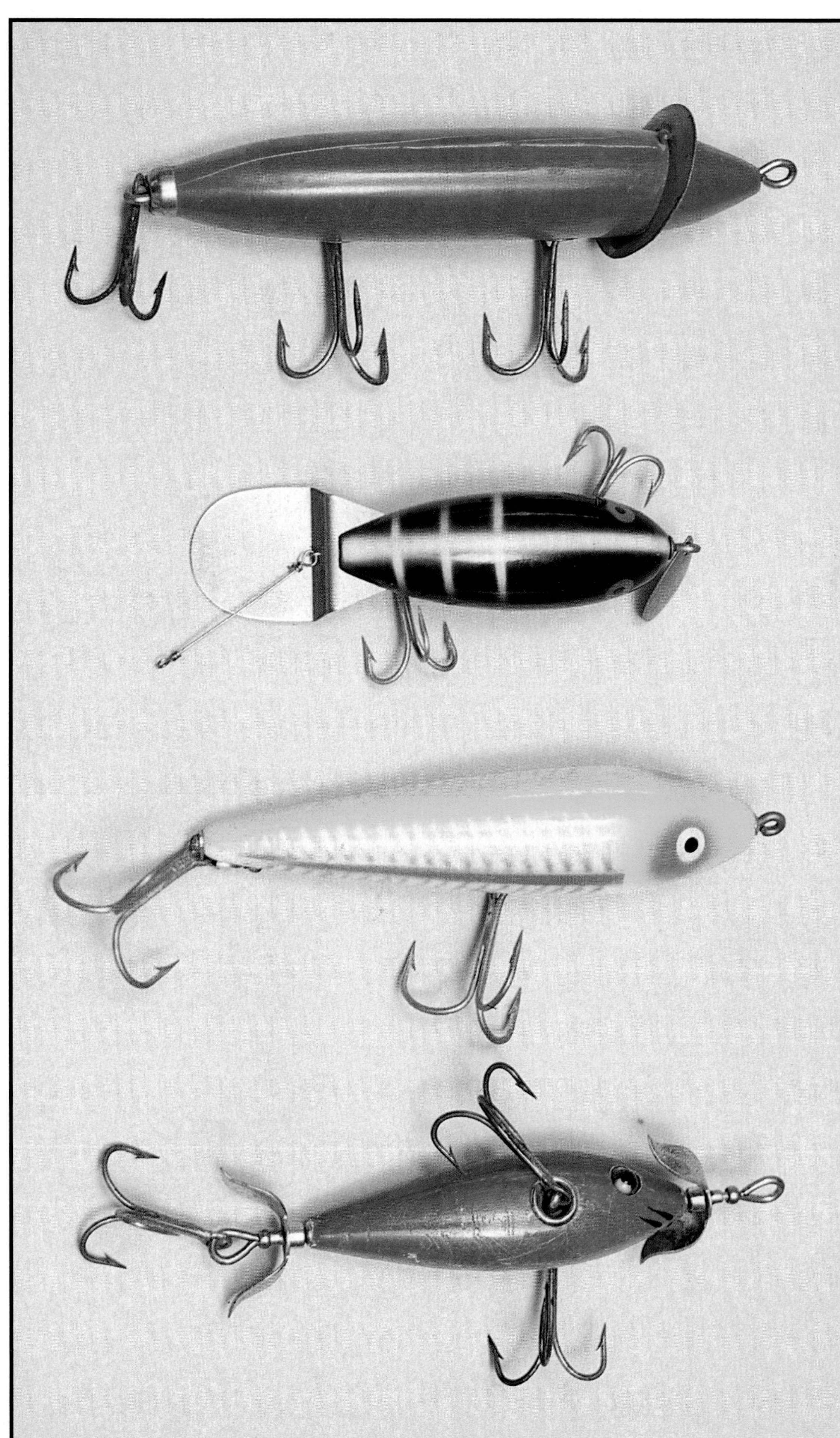

TOP to BOTTOM

A 4 3/4" classic Heddon EXPERT. It has a two pin collar attachment, a very deep almost cone shaped cup in the belly hook hanger and a tail hook insert.

A Heddon Series #D1900 GO-DEEPER CRAB measuring 3 1/2". The metal dive plane reads *Heddon Crab*.

A Heddon Series #6500 ZARAGOSSA marked *Heddon Wood Original Classic* on the belly. Heddon reissued this lure in wood in 1965 as a commemorative.

A Heddon #100 DOWAGIAC MINNOW with cup and screw eye belly hanger and the big propeller style with blade marked *Heddon Dowagiac*.

HOLLOWHEAD

R-K Tackle Company — Grand Rapids, Michigan

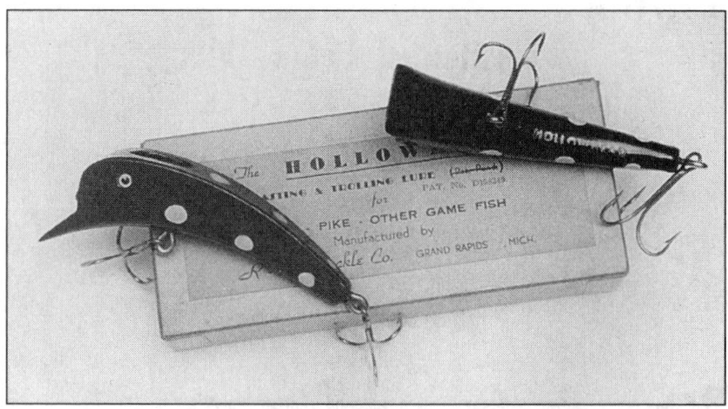

Note the hole in the top to the lure. The lure is made of wood but appears to be of fairly late vintage. Simple screw eye hook hangers.

The company operated only a short time (1948-1951). The name is derived from the first names of the owners, Ray and Kay Wiinika. The lures were made in only four colors. It is reported that several thousand were produced in the 3-4 years of operation. Collector value range: $10-$25.

THE HOODLER

Gilmore Tackle Company — Lurton, Arkansas

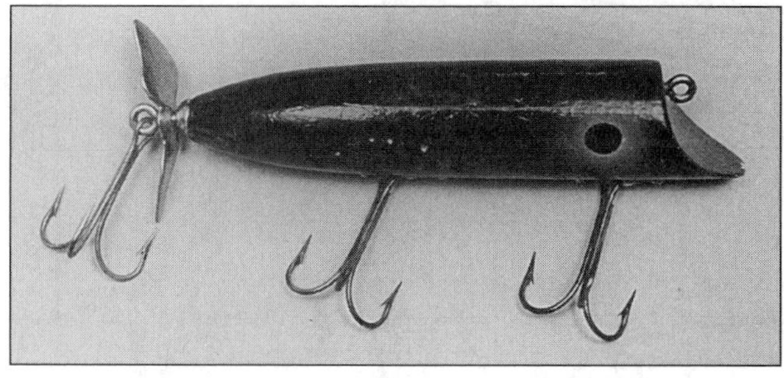

This 4" wooden lure has a floppy tail-mounted propeller spinner, one-piece surface hook hanger and painted eyes. I found no advertising fo̧r the company nor did I turn up any catalog listings for this company. Collector value range: $5-$12.

HOOKZEM

Hookzem Bait Company — Chicago, Illinois

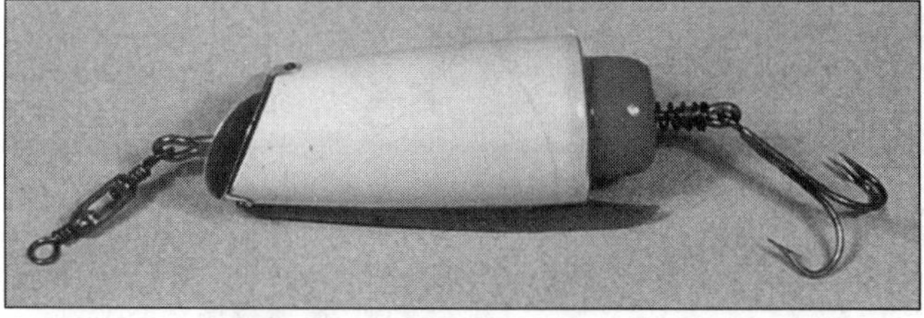

The photo shows this 3" lure in the sprung condition. When fished, the treble hook shank and hanger hardware is pushed up into the lure with the barbs against the body. This renders the lure weedless. When the fish bites down on the lure hitting the metal trigger on the belly, the hook snaps out. The lure was patented by Henry L. Gottschalk in 1919. Collector value range: $250-$400.

HOOTENANNA

The Montpelier Bait Co.,
a division of Manta-Ray Company, Inc. — Montpelier, Ohio

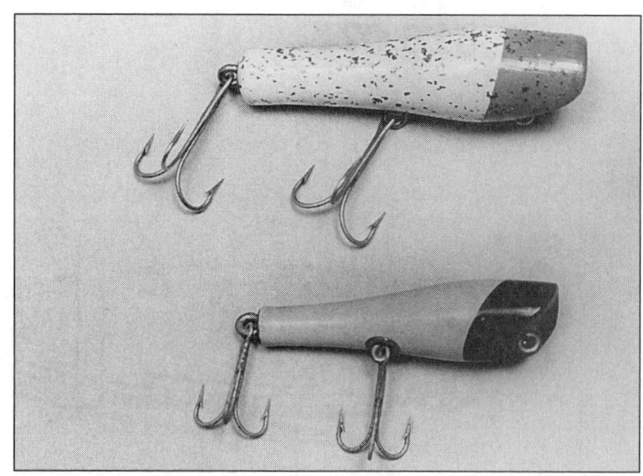

A c. 1934 advertisement by the Montpelier Company illustrated the lure and invited the reader to "Choose colors and styles from our handsome new catalog." Two years later, in 1936, the identical ad appeared. I am still looking for a copy of that catalog. I do have a copy of a 1977 brochure that says "Nationally famous since 1922." They were still being made of wood (northern Michigan white cedar) at the time and the brochure goes on to say the lures were finished with six coats of lacquer. The two in the previous photo represent two to the three sizes, but the sizes given were in weight, not length, 5/8 oz., 1/2 oz., and 1/4 oz. Collector value range: $12-$24.

COLOR OR FINISH: "Fishscale," blue back with white belly and red throat, white, red head, glitter, white with red throat and glitter, white with black head with cat eyes and glitter, yellow with black head, dark green with red head, white collar and glitter, cream with red head and cat eyes, solid black, blue/green back with white belly, red throat and glitter, "gray ghost" (gray with black head and cat eyes), black with white head, black with yellow head with white collar and cat eyes, "frog")dark green with light green belly, red head and cat eyes).

HOUSER HELL DIVER

The House of Houser — St. Louis, Missouri

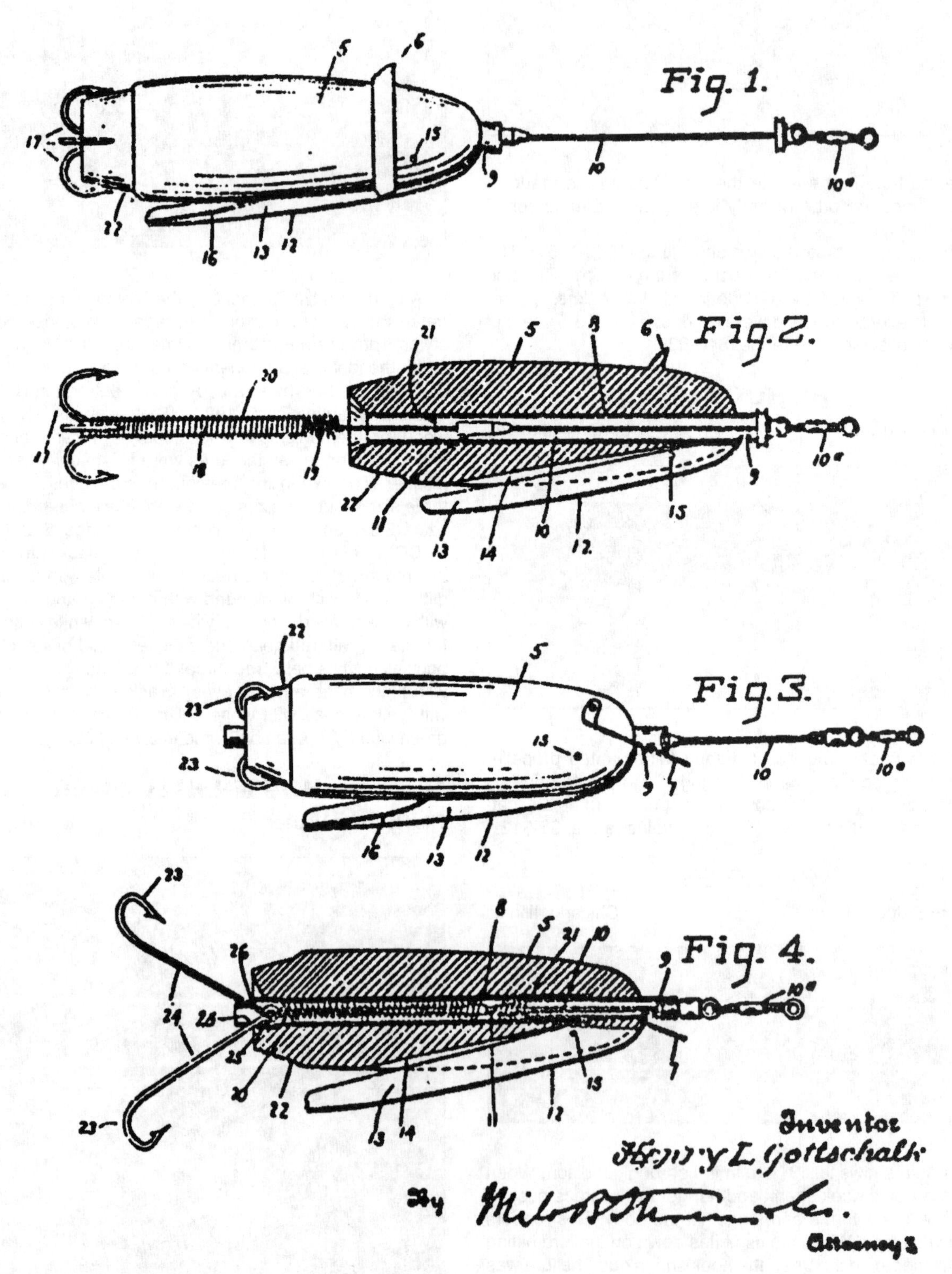

Gottschalk's 1919 patent drawing for the HOOKZEM. Photo courtesy Jim Muma.

The metal body of this spinner bait measures 1-1/4" and the lure overall, 4". There is no information beyond what the box provided. Note that the illustration of the lure on the box is upside down. The era is thought to be that of the late 1940s. Collector value range: $10-$20.

THE HOSMER MECHANICAL FROGGIE

J.D. Hosmer Company — Dearborn, Michigan

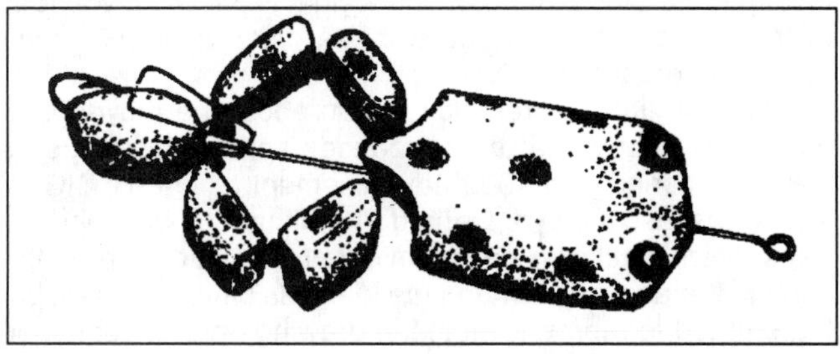

"IT FLOATS. ITS WEEDLESS. IT GETS 'EM." That's what it says on the box this clever lure came in. John D. Hosmer of Dearborn, Michigan began making them in the late 1920s and began making them commercially when, as the familiar story goes, they came into such demand by fishing buddies and others in his area. That was sometime in the early to mid-1930s. He crafted and painted them all himself. It is thought that he made only about 200 of them in the two years he was in business. It also is thought by some that the number could be higher. The wood components were carved from balsa, about 5-1/4" in length when assembled and had three weedless hooks, one at the feet and two on the belly. The colors available were yellow, green, silver and black with green being the most common. The frog spots were painted with a contrasting outer edge. Collector value range: $1,500-$2,500.

HOWE'S VACUUM BAITS

The Vacuum Bait Company — North Manchester, Indiana

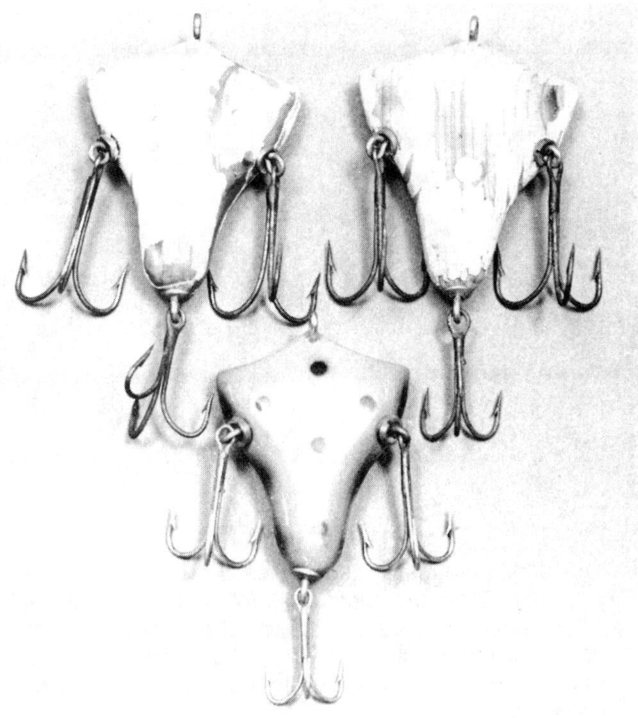

Of this wooden lure an old ad folder says "The development of the bait has been the result of years of experience in bass fishing by Professor Howe, of who it has often been said, can catch bass any time...". As you can see by the accompanying photo, the lure had a curious shape. One can only wonder about the curious name as well. The shape of the lure is suspiciously the same shape of some of the old upright vacuum cleaners of the same era, but an early promotional brochure attributes the name to the creation of a *vacuum* when reeled in rapidly, causing a spray over the top of the lure. It was a wooden surface plug with three swiveling treble hooks. These swivels were of great import to the designer and company as there was almost invariable use in all illustrations of a small hand pointing to them with the statement: "See that Swivel!" They originally came in a tin box.

The company was incorporated in 1909 in North Manchester, Indiana by Francis (Frank) O. Howe (Professor Howe), Charles W. Olinger and Jonas W. Warvel. The lure was developed by Howe. Often referred to as "Professor Howe" in their advertising, he was apparently a well-known student of scientific fishing credited with considerable prowess as a result of intense observation and study of fish, their habits and habitats, but the "professor" moniker is the result of his regular position as a teacher of music at the local Manchester College. Howe filed for his patent in 1908 and was granted it on October 5, 1909. A very important part of the patent was the special swiveling hook hanger mentioned above.

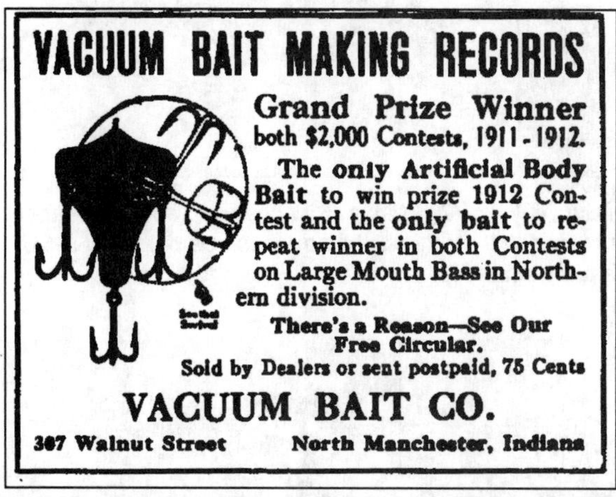

This advertisement from the August, 1913 issue of The Outer's Book magazine refers to the lure winning a $2,000 Grand Prize two years in a row, 1911 and 1912. Think what a prodigious sum of money that was for the time!

The lure was originally made available only in white with red stripes on the belly. A "V" shape or wedge of pork rind was a very popular bait of the time and indeed, early ads for the bait call it an artificial pork rind. The white body with streaks of red simulating marbling of the meat is a good mimic. The original was made in one size, 2 3/8". In 1913 they began making a second, smaller size at 2"and added five new color options. These were red, yellow, rainbow, frog and dragon fly. The red, yellow and rainbow are the most difficult to find.

Sometime around 1920-21, the company was dissolved and/or sold to South Bend. In either case the South Bend Company obtained the patent and the plug shows up in their catalogs in 1921-22. The South Bend version, however, exhibit some differences. The slant on the face is different, the swivels are not always the same as on the original. The most common South Bend version has regular cup and screw eye hook hardware. Many South Bend VACUUM BAITS also have tack-painted eyes or glass eyes. This latter characteristic was never the case with the Howe version. Collector value range: $50-$125. Please turn to the South Bend section for more information.

HUMPY PLUG

Humpy Bait Company — Algona, Iowa; Webster City, Iowa

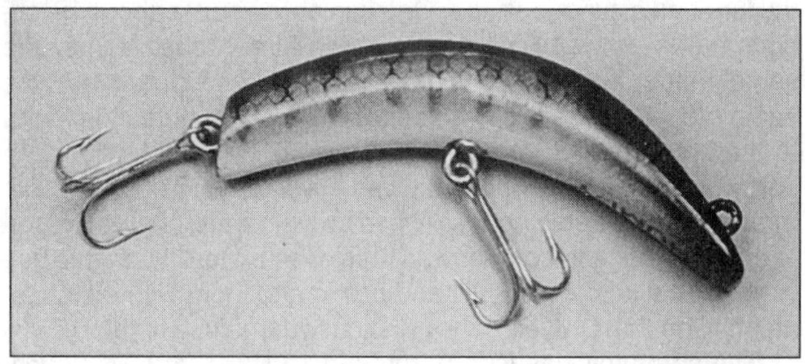

Information from the box is all we have with regard to the HUMPY PLUG. There was no explanation for there being two locations in Iowa. The lure was identified with the HUMPY under the lip and as a "#L3 160" on the box. It is a 2-5/8" plastic lure. The company is thought to have been doing business in the 1940s and 1950s. There is at least one other known HUMPY lure that also looks much like a LAZY IKE. Collector value range: $5-$10.

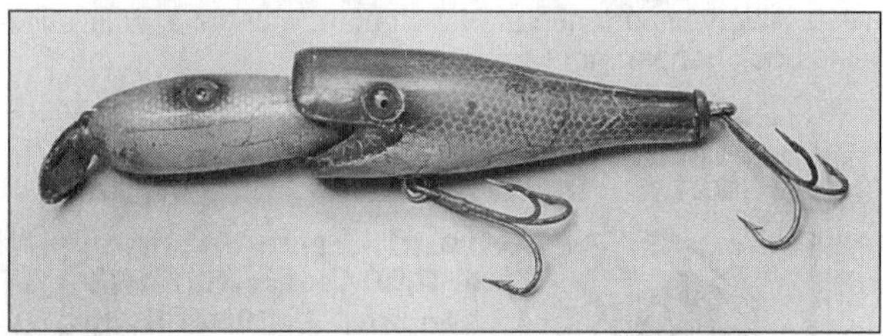

This HUNGRY JACK has a blunt nose and appears fatter when compared to the others. It also measures bigger at 5-5/8" and has red glass eyes.

Here is an example of the more commonly found shape. This one measures 4-1/2" and has amber glass eyes. Photo courtesy Jim Muma.

HUNGRY-JACK

Lloyd and Company — Chicago, Illinois

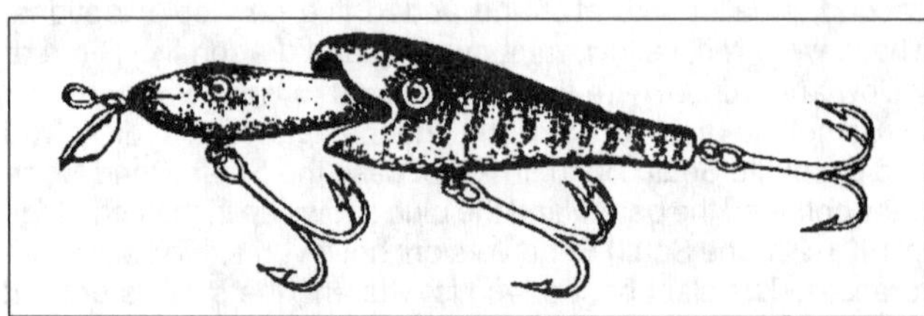

This most unusual, hard to find lure was available at least through the 1930s. A 1939 mixed tackle catalog listed it as available in "Natural scale finish only", but it was available as in the drawing above also. The finish seems to apply to the "eater" and not the "eaten." Almost all examples I have seen so far have the same light cream color finish on the smaller fish. I know of a dark blue scale finish that is applied to both the fish, a green scale finish and a brown scale finish. Both red and amber glass eyes occur. The two are articulated. So, on retrieval it looks as if the big fish is trying to gulp the little one down. They are cataloged at 4-3/4", but actually measure a bit less. Other references list them at both 4-1/4" and 4-1/2". This is related to the fact that they also made a 3-hook model. The weight is 3/4 oz. If you look at the photos carefully you will see differences. Collector value range: $200-$350.

Although little is presently known about the Lloyd Company, it is known that they produced some other lures as well. Mentioned in a 1939 advertisement for the HUNGRY JACK was also a Lloyd "Lighted Pirate Lure". It was made of transparent plastic with an illuminated red head. The photocopy of the ad was poor and the lure was difficult to see, but I attempted to reproduce it in the drawing here. It contained a small light bulb and a replaceable pen light battery. There was no size listed. Collector value range: $15-$40.

LIGHTED PIRATE LURE by Lloyd

HUNT LURE COMPANY

Dewey E. Hunt — Nashville, Tennessee

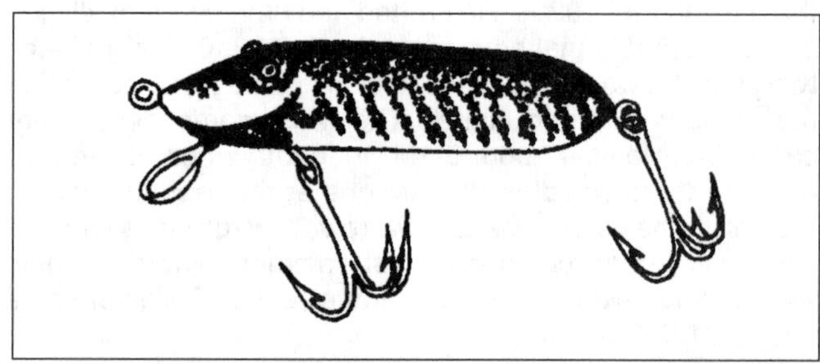

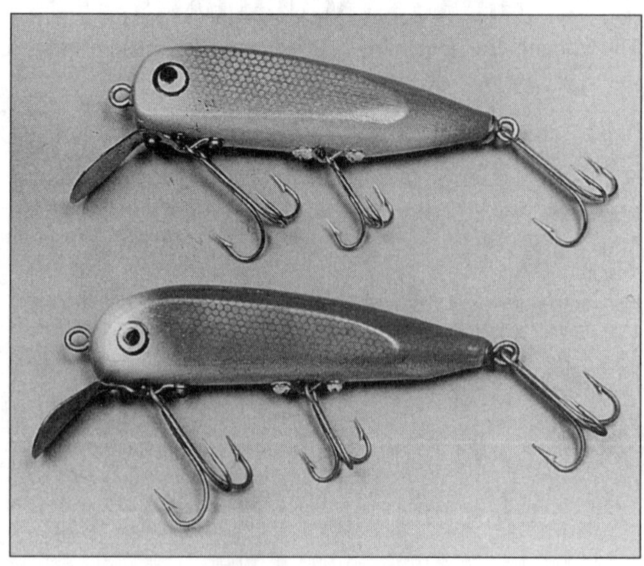

THE CHARMER

This 1950s company made at least three wooden lures, THE CHARMER in the photo at 3-1/4", THE HOOKER at 3" and THE ENTICER, size unknown. They all sport painted eyes and one-piece style belly hook hardware with the forward hanger being integrated with the dive plane. Collector value range: $8-$16.

THE HOOKER

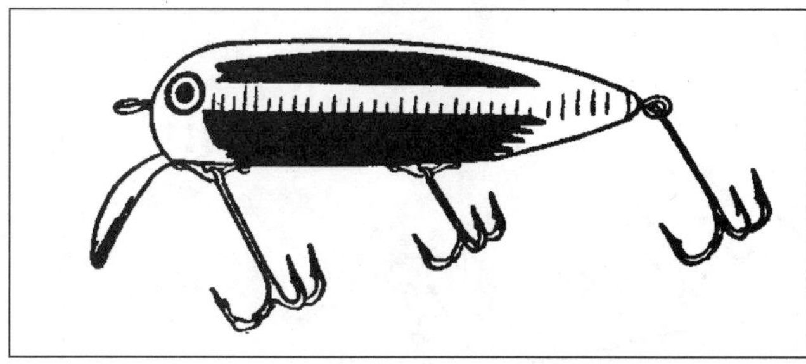

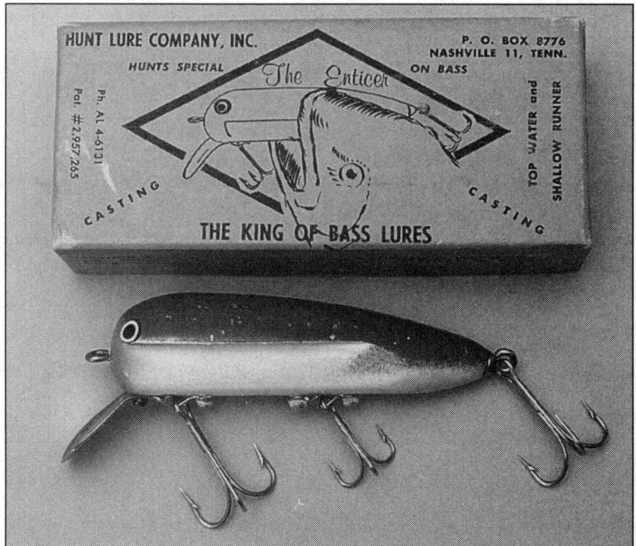

THE ENTICER with its original box.

Colors available for each model:

THE CHARMER

Black and Yellow
Green and Yellow
Green and Black
Black with White belly
Shad

THE HOOKER

Black and Yellow
Green and Yellow
Shad
Black and Green
Black and White

THE ENTICER

Green and Yellow with Yellow dots
Green and Black with Yellow dots
Black and Yellow Black and White
Shad

THE WEEDER

Ideel Fish Lures Company — Chicago, Illinois

This lure was in the Unknown Section of the third edition. A reader recognized it as like one in his collection. He had one in its original box with a pamphlet identifying it. There was also a metal spoon type listed, but no other lures. THE WEEDER was made in nine finishes. Collector value range: $10-25.

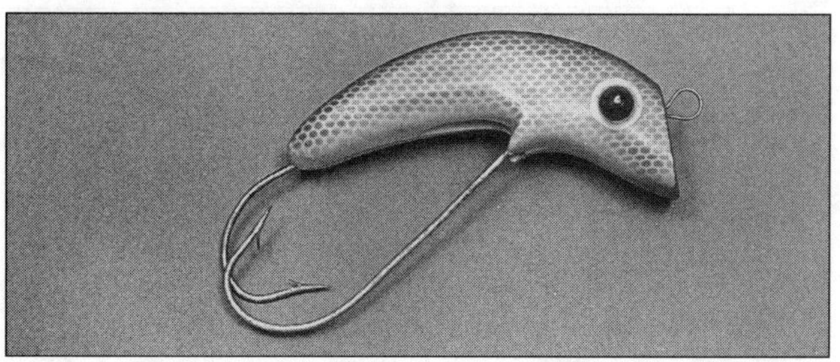

Small glass-eyed weedless lure with scale finish.

COLOR OR FINISH: Red head, red and white stripe, orange dot (I don't have the foggiest what that means), frog finish, pike finish, yellow scale, perch scale, aluminum scale, black scale.

IMMELL BAIT AND TACKLE COMPANY

Immell Bait Company — Blair, Wisconsin

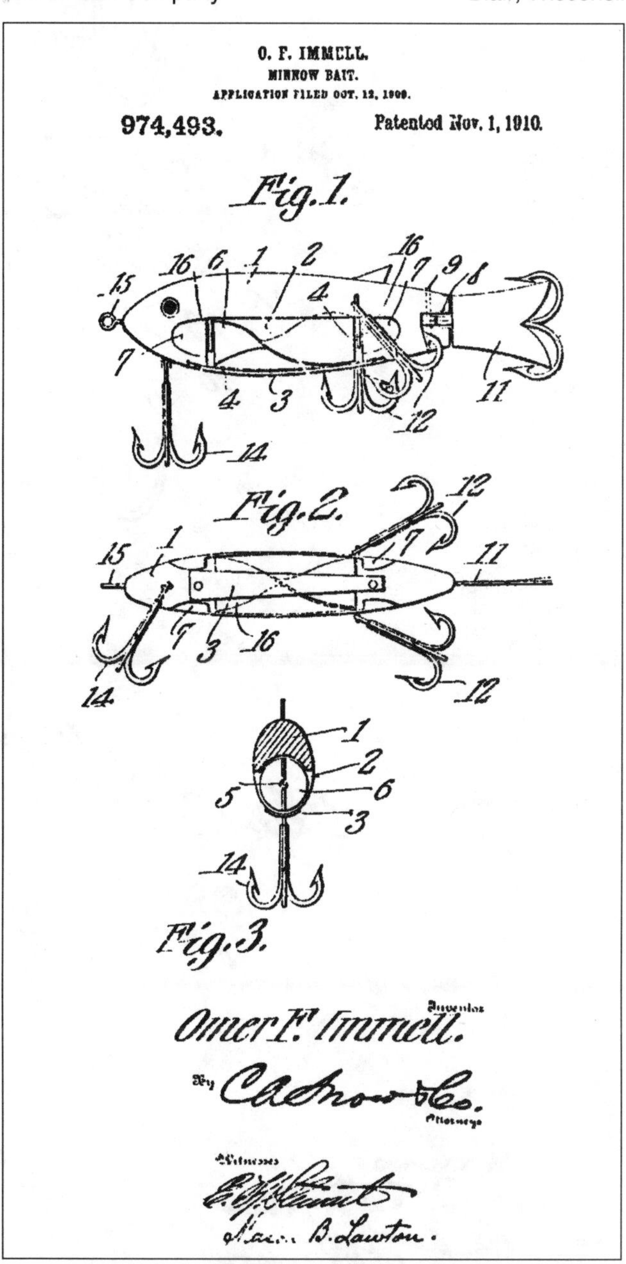

Illustration of original patent application for the CHIPPEWA by Omer F. Immell. Granted Nov. 1, 1910.

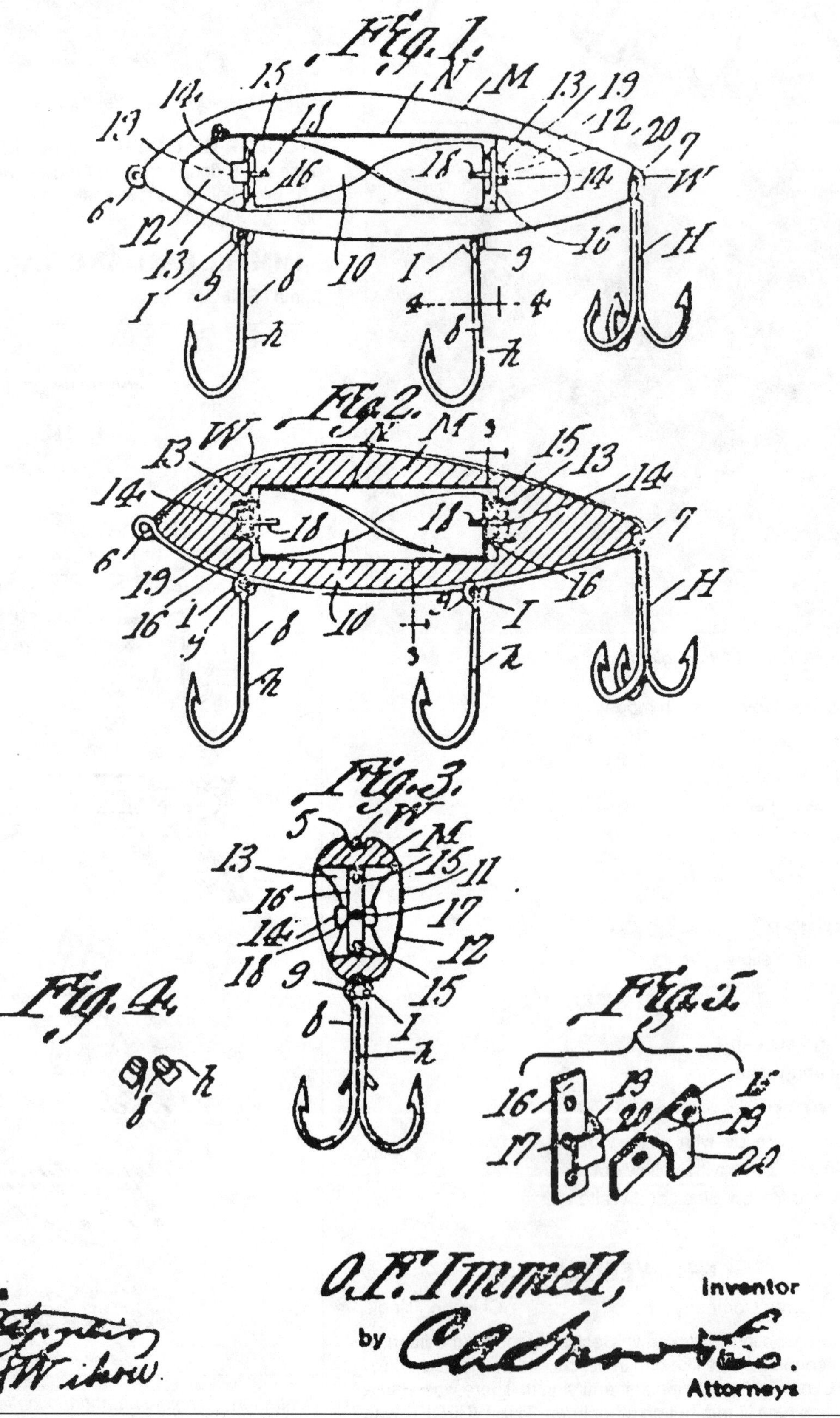

The second patent Immell filed. Resembles the lure more closely.

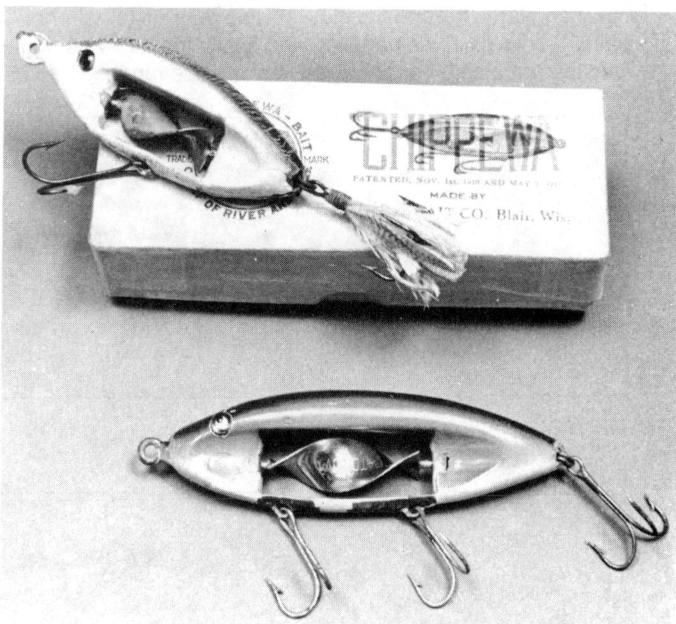

The Immell Bait Company CHIPPEWA Bait. Collector value range: $200-$300.

The Immell Bait Company has a short history and its products are highly sought. The most well known of these are the CHIPPEWA and the CHIPPEWA SKIPPER (made by C. J. Frost).

An original CHIPPEWA box.

The first lure, the CHIPPEWA was invented by Omer F. Immell, of Blair, Wisconsin, some time in or prior to 1909. He filed for its patent in October, 1909. It was granted in 1910. He was granted a second patent in 1911 that more closely resembles the lure he actually made. If you look at the patent illustration of the first you will see a metal tail fin that was never used on a production model. The second patent is without a tail. Prior to the application, Immell hand-made his lure and probably made several versions before settling on the final. These likely all had the tail fin. It is probable that he went into some small amount of production in the years 1910 and 1913. A 1910 issue of *National Sportsman Magazine* contained an advertisement for two CHIPPEWA style lures, the ECLIPSE and three sizes of the COMET. It is believed at this time that he attempted to go into commercial production then, but didn't quite make it. There can be no doubt that a few of these lures were made as it seems unlikely that he would have the advertising unless he was at least nominally prepared to go into production. In any case it was not until early 1913, it seems, that he was prepared once again to go into production. There were no further ads by him until the April, 1913 issue of *The Outers Book* magazine. Apparently Immell was able to reorganize his efforts and a corporation was formed in mid-1912 after which he prepared for and began manufacturing for distribution at some point thereafter and advertised to the public in the aforementioned 1913 ad. This ad was the first use of the trademark "Chippewa." It continued to be advertised in various periodicals until about 1915.

The actual manufacturing history of the lure is a bit clouded. It is generally accepted that he had the lure components manufactured elsewhere initially and assembled and painted by the Immell Company in Blair. There is some relationship between Immell and the C.J. Frost of Stevens Point, Wisconsin, located about 60 miles from Blair. They may have been the manufacturer of the components, but there is presently no real evidence to support this contention. Lending more weight to the supposition, however, is the fact that although Immell continued to advertise the CHIPPEWA in various publications until 1915, the last advertisement for it was an offering of it by the C.J. Frost Company. It was the one and only occurrence of the Frost Company advertising the CHIPPEWA I could find in a very large catalog and periodical collection. This also seems to signal the end of the Immell Bait Company as their advertisements disappeared altogether after that. Collector value range for Chippewas: $200-$300.

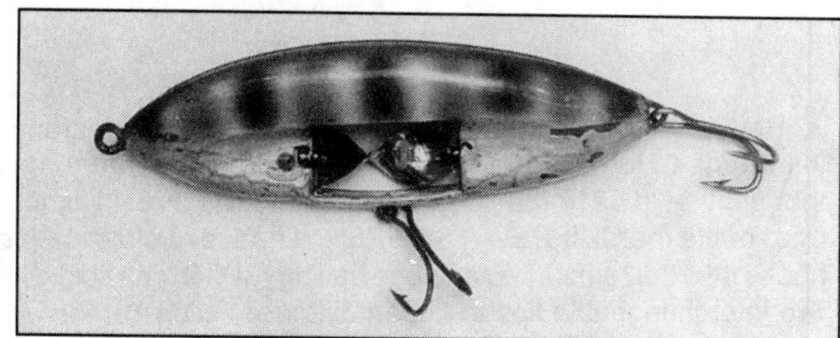

The Immell CHIPPEWA Floater, 4-1/2".

The Immell CHIPPEWA Bait was available in several sizes, floaters and sinkers. Sinkers are 3", 3-1/2", 4" and 5". Floaters were available in 4-1/2" and 5" sizes. It appears that all came with belly-mounted detachable double hooks and a trailing treble. All found so far have glass eyes except the 5" Floater. One of the ads breaks down the colors available as follows:

3-1/2" Size

Yellow Perch
Solid White
Red and Yellow
Fancy Sienna
Green back, spotted sides
Rainbow
Fancy Green back, spotted sides
Fancy Green back
Green back, white belly

4" Size

Red and Yellow
Fancy Sienna
Rainbow
Fancy Green back
Green back, white belly
Fancy Green back, spotted sides

5" Size

Red and Yellow
Rainbow
Fancy Green back
Green back, while belly
Fancy Green back, spotted sides

Colors available in the other sizes remain unknown, but one ad listed aluminum color and red. Solid yellow is also known to have been available.

THE CHIPPEWA SKIPPER

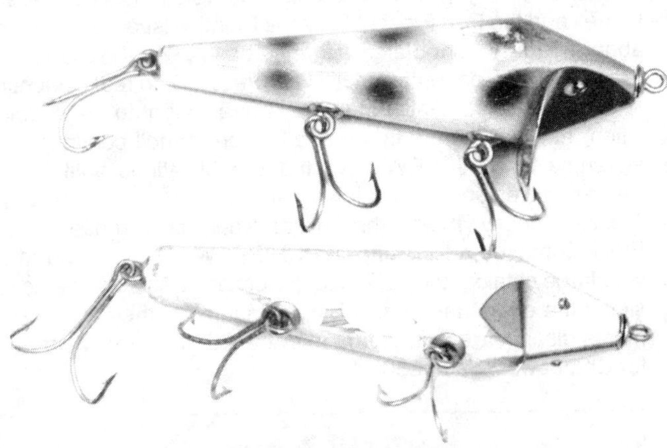

Before the demise of the Immell Company they apparently felt the need to expand their line to include another lure. It is thought that in 1914 they arranged with the C.J. Frost Company to make the CHIPPEWA SKIPPER. It had reversible double hooks, two belly-mounted and one trailing (3D). It was sold with two interchangeable lips to impart different actions at the anglers option. It is very unlikely the collector will find both unless he finds the plug in the original package. The lure was 4-1/2" long. Colors available were fancy spotted or green and white.

All advertisements by the C.J. Frost Company seem to have completely disappeared by 1919. Collector value range: $200-$400.

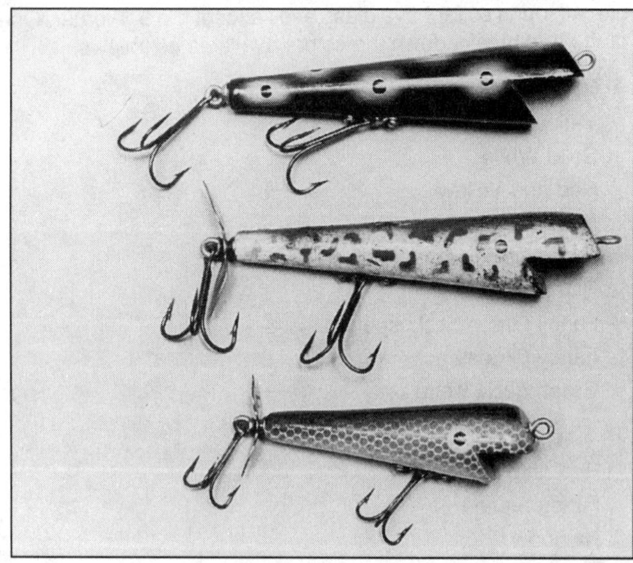

Immell INSTANT BASS. It has been reported, but not substantiated, that the Immell company made these lures also. They utilize one-piece surface hangers. Note the tail spinners on two of them. From top down: 3-5/8", 3-3/4" and 2-3/4".

ISLE ROYALE

Isle Royale Company — Jackson, Michigan

Isle Royale was in business from about 1940 to 1955. It is known that they made some lures for Shakespeare in the 1940s. Most of the Isle Royal lures I have seen have painted cup hardware. It appears that the cup was installed prior to painting, the paint was applied and finally the lure was rigged with the remaining hardware. Collector value range: $10-$25.

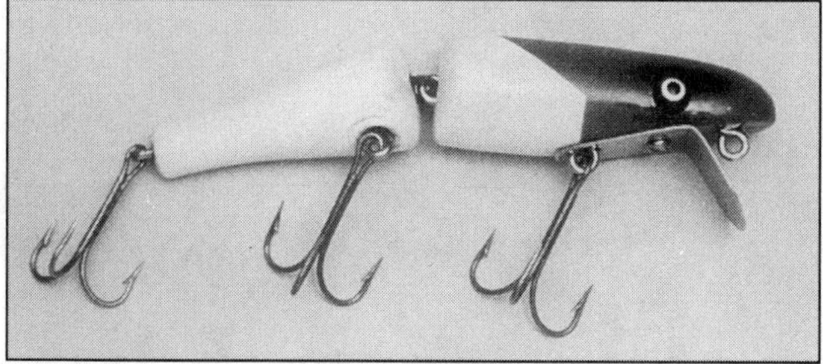

Isle Royale JOINTED PIKE.

Isle Royale JR. SOUTHERN BASSER #9999

Isle Royale POPPER #222

JACK'S DUAL SPINNER

Jack's Lures — Columbus, Indiana

This company was identified only by the information found on the lure box. The lure itself has a cast metal body, painted white. I have seen another in yellow. The overall measurement is 3-1/2". Collector value range: $20-$30.

JACK'S TACKLE MANUFACTURING COMPANY

Jack Lassiter Oklahoma City, Oklahoma

This company is thought to have been in business as early as the 1930s. A flyer describing two lures has at the bottom: "Write us for a color chart on Spinning and Fly Rod Lures. Ask us all about the all metal LUCK-E-LURE...". There is also another Jack's Tackle lure called the WIG-A-LURE. The latter is a feathered spoon wiggler.

JACK'S RIP-L-LURE

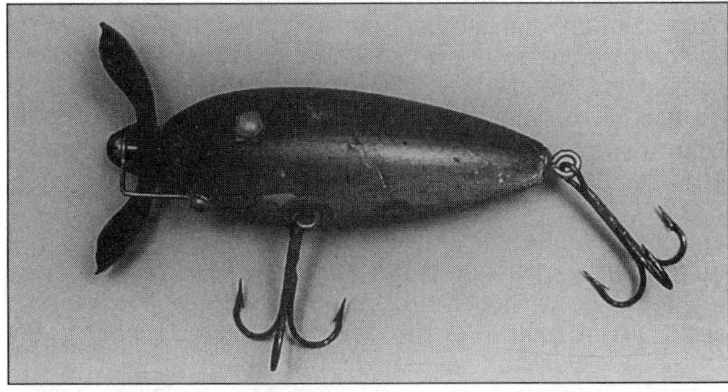

Most examples of the RIP-L-LURE found are made of plastic, however, this one is most assuredly made of wood. It has tack painted eyes, a tail cap and cup/screw eye hardware. The curious-looking blade at the nose of this 3" top water plug flips back and forth upon retrieve. There is a jointed version of this lure known to have been made. Colors for this lure were not found. It is likely that some of the colors for the following lures were used on it. Collector value range: $15-$20.

JAC-DIVER

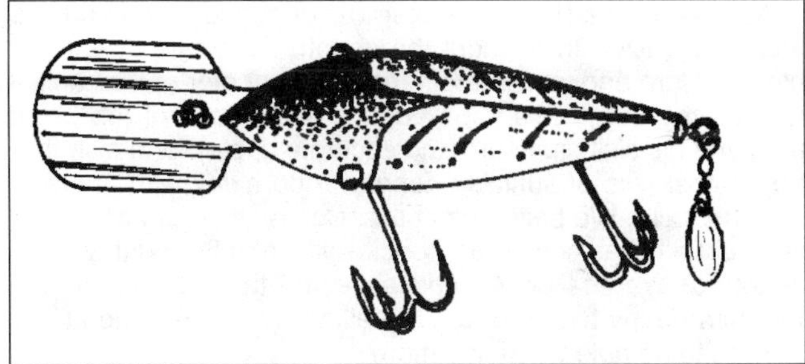

Designed for deep trolling and casting, this lure was made in two sizes. They are: 2-1/4", 3/8-oz and 4", 5/8-oz. There was a lengthy color listing. Collector value range: $5-$15.

COLORS FOR THE JAC-DIVER:

All Black
White with silver shaded eyes and silver bars on back
White with black rattlesnake pattern on back, bars on sides
Gray Shad pattern
Silver flash
Orange, black shading on back
Yellow and Green Perch
Yellow, silver markings on back and sides
Frog
White, red shadow line and dots
White, black shadow line and dots
White, black shadow eye and V rib
All white

JACK'S CRIPPLE MINNOW

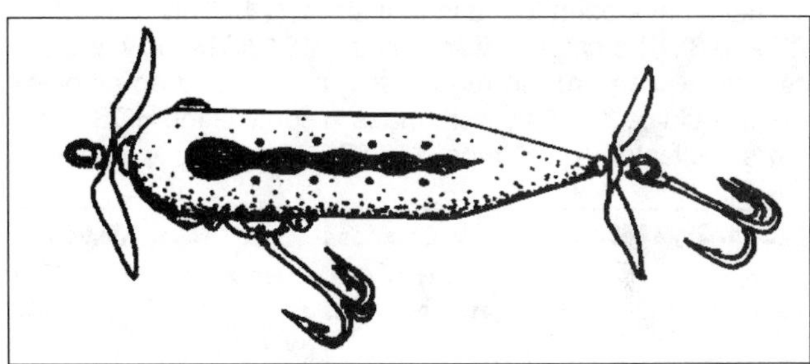

There was only a very small rendition of the lure on a poor photocopy of the flyer, but it looks like the lure may have been rigged with the strong through-body line tie/hook hanger hardware. There were two sizes given: "1/4 plus oz." and 1/2-oz. No lengths were given. Collector value range: $5-$15.

COLORS FOR JACK'S CRIPPLE MINNOW:

All black, red throat
Shad
Silver flash
Orange and black
Perch
Yellow and silver Frog
Red Head
Black shadow strip and dots

EDWARD LEE JACOBS

Vicksburg, Michigan

Jacob's specialty was fly rod lures, but he made a couple of highly sought wooden lures, the HOSS FLY and the POLLY-FROG. He patented both, in 1932 and 1941 respectively. Photo courtesy Jim Muma

JACOB'S HOSS FLY

The 2-1/4" HOSS FLY was somewhat complicated; the manner of attaching the wings in particular. The lure had a moveable metal collar to which the wings were attached. As you pulled the bait through the water the thin wings would flap. Unfortunately the thin metal wings were fragile and easily bent or broken when cast at a stump or rock. Collector value range: $250-$350.

COLOR OR FINISH

Bug
All black
All green
Gold body with red head
White body with red head
Yellow body with red head
Yellow body with black head

JACOB'S POLLY-FROG

These have been found in four sizes, 1-1/4" (fly rod), 2", 2-1/2" and 3". The patent was granted in 1942. The only two colors I have seen are the regular frog pattern and an all black one. It could be that they were made in some of the HOSS FLY colors. Collector value range: $50-$75

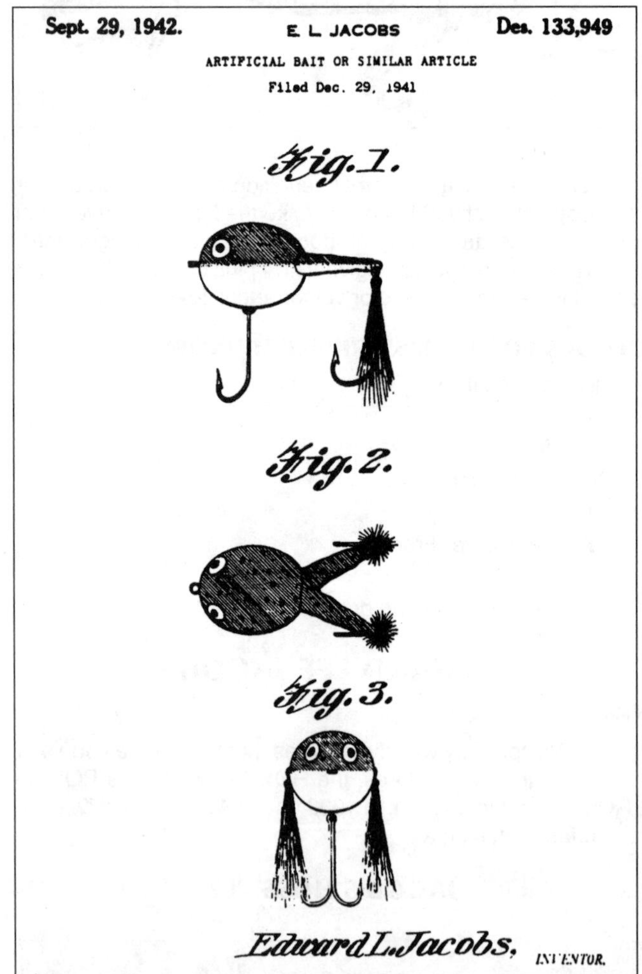

The illustration from Jacob's 1942 patent.

THE W.J. JAMISON COMPANY

Chicago, Illinois

Perhaps the most famous lure ever produced by Jamison is the COAXER (patented January 3, 1905), but there were several others manufactured. The company was established in 1904 and other than for the COAXER it was heavy into metal spinner and spoon type baits many of which are not covered here. Jamison continued into the 1940s and manufactured some of the early plastic lures then.

It is interesting to note the following account of a famous fishing contest between the COAXER and the Decker "Hopatcong" plug. It is taken from a W.J. Jamison Company, catalog printed circa 1910.

WE PROVED IT THE WORLD'S CHAMPIONSHIP BASS FISHING CONTEST WON BY THE "COAXER"

Desiring to prove in the most positive and satisfactory manner the "Coaxer" Surface Bait was superior to any other artificial bait on the market we issued a broad challenge in Field and Stream and National Sportsman to enter the "Coaxer" in contest with any other bait in the World. The contest to last three days and contestants to fish from the same boat, taking hourly turns in choosing fishing grounds and positions in the boat. The challenge found only one taker. Mr. Ans. Decker, of N.J., a professional bass fisherman and manufacturer of the "Decker Bait". The contest was brought off under the auspices of Field and Stream and the Congress Lake Club of Canton, Ohio, on the latter's private lake near Canton. There were three judges, each contestant selecting one, the third being Field and Stream's representative, Mr. Macy, who was sent from New York for that purpose. The date being set for June 16, 17 and 18, 1910, which was an unfortunate selection as the weather turned out very bad, there being two days almost absolute calm and intense heat. It was agreed that eight hours fishing would be done each day. Owing to these bad conditions and also that the lake is well fished by the club's 100 members and their friends and had not been stocked for many years, the catch was not exceptionally large, though it was considerably larger than the average on this lake.

The "Coaxer" not only won the event easily but also scored the largest number of fish landed without a miss, landing five one day and seven another day without a miss. It also hooked the most strikes without a miss, hooking fourteen strikes in succession on the last day of the contest, but losing four of the fish in the heavy weeds.

As Mr. Decker used a bait fitted with three treble hooks most of the time against a "Coaxer" with but two single hooks it proves rather conclusively that good single hooks will hook and hold better than trebles. The "Coaxer" showed its superiority in open water fishing as well as in the weeds by raising all the fish that were raised in strictly open water. There were but three of these, but one was hooked, which was apparently of about 5 pounds weight. However, he dived into the weeds and got free. All agreed that this was the largest fish hooked in the contest. All had a good chance to see as he leaped fully a foot clear of the water. The No. 1 Convertible "Coaxer" was used but without the double hook most of the time. 26 out of the 28 bass were caught on the trailer hook.

As the bait used by Mr. Decker was of a style that is and has been recognized throughout the country for years as a most excellent lure and was in the hands of an angler of rare ability both as regards to his knowledge of the habits of the black bass and his skill as a sure and accurate caster, and also that the contest was of sufficient length to do away with any element of "luck". We believe that the "Coaxer's" superiority over all other baits has been most conclusively and thoroughly demonstrated. We challenged and accepted the first comer and beat him nearly two to one. We believe we have done all we claimed to be able to do and more.

NO. 1 CONVERTIBLE "COAXER"

This is the lure used in the contest described. Most of the COAXERS had red felt wings but some are found with leather.

It is not known for certain if the leather was used in production or added by others later. The body was 1-7/8" long and made of cork. It has a single hook mounted in the tail and a second single hook attached to the first single hook. There was a removable belly-mounted double hook also. It was also available with a buck tail. Collector value range: $15-$32.

Left: Luminous buck tail COAXER. Right: feather tail model.

No. 1 WEEDLESS COAXER

This is the same as the No. 1 Convertible COAXER above, but does not have the detachable belly double hook. Collector value range: $10-$20

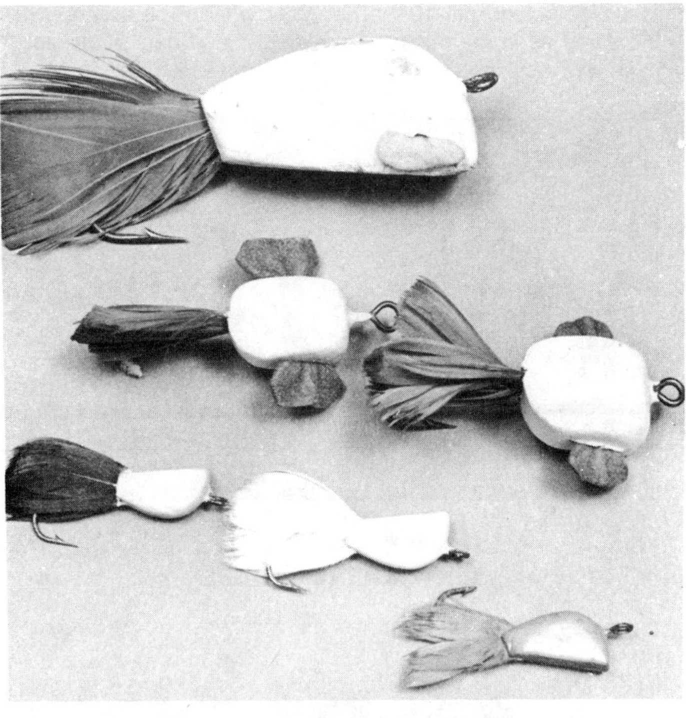

No. 1 WEEDLESS BOOKSTALL COAXER

Same as above but with a bookstall. Collector value range: $10-$20.

No. 2 WEEDLESS COAXER

Essentially the same as the above WEEDLESS COAXER, but smaller (1-1/8") body with a slightly different shape. Collector value range: $10-$20.

LUMINOUS BOOKSTALL "COAXER"

The same as the No. 1 WEEDLESS COAXER but with luminous paint. Collector value range: $15-$25.

No. 2 CONVERTIBLE COAXER

The same as the No. 2 WEEDLESS COAXER above with the addition of the detachable double hook on the belly. Collector value range: $10-$20.

No. 3 WEEDLESS COAXER

Made exactly the same as the No. 1 WEEDLESS COAXER only smaller. Collector value range: $10-$20.

No. 3 CONVERTIBLE COAXER

Exactly the same as above, but with the addition of a detachable belly-mounted double hook. Collector value range: $10-$20.

TEASER OR TANDEM COAXER

Two 1" body COAXERS mounted on a wire so as to make one run in front of the other. Collector value range: $60-$90.

THE MUSKIE COAXER

Another of the COAXER types this larger one is made for surface trolling. It has a 2-5/8" body length, a tail-mounted single hook (optional trailing single) and a belly-mounted double hook. Collector value range: $50-$75.

THE COAXER UNDERWATER

This is similar to the other COAXERS except the body is made of metal and has no wings. It has a tail-mounted single hook. It was also available with luminous paint. Collector value range: $20-$25.

FLY ROD WIGGLER

This plug came along about 1918 in three sizes and two hook type options. The sizes were 1-1/4", 1-3/4" and 2-1/2". They were available with double or single hooks and in eight colors. Collector value range: $40-$70.

COLOR OR FINISH: Silver shiner, golden shiner, red side minnow, red head, white body, yellow perch; solid white; solid red, solid yellow.

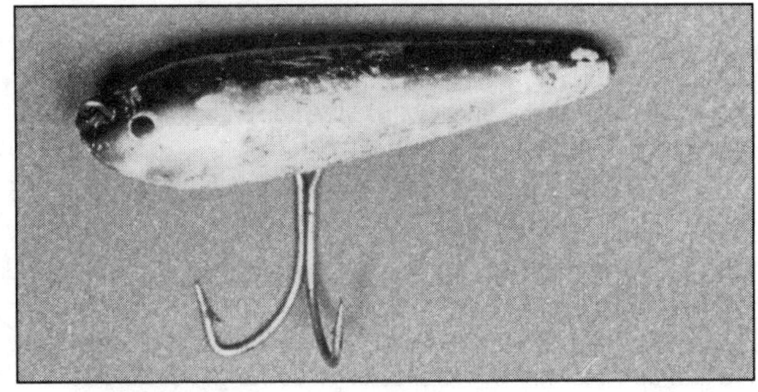

MASCOT

In 1916-17 Jamison introduced several versions of a new lure called the MASCOT. Collector value range of all: $80-$160.

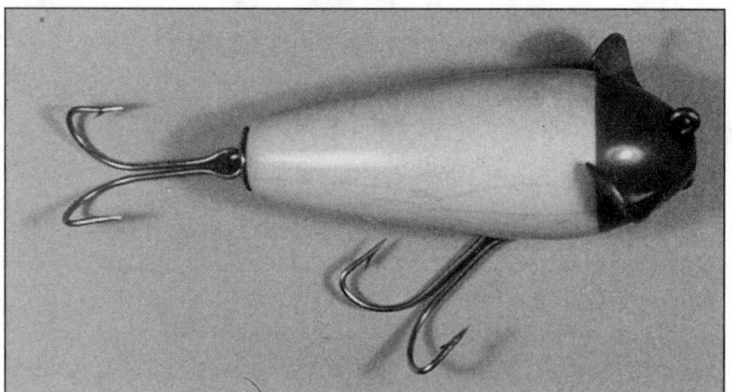

No. 1 WEEDLESS MASCOT

This lure was 4" long, had two belly hooks and a trailing double. It has two line ties at the nose and is reversible. Colors available were: White with red head, Solid red, White or Yellow.

No. 1 WINGED WEEDLESS MASCOT

Otherwise the plug is the same but slightly longer than the regular No. 1 MASCOT and has metal wings attached to the head.

No. 2 WINGED WEEDLESS MASCOT

Same basic body design as the other MASCOTS. It is 2-3/4" long, has wings, and only one belly double hook and a trailing double. It was available in luminous paint or white body with red head.

WEEDLESS MUSKELLUNGE MASCOT

Almost exactly the same as the regular No. 1 MASCOT but larger (5-1/2") and with stronger hooks and hardware.

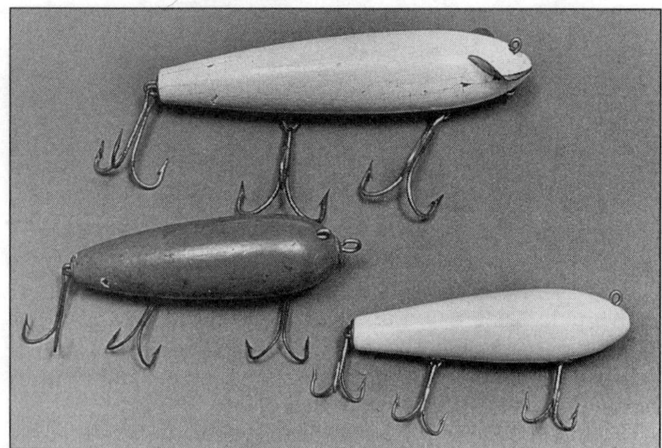

Top lure is the WEEDLESS No. 1 WINGED MASCOT. Deep running or surface lure choice (line tie at top and under head). Left is a 1915 vintage WEEDLESS MASCOT. Near or surface-running depending upon line tie choice (note nose-protecting washer at line tie). Top and left lures were available in solid red, white or yellow or with white body, red head. the lure at lower right is the CHICAGO WOBBLER.

CHICAGO WOBBLER

The lower lure in the previous photo showing three lures is the CHICAGO WOBBLER. Advertised as new in 1916 it is very similar in body style to the MASCOT series plugs. It had only one line tie (top of nose). Collector value range: $100-$200.

COLOR OR FINISH: Solid red, yellow or white; white body with red head.

HUMDINGER

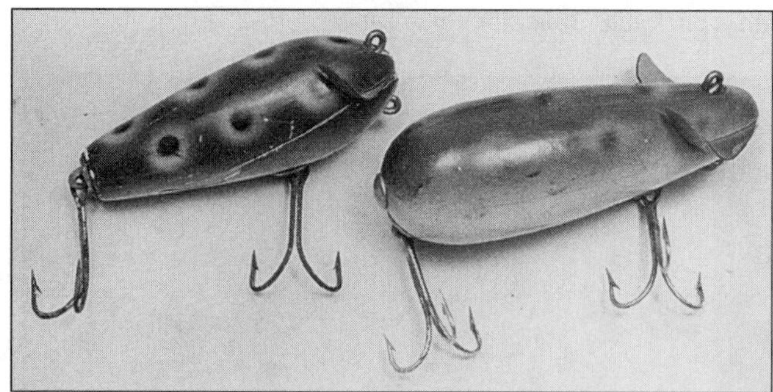

Left is a MASCOT. Right is a HUMDINGER.

New in 1916, this lure has a tear drop shape with the fat portion to the rear. Shown in the previous photo and the drawing above is the HUMDINGER. It has two line ties, two metal upswept wings on the head, a belly treble and trailing treble hook. Collector value range: $50-150.

SHANNON SPINNERS

Although the SHANNON TWIN SPINNER was in the line as early as 1917, this SHANNON SINGLE SPINNER wasn't found in catalogs until 1925. The TWIN SPINNER is essentially the same as in the photo here except that it had two wires, each with a spinner. Collector value range: $15-$25.

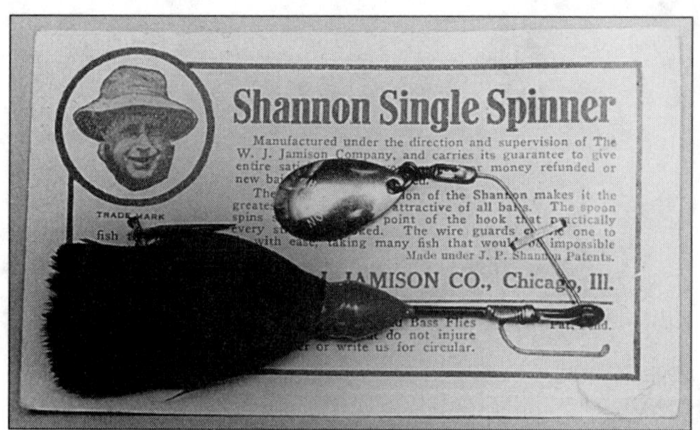

STRUGGLING MOUSE

This bait was newly introduced around 1919. It has a reversible metal wing affair at the nose to render it underwater or surface running. It was available with either one or two belly trebles and a trailing treble hook or all double hooks. Collector value range: $50-$150.

COLOR OR FINISH: Mouse color, crab; frog, white body with red head.

THE "NEMO" BASS BAIT

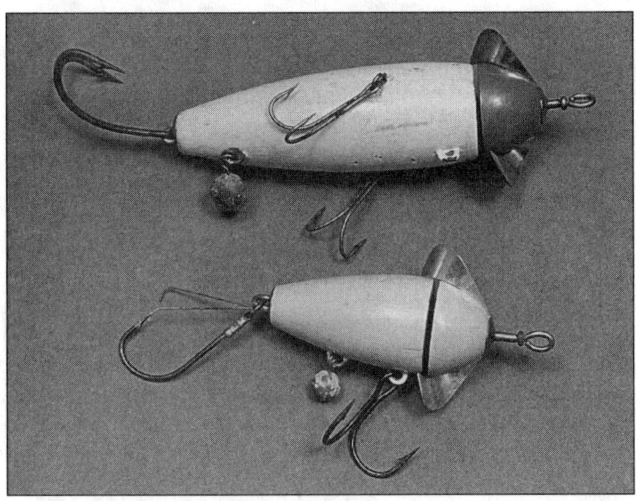

Top: The "NEMO" Muskie Bait. Lower. The "NEMO" BASS BAIT. Note the extra eye at bottom of the forward end. The feature allows the fisherman to move the external weight to make the lure run underwater.

This lure was introduced in 1910 as an underwater or surface plug. Made of wood, it has a revolving head, detachable belly-mounted double hook, trailing single hook with weed guard and a moveable weight. The lure length was 2-3/8". The colors available were white, red, yellow, blue or green and they could be ordered in any combination. Therefore, the collector may find the plug in one of the five solid colors or a combination of 20 mixed for a total of 25 possibilities. Collector value range: $400-$600.

THE "NEMO" MUSKIE BAIT

This is a larger version of the "NEMO" Bass Bait above. It has a trailing double hook, and a double hook mounted on each side of the body. The colors and combinations are the same. Collector value range: $500-$650.

HASTING'S WEEDLESS RUBBER FROG

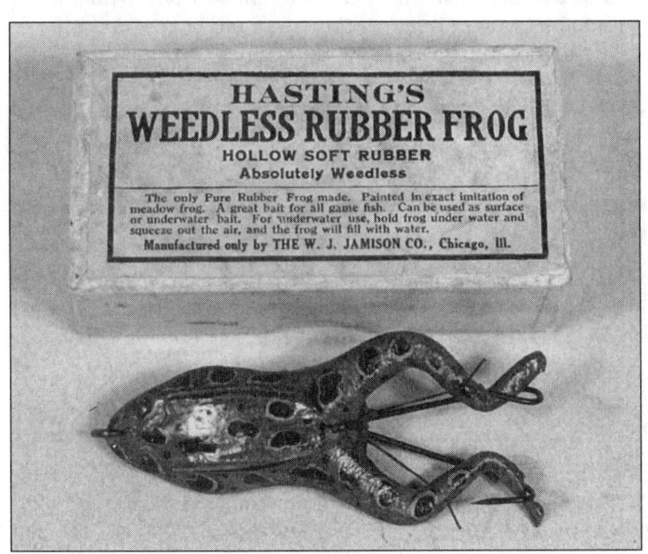

In the Jamison catalogs into the late 1930s, this was a lure made of "pure rubber" according to the entries. It was hollow and you could fill it with water to make it a sinker. Although this looks like the Hastings Floating cork frog, it plainly states on the box "Manufactured only by THE W. J. JAMISON CO." The lure was patented by James T. Hastings in 1895. Jamison must have secured the rights to manufacture it. Collector value range: $50-$75, with box add $100. Photo courtesy Jim Muma.

WIG-WAG (GEP BAIT)

This bait was made in three sizes. The bass size and musky sizes in the photo measure 4-1/2" and 6" respectively. The third size is 5-1/2". It was new in the 1930s and made with glass eyes. They were available in three color combinations: White body with red head, silver body with black head, yellow body and head with a brown back. Collector value range: $50-$100.

PLASTIC OR TENITE JAMISON LURES

Jamison began marketing molded plastic plugs in 1941. It was announced in the March, 1941 issue of *The Southern Sportsman.* The following listing of seven plugs are examples of this use of plastic. Some were made in wood first for a short time.

WIG-L-TWIN

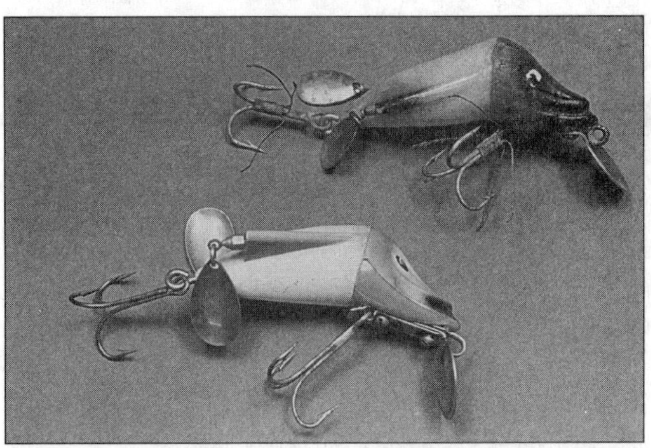

This bait is thought to be new around 1939. The WIG-L-TWIN was oddly shaped, with a deep-diving nose blade, two laterally mounted horizontal fins each with a small flashing spoon attached to the trailing edge. It has a belly treble and a trailing treble (2T). Collector value range: $15-$30.

CATALOG SERIES #	BODY LENGTH	LURE WEIGHT
1800	2-1/2"	5/8 oz.

COLOR OR FINISH (new in 1941): White body with red head and fins, black and white striped with white belly and black fins, golden brown scale finish, silver green scale finish.

COLOR OR FINISH (1951): Yellow perch, black and white, red and white, dace scale, rainbow, green scale, target spot, black and yellow, frog, natural crab, gold fish.

JAMISONS No. 1500

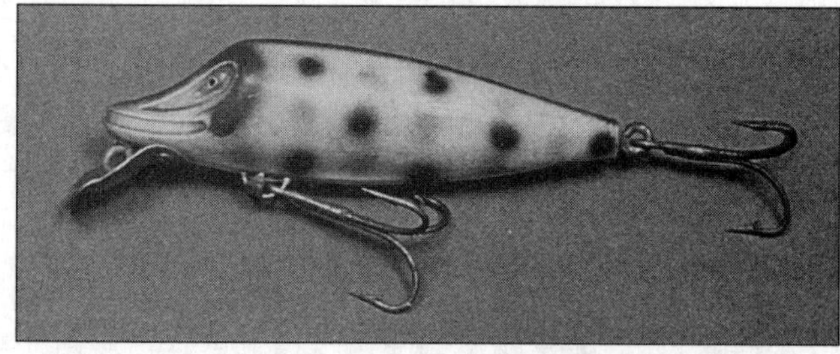

Made of plastic, this plug has a pointed-slope nose with line tie under it. There is a metal diving lip, a belly treble and trailing treble hook (2T). It was available in two sizes. Collector value range: $15-$30.

CATALOG SERIES #	BODY LENGTH	LURE WEIGHT
1500	3-1/4"	5/8 oz.
S1500	2-1/2"	1/2 oz.

COLOR OR FINISH: Red and white, black and white, target spot, frog, silver shiner, perch scale.

SURFACE WIGGLER

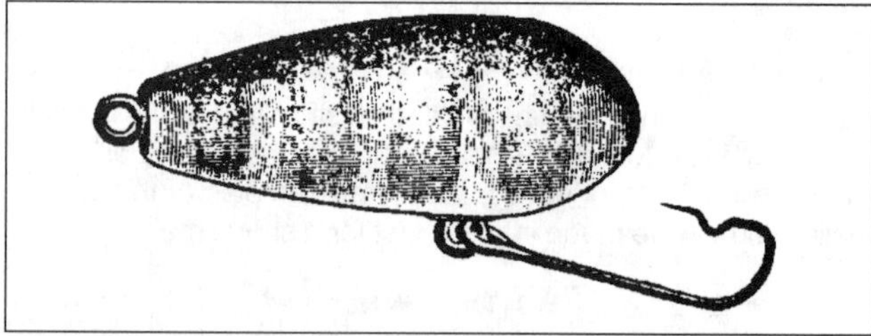

A 2-3/4" long tear drop shaped plug with the fat portion of the body to the rear. It was originally equipped with either a barbless single hook or a double hook mounted on the belly. Collector value range: $15-$25.

BEETLE PLOP

Another plastic plug (c. 1940). It has two metal fins, one on either side of the body and a single trailing treble hook (1T). Collector value range: $15-$25.

CATALOG SERIES	BODY LENGTH	LURE WEIGHT
2000	2"	1/2 oz.

COLOR OR FINISH: White body with redhead, white body with black head, white body with yellow head.

SHANNON TORPEDO No. 1900

This is a very similar lure to the No. 1500. Same hook configuration and metal diving lip. Made of Tenite and available in 14 different colors. Collector value range: $15-$30.

LUR-O-LITE No. 1950

Occasionally a company marketed a self-illuminated plug

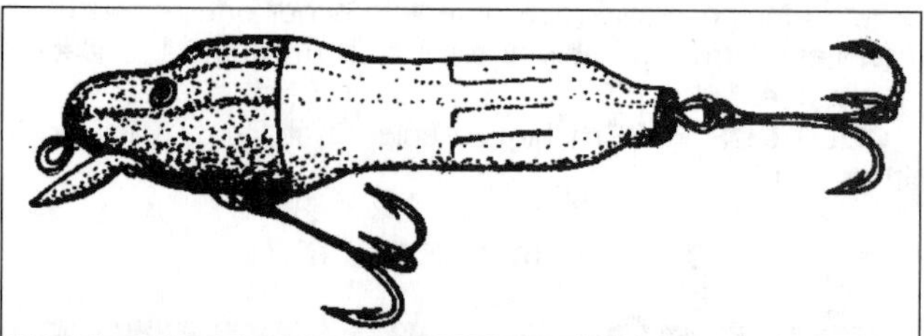

and Jamison was no exception. The LUR-O-LITE was made of molded plastic and had a battery-operated light inside. It was available only in a 4" size, 3 ounces in weight. The color was red head with white body. Collector value range:$40-$50.

QUIVERLURE c. 1940

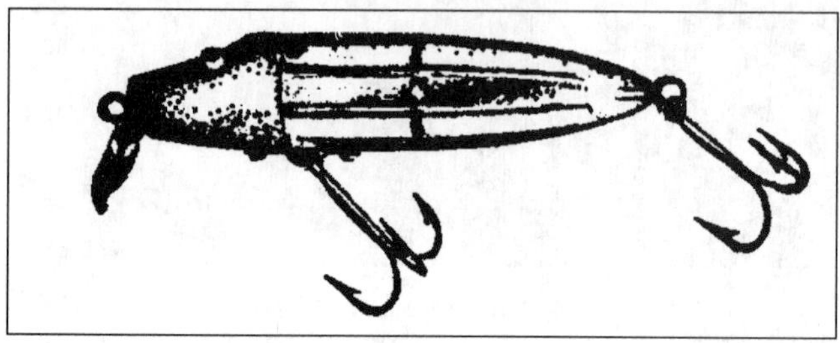

In previous editions this lure has been listed here in the Jamison section because they listed it in their catalogs with their series numbering system. Subsequently a 1940 advertisement has turned up where the Dillon Beck Mfg. Co. of Irvington, New Jersey advertised the same lure as their patented product. They must have had a licensing agreement with Jamison where they either supplied them or allowed them to manufacture the lure.

The plug was made of transparent plastic in the body and various head colors. The clear body allowed view of an internal shiny bar that appears to quiver on retrieve. The plug was made in three sizes. Collector value range: $10-$20.

CATALOG SERIES	BODY LENGTH	LURE WEIGHT	HOOKS
1900	3-1/4"	5/8 oz.	2T
1910	2-1/2"	1/2 oz.	2T
1920	4-3/4"	1 oz.	3T

COLOR OR FINISH: Red head, chrome bar; black head, chrome bar; yellow head, chrome bar, red head, red bar, yellow head, green bar.

JEMCO SONIC LURE

Jemco Bait Company East Gary, Indiana

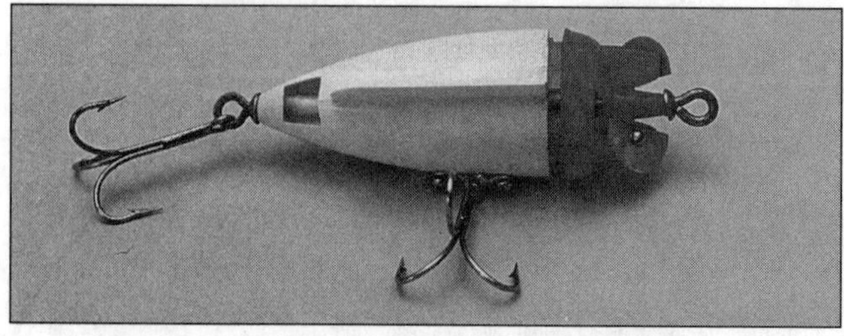

The mimeograph of the typed instructions that came with this lure was of such poor quality that the word SONIC actually appeared as SONIO. The latter may be the correct name. This is a hollow plastic lure with blades at the nose to turn the head. The paper stated there was a partition on the inside and a hole on each side "..permitting the water to flow alternately thru, giving it a wiggling action." The patent number given would have been granted in 1956. There were no colors given. The one in the photograph is 3" long with white body and red spinning head. The whole lure "...is coated with a luminous lacquer finish...". Collector value range: $10-$20.

JENNINGS FISHING TACKLE COMPANY

Olympia, Washington JENNINGS SURFACE MINNOW

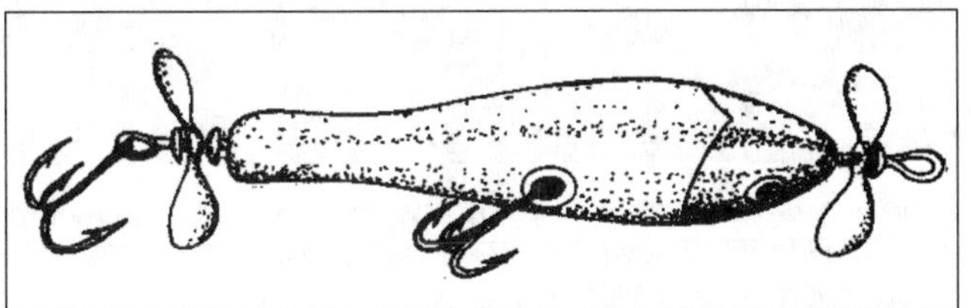

This is a shaped plug with propeller spinners fore and aft. It has painted eyes, a side treble and trailing treble hook. Length 3-1/4". Collector value range: $5-$10.

JENNINGS BULLFROG PLUG c. 1930

This 2-3/4" plug was designed for catching frogs, not fish. It has feathers concealing two single hooks and two wire antenna type appendages. Collector value range: $5-$10.

JENNY LIZ

Jenson Sporting Goods Austin, Texas

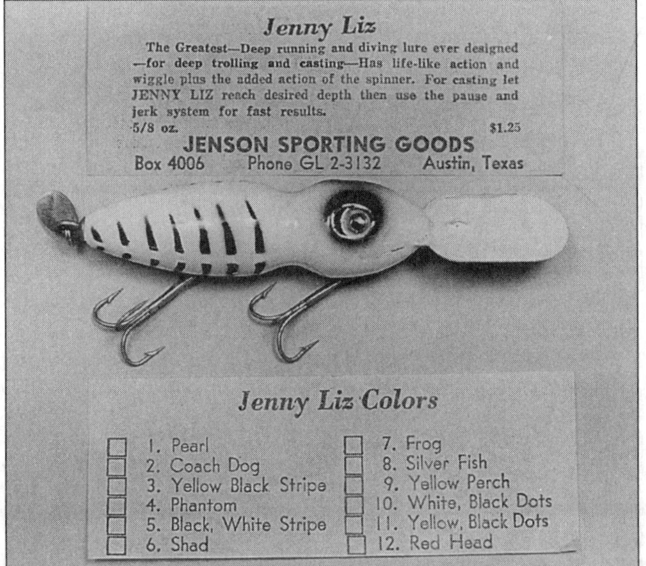

Except for the shape of the dive plane this wooden lure is an awful lot like Whopper Stopper's HELLBENDER; right down to the little flasher at the tail. It measures 3", weighs 5/8-oz. and utilizes one-piece surface hook hangers. These finishes listed below were copied right off a flyer that was packed in the box with the lure. It probably dates from the 1950s. Collector value range: $5-$10.

COLOR OR FINISH: Pearl, frog, coach dog, silver fish, yellow with black stripe, yellow perch, phantom, white with black dots, black with white stripe, yellow with black dots, shad, red head.

JERSEY EXPERT

E.C. Adams Morristown, New Jersey

IDEAL MINNOW

William E. Davis Morristown, New Jersey

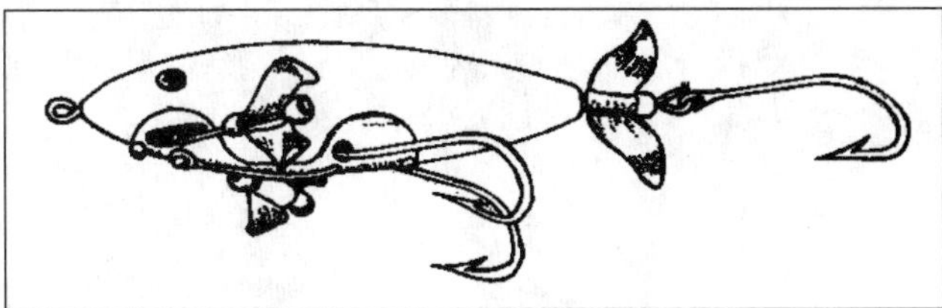

There is some amount of confusion surrounding these two very similar lures. Both of them were patented in 1907. Adams was first to get his patent with Davis getting his seven months later. The two were so close that there has to be some connection. The Davis patent was an improvement over the Adams patent in that there was a preventer device at the tail to keep the trailing hook from becoming entangled in the spinners and the hooks were readily removable. Because the two were so close in design, both men were from the same town, the second was an improvement over the first, and Davis is known to have offered both in advertising I think it reasonable to presume that the two struck some kind of deal. The drawing here was taken from an ad placed by Davis. It is the IDEAL MINNOW. If you will compare the drawing and the photo here to the two photos of the JERSEY

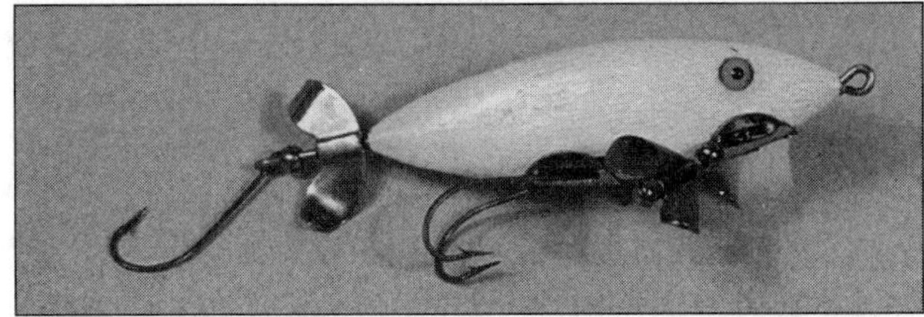

This is a W. E. Davis IDEAL MINNOW measuring 3-3/8". Photo courtesy Jim Muma.

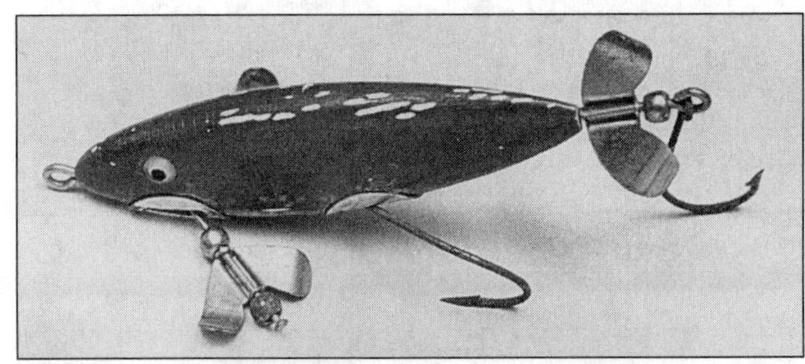

EXPERT(side and belly views) you will note that they are essentially the same lure. Now compare the two patent illustrations reproduced here and your own conclusions as to whether they are related. Each has a collector value range of $750-$1,000.

JOHNSON AUTOMATIC STRIKER

Carl A. Johnson — Chicago, Illinois

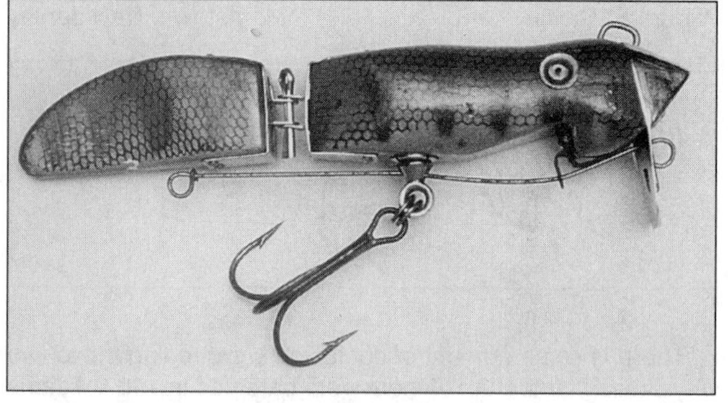

6-1/2" Johnson AUTOMATIC STRIKER.

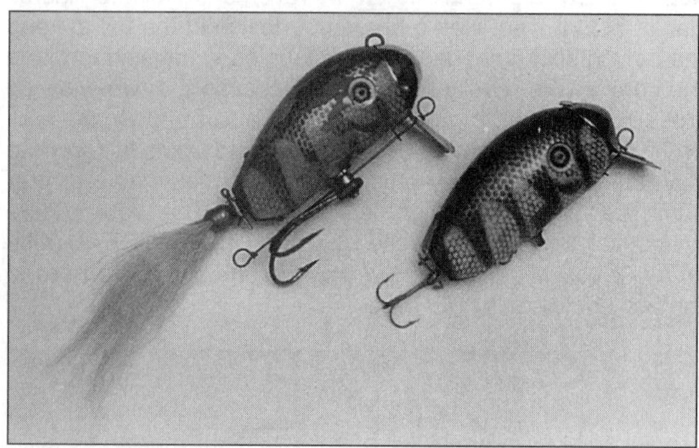

3" Johnson AUTOMATIC STRIKER. The one on the right is missing some hardware and has a rounded diving lip. The one on the left is complete and the lower lip is fluted and squared off.

2" Johnson AUTOMATIC STRIKER.

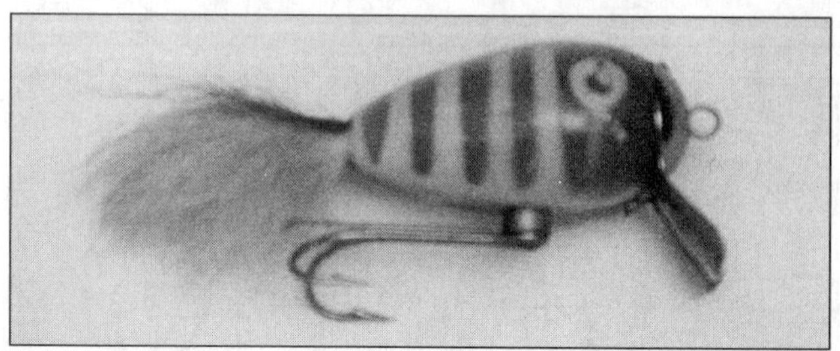

1-3/4" Johnson AUTOMATIC STRIKER JUNIOR.

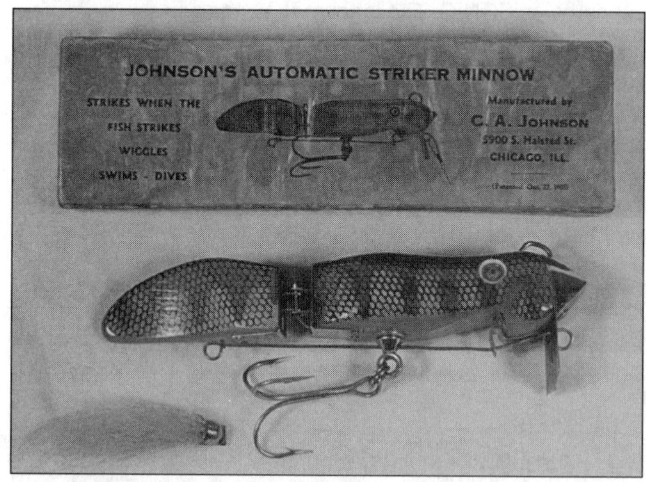

A new in the box example with a yellow bucktail. They were packed with the lure as interchangeable with the wooden tail. Photo courtesy Jim Muma.

Very little is known about Johnson, or product distribution of the AUTOMATIC STRIKERS. Patented in 1935, they are quality-made and somewhat complicated (see patent illustration). On all but the smallest size, the design allowed for the hook to swing away from the body upon strike. Ostensibly this allowed more reliable fish-holding capability. One small ad listed the following colors for the Junior size: Ivory body with red stripes; ivory body with black stripes; ivory body with green stripes and yellow tail; ivory body with green head. Only a silver scale finish was listed for the larger size in the ad. When found new in the box there is also a bucktail included that could be used at the tail instead of the wooden tail piece. Collector value range: $300-$500.

JOHNSON

Wisconsin

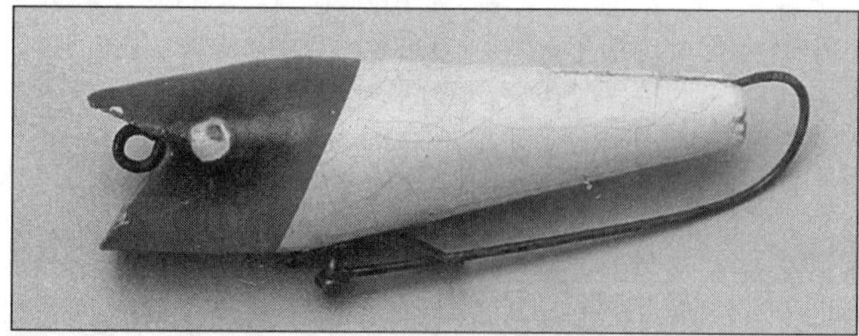

A Johnson DARTO. It measures 3-1/2". Note the weedless arrangement.

This is a Johnson WEEDO. It measures 3" body length and 4" overall. It bears a startling resemblance to the Fisher-Schuberth CAPTOR lure.

These wood lures might belong in the UNKNOWNS at the back of the book. We don't know much about them, but too much to place them there. Karl White has them in his fine book,

No. 849,622. PATENTED APR. 9, 1907.

E. C. ADAMS.

ARTIFICIAL FISH BAIT.

APPLICATION FILED JUNE 7, 1906.

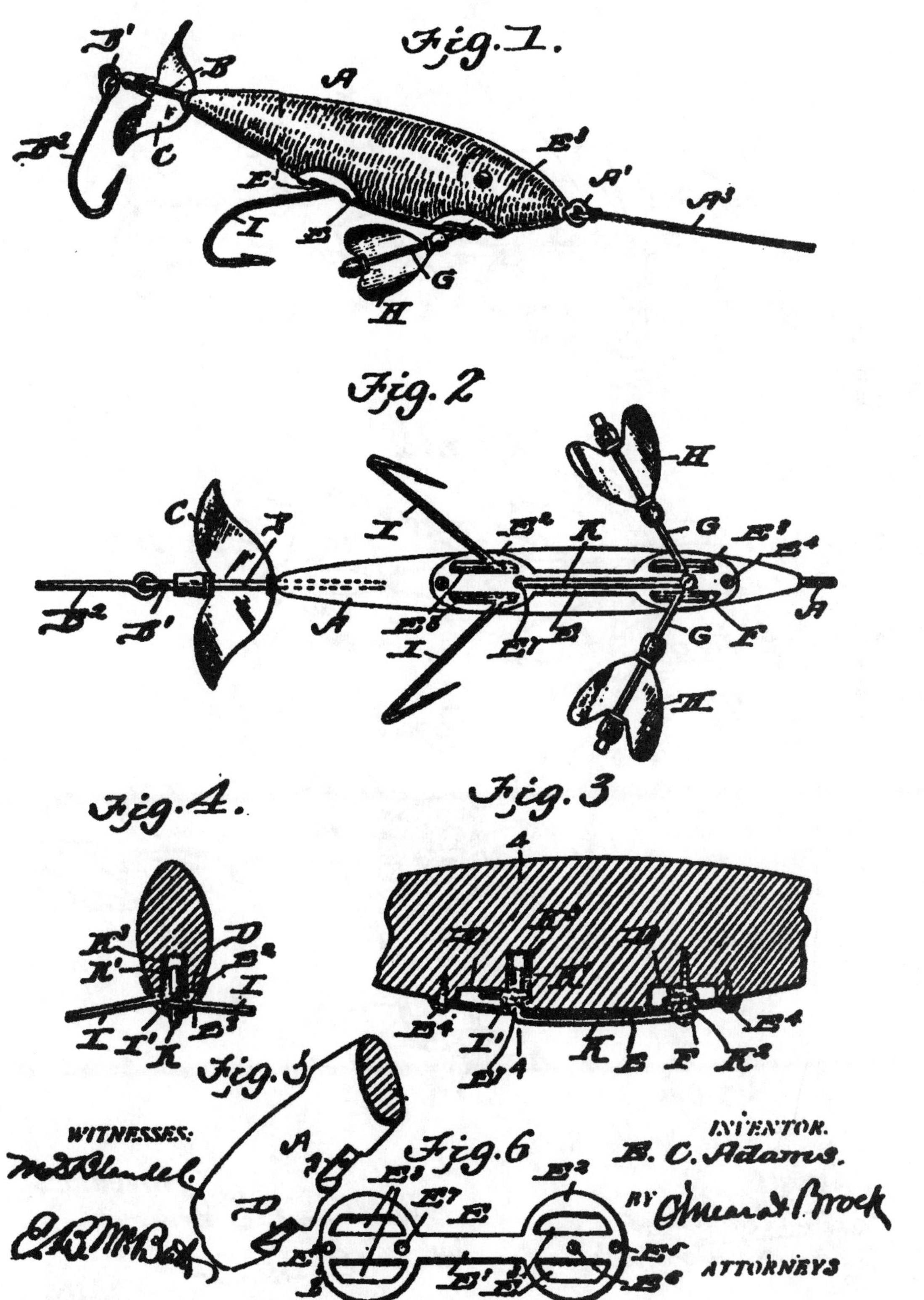

Patent illustration for the E.C Adams JERSEY EXPERT

No. 871,057. **PATENTED NOV. 12, 1907.**

W. E. DAVIS.

ARTIFICIAL BAIT.

APPLICATION FILED FEB. 2, 1907.

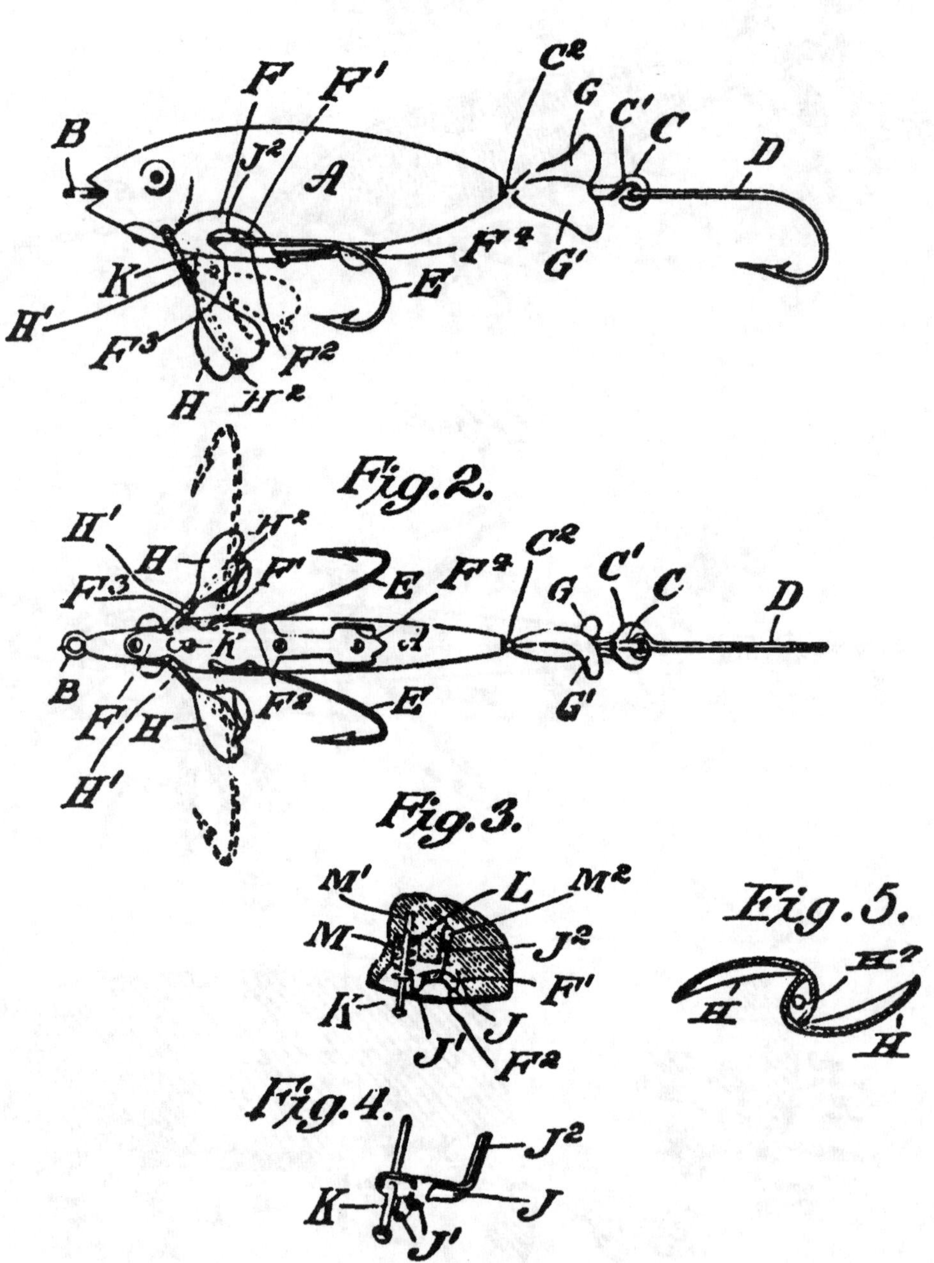

Attest: **Inventor:**

Edgeworth Greene William E. Davis.

Alan McDonnell by S. L. Cox. Atty.

Patent illustration for the W.E. Davis IDEAL MINNOW.

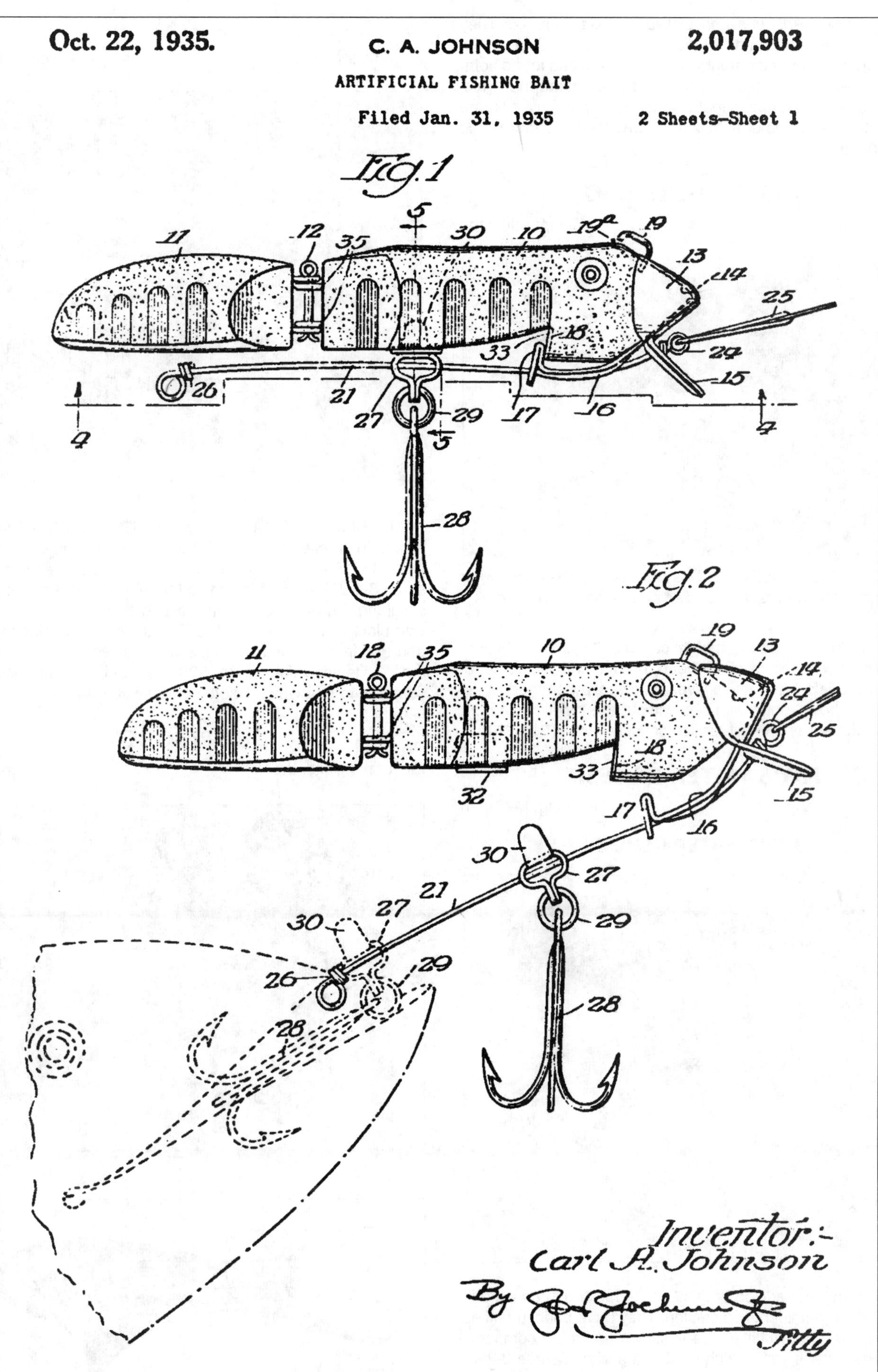

The illustration from the original Johnson AUTOMATIC STRIKER patent.

Fishing Tackle Antiques and Collectibles on page 76. They have names and the date 1947 is noted. I have made a search of a couple of hundred patents from the 1940s and found nothing. A collector friend had both of them so I photographed them for inclusion here in hopes that someone can give us a bit more information. No trade or auction data was found so there is no collector value here.

JOS. DOODLE BUG

Jos. Tackle Shop — Jasper, Indiana

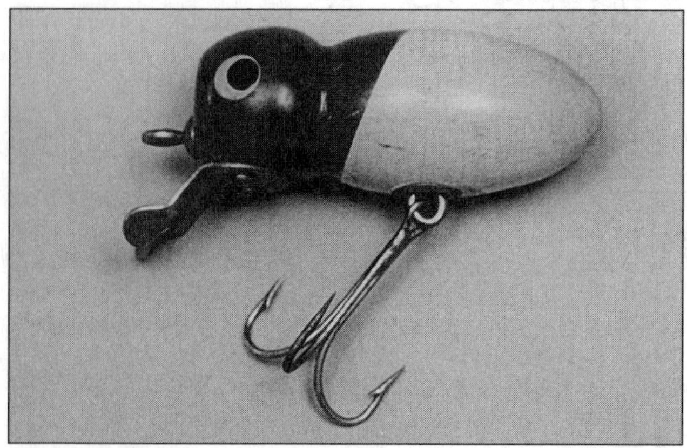

A 2-1/8" JOS. DOODLE BUG. This one has a red head and white body with painted eyes. Cup and screw eye hook hardware.

A c. 1930 lure made with eight color choices: black, brown, gray, white with red or black head, orange with black head. Earliest models have glass eyes followed by painted eyes. They have been found with and without the pigtail style pork rind attachment on the tail. Collector value range: $15-$20.

JOY'S WATER NEMESIS

Joy Bait Company — Lansing, Michigan

JOY'S WATER NEMESIS

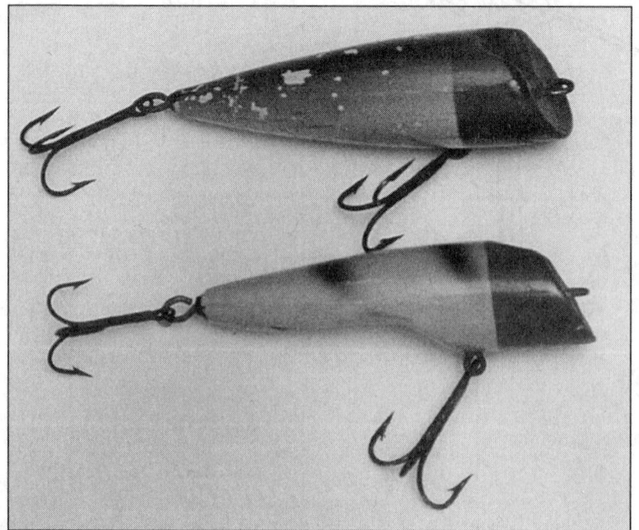

In the very first edition of this book these two lures were illustrated in the unidentified section. They have been identified as to maker, but still, little else is known about the company. The upper lure is yellow with red head and measures 3-3/4". The other is white with red head and black stripes and measures 3-5/8". Collector value range: $15-$30.

JUDAS

Sporting Industries — Chicago, Illinois

"THE FISH BETRAYER SUPREME" read a box flyer with fishing instructions. A search turned up one advertisement in the July, 1947 issue of *Sports Afield.* This plastic lure measures 3-1/2" long, not including the metal lip and it is listed as weighing 5/8-oz. The one in the photo here is colored green with black spots. The box flyer listed two colors: Spotted frog and Bull frog. It was also available weedless in the same colors. Collector value range: $20-40. The box would add substantially to that value. Photo courtesy Jim Muma.

JUMPING JO

Electronic Units, Inc. — Dayton, Ohio

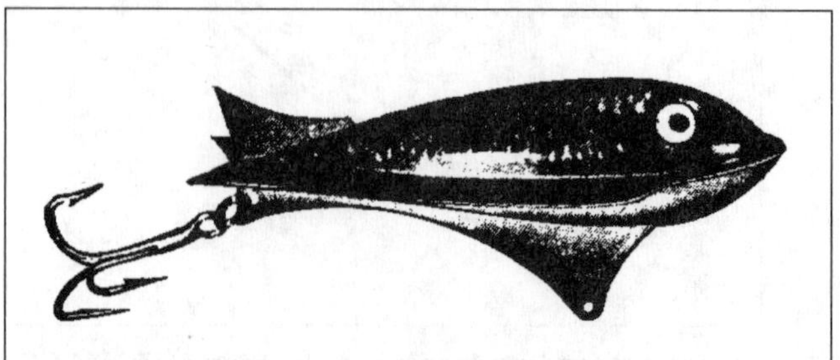

This is a 3-3/4" hollow metal top water lure with one treble hook. You can't see it in the photo, but the lure has a triangular shaped ventral fin that is also the line tie. The one in the photo has a frog finish. Other colors available were: Solid black, black scale, green frog with silver scale, perch, orange with black wavy line, red and white, silver and blue, yellow. These colors are from an auction list and a 1946 advertisement. The auction list had more colors than the ad list so this may not represent all that were available. Collector value range: $20-$40.

K-B SPOON

K-B Bait Company — Superior, Wisconsin

The box this lure came in stated that the K-B Bait Company was a subsidiary of Superior Metal Industries, Inc. and Superior Tool and Die Company. I also found an advertisement (1935) for them by the Superior Door Catch Company (Bait Division). Three sizes were listed, 2-1/2", 3-1/2" and 4-1/2". The box end stated "K-B FISHING SPOON, SIZE 3, COLOR, COPPER". It is a 3-3/8" metal spoon marked "K-B SUPERIOR, WIS PATENTED 3". Collector value range: $5-$15.

K & K MANUFACTURING COMPANY

Toledo, Ohio

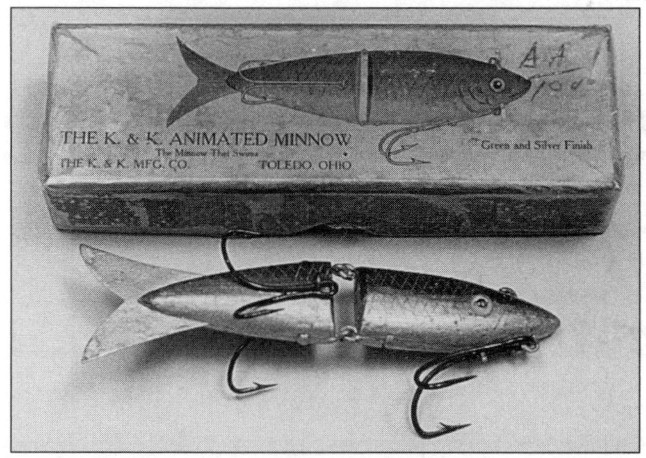

K & K ANIMATED MINNOW with original box.

Little is known about this Toledo, Ohio company, but it is generally accepted that they marketed one of the first, if not *the* first jointed animated minnows. Collector value range for any K & K lures: $750-$1,000. To find one in the box can as much as double that.

The following listing is from a 1907 K & K pocket catalog:

THE K & K ANIMATED MINNOWS

#1A GOLDEN SHINER (female type), 4-1/2", for black bass, 3 double hooks, jointed body.

K & K ANIMATED MINNOWS. The bottom lure has yellow back ground (iris) glass eyes.

#2A GOLDEN SHINER (male type), 4-/12", for sea bass or muskellunge, 3 double hooks, jointed body.

#1B Deep trolling, 4-1/2", for bass, 3 double hooks, jointed body.

#2C Deep trolling silver shiner, 4", for bass, large lake trout, land-locked salmon or striped sea bass, double hooks, jointed body. "THE MINNOETTE", 3", silver shiner, for small bass, rock bass, trout, small pickerel, white bass, etc., 3 double hooks, red devil finish, jointed body.

#3 King of Casting Bait (a surface bait). Swims about 3" under the surface, 3 double hooks, 4-1/2", jointed body, red devil finish (bright red and gold on back and side, silver belly).

UNJOINTED K & K MINNOWS

#1 RAINBOW GHOST - one double hook on body, feathered trailing treble, variegated colors.

#2 MOONLIGHT GHOST - same as above with white body and red stripes.

#4A THE WRIGGLER - one double hook mounted under the nose and a realistic tail fin. Also with 3 double hooks. Silver shiner.

There were several advertisements and catalog entries ranging from 1907 to 1916. A 1910 catalog listed a 5-1/5" GOLDEN SHINER. An Abercrombie and Fitch catalog from the same year did not list that particular size nor did they list any of the non-jointed models.

More about K & K Animated Minnows (taken from a 1909 Abercrombie and Fitch Catalog):

The numbers 1,2 and 5 each have three detachable double hooks and are sinking plugs.

#1	4-1/2"	Gold, silver, black and silver
#2	3-1/2"	Gold, silver, red, rainbow
#5	3"	Gold, silver, red

The numbers 3, 6 and 7 each have three detachable double hooks and are surface plugs.

#3	4-1/2"	Gold, silver, black & red, black & silver, white, rainbow
#6	3"	Gold, silver, red only
#7	3-1/2"	Gold, silver, red only

No. 857,883. PATENTED JUNE 25, 1907.

J. D. KREISSER.

ARTIFICIAL MINNOW FISHING BAIT.

APPLICATION FILED JAN. 8, 1906.

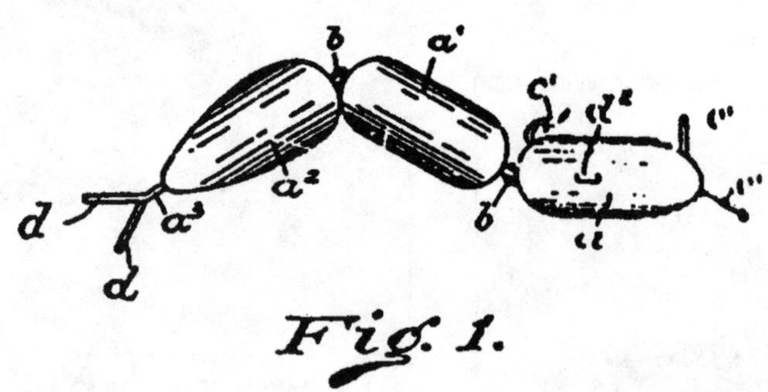

Fig. 1.

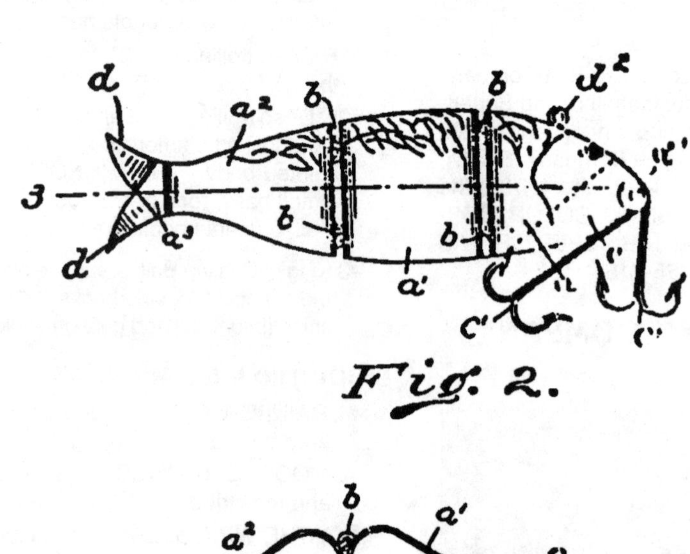

Fig. 2.

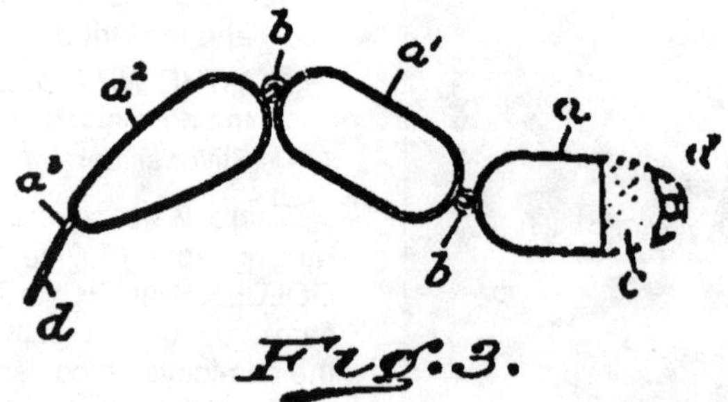

Fig. 3.

Witnesses
George H. Ricke
Geo. E. Heisel

Inventor
John D. Kreisser
By Edward Fischer
Attorney

KAUTZKY MANUFACTURING COMPANY

Joseph Kautzky — Fort Dodge, Iowa

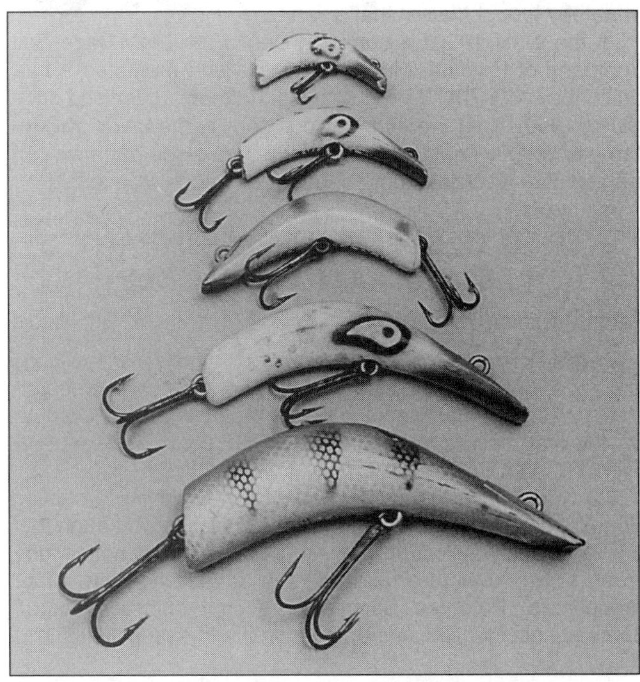

Five sizes of the LAZY IKE from top to bottom: 1-1/4", 1-3/4", 2", 3" and 3-1/2". Each is marked "LAZY IKE" on the belly.

I have a 1951 Kautzky catalog that states "THE KAUTZKY COMPANY IS IN ITS 54th YEAR." A little simple math puts the origin of the company around 1897 and that is a fact. Founded by Joseph Kautzky, an immigrant from Austria, it was originally primarily a gun and gunsmith shop and over the years expanded to include fishing and hunting supplies as well. The addition of Kautzky's sons Joseph, Jr., Rudy and daughter Marie made it a family business. Joseph, Jr. was an expert gunsmith and the Kautzky name is found on patents for many of the improvements in modern firearms.

We are here, however, more interested in what happened starting around the mid-1930s.

It seems there was a fisherman in the Fort Dodge area named Newel Daniels hand-carving a banana shaped lure that was apparently quite a fish-getter. *The story goes that the younger Joe Kautzky saw Daniels working the lure and remarked in part "...look at that lazy ike". One can only presume that the word "ike" meant fish or some such, in the local vernacular. Whatever the case, the name stuck.

*From the article The Legend of the "Lazy Ike" by Dr. Frank Kent, Des Moines, Iowa, 1991 issue of the *N.F.L.C.C. Gazette*, pages 17-18, 21, copyright 1991. Part of the information herein was gleaned from Dr. Kent's article.

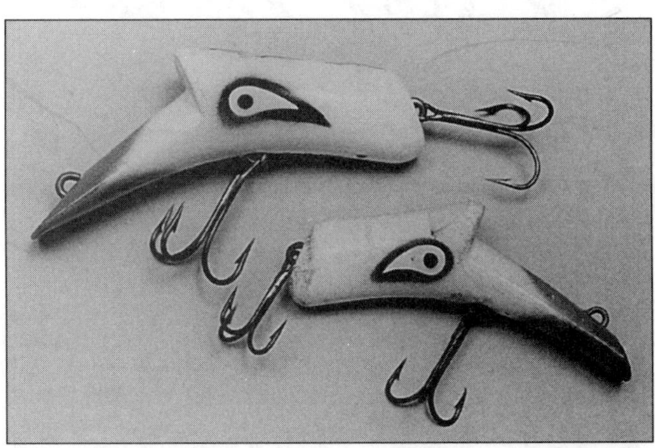

These are wooden TOP IKE's so identified on the belly of the lures. Measuring 3-1/2" and 3" the TOP IKE was placed in the line in the early 1950s. It was made in plastic from 1960 on.

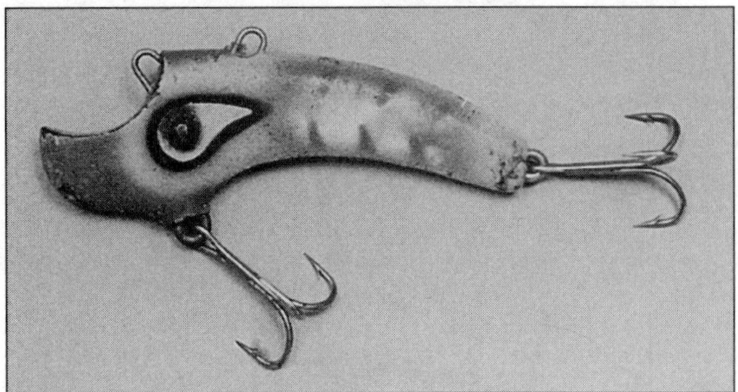

Although Kautzky placed this SKITTER IKE in the line in the 1950s in wood, this 2-7/8" example is a 1960s plastic model.

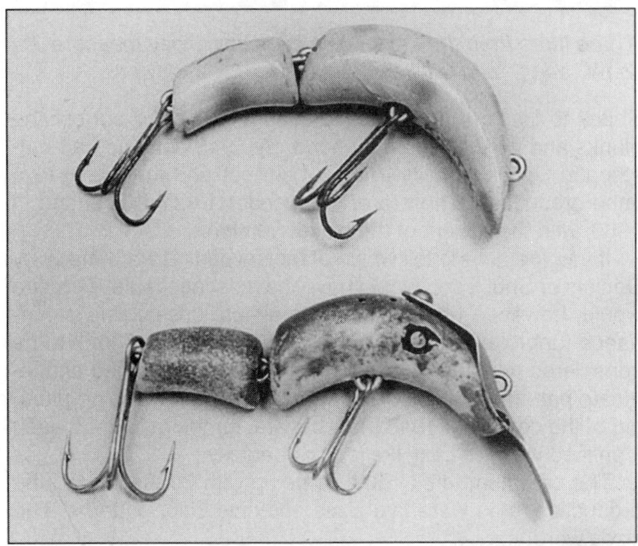

FLEX IKES. They were introduced in the 1950s in wood. These two are post-1960 plastic models. Note the metal dive plane on the lower lure. This is non-standard, but the plane matches those found on the DEEP IKE in the next photo.

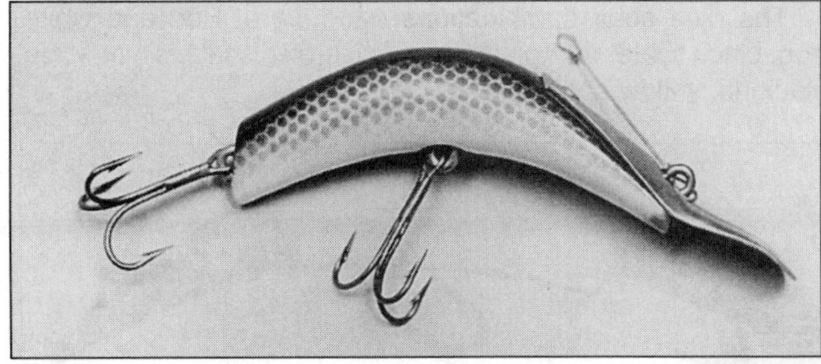

Kautzky DEEP IKES were available in 2-1/2" and 3-1/2" lengths. Made of wood when introduced in 1955, this is a 1960s plastic version.

There are three periods of LAZY IKE production. From 1938 to 1940 the entire production was hand-made by Newell Daniels. Daniels left the company in 1940, turning over rights to the lure to Kautzky. They then hired a man named "Pop"

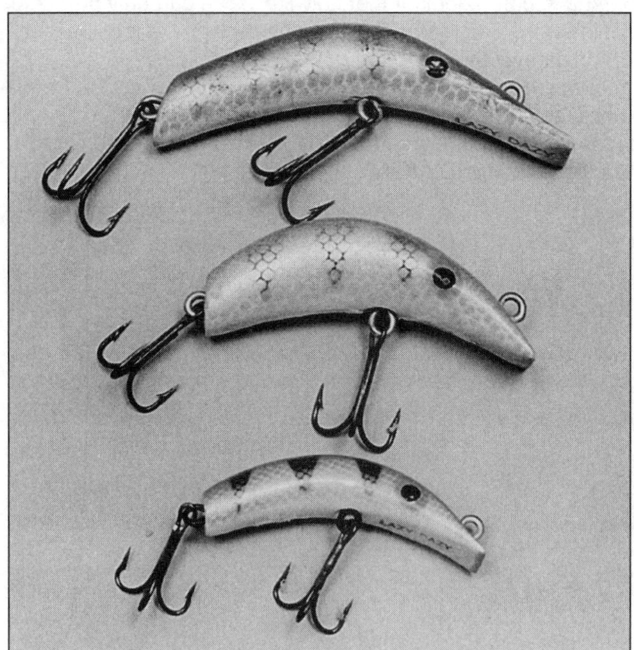

Three lures from the Lazy Daze company. They measure 3". 2-1/4" and 2" respectively.

Shuck to fashion the lures. He used a jig saw to cut out the blanks and finished them by hand. By 1945 demand had outstripped Shuck's ability to turn them out and they went to a lathe production. The era of the wooden LAZY IKE ended in 1960, with the advent of the plastic version.

If you are able to tell which of those you find were made by Daniels or Shuck you would have the most desirable. This find would, however, have to have an almost unshakable provenance (unbroken chain of ownership or attribution) for it to be considered genuine. Both men painted highly detailed and intricate patterns much too sophisticated for the machine painting of the day. After 1945 the lures are, for the most part, each identified with the Lazy Ike logo or Kautzky.

The best numbers I could come up with for the initial lathe production lures were five sizes and nine color patterns. The sizes were:

Tiny Ike Lure 1 -3/4", 1/1 5 oz. (fly rod size)
Lazy Ike, No. 1 2", 1/8 oz.
Lazy Ike, No. 2 2-1/2", 1/4 oz.
Lazy Ike, No. 3 3", 1/2 oz.

The nine color combinations listed were: Red and white, frog, black scale, orange spot, perch, brown scale, silver scale, black rib, yellow spot.

This is a copy of the illustration in the LAZY DAZY ad. Found in the June, 1950 issue of The Outdoorsman magazine.

The machine-made wooden LAZY IKE's were made literally in the millions so their collector value is limited and will not be addressed here. As far as the early, hand-made Daniels and Shuck products, there is virtually no trade data from which to determine a fair collector market value. It would be completely up to the proverbial willing seller and willing buyer to negotiate what they thought fair at that given time.

In the early 1950s a company called the Lazy Daze Bait Company of Preston, Minnesota made and marketed a lure called the LAZY DAZY in plastic. I found them advertised once (June, 1950). They were an obvious copy of the LAZY IKE. Inasmuch as they seemed to fall off the face of the earth we can surmise that Kautzky found them out and put a stop to it.

FRED C. KEELING AND COMPANY KEELING BAIT AND TACKLE

Fred C. Keeling Rockford, Illinois

Keeling came on the scene about 1914 and was in business until the 1930s when the company was sold to Horrocks-Ibbottsom. Keeling's early history is tied to the F.C. Woods Company, the first makers of wooden EXPERT minnows (see THE EXPERT WOODEN MINNOWS).

Many Keeling lures had spinners or metal diving/ wobbling planes that were made with holes in the blades. Although that is a very good way to identify a Keeling lure, it may not be foolproof. These holes are referred to in advertising copy rather vaguely as "Patented Spinners-The light shines through." Some almost identical ads do not contain this particular line

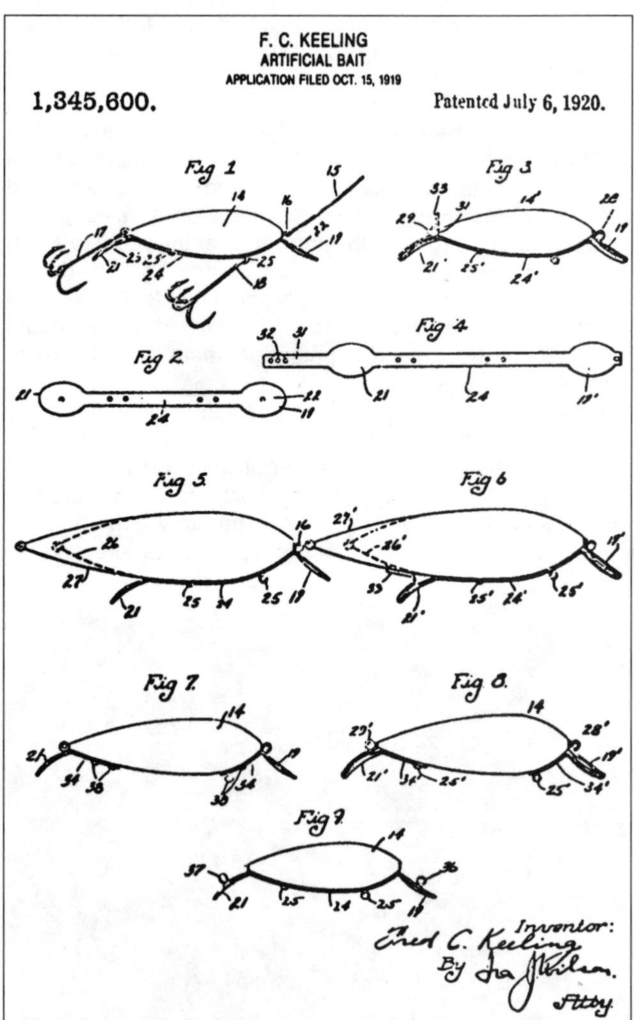

This patent illustration shows the typical Keeling metal under plate/dive and wobble plane. Note that the patent indicates they could be with or without the hole in the planes.

Keeling's King Bee Wiggle Minnow

Price.....................75 cents
Extra Wings........25c a pair
Colors A-W-C

No.	Length
20	2 -inches
25	2½-inches
30	3 -inches
35	3½-inches

The Minnow With Five Motions

The minnow with 5 movements—fingers only tools needed. 1. Wiggles 1 or 20 feet deep. 2. Up and down jump motion. 3. Spins like spoon hook for trolliing. 4. Throws spray on surface. 5. Wounded minnow surface wobble for bass. We bar no make of minnow when we say return and get your money back if anything on the market equals it in action. We offer copper colored minnows this year. Next year others will, as they are great for bass and muskie. In the meantime a copper Keeling expert will help you bring home some fish when other baits fail. For dark water we find aluminum or white best. Woods' patent the only detachable treble hook is part of our equipment. Special hooks used where laws allow 3 barbs only. You save by buying a set and get assorted colors, sizes also if you wish, as the King-bee small is only 2 inches long. Some little wiggler. Colors, copper, aluminum, white. Price, 75c prepaid. Set of three $2.00 prepaid.

FRED C. KEELING
128 N. First Street ROCKFORD, ILL.

A 1916 advertisement for the KING BEE WIGGLE MINNOW.

and the accompanying photos seems not to show the holes. There are a few lures without holes illustrated in these ads that are almost positively Keeling products.

The Keeling EXPERTS were just about identical to Woods or Clark EXPERTS at first, but they began to change a little, soon after the take-over. Keeling made them in 2-1/2", 3", 3-1/2", 4-1/2" and 5" sizes with hooks on the sides and in a few cases, on the belly. They were round, shaped, and flat-sided. All had holes in the propeller blades. In the 1930s they made what appears to be a cheaper version of the EXPERT with no-holes props, non-removable hooks and very simple paint jobs.

The Keeling baits are extensive. What is covered here are the most commonly known of them. There are many more. Any collector who wishes to gain more knowledge about Keeling needs to have Jack Looney's comprehensive book *Identification of Fishing Tackle Manufactured by the Fred C. Keeling & Company.* He is a Keeling specialist and you can't get a better book. Sources for books are listed toward the front of this book.

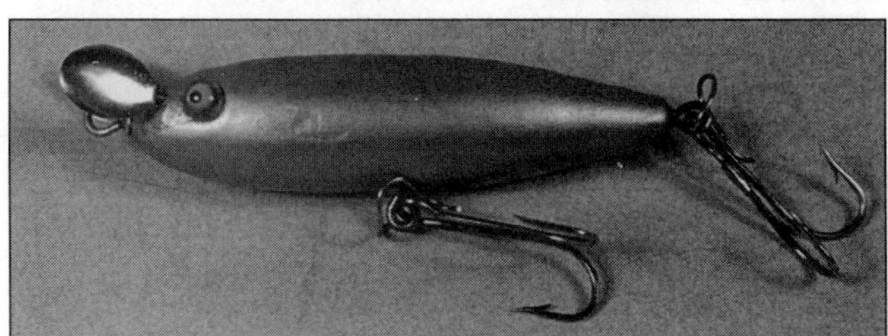

The KING BEE WIGGLE MINNOW. Photo courtesy Jim Muma.

KING BEE WIGGLE MINNOW.

This is the king of Keeling lures in the scarce department. The two blades were made adjustable allowing the fisherman to impart spinning, wiggling, wobbling, jumping, surface spray and deep-running motions. It was probably not around long with 1920 being an estimate of its demise.

It was made in four sizes: 2", 2-1/2", 3", 3-1/2". Collector value range: $250-$350.

This 3" round body lure has no eyes, one belly weight and twisted wire line tie and tail hook hanger. At close examination it appears that the tail hook hanger may have been modified. There may also have originally been a tail mounted propeller spinner. Collector value range: $60-80.

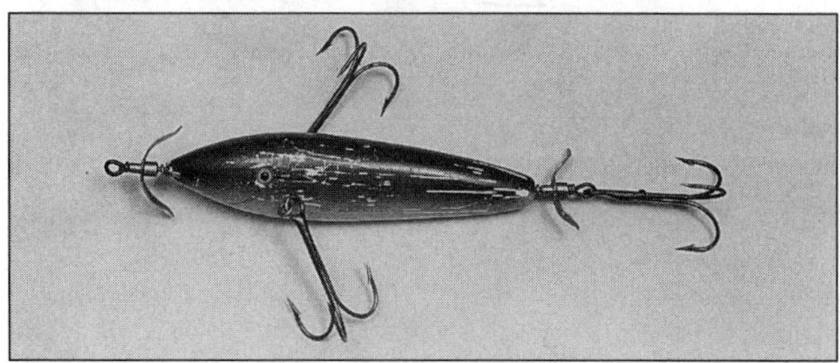

A Keeling shaped-body underwater EXPERT. Says "The Expert" on the side. The long 5" body is unusual. It has five belly weights, yellow glass eyes and a twisted through-body side treble hook hanger. Collector value range: $300-$400.

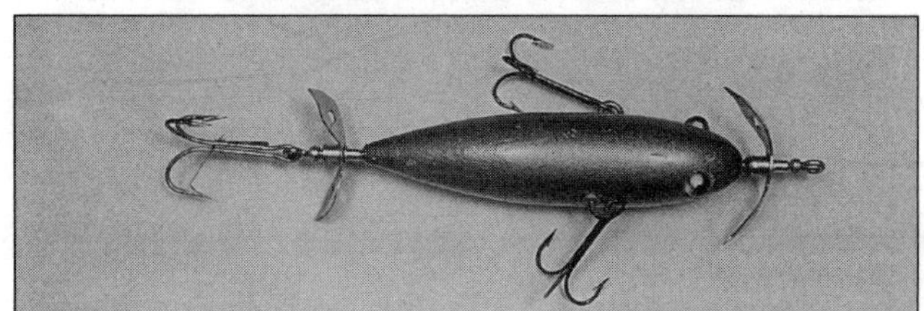

This 3-5/8" round-body EXPERT type has Keeling characteristics including the odd-ball spring-loaded side hook hangers. Collector value range: $200-$300.

A pair of Keeling unknowns. The one with the two propellers look something like the EXPERT above, but it has a tail somewhat reminiscent of the ST. JOHN'S WIGGLE below. Collector value range: $150-$225.. The other unknown Keeling is valued at $300-$400. Photo courtesy Jim Muma.

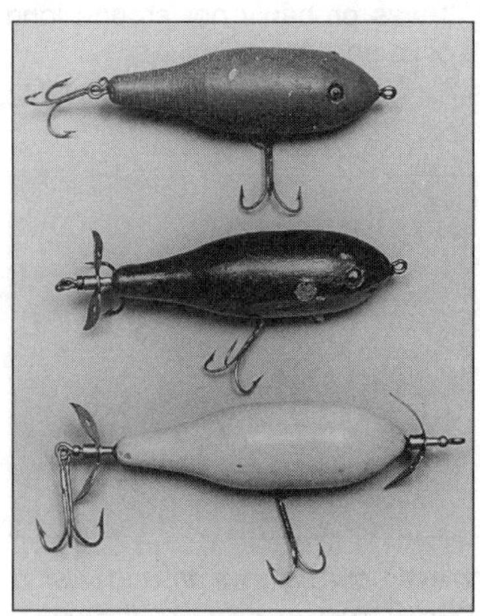

Keeling St. Johns Wiggle. This photo shows the three variations of the lure. Each is 3-3/4" long and has the typical Keeling spring loaded hook hanger. Top two have glass eyes and one internal belly weight forward of the belly hook. Center has five additional belly weights but it is obvious upon examinatin that they were added by fisherman. Collector value range: $150-$300.

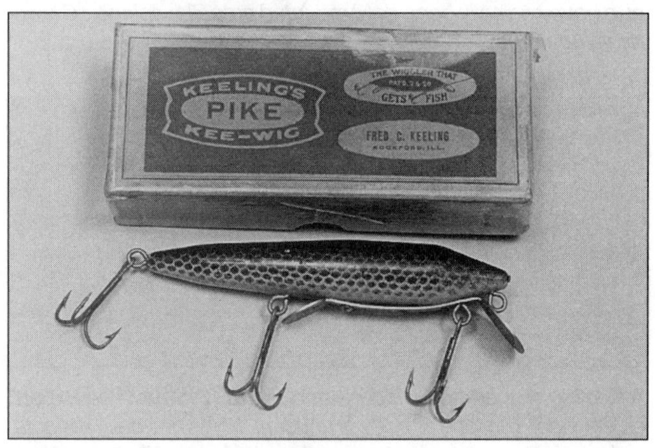

Keeling Pike KEE WIG with box. Measures 4-5/8" body length. No holes in the spoon-like portions of the metal. Box states the patent date as July 6, 1920. Collector value range: $50-$70.

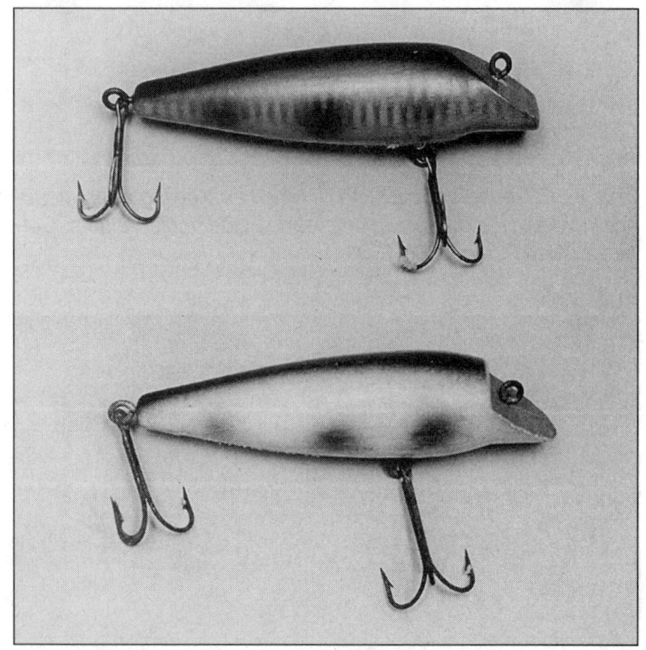

The upper lure in this photo is a BEARCAT. It is 3-7/8" and has plain screw eye hook hangers. The lower lure is the same size and shape and shares the same characteristics except for the slightly different lip design. Collector value range: $50-$60 each

This unidentified Keeling lure is the style of the Heddon ARTISTIC MINNOW and Pflueger SIMPLEX. It is 1-13/16" long and has both the Keeling prop with holes and spring-loaded hook hangers. Collector value range: $200-$300.

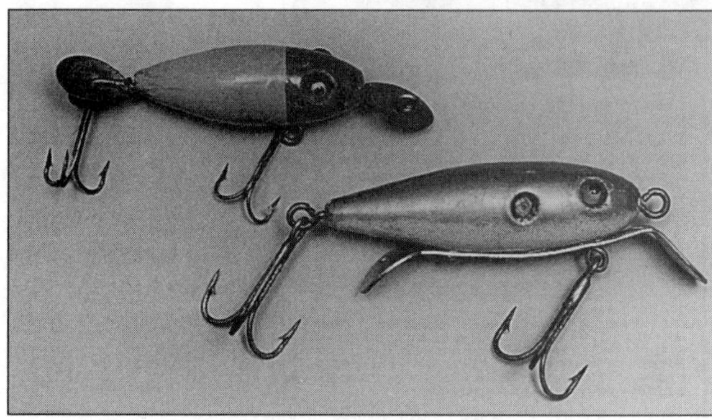

The lower lure is 2-5/8" long, has glass eyes and the Keeling belly fixture with holes. The apparent defect on the side appears almost as if it were done on purpose. The upper lure measures 2", is glass-eyed and sports brass spoons soldered to the line tie and tail hook hanger. It must have been a nightmare to tune for running true. Collector value range: $40-$50 each

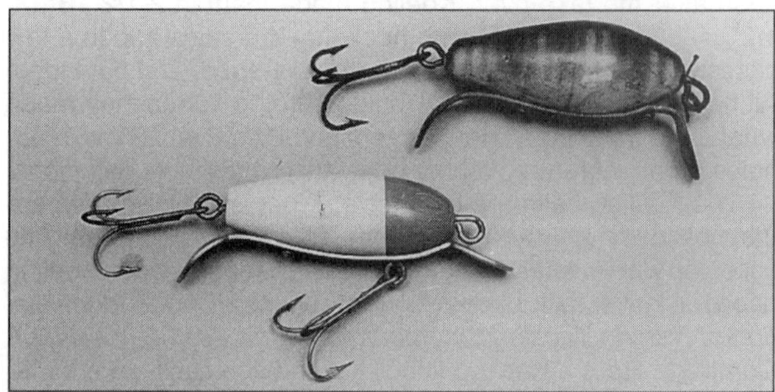

Two Keeling LITTLE TOMS measuring 2-1/2" and 2". Note the different body shapes. Both have the Keeling belly fixture with holes in the blades. Collector value range: $40-50.

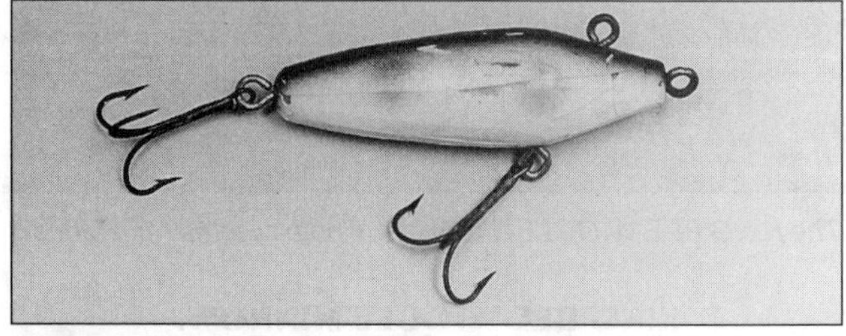

This lure is tentatively identified as a Keeling LITTLE FISH SPEAR. It is 2-3/4" long and has simple screw eye line tie and hook hangers. Collector value range: $40-50.

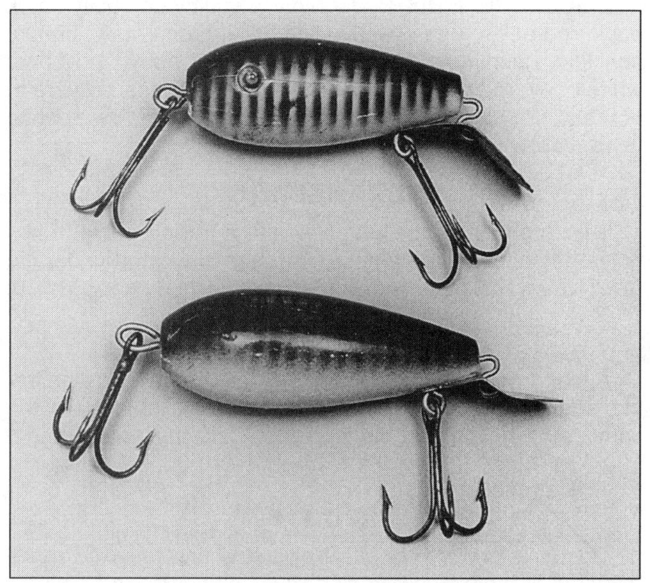

These two lures are probable Keelings. Both have the typical Keeling paint finish and unmarked metal diving lips. They measure 2-1/2" and 2-3/4". The larger one sports a double bend metal lip that is unmarked. The smaller one has glass eyes. The lip is painted red and marked "4 KEELING FLUTED SPOON". Collector value range: $65-$80.

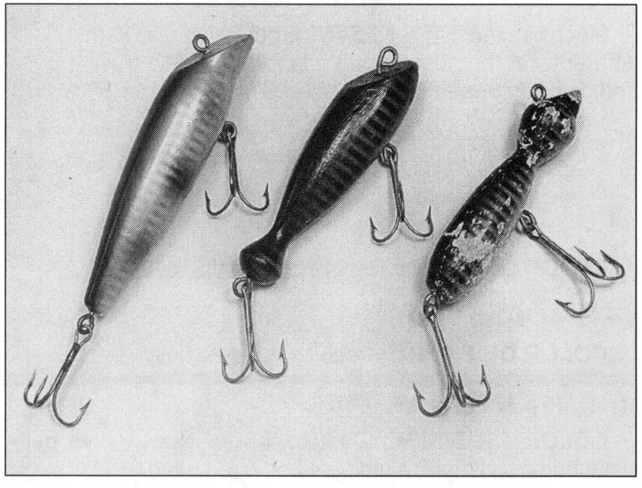

Three unknown lures attributed to Keeling because of their paint patterns. Top measures 4-1/2 and is an early BEARCAT. Center and bottom measures 3-1/3 and 3-1/4". Collector value range: $40-$50 each.

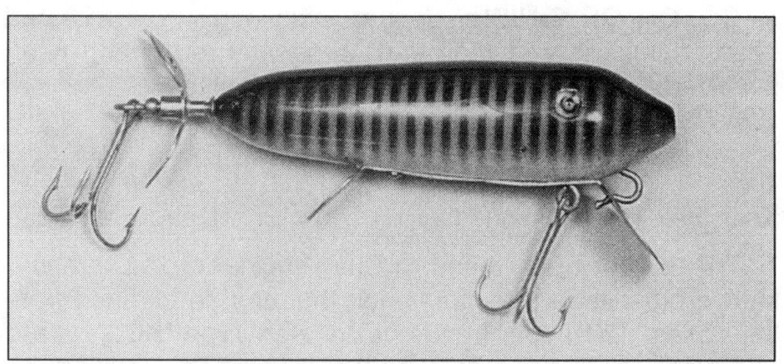

Typical Keeling paint pattern and blades. No holes in spoon-like portions of the metal, but the propeller does have the hoes. 5-7/8" body length. Similar to BASS-KEE-WIG. Collector value range: $30-$40.

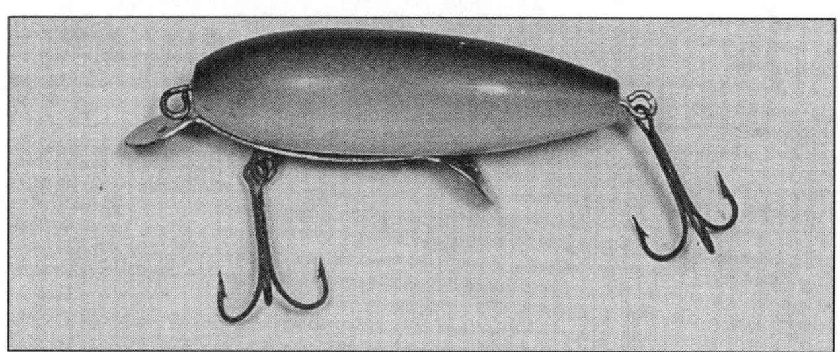

A probable Keeling TOM THUMB WIGGLER, the 3-1/4" SURFACE TOM. Metal body plate has "Keeling" stamped on it. Holes in lips. Actual measurement is 3-1/2". Collector value range: $30-$40.

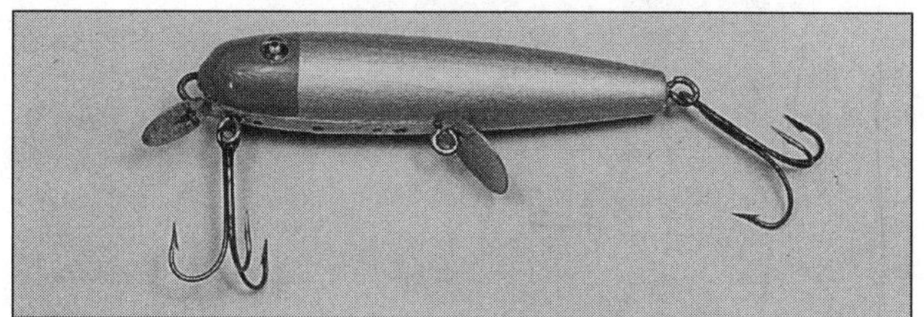

This lure measures 4" and has glass eyes and typical metal belly plate with lip at either end. The rear lip is stampled KEELING and the forward lip is stamped PAT'D 7-6-20. Probable PIKE-KEE-WIG. Collector value range: $30-$40.

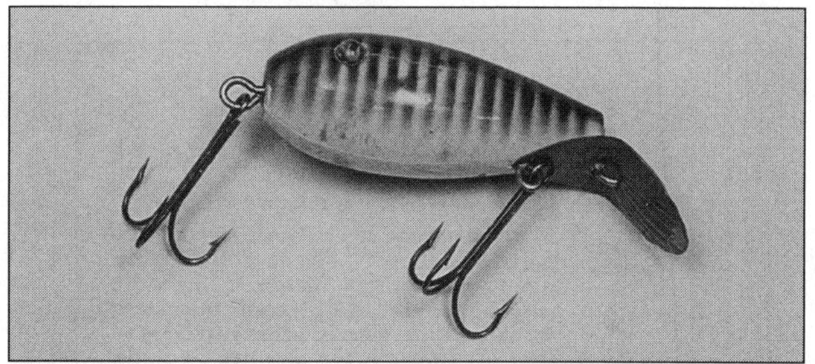

Unknown glass-eyed plug with typical Keeling paint job. Note the unusual fluted metal lip. Oollector value range: $40-$50.

An early Keeling SURFACE TOM in "beater" condition. 3-1/2" long it has no holes in the lips, but it is stamped Keeling.

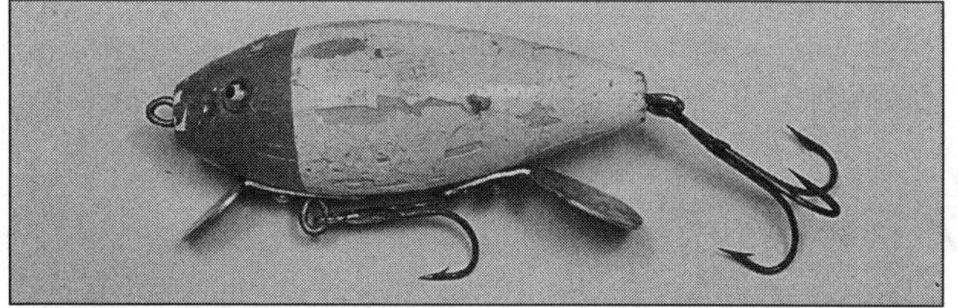

Unknown fat body, red headed lure. Has typical Keeling one-piece metal belly plate with for and aft lips. Collector value range: $25-$30

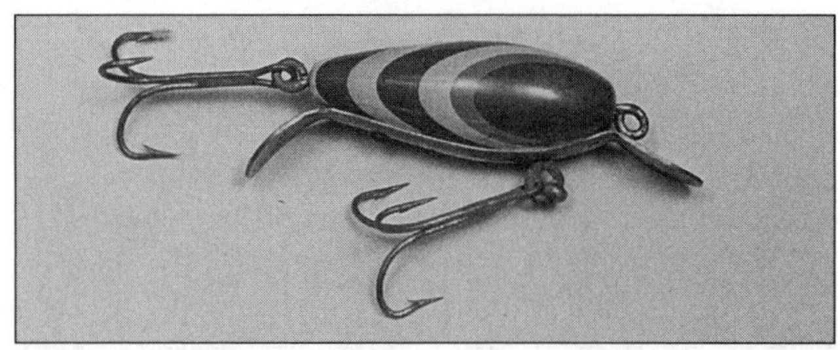

Keeling BABY TOM. Measure 2-1/2" and has holes in blades. Collector value range: $25-$35.

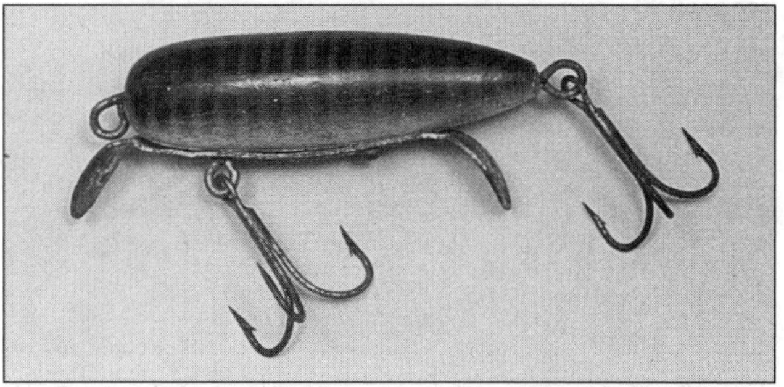

Probable Keeling LITTLE TOM. Measures 2-1/2" and has holes in blades. Collector value range $20-$30.

TOM THUMB WIGGLERS

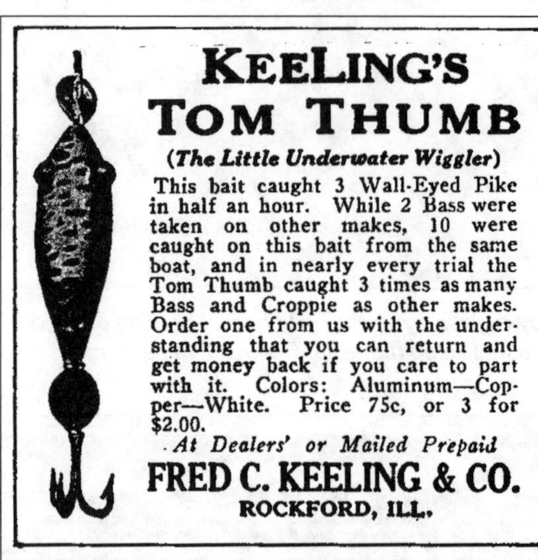

KEELING'S TOM THUMB

(*The Little Underwater Wiggler*)

This bait caught 3 Wall-Eyed Pike in half an hour. While 2 Bass were taken on other makes, 10 were caught on this bait from the same boat, and in nearly every trial the Tom Thumb caught 3 times as many Bass and Croppie as other makes. Order one from us with the understanding that you can return and get money back if you care to part with it. Colors: Aluminum—Copper—White. Price 75c, or 3 for $2.00.

At Dealers' or Mailed Prepaid

FRED C. KEELING & CO.

ROCKFORD, ILL.

A Keeling advertisement for the TOM THUMB WIGGLER from the May, 1918 issue of The Outers Book magazine.

This bait has a metal plate on the belly the front and rear portions ending in metal spoon shapes. These spoons have holes in the center and the metal belly portion has "KEELING" stamped in it. The lure came in five sizes, 12 colors and has one or two belly trebles and a trailing treble hook. Collector value range: $20-$30.

BODY

NAME	LENGTH
Baby Tom	2"
Little Tom	2-1/2"
Pike Tom	2-3/4"
Big Tom	3"
Surface Tom	3-1/4"

COLOR OR FINISH: Dark back, aluminum belly; dark back, red belly; green back, white belly; green body, bronze speckled; aluminum body, red head; gold body, red head; white body, red head; dark back, red sides, white belly; rainbow striped; yellow with red and green spots; black with white head; yellow with black head.

SURF-KEE-WIG

This lure has two belly trebles and a trailing treble. It has only one spoon-shaped metal plate and is located under the tail. Size and colors unknown. Collector value range: $20-$30.

TIP-TOP

A tear drop shaped plug with one belly treble, a trailing treble and tail mounted propeller. Colors available were the same as the Tom Thumb Wiggles. Collector value range: $20-$30.

RED-FIN

This is a lure with one trailing treble and tail- and nose-mounted propellers. It has glass eyes and came in an aluminum, copper, or white finish. Collector value range: $20-$30.

BASS-KEE-WIG

The same lure as the TOM THUMB WIGGLER except the metal belly plate/double spoon rig is reversed so that the larger spoon is forward. Collector value range: $20-$30.

PIKE-KEE-WIG

Much like the BASS KEE-WIG, but larger and shaped a bit differently at the nose. It had a belly treble and trailing treble and came in three models. Collector value range: $20-$30.

BODY

NAME	LENGTH
Baby	3-1/2"

COLOR OR FINISH: Dark back, aluminum belly.

Standard 4-1/2"

COLOR OR FINISH: Green back, white belly

Musky (heavy duty) 4-1/2"

COLOR OR FINISH: Dark back, red sides, white belly, white body, red head, aluminum body, red head.

SCOUT

The SCOUT has two belly treble hooks, line tie on top of the head, and a metal diving lip mounted directly on the front of the flat nose. Collector value range: $20-$30.

COLOR OR FINISH: Copper, aluminum, gold with red head, aluminum with red head, white with red head, green speckled.

KEEN KNIGHT

Keen Bait Manufacturing Co. Detroit, Michigan

These two lures, found in their original boxes, are unknown other than the information that can be gleaned from the boxes. The upper lure is designated Type "KC6", is red with black spots and measures 3-1/4" long. The smaller one is designated "KC-4", measures 1-5/8" and has red head and white body. The body may have originally been white and has yellowed with age. It's hard to say. Collector value range: $50-$150. Photo courtesy Clarence Zahn.

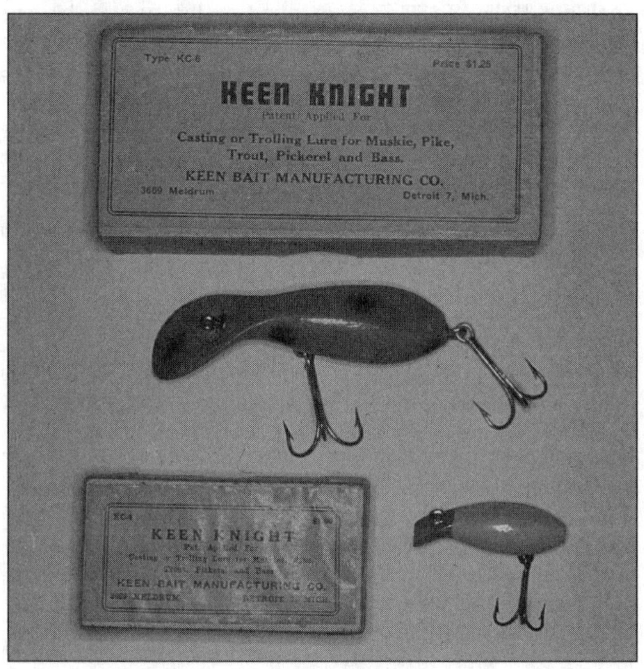

KELLER WEEDLESS SURFACE BAIT

Jim Keller — Wilmette, Illinois

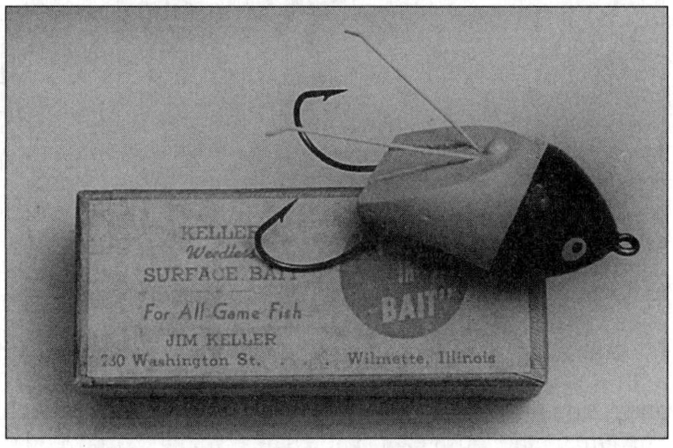

This wooden chunk of a lure is very similar to the Coldwater Bait Company's COMSTOCK CHUNK so don't confuse them if you come across one. The one in the photo measures 2-1/8" body and 3-1/4" overall including the hooks. The box states it is the 5/8 oz. size and that there was a 1/4 oz. size available. Presumably it was a bit smaller. It has a yellow body and black head with yellow and black painted eyes. Other available colors and vintage are unknown at this time. There was no trade data from which to draw a realistic value.

KENT FROG AND KENT DOUBLE SPINNER ARTIFICIAL MINNOW

F.A. Pardee and Company — Kent, Ohio
Samuel H. Friend — Kent, Ohio
Enterprise Manufacturing (Pflueger) — Akron, Ohio

F. A. Pardee and Co. was doing business at least as early as 1900. There was an advertisement in *Recreation* magazine that year, for the DOUBLE SPINNER ARTIFICIAL BAIT. This wooden plug is most likely the forerunner of Pflueger's TRORY UNDERWATER MINNOW or TRORY WOODEN MINNOW.

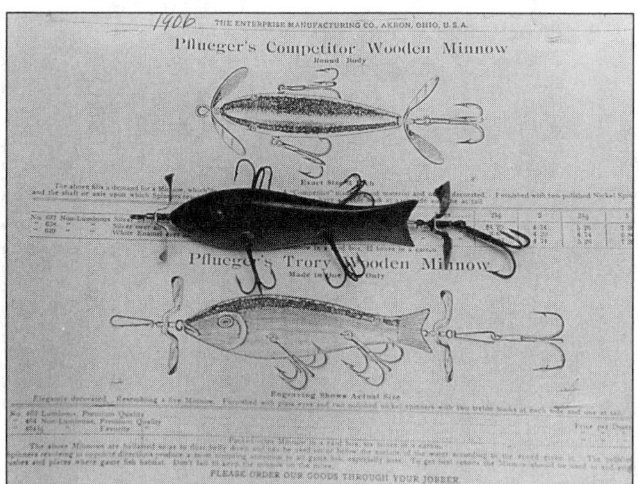

Similar ads for the same lure appear consistently until about 1904 and then seem to disappear from periodicals. By then Pardee was calling it the DOUBLE SPINNER ARTIFICIAL MINNOW. In 1906 a William Mills and Son catalog offered a "MANCO Wood Minnow" that is suspiciously similar to both the Pardee Double Spinner Minnow and the Trory Minnow by Pflueger which was offered in their early 1900s catalogs. The 1906 Pflueger catalog was the last to list it.

The photo of the lure on a catalog page here is of a lure that is probably a late Pardee or early Pflueger. It is either a TRORY or a DOUBLE SPINNER. The type of aluminum props on it were used by Pardee, but this prop was also one of the earliest types used by Pflueger. You will note the difference between the hook hardware on the lure and in the catalog illustration. The plugs are otherwise almost identical.

Top lure measures 3-7/8", has yellow glass eyes, red glass beads for bearings, internal belly weights, through-body twisted wire line tie/hook hangers and Friend patented split-ring hook eyes. Bottom lure measures 4" and exhibits the same characteristics as above. Poor paint is a result of improper cleaning of the plug. These two represent the transition from the KENT DOUBLE SPINNER (lower) to the PFLUEGER TRORY MINNOW (upper).

A 1906 advertisement announced that Samuel H. Friend had taken over the Pardee Company. The ad copy indicated that Friend had long been the manager of the company and took over upon Mr. Pardee's retirement. The ad also illustrated the top lure in the photo above. It was called "The KENT Double Spinner Bait." What is significant here is the elimination of the shaped tail fin visible in the lower lure and the use of newer type propeller spinners. Note the cone shape of the tube at the rear of the prop. Although the blades on the DOUBLE SPINNER are bow tie type now, most of the older style Pardee/Friend props had this same cone-shaped tube. The red bearing beads are also common to Pardee/ Friend products. All the hardware on this newer DOUBLE SPINNER is through-

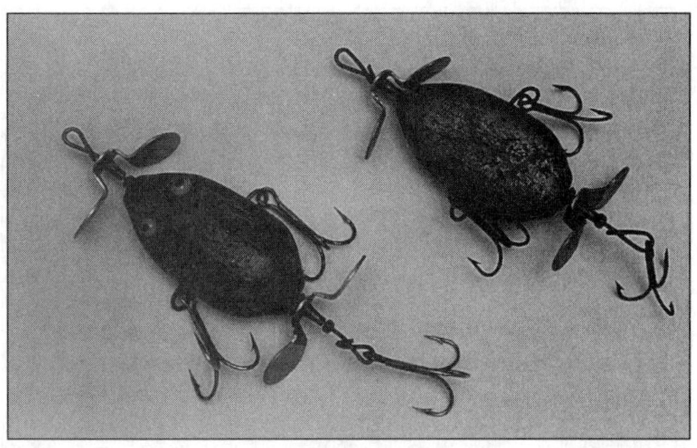

body and strong. There are heavy duty soldered side hook hangers also. Except for the beads and the cone-shaped tube type props this lure is almost a dead ringer for the Pflueger WIZARD that came along about 1906. Collector value range for the Pardee/Friend KENT WOODEN DOUBLE SPINNER MINNOWS: $1,500-$3,000.

Pictured here are two hand-made Samuel Friend KENT FROGS (as they are commonly known). They were listed in catalogs and ads variously as KENT CHAMPION FLOATER, KENT FROG FLOATER, KENT FLOATING BAIT, MANCO FLOATING FROG, and finally the "Pflueger KENT-FLOATER Bait." The one on the left is said to be hand-made by Samuel H. Friend. The earliest reference I found for the lure was as the "MANCO Floating Frog" in a 1906 William Mills and Son fishing tackle catalog. The one on the right closely resembles the Manco frog. It has two words stenciled on the belly, but only the first word is legible, "THE FROG." In the last edition I speculated that the four illegible letters on the bottom of the hand-made Samuel Kent frog might say "THE FROG". Since then, young Chris Crawford, of Ft. Wayne, Indiana sent me the following photos of his frog, where the letters are more readable and spell out "THE KENT". The lettering on the belly of his has been enhanced with pen and ink in the photo for clarity. The Samuel Friend Frogs in the previous photos all have glass eyes and twisted wire through-body hook hangers. Collector value range for KENT FROGS: $1,500-$2,000.

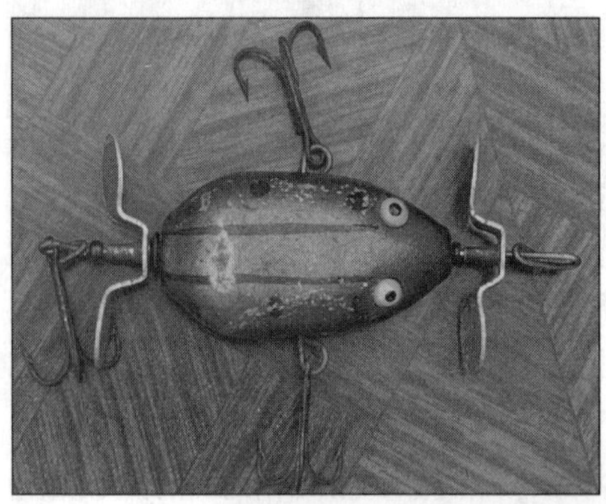

Photos courtesy of Chris Crawford.

Curiously, after the 1906 ad saying Friend had taken over operation of the Pardee Company, I found no subsequent advertisements by Samuel Friend. The KENT FROG did, however, appear often in various tackle company catalogs. In addition it appears that the Pflueger Company obtained the rights to the frog lure. There was a short reference with a drawing of the KENT FROG in the February, 1908 issue of *Field and Stream magazine* that said in part "...Kent Champion Floater manufactured by Samuel Friend, Kent, Ohio". It said further that it was made of red cedar and the sizes was 2-1/8" x 1/8", 3/4 oz.

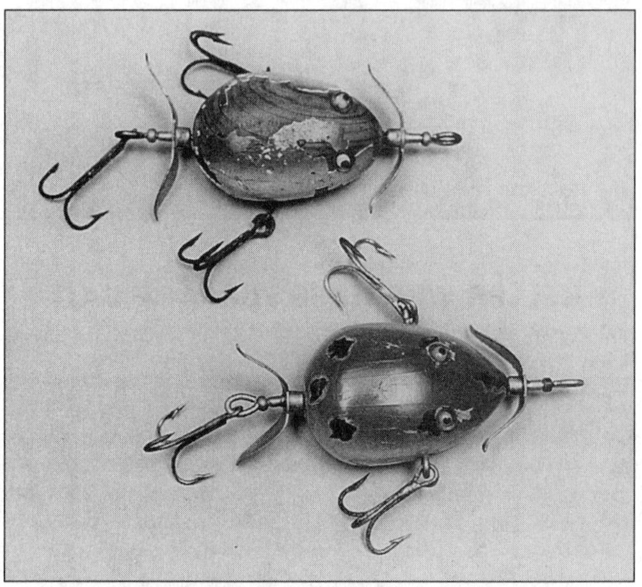

In the photo above are two that must represent the transition from Friend to Pflueger. The one on the bottom has glass eyes, through-body twisted wire side hook hangers and Pflueger style propeller spinners. The props are stamped with a "P" with in a diamond, but they are also stamped with an "R" and "L" on the blades. The latter is typical of Pflueger props. The lure on the top is exactly the same, with the exception of the use of the screw eye hook hangers. Apparently toward the end of the Pardee/Friend Company activity they were buying props from Pflueger. In any case the next development took place sometime prior to 1919. The Pflueger catalog collection I studied had a gap between the 1897 and 1919 issues. The fully "Pfluergerized" KENT FLOATER appears in the 1919 issue. Collector value range for the last PARDEE/FRIEND FROGS: $1,500-$2,000.

I came across a mail order catalog that contained an amazingly eclectic offering of goods, mostly cheap, that illustrated one very interesting item for $7.95. I tried to buy one, but the catalog was a year old and they didn't have any left. It was what they called the "AMAZING $2000 LURE". The illustration was of a KENT FROG. When I called about it the lady said "Oh yes, the Kent Frog." The words Kent Frog are never mentioned in the ad. The following is part of the ad copy; it's amusing. "Kept in Secret Vault By Fishing Genius-Now Available To The Public. Fabulous fishing lure was taken off the market in 1927 and kept in the hands of select private fishermen! One of the original lures was snapped up in an auction for an incredible $2,000!" We know about the auction, but who was the "Fishing Genius" and where was his "Secret Vault"?

THE KENTUCKY LEADER
Lex Baits

Hampton Fishing Lures — Louisville, Kentucky

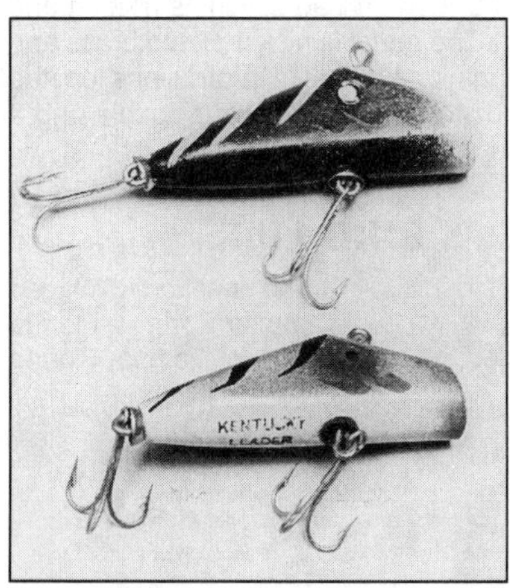

A pair of Lex Baits, KENTUCKY LEADERS. Each measures 2-5/8".

Thomas L. Hampton was the man who made the lure shaped like his home state. The story is a familiar one. Hampton was a fisherman who started making his own lure, using it and giving a few to fishing buddies. It was a fish-getter and the business was born out of demand. He went into the business in earnest in 1944 taking a partner named Irion, from across the river in Indiana. Hampton made the lures and Irion marketed them from his location in Indiana. The whole family was in the business of making and painting the lures. The lures all had indented painted eyes, cup and screw eye hook hardware. They were made in a 1/4 oz. spinning size and a 1/2 oz. casting size. All the lures had two red gill marks painted on each side of the head area. The company name changed to Hampton Fishing Lures a couple of years before Hampton's death in 1954. Collector value range: $20-$35.

COLOR OR FINISH: White body, black ribs with red nose; white body, black back with red nose*, yellow body with gray back and red nose*, yellow body with green back and red nose*, yellow body with black ribs, red back and red nose; yellow body with black ribs, green back and red nose; gray body with black ribs, back and nose; dark green body with yellow ribs and yellow nose; black body with yellow ribs and red nose; dark green body with light green back and red nose*.

**Spinning size only.*

THE KIMMICH MOUSE

Kimmich Bait Company — Ellwood City, Pennsylvania

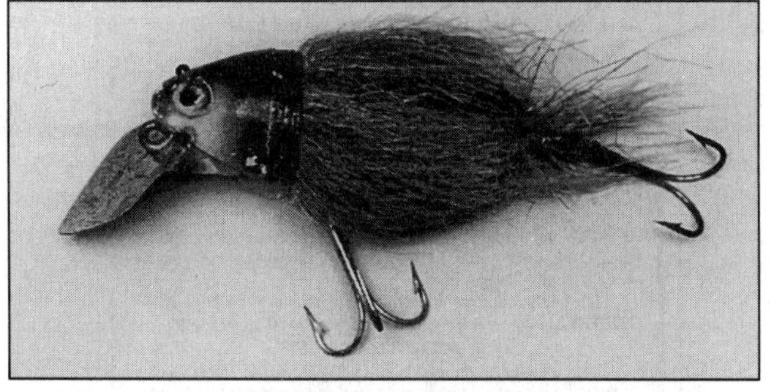

This lure is actually called the "Kimmich Special Mouse" according to the pamphlet packed in the box with the lure. It was patented by Harry Kimmich in 1929. The pamphlet said it was available in several colors, but did not specify what they were. Not known to many collectors is the lure was also available in wood body without the hair. Collector value range: $200-$300.

KIMMICH HAIRLESS MICE. Both lips marked patented January 22, 1929. The large one is 3-1/4" and the small one 2-1/4".

KING BINGO

Doug English Lure Co. — Corpus Christi, Texas

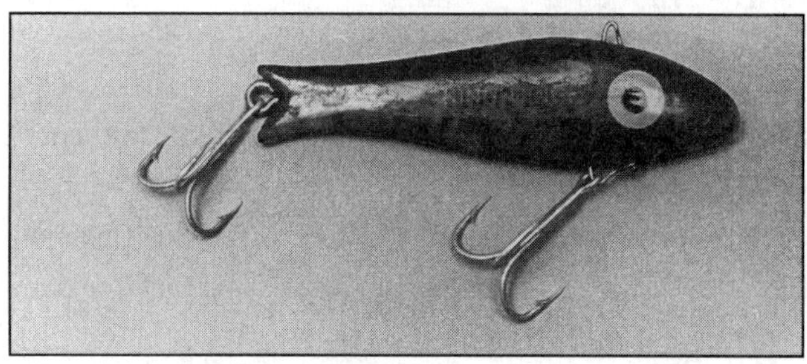

No advertising or catalog entries were found for this lure or company. It is a strong 3-5/8" translucent plastic lure. If you look hard you may be able to see the integrated hook hanger/line tie wire passing through the body just behind the eye. The words "KING BINGO" are also just barely visible. Collector value range: $5-$10.

KINGFISHER WOOD MINNOW

Edward K. Tryon — Philadelphia, Pennsylvania

This lure is actually a Pflueger 2-3/4" NEVERFAIL with unmarked propeller spinners. The Edward K. Tryon Company was a large fishing tackle dealer that did not manufacture any lures. They bought the products of other companies and sold them under their KINGFISHER house brand. It isn't obvious in the photo, but the box is made of wood with a paper label. Their were also cardboard boxes. The kingfisher birds are printed in red and the rest is printed in black. Collector value range: $50-$100, with the box $200-$300.

There were several other lures in the KINGFISHER line. They were all made by other companies. The following were listed in a 1939 Edward K. Tryon catalog:

KING FISHER LINE	SIZE	MADE BY
SURFACE LURE	3"	Heddon
BASS-A-LURE	3-3/4"	Shakespeare

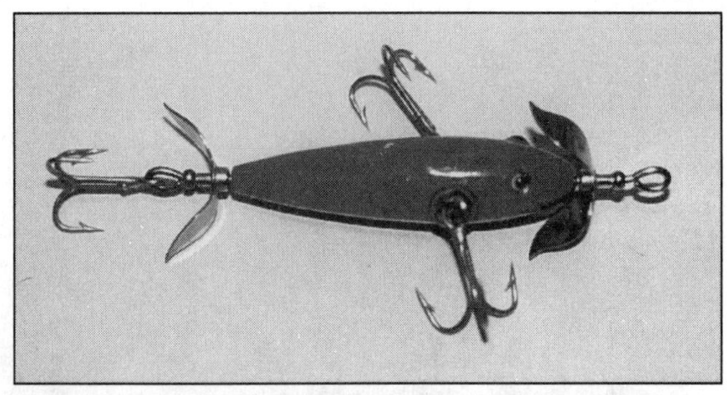

KING FISHER and original cardboard box. Made by Pflueger for the Edward K. Tryon company.

KING FISHER LINE	SIZE	MADE BY
BABY BASS-A-LURE	2-3/4"	Shakespeare
MIDGET BASS-A-LURE	2-1/4"	Shakespeare
SPECIAL MOUSE	3"	Shakespeare?
PIKE MINNOW	4"	Creek Chub Bait Company
JOINTED PIKE	3-1/4"	Creek Chub Bait Company
PIKE JUNIOR	3-1/4"	Creek Chub Bait Company
FLOATING INJURED MINNOW	3-3/4"	Creek Chub Bait Company
SMALL INJURED MINNOW	2-5/8"	Creek Chub Bait Company
TROUT PLUG	1-3/4"	South Bend
FLY ROD MINNOW	1"	South Bend
SINKING RIVER MINNOW	2-3/4"	Millsite

KING SPIRAL

King Spiral Company — Detroit, Michigan

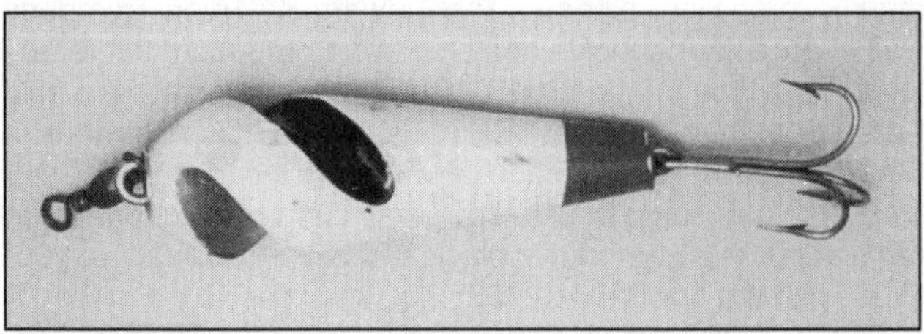

A strongly made 2-1/2" plug. Note the tail and nose reinforcing metal cup inserts. The lure is made of white birch and a man named L.A. Rose is associated with the King Spiral Company. It came in a cardboard tube. Little else is known about the company. Collector value range: $50-$100.

KING WIGGLER c. 1918

King Bait Company — Minneapolis, Minnesota

This is a hollow tubular metal lure with a rounded end cap and a sloped nose painted red. One ad says it is 3" long and another states it is 3-1/2". The metal is nickel-plated brass and there are two metal wings or blade-like protrusions on the sloped nose. Weight, 1 oz., one belly mounted double and a trailing hook. Collector value range: $75-$100.

KINNEY'S BIRD LURE

H.A. Kinney Company — Grand Junction, Michigan
Bangor, Michigan — Sulfur Springs, Florida
Old Hickory Rod & Tackle Co. — Tampa, Florida

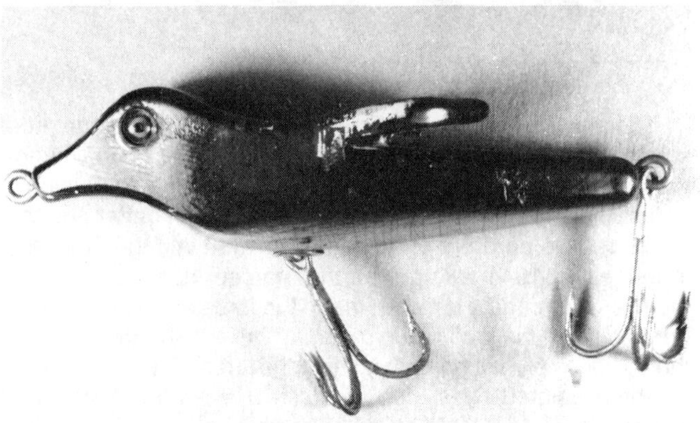

KINNEY'S BIRD LURES
FOR GAME FISH
Anglers, This Bird Don't "Sing"—It's a "Thriller"

THE WORLD'S FIRST BIRD LURE
For All Game Fish

ANGLERS know that a fluttering bird or fledgling on the water, is "desert" for all game fish. They strike it savagely. Our BIRD LURES positively imitate a fluttering bird on the water, when retrieved slowly, in short, "choppy" jerks, and if MR. BASS is around, "you got him." He don't "strike it," he "KILLS IT." **(No mistake about this.)**

Our BIRDS are each one finished and decorated in true AMERICAN BIRD colors, by one of the best artists in the Country.

PRICE $1.00 EACH, Postpaid
(STATE COLOR)

THE BEST DOLLAR'S WORTH YOU EVER GOT

This lure is the most expensive one made to sell at $1.00, but, anticipating an enormous sale—you get quality—we get ours in quantity.

Kinney's Famous BIRD LURES are proven BIG FISH GETTERS, and will give you Anglers "thrills" aplenty.

"THRILLS THAT LAST"

Just slip us a Dollar Bill, and get yours. State color of BIRD wanted, and pass this along to your fishing Buddy, (a sportsman's favor.) He will thank you.

ADDRESS
Old Hickory Rod & Tackle Company
Route No. 1, Box 137 A — Tampa, Florida

The KINNEY BIRD LURE was patented in 1927 by Herbert A. Kinney. They were painted fairly realistically, representing various species of birds. At some point there was some sort of connection to the Heddon Company. As you can see by the accompanying advertising flyer, the stamped words "HEDDON FINISH" at the upper left corner.

The above photo is of a KINNEY BIRD LURE painted like a red-winged black bird. It has cup hardware with the Heddon "L-rig" hook hanger. Collector value range: $400-$600.

KIRWAN'S BAD EGG c.1923

M.F. Kirwan Manufacturer — O'Neill, Nebraska

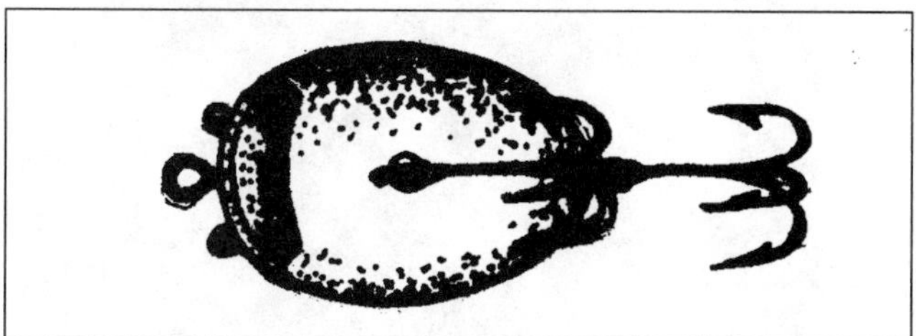

This plug was made in the shape of an egg. It had two small protruding eyes a belly treble and trailing treble hook. Made in white, yellow or silver. I found it advertised in a 1923 issue of *Outers' Recreation* magazine. Collector value range: $100-$200.

KLIPON LURES

Green-Wyle Company — Brooklyn, New York

These are two KLIPON lures. The upper measures 3-3/4", is multicolored and has glass eyes. There is a metal face plate that is marked "KLIPON". The smaller lure is 3" long. Both have peculiar hook hangers discussed in the text.

This c. 1930s company manufactured five different lures and they were available in 12 different finishes. This was stated in the only advertising I could find for the company. It did not list the colors. The advertisement illustrated an odd hook hanger that allowed attaching and detaching hooks at will. The ad stated "At Last-A Hookless Plug". Apparently they were sold without hooks so the fisherman could attach the hook of his choice. Collector value range: $100-$200.

THE KROKER

Mid North Tackle Company — Wells, Minnesota

This lure was mistakenly attributed to Jamison in the third edition. A collector recognized it for what he knew to be the KROKER, we now have it correctly identified. Although it is not dated, it is thought to be a 1930s lure. It is an unusual lure

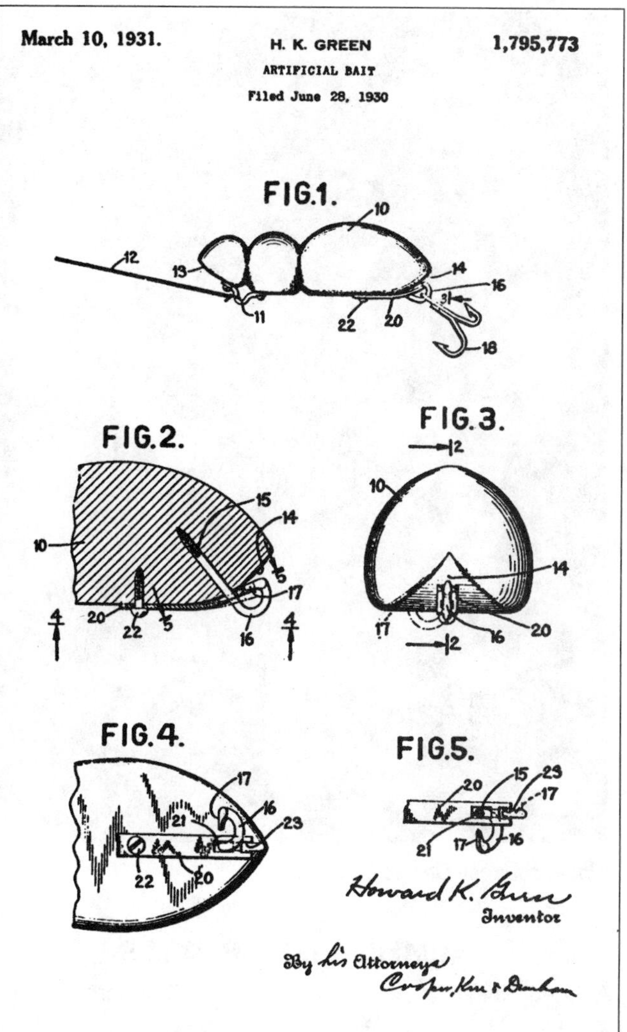

This patent was granted to Howard K. Green on March 10, 1931. While the lure is different from the ones in the photo, the tail hook hardware on the KLIPON LURES is exactly the same as the one in this patent illustration.

measuring 1-3/4" body and 4-3/4" overall. Note the smaller hook on the shank of the larger hook. It is attached in such a way as to adjust it up and down the shank to fit the live frog, minnow or other bait. The twin wire across the back filled a double purpose; that of holding the live bait on the lure and rendering it weedless at the same time. There is a protruding belly weight. They were available in red head, white body, solid red or solid white as far as can be determined presently. Collector value range: $20-$40.

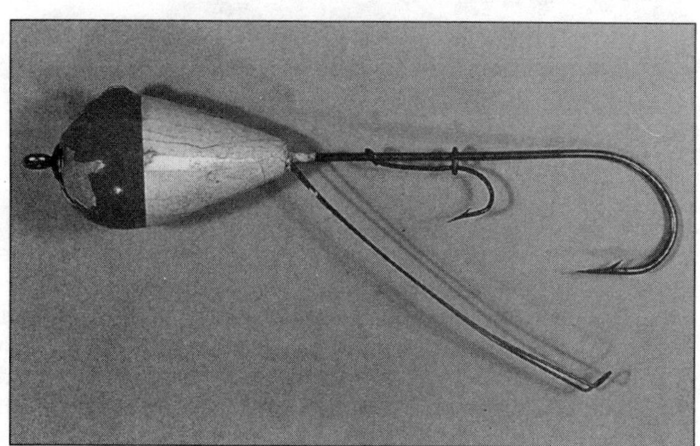

Photo courtesy Dennis Everson.

KUMM'S FISH SPOTTER

Arthur J. Kumm — Dearborn, Michigan

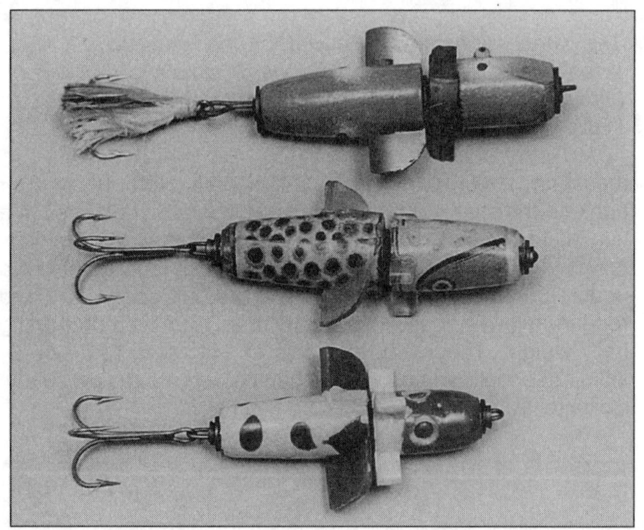

The top lure in the photo is the original wooden model of the FISH SPOTTER. The rear section rotates on retrieve by means of two metal blades attached to the front of that section. The one trailing treble was originally offered feathered as shown. It has yellow glass eyes and measures 2-7/8" long. The other two, as you have no doubt noticed, are later versions made of plastic. Kumm applied for the patent in 1933 and it was granted in mid-1935. The earlier wooden lures are valued at: $100-$300 while the plastic ones are worth: $20-$40. Both are difficult to locate.

KOEPKE LURE COMPANY

Frank L. Koepke — Ridgefield, Washington

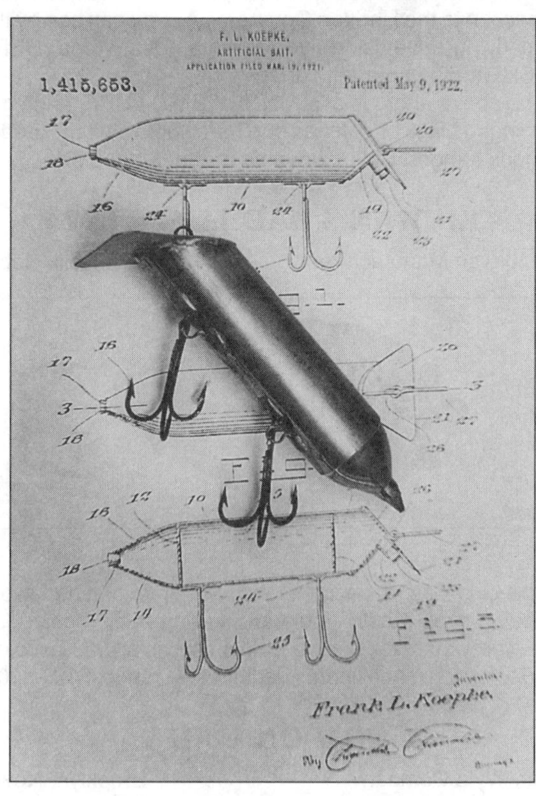

Frank Koepke obtained three patents for his lures. The first one shown in the patent drawing above. It was granted in May of 1922. Made of soldered brass, the lure was fashioned with three compartments. The forward or rear or both could be filled with water making it a floater, diver or imparting different action depending on how it was filled and the speed of retrieval. They were made in two versions. One was pointed in a cone shape at both ends. This one was available in four sizes, 2-1/4", 2-3/4" and 3-1/2" each with a single hook and the fourth, a 4" model available with either a single or double hook. The second version was available in a 3-1/2" single hooker and a 4" long double hooker.

The following picture is of three representatives of the second version. Essentially a double ender with a dive plane. The ones in the photo are 3-1/2", 3-3/4" and 4". The 3-3/4" may just be an anomaly of hand production.

The other two patents were for spinner type lures. The company closed sometime near the beginning of the Great Depression. Collector value range: $100-$150.

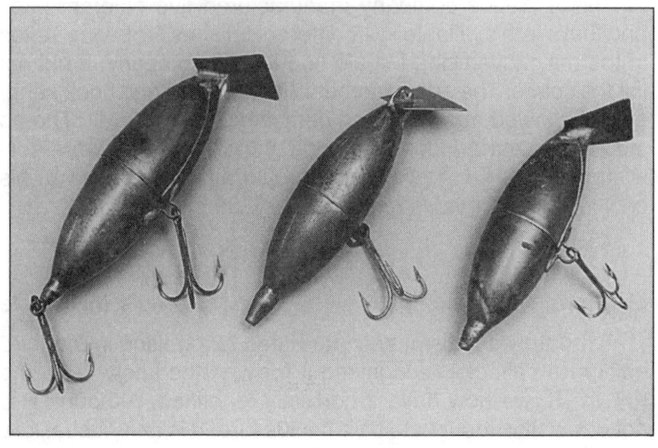

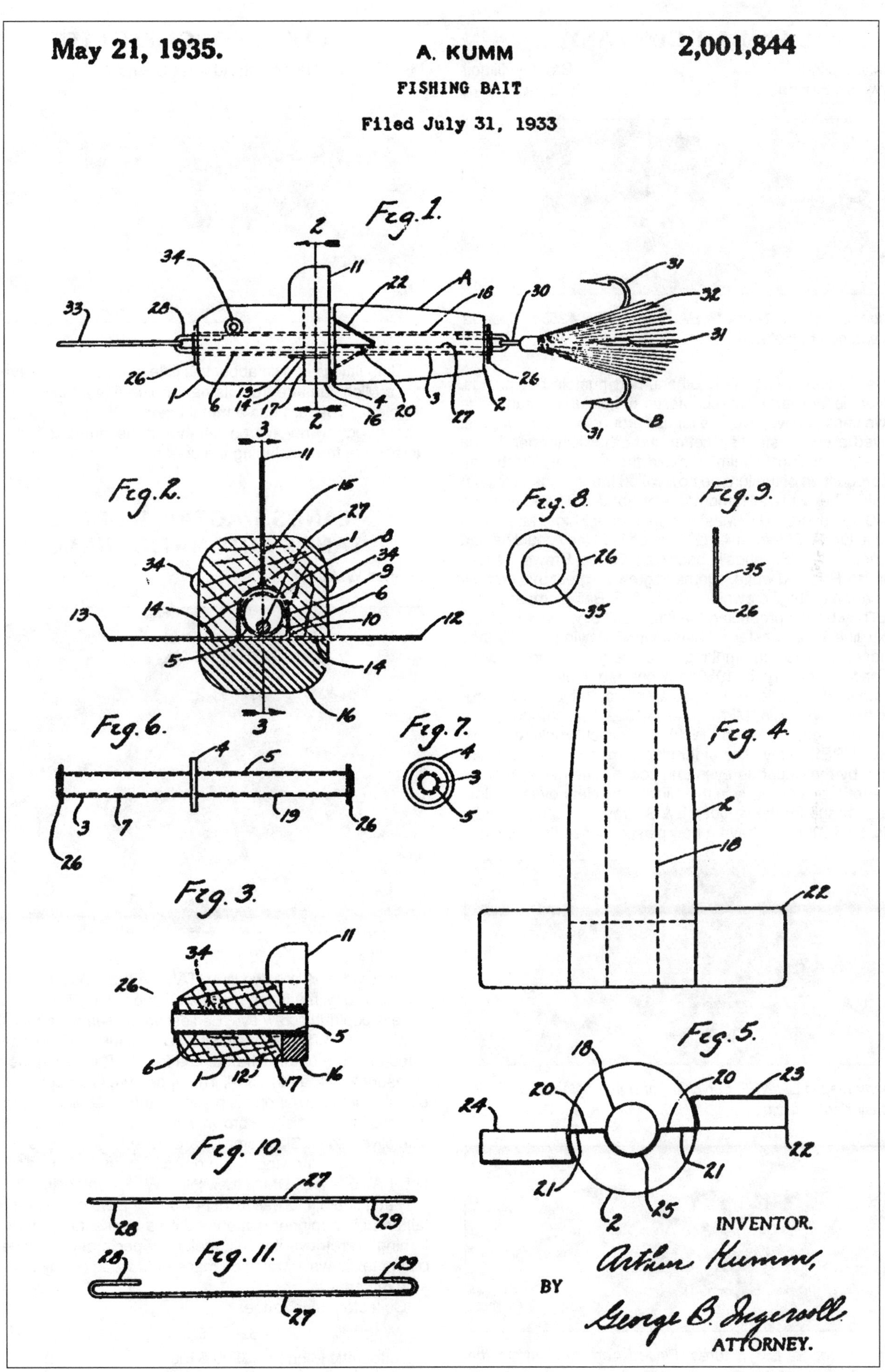

The original patent illustration for the KUMM'S FISH SPOTTER granted May 21, 1935 almost two years after it was filed.

L & S BAIT COMPANY

Kankakee, Illinois — Bradley, Illinois
Clearwater, Florida — Largo, Florida

An older 3-1/8" L & S plastic BASS MASTER #2534. Opaque eyes and non-reflective finish.

This company, like many others, had humble beginnings. The story is familiar. Harold LeMaster of Kankakee, had made his own bass and walleye lure for use around his home waters. It proved a successful fish getter and other fishermen in the area began asking for him to make them copies. He began hand production of the lure he now called the "LeMaster Shiner Minnow". They were all hand-made of wood and hand-painted. In 1940 he advertised LeMaster's Shiners, a Shiner Minnow at 3" and a Jumbo Shiner at 4-1/2". The ad said they could be had in "Four Beautiful Finishes in each size. Green, Brown, Yellow, (naturals), Red and white." Demand grew so great that he took on a partner, Phil Scrawnier. The L & S Bait Company was born. They began producing the lures, still of wood, on an assembly line in LeMaster's basement. Following WWII, they purchased plastic lure making machinery and the wooden lures became history. In 1950 they opened another operation in Clearwater, Florida to develop a saltwater line. They introduced the now familiar Mirro-Lures in 1952. The company was moved to Largo, Florida in the 1970s. It is still making plastic MIRROLURES today. The older plastic models can be distinguished by their opaque eyes and colors. The newer models have a reflective property in their finish and clear eyes. Collector value range for the wooden L & S lures: $10-$25, for older plastic: $5-$10, If you have a new plastic model, fish with it!

An early plastic SHINER MINNOW and its original box. Photo courtesy Ken Bernoteit.

Three late model L & S lures. Placed here to illustrate the shiny reflectivity of the new production lures. Photo courtesy Ken Bernoteit.

LAKE GEORGE FLOATER

Manufacturer Name and Address Unknown

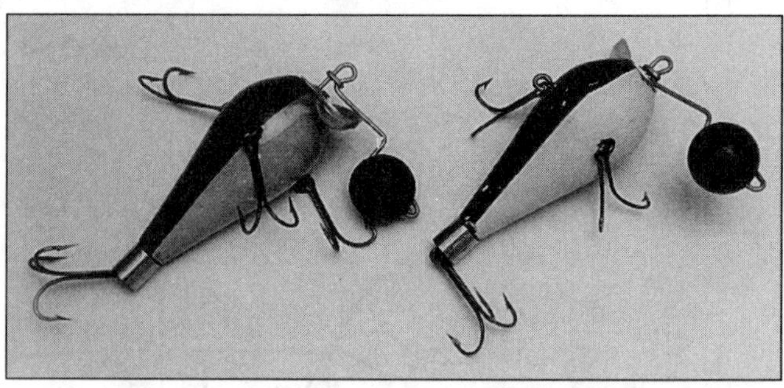

Very little is known about this little beauty. It is believed that it is a Michigan lure from its name. There is a Lake George in Michigan. The lure has a metal blade at the nose causing the whole body to revolve on retrieve. It measures 2-1/2" and 3" across the front including the cork ball. Collector value range: $150-$200.

LANE'S WAGTAIL WOBBLER
LANE'S AUTOMATIC MINNOW

Charles W. Lane — Madrid, New York

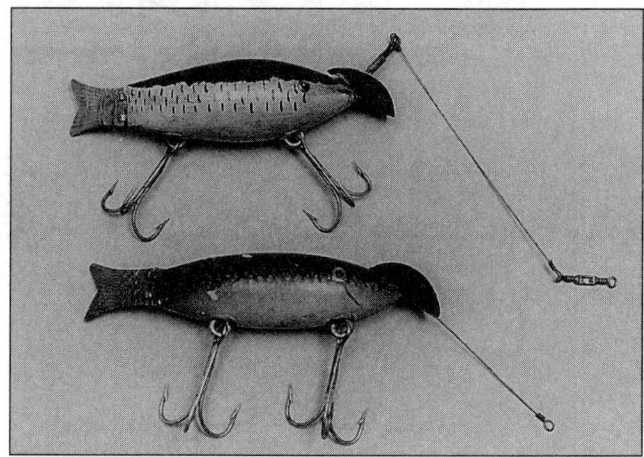

Pictured here are two WAGTAIL WOBBLERS. It is a wood-bodied lure with a fluted metal swinging tail fin. The hook hardware is cup and screw eye. Earliest advertisement I was able to find was 1924. The ad stated it was available in three sizes, but listed only the one illustrated. It is 2-7/8". The two in the photo measure 2-3/4" and 2-7/ 8". The upper lure is thought to be the oldest, but the lower one is presently the most difficult to locate. It came in two finishes, brown with gold sides and green back with silver sides. Sizes smaller are considered quite rare.

The patent drawing is the design for an earlier Lane product. LANE'S AUTOMATIC MINNOW. Patented in 1913, the only ad I could find was in 1914 issue of *Field and Stream.* The tail propeller spinner is mounted on a cam shaft so that when turning on retrieve it would make the pectoral fins move. The patent text says it was to be made of "...wood or any other suitable material."

Collector value range:

*Wagtail Wobbler - $200-$500.

Automatic Minnow - $500-$750.

**The smaller sizes of the WAGTAIL WOBBLER are considered quite rare.*

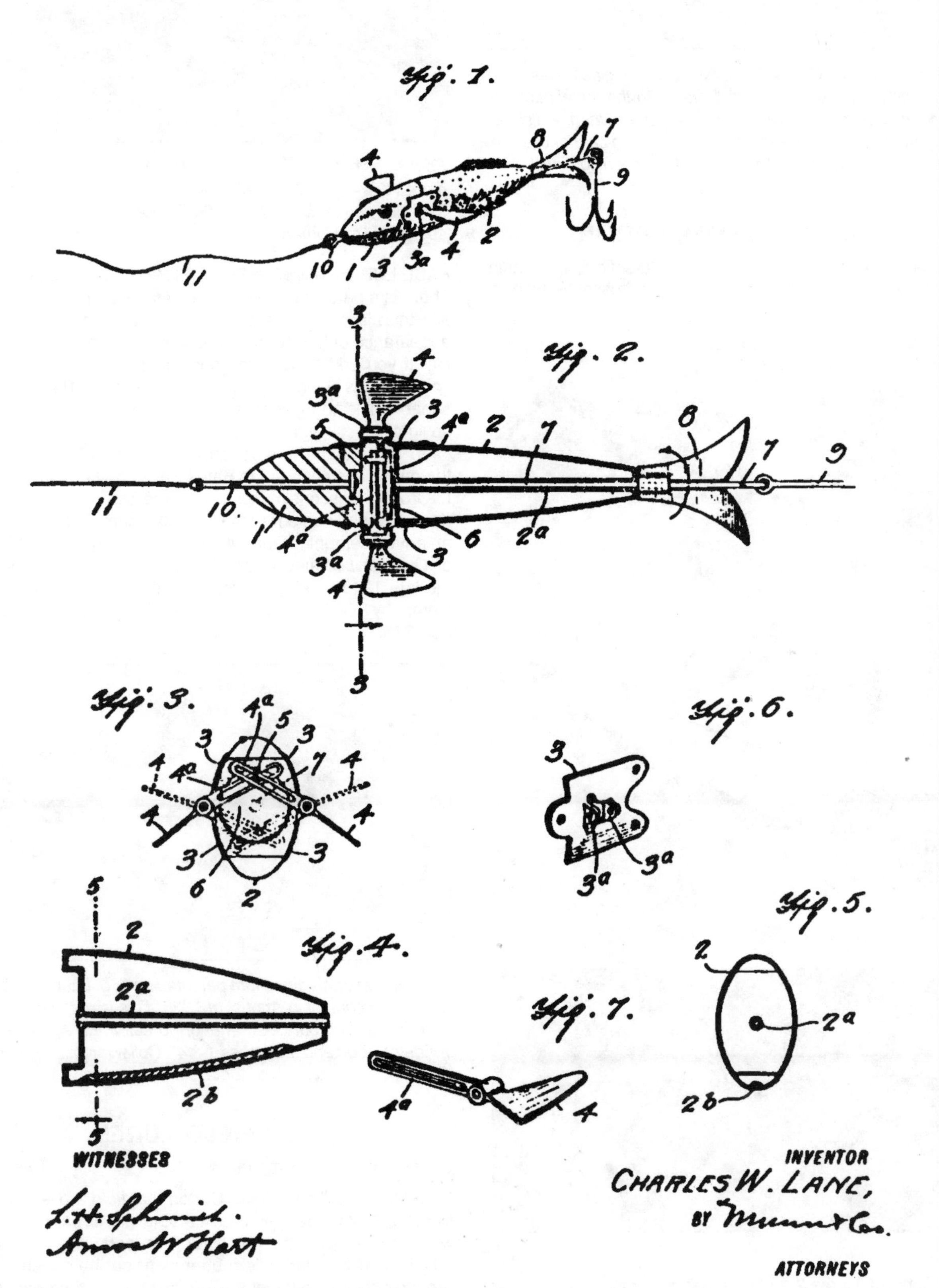

The patent drawing for Lane's AUTOMATIC MINNOW.

A wooden Lane AUTOMATIC MINNOW. It has glass eyes. The tail-mounted metal spinner is articulated with the metal pectoral fins and makes them "swim" upon retrieve. When a fish is hooked, the double hook swings free so the fish cannot use the weight of the lure to help sling the hook free when fighting.

LAUBY'S WONDER SPOON

Lauby Bait Company — Marshfield, Wisconsin
Bates Baits — LaCrosse, Wisconsin

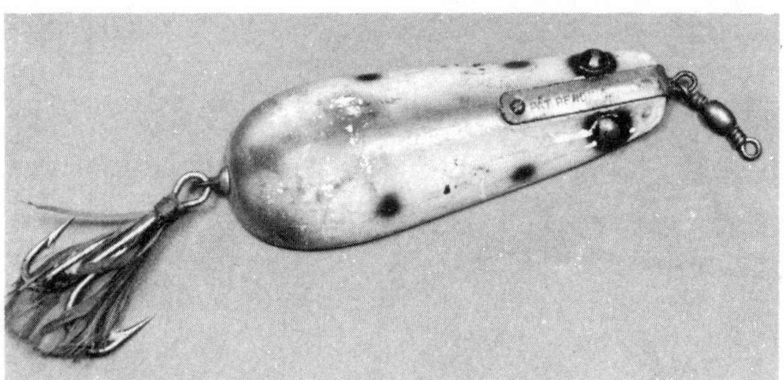

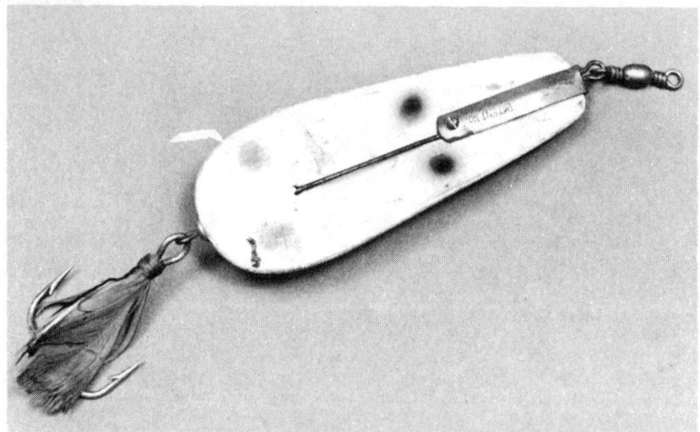

Four sizes of the c. 1939 LAUBY MINNOW. From top to bottom: 4-1/4", 3-1/4", 1-7/8", 1-3/8". The last two are fly rod sizes. Collector value range: $20-$40.; $40-$60. for the fly rod sizes. Photo courtesy Jim Muma.

This lure measures 2-15/16". It was found in its original box with a pamphlet. The pamphlet indicated that the company offered this lure plus "...WEEDLESS WONDER SPOONS SURFACE LURES-MINNOW FILES-FLY RODS-CASTING RODS." There is a patent number on the metal head plate, if taken literally, this places this lure around 1910. In no way does it have the appearance of having been made in that early era of lure making. If you add a "1" to the beginning of the patent number it comes out as being patented in the mid-1930s. That is more reasonable. The "1" must have either been left off or it was stamped so light, it just wasn't visible.

In 1938 Lauby was bought out by Albert Bates, Jr. Before the name was changed to Bates Baits, the company moved to LaCrosse, Wisconsin. Apparently the company remained under the Lauby name for a while, at the same address. There is an advertisement for the LAUBY LURE in the April 1939 issue of *Outdoor Life* magazine. The company ceased operation in the late 1940s and the patents were sold to the Paul Bunyan Company. Collector value range of the Lauby/Bates lures: $50-$75.

An unknown, un-named lure patented by A. J. Lauby in 1940. He filed for the patent in August of 1938. This is not exactly like the patent drawing, but close enough to call it the same lure. It is made of wood and measures 1-3/4". Collector value range: $20-$30. Photo courtesy Jim Muma.

LAYFIELD LURES

Sunnybrook Lure Company — Tyler, Texas

Jester "Jess" and Floyd "Cotton" Layfield are legends from Kerens, Texas. Jess started carving his lures in the 1920s with his wife doing the painting. Jess' early lure incorporated a Hawaiian Wiggler style rubber skirt, but he attached it to a groove cut into the top of the lure just behind the head. Cotton also developed a lure shaped somewhat like a banjo (wide at the head end) and a water churning paddle wheel at each

The left lure is an old wooden Layfield lure along with its more modern plastic counterpart and an original box. They are the #108 model, measuring 1-3/4" with cup and screw eye hook hardware.

side turning on a single armature. The single hook trailed, barb up so as to be fairly weedless.

The lure designs were patented and despite Jess' efforts, attempts at having a company manufacture them were unsuccessful (See patent illustration). Finally, Sunnybrook came along about 1950 and plastic versions of Jess's skirt bait were produced. Unfortunately this attempt was short-lived and Sunnybrook faded out before most fishermen even knew of their existence. If you find one of the original hand-carved and painted wooden Layfield lures you would have a treasure that is not only an explosive fish-getter, but a collectible as well. Collector value range:

Original Wooden Layfield $25-$50.

Plastic Layfield $10-$20.

COLOR OR FINISH: Red eyed pearl, black; blue-black eyes; clear, pearl black strip; green scale; red-head, yellow black eyes, pearl black scale; black with white dots; yellow black scale; white head with black body.

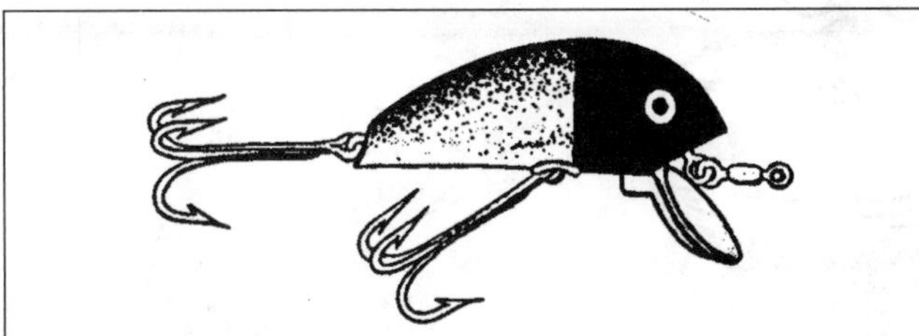

A plastic Layfield made by the Sunnybrook Lure Company. They are 1-7/8' long (body).

LEAPING LENA

Ralph Miller — Miami, Florida

Very little is known about the company or their well made lures. The two pictured here are with red heads and are 3-5/8" and 2" long. Notice the two different styles of the paint. The company was doing business in the 1940s and perhaps earlier. Collector value range: $15-$25.

Another with red head, green back and yellow belly. This lure measures 2-5/8" so we now know there are at least four sizes to be found. There is no mention of Ralph Miller on the boxes. Presumably he owned the Oceanic Tackle Shop in Miami.

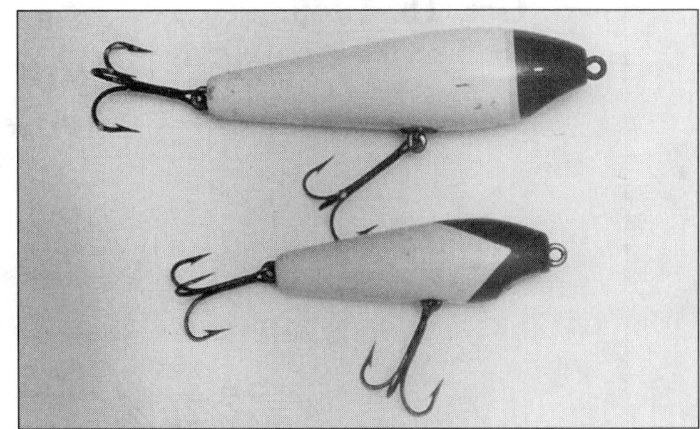

A LEAPING LENA and its original box. This one has a white body with red head and measures 3-1/2".

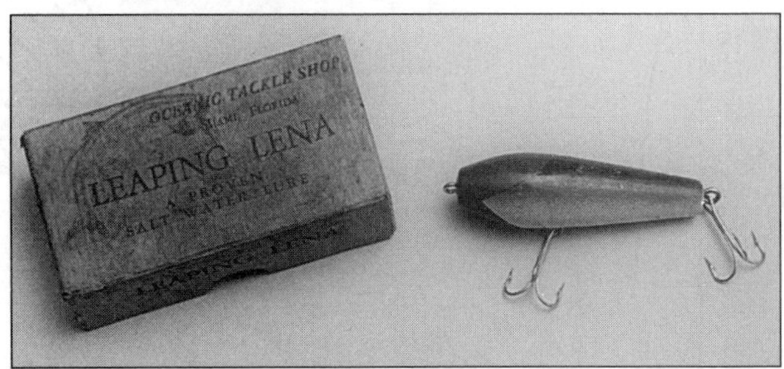

LED BOEUF CREEPER

Hew Plastic Sales — Erie, Pennsylvania

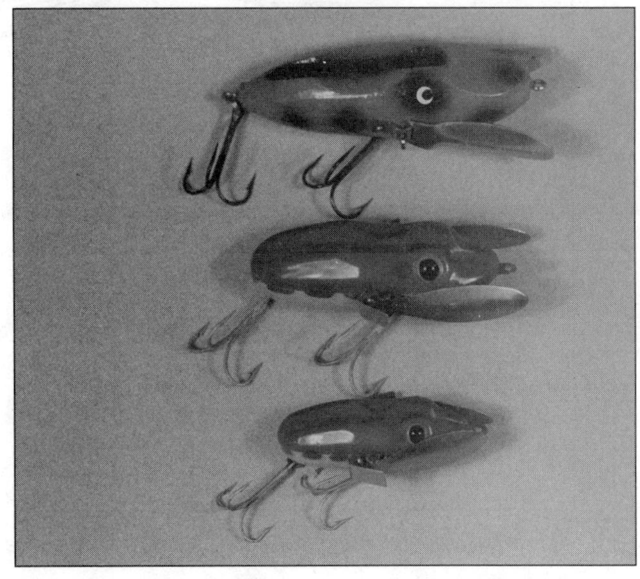

Oct. 18, 1949. **F. H. LAYFIELD** **2,485,053**

ARTIFICIAL FISH LURE

Filed Oct. 15, 1945

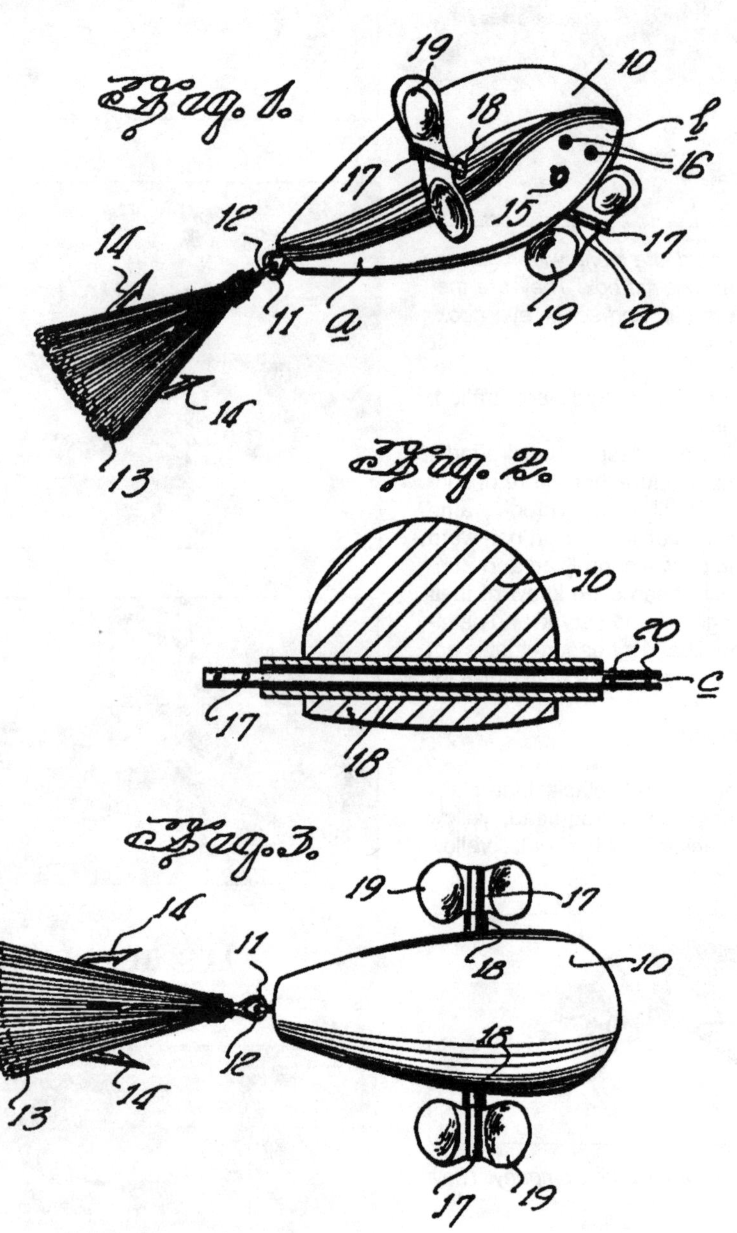

FLOYD H. LAYFIELD
INVENTOR.

BY

ATTORNEY

This is the patent drawing for Cotton Layfield's paddle wheel bait.

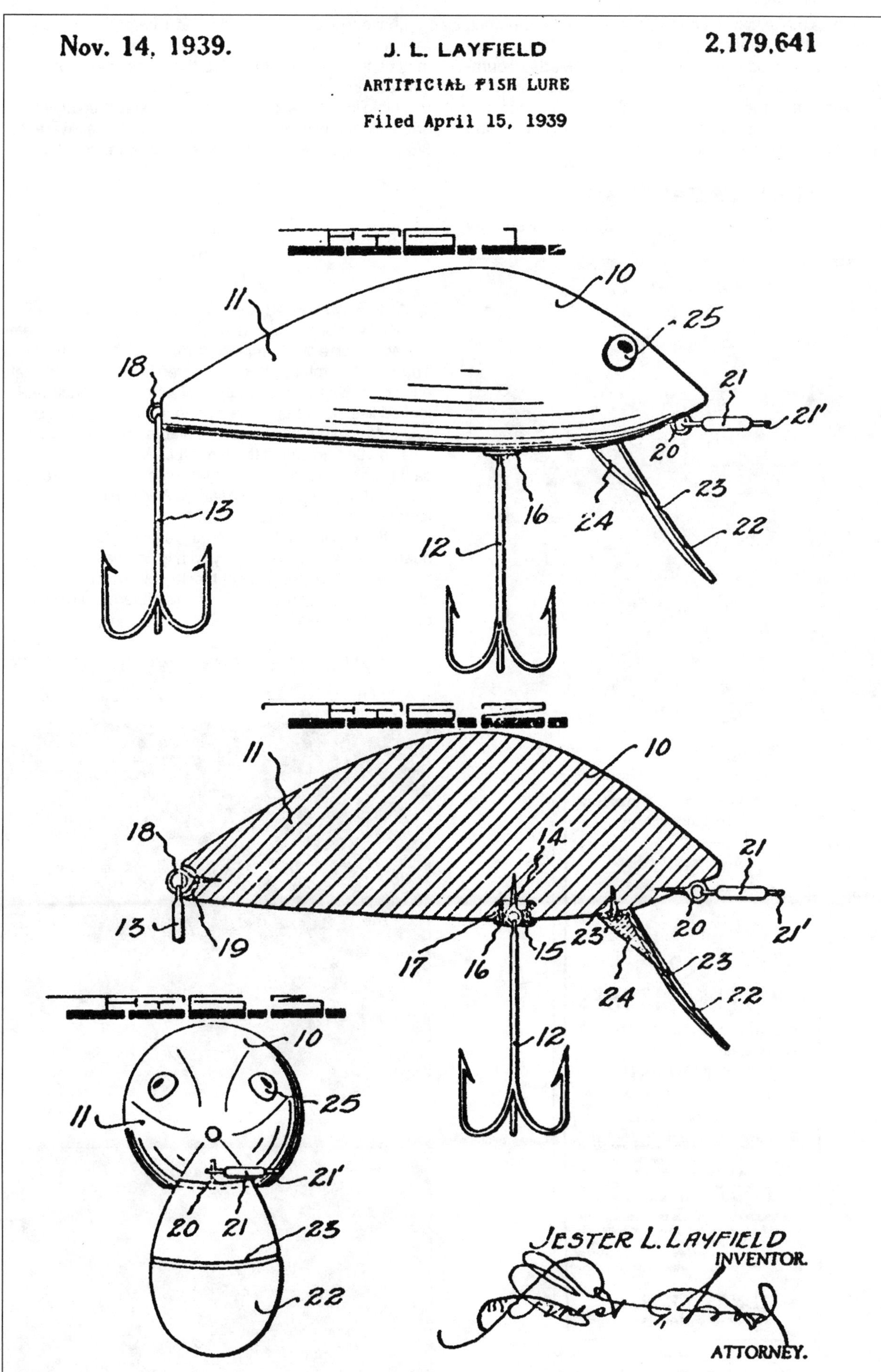

Nov. 14, 1939.
J. L. LAYFIELD
2,179,641
ARTIFICIAL FISH LURE
Filed April 15, 1939
JESTER L. LAYFIELD
INVENTOR.
ATTORNEY.

One of the patents granted for Layfield Lures.

This lure was made in wood and plastic. Only one reference was found, an advertisement in a 1949 issue of *Outdoors* magazine for the plastic model. It said the lure was "Made of durable green, brown and yellow plastics..." The lower two in the photo are plastic and measure 2-3/4" and 3-3/4". The top lure is a wooden model. Photo courtesy Jim Muma. Collector value range: $15-$30; for wood version: $40-$60.

LEEPER'S BASS BAIT

Henry Leeper — Fredonia, Kentucky

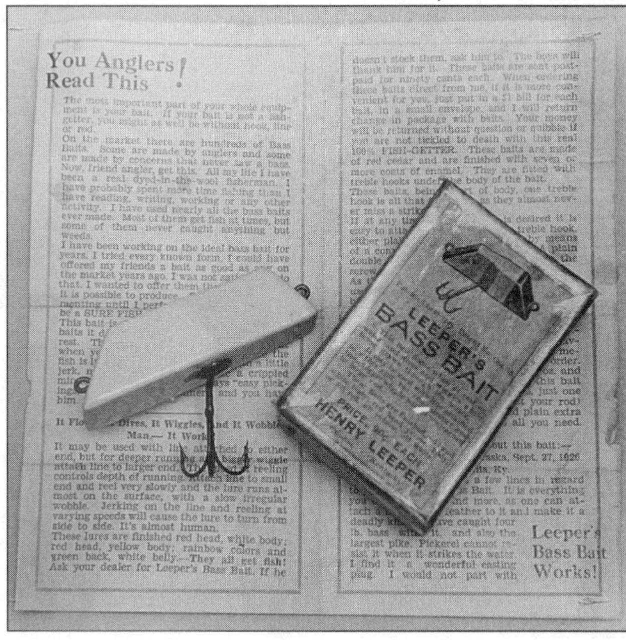

Bass forget their manners when they see—

OLD WHISTLEBRITCHES

it floats, it dives, it wiggles, it wobbles —

MAN, IT WORKS!

This plug resembles nothing that flies, crawls, walks or swims. It looks like hell to the fishermen—but it looks like heaven to the fish!

Attach your line to either end, put a small bucktail or small pork rind on the back and reel in with varying speeds. It's the durndest thing you ever saw in the water. A floater—it gets those big ones that watch the surface for feed. This plug has a North Carolina record of a 7¾ lb. bass.

Old Whistlebritches comes in three finishes: white with red head, yellow with red head, or white with green head. Sent postpaid for only fifty cents each, and here's my guarantee: Your money refunded if you are not perfectly satisfied with this lure. Write:

HENRY LEEPER
Fredonia, Kentucky

The 1941 advertisement in Southern Sportsman magazine.

I have found a 1919 and a 1921 patent date listed in separate places. I found the 1921 patent. It was filed in 1919 so that may be the source of the 1919 date. The latest date I found the lure advertised was 1941. A 1926 advertisement listed it as available in several sizes. Most were described only by number and weight. I was able to measure four. Those were 2-1/2", 2-3/8", 3" and 3-1/8". The weights listed were as follows:

#2 - 1/2-oz.
#4 - 3/4-oz.
#5 - 3/4-oz.
#7 - 3/16-oz.
#8 - unknown

As to why sizes #3 and #6 are omitted is anybody's guess. The #8 was described as being quite small in one reference, but actual size was omitted. It may have been a fly rod size. There were a total of 12 colors listed in ads and other references. There was no description of what the "Black and White" looked like. There is some evidence that suggests other sizes and colors might have been available on special order.

The 1941 ad called the lure OLD WHISTLEBRITCHES and said it was available on only three colors. They are white with red head, yellow with red head or Wwite with green head. Collector value range: $150-$200.

COLOR OR FINISH: Solid yellow, white body with red head, solid white; white body with green head, solid red, white body with black head, solid black; yellow body with red head, black and white; green body with red head, rainbow, aluminum body with red head.

LEHMAN'S WHITE WONDER BAIT

A.A. Lehman — Kalamazoo, Michigan

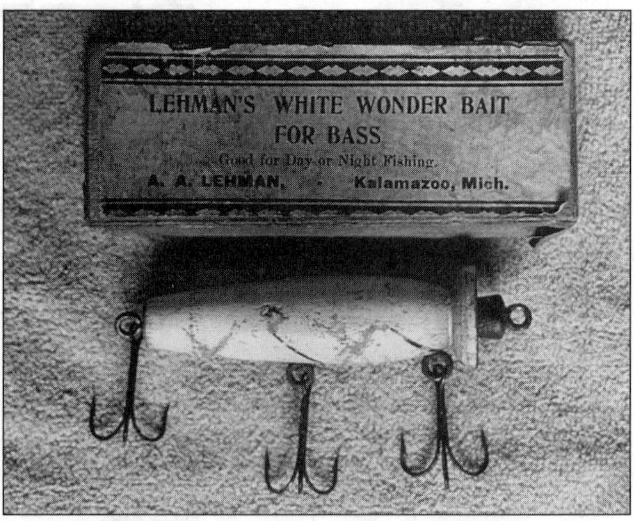

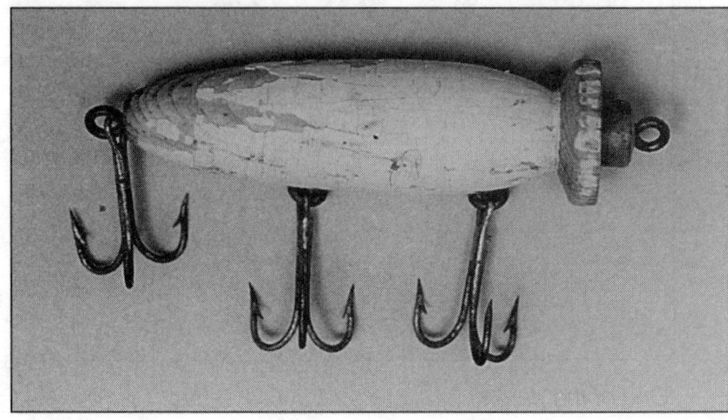

This 4" wooden lure looks a great deal like the Moonlight Bait Company's MOONLIGHT FLOATING BAIT #1 and is about the same vintage, c. 1910. No other information about the lure or A.A. Lehman was found. Collector value range: $200-$300.

LIVE ACTION FROG

Action Frog Corporation — Long Beach, California

There is little else known about this plastic lure. The information above came from the box. It measures 5-1/4" overall. When pulled through the water on retrieve, the propeller at the nose imparts kicking action to the legs. It is not readily visible, but there is also a treble hook on the belly. Collector value range: $75-$100. That is based upon only two occurrences of this lure being in price lists. What is incredible is that it, new in the box, brought $273 at auction in 1997. It would be best to consider that an aberration.

LIVE-LURE

Rice Engineering Company — Detroit, Michigan

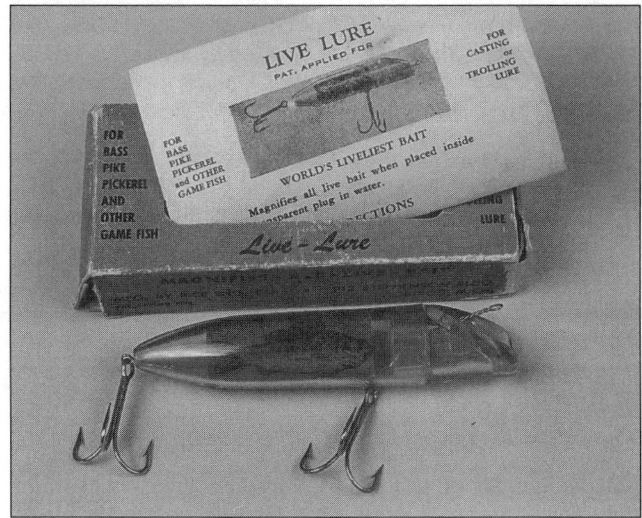

LIVE-LURE original box and papers.

This is another of the many attempts to make a minnow tube so one could "fish all day with but one minnow." Made of plastic, this lure was also supposed to magnify the minnow.

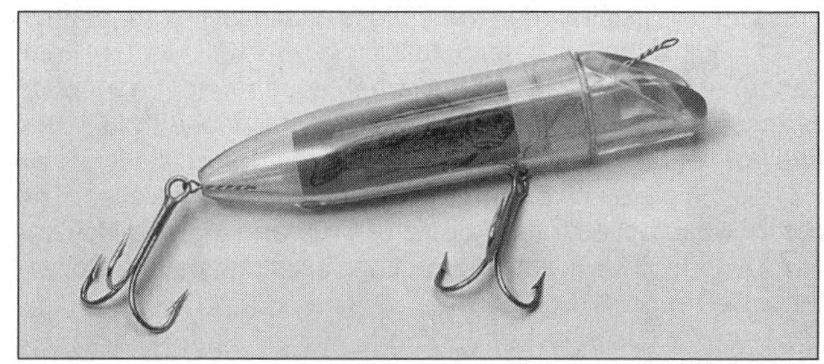

The head was removable for inserting the minnow and you could turn the head rendering the lure a top water or underwater runner. It measures 4" and is strongly rigged, with the line tie and hook hangers being one single continuous wire. It was found advertised in 1946 and 1947 in periodicals. Collector value range: N.A.

LISK M M U PLUG

Lisk Fly Manufacturing Co. — Greensboro, North Carolina

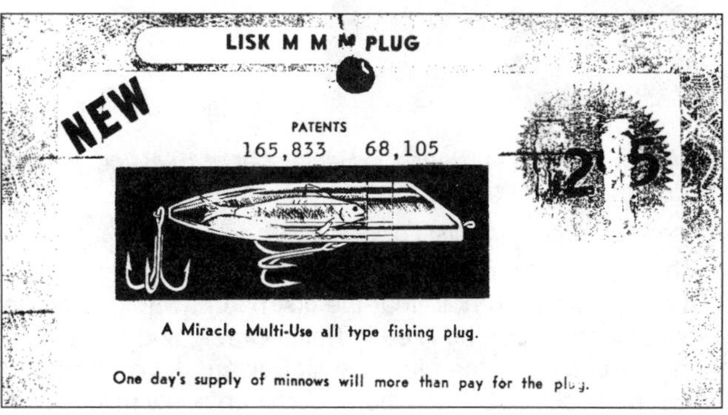

M M U stands for "Miracle Multi-Use." This lure seems almost identical to the LIVE-LURE. It's a wonder they were both able to secure a patent. This one has a patent number that places it as being granted in 1953, not long after the other was on the market. The inventor of this one had a lot more imagination. The literature said you could put live bait in it, but went on to suggest many other possibilities. Some of these were colored beads, luminous or fluorescent beads, painted cork or any other painted object or metal balls to make it rattle. They also suggested baking soda or Alka Seltzer to make it fizz, scented and/or colored oil, liver, dough, colored sponge or cotton. They even sold beads at 35 cents a tube. Colors of beads available: Assorted or one color, ruby red, fluorescent red, fluorescent yellow, pearl, gold, silver, black. Collector value range: N.A.

E.J. LOCKHART or WAGTAIL MINNOW MFG. CO.

Battle Creek, Michigan* — Galesburg, Michigan

A careful search through old catalogs, periodicals and patent records turned up a lot of new data that helps to shed a little more light than reported in the in previous editions. Eleven advertisements and references, and three patents were found. The earliest reference found was for the WAGTAIL WITCH in an article about new lures in a 1911 issue of magazine. It was illustrated and discussed briefly. The same article illustrated another Lockhart lure. It was captioned "The Lockhart Minnow", but no mention of it was made in the text. The lure pictured is actually the 4-1/2" WATER WITCH or POLLYWOG.

The WAGTAIL WITCH in the photo has to be a very early one because it doesn't have the typical Lockhart hook hangers. The one illustrated in the *Outer's* article lacked them also. If you look over the patent illustration you will see the hook hanger design. Look also at what appears to be a plate screwed on over the side body grooves of flutes. Although this has not yet been found, the lure in the *Outer's* article looks as if it has the plates on it. It also appears to have glass eyes. The patent was applied for in August of 1909 and granted November 11, 1911. This is actually Lockhart's second patent. Collector value range: $100-$200.

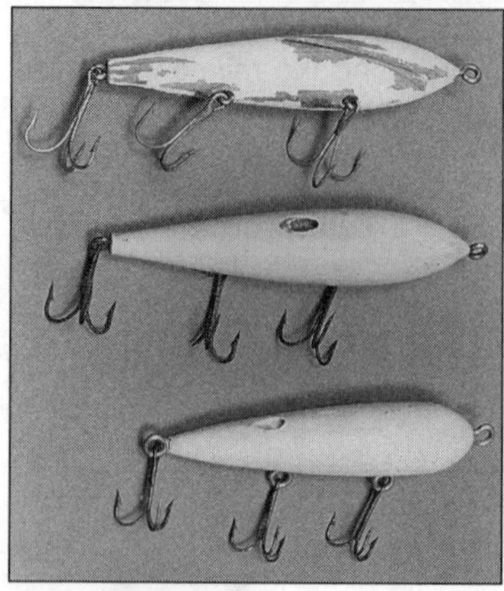

Upper: WAGTAIL WITCH. Center: 4-1/2" WATER WITCH or POLLYWOG. Lower: Unidentified Lockhart lure. Could be a different model, a forerunner or prototype of the above WATER WITCH.

The first patent was applied for in September of 1908 and granted to Lockhart June 1, 1909. It

**address given in the first Lockhart patent application.*

There are three sizes of the lure to be found.

It is interesting to note that the first patent was granted to Lockhart alone when he lived in Battle Creek, and the subsequent patents listed the grantees as Edward J. Lockhart and Evelyn M. Lockhart of Galesburg, Michigan a few miles down the road. Looks like Ed picked him up a wife and moved to the suburbs.

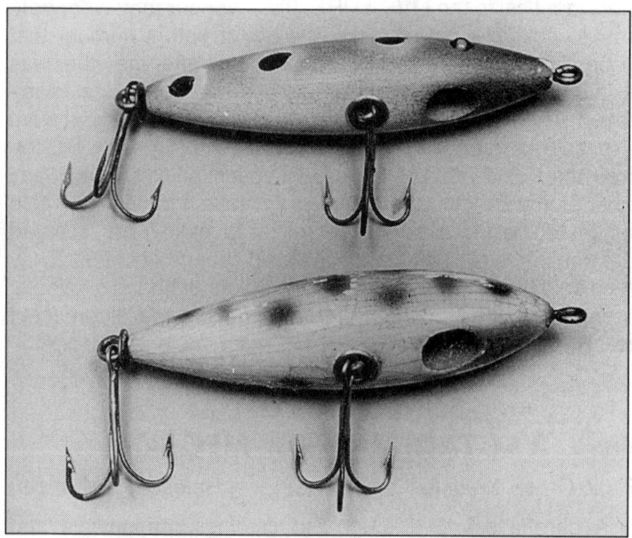

Two Lockhart WATER WITCHES. Note the shape variations. Both measure 4" long. They each have cup and screw eye belly hook hangers and tail protecting washer at the trailing treble hook. Upper lure sports glass eyes while the other has no eyes. Collector value range: $75-$100.

Illustrated above is the JERSEY SKEETER. No size or colors were found in any of the references. It came equipped with a single tail hook integral with the body and a belly double hook to comply with New Jersey hook restriction law. The ad stated that the double was detachable for replacement with a treble.

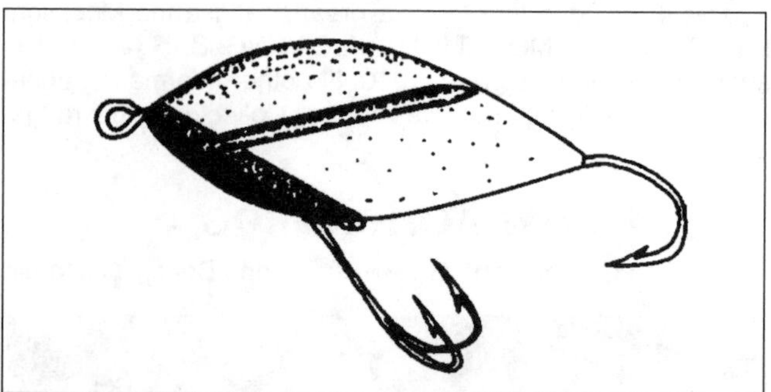

There are two Lockhart lures not pictured here; the WATER WASP and the WOBBLER WIZARD. The WATER WASP was advertised as being the same as the JERSEY SKEETER "... but twice as long. Can be had with or without weed guard." The WOBBLER WIZARD or WOBBLER SPECIAL has essentially the same body as the 4-1/2" Pollywog or Wagtail Witch, but has very wide flutes or grooves that are oriented more horizontally as opposed to the upswept, narrow flute or groove on the WAGTAIL WITCH. Collector value range: $200-$250.

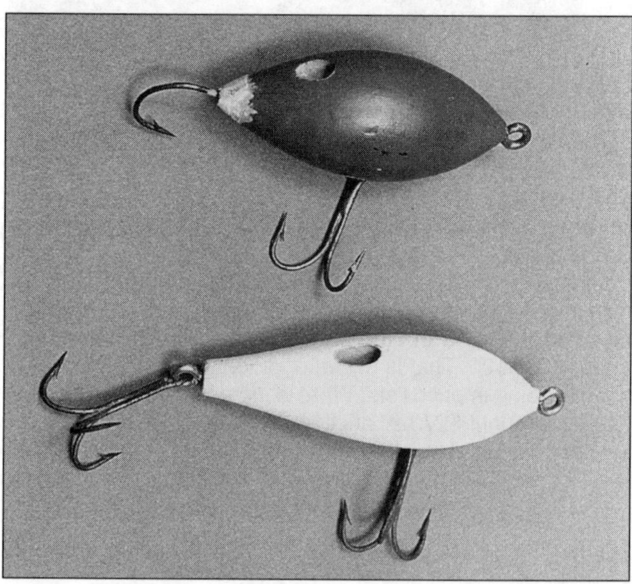

The 2-1/2" and 3-1/4" WATER WITCH or POLLYWOG. The smaller lure has apparently been modified by a fisherman as all advertising photos show a trailing treble hook. Collector value range: $60-$100.

It is important to note here, that there exists a lure made by another company that is very similar to the WATER WITCH. This lure is the EUREKA WIGGLER pictured and discussed with the Eureka company listing.

In all there are seven different Lockhart lures known presently:

WAGTAIL WITCH WATER

WITCH or POLLYWOG (3 sizes)

JERSEY SKEETER

WATER WASP

WOBBLER WIZARD or WOBBLER SPECIAL

Colors mentioned in various company advertisements are: White with red head, solid white, red or yellow. flutes or grooves are red or yellow.

FLASHER LURES

Long Island
Manufacturing Co. c. 1935 Long Island City, New York

E. J. LOCKHART.
FISH BAIT OR LURE.
APPLICATION FILED SEPT. 19, 1908.

923,670. Patented June 1, 1909.

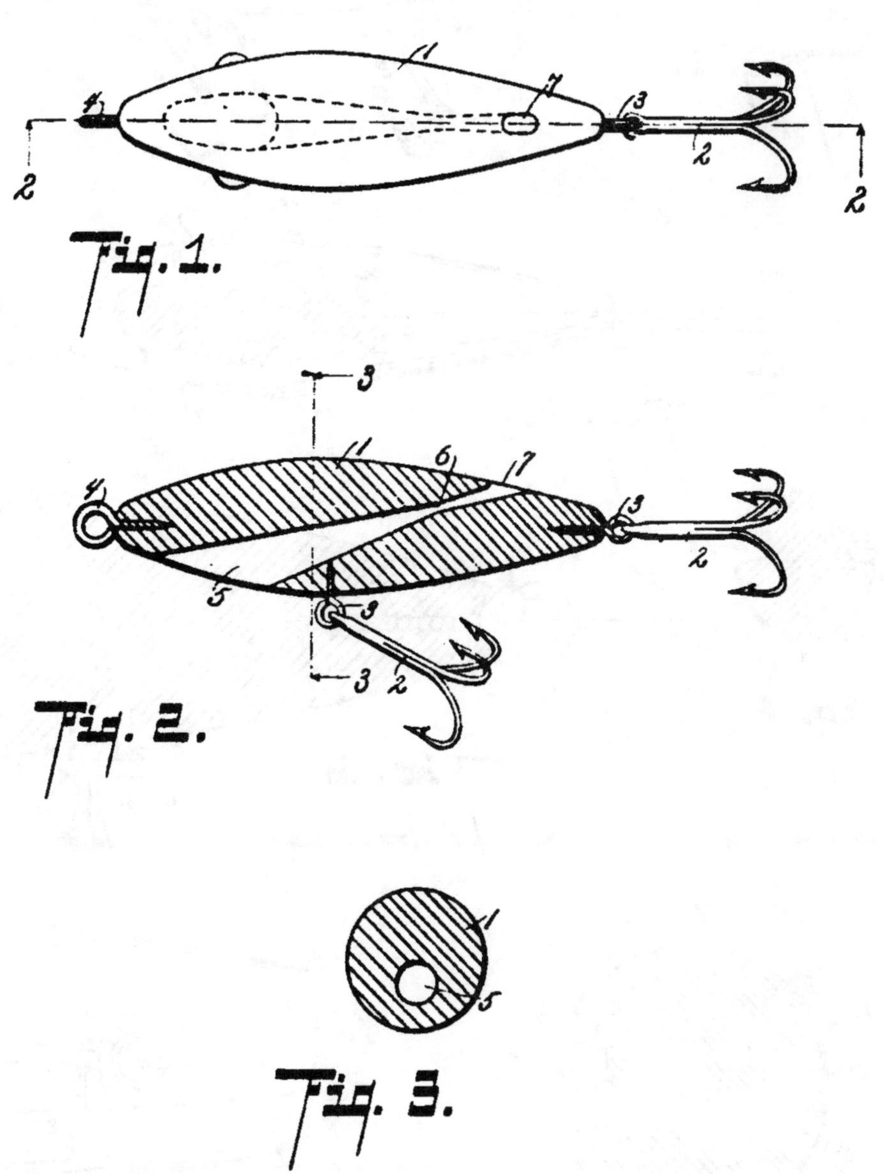

Inventor
Witnesses
Clora E. Braden
F. Gertrude Tallman
Edward J. Lockhart
By Chappell & Earl
Attorneys

A 1909 Lockhart patent drawing of the WATER WITCH or POLLYWOG.

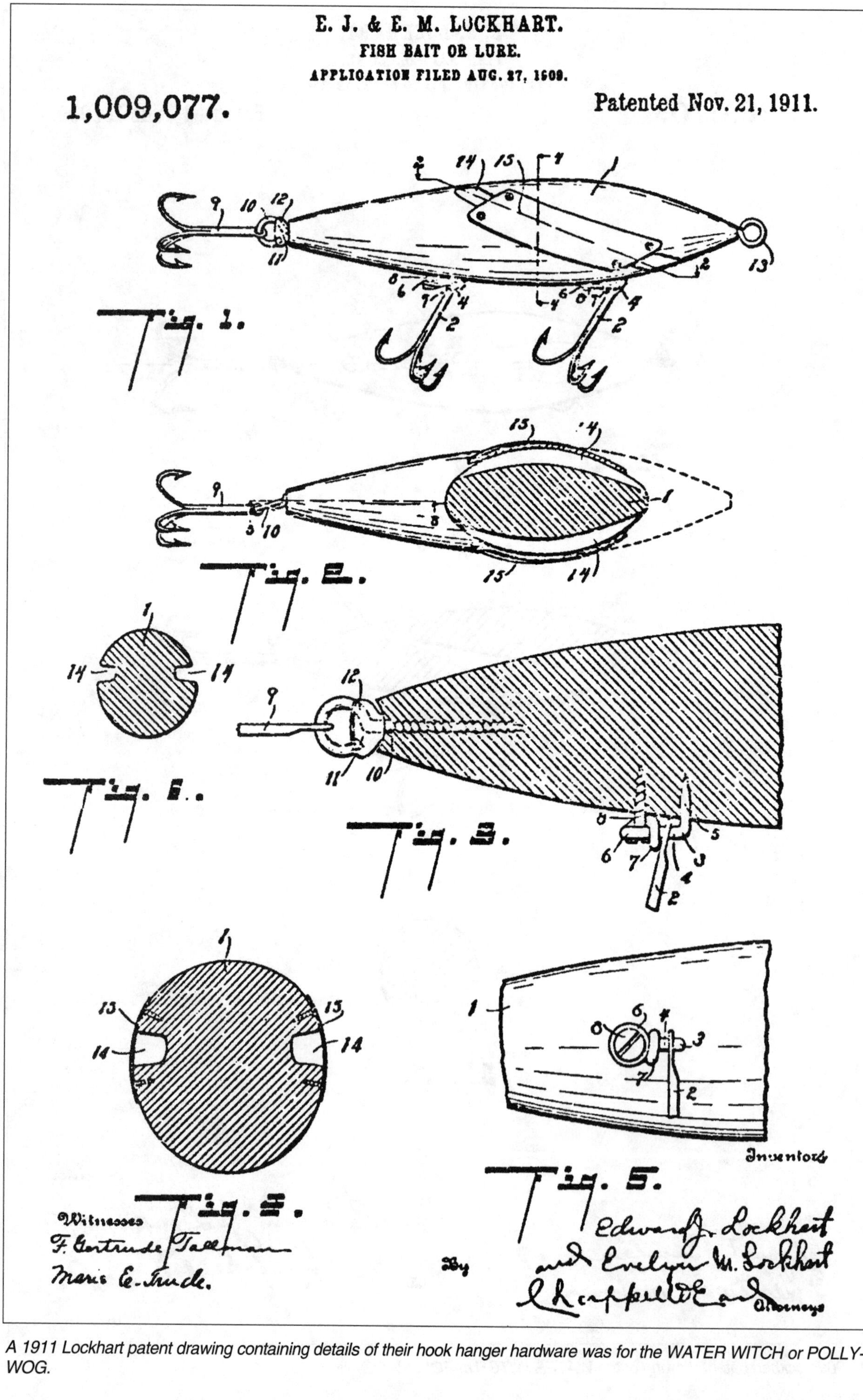

E. J. & E. M. LOCKHART.

FISH BAIT OR LURE.

APPLICATION FILED AUG. 27, 1909.

1,009,077. Patented Nov. 21, 1911.

Fig. 1.

Fig. 2.

Fig. 4.

Fig. 3.

Fig. 6.

Fig. 5.

Inventors

Witnesses
F. Gertrude Tallman
Marie E. Trude

Edward J. Lockhart
and Evelyn M. Lockhart
By Chappell & Earl
Attorneys

A 1911 Lockhart patent drawing containing details of their hook hanger hardware was for the WATER WITCH or POLLY-WOG.

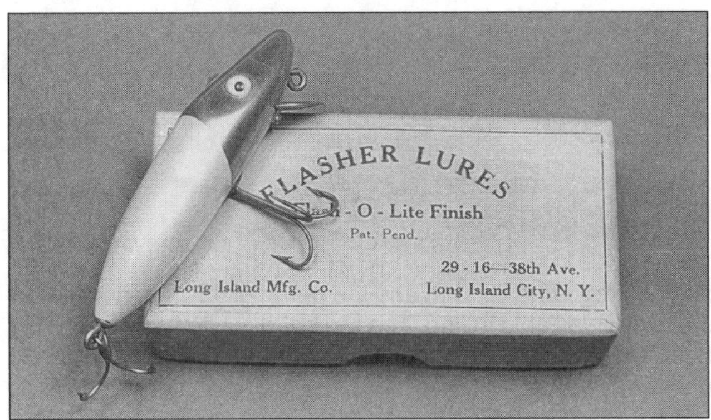

The lure illustrated here with the original box is mint. A 1936 William Mills & Son catalog listed two lures from this company. One of them appears to be the one in the photo here, a JUNIOR PIKE FLASHER. The other is a JUNIOR BASS FLASHER and is listed as 2-7/8", 3/8-oz., green back, yellow belly. In another advertisement (1934) it was said that the lures finishes were protected with a patented protective film known as "FLASH-O-LITE." It stated further that they were available in four freshwater and four salt water types and in "six color combinations." Collector value range: $20-$40.

LUCKY LADY WITH INNER GLOW

Luck Lady Tackle Co. — Los Angeles, California

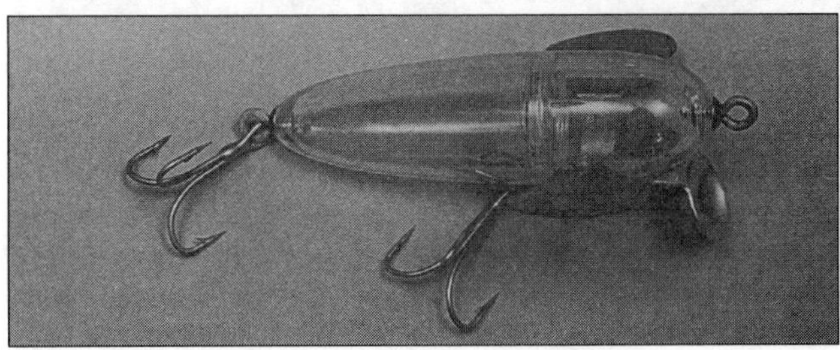

The name of this lure on the box is exactly as above. It measures 3-1/8" long and is made of clear plastic as you can see. The joint at back of the head is actually a screw joint allowing you to open the lure up. The name infers that there was something inside that made it glow or some such thing. The fact that you could open the lure indicates that whatever was inside would have to be replaced or renewed. They are not readily visible in the photo, but if you look closely you can see "wings" on the sides of the lure. Collector value is probably less than $10 as is. Perhaps more if whatever was supposed to be in it was found with the lure.

LUCKY LOUIE

Bill Minser — 'Minser Tackle Company
Seattle, Washington.

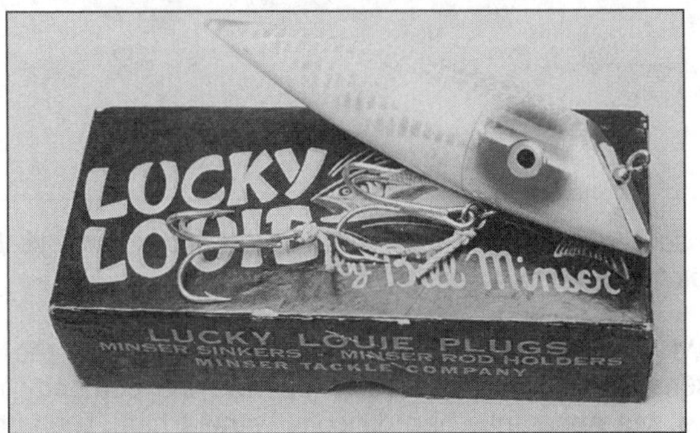

Another of the big northwestern salmon plugs. This 5-1/2" beauty was credited with being the lure that was used to catch the first place Tyee Salmon in the 1951 *Field & Stream* Fishing Contest. Collector value range: $15-$35.

LUMINOUS ART PRODUCTS

Lakefield, Canada

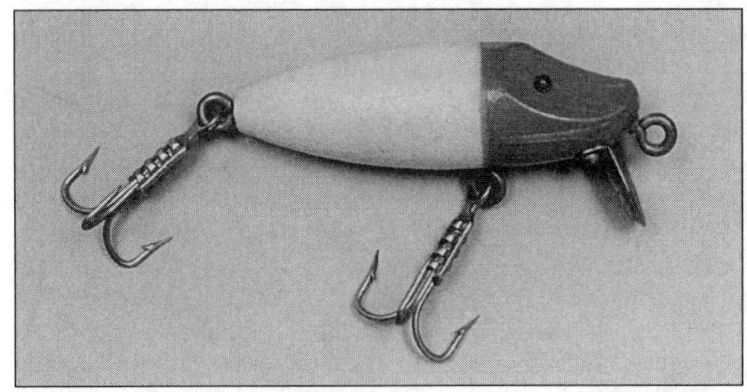

All that's known is the company and its location. The lure measures 2-1/2" and is made of plastic. It has a luminous white body with red head and unpainted tack eyes. It has simple screw eye line tie/hook hardware. Collector value range: No trade data found.

LURE-LITE

Lure Lite, Inc. — Junction, Texas

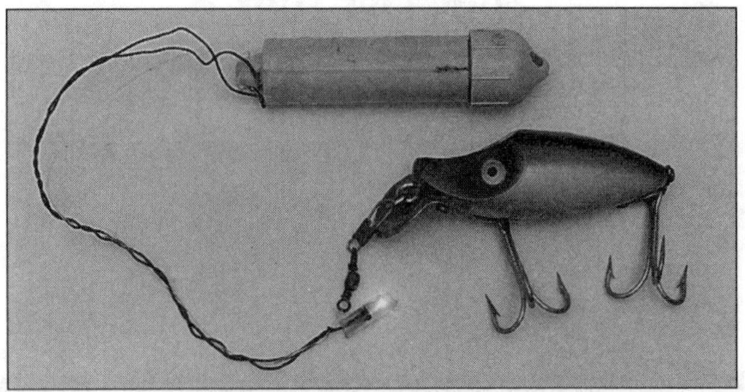

The lure in the photo above is a Heddon River Runt Spook. The LURE-LITE is actually a 2-3/4" watertight battery case with a leader and a tiny light trailing six inches behind. As you can see by the photo, it works. Just how effective it might be is anybody's guess. There was no trade information for this gizmo.

LUR-O-LITE

Sure Catch Lure Company — Irvington, New Jersey

The lure above is the only one so far that I can positively

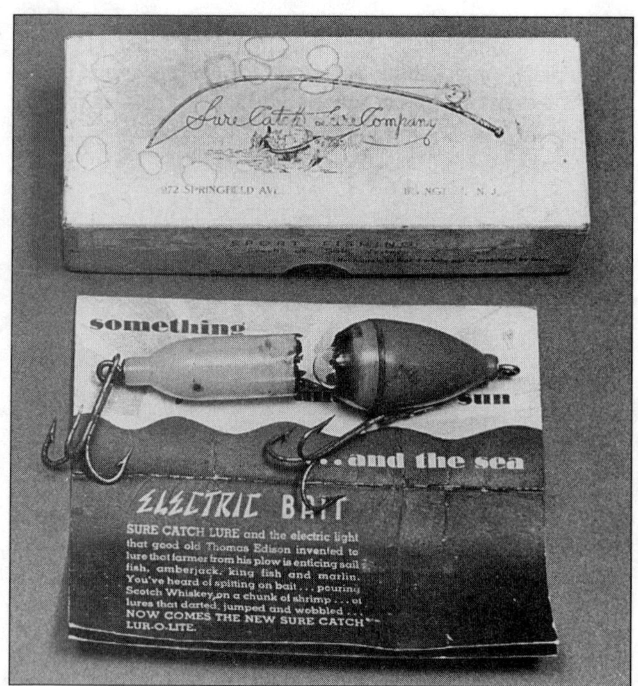

identify as from this company. It was a battery-powered electric light plastic lure. Looks like the last time it was used it was put back in the box while still switched on. The heat from the bulb melted it in two. Collector value range: $20-$30.

LURK LIVE LURE

Lurk Live Lures, Inc — 6241 Truman Road, Kansas City, Missouri

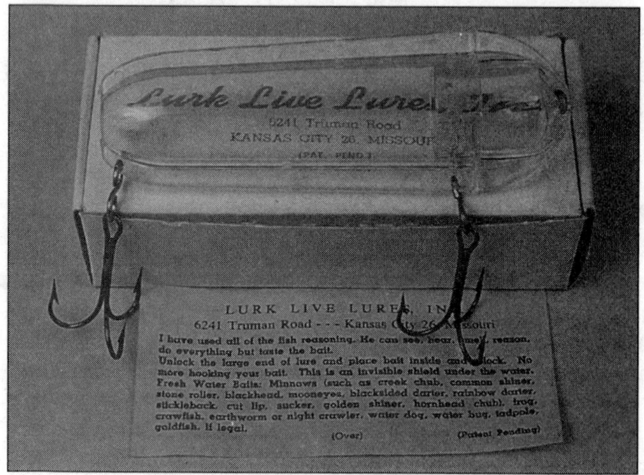

Measuring 4-1/4", this is another of the clear plastic lures in which you place a minnow or other live bait. A paper in the box lists no less than 30 suggestions for salt water fishing and 20 for freshwater fishing. "Unlock the large end of lure and place your bait inside and relock. No more hooking your bait. This is an invisible shield under the water." There are two line tie holes at the top and provision for adding another hook to the belly. Special thanks to Gene Abbey of Springfield, IL for this lure. Collector value range: No trade data found.

LUTON DUROFLASH LURE

Art Wire & Stamping Co. — Newark, New Jersey

The name and address of the above company was on the

box the lure came in. That and the name of this heavy 4" metal lure is all I was able to find. The red head, white body finish has a pearl-look. There was no trade information found from which to derive a value.

M & M TACKLE COMPANY

Memphis, Tennessee

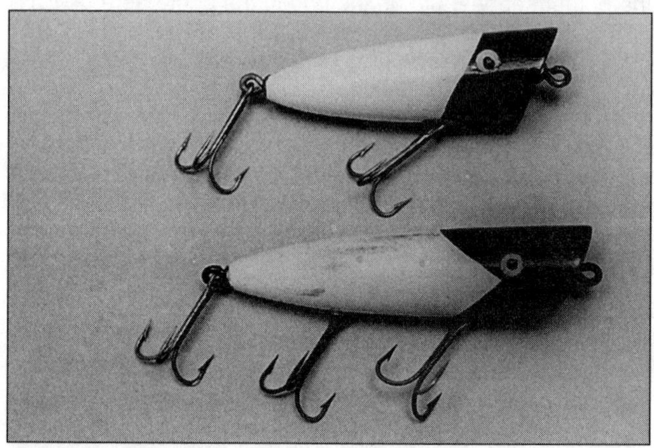

The only information found regarding this company and its products was from the boxes the lures were in. The smaller of the two in the photo above measures 3" and is called the SKIPPER. The other one measures 3-1/2" and is called the BLACK WIDOW. Both are wood body, have cup and screw eye hardware and tack/ washer eyes. Unable to assign a collector value due to absence of trade data.

McCAGG'S "BARNEY"

Mt. Kisco, New York

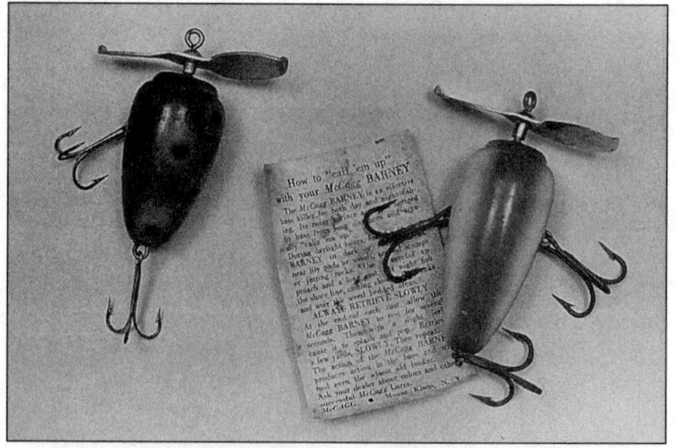

These SPINNING BARNEYS have cup and screw eye belly hook hardware and a protective tail cup insert.

When Jim Donaly of Jim Donaly Baits died in the mid-1930s, his family attempted to operate the company for a while, but apparently had difficulty without him. They began

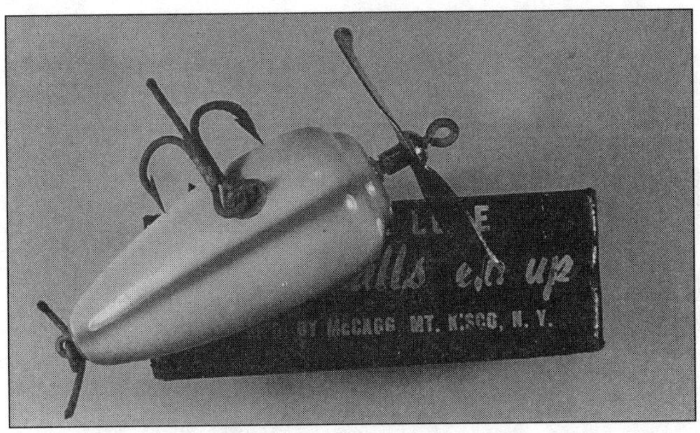

selling the rights to some of his patents to others. The most famous of these was a 1928 patent that eventually became the Heddon CRAZY CRAWLER. Around 1938 Barney McCagg, of Mt. Kisco, New York acquired the patent, the right to manufacture, some lure bodies and parts for the old Donaly REDFIN FLOATER. McCagg renamed the lure after his own nickname and began making and marketing the lure as the BARNEY. He assembled and painted them by hand and added a few more color patterns. The supply of Donaly bodies and parts were limited so he obtained equipment to turn the bodies, etc., but the entry of the U.S. into World War II put a halt to the operation. After the war was over he re-entered the lure making business and became successful enough that he turned to a fishing tackle manufacturer and distributor in New York City. How long he remained in business is not known for sure, but BARNEYS were still showing up in tackle catalogs in the 1950s.

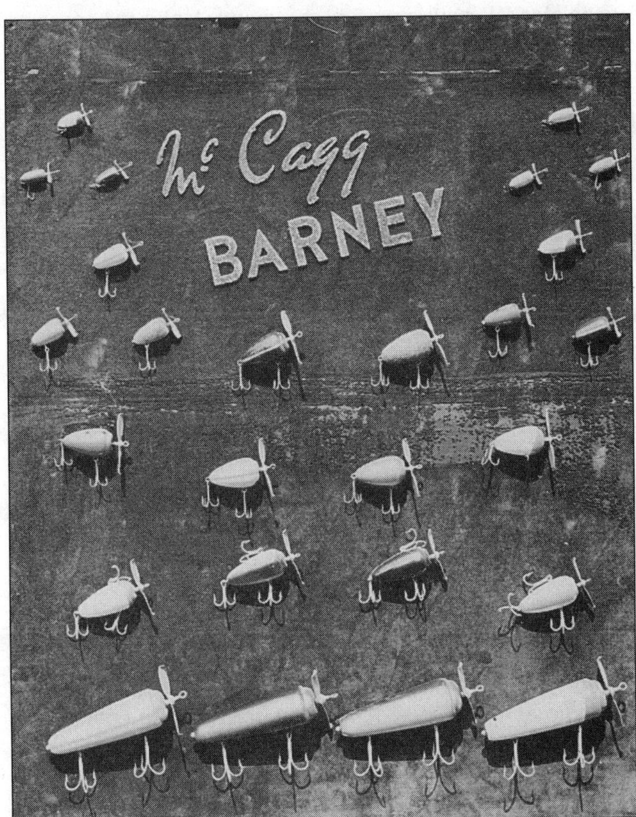

Salesman's sample board. Photo courtesy Harold G. "Doc" Herr.

I have seen 1-5/8", 2-1/4" and 2-3/4" sizes so far and a photo of a salesman sample board shows five different sizes ranging from 1-3/16" up to 5-3/4". There were six sizes of BARNEYS listed in a brochure, but the sizes were given in ounces not inches. They are listed following as they were in the brochure, except for the lengths I have added. They are approximate, but I believe to within an 1/8" tolerance.

BABY BARNEY (fly rod size)
1/1 6 oz. 1-3/16"

LITTLE BARNEY (spinning size)1/4 oz. 1-1/2"
BARNEY 5/8 oz. 2-1/2"
BIG BARNEY 7/8 oz.unk
SALTY BARNEY 1 oz. 5-1/2"
STRIPER BARNEY3-1/2 oz. unk

To help sort out the sizes of BARNEYS, collector and NFLCC member Harold G. "Doc" Herr of Ephrata, Pennsylvania has sent along a photo of a McCagg Barney salesman's sample board with a list of actual measurements of the bodies of the lures attached to it. The top row lures are 1-1/8"; second row, 1-5/8"; third row, 2-1/4"; fourth row, 2-3/4" and the bottom row, 5-3/4".

Color finishes for the lures are listed in the brochure:

*Red-White
*Rainbow
*Black
Mouse
Frog
Scale (Perch)
*Scale (Blue Mullet)

**These are the only colors listed for the saltwater models.*

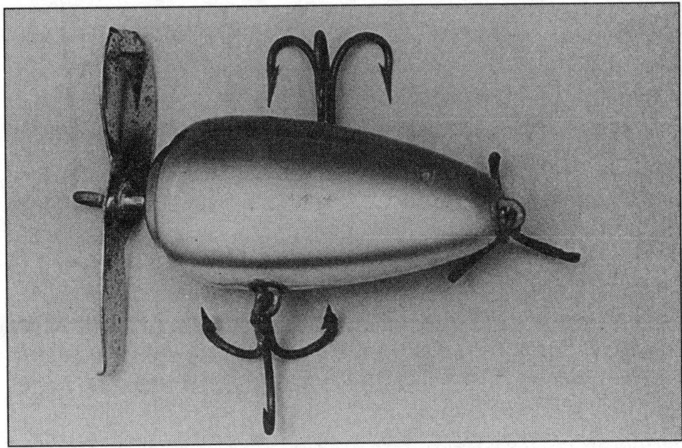

The propeller spinners were made of aluminum on the freshwater models and polished nickel plated brass spinners were used on the saltwater models. Collector value range: $25-$50.

THE McCORMIC MERMAID

McCormic Bait Company Kalamazoo, Michigan

This plug was found advertised in a May 1917 issue of *The National Sportsmans Magazine*. It has a 3-5/8" body, two belly trebles and a trailing treble. One unique feature is a small cupped-out area at the nose in which a short wire line tie is mounted (countersunk). The lure was apparently made for Shakespeare later or perhaps they bought the patent. In either case the same lure shows up in a 1920 Shakespeare catalog as the MERMAID MINNOW. Colors available from both companies are white, yellow, or red. It may also be found in white or black with a red head. The latter two colors were probably added by Shakespeare later. Collector value range: $75-$100.

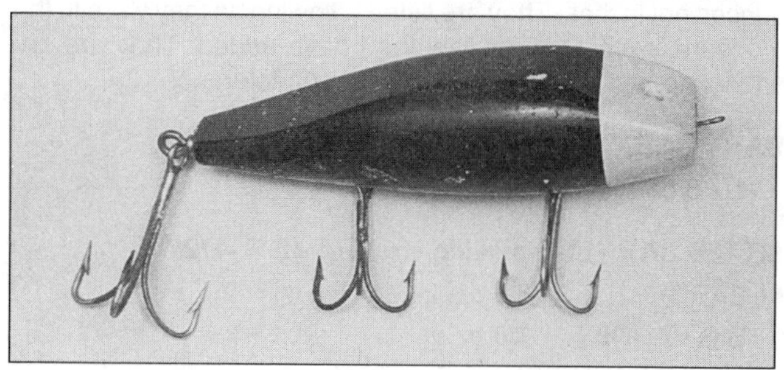

THE MAGICIAN

Bob-O Tackle Co. St. Petersburg, Florida

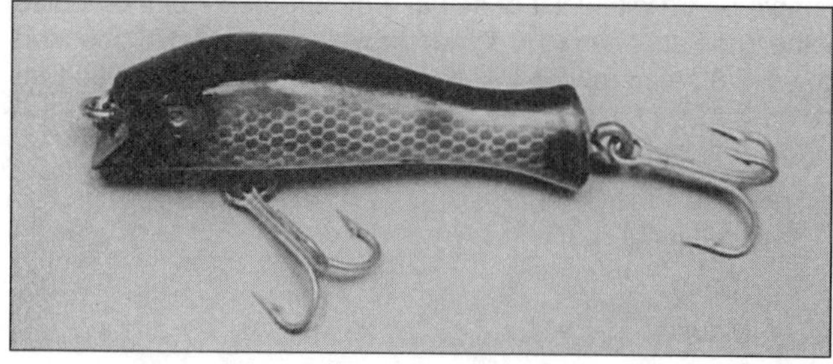

The only information I was able to turn up came from the box this lure came in. The lure is wooden, measures 2-5/8" and has a very nice finish. It is rigged with simple screw eye line tie and hook hanger. There was no trade data from which to derive a value.

MAKINEN TACKLE COMPANY

William Makinen Kaleva, Michigan

All I was able to find regarding Makinen was an undated lure box pamphlet, several advertisements from 1946-47 in three major magazines and a 1947 catalog. The catalog gave no hint of the time it had been in business, only that the president of the company was William (Bill) Makinen and the plant superintendent was Paul Bergstrom and an illustration of "THE NEW HOME OF MAKINEN TACKLE CO." They are thought to have been in business in the mid-1940s to the 1950s when they ended up in Heddon's hands.

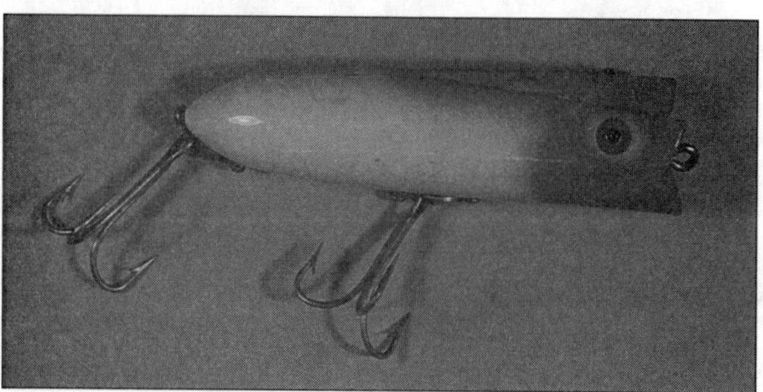

This interesting lure is a reworked Heddon LUCKY-13. It was apparently fashioned after the Heddon acquisition of the Makinen Tackle Company in 1951. It looks more Makinen than Heddon. It was obtained from a former Heddon employee. The body is the same shape as a LUCKY-13. It shows evidence of being a body pre-drilled for LUCKY-13 hardware, but the holes have been filled. It measures 3-1/2", has Heddon tack/plastic eyes and one-piece surface hook hanger hardware.

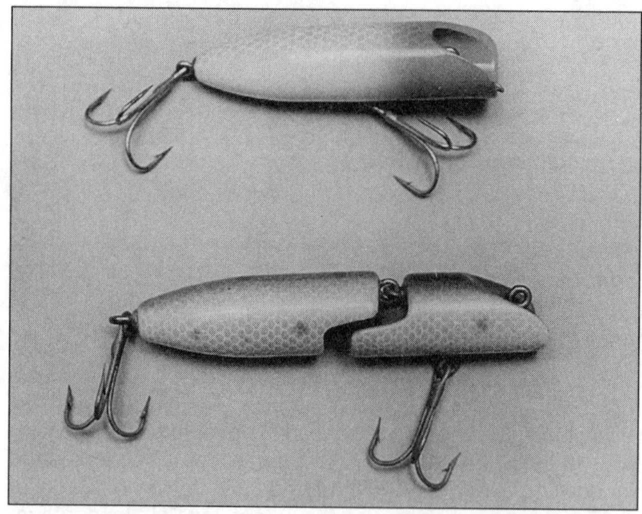

The upper lure is a 2-5/8" MAKILURE and the lower one, a 4" MERRY WIDOW actually measuring 3-7/8".

The catalog indicates they offered four styles of Tenite (plastic)lures, three styles of spoons and one spinner bait.

The Tenite lures are the MAKILURE, 3", 5/8 oz.; the MERRY WIDOW, 4", 3/4 oz.; the HOLI-COMET, 3-3/4", 5/8 oz. and 6-1/2", 1" in diameter; the WONDERLURE, 2-1/2", 3/8 oz. There is little difference between the Merry Widow and the Holi-Comet except where the joint in the Merry Widow is offset, the joint in the Holi-Comet is a straight cut across the body. The 1947 catalog does not list them, but they also made a 2-5/8" Makilure and a 1-7/8" Wonderlure. They may have come before or later. We now know that some early Makinen lures were made of wood; most notably the HOLI-COMETS and the MERRY WIDOW. These have both been found.

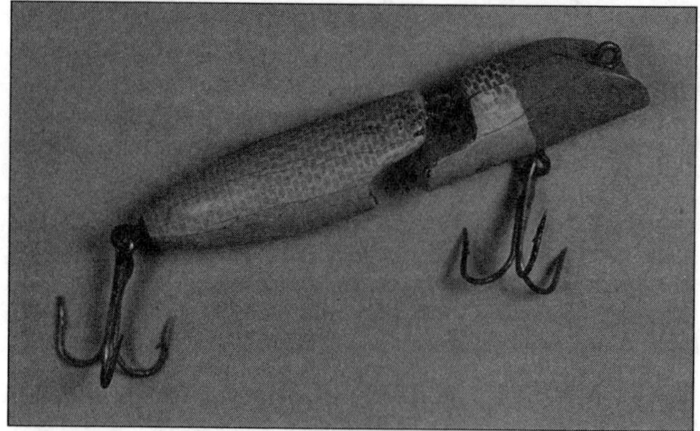

A wooden MERRY WIDOW.

There was a connection between Heddon and this company. It has been reported that Makinen made some lures for Heddon at some point. It is known the Makinen went bankrupt around 1949 and Heddon bought the remains of the company sometime around 1950-51. Heddon continued to operate the plant, making Heddon lures there, until 1955 when they closed the Kaleva operation down. This is probably the source of the idea that they made lures for Heddon.

The colors they offered were a bit sketchy in their description. Most of the colors except the Frog finish, also had a scale pattern. Here is a listing of them: Red head, white body; olive color with vertical stripes and scales on sides, back strip; white body, red spots and gold scale; yellow body with black stripe on back and red spots on sides; yellow body, black stripe on back, side and belly red spots; black body, scales on back;

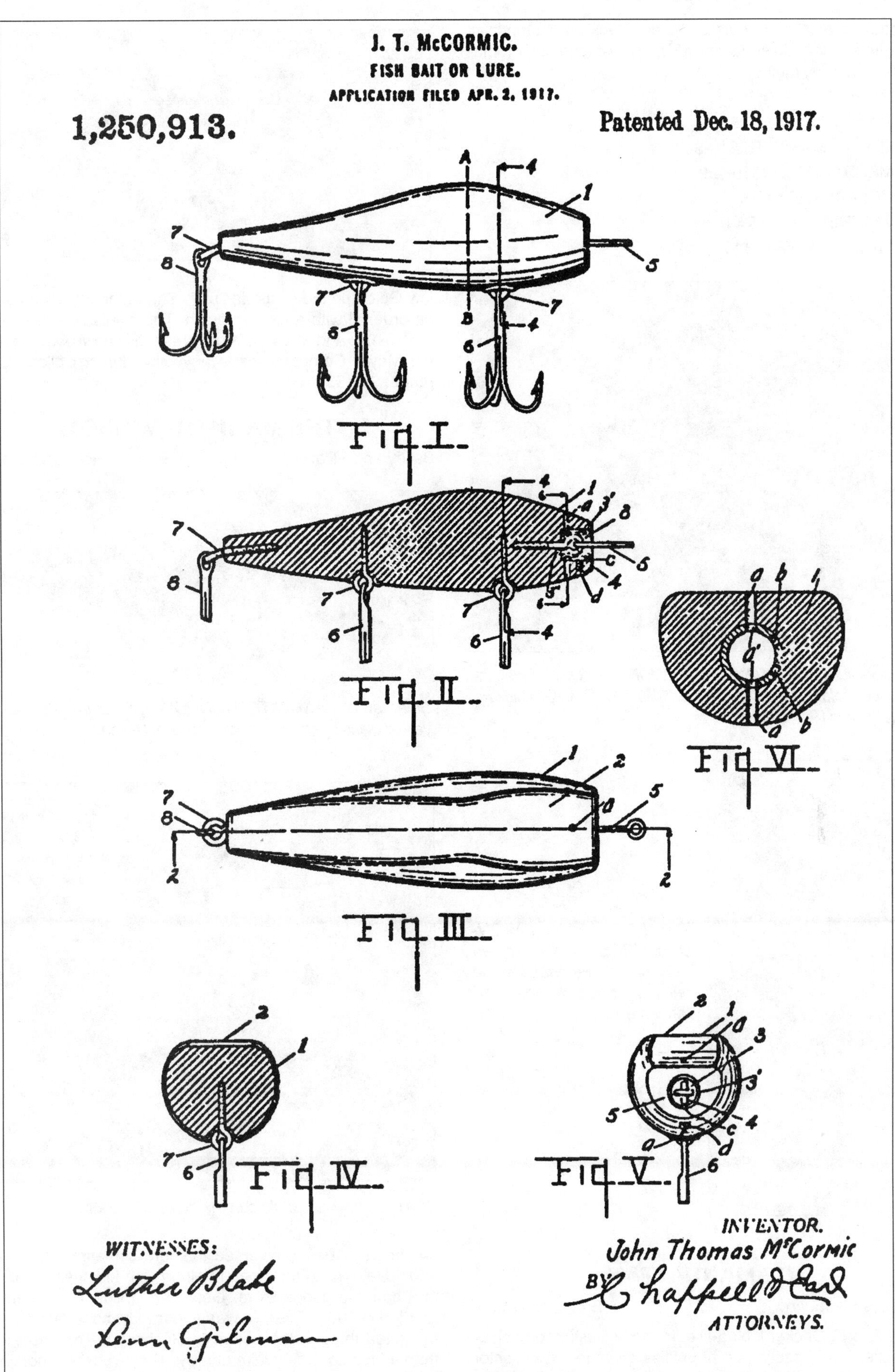

Original McCORMIC MERMAID patent. Granted to John Thomas McCormic December 18, 1917.

gray body, scales and spots on sides, black back stripe; all white with shaded red spots on sides; frog; orange color (goldfish); field mouse; mullet.

Collector value ranges:

MAKILURE $5-$15.
MUSKY MAKILURE$10-$20.
MERRY-WIDOW$10-$20.
HOLI-COMET$10-$20.
WONDERLURE$5-$15.
WADDLE BUG$5-$15.

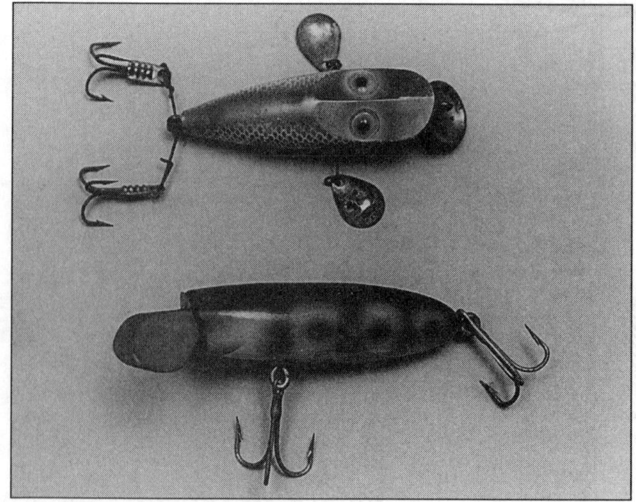

The upper lure is a 2-1/2" Makinen WONDERLURE. Flashers are copper color. The lower is a 2-5/8" WADDLE BUG. This lure was not in the 1947 catalog.

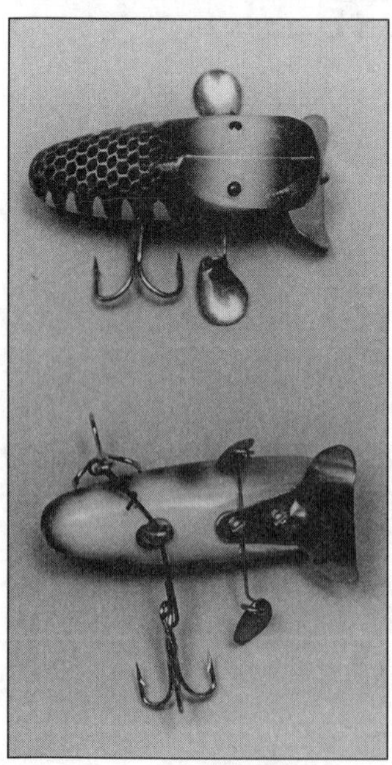

Two 1-7/8" Makinen WONDERLURES. One is shown belly up to demonstrate the unusual hook hanger arrangement.

THE MANHATTAN

S. J. Meyer Company — Bronx, New York

This Ans B. Decker look-a-like, formerly illustrated back in the Decker Lures section. is of unknown vintage. A collector found one, new in the box, in a rental house in New York and forwarded the information to me. The colors listed as available were: "White, Yellow, Mouse, White body with red head, Yellow Gold spotted or as desired". The latter implies they could be ordered with a custom finish. The available sizes were 2-3/4", 3-1/4" and 3-3/4". It is not presently known whether or not the Meyer Company made any other lures. Collector value range: $40-$50.

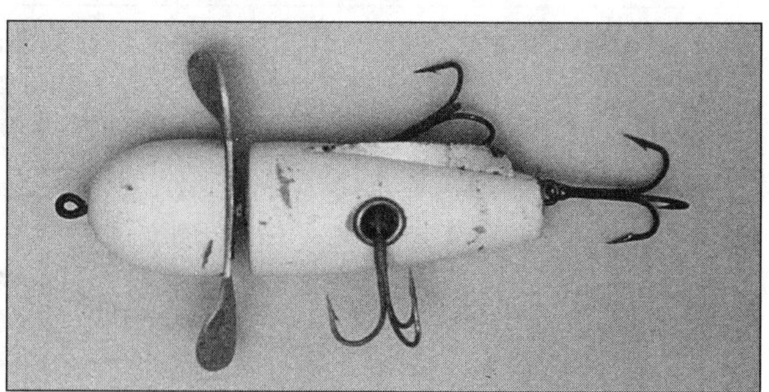

THE MANITOU MINNOW

Bailey and Elliot — Rochester, Indiana

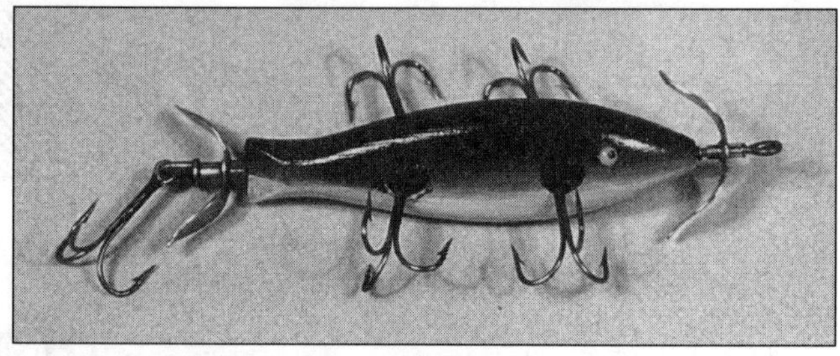

Side view of the MANITOU MINNOW. It measure 3-3/4" and has yellow glass eyes. Photo courtesy Jim Muma.

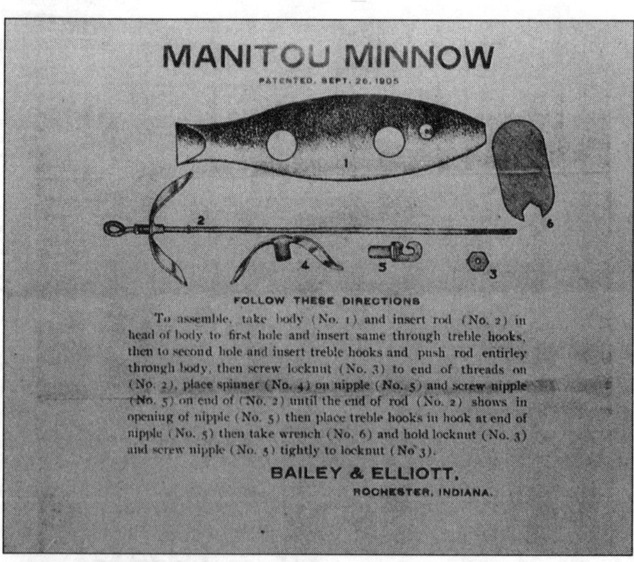

MANITOU MINNOW

PATENTED. SEPT. 26, 1905

FOLLOW THESE DIRECTIONS

To assemble, take body (No. 1) and insert rod (No. 2) in head of body to first hole and insert same through treble hooks, then to second hole and insert treble hooks and push rod entirley through body, then screw locknut (No. 3) to end of threads on (No. 2), place spinner (No. 4) on nipple (No. 5) and screw nipple (No. 5) on end of (No. 2) until the end of rod (No. 2) shows in opening of nipple (No. 5) then place treble hooks in hook at end of nipple (No. 5) then take wrench (No. 6) and hold locknut (No. 3) and screw nipple (No. 5) tightly to locknut (No 3).

BAILEY & ELLIOTT,
ROCHESTER, INDIANA.

The flyer that was packed in the box with the lure.

Simon K. Bailey invented this lure sometime in or before 1904. He applied for a patent along with his business partner in a sporting goods store, George A. Elliot. The patent was granted in 1905. The lure was apparently made by Bailey and marketed through their store in Rochester. The name came from a favorite fishing lake nearby. They were sold boxed with instructions for assembly using the little wrench shown in the photo. The lure was offered for only a short time. The story goes that it closely resembled a lure made by one of the larger

No. 800,536. PATENTED SEPT. 26, 1905.

S. K. BAILEY & G. A. ELLIOTT.

ARTIFICIAL BAIT.

APPLICATION FILED OCT. 18, 1904.

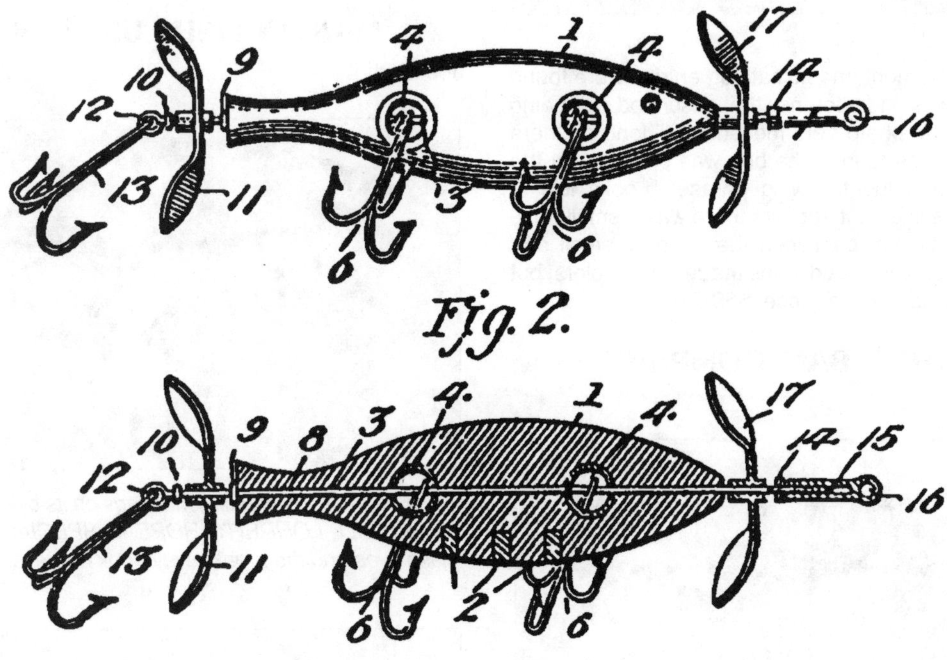

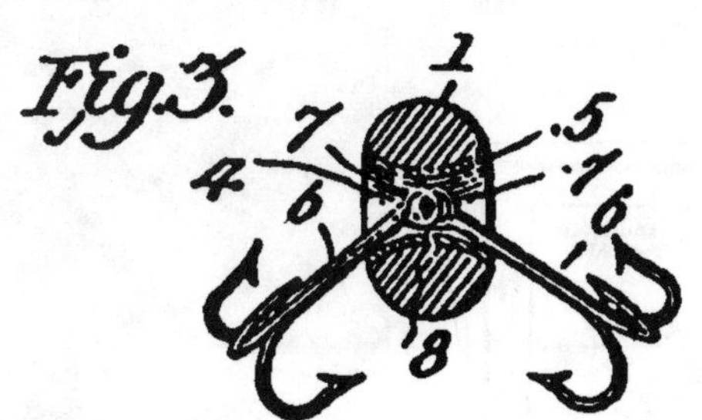

Inventors

Simon K. Bailey

George A. Elliott

Witnesses

By Victor J. Evans

Attorney

Original 1905 patent illustration for the MANITOU MINNOW.

companies and Bailey and Elliot were forced to cease marketing it. Collector value range: $600-$1,000.

COLOR OR FINISH: Solid red, dark green with yellow belly, pale green with white belly; dark green with white body.

MANNING'S TASTY SHRIMP LURE BAIT

Man's Shrimp Lure Company New Orleans, Louisiana

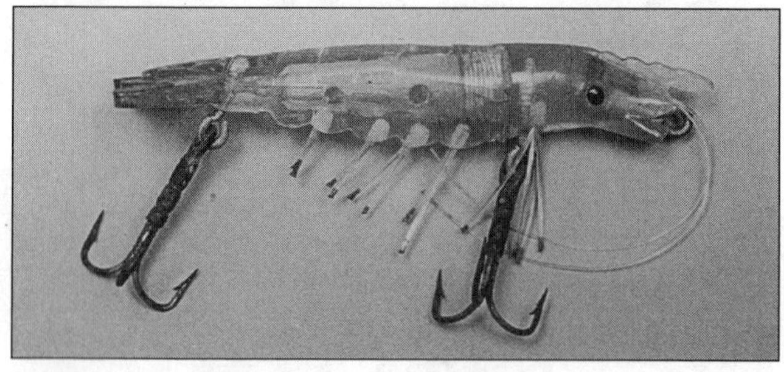

Only one advertisement and no catalog entries were found for this lure. There was one reference that described it as being 3-3/4". The one in the photo here measures 4" long so there may be two sizes to be found. The box was printed with the names as above and the following phrase: "Looks like it, Smells like it, Tastes like it". It appears there was a small refillable vial in the body that contained the shrimpy smell and taste. A 1954 advertisement said it was made in five colors, but didn't list them. Collector value range: $50-$75.

MARATHON BAIT COMPANY

Wausau, Wisconsin

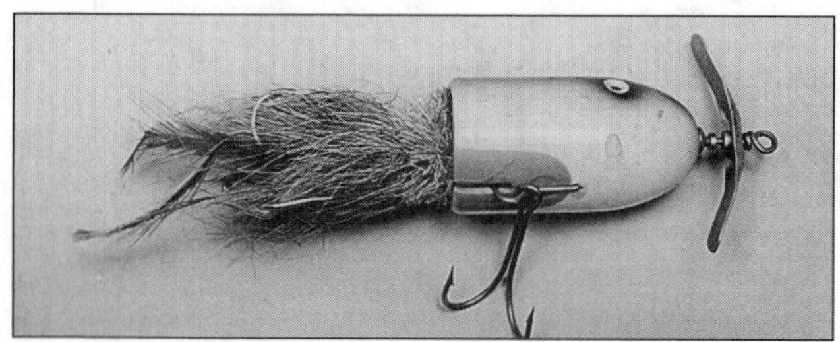

A Marathon wood body MUSK-E-MUNK, 2-1/4", 4" overall.

An original MUSK-E-MUNK box top.

The earliest reference found for Marathon was magazine advertising from 1931. They were in business at least into the 1960s. They offered mostly spoons and spinners, but they made at least two wood lures for northern muskie waters, the MUSK-E-MUNK and the MUSKIE-HUSKIE in the drawing below. Both lures have a treble hook almost completely concealed in the very generous buck tail and hackle tail or hook dressing and earliest versions had glass eyes. The finishes available for each were:

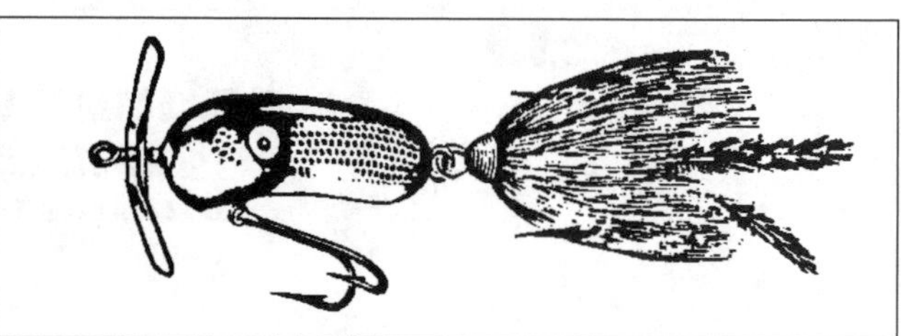

MUSK-E-MUNK	MUSKIE-HUSKIE
Natural	Red and white
White	Scale
Yellow	Brown
Black	Gray

Collector value range for either: $25-$50.

MARTIN FISH LURE COMPANY

Joe Martin Seattle, Washington

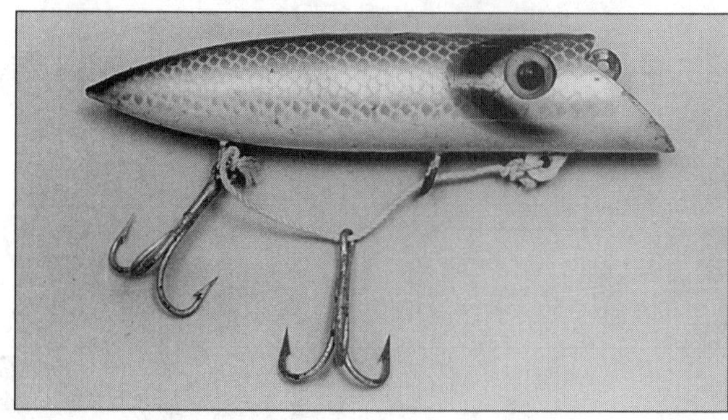

This 6" lure has interesting markings on its belly. It has "MARTIN 6" and "BILL LOHRER'S HOPE IS SPECIAL". It sports yellow glass eyes and the break-away hook harness.

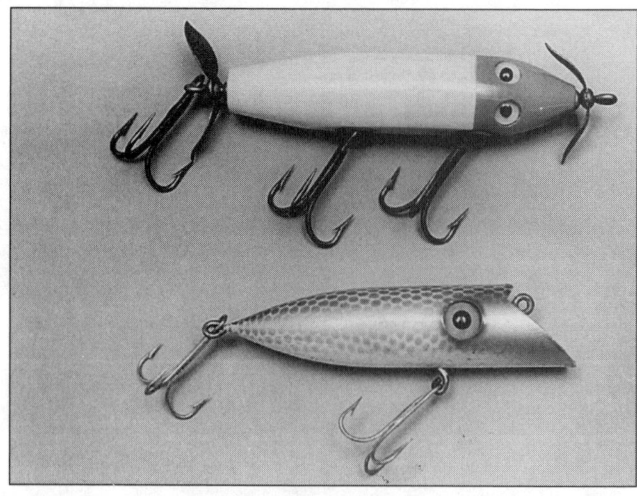

The upper lure is white with red head, has yellow glass eyes, cup and screw eye hardware. The lower lure has a scale finish and the same style hardware. Both have "Martin" stamped on the belly and measure 3-5/8" and 3-1/2".

One of the pioneer salmon lure makers of the Northwest, Martin products came on the market around 1927 and were made and marketed right up into the 1980s. They range in size mostly from 3" up to 7", but I have read of an 11" size also. In the 1930s Heddon began making large salmon plugs also. They obviously were copying Martin's lures. The Heddon KING BASSER was shaped quite similar to the Martin lure and indeed the break-away clips and the hook ties were almost identical. Martin got mad and sued the Heddon Company in 1937 and won what was a substantial dollar settlement in 1937. Collector value range: $20-$55.

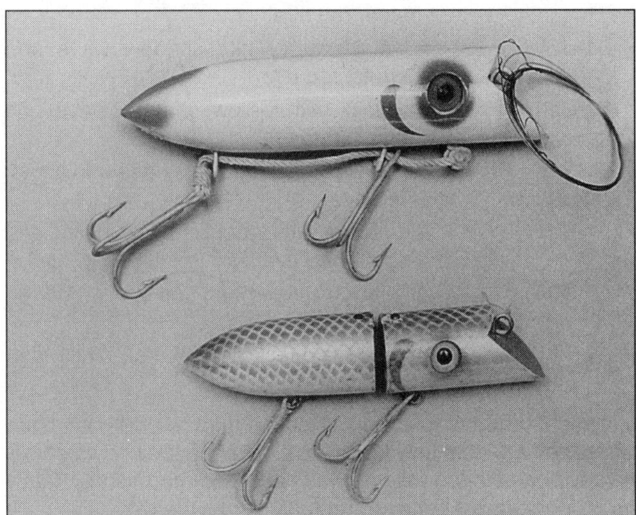

Two more Martin lures. The upper lure has the break-away hook harness and the lower example is jointed. Both are stamped with the name on the belly.

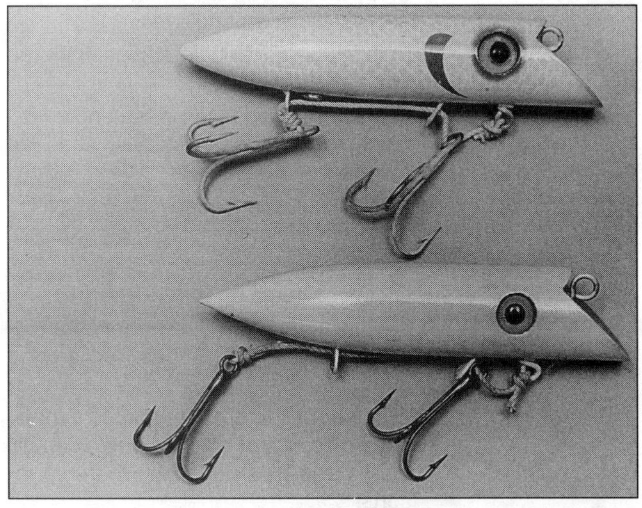

The upper, 6" lure here is yellow with a red gill slash. It has yellow glass eyes and the patent number on the belly. The jointed version also has yellow glass eyes and the patent number as well as "Martin" on the belly.

MARTIN'S LIZZARD

Jack H. Martin

Drumright, Oklahoma, 1946-1955
Stillwater, Oklahoma, 1955-1970

This lure is remarkably like the Whopper Stopper HELLBENDER lure. There were many smaller makers also making lures in this salamander shape so Mr. Martin didn't have a corner on the market. They measure 3-1/8" body length and 4-1/2" overall.

I have been privileged to have a lot of help sorting out this lure and its history. First I heard from Marc Dixon, NFLCC

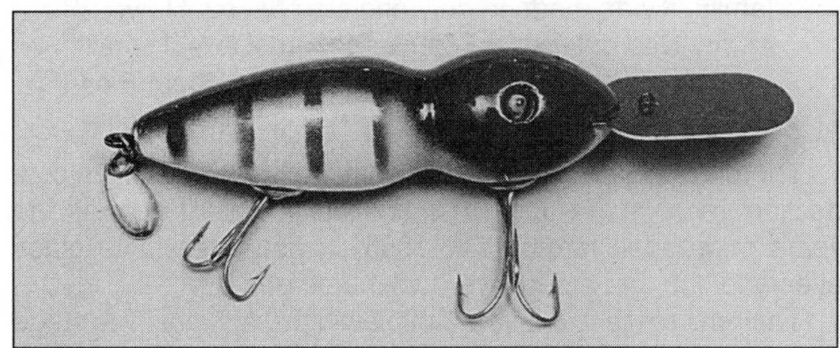

This MARTIN LIZZARD measures 4-1/4". It is made of wood and has glass eyes and has the cup and screw eye style belly hook hangers.

The upper lure is a wooden blank and the lower lure is a plastic MARTIN LIZZARD with molded in eyes.

member and LIZZARD specialist from Arkansa City, Kansas. He has provided me with invaluable information. Then I heard from Martin's son, Jack H. Martin, Jr. His historical information was welcome and invaluable. It follows here:

The following is a brief history of the Martin Lizzard, as told by Jack H. Martin Jr.

> The "Martin Lizzard" was perfected in 1946 by my father, Jack H. Martin, Sr., in Drumright, Oklahoma. Patents were applied for in the United States and Canada. The U.S. denied the full patent, but offered a patent pending classification, while Canada gave him a full patent.
>
> The body of the plug was of cedar and was turned on a wood lathe by hand. All paint was applied by air-brush guns. My mother placed the hooks, eyes, and tail spinner (flasher) on the plugs and placed them in individual paper boxes for shipping. The paper box was replaced by plastic in 1955 when we moved to Stillwater, Oklahoma. At that time the wooden bodies were also replaced by plastic.
>
> The hooks #4 and #6 were made by the Edgar Sealey Company in England and were a high grade of stainless steel. Paint, tail spinners, and glass eyes were purchased through the Herter's Company. The Lizzard was originally made in 48 different color combinations, however, upon request, my Dad would do special painting.
>
> My Dad made the plug until his death in 1970 in Stillwater. At that time I was living in Wichita, Kansas, and moved the Lizzard business there until 1973 at which time it was sold to Mr. Jerry Kincaid, Indianapolis, Indiana. During the time that I made the Lizzard, I reduced the color selection to 18 different color combinations. I am not sure what colors it is being offered in now. During production in the Martin

family, it was made in only one size 5/8 oz. However, my Dad did made a couple dozen of a real small size for me when I was a kid. I still have about 6 or 8 of these.

There are at least two readily identifiable periods in the production years of this lure. The first, as we have seen is the years of wooden lures, 1946-1955. These lures have glass eyes and cup and screw eye hook hardware.

The next stage is the years of plastic production. This stage broken down into three sub-stages:

Plastic bodies with glass eyes

Plastic bodies with painted eyes

Plastic bodies with pressed eyes (molded into the head)

The glass-eyed plastic lures are the earliest plastic LIZZARDS. They are likely to be the result of either remaining inventory or possibly it proved too difficult to use the glass eyes with the plastic bodies. None of the plastic models have ever been found with anything other than the simple screw eye in a molded depression. I believe the lures are still being made so I am not sure where the transition to the molded eye came. It may prove that this was done with the sale of the company in 1973. It would certainly be a more economical method of rendering eyes.

The two piece cardboard box is silver with green printing. It is very scarce.

Collector value range:

Wood with glass eyes: $20-$40.

Plastic with glass eyes: $30-$50.

Plastic with painted eyes: $10-$15.

Plastic with mold eyes: $4-$6.

The following is a list of 30 colors that were offered on the LIZZARD from Drumright, Oklahoma. That makes it a good list of wooden body colors. It is almost verbatim. Notice there are gaps in the numbers. If you assume the list started out at "12" and count the numbers not listed you come up with a total of 58 colors. Marc Dixon has almost that many in his collection and says he knows of more elsewhere. I think there may be over 60 to be found, making color collecting this lure a real challenge. Here's the list:

12-W	All white
12-B	All black
13-B	All black, white eye
14-B	All block, red eye
15-W	All white, block stripe down side, block eye
12-BW	Black head, white body, red eye
25-G	Light green with dark green down side, red eye
26-G	Dark green with red stripe on side, red eye
26-YP	Yellow, olive drab back, red eye
27-WB	White, black head and spots, red eye
28-WR	White, red head and spots, black eye
29-Y	Yellow with green and black spots, red eye
29-YFL	Yellow with green and red spots, red eye
30-Y	Yellow with black and red spots, red eye
30-YB	Yellow with black spots, red eye
31-BW	Black with white head, red eye
32-SF	Silver flash with black eye
35-D	Black back with green and red stripe on side, red eye
35-RS	Black back with red stripe on side, red eye
36-RW	White with red head, black eye
39-WRS	White with red spots and black eye
39-WBS	White with black spots, red eye
39-WBRS	White with black and red spots, red eye
40-BWS	All black with white stripe down side white eye
41-BWS	All block, white spots, red eye
44-T	Tan w/ olive drab stripe on back & down side, red eye
51-BSW	All black with white shadow wave and spots, red eye
51-BYWR	All black with yellow shadow wave and spots, red eye
51-SW	White with black shadow wave and spots, red eye
51-SWY	All yellow with block shadow wave and spots, red eye
56-B0	All black, orange head and spots, and red eye
58-0B	All orange, black head & tail, black ribs, orange eye

We can add the following 17 colors to the wood body color list as they are definitely known to exist. With the known colors the addition of these will make a total of 48; interestingly, that's the number Jack Martin, Jr. quoted. Here's the list:

FROG	with nine black spots w/ yellow around them, red around eyes, yellow belly.
GOLD	with five black stripes, red around eyes.
WHITE	with red blush head and lip, five black side stripes, black around eyes.
WHITE	with five blue-green side stripes, light red blush around eyes.
WHITE	with black blushed head, white under lip, black bumble bee stripes and red around eyes.
WHITE	with black blushed head and top of lip, white under lip, five blue-green stripes, red around eyes.
WHITE	with silver flitters.
BLACK	top, white bottom and sides, four pyramid-shaped black side stripes, red around eyes.
BLACK	with nine large cream colored spots, Cream color around eyes, red blush gill marks, red blush on chin where lip inserts.
YELLOW	with black head, five black side stripes, red around eyes.
YELLOW/BLACK	bumble bee finish with yellow head, yellow lip, red around eyes. The stripes end at the eye sockets.
YELLOW/BLACK	bumble bee finish with black head, black lip top, yellow lip bottom, four black stripes, red around eyes.
BLACK/WHITE	bumble bee. Six wide side stripes, black head and top of lip and red around eyes.
BLACK	top, cream color belly, four thin black side stripes, orange around eyes.
SILVER	top and sides, Cream color belly, 1/4" line from nose to tail, 14 gray spots, black spot on each side directly in line with lip 1/8" down from eye and 3/8" back from the eye. Red blush around eyes.

BLACK back, head and lip top. Five thin side stripes with red around eyes.

DARK green back, head and lip, tan belly, five green side stripes and orange around eyes.

The next step in the evolution is the glass-eyed plastic-bodied LIZZARD. There are 11 known colors in this variation. They are:

CLEAR body with scale finish on back, silver shore minnow pattern, silver lip, red around eyes and a painted red ventral fins.

BLACK all over with white around eyes.

BLACK with nine large white spots and white around eyes.

BLACK with five thin white side stripes, white around eyes.

BLACK back, sides and lip, gold belly with red painted ventral fins, nine orange spots on body, orange around eyes.

BLACK with silver flitters.

WHITE with clear belly, red painted ventral fins.

SILVER with clear belly, one black spot on each side behind and beneath the eyes, black around the eyes.

SILVER with clear belly, nine large black spots on body, red around eyes.

SILVER all over body with twenty black spots, red around eyes.

FROG with large black over yellow overlapping fade spots over entire body and top of lip, white under the lip and yellow around eyes.

The next generation is the plastic LIZZARD with *painted* eyes. There are only two patterns that have so far been found. They are:

WHITE back, belly and lip. Six gray side stripes beneath a silver scale side finish. Large orange eyes with black pupils.

BLACK blush head and lip top. Bottom of lip is silver, clear belly with red painted ventral fins, gold sides and back with four black pyramid shape stripes on each side that alternate and overlap resulting in a zig zag of gold on the back. Orange eyes with black pupils.

The last of the stages is the plastic lures with molded-in eyes. All of these eyes are yellow with black pupils. There are 23 patterns presently known to exist. These probably date from the sale of the company in 1974. The plastic lure with molded eyes may date from then to being contemporary

MARZ DOUBLE DUTY

Barnard Plating Company — Ann Arbor, Michigan

This metal lure measures 2-3/4" long and is apparently made so that you can pull it from either end depending whether you want to top water or underwater lure. It dates from sometime around the late 1930s to the early 1940s. Collector value range: $5-$15. Photo courtesy Clarence Zahn.

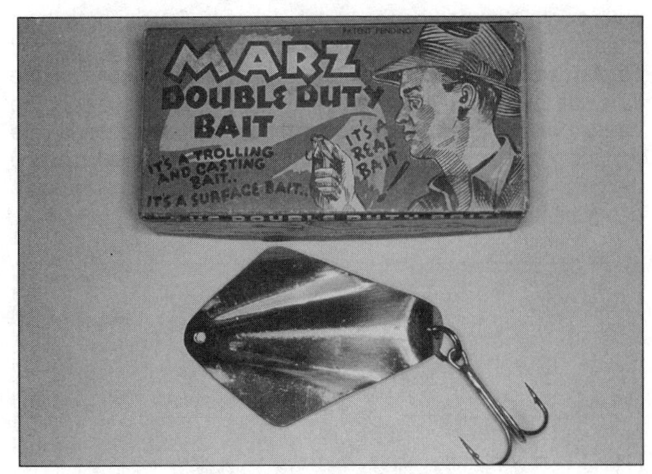

IMPORTANT NOTICE

The value ranges listed in this book are for lures in Very Good to Excellent condition. The values of those lures not in Very Good to Excellent condition can and probably will be worth considerably less. The values are meant to be a guide only.

MEDLEY'S WIGGLY CRAWFISH

F.B. Hamilton — Pasadena, California

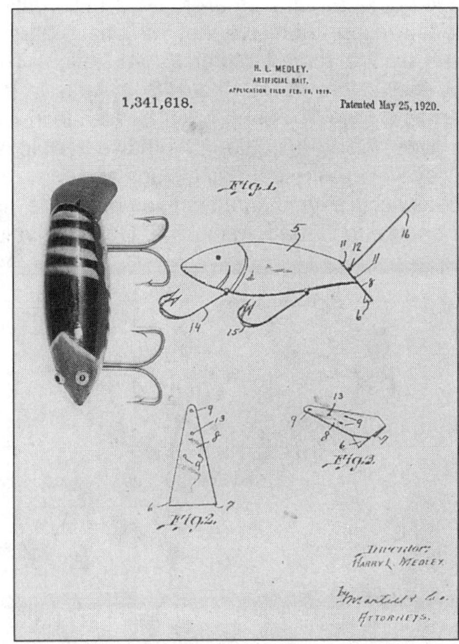

You will note in the photo that the patent date is May 25, 1920. There is another earlier patent dated August 5, 1919. Both show the same body, but the metal lip blade design is different. The earlier patent shows a metal lip much more like the actual product. The confusion lies in the fact that both patents were applied for on the same date, February 18, 1919. While both patents were filed for by Harry L. Medley of Los Angeles, California, the earlier one assigns one-third of the rights to Harry G. Hamilton of Youngstown, Ohio. The manufacturer of the lures was F.B. Hamilton Manufacturing of Pasadena, California and the patent date stamped on the metal lip was "8-5-19". There is an interesting story concerning the origin of the plug. It is said that Medley whittled the first plug out of a piece of pine and made the lip blade out of the tin from a Prince-Albert Tobacco can. He made it initially for his own use but the patents serve to indicate that the plug was successful for he did go to the trouble to secure the patent. Apparently somewhere along the line Hamilton came along with the wherewithal to manufacture them.

The lures were made in two sizes. The larger (3") has two belly double hooks and the smaller (2-1/2") has only one double. There is reason to believe they may have been provided with trebles by the manufacturer as an option. This is evidenced by the 2" lure in the photo. Both lures in the photos were given to a man in Youngstown by Hamilton himself. All had glass eyes and were equipped with two flexible rubber antennae. They were reverse running plugs and came in 12 color combinations according to an advertisement in the June, 1922 issue of *Forest and Stream* magazine. Collector value range: $75-$125.

A MEDLEY CRAWFISH measuring 2-1/4" on its original box. This lure has the two-piece surface belly hook hardware.

MEPPS

Sheldon's Inc. — Antigo, Wisconsin

By definition Mepps spinner baits are not particularly old nor is their history born in America. However, any veteran fisherman should know what a French spinner is and of those who do, most recognize the Mepps name as probably representing the best French spinner to be had. The Mepps spinners came along in the fairly early days of spin fishing in America and therefore important to its development. Hence their inclusion in this book. "...This inauspicious lure has earned itself a lasting place in the hearts and folklore of many thousands of loyal Waltonians."*

The lures originated in France in the early 1930s and were made by Andre Muelnard. The firm name was Manufacturier D'Engins De Precision Pour Peche Sportive. The first letters of the letters in the company's French name form the acronym "MEPPS". Mr. Todd Sheldon brought them to the United States in the early 1950s. The majority of the components of Mepps spinners sold in the U.S. are made in France and assembled in the Wisconsin plant. The illustrations on this page will help you to identify the earliest Mepps spinners. These earlier lures will be of interest to those collectors who are attempting to assemble a collection representing the evolution of metal spinners and spoons in American fishing history.

IDENTIFICATION OF EARLY MEPPS SPINNERS

Oldest Comets and Anglias have 'Brevete' on blades, French word for patent.

Twisted wire body was used on the first comets and continued in use until early 1970s.

Single-piece "Bell" is found on the oldest models.

Older Anglias in the #4 and #5 size had a red and yellow bead body.

1953 and older models will have sproat bend hooks.

Body style has changed substantially in the last 10 years.

**From Millions and Millions of Mepps by Roger Drayna. Autumn 1972 edition of Wisconsin Trails magazine.*

MERCURY MINNOW
Mercoy Tackle Company

4261 Buckingham — Detroit, Michigan
1359 Hollywood — Grosse Pointe, Michigan

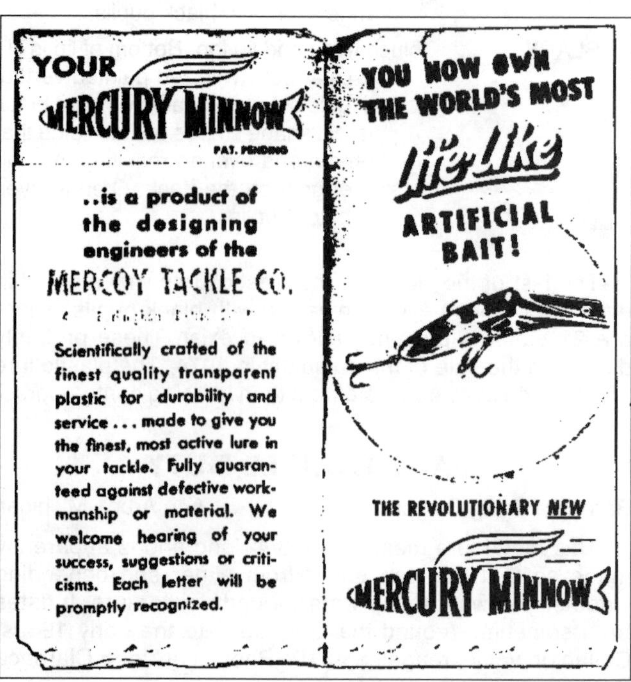

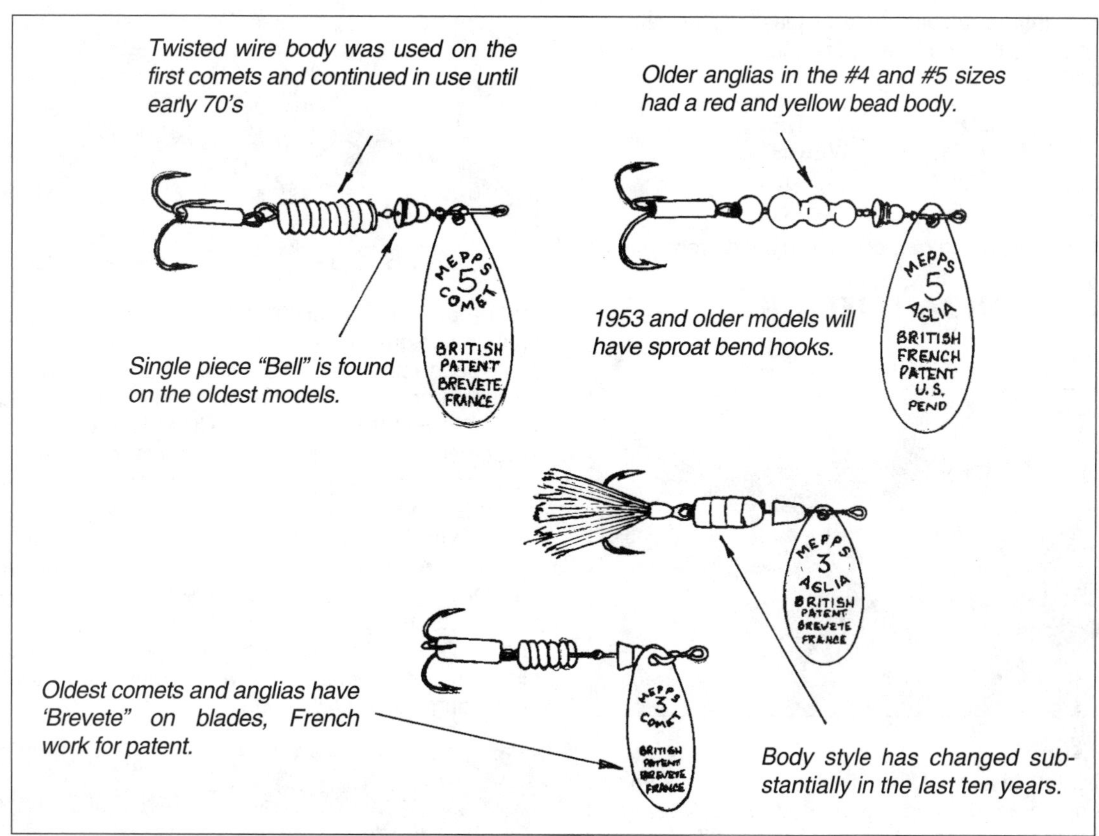
Twisted wire body was used on the first comets and continued in use until early 70's
Older anglias in the #4 and #5 sizes had a red and yellow bead body.
MEPPS 5 COMET
BRITISH PATENT BREVETE FRANCE
Single piece "Bell" is found on the oldest models.
1953 and older models will have sproat bend hooks.
MEPPS 5 AGLIA
BRITISH FRENCH PATENT U.S. PEND
MEPPS 3 AGLIA
BRITISH PATENT BREVETE FRANCE
Oldest comets and anglias have 'Brevete" on blades, French work for patent.
Body style has changed substantially in the last ten years.

One can speculate that the two addresses mean either the lure company was successful and had to move to bigger and better quarters or that the lack of success made a move to less expensive digs necessary. What ever the case this unique 4" plastic lure of the 1940s is interesting. It had mercury within the body that moved around on retrieve making it behave erratically, ostensibly "...imitating a wounded minnow escaping an attacking fish." There were two men, Lawrence Westerville and Howard Poe, involved in the invention and the company. It is reported that over 500,000 were made in 35 years of operation. Color options were: Red and white, perch, black and white, frog, pike, yellow and black, orange and black. Collector value range: $10-$15.

MERCURY WORM

Mer Worm Lure Company
Mercury Worm Lure Company — Angola , Indiana
K-L Company — Dallas, Texas

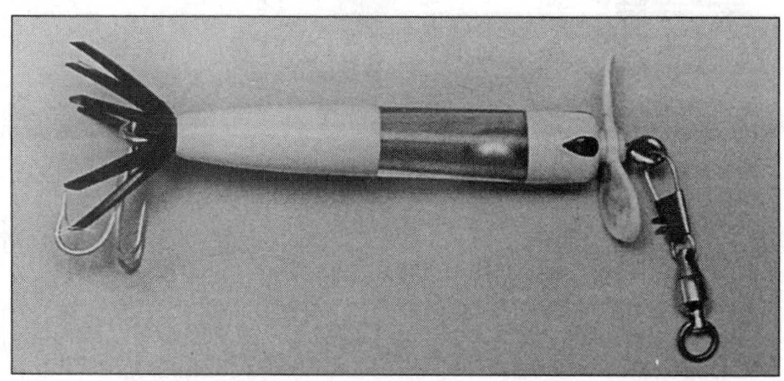

I found nothing in any catalogs or advertising that mentioned this lure. There was one other reference that attributed a 2-1/2" MER-WORM to a K-L Company in Angola, Indiana. The one in the photo here measures 3" and the Mer Worm company name was on the box. It is not known what is behind the two very distant locations of the company. A piece of literature dated 1965 says "it was in testing for twelve years." The patent number in the literature places the patent around 1956-57. It is a slim plastic lure with mercury in it, free to move back and forth. It has a plastic propeller spinner at the nose and one trailing treble hook. Collector value range: $8-$16.

SCATBACK

Mermade Bait Co., Inc. — Platteville, Wisconsin

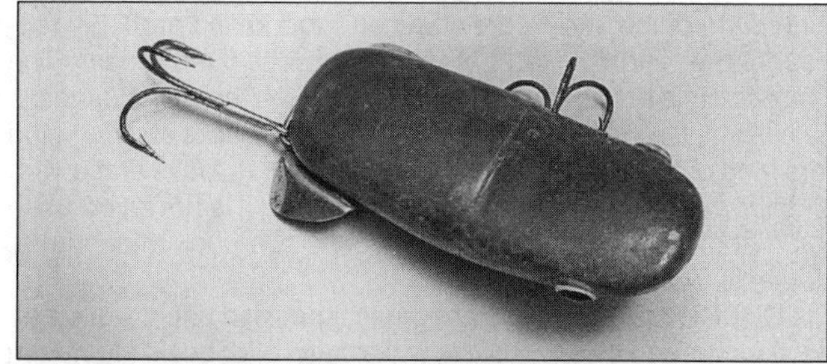

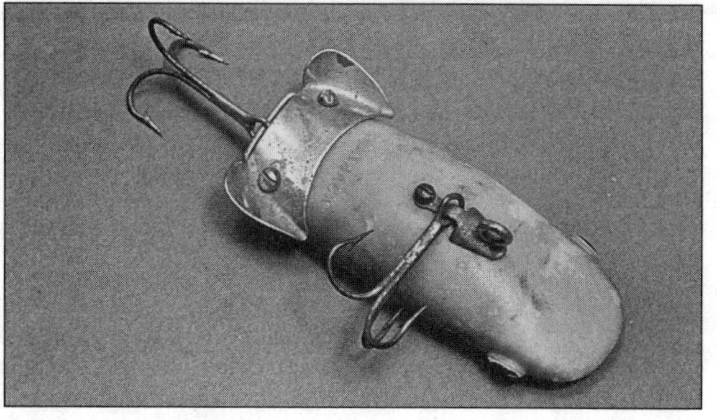

This 1940s vintage lure is made of plastic. The name is molded into the belly making it easily identified. Collector value range: $15-$35.

CATALOG TYPE	BODY LENGTH	LURE WEIGHT
Bass size	2-3/4"	5/8 oz.
Musky size	4"	1-1/8 oz.

COLOR OR FINISH: Shiner, perch; red head, frog; yellow.

MICHIGAN LIFE-LIKE

Adolph Arntz — Muskegon, Michigan

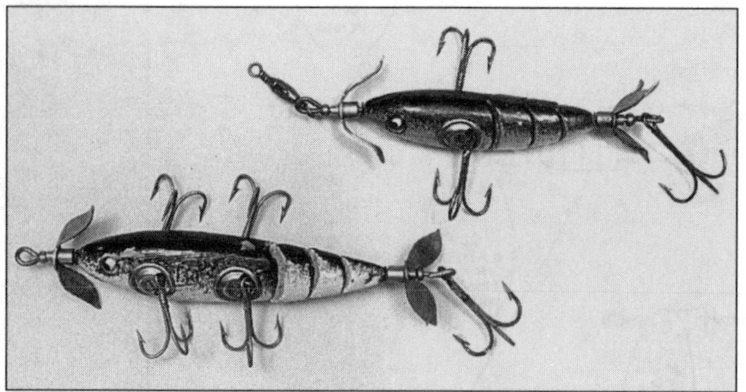

The origin and history of the Michigan Life-Like remains cloudy. The maker is in some way related to the Myers and Spellman confusion. The patent for the Michigan Life-Like was granted to Jacob Hansen of Muskegon, Michigan on February 28, 1908. It has been assumed that he was the manufacturer and a friend, Adolph Arntz, distributed the lure. Arntz was a sporting goods dealer in Muskegon. This assumption may or may not be true. The only advertisement I could find was in a 1910 issue of *The Angler's Guide*. It clearly stated: "Manufactured by Adolph Arntz." They are well made four-section jointed lures. The forward section is the largest, ending with three more smaller sections jointed so that there is a life-like motion to the plug. There are two sizes, 2-3/4" and 3-3/4". The smaller had three treble and the larger, five treble hooks. Both have glass eyes and propellers on the nose and tail. The tail propeller has three blades.

The side hook hangers shown on the lures in the above photo are of the style more commonly found and probably represent the oldest style. It is a more or less flush mount. The second style protrudes further and although the same principle is utilized, the design is different. The third style is shown in the drawing of the Hansen Underwater Minnow. It looks somewhat like the common one-piece surface hanger. It is however, used as a hook limiter and covers the screw eye hook attachment. Collector value range: $300-$600.

COLOR OR FINISH: Light green, speckled back, white belly, dark green, speckled back, white belly, dark back, aluminum color, brook trout, dark back, yellow belly; aluminum color, natural wood finish; perch; green bark, yellow sides, red belly.

MILLER'S REVERSIBLE MINNOW 1913-1920

Union Springs Specialty Company — Cayuga Springs, New York

This extremely rare lure can be found in two variations. The earliest model (c.1913) had simple screw eye or screw eye and washer hook hangers. It also had a slightly longer, much slimmer rear body section than the later version. The later one (c. 1916) utilizes the Pflueger type Neverfail hook hangers and a

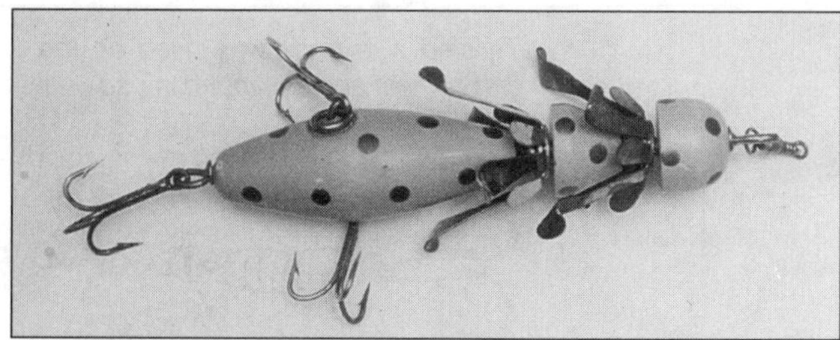

fatter rear body section. The 1916 lure seems much more refined in construction and finish. Examples of this latter model have been found new in a Pflueger box with the paper label (early maroon color with paper label) identifying it as a MILLER'S REVERSIBLE MINNOW. Clearly there was some sort of agreement struck between Pflueger and the Union Springs Company whereby Pflueger either bought the company or a license to produce the lures.

The lure is quite a wild looking contraption. Its propellers were colored gold and silver. The body was made of cedar, 4-1/2" long. It came in three color schemes: No. 1, yellow with gold spots; No. 2, white belly, blended red and green spots; and No. 3, white body, red head with gold spots. The one in the picture has the Pflueger "Neverfail Hook Hardware". Collector value range: $2,000-$2,500.

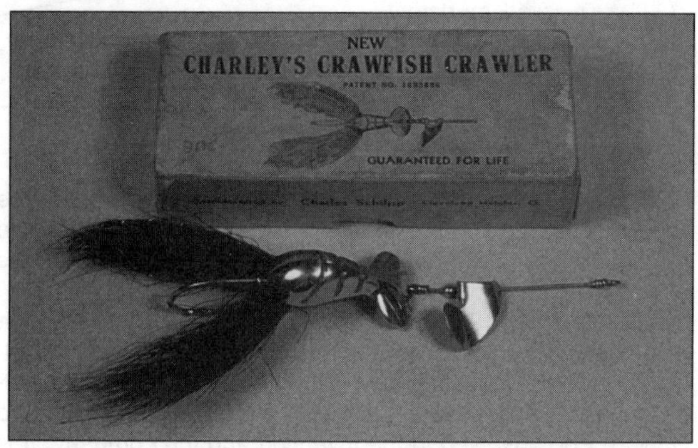

This is a 1-1/2" Charles Shlipp CRAWFISH CRAWLER. Printed on the box: "Manufactured by Charles Schlipp Cleveland Heights O." Collector value range: $20-$40. If found with the box that range could be as much a double. Photo courtesy Jim Muma.

THE MILL RUN PRODUCTS COMPANY

Charles P. Schlipp — Cleveland, Ohio

1948 ads in Sports Afield magazine for the WONDER MOUSE and the SILVER SHINER.

Schlipp is known to have been a lure designer for Al Foss. You can see the similarity in Shlipp and Foss baits. Shlipp seems to have begun his own business in the 1940s. His first lures came out only under his name as in the photo above. I have found several Mill Run Products Company advertisements for this and other lures in 1948 publications. What is puzzling is two patents dating 1929 and 1932. He must have been designing and patenting his own lures while working for Foss. The other lures advertised were Charley's Silver Frog, Charley's Silver Shiner and Charley's Wonder Mouse. All are valued at $15-$40.

MILLSITE TACKLE COMPANY

Howell, Michigan

It is generally believed that this company has been around since at least 1920, but I have never run across any catalogs earlier than the 1930s. I have, however, found a 1954 Millsite advertisement in *Field & Stream* magazine that clearly states "QUALITY TACKLE SINCE 1915". Although the company produced wooden plugs, the greatest majority of those observed by the author and listed here are made of plastics. Just about all that have metal lips are stamped on the lip with the company name.

RATTLE BUG

Called "NEW" in a 1940 catalog, this lure may be the first or, at the least, among the first to incorporate a loose metal ball internally so it would rattle on retrieve (see SEA BAT by Drake). It was made in the shape of a beetle, and has a diving lip and one treble hook. Collector value range: $10-$20.

CATALOG SERIES	BODY LENGTH	LURE WEIGHT
900	1-7/8"	5/8 oz.

COLOR OR FINISH: Black and red, natural, yellow and black, white and red, all red, red and yellow, *goldfish, *frog; *pike scale.

**These were not among the first six finishes offered in 1940.*

A 1-6/8" RATTLE BUG.

MILLSITE MINNOWS
The 99'R Series

Over the years there were a number of different finishes, transparent or opaque, and lip types used on the plastic minnows. There were three basic body sizes, but all were shaped about the same as in the photo. All had a belly treble and a trailing treble hook. The list of sizes and names follow here:

TRANSPARENT MINNOW (Floater)

3" 3/5 oz.

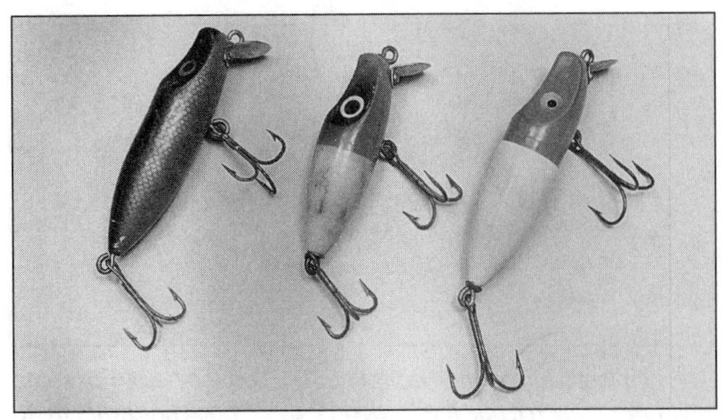

OPAQUE MINNOW (Floater)

3" 3/5 oz.

TRANSPARENT MINNOW (Baby Slow Sinker)

2-1/2" 1/2 oz.

OPAQUE MINNOW (Baby Slow Sinker)

2-1/2" 1/2 oz.

SINKING MODEL

3" 5/8 oz.

JOINTED FLOATING MODEL

3-3/4" 5/8 oz.

JOINTED SINKING MODEL

3-3/4" 3/4 o5z.

All were available variously with a deep-diving lip, or in floating or sinking versions with smaller diving lip. Collector value range: $10-$15.

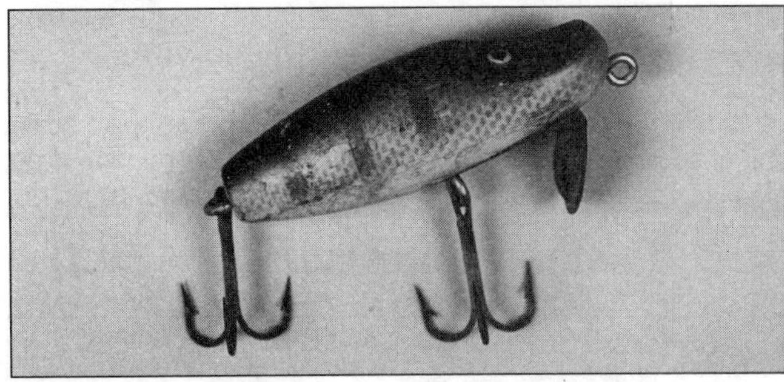

A wood body 99'R measuring 2-5/8" with tack-painted eyes. The metal lip is bent back.

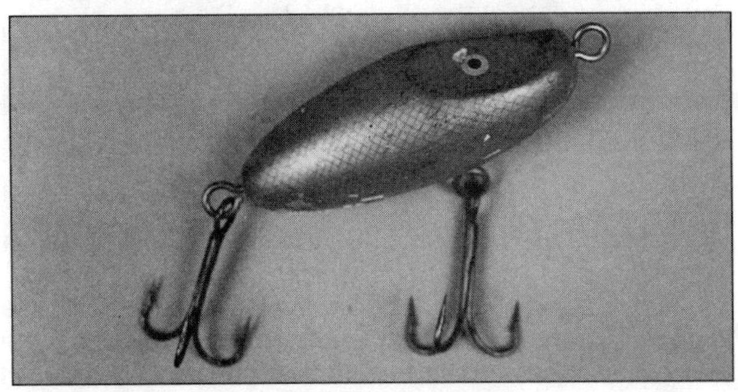

Another wood body Millsite lure. It appears to have a similar body style as the 99'R, but has no metal lip. It measures 2-1/2" and has painted eyes.

This 3" plastic lure is marked "MILLSITE" on the belly. For some unknown reason it has the Heddon 2-piece hook hardware making it look like a RIVER RUNT. Why would anyone go to all the trouble it took to do this?

MILLSITE COLORS

There were several colors used by Millsite, but which colors available on which plugs is not clearly indicated in most cases. The list of those colors found follows here. The list is probably not complete.

COLOR OR FINISH: Black and red; natural; red and white; goldfish; frog; pike scale; green scale, transparent, gold scale, transparent; silver scale, transparent; yellow scale, transparent; cardinal scale, transparent; shiner scale, transparent; orange and black spots.

These are two color charts from the 1940 catalog. Why they went to so much trouble separating out "Standard" from "Jointed" is anybody's guess. Perhaps these will help you sort out some of the Millsite lures.

STANDARD MODELS

White, red head; solid red; red, white head; solid black; silver speckle; rainbow; perch scale; silver herring; shiner scale; frog; green scale; white, red rib; pike scale; black rib; silver rib; green rib; yellow rib.

JOINTED MODELS

White, red head; perch scale; red, white head; pike scale; shiner scale; solid red; white, red rib; solid black; rainbow; frog; black rib; silver rib; yellow rib; green rib; silver herring.

PADDLE BUG

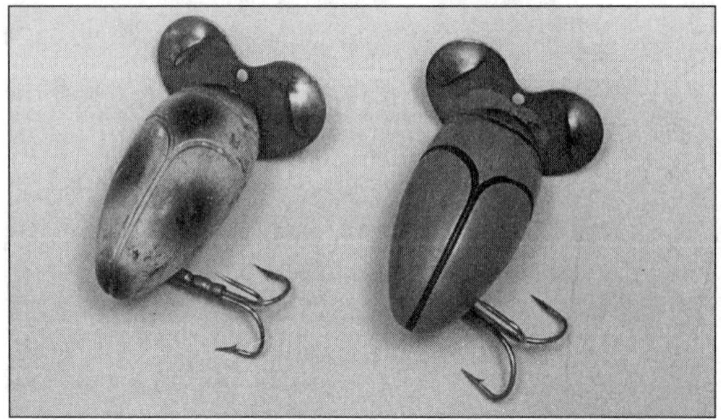

This is the same body design as the RATTLE BUG. It has a large metal mouthpiece much like the Arbogast "Jitterbug" but was slotted to allow water to pass through making bubbles. It has one treble hook, is 1-3/4" long, weighs 1/2 oz. and was available in the same colors as the "Rattle Bug." I have seen one that is the same design but with no slots in the mouth piece. Collector value range: $20-$40.

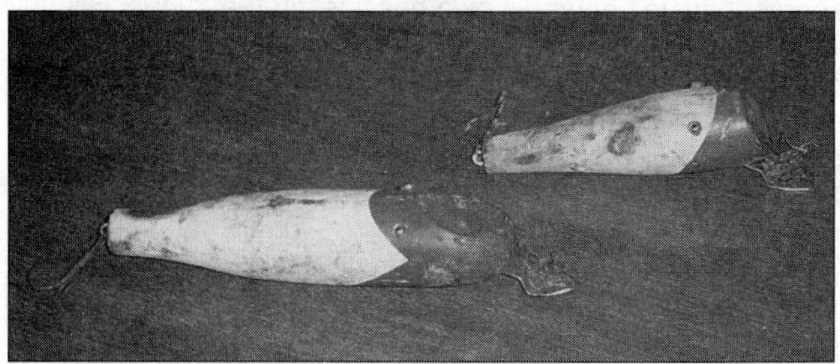

Collector Earl Keirstead of Madison, CT, sent along this photo of two wooden Millsite beaters. He said they are both identified as Millsite DEEP CREEPS on the metal dive lips. They measure 4-1/2" and 6" respectively.

DEEP CREEP

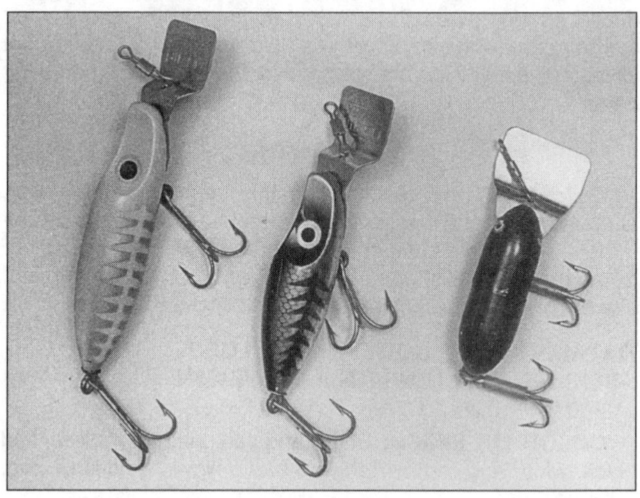

The two plugs on the left in the photo of three are positively identified as DEEP CREEPS. The far right plug is an unknown. There were no illustrations of it found in the catalogs. There were no sizes or weights listed for the DEEP CREEPS either. As far as can be determined DEEP CREEPS could be purchased in all Millsite colors. Collector value range: $5-$10.

DAILY DOUBLE

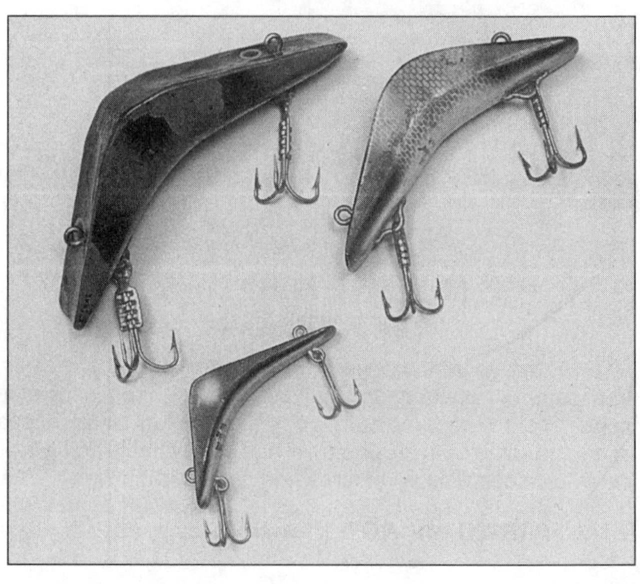

The photo shows the three sizes produced. They are double-ended so that the angler may choose shallow or deep running. Color list may be incomplete. Collector value range: $5-$12.

CATALOG SERIES #	BODY LENGTH	LURE WEIGHT
700	4"	3/4 oz.
800	2-1/2"	5/8 oz.
unk.	2"	unk.

COLOR OR FINISH: Red and white; silver speckle; perch scale; black and white spots; yellow and black spots; frog; orange and black spots; goldfish; silver and black spots; red and black spots; pike scale; black with white scales.

BASSOR BAIT

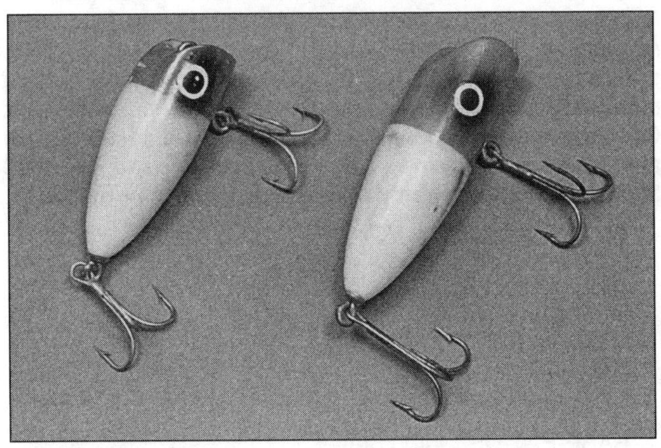

This lure was available in two sizes and only one color. The head is molded with a scooped out nose. Collector value range: $5-$10.

CATALOG SERIES #	BODY LENGTH	LURE WEIGHT
1200	2-3/4"	5/8 oz.
1300 (Baby)	2-1/4"	1/2 oz.
1400 (Jtd.)	3-1/2"	3/4 oz.

COLOR OR FINISH: Redhead, white body.

WIG WAG

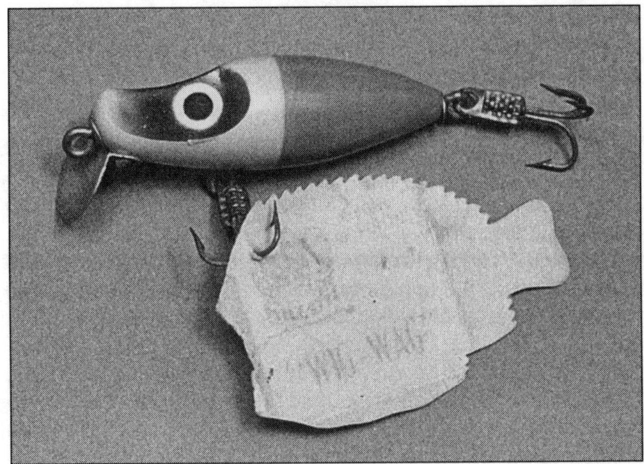

As you can see in the photo, this lure is identified as the WIG WAG on the fish-shaped tag attached. It weights 1/2 oz. and is 2-1/2" long. Colors produced are unknown. Collector value range: $5-$10.

WIG WAG with original box. Measures 3". Photo courtesy Jim Muma.

MILLSITE SPIN-E-BEE

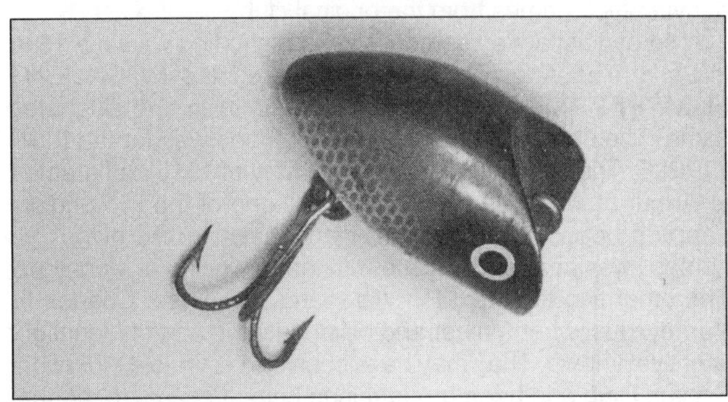

This bait is named on the belly as follows: "Millsite Spin-E-Bee 1/4 oz." No other information other than this is presently known. Let's hope more old catalogs surface soon. Collector value range: $5-$10.

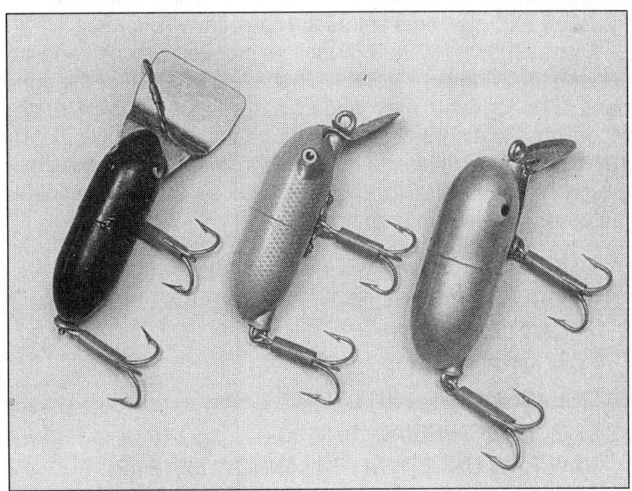

UNIDENTIFIED MILLSITE LURES

These three plastic plugs were not found in any of the available old catalogs. They are, however, identified as Millsite products on their diving blades. I have a letter from a collector who identifies these as being made by a W. C. "Slim" Crissy of Little Rock, Arkansas. It is confusing with the Millsite name on the blades. Perhaps time will sort this out.

THE MOONLIGHT BAIT COMPANY

Paw Paw, Michigan

The Moonlight Bait Company was formed by a legal agreement signed by Horace Emery Ball and Charles E. Varney on December 30, 1908 at Paw Paw, Michigan. A part of this document established Varney as the man who provided the start-up funds. The hand-written document is two legal pages long and after the signatures there is the beginning of a ledger starting in 1909. With this evidence we can now say with authority. that the Moonlight Bait Company began doing business in earnest in 1909.

The story behind this beginning is an interesting one. It seems there was a group of fishing friends who had little time for fishing in the daytime due to the constraints of employment so they began fishing at night. They soon discovered that night time was the time to hook the big ones. In 1906 they formed the appropriately named MOONLIGHT FISHING CLUB. The aforementioned Horace Emery Ball, it seems, had been fashioning a very successful lure and soon found himself providing them for other members of the club. One thing led to another and the result was the formation of the Moonlight Bait Company and its first lure, the MOONLIGHT FLOATING BAIT, both deriving their names from the original club.

The earliest advertisement I was able to find was in a 1910 issue of The Angler's Guide. It featured the MOONLIGHT FLOATING BAIT with a white luminous finish and illustrated same. The earliest Moonlight patent I found was for the FISH NIPPLE. The application was filed in May of 1910 and granted to Arthur R. Miller and Horace E. Ball one of the two original partners, both of Paw Paw, Michigan. These are two of the four names I was able to associate with the beginning of Moonlight. The other two are Ford R. Wilber and, of course, Charles E. Varney. Just when Wilber and Miller became part of Moonlight is not yet known. They may have been part of the old Moonlight Fishing Club and been brought in to help. It seems to me that Miller sharing the patent rights with Ball would probably mean he put some money into the company.

It has been reported elsewhere that the MOONLIGHT FLOATING BAIT was marketed as early as 1906. While we can accept its existence that early, we now know better. This report is apparently based upon the making and distribution of the lure by Ball to his fellow club members before the company was formed.

From 1909 to 1922-23 Moonlight enjoyed success and expanded their line considerably. In the two years after the company was founded they added a weedless version of the Moonlight Floating Bait, the Trout Bob and the Fish Nipple. By 1918 there were at least a dozen in the lineup. The following is a listing of those lures arranged, as best as I can determine, in the order of their appearance:

MOONLIGHT FLOATING BAIT (1908)
WEEDLESS MOONLIGHT FLOATING BAIT (1909-10)
TROUT BOB (1911)
FISH NIPPLE (1911)
DREADNOUGHT (1911-12)
THE "1913" SPECIAL (1912-13)
PAW PAW UNDERWATER MINNOW (1912-12)
PAW PAW PEARL WOBBLER (1912-13)
ZIG ZAG (1913)
PAW PAW FISH SPEAR (1914)
THE BUG (1915-16)
LADYBUG WIGGLER (1916-17)

In 1923 Moonlight began a transition period by merging with another lure company, the Silver Creek Novelty Works, becoming the Moonlight Bait and Novelty Works. This transition continued for the next five or six years with various acquisitions of the manufacturing rights to other lures until the company finally evolved into the famous Paw Paw Bait Company. The time between 1930 and 1935 is still a bit hazy as I have not been able to uncover any reliable information covering this period. The listing below approximates the transition through the years.

MOONLIGHT BAIT COMPANY 1909 to 1923
MOONLIGHT BAIT and NOVELTY WORKS
1923 to 1930-35
PAW PAW BAIT COMPANY 1930-35 to 1960s

The 1923 merging the Silver Creek Novelty Works of Dowagiac, Michigan resulted in a considerable expansion of their line. That company had been making POLLYWOGS, the SILVER CREEK WIGGLER and PIKEROONS among others. You may also run across several lures from SEA GULL (Schoenfeld-Gutter, NYC) that look like Moonlight lures. They were made by the Silver Creek Novelty Works and/or Moonlight for that company. The Sea Gull Company used the same catalog numbers as did Moonlight. About the time of the Silver Creek Company merger, Moonlight apparently had to reorganize their numbering system for their burgeoning lure line. The 1923 Moonlight Bait and Novelty Works catalog lists them as follows:

FLOATING BAIT #1
WEEDLESS FLOATING BAIT#2
FISH NIPPLE #4
ZIG ZAG BAIT #6
PAW PAW PEARL WOBBLER#7
BASS-EAT-US #300 Series
BABE-EAT-US #400 Series
TROUT-EAT-US #500 Series
POLLY-WOG #700 Series
POLLY-WOG JUNIOR#800 Series
PIKAROON #900 Series
BABY PIKAROON #1000 Series
CASTING BAIT (3", 3T)#1100 Series
CASTING BAIT (3", 5T)#1200 Series
LIGHT FEATHER MINNOW
(1 -3/4" overall, 1/3 oz.#1400 Series)
WEEDLESS FEATHER MINNOW#1500 Series
(3-1/2" overall, 1/6 oz.)
FEATHER MINNOW#1600 Series
(3-1/2" overall, 1/8 oz.)
WEEDLESS FEATHER MINNOW#1800 Series
(3" overall, 1/10 oz.)

You may note that the TROUT BOB, DREADNOUGHT, BUG, FISH SPEAR, UNDERWATER MINNOW, THE 1913 SPECIAL and the LADYBUG WIGGLER are all missing from the catalog listing. As far as I can determine they never showed up in the line again.

The #600 Series is conspicuously missing from the list, but it did show up in subsequent catalogs. About the same date as the above catalog. Moonlight obtained the rights to the lure patented by Frederick E. Comstock known as the COMSTOCK CHUNK. Comstock apparently worked for Moonlight for a time. The first listing of the #600 Series I found was in a 1926 Moonlight Catalog. It was called the 99% WEEDLESS. The same catalog listed the WILSON WOBBLER. It is known that Moonlight also obtained the rights to the WILSON WOBBLER and the WILSON CUPPED WOBBLER around 1926 also (see Hastings Sporting Goods Works). The Wilson's Cupped Wobbler became the BASS SEEKER in Moonlight catalogs. There is a two-year gap in my Moonlight and Paw Paw catalog collec-

A. R. MILLER & H. E. BALL.

BAIT.

APPLICATION FILED MAY 28, 1910.

981,454.

Patented Jan. 10, 1911.

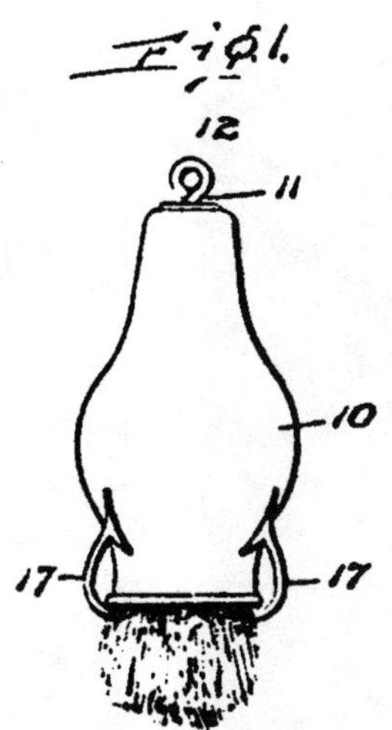

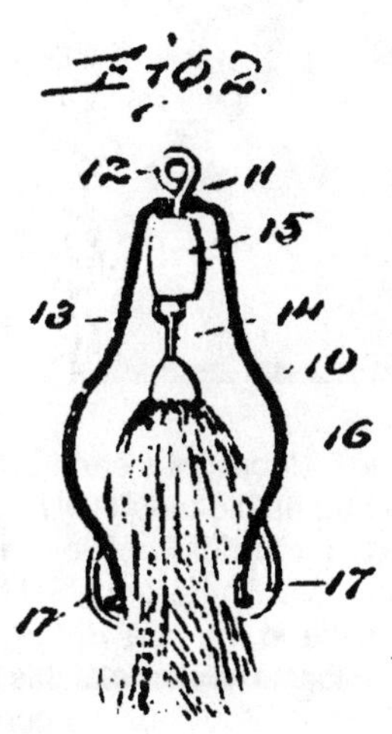

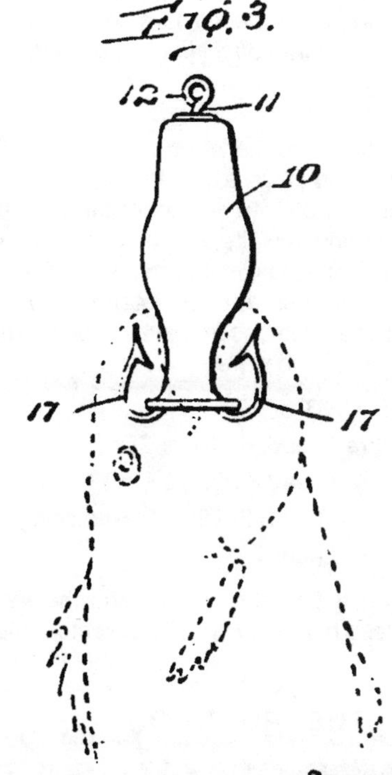

Inventors
Arthur R. Miller,
and Horace E. Ball,

Witnesses
J. M. Fowler Jr
G. M. Copenhaver

By Mason Fenwick & Lawrence.
Attorneys

The Moonlight FISH NIPPLE patent granted to Miller and Ball, January 10, 1911.

tion (1927 &1928). Perhaps the collection is simply incomplete. In any case it is the period in which Moonlight became the Paw Paw Bait Company. The 1929 edition is Paw Paw. Many of the same lures in the last Moonlight catalog are retained in the first (c. 1929) Paw Paw catalog I have. The Paw Paw Company remained in operation up into the 1960s. Please turn to the section on the Paw Paw Bait Company for more information.

THE MOONLIGHT FLOATING BAIT #1
THE WEEDLESS MOONLIGHT FLOATING BAIT #2

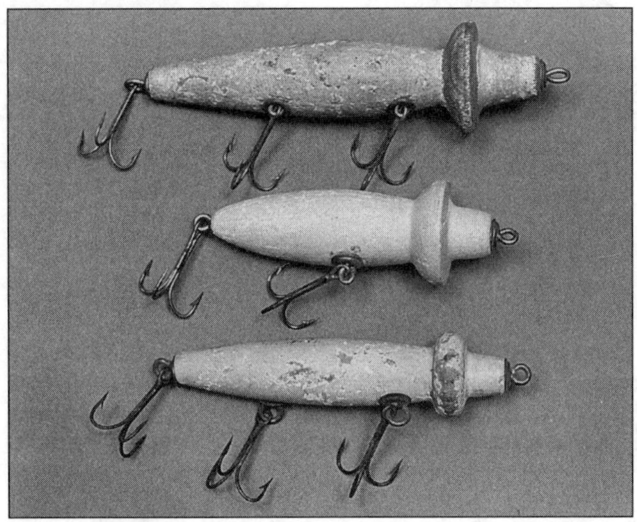

The upper lure is the FLOATING BAIT #1. The one in the middle was not cataloged, but is placed here because its similarity to the #1. The lower lure with offset hooks may not be a Moonlight product.

This plug was first mass-marketed by the company about 1909. The earliest versions were coated with a luminous paint and was 4" long with two belly trebles and a trailing treble hook. It was either solid luminous white or luminous white with a red head. It is not known for sure whether the weedless hook configuration was available then or came later. In any case soon after, a second, smaller size became available. The final sizes and configurations available were:

Luminous white, 4", 3T or 2T
Luminous white, red head, 4", 3T or 3D
Luminous white, red head, 3-5/8", 2T
Luminous white, red head, 3-5/8", 2T (weedless)
Luminous white, red head

The only difference between the #1 and the #2 was the presence of weedless hooks on the #2. Collector value range: $30-$60.

THE TROUT BOB

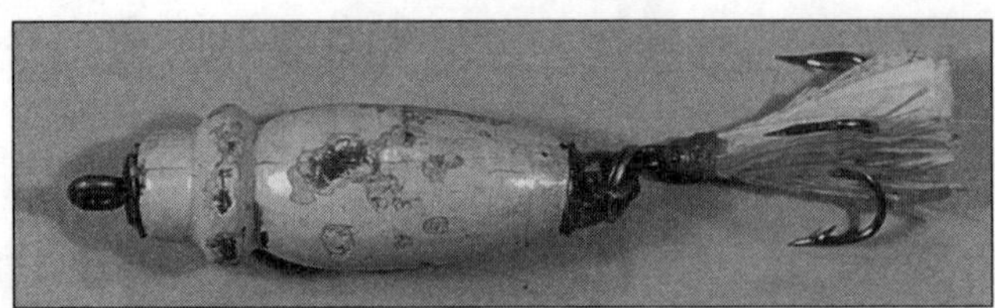

This small 1-1/8" plug first showed up in 1911 ad in *The Outer's Book* magazine. The only color known is solid white. It sports a feathered trailing treble hook. Sometimes known as the "Little Bob". Collector value range: $30-$60.

THE FISH NIPPLE

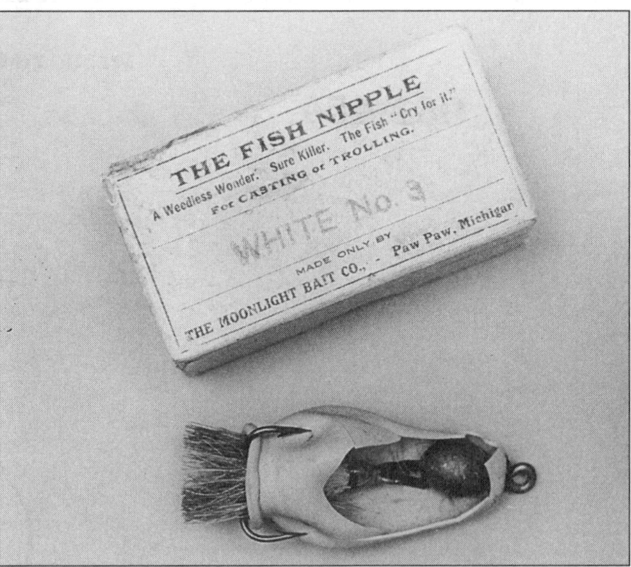

A 2-1/4" Moonlight FISH NIPPLE in white. The color choices are white and a rust red color. This one is damaged, but that allows you to see the internal construction.

This one has no evidence of ever having had the bucktail installed.

Another of Moonlight's earliest lures, it first appeared in the same 1911 ad as did the TROUT BOB. It was patented January 10, 1911 by Arthur R. Miller and Horace E. Ball, two of the original founders. There is a FISH NIPPLE look-a-like out there that was made in the late 1940s early 1950s with the brand name DuraFloat. The name of this lure is the OLD TIMER NIPPLE DIPPER. It is obviously a copy. One has to wonder why. Collector value range: $75-$125.

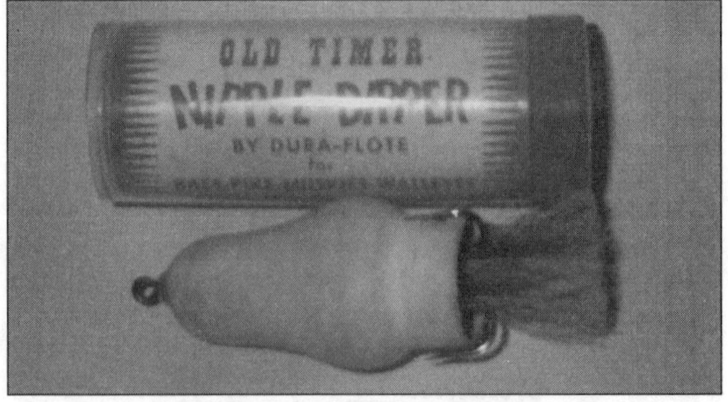

A 2-1/8" OLD TIMER NIPPLE-DIPPER with its original plastic tube. Collector value range: $25-$40.

THE "1913" SPECIAL

Apparently first available in 1913 (an ad said it had been thoroughly pre-tested in 1912) this plug was advertised as available

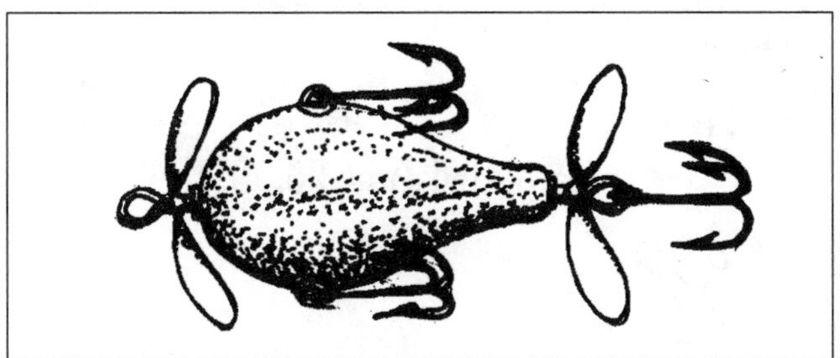

in only one finish. It was painted and covered with a glitter-like material to make it sparkle. It has a treble hook on each side and a trailing treble. There was one nose-mounted propeller and one tail-mounted. Collector value range: $500-$600.

THE PAW PAW FISH SPEAR

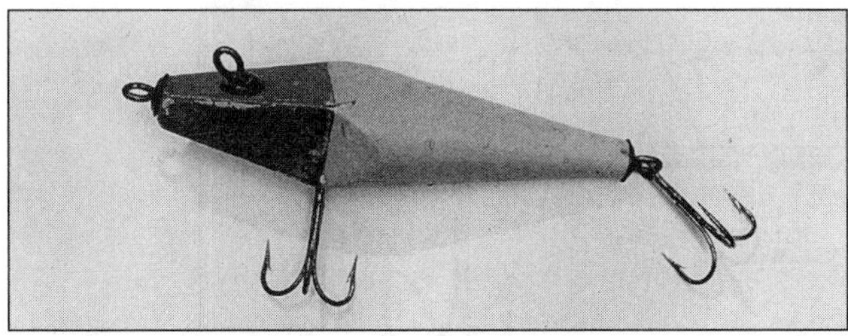

This plug was first found advertised in an August 1915 issue of *The Outer's Book* magazine. The size was not given, but colors were red, white, yellow or fancy spotted. Collector value range: $200-$400.

LADYBUG WIGGLER #800

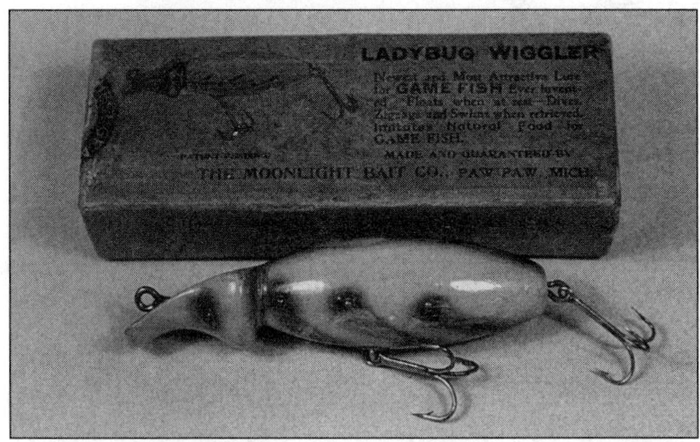

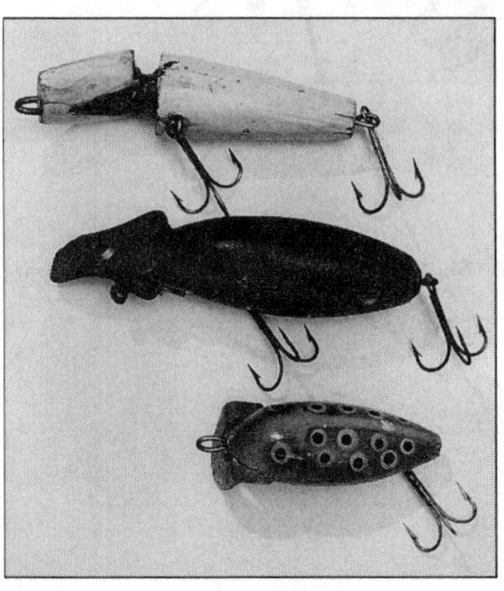

This is a photo of both models of the Moonlight LADYBUG WIGGLER.

The patent for this lure was applied for in late 1916 and granted June 26, 1917. It was first found advertised in the May, 1917 issue of *National Sportsman* magazine. The ad states "Newest and Most Attractive Lure for Game Fish Ever Invented." It had an odd-shaped diving plane head, a belly treble and trailing treble hook. It was available in three color finishes: White with red head and black legs, yellow with red head and black legs, green back with red and yellow decorations and black legs. The legs are broken off of the one in the photo here. You can see the remnants on the side of the body. Photo courtesy Jim Muma. Collector value range: $200-$400.

LADYBUG WIGGLER #1800

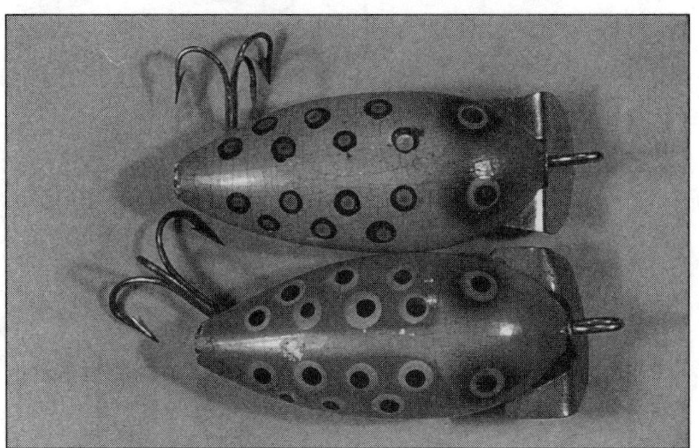

This lure was not listed in any of the Moonlight catalogs I have. The only place I was able to find it was, curiously, in a list of lures supposedly made by the Keeling Company that was published in a 1928 Shapleigh Hardware catalog. It was called a "Lady Bug Wiggler". The name was spelled as two words, not the one word LADYBUG as Moonlight always did. Whatever the reason, it was there and it is a Moonlight product. It measures 2-1/2". Collector value range: $100-$200.

POLLY-WOG
POLLY-WOG JUNIOR

The top lure here is a POLLY-WOG measuring 3-1/8". Though this size is not found cataloged there are so many of that size found that they must have been in regular production. This one may be a late Silver Creek or early Paw Paw product. The lower lure is a 4" Pikeroon. Both are painted simply and have painted eyes, suggesting that they are latter generation lures evolved to the most inexpensive production method.

A Silver Creek Novelty Works catalog was the first found to list the POLLY-WOGS. It is known from other ads that the Sil-

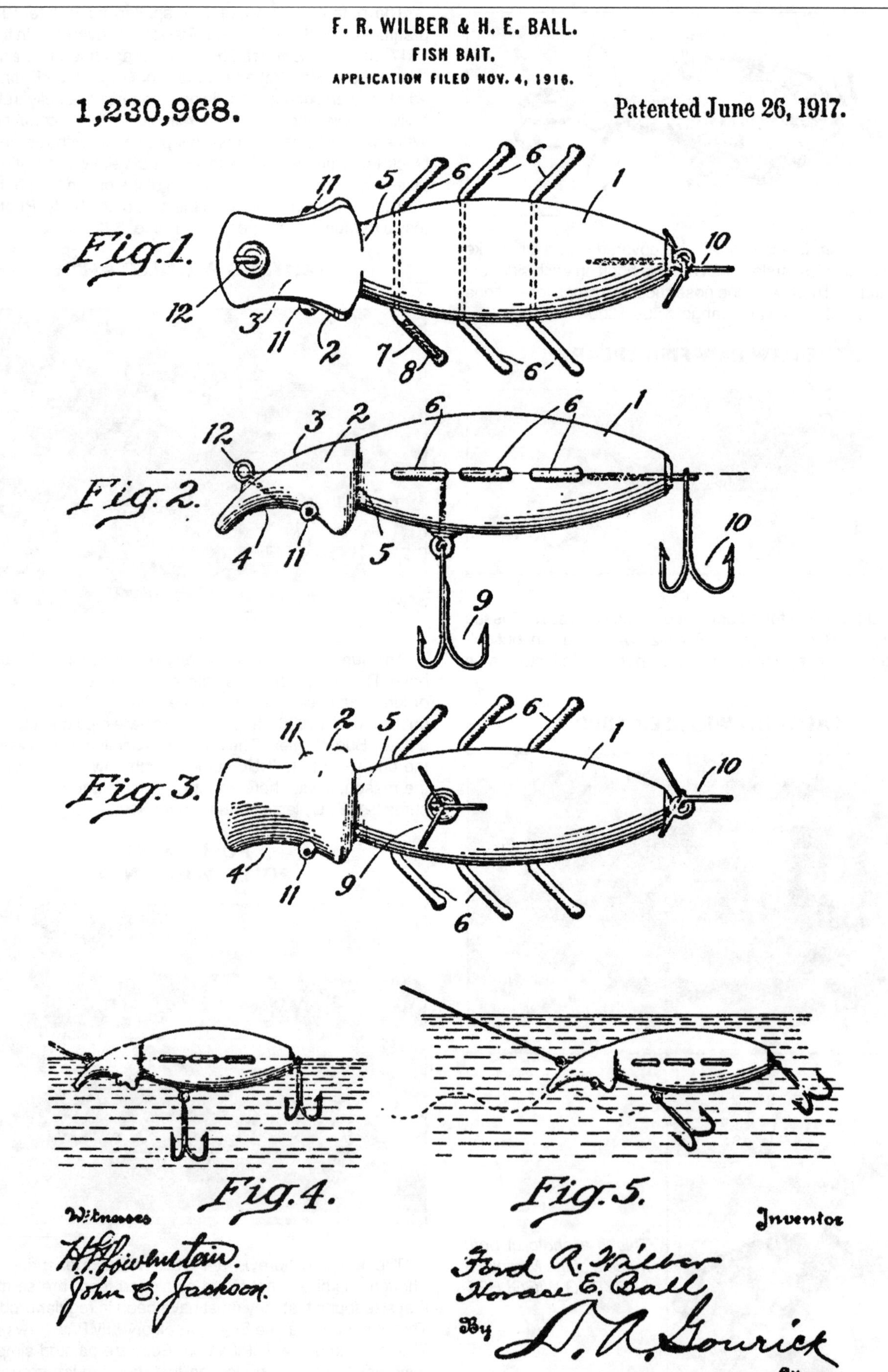

Original patent drawing for the LADYBUG WIGGLER #800.

ver Creek Novelty Works, Dowagiac, Michigan was the original maker of these plugs. A 1921 ad from that company stated: "Last year this bait made its debut in the angler's world". It is 4" long, weighs 4-3/4 oz. and colors listed are: Solid yellow, white with black spots, white with black stripes and moss back. A 1924 Moonlight catalog listed two sizes as available: 4", 3/4 oz.; and the Junior size was 2-1/2", 3/4 oz. The illustration showed glass eyes (as did the Silver Creek ad) and the copy listed nine colors as available. They were: Yellow; moss back; white, red striped; yellow, black spots; rainbow; white, black stripes; white; yellow perch; horned ace.

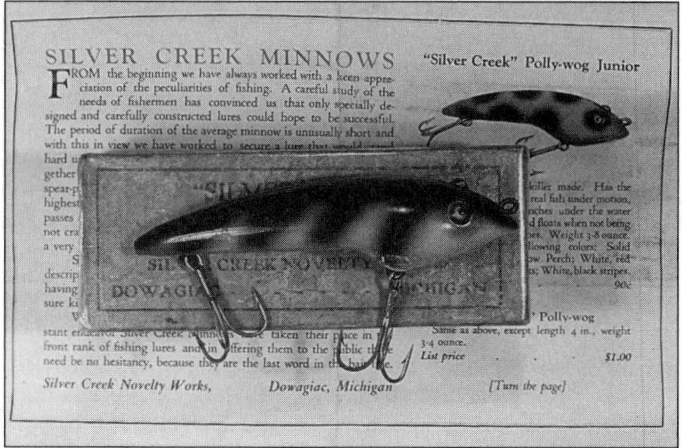

Sea Gull (Schoenfeld-Gutter, NYC) was also advertising the POLLY-WOGS for sale at about the same time. The oldest and rarest version has a notched mouth, but the lure was then a product of Silver Creek Novelty Works, not Moonlight. Collector value range: $60-$120.

THE 99% WEEDLESS

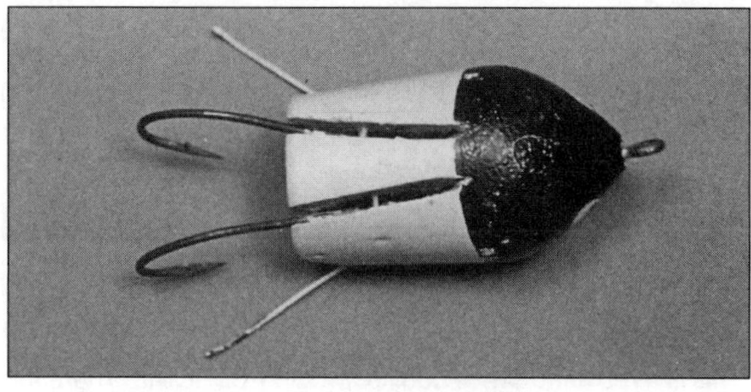

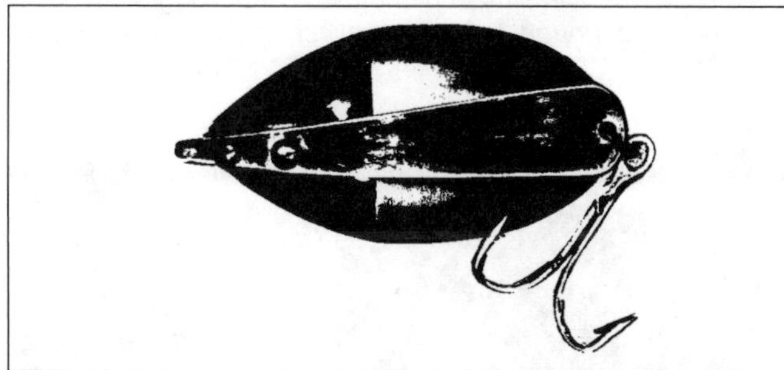

Here is a belly view of a strange version of the 99% WEEDLESS. It has a single metal piece screwed to the belly that acts as a line tie/hook holder.

A 1926 Moonlight catalog is the first to list this lure as available. It is actually the COMSTOCK CHUNK or a slightly modified version of it. Frederick Comstock applied for the patent on his lure in 1923 and it was granted to him in 1926. It was advertised as early as 1924 in catalogs and periodicals. It looks as if Moonlight obtained the rights from Comstock at about the time they were in transition to the Paw Paw Bait Company name. Moonlight listed it in six colors: White with green back, white, red head, luminous, white with black head, perch, all black. Collector value range: $15-$40.

BASS SEEKER AND BASS SEEKER JUNIOR

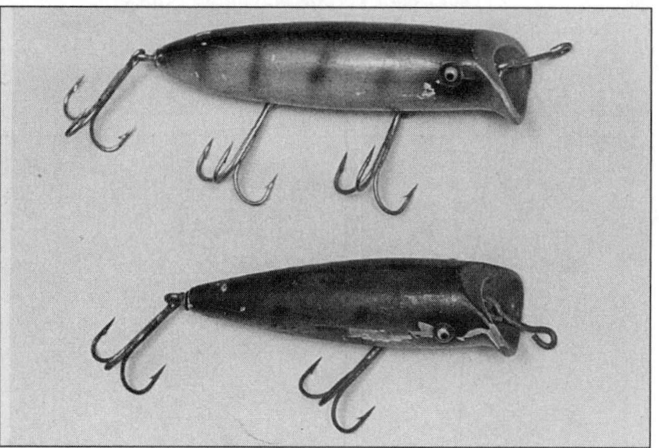

This is another acquisition of an outside company's lure during the Moonlight to Paw Paw transition period. The BASS SEEKERS were originally from the Hastings Sporting Goods Company who called them WILSON'S CUPPED WOBBLERS.

The lure has a scooped nose, heavy wire link leader, a belly treble and tailing treble. It was available in six color finishes: Gold color body with red head, white body with red head, green scale finish, gold scale finish, blue scale finish and perch finish. Collector value range: $25-$50.

MOONLIGHT WHIRLING CHUB c. 1929

This lure was made by Moonlight for Abbey and Imbrie. It measures 4-1/4". Photo courtesy Jim Muma. Collector value range: $100-$150.

MOONLIGHT CRAWDAD c. 1929

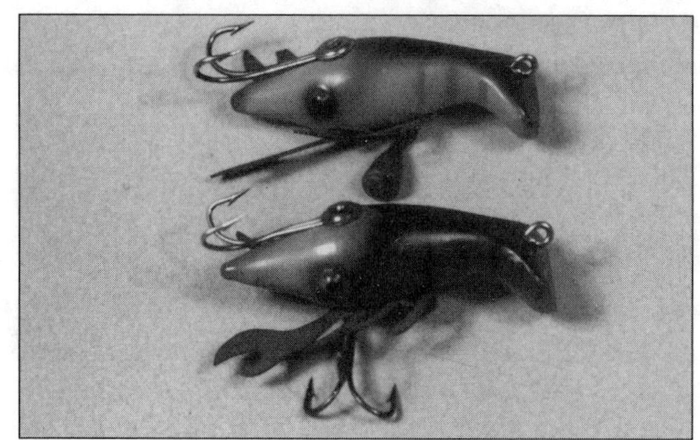

There are two different configurations represented in the photograph. They both have external belly weights hanging from the belly. There is no belly hook on the upper lures and a belly treble on the other. They both measure 2-7/8". Photo courtesy Jim Muma. Collector value range: $250-$400.

WILSON WOBBLER

This lure was originally made by the Hastings Sporting Goods people and acquired from them at about the time of the Moonlight to Paw Paw transition. The lure was actually WILSON'S FLUTED WOBBLER (see Hasting's listing for a photo). Collector value range: $30-$50.

LITTLE WONDER #2100 Series c1925

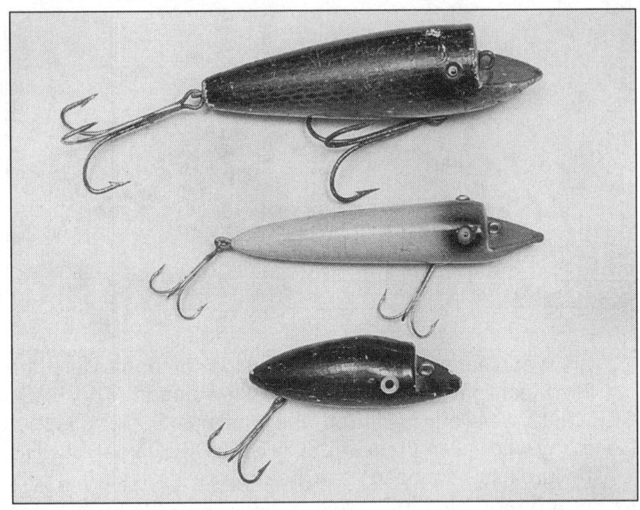

The lower plug in this photo is the LITTLE WONDER. The other two are here because of the similarity of the body design. They have not been found cataloged as yet, but are tentatively identified as a bass size and a musky size version of the LITTLE WONDER.

The Little Wonder was found in a Moonlight advertisement that stated: "BRAND NEW for 1925". No size or colors were listed in the ad but a 1926 catalog listing did contain six colors. They are: Red head with gold body; gold scale; green scale; blue scale; white body with red head; yellow perch. Collector value range: $50-$100.

PIKAROON

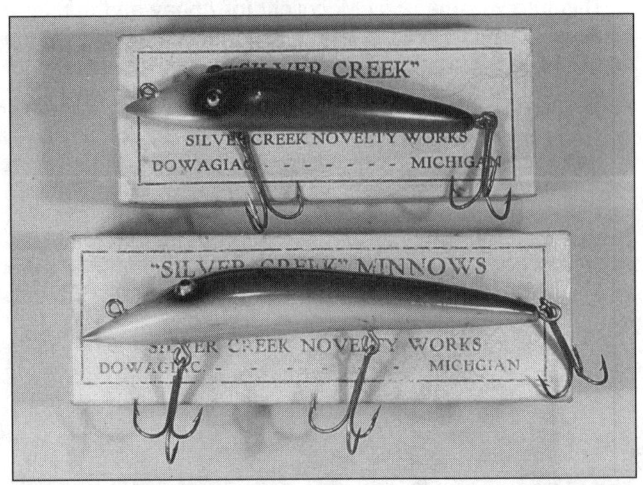

A pair of glass-eyed PIKAROONS made by the Silver Creek Novelty Works. They called them SILVER CREEK MINNOWS.

BABY PIKAROON
JOINTED PIKAROON

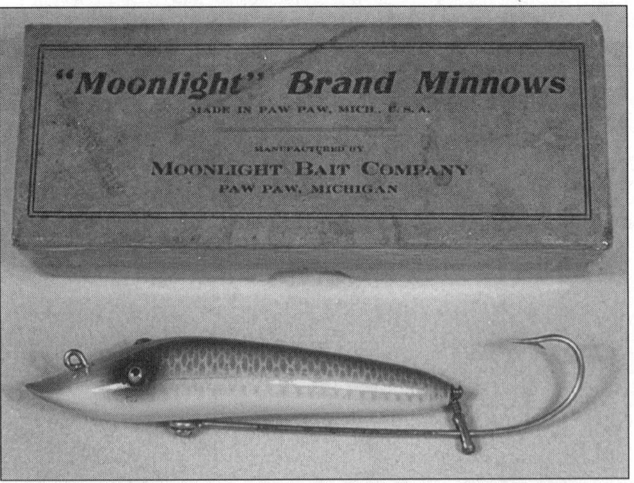

A 4-1/4" 2500 Series PIKAROON made for pikes and pickerels. Collector value range: $250-$350. Photo courtesy Jim Muma.

The following set of photos should help you to identify the various PIKAROONS that were available. If you were to compare these to the PIKAROONS in the Silver Creek Novelty Works section you may note a subtle difference in the style of the nose area. This is an unsubstantiated theory, but nevertheless one that is based on multiple observations; that the Moonlight versions have a little more refined looking, slightly turned up nose than those produced by Silver Creek before the 1923 Moonlight acquisition of the company. The PIKAROONS were made in a Baby size, 1000 Series at 4-1/4" with two trebles, a regular size at 5-1/4" found most commonly with two treble hooks and the jointed version.

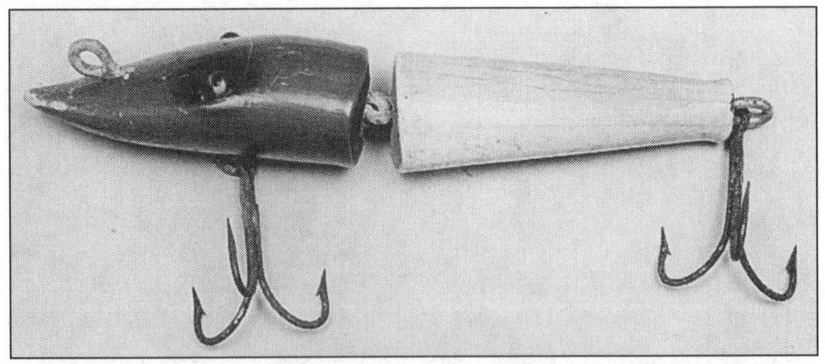

This is a red head, white body 6" MUSKY SPECIAL. There are three types of connecting hardware to be found on JOINTED PIKAROONS. The simple use of two connecting screw eyes on this lure is thought to be the earliest. Collector value range: $75-$150.

The above photo is a close-up view of two JOINTED PIKAROONS showing the second and third styles of connecting hardware. The one on the left has a large heavy wire loop from the trailing section wrapped around a heavy wire or brad placed laterally through the forward section. The one on the right has heavy cup and screw eye connectors.

This is a full side view of the JOINTED PIKAROONS in the previous photo. They each measure 4-1/8", have yellow glass eyes and screw eye hook hangers. Note the turned up noses. Collector value range: $75-$150.

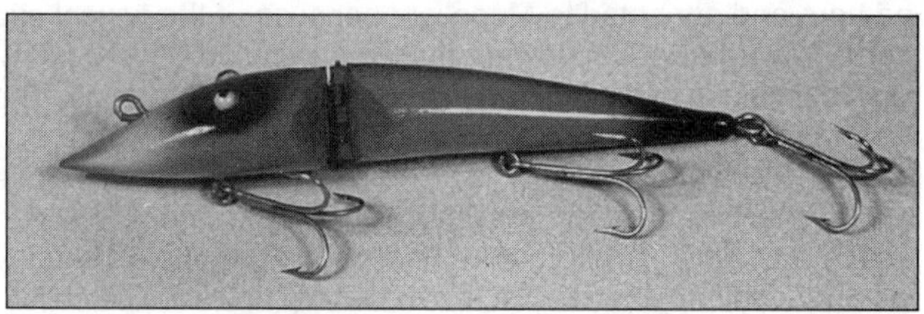

Note the very unusual use of a piano hinge at the joint. This may have been experimental and never put into production. Photo courtesy Jim Muma.

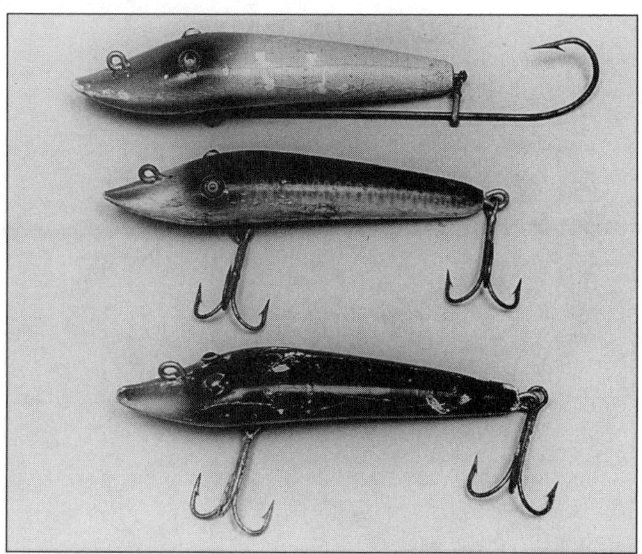

Note the typical Moonlight turned up nose on all three of these JOINTED PIKAROONS. They measure 4-1/16" at top and bottom with the middle plug at an even 4". Top and middle have glass eyes while the lower one sports tack painted eyes (TPE). Each has simple screw eye line tie and hook hangers. Collector value range for the upper lure: $150-$250. The other two are $60-$120.

BASS-EAT-US c. 1920

BABE-EAT-US c. 1920

TROUT-EAT-US c. 1920, 1926

BUG-EAT-US c. 1920

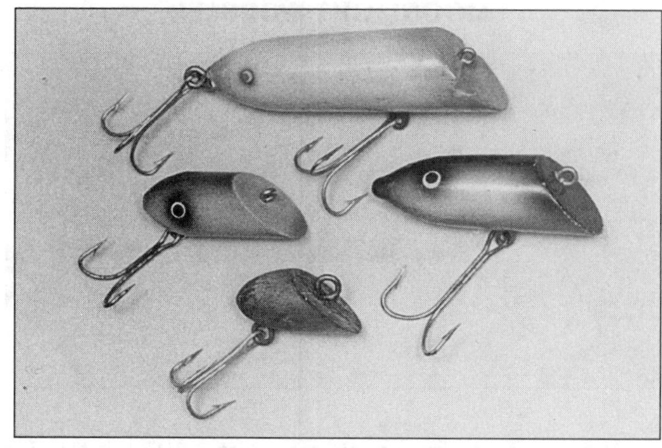

Three of these were found listed and illustrated in a c. 1920 Moonlight catalog. The TROUT-EAT-US was listed as 1-3/4" and a later (1926) catalog illustrated a TROUT-EAT-US, but no size was listed. The lure in the illustration is smaller than the 1920 version. It was described as a fly rod size in the 1926 catalog. The center two lures in the photo match the two catalog illustrations. The upper lure is a Silver Creek 3" BASS-EAT-US. The BABE-EAT-US is smaller version of the BASS-EAT-US at 2-1/2" with only two treble hooks. It is not pictured in the photo. The tiny lure at the bottom is the BUG-EAT-US. All four of the lures were part of the Silver Creek Novelty Works at the time Moonlight acquired the company. Collector value range: $25-$50. Colors listed in the c. 1920 catalog were: Yellow; white, green head; rainbow; yellow, black head; moss back; white, blue head; white, red head; yellow perch; yellow, red head; horned ace.

MOONLIGHT MOUSE #50

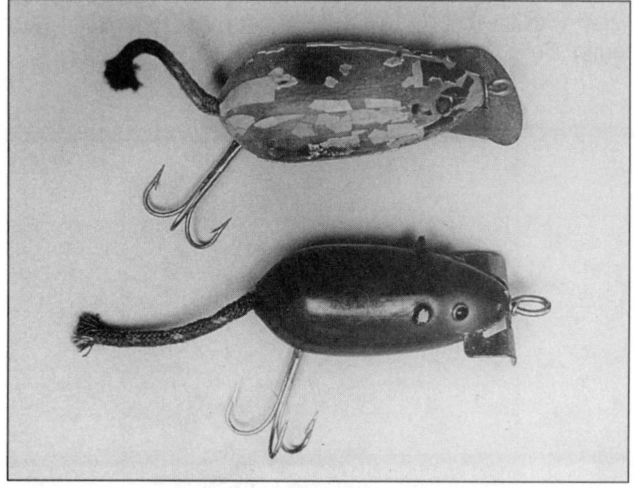

Both of these are MOONLIGHT MOUSE lures. They measure 2-3/8" and sport cup and screw eye hardware. The beat up one with the ears missing is the newer of the two. The other has the older style twisted wire line tie.

This little fellow first showed up in a 1926 catalog. It has a very distinctive metal lip that is attached to the body by sliding into a slot cut horizontally into the nose. A center portion of the blade is cut and bent up to cover the tip of the nose and is held in place by the screw eye line tie. The small lure at the bottom of the previous photo of LADYBUG WIG-

GLERS has the same blade. The MOUSE was available in white, gold, spotted or mouse color. Collector value range: $25-$55.

MOONLIGHT WOBBLER

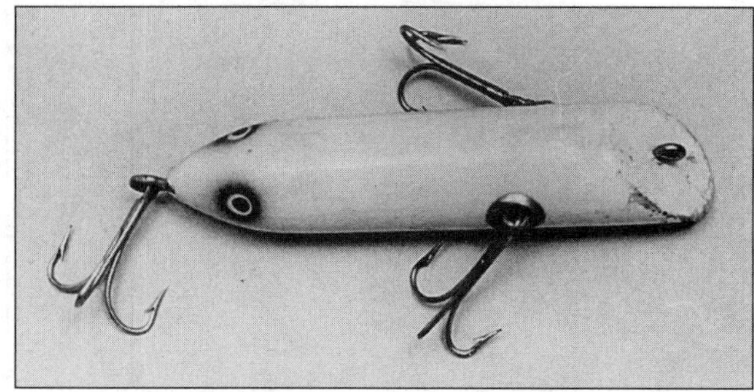

The lure in the above photo measures 3-3/4". It is the side hook model of the WOBBLER. There is another version where the two hooks are on the belly. Collector value range: $25-$75.

#1900 SERIES

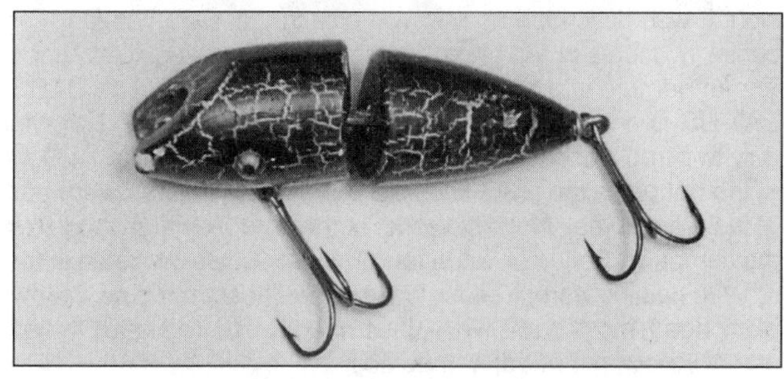

This un-named, jointed lure was listed and illustrated in a 1926 Moonlight catalog. It was available in the same six colors listed with the LITTLE WONDER. No other references were found. Collector value range: $35-$75.

#3300 SERIES

The #3300 is another un-named lure. No catalog or advertising references were found that included this lure. It is includ-

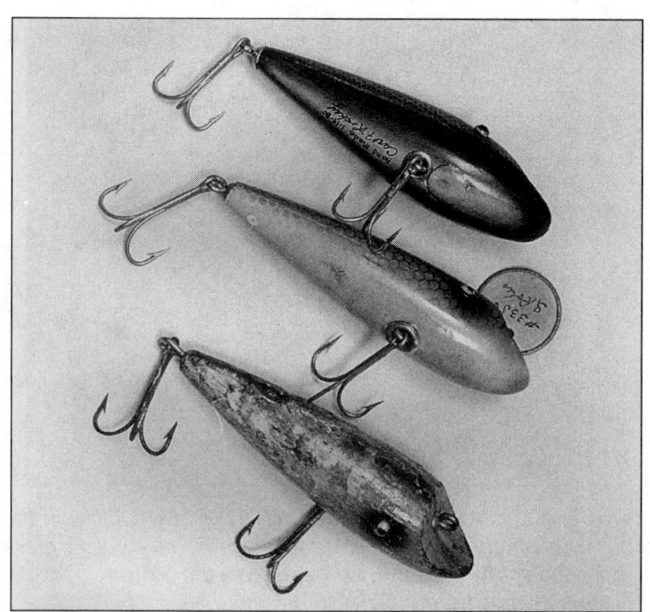

ed here and attributed to Moonlight because of the typical cup and screw eye hook hardware that was installed prior to painting, resulting in paint being found on the cup rim or flange. The lower two lures in both photos are yellow or white with green back and a rainbow finish. The top lure in both photos is a close replica that I made in my workshop as an experiment. You can see on the belly-up photo that I identified it as such. My copy wouldn't fool most collectors, but could trip up a novice collector. That's why all of us who fashion replicas should identify them as such, prominently and permanently. Collector value range: $30-$70.

CASTING BAITS

#1100 Series - #1200 Series

A Moonlight CASTING BAIT, Series #1100 with the original box.

These two Moonlight lures are truly beautiful examples of the classic, glass-eyed, floating, propeller spinner minnow style of Heddon, Shakespeare, South Bend and Pflueger. Found listed and illustrated in a c. 1924 Moonlight catalog only, they came in the two styles illustrated here. Both were listed as 3" in length, but the catalog illustrations don't appear to support that entry. The drawings here are exact copies of the illustrations right down to the hardware detail. There were also two underwater models of the CASTING BAITS. Collector value range: $80-$175.

Colors available were: Yellow; yellow body, black stripes; rainbow; white; moss back; yellow perch; white body, red stripes; horned ace; white body, black stripes.

LIGHT BAIT CASTING FEATHER MINNOW #1400 Series

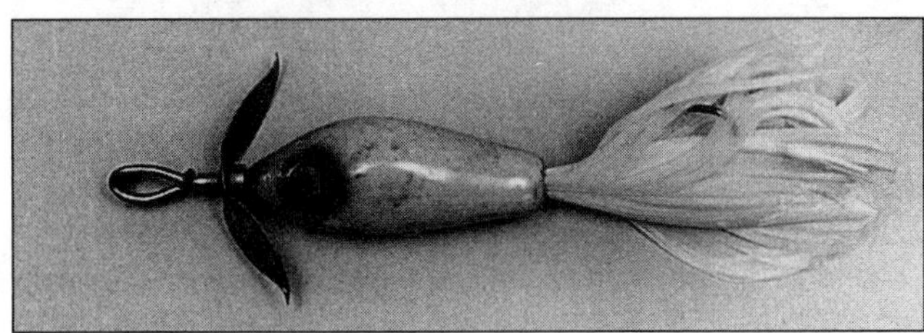

A c. 1920 and a 1926 catalog each list this lure and the small version of the WEEDLESS FEATHER MINNOW. The catalog entry reads as follows: "Light casting Feather Tail Minnow for light bait casting. No. 1-0 single hook, weight 1/3 ounce, length of body 1-3/4". Furnished in six colors: Yellow, white, orange, brown, red, gray.

There was no trade information found upon which an evaluation of worth could be derived.

WEEDLESS FEATHER MINNOW

#1500 Series - 3-1/2" overall, 1/6 oz.
#1800 Series - 3" overall, 1/10 oz.

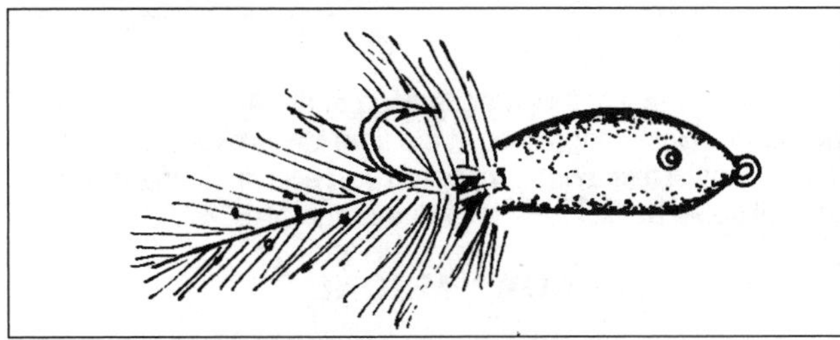

Colors available are the same as the #1400 Series. These two were also listed in the c. 1920 catalog, but only the #1800 was in the 1926. There was no trade information found upon which an evaluation of worth could be derived.

FEATHER MINNOW #1600 Series

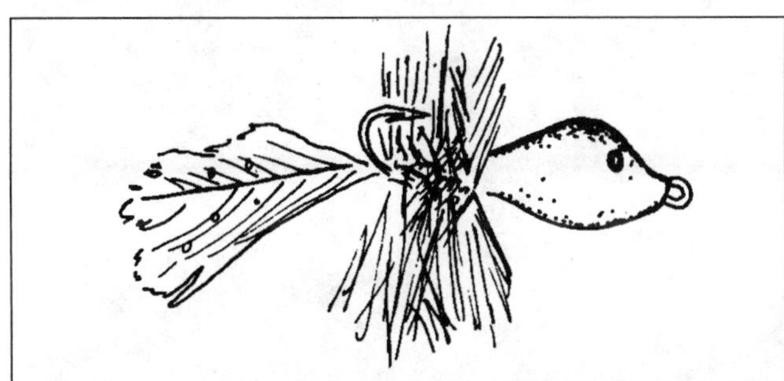

This lure was found in the c. 1920 catalog as were all the FEATHER MINNOW types. It was listed as 3-1/2" overall length, weight, 1/8 ounce. Available in the same six colors as the others. This little beauty came packed with a separate weight to be used on the line in front. The lure was so light that it needed the weight to swim correctly upon retrieve. The weight is painted in typical Moonlight style and has painted eyes. To find the lure with this weight is extremely rare. There was no trade information found from which to derive a collector value.

#2900 SERIES

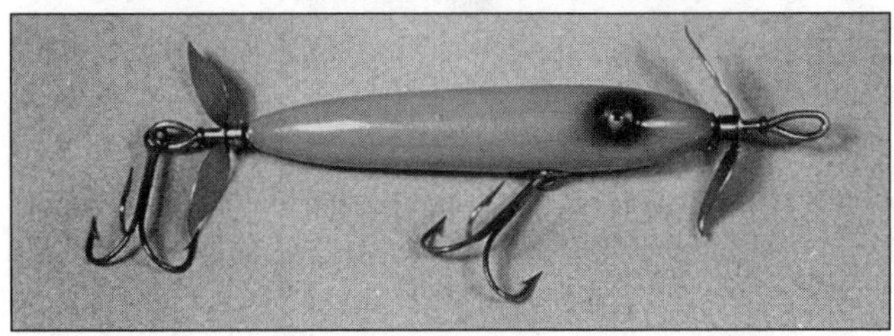

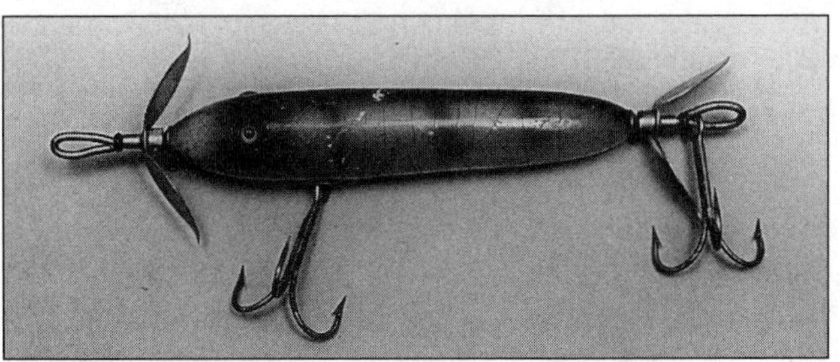

This lure was found only in the 1926 Moonlight catalog. It was illustrated with glass eyes and a propeller spinner at each end. There were no lengths given, but examples of the lures measure 3-1/2" and 4". It is the forerunner of the Paw Paw SLIM LINDY or TORPEDO. It is found with no propeller spinners. The eyes are glass and they are found with two types of propeller spinners, a Creek Chub Bait Company type floppy prop and a Heddon type. They are unmarked. Photo courtesy Jim Muma. Collector value range: $50-$80.

#3000 SERIES

This lure was found only in a 1926 Moonlight catalog. It was illustrated as having glass eyes with belly and trailing treble hooks and unmarked propeller spinners at each end. No colors, finishes or sizes were given. Examples of these measure 2-3/4". Photo courtesy Jim Muma. Collector value range: $50-$80.

THE ZIG ZAG BAIT

The Zig Zag was patented February 3, 1914 by Ford R. Wilber and Horace E. Ball. The first advertisement found for the ZIG ZAG was in a 1914 periodical. According to advertising copy it was only available with two belly trebles and a trailing treble hook (3T), but as you can see in the photo there was obviously one made with only one belly hook and the trailing hook (2T). The double hooks in the photo may have been added by a fisherman. Ads stated colors available as Red, White, Yellow, Luminous or Fancy Spotted. You can see there is one in the photo that is white with a red head. Perhaps the ad copy

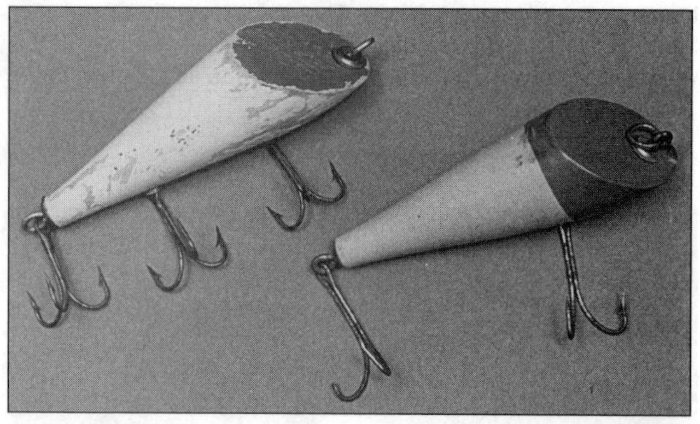

was a misprint and should have read "white or yellow bodies with red heads." There is also a 2-1/2" two-hook MIDGET ZIG ZAG, c. 1920 and a TOP WATER ZIG-ZAG, c. 1913. Collector value range: $25-$75.

A 3-1/4" TOP WATER ZIG ZAG. It has no eyes, has white body/red head and has a pork rind attachment on its back. They were normally packed with a leather strip in this attachment. The cup, of the cup and screw eye hardware is painted over.

THE "BUG" #8

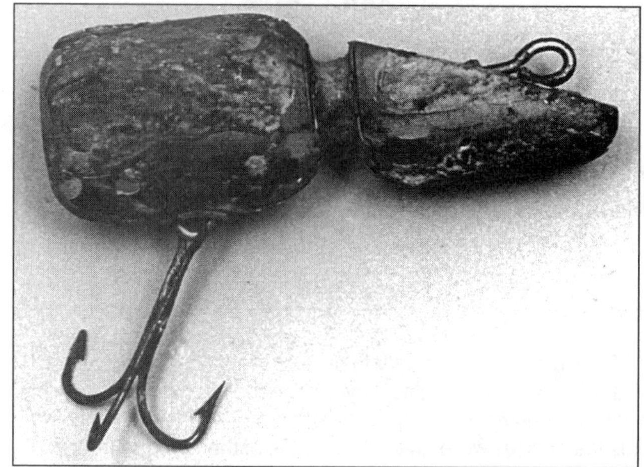

This little dude measures 2-3/4" long and has cup and screw-eye hook hardware.

This very curiously shaped plug has only one treble hook, mounted toward the tail, but on the belly of the lure. Colors were: Solid black; yellow and black with red head; yellow with red head; white with red head; white with red and black stripes; yellow striped white body. Collector value range: $300-$400.

THE DREADNOUGHT

First found advertised in 1912 and called a "Fish Pirate" it goes on to say it was a "...new departure in bait design" and

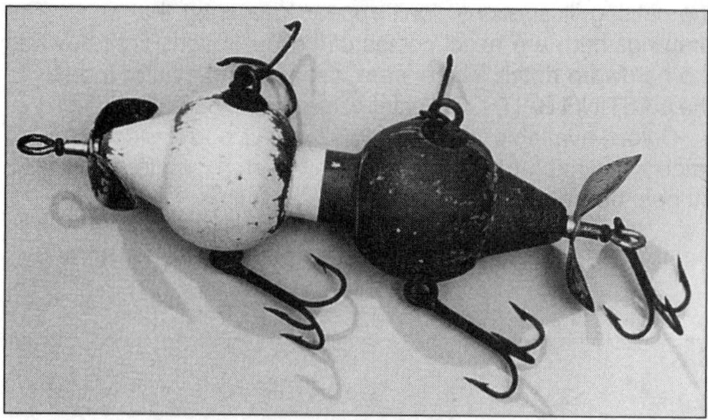

"makes a wake 'like a battleship'." I'll wager it didn't last long. More likely it scared all the fish out of the area. It had five treble hooks and two propeller spinners. The body was 4" long and was available in a red and white and a black and white finish. Collector value range: $500-$800.

THE PAW PAW UNDERWATER MINNOW

This lure was first found advertised in the April, 1913 issue of *The Outer's Book* magazine. At the time it was available in white, red or yellow. It has a nose-mounted propeller spinner and trailing buck tail treble hook. Collector value range: $150-$200.

UNKNOWN MOONLIGHT

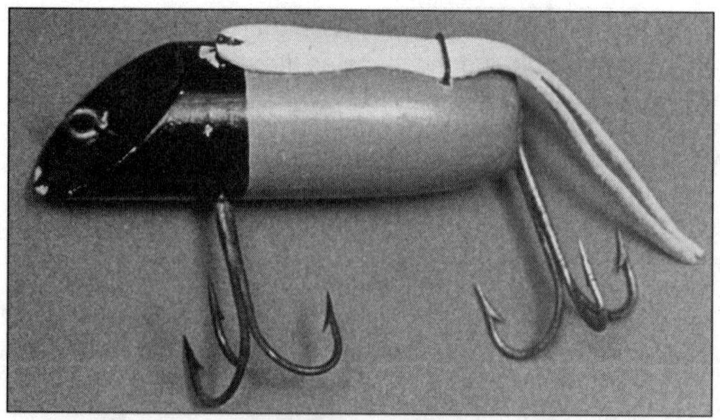

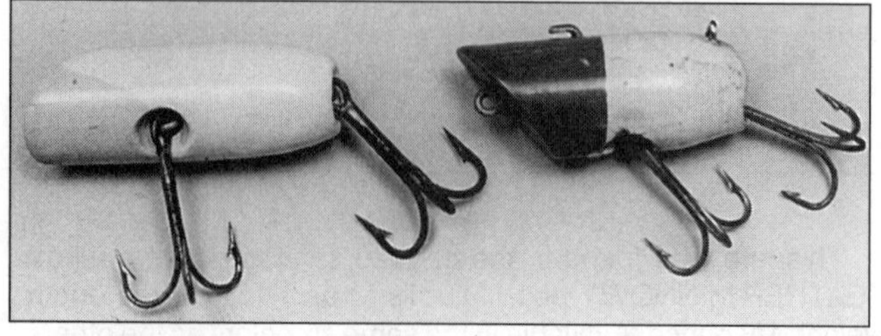

Two more Moonlight unknowns. The one on the right is a smaller, top water version of the previous lure. It measures 2-1/8".

F. R. WILBER & H. E. BALL.

ARTIFICIAL BAIT.

APPLICATION FILED SEPT. 8, 1913.

1,086,256. Patented Feb. 3, 1914.

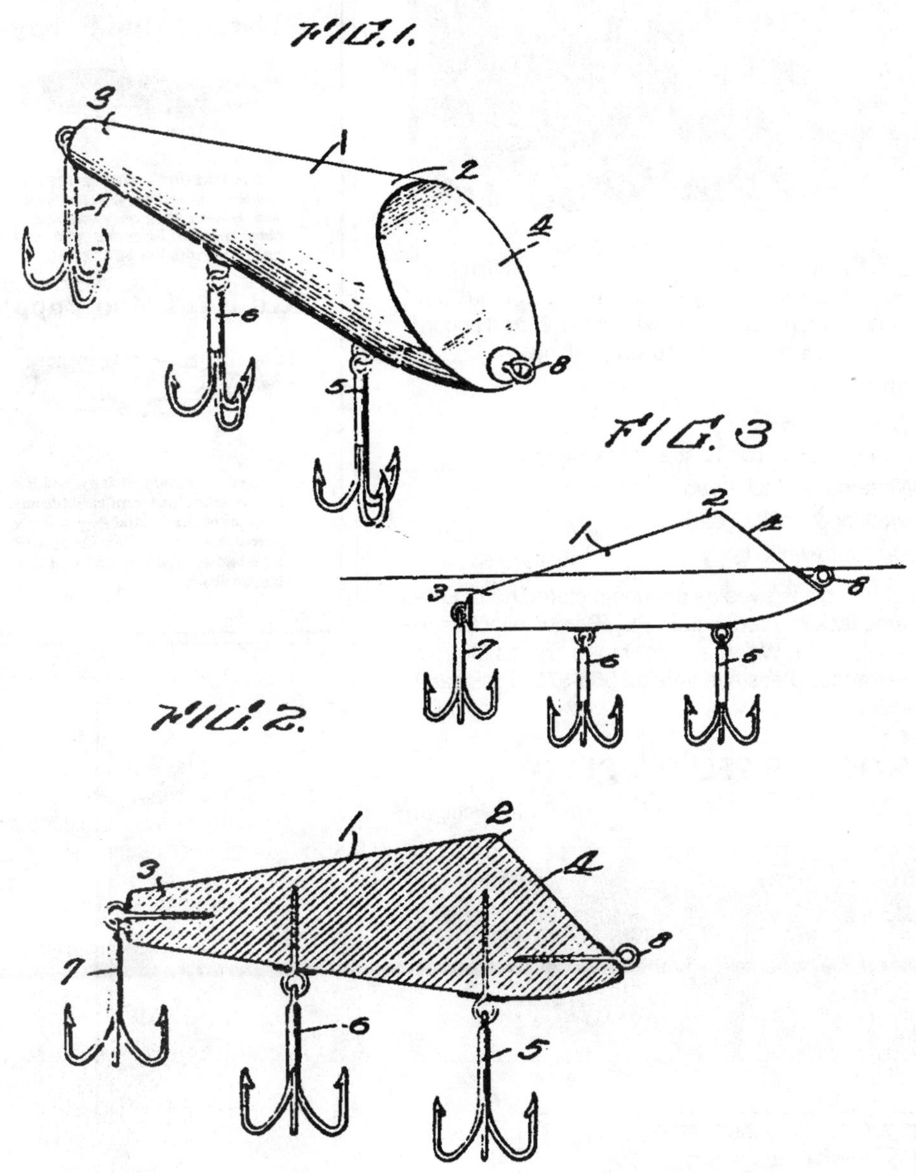

Ford R. Wilber Inventors
and
Horace E. Ball

Witnesses
R. S. Trogner
W. H. Wakefield

By Mason Fenwick & Lawrence
Attorneys

Original patent for the ZIG-ZAG BAIT.

The two previous lures are attributed to Moonlight because of their hardware, paint design and application. Not found in any catalogs or advertisements so far. No realistically derived value can be assigned at this time.

THE MOUSE

The Mouse Bait Company — Ft. Worth, Texas

A 1926 advertisement called this "The new game fish lure." It is a wood-bodied lure with a single treble hook, a unique bent metal dive lip and a leather tail. It measures 2-1/2" and according to the ad was available in the following finishes:

No. 100 White

No. 200 Natural Mouse

No. 300 Bloody Mouse (white streaked w/red)

No. 400 White body black head

No. 500 Black body white head

No. 600 Red head white body

The earliest had glass eyes as the one pictured here. Later the eyes became tack painted eyes (TPE). Some collectors refer to this lure as the "Ft. Worth Mouse" or the "Texas Mouse". Collector value range: Glass eye version $50-$75; Tack painted eyes $30-$60.

MOORE'S YELLOW PLUG

H.C. Moore — Ypsilanti, Michigan

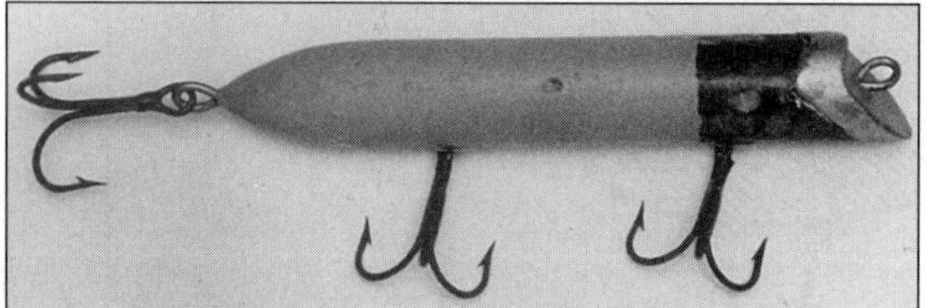

COPYRIGHT—1926 BY H.C.MOORE

Moore's YELLOW PLUG

PAT. APP'D FOR
MADE ONLY BY
H.C.MOORE
YPSILANTI, MICH.
PRICE $1.00

H. C. Moore, the inventor of MOORE'S YELLOW PLUG, which came into use December 1st, 1924, after a careful study and experiments on Fish Lure. It proved to be a wonderful success, so in the first two weeks in November, 1925, and to my surprise, I sold 100 of these Plugs to fishermen from all parts of the United States.

The demand for my YELLOW PLUGS was so great that I found it necessary to make them by hand to supply my customers, so I made and sold, all told, 400 up to March, 1926. I have seen 75 fishermen casting at one time and every one was using MOORE'S YELLOW PLUG. Patent applied for.

MOORE'S YELLOW PLUG has a weighted head, the proper weight to make it an under-surface bait, and gets down where the big fish are, and can be drawn through the water at any depth you desire, and gets the big fish that will not come to the surface.

MOORE'S YELLOW PLUG has seven distinct improvements over all other wooden bait:

FIRST—The yellow body and black head is positively the most attractive color under all conditions. Fishermen, kindly notice these colors on delivery wagons and especially on road curve signs. Why? Because they can be seen a greater distance.

SECOND—MOORE'S YELLOW PLUG, having a weighted head, will actually cast easily 20 to 30 feet further than any other Plug.

THIRD—Its weight in casting takes up the slack line, reducing backlash 30 per cent.

FOURTH—When cast it travels tail foremost, thus causing less wind resistance.

FIFTH—It casts easily against the wind.

SIXTH—Travels horizontally, under the surface, any distance you desire, by reeling fast or slow.

SEVENTH—MOORE'S YELLOW PLUG is positively the strongest plug made, and excellent for night fishing.

The fishermen who have used this YELLOW PLUG gave it its name, and it is a yellow body with a black head, the colors being original with me, and is the most attractive color in the water for any game fish. Has the strongest Rust Proof Treble Hooks. ACE of all Plugs. Use MOORE'S YELLOW PLUG and you will use no other. Price $1.00.

A strongly built, metal-head plug with cup and screw eye hook hangers. Collector value range: $75-$125.

MUD PUPPY

C.C. Roberts Bait Company — Mosinee, Wisconsin

Natural Mud Puppy

The NATURAL MUD PUPPY resembles the actions of a live sucker and is used to good advantage by those muskie fishermen who ordinarily fish with live bait.

Red Head Mud Puppy

The RED HEAD MUD PUPPY has all the action and results producing qualities of the Natural Puppy, but is colored in order to satisfy the demand for a bait adaptable to different fishing conditions.

How It Works

Put pin in nose of bait through ring in leader joint, pass hook end of leader across mouth and belly and press hook clasp into slot in bait and you are ready to fish.

CAUTION: Use leader, and keep hooks sharp.

Made in two sizes — LITTLE MUD PUPPY 5½ inches, 1¼ oz.; MUD PUPPY 7 inches, 2 oz.
Either size in Red Head or Natural finish.

This lure was first made in 1918 and the company is still in business today, 80 years later. Constance Charles Roberts invented the lure and filed for a patent on it in 1925 and granted it in 1928. At some point prior to his death in 1955 he took on a partner, Jim Rheinschmidt. He took over the operation at the time of Robert's death and is still making the lures in small quantities. This very unusual lure was designed so that the lure body would separate from the hook and line once the fish was hooked. This effectively removes the weight from the hook, thus making it more difficult for the fish to shake the hook out.

After you boated your fish you were then supposed to retrieve the floating lure body.

The lure was made in two basic sizes, the LITTLE MUD PUPPY at 5-1/2" and the regular size at 7". Each could be had in what they called "Natural" or white body with red head. For a short period of time, relative to the age of the company, a smaller version was made. In 1951-52 the PUPETTE was made. These are being made again in limited quantities.

Now to confuse the issue. Although the sizes and colors listed above are true, they are not the only sizes and finishes to exist. Early in the manufacture, the lures were all hand-carved and smaller at about 6-7/8". The sizes and colors listed reflect the evolution of the lure at the 1946 point. By sometime in the early 1930s the lures had grown to 7-3/4". At that point they developed mechanized construction for lure bodies and they became a standard 7" for the regular size.

The earliest MUD PUPPIES have a pin style hook release. This proved faulty and he quickly developed a spring style that was much more effective.

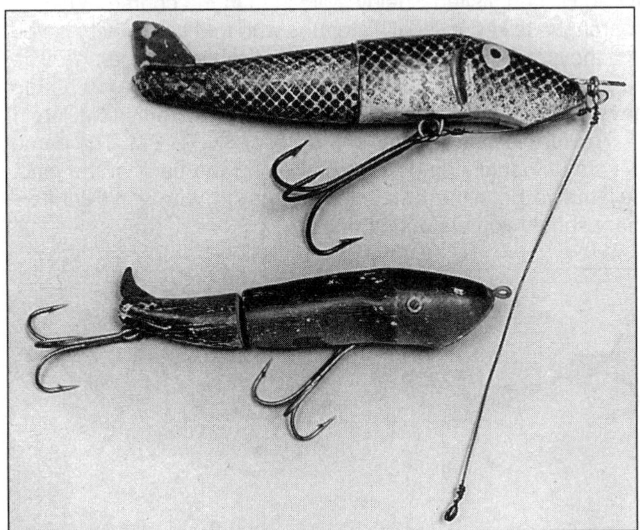

A pair of MUD PUPPY lures. Upper measures 6-1/2" and the lower 5-1/8". There can be little doubt that the upper lure represents a very early example with the pin in the nose, hook clasp and the painted eyes. The lower lure represents a later vintage.

A MUD PUPPY box.

It is thought that the earliest eyes were tack and/or painted. Then came glass and finally decals. The new PUPETTES have peel-and-stick eyes.

Hooks are usually trebles, but during the WWII years trebles were in short supply so they used just about any type they could lay their hands on. One unique hook that may be found on the lures made during the war years was a hand assembled treble made by soldering a single to a double and wrapping the shanks with wire for reinforcing.

Although the majority of the lures will be found in the basic colors above, there were many more as a result of dealer requests. One rare finish is the sucker scale. Roberts developed this finish early on, but there was apparently a patent infringement and he discontinued it. Other colors to look for are black, black and yellow, blue, gold, green, green perch, orange, purple, silver, tiger perch, yellow and yellow natural.

Over the 80 years they have obviously been extremely popular and successful. A lure pamphlet I read contained this testimonial, reading in part, "... catching two big muskies (24 and 28 lbs.) with your Mud Puppy." The testimonial was dated 1946, fully 18 years after the patent date. Collector value range: $25-$75. There was no trade information found for the older vintage MUD PUPPY.

I have an un-dated color brochure of the MUD PUPPY line of lures that has a Zip code in the address. That dates it after 1963 when the Zip Code was put in place by the postal service. In it are four sizes and styles of the lures and 15 color patterns. The styles are:

Number	Name	Size
0101	MUD PUPPY	7", 2 oz.
0103	MUD PUPPY RIVER MODEL	7", 2 oz.
0100	LITTLE MUD PUPPY	5-1/2", 1-1/4 oz.
0102	LITTLE MUD PUPPY RIVER MODEL	5-1/2", 1-1/4 oz.
0104	RIVER PUP4-1/2",	3/4 oz.
0105	PUPETTE2-7/8", 3	/4 oz.

COLOR OR FINISH: Yellow/red sucker, yellow sucker, natural sucker, yellow natural, yellow with black head, white with red head, yellow with red decoration, silver, black, green, yellow/red perch, perch, green perch, yellow/red natural.

MUK-CHOC-KO-FROG

Hub Company Beaver Dam, Wisconsin

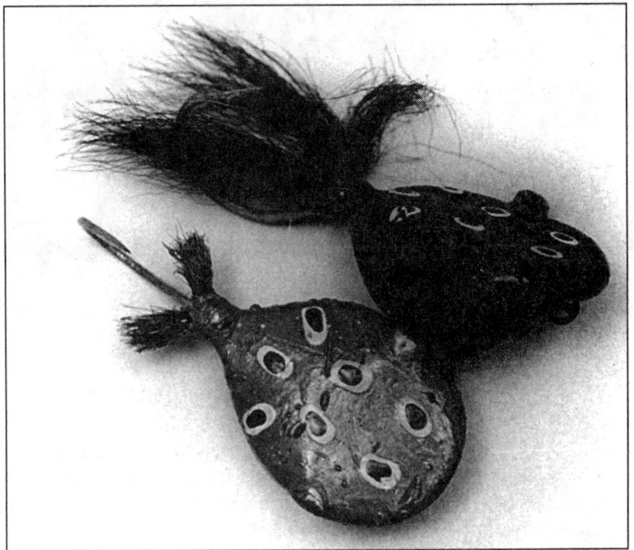

This plug has resided in the unknown section at the back of the book for many years. Finally we have an identification. There are two different styles they may be found in. The one in the photo has a rigid-mount single hook. The other style has a treble hook trailing in the traditional manner. It measures 2" long. Colors seen so far are: Black with white spots/black centers; white with black spots/yellow centers; yellow with black spots/red centers; green with black spots/yellow centers; light green with black spots/yellow centers. The eyes on the one in the photo are removable wooden pegs. They may not have actually been made to be removable; years of aging may be responsible. Collector value range: $30-$50.

MUSKOVIE-BOMB

Chicago, Illinois

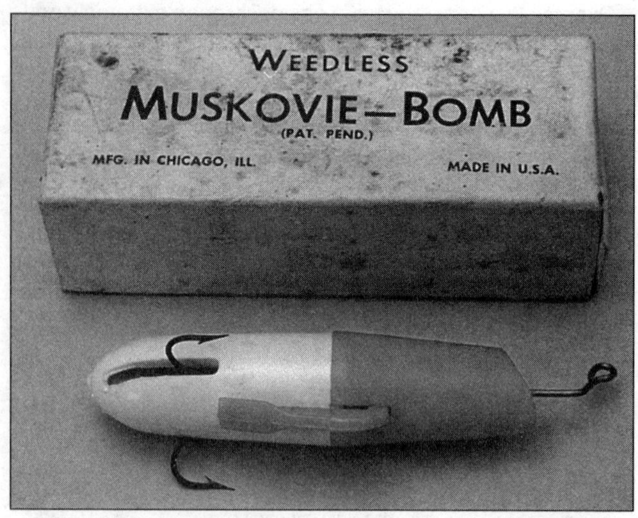

The name and city above came from the lure box. Beyond the measured length of 4" there is no other data regarding this plastic weedless lure. There was not even a company or manufacturer's name on the box. Collector value range unknown. No trade data found.

MUSHROOM BASS BAIT

J.A. Holzapfel — Jackson, Michigan

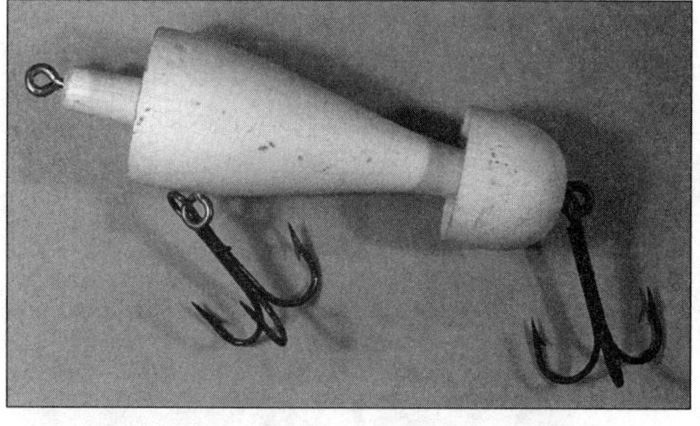

This unusual lure was made sometime around the 1910s. It is known to have appeared in at least three different paint patterns, all red, all white and a frog finish with some red. It has also been found in 3-1/2" and 3-7/8" sizes. All the line ties and hook hardware are large brass screw eyes. Collector value range: $300-$400. (see THE CROAKER)

MYERS AND SPELLMAN 1914-16

Edward D. Myers — Jack Spellman
Shelby, Michigan

These two have had the honor of having a dozen or so lures attributed to them over the years when in fact it is now thought they produced only one or two. Until now all the lures of Jacob Hansen and a man named Keller were erroneously lumped into one group under their name. It is easy to mistake a Myers lure for a Keller and vice versa unless they are stamped with the name on the back as the frequently are found. The following information regarding Myers and Spellman was unearthed by National Fishing Lure Collectors Club member Harold Dickert. They were not a full-time manufacturing company, but in fact they were partners in the local Ford automobile dealership. When Dickert visited Shelby, Michigan in the course of his research, he talked to local historians who told him they believed that the lures were actually made in the dealership garage. The number of them made is not known, but they certainly had to have made a fair bunch, because they did advertise the lure.

The lure is quite similar to the Keller GETS-EM. The name "Myers" is usually found stamped along the back of the plug. Be sure to note the other differences so you won't confuse them should you encounter one.

NATURALURE BAIT COMPANY

Pasadena, California

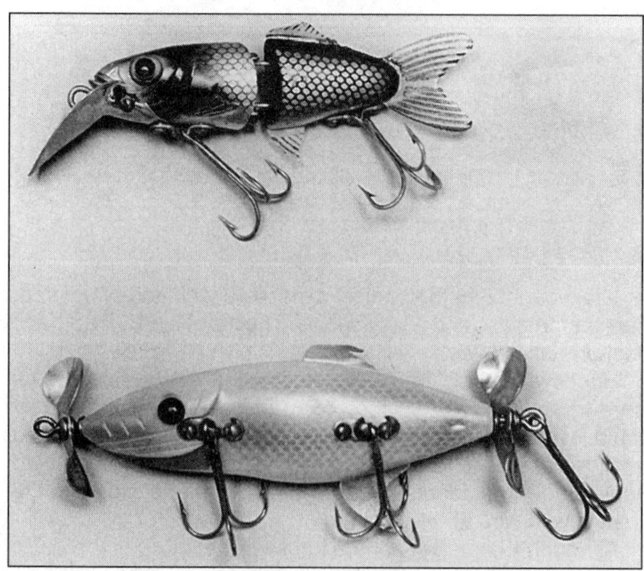

Top: A 3-7/8" STRIKIE MINNOW lure. Bottom: A 4" TROPICAL FLOATER.

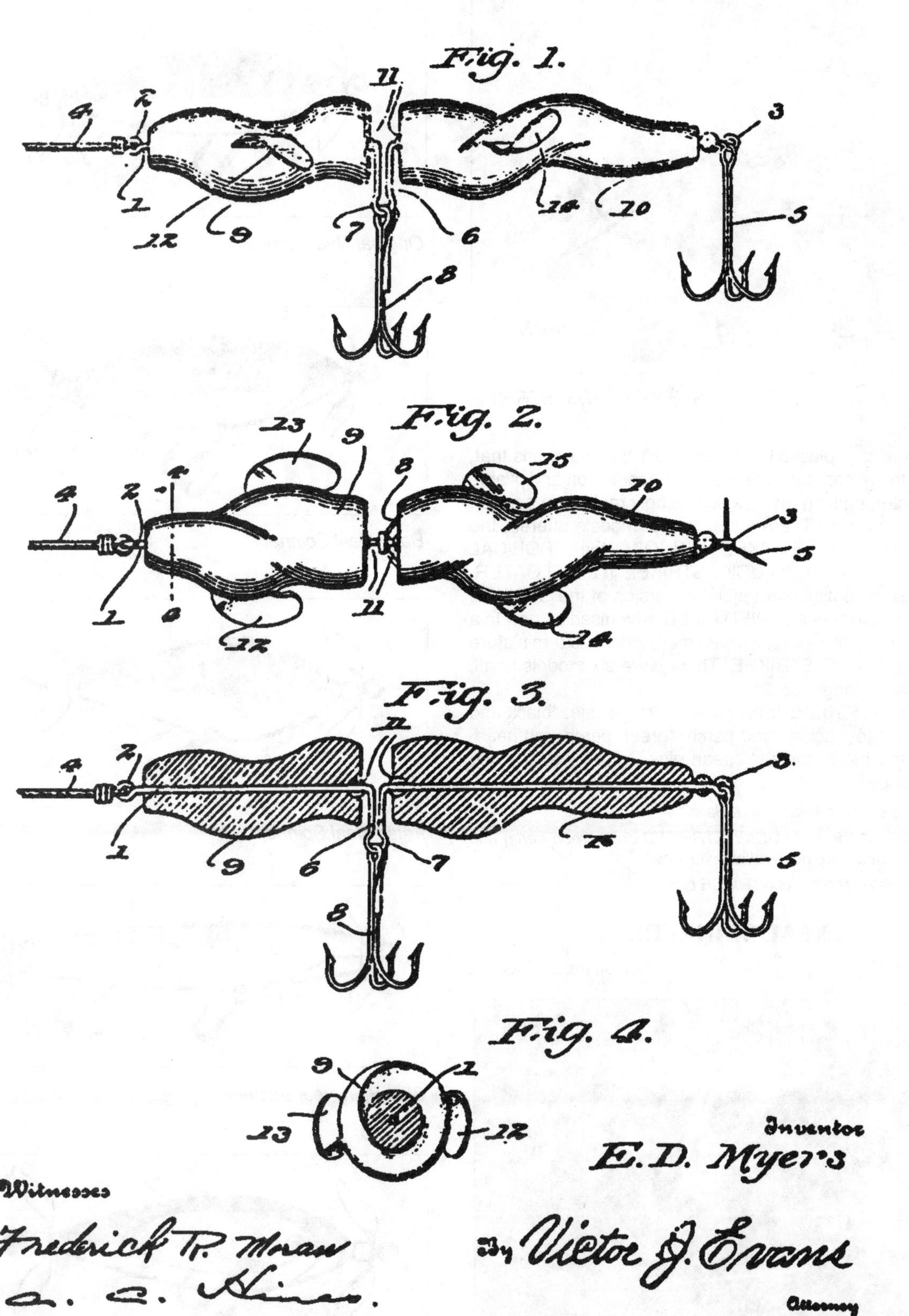

The patent illustration here is of a lure patented by Myers, but not yet found by collectors. It may not have never gone into production. Collector value range: $150-$250.

Top: A 3-1/2" STRIKEE FLOATER. Bottom: 3-7/8" STRIKEE MINNOW.

These unusual plastic lures from the 1950s have fins that, according to the company literature "...become soft and pliable when in water, making the lure surprisingly realistic in appearance and in action." There were several models offered, the KING STRIKEE or STRIKEE MINNOW, the TROPICAL FLOATER the tiny 1-1/2" LUCKY STRIKEE in a E FLOATER. The latter is essentially an unjointed version of the STRIKEE MINNOW. There was a 2" PIED PIPER advertised as new in a July, 1951 issue of *Field & Stream* magazine. It is a miniature version of the KING STRIKEE. There were six models in all. Collector value range: $5-$15.

COLOR OR FINISH: *Silver shiner, *frog scale, *black and silver scale, *gold scale, *red perch, *green perch, red head, **orange and black spots, ***pearl pink, ***sardine, ***flying fish, ***anchovy.

**Available on all the Naturalure Baits.*

***Available on the two LUCKY STRIKEES only. green perch and red perch finishes were not available on these.*

****Available on the KING STRIKEE only.*

NEAL SPINNERS

Carl Neal — Columbus, Indiana

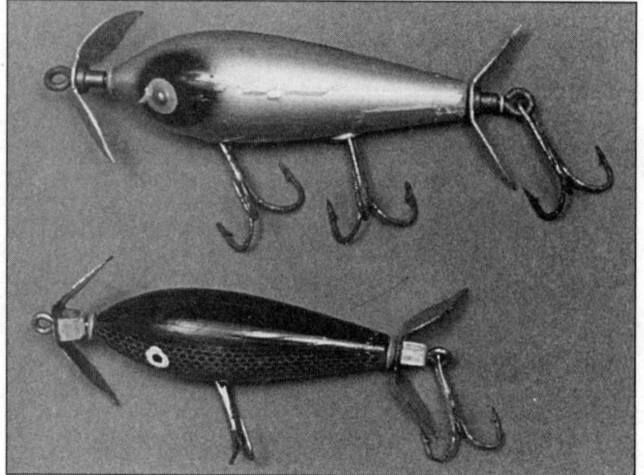

Several collectors have sent me flyers advertising that original Neal Spinners are now being "...Faithfully reproduced in high grade redwood with the highest quality finish we can use." The flyer is from the Tackle Service Center in Mooresville, Indiana. It illustrates six lures and they are illustrated here with the kind permission of the Tackle Service Center folks. They can be used to help identify the originals.

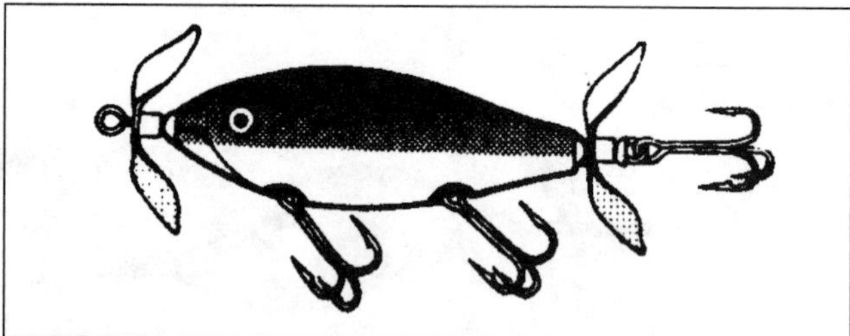

Original Neal Spinner

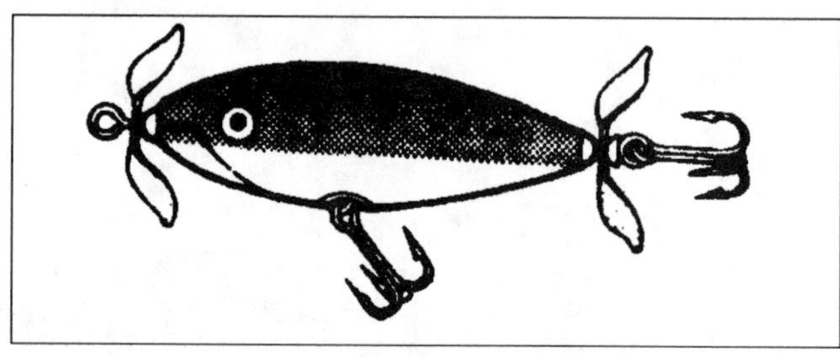

Baby Neal Spinner

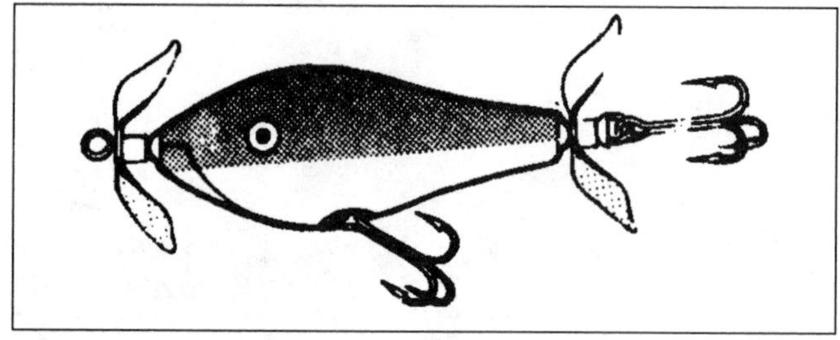

Fatso Neal Spinner

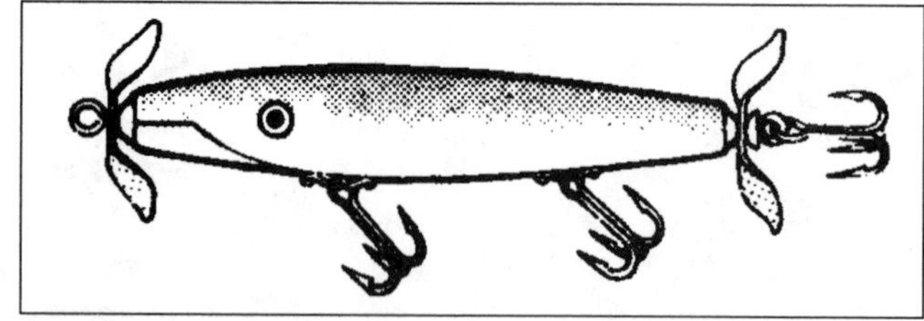

Slim Spin Neal Spinner

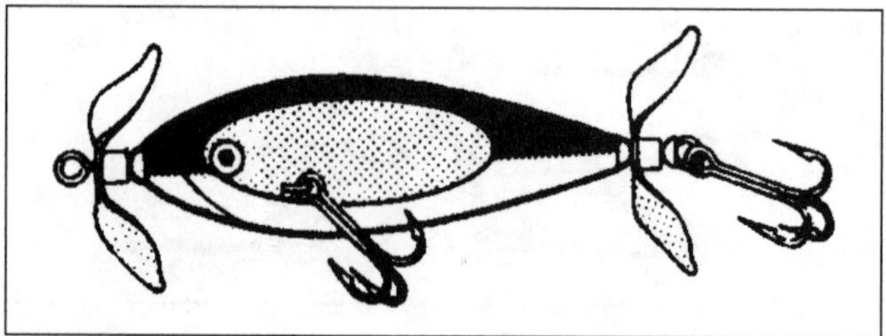

Sidewinder

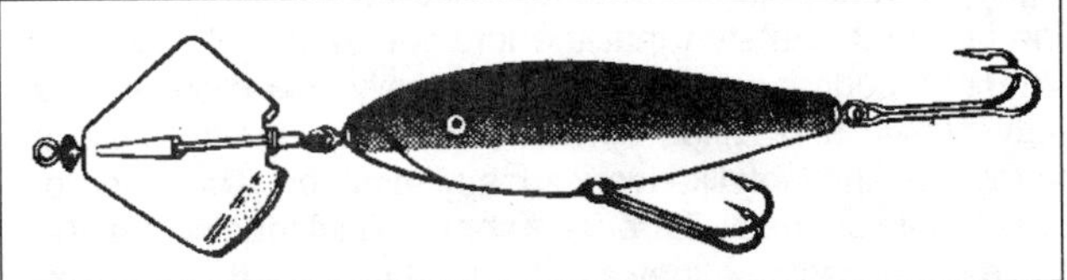

Tornado

Each of the reproductions are available in white, silver, chartreuse or black finishes. Weights, but not sizes were given. The two in the photo on the previous page are original NEAL SPINNERS at 3-1/4" and the BABY NEAL SPINNER measuring 2-3/4". The words NEAL SPINNER COLUMBUS, INDIANA are stenciled on their bellies.

I contacted the company twice asking for information regarding the history of the lures and information on how to tell them from the originals. They were very cooperative and attempted several times to contact the former owner of the lure rights to no avail. They were able to provide the following information regarding the differences between the old and the new lures. "The old NEAL SPINNER products were not ever offered with a scale finish and at the very least, the word NEAL was stamped on the underside of the body on the originals." Since then I have obtained an original catalog from the Neal Bait Manufacturing Company and they did indeed offer a scale finish. It is also known that the original Neal's used brass screw eye hardware and many had painted tack eyes. They are 1940s lures.

Something called a NEAL SPECO was sold at auction in 1995 for $28 and there was a 1997 auction sale of a pair of "Neal Spinners" for $31. Beyond this there was no trade data.

A 3-7/8" NEAL 2 IN 1 with the early cardboard box. Photo courtesy Jim Muma.

The early Neal boxes were cardboard with a jumping bass design as above. This is a newer, less elaborately designed, clear plastic box. The jumping bass is taken from the old design.

The following is a list of the various Neal lures offered in the catalog along with the colors available in each. Lengths were not give, only weights.

MEDIUM NEAL SPINNER	1/2 oz.
MIDGET NEAL SPINNER	1/3 oz.
BABY NEAL SPINNER	1/4 oz.

Colors for the NEAL SPINNERS: White, yellow, silver, orange, gold, red, black, green, brown, lt. pink, lt. orange, lt. red, lt. yellow, lt. green.

LARGE NEAL SKIPPER	1/2 oz.
MEDIUM NEAL SKIPPER	1/3 oz.
MIDGET NEAL SKIPPER	1/4 oz.
BABY NEAL SKIPPER	1/4 oz.

Colors for the NEAL SKIPPERS: White, yellow, orange, silver, black, red, gold, green.

MEDIUM NEAL 2 IN 1	1/2 oz.
MIDGET NEAL 2 IN 1	1/3 oz.
NEAL SPECO	1/2 oz.
NEAL FATSO	1/2 oz.
SLIM NEAL SPINNER	1/4 oz.

Colors for the 2 IN 1, SPECO, FATSO and SLIM NEAL SPINNER: White, yellow, orange, silver, black, red, gold, green.

They eliminated gold later and added chartreuse. Any of the lures were available in a scale finish.

NEON MICKEY BAIT COMPANY

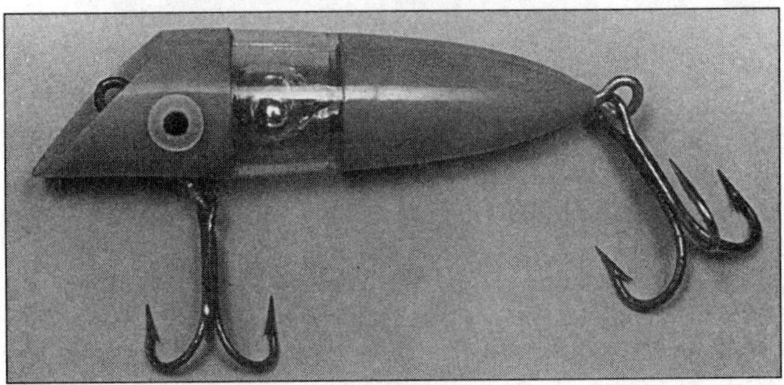

I was able to find only a single reference to the NEON MICKEY. It indicated that the lure was from around the mid-1950s and the company was based somewhere in the state of Oregon. The lure measures 4" long and has what appears to be a glass vial of mercury in the clear plastic mid-section. It is also filled with neon gas. When it wiggles, it actually lights up. It is red with indented painted eyes. This is a scarce bait difficult to find intact and operational. Collector value range: $50-$100.

NIFTIE MINNIE

Joseph M. Ness Co., Mfgrs. Minneapolis, Minnesota

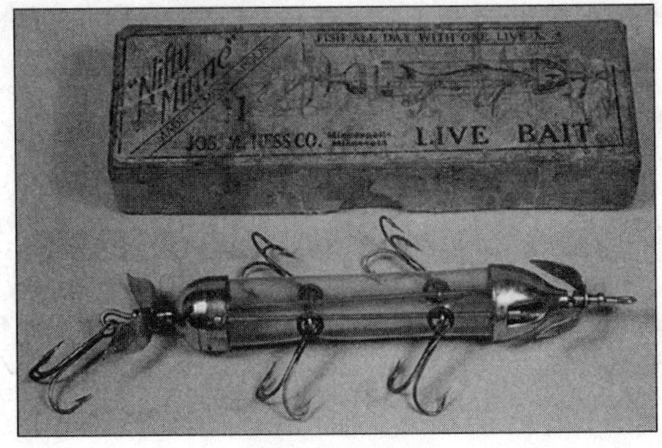

A 1915 issue of *The Outers Book* magazine has an advertisement for a lure heretofore thought to be another of the several different glass minnow tubes that have been found. Advertised by Joseph M. Ness, Co., Minneapolis it is called the NIFTIE MINNIE. It is a transparent tube with a metal cap and propeller spinner at the nose and tail. It sports two sets of opposite mounted side treble hooks, a trailing treble and the body is approximately 5-1/2" long. The ad states it was patented December 9, 1913 and that it had been available for "...Two seasons". It also said that the minnow was enclosed in a "...non-breakable flexible case." I believe this had to be plastic. Photo courtesy Jim Muma. Collector value range: $1,000-$1,500.

NIXON UNDERWATER c. 1914

Frank T. Nixon — Grand Rapids, Michigan

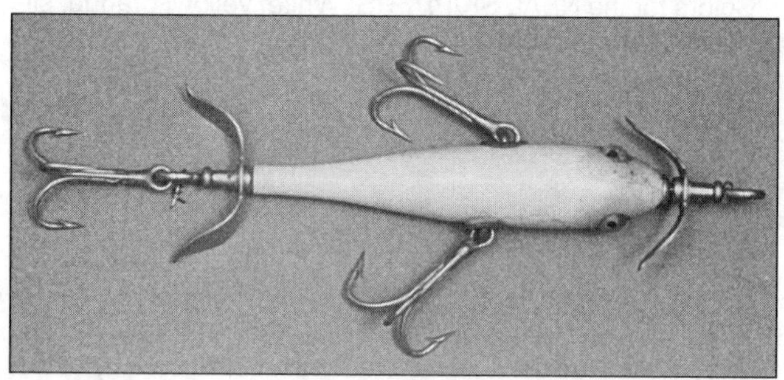

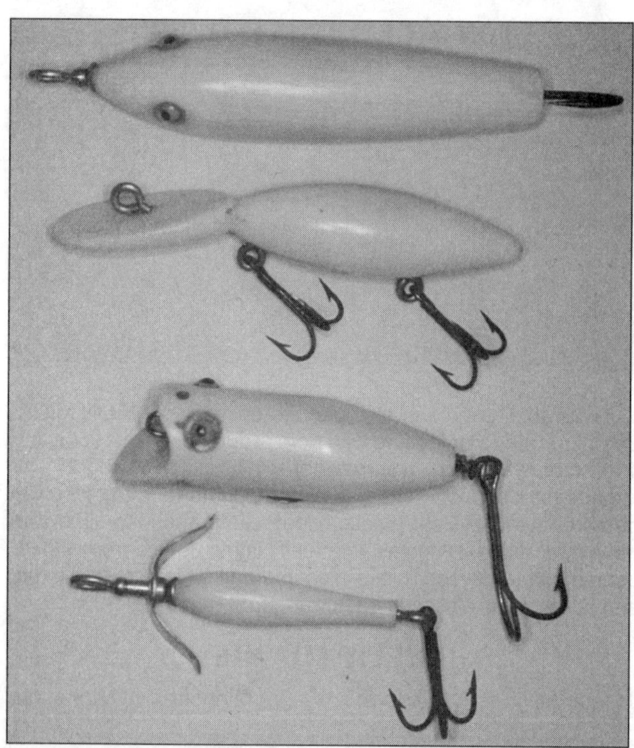

The lures in this photo are all unidentified as to name, but are Nixons and described as follows: The lure at top is glass-eyed, has a flat belly and rigid mount single tail hook. The next lure has no eyes, measures 3-3/8" and is very similar to a Rush Tango. The third lure down has glass eyes, a belly hook (missing), tail hook and is 2-3/8" long. The bottom lure is a tiny 1-1/2" and has no eyes.

This photo of a single lure is of the Nixon "THE ARISTOCRAT". It measures 3-1/4", has glass eyes and two propeller spinners.

THE ARISTOCRAT is known to have been offered by Nixon because it was found in its original box. The box has a 1914 copyright date giving us a pretty good handle on the vintage. The box further stated that the lure was made of "PERSIAN IVORY" though this seems highly unlikely. It is more likely an early plastic and Nixon simply coined the name. They are handsome and look like ivory so they might be. The other four lures (photo courtesy Clarence Zahn) are included here as Nixon products because they are made of virtually the same material and utilize the same type hardware. Collector value range: $450-$650.

NORTH COAST MINNOW

William Hoegee and Company — Location unknown

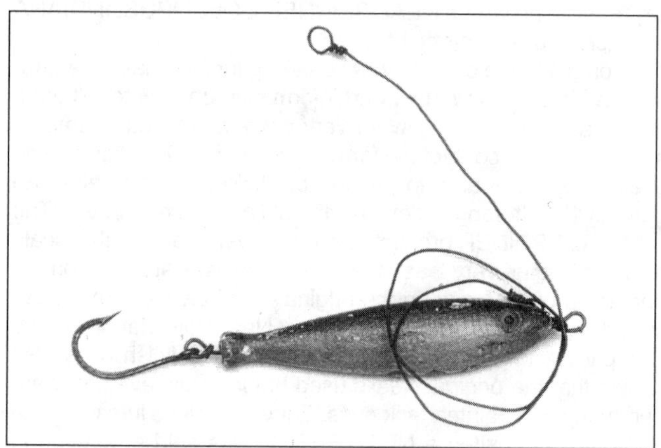

This 2-1/2" glass-eyed lure is extremely similar to three other lures listed in this book. They are the H. C. Royer SOUTH COAST MINNOW, the Pflueger CATALINA, and the South Bend COAST MINNOW. It has a through-body wire twisted on each end forming the line tie and the trailing hook hanger. There are three flush internal belly weights (visible in the photo). Collector value range: $175-$275.

NORTHERN KING WOODEN MINNOW

Marshall-Wells Company — Duluth, Minnesota

This beautiful 4-1/8" wooden lure is extremely similar to the Heddon 7500 Series VAMP. It has a bit longer snout, however, and there is no marking on the dive plane or anywhere else on the lure for that matter. It has cup and screw eye belly hook hangers and the same tail hook hanger as the Heddons. This one has glass eyes and a red head. What is so unusual about the lure is that the body behind the head is finished with real feathers apparently held to the body with the varnish or lacquer. It is hard to see it, but on very close examination you can see and feel the ridges. The box stated that the lure was "Made in Five Different Finishes". The box also listed the cities of Portland and Spokane in the U.S. and Winnipeg and Edmonton in

Canada as other locations presumably. The small square logo on the box says "Big Bill Tackle" and has what appears to be a pelican looking at a fish on a line. No trade data found.

ARTIFICIAL MINNOW

R. F. O'Brien — Location Unknown

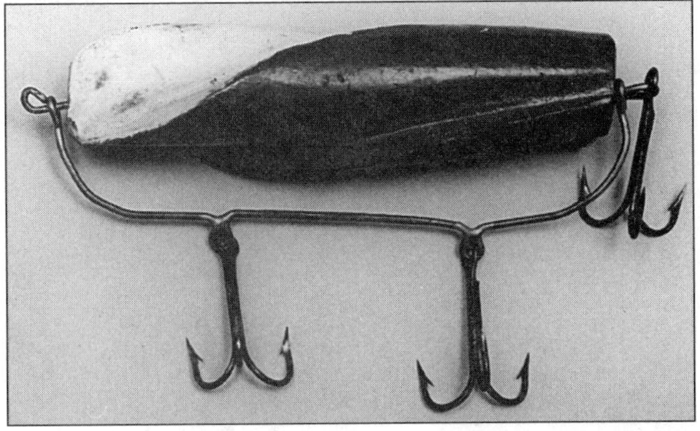

There is very little known about this interesting lure. We have the example in the photo and an incomplete patent application. We can't really even be absolutely certain the two match because there are differences. The lure and patent are so unusual and share so many characteristics, however, it is reasonable to match them up at this point. The body, painted red, white and black measures 3-5/8" and rotates around a through-body wire armature. The words "PAT APPD FOR" are etched into the lower wire hook hangers and painted white. Collector value range: $250-$500.

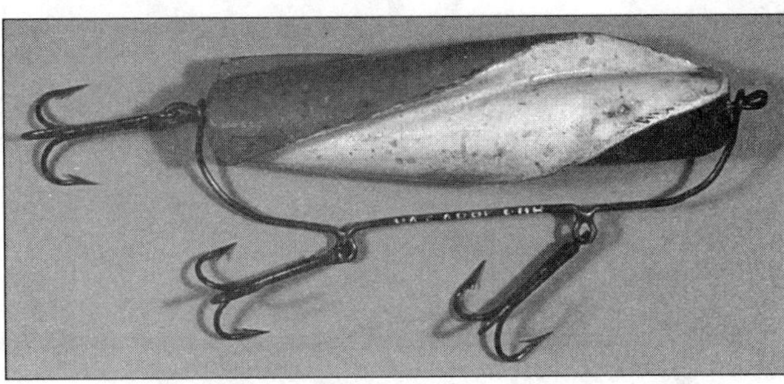

OGENE COMPANY

Abilene, Texas — THE ACRO-JET

This is a 2-1/2" wooden plug. It is one of only two found from this company so far. Perhaps some collectors have other information to share. Probably dated around 1943-44. Collector value range: $10-$20. That value is from the last edition. No additional trade data was found.

GLITTER BUG No. 2

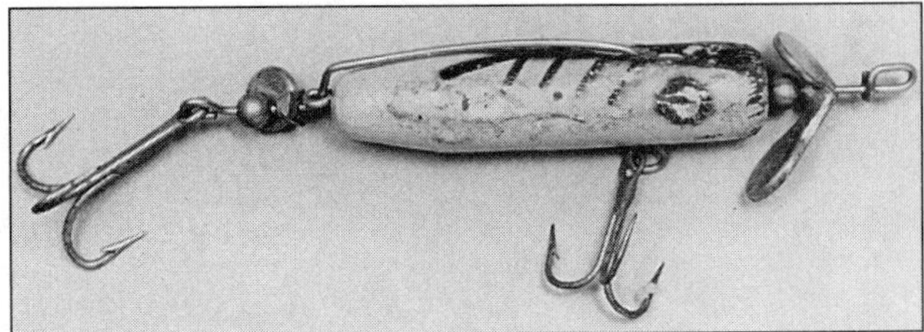

Actually called a GLITTER BUG No. 2 in a 1944 advertisement, this little glittering critter measures 2-1/4" long. The ad said "Assorted colors" and "Miniature Size". They did not clarify beyond that.

Unusual construction is the hallmark of this wooden plug from Texas. It is very strong. There is a single, heavy gauge wire starting at the nose (forming the line tie) proceeding into the body. It loops down to become the belly hook hanger then out and along the back, down through a screw eye at the tail and becomes the tail hook hanger. There is an asymmetrical spinner at each end. It measures 2-1/4" and, according to a 1944 advertisement, it came in "Assorted Colors." They did not list them. The ad also said "Miniature Size." That and the fact that the lure has a "No. 2" in its name infers that there is at least one other size to be found. Collector value range: $10-$18. That value is from the last edition. No additional trade data was found.

OL' BEN'S BAITS

Ridge Runner Lures, Inc. — Shreveport, Louisiana

When I first started writing this edition all I knew of this company was the name stenciled on the lures. I found an undated catalog, with the Shreveport address, called directory assistance and was pleasantly surprised to find I had connected with " Ol' Ben's" sons, Mike and Robert Bacon. They are still in the business he founded in 1926, but no longer make the wooden lures. They generously supplied me with a number of complete lures in their boxes, some painted lure bodies, some old advertising, photos, newspaper articles and another older catalog. The following was gleaned from that material.

R. F. O'BRIEN.

ARTIFICIAL MINNOW.

APPLICATION FILED MAY 21, 1917.

1,256,155. Patented Feb. 12, 1918.

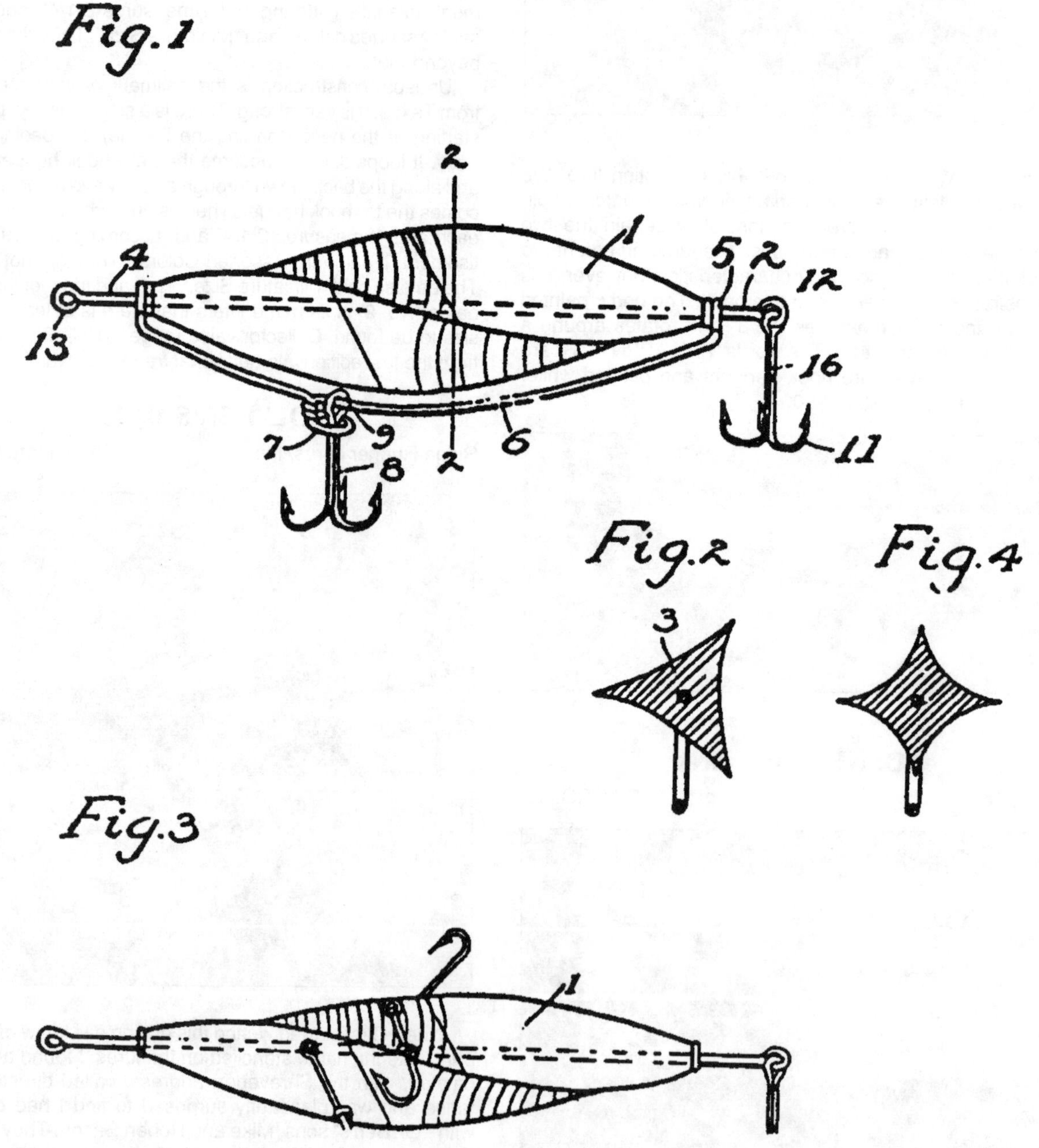

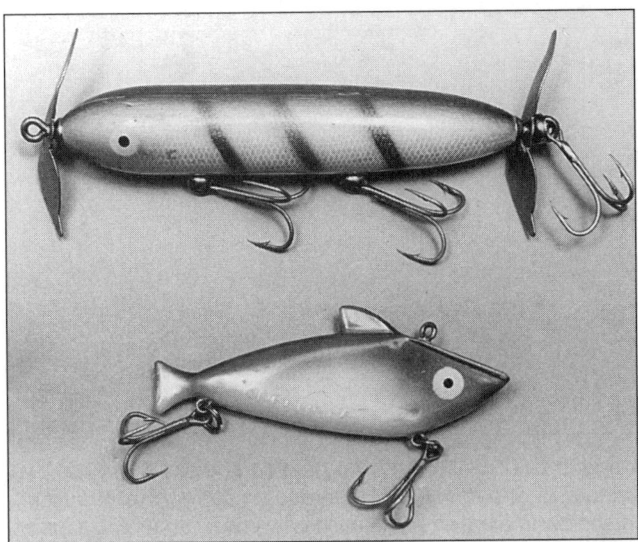

Upper lure is a wooden body OL' BEN'S BASS SNATCHER and is identified as such on its belly. It measures 4-1/4". The lower lure is a 3-1/4" plastic BASS TAKER. They also made a 2-1/2" size.

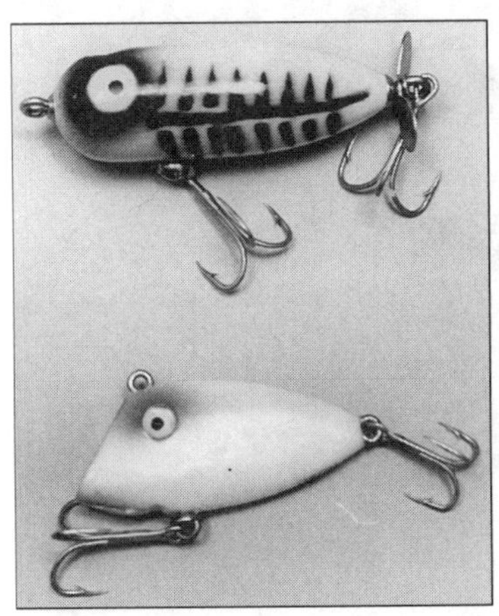

Upper lure is a wooden body, OL' BENS TOR-MAG measuring 2-1/4". Its name is marked on the belly. The other is a plastic HOBO measuring 2".

Benjamin Bacon, Sr. (1928-1993) worked with his father in the hardware and sporting goods business. Like many fishermen, he tinkered with tackle. In 1958, when a customer asked Ben if he could make an idea he had for a fishing lure a reality. After a little work the lure was born. This was the RIDGE RUNNER, the lure that is the namesake of the company that was founded that year. The company lasted until 1977 when the lure division was sold to Griffin Lures and was subsequently bought out by Luhr Jensen & Son. They retained the rubber skirt manufacturing business and market them under the 01' Ben's Rubber Skirts brand. In just under 20 years, the company produced over 30 different lures in as many as 54 different color combinations. Most of the designs were jigs with grubs, etc., plastic worms and spinners, but there were seven basic designs of wood lures and three of hard plastic. Most are represented in the following photos. The plastic BASSTAKER, incidentally, was introduced in 1971. That was the same year the PICO PERCH was picked by Sports Afield magazine to receive an award from their Angling Editor Homer Circle as one of the top 10 lures in the United States. The influence of the Pico lure and other lipless wiggler types on the BASS-TAKER is obvious. Many lure companies, including even Heddon, had jumped on the lipless vibrator band wagon. Ol' Ben's was just a little later than the others. The wood lures are very well made with high-quality, sometimes complicated paint finishes. The wooden lures were all made and painted by hand and are stamped with "Ol' BEN'S" and the model name on the back or belly. Sometimes the "Ol' BEN'S" is missing. The plastic lures have the name molded into the bodies. There was very little information found with regard to how these lures have been traded. This is probably because they are fairly late vintage products and not considered old enough to be of great interest to collectors. I can tell you from my handling of them that the wood lures, if not collectible now, will be. This is especially true now that collectors are looking at later vintage lures as collectible. Some near mint TOR-MAGS with no box were selling at $8-$10 in late 1997 and early 1998. That is the only trade data found.

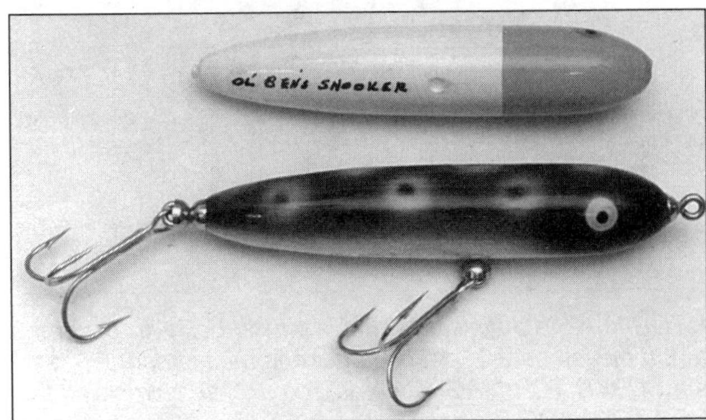

The lower lure is a standard 4-1/4" BASS STICKER. The lure body above it is exactly the same. Note, however, that the pre-drilled hole for the belly treble is farther back (by about 1/4") than that for the Bass Sticker and the hand-written words "OL' BEN'S SNOOKER". These were not found in the catalogs. It must have been a prototype.

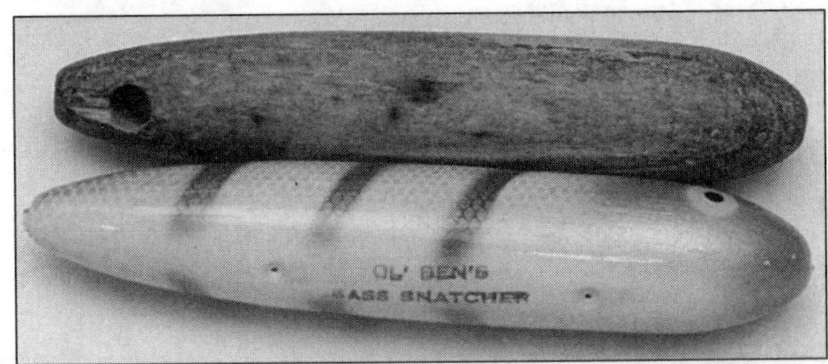

Among the Ol' Ben's lures that were sent to me was this unfinished, blank body. It is the same body used for the BASS STICKER and the BASS SNATCHER. It is a bit beat up as if it has been knocking around a long time. What makes it interesting is the deep, 3/8" hole bored in the tail end. It could be a prototype or unfinished experiment.

This 2-1/8" body is that of the SWISHER. The lure is normally rigged with propeller spinners fore and aft, a belly and tail treble hook. Called "NEW" in the newest catalog of the two undated ones I have.

A TOR-MAG in a typical Ol' Ben's plastic box with paper insert. It measures 2-1/4". The larger one measures 2-3/4" and is a SUPER TOR-MAG. There is also a 2" version called the TINY TORNADO.

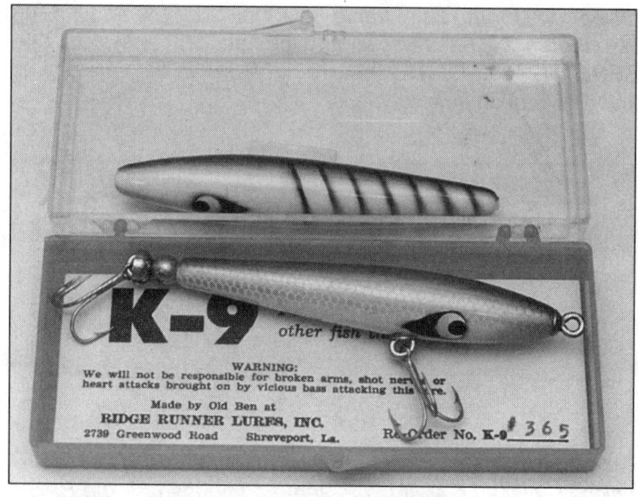

This K-9 measures 3-3/16" and is cataloged at 3-1/4". It is in a typical plastic box. I have seen them all clear or clear tops with red, pink and green bottoms. All are packed with the paper insert that identifies, the lure, its catalog/color code and the WARNING you see. If your eyes are like mine you can't read it so here goes: "We will not be responsible for broken arms, shot nerves or heart attack brought on by vicious bass attacking this lure." There is one other K-9, a 4-1/8". They came in Floating or Underwater models.

Two 2-1/8" HUSTLER bodies. They came rigged with belly and tail trebles with propeller spinners fore and aft or with only the tail spinners.

A rigged CRY BABY and two painted bodies. There are two sizes, a 2" and this 2-1/2". The one on the right is beautifully finished with a green scale finish on a yellow body with a green back stripe, white belly and yellow eyes over red flashes.

A 2-3/8" chugger-type Ol' Ben's BIG STUD. This lure was available also with a tail-mounted propeller spinner.

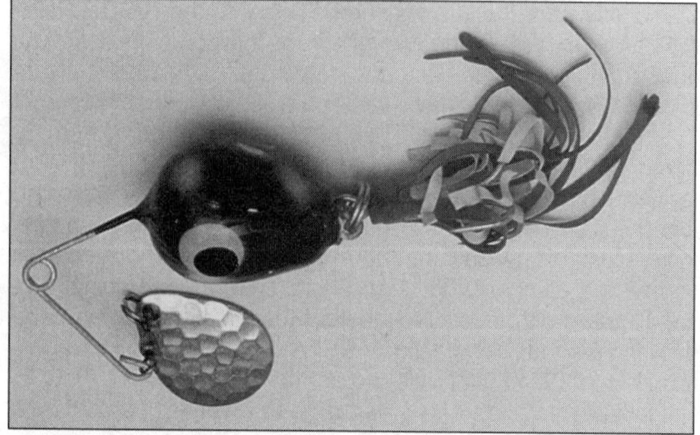

A FLOATIN' H & H with a 1" wooden body. The overall length measures 3-1/4" including the hook.

OLD FIGHTER

Beaver Bait Company — Ambridge, Pennsylvania

No information other than that on the original box was found

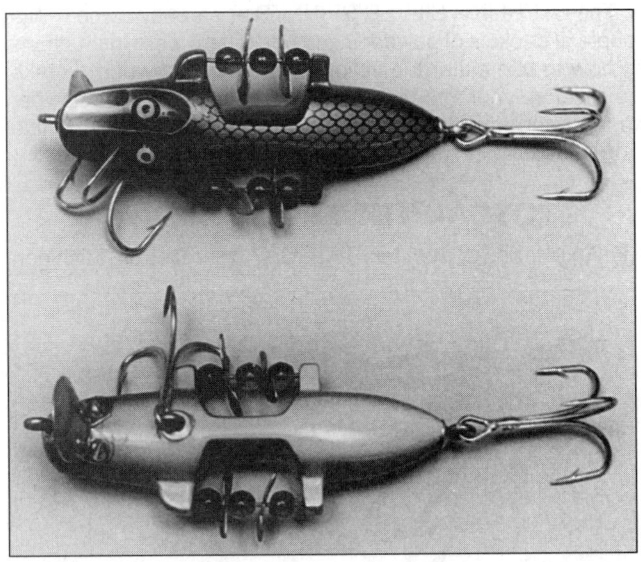

for this c. 1950 company or lure. It is a 3" plastic-bodied, complicated looking contraption, but seems well made. The photo shows back and belly views. Collector value range: $50-$70.

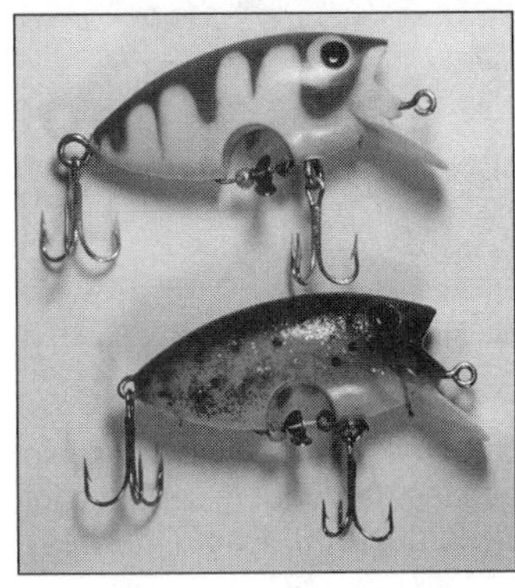

Here is a pair of unknown plastic lures that may be made by the same company. A similar bead and propeller flasher on a wire arrangement is used. These measure 2-1/2" overall including the dive plane. Photo courtesy Ken Bernoteit.

OLD LOBB

Floyd Ferris Lobb — Hamilton County, New York

This old copper spoon bait measures 4-1/4" overall, from swivel tip the end of the treble hook, and is stamped THE OLD LOBB. Nothing else beyond what is printed on the box top is known about the bait. The box text follows:

"Floyd Ferris Lobb was born early in this century, just when and where no one knows. In his youth he was a good musician, writer and tailor. When about 24 years of age, disappointed in love or for some reason best known to himself, he retired to Piseco Lake, Hamilton Co., New York, in the Adirondack forest, where he lived as a hermit until his death, in 1891. Part of this time was however enlivened by a wife. His later years were spent in a cabin quite alone. He was a hunter, trapper and fisherman, as eccentric as man can be. He designed this bait which bears his name. It has been used for years in Piseco Lake and is there unquestionably more killing than any other blade. In the belief that it will be generally taking it is offered to the fisherman in memory of 'Old Lobb.'"

The syntax is a bit taxing toward the end, but you get the idea. Collector value range: Insufficient trade data to determine.

OL' SKIPPER

Wynne Precision Company — Griffin, Georgia

An Ol' Skipper lure box top.

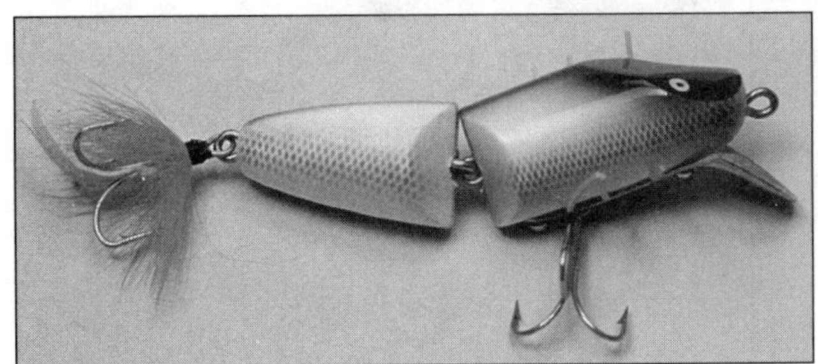

Ol' Skipper 4" jointed LUCKY TAIL WOBBLER.

Three different collectors within a couple of months in 1997 sent me photos of Ol' Skipper lures asking about them. Since then I have found only one reference. It was an advertisement in a may, 1949 issue of *Outdoors* magazine. The ad was for "OL' SKIPPER'S '1300' LUCKY TAIL 'CHUBBY'." I found a nearby collector who had the jointed version in the photograph. It is a high quality wooden lure with an excellent finish. While I have not yet found any more written material that which collectors have sent helps to begin sorting the company's products out.

There are at least three styles of these lures and a metal spinner to be found. There is evidence that at least one of the plugs was made in two sizes or more.

SERIES

NUMBER	NAME	SIZE
1300	Lucky Tail Chubby	?
?	Lucky Tail Wobbler	3-1/2"
1600	Jtd. Lucky Tail Wobbler	4"
?	Topwater Popper	2-3/8"
?	Sterling Silver Spinner	1-5/8"

The wooden lures have metal parts like dive lips or pork rind attachments that are well identified with the name of the com

This advertisement was found in a 1949 issue of Outdoors magazine.

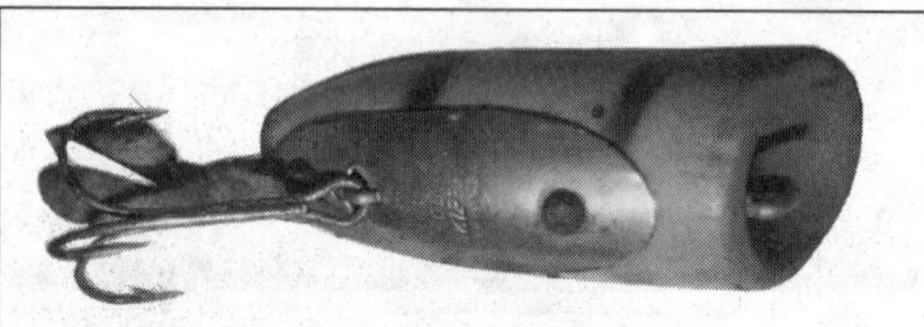

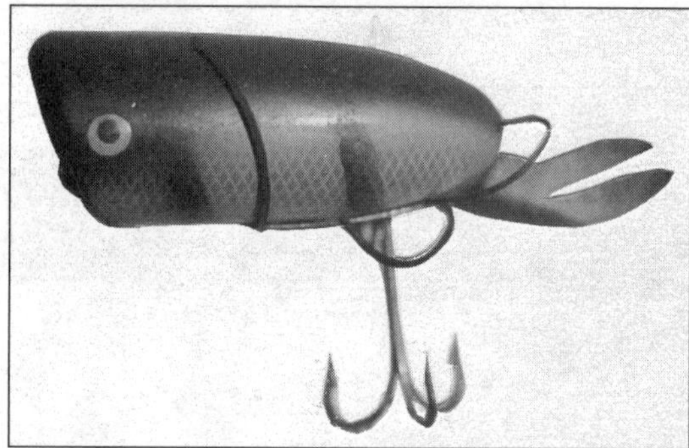

Two views of the TOPWATER POPPER showing the belly plate pork rind attachment and a few remnants of the rubber band legs. Ol' Skipper made and marketed their own white leather "pork rinds" called LUCKY TAIL FLIES.

A STERLING SILVER SPINNER and its original box.

pany. It also appears that each of them had spindly rubber legs, probably made of rubber bands. They are usually gone with only a little evidence of them found between the metal and the body. Collector value range: $20-$40.

The STERLING SILVER SPINNER apparently came with a couple of packets of powder in the box. There were instructions on how to use either the yellow or the white powder to make the silver spinner into different or multiple colors. The powder was missing from the box in the photograph. Collector value range: Insufficient trade data to determine.

OSCAR THE FROG c. 1947

T.F. Auclair and Assoc. Inc. Detroit, Michigan

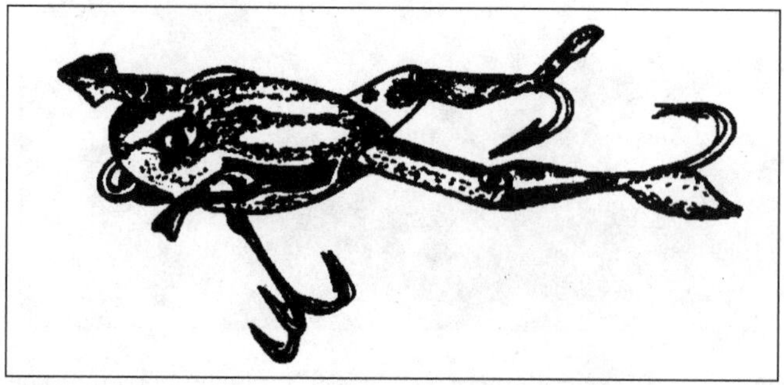

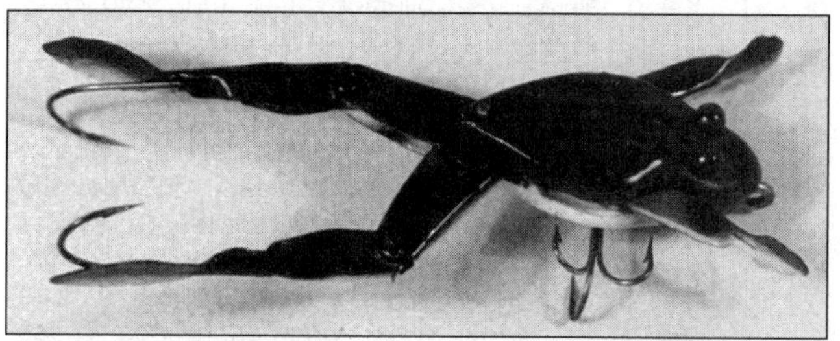

This is an animated frog made of metal. It has a belly treble and a single hook mounted in each leg. It probably caught a lot of weeds. Collector value range: $200-$300. Photo courtesy Jim Muma.

OSTER'S BAIT AND TACKLE

1241 East 59th Street Cleveland, Ohio

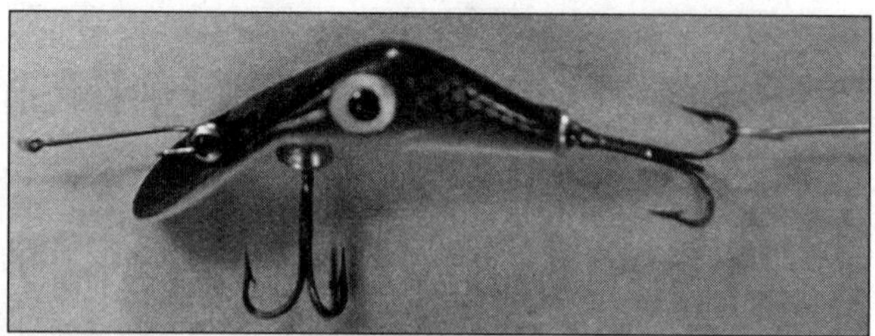

Model No. 400 TUFFE MINNOW. This product of Oster's Bait and Tackle is plastic and weighs in at 1/4 ounce.

A collector from Ohio wrote asking for information about this company. His research led him to Landis Machine, a division of Teledyne Specialty Equipment in Waynesboro, Pennsylvania. Oster was an old Cleveland company that made pipe threading machines. Oster merged with Landis Machine and apparently most of the Oster records were lost in the reorganization and move of the companies.

The box the TUFFE MINNOW came in contained a flyer listing four Oster baits as "Oster's Fish Getters Lures":

No. 200 STREAMER

No. 300 JOINTED

No. 400 STRAIGHT

No. 500 POPPER

I found nothing in 10,000 pages of research data, over 40 reference books and 4,000 patents. Collector value range: Insufficient trade data to determine.

OUTING MANUFACTURING COMPANY

Elkhart, Indiana

HEDDON OUTING

James Heddon's Sons Dowagiac, Michigan

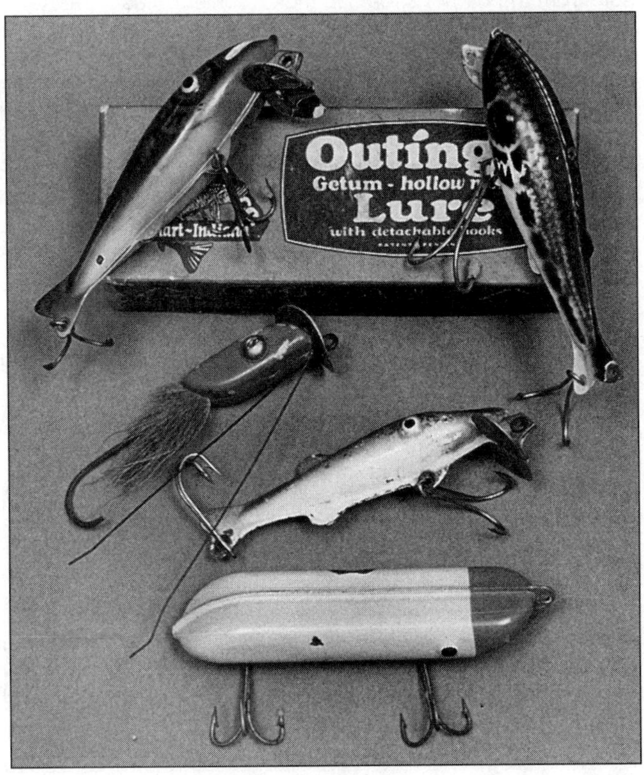

Top left on box: BASSY GETUM. Right: PIKEY GETUM without diving lip. The small lure is a BUCKY GETUM, then PIKEY GETUM (with diving lip). Bottom: FLOATEM GETUM.

Clarence L. Dewey is on record as the inventor of the FLOATER GETUM. He is probably the founder of the company. The Outing Company manufactured at least six different hollow metal lures made of bronze and painted in various patterns. They also manufactured a really nice tackle box a rod and reel combo, decoys, camping gear and more. The company was bought by Heddon in 1927 to get the rights to the tackle box. The lures came with the purchase and they were inventoried and sold until the supply was exhausted. Heddon never manufactured them.

DU-GETUM OUTING

CATALOG SERIES #	BODY LENGTH	LURE WEIGHT	COLLECTOR VALUE RANGE
700	3-1/8"	3/4 oz.	$90-$125
750	2-3/4"	1/2 oz.	$90-$125

COLOR OR FINISH: White with green head, white with red head, solid black, aluminum with red head, unpainted metal with green head.

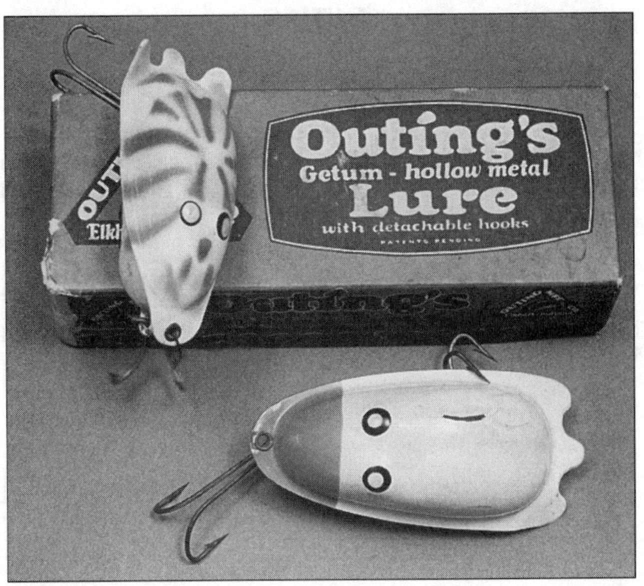

BASSY GETUM

Collector value range: $75-$125.

OUTING

CATALOG SERIES #	BODY LENGTH	LURE WEIGHT
1200	3-7/8"	5/8 oz.

COLOR OR FINISH: Black bass, largemouth bass, smallmouth bass, rock bass, calico bass, silver bass.

PIKY GETUM

Collector value range: $100-$200.

OUTING

CATALOG SERIES #	BODY LENGTH	LURE WEIGHT
1000	3-5/8"	1/2 oz.

COLOR OR FINISH: White and red, rainbow, red and green spots, green scale, pike scale, perch scale, silver shiner, red throat and silver back, mullet scale.

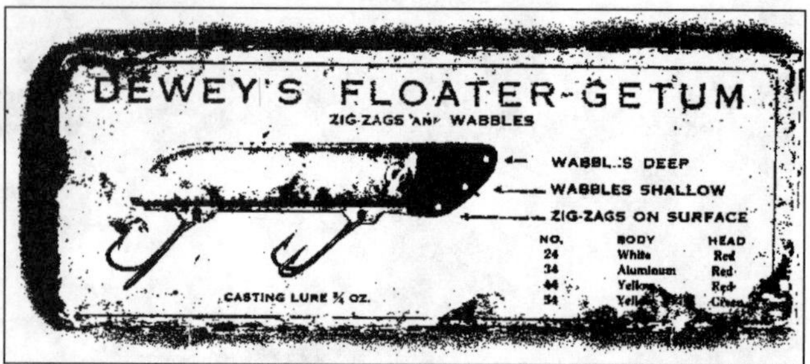

A FLOATER GETUM box. It lists four colors on the top, but on the side it says the lure came in five colors and that is so. (see list below).

FLOATER GETUM

Collector value range: $140-$200.

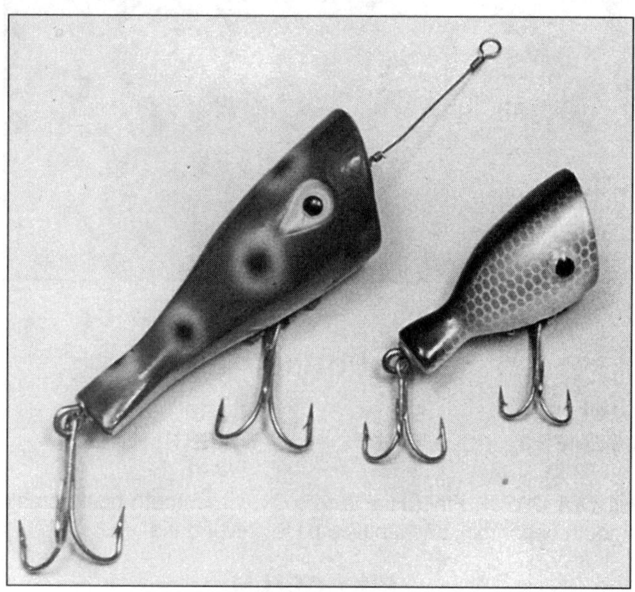

OUTING

CATALOG SERIES #	BODY LENGTH	LURE WEIGHT
400	4-1/8"	3/4 oz.

COLOR OR FINISH: White with red head, Yellow with red head, Aluminum color with red head, Black with red head, Yellow with green head.

BUCKY GETUM

See previous photo of five lures with box. Made in three sizes: 1/2 oz., 5/8 oz., 3/4 oz. Collector value range: $50-$75.

PORKY GETUM

FEATHER GETUM

LUCKY GETUM

These three use the same body as the BUCK GETUM. The FEATHER GETUM has a weed guard and attached feathers. The LUCKY GETUM has a trailing bucktail hook and the PORKY GETUM has a rigid-mount single hook with a tiny single hook pork rind attachment. Collector value range: $50-$75.

PACHNER AND KOEHLER, INC.

Momence, Illinois

The company is better known as P & K. It had its beginnings in 1933 when Mr. Leo C. Pachner had a barber shop in Illinois. He began by selling a minnow saver hook put together and sold from the barber shop. He took Koehler on as a partner in 1934. In 1936 Pachner and his family went on the road pulling a house trailer and selling the hook to tackle retailers. As they began selling more and more items of tackle they founded the P & K Corporation. They began manufacturing one of the first artificial lures made of rubber in 1939. World War II stopped their supply of hooks so they began manufacturing their own, eventually becoming the first U.S. manufacturers of treble hooks. The company blossomed into success, but Pachner & Koehler liquidated the company in 1966. Pachner retired afterwards, but like so many, sedentary life was not for him. He is alive and well today, publishing a successful periodical called the Farm Pond Harvest. He still resides in Momence, Illinois. The following listing of P & K lures will cover the wooden and plastic plugs up to the early 1950s.

WALKIE TALKIE

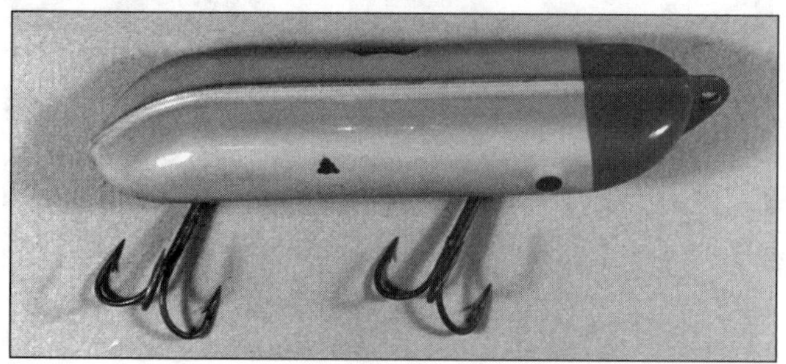

This is a plunker type lure made of Tenite. It has a belly treble and a trailing hook attached to a flared tail. It was available in two sizes (1-3/8" and 2-7/8"). By the 1950s the smaller size had been eliminated. Collector value range: $8-$12.

CATALOG SERIES #	BODY LENGTH	LURE WEIGHT
43	1-3/8"	unk
	2-7/8"	1/2 oz.

COLOR OR FINISH: Red and white; black and white; frog; yellow spot tail; yellow perch; pike; green scale; silver.

AMAZIN' MAIZIE

This is a 5/8 oz., 2-1/4" lure made of Tenite. It has a diving lip, a belly treble, and a trailing treble hook. It is thought that the lure was named in honor of Pachner's wife. Collector value range: $8-$12.

CATALOG SERIES #	BODY LENGTH	LURE WEIGHT
42	2-1/2"	5/8 oz.

COLOR OR FINISH: Red and white; frog; pike; yellow perch; black and white; yellow spot tail; green scale; silver, pike, rainbow.

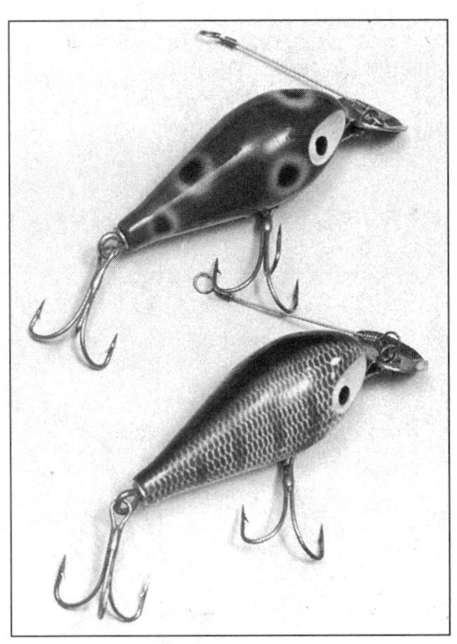

BRIGHT EYES

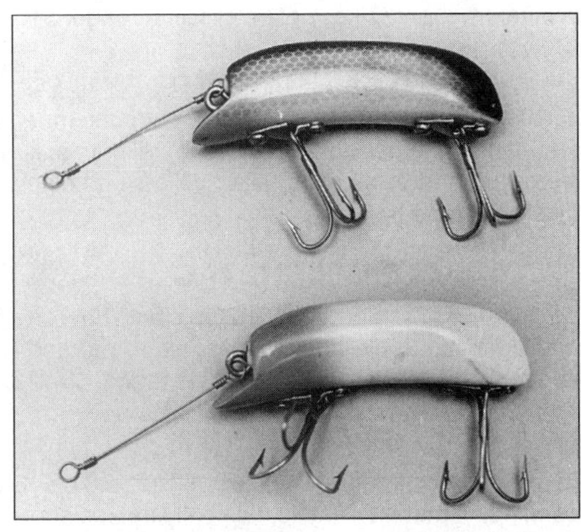

An oddly shaped Tenite lure with two belly-mounted trebles. It has a curved body and has a notch in the top of the head where the eyes and line tie are located. They were made available with a deep-diving blade later. The weight is 1/2 oz. and body length, 2-3/4". Same colors as the WALKIE TALKIE. Collector value range: $15-$20.

DEEP RUNNING BRIGHT EYES

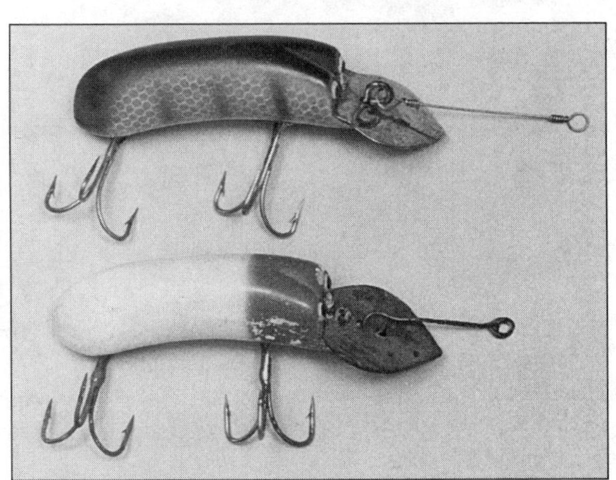

The same as the regular BRIGHT EYES, but with the addition of a deep-diving metal lip attached. Collector value range: $8-$12.

SPINNING MINNIE

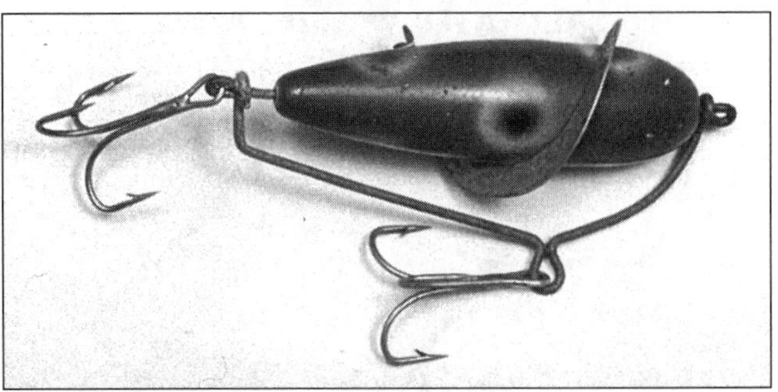

This is a Tenite plug with a small corkscrew ridge molded around the body to make it spin on retrieve. The hooks (2T) are mounted to a metal band attached to the nose and tail to allow the body to rotate freely maintaining the hooks in a down position. Available in two sizes, 1-1/2 and 3-1/4". Three colors observed are: Copper (metallic), aluminum color and frog spot. Collector value range: $20-$25.

WHIRL-A-WAY c. 1935

This is a fairly realistic looking plastic minnow with a trailing double hook. The body was fashioned with a hole through it lengthwise so that it could rotate on retrieve and slide on the hook shank and wire leader. When the fish struck the body it was supposed to slide forward leaving the fish to fight only the hook making it less likely to throw the lure. The leader was equipped with a rudder-like weight. They were also made with a single-barb hook. The length is 3" and the weight, 5/8 oz. The patent number found on a Whirl-A-Way lure pamphlet indicates the patent was granted in 1934. Collector value range: $15-$20.

COLOR OR FINISH: Red and white; black and white; yellow perch; black; pikie; green scale; spotted, spotted frog.

LIPPY

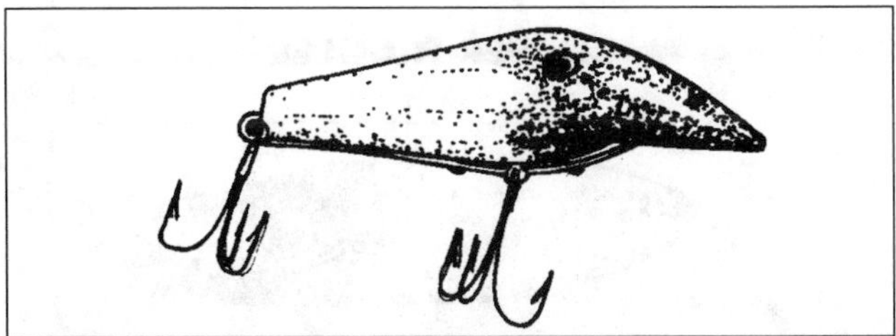

A strong salt water plug with a sloped, sharply pointed nose. It has a belly treble and trailing treble hook, both attached to a metal piece running on the surface underside of the lure. Collector value range: $8-$12.

CATALOG SERIES #	BODY LENGTH	LURE WEIGHT
63	7-1/2"	3-1/2"

COLOR OR FINISH: Red and white; brown scale; blue scale; silver.

SALTWATER WALKIE TALKIE

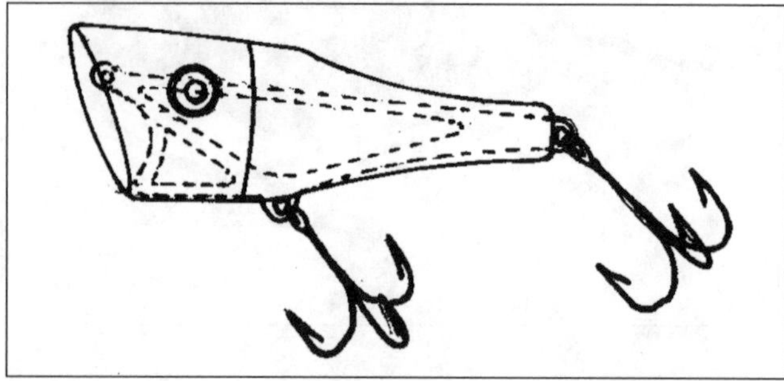

A very strong saltwater lure made of wood. There is a reinforced brass hook-holding device, riveted and cemented into the body. It has a belly treble and trailing treble hook. Collector value range: $10-$15.

CATALOG SERIES #	BODY LENGTH	LURE WEIGHT
62	5-1/2"	3-1/2 oz.

COLOR OR FINISH: Red and white; brown scale; blue scale; silver.

CLIPPER TOP KICK

This lure was a plunker type. It has one belly treble and a trailing treble hook. It was available in only one size (3", 1/2 oz.) and the color options were: Red and white; yellow perch; pike; silver flitter; and frog. Collector value range: $8-$12.

CLIPPER BASS WOBBLER

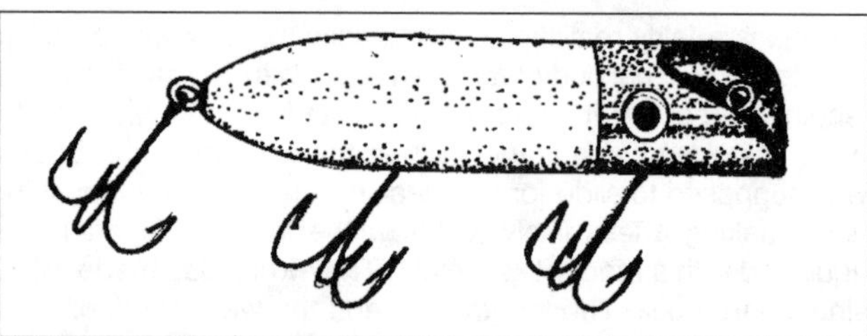

This lure has a scooped out nose, two belly trebles and a trailing treble hook. It came in two sizes: 2-1/2, 1/2 oz. and 3-3/4", 5/8 oz. The available colors were: Red and white; yellow perch; pike; silver flitter. Collector value range: $8-$12.

CLIPPER WIGGLER

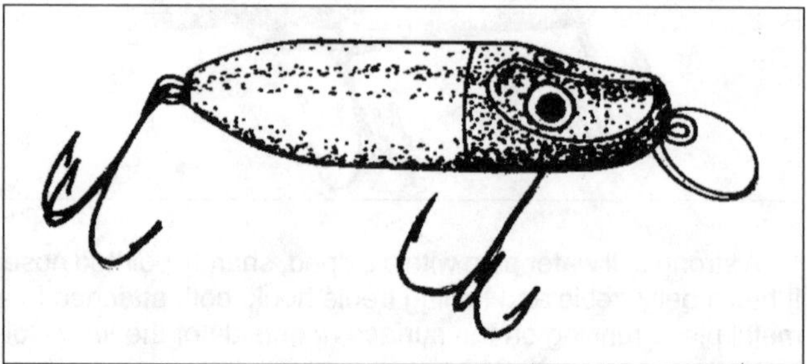

This plug was made in two sizes: 2-3/4", 1/2 oz.; smaller size unknown. It has two scooped out eye depressions rendering the nose slightly pointed. Both sizes have a round metal diving lip, a belly treble and trailing treble hook. Colors were exactly the same as the CLIPPER TOP KICK. Collector value range: $8-$12.

CLIPPER SURFACE SPINNER

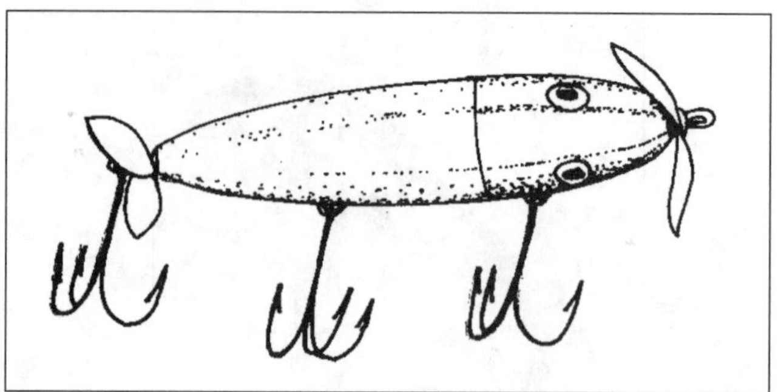

The SURFACE SPINNER has a 3-3/4" body and weighs 5/8 oz. It has two side trebles, a trailing treble hook, and fore- and aft-mounted propeller spinners. It was made in three finishes: red and white; frog; and pike. Collector value range: $10-$14.

CLIPPER TINY MITE

This lure was a small 1-3/4", 1/2-ounce plug with round metal diving lip. It has one belly treble and one trailing treble hook. Colors were: red and white; frog; pike; yellow and black. Collector value range: $6-$10.

CLIPPER ZIG ZAG

Made in two sizes (4", 5/8 oz.; 3", 1/2 oz.), both have two belly trebles and a trailing treble hook. Colors were: red and white; frog; pike; yellow and black. Collector value range: $6-$12.

CLIPPER MINNOW

The minnow was made in two sizes: 4-1/8", 5/8 oz.; 3-3/8", 1/2 oz. Each has a metal diving lip, two belly trebles and a trailing treble. Color options were: red and white; yellow perch; pike; and silver flitter. Collector value range: $6-$10.

SOFTY THE WONDER CRAB in its original box. Collector value range: $15-$20.

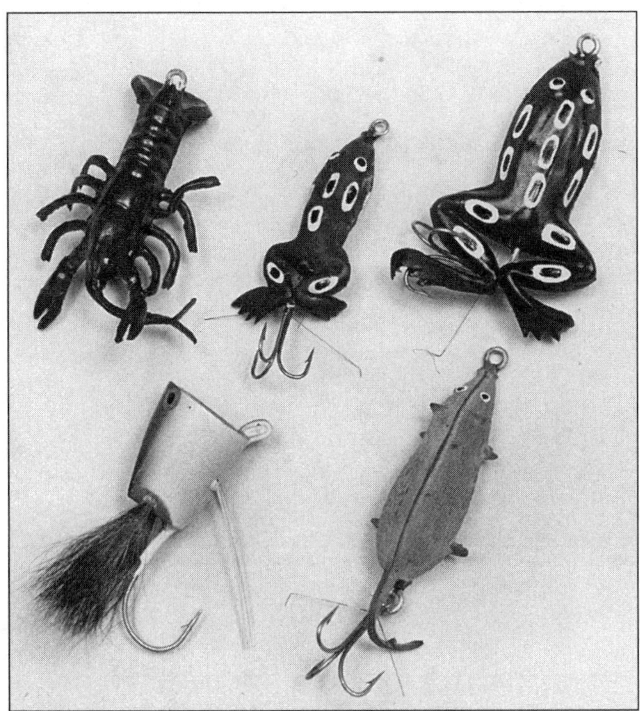

Top row; left to right: SOFTY THE WONDER CRAB, two sizes of SPOTTY THE WONDER FROG. Bottom left: a P & K fly rod popper. Bottom right: P & K MOUSE.

CLIPPER JOINTED PIKE

This is a jointed version of the CLIPPER MINNOW above. The hooks and colors are the same. The joint is between the belly treble hooks. Collector value range: $6-$12.

PAW PAW BAIT COMPANY

Paw Paw, Michigan

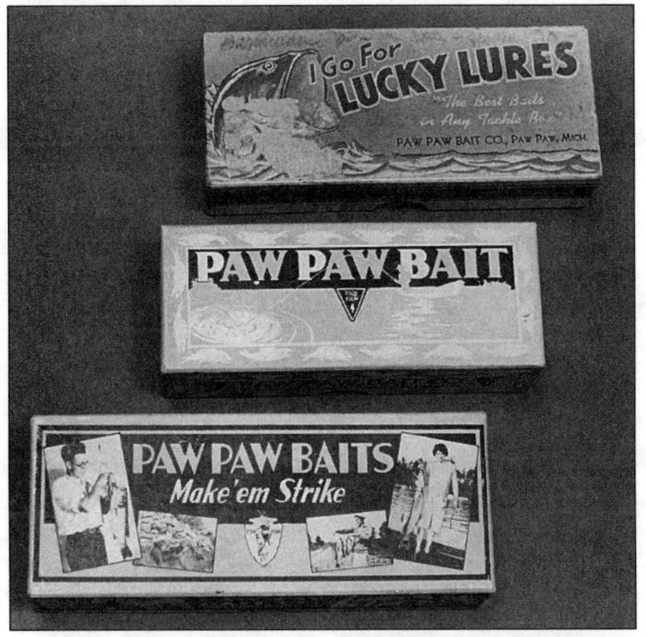

Paw Paw was in business continuously beginning around 1909 as the Moonlight Bait Company into the 1960s. In 1970 the Shakespeare Company bought out all Paw Paw rights and equipment, ending a long era of artificial bait production for the company. This apparently was not the end for Paw Paw lures, however, because I recently found a 1970s Shakespeare catalog that features a page of "PAW PAW FISHING LURES by Shakespeare".

Catalog and all advertising studies have established that a transition of the Moonlight Bait Company to the Paw Paw Bait Company took place somewhere around 1927. Please see Moonlight Bait Company for details leading up to the name change and early Paw Paw lures.

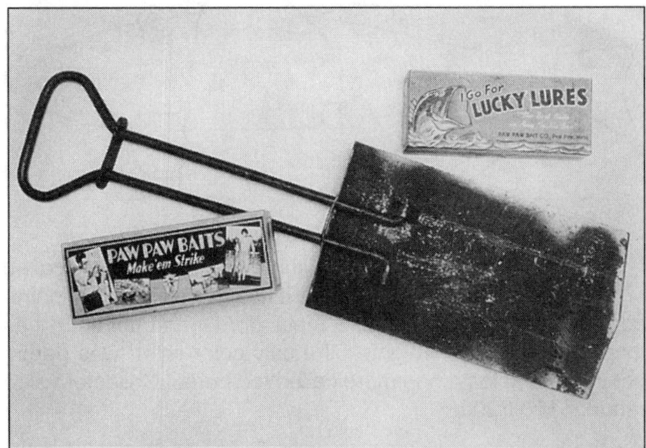

Here is an interesting piece of accessory fishing gear made by Paw Paw. They called it the Scout. It was a collapsible shovel measuring 18-1/4" in the extended position and 11-3/4" collapsed. A 1930 catalog offered it to help get your vehicle unstuck or for use around a fishing camp. It was patented by Paw Paw.

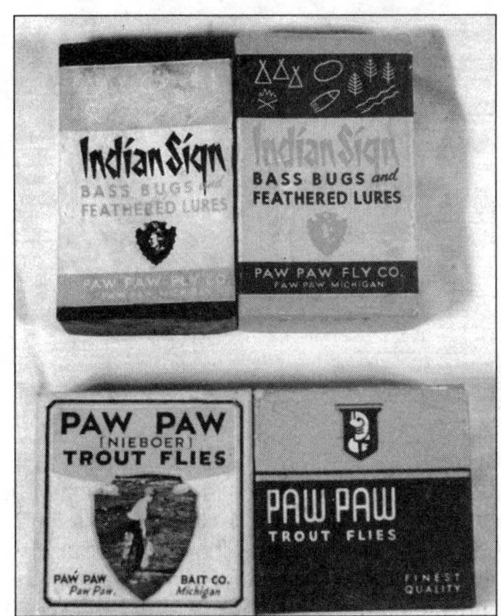

Four different Paw Paw fly rod lure boxes. Photo courtesy Jim Muma.

It is known that Paw Paw produced many fine plugs with glass eyes but most found so far have tacks or brads for eyes. They were installed before painting the body and the greatest majority of those found have had the paint knocked off through use. The metal shows through in this case.

To help recognize a Paw Paw lure look for the one-piece combination diving lip and forward hook hanger plainly visible in the photo of the Paw Paw Minnie Mouse.

There are a number of lures listed and illustrated at the end of the section that have been attributed to Paw Paw because of the recognizable hardware or paint and pattern styles. They were not found cataloged.

Paw Paw's catalogs have proved to be unreliable in identifying what may have been available from year to year. Some lures seem never to have been cataloged at all and others sporadically. Still others only appear in one year. This makes it difficult to pin down years of production for many of their lures.

PAW PAW FISH DECOY

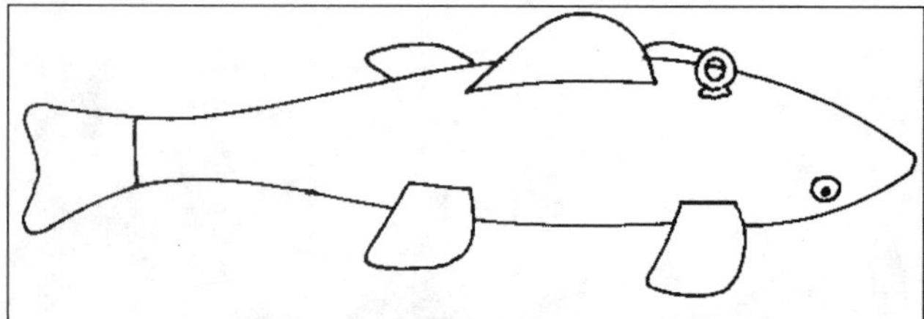

Found only in a 1929 catalog, this critter was actually called "The Greatest Spearing Minnow". It has glass eyes, two painted metal fins on each side, a metal dorsal and tail fin. It has three internal belly weights. The only color listed was perch, but there is at least one more called red horse. Collector value range: $100-$200.

BULLHEAD SERIES

The BULLHEAD was new in the 1929 catalog at 4-1/4" with glass eyes in the illustration. The lower plug in the photograph measures just a hair less than 4-1/2" in body length although all catalogs state 4-1/4". This BULLHEAD is probably of earlier vintage than 1931. They were gone from catalogs by the late 1930s. The lures above have tack or brad eyes (TPE). Collector value range: $100-$150.

CATALOG SERIES #	BODY LENGTH	LURE WEIGHT
3500	4-1/4"	3/4 oz.

COLOR OR FINISH: Silver perch, white with redhead, pearl finish with redhead, frog finish, dark brown (bullhead color), black with red spots.

THE CRAB

Not found in any of the available catalogs. This lure has a wooden body and two braided feelers trailing. The two lures shown here have glass eyes and measure 2-1/4" in body length. Dates and color finishes unknown. Collector value range: $50-$75.

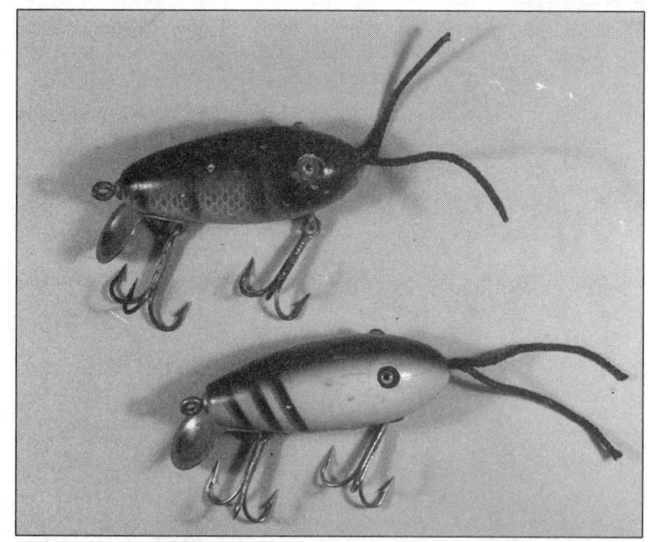

CRAWDAD

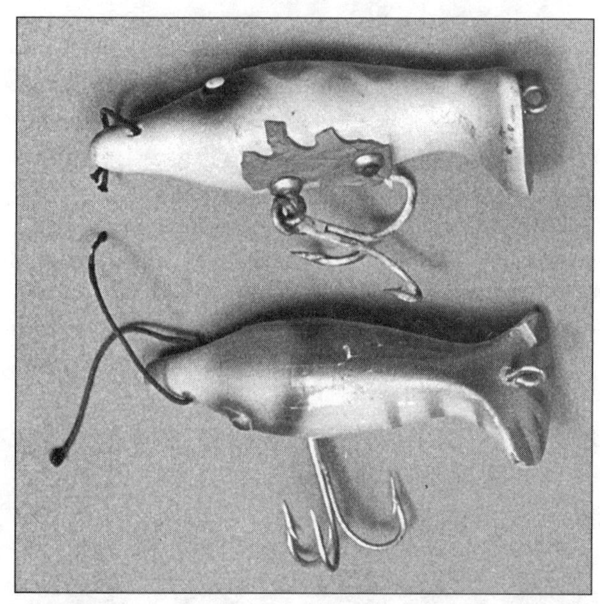

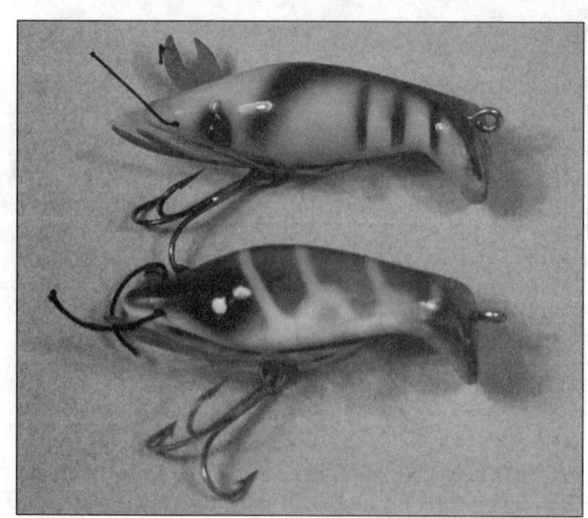

A pair of CRAWDADS in excellent condition. Photo courtesy Jim Muma.

The two plugs in the above photo illustrate the typical condition in which they are found. They were listed as "new" in the 1929 catalog. The lures both originally had two claws and six legs made of flexible rubber. Only a small piece of the rubber remains on the upper lure. Original models probably have glass eyes and occur only in a natural crawfish finish. Later models (c. 1931 and later) will have the tack painted eyes (TPE) and several other finishes as listed. Collector value range: $50-$75.

CATALOG SERIES #	BODY LENGTH	LURE WEIGHT
500	2-3/4"	3/4 oz.

COLOR OR FINISH: Yellow with black stripes, Solid black, Green with black stripes, Solid red, Brown with black stripes, Brown with red stripes. Black with yellow stripes.

CRIPPLED MINNOW

PAW PAW INJURED MINNOW 3400 Series

Sometimes called the CRIPPLED MINNOW in Paw Paw catalogs, this is an unusual lure that must have been difficult to make. It has glass eyes and two side-mounted trebles. I have not actually seen one, but a very good catalog illustration shows what appears to be a through-body wire with line tie at the nose ending in the aft treble hook hanger just forward of the tail. First found listed in a 1928 mixed tackle catalog of the Shapleigh Hardware Company. Collector value range: $75-$100. Photo courtesy Jim Muma.

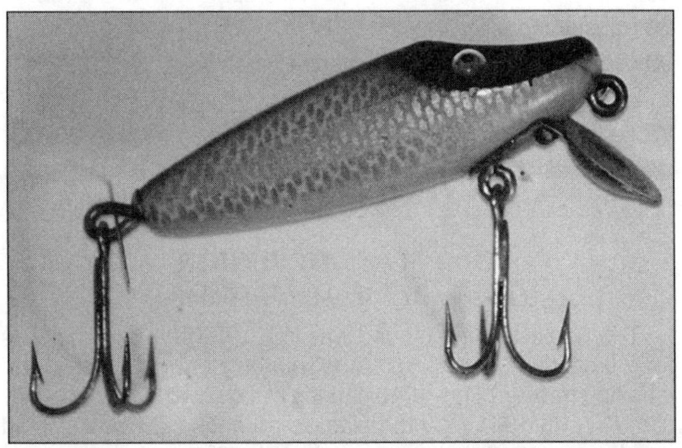

An early Paw Paw LIPPY SUE with glass eyes and in a really super Rainbow trout color pattern. Photo courtesy Ken Bernoteit.

CATALOG SERIES #	BODY LENGTH	LURE WEIGHT
3400	4"	5/8 oz.

COLOR OR FINISH: Green scale; white with redhead, pearl with red head, silver scale; gold scale; frog finish.

LIPPY JOE Series 6300

LIPPY JOE

LIPPY SUE

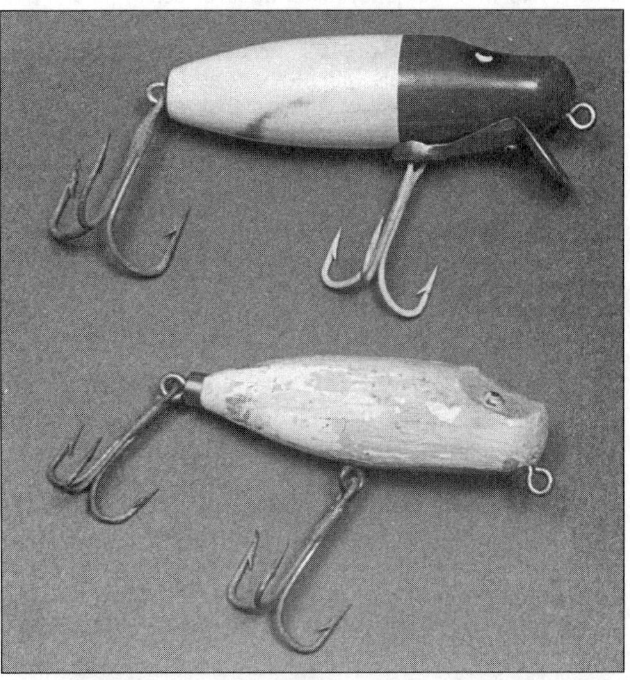

The upper lure in the photo of two lures here is a LIPPY JOE. The catalogs in the author's collection list only two sizes that were called LIPPY JOE, the regular and the BABY LIPPY JOE. They measure 3-1/8" and 2-3/4" respectively. Although only one matches the catalog size, the body styles seem to identify them. The smaller, light-colored plug with the tail cup and no lip may be an early model.

There are actually a number of sizes as well as jointed versions of this lure. Some were listed with no name and others seem to have been named by size. They all share the same body style. The LIPPY SUE seems to be no more than the standard lure with a feathered trailing treble; a "skirt" as it were.

Paw Paw introduce what they called "A NEW IRIDESCENT SCALE FINISH" IN 1940. At the same time and on the same page they said they were proud to "...present these sparkling new baits..." among other things and illustrated The #9100 Series and the #9300 Series in the chart below, in fourteen finishes. They were also in jointed versions.

They announced a plastic version in 1942 called the FLOATER-SINKER. Please turn to Paw Paw Plastics for an illustration. Even thought the made plastic versions the continued to produce them in wood into the 1960s Though the color choices had dwindled to five in number. Collector value range: $15-$25.

CATALOG

NAME	SERIES #	LENGTH	WEIGHT
None	6100	2-5/8	3/8 oz.
None	6300 (semi-floating)	3-1/8"	1/2 oz.

NAME	SERIES #	LENGTH	WEIGHT
MIDGET LURE	7100	1-1/2"	3/8 oz.
MIDGET LURE	7200	1-1/2"	3/8 oz
	(with feathered treble hook)		
None	9100	2-5/8"	3/8 oz.
	(seems to be same as the #6100)		
None	9100-J	2-5/8"	3/8 oz.
None	9300	3-1/4"	1/2 oz.
None	9300-J	3-1/4"	1/2 oz.

COLOR OR FINISH (1939): Yellow perch, green with gold dots, white with red head, rainbow, silver scale, natural pike, frog, silver flitters.

COLOR OR FINISH (1940): *Yellow scale with black head and stripes; *silver scale with red back and gray stripes; *gold scale; *natural gold scale; iridescent silver scale with gray back; silver scale with red head and stripes; yellow perch; *green with gold dots; white with red head; rainbow; silver scale; natural pike; frog finish; silver flitters.

**Not available in the 1942 catalog.*

COLOR OR FINISH (1963 catalog): Iridescent; white with red head; yellow perch; pike scale; dace.

PAW PAW MOUSE BAIT

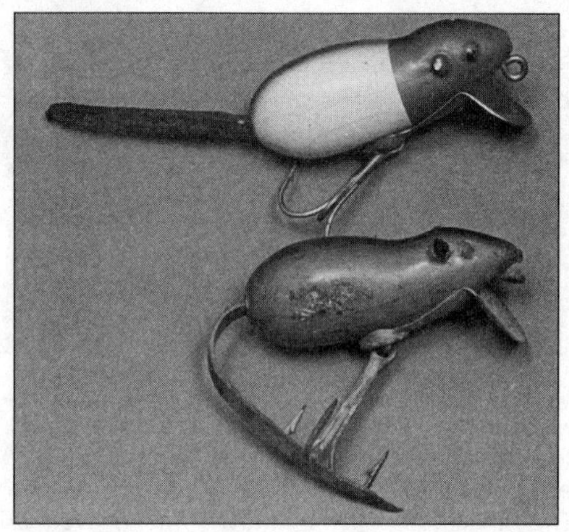

Newer vintage Paw Paw MOUSE BAIT (#40). Dates from about 1931 to the 1950s. Flexible leather tail, one-piece combination diving lip and hook hanger. Later called MINNIE MOUSE. Collector value range: $40-$55.

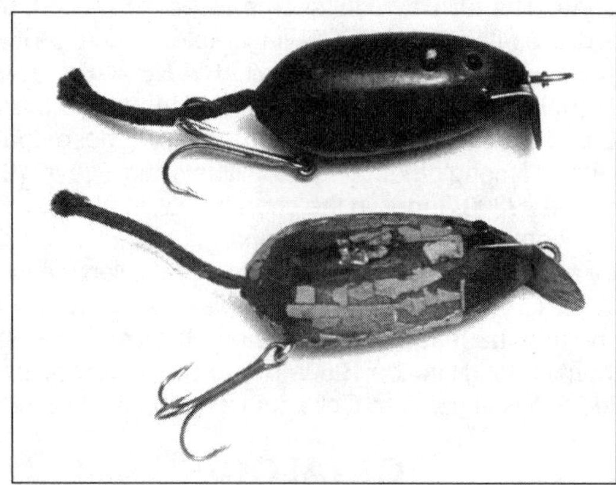

Oldest Paw Paw MOUSE or early Moonlight MOUSE (#50). Dates from around 1929 to 1930. Flexible braided tail, ears, simple screw-eye hook mount. Collector value range: $100-$200.

CATALOG SERIES #	BODY LENGTH	LURE WEIGHT
40	2-1/2"	5/8 oz.

CATALOG SERIES #	BODY LENGTH	LURE WEIGHT
*50	2-1/2"	5/8 oz.

COLOR OR FINISH: Mouse color (gray), black body with white head, white body with red head.

**Also available in brown, gray, or white fur finish by 1949.*

NATURAL HAIR MOUSE

Paw Paw NATURAL HAIR MOUSE. The uppermost lure is the design of the MUSKY MOUSE and the SEA MOUSE. The left middle is the 1928 3" model and the middle right is the 1930 2-1/2" model. Bottom is the fly rod model. Photo courtesy Jim Muma.

The earliest reference found was in a mixed tackle catalog of 1928 from the Shapleigh Hardware Company. It listed and pictured the #60 HAIR MOUSE at 3" and 1/2 oz. in Gray head or White head.

A 1929 catalog introduced the larger size as new. It was offered as the MUSKY MOUSE and SEA MOUSE, the latter being "..weighted for saltwater fishing. There is another model, but no reference to it has been found to date. It has an arrow-shaped metal diving lip that has the patent date "1-22-29" stamped on it. Collector value range: $75-$100.

CATALOG SERIES #	BODY LENGTH	LURE WEIGHT	COLLECTOR VALUE RANGE
Fly rod size	1-1/4"	?	$20-$30.
60	2-1/2"	1/2 oz.	$40-$50.
60	3"	5/8 oz.	$75-$100.
80 (Musky Mouse)	4-1/4"	?	$200-$300.
90 (Sea Mouse)	4-1/4"	heavier than #80	$100-$150.

COLOR OR FINISH: Gray head, Yellow head, Red head, White head.

OLD FLATSIDE

OLD FLATSIDE JUNIOR
(also called Wounded Minnow)

The earliest listing I found was in a 1939 catalog. This was for a flat side floater, 3-1/2" long with only one side treble and a trailing treble (2T). A 1940 catalog listed a two side treble version (3T). In 1941 only the single side hook (2T) was offered and then in 1942 they were back to the 3T version. Why this swapping back and forth is anybody's guess. By 1949 both were finally offered in the catalog. All of these were cataloged at 3-1/2" long but, as you can see in the photo, the 2T version was shorter. It actually measured 2-1/2". The 3T actual measurement is 3", not as the cataloged 3-1/2". As you can see in the photo, there are two distinctly different eye locations. Both types appear in catalog illustrations throughout the years. That probably represents the use of different cuts, regardless of design changes. Earliest Flatsides have glass eyes mounted at the sides of the head, then came tack painted eyes (TPE) on the sides, then TPE on top. Collector value range: $20-$30.

CATALOG SERIES #	BODY LENGTH	LURE WEIGHT
1500	2-1/2"	?
2500	3"	3/4 oz.

COLOR OR FINISH: Yellow perch, white with redhead, shad, pike scale, frog, silver flitters, dace, black with silver flitters, gold shiner scale, green with gold dots, rainbow, perch scale. It was made available covered in real frog skin in 1940.

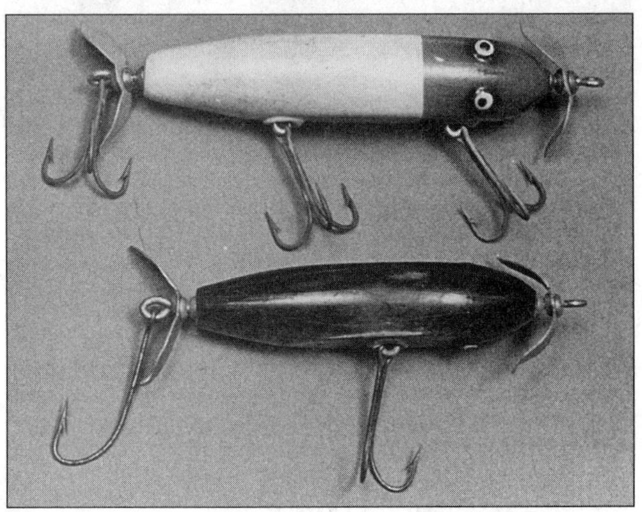

DARTER, Series 2500

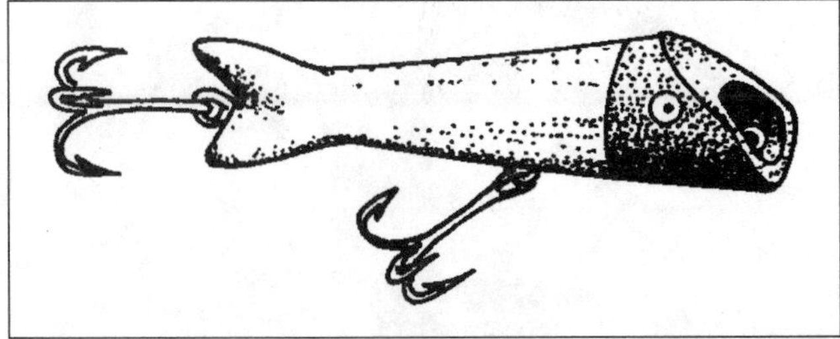

Paw Paw made a DARTER like just about all the lure makers of the day. This is a 1930s glass-eyed lure. It has a hollow in the face where the line tie is located. Collector value range: $20-$30.

CATALOG SERIES #	BODY LENGTH	LURE WEIGHT
2500	4"	3/4 oz.

COLOR OR FINISH: Green scale, white with red head, rainbow, silver scale, frog, perch.

DARTER, Series 9200

This Paw Paw DARTER is built in the more traditional body style, both straight and jointed. The straight DARTER could be bought with a tail propeller spinner if so desired. It was new in 1940. Just when the old style was changed to the new is not

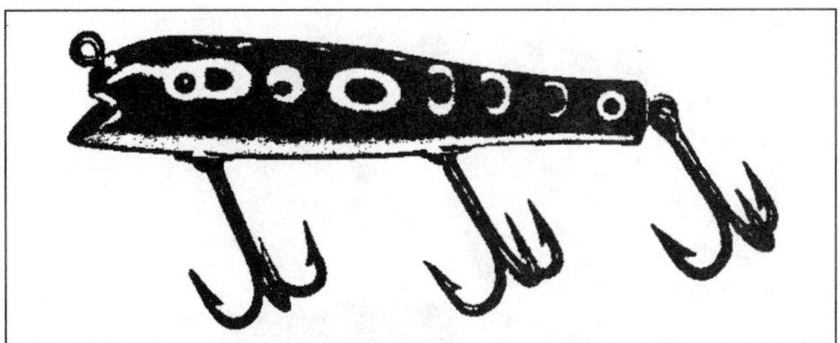

known, but probably in 1939-40. Neither one of them was in the 1939 catalog. They continued in production throughout the years. Collector value range: $10-$20.

The DARTER is one of a few Paw Paw lures that Shakespeare offered after they bought them out in 1970. It was made of wood also. They called it the DRAGON FLY for some peculiar reason.

PAW PAW

CATALOG SERIES #	BODY LENGTH	LURE WEIGHT
9200	3-3/4"	1/2 oz.
9200-J	3-3/4"	1/2 oz.

COLOR OR FINISH (Paw Paw): White with red head, pike scale, yellow with red and yellow spots, *frog special, *black with silver and red spots, *silver flitters.

**The only colors available in the 1963 catalog.*

CATALOG SERIES #	BODY LENGTH	LURE WEIGHT
9200	3-3/4"	1/2 oz.
9200-J	3-3/4"	1/2 oz.

COLOR OR FINISH (Shakespeare): Silver flitter, shad, yellow with red on black spots, frog, black with red on gold spots, white with red head.

BASS SEEKER

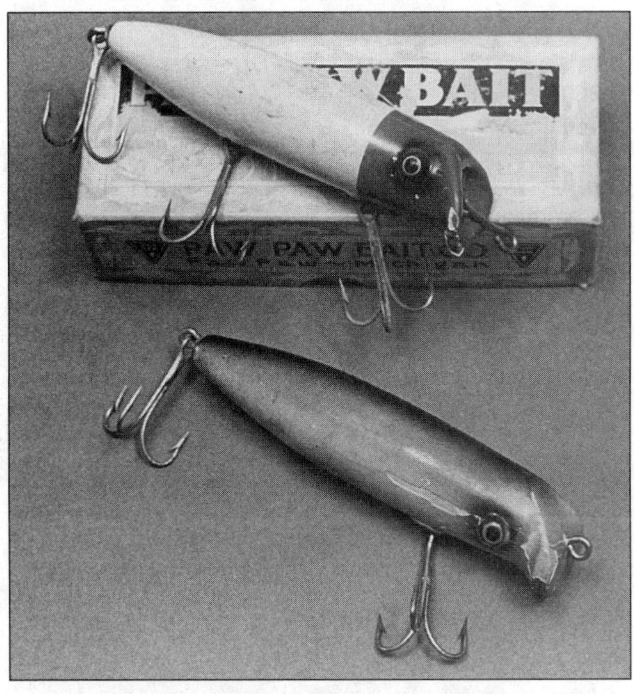

First found in a 1928 mixed tackle catalog, this is a lure retained from the old Moonlight Bait Company line. It has a cupped head with a short heavy wire line tie attached to the screw eye and a projecting lower jaw. They were first available with glass

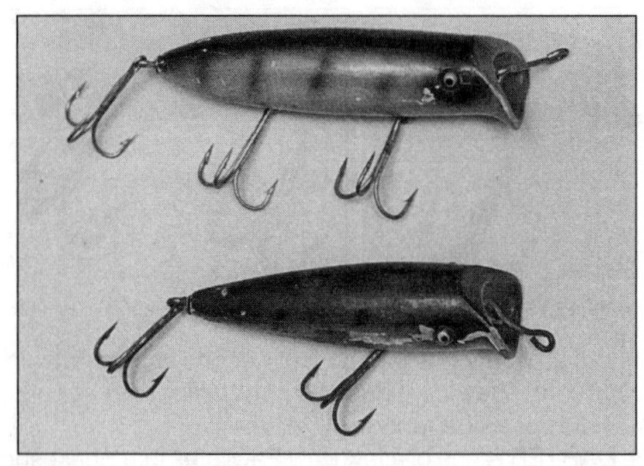

eyes, then tack painted eyes. They came equipped with either two or three treble hooks and were made in two sizes. The two lures in the photos that do not have cupped heads were not found in any catalogs or advertisements, but they are obviously the Bass Seeker bodies. Collector value range: $20-$30.

CATALOG SERIES #	BODY LENGTH	LURE WEIGHT
2600	4"	3/4 oz.
4600	3-1/4"	3/4 oz.

COLOR OR FINISH: Green scale; white with redhead, pearl finish with red head, gold scale; frog finish; perch; metallic glitters; red head, gold body, red head, green body, perch finish with green and silver metallic flitters; redhead, silver body.

PAW PAW RIVER TYPE

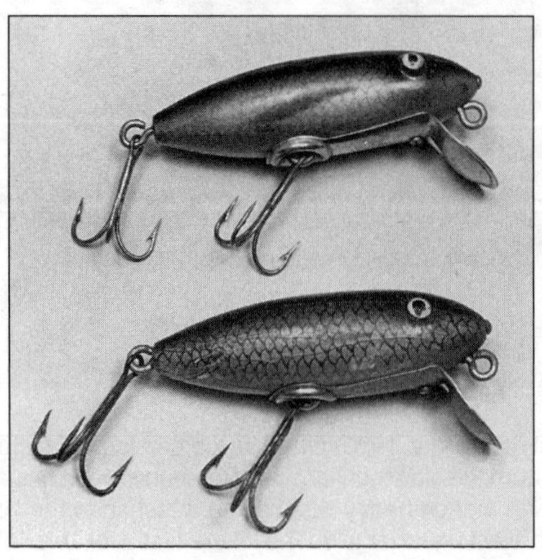

The photos above and below represent two slightly different body designs for this plug. The more tapered body and relatively blunt nose plugs are likely the oldest. The body measures for all four plugs in the photo is 2-1/2". Collector value range: $15-$25.

CATALOG SERIES#	BODY LENGTH	LURE WEIGHT
900	2-5/8"	1/2 oz.

COLOR OR FINISH: Perch scale; green scale; silver scale; pike scale; frog scale; white with red head, rainbow, silver flitters.

PIKE MINNOW LURE
No. 1600 Series

The photo above shows two body styles of this Paw Paw great. The upper plug in the photo is a dead ringer for the older model illustrated in a 1931 catalog. They were then available with only two treble hooks. Later models have three trebles and a groove on each side of the nose. All lures in the photos have the typical Paw Paw tack painted eyes (except where noted) and combination one-piece diving plane and forward hook mount.

This 6-3/4" strong jointed example is called THE DREADNAUGHT. Photo courtesy Jim Muma.

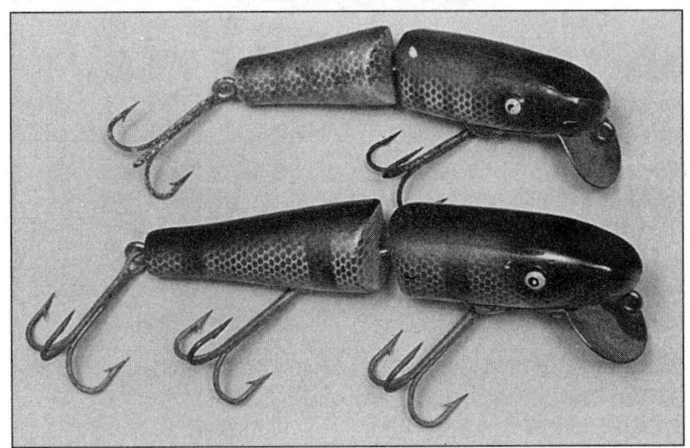

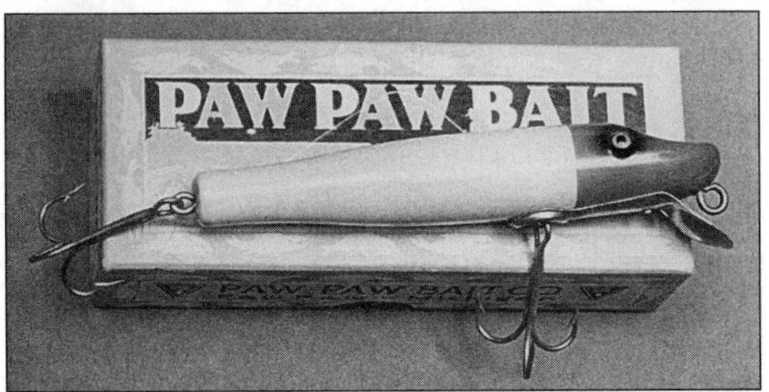

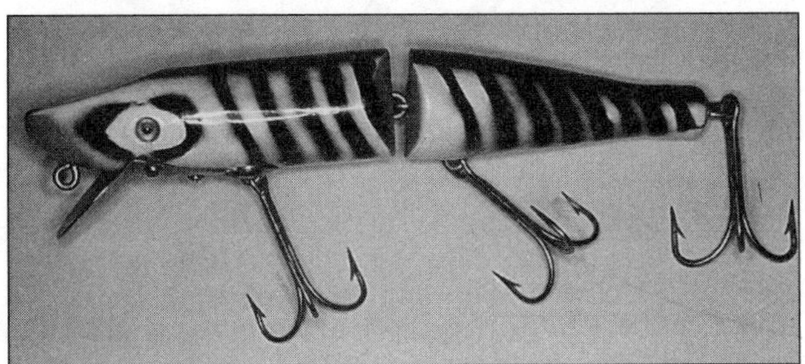

This is a rare glass-eyed version in the musky size 6-1/4".

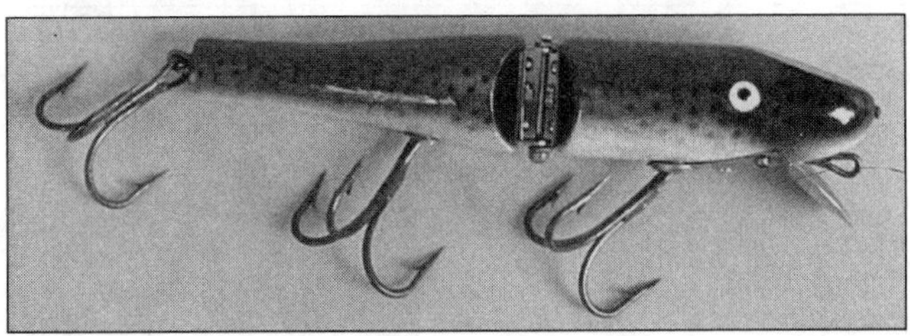

CATALOG SERIES NAME	BODY LENGTH	LURE WEIGHT	COLLECTOR VALUE RANGE
Dreadnaught	6-3/4?	?	$200-$300.
Musky	6-1/4"	2-3/8 oz.	$40-$60.
Musky Jtd.	6-1/4"	2-3/8 oz.	$40-$50.
Regular	4-1/2"	3/4 oz.	$20-$30.
Regular Jtd.	4-1/2"	3/4 oz.	$20-$30.
Baby	3-1/4"	1/2 oz.	$10-$20.
Baby Jtd.	3-1/4"	1/2 oz.	$10-$20.

COLOR OR FINISH: Green scale; gold scale; *white with red head, pearl finish; frog finish; *yellow perch; *pike scale; *silver flitters; **shad, **dace; **black with silver flitters; *gold shiner scale. the 4-1/2" straight pike minnow was made available covered in real frog skin in 1940.

**The only finish available by the late 1940s.*

***Added in 1949.*

PAW PAW WILSON WOBBLER

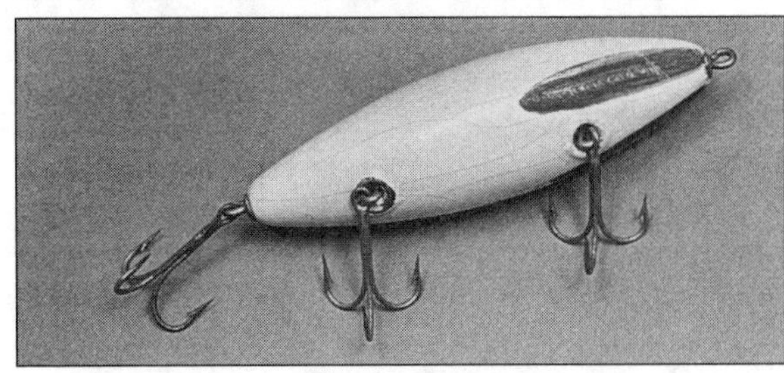

Carried over to Paw Paw from the old Moonlight line this lure was last listed in catalogs of the early 1930s. It is not certain if the one in the photo here is a genuine Paw Paw manufactured WILSON WOBBLER. It is pictured above because of the typical Paw Paw painted cup hardware. The catalogs listed it as 4" long, weight 3/4 oz. It comes with three trebles, two trebles or two double hooks. Collector value range: $20-$40.

COLORS OR FINISH: White with red flutes, red, yellow, rainbow, fox fire.

A Paw Paw WILSON WOBBLER with its original box. Photo courtesy Jim Muma.

BULLFROG

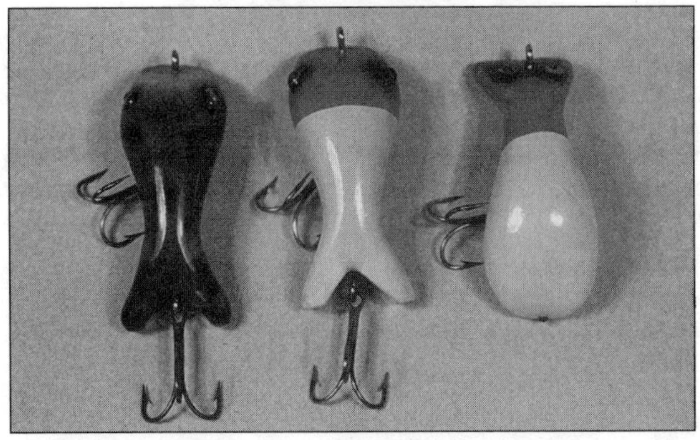

Three lures representing the two different versions of the BULL FROG that are found. Either version is rare. Photo courtesy Jim Muma.

A 1929 catalog listed and pictured this unusual tack-eyed lure. The drawing above is an exact copy of the catalog photograph. It was missing from catalogs by 1939. Size was not given, but colors listed were: Bullfrog finish and white with red head. The lure measures 2-3/4". Collector value range: $200-$300.

FOX FIRE

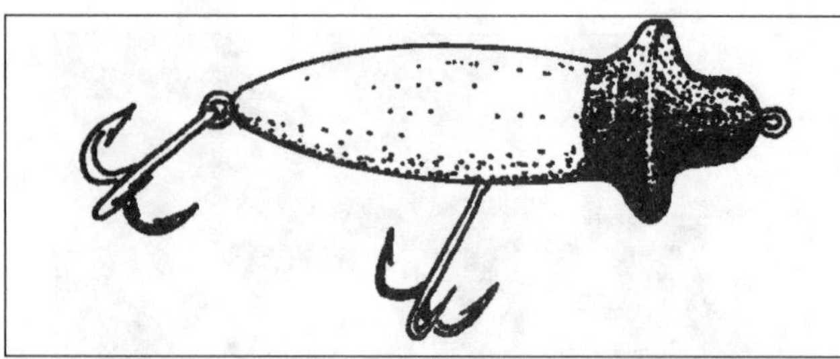

This is the famous MOONLIGHT FLOATING BAIT retained by Paw Paw from the old Moonlight line. They simply changed the name and continued to offer it in their catalogs until 1939 when it disappeared from the line. They are 4" long with a belly treble and trailing treble hook (2T) and two color options: Fox fire (luminous white)and white body with red head. Collector value range: $25-$40.

JUG HEAD

This is a 1-3/4" fly rod version of the FOX FIRE above. I has a double hook hung on the belly and was available in at least four color finishes. They are: White body with red head, green spotted, red spotted, rainbow. Collector value range: $100-$200.

SPINNING PICKEREL AND BASS LURE

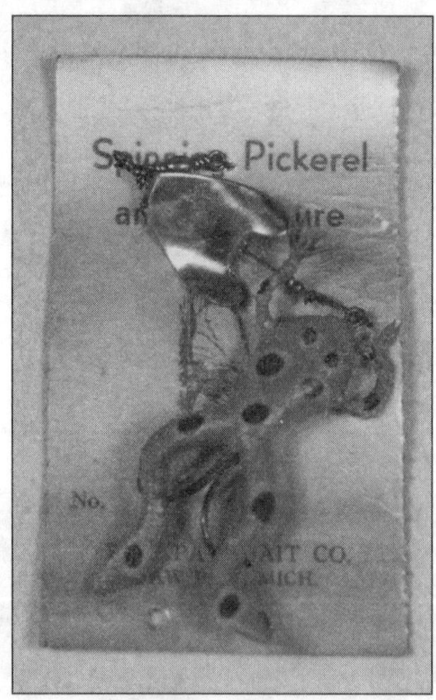

Not much is known about this little 2" lure. It is obvious there are more to look for from the box. It stated that you needed to look for Paw Paw's "BASS BUGS and FEATHERED LURES". Collector value range: $10-$20., with box: $30-$40.

PAW PAW POPPER

This Popper dates from about the early 1930s and was missing from catalogs by 1949. Earliest examples will have glass eyes. Collector value range: $10-$20.

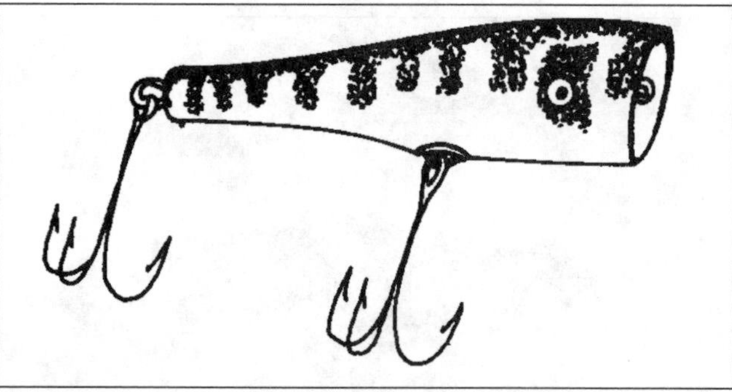

CATALOG SERIES #	BODY LENGTH	LURE WEIGHT
2200	3"	3/4 oz.

COLOR OR FINISH: Yellow perch, rainbow, green with gold scale, pike scale, perch scale, white with red head, frog, silver flitters, genuine frog skin covering (1940).

PLUNKER

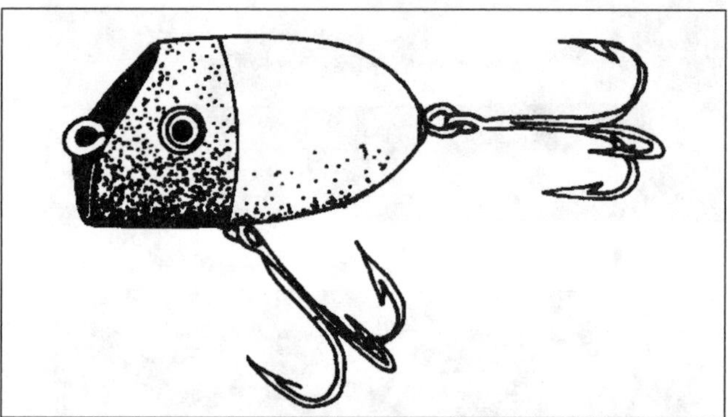

First found in a 1929 catalog this lure came in only one size: 2", 3/4 oz. Catalog copy says "It is the result of a years' experimenting ..." Collector value range: $20-$35.

COLOR OR FINISH: Yellow, white with red head, black with white head, silver, frog, perch.

CASTING LURE

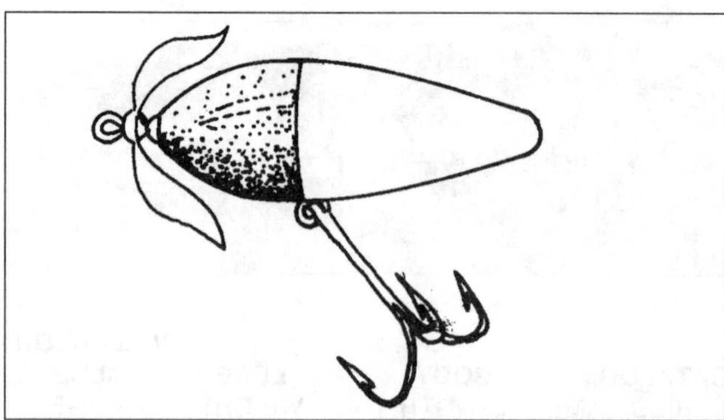

A 1930s propeller spinner bait that came only in white body and red head finish with no eyes. It had only one treble (belly mounted) and was 2" long weighing 1/2 oz. Collector value range: $25-$40.

CASTER BAIT SERIES

Paw Paw introduced these in 1940-41. All in the series, sometimes called "Nature Baits", are wood-bodied and all but the larger Saltwater/Muskie-size casters have the minnow tail shown in the photos. All also have the combination round diving lip/forward hook hanger. There are nine different lures in the series, each in small and/or large size with different hook configuration and some jointed version making a total of 23 for the entire line. Each was available in a choice of 13 paint finish patterns except for the BASS-CASTER and the DACE-CASTER. The former was made in 18 patterns and the DACE-CASTER was made in dace coloring only. This makes the collection of all these quite a challenge if you're so inclined. Add 1/4" to any sizes in the list for the length of the jointed version of the lure. Be careful not to mistake the WOUNDED TROUT for one of this series. The lures are similar, but have clearly different characteristics.

A comparison shot. Top lure is a BASS-CASTER. Middle: MUD MINNOW (note the curved, convex tail). The lower lure is a WOUNDED TROUT. Photo courtesy Jim Muma

The MUD MINNOW is not considered a CASTER-BAIT by some collectors. It is listed and illustrated in the same group, on the same catalog page. It is even called a MUD MINNOW CASTER in the list. It may be that it suffers from the same catalog mistake as did the WOUNDED TROUT. The fact that it is the only one with the rounded (convex) tail sets it apart. These subtle differences make collecting even more interesting. Collector value range: $40-$100.. The CASTER-BAITS are listed following:

PIKE-CASTER - Shape and action of a baby pike. Made in two sizes, 3-1/2" and 5-1/2", both straight and jointed. There were three treble hooks on the large size and two on the small ones.

PERCH-CASTER - Swimming and darting action. Made in two sizes, 3-1/2" and 5". Both in straight and jointed models. Hook configuration same as above.

CHUB-CASTER - Imitates a chub minnow. Iridescent finish. Made in two sizes, both straight and jointed, 3-1/2" and 5" with two treble hooks.

SHINER-CASTER - "Shimmering silvery markings like the live shiner minnow." Two sizes, 3-1/2" and 5" with two treble hooks.

DACE-CASTER - "Shimmering pearl finish." Made in two sizes, 3-1/2" straight and jointed and 5" straight only. Two treble hooks. Natural dace coloring only.

TROUT-CASTER - "True to nature shape and action." Made in two sizes, 3-1/2' and 5", both straight and jointed. Two treble hooks on small size and three on the large.

BASS-CASTER - One size at 2-1/2". Two treble hooks. "Shimmering pearl finish."

MUD MINNOW CASTER - One size at 3-1/4". Two treble hooks.

SALT WATER AND MUSKIE-CASTER - Sometimes called the DREADNOUGHT by collectors this lure was made in a 6-1/4" size, both straight and jointed. Three treble hooks.

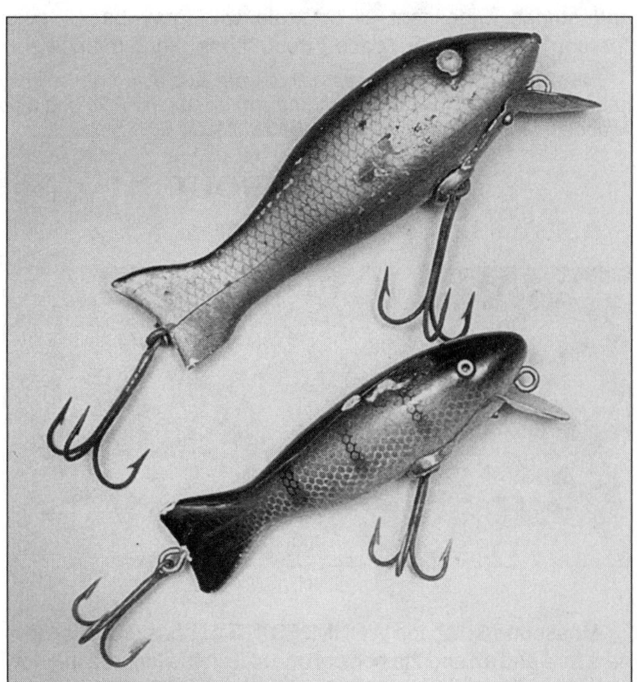

Upper lure is a SHINER-CASTER and the lower, a BASS-CASTER.

A 3-3/4" jointed CHUB-CASTER.

Two 2-1/2" BASS-CASTERS.

COLOR OR FINISH: Yellow perch, green with gold scale, white with red head, silver scale with green back, natural pike, green bach with silver flitters, yellow scale with black back and stripes, silver scale with red back and gray stripes, gold scale with red stripes, natural gold scale, silver scale with red head and stripes, iridescent silver scale with gray back, *pike, *perch, *chub, *shiner, *dace, *trout, *bass, *mud minnow.

With rare exceptions, these colors were available only on their namesake CASTER-BAITS. Each of them, except the Pike and Mud Minnow, were also available on the BASS-CASTER.

WOUNDED TROUT
7700-S Series

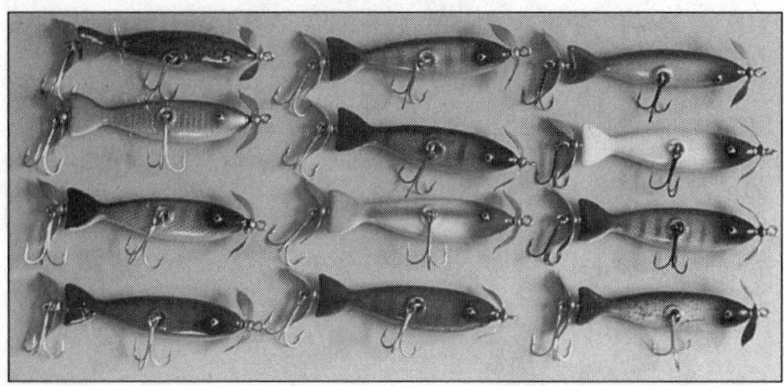

Measuring 3-1/2" the WOUNDED TROUT has propeller spinners fore and aft and the hook on the side in the "injured minnow' style as well as a tail treble. It dates to about 1939. It is often confused with a Paw Paw lure that uses the same body. As a matter of fact Paw Paw added to this confusion by listing it in their catalog with their CASTER-BAIT series listing where there was also a TROUT-CASTER. Here was its listing there:

WOUNDED TROUT-CASTER - A new surface bait, equipped with head and tail spinners. Action of a wounded minnow. 3 treble hooks. 13 popular patterns. That's all accurate data, but misleading because of where it was located. The picture accompanying is of 12 of the 13 patterns available. The color patterns are listed with the CASTER-BAIT Series. Again, do not confuse these with them. The colors are the same, but the characteristics are different. Collector value range: $300-$400.

UNDERWATER MINNOW
3300 Series

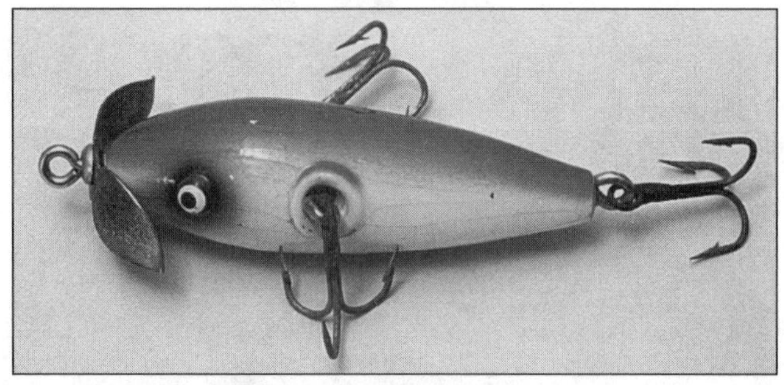

Found only in a 1939 edition of the catalogs. It measures 2-1/2" and has three treble hooks, typical painted cup hardware and a nose-mounted spinner. Colors listed were: Yellow perch, green with gold dots, white wit red head, rainbow, pike scale, perch scale, frog, silver flitters. Collector value range: N/A.

PUMPKIN SEED, No.1300 Series

First available sometime in the 1930s, these small lures have two propeller spinners, a trailing treble and belly-mount treble utilizing cup and screw eye hardware. Made only in a 1-7/8", 1/2 oz. size, the colors available were: Yellow perch; green, gold dots; white, red head; rainbow; pike scale; perch scale; frog; silver flitters. Collector value range: $20-$40.

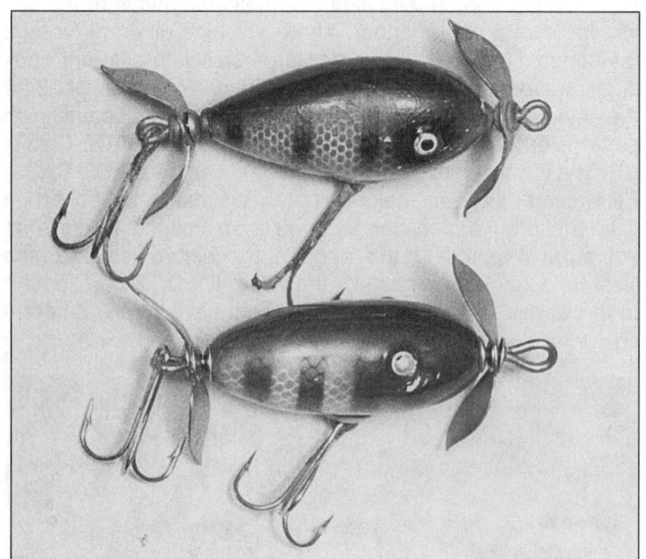

Upper left: The old model JIG-A-LURE with glass eyes. Lower right: The newer model.

JIG-A-LURE, No. 2700 Series

LITTLE JIGGER, No. 2600 Series

Described as new in the 1942 catalog, this lure underwent a metamorphosis by 1949 and was gone from the catalogs by the 1960s. Its first incarnation was as a handsome little plug with glass eyes. By 1949 they had been replaced in production by painted eyes. Both had a metal belly plate that was a dive or wobble plane at the nose and terminated at the tail as a another plane. The LITTLE JIGGER was listed and illustrated along with the JIG-A-LURE. It is the same lure with a feathered treble. Collector value range: N/A.

CATALOG SERIES #	BODY LENGTH	LURE WEIGHT
2700	1-5/16"	5/8 oz.

COLOR OR FINISH: Perch, red head with white body and silver metallic, *pike, red stripe and scale with gold sides and white belly, silver body with white scale and blue stripe, yellow body with red head and gold metallic, black with silver flitters.

**Missing from the 1949 color list. It was apparently replaced with the black with silver flitters finish.*

SHORE MINNOW
#2400 Series

This boxed, mint condition plug has #2407 on the box. The #2400 Series was not found in available catalogs. The #2400 in the photo above is white with a red head and measures 4-3/8" in body length. Collector value range: $15-$25.

PAW PAW PLENTY SPARKLE

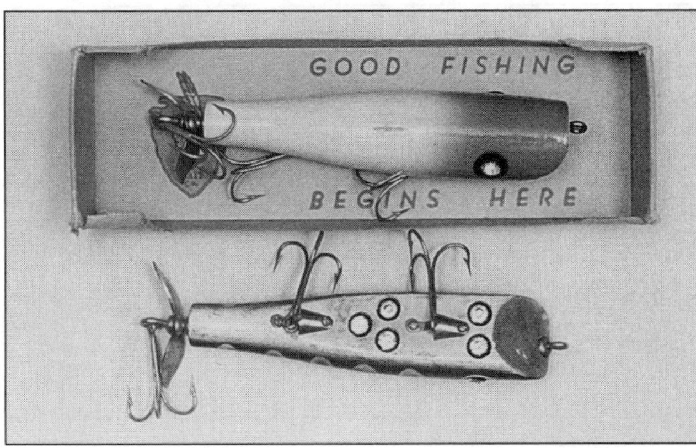

Aptly named, this wooden lure came in two sizes. The one in the photo is the larger (4") size and the other is the Plenty Sparkle Junior at 3-1/4". The larger size has five rhinestones on the belly as in the photo and the smaller has only three. Both have rhinestone eyes. Box marking identified the Series as No. 5500. Collector value range: $20-$30.

SKIPPY MINNOW

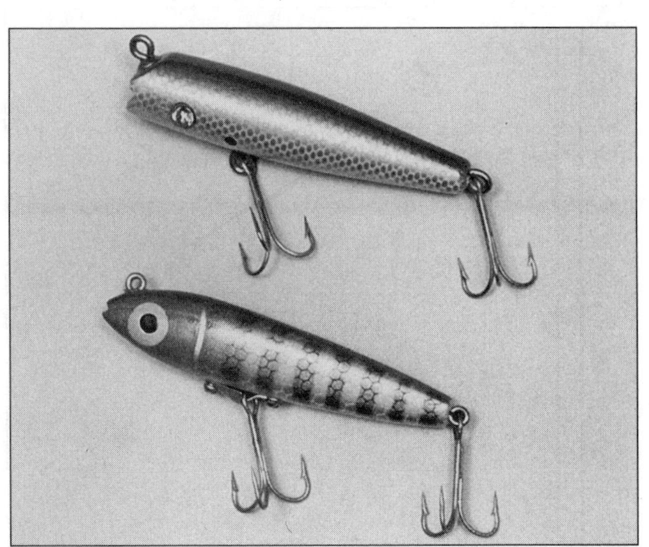

Neither of the two lures in the photo above actually match the illustrations in the catalogs and are otherwise unidentified. They are placed here because of their similarity to the catalog entries. Collector value range: $10-$15.

THE SHINER
THE LITTLE SHINER

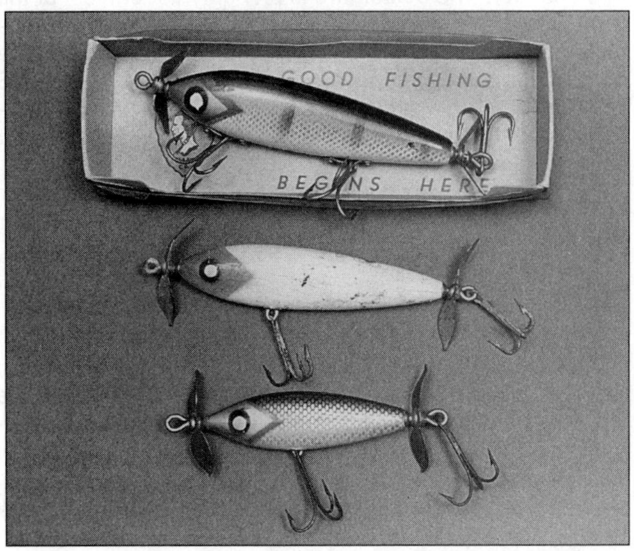

First available in a 1942 catalog. The boxed lure in the photo is the #8501 yellow perch finish. The lures were made in weighted and non-weighted models and in a "Jr." size.

Appeared in the 1949 catalog. THE SHINER was featured in a box with the TORPEDO headed "New Double-Strength Lures for Southern Fishing." It was made as a sinker and a floater. The LITTLE SHINER was made only as a floater. Collector value range: $10-$20.

CATALOG SERIES #	BODY LENGTH	LURE WEIGHT
8400 (Jr.)	2-3/4"	3/8 oz.
8500	4"	1/2 oz.
8600	4"	3/4 oz.

COLOR OR FINISH: Yellow belly with brown and silver back, yellow perch, green scale, white with red head, shad, pike scale, silver metallic, *shad, *frog, *black with silver ribs.

**Only on the LITTLE SHINER in 1963*

SLIM LINDY or TORPEDO
MIDGET SPINNING TORPEDO

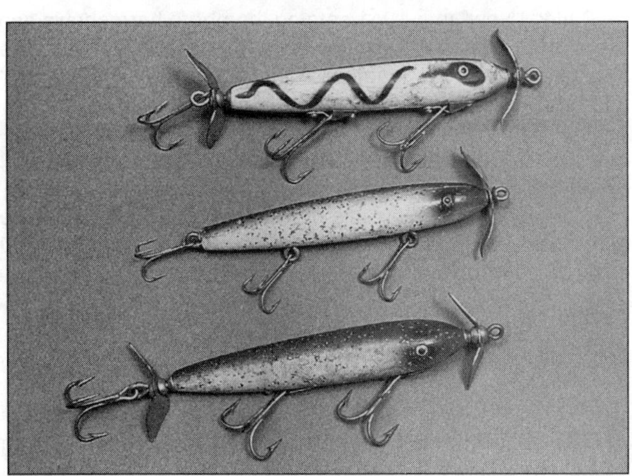

In a 1929 catalog this lure was called SLIM LINDY apparently in honor of Charles Lindbergh, who made his famous trans-Atlantic solo flight in May of 1927. It was the TORPEDO by 1939 or so. They were made in a sinking model only until the late 1940s when they added a floating version. The photo shows three hardware types to be found. The upper lure is the latest, having the one-piece hook hanger. The center lure is probably the earliest of the three because it has only the simple screw-eye hanger. The tail propeller has apparently been removed. The lure on the bottom has the cup hardware. Oldest of the SLIM LINDYS will likely have glass eyes. The MIDGET SPINNING TORPEDO didn't show up in catalogs until much later. Collector value range: $10-$20.

CATALOG SERIES #	BODY LENGTH	LURE WEIGHT
2400-S	4"	5/8 oz.
2400-F	4"	1/2 oz.
800	1-7/8	?

COLOR OR FINISH: *Green scale, *gold scale, *white with redhead, pike scale, silver flitters, white with black serpentine stripe, white with green serpentine stripe, green with black serpentine stripe, white with vertical black stripe, **yellow belly with brown and silver back, **yellow perch, **shad, **frog, **green with black serpentine stripe, **black scale with yellow belly, coach dog (new in 1949).

**The original finishes available on the Slim Lindy.*

***These were additional colors added in the late 1940s.*

WEEDLESS WOW

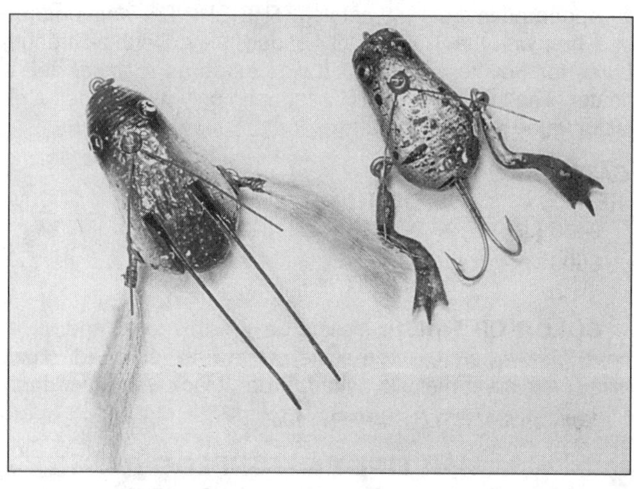

Called "New" in a 1941 catalog the photo here shows two sizes of Weedless Wows. The larger measures 21/4" and the smaller, 1-3/4" body lengths. They persisted in the line well into the 1960s. By the early 1960s they had modified the body by inserting a double hook into the tail end and hanging rubber legs from screw eyes on each side. Collector value range: $25-$45.

Be sure not to confuse this with another Paw Paw lure of the same name. The listing for this 1930s metal spinner No. 700 Series follows below.

CATALOG SERIES #	BODY LENGTH	LURE WEIGHT
600	1-3/4"	1/2 oz.
75 (newer)	2-1/4"	3/8 oz.

COLOR OR FINISH: Perch scale, pike scale, red head, frog finish, silver flitters, fluorescent.

WEEDLESS WOW No. 700(METAL)

First found listed in a 1929 Paw Paw catalog this spinner bait was listed at 5/8-oz. It is, however, reported to have been around as early as 1915. It was available with a red, white or black bucktail. Note the free swinging weight. They are not considered complete if this weight is missing. Collector value range: $50-$90.

CROAKER

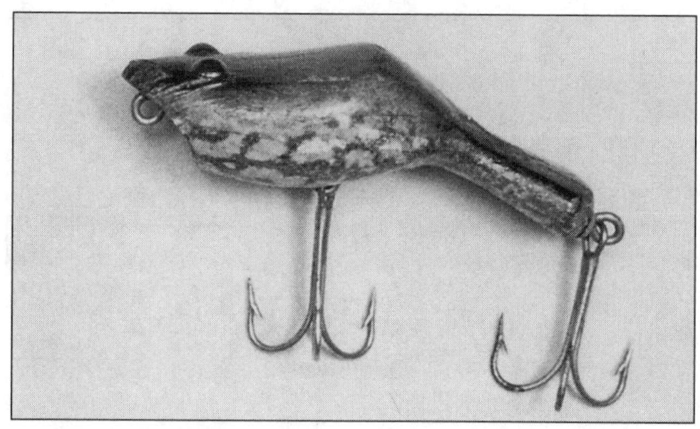

This frog plug was apparently new in 1940. It has a covering of genuine frog skin. It came in two sizes. The one in the photo is the larger (3"). The fly rod size (1-1/4") has a slightly different body design and only one integrated single hook. Collector value range: $75-$125., Fly rod size: $150-$200.

WOTTA-FROG
WOTTA-FROG, JR. (#74)

A catalog listing stated "New for 1941." As you can see in the photo, they had hair or modified bucktails tied to each of the trailing treble hooks. To find them with the hair/trebles intact is fairly unusual. The junior size was new around 1948-49. The WOTTA-FROG persisted on into the 1960s when it was offered without the dive lip also. Collector value range: $40-$75.

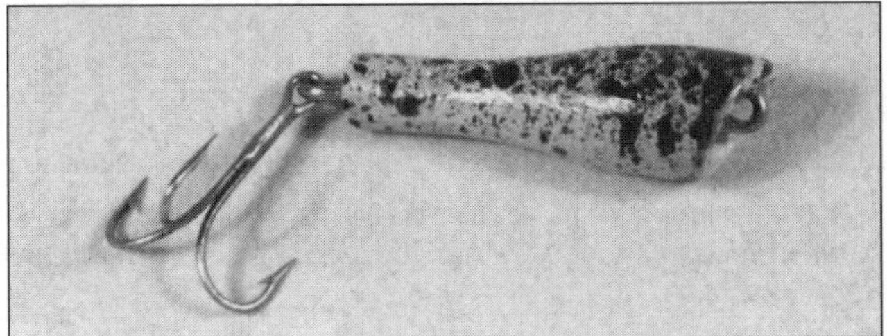

FROG LEG. Photo courtesy Jim Muma.

Another catalog entry for this lure illustrated one leg from the WOTTAFROG lure and called it the FROG LEG. The copy said that a fly fisherman wrote to tell of great success he had when he removed a leg for fly fishing. It apparently was a great success for a short time.

CATALOG SERIES #	BODY LENGTH	LURE WEIGHT	COLLECTOR VALUE RANGE
69F cork body	fly rod lure	N/A	$30-$40.
70F cork body	fly rod lure	N/A	$30-$40.
71F cork body	fly rod lure	N/A	$30-$40.
72GF wood body	fly rod lure*	N/A	$30-$40.
72YF wood body	fly rod lure*	N/A	No trade data
72	2-1/2"	1/2 oz.	No trade data
73	3-1/4"	5/8 oz.	$50-$80.
73L (leg)	1-3/4"	1/8 oz.	No trade data
74	4"	7/8 oz.	No trade data

COLOR OR FINISH: Found in green with paint spatter finish only.

**The wood body fly rod lure was made in green frog or brown frog finish.*

WOTTA-FROG fly rod lures. They measure 1/2" and 1/4" respectively. All have rubber legs. Photo courtesy Jim Muma

BELLY SPOON WOBBLER
BELLY SPOON

I did not find these in any of the 15 catalogs in my collection nor in any advertising. The BELLY SPOON WOBBLER is the upper lure in the photo. It measures a big 5-1/4" long and consists of the lure body attached to a polished metal belly plate. The metal

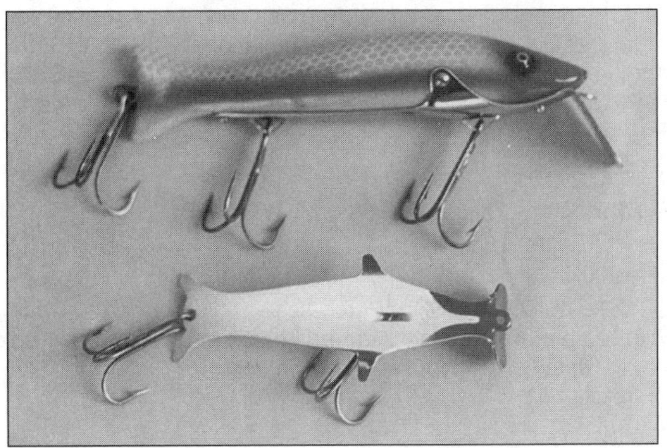

serves as the belly hook holder and the dive plane. Colors are unknown except for the one here which is white with gold scale, red head and stripe. Collector value range: $100-$200.

The lower lure in the photo is the BELLY SPOON. It is obviously a derivative of the metal portion of the other lure. It measures 3-3/4" long and is white with red head and fins. Other colors are unknown. Collector value range: $15-$25.

CENTIPEDE

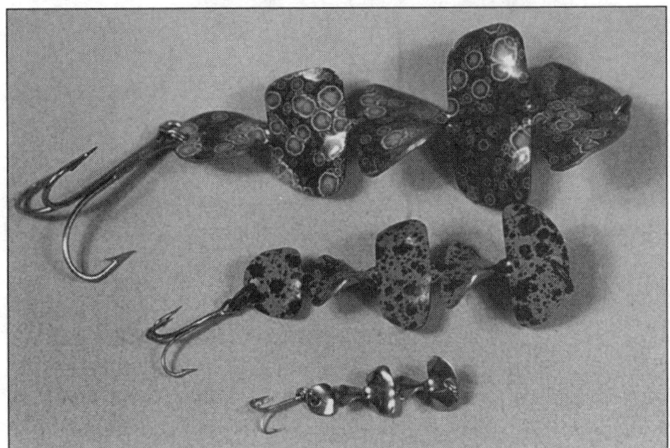

I have never seen anything in catalogs or advertising that lists this name, but some collectors refer to it as such. These three measure 5", 3-1/4" and 1-1/2" respectively. The are made of metal. The only two colors I have seen are the red with black splatter in the photo here, yellow with the same splatter and black with gold. It looks as if the black was not really splattered so much as dropped on the dry red or yellow paint. The Black one looks as if the gold was dropped onto the paint while still wet. It makes a unique pattern of gold spots. The fly rod size at the bottom is unpainted. Photo courtesy Jim Muma. Collector value range: $30-$60.

MISTER 13 Junior, #1800

MISTER 13 Senior, #1900

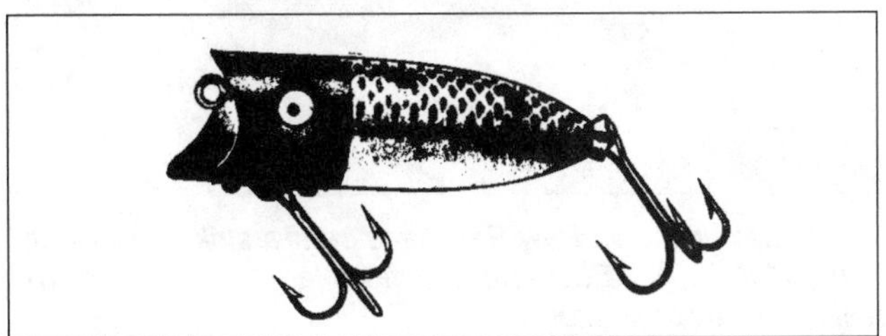

A 1963 catalog inferred this lure was new. It could be an older lure as under the name: "The Sensational 'MISTER 13'" is another phrase: "Now! Available in WOOD or PLASTIC (SPECIFY)". Collector value range in wood: No trade data, Plastic: $5-$15.

CATALOG SERIES #	BODY LENGTH	LURE WEIGHT
1800	2-3/4"	3/8 oz.
1900	4"	5/8 oz.

COLOR OR FINISH: *Perch scale, **yellow perch, white with red head, frog scale with red head, shiner scale with red head, white coach dog, yellow coach dog.

**Plastic only*

***Wood only*

UNIDENTIFIED PAW PAW LURES

None of the following lures were found in any of the Paw Paw catalogs in my collection. They each do, however, share one or more characteristics that make them certain or likely Paw Paw products.

Unidentified Paw Paw casting lure.

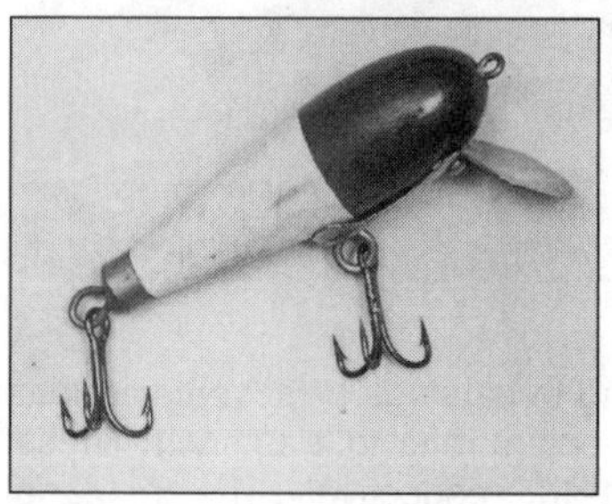

This little fellow has the characteristic Paw Paw combination diving lip and forward hook hanger hardware. It is otherwise dissimilar to any Paw Paw lure found in catalog and illustrations. It was not found in any catalogs.

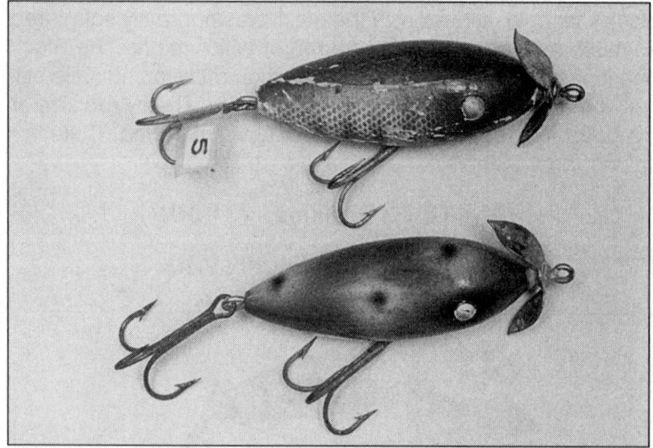

These two unknown Paw Paw lures bear a striking similarity to the PUMPKIN SEEDS but are much larger. Both have typical Paw Paw characteristics.

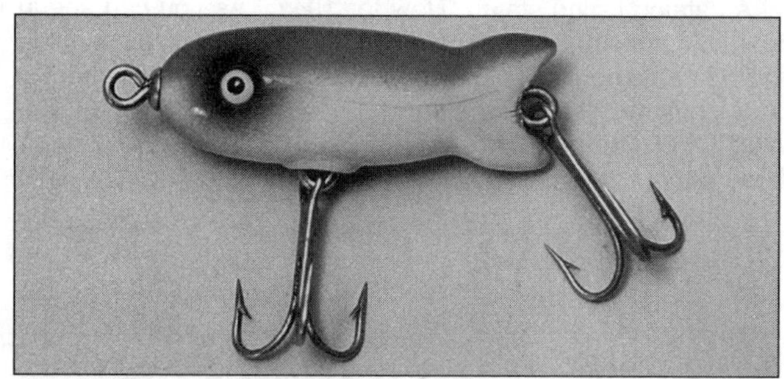

A little 2" minnow in an unmistakable Paw Paw paint finish. Was not found cataloged. It has the typical painted cup hardware also.

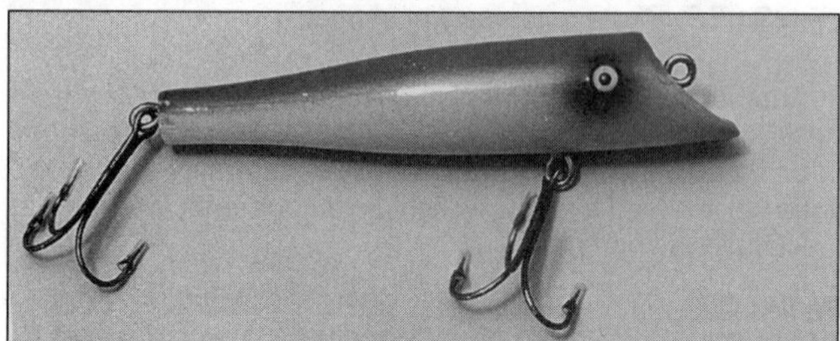

Another unidentified lure with the same paint and hardware as the previous bait. It measures 2-1/2" long.

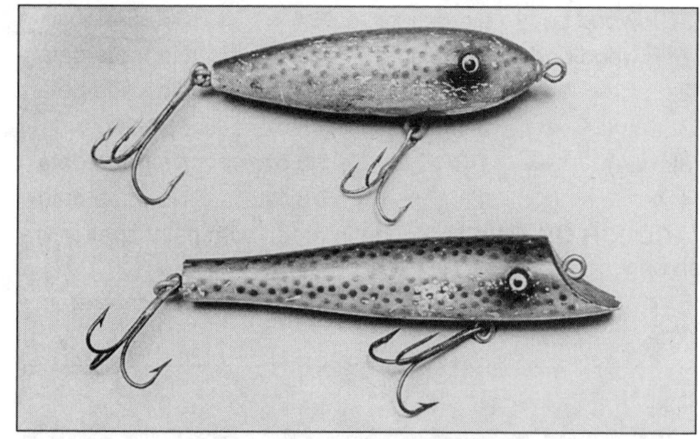

Two lures sporting Paw Paw's distinctive and beautiful Rainbow Trout paint finish. Not found in catalogs. They measure 3" and 3-7/8".

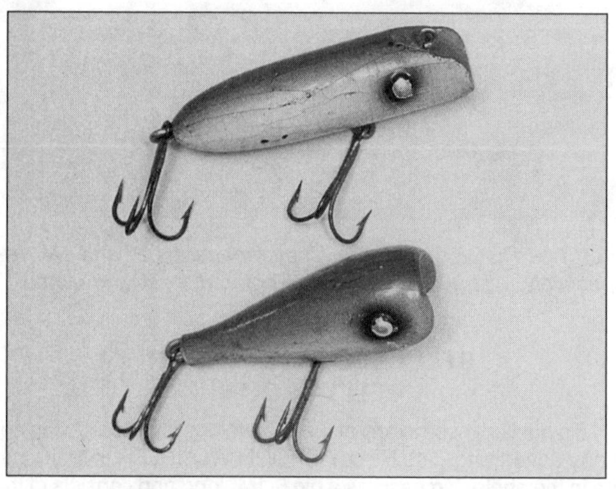

Two unidentified Paw Paw-type lures.

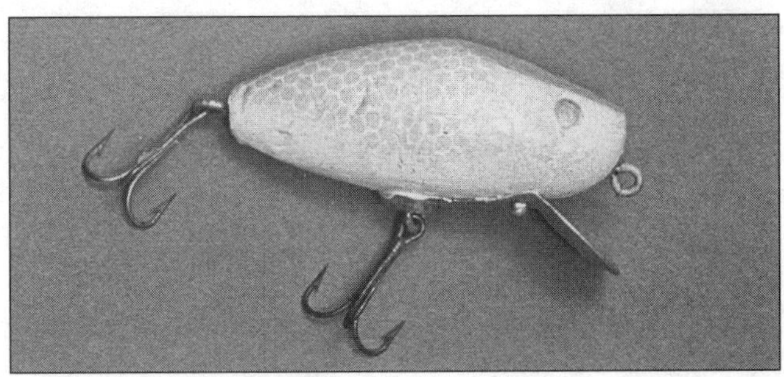

Unidentified Paw Paw lure.

Unidentified Paw Paw lures.

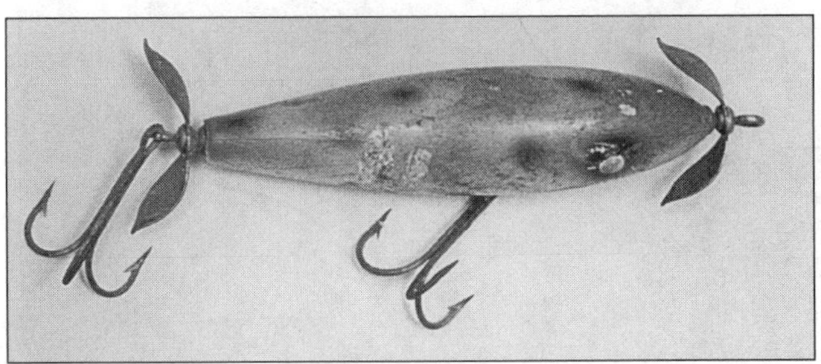

Unidentified Paw Paw lure.

PAW PAW'S "ECONOMY" LURES

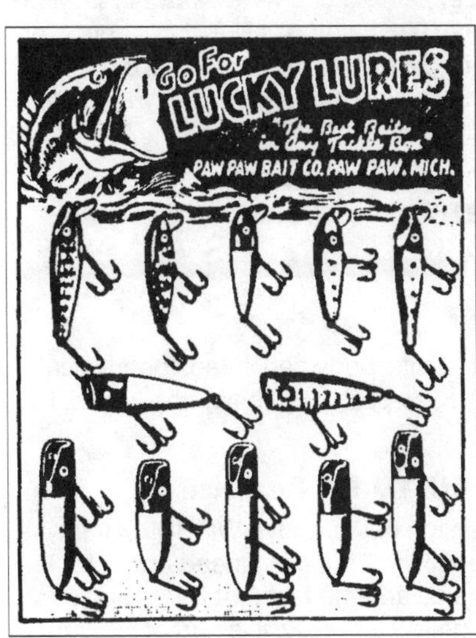

A point-of-purchase card display of Lucky Lures.

It appears that Paw Paw made a selection of lures that were not as expensive to make as their regular lures. These lines were sold at lower prices or, as they say in some of their ad copy, "Designed to meet the popular demand for a good wood minnow at a moderate price."

I think the first of these to come along were the "Zipper" lures in the late 1920s into the early 1930s. Shortly after this their line of carded "Lucky Lures" was offered to tackle dealers. In January of 1939 they introduced a series of 10 "Silver Creek Lures" that they said "Represents the biggest value attainable at such thrifty prices." They also marketed many display cards of up to nine different lures to dealers for point-of-purchase display in the early 1960s. These were called "Make 'em Strike" lures; "...Priced for Competitive Selling."

What would be really neat would be to find a complete card of LUCKY LURES or the boxed ZIPPER ASSORTMENT.

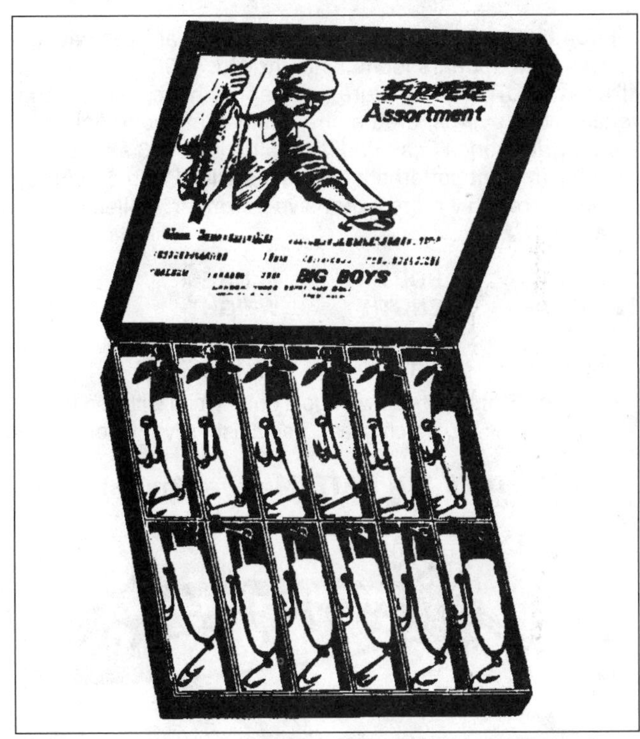

An assortment of 3-1/2" Zipper lures called Big Boys in a display box. The spinnered lure is called the BIG BOY SURFACE ZIPPER and the other is the BIG BOY SWIMMER ZIPPER.

Display card of Make 'em Strike lures by Paw Paw.

PIKE

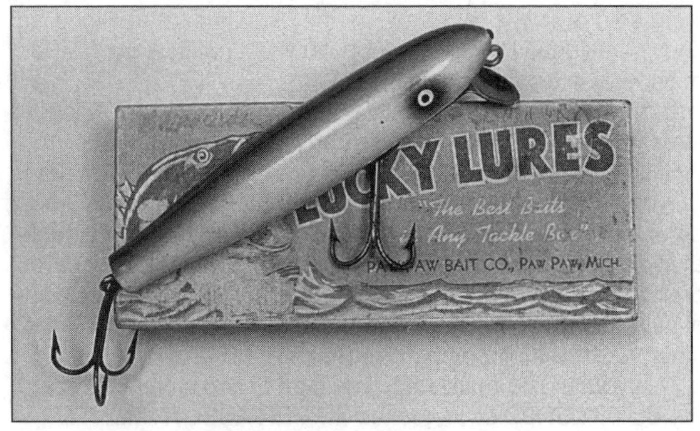

Found in its original box this lure is typical Paw Paw all the way. It is appears identical to the No. 1600 series PIKE MINNOW LURE. They were the same shape, length and weight. They even shared some of the same color finishes. The only difference I can find is that the No 1600 series was available in paint patterns, such as Metallic, Pearl and Frog, that were probably more expensive to render. Collector value range: N/A.

CATALOG SERIES #	BODY LENGTH	LURE WEIGHT
1400	3-1/4"	*1/2* oz.
1600	4-1/2	3/4 oz.

Color or Finish: green with gold dots, white with red head, rainbow, pike scale, perch scale, frog finish, silver flitters.

CLOTHES PIN BAIT (Make 'em Strike)

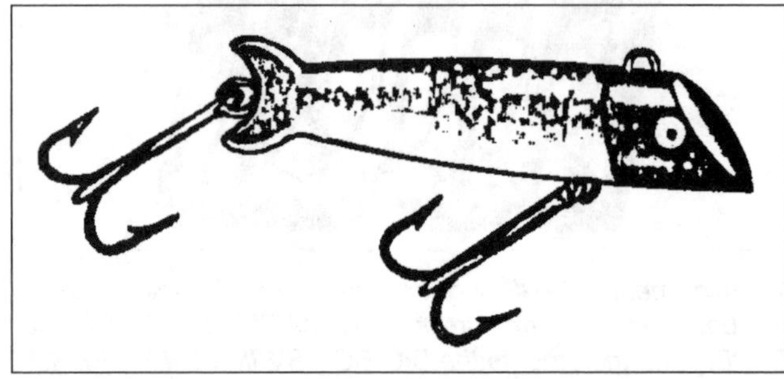

Almost all the major players in the lure business in the 1930s and 1940s had a clothes pin type lure. Paw Paw was no exception. It was listed as available in the 1939 and 1941 catalogs as part of the "Make 'em Strike" line. Collector value range: N/A.

CATALOG SERIES #	BODY LENGTH	LURE WEIGHT
2300S	1-1/2"	1/4 oz.
2300M	2-1/2"	*1/2* oz.
2300L	3-5/8	5/8 oz.

COLOR OR FINISH: Yellow body with red head and silver flitters, white body with red head, rainbow, silver flitters, red head with spotted body, Christmas tree (metallic).

McGINTY (Make 'em Strike)

A tiny 1-1/8" wood body brass wing lure. Its catalog listing said it was "A spinning Pickerel and Bass lure." Collector value range: $35-$45.

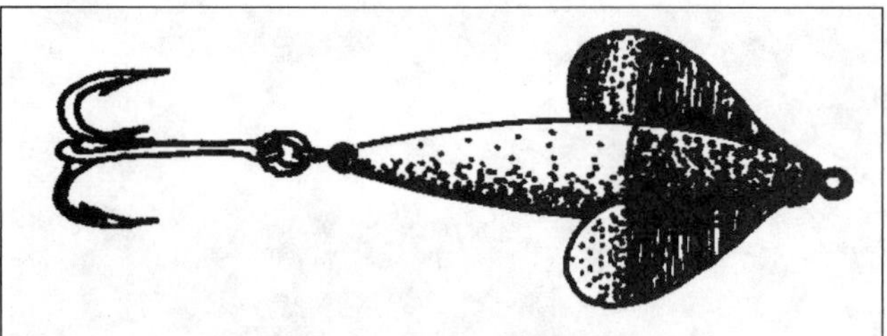

CATALOG SERIES #	BODY LENGTH	LURE WEIGHT
8000	1-1/8"	?

COLOR OR FINISH: Copper with red head, white with red head and flitters, rainbow trout, silver flitters, gold spotted, green and white spotted.

WOBBLER (Silver Creek Lures)

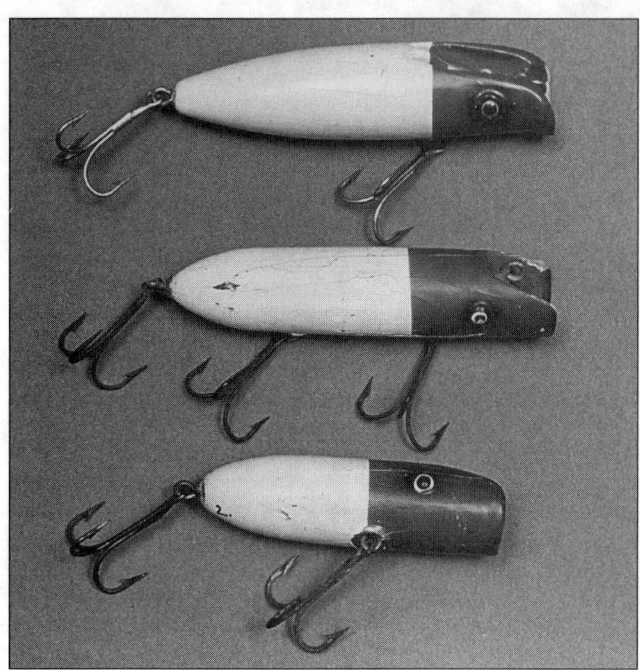

The photo above shows two of the three sizes to be found. The upper and center lures illustrate slightly different body designs. Each has the typical painted cup hardware. I first found the WOBBLERS listed in a 1938 catalog calling them new. Catalog copy says they were part of an extension of the line of lures "... lower in price, but lacking nothing in quality and workmanship..." Collector value range: $10-$20.

CATALOG SERIES #	BODY LENGTH	LURE WEIGHT
4100	2-1/2"	?
4200	3"	*1/2* oz.
4400	3-3/4"	3/4 Oz.

COLOR OR FINISH: White body red head; perch scale; pike scale; silver flitters; yellow perch; rainbow; frog; white, red and green spots.

GROOVE HEAD Fly Rod Lure

This is a tiny fly rod version of the above WOBBLER. It was not part of the "Silver Creek Line," but it is a dead ringer for the WOBBLER except for its size and the fact that it was equipped with a double hook at the belly. Curiously, it is part of the "Make 'em Strike" line. Collector value range: $10-$15.

CATALOG SERIES #	BODY LENGTH	LURE WEIGHT
700	1-5/8"	?

COLOR OR FINISH: Yellow perch, white with red head, rainbow, silver scale, natural pike, green scale, silver flitters.

PAW PAW PLASTIC LURES

The company marketed its first plastic lure in 1941 with the FLAP JACK and followed in 1942 with the Tenite FLOATER-SINKER. That was pretty much it until 1949 when their catalog ballyhooed "Sensational NEW PAW PAW PLASTIC BAITS." They introduced 12 lures as being newly offered in plastic. Three of them, however, were two models of the FLAP JACK and the FLOATER-DIVER introduced 7-8 years earlier. So it was really only nine new lures. At the same time they began offering a new finish on the plastics: FIREPLUG finishes. They are listed following: Neon red; fire orange; sodium yellow; saturn green; rainbow;

They added one more plastic lure, the WOGGLE BUG, in 1963. They continued production of many of the wooden lures right up until the Shakespeare purchase in 1970.

FLAP JACK, No. 3600 Series

FLAP JACK, JR., No. 6500 Series

MIDGET FLAP JACK, No. 6600 Series

FLAP JACK PHANTOM, No. 3400 Series

THREE HOOK FLAP JACK, No. 5300 Series

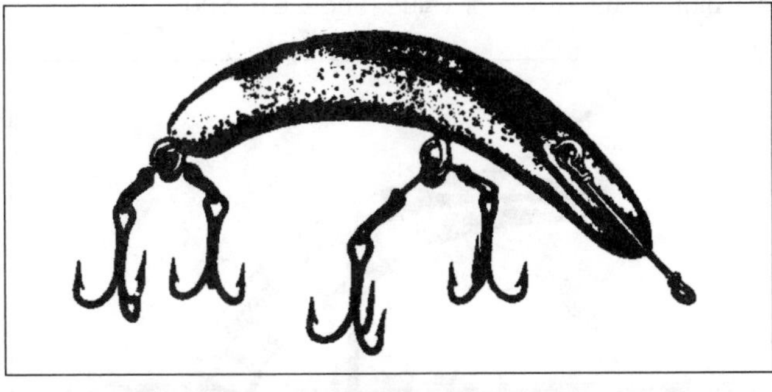

The lure in the accompanying drawing is of the "New Improved" FLAP JACK that was introduced in the 1963 catalog. The first one, introduced in 1941, was the same shape, but it had complicated "ball bearing" hook hardware where by four separate treble hooks hung from metal pieces located on each side fore and aft. The hooks dangled on wires attached to the inside of the metal piece. Presumably there was a ball attached to the end of the wire inside. Thus, ball bearing. This illustration was at the front of the catalog. Curiously the same shape of lure was offered in the interior of the catalog with fewer colors. It had simple cup and screw eye hardware with one belly treble and a trailing treble. I have never handled one, but I suspect this one is wood. In 1949, when they introduced the plastic lures there was another called the FLAP JACK PHANTOM that appeared to be fatter than the original. It had its own set of colors.

By the early 1960s the lure had evolved to the one in the accompanying photo and was available in a three hook version and two smaller sizes, the FLAP JACK, JR. and the MIDGET FLAP JACK. Collector value range: $5-$10. Photo courtesy Jim Muma.

The FLAP JACK is one of a few Paw Paw lures Shakespeare continued to offer after they bought the company. Unlike the others, they did not change the name. These are 1970s lures.

PAW PAW

CATALOG SERIES #	BODY LENGTH	LURE WEIGHT
3400	3-1/2"	3/4 oz.
3600	3-1/2"	3/4 oz.
5300	3-1/2"	3/4 oz.
6500	2-1/2"	1/4 oz.
6600	1-1/4"	1/16 oz.

COLOR OR FINISH (Original FLAP-JACK): Perch scale, white with red head, *pike scale, silver flitters, yellow and black with red spots, *orange with red and black spots, *light orange with red tip and black spots and top, *white with red tip and top and spots, *green frog, *yellow with red tip and black top and spots, *yellow with red and black spots, white with red and black spots, fluorescent, *white with red head.

**The only colors available in the 1949 catalog.*

COLOR OR FINISH (FLAP JACK PHANTOM): Yellow scale with silver ribs, green scale with silver ribs, white with red head and silver ribs, silver scale with black ribs, green with silver flash, orange scale with black ribs.

By 1963 there were only four color choices left for any of the lures. The FLAP JACK PHANTOM had disappeared. The colors left were: White with red head, frog, orange with red and black spots, yellow with red and black spots.

CATALOG SERIES #	BODY LENGTH	LURE WEIGHT
3600	3-1/2"	3/4 oz.
6500	2-1/2"	1/4 oz.
6600	2"	1/16 oz.

COLOR OR FINISH (Shakespeare): Silver flitter, perch scale, green shad, orange with black and red spots, yellow with black and red spots, frog, silver with black spots, chrome with blue scale, day glow orange, white with red head.

FLOATER-SINKER
DAPPER DAN (Shakespeare)

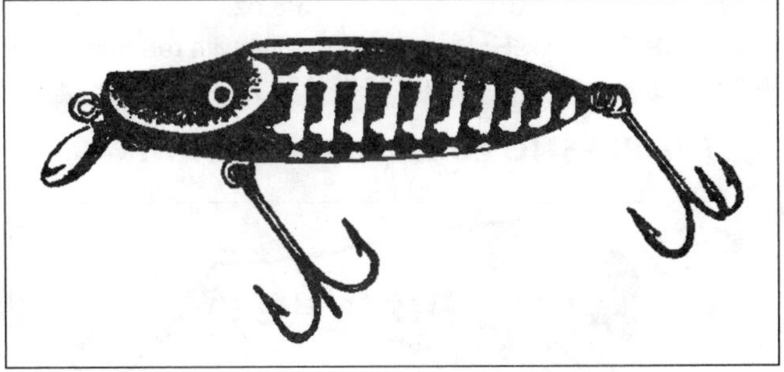

This bait was introduced in 1942. As the name indicates, it was made in two models, a floater and a sinker. The MIDGET was a smaller model of this plastic lure that was introduced as new in 1949. Please see that listing below for color patterns for the MIDGET Collector value range: $5-$10.

It was another of the Paw Paw lures that Shakespeare continued to offer after they bought them out in 1970. The had three versions: DAPPER DAN I, II and III.

PAW PAW

CATALOG SERIES #	BODY LENGTH	LURE WEIGHT
3700	3"	5/8 oz.
3800	3"	5/8 oz.
3900	2-1/4"	3/8 oz.

COLOR OR FINISH (Paw Paw): Yellow perch, white with red head, *red with white head, pike scale, black with white ribs, *silver with white ribs, silver with black ribs, yellow with white ribs.

**These two colors were no longer available by 1949.*

SHAKESPEARE

CATALOG SERIES #	BODY LENGTH	LURE WEIGHT
3700	3"	1/2 OZ.
3900	2-1/2"	1/2 OZ.
4000	2-1/4"	3/8 OZ.

COLOR OR FINISH (Shakespeare): Perch scale, black and white shore minnow, yellow shore minnow, rainbow, yellow coach dog white with red head.

WOGGLE BUG

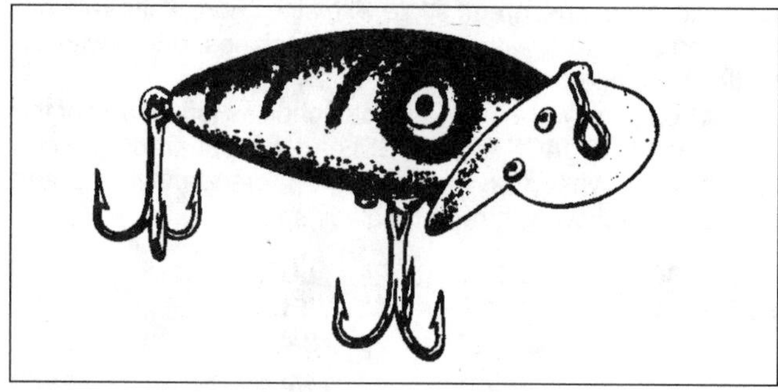

"Sensational NEW!" was the heading over this lure in the 1963 catalog. Looks like Paw Paw decided to get on the Arbogast JITTERBUG band wagon. This lure has exactly the same action. Collector value range: N/A.

CATALOG SERIES #	BODY LENGTH	LURE WEIGHT
WB-700	2-1/4"	1/4 oz.
WB-900	3"	5/8 oz.

COLOR OR FINISH: Perch scale, white with red head, pike scale, frog, silver flitters, black scale with yellow belly.

THE PLASTIC LURES RELEASED IN 1949

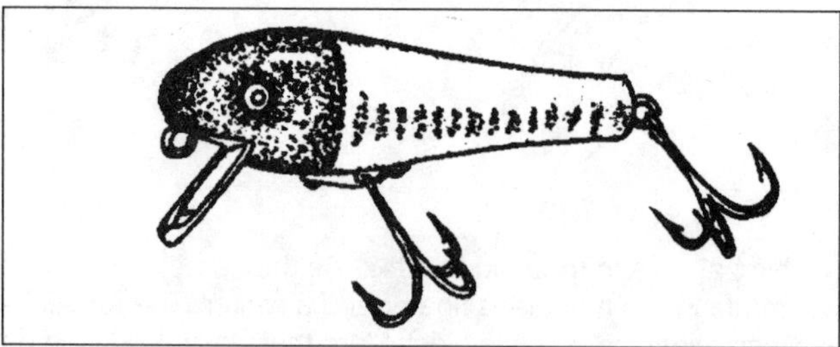

These are a group of lures that were illustrated on one page as newly released. There were no other details beyond size, weight and colors found.

SHORE MINNOW, No. 200 Series - 2-3/4", 1/2 oz. Collector value range: $5-$10.

COLOR OR FINISH: Yellow with belly scale and silver ribs, green with belly scale and silver ribs, dark red with silver metallic, white with red head and silver ribs and belly scale, black with silver metallic, orange with black ribs and belly scale, white with red ribs and belly scale, gold with gold metallic.

TRANSPARENT ZIGGER, No. 300 Series. This is the same lure as the ZIGGER below, in difference color patterns. It has exactly the same color choices as the SHORE MINNOW above. Collector value range: $10-$15.

ZIGGER, No. 400 Series - 3", 1/2 oz. Collector Value range: $10-$15.

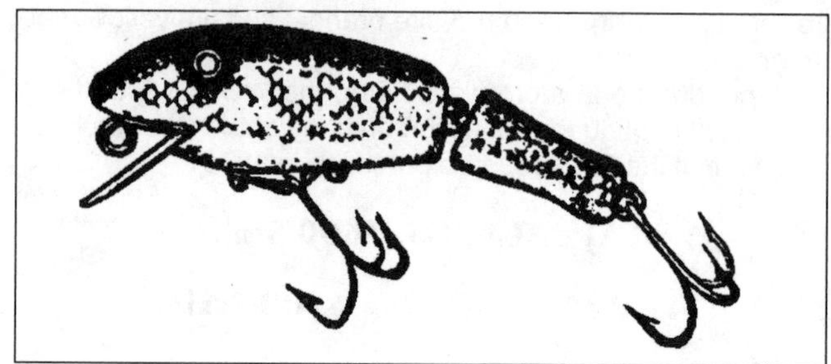

COLOR OR FINISH: White body with black back and scale, perch scale, white body with red head, shad scale, dace scale, pike scale.

CRAZY MIKE, No. 3300 Series - 3-1/2", 3/4 oz. Photo courtesy Jim Muma. Collector value range: $10-$20.

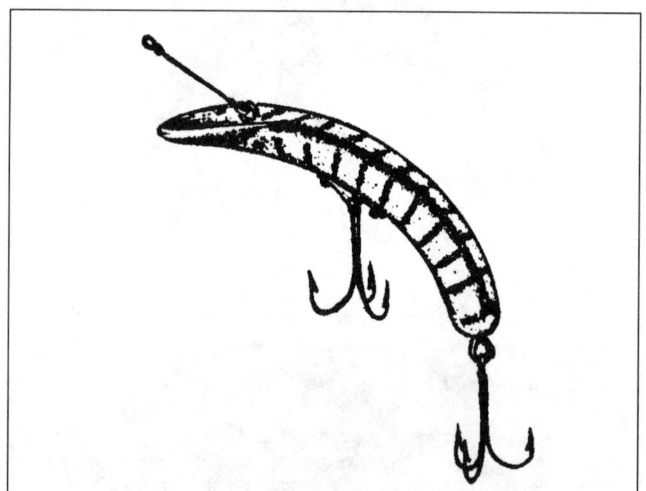

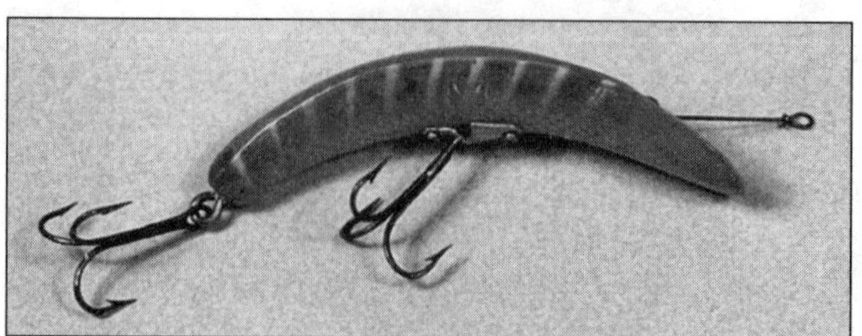

COLOR OR FINISH: Yellow scale with silver ribs, green scale with silver ribs, white with red head and silver ribs, silver scale with black ribs, green with silver flash, orange scale with black ribs, fireplug finishes above.

PLATYPUSS, No. 3500 Series - 3-1/2", 5/8 oz. Photo courtesy Jim Muma. Collector value range $10-$20.

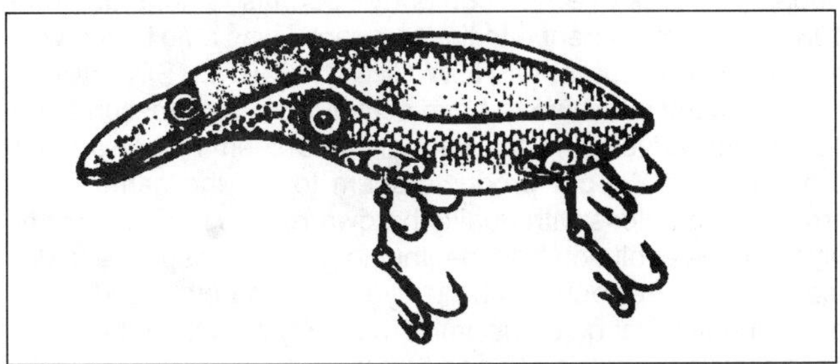

COLOR OR FINISH: Perch scale, white with red head, shad scale, pike scale, frog, dace scale, trout, orange with black spots, black with silver flash, yellow with black spots.

LIPPY JOE, No. 3000 Series

LIPPY JOE, No. 4000 Series

LIPPY SUE, No. 4100 Series

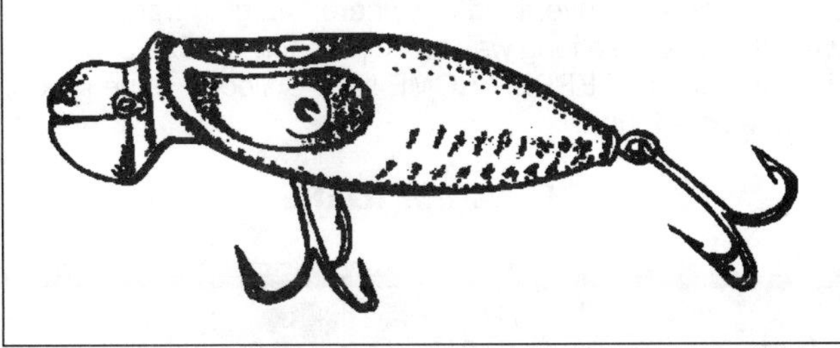

Don't confuse these two with the wooden lures of the same name. These are the plastic versions. the LIPPY SUE seems to be merely the standard lure with the addition of a feathered trailing treble hook. Collector value range: $10-$15.

CATALOG SERIES #	BODY LENGTH	LURE WEIGHT
3000	3"	*1/2* oz.
3100	3"	*1/2* oz. LIPPY SUE
4000	2-1/2	3/8 oz.
4100	2-1/2	3/8 oz. LIPPY SUE

COLOR OR FINISH: Yellow scale with silver ribs, green scale with silver ribs, white with red head and silver ribs, silver scale with black ribs, yellow perch, white scale with silver ribs, frog, black with silver flitters, *fireplug finish.

**No. 3000 and No. 4000 Series only.*

WIGGLE DEEPER, No. 7500 Series. This lure is exactly the same as the LIPPY JOE except it has a long deep diving lip. The colors were the same, including the fireplug finish. Collector value range: $10-$20.

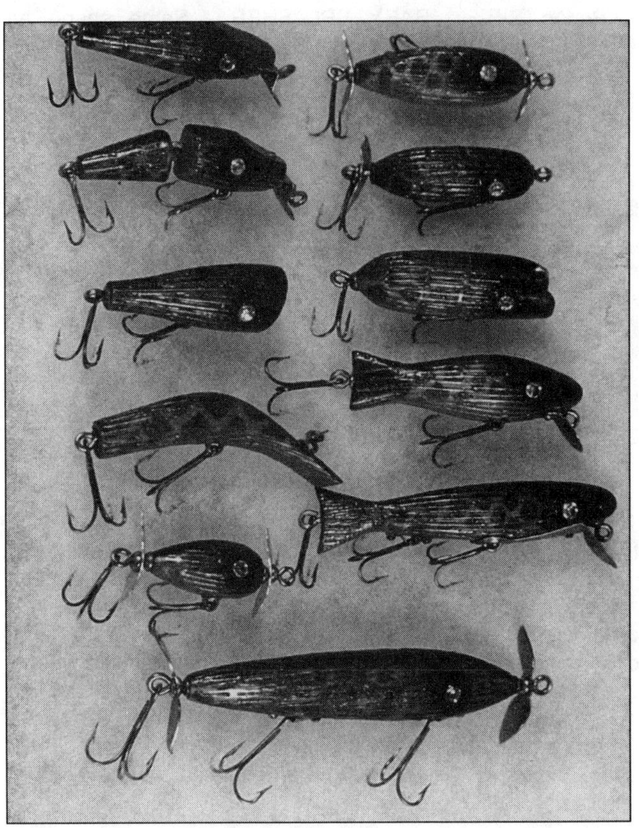

BONEHEADS. Left to right on Top row: SWAMP MINNOW, MISS FLATSIDE. Second row: JOINTED SWAMP MINNOW, TAIL SPLASHER. Third row: BRIGHT EYED POPPER, BONEHEAD WIGGLER. Fourth row: LAZY IKE, THE WOBBLER. Fifth row: BABY SPLASHER, STRUTTIN' SAM. Bottom: SOUTHERN TORPEDO. Photo courtesy Jim Muma.

BONEHEADS

This was a series of twelve different lures that came out in the 1960s. They have corrugated plastic on wood bodies that ostensibly caused them to leave a trail of bubbles behind upon retrieve. Its only finish was a gold body with brown spotting. It looks as if it was produced by spraying the large gauge netting of some sort. They have rhinestone eyes and various configurations. Eleven of them are in the accompanying photograph. All are listed following, with descriptions. Collector value range: $15-$35.

Series 12-a	NO NAME - Same shape as a FLOATER-SINKER. 2-3/4", 1/4 oz.
Series 8555	SOUTHERN SWAMP MINNOW (see photo). 4", *1/2* oz.
Series 12-B	JOINTED SWAMP MINNOW (see photo). 2-3/4", 14 oz.
Series 12-C	BRIGHT-EYED POPPER - Same shape as a POPPER. 2", 1/4 oz.
Series 12-D	MISS FLATSIDE - Same shape as a FLATSIDE. 2", 1/4 oz.
Series 12-E	TAIL SPLASHER - Same as above w/o tail spinner. 2", 1/4 oz.
Series 12-F	BONEHEAD WIGGLER - Same shape as BASS SEEKER. 3/8", 1.4 oz.
Series 12-G	WIGGLIN' MINNIE - Same shape as CASTER BAITS. 2-3/4", *1/2* oz.
Series 12-M	STRUTTIN' SAM (see photo). 3-5/8", 3/8 oz.
Series 12-N	THE WOBBLER (see photo). 3-3/4", *1/2* oz.

Series 12-S	BABY SPLASHER - Same shape as CASTING LURE. 1-7/8", 1/2 oz.
Series 2455	SOUTHERN TORPEDO - Same shape as TORPEDO. 4", 1/2 oz.

PAYNE'S HUMANE WOGGLE BUG

Payne Bait Co. — Chicago, Illinois

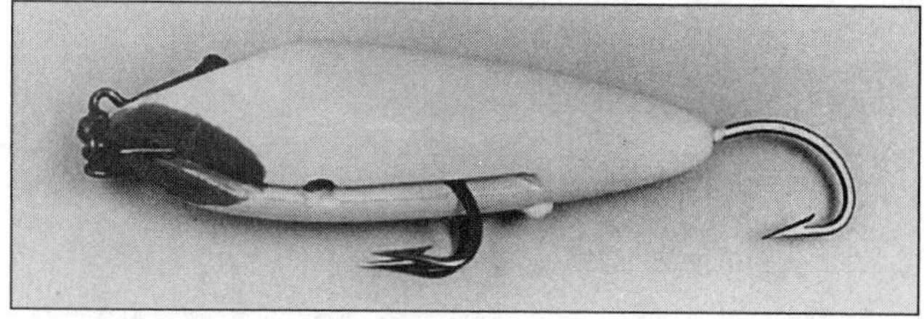

This 3-1/4" plug was available only in white body, red head finish. It was first found advertised in an April, 1915 edition of *The Outer's Book*, a popular outdoors magazine of the era, but seldom found advertised after. The same edition wrote the lure up along with five others as new for 1915. There were metal clips in the body slots to hold the hooks in until a strike whereupon the fish would pull the hook away from the lure body. The above mentioned article claimed that while fishing the lure a fisherman hooked a bass while fighting that fish a second bass struck the trailing lure resulting in a double catch. I have heard taller tales. Collector value range: $500-$1,000.

PELCAN

International Tackle Co. — South Bend, Indiana

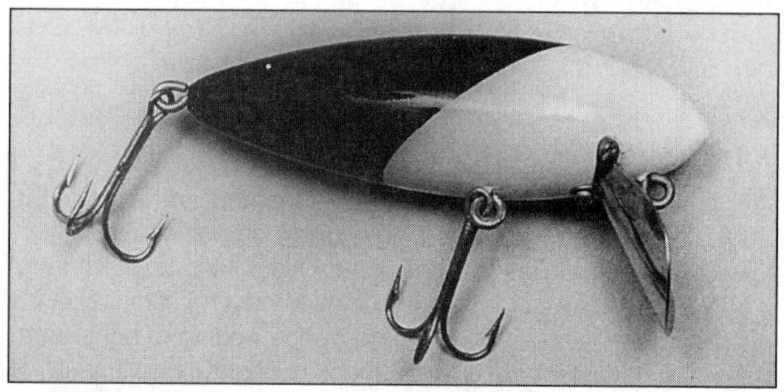

The company called this "THE IDEAL SURFACE LURE". The box was labeled "#201 WB". It has a simple screw eye belly hook hanger and line tie, is black and white in color and measures 3-1/2". It is a wooden lure. I was unable to turn up anything else about the company and its lures. Collector value range: $5-$15.

JOSEPH E. PEPPER

Rome, New York

It is difficult to sort out all known and suspected Joe Pepper lures. Some are readily identifiable as Pepper by obvious characteristics and/or the Pepper name stamped on metal parts. Others attributed to him are a result of his peculiar habit of painting gill strips on the lure opposite to the direction of actual fish gills; the method used by just about every other lure maker. See examples of this characteristic in some of the photos following.

The Pepper name is connected with fishing tackle all the way back to 1860 when Joseph Pepper's father John Pepper went into the rod-making business with Jay Hildreth and John B. McHarg. That business went through some changes over the years (bringing in his three sons). At some point in the late 1890s, son Joseph began his own tackle company. Joseph E. Pepper, Jr. took over the company upon his father's death in 1936. The first reference to the company I was able to find was a 1902 advertisement for NEW CENTURY BALL SPINNERS. The company is known to have continued in business into the 1950s, but advertising for Pepper lures seems to disappear around 1923. Pepper products seem to run the gamut from crude to high gloss with quality hardware. This may have simply been the evolution from beginning to end in response to demand. They are found with no eyes, painted eyes and glass eyes and several quite dissimilar body styles. Often the glass eyes are placed in the head so that the lure appears to be looking forward, forward and up or for some strange reason, cockeyed. This arrangement is, as far as I can determine, a uniquely Pepper characteristic. Many of the metal parts are stamped with his name and/or patent dates. The metal fins he used are most often found painted bright red. Pepper seemed to have used whatever propeller spinners were readily available, for many different types are found on his lures.

WOBBLER

A 2-3/4" wobbling spoon made of brass. I could not find this bait cataloged or advertised anywhere. Judging from the box swivel it does date a long way back; probably c. 1920 or before. It is stamped "JE PEPPER ROME NY". Collector value range: No trade data found.

ROMAN SPIDERS

Bass size.

Baby ROMAN SPIDER.

These came along sometime prior to 1915. The large (4-3/4") Musky size has no notched or split head as do the two smaller sizes. The Bass or Pickerel sizes is 3-1/4" and the BABY ROMAN SPIDER, 1-3/4". Most found have a crackle back finish. All will have string or twine legs or at least the holes through the body where they once were. Each has painted eyes. All are very scarce. Collector value range: $400-$500.

REVOLVING MINNOW

The REVOLVING MINNOW was introduced in 1911. They are extremely well made with high quality paint and hardware. A unique feature is the removable fins. If you didn't want the lure to revolve you simply unscrewed the fins. They are soldered to screw eyes to facilitate their removal without a screwdriver. The side hook hangers are twisted wire through-body. Both in the photos here have yellow glass eyes. The large size is 3-1/2" and the small, 2-1/2". Collector value range: $450-$500.

YANKEE AERO

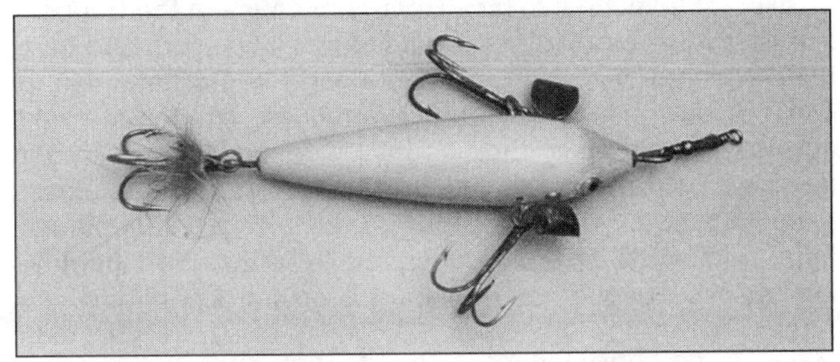

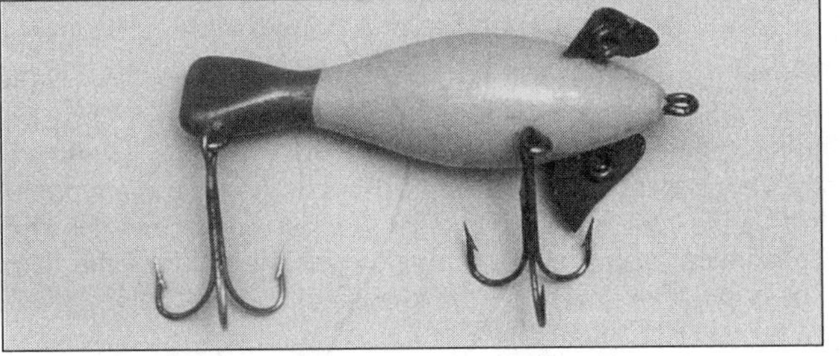

The photo is of the belly of the YANKEE AERO showing the method of providing adjustable or removable fins as discussed in the REVOLVING MINNOW previously. Note the fins are soldered to screw eyes. The lure was said to be available in four colors in an ad, but the only one listed was white with red tail. This very well made 4-1/2" plug was also available in a jointed version. Painted eyes or no eyes. Collector value range: $1,500-$2,000.

ROMAN REDTAIL MINNOW

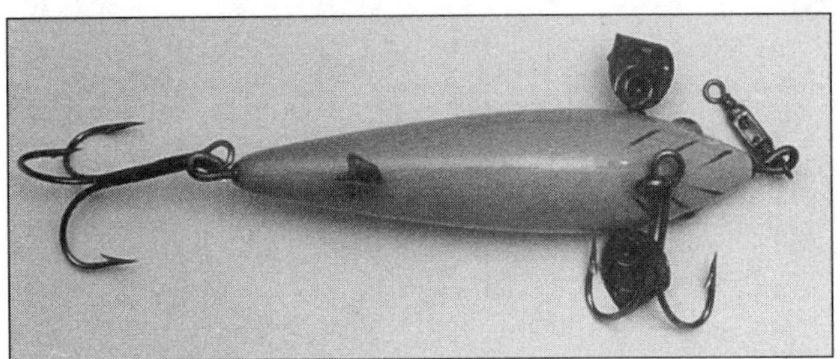

The REDTAIL came along about 1912. Another well made quality lure by Pepper, it too has adjustable side fins. In addition it has another fin fixed at the bottom of the tail. It was made in two sizes, 2-1/2" and 3-1/4", has glass eyes and through-body wire line tie and tail hook hanger. The belly view photo clearly shows the Pepper reverse gill marks. Collector value range: $400-$500.

THE ROAMER BAIT

Two 3" ROAMERS. They each have glass eyes and different styles of spinners. The one on the right has cut rubber bands inserted through the body holes to simulate the original 'legs'. The original 'Legs' were probably the same or similar.

A 1912 Pepper advertisement said that this was "The latest Bait on the Market." The ad text also said the legs were white. Some of these were made with a slant cut on the top of the head where eyes were painted. They were made in two sizes, the standard at 3" and the BABY ROAMER at 1-3/4". Colors available were: Yellow body with green head and green back with yellow belly. Collector value range: $400-$500.

Pepper's 1-3/4" BABY ROAMER BAIT

Pepper ROAMER BAIT body with a slant head.

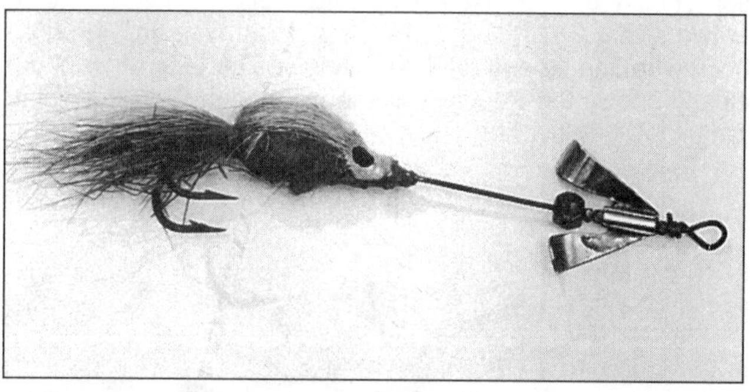

PEP'S DELTA BUG SPINNER. Collector value range: $30-$40.

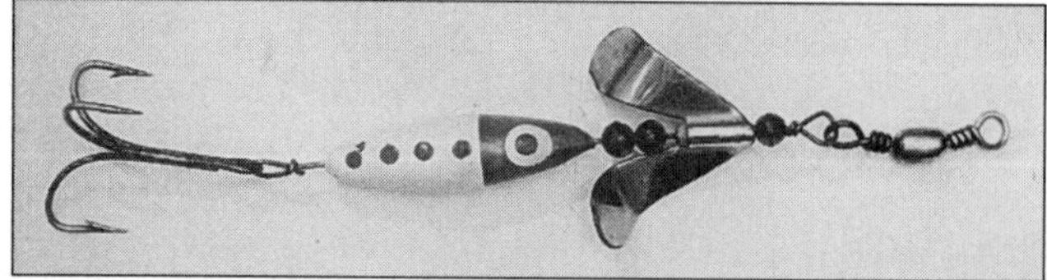

PEP'S STREAMLINE MINNOW. Lead body, red and white. Collector value range: $30-$40.

PEPPER UNDERWATER MINNOW

We can't be absolutely certain that the lures in the two photos here are Pepper products, but hardware and the reverse gill stripes make them likely candidates. Both have yellow glass eyes. The 5T model has cup and through-body wire hook hangers. Collector value range: $200-$300.

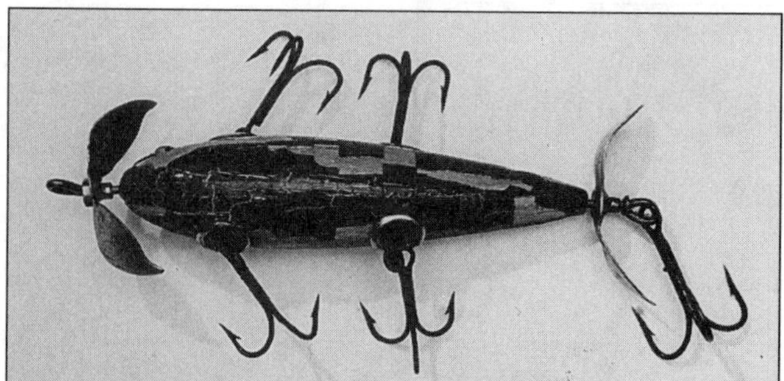

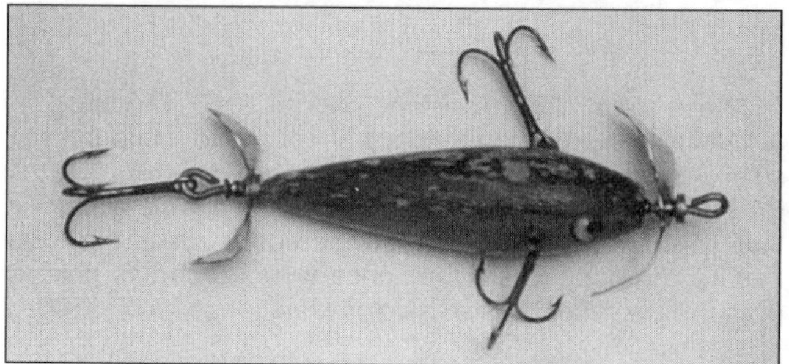

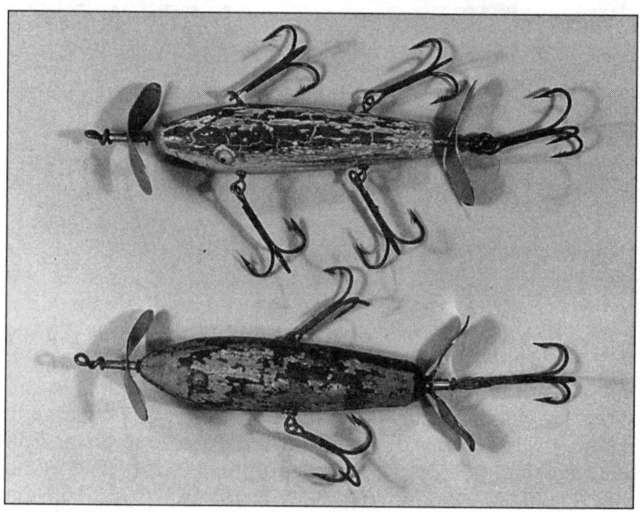

The upper lure in the photo is a known Pepper UNDERWATER MINNOW. The lower lure is not, but was bought by a collector thinking it to be a Pepper because of the Pepper-like hardware. Upon closer examination it was found to be a hand-whittled plug, with decidedly non-Pepper flat sides. It also sports unusual blue glass bead eyes. The latter would not necessarily be a surprise given Pepper's proclivity for using whatever materials were at hand, but the other characteristics say it isn't a Pepper product. This bait is placed here to illustrate how careful you need to be when identifying a possible purchase. If you bit on the lower lure you would have made a $150 to $200 mistake. Collector value range: $150-$200.

"FEATHERTAIL MINNOW"

The two little fellows here measure 1-3/4" and are made very much in the style of Heddon's "Artistic Minnow". The propeller spinner and the forward looking eye on the lower lure are very typical of Pepper lures. The gill marks and shape on the upper lure are also typical Pepper characteristics. he "tube" type prop armature flags this as the older of the two. The real Pepper name for the lure is not known. Collector value range: $600-$700.

No. 885,861. PATENTED APR. 28, 1908.

J. E. PEPPER.

ARTIFICIAL BAIT.

APPLICATION FILED SEPT. 20, 1907.

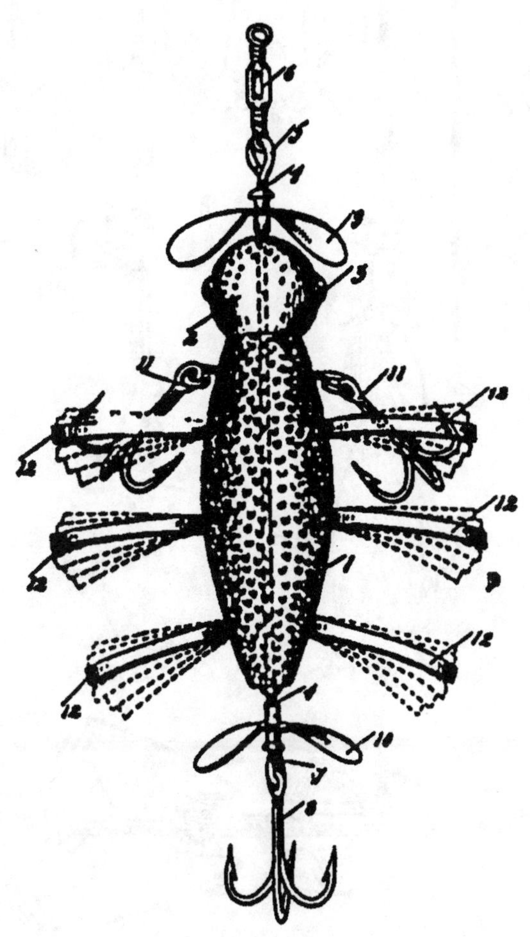

WITNESSES

Sarah E. Clark

INVENTOR

JOSEPH E. PEPPER

BY Robinson, Martin & Jones

ATTORNEYS.

The 1908 patent application drawing for the ROAMER BAIT.

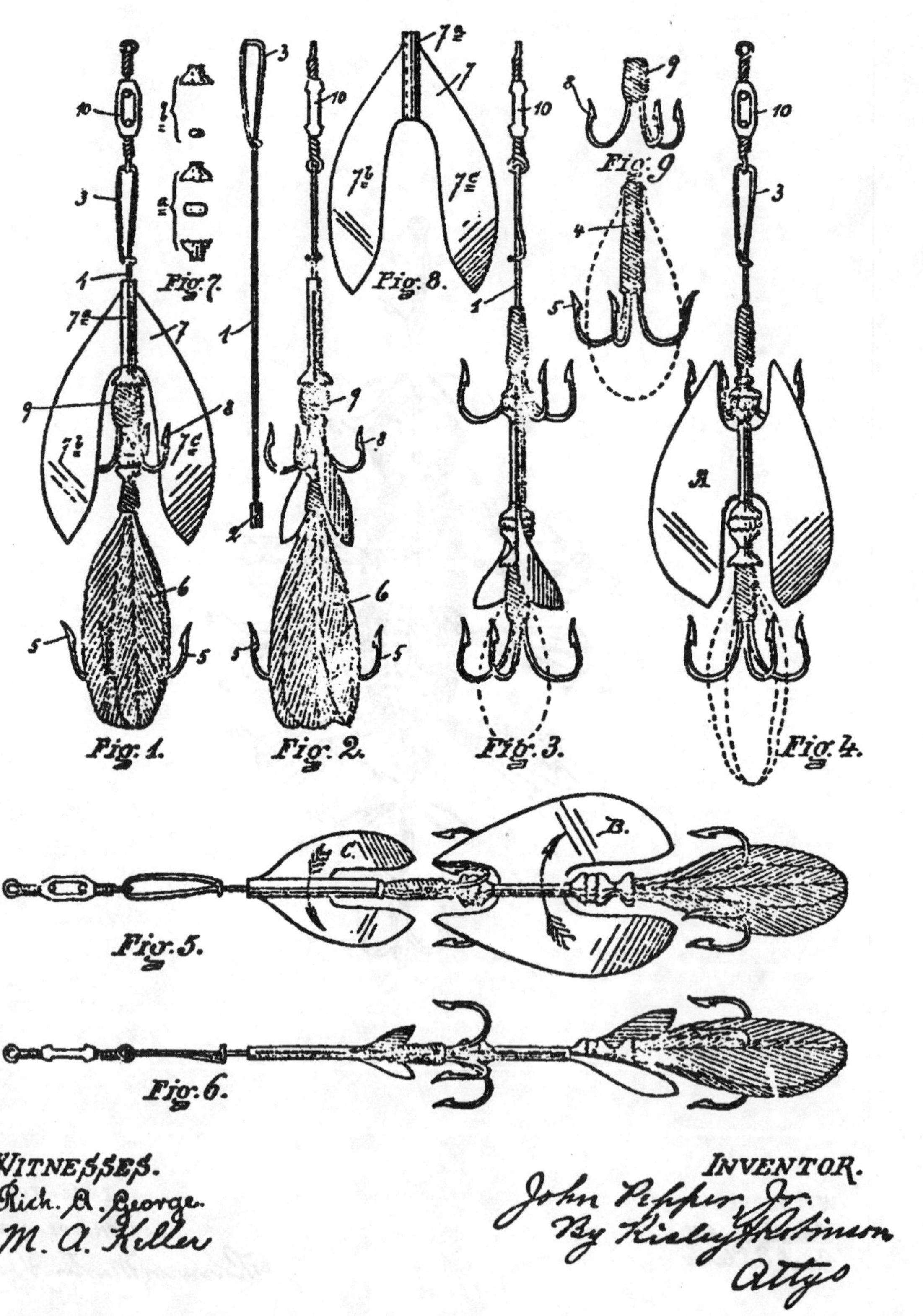

This patent was granted to John Pepper, Jr in 1893 when Joseph, and John, Jr. were in business with their father.

MISCELLANEOUS PEPPER LURES

The following photos are of mostly Pepper lures and a few other unidentified ones for comparison are offered as aid to Pepper identification. Because of the wide variety of styles, quality and hardware encountered with the lures, identification can sometimes prove difficult.

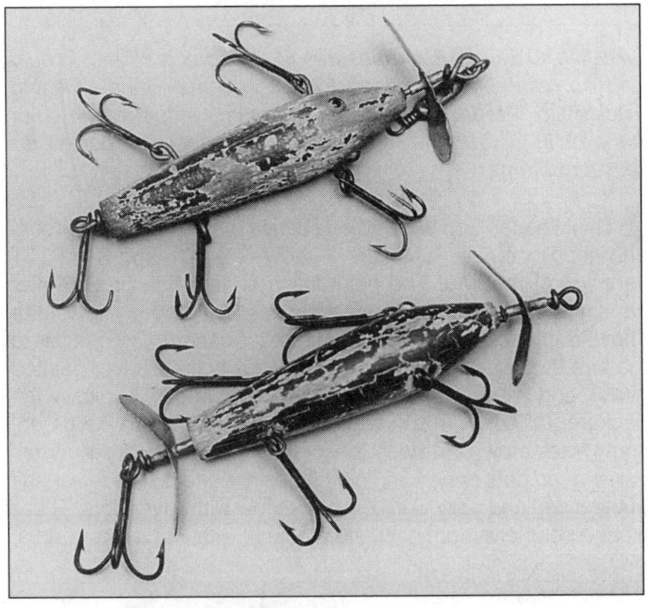

The 2-7/8" Pepper lures here share the same paint, same glass eyes and tube-type propeller spinners. The lower lure has through-body bent wire hook hardware and the upper, through-body twisted wire hardware. Both are found on Pepper lures. There are typical Pepper reverse gill marks visible on the upper lure. Collector value range: $175-$200.

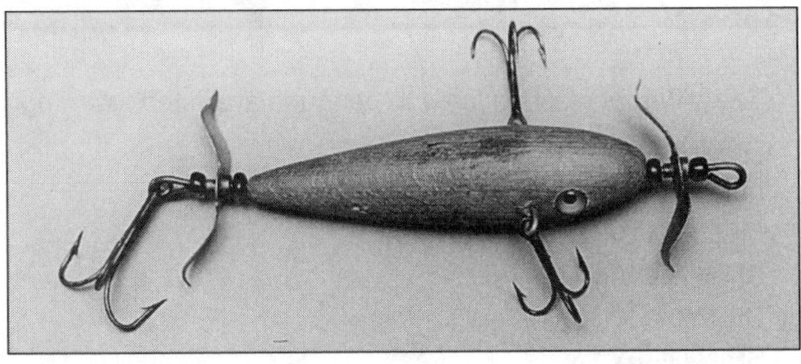

This plug has had the paint finish stripped off. It is a round body lure with big glass eyes. It has a pair of red glass bearing beads fore and aft and Pepper style through-body hook hangers. The second set of hooks is missing from this originally five-hook plug. Collector value range: $175-$200.

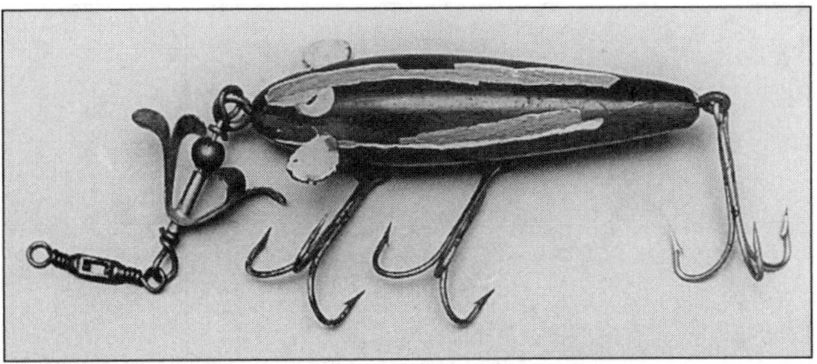

The photo above is of a 3-3/8" lure with painted eyes and a black back and red belly. The fancy propeller spinner is exactly like one on the illustration of the 20TH CENTURY WONDER MINNOW in a 1904 Pepper advertisement. The propeller spinners are unmarked. It has simple screw eye hook hangers. Collector value range: $400-$500.

The lure here measures 2-1/2". It has the same propeller spinner as the previous lure. The inscription "JE PEPPER ROME NY" is stamped on one of the blades. It has yellow glass eyes and has single red glass bearing bead at the nose. There was apparently a second hook, in the belly, for the hole is there. Collector value range: $700-$800.

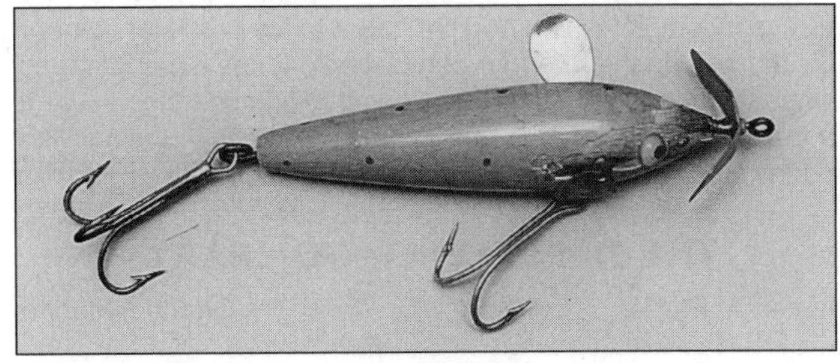

Although they are not easily seen in this photo, the body is decorated with gold dots. This was often used by Pepper. The lure is 3-1/4" and has forward looking yellow eyes. The two metal flippers are attached by a bent through-body wire with washers. One of the flipper blades is stamped "JE PEPPER ROME, NY". Collector value range: $400-$500.

This 3" plug is typical Pepper. It has forward looking yellow glass eyes, a single internalized belly weight and through-body wire hook hangers and line tie. Collector value range: $175-$200.

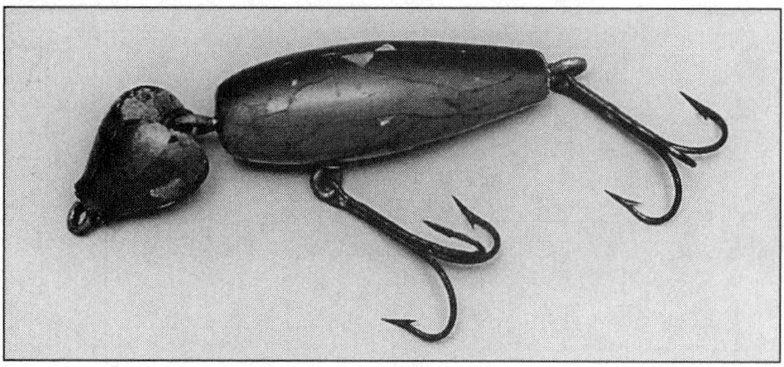

This jointed lure is 3" long. It is not found cataloged in any Pepper literature. It is attributed to Pepper because of the paint job and the fact that it was found in Rome, NY. It has a screw eye and washer belly hook hanger. Collector value range: $175-$200.

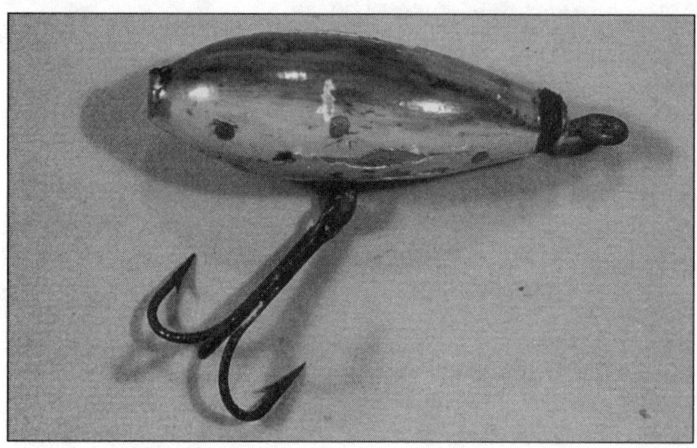

Reported as an unknown in a previous edition, but attributed to Pepper because of the paint finish and design. It is now known that it is definitely a Pepper product. The 1-11/16" lure here is incomplete. The original had a fancy propeller spinner like the one on the lure four photos back. It has a pair of fabric wings attached to its back. The wrapped line used to secure it to the lure can be seen in the photo. It makes the lure look like a June Bug. Collector value range: $250-$300.

THE JIM PFEFFER COMPANY

James A. Pfeffer — Orlando, Florida

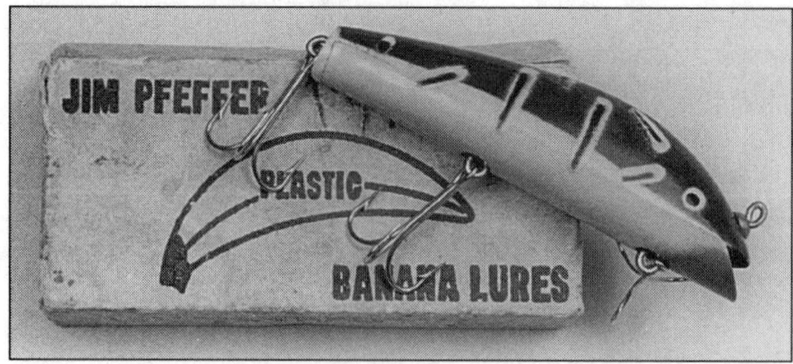

This is a 3-5/8" plastic Pfeffer BANANA LURE #220. It is identified as such on the belly. The box states it was distributed by Pat Woodall Specialties, West Palm Beach, Florida.

Jim Pfeffer carved the first of the famous BANANA LURES out of a piece of cedar in 1938, but the Pfeffer story starts ten years before that. In 1928 he first started carving and painting the ORLANDO SHINER.

Pfeffer hand-carved and the family painted the BANANA LURES up until 1957 when he and a friend, Pat Woodall, made an agreement for Woodall to produce it in plastic and to distribute them. The wooden lures were also hand carved and painted up until Pfeffer made another agreement wherein Woodall was given the right to produce them also, but only in wood. Woodall experimented with a process of coating the wood with aluminum and was successful only on his first attempt so the process was abandoned. It is estimated that there were some 1,000 of them aluminized and at least a few of them are bound to be out there somewhere.

ORLANDO SHINER. It measures 4". The box is wrong. I could find no connection between Pfeffer and the Florida Fishing Tackle Co. Pfeffer did have an enormous influence on color patterns in Florida. His colors were widely copied. Photo courtesy Jim Muma.

This wooden lure has cup and screw eye belly hook hangers and floppy propeller spinners. I know of 4", 3T and 3-1/2", 2T versions of the lure. The paint finish is very typical of Pfeffer lures. A color chart made by a successor company to Pfeffer showed thirteen different patterns, but most are very similar to the lure in the previous photo. They usually have silver painted heads and yellow painted eyes with black pupils. Typically the background color on the back and half the sides was green, sometimes brown, and were decorated variously with yellow, silver and red dots depending on the desired effect. The lower half of the sides and belly were usually yellow with silver dots. There were a couple without dots and a couple with just a row of dots.

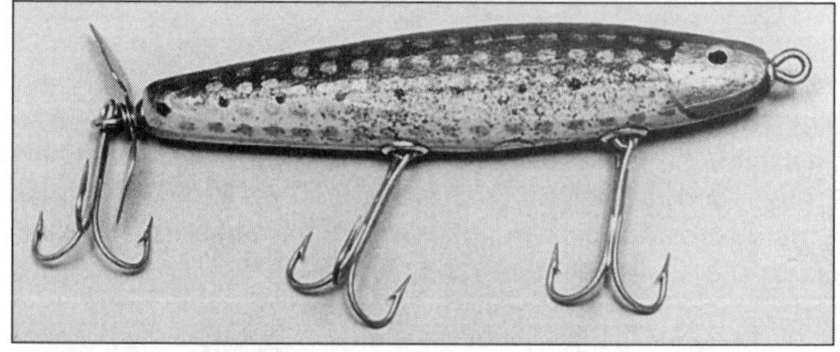

The different wooden lures to be found are listed following:

REGULAR BANANA
MIDGET BANANA
MEDIUM BANANA
SPIN BANANA
DILLY
SPIN DILLY
CAST TOP
SPIN TOP

MIDGET TOP
SAILFISH SHINER
ORLANDO SHINER
HUD-CHUG
CRIPPLE

Most Pfeffer lures are marked with its name on the belly. Collector value range for the Wooden lures: $25-$100, Plastic Banana lures: $8-$18.

PFEIFFER'S LIVE BAIT HOLDER

Pfeiffer's Live Bait Holder Co. Detroit, Michigan

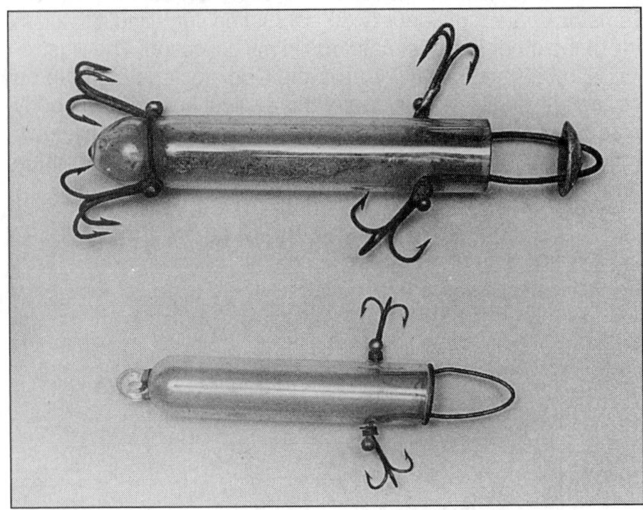

PFEIFFER'S LIVE BAIT HOLDER. It measures 4-1/4" including the metal stopper (cap). It is thought the smaller (3-1/4") one may be a Pfeiffer product also.

The only place I found this one advertised was in the August 1915 issue of *The Outer's Book.* The ad was illustrated and stated "None genuine unless Pfeiffer's name on stopper." The stopper is metal and it is stamped. The ad goes on to say "it is the original bait of its kind. Patented March 3, 1914." Except for the metal stopper (cap), this Pfeiffer lure is remarkably similar to the DETROIT GLASS MINNOW TUBE listed elsewhere in this book. The Pfeiffer bait is found in two sizes, the 4-1/4" size as in the photo and the more rare 3" size.

Other names to be associated with the glass minnow tube style lure are C.E. Henning, the c. 1911 Henning Minnow Tube and Charles C. Kellman.

Collector value range for the 3" size: $700-$1,000, 4-1/4" size: $450-$700.

PFLUEGER

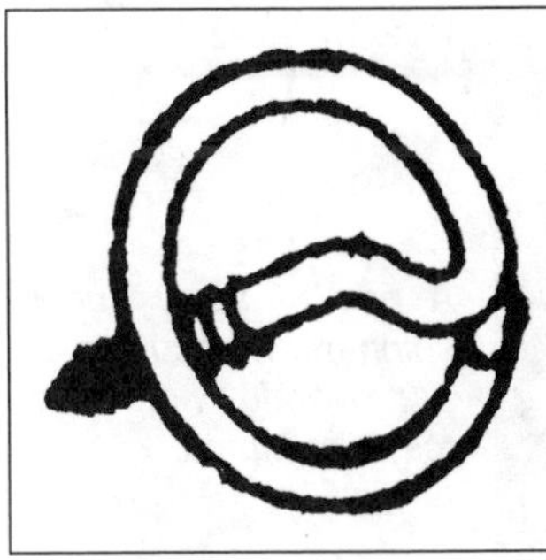

A detail of the 1911 Pflueger patent on their Neverfail hook hanger.

The company was established in 1886 by Earnest F. Pflueger, a German immigrant, as the Enterprise Manufacturing Company. Pflueger has always used 1864 as the establishment date for the company and this has been confusing. The explanation lies in their purchase of the American Fish Hook Company the same year. They were established in 1864. Apparently Pflueger thought that date would lend an air of expertise not given to brand new companies. They continued to use this date. In fact, a quote from their 1919 catalog boasts "..from a start in 1864 in the kitchen of a farm house in Akron, Ohio, through 55 years of earnest, honest endeavor and unremitting hard work, to a position today as the largest manufacturers of fishing tackle in America..". Over the years it continued to exist in the Pflueger family hands as The Enterprise Manufacturing Company, and finally, Pflueger Fishing Tackle. The company has almost always concentrated very heavily in reels and many types of metal spinner and spoon type artificial baits. These metal lures are numerous and most are not covered here. The following pages catalog the majority of the wooden plugs manufactured over the years to the early 1950s.

Pflueger patents include luminous paint on the fishing lures (first used on his lures in the mid-1880s). The patent was granted to him on February 12, 1883. Another important Pflueger patent was for the Neverfail hook hanger granted on October 29, 1911.

OBSERVATIONS REGARDING IDENTIFYING AND DATING PFLUEGER LURES:

1. Hook Hardware

a. First was a through-body twisted wire type. Some were bare and some had a small washer against the body. Neither lasted long.
b. There are a few very early Pflueger lures that used the see-through Gem-clip type hangers. Pflueger even patented this in 1910, but it was quickly abandoned due to the prior Rhodes patent in 1904, for about the same thing.
c. After the above problem, Pflueger developed their Neverfail hardware and it was patented in 1911.
d. Patent date for their one-piece surface hook hanger was 1922, so the transition from Neverfail to one-piece surface should be in the 1920-22 time frame.

NEVERFAIL wooden minnow in a Four Brother box. No explanation for the missing 'S'. Four Brothers was a brand used by the Enterprise Manufacturing Company. Photo courtesy Jim Muma. (see NEVERFAIL listing).

2. Propeller Spinners

a. First used propellers were both bow tie floppy and bow tie tube types.
b. By 1908 the propellers were more refined, smooth edge,

pointed blade ends. It has been reported they used a few one-notch blades at this point, but this was very limited.

c. They began marking their propellers sometime around 1910-12. The first ones were marked only with the word "PFLUEGER". The next mark was the Pflueger Bull Dog brand.

3. Eyes

a. Eye types are not a very good guide to dating Pflueger lures as they used glass eyes, no eyes and painted eyes at the same time through many years. Which they used depended upon which of the four grades of lures they made.

One last note about identification. If you find a lure in a FOUR BROTHERS brand box from the Enterprise company, it is going to date from the 1910s.

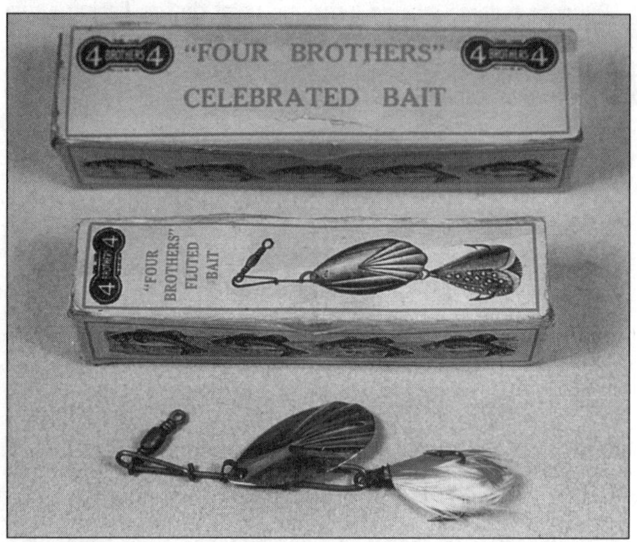

Unknown early Four Brothers (Enterprise Mfg. Co.) spinner and two boxes. Photo courtesy Jim Muma. Collector value range for the lure: $10-$20; for the boxes: $30-$60 each.

EXPERIMENTAL PFLUEGER LURE

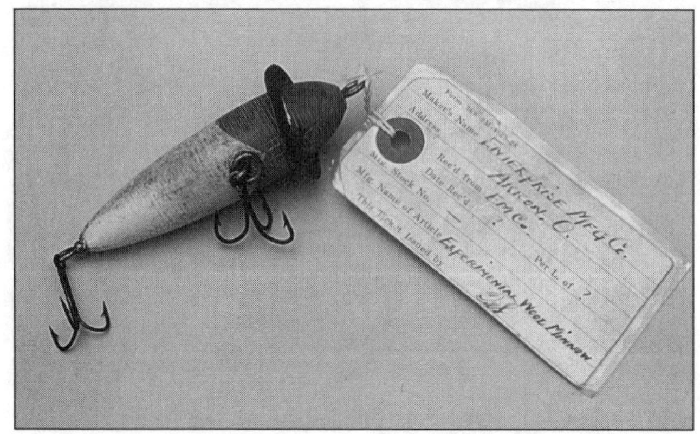

It looks as if Pflueger was looking into the possibility of competing with Heddon's No. 210 DOWAGIAC MINNOW. The lure never went into production. It has the Neverfail hardware so that dates it contemporary with the Heddon No. 210. The card attached to the lure was dated, but the year has been obscured over the years. Unique. No trade data from which to draw any conclusion as to collector value.

FLYING HELLGRAMMITE

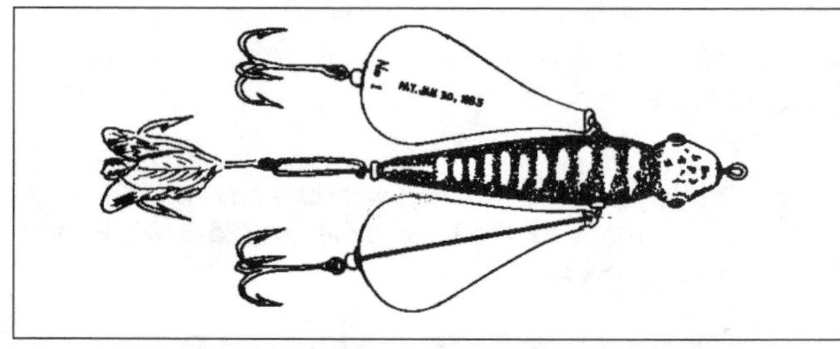

An 1885 catalog offers this very early, very rare wood body lure in four luminous models. It is obviously taken from the Comstock patent of January 30, 1883. I couldn't find it listed in any of the other Pflueger catalogs in my collection. The illustration with the entry clearly shows the Comstock patent date on the metal "wings." This is one of the earliest known wood body lures to be commercially produced. The only earlier one known is the 1876 Brush patent with a cork body. Collector value range: $2,500-$4,000.

BREAKLESS DEVON

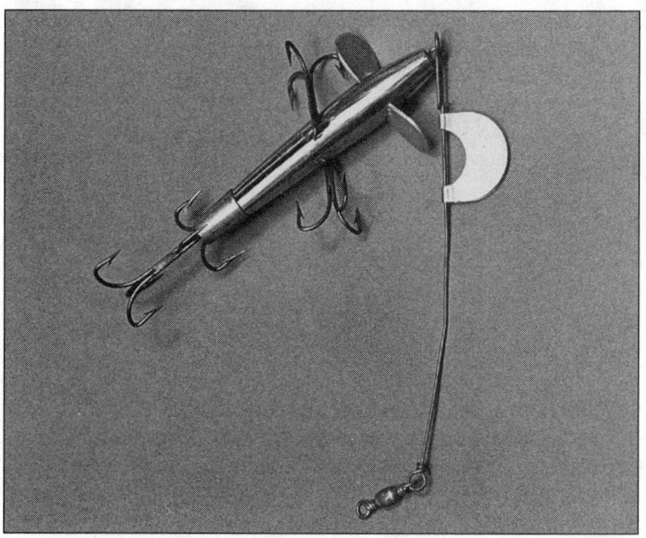

This all-metal lure was patented August 5, 1879 by Archer Wakeman of Cape Vincent, New York. It was routinely offered in the Pflueger catalog of 1897 (earliest in my possession) in five sizes. By 1906 the DEVON was available "Painted" in luminous and non-luminous or in "Brass, Nickel or Gilt." By 1919 the catalog entry was only "Polished Nickel Over All." In the 1920s it was Nickel and Copper only. It gained the single blade spinner in the photo about this time as well. The lure was offered continuously in those two finishes and five sizes right on into the 1950s. Sizes were: 2", 2-1/4", 2-1/2", 2-3/4" and 3". Collector value range: $40-$80.

A pair of fancy spoon spinners measuring 2-1/2" overall. Photo courtesy Jim Muma.

HEART SHAPED SPOON #661
EMPIRE SPOON

These are very early, extremely rare old spinning spoons. They date from around 1897 or before. The unusual sea shell pattern on the HEART SHAPED SPOON is illustrated in the 1897 catalog. The other is a guess based on the shape. The pattern on the spoon was unlike any I could find, but the shape and configuration are definitely Pflueger. Collector value range: $650-$800.

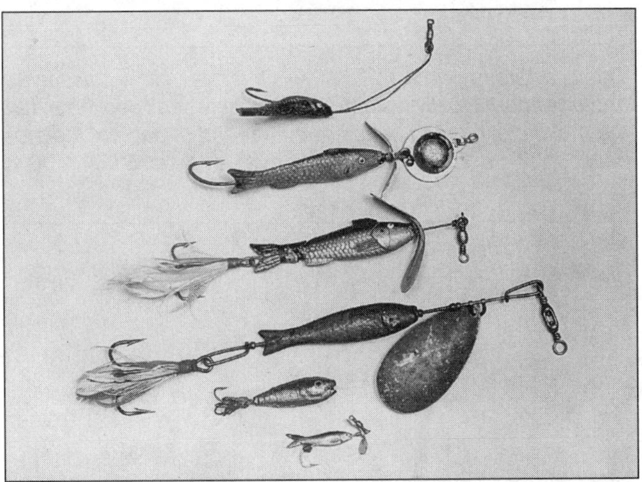

Top to bottom these rubber Pflueger lures are: SOFT RUBBER CASTING MINNOW c. 1897, RAZEM MINNOW, TEEL-AN c. 1930, unidentified rubber minnow, BIZ MINNOW #3400. Collector value range: $50-$200.

TANDEM SPINNER. These measure 2-1/4" and 4-1/4 respectively including the feathered treble hook.

This lure has been in the Pflueger catalogs from at least 1897. The ones in the photograph are not, however, that old. The older one was made in one size only, luminous or non-luminous. Look for the box swivel on the oldest. The newer style came along in the 1920s and have the beaded swivels from then on. Collector value range: $15-$20.

COLORADO SPINNER

This carded spinner is stamped "PFLUEGER COLORADO". The whole spoon is stamped with a star pattern. Pflueger bought the W. T. J. Lowe company in 1915 and carried the line for many years. The Lowe Star spinners were carried, but the catalogs I have don't show this pattern with the Star Spinner illustration. The card states the lure won the highest award for fishing tackle at the Philadelphia Sesqui-Centennial in 1926. It measures 3-1/2" overall including the treble hook. Photo courtesy Ken Bernoteit. Collector value range: $15-$25.

CHUM SPOON

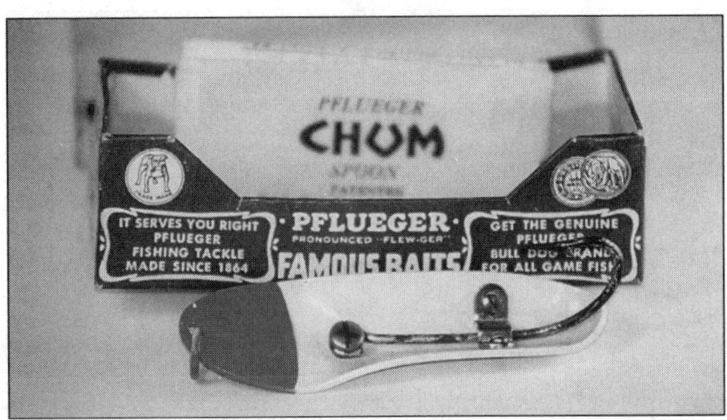

Showing up around the mid to late 1930s, there were several versions of this metal lure. They were available in two weedless models with the traditional wire weed guard as in the accompanying photo and in something called a "horse hair weed guard". The illustration of the latter didn't appear to be particularly weedless. There were five sizes of the spoon portion of the lure listed: 1-1/4" (fly rod size), 1-3/4", 2-11/64", 2-23/32" 3-3/8". One wonders why they were so precise with these measurements when they were so loose with the wooden bait sizes. Collector value range: N.A. The various versions to be found are listed as they were in the catalogs. Photo courtesy Ken Bernoteit

Plain with rigid mount single hook
Plain with rigid mount single hook with small trailing flasher
Plain with rigid mount single hook and trailing single
Plain with rigid mount single hook and trailing treble
Plain with rigid mount single hook and trailing buck tail treble
Plain with rigid mount single hook and trailing feathered treble
Weedless with rigid mount single hook
Weedless with rigid mount feathered single hook
Weedless with rigid mount single hook and trailing single
Colors were varied. The term "Diamolite" was used, but not described.
Polished Diamolite, both sides
Polished Diamolite, feathered
Polished Diamolite, white horse hair weed guard
White both sides, red head and yellow horse hair weed guard
Polished gold, both sides
Polished gold, feathered
Polished brass finish
White enamel, red head
Yellow, both sides, black head & black stripe, red horse hair weed guard

The colors for the fly rod size:

Nickel convex, copper concave, nickel flasher
White with red head and gold flitter, nickel flasher
Gold both sides with nickel flasher

FISH DECOYS

There was no illustration, but the 1906 catalog lists several "Fish Spearing Decoy Minnow(s)." There were three models made of soft rubber in four sizes: 2", 2-1/2", 3" and 7". They also offered one made of cedar. It was available in two sizes, 3-1/2" and 5". There were two finishes available: "Decorated" and "Plain Silver". Either one could be had in luminous or non-luminous. Collector value range: $250-$750.

WIZARD WOODEN MINNOW

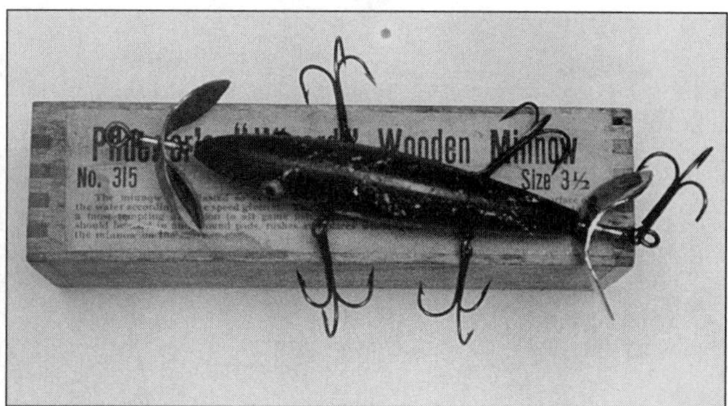

WIZARD WOODEN MINNOW #315 with its original wooden box.

This glass-eyed plug is another of the earlier ones manufactured under the Enterprise name. It was made in four different sizes (2-1/2", 3", 31/2" and 5"). All but the 2-1/2 had five treble hooks (two mounted on each side and one trailing). The 2-1/2" size had only one treble mounted on each side and one trailing (3T). All four had nose and tail mounted propellers rotating on a common wire shaft running through the length of the wedge-shaped body. It has glass eyes and finishes available are currently unknown. This plug does not appear in the 1925 or subsequent catalogs. Collector value range: $125-$200.

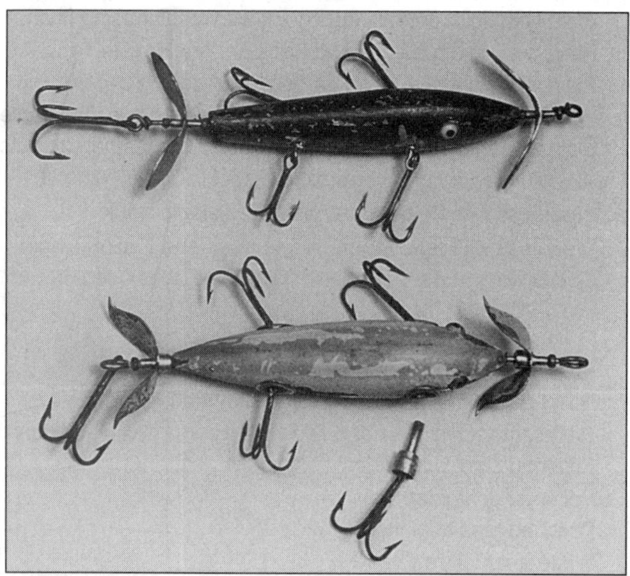

Upper is a WIZARD #315 5T. Note the old propellers and especially the through-body twisted wire side hook hangers. Lower bait has machine threaded screw-in hook hanger, is very strong and unique. These are not found often and probably represent experimentation while they were looking for a new strong hook hanger. They finally settled on the Neverfail.

This is a three hook 2-1/2" WIZARD. It has yellow glass eyes and one internal belly weight. You probably can't see them, but the metal ball bearing beads at the aft end of each of the propeller spinners is faceted. Collector value range: $125-$200.

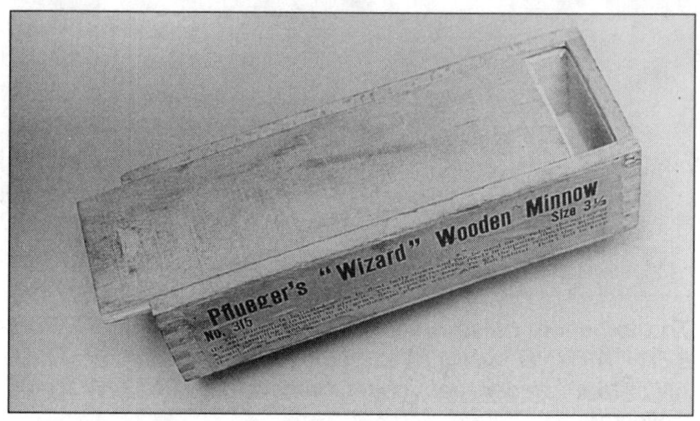

The original wooden box for a WIZARD WOODEN MINNOW.

COMPETITOR (WOODEN MINNOW)

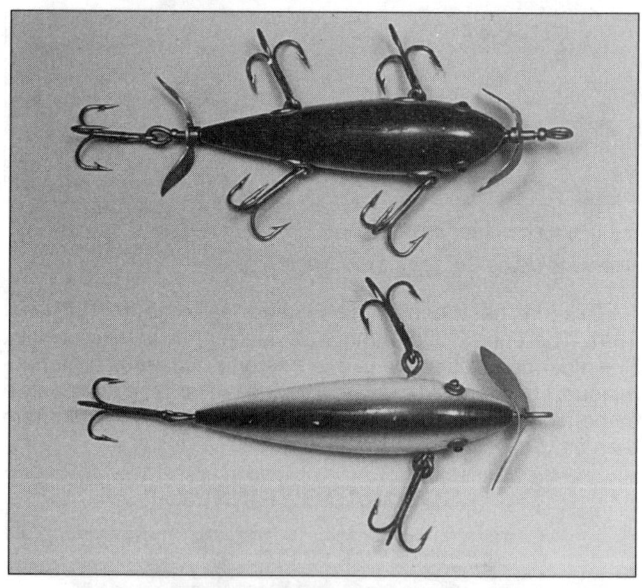

This is another early lure manufactured by Enterprise. It was produced in four sizes (2-1 / 2", 3", 3-1/2" and 5"). It has a round body with a wire shaft running through the length of the body connecting the line tie with the trailing hook link. It also had brass washer and tack eyes. It has a propeller mounted at the nose and the tail, one treble hook trailing, and one treble mounted on each side (3T). Colors available were: Silver belly with green back, Solid silver color. It does not appear in catalogs from 1925 on. Collector value range: $100-$175.

TRORY MINNOW

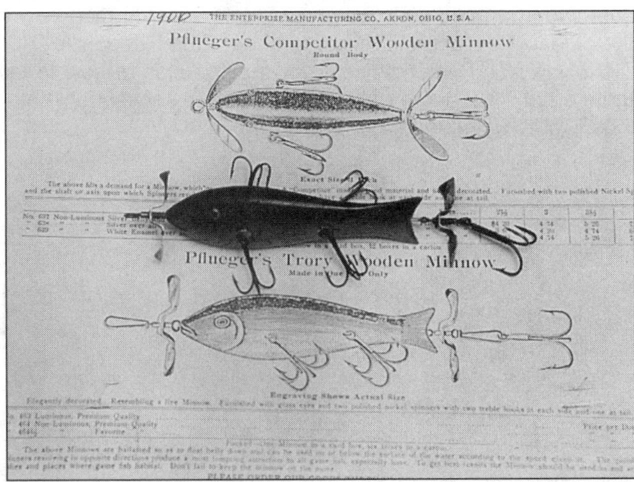

This is probably among the earliest (c. 1900) wooden plugs in the Pflueger line (manufactured by Enterprise). It is shaped like a minnow with propellers fore and aft. It sports five treble hooks, one trailing and two mounted on each side. It has glass eyes and the body is about 4" long. Color finishes available were not very specific in the early catalogs: Luminous Premium Quality, Non-luminous Premium Quality and Non-luminous Favorite. It does not appear at all in the catalog from 1925 on. Please read Kent section for detailed discussion. Collector value range: $2,000-$4,000.

CONRAD FROG

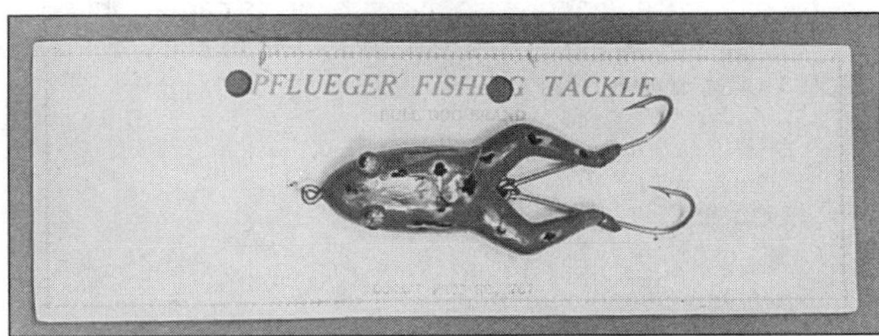

Mr. Frog first shows up in this model in 1905. It was available in a weedless version in the same style as the regular one in the photo here. Both were available in luminous and non-luminous finishes. The very first ones (pre-1905) were made of pressed ground cork, but subsequent to that they were made of rubber. Collector value range: $80-$100.

THE "MONARCH" MINNOWS (Pre-1925) (See Neverfail)

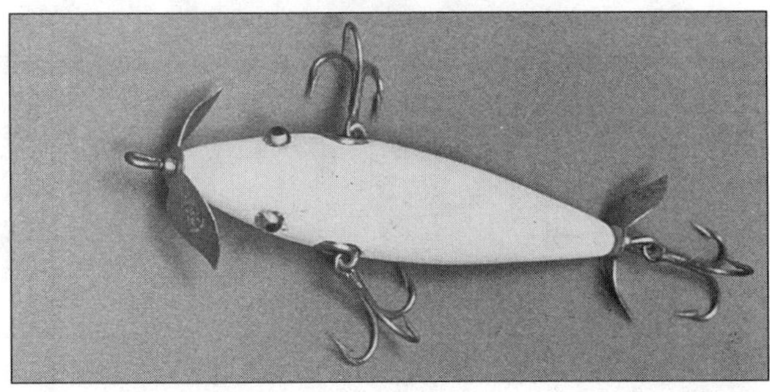

There were several types and sizes of plugs that were called "MONARCH". They were made as floating, underwater, and strong underwater especially for Musky fishing. It is known that the regular underwater and the floating versions came packed in wooden slide cover boxes. The collector will be fortunate indeed to find one in the very rare original packing box. None of these plugs are found in 1925 or later catalogs. Collector value range: $50-$200.

MONARCH Underwater Series 2100

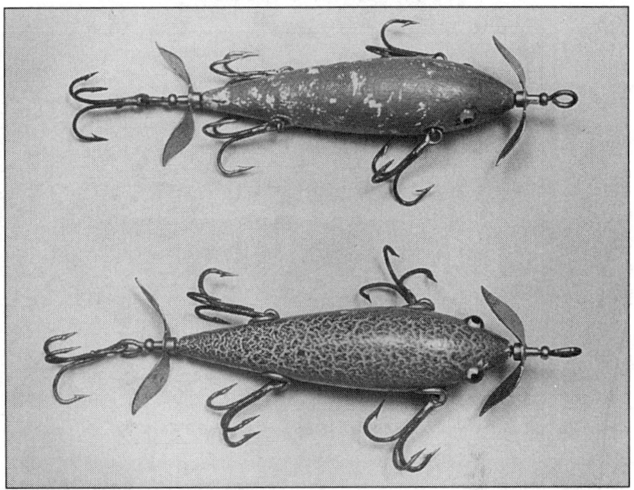

The Monarch Underwater was made in two different sizes: 2-3/4" and 3-5/8". The smaller has a side mounted treble hook on each side and one trailing (3T) and the larger size has two on each side and one trailing (5T). Both sizes had nose and tail propellers. Each size was available in the following twelve finishes: White belly, blended green back; White belly, blended slate back; Yellow belly, blended rainbow back; Yellow belly, blended brown back; Red belly, blended brown back; Silver belly, blended blue back; Silver belly, blended olive green back; Solid white; Solid red; Solid silver.

MONARCH Underwater Muskallonge Series 2200

The MONARCH Underwater Muskallonge (catalog spelling) was made in two sizes: 3-5/8" and 5" for heavy game fish. Each size has the through-body shaft on which was mounted the nose and tail propellers. The lures have one treble hook on each side (mounted to the shaft) and a trailing treble (3T). Both were available in one of only five finishes: White belly, blended green back; White belly, blended slate back; White belly, blended rainbow back; Yellow belly, blended brown back; Red belly, blended brown back.

MONARCH Floater Series 2300

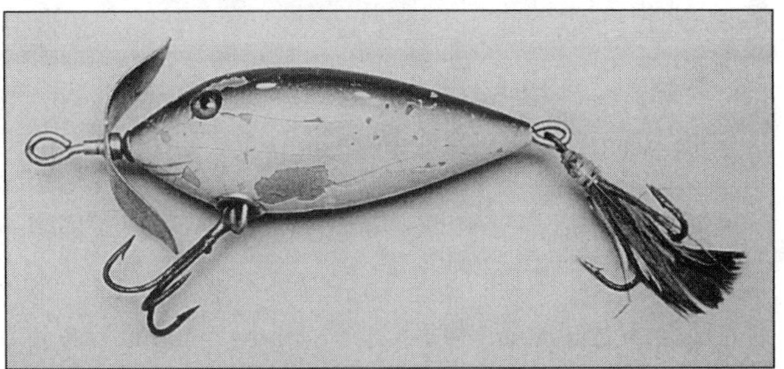

This is a MONARCH floater. It has a Gem clip style hook hanger, glass eyes and measures 2-3/4". Collector value range: $150-$175.

The MONARCH Floater was also available in two sizes: 2-3/4 and 4" with only the smaller being originally available with an optional buck tail trailing treble hook. The smaller has only a nose propeller, but the larger one also has a tail propeller. Both have a trailing and belly-mounted treble hook (2T). The available finishes were: White belly, blended green back; white belly, blended slate back; white belly, blended rainbow back; yellow belly, blended brown back; red belly, blended brown back; Silver belly, blended dark blue back.

SIMPLEX MINNOW. Lower is the accessory buoy.

SIMPLEX MINNOW. Belly view showing internalized weight.

SIMPLEX MINNOW (pre-1925)

Top: WHOOPEE SPINNER - 1930, Middle: O'BOY SPINNER - 1932, Bottom: RED DEVIL.

This is a beautiful little wooden minnow made in only a 1-3/4" size. They came in a small wooden box. These are sinkers, unless you use the accessory buoy to hold it close to the surface on retrieve. Earliest catalog I was able to find it in was 1909. It was available in two qualities, the Favorite and Premium. The Premium came with gold plated hardware. The Favorite quality had nickel plated hardware. They were made with one, two and three belly weights. The two weight models are the oldest. This lure is almost identical to the Heddon ARTISTIC MINNOW. See that listing for a discussion of how to tell them apart. They were not found in 1925 or subsequent catalogs. Collector value range: $75-$150.

RED DEVIL

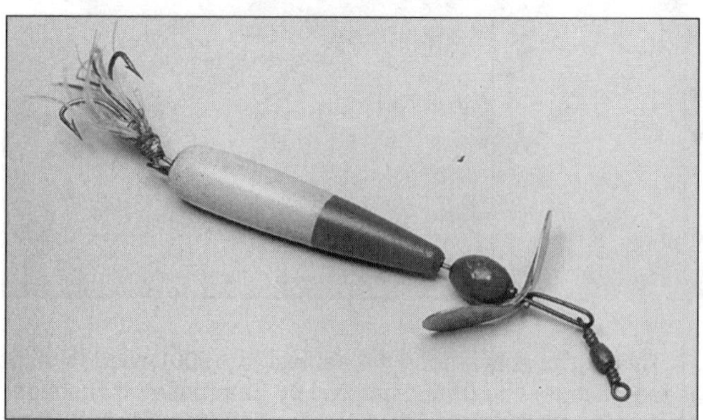

Pflueger brought this relatively hard to find lure into the line around 1920 and it disappeared from their catalogs in the 1940s. It was always available only in a red head, white body paint finish. Curiously, the catalog listing never referred to the size of the lure, only the spinner. The wood body portion of the one in the photo measures 2-5/8". The spinner blade on it is marked "PFLUEGER" on one blade and "2" on the other. In fact it was available in a spinner blade size 1 (1-9/16" x 15/32") and 2 (1-7/8" x 39/64"). Would you believe those very precise measurements came right out of the 1920 catalog listing? They refer to the length and width of the blade. Collector value range: $40-$50.

NEVERFAIL

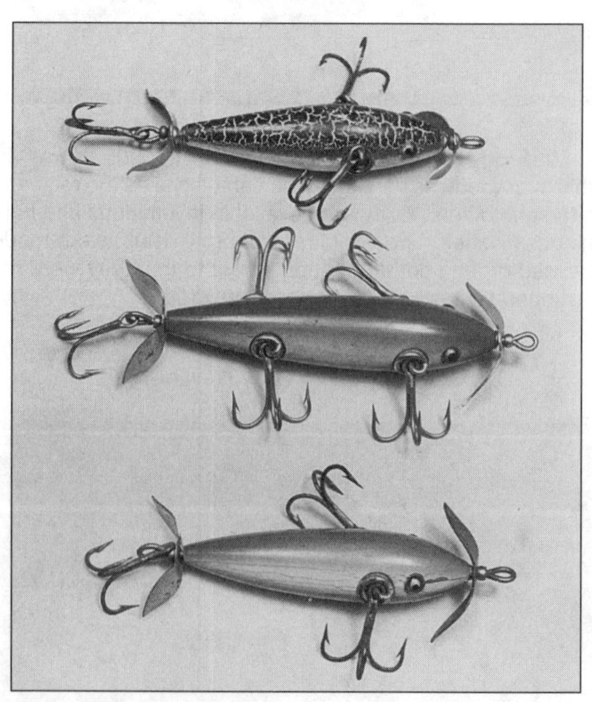

This name first appears in catalogs around the late 1920s, but the plug is remarkably similar, if not identical to some of the older MONARCH series plugs. It is known to have been produced by the Enterprise Manufacturing Company in the 1910s under the Four Brothers brand. The NEVERFAIL was made right on into the 1950s (3" only in 1955) in two sizes, both being underwater baits. The smaller has two opposite side mounted trebles and a trailing treble (3T) and the larger has two additional side trebles (5T). Both have fore and aft mounted propellers. Collector value range: $50-$120, Musky size: $350-$700.

A 2-3/4" NEVERFAIL and its box. The patent date of October 24, 1911 is printed on the box top. Photo courtesy Jim Muma. Collector value range: $50-$100, with box: $150-$200.

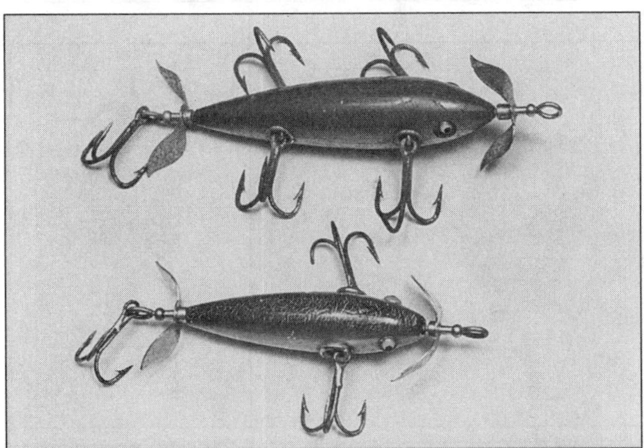

NEVERFAILS. The crackle back lure has the single word "Pflueger" stamped into the propeller blade. This is rare. The solid color plug has the Pflueger Bulldog trademark on the front propeller blade and is an older MONARCH with the see-through wire hook hangers. The crackle back model has Neverfail hook hanger.

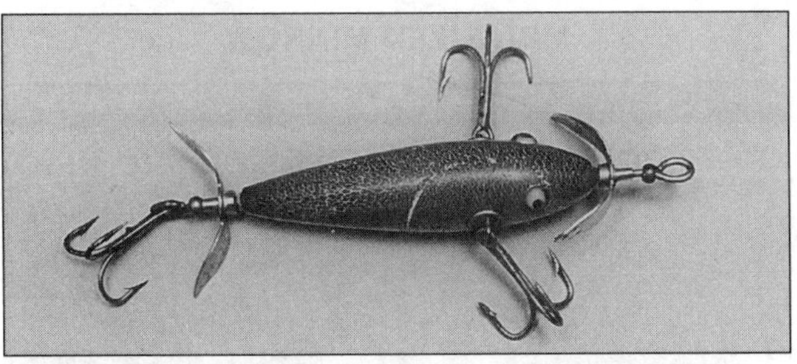

This is a very fine example of the NEVERFAIL. It measures 2-7/8", but the label on its box states it is "SIZE 2-3/4". The 2-3/4" size was not found in any catalog listing for the Neverfail. The label on the box says "THE ENTERPRISE MANUFACTURING COMPANY".

CATALOG SERIES #	BODY LENGTH	LURE WEIGHT
3100	*3"	3/4 oz.
	3-5/8"	1 oz.

COLOR OR FINISH: Luminous paint with gold spots, natural frog scale finish, *natural perch scale finish natural chub scale finish, white body with frog back, white body with green and red spots, yellow body with green and red back, *rainbow, solid red, *green cracked back, *yellow perch, white body with red head, *white body with red head and yellow and black spots.

*This size and these finishes were the only options available by 1955. The last finish on the list was new in the 1950s.

KETCH-EM WOODEN MINNOW c. 1912

These are the same lures as the NEVERFAILS above. As you can see by the boxes Pflueger made lures for other companies. KETCH-EM is the brand name of the Simmons Hardware Company of St. Louis, Missouri. The collector value range for the lure is the same as for the NEVERFAIL, but if found with one of the Simmons boxes, the value range is $200-$300. Photo courtesy Jim Muma.

KINGFISHER WOODEN MINNOW

Same story second verse of the KETCH-EM above. This is the same as the NEVERFAIL. Made by Pflueger for the Edward K.

Tryon company in Philadelphia to be sold under their Kingfisher brand. The collector value range for the lure is the same as for the NEVERFAIL, but if found with one of the Kingfisher boxes, the value range is $200-$300. Photo courtesy Jim Muma.

ELECTRIC WOODEN MINNOW

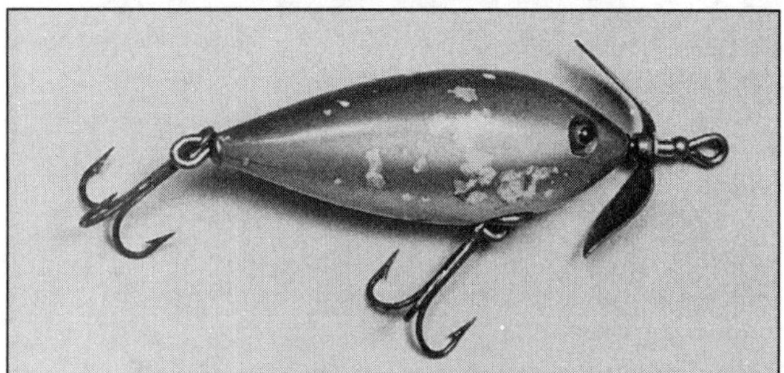

Small size 2-3/4" ELECTRIC MINNOW with Neverfail hook hangers.

This bait was first produced around 1920-21 in two sizes: 2-3/4" and 3-5/8". It has glass eyes, propellers mounted fore and aft, and a through-body wire shaft. The smaller version has two opposite side mounted trebles and a trailing treble (3T). The larger one has two additional opposite side trebles (5T). These lures did not appear in the 1925 or subsequent catalogs. Collector value range: $150-$200.

2-3/4" ELECTRIC MINNOW with Neverfail hardware. Propeller spinner is marked "Electric Bulldog".

COLOR OR FINISH: White belly, blended rainbow back; Aluminum belly, blended olive green back; White belly, fancy (cracked) green back; White belly, blended rainbow back; White belly, blended olive green back; White belly, fancy (cracked) green back.

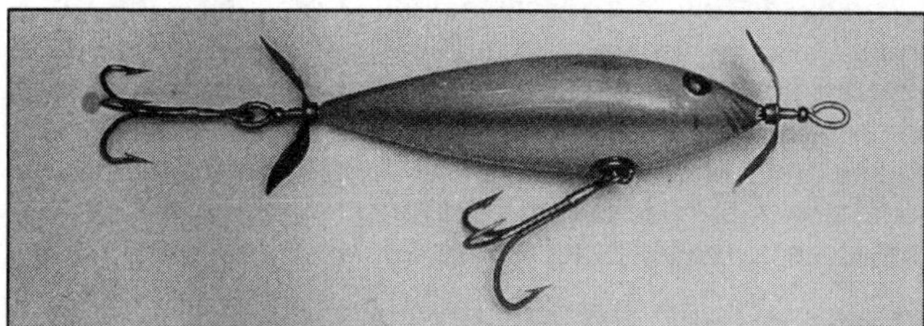

ELECTRIC MINNOW with propeller marked "Metalized Bulldog." Catalogs say 3-5/8", but this one measures 4. Neverfail hardware.

KENT FROG

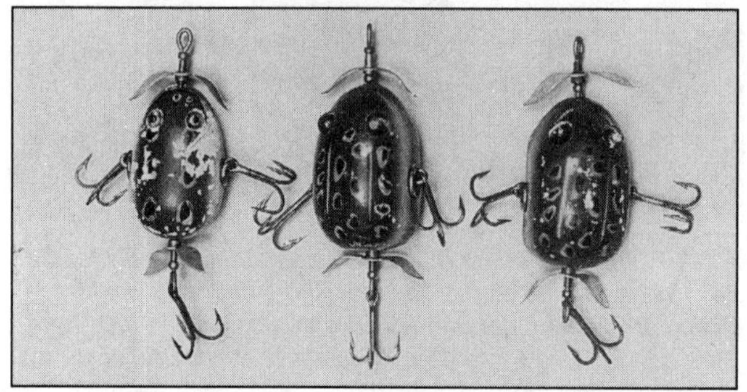

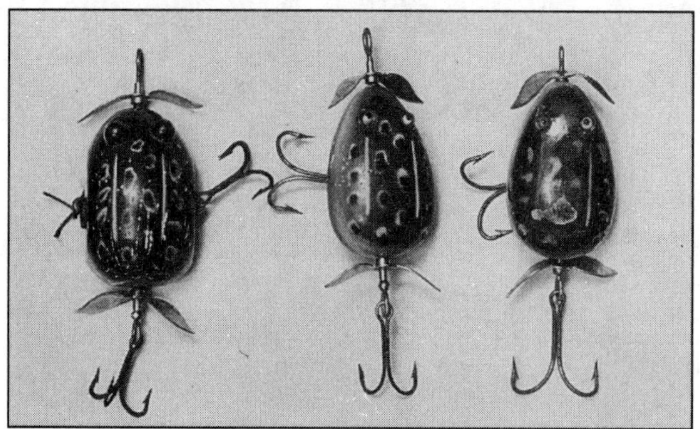

New for Pflueger around the late 1910s the six frogs in the photos illustrate changes in the Pflueger KENT FROG over the years. Read them left to right, top to bottom. Note changes in eyes, hook types and arrangements, and body shapes. The last version has a non-tube floppy propeller. Available only in the Meadow Frog finish as pictured. Collector value range: $300-$500. Please turn to the Kent section for detailed history of this lure.

METALIZED MINNOW

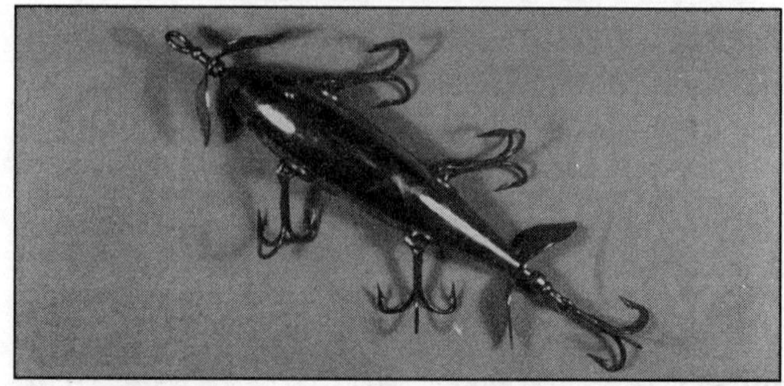

This METALIZED MINNOW has the Pflueger Bulldog trademark on the front propeller blade and the Neverfail hardware.

Patented around 1910-11 this plug doesn't appear in catalogs until sometime around the late 1920s. It was made in two sizes, the smaller with two opposite side mounted trebles and a trailing treble hook (3T). The larger has two additional side trebles (5T). Both sizes have fore and aft propellers. Collector value range: $150-$300.

CATALOG SERIES #	BODY LENGTH	LURE WEIGHT
2887	3-/58"	1 oz.

COLOR OR FINISH: Metalized (polished nickel).

MAGNET or MERIT
3600 Series

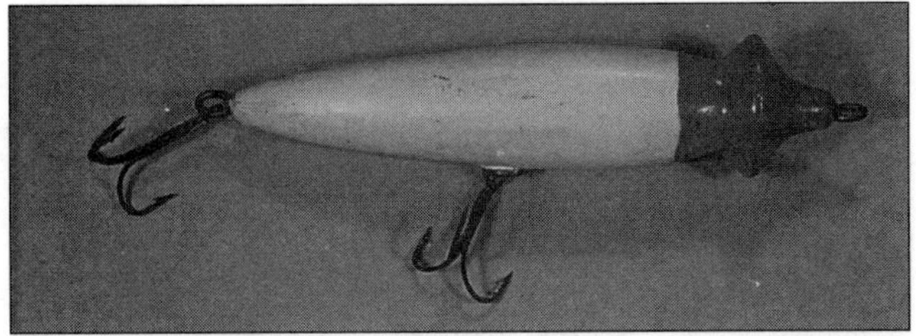

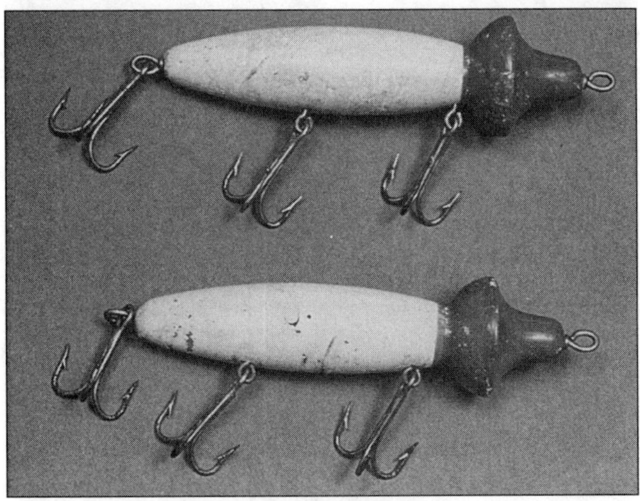

Upper lure is a Pflueger MAGNET. Lower is a Shakespeare SURFACE WONDER. See text for differences.

This is the first style of MAGNET or MERIT. Note the difference in the shape of the collar and the nose. This particular lure is a repaint. Collector value range: $50-$75.

The oldest reference to the MAGNET (first name) was a 1916 catalog entry with illustrations. There are a couple of significant things about this entry. First, the illustration is identical to a Shakespeare SURFACE WONDER except for one small detail. The forward hook hanger is extremely close to the collar whereas on the Shakespeare model the screw eye is located farther back (see photo for comparison). It looks as if Pflueger and Shakespeare were buying blank bodies from the same supplier at this time. The second observation comes from the text of the entry. It stated as follows: "Joint on the screw eye at head is soldered to prevent line from slipping out." By the early 1920s the body style had changed to that of the lures in the photo below. The name remained MAGNET until about 1935 when it was inexplicably changed to MERIT. The 1916 MAGNET was offered in 3 color choices: White luminous, plain white, white with red head. By 1925 the all white non-luminous white body with red head was offered and that was it from then on. So, if you have an all white or white with

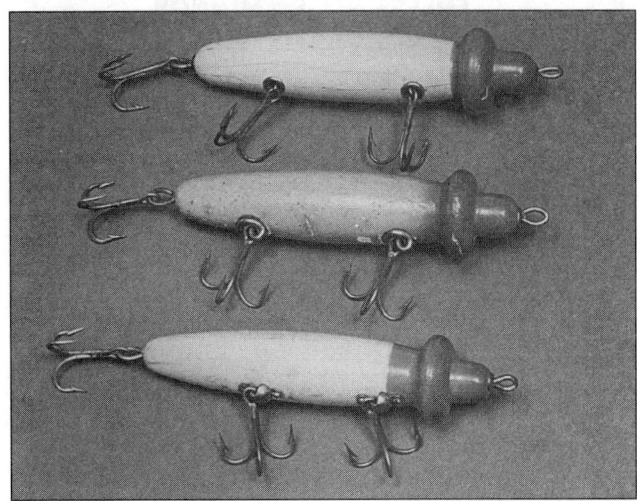

Three MAGNETS, oldest to newest. Top lure has thru-body wire line tie and tail treble hook hangers with paper clip type belly hook fasteners. Center lure has the Neverfail hook hanger and the lower plug has the one piece surface hanger.

gold spots, it's pre-1927 (if it's not a repaint). It was gone by the end of the 1940s. It was listed as 4-1/4" throughout the years. Collector value range: $40-$50.

PEERLESS

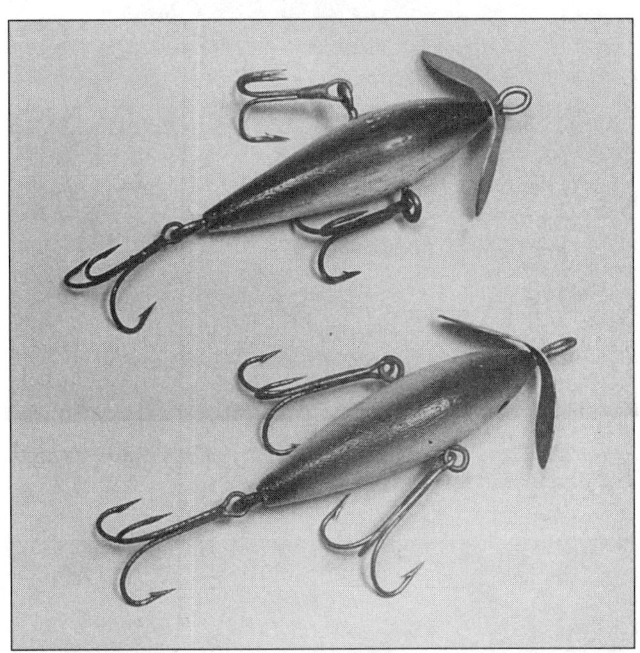

The PEERLESS minnow plugs were made as an inexpensive lure line with not quite the quality of the regular Pflueger line. All have opposite side trebles and a trailing treble hook (3T). They also have one nose mounted propeller. They came along in the late 1920s and apparently didn't stay in the line long after. Collector value range: $30-$50.

CATALOG SERIES #	BODY LENGTH	LURE WEIGHT
4100	2-1/2"	1/2 oz.
	2"	?
	3-1/2"	?

COLOR OR FINISH: White body, redhead, white body, green back, white body, red back.

PEERLESS or GEM MINNOW

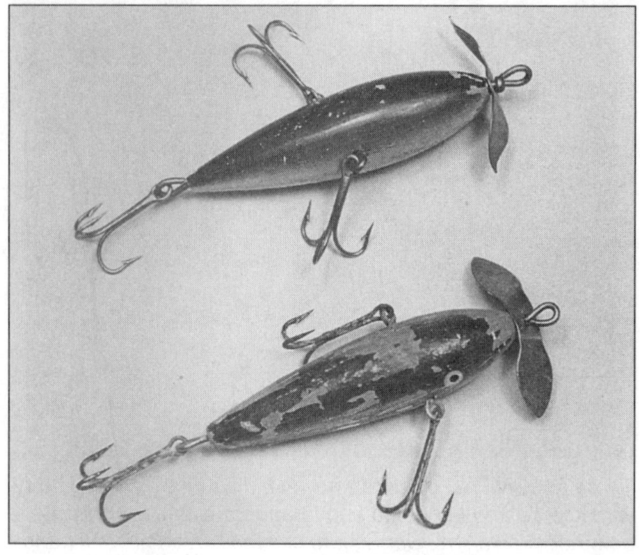

This is a very inexpensively constructed critter that looks like another contender for competing with the Shakespeare LITTLE PIRATE. Collector value range: $30-$40.

GLOBE

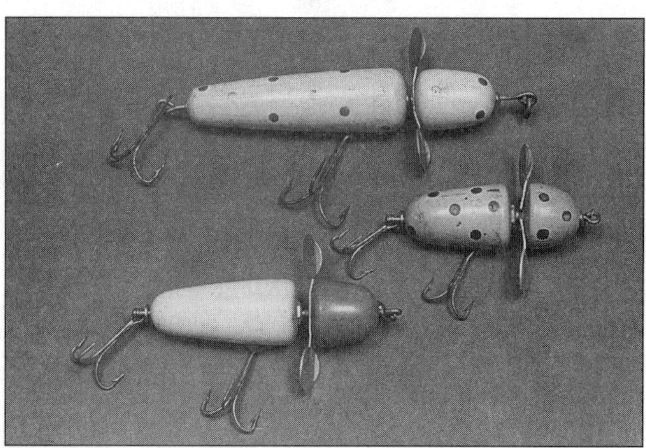

The three sizes of GLOBES, each with the one-piece surface hook hanger (latest).

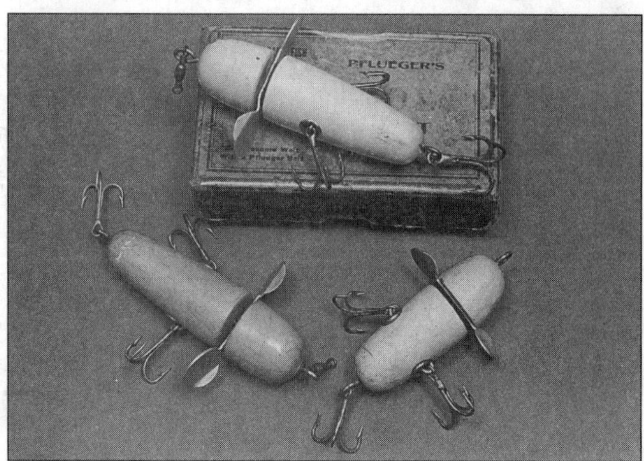

Three GLOBES and an original box. The one on the box is a 'Portage' and has the wire see-thru hook hanger (oldest). The remaining two lures have the Neverfail hardware.

One reference found was a photocopy of a catalog entry that said at the bottom to insert this entry in "...our catalog No. F26". I have not seen this catalog but I have seen F25 dated 1909. so, this entry must be a 1910 or later. In any case the 3-1/8" GLOBE pictured here is much like a Decker. The nose is a bit more pointed and rear body tapered more than a later Pflueger GLOBES. The next reference was in a 1916 Pflueger catalog. The 1916 illustration is the typical GLOBE shape, as in the photo. It was called the PORTAGE REFLEX BAIT in that entry. This one was available in two sizes, 2-3/4" and 3-5/8", and four finishes: Solid white, white with red head, yellow with gold spots, mouse color. A 1919 catalog offers only luminous white body and the yellow with gold spots. By 1925 the red head was back, making three choices.

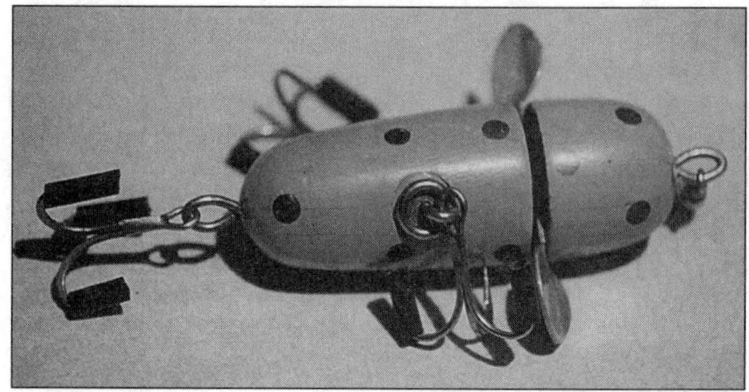

A Pflueger GLOBE with the screw eye rear hook hanger and the Neverfail on the belly (1914-1920).

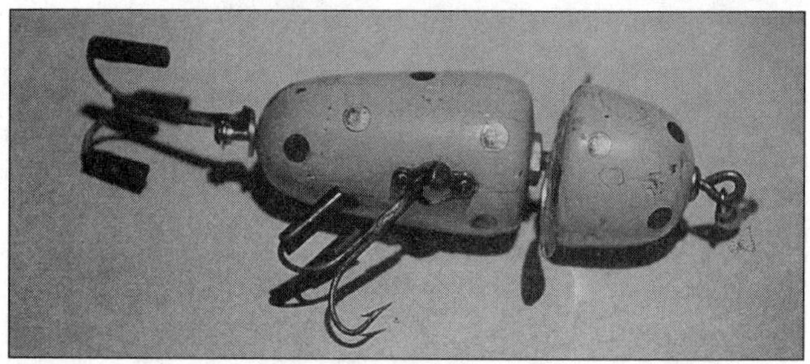

This GLOBE has the swiveling rare hook hanger, the two-piece surface hardware on the belly and the spring-loaded head (1930s-1940s).

1926 colors:

Luminous with gold spots
Yellow with gold spots
White with red head
Natural perch scale finish with red head
Natural chub scale finish with red head

Pike scale finish with red head was added in 1928 and in 1929 they added a larger size, 5-1/4". Black body with red head was added sometime in the 1940s. These color changes may be of some help in dating your Globes. However, changes pretty much reflect the typical evolution. One major change took place about 1930. They redesigned it so that the head could be pulled forward away from the body for easy weed removal. They were available into the 1950s. Collector value range: $30-$80.

CATALOG SERIES #	BODY LENGTH	LURE WEIGHT
3700	2-3/4"	5/8 oz.
	3-5/8"	3/4 oz.
	5-1/4"	1-1/3 oz.

A close-up photo of a blade on the newest(1967-1968) of the GLOBE lures showing the Pflueger Bulldog trademark and the "MADE IN HONG KONG" beneath it.

SPECIAL NOTE

Collector and N.F.L.C.C. member Phil Henderson of Garber, Oklahoma wrote an excellent article for the **N.F.L.C.C. GAZETTE* about dating Pflueger Globes. In it he included a chart of colors that is quite helpful in dating Globes. In addition to the color dating chart, Phil has developed a flow chart that is extremely helpful in dating. He sent along a copy with the color chart and has magnanimously granted permission for me to print both here for your use. He also furnished the last three photos.

**How Old Is That Pflueger Globe? Pages 12-14, December, 1993 issue, Volume 17, No. 59, copyright 1993.*

GLOBE COLOR DATING CHART
Developed by Phil Henderson

Here is a chart in order by model number showing the colors available, the dates these colors were used and the lure sizes these colors were available on.

There are several reasons for fixing the date on the "Black Lightning" and "Frog" at 1966. In the 1964 catalog these colors had yet to be offered. According to information provided by Trygve Lund, a retired engineer from Pflueger, Pflueger sold to Shakespeare on July 16, 1966 and in 1967 entered into a joint venture with Winpull Fishing Accessories Co. Ltd. of Hong Kong. During this time Globes were simplified (elimination of the spring-loaded head and swiveling rear hook hanger) and more colors added ("Black Lightning" and "Frog"). Some of these newer GLOBES have "MADE IN HONG KONG" stamped on the prop under the familiar Bulldog emblem.

FLOW CHART FOR DATING PFLUEGER GLOBES
Developed by Phil Henderson

Just answer the questions yes or no and follow the chart on the next page to the date of your Globe.

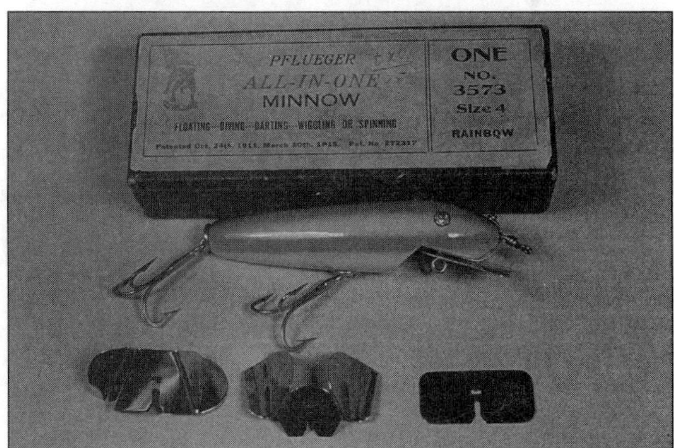

A Pflueger ALL-IN-ONE with all its parts and original box. Boxes for the lure have become as collectible as and almost as valuable as the lure. Their collector value range: $750-$1,000.

ALL-IN-ONE
(pre-1925)

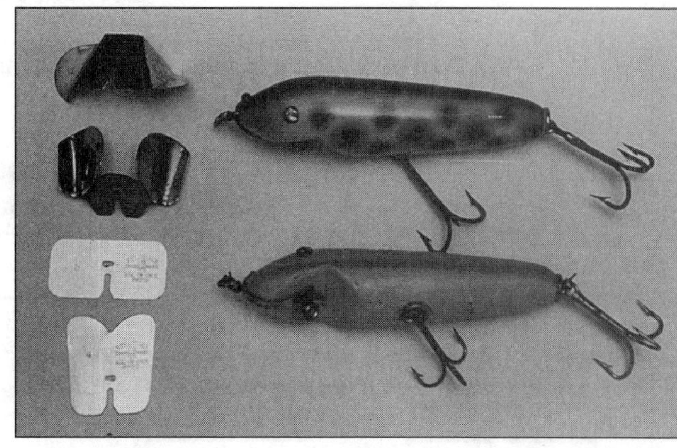

This interesting plug will probably be a very difficult item for the collector to find intact. It was furnished with four different interchangeable metal nose pieces. Each was different so that depending upon which you chose to use, the plug would rotate, dive shallow, deep dive or plane along the surface when retrieved. Because these metal planes were removable, it is not likely that you will find any but the one attached to the body unless you are lucky enough to acquire one new in the box. The plug has a belly-mount treble and a trailing treble hook. It was not found in catalogs of 1925 or after. Collector value range with all four planes: $1,000-$1,500, without extra planes: $250-$380.

COLOR OR FINISH: Luminous paint, solid white; white belly, blended green cracked back; white belly, blended rainbow cracked back; white belly, blended frog back; white belly, green and red spots.

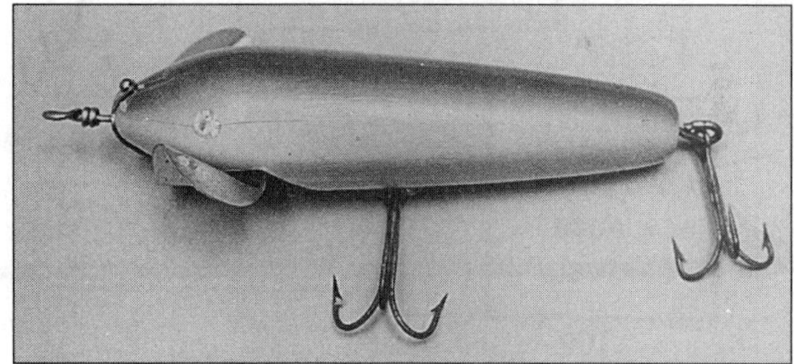

This 4" ALL-IN-ONE has the Pflueger patent Neverfail hook hanger for the belly hook and the very strong through-body line tie/tail hook hanger. Note that the rhinestone eyes have no metal retaining clips. They are simply glued in. The retaining clip is a later innovation.

BEARCAT

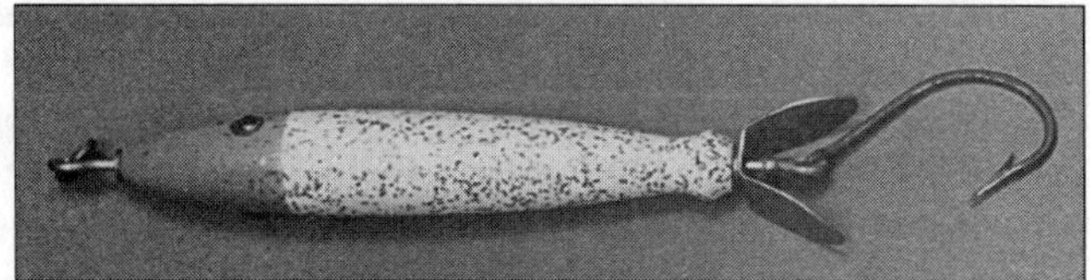

The BEARCAT is almost identical to the CATALINA (5500 series) except that it has a belly-mounted treble and a trailing treble hook. Patented in 1922, it appears in a 1925 catalog as available in natural mullet with scale finish, white with red throat, and white with a yellow and green back. It was missing from catalogs by 1930. Collector value range: $150-$250.

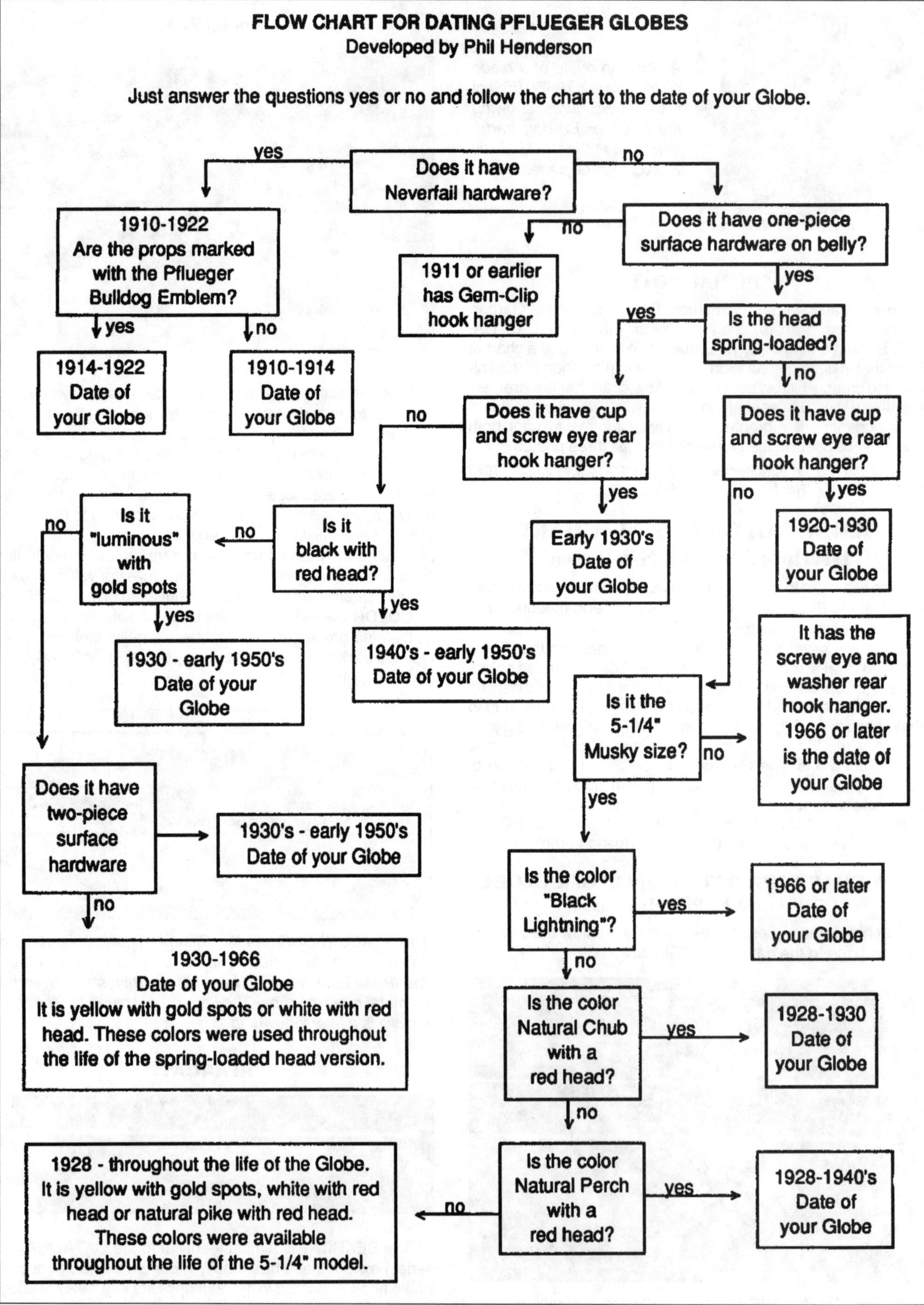
FLOW CHART FOR DATING PFLUEGER GLOBES
Developed by Phil Henderson
Just answer the questions yes or no and follow the chart to the date of your Globe.
Does it have Neverfail hardware?
yes
no
1910-1922 Are the props marked with the Pflueger Bulldog Emblem?
yes
no
1914-1922 Date of your Globe
1910-1914 Date of your Globe
Does it have one-piece surface hardware on belly?
no
yes
1911 or earlier has Gem-Clip hook hanger
Is the head spring-loaded?
yes
no
Does it have cup and screw eye rear hook hanger?
no
yes
Early 1930's Date of your Globe
Does it have cup and screw eye rear hook hanger?
no
yes
1920-1930 Date of your Globe
Is it black with red head?
no
yes
1940's - early 1950's Date of your Globe
Is it "luminous" with gold spots
no
yes
1930 - early 1950's Date of your Globe
Does it have two-piece surface hardware
1930's - early 1950's Date of your Globe
no
1930-1966 Date of your Globe It is yellow with gold spots or white with red head. These colors were used throughout the life of the spring-loaded head version.
Is it the 5-1/4" Musky size?
no
yes
It has the screw eye and washer rear hook hanger. 1966 or later is the date of your Globe
Is the color "Black Lightning"?
yes
no
1966 or later Date of your Globe
Is the color Natural Chub with a red head?
yes
no
1928-1930 Date of your Globe
Is the color Natural Perch with a red head?
yes
no
1928-1940's Date of your Globe
1928 - throughout the life of the Globe. It is yellow with gold spots, white with red head or natural pike with red head. These colors were available throughout the life of the 5-1/4" model.

GLOBE COLOR DATING CHART
Developed by Phil Henderson

Here is a chart in order by model number showing the colors available, the dates these colors were used and the lure sizes these colors were available on.

PORTAGE REFLEX	GLOBE	COLOR	DATES AVAILABLE	SIZES			pre-1913
				2-3/4"	3-5/8"	5-1/4"	3-1/8"
	3704	Natural Pike with red head	1928, through the life of the Globe			X	
	3706	Natural Perch with red head	1928 through late 1940's			X	
	3707	Natural Chub with red head	1928 through 1930			X	
	3742	Black body with red head	Introduced after 1941, disappeared before 1957	X	X		
	3745	Frog	First offered about 1966	X	X		
3850	3750	Yellow with gold spots	Throughout the life of the Globe	X	X	X	X
	3751	White enamel with gold spots	Used before 1916 only				
	3754	Black Lightning with silver sparks	Introduced about 1966		X	X	
	3770	Luminous Enamel	Discontinued before 1920	X	X		X
	3770	Luminous Enamel with gold spots	Introduced around 1920, dropped early 1950's	X	X		
3880	3780	White Enamel	Dropped by 1920	X	X		X
3896	3796	White enamel with red head	Life of the Globe except late teens and early 1920's	X	X	X	X
3898	3798	Mouse color enamel	Only known reference 1916. Note in catalog "...NOT carried in stock, but will be made to order."	X	X		

SURPRISE

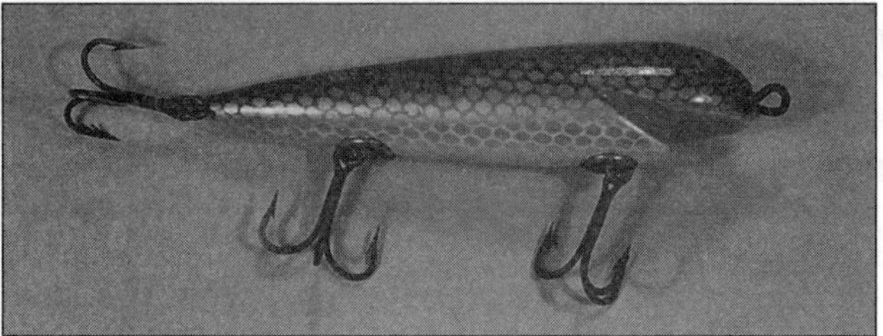

This beautiful mint condition 4" SURPRISE has no eyes of any sort. It is one of only two known to exist in private collections. Collector value range: $150-$200.

Another example with its original box. Photo courtesy Jim Muma.

The patent for the SURPRISE was applied for in 1913 and granted in 1915 so it must have been introduced around then. When first put in the line there was only a 4" size. It has two belly treble hooks and one trailing treble. By 1919 a 3" size two hooker had been added and the 4" size had become a two hook model also.

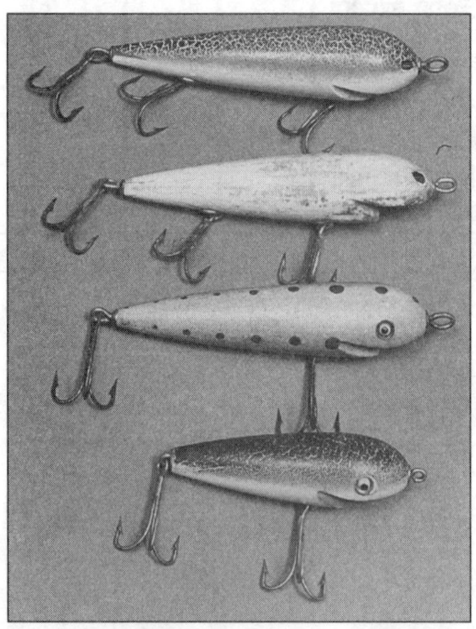

The top two here have empty eye sockets. The third one down has glass eyes as does the fourth down, a 3" SURFACE SURPRISE MINNOW.

The earliest models of the SURPRISE have empty eye sockets for eyes, just empty holes. This is a puzzling characteristic until you read the patent papers. It seems that someone thought they had a really bright idea. Ostensibly the sockets had a tendency to retain air when pulled under water in a diving motion. Further, it was thought that when you brought the lure to a horizontal position or stopped it, the air would be released in the form of tiny bubbles giving the appearance of the lure exhaling in a lifelike manner. By the early 1920s they were sporting the normal glass eyes of the time. I guess someone finally figured out that fish don't breathe air. The lure was absent from the Pflueger catalogs by the mid 1930s. Collector value range: $75-$150.

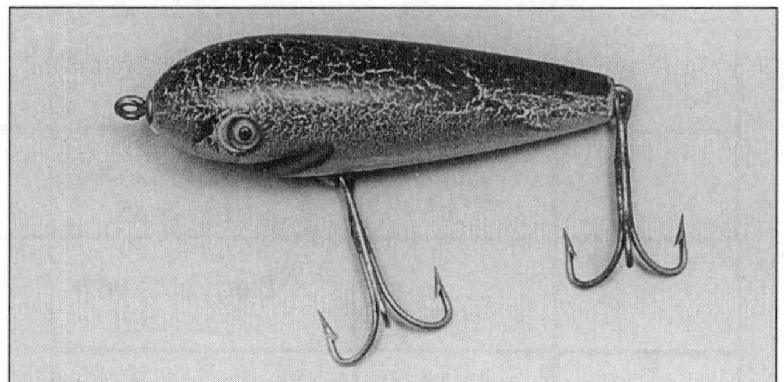

A 3" SURFACE SURPRISE with glass eyes.

CATALOG SERIES #	BODY LENGTH	LURE WEIGHT
3900	3"	1/2 oz.
	4"	5/8 oz.

COLOR OR FINISH: *Luminous paint with gold spots, golden shiner scale finish, natural mullet scale finish, natural frog scale finish, natural perch scale finish, *white body with red head, rainbow, *green cracked back.

**These were the only finishes available in 1931 and the 3" size had been eliminated.*

PAL-O-MINE

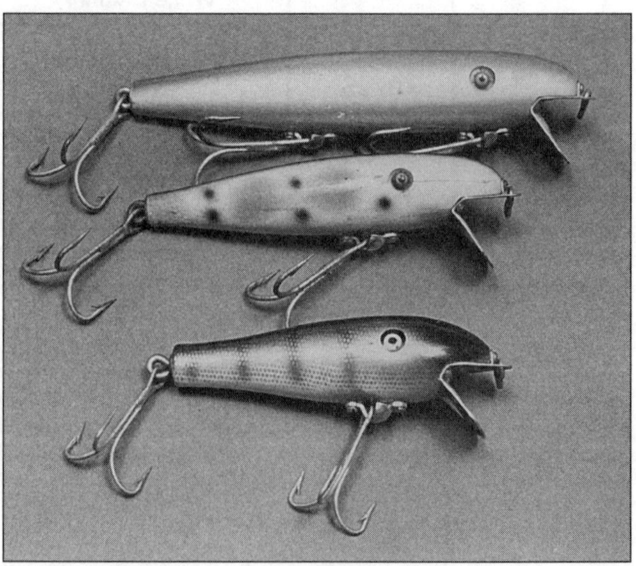

First introduced about 1925 the PAL-O-MINE continued to be offered throughout the years right into the 1950s. It was first available in only two sizes: 3-1/2" and 4-1/4". In 1932 a smaller (2-3/4") size was added. The basic design of these plugs didn't change but various color finishes were eliminated or added at particular year intervals. This will enable the collector to establish the approximate age of some of them (see listing).

The larger (4-1/2") has always been offered with two belly trebles and one trailing (3T). The 3-1/2" and 2-3/4" sizes have always sported only one belly treble hook and the trailing treble (2T). All have a metal lip fitted into a cutout notch at the nose. Collector value range: $15-$30.

CATALOG SERIES #	BODY LENGTH	LURE WEIGHT
5000	2-3/4"	1/3 oz.
	3-1/4"	1/2 oz.
	4-1/4"	3/4 oz.

COLOR OR FINISH: Golden shiner scale finish, red side scale finish, natural mullet scale finish, natural pike scale finish, natural frog with scale finish, natural perch scale finish, *solid black with white head, rainbow, +solid red, green cracked back, white with red head, **white with redhead and silver sparks, **red, green and yellow scramble finish; *solid white, red splash and gold specks; **solid white, red and green spots; ++redhead, pearl specks.

All finishes other than those listed above date the plug 1941 or later.

**Eliminated in 1931.*

***Added in 193 1, eliminated in 1938.*

+Eliminated in 1932.

++Added in 1932.

JOINTED PAL-O-MINE

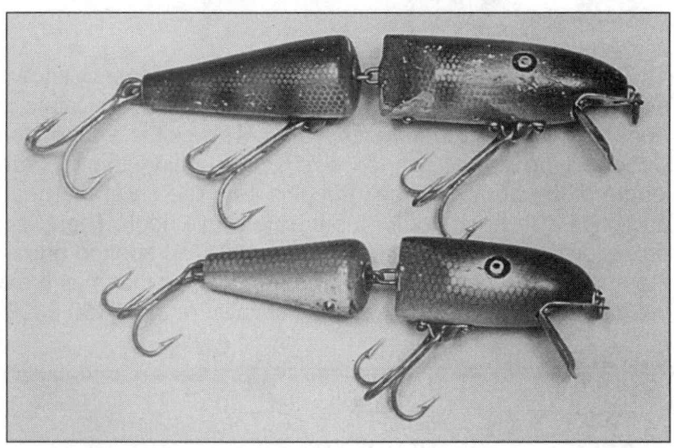

By 1936 the original PAL-O-MINE had become available in a jointed version. It was available in two sizes and the body design was the same as the unjointed version. Collector value range: $15-$30.

CATALOG SERIES #	BODY LENGTH	LURE WEIGHT
9000	3-1/4"	1/2 oz.
	4-1/4"	3/4 oz.

COLOR OR FINISH: Red side, scale finish; green mullet, scale finish; natural pike, scale finish; natural perch, scale finish; white with red head, silver sparks; rainbow blend.

O-BOY

The O-BOY came along around the mid 1920s and by 1931 it was no longer found in catalogs as a plug (the name was reused on a spinner bait). It was made in two sizes and three weights. The heavier stronger version was for big fish. All have a metal lip, a belly treble and trailing treble hook. Collector value range: $50-$150.

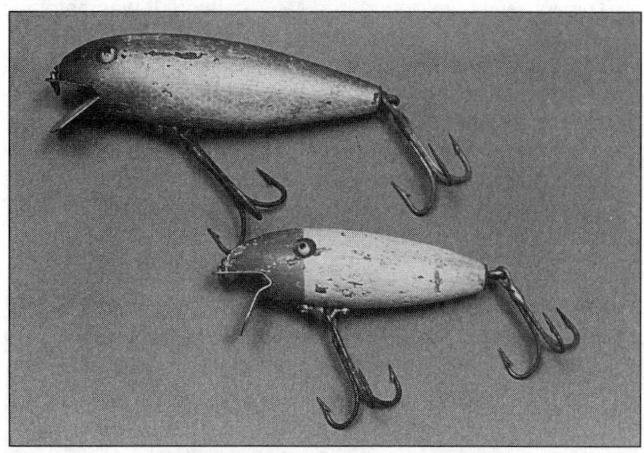

CATALOG SERIES #	BODY LENGTH	LURE WEIGHT
5400	2-1/4"	1/2 oz.
	3-1/2"	3/4, 7/8 oz.

COLOR OR FINISH: Golden shiner, scale finish; red side, scale finish; natural mullet, scale finish; natural frog, scale finish; natural chub, scale finish; black body, white head, white body, green and red spots; rainbow, green cracked back; white body, red head, red side, scale finish; natural chub, scale finish; silver color body, red head; rainbow.

WIZARD WIGGLER

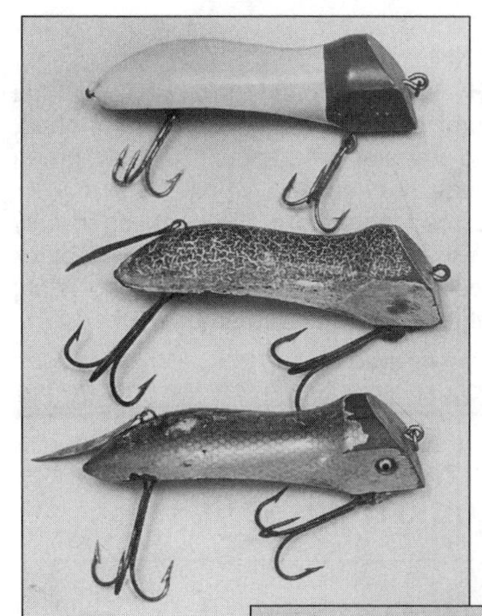

This lure was first found in a 1927 catalog. It was patented June 6, 1922. It had disappeared from catalogs by 1936. Although the patent drawing did not include it, it has a top tail-mounted metal flasher attached loosely so it would wiggle on retrieve. The top lure in the above photo is not like the regular production models. It is more like the patent drawing. Note the pork rind attachment on the tail (not in the patent). Interestingly, the Pflueger style one-piece surface hook hanger is part of this 1922 patent. Collector value range: $50-$150.

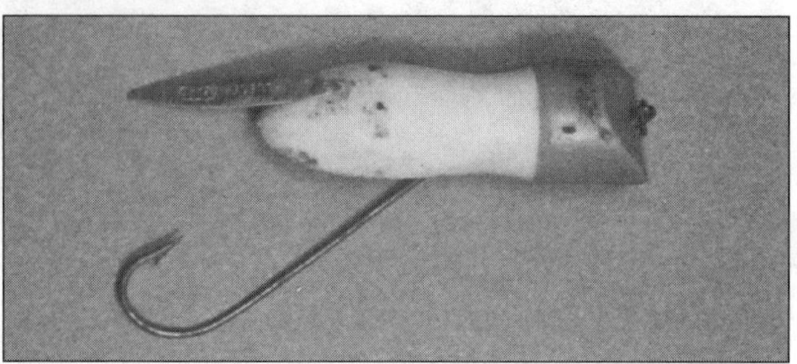

1-1/2" fly rod size.

CATALOG SERIES #	BODY LENGTH	LURE WEIGHT
4700	*1-1/2"	1/20 oz. (made with and without flasher)
	1-3/4"	1/10 oz. (made with and without flasher)
	2-1/4"	1/4 oz.
	*3"	1/2 oz.
	3-1/2"	5/8 oz.

COLOR OR FINISH: *Luminous paint, gold spots; *natural frog, scale finish; natural perch, scale finish; *natural chub, scale finish; white body, green and red spots; *rainbow, green cracked back; *white body, red head.

Note: The WIZARD reappeared in a 1938 catalog in only the 3" size and in six finishes: Natural perch, scale finish; black with silver lightning flash; luminous with red lightning flash; green cracked back; white body, red head and gray mouse.

**The only sizes and finishes available by 1929 and the 1-1/2" size was not available in Luminous paint or frog finish at this time. The frog finish was eliminated as an option in 1931.*

WIZARD MOUSE FLOCKED MOUSE

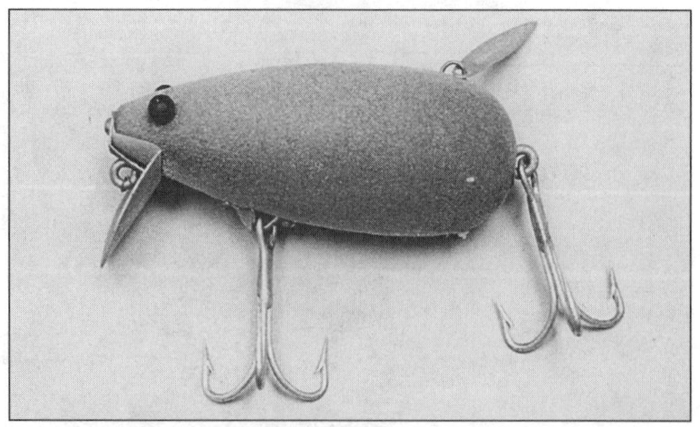

A thorough search through the Pflueger catalog collection turned up no mention of this lure. Collectors call it the WIZARD MOUSE or the FLOCKED MOUSE. It is placed it here because of the presence of a metal flasher on its back just like the one on the WIZARD WIGGLER. The blade does have "PFLUEGER WIGGLER" stamped on it. The body measures 1-5/8" in length and the finish is fuzzy brown with a white belly. The eyes are large black beads. Belly hook hardware is one-piece surface and the tail has a protective metal insert. Collector value range: $150-$200.

CATALINA (pre 1925)

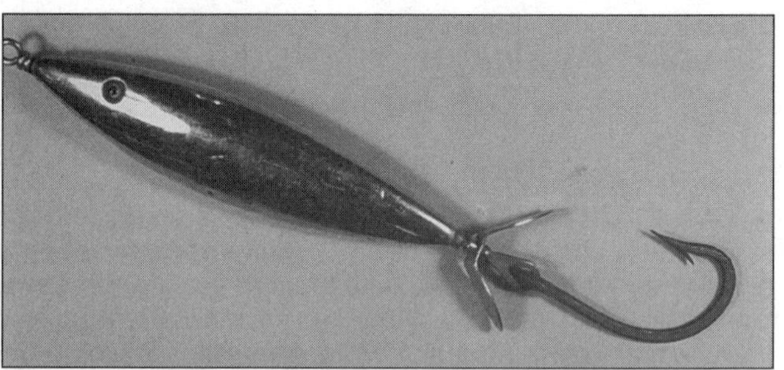

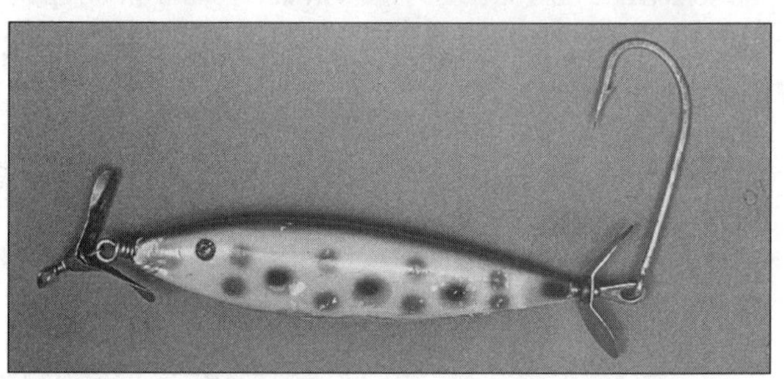

This plug was patented in 1910, but it is not presently known exactly when it entered the Pflueger line. It was in catalogs from 1925 to 1936 then disappeared. The bait is a long slim wooden type with a bronze wire shaft running through the length of the body. The shaft begins as a line tie at the nose and ends as a hook link for the trailing single hook. There is a propeller mounted on the shaft at the tail. The spotted one in the photo has a non-standard prop on the nose that may have been added by a fisherman. Collector value range: $100-$300.

CATALOG SERIES #	BODY LENGTH	LURE WEIGHT
5500	4-1/4"	?

COLOR OR FINISH: Natural Mullet, scale finish; White with red throat, White with yellow and green back; Solid red, Metalized (polished nickel-plate all over).

LIVE WIRE

Sometime around 1931 the LIVE WIRE appeared in only four color designs and two sizes. It is made of celluloid and very slim. It has a nose and tail propeller spinner, two belly trebles and a trailing treble hook (3T) on the larger size and only one belly treble on the smaller (2T). There is a dorsal fin very realistic in shape and appearance. By 1932 a saltwater version was in the line. It was a 4-1/2" body, with only the tail propeller and one trailing single hook (1T). By the 1937 catalog the plugs were still available in the saltwater version, but only one size of the regular lure was still being offered ,3-1/2". The 1941 catalog saltwater version was still offered in the original body design. Both had disappeared by 1955. Collector value range: old $35-$65, new $20-$25.

CATALOG SERIES #	BODY LENGTH	LURE WEIGHT	HOOKS
7600	5-1/2"	1 oz.	2T

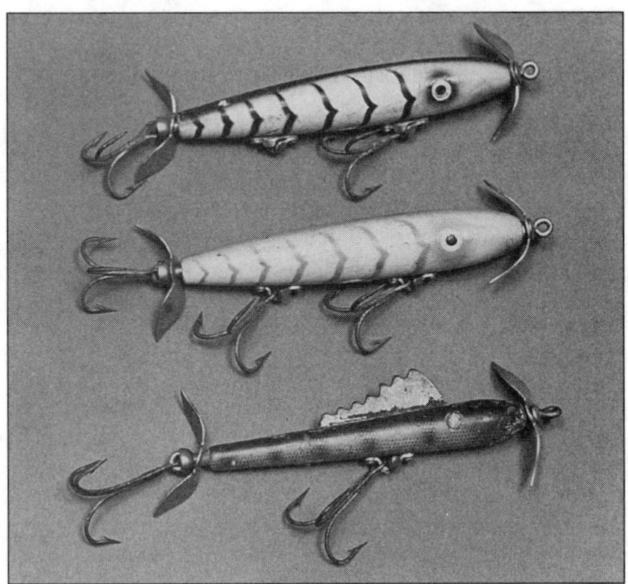

Oldest LIVE WIRE is at the bottom.

COLOR OR FINISH: *Natural Perch, scale finish; *green gar, scale finish; *silver sides, scale finish; *white body, red head, gold sparks.

7900
5-1/2"

COLOR OR FINISH: Green Mullet, scale finish, silver sparks; white body, red head, gold sparks; white body, yellow and green back; solid red, pearl sparks all over.

***9400 3-3/4" 3/4 oz.*

COLOR OR FINISH: Yellow body, red decorations; yellow body, black decorations; white body, black decorations; white body, red and green decorations.

**The four finishes available in the 1931 catalog.*

***The latest version.*

FRISKY

A 2-3/3" FRISKY with its original box. Photo courtesy Jim Muma.

Sometime in the mid 1930s this bait appeared in catalogs. It has a very unusual nose shape, one belly and one trailing treble hook (2T). By 1952 the FRISKY, as it was first designed, disappeared. The name was retained, but it applies to an entirely different lure. Collector value range for the original FRISKY: $25-$40. and for the new: $35-$55.

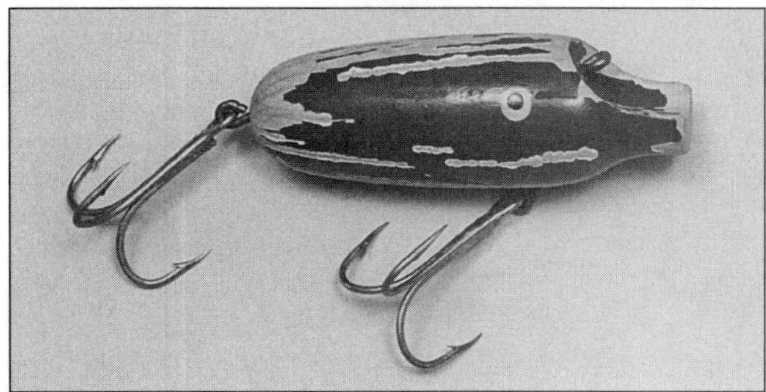

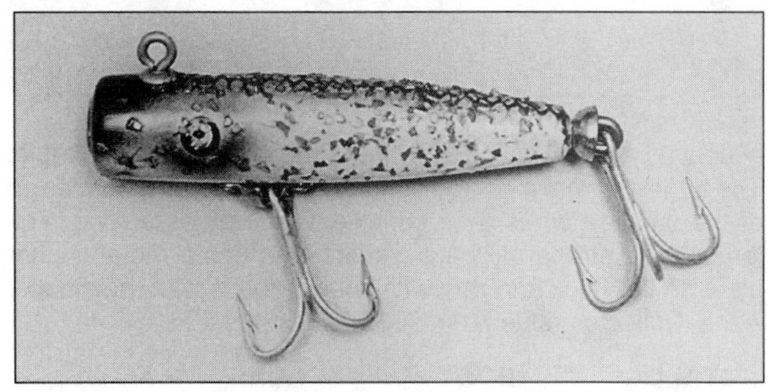

This is the new FRISKY appearing first in a 1952 catalog. It has unpainted eyes, one-piece surface hook hardware and measures 2-5/8".

CATALOG SERIES #	BODY LENGTH	LURE WEIGHT	HOOKS
8400	3"	1/2 oz.	2T

COLOR OR FINISH: White body with green back and red splash, white body with red head, mouse finish.

PAKRON

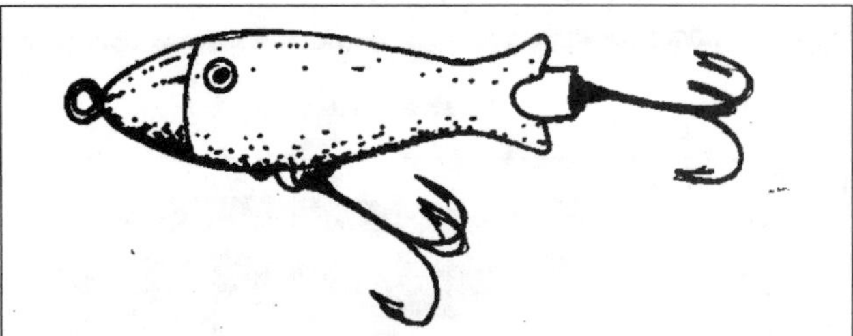

Appearing around 1931 this lure has a metal head with belly treble and a trailing treble. This trailing treble was hooked to a fastener that extended through the body to the metal head (2T). The lure was absent from catalogs by 1936. Collector value range: $75-$150.

CATALOG SERIES #	BODY LENGTH	LURE WEIGHT	
7000		2-3/4"	1 oz.

COLOR OR FINISH: Green Mullet, scale finish; white body, red head, gold sparks; white body, red head.

MUSTANG

This plug begins to appear in the catalogs about 1937. It can be found in four different sizes. The smaller three sizes are

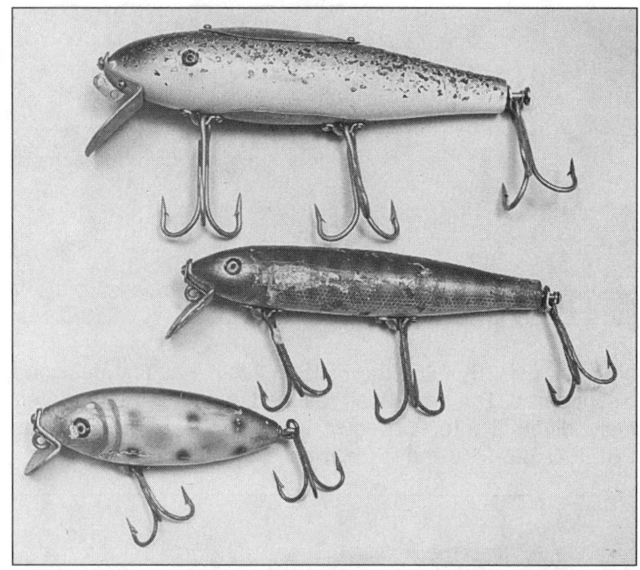

fitted with a metal diving lip, a belly treble and a trailing treble. The larger two have an additional belly treble. The body design of the smaller two is a bit chunkier than the larger one. The largest is a strong saltwater version and has a metal flasher plate on the back and belly. The photo above is of the smaller sizes. Collector value range: $25-$50.

CATALOG SERIES #	BODY LENGTH	LURE WEIGHT	HOOKS
*8600	2-1/2"	1/2 oz.	2T
8900	2-3/4"	1/2 oz.	2T
8900 (c. 1939)	4-1/2"	5/8 oz.	3T

COLOR OR FINISH: Red side, finish; green back, silver finish; natural pike, scale finish; natural perch, scale finish; white body, red head, silver sparks; black with silver lightning flash; white body, green and red spots; **sunfish, scale finish; **white body, red, yellow and black spots.

9500	5"	1-1/2 oz.	3T

COLOR OR FINISH: White body, red head only.

**The only size listed in 1937 and 1938.*

***New about 1941.*

POPRITE

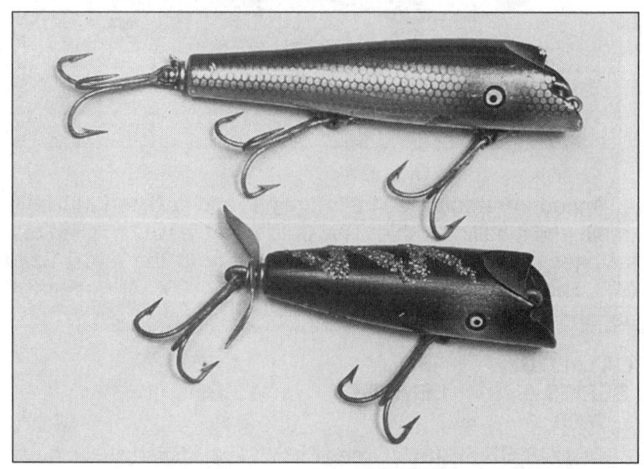

The POPRITE first appears around 1935-36 and stays in catalogs into the 1950s. It was first available in one size only (4"), but around 1940 a smaller size (3") was added. The larger sported two belly trebles and a trailing treble (3T) and the smaller has only one belly treble (2T). The 1955 catalog shows only the 3" size and there has been a tail propeller added. Collector value range: for older plugs $20-$50.

CATALOG SERIES #	BODY LENGTH	LURE WEIGHT
8500	3"	1/2 oz.
4"	5/8 oz.	

COLOR OR FINISH: *Red side, scale finish; *natural pike, scale finish; natural perch, scale finish; meadow frog; *white with silver sparks and red gills; *white with green and red spots; **green back, silver sparks; ** white with red head, silver sparks; **yellow with red stripes; **black with silver lightning flash.

**Eliminated by 1940-41.*

***Added in 1940-41.*

SCOOP

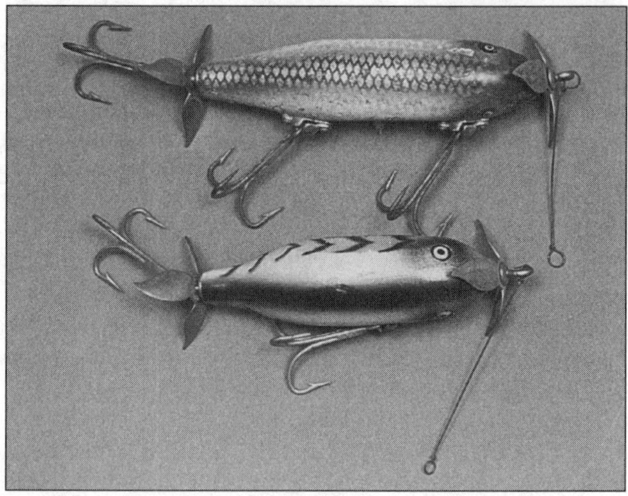

This is an unusual plug in that it has three-bladed propellers, fore and aft. Both sides of the body are slightly flattened and the body trebles are side mounted. New around 1937 it was first available in only one size (3-5/8"). By 1941 a second, smaller size (3") was available. The large size had two side trebles and a trailing treble (3T) and the smaller, only one side treble (2T). Both were removed from the line sometime in the late 1940s or early 1950s. They are very similar in body design to the Creek Chub Bait Company INJURED MINNOW except for the three blade propellers. Collector value range:$30-$60.

CATALOG SERIES #	BODY LENGTH	LURE WEIGHT
9300	*3"	1/2 oz.
3-5/8"	3/4 oz.	

COLOR OR FINISH: Red side, scale finish; silver sparks, green back; meadow frog, *natural perch, scale finish; *white with black stripes.

**Added around 1940-41.*

TNT

This all metal body plug was patented in 1929 and first observed in a 1931 catalog. It has a deep diving metal lip, a belly treble and a trailing treble. It had disappeared from catalogs by 1937. Collector value range: $50-$100.

CATALOG SERIES #	BODY LENGTH	LURE WEIGHT
6900	3-1/4"	1-1/10 oz.

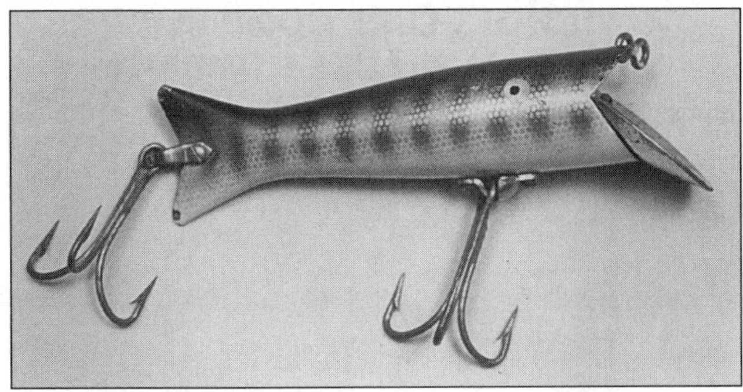

COLOR OR FINISH: Natural pike, scale blend; natural perch, scale finish; white with gold sparks, red head; spotlite finish with gold color lip; rainbow blend; polished nickel.

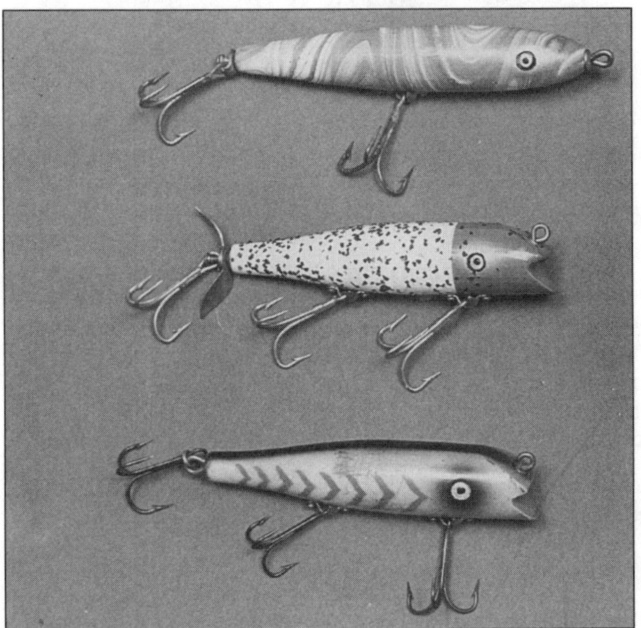

Three late 1940s Pflueger lures. Top is the BALLERINA #5400 Series. Middle is the TANTRUM #8400 and bottom is a painted eye DARTER of unknown vintage. Collector value range: $25-$50.

MILLER'S REVERSIBLE MINNOW

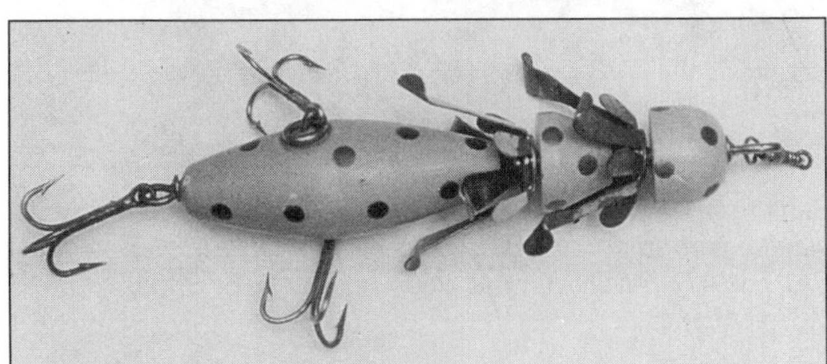

This extremely rare lure was first made by the Union Springs Specialty Company. It can be found in two variations. The earlier Union Springs model and the Pflueger model. The early (c. 1913) models had simple screw eye and washer hook hangers. It also has a slightly longer, much slimmer rear body section than the later version. The later one (c. 1916) utilizes the Pflueger type Neverfail hook hangers and a fatter rear body section. The 1916 lure seems much more refined in construction and finish. Examples of this latter model have been found new in a Pflueger box with the paper label (early maroon with paper label) identifying it as a MILLER'S REVERSIBLE MINNOW. Clearly there was some sort of agreement stuck between Pflueger and the Union Springs Company whereby Pflueger either bought the company or a license to produce the lures.

This lure is quite a wild looking contraption. Its propellers were colored gold and silver. The body was made of cedar, 4-1/2". It came in three color schemes: No. 1, Yellow with gold spots; No. 2, White belly, blended red and green spots; No. 3, White body, red head with gold spots. The one in the picture has the Pflueger "Neverfail Hook Hardware". Collector value range: $2,000-$2,500.

PFLUEGER UNKNOWN

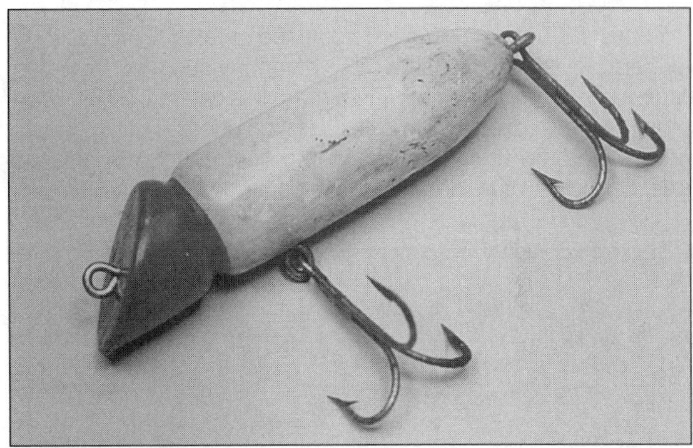

This is thought to be a Pflueger product. I have been unable to find it in any Pflueger publications. It measures 3-3/8" and has simple screw eye line tie/hook hanger hardware.

PHILLIPS FLY AND TACKLE COMPANY

Alexandria, Pennsylvania

Upper lure is a Phillips Series 1000 CRIPPLED KILLER. Lower lure is a Series 1600. It was not in the catalog so the name remains unknown.

I have an undated Phillips catalog "#53". The fact that there is a promotional photo in this catalog showing a happy George Phillips holding a fish he caught on one of his lures at Isle of Pines, Cuba and the catalog number lends credence to the supposition that this is a 1950s catalog. It has

11 plastic spinning and casting lures in it. The list follows:

Series 300 CRIPPLED KILLER Floater, 2-1/4"
Series 400 CRIPPLED KILLER Sinker, 1-3/4"
Series 900 MIDGET KILLER, 1-3/16"
Series 500 SPIN POPPER, 1-1/2" and 2"
Series 600 SPIN DEVIL, 2-1/4"
Series 700 WEIGHTED POPPER, 2-1/4" and 2-1/2"
Series 800 FLASH-O-MINO (underwater), 1-3/4"
Series 1000 CRIPPLED KILLER, 2-3/4"
Series 1100 SPINO-MINO, 3-1/2"
Series 1400 FAT BOY, 1-3/16" and 1-3/4"
Series 1500 BIG BOY, 2-1/2"
Series 1600 UN-CATALOGED, 2-1/4"
Series ISF INVINCIBLE STREAMER FLY for spinning, 3"

Series 1200 and 1300 were not in the catalog. Perhaps they were discontinued. The name of the company suggests they also made fly rod lures, but there were none in this catalog. I have seen some of them in price and sales lists at high prices. That suggests that the flies are more interesting to collectors than the plastic lures. Collector value range for the lures: under $10.

Two Series 1000 CRIPPLED KILLERS measuring 2-3/4" each.

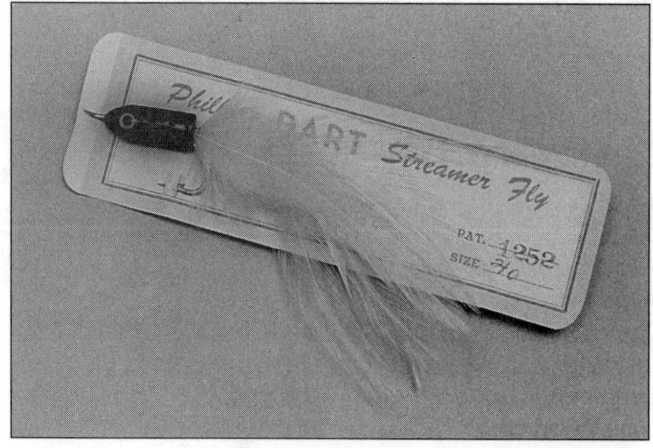

Phillips DART Streamer Fly #1252. Body measures 7/8" and the overall length is 4". Collector value range: No trade data found.

PICO LURES

Padre Island Company — San Antonio, Texas

NICHOLS LURE COMPANY
SPORTSMANS LURE COMPANY

Corpus Christi, Texas

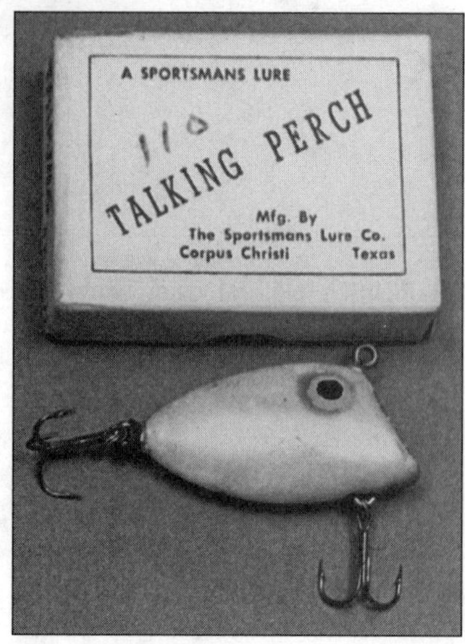

This present day company dates from 1933, but its roots are firmly in the 1920s when Fred Nichols was making his hand-carved red cedar lures. At some point he organized and formed the Nichols Lure Company. The box in the photo here has printed on its side: "Manufacturers of High Grade Fishing Tackle. Specializing in Wood and Plastic Lures." Nichols sold his company in 1947. After another sale the name became Pico.

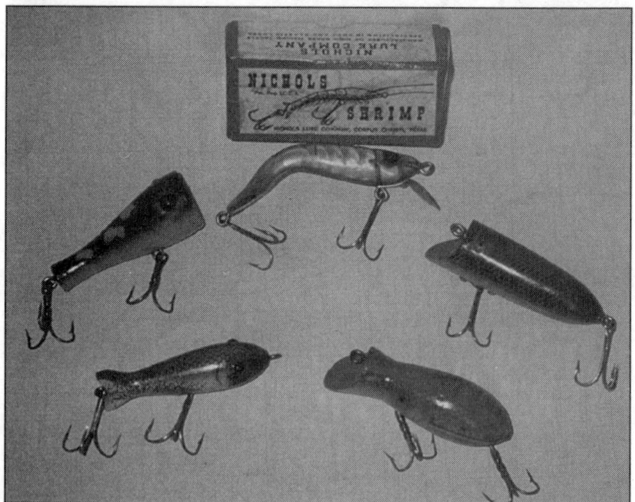

Baits from the Nichols Lure Company. Clockwise from top: a plastic shrimp lure, wood plug, wood CHIPMUNK, wood SALT WATER MINNOW, a wood popper type. Photo courtesy Jim Muma.

Just how the different names came to be and in what order is still unclear. There is some sort of connection, formal or informal, between Hawk Fish Lures, Pico and Whopper Stopper. In the last edition I reported that I had not yet found the written data to sort it out. It's still not, but I have made some progress. Please read the other lure company entries for what I have found.

I am indebted to Ed Henckel of Pico Lures for providing the first seven photos presented here. He gave me the photos almost twenty years ago. The lures are from the collection of Harvey Bowman.

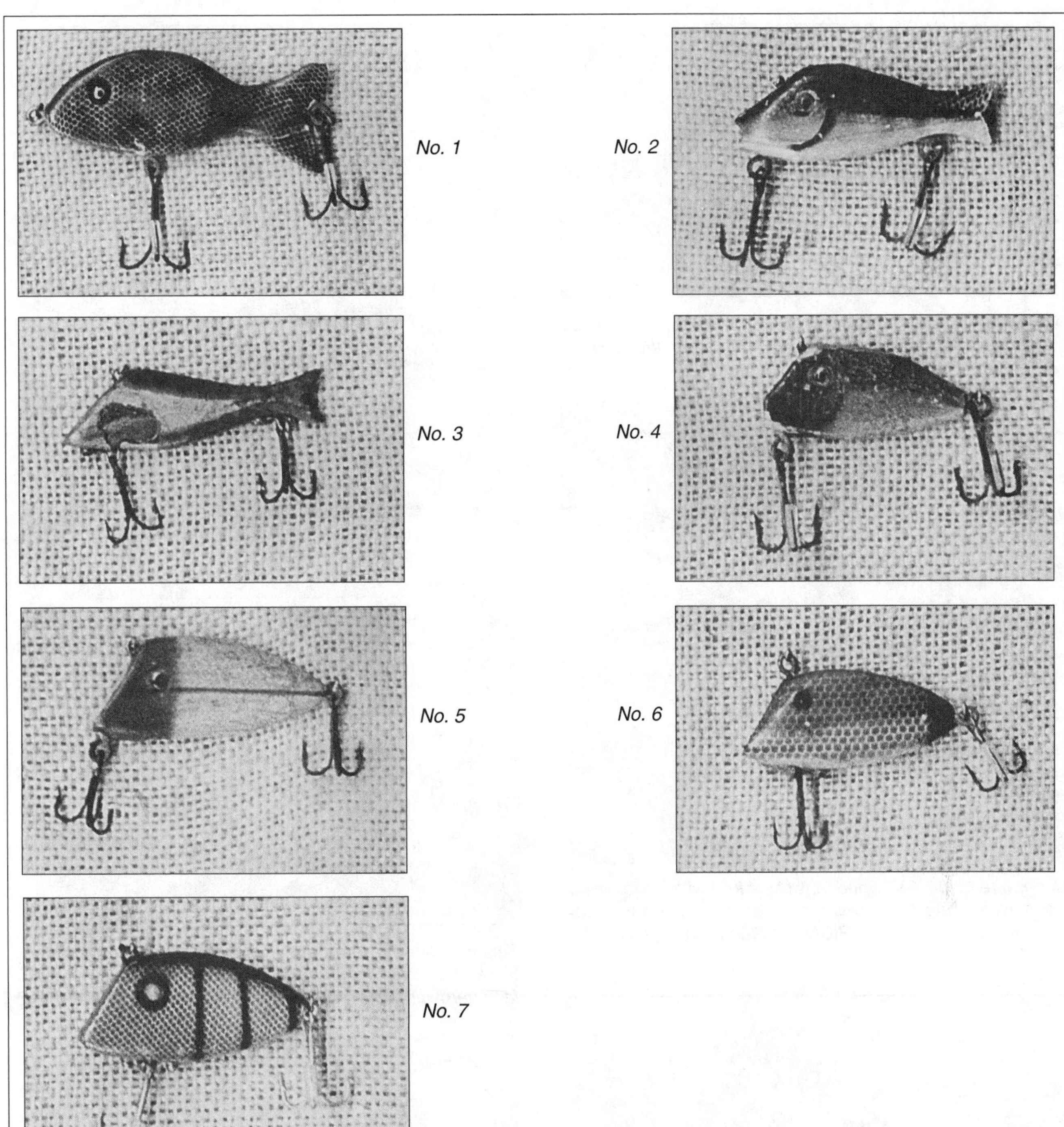

The photo marked No. 1 is of what is one of the earliest, but not the earliest, original vibrating lure designs. Called the PIGGY PERCH, it was hand-carved from red cedar by Fred Nichols in 1928 and it has glass eyes. Note the large tail fin. The earliest versions have a dorsal and ventral fin. The earliest also has a unique line tie arrangement where there were two parallel holes made through the body through which the wires were threaded, making a very strong line tie. No. 2 and No. 3 are also made of wood. This improved design was sold along with the older ones until the supply of the latter was exhausted. They were sold until about 1936. The primary improvement was making the tail fin smaller, although, like the original, they still had a tendency to get their tails broken or knocked off in use. The tailless No. 4 and No. 5 represents the last of the wooden PICO lures. The simplified design proved more durable and easier to carve. They were produced until the advent of plastic around 1946-1947. No. 6 represents the first of the plastic models and No. 7 is the present day lure. In 1971 Ed Henkel accepted a special award from Sports Afield magazine. Homer Circle, their Angling Editor, had named the PICO PERCH one of the ten best lures in the United States.

Nichols also made some shrimp lures. The early ones were also of wood and have glass eyes. They are rare and since no two of the few known to be in collector's hands are alike, they were apparently all handcrafted. Collector value range: Wooden Piggy Perch, $35-$50. No-Tail Wooden Pico, $25-$40. The Wooden Shrimp, $100-$200.

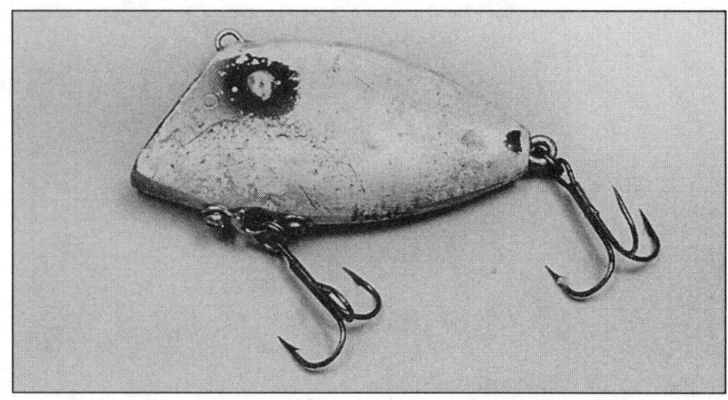

A 2-1/2" Pico with a black dot on its tail. This black dot is used to indicate a floating bait. It is marked "PICO" on the belly.

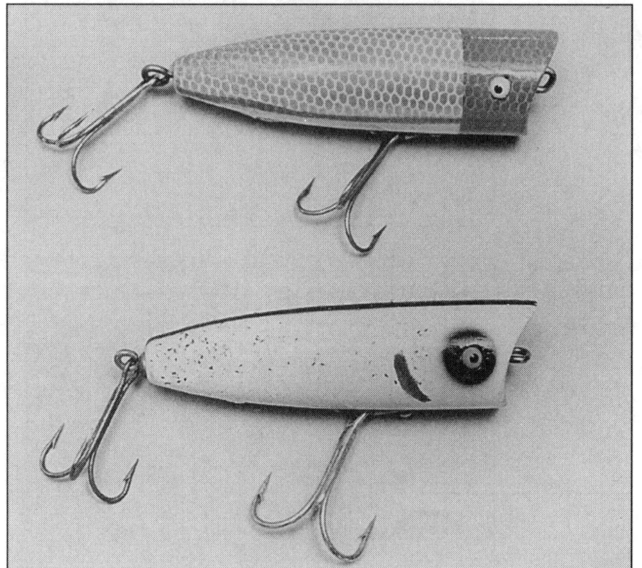

Upper lure is a 3-1/8" wooden Nichols lure with white beady glass eyes. The other measures the same, has yellow beady glass eyes and is marked PICO PLUNGER on the belly.

Both of these are wooden Nichols lures. Upper lure bears a remarkable resemblance of the Creek Chub Bait Company BOMBER. It is 3-1/4". The other, popper type, measure 2-3/8". Both have recessed screw eye belly hook hangers.

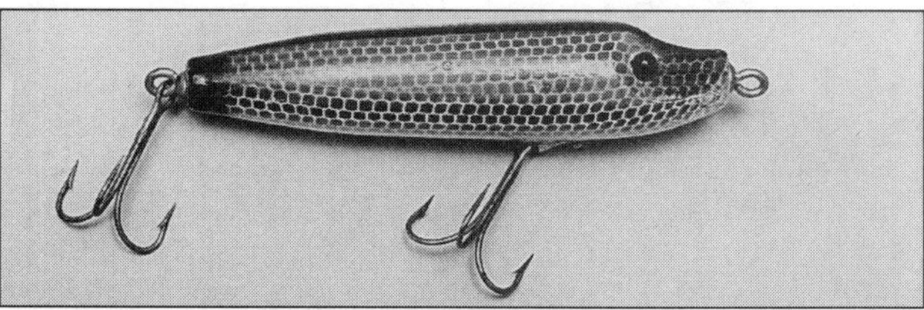

Wooden 2-5/8" VAMP-like PICO PAL with one-piece surface hardware and yellow beady glass eyes.

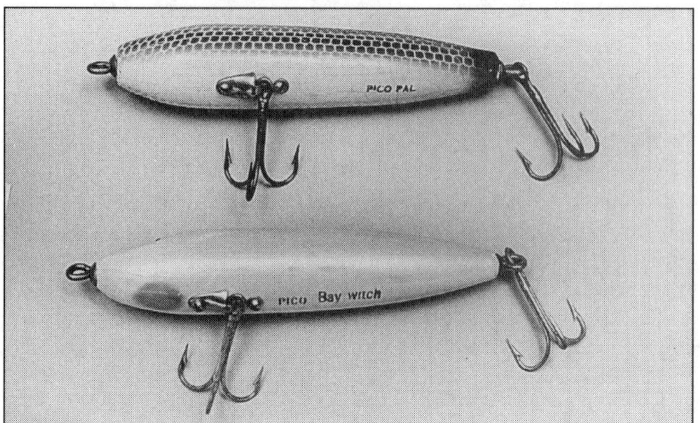

Belly view of the VAMP-like PICO PAL in the photo above. Note that one is marked "PICO Bay Watch". It is a bit longer the PICO PAL at 4" and it is also heavier. It is probably an underwater lure.

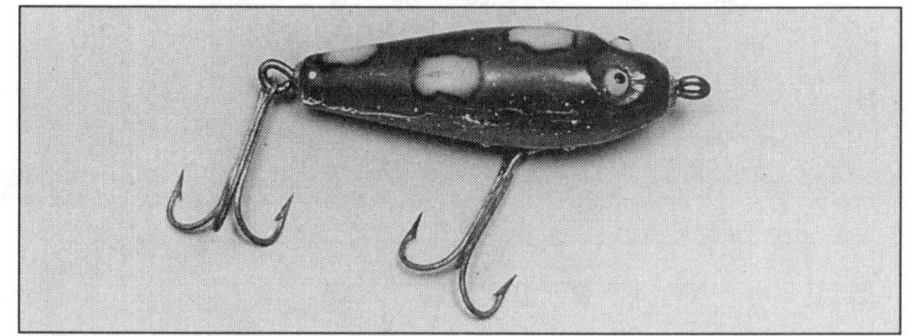

This wooden lure looks a bit like a Heddon VAMP. It has big black bead eyes, measures 3-3/4" and utilizes one-piece surface hardware. It is marked "PICO BAY WITCH" on its belly.

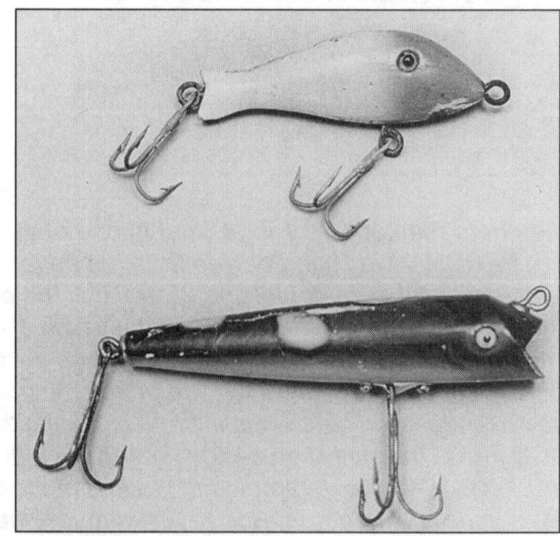

Upper wooden Nichols lure measures 2-3/4", has yellow glass eyes and simple screw eye hardware. Lower wooden Nichols darter type measures 3-3/4". It has a frog finish, beady white glass eyes and one-piece surface hardware.

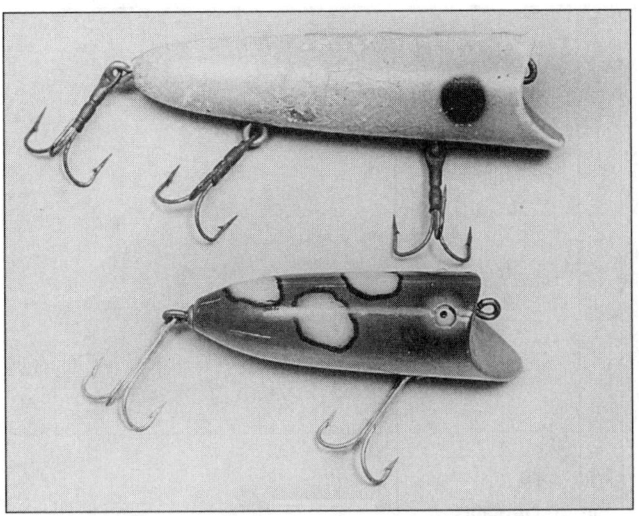

Two lures known to have been made by Fred Nichols. Upper lure measures 4, has simple screw eye hardware and a large blue spot for an eye. Lower has one-piece surface hardware and what appears to be glass eyes, but could be plastic taxidermy eyes.

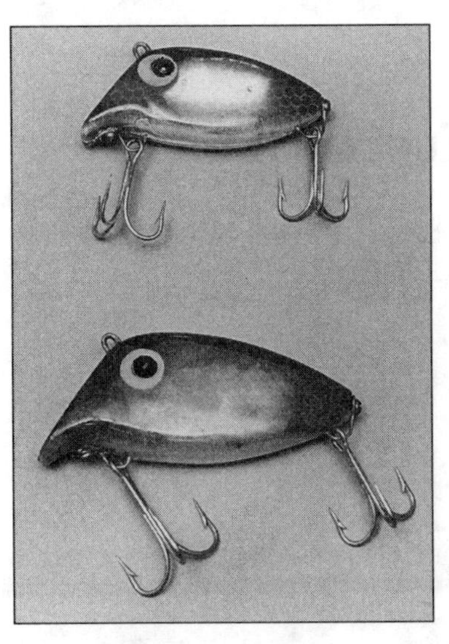

A 2" and 2-1/2" plastic PERKY PERCH from the Sportsman's Lure Company.

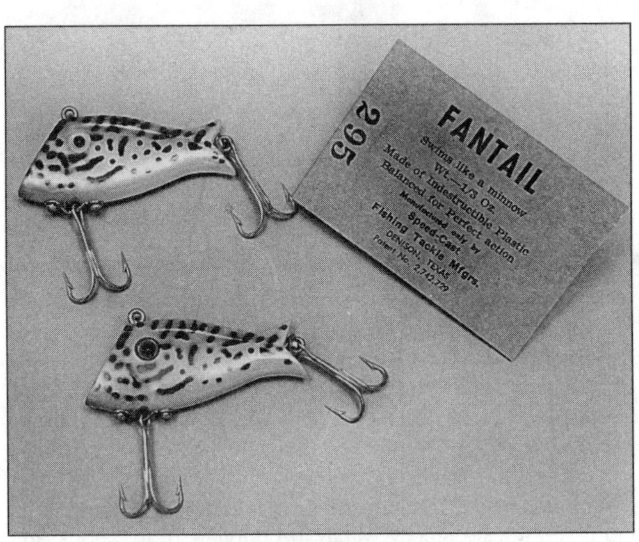

A pair of 2" plastic FANTAILS from the Speed-Cast Tackle Manufacturers, Dennison, Texas. PICO?

A Pico PLUNGER with the bead-like glass (?) eyes and one piece surface hardware.

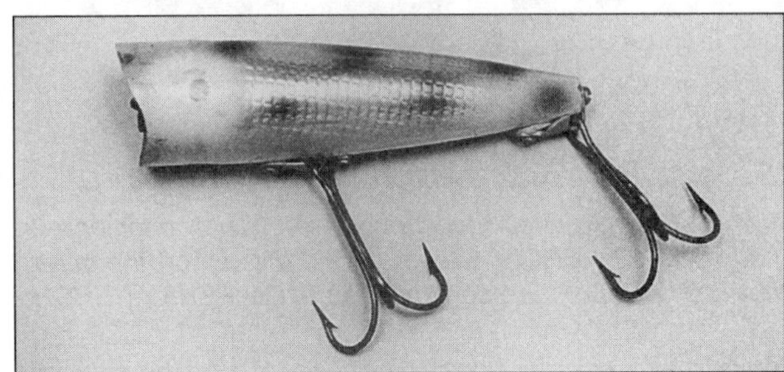

A 3-1/4" plastic PICO POP so marked on the belly.

A Pico SPLASHNIK measuring 3-3/8". This plastic lure has floppy pointed propeller spinners fore and aft.

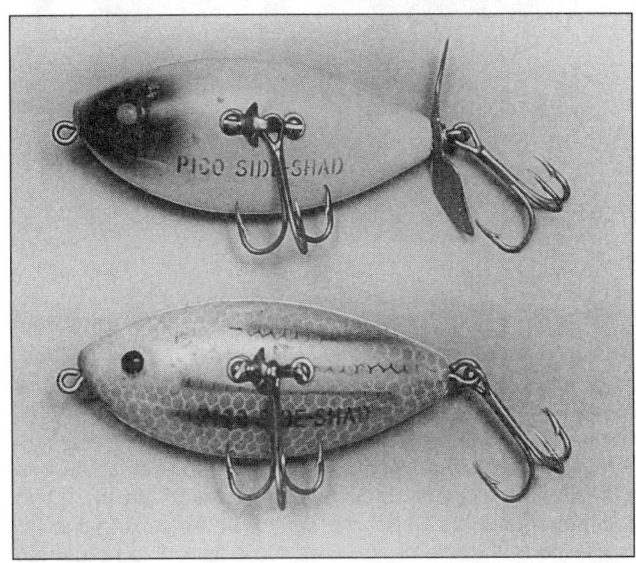

A pair of 2-1/2" plastic Pico lures stamped "PICO SIDE-SHAD". Note one has a tail propeller spinner and the other does not.

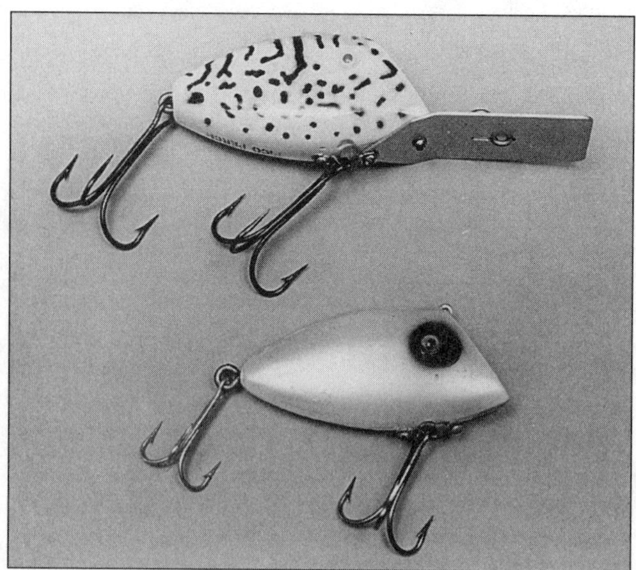

A pair of plastic lures measuring 2-1/4". The upper one is marked PICO PERCH. Except for the dive lip on the latter, they both look like the Sportsman's Lure Co. PERKY PERCH.

IMPORTANT NOTICE

The value ranges listed in this book are for lures in Very Good to Excellent condition. The values of those lures not in Very Good to Excellent condition can and probably will be worth considerably less. The values are meant to be a guide only.

PIRO'S WATER WHACKER

Piro Realistic Bait Company — Mangham, Louisiana

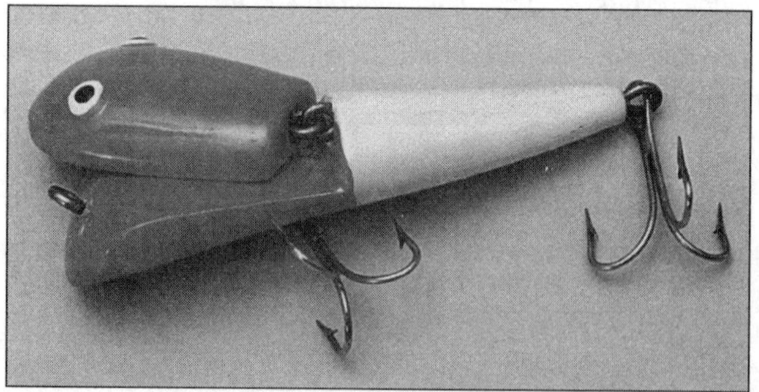

A search though all of my files, materials and references yielded no information about this company or the lure whatever. All there is, is the flyer that came with the new in the box wooden lure. It was patented in 1942. Measuring 3-1/2", this plug had a unique construction and line tie arrangement. You were supposed to thread your line through the lower screw eye and tie it to the upper screw eye. This was to put the "..two moveable members..under the control of the casting line". It was made in 12 different finishes. Collector value range: No trade data found.

Red Head
Shiner Scale

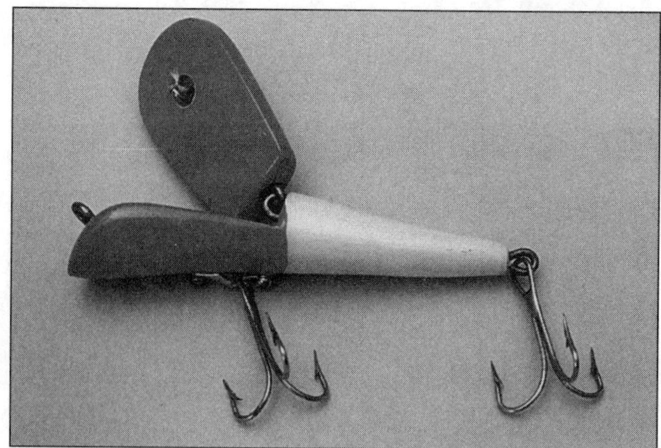

Pink Eye
Green Speckle
Yellow Speckle
Yellow Perch
Green Frog
Black and White
Insect Gray
Insect Blue Green
Black Eye
Red Mouth

PIPER LURE CO., LTD

John Pitts — Soren Sorenson
Grand Junction, Colorado

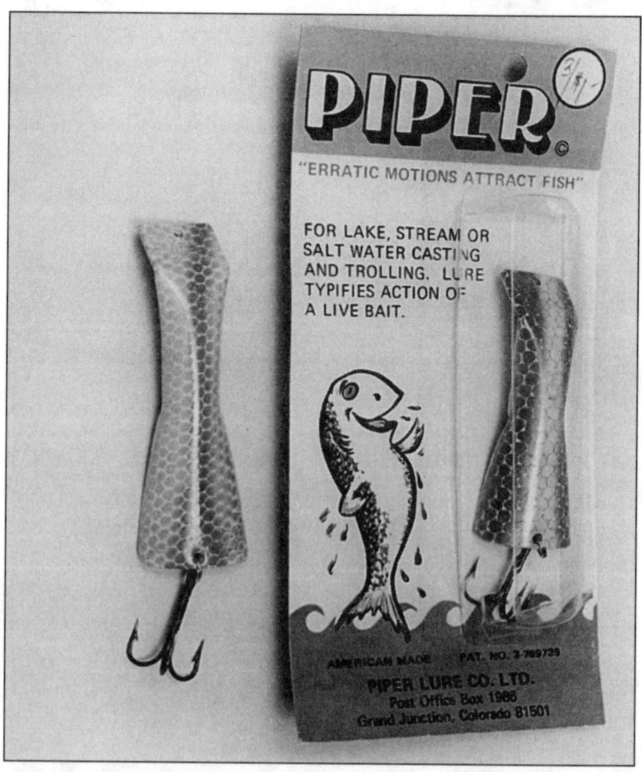

A Piper FISHTAIL.

Although this 1970s lure company is close to contemporary, and might not be strictly within the purview of this book, the company was short-lived and its lures interesting. Piper was in business from 1972 to 1978. The company was dissolved the year after John Pitts died. The lures were metal with beautiful finishes. There were four types, the 2-1/2", and 3-1/2" FISHTAILS and the 1-1/2" JIGGING LURE. The fourth type was a 4-1/2" FISHTAIL, but it was experimental and never went into production. What makes these lures interesting to the collector is the extremely limited number that were manufactured. The total production runs for each follows:

2-1/2" Fishtail - 600

3-1/2" Fishtail - 600

4-1/2" Fishtail - 100

1-1/2" Jigging lure - 1200

By the time of the company closing, all but 60 of the lures had been sold to the public.

Piper lures, according to a 1974 catalog, were available as follows:

"ALL LURES AVAILABLE IN SOLID OR SCALE FINISH IN THE FOLLOWING COLORS: Yellow, Red, Blue, Green, Orange, Black, White, Antique Brown.

FLUORESCENT COLORS: Yellow, Red Orange, Blue, Green.

Fluorescent colors are not available in scale finish.

Any two color combinations are available.

Special color orders are accepted on orders of 5 gross or more".

Collector value range:

1-1/2" Jigging Lure	$15-$25.
2-1/2" Fishtail Lure	$20-$30.
3-1/2" Fishtail Lure	$50-$75.
4-1/2" Fishtail Lure	$150-$200.

THE PONTIAC RADIANT THE PONTIAC MINNOW

Pontiac Manufacturing Co. — Pontiac, Michigan

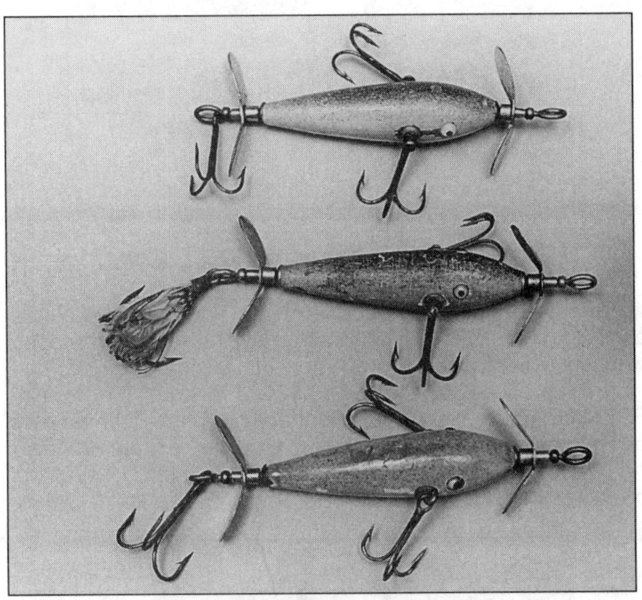

Upper 2-3/4" PONTIAC MINNOW has a screw and threaded tube hook fastener. The center lure has the so-called 'deluxe' style and the lower, the simple screw eye and hook arrangement. These are discussed in the text.

An article in a 1958 periodical takes an historical glance back 50 years to one of their 1908 issues and reprints an article headlined "1908-Luminous Lures Big News in Latest Lineup of Tackle Items." The article describes "The Radiant Minnow developed by the Pontiac Mfg. Company". Pontiac produced these lures in two sizes plus the same lures in other non-luminous colors.

There are three distinct and unique hook hanger hardware styles to be found. Each of them was designed to make the side hooks stand away from the body of the lure.

1. The earliest style was as threaded brass tube and screw that passed laterally through the body of the lure. The hook shank was bent and the tube and screw was a certain length so that when they were assembled and tightened down the hooks were allowed to rotate around the tube freely, but not touch the body.
2. In the second style, the so-called "Deluxe" style, the side trebles were mounted utilizing a screw placed through the eye of the hook and a raised or convex cup on the body. The screw is not tightened down against the hook and the shank of the hook is bent outwardly near the eye. This system allows the hooks to rotate through 360 degrees without touching the body or each other.
3. The third style utilizes a modified cup and screw eye arrangement that accomplishes the same thing. You can see that each stage in the evolution was simpler to make and less expensive.

Each example of Pontiac lures I have seen sport glass eyes and round propeller spinners fore and aft. There are two sizes to be found, a 2-7/8" and 3" three-hooker and a 3-3/4" five-hooker. The latter is the most difficult to find. Non-luminous colors available were Red, White, Yellow or Green. Collector value range: Three-Hooker, $200-$300.; Five-Hooker, $300-$400.

PORTER BAIT COMPANY

Dick Porter — Daytona Beach, Florida

I have an undated photocopy of a page from the Florida Antique Tackle Club newsletter that has a short article quoting Charles Waterman's column FISHING from a 1962 issue of Florida Wildlife. Waterman deducts from his historical information that the Porter Bait Company dates from about 1920. It was apparent from the article that the company was still in business in 1962.

Waterman was correct. Volume III *Florida Lure Makers and Their Lures* details the Porter company. Porter actually started making and selling Clothes Pin type baits about 1920. He continued this endeavor, part-time apparently, on into the 1930s. At some point he and a friend named Ray Johnson operated the Dixie Bait Company out of Daytona Beach, Florida. The Dixie lures are very rare. About the only way the average collector will be able to know he has found one is if it is in its original box. Johnson died and the Porter apparently decided he could reorganize with new people and began his Porter Bait Company in 1946.

Waterman's column on Porter was primarily singing the praises of the Porter SEA HAWK as a pier fishing lure second to none. He did allude to a couple of other Porter lures such as the SPIN HAWK, KILLER, RACKETEER and PIRATE, but there were many others. The Florida lure book features at least thirty-five different Porter lures. When you factor in different sizes and configurations of each over the years you can come up with dozens. Porter collecting can be a real interesting challenge. The following is a list of Porter names I came up with before seeing Volume III of *Florida Lure Makers and their Lures.* Many of them are illustrated herein.

OL CRIP

PIRATE

STIX

TOP-SPIN

ZOMBIE
POP-STOP
SPINDLE
SCOOTER POOPER
KILLER
RACKETEER
SEA HAWK
SPIN-POP
SMART ALEC
DUZ-BIZ

Those Porter lures I have handled and photographed all have imaginative colors and finishes and are superbly finished. Many of them are marked with the name of the lure or the name and the "PORTER" name, but this practice seems to have been initiated around 1940 so those older ones are probably not marked so. It appears that the hook hanger hardware type follows about the same evolution as other companies. The first seems to be a recessed screw eye with rimless cup followed by the common cup and screw eye hardware, then the one piece surface (beginning c. 1940) and finally the simple screw eye and washer arrangement.

Eyes were always painted, but some were rather elaborate, have three and sometimes four different rings of color. I have seen many Porter lures with a target painted on the belly, usually toward the throat, but have not yet been able to determine the significance of the mark if any.

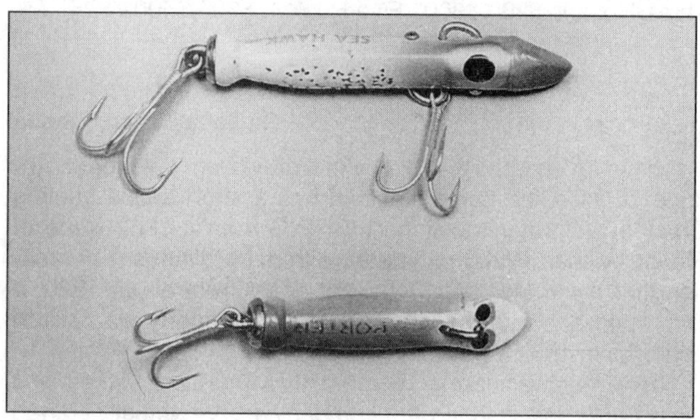

Above is a photo of two Porter SEA HAWKS, measuring 2-3/4" and 2" respectively. The Sea Hawk is a wood body lure with a molded metal (probably lead) head. Note the unusual line tie/belly hook hanger arrangement. This very strong rig consists of a single heavy gauge metal wire beginning at the metal head and penetrating the body making up the line tie or line tie and hook hanger. Collector value range: $10-$20.

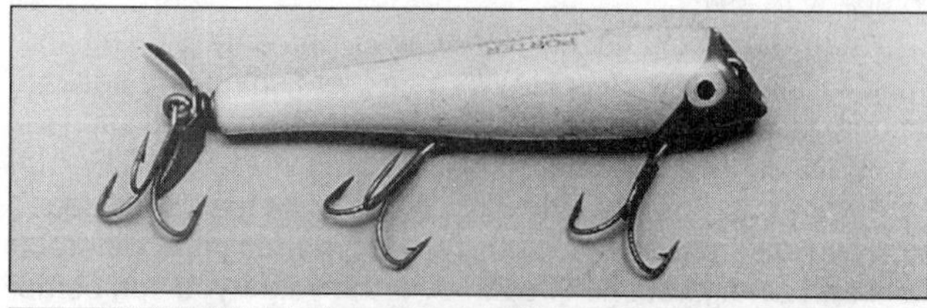

Above are two photos of the Porter POP-STOP (see SPIN-POP). They measure 4-1/4" and 4-1/8" respectively. Both have floppy propeller spinners and two-piece surface hook hanger hardware. The box in the photo is orange in color. This is a rare color making the box and the lure much more valuable than the lure alone. The less rare though certainly not commonly found color box is black with gold lettering. Collector value range: $10-$20.

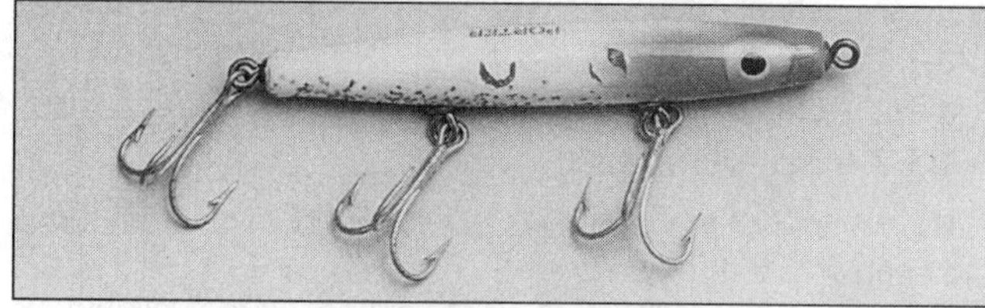

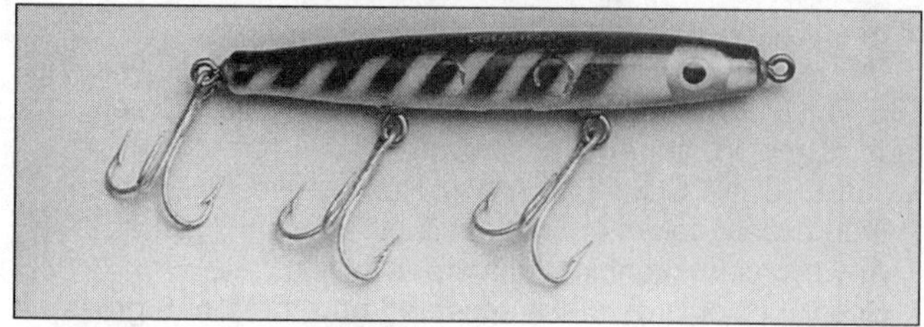

Porter PIRATES so marked on the back. Measuring 4", they each have six internalized belly weights, the screw eye and washer hook hanger/tail protector. Found in clear plastic boxes with paper inserts stating only the company name and address. Collector value range: $10-$20.

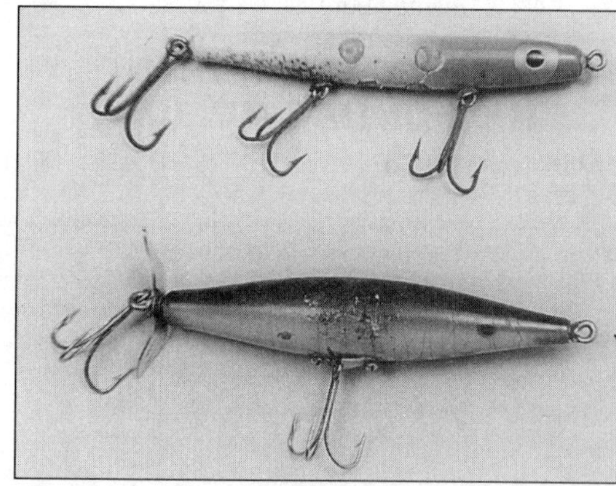

Upper lure is a Porter PIRATE, lower is a SPINDLE.

The upper lure in this photo is 4" long and is marked on the back PORTER PIRATE. It has screw eye hangers with cupped washers utilized as hook preventers. It has six internalized belly weights. Collector value: $10-$20. The lower lure is a 4" SPINDLE. It has the one piece surface hardware, four red dots on the belly and a rear floppy propeller spinner marked "SHAKESPEARE Made in U.S." Porter frequently use parts bought from other companies. Collector value range: $10-$20.

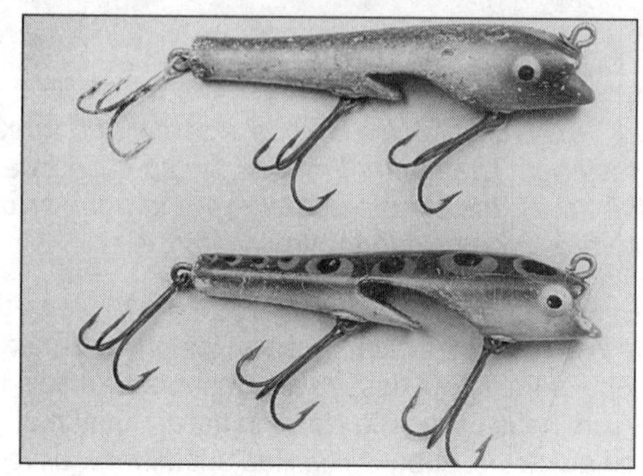

Here are two unusual Porter Company lures whose name remains unknown at the time. Collectors refer to it as the "Bottle Opener" for obvious reasons. Both of these sport the old cup and screw eye hangers and measure 4" long. When the tail hook hanger is removed it measures an unusually long 1-1/2" and has two washer bearings. There is also a hard material wrapped around the shank of the screw eye about 3/16" long behind the bearings and the body is bored out to accommodate the extra diameter caused by it. Collector value range: $10-$20.

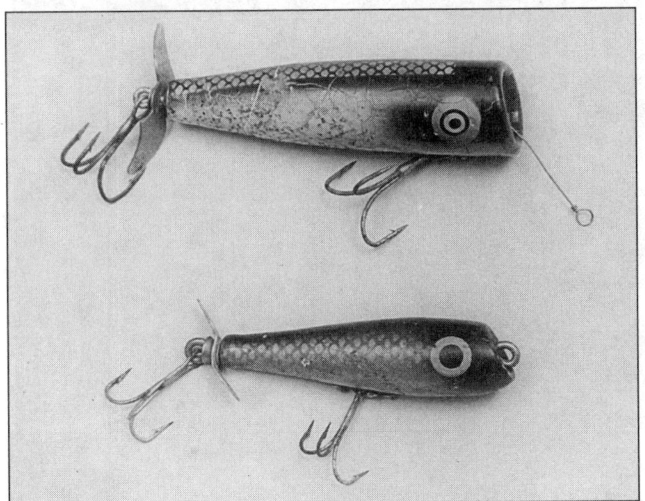

Upper lure is a Porter SMARTALEC, lower is a SPIN-POP

The c. 1940 SMART ALEC in the photo here measures 3-1/4", has a long wire leader and one-piece surface hook hanger hardware. It also has a target mark painted on its belly. Collector value range: $10-$20.

The SPIN-TOP is a smaller version of the POP-STOP illustrated earlier. It is 2-5/8" long, has one-piece surface hardware and an odd shaped rear mount aluminum propeller spinner. Collector value range: $10-$20.

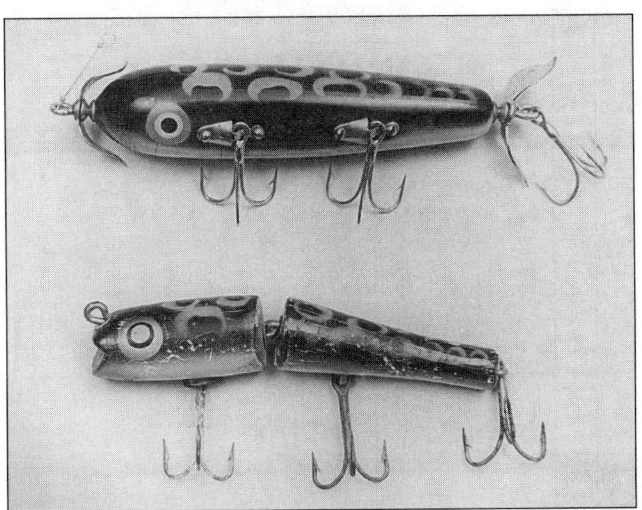

Upper lure is a Porter OL' CRIP and the lower one is a BROKEN BACK by Porter.

The OL' CRIP in the photo measures 4" long. I had two to examine and they were a bit different from each other. The one in the photo here has floppy propeller spinners bearing the "SHAKESPEARE, MADE IN U.S.A." oval logo and one-piece surface hook hanger hardware. The other one I examined was not nearly as well made. While both were flat-sided, the other one was decidedly thinner. The hardware was not as well made as the one in the photo and the Creek Chub Bait Co. style propeller spinners were unmarked. We can only surmise that it was a later model and made more economically for profit. Collector value range: $10-$20.

The other lure in the photo is a Porter BROKEN BACK measuring 4" long. It sports the old cup and screw eye hook hardware and a tail hook insert. Collector value range: $10-$20.

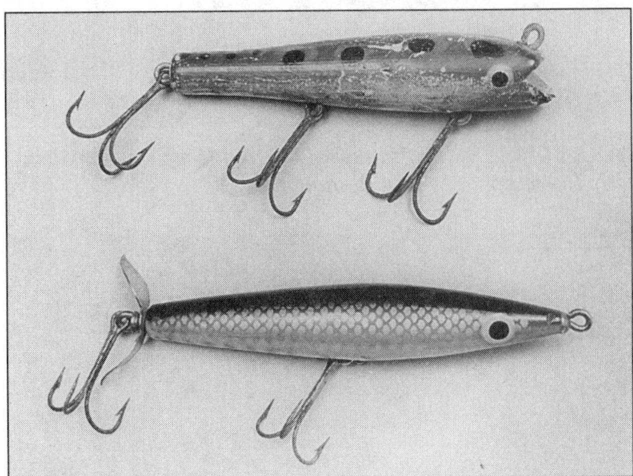

Upper lure is a 4" Porter DARTER and the lower lure is a SPINDLE measuring 4-1/4".

The DARTER in the photo has the oldest Porter rimless cup and screw eye belly hook hardware and a tail hook insert. Collector value range: $10-$20.

The Porter SPINDLE in the photo has the one-piece surface hardware, is marked "PORTER SPINDLE" on the back and an unmarked floppy propeller spinner. The belly has seven black stripes and a red slash mark painted on. Collector value range: $10-$20.

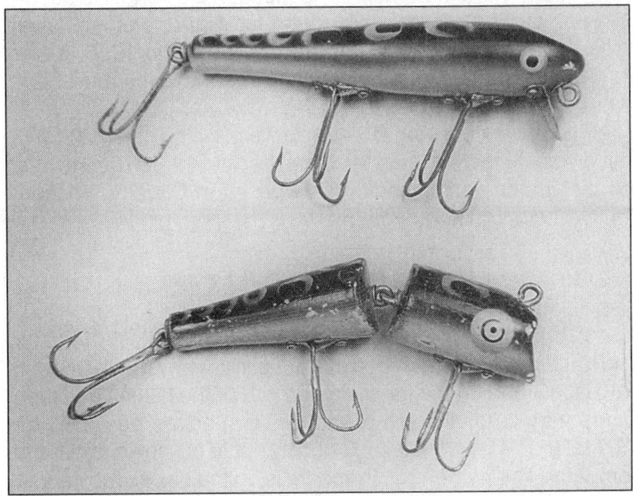

The upper lure is a Porter ZOMBIE measuring 4-1/4" and the other is a Porter 4" BROKEN BACK.

The ZOMBIE in the photo sports one-piece surface hardware. Note that there are two disc type washers at the tail with the concave sides facing each other. There seems to be no particular advantage to this configuration. It may have been an attempt at making a hook presenter or it may have been done inadvertently during assembly. Collector value range: $10-$20.

The BROKEN BACK is 1/8" longer than the one previously illustrated and has a more blunt face. It is a newer version, having the third style hook hanger hardware, the one-piece surface. It also has the tail hook insert. Collector value range: $10-$20.

A PULVERISER with its original box. It has a silver scale pattern. Photo courtesy Ken Bernoteit.

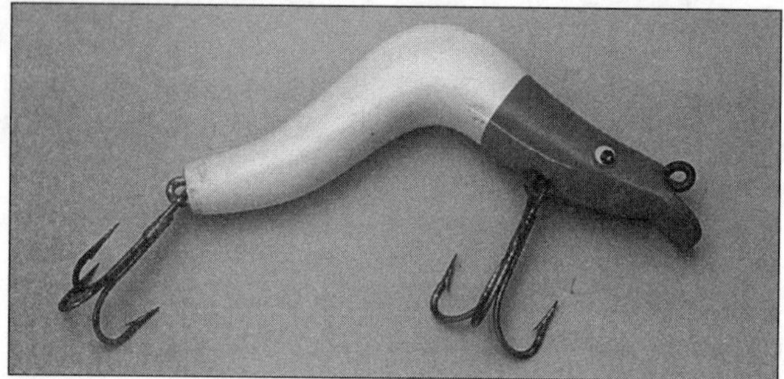

Red head and white body PULVERIZER.

PUL-V-RISER

Lynn E. Pulver Swea City, Iowa

Very little is known about Pulver or his lures. We do know that he applied for a patent on this one in 1951 and was granted it in early 1953. It is plastic and measures 3" long. No advertising or catalog entries were found for it or any other Pulver lures. I did find another patent granted to him in 1956. It was for a handsome metal spoon bait with beads so he must have serious about making his lures.

NFLCC member Ken Bernoteit tells of being given 20-30 of these lures to test on Lake Michigan back in the 1970s. He said the distributor was Spengler Enterprises in Cudahy, Wisconsin. Collector value range: $5-$7.

RAINBOW WIGGLERS

V. O. Pritchard Springfield, Missouri

These plastic lures are made of Lucite. They are molded in halves, painted on the flat inside on one of the halves and then joined very carefully with an adhesive specially designed for the material. The work is high quality. Little is known about the company. The name V.O. Pritchard is on the box as the maker. There is a connection between this company and an Anderson Bait Company also of Springfield. Dick Streater, in his *Streater's Reference Catalog of Old Fishing Lures* and Dean Murphy in his book, *Fishing Tackle Made in Missouri* both mention the Anderson Company as operating c. 1949. Streater has a "P. Anderson" notation and "A.B.C." in his reference. Murphy also notes that the Rainbow Lure Company was doing business in Springfield in 1992, but a call to directory assistance in Springfield revealed no such company in the telephone book in 1995. There was a letter postmarked in 1946, found in the basement Pritchard's old residence with some other papers that indicate that he and W.W. Anderson were planning a partnership in the lure business. The letter had a rough sketch of two halves of a plastic lure and description of the assembly process.

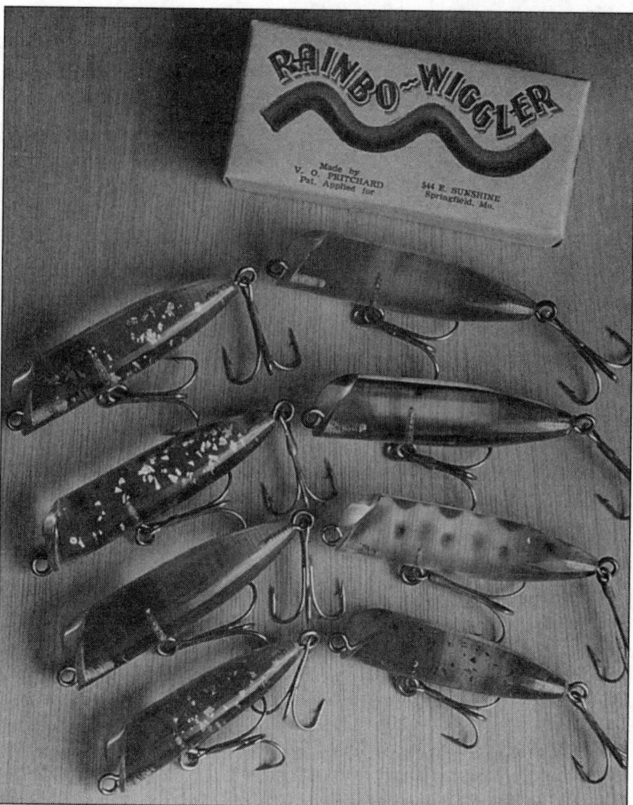

Photo courtesy Dennis "Doc" Hyder

The lures are found in two sizes, 2-1/2" and 2-3/4" in at least 15 different color patterns. They are extremely colorful. It's too bad I was unable to reproduce the photo in color. The colors are bright, almost vibrant. RAINBOW WIGGLER is a very appropriate name. The lures have been known to collectors for a few years, but it is only recently that the colorful boxes have been discovered. These boxes appear to be in short supply. Collector value range: $25-$30, new in the box: $75-$80.

REEAL LURES, INC.

Three Rivers, Massachusetts

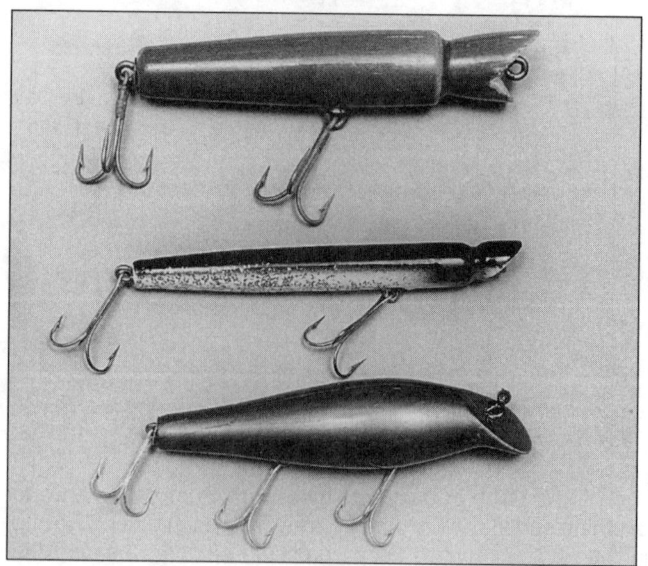

There is nothing known about these lures beyond the names on the boxes they came in and the company address from the same.

March 31, 1953 L. E. PULVER 2,632,973

FISHING LURE

Filed May 28, 1951

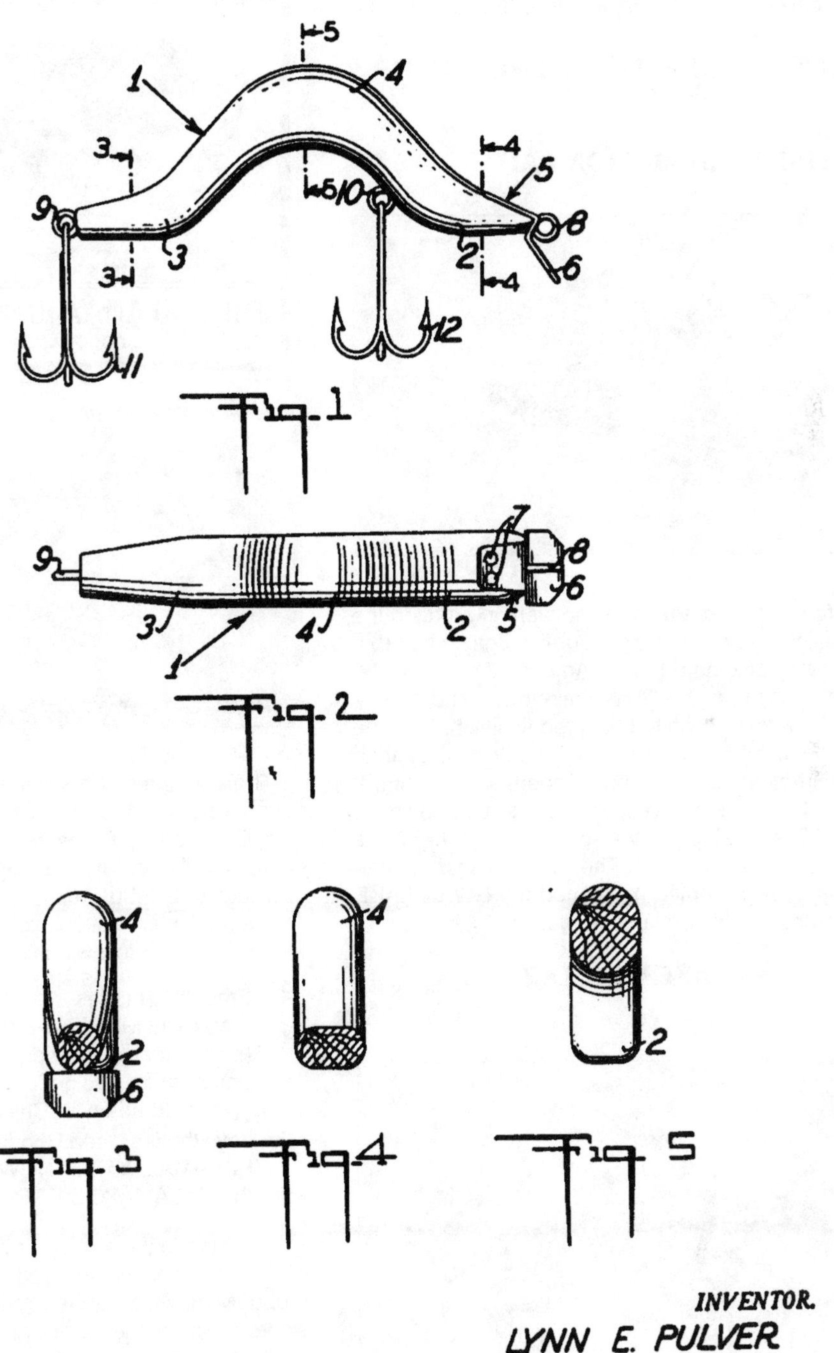

INVENTOR.
LYNN E. PULVER
BY
Robert U. Geib, Jr.
ATTORNEY

Top to bottom in the photo:

SIZZLER JR. 4-7/8" Cup and screw eye hook hangers.
FRESHWATER POPPER 4-5/8" Screw eye hook hangers.
FRESHWATER NIKE 4-3/8" Cup and screw eye hook hangers.

Each of these names was prefixed by the phrase "Famous Floyd Roman". There was no trade information from which to determine a value, but there was one reference to a Floyd Roman REEAL LURE 'SKIN DIVER" selling at auction in 1995 for $125 and interestingly, a FRESH WATER POPPER (Floyd Roman stick lure in the catalog) sold for only $15 in a 1997 auction.

J.W. REYNOLDS DECOY FACTORY

Chicago, Illinois

SPIKE-TAIL MOTION BAIT

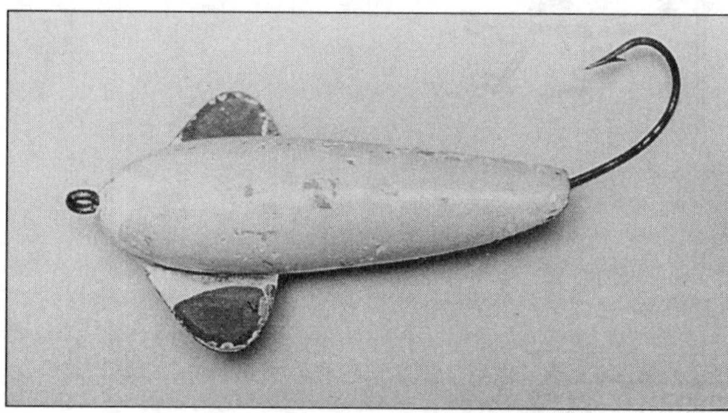

The only references I was able to find were in an ad in the April, 1915 edition of *The Outer's Book* magazine and a Schmelzer's catalog also dated 1915. Among other things the catalog stated that the lure was "A new minnow..." and it came in a red body, white fin or a white body, red fin finish. The one depicted in the photo here has a yellow body with a white head and red and white fins, but could be a fisherman's repaint. It measures 3-5/8" long, has no eyes, and sports cup and screw hook hardware. The catalog entry also states that the single hook is detachable and reversible. The 1915 ad said the lure was patented in 1914 and also mentioned the SWAN LAKE WIGGLER following. Collector value range: $150-$200.

SWAN LAKE WIGGLER

by Reynolds

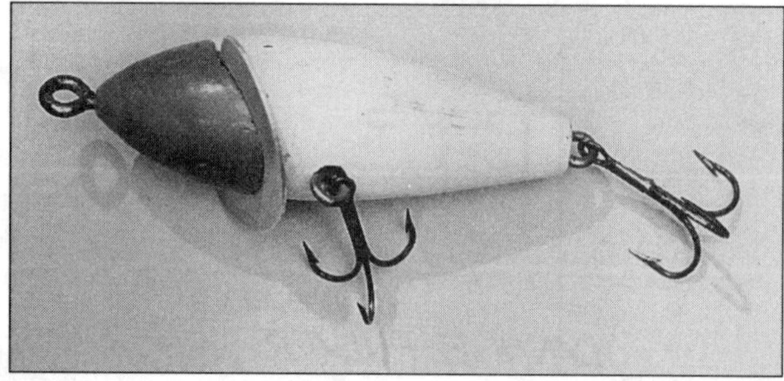

The one advertisement (1915) I was able to find said this lure was available "...in any color desired", that it was patented, and the hooks were detachable and reversible. The ad illustration shows a lure with double hooks. The metal flange is made of aluminum. Advertisement text indicated that they made other lures but did not specify. Collector value range: $150-$200.

RHODES

Bert O. Rhodes
Kalamazoo Fishing Tackle
Manufacturing Co.

Jay B. Rhodes

Fred D. Rhodes
Kalamazoo, Michigan

A 1904 advertisement.

There is some confusion when you try to sort out the relationship between Fred D. Rhodes, his uncle Jay B. Rhodes, Bert O. Rhodes, Frederick C. Austin and the Shakespeare Company. As you will see they are all tied to each other by way of a family or a business relationship of one sort or another. These particular relationships are a bit hazy in some instances. In any case, the following is what we do know.

1. Fred D. Rhodes was the inventor of THE PERFECT CASTING MINNOW and was granted the patent in 1904 (see patent illustration on page 115). The rights for the patent were assigned to Fred C. Austin of the Fred C. Austin Company of Chicago.
2. Jay Rhodes, Fred Rhodes' uncle, was the inventor of the KALAMAZOO MINNOW and his mechanical frog lure, the KALAMAZOO FROG.

Nowhere in the text of the patent application is any mention of just what material the frog lure was to be made from. It was probably made of rubber, but the drawings seem to suggest wood. Perhaps the patent model was made of wood and the production version was rubber.

3. It is known that Jay Rhodes worked for Fred C. Austin at the time of the 1904 St. Louis World's Fair. He apparently also worked at making and selling his own lures before, during and after his employment with Austin. In exactly what capacity he was employed is not known.
4. Bert O. Rhodes was probably a relative of the other two Rhodes. He was also granted a patent for a mechanical

No. 803,134. PATENTED OCT. 31, 1905.

J. B. RHODES.

FISH BAIT OR LURE.

APPLICATION FILED DEC. 5, 1904.

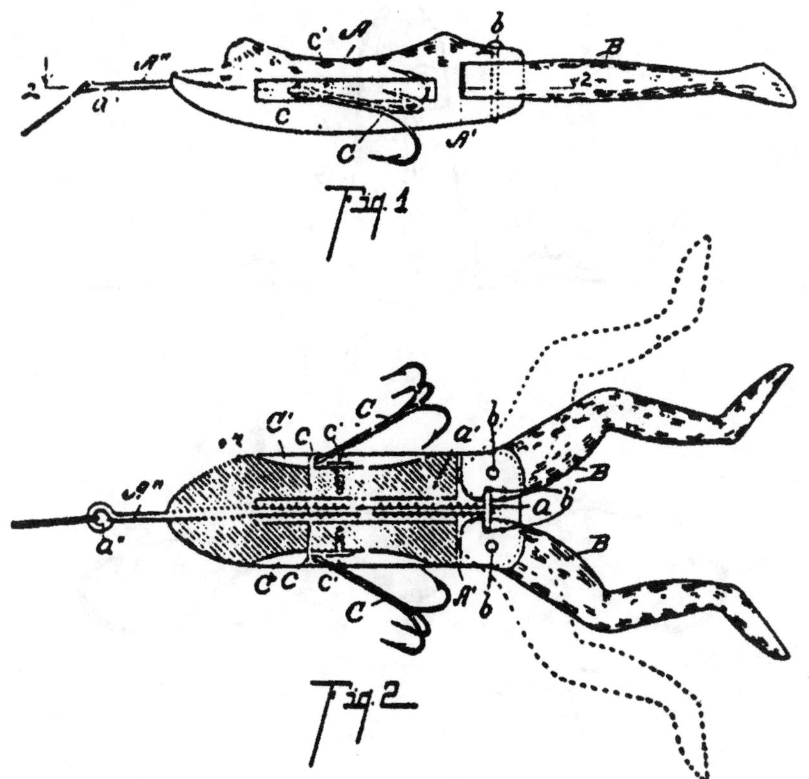

Witnesses:

Inventor,
Jay B. Rhodes
By Chappell & Earl
Att'ys

The 1905 patent for Jay Rhodes' mechanical frog.

No. 824 817. PATENTED JULY 3, 1906.

B. O. RHODES.

FISH BAIT OR LURE.

APPLICATION FILED OCT. 30, 1905.

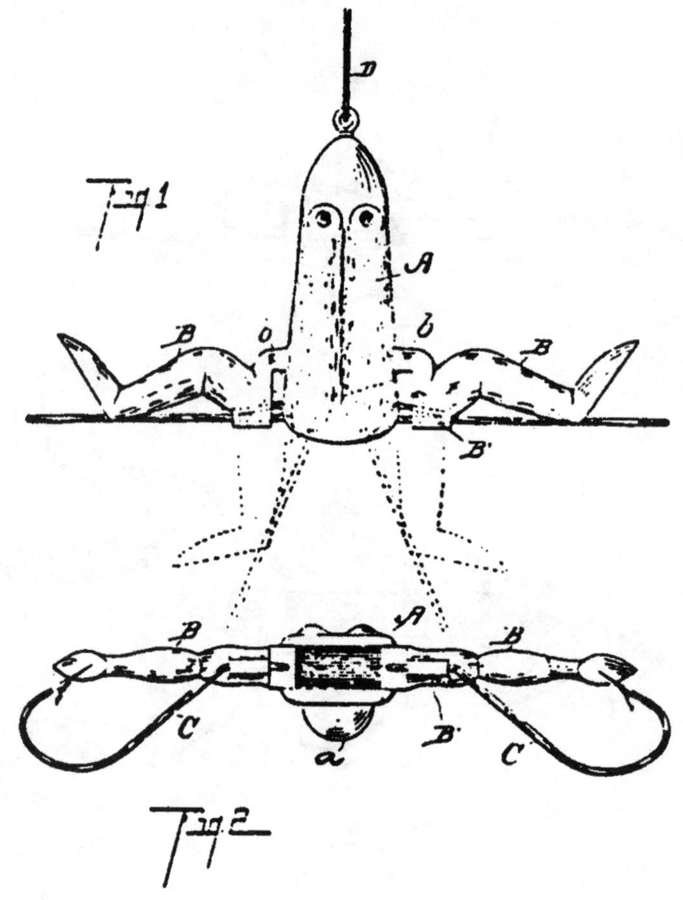

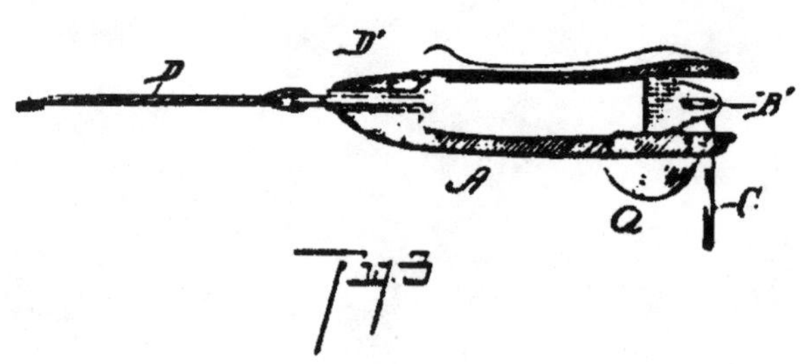

Witnesses:

Lulu Greenfield

Ethel L. Bradford

Inventor.

Bert O. Rhodes

By Chappell & Earl

Att'ys

Illustration in the 1906 Bert Rhodes patent.

rubber frog (see patent reproduced in part here and the drawing in the Shakespeare section). The patent was granted to him on July 3, 1906. What is interesting here is that at the time of granting the patent also says that all rights were assigned to William Shakespeare, Jr. More about this later.

5. Art and Scott Kimball reported in their book, Early Fishing Plugs of the U.S.A.(copyright 1985, Aardvark Publications, Inc.), that Jay Rhodes sold the rights to his KALAMAZOO FROG (Fred Rhodes' mechanical rubber frog) to Shakespeare in 1905. Since Bert Rhodes's frog was patented in 1906 (after the transfer of rights), it may be that Shakespeare asked him to patent a heretofore unpatented lure, assigning the rights to them for protection.
6. It is obvious from the above, that somehow Jay Rhodes had obtained the rights to Fred's lure from Frederick C. Austin and the rights to Bert's rubber frog at some point prior to 1905, but after the 1904 patent date of Fred's lure.

In conclusion, it would seem that most, if not all, the Rhodes lures ended up in the Shakespeare line early on in that company's development years. It is not certain whether all were eventually offered as a regular part of the line, but it is known that at least three were. These will be discussed in the Shakespeare section.

The following photos are of Fred D. Rhodes' PERFECT CASTING MINNOWS. Each of the three have five treble hooks (5T), but he made a shorter 3T model also. The 3T model seems to be in short supply as they are seldom found. Collector value range: $150-$500.

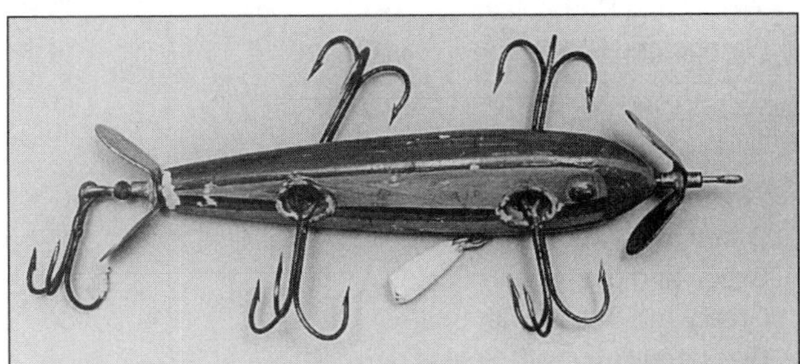

This 4" lure has the same hook hardware, marked props and staple hung external belly weight as the previous lure. The only significant difference is that this one has painted tack eyes.

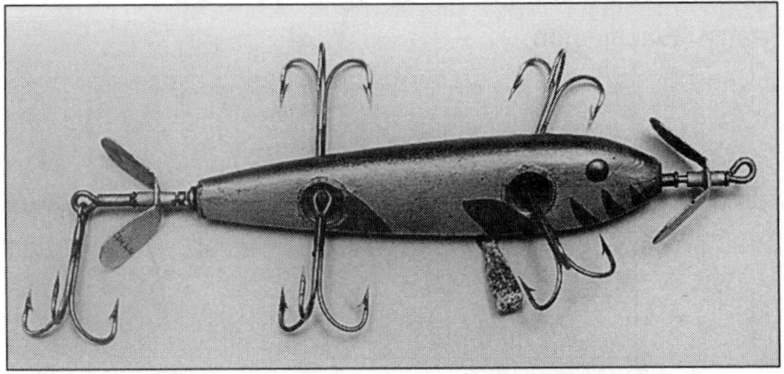

This lure is fairly typical of the early model PERFECT CASTING MINNOWS. The propeller spinners have stamped on the blade "PAT'S PNDG". It has an external belly weight with a staple hanger, brass tack eyes, and the side hooks are rigged two to a split ring around a through-body wire armature. Note the tube extender aft of the rear prop. The lure measures 4" exclusive of hardware.

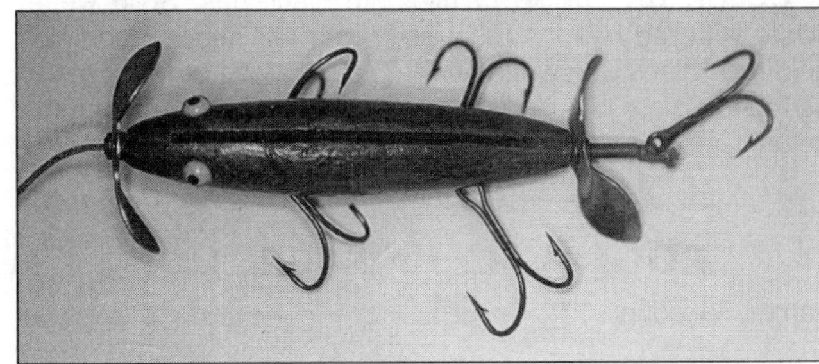

This 3-1/4" 5-hooker has glass eyes. Note the long brass tube placed at the tail end. This was to prevent the tail hook from contacting the tall propeller spinner. What makes this lure unique is the manner of hook attachment. It utilizes a string through the body. The slot along the back of the body enabled access to the string. Photo courtesy Clarence Zahn.

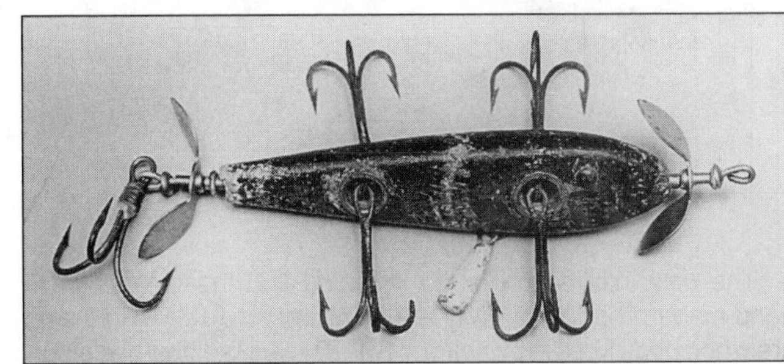

This 4-1/8" PERFECT CASTING MINNOW's principal difference from the previous two is that it is sporting early Shakespeare tube bow tie propeller spinners.

FRED RINEHART TACKLE COMPANY

Newark, Ohio

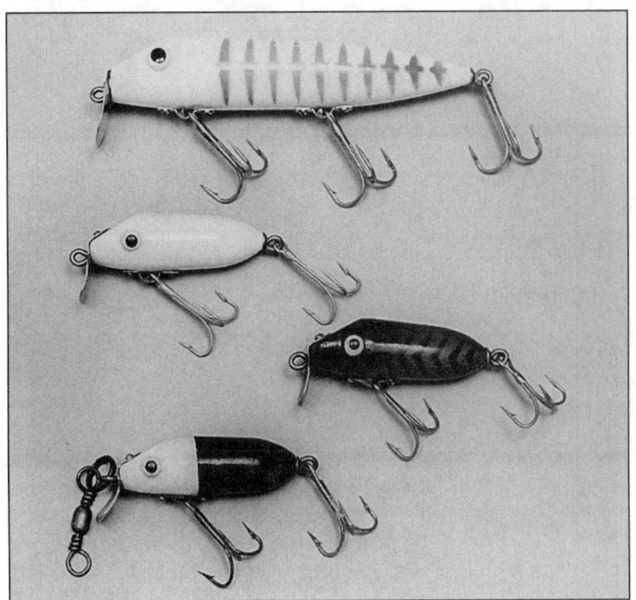

This company is known to have been doing business in the mid-1940s. The largest lure in the photo measures 4-3/4" and the others, 2-1/4". These plastic lures all utilize the one-piece surface style belly hook hangers. They are collectively known as RINEHART JINXES. Collector value range: $15-$30. Add $20 for new in the box.

COLOR OR FINISH: White with black ribs, Solid white, White with red head, Yellow body with red head, Black with gold ribs, Black with white head. There may be other colors to be found. There was no list. These colors are derived from the actual lures.

ROGERS FLY AND LURE CO.

Lamar, Missouri

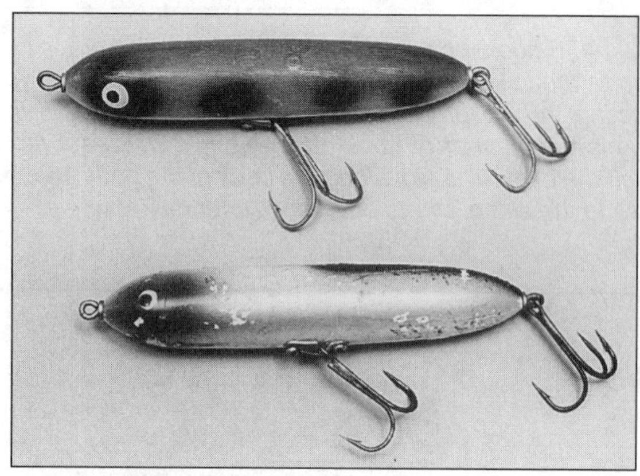

The only information found indicated that these lures were hand-made production. They are identified as JUMPER #1 and are wood body lures measuring 4-3/4". They utilize one-piece surface belly hook hangers. There was no trade information found that would allow a reasonable collector value to be determined.

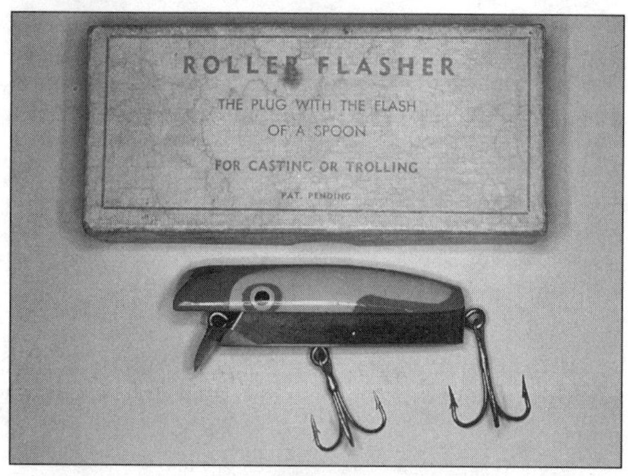

The wooden ROLLER FLASHER.

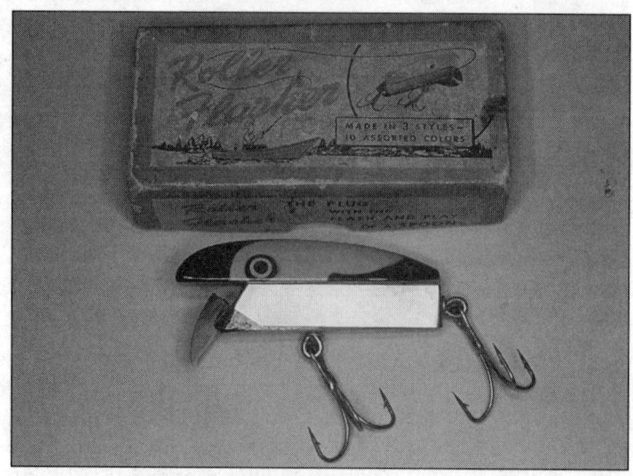

The plastic ROLLER FLASHER.

ROLLER FLASHER

B & J Tackle Company

Roller Flasher Company
Detroit, Michigan

The B & J Tackle Company is the name found on the plain, undecorated box in the photo. The lure that came in that box is made of wood, is 3" long, has painted eyes and a polished metal band extending all round the lower portion of the plug body. The lure with the decorated box has the same characteristics except that is only 2-1/2" long and is made of plastic. The lures are almost identical, obviously being made from the same design. The name change could signify the company changed hands and went to plastic construction at that time. The wood lure probably dates from the 1930s and the plastic one from the 1940s. I have a box paper for the plastic version that says the lure came in "...3 models and 10 different color combinations to please the exacting fisherman." There was no mention of sizes, but it lists ten different colors for each of the "Large Type Plug" and the "Small Type Plug". They are listed below *exactly* as the were listed on the papers. Photo courtesy Clarence Zahn. Collector value range: $20-$30.

LARGE TYPE PLUG

Red and White with Scales
Red and White - plain
Green and White with Scales
Green and Green
Green and Yellow with Scales
Black and Grey with Scales
Black and Grey - plain
Yellow and Black - plain
Yellow and Red - plain
Orange and Black

SMALL TYPE PLUG

White and Red with Scales
White and Red - plain
Green and White with Scales
Green and Green with Scales
Green and Yellow with Scales
Black and Grey with Scales
Yellow and Black
Yellow and Red
Black and Orange
Frog

ROSEGARD SALMON PLUG

Seattle, Washington

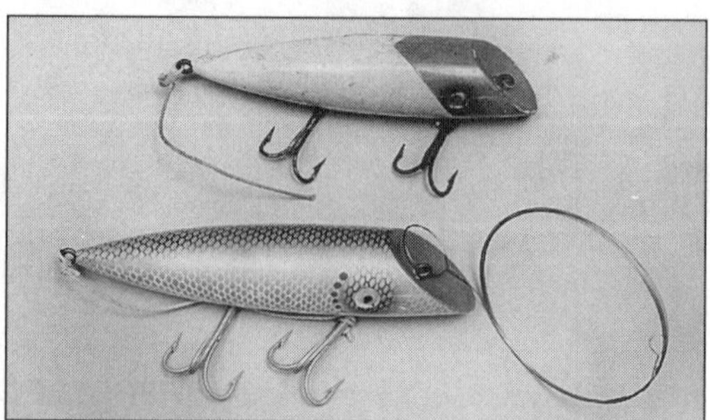

The smaller 5" lure has "ROSEGARD" on the belly and indented eyes. This particular lure has been modified with an embodied wire hook hanger instead of the standard string break-away hooks as on the longer 6" lure in the photo.

I was able to find very little information about this company. Other than it was operating in the late 1930s and the patent number placing the grant in 1941, and what information can be gleaned from the lures themselves. Collector value range: No trade date found.

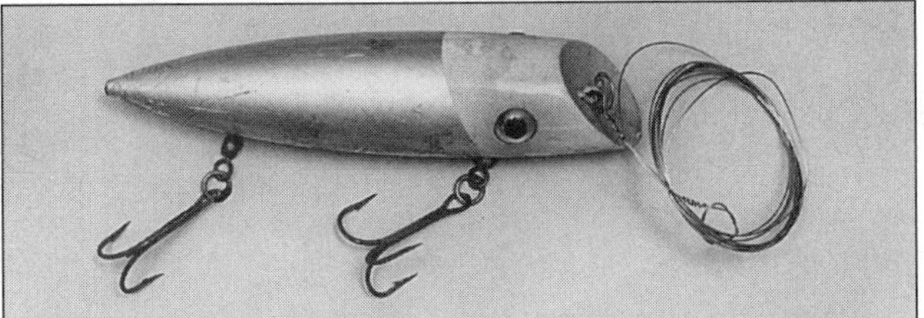

This 5-1/8" has a yellow scale finish, yellow glass eyes and one-piece surface type hook hangers with swivels. The word "BAUER" is found on the belly. The lure box stated that the lure was an Eddie Bauer product and that it was licensed under Rosegard patents. The patent number is one that was issued in 1941.

ROTARY MARVEL

Case Bait Company Detroit, Michigan

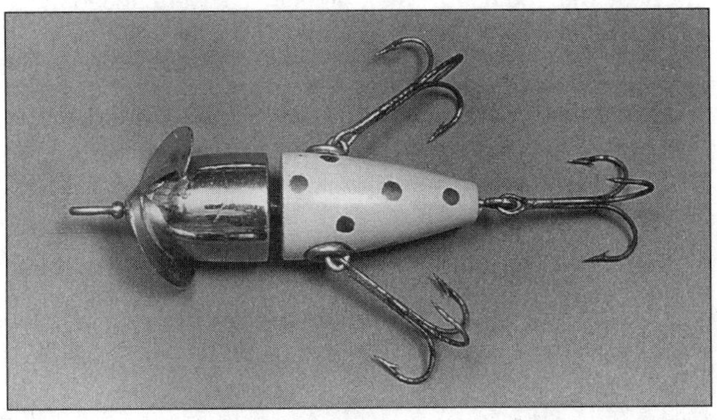

This strong well-made 3" lure has a nickel-plated rotating head. The one in the photo has the Pflueger Neverfail hook hangers. I have never seen the earlier version personally, but from all illustrations they appear to have had staple-type side hook hangers. Earliest reference I found was a 1914 advertisement in *Field & Stream* magazine. The ad said they were available in either red, yellow or white bodies. As you can see in the photo they must have added at least the polka-dot finish at some point. My research turned up no more exactly like this one. I did, however, find another very similar lure called THE ROTARY MARVEL. It was offered in a 1919 sporting goods catalog. The accompanying drawing is of the lure as it appeared in the catalog.

The ad text indicated it was made all of brass and was hollow. I don't know if there is any connection between the two. There does seem to be some sort of connection between the wooden ROTARY MARVEL and the MILLER'S REVERSIBLE MINNOW. When you examine them together it's easy to come to the conclusion that they were each made by the same people. The hardware and especially the paint job are remarkably alike. Collector value range: $250-$400.

RUSH'S TANGO MINNOWS

J.K. Rush Syracuse, New York

Early development of the RUSH TANGO MINNOW is mired in confusion. I reported in previous editions, one, that LeRoy Yakely was credited with the invention of the RUSH TANGO MINNOW and, two, that I would not (at that time) attempt to sort out the confusion surrounding its development. The first statement was wrong but, happily, the second can now be resolved to a greater degree.

It seems, as in many cases during early lure development, that there were several simultaneous individual revelations to occur regarding the invention of an at rest, floating plug with a sloped nose (flat planed) making it dive upon retrieve. This naturally gave rise to a dispute.

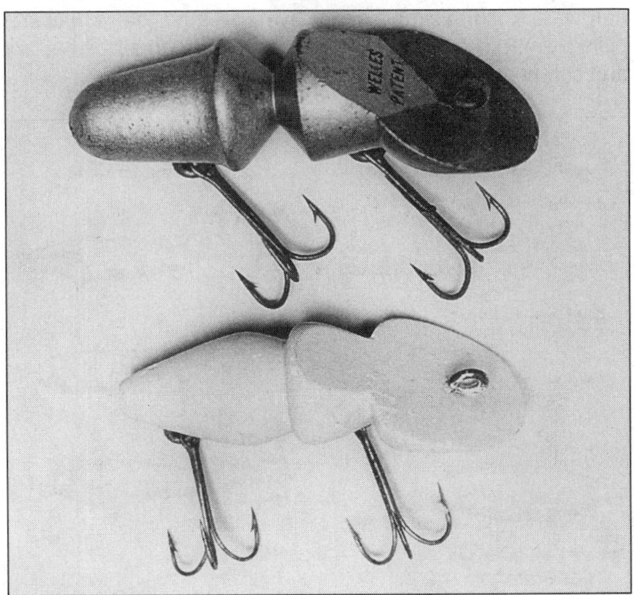

The upper lure measures 4" long, has simple screw eye hook hanger, is colored gold with a red head is stamped "WELLES PATENT". The lower 3-1/2" lure has the same characteristics as the other, but lacks the Welles patent stamp. It is white bodied and is placed here because of its similarity to the genuine article.

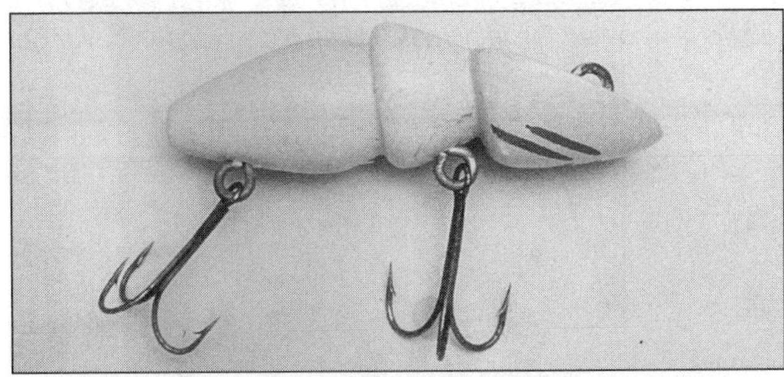

The Welles patent lure.

The design for the patent on the RUSH TANGO MINNOW was filed on September 4,1914 and granted to Le Roy Yakely of Syracuse, New York and assigned to Joseph K. Rush on December 22,1914. From this it would seem that Yakely was the inventor, but wait - the plot takes a twist here. The following patent apparently came swiftly to the attention of one Fillmore M. Smith. Smith held rights to two patents filed in 1912 and granted to a Henry S. Welles in 1913 and 1914 that described "...floating artificial baits ... which shall dive beneath the surface when drawn through the water ... ". Believing the RUSH TANGO MINNOW infringed upon his patents, Smith filed a law suit in 1915, seven months after the granting of the Yakely/Rush patent. The Welles patent lure was declared the first and from that point on RUSH TANGO boxes incorporated the words

"Fully recovered patents include Welles basic patents." Interestingly, I have seen a RUSH TANGO advertisement with the Welles name misspelled "Wells". One can only speculate whether that was accidental or on purpose. It could be that the licensing arrangement between Rush and Smith was less than friendly and that was one way of expressing animosity.

RUSH TANGOS continued successfully right up into the late 1920s. The earliest RUSH TANGOS had a unique line tie. It was a brass screw eye that was actually a machine screw eye that went all the way through the lip, secured on the bottom of the lip with a nut. This is reflected in the original patent. Hook hardware was the simple screw eye. Later the line tie was simplified to the regular screw eye and hook hangers were cup and screw eye type.

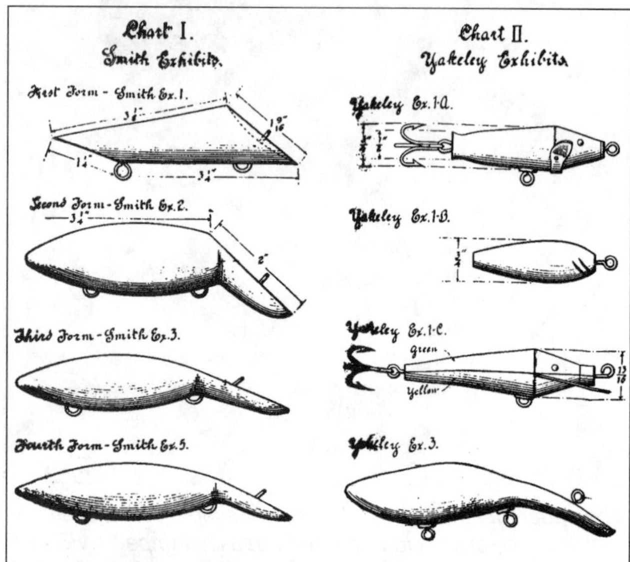

This illustration is a combination of two of the most important exhibits in the Smith vs Yakely/Rush lawsuit. The four side views of the lures in Chart I represent Smith's design transition from beginning to end Chart II is meant to illustrate Yakely's. When you see them side by side it becomes quite obvious who had the legitimate claim. It's a wonder it ever got to court.

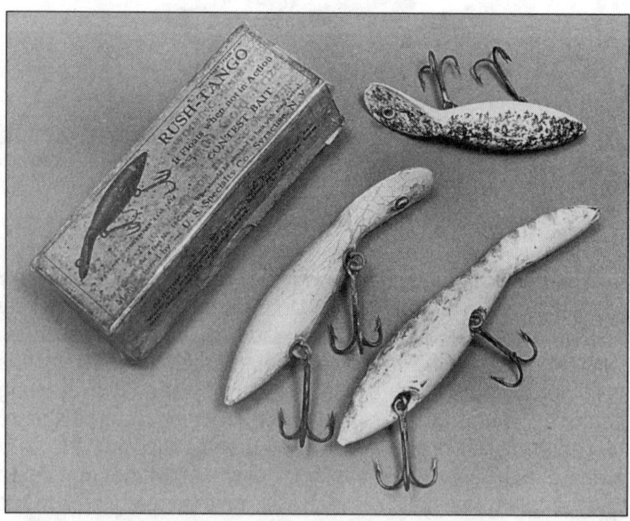

A 1916 or later Rush box for the SWIMMING MINNOW. Top lure exhibits the typical early mottled paint pattern. Middle lure shows the brass nut securing the line tie on the bottom of the lip. Lower lure shows recessed screw eyes without cup hardware.

RUSH TANGO MINNOW

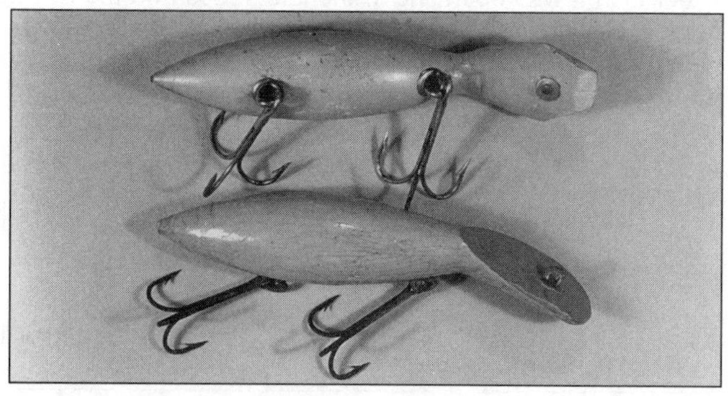

A pair of 5" RUSH TANGO SWIMMING MINNOWS. These have the line tie secured through the lip by the use of a machine threaded screw eye and a disk shaped nut at the underside. The hook hardware is a cup and screw eye arrangement, but the screw eyes are twisted in a way peculiar to Rush lures. The lip on the upper lure was modified by a fisherman.

Patented in 1914 a 1916 listing in an Abbey and Imbrie catalog calls this lure "Rush's Swimming Minnow". It was offered there, in two sizes (4" and 5") and three colors; white body with red head; white body, green and yellow mottled back; and yellow body with red head. Later, other colors were added. It has two belly trebles. Smaller and larger sizes were added to the line under different names. They will be discussed individually. Collector value range: $25-$75.

NAME	BODY LENGTH	LURE WEIGHT
Minnow	4"	?
	5"	oz.

COLOR OR FINISH: Luminous; White with red head, White, yellow and green mottled back; Yellow with red head,, Yellow, red and green mottled back; Red with white head, Solid white; White, red and green mottled back.

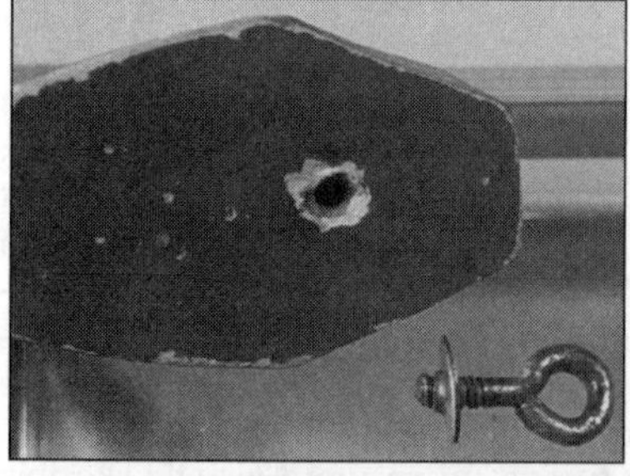

A close-up view of the machine threaded screw eye and nut described in the previous photo. If you pick up one of these don't be tempted to unscrew it. With age they tend to freeze up or corrode. You might damage or break it if you try.

These two RUSH TANGOS have the green and yellow mottled back finish. Note the subtle body shape differences. This is often the case with Rush lures. It may be that he just didn't control the body shape too stringently. The upper plug measures 5-1/16" and the lower, 5-3/16". Both have cup and regular screw eye hook hangers.

Upper lure here has the typical early RUSH TANGO twisted screw eye hook hangers. Lower lure is almost identical in body shape, however, it sports yellow glass eyes and smaller than usual cup and regular screw eye hook hardware. Both 4-1/8".

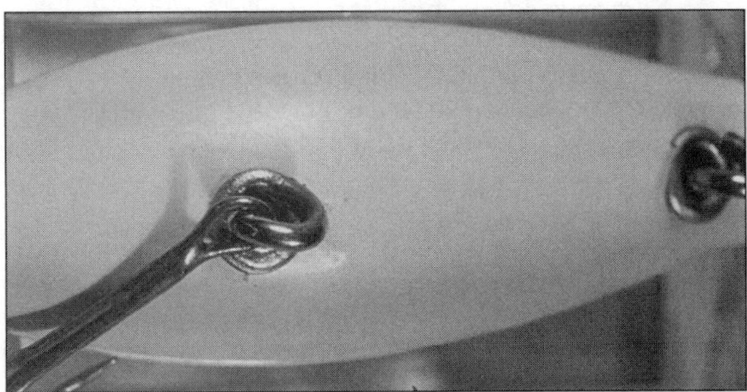

A close-up view of the belly of the previous lure showing the twisted screw eye described.

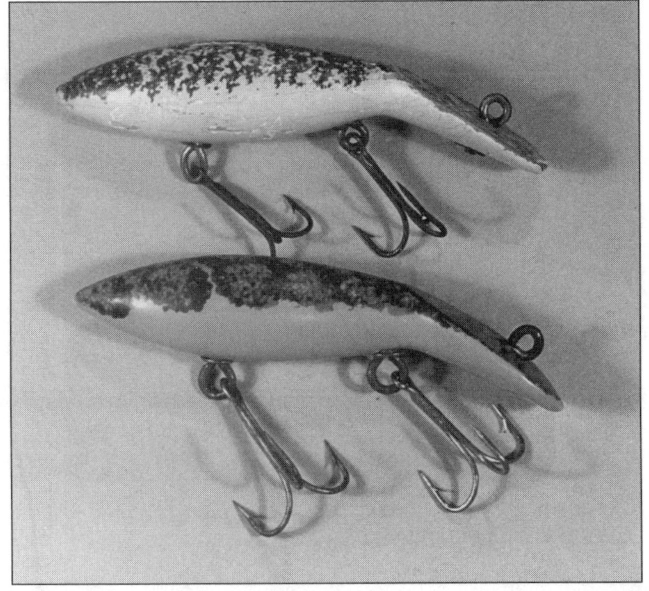

These two RUSH TANGO SWIMMING MINNOWS exhibit the two earlier style hook hangers. The upper lure (3-15/16") has the first style, the simple washer and regular screw eye. The lower (4-1/8") has the cup and twisted screw eye described previously.

A beautiful new RUSH TANGO MINNOW with its box. This is their Victory Finish. Difficult to find. Collector value range: $50-$75. Photo courtesy Jim Muma.

Two versions of the Deluxe RUSH TANGO MINNOW. Both have the metal head plate. Upper has no eyes and lower has glass eyes. Collector value range: $50-$90.

TANGO JUNIOR SWIMMING MINNOW OR RUSH TANGO JUNIOR

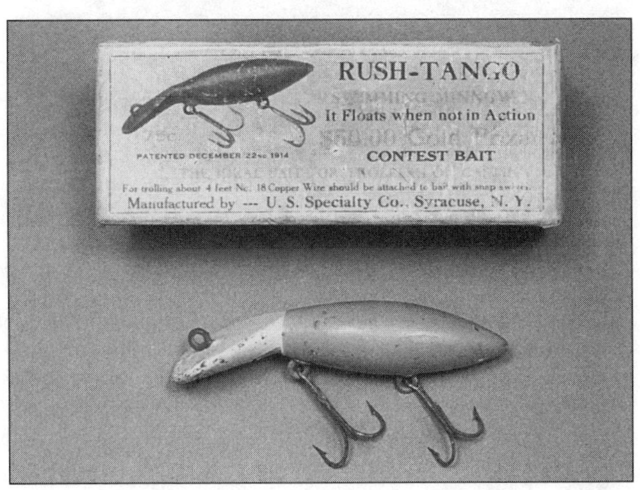

A RUSH TANGO box and standard RUSH TANGO JUNIOR bait.

A 1924 listing in a William Mills catalog states the size of the "Tango Junior Swimming Minnow" is 3-3/4" and 1/2 oz. A later ad in an undated catalog says there are two available, 4-1/2" 3/4 oz. or 4", but the name was "Rush Tango Junior". This may be a change in design or two different plugs. To help in determining which is which, the number, size and color finish listing below is separated into the two names. Both have belly trebles. Collector value range: $20-$50.

NAME	BODY LENGTH	LURE WEIGHT
Tango Jr. Swimming Minnow	3-3/4"	1/2 oz.

COLOR OR FINISH: Luminous white; white with red head, white, yellow and green mottled back; yellow, red and green mottled back; yellow with red head.

NAME	BODY LENGTH	LURE WEIGHT
Rush Tango	4-1/4"	3/4 oz.
Junior	4"	5/8 oz.

COLOR OR FINISH: White with red head; red with yellow head, red with white head; white, green and yellow mottled back.

MUSKY TANGO MINNOW AND FIELD SPECIAL MUSKY TANGO

This was the same basic body design as the other TANGOS, but is stronger and larger. Collector value range: $100-$250.

NAME	BODY LENGTH	LURE WEIGHT
Field Special	5-1/2"	?
Musky Tango	8"	?

COLOR OR FINISH: White with red head, white with yellow and green mottled back; red with white head.

MIDGET TANGO

The lure on the far right in the photo here is the MIDGET TANGO. It has been found advertised in a 1918 issue of *Outers' Book - Recreation.* It measures 1-13/16" and has the simple screw eye hook hanger. Collector value range: $20-$60.

The remaining lures in the photo reading from left to right:

#500 3-1/8" with the Victory finish and cup/screw eye hardware.

#400 3-1/8" with a recessed (no cup) hook hanger.

The third lure is a 2-3/8" unknown Rush Tango with the cup and twisted screw hook hardware. It has a very different, flattened squared off head plane. This is not visible in the photo. Collector value range: $20-$40.

NAME	BODY LENGTH	LURE WEIGHT
Midget	2-1/4"	?
	2-1/2"	?

S.O.S. TANGO

Same as above but slightly larger sizes at 3" and 3-1/8".

TIGER TANGO

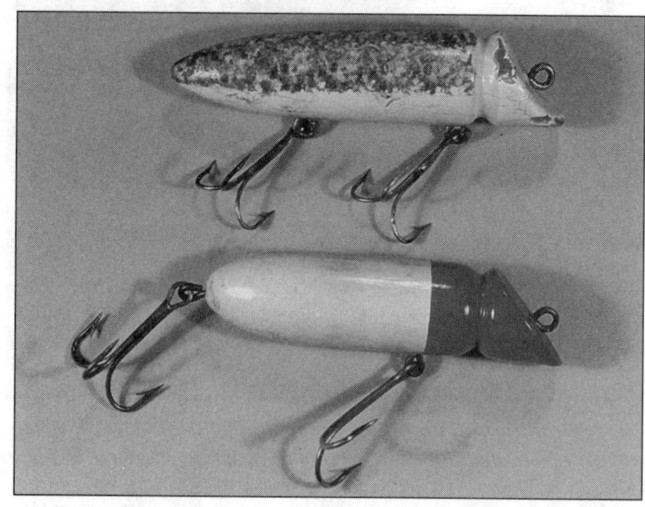

In a previous edition the lower lure was erroneously identified as the TIGER TANGO. It is now known that the upper lure here is the TIGER TANGO. The unknown measures 3-3/8" and is a Rush product. It could be a prototype. The TIGER TANGO measures 3-7/8". Collector value range: $50-$75.

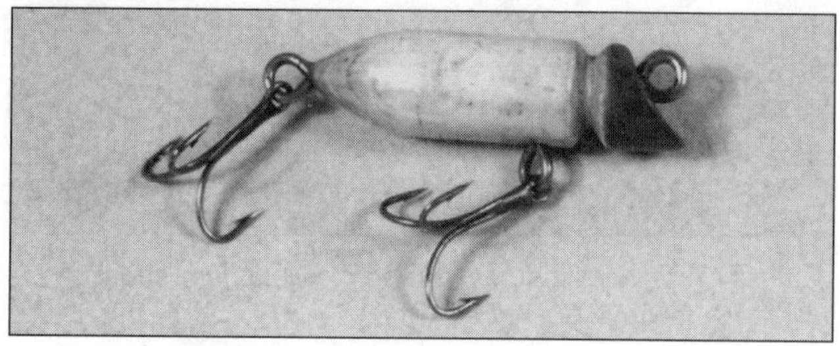

A fly rod-size TIGER TANGO measuring 1-7/8". Photo courtesy Jim Muma.

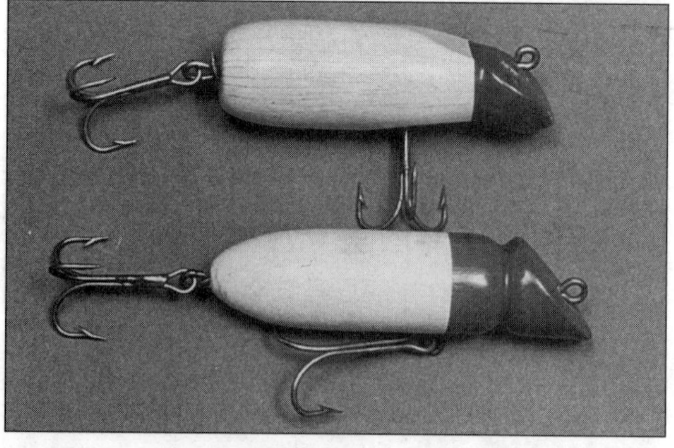

Upper lure may be an early prototype of the TIGER TANGO. The lower is the standard design.

SAF-T-LURE

Glenwillow Products — Cleveland, Ohio

This clever little plug derives its name from the fact that when in the closed position the fisherman could safely carry it in his pocket. It was made c. 1940s, measures 2-1/2" and is made of wood. Glenwillow apparently made another model flatter than this one. I have only seen a picture of it in the closed position, but it appears to have only a two-barbed hook. It is marked SAF-T-LURE on its back. Collector value range: $30-$50.

The SAF-T-LURE in the safe or closed position.

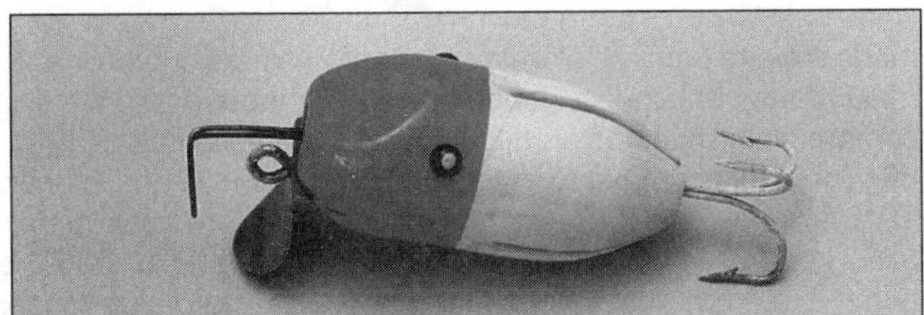

The SAF-T-LURE in the open position; ready to fish.

SAN LUCO LURES

San Luco, Inc. — San Diego Lure Company
San Diego, California

The only advertising reference found for this company was in a 1950 edition of *Sports Afield* magazine. It was not an advertisement for lures, but rather it was for San Luco, Inc. "TIGERGLAS" fishing rods. There was a small reference to lures: "Also the makers of famous TWO-TIMER LURES 'Twice the Fish'". The wooden lures in the photos are TWO-TIMERS. What appears to be four different lures are actually only two. The lures have a different pattern on each side. The upper lure in each photograph is a TWO-TIMER BASSIE measuring 4". It has a metal reinforcing plate on the lip much like the Heddon BASSER. The other lure is a TWO-TIMER MINNOW. It measures 3-3/4" and its box called it a "Collins TWO-TIMER MINNOW".

As intriguing the lures are it is also interesting to note the boxes are almost identical except for the name of the lure company. The biggest difference is the color. The San Luco box is a bit lighter than the other and is printed in blue. The San Diego Lure Co. box is printed in red ink. Collector value range: $25-$50.

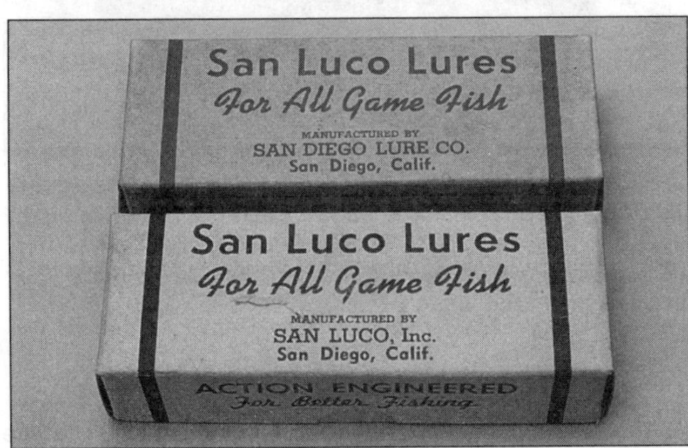

Note the different company names on the boxes. The upper is printed in red and the lower in blue ink.

The color on the TWO-TIMER BASSIE at the top is Red Shiner on one side and Yellow Perch on the other. The TWO-TIMER MINNOW has the same two colors.

The same lures as above turned to their other sides. Shows the different finishes.

SASSY SUSIE

Lakeside Lure Company — Dallas, Texas

This wooden lure from Texas was, according to the box, available in: "12 Color Patterns Two Models Surface and Medium Depth". There was no list of the colors of sizes of the models. The one in the above photo measures 2-1/2" long and is a yellow body with red stripes. It is identified on its back as "SASSY SUSIE". Collector value range: $10-$20.

A Schnell FISH-GETTER with its original box. Measures 2". Collector value range: $20-$30, with box: $40-$50.

SCHNELL BAIT COMPANY

Main & Charles Streets — Kankakee, Illinois

Schnell produced more than the one lure pictured above, but none were found. They ran an advertisement in 1936 and 1937 where they talked about two new patented lures in fly rod or casting size. The illustration was not a very good one, but it was a curved minnow-like with a rigid-mount single hook.

SCHOONIE'S SCOOTER

John Ray Schoonmaker — Kalamazoo, Michigan

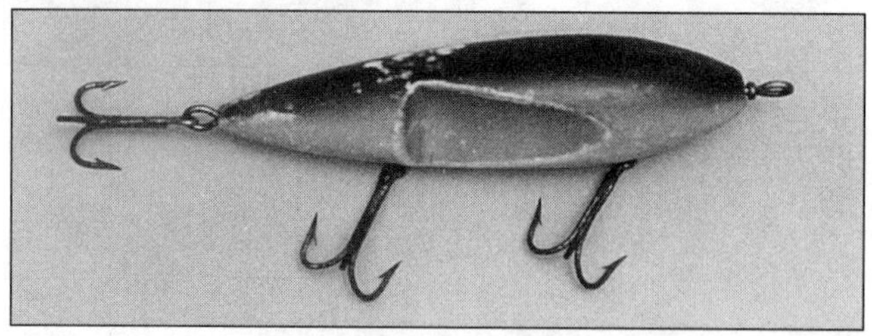

This lure was made in two sizes: 3-1/2", 5/8 oz. and 4-1/2", 1 ounce. It was a floater at rest, but on retrieve it rode just below the surface weaving from side to side. Patented in 1916 by Schoonmaker. I found it consistently advertised until about 1920 when it disappeared from periodicals. The photo above is a side view consequently doesn't show that the groove on the other side is located further up toward the nose. The Junior size has only one belly treble. They were available in a rainbow finish and white with a red head. Collector value range: $100-$200.

SCHROEDER'S WASHINGTON WONDER PLUG

Fred H. Schroeder — Tacoma, Washington

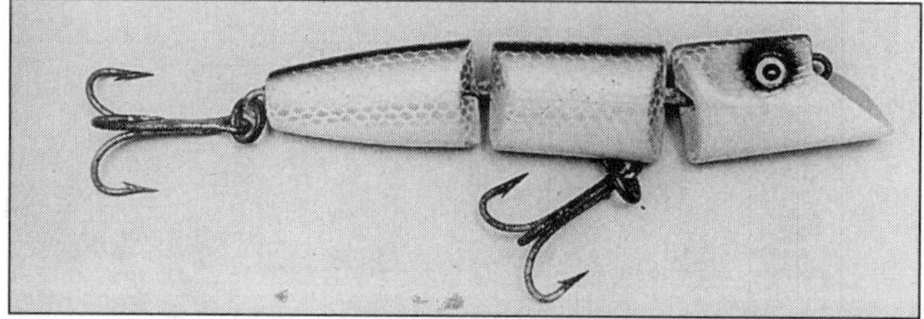

This high quality double-joint lure measures 5-3/16" in length. The patent was granted to Schroeder on February 9, 1937. It has yellow glass eyes and the heavy duty hardware illustrated in the patent drawing. The lure in the photo here has a shiner scale finish. Another example I know of is gold with red flecks. There are four other finishes reported to have been available: Silver with green flecks, White with red gill marks, Allen Stripey finish and a White with red eyes and tail, the latter reportedly available only with two single hooks. It is known that in addition to this lure Schroeder also made a single joint version and a regular unjointed version.

Little more is presently known about this company and its products. It is known that they also made some typical Pacific Northwest large break-a-way salmon plugs utilizing string type hook hangers. Collector value range: $100-150.

SCOOTERPOOPER

Scooterpooper Sales, Inc. — Columbia, South Carolina

This odd lure was born in a jewelry store. Alex Woodle first

made the lure from metal watch crystal containers or other round metal parts containers. The company was formed and the first commercially manufactured lures were made available in 1947-48. The earliest I have found them advertised is in an October, 1948 issue of *Field & Stream* magazine. They were again advertised in 1949 in *Sports Afield*. The lure measures 3" and the name is stamped on the spinner blade. Collector value range: $50-$75, with box: $175-$275. Photo courtesy Jim Muma.

SEARS, ROEBUCK AND COMPANY

Chicago, Illinois

The only information I have been able to dig up is the fact that they sold lures under the J. C. Higgins brand, Meadow Brook Lures and Winner Wooden Minnows. We know that Sears seldom, if ever, manufactured anything for sale in their stores. Who made these lures for them? We know that Creek Chub made some in the Shur-Strike line and sold under the Sears Meadow Brook Brand. We also know that Shakespeare made the WINNER WOODEN MINNOW below, but there were bound to have been more. Somebody out there is bound to have some in the boxes. When we see them, perhaps we can identify them.

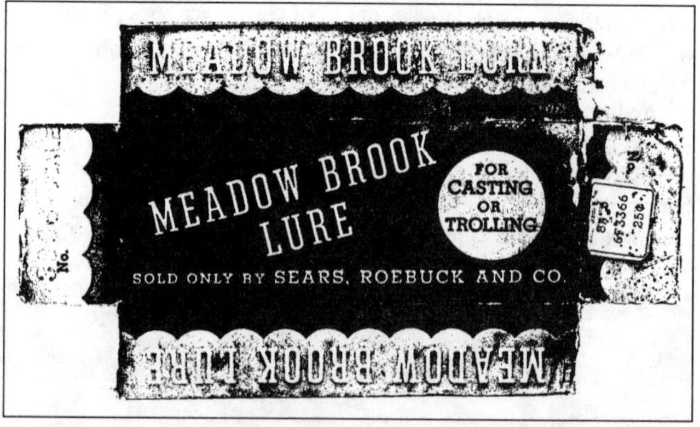

A MEADOW BROOK LURE box. It is not visible in the illustration, but the end of the box has stamped on it "3366 - SCALE". The box bottom states: "CASTING OR TROLLING LURES FOR BASS PIKE PICKEREL AND OTHER GAME FISH". Box courtesy Tom Bumbaugh.

THE WINNER WOODEN MINNOW

This lure presents something of a contradiction. The lure came in this wooden box. The problem arises when you read the entry for the lure in the 1908 Sears catalog. Complete with detailed illustration the entry reads in part "...New Winner

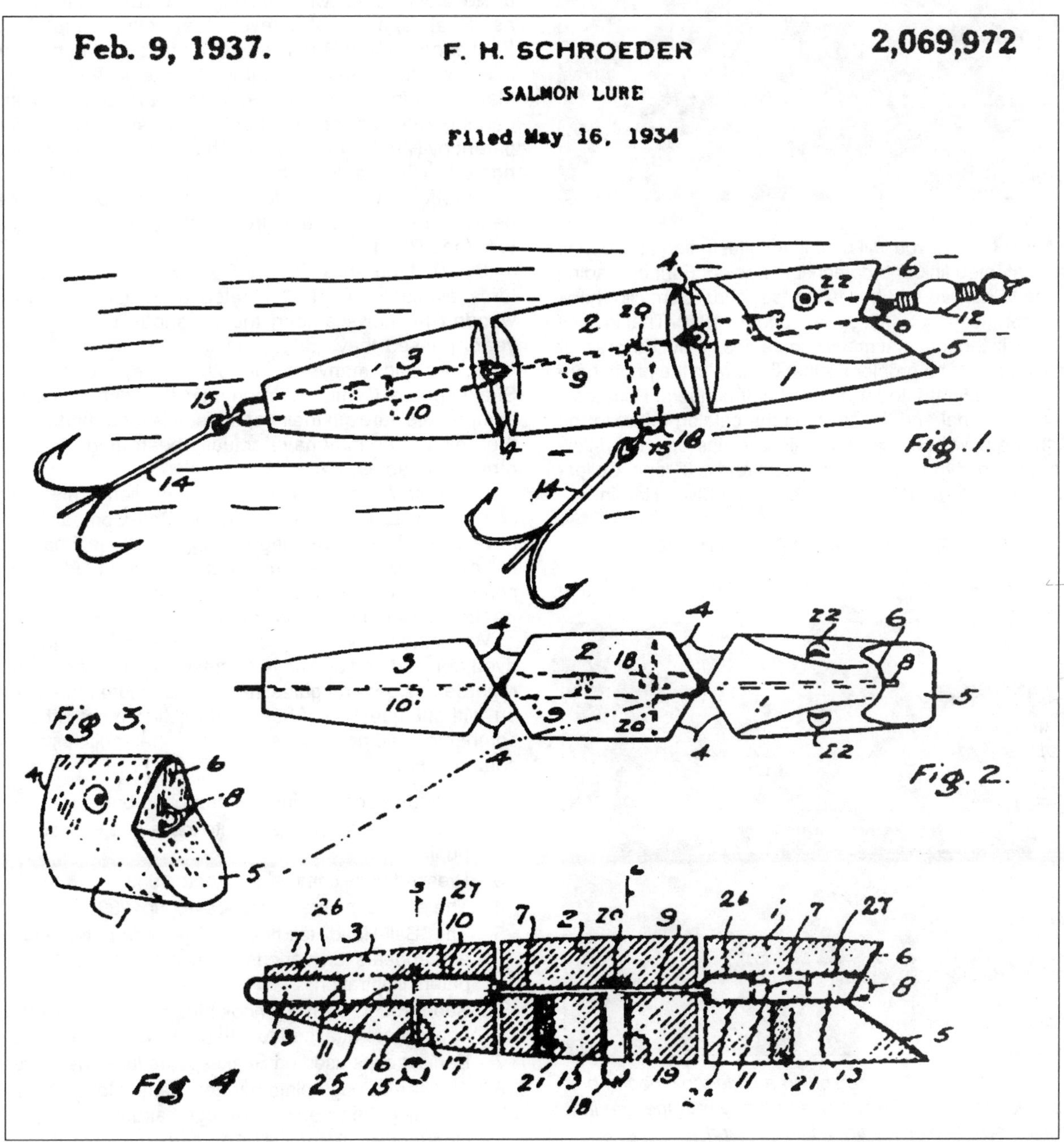

The illustration from the 1934 patent.

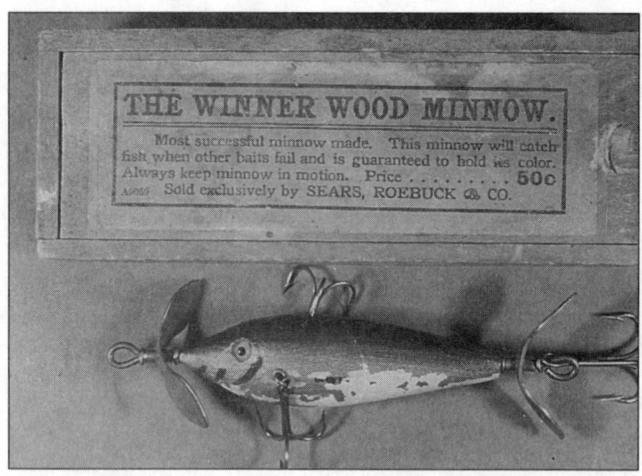

Wood Minnow ... as you will note in the illustration above, has the new patented link and detachable hooks." Further reading leads one to believe that this is the "see-thru, Gem clip" hook hanger often used by Shakespeare prior to 1910. That in itself is fine, for it is thought that many companies produced lures for Sears to market. The problem is that the lure in the photo here has through-body, twisted wire side hook hangers. Perhaps it is an earlier model and the "new" in the catalog refers to the lure with the new hook hanger. This one has opaque yellow glass eyes, tube type propeller spinners and is 3" long. Collector value range: $150-$250. Photo courtesy Clyde Harbin.

THE SHAKESPEARE LURES

William Shakespeare Kalamazoo, Michigan

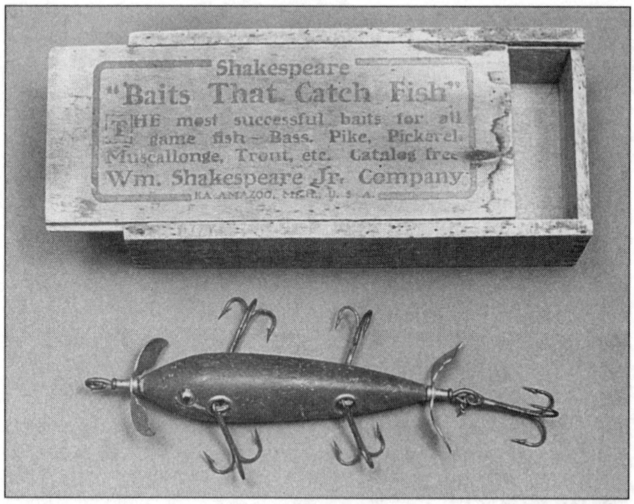

Many of the early plugs were sold in a slide-top wooden box such as pictured here. To find one of these with the lure in it or not is a fine catch. They are scarce indeed.

Shakespeare founded his tackle business in 1897. He invented and patented the first level-wind reel. It was so popular that he started the company to manufacture it. Shakespeare received the patent in 1896. The first lure he patented was for the wooden model of the REVOLUTION. The patent was applied for in July of 1900 and granted about 6 months later (February 5, 1901). It was granted jointly to Shakespeare and William Locher, both of Kalamazoo. Interestingly, one of the witnesses signing was an Andrew J. Shakespeare, Jr. Who was Mr. Locher? It is known that he owned a sporting goods establishment in Kalamazoo and that he was probably the dealer through whom Shakespeare sold his REVOLUTION bait (see the listing for that bait on the following pages). They obvious had a close business relations ship at the least. Locher shares the patent rights to the REVOLUTION equally. Locher, along with Tildon Robb, developed the Kalamazoo Short Casting Rod in 1905. Another name important in the early development of the company was Fred D. Rhodes, also of Kalamazoo. He and his uncle, Jay Rhodes, were making lures around the same time as Shakespeare. Whatever the relationship between Shakespeare and Rhodes was, it played an important role in a law suit. There was a patent dispute between Enterprise Manufacturing Company (Pflueger) and Shakespeare regarding the see-through hook fastener. It was originally patent by Rhodes in 1904 and Shakespeare had acquired all rights to Rhodes' lures by then and consequently won the lawsuit. Most or all Rhodes products ended up in Shakespeare's line and the name frequently used in lure nomenclature (see Rhodes).

By 1910 the Shakespeare Company had a large range of lures available. A 1910 catalog advertises a number of wooden minnows among these various offerings. As the years passed they added, deleted and modified their own baits. As did many of the other early companies, the Shakespeare Company frequently included some of their competitors' lures in their catalogs. It is thought that some of their own lures may have actually been made for them by other companies.

By 1952 William Shakespeare had died (1950) and the company was sold to Creek Chub Bait Company. It must have been the tail wagging the dog, because Shakespeare still exists today. They bought out Pflueger in 1956. Pflueger continued to operate as a separate entity.

Hints for Identifying Shakespeare Lures

While the following are observations and conclusions derived from catalog and advertisement studies, they should be regarded as general guidelines, not absolute facts to be taken without question. Shakespeare, like most other larger companies, did not always adhere to their policies regarding construction.

1. Rhodes wooden minnows are round-bodied
2. Earliest glass eyes had white irises and very small black pupils
3. Pressed eyes came along about 1933
4. The earliest painted eyes are about 1936
5. The "Ball-Head" tail hook hanger was patented in 1931 and appears on various lures through the 1930s (see patent illustration)
6. See-through Gem clip hook hangers were pre 1910. The hooks were attached to a through-body wire.
7. Earliest cups used on Shakespeare lures were brass
8. The see-through plate hangers came along about 1910, replacing the wired see-through hangers.
9. Cork-bodied REVOLUTIONS are probably the earliest Shakespeare production.
10. The photo of three 5T wooden minnows following and the drawing below show the evolution of the Shakespeare style propeller spinners.
11. See the SHAKESPEARE WOODEN MINNOWS for more detailed dating and identification guidelines.
12. In a 1941 catalog they announced a new luminous finish for two lures, the RIVER PUP and the SWIMMING MOUSE. The entry stated that the new luminous substance was molded into the lure. This can only mean they were plastic. This means that you need to examine any lure carefully.

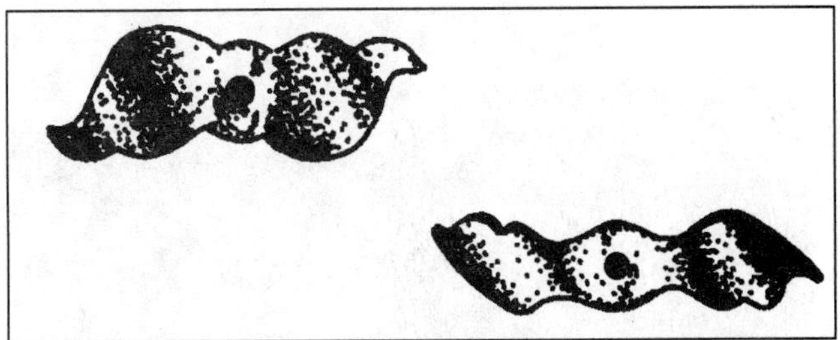

The propeller spinner on the left is the earlier style (c. 1907-08) referred to as the "A" style, "One-Hump" and sometimes the "Longhorn". The one on the right is the newer (c. 1916-17) referred to by collectors as the "B" style or the "Two-Hump".

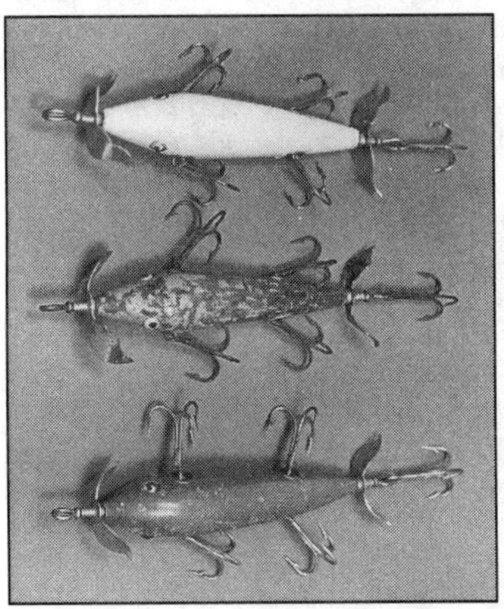

The white body lure has the first style propeller spinners sometimes called the "Longhorn" style. It was used from the beginning until about 1910. The lure in the center has the two-hump propeller used in the 1910'a and the last shows the smooth edge (no hump) propeller used thereafter. They also used a floppy bow tie type propeller on some of their less expensive lure lines.

SHAKESPEARE "REVOLUTION" BAIT AND SHAKESPEARE-WORDEN "BUCKTAIL SPINNER"

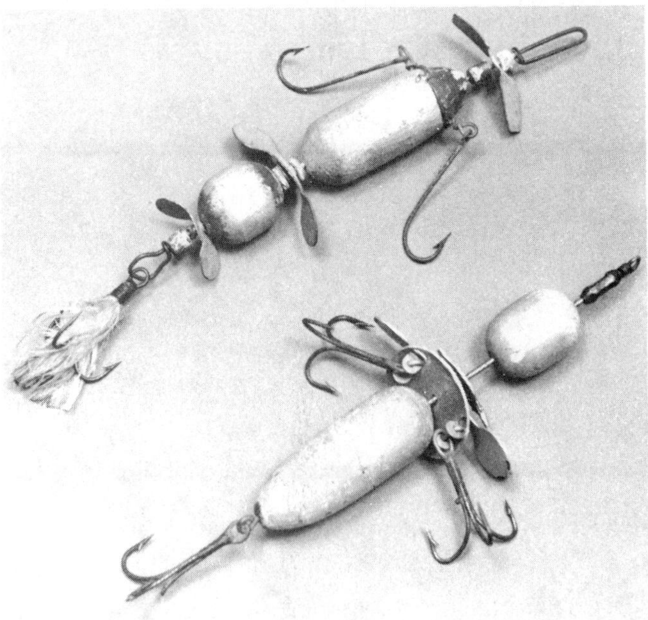

Lower lure is the wooden REVOLUTION. It matches the 1901 advertising illustration and the patent drawing for the wood REVOLUTION (first set of spinner blades broken off in photo). The Upper lure is thought to be the first BUCKTAIL SPINNER. All future aluminum models omit the small round second body section. Collector value range for the Wood Revolution: $750-$1,000.

The first patent (applied for July 6, 1900, granted February 5, 1901) was for a wood body REVOLUTION. An excerpt of a letter Shakespeare wrote to an printed in the July 2, 1900 edition of *The Sporting Goods Dealer* is of great interest with regard to the REVOLUTION bait:

"Together with the aid of our local sporting goods dealer, Mr. Wm. Locher, I have conceived an artificial bait...and I want to tell you about in calm and moderate terms, but it is quite impossible." The letter went on to tell about phenomenal demand for the lure in Kalamazoo for the previous six weeks. He went on to say: "...while the supply was no equal to the demand, you would then understand how this, together with the fact that this bait is the beginning of a *revolution* (my emphasis) in fishing, has so enthused me That I do not know how to tell you about it. Over 1,200 baits have been sold in this city alone, and the demand is increasing." He went on to describe the lure in great detail. It become obvious where the name for the lure came from now.

The lure was advertised in 1901, but apparently was quite brief in availability for it and the BUCKTAIL SPINNER in hollow aluminum were offered the same year. A 1901 edition of Rawlings Sporting Goods Company catalog offered of an aluminum 3-1/2" "Revolution Bait" (actually the BUCKTAIL SPINNER in the illustration). The 1902 Shakespeare catalog offered both in aluminum only (no mention of wood). The REVOLUTION was offered in three sizes, 3", 4" and 6" and the BUCKTAIL SPINNER in 4" only. The aluminum version was patented April 9, 1901.

By 1907 they were offered in the original aluminum, but also in three colors: green body with gold spots, white body with red head, yellow body with red head. Both had Acorn style body sections. Oddly, the illustration for the REVOLUTION shows the small second section reversed from the normal round part toward the nose of the lure. This shows up subsequent catalogs only occasionally. Few examples have shown up. Both also have acquired the first generation plain, pointed blade propeller spinners. The last catalog in which this was listed as available was in the 1921 edition.

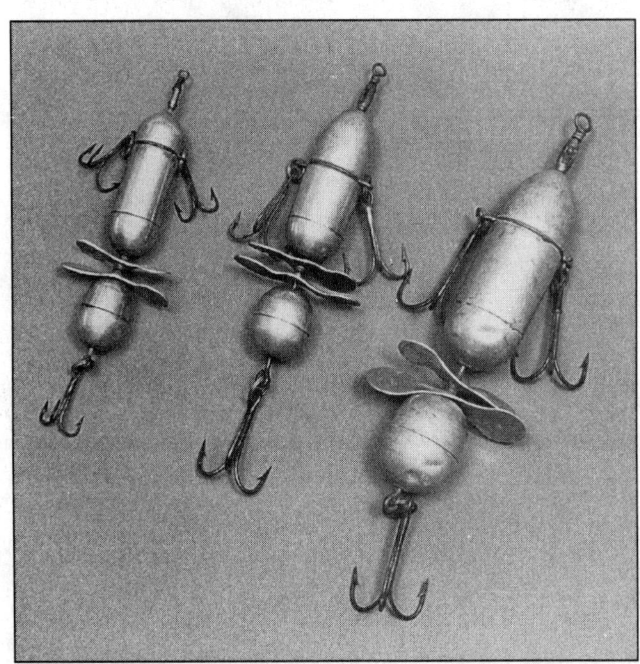

These three REVOLUTIONS match the illustration in the 1902 catalog. Note the rounded blade propellers (called Mickey Mouse props by some collectors). Blades are stamped "patent pending". Collector value range: $200-$300.

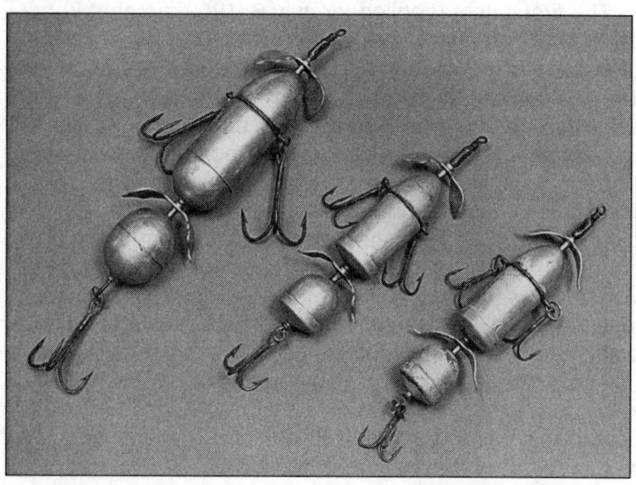

Left is a round end body style REVOLUTION with two-hump propellers. Center also has two-hump propellers. It is the acorn body style. The last sports the latest pointed propellers (no-hump). Collector value range: $150-$200.

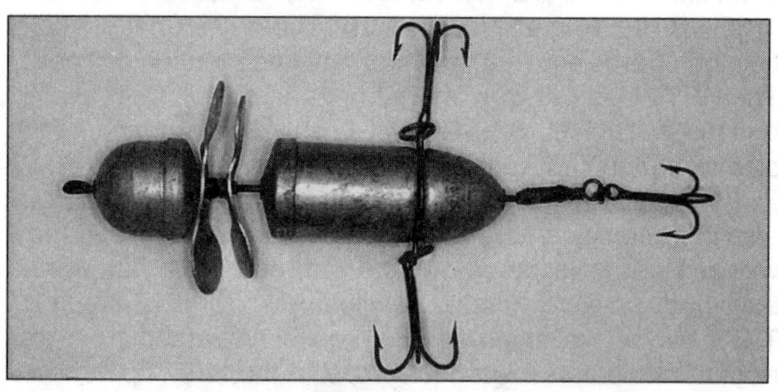

This is as close to the original patent as any I've seen so far. The only difference is in the location of the side trebles. The lure measures 3-1/2". Collector value range: $400-$500. Photo courtesy David Evans, Selma, AL.

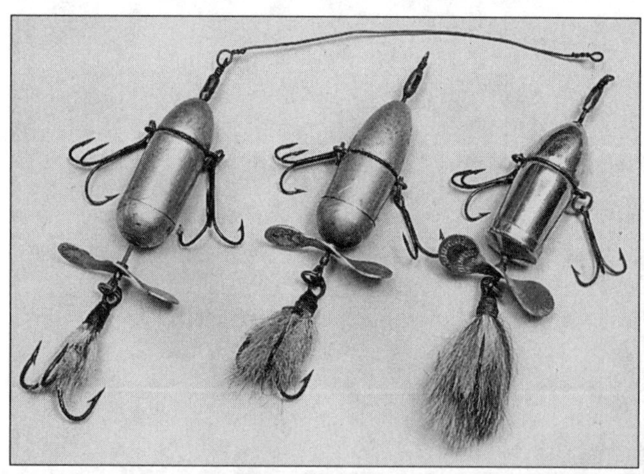

The BUCKTAIL SPINNER on the left (with wire leader) is a perfect match for the one illustrated in the 1902 catalog. Compare the shorter, rounder nose on it to the other two. This is the oldest version. The more pointed nose version was new in late 1901. A January, 1902 issue of the Sporting Goods Dealer illustrates this exact lure in an article. The nose, however, reverted to the shorter, rounder configuration and stayed that way. The last lure is a later, c. 1907 version with a cup closure at the end (called Acorn type by collectors). All these are marked as patent pending. Collector value range: $75-100.

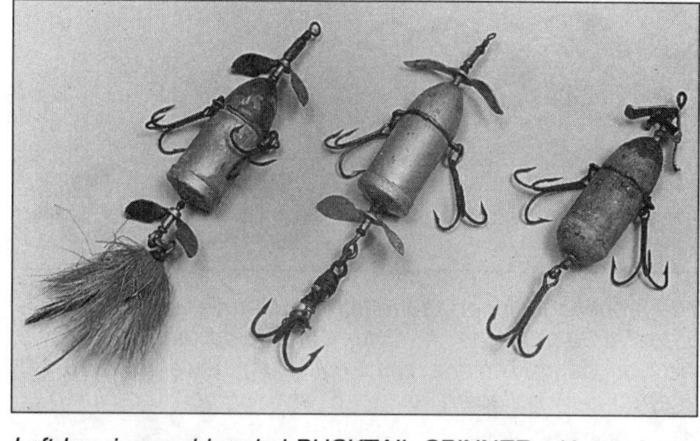

Left lure is a red headed BUCKTAIL SPINNER with two-hump propellers (acorn body style). Center is the same but with the later smooth edge (no-hump) pointed props. Right lure is an oddball. It is the original style body with the elaborate P & S Ball Bearing Company style propeller spinner used on the Joe Pepper 20th Century Wonder. May have been modified by a fisherman.

This is an odd ball REVOLUTION. Note that the ball is at the leading end of the lure. Someone may have monkeyed around with it, but it appears to have been made this way. It is painted yellow with gold dots and is 4-1/2" long.

THE "SURE LURE" WEEDLESS

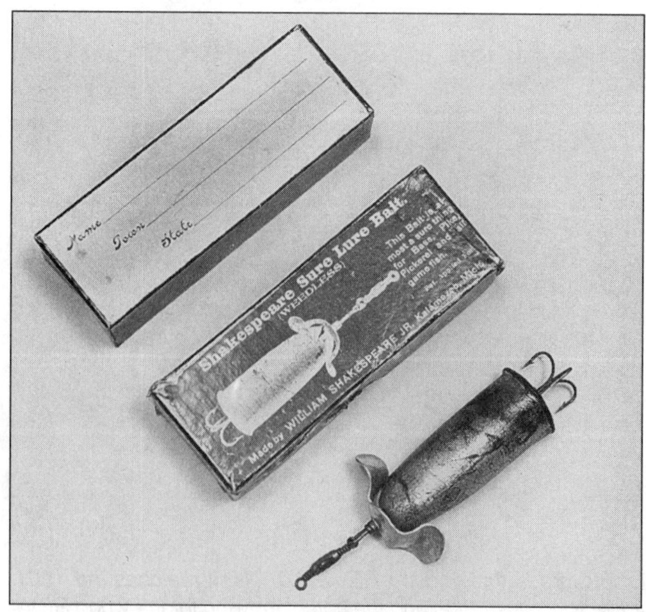

Appearing in the 1902 catalog this bait was made with a pure rubber tube surrounding the hook. This supposedly gave it its weedless character. The rubber tube was at first of a solid

No. 667,257. Patented Feb. 5, 1901.

W. SHAKESPEARE, Jr. & W. LOCHER.

MECHANICAL FISHING BAIT.

(Application filed July 8, 1900.)

(No Model.)

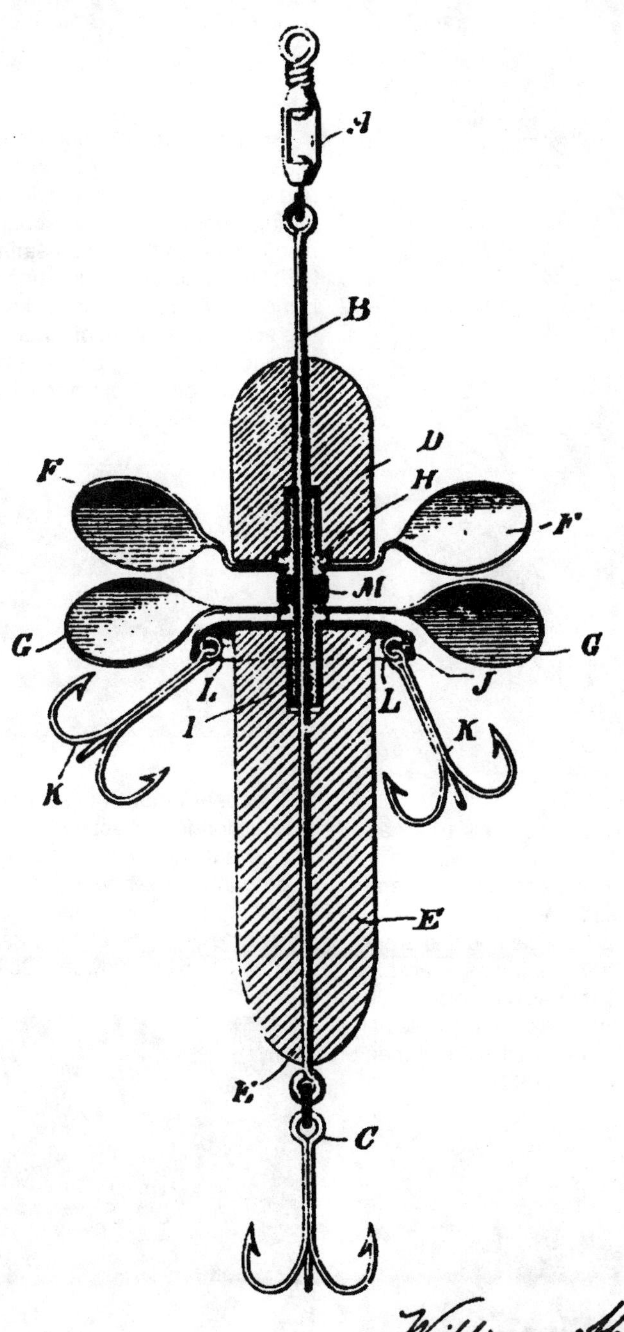

William Shakespeare Jr and William Locher.

Inventors.

Witnesses:

Geo. W. Naylor

William H. Snelling

By their Attorney Phillips Abbott.

The original patent illustration for the Shakespeare REVOLUTIONS.

aluminum color but later (c. 1910) gold spots were added. Available in one size only. Not found in post-1924 catalogs. Collector value range: $300-$400.

THE SHAKESPEARE "EVOLUTION BAIT"

The fourth and last bait to appear in Shakespeare's 1902 catalog is the EVOLUTION BAIT. The body is in the shape of a minnow and made of soft rubber. It has propellers on both ends and has three treble hooks. It was available in three sizes.

The EVOLUTION BAIT appears in a 1934 catalog and is essentially unchanged except that by the time it was available only in the 2-5/8" body length. The earlier ones were also available in 2-1/8" and 4" lengths. It apparently was not available after 1936 . The earliest models have "PAT PENDING" stamped on the propeller. Collector value range: $100-$200.

A 3-1/2" WOODEN MINNOW #43 with its original wooden box. Photo courtesy Jim Muma.

SHAKESPEARE WOODEN MINNOWS

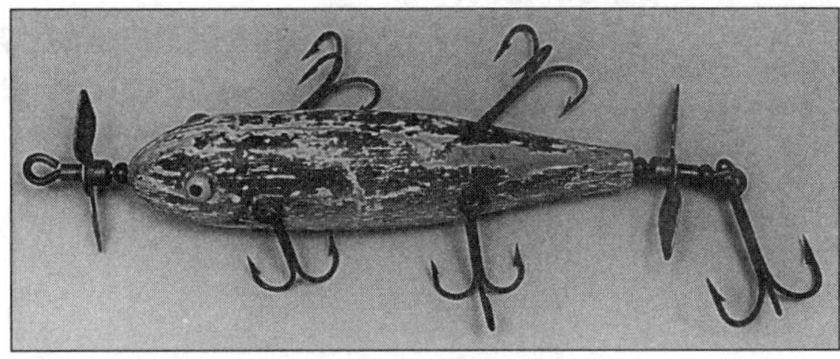

Sometime in 1905 Shakespeare acquired the rights to Fred D. Rhodes' patent for his wooden minnow. Prior to that they had been experimenting with various hook hangers. The following photos illustrate a couple of these experiments. Note also the use of the bead bearing fore and aft.

It isn't obvious, but the hooks are attached to a device that is made by clipping a cotter key and giving it machine threads. It is screwed in or out of a bullet shaped, rimless brass cup imbedded in the lure body so that some of the rim extends beyond the body. Collector value range: $150-$250, with an original wooden box it can easily double that.

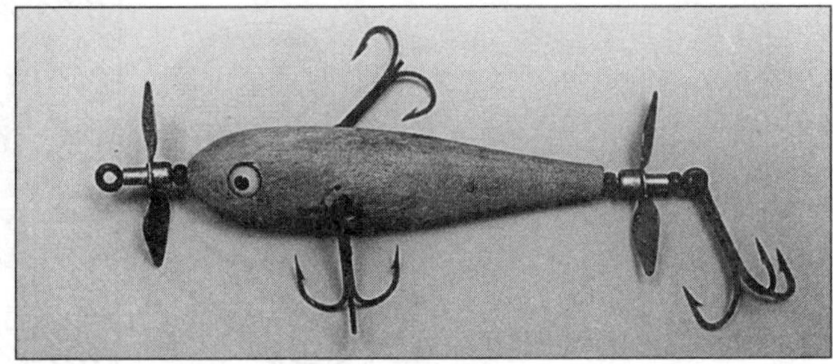

It appears that Shakespeare finally worked one out to his satisfaction for he applied for and was granted a patent for it. The patent and the lure bearing the hardware is shown above. It probably never went into production, however, for the Rhodes patent he acquired has much superior hook hanger hardware. Most Shakespeare WOODEN MINNOWS utilize use the Rhodes hardware. Collector value range: $200-$300.

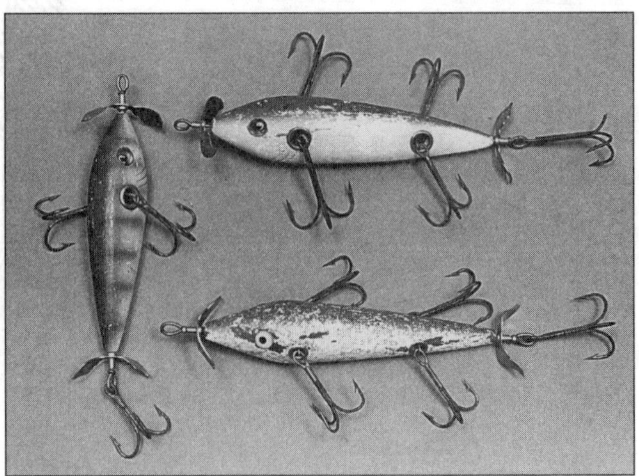

The following examples of the WOODEN MINNOWS date back to at least 1906 and probably represent some of the highest quality lures ever offered in the line.

They are of the highest quality offered in their line. They

No. 893,664. **PATENTED JULY 21, 1908.**

W. SHAKESPEARE, Jr.

FISH BAIT OR LURE.

APPLICATION FILED OCT. 23, 1905.

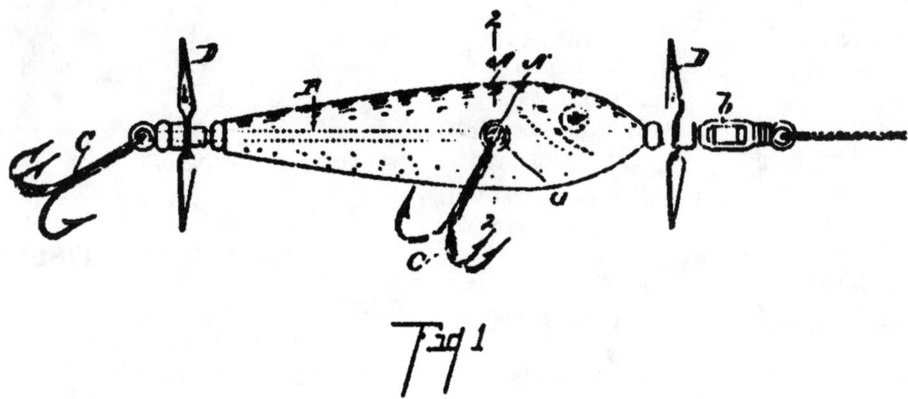

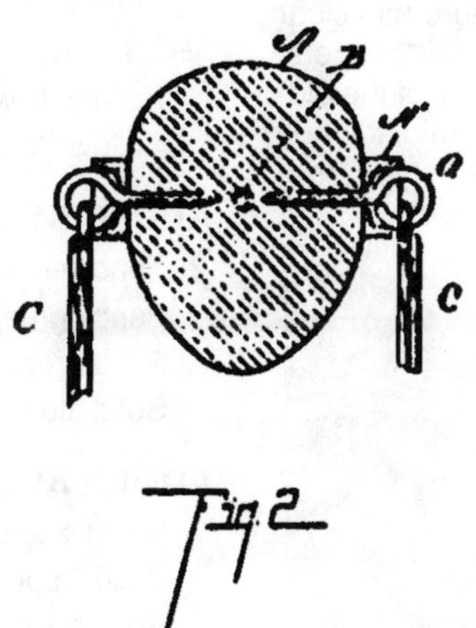

Witnesses:
Ethel A. Bradford
Amelia J. Alber

Inventor,
William Shakespeare Jr.
By Chappell & Earl
Att'ys.

Patent drawing for the new hook hardware.

were available in 5T (two on each side and one on the tail) and 3T (both belly and side mounts) at the time. They later added a 2T (single belly and one trailing). These were glass eyed and had the Gem-clip see-through hook hangers with brass cup hardware and Longhorn one-hump (or one notch) propeller spinners. This information comes from the catalog illustrations. It is known that earlier versions had the wired, see-through hook hangers. All of the earliest have a high forehead profile at the head of the body. Later this was not evident, being rounded off. All have shaped bodies.

The first sizes offered were 3", 3-1/2" and 4-1/2" bodies for each of the three hook styles. By 1910 they had added 1-3/4", 2-1/2", and 5-1/4" body sizes.

The following chart will help you with number of hooks and props.

SERIES No.	BODY LENGTH	PROPS	TREBLE HOOKS
00 (Floater)	1-3/4"	1 at nose	1T (tail)
03 (Sinker)	1-3/4'	2	3T (2 opp. side, 1 tail)
23 (Sinker)	2-1/2"	2	3T (2 opp. side, 1 tail)
31 (Floater)	3"	2	2T (1 belly, 1 tail)
33 (Sinker)	3"	2	3T (2 opp. side, 1 tail)
43 (Sinker)	3-1/2"	2	3T (2 opp. side, 1 tail)
44 (Floater and Sinker)	3-1/2"	2	5T (4 opp. side, 1 tail)
53 (Sinker)	4-1/2"	2	3T (2 opp. side, 1 tail)
64 (Floater and Sinker)	5-1/4"	2	5T (4 opp. side, 1 tail)

Any found with the see-through plate hook hanger hardware will be from the 1910s. See photos for more dating guidelines. The 3T lure on the left in the photo of three lures has the Rhodes 1904 patent Gem clip type hook hanger and the second style, two-hump propeller. The upper right lure has clear glass eyes and the same type propeller and hook hangers. Body is more rounded. The bottom right lure is one of the oldest of the WOODEN MINNOWS. It has the high forehead body profile, opaque yellow iris glass eyes, Longhorn style (one-hump) propeller, and wired see-through hook hangers.

The photo of five illustrates, among other things, the body style changes from earliest on (top to bottom). The white 3T model is the earliest body style with the high forehead profile. It has the Longhorn style (one-hump) propeller and glass eyes. The second from the top has the two-hump propeller. The third lure clearly shows the plate style hook hanger and the later smooth edge pointed propeller. The fourth lure shows a fatter body and the same propellers and the last shows the late style propeller with Shakespeare stamping on the blades. Colors found throughout the years are in the following list.

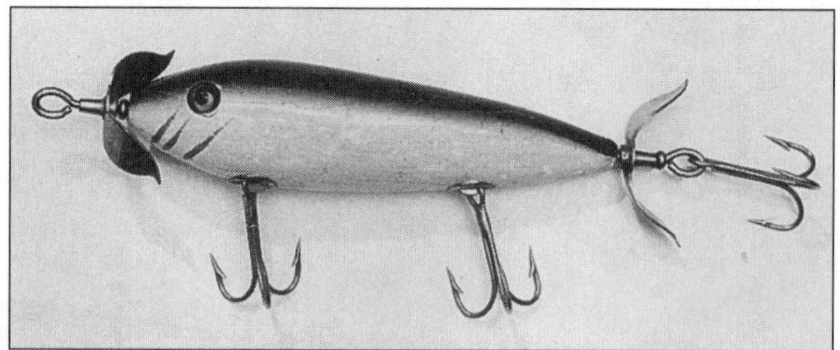

A really fine example of the lure.

COLORS ON THE FIRST THREE SIZES

1907

Green back, white belly
Red back, white belly
Green back, yellow belly
Red back, yellow belly
Green back, aluminum belly
Red back, aluminum belly
Solid white
Solid red
Solid yellow
Yellow Parch, shaded

ADDED BY 1910

Fancy sienna back, yellow belly
Fancy green back, white belly
Solid bronze green
Solid aluminum

ADDED BY 1917

Metallized or Metal Plated
Solid Copper
Solid Nickel
Solid Gold

ADDED BY 1920

White body, green and red spots
Frog colors
Rainbow
Cracked gold

By 1923 they were utilizing many of their scale finishes on the WOODEN MINNOWS. Collector value range: $10-$40.

SUBMARINE BAIT

For some unknown reason Shakespeare brought this lure out in 1925 as the SUBMARINE BAIT. It is essentially the same as their WOODEN MINNOW #42, underwater model. It appears as a separate offering sporadically through the years. It apparently was the last surviving member of the WOODEN MINNOWS and it disappeared from the catalogs in the late 1930s.

KRAZY KRITTER (plastic)

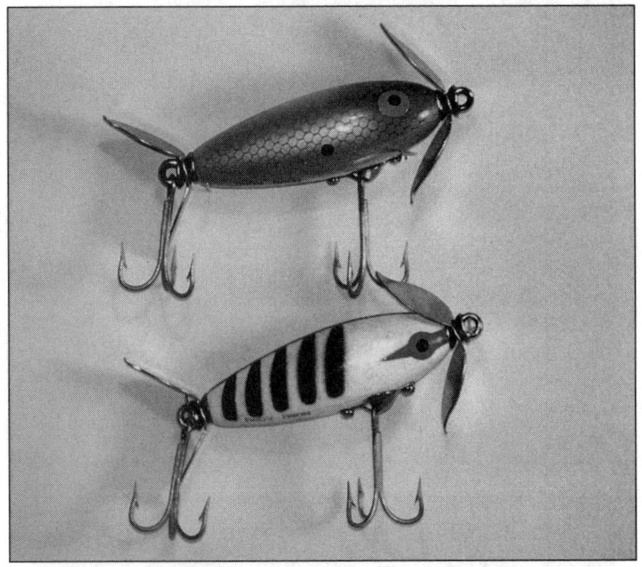

2" Plastic KRAZY KRITTER. Photo courtesy Ken Bernoteit.

It looks like Shakespeare resurrected the old wooden minnow in plastic form. This lure has to be post-1967. They entered into an agreement with a Hong Kong company to manufacture lures and other fishing tackle in 1967. These two lures are marked "Shakespeare Spinning Krazy Kritter Hong Kong" on their bellies. They measure 2" and the spinners are unmarked. Collector value range: $5-$10.

"RHODES" WOODEN MINNOWS

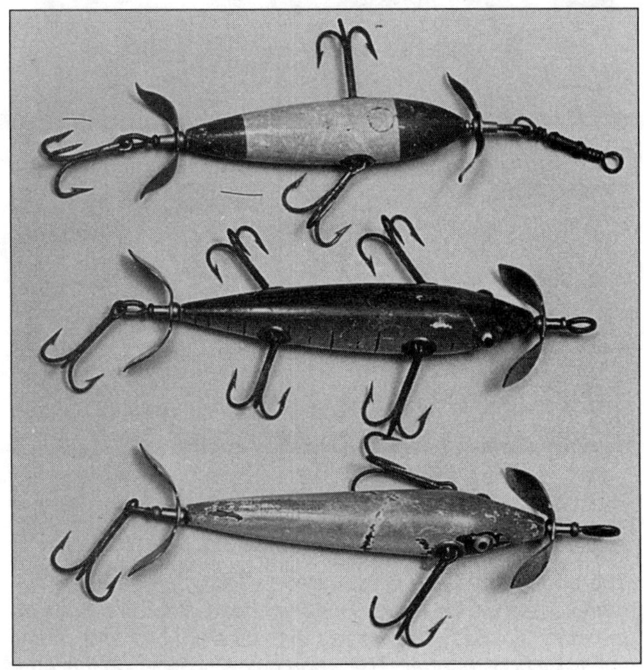

Upper lure in photo is a #33 Rhodes TORPEDO, white body with red head and tail. The TORPEDO was also available in a white body with red head only in 1910. The other two are #33 and #44 RHODES MINNOWS.

Regarding the RHODES MINNOWS a 1910 catalog states: "The 'Rhodes' Wooden Minnows are made of exactly the same high grade materials and with the same first class finish as the 'Shakespeare' Minnows". "They are identical in construction throughout except the Rhodes baits have round instead of shaped bodies."

Apparently Shakespeare was able to manufacture the Rhodes baits less expensively by utilizing a simpler round lure body. The catalog prices for a standard, shaped body Shakespeare 3" FANCY BACK MINNOW was 55 cents and that for a 3" round body Shakespeare Rhodes Minnow was 42 cents. Not a big difference at today's prices, but if we place a price of say $5. on the Shakespeare and set up a ratio we find that the Rhodes minnow would cost about $3.80. That represents a 23% savings or $1.20.

The earliest (c. 1907) Rhodes baits used a see-through type hook fastener and the 1910 catalogs depict this type in the lure illustrations. However, the text states that the "...hook link shown in the illustration has now been discarded for a newer one, the same as depicted in the representations of the various 'Shakespeare' Minnows." Those seen in the 1907 catalog are the early wired see-through type. The Rhodes patent that Shakespeare acquired was for, among other things, a Gem-clip type hook fastener, it must have been used on the Shakespeare RHODES WOODEN MINNOWS until then. It appears that Shakespeare began to equip the second-line Rhodes lures with the bar type fastener in 1910.

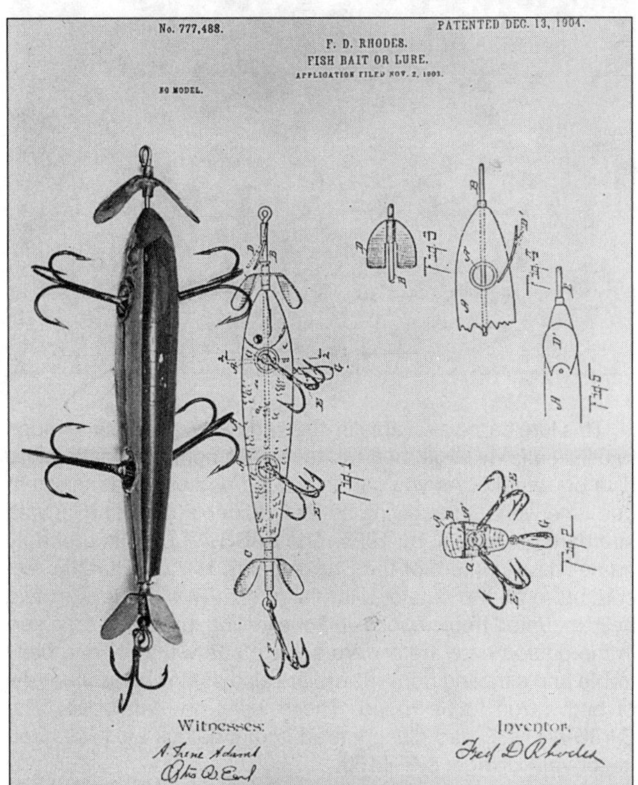

A RHODES WOODEN MINNOW and the patent drawing.

Basically there seem to be only three models of the RHODES WOODEN MINNOW offered. All versions have side mounted trebles and one trailing. Each has two propellers, nose and tail and all were available with or without a buck tail "...in place of the tail hook." One can only assume that the buck tail also has a treble hook. The lures are found with two side mounted treble hooks and a tail treble (3T) or four side-mounted and one trailing treble (5T). The RHODES WOODEN MINNOW had disappeared from Shakespeare catalogs by 1924. Collector value range: $150-$300.

CATALOG SERIES #	BODY LENGTH	HOOKS
*33f (Torpedo)	3"	3T
33R	3"	3T
43R	3-3/4"	3T
44R	3-3/4"	5T

COLOR OR FINISH: *Green back, white belly; *Red back, white belly; Brown back, white belly; *Solid red; *Solid yellow; *Solid white; Greenback, white belly, striped; Red back, white belly, striped; Brown back, white belly, striped.

**Torpedoes were available in the asterisked colors above plus Solid Aluminum color in 1920.*

THE BASS-A-LURE

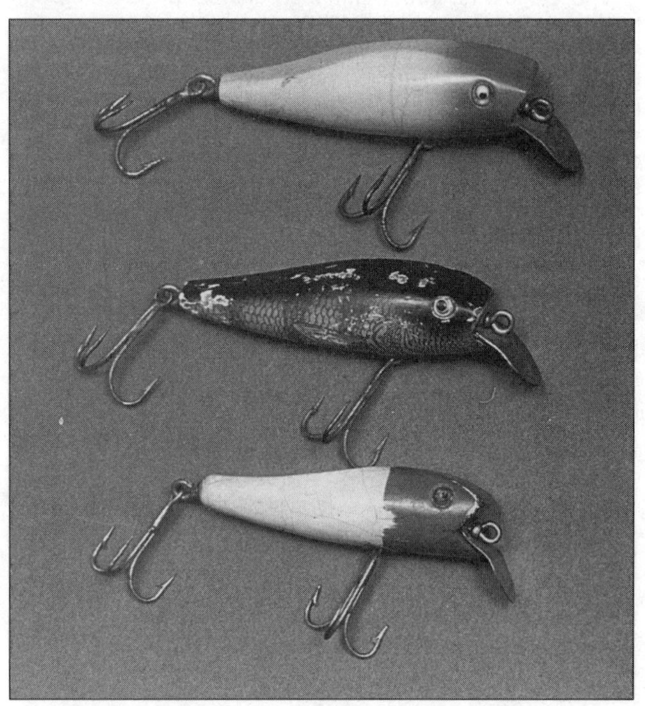

This lure came available in 1923 and is one of the first plugs to utilize a fairly large metal lip to make a normally floating lure dive on retrieve. As you can see in the photos it was made at one time without the diving lip (first model, 1923). The lip was standard equipment by 1925. The BASS-A-LURE is probably a later development of the Shakespeare HYDROPLANE. According to all the catalogs the large size was made with two belly mounted treble hooks and one trailing, but as you can see in the photos here there were some made with only one belly treble and a trailing hook. There are also some lipless versions of both sizes to be found. These were not cataloged. The BASS-A-LURE had disappeared from catalogs by 1949. Collector value range: $75-$150.

CATALOG SERIES #	BODY LENGTH
591	2-3/4"
*591-1/2	1-3/4"

COLOR OR FINISH (#591): Black body, white head; green "fancy back", scale finish; green back, yellow belly, scale finish.

COLOR OR FINISH (#591-1/2): Rainbow, scale finish; white body, redhead, yellow perch, scale finish.

**The 591-1/2 is the BASS-A-LURE JUNIOR. It is one inch shorter normally, has no blade lip, and has a trailing treble and only one belly mounted treble (2T).*

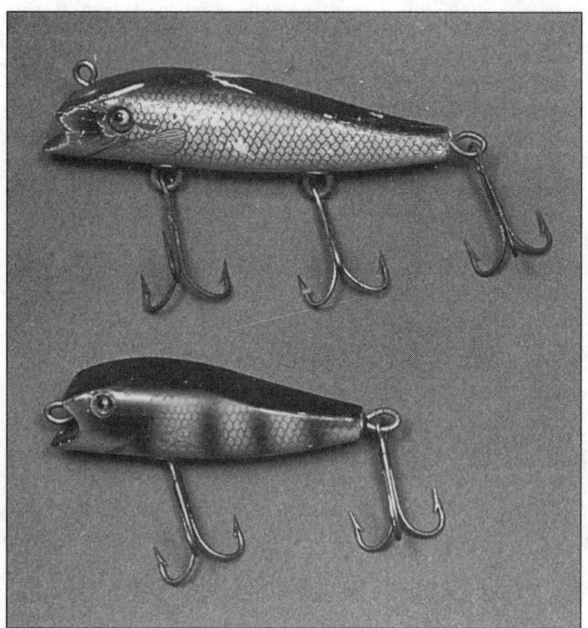

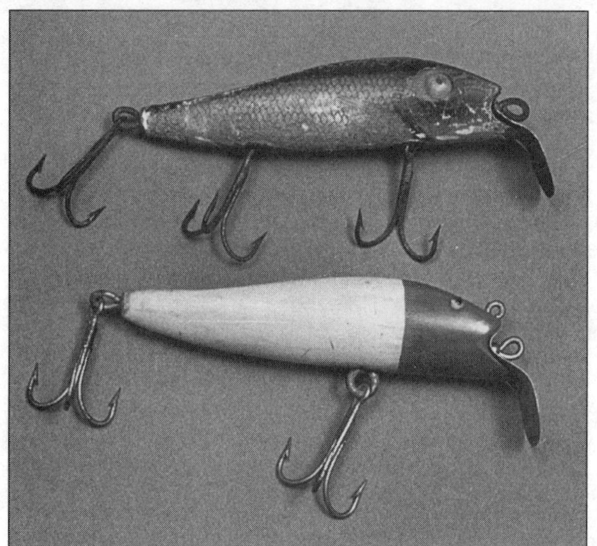

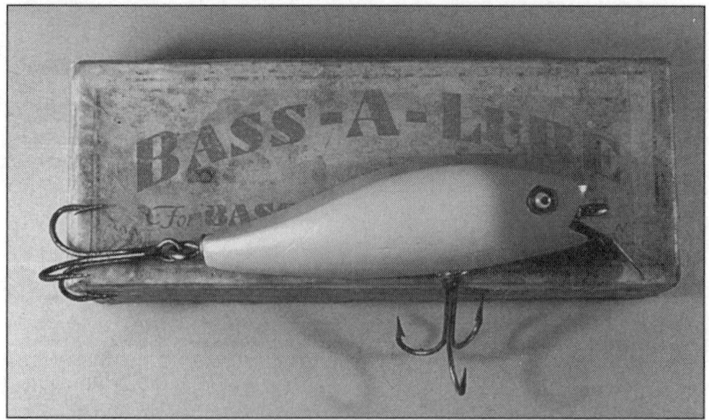

The body of this one is "squared-off" as you can see. The others are more rounded. The plug measures 3-1/4" without the metal lip, has yellow glass eyes and the cup and screw eye belly hook hanger. The wood box is scarce. On this one you can barely make out the word "SHAKESPEARE" under the words "For PIKE". There are also cardboard boxes with the same markings and additional art work of water and a jumping fish in the middle.

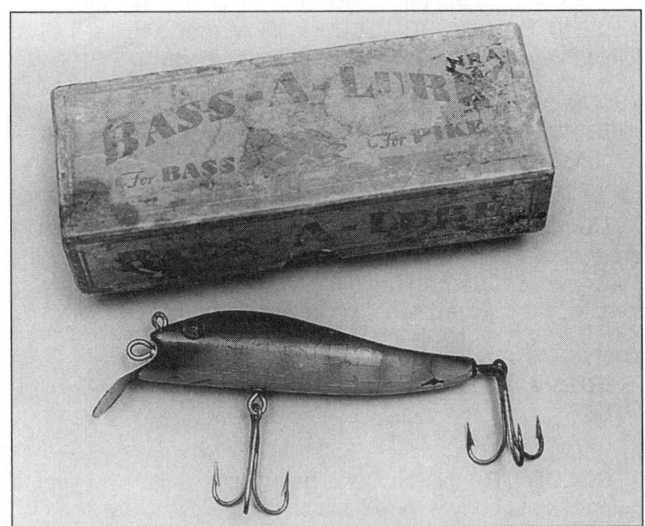

This is essentially the same as the above lure except for the more rounded body. This box has the addition of a fish jumping out of water (worn on the box and difficult to see in this photo).

Reading left to right: Shakespeare TANDEM SPINNER, WEEDLESS FEATHERED CASTING SPOON, MOOSE HAIR FRILL BASS BUG with a ponca style spinner, T. ROBB BASS FLY. All are from the 1920s. Collector value range: $20-$50.

T. ROBB WEEDLESS BASS FLY. Three examples with an original box. One lure in its original box is valued at $75-$100. Photo courtesy Jim Muma.

SHAKESPEARE T. ROBB WEEDLESS BASS FLY

This feathered weedless spinner showed up first in a 1923 catalog. It appeared consistently through the years until 1930 when it was gone from the catalog. The same four patterns were offered each year: Parmachene Belle, Black Prince, Scarlet Ibis and Yellow Sally. Collector value range: $20-$40.

SHAKESPEARE BASS-KAZOO

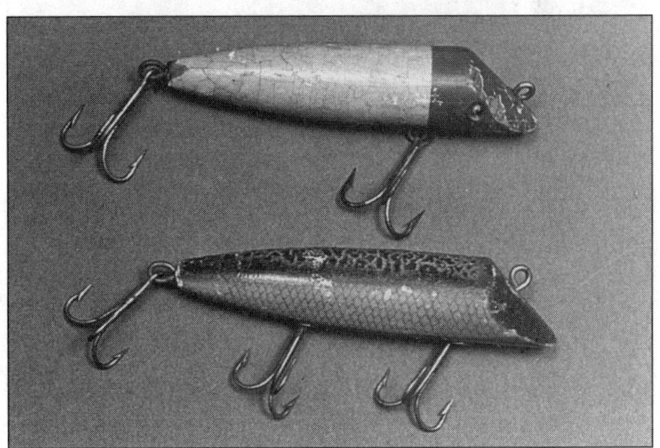

The 1924 catalog shows the BASS-KAZOO as being available in four colors and finish combinations and no eyes. This was reduced to two colors about 1935-36 which is the last year it was observed in catalogs in this form. The plug has two belly mounted treble hooks and one trailing treble (3T). The head is sloped to make it dive. Collector value range: $40-$80.

CATALOG SERIES #	BODY LENGTH
590	3-7/8"

COLOR OR FINISH: *Green "Fancy Back", scale finish; *Rainbow, scale finish; White body, red head; Yellow perch, scale finish.

**These two finishes had been eliminated by c. 1936.*

SHAKESPEARE BUDDY

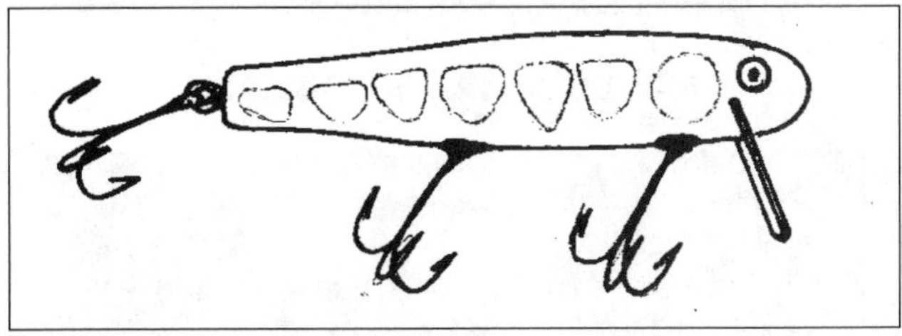

This wooden plug is unique in that it was advertised as having an "invisible lip". Upon close examination of the illustrations, it is apparent that the lip blade is made of clear plastic lip. This is the only occurrence of the clear plastic lip wooden lure in the Shakespeare portion of the author's catalog collection. The BUDDY has two belly mounted treble hooks and one trailing treble. The lure is included in a 1934 and a 1937 catalog but not from 1949 on. Collector value range: $30-$60.

CATALOG SERIES #	BODY LENGTH	LURE WEIGHT
6568	4-1/4"	3/5 oz.

COLOR OR FINISH: White body, red head, silver flitters; Spotted, Green perch, scale finish; Natural pickerel, scale finish; Silver flitter; Green mullet, scale finish.

THE DARTING SHRIMP

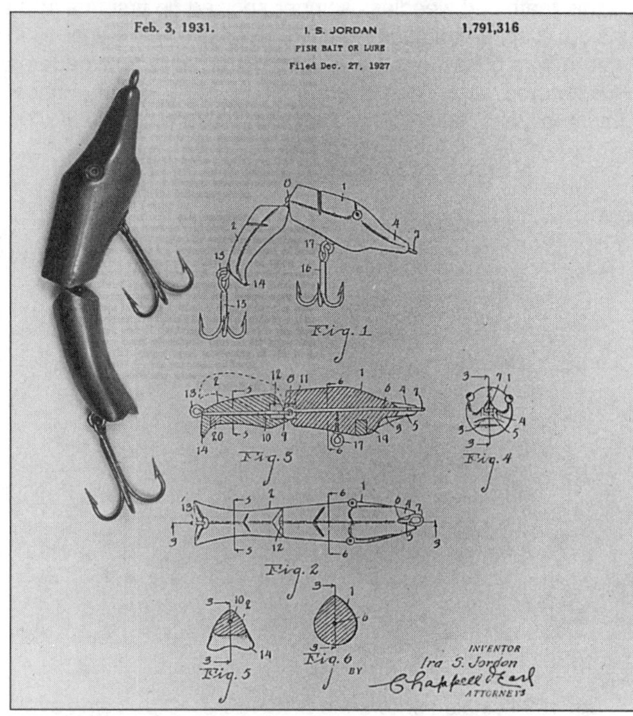

A DARTING SHRIMP photographed on its patent drawing.

This lure first appeared sometime around 1928-29, but was not fully patented until February 3, 1931. Looking sort of like a shrimp, it was jointed so that it would swim like one on retrieve. It has one belly-mounted treble hook and one trailing treble. Does not appear in catalogs from late 1930s on. Collector value range: $75-$100.

CATALOG SERIES #	BODY LENGTH	LURE WEIGHT
135	1-1/4"	7/10 oz.

COLOR OR FINISH: *Natural frog, *white body shaded red head, gold flitter; copper sides, dark back, silver belly, and a red flash at throat and tail.

**Earliest color combinations offered.*

THE EGYPTIAN WOBBLERS

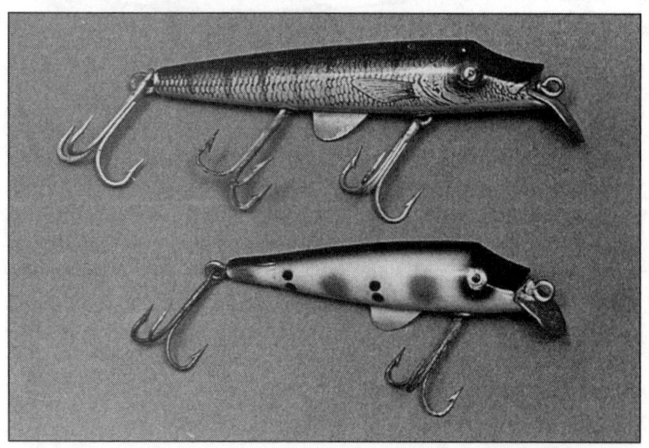

A 1934 catalog indicates that this plug had already been available for some time. The lure has a metal ventral fin, two belly treble hooks, a trailing treble, metal lip and has a gold colored hook finish for saltwater use. It is the same in subsequent catalogs and by the late 1940s and continuing into the 1950s an EGYPTIAN WOBBLER JUNIOR was offered as well as jointed versions of each. Collector value range: $75-$100.

CATALOG SERIES #	BODY LENGTH	LURE WEIGHT
*6636	4-7/8"	1 oz.
6635	3-5/8"	1/2 oz.

COLOR OR FINISH: Green "fancy back" with tangerine, green and white body; white body with red, black, and yellow spots and a black back stripe, silver flitters; yellow perch pattern; white body, red head, silver flitters; natural pickerel.

CATALOG SERIES #	BODY LENGTH	LURE WEIGHT
6677	5-1/2"	9/10 oz.
6676	4-3/4"	1/2 oz.

COLOR OR FINISH: Black back, scale finish and vertical stripes; white body with red, black, and yellow spots, silver flitters; white body, red head.

**Sometimes known as the STRIPED BASS WOBBLER.*

Collector value range for other wobblers: King Fish Wobbler, $75-$125.; Striped Bass Wobbler, $100-$150. and Kazoo Wobbler $50-$100.

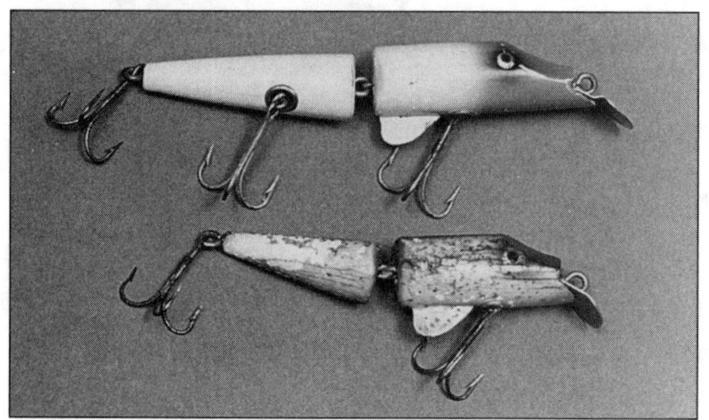

Jointed Egyptian Wobblers

THE "00" SIZE FANCY BACK AND METAL PLATE MINNOWS

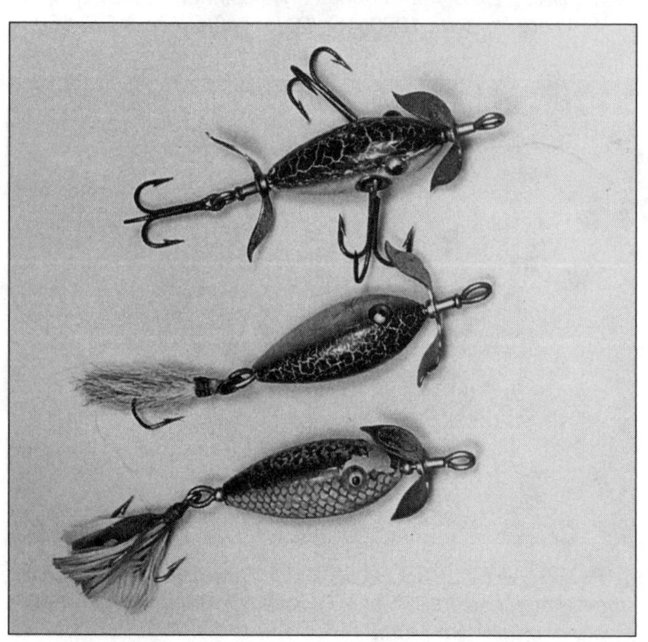

This small bait is almost exactly the same design as the Shakespeare PUNKIN' SEED minnow except made smaller. It was available in one body design and size only in the 1910 catalog, but several paint finishes were offered. The "Metal Plated" finish plugs were made by electroplating the body with copper, nickel, or gold, giving it a bright highly polished look. This finish was used on several other lures as well. The FANCY BACK MINNOW has a crackle-like finish. This finish was also used on other lures.

These plugs have a propeller on the nose and only one treble hook (1T) trailing. *Feathers were bound to the hook. The photo shows one example with a buck tail. It was apparently added later by an angler. Collector value range: $75-$125. The metallized versions are rare and can bring twice that or more.

This same lure is listed in a post 1934 catalog (probably between 1934-37) as "The Midget", available in "one finish only". The illustration shows a Fancy Back finish with natural scale sides. The feathers are multicolored and the lure body is 1-7/8" long. It is valued at $15-$25.

CATALOG SERIES #	BODY LENGTH
00s	1-3/4"

COLOR OR FINISH: "Fancy Back" in sienna, yellow belly; "Metal Plated" in copper, nickel & gold.

**The 3T plug in the photo is a #03 available in the 1910 catalog in fancy sienna back with yellow belly.*

RHODES "MECHANICAL SWIMMING FROG" #3GWF

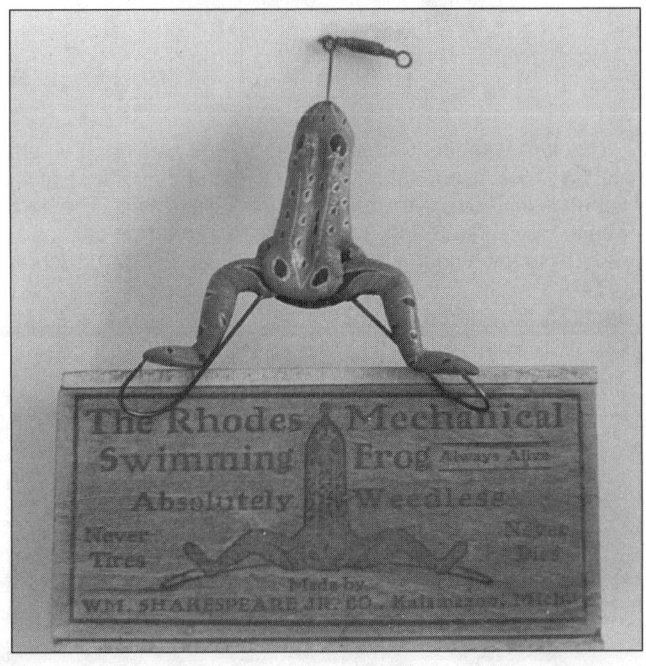

The MECHANICAL FROG with original wooden box. Photo courtesy Jim Muma.

This ingenious invention, offered in the 1910 catalog, was a rubber body frog that has flexible legs which kicked back each time the fishing line was tugged. Each leg has single weedless hooks and the belly has a removable double hook in order to render it weedless. The body length is 2-1/4" with legs extended, the overall length is about 4". The #3GWF does not appear in catalogs after the early 1920s. Collector value range: $350-$500. If found with the original wood box it could easily double that value.

THE "PIN HEAD" BAIT

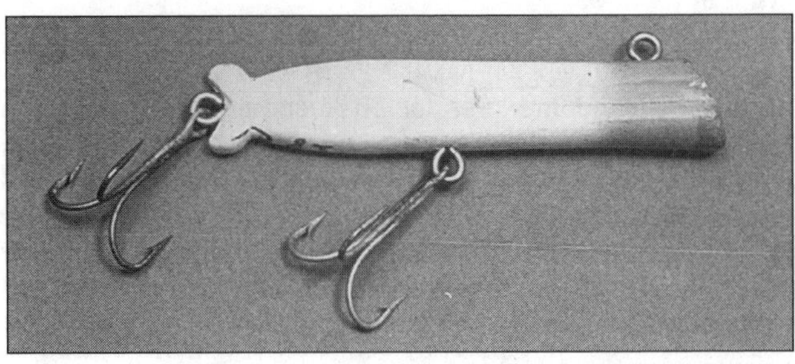

Appears in a 1934 catalog in one size, one weight. Heavily weighted in the head it was made for saltwater pier fishing. It has a belly treble hook and a trailing treble. The line tie is on top of the head (screw eye type). It was in continuous production until early 1950s. Collector value range: $10-$15.

RHODES TORPEDO #6540

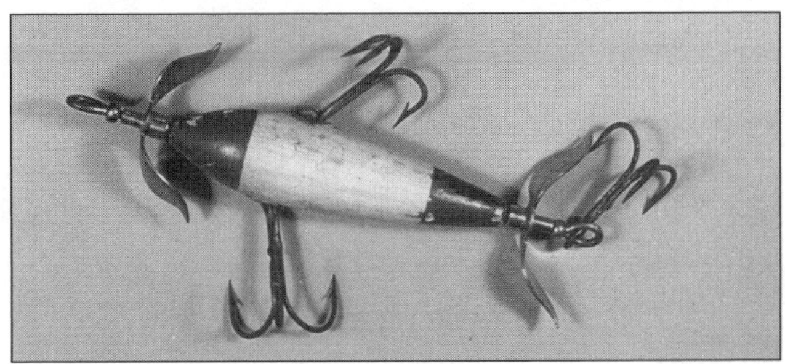

This 1934 catalog listing states that this "...two spinner underwater lure with side hooks was first put on the market by Shakespeare Company over 25 years ago...". The collector should be aware of the possibility of this newer TORPEDO being mistaken for the older one. Look at the hardware, size and body style closely if you find a TORPEDO, before deciding which you have. The propellers on the plug in the photo are marked with the Shakespeare name. Collector value range: $75-$150.

CATALOG SERIES #	BODY LENGTH	LURE WEIGHT
6540	3"	5/8 oz.

COLOR OR FINISH: Greenback, white sides, silver flitters; Spotted green frog; White body, red head.

"KAZOO" WOODEN MINNOW

Upper lure is an early KAZOO WOODEN MINNOW with simple screw-eye hook fastener (note off-set) and glass eyes. Lower lure is a later 3T model with tack and brass washer for eyes.

The KAZOO WOODEN MINNOWS were very inexpensively made, second line lures for Shakespeare. They appear in 1910 catalogs as available in several versions: floating or submerged; different hook numbers and positions, two sizes and several color designs. The body hooks (all treble) were attached by staples or a simple screw eye and now cup or cup hardware. All have a bow type tube propeller at the tail and nose and a trailing treble hook. Although this lure does not appear in catalogs from the early 1920s on, the name "Kazoo" is frequently used in connection with other Shakespeare lures. Collector value range: $75-$100.

CATALOG SERIES #	BODY LENGTH
31 GWK	3"

Floating style, 1 belly treble, 1 tail treble (2T), green back, white belly.

31 RWK3"

Floating style, 1 belly treble, I tail treble (2T), red back, white belly.

33 GWK3"

Submerged style, 2 side trebles, 1 tail treble (3T), green back, white belly.

33 RWF3"

Submerged style, trebles, 1 tail treble (3T), green back, white belly.

42 GWK3-3/4"

Floating style,2 side trebles, 1 tail treble (3T), red back, white belly.

42 RWK3-3/4"

Floating style,2 belly trebles, 1 tail treble (3T), red back, white belly.

43 GWK3-3/4"

Submerged style, 2 side trebles, 1 tail treble (3T), green back, white belly.

43 RWK 3-3/4"

Submerged style, 2 side trebles, 1 tail treble (3T), red back, white belly.

44 GWK 3-3/4"

Submerged style, 4 side trebles, 1 tail treble (5T), green back, white belly.

44 RWK 3-3/4"

Submerged style, 4 side trebles, 1 tail treble (5T), red back, white belly.

KAZOO CHUB MINNOW

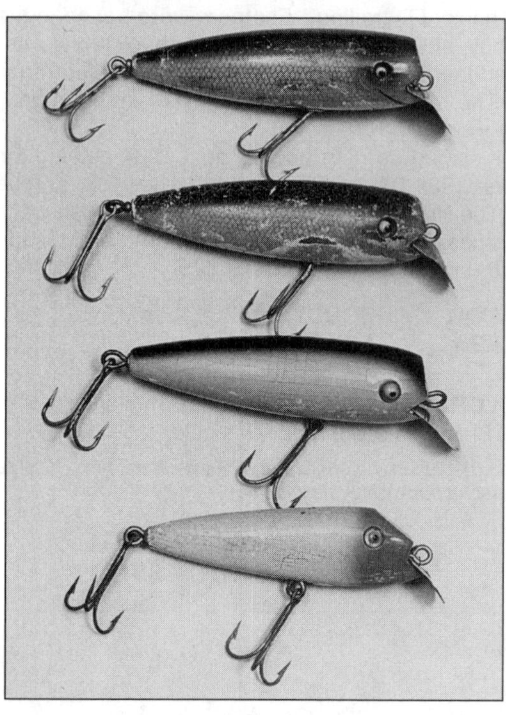

This lure was first found listed in a 1932 catalog. It wasn't listed in any subsequent catalogs. All four of these have glass eyes. The third one in the photo has pink glass eyes. The body of each measures 3-3/8", except for the shorter un-cataloged one. It may have been so similar to others in this line, such as the BASS-A-LURE that it was dropped from production. There seems to be a large number of very similar size and action plugs in their line. Collector value range: $75-$125.

MUSKIE TROLLING MINNOW OR KAZOO TROLLING MINNOW

Called a "new type of lure" in the 1924 catalog this plug has a reed body built around a treble hook. The three points of the hook protrude from the body. Another model has a single hook at the tail covered by a buck tail and moose hair tail, and fluted spoon forward of the body. The lure was available in three sizes, the smallest being the "Bass" and had no trailing hook. No actual sizes or weights were quoted. By 1929 the "Bass" size had disappeared from catalogs and by the late 1930s the lure disappeared from the catalogs altogether. Collector value range: $40-$100.

THE KAZOO WOBBLER

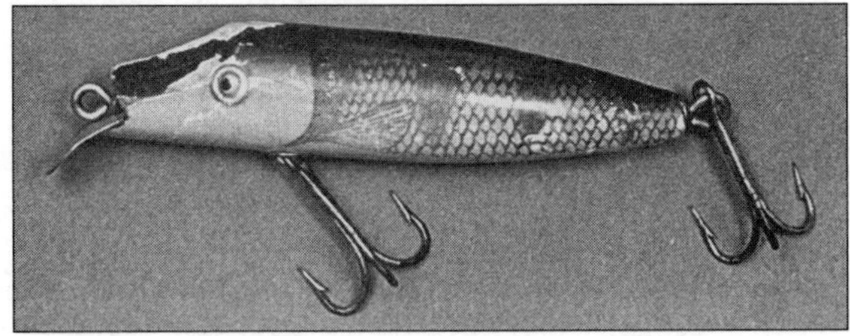

Called a "veteran bait" in the 1934 catalog, one would think it a later development of the BASS KAZOO or PIKIE KAZOO. Both continue to be offered in subsequent catalogs, however, so its original availability is presently hazy. The plug has a metal lip, belly-mounted fin, one belly-mounted treble hook and a trailing treble attached by regular screw eye or the Shakespeare "Ball Head Hook Retainer" used in the 1930s. Collector value range: $50-$100.

CATALOG SERIES #	BODY LENGTH	LURE WEIGHT
6637	4"	4/5 oz.

COLOR OR FINISH: Black back, tan and gold sides with vertical stripes; Black back, green & gold sides; Green back, golden yellow sides, white belly, Green back, Salmon pink and silver sides; Green back, white sides and silver flitters; White body, red head.

KAZOO WOBBLE TAIL #980

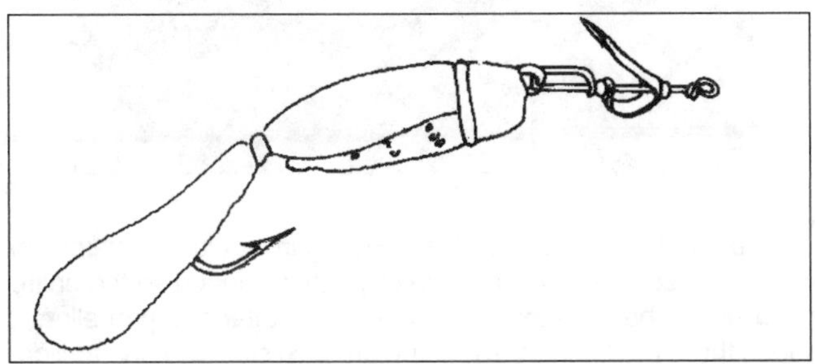

This lure was apparently short-lived for it appears only once in the catalog collection, a 1924 issue. It has a red body and highly colored scale finish, silk wound with a crude rubber flapper tail, one single tail hook, and a single blade propeller at the nose. Collector value range: $75-$100.

KAZOO FLAPPER WING #984

This lure is in the same category as the previous KAZOO WOBBLE TAIL. It was first observed in the 1924 catalog and one other later one, a 1926. The 1924 catalog lists it as being available in the three color patterns, but the 1926 listing says nothing about the available colors. The FLAPPER WING also had a reed body with scale finish. It has two rubber wings, a single blade nose propeller and a long trailing buck tail hiding a single hook. As with the WOBBLE TAIL, there was no size or weight listed. Collector value range: $75-$100.

THE PIKIE KAZOO

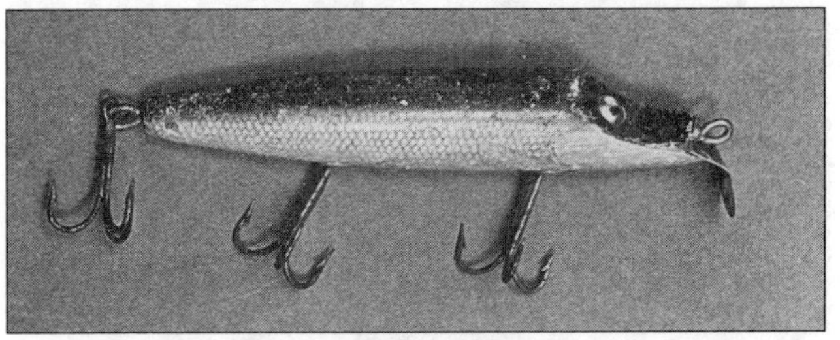

This lure, as depicted in a 1923 Shakespeare catalog, was available with two belly mounted treble hooks and a trailing treble. It is a long body pike lure with a metal lip which is "bendable" to vary the retrieve depth. Body length was 5-1/16" at first, but by 1924 it had shortened to 4-3/4". It was last observed in this form in catalogs from between 1934 and 1937. The same color and finish combinations were available from first to last. Collector value range: $50-$75.

CATALOG SERIES #	BODY LENGTH
637	5-1/16" & 4-3/4

COLOR OR FINISH: Green "fancy back" with scale finish; green back with scale finish; rainbow with scale finish; white body, red head, yellow perch with scale finish.

BABY PIKIE KAZOO

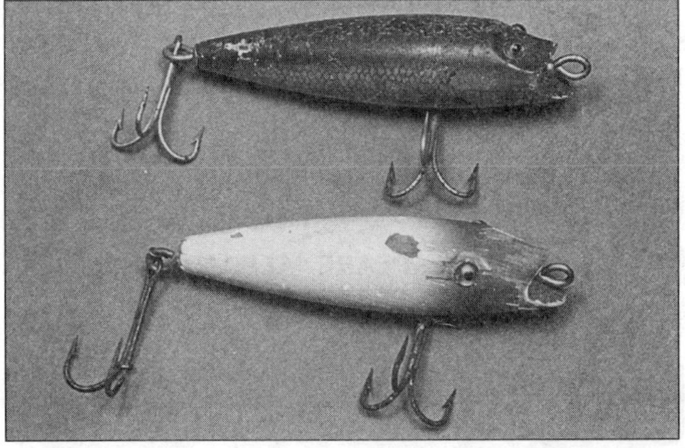

This lure, a smaller version of the PIKIE KAZOO, appeared in the same catalog (c. 1935) that the larger one was last observed in. It actually has a slightly different design in that there is no metal lip, rather the nose is designed to impart the same action. It has only one belly treble and a trailing treble (2T). The catalog number assigned to it was #637-1/2 and it was available in exactly the same finishes as the #637 above. Note eye location differences. Eyes on side is oldest version. Collector value range: $30-$50.

SHAKESPEARE "FAVORITE" FLOATING BAIT

I have found a small catalog calling this a new lure. Unfortunately it is not dated and all I have been able to do so far is pin it down to between 1910 and 1917 by using other catalog entries and catalog design style. It was offered in only one size. It has a double hook at the belly that is stabilized with a small pin. It is designed so that upon a fish striking the hook can pull of the pin and swing away from the lure body. This lure is very much like the Heddon ZARAGOSSA and the Creek Chub SARASOTA. It had disappeared from catalogs by the late 1920s. Collector value range: $250-$400.

This is a nose view of the FAVORITE showing the unique triangular shape of the body.

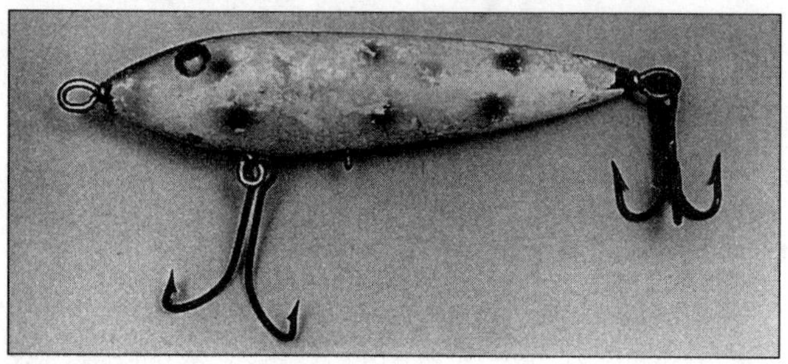

CATALOG SERIES #	BODY LENGTH
41F	3-5/8"

COLOR OR FINISH: Solid red, solid white, solid yellow, imitation frog color (later).

SHAKESPEARE "ALBANY" FLOATING BAIT c. 1913 No. 64

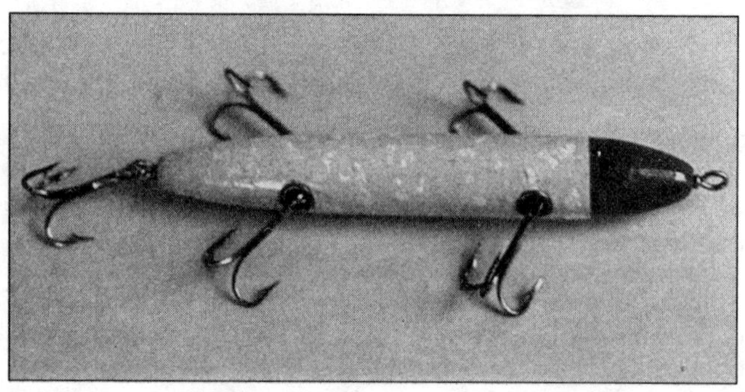

The earliest listing for this lure I was able to find was in a 1917 catalog. It was listed as available in a white body with blue head. It is known to exist with a red head also. It has plate hook hanger hardware and is 5-1/2" long. Collector value range: $1,500-$2,500. Photo courtesy Jim Muma.

THE FISHER BAIT

This floating plug was called a new lure in a 1940s catalog. It has a metal lip to make it dive on retrieve. Has a single belly-mounted treble hook forward of a ventral fin and one trailing treble. There was a smaller version of this plug called the JUNIOR FISHER BAIT. Collector value range: $60-$80.

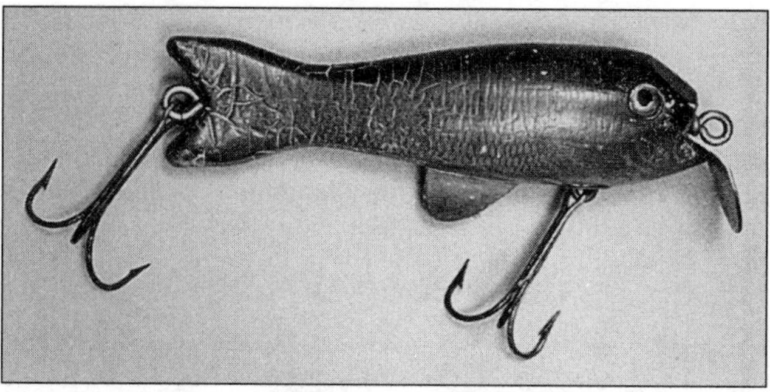

CATALOG SERIES #	BODY LENGTH	LURE WEIGHT
6508	2-7/8"	1/2 oz.
6509	3-3/4"	3/5 oz.

COLOR OR FINISH: Black and green, vertical stripes, scale finish; green bronze back, silver sides, white belly, scale finish; white body, spotted red, green and black, narrow green back; white body, green head, white body, red head, yellow perch scale finish.

SHAKESPEARE FLOATING "SPINNER"

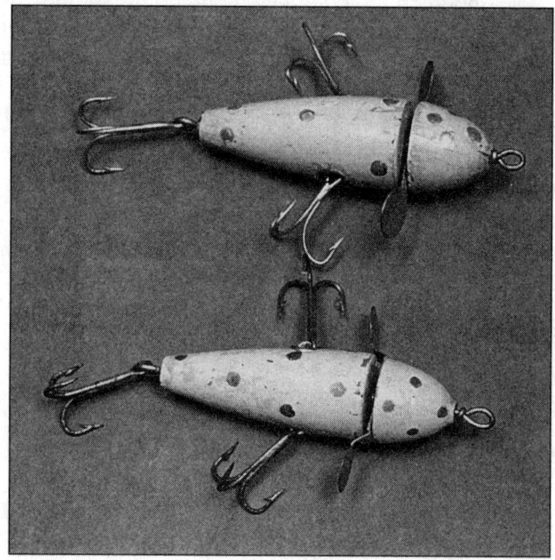

The 1910 catalog shows this wooden lure could be obtained in three color schemes. It was a floating bait designed so the entire head of the bait rotated by means of an attached propeller. It sports three treble hooks (3T), one on each side and one trailing.

The side hook fasteners in the lures photo are see-through plate type. The original was available only in a 3-1/8" size and three color designs, but the early 1920s a 2-7/8" size was offered and a fourth color had been added. 1924 and subsequent catalogs do not offer the plug. You may find this bait in a box from the Regal Bait Company. Shakespeare made their lures for other companies also. This is one of them. Collector value range: $50-$90.

CATALOG SERIES #	BODY LENGTH
3S	2-7/8"
4S	3-1/8"

COLOR OR FINISH: *white body with red head, *solid yellow with gold dots, *solid white with gold dots, solid white and variegated dots.

**The original finishes offered. The fourth was not offered until around 1920-24.*

FROG SKIN BAIT

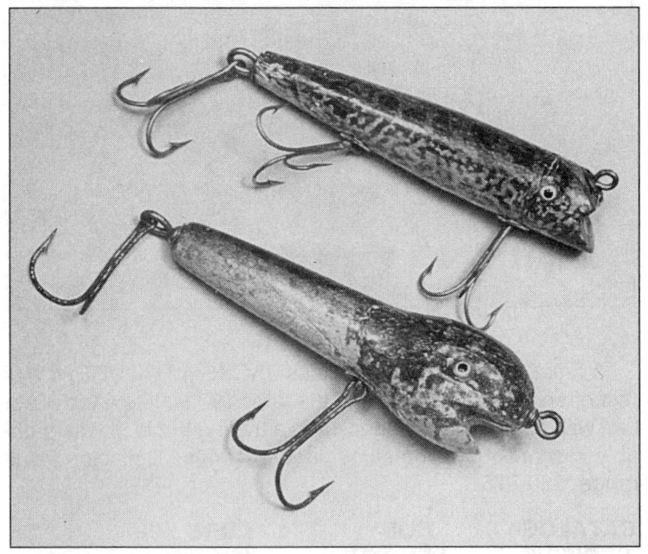

Upper lure is a Frog skin JERKIN by Shakespeare. Lower is the larger (3-3/4") FROG SKIN BAIT.

New sometime in the early 1930s, this was a wooden lure with actual frog skin stretched over the body. The first listing I found for it was in a 1936 catalog. It said nothing about it being new, just offered it as a routine matter-of-fact. It is thought by some that this lure was actually made for Shakespeare By the Eger bait Company. This is probably so because Eger actually held the patent, applied for in 1936 and granted in September of 1937. They are practically identical. A general rule for differentiating the two is that the Shakespeare version has white iris glass eyes and the Eger products supposedly do not. The lure disappeared sometime in the late 1930s. Collector value range: $50-$75.

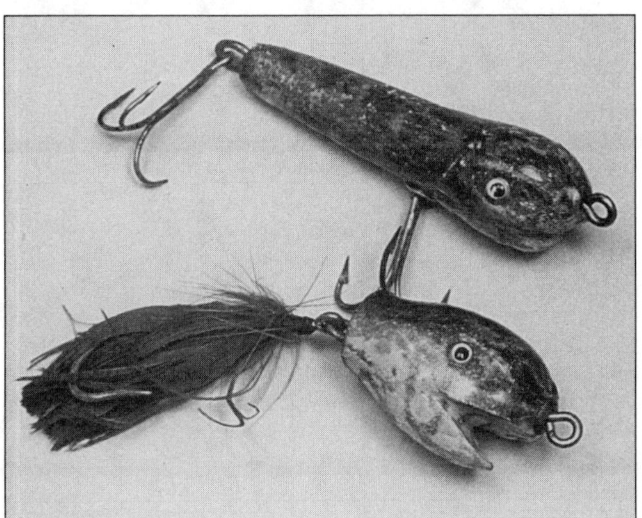

Upper lure is the small FROG SKIN BAIT. The lower was not found cataloged anywhere.

CATALOG SERIES #	BODY LENGTH
6505	3-3/4"
6505-S	3"

COLOR OR FINISH: All plugs have the natural frog skin stretched over the body.

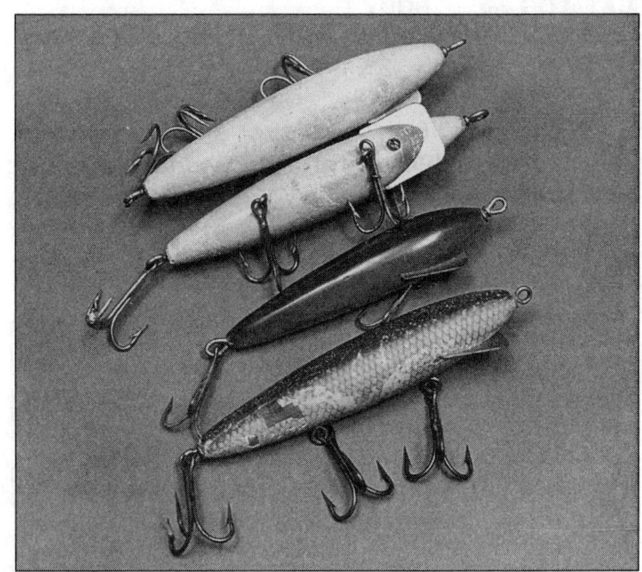

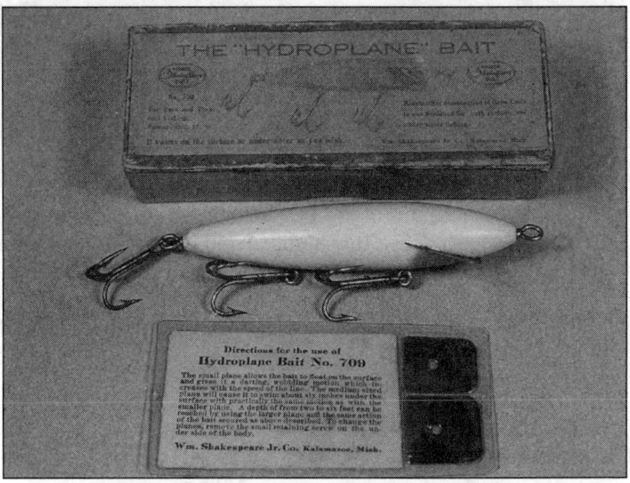

A Shakespeare HYDROPLANE BAIT new with its original box with extra planes and papers. There are only three complete sets known to be in collections. Super rare. No trade data was found. Photo courtesy Jim Muma.

THE HYDROPLANE

As shown in a 1920 catalog this bait was available in only one size, but shortly thereafter it was offered in three sizes. It has two simple screw eye mounted belly treble hooks and one tail treble. However, one shown in the photo obviously was made with only one belly treble. It was packed with three sizes of metal planes , each designed to run the lure at a different depth. The fly rod size has only one, permanent mount, plane. This bait was gone from the catalogs by the mid 1920s and is probably the forerunner of the Shakespeare BASS-A-LURE. Collector value range: $75-$175, Fly rod size, $100-$200.

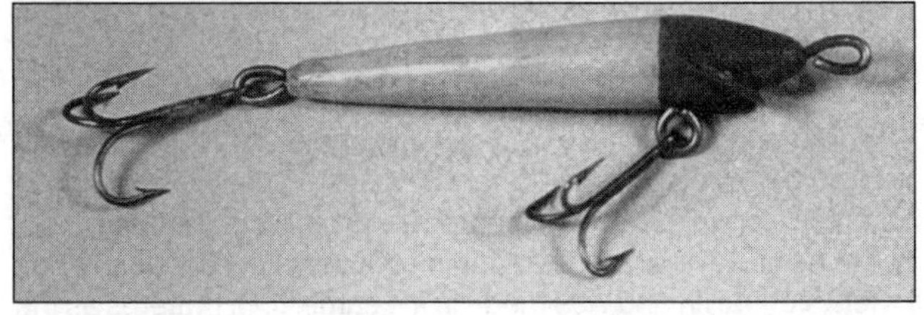

The fly rod size HYDROPLANE at 2-3/4". Photo courtesy Jim Muma.

CATALOG SERIES #	BODY LENGTH
709	4-1/2"
709 1/2	3"
?	2-3/4" fly rod size

COLOR OR FINISH: solid white, solid red, fancy green, frog back, spotted, rainbow, red and white, yellow perch.

INJUN JOE
LITTLE JOE

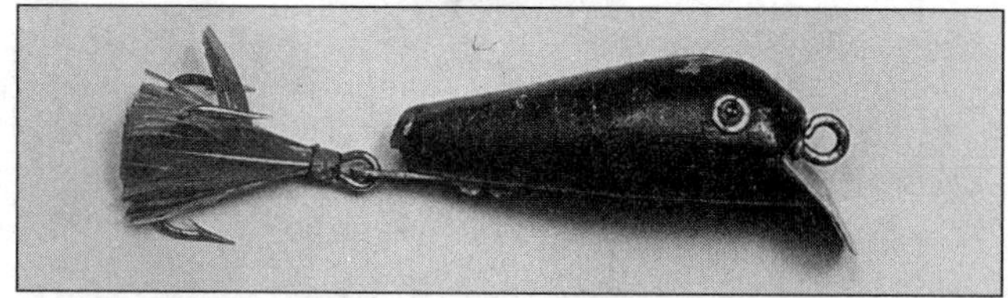

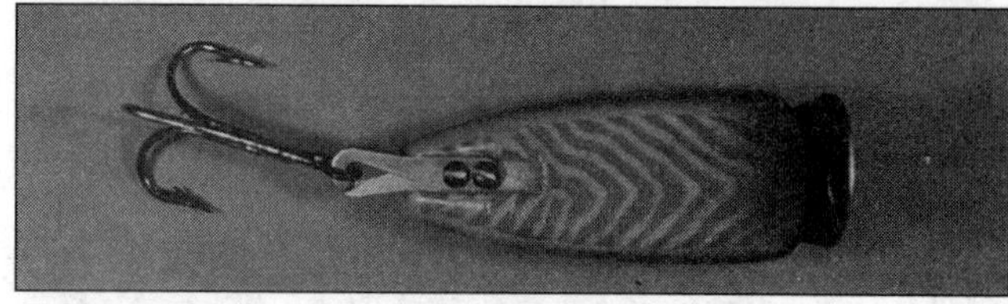

The photos here are of the LITTLE JOE. It is a smaller version of the INJUN JOE. They first showed up in a 1934 edition of the catalogs. Neither of these were found in subsequent catalogs. Both have metal diving lips and one trailing treble with or without fasteners. The larger, INJUN JOE, has an additional treble on the belly. Both have a unique scissor-type tail hook hanger. Collector value range: $40-$75.

CATALOG SERIES #	BODY LENGTH	LURE WEIGHT
6530	3"	1/2 oz.
6593	2-1/8"	1/2 oz.

COLOR OR FINISH: Rainbow with green back, green back with green and red sides, white body with red head, yellow perch, black body with yellow stripe, gray with tangerine striped belly, tangerine body with black back and black and yellow spots, black body with white head, lavender body with black spots.

JACKSMITH LURE

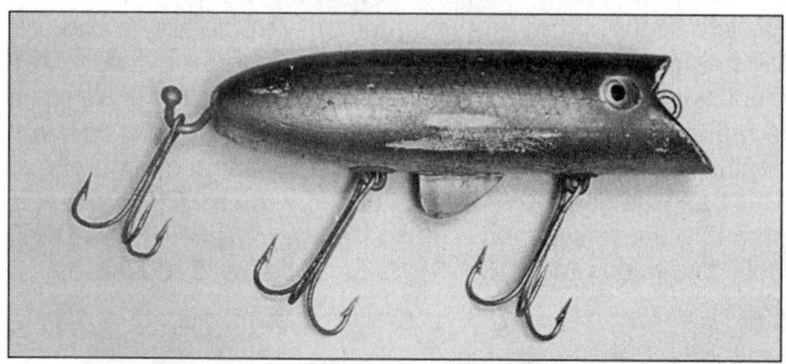

This is merely a heavy duty version of the JACK JR. below. It has two belly trebles instead of just the one. The 1934 catalog illustration shows the Shakespeare "Ball Post Hook Retainer", but by the mid 1940s it was the simple screw eye once again. It has a metal ventral fin and was made in the same color patterns as the JACK JR., but the white body, red head color combination does not have silver flitters. Collector value range: $50-$100.

THE JACK JR.

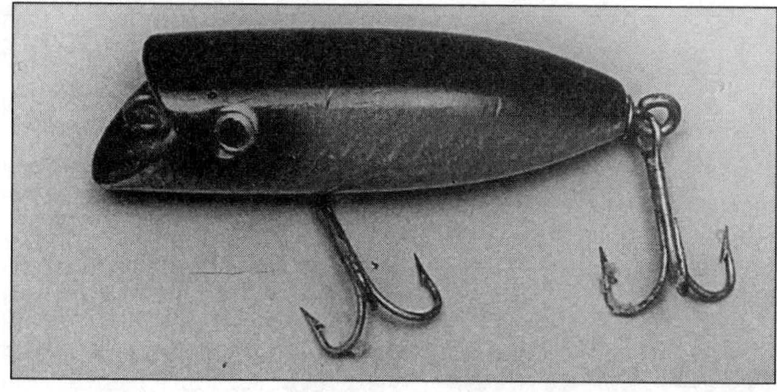

A small version of the previous JACKSMITH LURE, it was first offered sometime around the later 1920s. It is a top water bait with one belly treble hook and a trailing treble. It was probably discontinued sometime in the 1940s. Collector value range: $50-$75.

CATALOG SERIES #	BODY LENGTH	LURE WEIGHT
6560	2-3/4"	1/2 oz.

COLOR OR FINISH: *White body, red head, silver flitters; rainbow with green back; spotted, green and silver, scale finish; green "fancy back", scale finish; green perch, scale finish; white body, red head, black back, white belly, green and gold sides, scale finish; black back, tan and gold sides, with vertical stripes, scale finish.

**Later versions do not have silver flitters.*

JERKIN LURE

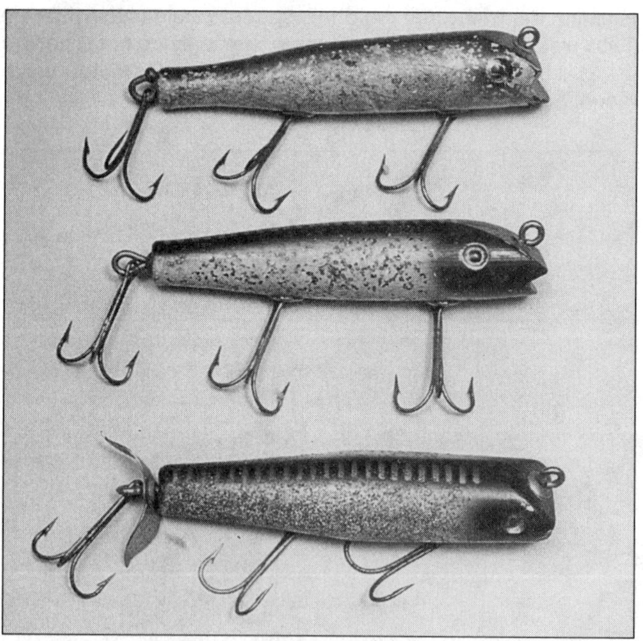

The 1934 catalog from the collection shows only one version of the JERKIN LURE available. By 1949 there was a second one offered that had a tail propeller. It was a surface popping plug and the 1934 illustration shows two belly trebles and a trailing treble attached by the Shakespeare "Ball Head Hook Retainer" (see upper plug). Collector value range: $15-$20.

CATALOG SERIES #	BODY LENGTH	LURE WEIGHT
6567	4"	3/5 oz.

COLOR OR FINISH: Frog; green and silver, scale finish; natural pickerel, scale finish; silver flitters; white body, red head; green back, red & white sides, scale finish; frog skin.

KING FISH WOBBLER

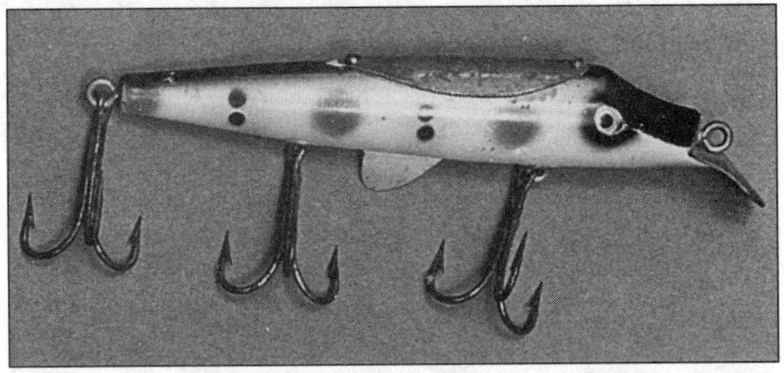

A 1934 catalog lists, but does not illustrate, this bait. It says it is the same body design as the Shakespeare EGYPTIAN WOBBLER. It is listed and illustrated in later catalogs, but disappeared from them by the end of the 1940s. This is a most unusual plug in that it has a chrome plated back plate and a gold colored hook finish. It has a metal ventral fin, two belly-mounted treble hooks, a trailing treble hook and a metal blade lip. Collector value range: $75-$125.

CATALOG SERIES #	BODY LENGTH	LURE WEIGHT
6535	4-7/8"	1-1/4 oz.
6601	1-7/8"	1/2 oz.
6510	3-3/4"	5/8 oz.

LUMINOUS FLOATING NIGHT BAIT

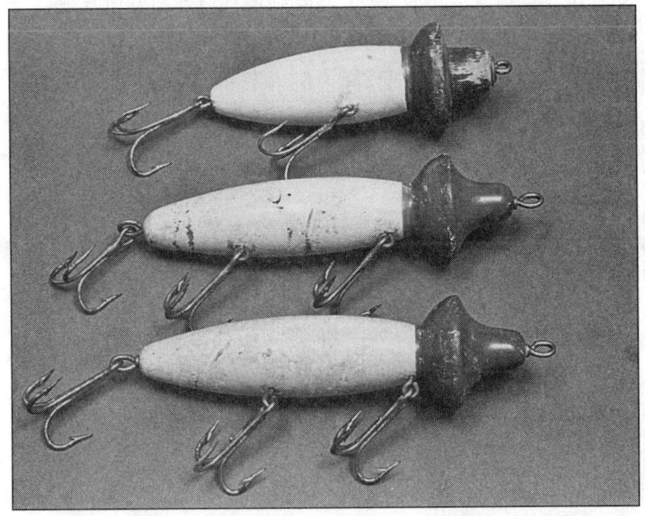

In a 1929 catalog this plug is advertised as being available in only one size. In a later one (1921-23) it is offered in two sizes. By the 1924 catalog there is but one size again. In addition one of the two belly treble hooks had been eliminated. Judging from the catalog illustrations, there was apparently a slight design change as well.

All the plugs were coated with a white luminous paint and until the mid 1920s. They have two belly mounted treble hooks and a trailing treble (3T). All those illustrated after the 1920s have only one belly and the tail mounted treble (2T) as in the photo here. In not a single instance were the actual sizes listed. The early models have a red head and white body, later ones were solid white. The Shakespeare catalog numbers were 680 for the larger one and 680 1/2 for the smaller one (see SURFACE WONDER). The Moonlight Bait Company also made one with the same size, shape, and hardware. Collector value range: $50-$100.

SHAKESPEARE MIDGET SPINNER

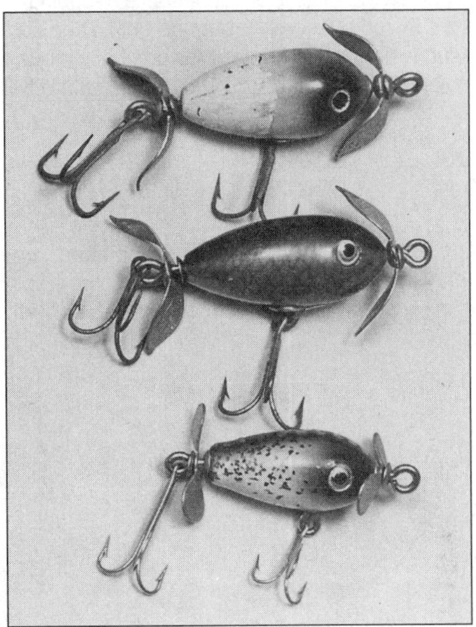

Probably a newer design of the old Shakespeare PUNKIN SEED. This plug has a propeller at the nose and tail, a belly treble hook and a trailing treble. Appears in the 1934 catalog and still present in the early 1950s catalogs. Collector value range: $75-$125.

CATALOG SERIES #	BODY LENGTH	LURE WEIGHT
6601	1-7/8"	1/2 oz.

COLOR OR FINISH: Shiner finish; sienna fancy, back, silver flitters; white body, red head, pickerel finish; green back, green & red sides.

NU-CRIP MINNOW

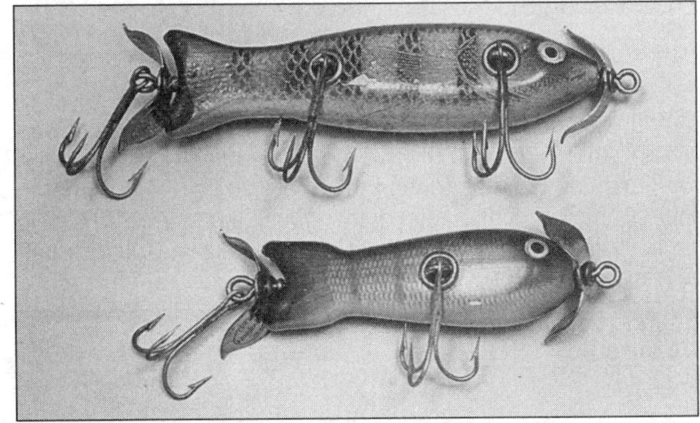

This plug, called new in the 1934 catalog, is shown in a minnow shape with a propeller spinner at the nose and tail. It has a trailing treble hook and two side mounted trebles (3T). It does not appear in mid 1940s catalog. Collector value range: $50-$100.

CATALOG SERIES #	BODY LENGTH	LURE WEIGHT
6510	3-3/4"	5/8 oz.

COLOR OR FINISH: Silver flitter; green frog; white body, red head, green back, red sides, scale finish; green back, golden yellow sides, scale finish; green back, tan and gold sides, dark vertical stripes, white belly, scale finish.

OREGON MIDGET

In the 1934 catalog this is described as a midget lure designed for use with a fly rod but some fishermen trolled and cast with it by adding a lead weight to the leader. Has one belly-mounted double hook. It looks like a miniature PIKIE KAZOO with a belly double hook. Collector value range: No trade data found

CATALOG SERIES #	BODY LENGTH	LURE WEIGHT
6377	1-3/4"	?

COLOR OR FINISH: White body, green head; green perch, scale finish; red, yellow and green spotted; green back, red & green sides, scale finish; yellow body, red head, white body, red head.

THE PAD-LER

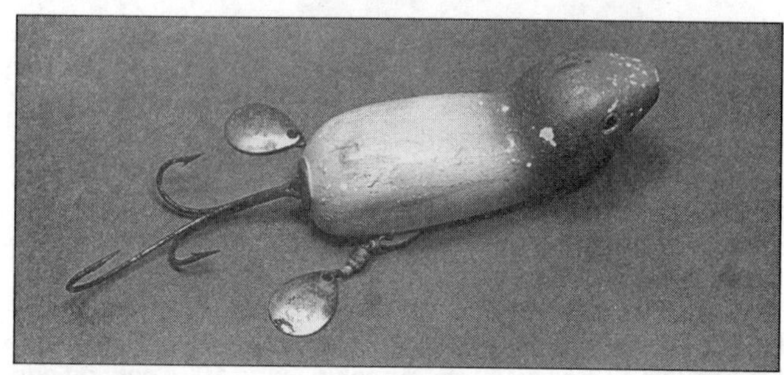

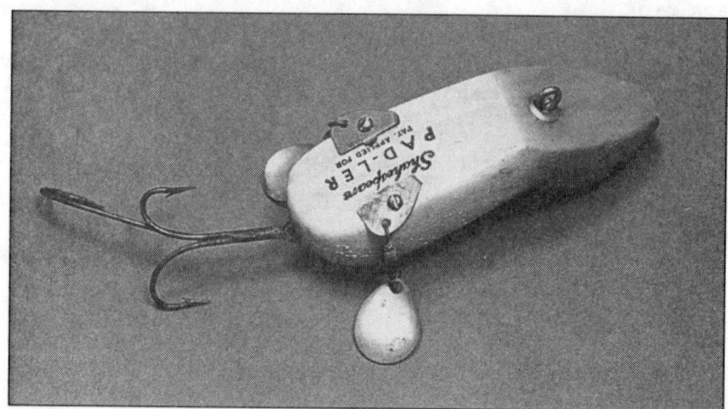

A Shakespeare catalog of 1936 calls this a new lure. It was made in the shape of a rodent, most particularly a mouse. The two small attached spoons in the photo above were meant to impart the swimming action of the mouse's rear legs. The plug has a trailing double hook. Found in three sizes. Collector value range: $70-$100.

CATALOG SERIES #	BODY LENGTH	LURE WEIGHT
6678	3-1/4"	1 oz.
6679	3-3/4"	1-1/2 oz.

COLOR OR FINISH: Green spotted frog, Gray body with white belly, White body with red head.

CATALOG SERIES #	BODY LENGTH	LURE WEIGHT
6680	2-7/8"	7/10 oz.

COLOR OR FINISH: Gray body with white belly, white body with black wavy stripe on sides, white body with red head.

"LITTLE PIRATE" MINNOW #23LP

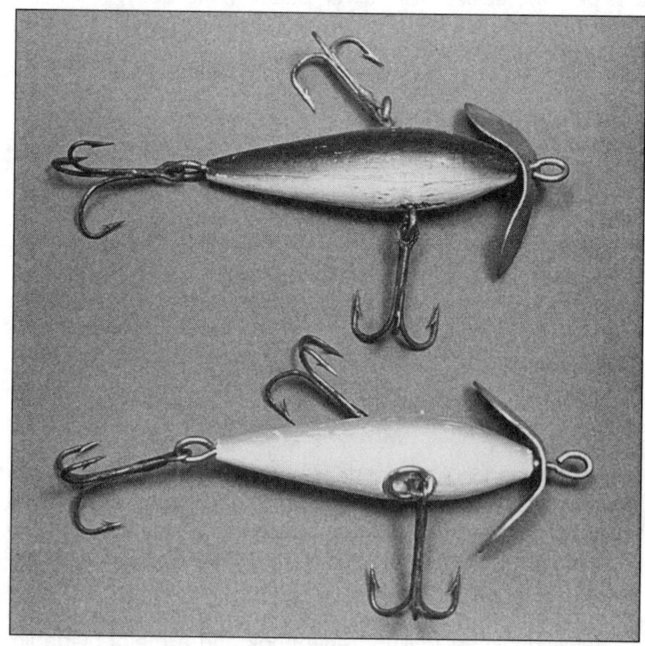

LITTLE PIRATE MINNOWS. Note the rather cheaply made propellers and simple screw eye hook hangars on upper Shakespeare lure. The lower lure is a Pflueger model with the Neverfail hook hanger (Pflueger PEERLESS).

This inexpensive lure appears in two pre-1920s catalogs at 15 cents and 17 cents respectively. They do not appear in later catalogs. The LITTLE PIRATE was available in white belly with either a green or red back. They are all 2-1/2" in length with one nose propeller spinner, two treble side hooks and one tail treble (3T). Collector value range: $25-$75.

THE PLOPPER #6511 OR #7-11

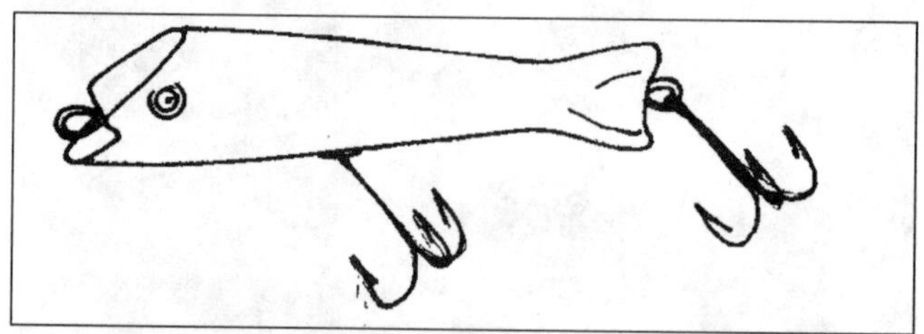

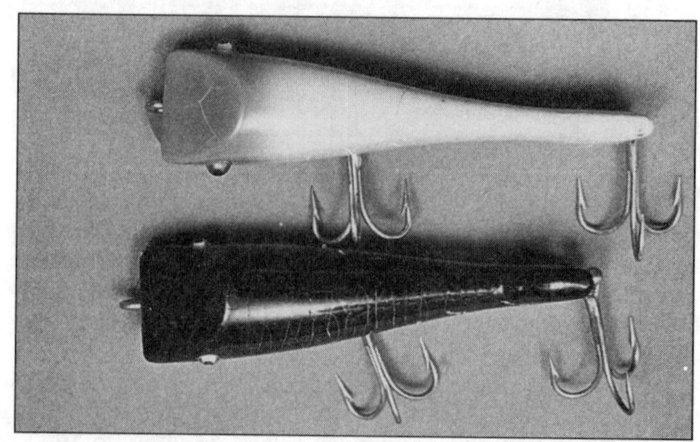

This lure is also known as the SEVEN-ELEVEN. It came along about 1926-27 and has been found with the 1930s Shakespeare Ball Head Hook Retainer. Named for the sound it

makes on retrieve, it has one belly mounted treble hook and a trailing treble. Listed as available in only one size and color, 3/5 oz., White body with shaded red head. The photo shows another color and body shape. Collector value range: $50-$100.

"POP-EYE"

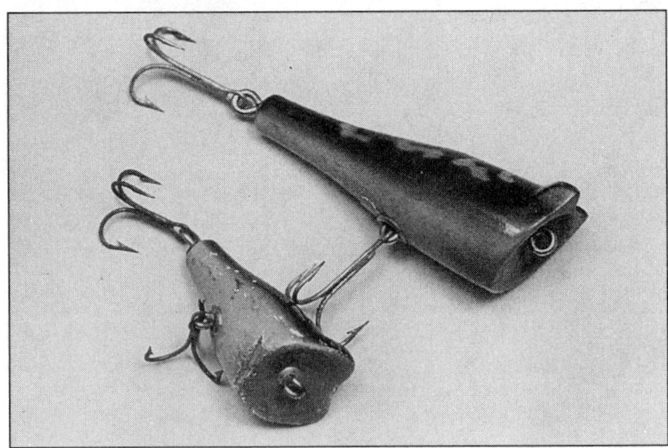

A 1949 catalog illustrates this as a top water plug. It is cone-shaped with two humps on the top of the larger and representing the Pop-Eyes. One belly treble and a trailing treble. Collector value range: $30-$50.

CATALOG SERIES #	BODY LENGTH	LURE WEIGHT
6575	3-1/2"	5/8 oz.

COLOR OR FINISH: Green spotted frog, Green back, white belly and silver flitters.

SHAKESPEARE "PUNKIN-SEED" MINNOW

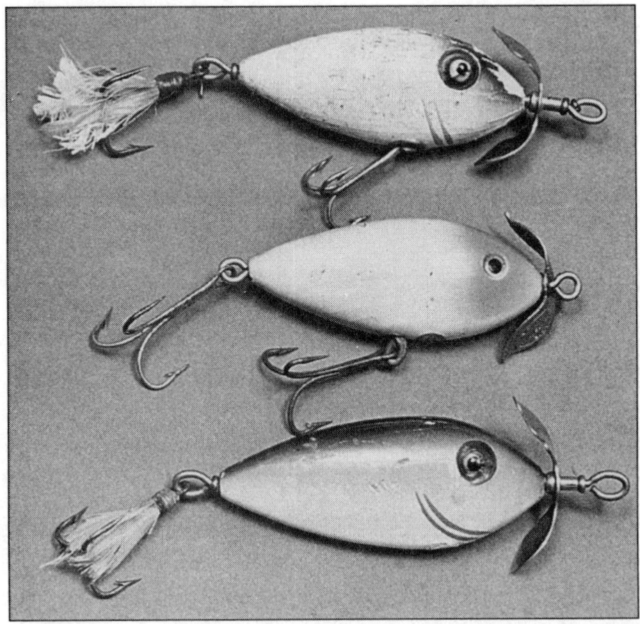

Upper lure with cup hardware is a floater with glass eyes and the early two-hump prop. Middle lure is a painted eye floater with the late model marked floppy propeller spinner. Lower is an early sinker (no belly hook). Has the two-hump prop and glass eyes.

The 1910 catalog offers these lures in one size, six color styles and in a floating and underwater version. The plug probably didn't last much past 1920 for I could not find it listed in that or subsequent catalogs with these catalog numbers or the exact design. It appears again as a #6601 in a 1937 catalog. There is later use of the same numbers in substantially different plugs. The floating version has two treble hooks (2T), one trailing with buck tail and one belly treble attached with the cup and screw eye hardware (CUP). The underwater version was available with or without the belly treble. Collector value range: $100-$200.

CATALOG SERIES #	BODY LENGTH
30P (sinker)	2-5/8"

COLOR OR FINISH: Green back, aluminum color belly; Green back, white belly, Red back, aluminum color belly.

31 P (floater)	2-5/8"

COLOR OR FINISH: Solid white with red on head, Solid white with green on head, Green back, white belly, Sienna Yellow "Fancy Back" with brown head.

SHAKESPEARE'S RIVER PUP

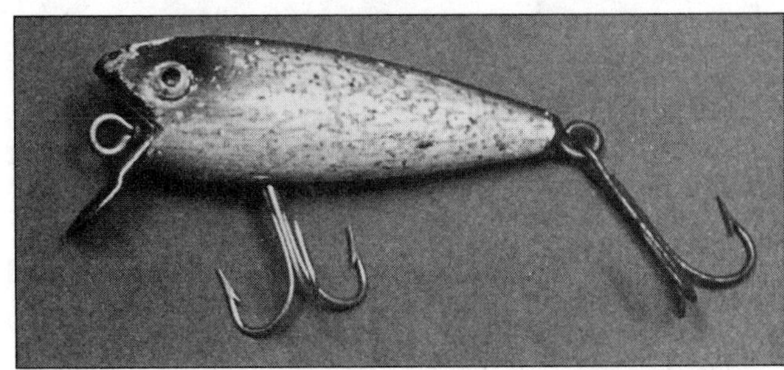

This smaller lure is weighted for deep running according to a 1934 catalog. It has a metal blade lip, one belly treble hook and one trailing treble (2T). The metal lip is notched on the early models and the later ones have no notch and the lip is longer and more squared off. See photo of GRUMPYS following for the later RIVER PUP. Collector value range: $10-$20.

CATALOG SERIES #	BODY LENGTH	LURE WEIGHT
6564	2-5/8"	1/2 oz.

COLOR OR FINISH: Rainbow with green back; pearl, spotted, white body, red head, silver flitters; green perch with red head, scale finish; *yellow body; *frog, *silver flitters.

**These were not among the first five color patterns to be offered.*

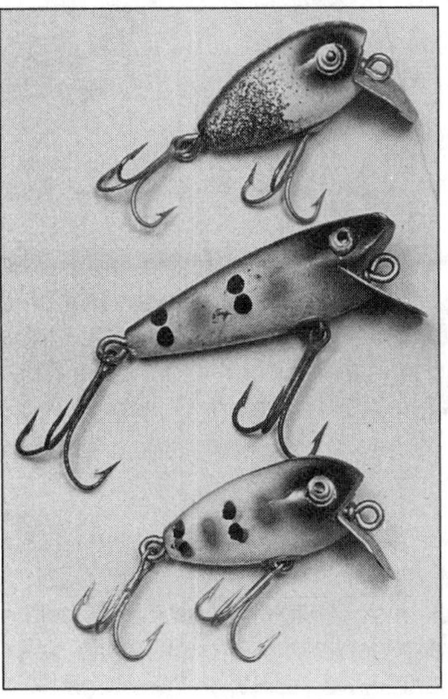

A later model RIVER PUP in center and two GRUMPYS.

SHAKESPEARE GLO-LITE PUP (plastic)

In 1941 Shakespeare devoted a lot of space to their new luminous finishes on the RIVER PUP. What is interesting is the wording describing the finish which reads in part "LUMINOUS SUBSTANCE IS MOLDED RIGHT INTO THE BAIT." That can only mean the lures were being made of plastic by then. How many other lures and when they had begun making in plastic is not clear. There was only one size listed. Collector value range: $5-$15.

CATALOG SERIES #	BODY LENGTH	LURE WEIGHT
6554	2-3/4"	5/8 oz.

COLOR OR FINISH: Frog with green spots, Green perch with red head, Mottled Pearl finish, White body with red head, White body with red head and silver flitters.

"GRUMPY" (see RIVER PUP photo above)

A 1941 catalog first illustrates this plug. It has a metal lip pointing very nearly straight down. A belly treble hook, and a trailing treble. Collector value range: $5-$15.

CATALOG SERIES #	BODY LENGTH	LURE WEIGHT
6602	1-3/4"	4/1 0 oz.

COLOR OR FINISH: Green spotted frog; green perch; white body, spotted red, green and black, narrow green back; green back, white belly, silver flitter; white body, redhead, yellow perch.

"DOPEY"

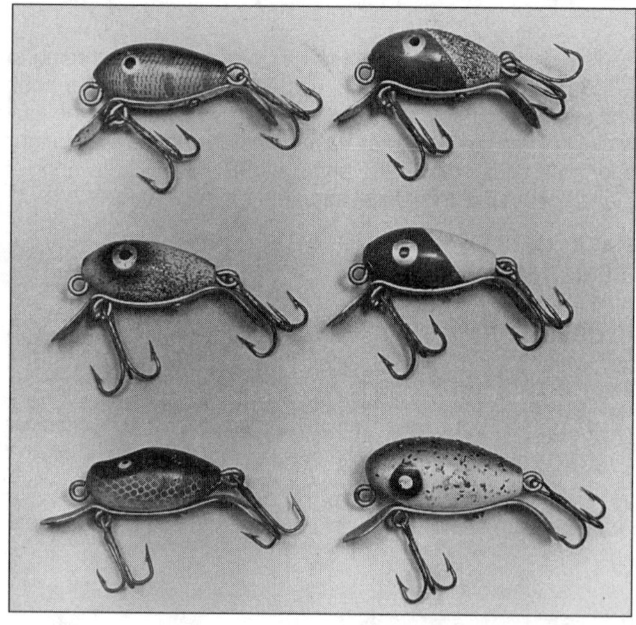

This is a very light, very small, deep-running plug. The DOPEY has a metal piece beginning as a blade lip and running down the belly extending into another blade just under the trailing treble hook. There is a second treble hook attached just behind the front lip. First seen in a 1941 catalog. Collector value range: $10-$20.

CATALOG SERIES #	BODY LENGTH	LURE WEIGHT
6603	1-5/16"	4/10 oz.

COLOR OR FINISH: Black body, white ribs; black body, white head, green spotted frog; green perch; green back, white belly, silver flitter, white body, red head, solid yellow, yellow perch.

SHAKESPEARE SARDINIA SALTWATER MINNOW #721

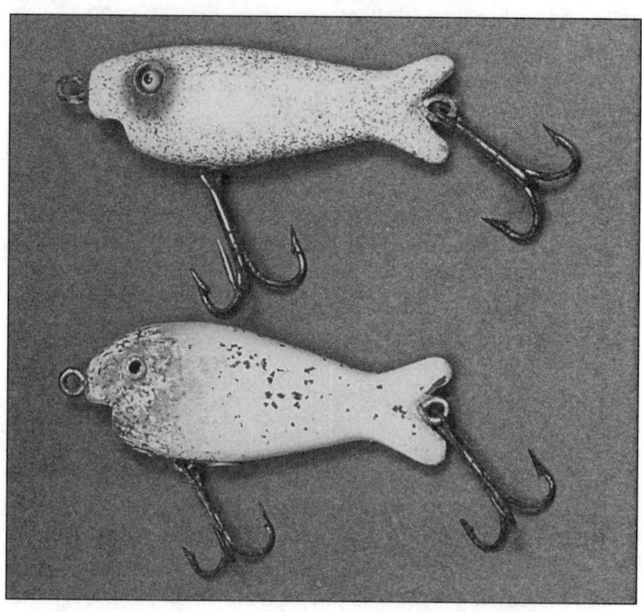

Upper lure is a glass eye #721 SARDINIA SALTWATER MINNOW. The lower appears much like the following Saltwater Special #722, but has a notched mouth and painted eyes. It could be, however, just a later version of the #721.

Although the first and last time this plug appears in the catalog collection is in 1924 and 1925, there can be no doubt that it was around longer than two years. It was made in the shape of a minnow, complete with tail and cut-out mouth. It has one belly mounted treble hook and one trailing treble (2T). Collector value range: $200-$300.

CATALOG SERIES #	BODY LENGTH
721	3"

COLOR OR FINISH: Solid white; Solid white with gold speckles.

SHAKESPEARE SALTWATER SPECIAL MINNOW #722

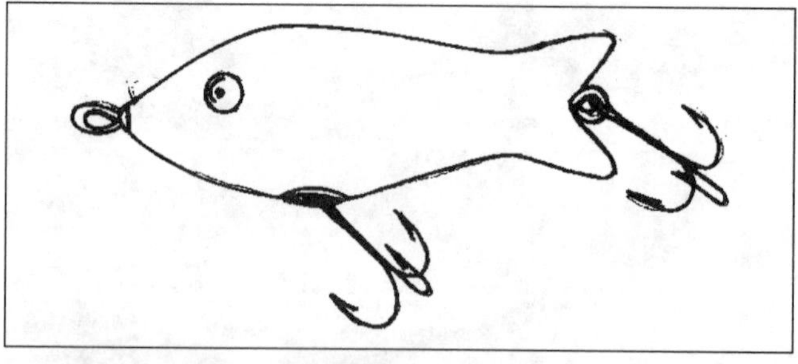

Essentially the same as the #721, the plug is only slightly different in body shape and has no mouth cutout. Available in same size and finishes. Collector value range: $200-$300.

THE SEA WITCH #133 & #6533

As far as can be determined this is an earlier version of the #6531 SEA WITCH. The length of the #133 is more but otherwise it appears to be essentially the same plug. The catalog states that the #6533 is the same lure as the #133 SEA WITCH the major difference being the addition of another line

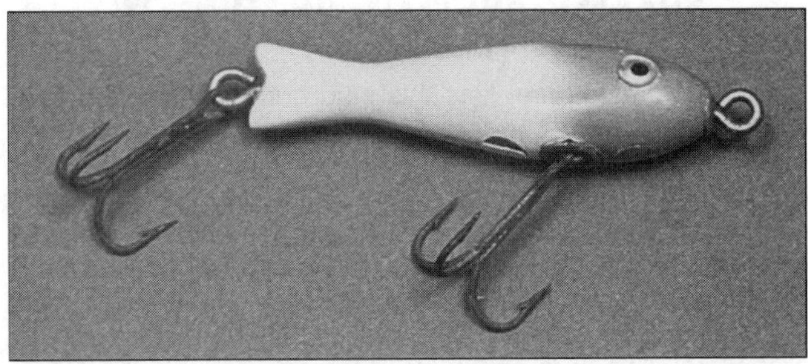

SEA WITCH. The tail hook has been altered by an angler. It is not known if the unusual tail hook hanger is production.

tie " ... in top of head". Thought to be of about 1928 vintage. Collector value range: $75-$125.

CATALOG SERIES #	BODY LENGTH	LURE WEIGHT
133	4"	3/4 oz.
6533	3/16"	1/2 oz.

COLOR OR FINISH: White body with redhead, White body with red head and gold flitters.

THE SEA WITCH #6531

THE SEA WITCH MIDGET #6534

The 1934 catalog describes these plugs as weighted and having "...special plated hooks'. They each have a belly treble and a trailing treble. Their differences are only in size, weight and color pattern availability, the body design being identical. Collector value range: $75-$125.

CATALOG SERIES #	BODY LENGTH	LURE WEIGHT
6531	3-3/4"	1 oz.
6534	2-3/4"	1/2 oz.

COLOR OR FINISH: Solid white; Solid white, redhead, solid white, red head, silver flitters, Solid white, red head, gold flitters; Spotted Pattern; Pearl luster finish.

BARNACLE BILL

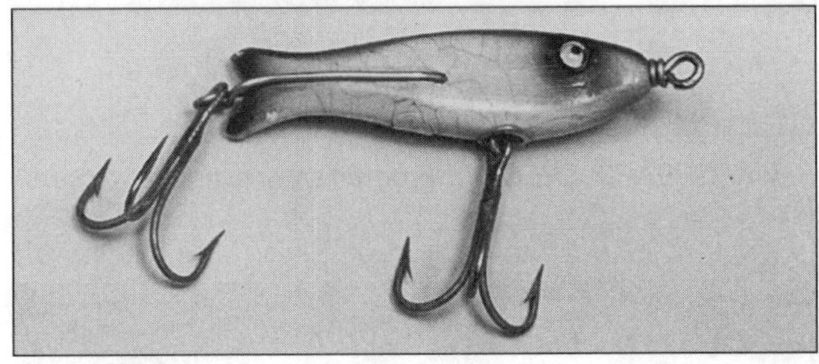

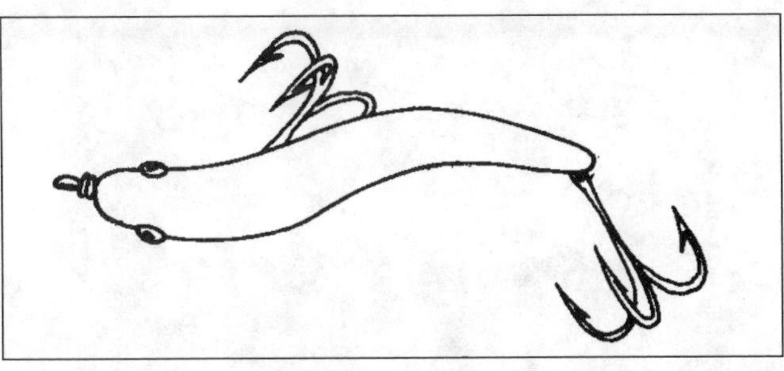

This very scarce saltwater lure is uniquely shaped. The photo here is a straight-on side view. The drawing is a top view showing the curved shape of the lure. The wire you can see in the photo is both internal and external. It is continuous forming both the line tie and hook hangers. It appeared first in the 1931 catalog. Collector value range: $100-$150.

CATALOG SERIES #	BODY LENGTH	LURE WEIGHT
6529	*3"	3/5 oz.

COLOR OR FINISH: White body, red head, gold flitters; white body, spotted red, yellow and black, gold flitters, black back, mud puppy (silver flitters); rainbow, blue, green, yellow, red and white: white body, eyes and tail shaded black.

**Actual measurement is 2-5/8".*

SHAKESPEARE "SHINER" MINNOW

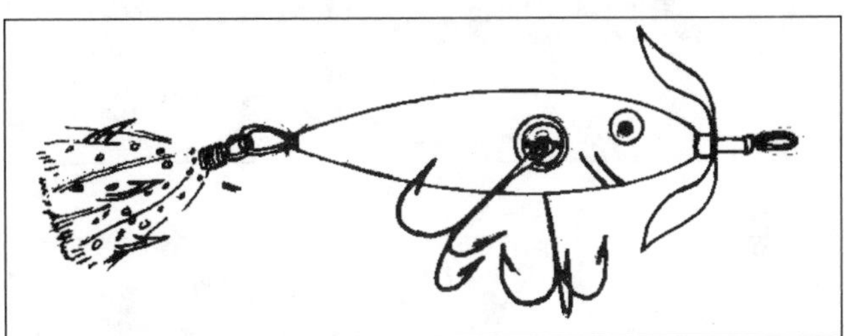

This crackle back SHINER is a bit beat up but still serves as a good lure for identifying any you may find. It measures 3-1/6" long, has white glass eyes, one internal belly weight and twisted through-body wire and see-through side hook hanger hardware.

This lure was offered in two sizes in the 1910 and subsequent catalogs, with or without a "fancy bucktail" on the trailing treble hook. It has two side treble hooks attached by the wire type "See Through" hook hanger. Both sizes has three treble hooks (3T) and a propeller spinner on the nose. Collector value range: $60-$120.

CATALOG SERIES #	BODY LENGTH
23 S	2-1/2"
43 S	3-3/4"

COLOR OR FINISH: Black back, white belly only.

SHAKESPEARE "SLIM JIM MINNOW"

This plug is one of the earliest Shakespeare baits to have painted thin vertical stripes along the body sides. The three photos are arranged in order from oldest, reading left to right in the photo of four lures and top to bottom in the other two photos. They show changes in body style, hook hardware, eyes and propellers. The 1910 catalog offers it in two sizes. Smaller models have only one propeller spinner and larger models have two. Both have two side mounted treble hooks and one tall mounted treble hook. The side hooks utilize the "See

Though" fastener on the earlier plugs. By 1920 only the larger size (3-3/4") seemed to be available. Although they continued to be a SLIM JIM bait offered, the side hook #43 had disappeared from Shakespeare catalogs by 1924. The original offering listed the same five color variations for each size. The last listing offered eight. Collector value range: $50-$100.

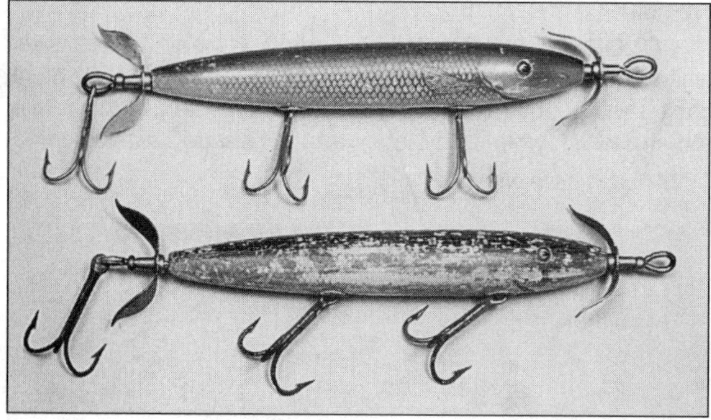

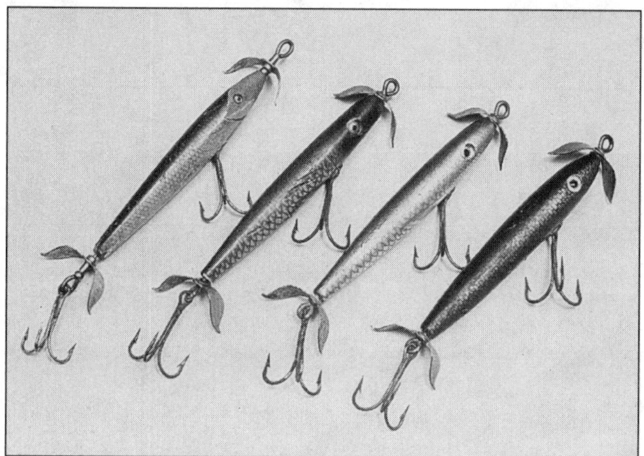

CATALOG SERIES #	BODY LENGTH
33	3"
43	3-3/4"

COLOR OR FINISH: blue back, white belly, striped; green back, white belly, striped; red back, white belly, striped; brown back, white belly, striped and spotted; solid white; *frog back, white belly, striped; *solid red; *solid yellow; *solid aluminum color.

**These colors were not offered in catalogs prior to early 1920s.*

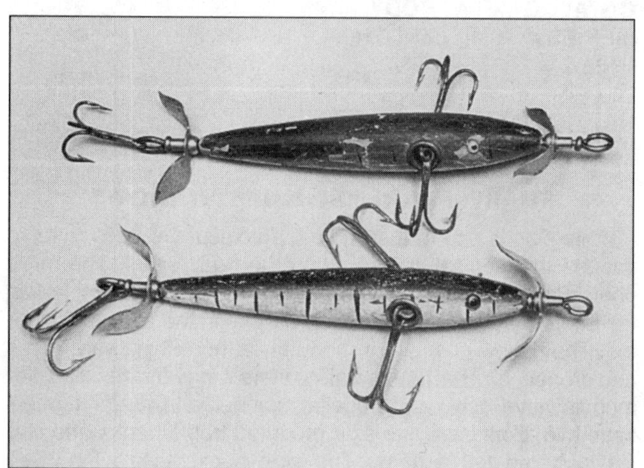

SHAKESPEARE "SLIM JIM" MINNOW (Underwater)

A 1924 catalog first lists this plug but a 1949 listing says they introduced the lure "...over 30 years ago". That dates the early ones around 1917-18 and they are very like the side hook #33 and #43. Similar to the earlier SLIM JIM minnow, but the configuration and catalog numbers are different. This newer one was offered in two sizes, the larger having two belly mounted treble hooks and a trailing treble. The smaller being the same except only one belly treble. Both have nose and tail propellers. This plug continues in production until the 1950s with very little change. The bodies are weighted and finishes have varied considerably through the years. Collector value range: $50-$100.

CATALOG SERIES #	BODY LENGTH	LURE WEIGHT
52 J or 6552	4-1/2"	4/5 oz.

COLOR OR FINISH: *Blue back, white belly, scale finish.

CATALOG SERIES #	BODY LENGTH	LURE WEIGHT
41 J or 6541	3-3/4"	3/5 oz.

COLOR OR FINISH: *Red back, white belly, scale finish; *rainbow, scale finish; *green back, yellow belly; green back, yellow belly, scale finish; *yellow perch, scale finish; gold body, red head, white body, red head, green back, silver sides, scale finish; natural pickerel pattern; green back, red and green striped sides; dark crackle back, maroon & silver sides; green back, golden yellow sides.

**Although these color patterns continue to be used through the years, they are the only finishes available from 1924 to around 1926-1932.*

SHAKESPEARE SPECIAL

SHAKESPEARE SPECIAL. Frog finish and natural pickerel finish.

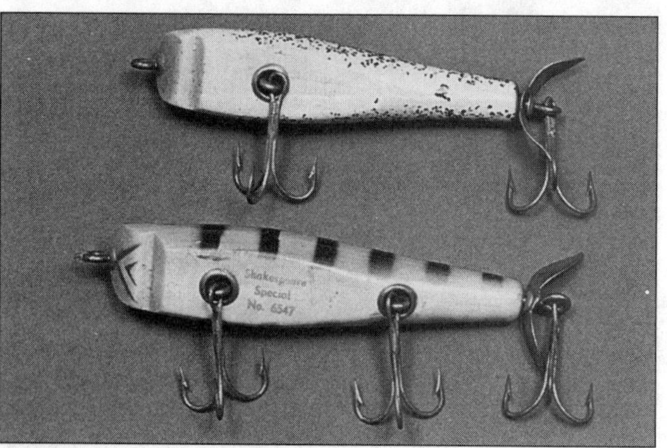

Belly view showing markings on SHAKESPEARE SPECIALS.

A surface lure with a tail-mounted propeller. It has a notched mouth below a forward sloping nose, one belly mounted treble hook and a trailing treble. The collector may easily become confused if he were confronted with the four different plugs represented by the accompanying photos. Three of them are unquestionably made by Shakespeare. Two, as you can see by the belly view photo, state SHAKESPEARE SPECIAL right on the body. In the other belly view the one on the bottom is made by Shakespeare, but the other is not. The one with the one-piece surface hook hanger was made by the Florida Fishing Tackle Company (Barracuda Brand) in St. Petersburg, Florida. Both can be found with either "Tampa" or St. Pete". (see Dalton Special).

CATALOG SERIES #	BODY LENGTH	LURE WEIGHT
6546	3"	1/2 oz.
6547	4"	5/8 oz.

COLOR OR FINISH: Frog finish, white belly; frog finish, yellow belly; natural pickerel with vertical stripes; solid yellow, black spots; green back, white belly, silver flitters; *yellow body, green stripes.

**Available only on the larger size, #6547*

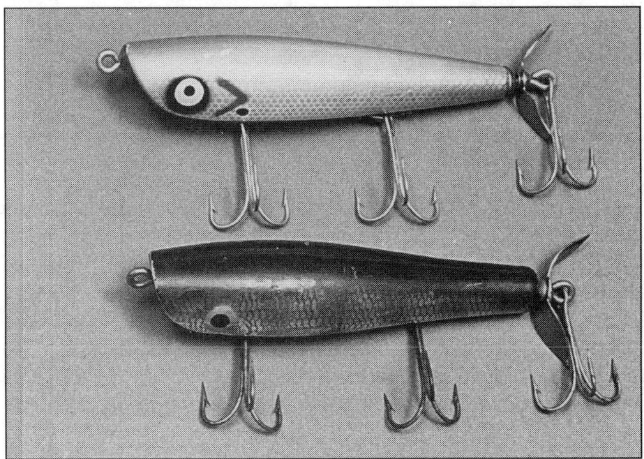

Upper plug us a Shakespeare product labeled Dalton Special. Lower plug is made by Florida Fishing Tackle Company.

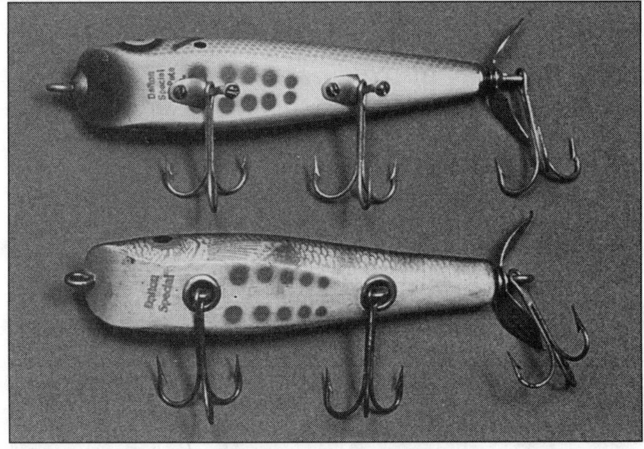

Belly view of the Shakespeare, (lower) and Florida Fishing Tackle Company (upper) Dalton Specials.

STRIKE-IT #6666

New around 1930 the STRIKE-IT is similar to the TANTALIZER. Note in photo here the STRIKE-IT has no metal diving lip. There were only three colors available in the 1930 catalog.

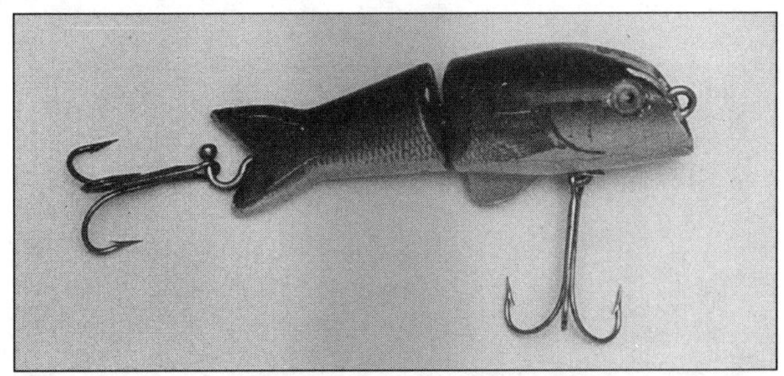

They are: Herring; Light grey back and sides, red at throat; White body, shaded red head. Missing from catalogs after 1931. Collector value range: $50-$80.

CATALOG SERIES #	BODY LENGTH	LURE WEIGHT
6666	4"	4/5 oz.

COLOR OR FINISH: (in addition to the above colors) Black body (white pickerel scale); bluish green body, spotted red and yellow, black back; mud puppy (light gray); white body, black head, white body, spotted red, black, and yellow, black back.

THE MERMAID AND THE LITTLE MERMAID

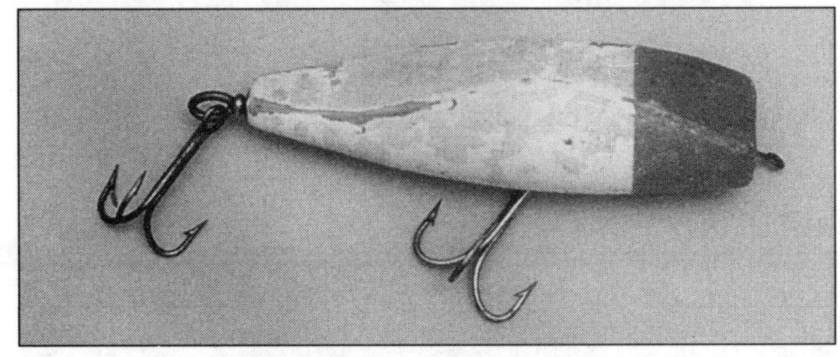

New for Shakespeare sometime in the early 1920s, it actually dates back to at least 1917. The McCORMICK MERMAID was patented by John Thomas McCormic of Kalamazoo, Michigan in 1917. The 1923 catalog was the only one in which I could find the Mermaid. Appears never to have been given eyes of any type. Collector value range: $50-100.

CATALOG SERIES #	BODY LENGTH	LURE WEIGHT
582	3-1/4"	?
583	3-5/8"	?

COLOR OR FINISH: Rainbow, scale finish; Yellow Perch, scale finish; Fancy green, scale finish; Frog back, scale finish; Green back, yellow belly, scale finish; White body, red head, Black body, white head.

THE SURE-LURE MINNOW

This familiar name was used for one of the first Shakespeare lures. This newer lure is made of molded rubber in the shape of a minnow. It is remarkably similar to the EVOLUTION

A later model, c. 1931 SURE-LURE MINNOW with its original box. It is called a Sure Lure-Perch. Photo courtesy Jim Muma.

MINNOW originally marketed around 1902. It appears in the 1931 catalog, but is gone from catalogs soon after. Collector value range: $75-$100.

CATALOG SERIES #	BODY LENGTH	LURE WEIGHT
6504	2-5/8"	1/2 oz.

COLOR OR FINISH: Shiner pattern; yellow perch pattern.

"SURFACE WONDER" #42 WW

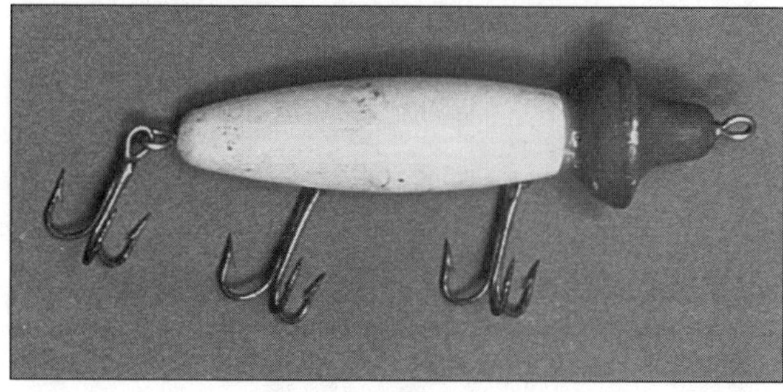

This plug was initially available in only one color design, a white body with a red head. An undated catalog (pre 1924) shows the SURFACE WONDER in a yellow body with red head and in "Imitation Frog Color" also.

A c. 1936 catalog lists the same lure as #42F, 3-3/4" body length, as available in one finish-only; white body with a red head. It is called "The Floater". Collector value range: $10-$20.

This plug is substantially similar to the LUMINOUS FLOATING NIGHT BAIT #680, but is not luminous. It has two belly mounted treble hooks and one trailing treble (3T). Collector value range: $50-$100.

CATALOG SERIES #	BODY LENGTH
42 WW	4"
42 Y.	4"
42 FEW	4"

COLOR OR FINISH: White body, red head; Yellow body, red head; Imitation frog color.

SHAKESPEARE SWIMMING MOUSE

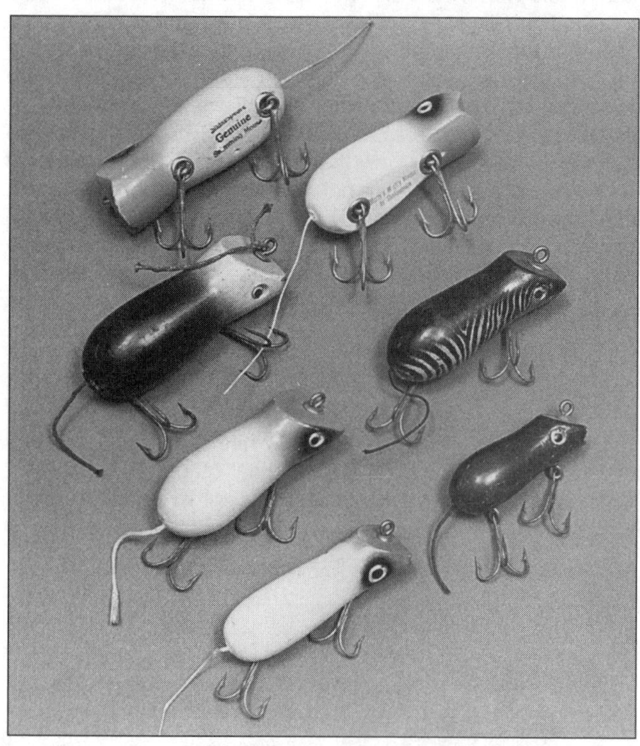

This lure appears in a 1924 catalog and in various versions continues all the way into the fifties. It has always been around 3-1/4" long with the exception of a 2-3/4" JUNIOR MOUSE which appeared sometime in the early 1930s and a 2-1/2" BABY MOUSE which is first observed by the author in a 1949 catalog. All have had two belly mounted treble hooks as in the photo. The lure is frequently found missing the tail. Has been found with only one treble hook (1T)(post 1934). Collector value range: $25-$55.

CATALOG SERIES #	BODY LENGTH	LURE WEIGHT
578	3-1/4"	?

COLOR OR FINISH: Solid black with white head, solid white with red head, yellow with white belly, black back & head; mouse gray with white belly, solid black.

CATALOG SERIES #	BODY LENGTH	LURE WEIGHT
6570	2-3/4"	5/8 oz.

COLOR OR FINISH: Gray body with white belly and black back, Gray body with white belly, Tiger stripe, Solid white, White body with black head, White body with red head. All are luminous.

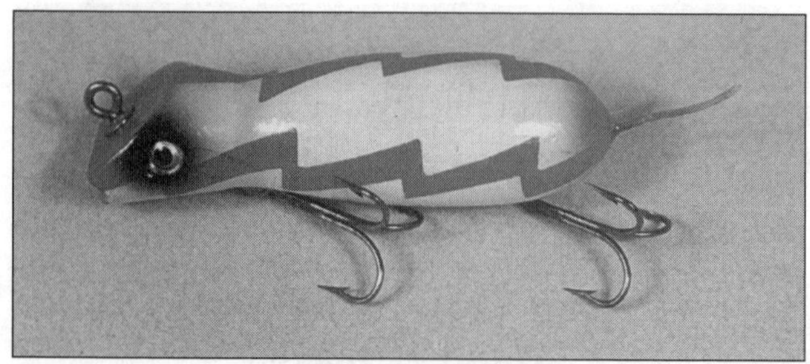

An un-cataloged SWIMMING MOUSE in an unusual pattern called Shazam. Age and origin unknown. It measures 3-3/8". Photo courtesy Jim Muma.

CATALOG SERIES #	BODY LENGTH	LURE WEIGHT
6577	2-1/2"	1/2 oz.

COLOR OR FINISH: Light gray, Imitation frog colors, Solid black, Black body with white head, Gray, Tiger stripe, White body with red head, Yellow body with red head.

CATALOG SERIES #	BODY LENGTH	LURE WEIGHT
6578	3"	8/10 oz.

COLOR OR FINISH: Black with shaded white belly.

CATALOG SERIES #	BODY LENGTH	LURE WEIGHT
6580	2-3/4"	5/8 oz.

COLOR OR FINISH: White with shaded red head, mouse gray with white belly, yellow with white belly, black shaded back and head; tiger stripe, black over yellow; yellow body with red head, black body with yellow back stripe, black body with white head.

SHAKESPEARE GLO-LITE MOUSE (plastic)

In 1941 Shakespeare devoted a lot of space to their new luminous finishes on the SWIMMING MOUSE. What is interesting is the wording describing the finish which reads in part "LUMINOUS SUBSTANCE IS MOLDED RIGHT INTO THE BAIT." That can only mean the lures were being made of plastic by now. How many others and when they had begun making in plastic is not clear. There was only one size listed. Collector value range: $5-$15.

CATALOG SERIES #	BODY LENGTH	LURE WEIGHT
6570	2-3/4"	5/8 oz.

COLOR OR FINISH: Black with white belly, black body with white head, gray body with black back and white belly, light gray body with white belly, tiger, white body with red head.

TANTALIZER

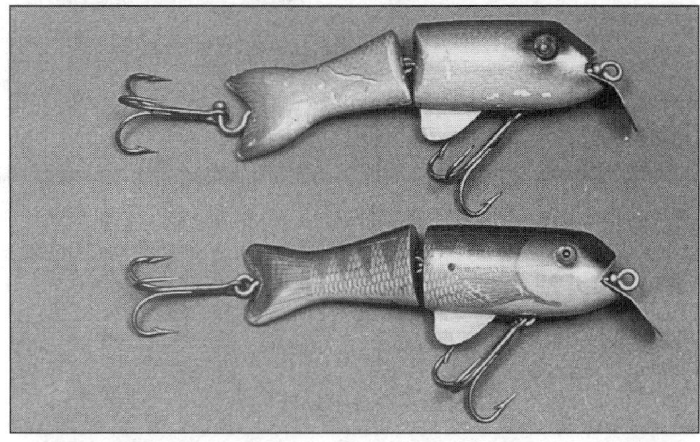

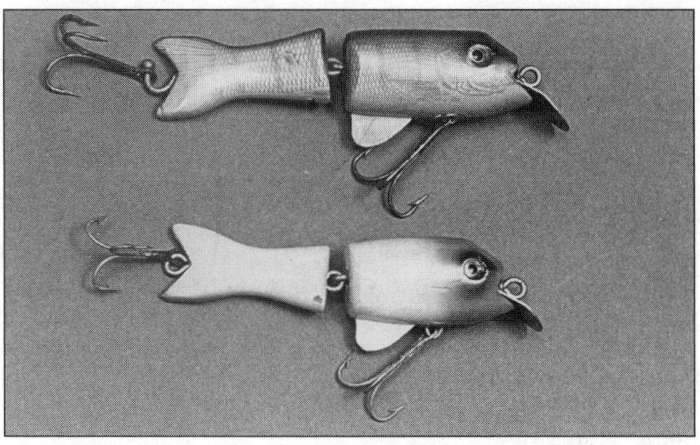

This is one of Shakespeare's first jointed baits. It appeared sometime around 1927-29 as did the DARTING SHRIMP. It is also one of the earliest of Shakespeare's use of the metal ventral fin. The plug has one belly-mounted treble hook and one trailing treble (2T). Found with glass or painted eyes, in one size and weight, and only in two color patterns initially. In a 1934 catalog the trailing hook fastener has been changed to the "Ball Head Hook Retainer" from the original simple screw eye (see photo). By 1937 this fastener had disappeared and again the screw eye came into use. The 1937 catalog also shows a slightly smaller "JR TANTALIZER" and both have gained a second belly treble (3T). Collector value range: $50-$150.

CATALOG SERIES #	BODY LENGTH	LURE WEIGHT
638 or 6638	4"	9/10 oz.

COLOR OR FINISH: *White body with shaded red head, *Natural pickerel.

**The color patterns first available.*

CATALOG SERIES #	BODY LENGTH	LURE WEIGHT
639 or 6639	4"	3/4 oz.

COLOR OR FINISH: Yellow perch with scale finish, shad finish, black back with tan and gold vertical side stripes, green back with silver and pink sides.

THE TARPALUNGE

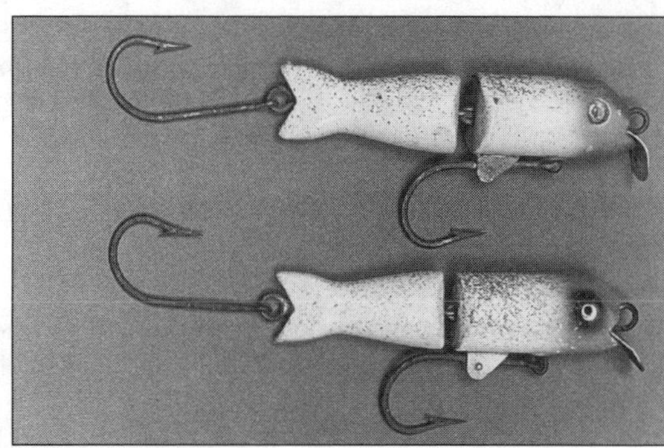

First observed in a 1930 catalog this is another jointed plug. It has a sloped head, ventral fin, a belly-mounted single point hook and one trailing. It was absent from catalogs by the late 1930s to early 1940s. Collector value range: $100-$300.

CATALOG SERIES #	BODY LENGTH	LURE WEIGHT
6640	5"	2-3/4"

COLOR OR FINISH: Shiner finish, mullet finish, red and white with silver flitters.

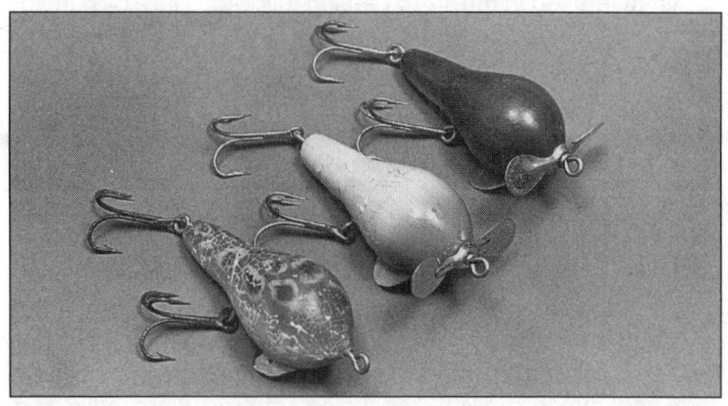

WAUKAZOO SURFACE SPINNERS. The lure with no propeller spinner is a mystery. It was ever cataloged this way. It shows absolutely no wear at the nose. If it ever had a prop it would have to show some wear if it was used.

WAUKAZOO SURFACE SPINNER

The earliest reference to this lure found so far was in an ad in the June, 1929 issue of *Field & Stream.* There is reason to believe it dates as early as 1924. It has a pear shaped body, ventral fin, one nose mounted propeller, a belly-mounted treble hook and trailing treble. "Shakespeare No. 1 is stamped on the propeller. It apparently wasn't too popular for it wasn't found in catalogs subsequent to 1931. Collector value range: $100-$150.

Note that each of these WAUKAZOO SURFACE SPINNERS have the patented Shakespeare ball-head hook hanger. Note also the different propeller spinners you may encounter. The plug on top has "Shakespeare Honorbilt" stamped into the blades.

CATALOG SERIES #	BODY LENGTH	LURE WEIGHT
6555	2-5/8"	3/4 oz.

COLOR OR FINISH: White body with shaded red head, natural frog finish, gray body with white belly and a flash of red at the throat.

SHAKESPEARE "WEEDLESS FROG" #4 WF

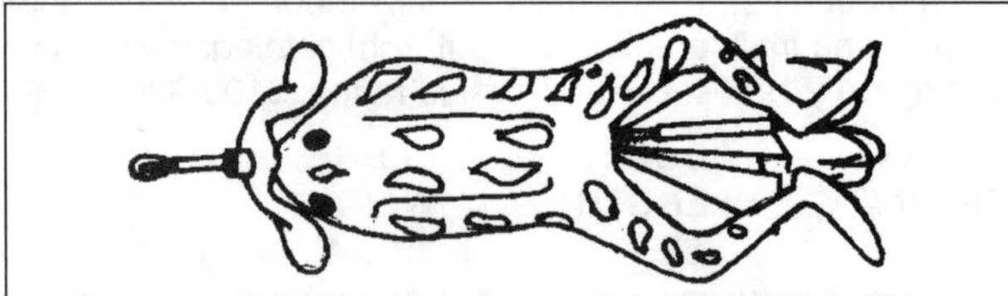

As advertised in the 1910 catalog this was a lure cast in soft rubber in the shape and marking of a frog. There were rubber guards protecting the single trailing treble hook (1T). It was 3-1/4" long and has a propeller on the nose. It apparently wasn't available long as subsequent catalogs offered weedless frogs made by others, and they do not list the #4 WF. Collector value range: $50-$100.

SHAKESPEARE "WHIRLWIND SPINNER" #65 W

This interesting plug apparently went out of production early on. By 1920 it was absent from the catalogs . It was listed in the 1910 catalog in one size only, 4" length overall with the body measuring 1-1/4". The colors offered were solid red, white, or yellow. All had a "Fancy feather buck tail" on the tail treble hook. The two side treble hooks were attached to the body with the see-through fastener (3T). There were two propellers, tail and nose. Collector value range: $100-$150.

The lure on the left has bow tie type propeller spinners. This is the earliest use prop.

BABY POPPER

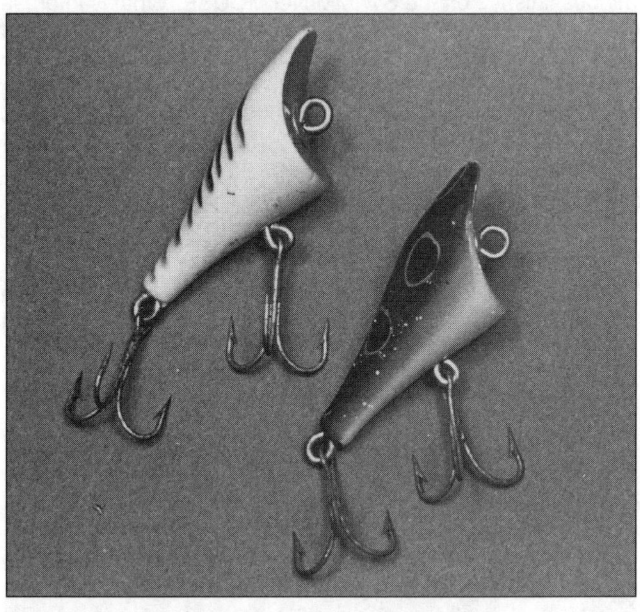

This little critter made its debut sometime in the early 1940s and had a short run as it had come and gone from catalogs in just a couple of years. Colors available unknown except for the two in the photo here. Collector value range: No trade data found.

GAD-ABOUT

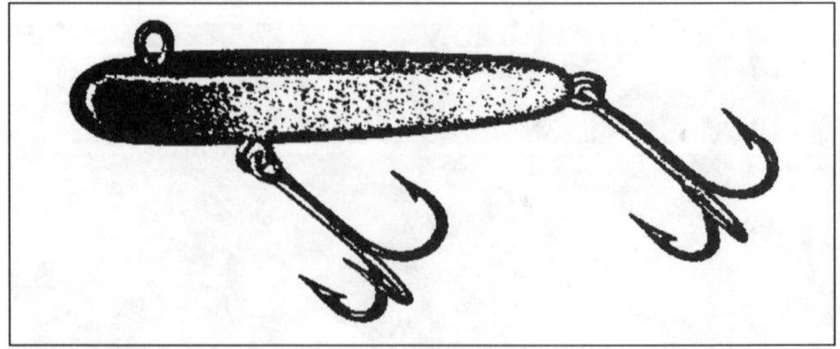

New in the 1941 catalog, the drawing above is taken from the illustration there. The entry said it was "A crazy actor in the water. Darts here, there and everywhere." Collector value range: N.A.

CATALOG SERIES #	BODY LENGTH	LURE WEIGHT
6562	3"	5/8 oz.

COLOR OR FINISH: White with red head, silver flitter side with narrow green back and white belly, mottled pearl finish.

WIGGLE-DIVER

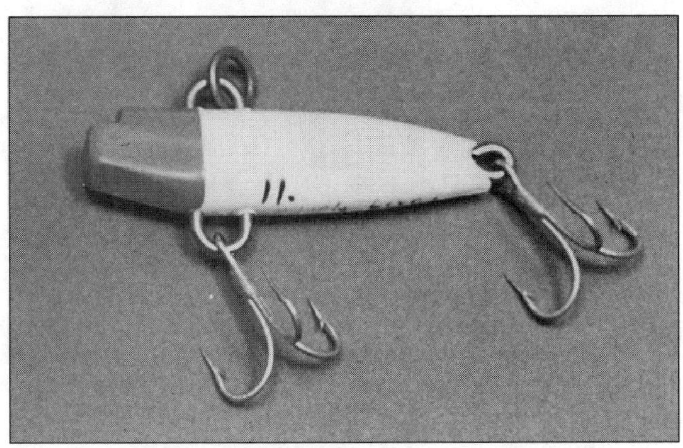

The later lure (1940s), the WIGGLE-DIVER, was made of molded plastic (Tenite). It is probable that earlier ones have wooden bodies. Some collectors dispute this, but the 1941 catalog clearly state that it was "Now Available in Indestructible Tenite." That infers it was previously made of wood. It could be, however, that the previous models were made of fragile plastic. Available in a 1940s catalog in three different sizes, each has one belly-mounted treble hook and a trailing treble. Collector value range: $10-$16.

CATALOG SERIES #	BODY LENGTH	LURE WEIGHT
6357	2-1/4"	1/2 oz.

COLOR OR FINISH: Green bronze back with silver sides, white belly and scale finish.

CATALOG SERIES #	BODY LENGTH	LURE WEIGHT
6538	3-1/2"	1 oz.

COLOR OR FINISH: Silver flitter with narrow green back and white belly.

CATALOG SERIES #	BODY LENGTH	LURE WEIGHT
6539	4-5/8"	1-1/4 oz.

COLOR OR FINISH: White body with redhead, yellow body with black head.

SHAKESPEARE JIM DANDY LURES

It is not known exactly when, but sometime around 1930 Shakespeare either bought or somehow obtained the rights to the lure designs of the Wise Sportsman Supply of Chicago and incorporated them into the line. Specific information regarding the lures is sketchy due to incomplete catalog listings. They were called Jim Dandys in the 1931 catalog, but the name was seldom mentioned in subsequent catalogs. The lures were simply integrated into the standard line. In 1936 and 1937 they sold something called the "Jim Dandy Casting Bait Assortment" that consisted of three FLOATERS and three SPOON BILL WOBBLERS. There was no mention of these being part of an inexpensive line. What is known so far follows.

JIM DANDY SPOON BELL WOBBLER

This glass-eyed Jim Dandy shows up first in a 1931 catalog and is never again listed in any I was able to study through the 1950s. The Jim Dandy line was an inexpensive selection of lures. Note the 1931 patent ball head tail hook hanger on the upper lure. The smaller size was not listed in the 1931 catalog entry. Collector value range: $50-$90.

CATALOG SERIES #	BODY LENGTH	LURE WEIGHT
6400	3-3/4"	3/4 oz.

COLOR OR FINISH: Greenback, red sides, white belly; Gray back, shading down to white belly; Red body, black head, black over yellow spots; White body, red head, Yellow body, red over black spots, black back.

JIM DANDY UNDERWATER

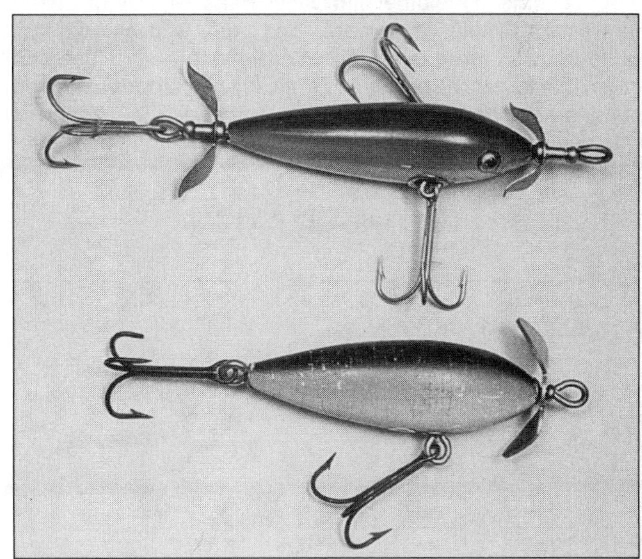

The upper glass eye 3T lure is the Jim Dandy UNDERWATER. The other is unidentified but is most likely the Jim dandy Surface. The Jim Dandy Baits was an inexpensive line of Shakespeare lures. I only found one reference to the line (in a 1931 catalog). Collector value range: $35-$75.

CATALOG SERIES #	BODY LENGTH	LURE WEIGHT
6406	3-3/4"	3/4 oz.

COLOR OR FINISH: Red body, black head, rainbow, white body, red head, greenish yellow sides, perch stripes with pink lower stripe, white belly and dark back.

JIM DANDY NUMBER 6503

A 1931 catalog entry is the first place this darter-type lure was found. Part of a Shakespeare line meant to be inexpensive, this lure was unnamed but looks something like a fat, unshaped BASS-A-LURE without the metal diving lip. They have pressed, painted eyes but might be found with glass eyes as some of the other Jim Dandy Baits. No size or weight was listed. Colors listed were: Red body with black head, white body with red head, green scale with silver sides and green back, yellow perch scale finish, black body with red head, orange and yellow body with red head. The latter color was never listed, but has been found. Collector value range: $30-$50.

JIM DANDY FLOATERS

This and the next photo are thought to be Jim Dandy floating lures because of their pressed, painted and zinc tack painted eyes. Also, the colors match one of those listed with the Jim Dandy UNDERWATER MINNOW previously listed. They sport the late smooth edge, pointed Shakespeare propellers. The upper lure in the photo has these propellers, marked Shakespeare. Collector value range: $40-$80.

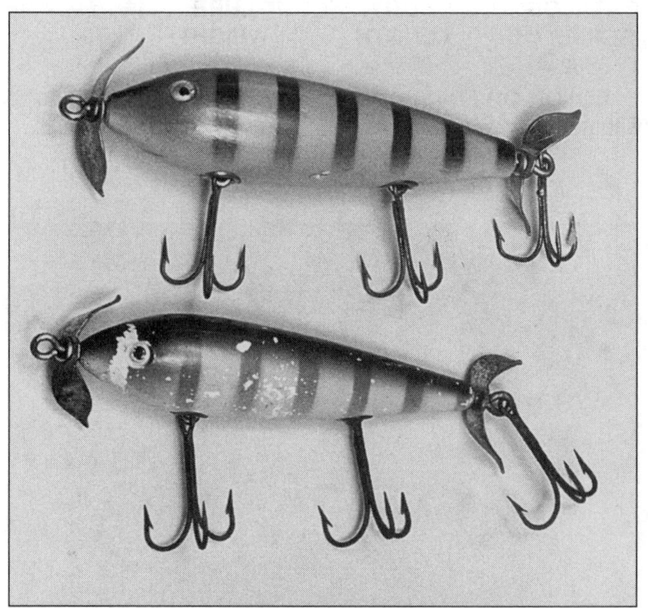

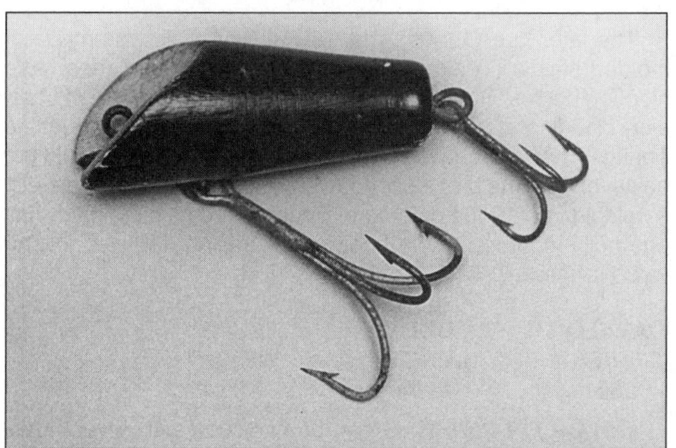

This is the original Schillinger patent Jim Dandy produced by Wise Sportsman Supply now owned by Shakespeare. It measures 2-1/2" and has simple screw eye and washer hook hanger hardware. Collector value range: $25-$40.

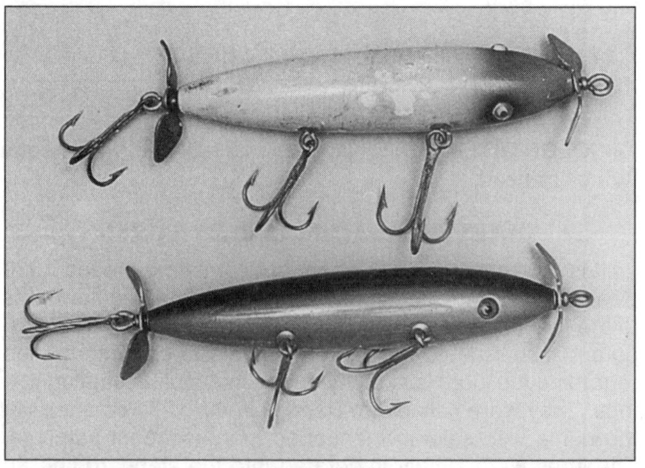

Two unidentified Jim Dandy lures. They each have the screw eye and washer hook hardware. The upper white body, red head lure has white iris glass eyes and is 4-1/4" long. The lower measures 4-5/16" and has yellow glass eyes. Collector value range: $45-$60.

Each of these is 4-1/8" long and has cup and screw eye hook hardware. The upper lure has white iris glass eyes white the lower sports embossed painted eyes. Note the latter has a scale finish. Collector value range: $45-$60.

SHAKESPEARE UNKNOWNS

The lower lure was not found cataloged either. It has an unmistakable Shakespeare paint finish and marked propeller spinner.

This glass eyed, 3" wooden lure came in a box that had "MACK'S DARTER #929" on it. There was no other information given or found. It has the Shakespeare SF paint finish with silver flitter sides, narrow green back and white belly. It measures 3".

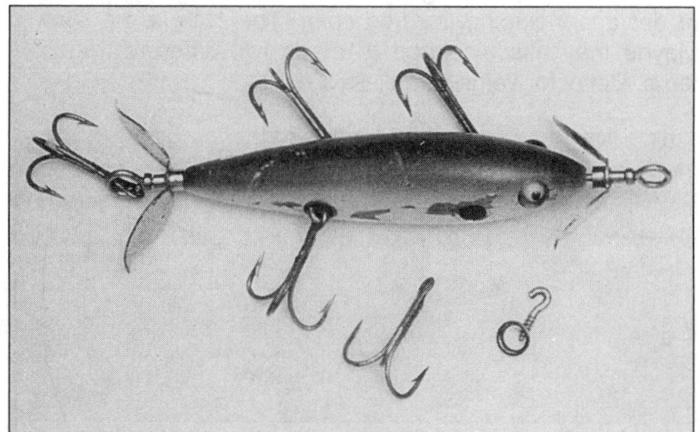

This is suspected to be a Shakespeare product. Has typical Shakespeare paint job, body style and propellers (unmarked). Note the flanged sleeve use instead of standard cup. Glass eyes.

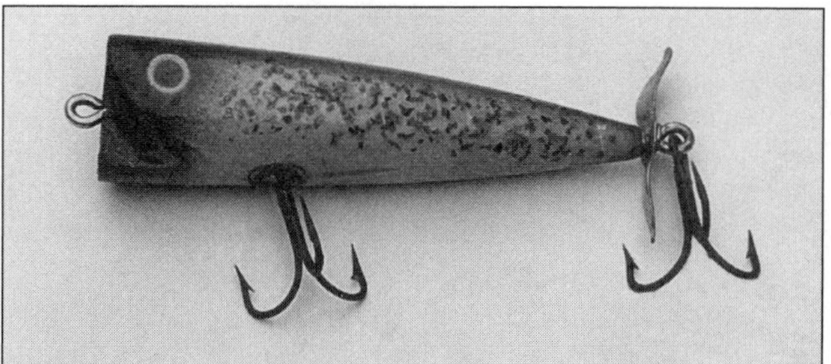

Here is another with the Shakespeare SF finish. The propeller spinner at the tail has "Shakespeare" stamped on it. It has a peculiarly shaped nose, painted eyes and two red painted fins (?) just behind the belly hook hanger.

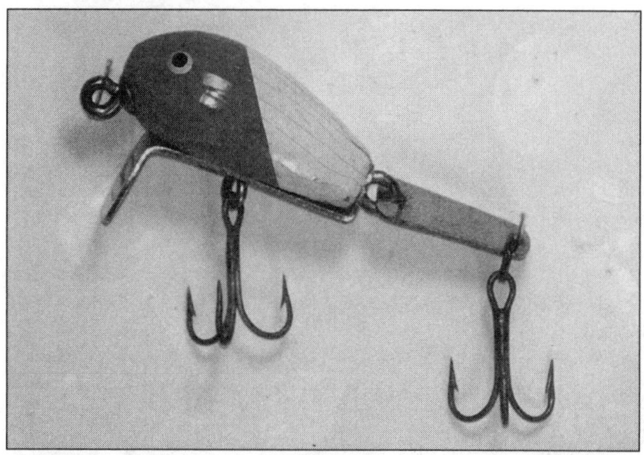

Here is a is a good one for you. This lure is absolutely identical to a #9100 Creek Chub Bait Company SPOONTAIL made for less than three years from 1954 to 1956. The metal lip plane is, however, stamped "SHAKESPEARE". As far as I can determine, it was never cataloged by Shakespeare.

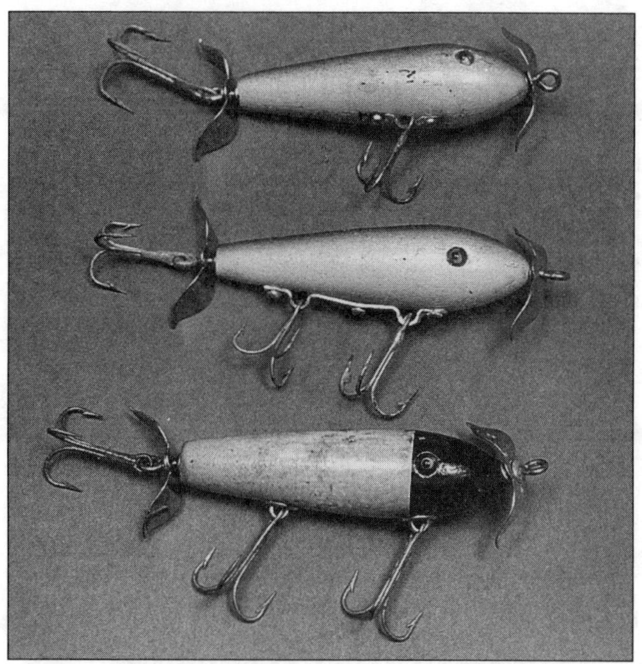

These three lures each have a wood body, glass eyes and Shakespeare propeller spinners. There are two types of props and each have "Shakespeare Honorbuilt" stamped on the blades.

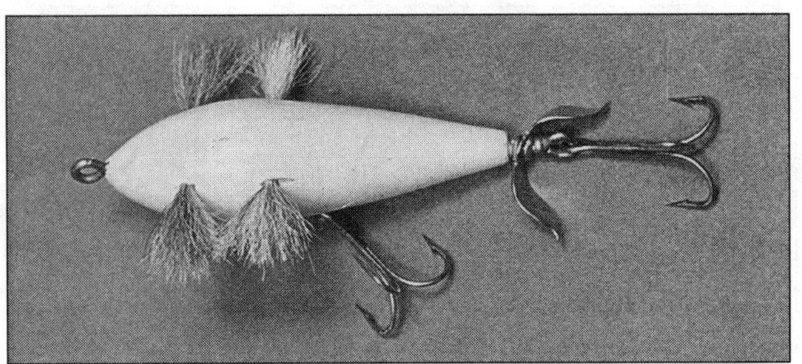

This strange looking plug is very well made and sports a marked Shakespeare propeller spinner.

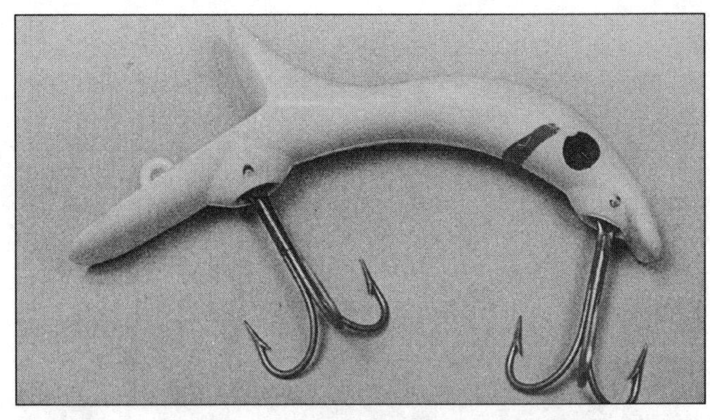

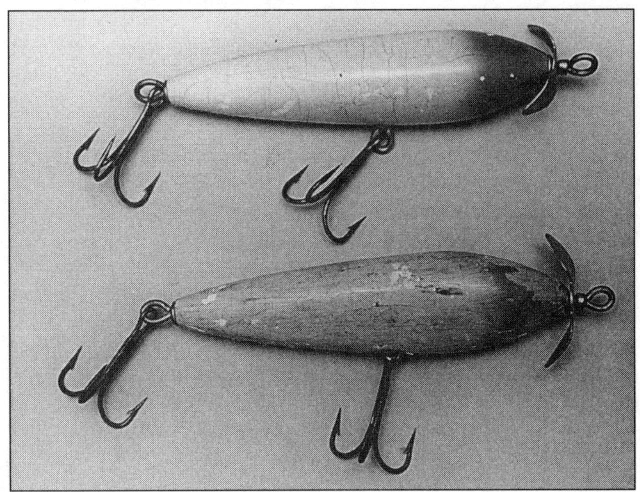

The upper lure was not found in any catalogs, but it has Shakespeare paint and hardware as well as the same unique triangular body shape as the Shakespeare FAVORITE. It measures 4-1/8" and utilizes screw eye and washer hook hanger hardware.

SHORE PATROL

John J. Fuelson & Assoc. Little Rock, Arkansas

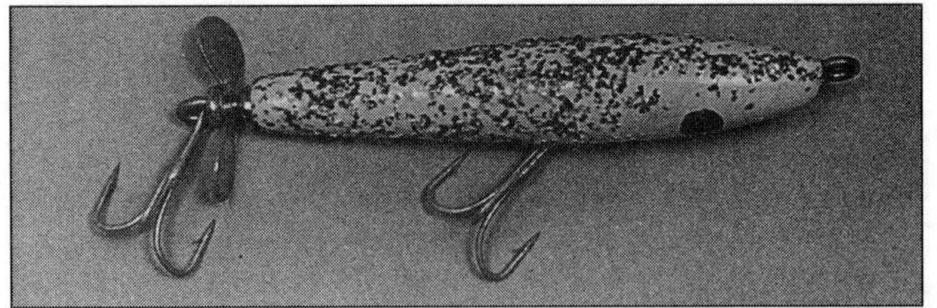

The is nothing known beyond this meager information found on the box. The lure has a round blade tail propeller spinner and measures 3-1/8" in length. Collector value range: $5-$15.

SHUREBITE BAIT COMPANY c. 1938

Bronson, Michigan

SHUREBITE ARTIFICIAL BAIT CO.

Lorain, Ohio Kokomo, Indiana

GENEVA MANUFACTURING

Bellwood, Illinois

Shurebite might have been named Suremove. They started out in Michigan, moved to Indiana, and ended up in Illinois to

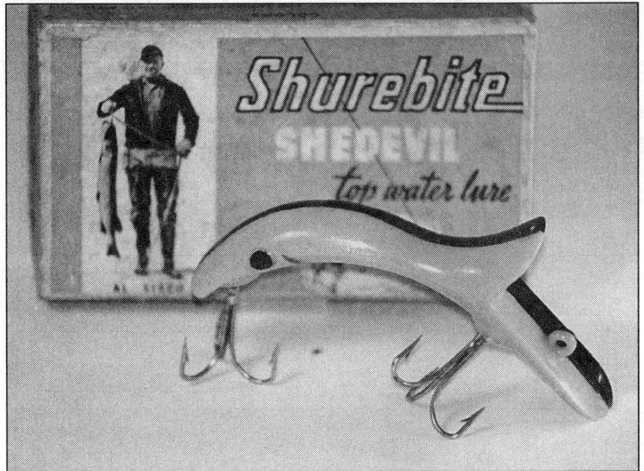

SHEDEVIL. Photo courtesy Ken Bernoteit.

the best of my knowledge. The president of the company was Al Sisco. His name is associated as the designer with several of their lures.

The odd Shaped lure pictured here is a 4" plastic SHEDEVIL. The box indicated that it was available in 18 different finishes. The box also has the Al Sisco name on it and the location was Bronson, Michigan. The earliest ad I found for the Bronson location was 1946. There were two 1949 advertisements found for this lure placed in periodicals by the Geneva Manufacturing Company. One of the ads listed some, but not all 18 colors. The colors listed were black, red, green, yellow, ivory, any combination of the two and also frog. If you calculate the combinations right you come up with 17 possible color designs including the frog color. The 18th is not known. Maybe they miscalculated or made two different frog patterns. Collector value range: $5-$15.

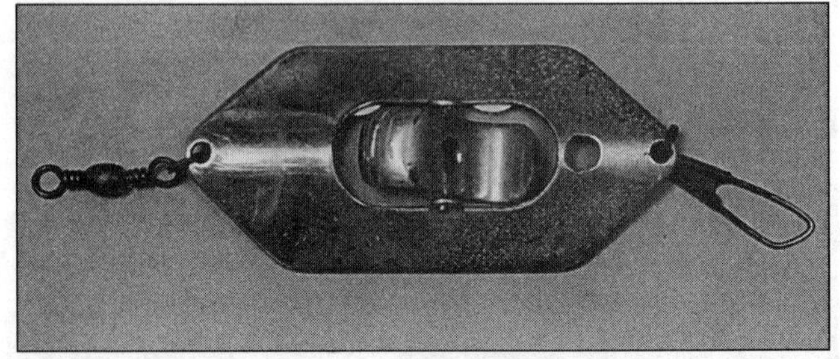

This 1-7/8" metal lure, the SHUREBITE SURFACE SPINNER, has a center spinning paddle wheel. It was also in a Al Sisco/Shurebite box, but this time the box says Lorain, Ohio. There was no way to ascertain a collector value for this lure.

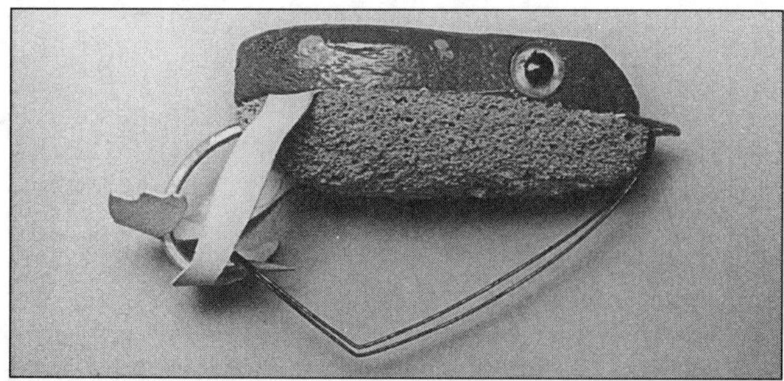

This is a 2-1/2" frog lure made of wood and sponge. The box was imprinted "SHUREBITE Top Water Weedless" and the company location was Bronson, Michigan. It was not possible to ascertain a collector value as there was no trade information available. There was one report of an auction sale in 1996 for $38.

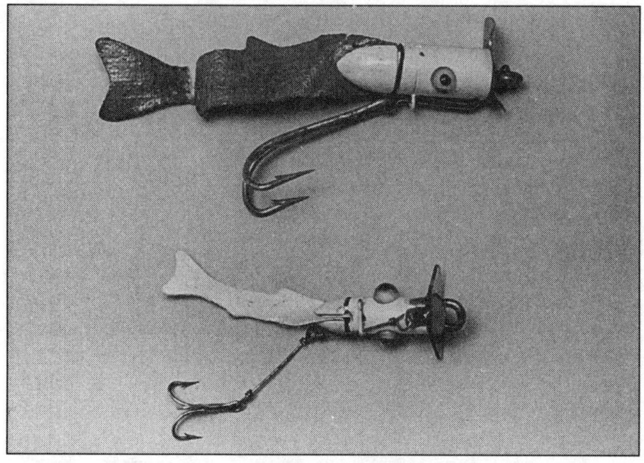

These two were in identical boxes imprinted "Artificial ShurEbitE Minnow" and "Al Sisco, Lorain, Ohio." They are both plastic and measure 3" overall and 1-7/8" overall. There was no trade data from which to draw a realistic collector value.

SHURKATCH BAITS

Shurkatch Fishing
Tackle Co., Inc. Richfield Springs, New York

There are 12 lures in this assortment. I found the same assortment listed in a 1939 Horrocks-Ibottson catalog. The company name and address came from the box in the photo. There was no other information found. Eye depressions and cup and screw eye hardware are common characteristics on these well made lures. Collector value range: $15-$50.

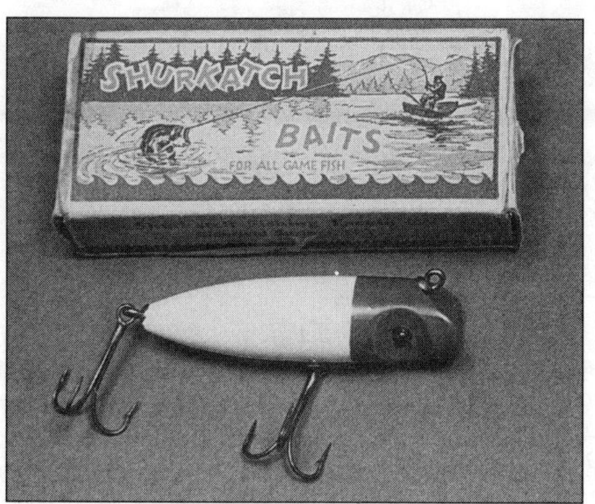

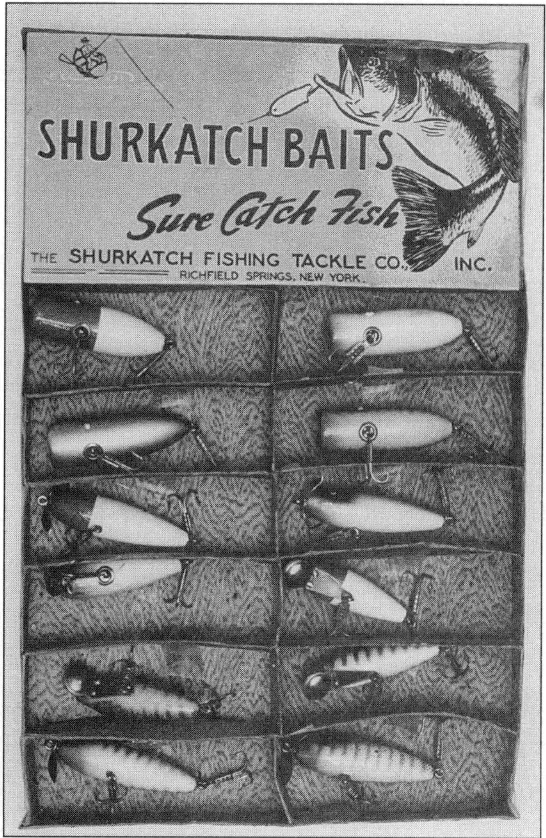

SILVER CREEK NOVELTY WORKS

Dowagiac, Michigan

Silver Creek Novelty Works started doing business sometime in the 1910s and continued until 1923 when the company and the Moonlight Bait Company merged. The merger resulted in that company changing its name to the Moonlight Bait and Novelty Works. Be sure to turn to the Moonlight section for further information. The Silver Creek Company was making a number of lures at the time and many were carried on in the Moonlight line. There were, I'm sure, many more made by Silver Creek that Moonlight didn't continue to make, but just what they were is not presently known. Those I have been able it identify as originally made by Silver Creek and continued in the Moonlight line are listed following:

WIGGLER, 3-1/2"

Colors and other size information unknown

POLLY-WOG, 4"

POLLYWOG JUNIOR, 3-1/4"

Both were made in solid yellow, moss back, yellow perch, white with red stripes, yellow with black spots, and white with black stripes.

BASS-EAT-US, 3"

BABE-EAT-US, 2-1/2"

TROUT-EAT-US, 1-3/4"

Each was available in yellow perch, rainbow, moss back, white body with red head, yellow body with red head, white body with green head and yellow body with black head.

BUG-EAT-US, 1-1/2"

Made in moss back, white with red head, yellow with red head, and white with a blue head.

PIKAROON MINNOW, 5-1/4"

BABY PIKAROON, 4-1/4"

Colors available were yellow, moss back, white with red back, yellow with black stripes, solid white and yellow perch.

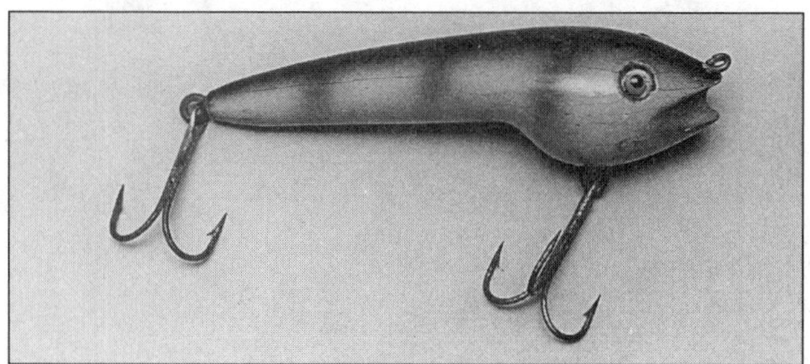

Silver Creek Novelty Works POLLY-WOG, 3-3/4". The notched mouth version shown here is very rare and found only in Silver Creek models. Collector value range. $300-$600.

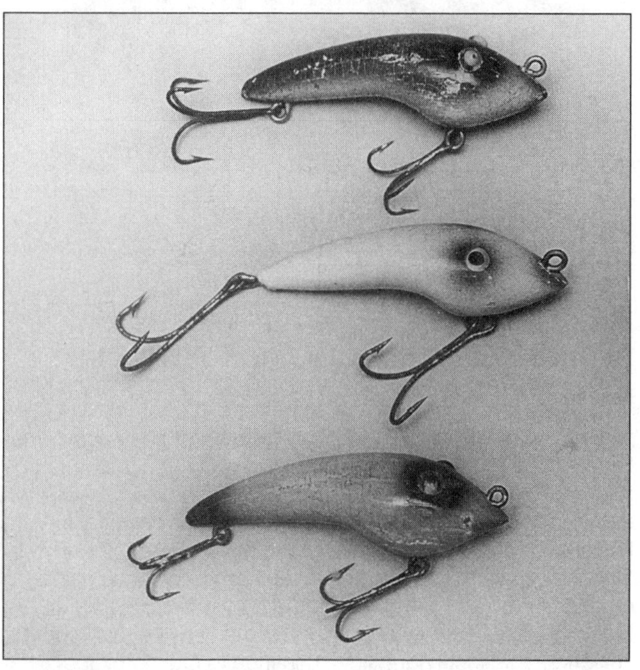

As you have seen in a previous photo, some Silver Creek Novelty Works s POLLY-WOGS came with a notched mouth (c. 1921). The top lure here is a Silver Creek POLLY-WOG without the notch. It measures 3-1/8" and has white glass eyes said to be found on Silver Creek lures, but not on Moonlight. The next two are Moonlight POLLY-WOGS. Note the fatter bodies. Collector value for Silver Creek POLLY-WOGS: $75-$100.

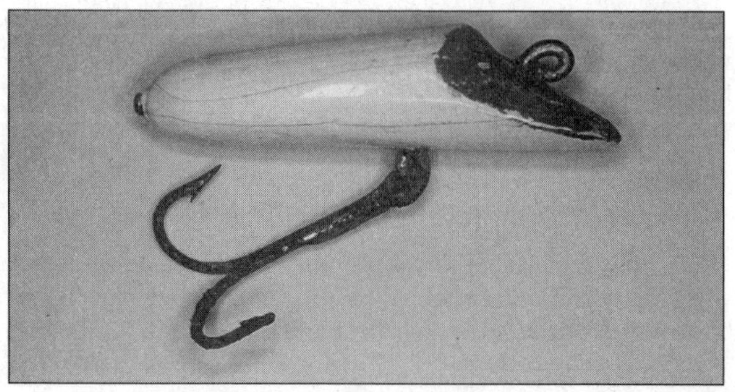

Silver Creek Novelty Works WIGGLER, 1-3/4". Collector value range: $200-$300.

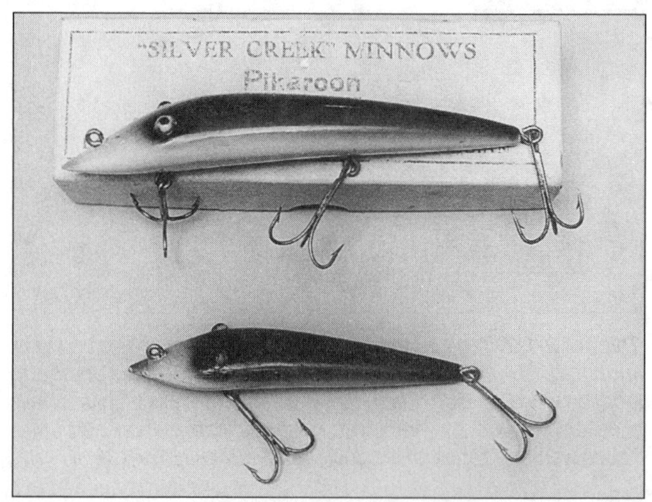

These two are the #1010 BABY PIKEROONS (bottom) and the #903 PIKEROON. Each has a screw eye line tie and hook hangers and glass eyes. Collector value range: $75-$100.

All baits float when at rest

Dive and dart when reeled

Moss back

"Silver Creek" Bass-Eat-Us

A near-surface bait, travels about fourteen inches under water, darts, wiggles and dives at an average speed of reeling. When reeled slowly, skims the surface with fluttering motion of a miller. Floats when not in motion. Average weight 1-2 oz. Length 3 in. Furnished in the following colors: Yellow Perch; Rainbow; Moss back; White body, red head; Yellow body, red head; White body, green head; Yellow body, black head. *List price, 80c*

White, red head

Yellow, red head

"Silver Creek" Babe-Eat-Us

Same as Bass-Eat-Us, but smaller, carries one set double hooks. 98% weedless. Average weight 3-8 oz. Length 2 1-2 in. Furnished in the following colors: Yellow Perch; Rainbow; Moss back; White body, red head; Yellow body, red head; White body, green head; Yellow body, black head. *List price, 75c*

White, red head

"Silver Creek" Bug-Eat-Us

Designed for fly rod, travels about twelve inches under water when reeled. Has a darting motion. Can be used for Trout and Bass. Length 1½ in. Weight ¼ oz. Furnished in four colors: Moss back; White, red head; Yellow, red head; White, blue head. *List price, 45c*

"Silver Creek" Trout-Eat-Us

A fly rod minnow. Designed for use on small and large streams, used equally as well on lakes for bass or trout, has the same motion as Bass-Eat-Us. Average weight 1-4 oz. Length 1 3-4 in. Furnished in the following colors: Yellow Perch; Rainbow; Moss back; White body, red head; Yellow body, red head; White body, green head; Yellow body, black head. *List price, 65c*

A brochure from the Silver Creek Novelty Works showing four of their smaller lures. Note the notch at the line ties. This is a characteristic not found on the Moonlight versions of these produced after the merger of the companies in 1923.

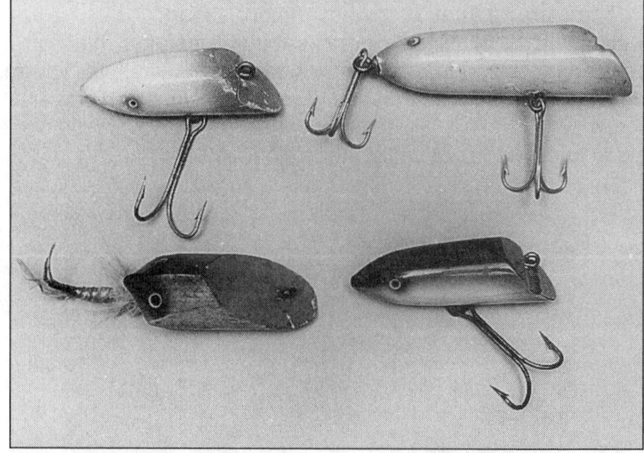

The 3" BASS-EAT-US and the two 2-3/8" BABE-EAT-US's are all Silver Creek made lures. Note the notches at the line tie areas. his is found only on the EAT-US type lures made by Silver Creek. he lower left lure appears to be a slightly larger BUG-EAT-US than the one found in catalogs. Collector value range for Silver Creek EAT-US types: $25-$75.

A new-in-the-box (NIB) BUG-EAT-US.

JACK K. SMITHWICK & SON, MANUFACTURERS SMITHWICK LURES

Jack K. Smithwick Shreveport, Louisiana

NOTE TO THE READER: Except where noted all photographs presented in the Smithwick section were provided by NFLCC member Ken Webb.

If you have read the OL' BEN's BAITS section you know of the happy accident I had connecting with the sons of the that company's founder. At the time I had little more than a few words about, and the location of Smithwick Lures. Just a short while after my first conversation with Mike Bacon in Shreveport, I received a telephone call from Ken Webb, also of Shreveport, saying that he had heard of my conversation with the Bacons and that he thought he would call to tell me that he was a Smithwick collector. Well the short of that is this: He spent a great deal of time putting together what he thought was a good representation of Smithwick Lures and got a friend who was a good photographer to shoot them and send them to me. What you see here is a result Ken's work.

Smithwick moved to the Shreveport area in 1946. He was a businessman who loved to fish. He began whittling lures from a broom handle in early 1947, for himself, his customers and fishing buddies. Quickly after that he was in the lure business, complete with brochures and an attractive box for the TOP-N-BOTTOM illustrating the lure in action in line drawing. This box was replaced by the newer, less specialized box around 1950. The new box was red and black and white and could be used for all their lures. The lure in the photo with the later box is a DANCER TOPWATER that was never cataloged and apparently made in very limited quantities. It has a drilled hole where a rubber

The right lure here is a TOP-N-BOTTOM and the left is a TWISTER. Both were among the earliest Smithwick offerings. The TWISTER was discontinued soon after around 1949.

Another of the earliest of Smithwick lures is the famous DEVILS HORSE. Bob McKinney, in his COLLECTIBLES column in the May/June, 1995 issue of *Sporting Classics* magazine said he never passes up a chance to buy a DEVIL'S HORSE because they remind him of a time in his life he likes to remember and in a testament to the lure itself, he says he also knows "...as long as I have a Devil's Horse and there's a largemouth bass left anywhere in the world, then my supper is assured..." The first DEVIL'S HORSE lures Jack Smithwick made were not marked that way, but rather the word "DEVIL" in the mark was spelled differently as in

DEVELS HORSE. He has said that he was afraid people wouldn't buy something with the word "DEVIL" on it. After a year or so of taking a lot of kidding he changed it. That is an easy way to tell if you have the earliest model. He never used the possessive apostrophe on the lure as in "DEVEL'S".

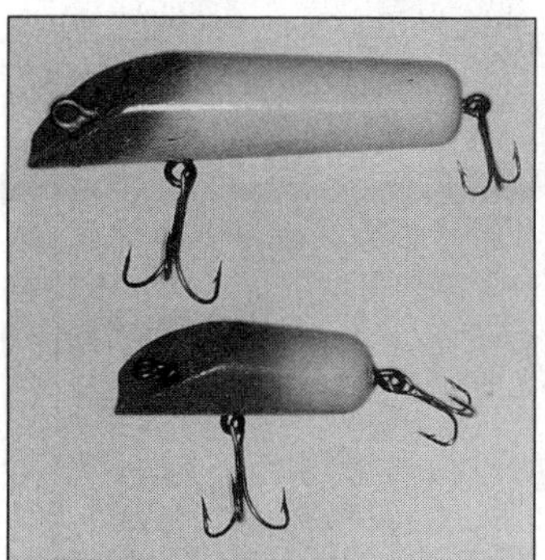

Two sizes of the TOP-N-BOTTOM, 3-3/8" and 2-3/8". Ken Webb says Jack Smithwick gave him the larger one in 1975 saying it was the last one he had. The bodies were turned on a lathe from a broom handle. skirt was pulled through.

Note the location of the eyes in the above photo of two DEVIL'S HORSE lures. They are practically on top of the hook hardware. In later models the eyes are found placed further forward. The eye location information is easiest utilized when studying stick-type baits. Early Smithwick lures have hand-painted eyes and at some point they began applying decal eyes. That time has not yet been pinned down sufficiently, but probably c. 1960.

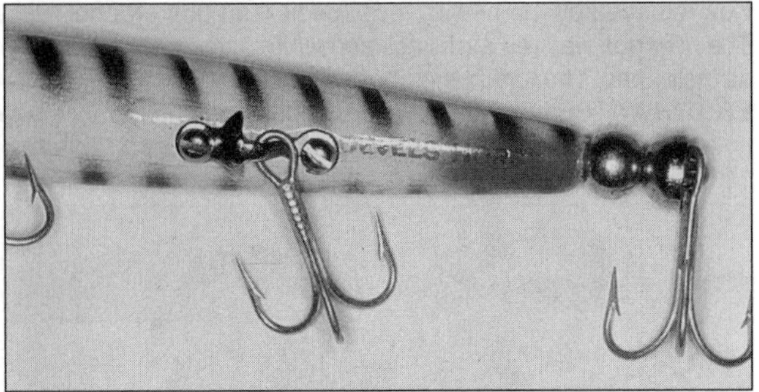

A DEVELS HORSE JUMPER showing the "DEVELS HORSE" mark and the ball weight at the tail.

The DEVILS HORSE was made in several sizes. The earliest were made in two sizes, 3-3/4" and 4-1/2". Then came the larger models, a 5-1/2" and in 1965 they brought out a musky or saltwater version at 6-1/2". There may have been a 7-1/2" size for a blank was found in the old factory, but one was not ever cataloged.

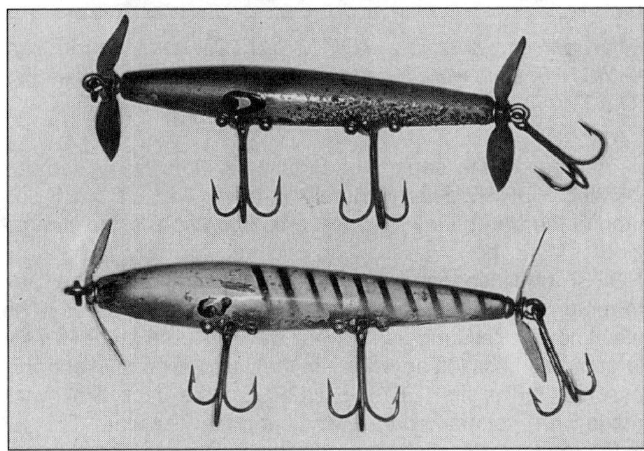

This is a pair of early DEVILS HORSE Slow Sinkers. They were made with heavier hooks, spinners and hardware.

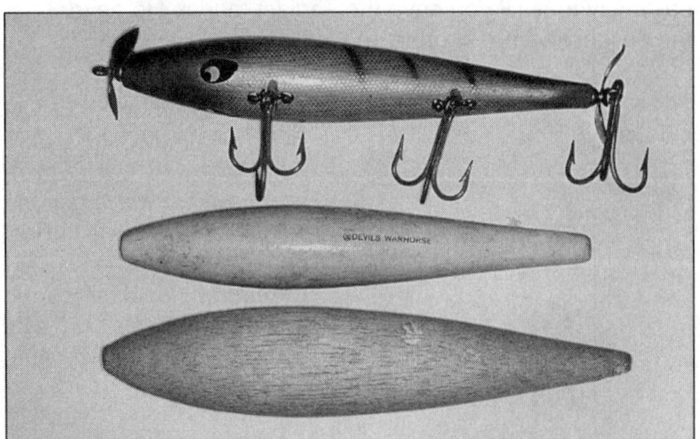

The upper lure is a later model of the DEVILS HORSE with the eye placement more toward the nose. The middle lure is an incomplete DEVILS WARHORSE and the lower blank appears to be of a KING SNIPE.

There were variations on the stick bait theme as well. There were models with no propeller spinners, one spinner, two spinners, weights and no weights and various numbers of hooks and sizes. What follows is a list of names, sizes and configurations:

MA SCOOTER - 3-3/4", 4-1/4", 1/4 oz., one tail spinner, 2T

PA SCOOTER - 3-3/4", 4-1/4", 1/2 oz., one tail spinner, 2T

PRANCER - 3-1/4", 1/4 oz., one tail spinner, 2T

DANCER - 3-1/4", 1/4 oz., round body, one tail spinner, 2T

DEVILS WARHORSE - 3-1/8", 4-1/8", 6-1/2", ball hooks on tail, 2T, 3T

DEVILS TOOTHPICK - 2-3/4", 3-1/4", 2T

DEVILS HORSE WEEDLESS - 3-1/8", 4-1/2".

This was a very short-lived version with a long shank single hook mounted at the belly with the hook curling up and through a screw eye at the tail thereby holding it semi-rigid. There was also a free-swinging flasher blade mounted to the hook shank.

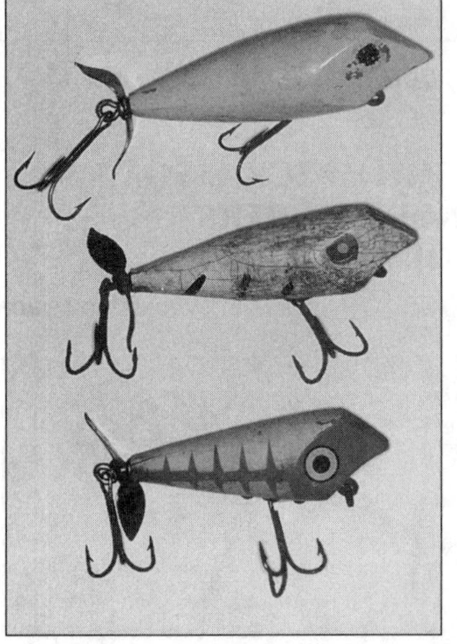

Here are three STUD DUCKS showing the transition from the relatively crude paint and eye details through to the fairly sophisticated pattern at the bottom.

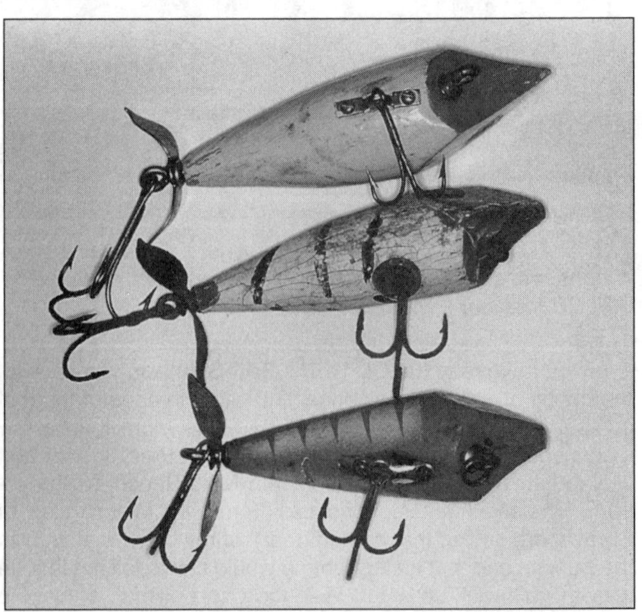

A belly view of the same three lures. You can get a better idea of the paint and the hardware. These are sometimes found factory-made without the tail propeller spinner.

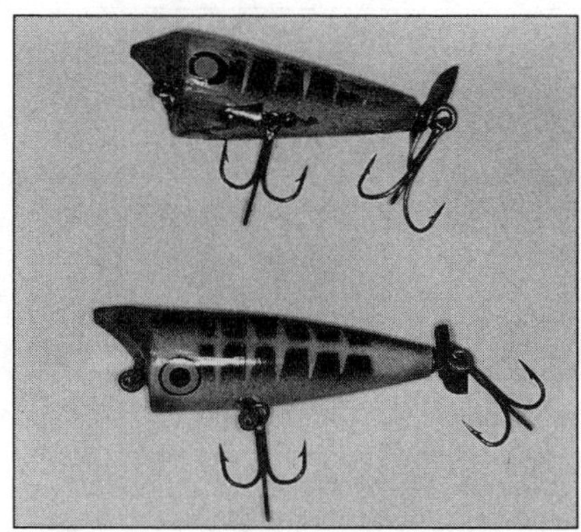

Two sizes of the Smithwick GANDY DANCER, 23/4" and 3-1/4" are shown in the above photo. The earliest have hand-painted yellow eyes with black rings. The lower lure has the decal eye. Many GANDY DANCERS are found with "Eger Bait Co." propeller spinners with the points snipped off. The lure was discontinued by 1949, but the name was resurrected in the 1970s on an entirely different lure. Names can be a problem with Smithwick for there seemed to be a tendency to hang on to a clever or neat name after a lure proved unsuccessful and discontinued and used on another later and totally unrelated lure. Another example is the BUCK-N-BAWL with not one, but two other unrelated lures bearing the same name. The original BUCK-N-BAWL is the upper lure in the photo below. It is marked on the belly thus: TOP & BOTTOM BUCK-N-BAWL.

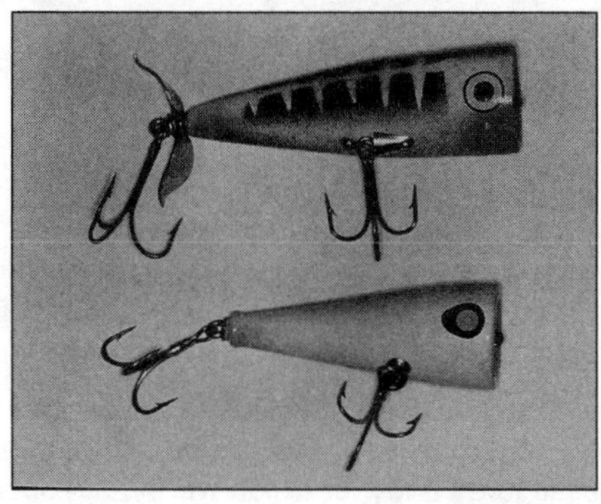

Measuring 3", it has a rear mounted propeller spinner from the Eger Bait company. There is another identical, but earlier version of this lure that bears the name HICK-N-HAWL. There is also a 2" BUCK-N-BAWL, JR., but it is an unrelated later vintage football shaped lure. The other lure in the photo is a SNAPPER. It measures 2-5/8" and is found with and without the tail spinner. This is an early model with the painted, yellow on black eye.

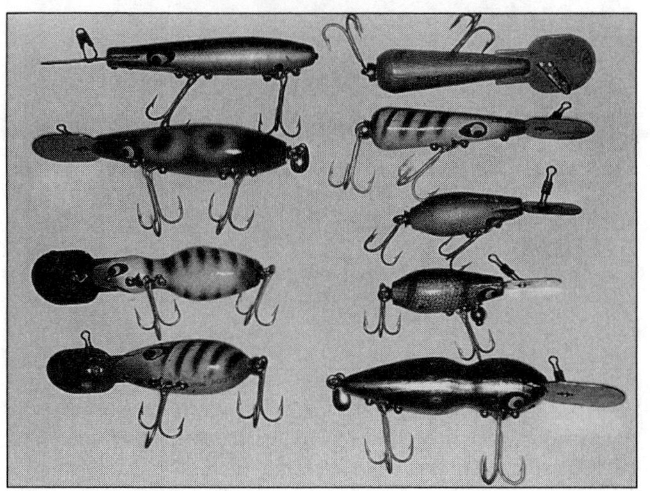

Here is a group Of seemingly unrelated (some of them) lures all bearing the name, ROOTER, along with other prefixes. If you look closely you will see that each of them shares a deep diving lip in common. They are arranged by age from the oldest at top left to the newest at bottom right.

Colors can be of some help in identifying the age of Smithwick lures because they started out with a fairly short list and added patterns periodically. The shortest list of colors I was able to find was in an undated flyer, but is probably fairly early. They are:

Pearl
Yellow with white rib
White
Shad
Red Head
Yellow with green back
Green Minnow
Black with white rib
Frog
Yellow with black rib
Silver flash
Silver shiner

You needn't try to pay any attention to numbers assigned to the finishes over the years for they changed often. The next list I found was a bit different: Solid white, red head, green minnow, silver flash, shad, yellow with green back and yellow with black rib had disappeared and the following patterns added:

Pearl with stripe
Gray shiner
Black smoke
Black head
Green with white rib
Rainbow
White with red rib
White with black rib

The next list used different descriptions that could be the same as some of the past colors listed. Any of the descriptions could have been changed with the result being the same color so this is not a terribly reliable method of dating. There were an incredible 62 colors listed for the DEVILS HORSE in a 1970s catalog.

Smithwick appears to have been tinkering, experimenting and changing things constantly so there is no telling what you might run across. Look for the eyes and there is also something rather distinct, but not particularly definable about Smithwick baits that experience will teach you.

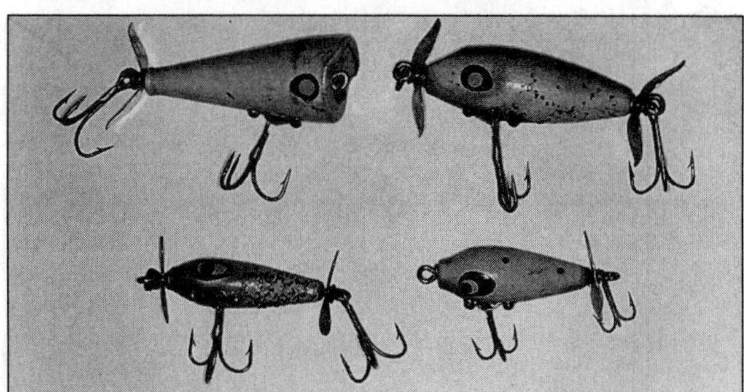

Upper left is a 2-1/2" SNAPPER with black eye spot with yellow iris. Upper right is a 2-3/8" MY PET. It has a flat top nose and was discontinued early in production. Lower left is a 1-3/4" JACK SPRAT sinker. The floater model has smaller spinners and hooks. Lower right is a DEVELS HORSE (HOSS) FLY measuring 1-5/8".

There was little or no useful trade data from which to draw a conclusion about any Smithwick lures save the DEVIL HORSE. Collector value range for them is $5-$10.

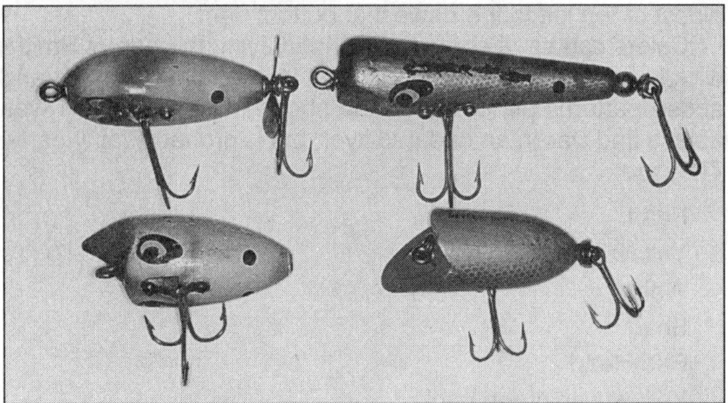

Upper left: A 1950s 2" SCOOTER. Notice the eyes on the flat belly. In production a very short time. Upper right: DEVELS WARHORSE measuring 2-3/4". Notice mouth cut at base of head. This lure was produced later without the cut and renamed CARROT TOP. Lower left: A 2-1/2" unknown Smithwick. Looks something like a short GANDY DANCER. Lower right: DEVELS HORSE STUD. Measures 2'. A rare, short-lived early production lure.

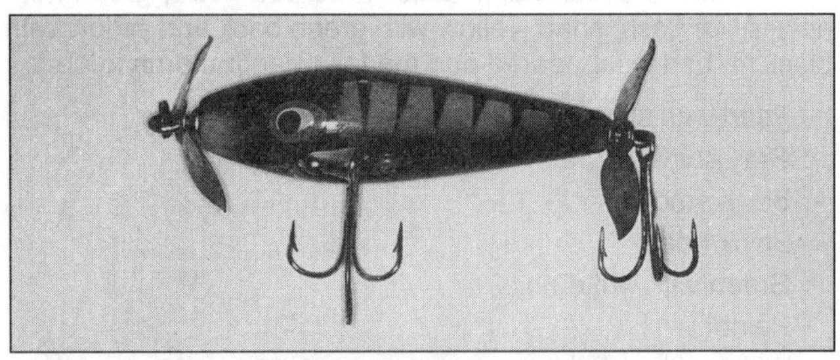

A 2-7/8" KING SNIPE. They are found with and without the propeller spinners. Notice the eyes at the bottom.

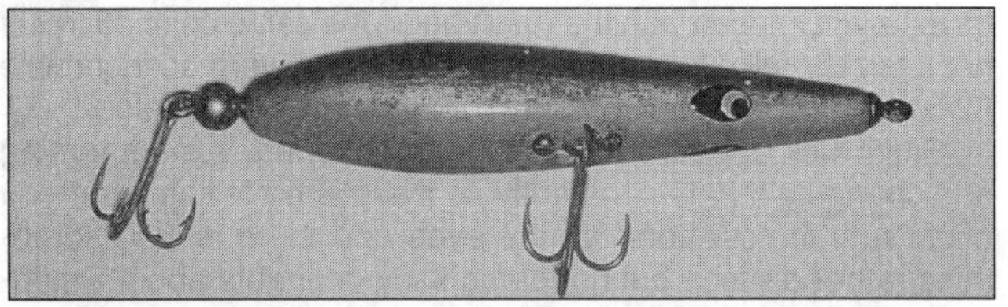

HIGH ROLLER. Measures 4-1/4". Notice the ball weight at the trailing end of the lure.

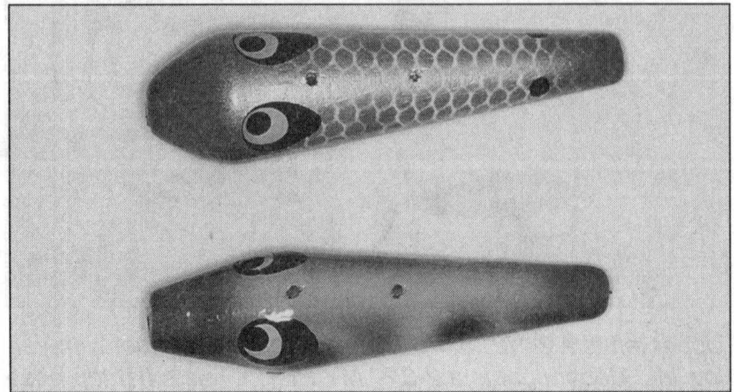

These are two different prototypes of the 2" MOUNTAIN LION, the last bait designed by Jack Smithwick. They were never put into production.

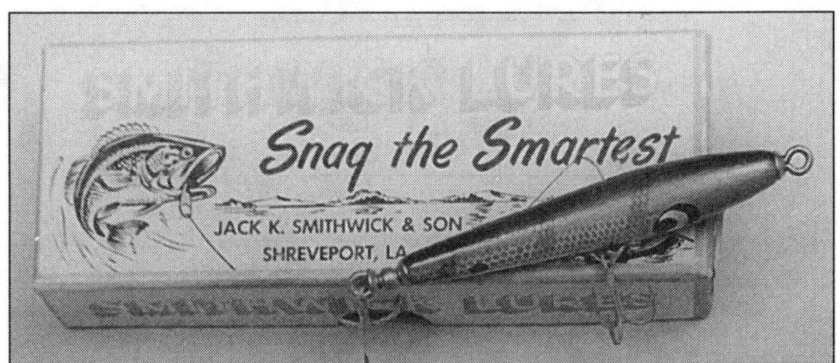

DEVIL'S TOOTH PICK and box. A 3" wooden bait. Two black dots on belly toward the tail. Photo from the author's files.

WALKING SCORPION c. 1950

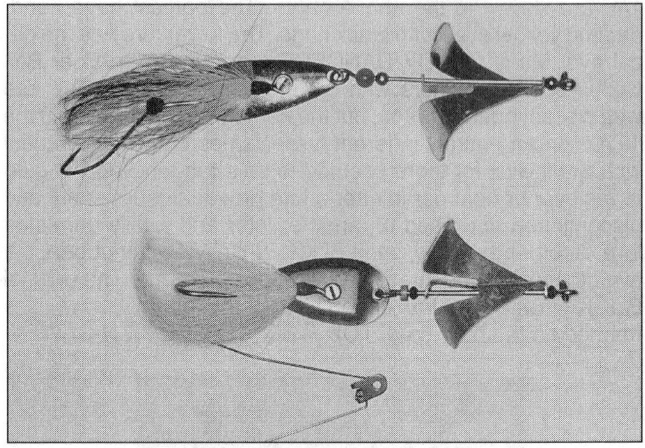

This is an early version of today's in-line buzz bait. The photo shows two different body styles to be found. It also came with a rubber skirt and a detachable weed guard.

PLASTIC SMITHWICK LURES

Up to here the Smithwick entry is all about their wooden lures. They produced at least one metal spinner bait and a number of plastic lures a few of which were quite successful.

BUTTERFLY

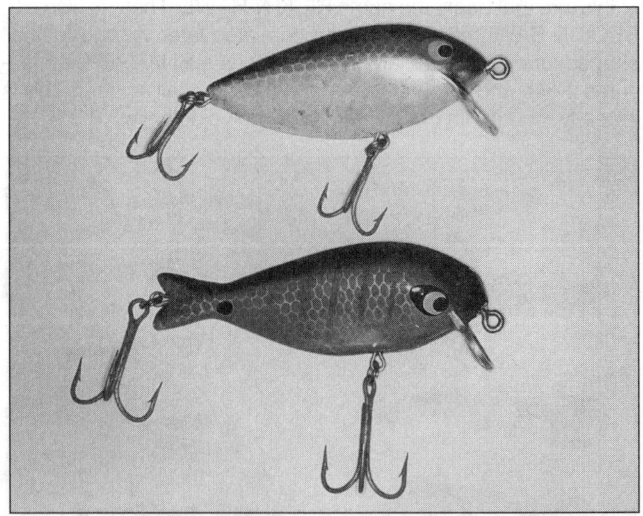

This was the first plastic lure for Smithwick. The lower lure in the photo is the earliest of the two. Apparently they found the forked tail difficult to make and changed to the more simple design.

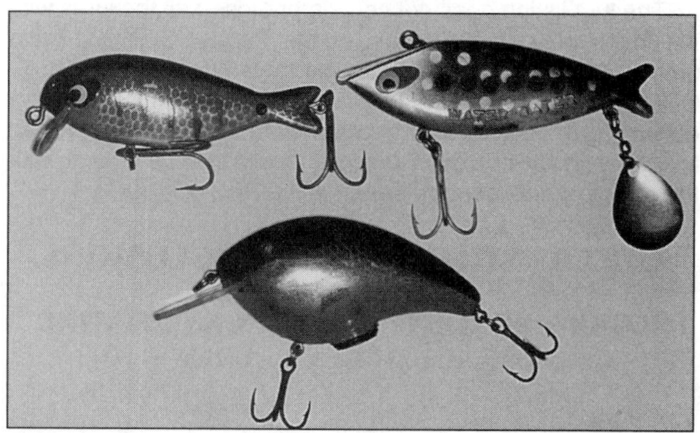

Top left: BUTTERFLY. Top right is a WATER GATOR and bottom is a BLINKER.

TAIL GATOR

WATER GATOR

The TAIL GATOR had a metal flasher rigged under the tail. Both of these lures were made in two sizes: 2-1/4" and 3-1/4". When the lure was rigged with a treble hook in place of the tail flasher it became the WATER GATOR.

BLINKER (Mid-1970s)

See previous photo. This is an ingenious lure with blinking eyes. It had built-in electronic circuitry powered by a small watch or clock battery. When the lure was placed in the water it was activated and the eyes blink. Removal from the water turns it off. It is said to have been unsuccessful. It would probably be more likely to have been too expensive. That technology is dirt cheap today, but in the 1970s it probably made the cost of the lure $15-$20. I have seen one. It really works.

BO-JACK

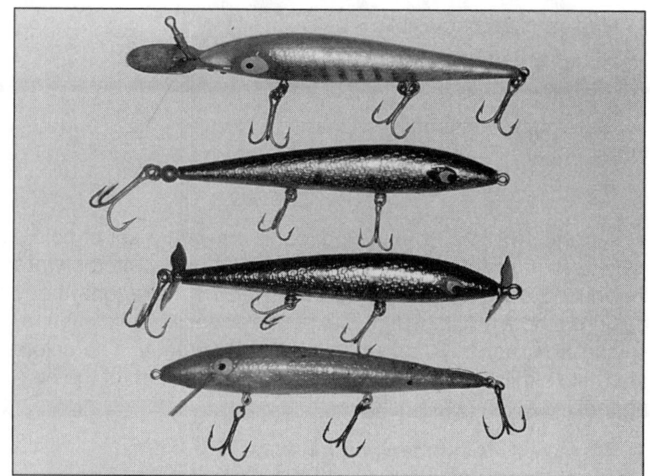

Reading top to bottom: DEEP DIVING ROGUE, SURFACE ROGUE, SPIN ROGUE, ROGUE.

It appears that when the BLINKER didn't make it, they used the bodies for another lure. The name is after Smithwick's son "Bo". The one in the photo measures 2-3/4". There were three sizes made: 3/16 ounce, 3/8 ounce and 1/2 ounce. Lengths were not given in their catalog. This was a fairly successful crank bait of the 1970s. Highly reminiscent of the BIG O.

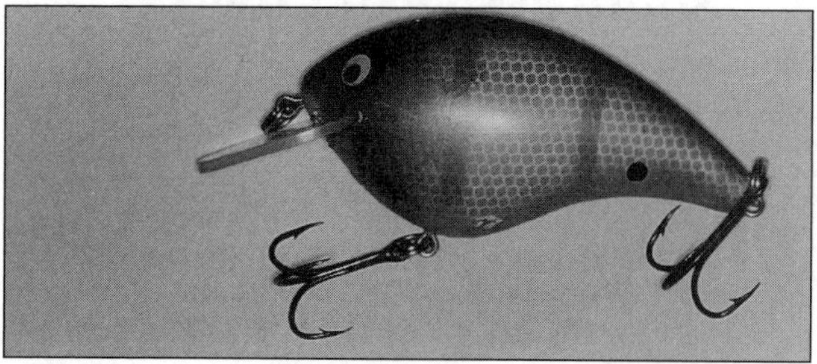

ROGUE

The various versions of this lure all measure 4-1/2" and 5 - 1/2". The ROGUES were released in 1964. Besides the four in the photograph there were the RATTLIN' ROGUE, a plastic lip DEEP ROGUE and DEEP RATTLIN' ROGUE as well as a plastic lip DEEP FLOAT RATTLIN' ROGUE.

SOCK-IT!

J. E. Groulx — Essexville, Michigan

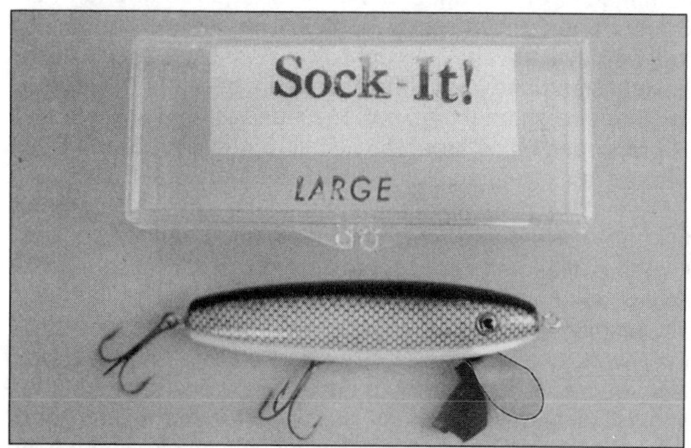

Probably made in the 1960s, this wood body lure is sometimes found with a red felt or red plastic attached to the lip to simulate blood. The metal lip was installed offset imparting a dying minnow motion on retrieve. It was apparently only made in one color, Black back and light gray scale blended to white belly. It is a quality lure. On wonders why so much pain was taken to make such a superior only to package it in a plastic box with a stamped label. They are also found in packaged in a sack with fishing instructions enclosed. Collector value range: $10-$15. Photo courtesy Jim Muma.

A beautiful metal 1/34 scale model of a 1957 International Harvester (IH) South Bend delivery van. It is painted red, white and yellow.

SOUTH BEND BAIT COMPANY

South Bend, Indiana

In 1895 F. G. "Bucktail" Worden, inventor of the buck tail lure started a small factory to manufacture fishing tackle in South Bend, Indiana. He began manufacturing with only one particular lure. This most famous lure was the WORDEN BUCKTAIL. Because of the widespread interest in his lure, he began making others. By 1905 he was operating as the Worden Bucktail Manufacturing Company, Inc. He had three men working for him. These gentlemen, F. L. Denis, F. A. Bryan and B. W. Olive, acquired the business from Worden and managed to attract enough capital to organize and form the South Bend Bait Company in 1909. The business did not do too well at first. They brought Ivar Hennings, a successful businessman and inveterate fisherman, in as the manager in 1910 to straighten things out. His management ability pulled the business out of trouble and into a success. South Bend ceased to exist when Gladding bought them out in 1965.

At first the company specialized in the production of buck tail baits. One of the early catalogs offered various buck tail spinners, flies and spoons, etc., but there were also eight or so wooden casting and trolling plugs. These early plugs usually employed one or more propellers and until around 1914 they were characterized by notched blades. Over the next few years several lures were added to the line and about the mid-1930s a new stronger hook-link hardware was introduced on the "Oreno" series plugs. It was an aluminum plate cemented and riveted inside the wood body. The metal eyes for attaching the hooks were the only parts to protrude from the body.

In 1938 the company introduced a series of "Obite" lures patterned after the "Oreno" plugs. The baits were molded of Tenite, a brand name for a plastic of the day. These employed a removable stainless steel wire running inside the length of the lure body instead of the aluminum plate mentioned above. This "Obite" series was meant to be less expensive line of plugs. There was no big fanfare or special announcement, but this is the first appearance of an all plastic lure in South Bend catalog. There were two: The BASS-OBITE and the TWO-OBITE. The metal TRIX-ORENO had a small plastic head piece.

In the remaining years to the present changing technology and fishing habits and knowledge have dictated changes, additions and deletions, in their lures.

The listing of lures in this section is primarily of South Bend wooden lures from inception to the early 1950s. Some early plastics, however, are listed. The metal products are numerous and not within the purview of this book, therefore they are not covered in any depth. a much more detailed study of the metal and all the wooden lures was undertaken and published by Jim Bourdon, *South Bend, Their Artificial Baits and Reels*, copyright 1985. This is highly recommended for the serious collector of South Bend. It was prepared primarily for members of the National Fishing Lure Collectors Club in a very limited number and was sold out quite soon. It has been reprinted in a limited edition of 1000 and will be available as long as the reprint edition is not exhausted. Turn to the section on recommended books for a source.

The lure listing does not contain photos of all the lures with the same basic body design of the BASS-ORENO. I have grouped them all together following the #973. The last BASS-ORENO style lure is the FISH-ORENO on page 713. With this exception, the entries are arranged more or less chronologically according to when each lure was new to the line, ending with the series of "inexpensive" lures called BEST-O-LUCK.

OBSERVATIONS AND CONCLUSIONS

REGARDING IDENTIFICATION AND DATING OF SOUTH BEND LURES

1. Colors

The earliest South Bend catalog (1912) in the author's possession illustrates eight wooden plugs as available in some or all of the 18 standard colors offered at that time. The body was of red cedar, the eyes were made of glass and counter sunk. Some were available in different hook configurations. The standard colors available at the time are listed below.

South Bend Standard Colors As Listed In The 1912 Catalog

Solid white
Solid red
Solid aluminum
Red head, white body
Red head and tail, aluminum body
Red head and tail, white body
Green back, white belly
Green back, yellow belly
Green cracked back, yellow belly
Green cracked back, white belly
Red back, white belly
Red back, yellow belly
Red cracked back, yellow belly
Red cracked back, white belly
Sienna cracked back, yellow belly
Slate back, white belly
Rainbow
Perch

Around 1921-24 South Bend came out with a set of colors collectors refer to as the HEX colors. The new patterns were introduced ostensibly to imitate the Heddon hexagonal body design without resorting to the expense or possible litigation resulting from actually making the hexagonal body. The colors are quite similar and create the illusion, somewhat, of the hexagonal body. They are listed as follows:

White body with green and red spots
Yellow body with green and red spots
Red body with black spots

There are shaded stripes oriented longitudinally on the body, helping to create the illusion. See photo of COMBINATION MINNOW on page 704 for an example.

They first offered three of their FIRE LACQUER colors in 1950, but the colors were officially introduced in the 1951 catalog in FIRE LACQUER for wood baits and the FISH-OBITE and FIRE MOLD for the other plastic lures. These were no longer an option in the 1953 catalog.

FIRE LACQUER

Neon Red
Fire Orange
Saturn green body with fire orange head

FIRE MOLD

Neon red
Fire orange
Saturn green body with fire orange head
Frog spotted Saturn green
Orange body with black and red spots
Orange body with black and yellow spots

Other than the above, colors and finishes are not a reliable tool for identification dating.

2. Eyes

a. Earliest South Bend lures had no eyes
b. Glass eyes came along sometime prior to 1921, probably 1913-14
c. The tack eye came along sometime around 1935-38. This period saw both glass eyes and tack eyes. Painted eyes (no tack) showed up on some of the very small lures such as the Ketch-Oreno in 1935.
d. Pressed eyes came along sometime in the late 1940s

3. Propeller Spinners

a. Notched propellers almost identical to the early Shakespeare notched propellers are the first to be used on South Bend wooden lures
b. The smooth blade, no notch propeller shows up around 1913-14. These are not marked with the South Bend name
c. Sometime around 1919-20 they began stamping the propellers with "South Bend".

4. Hardware

a. The first cup hardware was made of brass but soon it was nickel. The earliest are smaller than the next style. The next style was apparently made larger to accommodate the screw *hook*.
b. The 1930s Best-O-Luck series has painted cup flanges (lure painted after cup installation). Most older South Bend lures have screw eye and cup hardware. Only the very earliest will be found with screw eyes.
c. The only unique hook is called the Snap-Eye Detachable Single Hook (SD). First observed in a 1916 advertisement in *Forest and Stream* it was then listed in catalogs until 1925. The following dated lists of lures shows what lures they were available on and when they were an option.

1916 Advertisement

Bass-Oreno
Surf-Oreno
Woodpeckers

1921 Catalog

Underwater Minnows
Panatella
Surface Minnows
Panatella Wobbler
Woodpeckers
Combination Minnows
Minbucks
Surf-Oreno
Babe-Oreno
Bass-Oreno
Musk-Oreno

1922 Catalog

Underwater Minnows
Panatella
Woodpeckers
Surf-Oreno
Babe-Oreno
Bass-Oreno
Musk-Oreno

The 1925 catalog stated they were available on all wooden lures. This may not be much help, more of a matter of interest. Because they were detachable, a fisherman could change them around with great ease. If you find a lure with the SD hook, mint in its original box, it will be helpful.

A Worden KETCH-EM WOODEN MINNOW with original box. This bait measures 3-1/2", has glass eyes, an internal belly weight and cup/screw eye hook hardware.

THE WORDEN WOODEN MINNOW

One of the first lures made and marketed by Worden before his small company became South Bend. They can be tentatively identified by the shape of the propeller. So far they have all been the shape shown in the photograph here. The propellers almost always have the patent date of Dec. 29, 1903 stamped on the blade. The upper lure shown in the above photo is a #173 Wooden Minnow, 3" long. This and other Worden lures are rare. Collector value range: $200-$400.

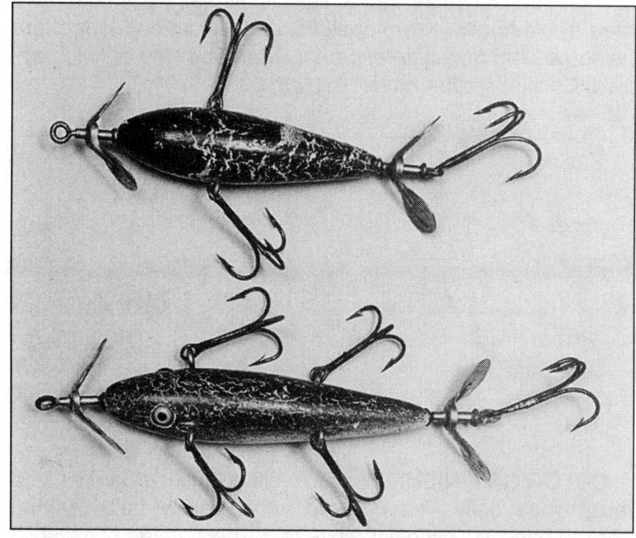

Upper lure is a #173 WORDEN WOODEN MINNOW. It is a 3" long, no eyes. Lower lure is a 3-3/4", 5T UNDERWATER WOODEN MINNOW.

MIDGET MINNOW #901

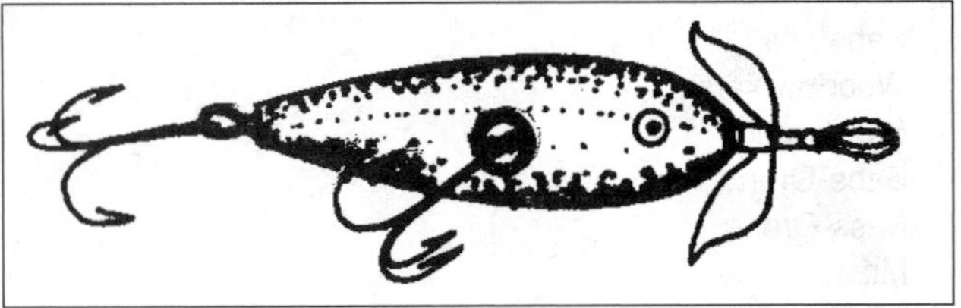

This is a very small version of the #902-#906 Underwater Minnows. It first appears in the 1921 catalog, but may have come along a bit before. They were gone by 1940. The plug is 2-1/2" weighing 1/2 ounce. The same colors as the #902-#906 were available on this plug. Collector value range: $30-$50.

UNDERWATER MINNOWS

Nos. 902, 903, 904, 905, 906 (c. 1912-1939)

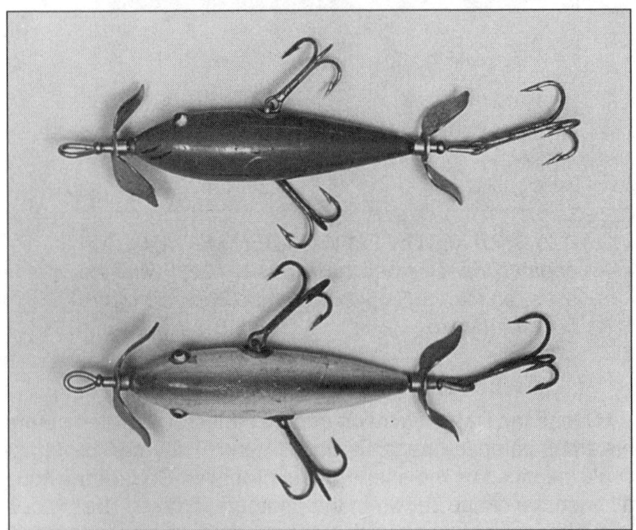

No. 903 and 904 underwater minnows.

The 1912 catalog illustrates several types of UNDERWATER MINNOWS as available. The No. 903 and 904 both have three treble hooks, two propellers, and weight and length are the same. The only difference appears to be type of finish applied. Collector value range: $100-$150.

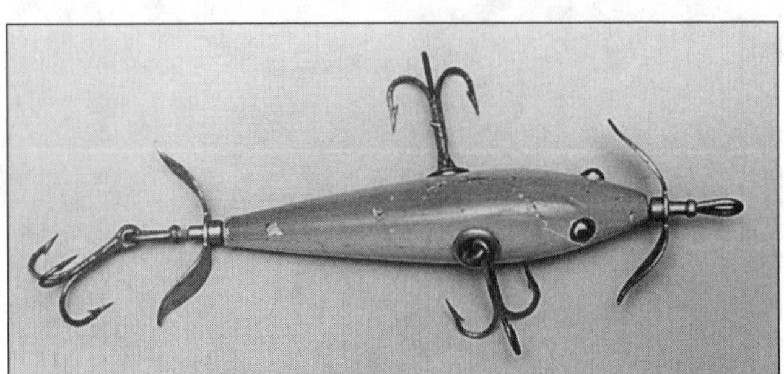

COLOR OR FINISH: Rainbow, yellow perch; green cracked back, white belly 'red cracked back, yellow belly' sienna cracked back, yellow belly' white body, dark shade back; solid white; white body, red head, white body, red head and tail, solid aluminum color, solid red, black nose; scale finish; scale finish, red blend, gold finish, redhead.

No. 9043"3/4 oz.3T

COLOR OR FINISH: White body, red and green spots; yellow body, red and green spots; red body, black spots; frog.

The No. 902 UNDERWATER MINNOW is essentially the same as the others but has only two trebles and they are weedless hooks.

No. 9023"3/4 oz.2T

COLOR OR FINISH: Rainbow, white body, dark shaded back, green cracked back, white belly.

The No. 905 and 906 are the same design as the others except they weigh more (1-1/4 oz.), are longer 3-5/8", and have five treble hooks. The colors are the same as No. 903 and 904 respectively.

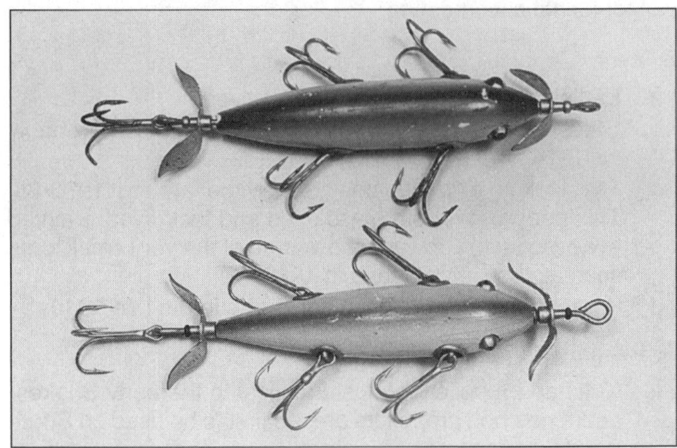

This is a No. 905 Underwater Minnow. It is identical to one illustrated in a 1918 South Bend catalog. It measures 3-1/2", has yellow glass eyes and cup/screw eye hook hangers. Note the c. 1918 notched propeller spinners.

UNKNOWN SOUTH BEND LURE

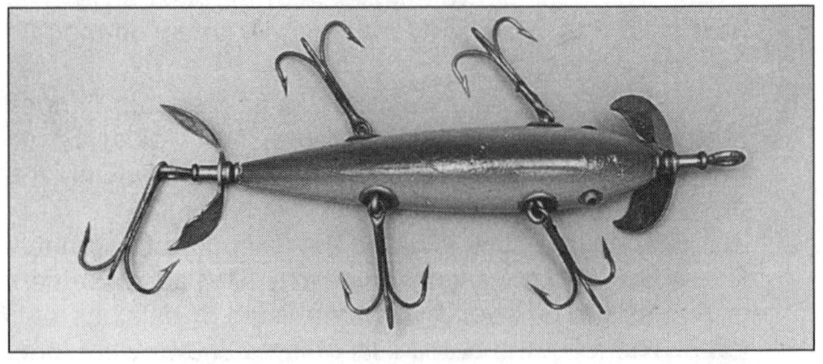

It is not known for certain that this lure is a South Bend product. It may not be apparent in the photo, but in handling this and the one above it becomes obvious that if South Bend didn't paint it then some other company did a remarkable job of copying their style. It's the same length and the eyes are yellow glass, but placed so that they are very cock-eyed. The cup and screw hook hardware is bigger and stronger than normal.

BEBOP

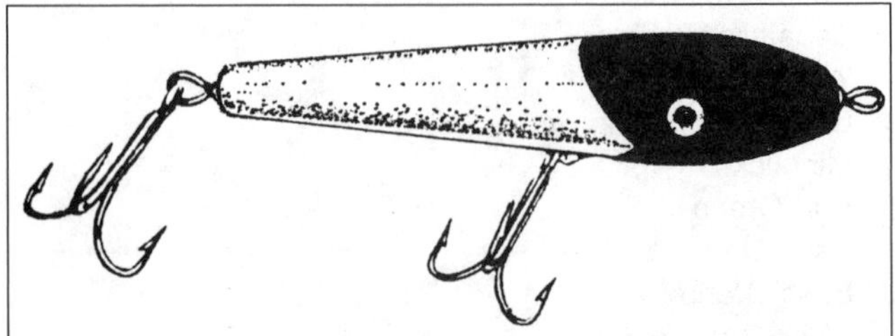

Announced as new in the 1950 catalog, this wood lure was offered in two sizes. The catalog name was printed "BeBop". They used model numbers that had been previously used on the now discontinued UNDERWATER MINNOWS. Collector Value Range: $5-$15.

CATALOG SERIES #	BODY LENGTH	LURE WEIGHT	HOOKS
902	3-3/8	1/2 oz.	2T
903	4-1/2"	58 oz.	2T

COLOR OR FINISH: White body with red arrowhead; yellow body with black tiger stripes and red arrowhead; silver speckled yellow body with black shad-o-wave stripe; yellow perch scale; yellow body with red and black spots, green stripe on back and red arrowhead; scale finish, green with silver speckles; blue mullet scale; orange body with black and red spots; light green frog, dark green frog with yellow belly.

CALLMAC BUGS

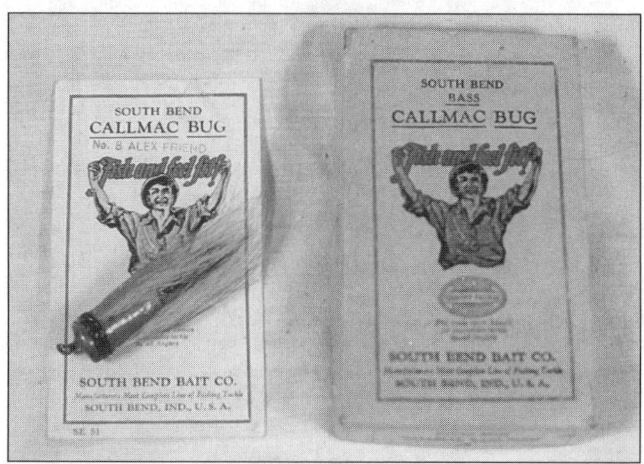

The earliest reference to the CALLMAC bugs I could find was in a 1923 South Bend advertisement. They probably date earlier than that. They are cork body, single hook floating fly rod baits. The 1923 ad said there were 12 colors available. By 1923 the list had grown to 24 for the bass size and 12 for the trout size. They are listed following. Those with a coloration listing were the only ones available in the 1926 catalog. Collector value range: $10-$15. If found in the box the value can as much as double or more. Photo courtesy Jim Muma.

BASS SIZE	COLORATION
Peet'e Favorite	
Dilg's Gem	Brown
Clark's Fancy	White
Wilder's Discovery	
Hadley's Choice	
St. John's Pal	Mallard
Chadwick's Sunbeam	Peacock
Alex Friend	Red and Yellow
Bob Davis	Yellow
ZaneGrey	Guinea
Carter Harrison	Squirrel
Dr. Henshall	Red and White
Brann's Ranger	Pheasant
Hank's Creation	
Miss Liberty	
Oriole	
Dixie Carroll	
Hampy Long	
Orange Drake	
Major Ensley	
Mills Special	
Buckingham Glory	
O'Reilly's Pet	
Ozark Ripley	Black

**Added by 1926.*

TROUT SIZE

Black Gnat
Parmer Bell
Cahill
McGinty
Coachman
Professor
Brown Hackle
March Brown
Gray Hackle
Squirrel Tail
Royal
Grizzly King

NIP-I-DIDEE

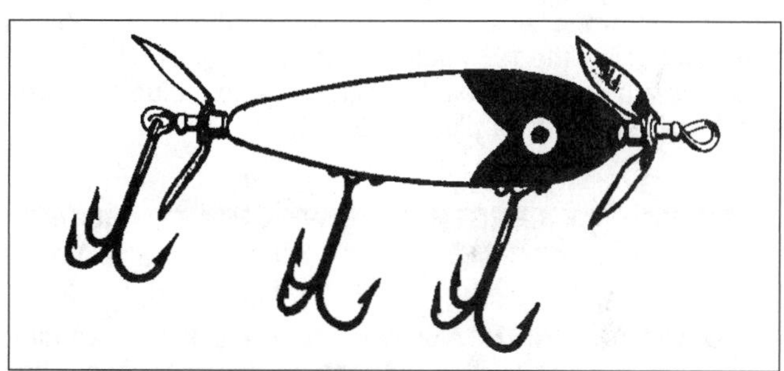

Introduced in 1947, this 3" lure was available in a floating model with double or treble hooks and an underwater model with treble hooks only. A collector sent a photo of a NIP-I-DIDEE that was inexplicably stamped OBSOLETE along the lower left side just above the rear hook hanger. The underwater model wasn't made available until 1951. Collector value range: $40-$60.

CATALOG SERIES #	BODY LENGTH	LURE WEIGHT	HOOKS
#910 (Floater)	3"5/8 oz.	3D, 3T	
#911	3"3/4 oz.	3T	

COLOR OR FINISH: *Aluminum color, aluminum color body with red arrowhead, *white body with red arrowhead, yellow body with red arrowhead, black body with white arrowhead, yellow perch scale; *dark green frog finish with yellow and black marking, *aluminum color body with red, green and black marking, *silver speckled body with green stripe on back, rainbow, **neon red, **saturn green, **fire orange.

**The only colors available in 1955-56. In 1947 the frog finish and rainbow were available only on the underwater model.*

***These were the first three Fire Lacquer colors made available in 1950.*

SPIN-I-DIDEE, #916

WEE-NIPEE, #912

A SPIN-I-DIDEE with surface hook hardware and measuring 2-1/2". Photo courtesy Ken Bernoteit.

Both of these lures came along about 1952. They are two small spinning versions of the NIP-I-DIDEE. They each have fore and aft propeller spinners. The WEE-NIPEE was absent from catalogs by the 1954 edition, but the larger SPIN-I-DIDEE remained along with its big brother. Collector value range for wood lure: $10-$20, for plastic: $5-$15.

CATALOG SERIES #	BODY LENGTH	LURE WEIGHT	HOOKS
912	2-3/8"	3/8 oz.	2D, 2T
916	2-1/4"	1/4 oz.	2T

COLOR OR FINISH: Aluminum color, black with red gills; dark green frog finish with yellow and black decorations; white body with red arrowhead; yellow perch scale; yellow body with red gills; *aluminum color body with red, green and black markings; *silver speckled body with green back.

**These two colors were added in the 1955 catalog.*

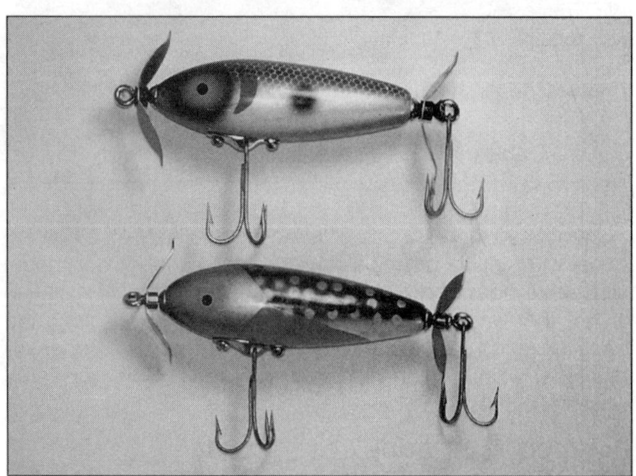

Two 2-1/4" SPIN-I-DIDEES. Upper is made of plastic and stamped "ORIGINAL SPIN-I-DIDEE. The lower lure is wood and stamped "SOUTH BEND SPIN-I-DIDEE WOOD LURE". Photo courtesy Ken Bernoteit.

THE PANATELLA MINNOW (c. 1912-1942)

A five treble Panatella Minnow with a "Barracuda Brand" propeller on the tail. May have been changed by a fisherman.

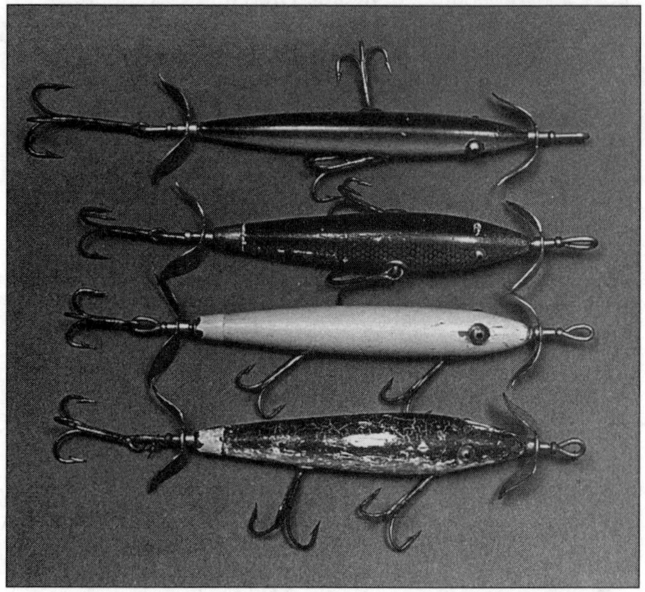

Plugs are arranged top to bottom, oldest to newest. Top lure has glass eyes, no tail cap and painted gill marks (not visible in photo) and no name on propellers. Second lure has tail cap, glass eyes and name pressed into props. Third lure has tail cap, large glass eyes and the propellers are different (may have been changed by an angler). Bottom lure is the strong saltwater version.

This plug was newly introduced in 1912* in the 3T model and was removed sometime around the 1940s. It first weighed about 9/10 ounce and body length was 4-1/4". The last ones available weighed a bit more (1-1/8 oz.), but the length remained the same. Earliest versions had either three or five treble hooks (one trailing and the others side or belly-mounted). Later catalogs made detachable single hooks an option. Collector value range: $50-$150.

**The 5T model is thought to be new in 1916.*

CATALOG SERIES #	BODY LENGTH	LURE WEIGHT	HOOKS
913	4-1/4"	9/10 oz.	3T
915	4-1/4"	9/10 oz.	5T

COLOR OF FINISH: **Green cracked back, white belly; **rainbow, yellow perch; white body, dark shaded back; red body, dark shaded back; white body, red head and tail; scale finish; redhead, aluminum color body; frog; **scale finish with red blend, gold finish with red head; **red head, white body.

***There were the only four finishes available by 1940.*

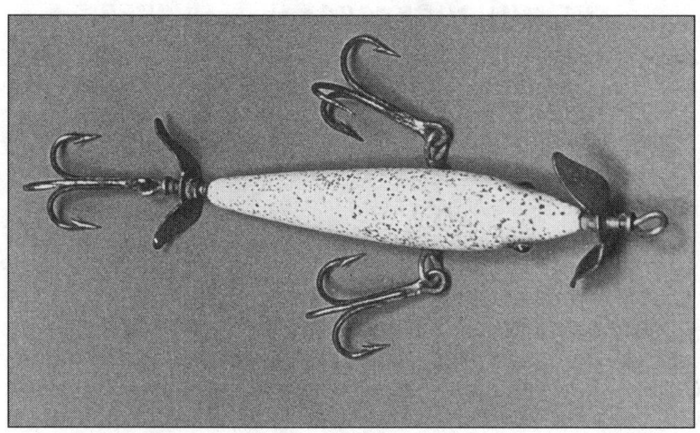

Salt water PANATELLA MINNOW with glass eyes and a strong rig.

SURFACE MINNOW

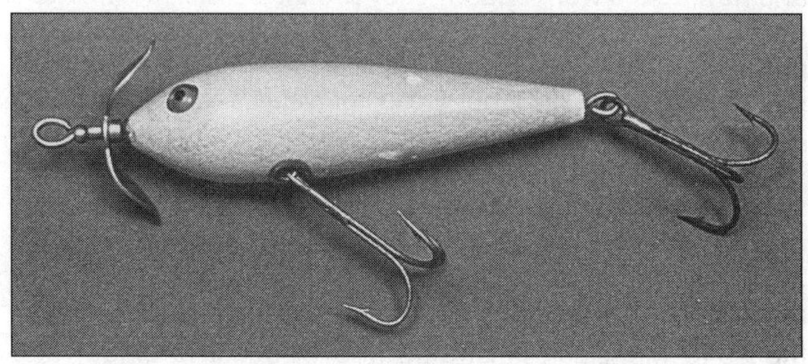

This particular plug shows up first in a 1912 catalog, the earliest South Bend catalog available I have. There were three versions first available there; The 920W and 920F, 921RH, and 922L. All have two trebles and one nose mounted propeller (notched until about 1914). The same numbers were used later for different lures. A 1939 catalog lists #920 as a "Wounded Minnow", #921 as a "Panetella Wobbler", and #922 as a "Darting Bait". All are completely different plugs. Collector value range: $100-$200.

CATALOG SERIES #	BODY LENGTH	LURE WEIGHT
920	3-1/2"	3/4 oz.
921	3-1/2"	3/4 oz.
922	3-1/2"	3/4 oz.

COLOR OR FINISH: Solid white; frog finish; white body, red head, luminous.

WEEDLESS SURFACE MINNOW

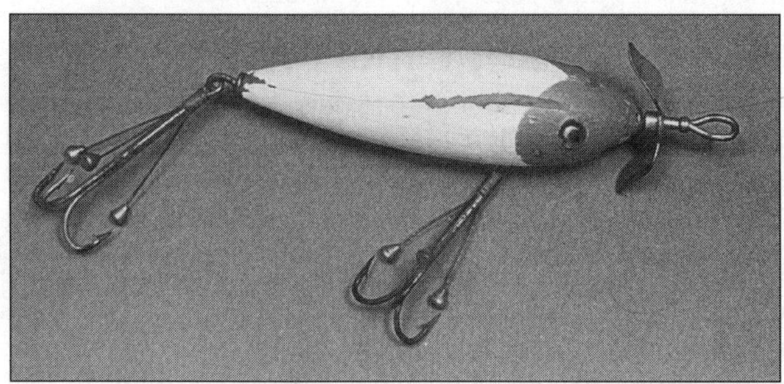

This is the same as 920 and 921 except that it was offered with weedless hooks. Available only in white body with red head or frog finish. Collector value range: $100-$200.

EXPLORER
JOINTED EXPLORER

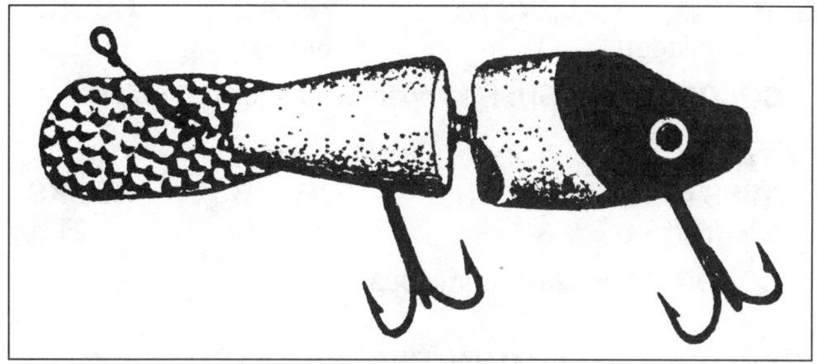

The 1922 catalog said these were "...brand new lures added to the South Bend line this year, designed for medium to deep traveling on a steady, fairly rapid retrieve." Neither one of them appeared in catalogs after the next year so it was a short two-year run for them. Collector Value Range: $5-$15.

CATALOG SERIES #	BODY LENGTH	LURE WEIGHT
920	3-3/4"	1/2 oz.
2920 jtd.	3-7/8"	1/2 oz.

COLOR OR FINISH: White body with red arrowhead; yellow body with green back, red and green spots; red blend scale finish; fire orange body wit black shad-o-wave stripe; neon red body with black shad-o-wave stripe; fire orange arrowhead; saturn green body with black shad-o-wave stripe.

THE WOODPECKER

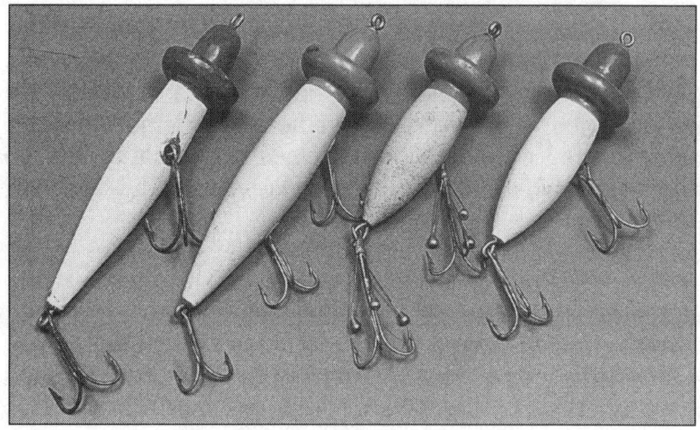

Found in a 1912 catalog as available in one design only; the body was white with red head. It had a distinct collar around the head (far left in photo). By 1921 it was available with a frog finish and weedless hooks if desired. A "midget" size was also made available about in the 1914 catalog. By the mid-1910s it was being offered with a luminous surface paint. It had disappeared from South Bend catalogs by the late 1930s. The large two treble hook model in the photo is rare. Collector value range: $40-$75.

CATALOG SERIES #	BODY LENGTH	LURE WEIGHT	HOOKS
923	4-1/2"	1 oz.	3T

COLOR OR FINISH: Red head with white body, Frog finish; All white

CATALOG SERIES #	BODY LENGTH	LURE WEIGHT	HOOKS
924	4-1/2"	1 oz.	3T

COLOR OR FINISH: Luminous

CATALOG SERIES #	BODY LENGTH	LURE WEIGHT	HOOKS
925 (midget)	3"	3/4 oz.	2T

COLOR OR FINISH: Red head, white body, All white

CATALOG SERIES #	BODY LENGTH	LURE WEIGHT	HOOKS
926 (midget)	3"	3/4 oz.	2T

COLOR OR FINISH: Luminous

COMBINATION MINNOWS, #931 through #934

These baits, sometimes known as WORDEN COMBINATION MINNOWS, appear in the 1912 catalog in two types (number of treble hooks). One has a single trailing treble and the other has the trailing treble and two more trebles, one mounted on each side. All types are in catalogs from then to the mid-1920s. Collector value range: $50-$150.

CATALOG SERIES #	BODY LENGTH	LURE WEIGHT	HOOKS
#931	2-5/8"	1/2 oz.	1T

COLOR OR FINISH: White body, red and green spots, natural buck tail; yellow body, red and green spots, natural buck tail, red body, black spots, natural buck tail, rainbow, natural buck tail, green cracked back, white belly, natural buck tail, yellow perch, natural buck tail; white body, dark shaded back, natural buck tail; red body, dark shaded back, natural buck tail, white body, red head, natural buck tail, luminous with white buck tail

CATALOG SERIES #	BODY LENGTH	LURE WEIGHT	HOOKS
#932	2-5/8"	1/2 oz.	1T

COLOR OR FINISH: White body, red and green spots, white buck tail, yellow body, red and green spots, white buck tail, red body, black spots, white buck tail.

CATALOG SERIES #	BODY LENGTH	LURE WEIGHT	HOOKS
#933	2-5/8"	1/2 oz.	3T
#934	2-5/8"	1 oz.	3T

COLOR OR FINISH: White body red and green spots, natural buck tail; yellow body, red and green spots, natural buck tail, red body, black spots, natural buck tail.

THE MIN-BUCK, #943 through #955

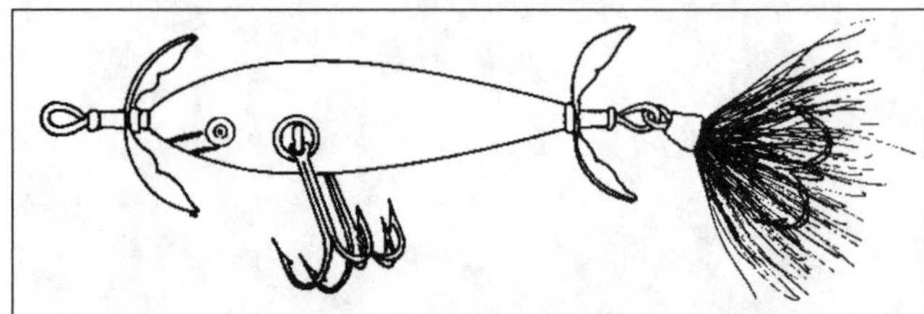

The 1912 catalog first offered the Min-Buck in "All Standard Colors". Two versions were available in the listing. The #943 with three trebles and the #945 with five trebles. The belly trebles were opposite side mounted. Both had trailing buck tail trebles. The illustration shows the early notched propeller. It is reproduced in the drawing above.

About 1914 two more, the #944 and the #946, were offered. These sport the smooth edge (no-notch) propeller spinners and new colors were added. They are the so-called "Hex" colors. They were 3" long in 3T and 3-5/8" in 5T. The #955 was a musky size Min-Buck, 5T at 5-1/4". No MIN-BUCKS were listed in catalogs from 1921 on. Collector value range: $90-$150; musky size $200-$300.

MUSKIE CASTING MINNOW, #953

This rare plug seems to have been offered for a very short time (c. 1914). Weighing in at 1-1/4 ounce, this fighter is 3-5/8" long. This lure is essentially the same body style as the #943 Min-Buck illustrated above, but it is bigger and heavier. It has the same hook configuration as well but is not supplied with a buck tail on the trailing treble. Collector value range: $300-$350.

MUSKIE TROLLING MINNOW, #956

This is the same lure as the #955 Min-Buck (5T) but does not have a Buck tail on the treble and is bigger at 5-1/4" and 2-1/4 oz. It has five trebles and was available in the 1912 catalog in all the standard colors. It was around until about 1922. Collector value range: $200-$300.

ICE FISHING DECOY, #258

This little known South Bend product showed up in only one of the catalogs, the 1923 edition. It is essentially the same body as the MUSKIE CASTING MINNOW, but is only the finished body with glass eyes and no hooks or hardware other than a screw hook/washer at the top with a swivel attached. It is 5" long and was available in on two finishes: Green Scale and Aluminum color body with red head.

There are only four presently known. There is no trade data from which to determine a realistic collector value.

SURF-ORENO #963

First appearing around 1916 this lure continued to be available throughout the years, but the color design options dwindled from 13 choices (1921) to only six by 1953. It sports two propellers and the later versions were available with only three trebles. Early versions were available with either two or three. Body length is 3-3/4" and weight is 1 ounce. The earliest #963 SURF-ORENOS had more elongated (TSB) bodies almost pointed at both ends and the later models were more rounded at the head. The original paint designs were: *Red head with white body; *frog design; rainbow; solid red, black nose; green cracked back with white belly; white body with green and red spotted decorations, blue head and aluminum color; *scale finish with red blend;

gold finish with red head. Collector value range: $20-$35.; The blue head version and scale finish are hard to come by and will bring $50-$140.

**The only colors available by 1953. There was an additional finish, yellow body with red painted gills available then.*

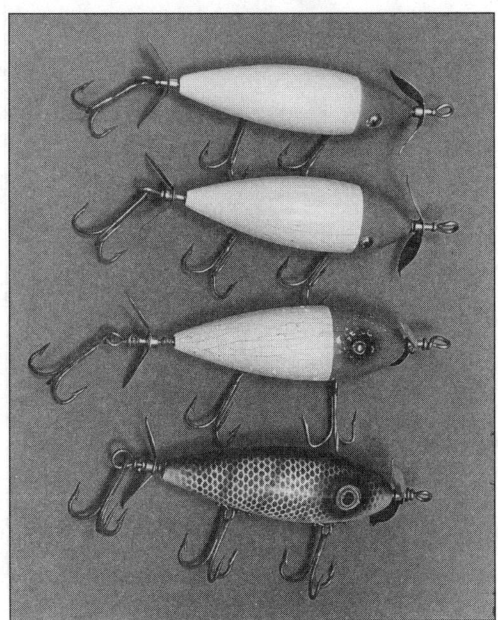

MIDGET SURF-ORENO

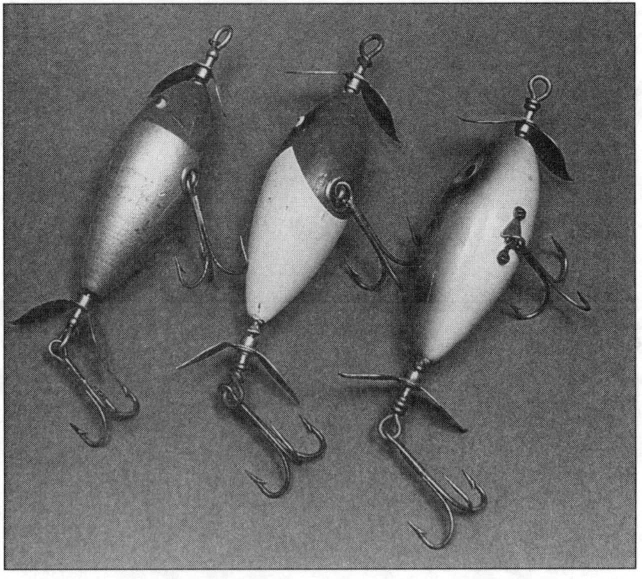

This plug appears around 1916 and is a smaller version of the #963 SURF-ORENO. It is 2-3/4" long and weighs approximately 1/2 oz. The same general comments made about the #963 apply to this #962 Midget Surf-Oreno. Collector value range: $15-$30.

FLY ROD SURF-ORENO #961

This is a tiny 1-1/2" version of the SURF-ORENO. It was around from the late 1920s until the early 1940s. Weight was cataloged as "1 pound per dozen". You figure it out. Colors listed in 1927 were: Red head, white body; rainbow; imitation frog; white body with red and green decorations; green scale finish; scale finish with red blend. Collector value range: $25-$40.

MUSKIE SURF-ORENO #964

Appearing first around 1925 this is a beefy version of the Surf-Oreno. It has nose- and tail-mounted propellers, two belly-mounted treble hooks and trailing treble. Had disappeared by the mid-1930s. Collector value range: $100-$300.

CATALOG SERIES #	BODY LENGTH	LURE WEIGHT
#964*	3-3/4"	1-1/18 oz.
#964	5-1/2"	1-1/18 oz.

COLOR OR FINISH: **Red head, white body, **rainbow, **scale finish with green blend, frog; scale finish with red blend, yellow perch scale finish.

**This size appeared for a few years in the late 1930s.*

***The first three finishes available.*

BASS-ORENO #973

The most famous lure in the South Bend line. This lure appeared in 1915 as part of their offerings, but it was probably available (in a slightly different design) before that. South Bend didn't invent the lure but rather bought the patent rights (J. S. Olds, December 19, 1915). Mr. Olds had been making and selling his lure before 1915. So if you see any weird looking plugs (the patent lure has an oval body) that seem much like the BASS-ORENO, it might be one of his. It underwent many changes through the years, but the overall design remained pretty much the same as the 1915 model. They have gone from no eyes to glass eyes (until 1927) to tack eyes (c. 1935) to pressed eyes (c. 1951) and last to painted eyes in the 1960s. A major change in construction was introduced in 1934. Called the BETTER BASS-ORENO, the body was sawed out longitudinally, making a slot from the belly in. A die-cut aluminum plate was inserted, glued and riveted in. The result was that only the three hook hangers and line tie (integral with the plate) protruded from the body. This lasted only until 1942. The standard cup rig continued to be available throughout this period also.

An intriguing fact is that the patent for the aluminum plate/sandwich construction belong, not to South Bend, but to Claude N. Rodgers and Louis A. Chapleau. Rodgers was one of the principles in the Bite-Em-Bate Company from the 1920s.

The BASS-ORENO was available in a large variety of finishes by 1921. They are: Red head, white body; yellow body, red and green spots; solid red, black nose; white body, red and green spots; rainbow; frog; red head, aluminum color body; luminous; scale; white body, blue head; scale with red blend; red head, gold color or body; solid black.

The famous BASS-ORENO survived throughout the years and offerings expanded to include many sizes and finishes for just about any type of fishing. Collector value range: $20-$50.

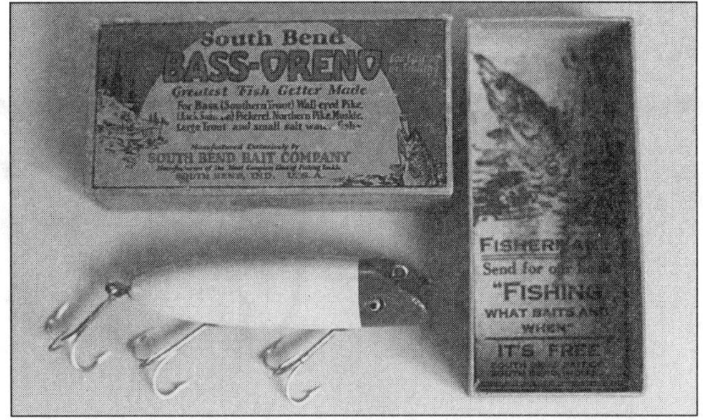

A glass eyed 1916 BASS-ORENO with its original box. Photo courtesy Jim Muma.

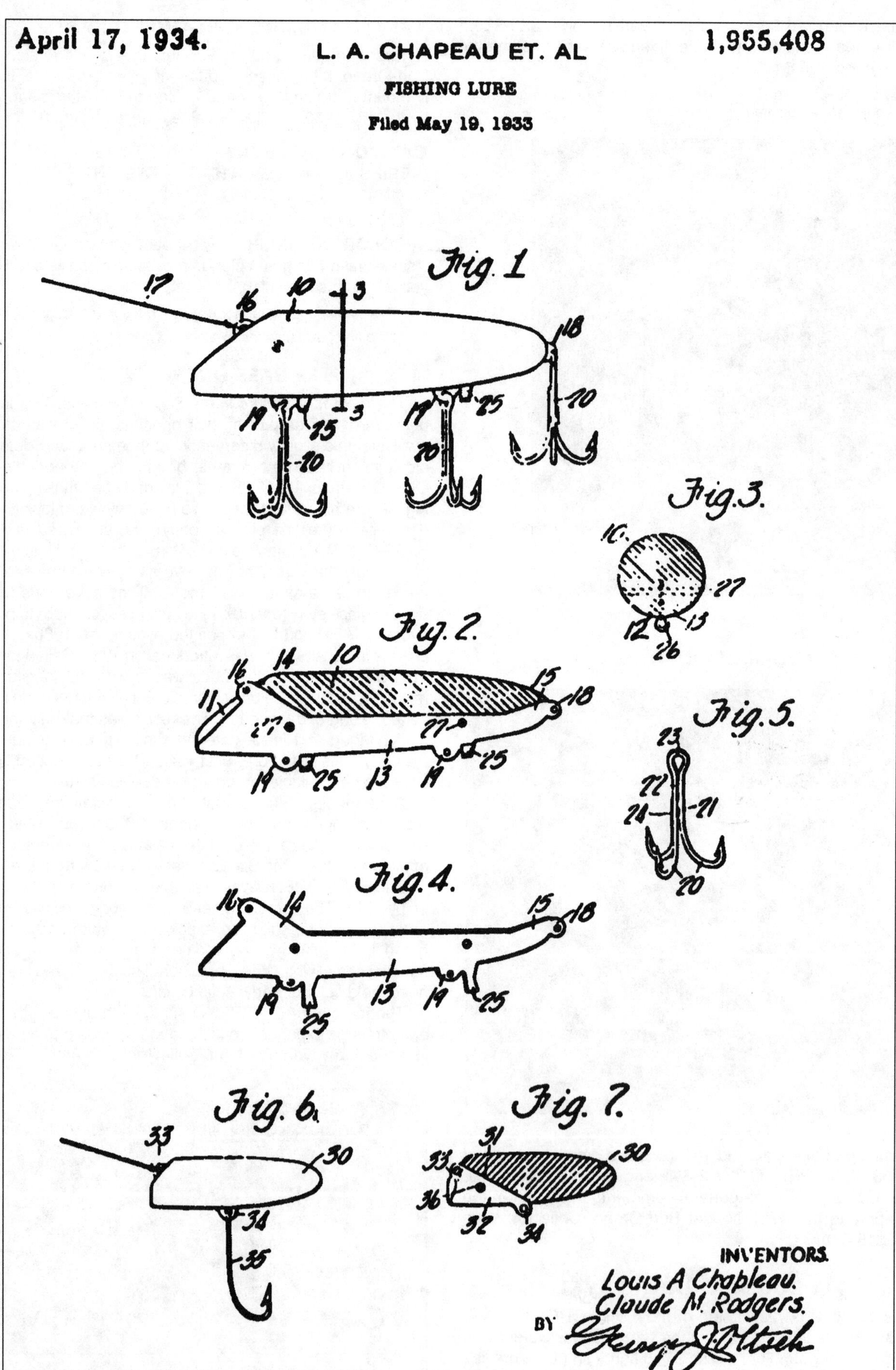

The patent illustration for the BETTER BASS-ORENO construction.

CATALOG SERIES #	BODY LENGTH	LURE WEIGHT	HOOKS
#973	3-1/2"	5/8 oz.	3T
#473*	3-3/4"	3/4 oz.	3T
#73**	3-3/4"	3/4 oz.	3T

**From 1934-35 this was the size listed in the catalogs.*

***This is the number for the Better Bass-Oreno.*

SALTWATER BASS-ORENO, #977

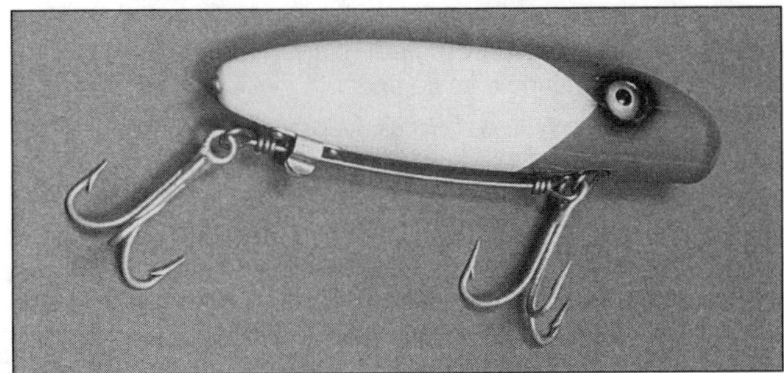

The lure in this photo is a 1950s SALTWATER BASS-ORENO type called the KING BASSER. The older models do not have this wire and clip rigged hardware.

This is the same lure as the regular BASS-ORENO except that it is built with much stronger hardware. It has only one belly treble and a trailing treble hook. It was made from about 1924 through 1942; however, it was constructed exclusively with the aluminum plate hardware (discussed with the regular BASS-ORENO) from 1934 on. Collector value range: $25-$50.

CATALOG SERIES #	BODY LENGTH	LURE WEIGHT	HOOKS
#977	3-1/2"	3/4 oz.	2T

COLOR OR FINISH: Red head, white body; red arrowhead, white body, *rainbow, *scale finish with green blend, 'scale finish with red blend; red head, aluminum color body, minnow scale finish; iridescent pearl,, dace scale finish; yellow perch scale finish; pike scale finish; yellow body, red and brown decorations; luminous.

**These were the first four finishes available. The others had been added by 1939.*

BABE-ORENO #972

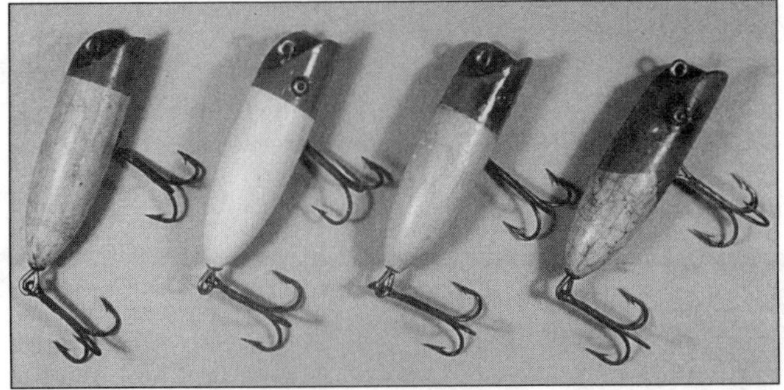

1916 is thought to be the birth date for this baby. It is continuously available into the 1950s. At birth it was 2-3/4" long, weighing 1/2 oz. It was available in at least 14 finishes by 1927. It is the same shape body as the BASS-ORENO and has one belly treble and a trailing treble. It was also available in the Better Babe-Oreno aluminum plate construction from 1934 through 1942.

The oldest ones had no eyes and a more shallow cupped head than the later versions and the paint line on the head was a straight vertical line. Size and weight has remained fairly constant through the years. Around 1926 eyes were added and a 1932 catalog illustrates it as available with detachable single hooks. By 1932-34 the paint design had changed to reflect an "arrow" or "arrowhead" design instead of the straight vertical paint line at the head. The above photo illustrates eye type and paint design changes from oldest to the last glass eye model. Collector value range: $15-$30. There is a rare red, white and blue model that will bring much more.

CATALOG SERIES #	BODY LENGTH	LURE WEIGHT	HOOKS
#972	2-3/4"	1/2 oz.	2T

COLOR OR FINISH: Red head, white body, yellow body, red and green spots, red body, black nose; white body, red and green spots; rainbow, frog; red head, aluminum color body, scale finish; scale finish with red blend, gold finish with red head, white body, blue head, luminous.

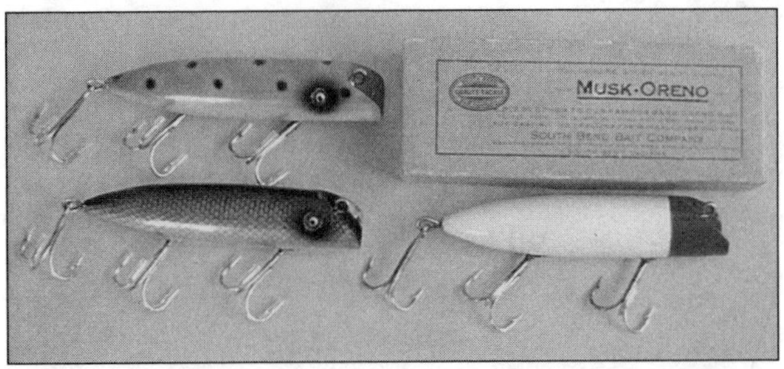

Three 4-1/2" MUSK-ORENOS with an original box. The box alone is valued at $20-$30. Photo courtesy Jim Muma.

MUSK-ORENO #976

This is a large version of the BASS-ORENO new about 1916. First found in a 1921 catalog supplement, it was offered with a "..5-inch piano wire leader having a snap arrangement, permitting easy removal if preferred." By 1930 this leader option was not mentioned. The earliest models have no eyes, but by 1925-26 eyes were present and sometime in 1934-35 the improved aluminum plate, hook-link was added. The plug has two belly-mounted trebles and one trailing. It was removed from the line sometime in the early 1940s. Collector value range: $40-$75.

CATALOG SERIES #	BODY LENGTH	LURE WEIGHT	HOOKS
#976	4-1/2"	1-1/8 oz.	3T

COLOR OR FINISH: Red head, white body, Yellow body, red and green spots; White body, red and green spots; Red body, black nose; Rainbow, Frog, Red head, aluminum color body, Scale finish; Scale finish with red blend, Gold finish with red head, white body, Luminous.

TROLL-ORENO #978

Called the "newest and latest number of the 'Oreno' baits" in the 1921 catalog. It was made of light cedar, has two belly treble hooks and one trailing treble. The same general comments concerning changes over the years that are made about the BASS-ORENO and BABE-ORENO apply here as well. Collector value range: $30-$60.

CATALOG SERIES #	BODY LENGTH	LURE WEIGHT	HOOKS
#978	6-1/2"	2 oz.	3T

COLOR OR FINISH: Green back, white belly; frog, scale finish with red blend, gold finish, red head, red head, white body, yellow body with red and green spots; white body with red and green spots; solid red with black nose; rainbow, red head with aluminum color body, white body, blue head.

TROUT-ORENO #971

The Trout-Oreno came along in 1920 and stayed in the line into the 1950s. It is the same shape as the BASS-ORENO, is 1-3/4" and has one belly-mounted double hook. Collector value range: $15-$50.

FLY-ORENO #970

This little bit of a wooden lure was new about 1921 and continues to be available into the 1950s. It is 1" with one belly-mounted double hook. Collector value range: $15-$50.

WIZ-ORENO #967

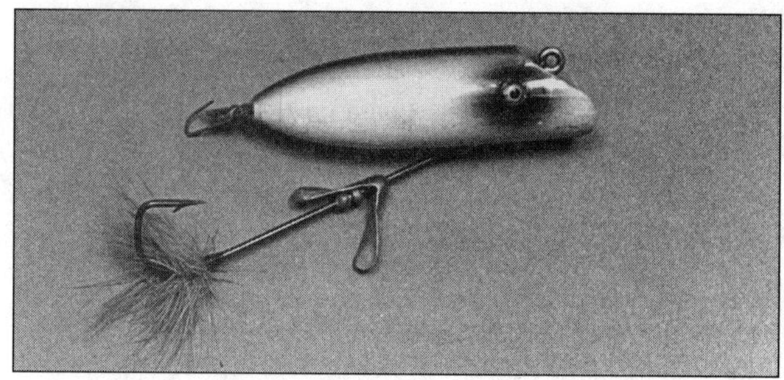

This is an unusual lure that utilized the BABE-ORENO body. There was a belly-mounted, long-shank, single-point hook with a special "swirling" propeller mounted on the hook shank and a gray hackle covering the point. There was a tail-mounted pork rind attachment also. New in 1925, this lure had disappeared from catalogs by 1930. Collector value range: $25-$40.

CATALOG SERIES #	BODY LENGTH	LURE WEIGHT
#967	2-3/4"	unk.

COLOR OR FINISH: Red head, white body, yellow perch scale finish; rainbow, scale finish with green, blend, red body, black nose; red head, aluminum color body, copper finish.

TARP-ORENO #979

Along about 1921-22 this large plug appeared. It is the same body design as the other "Oreno" type baits. In 1922 this plug was fitted with a belly-mounted double hook and a trailing double, but by 1925 and from then on the hooks were single point. Collector value range: $50-$70.

CATALOG SERIES #	BODY LENGTH	LURE WEIGHT
979	8"	5 oz.

COLOR OR FINISH: mullet scale finish; redhead, white body, redhead, aluminum color body, scale finish with green blend, scale finish with red blend, rainbow, iridescent pearl, minnow scale finish.

KING-ORENO, #986

This is the same design as the Tarp-Oreno but smaller (6-1/2" body length) and has only one single hook (belly mount). It first appears in the early 1920s and has disappeared from the line in the 1940s. Collector value range: $30-$60.

CATALOG SERIES #	BODY LENGTH	LURE WEIGHT
986	6-1/2"	2 oz.

COLOR OR FINISH: Yellow perch scale finish; red head, white body, *red arrowhead, white body, red head, aluminum color body, *scale finish with green blend, scale finish with red blend, rainbow, *minnow scale finish.

**These are the only three finishes available by the time it was discontinued.*

COAST-ORENO, #985

This bait is 4-1/2" in body length and weighs 1-1/2 oz. All comments made about the "KING-ORENO" #986 apply to this plug as well. Collector value range: $25-$50.

KETCH-ORENO, #909

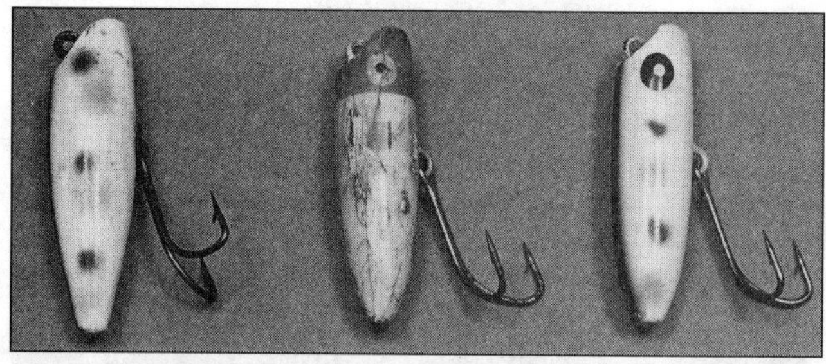

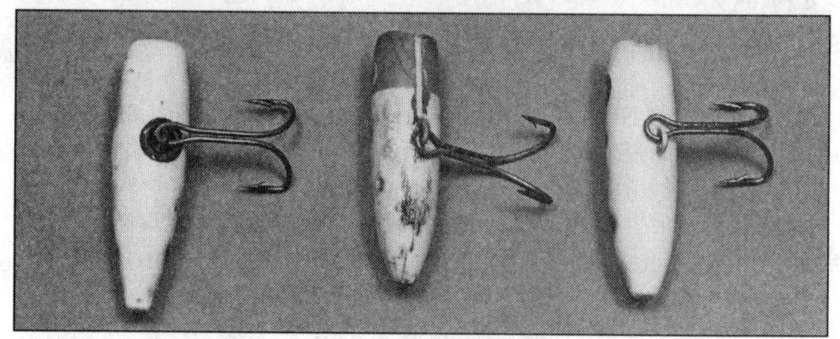

This small plug was first observed in a 1932 catalog. it has one belly-mounted double hook and was gone by 1940. Collector value range: $20-$40.

CATALOG SERIES #	BODY LENGTH	LURE WEIGHT
909	1-1/2"	1 oz. minus

COLOR OR FINISH: Red arrowhead, white body; red arrowhead, yellow body, scale finish with red blend, scale finish, green; pike scale finish; frog.

MIDGE-ORENOS showing hardware changes from oldest style at the top to the newest at the bottom.

MIDGE-ORENO #968

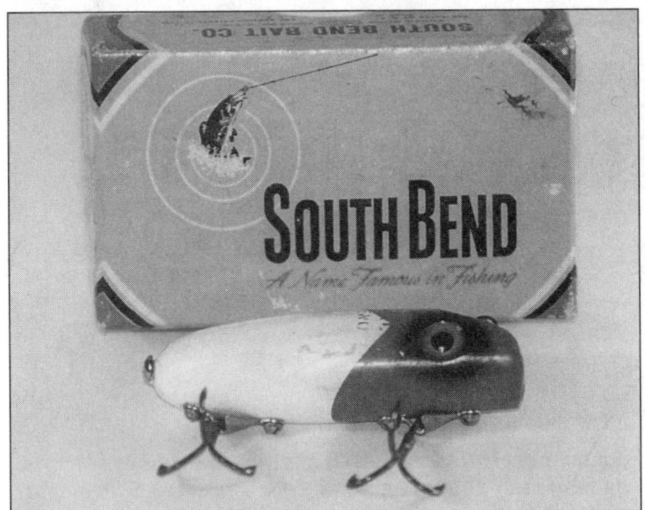

MIDGE-ORENO with original box. Photo courtesy Ken Bernoteit.

This plug was first found in a 1932 catalog and continued to be included from that point on. It has one belly treble and one treble mounted just under the tail end of the plug body. Collector value range: $15-$40.

CATALOG SERIES #	BODY LENGTH	LURE WEIGHT
968	2-1/4"	3/8 oz.

COLOR OR FINISH: **Red head, white body; red arrowhead, white body, **red arrowhead, yellow body; **black arrowhead, white body; yellow perch, scale finish; **green scale finish; *pike; silver speckled, white body, green back stripe; rainbow; copper scale finish; white head, black body, minnow scale finish, silver, black and red, dace scale finish.

**Available for only a short time after 1932.*

***These were the only colors available in 1932. Other added later.*

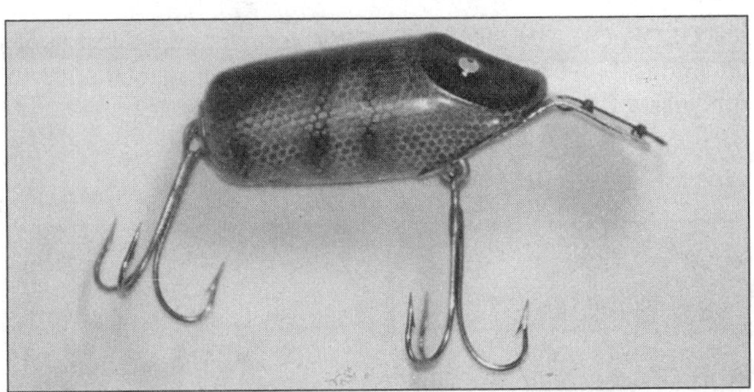

A DIVE-ORENO measuring 2-1/8". This size was not cataloged. Photo courtesy Ken Bernoteit.

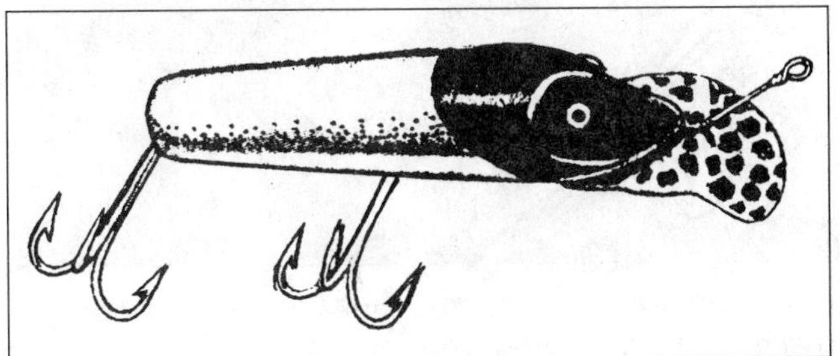

DIVE-ORENO

New in 1941 the two sizes of this lure remained in production (except for the war years) through 1952. They were stubby tail versions of the PIKE-ORENO. Collector Value Range: $15-$30.

CATALOG SERIES #	BODY LENGTH	LURE WEIGHT
952	3-1/4"	1-1/2 oz.
954	4"	5/8 oz.

COLOR OR FINISH: White body with red arrowhead, yellow perch scale, white body with silver speckles and green back, pike scale.

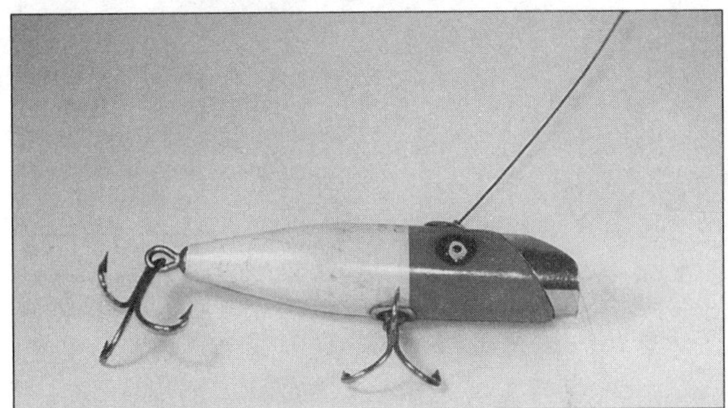

FISH-ORENO. Good view of the polished metal head. Photo courtesy Ken Bernoteit.

FISH-ORENO #953

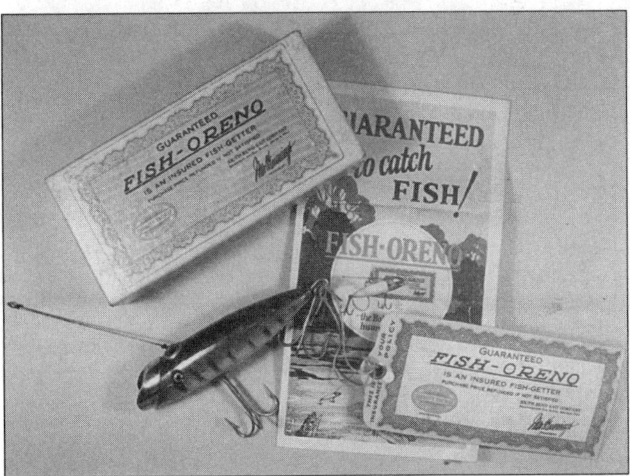

This interesting plug appeared in South Bend catalogs first in 1926, but there is evidence to suggest it was on the market at least at least as early as the previous year. The 1927 catalog states "The Fish-Oreno is the first lure ever produced that is guaranteed by the manufacturer to catch fish." It is covered by an insurance policy attached to the bait, that is backed by the resources of the South Bend Bait Co. "Can be sold to any angler with positive guarantee of 'money back' if not satisfied after one year's use."

The lure is similar to the BASS-ORENO but has a polished metal head, a wire leader permanently attached to a screw eye at the top of the head. One belly-mounted treble hook and a trailing treble. The guarantee tag and promotion of the guarantee had disappeared by 1939, but the bait was produced on into the early 1950s. Collector value range: $25-$50.

CATALOG SERIES #	BODY LENGTH	LURE WEIGHT
#953	3-1/2"	5/8 oz.

COLOR OR FINISH: White body, red head,, pike finish; scale finish; yellow body, green and red spots; copper scale finish; silver body, frog; rainbow, pike scale finish; silver speckled white body, green stripe; minnow scale finish, silver, black and red, yellow perch scale finish.

VACUUM BAIT

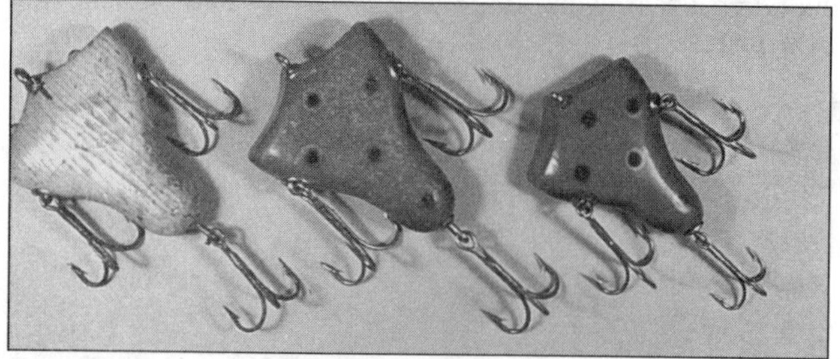

Belly view of three VACUUM BAITS. Left: Glass eyes. Center: No eyes; Right: Smaller size with no eyes and Howe's swivel hook hanger.

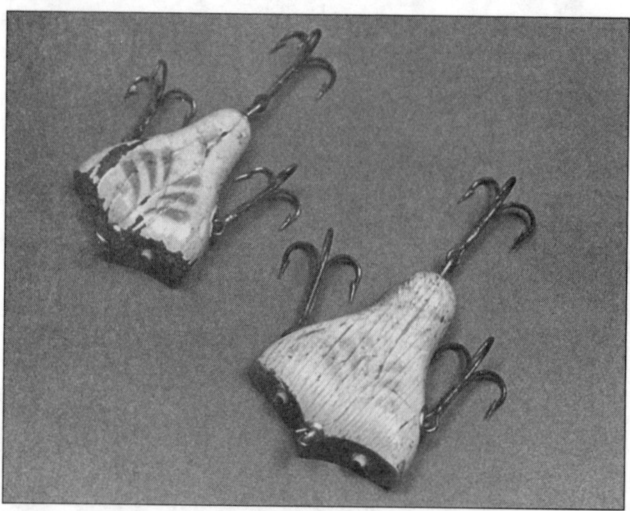

Belly view of two South Bend VACUUM BAITS with glass eyes.

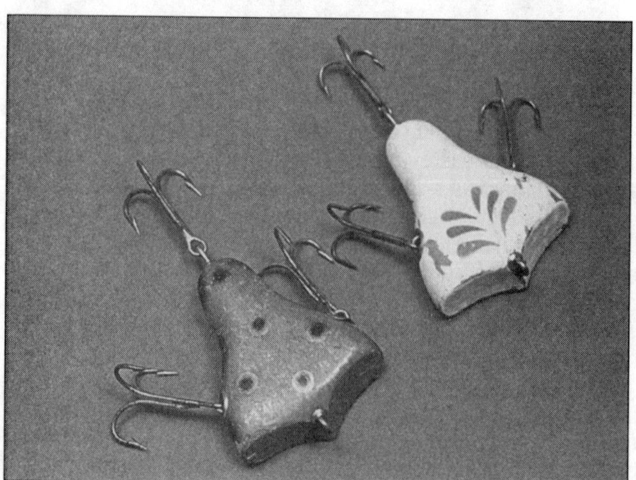

Belly view. Left: South Bend VACUUM BAIT. Right: Howe's Vacuum Bait.

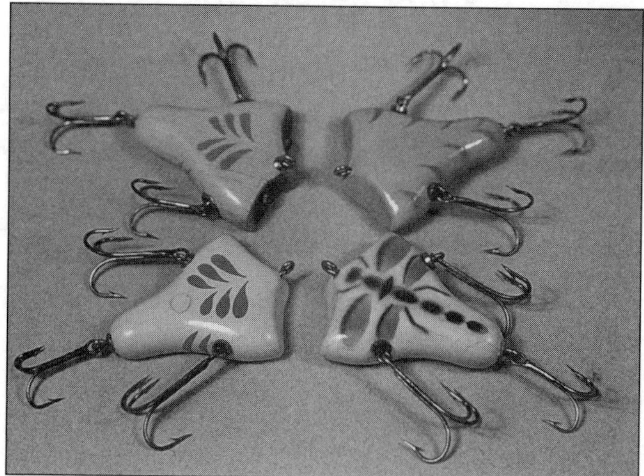

Four different VACUUM BAITS showing the various patterns. The dragon fly pattern on lower right is unusual. Photo courtesy Jim Muma.

This lure first occurs in a 1922 South Bend catalog but it was patented in 1909 by Francis O. Howe (see Howe's Vacuum Bait Company section). Apparently South Bend obtained the rights to the patent. As you can see by the photos here, the earliest South Bend versions used the original Howe swivel hook hanger hardware. What probably happened is that upon purchasing the right to manufacture the lure, South Bend also acquired some of Howe's inventory. As this was exhausted, South Bend began using their own hardware. Hence the mixture of hardware and possible bodies. At first South Bend only offered the larger size but soon after, a second, smaller size was added. Some of the earliest South Bend VACUUM BAITS have glass eyes and tack-painted eyes. The lure remained in catalogs until discontinued in the 1940s. Collector value range: $100-$200.

CATALOG SERIES #	BODY LENGTH	LURE WEIGHT
#1	2-3/8"	3/4 oz.
#21	2"	1/2 oz.

COLOR OR FINISH: White body, red stripes; yellow spotted with red and green; rainbow, dragon fly, frog; red spotted with yellow & black.

PIKE-ORENOS

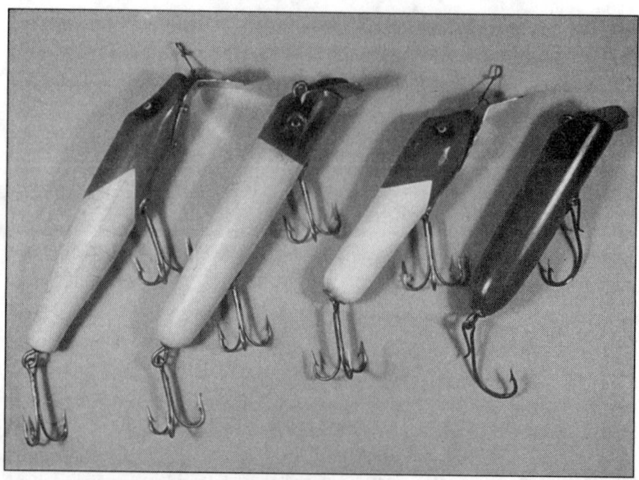

Left to right.- #957, #975, #956, #974. Shows major design changes discussed in the text.

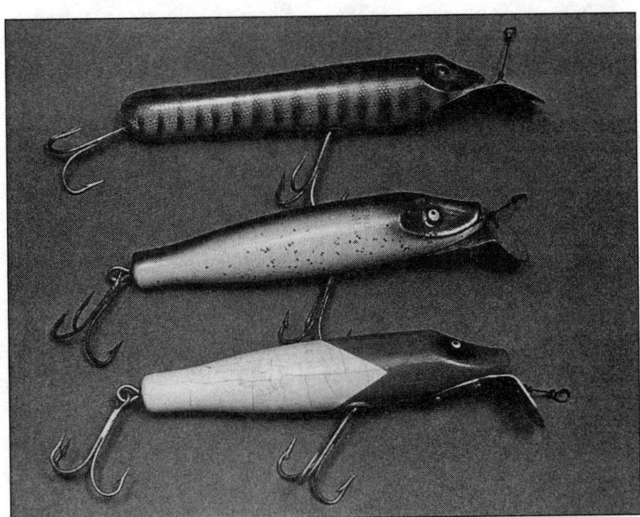
Shows three of the lip types. Top has long narrow lip with name on it. Middle has a hammered metal lip. Bottom has steep lip with no name. Shows body design changes.

An advertisement found in the February, 1951 issue of Sports Afield magazine. There was no mention of size, but it is definitely a PIKE-ORENO.

The first of the PIKE-ORENOS show up around 1922. They were nothing like the familiar two curved eye scoop model at first. It came out in two models, the regular at 4-1/4" and the MIDGET at 3". The first body style was the same as the BASS-ORENO. They fitted a metal plate into the nose scoop that extended down creating a lip (#974 and 975 in upper photo). They have no eyes. The next model has the curved eye scoops resulting in a fish-like face and nose. The body was slightly tapered but remained chunky. They continued to refine the body to the more familiar shape (c. 1932). Two more sizes were added that year, the BABY PIKE-ORENO (3-1/4") and the BIG PIKE-ORENO (5-3/8").

All three shared the same design. It had changed to a more pointed nose with eye depression scooped out of each side of the nose. The metal lip no longer covered the nose but was mounted beneath the nose and bent downward to impart the deep diving action. It has a 1" wire leader permanently fastened to the plate. One of the treble hooks has been removed and the belly position of the two remaining trebles changed.

By 1935 an even smaller one, the MIDGET PIKE-ORENO (2-1/2"), was offered and the newer arrowhead paint design was utilized on the three smallest versions. A third treble hook reappeared on the two largest sizes about 1935 also.

The PIKE-ORENOS were continuously available in one form or another throughout the years.

There is an exhaustive study by Jim Bourdon, entitled SOUTH BEND, Their Artificial Baits and Reels. It is a study of the company's catalogs from 1912 through 1953. Any collector of South Bend should have this book. It is listed with a source in the books section back in the front of the book.

CATALOG SERIES #	BODY LENGTH	LURE WEIGHT	HOOKS	COLLECTOR VALUE RANGE
*974	3"	?	2SD	$25-$40.
*975	4-1/4"	?	3T	$20-$50.
955 (Midget)	2-1/2"	1/2 oz.	2T	$20-$25.
956 (Baby)	3-1/4"	5/8 oz.	2T	$20-$40.
957 (Reg)	4-1/2"	3/4 oz.	3T, 2T	$20-$40.
958 (Big)	5-3/8"	1-1/2 oz.	3T, 2T	$15-$30.

COLOR OR FINISH: Red head, white body; red arrowhead, white body; iridescent pearl; green scale finish; yellow perch scale finish; pike scale finish; rainbow, **silver speckled white body, green stripe; scale finish with red blend, red head, aluminum color body, frog, red with black nose; white body, green and red spots.

**This was the first style Pike-Oreno.*

***This finish was not used with the 'Big Pike-Oreno'.*

JOINTED PIKE-ORENO #960

The jointed version of the PIKE-ORENO shows up first around the mid-1930s. It had undergone a design change by the 1950s and the number had changed to #2956. The old plug has a scoop taken out of the top of the head and was almost twice as long as the newer one. The newer version has two scoops in the head, one on either side making it more or less a pointed nose. The older one has two belly trebles and a trailer; new has the trailer but only one belly treble. Collector value range: $20-$40.

CATALOG SERIES #	BODY LENGTH	LURE WEIGHT
960	7"	2-1/8 oz.

COLOR OR FINISH: Red arrowhead, white body, scale finish, silver, black and red; green scale finish; red head, aluminum color body.

WHIRL-ORENO #935

New around the late 1920s this unusual surface lure had feathers mounted on a trailing treble hook. The body was 3-1/2" overall, 3" wide, and weighed in at 5/8 oz. It was available in three finishes: Red head with white body, Frog finish and Butterfly. The plug was available up to the early 1940s. Collector value range: $50-$100.

LI'L RASCAL

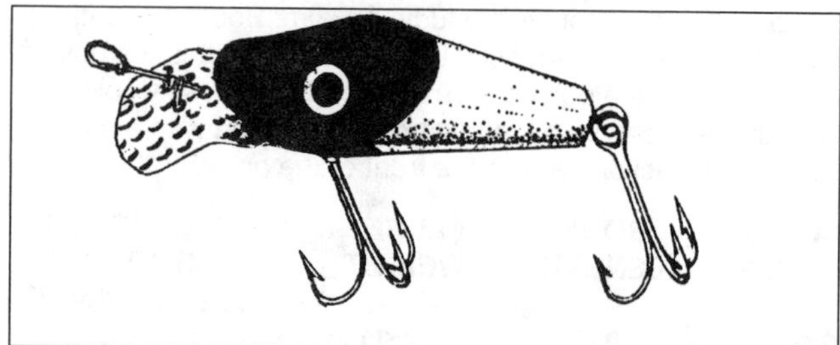

This little 2-3/4 inch light tackle lure was announced as a "NEW LURE" in the 1950 catalog going on to say: "It's Impudent Action Gets 'Em". It must have been a fairly successful lure for it stayed in the catalogs right into the late 1950s. Collector Value Range $5-$15.

CATALOG SERIES #	BODY LENGTH	LURE WEIGHT
955	2-3/4"	1/4"

COLOR OR FINISH: White body with red arrowhead, yellow perch scale finish, yellow body with silver speckles, black shad-o-wave stripe, rainbow with blue back, pike scale, white body with silver speckles and green back.

GULF-ORENO AND MIDGET GULF-ORENO

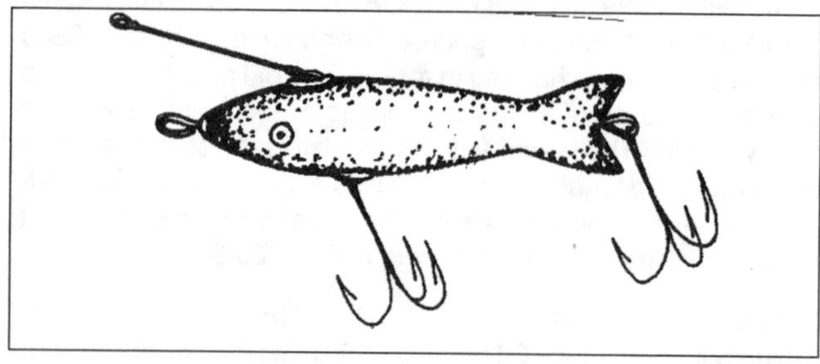

New around 1927 this plug was minnow shaped. It has a belly-mounted treble, a trailing treble, and a removable wire leader attached to the top, aft portion of the head. It had disappeared from catalogs by the early 1930s. Collector value range: $50-$100.

CATALOG SERIES #	BODY LENGTH	LURE WEIGHT
#983 (Reg)	3-1/2"	7/8 oz.
#982 (Midget)	2-3/4"	1/2 oz.

COLOR OR FINISH: White body, red around eyes, red gills; white body, gold speckled, red head, white body, silver speckled, black around eyes.

MINNOW #999

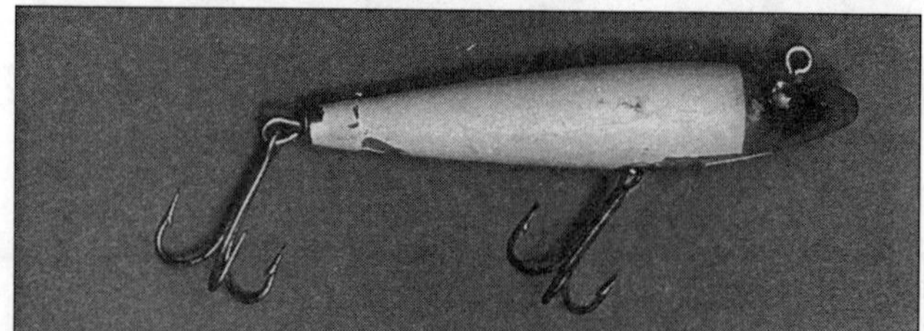

This slender plug was first found in a 1930 catalog. It has a line tie eye on top of the nose, a belly treble and a trailing treble hook. It is difficult to see in the photograph, but there is a small metal fin protruding from beneath the head. Collector value range: $40-$50.

CATALOG SERIES #	BODY LENGTH	LURE WEIGHT
#999	4" overall	5/8 oz.

COLOR OR FINISH: Red head, white body; green cracked back, scale finish; red head, black nose; yellow perch; musky finish.

PLUNK-ORENO #929

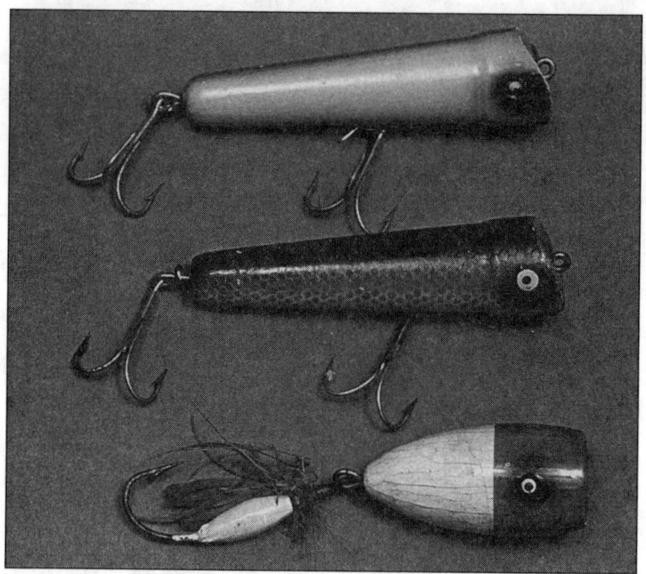

This plug shows up around the late 1920s and stayed in catalogs until 1932. It disappeared for several years to reappear as an entirely different design plug around 1939. The early plug was a long tapered body with a scooped head, one belly-mounted treble hook, a trailing treble, and glass eyes. It was 3-3/4" and weighed 5/8 oz. It came in three color finishes: Red head with white body, Green scale finish and Yellow perch scale finish. The new design was a short wood body with a tail mounted weighted single hook covered with fancy feathers. It weighs 5/8 oz. and is 4" long overall (body less than 2"). It was available in red head/white body, red head/black body, yellow perch, rainbow and frog finish. Collector value range: $30-$60.

TEASE-ORENO #940

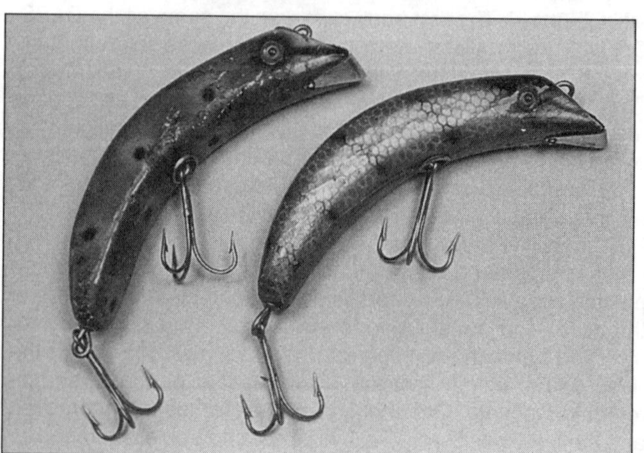

2-1/2" long, 1/2 ounce MIDGET TEASE-ORENOS.

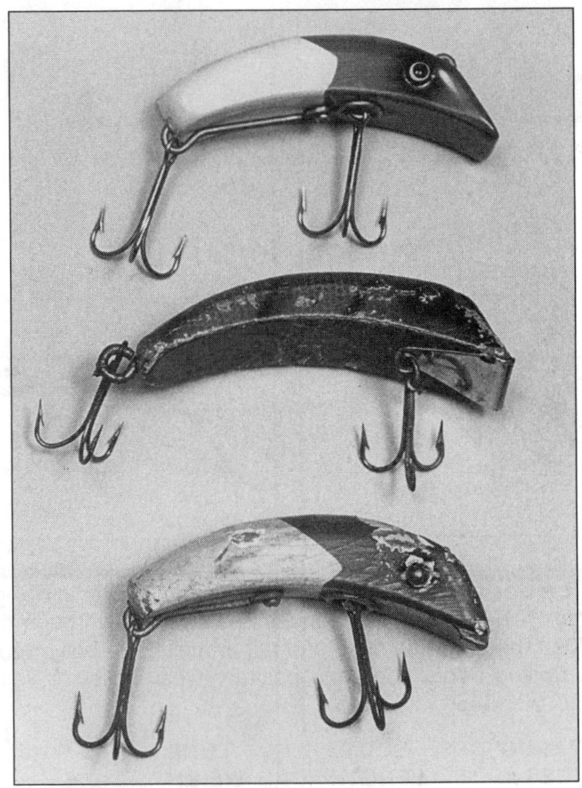

3-1/4" BABY TEASE-ORENOS.

This plug was introduced sometime prior to 1930. It has a chrome plated metal head plate, a trailing treble and a belly treble hook. It looks much like the Kautsky LAZY IKE of today. The MIDGET model didn't come along until about 1940. Collector value range: $20-$35.

CATALOG SERIES #	BODY LENGTH	LURE WEIGHT	HOOKS
936 (Midget)	2-7/8"	1/2 oz.	2T
939 (Baby)	3-1/4"	1/2 oz.	2T
940	4-1/8"	5/8 oz.	2T

COLOR OR FINISH: Red head, white body, rainbow, frog, green scale finish; yellow perch; minnow scale finish; iridescent pearl finish.

CRIPPLED MINNOW

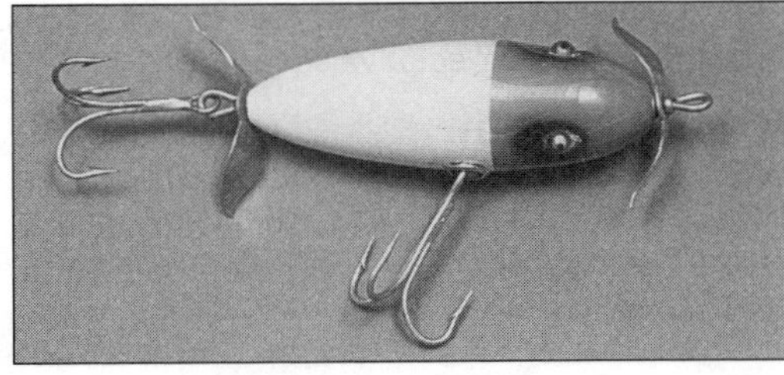

This plug first appears in a 1930 catalog but was gone by 1935. It has a belly-mounted treble* and a trailing treble hook. There are two propeller spinners, one nose and one tail mounted. Collector value range: $25-$50.

**Technically it is side mounted but the lure floats on its side therefore it is called belly-mounted.*

CATALOG SERIES #	BODY LENGTH	LURE WEIGHT
965	3-1/4"	5/8 oz.

COLOR OR FINISH: Redhead, white body, redhead, black nose; luminous; green scale finish; silver speckled, musky scale.

MOUSE-ORENO

New in the early 1930s this 2-3/4", 5/8 oz. mouse shaped plug has a flexible tail, a metal lip with wire leader attached and one belly mount treble hook. The original finishes available were: Gray mouse back with white belly, Solid black, and White body with Red blended eyes and gray stripes down the back. In 1934 a new finish was added. It was a fuzzy gray mouse-like skin finish. It replaced the first finish described above. The plug was available throughout the years after. There was a smaller fly rod version (#948) made as well. Collector value range for the regular size: $35-$50. The fly rod size: $40-$60.

PLUG-ORENO #959

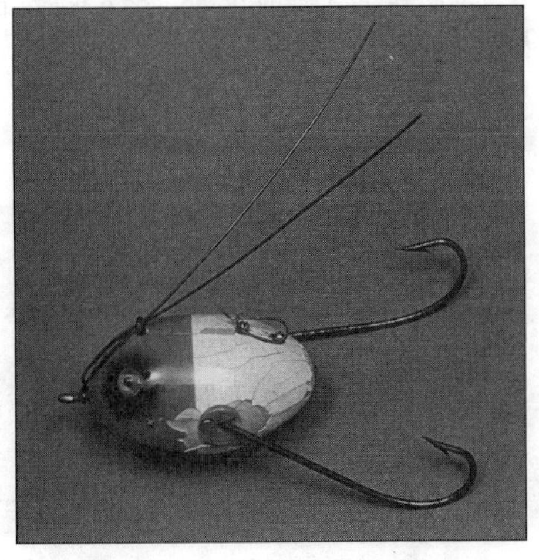

This is a weedless surface plug that was new in the 1930 catalog. It has two belly-mounted single hooks, a pork rind attachment on top of the body, and two wire weed guards. It was made into the 1940s. Collector value range: $100-$200.

CATALOG SERIES #	BODY LENGTH	LURE WEIGHT
#959	2"	5/8 oz.

COLOR OR FINISH: Red head, white body, frog, yellow body, red and green decorations.

MIN-ORENO

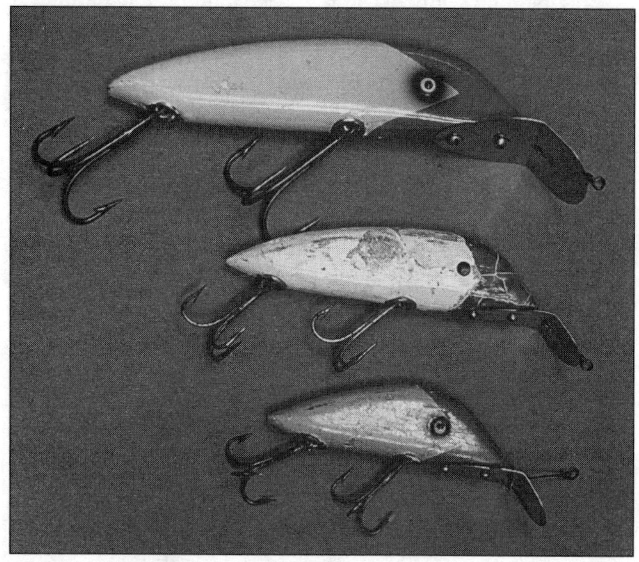

Three sizes of the Min-Oreno. Center lure has been poorly repainted.

A new lure for 1932 the MIN-ORENO was three years in designing according to the catalog. It is a departure from the usual shapes in the South Bend line. The lure was made in three different sizes, each available in six different finishes. It has an under-tail mounted treble, belly treble, painted eyes and a metal diving lip under the nose. It was made throughout the 1930s. Collector value range: $20-$30.

CATALOG SERIES #	BODY LENGTH	LURE WEIGHT
926	3"	3-1/2 oz.
927	4"	4-1/2 oz.
928	5-5/8"	6 oz.

COLOR OR FINISH: Red arrowhead, white body, red arrowhead, yellow body, yellow perch, scale finish; pike, scale finish; green scale finish; scale finish with red blend.

LUNGE-ORENO
MIDGET LUNGE-ORENO

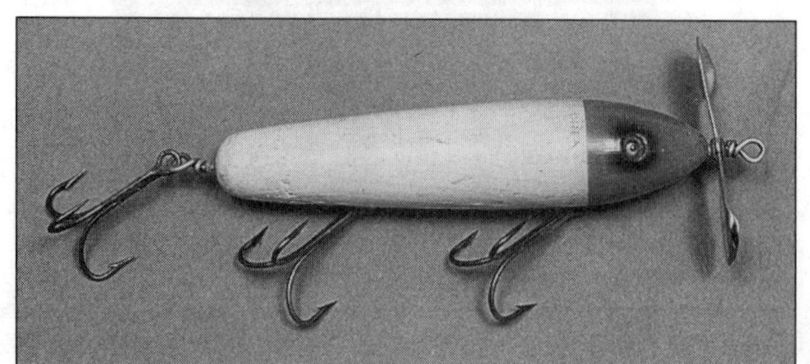

This large plug was new around 1930. The first version of it had two belly-mounted trebles and a trailing treble. There were two extra-large aluminum propellers, one at tail and nose. By 1932 the tail propeller had been eliminated for some reason. It remained this way all the way into the 1940s. The axis for the propeller was heavy wire passing all the way through the length of the body with the line tie incorporated at the front and the trailing treble at the back making a direct connection.

CATALOG SERIES #	BODY LENGTH	LURE WEIGHT	COLLECTOR VALUE RANGE
966	6"	2-1/2 oz.	$50-$150.
965 (Midget)	3-3/4"	1-1/8 oz.	$100-$200.

COLOR OR FINISH: Red head, white body, pike scale finish; yellow body, red and brown decorations; scale finish with red blend.

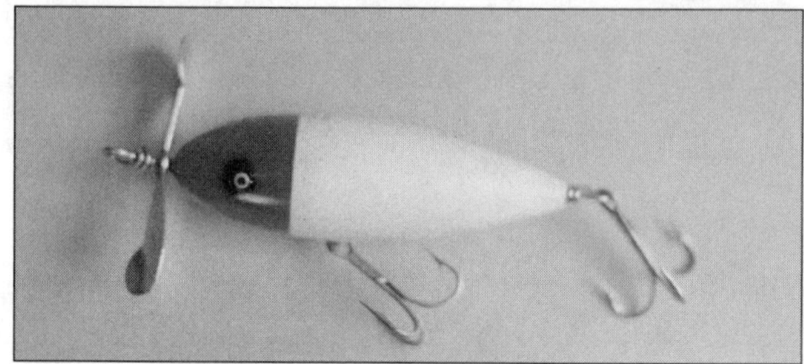

A 3-3/4" MIDGET LUNGE-ORENO. Photo courtesy Jim Muma.

SLIM-ORENO #912

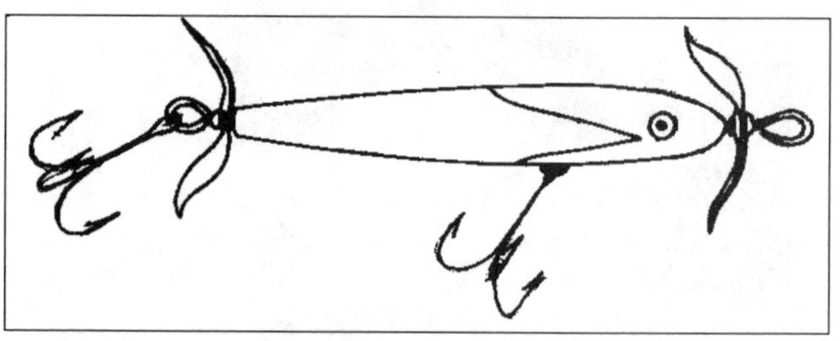

This was a new plug for 1932 that is very similar in design to the PANATELLA. It continues to be offered through the 1930s. The plug has nose and tail propellers, a belly treble and trailing treble hook and painted eyes. Collector value range: $30-$45.

CATALOG SERIES #	BODY LENGTH	LURE WEIGHT
912	3-3/4"	1/2 oz.

COLOR OR FINISH: Red arrowhead, white body; green cracked back, white belly, rainbow, yellow perch, scale finish; scale finish with red blend, green scale finish.

TRUCK-ORENO #936

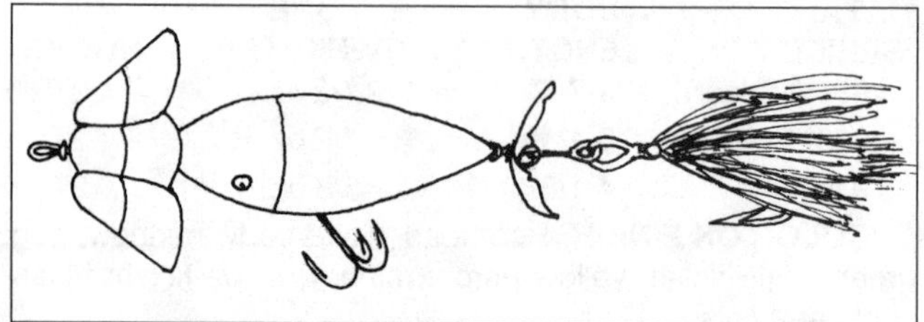

A new plug for 1938 and produced until sometime in the 1940s. This lure has an unusual head shaped so that it would turn like a propeller on retrieve. Please see WHIRL-ORENO for a picture of the head. The body is a SURF-ORENO with one belly treble and a small trailing spinner forward of a trailing feathered treble hook. Collector value range: $300-$450.

CATALOG SERIES #	BODY LENGTH	LURE WEIGHT
#936	9" overall	5 oz.

COLOR OR FINISH: Red head, white body, red and white feathers; frog, red and white feathers; yellow with black stripe, black and red dots, red and white feathers.

ENTICE-ORENO #991

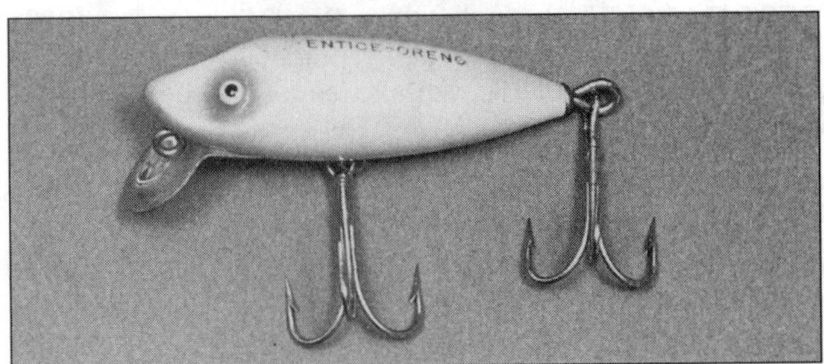

A new plug for 1938, it continued in production into the early 1940s. Apparently the FISH-OBITE, #1991 (Tenite body) was introduced in 1939 to replace the ENTICE-ORENO, #991 although the latter was still available at that time. The ENTICE-ORENO had one belly mount treble and a trailing treble hook. It has a metal lip and line tie under the nose. Collector value range: $15-$25.

CATALOG SERIES #	BODY LENGTH	LURE WEIGHT
#991	2-5/8"	1/2 oz.

COLOR OR FINISH: Red arrowhead, white body, white arrowhead, black body; black arrowhead, white body; silver speckle, white body, green back stripe; yellow perch scale; dace scale; pike scale; white body, red and green decorations; pearl finish; rainbow, blue back, minnow scale finish; red body, black shaded eyes.

TEX-ORENO

Sinker, #995
Floater, #996

Appearing in the late 1930s this plug was available with or without a weighted head. It has one belly treble and a trailing treble hook. Originally developed for trout fishing in the Houston/Corpus Christi Gulf waters. Collector value range: $40-$80.

CATALOG SERIES #	BODY LENGTH	LURE WEIGHT
#995 (Sinker)	2-3/4"	5/8 oz.
#996 (Floater)	2-3/4"	1/2 oz.

COLOR OR FINISH: Red arrowhead, white body, white arrowhead, yellow body, rainbow, blue back; pearl finish; silver speckled, minnow scale finish; dace scale.

TWO-ORENO, #975
BABY TWO-ORENO, #974

New in the mid- to late 1930s this unique plug came in two sizes. Each has two belly trebles, four eyes (2 each end), two line ties and a metal lip. The line could be tied to either end. It had been eliminated from the line by the 1940s. Collector value range: $30-$40.

CATALOG SERIES #	BODY LENGTH	LURE WEIGHT
975	3-3/4"	3/4 oz.
974	3"	1/2 oz.

COLOR OR FINISH: Red arrowhead, white body, rainbow with blue back; frog; yellow perch scale; pearl, green scale finish.

TWO-OBITE
BASS-OBITE

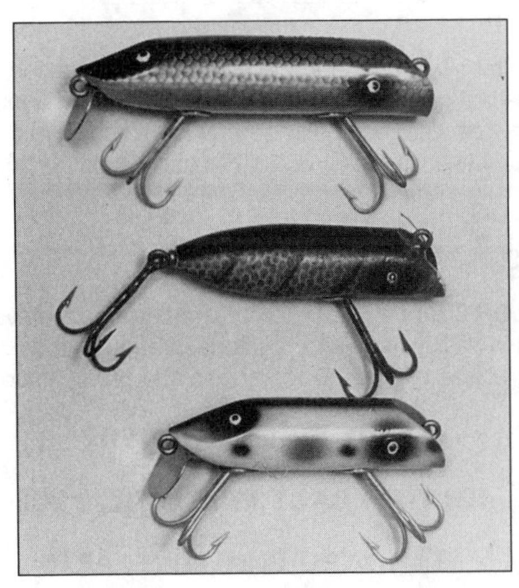

These are the same plugs as the TWO-ORENO and BASS-ORENO except that they are made of "Tenite". These came out about 1938 and the "Tenite" material was used more and more for these and other plugs as the years passed by. Collector value range: $20-$40.

DARTING BAIT

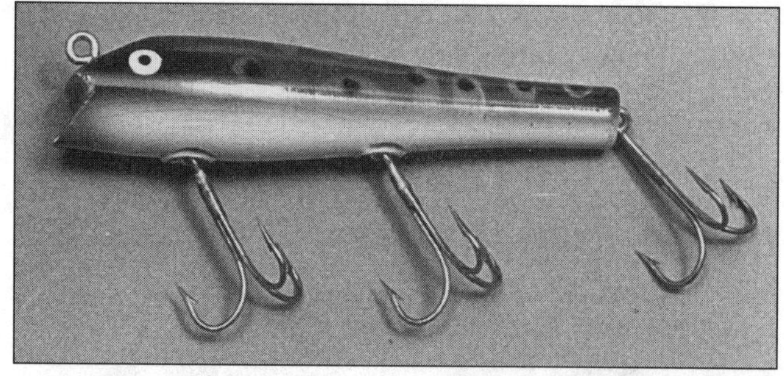

This part of series of low cost plugs marketed by South Bend in the 1930s and 1940s. It was the BEST-O-LUCK series. The lure has a "V" shaped mouth notch, two belly trebles and one trailing treble hook. Collector value range: $10-$20.

CATALOG SERIES #	BODY LENGTH	LURE WEIGHT
922	4"	1/2 oz.

COLOR OR FINISH: Splotch frog finish; redhead, white body, silver speckled white body, green back stripe; pike scale; yellow perch scale finish; white head, black body.

GOPLUNK

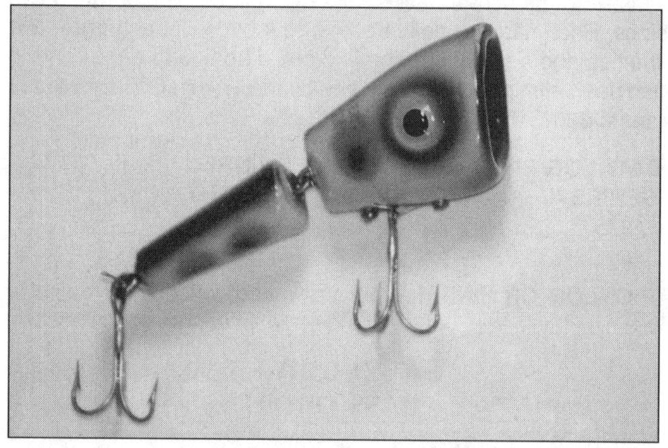

The first catalog I found the GOPLUNK in was the 1951 edition. The last catalog that listed it was in 1954. It is a jointed popper-type that was recommended for night fishing in the listings. Collector value range: $10-$20. Photo courtesy Ken Bernoteit.

CATALOG SERIES #	BODY LENGTH	LURE WEIGHT
2929	3"	3/8 oz.

COLOR OR FINISH: Black with red around the eyes; green frog finish with yellow and black decorations; white body with red arrowhead, yellow body with red and brown decorations.

BABY PIKE LURE, #907

JOINTED BABY PIKE LURE, #908

STANDARD PIKE LURE, #930

JOINTED STANDARD PIKE LURE, #931

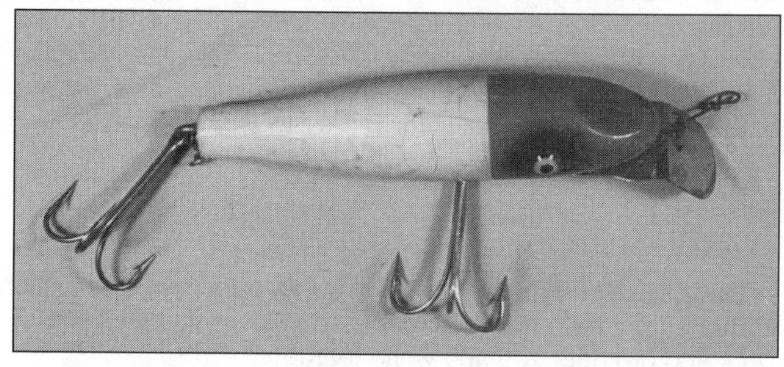

These four baits are part of the low cost series called "BEST-O-LUCK" lures marketed by South Bend in the 1930s and 1940s. All have a trailing treble, one belly-mounted treble, a slope nose, and metal lip with wire leader attached. Collector value range: $15-$20.

CATALOG SERIES #	BODY LENGTH	LURE WEIGHT
#907	3-1/4"	1/2 oz.
#908	3-1/2"	1/2 oz.
#930	4-3/8"	5/8 oz.
#931	4-1/2"	5/8 oz.

COLOR OR FINISH: Red head, white body; pike finish; pike scale finish; green striped, silver speckled body, green back stripe; yellow perch, scale finish; rainbow,, green scale finish.

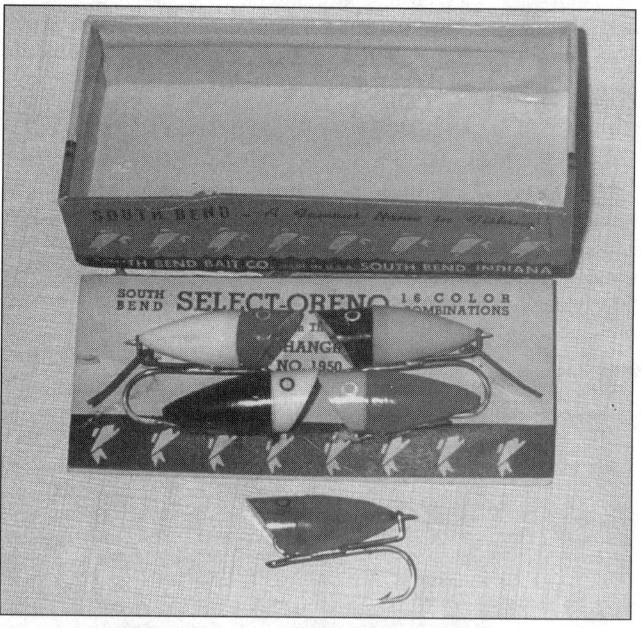

SELECT-ORENO. Complete set in the original box. The lure outside is the combination of the red head and body. Photo courtesy Jim Muma.

SELECT-ORENO #1950

This is an interesting 1-1/4" plastic fly rod lure. It came in the four pieces you see in the box. Each of the different heads and bodies came apart and were interchangeable. With that feature you could make 16 different combinations. I found a South Bend advertisement for it in a 1941 edition of *Hunting and Fishing* magazine. It said you could fill the body cavity with water to make it a sinker if you wished. Collector value range: $10-$15. each, Intact set with the box: No trade data found.

STANDARD WOBBLER, #943
BABY WOBBLER, #942

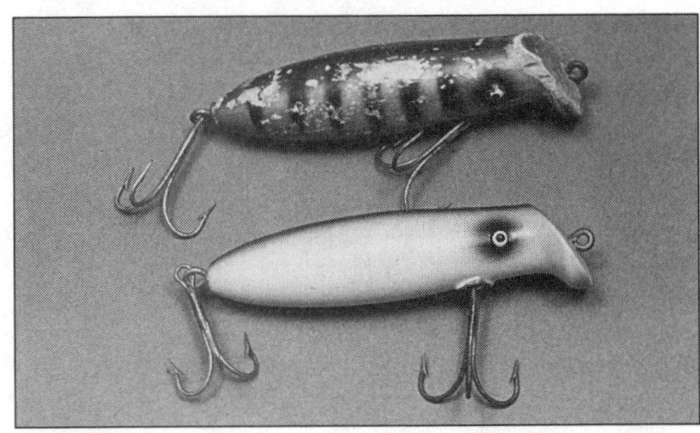

These plugs are part of the South Bend low cost series called BEST-O-LUCK and marketed through the 1930s and 1940s. They are the same design, the Baby Wobbler having one trailing treble and one belly treble hook and the larger having a second belly treble. Collector value range: $15-$20.

CATALOG SERIES #	BODY LENGTH	LURE WEIGHT
942	2-3/4"	1/2 oz.
943	3-3/4"	5/8 oz.

COLOR OR FINISH: Red head, white body; green striped,, pike finish; green scale finish; pike scale finish; yellow perch scale finish.

WEIGHTED WOBBLER, #941

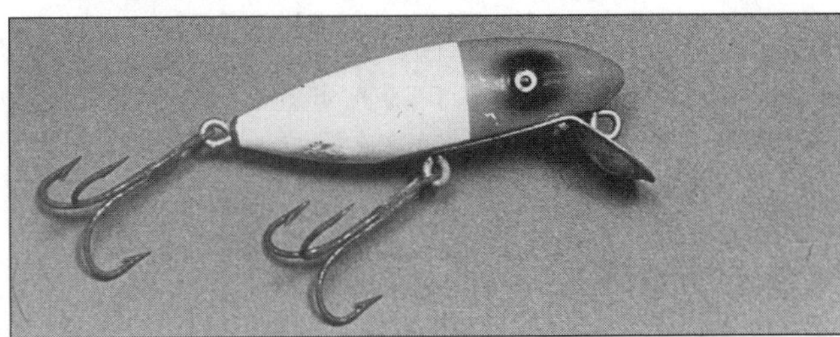

This lure is part of the "BEST-O-LUCK" series of low cost plugs marketed by South Bend in the 1930s and 1940s. It has a metal lip belly-mounted treble, and trailing treble hook. Collector value range: $15-$20.

CATALOG SERIES #	BODY LENGTH	LURE WEIGHT
941	2-5/8"	1/2 oz.

COLOR OR FINISH: Red head, white body; green striped, iridescent pearl finish; white silver speckled, greenback stripe; rainbow, blue back; red dace scale finish; pike scale finish; yellow perch scale finish.

BABY WOUNDED MINNOW, #914

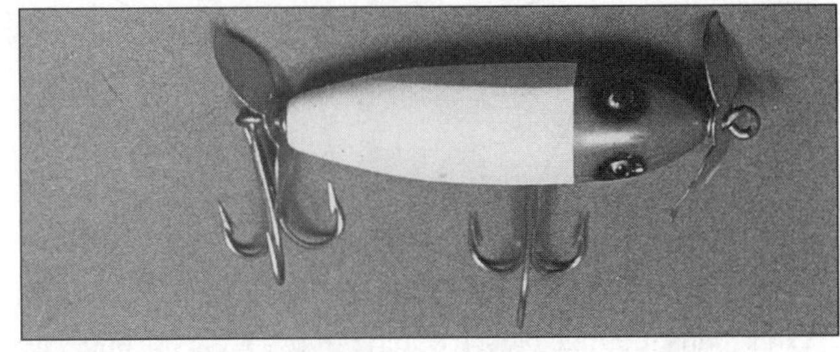

Note the flat sides on this BABY WOUNDED MINNOW.

This plug is part of a low cost line lures marketed by South Bend in the 1930s and 1940s called the "BEST-O-LUCK" series. It has a nose and tail propeller, a trailing treble hook, and belly-mounted treble hook. Collector value range: $15-$20.

CATALOG SERIES #	BODY LENGTH	LURE WEIGHT
914	2-3/4"	1/2 oz.

COLOR OR FINISH: Red head, white body, silver speckled body, red and brown stripes; pike finish; yellow perch, scale finish.

SURFACE LURE, #916

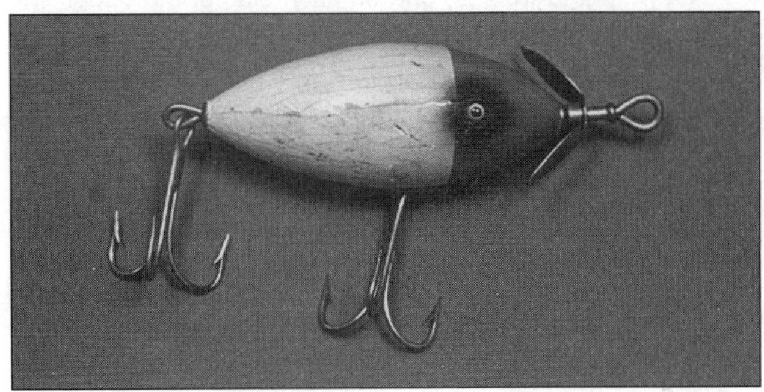

This is one of South Bend low cost line of lures marketed in the 1930s and 1940s. The lure was called "Best-O-Luck". This was an elongated egg shape plug with a propeller at the nose, a belly treble and trailing treble hook. Collector value range: $20-$25.

CATALOG SERIES #	BODY LENGTH	LURE WEIGHT
916	2-3/4"	5/8 oz.

COLOR OR FINISH: Red head, white body, frog finish.

SURFACE LURE, #950

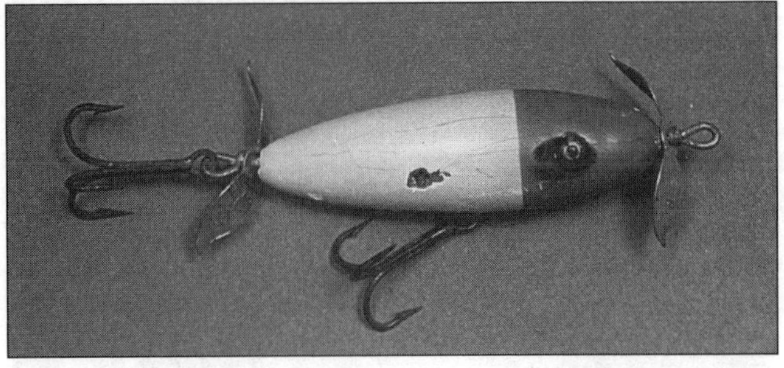

One of the "Best-O-Luck" bait series. This was a low cost line of lures marketed by South Bend in 1930s and 1940s. This plug has a front propeller, belly treble, and a trailing treble hook. Collector value range: $20-$25.

CATALOG SERIES #	BODY LENGTH	LURE WEIGHT
950	3-1/4"	1/2 oz.

COLOR OR FINISH: Redhead, white body, Greenback blending to white belly; Silver body, red throat, Yellow body, red back stripe.

WEIGHTED UNDERWATER LURE

#910 AND #918

Part of the South Bend low cost lure series called "Best-O-Luck" and marketed through the 1930s and 1940s. The #910

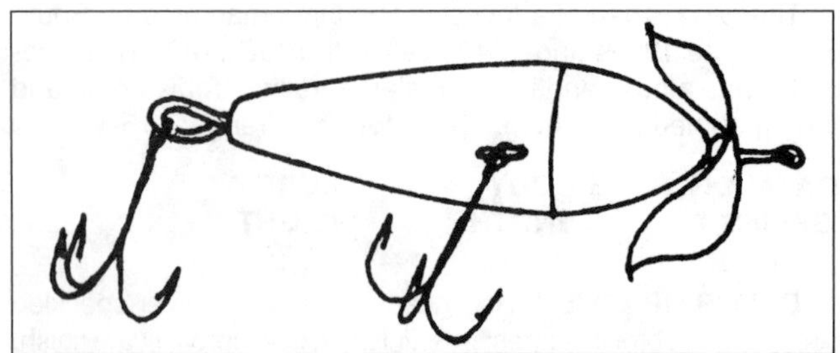

has one nose propeller spinner, one trailing treble hook and two side-mounted trebles, one on each side of the body. The #918 is the same except has one belly treble in place of the two side-mounted ones. Collector value range: $15-$25.

CATALOG SERIES #	BODY LENGTH	LURE WEIGHT
910	3"	5/8 oz.

COLOR OR FINISH: Red head, white body, greenback, white belly, yellow body, red back stripe; silver body, red throat

CATALOG SERIES #	BODY LENGTH	LURE WEIGHT
918	3"	5/8 oz.

COLOR OR FINISH: Red head, white body, rainbow with blue back; pike finish.

WOUNDED MINNOW, #920

BABY WOUNDED MINNOW, #914

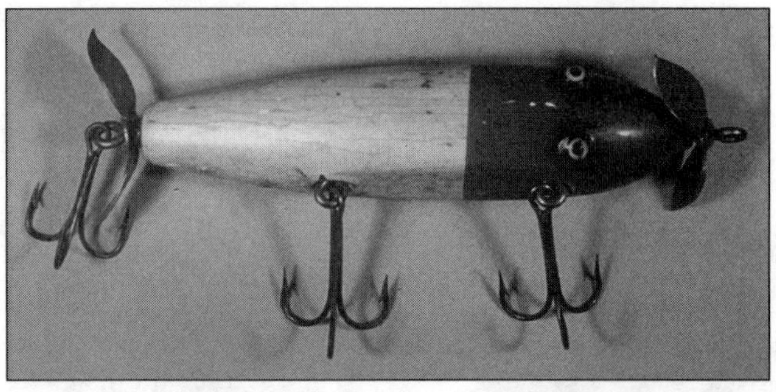

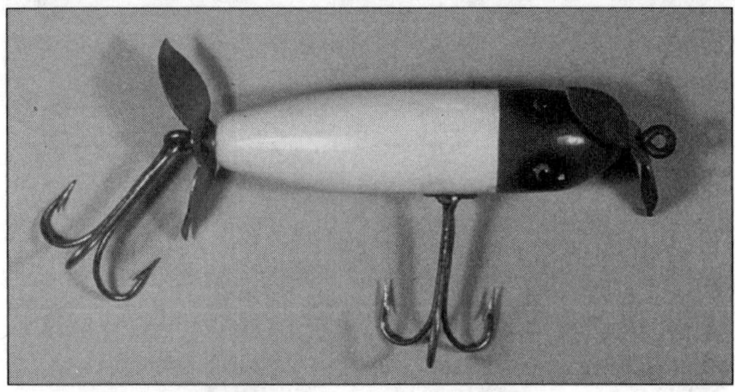

One of the "Best-O-Luck" series. This was a low cost line of lures marketed by South Bend in the 1930s and 1940s. It has a nose and tail propeller, two belly-mounted trebles, and a trailing treble hook. The smaller model has only one treble on the belly. Collector value range:$15-$25.

CATALOG SERIES #	BODY LENGTH	LURE WEIGHT
914	2-3/4"	1/2 oz.
920	3-5/8"	3/4 oz.

COLOR OR FINISH: Red head, white body; silver speckled body, red and brown stripes; pike finish; yellow perch, scale finish.

PANATELLA WOBBLER, #921

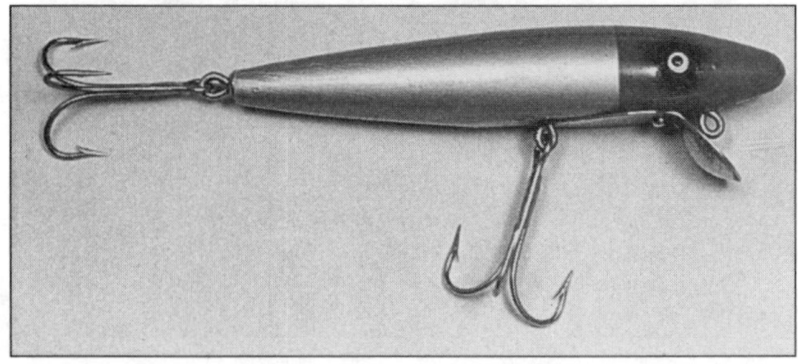

This plug is part Of the low cost South Bend series of lures called "Best-O-Luck" marketed in the 1930s and 1940s. It has a metal lip belly-mounted treble, and trailing treble hook. Collector value range: $15-$20.

CATALOG SERIES #	BODY LENGTH	LURE WEIGHT
921	4"	5/8 oz.

COLOR OR FINISH: red head, white body, red head, aluminum color body, green striped.

TRIX-ORENO

Fly Rod Sizes, #593, #594

Bait Casting Sizes, #595, #596

Salt Water Sizes, #597, #598, #599

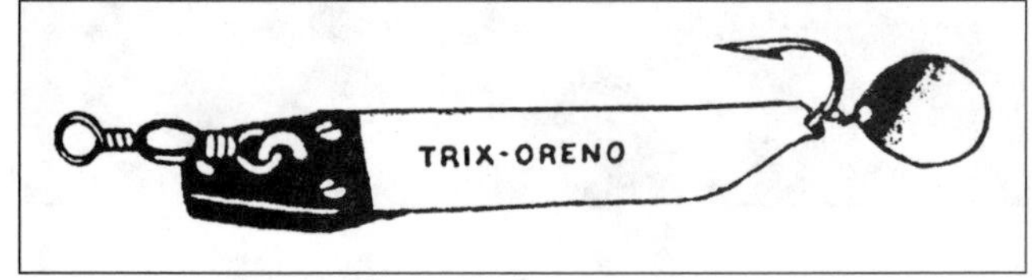

First found in the 1931 catalog they lasted throughout the years. Even though their first appearance in catalogs was in 1931, they were around before that. That particular catalog states that the TRIX-ORENO was "Endorsed by 100,000 Anglers the First Year!" Careful reading of the entry leads one to believe that the fly rod sizes were released some time before and the two bait casting sizes were new in 1931. Then along came three saltwater sizes in 1932. Collector Value Range: $5-$15.

CATALOG SERIES #	BODY LENGTH	LURE WEIGHT
593	1-1/8"	?
594	1-5/8"	?
595	2-1/4"	5/8 oz.
596	3-1/4"	7/8 oz.
597	4-3/8"	2 oz.
598	5"	2-3/4 oz.
599	5-5/8"	4 oz.

FIN-DINGO

This funny rounded plastic South Bend lure did not originate with them. The lure was regularly advertised by the Ropher

Tackle Company of West Los Angeles, California in 1950. They offered it in sinking and floating models in nine different colors. It first shows up as a South Bend product in 1953 in a sinker only. It was gone from the catalog by 1955. Another short run for one of their lures. Details of how they came to obtain the rights to the lure are presently unknown. Collector Value Range for Ropher Fin-Dingo: $30-$40, South Bend Fin-Dingo: $10-$20.

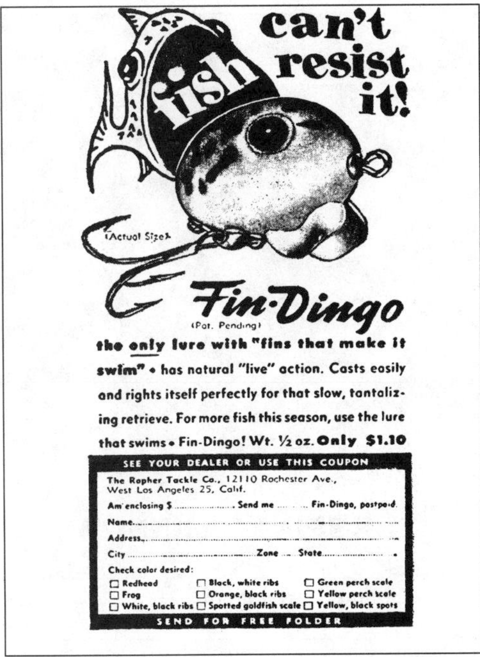

CATALOG SERIES #	BODY LENGTH	LURE WEIGHT
1965	1-5/8"	1/2 oz.

COLOR OR FINISH (Ropher Tackle): Red head, frog, white with black ribs, black with white ribs, orange with black ribs, spotted goldfish scale, green perch scale, yellow perch scale, yellow with black spots.

COLOR OR FINISH (South Bend): Frog, green perch scale, yellow with black spots, yellow perch scale, saturn green, white body with red arrowhead.

SUPER SNOOPER

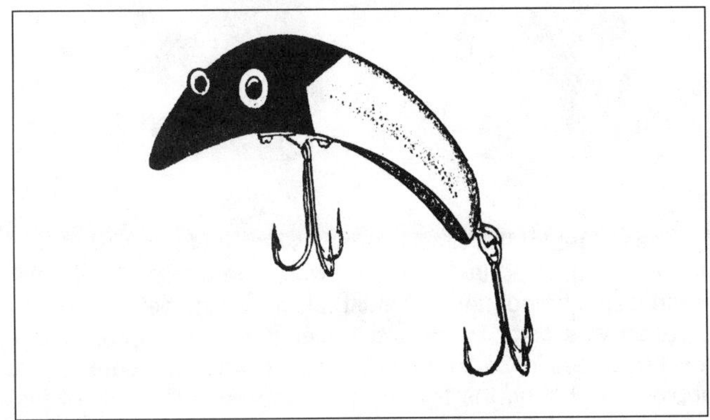

A new lure in the 1950 catalog described as "Molded of Plastic." It is a banana shaped bait. It is a floater at rest that travels a few inches below the surface upon retrieve. It was no longer available in the 1953 edition of the catalog. Collector Value Range: $5-$15.

CATALOG SERIES #	BODY LENGTH	LURE WEIGHT
1960	2-7/8"	1/2 oz.

COLOR OR FINISH: White body with red arrowhead, yellow perch, yellow body with red and brown decorations, white body with green back and silver speckles, green frog, orange body with red and black decorations.

SUN SPOT SPOONS

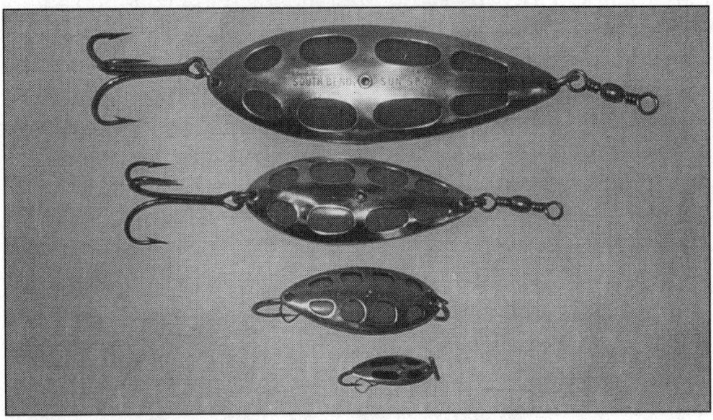

These were first listed in a 1941 catalog. There were 10 sizes ranging from a 1-3/16" fly rod size to a large 5". Sizes are overall with fixed hooks and spoon only with trailing hooks. The spoons are brass made available in a gold or chrome finish. The transparent plastic inner spoon is made in six different colors. They are red, yellow, green, orange, blue or white. Apparently the size influences the value. The fly rod size, as in the case of most, are the highest at $50-$75. With the others it's lowest with the smaller ones and highest with the larger ones. The range is $5 to $25. Photo Courtesy Jim Muma.

PEACH-ORENO

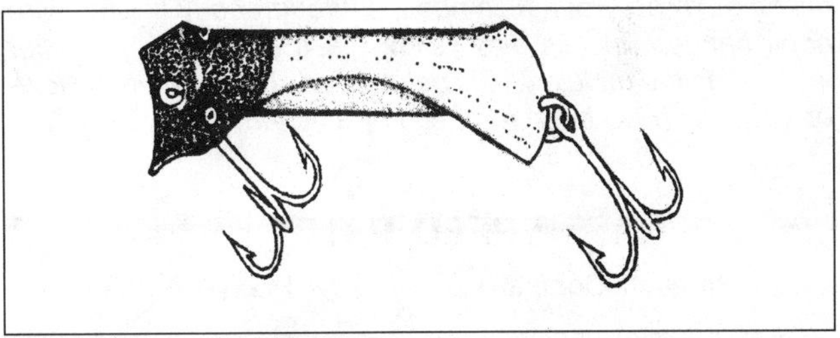

A hollow metal lure that was new in the 1941 catalog. It was made in seven styles. It must not have been a very good seller. It was soon gone from the catalogs. Collector value range: $5-$15.

CATALOG SERIES #	BODY LENGTH	LURE WEIGHT
501	2-1/2"	1/2 oz.
502	3-1/4"	3/4 oz.
503	4-1/8"	1-1/8 oz.
5030	4-7/8"	1-1/8 oz.
	(w/ No. 7/0 extra heavy single hook)	
504	4-7/8"	2 oz.
505	4-7/8"	2 oz.
	(w/ No. 7/0 extra heavy treble hook)	
5050	4-7/8"	2 oz.
	(w/ extra heavy single hook)	

COLOR OR FINISH: Chrome, gold finish, yellow perch scale finish, frog splotch, white body with red arrow head, silver herring scale finish, green scale finish, rainbow color with blue back.

SOUTH COAST MINNOW

H.C. Royer — Los Angeles, California

The SOUTH COAST MINNOW was first offered in advertising around 1910-11 with one of the advertisements commenting on their "..remarkable reception .. the last three years." A search turned up no patent, but the ads identified the inventor and source as a Dr. H. C. Royer of Terminal Island, Los Angeles, California. The ads disappeared after a couple of years. About then, roughly 1913, the Heddon Company began offering a very similar lure in their catalogs. They were continually offered, undergoing small modifications, until they disappeared from the line about 1927. The physical similarity of the Royer lure and the name leads to reasonable speculation that Heddon somehow obtained the rights to the lure around 1912-13, and renamed it the COAST MINNOW. Collector value range: $50-$75.

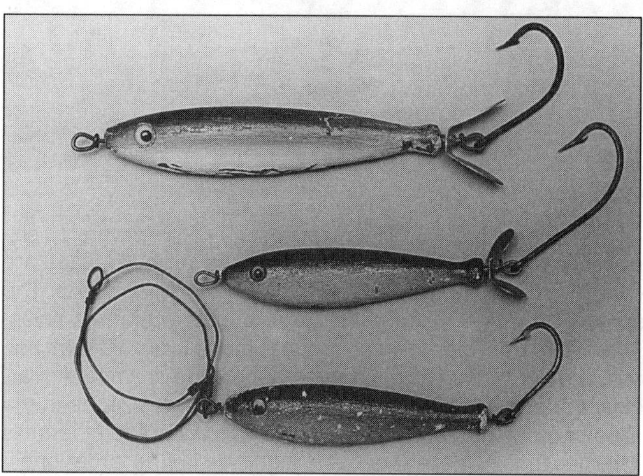

SOUTH COAST MINNOWS by H. C. Royer. The top lure is 4" long, has four internal belly weights. The lower two measure 3-1/8" and have three internal belly weights. Note the shaped tail on all three. Each also has the through-body twisted wire hook hanger/ line tie and yellow glass eyes. The propeller spinner on the middle lure is painted red. The prop on the lower lure may have been removed by a fisherman.

SPEED BAIT

Walton Products Company — Rochester, New York

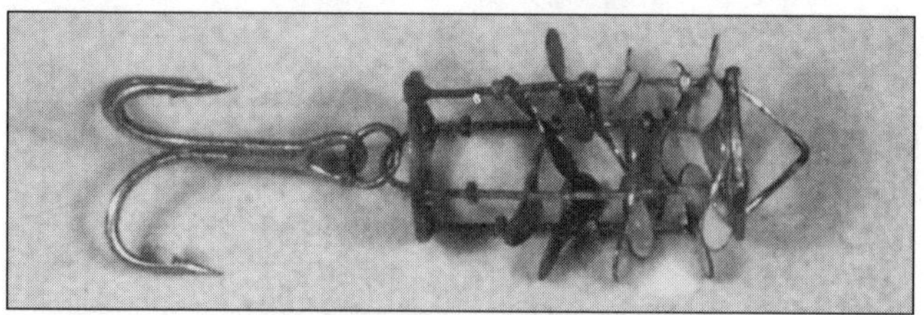

A crazy metal assemblage of 16 tiny propeller spinners all "..flashing, whirling and humming." according to a 1931 advertisement. They were made in three sizes: Trout at 1-1/4", Bass size at 2" and Musky at 4". They are all hard to find with the largest being the most difficult. The latter are valued at $200-$300. The two smaller sizes: $100-$150. Photo courtesy Jim Muma.

SPIDER LURE

The Turner Company — Ed and Delbert Turner, Hale, Missouri

A real contraption, this lure was developed by the Turners, father and son hardware store owners, around 1950. Delbert was the idea man and father Ed made them in a small machine shop at the store. Dean Murphy in his book, *Fishing Tackle Made in Missouri,* says that only about 150 were made and it didn't sell well. In fact, he says, son Delbert destroyed about 40-50 just before he retired. Simple math says there are only about 100 of these lures around at the most. They are 3-1/2" in diameter overall. Collector value range: $50-$75.

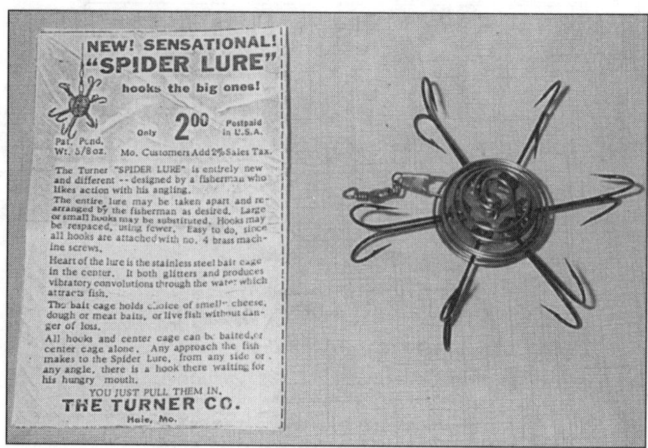

THE SPINNO MINNOW

Pecos River Tackle Company — Carlsbad, New Mexico
Uniline Manufacturing Corporation — Dallas, Texas

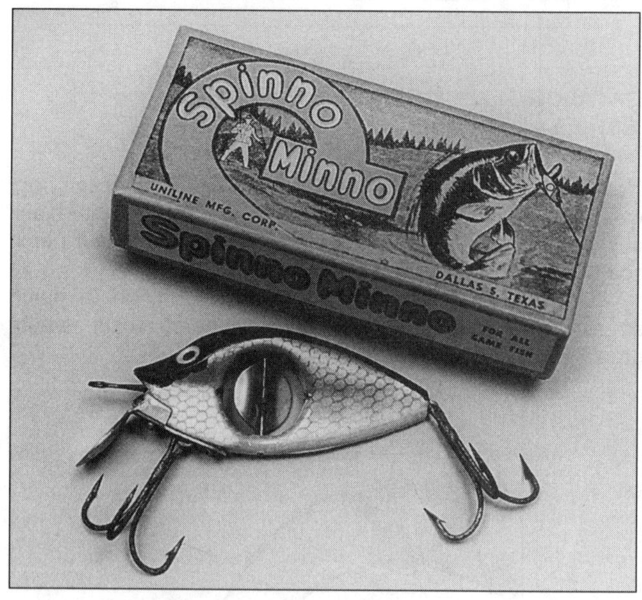

The patent for this plastic lure was applied for in early 1944 and it was granted in 1945, so it would be reasonable to assume it was being made at least a few months before the application was filed. Harry and Violet Van Buren were in the retail business in Carlsbad, New Mexico when the patent was applied for. Harry, the fisherman, is the likely inventor of the lure, but inexplicably, the patent is in his wife's name. The Pecos River Tackle Company in Carlsbad is the name found on some boxes. At some later time the company name and address on the box changed to "UNILINE MFG. CORP. DALLAS 5, TEXAS". This was a company owned by the Van Burens. The company ceased operation about 1950.

There are at least 20 different colors or finishes to be found.

They are listed following:

- Dark green
- White body with red head
- Gray rib
- Shiner
- Black body with white head
- Light green scale
- Blue bugger white rib
- Goldfish scale
- Perch
- Frog
- Solid black
- Rainbow
- Yellow rib

TRANSLUCENT "PASTEL SHADES OVER PEARL" INTRODUCED IN 1949

- Red
- Green
- Black
- Black
- Yellow
- Blue zebra

There is a variation with regard to the number of holes in the spinner disc. One has two and the other has three. Which came first is not known to me. There has been a glass-eyed wooden version found. This may be a unique early patent model. Collector value range: $20-$30.

SPLASH KING

Kala Lures Detroit, Michigan

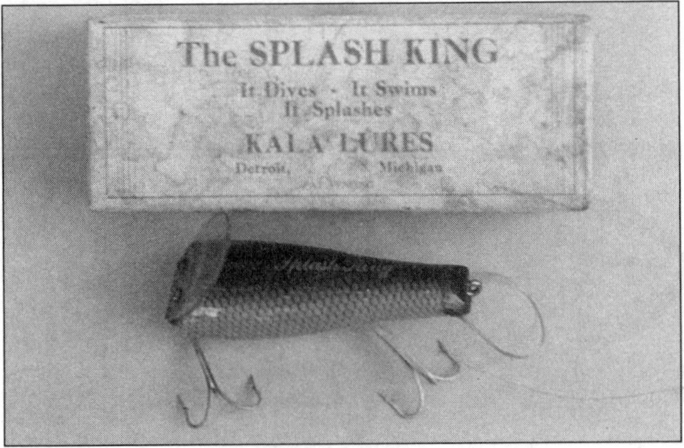

This is a quality lure. The body is wood with an excellent paint finish. It is unique with a clear plastic face plate and tail plain. The advertising describes them as "..leaving only the body of the lure visible in the water. It is identified with its name in script letters on the back and measures 3". This one has a yellow scale finish with black back. Other colors are not known. The lures was made in the 1940s and possible the early 1950s. Collector value range: $25-$50. Photo courtesy Jim Muma.

SPOONPLUG

Buck's Baits Hickory, North Carolina

All we have are the new in the box lures and what it says on

the light blue box. They are metal in two sizes: 3-3/4" and 4-1/2". There are at least the color patterns found: Green with yellow scale, Red with black dots and White with red head. There were two numbers found on the boxes "700 SERIES and "800 SERIES" corresponding to the two sizes of the lures. Collector value range: No trade data found.

SPRINGFIELD NOVELTY MANUFACTURING CO.

Springfield, Missouri THE "REEL" LURE

The Springfield Novelty Manufacturing Company was founded in 1932 by Stanley F. Myers and Adolph A. Kunz. They began operation in Myers' garage. With the help of Kunz's son and Myers' two sons they produced an astounding 8,000 lures in the first four months of operation. Even more amazing is that they worked only part-time, both hanging onto their regular jobs.

The photo accompanying shows seven different paint patterns on "REEL" lures. The other three are all what they called the "1/2 CHARMER". If you are familiar with the Charmer Minnow Company lures you may be struck by the similarity. Although it isn't likely that they would intentionally infringe on Charmer's patent, there is more to the story than coincidence. When Myers and Kunz first met, Kunz was an independent machinist in Springfield. However, prior to that he worked for the Charmer Minnow Company, also of Springfield, and was bound to have been influenced by his association with them. In any case Charmer apparently objected and Springfield Novelty suspended production of them. It is thought that only 40 or 50 1/2 CHARMERS were ever made, so to find one would be a real event.

Early in production Springfield Novelty used the rear sections of raw CHARMER MINNOW bodies (apparently Kunz had a bunch left over from his time at Charmer) for part of their lure, but they soon began turning their own on a lathe. This may account for the fact that the earliest REEL LURE bodies are 1/8" slimmer than those produced later. The lure body was 2" in length. They also started to make a musky size at 3-1/8", but for some unknown reason failed to place them into full-scale production and made only about a dozen examples. These, obviously, are very rare critters.

The lures made by Springfield Novelty were a very high quality product. They used select cedar, brass bushings, German silver hardware and imported hooks. Much work went into the fashioning and painting using multiple coats of enamel paint, each coat baked before the next. They did not advertise widely depending rather, on word-of-mouth. They were marketed only in Northeastern Missouri, east Oklahoma and east Texas so to find one outside that area would be unusual. There isn't sufficient trade data to establish a realistic collector value for either the MUSKY REEL LURE or the 1/2 CHARMER, but the collector value range for the 2" REEL Lure is: $75-$125.

Oct. 24, 1933. S. F. MYERS ET AL 1,931,932

ARTIFICIAL BAIT

Filed Oct. 29, 1932

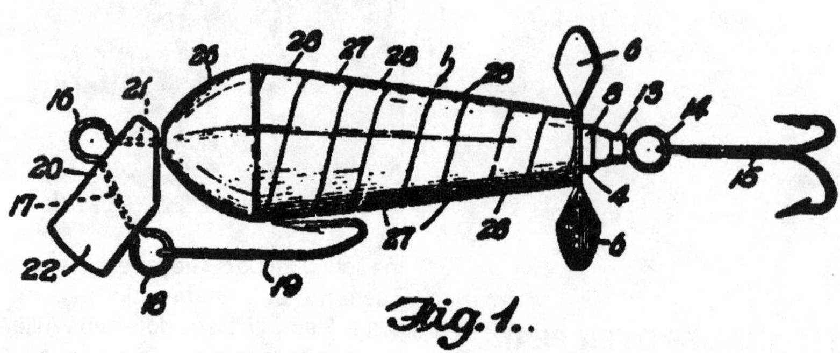

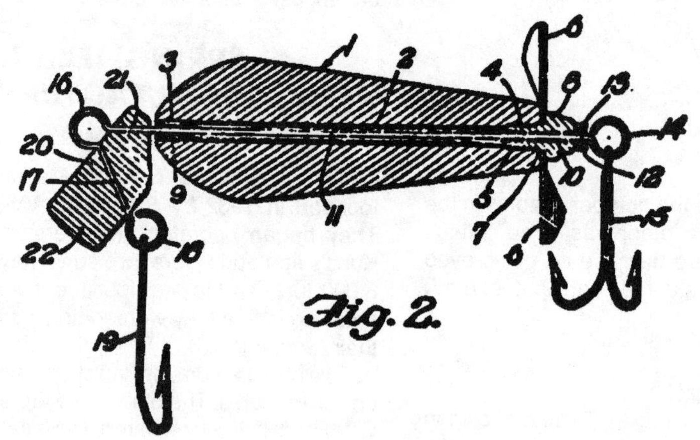

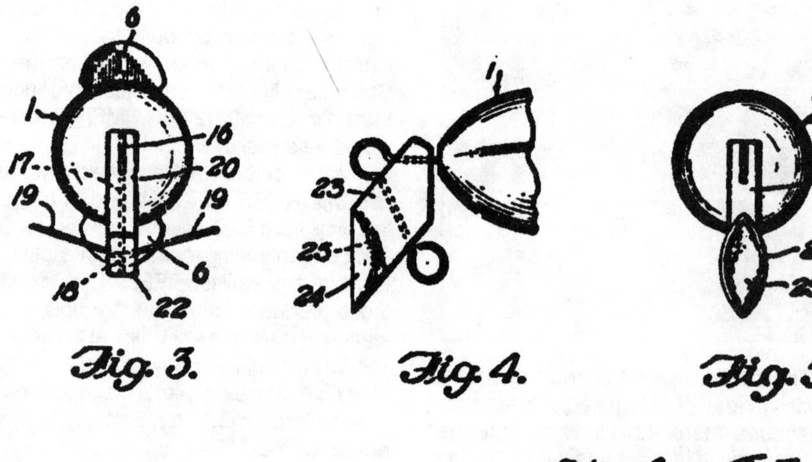

Inventors

Stanley F. Myers
Adolph A. Kung

By Frank H. Schwartz

Attorney

The illustration from the patent application.

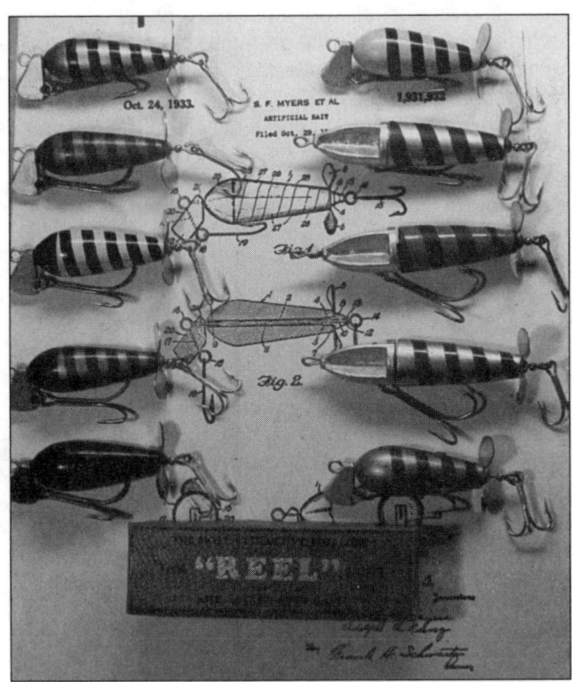

Left row shows five REEL LURES and right row shows two REEL LURES and three 1/2 CHARMERS. The box in the photo is the most common. It is red cardboard. The first was yellow and the second, white. Both have a picture of the lure on top.

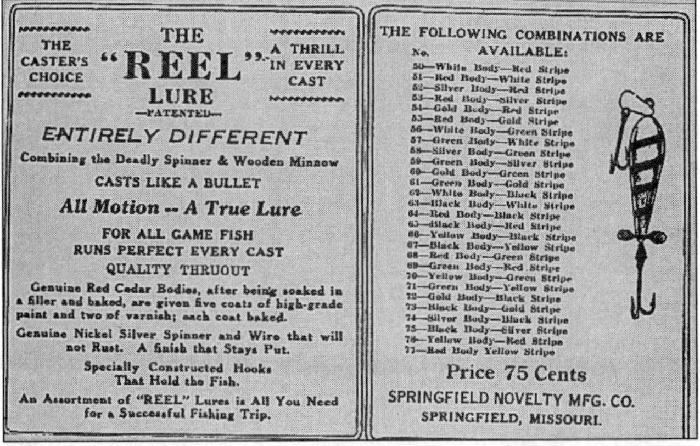

THE CASTER'S CHOICE

THE "REEL" LURE
—PATENTED—

A THRILL IN EVERY CAST

ENTIRELY DIFFERENT

Combining the Deadly Spinner & Wooden Minnow

CASTS LIKE A BULLET

All Motion -- A True Lure

FOR ALL GAME FISH
RUNS PERFECT EVERY CAST
QUALITY THRUOUT

Genuine Red Cedar Bodies, after being soaked in a filler and baked, are given five coats of high-grade paint and two of varnish; each coat baked.

Genuine Nickel Silver Spinner and Wire that will not Rust. A finish that Stays Put.

Specially Constructed Hooks That Hold the Fish.

An Assortment of "REEL" Lures is All You Need for a Successful Fishing Trip.

THE FOLLOWING COMBINATIONS ARE AVAILABLE:

No.
50—White Body—Red Stripe
51—Red Body—White Stripe
52—Silver Body—Red Stripe
53—Red Body—Silver Stripe
54—Gold Body—Red Stripe
55—Red Body—Gold Stripe
56—White Body—Green Stripe
57—Green Body—White Stripe
58—Silver Body—Green Stripe
59—Green Body—Silver Stripe
60—Gold Body—Green Stripe
61—Green Body—Gold Stripe
62—White Body—Black Stripe
63—Black Body—White Stripe
64—Red Body—Black Stripe
65—Black Body—Red Stripe
66—Yellow Body—Black Stripe
67—Black Body—Yellow Stripe
68—Red Body—Green Stripe
69—Green Body—Red Stripe
70—Yellow Body—Green Stripe
71—Green Body—Yellow Stripe
72—Gold Body—Black Stripe
73—Black Body—Gold Stripe
74—Silver Body—Black Stripe
75—Black Body—Silver Stripe
76—Yellow Body—Red Stripe
77—Red Body Yellow Stripe

Price 75 Cents

SPRINGFIELD NOVELTY MFG. CO.
SPRINGFIELD, MISSOURI.

This advertisement gives you all the available colors for the REEL LURE. Some were changed. The earliest Nos. 50 and 54 had red heads and the earliest No. 62 had a black head so there are 31 possible paint patterns to be found.

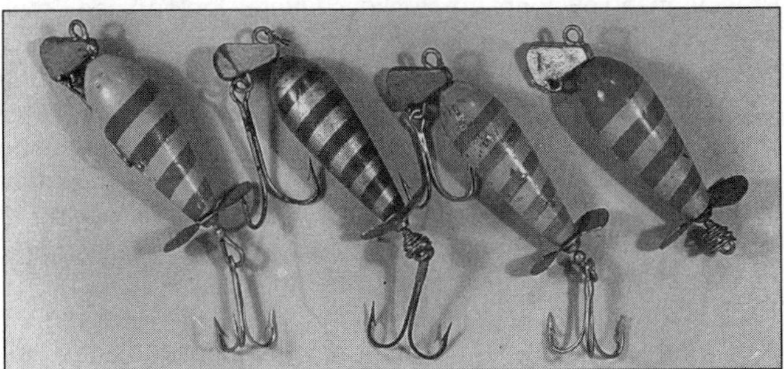

Four 2" REEL LURES. Left to right: Yellow body with red stripe, silver with green, yellow with green and red body with yellow stripe. The propeller spinner is attached to the lure body so that the whole body rotates around the wire armature on retrieve.

Two REEL LURES on a red box. The one on the right is missing its hooks. Note the hook guard on the lure at fight. It looks as if it is meant to prevent the hook from getting in the way of the spinner.

STEWART TACKLE COMPANY

Elman "Bud" Stewart — Flint, Michigan; Fenton, Michigan

Bud Stewart is a legend in his own time. That is an overworked phrase, but in this case an apt one. Stewart began making lures when he was 17, and was in the business commercially by the time he turned 20 back in the early 1930s. He retired in 1981 and has since been honored by having been designated a "Preeminent folk artist" by the Smithsonian and the people at Michigan State University who bestowed upon him the Michigan Heritage Award. He has also been inducted into the Fishing Hall of Fame.

Stewart's lures are characterized by bright and realistic colors, often looking wounded or bleeding. He has been quoted as saying "To be honest, I'm painting more for the fisherman than the fish. But it has to look natural and act natural."

He traveled the sporting and tackle show circuit hawking his wares for many years. He did hire a few people to help assemble his lures, at one point, but he says he painted them all himself. His products were not limited to lures; he produced ice fishing decoys as well. I could find very little in print about the lures and decoys. He apparently relied heavily on the circuit and word-of-mouth. If you want a really knock-out source of Stewart information and photos you need to get a copy of *Bud Stewart, Michigan's Legendary Lure Maker* by Frank Baron and Raymond Carver. The address for the book is listed elsewhere in this book. Stewart still makes lures, but they are limited and snatched up by collectors. The lures will not likely ever see water. About this Stewart says "I think they're nuts."

MUSKY DUCK. Collector value range: $100-$200.

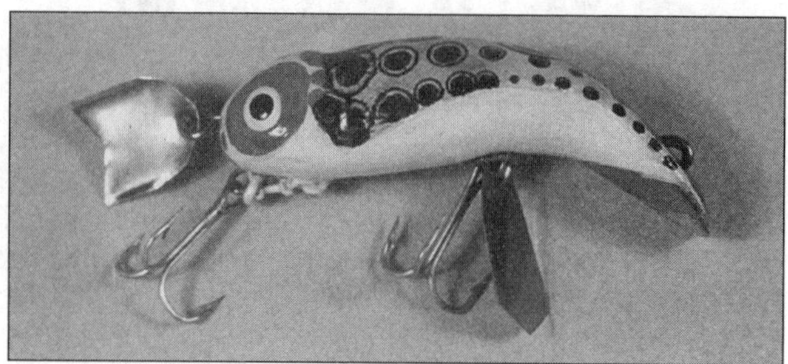

CRAB DIVER. Measures 3-1/4" and is signed by Bud Stewart. Collector value range: $100-$200. Photo courtesy Jim Muma.

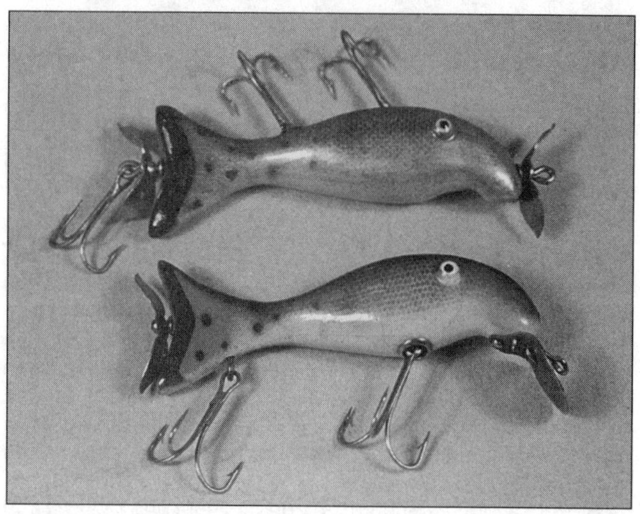

Upper is a SURFACE SUCKER and the lower lure is a DIVING SUCKER. Collector value range for either: $50-$70. Photo courtesy Jim Muma.

STRIKE-MASTER LURES

Strike-Master Tackle Company	Versailles, Ohio
Sure-Catch Bait Company	Versailles, Ohio

AUTHOR'S NOTE: This company has been a long time in getting sorted out. I tried for over 15 years, with little success. What follows here is an article prepared by Jim Bourdon of Croton-on-Hudson, New York. Jim is a man of extraordinary talent. He is an avid collector, but beyond that he approaches his collecting as a scholar, an artist and a writer. His careful research and preparation of the garnered material into eminently usable form for his fellow collectors is well known to members of the National Fishing Lure Collectors Club. What follows here was written by Jim Bourdon and finally resolves the confusion that bedeviled so many of us for so long.

Two STRIKE-MASTER HELLGRAMMITES on a box with Sure-Catch Bait Company on it.

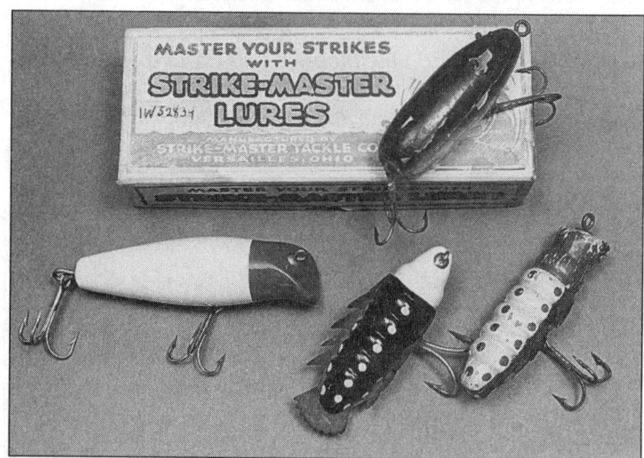

STRIKE-MASTER box with the name Strike-Master Tackle Company on it. The lures are the MOUSE (on box), BASS KING (left) and two HELLGRAMMITES.

During the late 1920s in Union City, Indiana, A.T. Death was producing lures under the name Sure Catch Bait. In 1928, he traveled to Versailles, Ohio to raise capital in order to open a lure manufacturing facility. Mr. Death succeeded in raising $10,000 from soon-to-be partners. Dr. John E. Gillette (Secretary), Dr. W.C. Guttermuth (President), August H. Grilliot (Vice President and owner of the Buckeye Overall factory) and Frank Ash (local banker) - an additional partner may have existed, possibly Charles Huber who was on the company's Board in 1929. The October 11, 1928 issue of The Versailles Policy proclaimed that a bait factory was coming to town and scheduled to start operations on November 1, 1928, with equipment transferred from Union City. This new factory was located at the corner of Water and Center Streets.

The start up was less than smooth, but by January 10, 1929, the local paper was reporting that the plant, "was now busy making baits to fill orders for several thousand lures", although operations had been delayed both in the transferring of old equipment and delivery of new equipment. This optimistic assessment evidently proved to be mostly hype. By October, A.T. Death was replaced as General Manager by C.O. Ellison whose forte was sales promotion. In 1930, the company's name was changed to the Strike-Master Tackle Co. Ellison's expertise proved temporarily positive as orders increased, and the company's work force was raised to 15-20 employees. This success was short-lived and the company finally shut down probably in 1931 when A.T. Death returned to Union City.

Although Strike-Master lures were produced for a very short period, numerous variations of the same lure appear from time to time. A partial explanation would be that A.T. Death produced many of these designs in Union City before and possibly after the Versailles facility's operation. Particular nuances to watch out for include:

Eye Styles

Some plugs can be found without eyes or with glass eyes - either standard or all black. The no-eye variations of a particular lure were generally the latest version.

Lip Styles

Those lures employing metal wobbling lips may have a cup-like depression stamped into them or be simply drilled for line-tie attachment. The simple lips appear to be earlier.

Head Styles

Certain baits with slanted wooden heads (i.e. Hellgrammite Crab) may sometimes appear with rounded (bullnose) heads. These bullnose plugs generally seem to be of later vintage than the slant-head.

Rubber Legs

Strike-master often utilized rubber legs or collars on its products. Variations have been noted as produced without these rubber appendages (later version).

Many examples of the company's product line are illustrated. The accompanying text, when required, will reference the Sure-Catch (pre-1930) name and/or model plus the later Strike-Master nomenclature separated by a slash mark. When available the color pattern number will be listed (parenthetically if Sure-Catch era).

It has only been in recent years that information has begun to surface regarding this company. With mounting interest by the Indiana collector community, many additional details should come to light in the next few years.

MR. DEATH

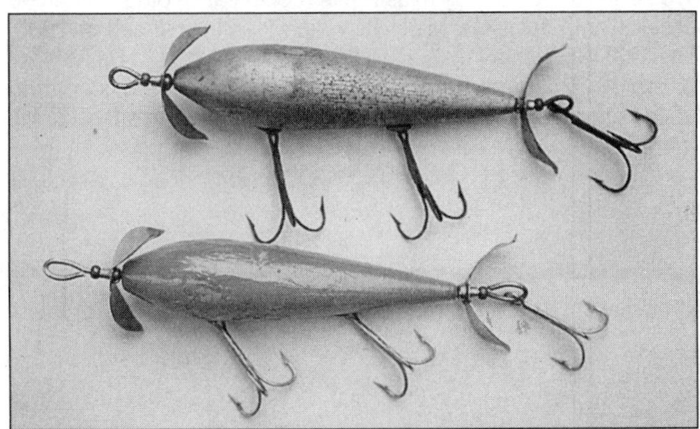

Although not found in any catalog or brochure, these 3-3/4" no-eyed lures have long been attributed to A.T. Death, dating to his early Indiana days. They utilize screw-eye hook-hangers around which are surface-mounted round wire bands. The top bait in silver (aluminum) and bottom in yellow are the only colors that have been noted. Collector value range: $75-$175.

SURFACE KILLER No. 45/45XX

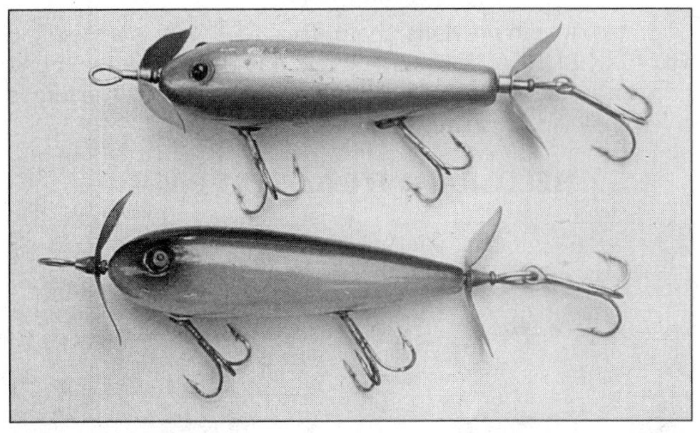

These 3-3/4" top water baits were a mainstay product of Mr. Death from his Union City days. The No. 4550 (top) has black glass eyes. Note the prop style on the No. 4549 (bottom). During the Sure-Catch period, this lure was also offered in a two-hook (No. 35) rendition. The No. 45 was listed as available in white with red head (No. 46), all silver with red head (No. 51) were added, and all yellow, deleted. The No. 35 series was offered in scaled and striped, all silver (No. 50) and white with red head (No. 46). Collector value range: $50-$150.

NIGHT HAWK No. 36XX

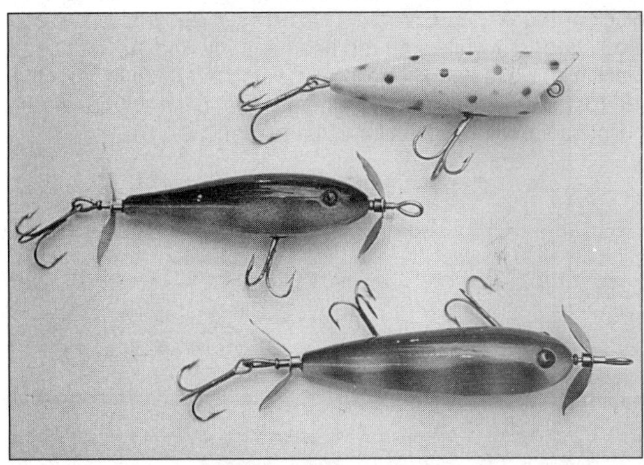

The top lure illustrated in the photo here is No. 6352 is 3-1/4" in length and has no eye detail. Note the notched mouth. During the Sure-Catch period, the company offered a similarly shaped model No. 63; however, the brochure shows glass eyes but does not illustrate the notched mouth. The No. 63XX was offered in colors No. 52 (white with black spots) and No. 46 (white with red head). Collector value range: $60-$160.

No. 33 SURFACE MINNOW-TYPE

Center bait in previous photo. Sure-Catch produced two groups of surface minnow-type lures. This style has a taped rear half and was described as "slightly underwater." The No. 45/45XX series was full bodied and referred to as "surface". The illustrated No. 33 (Perch) measures 3-1/2". A larger size was known as the No. 47 and the smaller No. 55. The No. 33 colors include Natural perch scale and White with red head. The No. 47 was offered in similar colors plus all silver and all yellow (see Mr. Death). The No. 55 was listed in white with red head, all silver and white with blue back. Collector value range: $50-$150.

INJURED SURFACE KILLER
(UN-CATALOGED)

Bottom lure in previous photo. This 3-5/8" lure is a modified No. 45XX SURFACE KILLER which has been shaved on one side and hooks mounted in injured minnow fashion. The lure is in Perch finish. Collector value range: $50-$150.

HELLGRAMMITE No 91XX Series

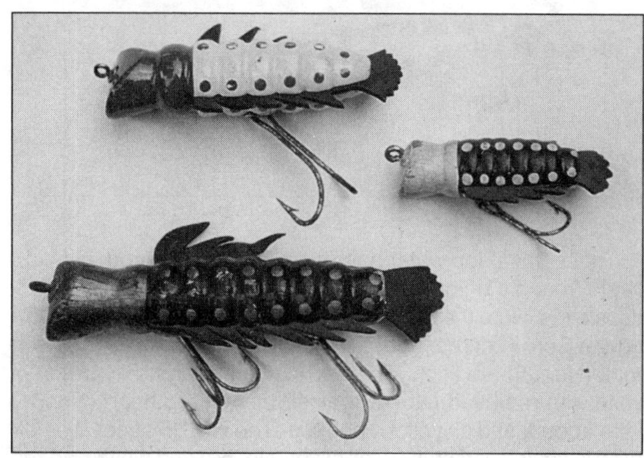

One of the company's most famous baits which was only offered during the Strike-Master era is the HELLGRAMMITE. Illustrated are three available sizes: Large No. 9153 (3-3/4") black with gold head, Medium No. 9146 (measures 2-3/8" catalog states 3") white with red head and Fly Rod No. 9147 (2") black with white head. This lure was also available in color No. 48 (orange with black head) and has been found in the bullnose variation. Collector value range: $50-$70.

CRAB No. 71/77XX Series

The Sure-Catch catalog reflects this lure with bead eyes, a metal lip, two trebles and available in one size only. The Strike-Master brochure reflects a no eye slant head model with a single double hook and available in two sizes: Large (3-1/4") and Fly Rod (2-1/8"). The lures pictured above date to the Strike-Master period. The large bait measures 3-1/4" and has black bead eyes. The smaller bait (2-3/4") has a "bullnose" and no eyes. The only available color is No. 23 natural crab (dark green). Collector value range: $50-$75.

No. 31

Only described as "slightly underwater", the No. 31 is a handsome wood-tailed lure with bulging (a SureCatch characteristic) glass eyes. This 3-1/4" lure is reflected in the catalog as having a single forward propeller only, although the lures above reflect additional variations. Note the prop style and typical Sure-Catch scale pattern. Available in the "scaled" color pattern only. Collector value range: $75-$175.

BUG NO. 19

This 3" wooden plug (top) was offered during the Sure-Catch period only. Depicted in the brochure and above with black glass eyes, it may have been produced with regular glass eyes as well. It was available in one size and three color patterns: White with red head (No. 46), black with gold head (No. 53), and all silver (No. 50). Collector value range: $75-$120.

MOUSE No. 65/65XX

This 2-1/2" lure (bottom lure in previous photo) with bead eyes and rubber ears is missing its rubber tail. Note similarity to Creek Chub's LUCKY MOUSE which was introduced in 1930. The MOUSE was available in three colors during the StrikeMaster era: No. 27 (natural mouse), No. 46 (white with red head) and No. 47 (black with white head). Collector value range: $80-$110.

FROG 67/67XX Series

The top lure (2-1/4" is missing its rubber legs but depicts the earlier glass-eyed version. The lower (23/8") is the later no eyed, no legged rendition. This lure was offered in one size and color (No. 25 green with black spots) only. Collector value range: $80-$120.

ROLLING DIVER No. 43/43XX

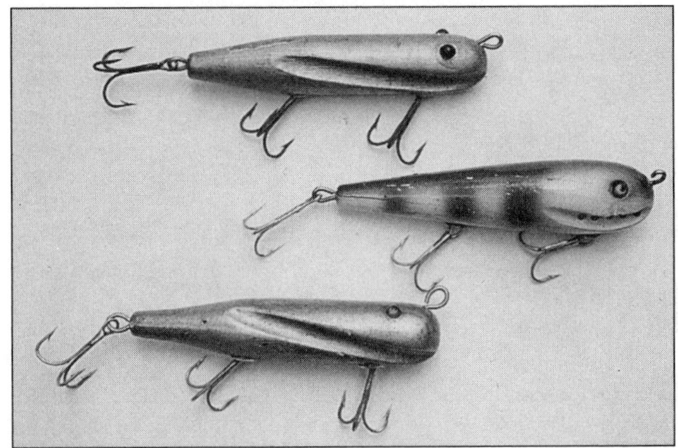

The above photo depicts three lures of this bait. The Perch (4-1/8") colored lure (center) has a short flute, standard glass eyes and red spots (a Strike-Master trademark) in the flute. The other two are all silver and measure 4". The upper plug (No. 4362) utilizes black glass eyes while the lower has standard eyes. The ROLLING DIVER was offered in one size only and in colors: No. 46 (white with red head), No. 15 (silver flecked natural perch), No. 49 (rainbow), No. 50 (all silver), No. 51 (silver with red head) and the un-cataloged No. 62 (above, white with green back, striped). Collector value range: $75-$100.

UNDERWATER LURES

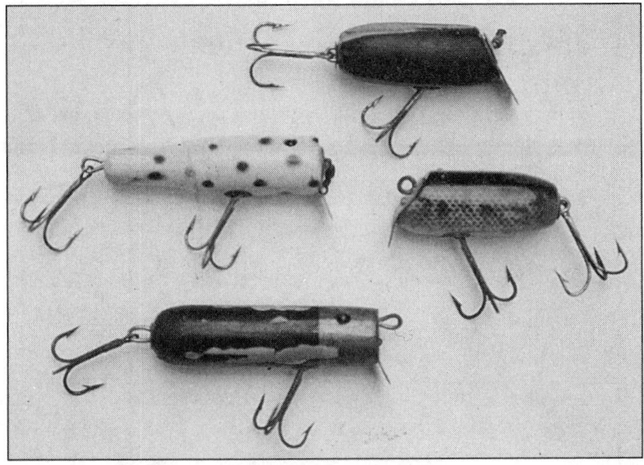

During the Sure-Catch era the company marketed a number of nameless underwater plugs. The photo here depicts the No. 23 and 53 series.

No. 23 (center left). This lure measures 2-7/8", has black glass eyes and employs a lip which is stamped with a cup like depression, very similar to those found later on Paw Paw lips. The barrel swivel on the line tie is typical of this manufacturer. Collector value range: $50-$75.

No. 23 (bottom lure). Except for its black glass eyes, and a slightly different lip shape, this 3" lure is a dead ringer for a plug found in a Sure-Catch Bait, Union City, Indiana box. Note the rounded tail compared to the tapered tail on the above version. This model was offered in three colors: Red with silver head, black with gold head (No. 53) and white with black spots (No. 52). Collector value range: $50-$75.

No. 53 (center right). This 2-1/8" bait with black glass eyes is identical to the Sure-Catch brochure illustration. The top bait is similar except that it utilizes a barrel swivel on the line tie. These lures were cataloged as available in white with red head (No. 46) and yellow with black spots and white with red spots. Other colors include all black and black scale with red spots as in photo. Collector value range: $50-$70.

DEATH'S PRIDE No. 29/29XX

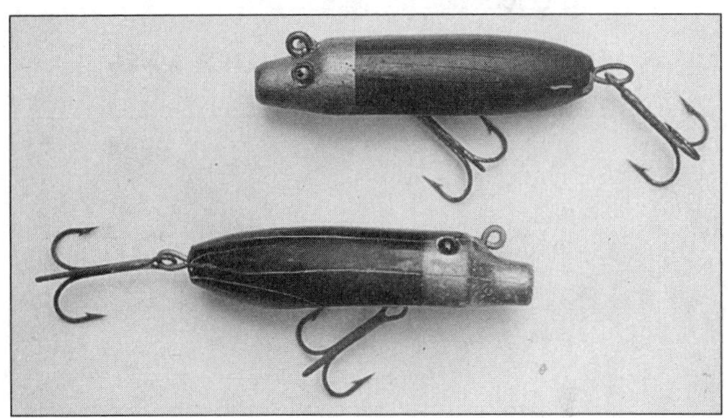

This lure provides an excellent example for comparison between Sure-Catch era (note the eye placement, next to line tie), eye usage (standard glass eye) and line tie (no washer). The No. 2953 (bottom) is also 3-1/2" but note its rear mounted black glass eye and washer line tie. The No. 29 was offered in white with red head (No. 46), black with gold head (No. 53) and all silver (No. 50). In addition to these colors, the NO. 29XX could be had in No. 15 (silver flecked, natural perch), No. 47 (black with white head) and No. 51 (silver with red head). Collector value range: $50-$160.

WATER WALTZER No. 19XX

The fattest version of this group (center), the 3" WATER WALTZER was available in colors: No. 46 (white with red head), No. 47 (black with white head), No. 48 (orange with black head), No. 51 (silver with red head), and No. 54 (all black). Collector value range: $50-$75.

BASS KING No. 85XX

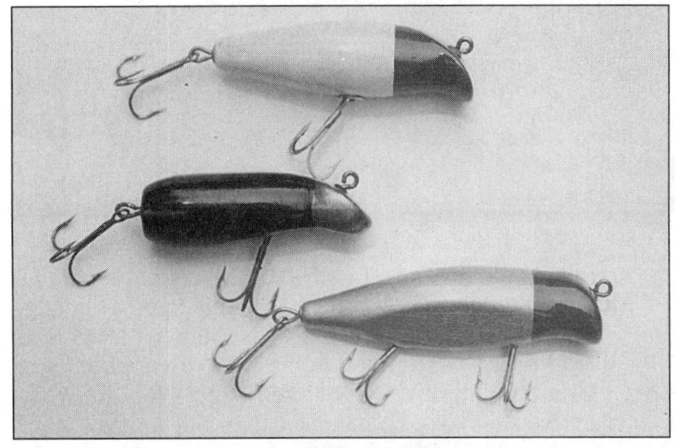

This 3-1/2" lure (top lure in previous photo)) is one of four similarly shaped Strike-Master products. It can be most readily confused with the 3-1/2" 89XX WITCH (not illustrated). The later has a more tapered rear and a grooved head. The BASS KING was offered in color patterns No. 46 (white with red head), No. 47 (black with white head), No. 48 (orange with black head), No. 49 (rainbow) and No. 53 (black with gold head). The No. 89XX was available in the same colors plus No. 62 (white with green back, striped). Collector value range: $50-$65.

MUSKIE MINNOW No. 75XX

The largest of these near surface swimmers, the MUSKIE MINNOW (bottom lure in previous photo), was available rigged for, either bass or musky (different hooks). The illustrated No. 7551 measured 3-7/8" and appears bass-rigged. It was offered in the same colors as the BASS KING plus No. 51 (silver with red head). Collector value range: $50-$75.

SURFACE SPRAYING GLIDER 8746

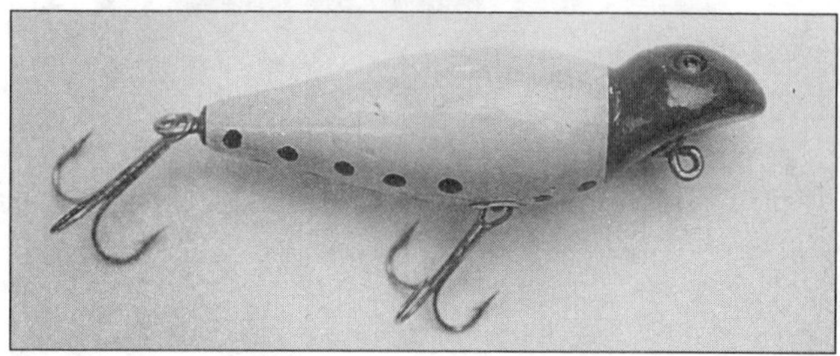

Most notable due to its similarity to the Creek Chub JIGGER (introduced in 1933), this 3-5/8" lure has standard glass eyes and bears characteristic Strike-Master spots on the belly. Available color patterns include: No. 46 (white with red head), No. 47 (black with white head), No. 48 (orange with black head), No. 51 (silver with red head) and No. 53 (black with gold head). Collector value range: $80-$120.

SURFACE TEASER No. 21/21XX

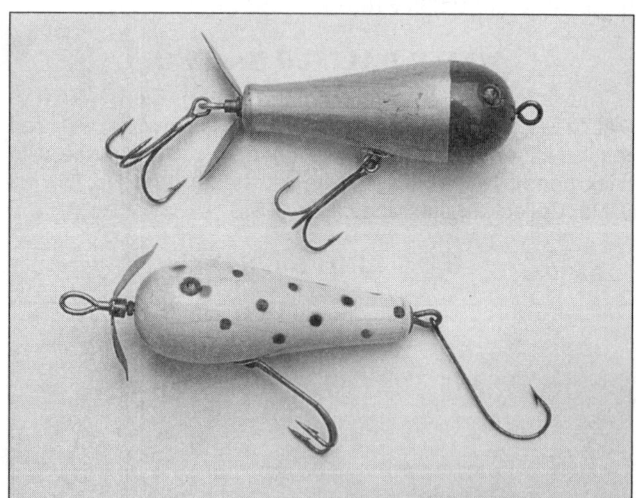

Offered in both the Sure-Catch and Strike-Master eras as a front prop plug, it was obviously available in other configurations. Generally measuring 2-3/4" (top lure No. 2151 is 2-7/8") this lure has been noted in the no eye variation. The No. 21 was offered in: White with red head (No. 46), white with black spots (No. 52), all silver (No. 50) and all black (No. 54). The No. 21XX series dropped color pattern No. 50 and added No. 47 (black with white head) and No. 62 (white with green stripes). The upper lures No. 2151 shows this bait as also available in silver with red head. Collector value range: $75-$100.

SMITH MINNOW OR THE WIGGLE TAIL BAIT

LaGrange Bait Company LaGrange, Indiana

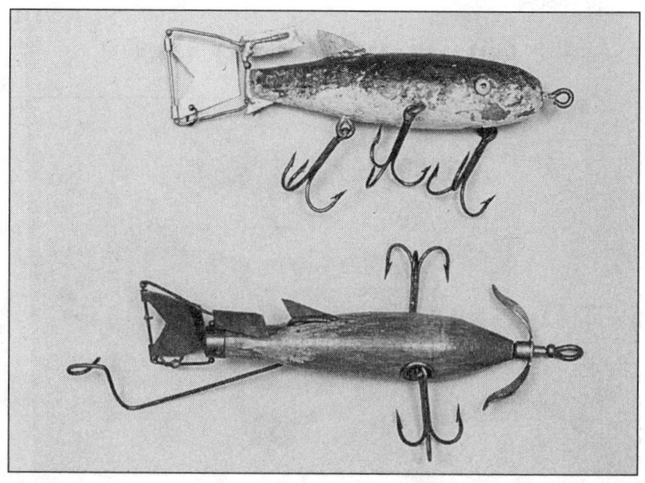

The Wiggle Tail Bait

Moves through the water in a zig-zag course, wriggling its tail, producing an exact imitation of a live minnow, swimming.

This movement makes a very attractive lure and it has been demonstrated that it will catch fish where all other baits fail.

SEE IT IN THE WATER AND YOU WILL BE CONVINCED

Each Bait nicely finished and packed in a wooden box.
PRICE--$1.00 each, post paid.

LaGrange Bait Company
LAGRANGE, IND.

Known as the SMITH MINNOW to most collectors, this rare little beauty sports glass eyes and a fairly complicated wagging tail fin. Smith was granted a patent for this lure February 7, 1905. The patent drawing shows the tail fin assembly clearly, but Smith apparently devised at least two variations. The two I have seen have tail fins that are slightly different so don't let that throw you if you are lucky enough to come across one.

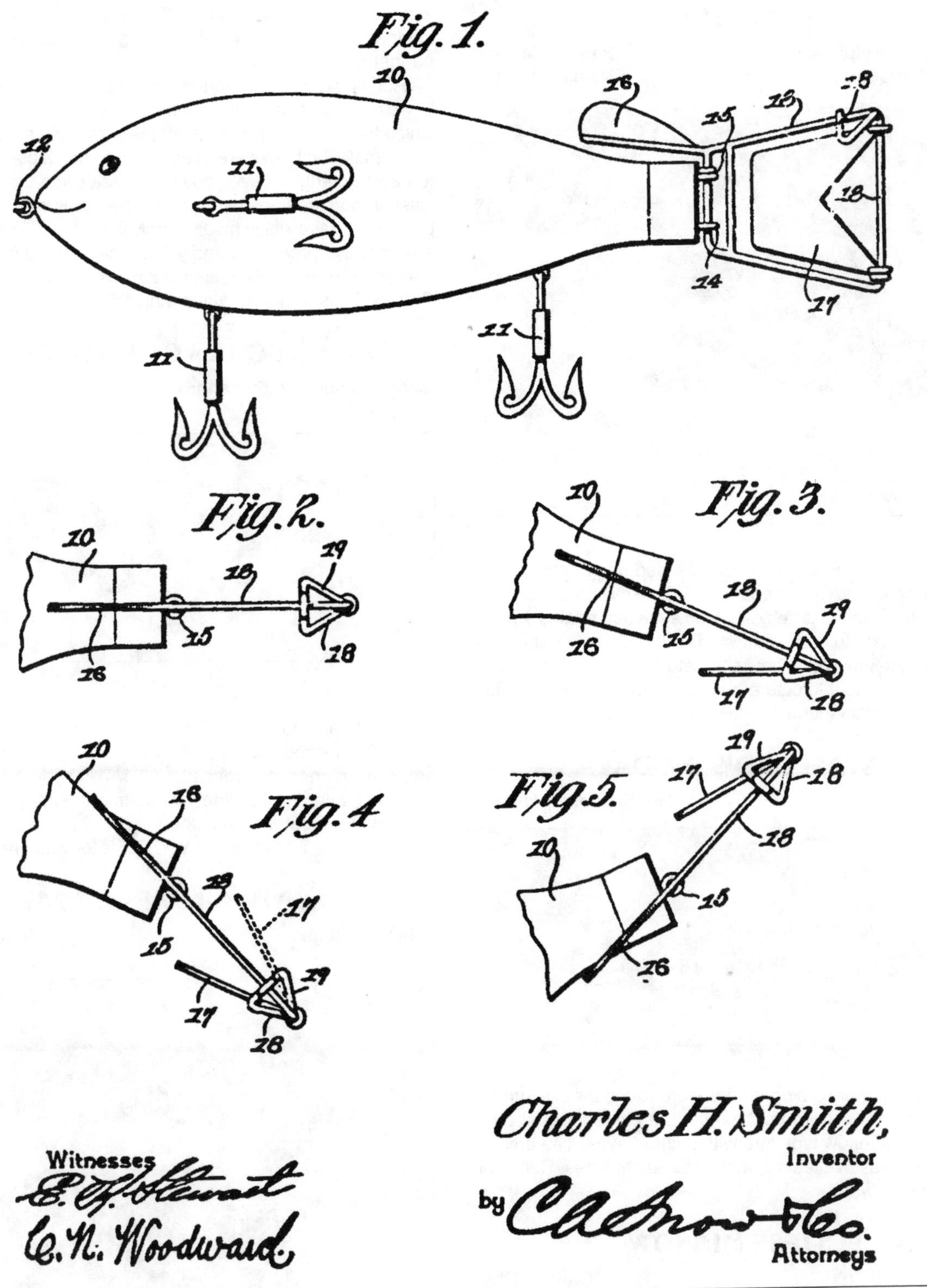
No. 781,794.
PATENTED FEB. 7, 1905.
C. H. SMITH.
ARTIFICIAL BAIT.
APPLICATION FILED JULY 27, 1904.
Fig. 1.
Fig. 2.
Fig. 3.
Fig. 4
Fig. 5.
Charles H. Smith,
Inventor
Witnesses
C. N. Woodward
by
Attorneys

Apparently Jim Heddon was interested in this particular lure. Clyde Harbin wrote of it in an article in the June 1987 issue of The *N.F.L.C.C. Gazette*, the club newsletter, that he has a slightly different lure, but nevertherless a copy, obtained from the Heddon factory, that has Heddon hardware. He also has a box pamphlet for SMITH'S WIGGLE TAIL BAIT that came from the personal scrapbook of Mr. Heddon. There is no doubt that the Heddon copy is one-of-a-kind, but it lends an interesting bit of side-line history to the story. Collector value range for the Smith WIGGLE TAIL BAIT. $1500-$2000.

SPIRAL-LURE

Calumet Tackle Company — Detroit, Michigan
Spiral Tackle Company — Detroit, Michigan

The first name and address was revealed upon removal of a paper label on the box in the photo here. These is no explanation for this as yet. The lure is fluted, has no eyes and rotates around a heavy wire armature on retrieve. The line tie and both hook hangers are integral with the wire armature. The plug measures 3" in length is thought to date around the 1930s. Collector value range: No trade data found. Photo courtesy Clarence Zahn.

STAFFORD'S DA-DA

Stafford's — Hot Springs, Arkansas

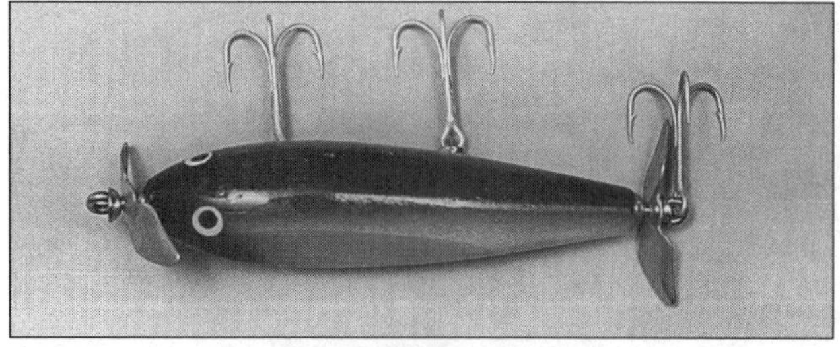

No advertising or catalog entries were found for this lure so what data is here is from the box the lure came in. It is a flat sided, injured minnow type lure with painted eyes. The box indicated that it was available in thirty different finishes. Collector value range: $10-$20.

ECLIPSE MINNOW

William Stuart & Co. — Canton, Ohio

The ECLIPSE is a wooden lure that was in production as early as 1905. It has been found with yellow glass eyes and un-

usual white glass eyes with black pupils. It was made in two sizes, 5T at 3-5/8" and 3T at 3". It sports fore and aft propeller spinners and a unique style of raised aluminum cup hook hanger hardware.

Regarding this hardware a 1905 Stuart advertisement states: "...we use a pressed aluminum washer with a raised ridge against which the hook rests, to prevent the point from striking the wood or enamel. The hooks are at all times in such a position so as not to become tangled .. We do not cut holes into the wood, as the washer is placed against the surface and is held in place by a brass screw eye which holds it firmly in position." They were available in white, green, red and yellow colors. It is thought to be the forerunner of an early Shakespeare plug. Perhaps they bought Stuart's rights. Collector value range: $300-$600.

SUGARWOOD LURES

Morgan Manufacturing and
Supply Company — Tulsa, Oklahoma

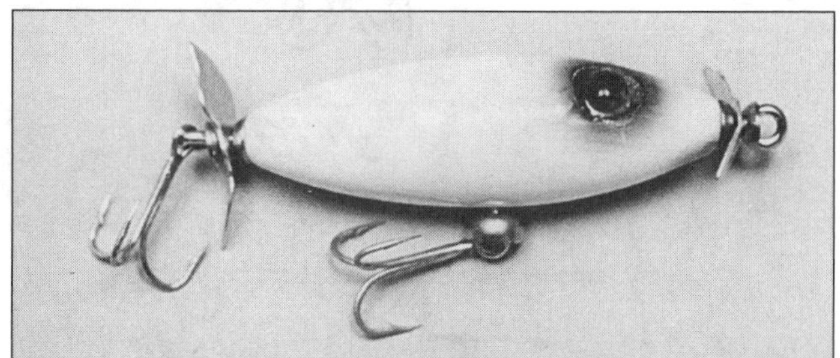

I was unable to find much information about this c. 1960 company. The wooden lure above has glass eyes, a pair of floppy propeller spinners and measures 2-1/4" in body length. Note the inverted cup/hook preventer arrangement. There are other Sugarwood lures, but the only one I know of is a 5" lure that looks very much like a Heddon VAMP. Collector value range: $5-$15.

SWIV-A-LURE, c. 1949

LaMothe-Stokes — Detroit, Michigan

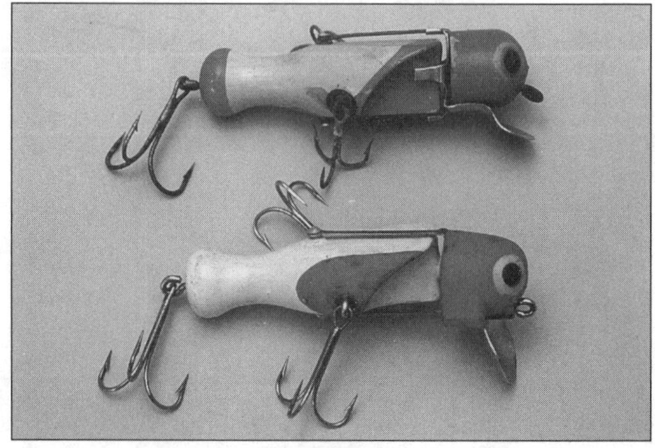

These peculiar lures were made by LaMothe-Stokes in Detroit. Beyond that little is known. The upper model in the photo is made of wood and the other is plastic. It appears as if they made the plastic model a bit less complex. Note that it also has a larger head and the metal lip is different. They are both difficult to find. The wood model is the hardest to find with most of its paint intact. It looks as if the wood bodies were painted raw, with no primer coat. This renders the finish fragile. They both measure 3-1/8" long. Collector value range: No trade data found.

SLIM SWEENEY'S TWINMINNOW

Twinminnow Bait Company — Fresno, California

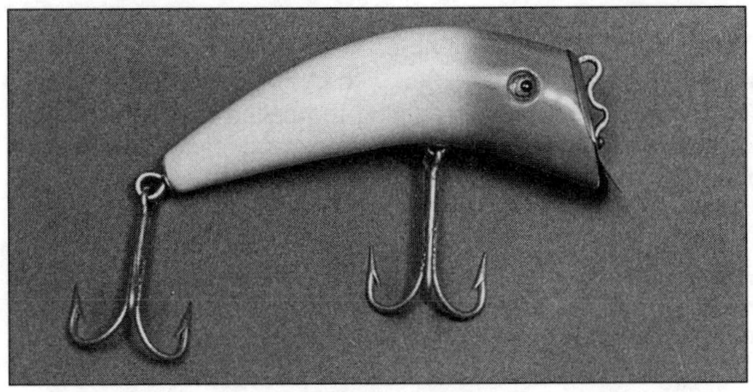

A c. 1939 glass eye, wooden lure. It is a surface or subsurface running lure depending upon which of the line ties used. 3-3/8" long, it was made in four finishes: Red head/white body, green perch scale, yellow perch scale, black back with gold sides and a white belly. Collector value range: $50-$100.

TANTA-LURE

Tanta-Lure Manufacturing Company — Youngstown, Ohio

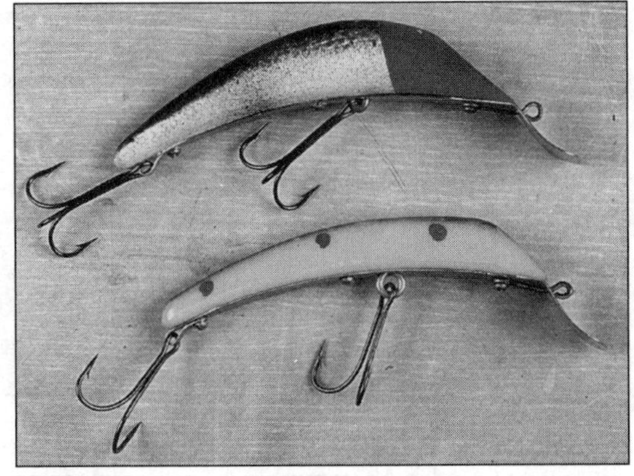

The wooden lure body measures 4" and 3/4" from belly to the top at its widest place. The stainless steel dive lip you see extends all the way down the belly of the lure ending as the tail treble hook hanger. The belly hook is attached by a simple recessed screw eye beneath the belly plate. There are no eyes. A very strong lure. The plastic version (lower lure in photo) is slightly shorter at 3-7/8" and the belly to top measurement is significantly slimmer at 1/2". Photo courtesy Galen Snyder. Collector value range: $15-$30.

TEMPTER FROG c. 1935

Tempter Bait Company — Pittsburgh, Pennsylvania; Akron, Ohio

Three references to this bait were found. Two put the company in Pittsburg and the other placed them in Akron. There are at least two sizes to be found. There is the 3-3/4" and the 2-1/4" fly rod size. One reference illustrates a "no leg" version at 2". This is the 3-3/4" size with no legs. It is not known if this was production or fisherman modification. Collector value range: $175-$375. Photo courtesy Jim Muma.

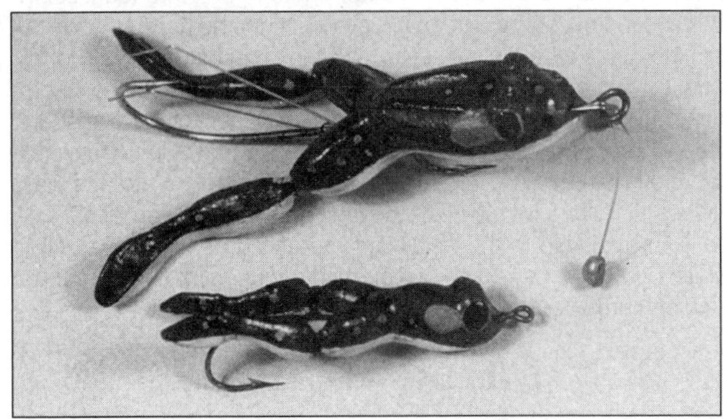

THOREN MINNOW CHASER

A. H. Thoren — Chicago, Illinois

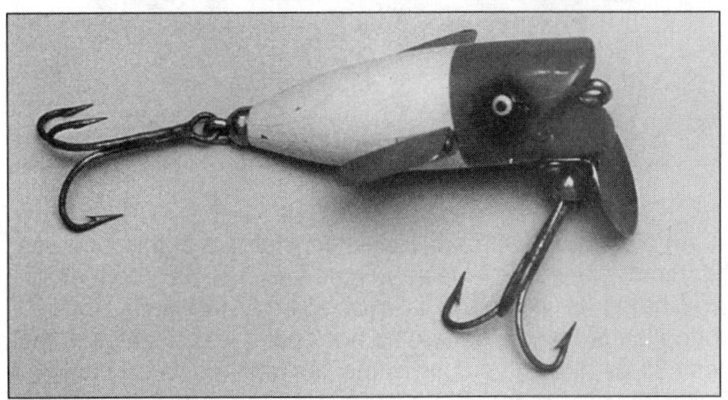

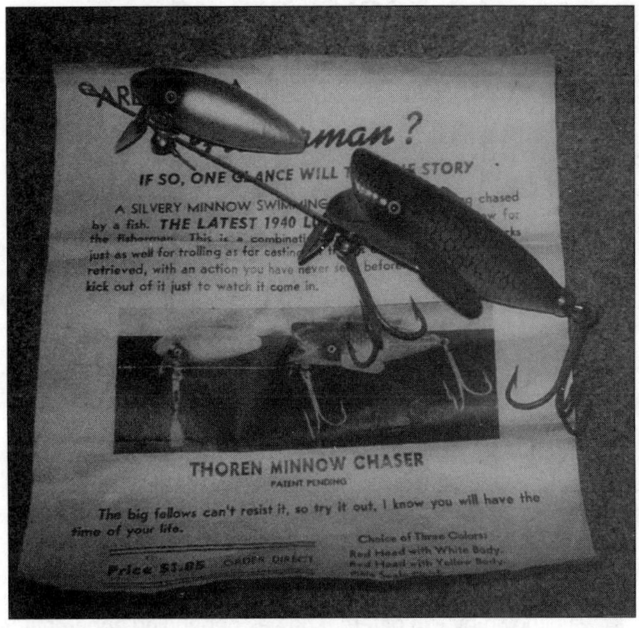

Listed as an unknown previously, thanks to three collectors who sent me a photo and photocopies of the box and box flyer, we now have a bit more information. The photo with the lure on the flyer was an instant photo type that didn't reproduce too well, but it helps. It is actually two lure bodies mounted on a wire. The flyer states: "A SILVERY MINNOW SWIMMING FOR DEAR LIFE, being chased by a fish." It also called the lure "THE LATEST 1940 LURE." What is puzzling is that the rear lure on the wire has hardware for attaching to the end of the wire fixture from the smaller forward minnow body. The other photo is of a lure identical in all ways to the other with one exception. It has no hardware for attaching to the wire; only a screw eye line tie in the mouth. Thoren must have made the lure both ways, one for fishing with the single lure and the other for the double. The smaller forward minnow measures 2", the rear measures 2-3/4" and the whole rig from tail to nose of the forward lure measures 51/4". The forward lure was always a "Silvery Minnow" as the flyer put it, but the larger "Chaser" was available in the following three finishes: Red head with white body; red head with yellow body; pikie scale finish. it has tack painted eyes. Collector value range: $200-$400.

TOLEDO WEEDLESS

Toledo Bait Company — Toledo, Ohio

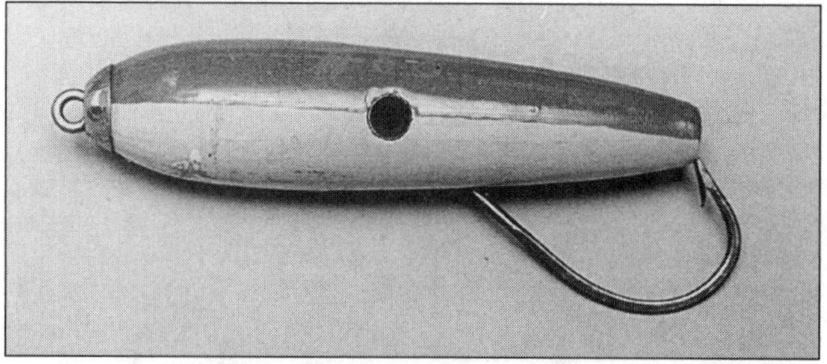

An old but undated advertisement states that this lure was "..famous.." and that it was patented May 12, 1925 so that approximates its vintage. It is a wood body lure with slot and spring loaded single hook. The hook point is concealed in the body so as to come out when the fish bites down on the lure. Collector value range: $100-$150.

L.J. TOOLEY TACKLE

Kalamazoo, Michigan — Detroit, Michigan

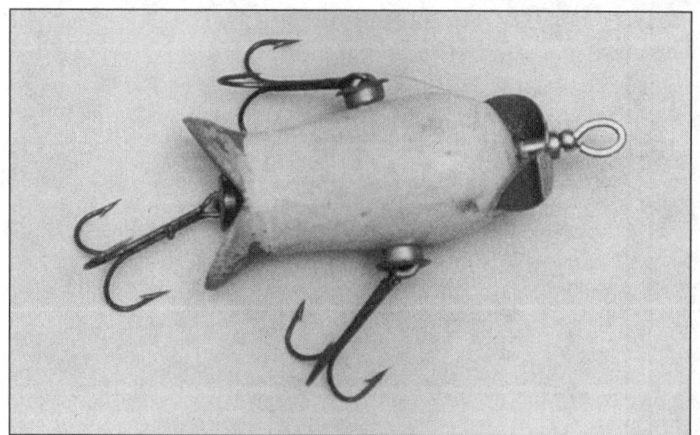

TOOLEY'S SURFACE BUNTY DARTER c. 1917. Note the unusual surface mounted cup and screw eye hook mounts.

It was known by two different names depending apparently upon when and where the company was doing business. They were also known as the L.J. Tooley Company at another Detroit address. Whatever the name or address, the company was owned by Lloyd J. Tooley of Kalamazoo and Detroit.

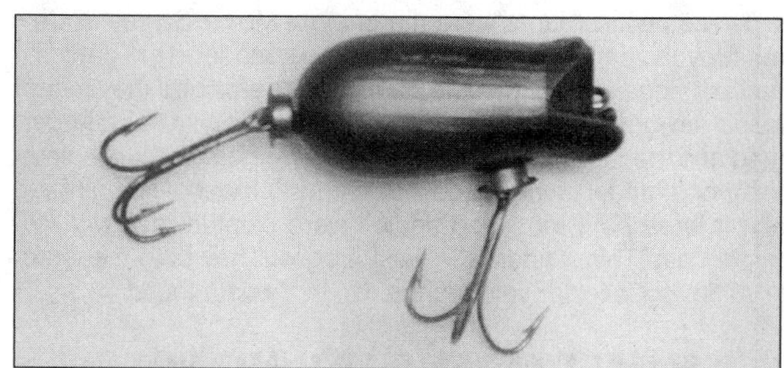

TOOLEY'S SPINNERED BUNTY. Also has the unusual surface mounted cup hardware.

Tooley was a champion bait caster in 1904, 1905 and 1906 setting a world record in 1905 with the then newly developed shorter Shakespeare bait casting rod called the "Kazoo" rod. The record was 199-2/3 feet, a prodigious distance even today over 90 years later!

The company manufactured silk lines and fishing rods as well as a few lures. The only references to lures other than the two here was to a "Tooley Minnow Tandem". The other two lures are the SURFACE BUNTY DARTER and the SPINNERED BUNTY. There are two sizes of the BUNTY DARTER 2" to 2-1/8" AND 2-1/4" long and was available in three finishes: Red head, white body; red head, gold body; white head, red body.

The second lure attributed to Tooley is 2-1/2" long with a nose mounted propeller spinner. We do not know its actual name so for now call it Tooley's SPINNERED BUNTY. If you find either of these bait handle them carefully. It seems that Tooley didn't prime them before painting. The finish is very fragile after over 90 years. Collector value range: $150-$250.

THE TORPEDO BAIT

George Jennings — Newark, New Jersey

This lure was found in Abercrombie & Fitch catalogs as early as 1907, but it is reported to date back to 1899 in an Abbey and Imbrie catalog. I have an 1898 A & I catalog and it is not listed there. The lure was called new in the 1907 catalog. They do not list any sizes, but they have been found in 2-1/4" and 2-3/4" lengths. The catalog also said the fins were drilled to attach extra hooks if desires. All came fitted with one feathered treble hook. Collector value range: $300-$400.

TORPEDO RAY

North American Tackle Company — Royal Oak, Michigan

John Irving Bell applied for the patent on his lure in 1943 and it was granted over four years later on March 16, 1948. This lure was listed in the second edition (1986) and over 12 years later more information about the North American Tackle Company has yet to turn up.

March 16, 1948

J. I. BELL

2,437,803

FISH LURE

Filed Dec. 1, 1943

FIG. 1

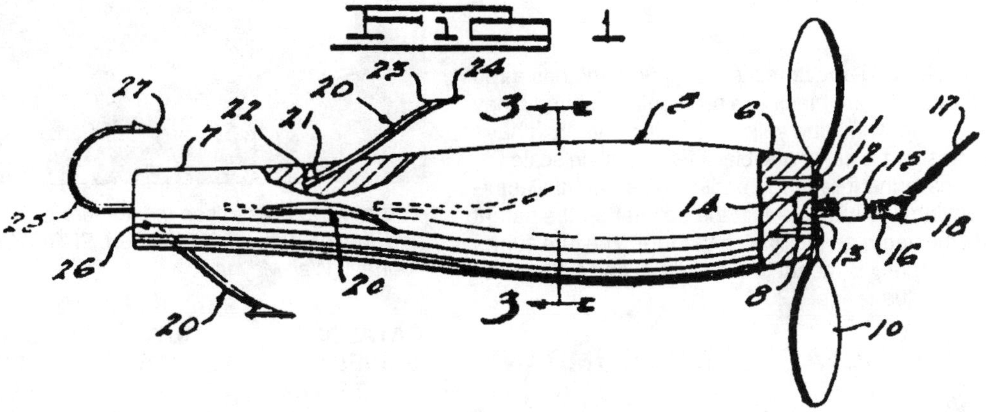

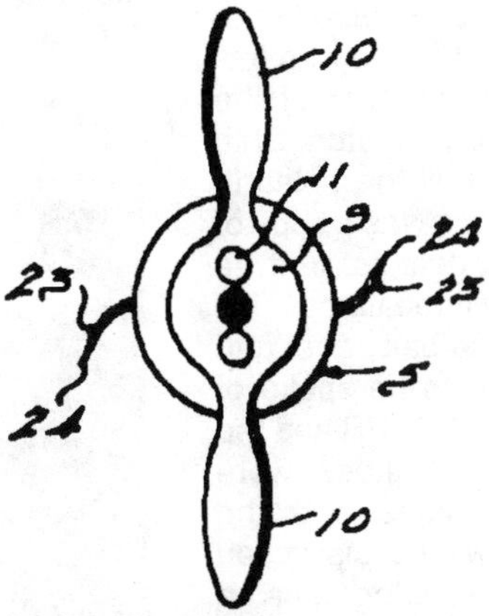

FIG. 2

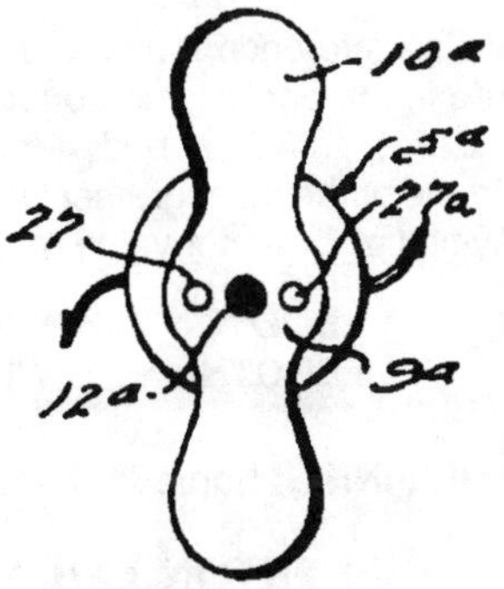

FIG. 4.

FIG. 3.

INVENTOR

J. Irving Bell.

BY

Barthel & Bugbee

ATTORNEYS.

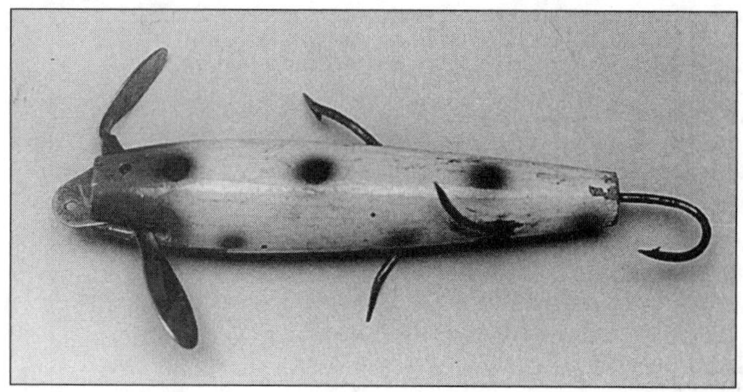

The lure in the photo above measures 3-5/8" and has a red head and yellow body with black and red spots. The body may have originally been white and yellowed over the years. I have seen another lure that is silver and black fish net style scale finish. If you compare the lure in the photo to the patent illustration accompanying you will note that the spinner on the patent drawing is not the same as the one on the lure. The lure sports a blade that apparently is meant to swing back and forth on retrieve. Collector value range: $20-$40.

TRENTON MANUFACTURING COMPANY

Walter H. Maynard — Covington, Kentucky

Trenton was in business in the 1940s. They advertised lures, cricket cages and a Trenton Inner-Lock Fly and Leader Box heavily in sporting magazines in 1947-48. I was fortunate to meet Walt Maynard, son of the founder of the company at the National Meet of the NFLCC in Dayton, Ohio in 1997. He provided some information to fill the holes in past editions. Among other things he gave me was a copy of a 1948 letter from their sales manager to dealers. In it he said "Last year we presented you with only three items. This year we have 14 - 9 lures, 3 tackle boxes, a bait cage, and a fisherman's thermometer." The three items he spoke of were the WHAM DOODLER, SURFACE DOODLER and the SPIN DOODLER. The names of each of these were changed because there was a conflict in names with the Wood's lure company DOODLER. They will be discussed with the individual lures. Walt also gave me photographs he had taken, but unfortunately only one was suitable for reproduction. I have included the 1949 catalog illustrations where I didn't obtain a photo.

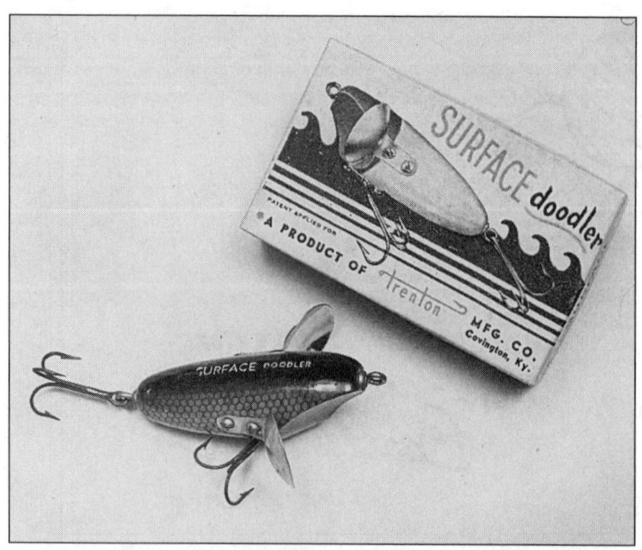

A original SURFACE DOODLER. It is brand new with its box.

SURFACE DOODLER or GURGLEHEAD

The lure was first called the SURFACE DOODLER, but in the 1949 catalog the name had changed to GURGLEHEAD. There was a conflict in names with the Wood's lure company DOODLER so the name was changed. You can find them with both names stamped on the back. When first manufactured the 'wings' were plated metal. They were later made of aluminum. Collector value range: $15-$35.

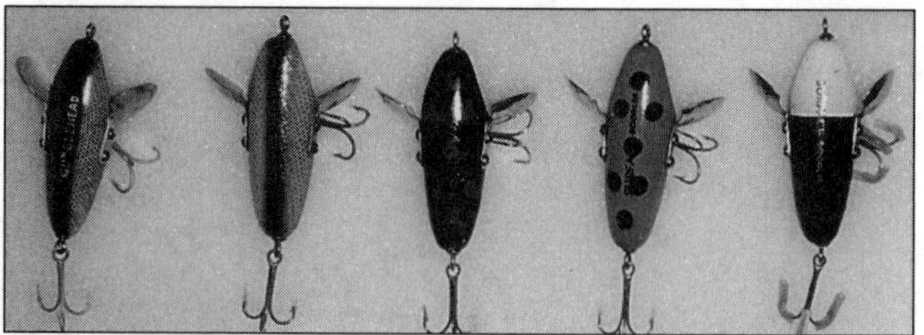

You may be able to see the left lure is marked GURGLEHEAD and the other four are marked SURFACE DOODLER. Photo courtesy Walt Maynard.

CATALOG SERIES #	BODY LENGTH	LURE WEIGHT
300 Series	3-1/4"	5/8 oz.

COLOR OR FINISH: White with red head, white with black head, green shiner, black shiner, golden scale, natural scale, spotted orange, black, frog, sparkle, gray.

MAD MOUSE

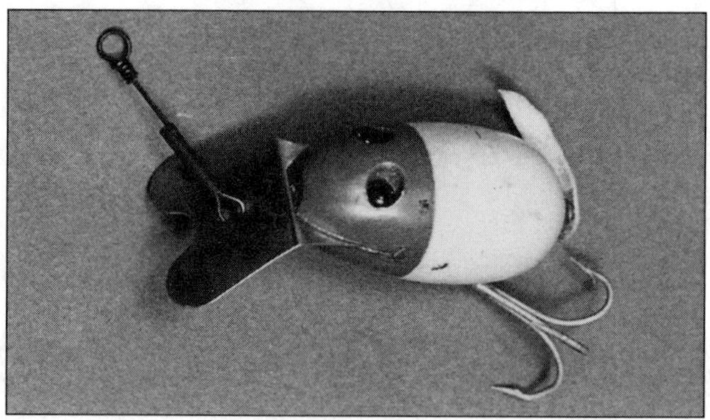

The only size reference found to this plug says it is 2-3/4" long. The lure in the photo is no doubt a MAD MOUSE, but it actually measures only 2" in body length. There may be two sizes to be found or the measurement in the reference included the metal diving lip. Collector value range: $15-$30.

CATALOG SERIES #	BODY LENGTH	LURE WEIGHT
600	2"	1/2 oz.

COLOR OR FINISH: Same as the GURGLEHEAD.

TRENTON TAIL SPIN

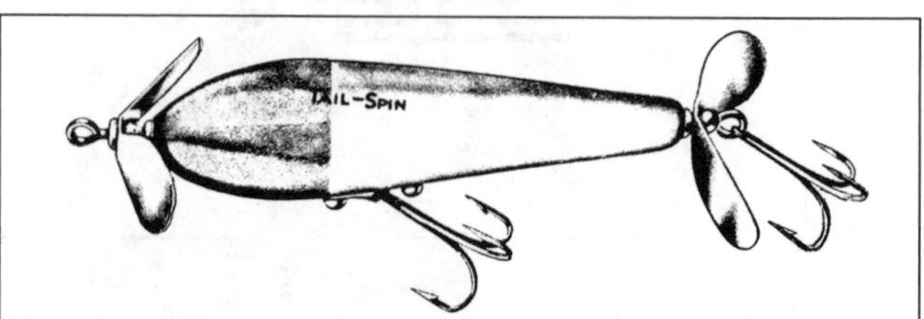

This wooden lure is 4-5/8" long and weighs 5/8 ounce. It has nose and tail propellers, a belly treble, and a trailing hook. It was new in the 1949 catalog. Collector value range: $15-$20.

CATALOG SERIES #	BODY LENGTH	LURE WEIGHT
1000	4-5/8"	5/8 oz.

COLOR OR FINISH: White with red head, red with silver head, silver, frog.

SPIN DIVER

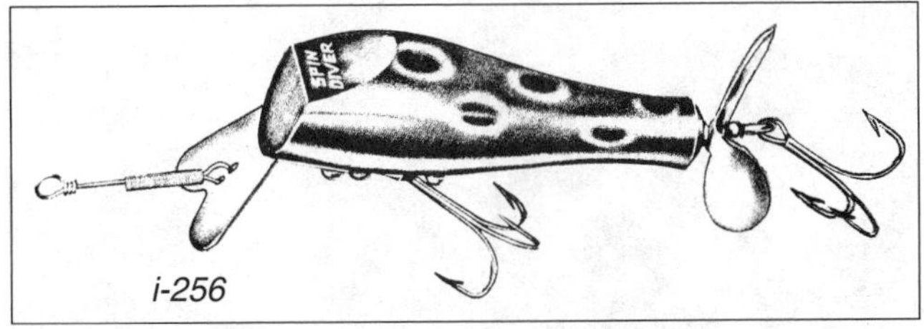

i-256

This is another of the new lures for 1949. It runs about 6" under water on retrieve. Collector value range: $15-$20.

CATALOG SERIES #	BODY LENGTH	LURE WEIGHT
900	2-3/4"	3/4 oz.

COLOR OR FINISH: Same as the GURGLEHEAD above.

SPIN DOODLER

SPIN TWIN Series 500

SPINNER Series 400

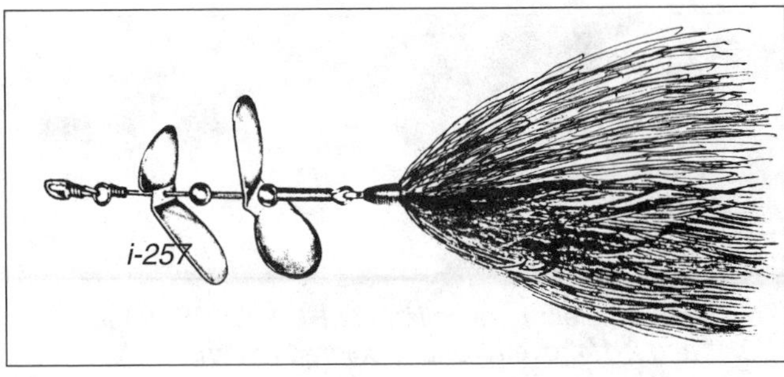
i-257

These were two spinners, one with one spinner and the other with two. The names was changed because of the conflict discussed above. The illustration from the catalog is of the TWIN-SPIN. Collector value range: $5-$10.

COLOR OR FINISH (buck tail): Red and white, black and white, black and yellow, yellow, white, red, natural.

WHAMTROLLER Series 800

WHAMCASTER Series 200

FLY WHAM Series 700

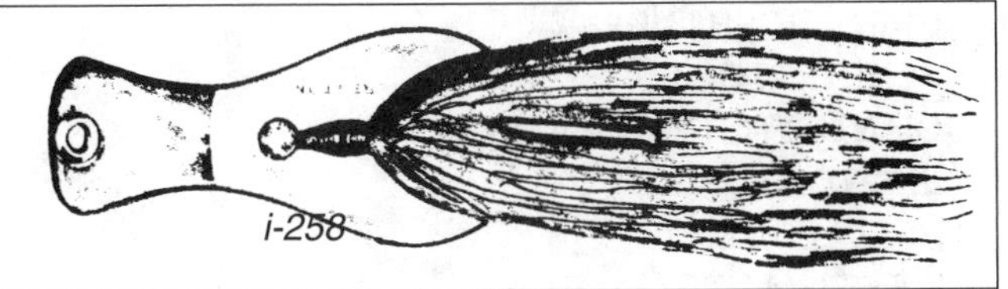
i-258

Metal spoon-types with buck tails. The FLY WHAM did not have the buck tail. The metal portion was available in brass, copper or stainless finishes. Sizes in the chart below are of the spoon and the rigid single hook inclusive. Collector value range: $5-$10.

CATALOG SERIES #	BODY LENGTH	LURE WEIGHT
200	2-1/2"	3/8 oz.
700	1-3/4"	1/16 oz.
800	3-1/4"	1 oz.

COLOR OR FINISH (Series 800 buck tail): Red, yellow, black.

COLOR OR FINISH (Series 200 buck tail): Red and white, black and white, black and white and yellow, black, black and yellow.

TROPICAL BAIT COMPANY

Indianapolis, Indiana

This goofy looking wooden top-water lure looks like an early PAC MAN. Called a STORMY PETREL, it measures 1-1/2" in diameter and is 1-7/8" overall. There was a brochure included in the box that illustrated a much smaller (5/8" dia.) version that has a 2-1/2" buck tail. It was called the BUGEYED BABBLER. Both were described in part as follows: "ACTION! With the slightest tip action the (lure) rotates on a transverse axis causing it to blow bubbles." Collector value range: $25-$50.

TRU-SHAD MFG. COMPANY

Monroe, Louisiana

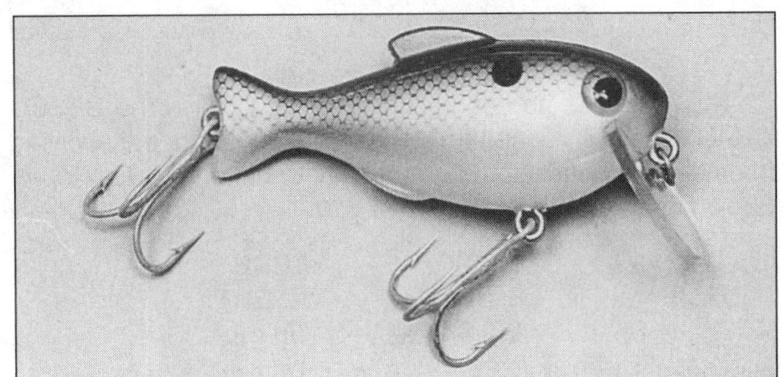

This is the only lure from this company I have found so far. The box identified the company and address. It also identified the lure as a top water "Tru-Shad #304". It measures 2-3/4", is made of plastic and has painted eyes. Collector value range: $5-$15.

TRUE TEMPER PRODUCTS

Geneva, Ohio

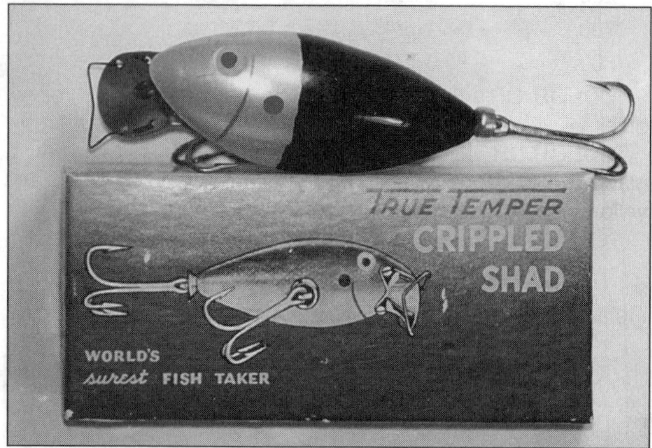

A True Temper SPEED SHAD with its original box. Photo courtesy Ken Bernoteit.

THE SPEED SHAD c. 1940

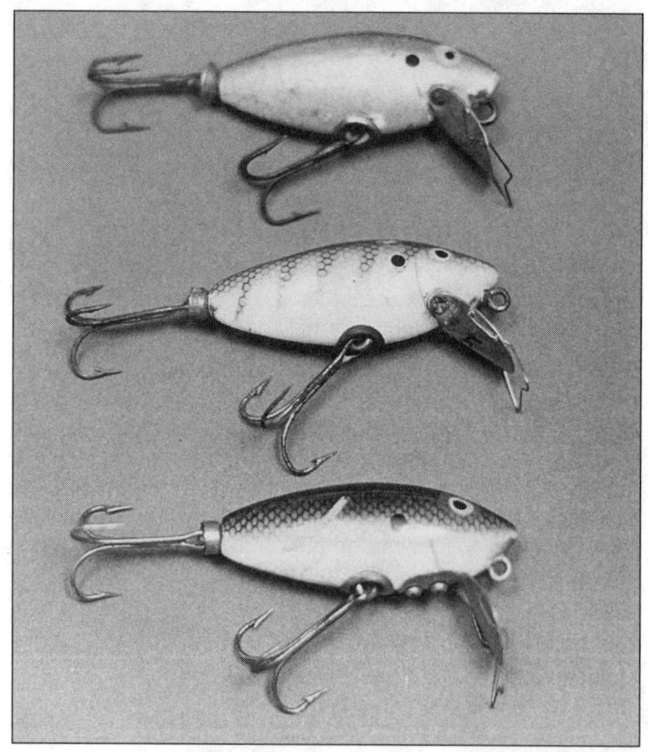

This lure also comes in a smaller size called the SPEED SHAD JUNIOR. Each has a wooden body and a metal diving lip under the nose. Both have a belly treble and trailing treble hook. Collector value range: $10-$20.

CATALOG NAME	BODY LENGTH	LURE WEIGHT
Speed Shad	2-3/8"	5/8 oz.
Speed Shad, Jr.	2"	1/2 oz.

COLOR OR FINISH: Natural shad, chub, pearl, perch, red and white, black and white.

CRIPPLED SHAD c. 1910

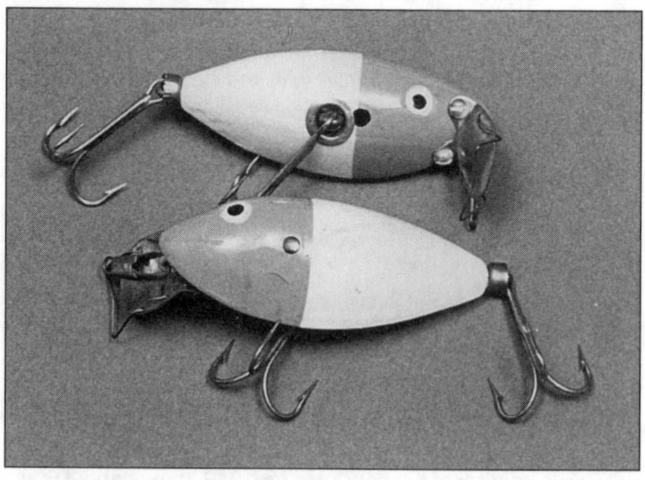

The originals were wooden floating plugs and then came plastic with a curved metal lip (shown in photo). It has one belly mounted treble* and a trailing treble hook. It weighs 5/8 oz. and the lure body length is 2-3/4". Collector value range: $10-$20.

COLOR OR FINISH: Natural shad, chub, pearl, perch, red and white, black and white.

**Technically it is a side-mount but the lure floats on its side therefore it is called belly-mount.*

TURBULENT FISHING LURES

Oscar C. Schaefer — Racine, Wisconsin

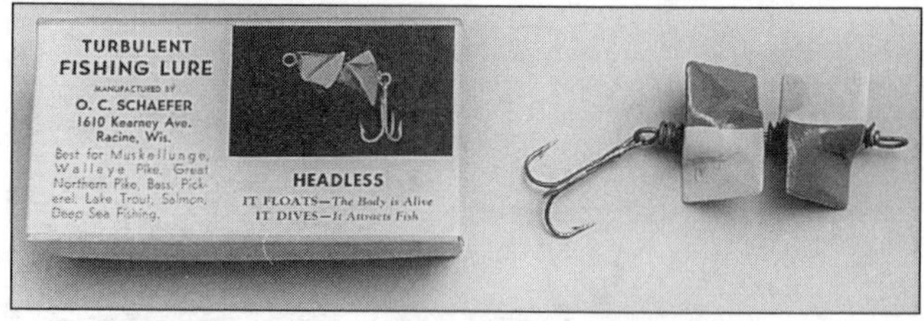

This is a Turbulent Lure called the HEADLESS. It measures 1-3/4" and 2-1/4" overall and is colored red and white.

The box that the above wooden lure came in had a couple of inserts. One was a comprehensive list of both salt water and fresh water game fish and which Turbulent Lures were best suited, how to rig them with bait such as worms, minnows, cut bait, crabs, mullet etc. It also included the maximum weight fish you could expect to encounter. The other listed 11 lures that were available:

SURFACE LURE
GIANT SURFACE LURE
DIVER LURE
GIANT DIVER LURE
TIGER LURE
GIANT TIGER LURE
PENETRATOR LURE
GIANT PENETRATOR LURE
EXCITOR LURE
HEADLESS LURE
WET FLY LURE

The color combinations available were listed as:

Red-yellow
Black dotted
Red-white
White dotted
Black-Yellow
Green Dotted
Black-White
Yellow Dotted

The TURBULENT GIANT lures were available only in red and white. There were no descriptions of the other lures. Collector value range: $35-$50.

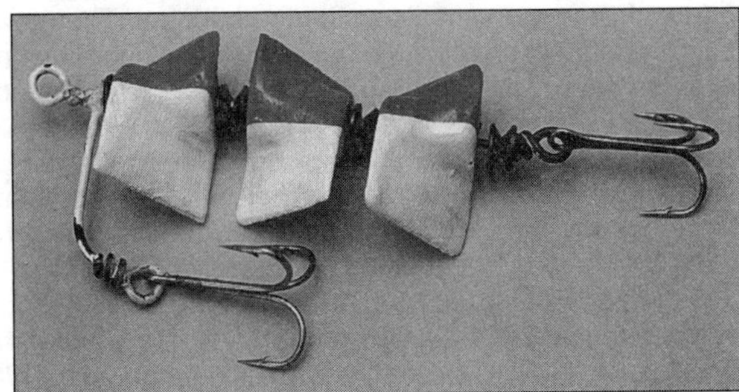

A 3" TURBULENT GIANT lure.

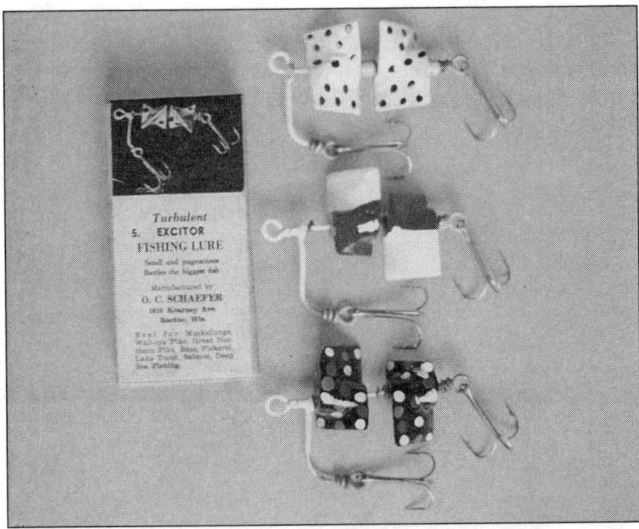

The TURBULENT EXCITOR. Photo courtesy Jim Muma.

The TURBULENT PENETRATOR. Photo courtesy Jim Muma.

TURNER CASTING BAIT
TURNER NIGHT CASTER

Zachary T. Turner — Coldwater, Michigan

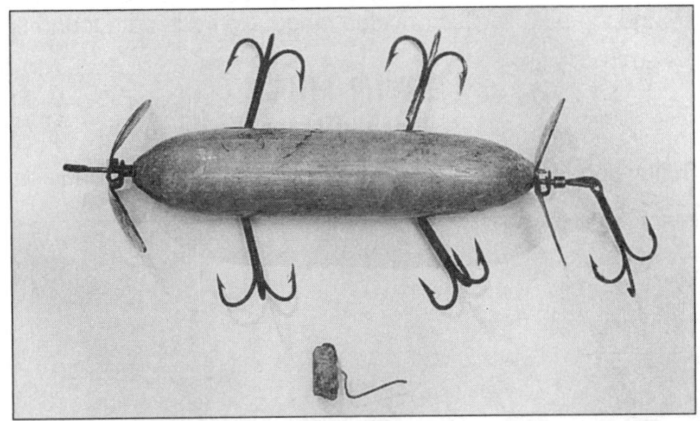

TURNER CASTING BAIT. Top view with belly weight removed.

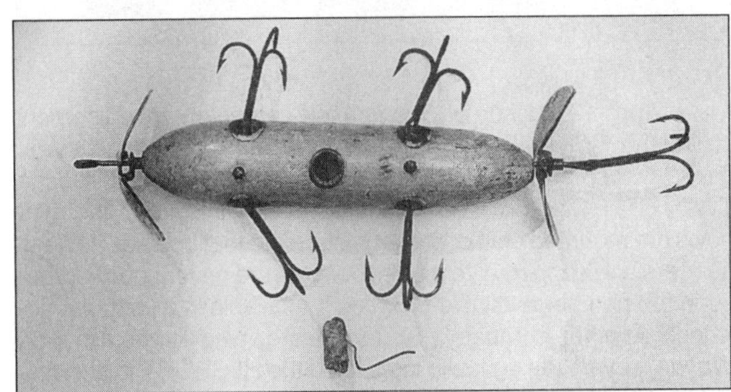

Belly view showing hook pins and hole for removable belly weight.

Father and son, the Turners were barbers. They ran their lure making business out of the back of their barber shop. The 4-1/8" wooden plug in the photos dates from around 1920s. A unique feature is the removable lead belly weight. The weight was cast with a spring wire so that it would have the weight firmly in the hole, but by squeezing the spring against the weight it could be removed. This feature made the plug a floater or sinker at will. Be very careful if you find one. The spring gets rusty and might break when you try to pull it out. There is a second, probably older, style where the belly weight is free swinging from the belly. The hook hardware was cup and see-through Gem-clip type hook hangers held fast by pins inserted from the belly. Colors were: frog back, orange and black, brown and white, mauve, dark back and orange belly, gold, aluminum, yellow white, orange, yellowish lemon and the NIGHT CASTER was luminous white. The company ceased operating in 1927. Collector value range: $250-$350.

TWINKLE BUG

F.M.F. Lures — 2322 Cansler Avenue, Gadsden, Alabama

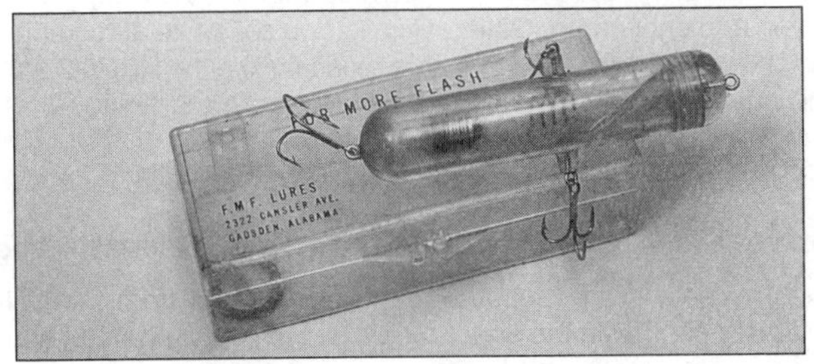

Measuring 3-1/2" this lure lights up under water. You can see the bulb. The battery has been removed. It came with flyer with an elaborate drawing, description and set of instructions for its use. Part of the instructions said the lure "..is designed for various colors by using different colors of cellophane around the bulb. Collector value range: No trade data found.

TWIN-MIN
TWIN-FINN

Staley-Johnson Manufacturing Co., Inc. Fort Wayne, Indiana

An April, 1947 issue of *Sports Afield* carried an advertisement calling the TWIN-MIN an "Amazing New Bait". Just the next year the same company was advertising the same bait, but called it a TWIN-FINN. Made of wood the lure measures 3". Both the minnows are mounted on a common metal plate that doubles as hook hangers and cupped dive plane. Colors were never specified beyond the number available (18) and "..available in all popular finishes." Another company, Staley Marine, also located in Fort Wayne, advertised a plastic lure called the HI-SPORT in the mid- to late-1950s. They are probably a later evolutionary step in the same company. Collector value range: $30-$50.

TWIRLING TWIRP

Watt Tackle Company Detroit, Michigan

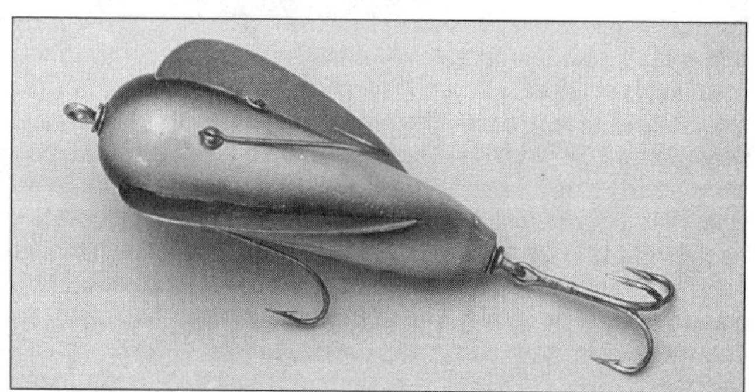

This 1940s wooden lure has three metal blades attached so as to make it revolve on retrieve. There is a single hook attached to the body between each of the blades for a total of three singles and a trailing treble. If a fish got near this one it was going to be hooked. The example in the photo was painted with three colors, yellow, green and dark green. Other colors known are white and orange, green and yellow. Although others report finding the lure in 2-3/4", this one measures 3" long. Collector value range: $20-$40.

UNDER-TAKER

Glen L. Evans, Inc. Caldwell, Idaho

A collector from Montana identified this lure from the UNKNOWN section in the second edition. He sent a photo of several lures in which an example of this lure appeared. His is new in the box. It has a red face, green body with yellow spray spots and bulging painted (tack?) eyes. The box yielded some information. On the box was printed "CRAFTSMAN Fishing Tackle. A product of Glen L. Evans, Inc., Caldwell, Idaho." There was also much printed information on how to fish the plug. The one in the photo here measures 3-7/8" and the one from the box measured 3-3/8".

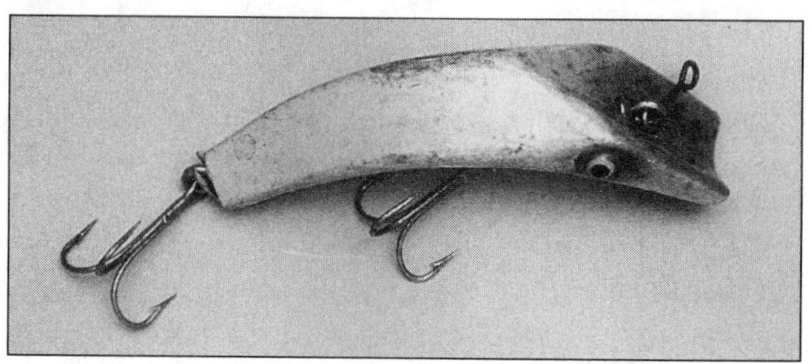

The Glen Evans Company began doing business from a basement operation in the 1920s and grew into a big company producing mostly flies, spinners, leaders and the like. The Gladding Corporation was running the operation when it finally sold to Luhr Jensen in the 1980s. The lures the company produced were the UNDER-TAKER and at least two others, the BURPER, a six-sided plunker style wooden lure and the TWO TIMER. The latter is exactly the same as the UNDER-TAKER except it was available in two paint patterns that were never used on the UNDER-TAKER, Frog and Perch. Collector value range for the three wooden lures: $40-$60.

COLOR OR FINISHES OBSERVED: Black with red face, pearl with red face, frog spot, white with red head and flitters, perch, red with black face, yellow with red head.

VAL-LUR

Val Products Company Chicago, Illinois

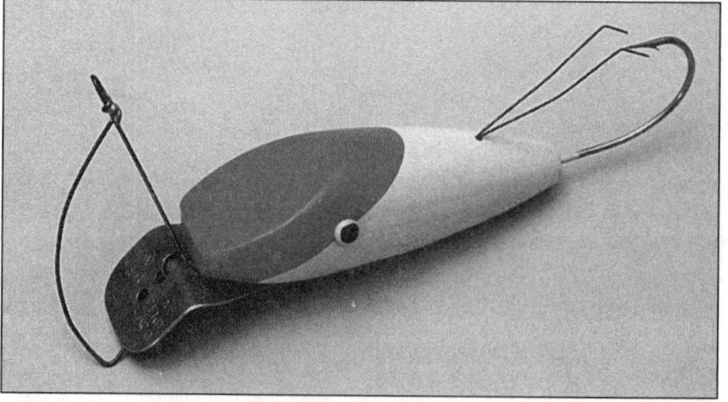

In actuality the lure pictured here is but one of a set of 10 called the VAL-LUR-SET. They were new in 1936. As you may be able to see in the advertisement reproduced here, there are three similar jointed VAL-LURS in the set. These are 4" long: The JOINTED MINNOW, JOINTED MINNOW with treble hook and MUSKY SPECIAL. Then there are four similar to the one in the photograph which measures 3-1/2", 4-1/4" overall. The four are the SKIDDER PLUG, HAIR TAIL PLUG, STRIP PLUG and SMALL-MOUTH WIGGLER. The other two are the NEW CASTING FLY and WEEDLESS PORK. There were only three colors listed as available: Red and white, perch scale or pike scale. I have seen the red head in a straight version as opposed to the slant version in the photo here. The metal dive lips are well marked with the company name. Collector value range: $20-$40.

10 PROVEN LURES MADE WITH THE VAL-LUR-SET $1

Gives you the most remarkable and **complete assortment of successful lures** for Bass, Musky, Pike, Pickerel, Trout, and pan fish. For deep, surface and semi-surface Equipped with the famous **"VAL SNAG-PROOF** and **Weedless NOSE GUARD."**

Enjoy real fishing this year with this great array of fish-getters: **1. Jointed Minnow**—single hook. 2. **Skidder Plug.** 3. **Hair Tail Plug.** 4. **Strip Plug.** 5. Small-Mouth **Wiggler.** 6. Wiggling **Chunk Plug.** 7. **Jointed Minnow-gang hooks.** 8. New Casting Fly. 9. **Weedless** Pork or Live-Bait Lure. 10. **Musky** Special. Our **LIMITED TIME** offer for this interchangeable set, which makes all above lures **$1 only.** Specify **ONE** finish **only:** Red and White, or Perch scale, or Pike scale. Order direct if dealer cannot supply you with VAL-LUR SET **"GET YOURS NOW—BEFORE SUPPLY IS EXHAUSTED."**

BIG PRIZES AWARDED: 1. Johnson Outb. Motor, 2. Savage 22 H.P. Rifle, 3. Quality Casting Rod, 4. High Grade **Fly Rod for best comments on VAL SNAGPROOF NOSE GUARD,** (accompanied by **Top of** VAL-LUR carton). Closing date, 10/1/1937. Other **valuable prizes to Every Entry. Particulars in all Val-Lur cartons and at your dealer.**

VAL PRODUCTS CO., 7239 Greenleaf Ave., Chicago, Ill., Dept. A-5.

A Val Products advertisement from the May, 1937 issue of Sports afield.

VAUGHN'S LURE

Vaughn's Tackle Company Cheboygan, Michigan

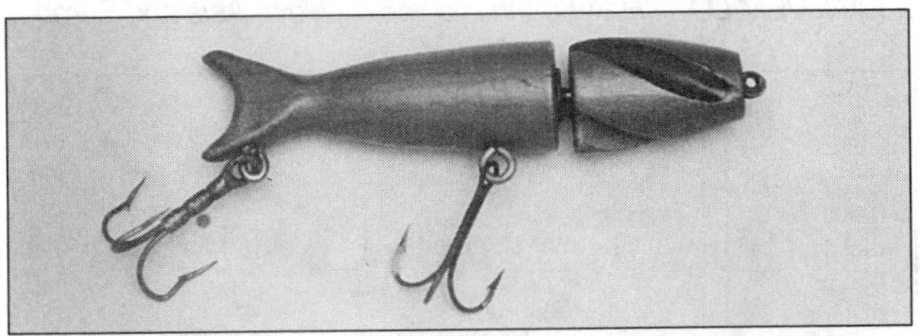

This lure appeared in the unknown section of the first edition of this book. It has since been identified. It has a green body and fully rotating head with three flutes. The flutes are painted red, yellow and white respectively. The body of this wooden lure measures 3-1/2". It dates from around the early 1930s. It was made "...in Six Different Colors, Red, White, Orange, Green, Black and Metallic Gray with contrasting colors in spiral." Collector value range: $90-$125.

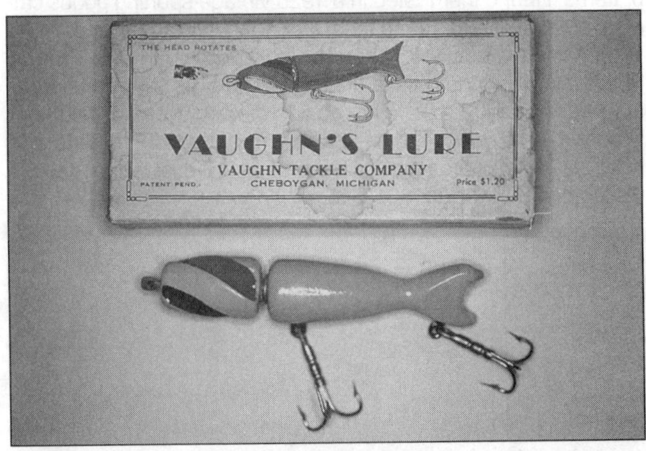

Listed as unknown in the first edition of this book this 3-5/8" lure was identified for the second edition. Nothing more has turned up in the 18 years since. This mint-in-the-box lure is yellow bodied with red and green flutes. Photo courtesy Clarence Zahn.

THE VEE-BUG

Martz Tackle Detroit, Michigan

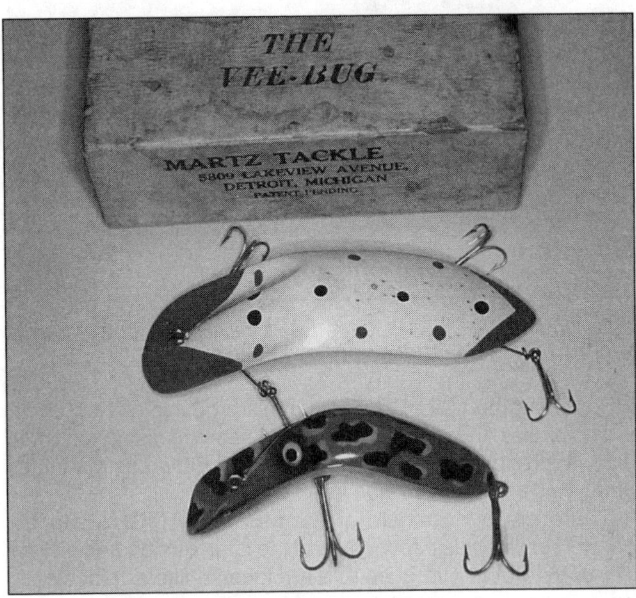

The upper lure in the photo is red and white and came in the box pictured. It is made of wood, measures 4-3/4" and was manufactured under a patent that was issued around 1937. The smaller, 3-5/8" version with a frog finish is a later model made of plastic. An advertisement in a 1950 issue of *The Outdoorsman* magazine said they were made in "Five Color Combinations..and Frog Coloring". That makes a total of six to be found. The ad was in black and white, but it appears the lure illustrated had a white body with a solid colored head. The other three colors are not known. The wooden model is difficult to find and has a collector value range of $20-$30; plastic: $5-$15. Photo courtesy Clarence Zahn.

VERMILION MEADOW MOUSE
(other Vermilion Lures)

Frank Knill Vermilion, Ohio

The slim body version of the VERMILION MEADOW MOUSE. Collector value range: $50-$75.

Earliest reference found was to a patent application filed by Frank Knill in 1922 for a lure unrelated to the MEADOW MOUSE. The earliest advertisement found was in a September issue of *Sporting Goods Journal* for Vermilion Spinners. Knill had a small operation, employing only a few part-time workers. The lures were assembled in his garage, the metal pieces being made by metal shops in Vermilion. He may have been a small operation, but he was serious, filing at least three patent applications, 1922,1924 and 1926.

As far as is known the MEADOW MOUSE was the only

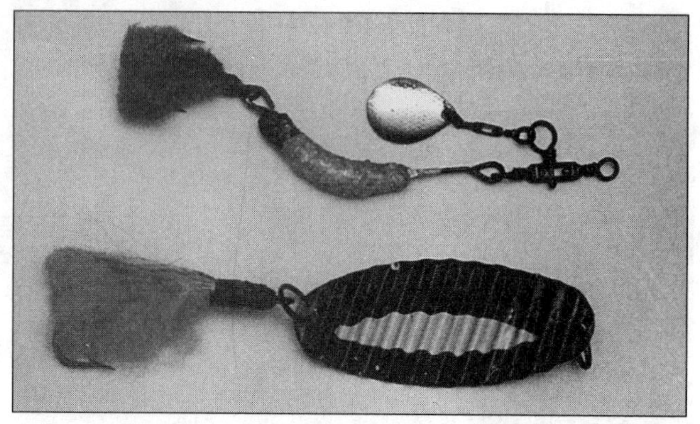

Upper lure is the VERMILION PEARL FLASHER. Lower lure is the VERMILION WOBBLER. Collector value range: $15-$20.

wooden plug he made. The rest of his products were spoons and spinners. Advertisements by Knill seem to disappear after 1933. It is reported that a company named Patterson Manufacturing made some Vermilion lures in 1949.

There are two models of the MEADOW MOUSE to be found. The oldest is a fat body and the later version has a slimmer body. Both have eyes that are faceted like a rhinestone, cup and screw eye hardware and leather tail as in the photo. They are 3-1/2" long.

THE VIKING FROG

Viking Bait and Novelty Company — Oscar Christiansen, St. Paul, Minnesota

This very rare wooden frog was patented in 1936. It is sometimes called the CHRISTIANSEN FROG by collectors. It measures 4-1/2" long. There is a variation where the first leg section behind the body is absent and the bent legs are attached to the body with the feet pointing inward instead of out as in the normal two joint model. Collector value range: No trade data found. Photo courtesy Jim Muma.

VOO-DOO

Reelon Corporation — South San Francisco, California

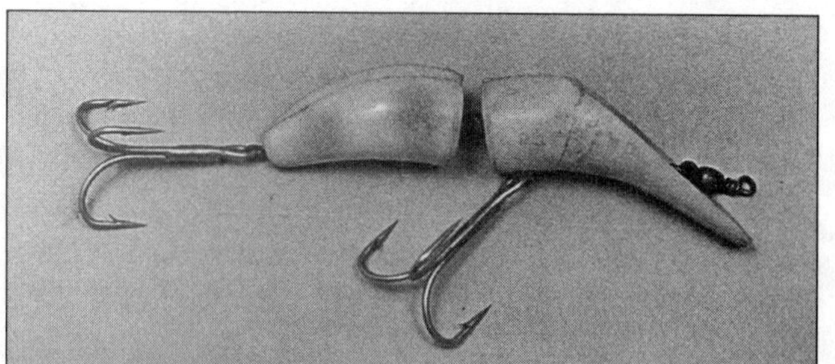

An advertisement in the July, 1950 issue of *The Outdoorsman* magazine lists three sizes of this jointed plastic lure: MASTER VOO-DOO at 5-1/4", the STANDARD VOO-DOO (photo) at 2-3/4" and the FLYROD VOO-DOO at 1-1/2". The 2-3/4" model always had two hooks, but the other two sizes could be bought with one or two hooks. It is reported to be available in nine colors. The ad said a "Wide selection of standard and fluorescent colors." I found a 1953 catalog listing of five colors. They are orange with black spots, yellow with red spots, frog with yellow belly, silver with black spots. Collector value range: $5-$10.

WADHAM NATURE BAITS

Percy Wadham — England

This 3-1/4" celluloid lure was in a Wadham box that identifies it as a LAND 'EM LOACH. A Loach is a fish native to Asia and Europe.

These lures are remarkable reproductions of minnows in beautiful colors. They were fashioned of celluloid. As you can see in the photo they were highly detailed. Readily identifiable, they were made in six sizes ranging from 1-1/4" to 3-1/2" and available in five patterns. I found them listed in a 1925 vintage sporting goods catalog, but nowhere did I find them independently advertised.

In previous editions I reported no address known. From a box I now know that this is an English lure. Its vintage is probably very early 1910s. The box I referred to also said that Wadhams came in "Nature, Land 'em and O.K." models and were "Made in sizes from 1-1/2" to 5" in 110 different patterns." Collector value range: $35-$45.

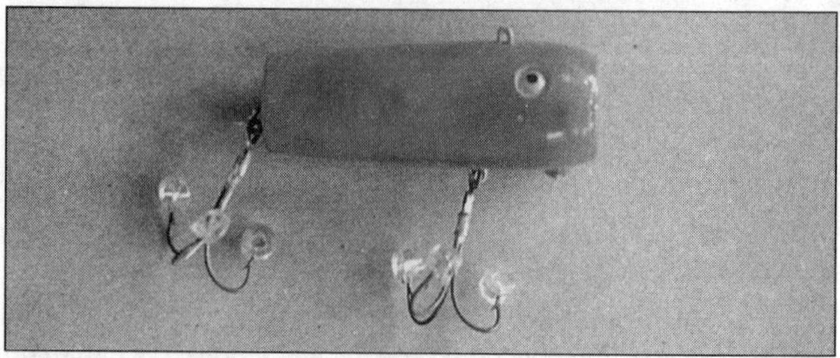

A Bill Warren MINNOW. This example is orange with red splotches. Not visible is a very large hole for the mouth.

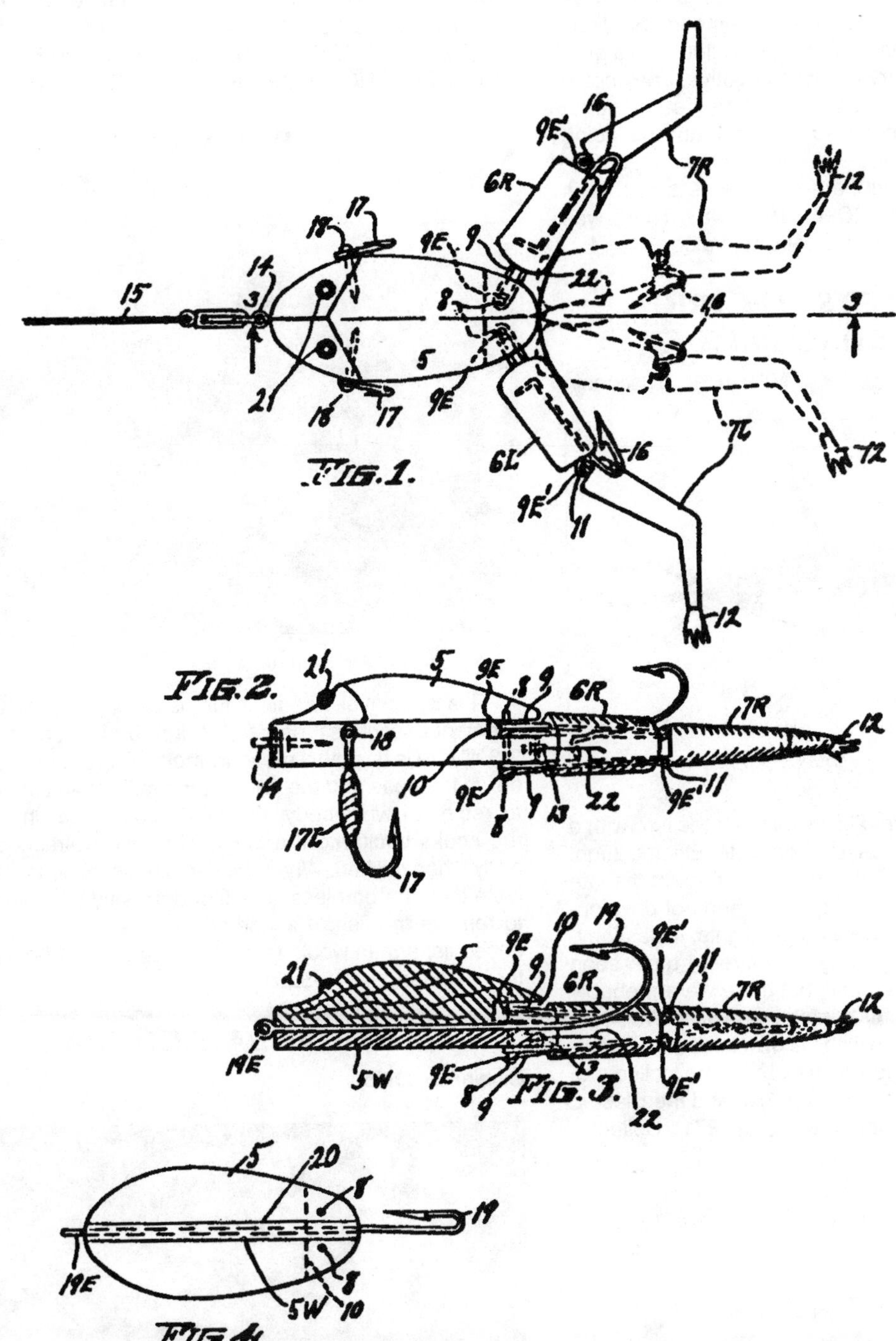

The drawing from the patent application by Oscar Christiansen.

BILL WARREN MINNOW

Pittsburg, Kansas

A collector sent me the photo here along with a request for any information I might have regarding the lure. Well, a thorough search of all the books and all my research files resulted in zilch. He measured the lure carefully and it is a small 2-11/16" long. It appears to be made of wood although he didn't say. Included with the lure was a letter that resulted from a query to the Pittsburg public library that was negative. They could turn up no records of anyone named Bill Warren at the street address on the box pamphlet. Looks like Mr. Warren is going to be elusive. Maybe one of you can help with some more information. The flyer did reveal that the lure was available in "EIGHT DIFFERENT COLOR COMBINATIONS." There was no trade data from which to derive a collector value.

DR. WASWEYLER'S ELECTRIC GLOW-CASTING BAIT

Dr. C. S. Wasweyler — Milwaukee, Wisconsin

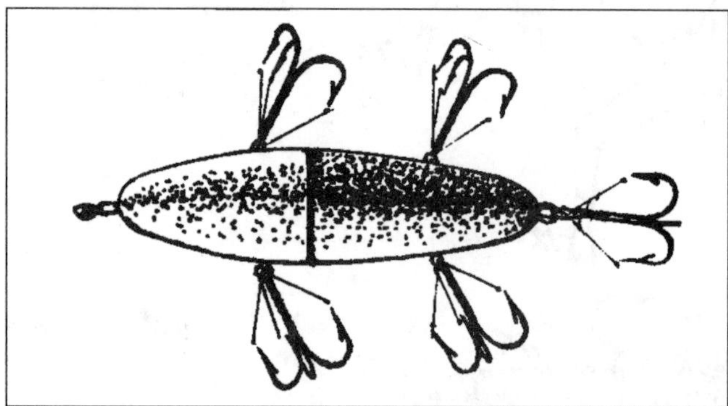

A 1914 advertisement offered and illustrated the lure with a battery operated light inside as "A Complete Electric Light Plant". Electric light was one of the great inventions of the late 1800s and by the 1910s there had been all sorts of developments including small battery-operated pen lights. It was inevitable that fishermen would try to light up lures. I have seen about a dozen different lighted lures, but there were probably more than that over the years. As a matter of fact Dr. Wasweyler seems to have experimented with his own as there is an altogether different lure attributed to him by some collectors. There may be some connection between him and the Electric Luminous Submarine Bait Company (see page 271). Collector value range: $500-$700.

WEBER

Stevens Point, Wisconsin

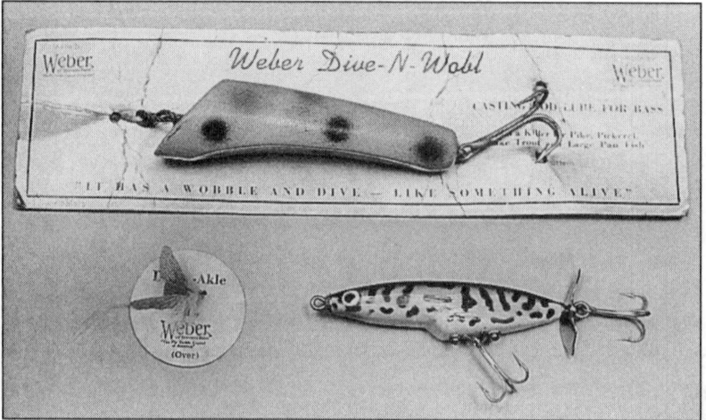

When the lures are found in the original packaging the package always has "WEBER of Stevens Point The Fly Tackle Capitol of America" on it. The DIVE-N-WOBBLE at top measures 3-1/2". The fly at bottom left is a DRAKE-ACKLE and the one on the right is a 2-3/4" SHADRAC. The company made fly rod lures and other lures for light tackle. Most of the lures have a collector value of less than $10, but some of their fly rod lures can go as high as $35-$40. Some names of other Weber lures are SUPER-DUPER, POP-ACKEL, VOO DOO BUG, POPPIN-FROG, BIG SHOT, FLIP-FROG, MOUSE and HAIR FROG.

WEED KING

Sevdy Enterprises — Worthington, Minnesota

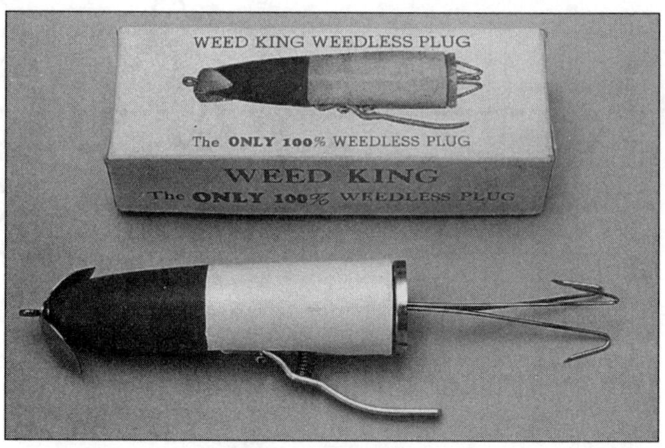

This is a clever weedless lure is 3-3/4" long. A 1953 Advertisement describes it as a 3-1/2" lure and others report 4". My 3-3/4" size is by actual measurement. There is a propeller spinner at the nose and the only color available was as in the photo, red head, white body. You prepared it for casting by pushing the hooks back into the body. The lever retracts toward the body when cocked. When the fish strikes, out come the hooks. Note they are barbless. The literature said this made it easier to remove the fish. If it worked I suspect any but the experienced fisherman would lose more fish than he boated. Collector value range: $15-$25.

WEEZEL BAIT COMPANY

Cincinnati, Ohio

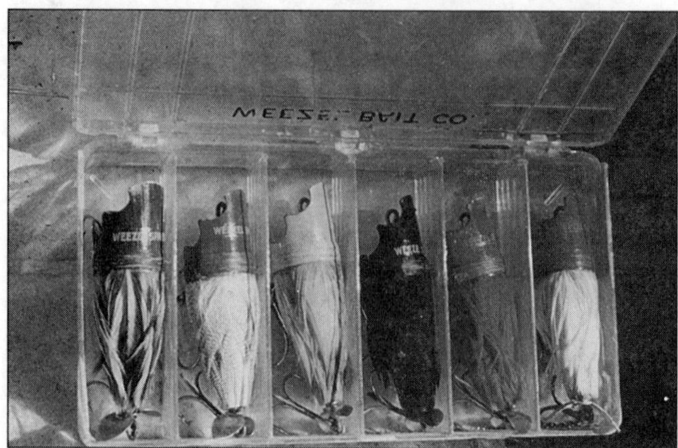

Photo courtesy Dennis Hyder

The best date I can come up with for this company is mid-1930s to the late 1940s. They manufactured at least 10 basic lure designs most of which were feathered metal spoon, spinner or jig types. The most sought after lures from this company are the WEEZEL SPARROW pictured above and the BOPPER which is essentially the same lure without the feathers. They are both wood-bodied 1/2 oz. lures manufactured under a patent number that dates about 1948. Collector value range: $15-$25.

The name Max Weesner is associated with this company. Some of their other products are WEESNER'S REX SPOON, WEESNER'S MUSKY WEEZEL, and MAX WEESNER'S BUCK SPINNER. The Weezel Company also made a crab shaped WEEZEL CRAB that was essentially a spoon with a rubber crab, and two versions of a light WEEZEL, a weighted feather minnow with a forward single blade "Ponca" type spinner or a metal surface plane at its head. It is called a WIGGLE DISH. There were also two very large SALTWATER MUSKIE WEEZELS, 5/8 oz. and 1 oz. weights, 9-1/2" long. They were available in 20 different color combinations.

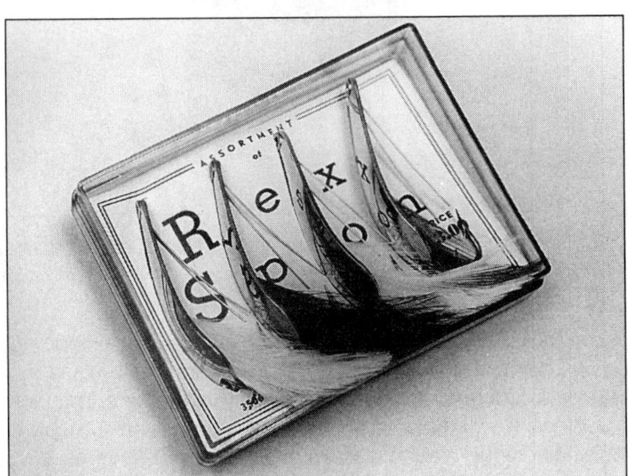

Four assorted Weezel REX SPOONS.

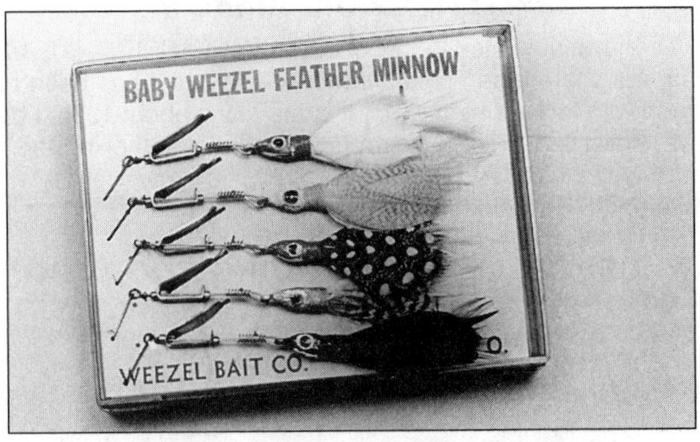

These FEATHER MINNOWS measure 3" overall.

The WEEZEL CASTING FEATHER MINNOW. Hook and body measures 2-1/2", 4-1/2" overall.

WELCH & GRAVES

Natural Bridge, New York

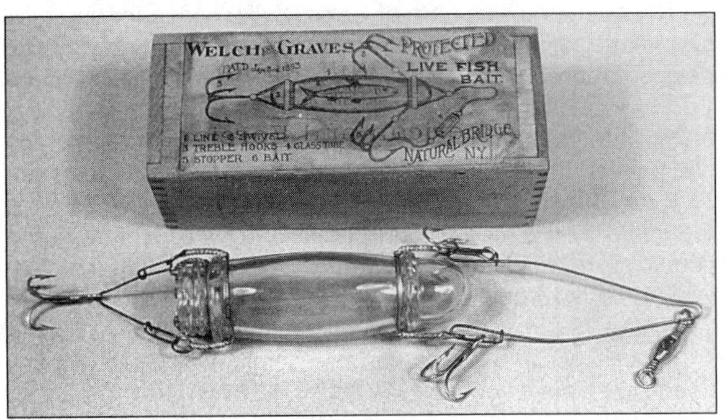

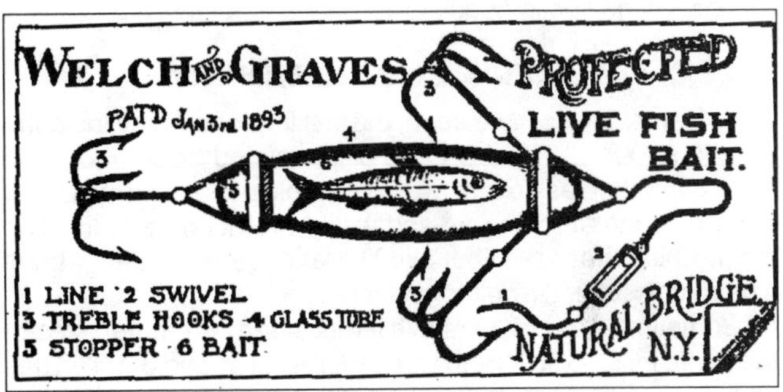

The glass minnow tube in the accompanying photo was invented by Henry J. Welch. He was granted a patent on it in January of 1893. An early advertisement called it an "...IMPROVED PROTECTED LIVE FISH BAIT . One minnow lasts a day...". One can only wonder at this word "IMPROVED". Does this mean he had made versions of this glass minnow tube earlier than the patented model? Whatever the case, this is certainly the earliest of this curious style of lure. You were supposed to put a live minnow in the glass tube and it would stay alive all day presumably catching fish over and over. A glass stopper was used to keep the minnow from escaping. The Graves in the name is Calvin V. Graves who manufactured the lures. His literature states that there were three sizes available, 3-1/2", 4-1/2" and 5-1/2". It has been reported, but unsubstantiated, that there was fourth size offered. Actual sizes that have been found are 3-1/8", 3-3/4", 4", 4-1/4", 4-3/8", 4-1/2" and 5". The box in the accompanying photo is an original. They were made of wood with a paper label. The label on this one is long gone. Collector value range: $450-$750. Identification of the lures is made easy by the clear identification molded into the side of the glass body stating:

WELCH & GRAVES
PAT. JAN 3, '93
NATURAL BRIDGE, N.Y.

Other names associated with the glass minnow tube style lure are: Detroit Glass Minnow Tube Co.; Pfeiffer's Live Bait Holder Co.; C. E. Henning, the c. 1911 Henning Minnow Tube and Charles C. Kellman. Photo courtesy Jim Muma.

An illustration from a Welch & Graves flyer. That same flyer had a rather strong admonition for users of any other glass minnow tube type lure. "Any transparent device for fishing without the name 'Welch & Graves, Patent Jan 3, 1893,' in the glass is an infringement and the users will be prosecuted?. One wonders what they would do to the maker.

WELLER'S CLASSIC MINNOW c. 1925

Erwin Weller Company — Sioux City, Iowa

The company was born of Erwin Weller's idea for a natural swimming action wooden minnow while fishing one day. He devised a three-piece articulated minnow. Thus was born the WELLER CLASSIC MINNOW. About 1920-21 he and his wife started turning out the lure in their home. He made them and she painted them. By 1924 the company had grown considerably, now making three sizes of the CLASSIC MINNOW. Over the years they added a fourth Classic, a MOUSE lure and a couple more, unjointed-wooden plugs. 1942 was the last year Weller made wooden lures, although they continued in operation. After 1942 the tackle they offered was all metal.

Anyone wishing to know more about the Weller company needs to obtain a copy of *History of the Erwin Weller Company* by Harold G. Dickert. It is the most complete Weller reference written to date. A source for it can be found in the recommended references section back toward the font of this book.

WELLER'S CLASSIC MINNOW

This was, as we have seen, the first lure offered by the company (1920-21). It had a three-piece jointed body (the joints were hinged), glass eyes, two belly trebles and a combination, one-piece metal lip/line tie and was 4-3/4" long, not including the flexible rubberized fiber tail. The latter had a tendency to rot away, hence are difficult to find intact.

Sometime around 1924 Weller included two more sizes of the jointed CLASSIC. Both were smaller at 4" and 3-1/4". They exhibit all the characteristics of the 4-3/4" lure, except they have only two-piece bodies.

A very typical Weller characteristic of jointed CLASSICS is the red-painted area of articulation to simulate injury. In fact, some of their advertisements featured the statement: "HORRORS! It Has Two Bloody Tooth Marks On Each Side."

Sometime around 1934 the rubber tail had disappeared from all sizes. That year saw the introduction of a fourth size, the NEW CLASSIC at 3-1/4". This one departed from the original style in two ways. The one-piece lip/line tie had changed to a screw eye line tie and a more standard screw-on metal diving lip was used. The hooks had changed from two belly trebles to one belly treble and one trailing treble. It still had glass eyes and hinged articulation. Finishes of the various CLASSICS found listed so far are: Chub, white body with red head, white body with blue head, brown pike, green pike, perch and red devil. Collector value range: $50-$100.

Hints for dating the CLASSIC:

1. 1920-21 to 1933 lures will have the flexible tail or the slot where it was once located.
2. 1934 to 1942 Wellers baits will have small pins or brads in tail and nose to fill up the holes made by the lathe. No tail fin.

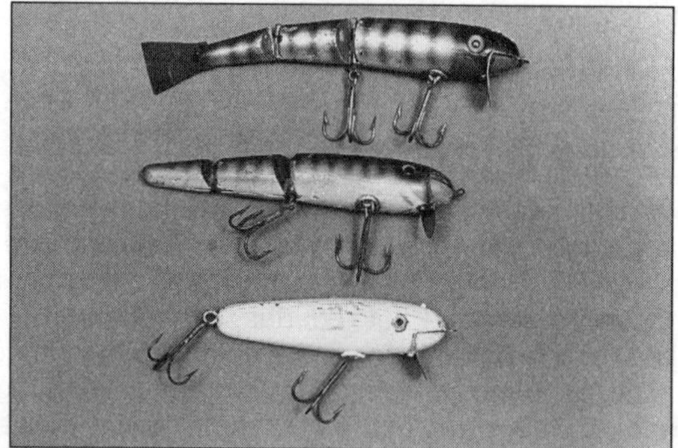

The two upper lures are Weller CLASSIC MINNOWS. The bottom lure is the SIMPLEX WIGGLER.

WELLER SIMPLEX WIGGLER

The lure was introduced sometime prior to 1933 when the metal diving lip style changed and continued in production, so presumably it may be found with both styles. The only one I have seen has the old style. It is 3-1/4" with treble and trailing treble hook. Finishes available were the same as the CLASSIC MINNOW. The one in the photo is solid white. It could be a repaint. Collector value range: $30-$90.

WELLER'S MOUSE

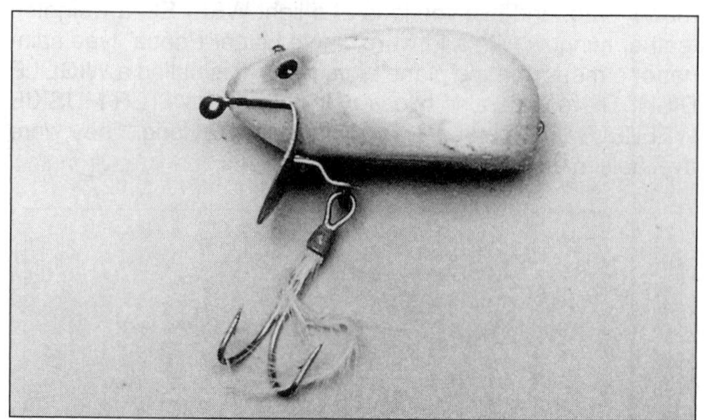

WELLER'S MOUSE. This one has black bead eyes, measures 1-13/16" and has one internalized belly weight. White in color.

The MOUSE was introduced in 1928 and continued in production until 1942. This is a mouse body shaped, 1-3/4" glass eyed plug with a double hook hidden in the fancy tail feathers. They were available with a single hook by "Special Order", so presumably the single hook model would be the hardest to find. Weight was 3/8 oz. and colors available were: Gray red and white, solid black, or solid white with pink eyes. Collector value range: $50-$100.

WELLER OZARK MINNOW

This is an unjointed model of the NEW CLASSIC. It is 2-1/2" long and shares the same characteristics, but it has been reported with tack painted eyes. It came along about 1934, I believe. Finishes available were: Brown pike, green pike, perch, chub, white with red head, blue with white head, yellow with white head. Collector value range: $10-$20.

WHOPPER-STOPPER SPORTING GOODS CO. WHOPPER-STOPPER BAIT COMPANY, INC. WHOPPER-STOPPER, INC.

Fred Eder — Sherman, Texas

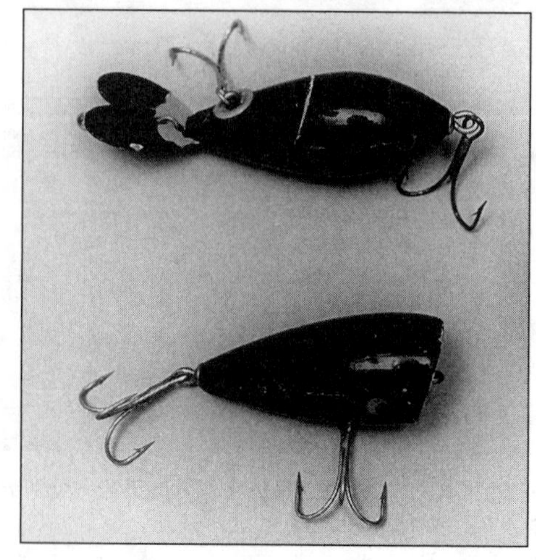

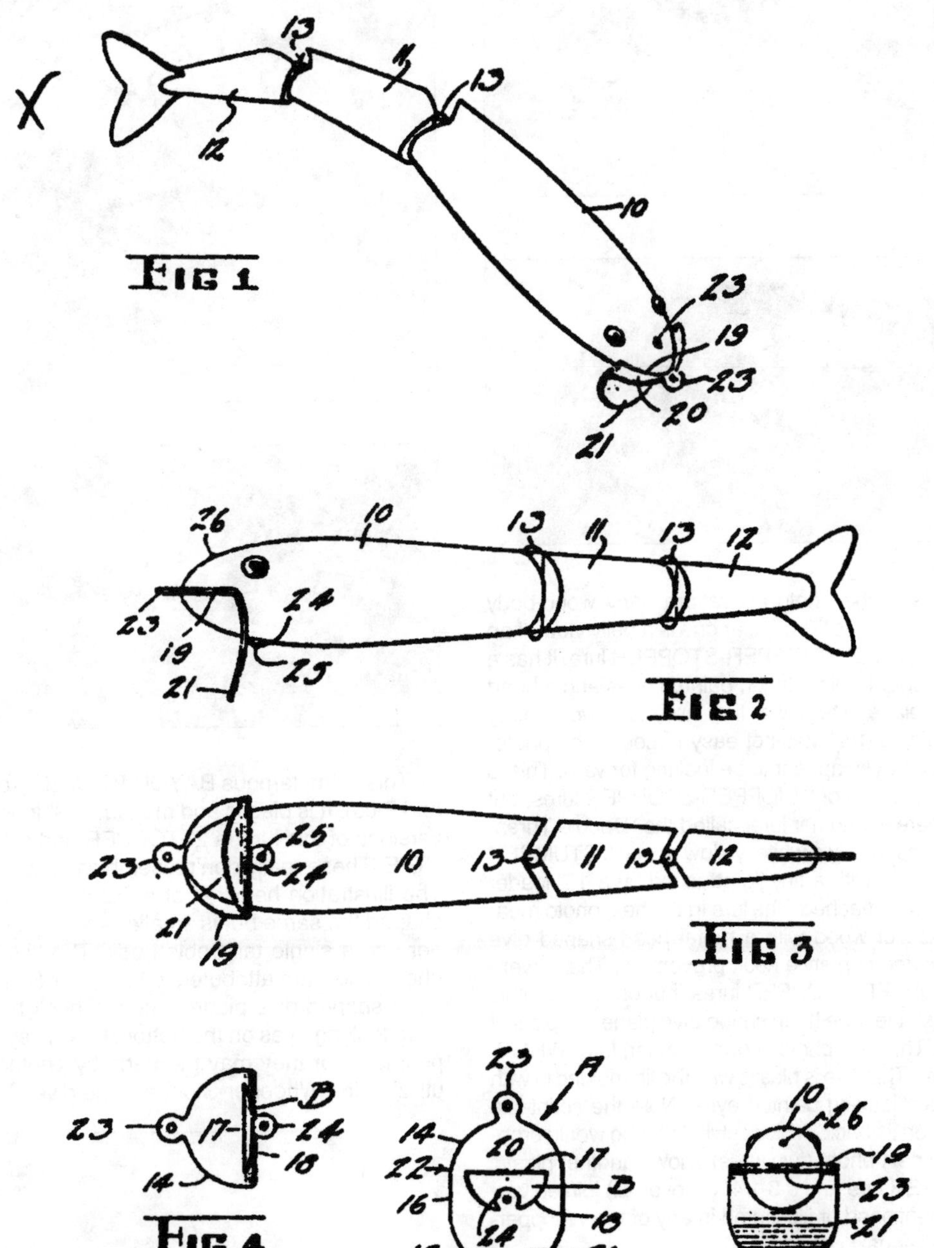

Patent illustration for Weller's CLASSIC MINNOW. Granted November 16, 1926, the patent actually claims only the metal mouth piece.

Fred Eder was a sales representative for a soap company before going into the lure business. One of his stops was the Bomber Bait Company in Gainesville, Texas. He began fishing with one of the founders and over time noticed the success that Bomber was enjoying. At some point this influenced him to found his own lure-making enterprise in the 1940s.

Both of the lures in the photo above are early wood-body WHOPPER-STOPPER lures. The upper one is a belly view of an original, back running 2-1/2" WHOPPER-STOPPER lure. It has a cup and screw eye belly treble hanger, painted eyes and a heart shaped metal dive plane. The lower lure here is a wood body STUMPER measuring 2-1/4". It is not easy to see in the photograph, but the painted eyes appear to be looking forward. This is a fairly typical characteristic of WHOPPER-STOPPER lures, but it is not the rule. There is another lure, called the "Double Threat POP 'N JIG" that is essentially a white, yellow or black STUMPER (without tail treble hook) with a tiny jig attached by a 15" leader where the tail hook was attached. The lure in the next photo measures 2-7/8" is made of wood with a metal heart-shaped dive plane. Note the inverted cup style hook preventers. These were often used on WHOPPER-STOPPER lures, but once again this in not a hard and fast rule. The heart shape dive plane is typical of the lures, however. The next photo shows another, later WHOPPER-STOPPER lure. This one is plastic with the lip molded in with the body and forward-looking painted eyes. Note the script-like style of the marking on its back. A block style lettering would probably be earlier. The next photo (two lures) shows another plastic WHOPPER-STOPPER lure and a 3-1/4" (4" over-all) jointed version that was not mentioned or illustrated in any of the Whopper-Stopper company materials I have.

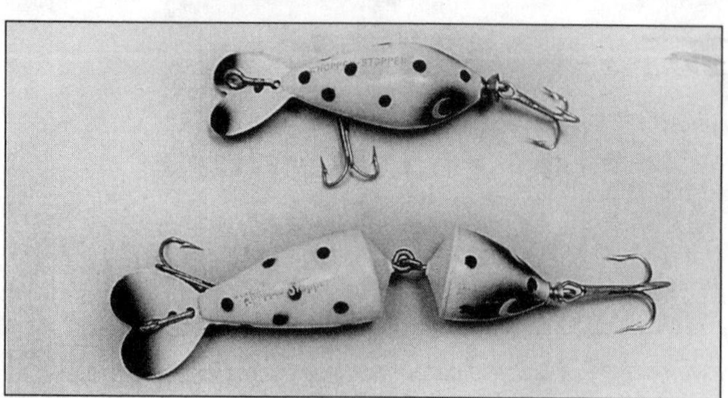

The next photo of three lures shows a HELLRAISER at the top and two other Whopper-Stopper lures that remain unidentified. The HELLRAISER measures 2-3/4" long, has a floppy tail prop and forward looking eyes. The unidentified lure in the middle is marked "Whopper-Stopper" on the back. The smallest one is placed here because of its forward looking eyes.

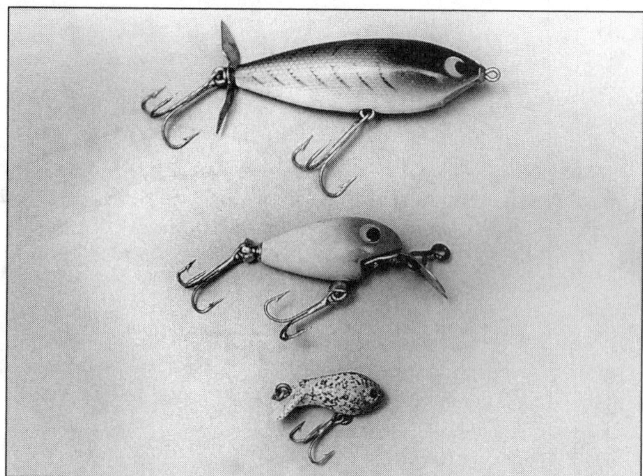

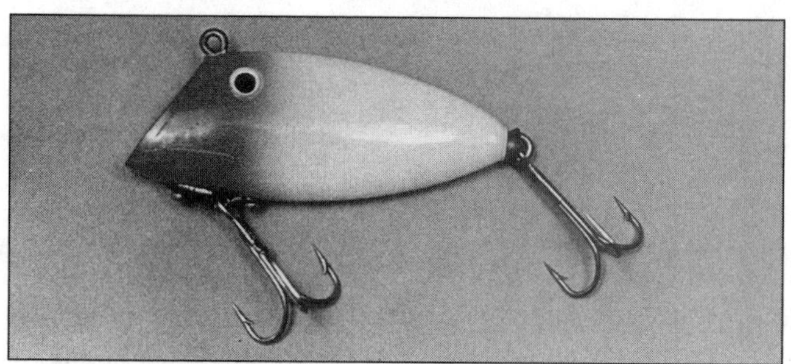

This is the famous BAYOU BOOGIE (see Hawk Fish Lures and Pico). It is plastic and measures 3" long. There are smaller versions of this lure, a 2" TOPPER and a 1 1/8" long FLY BOOGIE. These really don't resemble the BAYOU BOOGIE at all. The illustration below is of a TOPPER. The FLY BOOGIE is shaped the same but is smaller and has no tail propeller spinner and a single tail treble hook. The two plastic lures in the photo below are attributed to Whopper-Stopper because of the heart shaped dive planes and the hook hanger style and forward looking eyes on the bottom lure. They may have been experiments or they may be made by another company merely utilizing the Whopper-Stopper style dive planes.

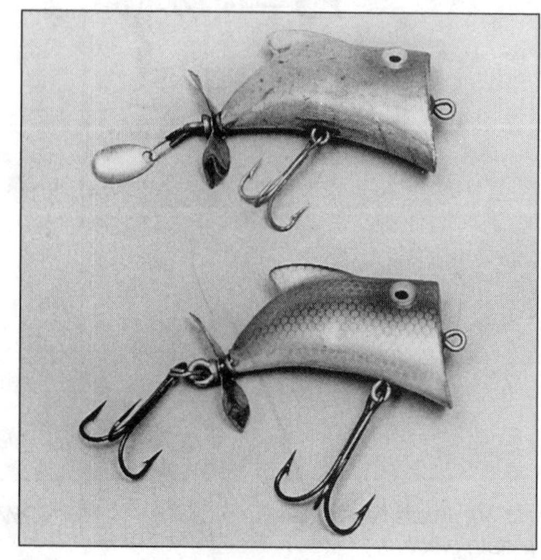

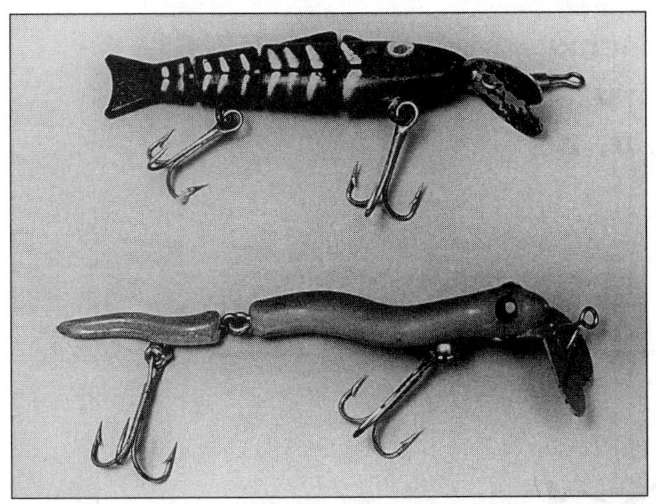

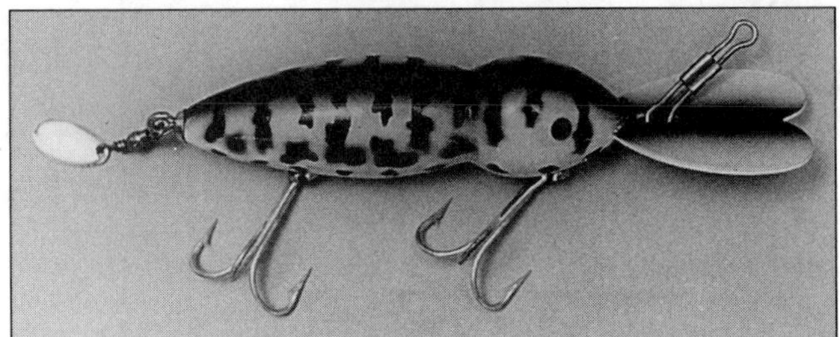

A Whopper-Stopper HELLBENDER.

COLLECTOR VALUE RANGES:

Wooden Whopper-Stopper	$12-$20.
Plastic Whopper-Stopper	$5-$12.
The Stumper	$5-$10.
Hellbender	$8-$14.
Hellraiser	$5-$10.
Pop 'n' Jig	$5-$10.
Bayou Boogie	$5-$10.
Topper	$5-$10.
Fly Boogie	$8-$15.

Colors or finishes that Whopper-Stopper lures may be found in the list following are not necessarily found on all the lures. Some listed are not descriptive at all.

Solid white	Pink eye ghost
Solid yellow	Solid black
Red head minnow	Yellow ghost
Yellow with black ribs	Gray ghost
White with black ribs	Ghost shore minnow
Black with white ribs	Green perch
Orange with black ribs	Shad
Pearl with red eyes	Bream
Pearl with blue eyes	Crappie
Silver	Garfish
Frog	Gray shad minnow
Silver flitter	Green shad minnow
White with black stripe	Brown shad minnow
White with black dots	Coach dog
Yellow with black dots	Coach dog-white & black
Yellow with black ribs	Shiner

1929 WIGGLER or POLLYWOG WIGGLER

Anthony J. Sobecki — South Bend, Indiana

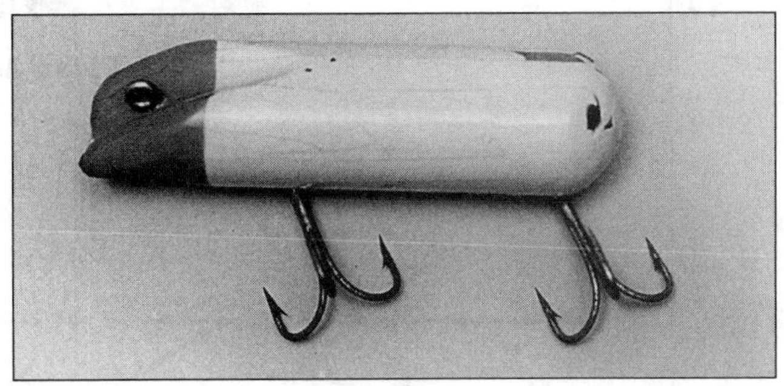

This odd-ball lure was patented in 1929. It measures 3-5/8" long and the hooks utilize the cup and screw eye hardware. This lure has a white body with red head. Little else is presently known about Sobecki or his lures. Collector value range: $75-$100.

WILCOX WIGGLER

Charles M. Wilcox — New Paris, Ohio

The upper WILCOX WIGGLER measures 3-7/16" has yellow glass eyes and see-through side hook hangers. The lower lure is a later, less complicated model. It has cup and screw eye hook hangers, glass eyes and is slightly broader and a bit longer.

I found two Wilcox advertisements for this lure. The earliest ad was for in a 1909 periodical. The ad copy said "JUST OUT". The other one was in a 1915 issue of *The Outer's Book* magazine that was actually placed by E. C. Campbell of Eaton, Ohio. Curiously, that 1915 ad also says the lure was new, six years later. The lures in the ads look the same to me, but there may be enough subtle differences to make it a new model. The exact wording in the ad was "The New 1915 WIGGLER".

The patent was granted November 5, 1907 to three people: Charles M. Wilcox of New Paris, Ohio, inventor; James E. Kirkpatrick of Anderson, Indiana, and Charles P. Kirkpatrick of New Paris, Ohio. The WILCOX WIGGLER in the photo matches the patent drawing. It is a very strongly constructed with single joint articulation, yellow glass eyes and one surface-flush internal belly weight. Collector value range: $2,000-$3,000.

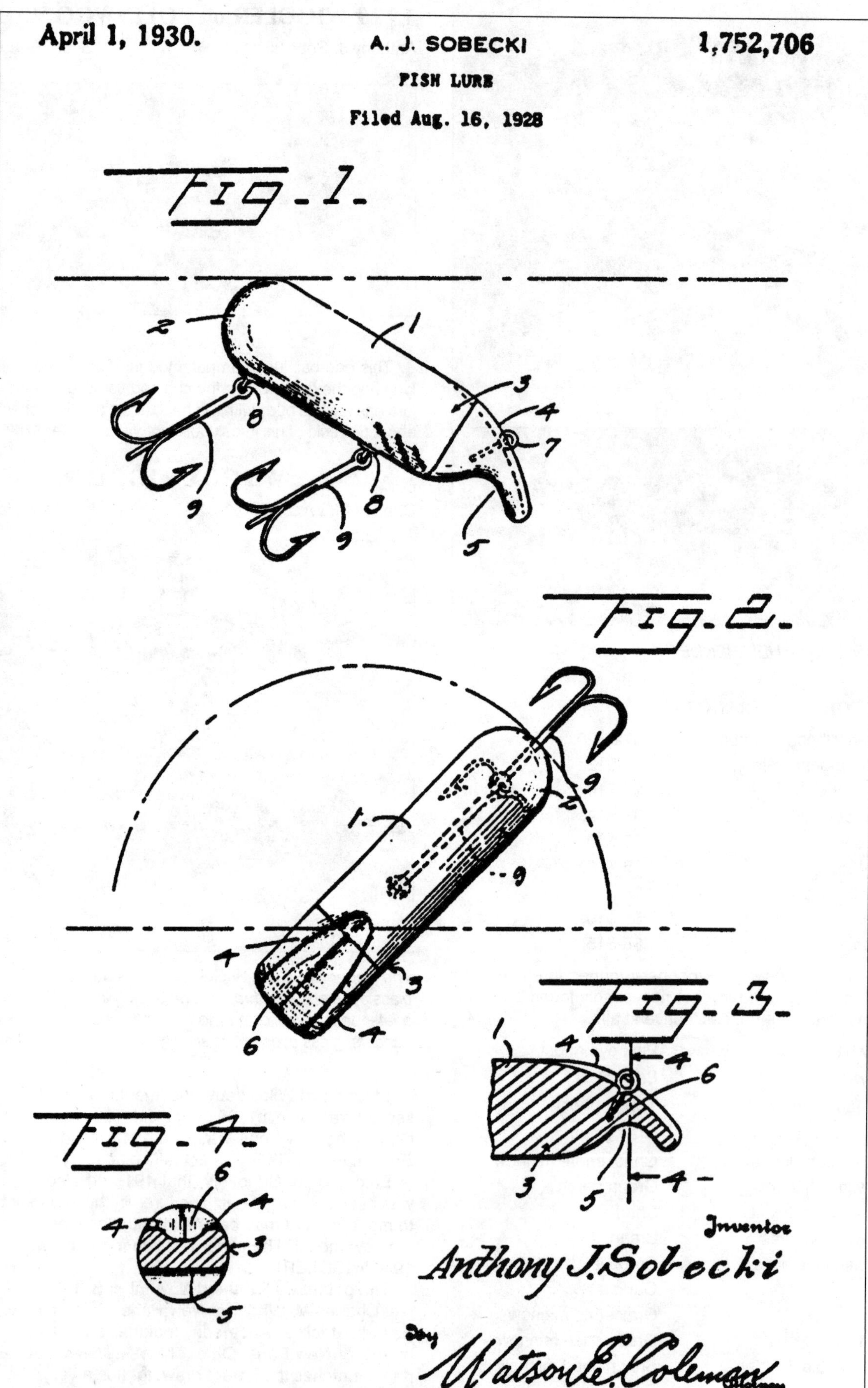

The illustration from the Sobecki patent illustration.

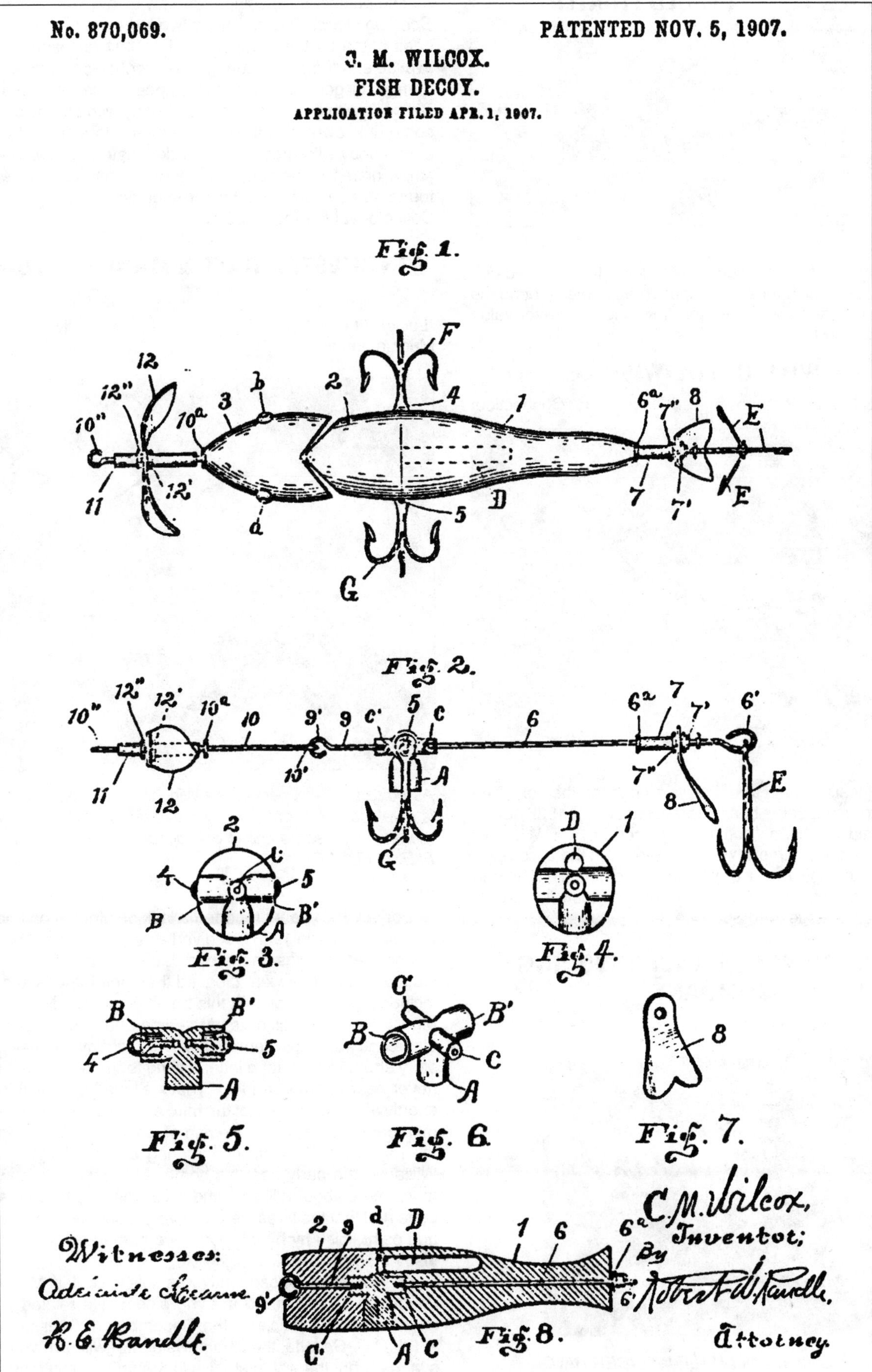

The drawing accompanying the patent, filed and granted to in 1907, for the WILCOX WIGGLER.

WILCOX RED HEADED FLOATER

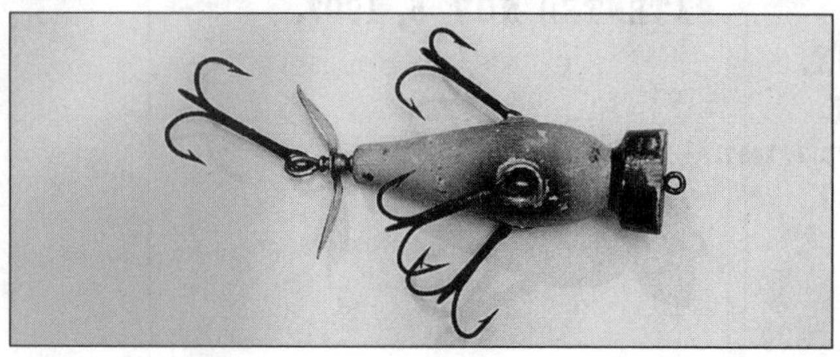

This very rare lure measures 2-7/8" long. It has raised cup and screw eye hook hanger hardware, three trebles around the body and one trailing with a propeller spinner. Collector value range: $300-$600.

WILL-O'-THE-WISP

Research & Model Company Glastonbury, Connecticut

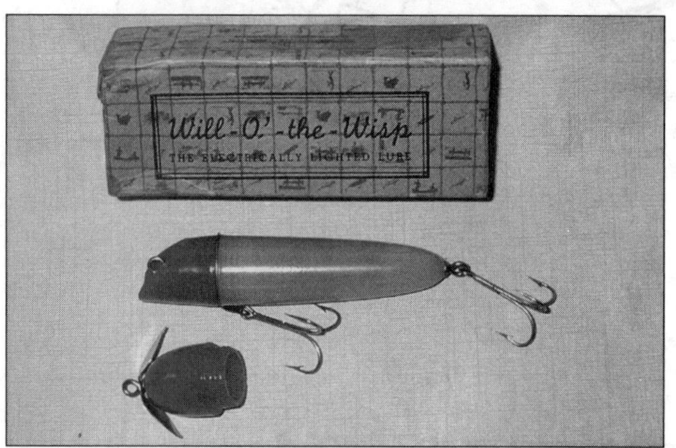

An electrically lighted lure. It says so right on the box. The lure has interchangeable heads as you can see. A 1936 advertisement said the heads could be ordered in Red, White or Black and the body came in white or yellow "..in the bass size." That seems to imply they were made in another size. The one in the photo here measures 4-1/4". Photo courtesy Jim Muma. Collector value range: $40-$60.

CLINTON WILT MANUFACTURING COMPANY

Springfield, Missouri

Lower. Clinton Wilt LITTLE WONDER BAIT #70, 2-1/8". Patent applied for in 1911, granted September 16, 1913. Upper: Clinton Wilt CHAMPION BAIT #50, 3-1/4".

The earliest advertising I found was in a 1922 issue of *The Sporting Goods Dealer*. These two lures are probably the only ones made by this company. When first released they were available in the following eight different color patterns: White, orange, or gold body with red stripes; white, orange, gold, or red body with green stripes; green body with orange stripes. At some unknown point they added three more finishes: Copper plated body with green stripe, nickel plated body with a green stripe or red stripe. So, there are at least 11 finishes to be found on each lure. Note the three-blade propeller spinners aft. Collector value range: $200-$350.

WINCHESTER BAIT & MANUFACTURING CO.

"Lucky Hit Bait" Oliver H. Williams
Muncie, Indiana Winchester, Indiana

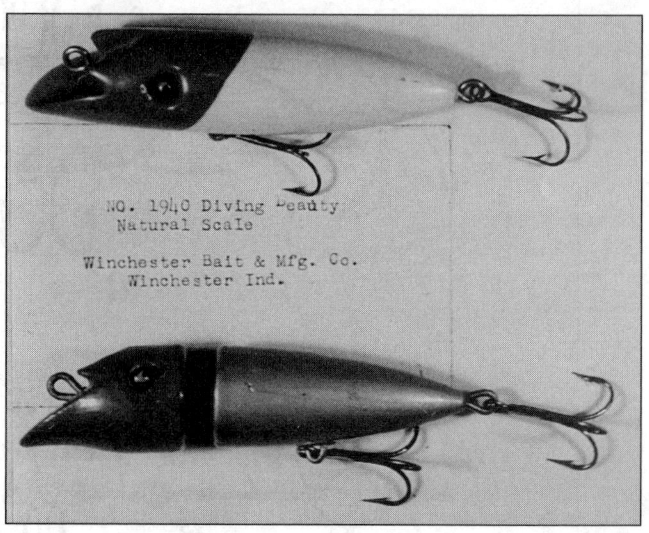

As indicated, the upper lure is a Winchester DIVING BEAUTY that is cataloged at 4, but actually measures 4-1/8". The lower lure measures the same and is cataloged at 4-1/4". It is a No. 2300 FLEXO FLOAT

For several years I reported a lack of information about this company. Back in 1986 I received a very nice letter from a lady saying that she was one of two daughters of a Mr. O. L. Williams and that they were pleased that their father's lures were included as collectibles in this book. She went on to say that Mr. Williams was still alive at the time and living in Elkhart, Indiana and about to celebrate his 97th birthday. To make a long story short, I wrote her a letter asking for more information and never heard from her again. That's all we knew until in 1991, shortly after the release of the third edition of this book. NFLCC member Dr. Jeremiah Holleman of Columbus, Mississippi had the happy accident of encountering a granddaughter of Mr. Williams at a party near his home. As a result we now know much more about Williams and his products. I had already ascertained that the lures were of a very high quality construction and paint finish by handling the two in the above photo. They also had glass eyes.

Dr. Holleman subsequently was able to contact Mr Williams' daughters and fill in the missing pieces. He related what he found out in an article in the December, 1991 issue of *The N.F.L.C.C. Gazette*, the club newsletter. I will give you a short synopsis, but the whole story is in the article. You may wish to obtain a copy.

The lures of the "LUCKY HIT BAIT" numbered 12 models. They were all hand-crafted wood floaters. The bodies were

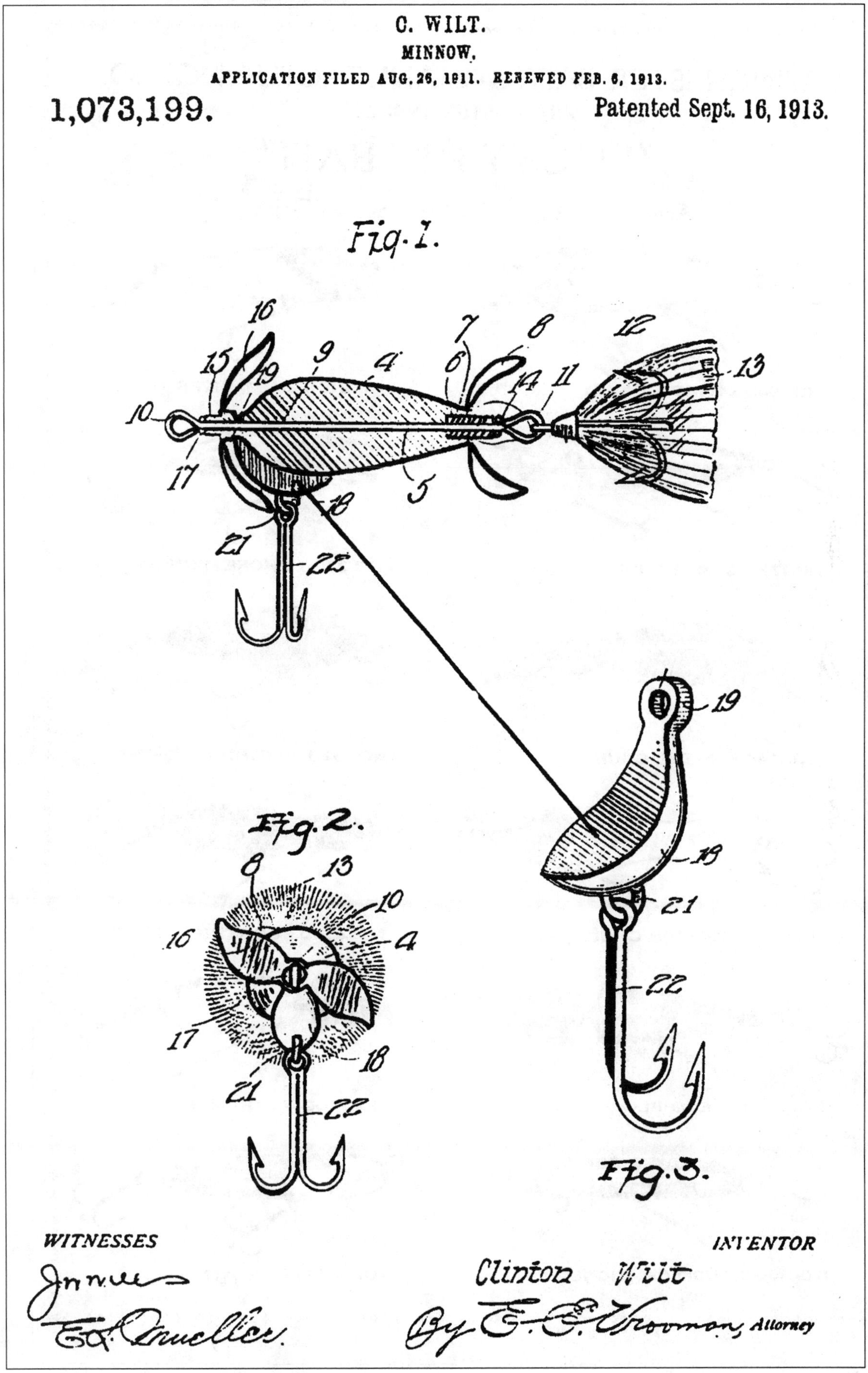

C. WILT.

MINNOW.

APPLICATION FILED AUG. 26, 1911. RENEWED FEB. 6, 1913.

1,073,199. Patented Sept. 16, 1913.

Fig. 1.

Fig. 2.

Fig. 3.

WITNESSES INVENTOR

Patent illustration of the Clinton Wilt Champion Bait. Granted Sept. 16, 1913.

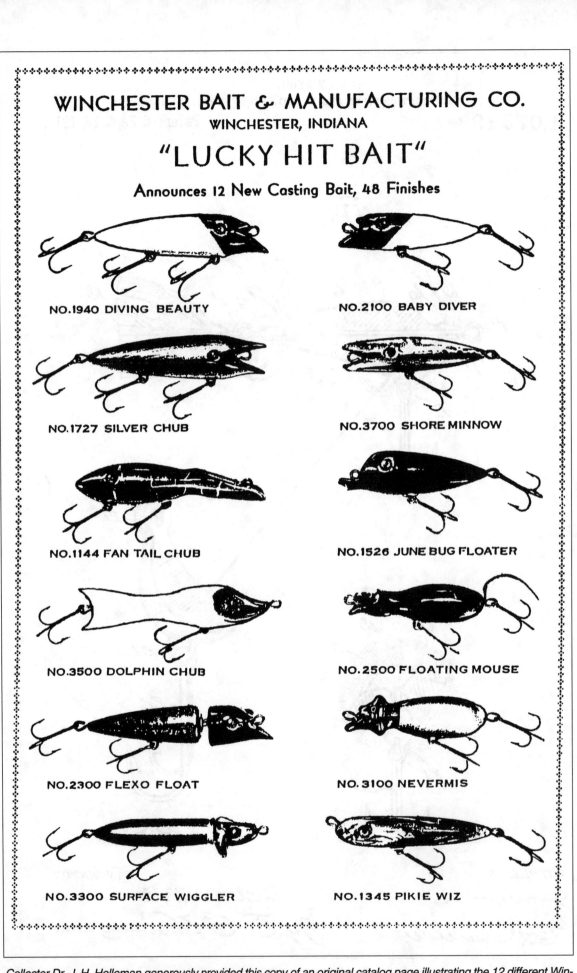

WINCHESTER BAIT & MANUFACTURING CO.

WINCHESTER, INDIANA

"LUCKY HIT BAIT"

Announces 12 New Casting Bait, 48 Finishes

NO.1940 DIVING BEAUTY

NO.2100 BABY DIVER

NO.1727 SILVER CHUB

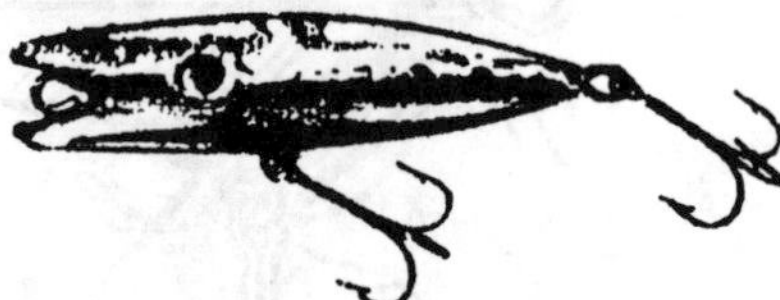

NO.3700 SHORE MINNOW

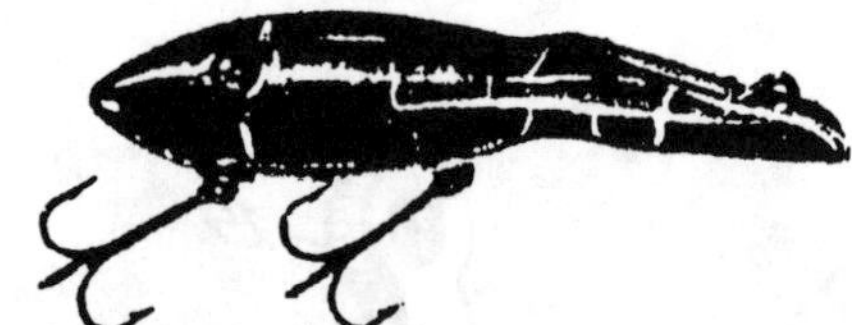

NO.1144 FAN TAIL CHUB

NO.1526 JUNE BUG FLOATER

NO.3500 DOLPHIN CHUB

NO.2500 FLOATING MOUSE

NO.2300 FLEXO FLOAT

NO.3100 NEVERMIS

NO.3300 SURFACE WIGGLER

NO.1345 PIKIE WIZ

Collector Dr. J. H. Holleman generously provided this copy of an original catalog page illustrating the 12 different Winchester Bait& Manufacturing Co. "LUCKY HIT BAIT" designs.

turned on a lathe, hand-detailed and painted in Williams' home in Muncie, Indiana. Williams and his daughters comprised the whole employee force. The lures were marketed from his father-in-law's home in Winchester, Indiana, hence the name of the company.

There were 17 different color finishes used on the lure, but not all colors were available on each lure. Each individual lure was available only in choices of four finishes. They are listed as follows:

*White body, red headRed body, black head
White body, black headGreen body, gold head
Silver body, red headSilver green stripe
Silver body, Black headSilver red stripe
Black body, red headRainbow finish
Gold body, red headYellow & green crackle
Gold body, green headRed & white crackle
Gray body, red headBrown &silver crackle
Brown body, red head

**This color combination will be found on all models except the #1144 FAN TAIL CHUB.*

Williams was employed full-time at a lamp company and worked on the lure business nights and weekends. He resigned from his job and discontinued lure making in 1937, when he founded a lamp business of his own. Collector value range: $200-$300.

Miscellaneous fly rod lures, carded leader and Winchester fishing tackle catalog. These catalogs are rare and can be worth more than $100.

WINCHESTER REPEATING ARMS COMPANY

New Haven, Connecticut

The famous Winchester Company got into the fishing tackle business in late 1919 and it ended with the purchase of a failed Winchester in 1931. Among other things they made many flies, metal spinner baits and a few wooden baits. They also bought out the Hendryx Reel Company. It is the wooden lures we will cover here. They are limited and because they marketed plugs for such a short time, almost any would be quite a find and a rare addition to your collection. There were only three basic styles. Most have the famous Winchester Trademark on them. Some have propellers and these are distinctly different from others, especially the aft propeller. The only list of color or finishes available seems to apply to all the plugs that were marketed. Only time will tell if this following list of eight colors is correct.

COLOR OR FINISH: White body, red head, green back stripes; green and gold back, yellow belly; green with silver sides; gold scale finish; silver scale finish; solid red, rainbow, green crackle back.

Any collector interested in Winchester will need to get a copy of Winchester Fishing Tackle, A Collector's Guide by Phil White. It is a very well-written, comprehensive guide to all of Winchester's tackle. Rods, reels, metal spinner baits, fly rod lures and the wooden baits. You will find a source for the book back toward the front of this book.

WINCHESTER MULTI-WOBBLER

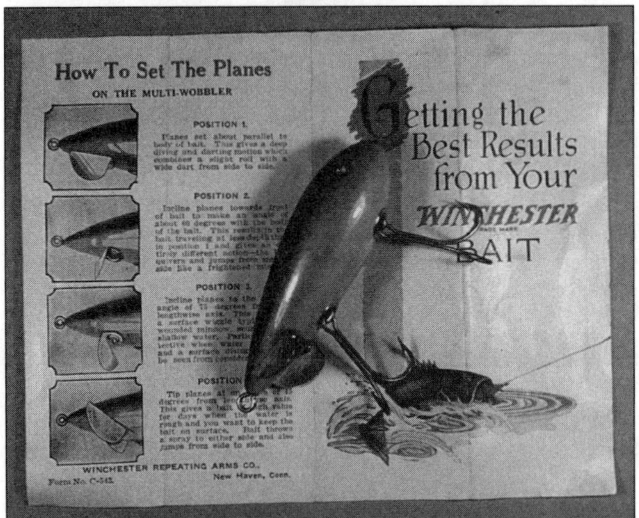

This is a tear drop shape, reverse running lure measuring 3-1/2". It sports two adjustable metal nose mounted side planes and has two belly mounted double hooks. It is a surface lure or under water swimmer depending upon how you adjust the planes. Collector value range: $100-$250.

WINCHESTER THREE/FIVE TREBLE HOOK MINNOW

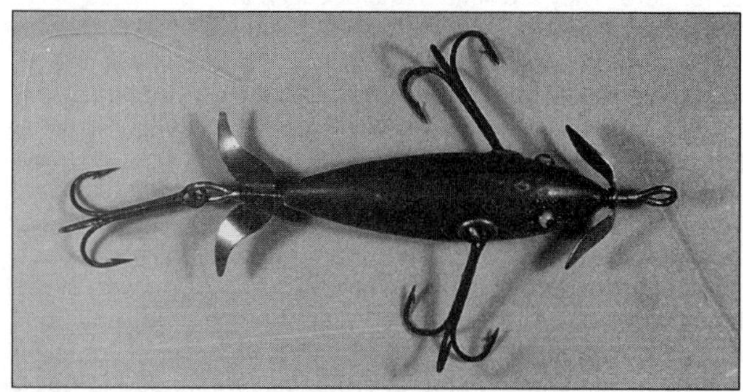

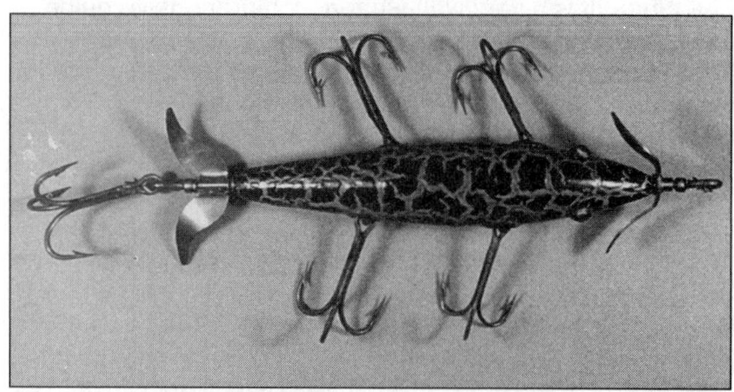

These lures have glass eyes and the distinctive Winchester nose and aft-mounted propeller shapes. The colors are the eight standard listed. They each have a trailing treble and opposite side mounted trebles 2 or 4). Collector value range: $300-$600.

WINNIE'S MICHIGAN STUMP DODGER

Albert Winnie — Traverse City, Michigan

Winnie was a barber in Traverse City who, by all accounts, hand-crafted all his lures on a lathe and painted them himself.

MICHIGAN STUMP DODGER with its original box. The box alone can bring over $100. Photo courtesy Jim Muma.

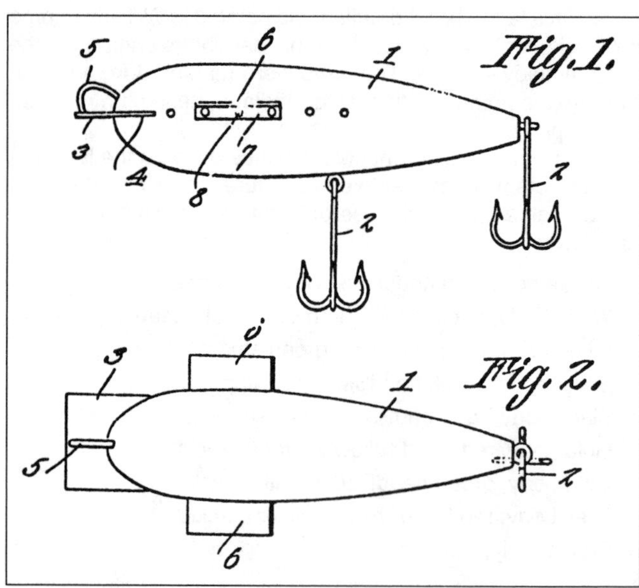

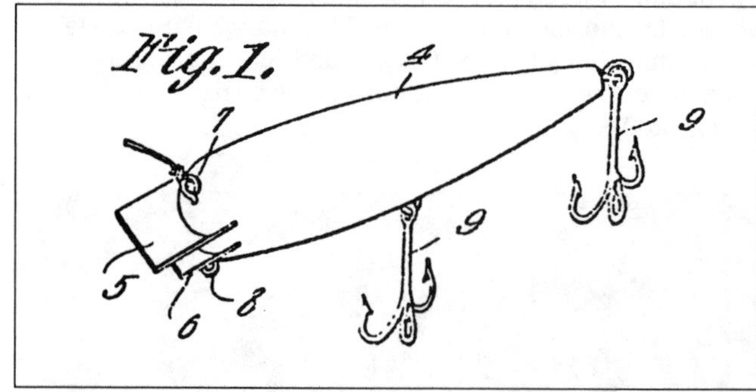

There is a tremendous variety of colors and sizes to be found as well as several different types of hardware. He first patented his STUMP DODGERS in 1914. As you can see by the detail from the patent reproduced here, there were two simple screw eye line ties, one at the top and the other beneath the head. This appears to be the first type he used. The lures in all the accompanying photos of various STUMP DODGERS each have the second generation line tie illustrated in the detail of a second (1916) Winnie patent reproduced here. This lure is made of metal with a cork interior body. Aside from the line tie style, the lure has never been seen. The line tie is sometimes found with two loops as in the lure pictured here.

Winnie made his lures mostly around 3-1/2" long, but they have turned up in 1/8" to 1/4" incremental sizes from as small as 2" to as large as 3-3/4". There is also a jointed version of the 3-3/4" size. Eyes were either absent or more often, consistently made with unpainted brass tacks through brass washers.

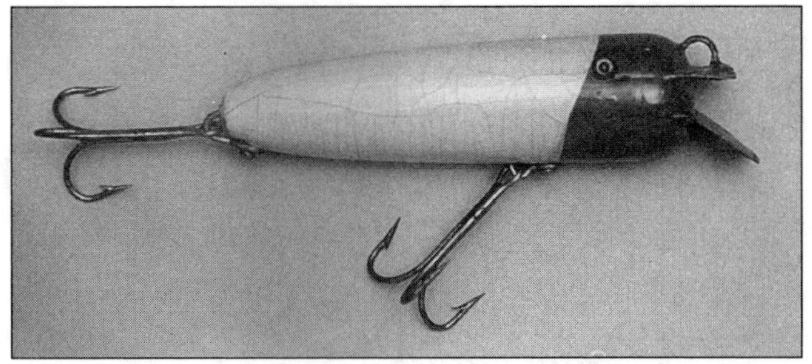

This bait illustrates the tack/washer eye and the L-rig with hump hook hanger.

These represent the greatest majority of those found. Occasionally he used various types of carpet tacks, painted and unpainted. Eye locations vary considerably. Hook hangers were of three types, a simple screw eye, a staple type hanger and an "L-rig" with a hump in it. Sometimes he combined different types on the same lure.

This example utilizes the simple screw eye hook hanger. Note the location of the eyes on top of the head.

The only two references I found in catalogs were in a 1916 Abbey and Imbrie catalog and in a mixed company section of a 1921 Shakespeare catalog. Both catalog listings stated a 3-1/2" size and the colors offered (combined from both catalogs) were:

Metallic finish

Rainbow

Green back, white belly

NFLCC member George Richey, in an article in the December, 1991 issue of the club newsletter, listed thirty five colors that have been found so far. Indeed, there may be more to find. A lure box enclosure states, among other things: "Any Color or Size Bait Made to Order 1-1/2 to 3-1/4 inches". Collector value range: $100-$300.

WINTER'S WEEDLESS SURFACE BAIT

N. G. Souther & Company — Chicago, Illinois

I found two advertisements for this lure. Both were in 1921 publications. They were made in two sizes and four color patterns. The sizes are 1-1/4" and 1-7/8". The colors were Green, white and red; yellow, red and black; tan, red and white; white, red and black. Collector value range: $300-$600. Photo courtesy Jim Muma.

JIM DANDY

Wise Sportsman Supply Co. — Chicago, Illinois

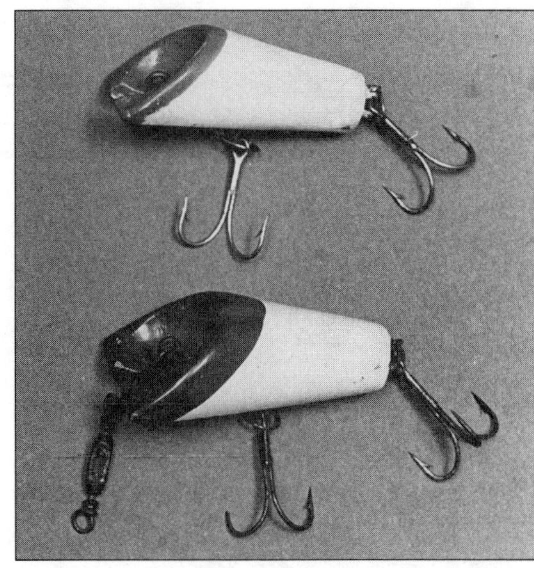

The JIM DANDY was new around 1915. Henry H. Schillinger, Paw Paw, Michigan, invented the lure, assigning rights to Wise Sportsman's Supply. The two in the photo are the bass size and the musky size, 2-1/4" and 3-1/2" respectively. It isn't too clear in the photo, but the lip is notched in the middle, resulting in two "wings". The sloped head is scooped out to create a concave head. The hook rings are distinctive, having metal guards to prevent the hooks from damaging the body. See Figure I and Figure II of patent drawing for this feature. The JIM DANDYS were available in solid white, white with red head or green spotted (frog finish). Collector value range: $30-$50. Please see the Jim Dandy lures in the Shakespeare section.

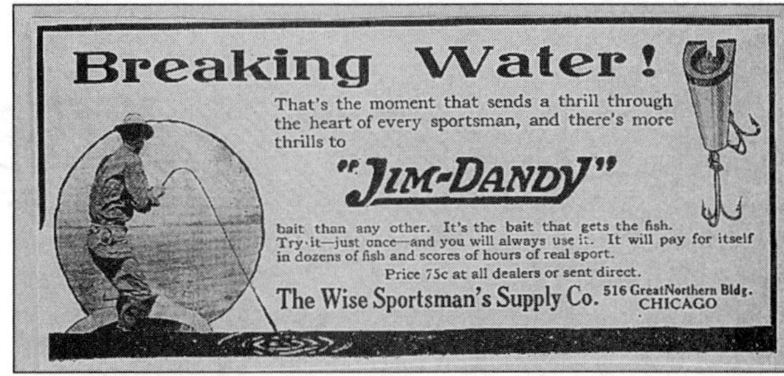

An advertisement in the May, 1918 issue of Outer's Book - Recreation magazine.

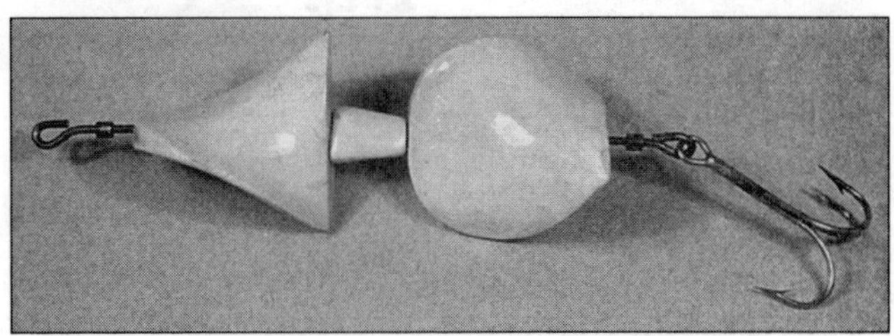

DOUBLE SPINNER. Photo courtesy Jim Muma.

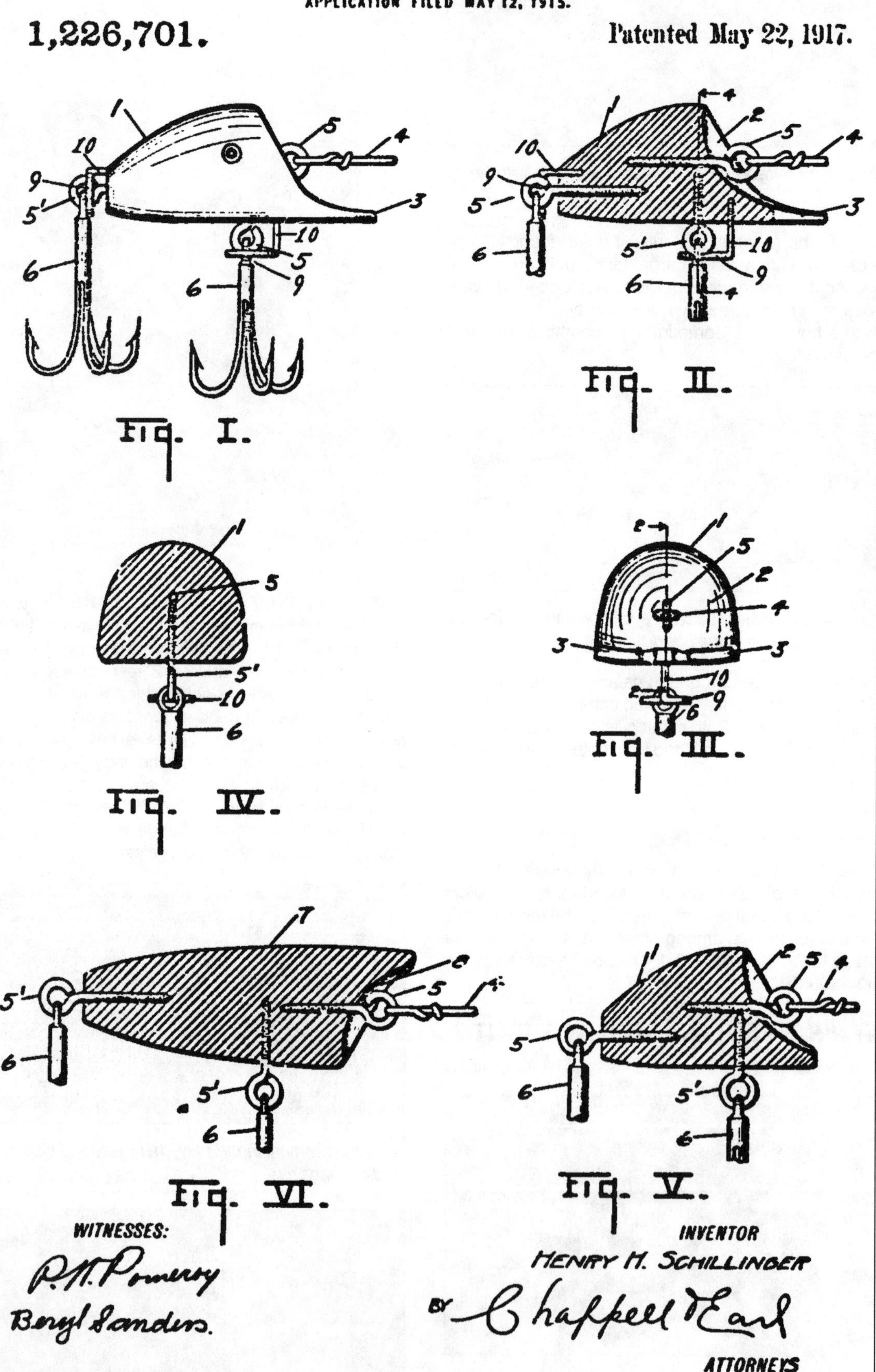

The patent drawing for the JIM DANDY.

This little 2" MOUSE lure is said to be a product of Leo Wise of Wise Sportsman Supply Company. It has large black bead eyes and is handsomely painted in very fine detail. The single trailing treble is attached by the use of a simple screw eye. Collector value range: $300-$600.

JIM DANDY DOUBLE SPINNER

I couldn't find any reference to this plastic lure. I have seen two different configurations. One like in the photo here and another. The other one has the triangular shape section reversed. It is the nose of the lure with the treble hook trailing behind the round shape section. Both measure 3-5/8". They came in red or white. Collector value range: $80-$120.

THE WONDER BUG

Mike Hildreth — Gunnison, Colorado

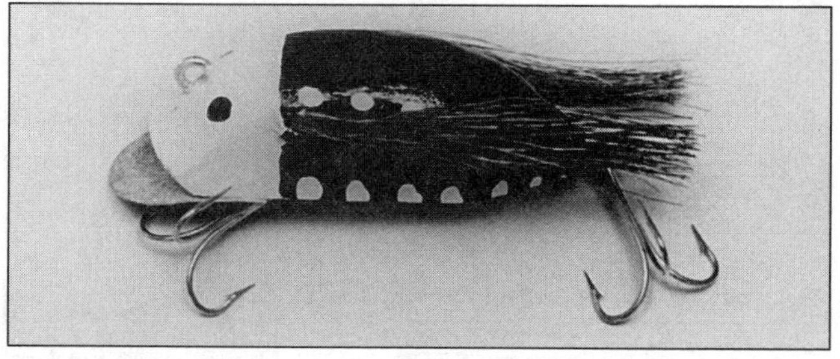

This 2-5/8" wooden lure is entirely hand-made by one man according to a flyer packed with the lure. Mike Hildreth packed his lure with that flyer in a clear plastic box with no markings. The flyer talks of his fishing in Mexico 36 years before in 1927. That makes the year 1963 when he wrote it. It is not clear, but apparently he had good luck fishing with a live Mexican bug down there and that this lure is a replica of that bug. Frankly, I wouldn't want to even pick up a bug that size, much less make it mad by trying to put it on a hook. His flyer says he makes them himself and that they '..will always be made by hand and in no other color." The color is black with white head, belly and spots.

According to Dean A. Murphy, in his fine book *Fishing Tackle made in Missouri,* copyright 1993, Hildreth was, at one time, a resident of Jacksonville, Missouri and that he and his children carved and made the lures in the winter to be sold in the next summer. Murphy interviewed Hildreth family members who told him that the Hildreths moved to Colorado in 1963 and employed three to five workers to produce the lures in a small factory making 10,000 the first year. The production only lasted four or five years after that. Collector value range: $10-$20.

WONDER STATE PRODUCTS COMPANY

Bill Monday, Harold Berry, Raymond Powell — Helena, Arkansas

This short-lived company lasted about one year. Formed by Monday, Powell and Berry in 1948, Wonder State was out of business just a year later. As true today as then, when you are undercapitalized and run out of money, the company just goes under. That isn't to say the lures were not good ones. They simply ran out of working capital.

They began with the BUG-R-BIRD. There were at least three different versions using the same body. The following photo depicts these three versions. They each measure 2-1/4". Note the leaders and line tie locations. They are often found with the name of the lure stenciled on the back. Collector value range: $50-$100.

Wonder State Products attempted to produce these in plastic with little success. A few rather crude ones were made, but they were never placed into production.

Colors the BUG-R-BIRDS may be found in are:

White body with red head
Solid black
Silver scale with red head and back
Silver scale with green head and back

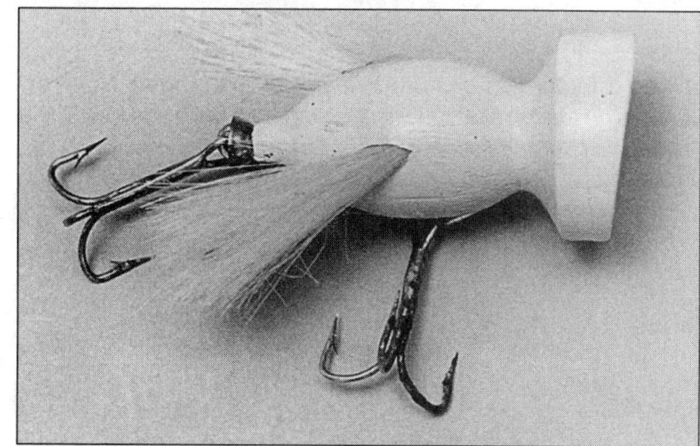

As short-lived as the company was they still experimented. This photo represents an attempt to make a popper version of the BUG-R-BIRD.

A measured 2-3/4"' long, this Wonder State Products BUG-R-BIRD has one-piece surface hook hardware. The lip on this one is brass and not shaped exactly like the regular nickel plated production lips. Could be a prototype.

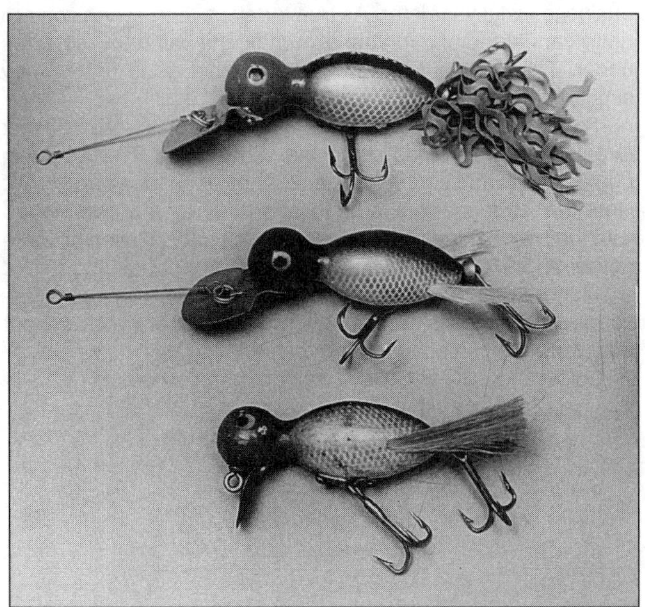

Three different versions of the lure with wood body. Note wire leaders on the top two and the different lip on the bottom example. These measure at a smaller 2-1/4".

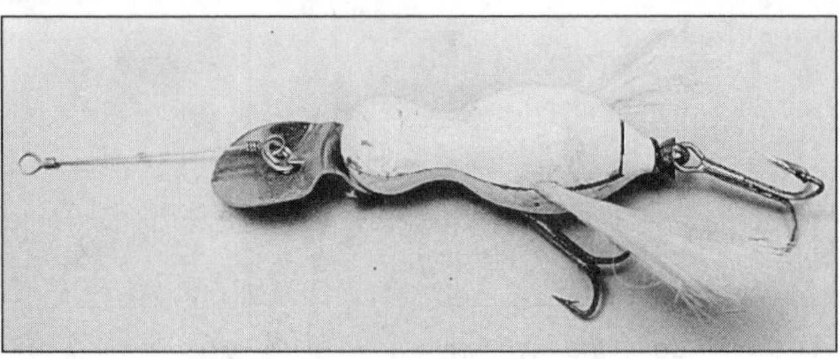

Plastic BUG-R-BIRD. White with one-piece surface hook hanger.

STEELHEAD

The other Wonder State Products production lure was the STEELHEAD. This was a 4" lure shaped much like a Heddon LUCKY-13 or a Clark DARTER SCOUT. These were packed with a polished shiny metal face (mouth) plate in the box for the fisherman to place on the face (mouth) if he so wished. Most must have liked the idea because just about all found have the plate attached. The photos following represent what was obviously a rapid series of changes to make the lures less expensive to produce by eliminating costly parts such as glass eyes and simplifying production. Collector value range: $50-$100.

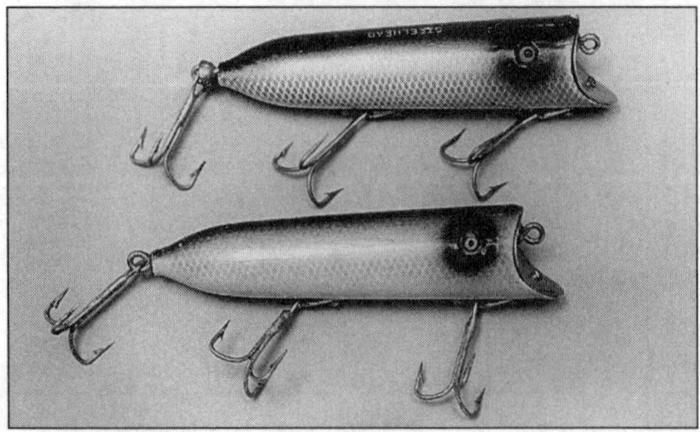

Two 4" STEELHEADS. The upper lure is an early one with glass eyes. The other has tack painted eyes (TPE). Each has the name on its back.

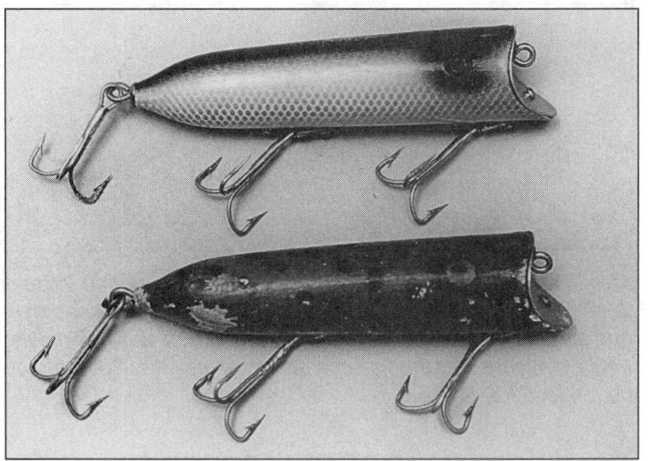

These two 4" STEELHEADS represent later versions. The upper lure has an indented eye and the name stenciled on its back. The lower lure has no name on the back and the eyes are painted.

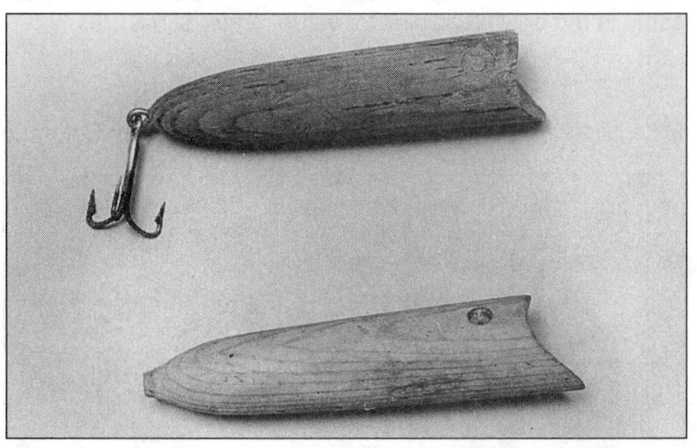

Two wooden blanks for the STEELHEAD. The upper has indented eyes and the lower one is drilled for glass eyes.

Colors that the STEELHEAD may be found in follows:

White with red head	Black with white head
Silver scale	Green frog
Gold scale with red head	Black with white ribs
Yellow perch	Silver with black ribs

A c. 1948 cardboard box from the Wonder State Company. Both of their commercially marketed lures were packaged in the same box.

WOOD'S LURES

Wood Manufacturing Co. Conway, Arkansas

The earliest I have been able to trace this company back to is 1937-40. They were listed in a McClean Sporting Goods Catalog of that approximate vintage.

The majority of Wood's plugs are found made of plastic, but some have been found made of wood, notably the POPPA-DOODLE. There may be others.

The following list of colors were available on almost all their lures. The first 10 on the list were the original finishes available. The last two were added at some later date.

COLOR OR FINISH: Pearl, Smoky Joe, chub; red head, shad, perch, yellow, shiner, black, frog, silver flash, grass pike.

DEEP-R-DOODLE

This lure was made in three sizes. Each has a metal diving plane, a belly and a trailing treble hook. Collector value range: $10-$20.

CATALOG SERIES #	BODY LENGTH	LURE WEIGHT
300	1-3/8"	1/6 oz.
800	2-1/4"	1/2 oz.
1000	3"	5/8 oz.

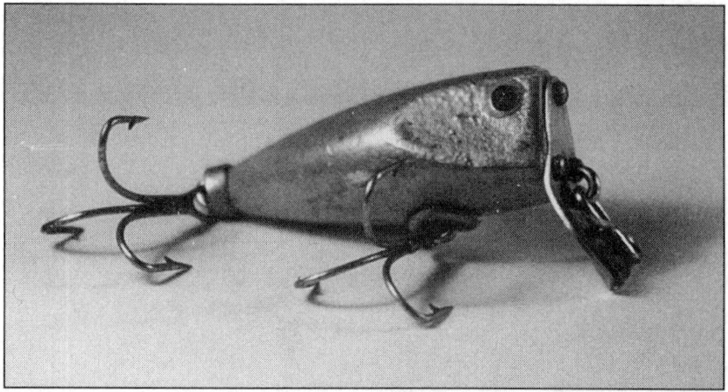

This is a wood body DIPSY DOODLE. It is gold in color. Gold was not a Woods option. Probably a repaint. Photo courtesy Ken Bernoteit.

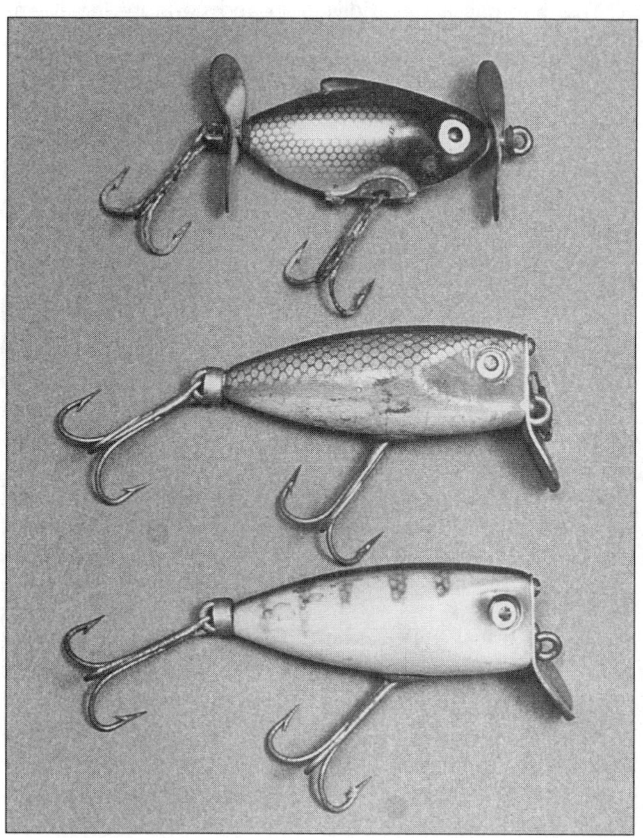

Top to bottom: The newer model of the DIPSY DOODLE. The next two are the older model with the flat nose and metal lip.

DIPSY DOODLE

There are two body styles for this lure the "old" (flat nose) and the new, a slightly rounded pointed nose and dorsal fin molded in. As far as can be determined the old style came in only a 1-3/4" size: #1400 (1/4 oz.), #1500 (3/8 oz.), and #1800 (1/2 oz.). The older model has a metal round spoon type diving lip blade. They have a belly treble and trailing treble hook. Found in all 12 finishes. Earliest models have wood bodies. Collector value range for wood: $20-$50, plastic: $10-$20.

DOODLER (Series #600)

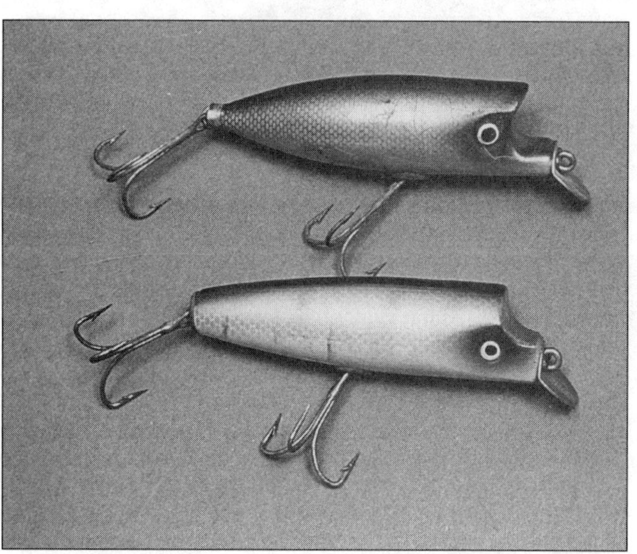

This bait has a metal diving lip and no propeller. It was made in two sizes: 3-1/4", 2T and 4", 3T. Collector value range: $10-$20.

DOODLER (Series #1600 & $1700)

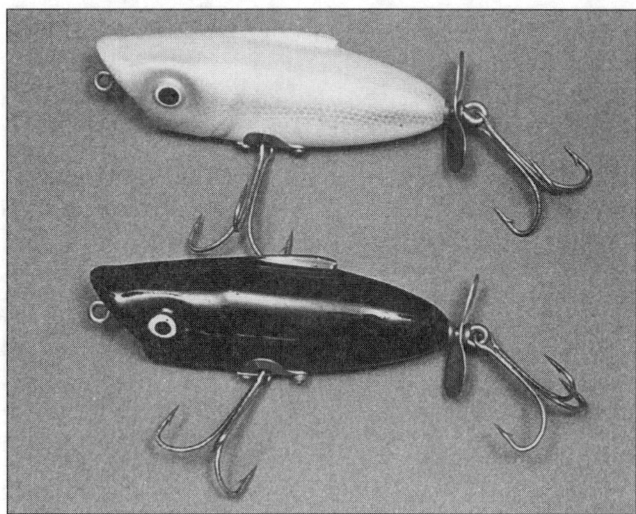

This is a different body style from the #600 DOODLER above. It is a surface lure available in two sizes: #1600 (1/2 oz., 2T) and #1700 (5/8 oz., 4", 3T). There is a tail-mounted propeller on each size. It was available in all 12 finishes. Collector value range: $10-$20.

SPOT TAIL MINNOW

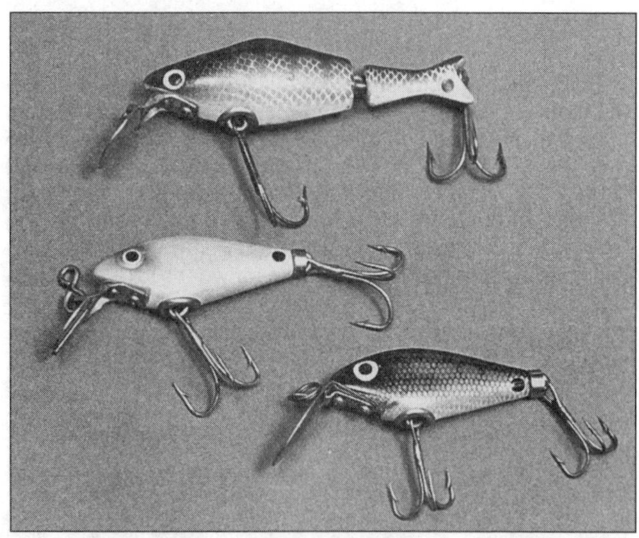

This lure was made in five styles. Each has a metal nose, a belly treble and a tail treble. One is jointed and one has a tail propeller. They were available in all 12 colors with a spot on the tail.

This lure is probably the forerunner to the Heddon SONIC. There is an interesting story about the SONIC. It was related to me by the famous "Uncle Homer" AKA Homer Circle, Angling Editor for *Sports Afield* magazine. He had run into the first lipless vibrators in Tennessee. It was called the CEDAR STUMP and you "..had to crank like blazes to get it to wiggle. I was with Heddon at the time and I said 'Well, that bait will never make it.'" He went on to say that when the PICO PERCH and THE BAYOU BOOGIE hit the scene, "Our salesmen at Heddon insisted we get in this market so we had Conrad Wood, the genius lure maker from El Dorado, Arkansas design the SONIC and SUPER SONIC which proved to be the hottest first-year seller Heddon ever made."

Collector value range for the SPOT TAILS: $10-$20.

CATALOG SERIES #	BODY LENGTH	LURE WEIGHT
700	2-1/4"	1/2 oz.
1100	2-3/4"	1/2 oz.
1300 (jtd.)	3"	1/2 oz.
2000	?	?
2000-S	?	3/8 oz.
	(propeller spinner at the tail)	

COLOR OR FINISH: Available in all 12 colors. #2000 also available in solid white.

POPPA-DOODLE

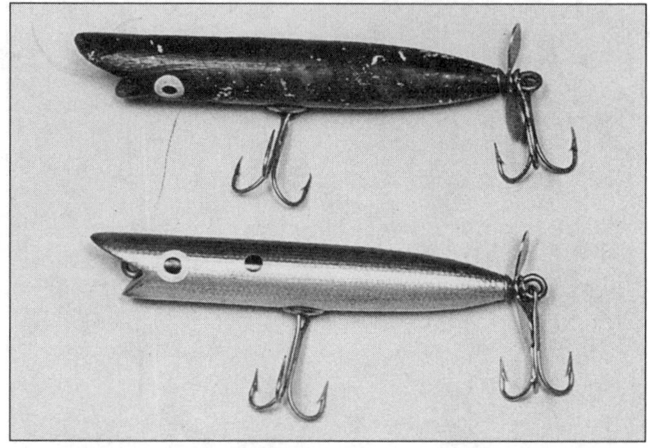

This is a surface plug with along slender 3-5/8" body weighing 1/4 oz. It has a belly treble, a trailing treble, and a tail mounted propeller. It was made in seven unknown colors plus solid white. These two are made of wood. It also was made in a larger size at 4" and a smaller 1/4 oz. size. Neither of the latter has the propeller spinner. Collector value range: $10-$20.

A 1930 vintage Wright & McGill catalog probably valued at about $75.

WRIGHT AND McGILL COMPANY

Denver, Colorado

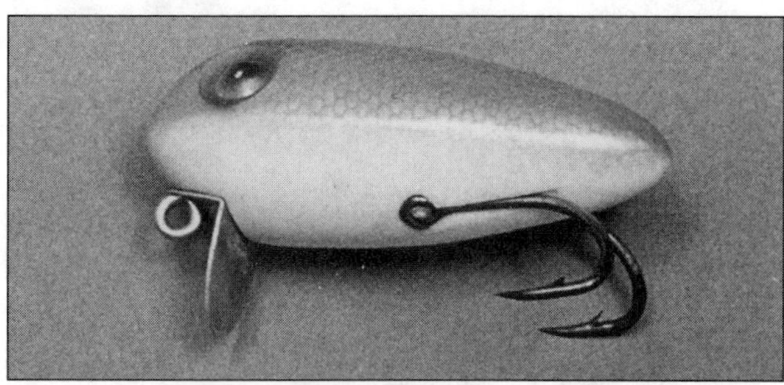

This Wright and McGill plug is 2-1/2" long and called BIG HAWK Collector value range: $10-$20.

This well known firm has been doing business continuously since 1925. Their "Eagle Claw" products are widely used and respected, but the number of artificial lures they have made is quite limited. They are heavily into fishing reels, rods, and hooks and presently produce no lures. I have a few miscellaneous ads and sporting goods catalogs from which to draw information as well as the 1930, 1951 and 1956 Wright and McGill Company catalogs. These represent the majority of the plugs marketed by the company.

BASS-O-GRAM

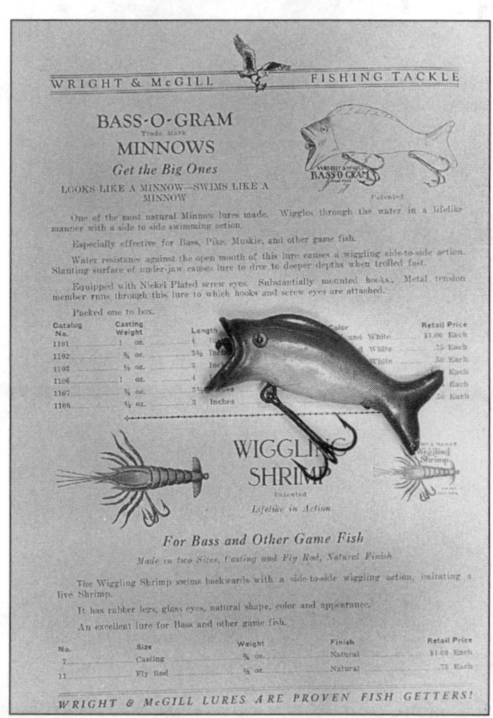

WRIGHT & McGILL FISHING TACKLE

BASS-O-GRAM
Trade Mark
MINNOWS
Get the Big Ones

LOOKS LIKE A MINNOW—SWIMS LIKE A MINNOW

Patented

One of the most natural Minnow lures made. Wiggles through the water in a lifelike manner with a side to side swimming action.

Especially effective for Bass, Pike, Muskie, and other game fish.

Water resistance against the open mouth of this lure causes a wiggling side-to-side action. Slanting surface of under-jaw causes lure to dive to deeper depths when trolled fast.

Equipped with Nickel Plated screw eyes. Substantially mounted hooks. Metal tension member runs through this lure to which hooks and screw eyes are attached.

Packed one to box.

Catalog No.	Casting Weight	Length	Color	Retail Price
1101	1 oz.	4 In[illegible]	[illegible] and White	$1.00 Each
1102	¾ oz.	3½ Inch[illegible]	[illegible]d White	.75 Each
1103	½ oz.	3 Inc[illegible]	[illegible]White	.50 Each
1106	1 oz.	4 [illegible]	[illegible]	[illegible] Each
1107	¾ oz.	3½ [illegible]es	[illegible]	[illegible] Each
1108	½ oz.	3 Inches	[illegible]	.50 Each

WIGGLI[illegible]
SHRI[illegible]
Patented
Lifelike in Action

For Bass and Other Game Fish

Made in two Sizes, Casting and Fly Rod, Natural Finish

The Wiggling Shrimp swims backwards with a side-to-side wiggling action, imitating a live Shrimp.

It has rubber legs, glass eyes, natural shape, color and appearance.

An excellent lure for Bass and other game fish.

No.	Size	Weight	Finish	Retail Price
7	Casting	¾ oz.	Natural	$1.00 Each
11	Fly Rod	½ oz.	Natural	.75 Each

WRIGHT & McGILL LURES ARE PROVEN FISH GETTERS!

This is a minnow like lure with a large open mouth and two belly treble hooks. It appeared in the 1930 catalog as available in three sizes and two finishes. Collector value range: $200-$300.

CATALOG SERIES #	BODY LENGTH	LURE WEIGHT
1101	4"	1 oz.

COLOR OR FINISH: Red and white.

CATALOG SERIES #	BODY LENGTH	LURE WEIGHT
1102	3-1/2"	3/4 oz.

COLOR OR FINISH: Red and white.

CATALOG SERIES #	BODY LENGTH	LURE WEIGHT
1103	3"	1/2 oz.

COLOR OR FINISH: Red and white.

CATALOG SERIES #	BODY LENGTH	LURE WEIGHT
1106	4"	1 oz.

COLOR OR FINISH: Natural.

CATALOG SERIES #	BODY LENGTH	LURE WEIGHT
1107	3-1/2"	3/4 oz.

COLOR OR FINISH: Natural.

CATALOG SERIES #	BODY LENGTH	LURE WEIGHT
1108	3"	1/2 oz.

COLOR OR FINISH: Natural.

BUG-A-BOO

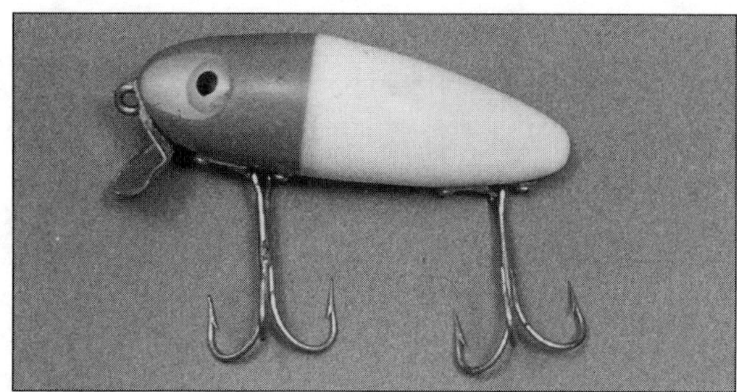

Here is a smaller version of the BUG-A-BOO sitting on its original box. The box indicated it is a "No. 302". It measures 2-5/8". A collector wrote to tell me that he has one new one in the box with a brochure identifying it as a BASS-ZOO-KA. Collector value range: $7-$14.

The BUG-A-BOO is a 2-3/8", 1 oz. plastic body lure with two belly trebles and a metal lip. It has scooped out (concave) eye sockets and the line tie is at the nose above the diving lip. Collector value range: $5-$15.

CATALOG SERIES #	BODY LENGTH	LURE WEIGHT
303	2-3/8"	1/2 oz.
467 (600)	1-3/4"	3/8 oz.

COLOR OR FINISH: Red and white, pike scale, perch scale, silver scale, gold scale, chub scale, yellow with silver scale, black and white, frog, rainbow, pearl, pearl with red stripe.

BASSKIL

This is almost exactly the same plug as the BUG-A-BOO but longer (3"). Colors unknown, but probably the same. Collector value range: $5-$15.

CRAWFISH

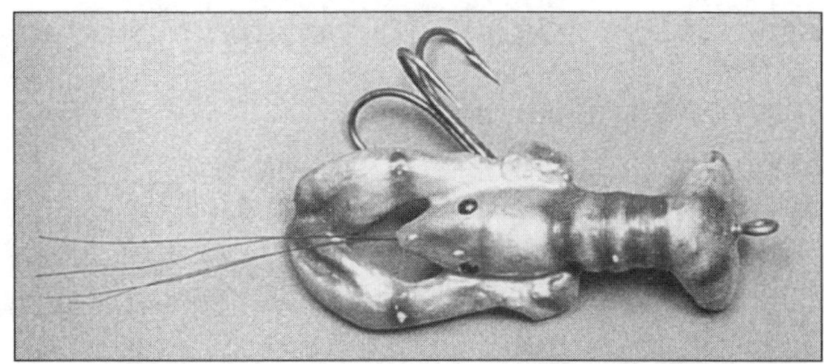

This lure was found in the 1930 catalog as available in only one size (2-3/4", 1/2 oz.). It was a reverse running plug with rubber legs and bristle antennae at the nose of the crawfish body. It has one belly treble. Collector value range: $100-$150.

DIXIE DANDY

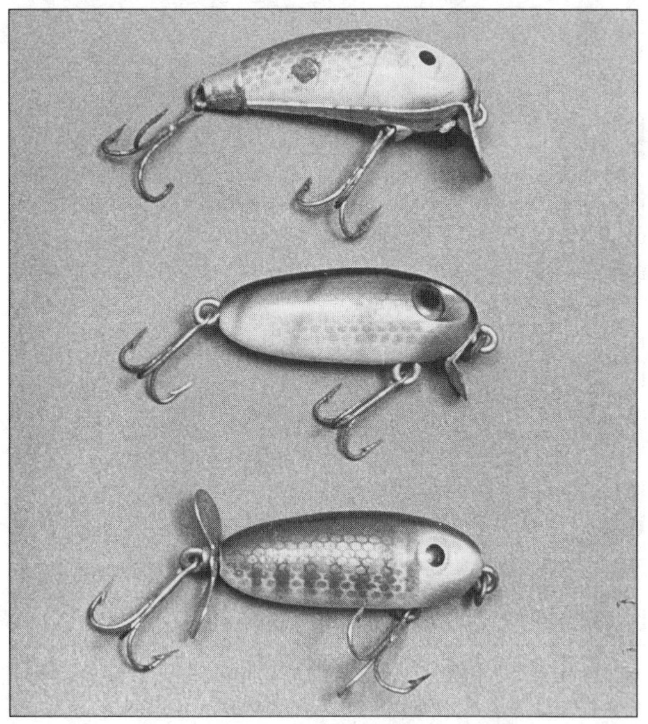

Top: #470 Series MIRACLE MINNOW with metal belly plate. Center: #600 DIXIE DANDY. Bottom: BUG-A-BOO.

This is a surface spinning plug with a belly treble, trailing treble hook and a tail-mounted propeller spinner. Size and colors unknown. Collector value range: $6-$12.

THE FLAPPER CRAB

Pictured here is a side/under and top view of the FLAPPER CRAB. One of the rubber pinchers is missing from the nose area and two or three of the rubber legs are also missing. Found in the 1930 catalog this lure was made in two sizes, one color. They have glass eyes, one treble and were reverse running. Small fly rod size: 1/2 oz. Large, casting size: 1 oz., 2-1/2". (see patent drawing). Collector value range: $50-$75. Box alone: $80-$120.

FLAPPER CRAB with original box. Photo courtesy Jim Muma.

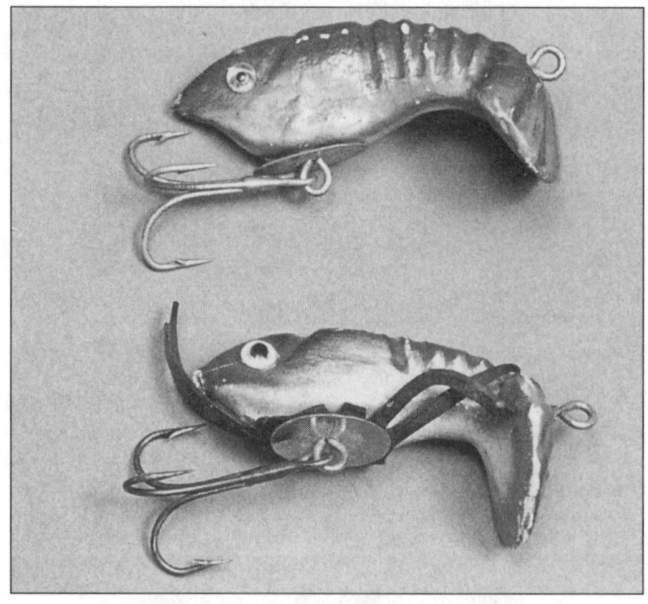

HIJACKER

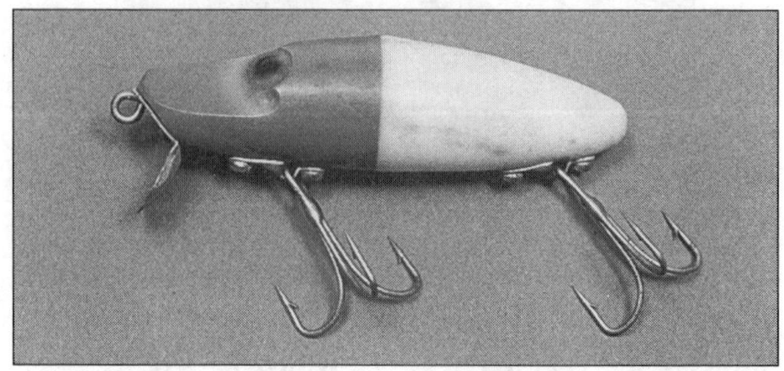

This is a plastic body plug weighing 5/8 oz. and 3-1/2" and has scooped out eye sockets extended to the nose making it more or less pointed. There is a metal lip and two belly treble hooks. It came in the same colors as the Bug-A-Boo. Collector value range: $5-$15.

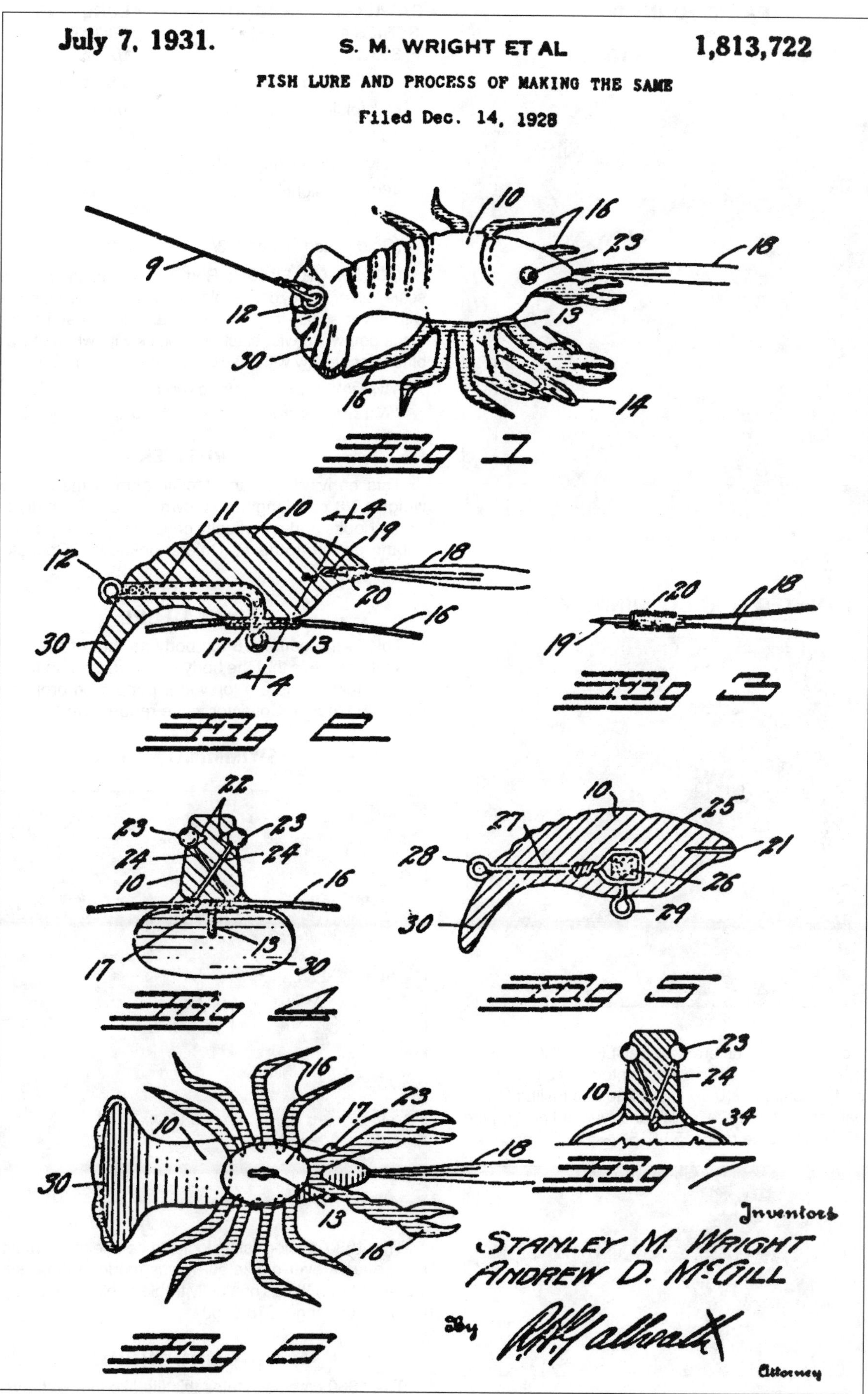

Illustration accompanying the patent application for the FLAPPER CRAB. Granted July 7, 1931 to Stanley M. Wright and Andrew D. McGill of Denver, Colorado.

MIRACLE MINNOW

MIRACLE MINNOW MIDGET

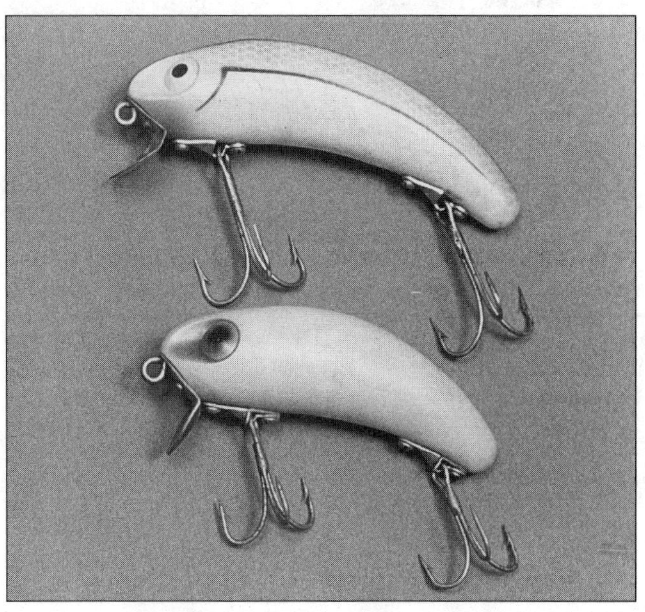

JOINTED MIRACLE MINNOW

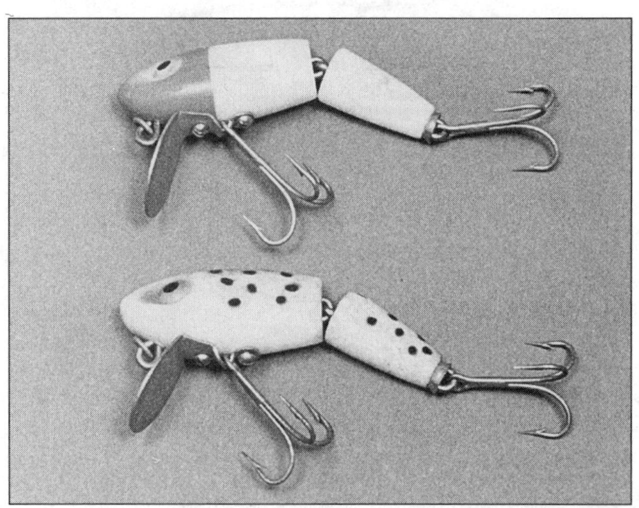

There are at least six different MIRACLE MINNOW styles the collector may encounter. One was jointed, but all five have the same body design, one belly treble and one trailing treble. The principal differences were in size and type or finish on the hardware. Collector value range: $5-$15.

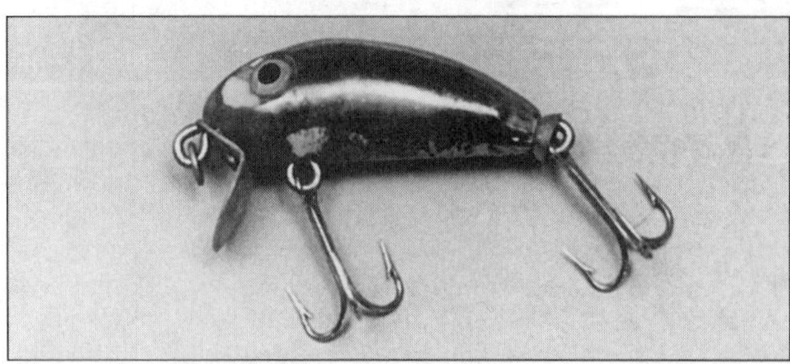

A 1-1/2" metallic finish with MIRACLE MINNOW stamped in the metal lip.

CATALOG SERIES #	BODY LENGTH	LURE WEIGHT
305	3"	1/2 oz.
472 (jointed)	2-1/2"	3/8 oz.
601 (plain)	1-3/4"	1/8 oz.
407-W		
(Silver bright fitting)1-3/4"		3/8 oz.
466-W (weighted)1-3/4"		1/4 oz.
471-W		
(Gold plated fittings)1-3/4"		3/8 oz.

COLOR OR FINISH: Red and white, pike scale, perch scale, silver scale, gold scale, chub scale, *brown scale, yellow with silver scale, frog, pearl, white with red stripe, white with black dot, white with black rib, *black with white rib, white with black dot, yellow with black dot, **metallic finishes.

**Available only on the jointed versions.*

***Not available on the lures with "silver bright" or "gold plated fittings".*

RUSTLER

This early Wright and McGill plug is made of wood. It weighs 3/8 oz., length unknown. It has two belly-mounted treble hooks and a vertically concave face sloped to make it submerge on retrieve. Colors unknown. Collector value range: $5-$15.

POP-A-LURE

This is the same 3/8 oz. body as that of the RUSTLER. The difference is that the body is turned over so that the face would make the lure a top water popper on proper retrieve. Colors unknown. Collector value range: $5-$15.

SWIMMING MOUSE

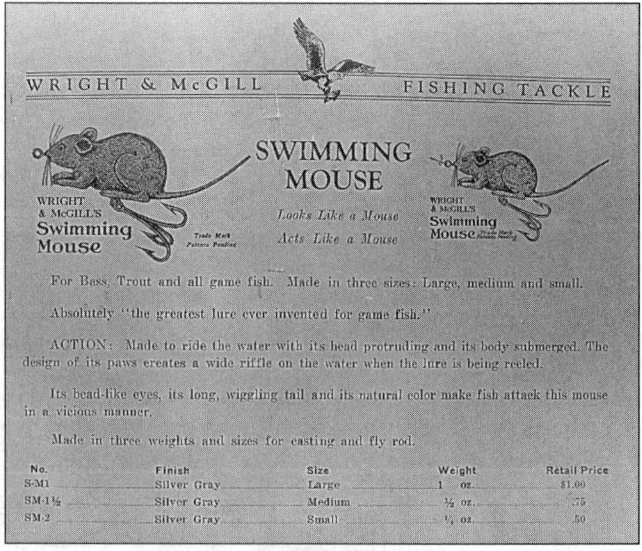

WRIGHT & McGILL FISHING TACKLE

SWIMMING MOUSE

Looks Like a Mouse

Acts Like a Mouse

For Bass, Trout and all game fish. Made in three sizes: Large, medium and small.

Absolutely "the greatest lure ever invented for game fish."

ACTION: Made to ride the water with its head protruding and its body submerged. The design of its paws creates a wide riffle on the water when the lure is being reeled.

Its bead-like eyes, its long, wiggling tail and its natural color make fish attack this mouse in a vicious manner.

Made in three weights and sizes for casting and fly rod.

No.	Finish	Size	Weight	Retail Price
S-M1	Silver Gray	Large	1 oz.	$1.00
SM-1½	Silver Gray	Medium	½ oz.	.75
SM-2	Silver Gray	Small	¼ oz.	.50

This 1930 catalog listing looks to be one of the most life-like mouse lures ever marketed. It was made in three sizes (1/4, 1/2, and 1 oz.). It has one belly treble hook and lead eyes. Collector value range: $75-$100.

WIGGLING SHRIMP

The 1930 catalogs states this life-like lure was available in two sizes (3/4 oz. and 1/2 oz.). It has rubber legs, glass eyes and one treble hook. Collector value range: $75-$125.

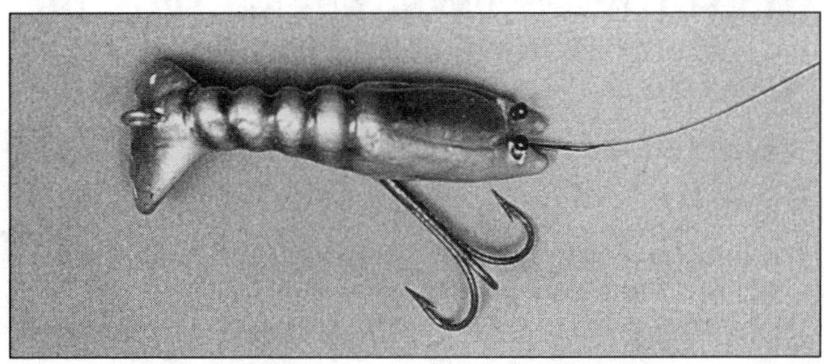

FLASHER MINNOW

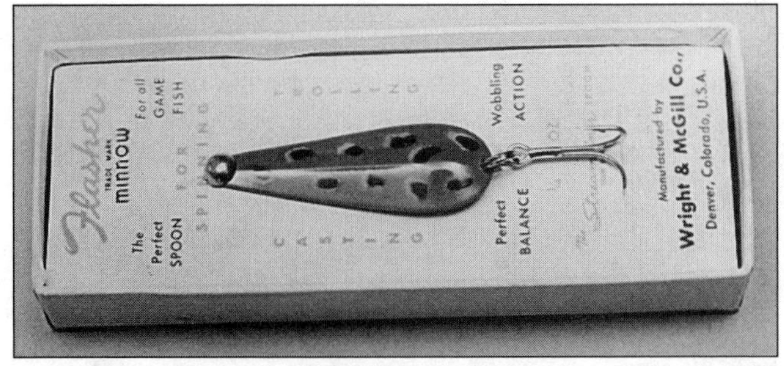

The FLASHER MINNOW was not found advertised or in any catalogs. The one in the photo measures 2-3/4" overall and is in a frog finish. Collector value range: No trade data found.

NAPPANEE "YPSI" BAITS

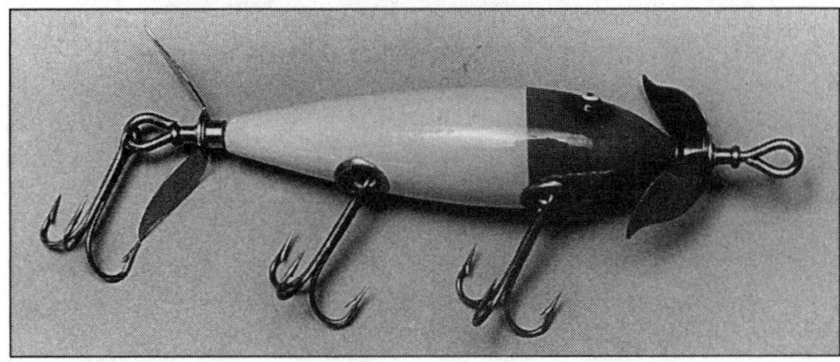

J. O. Kantz — Nappanee, Indiana

The NAPPANEE YPSI pictured here measures 3" in length and utilizes cup and screw eye hook hardware and has a yellow body with red head and tack painted eyes.

In the third edition I presented a possible scenario outlining a theory of the origin and evolution of this bait attributing it exclusively to the Ypsilanti Minnow Bait Company in Hillsdale, Michigan. Some of my data was right, but more importantly, much was wrong. I did admit that it might be far-fetched for some collectors, but I believe some of the lures in the photos belonged there. Finally some well researched material was published. National Fishing Lure Collectors Club (NFLCC) member Dave Culp of Huntington, Indiana wrote an article in the September 1991 issue of *The N.F.L.C.C. Gazette*, the club newsletter that sorted out the confusion. The article is comprehensive and the following is but a brief summery. If you wish to get a copy, talk to a member or better yet, join the club and get the back copy of the newsletter. I used it to straighten out the confusion in the fourth edition.

According to information Dave Culp found, J. O. Kantz, a lawyer in Nappanee, hand-crafted a successful "fish-getter" in the early 1900s that became highly sought by his buddies and other fishermen in the area. As the familiar story goes he decided to go into production. Being a busy lawyer, however,

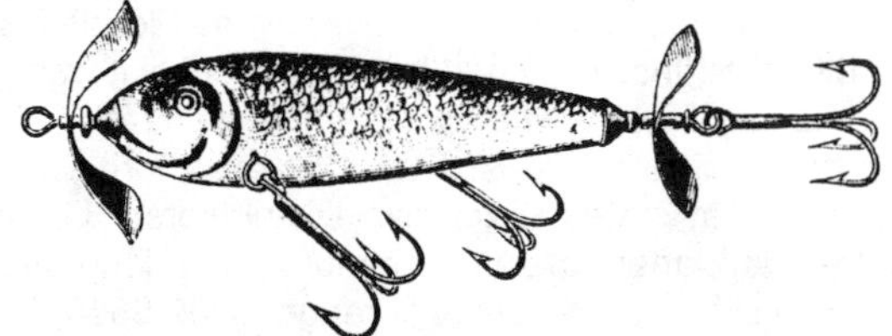

THE NEW YPSILANTI BAIT

The Only Bait With the Hooks in the Right Place

In introducing this bait I give the purchaser a bait for fishing on the surface as well as under the water. Every fisherman knows that in the early spring fishing, a bass will strike a fluttering object on top of water quicker that it will take it under water. This bait in reeling in, flutters on top and represents a wounded minnow, making the best lure out.

Later in the season as the bass get more shy, put sinker on line close down to nose of bait and go under water to any desired depth.

It is not only the best finished bait but the best lure on the market, and the new feature is the HOOKS stand OUT from the sides of the bait when in motion while with other baits the hooks lay up close along the sides and only one hook out of every set is of any use at all, while the fish can't bunt this bait without getting hooked and hooks don't tangle in casting.

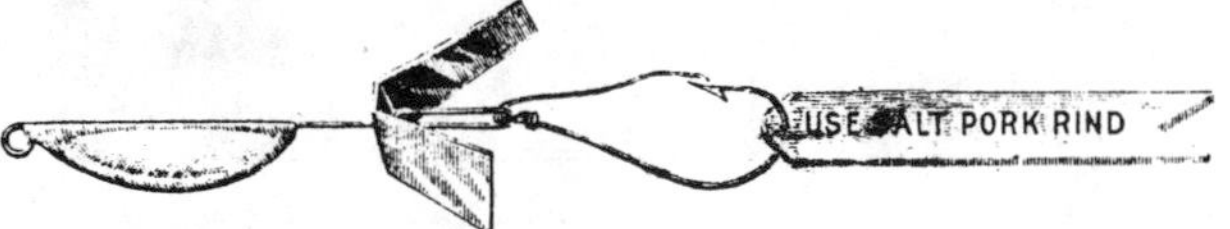

First of all, fishing is a science, and it is necessary to have a hook so arranged that one is able to fish among the weeds and rushes without getting fast. In this hook you will get the desired article. This being a casting hook, will not twist your line. The anchor as well as the casting weight do not turn over in water, and being baited as shown in cut with pork rind (which is an excellent bait for bass and pickerel), keeps the hook weedless, and the wire spring does not allow the fish to shake the hook out of its mouth, operating as a snap

Remaining in deep water casting towards shore, and drawing hook through weeds toward deep water, not allowing bait to settle when striking water but to start instantly.

In fishing with artificial bait KEEP OUT OF SIGHT OF YOUR GAME.

made it impossible for him to run a company such as this, so he made arrangements through a fishing buddy who was also connected to a hardware and paint business in Nappanee, to arrange manufacture and distribute the lure on a royalty basis. The company was the A. H. Kaufman and Company. This happened around 1910. The first company to manufacture the lure was the Ypsilanti Minnow Bait Company or the Ypsi Bait Company. There is a short write-up with illustration in the May, 1910 issue of *Field & Stream* that calls it "The New Ypsi Bait" from the Ypsi Bait Company in Hillsdale, Michigan. There is no way to be sure that this small flyer or lure box enclosure matches the lure here, but it does describe the lure in part as follows: "..the HOOKS stand OUT from the sides of the bait..". Apparently the hooks or hangers were fitted with a "preventer" of some sort and the hooks were offset to either side of the belly. I believe these to be characteristics of the early "YPSI" lures. I may be proven wrong. Whatever the case over the years they were made in two general lengths, 3" and 3-1/4" and in three models, an underwater, a semi-surface and a surface model. The earliest has tack eyes and then came indented eyes. The colors it was available in were: Solid black, solid red, solid aluminum color, solid yellow, yellow body with red head, aluminum color with red head. There were none produced with decorations such as scales, stripes, etc.

The lure was produced by the Ypsilanti Company until 1915 when the Paw Paw Bait Company took over the task. They had it until 1925 when the South Bend Bait Co. took over the production. They manufactured the lure for 20 years and in 1945 production was taken over by the Florida Fishing Tackle Mfg. Co., Inc. They had the contract until it was given over to Richard Pippen who was the manufacturer until production ended in the 1960s. I also have a Florida Fishing Tackle flyer that states "Exclusive Distributors - Lehman's Hardware, Nappanee, Indiana. The lure has a long and distinguished history. Collector value range: $200-$300.

ZINK SCREWTAIL

Zink Artificial Bait Company Dixon, Illinois

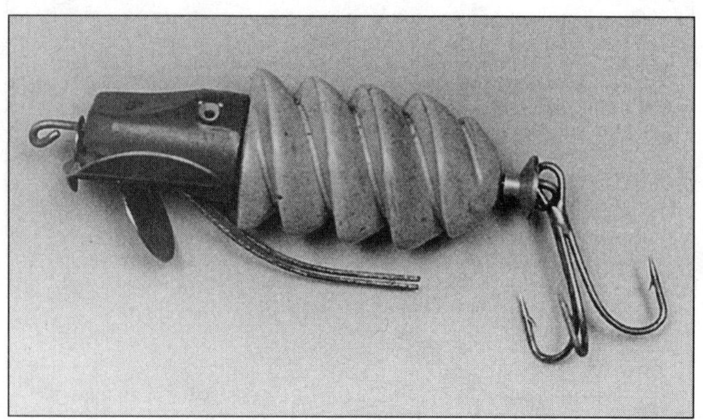

This peculiar looking dude measures 2-1/2". The body rotates around a wire armature that makes up the line tie and tail hook hanger. The metal device at the head is adjustable rendering it a surface or diving plug. The eyes are painted and located in a depression. It is a 1940s era lure. The only advertisement found stated that it was available in four colors, but did not list them. The one in the photo here has a pearl white body and a red head. Other colors observed are orange, brown and black; yellow and green, black and silver gray. Collector value range: $20-$40.

IMPORTANT NOTICE

The value ranges listed in this book are for lures in Very Good to Excellent condition. The values of those lures not in Very Good to Excellent condition can and probably will be worth considerably less. The values are meant to be a guide only.

UNIDENTIFIED OLD LURES

In the first four editions there were a number of these unknowns that are now known, thanks to collectors who either recognized them or did a little detective work. A little over one-half of them were identified and they have been placed appropriately in this book with what was learned about them.

Following here is a new and more extensive challenge. Hopefully we can get them identified. There are some left from the first editions. Those have remained unknown for almost 20 years now. Where there is anything known or suspected, it is noted. If you can help, by all means drop the publisher a line. Your contribution will be shared with other collectors in subsequent editions.

THE FOLLOWING UNKNOWNS ARE FROM THE COLLECTION OF KEN BERNOTEIT. THE PHOTOGRAPHS WERE FURNISHED BY KEN.

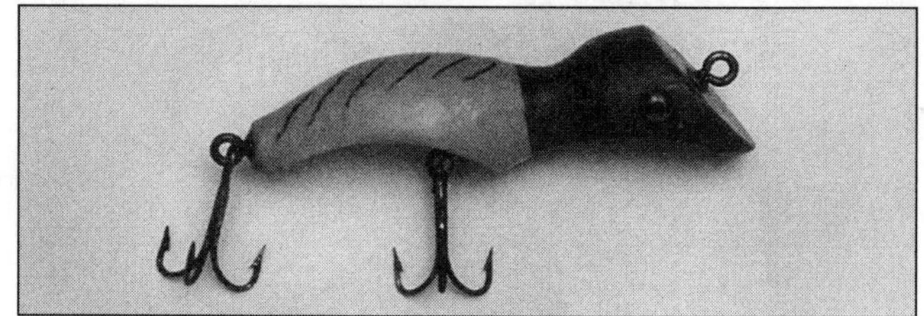

White with red head, 3-3/4" long. Cup and screw eye hardware. No eyes.

White body with red head, 4" long. Tail hook is rigid. Glass bug eyes.

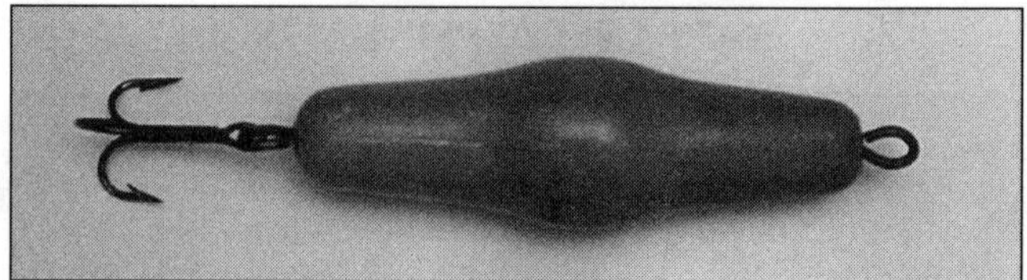

Solid yellow, 3-1/8" long. Has internalized belly weight.

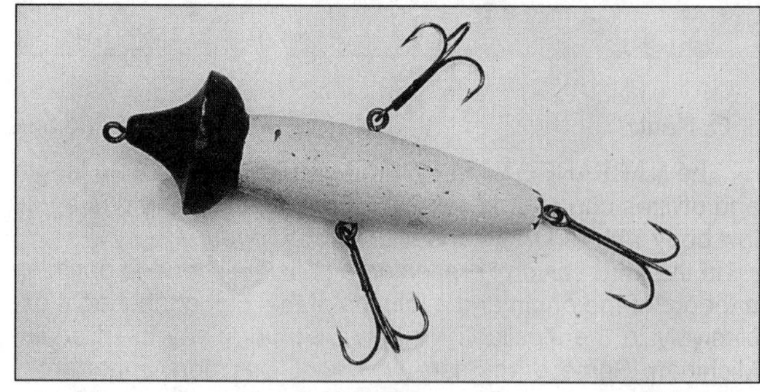

This woodpecker type lure is 4-1/2" long with brass screw eye hook hangers. It is extremely nose heavy, but a dunking in the sink showed me it floats beautifully.

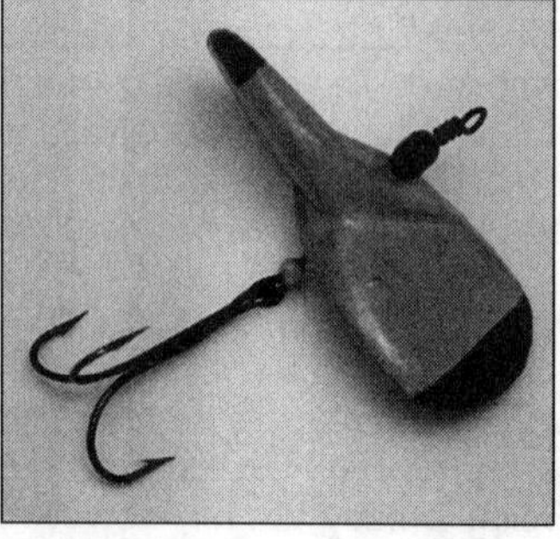

A very unusual wooden lure carved in the shape of a propeller 2-1/2" across. PAT PEND is stamped into the wood. Note glass bead at aft end. There is a tube forced through the center so that the propeller will spin easily around the armature.

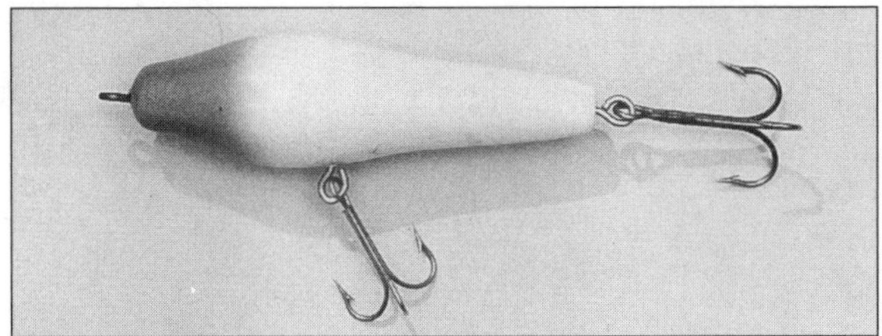

White body with red head, 3-1/2".

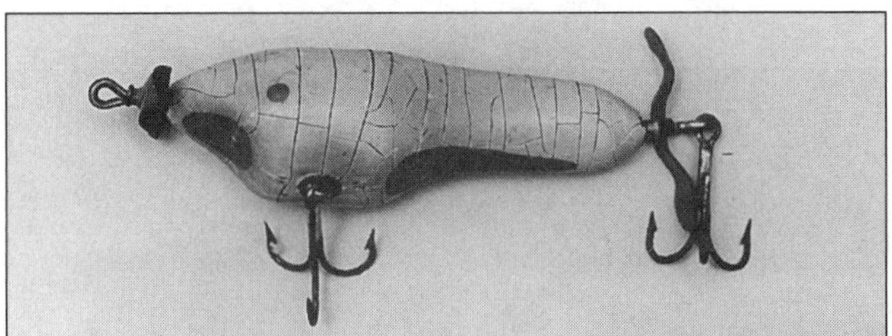

Body has yellowed with age but was originally white. Other markings are red. Deep brass cup with no bottom and screw eye hook hardware and brass propeller spinners. Line tie and tail hook hanger is not through-body.

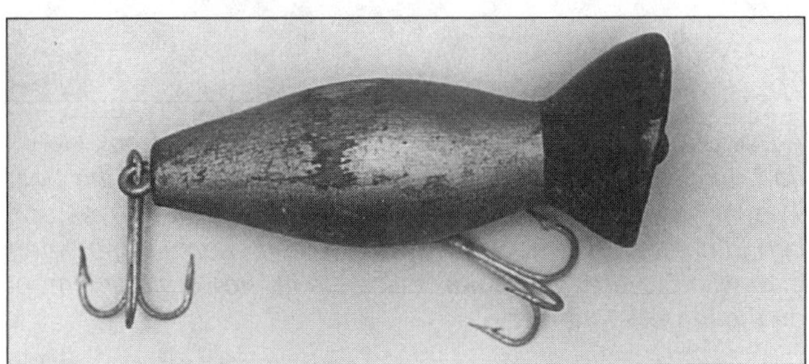

This unknown lure has a gold body with black head and measures 3-1/8". It has brass cup and screw eye belly hook hardware and a tail hook insert.

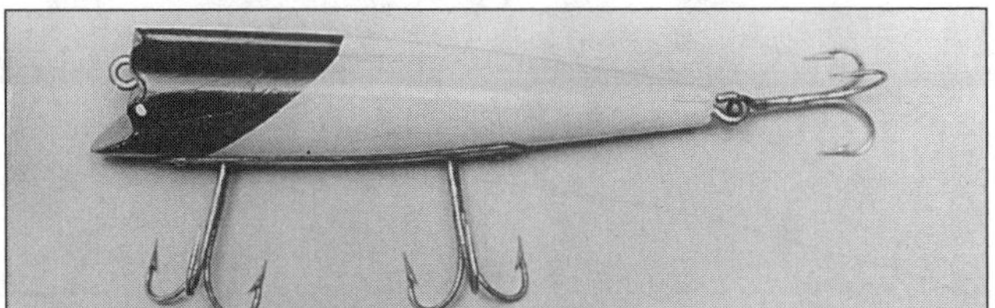

White body/red head. Measures 4-3/8". There is a metal plate over a wire belly hook hanger. Note the metal protective plate shaped to fit the odd shaped face.

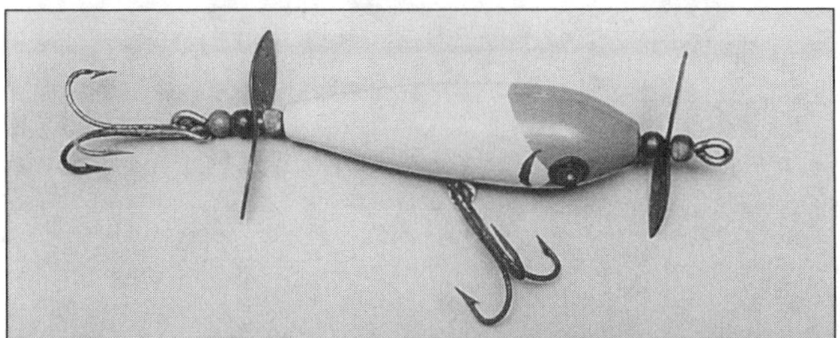

This unknown white-bodied, red-headed lure measures 2-3/4" and has brass floppy propeller spinners. The red and black bearing beads are wooden. Eyes are made by the placement of a plastic washer, brass washer and black bead in that order.

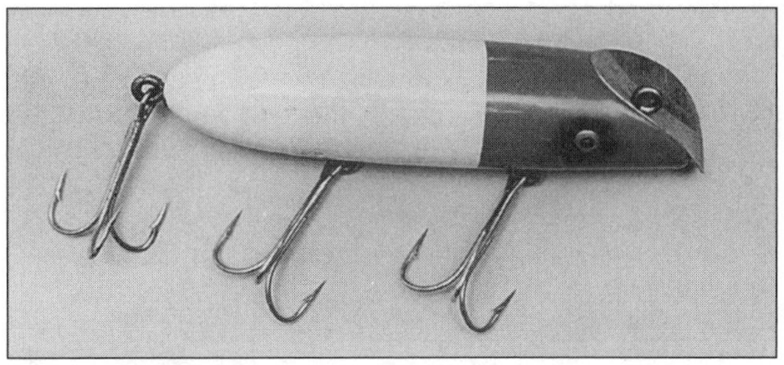

This lure appears to be a South Bend product due to its hook hangers, eyes and paint job, but the metal face plate/diving lip is decidedly not. There is a narrow strip of silver scale finish along the belly of this white body, red head lure. It measures 4".

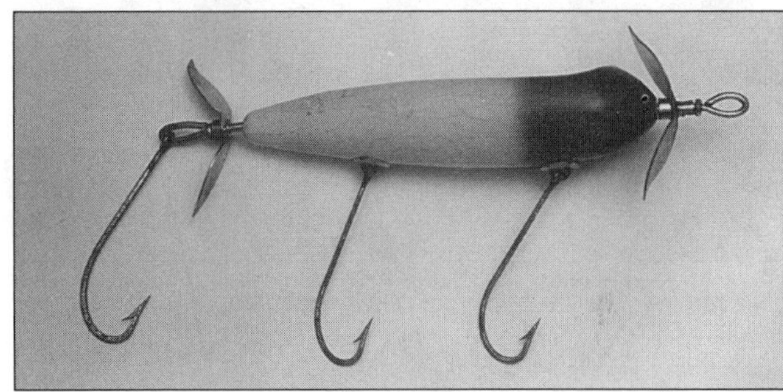

White with red head, 3-3/4". Painted eyes. Belly hooks are mounted on a wire bridle extending the hooks out to either side.

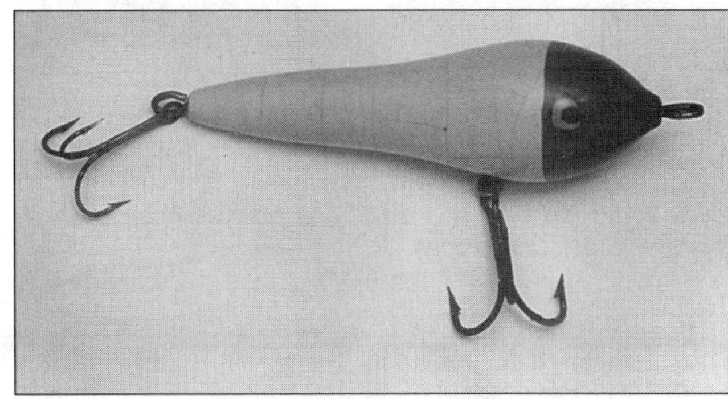

May have been solid white. The head appears to have been painted red by a fisherman. Has painted eyes (gold with black pupil) and is 4" long. Screw eye only, hook hanger.

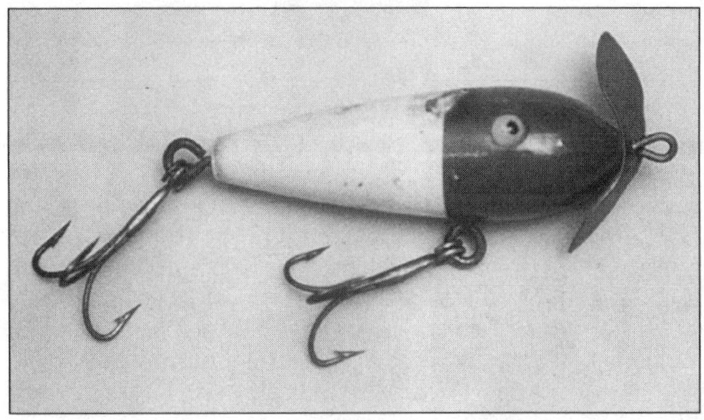

White with red head, 3" long. Note the double ring eye treble hooks. Unmarked floppy propeller forward spinner. Has opaque yellow glass eyes.

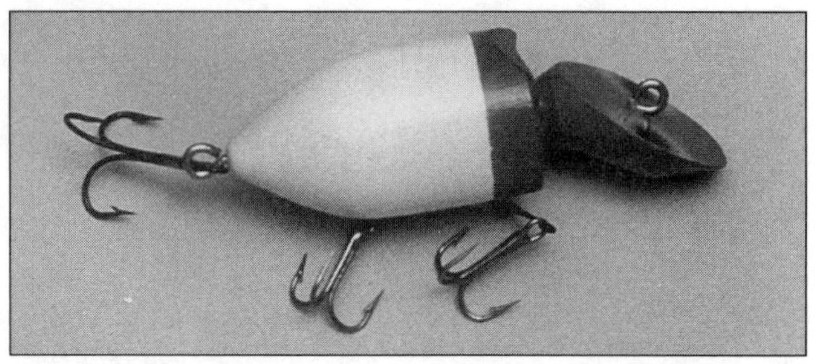

White with red head, 3-3/4". Painted eyes. Belly hooks are mounted on a wire bridle extending the hooks out to either side.

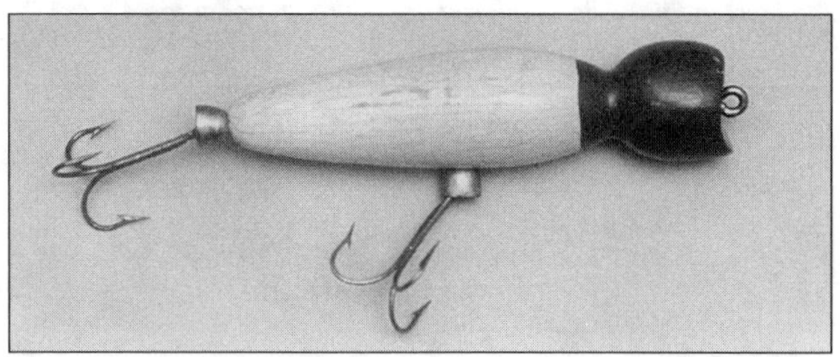

This red head, white body lure has the same hook limiter hanger patented by O. L. Strausborger in 1932. Could by a Strausborger not nothing also is known.

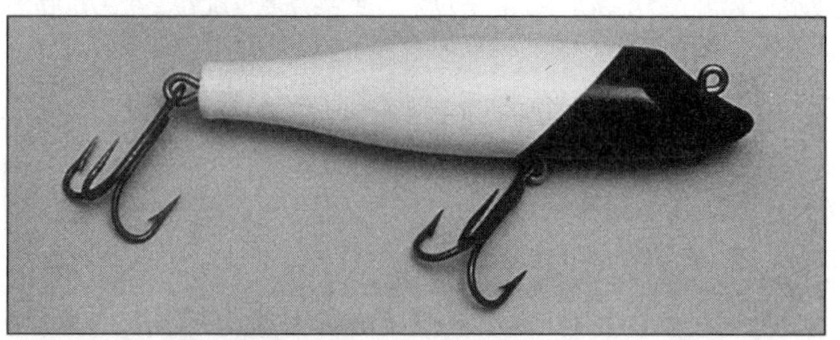

White body with black head, 4-1/2" long. No eyes. Nose and body similar to Creek Chub Pikies.

Head and belly covered with metal. The head plate has big, bright red glass eyes set in it. Green with frog spots. Rigid mounted single hook with wire and guard. 2-1/2" long.

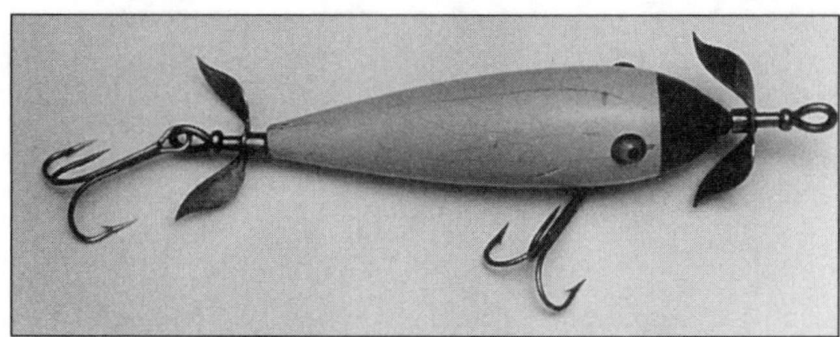

White body with red head, 3-1/2" long. Glass eyes. Cup and screw eye hook hanger and unmarked propeller spinners.

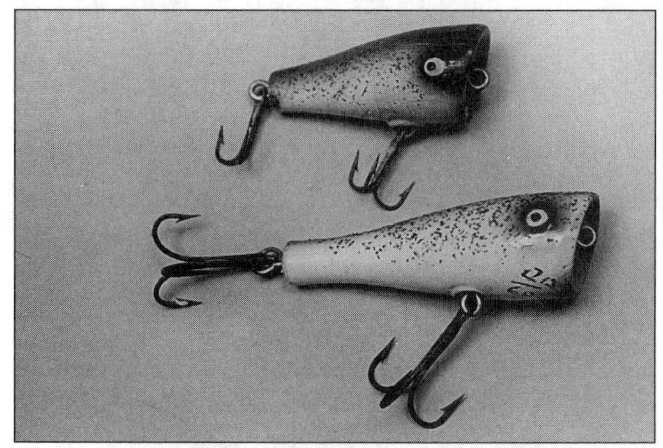

A pair of nicely made wood popper type lures. The box identified one of them as a "2112" nothing more was on the box. They measure 2-1/4" and 2-3/4", have tack painted eyes and cup and screw eye hook hardware. The cup rims are painted over with the lure body paint Notice the tail hook reinforcement on the larger of the two.

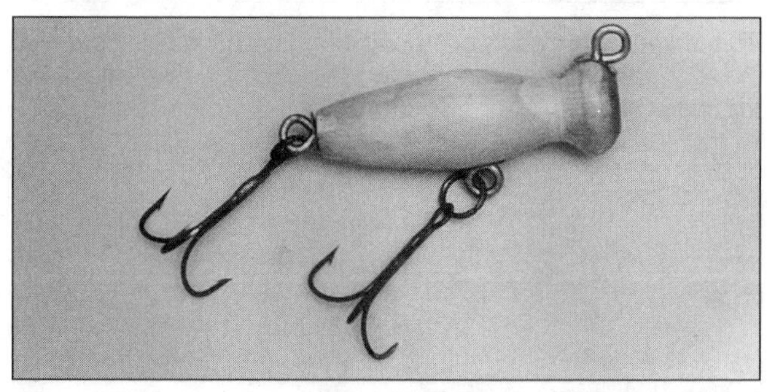

Solid white, 2-1/2" long. Note small metal plate on top of head underline tie. Screw eye and washer hook hangers. O-ring hook fasteners.

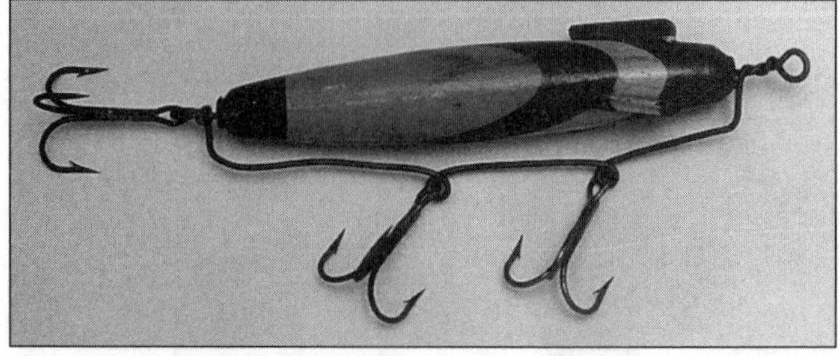

Yellow body with black tail and red, white and green stripes at the head. Metal (brass?) fins at head to make the lure rotate. The body rotates around a one-piece brass wire that incorporates the hook hanger method. 4" long.

Solid black body, 4-1/4" long. Woodpecker type lure with a# brass hardware. Screw eye and cone shaped inverted cup on surface (not counter sunk as regular cup hardware),

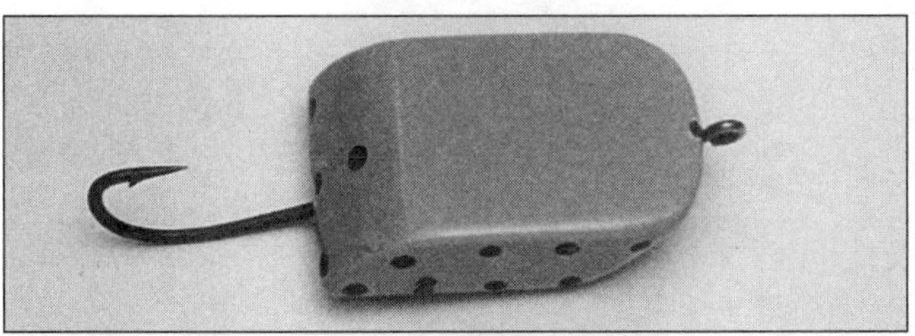

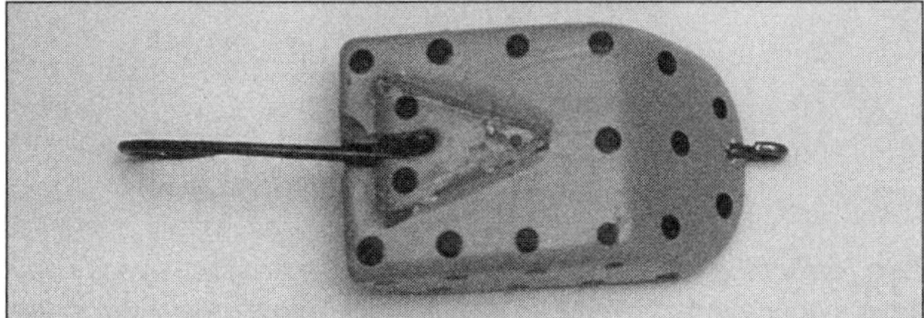

Top and belly view yellow with black spots. Has brad inserted through the side for the single hook to swing on. Triangular lead weight on belly.

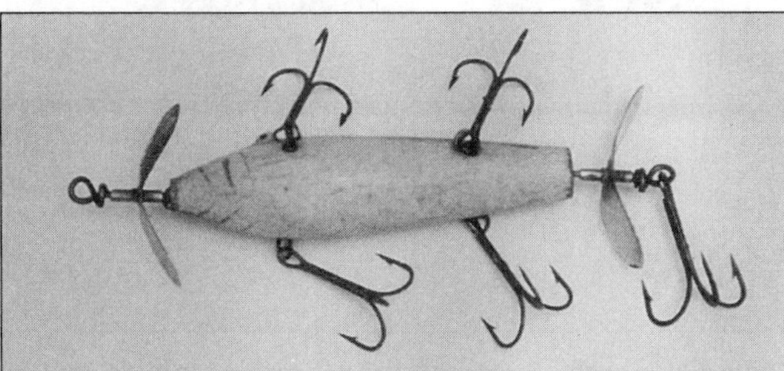

Top and belly views of a lure with reversed gill stripes typical of Joe Pepper lures. Has yellow glass eyes, through-body twisted wire hook hangers and line tie/trailing hook hanger. Tube-type bow tie propellers.

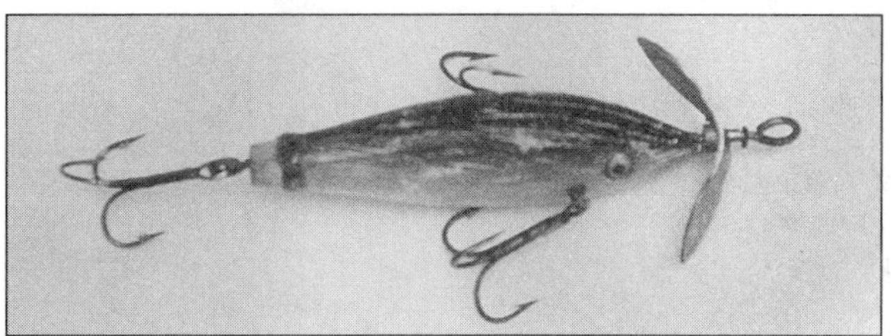

This green back lure has a brass bow tie type non-floppy propeller spinner. Yellow glass eyes and two very small internal belly weights. The knob on the and is wrapping that used to hold a buck tail like the South Bend Combination Minnows.

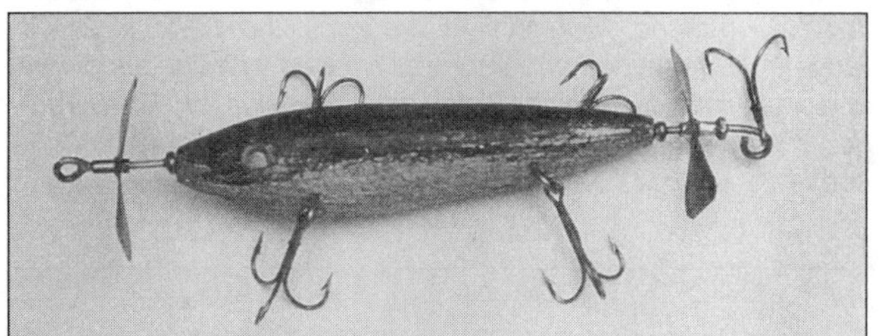

Unusual shaped blades on tube-type propeller spinners. Through-body twisted wire hook hangers and line tie/trailing hook combination. Painted eyes.

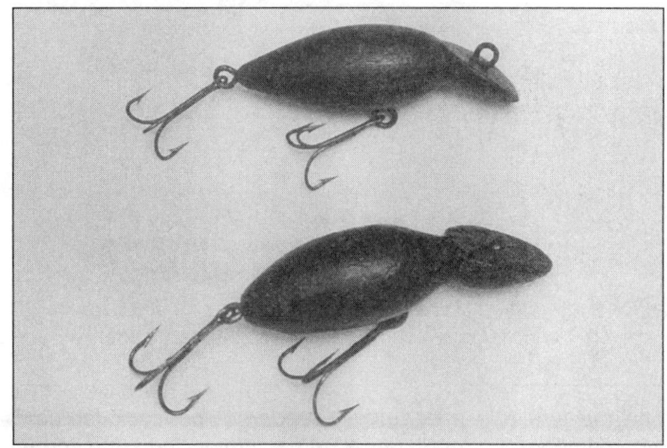

Upper lure is natural unvarnished wood. The lower is similar in shape and is crudely repainted black. Simple screw eye hardware.

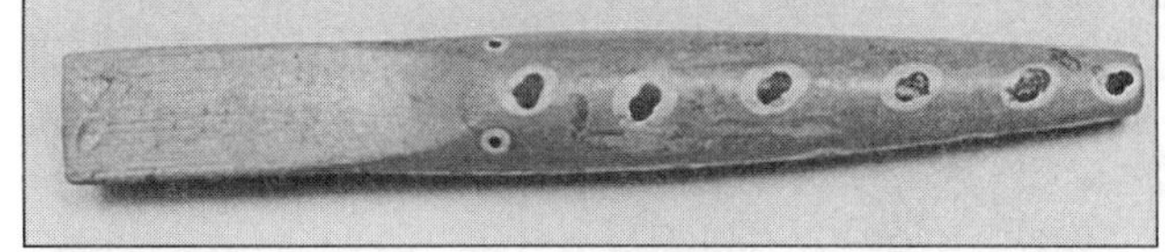

This 5-3/8" wooden gar shaped minnow was sent to me by a collector. He said it and over one hundred-fifty others in 14 different variations, color, size, etc. were bought at an estate auction in Jacksonville, Florida. None were equipped with any hardware, but all have an internal belly weight. The photos are of a top and belly view. Note the name BURKAM on the nose. He said the green ones were the only ones so marked. This one is green with black spots with yellow perimeters.

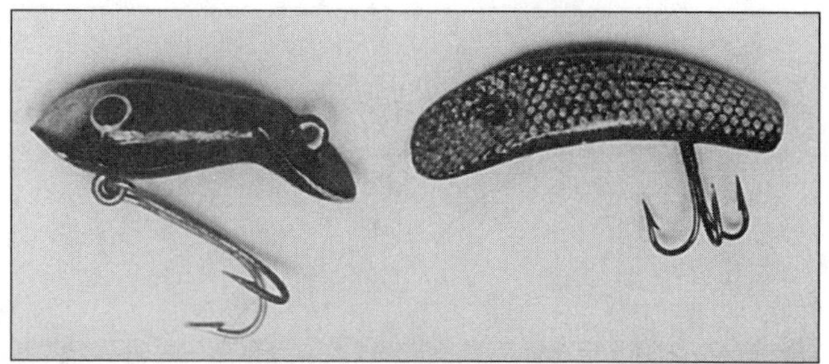

These two little fellows measure 1-1/2" and 2". They are from a lot of over 300 given to a collector in Florida. He said the man who gave them to him obtained them back in the late 1960s and told him they were made in the late 1930s and early 1940s, possible in Mt. Clemmons, Michigan. All are within the 1-1/2" to 2-5/8" range, made of wood and very well finished with various colors and scale finishes. They all look much like Helins and Rush Tangos in miniature. The Helin-like lures have very unique through-body wire line tie/hook hangers.

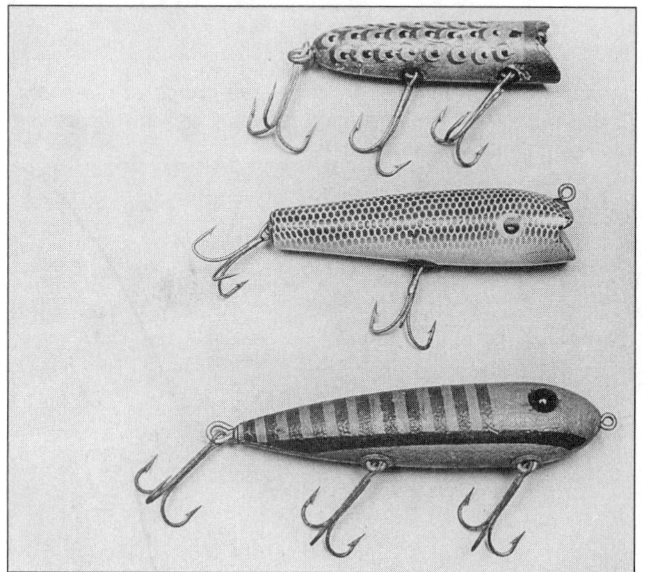

The top lure has a beautifully rendered "peacock feather" type paint pattern measures 3". It has rimless cup and screw eye hook hardware. The middle lure, measuring 3-1/2" is a "stump knocker" style lure with a very nice green scale finish. It utilizes cup and screw eye hook hangers. The lower lure measures 4-1/2" and has cup and screw eye hook hangers. It has unusual brown glass eyes.

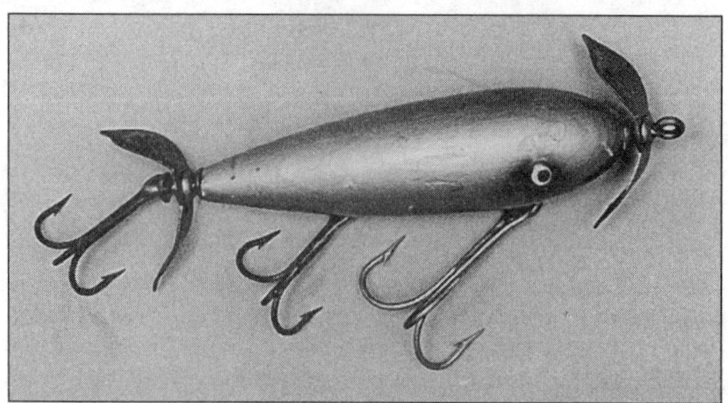

This copper-colored 3-1/8" wood lure has tack-painted eyes and cup/screw eye hook hardware. There was a tag attached that had "Ed Hill Colon, MI" on it.

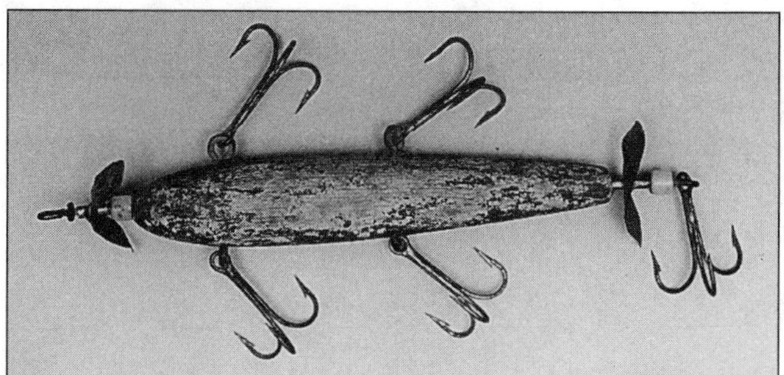

The green finish on this 4-1/2" unknown is just about worn off. There is a rectangular internal belly weight measuring 1/8" wide and 1-1/4" long. Note the bearings fore and aft. They are cylindrical shaped, made of what appears to be porcelain and are pink in color.

Two really nice wooden poppers. Notice the unusual eyes. They have a concave face and the hook is glued into a groove cut in the belly. The body measures 1-1/4" with the overall length being 2".

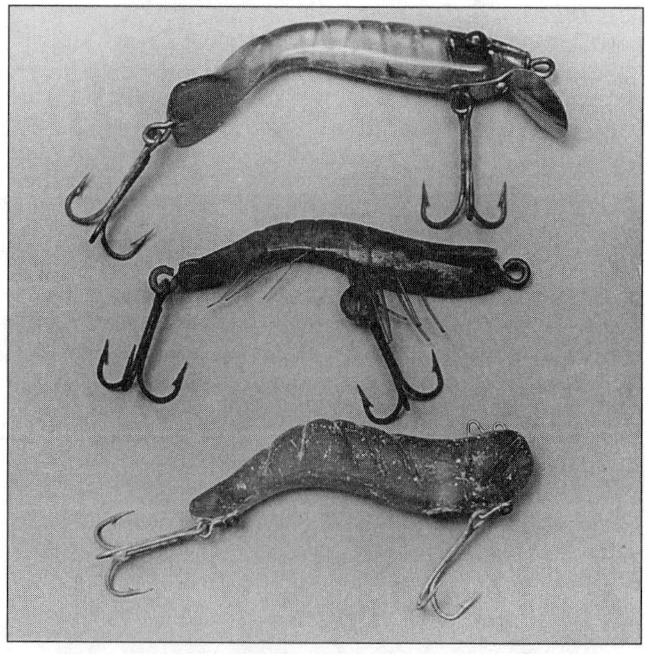

Three plastic shrimp lures measuring 3" for the top and 2-3/4" for the other two. The top lure has been identified as a Nichol SHRIMP. Please turn to the PICO section for more information. The third from the top has now been identified as a Bing PLUG IN' SHORTY made by the Doug English Lure Company in Texas.

This well-made 5-3/4" x 1-1/2" (dia.) wooden lure has recessed screw eye hook hangers. Note the flattened head. No identification marking anywhere on the body.

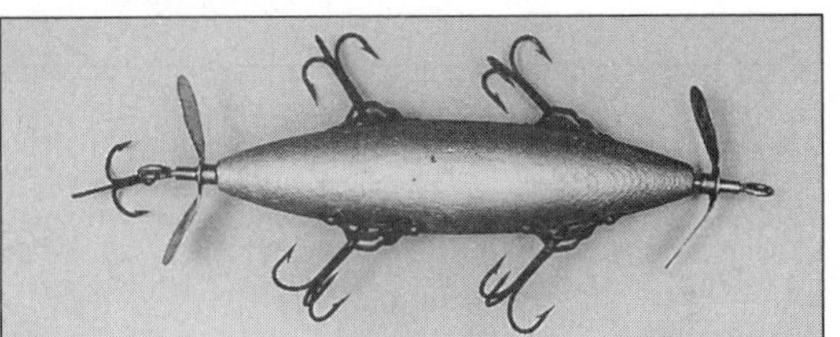

This 4-1/4" unknown wooden lure is painted an aluminum color. It has tube type propeller spinners and odd hook hangers apparently designed to hold the hooks straight out to the side, but still able to pivot fore and aft.

A 4-1/2" wooden lure with green body and white belly. The fish tail at the rear is made of metal and the nose propeller spinner is brass. It sports four single hooks.

This 3-1/2" unknown has a white body, red head and tail and red spots. Notice how the two single hooks are hold against the body by clips at the rear.

This wood body lure measures 2-1/2". It has twisted wire, through-body hook hangers and unusual propeller spinners. There are three red glass bearings, one at the nose and two at the tail, fore and aft of the propeller.

This egg-shaped plug has a frog finish and measures 2" long. The nose mounted dive plane is triangular in shape and made of brass. It appears to have had glass eyes.

Measures 3". Note the carved-in grooves. Cup and screw eye hardware. The eyes were carved before painting.

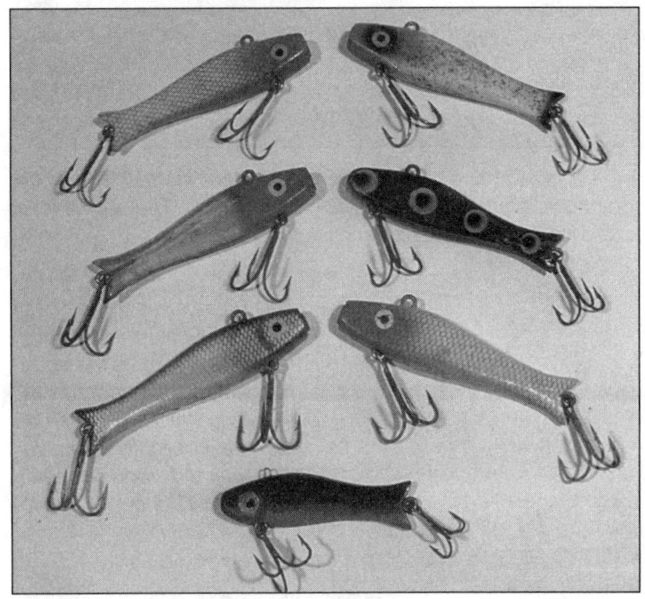

Seven unknown plastic lures thought to date sometime in the 1940-50s era. The photo was sent to me with no other information.

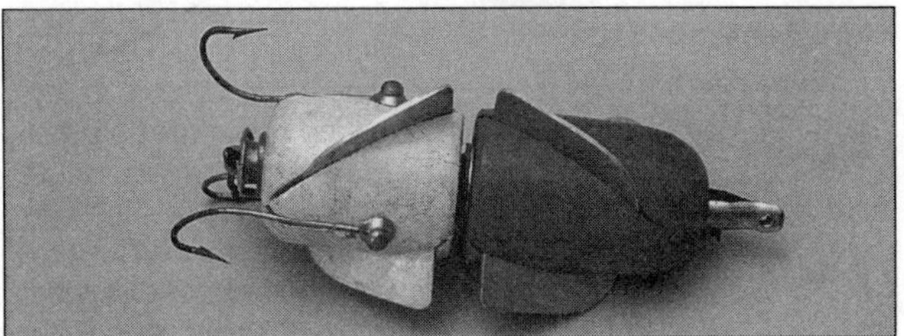

This wood bait with metal fins measures 3-1/2" overall. It is red and white. There is a mechanism in the lure whereby it can be wound up by turning one of the halves. It would move around by itself in the water.

This a fairly large wooden bait measuring 4" body length and 9" overall including the metal lip and the buck tail. It is very colorful with green back, yellow sides and glowing red belly. The buck tail is in matching colors. The eyes are bright red with black pupil.

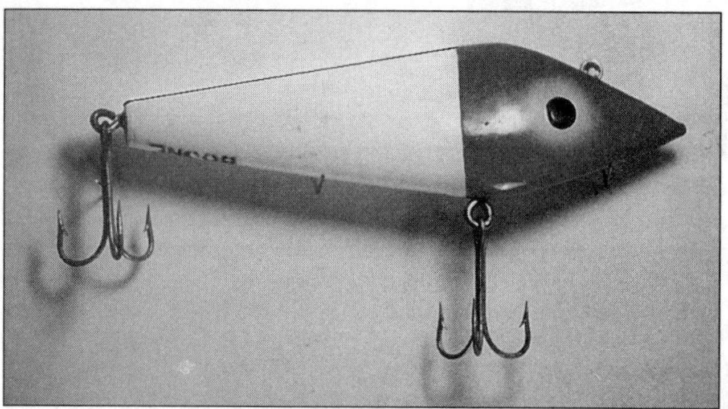

A 3-1/2" plastic lure marked "BOONE" under the tail. The white body blended into the background in the photo. The outline was added to the back with pen and ink for definition.

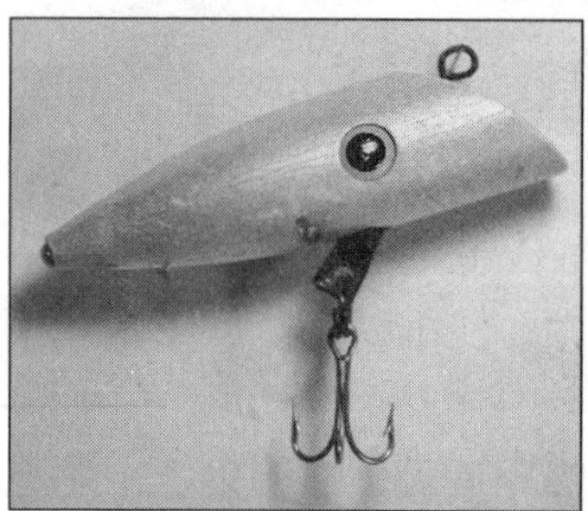

This unusual wood bait has a metal tube running from top to belly. It forms the hook hanger and incorporates a swiveling line tie. The face of the lure is slightly concave and painted red. It measures 2-3/4" long.

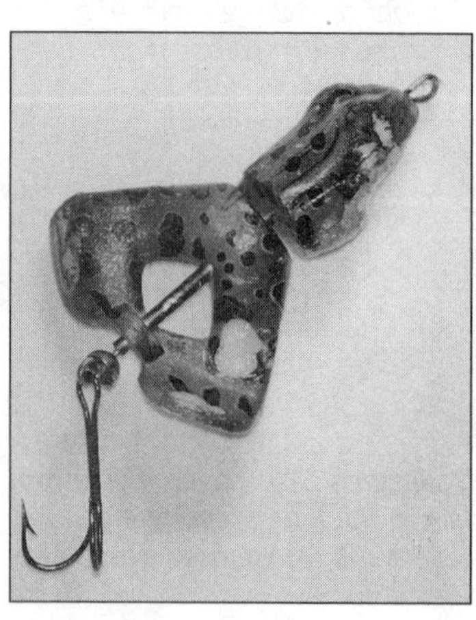

Measuring 3", this wood lure has an internalized weight just behind the cup and screw eye belly hook hanger. Its difficult to tell, but the eyes may be glass. They are opaque yellow with black pupils. The legs on this plastic frog lure rotate upon retrieve. It measures 3" and is colored brown with black frog spots.

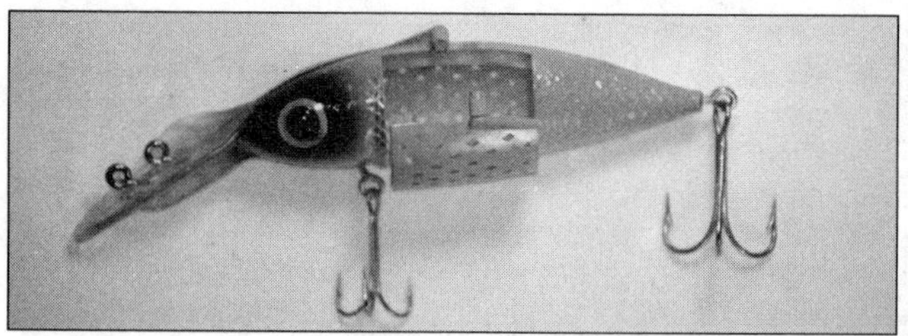

This is a very unusual plastic lure. It is hollow with holes in the body and a hinged door in the side. I suppose you could put anything in it, but I suspect it is for chum or some other smelly substance. It measures 4-1/4" overall.

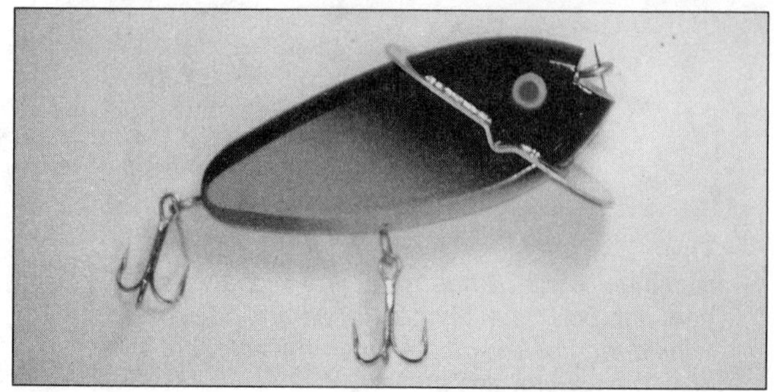

A flat-sided wood lure with an aluminum collar. The body measures 1/2" wide and 3" long. It is painted yellow with a black head and back and a spray of bright red under the tail end. Red eye with white iris.

A silvery white finish plastic lure with great big plastic eyes. It measures 3-1/2" long.

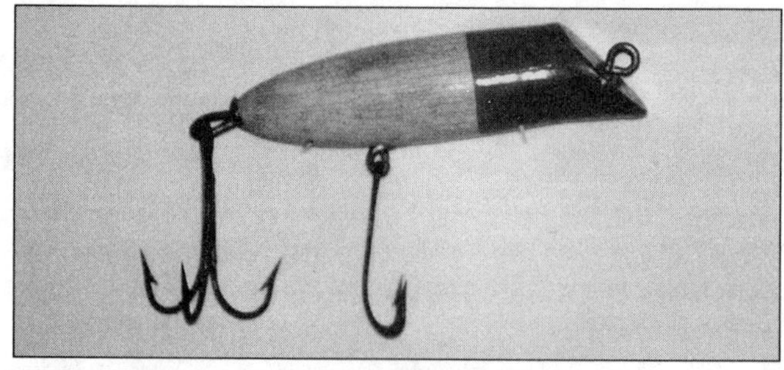

This wood lure is white with a red head and measures 2-3/4". Notice the flare toward the slant face.

A reverse-running wooden lure measuring 2-1/4". It is black and white.

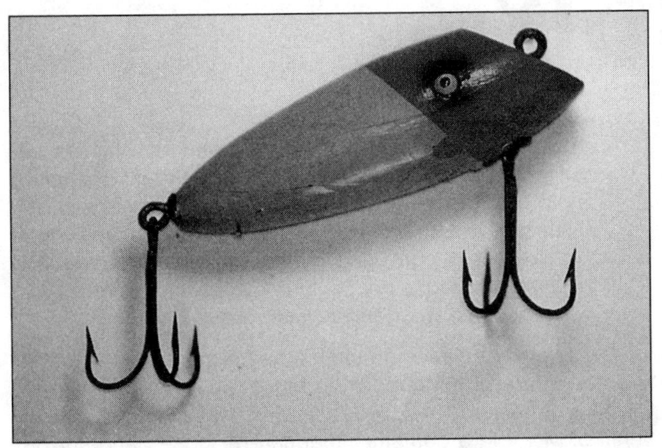

Sporting opaque yellow glass eyes, this red and white wooden lure measures 3" long. It also has an internalized belly weight just aft of the belly treble.

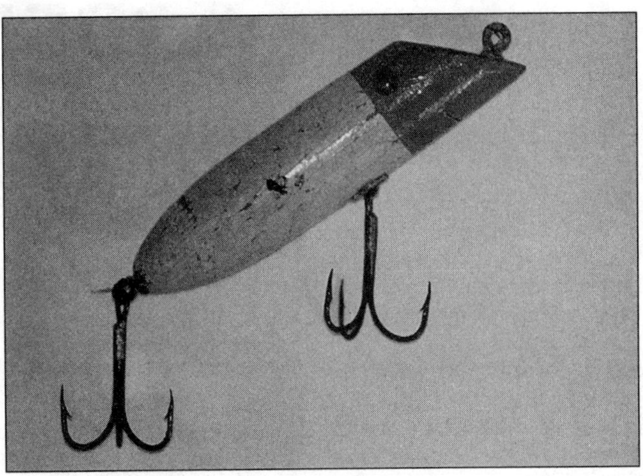

A wooden lure measuring 3-5/8". It has glass eyes and cup/screw eye belly hook hanger. Red and white in color.

APPENDIX A

CLEANING AND RESTORING OLD FISHING LURES

First of all, lure collectors don't legitimately restore old lures to original or mint condition most of the time. We have already briefly discussed repaints and the need for plainly marking them as such. It might be interesting and for a legitimate reason to restore a lure to original or mint condition, but once again the need for marking them as such is of paramount importance. Back in 1988, NFLCC member Phil Smith reported in the club newsletter that he had found a authentic looking Moonlight Bait Company "Dreadnought", being represented as the real thing. It was decidedly not so. He noted that the cups in the hook hardware were not right and that the propeller spinners were actually from a Creek Chub Bait Company lure. This lure may have been born honestly, but we have no way of knowing without a mark of some sort indicating it. When lure collectors "restore" what we really mean is clean and renew. We restore the brightness or luster of the paint or finish for instance. We can straighten out hardware or even replace it with parts from a like plug or other lure from the same vintage and lure maker. Remember the comments regarding saving old beat-up lures or "Beaters" for their hardware? The following are some "do's and don'ts" for the "renewing" of old lures:

1. The first and paramount rule is to approach this with great care and caution. You don't want to render further damage to the lure. I have handled hundreds in various stages of deterioration and believe me, you can do great harm if you do the wrong thing. If you are unsure, the best approach is to do nothing.
2. Some collectors advocate a coating of some sort, ostensibly to preserve what there is. I oppose anything other than a light coating of linseed oil or fine furniture paste wax applied with the fingers or a cotton swab.
3. If paint is flaking, but limber enough to press back against the lure body, you might take a toothpick and apply a little white glue under the paint. This may help slow or prevent further damage.
4. Crazing is the appearance of lots of tiny cracks all over the surface. Nothing can be done to prevent this from happening, but the application of a small amount of linseed oil rubbed in with the fingers may "feed" the paint and impede or stop further crazing.
5. Cleaning the body should be approached with care. First try to use as little water as possible on wooden lures with cracked or missing paint. Water can be absorbed by the wood and exacerbate the already-present damage. Instead, you might experiment on a beater. Dilute a small amount of a mild liquid dishwashing detergent such as Ivory. Don't make the mistake of rinsing it under water after. Try to use it in small amounts with a cotton swabs or soft bristle tooth brush and then use damp swabs or soft cotton cloth to rinse, progressing to a dry swab or cloth to remove the cleanser and to dry the lure. This is not so critical with well-preserved wooden lure with paint finish intact.

A really great cleaning solution is the mix that is used for fine furniture at the Metropolitan Museum of Art in New York City. It is equal parts of boiled linseed oil, white vinegar and turpentine. Mix it in a container that can be closed and shaken vigorously to mix. Apply it as above.

6. Plastic lures usually are a bit more durable, but don't assume this. Often, especially in the early days, plastics were painted just as the wooden ones. Be very aware, however, that early plastics were sometimes unstable and plastics of any era can be subject to great damage if a solvent of the wrong type is used.
7. Cleaning the metal parts need not usually be approached with such care as the paint finishes unless some of the metal is painted and you wish to preserve the paint. Carefully remove parts and boil them for a few minutes in plain water and pat dry in a towel. Any stubborn crud can then be removed with a toothbrush or fine brass bristle brush. Any remaining might be popped off with the tip of a small knife or Exacto tool. Finally, all else failing, you can soak the parts in a 50/50 solution of distilled white vinegar and water for about five minutes, but no more than ten minutes depending on how well it works for you. If none of this works, you'll probably just have to live with it.
8. If you are cleaning brass or copper parts get some household ammonia. Do this outdoors or in a well ventilated garage or shop area. Place the parts in a container and cover with the ammonia. You should see the results in two to 24 hours. Wear rubber gloves when removing the parts. Some collectors say to avoid using sudsy ammonia in this process. I have never used it on lure parts, but have used it successfully on large antique brass and copper pieces. It is probably best to err on the conservative side. You should avoid any stronger solutions such as toilet bowl cleaners. Most of this type of cleaners contain muriatic acid that can etch your metal parts thereby ruining them.
9. A note about the small lengths of plastic tubing some collectors use to guard the points and barbs of hooks. These tend to deteriorate over the years and stick to the lure body causing damage to the paint finish.

APPENDIX B

PHOTOGRAPHING YOUR LURES

There are three very good reasons for photographing your collection. First and foremost is for insurance purposes. Should you experience theft, fire or any other disaster that results in the loss of your collection, you have a good record of what you had. Insurance companies are loathe to accept your word that your missing or destroyed "Green Eyed Goggler" had glass eyes and was worth 20 times as much as one with painted eyes that could be purchased for five bucks at a show today. In the case of theft, you have little chance of identifying it as yours in most instances in the event of a recovery. Law enforcement authorities often recover stolen property that can't be identified as to owner. If you have photos and documentation such as detailed descriptions of unique marks, etc., they can help you positively identify what is yours. A second good reason is for sales and trades through the mail without risk of loss or damage. The third reason is to help you and me. I get hundreds of photos every year, more than one half of which are useless. You send me photos with your questions and all I can see is a crowd scene at a football game or what appears to be a scarecrow in the middle of a 40-acre field. In addition to the lure(s) being about a quarter of an inch long in the photo, about half the time it is out of focus. Can't help much there. So, are you ready for your photo lesson?

This will be simple and a little fun for most of you. It won't make you America's next Ansel Adams, but it will make you a better photographer of lures. You experts and pros can skip this.

THE CAMERA

The two most common cameras most of us use today are the 35mm single lens reflex (SLR) and the very common automatic "point and shoot" cameras that use the mini negative disc or regular 35 mm film. Forget the Polaroid or other instant cameras. Unless you have the very expensive special application versions, they are useless in this application. The method for taking the picture differs with the types of cameras so I will go through the basic set-up to get your lures ready to shoot and then describe the method for each of the camera types.

SETTING

A simple table top or any flat or slightly inclined surface will do. Avoid concrete, wood or any textured surface, however. I recommend that you use simple poster board or mat board as a background. The color should be a light shade of yellow, gray, beige or blue.

LIGHTING

There are two types of light, natural or artificial.

NATURAL LIGHT - The simplest and best light is natural light outdoors and the best of this is found on an overcast day or in the shade on a bright sunshiny day. This eliminates harsh shadows. You can get almost the same light indoors if you shoot your pictures at a large window that is letting lots of light, but not letting direct sunlight in.

ARTIFICIAL LIGHT - If you wish to shoot indoors under artificial light, you can do so in a bright, well-lighted room. You must be careful, however, about the type of light you have there. Fluorescent lighting will produce pictures with a decidedly greenish cast. Incandescent light, ordinary light bulbs, will result in photos with a red or yellowish cast. The two problems described above happen when you use ordinary, daylight color film designed for outdoor use or with a flash or strobe indoors. Most modern film processing labs can utilize filters to correct this problem, but you must tell them about the type of light you used, before they make the color prints. Slides present more difficulty, but they can also be color corrected (prints from the slides only). To avoid all this, it is best to shoot under natural light.

A third possibility is to use a flash or strobe, but ordinarily this produces a severe, flat photo with harsh shadows. If you can devise a way of filtering the flash, diffusing or "bouncing" it, the results are generally more satisfactory. The best use of flash is for "fill light" when shooting outdoors. This fills in shadows, all but eliminating them if properly done.

CHOICE OF FILM

Film comes in different speeds (ASA ratings). The higher the ASA, the faster the speed of the film. The faster the speed, the less light needed to make a good photo. There is a trade-off, however. The faster the film speed, the grainier the resulting picture. This should not be an important factor to you unless you intend to enlarge the picture or submit it for publication where the publisher may need to do the same thing. I recommend that you use film with an ASA of 200, but if you have a poor light situation, an ASA of 400 will give satisfactory results. Those of you with modern automatic cameras shouldn't need to worry about switching these various ASA rating around because your camera will automatically adjust itself to the ASA of the film you load it with. Be sure to read your cameras instruction manual about this (You did read your manual didn't you?). Those of you with the more complicated SLR's already know what to do.

GENERAL TECHNIQUES

First, you have a choice of methods. If you are shooting the pictures for insurance inventory purposes and will write detailed descriptions of each lure, you may choose to make a "gang" shot; that is shooting a number of lures in the same frame or shooting your display board or cabinet (if there is a glass door, be sure to open it first). This is really less desirable because of the loss of photographic detail you may need or may be required for identification. If you don't wish to shoot each individual lure, then shoot them in groups of no more than three or four.

When you take the picture, try to get down as close to the lures as you can, filling the frame. Watch that your own shadow doesn't shade the lure(s) and ruin the picture. Remember also that you want to show the best features. You may want to take more than one photo if there is a special feature that would not show in a careful arrangement of the lure. Close-up lenses or zooms are available for some of the automatic cameras and are available for virtually all SLR's. You may find a tripod very useful also. More about tripods later.

TECHNIQUES FOR AUTOMATIC CAMERAS

Most of the automatic cameras available today are made for landscape and portraiture and come with fixed focus lens or an automatic focus feature. Some even have a zoom or "macro" feature allowing you to get a little closer to your subject. This feature allows a little nicer close-up portraiture, but unless it is a very unusual automatic camera, it will not be of much use for the purpose at hand. The average automatic will not allow you to get any closer than three feet from your subject. If you attempt to get any closer everything will be out of focus. The field of view of these cameras at three feet is about 20" x 24". If you put one 6" lure in the middle of that, take the picture and process it, you will get a snapshot about 4" x 5" in size and a lure less than 1-1/4" long, a lonesome trifling tidbit in the center. Remember the scarecrow in the 40-acre field? It would be of little use in identification. A few of these cameras have close-up attachments that may make them more suitable for this type of photography so check your manual and the dealer. Chances are that this type of camera will only be suitable for group pictures, but some will do better than others and a few may even do better than the manual indicates. You might want to experiment with one roll of film to see what yours will do. If the experiment is a failure, I suggest you prevail upon a friend or relative who has a better camera to help you out. Better yet, go out and buy one. They are not nearly so complicated as they look.

TECHNIQUE FOR THE SINGLE LENS REFLEX (SLR) CAMERA

Chances are, many of you who own SLR's have never tried macro photography. That is what small object photography is called. If you have perfected the art, skip the rest of this section. It will only serve to bore you. For the others, it will prove to be fascinating when you master it.

Macro photography is a big word for a relatively simple technique, the results of which can be quite rewarding. In fact many of the photos in this book were shot with a manual Honeywell Pentax SLR with a standard 55mm lens that I bought over 20 years ago. Many of you will probably have much newer and better cameras than mine. Yours should do at least as well as mine which will focus down to about 13" from the subject with a 5" x 7" field of view. With a set of relatively inexpensive (about $30-$40) set of stacking closeup lenses, you can get some spectacular close-ups. Remember though, the more magnification you get, the less depth of field you will have. I may have lost some of you there. Depth of field is simply the area in front of the camera that will photograph with acceptable sharpness. Said another way it is the distance or area between the nearest and farthest point in the scene to be photographed that will be in focus in the resulting picture.

Focusing and Depth of Field - The depth of field you need is a function of the f-stop selected for the photograph and to a lesser extent, the distance from the lens to the subject. The f-stop represents the size of the aperture of the lens. Unless you wish to understand it further, all you need to know is, that the higher the f-stop number selected, the more the depth of field you will have. It varies with the lens, but the depth of field with my camera is about 3" when it is focused as close as possible. When I focus on an object, I try to focus about midway into its depth. This way, if you are shooting from the side (at an oblique angle) all will be in focus, from the hooks to the back. You may be able to do a little better or a little worse, depending upon your lens. Although you will be working as close to your subject as you can, you should also know that the further the camera gets from the subject, the greater the depth of field.

Shutter Speeds and f-stops - I have already noted that you will want to use a high f-stop number to get the depth of field you want. The higher the f-stop, the smaller the aperture. Aperture refers to the hole through which the reflected light from your subject passes on its way to the film surface. The smaller that hole, the longer it takes light sufficient enough to form a good image on the film to get through ft. It follows then, that the smaller the hole, the longer the shutter must remain open. Since you want good depth of field you will have to trade off for time. This may mean that the shutter speed may be too slow for you to hand-hold your camera. You need to experiment a bit to see if you will need a tripod. Generally speaking if your shutter speed is 1/50th of a second or faster, you can probably hand hold the camera although some people are steady enough to do it at 1/30th a second; any slower will require a tripod. If you find you need to use a tripod, you may also need to get a cable release to keep from shaking the camera when tripping the shutter. Cable releases are inexpensive and, if you shop around, tripods can be relatively inexpensive also.

Shooting the Picture - Here is a good starting set-up for your experimental role:

Film speed........ASA 100 to 200

Shutter speed.....1/15 to 1/60

f-stop............f-11 to f-16

Focal distance....14" to 18" (approximately) As close as you can or need to be.

You will likely need to experiment a bit until you find the settings that give you the results you want. There are 12-exposure rolls of film. You may wish to shoot a few and have them processed before trying some new settings. Most processors charge only for the prints made. The best way to find the ideal set-up for your particular light conditions is to shoot at different f-stops leaving everything else constant, placing a piece of paper in the shot with the subject identifying the setting. You will then have a set of photos from which to pick the best and have the camera setting right there in the picture.

SOME LAST NOTES ON PHOTOGRAPHING YOUR COLLECTION

Now you have your photograph(s). First, especially if this is an insurance inventory, you should have two sets of photos. One set is for you to keep at home to work with or send to other collectors for sale or trade and the other in a safe deposit box or other safe place away from where you keep your collection. This is in the event you have a fire or other happenstance resulting in the loss of your collection and the photo record kept at home. Second, you should have a written record of things such as measurements, distinguishing marks, when and from where you obtained it and how much it was valued then and at present. An easy way to keep track of the data for each lure is to use pressure sensitive labels to record it and apply the label to the back of the photo. If you use a ball point pen to write on the back an impression of the writing will show through on the image side of the photo. Likewise using an ink pen runs the risk of not-quite-dry ink transferring to the face of the photo placed under it. The photo and data can leave little doubt as to ownership and value. One last comment: If you are photographing the lure to send to me - give me the same information. If you learn the photo lesson well, you might end up with a photo credit in the next edition.

Index

A

B

C

D

E

F

G

H

I

J

K

L

M

N

O

P

R

S

T

U

V

W

Y

Z